New

**Current biography
yearbook.**

3248   83

WITHDRAWN

Current Biography. Yearbook 2007

EDITOR
Clifford Thompson

SENIOR EDITORS
Miriam Helbok
Mari Rich

PRODUCTION EDITOR
Julia Weist

ASSISTANT EDITORS
Jennifer Curry
Christopher Mari
Albert Rolls

CONTRIBUTING EDITOR
Kieran Dugan

STAFF WRITERS
Matt Broadus
Forrest Cole
Christopher Cullen
Sara J. Donnelly
Ronald Eniclerico
David J. Kim
Nicholas W. Malinowski
Bertha Muteba
Kenneth Partridge
David Ramm
Claire Stanford

CONTRIBUTING WRITERS
In-Young Chang
Dan Firrincili
Selma Yampolsky

EDITORIAL ASSISTANT
Carolyn Ellis

THE H. W. WILSON COMPANY
NEW YORK   DUBLIN

SIXTY-EIGHTH ANNUAL CUMULATION—2007

PRINTED IN THE UNITED STATES OF AMERICA

International Standard Serial No. (0084-9499)

International Standard Book No. – 978-0-8242-1084-7

Library of Congress Catalog Card No. (40-27432)

Table of Contents

PREFACE

The aim of *Current Biography Yearbook 2007*, like that of the preceding volumes in this series of annual dictionaries of contemporary biography, now in its seventh decade of publication, is to provide reference librarians, students, and researchers with objective, accurate, and well-documented biographical articles about living leaders in all fields of human accomplishment. Whenever feasible, obituary notices appear for persons whose biographies have been published in *Current Biography*.

Current Biography Yearbook 2007 carries on the policy of including new and updated biographical profiles that supersede earlier articles. Profiles have been made as accurate and objective as possible through careful researching of newspapers, magazines, the World Wide Web, authoritative reference books, and news releases of both government and private agencies. Immediately after they are published in the 11 monthly issues, articles are submitted to biographees to give them an opportunity to suggest additions and corrections in time for publication of the *Current Biography Yearbook*. To take account of major changes in the careers of biographees, articles are revised before they are included in the yearbook.

Classification by Profession–2007 and *2001–2007 Index* are at the end of this volume. *Current Biography Cumulated Index 1940–2005* cumulates and supersedes all previous indexes.

For their assistance in preparing *Current Biography Yearbook 2007*, I thank the staff of *Current Biography* and also the staffs of the company's Computer and Manufacturing departments.

Current Biography welcomes comments and suggestions. Please send your comments to: The Editor, *Current Biography*, The H. W. Wilson Company, 950 University Ave., Bronx, NY 10452; fax: 718-590-4566; E-mail: cthompson@hwwilson.com.

Clifford Thompson

List of Biographies

Current Biography Yearbook 2007

Courtesy of Jessica Abel

Abel, Jessica

Nov. 15, 1969– Comic-book writer and artist

Address: c/o Fantagraphics Books, 7563 Lake City Way, N.E., Seattle, WA 98115

"I have nothing against the mainstream," the alternative-comics artist Jessica Abel said in an interview for the Web site SilverBulletComic-Books.com. "It just isn't inherently interesting to me." Abel's comic-book series *Artbabe* launched her to stardom in the world of alternative—or underground—comics, which take a literary approach to the medium, often addressing complex social issues as well as the minutiae of everyday life. Rather than formulaic story arcs featuring buxom super-heroines in revealing costumes, *Artbabe* focused on a realistic depiction of the trials and tribulations of young adults. *Artbabe*, which ran in serialized form from 1992 to 1999, was embraced by a new generation of comic-book readers, many of whom were adolescent and 20-something females. The success of *Artbabe* led to comics-journalism assignments for Abel, including a book co-written with the popular public-radio host Ira Glass of *This American Life*. Old and new fans welcomed her second major series, *La Perdida*, which ran from 2001 to 2005 in serialized form and ap-

peared as a graphic novel in 2006. In addition to her work as an artist and writer, Abel teaches a course on drawing and writing comics at the School of Visual Arts in New York City. She has also taught and lectured at the Wexner Center for the Arts at the University of Ohio; the Institute of Contemporary Arts, London; Syracuse University; and Parsons School of Art.

Jessica C. Abel was born on November 15, 1969 and spent her childhood and adolescence in the Chicago, Illinois, area, primarily in the city of Evanston. As a child she read comic books and was particularly fond of a *Ms.* magazine publication from the early 1970s that collected some of the 1940s *Wonder Woman* comics by Charles Moulton and H. G. Peters. The publication included an introduction by the noted feminist Gloria Steinem and critical essays from other authors; Abel's interest, however, lay strictly with the stories and artwork of the comics themselves. She sometimes sneaked glances at her stepbrother's comic books, including *Daredevil* and *Electra*, which he kept in his room, and also developed an intense love for Saturday-morning TV cartoons. She made several illustrated books as a child, including one about a monster who ate her beloved gym teacher. When she entered early adolescence, Abel lost interest in comics for a time. Then, at 15, when she was working at a local hardware store, she began reading the comic books in the racks at the convenience store where she went for lunch. "I thought it was pretty rebellious and 'punk' to be a girl and yet reading comics . . . ," she recalled for her Web site, JessicaAbel.com. "However, I was still pretty lost in a comics store at that point; I didn't have much of a clue what I liked. I also didn't know anyone else who read comics, so didn't have anyone to talk to about it." At around that time, such "serious" comics as Art Spiegelman's *Maus* began to appear, with the result that "there was a huge buzz in the mainstream media about 'comics aren't just for kids anymore,'" as Abel recalled for her Web site. "Of course I got those books, and they kept me going deeper into comics."

At Evanston Township High School, Abel became the news editor of the school paper, the *Evanstonian*. That job led to her first attempt at comics-style illustration. She recalled for JessicaAbel.com, "It depicted me and my best friends as members of a hypothetical though extremely cool band, the Liliputians. We were doing something or other that involved being in a hole in the ground. I can't remember what." After graduating, Abel went on to Carleton College, in Northfield, Minnesota. As a freshman, she stated on her Web site, she encountered what was, "without a doubt, the most important influence on my comics, my conception of what comics are and can be, and my choice to become a cartoonist": *Love and Rockets,* by Jaime, Gilbert, and (occasionally) Mario Hernandez. That series "totally blew me away, and more importantly blew away all the limits I had known up to that point as to what could be done in comics." *Love and Rockets,* begun in 1981 and published by Fantagraphics Books, led the underground comics movement of the 1980s, providing an alternative to the traditional superhero tales offered by the mainstream publishers Marvel Comics and DC Comics; the series, which is still published, was considered highly unusual at first, as all of its main characters were female, while the authors were men. Abel told Neda Ulaby for National Public Radio's *All Things Considered* (March 31, 2002), "Both Jaime and Gilbert are incredibly sensitive to the way it feels to be female, and I still have no idea why that is, why they're able to do that."

Inspired by her rediscovered love for comics, Abel proposed that she create for her course in ancient Greek literature a comic in place of a traditional final paper. Her professor agreed, and Abel received an "A" for her comic-book version of Euripides' *Medea,* set in outer space. That work was Abel's first sequential-art comic. She transferred to the University of Chicago in her sophomore year; during that fall semester she noticed a flyer put up by a student-run comics club that was soliciting submissions of original comics to be published in an anthology. At the organizational meeting, she met a fellow student, Ivan Brunetti, then the writer of a comic strip in the *Chicago Maroon,* the University of Chicago's student newspaper. (Brunetti later went on to publish a wide array of work, including the critically acclaimed autobiographical comic-book series *Schizo.*) The first volume of the student anthology, *Breakdown,* was edited by Brunetti and included the first half of Abel's story "The Junkie." The story was based in part on erotic writing by Abel's best friend from Evanston Township High School. Abel recalled for her Web site, "Looking at it now, it's a bit embarrassing for both of us, but at the time, it felt really powerful." In her junior year Abel served as the editor of *Breakdown.* She graduated with a bachelor's degree in English, with honors, in 1991.

In 1992, on her own, Abel began publishing *Artbabe,* a comic-book series about young adults. Each cover of *Artbabe* featured a portrait of a bespectacled 20-something female artist who did not appear as a character in any of the stories. From the first issue, readers speculated that Abel, herself a bespectacled 20-something artist at the time, was the model for the character. Abel has repeatedly refuted the theory. She stated for JessicaAbel.com, "Artbabe is a fictional character who graces the front covers of my comic book series *Artbabe* . . . but so far, never in *Artbabe* itself. She is a painter. She is based on a real person I once knew. . . . That said, even my closest friends insist that I am Artbabe, even though I look nothing like her. . . .

They're very adamant about it. But, I mean, a lot of people wear glasses, for god's sake!"

Abel won a contest to meet Peter Bagge, an artist with an enormous following in the alternative-comics community. Bagge, the author of the cult-hit comic-book series *Hate,* arranged to meet Abel at a comic-book convention in Chicago. Abel brought 50 copies of *Artbabe* #1 with her and showed them to Bagge and his editor, Gary Groth of Fantagraphics Books. While Groth was not particularly impressed, Bagge wrote favorably about the comic book in *Hate* #10. That publicity, combined with word-of-mouth advertising, allowed Abel to continue self-publishing *Artbabe* with her earnings from orders and from her day job in the administration department at the School of the Art Institute of Chicago. As *Artbabe* grew in popularity, Abel became something of an icon in the latest wave of the alternative-comics movement, with her books selling in independent bookstores and in some comic-book stores. As Joy Press observed for the *Village Voice* (March 21, 2006), "Influenced by the likes of *Love and Rockets* and dominated by clever glam-rock chicks wrangling with angsty romantic entanglements or hanging out with girlfriends in grungy bars, *Artbabe* became a hot underground comic at a moment when few other women were drawing them."

In 1996 Abel began drawing the comic strip *Chicagophile* for the *University of Chicago Magazine,* the alumni publication of her alma mater. Later that year she won a grant from the Xeric Foundation, a nonprofit organization founded by Peter Laird, co-creator of the popular comic-book series *Teenage Mutant Ninja Turtles.* Abel used the grant to put out the first full-sized, professionally printed issue of *Artbabe.* That issue attracted the attention of Groth, who signed Abel to publish *Artbabe* with Fantagraphics.

In 1997 Abel won the prestigious Harvey Award for Best New Talent in Comics, named for the cartoonist Harvey Kurtzman, the founding editor of the comic book *Mad.* That year Abel also won the 1997 Lulu Award for Best New Talent, whose name comes from *Little Lulu,* the 1930s comic-strip character created by Marjorie Henderson Buell; Lulu Award winners are chosen by members of the Friends of Lulu, a nonprofit organization that works to involve more women in the male-dominated comics industry.

In 1998 Abel moved to Mexico with her boyfriend, the cartoonist Matt Madden. While there, she decided to end the *Artbabe* series. She told Carla Garcia for the Web site OstrichInk.com (December 2003), "I felt like, I'm done with this. I've had these experiences [depicted in the *Artbabe* stories] or something like them in the past, and now I'm not living there and not doing these things, so why am I still writing about it? And it felt sort of weird, so I stopped at that point, and I figured that maybe some time I'll be inspired again to do stuff with sort of that milieu I was using in *Artbabe,* but it seems sort of unlikely because I'm not going to go backward in my life." While in Mexico she continued working on the comic strip *Chicagophile*.

During her two years in Mexico City, Abel reassessed her drawing style and set out to make distinct changes in the way that she created images. In an interview for the Web site of the PBS television series *POV* (2006), Abel told Rebecca Bengal, "Among other things, I realized that when you draw in such a tight, controlled style, you open yourself up to (in my case, my own) criticism that things aren't quite right. If [a] room is drawn so carefully, when a detail is wrong or missing, it's wrong or missing. The reader's imagination doesn't add the detail in. . . . Then, of course, there's the time issue. Those pages took me forever, and gave me major hand/arm pain. So when I was living in Mexico, I . . . plunged into a period of doing exercises and research to develop a new way to draw. The result was a style that implies more than it shows, and so, ironically, feels more 'true' to the scene I want to draw than a style that is more specific. It seems to me that the reader's imagination is able to fill in the gaps more effectively than I ever could."

In 1999 Abel was contacted by Ira Glass, the host of the popular Public Radio International program *This American Life*. Glass had not seen much of Abel's work but had clipped and saved one of her stories years earlier; wanting to speak with her about a possible assignment, and discovering that she no longer lived in Chicago, he found her telephone number in Mexico and called her with his offer. The result was *Radio: An Illustrated Guide*, a 32-page "inside" look at radio. Illustrated by Abel, and co-written by Abel and Glass, the book was used as a premium for *This American Life*'s winter 2000 fund-raising drive. Abel told Greg Stump for *Comics Journal* #270 (August 2005) about the work, "That was a good and satisfying book, but it took me three or four months of back-breaking work to put it together. Not that I wouldn't do it again for the right piece, but it would have to fall in my lap. I'm not looking for it."

In 2000 Madden and Abel moved back to the U.S. They were married that July and moved to Brooklyn, New York, later in the year. Also in 2000 Fantagraphics Books published *Mirror, Window*, a volume of *Artbabe* stories. Eric Searleman wrote for the *Arizona Republic* (December 7, 2000), "Whether she's working in fiction or nonfiction, Abel is struggling to make sense of the cold, uncaring universe. Her best story brings together two women who, despite being friends, seem to live in different worlds. In another story, she playfully juggles the points of view of her two love-smitten protagonists. One thing is certain: The universe is a better place when Abel is at her drawing table." In 2001 Fantagraphics Books brought out *Soundtrack*, a compilation of Abel's earlier work.

That same year Abel began teaching in the Cartooning Department at the School of Visual Arts in New York City; she told Joy Press in 2006 that women make up 30 to 40 percent of her students.

"My age and above," Abel said, "I could count the active female cartoonists on one hand. But there are a *ton* of young women starting now." She told Stump, "I'm very proud to say that my students do not come out of my class looking like me, none of them have. They come out looking more like *themselves*. I think I can teach them a lot of stuff. I can't teach them to be artists; I can't teach them the central spark."

From 2001 to 2005 Fantagraphics published Abel's comic *La Perdida* in serialized form. *La Perdida* follows the adventures of an American woman, Carla, who moves to Mexico City on a journey of self-discovery. For that series Abel employed the new, more fluid style of drawing she had developed during her time in Mexico. In 2002 Abel won the Harvey Award for Best New Series for *La Perdida*. In 2006 *La Perdida* was published in a single volume by Pantheon.

Life Sucks, a graphic novel co-written by Abel and Gabriel Soria and illustrated by Martin Pleece, was slated for publication by First Second in early 2008. Abel's first prose novel for teens, *Carmina*, will be published by HarperCollins. Abel and her husband, Matt Madden, are writing a textbook about creating comics. The couple live in Brooklyn.

—S.J.D.

Suggested Reading: *Comics Journal* #190 Sep. 2006, #270 Aug. 2005; JessicaAbel.com; *Village Voice* (on-line) Mar. 21, 2006

Selected Books: *Radio: An Illustrated Guide*, 1999; *Mirror, Window*, 2000; *Soundtrack*, 2001; *La Perdida*, 2006

Acocella, Joan

Apr. 13, 1945– Writer; critic

Address: The New Yorker, 4 Times Sq., New York, NY 10036-6592

Joan Acocella is best known as a dance critic, a label that belies the widely varied topics about which she has written. While covering dance for numerous publications, including, since 1998, the *New Yorker*, Acocella has also produced acclaimed works of biography and literary criticism as well as volumes on psychology and psychiatry. *Mark Morris* (1993), a biography of the dancer and choreographer, was followed in 1999 by *Creating Hysteria: Women and Multiple Personality Disorder*, in which Acocella scrutinized the trend among psychotherapists of arriving at diagnoses of multiple-personality disorder. *Willa Cather and the Politics of Criticism* (2000) represents Acocella's attempt to point out the timeless felicities of Cather's fiction while engaging those academics

Joyce Ravid, courtesy of Random House
Joan Acocella

who have alternately elevated and denigrated Cather as a feminist, rightist, or lesbian writer. For *Twenty-Eight Artists and Two Saints*, a volume published in early 2007, Acocella gathered many of the essays she had published in the *New Yorker* and the *New York Review of Books*. The collection's 31 pieces shed light on the lives and work of such comparatively obscure writers as Marguerite Yourcenar, Italo Svevo, Joseph Roth, and Stefan Zweig; provided portraits of geniuses in the field of dance, including Vaslav Nijinsky, Mikhail Baryshnikov, Suzanne Farrell, and George Balanchine; and sought to correct what Acocella regards as the mistaken views of biographers of such figures as the writer Primo Levi. Kathryn Harrison, writing for the *New York Times Book Review* (February 16, 2007), called Acocella's essays "highly readable" and added that Acocella is "knowledgeable without being a show-off, meticulous in her research and energetically conversational."

The writer was born Joan Ross on April 13, 1945 in San Francisco, California, to Florence (Hartzell) Ross and Arnold Marcus Ross. She grew up in nearby Oakland and was educated at the University of California at Berkeley, receiving her B.A. degree in English in 1966. In that year she married Nicholas Acocella (they were divorced in 1991), using his surname from then on in her professional capacity. In 1968 she and her husband moved to New York City; she continued her education at Rutgers University, in New Brunswick, New Jersey, studying comparative literature. (She received her Ph.D. degree in 1983.) In New York she was exposed to the choreographer George Balanchine's work for the New York City Ballet, which, as she told Alden Mudge for *BookPage* (February 2007,

on-line), was "a transforming experience" for her. "I saw the works of Balanchine when he was healthy and when the company was simply wonderful, and I really lost my heart." She then made what she described to Mudge as her "swerve to dance," or, rather, dance writing, a field she entered largely self-taught. She lectured in literature only briefly, as a teaching assistant at Rutgers, before teaching dance history and dance criticism. Subsequently—in part because "I had a child, we needed money," as she told Mudge—Acocella turned to journalism. While teaching intermittently at the State University of New York at Purchase in the 1980s, she served as an editor at *Dance Magazine* from 1983 to 1985 and as a dance critic for *7 Days* from 1988 to 1990. She wrote for the New York *Daily News* for three years in the early 1990s and covered dance for the London *Financial Times* from 1993 to 1996. From there she moved to the *Wall Street Journal* in 1996 and to the *New Yorker* in 1998.

While writing chiefly about dance for those high-profile publications, Acocella devoted time to others of her eclectic interests, as well. Her first book, published in 1977, was *Abnormal Psychology: Current Perspectives*, co-written with James F. Calhoun and Leonard D. Goodstein. Acocella and Calhoun also collaborated on *The Psychology of Adjustment and Human Relationships* (1978). *Physical Anthropology and Archeology*, which she co-authored with Clifford J. Jolly and Fred Plog, appeared in 1979. In the mid-1980s Acocella—by then a recognized dance critic—collaborated with Lynn Ager Wallen to edit *The Spectrum of World Dance: Tradition, Transition, and Innovation: Selected Papers from the 1982 and 1983 CORD [Congress of Research in Dance] Conferences* (1987). In 1988 she contributed to *The Art of Enchantment: Diaghilev's Ballets Russes, 1909–1929*, compiled by Nancy Van Norman Baer. The practice of dance criticism was the topic of *Andre Levinson on Dance: Writings from Paris in the Twenties*, edited by Acocella and Lynn Garafola and published in 1991.

Acocella's first book-length solo venture as a dance writer was *Mark Morris*, a biography and appreciation of the noted choreographer, which appeared in 1993. The book won unanimous praise. Janice Berman declared in *Newsday* (December 5, 1993), "Acocella comes quite close to giving us a key to Morris' dances. She builds her theory on the time he spent as a young dancer with a folk-dance company called Koleda. It was like a '60s commune. The emphasis was on the community; individual differences didn't matter when the dancing was going on. . . . Acocella sees Morris' dances not as mere choreography but as the microcosm of an ideal, and when she says of Morris, 'It's wonderful to think what he may do,' readers will be hard put not to share her enthusiasm." The "mere fact that Mr. Morris could inspire a book as good as this is a credit to him," John Rockwell wrote for the *New York Times Book Review* (January 23, 1994).

Rockwell called *Mark Morris* "a deft blend of biography, dance history, backstage detail and critical analysis. . . . What is especially impressive in Ms. Acocella's book is how everything in it supports everything else; there is no waste. Biographical information contributes to analytical insight. Particular dances are discussed in themselves, but also in relation to larger themes in Mark Morris's work and times: his spirituality and simultaneous celebrations of the body; his preference for the love of community over heterosexual monogamy as idealized in the balletic pas de deux; his unusual involvement with text, narrative and the inner workings of music; and his shifting balance between irony and sincerity. The author maintains a tempered tone, a prevailing judicious adoration that only occasionally breaks into outright rapture." Margo Jefferson noted for the *New York Times* (January 5, 1994) that Acocella "navigates the life" of Morris "competently and the work terrifically."

The Diary of Vaslav Nijinsky (1999), edited and with an introduction by Acocella, offered a view into the mental deterioration of the great Russian dancer and choreographer. Nijinsky, world famous in the early part of the 20th century, partnered with Sergei Diaghilev—in life as well as in the creation of radical ballets—to bring Russian ballet to its greatest modernist flowering. Then, in 1919, married and with a small child, Nijinsky left the world of dance. He wrote continuously for nearly two months, chronicling his descent into what was diagnosed as schizophrenia, and was then hospitalized almost until the time of his death, in 1950. Nijinsky's wife, Romola, who published her husband's diary in 1936, had a vested interest in cutting and reshaping it to create a more favorable portrait of herself and to blur the truth about Nijinsky's sexuality. With her annotations and introduction to Kyril FitzLyon's translation of the unexpurgated diary, Acocella presented what she called, according to Janice Ross in the *Los Angeles Times Book Review* (March 14, 1999), "the only sustained, on-the-spot (not retrospective) written account, by a major artist, of the experience of entering psychosis." Ross concluded that "with Nijinsky's diary at last available in its entirety, in a richly literate and annotated translation, his final tortured effort to communicate his inner demons is complete. Acocella is a masterful midwife to this extraordinary tale."

In *Creating Hysteria: Women and Multiple Personality Disorder* (1999), Acocella used her background in psychology, acquired through writing textbooks in the field, and her critical acumen to scrutinize the newly popular diagnosis of multiple-personality disorder and the recovered-memory movement in psychotherapy—the latter a form of therapy whose practitioners seek to uncover blocked memories of childhood sexual abuse. In the 1980s the idea that childhood sexual abuse was so painful that it caused its victims to "dissociate" themselves from the memories, and therefore develop multiple personalities, became prevalent among some groups of therapists. *Creating Hysteria* is a strong polemic against those therapists, whose patients have often been women of lower socioeconomic status who are easily hypnotized. Those women "almost always meet criteria for other, better-established mental disorders. M.P.D. [multiple-personality disorder] provides a particular form for suffering, one that is more compelling, for both patient and doctor, than run-of-the mill depression or anxiety, " the psychiatrist and writer Peter Kramer noted in his assessment of *Creating Hysteria* for the *New York Times Book Review* (November 21, 1999). "Acocella traces that form to the 1974 best seller *Sybil*, an account of . . . early sexual abuse in the case of a housewife with 16 alters [alternative personalities]." The psychiatrist who treated "Sybil," rather than merely observing her personalities, seems to have pushed her into acting them out, as Kramer noted. "Acocella identifies psychiatrists who played a lead role in this fiasco," he added. "But her story's hero is also a psychiatrist . . . who wrote: 'Close the dissociation services and disperse the patients to general psychiatric units. Ignore the alters. . . . Pay attention to real present problems.'" Kramer concluded, "Acocella sees the furor as having lessened the pressure for substantive solutions to the problems of disadvantaged women and children. For her, the crucial target is not sexual abuse but poverty." The *Publishers Weekly* (August 9, 1999) reviewers, Jeff Zaleski and Paul Gediman, noted that "Acocella builds a highly convincing case against mental health professionals whom she portrays as exploiters who prompted the mass hysteria and witchhunts that have resulted from recovered memory syndrome and the MPD diagnosis. . . . However, she proceeds to undercut her own argument by destroying all in her path: the child-protection movement, the credibility of women who say they were abused as children, the self-help (AA) movement, the feminist movement, insight-based psychotherapy, 'New-Age spirituality' and postmodern theory are just a few of the victims of her sweep."

Acocella has been viewed not only as a master critic of dance but also as a master of the analysis of criticism itself. She reinforced that view with the 94-page *Willa Cather and the Politics of Criticism* (2000), in which she attempted to restore the American writer of the title to a place of honor in the literary canon, by pointing out the beauty of her style and of her conscious restraint. The book, which grew from an article Acocella had published in 1995 in the *New Yorker*, is "both a brisk appreciation of Cather's artistic achievement and a stern, even cutting assault on modern Cather scholarship . . . ," according to Terry Castle, writing for the *London Review of Books* (December 14, 2000). "The original article was a fairly devastating attack on the various ways in which Cather—in Acocella's view the only American novelist besides [Henry] James to rival Tolstoy and Flaubert for beauty of style and moral depth—had been manhandled by contemporary academic critics." Discussing the original essay, Castle credited Acocella with having "cut through the [academics'] verbiage to offer a purified, if somewhat old-fashioned, model of literary appreciation: one distinguished, like Cather's fiction itself, by modesty, tact and unshakable common sense." Reviewing the expanded work, Castle called Acocella a "marvelous, canny writer" but faulted her for going too far in attacking scholars who had embraced or disdained Cather for extraliterary and perhaps misguided reasons—from those who accused her of being oblivious to social forces to those seeking to "out" her as a lesbian. "Acocella swells with righteous anger at those theory-mad pigeonholers . . . ," Terry Teachout wrote in an assessment of the book for the *National Review* (March 20, 2000). "Out of that anger, she has made this eloquent, wholly admirable book."

Acocella collected essays originally published in the *New Yorker* and the *New York Review of Books* for her volume *Twenty-Eight Artists and Two Saints* (2007). The 31 pieces in the book include essays on nine figures from the world of dance, among them Jerome Robbins, Martha Graham, Bob Fosse, and Twyla Tharp; 17 writers, including Italo Svevo, Stefan Zweig, Simone de Beauvoir, Primo Levi, Saul Bellow, and Susan Sontag; the biblical figure Mary Magdalene; and the 15th-century French freedom fighter Joan of Arc. (The two last-named figures are the saints of the title.) Acocella noted in her introduction to the book, as quoted by Joyce Carol Oates in the *New York Review of Books* (March 15, 2007, on-line), that a theme running through the essays is "difficulty, hardship"; the individuals under examination demonstrate that while "many people are brilliant," what "allows genius to flower" is—contrary to the beliefs of some—"not neurosis, but its opposite, 'ego strength,' meaning (among other things) ordinary, Sunday-school virtues such as tenacity and above all the ability to survive disappointment." "Acocella casts a sympathetic eye on the lives and misfortunes of her subjects, one by one, and tries to trace connections to their work," Julie Phillips commented for *Newsday* (February 4, 2007). "Basically, that's the project of biography, and in fact these essays, like all good biographies, aren't really held together by theories. The threads that run through them are Acocella's intelligence, intellectual curiosity, empathy and wonderful prose." Oates called the essays in the book "exemplary," adding, "Acocella's enthusiasm for certain of her subjects makes the reader want to seek out their work immediately, to read and to reread."

Despite the eclecticism reflected in her body of work, Acocella remains best known as a dance critic. In one piece representative of her work for the *New Yorker*, she wrote for the November 22, 1999 issue, "However New York City Ballet, founded by George Balanchine, is doing with his work (often, miserably), several other companies, not founded by him, are doing very well. Last month, Miami City Ballet brought to Newark's New Jersey Performing Arts Center three Balanchine ballets, including the evening-length *Jewels*, and suddenly we saw again the thing that N.Y.C.B. had in the past and doesn't have in the present—that shivering hyper-aliveness. You look at it, and your hair stands on end." In another, discussing the state of the Bolshoi Ballet, she wrote for the August 7, 2000 issue, "Of the three young men who led the Lincoln Center season, not one is a finished classical dancer. Sergei Filin, though handsome and stylish, needs to get a lot stronger. Andre Uvarov . . . doesn't plié when he lands. Nikolai Tsiskaridze, a big, grinning Georgian, has a lovely jump, but in smaller steps he takes a long time to figure out where his feet are supposed to be." For the March 18, 2002 issue, she wrote about Mark Morris, "Morris's concern with music has resulted in some choreographic curiosities. All his work hews close to its music, but every now and then he creates a piece so faithful to its score, and so devoid of any other reference, as to deserve the term 'music visualization' . . . . As far as I can tell, Morris's effort, in his music-visualization pieces, simply to reflect the score is not an evasion of emotion; it is an act of deference to the emotion contained in the music."

In 2002 Acocella participated in a panel discussion, called "Criticism and/or Journalism," which was sponsored by Columbia University's National Arts Journalism Program. During the discussion she expressed her wish that "when I'd started out" as a critic, "I hadn't been so mean and so arrogant. I was so insecure, and I really didn't know what the hell I was talking about. I'm from the one art that is not taught in the university. I was a literature student, and I was self-taught in dance. But it's one thing to read a lot of dance history, and another thing to go and see the Alvin Ailey [company] or the Merce Cunningham company for the first time and will yourself to pretend that you can write about this. You read others—of course, the reason I became a dance critic was I read dance critics who I admired. But in the beginning, I was really mean, because I was trying to have authority. . . . Sometimes I think I was more fun then. Wooh, the things I said! I was really a tough cookie."

Joan Acocella lives in New York. She has one son, Bartholomew Acocella.

—S.Y.

Suggested Reading: *Atlanta Journal-Constitution* L p11 Mar. 7, 1999; *Book Page* (on-line) Feb. 2007; *Boston Globe* E p1 Feb. 14, 1999; *London Review of Books* (on-line) Dec. 14, 2000; *Los Angeles Times Book Review* p12 Mar. 14, 1999; *National Review* (on-line) Mar. 20, 2000; *New York Review of Books* p31+ Mar. 15, 2007; *New York Times* C p21 Jan. 5, 1994; *New York Times Book Review* p9 Jan. 22, 1994, p82 Nov. 21, 1999, p23 Apr. 2, 2000, (on-line) Feb. 16, 2007; *Newsday* C p30 Feb. 4, 2007; *Salmagundi* p90+ Fall 2002

Selected Books: *Mark Morris*, 1993; *Creating Hysteria: Women and Multiple Personality Disorder*, 1999; *Willa Cather and the Politics of Criticism*, 2000; *Twenty-Eight Artists and Two Saints: Essays*, 2007; as editor—*The Spectrum of World Dance: Tradition, Transition, and Innovation: Selected Papers from the 1982 and 1983 CORD Conferences* (with Lynn Ager Wallen), 1987; *Andre Levinson on Dance: Writings from Paris in the Twenties* (with Lynn Garafola), 1991; *The Diary of Vaslav Nijinsky*, 1999

David Bohrer, courtesy of the White House

Addington, David S.

Jan. 22, 1957– Lawyer; vice-presidential aide

Address: The White House, 1600 Pennsylvania Ave., N.W., Washington, DC 20500

In the years since the administration of George W. Bush began coming under harsh criticism for what are widely considered as abuses of executive power, a relatively little-known White House lawyer, David S. Addington, has emerged as the person many hold most responsible for promoting those abuses. A career government lawyer who has never run for elective office, Addington has worked closely with Vice President Richard B. "Dick" Cheney since the 1980s, when the latter was the ranking Republican on a House of Representatives select committee investigating the Iran-Contra scandal. In 2005 Addington became Cheney's chief of staff, succeeding I. Lewis "Scooter" Libby, who resigned after he was charged with perjury and ob-

struction of justice in a matter involving the leak of classified information—specifically, the identity of Valerie Plame, who was then working for the Central Intelligence Agency (CIA). Since the terrorist attacks of September 11, 2001, according to knowledgeable sources, Addington has been the dominant member of an insular group of top Bush administration officials overseeing the U.S.'s controversial counterterrorism measures, among them the indefinite detention of terror suspects who have no legal recourse, aggressive interrogation methods (including what the Geneva Conventions define as torture), and warrantless wiretapping of domestic phone calls. Addington's unusual influence may stem from his being an expert on national-security law in an administration that includes few other lawyers. He is also a dedicated advocate of heightened executive power, and together with Cheney he has sought to return greater authority to that branch of the government, in the belief that it has been increasingly marginalized since the Vietnam War era. Jane Harman, a ranking Democrat on the House Intelligence Committee, speaking of Cheney and Addington, told Jane Mayer for the *New Yorker* (July 3, 2006),"They're focused on restoring the Nixon Presidency. They've persuaded themselves that, following Nixon, things went all wrong."

Addington is also known for his belief that the executive branch has the right, if not the duty, to conduct much of its work in secrecy. He insists on maintaining his personal privacy as well. He does not give interviews and refuses to be photographed for news stories. Colleagues of his told Mayer that, as she wrote, he "keeps the door of his office locked at all times . . . because of the national-security documents in his files." "David can be less than civilized. He can be extremely unpleasant," an unnamed official told Chitra Ragavan for *U.S. News & World Report* (May 29, 2006), and a former high-ranking national security lawyer told Mayer, "He's a bully, pure and simple." "He's powerful because people know he speaks for the Vice-President, and because he's an extremely smart, creative, and aggressive public official," a former White House lawyer, Bradford Berenson, told Mayer. "Some engage in bureaucratic infighting using slaps. Some use knives. David falls into the latter category." Addington famously carries in one of his pockets a copy of the Constitution and sometimes cites it in arguments.

The youngest of the four children and the only son of Jerry Addington, an electrical engineer with the U.S. Army, and Eleanore Addington, a homemaker, David S. Addington was born on January 22, 1957 in Washington, D.C. "A traditional Catholic military family," as Mayer wrote, the Addingtons moved often; for a while they lived in Saudi Arabia. Jerry Addington retired from the military with the rank of brigadier general in 1970, when David was 13, and, after settling in a middle-class community in Albuquerque, New Mexico, he began teaching middle-school math. David Addington attended Sandia High School, in Albuquerque. His high-school friend Leonard Napolitano (whose sister, Janet, is currently the Democratic governor of Arizona) told Mayer, "I don't think that in high school David was a believer in the divine right of kings." He added, though, that Addington was "always conservative." Napolitano also said that he and Addington were "the brains, or nerds" in school and were fond of all-night poker sessions; unlike many of their peers, they were not out to "challenge authority." Irwin Hoffman, one of Addington's history teachers, told Mayer that Addington believed that the U.S. "should have stayed and won the Vietnam War, despite the fact that we were losing." He also said, "The boy seemed terribly, terribly bright. He wrote well, and he was very verbal, not at all reluctant to express his opinions. He was pleasant and quite handsome. He also had a very strong sarcastic streak. He was scornful of anyone who said anything that was naïve, or less than bright. His sneers were almost palpable." Many have speculated that Addington's personal crusade to increase the power of the president stems from his reaction to events that occurred around the time he graduated from high school, when a series of congressional hearings made public various legal transgressions of the Central Intelligence Agency (CIA) and the administration of President Richard Nixon. (The hearings followed events triggered by the Watergate scandal, which refers to break-ins by Republican operatives at the Democratic National Committee headquarters at the Watergate complex, a mixture of commercial and residential spaces in Washington, D.C.) At that time, Mayer wrote, "Congress passed a series of measures aimed at reinvigorating the system of checks and balances, including an expanded Freedom of Information Act and the Foreign Intelligence Surveillance Act, the law requiring judicial review before foreign suspects inside the country could be wiretapped." In addition, congressional oversight of the CIA was greatly increased, with the creation of the House and the Senate Intelligence Committees.

After Addington graduated from high school, in 1974, he briefly attended the U.S. Naval Academy, in Annapolis, Maryland. He quit before he completed his freshman year, because "the academy wasn't academically challenging enough for him," as Napolitano told Mayer. He next enrolled at Georgetown University, in Washington, D.C., where in 1978 he earned a B.S. degree summa cum laude from the Edmund A. Walsh School of Foreign Service. In 1981 he received a J.D. degree from the Duke University School of Law, in Durham, North Carolina. At around that time Addington married his first wife, Linda Werling, who was then a graduate student in pharmacology; the couple later divorced.

Addington began his professional life as an assistant general counsel at the CIA. He spent two years there, devoting his efforts to "curtailing the ability of Congress to interfere in intelligence gath-

ering," as Mayer wrote. He then worked on Capitol Hill as counsel to the House Intelligence and Foreign Affairs Committees. In that position he met Cheney, who was then a congressman from Wyoming and a member of the Intelligence Committee. Cheney shared Addington's views about the erosion of executive power as a result of Watergate and the Vietnam War. As the ranking Republican staff member on the congressional committee investigating the Iran-Contra affair, Cheney commissioned a report on President Ronald Reagan's activities. (Members of the Reagan administration, defying the will of Congress, had secretly sold arms to Iran, an enemy of the U.S., and used the proceeds to support the Contras, an insurgent, anti-Communist guerrilla group who were fighting the leftist, Sandinista government in Nicaragua.) Addington helped write that document—the Minority Report (1987)—which Mayer described as "scholarly-sounding but politically outlandish." It expressed the view, held by Addington and Cheney, that the law prohibiting aid to the Nicaraguan contras was unconstitutional and improperly interfered with executive power. "The report . . . defended the legality of ignoring congressional intelligence oversight," Mayer wrote, "arguing that 'the President has the Constitutional and statutory authority to withhold notifying Congress of covert actions under rare conditions.'" Cheney has since cited the report as a reference for those who wish to understand his views regarding the importance of executive power. According to Jane Mayer, many consitutional experts question Addington's interpretation of the parts of the Constitution that deal with the powers of the president.

Starting in 1987 Addington served as a special assistant to President Reagan for about one year and as his deputy assistant for roughly another year. In 1989, after Reagan's successor in the White House, George H. W. Bush, named Cheney secretary of defense, Cheney hired Addington as his special assistant and later named him deputy secretary of defense. In 1992 Addington assumed the job of general counsel—chief lawyer—for the Defense Department, a position in which he was regarded by many as Cheney's "gatekeeper," a zealous defender of the secretary's interests. David Gribben, who at that time served as Cheney's chief of staff, told Ragavan that Addington "became the most powerful staffer in the Pentagon" (the Defense Department's headquarters), reviewing all the papers that passed to and from Cheney and the deputy defense secretary (the department's second-highest-ranking official), Donald J. Atwood. "Using a red felt-tipped pen, he covered his colleagues' memos with comments before returning them for rewrites," Mayer wrote; she quoted a former military official who had worked with him as saying, "His editing invariably made arguments sharper, smarter, and more firm in their defense of Cheney's executive powers." During that period Addington became embroiled in a power struggle with the judge advocates general (JAGs). (Each arm of the U.S. military—the army, air force, navy and marine corps, and coast guard—has a judge advocate general, who is both an officer and a lawyer, and a staff of officer/lawyers, who provide the secretary of the relevant military branch with legal advice in all matters not under the purview of the general counsel to that branch.) The power struggle began when Addington wrote a memo requiring each JAG to report to the general counsel of his service branch. A retired navy JAG, Rear Admiral Don Guter, told Ragavan that the JAGs opposed a requirement that "came under the rubric of civilian control of the military. It's centralization. It's control." The JAGs, aided by Congress, successfully fought the measure. Addington responded with a memo stipulating that the general counsel of each service, not the JAGs, had the authority to issue final legal opinions. When Addington joined the administration of George W. Bush, Guter warned his fellow JAGs that the conflict would flare up again. Indeed, Addington and his associates in the administration have found some of their harshest opposition among the JAGs, who have been "marginalized from the decision making on military tribunals and detainee treatment policies," as Ragavan wrote.

During the presidency of Bill Clinton, from 1993 to 2001, Addington worked as a lawyer for several firms and organizations, among them the American Trucking Associations, in all of which he held "high-level management positions," according to his biography on American President.org. In the mid-1990s he also headed a group set up to explore the possibility of Cheney's running for president. After the election of Bush and Cheney in 2000, Mayer wrote, "Addington helped oversee the transition, setting up the most powerful Vice-Presidency in America's history"—one in which, as Addington reportedly told Napolitano, the president and vice president would be symbolically united in a single "executive office." As Cheney's legal counsel, Mayer wrote, Addington arranged that "virtually all important documents relating to national-security matters were seen by the Vice-President's office." Addington still held considerable sway at the Defense Department, and he "helped his protégé William J. Haynes secure the position of general counsel" there, according to Mayer. A former White House lawyer told Mayer, "It's obvious that Addington runs the whole operation" at the Pentagon's legal office.

Nancy P. Dorn, who served Cheney as an assistant for legislative affairs before she became the deputy director of the Office of Management and Budget, in 2002, told Ragavan that Addington and Cheney are so close that they "hardly even have to communicate with words." In 2001 Cheney convened at the White House a series of secret meetings of an energy task force, attended by influential energy-industry lobbyists. The lobbyists participated in the drafting of energy policy, and Cheney "suggest[ed] a package of tax breaks and other incentives for their companies," as Charlie Savage

wrote for the *Boston Globe* (November 26, 2006). The meetings led to an outcry from environmentalists, who were left out of them. Cheney and Addington rebuffed attempts by members of Congress and watchdog groups to obtain the names of the lobbyists and records of what was discussed at the meetings; in legal battles that reached as high as the U.S. Supreme Court, the refusal of Cheney and Addington to release any information was upheld. In letters to David Walker, the comptroller general of the Government Accountability Office, Congress's investigative arm, Addington asserted that it was important that neither Congress nor the courts "intrude into the heart of executive deliberations," to avoid suppressing the "candor" needed for "effective government," according to Ragavan.

Addington is best known for his role in the creation of the post–September 11 national-security measures that gave unprecedented control in a broad sphere to the executive branch. "In the months after the attacks," Ragavan wrote, "the White House made three crucial decisions: to keep Congress out of the loop on major policy decisions like the creation of military commissions, to interpret laws as narrowly as possible, and to confine decision making to a small, trusted circle." That circle included Addington; the current attorney general, Alberto Gonzales; Gonzales's deputies Timothy Flanigan and David Leitch; William Haynes; and John Yoo, a lawyer for the Justice Department's Office of Legal Counsel (OLC). "Traditionally, OLC staffers tend to be longtime career lawyers who ensure that the tenor of the legal opinions rendered is devoid of political overtones," Ragavan wrote. "After 9/11, however, OLC lawyers drafted a series of opinions that many career Justice Department attorneys viewed as having traduced the office's heritage of nuanced, almost scholarly, legal analysis. Addington, according to several Justice Department officials, helped Yoo shape some of the most controversial OLC memos."

"It seems clear," Mayer wrote, "that Addington was able to promote vast executive powers after September 11th in part because he and Cheney had been laying the political groundwork for years." After September 11, 2001 the Pentagon and Joint Chiefs of Staff suggested that authorization of military force in response to the terrorist attacks be limited to actions against the terrorist organization Al Qaeda and its offshoots, as well as Afghanistan's Taliban regime. Scott Horton, the chairman of the Committee on International Law of the Bar Association of the City of New York and an expert on the interrogation of terror suspects, told Ragavan that Addington and Cheney wanted the meaning of "authorization of military force" to be "defined more broadly, because it provided the trigger for this radical redefinition of presidential power." In response to the Pentagon and Joint Chiefs' suggestion, the OLC issued a memo asserting that Congress could not "place any limits on the president's determinations as to any terrorist threat, the amount of military force to be used in response, or the method, timing, and nature of the response." The statement, which, according to many observers, clearly showed Addington's influence, was written by Yoo, who would draft several such memos and would also make controversial statements affirming the legality of the torture of, and denial of rights to, "unlawful enemy combatants"—the broad label with which the administration identified its detainees.

The handling of war criminals became one of the most controversial of the policy issues that arose following September 11. In discussions about it held by government officials, Timothy Flanigan, one of Gonzales's deputies, represented the Addington/Cheney inner circle. After an interagency group within the administration, led by Pierre Prosper, the State Department's ambassador at large for war-crimes issues, examined various options for the treatment of those captured in battle, Ragavan wrote, Flanigan "wrested away the group's work product," which dealt with military tribunals—military courts designed to try members of enemy forces during wartime. With Addington's help, Ragavan continued, "Flanigan wrote a draft order for the White House, based on an OLC memo arguing that the president had the legal authority to authorize military commissions—period." Bush thus felt empowered to authorize the secretary of defense to create military commissions applying to all people characterized as "unlawful enemy combatants." According to Ragavan, "The Pentagon's entire corps of JAG officers was kept in the dark" about the creation of the commissions, as were Prosper, Condoleezza Rice, who was then the national security adviser, and Colin L. Powell, who was then secretary of state. Furthermore, Addington's circle rejected the idea, proposed by Prosper and others, that the creation of military commissions be subject to an independent review, possibly led by civilians, to allay "the distrust of European governments toward all things military," in Ragavan's words, and some of the public's uneasiness regarding the administration's controversial actions.

In early 2002 Flanigan wrote a memo, reportedly with Addington's input and signed by Gonzales, expressing the view that the war on terrorism represented a "new paradigm," as quoted by Ragavan, that "render[ed] obsolete" the Geneva Conventions' rules regarding the treatment of prisoners—including limits on the handling of interrogations and other legal protections the Conventions afforded prisoners. Addington and Yoo also produced a second memo, in August 2002, which the head of the OLC, Jay Bybee, signed. The memo interpreted a prior U.S. law that both prohibited torture and implemented the U.N. Convention Against Torture, deeming those precedents to be "unwarranted infringement on executive-branch power," according to Ragavan. Ragavan wrote that in the memo, "the three lawyers agreed that the president could override or ignore the statute, as needed, to protect national security. And they concluded that those who engaged in conduct that might violate the law might nevertheless have an appropriate legal defense based on 'self-defense' or 'necessity.'" That unprecedented defiance of the torture statute sparked consternation among Justice Department lawyers, many of whom were politically conservative. When Jack Goldsmith replaced Bybee as head of the OLC, in 2003, the memo that Bybee had signed was withdrawn. Instead, according to Ragavan, another OLC lawyer, Daniel Levin, drafted a more limited legal opinion "that scrapped whole sections of the Bybee memo." Levin distributed this memo more widely than Bybee had and revised it along lines suggested by Justice Department officials and State Department lawyers.

Goldsmith, determined to return the OLC to "its more traditional role" as a provider of nonpartisan legal advise, as a former Justice Department attorney told Ragavan, insisted that more consultation among agencies was necessary, and he ordered that all the "war on terror" memos written by Addington, Bybee, and others be reviewed. Goldsmith, along with the Justice Department lawyer Patrick Philbin (both of whom Ragavan described as "extremely conservative and pro-presidential power"), also expressed doubts about the legality of the National Security Agency's conducting of electronic surveillance inside the United States without taking the precautions mandated by the Foreign Intelligence Surveillance Act—another controversial activity that President Bush approved after the events of September 11. According to Ragavan, Addington and other conservative administration lawyers argued that Bush "had the authority to order the secret surveillance under his constitutional authority as commander in chief and by the authority granted to him by Congress's use-of-force resolution before the invasion of Afghanistan." But Goldsmith and Philbin, Ragavan wrote, "found Addington and Yoo's legal analysis and opinions to be sloppy and overreaching." Administration officials, Ragavan, wrote, reported to her that Addington, rejecting that finding, "excoriated Goldsmith over what he viewed as his betrayal."

Most recently, Addington has been identified as chiefly responsible for the Bush administration's frequent use of signing statements—statements added to bills passed by Congress and signed by the president, in which, as an alternative to vetoing the legislation (which would make it possible for Congress to override the vetoes), the president offers his own interpretation of what the laws stipulate. "The statements assert the president's right to ignore the laws because they conflict with his interpretation of the Constitution," Charlie Savage wrote for the Boston Globe (May 28, 2006). Signing statements were originally created to clarify a president's understanding of ambiguous laws, but in the Bush administration they have reportedly been used to circumvent, change, or abandon specific parts of laws. As of May 2006 Bush had appended more than 750 signing statements since he entered the White House, significantly more than all previous presidents combined, while he has not issued a single veto. In effect, he has used signing statements as line-item vetoes—that is, a veto of part of a piece of legislation rather than the whole piece, a step that the Supreme Court has ruled unconstitutional.

Addington lives with his second wife, Cynthia, and their three daughters in Arlington, Virginia. According to Jane Mayer, he is "a tall, bespectacled man . . . who has a thickening middle, a thatch of gray hair, and a trim gray beard, which gives him the look of a sea captain." He has been described as courteous and family-oriented and as having a fiery temper. Unlike most other high-ranking administration officials, who are chauffeured to work, he commutes to his job using the Metro train. According to Chitra Ragavan, he has often spent weekends "cheering at his daughters' soccer games."

—M.B.

Suggested Reading: *Boston Globe* A p1+ May 28, 2006; *New York Times* A p22 Nov. 2, 2005; *New Yorker* (on-line) July 3, 2006; *U.S. News & World Report* (on-line) May 29, 2006

Michael Buckner/Getty Images

Agatston, Arthur

Jan. 22, 1947– Cardiologist; writer; nutrition researcher

Address: c/o Author Mail, Rodale, 33 E. Minor St., Emmaus, PA 18098

"If a patient of mine has a heart attack, I ask myself: 'What have I done wrong?,'" the cardiologist, nutrition researcher, and writer Arthur Agatston said to John Tanasychuk for the Fort Lauderdale, Florida, *Sun-Sentinel* (April 11, 2004). For the past several years, the Miami Beach, Florida–based Agatston has been widely known as the "South Beach diet doctor," a moniker that refers to the eating regimen he created with the help of the dietitian and nutritionist Marie Almon, a colleague of his at Miami's Mount Sinai Medical Center, where he has headed the division of noninvasive cardiology for many years. The label also links him with his books, all of which contain the words "South Beach diet" in their titles. He wrote them, as he has often said, not to enable people to look good in bathing suits or drop a clothing size or two in a few weeks but to help them avoid getting heart disease or having strokes. The first of Agatston's books, *The South Beach Diet: The Delicious, Doctor-Designed, Foolproof Plan for Fast and Healthy Weight Loss* (2003), has sold more than nine million copies and has been translated into some three dozen languages. Among his other books are cookbooks (one of which landed on Amazon.com's top-five sellers before its publication date), a manual for maintaining a healthy heart, and a guide to "good" fats and "good" carbohydrates (carbs, as they are called colloquially), which rank low on the so-called glycemic index, a scale, devised by a Canadian scientist, that Agatston used in developing the South Beach diet. "It has been a great revelation to me that weight loss is not about low carbs or low fat, but the right carbs and the right fats . . . ," Agatston has said, as quoted by *Market Wire* (April 25, 2005). "I am seeing a growing consensus among nutrition experts about the importance of the right carbs like whole grains, fruits and vegetables in the diet, as well as including unsaturated fats like olive and canola oils—all consistent with The South Beach Diet." In 2004 Agatston used part of his earnings from *The South Beach Diet* to set up the Agatston Research Institute, in Miami, whose goal is to find ways to prevent obesity and heart disease. In 2005 he signed a contract with Kraft Foods, which launched a line of South Beach Diet prepared meals and other items. He also maintains the South Beach Diet Web site, which as of early 2007 had half a million subscribers; for a fee of $5.00 per week, they have access to recipes, meal-planning tools, and "private discussions" with on-line nutritionists.

Agatston's approach to healthful eating is not without critics. "What it comes down to," Marion Nestle, a professor of nutrition, food studies, and public health at New York University, said to Abby Goodnough for the *New York Times* (October 7, 2003), "is that this is a standard 1,200- to 1,400-

calorie-a-day diet, so of course people are going to lose weight. I do think there's something to the glycemic index, but I just don't think it's the be-all and end-all, and that it's the root of obesity." In a conversation with Alex Witchel for the *New York Times* (April 14, 2004), Nestle said that the South Beach diet does not address the fundamental issue of overeating. "I don't understand why it's gotten the attention it has," she said. "For the first two weeks it's a standard low-carbohydrate diet. It's very hard to argue with restricting bread, white rice, pasta, soft drinks, all great ideas when trying to lose weight. But the hype is [Agatston] never talks about quantity. It's calories that make a difference in losing weight or not." Robert Eckel, the president of the American Heart Association, told reporters for *People* (April 16, 2004) that Agatston is "respected in cardiology," but he voiced concern that Agatston was "playing into the carbohydrate message." "Obesity is calories—there is nothing magic about carbs versus fat," Eckel added. In response to such criticism, Agatston told Witchel, "When choosing the right fats and the right carbohydrates, in general, the quantity takes care of itself." Thus, he explained, weighing one's foods, as people following certain diets must do, is unnecessary. "Also," he said, "I'm not claiming any unique vision; I've learned a lot from other people. The diet is a consensus of current opinion." He repeated that point in his conversation with Tanasychuk, saying, "The country was ready for [the South Beach diet]. Because a lot of what we have in the book has been percolating through doctors and the public. . . . Everything in there was kind of obvious. If you've really been on top of nutrition, there's nothing in there that's really controversial. There's no substance to the criticism as far as I'm concerned."

Arthur Stephen Agatston was born on January 22, 1947 in New York City to Howard James Agatston and Adell (Paymer) Agatston. He has two sisters and one brother. His paternal grandfather, Sigmund Agatston, had the surname "Agatstein" when he immigrated to the U.S. from Poland; fearing anti-Semitic prejudice, he changed his name when he applied to medical school. He graduated from Columbia Presbyterian Medical School in 1903 and became an ophthalmologist; his innovative technique for early detection of eye disease became standard in the field. Arthur Agatston's father, Howard James Agatston, was also an ophthalmologist; he practiced in Roslyn, New York, on Long Island, where Agatston grew up. "I knew since I was in elementary school that I wanted to be a doctor," Agatston said to Marie Guma-Diaz for the *Miami (Florida) Herald* (December 10, 2005). "I watched my dad's work in the community, and learned to like the doctor-patient relationship. The love for the academic studies came later."

Agatston earned a B.A. degree from the University of Wisconsin at Madison in 1969 and an M.D. degree in 1973 from the New York University (NYU) School of Medicine, in New York City. He completed his internship and residency in internal medicine at the Montefiore Medical Center, which is affiliated with the Albert Einstein College of Medicine, in the New York City borough of the Bronx. From 1977 to 1979 he was a cardiology fellow at NYU Medical Center. The next year he joined the staff of the Mount Sinai Medical Center, in Miami, which is associated with the University of Miami School of Medicine. He has headed the center's division of noninvasive cardiology for many years.

In 1988, with his colleague Warren Janowitz, a radiologist, Agatston began working on a way to determine the amount of calcium present in people's coronary arteries. Excessive levels of calcium often lead to arteriosclerosis, a chronic disease that impairs blood circulation and places people at risk for heart attacks or strokes. Agatston and Janowitz were later members of a team that developed electron beam tomography (EBT), a fast, noninvasive technique for scanning every part of the body; with EBT, doctors can detect and quantify even small calcium deposits in the arteries that carry oxygenated blood to the heart. The so-called Agatston score is a measure of the amount of calcium in the coronary arteries. In a conversation with Soriya Daniels for the *Cleveland (Ohio) Jewish News* (February 13, 2004), Agatston said that the widespread adoption of EBT was his "most rewarding experience."

Beginning around the late 1980s, Agatston noticed that among his patients who suffered from hypertension and other heart-related ailments, a majority were gaining weight and were developing abnormal blood chemistries. He, too, had become a little fatter around his midsection, and in the U.S. as a whole, obesity was becoming increasingly common. Agatston thought that the problem might be related to the growing popularity of low-fat, high-carbohydrate diets, such as the one that the American Heart Association had been recommending. "If it was low-fat, [we thought] you could eat with impunity, and I did, as did the country in general," Agatston told an interviewer for *People* (April 26, 2004). Agatston feared that U.S. food companies, reacting to the advice of the American Heart Association and others, were selling too many items containing processed carbohydrates. Foods of that kind contain large amounts of flour, sugar, and high-fructose corn syrup. "Nobody in the history of man ever ate complex carbohydrates like we have," Agatston said to Abby Goodnough for the *New York Times* (October 7, 2003).

Agatston began investigating how the body processes carbohydrates. "My concern was not with my patients' appearances," he told Soriya Daniels. "I wanted to find a diet that would help prevent or reverse the myriad of heart and vascular problems that stem from obesity." During his research he learned about the glycemic index (GI), developed in the late 1970s by David J. A. Jenkins, a specialist in the nutritional sciences at the University of Toronto, Canada. The glycemic index ranks foods, on a scale of zero to 100, according to how much the quantity of glucose in an individual's blood increases within two to three hours of eating those foods. Foods with a high GI score include baked potatoes, white bread, and most pastas; those with low scores include foods rich in fiber, such as whole- and multi-grain bread, lean meat, and most vegetables. Foods with high scores (over 55) are digested more quickly than those with low scores, and people often feel hungry much sooner after eating the former than after consuming the latter. Using that information Agatston drew up what he called the "modified carbohydrate diet"—the precursor to the South Beach diet. He and a select group of his private patients who tested the diet began to lose weight.

In about 1996 Agatston, in collaboration with Marie Almon, the chief clinical dietitian at Mount Sinai, worked out a more detailed diet, one that did not need to be supplemented with exercise. They printed instructions for following the diet and distributed them to a greater number of people than had tested the diet earlier. In addition to weight, the cholesterol levels decreased in most of the people in the new sample. Agatston presented his findings at national meetings of the American College of Cardiology and the American Heart Association. Meanwhile, word of the diet had spread in the Miami area and reached the media, which dubbed it the South Beach diet, referring to an upscale section of Miami Beach. Several Miami eateries changed their menus to appeal to diners on the diet. What had "started as research . . . got the glitz added to it by the local media," Agatston commented to Howard Cohen for the *Miami Herald* (May 1, 2003).

In April 2003 the health-and-fitness publishing house Rodale, based in Emmaus, Pennsylvania, published Agatston's first book, *The South Beach Diet: The Delicious, Doctor-Designed, Foolproof Plan for Fast and Healthy Weight Loss*. The book remained on the *New York Times* best-seller list for 38 consecutive weeks. Among Agatston's other books are *The South Beach Diet Cookbook: More than 200 Delicious Recipes that Fit the Nation's Top Diet* (2004), which had a first-run printing of 1.5 million copies—a record for a cookbook; *The South Beach Diet Good Fats/Good Carbs Guide: The Complete and Easy Reference for All Your Favorite Foods* (2004), which was *Publishers Weekly*'s number-one best-seller for 18 weeks; *The South Beach Diet Dining Guide* (2005); and *The South Beach Heart Program: The 4-Step Plan that Can Save Your Life* (2006).

The South Beach diet is divided into three stages. In phase one, which lasts two weeks, no foods rich in carbohydrates—pasta, potatoes, fruit, bread, cereal, and rice—are permitted; alcoholic beverages are also off-limits. Meals consist of "normal-size portions of lean meat, fish, eggs, reduced-fat cheese, nonfat yogurt, nuts, and plenty of vegetables." According to Agatston, dieters can lose as many as 13 pounds in those first two weeks. (The

Web site factsaboutfitness.com reported that in one study of the diet, the results of which were published in the *Archives of Internal Medicine*, the "average weight loss among the subjects was 13.6 pounds in 12 weeks, . . . not the first two weeks.") In phase two, dieters may eat certain fruits and carbohydrate-laden foods having low GI scores (whole-grain items, for example); they are advised to remain in that stage until they reach their desired weights. Alex Witchel characterized the final stage of the diet, meant to be adopted permanently, as "a more lenient version" of the second phase.

The South Beach diet has often been compared with another popular regimen, introduced in 1972 in the book *Dr. Atkins' Diet Revolution*, by Robert Atkins, who maintained that the harmful effects of saturated fats had been highly exaggerated and that high-carbohydrate diets were far more harmful than diets consisting mostly of proteins and fats. People who maintain the Atkins diet avoid refined sugar, milk, white rice, white potatoes, or white flour (found in white bread, most cakes, cookies, and pastries, and most pasta). They may eat virtually unlimited amounts of meat, poultry, fish, eggs, cheese, and cream, and, after the first two weeks on the diet, limited amounts of fruits, vegetables, and whole-grain foods. One major difference between the Atkins diet and the South Beach diet, according to experts, is that Atkins practitioners enter a metabolic state known as ketosis, in which the body, lacking sufficient carbohydrates, converts stores of fat into energy. Agatston has said that when he designed his diet, he consciously tried to avoid triggering ketosis in his patients, because, in hypertensives, it can cause serious adverse effects.

The popularity of *The South Beach Diet* led to Agatston's alliance with Kraft Foods, one of the world's largest food and beverage companies. In 2004 Kraft began placing the South Beach Diet trademark on some of its products. The next year the company introduced a line of South Beach Diet products, among them frozen entrees and snacks. "Things can be nutritious and come from a package," Agatston's collaborator Marie Almon said to Lisa Belkin for the *New York Times Magazine* (August 20, 2006). "It depends what's in the package, not the fact that there is a package." Some of Kraft's South Beach items came under attack because of their high levels of sodium; daily ingestion of sodium in greater than moderate amounts has been linked with hypertension. Speaking with Howard Cohen and Kathy Martin for the *Miami Herald* (May 5, 2005), Agatston acknowledged that he would not recommend some of the new Kraft products to patients suffering from heart disease or high blood pressure, but he defended the South Beach diet's overriding principle. "America is overfed . . . ," he said. "If you lose weight and reverse the metabolic syndrome, blood pressure comes down."

Thanks to his book, Agatston told Lisa Belkin, he gained "a bully pulpit and an opportunity to change the way Americans eat. One of the obvious places to start is with children. And that means schools." In July 2004 Agatston, as the head of the Agatston Research Institute, signed a contract with the Osceola County School District, in Florida, that allowed him to take control of the meals supplied by cafeterias in four elementary schools, all in Kissimmee, a city whose population is about 50,000. Starting in the fall of 2004, he began testing a program called HOPS—Healthier Options for Public Schoolchildren—in which more nutritious and fewer high-fat foods were on the schools' menus, and some items (among them white bread, turkey or pork with gravy, sweetened breakfast cereals, and Tater Tots—deep-fried, small cylinders of grated potatoes) are banned. Currently, the HOPS program reaches 9,000 students in the Miami-Dade County School District, and Agatston plans to introduce it to schools outside Florida. In terms of the effectiveness of the program, as measured by a decrease in the number of overweight children in the test schools, Agatston told Belkin that "true trends" will be discernible only after HOPS has been in place for five years. "If the data don't show what we want to see," he said, "we aren't going to throw up our hands and say, 'Let them eat what they want.' All that will mean is that we aren't doing this as well as we can, so we will have to find a way to do it better."

In addition to his duties at the University of Miami School of Medicine, where he serves as an associate professor of medicine, Agatston has maintained a private practice as a partner with South Florida Cardiology Associates, in Miami. He lectures on nutrition nationally and internationally, serves as a consultant for the Clinical Trials Committee of the National Institutes of Health, and co-directs the Symposium on Prevention of Cardiovascular Disease, which meets annually.

Agatston and his wife, Sari Agatston, a lawyer, married in 1983. Sari Agatston has assisted her husband with all his books, which is why he often uses the first-person plural when talking about them, and she handles the financial and other aspects of his businesses. The Agatstons are the parents of two sons, Adam and Evan, and live in Sunset Island, a section of Miami Beach. Interviewers have described Agatston as approachable, self-effacing, and friendly and as trim but not buff. In his leisure time he enjoys reading books about history and politics and playing golf.

—D.F.

Suggested Reading: *Boston Globe* B p7 Sep. 22, 2003; *Cleveland Jewish News* p40 Feb. 13, 2004; (Fort Lauderdale, Florida) *Sun-Sentinel* Health and Family D p1+ Apr. 11, 2004; *Miami (Florida) Herald* Living E p1 May 1, 2003, A p1+ May 5, 2005, WW p13 Dec. 10, 2005; *New York Times* F p1+ Oct. 7, 2003, F p1+ Apr. 14, 2004; *New York Times Magazine* p30+ Aug. 20, 2006; *People* p65 Apr. 26, 2004; WebMd.com

Selected Books: *The South Beach Diet: The Delicious, Doctor-Designed, Foolproof Plan for Fast and Healthy Weight Loss*, 2003; *The South Beach Diet Cookbook: More than 200 Delicious Recipes that Fit the Nation's Top Diet*, 2004; *The South Beach Diet Good Fats/Good Carbs Guide: The Complete and Easy Reference for All Your Favorite Foods*, 2004; *The South Beach Diet Dining Guide*, 2005; *The South Beach Diet Quick and Easy Cookbook: 200 Delicious Recipes Ready in 30 Minutes or Less*, 2005; *The South Beach Diet Parties & Holidays Cookbook: Healthy Recipes for Entertaining Family and Friends*, 2006; *The South Beach Diet Heart Program: The 4-Step Plan That Can Save Your Life*, 2006; *The South Beach Diet Taste of Summer Cookbook*, 2007

Aitken, Doug

Mar. 18, 1968– Video and multimedia artist

Address: 303 Gallery, 525 W. 22d St., New York, NY 10011

In January 2007 *Sleepwalkers*, a work by Doug Aitken, a multimedia artist who specializes in video, debuted at the Museum of Modern Art (MoMA) in New York City, one of the world's most prestigious showcases for contemporary art. Comprising carefully synchronized short films that depict daily routines of five city dwellers, *Sleepwalkers* was projected onto the surfaces of the museum's shiny exterior walls, transforming them into palettes of color and light visible to pedestrians. With a "soundtrack" composed only of ambient noises in Midtown Manhattan, *Sleepwalkers* was, in Aitken's words, a "silent film for the 21st century," according to Sia Michel in *New York Magazine* (January 15, 2007), one that "vaults humans into an architectural scale," as Simon Houpt wrote for the Toronto *Globe and Mail* (January 15, 2007). "Our way of living today is expanded, fragmented, kaleidoscopic . . . ," Aitken said to Jori Finkel for the *New York Times* (January 7, 2007). "A film that takes place simultaneously with multiple projects in different combinations every time it runs is closer to our human experience than a traditional film. I don't think we really see life as a novella. I don't think we see life in ways that have clear beginnings and ends." "Cinema has reached stalemate," Aitken said to Clare Henry for the *Financial Times* (January 19, 2007). "Directors resort to more violence, more sex. I aim to open things up, take moving images out of the cinema into a nocturnal space. I want to make challenging work accessible to pedestrians, to the general public, yet transform people's experience and concept of the city." Aitken's fascination with fractured narrative, time, space, and memory informed his earlier works as

Roger Kisby/Getty Images

Doug Aitken with singer Cat Power (Chan Marshall) onstage at MoMA

well. After honing his skills as a music-video and commercial director, he produced polished video installations that used exterior and interior spaces, among them *Dawn* (1994), *Monsoon* (1995), and *Electric Earth* (1999), the last of which earned the Golden Lion International Prize at the Venice Biennale. (In some sources the names of his works are spelled without capitals.) "On some level, all of my work is related to what I see as certain new tendencies in the culture," Aitken told Jeffrey Kastner for the *New York Times* (October 6, 2002). "Accelerated nomadicisim, self-contained, decentralized communication—these things are at the core of this space we're living in, a terrain that is radically different from the past." "What I like about his work," Mary Spirito, the director of the 303 Gallery, Aitken's New York representative, told Jacob Bernstein for *WWD* (March 13, 2006), "is that he's able to take a very Hollywood or commercial language and apply it to ideas that have a home in the art world, that you would never see in a larger popular context." Connie Butler, a curator for the Museum of Contemporary Art in Los Angeles, told Amy Gerstler for *Los Angeles Magazine* (November 1, 2000) that Aitken "has taken on the challenge of trying to work in an area somewhere between popular video and art video. . . . He's trying to find a kind of in-between space." Aitken's work has been displayed in more than three dozen solo exhibitions, overseas (in Austria, the Czech Republic, Denmark, England, France, Germany, Italy, Japan, Spain, and Switzerland) as well as in many American cities; his work has also been included in nearly 100 group exhibitions. "Like everyone else, I'm just a satellite dish with roots," he told Kristine McKenna for *LA Weekly* (March 17, 2000). "The

amount of information that surrounds us is absolutely staggering—and that's one of the things my work is about."

An only child, Doug Aitken was born on March 18, 1968 in Redondo Beach, California. His mother was a journalist, his father a lawyer. "Some of my earliest memories are of trying to find ways to steal notepads from one of my parents' offices so I could draw when they'd drag me to work with them," he told Amy Gerstler. He has traced his lack of interest in nostalgia or romanticism to his growing up in Southern California, "where there is virtually no sense of history, not like you have in Europe," as he told Simon Grant for the London *Evening Standard* (October 8, 1999). "When people talk about things that are historical they might be talking about a building that is four years old. We live in a present and this is what I look at in my work" Aitken attended Marymount College, a two-year school in Palos Verdes, California, in 1986–87, then enrolled in the illustration program at the renowned Art Center College of Design, in Pasadena, California. Less concerned with developing personal aesthetics than with "learning the language of mass communication," as he said to Kristine McKenna, Aitken quickly grew disillusioned with the limitations posed by drawing and illustration. Referring to "forms of communication and concepts and finding ways of stretching them apart," he told Jeffrey Kastner, "I found myself frustrated trying to bring these ideas to life. . . . I felt that I wasn't able to activate the mediums I was working in." He gravitated instead toward film and video, according to Kastner, as a means to document "stray moments of perpetual poetry." He graduated with a B.F.A. degree in 1991.

For his first work after college, entitled *Inflection* (1992), Aitken "mounted a surveillance camera inside a high-powered rocket, and launched it above the neighborhood where it was created," as he told McKenna. In his essay "Building Images" for the *Sleepwalkers* catalog (2007), Klaus Biesenbach, the chief curator of MoMA's Department of Media, wrote that the images recorded by the airborne camera "recall the perspective of an orbiting satellite, revealing patterns and topographic rhythms in the suburban structures." To produce *Superstar* (1993), Aitken climbed the letters of the famous "Hollywood" sign, on Mount Lee, in Los Angeles, photographing his movements with a camera mounted on his back. According to Biesenbach, *Superstar* reflected the "spatial and temporal pairing of the camera's moving and the action it records."

Over the next few years, Aitken filmed in a variety of exotic locations, experimenting at times with character studies. He also accepted a series of commercial art projects, most notably as music-video director for Fatboy Slim, a British hip-hop dance artist, and for the Barenaked Ladies, a Canadian alternative rock band, and as director of television advertisements for Budweiser and Converse. Commercial videography refined Aitken's production skills and visual grammar (also called film grammar, referring to such aspects of filmmaking as technique and style), evident in later video works that critics deemed "cinematic" and "visually seductive," according to Gerstler. Meanwhile, in the early 1990s Aitken had moved to New York City, where he began trying to stretch the bounds of traditional two-dimensional video exhibition by incorporating more elaborate, multi-screen showcases for "reimagined" spaces—a technique he dubbed "exploded cinema." "I wanted to find a way to expand the work into something that became more topographical," Aitken told Kastner, "that became a kind of psychological space, with less of a distance for the viewer. I didn't want that glass barrier of the single screen—that frame, like a painting. I wanted to see if it was possible to blow that open and create a space of pure content and communication." The notion of video and space—or, rather, video *in* space—was explored in *Dawn* (1994), Aitken's first solo show in New York, in which three suspended television monitors showed a montage of images extracted from commercial teenage "angst" films. "Paced like a movie trailer but read[ing] more like a riddle," as Jerry Saltz wrote for *Art in America* (April 1994), *Dawn* refashioned the Hollywood teen film genre into a subtle, mythical autobiography.

Aitken next turned to photographing the "entropy of landscapes . . . ," as he told Kristine McKenna, or documenting "the way landscape can transform into something else." He traveled to Jonestown, Guyana, in 1995, to film at the site of the mass suicide committed in 1978 by members of the People's Temple, a religious cult founded by Jim Jones. The resulting work, *Monsoon*, was, Aitken

told McKenna, "extremely quiet, and I hope it conveys some sense of the stillness and silence of the place." The following year Aitken journeyed to Namibia, in southern Africa, to investigate a 75,000-square-mile diamond-mining region that had remained off-limits to the public since 1908. The fruit of Aitken's journey—*Diamond Sea* (1997)—is as "sensual and vivid as any IMAX film," in Gerstler's words. "Picturesque footage is intercut with shots of ghostly, decimated structures and junked equipment that the desert sands are reclaiming." Susanne Weaver, the assistant curator of contemporary art for the Dallas Museum of Art, in Texas, described the three-wall projection of *Diamond Sea* at that museum as "a spellbinding and breathtakingly beautiful journey into the true nature of reality and the mystery of perception at the end of the century," as quoted by Janet Kutner in the *Dallas Morning News* (June 20, 1999). Kutner herself was less impressed, calling Aitken's installation "disorienting in a frustrating sort of way. We never get a feel for where we are or why—merely a jumble of quick impressions that are all but impossible to piece together."

Aitken's breakthrough in the international art world came in 1999, with *Electric Earth*, an eight-screen video installation divided among four different rooms, which chronicled the nocturnal journey of a solitary man making his way across a deserted urban landscape, accompanied by the pulsating beats of a techno-music soundtrack. As the protagonist jerked, twitched, and danced past vending machines, laundromats, gas stations, and other familiar structures, intoning all the while that "I dance so fast that I become what's around me," the images blended into an ethereal, neon-lit fantasy. "Sometimes in my work a literal physical space will start to transform itself into psychological space. Places start to become fictions," Aitken told Gerstler. Elaborating on the protagonist's attempts to synchronize with his surroundings, Aitken said to Hugh Hart for the *Los Angeles Times* (March 26, 2006), "Are we moving faster, or are our surroundings just moving faster? Do we harmonize or are we left behind, or are we constantly between the two?" Aitken described the plight of the protagonist—and in turn that of the engaged viewer—in another way for Jeffrey Kastner: "The character finds himself caught between consciousness and subconsciousness—it's like he's the only person on earth, and things begin to open up, experience begins to expand, and perception becomes more omnidirectional." The precisely choreographed interplay of image, rhythm, light, and character in *Electric Earth* drew rave reviews at the 1999 Venice Biennale, a major international art showcase, where it captured the Golden Lion International Prize. Critics specifically praised Aitken for his ability to draw viewers into the cinematic space, so that they become "part of the experience," as the art curator Francesco Bonami told Gerstler. Assessing *Electric Earth* in "Building Images," Klaus Biesenbach wrote, "Typical pop-culture encounters tend to be with short narratives, such as music videos; *electric earth* translates and refines such encounters into an accomplished, precise form, connecting them to the cinematic and museum practices of contemplation, observation, and experience."

In the work *Glass Horizon* (2000), Aitken projected the image of a pair of eyes onto the exterior of the Vienna Secession Building, in Austria (associated with Gustav Klimt and others who introduced what is known as Art Noveau, in the late 19th and early 20th centuries). The effect of eyes peering at Viennese cityscapes reflected Aitken's notion of art as "urban interruptive."

Aitken's next major piece, *New Ocean* (2001), was shown at the Serpentine Gallery in London, England. It presented images of water droplets, snowy landscapes, waterfalls, icebergs, and oceans photographed in places as far-flung as the Arctic and Argentina, interspersed with images of urban sojourners (in one instance, a female trapeze artist swinging against the backdrop of a dark metropolis) in a liquid apocalypse; the basement, roof, and other parts of the gallery building served as a "blank canvas" for the work. "We live in a temporal landscape where everything about our being is constantly in flux," Aitken said to Hugh Hart. "In that sense, it's a fraud that so many films and so much literature feels this necessity to create a conclusion, a beginning and an end. It denies a lot of the mystique of life." In his review of *New Ocean* for the London *Guardian* (October 16, 2001), Adrian Searle wrote that Aitken's imagery "implies a very modern, apocalyptic kind of drowning," while Richard Cork, writing for the London *Times* (October 17, 2001), argued that "Aitken offers us a salutary reminder, in the midst of our terrorist-haunted trauma, that we have ourselves imperilled the world with the spectre of unchecked solar meltdown and rising floods." By contrast, William Packer, a critic for the London *Financial Times* (October 16, 2006), wondered whether the semblance of narrative in *New Ocean* amounted to anything more than "a banal restatement of the old truth, of man's insignificance and puny aspiration in the face of the grand, implacable immensity of nature, and the passage of time."

In *New Skin* (2002) Aitken examined the notions of memory, sight, and perception in a multi-screen video that showed a Tokyo woman descending into blindness. The narrative of *New Skin*, as Aitken explained to Hugh Hart, "moved around constantly, almost like a lotus blossom expanding, so that the piece wouldn't dictate to the viewer when it began and finished. You could walk in at a different time and pick up the story in a different place." To create the illusion of circularity, Aitken employed four oval screens, placed in a petal-like formation, which showed the woman indoors and outside, struggling to retain the images fading from her vision while reciting "The more I see, the less I believe in the images I find." An electronic countdown, which periodically interrupted

the visual narrative, served as the marker of inevitability for both the protagonist, facing total darkness, and the viewer, witnessing it from the outside. In another piece, *Interiors*, exhibited in the same year at the Henry Art Gallery, in Seattle, Washington, Aitken offered four visual narratives filmed in Mexico, Japan, Los Angeles, and a U.S. helicopter factory, respectively, with each projected in one of four square rooms arranged in the shape of a Greek cross. *Interiors* invited viewers to recombine the characters and settings (all of them urban) and form their own narratives. "It is about the idea of chaos and order, harmony and disharmony," Aitken noted for the Henry Art Gallery press kit, as quoted by Tracey Fugami in *Afterimage* (July 1, 2005). "It looks at how moments in time come together and then separate. It is a composition in the musical sense, like a piece of cacophonic music in which rare moments collide to create larger meanings. It is a piece about time." The effect, Klaus Biesenbach wrote, was "less about duration than it is about simultaneity, symmetry, lack of hierarchy, and the validity of any given scene at any given time."

Aitken has traced the genesis of *Sleepwalkers*, his first public art showcased in the U.S., to an evening walk he took through Midtown Manhattan in the early 2000s. "I had this kind of vision at that moment," he recalled to Simon Houpt, "and I was imagining: if only there was a way the skyscrapers could communicate with each other, if they could contain narratives, if they could somehow become flesh and blood, pulsing, breathing." "This is a city that resembles a human body in every way, from the sidewalks, Internet cables, and subway tunnels that are its veins, to the people and vehicles, fueled by gasoline, coffee, and alcohol, that surge through the veins like blood," he wrote for the *Sleepwalkers* catalog (2007). "The city's heart pulses to the rhythm of the street noise and flashing traffic lights, but it's the mind that drives everything. The city's visceral human nature—its passion, violence, and lust—is obsessed with time, as the city, like the body, constantly replenishes itself. The city lives nowhere more strongly than the present." Later, when Aitken saw the reflective façades of the newly renovated MoMA—a "brilliant, glowing light box," as he described it to Jori Finkel—he envisioned a "kind of hybrid space between architecture, film and sculpture . . . ," as he told Kevin West for *W* (January 1, 2007). "I think I've seen this project as a way to try to create a liquid architecture, by turning architecture into a waterfall of changing, shifting narratives." With support from MoMA and Creative Time, a New York–based public-arts organization, Aitken turned his ideas into reality.

Sleepwalkers debuted at MoMA on January 16, 2007 and was exhibited nightly from 5 p.m. to 10 p.m. throughout its highly publicized four-week run. Consisting of seven vast projections on the outer walls of the museum (some of them in its enclosed courtyard), it featured five archetypal city inhabitants—a business executive, a postal clerk, a bike messenger, an electrician, and an office worker—engaged in mundane activities. "I saw the characters almost as signifiers," Aitken explained to West, "as vehicles for this movement and flow of the city running through you." As each narrative ended, the characters reappeared on different façades. By using the visual and aural backdrop of Manhattan—adjacent structures and street sounds—*Sleepwalkers* transcended the conventions of two-dimensional theatrical viewing to achieve an "expanded cinema," as Peter Eleey, then with Creative Time (and now the visual-arts curator at the Walker Art Center), wrote in his essay "The Exploded Drive-In" for the *Sleepwalkers* catalog. Reviewing *Sleepwalkers* for the *New York Times* (January 18, 2007), Roberta Smith wrote, "It is an outstanding example of what might be called archivideo or videotecture," and she praised Aitken for "creating a postmodern Cubist symphony for the house [that is, MoMA] that Cubism built." (Cubism was a 20th-century art movement whose adherents rendered subjects from multiple viewpoints.) A. M. Homes, writing for *Vanity Fair* (December 2006), described *Sleepwalkers* as a "cinematic wonderland . . . a transcendent love letter where memory and narrative come together and then part" and credited Aitken with redefining "pop culture and high art with images that are accessible to all and sublime to those in the know." Those less enthusiastic or not at all impressed with *Sleepwalkers* included Ariella Budick, who wrote for *Newsday* (January 19, 2007) that Aitken's vision was "cliched, unsatisfying, and even false."

Aitken's other video installations include *Moment* (2005), which employed a hall of mirrors; *Eraser* (1998), a video work that showed his journey across the Caribbean island of Montserrat; and *Into the Sun* (1999), his exploration of the Bollywood film industry, in India. Aitken has written texts that accompany some of his video pieces, including *I Am a Bullet: Scenes from an Accelerating Culture* (2000, co-written by Dean Kuiypers), *Notes for New Religions, Notes for No Religions* (2001), and *Doug Aitken: A-Z Book (Fractals)* (2003). *Broken Screen: Expanding the Image, Breaking the Narrative: 26 Conversations with Doug Aitken* (2006) contains transcriptions of talks between Aitken and some of his contemporaries about nonlinear narratives in art.

"Aitken's a fascinating guy," Peter Eleey told Sia Michel. "He has a kind of sensitive, poetic attention to the world, and to be able to balance that with the [managerial] demands of the large-scale productions he does is a very rare gift." After residing in New York City for many years, Aitken moved to Venice, California, where he lives with Elizabeth Paige Smith, a furniture designer. "In my work, I like to create spaces that are in between departure and destination," he told Amy Gerstler. "I've always had wheels for feet. I'm gone about sixty percent of the time, but these days, I'm in L.A. more than anyplace else."

—D.J.K.

Suggested Reading: *Art Review* p68+ Jan. 2007; *Financial Times* (U.S. edition) p10 Jan. 19, 2007; *LA Weekly* p59+ Mar. 17, 2000; *Los Angeles Magazine* p122+ Nov. 1, 2000; *Los Angeles Times* E p14 Mar. 25, 2006; *New York* p64+ Jan. 15, 2007; *New York Times* II p35 Oct. 6, 2002, II p22 Jan. 7, 2007, E p5 Jan. 18, 2007; *Sleepwalkers* (MoMA catalog), 2007; (Toronto) *Globe and Mail* R p1 Jan. 15, 2007; *W* p112+ Jan. 1, 2007

Selected Installations: *Electric Earth*, 1999; *New Ocean*, 2001; *New Skin*, 2002; *Sleepwalkers*, 2007

Selected Books: *Metallic Sleep*, 1999; *I Am a Bullet: Scenes from an Accelerating Culture* (with Dean Kuiypers), 2000; *Notes for New Religions, Notes for No Religions*, 2001; *Doug Aitken: A-Z Book (Fractals)*, 2003; Daniel, Noel, ed. *Broken Screen: Expanding the Image, Breaking the Narrative: 26 Conversations with Doug Aitken*, 2006

Ajami, Fouad

Sep. 19, 1945– Professor of Middle East studies; political adviser; journalist

Address: Johns Hopkins University, Nitze Bldg. Rm. 200, 1740 Massachusetts Ave., N.W., Washington, DC 20036

In 1990, when Iraqi troops invaded Kuwait, Fouad Ajami was recognized among academics, government advisers and decision makers, and political pundits as an authority on the Middle East, in particular the Arab world, but he was little known among the general public. Then, in 1991, during the brief war in which a U.S.-led coalition ousted the Iraqis from their neighbor's land, media demand for Ajami's analyses and views grew manyfold; with his frequent appearances on *CBS News* and other television news broadcasts and current-events talk shows, untold numbers of lay viewers, too, came to perceive him as an expert on Middle East affairs. Since that time Ajami has established himself as an influential—and highly controversial—voice in the evolving discourse on the Middle East and its future. Ajami's convictions have changed since his teenage years, when he was attracted to pan-Arabism, which calls for cultural and political unity among Arab nations. A native of Lebanon, Ajami is a descendant of Iranians, or Persians, who are not considered Arabs; readily available sources do not reveal whether he regards himself as Arab, but he is usually identified as such—and by some detractors as a "self-hating" Arab. Ajami has lived in the U.S. since 1963, when he began his undergraduate education. In 1980,

Fouad Ajami

Courtesy of Keppler Speakers

less than a decade after he earned his doctorate, he became the Majid Khadduri professor and director of Middle East Studies at the Johns Hopkins University's Paul H. Nitze School of Advanced International Studies (SAIS), in Washington, D.C. Ajami's support for the U.S.-led war in Iraq launched in 2003, and his optimistic predictions regarding its outcome, have earned him plaudits from American government officials including Secretary of State Condoleezza Rice, politically conservative or neoconservative commentators and politicians, and some more-neutral observers. Salim Mansur, for example, who teaches political science at the University of Western Ontario, in Canada, and is a board member of the Center for Islamic Pluralism, in Washington, D.C., described him in a column for the *Toronto (Canada) Sun* (on-line) as a "penetratingly astute observer of Arab politics." Among many in the Arab world, however, and many American observers, he is seen as harboring anti-Arab bias and pro-Israel sentiment. "His unpardonable sin is to write disparagingly of Arab culture, especially in its nationalist mode," Edward Mortimer wrote for the *Los Angeles Times* (February 22, 1998). In a review of Ajami's most recent book, Noah Feldman, a professor of law at New York University and a senior fellow at the Council on Foreign Relations (of which Ajami is a member), wrote for the *New York Times Book Review* (July 30, 2006, on-line), "Respected by politicians who disdain most academics, and excoriated by antiwar academics who detest the present [U.S.] government, Ajami richly deserves the attention of both camps."

A naturalized American citizen, Ajami has written many op-ed pieces and other essays for the *New Republic, U.S. News & World Report*, the *Wall Street Journal*, and other widely read periodicals. He is also the author of seven books, including *The Arab Predicament: Arab Political Thought and Practice Since 1967* (1981); *The Vanished Imam: Musa al Sadr and the Shia of Lebanon* (1986); *Beirut: City of Regrets* (1988); *The Dream Palace of the Arabs* (1998); and *The Foreigner's Gift: The Americans, the Arabs, and the Iraqis in Iraq* (2006). To understand the Middle East, he has said, according to the SAIS Web site, "you have to find the magic of the middle ground between that which passes under the name of policy analysis and that which passes under the name of cultural analysis—the study of history and civilization." In 1982 Ajami received a John D. and Catherine T. MacArthur Foundation Fellowship, often called the "genius grant." His other honors include a National Humanities Medal, awarded at a White House ceremony in 2006. Also in 2006 he won a Bradley Prize, from the Lynde and Harry Bradley Foundation, for his achievements in promoting "liberal democracy, equality and democratic capitalism."

Fouad Ajami was born on September 19, 1945 in Arnoun, a village in southern Lebanon, to parents of Iranian descent. (The name "Iran" means "land of the Aryans," which refers to a nomadic, Indo-European tribe who migrated to the Middle East from what is now southern Russia and Turkistan. Iranians speak Farsi, not Arabic.) Ajami's mother and father were tobacco farmers and devout followers of Shii Islam. (The second-largest sect among Muslims, Shiites are also called Shi'ites, Shias, and Shi'as. Although the U.S. media often refer to them as a monolithic bloc, they are not a single, cohesive group, and their religious beliefs vary.) With limited acreage, Ajami's parents found themselves unable to provide adequately for their growing family, and when Fouad was four, the family settled in a semi-rural Armenian community in Beirut, Lebanon's capital city and chief seaport. The Ajamis were eager to assimilate into the local culture, which was mostly Sunni Muslim and Maronite Christian. "We were strangers to Beirut's polish, to her missionary schools, to her Levantine [eastern Mediterranean] manners. We wanted to pass undetected into the modern world of Beirut, to partake of its ways," Ajami wrote in an op-ed piece for the *Washington Post* (September 11, 1988). In Beirut as a whole at that time, Christians lived apart from Sunni Muslims, and both lived apart from residents of the upscale enclave whose culture, in Ajami's words, was "Anglo-Saxon, self-consciously so." Outside his own community, Ajami discovered, "anything Persian, anything Shia, was anathema. . . . Speaking Persianized Arabic was a threat to something unresolved in my identity," as he once wrote, according to Adam Shatz, writing for the *Nation* (April 28, 2003). An unidentified friend of Ajami's told Shatz that in school, among his mostly Sunni classmates,

"Fouad was taunted for being a Shiite, and for being short. That left him with a lasting sense of bitterness toward the Sunnis." During the 1950s Ajami identified with sympathizers of the pan-Arabist ideology championed by the president of Egypt, Gamal Abdel Nasser; a revered symbol of Arab pride and dignity, Nasser called for ethnic and religious unity among Muslim and Christian Arabs. (The concept became known as Nasserism.) At the same time Ajami harbored a secret fancy for American popular culture, as depicted in American-made films.

In 1963 Ajami immigrated to the United States and enrolled at Eastern Oregon College (now Eastern Oregon University), in LaGrande, where he earned a bachelor's degree. He later matriculated at the University of Washington at Seattle to pursue doctoral studies in political science and international relations. His dissertation was entitled "The Multinational Corporation: Expanding the Frontiers of World Politics." In 1973 Ajami joined the faculty of the Department of Politics and the Center of International Studies at Princeton University, in Princeton, New Jersey, where he won two postgraduate fellowships. His monograph *Global Populists: Third-World Nations and World-Order Crises* was published by Princeton's Center of International Studies in 1974. In that work Ajami provided an economic history of recent years, a description and analysis of economic conditions in developing nations, and a discussion of world politics beginning at the end of World War II. Another monograph, *Human Rights and World Order Politics* (1978), was published by the Institute for World Order (now the World Policy Institute, a part of the New School).

In academic circles during that period, Ajami became known as a progressive thinker and advocate for Palestinian self-determination. While he outspokenly opposed what was widely perceived as aggression (political and social as well as military) on the part of Israel, he criticized what he viewed as the shortcomings of the Arab nations. In "The Fate of Nonalignment," published in *Foreign Affairs* (Winter 1980/1981), Ajami challenged Third World societies to reexamine their dependence on the global superpowers—namely, the United States and what was then the Soviet Union—and forge renewed alliances with one another: "Overwhelmingly, the cultural and economic traffic from the Third World has been in the direction of Europe, or of America, or of the Soviet bloc," he wrote. "Third World societies need more sustained traffic among themselves. To do so they have to shed some of the self-contempt that the once-colonized bring into the world and project onto people more or less like themselves. There have to be alternative sources of aid to what the superpowers promise."

In 1980 Ajami moved to Washington, D.C., and took the position of Majid Khadduri professor and director of Middle East Studies at the Johns Hopkins University School of Advanced International Studies. Meanwhile, he was becoming more prominent as a writer, with articles in such periodicals as *Harper's*, *Foreign Policy*, the *Nation*, *Maclean's*, *U.S. News & World Report*, the *New Republic*, and the *New York Times Book Review*; he also appeared with increasing frequency on television as a commentator, most notably, beginning in 1985, for *CBS News*.

Ajami's book *The Arab Predicament: Arab Political Thought and Practice Since 1967* was published in 1981. In tracing the rise and collapse of various Arab ideological movements since the late 1960s, while expressing his own disillusionment over the demise of Nasserism, Ajami produced a poetic, elegiac account of "shattered dreams," as Jacquelyn S. Porth wrote in a review for *Defense & Foreign Affair*s (January/February 1983). In his book he warned Arabs of the dangers of their "desire to escape from politics, to trust it all to grand schemes—at times liberal schemes, for others, Marxist schemes, more recently, fundamentalist, restorationist schemes." Porth praised *The Arab Predicament* as "the most important work written by an Arab in this generation . . . a thoughtful book, thoroughly informed, and courageously presented." Arab critics in the West, however, accused Ajami of "papering over the injustices of imperialism and blaming the victim," as Adam Shatz wrote, and faulted him for favoring Israel. *The Arab Predicament* positioned Ajami as the rare Middle Eastern émigré intellectual who analyzed Middle Eastern politics with an outsider's eye. Many pro-Israel intellectuals hailed Ajami's conservative leanings and anticipated his becoming a formidable rival to the noted Columbia University scholar Edward W. Said, a prominent and controversial Arab-American advocate of the Palestinian cause.

Ajami recognized that his views straddled both sides of the ideological spectrum. On one hand, he opposed Israel's invasion of Lebanon in 1982, arguing in an op-ed piece for the *New York Times* (June 21, 1982) that it "came with a great delusion: that if you could pound men and women hard enough, if you could bring them to their knees, you could make peace with them." Ajami also criticized the U.S.'s involvement in the Lebanese conflict, telling a writer for United Press International (December 6, 1983), "What we've done is we've placed enough presence there to make the Syrians look heroic, to make us look like enemies of the Arab world and to implicate us in Israeli policies in the region. It's a long-time presence and it's an exposed presence." On the other hand, Ajami also criticized the Palestinian guerrillas in Lebanon and cast his sympathies with the Lebanese Shiite minority. He also distanced himself from Said, with whom he had once shared a litany of criticisms against American foreign-interventionist policies. The Lebanese journalist Hisham Milhem described to Shatz the fundamental difference between Ajami and Said by referring to a favorite writer of both—the Polish-born English-language novelist

Joseph Conrad (1857–1924): "Edward and Fouad are both crazy about Conrad, but they see in him very different things. Edward sees the critic of empire, especially in *Heart of Darkness*. Fouad, on the other hand, admires the Polish exile in Western Europe who made a conscious break with the old country."

In 1982 Ajami received a John D. and Catherine T. MacArthur Foundation Fellowship. The following year, by invitation, he became a member of the Council on Foreign Relations, a New York City–based foreign-policy think tank. His next book, *The Vanished Imam: Musa al Sadr and the Shia of Lebanon* (1986), is about an Iranian-born philosopher who became a religious and political leader of Lebanese Shiites. Al Sadr disappeared in 1978, after arriving in Libya to talk with officials in the government of the dictator Muammar Al-Qaddafi; his fate remains unknown. In the introduction to the book, Ajami explained why he had chosen to write about al Sadr: "Now and then a man, through no act of premeditation on his own part, serves as some kind of refractor. Standing at some remove from him, we see many lights converge on him; and then we see him illuminating the landscape around him." In an assessment of *The Vanished Imam* for the *New York Times Book Review* (May 25, 1986), the cultural anthropologist Mary Catherine Bateson commended Ajami for achieving "fairness without abandoning his own background as a source of insight, drawing the reader close to the passion and particularity of a most beautiful and battered country. . . . This work celebrates one of the paramount facts of the Middle East, the fact of pervasive ambiguity." Elizabeth R. Hayford, in a critique for *Library Journal* (July 1986), wrote, "What begins as a narrow study of a relatively minor figure becomes a sensitive and probing analysis of current Middle Eastern society." The *New York Times Book Review* listed *The Vanished Imam* among the 10 best books of 1986.

Ajami wrote the text that accompanies Eli Reed's photographs in *Beirut: City of Regrets* (1988). In what ended up as a sentimental ode to the city of his youth, Ajami conjured old Beirut, an exemplar of religious and ethnic diversity until 1975, when civil war broke out. During the next 15 years, fighting among sectarian Lebanese groups and military actions by Syrian and Israeli troops devastated the city. In the *Washington Post* (December 25, 1988), David Ignatius described Ajami's text as "probably the best brief explanation available of the Lebanese paradox—and of why the country continues to exert such a powerful fascination for those who at one time or another fell in love with the place. Ajami . . . has written an elegy for the Beirut of his memory, a charming, seductive but ultimately impossible city that is now as dead as ancient Phoenicia."

In 1991, in what became known as the Gulf War, the United States led a 20-nation coalition mandated by the United Nations to liberate Kuwait from an Iraqi takeover masterminded by the then-

dictator Saddam Hussein. Many in the media turned to Ajami to elucidate American foreign-policy matters for the Arab world. "We want to make sure—we just want to liberate Kuwait," he said in one broadcast, as transcribed for *CBS News* (January 17, 1991, on-line). "We're not here to conquer Iraq. We're not here to annex Iraq. We're not here to impose our order of things on Iraq." According to Shatz, Ajami's academic reputation, as well as his media cachet, soared during the fighting and in the following months. Administrators at Harvard University, in Cambridge, Massachusetts, for example, courted Ajami, without success, for a departmental chairmanship; in June 1992 the members of the Council on Foreign Relations elected him to a five-year term on the group's board of directors. Augustus Richard Norton, a professor of anthropology and international relations at Boston University, told Shatz that Ajami, an immigrant to the United States from "a place no one had heard of" in Lebanon, had "reached the peak of power." "This was a true immigrant success story," Norton continued, "one of those moments that make an immigrant grateful for America. And I think it implanted [in him] a deep sense of patriotism [for the U.S.] that wasn't present before."

In 1993 Ajami sparked heated debates in foreign-policy circles with his fierce rebuttal to "The Clash of Civilizations," an essay by the Harvard University professor Samuel P. Huntington for *Foreign Affairs* (Summer 1993). In his essay Huntington wrote that he envisioned the post–Cold War geopolitical landscape as being divided into eight major civilizations (Western, Confucian, Japanese, Islamic, Hindu, Slavic-Orthodox, Latin American, and African) and argued that international conflict would be framed as the collision of civilizations rather than nation states. "It is my hypothesis that the fundamental source of conflict in this new world will not be primarily ideological or primarily economic. The great divisions among humankind and the dominating source of conflict will be cultural. . . . The principal conflicts of global politics will occur between nations and groups of different civilizations. The clash of civilizations will be the battle lines of the future." In his response for *Foreign Affairs* (Fall 1993), Ajami expressed the view that Huntington's scenario "underestimated the tenacity of modernity and secularism in places that acquired these ways against great odds," citing as an example Indian secularism and the rise of the Indian middle class, which led to the overthrow of British rule and the formation of the modern Indian nation-state. "They will not cede all this for a kingdom of Hindu purity," Ajami wrote. He ended with the contention that "civilizations do not control states, states control civilizations." Reactions to Huntington's and Ajami's arguments came from foreign-policy experts all over the world. Kishore Mahbubani, for example, a longtime Singaporean career diplomat who is currently Singapore's ambassador to the United Nations, agreed with Huntington, telling John Shiry for the Toronto, Canada,

Financial Post (October 12, 1993), "The West seems to be almost deliberately pursuing a course designed to aggravate the Islamic world." The Georgetown University professor and former U.S. ambassador to the U.N. Jeane Kirkpatrick supported Ajami's view. "The most important and explosive differences involving Muslims are found within the Muslim world itself," she told Shiry.

Ajami's book *The Dream Palace of the Arabs: A Generation's Odyss*ey (1998) is a tribute to the generation of Arab writers and intellectuals who wrestled with the transition from Arab traditionalism to modernism. The title comes from the book *Seven Pillars of Wisdom*, by T. E. Lawrence (known as Lawrence of Arabia), in which Lawrence confessed to his failed attempts, on behalf of the Arabs, to "build a dream palace of their national thoughts." In the introduction to *The Dream Palace of the Arabs*, Ajami wrote, "I am a stranger, but no distance could wash me clean of that inheritance," as quoted by Edward Mortimer in the *Los Angeles Times* (February 22, 1998). Devoting several chapters to influential intellectuals in the Arab modernist movement, such as the revolutionary Lebanese poet Khalil Hwai and the Syrian writer Ali Ahmad Said, Ajami, as Mortimer wrote, seemed to "share the pain, and even some of the shame, that other Arab intellectuals feel about the shipwreck of the nationalist dream, even if he is not prepared to join them in what he would consider futile denunciations of Israeli or American policy." Adam Shatz asserted that *The Dream Palace of the Arabs* reflects Ajami's "sympathy for the world he left behind, although there is something furtive, something ghostly about his affection, as if he were writing about a lover he has taught himself to spurn." Andrew Rubin, also in the *Nation* (March 23, 1998), offered a harsher view: "For Ajami to reduce modern Arab intellectual history to a series of generational (and highly gendered) conflicts between the old and the new, between fathers and sons, between modernists and traditionalists, between secularists and clerics, is to ignore the complexity, the sophistication and above all the possibilities of renewal that exist in other spheres of civil society that Ajami does not even recognize as modern."

Following the September 11, 2001 terrorist attacks, and continuing after the U.S. invasion of Iraq in 2003, the American media and members of the administration of President George W. Bush frequently consulted Ajami for his political insights. A strong supporter of President Bush's Middle East policies—in particular, Bush's proposals for creating conditions for a democratic Iraq—Ajami argued in *Foreign Affairs* (January/February 2003), "Above and beyond toppling the regime of Saddam Hussein and dismantling its deadly weapons, the driving motivation of a new American endeavor in Iraq and in neighboring Arab lands should be modernizing the Arab world." He told Michael Douglas for the *Akron (Ohio) Beacon Journal* (March 2, 2003), "The very brutality that the Iraqis have endured under Saddam may be Iraq's saving grace if

redemption comes its way. There may come relief after liberation—and a measure of realism." Ajami's pro-American and, many argued, pro-Israeli stance drew heated criticism from Arab scholars who saw Ajami's perspectives on the modern Arab world as unflattering and simplistic. "I think most of the time what Fouad Ajami does is tell an American audience, and very often a Jewish American audience, what it wants to hear about Arabs," Hussein Ibish, the national communications director of the American-Arab Anti-Discrimination Committee, told Eric Boehlert for *Salon* (December 21, 2001). In the same article, James Zogy, head of the Arab-American Institute, attributed Ajami's rise to prominence to "his basic willingness to deconstruct legitimate Arab positions in public opinion here [in the U.S.]." More recently, with mounting evidence suggesting flaws in U.S. intelligence and foreign-policy strategies, Ajami has tempered his views concerning the U.S. mission in Iraq, while remaining hopeful for its success. During the July 14, 2006 broadcast of the *Charlie Rose Show*, Ajami said, "I'm a total hawk. We owe the Arab world no apology for anything. . . . The terror attacks of 9/11 . . . emanated right from the heart of Arab society." But he also said that although he regarded the war in Iraq as "noble," it might turn out to be a "noble failure." "Sometimes a noble effort can fail," he acknowledged.

Ajami's latest book, *The Foreigner's Gift: The Americans, the Arabs, and the Iraqis in Iraq*, is a collection of vignettes, interviews, and reflections that reveal his guarded optimism concerning U.S. involvement in Iraq and the Middle East. Highly critical of Iraq's indigenous Sunni Muslims for their spread of sectarianism and violence, Ajami argued that Iraq's primary challenge was to "build an inclusive form of national identity that could subsume the country's traditional sectarian, ethnic and tribal loyalties," according to R. Stephen Humphreys in a review for the *Washington Post Book World* (August 6, 2006). Humphreys called Ajami "eloquent and sometimes moving, but his struggle to convey the complexities of Iraq heightens the sense of ambivalence that infuses the book."

Ajami and his wife, the former Michelle Saltmarsh, live in New York City.

—D.J.K.

Suggested Reading: *Nation* (on-line) Apr. 28, 2003; *New York Times* VII p5 May 25, 1986; *Salon.com* Dec. 21, 2001; *Washington Post* C p5 Sep. 11, 1988, T p8 Aug. 6, 2006

Selected Books: *The Arab Predicament: Arab Political Thought and Practice Since 1967*, 1981; *The Vanished Imam: Musa al Sadr and the Shia of Lebanon*, 1986; *The Dream Palace of the Arabs: A Generation's Odyssey*, 1998; *The Foreigner's Gift: The Americans, the Arabs, and the Iraqis in Iraq*, 2006

Mario Tama/Getty Images

Alterman, Eric

Jan. 14, 1960– Journalist; historian; media critic; teacher

Address: Brooklyn College, Dept. of English, 2308 Boylan Hall, 2900 Bedford Ave., Brooklyn, NY 11210

The historian and unapologetically liberal media critic Eric Alterman has become a favorite target for conservatives because of his politically charged books, which have questioned the existence of the so-called liberal media bias and condemned the George W. Bush presidency, among other stands. Alterman is a columnist for the *Nation* magazine and the author of a Weblog (more commonly known as a blog) called "Altercation," which was featured for several years on MSNBC.com and can now be found on mediamatters.org. He is also a senior fellow at the liberal think tank Center for American Progress, for which he writes and edits the column "Think Again," and a professor of English and journalism at Brooklyn College and the Graduate School of Journalism at the City University of New York. Alterman first came to widespread notice with the book *Sound and Fury* (1992), an indictment of the attention and authority granted right-wing pundits by the media and the public. In subsequent years Alterman, who went on to write *What Liberal Media?* (2003) and *When Presidents Lie* (2004), among other books, has inspired considerable attention himself—generating heated attacks from those on the right and equally passionate defenses by his supporters. "My audience is the universe of sensible people," he told Elisabeth Eaves for *Publishers Weekly* (January 27,

2003). "You don't have to see the world my way to agree with what I'm saying. I make the argument—I give you the evidence."

Eric Ross Alterman was born on January 14, 1960 in the New York City borough of Queens; he grew up in Scarsdale, New York, an upper-middle-class suburb of New York City. Alterman's mother, the former Ruth Weitzman, was a school psychologist, and his father, Carl, was a salesman and engineer. According to George Gurley, in an article for the *New York Observer* (April 14, 2003), Alterman worked at the Bronx Zoo for a time while a student. Alterman described himself in an article for the *Nation* (March 9, 2005, on-line) as "a pretty serious Jew—bar mitzvah, educated in Israel, lights candles on Friday night, goes to shul, sends the kid to Hebrew school, contributes to [the Jewish periodical] the *Forward*." (Despite such a background, Alterman is frequently called on to defend himself against charges of anti-Semitic or anti-Israel bias, because of what has been construed as his strong support for Palestinian rights. He wrote to *Current Biography* that he is, rather, "a strong defender of the Israeli peace movement and of the necessity of a just peace between Israel and the Palestinians, rather than of Palestinian rights per se.")

Alterman attended Cornell University, in Ithaca, New York, earning his B.A. degree in history and government in 1982. In 1986 he earned a master's degree in international relations from Yale University, in New Haven, Connecticut, and then went on to study for a doctoral degree in U.S. history from Stanford University, in Palo Alto, California. During his student years he wrote on a freelance basis for such publications as *Mother Jones*, the *Nation*, the *New Republic*, *Harper's*, *Vanity Fair*, and the *New York Times*. His first book, *Sound and Fury: The Washington Punditocracy and the Collapse of American Politics*, was published while Alterman was still at Stanford. (Later editions featured a different subtitle, *The Making of the Punditocracy*.) In the book Alterman, who graduated from Stanford in 1993, described what he saw as a decline in the nation's public discourse, which he attributed to the rise of right-wing pundits—opinionated print and television personalities including Pat Buchanan, Robert Novak, and George Will—and to an eclipse of journalistic values by what he described to *Current Biography* as "entertainment values." Alterman took as his starting point the year 1896, when the publisher Adolph S. Ochs championed a policy of objectivity at the *New York Times*. At that time such a policy was an exception—most papers freely featured the opinions of their writers. As objectivity progressively became the media standard, pundits appeared, according to Alterman, to supply the missing opinions. Unlike today's "talking heads," the early pundits, Alterman contended, used their positions not to argue endlessly but to champion bipartisan views. That changed in the 1960s, when many of the most influential political commentators began voicing their distrust of government officials. In order to balance its content in the face of criticism from President Richard M. Nixon's Republican administration, the *New York Times* hired such conservative op-ed writers as George Will and William Safire, and other publications followed suit. Those men, Alterman argued, had little background in journalism but were employed because they were the only conservatives available. That scenario eventually led to what Alterman saw as the control of the media by "the punditocracy," right-wing figures whose visibility and influence were detrimental to political discourse. Many reviewers of *Sound and Fury* noted Alterman's insightful points but complained about his angry tone and his exaggeration of the pundits' power. Alterman was invited to appear on several popular television talk shows to promote the book, which, he told Gurley, he had hoped would make at least some of the right-wing pundits "afraid to show their faces in public again, because I had so humiliated and revealed them for the charlatans that they were—but, in fact, nothing changed at all. Everything went back to the way it was." Alterman began appearing as a regular commentator on the MSNBC cable channel in 1996. (His association with the company—first as a television personality and columnist, then as a blogger—would last for a decade.)

In *Who Speaks for America? Why Democracy Matters in Foreign Policy*, published in 1998, Alterman argued that American foreign policy reflected too little participation on the part of the public. He contended that the country's system of diplomacy had become increasingly corrupt and ineffective, due to the government's progressively sinister policy of expansionism, willingness to make covert deals that bypassed the Constitution, and susceptibility to the influence of special-interest groups. Alterman suggested that those problems could be remedied by calling on foreign-policy advisory committees—composed of ordinary citizens—to make recommendations to Congress and the White House. Many critics, while questioning whether the American public was as well suited and eager to guide the country's actions abroad as Alterman implied, still found the book valuable. Gregg Easterbrook wrote for the *Washington Monthly* (December 1998), "*Who Speaks for America?* sits square in the tradition of the book that should be read precisely because it's full of material we think we do not need to read. Alterman has produced a volume that is well-written, vigorous and perceptive." "Alterman paints with a broad brush. . . . More a successful polemic than a judicious analysis, [the book] should nonetheless be widely read and its arguments heeded," John Dumbrell wrote for *Perspectives on Political Science* (Summer 1999).

In 1999 Alterman, by then widely known as a regular columnist for the *Nation*, published the nonpolitical *It Ain't No Sin to Be Glad You're Alive: The Promise of Bruce Springsteen*. The book, which took its title from a line in the Springsteen song "Badlands," examined the iconic rock musician's New Jersey childhood and relationship with his father, his rise in the music industry, and his breakthrough success with the 1975 album *Born to Run*. Springsteen had been a powerful influence on Alterman's teenage years; Gurley quoted Alterman as writing that the title single of *Born to Run* "exploded in my home, in my mind and changed my life." Miriam Longino, in a review for the *Atlanta Journal-Constitution* (January 23, 2000), wrote that "as a 15-year-old ticked off at the world, Alterman hung out on the high school football field drinking Miller eight-packs, boom box turned up loud, shouting [Springsteen lyrics] to the sky." She continued (drawing on the lyrics of the song "Born to Run" herself), "[Alterman's] analytical, middle-aged mind, combined with an almost teenlike worship of Springsteen, makes this music bio much more than gossipy patter. For the Springsteen fan, it's an insightful, fuel-injected ride on a runaway American dream."

Alterman returned to the familiar realm of politics for his next book. In the exhaustively footnoted *What Liberal Media? The Truth About Bias and the News* (2003), he countered the claims of left-wing bias in the media that had been made in such widely read titles as Bernard Goldberg's *Bias: A CBS Insider Exposes How the Media Distort the News* (2001) and Anne Coulter's *Slander: Liberal Lies About the American Right* (2002). Regarding the success of his opponents' books, Alterman told Eaves, "There's a conservative movement in this country and it's big. One of the opening quotes of [my] book is [the musician] Paul Simon's 'A man hears what he wants to hear and disregards the rest.' I think people like to buy books that confirm what they believe they already know, and there are a lot of them on the conservative side. They're very good at getting the word out." He explained to Eaves that he had written the book because of his "frustration at the power of a dangerous and destructive myth [of liberal media bias]. . . . You say the words 'liberal media' and it conjures up a whole host of images and alleged facts that make it possible to make a case without actually making the case. It's a kind of shorthand and substitute for careful thinking, to say nothing of actual journalistic proof." As evidence that the media more often tilted not to the left but to the right, Alterman pointed out that many journalists had called for the impeachment of Democratic president Bill Clinton, who had lied under oath about his extramarital affair, and largely remained silent in the wake of the Republican George W. Bush's controversial 2000 election victory after the Florida recount. Some critics saw Alterman's claims that the media favored the right to be the inevitable convictions of a passionate liberal, while others found the book a refreshing alternative to the right's rhetoric. Chauncey Mabe, in one representative review, wrote for the Fort Lauderdale, Florida, *Sun-Sentinel* (April 13, 2003), "While it comes as no surprise that an out-and-out liberal scribe like Alterman finds little liberal bias, he reaches his conclusions in ways that are difficult if not impossible to refute."

The Book on Bush: How George W. (Mis)Leads America (2004) is a broad critique of Bush's presidency, co-authored by Alterman's fellow New Yorker Mark Green, who had been the Democratic nominee against Michael Bloomberg in the city's 2001 mayoral election. The book attacked, among other things, the Bush administration's energy policy and the president's invocation of God to defend his foreign policy. The authors also exposed inconsistencies between the president's public image and his actions in office; they contended that Bush had presented himself as moderate in his 2000 campaign but, once elected, had introduced policies reflecting the interests of the extreme right. An anonymous critic for *Kirkus Reviews* (February 9, 2004) called the book "carefully researched and plenty passionate: a veritable bible for Bush-bashers." Other critics were impressed by the scope of the book, though they questioned whether that comprehensiveness helped the authors' case. While acknowledging that Alterman and Green "stay above . . . the snobbish preoccupation with malapropisms that cheapen[s] so many critiques of the Oval Office occupant," James P. Pinkerton wrote for the *Washington Post* (February 1, 2004) that the book still failed to account for Bush's popularity.

Alterman's next book, *When Presidents Lie: A History of Official Deception and Its Consequences*, also published in 2004, examined four examples of presidential deception in the 20th century. It covered Franklin Roosevelt's secretive deals with the Soviet dictator Joseph Stalin; John F. Kennedy's unpublicized compromises with Russia during the Cuban missile crisis; Lyndon B. Johnson's distortion of the Gulf of Tonkin incident, which led to the increased presence of the U.S. in Vietnam; and the Ronald Reagan administration's cover-up of arms sales in the Iran-Contra scandal. John W. Dean wrote for the *Washington Monthly* (November 2004) that *When Presidents Lie* is "an astute study of presidential decision-making—if lying instead of telling the truth can be so dignified—along with critical examination of the news media's unfortunate but recurring role in facilitating presidential lying." Viking Press is slated to publish Alterman's seventh book, *Why We're Liberals: A Political Handbook to Post-Bush America*, in 2008.

In 1992 Alterman won the George Orwell Award, given by the National Council of Teachers of English to honor honesty and clarity in the public use of language, for *Sound and Fury*, and in 1999 he received the Stephen Crane Literary Award for *It Ain't No Sin to be Glad You're Alive*. Besides his fellowship at the Center for American Progress, Alterman holds fellowships at the New School's World Policy Institute and the organization Media Matters for America, the latter of which agreed to post the blog "Altercation" on its own Web site (mediamatters.org) after MSNBC decided

in 2006 not to retain Alterman. (Although the company claimed that his dismissal was purely a business decision, some of Alterman's supporters have theorized that it was actually an attempt by management to censor his viewpoints.) Alterman is also a professor of English at Brooklyn College, part of the City University of New York (CUNY). In 2003 he was asked to audition for the role of a reporter on the HBO series *The Sopranos*, but he did not win the part. He was later hired as a historical consultant for HBO.

Alterman, whose first marriage ended in divorce, has lived for more than 10 years with Diana Silver, who teaches at New York University, where she also earned her doctorate in public administration. They live in Manhattan and have a daughter, Eve Rose. Alterman is sometimes reported to have a demanding, mercurial personality. "Eric is difficult," Katrina vanden Heuvel, one of Alterman's editors, told Gurley. "But behind that difficult, gruff exterior is someone who cares deeply about progressive ideas and democracy in this country."

—M.B.

Suggested Reading: Eric Alterman Web wite; *Nation* (on-line) Mar. 9, 2005; *New York Observer* p1+ Apr. 14, 2003; *Publishers Weekly* p247 Jan. 27, 2003; *Who's Who in America*, 2006

Selected Books: *Sound and Fury: The Washington Punditocracy and the Collapse of American Politics*, 1992 (later editions subtitled *The Making of the Punditocracy*); *Who Speaks for America? Why Democracy Matters in Foreign Policy*, 1998; *It Ain't No Sin to Be Glad You're Alive: The Promise of Bruce Springsteen*, 1999; *What Liberal Media? The Truth About Bias and the News*, 2003; *The Book on Bush: How George W. (Mis)Leads America* (with Mark Green), 2004; *When Presidents Lie: A History of Official Deception and Its Consequences*, 2004

Ames, Jonathan

Mar. 23, 1964– Writer; performance artist

Address: 181 Wyckoff St., Brooklyn, NY 11217

"All writers have to provoke a reaction," Jonathan Ames said to Sarah Stodola in an interview for *Me Three* (June 2004, on-line). "You have to hold the reader's attention. My first goal as a writer is not to bore." With the novels *I Pass Like Night* (1989), *The Extra Man* (1998), and *Wake Up, Sir!* (2004) and essay collections including, most recently, *I Love You More Than You Know* (2006), Ames has provoked reactions that range from admiration and raucous laughter to discomfort and revulsion—but probably not, to date, boredom. A chief feature of both Ames's fiction and nonfiction is the unflinch-

Travis Roozée, courtesy of Jonathan Ames

Jonathan Ames

ing openness he brings to topics usually referred to euphemistically or not mentioned at all, such as sexual obsession and perversion or various body ailments (irritable bowel syndrome is just one example). While the characters and themes of his novels have led Ames to be compared to such past prose masters as F. Scott Fitzgerald and P. G. Wodehouse, his nonfiction pieces have been likened to those of his contemporary David Sedaris. "I steal from all the writers I love," Ames admitted to Stodola. "It probably doesn't show since I'm a slug and they're gods, but I steal from them."

The only son of Irwin Ames, a salesman of textile chemicals, and Florence Mann, a special-education teacher, Jonathan Spencer Ames was born on March 23, 1964 in New York City. He grew up 40 miles outside the city, in the middle-class New Jersey town of Oakland. His parents instilled in him a love of reading. Each month Ames's mother, who wrote poetry, would order a wide variety of books and magazines, including sports biographies and comic books, through a school-affiliated catalog, allowing Ames to choose whatever he wanted. He recalled to *Current Biography*, "We weren't rich, but when it came to books there seemed to be no cutting corners." Edgar Rice Burroughs's Tarzan books and the novels of J. R. R. Tolkien sparked Ames's desire to be creative and have adventures. In addition to making up games that involved running through the woods, Ames and his friends channeled much of their energy into fishing, swimming, and playing a variety of sports.

Ames attended Valley Middle School and Indian Hills High School. In those years he read the offbeat novels of Kurt Vonnegut as well as Hunter S. Thompson's nonfiction work *Fear and Loathing in Las Vegas*, the latter of which fed Ames's desire to be, as he put it to *Current Biography*, a "crazy journalist." During his sophomore year of high school, under the tutelage of a teacher, Anne Peters, he began writing sports pieces for the school newspaper, *Drumbeats*; he also contributed sports articles to a weekly town paper, the *Wyckoff News*. In addition, he had humorous pieces printed in the Bergen County, New Jersey, *Record*, a major daily in the area. In 1981, when he was 17, he purchased a copy of Jack Kerouac's novel *On the Road*, whose first chapter contained a line that would serve thereafter as a reference point for Ames: "I was a young writer and I wanted to take off." Ames became the editor of *Drumbeats*, graduated among the top 15 students in his class, and earned five varsity letters in sports including soccer, cross-country running, and tennis. He was also one of the top three saber fencers in the state and among the top 12 in the country.

The latter achievement helped Ames to win admittance to Princeton University, in Princeton, New Jersey, where he enrolled in September 1982. During his college years, as he informed *Current Biography*, he "fell in with the artists and the nuts and the malcontents." In 1986 the esteemed novelist Joyce Carol Oates, who was Ames's thesis adviser, gave him a copy of Hubert Selby Jr.'s cult novel, *Last Exit to Brooklyn*, as he was starting work on his thesis, a novella entitled "I Pass Like Night." Selby's novel, along with the works of Raymond Carver, Ernest Hemingway, and Jerzy Kosinski (particularly his 1968 novel, *Steps*), served as the main influences for the novella. Ames graduated from Princeton in 1987. In the following year he expanded his novella into a full-length novel, which was published in 1989. Ames, who had been living in Paris, France, for several months, returned to the U.S. in time for the book's publication.

Reviewers of *I Pass Like Night* found much promise in the fledgling author's debut, noting that its scenes of urban decay were reminiscent of such films as *Midnight Cowboy* and *Taxi Driver*. The coming-of-age novel's narrator and protagonist, Alexander Vine, defies his Jewish family's expectations that he will attend college and enter a prestigious profession; instead, he ekes out a living in the harrowing streets of the Bowery, mostly from tips acquired as a hotel doorman. When night falls, Vine, chiefly out of ennui, engages in drunken homosexual affairs and visits prostitutes. Critics were quick to compare Vine to Holden Caulfield, the teenage narrator of J. D. Salinger's much-celebrated novel *The Catcher in the Rye*. Hugo Giles, assessing Ames's novel for the *Hobart (Australia) Mercury* (December 23, 1989), wrote, "In the jaded 80s *I Pass Like Night* is unlikely to achieve the same shock impact as *Catcher* but it is a moving and anguished reflection of a generation in crisis." Some complained that because Vine was not given to introspection, readers were prevented from developing an attachment to the character. For the most part, however, the debut was well-received.

Despite the acclaim, Ames would spend most of the next decade, as he recalled to *Current Biography*, leading "a hand-to-mouth existence." For two years beginning in 1990, finding himself with little money, he drove a taxi in Princeton; meanwhile, he worked on a second novel. In 1992 he enrolled in the graduate writing program at Columbia University, in New York, earning an M.F.A. degree in 1995 with the aim of securing a teaching position. In addition to other jobs he held during that period, Ames taught composition at a business school and creative writing at the Gotham Writer's Workshop. He also launched his oral storytelling career with a monologue at New York's Fez nightclub and other venues. Ames completed his novel *The Extra Man* in September 1996 and began shopping it around to prospective publishers; the book was rejected by 20 houses before Scribner accepted it. Published in 1998, *The Extra Man* follows the adventures of Louis Ives, who, after getting fired from a teaching position at a Princeton prep school because of a cross-dressing incident, goes to New York and meets up with an eccentric, asexual playwright, Henry Harrison. Henry, who serves as an "extra man" for elderly high-society women at dinner parties, schools Louis in everything from maintaining chivalrous behavior and dressing in a sophisticated manner to sneaking into Broadway plays and escaping notice while relieving himself in the street.

Ames's comedy of manners got a warm reception, with Scott Eyman writing for the *Seattle Post-Intelligencer* (November 2, 1998), "In Henry and Louis, Ames has created—or transcribed—two of the most startlingly human characters in recent fiction." Francine Prose wrote for the *New York Observer*, as posted on Amazon.com, "Ames has the one thing [F. Scott] Fitzgerald lacked: a sense of humor. . . . *The Extra Man* wins us over with its sheer energy and good will, its confidence in the ability of its own humor and intelligence to widen our ideas about the possibilities of love, and about the permissible range of inner and outer lives to which today's young gentleman may properly aspire." The novel won comparison to such classic odd-couple tales as the movie *Harold and Maude* and John Steinbeck's novel *Of Mice and Men*; Ames, for his part, has said that he based Louis Ives in part on the man-about-town characters of Fitzgerald and Oscar Wilde. (Like some of Wilde's sexually adventurous characters, Ives enjoys the company of the transgendered.) Ames's own fascination and personal experiences with transvestites were reflected in a passage in *The Extra Man* that finds Ives in one of his favorite bars, where a drag queen tells him, "You're not really straight, but you're not really gay. You're straightish." Ames told Matthew Flamm for *Newsday* (August 30, 1998), "I don't know what straight people think of me." He described himself as "probably the gayest straight writer in America" and added, "I don't know what I think of me."

In 1999 Ames received a Guggenheim fellowship and mounted a one-man, Off-Off-Broadway show, *Oedipussy*—a cocktail of self-deprecation, surrealism, and sex that made references to figures ranging from Sigmund Freud and Marcel Proust to Porky Pig. Some critics praised the show, likening Ames's storytelling style to those of Woody Allen and Lenny Bruce, while others were less favorably impressed. A reviewer for the *Village Voice* (February 16, 1999) wrote, "There are some hilarious moments in Jonathan Ames's *Oedipussy*, but his . . . shtick is utterly cliched." In a reference to a radio "shock jock," the reviewer added that *Oedipussy* seemed like "a master's thesis from the creative writing program at Howard Stern University."

In late 1996, meanwhile, Ames had begun writing essays for *New York Press*; he was given his own column there in the fall of 1997, attracting a cult following with his humorous, self-deprecatory style. In 2000 he left *New York Press* to teach creative writing for two semesters as a visiting professor at Indiana University. While there he published a book of his "City Slicker" columns from the *New York Press*, titling the collection *What's Not to Love?: The Adventures of a Mildly Perverted Young Writer*. The book's largely autobiographical subject matter ranges from sex and venereal disease to bodily sensations not generally mentioned in print or polite conversation. "Like any good (albeit shticky) performer—[Woody] Allen, [Jerry] Seinfeld, and a thousand Catskills comedians before them—Ames openly provokes the reader to have fun at his own expense, even as he admits to thoughts of suicide," Maya Kremen wrote for the *Village Voice* (June 27, 2000). In 2004 *What's Not to Love?* inspired a Showtime television network pilot in which the humorist played himself; the pilot did not develop into a series.

Ames returned to New York in 2002. That year he followed up *What's Not to Love?* with a second autobiographical work, *My Less Than Secret Life*, comprising five short stories and 42 essays, the latter including past *New York Press* installments, book reviews, and e-zine contributions. As posted on Amazon.com, a contributor to *Publishers Weekly* noted about the book, among whose pieces are "Booty and the Beast," "The Orgy," and "The Nista Affair," that Ames is "like the dirtiest, smartest kid on the playground: you might cringe, but you can't help being transfixed." In 2003 the late-night talk-show host David Letterman came across one of Ames's books, and afterward the writer appeared on Letterman's *Late Show* three times in 18 months.

Ames's third novel, *Wake Up, Sir!* (2004), paid homage to the humor novelist P. G. Wodehouse. (Ames has said that rediscovering Wodehouse's works in the early 2000s helped to lift him from a bout of depression.) The novel's main character, a talented, alcoholic writer named Alan Blair, goes to an artists' colony, where he falls in love with a mannish female sculptor. Blair is helped throughout by his discreet, preternaturally efficient butler,

Jeeves (one of Wodehouse's most memorable characters). Reviewers of the novel compared Ames to his fellow humorist David Sedaris, with D. K. Row writing for the *Oregonian* (July 18, 2004), "Ames is a better writer than the more famous Sedaris. . . . Ames is more genuine, daring and unabashed than other humorists he's often grouped with, tackling everything from homosexual impulses to Jewish self-loathing. He exposes himself more, literally and figuratively, leaving no thought, person or psychosis unexamined. And he does so with a humanity and a style that, on a phrase level, is rarely matched by many essayists and humorists today." In another assessment of *Wake Up, Sir!*, Ben S. Pollock, writing for the *Arkansas Democrat-Gazette* (September 19, 2004), hailed Ames as "a humorist for our age."

In 2005 Ames brought his fascination with transsexualism to the editing of a book, *Sexual Metamorphosis: An Anthology of Transsexual Memoirs*. The volume is comprised of excerpts of writings by transsexuals, taken from books and manuscripts housed at Indiana University's Kinsey Institute. (The institute is named after its founder, the famed sex expert Alfred Kinsey.) Jim Nawrocki, writing for *Gay & Lesbian Review Worldwide* (January 1, 2006), called Ames's choice of material "very good," adding that it is "fairly representative of the range of transsexualism." The anthology begins with case studies from the late 19th century and ends with memoirs from as recent as 2003.

In early 2006 Ames published his third collection of autobiographical essays, *I Love You More Than You Know*. The collection juxtaposes the outrageous and the sentimental; in one piece, for instance, he recalls leaving the library, where he is supposed to be working while his mother looks after his young son, to visit a dominatrix; in another, he gives a sweet account of visiting his 90-year-old great-aunt, Doris, in her Queens, New York, apartment. That essay includes the passage, "I love her desperately and as she gets older—especially of late, as she becomes more feeble—my love seems to be picking up velocity, overwhelming me almost, tinged as it is with panic: I'm so afraid of losing her." D. Grant Black wrote for the Toronto *Globe and Mail* (March 18, 2006), "When you think all this guy can be counted on is to deliver toilet and pervert humour, he changes gears with a sentimental vignette." Ames explained to Ruth Graham for *New York Sun* (April 22, 2005) about his work, "I tend to find that I work best from a first-person vehicle, taking a weird aspect of my personality and then expanding it into a character—kind of like those shrinky dolls that might be tiny and then you pour water on them and they grow."

Ames, whom D. Grant Black described as "a prematurely bald man with the health afflictions of a senior," lives in Brooklyn, New York. He has a number of projects underway or recently completed, including a cover story on the musician Marilyn Manson for the June 2007 issue of *Spin* magazine and a graphic novel, *The Alcoholic*, which will be published in 2008 by DC Comics, with illustrations by Dean Haspiel. Ames has written screenplay adaptations for *The Extra Man* and for Darcy O'Brien's novel *A Way of Life, Like Any Other*. He is an occasional orator and host of a storytelling series called "The Moth," organized by a nonprofit group based in New York City that is dedicated to fresh takes on the art of storytelling. Retaining his interest in sports, Ames has developed a passion for boxing and has even competed in amateur matches. On July 26, 2007 he defeated the Canadian writer Craig Davidson in a bout at Gleason's Boxing Gym in Brooklyn. In the press Ames has been linked romantically to the singer-songwriter Fiona Apple.

—C.C.

Suggested Reading: *Identity Theory* (on-line) Sep. 22, 2004; Jonathan Ames official Web site; *Modernist* (on-line) 2003; *New York Sun* p24 Apr. 22, 2005; *Newsday* B p11 Aug. 30, 1998; *Village Voice* p159 Feb. 16, 1999, p135 June 27, 2000, p69 Oct. 31, 2000, p50 May 6, 2003

Selected Books: fiction—*I Pass Like Night*, 1989; *The Extra Man*, 1998; *Wake Up, Sir!*, 2004; nonfiction—*What's Not to Love?: The Adventures of a Mildly Perverted Young Writer*, 2000; *My Less Than Secret Life*, 2002; *I Love You More Than You Know*, 2006; as editor—*Sexual Metamorphosis: An Anthology of Transsexual Memoirs*, 2005

Anderson, Tom and DeWolfe, Christopher

Co-founders of MySpace.com

Anderson, Tom
Oct. 13, 1975– Co-founder of MySpace.com

DeWolfe, Christopher
1966(?)– Co-founder of MySpace.com

Address: Fox Interactive, P.O. Box 900, Beverly Hills, CA 90213

In 2003 Tom Anderson, a former film student and struggling musician, and Christopher DeWolfe, an on-line marketing executive, started the social-networking site MySpace, which had its official launch the following year. Setting out to establish a Web site that would evoke a nightclub atmosphere, Anderson and DeWolfe enlisted as its first users acquaintances from the club scene in and around Santa Monica, California, where they were based. The site, as Saul Hansell wrote for the *New York Times* (April 23, 2006), tapped into "three passions of young people: expressing themselves,

Tom Anderson (left) and Christopher DeWolfe. (Photo: Evan Agostini/Getty Images)

Tom Anderson and Christopher DeWolfe

interacting with friends and consuming popular culture," and it quickly became, as Matt Krantz wrote for *USA Today* (February 13, 2006), "a cultural phenomenon for the under-30 set, much as MTV captivated the generation before." The most significant aspect of MySpace.com, however, seems to have been the greater freedom it gave users. Reflecting Anderson and DeWolfe's professed—if vague—dislike of rules, MySpace lured users away from on-line social networks that had more limits on what their members could do. Now, MySpace "is home to [more than] 2.2 million bands, 8,000 comedians, thousands of filmmakers, and millions of striving, attention-starved wannabes—100 million actually," Patricia Sellers wrote for *Fortune* (September 4, 2006), adding that "on a typical day, it signs up 230,000 [new users]— roughly the population of Scottsdale [Arizona]."

Tom Anderson was born on October 13, 1975. His father was an entrepreneur who "had one crazy idea after another," Anderson noted on his MySpace page, as displayed on *Fortune.com* (September 4, 2006). He attended the University of California at Berkeley, where he earned a B.A. degree in English and rhetoric in 1997. After his graduation he played in a series of bands, among them Swank, for which he sang and played guitar. He next enrolled in the film school at the University of California–Los Angeles (UCLA), from which he graduated in 2000. Unprepared by his education or professional background for any well-paying career, Anderson was, he told Sellers, "rescued . . . from a lifetime of unemployment" by Christopher DeWolfe, who was the vice president of sales and marketing at Xdrive Technologies, a company that offered users extensive free on-line storage.

DeWolfe was born in Portland, Oregon, in the mid-1960s—sources date his birth as early as 1963 and as late as 1967; his 2006 profile in *Fortune* gave his age as 40, leading many to give his birth year as 1966. His parents were teachers. He studied business at the University of Washington, earning a B.A. degree in finance in 1988. After college DeWolfe went into sales and later entered the M.B.A. program at UCLA, earning his degree in 1997. In the same year he took a position as the vice president of marketing at the First Bank of Beverly Hills (FBBH).

In 1999 DeWolfe left FBBH to join Xdrive. It was in that capacity that DeWolfe, in 2000, met Anderson, who answered an ad to earn $20 by testing an Xdrive product. Anderson hated the product, "but DeWolfe . . . liked Anderson's candor and offered him a job" as a copy editor, Sellers reported. Anderson enjoyed working with DeWolfe because of the independence the job afforded him. "I remember, I asked Chris, 'What do I do?' He said, 'Go figure out how to make money.' . . . It was never, 'Here's the job I want you to do.'" The men offered different accounts on ABC's *Nightline* (May 10, 2007), telling Mary Fulginiti that Anderson was about to quit his job with Xdrive because he disliked his boss. "And then Chris, kind of, rescued me and pulled me into his department. He said, 'Don't leave.' And that's sort of where we started off." In any case, when Xdrive went bankrupt, in 2001, and the two were laid off, DeWolfe and Anderson formed the Internet marketing firm Response Base, which devised marketing strategies with the help of Spam, pop-ups, and other aggressive forms of on-line advertising. The business took off, and the next year they sold it for several million dollars to eUniverse, a larger on-line marketing company. Later in the year DeWolfe was appointed to the board of directors at Fog Cutter Capital Group, a real-estate firm.

Around that time Anderson began thinking about developing a social networking site. Both Anderson and DeWolfe, as well as other employees of eUniverse, had accounts with Friendster, a popular on-line social network that was launched in 2002. "I had looked at dating sites and niche communities like BlackPlanet, AsianAvenue, and MiGente, as well as Friendster," Anderson told Sellers. "And I thought, 'They're thinking way too small.'" Anderson and DeWolfe persuaded eUniverse's CEO, Brad Greenspan, to let them create their own social-networking site. "Recognizing the potential of the Friendster concept," Trent Lapinski wrote for the computer-industry blog *Valleywag* (September 11, 2006), "a plan was hatched to quickly mimic the appealing features of the site, rebrand it as MySpace [a name apparently stolen from a competitor of Xdrive that went out of business in 2001], and then out-market them using eUniverse's resources." The first version of MySpace was ready within 10 days. Anderson and DeWolfe changed more than just their competitors' marketing strategy, however; despite doubts about

ANDERSON and DeWOLFE

the profitability of their model, they insisted on building an open site—that is, one that gave users almost complete control over the content. Local bands and club owners whom Anderson and DeWolfe recruited were the first to create pages, establishing from the start MySpace's value as both a promotional tool for bands and a forum for fans. Music has remained an important element of the site, and since its launch such bands as R.E.M., Black Eyed Peas, and Weezer have streamed new albums onto it before releasing them.

"We didn't do traditional marketing, but we did try to find photographers and creative people because we thought that would make the site more interesting," Anderson told Natalie Pace for *Forbes* (January 4, 2006). "In the beginning, it was all Los Angeles—actors, photographers and musicians. That made for an interesting community, and brought in a lot of people. A lot of the early growth, however, had to do with the features and what our competitors were not allowing people to do." MySpace, for example, allowed pages to be dedicated to such entities as cities, dogs, or even ideas, while Friendster deleted such pages. The absence of such rules proved popular, and people began switching from Friendster to MySpace. The development of MySpace went "remarkably easy for us," Anderson told Pace. "I can't say that we struggled for a long time; we only struggled for about a month. When we were about a month into it, I remember thinking, 'This may not work out.' . . . One day . . . we saw this huge spike because of people telling each other. It just went crazy from there." Anderson, who emerged as the face of the site, is the one whom users are most likely to know; he is the first "friend," so his is the first user photograph a new subscriber will see. "Peering coquettishly over his shoulder from every profile page, he has attained an almost mystical status—somewhere between Jim Morrison and Steve Jobs," James Verini wrote for *Vanity Fair* (March 2006). Jeff Phillips, the singer for the band Hollywood Undead, who achieved popularity on MySpace, told Alex Williams for the *New York Times* (August 28, 2005), "Tom is a god. Literally, anywhere I've seen him, when we're out with him, people just stop on the street. They're like, 'Tom!' They want his autograph, pictures taken with him. It's like he's a rock star." By contrast, DeWolfe, who is regarded as the brains behind the business, has worked mostly behind the scenes. His MySpace page, for instance, is private; users can view it only with his permission. "Tom and I . . . have gotten to know each other's strengths and weaknesses," he told Fulginiti. "So, he focuses a lot more on, you know, the front-end user experience. And I focus more on building the organization and growing the business, and in making sure that this . . . becomes a global empire."

Commentators have voiced varying degrees of skepticism about the authenticity of the two men's public profiles. Verini noted that DeWolfe and Anderson are "almost too perfectly cast for their roles as elder business-school pragmatist and young vi-sionary with a film degree and guitar." Lapinski challenged their story outright: "Most users don't know that Tom Anderson is more of a PR scheme than anything else—the mascot designed to give a friendlier feel to a site created by a marketing company known for viral entertainment website, pop-up advertising, spam, spyware, and adware . . . ," he wrote. "With his almost alternateen good looks, Tom Anderson has served as an exceptionally convincing distraction" from the parent company's unappealing advertising practices.

In September 2005 NewsCorp., owned by the Australian media mogul Rupert Murdoch, purchased eUniverse—which, by that time, had been renamed Intermix Media—for $580 million. The acquisition, Sellers wrote, "puts the MySpace guys in an awkward spot. They founded their website on the principles of user control, grass-roots growth, and authenticity. . . . But now [they] have NewsCorp.'s financial targets to hit, a 'chief revenue officer' to contend with and serious pressure to make MySpace safe for advertisers." Murdoch admitted to Sellers that Anderson and DeWolfe initially "weren't too keen on the deal," explaining, "They could get more money later, if they waited to sell. And they had a reluctance about being corporatized." The transaction brought them an estimated $15 million each in bonuses, and Murdoch "provided them with the cash to reinforce MySpace's shaky computer system and to hire armies of sales representatives to bring in more money from the banner ads and sponsored pages that MySpace sells," Hansell reported. Anderson and DeWolfe have described the deal in mostly optimistic terms, with Anderson telling Williams that it would change little about how MySpace operated. "We get to keep doing what we're doing, and have more money to do it," he said. "We're not moving over there, they're not coming over here. We just kind of go talk to them once a month and let them know what's up."

Murdoch, however, made changes. Over Anderson's protests that moving the company would damage its laid-back culture, MySpace headquarters relocated from Santa Monica to Beverly Hills, where NewsCorp. was consolidating its Internet properties. Murdoch also made plans to tap into the site's tremendous advertising potential, something its creators had strategically ignored. When the site began, "although its scrappy backer was hungry for cash," as Hansell observed, DeWolfe "resisted pressure to flood MySpace with advertising and to turn all of its members into money." MySpace's advertising potential rested in part with its enormous number of user pages. While NewsCorp.'s emphasis on advertising risked alienating MySpace's users, it also increased the business possibilities, and a number of projects are being considered, are in development, or have already been launched, including pacts with Google and eBay; a record label; a service that would allow users to call each other; and a sports site, to name a few. "Anything you can do on the Internet, I want you to be able to do on MySpace," Anderson told Steven Barrie-Anthony for the *Los Angeles Times* (May 10, 2006). "That's the goal and ambition. Almost all the things you can do online can be enhanced by the social structure of MySpace."

In June 2007, in an effort to compete with YouTube, the Internet's leading provider of video content, MySpace launched MySpace TV. DeWolfe told Brad Stone for the *New York Times* (June 27, 2007) that "no one has really pointed out that MySpace has been focused on video and has quietly come within striking distance of YouTube."

In his on-line profile Anderson has listed among his interests weight lifting, hiking, traveling, studying the history of communism, and listening to music. Asked by Krantz what he does in his spare time, he said, "I do nothing else but work." His marital status, as noted on MySpace.com, is "single." DeWolfe is married to a former record executive; the couple became first-time parents in 2006. According to a mockup of his MySpace Web page, as created by Fortune.com, he spends "weekends at a beach a little north of LA (Hint: a downmarket rental in Malibu). In the winter, I ski in a chic Colorado town (Hint: it begins with an A)."

—M.B.

Suggested Reading: *Fortune* p66 Sep. 4, 2006; *New York Times* III p1 Apr. 23, 2006, IX p1 Aug. 28, 2005; *USA Today* B p13 Feb. 13, 2006; *Valleywag* (on-line) Sep. 11, 2006; *Vanity Fair* p238 Mar. 2006

Paul Fetters, courtesy of HHMI

Anderson, Winston A.

July 26, 1940– Cell biologist; cancer researcher; educator; historian

Address: Howard University Dept. of Biology, 415 College St., N.W., Washington, DC 20059

Over the last several decades, the Howard University biology professor Winston A. Anderson has led a triple life. He has built an impressive career as a cell biologist and as a researcher specializing in the growth of cancer cells; he has been heavily involved in efforts to improve the education of minority students, heading, among other committees, the Fogarty International Center's Minority International Research Program, which supports the global training of minorities in the biomedical sciences; and he is best-known to some as the co-founder of the Sandy Spring Slavery Museum and African Art Gallery, in Maryland, devoted to chronicling the past experiences of Africans and African-Americans. In 2006 the Howard Hughes Medical Institute (HHMI) presented Anderson with a $1 million grant, with which he plans to expand the scientific research and learning facilities at Howard and to place carefully selected honor students from Howard in mentoring programs at leading research centers. "If it sounds a little like an academic version of the Marine Corps," as the HHMI Web site put it, "that's not far off." The Jamaican-born Anderson has long stressed the importance of being a mentor and has urged others to undertake that role. In the lecture he gave in 1999 upon receiving the E. E. Just Award, presented by the American Society for Cell Biology (ASCB), he said, "It is a good feeling to wake up to *Good Morning America* to see your student being interviewed for making major advances in breast cancer research or in the biomedical sciences; so by influencing the lives of students you will receive rewards that money cannot buy."

Winston A. Anderson was born on July 26, 1940 in rural Jamaica, into a family "that pushed race-consciousness when I was growing up," as he explained to Michael H. Cottman for the *Washington Post* (January 11, 2001). He attended Calabar High School, in Kingston, Jamaica, from 1952 to 1959; in 1958 he completed the University of London, Higher School Certificate Examination in Jamaica. (Jamaica is a former colony of the United Kingdom; a number of universities and other bodies in the U.K. offer exams overseas, particularly in former colonies, through which students qualify to pursue higher education.) At 17 Anderson went to Washington, D.C., where he studied at the historically black Howard University, earning a B.S. degree in zoology in 1962 and an M.S. degree in the same subject in 1963. Anderson studied in the U.S. during some of the key events of the civil rights movement, including the 1963 March on Washington, and he was exposed to the rhetoric of civil rights and black-power advocates including Stokely Carmichael. Those developments fed what Anderson described to Cottman as his "great interest in race relations," one that led him to begin collecting historical items related to the African-American experience—such as shackles used for slaves, emancipation papers, and Ku Klux Klan artifacts—which now fill his home and are displayed at the museum he co-founded.

Anderson won the Beta Kappa Chi Award for Academic Excellence at Howard before continuing his education at Brown University, in Providence, Rhode Island. He has credited his teachers at Howard with guiding him toward a career in biomedical science and with encouraging him to attend Brown, since "it was in my best interest not to get three degrees from the same institution," as Anderson recalled in his E. E. Just Award lecture. He studied cell biology at Brown, where, he said in his lecture, he was one of a tight-knit group of 11 graduate students who considered themselves "cytonauts," or explorers in the field of cytology, the area of biology concerned with the structure and function of cells. He and the other students set about "discovering and defining, rediscovering, and redefining the structure and functions of organelles," which are distinct parts of cells. While taking part in the emerging study of mitochondrial DNA (that is, DNA found in the mitochondrion, the organelle that converts food molecules into energy), Anderson and his fellow students presented a paper on what he termed "the greatest mitochondrial DNA repository," located in the kinetoplast of a trypanosome. (A trypanosome is any parasitic protozoa in an animal or human, usually transmitted through an insect bite; a kinetoplast is a DNA-bearing organelle within the mitochondria of the trypanosome.) Anderson called his group's paper on mitochondrial DNA his "first citation classic." From 1963 to 1966, during his graduate-school years, he published 10 papers in prestigious journals including the *Journal of Cell Biology*, *Experimental Cell Research*, and *Zeitschrift für Zellforschung*. Since then Anderson has contributed to such journals regularly, usually with one or more co-authors.

Anderson earned a doctoral degree in biomedical sciences from Brown in 1966. He then spent two years in France as an American Cancer Society postdoctoral fellow, studying with Jean Andre in the Faculty of Sciences, University of Paris. There, he said in his E. E. Just Award lecture, he assisted in the effort to visualize the production of mitochondrial DNA and RNA through autoradiography (the creation of photographic images through radiation). The scientists also studied energy sources in cells. In his E. E. Just lecture, Anderson called his time in France "a most fascinating chapter in my life," which "provided lifetime links with several leading scientists of the time." In 1968 Anderson served as a postdoctoral fellow with the cell-

biology pioneer and first ASCB president, Don Fawcett, in the Department of Anatomy at Harvard Medical School, in Boston, Massachusetts. In the 1969–70 academic year, Anderson worked as an instructor in anatomy there. "At Harvard," Anderson said in the Just lecture, "it was possible to realize many of my aspirations in teaching and research." He learned from Fawcett and others that "good research was an important key to success in the academic profession; however, only as a responsible mentor can one ever become a good university professor. I believe that my career was launched at that time."

Having to, as he said in the lecture, "grow up and find a real job," Anderson next took an assistant-professor post in the Department of Anatomy at the University of Chicago's Pritzker School of Medicine. For two years beginning in 1973, he was an associate professor of anatomy there. In 1975 Anderson received the prestigious Anne Langer Award for Cancer Research, for his studies of breast cancer and uterine physiology. He also earned the first Distinguished Teacher Award at the Pritzker School of Medicine, recommended by the freshman and sophomore medical classes. Anderson began teaching at Howard University in 1975, serving from that time until 1984 as chairman of the school's Department of Zoology. In 1983 he received the College of Liberal Arts Award for Academic Excellence, and in 1984 he was presented with the Citation for Excellence in Graduate Education from the Graduate School of Arts and Sciences. Much of Anderson's recent research has centered on identifying the causes of cancer, specifically the role of estrogen, the naturally occuring or synthetic steroid that contributes to the growth and maintenance of the female reproductive system; he is also concerned with identifying triggers of cancer at the subcellular level.

While Anderson's research has been well documented in science journals over the past several decades, his activity outside academia has received more mainstream press coverage. In 1988 he and his brother Bernard, a surgeon at D.C. General Hospital, bought an acre of land in Sandy Spring, Maryland; that area was home to the earliest free black community in Montgomery County, Maryland, and an important "stop" on the Underground Railroad, the network through which many blacks escaped slavery. Anderson learned about the history of Sandy Spring by talking to older African-American residents who grew up there and had ancestors in the area. In Sandy Spring he and his brother co-founded the Sandy Spring Slavery Museum and African Art Gallery. "We were fascinated by this area," Anderson told Cottman. "It is steeped with history, and the black experience was overshadowed by the greater community, but we decided to focus on the heritage of black people, and we wanted to put the museum in the center of the hidden or neglected part of Sandy Spring." The town was settled by Quakers, who either did not own slaves or freed them long before the Emancipation Proclamation of 1863; the Quakers taught many local African-Americans to read and write.

The museum includes a 25-foot-tall replica of a slave ship, built by Anderson, with 50-foot sails. "In the hull of the ship . . . are models of slaves from various tribes, chained and sitting in a tight, confined area, much the same way they were on the months-long passage from Africa," Cottman wrote, noting that Anderson had made many of the models out of papier-mâché and given them faces resembling those of people he knew. Using thousands of dollars of his own money, and with help from his brother, Anderson built the replica over a span of 18 months in the early 1990s. "People were skeptical at first when I started building it," Anderson told Barbara Ruben for the *Washington Post* (March 30, 2000). "They'd say, 'You think you're Noah or something?' But pretty soon neighbors whose families had lived here for generations began stopping by and bringing me glasses of water." The museum is located on Brooke Road in Sandy Spring, along which, in the 19th century, many of the area's free blacks built their houses. In the decade after the completion of the slave ship, the Anderson brothers added to the museum a log cabin that had been dismantled and relocated from a nearby estate; the cabin exemplified the simple, poorly furnished slave dwellings in Maryland and the southern United States in the 1850s. The cabin "is only big enough for a bed and a table on its first floor and a loft above, but it was home to 13 people at one time," Ruben wrote. "The cabin has no windows on its first floor, and the one oil lamp cast barely enough murky light to see the drying tobacco hung from the ceiling and the burlap-covered straw bed." An artifact-filled pavilion, also part of the museum, was built to resemble a round African hut called a tukul; items from Africa and the African diaspora, including beaded skirts from South Africa, Haitian sculptures, and Ethiopian tapestries, are displayed there. Anderson taught himself the art of stained glass in order to create the building's windows, which depict several historical scenes. A more recent addition to the museum is a building to house civil rights artifacts and slavery memorabilia; it consists of four galleries as well as a gathering space for lectures and other events. In all, Anderson told Cottman, he spent roughly $90,000 of his own money on the museum, in addition to small donations. "It has brought a sense of accomplishment and pride," he said. Cottman wrote that Anderson is "soft-spoken, but when it comes to his love of history, particularly about African Americans, he speaks with a quiet power."

Anderson has presided over numerous committees, and secured an impressive number of grants, in his efforts to improve career preparation for minorities in the sciences. For 10 years beginning in 1977, he directed Life Science Careers for Minority High School Students in the United States, funded by Howard University and the Rockefeller Foundation. The program provided summer research opportunities at sites around the country for more than 800 high-school students, of whom 70 to 80 percent subsequently enrolled in college. Another program overseen by Anderson, and supported by the Pew Charitable Trust, recruited and trained more than 50 Washington-area high-school students in science and mathematics at Howard's labs and more than 35 others at the labs of Yale, Brown, and other universities. An award from the National Science Foundation sponsored the Research Careers for Minority Scholars in Sciences, Engineering and Mathematics program (RCMS), through which 33 undergraduates performed specialized research in 12 laboratories, from 1991 to 1994. Anderson noted on his résumé that during that time 12 RCMS students graduated with B.S. degrees— six cum laude, five magna cum laude, and one summa cum laude; six were inducted into Phi Beta Kappa. In addition, nine students enrolled in Ph.D. programs: one in astrophysics at the University of Michigan, one in biochemistry at Purdue University, one in chemical engineering at Stanford University, two in mathematics at Howard, one in medicinal chemistry at Howard, and three in medical school. One student, after earning an engineering degree, went to work for the Xerox Corp. The program also awarded advanced teaching certificates and offered a master's degree program in education for high-school science teachers. Through another program, funded by an anonymous donor to Howard University, Anderson has assisted in training 300 ninth- and 10th-grade high-school teachers in Ethiopia.

In 2006 Anderson was one of 20 scientists who each received $1 million from the Howard Hughes Medical Institute, to be spent at their discretion. The award was given to individuals, selected from more than 100 research universities, who had outstanding records of helping to place graduates in medical or graduate schools. According to a profile of Anderson on the HHMI Web site, his plans for the money include helping Howard establish core research labs with state-of-the-art facilities for work in computational mathematics, biophysics, cell and molecular biology, DNA research, and research into proteins. Intensive training in those disciplines, he proposed, would give minority students entering biomedical research fields the "competitive edge" that insufficient funding had previously made unattainable for them. Anderson was quoted on the site as saying that at present, "students cannot be adequately trained at our institutions because of a lack of resources." Despite those conditions, science is popular among students at Howard; by contrast, there has been a nationwide decrease in interest in science among high-school and college students. "We don't have a problem [with that] at Howard," Anderson maintained, according to the HHMI site. "We have 700 science majors"—roughly 10 percent of Howard's undergraduates. As part of his proposal for using the $1 million award, Anderson intended each year to choose 20 juniors and seniors from among his honors science undergraduates to take part in various mentoring programs at research centers and have their work published in peer-reviewed journals. Also, a proposed summer exchange program would take students to African countries including Ghana, Ethiopia, Mali, and Nigeria, to study tropical diseases and ethnopharmacology, the use of indigenous plants for medicinal purposes. To cultivate younger talent, Anderson intended to upgrade introductory science courses to prepare honors sophomores for the junior and senior honors research program, and to grant admission to Howard courses to advanced-placement science students in local high schools. "If you provide these core units, identify the students early, and get them trained the right way, then they can be competitive," Anderson said.

Among his many distinctions, Anderson is the first minority scientist ever elected to the prestigious American Society for Cell Biology Council, and he is a founding member of the ASCB's Minority Affairs Committee. Other honors Anderson has received include the 1988 F. E. Mapp Biomedical Research and Service Award from Morehouse Col-

lege, in Atlanta, Georgia, and selection as the King, Chavez, Rosa Parks Scholar at Oakland University, in Rochester, Michigan, in 1990. In 1992 he received Brown University's Outstanding Graduate Alumnus Award. That same year Howard awarded him the Certificate of Appreciation from the Division of Academic Affairs on behalf of Research Careers for Minority Scholars. In 1999 he received the Outstanding Doctoral Student Trainer in Biology award from Howard's Graduate School of Arts and Sciences. In 2002 he received a White House Millennium Award for outstanding achievement in research.

Anderson's wife, Carol, was born and raised in Kansas City, Missouri. He has two daughters, Laura and Lea, and a son, Michael.

—M.B.

Suggested Reading: Howard Hughes Medical Institute Web site; Howard University Web site; *Washington Post* T p16 Jan. 11, 2001, M p1 Mar. 30, 2000

Athey, Susan

Nov. 29, 1970– Economist; educator

Address: Dept. of Economics, Harvard University, Cambridge, MA 02138-3001

"When I'm working on a mathematical or conceptual problem in economic theory, there is a sense of creating another world inside my mind. I'm not aware of the world around me. If I have to run an errand, I'll bring my notes, and anything that comes into my life is an unwanted distraction. . . . I work all the time." The economist Susan C. Athey offered those observations about herself to John Koch during an interview for the *Boston Globe* (August 2, 1998) conducted three years after she earned her doctoral degree and joined the faculty of the Massachusetts Institute of Technology (MIT). The theory Athey had presented in her Ph.D. dissertation, in 1995, had struck economists in academia as so extraordinary that she had received offers of jobs from 23 colleges and universities in addition to MIT—and might have received more, had she not announced that she would not consider any others. "We fought really hard to get her," Bengt Holmstrom, the Paul A. Samuelson professor of economics at MIT, told Sylvia Nasar for the *New York Times* (April 21, 1995), in a front-page article in the Business section that identified Athey as "the hottest prospect among the new Ph.D.'s in economics" that year. "I've rarely seen somebody about whom there was as much unanimity," Holmstrom added. After working at MIT for six years, Athey became an associate professor at Stanford University; she held the title of profes-

Courtesy of Harvard University

sor there when she left, in 2006, to assume the same post at Harvard University. The next year Athey received the John Bates Clark Medal; given every two years by the American Economic Association (AEA) to the most promising economist under the age of 40, the award is second in prestige only to the Nobel Prize for economics. Among the 30 economists so honored to date (11 of whom went on to win the Nobel Prize), Athey is the only woman. "Susan's work on the foundations of economic theory is of fundamental importance," the Oxford University economist Paul Klemperer told a reporter for the *Economist* (April 28, 2007), "showing economists when they can have confidence in their 'equilibrium' theories and when they can't."

"Economics lets you rigorously analyze something and come back with insights and answers you didn't have before," Athey told Alvin Powell for the *Harvard University Gazette* (November 9, 2006, on-line). "I will sometimes go into a topic very deeply and abstractly, but eventually there's going to be a link to changing the world in some way, even if it's sometimes indirect." Athey's specialties are microeconomic theory, which focuses on decisions made by consumers (individuals, families, and businesses) and producers regarding purchases, investments, and other matters related to economics; industrial organization, a branch of microeconomics that deals with competition and other behavior of companies and government agencies acting as consumers; and econometrics,which involves the use of quantitative and statistical tools to analyze economic data and make predictions. According to the AEA's Web site, Athey is "an applied theorist"; she has formulated economic theories and also applied those theories to real-world problems and situations in strikingly original, eminently useful ways. Writing for the Web site Economicprincipals.com (April 22, 2007), David Warsh described Athey's theoretical work as "complicated in the extreme"; with few exceptions, laypeople would find it incomprehensible. Her applications, however, involve such familiar matters as diversity and affirmative action in organizational settings (including schools and businesses); 911 emergency-response systems; and auctions held by private concerns (for items ranging from fresh fish and flowers to real estate and antiques) and governments (for items ranging from treasury bills, auctioned by the U.S. Treasury Department, to natural resources, including timber, auctioned by the U.S. Forest Service, and oil and gas leases, auctioned by the Bureau of Land Management of the U.S. Department of the Interior).

In awarding the Clark Medal to her, the AEA cited as groundbreaking contributions to economics several papers written or co-authored by Athey that appeared in the *Quarterly Journal of Economics*, the *Journal of Political Economy*, the *Review of Economic Studies*, and *Econometrica*; she has also published articles in the *American Economic Review*, the *International Economic Review*, and the *Rand Journal of Economics*. Athey's work has been supported by funding from MIT, Stanford University, and, continuously since 1995, the National Science Foundation. Since 2001 Athey has been a research associate with the National Bureau of Economic Research, which describes itself as "a private, nonprofit, nonpartisan research organization dedicated to promoting a greater understanding of how the economy works." She is a principal with the firm Market Design Inc., which, according to

Alvin Powell, "advises governments on the design of auctions for items as varied as public resources, pollution permits, and the procurement of electricity." Several times in 1999, 2000, and 2001, she served as a consultant to the Research Department of the Federal Reserve Bank of Minneapolis, in Minnesota. She has been a senior consultant to Criterion Auctioneers of London, in England, since 2006.

"I love being in the middle of the research process, or the beginning," Athey told Rachel Croson for the *CSWEP Newsletter* (Spring/Summer 2001), published by the AEA's Committee on the Status of Women in the Economics Profession. "Coming up with a new theory, and developing a model, and proving some results, and then changing the model, and getting to the point where you have just the right model and into discovering how it works— just the moment when the model really 'sings' to you—is just a 'high' that it's hard to match anywhere else." By her own account, Athey regards one of the most important—and gratifying— aspects of her work the mentoring of students. "That gives me a lot of meaning—it feels like the impact that I have there will outlast a lot of the other things that I do," she told Croson. Athey hopes to influence her female students not only as an accomplished woman in the field but as one of the first at the top of the profession to enjoy marriage and motherhood along with her career.

The younger of the two daughters of Elizabeth Johansen, an English teacher, and Whit Athey, a physicist, Susan Carleton Athey was born on November 29, 1970 in Boston, Massachusetts, and grew up in Rockville, Maryland. Her sister, Jennifer Athey, is a psychiatrist. Her father worked for the U.S. Food and Drug Administration; after he retired, he co-founded the free on-line magazine *Journal of Genetic Genealogy*, which he edits. Whit Athey tried to imbue in his daughters his love for math and science, while his wife inspired in them an energetic optimism and a feeling for language. Athey's father has suggested that having a precocious older sister who earned many "kudos" made Susan "determined that she could do just as well," as he told Sylvia Nasar for the *New York Times* (April 21, 1995). A gifted student, Susan Athey sometimes purposely got poor grades so that she would fit in among her classmates. During her teens she played field hockey and other sports and had a series of odd jobs, among them telemarketing for a lawn service and working in pizza eateries. Unlike the vast majority of her peers, she read a newspaper (the *Washington Post*) daily. When John Koch asked her whether she was a nerd in high school, Athey replied, "No. I partied a lot. I found it hard to be a teenage girl and be real serious about math and school at the same time. I ended up not paying much attention to academics for a couple of years, but I knew that I wanted to achieve a lot in my life, so I decided to graduate early." Athey completed high school in three years and at 16, along with her sister, enrolled at Duke University, in Durham, North Carolina. According to economicprincipals.com, her parents divorced around that time.

At Duke Athey relished being in an environment in which intellectual pursuits were highly valued. She chose as her majors math and computer science, taking a few economics courses with the idea that she might someday enter the computer business. In her sophomore year a sorority friend of hers introduced her to Duke's microeconomics specialist Robert Marshall, and she became his full-time research assistant that summer. Earlier, she had worked for a computer business that had acquired a contract with the federal government through what is known as a procurement auction. Under Marshall's guidance Athey studied a flaw she had noticed in the auction system: the low cost of disputing the government's decision appeared to encourage losers to protest an inordinate number of outcomes. They would then receive payments from the winners through legal settlements. In what Marshall and Athey termed "procurement oversight by protest," the winners and losers were actually cooperating on bids. Athey wrote a paper about the problem, and later, in June 1991, she was present when Marshall testified before a subcommittee of the U.S. Senate Committee on Government Affairs about the need to change the auction process. "It was a neat chance to see how theoretical research in economics could influence public policy," she told Rachel Croson. Athey added economics to her majors at Marshall's urging and after she attended a seminar on game theory and industrial organization that fascinated her. (Game theory, a branch of applied mathematics and economics, is concerned with ways to make the best possible decisions, usually to maximize gains or minimize losses, in situations in which specific information is known and in which others are similarly engaged.) "What I liked about economics, early on, was that it was very rigorous and analytical, yet it could be applied to real-world policy problems," she told Croson. Athey graduated magna cum laude from Duke in 1991 with a B.A. degree in economics, math, and computer science. She was elected to the honor society Phi Beta Kappa.

Athey next enrolled at the School of Business at Stanford University, in Palo Alto, California, to pursue a Ph.D. in economics. As she wrote for the Harvard Department of Economics Web site, in what was labeled "a (somewhat) less technical introduction" to her research, at Stanford Athey observed that only tall, athletic male students were invited to join the informal departmental basketball team; women (even if they had basketball skills, as she had) as well as short or unathletic men were unwelcome. Moreover, faculty members who played with the team recruited their research assistants only from among the students on the team; the latter thus benefited professionally from their suitability for that particular recreational activity. When Athey learned that her fellow students also enjoyed weightlifting, she took up that

sport, solely to advance her career. That tactic worked: "I wasn't left out of the networking and informal conversations that can sometimes lead to collaborations," as she wrote. After those experiences, she continued, "I was left puzzling over what economic theory would have to say" about them. "What was missing from standard models that would account for these real effects of being a minority?" Working with two other students, Christopher Avery and Peter Zemsky, she constructed what she called "an 'applied theory' model of diversity in organizations that captured the idea that similarities among workers of different 'types'—gender or race, for example—make mentoring more productive." In her "first economic paper," "Mentoring and Diversity," which (because of publication delays) appeared in American Economic Review in September 2000, Athey, Avery, and Zemsky wrote, as paraphrased by Athey, "Firms face a tradeoff between maximizing the mentoring that goes to the majority type—where type-biased mentoring implies majorities are more likely to be promoted—and implementing voluntary affirmative action programs that lead the firm more quickly to full diversity, which allows the firm to provide intermediate amounts of mentoring to the best and brightest workers of both groups."

In her doctoral dissertation Athey presented new mathematical methods for analyzing risky business decisions involving, for example, foreign investments or technological advances. The tools she created, which have become standard in economic research, were outstandingly original. "I remember being just totally stunned," the economist Paul Milgrom, one of her doctoral advisers, told Mark Whitehouse for the Wall Street Journal (April 21, 2007). "This was a problem that had occurred to me that I thought was just too hard."

Athey's work at Stanford led to unprecedented interest in her on the academic job market. The economist John Roberts, another of her Ph.D. advisers, told Elizabeth Kelleher for USInfo.state.gov (May 1, 2007) that when she completed her Ph.D., Athey was "the hottest thing ever. Normally, a graduate of a good program in economics might have two or three [job] offers. She stopped accepting requests to interview when she had 24 offers." Roberts also said of her, "She is very dedicated and ambitious in a good way. But ultimately, what it is all about is just how smart she is." In 1995 Athey joined the faculty of MIT as an assistant professor; from 1997 to 1999, when she was promoted to associate professor, her titles bore the prefix Castle Krob Career Development. She won tenure before she turned 30—a rarity in her field. In 1997 and 1998 Athey was a Cowles Foundation visiting assistant professor at Yale University, in New Haven, Connecticut. In 2001 she left MIT, returning to Stanford as an associate professor in the Economics Department; she became a full professor in 2004, teaching students in the Graduate School of Business as well as undergraduates.

According to the great British economist John Maynard Keynes (1883–1946), "The master-economist must possess a rare combination of gifts. He must reach a high standard in several different directions and must combine talents not often found together. He must be mathematician, historian, statesman, philosopher—in some degree. He must understand symbols and speak in words. He must contemplate the particular in terms of the general, and touch abstract and concrete in the same flight of thought. He must study the present in the light of the past for the purposes of the future. No part of a man's nature or his institutions must lie entirely outside his regard. He must be purposeful and disinterested in a simultaneous mood; as aloof and incorruptible as an artist, yet sometimes as near the earth as a politician." In an example of a concrete application of Athey's work, in 2004 she was hired to assist Bob Friesen, an official with the British Columbia, Canada, Ministry of Forests, in constructing an auction-based system for selling government-owned timber (trees that are potential sources of lumber). "We wanted to make sure that we had a world expert so the system would be a sound system that wasn't under attack," Friesen later told Lisa Priest for the Toronto, Canada, *Globe and Mail* (April 23, 2007). Forestry is a major industry in British Columbia; currently, income from wood and paper products amounts to about 10 percent of the province's gross domestic product. For years, in setting the fees that lumber companies paid to the province in return for the right to harvest trees, British Columbia had relied on a comparative-value pricing system. Athey, who had studied timber auctions beginning during her years at Duke, used a statistical model to analyze data from past British Columbian timber auctions to determine prices that more accurately reflected market values. "Once you have those prices [at auction], those prices can be used as a benchmark for setting prices on timber that cannot be sold by auction," Athey explained to Priest. "What you want is something that reflects the price that a private landowner might receive." The new system helped to settle a trade dispute between Canada and the United States, which had accused its northern neighbor of subsidizing timber exports. Athey has also worked with the Australian government regarding timber auctions.

Athey has remained in academia rather than taking a full-time job in the corporate world, where she could earn far more, because she regards the mentoring of students as essential to her work. "I tend to have close relationships with students," she told Kelleher. "It helps humanize the leadership of the profession to them." She told Rachel Croson, "I feel lucky that I've already had the chance to see the effect that I've had on a few students' lives." Although women are not nearly as rare in economics as they were in the recent past, they are still underrepresented. Currently, women earn about one-third of the bachelor's degrees and one-third of the Ph.D. degrees awarded annually in economics, but at the universities that grant those Ph.D.s, only 8 percent of full professors in economics are women, according to the *CSWEP Newsletter* (2006, on-line). When Athey taught at Stanford, she was the only female tenured faculty member in the Economics Department. As of the spring of 2007, she was one of only three tenured women in Harvard's Economics Department. Athey told Kelleher that her selection as a Clark award winner had generated an "overwhelming response" from women in the profession. "To the extent that I become a role model for younger women, that's really exciting," she told Lisa Priest.

Athey's honors include her winning a half-dozen scholarships and fellowships, among them the Duke University Alice Baldwin Memorial Scholarship (1990–91), a National Science Foundation Graduate Fellowship (1991–94), and the AEA's Elaine Bennett Research Prize (2001). In January 2007 she delivered the Toulouse Lectures in Economics, in France; her subject was "Dynamic Contracts and Games with Hidden Information." Athey and her husband, Guido Imbens, a native of the Netherlands and Harvard professor of economics, have collaborated professionally on two papers, on the subjects of what economists call discrete-choice models and difference-in-difference models. The couple live in Cambridge, Massachusetts, with their son, Carleton, born in 2004, and daughter, Annalise, born in 2006. Before she became a mother (and had a bit more leisure time), Athey's recreational interests included running, biking, and in-line skating.

—N.W.M.

Suggested Reading: American Economic Association Web site; *Boston Globe Magazine* (on-line) Aug. 2, 1998; *CSWEP Newsletter* (on-line) Spring/Summer 2001; *Economic Principals* (on-line) Apr. 22, 2007; *Harvard University Gazette* (on-line) Nov. 8, 2006; Harvard University Department of Economics Web site; *New York Times* D p1+ Apr. 21, 1995; Susan Athey's home page on Harvard University's Web site; (Toronto, Canada) *Globe and Mail* A p6 Apr. 23, 2007; USInfo.state.gov May 1, 2007; *Wall Street Journal* A p1+ Apr. 21, 2007; *Who's Who in America, 2007*

Atkinson, Kate

Dec. 20, 1951– Writer

Address: c/o Little, Brown & Co., 1271 Ave. of the Americas, New York, NY 10020

The English-born, Scottish-based writer Kate Atkinson was 44 when her first novel, *Behind the Scenes at the Museum* (1995), captured Britain's prestigious Whitbread Award, winning out over

Courtesy of Peter Ross

Kate Atkinson

the works of more established writers. With that book and her two follow-up novels, *Human Croquet* (1997) and *Emotionally Weird* (2000), Atkinson, a onetime Ph.D. candidate in literature, established a reputation for works whose sometimes deliriously comic tone belied the seriousness of their themes: bleak family histories, parents' betrayals of children, and irreparable loss. Following the publication of her 2002 story collection, *Not the End of the World*, Atkinson turned to the mystery/thriller genre, to write the well-reviewed novels *Case Histories* (2004) and her most recent work, *One Good Turn* (2006). In the London *Telegraph* (August 29, 2004, on-line), Helen Brown expressed the view that the writing of mysteries is well-suited to Atkinson's talents. Referring to Jackson Brodie, the detective-protagonist of *Case Histories*, Brown wrote, "Considering the intimate details of other people's lives for a living is something Jackson and Atkinson have in common."

An only child, Kate Atkinson was born in York, England, on December 20, 1951. Her parents ran a surgical-supplies store, and the family lived in an apartment above the store until Atkinson was two years old. Atkinson read voraciously as a child; among her favorite books were Richmal Compton's 1922 comic novel *Just William* and the works of Lewis Carroll, including *Alice's Adventures in Wonderland*, which she has recalled reading once a week between the ages of five and 10. She attended a private elementary school and the Queen Anne Grammar School for Girls before enrolling at Dundee University, in Scotland; she matriculated there after failing the entrance examinations at Oxbridge University and the University of Edinburgh. (Between secondary school and college she

worked briefly as a maid in a hotel, a fact that the press would later publicize widely. She has also, by her own account, worked as a legal secretary, headed a welfare-benefits office, run a youth program for visiting the elderly, and served as a home aide, among other jobs. "The more experience you get the better," she wrote for the Web site Write Words, with reference to becoming a writer.) Atkinson graduated from Dundee with an M.A. degree in English literature in 1974, and thereafter she made Scotland her home. In 1973 she had married another Dundee student; her first daughter, Eve, was born in 1975, and Atkinson was divorced soon afterward. She remained at Dundee, where, having become fascinated by the work of American writers including Donald Barthelme and Kurt Vonnegut, she studied for a Ph.D. degree in American literature and completed a dissertation, "The Post-Modern American Short Story in Its Historical Context." She failed her oral examination, however, and fell short of obtaining her degree. Having done so, she "suddenly had no creative outlet" and was "very unhappy," as she stated for Write Words. She added, "Unhappiness is a great kick start to writing."

Atkinson married for the second time in 1982, giving birth to her second child, Helen, the same year. After five years that marriage, too, ended. Meanwhile, she had begun working part-time and writing fiction. One of her short stories won the *Woman's Own* magazine prize in 1988, and two years later she was runner-up for the Bridport Short Story Prize. She told Wendy Smith for an interview in New York *Newsday* (June 22, 1997), however, that she did not make a conscious commitment to a writing career until she was 40. Her career took off in earnest when she won the prestigious Ian St. James Award for her story "Karmic Mothers—Fact or Fiction?"

Atkinson's first novel, *Behind the Scenes at the Museum*, appeared in 1995. She has recalled that the inspiration for the book came in part from a dream she had; in it, she was visiting the Castle Museum of Yorkshire Life, in York, when the displays came to life. The novel brought its author the Whitbread Book of the Year Award, winning over the celebrated novelist Salman Rushdie's *The Moor's Last Sigh*, among other books by better-known writers. (In response, one British newspaper ran a headline reading, "44 Year Old Chambermaid Wins Whitbread.") Ruby Lennox, the narrator and protagonist of *Behind the Scenes at the Museum*, mainly presented as a teenager, describes a century of events in her family prior to—and including—her own birth. She also tells of her life in York, spent above the family pet shop with her two older sisters and her bickering parents—a philandering father and a mother who admits to not liking children. While the novel is in some respects reminiscent of the York author Laurence Sterne's 18th-century comic tour de force *Tristram Shandy*, Ben Macintyre noted for the *New York Times Book Review* (March 31, 1996) that even "by traditional standards of Yorkshire gloom, what happens to the intervening generations of Ruby's family is pretty dire. Most end up married to people they cordially detest or with children they did not expect or much want; many die violent, early deaths and almost all are miserable, some quite happily so. . . . . Like Yorkshire itself, *Behind the Scenes at the Museum* is all sharp edges; it is a caustic and affectionate portrayal of a world in which bleak but nourishing wit is the only safety net." Georgia Jones-Davis, writing for the *Los Angeles Times* (December 27, 1995), called the novel "a powerhouse of storytelling, a treasure chest bursting with the painful, pitiful, sad, always fascinating details of the most ordinary of lives." In addition to the Whitbread, *Behind the Scenes at the Museum* earned Atkinson the Lire Book of the Year prize, from France, and the *Yorkshire Post* Book Award for best first work. Atkinson was presented with the E. M. Forster Award from the American Academy of Arts and Letters in 1997.

Stung by assumptions that *Behind the Scenes at the Museum*, set in her native York, was the story of her own life, Atkinson deliberately made *Human Croquet*, her 1997 novel and the second in what she termed a trilogy, "purely a product of the imagination," as she said to Wendy Smith. Isobel Fairfax, the main character in *Human Croquet*, slips "in and out of linear time" and "experiences Christmas Eve and Day, 1960, over and over again, with increasingly and hilariously disastrous results," in Smith's words. Isobel and her older brother, Charles, grow up without their mother, who "ran off with a fancy man," according to the children's aunt; the novel's humor aside, its "central motif," as Rosemary Goring noted in *Scotland on Sunday* (March 9, 1997), is "a profound sense of loss." Claire Harman, writing for the *Independent* (March 9, 1997), called *Human Croquet* "interestingly confusing" and noted that "the device of time-warping . . . is taken very much further than the reader anticipates, beyond the point at which it appears fanciful and into a region where all sorts of possibilities open up. . . . Once you've given up trying to follow the real plot—if there is one—the problem of the book having no message becomes irrelevant; the author makes you attend to her contradictory stories for their own sake." Rosemary Goring observed, "Atkinson stirs together her cast like a witch flavouring her cauldron, the result a faintly gothic and beguiling concoction that is inimitable. One of her talents is to invest mundane detail with surreal significance, while at the same time deflating horrors, such as violence or abuse, by the clarity of her observation, unloaded with comment, but seen as through a youngster's camera eye. . . . The joists of life, where farce and dullness and cruel despair lie beneath a placid surface, are Atkinson's terrain."

In her novel *Emotionally Weird* (2000), set in the early 1970s, Atkinson again explored the themes of family history and mother-daughter relationships. Effie, while studying at Dundee University and maintaining her relationship with her drug-addled boyfriend, shares a house—and trades dubious autobiographical stories—with Nora, the woman she believes at first to be her mother. Meanwhile, Effie realizes that she is being followed. Rosemary Goring noted in *Scotland on Sunday* (February 20, 2000) that *Emotionally Weird* forms a continuum with *Behind the Scenes at the Museum* and *Human Croquet*. Each of the first two novels, she wrote, "took the form of family archaeology, the narrator prying into secrets, digging up the past and piecing together the fragments until a whole, if cracked, picture emerges. In both books we were drawn into the past as well as watching the unfolding present, Atkinson slipstreaming into history with the ease of a greased diver cutting through the waves." Goring found that with *Emotionally Weird*, Atkinson had used the same approach, and taken on similar themes, less successfully. "The design and central issues of *Emotionally Weird* are identical, but where the earlier books held their plot tightly controlled, and with it your interest, this time the structure is stretched so thin it's transparent. . . . Atkinson's cast of hundreds and attention to specifics is a good idea that runs out of control." Stephanie Zacharek, writing for the *New York Times Book Review* (June 25, 2000), arrived at much the same conclusion, noting that *Emotionally Weird* starts with "lively, crackling prose" and "deft character descriptions" but ultimately finding that "a problem with too much clever wordplay and so many enticingly detailed descriptions" is that "they can build you up just to let you down. . . . Atkinson is so good at describing her characters that she introduces altogether too many of them, and many of the better ones don't have much to do. . . . *Emotionally Weird* is clearly supposed to be a rumination on the bond between mothers and daughters, and Effie's shaggy-dog story is most likely intended as a metaphorical reflection of her emotional state. Too bad it untwirls itself halfway through."

Atkinson explained to Kim Bunce for the London *Observer* (March 12, 2000) her realization that her first three books were "based on *Alice in Wonderland* in one way or another but the young girl has now reached 21 and is grown up." She added, "I've had enough of that kind of writing." Accordingly, she next wrote *Not the End of the World* (2002), a short-story collection. The 12 stories each stand alone, but there are recurring characters among them; the first and last stories, both of which are set in a drastically decayed London and feature the characters Charlene and Trudi, fully reveal the thread running through the book. "These jazzy, offbeat stories studded with pop cultural references will appeal to Atkinson's fans and all readers of smart, trendy fiction," Barbara Love wrote in a review of *Not the End of the World* for *Library Journal* (September 1, 2003).

Case Histories, Atkinson's 2004 novel, marked another departure for the writer. That book, her first crime novel, centers on the policeman-turned-private-detective Jackson Brodie, who attempts to solve the mysteries surrounding three events of years past: the disappearance of a three-year-old girl; the killing of a young woman; and the ax-murder of a young husband and father, apparently by his wife. In describing her choice of a protagonist, Atkinson said to Helen Brown, "I wanted to write about a man man, who's interested in cars . . . you know? A man man. It's been said that the men in my books have been absent, or weak, or creepy. Jackson is 'the last good man standing.'" Carrie O'Grady wrote for the London *Guardian* (October 2, 2004), "*Case Histories* is essentially a balancing act, with evil and ignorance stacked opposite truth and healing. In this aspect the book is more satisfying than many detective novels—not just because it is so well written, but in its defiant refusal to let the dark side win the day merely for the sake of looking gritty and 'real.' Of course, *Case Histories* is not all sunshine and trite happy endings, but this is a book that rests on a strong and well-constructed moral framework, and is all the more powerful for it." Katie Owen, writing for the London *Daily Telegraph* (August 29, 2004, online), pronounced *Case Histories* to be Atkinson's "best book yet."

In *One Good Turn* (2006), her most recent book, Atkinson again turned to the crime/mystery genre—this time to tell the story of Martin Canning, a 50-year-old, sedentary mystery writer who performs an uncharacteristic act of physical bravery that makes him the target of a killer. Assessing the novel for the *New York Times Book Review* (October 29, 2006, on-line), Liesl Schillinger observed that prior to Atkinson's forays into crime fiction, "her novels and stories were puzzles of interpersonal connection: sometimes homey and nostalgic, like a jigsaw, sometimes experimental, like a Rubik's Cube, but always recognizable once assembled. Paradoxically, murder has given her a framework that helps liberate her insights on the living, as the lurking presence of corpses reminds readers that there are worse offenses than bad parenting and worse fates than unhappy marriages." Once, Schillinger concluded, "domestic dynamics were Atkinson's whole subject. Now they're her fuel tank."

Atkinson lives in Edinburgh. Catherine Lockerbie reported in the *Scotsman* (February 3, 1996) that contrary to an article in the *Daily Mail* describing Atkinson as being "pale" and "rather pimply" with "unwashed" hair, and as looking "like any tired London tourist," the novelist is "a strikingly beautiful and vivacious woman—with very well-washed hair." In addition to publishing fiction, Atkinson has written dramatic works. Her short 1996 play, *Nice*, was written for the Traverse Theatre, in Edinburgh. Her play *Abandonment* was published in 2000 and opened at the Edinburgh Festival in the same year.

—S.Y.

Suggested Reading: (Glasgow) *Herald* p12 Nov. 2, 2002; *Kirkus Reviews* p755 Aug. 15, 2004; (London) *Daily Telegraph* p12 Aug. 28, 2004, (on-line) Aug. 29, 2004; (London) *Independent* p29 Mar. 9, 1997, (on-line) Sep. 10, 2004; (London) *Observer* p13 Mar. 12, 2000; *Los Angeles Times* E p5 Dec. 27, 1995; *New York Times Book Review* p13 Mar. 31, 1996, p5 June 25, 2000; *Newsday* G p11 June 22, 1997; *People* (on-line) Jan. 12, 2004; *Scotland on Sunday* Spectrum p13 Mar. 9, 1997, p12 Feb. 20, 2000; *Scotsman* p16 Feb. 3, 1996

Selected Books: *Behind the Scenes at the Museum*, 1995; *Human Croquet*, 1997; *Emotionally Weird*, 2000; *Not the End of the World*, 2002; *Case Histories*, 2004; *One Good Turn*, 2006

Selected Plays: *Nice*, 1996; *Abandonment*, 2000

Baker, James A. 3d

NOTE: An earlier article about James A. Baker 3d appeared in *Current Biography* in 1982.

Apr. 28, 1930– Organization official; former government official

Address: James A. Baker III Institute for Public Policy, 6100 Main St., Rice University, Baker Hall, Suite 120, Houston, TX 77005

Few figures in American politics have had as much influence over the events of the last quarter-century as James A. Baker 3d. Baker served most recently as the co-chair of the Iraq Study Group, the bipartisan blue-ribbon commission charged in 2006 with making recommendations to President George W. Bush and Congress for a new direction in the Iraq War. The son of an old-money family in Houston, Texas, Baker is an unusual political figure, known for his prowess as both a Republican partisan, capable of doing whatever is needed to win elections, and a dealmaker, prepared when necessary to reach across a domestic or international divide. Baker first became well-known through his work on Gerald R. Ford's unsuccessful 1976 presidential campaign; his closest political association—dating back nearly four decades—has been with former president George H. W. Bush, for whom he served as campaign manager, chief of staff, and secretary of state. Frequently called the elder Bush's *consigliere*—the Italian word for adviser or counselor—Baker was instrumental in getting Bush to serve as Ronald Reagan's running mate in the 1980 presidential election and in guiding Bush's own successful campaign for the White House in 1988. Baker's association with the Bush family remains close; he led George W. Bush's

Alex Wong/Getty Images
Baker addresses the media after discussing federal election reform with congressional leaders

team during the ballot recount in Florida, following the 2000 presidential election, and aided the current president on the issue of Iraqi debt in 2003.

As the face of the Republican Party during the 2000 vote recount, Baker saw the erosion of the above-the-fray image he had crafted as secretary of state from 1989 to 1992. Once known for helping to forge the deals that controlled the former Soviet Union's nuclear stockpile, reunified Germany in 1990, and created the international coalition that drove the Iraqi army from Kuwait in 1991, Baker came to be regarded by some after the 2000 election as little more than a Republican hatchetman. Since the December 2006 release of *The Iraq Study Group Report*, which was highly critical of the current Bush administration's policy in Iraq, Baker has begun once more to be perceived as a pragmatic internationalist willing to achieve peace in the Middle East through negotiations with nations in the region, whether they are friendly or antagonistic toward the United States. While warning that "there is no magic formula that will solve the problems of Iraq," as quoted by a writer for the Agence France-Presse (December 6, 2006), Baker recommended that the U.S. open talks with Iran and Syria—two nations suspected of stirring up sectarian violence in Iraq as well as supplying and arming fighters there. "You don't just talk to your friends, and it's not a sign of weakness to talk to somebody," Baker said in an interview broadcast on MSNBC in October 2006, as quoted by the Agence France-Presse reporter. "It's not necessarily appeasement, provided you do it in the right way and you just don't roll over and give something, that you're hard-nosed and tough about it."

James Addison Baker 3d was born in Houston on April 28, 1930, the son of a well-to-do attorney nicknamed "the Warden" by his children. A strict disciplinarian, James A. Baker Jr. was known to throw a bucketful of ice water on his children if they were not awake by seven o'clock in the morning. As the younger James Baker explained to Tony Kornheiser for the *Washington Post* (January 18, 1981), at an early age he was "made conscious of the fact that I sort of had a heritage to live up to." His great-grandfather was a founder of Baker & Botts, one of Houston's first legal offices, and his grandfather, "the Captain," built it into the largest and probably the most prestigious law firm in the city through his connections in banking, real estate, and brokerage as well as his own investments. The Bonners, Baker's mother's family, made their fortune in the oil business. Like his father, Jim Baker, as he prefers to be known, attended the Hill School, a college prep school in Pottstown, Pennsylvania, then enrolled at Princeton University. Although he was a classics major, he wrote his senior thesis on the British Labour Party from 1945 to 1952. After receiving his B.A. degree from Princeton, in 1952, he spent two years on active duty in the United States Marine Corps. Having learned to shoot when he was a child, he became an expert marksman and was a member of the pistol and rifle team at Camp Lejeune, North Carolina. At his father's insistence, Baker returned to his home state upon completion of his military service to study law at the University of Texas at Austin.

Prevented by a company rule against nepotism from joining the family business, Baker went to work for Andrews, Kurth, Campbell & Jones, another high-powered corporate law firm in Houston, immediately after earning his J.D. degree, in 1957. "It was one of the best things that ever happened to me," he said years later, as quoted in *Newsweek* (September 6, 1976). "I always would have wondered if I would have made it on my own." He began his career in trial law, quickly growing disenchanted with the work and taking up business law instead. Within a decade he was made a partner at the firm. Baker found that he had a knack for making money in other ways, as well. In addition to making profitable investments, he succeeded as the head of a real-estate firm and the co-founder of both a brokerage house and a company that serviced oil wells; he and others sold the latter business for a substantial sum.

Although he was nominally a Democrat, Baker was by his own account "totally apolitical" during those years—in part because, as has been widely reported, his family saw politics as a corrupt profession. Meanwhile, his wife, the former Mary McHenry, was an active member of the Republican Party in Texas, who most notably contributed to the congressional campaigns of George Herbert Walker Bush. It was not until 1970, following the death of his wife that February from breast cancer, that Baker became actively involved in politics. In that year Bush, a longtime friend who had recently announced his candidacy for the U.S. Senate, asked Baker to run his Harris County, Texas, campaign. In interviews Baker has expressed his belief that Bush made the request in order to help him come to terms with his bereavement, to "give me something to do," as he once put it. Bush lost the race to Lloyd Bentsen, but largely because of Baker's organizational ability, he easily carried Harris County, which includes Houston, taking 61 percent of the votes cast. As a result of that experience, Baker switched parties to become, in his words, "absolutely, totally, pure Republican."

In 1972 Baker ran the campaigns in 14 Texas counties for the victorious Republican national ticket, headed by the incumbent president, Richard M. Nixon. A few months later he was named state Republican finance chairman. Reportedly on the recommendation of Bush, in 1975 he was offered a post as under secretary of commerce in Gerald R. Ford's administration. The following year, President Ford persuaded him to relinquish that position to become chief delegate hunter for the Ford campaign at the 1976 Republican National Convention, held in Kansas City, Missouri. Contrary to the predictions of many old-line political professionals, the personable and energetic Texan rounded up the final 200 or so delegate votes that pushed Ford over the top and won him his party's presidential nomination on the first ballot. Just a week after the convention, on August 25, 1976, Baker succeeded Rogers C. B. Morton as chairman of the President Ford Committee. He was the third man to head the campaign in five months. At the time of Baker's appointment, Ford was trailing Jimmy Carter, the Democratic standard-bearer, by some 30 points in most public opinion polls. In-

sisting that "people have been selling us and this President short for months," Baker devised a rather unorthodox game plan. According to Kandy Stroud, a political correspondent and the author of the book *How Jimmy Won* (1977), an analysis of Carter's 1976 presidential campaign, Baker advised Ford to emphasize his "presidential" image by spending most of his time at the White House until the last few weeks of the campaign. For the closing days of the campaign, he recommended an all-out personal appeal by the president, accompanied by a media blitz. The unorthodox strategy worked so well that Ford made up almost the entire 30-point deficit, but it was not quite enough. The incumbent president lost the national election on November 2, 1976 to Carter by just over 1 percent of the total vote. Despite his candidate's loss Baker earned a reputation as a campaign tactician of uncommon ability. As Stroud wrote, "Not until the bitter end, when James Baker took over, was there the slightest semblance of order or direction in the Ford campaign."

After the election Baker returned to his law practice in Texas, but, as he told Tony Kornheiser, "it didn't hold the same fascination for me anymore." In 1978 he announced his candidacy for the office of state attorney general. Despite the help of such high-powered Republicans as George H. W. Bush, Gerald Ford, Jack Kemp, John B. Connally Jr., and Ronald Reagan, who stumped the state in his behalf, and a campaign chest of over $1.5 million, he was beaten in that contest, his one and only bid for elective office to date, by a conservative Democrat. Nevertheless, he managed to garner about 46 percent of the vote, the highest total ever for a Republican running below the first line on a statewide ticket in what was then an overwhelmingly Democratic Texas.

The following year Baker agreed to manage George H. W. Bush's campaign for the Republican presidential nomination. To the astonishment of most veteran campaign watchers, Baker guided Bush, who was generally considered to be the underdog in the crowded Republican field, to a stunning political upset in the Iowa caucuses. Because they were the first political event of the year, the caucuses attracted heavy press coverage. Bush's victory, and the accompanying media splash, made him the front-runner going into the snowbelt primaries and aided him in winning six straight primaries. In the New Hampshire primary campaign, however, Bush made a costly mistake when he stubbornly refused to allow other candidates to participate in a televised debate that had originally been scheduled to include only Bush and his most serious challenger for the nomination, Ronald Reagan. A few months later, just before the crucial California primary, Baker persuaded Bush to withdraw from the race. He later admitted that Bush's taking the vice-presidential spot on the Republican ticket was "in [his] mind always as a fallback."

The timing and grace of the withdrawal decision undoubtedly made it easier for hardcore conservatives to accept Bush—a comparatively moderate Republican—as Reagan's running mate at the Republican National Convention. At Bush's suggestion Baker joined the Reagan campaign team as a senior adviser. Responsible for drawing up the budget for the final weeks of the campaign, he successfully argued in favor of cutting salaries and other personnel costs and putting that money into media advertising. He was also involved in the negotiations for the television debates with President Carter and with John B. Anderson, the Independent candidate. Against the advice of Edwin Meese 3d, Reagan's longtime associate, Baker pressed for a showdown debate with Carter. "I knew Reagan wipes people out in debates . . . ," he explained to Tony Kornheiser. "I knew that there were people on the fence about Reagan, people who'd heard he was a bomb-thrower"—that is, a trigger-happy political extremist. "The only way to overcome that impression was to get him on TV. . . . I knew Reagan would show better than Carter. Reagan never loses a debate." Baker was one of several aides who helped coach Reagan for the final television confrontation with Carter. In the opinion of many political analysts, that debate clinched the election for Reagan.

Ten days after Ronald Reagan's election to the presidency, on November 14, 1980, Baker was named White House chief of staff. His main duty in that post was to supervise the activities of nearly 1,300 White House employees; he also served as a trusted senior adviser to President Reagan, particularly in the area of legislative affairs. Baker's appointment surprised Washington insiders, many of whom had predicted that the new president would choose Ed Meese, the chief of staff during Reagan's tenure as governor of California. Moreover, Baker was considerably more moderate politically than the other members of Reagan's inner White House circle. In addition to managing the White House personnel office, he oversaw the operations of the legislative-affairs, public-liaison, press and communications, political-affairs, and speechwriting offices. Baker had further responsibilities as a member of the National Security Council and as a senior foreign-policy adviser. "It's a managerial job," he explained to Louise Sweeney for the *Christian Science Monitor* (December 30, 1980). "I think you've got to be able to make that train run efficiently, or the President will not appear to have it all together. You've got to be low key and low visibility because your own role is that of an honest broker. . . . I have to refrain from . . . suggesting policy options to the President." "You see," he went on, "I have to make sure that he gets all sides of every question, and that everybody who should have a chance to contribute to that decision has a chance."

In Washington circles Baker, presidential counselor Ed Meese, and Michael Deaver, the deputy chief of staff, quickly became known as the "Big Three" or the "Troika" of the Reagan administration. The extent of the authority exercised by those three men was perhaps first revealed to the public on March 30, 1981, when the president was wounded in an assassination attempt. In the harrowing hours following the shooting, they made almost all of the crucial decisions. For example, once they knew that President Reagan's life was not in immediate danger and that the international situation was stable, the three decided it was not necessary to invoke the 25th Amendment, which would have transferred power to Vice President Bush. During his 12-day hospital stay, Reagan relied heavily on his daily meetings with Baker, Meese, and Deaver for briefings and for help in decision-making.

During Reagan's first few months in office, Baker concentrated on securing congressional passage of Reagan's controversial supply-side tax and budget package. A firm believer that supply creates its own demand, Reagan advocated an economic policy of lower taxes and increased production, as opposed to the classical economic model that attempts to stimulate demand by first improving economic conditions. According to Secretary of the Treasury Donald T. Regan, as quoted in *People* (August 31, 1981), "Baker never left his desk, but he told the President when to play the good guy, when to play the bad guy, when to call a Senator or a Congressman" who might be wavering in his or her support for the president's plans. Representative Jack Kemp, the co-author of the Kemp-Roth bill, a comprehensive federal tax-cut proposal, added, "With all due respect to the President and Secretary Regan, it was Baker who got the budget and tax package passed."

Although he had long contended that "you can't be an honest broker and push policy," Baker nonetheless worked closely with Meese and other advisers on policy formulation and legislative strategy. (During his time as Reagan's chief of staff, Baker was nicknamed the "Velvet Hammer" for his ability to beat political opponents without making enemies.) In planning sessions he argued against the creation of a so-called "super Cabinet" in which some department secretaries would have had to report to others. Fearing a "power play" by Secretary of State Alexander M. Haig Jr., Baker successfully urged that Vice President Bush be named to head the National Security Council's crisis-management committee. He also helped smooth over the objections of right-to-life groups to President Reagan's nomination of Sandra Day O'Connor as the first female associate justice of the United States Supreme Court. In addition, in 1982 and 1983 Baker helped to secure a deal with the Democratic-controlled Congress on Social Security reform, which created the first-ever trust fund guaranteeing benefits for future senior citizens. Reagan signed the 1983 law accelerating an increase in the payroll-tax rate, adding employees to the Social Security system, and slowly increasing the age for receiving full retirement benefits—measures that, in the face of predictions that Social Security benefits would soon disappear, ensured their continuation for the next 20 years. (As of early 2007, however, many experts were forecasting a shortfall in the Social Security program, as the "baby boom" generation begins to retire.)

Though the Baker-supported tax-cut package did not initially produce results sufficient to lift the country out of recession, by November 1984 the American public was feeling secure enough in the nation's economic outlook to give Reagan a landslide victory over former vice president Walter Mondale, his Democratic challenger, in that year's presidential election. As for Baker himself, the successes of Reagan's first term—as well as his skillful management of Reagan's reelection campaign—had brought him virtually unchallenged authority in the White House.

In February 1985 Baker and Don Regan switched jobs, with the former becoming secretary of the treasury and the latter chief of staff. When he took over the Department of the Treasury, Baker had very little experience in the realm of tax and finance, apart from having helped to steer Reagan's economic stimulus and tax-cut package through Congress. In order to achieve Reagan's goals at the Treasury Department, Baker brought with him from the White House Richard Darman, who would serve as his economic adviser while Baker negotiated compromises with Congress.

During Baker's first year as treasury secretary, the greatest challenge he faced was to push through Congress an overhaul of the tax system. Defying predictions, his efforts led to the Tax Reform Act of 1986, which simplified the income-tax code, expanded the tax base, and eliminated a number of tax shelters. Today, the passage of that legislation is considered to be the last domestic success of Reagan's presidency. Though tax reform is now considered one of Baker's major achievements as head of the Treasury Department, his initial successes came in the international arena, when he negotiated an agreement that drove down the dollar's value for the sake of increasing trade and introduced a program to aid indebted nations in the developing world. At the halfway mark of Baker's term as treasury secretary, Lenny Glynn wrote for the *Globe and Mail Report on Business Magazine* (November 1986), "There is ample reason to argue that . . . Baker has already made more of a mark on the U.S. dollar—and world finance generally—than any U.S. treasury secretary since flamboyant fellow Texan John Connally orchestrated the last gasp of the gold standard in 1971–73." In addition to his work as secretary of the treasury, Baker was also assigned to serve as chair of the President's Economic Policy Council.

Baker left the Treasury Department in 1988 to manage George H. W. Bush's campaign for the presidency that year. After helping to fend off attacks from the right wing of the Republican Party, which criticized Bush's positions on such hot-button social issues as abortion and flag burning,

Baker secured Bush's overwhelming, come-from-behind victory against the Democratic challenger, Governor Michael S. Dukakis of Massachusetts, in the general election. The 1988 presidential campaign is generally remembered as one of the most brutal of recent times. As head of Bush's campaign team, Baker was criticized for his use of mudslinging tactics, in particular a number of attack ads focusing on Dukakis's character and his actions as governor.

Shortly after Bush took office, in January 1989, he named his old friend to the post of secretary of state, a position Baker had long desired. As the nation's chief diplomat, Baker soon found himself challenged by a shift in global politics. Foreign policy during the Reagan administration had been directed at confronting communism—both its existing form, in the Soviet Union, and its possible emergence in other areas of the world, such as Latin America. Reagan's doctrine had mandated that the United States negotiate with the Soviets only from a position of strength, achieved through a massive buildup of conventional and nuclear arms. By his second term, Reagan had become more willing to sign accords with the Soviets to control the proliferation of nuclear weapons. In 1988 the Soviet Union officially declared that it would no longer intervene in the affairs of its satellite nations in Eastern Europe. A year later Soviet troops withdrew from Afghanistan, where they had been waging a war of aggression since 1979.

Though it was not common knowledge at the time, communism in the Soviet Union and Eastern Europe was in its death throes when George Bush became president. Battered by a poor economy, an overstretched military, and poor infrastructure, the Soviet Union faced the first public recognition of its weakening grip on power on November 9, 1989, when masses of East Berliners, cut off from the rest of the city since the early 1960s by the Berlin Wall, were allowed by East German and Soviet authorities to cross the border and take part in a jubilant celebration with their brethren in the West. The wall was destroyed over the next several weeks by a euphoric German public who longed for reunification, which was officially declared on October 3, 1990. Baker, in his position as secretary of state, was the key negotiator in the reunification process.

Meanwhile, knowing that little was to be gained by further confrontation with the West, the Soviet premier, Mikhail Gorbachev, had met President Bush in Malta in December 1989 to declare a formal end to the Cold War. Shortly thereafter, the Warsaw Pact nations of Eastern Europe, as well as Soviet republics including Lithuania, began declaring their independence from the Soviet Union, as their citizens called for elections. In the Soviet Union itself the Communist regime was collapsing, despite hardliners' resistance to Gorbachev's reforms. A 1991 coup attempt against Gorbachev failed, leading the way for Boris Yeltsin and others to advocate the dissolution of the Soviet Union. In December 1991 the Soviet Union was voted out of existence by its own legislature, and its 15 republics became independent nations. Yeltsin subsequently became president of a newly democratic Russia.

One of the major challenges Baker faced during that remarkable period was helping to secure the former Soviet Union's nuclear weapons, which had been stationed throughout its 15 republics and in parts of Eastern Europe. In early December 1991, following a Ukrainian vote that supported the nation's full independence from Russia, Baker traveled to the capital, Kiev, to discuss the control of nuclear weapons in Ukraine. As other former Soviet states became independent, the Bush administration expressed concern that those states could threaten one another—or other nations—with the nuclear weapons on their soil. In order to guard against such a threat, Baker and other White House officials negotiated with their Russian counterparts the Strategic Arms Reduction Treaty (START) of 1991 and the Nunn-Lugar Cooperative Threat Reduction of 1992, which reduced the number of nuclear weapons and brought the remainder under the control of the Russian government. During the negotiations Baker played a key role in ensuring that all former Soviet republics were free of nuclear weapons. He also helped to provide aid packages to the former Soviet republics, as they made the transition to democratic government.

The other major foreign-policy crisis faced by the Bush administration erupted on August 2, 1990, when Iraq's then-president, Saddam Hussein, sent 120,000 troops to invade neighboring Kuwait, whose forces quickly capitulated. Declaring Kuwait to be a reclaimed province of Iraq, Hussein now personally controlled one-fifth of the world's oil reserves. Some speculated that Hussein would keep supplying oil and reap even greater profits than before, others that he would cut back the flow of oil and make up the difference in increased prices. There were fears among world leaders that Hussein would press on to Saudi Arabia or other oil-producing countries—perhaps in an attempt to unite all Arab countries under his rule—and initiate a final confrontation with Israel.

The Bush administration asked the United Nations to enforce economic sanctions against Hussein's regime, demanding a worldwide boycott of Iraqi oil. Well known for his pragmatic approach, Baker was an early and strong advocate of imposing sanctions on Iraq, hoping that economic pressure alone would force Hussein to cede control of Kuwait. The U.N. implemented the sanctions, which failed to persuade Hussein to recall his troops from Kuwait. After negotiating with other world leaders, Bush and Baker then proceeded to amass a large coalition of United Nations forces in the region—led mainly by the U.S. and composed primarily of U.S. troops—to demand Iraq's withdrawal from Kuwait. Iraq failed to comply with the January 15, 1991 deadline; the next day, coalition forces commenced air attacks on Iraq, followed by an invading ground force of about half a million

troops five weeks later. Four days after that, Iraq agreed to a ceasefire and to the terms of disarmament stipulated by the U.N.

Baker spent the latter half of his time as secretary of state working on a wide variety of issues. In addition to hammering out nuclear-weapons treaties with Russia, he attempted to enact a peace agreement between the Israelis and the Palestinians. He also increased trade with China, at the same time pressing that Communist regime to ease its suppression of human rights and limit its missile sales. Chinese officials only grudgingly gave him a promise to curtail missile sales and to allow dissidents to leave the country. The country's human rights record remains a source of tension between China and the U.S.

In 1992 President Bush encountered serious challenges to his reelection from the Democrat Bill Clinton, who was then the governor of Arkansas, and H. Ross Perot, the maverick billionaire businessman who had launched a strong third-party candidacy. Saddled with a sluggish economy and sagging poll numbers, Bush asked Baker in the summer of 1992 to come back to the White House as his chief of staff and campaign strategist. Leaving the State Department was difficult for Baker, who loved working there. "I hated to leave that job," Baker told John Spong for Texas Monthly (December 2003). "The only time I can ever remember losing my composure was when I said good-bye to the people at State. It was an emotional moment." Baker took charge of Bush's reelection campaign in August 1992, shortly after the Republican National Convention was held in Houston. His efforts failed: the voting public, apparently weary of the president's focus on foreign affairs at a time when the country was in an economic downturn, elected Clinton—who won with a minority of the popular vote (43 percent) but a majority of votes in the Electoral College. (Perot drew 19 percent of the popular vote, most of it, analysts generally agree, coming from citizens who would otherwise have voted for Bush.)

With the failure of Bush's reelection bid, Baker found himself out of Washington politics for the first time in 12 years—and, at age 62, out of a job. He did not remain unemployed for long. He became a senior partner at his family's firm, Baker & Botts, while devoting much of his time to the establishment, in 1993, of the James A. Baker III Institute for Public Policy, which he continues to serve as honorary chairman. According to its Web site, the Baker Institute "is strictly non-partisan and dedicated to the highest standards of intellectual excellence and integrity with the goal of helping bridge the gap between the theory and practice of public policy by drawing together experts from academia, government, the media, business, and non-governmental organizations. By so doing, the institute will broaden the professional perspective and personal understanding of all those involved in the study, formulation, execution, and criticism of public policy." The institute publishes policy papers, sponsors research fellowships, and organizes gatherings of eminent public officials to discuss government policy concerning such diverse topics as energy consumption, space exploration, global climate change, Latin America, and the current crisis in Iraq. A variety of world leaders have spoken at the behest of the Baker Institute, including Russian president Vladimir Putin and former South African president Nelson Mandela.

In addition to his work with the institute, Baker served as a consultant for the energy giant Enron, mainly writing papers on the political situations in nations where Enron conducted business. He left Enron in 1994, long before the company's name became synonymous in the public mind with corporate irresponsibility. Somewhat more controversially, the former secretary of state also worked for the Carlyle Group, a Washington, D.C.-based private equity firm that facilitates the purchases of companies, among other activities. Widely reported to be, in effect, the 11th-largest defense contractor in the United States, the Carlyle Group has a client base that extends to nations including Saudi Arabia and has had a number of former politicians, including George H. W. Bush and former British prime minister John Major, on its payroll; the Carlyle Group has drawn criticism for its mingling of political, business, and national-defense interests. Baker has dismissed such criticism, while stressing in interviews that his Carlyle Group work has mainly consisted of giving speeches on world politics.

In 1997 Baker was named as the personal envoy of U.N. secretary-general Kofi Annan to Western Sahara, where it was hoped that he could hammer out a peace accord between the Moroccan government and the Polisario Front, which sought Western Sahara's independence from Morocco. Unable to make headway in the negotiations, Baker resigned from the position in 2004, leaving behind a plan that has been endorsed by the United Nations Security Council.

Baker's return to partisan politics came about shortly after the November 7, 2000 presidential election, when he received a call from the Republican candidate, Texas governor George W. Bush, the oldest son of the former president. The younger Bush had run against Vice President Al Gore; the election hinged on a recount of votes in Florida, where the initial count gave Bush the victory by only a few hundred votes. Bush asked Baker to take charge of the Republican team helping to monitor the recount, while Gore tapped former secretary of state Warren Christopher to handle matters on the Democratic side by contesting the results of the election in the Florida courts. Baker countered through his team of 100 lawyers with a motion to stop the recounts altogether and allow the original count to stand. He also devised the strategy of taking the recount fight all the way to the United States Supreme Court, where he felt that the Bush team would get a fairer hearing than in the mostly Democratic-appointed state courts. The Supreme Court put an end to the recounts, giving Bush the presidency. Baker, meanwhile, saw his nonpartisan image tarnished. Following the recount fight, he returned to private life. In the hope of preventing another episode of the kind that had occurred in Florida, he agreed to co-chair, with former president Jimmy Carter, a commission to recommend changes in the voting process in national elections.

In early 2006 George W. Bush called on Baker again, to help him with a seemingly insurmountable problem—the Iraq war. (The original justification for the war was to rid Iraq of so-called weapons of mass destruction; no such weapons were found there.) Though the initial phase of the war—beginning with the invasion by U.S.-led coalition forces on March 20, 2003 and culminating in the capture of Saddam Hussein—was thought to be successful, the period of U.S. occupation has been marked by increasing violence between Sunni and Shiite factions, as each Muslim group vies for power in Iraq. As the growing insurgency against Iraq's fledgling democratic government threatened throughout 2005 and early 2006 to destabilize the country, Congressman Frank Wolf, a Republican from Virginia, proposed that a 10-person bipartisan commission be established to study the situation and suggest military and political options. With matters in Iraq worsening, President Bush saw his approval rating plummet, taking with it the fortunes of the Republican Party, which had majorities in both houses of Congress. In the midterm elections of November 2006, voters gave the Democratic Party majorities in both houses for the first time since 1994.

Earlier, when Congress approved funds to establish the Iraq Study Group, in March 2006, two men were asked to co-chair it: Baker and former congressman Lee Hamilton, a Democrat. (Baker had worked with the second Bush administration in 2003, serving as the president's envoy on the issue of Iraqi debt.) With the other eight members of their bipartisan commission, Baker and Hamilton worked from March through early December 2006, interviewing both U.S. and Iraqi officials, visiting Iraq to get a better understanding of the insurgency, and contacting world leaders with a vested interest in Iraq. When they completed their work, they unanimously approved 79 recommendations to be presented to the president and Congress. After the release of their 100-page report, on December 6, Baker publicly urged that the administration embrace it in its entirety. "I hope," he said at the time, as quoted by Michael Duffy and Mike Allen in *Time* (December 18, 2006), "we don't treat this like a fruit salad and say, 'I like this, but I don't like that.'"

Eschewing the ideal of democracy that the Bush administration had called the only true measure of victory in Iraq, the Iraq Study Group characterized the situation there as "grave and deteriorating" and presented a pragmatic approach that favored stability for the country above all else. Among the Baker-Hamilton commission's recommendations were a withdrawal of U.S. forces from combat operations by the first quarter of 2008; an increase in the number of embedded U.S. trainers in the Iraqi army and police forces; an aggressive new diplomatic push to solve the Israeli-Palestinian issue, which would include direct negotiations with Iran and Syria; and a timetable for accomplishments by the Iraqi government, complete with penalties for noncompliance. The commission's highly anticipated report got a mixed reception. Opponents of the war felt that the report did not go far enough in its recommendations for withdrawal, while advocates of the war argued that the recommendations to engage Syria and Iran—two nations long suspected of helping to stir up sectarian violence in Iraq—were misguided. Baker's hope that the Bush administration would adopt all of the report's recommendations appears to have been dashed: after studying the Baker-Hamilton commission's report and consulting with other advisers, the president called in January 2007 for the deployment of more than 20,000 additional U.S. troops in Iraq.

After the death of his first wife, Mary (McHenry) Baker, whom he had wed in 1953, Baker married Susan Garrett Winston, one of Mary's best friends and the daughter of a Texas rancher, on August 6, 1973. He has four sons—James IV, Stewart, John, and Douglas—by his first wife, and three step-children from Susan Baker's first marriage, which ended in divorce. The Bakers' youngest child, Mary Bonner Baker, was born in 1977. The recipient of the 1992 Presidential Medal of Freedom, bestowed on him by the first President Bush, Baker is the author of two books: *The Politics of Diplomacy* (1995), a reflection on his time as secretary of state, and *"Work Hard, Study . . . And Keep Out of Politics!"* (2006), a memoir.

—C.M.

Suggested Reading: Baker Institute Web site; *New York Times* A p9 Nov. 19, 1991, A p8 Dec. 8, 1991, A p1+ July 22, 1992, A p1+ Aug. 14, 1992, D p5, Feb. 23, 1993; *New York Times Magazine* p14+ Apr. 18, 1981; *Newsweek* p38+ Nov. 20, 2006, p35+ Nov. 27, 2006; *Texas Monthly* p151+ Dec. 2003; *Time* p39 Mar. 22, 1993, p40+ Dec. 18, 2006; (Toronto) *Globe and Mail Report on Business Magazine* p64+ Nov. 1986; *U.S. News & World Report* p38+ Dec. 18, 2006

Selected Books: *The Politics of Diplomacy*, 1995; *"Work Hard, Study . . . And Keep Out of Politics!": Adventures and Lessons from an Unexpected Public Life*, 2006; *The Iraq Study Group Report* (with Lee H. Hamilton and others), 2006

Banks, Tyra

Dec. 4, 1973– Model; actress; television host

Address: c/o Studio Fan Mail, 1122 S. Robertson Blvd., #15, Los Angeles, CA 90035

For the model, actress, and TV-show host Tyra Banks, being "fierce"—the word on which Banks has put her personal stamp, one that she uses to mean strong, bold, and confident—is the most valuable trait a woman can have. Banks, who has gone from a middle-class upbringing in Los Angeles, California, to supermodel status, to a new role as a burgeoning television tycoon, has often had to be fierce, as she defines it, to succeed in her field. As a rising model in an industry often biased toward white women, Banks had to fight to get on the runway. Her 1991 Paris debut instantly garnered her offers for 25 runway shows, an unprecedented number for a new model; even with that success, Banks continued to struggle with the undercurrent of discrimination in the fashion world, being offered lower pay than her white counterparts and facing fewer modeling opportunities. "I'm used to hearing the word 'no' because people say that to me all the time," she told Aldore Collier for *Ebony* (May 2004). "When people say 'no' or that I should stay away from certain things, I take it as 'Oh, okay you're telling me to stay away from that. I'm going after it.'" Realizing that her pursuit of runway mod-

Scott Gries/Getty Images

eling would limit her options, Banks sought work in print ads, signing exclusive contracts with Cover Girl Cosmetics and Victoria's Secret, and in 1997 she became the first African-American to pose solo on the cover of the celebrated annual *Sports Illus-*

trated swimsuit issue. In 2003 Banks, who had always had ambitions beyond modeling, expanded into television as the host of the show *America's Next Top Model* (*ANTM*), which recently began its ninth 10- to 14-episode season. "The minute you meet her, you understand why she's a supermodel," Ken Mok, an *ANTM* producer, said about Banks to Marc Peyser and Allison Samuels for *Newsweek* (March 15, 2004). "She has such a big-picture sense about herself. If she was a doctor, she'd be chief of surgery at Cedars." The show's tremendous success, especially among the highly coveted 18-to-34-year-old female viewership, led to the creation of Banks's own daytime talk show, in 2005. Though it has met with mixed critical reviews, *The Tyra Banks Show* has been a hit with the same group of young women who faithfully watch Banks doling out judgments on *ANTM* every week. Banks's entry into the arena of prominent media figures has led her to be compared, inevitably, to the phenomenally successful African-American media personality Oprah Winfrey—comparisons that Banks says are premature but that she hopes to make appropriate. "I want to be successful across the board," Banks told Peyser and Samuels. "I want an empire like Oprah's. I may do it with a little more cleavage, but I plan to get there."

Tyra Lynne Banks was born on December 4, 1973 in Los Angeles to Carolyn London, a medical photographer for the Jet Propulsion Lab at the National Aeronautics and Space Administration (NASA), and Donald Banks, a computer consultant. After her parents divorced, when she was six years old, Tyra and her older brother, Devin, lived with their mother; the family remained on good terms. Growing up in Inglewood, California, Banks originally considered becoming a veterinarian; she was also interested in media. "I used to watch commercials on television and be like 'Mama, the punch line wasn't right,'" she recalled to Alisa Gumbs for *Black Enterprise* (September 2006). "I would rewrite the commercials, and she would encourage me. So it started with me wanting to be in advertising. And then it just developed into film and television." When Banks enrolled at Immaculate Heart High School, a Catholic girls' school, she had already reached her statuesque height of five feet 11 inches. At all of 110 pounds, she was often the target of jokes, some comparing her to Ethiopian famine victims, and she was frequently called names such as "lightbulb head" because of her large forehead. Not surprisingly, Banks had no plans to base a career on her looks—until one of her best friends suggested that she pursue modeling. With a portfolio shot by her mother, Banks began going to interviews at Los Angeles modeling agencies, which consistently turned her down. "The market for black models was not good," London told Tom Gliatto and Bryan Alexander for *People* (April 11, 1994). "They would say, 'We have this many black girls already.'" After receiving many rejections, Banks decided to give up on modeling

and enrolled at Loyola Marymount University, in Los Angeles, to study film.

Two weeks before her classes were to start, a French modeling scout spotted Banks walking down the street and immediately offered her a spot in the upcoming haute couture shows in Paris, France, where she enjoyed immediate success. *People* magazine (May 9, 1994), in a profile of Banks for its 1994 "50 Most Beautiful People" issue, noted that in Paris Banks's "sensual lope and sleek, space-age frame gave her instant catwalk charisma." After appearing in Paris, Banks was booked for 25 fashion shows—a feat no first-time model, black or white, had ever achieved. She reflected on her struggle to break into the business to Margena A. Christian for *Jet* (May 26, 2003): "There's a lot of people who will tell you no. A lot of people who will tell you that you're too this and too that. I had people tell me that I'm 'too Black, not Black enough, my lips are too big, forehead too big, hair too this,' just so many things," she said. "Finally one agency said yes. All you need is for one person to say yes."

Even with that success, the modeling community in the U.S. and abroad had yet to fully embrace Banks. As a relatively curvaceous—if slender—black woman in an industry of stick-straight white models, Banks had to contend with both her perceived physical deficiencies and a culture of underlying discrimination against nonwhite models, which led to fewer jobs and lower pay. Comparisons in the press between Banks and Naomi Campbell, the other prominent black model at the time, led to an intense rivalry between the two women. Campbell, who was long-established in the industry, reportedly refused to model in the same Chanel show as Banks, forcing out the less experienced model. The tension between the two eventually led Banks to leave their shared modeling agency, Elite Modeling Agency, for IMG. "No model should have to endure what I went through at 17," Banks told Deborah Gregory for *Essence* (February 1995). "It's very sad that the fashion business and press can't accept that there can be more than one reigning Black supermodel at a time."

In 1991 Banks formed Tygirl Inc. to manage her growing career. Two years later she signed an exclusive deal with Cover Girl Cosmetics, making her only the third black model to be offered a long-term contract with that company. That year she also began expanding beyond modeling with appearances on the sitcom *The Fresh Prince of Bel-Air* as Jackie Ames, the love interest of Will Smith's character. Though she was interested in pursuing acting further, she left the show after only seven episodes, concerned that she would become typecast as a beautiful but superficial woman. She also turned down a role as a woman who has a one-night stand with Tom Cruise's character in the suspense blockbuster *The Firm*, because she did not want to portray a purely ornamental character. By that point in her career, Banks had begun appearing on magazine covers as well as at fashion shows. One such cover—a 1993 shot for *Essence*—caught the eye of the film director John Singleton, who became interested in casting her in his upcoming movie *Higher Learning*. While she received some praise for her portrayal of Deja, a track star who meets a tragic end, Banks continued to concentrate on modeling.

Banks had long been advised to stick to runway modeling, with agents telling her that her forehead was too large for the close scrutiny her face would receive in print ads. Banks, however, had a different vision for her career. One day, tired of dieting to maintain the preferred look of the runway model, she saw the supermodel Cindy Crawford hosting a television program and felt inspired to take charge of her own career. "I knew I wanted to be in control like her," Banks recalled to Collier. "There's never been a Black model with that kind of mass appeal, and I wanted to be like that." Banks informed her agent that she wanted to move away from haute couture and toward the more mainstream—and more lucrative—print ads. In 1996 she became the first black model to pose for the cover of *GQ* and also the first to do so for the cover of the *Sports Illustrated* swimsuit issue, appearing on the latter alongside the white model Valeria Mazza. The following year she made history again, when she appeared on the swimsuit issue by herself, becoming the first black model to pose solo for the cover in the famed issue's then-31-year run. Victoria's Secret put Banks on the cover of its 1997 swimsuit catalog, subsequently signing her to a long-term contract that included both print and television ads. Still, Banks had greater aspirations. "I was the girl that on every commercial was talking to everybody: the director, the grips, even the line producer. I tried to educate myself as much as possible when I was on set," she recalled to Gumbs. In another triumph for minority models, in 1997 she was also named supermodel of the year at the Michael Awards, the fashion industry's annual awards ceremony. With Vanessa Thomas Bush, she wrote *Tyra's Beauty Inside & Out* (1998), a book on maintaining beauty and self-esteem. In 2000 she appeared with Lindsay Lohan in the Disney made-for-television movie *Life-Size* and had roles in the films *Coyote Ugly* and *Love & Basketball*. In 2002 she co-starred in the horror film *Halloween: Resurrection*. During those years she also appeared in several television shows, including *New York Undercover*, *The Hughleys*, and *Felicity*.

Banks came into greater prominence with her creation of *America's Next Top Model*, which debuted in 2003 with Banks as host. "I was in my kitchen in my underwear looking out the window, and just saw the words 'America's Top Model' in my head," she recalled to Peyser and Samuels. "I wanted to do a show where people were striving for a goal, winning something that you've worked hard for." Each season of the show begins with 10 or so contestants, who compete over the course of the season for a modeling contract and the title of America's Next Top Model. On each installment,

one contestant is eliminated. UPN's president, Dawn Ostroff, approved the program only hours after Banks presented her idea: to show the public that it takes more than just good looks to make it in the modeling industry. "There are pretty faces everywhere. . . . Supermodels are the ones that have personality . . . ," Banks told Christian. "I think you have to have a combination of accessibility where everyone in America can feel like they know you. You need a certain sense of beauty, a beauty that's not too intimidating where it doesn't scare people. You need a personality that's fun. You should be a person who can speak well and represent products. . . . Our winner is a true model because she passed all the tests."

America's Next Top Model, which finished its seventh season as the number-one show on its network (now called the CW), revolves around Banks, whose company, Bankable Productions, owns a 25 percent stake in the show. "The aspiring models view her both as the bearer of a magic ticket out of poverty, obscurity, stripping, or waitressing and as a comforting, maternal, Oprah-like figure," Nancy Franklin wrote for the *New Yorker* (March 14, 2005). "Even while she is pondering which chick will be thrown out of the nest each week, Banks dispenses plentiful hugs to her charges, at one point getting down on a bathroom floor to console a distressed girl."

Banks's colleagues on the set of *ANTM* have agreed that, as Banks has put it, there is a "nighttime Tyra" and a "daytime Tyra." The former, a caricature of the diva-like behavior that viewers expect from a supermodel, is on display on *ANTM*. The latter, according to Banks and her colleagues, is the true, unpretentious Banks, who appears at all other times. "Daytime Tyra" found an outlet in 2005, when Banks signed on to host her own daytime talk show in addition to *ANTM*. She had been offered a chance to host a talk show a few years earlier, after she had impressed network executives with a two-year position as a youth correspondent on *Oprah*, but she had turned it down. Having gotten a little older, though, she felt she had reached the right point in her life to create the kind of show she wanted. "Because I've been hurt and I've been stupid and I've stayed in a destructive relationship for way too long, now I feel I can talk to people about their problems," she told Celeste Fremon for *Good Housekeeping* (October 2005). Banks envisioned her program as being different from other talk shows, explaining to Andy Serwer for *Fortune* (February 20, 2006), "It's not really a talk show. It's a woman's guide to life. It's topical, connected to the news, but we do fashion and fun stuff. It's like different pages or sections in a women's magazine. They're unique, but they all fit together under one cover." *The Tyra Banks Show* debuted on September 12, 2005. Dick Robertson, the president of Warner Brothers Domestic Television Distribution, explained to Kimberly Speight for the *Hollywood Reporter* (September 30, 2004) why the company was so eager for the distribution rights to the show:

"Tyra is a very impressive person; she's obviously more than a model," he said. "It's her appearances on *Oprah* that we looked at and said, 'If there's ever a future Oprah, she could be the one.'"

Deciding to leave modeling while she was still successful in the industry, Banks officially retired from the runway in December 2005, after her last Victoria's Secret show, and focused her energy on her television shows. One of her first moves was to hire an interview coach, to help improve her hosting skills. "For the first season of the talk show, I would scream high-pitched and do a lot of stupid things," she said to Collier. "Or, I'd interview someone and they'd say something poignant, but I wouldn't hear because I was so focused on my next question. So I learned to listen and have it be a conversation." Still, many critics continued to pan the show, calling it a way for Banks to work through her own psychological issues while turning her name into a brand. "An *Oprah* for a younger crowd, the talk show ostensibly focuses on 'the dreams, hopes and challenges of today's young women,'" Alyson Ward wrote for the *Fort Worth (Texas) Star-Telegram* (March 8, 2006). "But you know what it really focuses on? The dreams, hopes and challenges of Tyra Banks." For one show, Banks brought on a doctor who gave her an on-camera sonogram, to prove that her much-discussed breasts had not been surgically enhanced. On another, Banks confronted a porn star using the name Tyra Banxxx. On still another, she invited her former rival, Naomi Campbell, to talk about their past adversarial relationship. The popular success of the show—and particularly of those installments—rests on Banks's persona. In everything she does, Banks says, she strives to be "fierce"; for many critics, however, that trait is not enough to warrant comparisons to the heavy hitters of daytime TV. "She may be fierce, but unfortunately Tyra isn't as smart or as dynamic or as quick or as sensible as Oprah, and she's not as insightful or as instructive or as commanding a presence as Dr. Phil," Heather Havrilesky wrote for *Salon.com* (October 2, 2005). "In the end, when she's interviewing a young woman about cheating or asking another woman how she feels about commitment, it just sounds vapid and rambling and you feel like you're overhearing two teenage girls gossiping aimlessly on the bus." Nonetheless, *The Tyra Banks Show* has been a hit, especially with the highly-sought-after 18-to-34-year-old female viewers. Currently in its third season, the show has been renewed through 2009. Banks told Juan Morales for *Redbook* (April 2006) that she is working hard to take some of the advice that she doles out so readily on *ANTM* and on her talk show. "I have goals and ambitions, and I'm a perfectionist. I look at my talk show ratings and think, 'This is good, but we can do better.' I'm always pushing myself. But I'm learning to pull back," she said. "I always tell my models [on *ANTM*] that perfect is boring. Sometimes I have to remind myself of that—that it's okay if there are flaws here and there. I used to stay up all night if something didn't go right on my talk show. Now, I'm like, 'You know what? We're a new show, and we're going to get there.'"

Banks recently moved to New York, where *The Tyra Banks Show* is now filmed. Her company, Bankable Productions, has five television shows in development, as well as a film that Banks will both act in and produce. Banks has formed her own licensing firm, which is looking to branch into the lingerie market. She is also working on a fashion-related Internet site. In 1992 she established the Tyra Banks Scholarship at the private Los Angeles high school that she attended. In 1999 she founded TZone, a Los Angeles–based summer camp focusing on building confidence in teenage girls. She hopes to establish more camps like it around the country.

—C.S.

Suggested Reading: *Ebony* p154+ May 2004; *Essence* p60+ Feb. 1995; *Fort Worth (Texas) Star Telegram* F p1 Mar. 8, 2006; *Jet* p56+ May 26, 2003; *New Yorker* p 143 Mar. 14, 2005

Selected Films: *Higher Learning*, 1995; *Coyote Ugly*, 2000; *Halloween: Resurrection*, 2002

Selected Books: *Tyra's Beauty Inside & Out* (with Vanessa Thomas Bush), 1998

Selected Television Shows: *The Fresh Prince of Bel-Air*, 1993; *America's Next Top Model*, 2003–; *The Tyra Banks Show*, 2005–

Barber, Patricia

1956– Jazz singer, songwriter, and pianist

Address: c/o Spire Artist Management, 5438 Boyd Ave., Oakland, CA 94618

Being a jazz musician "is such a difficult lifestyle—the late nights, the smoke, the insecurity, the lack of health insurance—and I wanted to be a nice middle-class girl," the jazz pianist and singer Patricia Barber told the music critic Terry Teachout during an interview for the *New York Times* (June 23, 2002), in recalling her undergraduate years, in the mid-1970s. "My father was a musician, and he died an alcoholic, and my mother was afraid that something bad would happen to me, too. I was going to go to law school, medical school, anything other than music, and finally I called my mother during my senior year in college and said: 'Mom, I'm going to be a jazz musician. I can't help it.' And she cried. . . . She was just afraid. And so was I. It's only been very, very recently that I haven't almost hated what I was doing." One night, during a performance, Barber continued, "I made myself look out at those wonderful people who'd come to

Pierre-Franck Colombier/AFP/Getty Images

Patricia Barber

hear me, and I thought: 'My God, they're paying $20 a ticket. What could they possibly be paying for? Why are they coming? There must be a reason.' And all at once I felt able to embrace the fact that this is who I am, this is where I am."

"Nobody else today is doing what Barber does," Bob Young wrote for the *Boston Herald* (February 20, 1999). "Her smart, often oblique lyrics are delivered with a clean-lined, sensual vocalizing and unique arrangements that twist and turn in unexpected directions like the best jazz always does." Described as one of the most skilled, inventive, literate, and droll songwriters, vocalists, and pianists in present-day jazz, Barber has given upwards of 1,000 performances since the early 1980s, many of them at two clubs in Chicago, Illinois: the Gold Star Sardine Bar, where she appeared from 1984 to 1992, and the Green Mill, beginning in 1994. Most of the nine albums she has recorded since 1989 offer a mixture of jazz standards, pop covers, and original songs, some with music set to works written by others (among them such poets or writers as Paul Verlaine, e. e. cummings, Maya Angelou, and Virginia Woolf), and some whose music and lyrics she composed herself. Her most recent album, *Mythologies*, created with the support of a 2003 Guggenheim fellowship—the only one ever to be awarded to a songwriter—is a song cycle inspired by characters from Greek myth described in *The Metamorphoses*, by the Roman poet Ovid (43 B.C.–17 A.D.). "The artistic heights to which Barber aspires in *Mythologies* may make this release more endearing to serious listeners than to the vast commercial audience, which has made icons of far lesser talents, such as Norah Jones, Diana Krall and Jane Monheit," the veteran jazz critic Howard Re-

ich wrote for the *Chicago Tribune* (August 13, 2006). "While these artists have triumphed commercially by reviving role models of the distant past—particularly the seductive, purring chanteuse of the 1940s and '50s—Barber has ventured into fresher territory. To her, the female singer-pianist is not necessarily an object of nostalgia and romance but a contemporary thinker with intellectual firepower to burn."

"In an age when pipsqueak voices and easy-listening sensibilities routinely draw critical praise and commercial success, Barber has emerged as the anti-diva: a singer uninterested in assuming the usual romantic poses, a songwriter unwilling to pen cloyingly sweet love songs, a pianist who actually has something distinctive to say at the keyboard," Reich declared in the *Chicago Sun-Times* (September 13, 2004). Barber's voice has been described as having "the confidential purr of a bass flute" (by Terry Teachout); as having an "alluring liquidity" (by Reich); as "deep" and "winsome" (by the jazz journalist R.J. DeLuke, in AllAboutJazz.com, March 1, 2004); as "instantly appealing and often downright sexy" (by the music journalist and broadcaster George Graham, on his Web site, 2002); as "coolly understated" (by Bill Beuttler, in the *Boston Globe*, October 1, 2004); and as "a low-vibrato alto on perpetual rhythm and timbre alert" (by Margo Jefferson, in the *New York Times*, October 16, 2000). Barber's lyrics in her 2002 album, *Verse*, struck Graham as "some of the most absorbing I have heard on record in a long time." Barber, he continued, "writes in part from experience, often metaphorically, and takes on some familiar subjects by casting an entirely new light on them. But most impressive is her sheer power of language. She puts words and phrases into songs the likes of which have rarely been heard, and at a more poetic level than some of the best folkies. She is also not without a sense of dry wit." According to Mike Joyce, writing for the *Washington Post* (February 12, 1999), some of Barber's lyrics "bring to mind Joni Mitchell's gift for metaphor and imagery, while others reflect a decidedly sardonic view of contemporary life." "People need music now," Barber said to Michael Friedman during an interview for AllAboutJazz.com (November 1998). "They need music that speaks to their souls, not just their heads. . . . They need music that grabs them where they didn't know they needed to be grabbed. . . . They need art desperately. Jazz could give them what they need."

Patricia Barber was born in 1956 in Illinois and spent her early years in a suburb of Chicago. A sister, Ann, died of cancer in 1999. (Barber wrote "Love, Put on Your Faces," based on a poem by e. e. cummings, in honor of Ann; backed by the Choral Thunder Vocal Choir, the song is on her album *Modern Cool*.) Barber's mother was an amateur blues singer. Her father, Floyd "Shin" Barber, was an alto saxophonist who occasionally played with Glenn Miller's band, among others, and also led a

Chicago-area ensemble. Unable to support his family adequately as a musician, he became a pharmacist. He started to teach Patricia piano when she was five and continued to instruct her until his death, when she was nine. After her mother became widowed, she settled with her daughters elsewhere in the Midwest (in Iowa or Nebraska, according to various sources). During Barber's adolescence, in the late 1960s, as she recalled to DeLuke, she had no interest in the Beatles, the Rolling Stones, or other groups popular at that time. "I was listening to what I guess you call the classic American songsters. Frank Sinatra. I wasn't really into the really hip people, like Sarah Vaughn, until high school. And Miles Davis." Barber played several instruments in her high-school band and had a singing part in a student musical. She attended the University of Iowa, where she majored in both classical piano and psychology. During her college years, she told DeLuke, she sang with a local band, solely to earn some pocket money. She earned a B.A. degree in 1977. Nearly two decades later, in 1996, armed with a scholarship, she earned a master's degree in music from Northwestern University, in Evanston, Illinois.

Earlier, in 1979, having resolved to pursue jazz as a profession, Barber had moved to Chicago and begun performing in clubs on the city's jazz circuit. In considering where to start building her career, she had ruled out New York and Los Angeles, because in those cities, as she explained to Lloyd Sachs for the Los Angeles Times (August 15, 1999), "you start second-guessing yourself too soon. You ask yourself, am I hip enough to be here? Is this what's gonna get me attention? In Chicago, you don't have that. The music develops in rather an unfettered way." For the next five years or so, Barber entertained whenever she could in Chicago clubs. At times she faced tough audiences. "There were real bad jobs like one club in a neighborhood so bad the owner had to walk me out through the bar each night," she told Steven Pratt for the Chicago Tribune (November 9, 1988). "One time a drunk broke a beer bottle and started climbing right over the piano threatening to rape me." She also locked horns with some club owners. "They wanted me to smile at the male customers and talk to them between sets," she told Sachs for the Chicago Sun-Times (June 4, 1995). "I wanted to read books instead." Nevertheless, as she recalled to DeLuke, her experiences during that period left her with "some of my best memories. All of the musicians helped me. Sometimes I would need a certain lesson from a certain pianist and I would call and have a lesson or two, or they'd help me on a gig; tell me what to study, what to listen to. Tell me what I was bad at."

In 1984, at the suggestion of the longtime jazz critic and broadcaster Neil Tesser, Barber auditioned successfully for a five-night-a-week, semi-permanent gig at the Gold Star Sardine Bar, a tiny, very popular Chicago cabaret that was usually packed with patrons (hence the name "Sardine")

and, on weekends, often had long lines of people outside awaiting entrance. At the beginning of what turned into an eight-year association with Gold Star (which closed in 1997), the club's owner, Bill Allen, paid her $300 a week; according to Sachs (June 4, 1995), "what began as little more than a tax writeoff" for him "became a national attraction." "I always have had this ability to draw crowds," Barber told Sachs. "Some people say that's because of charisma, but I can't see that. I mean, the way the trio is set up, I play with my back to the audience most of the time. I think it has to do with my sincerity. People know I'm not faking anything."

In 1989 Barber released her first album, Split, which she produced and released on her own on what she dubbed the Floyd Records label. A mix of jazz standards and Barber originals, it was described on the Web site allmusic.com as offering "a dramatic cabaret vocal style and complex harmonic post-bop passages—a template that longtime fans will recognize." Barber's second album, A Distortion of Love (1992), was released on the PolyGram label. Because PolyGram's parent company was in financial difficulties at the time, the record was not promoted, and it "quickly sank into oblivion," according to Sachs (June 4, 1995). Soon afterward Barber received an offer to record an album on which her piano playing would be processed through a computer. "I was so desperate for a little financial security, I accepted," she told Sachs. "But I woke up the next morning feeling so depressed, I called back and turned them down. There was no way I could have made that album and lived with myself." For months afterward Barber continued to suffer bouts of depression, and she stopped performing. She resumed entertaining publicly at the urging of Dave Jemilo, the owner of the Green Mill, a jazz club in Uptown Chicago and the site of the Uptown Poetry Slam. Since then, except when on the road, Barber has performed there with the other members of what is now the Patricia Barber Quartet once or twice a week. Currently, the other members of her ensemble are the bassist Michael Arnopol, with whom she has worked virtually from the start of her career; the guitarist Neal Alger; and the drummer Eric Montzka. Others with whom she has collaborated, in the studio and/or in concert, include the drummers Mark Walker, Adam Cruz, Adam Nussbaum, and Joey Baron; the percussionist Ruben P. Alvarez; the guitarists Wolfgang Muthspiel, John McLean, and Charlie Hunter; the bassist Marc Johnson; and the trumpeter Dave Douglas.

Barber began writing songs, she told Bill Beuttler, "out of desperation. I was singing six nights a week at the Gold Star Sardine Bar, and I was just tired of the repertoire. And I wanted music that spoke to contemporary events and new feelings and this and that, so I had to give it a shot. And it turned out I had a facility for it." Café Blue (1994), which Barber recorded for the independent Premonition label, contains such original compositions as "Too Rich for My Blood," "Yellow Car III,"

"Mourning Grace" (based on a poem by Maya Angelou), and "Wood Is a Pleasant Thing to Think About" (whose title she took from an essay by Virginia Woolf). Also on the album are such jazz standards as Miles Davis's "Nardis" and songs including "The Thrill Is Gone," written by Roy Hawkins and Rick Darnell and popularized by B. B. King, and "Inch Worm," by Frank Loesser—her rendition being "the only sexy version of this song ever recorded," in the opinion of the jazz critic Matt Cibula in PopMatters.com (December 2, 2004). *Café Blue* attracted a great deal of attention from critics, some of whom hailed it as one of the best jazz albums of the year, and it significantly boosted Barber's drawing power in big cities in the U.S. and Canada.

Michael Friedman, the founder of Premonition, aggressively promoted Barber's next album, *Modern Cool* (1998), and it sold uncommonly well for a work of its kind. Of its 12 tracks, all but three are original songs. In 1999 Blue Note Records, which had bought Premonition the previous year, released *Companion*, a compilation of unusual renditions of popular material that Barber recorded live at the Green Mill. Her next disk, *Nightclub* (2000), is comprised entirely of jazz standards. Earlier, she had refused requests from major labels to record such a collection, she told Martin Johnson for *Newsday* (October 13, 2002), "because I had some feeling that I could create an individual sound in doing those songs. And I didn't want to get stuck doing standards record after standards record; I knew that if you did a standards record and it was successful, that would happen." Thanks to the enthusiastic reception that greeted her last several albums, though, she felt "I'd established myself as an idiosyncratic artist, and I could go ahead and do standards, which is a huge part of our repertoire. Also, it was for my mother; she wanted to hear those songs. . . . Also, I knew I would be doing *Verse*, and I wanted to draw a line to the past before I drew a line to the future."

With the exception of "Dansons la Gigue," whose lyrics, sung in French, are from a poem by Paul Verlaine, every track on *Verse* (2002) is an original Barber song. Steve Greenlee, writing for the *Boston Globe* (September 20, 2002), called the album "among the smartest records of jazz vocals—and lyrics—ever produced." Mark Ruffin, who hosts a jazz radio show with Neil Tesser, was similarly impressed; in a review for Amazon.com, he wrote, "With Dave Douglas dancing his trumpet around her witty and literate tales, these 10 scholarly vignettes are reminiscent of the way the great Cole Porter educated his listeners while thoroughly twisting the English language in an irresistibly entertaining way. 'I Could Eat Your Words' is about philosophy, cooking, and falling in love with your college professor. In it [Barber] somehow can 'suck the salt from erudition, drink remorse like a cabernet, sweeten with equivocation' and still swing. Many singers would still be stuck on 'erudition' while Barber—all sly, darkly slick, and witty—

continues to compose from a high artistic perch. Mentioning David Hockney, Edward Hopper, and Goya in the text of 'If I Were Blue,' and Baudelaire in 'You've Gotta Go Home,' ain't no easy trick."

Barber recorded *Live: A Fortnight in France* (2004) with Neal Alger, Michael Arnopol, and Eric Montzka during a two-week tour of the French cities La Rochelle, Metz, and Paris; its tracks include five original songs and five covers. In a critique for the *Iowa Alumni Magazine* (December 2004, online), Michael Tracy wrote, "Barber's presence as a witty songwriter and lyrical singer come to the forefront on this live album. But what may be more impressive is her prowess on the ivory keys. She struts her stuff with show-stopping performances. She's not afraid of taking chances, either, bravely transforming the classic Beatles' 'Norwegian Wood' from a two-minute ballad originally played on acoustic guitars into a sleek seven-minute jazz number full of tempo changes, piano and electric guitar solos, and driving percussion. It's a measure of her skill and artistry that Barber successfully turns this 'Fab Four' hit into her own."

Supported by a Guggenheim fellowship, Barber devoted more than a year to reading and other research that culminated in the creation of *Mythologies* (2006). The project was inspired by Ovid's *Metamorphoses*, an anthology of Greek and Roman myths retold in verse, and by a stage play, based on the same work, by the Chicago theater director Mary Zimmerman, which was mounted at the Lookingglass Theatre, in Chicago, in 1998. The album's tracks are "The Moon"; "Morpheus"; "Pygmalion"; "Hunger"; "Icarus (for Nina Simone)"; "Orpheus/Sonnet"; "Persephone"; "Narcissus"; "Whiteworld/Oedipus"; "Phaethon"; and "The Hours." The descriptions of the tracks that she wrote for the "Discs" portion of her Web site reveal some of the impulses, emotions, and interests that led to her choices of subjects. Barber wrote, for example, that "The Hours"—in Ovid's work, two goddesses who simply observe humanity—"is an homage to human courage in the face of Death. I read the writing of Primo Levi, an Auschwitz survivor, to try to understand what it feels like knowing death is coming soon. I also consulted my doctor, who took me through the University of Chicago hospitals and talked to me about life and death. . . . 'The Hours' . . . is about time, life and death. But it's also about life as a performance, or more accurately, a performer, writing about our life as a performance." In a representative assessment of *Mythologies* for the *Boston Globe* (August 15, 2006), the music critic and culture reporter Siddhartha Mitter called the album "undeniably heady" but "also genuinely liberal in its interpretations of the stories and its overall musical sensibility, making it not just one of the year's most enjoyable releases but also one of the most thought-provoking." Barber's lyrics, he added, "are as beautiful and complex as you'll find in jazz today."

Barber, who suffered from stage fright for many years, usually performs barefoot. She is over six feet tall. "Off stage, Ms. Barber is . . . precisely spoken, slightly shy and instantly likeable . . . ," Terry Teachout wrote, "far more a down-to-earth jazz musician than the angst-ridden egghead some of her fans take her to be." In the fall of 2007, as the winner of a Townsend resident fellowship from the University of California at Berkeley, Barber will spend a month at the school, sharing her expertise with students and faculty members. Openly gay, she has lived since the late 1990s with the musicologist and music historian Martha Feldman, who teaches at the University of Chicago. She maintains a home in Chicago and owns a farm in Michigan.

—M.B.

Suggested Reading: *All About Jazz* (on-line) Nov. 1998, Mar. 1, 2004; Blue Note Web site; *Chicago Sun-Times* Show p11 June 4, 1995; *Chicago Tribune* C p9 July 6, 2003, C p9 Aug. 13, 2006, Tempo p1 Sep. 13, 2004; *Los Angeles Times* Calendar p4 Aug. 15, 1999; *New York Times* II p27 June 23, 2002; *Newsday* D p3 Oct. 13, 2002; patriciabarber.com; popmatters.com Dec. 2, 2004; *Washington Post* C p5 Aug. 28, 2002

Selected Recordings: *Split*, 1989; *A Distortion of Love*, 1992; *Café Blue*, 1994; *Modern Cool*, 1998; *Companion*, 1999; *Nightclub*, 2000; *Verse*, 2002; *Live! A Fortnight in France*, 2004; *Mythologies*, 2006

Selected Films: *Live! France 2004*, 2005

Courtesy of Southend Press

Barsamian, David

[bar-SAHM-yahn]

June 14, 1945– Founder, director, and host of the program Alternative Radio; *writer*

Address: Alternative Radio, P.O. Box 551, Boulder, CO 80306

"The U.S. is not lacking in people with a diversity of opinion, but the mainstream media have a golden Rolodex that they go to time and time again. And most of these authorities are people who haven't had an original idea in fifty years," David Barsamian, the founder, longtime director, and host of

Alternative Radio, told Michael Roberts for *Denver (Colorado) Westword* (August 17, 2000). Barsamian's career in radio began in 1978, when he became the host of an international-music program on the Boulder, Colorado, station KGNU. With the addition of remarks and interviews about public affairs, his program metamorphosed during the next eight years into the all-talk *Alternative Radio*, an hourlong, weekly program that "provides information, analyses and views that are frequently ignored or distorted in other media," according to its Web site. With few exceptions, Barsamian has confined his guests to intellectual writers and social activists whose political views are left of center. His award-winning series, which has no corporate sponsors, is currently carried by more than 125 stations in the United States, Canada, Europe, South Africa, and Australia as well as on short-wave radio and the Internet. Barsamian told Dale McGarrigle for the *Bangor (Maine) Daily News* (July 22, 2004) that *Alternative Radio* succeeds "because of the deplorable job that corporate media and public broadcasting have done" in providing "alternative views" to mainstream news sources. "There's a huge amount of interest in independent analysis," he told McGarrigle, and while public radio programs could offer it, he maintained, they rarely do, because the directors of those programs are "timid, skittish, and won't air anything that will rock the boat."

Barsamian has interviewed hundreds of public figures on *Alternative Radio*, some at least half a dozen times. They include Ralph Nader, the 1996 and 2000 Green Party presidential candidate, who has founded many advocacy groups, among them the Center for the Study of Responsive Law, the Center for Auto Safety, and the Project for Corporate Responsibility, and whose writings include the highly influential 1965 book *Unsafe at Any Speed: The Designed-In Dangers of the American Automobile*; Eqbal Ahmad, a professor of international relations and Middle Eastern studies, who served as a managing editor of the quarterly *Race and Class*; Ben Bagdikian, a journalist and educator, whose books include *In the Midst of Plenty: The Poor in America* and *The Media Monopoly*; Angela Davis, a former member of the Communist and Black Panther Parties, a founder of the organization Critical Resistance, which opposes the "prison-industrial complex," and a professor in the History of Consciousness Department at the University of California at Santa Cruz; Michael Parenti, a political analyst, whose books include *The Terrorism Trap: 9/11 and Beyond*, *Superpatriotism*, and *The Culture Struggle*; Tariq Ali, an antiwar activist, novelist, historian, filmmaker, and member of the editorial committee of the British publication *New Left Review*; Arundhati Roy, a Booker Prize–winning novelist who now devotes herself to fighting neo-imperialism, globalization, the testing of nuclear weapons, and the building of massive dams in densely populated parts of India; and Edward Said, a professor of English, postcolonial theorist, champion of Palestinian rights, and author of *Orientalism* and *Covering Islam: How the Media and the Experts Determine How We See the Rest of the World*. Barsamian's most frequent guests have been Howard Zinn, a historian, social critic, and political scientist and the author of *A People's History of the United States*, who has been on *Alternative Radio* four dozen times, and Noam Chomsky, a prolific author and linguistic philosopher, who ushered in a revolution in the study of language and has long been a fierce critic of U.S. foreign policy; he has joined Barsamian on the air nearly 200 times. Transcriptions of Barsamian's conversations with Ahmad, Ali, Said, Roy, Zinn, and Chomsky, conducted on *Alternative Radio* and elsewhere, appear in a dozen books. Among Barsamian's other books is *The Decline and Fall of Public Broadcasting* (2001). In a review of *The Checkbook and the Cruise Missile: Conversations with Arundhati Roy* for the South African newspaper the *Sunday Times* (January 9, 2005), Loren Anthony wrote, "Sometimes—it's not too often—the interviewer threatens to outshine the interviewee. Barsamian asks those kind of questions. He offers staggering insights of his own. This is sharp, fast-paced stuff."

Zinn has characterized Barsamian as the "Studs Terkel of our generation," a reference to a renowned Chicago-based radio host, historian, and writer whose interview program aired for 45 years, beginning in 1952. The Institute for Alternative Journalism listed Barsamian among the "Top Ten Media Heroes" of 1994. He received the Upton Sinclair Freedom of Expression Award from the American Civil Liberties Union in 2003 and the Rocky Mountain Center's Peace and Justice Award in 2006. Also in 2006 the Lannan Foundation awarded him its Cultural Freedom Fellowship.

David Barsamian was born on June 14, 1945 in New York City. His parents, who were born into Armenian peasant families on the Anatolian Peninsula in what is now Turkey, fled their ancestral homes during the Armenian Genocide of 1915–17, eventually immigrating to New York in 1921. Nearly all of the relatives of Barsamian's parents were killed during the ethnic violence in their native land. Barsamian's parents had been young at the time, as well as uneducated, and they had not fully understood the reasons for their families' evictions from their respective hometowns when they arrived in New York. As Barsamian became more knowledgeable about the experiences of his family, he was profoundly affected by the history of violence in their pasts. "It's influenced me in terms of being very skeptical and doubting, particularly of authority," Barsamian explained to *Mediatribe* (February 7, 1995, on-line). After graduating from high school in New York City, in about 1963, Barsamian attended San Francisco State University, in California, for one year; he then dropped out, because, as he told Michael Roberts for the *Denver Westword* (August 17, 2000), "I was so bored out of my mind." He spent the next five years abroad. For three of those years, he lived in India, where he studied music and learned to play the sitar. His experiences during that period were "very radicalizing," as he put it in a conversation with Shandra Jordan for the Fort Collins, Colorado, *Rocky Mountain Collegian* (October 25, 2001). Barsamian returned to New York City in 1970, and for the next eight years he worked odd jobs, giving sitar lessons, teaching English to immigrants, and, for a while, working in the government of India's tourist office. In 1978 he moved to Boulder, where his sister was living.

Though he had never worked in the radio industry, Barsamian successfully pitched an international-music program to executives of KGNU, a community radio station in Boulder, and earned a one-hour timeslot. His show debuted in 1978. After Iranian student militants seized the American Embassy in Tehran, Iran, in November 1979, and took American staff members hostage, Barsamian began to inject comments about current events between songs. "There was an enormous amount of distortion and misinformation about Muslims, Islam and the Middle East" in the U.S. media at that time, as Barsamian recalled to Roberts. "I started to introduce political information trying to counter the kind of carpet-bombing of propaganda that was feeding Islamophobia in the country." Feedback from listeners revealed that they found his comments interesting, so he broadened the scope of his show to include interviews with political thinkers and social activists.

In 1986 Barsamian renamed his program *Alternative Radio* and filled it almost entirely with interviews. In a conversation with Colin Wright for the *Washington Free Press* (February/March 1995, on-line), he said that he focused on such topics as "the media themselves, which I believe to be a major source of disturbance and propaganda in the political and social culture. Also, the environment, Native American issues, human rights, and those kinds of things." He soon discovered that progressive or radical thinkers who were eager to discuss such subjects on the air rarely hesitated to submit to interviews in his studio. Meanwhile, it had become increasingly apparent to him that many radio listeners outside his broadcast area felt dissatisfied with conventional news sources but had no access to alternatives. To reach those people, in 1986 he began disseminating his program via satellite, which he had found, to his surprise, to be inexpensive. Barsamian was promoted to news director of KGNU in 1987; he left that position in 1991 to concentrate on *Alternative Radio,* which had become one of KGNU's most popular shows. Marty Durlin, KGNU's station manager, told Roberts in 2000, "If someone had told me, 'I'm going to make a living out of recording dissident intellectuals and putting them on the air uninterrupted,' I would have said, 'Right—good luck.' I'm amazed that there's that big of a market out there for this. But David has found it." She continued, "*Alternative Radio* really flies in the face of all the research that the marketers and focus groups in Washington have done. They talk about how people have such a short attention span that you have to measure audiences in increments of 15 minutes. What David does couldn't be more opposite of that, but he's got an awful lot of people out there, of all ages, who really appreciate what he's doing." *Alternative Radio* is available for broadcast by other stations free of charge; it is supported entirely by sales of Barsamian's books and recordings and transcripts of individual shows and the fees he receives at some of his talks in the U.S. and abroad. For a while Barsamian sold cassette recordings of his shows for $1 apiece; currently, such recordings are available on CDs as well as cassettes for $15 each and for download in mp3 format from his Web site, alternativeradio.org. Printed transcripts cost $9.

Many public radio stations do not carry *Alternative Radio* because programmers object to the bias of the show, which they argue runs contrary to the preference of their listeners for multiple points of view. Barsamian has contended that it is the programmers themselves, rather than their listeners, who do not agree with the political stance of *Alternative Radio.* He argues further that by refusing to offer *Alternative Radio,* such stations fail to honor the intentions of the Public Broadcasting Act of 1967, which states that public radio and television, which would be supported in part by federal funds, should "address the needs of unserved and underserved audiences." The legislation was inspired by a report, "Public Television: A Program for Action," prepared by a commission created by the Carnegie Corp. of New York, a charitable foundation, and made public in early 1967. "One of the things [*Alternative Radio*] is about that makes some public-radio stations very uncomfortable is that it's dedicated to the founding principles of public broadcasting," as embodied in the Carnegie Commission's report, as Barsamian told Roberts. "The report said public radio was intended to serve 'as a forum for debate' and to provide 'a voice for

groups that may otherwise be unheard.' That may not be the mission of a lot of public radio anymore, but it's still ours." According to Barsamian and others, public radio stations have succumbed to the demands of corporate underwriters, who pressure them to gear programming to mainstream audiences. In his book *The Decline and Fall of Public Broadcasting,* Barsamian reminded readers of the goals of public programming as described by the 1967 legislation. Barsamian blames the "fall" of public broadcasting on insufficient federal funding and viewer donations, which has driven public radio and television "into the outstretched arms of corporate advertisers," as he told Ron Simon for the *Television Quarterly* (Spring 2002). In the book Barsamian pointed out that programs hosted by such politically conservative pundits as William F. Buckley Jr., Ben Wattenberg, and John McLaughlin received public broadcast air time, as do such pro-business programs as *Wall $treet Week,* whereas the Public Broadcasting Service rejected the airing of such documentaries as *Out at Work,* about homosexuals in the workplace, and the Academy Award–winning *Defending Our Lives,* about the prevalence of domestic violence in the U.S., which featured four women who were behind bars for killing the men who had battered them. Similarly, representatives of public-interest organizations and other citizens' groups are generally absent from public TV and radio. Barsamian also argued that corporate underwriting undercuts the ability of public broadcasting to present objective accounts of current events. As an example, he cited the case of Archer Daniels Midland (ADM), one of the world's largest processors of grain, whose top executives were indicted in 1995 for alleged price fixing (and were subsequently found guilty); no mention of their indictment was made on PBS's popular program *NewsHour with Jim Lehrer,* whose underwriters included ADM. "It was a major business story—they could not have missed it," Barsamian told Jeff Wright for the *Register-Guard* (May 2, 2002), an Oregon newspaper.

Barsamian has also charged that National Public Radio (NPR) programs such as *All Things Considered* and *Morning Edition* are different from commercial radio shows only in their "level of civility," as he put it to Colin Wright. "They are bastions of politeness, but they're still not giving people perspectives from A to Z." Barsamian told Dale McGarrigle that community radio stations such as KGNU represent "one of the islands of audio independence in a sea of corporate control." Referring to the war in Iraq launched by the U.S. in 2003, he said, "It's important, especially in a time of war. We need to have a clear explanation from the media of why these wars are necessary. When the evidence was completely distorted, as a result of government lying being repeated by corporate media, community radio is the oxygen of democracy, where listeners can turn for independently verified information." Approximately 200 of the 800 NPR stations in the U.S. do not broadcast *Alternative*

Radio. Barsamian told Colin Wright that he believed that those 200 stations find the ideas expressed on *Alternative Radio* "very threatening to the existing arrangements of power and privilege in this country, which, more and more, these stations have come to reflect." Barsamian himself has been criticized for providing a platform for many supporters of Palestinian rights but virtually never inviting sympathizers of the Israeli point of view as guests. In answer to such criticism, he has said that the U.S. media overwhelmingly favor Israel in covering events in the Middle East and downplay the plight of the Palestinians, and that he is simply trying to redress that imbalance.

While maintaining his responsibilities regarding *Alternative Radio*, Barsamian has also been very active in pursuing longer discussions with some of his subjects. Transcripts of his interviews with Howard Zinn appear in *The Future of History* (1999) and *Original Zinn: Conversations on History and Politics* (2006); with Noam Chomsky, in *Chronicles of Dissent* (1992), *The Prosperous Few and the Restless Many* (1993), *Secrets, Lies, and Democracy* (1994), *Keeping the Rabble in Line* (1994), *Class Warfare* (1996), *The Common Good* (1998), *Propaganda and the Public Mind* (2001), and *Imperial Ambitions: Conversations on the Post-9/11 World* (2005); with Ali Tariq, in *Speaking of Empire and Resistance*; with Arundhati Roy, in *The Checkbook and the Cruise Missile* (2004); with Edward Said, in *The Pen and the Sword* (1994) and *Culture and Resistance* (2003); and with Eqbal Ahmad, in *Confronting Empire* (2000) and *Terrorism: Theirs and Ours* (2001). Barsamian's 2004 volume *Louder Than Bombs: Interviews from the* Progressive *Magazine* includes discussions he held between 1997 and 2004 with Vandana Shiva, Kurt Vonnegut, Angela Davis, Edwidge Dandicat, Amartya Sen, Kevin Phillips, Taylor Branch, and others. A reviewer of *Louder than Bombs* for Powells.com wrote that Barsamian "converses with some of the best minds of our time, and skillfully weaves their analyses and personal insights into a digest of the world's most pressing issues." Barsamian's book *Targeting Iran*, published in 2007, contains transcripts of interviews with Chomsky; Ervand Abrahamian, the author of *Iran Between Two Revolutions*; Shirin Ebadi, the Iranian lawyer and human rights activist who won the Nobel Peace Prize in 2003; and Nahid Mozaffari, who edited *Strange Times, My Dear: The PEN Anthology of Contemporary Iranian Literature. What We Say Goes: Conversations on U.S. Power in a Changing World*, also published in 2007, is another collection of interviews that Barsamian conducted with Chomsky. Among the topics discussed are the ongoing wars in Iraq and Afghanistan, the Israeli-Palestinian conflict, and the 2006 U.S. midterm elections.

Barsamian's busy speaking schedule includes events in theaters and elsewhere that are held as benefits (and at which his books and CDs are offered for sale). In his January 2007 appearances, his beneficiaries included the Colorado Coalition for the Prevention of Nuclear War and the Tucson, Arizona, radio station KXCI. His articles and interviews appear regularly in *Z Magazine*, the *Progressive*, and the *Nation*. Barsamian lives in Boulder. Readily available sources do not indicate whether he is or has ever been married.

—N.W.M.

Suggested Reading:*Alternative Radio* Web site; *Aztag Daily* (on-line) Feb. 12, 2004; *Bangor (Maine) Daily News* C p1+ July 22, 2004; *Denver (Colorado) Westword* (on-line) Aug. 17, 2000; (Oregon) *Register-Guard* May 2, 2002; *Santa Fe New Mexican* P p34 Feb. 25, 2000; (South Africa) *Sunday Times* p14 Jan. 9, 2005; *Television Quarterly* p86+ Spring 2002; *Washington Free Press* (on-line) Feb./Mar. 1995

Selected Books: *Stenographers to Power: Media and Propaganda*, 1992; *The Decline and Fall of Public Broadcasting*, 2001; *Louder Than Bombs: Interviews from the* Progressive *Magazine*, 2004; *Targeting Iran*, 2007; with Eqbal Ahmad—*Eqbal Ahmad, Confronting Empire*, 2000; *Terrorism: Theirs and Ours*, 2001; with Tariq Ali—*Speaking of Empire and Resistance*, 2005; with Noam Chomsky—*Chronicles of Dissent*, 1992; *The Prosperous Few and the Restless Many*, 1993; *Secrets, Lies, and Democracy*, 1994; *Keeping the Rabble in Line*, 1994; *Class Warfare*, 1996; *The Common Good*, 1998; *Propaganda and the Public Mind*, 2001; *What We Say Goes: Conversations on U.S. Power in a Changing World*, 2007; with Arundhati Roy—*The Checkbook and the Cruise Missile*, 2004; with Edward W. Said—*The Pen and the Sword*, 1994; with Howard Zinn—*The Future of History*, 1999; *Original Zinn: Conversations on History and Politics*, 2006

Bawer, Bruce

(BOW-er)

Oct. 31, 1956– Writer; critic

Address: c/o Talbot Fortune Agency, 540 Boston Post Rd., PMB 266, Mamaroneck, NY 10543

The social and political commentator Bruce Bawer is known for setting off alarm bells with his writing. In *A Place at the Table: The Gay Individual in American Society* (1993), Bawer, who is gay, argued that homosexuals would never earn their place "at the table"—that is, be treated as equals under American law—until more militant gays allowed themselves to be assimilated into American society rather than emphasizing their differences from it. In his 1997 book, *Stealing Jesus: How Fundamentalism Betrays Christianity*, he expressed

Courtesy of Bruce Bawer

Bruce Bawer

the belief that fundamentalist Christians were gaining undue control of many aspects of American life, including political decision-making. And in his most recent—and even more controversial—book, *While Europe Slept: How Radical Islam Is Destroying the West from Within* (2006), Bawer pointed to what he saw as the dire effects on Europe of its unassimilated Islamic communities, whose values, he argued, conflict with those of their adopted countries. In addition to his 11 books of literary, social, and political criticism, Bawer has contributed essays, reviews, and travel pieces to a number of publications, including the *New Republic*, the *Nation*, *Newsweek*, the *Wall Street Journal*, and the *New York Times*. He remains best known for his thought-provoking and category-defying views on politics. "Over the years, I've seen just about every possible label from across the political spectrum attached to my name," he wrote for his Web site. "In fact I've always considered myself a centrist or a classical liberal and I've always been a registered Democrat, though for a time in the 1980s I usually didn't protest when others labeled me a 'neoconservative.'" The ambiguities in his personal political philosophies often perplex both his readership and the media, with the latter pegging him as a diehard liberal one moment and a devout conservative the next. The threads running through Bawer's work are a willingness to voice an unpopular—and, at times, never-before-stated—opinion and his refusal to hew to any party line. "In any case I've never sought to serve any ideological establishment in my writings, only to express my own sense of things—which includes reserving the right to criticize undemocratic tendencies on both the right and the left," he wrote for

his Web site. "From time to time this apparent want of ideological purity has caused confusion or even indignation among readers who expect one to fit into a neat right-or-left dichotomy. So be it."

Theodore Bruce Bawer was born on October 31, 1956 in New York City to Theodore Bawer, a physician, and Nell Carol Thomas. He grew up in the borough of Manhattan, attending Public School 49, Junior High School 119, and Newton High School. After graduating from high school, Bawer enrolled at the State University of New York (SUNY) at Stony Brook, on Long Island, where he earned his bachelor's, master's, and Ph.D. degrees in English. He subsequently taught classes at SUNY in literature and composition. Other positions he held in the years immediately after he obtained his doctorate included literary editor for *Arrival* magazine, writing tutor for honors students at Adelphi University, on Long Island, and board member of the National Book Critics Circle (NBCC), whose publication, the *NBCC Journal*, he edited.

In 1983 Bawer began to contribute literary criticism to the *New Criterion*, which is now known as a politically conservative magazine but was devoted while he was there to literature and the arts. He also contributed to *American Spectator*, a Washington, D.C.–based political monthly magazine, as a movie critic. His first full-length work, *The Middle Generation: The Lives and Poetry of Delmore Schwartz, Randall Jarrell, John Berryman, and Robert Lowell* (1986), a revised version of his dissertation, was awarded *Choice* magazine's 1987 Outstanding Academic Book Award and chosen as the American Library Association's Academic Book of the Year; it was also a finalist in the NBCC's Reviewer's Citation category. He followed that success with a collection of arts criticism, *Diminishing Fictions: Essays on the Modern American Novel and Its Critics* (1988). *Coast to Coast* (1992), Bawer's first foray into poetry, was named the year's best first book of poems by the *Dictionary of Literary Biography Yearbook*. Also in the early 1990s, Bawer published two volumes of previously collected pieces—*The Screenplay's the Thing: Movie Criticism, 1986-1990* (1992), comprising reviews from the *American Spectator*, and *The Aspect of Eternity: Essays*, a collection of 15 of his pieces from the *New Criterion*. The essays in the latter book examine the work of a number of modern novelists, with frequent and often harsh criticism of those Bawer judged to be guilty of anti-Americanism or other faults. Whether or not reviewers of the collection agreed with his opinions, they largely admired his presentation. "Bawer states his positions bravely. He has read these novelists with care and, usually, with discernment, and he writes about them lucidly and elegantly," Michelle Harris wrote for the *Los Angeles Times* (August 9, 1993).

With *A Place at the Table: The Gay Individual in American Society*, Bawer established himself as a social and political critic. Adopting a phrase of President Bill Clinton's, Bawer argued for the mainstreaming of homosexuality—for creating "a place at the table" for the homosexual man or woman. "My point throughout this book," he wrote, as quoted by Jonathan Yardley in the *Washington Post* (November 7, 1993), "is not that homosexuals deserve preferential treatment of any kind because they belong to a victim group, but rather that gay individuals do not deserve to have their lives, careers and committed relationships treated differently from those of heterosexuals simply because they are gay." Controversially, however, he asserted that the lack of equal rights for gays was due in part to some homosexuals' own unwillingness to assimilate into heterosexual America. "Don't ask for a medal; don't feel sorry for yourself," he wrote. "Being gay is an inconvenience; so are a lot of things; get on with it; if others have a problem with it, that's their problem." In particular, Bawer argued that what he described as the promiscuous behavior of gay men was undermining efforts to earn equal rights for the gay and lesbian community. "Above all, don't use your homosexuality or their contempt for it as an excuse to lower your moral standards," he advised. "The important thing is to behave in such a way as to keep your own respect and that of people whose respect means something." Throughout *A Place at the Table*, Bawer attempted to prove that political conservatism and homosexuality are not incompatible but, in fact, complementary. If conservatives did not alienate the homosexual population by mixing religious dogma with political beliefs, Bawer argued, there would be no inherent reason for gays to be more drawn to liberalism than conservatism, especially considering true conservatism's emphasis on privacy. "The sensible—and truly conservative—way of dealing with the fact of homosexuality would be to arrange society in such a way that homosexuals can grow into well-integrated and productive members of it as easily as their heterosexual counterparts," Bawer wrote.

The book's message, with its assignations of blame and responsibility, provoked widespread discussion, especially within the gay community. "Bruce Bawer's *A Place at the Table* now appears to be the first important work in the evaluation of gay culture by gay men," David Bergman wrote for the *Harvard Gay & Lesbian Review* (January 31, 1998), five years after the book's publication. Many reviewers pointed out what they saw as flaws in Bawer's argument but nonetheless applauded him for his sophisticated writing and his willingness to tackle a potentially uncomfortable issue. "To be sure *A Place at the Table* is imperfect," Jonathan Yardley wrote. "Bawer has a regrettable penchant for sweeping generalizations, he expresses a surprisingly rancorous view of conventional heterosexual marriage, and at times his pleas for acceptance and mutual understanding carry an angry edge." But Yardley also praised the quality of the prose and the motivation behind the book: "His own writing invariably is lucid, measured, witty and authoritative; he seems to take more pleasure

in giving praise than damnation, but he does both with style and verve."

For two years following the book's publication, Bawer continued to focus primarily on the theme of homosexuality in America. In his much-discussed essay "Notes on Stonewall," published in the *New Republic* on June 13, 1994, Bawer presented a condensed version of his thesis from *A Place at the Table*. The title referred to the 1969 Stonewall riots, a series of violent conflicts between the New York City police and a large number of homosexual and transgendered people following a police raid of a gay bar in Greenwich Village. The riots represented a turning point in the gay rights movement, with an unprecedented display of unified force on the part of homosexuals. In the essay Bawer argued that such dramatic displays were no longer necessary in the fight for full acceptance of homosexuals in American society, and that those strategies—and the homophobic knee-jerk reaction to them—were relics of the past. "It seems to me," Bawer wrote, "that both sides of the gay rights struggle are trapped in what may well be characterized as a politics of nostalgia." Rather than the aggressive behavior of the Stonewall riots, Bawer advised patience and moderation, placing the burden of responsibility on the shoulders of homosexuals to demonstrate their acceptability. "Getting America to accept homosexuality will first be a matter of education. The job is not to shout at straight Americans, 'We're here, we're queer, get used to it,'" Bawer wrote. "The job is to do the hard, painstaking work of getting straight Americans used to it. This isn't dramatic work; nor is it work that provides a quick emotional release. Rather, it requires discipline, commitment, responsibility." Even more controversially, Bawer suggested that many gay men were reluctant to adopt a moderate approach because they were so accustomed to their marginalized position in society that they did not want to change it. "What these reactions signify to me is a powerful tendency among some homosexuals to recoil reflexively from the vision of an America where gays live as full and open members of society, with all the rights, responsibilities and opportunities of heterosexuals," Bawer wrote.

After *Prophets and Professors: Essays on the Lives and Works of Modern Poets* (1995), which discusses what he viewed as the commercialization and concurrent decline of modern poetry, Bawer returned the next year to the theme of gay conservatism as the editor of *Beyond Queer: Challenging the Gay Left Orthodoxy*. The book contained nine essays by Bawer himself, as well as 30 essays by 16 other contributors (straight and gay), including the *New Republic* editor Andrew Sullivan, the *Chicago Tribune* columnist Stephen H. Chapman, the novelist John Weir, and the Washington, D.C., attorney John W. Berresford. In the book, whose title is meant to criticize homosexuals' reclamation of the pejorative term "queer," Bawer again expressed his frustration with contemporary equivalents of the Stonewall riots—acts that, he argued, make big statements but have little practical value. He and many of the other contributors were "impatient with the queer left's abiding fascination with aimless utopianism," he wrote, as quoted by Jameson Currier in the *Washington Post* (June 9, 1996). "We're impatient with the models of activism that involve playing at revolution instead of focusing on the serious work of reform." As usual, critics found some of the essays' positions untenable (and this time, in a book not written solely by Bawer, they found some of the prose mediocre) but applauded the book nonetheless for the authors' willingness to take potentially unpopular stands. "Though it seems improbable to agree with every opinion put forth in *Beyond Queer* (and a few are down-right whiney), most of the writing is thought-provoking," Currier wrote. That year, Bawer also co-authored *House and Home* with the Republican congressman Steve Gunderson and Gunderson's partner, Rob Morris; the book follows Gunderson's career as a gay politician and his relationship with Morris in a time of an increasingly political—and particularly religious—debate over sexual preference.

In 1997 Bawer directly tackled the subject of religion with *Stealing Jesus: How Fundamentalism Betrays Christianity*. Bawer is himself a regular churchgoer (he belongs to the Episcopalian church, a denomination of Christianity that has been comparatively welcoming to homosexuals), and the book is not an attack on Christianity as a whole. Rather, he divided Christians into two camps, "legalistic" and "nonlegalistic." The legalistic Christians—primarily evangelicals and fundamentalists—emphasize the exact wording in the Bible; nonlegalistic Christians emphasize the general philosophy behind Jesus's teachings, particularly focusing on love and acceptance. Bawer argued that the legalistic Christians have begun to hijack not only American Christianity but also America itself—from its politics to its culture. The book, which Chris Bull described for the *Washington Post* (December 21, 1997) as "an earnest and at times eloquent entreaty" for a return to nonlegalistic Christianity, went into multiple printings. Still, while reviews praised Bawer's thorough analysis of the current American religious climate, many argued that Bawer was spouting the very same kind of demagogy against which he was preaching. "Like other critics of the religious right . . . Bawer undermines his noble cause by resorting to a form of religious bigotry and political stereotyping," Bull wrote, noting that while Bawer was careful early on to distinguish among different sects within the religious right, he abandoned that discernment later in the book, making all of the religious right—fundamentalists, evangelicals, and others—into the same enemy. "By lumping religious conservatives into an anti-intellectual monolith, Bawer makes it easier to dismiss the movement's gains but harder to understand the deep-seated economic and social uncertainties that animate it," Bull wrote.

Disillusioned with the lack of tolerance he saw in America—as well as with the country's levels of education and commitment to social safeguards, which he found to be low for a Western nation— Bawer moved from New York to Amsterdam, the Netherlands, with his longtime partner, Chris Davenport, in 1998. Finding the Netherlands to be superior in many ways to the U.S. but not the social utopia they had envisioned, the next year Bawer and Davenport moved to Oslo, Norway, where they registered officially as partners. Bawer began translating books from Norwegian to English and writing travel pieces on the Netherlands and Scandinavia. At the same time, he grew interested in the European political climate. Following the September 11, 2001 terrorist attacks on the U.S. and the 2005 bombings in London, England, Bawer noticed a shift in societal attitudes toward Muslims in both his Norwegian neighborhood and in Europe as a whole. Muslims were immigrating to European countries in greater and greater numbers, he said, frequently segregating themselves within cities and creating a drain on their new countries' social resources while giving little in return. Meanwhile, Europeans were becoming more and more reluctant to tighten immigration policies, or to say anything at all about the problem of Muslim immigration, out of what Bawer called a misguided sense of political correctness. One of the examples Bawer frequently cited was the expulsion of the Dutch politician Pim Fortuyn, the author of *Against the Islamicization of Our Culture*, from his own party for his hardline stance against Islam; Fortuyn was later assassinated by a Dutchman who disagreed with his views. In 2004 the Dutch film director Theo van Gogh, whose most recent film had criticized Muslims' treatment of women, was killed by a member of a radical Muslim network. In the days following van Gogh's killing, Bawer traveled to the Netherlands, writing a piece for the *New York Times* (November 14, 2004) that expressed his concern that van Gogh's murder would elicit the same overly politically correct reaction that Fortuyn's had. Bawer reflected on the divide between the native Dutch and Muslim populations in the Netherlands. "Instead of addressing this issue, Dutch officials (like their counterparts across the continent) churned out rhetoric about multicultural diversity and mutual respect," Bawer wrote. "By tolerating Muslim intolerance of Western society, was the Netherlands setting itself on a path toward cataclysmic social confrontation?"

In Bawer's view, not only the Netherlands but all of Europe was headed toward such disaster—a position on which he elaborated in 2006, with *While Europe Slept: How Radical Islam Is Destroying the West from Within*. Bawer asserted that Europe is at a "Weimar moment," a point at which it has to decide whether it will capitulate to Islamic fundamentalists or resist their growing power over European society and politics. Criticizing Europe's "self-destructive passivity, its softness towards tyranny, its reflexive inclination to appease," Bawer cited data in seeking to demonstrate the drain on European countries' resources caused by Muslims: 70 percent of the inmates in French prisons, he pointed out, are Muslim; four out of five residents of the main women's shelter in Oslo are non-Norwegian Muslim women seeking protection from male family members; in Denmark, Muslims make up 5 percent of the population but receive 40 percent of its welfare payments. Bawer argued that unlike the U.S., which places a heavy emphasis on assimilating its immigrants, Europe has allowed its immigrant populations—especially Islamic immigrants—to exist separate from the rest of society and maintain practices and belief systems that clash with the greater ideology of their adopted countries. While giving particular attention to the hatred of homosexuality ingrained in fundamentalist Islamic beliefs, he also cited the poor treatment of women, with examples including forced marriage, polygamy, and marital rape. The communities Bawer discussed in his book are those that tourists rarely visit and journalists do not often write about, leaving the vast majority of the American public ignorant of how severe the situation really is, Carlin Romano wrote for the *Philadelphia Inquirer* (February 20, 2006). Romano called *While Europe Slept* a "must-read book," saying that it "raises profound challenges to standard ideas of democracy, authority, and free expression." He added, "Accept his analysis or not, Bawer and his details startle."

The book, currently in its eighth printing, has provoked strong reactions. Bawer "has an acute eye for how such fragile societies fall prey to unscrupulous extremists and opportunistic, welfare-addicted outsiders," Clive Davis wrote for the *Washington Times* (March 26, 2006). "He also provides a fine overview of the way elite opinion across the continent has lapsed into a default mode of blaming the evils of American-style capitalism for almost every social ill on the planet." Some criticized Bawer for making generalizations based on data gathered almost entirely in Norway and the Netherlands; others, including Mark Steyn, writing for the *Jerusalem Post* (April 9, 2006), complained about the book's "overwrought" prose. For the most part, though, detractors disagreed with the general message of the book. When Eliot Weinberger, a onetime finalist for the National Book Critics Circle Award, announced *While Europe Slept* as a nominee in the NBCC's criticism category, he accused Bawer of engaging in "racism as criticism." The NBCC board president, John Freeman, also commented on the organization's blog on the nomination, writing, "I have never been more embarrassed by a choice than I have been with Bruce Bawer's *While Europe Slept*. Its hyperventilated rhetoric tips from actual critique into Islamophobia." Responding to Weinberger's comments in the January 29, 2007 entry of his blog, Bawer pointed out that Islamic fundamentalists—the group he opposed—were not a race in and of themselves. "It's easy—and, in some circles, highly effective—to

fling the 'R' word instead of trying to respond to irrefutable facts and arguments," he wrote. "One of the most disgraceful developments of our time is that many Western authors and intellectuals who pride themselves on being liberals have effectively aligned themselves with an outrageously illiberal movement that rejects equal rights for women, that believes gays and Jews should be executed, that supports the coldblooded murder of one's own children in the name of honor, etc., etc. These authors and intellectuals respond to every criticism of that chilling fundamentalist code—however cogent and correct the criticism may be—by hurling the 'R' word." He concluded, "I will not be cowed by such disgraceful, duplicitous rhetoric. Civilized, tolerant, pluralist values are at stake—values that affect freedom-loving individuals of all races."

Bawer lives in Oslo with his partner, Chris Davenport.

—C.S.

Suggested Reading: brucebawer.com; *Hudson Review* Vol. LVII, No. 1, Spring 2004; *New York Times* E p1 Feb. 8, 2007; *Philadelphia Inquirer* Entertainment News Feb. 20, 2006

Selected Books: *The Middle Generation: The Lives and Poetry of Delmore Schwartz, Randall Jarrell, John Berryman, and Robert Lowell*, 1986; *Diminishing Fictions: Essays on the Modern American Novel and Its Critics*, 1988; *The Screenplay's the Thing: Movie Criticism, 1986–1990*, 1992; *A Place at the Table: The Gay Individual in American Society*, 1993; *Stealing Jesus: How Fundamentalism Betrays Christianity*, 1997; *While Europe Slept: How Radical Islam Is Destroying the West from Within*, 2006

Beck, Kent

Mar. 31, 1961– Computer programmer

Address: Three Rivers Institute, P.O. Box 128, Merlin, OR 97532

Kent Beck is famous among computer programmers for spearheading the creation of the Extreme Programming (XP) process for software development—a method, as Lesley Stones wrote for the South African *Business Day* (July 7, 2005), that "turns upside down the usual image of uncommunicative geeks beavering away in cubicles awash with coffee and junk food." Beck's XP system, which he described to Lee Copeland for *Computerworld* (December 3, 2001) as a "lightweight methodology," differs radically from conventional systems, which often begin with a list of requirements given by a client or manager to programmers, who then design, code, and test the software. With that traditional process, sometimes called the waterfall

Courtesy of the Three Rivers Institute

Kent Beck

method, the gulf between what the client envisions and what the developer produces can be quite large, and testing software only after the bulk of the code has been written can create a wealth of errors. Julie Pitta, writing for *Forbes* (July 9, 2001), pointed out some of the waterfall method's shortcomings: "Typically, chunks of code written by individual programmers are glued together and then handed off to testers, who look for bugs. But finding all the bugs in a large program is brain-curdling work. Worse, even great code can accidentally become irrelevant: Once an independent team clinches a deal to develop code, the programmers have little contact with the final customers." Danny O'Brien, writing for the *Irish Times* (November 29, 2002), noted that some estimates suggest that only 10 to 40 percent of the software that companies develop for internal use actually runs successfully, adding: "In the 1960s, this ongoing statistical disaster was ascribed to programming's lack of rigour compared to other, more mature technical skills, like engineering. But as layer after layer of sadistic rules have been created for creating programs, carefully documenting requirements, and meticulously plotting every detail of the schedule before it happens, the delays have merely got longer, and the failures more spectacular."

Beck formalized XP during the mid-1990s, when he and Ron Jeffries, one of his collaborators, consulted on a major software project for the Chrysler Corp. Since then XP has been used at such companies as Ford, IBM, Symantec, and GlaxoSmithKline and has led many small- to medium-size companies to revise their software-development processes. The tenets of XP are, Copeland wrote, to "keep the code simple, review

it frequently, test early and often, and work a 40-hour week." Not tied to any particular technology or programming language and unrelated to the popular Microsoft Windows XP operating system that followed it, XP attempts to bring a company's business and technical teams together by stressing four core values: communication, simplicity, feedback, and courage. With XP, Beck told Stones, "the people who really matter to the development come together, so people on the team are not just programmers, but a wide mix of people who will use the software, managers, testers, analysts and graphic artists. It's a challenge because it requires interpersonal skills—which developers aren't known for having." Part of what makes XP unusual is Beck's attention to the social and spatial arrangements of the workplace. One of the fundamental aspects of XP, and one of the most controversial among programmers, is the idea of pair programming—coders working side by side on the same computer, sharing a single keyboard. Beck, in introducing XP, maintained that pair programming leads to higher-quality code that requires less time to test and debug, and that it helps to make the code less opaque to the programmers who later need to maintain the software. Paired programming flows naturally out of Beck's conviction that, as he wrote in response to a questionnaire from the computer magazine *EXE* (March 1, 2000), "who you work with is more important than what you work on." Developers following the XP process are also expected to code in close proximity to one another, preferably in open rooms. Recounting an experience he had while consulting with a company in Chicago, Illinois, Beck told Malcolm Gladwell for the *New Yorker* (September 5, 2005) that his advice was largely restricted to urging the development team to work in the same space. "They hired me for my technical expertise," Beck told Gladwell. "And I told them to rearrange the office furniture, and that was the most valuable thing I could offer them."

An experienced programmer and independent consultant, Beck has written extensively on XP and other subjects related to programming. He has also been instrumental in developing a number of software-development tools, including the JUnit testing framework, which he created with a fellow programmer, Erich Gamma, and which has become perhaps the world's most widely used testing framework for the programming language Java. Beck is a pioneer of test-driven development, a method that inverts the prevailing approach to writing code. Instead of developing a program to accomplish a given task and then testing it afterward, a programmer following the test-driven development method first writes a test for a specific task and then writes the code to match the test. Beck's radical prescription for creating better code has provoked strong criticism from many programmers, who often argue that Beck's intensely collaborative model slows the development process and that many details of the XP process make it impracticable for large-scale projects. "XP is not for everybody," Beck admitted to Linda Tischler for *Fast Company* (October 2001). "It's like programming naked. You are exposed. But if you work together, you have twice as many ideas, and you get fewer defects."

Kent Lynden Beck was born on March 31, 1961 in San Jose, California, to Doug and Bernadette Beck. Beck's father was an electrical engineer who worked on some of the building blocks of computer hardware, including discrete components for individual circuits and integrated circuits, and Beck began programming at the age of 12—evidence of the extent of his access to technology at that time, unusual even in the Silicon Valley area, where he was raised. In his correspondence with ESE, Beck described the first computer he ever used as an "85-pound Philco desktop calculator" that displayed its output using a cold-cathode device called a nixie tube. ("The demise of nixie tubes," Beck added, tongue-in-cheek, "was the first step in the tragedy that is modern technology.") A devoted guitar and banjo player from an early age, Beck told *Current Biography* that he "was always interested in music" and that, while in college at the University of Oregon, in Eugene, he "alternated majors every year between computer science and music (classical guitar)." Beck earned his B.S. and M.S. degrees in computer science from Oregon. The thesis for his master's degree, which he received in 1987, was titled "A Relational Database Interface Scheme."

Before earning his master's, Beck had begun working at the company Tektronix, based in Beaverton, Oregon. There, he met Ward Cunningham, who became an important collaborator, in part because of their shared interest in object-oriented programming. (A method for coding that breaks larger programs into discrete units, termed objects, each of which possesses a narrow function and a degree of independence and interchangeability, object-oriented programming is distinct from earlier styles of programming—which treated code as a series of linear procedures, each of which might serve multiple functions.) Beck and Cunningham were also among the early advocates of applying to software development so-called pattern languages—an approach to formalizing decision-making in architecture and urban design first advanced by the Austrian-born architect Christopher Alexander. In September 1987 they co-authored the paper "Using Pattern Languages for Object-Oriented Programs," which they delivered at the second annual OOPSLA (Object-Oriented Programming, Systems, Languages, and Applications) conference in Orlando, Florida. By the time of that conference, Beck had already left Tektronix for Apple Computer, based in Cupertino, California. After working to develop applications for Apple's then-revolutionary Macintosh computer system, Beck moved to another Silicon Valley company, the minisupercomputer maker MasPar, before becoming a private consultant and the founder of

First Class Software, which distributed some of the software he created, including the programming utilities Profile V and Object Explorer, both of which draw on Beck's years of experience in programming in the language Smalltalk.

In the late 1980s and early 1990s, Beck and Cunningham became known in object-oriented programming circles for their advocacy of a programming technique called Class, Responsibility, and Collaboration (CRC) cards. Cunningham first suggested CRC cards as a way of recording key information about some of the objects in a planned program while also controlling the scope of that information, since it had to fit on the front of a single index card. CRC cards have since become widely used as a brainstorming and organizational tool, but Beck and Cunningham also saw them as a way of explaining to novices how object-oriented programming works and of freeing up the development process. "The cards are being used as props to aid the telling of a story of computation," Beck and Cunningham wrote in a paper delivered at the 1989 OOPSLA conference and available on the Web site of Cunningham's consulting company, Cunningham & Cunningham Inc. "The cards allow its telling without recourse to programming language syntax or idiom." In the paper Beck and Cunningham drew attention to the success of CRC cards, particularly in groups, and remarked on "the value of physically moving the cards around. When learners pick up an object they seem to more readily identify with it, and are prepared to deal with the remainder of the design from its perspective. It is the value of this physical interaction that has led us to resist a computerization of the cards."

The idea of individual parts of a program as stories, and the emphasis on groups and physical presence in the development process, became key parts of XP, which Beck began to develop in detail in 1996, when he started consulting on a project for the Chrysler Corp. Known as the Chrysler Comprehensive Compensation System (C3), the project sought to replace a variety of older software with a single payroll application that could successfully write paychecks for all of the company's employees—a formidable task given Chrysler's roster of nearly 90,000 workers and the wide variety of taxes, deductions, and payment plans that had to be factored into the amounts of the checks. "They had a crying business need; it had to work," Beck told Scott Plamondon for IBM's on-line DeveloperWorks (June 17, 2003). Despite about a year's development work, the project was in disarray when Beck arrived, prompting him to tell the company's chief information officer at that time, Sue Unger, as Beck explained to Plamondon, "that [Unger] had three options: keep going, which no one wanted; cancel the project and fire everyone; or give everyone a week off and start over. She picked option 'c' and said 'but you're in charge.'" ("I said, 'You don't understand. I'm a consultant. I don't do in charge,'" Beck told Sam Williams for a May 29, 2002 article in the on-line magazine *Salon*. "She said, 'You don't understand, I'm Sue Unger. You're in charge.'") When the employees returned from their week off, Beck interviewed each of them and began developing a plan for managing the project. "I told the first guy that we'll divide the project into three-week intervals called, say, *iterations*," Beck told Plamondon. "In each iteration we'll implement a few new features called *stories*. We'll write down all the stories we need, slot them into the iterations, then do it. I told the next guy [I interviewed] that we have these three-week iterations divided into stories. For each story we'll write these . . . *acceptance tests* to demonstrate that the stories meet the customer's expectations. With each person I interviewed I added a little more. By the end of the day, I'd interviewed 20 people and had laid out Extreme Programming's basics."

Beck told Danny O'Brien that the biggest problem he attempted to solve through XP was "the difficulty of measuring the intermediate states of a project." Beck's idea to break projects down into stories became known as the "planning game." Under that model the number of stories can be adjusted as the deadline allows. Each story is written on a story card and has an estimated time of completion. Programmers enjoy using stories, O'Brien explained, "because they're never stuck with an unrealistic deadline. Everything is broken down into simple chunks that need just a few days to code and test. And a test for every task is written by the paired programmers before they code it up." Writing tests before coding, rather than after, is another of Beck's innovations. It allows clients to see the progress being made prior to the project's completion and, if necessary, to adjust features of the programming. With XP, clients are even included on the working teams. Before he came on board at Chrysler, Beck told Plamondon, the team working on C3 "treated the requirements as a fixed set of tasks. The tasks would grow over time, like a mirage. At some point the project recedes as fast as it progresses. Instead, we made the project's scope visible with stories with costs and a fixed budget." The first release of Beck's version of the C3 system came out roughly on time, but subsequent releases failed to match that early success, and the program wrote checks for only about 10,000 employees; still, that in itself was considered a substantial achievement. (In 1998 Chrysler merged with the European automaker Daimler-Benz to create DaimlerChrysler, and two years later the C3 project was terminated altogether.)

Beck gave his methodology the name Extreme Programming while still at Chrysler, taking his inspiration from extreme sports. "I wanted my teams to have that same sense of fearlessness in the face of challenge," Beck told Sam Williams. "People who are serious about extreme sports are prepared," Beck explained to Alan Goldstein for the *Dallas Morning News* (March 20, 2003). "They have the best possible equipment. If they're going whitewater rafting, they carefully map the bottom. They don't just go, 'Oh cool, nobody's done this be-

fore,' and jump in a raft." In 2000 Beck published his first book on the topic, *Extreme Programming Explained: Embrace Change*, and after that acolytes for XP emerged from all over the world, particularly in Europe and Japan. (Published in late 1999 but carrying a copyright for the following year, *Extreme Programming Explained* is sometimes listed as *eXtreme Programming eXplained*.) In 2000 Beck collaborated with Martin Fowler on a more technical guide to XP, *Planning Extreme Programming*, and that same year the first international conference on XP was held in Cagliari, on the Italian island of Sardinia; conferences on XP have been held in every subsequent year thus far. In 2000 Beck also founded The Three Rivers Institute, in Merlin, Oregon, to study the interaction of business and technology and to promote XP. The following year Beck joined more than a dozen other influential programmers in signing a "Manifesto for Agile Software Development." Now seen as the larger movement of which XP is a part, agile programming is described in the manifesto, reproduced on Agilemanifesto.org, as valuing: "Individuals and interactions over processes and tools / Working software over comprehensive documentation / Customer collaboration over contract negotiation / Responding to change over following a plan."

If fans of XP "cropped up like kudzu," as Lee Copeland wrote, the book also "sparked a maelstrom of debate among programmers and project managers who either love or love to hate [Beck's] ideas." XP goes against the habits of many in the field by stipulating that programmers not work more than 40 hours per week, and it promotes greater communication between programmers and company managers, while at the same time deemphasizing the process of documenting, within the code itself, what individual parts of a program are intended to do. Beck also advocates leaving programs open to change by any member of the development team. That gives everyone the power to correct an error, but it also leaves projects more vulnerable than some companies would like. Perhaps the greatest point of resistance to XP concerns pair programming, a method that Beck has said grew out of his experiences with Cunningham. "I'm a poor programmer, compared to Ward," Beck told O'Brien. "But we worked out a way that that didn't matter." While sharing one computer and taking turns using the keyboard worked for Beck and Cunningham, many other programmers have found it awkward. "Programmers consider themselves masters and artists," Jim Duggan, now a vice president at the consulting firm Gartner Inc., told Copeland. "And if you have two artists at the same palette, they're going to fight over the brush."

In addition to his books about XP and other texts, Beck has written *Smalltalk Best Practice Patterns* (1996), *Kent Beck's Guide to Better Smalltalk: A Sorted Collection* (1999), *Test-Driven Development: By Example* (2003), *JUnit Pocket Guide* (2004), and *Implementation Patterns* (2006).

Beck lives on a 20-acre property near Merlin, Oregon, with his wife, Cynthia Andres, a psychologist who is also Beck's co-author for the second edition (2004) of *Extreme Programming Explained*. They have five children: Bethany, Lincoln, Lindsey, Forrest, and Joelle.

Beck enjoys a worldwide demand for his services as a consultant, telling *Current Biography* that at present he is "on contract with companies in Canada, Europe, and Asia"; he is also continuing to work on JUnit. Asked by *EXE* whether the best software developers are born or made, Beck responded, "Made, clearly. If you're a techno-whiz, you have to learn the people stuff the hard way. If you're a people person, you have to work hard on technical skills. If you're like me, you have to climb both mountains at once."

—M.B.

Suggested Reading: *Computerworld* p48 Dec. 3, 2001; Cunningham & Cunningham Web site; *Economist* p7+ Dec. 7, 2000; *Forbes* p142 July 9, 2001; *Irish Times* p55 Nov. 29, 2002; *Salon* (on-line) May 29, 2002; Three Rivers Institute Web site

Selected Books: *Smalltalk Best Practice Patterns*, 1996; *Kent Beck's Guide to Better Smalltalk: A Sorted Collection*, 1999; *Extreme Programming Explained: Embrace Change*, 2000; *Planning Extreme Programming* (with Martin Fowler), 2000; *Test-Driven Development: By Example*, 2003; *JUnit Pocket Guide*, 2004; *Implementation Patterns*, 2006

Stephen Shugerman/Getty Images

Bergeron, Tom

(BER-jer-on)

May 6, 1955– Television host

Address: c/o IMG, 1640 S. Sepulveda Blvd., Suite 222, Los Angeles, CA 90025

"I'm responsible for what I am and what I want to be," the television personality Tom Bergeron told Keith Nelson and J. P. Smith during an interview for the *Exeter High School* student newspaper (October 1981, on-line), shortly before he landed his first job on TV. "I'm not trying to live by another's standards." Known for his quick wit and affability,

Bergeron began his career as a local radio deejay in Massachusetts in 1972, when he was still in high school. A trained mime, he became a fixture in Boston-area radio and television during the 1980s, then gained national exposure as the co-host of the daily television show *Breakfast Time* for five years beginning in 1993. His improvisational skills were particularly valuable on *Breakfast Time* which was almost entirely unscripted. (The show was renamed *Fox After Breakfast* after it moved from the FX channel to the Fox network, in 1996.) Bergeron, Dean Johnson wrote for the *Boston Herald* (February 2, 1997), was "unafraid to sacrifice himself or make himself look bad for the overall success of a particular show. Not many TV hosts take that road these days." In 1998 Bergeron served briefly as an anchor on the ABC show *Good Morning America*. "I came away from that experience sort of reaffirming that my own comfort zone is in entertainment and less in news," he told Lesley Creegan for CNN (December 22, 2000, on-line). Bergeron hosted the third incarnation of the game show *Hollywood Squares* from 1998 until its demise, in 2004. In 2000 he shared (with Bob Barker, the host of *The Price Is Right*) the Daytime Emmy Award for outstanding game-show host. Since 2001 Bergeron has hosted *America's Funniest Home Videos*, which has run longer than any other prime-time entertainment program in ABC's history. Since 2005 he has co-hosted *Dancing with the Stars*, another of ABC's most popular programs. As he told Creegan, Bergeron regards himself as "somebody who treats what he does as a job that's fun, that he enjoys, but that doesn't define him."

Tom Bergeron was born on May 6, 1955 to Kay and Ray Bergeron. He and his sister, Maureen, grew up in Haverhill, Massachusetts, a town of 60,000 on the New Hampshire border. At Haverhill High School, Bergeron was elected president of the student council and editor of the student newspaper. One of his teachers moonlighted as a newsman for WHAV and set up an interview for him at the radio station, in nearby Methuen. Bergeron was hired immediately and, at 17, became the youngest deejay in the state. His other extracurricular activities included contributing editorial cartoons to the *Haverhill Gazette* and other local newspapers. After his high-school graduation, Bergeron opted to continue his career in radio rather than attend college. "I didn't see the use of going to college to learn about how to get a job in broadcasting when I already had a job in broadcasting," Bergeron explained to Nelson and Smith. "I regret not going, from a social standpoint, but I think it was a career-wise move." He took courses in theater arts at night at Northern Essex Community College, which has campuses in and around Haverhill.

In the mid-1970s Bergeron moved to New York City to pursue a career on the stage, on the strength of a nightclub show he had created, which incorporated mime and a monologue. He soon returned to New England. Next, he trained under the famous mime Tony Montanaro at the Celebration Barn Theatre, in South Paris, Maine. (In 2004 Bergeron participated in a tribute concert for Montanaro that was filmed for the documentary *Tony Montanaro, The Miracle of Inspiration*, made by James "Huey" Coleman, Leland Faulkner, and Richard Serls.)

In 1980 Bergeron returned to radio work, as the host/deejay of a comedy, talk, and music program that aired between 7:00 p.m. and midnight on WHEB in Portsmouth, New Hampshire. He considered his role on *The Tom Bergeron Show*, as it was named, to be that of a performer; on it, he cultivated his sardonic yet affable style of humor and on occasion placed phone calls to people around the world whom he thought his audience would find interesting. Bergeron has said that the most difficult part of being a deejay, for him, was having to maintain at all times the impression that he was enjoying himself; when he was not, he relied on his acting skills to cover up his feelings. *The Tom Bergeron Show* became very popular; according to a biography of Bergeron on the Web site of the lecture bureau Speakers-Network, it led to a tripling of WHEB's listenership. During that time Bergeron, along with his fellow deejay Bill McDermond, campaigned publicly for jobs on the popular NBC television show *Saturday Night Live*. Fans of Bergeron and McDermond made phone calls, produced buttons, and wrote letters urging NBC to hire them, all to no avail.

During one vacation from his radio job, Bergeron wrote, directed, hosted, and starred in *For One Night Only, All Week Long*, a four-day variety-show marathon mounted at Theatre by the Sea, a small venue in Portsmouth. His performance, in which he mimed, sang, and acted in serious and comic skits, drew positive responses from critics and the public. It helped him get a job in television, in 1982, as the host of the local PBS quiz show *Granite State Games*, in which New Hampshire high-school students competed in such areas of expertise as math, science, and social studies. Later, Bergeron joined WBZ-TV, in Boston, Massachu-

setts, as an "on-air personality." He first hosted broadcasts of *Lottery Live*, drawings for the Massachusetts state lottery. He then served as host of the Emmy Award–winning, magazine-style children's program *Super Kids*; the multi–award-winning series *Rap Around*, in which adolescents and teens talked about their problems and issues that affected them; and the news program *4 Today*. He continued to host *The Tom Bergeron Show* on the radio until 1987, when he began a six-year stint as the host of a widely viewed morning talk show, *People Are Talking*, on WBZ-TV. By that time he had become a well-known figure on Boston-area television. "Glib without being smarmy, smoothly ranging from substance to fluff and back to substance again, Bergeron emerged as one of the easiest-to-take TV personalities Boston has ever had," Don Aucoin wrote for the *Boston Globe* (September 14, 1998). In 1990, in addition to his television duties, Bergeron returned to radio to host Boston's top-rated morning show on WBZ-AM.

Three years later, turning his back on radio permanently, Bergeron won a co-host's position on the morning show *Breakfast Time*. Aired on the upstart cable channel FX, the show brought Bergeron his first national exposure. Set in a fancy, 6,500-square-foot Manhattan apartment, *Breakfast Time* offered an informal variation on the standard morning-TV format. Along with his co-host, Laurie Hibberd, and a cast of regulars, including Bob, a large puppet (voiced by Al Rosenberg), Bergeron entertained guests at the apartment; everyone would walk from room to room and then sit down for breakfast, conversing as they ate. A crew with handheld cameras followed the action, which was unscripted. "It was designed to be a live, flexible environment and—given that it had an entertainment base—I loved it. It was like breathing pure oxygen . . . ," Bergeron told Lesley Creegan. Listing famous entertainers who appeared on *Breakfast Time*, he said, "One show, Gladys Knight was my co-host. Garth Brooks was there, and Martin Sheen, Emilio Estevez and Beau Bridges were all just hanging around chatting." In effect, he continued, viewers became "Peeping Toms at this incredible party." He added, "For someone like myself, it wasn't like work." "People in the business really took to the show," Bergeron told Nancy Imperiale Wellons for the *Orlando (Florida) Sentinel* (March 16, 2000). "We were doing something different, with a lot of improvising. What made it exciting for me was you didn't know what was going to happen. You had to trust you had enough resources to make it work, or roll with whatever went wrong." The "energetic" Bergeron, as Peter M. Nichols described him for the *New York Times* (September 8, 1996), proved to be a capable facilitator, and in early 1996 the show, renamed *Fox After Breakfast*, moved to the Fox network, with a far larger potential audience. Fox decision-makers cut the show from two hours to one and dropped some of its stock characters, and without them the show lost some of its liveliness and quirkiness. It was also pitted against tough competition, notably the morning staple *Live with Regis and Kathy Lee*. Contrary to the hopes of *Breakfast's* producers, its increased exposure did not bring better ratings. In mid-1997, after several attempts to streamline *Fox After Breakfast* failed to increase its audience, Bergeron was fired. (The show was soon canceled.)

In 1998 ABC hired Bergeron as a fill-in anchor for Charlie Gibson on *Good Morning America*. Gibson had announced that he planned to leave the show that year, and many speculated that Bergeron would be named to replace him. Instead, the position went to Kevin Newman, an ABC news correspondent who had also hosted ABC's series *World News Now*. "Clearly, without a journalism background, I was regarded, justifiably to some extent, as an outsider," Bergeron told Creegan. Not long afterward King World Productions, which had acquired the rights to *Hollywood Squares*, tapped him to be the host of a new version of that classic game show, which had had two runs between 1966 and 1981. Based on tic-tac-toe, *Hollywood Squares* was designed as a quiz involving questions presented to nine celebrities (each of whom faced the audience from a tic-tac-toe square); the celebrities offered answers to contestants, who had to determine if the answers were true or false. Bergeron had established himself as a reliable improviser who could joust skillfully with laugh-grabbing celebrities, but he was hesitant to host a game show in which his main function would be to keep the repartee from flagging rather than to jump into the fray with the guests himself. He decided to accept the job when he learned that Whoopi Goldberg had signed on to co-produce the show and participate in it as the "center square." Bergeron had met Goldberg when she appeared as a guest on *Fox After Breakfast*. "The two of us kind of hit it off," Bergeron recalled to Mel Bracht for the *Daily Oklahoman* (March 19, 2000). "We were like a couple of bad kids in daycare."

The new *Hollywood Squares* debuted in September 1998, and thanks to "the chemistry of the people involved," as Bergeron put it to Creegan, and the many laughs they generated, it was a solid success; for some years it usually placed among the top 15 nationally syndicated shows. "We can't forget that the contestants are the representatives of the viewers at home," Bergeron told Creegan, "and if we make it too much of a yuk-fest at the expense of the contestants, that turns off the viewer." *Hollywood Squares* gave Bergeron his widest exposure up to that time; he won an Emmy Award for his work on the show and received nominations on two other occasions. Twice a month in Los Angeles, California, up to 10 installments of the show were taped during a few days, a schedule that enabled Bergeron to spend more time with his wife and children and to pursue other projects in and outside television. He wrote a novel (it was never published), appeared as himself on a 1998 episode of the CBS sitcom *The Nanny*, and guest-hosted CBS's *The Early Show* the next year. The last installment of *Hollywood Squares* aired in September 2004.

Earlier, in 2001, Bergeron had signed on as the temporary host of the long-running comedy show *America's Funniest Home Videos*, which had been added to the network's prime-time lineup. The series, which premiered in 1989, offers clips of videos made by ordinary people, many of them showing pratfalls, results of practical jokes, or the clownish behavior of children or pets. After the departure of its original host, Bob Saget, in 1997, the popularity of the program had declined. *America's Funniest Home Videos* provided Bergeron with a showcase for his gifts for dry humor and ad-libbing. With his help the show's ratings began to improve, and later in 2001 Bergeron was hired as the full-time host. In one recurring bit that he introduced, "Tom's Home Movies," images of his head were superimposed on those of people in the videos. "I'm very privileged to have become a part of this classic, this institution," Bergeron told Ray Richmond for the *Hollywood Reporter* (November 5, 2003). "It's great because, as a dad, I have a particular appreciation for videos where it looks like parents have surrendered all parental responsibility: You know, like the kid in the backyard, being dragged by the self-propelled mower all over the grass and into the woods, as you hear mom on-camera laughing hysterically. You wonder at what point maternal instinct kicks in, and the mother finally says, 'You know, maybe we should save Skippy from the forest.' I now get to be the guy who introduces that video—and that's pretty special. It's like I get to oversee a video buffet, where people can go several times an hour and be guaranteed a good laugh. How many places on TV can you go where that's still true?" He told Dan Snierson for *Entertainment Weekly* (May 17, 2007), "When you're looking at nuclear Armageddon and global warming, a good crotch hit is like a cool breeze on a hot summer day." With the exception of *The Simpsons* on Fox, no current prime-time network comedy series has aired longer than *America's Funniest Home Videos*. The program attracted an average of nine million viewers a week in 2006. As of mid-October 2007, Bergeron was still hosting the show.

Concurrently, in 2005, Bergeron was recruited to co-host *Dancing with the Stars*, an American version of the BBC series *Strictly Come Dancing*. The program, which debuted on ABC in June of that year, features dance competitions, in which the contestants are couples, each made up of one celebrity and a professional dancer; the "stars" have included the model Kelly Monaco, the actor and singer Drew Lachey, the singer Joey Fatone of the band 'N Sync, the former football player Emmitt Smith, the boxing champion Laila Ali, and the speed skater Apolo Ohno. One of ABC's top shows, *Dancing with the Stars* has drawn Nielsen ratings of as high as three and never lower than 18.

In 2002 Bergeron made his TV debut as a dramatic actor on *Star Trek: Enterprise*, as the Alien Trader D'Marr. (He returned to that show for one episode in 2005, in the role of a Coridan ambassador.) He co-hosted the 49th Miss America beauty pageant in 2003. In 2006 he hosted the New England Emmy Awards, and the next year he hosted the Academy of Television Arts & Sciences Foundation's 28th Annual College Television Awards, which honored student achievement. He has appeared as a guest on TV programs including *The View*, *Larry King Live*, *Entertainment Tonight*, and *The Nanny*. In 2007 he was inducted into the newly founded Massachusetts Broadcasters Hall of Fame.

A longtime volunteer for the March of Dimes, Bergeron served as the 2007 national WalkAmerica spokesperson. In 2005 and 2006 he co-hosted the Jerry Lewis Muscular Dystrophy Association Telethon, and since May 2007 he has been a national vice president of that organization. Bergeron and his wife, Lois, a former TV producer, have homes in Old Greenwich, Connecticut, and Lee, New Hampshire. The couple have two teenage daughters, Jessica and Samantha. "There were a lot of years when I was up at 3:30 a.m. and never saw them until briefly in the afternoon and I was in bed before they were," he recalled to Lesley Creegan. "I was sort of this shadowy presence. Lois got them a game one year called 'Don't Wake Up Daddy.'" He also said to Creegan, "I'm never happier than when I'm at our house in New Hampshire, sitting on the back deck with a cup of coffee, reading the paper. It's all about being with my family and living my life."

—N.W.M.

Suggested Reading: *Boston Globe* p31 Feb. 26, 1996, C p7 Sep. 14, 1998; *Boston Herald Television* p6 Feb. 2, 1997, C p7 Sep. 14, 1998; CNN (on-line) Dec. 22, 2000; *Entertainment Weekly* (on-line) May 17, 2007; *Hollywood Reporter* (on-line) Nov. 5, 2003; (New Orleans) *Times-Picayune* T p6 Sep. 1, 1996; *Orlando (Florida) Sentinel* E p1+ Mar. 16, 2000; tv.com

Selected Television Shows: *Breakfast Time* (later known as *Fox After Breakfast*), 1993–97; *Hollywood Squares*, 1998–2004; *Good Morning America*, 1998; *America's Funniest Home Videos*, 2001– ; *Dancing with the Stars*, 2005–

Blitzer, Wolf

Mar. 22, 1948– Anchor of the CNN program The Situation Room; *former senior CNN White House correspondent*

Address: CNN Washington Bureau, 820 First St., N.E., Washington, DC 20002

"What you see on TV is what you get if you speak to me," the journalist and television-news anchor Wolf Blitzer said to Jim Bisco for *UB Today* (Winter 2004, on-line), the alumni magazine of the State University of New York at Buffalo. "I don't put an air on, and I try not to talk down to the viewers. . . . I'm going to give them the news and do it in a way that I try to make as understandable and as easy for the viewers as I possibly can." Blitzer currently appears on the news channel CNN as the anchor of two programs: *The Situation Room*, which airs for three hours every weekday, and *Late Edition with Wolf Blitzer*, which airs for two hours every Sunday night. For two years after he joined CNN, in 1990, Blitzer reported from the Pentagon on U.S. military affairs. During the round-the-clock, live television coverage of the Persian Gulf War of 1991, which followed the invasion of Kuwait by Iraqi troops, Blitzer's face became one of the most recognizable among those of front-line reporters. The events in Kuwait "changed my life from an unknown journalist and made me known because of CNN's reach," Blitzer told an interviewer for Journalismjobs.com (March 2000). "It almost

Evan Agostini/Getty Images

made me a household name." His coverage of the September 11, 2001 terrorist attacks earned him and other CNN journalists an Edward R. Murrow Award. From 1992 to 1999, during Bill Clinton's presidency, Blitzer served as CNN's White House correspondent. Later, he covered the American presidential races of 2000 and 2004 and the destruction caused in Southeast Asia by a tsunami in 2004 and in the Gulf States of the southern U.S. by Hurricane Katrina in 2005; for his work on the tsunami and hurricane disasters, he and his CNN team won an Alfred I. DuPont Award and a George Foster Peabody Award, respectively. Since 2003 Blitzer has traveled to the Middle East several times to report on the war in Iraq; for a few days in 2005, he accompanied American ground troops there. Over the years he has interviewed dozens of major political figures, including many heads of state.

Blitzer began his career in print journalism. For 18 months beginning in 1972, he served as the Reuters News Agency's correspondent in Israel. For the next 16 years or so, he was based in Washington, D.C., and wrote news analyses and reports for the *Jerusalem Post*. He has written two books, the first about his experiences as an American Jew reporting on Israel and the second about Jonathan Jay Pollard, an American Jew who is serving a life sentence in the U.S. for supplying American military secrets to Israel; the latter book also concerns U.S.-Israel relations and what the Pollard case revealed about them. Blitzer has been criticized for allowing a bias toward Israel to color his reporting and also for being "a reliable weather vane for conventional wisdom," as Eric Alterman put it in the *Nation* (February 6, 2006). But he is widely respected for his determination to be accurate and precise. When Patricia Sheridan, a reporter for the Pittsburgh, Pennsylvania, *Post-Gazette* (October 3, 2005, on-line), asked him, "How would you change news coverage if you could?," he answered, "The facts: who, when, where and why. You tell the people the stories the best you know. If there is something you don't know, you be up front and make that clear. You always give the aggrieved party the chance to respond before you publish or go to air. That's just my kind of old-fashioned news values." Blitzer's recent honors include the 2003 Daniel Pearl Award, from the Chicago Press Veterans Association, and the 2004 Journalist Pillar of Justice Award, from the Respect for Law Alliance.

The son of David Blitzer, a home builder, and the former Cesia Zylberfuden, a homemaker, Wolf Blitzer was born on March 22, 1948 in Augsburg, in what was then West Germany. His parents were both natives of Poland who had survived the Holocaust. When Wolf was a year old, the Blitzers immigrated to the United States and settled in Buffalo, New York. Blitzer's given name—a frequent source of humor in his professional life—was that of his maternal grandfather. Raised in a traditional Jewish home, he learned about international political affairs, particularly regarding Israel, starting at an early age. He made his first visit to the Jewish state in 1961, after his bar mitzvah.

Blitzer graduated from Kenmore West Senior High School, in Buffalo, in 1966, and then enrolled at the State University of New York at Buffalo (SUNY-Buffalo). The Vietnam War was raging, and the campus, as Blitzer told Jim Bisco, was "very po-

litically charged." As an undergraduate Blitzer joined the Alpha Epsilon Pi fraternity and majored in American history. In one class, Blitzer told Bisco, he learned about "the whole notion of revisionist history—that there's a conventional wisdom of what happened, and then a group of historians will come out and start revising that history and come up with a totally different explanation for what happened and back it up with original research and sources." In the summer of 1968, Blitzer took courses at the Hebrew University of Jerusalem, where his interest in world affairs intensified. He earned a B.A. degree in history from SUNY-Buffalo in 1970. As an invited speaker at the college in 2003, Blitzer said that the school had "helped shape me, it developed a curiosity," as quoted by Sue Wuetcher in the *University of Buffalo Reporter* (October 9, 2003).

Blitzer next enrolled at the Johns Hopkins University School of Advanced International Studies, in Baltimore, Maryland, where he earned an M.A. degree in international relations in 1972. He then "fell into" journalism, as he put it to Bisco, taking an 18-month assignment as a junior reporter at the Tel Aviv bureau of the Reuters News Agency. "I didn't have any college experience in journalism," he told an interviewer for Journalismjobs.com. "I never took a course. . . . It was a challenge learning to type. I self-taught myself how to touch type. I was blessed with some excellent senior journalists who trained me patiently and taught me the basic skills of being a reporter." At the same time, Blitzer wrestled with doubts about his long-term prospects in journalism, while enduring ruthless, ritualistic needling by the bureau's British journalists. "They berated me, they taunted me, they cajoled me . . . ," Blitzer recalled to Betsy Rothstein for the *Hill* (September 7, 2005). "It was a hazing experience. It was almost like joining a fraternity."

In 1973, after completing his Reuters internship, Blitzer returned to the U.S. and got married. He worked briefly as the editor of the *Near East Report*, a publication of the American Israeli Public Affairs Committee (AIPAC), a pro-Israel lobby. Later in 1973 he began working as the Washington, D.C., correspondent for the *Jerusalem Post*, an English-language daily widely read by members of the Israeli government and foreign service as well as by many Jewish Americans. Blitzer quickly gained a reputation as a fair-minded reporter with a good grasp of Israeli politics, and in time he was given the title of Washington bureau chief. His analyses for the *Post* were reprinted in some three dozen other newspapers in the U.S. and abroad, among them the *Atlanta (Georgia) Jewish Times* and its sister paper in Baltimore; the *London (England) Jewish Chronicle*; and several Israeli newspapers. (In the Israeli papers he published under the byline Ze'ev Barak, "Ze'ev" meaning "wolf" and "Barak" meaning "lightning" in Hebrew, as "Blitzer" does in German.) During his 16 years with the *Jerusalem Post*, he covered such events as the trip by the German chancellor Willy Brandt to

Israel, in 1973—the first visit by a German head of state to Israel; the first Israeli-Egyptian peace conference, in 1977, which culminated in the signing of the Camp David peace agreement, signed by President Anwar Sadat of Egypt and Prime Minister Menachem Begin of Israel, and witnessed by the U.S. president, Jimmy Carter, in 1978; and the withdrawal of the Syrian and Palestine Liberation Organization's military forces from Beirut, Lebanon, in 1982, which ended a conflict involving Israel as well.

Periodically, Blitzer was accused of pro-Israeli bias in his reporting for the *Jerusalem Post.* "I'm an American Jew who writes for an Israeli newspaper," he said to Anne E. Rumsey for the *National Journal* (April 25, 1987). "I'm not an Israeli, but I speak Hebrew. Since I do sort of have one foot in each camp a little bit, I am in a unique position to try to interpret Israel to the American Jewish community, and the American Jewish community to Israel." In his book *Between Washington and Jerusalem: A Reporter's Notebook* (1985), Blitzer talked about the difficulties inherent in his position. In addition to delineating the economic, political, and military ties between the U.S. and Israel, the book devoted many pages to "analyzing the psychological reactions [of Israel] to hypothetical expectations [set by the U.S.]," as J. Robert Moskin wrote in a review for the *Washington Post Book World* (December 29, 1985). Peter Grose, in the *New York Times Book Review* (March 9, 1986), described *Between Washington and Jerusalem* as a "rich lode of source material, considering [Blitzer's] intimacy with Washington, his sensitivity in posing the right questions and his faithful recording of the answers. . . . This is not a book for ideologues or for those who may question the wisdom of an American-Israeli alliance. . . . But for those who always suspect an ineluctable conspiracy between the United States and Israel, this book shows how things really happen."

Blitzer's second book, *Territory of Lies: The Exclusive Story of Jonathan Jay Pollard, The American Who Spied on His Country for Israel and How He Was Betrayed* (1989), was inspired by the criminal behavior and fate of Pollard, an American Jew and passionate Zionist, who, in the early 1980s, as an analyst for the U.S. Office of Naval Intelligence, had smuggled top-secret U.S. military documents to the Israeli government. When his clandestine activities were discovered by U.S. counterintelligence officials, he fled to the Israeli Embassy in Washington, D.C., for safety, but Israeli officials, who had denied involvement in Pollard's illegal actions, turned him over to U.S. authorities. In 1986 Pollard pleaded guilty to spying and was sentenced to life in prison. According to Steven Luxenberg in the *Washington Post* (May 21, 1989), the discovery by the U.S. of Pollard's transactions "triggered one of the most significant crises in more than 40 years of U.S.-Israel relations." Blitzer, who had two exclusive interviews with Pollard during Pollard's sentencing trial, began his

research for the book with the goal of determining whether Pollard was, as he wrote in his book, "the destructive, dangerous spy" portrayed by U.S. officials or "simply an over-bright young man who led a rich fantasy life that centered on his becoming a superhero of the country that he idolized"—Israel. In addition to giving an account of Pollard's detection and arrest and his motivations, Blitzer focused on the implications of Israel's purported (though adamantly denied) involvement in espionage against the U.S., a longtime ally. "In espionage, you hardly ever know what's really going on . . . you sometimes find that a light at the end of the tunnel leads only to a tunnel at the end of the light," he wrote. Blitzer's views clashed with those of some factions in the American Jewish community. "[Blitzer] believes the Israeli government did Pollard a wrong when they didn't get him out of the country. He looked like an apologist for Pollard," one prominent Jewish political activist complained to Anne Rumsey. In a critique for the *New York Review of Books* (October 26, 1989), the investigative journalist Robert I. Friedman, who in the *Nation* had often criticized Israeli policies as contrary to the principles of ethical humanism, described Blitzer's book as "often fascinating, sometimes apologetic"; he later wrote, also for the *New York Review of Books* (February 1, 1990), that the book was "a slick piece of damage control that would make [Blitzer's] former employers at AIPAC (not to mention Israel's Defense Ministry) proud." Praise for *Territory of Lies* came from Gary Thatcher, writing for the *Christian Science Monitor* (May 17, 1989), who called it "thorough and authoritative," and from Walter Laqueur, who, in the *New Republic* (June 5, 1989), described it as "exceedingly well researched, but also well written and eminently fair." "Blitzer is at his best in the more dramatic parts of his narrative, particularly his reconstruction of Pollard's detection and arrest . . . ," Luxenberg wrote. "But the most compelling part of the book is Blitzer's struggle to make sense out of Pollard's complicated personality."

While on the staff of the *Jerusalem Post*, Blitzer occasionally appeared on such television news programs as *Nightline* and *The MacNeil/Lehrer Report* (renamed *The MacNeil/Lehrer NewsHour* in 1983). By the end of the 1980s, he felt ready to leave print journalism, in part, as he told Scott Williams for the Associated Press (February 4, 1991), because "I could see that I was writing the same old stories with different names." According to the *Atlanta Jewish Times* (July 16, 1999, on-line), the sale of the *Jerusalem Post* to a new owner, and its adoption of a more right-of-center political slant, also pushed him to make a change. In 1990 Blitzer joined the Cable News Network (CNN) as the military-affairs correspondent at the Pentagon. "I thought the Pentagon was going to be a quiet little beat," he recalled to Williams. "I really thought it was going to be two or three times a week that I'd get on the air." Iraq's invasion of Kuwait in August 1990 and the subsequent U.S.-led attack on Iraqi troops transformed Blitzer's job dramatically. Calling Iraq's aggressive action "bad for Kuwait and good for my career," Blitzer told the *Atlanta Jewish Times* interviewer, "Here was a story that I knew a lot about, covering the Middle East for so many years. Here was a story that the whole world was watching, that I could use sources that I had used for many years." The war in the Persian Gulf was the first to be covered live and nonstop on television—in particular, by CNN. Blitzer, who reported from the field as many as a dozen times a day, became an instant star and helped to make CNN the top-rated news channel. "When you are in the right place at the right time and you do something about it, and you do it right, you get lucky," Blitzer told the *Atlanta Jewish Times* interviewer. For their coverage of the Gulf War, Blitzer and other CNN reporters shared a Golden CableACE Award, given by the National Academy of Cable Programming. In August 1991 Blitzer became one of the first Western journalists invited to report from Moscow, Russia, on the inside workings of the KGB—the acronym of the security, secret police, and intelligence agency of the USSR (Union of Soviet Socialist Republics); the following December he returned to Moscow to cover the Soviet Union's dissolution.

For seven years beginning with the election of Bill Clinton as president, in November 1992, Blitzer served as CNN's senior White House correspondent. He earned the Best in Business Award in 1994 from the *American Journalism Review* for his coverage of the first two years of the Clinton administration and an Emmy Award in 1996 for his reporting on the bombing by American terrorists of the Alfred P. Murrah Federal Building in Oklahoma City, Oklahoma, which left 168 people dead. He also reported on the sex scandal involving President Clinton and a onetime White House intern, Monica Lewinsky, which led to President Clinton's impeachment and trial by the U.S. Senate on charges of perjury and obstruction of justice. The impeachment proceedings and subsequent trial, in early 1999, and the media's coverage of them disgusted Blitzer. "Here was a criminal investigation of the president and a trial in the Senate, and the impeachment process in the House. So we had to cover it, but it seemed like such a terrible waste that we had to go through. Specifically, it drained a lot of attention away from where our focus should have been," he told the *Atlanta Jewish Times* interviewer, citing as one example the bombing of Kosovo and other parts of the former Yugoslavia by NATO (North Atlantic Treaty Organization) forces, after the massacre of ethnic Albanians by Serbians with the encouragement of the Yugoslav president, Slobodan Milosevic.

Earlier, in 1998, Blitzer began to host his own political talk show, *Late Edition with Wolf Blitzer*, broadcast on CNN on Sunday nights; according to the CNN Web site, the program airs in 200 countries. He co-anchored *The World Today* from 1999 to 2000, when he debuted as the sole anchor of CNN's *Wolf Blitzer Reports*. In 2005 that program

was replaced with *The Situation Room*, which Blitzer continues to host. "*The Situation Room* is a buzzing hive of news activity that the viewer can just leave on in the late afternoon," Jon Klein, CNN's president, told Linda Moss for *Multichannel News* (June 13, 2005). "It focuses all of the newsgathering, reporting and analytical capabilities of CNN." Blitzer thus appears on air 17 hours every week. His job, he told Paul Bedard for *U.S. News & World Report* (August 7, 2006, on-line), is "very physical and demanding." "You've got to be in good shape," he noted. Toward that end, he tries to sleep seven hours each night, exercises on a treadmill every morning for an hour when he is not away from home, and makes sure that he drinks plenty of water and eats healthful meals. According to Bedard, the ratings his shows have earned are "much better" than those of the programs that used to air in their time slots. And despite his long hours, Bedard wrote, "he's still got time to phone and E-mail his family and pals during commercials and attend baseball and basketball games." "You try to have a balanced life," Blitzer told him, "and make sure you're not just obsessed with one part of it."

In addition to those already mentioned, Blitzer's honors include the International Platform Association's Lowell Thomas Broadcast Journalism Award, for contributions in his field (1999); the Anti-Defamation League's Hubert H. Humphrey First Amendment Freedoms Prize (2000); the American Veteran Awards' Ernie Pyle Journalism Award, for excellence in military reporting (2002); and four honorary doctorates.

Blitzer and his wife, the former Lynn Greenfield, have one daughter, Elana. The couple live in Bethesda, Maryland. As of September 2005, when Betsy Rothstein wrote about him, his wife was a professional shopper at the Chevy Chase, Maryland, branch of Saks Fifth Avenue, and his daughter was the assistant beauty editor at *Self* magazine in New York City. Blitzer's recreational interests include playing tennis.

—D.J.K.

Suggested Reading: Associated Press Feb. 4, 1991; *Atlanta Jewish Times* (on-line) July 16, 1999; *Atlanta Journal-Constitution* H p1 Sep. 13, 1999; CNN.com; *National Journal* p1013 Apr. 25, 1987; *Washington Post Book World* p4 Dec. 29, 1985, p11 May 21, 1989

Selected Books: *Between Washington and Jerusalem: A Reporter's Notebook*, 1985; *Territory of Lies: The Exclusive Story of Jonathan Jay Pollard, the American Who Spied on His Country for Israel and How He Was Betrayed*, 1989

Selected Television Shows: *Late Edition with Wolf Blitzer*, 1998– ; *The World Today*, 1999–2000; *Wolf Blitzer Reports*, 2000–05; *The Situation Room*, 2005–

Susan Grace, courtesy of Common Courage Press

Blum, William

(bloom)

Mar. 6, 1933– Writer; political dissident

Address: 5100 Connecticut Ave., N.W., #707, Washington, DC 20008

"If I were the president, I could stop terrorist attacks against the United States in a few days. Permanently," William Blum, a writer, public speaker, and outspoken political dissident, asserted in a speech given in Boulder, Colorado, on October 21, 2002, as transcribed on the Third World Traveler Web site. "I would first apologize—very publicly and very sincerely—to all the widows and orphans, the tortured and impoverished, and all the many millions of other victims of American imperialism. Then I would announce that America's global interventions have come to an end and inform Israel that it is no longer the 51st state of the union but—believe it or not—a foreign country. I would then reduce the military budget by at least 90% and use the savings to pay reparations to our victims and repair the damage from our bombings. There would be enough money. Do you know what one year's military budget is equal to? One year. It's equal to more than $20,000 per hour for every hour since Jesus Christ was born. That's what I'd do on my first three days in the White House. On the fourth day, I'd be assassinated." Blum was largely ignored by the mainstream media until January 2006, when Osama bin Laden, the leader of the terrorist organization Al Qaeda, suggested in an audiotape that it would be "useful" for Americans to read Blum's book *Rogue State: A Guide to the*

World's Only Superpower (2000; updated in 2005), in which Blum argued that while he totally opposes the murderous actions of terrorist groups, they can be explained as responses to what he views as the imperialistic, amoral foreign policy of the current U.S. government—and those of its predecessors going back several decades. "The attacks are not going to end until we stop bombing innocent people and devastating villages and grand old cities," Blum said in another speech, on October 22, 2002, as partially transcribed for the Australian journal *On Line Opinion* (March 17, 2003). "And they are not going to end until we stop supporting gross violators of human rights who oppress their people."

Bin Laden's reference to Blum became the subject of news reports in the U.S., which led to an immediate increase in sales of *Rogue State*. It also spurred some people to send Blum e-mail messages in which they accused him of "giving aid and comfort to the enemy," as he told an interviewer for the C-SPAN TV program *Washington Journal* (January 28, 2006, on-line). Blum continued, "I'll give you my answer, which I give to them. My answer is on the one hand, I have nothing but intense dislike for religious fundamentalism and the kinds of societies spawned by such fundamentalism, like the Taliban in Afghanistan. That should be clear. I have total distaste for them. On the other hand, I'm a member of a movement, which has the high ambition of slowing down, if not stopping, the American empire and hoping to cease its continuation of very hostile actions all over the world . . . that's been going on for a long, long time. And we're committed to slowing that down. And to do that, we have to have access to the mass media, which we normally don't. I mean I certainly don't. And so because of what happened"—that is, bin Laden's mention of his book—"I've had much more access to the mass media than I ever imagined I would. And for that reason, I'm glad it happened."

Rogue State and Blum's other books have been translated, all told, into more than a dozen languages, among them Arabic. In those volumes as well as in the many articles he has written, mainly for alternative publications and for the *Anti-Empire Report*, his free monthly on-line newsletter, Blum has attempted to dispel the widely held notion that the U.S. government is a benign guardian of freedom at home and abroad. In often-quoted lines from *Rogue State*, he wrote, "From 1945 to the end of the century, the United States attempted to overthrow more than 40 foreign governments"—50 by 2007, he currently maintains—"and to crush more than 30 populist-nationalist movements struggling against intolerable regimes. . . . In the process, the U.S. caused the end of life for several million people, and condemned many millions more to a life of agony and despair." In his October 22, 2002 speech, made five months before the U.S. invaded Iraq, Blum said, "U.S. foreign policy has no moral factor built into its DNA. It's not easy for most Americans to accept this. They see our leaders on TV and their photos in the press, they see them smiling or laughing, telling jokes; see them with their families, hear them speak of God and love, of peace and law, of democracy and freedom, of human rights and justice and even baseball. . . . How can they be called immoral? . . . But our leaders are perhaps not so much immoral as they are amoral. It's not that they take pleasure in causing so much death and suffering. It's that they just don't care [as] long as the death and suffering advance the agenda of the Empire, as long as the right people and the right corporations gain wealth and power and privilege and prestige, as long as the death and suffering aren't happening to them or people close to them. They just don't care about it happening to other people, including the American soldiers whom they throw into wars." He also said, "Our leaders have been telling us one story after another about why Iraq is a threat, a nuclear threat, a terrorist state, tied to al Qa'ida—only to have each story amount to nothing. They told us for a long time that Iraq must agree to having the weapons inspectors back in, and when it agreed to this they said 'No, no, that isn't good enough.' And now that the inspectors can't find any prohibited weapons, is that good news for our peace-loving government leaders? Of course not. They hate it. Does this sudden urgency of fighting a war in the absence of a fight make sense? It does, I suggest, only if you understand that this is not about Saddam Hussein but about ambitious U.S. leaders with Iraq and its oil in their sights, needing a pretext to satisfy gullible people. Oil would not be the only reason for taking over Iraq. The country would be opened up for globalisation and the multinationals would march in and privatise everything in sight, not to mention the further benefit of disabling Israel's arch enemy." He concluded his speech with what he called "two laws of politics, courtesy of the Watergate scandal of the 70s": "No matter how paranoid you are, what the government is actually doing is worse than you imagine," and "Don't believe anything until it's been officially denied."

The son of Jewish immigrants from Poland—Isadore Blum, a factory worker, and the former Ruth Katz—William Henry Blum was born on March 6, 1933 in the New York City borough of Brooklyn. He graduated from Erasmus Hall High School, a Brooklyn public school, and then enrolled at City College (now part of the City University of New York), where he studied accounting. He earned a B.B.A. (bachelor of business administration) in 1955. For the next five years, he held jobs in accounting in New York City. In 1960 he joined IBM, for which he worked until 1964 as a systems analyst and programmer. For the next three years, Blum held that title as an employee of the U.S. State Department, in Washington, D.C. In a profile of him for *Salon.com* (January 21, 2006), Michael Scherer wrote that Blum was "an avowed anti-Communist" when he began working for the

federal government; indeed, by Blum's own account, he hoped to become a Foreign Service officer. His opposition to the U.S. involvement in the Vietnam War led him to abandon that goal and to quit his job at the State Department, in 1967. During that period he organized and participated in demonstrations against the war.

In 1967, with other opponents of the war, Blum founded the *Washington Free Press*, based in Washington, D.C. (An unrelated bimonthly with the same name has been published in Seattle, Washington, since 1993.) The *Washington Free Press* was among the first alternative or underground newspapers in the nation's capital in modern times. Blum, who served as its editor until sometime in 1969, has said that others on the paper's staff rejected what they termed "intellectualism"; they "thought that editing was bourgeois," he told Scherer, and as a consequence, sloppy writing marked many of their articles. Also in 1969 Blum and a dissident friend of his, Sal Ferrera, found out, by tracing the license-plate numbers and letters on cars on a road next to the CIA's headquarters, the names and addresses of many CIA employees. They published that information in the alternative weekly *Quicksilver Times*.

Blum spent the first six years of the next decade as a freelance journalist in the U.S., South America, and Europe. In the early 1970s he lived in Chile, where in 1970 Salvador Allende, identified as a Marxist or Socialist, had won the presidency in a democratically held election. Fearful of the spread of communism in South America, the U.S. government launched an economic blockade against Chile, leading to mounting tensions within the country and increasing polarization of political factions on the left and right. Exacerbating those problems, as Blum and others suspected at the time and as later became publicly known, were undercover activities carried out by the CIA with the aim of destabilizing the country. On September 11, 1973 a CIA-supported coup led by members of the Chilean armed forces took place, resulting that day in Allende's death. A military junta led by the Chilean army general Augusto Pinochet took over the government, which became a brutal dictatorship and remained so for the next 17 years. Those events in Chile increased Blum's awareness of the reach of the CIA. For a while starting in about 1974, Blum worked in London, England, with Philip Agee, a former CIA officer, who, in his book *Inside the Company: CIA Diary* (1975), exposed some of the CIA's clandestine attempts to overthrow the legitimate governments of several Latin American countries. In the book Agee revealed that Sal Ferrera was a CIA informant who focused on demonstrations held at colleges.

From 1976 to 1980 Blum worked at the radio station KPFA in Berkeley, California, as business manager and news writer. He next served, in 1981 and 1982, as general manager and writer at the *Daily Californian*, an independent newspaper published at the University of California at Berkeley.

He then returned to freelance writing. His first book, *The CIA: A Forgotten History: U.S. Global Interventions Since World War II*, was published in 1986. In a review of the book for *Choice* (May 1987), R. H. Immerman wrote, "Using an impressive but indiscriminate array of materials, Blum chronicles [American intervention abroad], beginning with China in 1945 and ending with present-day Nicaragua. His case studies are superficial and simplistic, but should not be dismissed; taken together . . . they constitute a damning indictment." Julian Symons, the *Times Literary Supplement* (January 30, 1987) reviewer, wrote that the book contained "a relentless listing of the Agency's overt and covert interventions in the affairs of other countries"; he also complained that Blum was "given to rhetoric that does not help what is sometimes a well-presented argument." Several updated and expanded editions of *The CIA: A Forgotten History* have been published, with the title *Killing Hope: U.S. Military and CIA Interventions Since World War II*. In the late 1980s Blum collaborated with the filmmaker Oliver Stone on a screenplay for a documentary based on *The CIA: A Forgotten History*. The project never came to fruition. Blum later wrote several other screenplays, none of which has yet been made into a movie.

On the January 28, 2006 installment of *Washington Journal*, Blum referred to his book *Rogue State: A Guide to the World's Only Superpower* as a "mini-encyclopedia of the many kinds of unhumanitarian policies of U.S. foreign policy." "What Blum has done is to analyse American foreign policy since the end of the Second World War as if the U.S. were any other nation state," Will Self wrote in a review of the book for *New Statesman* (January 14, 2002). "Hence the title *Rogue State*, because if the actions of the U.S. government are assessed by any of the standards it brings to bear in its employment of the term, then the U.S. itself is revealed as the biggest rogue of them all." Self also noted, "We find in these pages, meticulously detailed and annotated, all the instances of assassination, covert and overt destabilization, election-rigging, sponsorship of terrorism, secret surveillance, brainwashing and provocation that the U.S. has employed to further its burgeoning corporate empire (otherwise known as the 'new world order')." Donald K. Gutierrez, in a critique for the *Bloomsbury Review* that was posted on *North Coast Xpress* (Fall 2001, on-line), wrote, "*Rogue State* is a guide indeed to ample and convincing evidence that the United States, citadel of global democratic idealism, has for over fifty years been—and remains— the most terrifying military force in the world to many nations."

Blum's book *West-Bloc Dissident: A Cold War Memoir*, which is both historical-political journalism and autobiography, was published in 2002. Along with accounts of public events, such as the October 21, 1967 March on the Pentagon, its contents range from anecdotes about the many well-known people Blum has met, among them the activist Jerry Rubin, the writer Norman Mailer, and the poet Allen Ginsberg, to reminiscences about his romantic involvements and the many occasions on which he felt disillusioned and heartsick about the course of modern history. In reviews for Amazon.com, readers described *West-Bloc Dissident* as a down-to-earth, jargon-free, and witty book by a "courageous idealist" who "cares very much about his world and the people in it," in the words of two of them.

Freeing the World to Death: Essays on the American Empire (2004), Blum's most recent book, is a collection of two dozen original or previously published essays. They bear such titles as "Myth and Denial in the War on Terrorism"; "Peru: Their Terrorists, Our Freedom Fighters"; "Before There Were Terrorists, There Were Communists and the Wonderful World of Anti-Communism"; "Cuban Political Prisoners in the United States"; "The Myth of America's 'Booming Economy'"; and "The Election Circus." In one essay, "Needless Slaughter, Useful Terror: Atomic Diplomacy," which originally appeared in 1995, Blum argued that the dropping of atom bombs on the Japanese cities of Hiroshima and Nagasaki in August 1945 was without justification. He cited published evidence— including, for example, a section of Dwight D. Eisenhower's memoir *The White House Years: Mandate for Change, 1953-1956* (1963)—that during World War II, Japan had indicated its willingness to surrender to the United States on several occasions beginning in 1943, and that, in Blum's words, "by 1945, Japan's entire military and industrial machine was grinding to a halt as the resources needed to wage war were all but eradicated. . . . When, in the spring of 1945, the island nation's lifeline to oil was severed, the war was over except for the fighting." Nevertheless, he wrote, the United States dropped the bombs, because U.S. leaders wanted to scare the leaders of the Soviet Union. "In the State Department there developed a tendency to think of the bomb as a diplomatic weapon," the U.S. secretary of war at that time, Henry L. Stimson, wrote, as reported by Blum. And in the book *Meeting at Potsdam* (1975), the historian Charles L. Mee Jr. wrote, as quoted by Blum, that the bombings' psychological effect on Joseph Stalin, the head of the Soviet Union, "was twofold. The Americans had not only used a doomsday machine; they had used it when, as Stalin knew, it was not militarily necessary. It was this last chilling fact that doubtless made the greatest impression on the Russians."

In another essay in *Freeing the World to Death*, "Conversations (Sort of) with Americans," Blum answered questions typical of those that he has received in e-mail messages or on radio interview programs from people who disagree with his views. To the question "Are you glad that Saddam Hussein is out of power?" he responded, "No. Tell me, if you went into surgery to correct a knee problem and the surgeon mistakenly amputated your entire leg, what would you think if someone then asked you: Are you glad that you no longer have a knee problem? Of course you wouldn't be glad. The cost to you would not be worth it. It's the same with the Iraqi people, the cost of the bombing, invasion, occupation, and daily violence and humiliation has been a terrible price to pay for the removal of Hussein, whom many Iraqis actually supported anyhow." To the question "Don't you realize that the wars you criticize give you the freedom to say all the crap that comes out of your mouth?" he responded, "Oh that's just a conservative cliché. Our wars are not fought for any American's freedom. There's been no threat to our freedom of speech from abroad, only at home, like the Red Scare, McCarthyism, Cointelpro [an FBI program aimed at investigating and disrupting dissident organizations], and the Patriot Act." To the question "Do you regard yourself as patriotic?," he responded, "Well, I guess you're speaking of some kind of blind patriotism, but even if you have a more balanced view of it, what you're thinking about me would still be correct. I'm not patriotic. In fact, I don't want to be patriotic. I'd go so far as to say that I'm patriotically challenged. Many people on the left, now as in the 1960s, do not want to concede the issue of patriotism to the conservatives. The left insists that they are the real patriots because of demanding that the United States lives up to its professed principles. That's all well and good, but I'm not one of those leftists. I don't think that patri-

otism is one of the more noble sides of mankind. George Bernard Shaw wrote that patriotism is the conviction that your country is superior to all others because you were born in it."

Blum supported the presidential candidacies of the social activist Ralph Nader in 1996, 2000, and 2004. He is separated from his wife, Adelheid Zöfel, a professional translator. The couple, who married in 1979, have one son, Alexander. Known as Bill among his friends and associates, Blum lives in Washington, D.C. He devotes a substantial amount of time to responding to the many e-mail messages that he receives daily. In 1999 he received an Excellence in Journalism Award from Project Censored, an organization that promotes independent journalism.

—D.F.

Suggested Reading: Killinghope.org; onlineopinion.com Mar. 17, 2003; Salon (on-line) Jan. 21, 2006; Third World Traveler Web site; *Washington Post* C p1+ Jan. 21, 2006

Selected Books: *Killing Hope: U.S. Military and CIA Interventions Since World War II*, 1995; *Rogue State: A Guide to the World's Only Superpower*, 2000; *West-Bloc Dissident: A Cold War Memoir*, 2002; *Freeing the World to Death: Essays on the American Empire*, 2004

Booker, Cory

Apr. 27, 1969– Mayor of Newark (Democrat)

Address: Newark City Hall, 920 Broad St., Newark, NJ 07102

The contentious and nationally watched 2002 mayoral campaign in Newark, New Jersey, pitted the wily, 66-year-old four-term incumbent, Sharpe James, against Cory Booker, a Rhodes scholar, lawyer, community activist, and one-term city councilman representing the city's Central Ward. The challenger, who was then in his early 30s, cast himself as a reform-minded candidate who would take the necessary steps to reduce gang violence and other crime, improve the city's failing schools, and root out cronyism and corruption in city government. The acrimonious campaign (captured in the Academy Award–nominated documentary *Street Fight*) ended with Booker narrowly defeated at the polls but still determined to head Newark's government someday. Toward that end, he redoubled his efforts to forge relationships with union officials, the police, and others who had not supported him in his attempt to unseat James. In 2006, having broadened his support base, he won the election for mayor, this time in a race with a challenger far less formidable than Sharpe (who had

Paul Hawthorne/Getty Images

decided against running for a sixth term). On July 1, 2006 Booker was sworn in as Newark's first new mayor since 1986. While he is a Democrat, many argue that his politics defy classification. According to Ellis Cose, writing for *Newsweek* (May 13, 2002), he has come to represent "a post-racial man for an increasingly diverse Newark who believes in multiracial, multiethnic coalitions and nondoctrinaire thought." In April 2006 *U.S. News & World Report* included Booker in its profiles of America's best leaders. "[People] can't believe he's for real," Shmuley Boteach, a rabbi and friend of Booker's, said to Damien Cave and Josh Benson for the *New York Times* (May 4, 2006). "But it's rare that a man of the level of sincerity and authenticity of Cory Booker comes into politics and, God willing, as he goes through the process, those incredible qualities will remain."

The younger of the two sons of Cary Booker Sr. and Carolyn Booker, Cory Anthony Booker was born on April 27, 1969 in Washington, D.C. His older brother, Cary, is a professor of education at Rutgers University at Newark and an associate dean in charge of the New Jersey Educational Opportunity Fund on that campus. Booker's parents were among the first African-Americans to hold executive positions with IBM, his father as a salesperson and his mother as a personnel director. Around the time of his birth, his mother and father bid on a house in Harrington Park, New Jersey, an affluent neighborhood, roughly 20 miles northeast of Newark, that was then made up entirely of white families. A real-estate agent spurned the Bookers' offer, telling the couple, falsely, that the house had already been sold. The Bookers, sensing discrimination, contacted the New Jersey Fair Housing Commission. On the family's behalf the organization sent a white couple to make an offer on the house, which was promptly accepted. With the realtor's discriminatory behavior exposed, the Bookers were soon allowed to purchase the house, where they raised their sons. Cary and Carolyn Booker were also actively involved in the civil rights movement of the 1960s and 1970s, often taking their children along to rallies. Mayor Booker has recalled listening to, even memorizing, his father's recordings of speeches by the civil rights leader Martin Luther King Jr. Booker has often said that he was inspired by the story of his parents' actions and, in general, by the previous generation's fight to end racial discrimination. He said to David Segal for the *Washington Post* (July 3, 2006), "I feel like I was born on second base. My parents, they weren't even born in the dugout. They couldn't afford tickets to the stadium. They gave me everything I could dream of, raised me in one of the country's wealthiest suburbs, rooted me in the culture of this country, black culture. I would have betrayed all of the opportunities I've had if I didn't give something back." He told Susan Headden for *U.S. News & World Report* (April 24, 2006), "The stories I would hear from my parents were often of the ugliest pictures of America, but my parents raised me to believe that I had to be a part of this unfolding story, and that the best way to do that was to be a part of the struggle."

By all reports, as a youth Booker was extremely well-behaved, bright, and even-tempered. Those close to him predicted a political career for him. He attended Northern Valley Regional High School, where he and his brother were among a small number of black students. In high school he played football, becoming a high-school All-American and winning Player of the Year honors; he also became class president in his senior year. By that time, by virtue of his gregariousness, those who knew him well at Northern Valley took to calling him "the Mayor." "He was the kind of guy who slowed you down when you hung around him because he'd say 'hi' to everyone," Chris Magarro, a friend of Booker's since grammar school, said to David Segal. "The kids, the teachers, the janitors. Everyone."

Booker received a full scholarship to play football (tight end) at Stanford University, in California. He maintained high grades and played a key role in student government. In his free time he volunteered at a crisis-counseling hotline serving the disadvantaged neighborhood of East Palo Alto, near the campus. While working there during his senior year, he took a phone call from a person threatening to jump off a building. "I remember having this profound conversation on the side of the ledge about why he shouldn't jump, and it was almost like a gift to me," Booker said to Susan Headden. "I'll never forget the power I felt when he touched hands for me to pull him over. And at that moment, I realized, 'What am I doing? I don't want to be a football player. I want to get back to the business of making connections with people through my work.'"

Booker earned a bachelor's degree in political science from Stanford in 1991 and a master's degree in sociology from the school in 1992. He then won a prestigious Rhodes scholarship to attend Oxford University, in England, where he earned a degree in modern history, with honors, in 1994. While there, to the consternation of many, Booker—a Baptist—joined the l'Chaim Society, a Jewish student group. He explained to Headden that he became "more Christian" by learning about other religions, adding, "You see the divine core in all these religions, you see the beauty and the power and the possibilities, then you yourself gain a deeper reverence for God." He has also said that his interest in the l'Chaim Society stemmed from its emphasis on serving others. After he befriended Rabbi Shmuley Boteach, its founder, Booker was instrumental in organizing, in the group's name, some of the most popular events on campus. Booker later became the group's president, which led to an increase in the number of non-Jewish students who joined the organization. As Headdon reported, one member of the l'Chaim Society said that Booker had made him a better Jew. According to the *New York Times* (April 24, 2002), when a faction of the group's leaders demanded Booker's dismissal, the British press caught wind of the controversy and covered it extensively; both Booker and Rabbi Boteach were later forced to leave the organization. After he returned to the U.S., Booker attended Yale University Law School, in New Haven, Connecticut, graduating in 1997. While in law school Booker volunteered in a local Big Brother program, ran a student legal clinic, and was a founding member of the Yale Chai society.

It was in 1995, while in law school, that Booker began his association with Newark, a scene of urban blight where he hoped to make positive contributions to the community; he had relatives in Newark and connections to some of the city's churches. He began by serving as a volunteer with children and working as a legal adviser for an association of low-income tenants. "At the time I had a very negative view of politics and politicians," he said to Cave and Benson. "So I was going to be the great sort of social activist—a person that makes politicians move toward social justice." To get to know the tenants he was representing, Booker rented an apartment in a dilapidated housing project called Brick Towers. He organized a letter-writing campaign among the tenants, then took their management company to court over the substandard conditions of the dwellings. Meanwhile, he served as a staff attorney for the Urban Justice Center and as a coordinator of the Newark Youth Project. In 1998, at age 29, Booker—at the urging of the tenants—ran successfully for a seat on Newark's Municipal Council, becoming the youngest person ever elected to that body. He defeated George Branch, a 16-year incumbent and well-entrenched member of Newark's political machine. In the following year, in a protest against dangerous conditions in Newark's poor neighborhoods—symbolized by open-air drug dealing outside an apartment complex where a violent crime had recently occurred—and against the city government's seeming unwillingness to address the problem, Booker staged a 10-day hunger strike. During the strike he lived in a tent in front of the complex, where dozens of people soon joined him. "It transformed my life," Booker said to Segal.

For much of the 19th century, Newark stood as one of the U.S.'s most vibrant industrial centers. Among other industries, manufacturing, shipping, and insurance businesses flourished there, and some of the country's most prominent inventors and businesspersons called the city home. In the 1920s the bustling city's population had reached nearly 415,000. To accommodate that growth, one of the country's first subway lines opened there in 1935. The city's decline was due to a number of factors. As a result of the Housing Act of 1934, the Federal Housing Administration "redlined" virtually all of the city's land—that is, it divided neighborhoods according to their residents' races and socioeconomic status; the intention was to improve housing for poor residents, but the effect was to segregate the city, with poor and/or minority citizens able to obtain mortgages only in certain areas while, in other areas, mortgage loans were not available. It became easier to secure mortgages in the suburbs than in the city, thereby leading to a "white migration" out of Newark. The building of several major highways that intersected the city, including the New Jersey Turnpike and Interstate 280, enabled middle-class people to live in the suburbs and commute to the city for work. People fled Newark in droves: according to Kit R. Roane, writing for *U.S. News & World Report* (May 13, 2002), from 1950 to 1990 Newark's population fell from nearly 439,000 to about 275,000. At the same time, lower-wage jobs became more prevalent in Newark. By 1966 Newark had a black majority, but its political institutions and economic power remained white-controlled. On the night of July 12, 1967, during a time of pervasive poverty, high unemployment, instances of police brutality, and a feeling of disenfranchisement among the city's black population, John Smith, a black cab driver, was arrested and beaten by police who had accused him of tailgating a police car. Rumors spread that the police had killed Smith, setting off six days of riots, looting, and violence in Newark that led to 26 deaths and more than 1,000 injuries. The National Guard was brought into Newark, and reports about the unrest were broadcast on national television. As Kit R. Roane put it, "Newark came to symbolize America's worst nightmare of urban decay."

In the 1990s, under the administration of Sharpe James—who had come to prominence during the civil rights movement and become the city's mayor in 1986—Newark's social indicators steadily declined. The city lost 20 percent of its tax base and collected only 83 percent of the taxes it was owed. Its infant-mortality rate and unemployment rate climbed at one point to twice the state averages; 80 percent of the city's public-school students qualified for free or reduced-cost lunch programs; and Newark's murder rate skyrocketed, to three times those of the nearby urban centers of Paterson and Jersey City. In the mid-1990s New Jersey's state government took control of the city's underachieving schools. According to the *New Republic* (June 3, 2002), a poll taken in 1999 ranked Newark "the worst place in the United States to raise a child." In 1997 James's chief of staff was convicted of bribery; also that year, the city's police chief was found guilty of embezzlement. James's defenders, claiming that the city was undergoing a "renaissance," pointed to such achievements as the completion, in 1997, of the sprawling New Jersey Performing Arts Center, in the heart of downtown, and to the construction of a new minor-league baseball stadium.

Such were the conditions in Newark when, in 2002, Booker announced his mayoral candidacy. Having raised some $3 million in contributions, Booker campaigned aggressively on a platform of change that included strengthening the police force, requiring the state to channel more money to the city's schools, and making job training available to ex-convicts. James, meanwhile, attempted to cast Booker as an interloper, someone not "black enough" to lead Newark's mostly African-

American population. The incumbent enjoyed the support of such popular Democrats as then–U.S. senator Jon Corzine, the Reverend Al Sharpton, and the Reverend Jesse Jackson. Directly or indirectly, James accused Booker, at various stages of the extremely negative campaign, of being everything from a closeted homosexual to an instrument of Jews, Republicans, and the Ku Klux Klan. (Booker spoke favorably during the campaign of school vouchers, a stance that is supported most often by Republicans.) Arianna Huffington, writing for *Salon.com* (April 30, 2002), noted that the mayoral race had "become a case study in the nationwide clash pitting reformers vs. the establishment, the afflicted vs. the comfortable, the politics of ideas vs. the politics of dirty tricks." James edged out Booker by a margin of 3,494 of the roughly 53,000 votes cast in the nonpartisan election, held on May 14, 2002. After the election Booker turned down a job offer from CNBC to host a talk show as well as an opportunity to work in New Jersey's state government.

In his 2005 documentary *Street Fight*, Marshall Curry captured events connected with the hostile 2002 election between Booker and James. *Street Fight*, which was nominated in 2006 for an Academy Award in the documentary-feature category, examined a campaign that the film critic David Denby, writing for the *New Yorker* (March 6, 2006), called "a testing ground for the political weight of 'blackness.'" In the film, which covers the month leading up to the election and ends after voting day, Curry, a Booker supporter, encounters aggression on the part of some of James's supporters. After describing a scene in which Curry is treated aggressively by Newark police, Denby wrote, "In the middle of the fracas, [Curry] holds the camera at his waist and keeps it running, as angry faces loom over him. James's people, in their dealing with the filmmaker, reveal a good deal about their customary way of doing business."

Following his defeat by James, Booker remained active—and visible—in Newark. He co-founded a law firm, located in downtown Newark, that specialized in bankruptcy cases, municipal law, and tenants'-rights issues. He also started Newark Now, a not-for-profit organization whose mission is "to equip and empower Newark residents with the tools and resources needed to transform their communities through neighborhood-based associations and tenant organizations," according to its Web site. Booker also took time to respond to his critics, particularly those who had charged that he was "not black enough" to be Newark's mayor. In an article for *Esquire* (December 2002), he wrote: "Each time I ran for office, as soon as I announced my candidacy, I was loudly reviled by my opponents as the white candidate, not black enough, the tool of the Jews or a pawn of white society trying to take over Newark. Jesse Jackson, whom I have greatly admired, came to town and called me a 'wolf in sheep's clothing.' Leaders who ascended to office during times of great racial strife, who

themselves overcame great racial obstacles, now used a racial bludgeon to protect themselves from (in both cases) their first real electoral challenge. Moreover, they sought to appeal to a narrow essentialism that is an affront to the very racial expansiveness and diversity their generation fought to obtain. My generation and the increasingly diverse black experiences we know owe a terrific debt to the previous generation's historic struggles. But many in the political establishment in Newark labeled us as pawns of others, as disloyal to their struggles for black advancement, or worse, as co-opted traitors. Well, as much as the epithets enraged my civil-rights-activist parents, they can call me what they will. I know who I am. I know what has to be done."

To appeal to a greater number of voters in Newark as he prepared for his next mayoral run, Booker worked to make himself appear less of an outsider. His daily appointments included meetings with union heads and other political insiders. He also hired a media-consulting firm that had recently helped elect Jon S. Corzine to the governorship of New Jersey, and he even chose as an adviser a former Sharpe James employee. Booker was gambling that he could broaden his support among Newark's powerful political establishment without alienating his original supporters. Joseph Marbach, chairman of the Political Science Department at Seton Hall University, said to Terry Golway for the *New York Times* (September 26, 2004), "If you want to have a significant impact, you have to operate within the established rules. It looks like Cory Booker has figured that out. You have to be pragmatic. Last time, he had the support of many intellectuals, but on the ground, the people who vote were blue-collar union workers and churchgoers." For his part, Booker said to Golway, "What we're trying to do is create a transition in governance in Newark. We're not using terms like 'clean house' or worse. The goal is not to beat Sharpe James or punish his supporters. The goal is to create a strong, vibrant city."

In April 2003 Booker received a political boost when supporters of Newark's state-appointed school superintendent, Marion Bolden, won election to the local school advisory board, defeating incumbents who were political allies of James. Golway described that development as indicating a change in voters' attitudes and as a sign that James "would be vulnerable if he tried for a sixth term." In what was perhaps a related development, on March 27, 2006 James announced that he would not run again for mayor. (James said at the time that he preferred to concentrate on defending his seat in the New Jersey State Senate, which he held simultaneously.) On May 9 Booker defeated Ronald L. Rice Sr., Newark's deputy mayor under James from 2002 to 2006—whom he had outspent by a substantial margin—to win election as mayor, taking 72 percent of the vote. Six of Booker's supporters were elected to the City Council, promising the incoming mayor a secure grasp on the city government. In the days leading up to his swearing-in ceremony, state and local investigators uncovered a plot, coordinated by incarcerated members of a Newark street gang, to assassinate Booker. As a result of the discovery, Booker has been placed under 24-hour protection by the Newark Police Department. The threat is believed to be a reaction to Booker's hardline stance against violence and other gang activity.

Since he took office, on July 1, 2006, Booker has moved swiftly to make changes in Newark's government. He announced the hiring of Bo Kemp, the co-founder and former executive vice president of the publishing company Vanguarde Media, as the city's business administrator, and promoted Anthony Campos, previously the city's deputy police chief, to the position of acting police chief. He also delivered an ambitious 100-day plan to address the issues of public safety, economic empowerment, programs to support families, children, and seniors, and government reform. The plan includes the creation of the Department of Child and Family Well-Being, which will bring a number of already existing agencies under one umbrella; the creation of a new post whose occupant will focus exclusively on helping ex-convicts to train for and find jobs; and a refurbishment of the city's police department, which will include a more visible street-level police force and the renovation of several precincts. In addition, Booker announced that land owned by the city would no longer be sold at a discounted rate to the politically influential, a practice of the James administration that had long been a target of criticism from Booker. In announcing the bold reforms, Booker said that he wants Newark to represent "America's leading urban city in safety, prosperity, and the nurturing of family life," as quoted by the *Philadelphia Inquirer* (July 11, 2006). He added, "We all as Newarkers have to start thinking of ourselves in these larger terms. . . . It's time for this city to get up again and lead our nation at a time when there is darkness in America." Putting Newark on fiscally sound footing is also a major goal of his administration.

While Booker initially opposed the construction of a $210-million sports arena in Newark, he changed his mind in October 2006, after the proposed facility's main tenant, the New Jersey Devils of the National Hockey League, agreed to hire a greater number of minority-owned vendors and help fund projects throughout the city. The team also agreed to give the city a nearby lot, which it had originally intended to use for retail development.

In July 2007 statistics were released showing that during the first half of the year, Newark had experienced a 20 percent drop in crime since the same period in 2006. Looking specifically at a 30 percent decline in shootings, Booker attributed the favorable data to new police tactics, including efforts to fight drug trafficking, loitering, and prostitution. The study also showed that there were 48 murders committed in the first half of the year, down from 51 in 2006. "It's not satisfactory yet, but we are making progress," Booker said, according to David Porter of the Associated Press (July 6, 2007).

Some observers have maintained, however, that the city is not making enough progress—an argument that gained strength in the wake of the execution-style slayings of three college students on August 4, 2007. Less than two weeks after the killings, which took place in a Newark schoolyard, Booker announced the launch of a new crime-fighting initiative, in which more video cameras would be installed throughout the city. The cameras were to be equipped with sensors that alert police whenever shots have been fired. "In case I haven't said it plainly enough, this leadership is asking for help from the community," Booker said, according to Brad Parks and Jeffrey C. Mays, writing for the Newark *Star-Ledger* (August 15, 2007).

Booker's critics have charged that he is merely attempting to use Newark as a springboard to higher political office. Booker, who takes great offense at that suggestion, said to David Segal, "It frustrates me because it's as though this challenge isn't important." Booker has indicated that inner-city Newark, and U.S. inner cities in general, represent "the greatest challenge facing this country." He said, "If you think about it, besides some rural areas, inner cities are the last great challenge to this country, to be what [the country] says it is." The mayorship of a U.S. city, Booker said in an interview with Lawrence Aaron for the Bergen County, New Jersey, *Record* (June 25, 2006), represents "the most powerful position in the country for dealing with America's unfinished business." Elaborating on that idea, he said that crime and urban decay are problems "for a mayor—to manage change, to make an impact. This is the most enviable position to be in if that's your goal and your dream."

Booker, who stands six feet three inches tall, has often been described as handsome and telegenic; he is known for his "perpetual smile and gregarious earnestness"—attributes that initially gave residents of Newark the impression that he "seemed too polished to be sincere," according to Damien Cave and Josh Benson. Booker, they added, "seemed almost like a caricature of a politician." A vegetarian, Booker exercises and meditates regularly and does not drink alcohol. He is a fan of science fiction, *Star Trek* in particular. Booker, who is single, has maintained his residence on the top floor at Brick Towers. He is a member of the Executive Committee of Yale Law School; the Columbia University Teachers' College board of trustees; and the boards of the Black Alliance for Educational Options, the North Star Academy, Integrity Inc., and the International Longevity Center. *Esquire* listed him among the 40 "Best and Brightest" in 2002; in 2005, *New Jersey Monthly* named him among the state's "Top 40 Under 40," and *Black Enterprise* hailed him as one of "America's Most Powerful Players Under 40."

—D.F.

BOROWITZ

Suggested Reading: (Bergen County, New Jersey) *Record* O p1 June 25, 2006; *Esquire* p 162+ Dec. 2002; *New York Times* A p1+ Apr. 24, 2002, A p1+ May 4, 2006; *U.S. News & World Report* p35+ Apr. 24, 2006; *Washington Post* C p1+ July 3, 2006

Bowers/Getty Images

Borowitz, Andy

Jan. 4, 1958– Comedy writer

Address: c/o Hyperion Books, 77 W. 66th St., 11th Fl., New York, NY 10023

Andy Borowitz is an entertainment-industry jack-of-all-trades. He has been a television writer, a film producer, an actor, an author, a fake-news journalist, and a stand-up comedian, and his career path has taken him from the presidency of the legendary humor magazine the *Harvard Lampoon* to recognition in Hollywood and New York. His first major professional success was the creation of the television series *The Fresh Prince of Bel-Air*, starring Will Smith (who was then known primarily as a young rap star). Borowitz has also established himself as a major presence on the Internet and radio: he currently writes fake-news articles five days a week for his satirical on-line publication, the *Borowitz Report*, and is a regular guest on National Public Radio's *Weekend Edition*. Additionally, he writes humorous pieces for the *New Yorker* and other print publications. "Safe to say I'm the only person who has both written for the *New Yorker* and created a sitcom for a rapper," he told Lynn Harris for MediaBistro.com (June 13, 2003).

Andrew S. Borowitz was born on January 4, 1958 in Shaker Heights, a leafy suburb of Cleveland, Ohio. In an interview with CreativeParents.com, Borowitz said, "I'm told I was funny as a kid. Although I'm the first professional comedian in my family, my Dad has always been very funny, and my Mom has her moments, too. It was a funny dinner table with a lot of jokes flying back and forth. Plus, my Dad often took me to a movie theater . . . that showed old movies, where I first saw the Marx Brothers, W.C. Fields, etc. It was a valuable education." As a child Borowitz was fond of books by the author Beverly Cleary. "I think the books you read and love as a child always stay with you," he told Claire Zulkey for the Web site Zulkey.com. "I loved *Henry and Ribsy* [by Cleary], in part I suppose because it was about a boy and his dog and I never had a dog. . . . Conversely, the books you hated as a kid will always hate. I know people will kill me for saying this, but I never saw the appeal of Dr. Seuss. I despised *Hop on Pop*—I found the similarity of the rhyming words in it maddeningly confusing. It probably made it harder for me to learn how to read. I'm still playing catch-up today." As Borowitz grew older, he began to admire the humorous prose of Mark Twain and Woody Allen. He began making his own amateur films at the age of 13. When he was 17 the Cleveland Museum of Art hired him as a filmmaking instructor. (His early films were lost during a cross-country move.)

Borowitz graduated from Shaker Heights High School before enrolling at Harvard University, in Cambridge, Massachusetts. While at Harvard he performed stand-up comedy and wrote for the Hasty Pudding Theatricals, a student-run theater group founded in 1795. (The group's shows are noted for their use of male actors in drag.) Borowitz, who studied with the playwright William Alfred and wrote his senior thesis on Restoration comedy, was also president of the hugely influential *Harvard Lampoon*, which has counted among its writers such luminaries as William Randolph Hearst, George Santayana, Robert Benchley, John Updike, George Plimpton, and Conan O'Brien (also a former president of the publication), as well as many of the writers and producers for the TV series *The Simpsons, The Office, Futurama, Saturday Night Live, Seinfeld,* and *Late Night with David Letterman.*

The *Lampoon* has a longstanding tradition of pulling practical jokes on the staff of the mainstream campus newspaper, the *Crimson*. In an interview with *Current Biography*, Borowitz said, "We did really mature things, like stealing furniture from their building. But we also did *Crimson* parodies—complete issues of the *Crimson* that we published on days that they didn't. We published one that we sent out to all of the incoming Harvard freshmen one summer. The Harvard administration wasn't too happy with me." (The *Lampoon*'s parodies of the *Crimson* frequently featured irreverent humor and obscene language.)

Borowitz worked during two summer breaks at a law firm, which helped to convince him that he did not want to become an attorney. After graduating from Harvard magna cum laude, in 1980, he moved to Los Angeles, California, to work for Bud Yorkin, a TV producer, who had been impressed by a stand-up comedy performance of Borowitz's in Cambridge. Yorkin was a producing partner of the famed entertainment-industry figure Norman Lear, and Borowitz's first job found him working on a spin-off of Lear's innovative series *All in the Family*, which featured the now-iconic character Archie Bunker (played by Carroll O'Connor), a loud-mouthed bigot who lived in a working-class neighborhood in Queens, New York. Unlike the original show, the spin-off, called *Archie Bunker's Place*, proved unpopular with audiences and critics, and the experience of working with O'Connor—by many accounts a hard-to-please, stubbornly opinionated man—was harrowing for Borowitz.

From 1982 to 1983 Borowitz wrote for *Square Pegs*, a short-lived TV series about a group of misfit teens, starring Sarah Jessica Parker. During the 1983–84 season he wrote for the popular show *The Facts of Life*, which chronicled the adventures of a diverse group of girls at a boarding school called Langley. "That was the worst year of my professional life," he told Harris. "I may have been the worst writer in the history of that show. . . . The same company [responsible for *Square Pegs*] said, 'Come apply your hip, edgy sensibility to *The Facts of Life*.' I mean, I was 24 and I listened to [the punk-rock band] The Clash and they thought I could spice up the girls at Langley with my 'sensibility.' But it turned out I was a dismal failure. . . . They never wanted to use my jokes." For Annabelle Gurwitch's book *Fired!: Tales of the Canned, Canceled, Downsized and Dismissed* (2006), Borowitz described being fired from *The Facts of Life* after being told that he just didn't "get" one of the main characters, Tootie, a mischievous wisecracker (and seemingly one of Langley's few black students). Borowitz appeared in Gurwitch's 2007 documentary film, *Fired!*

Throughout the 1980s Borowitz wrote for a variety of television and film projects, including the TV series *Day by Day* and *Easy Street*. In 1990 he and his then-wife, Susan, co-created *The Fresh Prince of Bel-Air*, a show about the exploits of a young fish out of water, Will (played by Will Smith), who is sent from the tough streets of West Philadelphia to live in luxury and safety with his uncle's well-to-do family in California. Borowitz had gained inspiration for the show after a visit to the home of the black music producer Quincy Jones, who told him about his children's privileged upbringing and consequent feelings of entitlement. Borowitz earned an NAACP Image Award for co-creating the series, which was a critical and commercial hit. Borowitz is credited as either writer or executive consultant on several episodes of the series, which launched Smith's successful acting career. *The Fresh Prince of Bel-Air* aired for six seasons on NBC and continues to be shown in syndication in more than 100 nations.

Despite the popularity of *Fresh Prince*, Borowitz was relieved to leave the world of TV sitcoms. He told CreativeParents.com, "What often passes for collaboration in TV is really just a kind of crushing group-think process, not altogether different from focus groups in advertising." In 1998 he co-produced the well-received film *Pleasantville*, starring Reese Witherspoon, Tobey Maguire, William H. Macy, Joan Allen, and Jeff Daniels. The movie, like *The Fresh Prince of Bel-Air*, has a fish-out-of-water scenario; it follows two siblings who are magically sucked into their TV set after squabbling over a mysterious remote control and find themselves trapped in an old-fashioned TV show similar to *Leave It to Beaver* or *Father Knows Best*. *Pleasantville* was nominated for three Academy Awards, in the categories of art direction and set decoration, costume design, and original dramatic score.

After *Pleasantville* Borowitz turned his attention to writing satirical commentary for print publications and for his *Borowitz Report*. Borowitz explained the genesis of the *Borowitz Report* to Allen Voivod for the Bitter Cup Weblog: "I had started writing fake news when I was an editor of the *Harvard Lampoon* in college. When I started going online (shockingly late, in 1997 or so) I started writing fake news stories and sending them to friends. I started the [*Borowitz Report*] site in 2001 just to make it easier to send the stories out. I was really just doing it for me and my friends." One of his most-forwarded pieces is an article headlined "Osama Bin Laden's Wives 'Really Pissed' at Him, Sources Say," in which "Debbie Bin Laden," purportedly one of the Saudi terrorist's four wives, complains, "The world knows how evil Osama is. . . . What they don't know is how cheap he is." She continues, "The day the allied bombers knocked out all of the power plants in Kandahar was the happiest day in Osama's life, because he knew it would bring down our electric bill. [He told the Taliban to ban all movies] just so he wouldn't have to take us to any." Another popular *Borowitz Report* piece, about the possible Republican presidential candidates for 2008, has the men "engaged in a battle royal, with each candidate staking his claim to the title of the whitest white male in the G.O.P. race." Borowitz told Zulkey, "The great (or terrible) thing about *The Borowitz Report* is that through some insanity of my own I've committed myself to writing it five days a week. No one pays me to do it, but thousands of readers get pissed at me (and tell me) if I miss a day. . . . What this means is that even if I feel [terrible] I have to power my way through writing a 250 word column. 250 words doesn't sound like much but if you're feeling down or lonely that day, it's still a pain."

Meanwhile, Borowitz had also written several books. In 2000 he published *The Trillionaire Next Door: The Greedy Investor's Guide to Day Trading*, a parody of get-rich-quick books. In tongue-in-cheek fashion, he dedicated the book to Oprah Winfrey, expressing the hope that she would endorse his book on her TV talk show. In 2003 he published *Who Moved My Soap?: The CEO's Guide to Surviving in Prison*, a parody of such business books as Spencer Johnson's *Who Moved My Cheese?* (1998). Borowitz told Harris, "As a satirist, I am always looking for fair game. And CEOs have had so much fun at our expense, now it's time for us to have fun at theirs. . . . Whenever I wrote about Tyco or Enron I got a tremendous response from readers who'd say, 'Go get 'em!' When you have millions of people who have lost their jobs or their life savings because of these guys . . . the reason the book is priced at a low $9.95 is because if you were a shareholder that may be all you have left." Dishonest executives have long been a favorite target for Borowitz: in an August 8, 2002 *CNN American Morning* interview, for example, he told the anchor Paula Zahn, "I was quite offended . . . because I read in the *Wall Street Journal* that [disgraced Tyco CEO] L. Dennis Kozlowski had a $6,000 shower curtain. And I think a CEO should be able to make do with a $3,000 shower curtain."

In 2004 Borowitz published *Governor Arnold: A Photodiary of His First 100 Days in Office*, a volume of photos of the actor-turned-politician Arnold Schwarzenegger, with humorous captions. That year he also published a collection of his columns from the Web, *The Borowitz Report: The Big Book of Shockers*. In 2006 *The Republican Playbook*, purported to be a secret guide to political strategy stolen from the Republican Party, was published. Borowitz claimed that President Richard Nixon had "commissioned" the first edition back in 1972. The book counseled Republican strategists to use such tactics as disseminating doctored photos of Supreme Court justices—with the justices replaced by such left-wing celebrities as Michael Moore and Barbra Streisand—in order to spread panic. Borowitz told Jane Borden for *Time Out New York* (October 5, 2006, on-line), "I've been doing fake journalism for five years, so I thought fake investigative journalism would be a good career move."

Borowitz has never confined his barbs to one political party. During an August 29, 2003 appearance on *CNN American Morning*, for example, he discussed the massive blackout that had recently struck the Northeast and Upper Midwest, telling the anchor Soledad O'Brian, "I think we can expect the Democrats and Republicans to roll up their sleeves and start blaming each other for the blackout." Still, he is sometimes accused of being biased against Republicans and conservatives. When asked about such a tendency during an October 6, 2004 live chat posted on MSNBC.com, he replied, "It may seem that way, but only because they're in power at the moment. If [John] Kerry gets elected [in 2004], my liberal readers will be in for a shock, because I'm going to be ridiculing him then. My only agenda is to make fun of the guy who's running the show." He elaborated, "I try to stay away from making fun of the little guy. To me, it's the wealthy, powerful and famous who are the only worthy targets for satire. If you make fun of ordinary people, that's not satire, that's just picking on someone. Fortunately, there's no shortage of Paris Hiltons, Bushes, Kerrys, etc.—it's what the Pentagon calls a target-rich environment."

In 2006 Borowitz joined the Rock Bottom Remainders, a rock band made up of best-selling authors. Among the other members are Dave Barry, Ridley Pearson, Stephen King, Amy Tan, Barbara Kingsolver, Mitch Albom, and Scott Turow. Borowitz told *Current Biography*, "My signature song is 'I'm Not Your Steppin' Stone' by the Monkees, which I do as an angry punkish rant."

Borowitz has taught screenwriting and humor writing in the U.S. and Europe and is currently on the guest faculty of the Maurits Binger Film Institute, in Amsterdam, the Netherlands. He often hosts the Moth, a storytelling event based in New York City. Borowitz told *Current Biography*, "I met a woman at a party (I think it was 1999) who had worked with the Moth and thought I might be a good storyteller. . . . I now host about half their shows. So much art and entertainment is packaged and polished now—it's great to get back to something as simple and primal as standing up and telling a story from memory. The fact that things can and do go wrong is one of the valuable things about it, because so many of the imperfections in other forms of entertainment these days are sanded down or eliminated."

In 2001 Borowitz was a finalist for the James Thurber Prize for American Humor (given by the Thurber House, a nonprofit literary center in Columbus, Ohio, Thurber's hometown), and the following year he was inducted into the Friars Club of New York, an elite society of comedians and celebrities founded in 1904. In 2004 the National Press Club awarded him its first-ever prize for humor, the Angele Gingras Humor Award (named for a press-club member who wrote humorous pieces for magazines and newspapers).

In 2004 Borowitz turned briefly to acting, landing small roles in Woody Allen's *Melinda and Melinda*, which starred Will Ferrell, and in *Marie and Bruce*, which starred Julianne Moore and Matthew Broderick and was co-written by the noted playwright, screenwriter, and actor Wallace Shawn. Borowitz told CreativeParents.com, "I don't have much of a desire to be taken 'seriously' in a conventional sense of that word. I'll never play Hamlet, for example. . . . The most serious reaction I ever aspire to is a good strong belly-laugh. Then I know I've made my point."

Borowitz has two children: Max and Alexandra. He currently lives in Tribeca, a neighborhood in downtown New York City.

—S.J.D.

Suggested Reading: BorowitzReport.com; CNN.com Aug. 8, 2002, Aug. 29, 2003; CreativeParents.com; MediaBistro.com June 13, 2006; MSNBC.com Oct. 6, 2004; *Time Out New York* (on-line) Oct. 5–11, 2006; Zulkey.com

Selected Books: *The Trillionaire Next Door: The Greedy Investor's Guide to Day Trading*, 2000; *Who Moved My Soap?: The CEO's Guide to Surviving in Prison*, 2003; *Governor Arnold: A Photodiary of His First 100 Days in Office*, 2004; *The Borowitz Report: The Big Book of Shockers*, 2004; *The Republican Playbook*, 2006

Selected Films: as actor—*Melinda and Melinda*, 2004; *Marie and Bruce*, 2004; *Fired!*, 2007

Jim McIsaac/Getty Images

Brown, Troy

July 2, 1971– Football player

Address: c/o Premier Sports Management, 1401 Ocean Ave., Suite 302, Santa Monica, CA 90401

"Oh, man, he is some football player," Bill Belichick, the head coach of the New England Patriots, said to Josh Elliott for *Sports Illustrated* (February 13, 2002) about the veteran Troy Brown. "He returns kicks, blocks on running plays. . . . You just love to have guys like that on your team. He puts the team first. That's really a great example he sets for our younger players because he's so team oriented. A lot of things have come his way because of hard work and determination." At five feet 10 inches and 196 pounds, the multifaceted Brown, a

wide receiver who has also served the Patriots as a punt returner and defensive back, has overcome others' misgivings about his size and speed to build a storied 14-year career in the National Football League (NFL). "It's been a constant battle for me," Brown told Ron Borges for the *Boston Globe* (August 29, 2005). "I never have felt like I had a job my whole career. It's always like I've got to prove it to them." Criticism over Brown's athleticism has fueled his determination to succeed, which in turn has earned him championships at both the high-school and collegiate levels, three coveted Super Bowl titles with the Patriots, and the unbounded respect of coaches, teammates, and rivals. "He's incredible," Tom Brady, a quarterback for the Patriots, told Jim Donaldson for the *Providence (Rhode Island) Journal* (October 4, 2006). "He's just the ultimate football player."

An eighth-round draft pick of the Patriots in 1993, Brown saw limited play during his first years in the NFL, as a punt-return specialist on special teams. Slowly and methodically developing his reputation for both versatility and reliability, Brown emerged in 2000 as the mainstay of the Patriots' offense, under the leadership of Belichick. From 2000 to 2002 Brown flourished as the Patriots' primary wide receiver, making 281 receptions for 3,033 yards. (His 101 receptions in 2001 set a franchise mark for most catches in a single season.) Still a feared punt returner on special teams, Brown further expanded his repertoire when he began playing cornerback for the injury-plagued Patriots at the start of the 2004 season. With his solid and consistent play on both sides of the line of scrimmage, Brown served as the cornerstone for a Patriots franchise that went on to capture Super Bowl titles in 2001, 2003, and 2004. "Troy is a player for the ages," the former Patriots receiver and kicker Gino Cappelletti told John Tomase for the *Boston Herald* (November 22, 2006). "He could have played in any era." "There are some players that are really smart intellectually, but football doesn't come that easily to them. Then there are other guys who maybe wouldn't do that well on some type of test, but they really understand concepts," Belichick noted to Michael Parente for the *Pawtucket (Rhode Island) Times* (October 12, 2006, on-line). "[Brown] does all of those. He's smart. He's instinctive. . . . He can play offense or defense. He's tough. He's strong for his size. He's quick. He has good playing speed. He can do a lot of things." Brown ranks first on the Patriots' all-time receptions list, with 557 catches, and holds the team's all-time yardage mark for return specialists, with 4,386 total combined yards. In November 2004 he achieved the rare feat of recording a reception and an interception in the same game, a first in franchise history. When asked by Donaldson whether he considers himself an offensive- or defensive-minded player, Brown responded, "I think of myself as a football player."

BROWN

Troy Fitzgerald Brown was born on July 2, 1971 in Barnwell, South Carolina, the second of the three children of Richardean Brown, a single mother, who worked for a manufacturer of outdoor appliances. He saw his father on rare occasions as a child. Brown grew up in the small farm town of nearby Blackville, where there were "lots of cotton, corn, peanuts, and soybeans," as he told Sandy Wells for the Charleston (*West Virginia*) *Gazette* (July 10, 2006). "I'm not far removed from picking cotton. My grandma picked cotton. My momma and my uncles picked cotton. I didn't have to go through that." Instead, Brown helped the family financially by picking watermelons, cantaloupes, and cucumbers and loading them onto trucks. "If I could go out there at that age and bear that heat that long and the fumes from the trucks and load three 18-wheelers in a day, it just hardens you," Brown said to Elliott. "There ain't too much I don't think I can do." At the age of seven, Brown joined a peewee-league football team as an undersized running back. "I knew he was going to be something . . . ," Richardean Brown told Thomas Grant Jr. for tandd.com (February 1, 2004, on-line), published by the Orangeburg, South Carolina, *Times and Democrat*. "It was just something about him. The little kid on the field." She added, "He would never sit on the sidelines and do a lot of talking. He was always very observant. . . . He would be standing off to himself just watching everything that the coach did and everything the other players did." Brown continued to excel in football as a member of the Hawks at Blackville-Hilda High School, playing as wide receiver, running back, defensive back, and kick returner. In 1988 Brown earned all-state honors for his achievements on the football field, where he made 44 receptions for 706 yards and scored 11 touchdowns on offense, made 55 tackles and four interceptions on defense, and returned four punts for touchdowns as a punt returner on special teams. The Hawks went on to amass a 14–1 record and the state Class A championship. Meanwhile, Brown also lettered in track.

Despite his standout career in high school, Brown initially received little interest from major college-football programs, due mainly to his relatively small stature. At five feet nine inches, Brown had been dismissed as an undersized wide receiver of only average speed. With no formal offers from Division I-A schools (Division I-A represents the highest level of competition in the National Collegiate Athletic Association, or NCAA), Brown enrolled for two years at the little-known Lees-McCrae Junior College, in Banner Elk, North Carolina, and worked summers to pay for his education. Matters changed when he caught the attention of Chris Scelfo, then the assistant football coach at the Division I-AA Marshall University, in West Virginia, who visited Lees-McCrae to scout another athlete and discovered Brown by chance. Scelfo told Elliot, "We weren't in need of a receiver. Troy was . . . 175 pounds at the time. He wasn't the fastest guy on the team, but he had an air about him." On

Scelfo's recommendation, Brown transferred to Marshall, in 1991, and starred as both wide receiver and kick returner, emerging as "the most dangerous scoring threat in all of I-AA football," according to Joann C. Elmer, writing for the South Carolina *State Journal* (September 24, 2004). As a junior Brown boasted promising numbers at several positions: 38 receptions for 822 yards as a receiver; a 14.8 yards-per-return average as a punt returner, which placed him second nationally; and a stellar 39 yards-per-return average as a kickoff returner. That season Marshall reached the championship game, which they lost to Youngstown State. In 1992 Brown capped his two-year stint at Marshall in impressive fashion, finishing the season with 101 catches for 1,654 yards and 16 touchdowns and earning All-American and National Player of the Year honors. On the strength of Brown's play, Marshall steamrolled through the Southern Conference en route to a rematch against Youngstown State, this time beating their rivals to capture the I-AA championship. Brown finished his college career as the NCAA's career leader in kickoff return average (29.69 yards per return). He also tied the NCAA record for most touchdowns on kick returns (four) in a single season and had a career average of one touchdown for every eight times he made contact with the ball. Brown graduated from Marshall in 1993 with a degree in sports management.

At the time of the 1993 NFL draft, doubts about Brown's athleticism resurfaced. Echoing past criticism, professional scouts deemed Brown too slow and small to succeed as an NFL wide receiver. As a result Brown went undrafted until the eight round, when the New England Patriots, led by then–head coach Bill Parcells, made him the 198th overall selection. "If you watched the tape of him, you'd be like our special teams coaches, just drooling," Parcells said to Dick Cerasuolo for the Worcester, Massachusetts, *Telegram & Gazette* (April 27, 1993). "He led the nation in returns two years ago. He's a return man with 109 catches. Donnan [the head coach at Marshall] told me this is a guy I'd better keep an eye on." Brown did not find his transition to the professional ranks to be particularly difficult, explaining to Sandy Wells that at Marshall "I had done everything—special teams, returning kicks, kickoffs, blocking kicks, field goals. A lot of guys don't make it because they're used to being the man in school, then they go to a league where guys have to be able to do different things to save space on the team." During rookie mini-camps Brown showcased his all-around skills, impressing another rookie, Drew Bledsoe, the Patriots' future star quarterback, who said of Brown to Elliott, "He was amazing, making play after play. I thought to myself, How did this guy last until the eighth round?"

In his first full season in the NFL, Brown played on special teams as a kick- and punt-return specialist, averaging 9.0 yards per return; in a few instances he played reserve receiver, averaging 11.0 yards per carry. Brown told Jeff D'Alessio for the

Charleston (*West Virginia*) *Daily Mail* (March 11, 1994), "Special teams is my meal ticket, like any late-round draft pick. The more you can do on special teams, the better the chance you have of sticking around." "He's got a place in this league," Ray Perkins, then the team offensive coordinator, said to D'Alessio. "It's just a matter of us finding where that place is." While Brown's rookie campaign was successful, his second season, beginning in 1994, got off to a shaky start. In a preseason game against the Green Bay Packers, Brown committed a costly turnover by fumbling a punt return, leading to a Packers' victory; days later he was unceremoniously released from the team. "It wasn't just that one play . . . ," Parcells explained to a writer for the *Telegram & Gazette* (August 29, 1994). "He just didn't do enough in the preseason." Brown blamed his sluggish start on "that fatal mistake of going home after that first year and acting like a star and hitting every party in town . . . ," as he told Wells. "Funny how getting cut humbles you." Brown returned home to Huntington, West Virginia, for the first part of the season, working at a local boys' club and maintaining his fitness through private workouts. At midseason Brown rejoined the Patriots to replace a struggling punt returner who had been released from the team; he finished the season with a team-high 24 punt returns. In 1995 Brown secured a permanent spot on the Patriots' roster with a solid performance in the preseason, which impressed the demanding Parcells. "He fought his way every day. He didn't miss anything. Every time we gave him the ball in the preseason, he had an opportunity and he took advantage of it," Parcells told Jim Greenidge for the *Boston Globe* (August 28, 1995). "I'm trying to make the best of my chances," Brown said to Greenidge for the *Globe* (October 7, 1995). "I just want to go down and make some plays that will help our team win."

Brown played in every game during the 1995 season, making noticeable strides toward becoming the versatile playmaker the Patriots had envisioned when they drafted him. Among other highlights that season, Brown scored his first career touchdown off a 75-yard kickoff return in a game against the New York Jets. He finished the year with career highs in kickoff returns (31), kickoff returns yardage (672), receptions (14), and receiving yards (159). In 1996 Brown established himself as a mainstay on special teams, handling 29 kickoff returns for a career-high average of 21.9 yards per return. As wide receiver he caught 21 passes for 222 yards and made one of the more acrobatic catches of the year in the Patriots' season-ending game against their division rivals, the New York Giants. During the team's final drive in the fourth quarter, Brown, while lying on the ground, extended his arms to snag a 13-yard pass from Drew Bledsoe, which led to the Patriots' 23–22 victory, securing the American Football Conference (AFC) East title. "I try to make up for [my lack of speed] by using . . . my hands," Brown told Greenidge (October 7, 1995). "I try not to let it stop me from going

out and making plays." In Super Bowl XXXI the Patriots were defeated by the Green Bay Packers, 35–21. Due to a hernia injury, Brown remained inactive for the entire game. "That was extremely difficult to watch," Brown said to Barry Wilner for the Associated Press (January 30, 2002). "It was a Super Bowl, man. At one point, I probably would've preferred to be at home than on the sideline." (After New England's loss, Parcells resigned to become the head coach and general manager of the New York Jets. He was succeeded by Pete Carroll.)

In 1997, his fifth season, Brown replaced the injured starter Terry Glenn at wide receiver and performed impressively, posting a career-best 41 catches for 607 yards (an average of 14.8 yards per catch) and six touchdowns. He also led all receivers on the team in games in which he received for 100 or more yards. Over the next few seasons, Brown shuttled between special teams, his mainstay, and wide receiver, emerging as one of the Patriots' more versatile backs. In 2000, after Carroll was fired, Bill Belichick became the Patriots' head coach; widely admired around the NFL for his strategic prowess and sharp eye for talent, Belichick made Brown one of the focal points of the Patriots' offense, using him as both starting wide receiver and primary punt returner on special teams. With Belichick's vote of confidence, Brown flourished during a three-year span, from 2000 to 2002, capitalizing on his deceptive strength and keen on-the-field instincts to become one of the NFL's most accomplished receivers. "[Brown is] a crafty guy who knows what defenses want to do against him," Ashley Ambrose, a former cornerback for the Atlanta Falcons, told writers for *Sports Illustrated* (December 24–31, 2001). "People think receivers need to be big and fast, but look at Troy—that's just not true. He's always been tough to cover one-on-one." Similarly, Brent Alexander, a onetime free safety for the Pittsburgh Steelers, explained to Dan Pompei for the *Sporting News* (February 4, 2002) that "unless you've lined up against [Brown], you wouldn't know how strong he is. He really plays with power for his size. . . . You can't always see it on film." Brown's offensive statistics confirmed those statements. In the 2001 season, for example, Brown achieved career-best marks at wide receiver with a team-record 101 receptions (for 1,199 yards), and as punt returner he led the NFL with an average of 14.2 yards per return. "I always believed in myself, that I could be a playmaker if I just got the chance," Brown said to Elliott. "I've always been thought of as too small or too slow, but I knew that stuff didn't matter so much if you wanted it bad enough."

In the 2001 postseason Brown played an integral role in the Patriots' drive toward their third Super Bowl appearance in team history. Against the Pittsburgh Steelers in the AFC Championship game, Brown returned a 55-yard punt return for the game's first touchdown; in another play he scooped the ball following a blocked field-goal attempt by the Steelers and made a lateral pass to his teammate Antwan Harris, who scored. The game, which the Patriots won, 24–17, had shown Brown at his best. "Mr. Reliable," Brown's teammate Ty Law said of Brown to Skip Wood for *USA Today* (December 11, 2001). "When it comes down to crunch time, you can count on him. You know he's going to be there." The Patriots advanced to face the St. Louis Rams, the NFC champions, in Super Bowl XXXVI, "a game we weren't supposed to win," Brown said to Wells. With Tom Brady at quarterback and a cadre of veteran playmakers led by Brown, the Patriots offset the Rams' potent offense in part through cohesiveness. "When we came out for the game, we chose not to be announced individually," Brown told Wells. "We weren't going to play as individuals; we wanted to come out as a team." For his part Brown netted six catches for 89 yards, including a pivotal 23-yard reception during the game's final drive to set up the kicker Adam Vinatieri's field goal, which brought the Patriots a 20–17 victory and their first Super Bowl title. "Without Troy Brown, I don't know what our record would be this year, but we certainly would not be standing where we are right now," Bledsoe said to Pompei. "I would say he's by far the most valuable player on our team." "Maybe [Brown has] been this good the whole time," Charlie Weis, then the Patriots' offensive coordinator, said to Barry Wilner for the Associated Press Worldstream (January 30, 2002),"and it just took a long time for us to figure it out." Brown capped his breakout season with his first appearance in the Pro Bowl.

With a record of 9–7 in 2002, the Patriots fell short of winning the division title. In the wake of their second Super Bowl title (a 32–29 victory over the Carolina Panthers in Super Bowl XXXVIII), which capped their 2003 season, the Patriots began the 2004 campaign with a view toward capturing a third championship and building an image as a modern NFL dynasty. With injuries early in the season decimating the team's defensive roster, Belichick tabbed Brown during the preseason to take on double duties as wide receiver and defensive back. "Everyone else thought it was a joke," Brown said of his assignment to Tom Pedulla for *USA Today* (December 20, 2004). "But when I do something, I do it as well as I can." That November Brown made his defensive debut against the St. Louis Rams, known for its squad of talented wide receivers, and performed impressively, with three solo tackles. As the season progressed Brown's play at cornerback increased while his offensive role diminished; in fact, he finished the season with the same number of tackles (17) as receptions, along with three interceptions. "After 12 years, you don't think of yourself as being able to go over and play defense," he told Jennifer Toland for the *Telegram & Gazette* (January 15, 2005). "But they asked me to do something, and I said I would give it a shot and give it my best effort. It's just another example of not being afraid to take chances and seeing what you have. I wouldn't have known I could

have done it if I hadn't tried." "You can't exaggerate the difficulty of what Troy has done," the former NFL quarterback Joe Theismann, an analyst for ESPN, told Paul Attner for the *Sporting News* (February 11, 2005). "As a slot corner[back], it is really hard. You are on an island, the receiver is in the middle of the field, and you don't have the sideline to help you. To do this at his age, and with the specific skill set it takes, he is just a phenomenal athlete."

In the 2005 season, while the Patriots amassed a record of 10–6, Brown made 39 receptions for 466 yards; the team claimed the AFC East title before losing in the second round of the play-offs to the Denver Broncos. In an August 2006 exhibition game against the New York Giants, Brown added quarterback to his list of on-the-field accomplishments. During the 2006 regular season, his 14th in the NFL, Brown continued to impress with his stellar play on both offense and defense. In one highlight early in the season, he helped shut down the Green Bay Packers' offense by limiting their star receiver Donald Driver to just two catches (Driver averaged seven per game). Brown's fellow cornerback Chad Scott credited his defensive instincts to his experience on offense. "Troy understands—being the type of good receiver he is—what receivers are trying to do," Scott said to John Tomase. "He understands leverage. He knows what they're thinking. He knows where they're trying to go." During the Patriots' divisional play-off game against the San Diego Chargers, with the Patriots down 21–13 in the waning moments of the fourth quarter, Brown stripped the Chargers' safety Marlon McCree's interception of an errant pass by Tom Brady, preserving a Patriots possession and leading to a game-tying score. "That play . . . was the best play I've ever seen," Brady told Reiss for the *Boston Globe* (January 20, 2007). "It saved our season." Though the Patriots' season came to an end with a loss to the Indianapolis Colts, 38–34, in the AFC Championship game, Brown finished the 2006 campaign having achieved another career milestone. With season-ending totals of 43 catches for 384 yards at wide receiver (in addition to his duties at cornerback), Brown became the Patriots' all-time receiving leader, with 557 for his career, breaking Stanley Morgan's total of 534 catches, set in 1989. Though there had been talk of Brown's retiring after the 2006 season, in July 2007 he signed a one-year contract with the Patriots. At the beginning of the season, he was placed on the team's reserve/physically-unable-to-perform list, as he had undergone knee surgery in the off-season; it was expected that he would be sidelined for the season's first six weeks.

Brown is married to Kim Courts Brown. The couple have two sons, Sir'mon and SaanJay, and make their home in Huntington, West Virginia, where Brown is active in the community—serving as a youth tee-ball and soccer coach and as host of an annual football camp for children. In March 2006 Brown launched the first Troy Brown Fantasy

Football Camp, a fund-raiser for Marshall University's Child Development Academy.

—D.J.K.

Suggested Reading: Associated Press (on-line) Jan. 30, 2002; *Boston Globe* D p1 Aug. 29, 2005; *Boston Herald* p71 Nov. 22, 2006; *Charleston* (*West Virginia*) *Gazette* C p1 July 10, 2006; NFL.com; Patriots.com; *Sports Illustrated* p66 Feb. 13, 2002; Thetandd.com Feb. 1, 2004, Feb. 13, 2005; *USA Today* C p4 Dec. 11, 2001

Ethan Miller/Getty Images

Brunson, Doyle

Aug. 10, 1933– Poker player; writer

Address: c/o Cardoza Publishing, P.O. Box 1500, Cooper Station, New York, NY 10276

"Doyle Brunson is a poker revolutionary in too many ways to count, but his decision to put all of his knowledge into print nearly 30 years ago changed the face of poker forever," Chuck Blount declared in the *San Antonio (Texas) Express-News* (May 25, 2006). Blount was referring to Brunson's book *How I Made $1,000,000 Playing Poker*, later retitled *Super System: A Course in Power Poker*. Considered a players' bible, the book appeared in 1978, the year after Brunson won the World Series of Poker (WSOP) for the second year in a row. Altogether, he has won 10 championships (in various types of poker) at the WSOP, a feat matched by only one other player (Johnny Chan) and surpassed by only one (Phil Hellmuth Jr.). "If you consider the creation of the World Series of Poker in 1970

as the beginning of modern-day poker, then Brunson is the game's equivalent of Babe Ruth, Michael Jordan and Jack Nicklaus rolled into one," Marc Schwarz wrote for the Bergen County, New Jersey, *Record* (December 25, 2005), referring to legends of baseball, basketball, and golf, respectively. Nicknamed "Texas Dolly," Brunson has been a dominant player in professional poker since the late 1950s, when he participated in illegal games throughout Texas. In *Super System* and his other books, he has not only offered poker neophytes insights into how professionals win but has stressed the importance of honor, trust, and responsibility at the poker table. As one of the first respected voices in the game to do so, he has come to personify the notion that gambling can be a respectable profession. Brunson has his own Web site, DoylesRoom.com, and although he prefers cash games—that is, games in which the winners take home unlimited sums of money—he has appeared in many celebrity poker tournaments in the U.S. and overseas. "He's the godfather of the game," the professional player Phil Gordon told Jeff Wilson for the *Fort Worth (Texas) Star-Telegram* (June 13, 2004). "He's certainly in the top 10 that have ever played the game, and he's probably in the top three of people who have made a real difference in the game and brought it from the back rooms of Texas to mainstream television." Brunson is associated most frequently with Texas Hold 'Em, one of the hundreds of poker variants and currently the most popular one in the U.S. Now 74, he remains active at poker events and often defeats opponents decades younger than he is. He told Marc Schwarz that because of age, "I've lost 10 percent of my game, but fortunately I was 20 percent ahead to start with."

The second of three children, Doyle Brunson was born on August 10, 1933 in Longworth, a tiny town in Texas. He reportedly got his nickname, Texas Dolly, as an adult, when Jimmy "the Greek" Snyder, a Las Vegas bookmaker, mispronounced "Doyle" during an announcement for a poker game. He and his siblings grew up in a four-room house with an outhouse in the backyard. His father worked for the Planters Gin Co., which produced cottonseed oil; he held a second job as the manager of a local gymnasium, whose facilities young Brunson used often. Brunson's parents were Baptists, and the family attended church regularly. Brunson began his education in a one-room school in Longworth. After he entered the regional high school in Sweetwater, Texas, he would run the 10 miles or so to and from school with two friends of his. "I knew the only way to leave Longworth and go to college was on an athletic scholarship," he told Nolan Dalla for the Web site Pokerpages.com (June 17, 2003). Brunson and his friends became the stars of Sweetwater High's basketball team, and Brunson became a standout in track. During his senior year he won the mile race at the Texas Interscholastic Track Meet with a time of 4:38—faster than any other high schooler in the state that year. When he graduated Brunson was ranked as the top high-school miler and among the five best high-school basketball players in Texas. He then enrolled at Hardin-Simmons University, in Abilene, Texas, a Baptist-affiliated university 40 miles from Longworth, one of the dozens of colleges that had offered him scholarships. During his junior year at Hardin-Simmons, Brunson was voted the Border Conference's Most Valuable Player in track and basketball. By then he had trimmed his mile time to 4:18, and *Dell Basketball Magazine* had ranked him among the nation's top 10 college basketball players. He began to attract interest from professional basketball teams, notably the Minneapolis Lakers (now the Los Angeles Lakers), and considered trying out for the U.S. National Track Team.

Brunson had been introduced to poker while in high school, playing Five-Card Draw. In college, although playing poker for money was illegal in Texas then, he played on Saturday nights. "I got caught once or twice and was disciplined for gambling . . . but since I was one of the basketball stars nothing much came of it," Brunson recalled in an essay posted on DoylesRoom.com. During the summer following his junior year, Brunson got a job at the U.S. Gypsum plant in Longworth. One day, while he was unloading sheetrock from a truck, a 2,000-pound stack of the material fell on his leg, breaking it badly. Unable to run or play basketball while the leg healed (a process that took nearly two years and left him with a permanent limp), Brunson spent his free time playing poker at his college and others, in part as a way to exercise his extreme competitiveness. He learned many of the hundreds of variations of poker, enabling him to compete in whatever games he happened upon, and he often won. In his senior year, with his leg in a cast, he feared that a career in sports might no longer be possible for him, and he became more studious. After he completed college, in 1954, he entered a one-year master's-degree program in administrative education at Hardin-Simmons. During that period he also began to play poker more seriously. After he earned his master's degree, Brunson sought work at schools. The salary for the highest-paying job he was offered, that of high-school basketball coach, was $4,800 a year—an amount he considered far too low. (In 1954–55 the average salary for teachers in the U.S. was $3,950.) Instead, Brunson took a job as a salesman for the Burroughs Corp., selling bookkeeping equipment. While on the road one day, he spent the afternoon in a back-room poker game with a potential customer. In only three hours he pocketed as much money as he earned at Burroughs in a month. He promptly quit his job to play poker full-time.

Brunson began his professional career in poker on Exchange Street in Fort Worth, Texas, a part of the city notorious for "shootings, muggings, robberies, and just about every kind of violence imaginable," as he described it in *Super System*. In addition to the danger of arrest, poker players had to grapple with cheaters and gamblers who balked at paying what they owed. People with partners seemed to be somewhat less vulnerable to trouble, so Brunson traveled with another man. In the lawless and perilous atmosphere that prevailed, Brunson has said, he gained the ability to concentrate under any circumstances. In time he developed friendships with two like-minded gamblers—Brian "Sailor" Roberts and Thomas "Amarillo Slim" Preston. When his original partner gave up road games, Brunson teamed up with Roberts and Preston. For nearly six years, the three traveled together, playing for ever-higher stakes; they shared not only hotel rooms but their money, so that the successes of one would make up for the losses of the others. Away from games, they talked endlessly about strategies, odds, and the psychology of poker. As their reputation as tough professionals grew, the trio began to get invited to private games at clubs, environments in which they felt safe and where their opponents often included wealthy oilmen and cattlemen who wanted to match wits with professional gamblers. After a trip to Las Vegas, Nevada, during which they lost all their money, Brunson, Roberts, and Preston went their separate ways.

Brunson returned to the poker circuit in Texas and also began gambling on sports events. In 1962, a few months after he had gotten married, doctors discovered a malignant tumor in Brunson's neck. Brunson underwent surgery and was told that he had less than six months to live. But after a second operation, the cancer disappeared completely. "I returned to the poker circuit with a zest and appreciation for life I never had before," Brunson recalled in *Super System*. He won in his next 54 sessions, a feat that he has never matched. One result of that remarkable winning streak was that he stopped getting invited to games. Unable to maintain his livelihood in Texas, in 1973 Brunson moved with his family to Las Vegas, known as the nation's gambling center.

Las Vegas was the home of Binion's Horseshoe (known since 2005 as Binion's Gambling Hall and Hotel), a casino where the World Series of Poker was held annually from 1970 through 2004. The first series included a half-dozen poker variants, and the winner was elected by all the players at the end of the events. In 1971 the tournament was changed to one winner-takes-all No-Limit Texas Hold 'Em series. In later years other events were added. Thanks to the WSOP and tournaments of its kind, Texas Hold 'Em is now the most popular form of poker in the U.S., and the matches are third in popularity among televised sports nationwide, after pro football and NASCAR races. In Texas Hold 'Em, each player receives two cards dealt face-down (the "hole cards"). After a round of betting, the dealer turns over three "community cards" (so-called because the players share those cards)—the stage of the game called "the flop." Another round of betting ensues, followed by the dealing of a fourth community card, or "turn card"; the turning of the fifth and final community card, or "the river," is preceded and followed by a round of betting. The winner is the player who holds the best five cards—using any combination of community and hole cards.

Already well-known in gambling circles, Brunson became a national celebrity in poker circles through the World Series of Poker. In 1976 he bested 22 players to win the main event and a pot of $220,000; he also earned $80,250 by winning the deuce-to-seven draw game. At the 1977 WSOP, Brunson won the seven-card-stud split event (and $62,500) and the main event, defeating 34 challengers and taking home $340,000. He is one of only four players who have won the main event more than once. Improbably, Brunson won in 1976 and 1977 with a full house consisting of three 10s and two deuces, now known in poker circles as the "Doyle Brunson." Throughout the 1980s he entered multiple events at the WSOP. In 1980 he placed second in both the main event and the deuce-to-seven draw tournament. In 1982 he placed fourth in the main event and third in the ace-to-five draw. The following year he placed third in the main event, and in 1986 he placed fourth in the Omaha pot-limit event. ("Limit" refers to the amount of the bets permitted in a particular game, both in opening the game and in raising the ante during the game. Common forms are called no limit, pot limit, fixed limit, and spread limit.) Brunson's only other top finishes in the main event came in 1997, when he came in 16th, and in 2004, when he ended in the 53d position. Brunson has won 10 gold-and-gem–studded bracelets, awarded for a first-place finish in any event. He won his most recent bracelet in 2005, in a short-handed no-limit Texas Hold 'Em game. (In short-handed games, six players sit at each table, rather than the usual nine or 10.)

In 1978, on the heels of his two WSOP main-event titles, Brunson self-published *How I Made $1,000,000 Playing Poker*. Written "as told to" Allan Goldberg, it contains chapters by Brunson; Bobby Baldwin, the 1978 WSOP champion; and four men considered to be top poker theorists: David "Chip" Reese, Mike Caro, David Sklansky, and Joey Hawthorne. Other poker experts whom Brunson had approached as potential contributors to the book balked at the idea of exposing their "secrets." In his own chapters, in addition to describing the mechanics of poker variants and suggesting what to do in specific situations, Brunson discussed money management, opponents to avoid, and ways of finding the right game for one's particular style of play. He also wrote that being very aggressive and taking advantage of weaker players are keys to success. "You will be playing mostly against unskilled gamblers," he wrote. "Their minds are not particularly sharp and often they haven't lived life very successfully. They're financially troubled or psychologically battered. . . . You might as well know the truth, sad as it is—they've come to escape the pain." He revealed that some of his fiercest battles had been with players whom he liked and respected, in games in which all involved did whatever they could—within the rules—to win.

For nearly a quarter-century, *Super System* was sold only in casinos and card rooms and priced at $100. In 2005 the New York City firm Cardoza made available a new, less expensive edition of the book, as well as *Doyle Brunson's Super System 2*, which contains chapters by such poker luminaries as Crandall Addington, Lyle Berman, Johnny Chan, Steve Lipscomb, Daniel Negreano, and Steve Zolotow as well as Brunson, Baldwin, and Caro. Earlier, in 1984, Brunson had published the book *According to Doyle*, a collection of articles that he had written for the newspapers *Gambling Times* and *Poker Player*. Mainly stories or reminiscences, each article "has a message for poker players using one or more examples from Brunson's past," Nick Christenson wrote for jetcafe.org (February 7, 2002). Christenson recommended the book for any player who "wants to get inside the mind of a poker champion." Among Brunson's other books are *Poker Wisdom of a Champion* (2003); *Online Poker: Your Guide to Playing Online Poker Safely & Winning Money!* (2005); and *My 50 Most Memorable Hands* (2007).

Brunson has often played in the biggest cash games in the world—contests in which the stakes climb into millions of dollars—as well as in tournaments. He has participated in many events in the World Poker Tour (WPT), which was launched in 2002 and is hosted by the Travel Channel. In 2004 he won the WPT's Legends of Poker event, at the Bicycle Casino, in Los Angeles, California, and earned $1.2 million. He was among the first players to be honored on the WPT's Walk of Fame, on the sidewalk outside the Commerce Casino in Los Angeles. According to the WPT's Web site, the Walk of Fame recognizes "the men and women who have played the game at its highest level; contributed to its evolution and popularity; celebrated poker in film, television, and literature; and are making the game appealing for a new generation of poker fans."

Brunson told Joe Drape for the *New York Times* (July 10, 2005) that the best poker players "have absolutely no regard for money. You have to look at it as action and the money as units. What you're trying to do is win as many units as possible." Brunson lives in California with his wife, Louise. He has two daughters, Pam and Cheryl, and a son, Todd, who in 2005 won the Omaha high-low split event at the WSOP. A third daughter, Doyla, died of heart disease at age 18 in 1980.

—N.W.M.

Suggested Reading: *Chicago Tribune Magazine* p33 Apr. 23, 1989; DoylesRoom.com; *Fort Worth (Texas) Star-Telegram Magazine* p1+ May 6, 2001; *New York Times* VIII p1+ July 10, 2005; *San Antonio (Texas) Express-News* C p3 July 14, 2005, C p7 May 25, 2006

Selected Books: *How I Made $1,000,000 Playing Poker* (with Allan Goldberg), 1978, retitled *Super System: A Course in Power Poker*, 2003; *According to Doyle*, 1984; *Poker Wisdom of a Champion*, 2003; *Doyle Brunson's Super System 2*, 2005; *Doyle Brunson: No Limit* (with Mike Cochran), 2005; *Online Poker: Your Guide to Playing Online Poker Safely & Winning Money!*, 2005; *My 50 Most Memorable Hands*, 2007

Courtesy of William Taufic

Burns, Ursula M.

Sep. 20, 1958– President of the Xerox Corp.

Address: Xerox Corp., 800 Long Ridge Rd., Stamford, CT 06904

"My perspective comes in part from being a New York black lady, in part from being an engineer. I know I'm smart and have opinions that are worth hearing," Ursula M. Burns, the president of the Xerox Corp., told Claudia H. Deutsch for the *New York Times* (June 1, 2003). Her self-confidence and determination enabled Burns to lift herself out of the impoverished conditions of her upbringing, enter an Ivy League graduate program, and eventually become a top executive at a multibillion-dollar corporation. Placed on *Black Enterprise*'s list of the most powerful African-Americans in the U.S. corporate world in both 2005 and 2006, Burns is now the highest-ranking black executive at Xerox, a firm founded in 1906 in Rochester, New York, as the Haloid Co. Burns's ascension to power at Xerox began with a summer internship after she completed college. She has earned a reputation for finan-

cial wizardry, which was cemented when she helped save Xerox from bankruptcy. The corporate business consultant David A. Nadler, referring to the corporation's chief executive officer (CEO), told Deutsch, "When you think about who will follow Anne Mulcahy, you can't not consider Ursula Burns. . . . Even in her 30's, she was a smart, unconventional thinker who'd embrace new ideas even while older executives at the table were rejecting them."

Ursula M. Burns was born on September 20, 1958. She was the second of her mother's three children, who had two different fathers, neither of whom participated in the children's upbringing. Burns and her siblings grew up in a public housing project on Delancey Street in New York City. "There were lots of Jewish immigrants, fewer Hispanics and African-Americans, but the common denominator and great equalizer was poverty," Burns told Deutsch. Her mother, Olga, ironed laundry and set up a daycare facility in their home, doing "whatever the hell she needed to keep us all going," as Burns told Betsy Morris for *Fortune* (January 24, 2006, on-line). Despite the meagerness of her mother's income, Burns and her siblings attended Catholic schools. Her mother, Burns told Deutsch, "felt it was the only way to get us good educations, and keep us safe." Burns excelled at math. She was accepted into a few Ivy League colleges but chose instead to attend the Polytechnic Institute (now Polytechnic University) in Brooklyn, New York. She qualified for the New York State Higher Education Opportunity Program, which offers disadvantaged students scholarships and tutoring to help them succeed in college. The director of the program at Polytechnic, Connie Costa, recognized Burns's potential and encouraged her to become a tutor.

Burns graduated from Polytechnic in 1980 with a B.S. degree in mechanical engineering, a subject that she embraced because she believed it would lead to a high-paying job. She then pursued a graduate degree at Columbia University, in New York City. During the summer she served as an intern at Xerox, a company that attracted her "because of its respected reputation for research and engineering," as she told the *EFY Times* (September 5, 2007, on-line). She impressed her supervisors enough to get work there as an independent consultant when her internship ended; she became a full-time Xerox employee shortly thereafter. While still new to the company, Burns caught the attention of a Xerox executive, Wayland R. Hicks, when she argued with him at a staff meeting. Their dispute involved a question posed by another participant in the meeting—in what Burns considered an accusatory tone—about the company's commitment to diversity; the question suggested that Xerox was hiring unqualified people for the sake of filling quotas. When Hicks responded in a manner that Burns thought was "overly diplomatic," as a reporter for Womenworking.com (June 2003) put it, Burns "basically told him that he was wrong," as she recalled to that reporter. Hicks was impressed with the way Burns had conducted herself and took her under his wing.

In the meantime, in 1981, Burns had obtained an M.S. degree from Columbia, having received financial help through a Xerox initiative created to encourage minorities to take graduate courses in mechanical engineering. That year she also began dating a Xerox scientist, Lloyd F. Bean, who was 20 years her senior. She and Bean married in 1988.

During the 1980s and early 1990s, Burns was repeatedly promoted at Xerox as a product developer and manager. In 1990 she became the executive assistant to Xerox's executive vice president of marketing and customer operations; the following year she became the executive assistant to Paul A. Allaire, who was then the CEO and chairman. Thereafter, she was given steadily increasing responsibilities. In 1995 she was made the vice president and general manager of Xerox's work-group copier-business unit, a position that, among other duties, put her in charge of marketing a copier machine designed to keep possible damage to library books at a minimum when people photocopied from them. Two years later she was named the vice president and general manager of the departmental business unit. In that position she oversaw the development and construction of large workgroup digital copiers and light lens copiers as well as their sales and service.

In 1999 Burns became Xerox's vice president of worldwide manufacturing and also joined the company's board of directors. The following year she was named senior vice president of corporate services, with responsibility for manufacturing and supply-chain operations—"just in time to play a big role in helping Mulcahy keep Xerox from going off a cliff," as Morris wrote. Beset by financial woes and losing out to competitors—Canon and Ricoh—the company nearly went bankrupt in 2000 and 2001. During that period, while Mulcahy traveled frequently in attempts to reassure stockholders and meet with corporate clients, Burns managed activities behind the scenes. To cite one important area, she negotiated with representatives of the Rochester unit of the Union of Needletrades, Industrial and Textile Employees (UNITE), which represents Xerox's manufacturing workers. After those talks Burns was able to hire an outside contractor, Flextronics International, to manufacture Xerox products, and the company began to downsize its manufacturing staff, a move that reportedly led to a $2 billion cut in costs over the next few years.

In December 2002, while she was helping Xerox move toward financial health, Burns was appointed president of the company's business-group operations. She thus became responsible for "global research, engineering, marketing and manufacturing of Xerox technology and supplies," according to the Associated Press Financial Wire (April 3, 2007). Burns's style and methods earned her the respect of many Xerox stockholders and executives.

Her detractors included Gary Bonadonna, director of the Rochester branch of UNITE, who told Deutsch, "It's hard sometimes to persuade her that the right thing to do is not always apparent from the financials." James J. Miller, president of the Xerox Office group, accused her of micromanaging, telling Deutsch that Burns "sometimes asks for signature authority over things I think should be my decision."

By the middle of 2003, after having laid off 25,000 workers, Xerox was no longer in financial trouble. "Ten percent of that was Anne, 90 percent was me," Burns told Deutsch. "Essentially, I'm the Ms. Inside for the operational side of the business." Xerox began to produce copiers without the expensive accessories that had previously been standard and thus lured back customers who had not wanted such accessories and had turned to Xerox's competitors to avoid paying for them. "Being a strong player here [in the office market] is critical for Xerox," Burns told Barnaby J. Feder for the New York Times (May 1, 2003). "Stabilizing our operations has made it possible to participate more broadly in this market. Now customers can buy only what they need."

Xerox next set out to increase its share of the color-printing market, specifically the digital market, investing in research to enhance its product line. Competitors viewed the move with skepticism. Sam Yoshida, a Canon USA executive, for example, as paraphrased by Nanette Byrnes in BusinessWeek (December 13, 2004), said that "Canon can leverage its color research across a variety of digital products, including cameras, video, and copiers. That gives the company more bang for its research buck." Burns discounted such concerns, arguing, as paraphrased by Byrnes, that "color innovations hatched originally for one machine migrate up and down Xerox's 30-product color line." Burns's optimism proved to be well founded. In 2005 and 2006 Xerox released 19 color products—among the most important of which was the Phaser solid ink printers and the iGen3, a digital printer that can be used for producing books, catalogs, and flyers—and increased its revenues from color-copier sales by 14 percent. Such sales accounted for 34 percent of the company's revenue by the end of 2006; by the second quarter of 2007, the figure had climbed to 40.3 percent.

In April 2007 Burns was promoted to president of Xerox, making her Mulcahy's second-in-command. That same month she was elected to the company's board of directors. Mulcahy, according to the New York Beacon (April 12, 2007), said that Xerox's recent progress "happened on Ursula's watch as she drove a technology strategy that launched more than 100 products in the last three years. At the same time, Ursula led activities that strengthened Xerox's business model so we're more efficient, competitive and profitable. This organizational change is a logical next step for our company and for Ursula. She brings deep knowledge and experience to the president role, where she'll work closely with me and our leadership team to accelerate our growth in color, services and new business markets." For her part, Burns said that she had remained with the company "because of the people and to be part of a values-based culture with a passion for innovation and a deep commitment to customers. . . . I have tremendous pride in this company." Burns retained the responsibilities of her previous position and took over the company's information-management organization; its corporate-strategy, human-resources, and marketing operations; and its global accounts. She kept her office in Rochester, New York, and set up another one at the company's headquarters, in Stamford, Connecticut.

Burns's honors include the Athena Award of the Women's Council of the Rochester Business Alliance for her professional accomplishments and community service. She sits on a number of boards of directors, among them those of American Express; Boston Scientific, a manufacturer of medical devices; the Center on Addiction and Substance Abuse (CASA); the University of Rochester; For Inspiration and Recognition of Science and Technology (FIRST), a nonprofit organization founded by the inventor Dean Kamen to inspire students to pursue engineering and technology studies; and the National Association of Manufacturers. In October 2007 *Fortune* magazine placed Burns 11th on its list of most-powerful women in business. (Mulcahy was second.) Burns ranked 27th the previous year.

Burns lives in Rochester with her husband, who is now retired, and their teenage children, Malcolm and Melissa. She strives to maintain a full life outside the office, keeping her weekends free for her family, tackling home-related tasks only after her children have gone to bed, running for 35 minutes a day, and employing the services of a personal trainer twice a week.

—S.J.D.

Suggested Reading: *Fortune* (on-line) Jan. 24, 2006; *New York Beacon* p16 Apr. 17, 2007; *New York Times* III p2 June 1, 2003

Carell, Steve

Aug. 16, 1962– Comic actor

Address: NBC Entertainment, 30 Rockefeller Plaza, New York, NY 10112

With a hit television show, a starring role in one of the biggest blockbuster movie comedies of 2005, and a critically acclaimed independent film in 2006, Steve Carell has become—in the words of Josh Wolk, writing for *Entertainment Weekly* (February 24, 2006)—"the go-to comedy property of Hollywood." Early in his career, despite a promising start with the storied Second City troupe, the actor struggled to find his niche in the industry, suffering through a number of failed projects before winning a spot as a faux news correspondent on *The Daily Show* in 1999. In 2003 Carell got his first break in feature films, with a memorable role in *Bruce Almighty*, which he followed with supporting parts in *Sleepover* and *Anchorman: The Legend of Ron Burgundy* the following year. In 2005 Carell scored his first starring film role, in *The 40 Year Old Virgin*, as well as the lead role, that of a clueless middle manager, in *The Office*—NBC's remake of the British television series. By the end of 2005 Carell had ascended to Hollywood stardom, been pronounced the Funniest Man in America on the cover of *Time* magazine, and hosted the 2005-06 season premiere of *Saturday Night Live*. *Entertainment Weekly* named Carell the number-two entertainer of 2005 (second only to the cast of the TV series *Lost*), and Carell, along with his frequent co-star, Will Ferrell, presented an award and performed at the 2006 Academy Awards cere-

Evan Agostini/Getty Images

mony. Later that year he earned praise for his role in the movie *Little Miss Sunshine*. The writer and director Peter Hedges, who cast Carell in the film *Dan in Real Life* (2007), told Wolk that Carell is "the rare actor who can make you laugh and break your heart, sometimes within seconds."

Steven John Carell was born on August 16, 1962 in Concord, Massachusetts, into an Italian-American family. He gave his first acting performance at age six, in a school Thanksgiving play called *The Roar of the Greasepaint, the Smell of the Turkey*, in which he played a Native American canoeist. He was educated at the private, all-boys Fenn School and at the Middlesex School, in Concord, before attending Newton South High School, in Newton, Massachusetts. There, he wrote for the school newspaper and acted in several musicals. He enrolled in, and graduated from, Denison University, in Granville, Ohio, and briefly considered attending law school before moving to Chicago, Illinois, in 1985 to pursue a career in acting.

For several years Carell struggled to find steady employment. He received a small role in John Hughes's comedic film *Curly Sue*, which was released in 1991, and landed a few parts in television commercials. Carell got his first break in 1990, when he earned a spot in Second City—the improvisational school and troupe, based in Chicago, that had launched the careers of many television and film stars, including John Belushi, Bill Murray, Dan Aykroyd, Shelley Long, and Chris Farley. After cutting his teeth with satellite groups for several months, Carell appeared on Second City's main stage in May 1991 for a production of *Winner Takes Oil*. For the next five years, he performed with Second City and taught improvisation classes for the company. While many of his colleagues viewed Second City as a step along the acting career path (the reputation of the group drew television and film-talent scouts to performances), Carell found that his work with the troupe was enough in itself to satisfy him. "I already felt like I'd made it, just being at Second City . . . ," he explained to Nathan Rabin for the *A.V. Club* (August 23, 2005, on-line). "When I was there, I thought, 'If I could just do Second City and do a couple of television commercials . . .' Man I was set. There was nothing in my mind better than that." Most of his work with Second City was comedic, which Carell—who has said that he does not consider himself a particularly funny person—explains as a product of his environment at Second City. "Comedy just sort of was a byproduct of what I was hired to do," Carell told Rabin. "I never had the preconceived notion, 'I will be a comedic actor.' I just thought, 'I'll go into acting and see what kind of work I can get.'"

In 1995 Carell married Nancy Walls, whom he had met while she was a student in an improvisational class he was teaching at Second City. The following year, Walls, a talented comedian in her own right, joined the cast of *Saturday Night Live*, and the couple moved to New York City, where that show was recorded. Looking for work in New York, Carell auditioned for a new sketch-comedy series, the *Dana Carvey Show*, and was hired as a writer and performer for the program, which aired on ABC in the spring of 1996. Along with Carvey and Carell, the show also featured, among others, Robert Smigel and Stephen Colbert, both of whom had worked with Carell at Second City. Sabotaged partly by its family-oriented time slot, the show was unable to sustain a consistent audience and

was pulled after only eight weeks, a development that "floored me," Carell told Josh Wolk. "How could it not work? It was too funny for people not to watch it." One installment that Carell sees as having contributed to the show's demise had Carvey performing an impression of President Bill Clinton, who in the sketch describes himself as a nurturing president while breast-feeding a litter of golden retriever puppies. "People were so outraged," Carell explained to Rabin. "That was pre–Monica Lewinsky [with whom Clinton had an extramarital affair], that was before his public fall from grace, so people were so offended that we would be poking fun at the President that way. A year or two later, it would've been no problem, but at the time, it was perceived to be in extremely bad taste." After the cancellation of the *Dana Carvey Show*, Carell and his wife moved to Los Angeles, California, where for three years he braved audition after audition. "I was just trying to keep my head above water and get what I could get," Carell told Rabin. During that period he earned a role in a very short-lived 1997 sitcom, *Over the Top*, which starred Tim Curry and Annie Potts, and a few uncredited roles in unsuccessful films.

Carell's luck changed in 1999, when he landed a role on *The Daily Show*, a fake-news program that airs on Comedy Central. At the time the program was in a transitional period, following the arrival of a new host, Jon Stewart, and the producers were looking for new talent. Stephen Colbert, who had been appearing on the show since 1997, suggested Carell, who was hired to play a field correspondent for the show; Carell also appeared in a recurring role as Produce Pete, and with Colbert he took part in an ongoing point-counterpoint sketch called *Even Stephven*. Carell received positive reviews for his work on *The Daily Show* and became known for his deadpan on-air demeanor. He told a reporter for *Daily Variety* (April 21, 2005) that he thought of the correspondent he portrayed as "a guy who used to be a national news reporter and had been demoted to this Podunk local show and had kind of a chip on his shoulder. Clearly out of his league in national news and probably local news, too." Carell's first assignment on the program was to interview a real-life Elvis Presley impersonator who also managed a snake-venom research facility. "There's very little you could do to prepare to be a correspondent on *The Daily Show*," Carell explained to Rabin, "because it's not being a journalist, it's not being an actor. It involves elements of both those things, but they're not required necessarily as job experience." Carell told Rabin that he sometimes feared that the show had a "self-satisfied quality," as if "we're the smart ones and we're so much smarter and better than the people we're interviewing"—who did not always understand the humorous nature of the show—"and I didn't like that." To address that problem, when he interviewed subjects he tried to ask idiotic questions, to make it clear to viewers that the interviewer, and not just his subjects, was supposed to be part of the joke. Carell's favorite sketches were those in which "no one looked like an idiot other than me," as he explained to *Daily Variety*.

During the 2000 presidential election season, *The Daily Show*, for the first time, joined members of the press corps to cover the campaigns. By asking often impertinent questions that ranged from awkward to abusive, *The Daily Show* correspondents hoped to reveal the candidates' senses of humor. Carell particularly enjoyed spending time with the U.S. senator and presidential candidate John S. McCain of Arizona, who seemed to Carell to be genuinely interested in the theme of the show rather than in proving that he himself was funny. "I think people want to see this human side of the candidates," Carell remarked at the time to Edward Stubenrauch for the Ohio University *Post*, as quoted by University Wire (March 8, 2000). "Today . . . people are a lot more interested in sense of humor and character. They like to see that these people are human beings and people they can identify with." Performing on *The Daily Show* gave Carell national exposure and vital experience. He has said that the culture of the program, which allowed him and other contributors the freedom to fail, enabled them to attempt riskier gags and improved his ability as a performer.

Carell left *The Daily Show* in 2002 to take a recurring role in the sitcom *Watching Ellie*, starring Julia Louis-Dreyfus. Carell starred as the title character's passive-aggressive ex-boyfriend on that short-lived series. Following its cancellation, he received his largest screen role up to that time, as Evan Baxter in the comedy *Bruce Almighty* (2003), starring Jim Carrey. Carell received rave reviews for his brief but memorable portrayal of Carrey's on-screen nemesis, a smirking newscaster. In 2004 Carell starred in two films that opened on the same day, July 9. In *Anchorman: The Legend of Ron Burgundy*, he played Brick Tamland, a mentally handicapped weatherman, opposite Will Ferrell in the title role. The film was successful, grossing over $90 million worldwide. While some critics thought that Carell's performance upstaged Ferrell's, a reviewer for the New Orleans *Times-Picayune* (July 9, 2004) found "the running gag about Carell's character's mental retardation" to be "borderline offensive." *Sleepover*, a family comedy in which Carell played a child-hating security guard, was decidedly less successful than *Anchorman*, pulling in about $10 million in limited distribution. On the strength of his performance in *Anchorman*, Carell quickly earned more film opportunities. He had supporting roles opposite Ferrell in two other films: *Melinda and Melinda*, directed by Woody Allen, and *Bewitched*, a 2005 homage to the popular 1960s sitcom of the same name. In *Bewitched* Carell took the role of Uncle Arthur, played in the TV series by Paul Lynde. Carell was drawn to the film because he enjoyed working with Ferrell and was a fan of the film's director, Nora Ephron. *Bewitched*, while universally panned by critics, was successful at the box office. Though

Carell's role was not a major one, he thought that the project was "kind of silly and fun to do," as he told Rabin.

While he was filming *Anchorman*, Carell's brand of humor impressed one of the film's producers, Judd Apatow. "I was constantly amazed how funny Steve was on the set of *Anchorman* and wanted to create an opportunity where he was the lead," Apatow explained to Borys Kit for the *Hollywood Reporter* (October 20, 2004). Carell pitched Apatow a story idea that was loosely based on a sketch that he had performed with Second City. The premise involved a group of men sharing risqué stories; in the group was "one guy who just couldn't keep up," Carell told Devin Gordon for *Newsweek* (August 15, 2005). "It becomes quickly apparent that he's never done *any* of the things he's talking about." Apatow liked the idea and hired Carell to co-write and star in the film *The 40 Year Old Virgin*. In portraying the title character, Andy Stitzer, Carell strived to avoid one-dimensionality as well as clichés about middle-age loners. "We didn't want to make the guy a creep, or someone who's emotionally damaged, or some crazy uber-nerd. He's just a normal guy who missed out on some opportunities, and we didn't want to retread the cliché of who a virgin might be. We actually did a lot of reading about case studies of middle-aged virginity, and the people we read about were not unlike the character. They were just normal people functioning in our society who for one reason or another gave up. And it's not because they didn't want to, or weren't capable of it, they had just given up on the whole notion," Carell told Nathan Rabin. In the film Stitzer's co-workers try to arrange a date for him, and through a series of misadventures, he becomes romantically involved with a single mother (played by Catherine Keener) with her own sexual idiosyncrasies. In *Entertainment Weekly* (August 17, 2005, on-line), Owen Gleiberman called the film "buoyantly clever and amusing, a comedy of horny embarrassment that has the inspiration to present a middle-aged virgin's dilemma as a projection of all our romantic anxieties." Gleiberman applauded Carell's efforts as a leading man as well, remarking: "Andy may be a light caricature of a clueless, repressed loser . . . but Carell plays him in the funniest and most surprising way possible: as a credible human being." The film became a summer blockbuster, opening at number one in the United States, Canada, England, and 10 other countries and eventually grossing over $170 million worldwide. The American Film Institute chose *The 40 Year Old Virgin* as one of the top 10 movies of 2005, and the Broadcast Film Critics Association named the film best comedy of that year.

The success of *The 40 Year Old Virgin* brought Carell a reputation as one of Hollywood's brightest new film-comedy stars. It had the added effect of drawing viewers to his concurrent work on television, where, in the spring of 2005, he had debuted in the starring role in NBC's remake of the BBC comedy series *The Office*. He plays Michael Scott, a manager in a paper company, whose delusions of competence and coolness lead him to make wince-inducing decisions and attempts at humor. The BBC program had been very popular in England and had developed a cult following in the United States during its run on BBC America, which made Carell fear that the NBC project would suffer by comparison. Indeed, the show was not an instant hit in the U.S., as uninitiated viewers had a difficult time adjusting to the style and humor of the series, which does not use a laugh track and is marked by uneasy silences between characters. Critics, by contrast, were enthusiastic about the series from the outset. Joel Stein, writing for *Time* (March 13, 2005), described Michael Scott as a "confident, articulate buffoon who has no idea he's messing things up" and found that Carell played the part brilliantly: "With his serious, *Father Knows Best* demeanor, Carell maintains self-assurance in the face of obvious failure; he's a pompous but lovable loser." Carell joked to Stein that he did not have to do much research for the character, as Michael reflected elements of the actor himself. "I myself am a lovable loser. So it's an easy transition," he said. "I'm more loser than lovable, but I bring lovable to the screen." Greg Daniels, the executive producer of *The Office*, said to Stein that Carell brought unusual nuance to his character: "A lot of people play dumb people. But Steve has a way of playing intelligent, articulate people who make foolish choices. People who on the face of it seem smart but once you look deeper have no clue. Which is cool for comedy that's more subtle." Carell won a Golden Globe Award for best performance by an actor in a television series (musical or comedy) from the Hollywood Foreign Press in 2006.

With the critical and popular success of *The Office* and *The 40 Year Old Virgin*, Carell emerged rather suddenly as a major Hollywood draw, and NBC found it necessary to grant him a flexible shooting schedule, so that he could continue to act in films while remaining on the program. Carell's celebrity has led many to speculate that he will not remain on a television show for long. Carell has refuted that notion, telling Wolk, "This sort of [show] only happens once in an actor's life. I'm proud of it and lucky to be working with the people I am." In 2006 Carell lent his voice to the Dreamworks animated production *Over the Hedge* and starred as Frank Hoover, a suicidal Proust scholar, in the independent dark comedy *Little Miss Sunshine*. David Edelstein, in his review of the latter film for *New York* (August 7, 2006, on-line), remarked that Carell offered a "superb interior performance."

In 2007 Carell starred in the sequel to *Bruce Almighty*. In *Evan Almighty* he reprised his broadcast-journalist character—this time in the title role, opposite Morgan Freeman and Lauren Graham. Later that year Carell appeared as the title character in *Dan in Real Life*. In 2008 he is slated to play Maxwell Smart in *Get Smart* and provide the voice

for the mayor of Whoville in *Horton Hears a Who*. Although he has said that his current schedule sometimes tires him, he has refused to complain about his workload, telling Wolk, "You hope and dream for so long that you'll actually become employed, and when you do, the last thing you want to do is whine about it."

Carell currently lives in Los Angeles with his wife, Nancy Walls. The couple have two children: Elisabeth, born in May 2001, and John, born in June 2004. Carell is a longtime member of a Burbank, California, amateur hockey league. "Because my wife . . . was on *Saturday Night Live*," Carell said to Nathan Rabin, "and she's very smart and funny, people sometimes ask whether our home life is a continuous laugh riot, and it couldn't be further from that. We enjoy each other, we make each other laugh, but it's not George Burns and Gracie Allen banter constantly. It's changing diapers and chasing kids and . . . you know. We're very normal."

—N.W.M.

Suggested Reading: *Baltimore Sun* E p1 June 13, 1996; *Entertainment Weekly* p20 Feb. 24, 2006; (New Orleans) *Times-Picayune* Lagniappe p4 July 9, 2004; *Newsweek* (on-line) Aug. 15, 2005; *Playboy* p84 Nov. 1, 2005; *Time* p72 Mar. 13, 2005

Selected Films: *Curly Sue*, 1991; *Bruce Almighty*, 2003; *Anchorman: The Legend of Ron Burgundy*, 2004; *Sleepover*, 2004; *Melinda and Melinda*, 2004; *Bewitched*, 2005; *The 40 Year Old Virgin*, 2005; *Dan in Real Life*, 2007; *Evan Almighty*, 2007

Selected Television Shows: *The Office*, 2005–

Carter, Majora

Oct. 27, 1966– Environmental activist; founder of Sustainable South Bronx

Address: Sustainable South Bronx, 890 Garrison Ave., Fourth Fl., Bronx, NY 10474

The activist Majora Carter was born and raised and now works in the South Bronx, an environmentally challenged area of one of New York City's boroughs. Guy Trebay described that region for the *Village Voice* (January 25, 2000): "When the wind clocks south from the waste recovery facility, it carries a stink that, as a friend once put it, could gag a maggot. Compacted sludge from a nearby city sewage treatment plant is fired here at high temperatures to form fertilizer pellets. Compared to the smell this process generates, the adjacent sewage plant seems almost perfumed. . . . It doesn't take much to dismiss this desolate place out of hand."

Majora Carter

The founder of the activist group Sustainable South Bronx (SSBX), Carter is devoted, according to the organization's Web site, to issues of "land-use, energy, transportation, water and waste policy, and education in order to advance the environmental and economic rebirth of the South Bronx," and she hopes "to inspire solutions in areas like it across the nation and around the world." All her work, Carter told Amanda Griscom Little for *Grist* (September 28, 2006, on-line), "is an effort to help people in the South Bronx understand that we're not this awful, awful, monstrous place, but we're people like everybody else, and we can feel pride in our neighborhood."

The youngest of 10 children, Majora Carter was born on October 27, 1966 to parents whose formal education ended with elementary school. Carter's mother and father had moved to the Hunts Point section of the South Bronx in the 1940s, when it was a mostly white, working-class enclave. They had been among the first African-Americans to buy a home there. By the time Carter was born, most of the neighborhood's Caucasian residents had moved to the suburbs, and the area had become a predominantly black and Latino ghetto, characterized by high rates of unemployment and violent crime. In the 1970s a rash of arson solidified Carter's resolve to escape the neighborhood. She told Krista Tippett for the American Public Media radio program *Speaking of Faith* (January 11, 2007) that she grew up "when the South Bronx in and of itself was burning. . . . Lots of landlords were torching their buildings in order to collect insurance money, and if you had, you know, any kind of intellectual acumen, then . . . your duty to yourself was to leave an area like the South Bronx as soon as you

could." One of her earliest memories is of watching the buildings on either side of her family's building burn down. She told Tippett, "I was about seven or eight. . . . And then at the end of [that same] summer my brother was killed, you know, as a result of a drug war. And I just remember thinking, 'I've got to get out of here.'"

Carter excelled at Primary School 48 and Intermediate School 74 and was accepted into the fiercely competitive Bronx High School of Science, one of the top public high schools in New York City. She graduated in 1984 and then attended Wesleyan University, in Middletown, Connecticut, where she earned a bachelor's degree in film studies in 1988. She then moved back to New York City, choosing to live in the borough of Brooklyn. She had married and divorced by the time she entered the highly selective master-of-fine-arts program at New York University; in 1997 she earned an M.F.A. degree in creative writing.

Graduate school proved expensive, so Carter moved back to her parents' home in the South Bronx in order to save money. She returned to find a neighborhood polluted by the effluents from sewage-treatment plants and the exhaust gases of diesel trucks traveling to and from the nearby Hunts Point Cooperative Market—where nearly all the city's produce and much of its meat arrives before being transported to businesses in the city. The neighborhood, which also contained numerous construction- and demolition-waste yards, was among the poorest in the country. Carter told Steve Inskeep for the National Public Radio program *Morning Edition* (September 20, 2005), "The South Bronx was the poster child for urban blight for many, many years, and I hated it. . . . But coming back, it was also one of the best things in the world that happened to me because I actually got very politicized, you know, in terms of understanding . . . burdens that the community was dealing with."

Carter initially became involved in arts-based community projects. "One of the projects I ran was called Street Trees, which exhibited artists' interpretations of the lack of street trees in the neighborhood—sculptures made, you know, from scrap metal and found objects," she told Little. Her priorities changed when she learned of city officials' plan to send 35,000 tons of residential refuse each week to transfer stations in the South Bronx, from which it would then be shipped to distant landfills. "One day I heard about the mayor's plan to privatize waste handling in the city," she recalled to Little. "They were going to shut down the Staten Island landfill without any environmental review and divert the waste handling to our neighborhood. I thought, 'Wait, we already handle 40 percent of the city's commercial waste, and that would bring in another 40 percent of the city's municipal waste.' As I researched, I began to realize that if we're not actively meeting the environmental needs of our community, then all the art in the world isn't gonna help." She began to knock on doors to educate her neighbors about the plan; she also spoke at local community meetings and formulated an alternative proposal that would divide the trash more equally among New York City's boroughs. After a groundswell of grassroots pressure from the community, the mayor's plan was scrapped.

In 1997 Carter became an associate director of the Point Community Development Corp., a nonprofit organization devoted to improving social, economic, and environmental conditions in the South Bronx. One of her first successes was in securing funding so that the Hunts Point Cooperative Market could install electrical truck bays that allowed parked vehicles to avoid idling their engines, thus reducing the diesel fumes in the surrounding area. While working at the development corporation, Carter met a city parks official who offered her $10,000 in seed money for a Bronx River restoration project. Because access to the river in the South Bronx was blocked by massive industrial plants, Carter could not immediately conceive of a use for the money. Then, "while jogging with my dog one morning, she pulled me into what I thought was an illegal garbage dump," she wrote for the SSBX Web site. "There were weeds, piles of garbage, tires, and other stuff that I won't mention here. But she kept dragging me through all this and lo and behold at the end of this lot, was the river. It was beautiful in the early morning light, it was inspiring; and I knew that this forgotten little street end, abandoned like the dog that brought me there, was worth saving. I knew it would grow to become the proud beginnings of the community-led waterfront revitalization of Hunts Point. And just like my new dog [a former stray that had grown into a healthy, 80-pound animal], it was an idea that got bigger than I had imagined."

Carter used the seed money to turn the area into a small park. (In later years she helped raise $3.2 million to enhance the park, which was completed in 2006.) Her lobbying led to the allocation of $30 million in city, state, and federal aid to build additional parks, connect bicycle paths, and restore wetlands and wildlife habitats along the river. In 2001 the New York *Daily News* named Carter one of "50 New Yorkers to Watch." She considered a run for the City Council but instead started Sustainable South Bronx, with the mission of achieving what has been termed "environmental justice" by improving social, economic, and environmental conditions in the South Bronx. In 2003, to name one initiative, SSBX launched the Bronx Environmental Stewardship Training Program, to prepare local residents for "green-collar" jobs in environmental fields. The group is also working to demolish the Sheridan Expressway, a short stretch of road that, according to the SSBX Web site, has "contributed to the blight, disinvestment and public health problems plaguing the South Bronx." (Carter has explained to journalists that although the South Bronx has a low rate of car ownership, the area's asthma rates are many times the national average, in part because of the heavy commercial traffic.)

Carter initiated the installation of New York City's first so-called green- and cool-roof, on the roof above SSBX's offices in the American Banknote Building. Unveiled in September 2005, the roof has a reflective surface, which does not absorb heat, and an abundance of greenery, which soaks up most of the rain that falls on it. Normally, rain drains into the city's sewers, many of which cannot accommodate all of the rainfall. Carter has since set up a company, SmartRoof, to install and maintain green roofs in and around the city.

In February 2006 Carter caused a minor stir at the Technology Entertainment Design (TED) conference, in California, when, during a speech, she recounted how she had tried to talk to former vice president Al Gore earlier in the day about grassroots efforts to combat global warming. Gore had disregarded her, simply suggesting that she send him a grant proposal. "I wasn't asking him for money," she explained. "I was making him an offer." After the public rebuke Gore acknowledged Carter's work and asked her to join the board of his Alliance for Climate Protection. To date, she has not done so.

On November 20, 2006 Mayor Michael Bloomberg of New York City unveiled a master plan for the South Bronx Greenway, designed jointly by Sustainable South Bronx, the Point Community Development Corp., and the New York City Economic Development Corp. It included plans for the creation of 1.5 miles of new waterfront green space, 8.5 miles of streets with foliage and wide pedestrian walking spaces, and nearly 12 acres of new open space on the waterfront. The South Bronx Greenway plan was the culmination of nearly a decade of lobbying by Carter and her fellow activists. In April 2007 *The Green*, a weekly, three-hour lineup of environmental-education programs, premiered on the Sundance Channel. Carter co-hosts *The Green* with the journalist Simran Sethi.

Currently, Carter is engaged in a battle with the New York City officials over the proposed placement of a 2,000-inmate jail at Oak Point in the South Bronx. The 25-acre site, which lies between the East River and a major railway line, is "ideally suited for the kind of clean-tech industry that our economy is falling behind in—the kind that can clean up the way we handle waste, adding value and employment prospects at the same time," Carter told *Current Biography*.

Carter has been honored many times for her activism. In 1999 the U.S. Environmental Protection Agency gave her its Environmental Quality Award for her service to the community, and in 2004 she won the Women with Organic Style Award from *Organic Style* magazine. In September 2005 Carter attracted international attention after the John D. and Catherine T. MacArthur Foundation awarded her its "genius grant," a stipend of $500,000 paid in five annual installments. In 2006 she won the Earth Day Environmental Advocates' Award from the Natural Resources Defense Council, a nonprofit environmental-rights organization. In December

2006 *Newsweek* named Carter, who had been a featured panelist at the Clinton Global Initiative (CGI) summit that year, a person to watch in 2007. Shortly thereafter New York University awarded her its Dr. Martin Luther King Jr. Humanitarian Award, and she also received the New York State Women of Excellence Award from Lieutenant Governor David Patterson. Later in 2007 she was named one of the 50 most influential women in the city by the *New York Post*, appeared on *Ebony*'s "Power 150" list, and was deemed a member of the "New Power Generation" by *Vibe*. In June 2007 Carter was named to New York's Renewable Energy Task Force, a group charged with identifying "ways of expanding the state's use of renewable energy and alternative fuels," according to the States News Service (June 24, 2007). The task force was expected to complete its first report in December 2007.

"There's this big fear that environmental justice is fiscally irresponsible, that communities like ours need all kinds of money and assistance," Carter told Little. "The irony is that our public-health problems—our rampant asthma and other environmental illnesses—do need such resources. Our sustainability strategy, on the contrary, does not. Our organization is beginning to prove that we can implement our strategy in a pretty darn economically and fiscally responsible way. Things like parks and green roofs and decent zoning policies and green-collar jobs and public transportation don't cost a huge amount, but can make a tremendous difference that has long-term economic advantages both locally and nationally."

Carter lives in the Hunts Points section of the South Bronx with her second husband, James Chase, a communications specialist. The two were married in October 2006, in the park on the Bronx River that she helped to develop.

—S.J.D.

Suggested Reading: *Chronicle of Philanthropy* p44 Oct. 27, 2005; *Essence* p24 Jan. 2005; Grist (on-line) Sep. 28, 2006; (New York) *Daily News* p72 Oct. 16, 1998, p12 Mar. 12, 1999, p1 Aug.13, 2001; *New York Times* XIV p1+ Dec. 3, 2000, B p2 Aug. 15, 2001; *Organic Style* p73 May 1, 2004; Sustainable South Bronx Web site; *Village Voice* p34 Jan. 25, 2000

Carter, Matthew

Oct. 1, 1937– Typographer

Address: Carter & Cone Type Inc., 2155 Massachusetts Ave., Cambridge, MA 02140

The typographer Matthew Carter is an artist, but his work rarely appears in the traditional venues of museums and galleries. Rather, the two dozen typefaces he has designed—among them ITC Galliard, Bell Centennial, Helvetica Compressed, Skia, Verdana, Georgia, Cochin, Big Caslon, Bitstream Charter, and Snell Roundhand script—are almost everywhere in the printed materials of everyday life and on computer screens. The British-born Carter "commands a wider audience for his work than most artists ever dream of," Johanna Drucker wrote in an essay about Carter's creations, as quoted by John D. Berry for creativepro.com (November 4, 2002). "Open a book catalog from any major publisher and you will see ITC Galliard. Browse a newsstand and some version of Miller News will pop into view. Go online and you'll find Verdana everywhere on the Web. Use a reference book. Find a telephone number. Buy a ticket for an event. Read an announcement in a digital source. Carter's work pervades the media through which the messages you receive are being conveyed." Carter has designed type for some of the most prominent magazines and newspapers in the world, including the *New York Times*, the *Washington Post*, the *Philadelphia Inquirer*, the London *Guardian*, *Time*, *Newsweek*, *Sports Illustrated*, *U.S. News & World Report*, *Wired*, and Na-

Steve Marsel Studio, courtesy of Carter & Cone Type Inc.

tional Geographic. He also created the on-screen font for Microsoft and the font used in AT&T phone books.

Since the mid-1950s, when he began his professional life, Carter has witnessed the technological evolution of his craft—one that now increasingly relies on computers, after hundreds of years during which metal type was set by hand and then by machines so noisy that their operation was considered an ideal job for the deaf. "I'm lucky because I must be the last generation of people who could have made type all the ways type could have been made," he told Quendrith Johnson for the *Boston Business Journal* (March 19, 1990). "We're in the throes of the greatest technical revolution that has ever overtaken us. Through most of type's history you would have been born and died with the same technology." With those advances in technology has come an increased interest in typography. A half-century ago only a few fonts existed; today there are more than 40,000. "I used to hate social gatherings and such," Carter told Johnson. "When you say you're a type designer people would say, 'I thought they were all dead.' The level of awareness of types and typography has grown enormously." Called "the king of contemporary type design" by Alice Rawsthorn in the *New York Times* (February 26, 2006), Carter encourages members of the public to trust their instincts regarding fonts and to use type as a functional art form. "Type is a way in which people can express their personality or point of view or taste, even in humdrum office communications," Carter told Jon Pepper for *Lotus* (September 1989). "Choice of type isn't much different from choice of clothing or choice of food."

Matthew Carter was born on October 1, 1937 in London, England, to Harry Graham Carter and Ella Mary (Garratt) Carter. He has a younger brother. His father, who earned the title Officer of the British Empire (OBE), was a distinguished typographer, book designer, linguist, and printing historian; he created the font Cyrillic Baskerville and, while stationed in what was then Palestine during World War II, a Hebrew typeface. He was the author of several books, including *A View of Early Typography Up to About 1600* (1969) and *A History of the Oxford University Press* (1975), and is the subject of *Harry Carter, Typographer* (2005), by Martyn Thomas and others. Matthew Carter's mother studied architecture but never completed the qualifications necessary to become a certified architect; instead, she worked as a draftsman. After the Germans began to bomb London, in 1940, a year after the outbreak of the war, the Carters bought a house in Croydon, about nine miles south of central London. The family later had to evacuate Croydon, leaving most of their possessions behind. In one of Matthew Carter's earliest memories, his mother cut letters of the alphabet out of linoleum to teach him how to read; the letters, he has recalled, were in the font Gill Sans. (Eric Gill was a renowned early-20th-century British type designer; "sans" refers to the absence of serifs, the small, nonstructural appendages on letters, such as the horizontal lines at the tops and bottoms of the verticals in the font used in *Current Biography*.) When Carter was seven he began attending a boarding school, where his interests in art and jazz made him feel like an outsider. Carter recalled to Alec Wilkinson for the *New Yorker* (December 5, 2005) that his housemaster, assuming that he would never become fit for a high-status job in, for example,

the law or finance, repeatedly told him, "Carter, you'll never be a gentleman."

In 1955, when Carter was 17, he won acceptance to Oxford University, in England. Many college freshmen in England at that time had already served in the armed forces. Carter could not enter the military, because he had asthma, and thus he was younger than most college-bound students. For that reason, Oxford officials advised him to take a year off before beginning his undergraduate studies. His father arranged an internship for him at Johan Enschede & Zonen Printing Works, an esteemed printing company in Haarlem, in the Netherlands. Though most printing houses had switched to mechanically produced type in the late 19th century, Enschede still employed a manual technique, called punch cutting, that was hundreds of years old. "There was a very tactile aspect to the whole thing," Carter recalled to Christopher Cox for the *Boston Herald* (June 15, 1999). "I enjoyed getting my hands dirty." Carter's talents lay not in his dexterity but in his artistic imagination. "Although I couldn't write particularly well . . . ," he told Margaret Re in an interview published in *Typographically Speaking*, quoted by Wilkinson, "I could see in my mind's eye what I wanted the letter to look like, and I could perfectly understand the sequence of the pen strokes that went into making the letter. I just couldn't make the pen do it." After apprenticing under P. H. Raedisch at Enschede for a year, Carter decided not to enroll at Oxford but to pursue a career in type design full-time.

In 1956 Carter returned to England and, while living with his parents, painted signs and lettered other items. The next year he moved to an aunt's residence in London and found work with a group of progressive designers who were trying to modernize the look of type styles used in England. In 1959, while still freelancing, he became the subject of a cover article in the *New Mechanick Exercises*, a journal about typography and printing. "*Mirabile dictu*" ("wonderful to relate"), the article stated, as quoted by Wilkinson, "a new and extremely promising hand-punchcutter has lately emerged and set up business as an engraver of steel punches, lettering artist and typographical designer. His name is Matthew Carter." Around that time a friend of his father's took Carter to lunch and asked him if there was anything he wanted; Carter answered that he wanted to go to New York. The family friend gave Carter £300, and in April 1960 Carter arrived in New York. The city—and its design culture—was a revelation for Carter. "I was made abruptly and forcefully to realize that I knew nothing," he told Wilkinson. "The cowardly part of me could have gone back to England and pretended I hadn't seen all of this design. Or I could decide, 'Wake up, Matthew, you've been living in a fool's paradise. You crossed the Atlantic and found something that knocked you sideways, now it's your move.'" Unable to find a job in New York, Carter went back to England, where in 1963 he began working as a typographical adviser for Crosfield Electronics, the British manufacturer of Photon/Lumitype, a phototypesetting machine. While at Crosfield, Carter designed a few fonts, including one for a new terminal at Heathrow Airport, which serves London. "That was not wasted time, but I didn't really produce any work in that first decade that stood the test of time," he said to Simon Esterson for *Creative Review* (April 6, 2005). "There was a big gap before I could get myself in a place where I could do some work."

In 1965 Carter got a job with Mergenthaler Linotype, in the New York City borough of Brooklyn. The Linotype machine, invented by Ottmar Mergenthaler in 1886, set type mechanically, doing away with the laborious method of setting each letter in a line of type by hand. Within his first year there, Carter designed the font Auriga; the following year, he designed Snell Roundhand, one of the first fonts to connect letters written in cursive script. During the next five years, Carter designed Helvetica Compressed, Olympian, ITC Charter, and Greek and Korean typefaces, among others. In 1971 Carter moved back to London to work for the British division of Mergenthaler Linotype. During his 10 years there, he designed the fonts Balliard and Shelley script and fonts for characters used in printed Hebrew, Greek, and Devangari (a script used for a number of Indian languages, including Hindi and Sanskrit). In 1974 Carter received a commission from AT&T to create a new font for the company's telephone books. The assignment was very specific: AT&T (then known as the Southeastern Bell Corp.) wanted the smallest possible type that could be printed legibly on the low-grade paper used for the books. That limitation did not trouble Carter. "I like to work in a situation that has some constraints," he told Cox. "If you put a big blank canvas in front of me on a Monday morning and say, 'Make an amazing design,' it would be blank come Friday. I wouldn't know where to start." Carter completed the design of Bell Centennial in 1978. He had increased the phone directories' readability by making the typeface for addresses slim and the face for names and numbers wide and heavy—that is, boldface—enhancing the contrast while saving space and the corresponding printing costs. From 1980 to 1981 Carter was a consultant for the Printer Planning Division of IBM. For four years beginning in 1980, he also served in Great Britain as the typographical adviser to Her Majesty's Stationery Office, whose activities include the printing of legislation. In 1982, also in Britain, the Royal Society for the Encouragement of Arts, Manufactures & Commerce (RSA) named him a Royal Designer for Industry, a designation that, according to the RSA's Web site, recognizes "people who have achieved sustained excellence in aesthetic and efficient design for industry."

In addition to becoming known for his emphasis on functionality, Carter made a name for himself with his ability to modernize historic fonts, making them look both classic and contemporary. An

example is ITC Galliard (ITC is the acronym of the New York–based International Typeface Corp., which issued the new typeface). After working sporadically on it since the 1960s, Carter completed the design of ITC Galliard in 1978. Based on a typeface created in the 16th century by the French punchcutter and printer Robert Granjon, the font became popular almost immediately and is considered a great achievement not only in typography but in design in general.

In 1981, with three of his Linotype co-workers—Cherie Cone, Mike Parker, and Rob Friedman—Carter founded Bitstream Inc., in Cambridge, Massachusetts. The first digital-type company, Bitstream offered fonts appropriate for computers and laser printers, whose requirements differ from those of Linotype or phototypesetting machines. The advent of the computer led to an unprecedented evolution in type design, because it enabled typographers to create fonts electronically rather than through the painstaking hand-carving that had characterized the art for so long. "I'm sometimes a bit nostalgic about the time when it was a tiny club, when you had to go through painful initiations in order to be a type designer," Carter told Esterson, "but on balance, I'm glad the whole thing got blown wide open by the computer. . . . If I had my choice of period in which to have worked in this business I would choose exactly the one that I happen to have lucked into, precisely because of all these changes. I'm endlessly glad to have survived into the digital era because I regard that as the best technology we've ever had. There are some drawbacks, there have been some losses, but for me, it's just a dream." Acting as the vice president and director responsible for design standards at Bitstream, Carter designed many of the company's most popular fonts, including Bitstream Charter in 1987. Other fonts produced at Bitstream during Carter's decade with the firm include Swiss 721, Arrus BT, Oz Handicraft BT, Gothic 821, and Iowan Old Style BT.

As Bitstream expanded into other areas of software development, Carter wanted to focus his energy on design. To that end, he and Cherie Cone left the company in 1991 and founded Carter & Cone Type Inc. Based in Cambridge, Massachusetts, Carter & Cone became the exclusive studio for Carter's designs. The fonts Carter has created while at Carter & Cone are considered some of his most beautiful and innovative: Elephant (1992, renamed Big Figgins in 1998); Mantinia (1993); and Big Calson and Skia (1994), the latter of which was a commission for Apple Computer Inc. In 1995 he created Walker, for the Walker Art Center in Minneapolis, Minnesota, and Sophia, for the Museum of Fine Arts in Boston, Massachusetts, whose design was influenced by the lettering on a Roman chalice in the museum's collection. In 1994 Carter began work on a commission from Microsoft for an on-screen font that would be of the utmost readability. "That whole episode with Microsoft is something that I very much enjoyed and was interested in, because it did have constraints, and a lot of difficulties," Carter told Esterson. The resulting font, Verdana, has been widely praised for its legibility at both large sizes (at which many other fonts get jagged edges or become blurred) and small (at which letters such as the lowercase "i" and "l" may become indistinguishable). Microsoft released Verdana in 1996 with its software and also offered free downloads of the font from its Web site, encouraging its wide distribution. In the same year, also for Microsoft, Carter completed the design of Georgia, a font considered Verdana's equal in on-screen readability. Verdana has become one of the most widely used fonts on the Internet, and Microsoft has said it will keep both Verdana and Georgia available without charge.

Carter wrote the introduction for *Type Graphics: The Power of Type in Graphic Design* (2001), by Margaret E. Richardson. The following year his work was the subject of an exhibit at the University of Maryland, called Typographically Speaking: The Art of Matthew Carter. The exhibit, which later traveled to universities around the country, included dozens of drawings, sketches, and printed examples documenting Carter's creation of various fonts. The show's catalog was published as a book with the same title in 2003. Reviewing it for *Library Journal* (October 15, 2003), Phil Hamlett called the volume "handsome." "Essential for those interested in typography, the book also contains rewards for a general public coming into a wider appreciation of type and typesetting by virtue of the proliferation of desktop publishing," he wrote. Also in 2003 the Museum of Modern Art in New York, commonly called MoMA, asked Carter to "refresh" the typeface—Franklin Gothic No. 2—used for its logo and all its printed matter, including its name on coffee mugs. "That opportunity to really study these letterforms and capture them as faithfully as I could was sort of an education to me," Carter told Andrew Blum for the *New York Times* (September 21, 2003). Museum executives, Blum wrote, "spent eight months scrutinizing every tiny step in the process" through which Carter made extremely subtle changes. "You would have to look rather closely" to see them, Blum reported. "Extremely closely. In fact, someone could set the old logo and the new logo side by side and stare for some time before detecting even the slightest distinction." He added, "The folks who led the exhaustive makeover process couldn't be more pleased." In 2004 Carter redesigned a family of typefaces for Yale University; with names including Yale Administrative Roman and Italic, Yale Design Roman and Italic, Yale Small Capitals, and Yale Web Small Capitals, the fonts are used for everything from school catalogs and annual reports to signs that must be visible from a distance.

Carter is a member of the Alliance Graphique Internationale and chairman of the type designers' committee of AtypI (Association Typographique Internationale). He has received the Frederic W. Goudy Award in Typography from the Rochester Institute of Technology for outstanding contribution to the printing industry; the Middleton Award from the American Center for Design; the Chrysler Award for Innovation in Design; the Vadim Award from the Moscow Academy of Graphic Design; and medals from the AIGA (originally, the American Institute of Graphic Arts) and the Type Directors Club. Carter has been a senior critic on Yale University's Graphic Design faculty since 1976. He has received honorary doctor of fine arts degrees from the Art Institute of Boston and the Minneapolis College of Art and Design.

When Andrew Blum visited him in 2003, Carter's home was a third-floor walk-up apartment in Cambridge, Massachusetts. Carter lives with the artist Arlene Chung.

—C.S.

Suggested Reading: aiga.org; *Boston Herald* Arts & Life p43 June 15, 1999; *Creative Review* p42+ Apr. 6, 2005; designmuseum.org; graphicdesign.com; *New Yorker* p56+ Dec. 5, 2005; *U.S. News & World Report* (on-line) Aug. 24, 2003; Re, Margaret. *Typographically Speaking: The Art of Matthew Carter*, 2003

Cat Power

Jan. 21, 1972– Singer; songwriter

Address: Matador Records, 625 Broadway, 12th Fl., New York, NY 10012

Over the last dozen years, Chan Marshall, better known as Cat Power, has built a reputation for writing and performing songs whose melancholy is enhanced by what has been called the "yearning" quality of her rough-edged voice. "A lot of people think my music is sad. It's not sad, it's triumphant. I'm triumphant," she said to Cynthia Joyce for *Salon.com* (September 30, 2006). "If people can be open enough with themselves to be creative and let things like that come out, you know, allow themselves to feel things enough to be that honest with themselves I feel that's really positive. Even though that might sound sad." Cat Power is nearly as well known for her eccentric onstage style as for her music, with shows that often involve as much self-criticism and ill temper as performance—and that seem to have only added to her mystique and the size of her following. She is "one of those rare enigmas in the entertainment industry. She hates to perform," Benjamin Law wrote for the Queensland, Australia, *Courier Mail* (August 16, 2003). "Worse still, when she does perform she's prone to dissect her own performance even before she's left the stage." Cat Power has charmed critics and ordinary music fans alike with songs that combine elements of rock, folk, punk, soul, and blues. Her albums include *Dear Sir* (1995), *Myra Lee* (1996),

Stefano Giovannini, courtesy of Comerica CityFest
Cat Power

Moon Pix (1999), *You Are Free* (2003), and *The Greatest* (2006), which received the coveted Shortlist Music Prize. Her album *Jukebox* was due for release in early 2008.

Cat Power was born Charlyn "Chan" (pronounced "Shawn") Marie Marshall on January 21, 1972 in Atlanta, Georgia, to Charlie and Myra Lee Marshall. Because her father was an itinerant blue pianist, Marshall led a peripatetic existence, never staying in one place long enough to form long-term friendships. During Marshall's childhood her parents divorced, and both remarried, forcing Marshall and her sister to move constantly to and from the homes of their mother (a self-described hippie) and grandmother; little of the songwriter's early life was spent with her biological father. Her stepfather's job also kept the family on the move, with the result that Marshall attended 10 different schools, in cities that included Memphis, Tennessee, and Greensboro, North Carolina. Marshall's family had a history of alcohol abuse and psychological problems, and she herself began drinking at an early age.

As a girl Marshall listened to the music in her stepfather's collection, which included records by Creedence Clearwater Revival, the Rolling Stones, and Otis Redding (her favorite singer). She wrote her first song, "Windows," when she was in fourth grade. On that occasion, as she explained to an interviewer for *Spin* (November 22, 2006, on-line), "I felt like I had a secret, like I had made a life for myself." (She noted to the *Spin* interviewer that the song is "very similar" to one of her later compositions, "Norma Jean.") As she became passionate about music, she started listening to the songs of the legendary singer-songwriters Bob Dylan (who

became her favorite songwriter), the southern rockers Lynyrd Skynyrd and the Allman Brothers, the soul diva Aretha Franklin, and the pop / jazz singer Roberta Flack. At 16 she became estranged from her mother and went to Atlanta to live with her father, with whom she also had a strained relationship. Her father did not allow her to touch his baby grand piano, but whenever he left the house, she would use the opportunity to teach herself to play. During that time she also bought her first guitar, a 1950s-era Silvertone, but left it untouched in the corner of her room for two years before attempting to play it.

Marshall dropped out of high school during her senior year, in the late 1980s, and moved out of her father's house. (The two are no longer on speaking terms.) She went to live with friends who were part of Atlanta's underground music scene, similar in many respects to Seattle's grunge / indie rock movement of the same period. An early mentor introduced her to such seminal underground bands as Rocket from the Tombs and to modernist literature, including James Joyce's novel *Ulysses*. After forming bonds with other musicians through a number of impromptu basement jam sessions, Marshall became the lead singer of a group that included the local musicians Glen Thrasher and Mark Moore. On the day of their first show, Marshall, who was working as a cashier at a pizzeria, received a last-minute call from Moore, who needed a name for their band. Staring at the long line of customers before her, Marshall saw an elderly man wearing a cap emblazoned with the words "Cat Diesel Power," and she yelled "Cat Power" into the telephone before hanging up.

As Marshall was attempting to launch her music career, her friends succumbed to the effects of drug use. "I was working as a waitress in Atlanta when my boyfriend passed away and I completely lost my mind. Then my best friend died of AIDS. Everyone I loved in Atlanta was on heroin," she recalled to Will Hodgkinson for the London *Guardian* (May 23, 2003). In 1992, to escape that environment, Marshall—all but penniless—moved with Thrasher to the East Village section of New York City.

The two shared a room in a cheap apartment and found gigs in the Lower East Side clubs ABC No Rio and Brownies, among other venues. Marshall continued to support herself through waitressing and working numerous odd jobs, which included organizing the apartment of a woman who had obsessive-compulsive disorder and unloading trucks in the meat-packing district for $25 per day. She and Thrasher performed as Cat Power for six months before Thrasher quit the act and went back to Atlanta. Thinking that the act had come to its end, Marshall was surprised when an art-punk group called God Is My Co-Pilot booked her to play solo as its opening act at the legendary punk mecca CBGB's. It was at that point that Marshall took "Cat Power" as her stage name. Several days later she was asked to be an opening act for her fellow fledgling indie rocker Liz Phair. Her performance impressed Sonic Youth's drummer, Steve Shelley, and Tim Foljahn of Two Dollar Guitar, who agreed to back her in the studio, helping Marshall to record her first two albums, *Dear Sir* (1995) and *Myra Lee* (1996) in a single day. The two albums (the latter named for her mother) were noted for Marshall's unpredictable, stream-of-consciousness lyrics. Heather Phares, reviewing *Myra Lee* for the All Music Guide (on-line), wrote that Marshall's "yearning voice lends extra emotion to her songs" and that the album's "raw, overheard sound" gave it "a sonic honesty" that paralleled the raspy-voiced singer's writing. In the mid-1990s Marshall developed a strong underground following for her exciting, sometimes bizarre live shows.

On the strength of the acclaim her first two albums had received, Marshall signed with the Matador label in 1996. That year she released *What Would the Community Think*, a departure from her first two albums, offering a personal approach to songwriting in place of the detachment that marked *Dear Sir* and *Myra Lee*. The album's opening track, "In This Hole," which tells the tale of poverty-stricken, star-crossed lovers, includes the lyrics, "One absence of truth / One horrible thing you saw / What you truly wanted to become / And who you thought I was / Who you thought I was / In this hole we have fixed / We get further and further / Further from the world / We must do / We must do." The album also highlights Marshall's strengths as a soul singer, particularly in the songs "They Tell Me" and "Taking People."

During the three-month tour—co-headlined by the alternative rock band Guv'ner—that she undertook in support of her album, Marshall became notorious for her onstage behavior. Alternately contrite and belligerent, she would apologize repeatedly to the audience for mistakes, make startlingly abrupt transitions between songs, perform with her back to the audience, or simply walk out in the middle of a set. Much of that behavior was attributed to drunkenness. Instead of driving fans away, Marshall's erratic behavior added to her cult status, and critics embraced her as a tragic heroine. Ben Ratliff, reviewing a Cat Power show for the *New York Times* (January 5, 1999) a couple of years later, wrote, "Gone was the idea of exultation, or of showing what one can do; in its place was outrageously passive-aggressive behavior and nonmusicianship. The show was a meaningful comment on current indie-rock esthetics: Ms. Marshall makes music that's the equivalent of a lifeless handshake, but she has enough artistic credibility to sell out the medium-size hall." After the tour Marshall took a hiatus from the music world, working as a babysitter in Portland, Oregon, and spending time in Prosperity, South Carolina, with her boyfriend at the time, Bill Callahan, of the music group Smog. It was there that she wrote the material for her fourth studio album, *Moon Pix*.

The story behind the inspiration for that album has been the subject of much rumor. In an interview with Matt Dorman for *Comes with a Smile*

magazine (Winter 1998/1999), Marshall recalled that in South Carolina, "I had a dream that somebody was telling me to come into the field—'cause I live behind a field—basically to die, or something. I realised that I didn't want to die so I woke up and didn't meet the voice in the field and then I went and wrote this record. And then two close friends of mine died the next day." Soon afterward Marshall persuaded Matador to fly her to Melbourne, Australia, with Callahan (who was already heading there), to record *Moon Pix* at Sing Sing Studios with the Dirty Three members Jim White (on drums) and Mick Turner (on guitar). "On *Moon Pix* I had no idea what I was doing," Marshall explained to Brian Garrity for *Billboard* (March 11, 2000). "I didn't know what I wanted when I walked into that studio. . . . Everything was just impulsive and just making stuff up." While Marshall considered the record unfocused and spontaneous, critics hailed it as being her most accomplished to date. Ryan Schreiber, in a review posted on the Pitchfork Media Web site (November 1, 1998), wrote, "Her sound is like Liz Phair on Valium mixed with the lonesome, desert highway tone of Modest Mouse. It's pretty, clever, and terribly depressing—all of which are common traits in any classic statement-making album." Standout songs on the album include "Cross Bones Style," inspired by Madonna's "Lucky Star"; "American Flag," which used the drum loop from the Beastie Boys' "Paul Revere"; and the melancholy "Say." One critic remarked that a line from the last-named song, "If you're looking for something easy, you might as well give it up," summed up the nature of the album.

In November 1999, following the *Moon Pix* tour, Marshall entered the studio to make her next album. She chose to record the covers of other artists' songs that she had been playing during live shows. (Marshall has explained that she often feels more comfortable playing others' songs than performing her own, much like an actress who, ill at ease in her own skin, prefers to portray a character.) *The Covers Record* (2000), which featured Marshall's versions of songs by the likes of the Rolling Stones, Bob Dylan, the Velvet Underground, Moby Grape, and Lou Reed, received widespread critical acclaim.

After three years of touring the world, Marshall returned to the U.S. to record original material for *You Are Free* (2003). Perhaps her most celebrated album to date, the diverse *You Are Free* juxtaposed Marshall's quiet solo work with traditional rock and included work by the guest musicians Dave Grohl (of Nirvana and Foo Fighters), Eddie Veder (of Pearl Jam), and Warren Ellis (of Dirty Three). On songs such as "I Don't Blame You," the singer reflected on her own flaws, with lyrics that include, "Last time I saw you, you were on stage / Your hair was wild, your eyes were red / And you were in a rage / You were swinging your guitar around / Cause they wanted to hear that sound / But you didn't want to play / And I don't blame you." In the song "Free," she attempted to separate music from the trappings of being a rock-and-roll celebrity, with lines such as, "Don't be in love with the autograph / Just be in love when you love that song on and on." In the bleak "Names," Marshall sang about child abuse and lost loved ones. With *You Are Free*, Cat Power gained mainstream success, including a high-profile appearance on *The Late Show with David Letterman* and moderate exposure on MTV2's weekly music show *Subterranean*.

Such success did not prevent Marshall from entering a period of depression. Due in large part to her breakup with her long-term boyfriend, she began drinking heavily. Her musical output in the months that followed was limited to the 2004 release of a DVD / CD package, called *Speaking for Trees*. The DVD portion, filmed by Mark Borthwick, featured a nearly two-hour, static shot of Marshall singing and playing electric guitar in the countryside; the CD contained only a single, 18-minute song, "Willie Deadwilder." *Speaking for Trees* received mixed reviews. In early 2005 Marshall started touring again, winning new fans with sold-out solo shows despite—or because of—her instability.

At Ardent Studios in Memphis, Tennessee, backed by musicians who included former members of Al Green's band, Teenie and Flick Hodges, Marshall recorded her seventh studio album, *The Greatest*, in the summer of 2005. Two weeks prior to the album's January 2006 release, Marshall had a nervous breakdown and was committed to Mount Sinai Medical Center in Miami, Florida, for psychiatric treatment. *The Greatest* received glowing reviews; centering on the theme of love and featuring brass and string sections on a number of songs, the album is considered her most uplifting to date. Christian Hoard wrote in a review for *Rolling Stone* (February 9, 2006), "*The Greatest* works up subtly atmospheric, sweet-and-sour country folk, propelled by a voice that sounds weathered by bad love and two packs a day—but determined to make autumnal beauty out of her bad memories." Notable songs included the record's title track, a ballad about a boy who dreams of becoming a boxer, and the closing song, "Love and Communication," which mixes lyrical poetry with ominous guitar grooves and string arrangements.

Currently sober, Marshall has written her next album of original material, *Sun*, which was due for release in the spring of 2008. Before that, she planned to release *Jukebox*; the highly anticipated follow-up to her 2000 covers album, it was to feature renditions of songs by James Brown, Billie Holiday, and Bob Dylan, among others, and an original piece, "Song for Bobby." Marshall supports numerous charitable groups, among them the Bereaved Israeli and Palestinian Parents' Circle and PETA (People for the Ethical Treatment of Animals). She has also shown an interest in acting, having recently had a part in the director Wong Kar Wai's *My Blueberry Nights*, which stars Rachel

Weisz and Jude Law and debuted at the 2007 Cannes Film Festival.

—C.C.

Suggested Reading: All Music Guide (on-line); *Harp* (on-line) Jan./Feb. 2006; (London) *Guardian* (on-line) May 23, 2003; *New York* (on-line) Jan. 23, 2006; *New York Times* E p1+ Sep. 20, 2006; *New Yorker* p147+ Aug. 18, 2003; (Queensland, Australia) *Courier Mail* M p1+ Aug. 16, 2003; *Rolling Stone* p59+ Feb. 9, 2006; *Salon.com* Sep. 30, 2006; *Spin* (on-line) Nov. 22, 2006

Selected Recordings: *Dear Sir*, 1995; *Myra Lee*, 1996; *Moon Pix*, 1999; *You Are Free*, 2003; *The Greatest*, 2006

Chen, Steve; Hurley, Chad; and Karim, Jawed

Co-founders of YouTube

Chen, Steve
1978(?)– Information-technology executive; entrepreneur

Hurley, Chad
1977(?)– Information-technology executive; entrepreneur

Karim, Jawed
1979– Entrepreneur; computer scientist

Address: YouTube Inc., 1000 Cherry Ave., 2d Floor, San Bruno, CA 94066

YouTube, the Internet video-sharing application that has become one of the fastest-growing Web sites ever, was started in 2005 by three former coworkers—Jawed Karim, Steve Chen, and Chad Hurley—who were frustrated by their inability to share their home videos over the Internet. Less than two years after its creation, YouTube had become one of the most popular Web sites on the Internet: according to the Web-traffic monitor Alexa Internet, YouTube, as of late 2006, was the seventh-most-trafficked site on-line. It commands a 46 percent market share of all visits to video Web sites in the U.S., and *PC World* magazine named it the ninth-best product of 2005. When the Internet giant Google bought YouTube at the end of 2006 for $1.65 billion in stock, the three founders—who, in what has become a dot-com cliché, literally started the company in one of their garages—made millions of dollars and became Internet celebrities, virtually overnight.

YouTube is considered to be the quintessential example of the movement known as "Web 2.0"—a term often used to describe a new generation of In-

Robyn Beck/Getty Images

YouTube co-founders Chad Hurley (left) and Steve Chen

ternet-based computer services that emphasize collaboration and sharing among users. YouTube, like the social networking site MySpace, is an enabler; the content for the site is supplied by the users, rather than those who run the site. By putting the programming in the hands of the audience, YouTube has become "the TV station you always dreamed of," according to a reporter for *BusinessWeek* (April 10, 2006, on-line): "YouTube offers mainstream shows from the current season, clips from TV's earliest days, and homemade movies from around the world. You watch what you want when you want, whether it's highlights from Los Angeles Laker Kobe Bryant's 81-point outburst in January or a 1968 clip of Johnny Cash performing 'Ring of Fire.'" Though analysts initially speculated that YouTube might be the new Napster—a highly successful file-sharing service that was shut down by court order for its inability to prevent users from exchanging copyrighted material—such traditional content providers as record labels and television networks have begun to realize that YouTube, rather than competing with them, can be used as a tool to attract new customers. "We want to be a destination that promotes the entertainment offered by these guys . . . ," Hurley told the reporter for *BusinessWeek*, referring to networks, record labels, and content providers. "We started this to solve a personal problem. Now we're creating a new way to reach audiences in an era where the traditional TV time slot doesn't exist anymore." Explaining why the editors of *Time* (online) chose YouTube as the best invention of 2006, Lev Grossman wrote, "YouTube created a new way for millions of people to entertain, educate, shock, rock and grok one another on a scale we've never seen before."

Jawed Karim was born in East Germany in 1979. His family moved to West Germany soon after Karim's birth, and then to St. Paul, Minnesota, in 1992. His father, Naimul, is originally from Bangladesh and works as a researcher at 3M; his mother, Christine, who is German, is a professor of biochemistry at the University of Minnesota at Minneapolis–St. Paul. Karim developed an interest in science and technology at an early age: his parents had trouble finding child care and often brought him to their labs, providing him with beakers and other lab equipment to keep him occupied. When Karim was 10 years old, his father bought him a used Commodore computer, and the precocious child quickly learned to write software code. While a student at St. Paul's Central High School, Karim created an e-mail system for the teachers, and during his senior year, he was hired by his mother's lab to create a Web site for it. While working on the site, he became interested in some of the research problems that his mother and her colleagues were studying, and he was inspired to map the atomic structure of a protein that was crucial to their work. He did so by creating a complex computational process that is now a standard in the field. After graduating from high school, in 1997, he enrolled at the University of Illinois at Urbana-Champaign to study computer science. He selected that school because it was the alma mater of Marc Andreessen, the co-founder of Netscape Communications Corp., the Internet company that popularized an early Web browser. In 2000, during his junior year in college, Karim dropped out and accepted a position at the Palo Alto, California, Internet company PayPal—which was then a fledgling payments-processing company and is now the world's largest on-line payment service.

Steven Chen was born in August 1978 (some sources say 1979) in Taiwan. His family moved to the U.S. in 1986, and he was raised in the northwest Chicago suburb of Prospect Heights. Chen, who was interested in math and science from an early age, attended John Hersey High School, in nearby Arlington Heights, for his freshman year. He then transferred to the prestigious Illinois Mathematics and Science Academy, in Aurora, where he learned about computer programming, for his sophomore and junior years. He returned to Hersey for his senior year. John Novak, Chen's tennis coach and calculus teacher at Hersey, told Shamus Toomey for the *Chicago Sun-Times* (October 12, 2006, on-line) that Chen "was a pretty solid 'B' student. He didn't do anything to really stand head and shoulders above everybody else." Chen enrolled in the same computer-science program as Karim at the University of Illinois at Urbana-Champaign; Chen, too, left the program before graduating to join PayPal.

The second of Donald and JoAnn Hurley's three children, Chad Hurley was born in about 1977 and grew up in suburban Philadelphia, Pennsylvania. He has an older sister, Heather, and a younger brother, Brent, who was hired by YouTube in 2006. Hurley got his entrepreneurial start when, as a five-year-old, he attempted to sell his paintings from his front yard. After graduating from Twin Valley High School, in Elverson, Pennsylvania, Hurley attended Indiana University of Pennsylvania (IUP), studying both print and Web design. Hurley earned a bachelor's degree from IUP in 1999. He submitted his resumé to PayPal after reading an article about the company in *Wired* magazine. During his interview with PayPal managers, he impressed his questioners by designing a T-shirt for the company on the spot. While with the company, he designed its first user interface and company logo.

Karim, Hurley, and Chen earned millions when the Internet shopping portal eBay bought PayPal for $1.5 billion in 2002. Like many of their colleagues, Hurley and Karim left PayPal shortly afterward; Chen stayed on until early 2005 to help the company launch its operations in China. Between 2002 and 2005 Hurley worked as an independent consultant in the Silicon Valley region of California, and Karim completed his bachelor's degree in computer science by taking courses on-line and at Santa Clara University, in California. Although the three were no longer working together, they stayed in touch and saw each other at PayPal reunions. (PayPal alumni are a famously close-knit group, and many have worked on projects together after leaving the company. They are sometimes called the "PayPal mafia.") By 2005 Hurley, Chen, and Karim had begun talking about forming their own Internet start-up. They often met for late-night brainstorming sessions at one another's homes or at 24-hour diners.

Inspiration struck the three following a party at Chen's San Francisco, California, home. Several people at the party, including Hurley, Chen, and Karim, had recorded digital videos during the event. The three friends discovered a mutual frustration in their inability to share those clips over the Internet. The files were too large to be e-mailed, and posting them on Web sites was a tedious process that often required users to install or update software. The three friends quickly realized that many people were likely facing the same problems. YouTube was developed over the course of the next few months in the garage of Hurley's Menlo Park, California, home. The team designed the site so that visitors can upload video to the YouTube server in a variety of video formats, including QuickTime, WMV, or AVI. Once uploaded, a visitor's file is then automatically converted into the FLV format, which is played using Adobe Flash Player software. Most Internet browsers come with a Flash plug-in already installed; it is standard in the top three browsers—Microsoft Internet Explorer, the open-source browser Firefox, and Apple's Safari—which, according to the HitsLink Web site, have a combined market share of 98 percent. Consequently, the vast majority of visitors to YouTube do not need to download new software or update their current software in order to view the available clips.

The domain name YouTube.com was activated in February 2005. Karim uploaded the first video—an 18-second clip of himself standing in front of the elephant pen at a California zoo—to the YouTube site on April 23, 2005. By that point the founders had agreed that Karim would not accept a formal title or salary from the company, remaining only a consultant while he pursued his master's degree in computer science at Stanford University, in Palo Alto. He remained one of the company's largest individual shareholders, though he retained fewer shares than Chen and Hurley. Hurley became the chief executive officer, and Chen became the chief technical officer. The two divided their tasks according to their abilities and interests, with Hurley concentrating on the user interface of the site and Chen coordinating the architecture and the technical aspects of their company. As CEO, Hurley, who was more familiar with technology and design than with the rudiments of running a company, had to acquire general business skills on the job.

In an effort to expand the capabilities of the Web site, the founders searched for investors and ultimately turned to Roelof Botha, a former chief financial officer at PayPal, who had become a partner at Sequoia Capital—a venture-capital firm that had previously scored dot-com success with Google, Yahoo!, and PayPal. Botha negotiated Sequoia's initial offering of $3.5 million, adding $8 million in April 2006. The funds were used to enhance product development and expand the Web site's sales and marketing efforts. Within a year of its inception, YouTube became one of the most trafficked Web sites on the Internet; by late 2006 YouTube was drawing nearly 100 million viewers each day.

Though many YouTube visitors post home videos or other original content on the site, others post such pirated materials as clips from their favorite sporting events or television shows. YouTube's terms of use explicitly state that users should not post copyrighted material without permission, but its administrators do not review each post, and remove copyrighted material only when the owners complain. In February 2006 NBC asked YouTube to remove from its site a two-and-a-half-minute segment called *Lazy Sunday: The Chronicles of Narnia*, which featured a rap by *Saturday Night Live* cast members Chris Parnell and Andy Samberg, from its site. The clip originally aired on the network on December 17, 2005 and later created considerable buzz on-line, particularly on YouTube, which hosted multiple copies of the segment, with one version prompting more than five million downloads. *Lazy Sunday* was also available on the show's official site, but, according to Anne Broache for *CNET News* (February 17, 2006, on-line), "its embedded video player appears to work only with Windows."

Ironically, NBC's demand that YouTube remove *Lazy Sunday*, as well as the network's coverage of segments from the 2006 Olympic Games, won even greater publicity for the Web site. In June 2006 the network, recognizing the marketing potential of allowing portions of its programs to air on-line, took the unusual step of creating a strategic partnership with YouTube; NBC agreed to promote the Web site on some of its shows and bought ad space and uploaded promotional videos for its programming. YouTube has since reached agreements with other content providers, including the National Hockey League and such recording labels as Sony BMG, Warner Music Group, and EMI. CBS executives also came around, after YouTube's posting of a CBS News story about an autistic teenager who made six three-point shots in a high-school basketball game generated enough buzz on-line to win the youth a visit from President George W. Bush and a contract to create a film based on his life. "You've got to find the fine line between the great promotion YouTube gives a network, and protecting our rights," Sean McManus, the president of CBS News and Sports, was quoted as saying by a reporter for *TelevisionWeek* (July 16, 2006, on-line). "Our inclination now is, the more exposure we get from clips like that, the better it is for CBS News and the CBS television network, so in retrospect we probably should have embraced the exposure, and embraced the attention it was bringing CBS, instead of being parochial and saying 'let's pull it down.'"

YouTube has made several changes to its structure to help combat the existence of pirated material on the site. Clips are now limited to 10 minutes to prevent users from uploading entire episodes of shows. (That regulation is commonly circumvent-

ed by splitting longer pieces into several 10-minute clips.) The YouTube team is also working to develop software that will prevent users from reposting videos that were previously removed from the site. Still, some content providers argue that YouTube has not done enough to restrict copyrighted material and is, in fact, using such content to attract visitors.

At the end of 2006, Google bought YouTube for a reported $1.65 billion in stock. That news came as a surprise to both industry insiders and users of the site—some of whom have disparagingly referred to the collaboration as GooTube. While some business analysts questioned Google's decision to spend so much on a company that had yet to turn a profit, others viewed the purchase as a strong move for Google. According to Andrew Ross Sorkin, writing for the *New York Times* (October 10, 2006), Benjamin Schachter, a UBS analyst, wrote in a note to investors, "The price tag of about $1.6 billion is difficult to justify on a spreadsheet and may be somewhat of a throwback to the days of paying for eyeballs and page views, but this is a strategic bet that Google would be placing for a long-term objective: to be the technology and distribution partner for content owners and publishers." A conservative estimate lists YouTube's regular users at 50 million, which puts Google's purchase price at around $33 per user.

Some YouTube users criticized Chen and Hurley for selling out just months after Hurley announced that he had no intention of ending YouTube's independence. For their part, Chen and Hurley believed that the deal, which allowed them to retain control over the company, would be beneficial to YouTube's future. "We quickly realized that with Google's resources, we would have access to more resources and talents to drive towards our goal faster without needing to make sacrifices on product decisions," Chen explained to Toomey. "There's a long list of product ideas that we've had swimming in all our heads but we simply didn't have the resources to execute them." Reportedly, Chen and Hurley, who together owned an estimated 40 to 45 percent of the company, each received Google stock worth several hundred million dollars. Karim received less, though still a significant amount of money.

In October 2007, after being sued by a number of media companies (including the industry giant Viacom, which was seeking $1 billion in damages), YouTube unveiled its "Video Identification" content-filtering tool. The technology, intended to stop users from uploading copyrighted material, compares posted videos to samples contained in a database. When pirated material is found, the copyright holder will have the choice of removing the content or profiting from ads placed alongside the videos. "We're delighted that Google appears to be stepping up to its responsibility and ending the practice of profiting from infringement," Mike Fricklas, Viacom's general counsel, said, according to Eric Auchard, a Reuters (October 15, 2007) reporter. Attorneys for Google said the company was doing more than it was legally required to do to stop the spread of copyrighted materials, adding that the new filter had nothing to do with the lawsuits.

Hurley invested in the satirical film *Thank You for Smoking* (2006), which was produced by Room 9 Entertainment, a company founded by another member of the "PayPal mafia," David Sacks, the company's former chief operations officer. Karim—who, despite his success, reportedly lives in a student-residence hall at Stanford—has expressed an interest in becoming a university professor, but he has not ruled out developing another Web site.

In May 2007 *Time* magazine placed Chen and Hurley on its list of the 100 most influential people on the planet. The next month Chen and Hurley announced that YouTube would debut in seven new languages: Japanese, Polish, Dutch, French, Spanish, Portuguese, and Italian. In July YouTube become involved in the 2008 presidential race, as the Web site, in conjunction with CNN, hosted a debate in which the Democratic candidates answered questions submitted by users in video form. A similar debate for Republican presidential hopefuls was scheduled to take place in November 2007.

—N.W.M.

Suggested Reading: *Business Week* (on-line) Apr. 10, 2006; *Chicago Sun-Times* (on-line) Oct. 12, 2006; *Oakland Tribune* (on-line) Oct. 10, 2006; *New York Times* A p1+ Oct. 10, 2006, C p1+ Oct. 17, 2006; *Newsweek* (on-line) Oct. 9, 2006; *Pittsburgh Tribune-Review* (on-line) Oct. 12, 2006

Courtesy of Opus 3 Artists

Chung, Kyung-Wha

Mar. 26, 1948– Violinist

Address: c/o International Creative Management (ICM), 40 W. 57th St., New York, NY 10019

The Korean-born violinist Kyung-Wha Chung was among the first classical musicians from Asia to gain prominence in Europe and North America. In 1960, at age 12, Chung left her native land to study with the highly influential and respected violin teacher Ivan Galamian at the Juilliard School, in New York City. Seven years later she shared the first prize in the Leventritt International Competition—one of the world's most prestigious contests for violinists—with Pinchas Zukerman. In 1970 her career received a tremendous boost, when, substituting on a few days' notice for another up-and-comer, Itzhak Perlman, she performed the Tchaikovsky Violin Concerto with the London Symphony Orchestra under André Previn, in England. Thanks to the rave review written by a London *Financial Times* critic, she immediately received invitations to appear as a soloist three more times with the same orchestra and, soon afterward, with many other distinguished groups. She has since performed with virtually every major orchestra and conductor, as well as in duos with such pianists as Radu Lupu and Krystian Zimerman and with chamber groups, among them the Chung Trio, whose other members are her brother Myung-Whun Chung, a pianist and conductor, and her sister Myung-Wha Chung, a cellist. She has made recordings for London Records, EMI, Decca, Angel, RCA, and Deutsche Grammophon. In addition to 18th- and 19th-century standards, Chung's repertoire includes extremely difficult 20th-century violin concertos that many accomplished musicians never attempt to tackle, among them those by Edward Elgar, Alban Berg, Béla Bartók, and William Walton. Chung played at the concert held at Royal Festival Hall, in London, England, to mark the 80th birthday of Walton, in 1982, and she has performed at the Salzberg, Vienna, and Edinburgh music festivals.

Chung's playing has often been described as unique. It has also been characterized as, by turns, passionate, fiery, tempestuous, and intensely exciting and also precisely articulated, sweet, smooth, and aristocratic. Chung told Mary Campbell for the Associated Press (February 14, 1999), "In every stage appearance I try to give a performance out of that moment, of utter conviction. It's unbelievably exhausting. The public can share and witness it." In an article for the London *Times* (May 5, 1990), Richard Morrison wrote that Chung "has always had an extraordinary ability to startle the ear with unexpected tonal colourings, to move from a burning brightness of timbre to dark intimacy in the course of a single bar, and"—referring to the renowned British classical actor John Gielgud—"to use a highly-developed bow control to articulate a passage with the subtlety of Gielgud reading a Shakespeare sonnet." "One strives for certain phrases or colours for years," Chung told Morrison. "You know inside your mind what you want, but it doesn't come. I can work for hours to get a precise colouring on just one note."

As a Juilliard student and for years afterward, Chung heeded Ivan Galamian's command, repeated countless times, to remain single and devote herself entirely to her career. A few years after Galamian's death, in 1981, she married; after the arrival of the second of her two sons, she reduced her concert schedule from approximately 120 appearances annually (an average of three per week during the nine-month concert season) to about 60, so as to have more time at home with her children. By her own account, motherhood has enriched not only her life as a whole but her playing as well. "This is exactly how . . . I'd like [my life] to be. I am living . . . my dream of what . . . I always wanted to be," she told the flutist Eugenia Zukerman during an interview for the CBS television program *Sunday Morning* (June 2, 1991).

Kyung-Wha Chung was born on March 26, 1948 in Seoul, South Korea, the fourth of the seven children of Chun Chai Chung, a Seoul police officer, who later became a restaurateur with his wife, Won Sook Chung. (Some sources list the name of Chung's mother as Yi-Suk Chung; a few mention an eighth child, who died in infancy.) *Time* (November 18, 1974, on-line) reported that Chun Chai Chung also managed a mushroom plantation after immigrating to the U.S. According to Anna S. Roh, writing for *koreana.or.kr* (Spring 2004), Chung's mother wrote her autobiography, which is largely about her children and became a best-seller in Korea. During the Korean War (1950–53), much of Seoul was destroyed, and the Chung family fled to the southern harbor city of Pusan. (Chung's father found temporary refuge in Japan. According to one source, the whole family eventually returned to Seoul.) Accounts of Chung's childhood differ slightly in terms of chronology and in other ways. From an early age Chung and her siblings were exposed to classical music, most of which was composed by Europeans. "Both my parents were music lovers," she told a writer for Asiaweek.com (1995). "Music was part of our education, and there was always music-making at home." Chung's younger brother, Myung-Whun Chung, told Howard Reich for the *Chicago Tribune* (November 27, 1988), "Western music . . . is an art form that's learnable—it's simply a language. One is not born with a talent for Western music or Eastern music. One

is born with a sensitivity for music in general, and then it's a question of what you do with it." Kyung-Wha Chung began singing when she was two years old and performed in several singing contests as a child. At age five or so, like each of the Chung children in turn, she began to take piano lessons; later, she, like them, was encouraged to experiment with other instruments as well. She and her siblings showed remarkable ability and tenacity as budding musicians. "I think Oriental children have the drive to excel very early—they work with tremendous discipline," Chung told Reich. "Maybe it's because Korean society is still based on teaching and philosophies of [the Chinese sage] Confucius, which stress the beauty of living up to the expectations of your elders and your society." When a family friend (or relative, according to some sources) gave the Chungs a quarter-size violin, Kyung-Wha, who was then about six, immediately felt drawn to the instrument and its tones, which she has likened to those of the human voice. "I could make any kind of melody I wanted. . . . On the piano, my little fingers couldn't get around at all," she told Catherine Reese Newton for the *Salt Lake (Utah) Tribune* (April 27, 2003). She also told Newton, "My love of the instrument and love of music continue to grow." Within weeks, Chung had begun to play pieces by ear. "I had burning ambition. As a child I wanted to conquer the world, to become the biggest star in the whole world. You live in your dream; reality wasn't something I wanted to accept," she told Mary Campbell.

Chung has credited her parents with consistently supporting her musical goals and helping her to persevere through early setbacks, such as failure to advance past the preliminary round of a violin competition when she was eight. She won other contests in South Korea, however, and attracted much attention there. In 1961 she and her older sister Myung-So, a flutist, gained admission to the Juilliard School, with scholarships. (The next year the rest of the Chung family settled in Seattle, Washington, where Chung's parents operated a Korean restaurant at the 1962 World's Fair.) Kyung-Wha also took classes in a public school, where, as she recalled to Leslie Rubinstein for the *New York Times Magazine* (November 23, 1980), "I was afraid to speak English because I am a perfectionist, so for three years I barely spoke." At Juilliard she was shocked to discover how skillful and talented many of her fellow students were, and how large their repertoires were compared with hers. Her violin teacher there, Ivan Galamian, was extremely demanding; as Chung told Rubinstein, he "drove" her, and she "feared him like people feared God." "His biggest worry was that I would have a boyfriend, be distracted. He would tell me in the lesson, 'You won't marry?' I'd say, 'Oh, of course not, Mr. G." (Even years later, when Chung was performing extensively, Galamian told her repeatedly, "You are not a girl. You are my boy-girl," according to Barbara L. Sand, writing for the January 1, 1999 edition of the *American Record Guide*.)

Chung also pushed herself relentlessly, believing that she "had this obligation to my parents, my country, my six brothers and sisters, and always felt pressured and afraid of disappointing them," as she recalled to Rubinstein. In 1967 Chung participated in the Leventritt violin competition, held at Carnegie Hall, in New York City. Both she and the Israeli-born Pinchas Zukerman impressed the Leventritt jurors equally, and after trying in vain to decide which violinist deserved the top honor, the jury awarded the gold medal to both of them. During the next two years, Chung performed with the New York Philharmonic, the Chicago Symphony Orchestra, and other orchestras in the U.S. and Europe.

In her first New York City recital (a benefit concert for the Professional Children's School, in New York), Chung performed works for violin and piano (Jean-Marie Leclair's Sonata no. 3, Brahms's Sonata in D minor, Arnold Schoenberg's Fantaisie Opus 47, and Saint-Saëns's Introduction and Rondo Capriccioso) with her brother Myung-Whun, and Anton Arensky's Trio in D minor, with Myung-Whun and her sister Myung-Wha. After describing Chung and her siblings as "truly remarkable," Allen Hughes wrote in a review for the *New York Times* (February 25, 1970) that as the violinist played, "it seemed that she was probably incapable of producing an unattractive tone on the instrument. And she did not appear to be playing extra carefully, or gingerly, to keep the sound agreeable."

One day in the spring of 1970, Chung was asked to play Tchaikovsky's Violin Concerto in D major with the London Symphony Orchestra, under the baton of André Previn, at the Royal Festival Hall, in London; she was to replace the Israeli virtuoso Itzhak Perlman, who had suddenly become unable to fulfill his commitment to perform with the orchestra in a concert scheduled for a few days hence. "Sometimes one person's mischance becomes another person's chance. For a young player, replacing another artist can be the first stepping stone to a career," Chung observed to Edith Eisler for a 1990s interview posted on Amazon.com. "At first everything seemed to be against me," she recalled to Eisler: "I had stepped in at the last moment, and there was so much confusion that I hardly had any rehearsal, but as a result the musicians were all the more concentrated at the performance. The communication with the audience was very strong, so the event was a wonderful experience." A critic for the London *Financial Times*, as quoted by Mary Campbell, praised "the expressive force of [Chung's] performance: sweet, silken phrasing, soft and tender in the slow movement; beautiful playing, immeasurably mature." Recalling the review to Eisler, Chung called it "one of the best . . . I have ever received in my life. It was really quite embarrassing—[the critic] simply said I was better than everybody else, mentioning a lot of names." Soon after that concert, Chung got more than two dozen invitations to perform with major orches-

tras. During that period she also received instruction from the famous violinist Joseph Szigeti, and, following his advice, she began to visit art museums and galleries and to read great works of literature. Those activities, she has said, deepened her understanding of music and enriched her musical sensibilities.

Also in 1970, after illness prevented the singer Renata Tebaldi from attending a recording session for London Records, the company invited Chung to come to its studios to record both the Tchaikovsky and the Sibelius Violin Concertos; afterward, Chung signed a contract with the label. In 1972 the South Korean government awarded her the Order of Civil Merit, the nation's highest civilian honor. "Until she became a world-class violinist, it was only remotely possible for a Korean to achieve that kind of success," the conductor Kyung Soo Won told an interviewer for *Asiaweek.com* (1995). "It was like a dream in the clouds. But she showed it was possible."

Throughout the 1970s and the first half of the 1980s, Chung made about 120 appearances every year. She also continued to perform with Myung-Whun and Myung-Wha, as a member of the Chung Trio. According to the writer for *Time*, "Myung-Whun is intense, Kyung-Wha is fiery, and Myung-Wha pacific. . . . When family frictions do arise, the Chungs may find their strongest bond in their individual ability to make shafts of sound seem more vivid than anything else in life." In a critique of a Chung Trio performance at the Academy of Music in Philadelphia, Pennsylvania, Hubert Saal wrote for *Newsweek* (November 29, 1976), "Their teamwork and instrumental balance were razor-sharp, yet there was no sacrifice of individual voices, of the effervescent Kyung-Wha, the smoldering Myung-Wha, the deliberate Myung-Whun. To hear the Chungs make music together is to hear an ensemble whose members have played together all their lives." The Chungs have recorded trios by Beethoven, Dvořák, Tchaikovsky, and Shostakovich, as well as Beethoven's Triple Concerto, the last with the Philharmonia Orchestra of London, for the Deutsche Grammophon label.

In 1978 Chung took a six-month sabbatical from performing, to think about her life. "It's [a] very, very difficult thing to do, which I didn't realize," she told Eugenia Zukerman in 1991. "I just wanted . . . to just face—Where am I going?" When she began concertizing again, she was still "determined to be single," as she told Thor Eckert Jr. She would tell members of her family, as she recalled to Eckert, "Look, I've thought about marriage. I realized it's not possible, because I'm committed to my profession, and it would be unfair for me to have a family, because I won't do them justice." She added, "I suppose that was because a right person didn't come along." In 1984 Chung married a British businessman; over the next few years, she became the mother of two sons and cut her touring schedule by half. "I'm faced with, actually, what [a] normal human being faces: life," she told Eugenia Zukerman. "It isn't just something I read about or I sort of see from [the] side. I'm . . . actually living it." Chung told Frank Magiera for the Worcester, Massachusetts, *Telegram & Gazette* (January 17, 2000), "When you become a mother, you're an entirely different person. I have really nothing to do with what I used to be. My musical outlook grows and is nurtured by my surroundings. Now my family is the most important thing for me." She told Barbara L. Sand in 1999, "The whole hysterical issue of 'Where do I stand in my career? Am I going to get this date or that date?' no longer exists. I am just making music."

In the late 1980s Chung and her husband, who had been living in England, established a second home, in New York City. In 1988 Chung signed an exclusive contract with EMI Classics, to record a new series of albums and re-record earlier pieces produced for London Records. "Recordings are so personal for me," she told Marc Shulgold for the *Rocky Mountain News* (January 25, 1998). "Nothing is ever permanent in an interpretation—but that's not the case with a record. You have to leave something of your soul on that compact disc. The problem is, your soul is not perfect, so a recording never will be." Chung's rendering of Béla Bartók's Violin Concerto no. 2, recorded with the City of Birmingham Symphony Orchestra under Simon Rattle (on a disc that also contained Bartók's first and second Rhapsodies), won the 1988 Gramophone Award (often dubbed the Oscars of the classical-music world) for best concerto recording. She won a second Gramophone Award, 10 years later, for best chamber-music recording, for an album made with Krystian Zimerman, of violin and piano sonatas by Ottorino Respighi and Richard Strauss. Others among her albums include recordings of the Mendelssohn and Tchaikovsky Violin Concertos, with the Montreal Symphony Orchestra under Charles Dutoit (1990); Dvořák's Violin Concerto and Romance in F minor, with Riccardo Muti and the Philadelphia Orchestra (1990); Bartók and Berg's Violin Concertos, with the Chicago Symphony Orchestra under Georg Solti (1990); Beethoven's Violin Concerto and Bruch's Violin Concerto no. 1, with the Concertgebouw Orchestra Amsterdam under Klaus Tennstedt (1992); concertos by Prokofiev and Stravinsky, with the London Symphony Orchestra under André Previn (1998); *Souvenirs*, solo violin pieces by Bach, Debussy, Dvořák, and Jacques Ibert (1999); Vivaldi's *The Four Seasons*, with the St. Luke's Chamber Ensemble (2001); and *Con Amore: Violin Encores* (2006), which offers pieces by Chopin, Brahms, Debussy, Elgar, Wieniawski, Fritz Kreisler, and Eduard Poldini. Chung played several pieces for the album *Essential Violin* (2003). In 1999 the Decca Music Group reissued Chung's earlier recordings of Bruch's Violin Concerto no. 1 and Mendelssohn's Violin Concerto, as part of its Legends recording series.

In recent years Chung has performed with the Munich Philharmonic, the Helsinki Philharmonic, the Vienna Philharmonic, the Toronto Symphony Orchestra, the Philadelphia Orchestra, and the Boston Symphony Orchestra, among others. She plays an instrument produced in 1734 by the Guarneri family, famous for the extraordinary quality of their violins. Although she has spent relatively little time in South Korea in the past 46 years, Chung has told interviewers that she still regards herself as wholly Korean. She and her husband are the parents of two sons, Frederick and Eugene. The couple live in New York City and also maintain a home in southern England, where Chung enjoys gardening.

—D.J.K.

Suggested Reading: *American Record Guide* p5 Jan. 1, 1999; *Asiaweek.com* 1995; Associated Press Feb. 14, 1999; *Chicago Tribune* C p4 Feb. 1, 1987, C p18 Nov. 27, 1988; *Christian Science Monitor* p11 May 4, 1989; ICM Artists Web site; (London) *Times* May 5, 1990; *New York Times Magazine* VI p30+ Nov. 23, 1980; *Time* (on-line) Nov. 18, 1974

Selected Recordings: *Béla Bartók: Violin Concerto No. 2; Rhapsodies Nos. 1 & 2*, 1994; *Brahms: Violin Sonatas Nos. 1-3*, 1998; *Vivaldi: The Four Seasons*, 2001

Cohen, Richard

Feb. 6, 1941– Columnist

Address: Washington Post, 1150 15th St., N.W., Washington, DC 20071

As a *Washington Post* reporter for eight years beginning in 1968, and as a columnist at the paper since 1976, Richard Cohen has written about every presidential race in the United States since the Republican Richard Nixon ran against the Democrat Hubert H. Humphrey, and he has offered his opinions on a multitude of other topics and events thousands of times. Now 66, Cohen was born at the start of the third term of President Franklin D. Roosevelt, during World War II, and he has identified himself as a member of the generation that "went from radio to television, from party-line phones to poolside portables and from typewriters to computers," as he wrote in his October 7, 1990 *Washington Post* column. Currently published twice weekly and syndicated worldwide, Cohen's columns are generally viewed as having a liberal slant, but they are not amenable to rigid pigeonholing. In them he has expressed his thoughts on matters ranging from the mundane—whether or how much to tip an unsatisfactory waiter, for example—to life-and-death issues of national or interna-

Courtesy of Washington Post Writers Group

Richard Cohen

tional import, among them the current war in Iraq and the ever-present armed or verbal hostilities between Jews and Arabs in the Middle East; occasionally, his pieces have thrust him into the center of contentious debate. Cohen's investigative reporting earned him awards from Sigma Delta Chi (the Society of Professional Journalists) and the Washington-Baltimore Newspaper Guild, and he was a finalist for the Pulitzer Prize three times, in 1987, 1989, and 1990, for his "eloquent" and "clear and controlled" commentary on social, political, and other national issues.

Richard Martin Cohen and his twin sister were born to Harry Louis Cohen and Pearl (Rosenberg) Cohen, a Jewish couple, on February 6, 1941 in New York City. His father, who was orphaned as a youngster, and his mother, who immigrated to the U.S. from Poland at age seven, both endured prolonged hunger and other hurtful circumstances in childhood. As Cohen wrote for the *Washington Post* (December 24, 2002), his father "marveled at the term 'job satisfaction.' To him, to his generation, it was satisfaction enough just to have a job." His mother as well as his father worked outside the home while he was growing up. Beginning in elementary school, Cohen often felt anxiety and even terror in his classes. In the *Washington Post Magazine* (November 15, 1987), he wrote, "When I was a student, I believed in the conspiracy theory of parenthood. I thought all parents had gotten together to lie about school, to say it was the best time of their lives. . . . What were these people talking about?"

After he graduated from Far Rockaway High School, in the New York City borough of Queens, Cohen entered Hunter College, in Manhattan, and

later transferred to New York University. He attended classes at night and worked during the day; for that reason he was several years older than the average college senior when, in 1967, he earned a B.S. degree. He then enrolled in the graduate program in journalism at Columbia University, also in New York City, where he received an M.S. degree in 1968. Meanwhile, he had joined the staff of the *New York Herald Tribune* as a copy aide and then worked as a reporter for United Press International. After he left Columbia he completed military service (the universal draft was then in effect) at facilities within the continental U.S.

In 1968 Cohen moved to Washington, D.C., and began working for the *Washington Post* as a general-assignment reporter. Initially, he covered local politics, police activity, and other news of possible interest to residents of the nation's capital. Next, he was promoted to chief Maryland correspondent. With his fellow reporter Jules Witcover, he broke the story of the criminal investigation into the activities of Vice President Spiro T. Agnew when Agnew had served as governor of Maryland. In 1973 Agnew, who served under President Richard M. Nixon, resigned and pleaded no contest to criminal charges of money laundering and tax evasion. Cohen and Witcover wrote about Agnew's career and downfall in their book, *A Heartbeat Away: The Investigation and Resignation of Spiro T. Agnew* (1974). The book earned plaudits from reviewers on both the left and the right sides of the political spectrum. Writing for the *New Republic* (April 27, 1974) three months before Nixon's resignation, Ernest Gruening, a former Democratic U.S. senator from Alaska, described *A Heartbeat Away* as "a complete account of the single greatest political scandal in American history: the first time a Vice President was forced from office for malfeasance. It should be required reading for the many who, noting the parallels in the performance of the two men elected to the first and second highest offices in the land, anticipate a possible similar denouement in the case of the higher official on whom judgment has not been as yet officially and legally pronounced." In an assessment for the *National Review* (May 24, 1974), the conservative commentator Robert D. Novak wrote, "The story is as readable and engrossing as the best detective fiction."

In 1976 Cohen became a *Washington Post* columnist. His opinion pieces, which appeared on the first page of the Metro section three times a week, soon attracted a large readership. In a one-month period in May–June 1978, Cohen published articles with titles including "Walking Amid History at Arlington Cemetery"; "Kennedy: Alternative for All Seasons," about Larry O'Brien, a former chairman of the Democratic National Committee; "The Realities of Death: A Funeral for Pet Fish"; "The Issue at Skokie: It's a Matter of Law," about the controversy surrounding a planned march of Nazis in Skokie, Illinois; "The Puzzle of People Who Hate Homosexuals"; "The Voices She Heard Were Not in Courtroom," about the sentencing of the murderer David Berkowitz, known as the Son of Sam, and others like him, who hear imaginary but compelling voices telling them what they must do; "Childhood Memories of the Rosenberg Case," about the execution of Julius and Ethel Rosenberg in 1953 on charges of spying for the Soviet Union; and "For the Divorced Woman, [Life Is] Not Like the Movies."

In 1981 the *Post* made Cohen a member of the *Washington Post* Writers Group, whose columns or articles for that newspaper are syndicated around the world. In 1984 Cohen's column was moved to the *Post*'s op-ed page, where, in the following year, it offered his views on such subjects as President Ronald Reagan's visit to a cemetery in Bitburg, West Germany, in which Nazi officers were buried ("What, Exactly, Is Reagan Honoring?"); the bombing by Philadelphia, Pennsylvania, police officers of a house occupied by an armed, radical group called Move, in which 11 people were killed and dozens of other houses were set afire ("Who's to Blame?"); the lack of knowledge and interest among most Americans about affairs in foreign lands ("Victim of Ignorance"); the Boy Scouts of America requirement that scouts believe in God ("A Scout Badge for Hypocrisy"); and point shaving and other illegal activities in college sports ("The Losers' Championship").

"Closing the Door on Crime," an article of Cohen's that appeared in the first issue of the *Washington Post Sunday Magazine* (September 7, 1986), sparked fierce controversy. For that piece Cohen had interviewed two Washington, D.C., retail-store owners and learned that they either refused to admit young black men into their shops or quickly hustled them out after they entered. Cohen wrote that the store owners were "reacting out of fear to a combination of race, youth, and sex. . . . Young black males commit an inordinate amount of urban crime." Cohen argued that since not only their race, but also their ages and sex figured in the store-keepers' decisions to bar the men, their actions could not be labeled racist. "And while race is clearly the most compelling factor," he also wrote, "ask yourself what their policies would be if young white males were responsible for most urban crime." Cohen's column drew a flood of angry phone calls and letters from people who accused him and the *Post* of projecting blacks in an unconscionably bad light and of reinforcing negative stereotypes. (The cover article of that issue of the magazine, about a black rap artist accused of murder, along with the absence of any advertisements containing images of blacks, drew further condemnation.) Cohen responded to that criticism the next week, writing for the *Post* (September 14, 1986), "Now I am being accused of racism. The accusation stings if only because there is no way to prove otherwise. It is said that in describing the situation and empathizing with the merchants, I am either somehow responsible for it or, worse, have abetted it. But I was attempting to point out . . . that what seems like racism—the refusal to admit or serve

young blacks—is often more complicated than that. . . . A cabdriver who passes up a young black male is seeing more than race. He is also seeing sex and age. The three together fit the profile of the most common type of Washington criminal, and the cabdriver acts accordingly. . . . In a different city, a different kind of person would be passed up." Years later Cohen said to Erin Moriarty for the CBS News program *48 Hours* (January 5, 1994), "Is a single column worth . . . hundreds of phone calls, tons of letters, pickets outside of the *Washington Post*, the vilification that I got? There must be columnists out there who love that kind of controversy. My instinct was to go under the desk. . . . Black political leaders in Washington were upset to one extent or another and I felt besieged . . . It was an educational experience, like getting kicked in the teeth is an educational experience." On the *Post*'s op-ed page on October 6, 1986, the paper's executive editor, Benjamin C. Bradlee, apologized for causing offense with Cohen's article and the cover story.

During the 1990s Cohen often appeared on the CNN TV series *Crossfire*, debating current issues with the program's hosts, Robert Novak and Michael Kinsley. In his columns he discussed such issues as the death penalty, abortion and gay rights, the Israeli-Palestinian conflict, and affirmative action. When President George H. W. Bush nominated Clarence Thomas, an African-American, to fill the seat of the recently retired justice Thurgood Marshall on the Supreme Court, Cohen wrote for the *Washington Post* (July 4, 1991), "Thomas is not 'the best.' He is only the best of a certain category, and we all know it. He might be the best black nominee or, to be even more specific, the best black conservative nominee. . . . Thomas was picked because he's black. That's not to say that he's not smart and not learned and not . . . the most wonderful of all people. It's simply to say that if he were white, he never would have been summoned to Kennebunkport"—the site of Bush's summer home, in Maine—"and anointed the most meritorious of all people with merit."

Cohen was in New York City on September 11, 2001 and witnessed firsthand the events surrounding the terrorist attacks on the World Trade Center. The fall of the first of the twin towers, he wrote for the *Washington Post* (September 12, 2001), produced "a noise unlike any I've ever heard. It was a roar wrapped in thunder followed quickly by the feel of sound on your face. . . . I looked into the sky, but there was nothing there. Suddenly, a blizzard hit, and the quaint streets of lower Manhattan were turned white with powdered building material. . . . The World Trade Center had collapsed. I could not see and I could hardly breathe . . . Where is it safe? Nowhere. Nowhere, anymore." A few days later he wrote for the *Washington Post* (September 15, 2001), "New York and Washington grieve because we failed, and failed badly, at the business of intelligence. Republicans were at fault and Democrats were at fault and so, in a way, were we all. Most of us believed that high-tech could do the work of people and that war could be waged without the loss of life. On Tuesday, in the rubble somewhere, was an uncounted victim: our innocence."

In his column of January 17, 2006, Cohen discussed the talk-show host Oprah Winfrey's defense of James Frey's book *A Million Little Pieces* (2005) after the public revelation that it contained significant distortions and lies, making it more a work of fiction than a memoir, as its publisher, Doubleday, had described it in publicity material and advertisements. Purportedly an account of Frey's experiences as a recovering alcohol and crack-cocaine addict, *A Million Little Pieces* had enjoyed enormous commercial success after Winfrey featured it on her program the previous September. Several million copies were purchased before staff members of the investigative Web site the Smoking Gun posted evidence that important parts of the book were complete fabrications. Winfrey gave short shrift to that news, maintaining that Frey's failure to stick faithfully to fact did not diminish the value of the book as a story of redemption. In a column entitled "Oprah's Grand Delusion," Cohen wrote, "No one expects Oprah to fact-check every book she urges her audience to read. Sticking by it is quite another matter. . . . Fame and wealth has lured her into believing that she possesses something akin to papal infallibility. She finds herself incapable of seeing that she has been twice fooled—once by Frey, a second time by herself." To Cohen's surprise, Winfrey invited him to join a panel of journalists and others for the January 26, 2006 installment of her show, during which, under Winfrey's blunt questioning, Frey admitted that he had consciously included falsehoods in his book. Winfrey told Cohen that she appreciated his assertion that she had been "deluded" with regard to Frey. "I was impressed with that because I thought sometimes criticism can be very helpful," she said. "So thank you very much. You were right. I was wrong."

Cohen himself was subjected to intense disapproval during a period of violent conflict between Israel and the Muslim anti-Israel paramilitary group Hezbollah in 2006. The brouhaha began after the publication of a column entitled "Hunker Down with History" (July 18, 2006), in which Cohen wrote, "The greatest mistake Israel could make at the moment is to forget that Israel itself is a mistake. It is an honest mistake, a well-intentioned mistake, a mistake for which no one is culpable, but the idea of creating a nation of European Jews in an area of Arab Muslims (and some Christians) has produced a century of warfare and terrorism of the sort we are seeing now." Cohen expressed no opinion as to whether ownership of the land that is now Israel rightfully belongs to Jews or Arabs; referred to Hezbollah as a group of zealots that, as such, is "not amenable to reason," and another Arab organization, Hamas, as "a fetid, anti-Semitic outfit whose organizing principle is hatred of Isra-

el"; and noted that "the underlying, subterranean hatred of the Jewish state in the Islamic world just keeps bubbling to the surface." After referring to the "horrific history of the Jews in 19th- and 20th-century Europe," he wrote, "Little wonder" that many Jews "embraced the dream of Zionism and went to Palestine, first a colony of Turkey and later of Britain. They were in effect running for their lives. Most of those who remained [in Europe]— 97.5 percent of Poland's Jews, for instance—were murdered in the Holocaust." Cohen's article nevertheless drew hundreds of condemnations from defenders of Israel, on blogs, in the mailbox of the *Washington Post*, and, perhaps most prominently, in an article by Alvin H. Rosenfeld, a professor of Jewish studies and the director of the Institute for Jewish Culture and the Arts at Indiana University. In that article, called "'Progressive' Jewish Thought and the New Anti-Semitism," which was published by the American Jewish Committee, Rosenfeld criticized as examples of "the new anti-Semitism" the views of Cohen and a few other prominent Jewish intellectuals who had expressed misgivings about the establishment of the state of Israel in the Middle East. "Cohen is right about the never-ending violence, but wrong about its causes," Rosenfeld wrote. "Instead of placing the responsibility for terrorism squarely where it belongs, he dodges the issue. . . . Instead, he blames the agents of an abstract and errant 'history' for having brought the Jewish state into being in the first place."

In an opinion column for the *Jerusalem Post* (February 6, 2007), David A. Harris, the executive director of the American Jewish Committee, wrote that Cohen was an "exception" among the Jewish intellectuals criticized by Rosenfeld, because Cohen's "disturbing comments" in his controversial column "do not reflect the totality of his occasional writings on the Middle East." In response to his critics and Harris's comments, Cohen wrote for the *Washington Post* (February 6, 2007) that within a year of his being hired by that newspaper, he wrote his "first column about anti-Semitism. Since then, I have written about 90 more, most of them full-throated condemnations of the hatred that killed fully one-third of all Jews during my own lifetime. So it comes as a surprise that has the force of a mugging to be accused of aiding the very people I so hate—of being an abettor of something called 'The New Anti-Semitism.'" He also wrote, "My 'occasional writings' [on the Middle East] include at least 30 datelined columns from the region and a near-obsessive attention to the subject. . . . It's sad that the American Jewish Committee commissioned and published Rosenfeld's report. I can't imagine what good will come out of it. Instead, it has given license to the most intolerant and narrow-minded of Israel's defenders so that, as the AJC concedes in my case, any veering from orthodoxy is met with censure."

More recently, in his column of July 17, 2007, Cohen found fault with Richard Carmona, who served as the U.S. surgeon general (2002–06), for waiting until he had left office before he revealed publicly the extent to which he had been muzzled by the administration of President George W. Bush with regard to such controversial topics as stem-cell research and sexual abstinence among teenagers. Cohen's September 18, 2007 column criticized Democratic U.S. senator and presidential hopeful Hillary Rodham Clinton of New York for failing to comment on an ad placed in the *New York Times* in which the organization MoveOn labeled General David Petraeus, the commander of the U.S.-led forces in Iraq, "General Betray Us." Writing on September 25, 2007, Cohen agreed with the proposal, offered by the Democratic U.S. senator and presidential hopeful Joseph Biden of Dela-

ware and Leslie Gelb, the president emeritus of the Council of Foreign Relations, that Iraq be divided into three parts: a Shi'ite south, a Sunni center, and a Kurdish north.

Married three times and divorced twice, Cohen lives in Washington, D.C., and New York City. He has one son, Alexander.

—S.J.D.

Suggested Reading: postwritersgroup.com; *Washington Post* R p4 Oct. 7, 1990, A p15 Dec. 24, 2002; *Washington Post* (on-line); *Washington Post Magazine* W p5 Nov. 15, 1987; *Who's Who in America*, 2007

Selected Books: *A Heartbeat Away: The Investigation and Resignation of Spiro T. Agnew* (with Jules Witcover), 1974

Alex Wong/Getty Images

Coleman, Mary Sue

Oct. 2, 1943– University president; educator

Address: Office of the President, University of Michigan, 503 Thompson St., 2074 Fleming Bldg., Ann Arbor, MI 48109

"Being president of a university is a hard job, equally tough for men and women. The pressures are no different," Mary Sue Coleman, who began her academic career as a biochemist at the University of Kentucky, told Mark Clayton for the *Christian Science Monitor* (July 23, 2002), shortly after she was appointed the first female president of the

University of Michigan (U.M.), in May 2002. Coleman, however, has had a particularly challenging tenure at Michigan—though her gender has had little to do with her difficulties—as she has found herself embroiled in a series of high-profile legal battles, one involving illegal payments that were made to U.M. basketball players during the late 1980s and throughout the 1990s, another centering on the university's use of affirmative action in its admissions process for its undergraduate and law schools, and still another concerning its decision to grant the search engine Google permission to scan and make available on the Internet every volume in its library. Coleman, who had anticipated some of those problems as well as the need to work on solving U.M.'s budgetary difficulties, was particularly well-prepared for dealing with the issues facing the university when she assumed her position. As the University of Iowa's president over the preceding seven years, she had not simply earned a reputation for being a skilled fundraiser—one of the factors that led to her being hired at Michigan—but had also shown a deep concern for making public education accessible to all and for preserving a diverse campus, issues central to the Google and affirmative-action cases, respectively.

Born Mary Sue Wilson on October 2, 1943 in Madison County, Kentucky, Coleman was the middle child of Leland and Margaret Wilson. Her father, who had grown up in rural Kentucky, had earned a doctorate through the G.I. Bill and worked as a professor at public colleges. (His background, many have noted, likely influenced Coleman's strong commitment to public institutions.) Her family later moved to Georgia, where Coleman received much of her elementary education. When she was 12 her father took a position at the University of Northern Iowa (UNI), and the family moved again. In Iowa Coleman's teachers feared that her strong southern accent would be a social detriment for her; in order to "correct" it, they saw to it that she received speech therapy, which was not wholly successful. "'The teachers were so kind,' Coleman says, still amused," Michael H. Hodges wrote for the *Detroit News* (October 25, 2002). "'I had a fabulous childhood. I can't describe it any other way.'" Hodges added, "It was, in fact, a classic 1950s small-town upbringing—*Leave It to Beaver* with pigtails, defined by sleepovers, softball games and camping out. And petri dishes." Those last items helped sustain the love for science that she developed early in life. She was not, she has claimed, influenced in that regard by her father, even though she took chemistry courses that he taught at UNI when she was still a high-school student. During her senior year Coleman was a finalist in the Westinghouse Science Talent Search, which led to her meeting President John F. Kennedy in the Oval Office. Following high school she attended Grinnell College, in Iowa, where she earned a bachelor's degree in chemistry, in 1965, and met her future husband, Kenneth Coleman, a political-science student. The two went on to attend graduate school at the University of North Carolina (UNC) at Chapel Hill, where they both earned doctorates, he in political science and she in biochemistry.

After completing graduate school, in 1969, Coleman followed her husband to the University of Kentucky. He had found a tenure-track faculty position there, and she took a job as a research associate in the university's medical-school laboratory. Her work led to her getting a faculty position in the Biochemistry Department. She was later given a top position at the university's Markey Cancer Center—where she did research on the effect of the immune system on malignancies—and was elected by her colleagues to represent them on the board of trustees. She remained at Kentucky until 1990, when she returned to UNC to take an administrative post, serving as the associate provost and dean of research between 1990 and 1992 and as the vice chancellor for graduate studies and research during the 1992–93 academic year. The move altered her perception of university campuses. When she had attended UNC, Coleman told Clayton, it was "really a pretty homogeneous place, not many women on the faculty, mostly Caucasian. . . . It was a good education, and I was happy with it, but then 25 years later I had the opportunity to go back and join the administration there. By then, it was a far more diverse place, faculty and students. It was just a much more intellectually vibrant place, and I've taken that [awareness of the value of diversity] with me." Coleman then moved to the University of New Mexico, where she was a provost and vice president for academic affairs between 1993 and 1995.

In what she predicted would be her final career move, in 1995 Coleman accepted a position as president of the University of Iowa, assuming her responsibilities in the middle of the 1995–96 academic year. There, she cultivated a spirit of collaboration between students and administrators,

holding regular fireside chats to address students' concerns. She also devoted much energy to raising money, which was necessary to balance a budget that was continually shrinking due to cuts in state funding. In 2001, for example, the university faced a budget cut of $21.9 million. Coleman had prepared the school to absorb the loss, having raised $172 million in 2000. Indeed, during her tenure, the university saw an average annual increase in donations of 22 percent. To offset further its loss of state funding, Coleman cut deeply into the university's administrative costs (eliminating, for instance, a vice-president position), did not replace many of the faculty who had retired, and scrapped many course offerings. Despite such measures, the university was forced to increase its tuition. Worried that such increases threatened students' access to a public education, Coleman designated more money for financial aid. Her other great success at Iowa was her ability to raise money for research purposes, increasing the amount of money that Iowa held for research from $178 million to $300 million. During that time Coleman also remained active in the sciences, working as a professor of biochemistry at Iowa's College of Medicine and as a professor of biological sciences at its College of Liberal Arts. For that work she was elected to the National Academy of Sciences' Institute of Medicine, in 1997.

Upon assuming her position as the University of Michigan's president, in 2002, Coleman became the first woman to have attained the presidency of two Big Ten schools (the other being Iowa) and the first president at Michigan since 1979 who had no prior ties to the university. She signed a five-year contract with a starting salary of $475,000 per year—$200,000 more than she had earned at Iowa—making her one of the highest-paid public-university presidents in the country. Coleman immediately had to deal with the school's budget problems as well as two other major crises. While the cost of operating public universities in the state had risen dramatically, due mainly to health-care and utility expenses, state funding for the schools had remained flat. That led to an 83 percent increase in tuition between 1992 and 2002—more than double the rate of inflation during that period. To control further increases in tuition, the governor of Michigan had reached an agreement with Michigan's 15 public universities to continue current funding levels (rather than decrease them), provided they held tuition increases to 8.5 percent or lower. University presidents, pressed for further sources of income, had begun focusing on private donations, and as the U.M. president, Coleman began working hard to solicit private support as well as convince the public that the university is a valuable public asset. "I've made the argument that investment by the states is crucial," she told Clayton. "Having a great public university is more than just the private good that comes to those who seek education there. We're a big resource. I want to make the case to the residents of Michigan that they have a jewel here that's worth supporting."

The most immediate crisis that Coleman faced as president—and also the biggest sports scandal in the school's history—was over illegal loans that had been given to Michigan basketball players by a retired Ford Motor Co. electrician and local basketball booster named Ed Martin between 1988 and 1999. Martin had spent more than $600,000 on U.M. players—including the future National Basketball Association (NBA) star Chris Webber—using money that he earned by running an illegal lottery in Detroit auto plants. In June 2002 Martin pleaded guilty to a federal charge of conspiracy to launder money. That November, partly in an effort to avoid more serious penalties from the National Collegiate Athletic Association (NCAA), Coleman and the university imposed heavy penalties on its basketball program, including banning its team's participation in that year's postseason and forfeiting every game won while the four players who received money were on the team. (Those included the team's two appearances in NCAA championship games in the early 1990s.) "This is a day of great shame for the university," Coleman said at a news conference, as Danny Hakim reported for the New York Times (November 8, 2002). "I am determined nothing like this will ever happen again at Michigan." Several commemorative banners were removed from the school's sports arena, and the basketball program was placed on probation for two years. Coleman was especially aware of the potential harm of the scandal, having served on the board of trustees at Kentucky in 1989–90, when that school's basketball program was penalized, and its basketball coach and athletic director forced to resign, over illegal recruiting practices. "That experience made me very cognizant of this issue," she said at the news conference, as Maryanne George reported for the Detroit Free Press (November 8, 2002). "No one had to convince me about what can happen if you don't get to the bottom of these situations."

The other crisis Coleman faced involved admission policies at U.M.'s undergraduate and law schools. In 1997 two individuals who were denied admittance to those schools had filed separate lawsuits in which they claimed that the university's use of race as a factor in its admissions process was illegal under the 14th Amendment, specifically its Equal Protection Clause, and that Michigan's admissions policy relied on racial stereotyping. The cases brought renewed attention to Regents of the University of California v. Bakke, a 1978 U.S. Supreme Court case in which it was decided that race could be used as a factor in admissions but that quota systems to ensure racial diversity were prohibited. Lawyers for the individuals who had been denied admittance to U.M.—who themselves received the support of lawyers working for the administration of President George W. Bush—claimed that Michigan's practice of awarding "points" to minority applicants amounted to the use of quotas. "The enormous size of the preferences is what creates the 'two track' or 'dual' ad-

missions system that enables the Law School to achieve its quota," one of the student's lawyers wrote in a brief, as Maryanne George reported for the Detroit Free Press (January 17, 2003). Coleman had been observing the proceedings while still at Iowa and discussed the issue in her meetings with the presidential-search advisory committee. "One of the questions I asked [during the interviews]," Coleman said, as Tamar Lewin reported for the New York Times (May 30, 2002) "was how people on campus feel about the court cases. And one of the things that impressed me was what a passionate discussion I heard of how people felt they were engaged at an important point in history, working for something that could influence all of higher education."

As Michigan's president, Coleman quickly began to defend the university's support of affirmative action, both in faculty appointments and student admissions, leading the fight against the lawsuits. In June 2003 the Supreme Court ruled that admissions processes that use mechanical formulas to weigh applicants' race were unconstitutional but upheld the legality of affirmative action. Thus, Michigan's undergraduate point system for admissions had to be changed, while the law school's practice of judging every applicant on an individual basis was allowed to remain the same. Colleges around the country had to make similar adjustments. For Coleman, the ruling meant that more money was needed for additional undergraduate-admissions staff to screen each individual applicant. She nonetheless remained committed to the ideal of diversity, telling Judy Woodruff for CNN (June 23, 2003): "I want to let students know that now we'll be looking, using a slightly different policy, but we're going to give every application a fair look. And we're going to build a diverse class because we think that's the best educational opportunity for students, both minority and non-minority. And we're going to be tailoring our policies in a way that the court says is constitutional." Over the next three years, Coleman worked vigorously at boosting diversity on Michigan's campus, investing "considerable time in personal admissions recruiting and outreach visits," as US States News (June 16, 2006) reported when it was announced, in 2005, that she had signed a new five-year contract with U.M. The report went on to note that she "also launched a major new commitment to financial aid in 2005 with the M-PACT program, which provides additional grants to approximately 3,000 Michigan undergraduates each year. Total student enrollment at the Ann Arbor campus has grown from 38,972 in fall 2002 to nearly 40,000 in fall 2005, with the majority of that growth in undergraduate enrollment."

It may have been Coleman's deep belief in public education's importance that led her into another controversy. In 2005 she announced that she had secured a deal with Google that would allow the search engine to scan the university's entire library and place electronic copies of its books on the

Google Library Project. Claiming copyright infringement, numerous authors and publishers, including five member groups of the American Association of Publishers (AAP), filed lawsuits against Google. The AAP accused the company of profiting from copyrighted material without the authors' permission. Coleman maintained that making books searchable on-line would only help sales. "I can't understand why any bookseller or publisher, especially scholarly presses with such narrow audiences, would oppose an approach that all but guarantees increased exposure," Coleman said in a speech given to the annual conference of the professional and scholarly division of the AAP, as Gabe Nelson reported for the *Michigan Daily* (February 7, 2006). Only excerpts, and not full texts, would be viewable to students, along with links to sites enabling students to buy the books or borrow them from libraries. Still, many were upset over Google's intention to sell advertising space on the Web pages on which access to the books would be available. "What gives [Google] the right to digitize my book without my permission?" one of the AAP members said in a question-and-answer session following Coleman's speech, as Andrea L. Foster reported for the *Chronicle of Higher Education* (February 17, 2006). "In most cases, that would be considered stealing." Coleman argued that digitization was necessary as research was increasingly being done on the Internet. "We must change with our students," she said, according to Foster. "And that means embracing the Internet for all it can, and does offer."

The admission policies that had been instituted to conform to the 2003 Supreme Court ruling were threatened in 2006, when Michigan's voters approved an amendment to the state's constitution called the Michigan Civil Rights Initiative (MCRI), which banned public agencies, including state schools, from using any form of racial preferences. Coleman was unmoved by the approval of MCRI, saying in a speech the day after the vote, as Steve Chapman wrote for the *Chicago Tribune* (November 23, 2006), that U.M. would do "'whatever it takes' to delay, frustrate and circumvent" the amendment, accusing voters, Chapman went on to report, "of opposing 'a community that is fair and equal for all.'" Coleman, Chapman added, "said California's 1996 ban on racial and gender preferences 'has been a horribly failed experiment' that 'we cannot, and will not, allow to take seed here in Michigan.' And she assured her campus audience . . . 'We will find ways to overcome the handcuffs that Proposal 2 [that is, the MCRI] attempts to place on our reach for greater diversity.'"

In September 2007, as Coleman began her second five-year term as president, she received a 3 percent raise in salary, bringing her annual pay to $532,000. Bonuses and other forms of monetary compensation brought her total compensation to $757,643—the third-highest salary among American public-college heads. Coleman announced that she would donate her additional $15,500 per year

in earnings to the university, for scholarships for graduate and professional students.

In addition to serving as president, Coleman is a professor of biological chemistry in U.M.'s medical school and a professor of chemistry in its College of Literature, Science and the Arts. "Her manner," Hodges notes, "is breezy and engaging, her conversation punctuated with Iowaisms like 'Oh, gosh' and 'Oh my heavens.'" She and her husband have one son, Jonathan, who works as a mutual-funds manager in Denver, Colorado.

—M.B.

Suggested Reading: *Christian Science Monitor* p16 July 23, 2002; *Chronicle of Higher Education* p40 Feb. 17, 2006; *Detroit News* C p1 Oct. 25, 2002; *New York Times* A p22 May 30, 2002, A p22 June 25, 2003

Matthew Peyton/Getty Images

Coleman, Ronnie

May 13, 1964– Bodybuilder

Address: c/o International Federation of Bodybuilding & Fitness, 2875 Bates Rd., Montreal, Quebec, Canada H3S 1B7

"I'll continue working out, regardless of whether I'm competing, because it's my hobby. I love it. I train with those weights not because I feel that's what's required in order to beat everyone else, but because it's fun, and part of the reason it's fun is that, when I'm in the middle of an extremely heavy set, my attitude is the same as it is with anything else I take on in life: I can do anything I want to do.

Nothing can prevent me." Those words, quoted by Julian Schmidt for *Flex* (April 1, 2004), were spoken by the bodybuilder Ronnie Coleman, who tied one of his sport's all-time records by reigning for eight years as the holder of the Mr. Olympia title. Coleman began training for bodybuilding contests in the early 1990s, while working as a police officer in Texas (a job he still holds). Not an "overnight" success in the world of professional bodybuilding, he followed his early victories in amateur competition with finishes of sixth place or lower in a string of Mr. Olympia professional contests. With his upset win over Flex Wheeler in the 1998 competition, he began his long series of first-place finishes, a run broken only in 2006 by Jay Cutler. Along the way Coleman set a record for most wins in International Federation of Bodybuilding & Fitness (IFBB) competition.

The oldest of four children, Ronnie Dean Coleman was born on May 13, 1964 in Monroe, Louisiana, and raised in nearby Bastrop. Because he was shy as a boy, his classmates occasionally bullied him during his grade-school years, despite the fact that he "was always the biggest kid in school," as his mother, Jessie Benton, said to Nancy Kruh for the *Dallas Morning News* (October 3, 1999). His mother forbade him from fighting back. Instead, as early as junior high school, he began lifting the weights his mother had purchased for him, in order to build his strength and confidence. Lifting weights soon "became a part of his life," as his mother said to Kruh.

The commitment to intense training for which Coleman is known began during his years at Bastrop High School. While playing football there, and also working various jobs after school, he always found time to lift weights. He said to Kruh that his teammates in high school "always vote[d] me 'most dedicated' because I was the only one in the summertime who would go to the weight room and work out." After graduating he enrolled at Grambling State University, in Grambling, Louisiana, majoring in accounting and playing on the football team there as well. At Grambling he earned the nickname "Big Arm" and won a campus-wide contest for the best male physique. Coleman earned a spot on the team's starting lineup in his junior year but realized that his chances of playing the sport professionally were small. He said to Ellen Mazo for the *Pittsburgh Post-Gazette* (May 1, 1999), "I wasn't given the genetics for football. This [bodybuilding] is my gift right here. I was always well-built." He added, "You can't do certain sports without the genetics, and talent, too, of course."

After graduating with honors from Grambling, in the late 1980s, Coleman headed to Dallas, Texas. In part because the national economy was sluggish at the time, Coleman had trouble finding work that interested him, and he took a job at a Domino's Pizza restaurant, serving at different times as delivery person, pie maker, and manager. "Domino's was the hardest job I ever had," he said, according to his Web site. "I dreaded every day working there, but I knew I was destined for something better." After working for roughly two years at Domino's, he responded to a newspaper recruitment ad placed by the Arlington, Texas, Police Department and trained to become a police officer. He enjoyed the varied nature of his new job; he was also happy that his schedule left him plenty of time to lift weights. After joining the MetroFlex Gym, in Arlington, at the suggestion of a fellow officer, he was approached by the gym's owner, Brian Dobson, an amateur bodybuilder, who offered Coleman a free lifetime membership if he would agree to let Dobson train him for the upcoming Mr. Texas bodybuilding competition. "As soon as he walked in, I could see the unbelievable potential," Dobson said to Kruh. "I could see his veins through his sweatpants. He didn't train very seriously, and I told him he could make a good living at this. He didn't believe me at first." Dobson added, "When he first started, he didn't know 'super-setting' [combining more than one exercise with no rest in between] and everyone used to make fun of how small his calves were. He knew all the basic lifts, but there are a lot of tricks—different ways to position the feet or your wrists to bring your peaks."

Bodybuilding competitions are usually based on a system of points awarded by a panel of judges. Most contests are divided into rounds: the Standing Relaxed (or Symmetry) Round, in which judges evaluate the symmetry of each competitor's physique; the Comparison (or Muscularity) Round, in which the bodybuilders flex their biceps, triceps, and other muscles in a series of standard poses; and the Free Posing Round, during which the contestants display their muscles in whatever manner they wish. (That round often includes music.) Accepting Dobson's offer to train him for the Mr. Texas competition, Coleman increased the intensity of his weightlifting regimen. Despite his initial reservations, he followed the common practice of donning bikini briefs and slathering oil over his body prior to competition. (He explained to Kruh that once onstage, "you get over your shyness real quick.") In April 1990 Coleman entered and won the Mr. Texas bodybuilding contest in both the heavyweight and overall categories, defeating Dobson, among others. Also in 1990 Coleman took the heavyweight and overall titles at that year's National Physique Committee (NPC) Texas Championships. In 1991 Coleman won the most prestigious competition in amateur weightlifting, the Mr. Universe contest. That victory qualified him to enter the professional contests sponsored by the IFBB, the sport's largest sanctioning body.

Coleman's rise to the top ranks of the professional bodybuilding circuit was gradual. In his first half-dozen years (starting in 1992) of competing in the Mr. Olympia contest, an invitation-only event, he placed sixth or lower. His slow ascent was uncharacteristic for champion bodybuilders. "Most Mr. Olympias are prodigies," Peter McGough, the editor in chief of *Flex*, said to Nancy Kruh. "If they're great, they come through very quickly. Ronnie came through slowly, bit by bit. It was a real study in perseverance." Making it particularly difficult for Coleman—and most of his competitors—to win during that period was the presence of the British bodybuilder Dorian Yates, who won the Mr. Olympia contest six consecutive times, from 1992 to 1997. A bright spot during those years came in 1995, when Coleman won his first competition as a professional—the Canada Pro Cup. He took first place in that contest again the next year, and in 1997 he won the Russian Grand Prix. Nonetheless, even with Yates's retirement, following his 1997 victory, Coleman was regarded as a long shot when he entered the 1998 Mr. Olympia contest, held in New York City's Madison Square Garden. Flex Wheeler, an American bodybuilder, was considered the favorite in the event. Coleman had finished second behind Wheeler in two 1996 contests: the Florida Pro Invitational and the Night of Champions. To prepare for the 1998 Mr. Olympia competition, Coleman enlisted the aid of the nutritionist Chad Nicholls; at Nicholls's suggestion, he experimented with lesser or greater amounts of liquids, protein, and carbohydrates, to see how his body would respond. "It's really a matter of trial and error," Nicholls admitted to Nancy Kruh. "But we got lucky." That was evidently true, as Coleman, by all accounts, arrived at the competition no larger than before but with a firmer physique. At the end of the contest, when he was declared the winner (Wheeler placed second), Coleman collapsed onstage and burst into tears. "I still haven't recovered," he told Kruh nearly a year later. "I can watch the tape now and start crying. It's so overwhelming. It's almost better than winning the lottery, because you worked for it. It's like something you want all your life, but you never thought it would happen, and all of a sudden it did."

Coleman defended his title successfully over the next seven consecutive years. In recent years his chief competition has come from the German bodybuilder Gunter Schlierkamp and the American Jay Cutler—who defeated Coleman in competition on September 30, 2006 to take the Mr. Olympia title. Coleman, who finished second, is thus tied with Lee Haney for the most consecutive Mr. Olympia titles, with eight. (Haney won the contest from 1984 through 1991.) Coleman has won 26 IFBB competitions during his career; his victories have come in contests held in Russia, Holland, New Zealand, and England. Speaking with Evan Rapp in a videotaped interview for *ProSource* (October 30, 2006) after his controversial loss to Cutler, Coleman said that the defeat was "hard at first" to accept but that he planned to "put it behind" him and continue to compete. The 42-year-old added, "I'm having too much fun to retire."

On September 29, 2007 Coleman finished fourth in the Mr. Olympia competition, losing to Cutler, who again captured the title. Prior to that event, Coleman had announced that that year's Mr. Olympia appearance would be his last.

According to a profile of Coleman appearing in *Muscle & Fitness* (March 1, 2003), in the 10 weeks prior to tournament competition, the bodybuilder consumes about 50 pounds of steak, 210 pounds of chicken, 96 pounds of potatoes, and ample portions of grits and rice. In addition, at 2 a.m. he drinks a "meal-replacement" shake packed with as many as 80 grams of protein. Coleman has parlayed his success as a professional bodybuilder into numerous product endorsements and other opportunities. His schedule includes a great deal of travel—up to nine months per year. On the road Coleman makes guest appearances at gym openings in the U.S. and frequently visits countries including China, Brazil, and Australia, where he is equally admired. Since 1997 he has released several training videos: *Ronnie Coleman's First Training Video*; *The Unbelievable*; *The Cost of Redemption*; and *On the Road*. In the videos Coleman dispenses tips for more experienced weightlifters, while cautioning against overexertion and improper form. Coleman said to Julian Schmidt, "Strength is my goal in training and the basis of my muscle gains, but it's never at the expense of getting a full range of motion with every repetition. Anytime someone asks me what I feel is the most important technique in the performance of an exercise, that's always my answer. In order to work ever fiber in a muscle and allow it to pump itself to its maximum capacity with blood, it must be fully stretched, then fully contracted. Feel that stress all the way, and that muscle has choice but to grow." He also said to Schmidt, "People seem to be awed at how strong I am, but my lifts . . . on my video are not my max. I can always do more, but I would have to strain and cheat, which does not necessarily build strength or mass. Furthermore, I would be risking injury."

When working out, Coleman uses free weights rather than machines in order to maximize his flexibility and range of motion. He lifts weights six days per week. "Regardless of how heavy I lift, the preeminent principle in all of my training is to work the muscle as best I can," he said to Schmidt. "That is efficiently accomplished by applying maximum resistance [weight], so the muscle is exhausted as quickly as possible and the target muscle—not the ancillary muscles or leveraged joints—do the work. Every rep is therefore performed in a very strict manner, and the success of this is gauged by the fullness of the pump in that muscle."

Ronnie Coleman stands five feet 11 inches tall. His top-form measurements, in inches, are as follows: biceps, 24; chest, 60; and thighs, 34. In the words of Nancy Kruh, Coleman is "5 feet 11 inches of perfectly molded muscle mass that makes just about every other male specimen of the species look like the 'before' picture in the old Charles Atlas ads." During competition Coleman tips the scales at 280 pounds; in the off-season his weight is closer to 315 pounds. He is able to shed weight quickly in the weeks leading up to competition by adding cardiovascular exercise to his daily workout routine.

Coleman is devoutly religious and is known for his humility. He lives in Arlington, Texas, where he remains a reserve officer of the Arlington Police Department. (He requires specially tailored uniforms.) Coleman enjoys listening to hip-hop music, especially during weight training.

—D.F.

Suggested Reading: *Dallas Morning News* E p1 Oct. 3, 1999; *Flex* p66+ Apr. 1, 2004; *New York Times* VIII p13 Oct. 11, 1998; *Playboy* p64+ Feb. 1, 2006

Selected Videos: *Ronnie Coleman's First Training Video*; *The Unbelievable*; *The Cost of Redemption*; *On the Road*

Frazer Harrison/Getty Images

Craig, Daniel

Mar. 2, 1968– Actor

Address: c/o Creative Artists Agency, 9830 Wilshire Blvd., Beverly Hills, CA 90212

The average celebrity is probably unable to identify the moment he or she became a star as exactly as the British actor Daniel Craig can. On October 14, 2005, after months of speculation over who would next portray the suave, high-living master spy James Bond, Craig showed up at a press conference held on the banks of the River Thames. The manner of his arrival—he sped up on a military boat, wearing a dark, tailored suit and dark glass-

es—made his announcement clear to the press before he even alighted. By the time Craig's feet were on solid ground, all present knew they were looking at the man who would be the sixth Agent 007. Debonair, self-possessed, used to playing emotionally complex characters, Craig seemed fully prepared to play the main character in arguably the most successful film franchise of all time. With his blond hair, lesser height, and—as he admits—craggy features, Craig is a physical departure from past Bonds, played by Sean Connery, George Lazenby, Roger Moore, Timothy Dalton, and, most recently, Pierce Brosnan; but Craig's Bond was not meant to be like those of the past—he was to be a tortured character, more suited to the 21st century and its fraught international climate. Craig's attraction to elusive and not-always-likable characters made him an appropriate choice to personify the new Bond. "On screen, [Craig] exerts a supreme amount of control, releasing emotions in the most subtle of ways," Gaby Wood wrote for the London *Observer* (April 27, 2003), over two years before the announcement that made Craig a recognizable name. "His face is slightly rugged without being steely—in some lights it looks handsomely sculpted, in others that of a life-worn boxer. His eyes are a lethal blue—when you see them on celluloid they seem too pale and too strange not to carry some meaning. . . . Craig is a commanding, powerful actor. Seen back to back, his film roles show off an extraordinary range, and an exceptional grasp of rawness and complication." Now hailed as one of the best Bonds in the series, Craig initially met with a great deal of skepticism when he first stepped into the role, though those who knew him well insisted that he would make a good 21st-century Bond. "The thing that is really exciting is that he is a proper actor," Clive Owen, who was also rumored to have been considered for the part, told the BBC News (September 19, 2006) of his fellow Brit. "He is not shallow or posing, they have cast a really serious actor and I think when the film comes out everyone will see what a great choice he was." *Casino Royale* (2006), the first film to star Craig as Bond, represented an opportunity for the actor to play the kind of character in which he had come to specialize: a man in the process of understanding his own identity and confronting his "demons." "I just look for characters who are trying to change or are in the process of changing," Craig told Lawrie Masterson for the Queensland, Australia, *Sunday Mail* (August 7, 2005), "who are maybe on the edge."

Daniel Wroughton Craig was born on March 2, 1968 in Chester, England. His father, Timothy James Craig, held various positions as a merchant seaman, steel erector, and landlord of Ring O'Bells, a pub in Frodsham, Cheshire. His mother, Carol Olivia Williams, was an art teacher. The couple, who also had a daughter, Lea, divorced when Craig was four, and he moved with his mother and sister to Liverpool. There, Craig's mother spent considerable time at the city's famously left-wing Everyman

Theatre, which served as a base for her artsy, politically active social circle. Growing up in that environment contributed to Craig's decision, made when he was six, to be an actor. At Hilbre High School Craig played rugby and also starred in many of the school's theatrical productions, including *Oliver*, *Romeo and Juliet*, and *Cinderella*. Never a stellar student, he had by age 16 fallen behind in the rigid British school system and had decided to drop out. His mother encouraged his acting ambition, applying to the National Youth Theatre (NYT) on his behalf and sending him to its auditions, in Manchester, in 1984. After succeeding there, Craig moved to London to perform with the NYT. He recalled to Jasper Rees for the London *Times* (January 17, 2004), "I was always going to move to London. I always wanted to be an actor. I had the arrogance to believe I couldn't be anything else." In London he worked in restaurants as a cook and a waiter to make ends meet—sometimes barely. "When you first come here you have to survive," he told Rees. "You tend to end up being selfish. You have to live off people's floors and rent property and you end up doing runners"—that is, he left dwellings while still owing rent money. Craig has recalled that his youth was, in some ways, a distinct advantage in coping with life in London. "When you're 16, bravery doesn't come into it," he explained to Lottie Moggach for the *Times* (September 18, 1999). "You do what you do. You either come here and fall flat on your face, or you survive and become successful." While with the NYT Craig made his stage debut, as Agamemnon in Shakespeare's *Troilus and Cressida*; he also toured with the company in Spain and Russia. In 1988, after repeated rejections, Craig was accepted at the prestigious Guildhall School of Music and Drama, from which he graduated in 1991. (He studied alongside a young Ewan McGregor.)

While still in school, Craig had been cast as a bullying South African neo-Nazi in the high-budget film *The Power of One* (1992). Next, he played a German officer in *The Adventures of Young Indiana Jones: Daredevils of the Desert*, which went straight to video. A small part in the television show *Boon* in 1992 was followed by a role in the play *No Remission*, with the Midnight Theatre Company, in which Craig played a vicious paratrooper. Despite strong reviews that noted Craig's ability to convey latent fury—Georgina Brown, reviewing *No Remission* for the London *Independent* (July 24, 1992), wrote that the actor "contains his violence like an unexploded mine"—Craig was becoming frustrated with what he saw as the limited parts available to young British male actors at the time. He later told Moggach, "I was getting all these parts of terribly posh boys and I'm not posh. It was a great lesson, because I can't play posh. Posh is breeding. I'm not interested in that kind of stuff. It's lovely, and it may have relevance somewhere but it has no relevance to me whatsoever. . . . Films should be about everybody." In 1992 he took a role in the television series *Covington*

Cross, a medieval family drama, which aired for only a short time. The next year saw parts in several British television series: the news satire *Drop the Dead Donkey;* the police drama *Between the Lines*; and the comedy *Heartbeat*. Craig also starred in a staging of Tony Kushner's *Angels in America* at the Royal National Theatre and in the television movies *Sharpe's Eagle* and *Genghis Cohn*. In 1994 he was seen onstage in *The Rover*, a production of a play by the 17th-century dramatist Aphra Behn, mounted by the Women's Playhouse Trust, and in 1995 he made perhaps his most prominent appearance up to that point, as the love interest of the character played by a then-unknown Kate Winslet, in the film *A Kid in King Arthur's Court*.

Craig got a bigger break the following year, with a role that suited his preference for gritty, streetwise characters. Playing Geordie Peacock—a man who sold drugs to corrupt police officers, committed arson, was sentenced to life in prison, and then escaped—in the popular, nine-part BBC2 television series *Our Friends in the North*, Craig became a minor heartthrob in England. By the time he appeared as a highwayman in the 1996 made-for-TV film *The Fortunes and Misfortunes of Moll Flanders*, Craig had become a legitimate star in his native country. That year he also appeared in *Saint-Ex*, a BBC film about the French author Antoine de Saint-Exupery. In 1997 he appeared in the little-watched television movie *The Ice House* and in the British film *Obsession*, on the set of which he met the German actress Heike Makatsch, whom he dated for seven years.

In the 1990s Craig appeared only infrequently in films that gained wide notice in the U.S. In 1998 he had a small role in *Elizabeth* and also starred in the considerably less-noticed Irish film *Love and Rage*, as the real-life James Lynchehaun, a would-be murderer, on whom J. M. Synge based his play *The Playboy of the Western World*. Craig also took on a risky role in the film *Love Is the Devil*, about the British writer Francis Bacon; Craig played Bacon's lover in a story complete with violent, graphic love scenes. In 1999 Craig starred in William Boyd's World War I saga *The Trench*. "His screen presence is, quite simply, breathtaking," Moggach wrote. Boyd told Wood that he was impressed by Craig's ability not only to portray aggression but to harness and modulate it. He added that Craig has "an amazing ability to express emotion of the most poignant kind as well as the most vehement kind. Not all leading men have that—they can do the tough stuff, but they can't always do both." Still not particularly well-known in Hollywood, Craig told Moggach that he was nonetheless happy with his career, portraying the kind of emotionally conflicted, and often disturbed, characters to which he was so drawn. "The most important thing for me is that I'm really enjoying my work at the moment," he said. "I'm having a good time, and I want to maintain this feeling for as long as possible."

In 2000 Craig starred opposite Kim Basinger as a land manager in 1970s Kenya in *I Dreamed of Africa*, which garnered little notice in the U.S. The same year he was seen in a role more characteristic of his past work, as a schizophrenic in the independent film *Some Voices*, whose script required him to run naked down a busy London street. In 2001, after an acclaimed turn as Guy Crouchback in an adaptation of the novelist Evelyn Waugh's *Sword of Honour* trilogy, Craig made a mark in Hollywood—the place he had been so ambivalent about—with exactly the kind of role he usually avoided, that of the title character's love interest in the big-budget film *Lara Croft: Tomb Raider,* starring Angelina Jolie. He explained to James Mottram for the London *Sunday Express* (July 1, 2001) that while the part was not ideal for him, it would allow him greater latitude as an actor in the future. "I'd hate to think I was nailing my colors to the mast with something I didn't believe in," he said. "I had to do it because it is an experience. I'd never done something on this scale before. It will be nice to think that if I do this film, I'll have more of a choice as to what I do here." Ironically, Sam Mendes, the director of Craig's next major film, *Road to Perdition* (2002), cast Craig not because of the actor's exposure from *Lara Croft* but on the strength of his performance in *Sword of Honour*. *Road to Perdition* was highly acclaimed, and Craig, as the deranged, vengeful son of the gangster played by Paul Newman, began to receive wider critical notice. Also in 2002 Craig returned to the London stage in two plays: Michael Frayn's Pulitzer Prize–winning *Copenhagen* and Caryl Churchill's *A Number,* which addressed the controversial issue of human cloning. Michael Gambon, Craig's co-star in *A Number*, told Matthew Sweet for the London *Independent on Sunday* (September 22, 2002), "I've never worked with a young actor so smoothly. He's so intelligent and sharp and clever. And I'm not just saying that, he's just perfect. He can do anything."

The truth of that statement was tested to a degree the next year, with Craig's decision to portray one of the most controversial figures in contemporary English literature, the poet Ted Hughes. Opposite Gwyneth Paltrow as Hughes's wife and fellow poet, Sylvia Plath, in *Sylvia*, Craig came under fire from fans of Plath, who still accuse Hughes of being responsible for Plath's suicide and opposed any effort to represent Hughes in anything but a negative light. Craig strove to portray Hughes as a man who was deeply conflicted about commitment but nonetheless passionately in love with his wife. Although the movie got a lukewarm reception, Craig got rave reviews for his success in conveying his character's stony façade as well as the sensitivity underneath. Also in 2003, again making a risky choice, he starred in *The Mother*, as a carpenter who beds both his client and her mother, who is 30 years his senior.

In 2004 Craig received more attention for his personal life than for his professional achievements. He starred in the gangster film *Layer Cake* as the unnamed narrator; his much-lauded performance ("Daniel Craig really owns the film," Liz Braun wrote for the June 10, 2005 edition of the *Toronto Sun*) was overshadowed in the press by his successive romantic relationships with his co-star, Sienna Miller; the British supermodel Kate Moss; and the film producer Satsuki Mitchell, his current girlfriend. In 2005, with his personal life apparently sorted out, Craig starred in *The Jacket*, with Adrien Brody; the little-noticed television thriller *Archangel;* and Steven Spielberg's high-profile film *Munich,* for which he underwent an unusually easy audition process. "I had a meeting with Steven Spielberg that was 10 minutes long," Craig told Masterson. "He offered me the job. I walked out and went and had a drink."

Craig joked that he also indulged in a drink—James Bond's favorite: a martini—when he found out he had been chosen to play the spy in *Casino Royale*, a new film version of Ian Fleming's same-titled first Bond novel, published in 1953. "I had never even *considered* [the role]," he told David Katz for *Esquire* (September 1, 2006). "Well, of course, as a child I considered it. But once I started acting, it was never an agenda." Few diehard fans of the Bond series had predicted that a blond actor would follow in the footsteps of the prototypical—and, in the opinion of many, definitive—screen Bond, Sean Connery. Immediately after the announcement, Bond devotees created vitriolic anti-Craig Web sites, such as one called Daniel Craig Is Not Bond, railing against the actor's perceived physical shortcomings. "It was a big risk . . . ," *Casino Royale*'s director, Martin Campbell, told Nick Curtis for the London *Evening Standard* (November 15, 2006) of casting Craig. "And with a new Bond, you never know if it's going to work. Even if you've got the best actor in the world, you don't know until the last minute if he will connect with the public as Bond." While the announcement of a new Bond has always been met with some skepticism among fans, the attacks against Craig were especially personal. "I knew there would be criticism because he is not your stereotypical, pretty-boy Bond," Campbell told Curtis. "He's sexy but he's not poster pinup goodlooking." Despite the public's reaction, the choice of Craig had the overwhelming support of the actor's co-stars and predecessors—even Connery, who told Richard Price for the London *Daily Mail* (November 15, 2006), "He's a great choice, really interesting—different." "You lose your sense of humor very rapidly . . . ," Craig told Katz about the period when the criticism started being posted on the Internet. "I had a very dark two or three days. I was very despondent. But . . . I vowed to work twice as hard and get it right. Get it *beyond* right."

Critics and fans unanimously agreed that Craig had achieved that goal, breathing new life into the Bond series as a younger, more conflicted secret agent who has just earned his "double-0" status (meaning that he is, in a phrase well-known among Bond fans, "licensed to kill"). In the *Atlanta Journal-Constitution* (November 16, 2006), Eleanor Ringel Gillespie wrote, "Craig is definitely the Real Thing—dangerous, seductive, with a wired intensity that, along with his irradiated blue eyes, calls to mind Connery's sex-symbol contemporary, Steve McQueen." Price noted that Craig's idiosyncrasies had turned out to be great advantages in reviving the image of Bond. "With his impeccable pedigree as a serious actor he has immediately made the role his own, introducing an edgier appeal which harks back to the original Bond novels." Noting Craig's muscular build, Katz wrote, "Connery may have been vaguely menacing, but Daniel Craig looks like he could actually hurt you." While *Casino Royale* represented a departure in some ways from past Bond films—with fewer gadgets, the absence of the recurring characters Moneypenny and Q, and more intense violence—Craig said that he was well aware of the tenets of success for the character and the film. "I'm a Bond fan," Craig told Jo Walker for the Liverpool, England, *Daily Post* (November 11, 2006). "If I go and see a Bond movie there are certain things I think should be in it. And they're there. We've got them in spades. Nobody knows more than I do how important this is, and it's my job to get it right." *Casino Royale*, the 21st movie in the series, went on to become the highest-earning Bond film of all time, bringing in $454 million by late December and surpassing the record of $431 million set by *Die Another Day* (2002). Craig is currently filming the next Bond movie, which is scheduled for release in 2008 and has the working title "Bond 22."

In 2006 Craig also starred in *Infamous*, about the writer Truman Capote, as one of the murderers Capote profiled in his nonfiction classic *In Cold Blood*. In 2007 Craig starred opposite Nicole Kidman in *Invasion*, a remake of *Invasion of the Body Snatchers*. He also appeared, again opposite Kidman, in *The Golden Compass*, the first in an intended trilogy based on Philip Pullman's best-selling fantasy series His Dark Materials. In addition to the next Bond film, Craig was cast in at least three motion pictures scheduled for release in 2008, including *Flashbacks of a Fool*, *Defiance*, and *I Lucifer*.

In 2007 Craig was invited to join the Academy of Motion Picture Arts and Sciences, an honor given to those who have "distinguished themselves by their contributions to theatrical motion pictures," according to an academy press release. Craig has one daughter, Ella, from his 1992 marriage to the Scottish actress Fiona Loudon; the couple divorced in 1994. He is the chairman of the honorary board of directors of STOP (Stop Trafficking of People), an organization devoted to combating the sexual and economic exploitation of women and children.

—C.S.

Suggested Reading: *Atlanta Journal-Constitution* E p1 Nov. 16, 2006; *Esquire* p200 Sep. 1, 2006; (London) *Observer* p16 Apr. 27, 2003; (London) *Times Magazine* p21 Jan. 17, 2004

Selected Films: *Our Friends in the North*, 1996; *The Fortunes and Misfortunes of Moll Flanders*, 1996; *Love and Rage*, 1998; *Love Is the Devil*, 1998; *The Trench*, 1999; *Lara Croft: Tomb Raider*, 2001; *Sword of Honour*, 2001; *Road to Perdition*, 2002; *Sylvia*, 2003; *Layer Cake*, 2004; *Infamous*, 2006; *Casino Royale*, 2006

Win McNamee/Getty Images

Crocker, Ryan

June 19, 1949– U.S. ambassador to Iraq

Address: Embassy of the U.S., APO AE 09316, Baghdad, Iraq

As demonstrated by his successive posts as U.S. ambassador to Lebanon, Kuwait, Syria, and Pakistan, Ryan Crocker is "a man who doesn't mind the hot spots," as Greg Palkot put it for the Fox News Network (March 28, 2007). "In fact, his resume reads like a timeline of terrorism and conflict during the last four decades." In March 2007 Crocker took on what is widely considered to be his most difficult assignment yet, when he became the U.S. ambassador to Iraq. U.S. secretary of state Condoleezza Rice told reporters at a press conference on January 8, 2007, on the occasion of Crocker's nomination to the post, "Few diplomats have the kind of experience in the broader Middle East that Ryan has amassed in his three decades of service. . . . Ryan Crocker is known and respected throughout our government, throughout the Middle East, and throughout the world. He knows the language and culture of the region, as well as the leaders and the societies that they lead. . . . Ryan will be a demanding boss in our embassy, you can be sure of that, but a fair and inspiring one." Crocker has worked with the heads of the Iraqi government and U.S. military officials in an attempt to bring stability to Iraq, which has been riven by sectarian violence since the American occupation that began in 2003. A former colleague of Crocker's, speaking with Scott Shane for the *New York Times* (January 6, 2007), called the ambassador "incredibly hard-working, very serious, a little introverted. I'd say he's more respected than loved in the State Department, but he certainly is respected. He's done the dirtiest, hardest assignments you can imagine."

Ryan Clark Crocker was born on June 19, 1949 in Spokane, Washington. Because his father was an officer in the U.S. Air Force, he lived in several countries as a child, attending schools in Morocco, Canada, and Turkey as well as the United States. He studied at University College Dublin, in Ireland, and Whitman College, in Walla Walla, Washington, obtaining a B.A. degree in English literature from the latter school in 1971. Intent on a career in the Foreign Service, he entered Persian-language training through the State Department, in 1972, and was assigned to work at the American Consulate in Khorramshahr, Iran, later that year. In 1974 he was assigned to the American Embassy in Doha, Qatar, as an economic-commercial officer. In 1976 he returned to Washington, D.C., to begin Arabic-language training, completing a 20-month program at the Foreign Service Institute's Arabic School in Tunis, Tunisia, in June 1978. At one point during Crocker's training, he spent two weeks with a Bedouin desert tribe in Jordan, practicing Arabic and helping to herd sheep.

In 1978 Crocker was assigned to be chief of the economic-commercial section at the American Embassy in Baghdad, Iraq. At the time Saddam Hussein was on the verge of taking over that country's presidency and beginning the 24-year authoritarian rule that has often been called a reign of terror. During his swearing-in ceremony as the United States ambassador to Iraq, on March 29, 2007, Crocker recalled his earlier days in Baghdad, saying, "There was no security. Iraqis everywhere lived in terror of the midnight knock on the door. Neighbors were afraid to talk to neighbors. It truly was the republic of fear." Beginning in 1981 Crocker served in the political section at the U.S. Embassy in Beirut, Lebanon. He told Greg Palkot, "Lebanon in the early '80s was just awful." Lebanon underwent a civil war from 1975 to 1990, during which neighboring countries aided the various factions seeking to win control of the nation. In June 1982 the Israeli Defense Forces (IDF) invaded northern Lebanon; the following August another of the armed groups fighting in Lebanon's civil war,

the anti-Israel Palestine Liberation Organization (PLO), agreed to leave Lebanon, and Israel agreed not to move its troops further south into Beirut. Later that summer the Lebanese president-elect, Bachir Gemayel, an ally of Israel, was assassinated. In September the IDF advanced into West Beirut and sent members of a pro-Gemayel Christian militia group, the Lebanese Forces, into the Sabra and Shatila refugee camps, near Beirut, which housed Palestinians who had been displaced from their homes during various Israeli military actions. According to Israeli officials, the militia was instructed to capture any PLO fighters remaining in the camps. Instead, over a three-day period, the militia tortured, raped, and killed hundreds of men, women, and children in what came to be known as the Sabra and Shatila Massacre. Images of the massacre were broadcast all over the world, sparking international outrage.

The Sabra and Shatila killings presented a diplomatic challenge for the United States, which had strong military, economic, and cultural ties to Israel. Beth Jones, who served as Crocker's contact at the State Department at the time, told Renee Montagne for the National Public Radio (NPR) program *Morning Edition* (February 7, 2007) that Crocker "was one of the first on the scene, and there was no cell phone, there was no Blackberry, there was no anything. So there were plenty of periods of time where we didn't know where he was or whether he was safe. And mind you, this was a horrific set of scenes that he was looking at. He went through all of it for me on the phone, but at the same time was working with the rescue workers and others, and the survivors, to try to help them sort out who was still alive, who needed urgent medical care and what else needed to be done."

In the aftermath of the massacre, the U.S. sent troops to Lebanon to quell uprisings from anti-Israeli groups in the country. The U.S. backed the parliamentary election in which Bachir Gemayel's brother, Amine Gemayel, was elected president. On April 18, 1983 a suicide bomber drove a van into the United States embassy, causing an explosion that killed 63 people. Jones told Renee Montagne that Crocker "was blown across his office. I was in touch with him pretty quickly after that and then out of touch with him because he was down on the rubble, pulling people out . . . and trying to help us identify who had been hurt and who hadn't made it through." Anti-U.S. attacks continued in Lebanon throughout the early 1980s. Crocker left the country in 1984.

Crocker spent the 1984–85 academic year at Princeton University, in Princeton, New Jersey, pursuing coursework in Near Eastern studies. From 1985 to 1987 he served as the deputy director of the Office of Israel and Arab-Israeli Affairs at the State Department, in Washington, D.C. From 1987 to 1990 he worked as a political counselor at the American Embassy in Cairo, Egypt. In 1990 he returned to Beirut to serve as the U.S. ambassador to Lebanon. Augustus Richard Norton, the author of

Hezbollah: A Short History and other books, told Barbara Slavin for *USA Today* (September 9, 2007), "While most officials in the U.S. Embassy were clueless about developments in the Shiite community [in Lebanon], Ryan proved to be a different story. He immediately grasped that something important was going on and as a result pursued his own contacts in southern Lebanon." Scott Shane reported that at that time Crocker, a marathon runner, ran "several miles early every morning, even in . . . Beirut, where he was trailed by burly security guards who sometimes had to hop on bicycles to keep up."

Following the Iraqi invasion of neighboring Kuwait, in August 1990, Crocker also became the director of the Iraq-Kuwait Task Force, which advised the State Department during the Persian Gulf War of 1991—in which the U.S. and its allies drove Iraqi forces from Kuwait. In 1993 he stepped down from his post as ambassador to Lebanon, and in the following year he received the Presidential Distinguished Service Award from President Bill Clinton. From 1994 to 1997 Crocker served as the U.S. ambassador to Kuwait. In 1997 he received the Department of Defense Medal for Distinguished Civilian Service.

Crocker became the U.S. ambassador to Syria in 1998. After President Clinton nominated him for that post, Crocker testified before the Senate Committee on Foreign Relations (May 7, 1998), stating, "As you know, our relationship with Syria is complex and touches on our core foreign policy interests in the region. The United States has serious policy differences with Damascus [Syria's capital] over Syria's continued support for terrorist groups [including Hezbollah] and its human rights record. You have my firm commitment to continue the fight against terrorism and to press the Syrian government to improve its human rights treatment of the Syrian people." Crocker's tenure in Syria included an incident in which an armed Syrian gang breached embassy security and ransacked the ambassador's residence. U.S. senator Charles Hagel, Republican of Nebraska, told the Senate Foreign Relations Committee (September 29, 2004), as quoted by the Federal News Service, "I recall arriving in Syria one afternoon when Ambassador Crocker was there. It was the day after the United States embassy in Damascus had essentially been sacked. And in a very low-key way, as we went into the ambassador's residence, I asked how his family was, and he said, well, it had been a bit harrowing for his wife, who had locked herself in a room on the second floor of the ambassador's residence as this group of thugs was . . . stealing what they could from the house, and shooting up the house. A rather hectic time in the life of an ambassador and his family. But Ambassador Crocker . . . did not blink. He stayed with the schedule we had." Ultimately, Crocker and his team were not able to end Syria's financing of Hezbollah, which continued to operate in southern Lebanon and beyond. In 1999 Crocker was given the Presidential Meritori-

ous Service Award by President Clinton. He ended his ambassadorship to Syria in 2001.

In May of that year, Crocker received an honorary doctor of laws degree from his alma mater, Whitman College. In August he became deputy assistant secretary of state for Near Eastern affairs, a post that enabled him to live in the United States, though he was still required to travel frequently. (According to Shane, Crocker "prefers working overseas.")

After the September 11, 2001 terrorist attacks on the United States, Crocker's Middle East expertise and language skills were in high demand. In January 2002 President George W. Bush appointed Crocker to be the interim envoy to the new government of Afghanistan, which was formed after the United States military invasion captured, assassinated, or drove into hiding members of the Islamic fundamentalist Taliban government. While the United States was able, with Crocker's help, to facilitate the transition to a nominally democratic government, the Taliban retained power in many parts of the country, particularly along the rural Pakistan-Afghanistan border. Crocker received the Robert C. Frasure Memorial Award from the U.S. State Department for "exceptional courage and leadership" in Afghanistan. (The award was named for a U.S. diplomat who died in an automobile accident while on a peacekeeping mission in Bosnia in 1995.)

Near the end of 2002, Crocker sent a memo to then–Deputy Secretary of State Richard Armitage and then–Secretary of State Colin L. Powell. At the time the Bush administration was preparing to go to war in Iraq, for the stated purpose of ridding that country of so-called weapons of mass destruction, which were not subsequently found there. Armitage told Montagne that Crocker's memo pointed out "the tremendous difficulties that would ensue after an invasion of Iraq. The decision to invade is one thing, but the management of the post-invasion process is fraught with some difficulties that are rooted in history. Lack of a homogeneous population, the sectarian strains, the tribal nature of the society—all led to a very difficult equation. . . . From my point of view [the memo] was dead on the money." Montagne, speaking in early 2007, noted that the memo had "become a touchstone . . . about pre-war planning."

In May 2003 Crocker left his position in Afghanistan to become the first director of governance for the Coalition Provisional Authority in Iraq, a post in which he oversaw political reconstruction in the country following the U.S. invasion. Many observers in the Iraqi and international press opined that Crocker made a mistake in helping to create Iraq's first government council with certain numbers of seats reserved for members of various ethnic or religious affiliations; indeed, some later blamed that decision for the increased sectarian tension and violence in Iraq. Crocker reportedly had a tense relationship with then-ambassador to Iraq L. Paul Bremer, as they disagreed on the direction that political reconstruction should take. Crocker told the Iraqi journalist Aziz Al-Haff for Al-Iraqiya Television (April 19, 2007), "Clearly after the fall of Saddam we all faced a very complex situation in Iraq. And it was one without a roadmap. We had to deal with the reality as we and the Iraqis found it. And the reality is . . . that there were a number of parties that defined themselves in Islamic terms. And they were represented on that initial governing council. . . . We—the United States and the Coalition—did not create these parties. We recognized their existence. We recognized their weight on the political stage, and we worked together to try to build a governing mechanism that would advance the cause of Iraq." In August 2003 Crocker left his position in Iraq and returned to the United States, where he became the international-affairs adviser at the National War College, part of the National Defense University. Many senior military and government officials study at the National War College in order to prepare for more advanced positions. Also in 2003 Crocker received the Presidential Meritorious Service Award again, this time from President Bush.

In September 2004 Bush awarded Crocker the rank of career ambassador, the highest level attainable in the Foreign Service. The Bush administration then nominated Crocker to be the next U.S. ambassador to Pakistan. On September 29, 2004 Crocker told the Senate Foreign Relations Committee, "If confirmed, I will place particular emphasis on our education programs, where we are working with the Pakistani government to improve the quality and affordability of Pakistan's public schools so that parents of limited means have an alternative to narrow, religiously oriented education." He added that while he had more experience in the Middle East than in South Asia, he had "extensive experience with the issues that shape that area [South Asia] as well: the problem of global terrorism, the problem of Islamic extremism, the problem of underdevelopment, the problem of bad governance, the problem of regional conflict. These are all issues that I wrestled with in the Middle East dimension my entire career." Crocker was confirmed as the ambassador to Pakistan and served there from 2004 to 2007.

In January of the latter year, Secretary of State Condoleezza Rice announced President Bush's decision to nominate Crocker to be the new ambassador to Iraq, replacing Zalmay Khalilzad, who had been appointed in April 2005. Armitage told Montagne about Crocker, "He's the best field man, I think, that we've got in the Foreign Service . . . someone who is always reveling in the dirty, hard and dangerous jobs." The Senate confirmed Bush's choice on March 7, and Crocker left his post in Pakistan to prepare for his job in Iraq. On March 29 he officially took over ambassadorial duties at a swearing-in ceremony in Baghdad. While such ceremonies generally take place in Washington, D.C., Crocker requested that his be held in the country where he would serve; he told those assembled on

that occasion, as quoted on the Web site of the U.S. Embassy in Iraq, "It was very important to me to have this ceremony here, not just in the interest of time, but because here in Iraq America faces its most critical foreign policy challenge. . . . The Iraqi people themselves face a historic test—one rooted in a shared view of common humanity as the grounds on which to base sometimes very difficult compromises. Turning the tide from oppression to freedom does not come overnight. It does not come without high costs. . . . We must stand by . . . all Iraqis who seek a better future and remain committed to their success." In Baghdad Crocker has worked closely with Iraqi president Jalal Talabani, Prime Minister Nuri Kamal Al-Maliki, and the top U.S. military commander in Iraq, General David H. Petraeus. Crocker told Renee Montagne for Morning Edition (June 6, 2007), "If my day starts with the alarm going off, rather than an overnight phone call, nothing really, really bad has happened overnight. My first thought every morning is, did we have casualties?"

The situation in Iraq is complicated by numerous factors. Though the arrest and execution of Saddam Hussein ended a nearly quarter-century-long, murderous dictatorship, they did not eliminate the deep-seated sectarian tensions dividing various ethnic and religious factions in Iraq. The majority of Iraqis are Muslim, but they are not united. Members of the largest sect, the Shi'ites, follow a theological tradition different from that of the members of the second-largest group, the Sunnis. There exist both interdenominational and intradenominational fighting, the latter often based upon ethnic tribal allegiances. In January 2007 President Bush announced a plan for a "surge," or increase, in the number of American troops sent to Iraq, in an effort to quell the extensive violence; 30,000 more troops and support personnel were committed to active service. According to NPR.org, U.S. troop fatalities from March 2003 through August 2007 numbered 3,740. The number of Iraqi civilian casualties, while disputed, was far greater.

Since he assumed the top U.S. diplomatic post in Iraq, Crocker has often, in press conferences and speeches, stressed the need for patience with regard to conditions there. He has often used the terms "Washington clock" and "Baghdad clock" to refer to the desire of the American public and U.S. government officials for quick action—a desire that is at odds, he feels, with the reality of slow progress on the ground in Iraq. At a press roundtable in Baghdad on May 18, 2007, Crocker told journalists, "I think we are seeing some progress, as it were, at the strategic level, but there's a tremendous amount of damage out there that's got to be repaired. I mean, the sectarian violence over the last year has been hugely corrosive. And you just don't wave a wand over it and make that go away in a day, a week or a month." He told Renee Montagne for Morning Edition (June 6, 2007), "Sometimes I think that in the U.S. we're looking at Iraq right now as though it were the last half of a three-reel movie. For Iraqis, it's a five-reel movie and they are still in the first half of it. I don't see an end game, as it were, in sight. . . . You know, if we were to scale back our engagement here in a major way before there has been a major change in circumstances on the ground, what are the consequences? My experience—three-and-a-half decades in this part of the world—suggests to me that things could get very much worse." On September 10, 2007 Ambassador Crocker appeared with General Petraeus before a joint session of the U.S. House Committee on Foreign Affairs and the House Armed Services Committee; in that eagerly anticipated session, Petraeus described what he called slow progress in Iraq and said that the U.S. should be able to return to its "pre-surge" troop level of about 130,000 soldiers in that country. Crocker, for his part, again sought to discourage a quick withdrawal of all U.S. troops from Iraq.

Crocker is married to Christine Barnes, whom he met in 1979, when she was a secretary for the Foreign Service.

—S.J.D.

Suggested Reading: (London) *Daily Mail* p4 May 29, 2007; *New York Times* (on-line) Jan. 6, 2007; *Newsweek* p46+ June 18 2007; NPR *Morning Edition* (on-line) June 5, 2007; Web site of the U.S. Embassy in Iraq

---

Getty Images

Culpepper, Daunte

(DAN-tay)

Jan. 28, 1977– Football player

Address: Oakland Raiders, Network Associates Coliseum, 7000 Coliseum Way, Oakland, CA 94621

In the 2007 season of the National Football League (NFL), the quarterback Daunte Culpepper has been attempting a professional comeback, a return to the spectacular play that preceded a series of career-derailing injuries. With his speed, agility, strong throwing arm, and pinpoint accuracy, Culpepper was touted at the outset of his career as one of the most talented quarterbacks in football, despite a six-foot four-inch, 260-pound frame not traditionally associated with his position. Over the course of his four years at the University of Central Florida (UCF), Culpepper threw for 84 touchdowns and more than 11,000 yards, shattering a 15-year National Collegiate Athletic Association (NCAA) record for completion percentage in a single season and becoming one of only three players in NCAA history to reach 10,000 passing yards and 1,000 rushing yards. Drafted in 1999 by the Minnesota Vikings, Culpepper went on to set single-season team records in touchdowns and rushing yards and to appear in three Pro Bowls. Following the 2005 season—the second of his professional career to be cut short by injury—he was traded to the Miami Dolphins, spending only one, incomplete year with that team before undergoing knee surgery. Released from the team in June 2007, Culpepper signed a contract two months later with the Oakland Raiders.

Daunte Richard Culpepper was born on January 28, 1977 in Ocala, a town in north-central Florida, 30 miles south of Gainesville. The identity of his father has not been publicly divulged. At the time of Culpepper's birth, his mother, Barbara Henderson, was a resident of the McPherson School for Girls, a state-run juvenile-reform institution, and was headed to prison. Determined to prevent the state from placing her son with a family she did not know, Henderson asked Emma Culpepper, a McPherson School house parent, to adopt the boy. Emma Culpepper had raised 14 children (none of them her biological offspring), including her late brother's four children and the sons and daughters of other McPherson School girls. Emma Culpepper, who was 62 years old then, "said no to Barbara. Two or three times," as she recalled to Marcus Hayes for the *Philadelphia Daily News* (February 2, 1999). "I know it was the Lord who told me to take him, because I was sick of kids. Sick of 'em." As quoted on *Culpepper Connections!* The Culpepper Family History Site (on-line), she said, "I'm so glad I said yes. . . . He was a blessing from God." Daunte had been living with Emma Culpepper for about five years when Henderson, who had been released from prison, came to take him home with her. Daunte Culpepper told Michael McLeod for the *Orlando Sentinel* (October 18, 1998), "All I remember is: I didn't like it. My biological mama tried everything to calm me down, but I just wouldn't stop screaming and carrying on. Finally, [Emma] came back for me. I was never so happy as I was when I saw her." Daunte, who regularly visits Henderson (the mother of several other children), continued to live with Emma. "I'm just glad that [Henderson] had enough in her heart to give me up," he said for the *Culpepper Connections!* site. "Actually, she gave me up twice. . . . I knew she was my mom, but I didn't want to live with anybody but Emma." Culpepper grew up with three older boys, whom he considered his brothers. "We slept in bunk beds in the same room every night," he told Bruce Lowitt for the *St. Petersburg (Florida) Times* (September 30, 1998). "We were pretty happy all the time, fighting and arguing. That's what boys do. I was always bigger than anyone my age, so I didn't get picked on much at school. But I was the baby at home. I got it all the time. I think my competitive nature came from living with those guys." As a child Culpepper demonstrated musical talent at an early age; he learned to play the cello, violin, and bass violin while attending elementary school and became so proficient that he was invited to play with a community-college orchestra.

Culpepper abandoned his music lessons when he became involved in football, during middle school. At 12 he started as a wide receiver in the Marion County Junior Football League; one day during practice, after retrieving a ball that had been thrown too far down the field, he threw it to the coach, who was so impressed with Culpepper's strong arm that he moved the young athlete to the quarterback position. At Vanguard High School, in Ocala, Culpepper lettered in baseball and basketball in addition to football. He was not as accomplished in the classroom. "My freshman and sophomore years, I didn't do anything," he told Rana L. Cash for the *Miami Herald* (January 27, 1995). "I was lazy. It wasn't that I couldn't do it, I just didn't apply myself." At the end of Culpepper's junior year, his cumulative 1.5 grade-point average (GPA) was below the 2.0 average required by the NCAA to qualify for an athletic scholarship. Amid waning interest from Division I schools that had sought to recruit him, including Florida State University, the University of Miami, and the University of Florida, and media speculation that he would have to attend junior college, Culpepper worked hard to improve his GPA. With the help of Phil Yancey, his high-school coach, and Paul Lounsberry, a former high-school teacher and the offensive-line coach for the Golden Knights football team at the University of Central Florida (UCF), a school that still had interest in recruiting Culpepper, he improved his study habits and his grades. He met the NCAA's academic requirement with a 3.4 average in his final year of high school, which raised his overall GPA

to 2.03, and he earned a qualifying score of 17 on the ACT (American College Test), a standardized college-entrance exam, on his third attempt.

In his senior year of high school, 1994–95, Culpepper led the Vanguard Knights football team to its first undefeated regular-season record and to the Class 5-A state title game, which they lost to Bradenton Southeast, 19–17. His 3,070 passing yards, 602 rushing yards, and 31 touchdown passes garnered Culpepper All-American honors and the title "Mr. Football" from the Florida Athletic Coaches Association. Over his three seasons at Vanguard, Culpepper passed for 6,107 yards, throwing 57 touchdowns and only 29 interceptions while rushing for 927 yards and 26 touchdowns; his eight completed passes for 137 yards propelled Florida to a victory in the annual Florida-Georgia High School All-Star Classic. He posted equally impressive numbers in baseball and basketball that year. Although he was drafted by the New York Yankees in the 26th round of the 1995 Major League Baseball June amateur draft, he turned down that opportunity in order to attend the University of Central Florida on an athletic scholarship, despite renewed interest from several Division I-A schools. He explained to Larry Guest for the *Orlando Sentinel* (August 6, 1995), "UCF stayed with me all the way, so I felt I should stay with them." Another factor in Culpepper's decision was that he was slated to be the cornerstone of UCF's Golden Knights, a team that was preparing to make the leap from the NCAA's Division I-AA to Division I-A, the highest level of competition, in 1996, during Culpepper's sophomore year.

As a UCF freshman, Culpepper faced an immediate challenge, taking over the offense from Darin Hinshaw, whose 9,000 career passing yards and 82 touchdowns made him the most accomplished quarterback in the Knights' history. He reportedly also encountered resistance from UCF fans over Coach Gene McDowell's decision not to start the returning backup quarterback Kevin Reid. Culpepper demonstrated poise in his debut against the ninth-ranked Division I-AA team Eastern Kentucky, leading his team to a 40–32 victory; in that game he was successful in his first 12 pass attempts, ultimately completing 20 of 25 passes for three touchdowns and 254 yards and earning national offensive player-of-the-week honors in the division. In describing his performance, McDowell told Jerry Greene for the *Orlando Sentinel* (November 20, 1998), "Neither 'spectacular' nor 'extraordinary' begin to describe it. My guess is that it was the best first-time performance ever by a freshman quarterback." Culpepper was even more impressive in his second game of the season, against Carson-Newman College, throwing 22 of 30 completions for two touchdowns and 307 yards. Completing 14 of 16 passes in an October 1995 game against Alabama's Samford University, Culpepper set a school record for completion percentage (.875) in a game. Despite the departure of the defensive leaders Travis Cooper and Greg Jefferson (both of whom graduated) and the loss of two starting wide receivers, Todd Cleveland and Rufus Hall (because of academic failure and a knee injury, respectively), Culpepper led the Golden Knights to a 6–5 record, closing out the final game of the 1995 season with a two-touchdown, 184-yard performance in Central Florida's 37–17 victory over Maine. At the end of his freshman season, Culpepper, who had thrown for 2,071 yards and 12 touchdown passes, was ranked 28th in the U.S. in passing efficiency (122.9) and 40th in total offense (189.9). He received the Most Outstanding Offensive Rookie of the Year Award from UCF and was named third-team I-AA All-American and Freshman Offensive Player of the Year.

Culpepper got off to a strong start in 1996, in his sophomore season—and Central Florida's first season at the Division I-A level—leading the Golden Knights to a 39–33 comeback victory in the Florida Citrus Bowl with a 13-play, 79-yard scoring drive in the fourth quarter of their opening game, against William and Mary College. However, he was unable to finish the second game of the season, completing 14 of 23 passes for 159 yards and two touchdowns in a loss against South Carolina's Gamecocks before suffering an ankle sprain in the third quarter, which kept him off the football field for a month. In October 1996, in his return game against the Division I-AA's Samford, his two-touchdown, 162-yard passing performance propelled the Knights to a 38–6 victory—and only their second win of the season. Following a 39–38 loss to Northeastern Louisiana, Culpepper suffered a setback in a game against Georgia Tech when he separated the shoulder of his non-throwing arm in the second quarter and was replaced by Jason Thorpe. (UCF lost, 27–20.) Despite media speculation that Thorpe would take over at the starting-quarterback position, Culpepper led UCF's offense to wins in the remaining three games, against Illinois State (42–15), the University of Alabama at Birmingham (35–13), and Bowling Green (27–19), during which he threw for 1,008 yards and eight touchdowns and completed 60 of 95 passes with only two interceptions. While the Golden Knights finished the 1996 season with a 5–6 record and a passing offense ranked 16th nationally, Culpepper, who was named Offensive MVP by UCF, improved his rankings in the categories of total offense (242.5) and passing efficiency (138.6).

Nineteen-ninety-seven was arguably Culpepper's breakthrough season. Following UCF's losses in the first three games, the Golden Knights, with Culpepper at the helm, rallied to win the next five of their eight remaining games and to match their 1996 record of five wins and six losses. Culpepper's best performance came against Northeast Louisiana, a game in which he recorded 385 passing yards, 95 rushing yards, and five touchdowns while setting a school record with 480 total offensive yards. He also rose to the occasion against established Southern Conference teams in Division I-A. Central Florida's game against the then–sixth-

ranked Nebraska Cornhuskers represented Culpepper's debut on a national stage; he completed 24 of 35 passes for 318 yards and one touchdown, giving the Golden Knights a 17–14 halftime lead before they were outscored, 24–7, in the second half. Against eighth-ranked Auburn University, Culpepper's 19-pass, 210-yard performance—with one touchdown—was good enough to lead the Knights to a 14–14 tie through the first two quarters, after which Auburn scored 27 unanswered second-half points. Culpepper finished fourth in the nation in total offense, with 320 yards per game, and 15th in passing efficiency, with a 146.91 rating; he set 15 new school records, including total passing yards (3,086) and total offensive yards (3,524). In addition to his being named as a finalist for the Davey O'Brien National Quarterback Award and First-Team All-American by the NFL Draft Report, Football News selected him as a semifinalist for Offensive Player of the Year and gave him All-American honorable mention.

Despite his dominating performance during the 1997 season, Culpepper did not declare himself eligible for the 1998 NFL draft, deciding to return to the University of Central Florida for his senior season. "My mom always taught me about loyalty. UCF stood by me. They helped me when I needed it, and now I feel the program's at a point where maybe I can help them," he told Philip Singerman for Sport (September 1998). He adapted well to the new, professional-style offense implemented by the team's new head coach, Mike Kruczek. His stellar performances in the first two games of the season, victories against Louisiana Tech (64–30) and Eastern Illinois (48–0), began talk about him as a possible Heisman Trophy candidate. Culpepper followed a 35–7 loss to Purdue in his national debut on ESPN with five consecutive wins, highlighted by a winning 320-yard performance against Bowling Green (38–31) that made him the school's all-time leading passer and a 438-passing-yard performance against Southwestern Louisiana, which set a school record. His CFU career statistics of 11,412 passing yards and 1,020 rushing yards made him one of three players in the history of the NCAA, along with Steve McNair of Alcorn State University and Doug Nussmeier of the University of Idaho, to reach 10,000 passing yards and 1,000 rushing yards. Culpepper also set a new NCAA mark with his pass-completion percentage (73.6), breaking Steve Young's previous record of 71.3 at Brigham Young University in 1983. Culpepper's numbers for the season in passing yards (3,690) and touchdowns (28) garnered him five first-place votes and a ranking of sixth overall in the balloting for the Heisman Trophy, which was awarded to the running back Ricky Williams.

After graduating from Central Florida with a degree in secondary education, Culpepper—who made himself eligible for the 1999 NFL draft—was projected to be one of a group of five quarterbacks, including Donovan McNabb and Tim Couch, to be selected in the draft's first round. While his speed, arm strength, and exceptional mobility made Culpepper attractive to team officials, his relative lack of experience against the higher-seeded teams in the division was a concern for NFL teams. (Central Florida's schedule included several games against some of the lower-seeded Division I schools.) As a result he ended up the 11th pick overall, getting drafted in April by the Minnesota Vikings. Despite skepticism from Vikings fans, Culpepper was given a five-year, $7 million contract.

In his rookie season with the Vikings, Culpepper served as the third-string quarterback behind Randall Cunningham, who had long been his role model, and the backup quarterback Jeff George. After the Vikings' 1999 season, Cunningham and George were released, and the starting-quarterback reins were turned over to Culpepper, who ended fans' and critics' doubts with victories in the first seven games, helped in part by his scrambling and by the receiving corps of Randy Moss, Cris Carter, and Robert Smith. "The game is changing so much, it's forcing the [quarterback] position to be played by somebody like me," Culpepper had said the previous year to Mike Bruton for the *Philadelphia Inquirer* (April 11, 1999). "Somebody that's big, because the defense is getting faster. The defense is getting bigger and stronger, and you've got to have a quarterback that's getting bigger and stronger along with them." The Vikings finished the 2000 season with an 11–5 record and defeated the New Orleans Saints to advance to the National Football Conference (NFC) Championship Game, in which they lost to the New York Giants, 41–0. Culpepper ranked third in Vikings history in passing yards for the season (3,937), third overall in the NFC in quarterback rating (98.0), and fourth overall in the NFL in the same category. He was also selected to his first Pro Bowl.

Culpepper failed to repeat that success in the 2001 season, hampered by Smith's unexpected retirement, the ineffective play of an aging Cris Carter, and the loss of the offensive tackles Todd Steussie, a free agent, and Korey Stringer, Culpepper's close friend, who had died after suffering heat stroke during training camp. With a dearth of offensive playmakers, Randy Moss became Culpepper's main offensive ally and drew double and even triple coverage from opposing teams. In the first 11 games, Culpepper completed 64.2 percent of his passes, throwing 235 completions for 2,612 yards, 14 touchdowns, and 13 interceptions before undergoing surgery for a sprained ligament in his left knee, which ended his play for the season. He endured the loss of Head Coach Dennis Green after that year, during which the Vikings posted a 5–11 record. Culpepper's problems with overthrows, fumbles, and turnovers continued during his 2002 season with the Vikings, the first under the team's new head coach, Mike Tice. Halfway through the season, Culpepper, with the wide receiver Moss as his sole target, had thrown only eight touchdowns, with 14 interceptions; after 13 games, the Vikings had three wins and 10 losses. In a home game

against the New York Giants, Culpepper was booed by fans and benched in the third quarter in favor of the backup Todd Bouman; the Vikings lost, 27–20. "Driving home that night, I made up my mind. I would never play like that, ever again," Culpepper recalled to Josh Elliott for *Sports Illustrated for Kids* (January 2005). He remained the starter and worked with the offensive coordinator Scott Linehan on improving his footwork, ball handling, and accuracy. In the final three games of the season, Culpepper completed 67 of 94 passes for 868 yards and four touchdowns, and the Vikings finished the season with a 6–10 record. He ended the 2002 season as the second-ranked passer in the NFC, with 3,853 passing yards, and set team records in rushing yards (609), attempts (106), and rushing touchdowns (10); his rushing-yards total qualified as the eighth-highest by a quarterback in NFL history, and his rushing-touchdowns total was the fourth-highest. Despite an up-and-down 2002 season, the Vikings' then-owner, Red McCombs, signed Culpepper in July 2003 to a 10-year, $102 million deal.

Culpepper's throwing accuracy continued to improve in the 2003 season, as the Vikings recorded victories in their first six games. Despite his cutting his number of interceptions by half (from 23 in 2002 to 11 in 2003), the team managed only three victories in the remaining 10 games, finishing the season with a record of 9–7 and failing to make the play-offs. In 2004 the Vikings were among the NFC's favorites to appear in the Super Bowl. Culpepper's 18 touchdowns over a month-long period, including three games in which he threw five touchdowns each, brought the team a 4–1 record and put him on pace to break Dan Marino's record of 48 touchdowns in one season (which has since been surpassed by the Indianapolis Colts' quarterback Peyton Manning, who completed 49 touchdown passes during the 2004 season). The Vikings' defense struggled the rest of the season, and the team won only one of their last five games; they made the play-offs, however, with a record of eight wins and eight losses. In the first round, against the Green Bay Packers, Culpepper made 19 completions for 284 yards and four touchdowns to lead the Vikings to a win, 31–17. The Philadelphia Eagles' defense proved to be a greater challenge for Culpepper, who, despite an injured Moss, managed to keep the Vikings in the game until the fourth quarter before losing 27–14. Culpepper posted league-leading statistics of 4,717 passing yards and 39 touchdowns (a Vikings' record) with only 11 interceptions and a quarterback rating of 110.9, which also earned him his third Pro Bowl appearance. His total offensive yards (5,123), passing and rushing, surpassed Marino's NFL record.

Culpepper's 2005 season got off to a shaky start, following the departures of Linehan and Moss and a season-ending injury suffered by the Pro Bowl center Matt Birk. The quarterback failed to complete a touchdown pass in either of the first two games, which the Vikings lost. He managed a three-touchdown, 300-yard performance in a 33–16 home win against the New Orleans Saints but was plagued by two interceptions and a fumble in Minnesota's 30–10 loss to the Atlanta Falcons. The Vikings' season was further marred by charges of sexual misconduct by team players during a charter-boat cruise on which Culpepper was reported to be a passenger. (In April the case against Culpepper was dismissed. Three of his teammates received fines and were ordered to perform community service.) Culpepper managed only two interceptions in a losing 28–3 effort against the Chicago Bears, then suffered knee-ligament damage in October during the Vikings' loss to the Carolina Panthers—marking the second time in six years that Culpepper's season was cut short by injury. He finished 2005 with only six touchdowns and a quarterback rating of 72.0, while leading the league with 12 interceptions; he underwent surgery the next month and was replaced by Brad Johnson.

Prior to the 2006 season, Culpepper was traded to the Miami Dolphins. His year with that team was marked by disagreements—including heated exchanges—with the head coach, Nick Saban, and by injuries: after winning only one of the four games in which he played, he underwent arthroscopic surgery at the end of November and was placed on the injured-reserve list the following month, ending his season. In June 2007 Culpepper asked to be released from the Dolphins. In August he signed a one-year contract with the Oakland Raiders. "All I want is an opportunity," he said to Jarrett Bell for *USA Today* (August 15, 2007, on-line). "Then the rest is on me. I feel like I'm a starter in this league. When that happens, who knows? But I know I have a lot to contribute."

Culpepper made his Raiders debut in the third week of the 2007–08 season, when he replaced the first-string quarterback Josh McCown to start the second half of a game against the Cleveland Browns. Culpepper completed eight of 14 passes for 118 yards, helping Oakland hang on for a 26–24 win. The following week, on September 30, in a game against the Miami Dolphins, he earned his first start of the season. Culpepper scored five touchdowns, rushing for three and passing for two, as the Raiders posted a 35–17 win. After the game he insisted that he had no hard feelings toward his former team. "The only thing I felt bad about is I didn't have a chance to show the fans here me healthy as a Dolphin," he said, according to the Associated Press (October 1, 2007). "But now I had a chance to show them today, and I'm glad I was able to do that." Culpepper was named AFC offensive player of that week.

Culpepper was less successful in his second start, on October 14, 2007, as the Raiders lost to the San Diego Chargers, 28–14. In the course of the game, he fumbled once, threw two interceptions, and was sacked six times. Despite his spotty play, he was slated to start against the Kansas City Chiefs in the Raiders' next game. Observers speculated that McCown, who was getting ready to return after breaking a toe, might regain his first-string quarter-

back job the following week, in a road game against the Tennessee Titans. "I don't know because Josh isn't healthy," the Raiders coach, Lane Kiffin, told David White for the *San Francisco Chronicle* (October 18, 2007). "He's not all the way back, so Daunte's our starter right now."

Culpepper and his wife, Kimberly Rhem, his high-school sweetheart, have three children.

—B.M.

Suggested Reading: Associated Press Aug. 1, 2007; NFL.com; *Orlando (Florida) Sentinel* p6 Oct.18, 1998; *Sports Illustrated for Kids* p22 Jan. 2005; *St. Petersburg (Florida) Times* C p1 Sep. 30, 1998; Stewart, Mark. *Daunte Culpepper, Command and Control*, 2002; Thornley, Stew. *Super Sports Star Daunte Culpepper*, 2003

Geraldine Dallek, courtesy of HarperCollins Publishers

Dallek, Robert

May 16, 1934– Historian; biographer

Address: c/o Author Mail, Seventh Fl., HarperCollins, 10 E. 53d St., New York, NY 10022

According to the historian and writer Robert Dallek, no biographer can fully understand his or her subject. "I don't think any historian worth his or her salt would dare argue the production of a definitive study of any major historical figure . . . ," he told Jeff Guinn for the *Fort Worth (Texas) Star-Telegram* (May 17, 1998). "There is no definitive history, ever—just better-informed history." Dallek, who has taught at Columbia University, the

University of California at Los Angeles, Boston University, and Dartmouth College, is renowned for his meticulously researched biographies of American presidents—studies that, with few exceptions, his peers view as among the best-informed in that genre and as outstanding for their distinctive readings of people and events. In most of his biographies—notably, an 848-page tome on President John F. Kennedy and a two-volume work on Kennedy's successor in the White House, Lyndon B. Johnson—Dallek has applied his psychoanalytic training to analyze his subjects' characters and motivations. As someone who loves the American presidency as an institution, he has often been praised for his fairness, avoiding both the idolization and the belittlement of his subjects. "Robert Dallek's passion for history, politics and the presidency seems to fuel him—that and his Brooklyn skepticism not only about politicians, but also about half-baked political theory," Patrick Butters wrote for the *Washington Times* (June 9, 1998). "Sometimes," Butters added, "he's so emphatic [when he speaks] that he runs out of breath." Engagingly written and accessible to interested lay readers as well as specialists, Dallek's books have transcended the niche market of biography. "Quality writing can still find a wide audience. So can the kind of quality leadership historians love to write about," he told Guinn. "I'm certain of that."

Robert Dallek was born to Rubin and Esther Dallek on May 16, 1934 in the New York City borough of Brooklyn. He received a B.A. degree in history with high honors from the University of Illinois in 1955. He earned an M.A. degree, in 1957, and a Ph.D, in 1964, both in history, from Columbia University, in New York City. His doctoral dissertation, entitled "Roosevelt's Ambassador: The Public Career of William E. Dodd," was about the historian and biographer who served as President Franklin D. Roosevelt's ambassador to Germany from 1933, when Adolf Hitler became Germany's chancellor, to 1938, the year that nation invaded Austria. While working toward his doctorate, Dallek lectured in history at the City College of New York from 1959 to 1960 and in the same subject at Columbia from 1960 to 1964. Immediately after he completed his formal education, Dallek took a position as an assistant professor of history at the University of California at Los Angeles (UCLA); he later became a full professor there. From 1972 to 1974 he served as vice chairman of the school's History Department. In 1984 he earned UCLA's Henry L. Eby Award for the Art of Teaching.

In 1968 Dallek published his first book, *Democrat and Diplomat: The Life of William E. Dodd*, which grew out of his Ph.D. dissertation. His next, *Franklin D. Roosevelt and American Foreign Policy 1932–1945* (1979), won the Bancroft Prize (awarded by Columbia University) and was nominated for the American Book Award in history. (It was reissued in 1995 with a new afterword by Dallek.) The reviewer for the *Economist* (September 8, 1979) called the book "an able and even exhilarat-

ing vindication of Roosevelt's policy. Its chronological narrative gains in lucidity as events themselves gather momentum. . . . The author provides a balanced defence of Roosevelt's policy at the Yalta conference . . . in which he shows an exceptional talent for advocacy." From 1981 to 1985, concurrently with his work at UCLA, Dallek was a research associate at the Southern California Psychoanalytic Institute, in Beverly Hills.

Dallek's third book, *The American Style of Foreign Policy: Cultural Politics and Foreign Affairs* (1983), was his first to receive widespread notice. In examining U.S. foreign policy from the last years of the 1800s through the presidency of Richard Nixon, Dallek argued that the international dealings of the U.S. served primarily as an outlet for domestic concerns; in effect, they represented battles within the national psyche between conformity and individualism played out on the world stage. The Spanish-American War, for example, according to Dallek, served as a psychological release for a populace that felt oppressed by increasing industrialization. Mark Garrison, who reviewed *The American Style of Foreign Policy* for the *Washington Post* (May 8, 1983), found that Dallek did not have sufficient evidence to back up some of his assertions, but he praised the writer "for consciously stepping off into uncharted territory, offering his own controversial interpretations of domestic sources of American foreign policy in order to stimulate discussion and further investigation." He continued, "Studies like Dallek's should help us face up to our own shortcomings." The *New York Times Book Review* selected *The American Style of Foreign Policy* as one of 200 notable books of 1983.

In the middle of the Reagan presidency, Dallek published *Ronald Reagan: The Politics of Symbolism* (1984), an analysis of Reagan's ideology and its popularity within the U.S. In Dallek's "interesting but not entirely convincing" argument, as Gaddis Smith put it in a critique of the book for *Foreign Affairs* (Summer 1984), Dallek tried to show that Reagan's opposition to all forms of dependency—including welfare in the U.S. and the dependency on the government of citizens in the Soviet Union—stemmed from the president's growing up with a dependent, alcoholic father. The book was reissued in 1999 with a new preface in which Dallek discussed the then-upcoming 2000 presidential election.

In 1991 Dallek published *Lone Star Rising: Lyndon Johnson and His Times, 1908–1960*, the first volume of a planned two-volume biography. By his own account, his research at the Southern California Psychoanalytic Institute helped him to recognize that Johnson's self-regard was so extreme that it could be considered a psychiatric disorder. "One doesn't simply write about Lyndon Johnson," Dallek told James Willwerth for *Time* (July 29, 1991). "You get the Johnson treatment from beyond the grave—arm around you, nose to nose. I should admit that he also reminds me of my father, quite an overbearing and narcissistic character. And in some ways, he reminds me of myself. Another workaholic." Coincidentally, the publication of Long Star Rising, which Dallek had been working on for seven years, closely followed that of Means of Ascent, the second volume in a projected three-volume biography of Johnson by the best-selling biographer Robert Caro. While Caro's account was considered more readable than Dallek's, Dallek's was widely praised as a more accurate and more penetrating portrayal of Johnson. "On balance, as a historian seeking to place his subject in context and as a biographer sensitive to the full range of Johnson's stupefyingly complex character, Dallek has Caro beat all to feathers," David M. Kennedy wrote for the Atlantic (September 1991). Kennedy also expressed his admiration for Dallek's willingness to confront the "unsavory" elements of Johnson's life and those of his other subjects as well as those of the times in which they lived: "Dallek is not a cartoonist but a scrupulously faithful portraitist. He appreciates how tangled is the skein of history, and how mysterious is the human heart—especially Lyndon Johnson's heart. He gives us Johnson warts and all. . . . If understanding Johnson's life is in fact the key to understanding the 1960s, in Dallek's telling neither the puzzle nor the solution will be a simple matter."

In the spring of 1993, Dallek was a visiting professor at the California Institute of Technology, in Pasadena. The following year, prompted by cutbacks in the University of California system, he took early retirement. He was a visiting professor at Oxford University, in England, from 1994 to 1995 and at the Lyndon B. Johnson School of Public Affairs at the University of Texas in the spring of 1996. In September of that year, he joined the faculty of Boston University, in Massachusetts, as an adjunct professor in the History Department, a position he held until 2002. Also in 1996 Dallek published Hail to the Chief: The Making and Unmaking of the American Presidents, described by Fritz Lanham in the Houston (Texas) Chronicle (October 13, 1996) as "rather schematic but thought-provoking." Dallek explained to Lanham that he wrote the book because he had felt "distressed at how cynical people have been in the country about the presidential office and our political institutions. And what I wanted to say was that the institution has worked well in the past and can work well in the future."

The second volume of Dallek's Johnson biography, Flawed Giant: Lyndon Johnson and His Times, 1961–1973, was published in 1998. Again, Dallek received wide praise for his willingness and ability to view Johnson and his presidency in a balanced fashion, especially the administration's handling of the Vietnam War. Dallek said he thought that the book, published during the events leading up to the impeachment trial of President Bill Clinton, in early 1999, came at a time when both historians and the American public were beginning to view Johnson differently—as a president who, for

all his flaws, at least knew how to give the illusion of authority. "We currently sense a vacuum of political leadership in this country and, I think, a yearning for strong leadership," Dallek told Jeff Guinn for the Fort Worth (Texas) Star-Telegram (May 17, 1998). "There are no political heroes anymore. Politicians are seen as questionable folks. LBJ, by God, was a man who acted like he was in charge." In Flawed Giant Dallek concluded that Johnson's narcissism and occasional paranoiac behavior led to his downfall as president, causing him to be deeply troubled and incapable of making the decisions necessary to get the United States out of Vietnam. Most reviewers lauded Flawed Giant, though with reservations. Milton Rosenberg, for example, wrote for the Chicago Tribune (April 12, 1998), "Dallek has given us a great narrative history, superbly researched, richly detailed, sensitively nuanced and compellingly told. But the narrative method works against the clear assignment of responsibility, the precise location of cause."

For his next subject, President John F. Kennedy, Dallek had to contend with a considerably larger amount of source material. After gaining exclusive access to Kennedy's previously unseen medical files, he decided to focus on the president's struggles with Addison's disease, colitis (also called irritable bowel syndrome), and severe back pain. In An Unfinished Life: John F. Kennedy, 1917–1963 (2003), Dallek revealed that Kennedy led not the charmed life many Americans imagined, but rather one seldom free of extreme pain or heavy medication. "It's a complicated portrait—and yes, in the end, a positive one—but its greatest achievement is the way it avoids both myth-making and myth-breaking, while exposing us to the complicated life within," David Ulin wrote for Newsday (June 22, 2003). Other reviewers, however, found fault with the medical drama presented in the book. "It doesn't rise to the level of magisterial, nor does it move along in a sprightly way. . . ," Jack Ohman wrote for the Oregonian (June 8, 2003). "An Unfinished Life is neither grossly titillating nor studiously academic; it merely chugs along through the now-familiar JFK curriculum vitae." Many other reviewers also commented on the familiarity of the story but expressed the opinion that Dallek may have produced as near to a definitive biography of the 35th president as may be possible. "With his personal knowledge of the Kennedy years and with his deep scholarship, Robert Dallek has produced a biography of John F. Kennedy that will not be easy for any future author to surpass," Lewis Gould wrote for the Chicago Tribune (September 7, 2003). The book, which was excerpted in the December 2002 issue of the Atlantic, became a number-one New York Times best-seller and remained on the best-seller list for two months.

Over the next few years, Dallek revised his first book on Johnson and delved further into his study of Kennedy. In 2003 he published Lyndon B. Johnson: Portrait of a President, a condensed version of his two-volume biography. Dallek co-wrote, with the historian Terry Golway, essays that accompanied the CD *Let Every Nation Know: John F. Kennedy in His Words* (2006). In 2004–05 he was a guest professor and Montgomery fellow at Dartmouth College, in Hanover, New Hampshire.

Dallek's most recent book, *Nixon and Kissinger: Partners in Power* (2007), describes and analyzes the relationship between President Nixon and his national security adviser and, later, secretary of state, Henry Kissinger, each of whom had been the subject of extensive scrutiny. Dallek argued that many of the successes and failures of the Nixon administration resulted from the competitive yet symbiotic partnership the men maintained. In writing the book, more than 30 years after the Nixon presidency, Dallek made use of a large amount of recently declassified material: 20,000 pages of transcripts of Kissinger's telephone conversations, 2,800 hours of Nixon's tape recordings, and millions of pages of national-security documents. Though Dallek did not draw extended parallels between the administrations of Nixon and George W. Bush within the text, in the preface he noted that certain similarities presented fodder for future study. "Arguments about the wisdom of the war in Iraq and how to end U.S. involvement there, relations with China and Russia, what to do about enduring Mideast tensions between Israelis and Arabs, and the advantages and disadvantages of an imperial presidency can, I believe, be usefully considered in the context of a fresh look at Nixon and Kissinger and the power they wielded for good and ill," he wrote, as quoted by Michiko Kakutani in the *New York Times* (April 24, 2007). In an interview with Terry Gross for the National Public Radio program *Fresh Air* (April 25, 2007), Dallek said, "What I find interesting with this material on Nixon and Kissinger is that this was the most secretive administration in American presidential history until maybe this current administration."

In an assessment of *Nixon and Kissinger* for the *Boston Globe* (May 6, 2007), Martin Nolan called the book "admirable and important," while Kakutani described it as "engrossing." Mark Atwood Lawrence, however, writing for the *New York Times Book Review* (May 13, 2007), claimed that Dallek had led the reader astray. "Dallek's attention to personalities makes *Nixon and Kissinger* remarkably engaging for a 700-page study of policy making," Lawrence wrote. "But this emphasis also underlies its chief weakness: the implication that foreign policy devised by Nixon and Kissinger lacked intellectual coherence" and seemed haphazard. In reality, Lawrence asserted, the two men had followed a coherent strategy of realpolitik. Other reviewers applauded Dallek's focus on "psychobiography"—a subset of biography that seeks to understand the subject through psychological theory. Writing for the *Los Angeles Times* (May 13, 2007), Tim Rutten admired Dallek's dissection of the often-fraught relationship between Nixon and Kissinger. "What sets Dallek's work so forcefully apart from others who have attempted it is his care-

fully sourced insight into the psychodynamics of their relationship," he wrote. That insight—in addition to Dallek's extensive scholarly legwork and his fluid writing—Rutton wrote, made the book the ideal biography. "Dallek's *Nixon and Kissinger* is everything one could want in a contemporary history—a meticulously researched story, written with unobtrusive elegance, unsparing in its judgments, but tempered by sobriety and a genuine compassion for its compelling yet breathtakingly flawed subjects," he wrote. Rutten also expressed the view that *Nixon and Kissinger* surpassed Dallek's books on Johnson and Kennedy—which he described as "magisterial" and "deservedly best-selling," respectively—and set "a new benchmark for the field." It "surely will come to be regarded as a classic work of contemporary American history," he concluded.

Among other honors, Dallek was a John Simon Guggenheim fellow in 1973–74; a senior fellow of the National Endowment for the Humanities in 1976–77; and a Humanities fellow of the Rockefeller Foundation in 1981–82. In 1994 Dallek was elected a fellow of the American Academy of Arts and Sciences, and in 1995 he served as president of the Society for Historians of American Foreign Relations. He has lectured at schools including University College London, the University of Wyoming, Vassar College, and the University of Texas at Austin. He has served as a consultant for several television documentaries and has been a member of many prize committees, among them the committee for the 1985 Pulitzer Prize in history.

Dallek's first marriage, in 1959, to Ilse Shatzkin, ended with her death three years later. Since 1965 he has been married to the former Geraldine Kronmal, a health-policy consultant; the couple live in Washington, D.C. Their son, Matthew Dallek, a historian and speechwriter, is the author of *The Right Moment: Reagan's First Victory and the Decisive Turning Point in American Politics* (2000). Their daughter, Rebecca Dallek, is a specialist in technology in education.

—C.S.

Suggested Reading: *Boston Globe* C p1+ Apr. 22, 1998; *International Herald Tribune* (on-line) Apr. 18, 2007; *Who's Who in America, 2007*

Selected Books: *Franklin D. Roosevelt and American Foreign Policy 1932–1945*, 1979; *The American Style of Foreign Policy: Cultural Politics and Foreign Affairs*, 1983; *Ronald Reagan: The Politics of Symbolism*, 1984; *Lone Star Rising: Lyndon Johnson and His Times, 1908-1960*, 1991; *Hail to the Chief: The Making and Unmaking of the American Presidents*, 1996; *Flawed Giant: Lyndon Johnson and His Times, 1961-1973*, 1998; *An Unfinished Life: John F. Kennedy, 1917-1963*, 2003; *Nixon and Kissinger: Partners in Power*, 2007

Christian Steiner, courtesy of Antonio Damasio

Damasio, Antonio R.

Feb. 25, 1944– Neurobiologist; writer; educator

Address: Health Sciences Campus, Neurobiology Division, University of Southern California, Los Angeles, CA 90033

The story of a horrific accident that severely injured a railroad-construction foreman in mid-19th-century Vermont played a large role in attracting Antonio R. Damasio to a career in research—a career that has placed him among the world's most accomplished neuroscientists. The foreman, Phineas Gage, a smart, well-mannered, personable man, was on the job when an explosion drove a 13-pound, three-foot-long, one-and-a-quarter-inch-diameter iron bar upward into his skull just below his left cheekbone. The bar passed through one or both of the frontal lobes of his brain and emerged from the top of his head with a tremendous force that carried it 90 feet (the distance from first base to second on a baseball diamond). Much to his doctor's surprise, within about two months Gage had regained his ability to walk and talk, but his personality had changed irreversibly, leaving him hot-tempered, foul-mouthed, unpredictable, and unable to conduct himself responsibly. "At first I was interested in all types of neurological injuries," Damasio recalled to Manuela Lenzen during an interview for *Scientific American Mind* (April 2005). "If one area of the brain would lose its ability to function, the patient's behavior could change either dramatically or only subtly. One day I asked myself, 'What is missing in a person who can pass an intelligence test with flying colors but can't even organize his own life?' Such patients can hold their

own in completely rational arguments but fail, for example, to avoid a situation involving unnecessary risk. These kinds of problems mainly occur after an injury to the forebrain. As our tests prove, the result is a lack of normal emotional reactions. I continue to be fascinated by the fact that feelings are not just the shady side of reason but that they help us to reach decisions as well."

Damasio is among the vanguard of scientists who have expanded neuroscience to include not only biology and medicine but psychology, philosophy, and literature. Fundamental to his work is the distinction between emotion and feeling—terms that most laypeople use interchangeably. For neuroscientists, as Damasio told Lenzen, emotions are "more or less" the complex automatic and unconscious reactions of the body to particular stimuli; feelings, he explained, "occur after we become aware in our brain of such physical changes." A racing heart, dry mouth, sudden copious sweating, constriction of the throat, trembling, and loss of bowel or bladder control are all *emotional* (bodily) reactions to intense fear. The *feeling* (mental awareness) of fear is what we experience when the brain recognizes those physical changes. As a gatherer of information, the brain relies on signals from the body's sensory and motor nerves and on chemical signals that circulate through the bloodstream, and its stored data change constantly along with changes in those signals. Damasio has identified specific areas of the brain that are involved in the processing of emotions, and he has found evidence that casts doubt on the long-held belief that logic and rational thought require the control and suppression of emotion; rather, as his research has shown, emotion is essential to logical reasoning and integral to sound decision-making. He has also proposed that humans' internal processes not only preserve life but also motivate and shape the development of cultures and systems of morality. In a related area, Damasio has constructed a theory about levels of consciousness.

In an interview posted on the Harcourt Books Web site in 2002, Damasio said that recent neurological research had enabled scientists to "speak with confidence about 'what feelings are'—where they come from, how they happen, what they are made of biologically. . . .We have identified brain areas and brain pathways necessary to feel emotions. Armed with the new knowledge we can even venture to say what feelings are for. The new knowledge broadens our view of human nature. We can not really know who we are if we do not understand the brain mechanisms behind emotion and feeling—what causes emotions, what leads to feelings, how they affect our decisions, social behavior, and creativity, and where they fit in evolution." Damasio also said to the Harcourt interviewer, "Interestingly, the moral behaviors are emotional—compassion, shame, indignation, dominant pride or submission. As in the case of culture, the contribution of everything that is learned and created in a group plays a major role in shaping moral behaviors. Only humans can codify and refine rules of moral behavior. Animals can behave in moral-like ways, but only humans have ethics and write laws and design justice systems." Damasio believes, as he told the same interviewer, that "knowing about the workings of mind and brain can help us deal more effectively with the social problems we face today. Part of our failures in the past may well be due to underestimating the positive and negative power of emotions. On a purely practical level, the new knowledge will also let us develop new medications to cure causes of human suffering such as pain and depression."

In 2005 Damasio, a native of Portugal, joined the faculty of the University of Southern California (USC), after working at the University of Iowa for 30 years. According to information about him on USC's Web site, his major contributions to neuroscience also include discoveries about the roles that the parts of the brain known as the cortex and subcortex play in humans' ability to recognize faces and objects, and about pathological changes in victims of Alzheimer's disease. Damasio has written or co-authored hundreds of scientific papers, many of them with his wife, Hanna Damasio, a highly accomplished specialist in neurological imaging, who, like him, holds an endowed chair at USC. Antonio Damasio has also written three widely praised books for knowledgeable laypeople that have been described as both surprisingly accessible and entertaining and as daunting for the average reader: *Descartes' Error: Emotion, Reason and the Human Brain*, which has sold more than 500,000 copies, been translated into 18 languages, and earned Damasio a *Los Angeles Times* Book Award nomination; *The Feeling of What Happens: Body and Emotion in the Making of Consciousness*, which the *New York Times* chose as one of the 10 best books of 1999; and *Looking for Spinoza: Joy, Sorrow and the Feeling Brain*. According to Damasio, neuroscience is developing so rapidly that many of his conclusions may soon become outdated. In his introduction to *Descartes' Error*, he wrote, "I have a difficult time seeing scientific results, especially in neurobiology, as anything but provisional approximations to be enjoyed for a while and discarded as soon as better accounts become available."

Antonio R. Damasio was born on February 25, 1944 in Lisbon, the capital of Portugal. He received an M.D. degree in 1969 and a Ph.D. in 1974, both from the University of Lisbon. From 1971 until 1975 he served as chief of the Language and Research Laboratory at the Centro de Estudos Egas Moniz, in the same city. His interest in neuroscience deepened following a year (1974–75) at the Aphasia Research Center in Boston, Massachusetts. There, he studied under Norman Geschwind, a trailblazer in behavioral neurobiology. After he returned to Lisbon, Damasio became an auxiliary professor in the Neurology Department at the University of Lisbon Medical School. Also in 1975 he settled in the U.S., where he became a naturalized citizen.

From 1975 until 2005 Damasio taught at the University of Iowa in Iowa City, a leading center for the study of the nervous system and behavior. He was promoted to associate professor in 1976 and full professor in 1980. Beginning in 1977 he chaired the division of Behavioral and Cognitive Neuroscience within the Department of Neurology, and from 1986 until his departure from the university, he headed the Neurobiology Department. Between 1985 and 2005 he also directed the Alzheimer's Disease Research Center, an arm of that department. While at the University of Iowa, Damasio helped to establish, with his wife, one of the world's largest databases of brain injuries; it contains thousands of diagnostic images and information about hundreds of studies of brain lesions. He also helped to set up a world-renowned laboratory for research on a wide range of brain injuries. In 2005 Damasio left Iowa to join the faculty of USC, in Los Angeles, where he holds the David Dornsife professorship in neuroscience and directs the school's Brain and Creativity Institute. He also teaches at the University of Iowa part-time. In addition, since 1989 he has been an adjunct professor at the Salk Institute for Biological Studies, in La Jolla, California.

As recently as 20 years ago, neuroscientists generally viewed the brain as a glorified computer or calculating machine. Brain research focused on the biological underpinnings of perception, memory, and other cognitive processes. Damasio has found evidence that, like perception and memory, emotions and feelings can be defined biologically; specifically, he has discovered, so-called gut reactions have biological foundations, and humans rely on emotional cues when they make decisions. Through work with patients with brains damaged as a result of strokes, trauma, or disease, including severe epilepsy, he has shown that a person who lacks the faculty to process emotion has difficulty in making rational decisions. People who lack functional amygdalas, for example, as he explained to Alexander Star for the *New York Times Magazine* (May 7, 2000), "cannot recognize fear in people's expressions, and they cannot experience fear themselves." Damasio is also studying the role of emotion in feelings related to social relations, among them sympathy, shame, and pride, thus using neurobiology to develop theories about human nature as well as human interactions. Damasio believes that his research on emotions has practical implications for the treatment of psychological maladies. "Emotional disorders form the core of most psychological illnesses—a good example of this is depression," he told Lenzen. "Specific treatments will be developed in the future, such as new types of medicine that target distinct cellular and molecular systems. Other forms of therapy are also sure to benefit, from traditional psychotherapy to social intervention."

Damasio's first book, *Lesion Analysis in Neuropsychology*, was published by Oxford University Press in 1989. Written with Hanna Damasio, it was named the outstanding book of the year in biology and the medical sciences by the Professional and Scholarly Book Division of the Association of American Publishers. The Damasios have often conducted joint research; together, they have written more than 60 book chapters or articles for scientific journals. Hanna Damasio's career has closely paralleled her husband's: she graduated from the same medical school in the same year that he did and joined the faculty of the Department of Neurology at the University of Iowa in 1976. At that school she directed the Laboratory for Neuroimaging and Human Neuroanatomy from 1982 to 2004 and co-directed the Division of Cognitive Neuroscience from 1985 to 2004. She was named the Dana Dornsife chair in neuroscience and professor of psychology at USC in 2005. Like her husband, she is an adjunct professor at the Salk Institute for Biological Studies and at the University of Iowa. At USC she also directs the Dornsife Cognitive Neuroscience Imaging Center. She pioneered the use of computerized tomography, nuclear magnetic resonance, and other methods for producing images of the brain—important tools in the diagnosis of neurological diseases. Her book *Human Brain Anatomy in Computerized Images* (1995) has become a standard reference.

Antonio Damasio's next book was *Descartes' Error: Emotion, Reason and the Human Brain* (1994). René Descartes (1596–1650) was an enormously influential French philosopher, scientist, and mathematician. The error to which Damasio referred was Descartes' formulation of a mind-brain duality. Descartes conceived of the brain as a tangible machine that obeys the laws of physics and has as its defining attribute "spatial extension." The mind, in Descartes' view, is an intangible entity that does not obey those laws; its defining attribute is thought. Cartesian dualism, as that idea is known, posits that the brain and the mind are profoundly different and have nothing in common; according to Descartes, they interact only in the pineal gland, a pea-sized part of the brain. The deeply puzzling question of how the nonmaterial mind and the material brain interact is known as the mind-body problem. In the quarterly journal *Independent School* (Fall 2005), Richard Barbieri wrote that in *Descartes' Error* (and *Looking for Spinoza*), "Damasio takes on the issue of mind-brain dualism, not as a militant materialist, but as a believer in the absolute interconnectedness and interdependence of brain and body experiences. In this dense and difficult book . . . Damasio connects the quests of philosophers, playwrights and poets to the modern efforts of neuroscientists. . . . For all his technical language of somatic markers and skin conductance, Damasio sides with the saints and poets, as when he observes that 'Emily Dickinson was right, one single brain, being wider than the sky, can comfortably accommodate a good intellect and the whole world besides.'"

In *Looking for Spinoza: Joy, Sorrow and the Feeling Brain* (2002), Damasio drew upon scientific discoveries made during the previous eight years to expand upon the content of *Descartes' Error* and discuss aspects of the philosophy of Baruch (also known as Benedict) Spinoza (1632–77), a descendant of Portuguese Jews living in exile in Amsterdam, the Netherlands. Spinoza, whose heretical beliefs led the Dutch Jewish community to excommunicate him, wrote that mind and body are not separate entities but are different manifestations of the same thing (nature or God). "Spinoza fascinates me not only because he was ahead of his time with his ideas on biology but also for the conclusions he drew from these ideas about the correct way to live life and set up a society," Damasio told Lenzen. "Spinoza was a very life-affirming thinker. He recommended contrasting the negative emotions such as sadness and fear with joy, for example. He understood this kind of practice as a way to reach an inner peace and stoic equanimity." Damasio told the Harcourt interviewer, "The book shows how Spinoza, alone and marginalized, was able to achieve happiness by cultivating curiosity, knowledge, and goodness of character." In a critique of *Looking for Spinoza* for *Scientific American* (March 2003), Erica Goode wrote, "Scientists who write books come in two varieties: those who are cautious, reluctant to stray beyond the data before them, and those who are bold and synthetic, using what is known as a springboard for journeys into unproved theory. Damasio, whom some have accused of leaping ahead of what scientists actually know in order to construct convincing narratives, obviously belongs to the latter group. Some readers will fault him for it; others will see it as a strength. It is through such speculative leaps, after all, that understanding often advances. Those who have read Damasio's popular works *Descartes' Error* and *The Feeling of What Happens* will find [in *Looking for Spinoza*] much that is already familiar. Still, *Looking for Spinoza* is compelling, in part because it so strongly conveys the feel of a personal expedition: the neurologist sifts through what is known about the philosopher's life as if pursuing a lost relative."

The Feeling of What Happens: Body and Emotion in the Making of Consciousness (1999), written after *Descartes' Error* and before *Looking for Spinoza*, offers Damasio's assessment of a phenomenon usually relegated to the realm of philosophy. While many scientists have studied the ways in which the brain processes what our senses tell us, in *The Feeling of What Happens*, Damasio concentrated on the ways in which those sensations contribute to the creation of the "autobiographical self"—an individual's notion of him- or herself. (Our sensations include not only what we see, hear, smell, touch, and taste but also what we learn from our awareness of pain, for example, as well as of temperature, balance, movement, and the positions of our arms, legs, and other body parts at any moment, and such sensations as nausea and blushing.) Damasio explained that philosophers and scientists have traditionally located humans' center for consciousness at the sites connected with the brain's greatest attributes or products—language, memory, creativity. He has learned from his studies of people with crippling epilepsy and other forms of brain damage that individuals who cannot speak or understand speech, lack long- or short-term memory, and show no creativity nevertheless often exhibit some form of consciousness, and he has theorized that consciousness arises from activity in scattered parts of the brain. Based on clinical research, he constructed a theory according to which there are three levels of consciousness: proto-consciousness, which monitors our bodily states (in essence, what is known as homeostatic regulation) and of which we are mostly unaware; core consciousness, which arises from our moment-to-moment awareness of outside objects, events, feelings, or memories; and extended consciousness, "in which there are many levels and grades, providing an elaborate sense of self—an identity and a person, you and me . . . ," as David Walton wrote for the *Dallas Morning News* (September 19, 1999). Damasio, describing the constantly changing "autobiographical self," wrote in *The Feeling of What Happens*, "It is astonishing that we have a sense of self at all, that we have . . . some continuity of structure and function that constitutes identity, some stable traits of behavior we call a personality." He also wrote, "The drama of the human condition comes solely from consciousness." But the price we pay for consciousness "is not just the price of risk and danger and pain. It is the price of knowing risk, danger and pain . . . the price of knowing what pleasure is and knowing when it is missing or unattainable." According to the neuroscientist William H. Calvin, writing for the *New York Times* (October 24, 1999), *The Feeling of What Happens* "is a must-read book for anyone wanting a neurologist's perspective on one of the greatest unsolved mysteries, human consciousness and how it exceeds that of the other apes."

Currently, Damasio is co-leading a project, supported by USC's Annenberg Center for Communication, that explores "the systematic investigation of facial, postural, and vocal behaviors during social interactions across different ethnic/cultural groups," according to the center's Web site. The study grew out of the observation that ethnic or cultural groups often misread the social communications of other groups.

In the *New York Times* (April 19, 2003), Emily Eakin described Damasio as "a slight, fine-featured man with elegant manners and a shock of white hair . . . [who] exudes old-world charm. His conversation is a velvet murmur that hints at his Portuguese roots; his passion is in his hands, which slice the air in quick, graceful movements as he speaks." Damasio's curriculum vitae lists 32 honors and awards. With his wife and Yves Christen, Damasio edited the book *Neurobiology of Decision-making* (1996); with three others, he edited *Unity of Knowl-*

edge: *The Convergence of Natural and Human Science* (2001). Antonio and Hanna Damasio live in Los Angeles.

—N.W.M.

Suggested Reading: *New Scientist* p469 Mar. 11, 2000; *New York Times* C p1+ Dec. 6, 1994, C p5 Mar. 4, 1997, VI p31 May 7, 2000, D p7 Apr. 19, 2003; *New York Times Magazine* p31 May 7, 2000; *Scientific American* p104+ Mar. 2003; *Scientific American Mind* (on-line) Apr. 2005; usc.edu; *Washington Post* A p2 Sep. 20, 2000

Selected Books: *Descartes' Error: Emotion, Reason and the Human Brain*, 1994; *The Feeling of What Happens: Body and Emotion in the Making of Consciousness*, 1999; *Looking for Spinoza: Joy, Sorrow and the Feeling Brain*, 2002

William Thomas Cain/Getty Images

Davis, Evelyn Y.

Aug. 16, 1929– Shareholder activist; publisher of Highlights and Lowlights

Address: Highlights and Lowlights, *Watergate Office Bldg., Ste. 215, 2600 Virginia Ave. NW, Washington, D.C. 20037*

The editors of *People* (May 20, 1996) dubbed Evelyn Y. Davis "America's most dreaded corporate gadfly." The metaphor of the gadfly is frequently applied to Davis, who has made it her mission to represent the small investor at the numerous shareholder meetings she attends every year. A colorful figure, whom even those sympathetic to her cause describe as abrasive, Davis is known for haranguing company heads about their performance, credibility, or even appearance. (She famously told Lee Iacocca, then the widely respected chairman of Chrysler, that he needed to watch his diet.) She has agitated for more transparent corporate governance and increased accountability, among other measures, and while some observers argue that Davis, who owns shares in some 100 companies, has undermined the cause of shareholder rights with her antics, others have acknowledged her great positive impact. Michael Rosenzweig, a corporate attorney and law professor, told Mike Tierney for the *Atlanta (Georgia) Journal-Constitution* (May 22, 2005), "My view . . . is she was something of a visionary. Evelyn was one of the earliest proponents of shareholder democracy. In a sense, the market has come to her." "She's one of a kind," Ray Smith, the former chief executive of Bell Atlantic, told Amy Feldman for the New York *Daily News* (May 24, 1998). "She's not a gadfly . . . she's a gad-eagle."

Davis was born Evelyn Yvonne DeJong on August 16, 1929 in Amsterdam, the Netherlands. Her father, Herman DeJong, was a prosperous neurologist, and her mother, Marianna, was a psychologist. The family employed a French governess for Davis and her older brother, Rudolph, as well as two maids to care for their large home. Although she has told journalists that her parents sometimes favored Rudolph over her, she has also said that her childhood was generally happy. (She has credited some of her drive and ambition to her rivalry with her brother, who pursued a career in medicine.) One day in December 1942, while her father was lecturing in the United States, Nazis arrested Davis, her mother, and her brother. Along with some 650 other wealthy Dutch Jews, they were sent to an old castle in Barneveld, a suburb of Amsterdam, where they were imprisoned for nine months. "Compared to other places, [Barneveld] was a country club," Davis told Jack Kelley for *USA Today* (May 5, 1997).

In the fall of 1943, the three DeJongs were sent to a small concentration camp called Westerbork, in the Dutch province of Drenthe. (Westerbork is perhaps best known as the camp in which Anne Frank was imprisoned before being transported to Auschwitz.) There, Davis labored picking potatoes and, during a mortar attack, was hit by shrapnel that left a deep scar on the back of her right calf. Conditions worsened the following year when she and her mother and brother were sent by railway car to Theresienstadt, a concentration camp in the former Czechoslovakia, where she was forced to split mica in a factory for several hours a day. Unafraid, even then, to speak her mind, she once got into an argument with a female guard and was severely beaten as punishment. Food was scarce—inmates were served mainly meager portions of thin soup and potatoes—and she often dreamed at night of chocolate pudding. As a further form of mental escape, Davis began constructing romantic

fantasies about the director of the mica factory, a Czech Nazi. She told Peter Carlson for the *Washington Post* (April 20, 2003), "I'd look forward to going to the factory because I'd see this guy. Nothing happened: I was still an innocent girl. But it made the whole thing bearable for me. Ever since then, I've had infatuations with what you'd call very prominent authority types." In May 1945 Russian troops liberated Theresienstadt. Davis believes that if the war had continued much longer, she would have died before being freed. "But I don't want people to feel sorry for me," she told Kelley. "Every person has a tragedy in their past. This is mine."

Davis's parents divorced after the war. Her mother stayed in the Netherlands, while Davis and her brother moved to Catonsville, Maryland, to live with their father, who had remarried and was teaching at Johns Hopkins University, in Baltimore. In 1947 Davis graduated from Catonsville High School. With the intention of pursuing a degree in business, she attended Western Maryland College for a semester and then transferred to George Washington University, in Washington, D.C., where she studied for two years. She then dropped out of school, for reasons she is unwilling to discuss with reporters, and began to take a series of secretarial jobs.

After being jilted by a lover (reportedly a high-level government official) with whom she had had a five-year relationship, Davis wanted to spite him, as she has related to reporters, by getting married to someone else. In 1957 she married William Henry Davis III, an accountant from a wealthy North Carolina family. She has kept his name ever since, although they divorced in 1958. Davis then moved to New York City with money she had won in the divorce settlement. Her father, who had died in 1956, had left her several thousand dollars in securities, which Davis used to invest in the stock market.

In 1959 Davis attended her first stockholders' meeting, held by International Business Machines (now commonly known as IBM). When she stood up to ask a question, she was "shaking like a leaf," as she recalled to Pamela Moore for the *Charlotte (North Carolina) Observer* (April 26, 1995). Davis strengthened her confidence by means of a $20 course in public speaking at a YMCA. "Then I became like a fish in the water," she told Moore. Emboldened, she started taking classes in securities analysis at the New York Institute of Finance.

Davis traveled all over the country to attend shareholder meetings and parties. In the early 1960s, for the first time, she proposed a shareholder resolution, challenging the wisdom of the charitable contributions made by R. H. Macy and Co. While her resolution did not pass, it attracted attention to an important issue: federal securities laws prevented shareholders from knowing the amount of a company's contributions and prevented them from learning who was receiving a company's largesse.

At about that time Davis started her own business, Shareholder Research, which operated out of a hotel room not far from United Nations headquarters, in New York City. She frequented the U.N. delegates' lounge and managed to obtain a temporary U.N. press pass. In 1963, in a widely reported incident, she was arrested at the hotel and charged with prostitution. (Tabloid reporters speculated that she was running a call-girl ring frequented by U.N. officials.) Davis was convicted and received a 30-day suspended sentence. She has refused to talk about the scandal. When asked about it, she told Amy Feldman, "I don't comment. It's all garbage."

In 1965 Davis moved her one-woman enterprise to an office in the Watergate Building, in Washington, D.C., and began to publish a newsletter, *Highlights and Lowlights*. The newsletter included business analysis along with Davis's views on politics, travel, and other topics. Adopting the mantle of a muckraker, Davis wrote it in the style of a gossip column with an idiosyncratic use of punctuation. "The corporate secretary at Safeway is no longer there, thank goodness!!! We don't care whether she got fired, quit or retired. She is gone—hoorah!!!" read a typical entry, as quoted by Carlson. Another, as quoted by John M. Doyle in the *Chicago Tribune* (April 22, 1990), read: "At one of the most important meetings of the year only ONE 'outside' director, the son of the founder, attended!!! Time Inc.!!!! This showed disrespect for the chairman, the stockholders and other attendees!!"

Highlights and Lowlights initially sold for about $20 per copy. As Davis's profile rose in the corporate world, she repeatedly increased the price. It is currently sold—only to CEOs and presidents—for almost $600 a copy, with a two-copy minimum required. Detractors, who charge that Davis is less likely to attack a newsletter purchaser at a shareholders meeting, have criticized her for browbeating executives into buying the publication. When questioned about her tactics, Davis asked Susan Decker, writing for the *Seattle (Washington) Times* (August 11, 2000), "I bully them?" and then added, "More power to me if I can, right?" In November 1969 Davis married her second husband, a stockbroker named Marvin Knudsen; the union ended in divorce three months later.

Throughout the 1970s Davis got increasing attention with her stunts. During one General Motors meeting, she strutted around the room in a bathing suit, waving the American flag. At a *Washington Post* company meeting, Davis criticized the paper for not giving her enough publicity. In 1977 she was assaulted by a fellow stockholder and sent to the hospital with an injury that required five stitches. Undaunted, she returned an hour later to attend another meeting. By the late 1970s she had been granted access to White House press conferences. Even in that rarefied atmosphere, Davis did not modify her behavior: once, when she was excluded from a conference with Mikhail Gorbachev, she buttonholed Gorbachev's press secretary for foreign affairs and ended up getting a short private meeting with the Soviet leader. During the administration of President Bill Clinton, after being forced to stand at one press conference, she screamed that seats should be assigned according to income level.

Most of Davis's proposals called for the disclosure of a company's legal fees; for annual elections of auditors; or for the disclosure, limiting, or cessation of corporate contributions to charities and politicians. In 1980 the Securities and Exchange Commission (SEC) supported claims that Davis's habitual heckling was meant merely to draw attention to herself and agreed to let several major corporations ignore her resolutions. Spurred by Davis's prolonged diatribes, Citicorp passed a resolution that allotted just three minutes for individual shareholders to air their grievances at annual meetings. Still, Davis continued to behave in a manner designed to irritate. In 1984, for example, she began pushing for an anti-greenmail policy in response to General Motors' $700 million payment to the shareholder and onetime presidential candidate H. Ross Perot. (A twist on blackmail, greenmail is a company's repurchase of its stock from an undesirable shareholder at a greatly inflated price.) After years of resistance, General Motors adopted an anti-greenmail policy in 1990.

When Davis got her first driver's license, in 1984, she asked Lee Iacocca to deliver a car to her personally. When he declined to do so, she approached the head of Ford, Philip Caldwell, who delivered the keys to a Ford model to her himself. (Since then, whenever Davis has bought a new car, the manufacturer's chief executive officer has delivered the keys in person.)

In 1985 Davis started fighting for the elimination of staggered elections for company directors. In staggered elections only a portion of a board is elected each year, which makes it more difficult for outsiders to mount successful takeovers. While many companies insist that staggered elections provide necessary continuity, some others, including the pharmaceutical giant Bristol-Myers Squibb, have eliminated such elections in response to Davis's resolutions.

In 1989 Davis established the Evelyn Y. Davis Foundation; she currently donates millions each year to business schools, museums, and hospitals. The foundation recently endowed a scholarship fund for students interested in business or political journalism. (By her own admission, Davis requires institutions to which she has given funds to mount conspicuous plaques bearing her name.) In 1991 Davis married her third husband, the economist Walter Froh, whom she had met at a U.S. Senate Banking Committee hearing. They divorced three years later. "I'm a beautiful woman. Men find me extremely intriguing. But I have been unlucky in love," she told Gary Strauss for *USA Today* (April 28, 2003).

DECEMBERISTS

Age has not tempered Davis's behavior. In 1991, for example, the year she turned 62, she asked the chairman of the struggling U.S. Airways, as reported by Robert Trigaux for the *St. Petersburg (Florida) Times* (May 22, 2002), "Are you going to stay or jump out and leave us holding the bag?" Later in the 1990s, when Chrysler's chairman, Robert Eaton, endorsed his company's sale to Daimler-Benz (a firm that had contributed greatly to the German war effort during World War II), she attacked him, saying, according to Trigaux, "You'll always have that on your conscience, Bob. Remember that."

When a number of high-profile corporate corruption scandals surfaced in the early 2000s (with the Enron debacle being a prime example), even Davis's foes were forced to admit that rigorous shareholder oversight was needed in the corporate world. Davis has continued to propose several resolutions each year, many of them relating to the elimination of staggered elections or the need for greater fiscal disclosure. "What else would I do with myself?" she asked Strauss. "I love the challenges, the conflict, and the intrigue."

Davis, who divorced her fourth husband, John E. Patterson, in 2006, is known for her vibrantly colored hair, designer suits, and distinctive Dutch accent. She has no offspring. "Stocks are my children," she told Strauss. Davis has purchased a burial plot and headstone at Rock Creek Cemetery, in Washington, D.C. The headstone, which mentions only two divorces and lacks only the as-yet-unknown date of death, reads, in part, "Power is greater than love, and I didn't get where I am by standing in line and being shy."

—C.C.

Suggested Reading: *Chicago Tribune* D p14 Apr. 22, 1990, C p5 Sep. 5, 1994; (New York) *Daily News* p50 May 24, 1998; *People* p69 May 20, 1996; *Seattle (Washington) Times* C p2 Aug. 11, 2000; *St. Petersburg (Florida) Times* E p1 May 22, 2002; *USA Today* B p5 May 5, 1997, B p4 Apr. 28, 2003; *Washington Post* B p1 Dec. 31, 1995, F p1 Apr. 20, 2003

Decemberists

Music group

Meloy, Colin
Oct. 5, 1974– Songwriter; singer; guitarist

Query, Nate
June 7, 1973– Bassist

Funk, Chris
1971(?)– Multi-instrumentalist

Conlee, Jenny
1971(?)– Keyboardist

Moen, John
1968(?)– Drummer

Address: c/o Capitol Records, 1750 N. Vine St., Los Angeles, CA 90028-5209

"Among the current crop of skinny emo boys whining about unattainable love and blinged-out divas searching for street credibility, the Decemberists stand out like a skull and crossbones on an empty blue horizon," Abigail Clouseau proclaimed in *SF Weekly* (January 14, 2004). "Where most bands play chord changes, rhythms, and melodies, the Decemberists score short musical films. Where most write lyrics about a disenchanted girlfriend or flowery, musical self-help manuals, this band crafts meticulous fables, creating curious characters . . . with words that give us glimpses of their personalities and music that fills in the gaps." Led by the songwriter, vocalist, and guitarist Colin

Meloy, the Portland, Oregon–based Decemberists are distinguished by their unusually literary lyrics, which contain archaic or arcane words, and their penchant for story songs, which have been described as simultaneously beautiful and creepy. Seldom about contemporary events, most of them feature pirates, ghosts, or wandering soldiers and tell of a love that ends with death. "Mr. Meloy has lovingly created his own alternate universe, and he draws his hapless characters with enormous wit and tenderness," Kelefa Sanneh wrote for the *New York Times* (March 30, 2004). Since its formation, in the wake of the September 11, 2001 terrorist attacks on the U.S., the group has released four full-length albums: *Castaways and Cutouts*, *Her Majesty the Decemberists*, and *Picaresque*, all on the independent label Hush Records, and *The Crane Wife*, which bears the Capitol label. In an on-line poll, listeners of National Public Radio programs ranked *The Crane Wife* number one among CDs released in 2006. In addition to Meloy, the current members of the Decemberists are Chris Funk, multi-instrumentalist; Jenny Conlee, keyboardist; Nate Query, bassist; and John Moen, drummer. Past members include Jesse Emerson, guitarist; Ezra Holbrook, drummer; and Rachel Blumberg, drummer and vocalist.

Colin Meloy, who plays the most prominent part in shaping the direction of the Decemberists and usually acts as the band's spokesperson, was born on October 5, 1974 and raised in Helena, Montana. His mother works in the field of public health; his father, Peter Michael "Mike" Meloy, is a lawyer who in the 1970s served in the Montana state legislature. Meloy's older sister, Maile, is the prize-winning author of the books *Half in Love*, *Liars and*

Autumn De Wilde, courtesy of Capitol Records
The Decemberists (l. to r.): J. Conlee, C. Funk, C. Meloy, J. Moen, N. Query

Saints, and *A Family Daughter*. His great-uncle Henry Meloy was an accomplished 20th-century artist; a gallery is named for him at the University of Montana. Speaking of his great-uncle, Colin Meloy told Terry Gross for the National Public Radio program *Fresh Air* (January 29, 2007, on-line), "Even though I never met him . . . just knowing that he had been a part of the family and had been a successful painter, . . . in a family of mostly . . . attorneys and judges . . . [showed me that] it was a possible thing." A drawing by Henry Meloy is on the cover of an album Colin Meloy made with his alternative-country band Tarkio.

During his childhood, Meloy told Sara Scribner for the Westchester County, New York, *Journal News* (October 23, 2003), "my parents' friends used to call me 'Underwater Boy' because I was constantly wandering around sort of in my own head, sort of floating in water. I was always lost in my own imagination." He felt like an outsider among his peers, in part because he lacked interest and talent in sports but enjoyed reading. His musical tastes, too, differed from those of others his age. "Finding records for me was an epic struggle, a Herculean struggle that involved a lot of trying to talk record stores into carrying a certain kind of record," he told Scribner. "It wasn't an environment that fostered my sort of person." A turning point came when he joined the theater group in his high school and won parts in student musicals. "Theater, for me, was an important outlet and really the first thing I discovered that gave me a community of friends . . . doing something expressive," he told Michael Roberts for the *Denver (Colorado) Westword* (March 11, 2004).

Meloy attended an Oregon college briefly before transferring to the University of Montana at Missoula. He rejected his father's advice that he study a subject that would lead to an assured steady income and instead majored in creative writing and minored in theater. But he heeded the suggestion of professors of his that he not enter a master's degree program immediately after his graduation. Before he completed his college education, he formed Tarkio, named for a town near Missoula. In 1999, reportedly unhappy with the types of audiences Tarkio attracted, he left Missoula and moved to Portland, Oregon.

The Decemberists formed in Portland in 2001. Meloy named the band partly in homage to the Decembrists, a group of early 19th-century Russian revolutionaries who wanted to establish representative democracy in their country; in December 1825 soldiers loyal to Czar Nicholas I crushed the attempt by 3,000 of the rebels to force the czar's removal. Meloy told Scribner that the name of the band also refers to people who like "wintry climes." In addition to Meloy, the founding members were Nate Query, born on June 7, 1973; Chris Funk and Jenny Conlee, both born around 1971; and the vocalist Ezra Holbrook, a fixture of the Portland independent-music scene. Funk, an Indiana native, joined the Decemberists after attending Coe College, in Iowa. Conlee and Query had played in the Portland band Calobo during the 1990s.

In 2002 the small independent label Hush Records, located in Portland, released the Decemberists' first full-length album, *Castaways and Cutouts*, "a smattering of songs we'd been performing live for the past year or so—it was done so innocently, there were absolutely no expectations whatsoever . . . ," as Meloy told Devon Powers for popmatters.com (September 25, 2003). "We were [recording the album] merely to create something to give to the world." *Castaways and Cutouts*, and in particular its song "Odalisque," attracted much attention in the Portland area, and in May 2003 a larger label, the Olympia, Washington–based Kill Rock Stars, re-released the album. "Second chances in life can be rare, but almost all of us deserve them. Especially the Decemberists . . . ," Mark Woodlief wrote for the *Oregonian* (April 25, 2003). "If you missed *Castaways and Cutouts* the first time around, this is a second chance you shouldn't pass up." Joshua Klein, a reviewer for the *Chicago Tribune* (August 18, 2003), reacted quite differently. "The Decemberists . . . are pretentious Portland musicians led by Colin Meloy, who has no problem packing his self-consciously literate lyrics with enough references to exotic places and events to shame even the shameless Sting," Klein wrote.

Later in 2003 Kill Rock Stars released the band's next album, *Her Majesty the Decemberists*. Its 11 tracks include "Shanty for the Arethusa," "The Gymnast, High Above the Ground," "Los Angeles, I'm Yours," "The Chimbley Sweep," and "Song for Myla Goldberg," the last of which is dedicated to the author of the novel *Bee Season*. Meloy told Powers that while he had been responsible for most of the writing, arranging, and producing of *Castaways and Cutouts*, *Her Majesty* was "much more collaborative." A number of reviews of *Her Majesty* cited the Decemberists' similarity to another critically acclaimed indie band, the Jeff Mangum–fronted Neutral Milk Hotel. Dylan Siegler, for example, wrote for the *Dallas (Texas) Observer* (September 25, 2003), "If you are one of the 75,000-plus people who bought Neutral Milk Hotel's last album, the first thing you will think when you hear the Decemberists is this: Damn, that guy sings like Jeff Mangum from Neutral Milk Hotel. . . . Acoustic guitar makes way for bells, strings, horns and accordion, and here and there, schmaltzy '70s AM-radio flourishes add an ironic smirk to offset the endemic seriousness of Meloy's vocal. If upping the irony quotient pulls those theatrics into even more confusing territory, it's really the only barrier to enjoying this varied record. That is, if you haven't heard Neutral Milk Hotel." Similarly, Jesse Jarnow wrote for *Salon.com* (September 16, 2003), "I have an instant affection for Meloy and the Decemberists. And the reason for my instant affection, which is admittedly unfair to all parties, is that they uncannily resemble an entirely different band: Neutral Milk Hotel. . . . They sound like them right down to the smallest of mannerisms: the nasal faux-English accent, the ragtag marching rhythms, the fascination with the Old World, the songs about dead European girls. It's forgivable, because it doesn't sound exactly intentional."

Reviewers of *Her Majesty the Decemberists* also mentioned the band's penchant for old-fashioned language. Scribner wrote of their use of archaic terminology, "It's worth it to look up the words: otherwise, how would you know that 'bombazine' is a fabric using silk and cotton and used for mourning clothes?" Meloy told Scribner, "I don't think I use any words that I wouldn't relish to use in a conversation. There are words in the English language that are so amazing and so beautiful and so underused it's a bit of a crime, so it's not like I'm going through the dictionary looking for these words." He told Clouseau, "I come at it from a historian's perspective. The characters that appear in the songs, if you really boil it down, are pretty much anachronistic stereotypes or just literary motifs or figures that have popped up in literature since the 19th century."

In 2004 the Decemberists recorded a five-part, 18-minute operetta called *The Tain*, produced by Chris Walla, the guitarist and producer for the indie band Death Cab for Cutie. Released on Acuarela Discos, a Spanish label, the operetta was loosely based on the late-11th-century/early-12th-century Irish epic *Táin Bó Cúalnge* (*The Cattle Raid of Cooley*) about the attempt by the teenage Ulster hero Cúchulainn to prevent Queen Medb and her husband, Ailill, from stealing a stud bull. Kelefa Sanneh, the *New York Times* critic, described *The*

Tain as "an appealing (if sometimes exhausting) homemade epic, full of intriguing narrative fragments and nimble musical U-turns." Sanneh, who attended the band's sold-out show at the Bowery Ballroom, in New York City, on March 25, 2004, wrote that the *Tain* songs "never curdle into mere parody" and noted, "As if to offset the willful obscurity of his lyrics, Mr. Meloy often seizes on bright, sometimes maddeningly catchy tunes." In an assessment of the Decemberists' performance at the Troubadour, a club in West Hollywood, California, on April 7, 2004, Steve Hochman wrote for the *Los Angeles Times* (April 9, 2004) that *The Tain* "went from a heavy blues riff to a [Kurt] Weill-like waltz and back—something that might appeal to fans of Belle & Sebastian and Jethro Tull." Of the concert as a whole, he wrote, "Yes, it can get a bit precious at times, even with the encore-closing cacophony in which Meloy smashed not a guitar, but a mandolin. But it's a worthwhile price for an entertaining evening of smarting up rather than the standard dumbing down."

During the winter of 2004–05, Meloy embarked on a solo tour. He told Annie Zaleski for the *Phoenix (Arizona) New Times* (October 20, 2005), "It was just great to play because it was smaller audiences. It seemed like, in each city, it was your normal Decemberists audience boiled down to the core 150, 200 people. It was a lot of fun in that respect . . . and everyone who was there knew all the songs, and inevitably [it] turned into this big sing-along thing. . . . We're very lucky to have won over such sweet people."

In Portland on March 17, 2005, the trailer containing the band's instruments and equipment was stolen—a loss totaling approximately $70,000. In the next few weeks, fans raised over $8,000 to assist the band. Thanks to an anonymous tip and the help of the police, the Decemberists eventually recovered about $50,000 worth of their instruments.

The Decemberists' next album, the 11-song *Picaresque* (2005), was the last to be released by Kill Rock Stars, as specified in the band's contract. Its tracks include "Sixteen Military Wives," "Eli, the Barrow Boy," "The Bagman's Gambit," "The Mariner's Revenge Song," and "Of Angels and Angles." "Like its predecessors, it's filled with allusions to rogues and prostitutes, sailors and kings," Jim Farber wrote about that album for the New York *Daily News* (April 1, 2005), adding that the melange of instruments included the shofar, made from the horn of a ram or other animal and blown during certain Jewish ceremonies. Yeow Kai Chai, reviewing *Picaresque* for the Singapore *Straits Times* (August 12, 2005), wrote, "Musically, it's invigoratingly cavalier, ranging from Tin Pan Alley to nighttime balladry to operetta, with the group adding saxophones, trombones and violins to their delicious chop suey." Praise for the CD also came from Jessica Grant, who wrote for the *Kansas State Collegian* (May 3, 2005), "It is impossible to capture the moving and cohesive power of this album"; Thor Christensen, who opined in the *Dallas (Tex-*

as) Morning News (April 10, 2005), "It's hard not to get sucked into these tragic-yet-hummable tales"; and Jen Carlson, who enthused on Gotha-mist.org, "*Picaresque* delivers gem after gem of epic songcrafting, making it one of those rare abums we can listen to straight through (and re-peatedly, at that)." The few dissenting voices in-cluded that of Scott Faingold, who complained in the *Houston (Texas) Press* (September 22, 2005), "The sound of the Decemberists is not unlike Nick Cave's Bad Seeds, if that band were drained of all testosterone and fronted by [the nerdy] Arnold Horshack from [the 1970s sitcom] *Welcome Back, Kotter.*"

Prior to recording *Picaresque*, Meloy had told a *Grand Rapids (Michigan) Press* (September 21, 2004) reporter that Kill Rock Stars had "a com-pletely hands-off approach" to the band's work, and he characterized the Decemberists' relation-ship with the label as "great." Nevertheless, he said that the band was hoping to move to a larger label, and in 2005 the band signed a contract with Capi-tol Records. "The idea of reaching a wider audi-ence has become really attractive," Meloy told Amy Phillips for pitchforkmedia.com (December 12, 2005). "It just felt like we had tapped out the resources of Kill Rock Stars. We could have stayed on that label until the end of time, putting out proper Decemberists records that sold x amount of copies. But there was a general thought after this last tour that the music and the stage show were evolving. We felt like there was an opportunity for something bigger." He added, "We've never been the sort of group that has lived and breathed indie-ness."

In late 2005 John Moen (born around 1968) joined the Decemberists. The next year the band re-leased *The Crane Wife*, produced by Chris Walla and Tucker Martine. The title track offers Meloy's take on a traditional Japanese tale. "There was a real strong sense among the band that we were not going to try to make a record that somebody would typically make for a major label," Meloy told NPR.org. "We didn't want the fact that we had signed onto a major label [to] change our approach or aesthetic. In some ways, I think it pushed us far-ther to the left, farther out of the comfortable De-cemberists zone." Simon Cosyns wrote for *MX* (February 8, 2007), a magazine published in Aus-tralia, where *The Crane Wife* arrived in early 2007, that "without doubt," *The Crane Wife* "is the first truly great record of 2007." Stephen M. Deusner wrote on PitchforkMedia.com, "Given the band's graduation from minor to major leagues, *The Crane Wife* may prove to be the most crucial record the Decemberists will release in their lifetime. Fortu-nately, their fourth album further magnifies and re-fines their strengths. . . . Here the band gels into a tight, intuitive unit. The musicians give each song a particular spark and character, not just rein-forcing the lyrics but actively telling a story."

The Decemberists received unexpected publici-ty in November 2006 when Stephen Colbert, on his fake-news TV program *The Colbert Report*, de-nounced the band for allegedly copying a segment of an installment of his show in a music video in which they made use of so-called green-screen (or bluescreen) technology. The denunciation came in a full-length *Colbert Report* installment that fea-tured appearances by the TV journalist Morley Safer, former secretary of state Henry Kissinger, and the British musician Peter Frampton.

Meloy is the author of "Let It Be," a long essay in which he described the influence on him during his childhood of the Replacements' 1984 album of the same title; the essay was published in 2005 by Continuum International as part of a series about landmark rock-and-roll albums. In 2006 Meloy and the artist Carson Friedman Ellis, who has illustrat-ed the covers for all of the Decemberists' albums, became the parents of a boy, Henry "Hank" Meloy.

—S.J.D.

Suggested Reading: believermag.com June 2004; *Boston Globe* D p12 June 11, 2004; (Queensland, Australia) *Courier-Mail* p52 Feb. 8, 2007; Decemberists Web site; *Denver (Colorado) Post* F p4 Mar. 9, 2004; *Denver (Colorado) Westword* Music section Mar. 1, 2004; (London) *Guardian* p14 July 26, 2005; *MX* p24 Feb. 8, 2007; pitchforkmedia.com Dec. 12, 2005; *SF (California) Weekly* Music section Jan. 14, 2004; *Virginian-Pilot* E p7 Mar. 29, 2007

Selected Recordings: *Castaways and Cutouts*, 2002; *Her Majesty the Decemberists*, 2003; *Picaresque*, 2005; *The Crane Wife*, 2006

Desai, Kiran

Sep. 3, 1971– Writer

Address: c/o Grove/Atlantic, 841 Broadway, New York, NY 10003

"Writing, for me, means humility," the Indian-born novelist Kiran Desai told an interviewer for *Rediff* (January 30, 2006, on-line). "It's a process that in-volves fear and doubt, especially if you're writing honestly." Such doubt and humility notwithstand-ing, Desai—the daughter of the noted writer Anita Desai—has won a great deal of praise for her two novels. The first, *Hullabaloo in the Guava Orchard* (1998), drew comparisons to the work of her fellow Indian-born writer Salman Rushdie, for the rich-ness of her writing, characters, and multiple plots, and she won Britain's Man Booker Prize for her 2006 novel, *The Inheritance of Loss*, a multigenera-tional story set in India and New York. Those ac-complishments have apparently not altered her at-titude about writing fiction. "Each book is its own

Katja Lenz/AFP/Getty Images

Kiran Desai

challenge," she explained to the *Rediff* interviewer, "and I find myself at exactly the same level of trepidation and doubt as when I began the last time around."

Kiran Desai was born on September 3, 1971 in New Delhi, India, one of the four children of Anita Desai, whose novels include *Voices in the City* (1965), *Clear Light of Day* (1980), and *Baumgartner's Bombay* (2000), and Ashvin Desai, a businessman. Anita Desai's mother was German, her father a refugee from what later became Bangladesh; Ashvin Desai's parents were from the western Indian region of Gujarat. Kiran Desai was raised in India, sometimes living outside New Delhi and sometimes in Kalimpong, in the Himalayas, where her family had a house "that was named Chomiomi after a snow mountain in Tibet," as Desai told the interviewer for *Rediff*. She had a happy childhood. Her earliest memories, she said to the *Rediff* interviewer, are of "sitting under the table pulling the toes of all my older siblings and parents in turn. Utter happiness. I remember my father whistling in his bath," and, she said, she recalls "sitting, a very little girl, in my mother's lap, layers of soft, old Bengali striped sari, playing with the bangles she wore, one on each wrist, a book in front, and her voice which is an utterly beautiful voice, reading." She added, "Human warmth is such an innate part of India, and good humour." At the same time, as Desai explained for *Rediff*, "Kalimpong has a population of Tibetan refugees and a majority population of Nepalis who were brought generations ago to work on British tea plantations. It is a very beautiful place, but the strains were obvious even when we were living there." Long-festering class tensions led to unrest in the area.

Desai received part of her education at St. Joseph's Convent in Kalimpong and then, when she was 15, moved to England to continue her schooling. (Some sources say that she was 14 at the time; Desai herself, in different interviews, has said both.) After a year in England, Desai moved to the United States. She attended high school in Massachusetts before enrolling at Bennington College, in Bennington, Vermont. She studied for a time at the writing program at Hollins University, in Roanoke, Virginia, and later went to Columbia University, in New York City, where she obtained an M.F.A. degree.

It was at Hollins that Desai began writing her first novel, *Hullabaloo in the Guava Orchard*, published in 1998. In an interview for the Random House on-line publication *Bold Type* (May 1999), Desai revealed that she had gotten the idea for the novel after reading an account in an Indian newspaper of a hermit who lived for many years, until his death, in a tree. "So I began to wonder about what it was about someone like this who would do something as extreme as to spend his life in a tree," Desai said. "So it started really with that character, and then the story built up around it." She began writing, she added, with "no idea what the story would be" and "no idea of the plot. It sort of gathered momentum and drew me along. It was an incredibly messy process." *Hullabaloo in the Guava Orchard* tells the story of Sampath, a misfit young man in an Indian village whose life lacks direction until he becomes a tree-dwelling guru, attracting followers from far and near. Sampath's traditionalist father, disconcerted at first by his son's actions, is ultimately not above making profits from the sale and resale of objects of devotion that are to be placed at the foot of the tree; the novel follows many others among Sampath's family members and fellow village dwellers, as well.

"Although the publishers of *Hullaballo in the Guava Orchard* have been comparing the book to Arundhati Roy's award-winning novel *God of Small Things*, 27-year-old Kiran Desai turns out to have less in common with Ms. Roy or Salman Rushdie than with an older generation of Indian writers, including her mother, Anita Desai, and R. K. Narayan," Michiko Kakutani wrote for the *New York Times* (June 12, 1998). "There are no grand, mythic visions at work in *Hullabaloo*, no ambitious displays of magical realism. Rather, the novel stands as a meticulously crafted piece of gently comic satire—a small, finely tuned fable that attests to the author's pitch-perfect ear for character and mood, and her natural storytelling gifts." Reviewing the novel for *Newsday* (June 1, 1998), Lise Funderburg wrote that Desai "has attacked classic themes: women's roles, worship of false idols, intolerance, generation gaps. Couched in the broad comedy that relies on the familiarity of each subplot, these issues ambush the reader. What seems merely to be the lead-in to a good laugh and nothing more actually lingers, leaving questions that are, for all their familiarity, no less profound." For

Hullaballo in the Guava Orchard, Desai was presented with the Betty Trask Award, given by the Society of Authors, a British organization.

Asked why eight years had passed between the publication dates of her first and second novels, Desai said to an interviewer for *Jabberwock* (January 20, 2006, on-line), "I suppose I was working and reworking the second book a lot." Most critics seemed to feel that her second book was worth the wait. "If *Hullabaloo in the Guava Orchard* established Desai as an expert storyteller, *The Inheritance of Loss*," Desai's 2006 novel, "distinguishes her as a writer of note," Jenifer Berman commented in the *Los Angeles Times Book Review* (January 22, 2006). Set mainly in Kalimpong, where Desai spent much of her childhood, *The Inheritance of Loss* follows the lives of a retired, English-educated judge, whose time abroad has caused him to feel permanently out of place in his homeland; the judge's granddaughter, Sai, an orphaned teenager who lives with him; the judge's cook, who dotes on Sai; the cook's son, Biju, who earns subsistence wages as a waiter in New York; and Sai's tutor and romantic interest, Gyan, an ethnic Nepalese who becomes involved with a rebel group and thereafter rejects what he sees as Sai's bourgeois lifestyle.

"Although it focuses on the fate of a few powerless individuals, Kiran Desai's extraordinary new novel manages to explore, with intimacy and insight, just about every contemporary international issue: globalization, multiculturalism, economic inequality, fundamentalism and terrorist violence," Pankaj Mishra wrote in an assessment of *The Inheritance of Loss* for the *New York Times Book Review* (February 12, 2006). "Despite being set in the mid-1980's, it seems the best kind of post-9/11 novel." The book, according to Marjorie Kehe's review for the *Christian Science Monitor* (January 24, 2006), "is populated by characters who are mostly either exiles, eccentrics, or both. It is a work full of color and comedy, even as it challenges all to face the same heart-wrenching questions that haunt the immigrant: Who am I? Where do I belong? . . . Nothing sours the warm heart at the center of this novel. Desai is sometimes compared to Salman Rushdie, and the energy and fecundity of imagination in her works do make them somewhat akin to his. But the tenderness in her novels is all her own." In 2006 Desai won the Man Booker Prize, awarded to writers who are British or Commonwealth citizens, for *The Inheritance of Loss*, becoming the youngest woman ever to receive the prize. (As quoted by Dwight Garner in the December 3, 2006 edition of *New York Times*, Desai said that "in an odd way" she owes her award to U.S. president George W. Bush, as it was his 2004 reelection that led her to put off becoming a U.S. citizen.)

Desai said during her interview for *Bold Type*, "There are all kinds of theories that you get told in writing workshops—'Write what you know,' and that sort of thing, which I don't believe at all. I think one of the great joys of writing is to try and explore what you don't know, that's exciting to me. There are all kinds of little [rules]—show, don't tell—I just wouldn't pay attention to any of that really." Asked by the *Bold Type* interviewer about her mother's influence on her own writing, Desai said, "I'm sure she did have a big influence, because all my life I've grown up hearing her talk about writing and literature and books. It was wonderful to have her around when I was writing [*Hullabaloo in the Guava Orchard*]. . . . She was very good through that whole time, not providing critical support as much as emotional support. A very motherly role, really."

Kiran Desai lives in Brooklyn, New York. Each year she visits India, where much of her immediate family live. Her connection with India, she commented to the *Rediff* interviewer, "was never broken."

—S.Y.

Suggested Reading: *Christian Science Monitor* F p13 Jan. 24, 2006; (London) *Times* (on-line) May 2, 1998; *Los Angeles Times Book Review* p5 Jan. 22, 2006; *New York Times Book Review* p12 July 19, 1998, p11 Feb. 12, 2006; *Rediff* (on-line) Jan. 30, 2006;

Selected books: *Hullabaloo in the Guava Orchard*, 1998; *The Inheritance of Loss*, 2006

Deutsch, Linda

1943– Associated Press trial reporter

Address: Associated Press, 221 S. Figueroa St., Third Fl., Los Angeles, CA 90012-2553

"I am the eyes and ears of the public," the courtroom reporter Linda Deutsch said to Nancy Mills for the *Spirited Woman* newsletter (December 2003, on-line). "I'm there to say what happened, not to give any opinions on why it happened or who's responsible. I am an unbiased observer. TV cameras are not always there and even when they are people do not sit and watch every minute, they depend on the reporter to sum up what happened. . . . I fill two notebooks a day and bring it down to a manageable size where people can know what was said, what was important, what's happened, and if possible, how it felt to be in the courtroom when all this happened." Deutsch has been on the staff of the Associated Press (AP) for the past 40 years, and for much of that time, she has been ranked among the foremost American courtroom journalists of modern times. When she joined the AP, where speed, accuracy, objectivity, fairness, and the ability to cover varied subjects are highly valued, Deutsch welcomed the rush of adrenaline that deadline pressures stirred in her. Her articles have appeared in newspapers and on Web sites

Damian Dovarganes-Pool/Getty Images

Linda Deutsch

worldwide, and her work has occasionally taken her overseas—for example, to Guam, in 1975, when she wrote about the fall of Saigon, which marked the end of the Vietnam War. Among the wide array of events she has witnessed, she is best known for her detailed, objective reporting on some of the most sensational, newsworthy, and influential trials of recent decades, including those of Sirhan Sirhan, Charles Manson, Patty Hearst, Angela Davis, Daniel Ellsberg, Lynette ("Squeaky") Fromme, Claudine Longet, Joseph Hazelwood (the skipper of the *Exxon Valdez*), the four Los Angeles police officers who beat Rodney King, John Z. De Lorean, Michael Jackson, and O. J. Simpson. At the end of Simpson's criminal trial, in 1994, the AP awarded Deutsch its Oliver Gramling Reporter Award for her outstanding work. Two years earlier the AP had named her a special correspondent, a title she shares with only 18 past and present AP journalists. Patt Morrison, the president of the Los Angeles Press Club, described Deutsch to the PR Newswire (March 24, 2005) as "an irreplaceable and irreproachable source of information to the millions who read her reportage, truly free from spin or slant" and as "a supremely and scrupulously thorough, accurate, fair and honest reporter who has the respect and regard of both sides in any trial she covers—before, during and after." "I can't think of anything I would rather do," Deutsch told Michele Norris, who interviewed her for National Public Radio (January 15, 2007). "It's like being in a theater everyday. It's like being in the front row seat to history. . . . No other beat offers this kind of access to human emotion. You get at the heart of what people are about. And I think that the murder trial, whether it has any historical significance

or not, is always of interest because people wonder: Could I do that? And I sit there and have to listen to both sides, put the pieces together, and present them to an audience. It's the most exciting thing I can think that any reporter could do."

Linda C. Deutsch was born in 1943 in New Jersey. Her mother was a writer. Deutsch began writing poetry and prose at an early age. On her ninth birthday she received her first typewriter, from her father (who died before she reached her teens). Her first attempt at reporting sprang from her interest in the rock-and-roll star Elvis Presley. "I got the idea that I could start an Elvis fan club and I could put out a newspaper," she told Lesley Visser for CBS News (August 15, 2002). "And that's what I did. I published the *Elvis Times*, which went all over the world." In 1958, while Presley was serving in the U.S. Army, thousands of people signed a petition that Deutsch had organized, urging Dick Clark, the host of the popular TV show *American Bandstand*, to promote his music. At about the same time, Deutsch began working for a local newspaper, the *Asbury Park Press*, writing a weekly column about area high schools and, occasionally, other subjects and events. One of her uncles, a newspaper editor, encouraged her to take up journalism as a career, telling her that it was exciting and would offer a stable income and opportunities to meet many people.

Deutsch attended Monmouth University (called Monmouth College then), in West Long Branch, New Jersey, where she majored in journalism. "I was interested in history and the way social trends evolve and journalism gave me a front row seat at history," she told Nancy Mills. Bank loans and earnings from part-time jobs enabled her to pay for her tuition and expenses. Deutsch wrote for the campus weekly and spent her summers interning at local newspapers. In the summer of 1963, she worked the night shift at the *Evening News* in Perth Amboy, reporting on municipal meetings and gathering information for obituaries. One day that summer she learned that a major civil rights march was to take place in Washington, D.C., on August 28. Although she was eager to attend, she "wouldn't dare have had the guts to say something [to the editor]," as she recalled to John Hughes for the *Orange County (California) Register* (November 14, 1995). "So I left him a note saying I thought the march was something the paper should cover. He called me the next day and said, 'OK, if it won't cost us anything, you can go.'" Deutsch hitched a ride to Washington with members of the Perth Amboy branch of the NAACP (National Association for the Advancement of Colored People), and, with an estimated 250,000 others, she witnessed Martin Luther King Jr. giving his historic "I Have a Dream" speech in front of the Lincoln Memorial. The next day her account of the march appeared on the front page of the *Evening News*. "After you do something like that, there's no turning back," Deutsch told Michelle Sahn for the East Brunswick, New Jersey, *Home News Tribune* (July 8, 2004). "I knew then that journalism was my life." In November of that year, when John F. Kennedy was assassinated, she volunteered to help workers at the *Asbury Park Press* prepare articles for the next day's edition, as a way of conquering the helpless feeling she experienced after hearing of the president's death. Her assignment—to make a list of all the local businesses and services that would be closed the day of Kennedy's funeral—made clear to her the public-service aspect of journalism. "It gave us a role in history," Deutsch told Hughes. "It was so amazing to realize that we could do something."

After she earned a bachelor's degree, in 1965, Deutsch covered entertainment news for several New Jersey newspapers. In 1967 she moved to Los Angeles, in order to be close to Hollywood, where many such stories originated. After a brief stint with the *San Bernardino Sun*, she got a job as a general-assignment reporter with the Associated Press. (Founded in 1846, the AP is the oldest news-gathering organization in the world. It is a not-for-profit cooperative that is owned by the American daily newspapers—currently, there are 1,500—that are among its members. A board of directors, elected by its U.S. members, directs its operations. Some 200 weekly, non-English, and college newspapers are also members. Five thousand radio and television outlets, too, use its services, and it maintains a radio network, called AP Radio News, that has 850 affiliates. Currently, the AP's staff includes approximately 2,730 journalists, associated with 243 news bureaus in 97 countries. In addition to written, audio, and visual news reports, the AP supplies photos and graphics.) Whenever she could, Deutsch wrote about the entertainment industry, with the thought of making it her area of expertise. Along with many other AP reporters, she covered the assassination of Senator Robert F. Kennedy of New York, in June 1968, during his bid for that year's Democratic presidential nomination. Her assignment as a "backup" reporter at the trial of the senator's killer, Sirhan Sirhan, was her "first huge, huge story in the L.A. bureau [of the AP]," and, in leading her to decide on court reporting as her specialty, "it changed my life," as she told Michele Norris. Her decision was reinforced in 1970, when she became the AP's principal reporter during the highly publicized, sensational trial of the cult leader Charles Manson and several of his followers, who had murdered the actress Sharon Tate (the pregnant wife of the filmmaker Roman Polanski), four of her friends, and two others in 1969. Deutsch has referred to her experiences during the nine-month trial (1970–71) as her own "trial by fire." "It was exhausting, and it was mind-bending . . . ," Deutsch explained to Norris. "You lived in a different reality, because you were suddenly in this world of this commune that [Manson] ran." She told Hughes, "At some point I realized that [a courtroom trial] was the greatest theater in the world. This was true theater, the morality play for our times. . . . And it is the one story [in journalism] that has a beginning, a middle and an end."

Deutsch has attended many of the hearings at which Susan Atkins, Leslie Van Houten, and Patricia Krenwinkel, the women convicted of murder in the Charles Manson trial, have unsuccessfully applied for parole. (The women's death sentences were changed to sentences of life imprisonment after California abolished the death penalty, in 1972. The state reinstated the death penalty in 1977.)

During the Sirhan and Manson trials, Deutsch had many conversations with the highly respected trial reporter Theo Wilson of the New York *Daily News*. Wilson became her "mentor, teacher, sister, and best friend," as Deutsch told Jeff Baker for the *Oregonian* (April 12, 1997), and before long their peers began referring to them as "Thinda" or "the Snoop Sisters." From Wilson, Deutsch learned that good trial reporters are always the last people to leave the courtroom, pay close attention only to what is said inside the courtroom (on the witness stand, by the judge, and by the lawyers), disregard anything lawyers or others say outside it (which is often "spin"), and never make up their minds about defendants' guilt or innocence until the trials end. "Theo believed in observation and description," Deutsch told Baker. "She always said, 'Keep writing, no matter what, and don't leave the courtroom unless you have to file.'" As an example of what one might miss by not following that rule, Deutsch mentioned that during the Manson trial, while some reporters were smoking outside the courtroom, Manson "leaped at the judge with a pencil in his hand"—an incident bound to interest many newspaper readers. Theo Wilson died in 1997, a few days after she began a promotional tour for her book, *Headline Justice: Inside the Courtroom: The Country's Most Controversial Trials* (1996). Deutsch toured in her stead, between her AP assignments.

In addition to the Manson trial, well-known trials that Deutsch has covered include those of Patty Hearst, a granddaughter of the newspaper magnate William Randolph Hearst, who in 1976 was found guilty of taking part in a bank robbery along with members of the Symbionese Liberation Army, an urban guerrilla group that had kidnapped her in 1974; Angela Davis, a one-time member of the Black Panther and Communist Parties, who was acquitted in 1972 of murder, kidnapping, and criminal-conspiracy charges in a case involving the killing of a judge during the attempted escape from a California courtroom of three prisoners in 1970; Daniel Ellsberg, whose 12 counts of felony, stemming from his giving to the *New York Times* a copy of the *History of Decision Making in Vietnam, 1945–1968*—a classified government report better known as the Pentagon Papers, which he had helped to write—were dismissed by a judge in 1973, on the grounds of government misconduct; Lynette ("Squeaky") Fromme, a follower of Charles Manson, who in 1975 was convicted of the attempted assassination of President Gerald R. Ford; the entertainer Claudine Longet (the ex-wife of the singer Andy Williams), whose killing of the champion skier Vladimir ("Spider") Sabich was deemed criminally negligent homicide and earned her, in 1979, a 30-day jail sentence; the automobile executive and designer John Z. De Lorean, who in 1984 was acquitted, on grounds of entrapment, of charges of selling cocaine to undercover police and conspiring in money laundering; Joseph J. Hazelwood, who in 1990 was found guilty of misdemeanor negligence in connection with the spillage into Alaskan waters of more than 11 million gallons of oil from the *Exxon Valdez* in 1989, when he was the ship's captain; the criminal (1991) and civil (1993) trials of the four Los Angeles police officers who beat Rodney King, a black man, with the first trial ending in the nearly all-white jury's verdict of not guilty, which sparked days of riots in Los Angeles that left several dozen people dead, thousands injured, and as much as $1 billion in property damage; the former football star O. J. Simpson, who in 1994, in a criminal trial, was acquitted of the murder of his ex-wife Nicole Brown Simpson and her friend Ronald Goldman and in 1997, in a civil trial, was found liable for their deaths; and the singer Michael Jackson, who was charged with child molestation and was acquitted on all counts in 2005. Deutsch told Michele Norris, "I always say that trials mirror history. That if you wanted to know what was going on in America at a specific time, you needed to walk into a courtroom and look around and listen to what was happening. And you would see, for instance in the Ellsberg trial, you saw the Vietnam War. In the Angela Davis trial, you saw the story of the Black Panthers. In the Patty Hearst trial, we had post-Vietnam alienation. . . . You go on and on, and you come up to the more present time with the O.J. Simpson trial, which . . . had all the elements of celebrity and racism and domestic violence—a lot of issues."

At the outset of Simpson's criminal trial, Deutsch's peers chose her to be the sole journalist in the courtroom during jury selection. Laurie L. Levenson, a former senior trial attorney and assistant chief of the Criminal Division of the Los Angeles district attorney's office, told Nerissa Young for the *Quill* (October 1, 1998) that Deutsch "can watch jury selection, which is like watching paint dry on the wall, and she makes it interesting." Simpson's defense attorney Johnnie Cochran told Young that he considered Deutsch "without peer" and revealed that she was the only reporter to whom he had given both his home and office telephone numbers. On one occasion another of Simpson's lawyers, Robert Shapiro, interrupted Deutsch's daily wrap-up of courtroom events to the media pool outside the courthouse to accuse her of being "too objective." "I try to put myself in the position of the juror," Deutsch told Hughes. "I've always believed that if you told the public what came out in a court, they could make their own decision." Deutsch's reporting of the Simpson trial earned her a Pulitzer Prize nomination—as well as a personal telephone call from Simpson at the conclusion of the trial, thanking her for remaining im-

partial throughout. *Verdict: The Chronicle of the O.J. Simpson Trial*, co-authored by Deutsch, other AP reporters, and the true-crime writer Michael Fleeman, was published in 1995.

In recent years Deutsch has become an advocate for greater media access to the courts. "It is a fight to cover the courts because a lot of people try to keep you out . . . ," Deutsch said, as reported by City News Service (May 7, 2001). "It is a daily First Amendment battle." She is also battling what she views as a decline in journalists' objectivity and has argued that sensationalistic media coverage hurts journalists who seek to cover trials objectively. "The Simpson trial was a huge setback, not just for TV but for media in general," Deutsch told Michael Ollove for the *Baltimore Sun* (October 7, 1998). While she has no objection to having cameras in courtrooms, she felt that television coverage of the Simpson trial was often inaccurate, poorly researched, and inconsequential to the outcome of the trial and often presented to the public a scene different from that experienced by the jurors. Also contributing to the decline in media objectivity, Deutsch has said, is the desire of many television journalists to be celebrities. At a lecture she gave in 2005, as reported by Keith Brown for the *Asbury Park Press* (September 23, 2005), she complained that journalists sometimes forget that their primary concern should be reporting the facts. "That's what being a reporter is all about," she said. "[The public] should never know what you are thinking." At the same time, she said, "Journalists have always had soul. It's their business to have soul, to care." Coverage of the devastating effects of Hurricane Katrina, in her opinion, demonstrated that element of journalism powerfully.

With the AP's court reporter Dick Carelli, Deutsch wrote *Covering the Courts: An Associated Press Manual for Reporters*. Her awards include the Honor Medal for Distinguished Service in Journalism from the University of Missouri School of Journalism and the First Amendment Award from the Society of Professional Journalists.

—N.W.M.

Suggested Reading: *Baltimore Sun* E p1+ Oct. 7, 1998; (East Brunswick, New Jersey) *Home News Tribune* H p9 July 8, 2004; *Los Angeles Times Magazine* p5 June 6, 2004; *Orange County (California) Register* E p1+ Nov. 14, 1995; *Quill* p6 Oct. 1, 1998; *Spirited Woman Newsletter* (online) Dec. 2003

Selected Books: *Verdict: The Chronicle of the O.J. Simpson Trial* (with Michael Fleeman and Associated Press reporters), 1995

Courtesy of Dartmouth College

Dodge, Charles

June 5, 1942– Composer; educator

*Address: Dartmouth College, Music Dept.,
Hanover, NH 03755*

The often-performed piece *Any Resemblance Is
Purely Coincidental* and many other compositions
by Charles Dodge, a major figure in the realm of
computer music, "toy with sounds of speech, tease
them, twist them and toss them about with acrobatic virtuosity," as Edward Rothstein wrote for the
New York Times (April 19, 1982). According to an
unnamed writer quoted on the Web site of New Albion Records, which released an album containing
Any Resemblance Is Purely Coincidental in 1998,
"If there is one piece identified with Dodge, a 'signature' piece if you will, it would have to be *Any
Resemblance . . .*, which has those qualities that
seem to imbue his work in general—charm, wit,
poignancy and technical brilliance." Classically
trained in music, Dodge studied under such 20th-
century luminaries as the composers Darius Milhaud and Gunther Schuller. As a graduate student
in the 1960s, he gained attention for his orchestral
and chamber-ensemble pieces, winning a Woodrow Wilson fellowship and four Broadcast Music
Inc. (BMI) awards between 1963 and 1967. Beginning during that period, his fascination with synthesized speech led him to gain enough technical
knowhow to experiment with state-of-the-art computerized sound, in such compositions as *Earth's
Magnetic Field* and *Speech Songs*. In the opinion
of the composer and music critic Tom Johnson,
writing for the "Musical America" section of *High
Fidelity* (October 1975), those compositions as well

as his *In Celebration* and *The Story of Our Lives*
showed that Dodge was the only person who, by
the mid-1970s, had "really grasped the medium
and produced computer music which compares
with the finest instrumental and vocal music."
While "conventional classical-music lovers
quaked at the prospect of diabolical scientist-
composers coaxing squat and ominous metal boxes
into musical life," as John Rockwell wrote for the
New York Times (September 22, 1985), Dodge has
long regarded the computer as "just another instrument, albeit a very important one," as he said during an interview with Tim Page for the *New York
Times* (October 10, 1983). "We are not making the
instruments of the past obsolete, only adding one
more contemporary sound." Before he became a
visiting professor at Dartmouth College, in 1993,
Dodge taught at Columbia and Princeton Universities and at Brooklyn College. His compositions include works written on commissions from the National Endowment for the Arts, the Koussevitzky
Music Foundation, the Contemporary Music Society of New York, Swedish National Radio, the São
Paulo Bienale, the Los Angeles Philharmonic Orchestra, and the American Guild of Organists,
among other sources, and they have been performed at many musical festivals and other sites.
With Thomas A. Jerse, he is the co-author of *Computer Music: Synthesis, Composition, and Performance* (1985; second edition, 1997). Dodge was the
composer-in-residence at the 16th annual Florida
Electroacoustic Music Festival, held at the University of Florida at Gainesville in April 2007.

Charles Malcolm Dodge was born in Ames,
Iowa, on June 5, 1942 to Albert Francis Dodge and
Constance Dodge. In 1960 he entered the University of Iowa, whose school of music is considered
among the finest in the U.S. At the end of his freshman year, he studied at the summer school run in
conjunction with the Aspen Music Festival, in Colorado; his instructor was the French composer Darius Milhaud. Dodge earned a B.A. degree with
honors and high distinction in music from the University of Iowa in 1964. That summer he studied
under the composer Gunther Schuller at the Berkshire Music Center (now known as the Tanglewood Music Center), in Tanglewood, Massachusetts. A composition in five parts that he wrote for
cello and piano in 1964 is the first in his official list
of creative works. That year he enrolled at Columbia University, in New York City, where his instructors included Otto Luenig, an electronic-
music pioneer; Richard Hervig, the founding director of the University of Iowa's Center for New Music; Jack Beeson, who has composed operas, choral
music, and chamber works; and Chou Wen-chung,
whose special interest is the integration of music
from Asia and the West. Dodge held a Woodrow
Wilson fellowship in 1964–65 and, the following
year, a Lydia C. Roberts fellowship (available only
to Iowa natives who earned bachelor's degrees
from Iowa colleges). Dodge received an M.A. degree in 1966 and a D.M.A. (Doctor of Musical Arts)

degree in musical composition in 1970, both from Columbia. Nonesuch released his long-playing record *Computer Music* in the latter year. Dodge taught at Columbia from 1967 to 1969, then spent a year teaching at Princeton University, in New Jersey. At Princeton he studied computer music with Godfrey Winham, an influential music theorist during the 1960s and 1970s. In 1970 Dodge returned to Columbia, where he held the title of assistant professor of music for the next seven years. During that time he introduced a graduate program in computer music there.

Dodge used equipment at the Columbia University Computer Center to record his album *Earth's Magnetic Field: Realizations in Computed Electronic Sound*, for which he "translated" into music the data in scientific charts tracking the sun's effects on Earth's magnetic field. The graphic depictions of the measurements, compiled by the geophysicist Julius Bartels, resembled musical notation—so much so that the charts were known among scientists as "Bartels's musical diagrams." In a critique for the *New York Times* (November 8, 1970) of *Earth's Magnetic Field*, Donal Henahan wrote that the music sounded "astonishingly simple and atonal." "For one reason or another," he also wrote, "the music tends to 'go nowhere,' as a listener trained to expect development in musical ideas might say. But no doubt we would say the same of the magnetic-field phenomenon itself, while a geophysicist would easily deduce patterns." Although Henahan questioned the effectiveness of Dodge's reliance on Bartels's charts, he acknowledged that "there is, at any rate, a great deal of pleasing sound on this record, even if interest flags long before its half hour of life."

Concurrently with his duties at Columbia, Dodge conducted research after-hours on computerized speech and electronic music at the Behavioral and Acoustic Research Center at Bell Telephone Laboratories, in Murray Hill, New Jersey. The center was directed by Max V. Matthews, who made recordings of computer music in the 1950s and is considered to be the inventor of that genre. In an essay for a series about the early "gurus" of electronic music gathered by Jason Gross and posted on the on-line magazine *Perfect Sound Forever* (April 2000), Dodge recalled that the research on electronic speech carried out in Matthews's lab fascinated him. "I was . . . struck how much more interesting the sounds of synthesized speech which were made by the researchers were than the attempts at musical sounds that my friends and I were making," he wrote. With Matthews's permission, Dodge used the lab's equipment at night to create a computer program that would produce compositions incorporating synthetic speech. Joseph Olive, one of Matthews's programmers, and several other computer experts—among them Kenneth Steiglitz of Princeton University and two of Dodge's Columbia colleagues, Howard Eskin and Richard Garland—helped him to write the program. As text, he used four "almost dreamlike," "surreal" poems, as he described them, that were written by the poet Mark Strand, a Columbia professor and friend of his. "I'd never been able to write very effective vocal music and here was an opportunity to make music with words," Dodge explained for *Perfect Sound Forever*. "I was really attracted to that. It wasn't singing in the usual sense. It was making music out of the nature of speech itself." The new software enabled him to retain the pitch of a recorded voice while making the words speed up or slow down, or retain the rhythm of the speech while changing the pitch—changes not possible with audiotapes at that time. In an undated entry posted on CDeMusic.org, the Web site of the Electronic Music Foundation, Dodge was quoted as saying, "The first stage was to reproduce the spoken voice as accurately as I could. I made one run through the poem that way. Then I made another run through the poem making continuous glides through the vowel sounds. Then I made another run where the natural pitch contour of the voice was replaced by a melody. And there were a couple of other runs, one where I replaced the vowel part of the speech with noise so that it sounded whispered. . . . The piece went together by cutting between them." The resulting album, *Speech Songs*, released in 1972 on Nonesuch Records, was Dodge's first published work for synthesized voice. The pieces sounded to Edward Rothstein like "heightened speech that nearly qualified as song." *Speech Songs* "astounded the computer experts almost as much as it has delighted musical audiences . . . ," Johnson wrote. "The quality of the computer's voice does not hold up very well against Sills"—a reference to the soprano Beverly Sills—"but it sings tricky atonal passages far faster than she could, and with immaculate intonation and a sense of humor to go with it. And its diction is at least as comprehensible as that of most opera stars."

In subsequent works that contained synthetic speech, Dodge included live instrumentation and randomly generated musical passages. *In Celebration* (1975), another synthesis of a poem by Mark Strand, also offers echo and whisper effects. "Throughout this work you'll hear slithering motifs and drunken-sounding chords seeming to fade in and out of a unique, bizarre sound-scape, all to subtly encompass the feeling—and perhaps the elusive meaning—of Mark Strand's esoteric poem," Robert Cummings wrote for *Computer Music Journal* (Summer 1997). For *Cascando* (1978), Dodge added music to a radio play in places selected by its creator, Samuel Beckett. Dodge also had a speaking part, accompanied by two computerized sound sources, dubbed "Voice" and "Music." According to Joan Reinthaler, a *Washington Post* (November 20, 1984) reviewer who attended a concert featuring Dodge compositions in Bethesda, Maryland, in 1984, *Cascando* "sets a vintage Beckett thesis in a perfect context of mechanically droning voices and intermittent aimless sounds, some musical and some not, all electronic." She added,

"Some might dispute that what Dodge is creating is music, but whatever it is, it's interesting, it's imaginative, and it's part of our future."

Dodge won fellowships from the Guggenheim Foundation twice in the 1970s (1972–73 and 1975–76). He left Columbia in 1977 to teach music as an assistant professor at Brooklyn College, a division of the City University of New York. He held the title of professor from 1980 to 1995 and founded and directed the school's Center for Computer Music. Much of Dodge's work in the 1980s explored "the confrontation between new, often dehumanizing technology and the musical expression of human thought and feeling," according to his profile in the *New Grove Dictionary of Music and Musicians* (2001). In his eight-minute piece *Any Resemblance Is Purely Coincidental* (1980), written for live piano and tape, Dodge used what he identified as a "computer restoration and resynthesis" of a 1907 recording of the great Italian tenor Enrico Caruso (1873–1921) singing the aria "Vesti la giubba" ("Put on the Costume"), from Ruggiero Leoncavallo's opera *I Pagliacci*; the resynthesis dated from the early 1970s and was the work of Thomas G. Stockham, a pioneer in digital audio recording, and his University of Utah student Neil J. Miller. "In the course of the work," Dodge wrote, as quoted in an undated entry on the Web site Art of the States, "the voice searches for an accompaniment and is heard at different times with the original band, with electronic sounds, with copies of itself, with the live piano, and the combinations of them all. There is a surrealistic, dreamlike aspect to these apparent dislocations. The initial efforts are humorous; as the work progresses other emotions come into play." Along with works by other contemporary American composers, among them Milton Babbitt and John Cage, *Any Resemblance Is Purely Coincidental* premiered in 1981 at the Carnegie Recital Hall, in New York City. In a review of the concert for the *New York Times* (May 16, 1981), John Rockwell described the piece as "really successful"; it "alternates between the funny and the eerie and . . . is mostly very charming," he wrote. The CD *Any Resemblance Is Purely Coincidental*, recorded for the New Albion label in 1994, offers six works composed by Dodge in the 1980s in addition to the title piece: four "Speech Songs," "sung" by Dodge; "The Waves," with text by Virginia Woolf and electronic permutations of the voice of the soprano Joan La Barbara; and "Viola Elegy," for which Dodge's son, Baird, played the solo instrument.

From 1971 to 1975 Dodge served as president of the American Composers Alliance, which publishes scores of concert music composed by its approximately 200 members, and from 1979 to 1982 he was the president of the American Music Center, which, according to its Web site, is dedicated to "building a national community for new American music." In 1974 he organized the first International Computer Music Conference; sponsored since 1979 by the International Computer Music Associ-

ation, the annual event includes concerts, lectures, and workshops.

Dodge's son, Baird Dodge, a violist with the Chicago Symphony Orchestra, and his daughter Samantha are his children from his first marriage, which ended in divorce in 1971. Since 1978 he has been married to the former Katherine King Schlefer, with whom he has one daughter, Margaret. The couple live in Putney, Vermont.

—M.B.

Suggested Reading: *Computer Music Journal* p11+ Spring 1995; *High Fidelity* Musical America p10+ Oct. 1975; *New York Times* Arts and Leisure p138 Nov. 8, 1970, II p21 Sep. 22,1985; *Perfect Sound Forever* (on-line) Apr. 2000; *New Grove Dictionary of Music and Musicians*, 2001; *Who's Who in America, 2006*

Selected Compositions: *Earth's Magnetic Field*, 1970; *Speech Songs*, 1972; *Cascando*, 1978; *Any Resemblance Is Purely Coincidental*, 1980; *Viola Elegy*, 1987

Selected Books: *Computer Music: Synthesis, Composition, and Performance* (with Thomas A. Jerse), 1985, second edition, 1997

Donovan, Billy

May 30, 1965– College basketball coach

Address: University Athletic Association, P.O. Box 14485, Gainesville, FL 32604

Billy Donovan coached the University of Florida men's basketball team to the NCAA (National Collegiate Athletic Association) Division I championships in both 2006 and 2007, thus becoming only the third college coach (after John Wooden of the the University of California at Los Angeles and Mike Krzyzewski of Duke University) to win back-to-back titles. He is also one of very few in college basketball to appear in the Final Four as a player and later win a title as a coach. Donovan first gained national attention in 1987, while playing with the Providence College basketball team and helping to lead them on a surprising run to the Final Four. After a brief career as a professional, Donovan began working as a coach. He earned the title of head coach for the first time in 1994, at Marshall University. As the head coach at the University of Florida since 1996, he has turned that school's basketball team into one of the most consistently successful in the nation. Donovan is well known for his fierce work ethic, his unusual skill as a recruiter, and his boyish infatuation with the game of basketball. "I really felt, as a player, in order for me to play at the level I played at, obviously I had to be a student of the game," he explained to Michael

Brian Bahr/Getty Images

Billy Donovan

work harder than his competitors. "A lot of what I did was out of fear," Donovan told S. L. Price for *Sports Illustrated* (November 23, 1998). "Fear of someday looking back on my career and seeing I hadn't done the best I could. Fear of knowing I wasn't overly talented. It came from my dad. He made me realize who I was." Donovan often honed his basketball skills in his backyard alone at night. His mother would receive phone calls from neighbors at 11 o'clock, complaining about the noise. "I used to call from the bedroom window, 'Billy, come in now! The neighbors are tired of hearing that basketball bounce . . . they want to go to sleep!'" she told Chris Harry for the *Orlando Sentinel* (October 27, 1996). Donovan eschewed typical teenage social events in order to concentrate on basketball; sometimes he broke into his high-school gymnasium to work out after the building had closed. His father recounted a now-famous story to Michael Vega for the *Boston Globe* (March 28, 2000), about a night when Donovan never came home. "His mother and I went over to the gym and found him there, and we were like, 'Billy, do you have any idea what time it is?' and he says 'I just lost track of time.'" Donovan's efforts paid off: he starred at point guard in his junior and senior years at St. Agnes, leading the team to a 51–5 record over the course of two seasons. A handful of Division I basketball programs recruited Donovan, among them Seton Hall, Temple University, and Providence College, in Rhode Island. After showing Donovan game tape of the legendary point guard Ernie DiGregorio, a Providence star in the early 1970s who went on to play in the NBA, the Providence coach at that time, Joe Mullaney, told Donovan that he could be the next "Ernie D." The stocky, barely six-foot-tall Donovan agreed to attend Providence and join the Friars, the school's basketball team.

Vega for the *Boston Globe* (March 28, 2000). "I love watching games as a basketball junkie, and I still am. . . . I love watching film. I love being at practice. I love being on the floor with these guys, and I love trying to find innovative ways to try to motivate them and try to bring out the best in them." He added, "In life, very few people are fortunate to be able to do something that they love, and I feel very privileged to do that." Donovan's honors include being named Southern Conference Coach of the Year in 1994 and ESPN.com National Coach of the Year in 2001. In 1999 he was enshrined in the Providence Hall of Fame for his efforts as a player and coach.

The eldest of the three children of William J. Donovan and his wife, Joan, William John Donovan was born on May 30, 1965 in Rockville Centre, New York, a Long Island suburb of New York City. His father played basketball at Boston College during the 1960s; he worked for J. P. S. Yarn and Converter as a salesman and after 22 years became the company's president. The younger Donovan started to play basketball at an early age; one of his first heroes was Walt Frazier of the New York Knicks. When Donovan, as a sixth-grader, wrote an essay about his dream of playing basketball professionally in the National Basketball Association (NBA), his teacher told the class that he had a better chance of getting struck by lightning. Short, chubby, and not a gifted athlete, Donovan had a difficult time making it onto the St. Agnes High School basketball team and did not earn consistent playing time until his junior year. His father challenged him to work harder at becoming a better basketball player, and in response he adopted the motto "Do more," promising himself that he would always

Donovan did not excel in Mullaney's slow-paced, half-court system, and in his first two seasons, he had little playing time and grew bored. He also struggled with his weight, and he fell out of favor with the coaching staff. He averaged only 2.7 points per game in his first two seasons, and many, including Donovan himself, thought that he was overmatched in the Big East Conference, one of the toughest divisions in the country. After the 1984–85 season, in which Providence earned 11 wins and 20 losses, Mullaney resigned and was replaced by Rick Pitino, a young coach who had recently been an assistant coach in the NBA. Donovan had considered transferring to another school, but he changed his mind after Pitino told him that in the upcoming season, they would play a fast-paced offense that would use four guards, and that if Donovan got into better physical condition and increased his mobility, he would have a chance to earn more playing time. Donovan returned home after his sophomore year intent on becoming one of the four starting guards. "I always had worked hard," Donovan told Chris Harry. "But Coach Pitino taught me the right way to work." Again using his high-school gymnasium after dark, Donovan worked tirelessly to improve his conditioning and his jump shot. He also began joining pickup games in New York City playgrounds, where competition was intense. "It was great playing with those guys," Donovan told Michael Wilbon for the *Washington Post* (March 27, 1987). "I learned how to get my shot off, use different dribbles. And you just got an appreciation for winning. On the playground, if you lose, you have to sit an hour to get back on the court because there's about 15 guys [in teams of five] waiting for winners." He entered his third year at Providence 18 pounds lighter, faster on his feet, and with a better understanding of the game. As a junior he averaged 15.1 points per game as the Friars' starting point guard. At Pitino's urging, he practiced diligently over the summer.

During the 1986–87 season, Donovan again flourished under Pitino's high-octane offense system, averaging 20.6 points and 7.1 assists per game and gaining recognition as one of the best guards in the Big East Conference. The Friars achieved a record of 25–9, fourth-best in the league, and earned an invitation to the NCAA Tournament. Over the course of the tournament, Donovan and Pitino garnered national praise for leading Providence, a small, Catholic college with a student body of 3,600, to victories over some of the most successful teams in the country, among them the University of Alabama and Georgetown University. With an approach that favored the three-point shot, full-court pressure, and a frantic pace, Providence won four games to reach the Final Four. Led by Donovan, who had averaged 26.5 points per game during the four games preceding the Final Four, the Friars became the "feel-good" success story of the season. Sportswriters referred to the three-point arc as the "Friar Patch" because of the frequency with which Donovan's team made the long-range shots, and they called Donovan "Billy the Kid," after the Old West gunfighter, a reference to his quick release and accurate shots. Although the team lost to Syracuse University in the national semifinal match, their improbable run to the Final Four earned a permanent place for Providence College in NCAA basketball lore. Looking back on that success, Pitino told Harry, "Billy Donovan went from being the Pillsbury Doughboy to taking a middle-of-the-pack team to the Final Four. He's one of the greatest rags-to-riches stories I've ever been associated with."

After he graduated from college, with a B.A. degree in general social studies, in 1987, the Utah Jazz selected Donovan in the third round of the NBA draft. He was unable to make the team, however, and joined the Wyoming Wildcatters of the Continental Basketball Association (CBA), a weaker professional league. He performed well, and during the season the New York Knicks of the NBA offered him a contract. Skeptics wrote that that opportunity came his way only because of Rick Pitino, who had become the Knicks' head coach the previous summer. Gary Binford, writing

for *Newsday* (February 2, 1988), described Donovan as "too small and too slow" and as "a liability defensively," but acknowledged that he was "adroit at feeding the ball to the pivot—a skill that no other Knick possesses with the exception of Mark Jackson." Overall, as a member of the Knicks, Donovan was ineffective, and he was cut from the team after 44 contests. The following season Donovan got another chance to play with the Utah Jazz, but he performed poorly and soon found himself back in the CBA, playing for the Rapid City Thrillers. In February 1989 Donovan ended his career as a player, because no professional teams were interested in hiring him. "I left without any excuses," Donovan told Harry. "I had my shot. I wasn't good enough and I could live with that."

His impending marriage, planned for that summer, led Donovan to take a job as a broker with a Wall Street investment firm. He soon realized that such work did not suit him. "I hated it," he told Monte Burke for *Forbes* (March 19, 2001). "I was cold-calling all day, trying to drum up leads, studying for the Series 7 broker test. I'd played basketball my whole life, and there I was calling some guy in Texas, trying to get him to give me money like I knew what I was doing." Although he passed the test, after three months on Wall Street, Donovan decided that he would look for a job as a basketball coach. By his own account, he had always wanted to be a coach but had been deterred by the long hours and low pay. He telephoned Pitino, who told him that he was taking the head-coach position at the University of Kentucky the following season and could hire Donovan as a graduate assistant with a salary of $370 a month. Donovan's father, who was present during the conversation with Pitino, saw his son's face "[light] up like a Christmas tree," as he told Price. Donovan accepted the offer, buoyed by his father's advice to pursue his dream. Although Pitino had "never thought of Billy as a coach," as he told Price—"I guess I just thought he was too nice a kid," he explained—Donovan worked his way to the top assistant position. "I'd always prided myself in working 16-hour days," Pitino explained to Harry. "Billy was a guy who took that to another level. He camped out in the office." Donovan's dedication to his work took a toll on his home life. His wife, the former Christine Hasbrouck D'Auria, "fought his job for two years . . . ," as she told Price. "All of a sudden it was just Coach Pitino and 20-hour workdays. No joke."

After five seasons with Pitino and his team, the Wildcats, Donovan accepted the head-coach position at Marshall University, in Huntington, West Virginia; at 28 he became the youngest head coach in Division I. During the previous season, 1993–94, Marshall's basketball team, the Thundering Herd, had won only nine games, and students' interest in the team had waned. Under the breakneck-paced system, similar to Pitino's, that Donovan introduced—it was nicknamed "Billy Ball" by the local media—the players' performance improved markedly; the team won 18 games and earned a berth in the Southern Conference tournament. Although they lost in the first round of the tournament, the team had won back many of their previous fans and earned many new ones. Two days after the 1994–95 season ended, Donovan was hospitalized for several days with exhaustion. The following year the team won 17 games and lost 11.

After the 1995–96 season Donovan left Marshall to become the head coach of the University of Florida's team, the Gators. He took the position against the advice of Pitino, who compared the Gators unfavorably with the Thundering Herd and all the teams in the Southeastern Conference (SEC) and warned Donovan that the school's football team, under the venerated Steve Spurrier, captured the lion's share of attention on campus; indeed, Florida was widely perceived as a "football school." Nevertheless, Donovan welcomed the challenge. Determined to build a talented team, he made his top priorities the recruitment and the development of relationships with top basketball high schools— tasks his predecessor, Lon Kruger, had largely neglected. "Recruiting good players is obviously the key to any successful program," Donovan told Matt Hayes for the *Florida Times-Union* (August 3, 1997). "But there's a lot of hard work and commitment involved, too—from the players and coaches. You can't just assume if you walk on the court with these great high school numbers that it's going to translate to the college level. You have to recruit players to fit your system, and everyone has to work as hard as they can to get where they want to be. It's a never-ending process." Twelve hours after he was installed as the Gators' head coach, Donovan called Frank Martin, who was then the coach at Miami Senior High School, one of the top basketball schools in Florida, to discuss ways to attract basketball players from all over Florida. "Billy and his staff have been working their tails off since the day they were hired," Martin told Matt Hayes for the *Florida Times-Union* (August 3, 1997). "As a high school coach, you're impressed with a group of people that get after it like that." Within a few months Donovan had persuaded Brindley Wright of Miami Senior, one of the highest-rated players in the state, to enroll at the University of Florida.

During his first year at Florida, Donovan installed his "Billy Ball" system, but he had difficulty motivating players who had been recruited by Kruger; seniors in particular had grown disenchanted as the Gators' fortunes had worsened. A low point for Donovan came at the end of January 1997, when the Gators lost a game against Rick Pitino's Wildcats, 92–65. The team struggled for the remainder of the season, finishing with a record of 13–17, but Donovan believed that he had established an effective system. During the 1997–98 season the team—led by a former Marshall student, Jason Williams, who had followed Donovan to Florida—won 14 games and lost 15, and they participated in the National Invitational Tournament at the conclusion of the regular season. In 1998–99 the

team, fortified by Donovan's young recruits, racked up 22 wins, a Florida record. They finished the season 17th in the nation and made it to the third round of the Men's Division I NCAA Tournament.

The 1998–99 Gator team featured Donovan's first full class of recruits. Before that season he had attracted four of the state of Florida's top players and Mike Miller, a two-time South Dakota high-school Player of the Year, who chose Florida over several traditionally more successful basketball programs. Donovan's ability to attract Miller to Florida made considerable waves on the national basketball scene. Miller was counted among the elite high-school basketball players in the country and had been strenuously courted by some of the most celebrated programs in the U.S. Speaking of his recruitment efforts, Donovan explained to S. L. Price, "We don't have the tradition of Kentucky or Kansas. We have to be innovative. We have to call at midnight. We've got to have a different type of relationship with the kids. We've got to watch them play every day during the July period [when NCAA-sanctioned evaluations occur]. Hopefully, all that stuff means something in the end." He also said, "We take the rules to the extreme, but we're doing things the right way. I realize more and more in this recruiting game that there is a perceived hierarchy: Certain programs are supposed to get certain players, then the next tier schools fall in and then the next. We've ruffled feathers going after guys that maybe we weren't supposed to be in on, much less get. But we've been nothing but aboveboard." Lauded by some coaches, Donovan's recruitment efforts angered those who complained that he was "stealing" prime prospects. At the request of Roy Williams, the head coach at the University of Kansas, an NCAA committee began to investigate Florida for possible recruiting violations. Ten months later the committee cleared Florida of any wrongdoing. Mike Miller attributed Donovan's success as a recruiter to his age and personal attributes. "Coach Donovan is younger than most head coaches, he's got a lot of enthusiasm," Miller explained to Price. "That's what sells him to a lot of recruits. He relates to us better than the older coaches, he knows how we feel and what we want out of basketball."

In 1999–2000, led by Mike Miller and Donovan's other second-year stars, the Gators made their second-ever Final Four appearance, defeating the University of North Carolina in the semifinals before falling to Michigan State in the championship game. In just four years Donovan had established Florida as one of the top basketball schools in the United States. Since the 1998–99 season, the team has reached the NCAA Tournament in every year—currently, a streak of eight consecutive times. (Prior to Donovan's arrival, the school had never reached the tournament in more than three consecutive years in eight decades.) During the 2002–03 season the Gators achieved a number-one ranking in the ESPN/*USA Today* poll for the first time in school history, and they earned the number-one ranking the next year as well. Nevertheless, Donovan was criticized for his inability to lead the team to victories in the postseason. After their 2000 Final Four appearance, the Gators were perennial contenders for the national championship yet seemed to play at their worst in the most important games; they never made it past the second round and often lost to far inferior teams. With all the new talent Donovan had brought in, expectations had risen, and for the first time in his life, he was labeled an underachiever. Some detractors believed that Donovan pushed his players too hard, so that by the end of the season, they were burnt out and ineffective. Others questioned his system and suggested that though he was a top-notch recruiter, he seemed to be unable to coach the game at the highest level.

Donovan reversed that trend partially during the 2004–05 season, when Florida won its first SEC Tournament championship but again fell in the second round of the NCAA Tournament. At the conclusion of the season, the Gators' top three players left for the NBA, and Florida began the 2005–06 season absent from the ESPN/*USA Today*'s list of top-25 ranked schools. The team surprised many by winning their first 17 games, rising to the number-two ranking during that streak. Florida again won the SEC Tournament and was seeded third in their region for the NCAA Tournament. With the help of their star player Joakim Noah, the Gators beat every team they played in the NCAA Tournament by considerable margins. The only close score was their 57–53 third-round victory over Georgetown University. On April 3, 2006 the Gators beat the University of California–Los Angeles for the national championship by a score of 73–57. At 40 years of age, Donovan thus became the third-youngest basketball coach to win the NCAA Tournament. Pitino, who had watched his protégé from the stands during the championship game, said to Pat Forde for ESPN.com (April 4, 2006), "Billy was well prepared tonight. That was a coaching clinic." In an example of the strength of the players' team-first mentality, three of the Gators' stars chose to return to Florida for the 2006–07 season, despite the assumption that they were certain to be NBA draftees. On December 20, 2006 Donovan won his 236th game at Florida, surpassing Norm Sloan to become the winningest coach in Florida basketball history.

In 2007 the Gators were SEC Regular Season and SEC Tournament champions and received the number-one overall seed in the NCAA Tournament, reaching the Final Four. On March 31, taking on UCLA for the second year in a row, they won by a score of 76–66. Then, on April 2, they defeated the Ohio State Buckeyes, 84–75, to secure their second national championship in two years. In a testament to the strength of the players' team-first mentality, three members of the Gators—Joakim Noah, Al Horford, and Corey Brewer—had postponed their availability for the NBA draft in order to have the chance to win the NCAA title two years in succession.

In June 2007, much to the surprise of many fans and participants in college basketball, Donovan agreed to a five-year, $27.5 million deal with the Orlando Magic of the NBA. Six days later he changed his mind and signed a six-year contract with the Gators worth $3.5 million per year. In an Associated Press article posted on msnbc.com (June 7, 2007), Donovan was quoted as saying, "As long as the University of Florida would like to have me here, this is where I want to be. For my part, I want to be at the University of Florida for the rest of my time coaching."

Donovan and his wife married in 1989. For some years Christine Donovan taught fourth grade. The couple live in Florida with their four children: William, Hasbrouck, Bryan, and Connor.

—N.W.M.

Suggested Reading: *Boston Globe* F p1 Mar. 28, 2000; *Chicago Tribune* C p7 Mar. 27, 1987; *Newsday* p115 Feb. 2, 1988; *Orlando Sentinel* C p18 Oct. 27, 1996; *Sports Illustrated* p122 Nov. 23, 1998;

Scott Halleran/Getty Images

Dungy, Tony

(DUN-jee)

Oct. 6, 1955– Football coach

Address: Indianapolis Colts, 7001 W. 56th St., Indianapolis, IN 46254

In the fall of 2007, Tony Dungy embarked on his sixth season as the head coach of the Indianapolis

Colts of the National Football League (NFL). In his first five years with the Colts, Dungy directed the team to more than 10 wins per season, a 60–20 regular-season record, five play-off appearances, four American Football Conference (AFC) South titles, two AFC championship-game appearances, and, most recently, a 29–17 victory over the Chicago Bears in Super Bowl XLI—which made Dungy the first African-American head coach to win the Super Bowl and just the third person to do so as both a player and a head coach. (The others are Mike Ditka and Tom Flores.) The 2007 season marked Dungy's 12th as an NFL head coach, a post in which he has established himself as an innovator and as one of the brightest defensive minds in the league. His coaching excellence is illustrated by a 120–62 career regular-season record (as of mid-October 2007) and an overall mark of 129–70; in nine of his 11 seasons as an NFL head coach, his teams have made play-off appearances. The .648 regular-season winning percentage he had achieved by the start of the 2007 season was the best among active NFL coaches with more than 50 regular-season victories. In 2005 Dungy became the 35th coach in NFL history to earn 100 victories. Dungy's success in both the National Football Conference (NFC) and the AFC has earned him the distinction of being the only NFL coach to defeat each of the 32 franchises in the league.

Prior to becoming a head coach, Dungy was a defensive assistant or defensive coordinator with the Pittsburgh Steelers, Kansas City Chiefs, and the Minnesota Vikings, all of the NFL, as well as a defensive assistant for the University of Minnesota football team. Dungy's teams have been characterized by their preparation, strong grounding in fundamentals, and attention to detail. His quiet coaching style and professorial image are atypical for an NFL head coach, but his calm demeanor belies strong convictions. While some have suggested that Dungy would be more effective if he raised his voice more often, Dungy has refuted that assertion. "I think there are people who want coaches to rant and rave," Dungy said to Bob Glauber for the *Sporting News* (February 27, 1995), "but there are a lot of coaches who don't. . . . I think there are a lot of different ways to be successful." Dungy also has gained a reputation as a "player's coach" through his willingness to listen to his players' suggestions. "I hear people say, 'Well, he doesn't holler at the guys,'" Dungy told Gwen Knapp for the *Philadelphia Inquirer* (January 1, 1995). "It's hard for me to understand that grown men can't understand simple directions. I never felt that I had to curse at a guy to make him understand that something needs to be done a certain way. If I reach the point where I have to say 'You SOB, what were you doing there,' we're already in trouble." "You have to make them believe that what you're doing is going to help them to win football games," Dungy told Alan Robinson for the Associated Press (September 19, 1984). "You have to appeal to their intellect." When he is confronted with a player who is unable or unwilling to take instruction, Dungy's solution, rather than belittling the player, is to replace him with another—which has proved to be an effective means of motivation. The Colts' defensive lineman Anthony McFarland told James Patrick for the *Salt Lake (Utah) Tribune* (February 4, 2007), "[Dungy's] a laid-back guy, but he's also a very firm guy. He has expectations and he presents them to you in a manner that's easy to follow, and he expects you to be a man about it."

The second of Cleomae and Wilbur Dungy's four children, Anthony Kevin Dungy was born on October 6, 1955 and grew up in Jackson, Michigan, 100 miles west of Detroit. His mother taught English and speech courses at Jackson High School, where she also coached the cheerleading squad for a time; his father taught surgical anatomy at Delta Community College. Dungy's parents, who raised their children in the Baptist faith, "were very supportive," Dungy told Mick McCabe for the *Detroit Free Press* (September 6, 1996). "They created an atmosphere where we thought it was important to study and do things right. They set a good example for us." Ray Hill, a former student of Dungy's mother, told Martin Fennelly for the *Tampa Bay (Florida) Tribune* (January 7, 2002) that Cleomae Dungy "never yelled or raised her voice. She just had a way of saying things, of looking at you, that commanded respect. She was low key, but in control." Alluding to Tony Dungy, Fennelly wrote, "Sound familiar?" Dungy's father, who had taught high-school biology in an all-black school in Virginia during the 1950s, also pushed his children to pursue their dreams despite the racial prejudice they might face. Tony Dungy said to S. L. Price for *Sports Illustrated* (June 10, 1996), describing the family's attitude toward racial discrimination, "Don't use it as an excuse, don't let it beat you, don't give up." In his youth Dungy nonetheless let his frustration get the better of him on occasion. As Price reported, in ninth grade Dungy was expelled from a basketball game for fighting. That episode taught him a lesson. "I realized that because I got out of control, I satisfied a little anger but I was out of the game," he said to Price. "Now I wasn't playing, and what good did it do?"

As a youngster Dungy proved to be a natural athlete and often played sports with older children. "I enjoyed the challenge of being the worst player on a good team rather than the best on a bad team," Dungy explained to Jerry Green for the *Seattle Times* (November 30, 1997). When he was 14 and playing as a quarterback at Frost Junior High, a photograph of him appeared in the "Faces in the Crowd" section of *Sports Illustrated*. The next year, as a sophomore, he was the starting quarterback at Parkside High School. Dungy was successful at other sports as well: in his three years at Parkside, playing football, basketball, and baseball at the varsity level, he helped win eight out of a possible nine league championships. His coaches were impressed by his leadership, preparation, and intelligence as well as his playing ability. "His vocabulary is unbelievable," Dungy's high-school football coach, Dave Driscoll, told Jerry Green. "He could talk with the most intelligent people at Parkside High School and did quite often, teachers. . . . Then he could talk to the kids on the street, talk at that level, and make everybody feel comfortable. I don't know what his IQ is, but I'll bet you it's close to 200. He had a sense of humor, particularly with his peers. When he talked with me and others, he was serious. He had a tremendous desire for knowledge in all areas. He could have been a businessman. He could have been a lawyer, a doctor." In an interview with Mick McCabe for the *Detroit Free Press* (September 6, 1996), Driscoll called Dungy "a once-in-a-lifetime young man." Dungy graduated from Parkside High School in 1973 with a 3.74 grade-point average.

Dungy entered the University of Minnesota in 1973 on an athletic scholarship and played on both the football and basketball teams in his freshman year. After averaging 2.6 points per game as a reserve shooting guard, Dungy quit the basketball team in his sophomore season in order to concentrate on football—the sport at which he showed the most promise. He starred at quarterback for the Golden Gophers, emerging as a threat at both running and passing. He finished his years at the school as its career leader in pass attempts (576), completions (9,274), passing yards (3,577), and touchdown passes (25). Additionally, he rushed 413 times for 1,345 yards and 16 touchdowns and twice earned the team's Most Valuable Player award. As a senior he played in the East-West Shrine game, the Hula Bowl, and the Japan Bowl, all postseason all-star games. After graduating in 1976, with a bachelor's degree in business administration, Dungy ranked fourth in Big Ten conference history in total offense, behind Mike Phipps, Archie Griffin, and Bob Griese.

Dungy hoped his success would lead to an opportunity to play quarterback in the NFL, but despite his impressive college statistics, he was not drafted by an NFL team. In May 1977 he signed as a free agent with the Pittsburgh Steelers; the team did not intend for him to play quarterback, instead making him a wide receiver and, finally, a safety—the first time since grade school that he had played a defensive position. At first Dungy believed the team's assertion that, at just an inch over six feet, he was too short to be a quarterback in the NFL. As he spent more time in the league, however, he began to believe that teams were biased against African-American quarterbacks. "I'd stand next to [quarterback] Bob Griese and look him right in the eye, and stand next to [quarterback] Fran Tarkenton and look him right in the eye," Dungy told Price. "I'd watch some of the backups throw and say, 'These guys are not very good.' It wasn't until I played a couple years that I started thinking that maybe there was something to this," he continued, referring to racial discrimination. Still, because his role as a defensive player allowed him to stay in the league, Dungy dedicated himself to watching

many hours of film in order to learn the nuances of the position. He played in 14 games as a rookie and intercepted three passes. He also was the Steelers' emergency option at quarterback. In one game, after the quarterbacks Terry Bradshaw and Mike Kruczek had both been injured, Dungy played his former position, completing three of eight passes for 43 yards while rushing three times for eight yards. In that game Dungy became the only player in NFL history to throw an interception and make a defensive interception in the same game. The following year, 1978, Dungy played in 16 games, starting in two at safety, and ranked second in the AFC in interceptions, with six. That season he appeared in Super Bowl XIII, in which Pittsburgh defeated Dallas, 35–31. He was then traded to the San Francisco 49ers, playing in 15 games for them during the 1979 season before being traded once more, this time to the New York Giants. Cut from the Giants during training camp prior to the 1980 season, he retired as a player.

Dungy was not out of work long. He began his coaching career in the fall of 1980, as the defensive backs' coach for the University of Minnesota. The following year, on the recommendation of the Giants' owner, Wellington Mara, Dungy was hired as a defensive assistant by the Steelers. At just 25 years of age, Dungy was the youngest assistant coach in the NFL. In 1982 the Steelers promoted Dungy to defensive backs' coach, a position he held for two seasons before being promoted again, to defensive coordinator, in 1984. At the time Dungy was the only African-American coordinator in the NFL, and the youngest; in fact, he was younger than many of the players he instructed. In his five seasons as defensive coordinator of the Steelers, Dungy's defenses averaged 24 interceptions and 37 takeaways and scored 20 touchdowns—and were considered among the league's best. In 1988, following a disappointing season, the Steelers restructured their coaching staff, firing four assistants and reassigning several others. Rather than accepting a demotion, Dungy resigned.

During his time with the Steelers, Dungy was considered one of the rising coaching stars in the NFL, and many speculated that he would become the first African-American head coach in the modern NFL. (At the time Frederick "Fritz" Pollard, who became the head coach of the Hammond Pros in 1921, was the only African-American coach in NFL history.) Dungy was not considered for many head-coaching positions, however, though he had at least two interviews for such posts, with the Philadelphia Eagles in 1985 and the Green Bay Packers three years later. Referring to the latter, Dungy said to G. D. Clay for New York *Newsday* (January 9, 1994), "I think it was just something to keep the NAACP and Jesse Jackson off their back. I don't consider that interview an interview." At the time many sportswriters offered their points of view as to why Dungy had not gained a head-coaching position. Some suggested that his quiet demeanor and humility, which made him ill-suited for self-promotion, slowed his ascent up the coaching ladder. Many more suggested that the lack of an African-American head coach in the league, despite the fact that a majority of the players were African-American, was a clear sign of discrimination. Dungy was among those who suggested that the situation stemmed from the league's historical discrimination and the insularity of its network of owners, all of whom were tradition-oriented, conservative, elderly white men. (In 1934, through a "gentlemen's agreement," NFL owners had colluded to phase African-American players or coaches out of the NFL, and the league remained all-white until 1946.) "[The owners] just don't know very many minority guys to talk to," Dungy said, as reported by Sid Hartman for the Minneapolis, Minnesota, *Star Tribune* (January 24, 1993). "I don't think it is any kind of blatant discrimination because they want to win. But I just don't think it occurs to them that some of the black coaches could by very effective." "Most owners, when they visualize their head coach, they have trouble visualizing someone black because they haven't seen many of those," Dungy told Ron Lesko for the Associated Press (October 31, 1994). "Myself, when I think of head coaches, I think of Vince Lombardi, Don Shula, Tom Landry, Chuck Noll. All your role models have been white coaches. You have to reassess your thoughts and try to open it up to everybody who's out there, and that's where I think the system's been slow." Dungy also believed that because owners were often removed from developments on the field, they had to rely on publicity and name recognition when hiring coaches—a process that did not favor the NFL's few black assistants, who were not in a position to have their successes noticed. "What we're looking for is a day when a black coach can be interviewed, hired and lose their jobs and it's not newsworthy," Dungy told Gary Shelton for the *St. Petersburg (Florida) Times* (June 2, 1991).

After leaving the Steelers, Dungy served as the defensive backs' coach for the Kansas City Chiefs from 1989 through 1991, helping the Chiefs earn a play-off berth in each of his final two seasons. In 1989 the Chiefs finished first in the AFC and second in the NFL overall in pass defense. In 1989 and 1990 Dungy's defensive backs allowed the second-fewest completions in the NFL and the second-lowest completion percentage in the league. Under Dungy's tutelage the defensive backs Albert Lewis and Kevin Ross were both selected twice for the Pro Bowl. Following the 1991 season Dungy took the defensive coordinator's position with the Minnesota Vikings under head coach Dennis Green, who in January 1992 had become just the third African-American head coach in the NFL. (Art Shell had become the head coach of the Oakland Raiders in October 1989.) In his new position—just below head coach in the leadership hierarchy—Dungy once more put himself in a position to be considered for a head-coaching job. Taking over a veteran-heavy squad was not an easy task for the young

coach, but in one year, through his innovative strategies, Dungy turned a mediocre defense into one of the league's best. He experimented with different lineups, changed the positions of many of the players, and displayed a gift for placing athletes in positions that would allow them to anticipate the play of the opposing team. He also promoted a ball-hawking style of defense and demanded that his players try on each possession to take the football from the opposing team's offense. That tactic made the Vikings one of the best teams in the NFL at forcing turnovers. Dungy tried to confuse offenses by switching from zone to man-to-man defenses and presenting unusual defensive alignments. During his tenure as Minnesota's defensive coordinator, Dungy reestablished himself as one of the top defensive minds in the NFL. In four seasons his defenses intercepted a league-high 95 passes, and his players spurred the team to three play-off appearances. The Vikings' defenses under Dungy ranked eighth in the NFL in 1992, first in 1993, fifth in 1994, and 20th out of 30 in 1995. "One of the keys to our defense is Tony being such a smart guy," the defensive tackle John Randle told Jeff Lenihan for the *Star Tribune* (January 7, 1994). "To me, it's like he goes into the future to the next game, sees what is going to happen, and then comes back to practice and tells us. When we're in practice, it's like he's already been in the next game. It's amazing." Randle's teammate Jack Del Rio concurred, telling Lenihan, "He's the best football mind I've ever been around. . . . I have a tremendous amount of respect for him."

In 1996 Dungy fulfilled his dream of becoming an NFL head coach, when he was hired by the Tampa Bay Buccaneers. The team had one of the worst franchises in the NFL—including an all-time win-loss ratio of 94–213 and just three play-off appearances in its 20-year history. Dungy employed a defense in Tampa that came to be known as the Tampa 2. With roots in the two-deep coverage schemes Dungy had used in Pittsburgh in the 1970s, the Tampa 2 placed a premium on speed and thus on players who were fast but undersized by NFL standards. The strategy is now used widely in the NFL. Under Dungy's watch the Buccaneers' defense quickly became one of the NFL's tightest. In just his second season in Tampa Bay, Dungy guided the team to a 10–6 record and a wild-card berth in the play-offs, where they earned a first-round victory over the Detroit Lions. Dungy was named Professional Coach of the Year by the Maxwell Football Club for his efforts that season, and the team sent a league-high eight players to the Pro Bowl. The Buccaneers slumped in 1998, finishing with an 8–8 record and out of contention for the play-offs, but Dungy received a vote of confidence from the organization, earning a new contract. In 1999 the Buccaneers rebounded, winning the NFC Central Division title, their first division championship since 1981 and just the third in franchise history. They advanced to the NFC Championship game, where they lost to the eventual Super Bowl champion St. Louis Rams, 11–6. In 2000 Tampa Bay again displayed a ferocious defense, which recorded a club-record 55 sacks and sent nine players to the Pro Bowl, but the team finished the season with a disappointing 21–3 loss to the Philadelphia Eagles in the first play-off round. In 2001 Tampa Bay finished sixth in total defense and eighth in the NFL in points allowed and sent six players to the Pro Bowl, but again lost in the first play-off round. Dungy designed some of the best defenses of the era during his time with Tampa Bay, but although he employed several offensive coordinators during those years, he was never able to generate an offense good enough to make Tampa Bay into a genuine championship contender. When the Buccaneers lost to the Philadelphia Eagles in the first play-off round of 2001 by a score of 31–9, the occasion marked the third consecutive play-off game in which Tampa Bay was unable to score an offensive touchdown. Despite the players' loyalty to Dungy, he could not overcome the team's offensive woes and was fired at the end of the season. (Following Dungy's dismissal, Tampa Bay hired the offense-minded John Gruden, and the Buccaneers, using many of Dungy's defensive strategies, won the Super Bowl the following year.) As head coach Dungy had compiled a 54–42 regular-season record and led the Buccaneers to four play-off appearances, leaving as the most successful coach in Tampa Bay history. The former Tampa Bay player Hardy Nickerson told S. L. Price that Dungy was a quiet but effective motivator. "He's a man of integrity, he has a great deal of character," Nickerson said. "He has that aura. You want to do your best because of the type of guy he is."

A variety of teams expressed interest in hiring Dungy, impressed with what he had accomplished with the Tampa Bay players both on and off the field. In January 2002 he was hired as the head coach of the Indianapolis Colts. The team had a potent offense but a marginal defense; in his first three seasons with the Colts, Dungy made improvements on defense a priority—employing the Tampa 2 approach—without altering many of the offensive schemes. The effects were immediate: in 2002 the team won 10 games while losing just six. In 2003 the Colts, for only the eighth time in franchise history, went for the whole season without losing consecutive games. The team won 12 regular-season contests before falling to the New England Patriots in the AFC Championship Game. In 2004 the offense scored 522 points, the fifth-highest in NFL history, led by quarterback Peyton Manning. The defense contributed to the success by forcing 36 turnovers, tied for third in the NFL, and 45 quarterback sacks, led by Dwight Freeney's NFL-leading 16. Freeney became the first Colt to win the sack title since the category became an official statistic, in 1982. After again winning 12 games while losing just four, the Colts lost to their rivals the Patriots in the second play-off round.

In 2005 the Colts set an NFL record by winning 13 consecutive games by a margin of seven or more points. Dungy's defensive strategies had gelled, and the team, with a similarly effective offense, had achieved a greater balance than in the past. The Colts, who ranked second in the NFL in both scoring offense and scoring defense, trailed in only four games all season—for a total of 148 minutes and 16 seconds—and finished with 14 wins and two losses. That record earned them a first-round bye in the play-offs, and they were a favorite to advance to the Super Bowl. They were defeated by the Pittsburgh Steelers, however, in their first play-off game. The loss brought questions about Dungy's ability to win in the postseason.

In the following season Dungy silenced his critics. The Colts were undefeated in their first nine games, earning a perfect home record en route to a 12–4 season finish. Despite their regular-season success, previous postseason failures led the Colts to be considered underdogs in the play-offs. In the first round they faced the Kansas City Chiefs, in a game billed as a shootout between two high-scoring clubs. With a dominant defense, the Colts won easily, 23–8. Next, in a match against the Baltimore Ravens, another stirring defensive effort—and five field goals from the kicker Adam Vinatieri—led to a 15–6 Colts victory. In the AFC Championship game, against the New England Patriots, the Colts had fallen behind 21–6 by half-time but scored 32 second-half points to notch another victory—and a long-awaited berth in the Super Bowl. The Colts faced the Chicago Bears, a team that relied on a stout defense and a conservative offense. The game pitted Dungy against Lovie Smith, who had worked under Dungy at Tampa Bay; the matchup, on February 4, 2007, brought added attention because both coaches were African-American, and the victor would be the first black head coach to win the Super Bowl. Dungy prevailed, and the Colts won the game by a score of 29–17.

In August 2007 President George W. Bush appointed Dungy to his Council on Service and Civic Participation, a 25-member group established in 2003 to "help recognize outstanding volunteer service, and in so doing, foster even greater participation among all Americans to answer [the president's] call to service," according to Joe Oehser, writing for the official Colts Web site (August 14, 2007). That month Tyndale House Publishers brought out *Quiet Strength: The Principles, Practices, and Priorities of a Winning Life*, a memoir Dungy wrote with Nathan Whitaker. The book reached number one on the *New York Times* nonfiction best-seller list, marking the first time an NFL-related book had attained that position. The publishing company Simon & Schuster announced in September 2007 that Dungy had signed on to write *You Can Do It*, a children's book, due out in July 2008.

Dungy and the Colts started the 2007 season with six straight wins. By mid-October the Patriots, their longtime rivals, were the only other undefeated team in the NFL, having won their first seven games. The two teams were scheduled to play each other on November 4, 2007.

Throughout his career Dungy has been active in community organizations in the cities where he has lived and worked. While with the Buccaneers, he served as a public speaker for the Fellowship of Christian Athletes and Athletes in Action. He launched Mentors for Life, a program that provided area youths and their mentors with tickets to Buccaneers home games. He was also a supporter of charitable programs for children, such as Family First, Big Brothers/Big Sisters, Boys & Girls Clubs, the Prison Crusade Ministry, and foster-parenting organizations. In Indianapolis Dungy helped implement a local Baskets of Hope program that benefits the Riley Hospital for Children. He has been a spokesperson for All-Pro Dad, a family-themed organization; Arby's Combo, which benefits Big Brothers/Big Sisters; and the Boys & Girls Club. He also appeared at the Black Coaches Association National Convention and Indiana Black Expo. He participates frequently in local faith-based events and at family football clinics.

Dungy and his wife, Lauren, have five children—Tiara, Eric, Jade, Jordan, and Justin—the last three of whom are adopted. Justin joined the family as an infant in mid-2006, a half-year after the Dungys' son James committed suicide. "It's human nature to grieve, and you're going to have some pain," Dungy told Jarrett Bell for USA Today (August 31, 2006, on-line). "But then the choice is how you handle the pain. You can choose to go on and fight through it, or you can choose to succumb to it. . . . You can't make the feeling go away. There's no Novocain or anything that can just take it away. You begin to realize that you can still function, you can still move forward."

—N.W.M.

Suggested Reading: *Chicago Tribune* C p5 Nov. 3, 1992; *Detroit Free Press* C p1 Sep. 6, 1996; (Minneapolis, Minnesota) *Star Tribune* C p1 July 31, 1992, C p1 Dec. 17, 1992; *Newsday* p20 Jan. 9, 1994; *Philadelphia Inquirer* C p6 Jan. 21, 1994, C p10 Jan.1, 1995; *Seattle Times* C p7 Nov. 30, 1997; *Sports Illustrated* p68 June 10, 1996; *St. Petersburg Times* C p1 June 2, 1991; *Washington Post* D p1 Dec. 27, 1985

Selected Books: *Quiet Strength: The Principles, Practices, and Priorities of a Winning Life* (with Nathan Whitaker), 2007

Dwight, Ed

Sep. 9, 1933– Sculptor

Address: Ed Dwight Studios, 3824 Dahlia St., Denver, CO 80207

When Ed Dwight began his career as a sculptor, in the early 1970s, he knew virtually nothing about such prominent figures in African-American history as Harriet Tubman, Sojourner Truth, and Frederick Douglass. Now—more than 2,500 sculptures later—Dwight has made a name for himself with statues of those and many other historically important African-Americans. In the 1960s Dwight himself had come close to becoming a historic first: the United States' first black astronaut. Passed over for that job after years of training, he turned to art, and he has since created more than 80 publicly commissioned monuments. "Anything that has to do with black folks' accomplishments, I am interested in," he told Fahizah Alim for the *Sacramento (California) Bee* (April 11, 2003). "I go through a metamorphosis and become [the subjects]." In his 30,000-square-foot studio in Denver, Colorado—one of the largest privately owned, single-artist production facilities in the western U.S.—he has produced works that in some cases have earned him more than $250,000 apiece. Dwight has been credited with introducing significant innovations

Ed Dwight (left) with Bill Dixon, owner, Atlanta Art Gallery. (Photo: Courtesy of the Atlanta Art Gallery)

in the "negative space" technique, which focuses on the spaces around and between the elements of a sculpture as well as on its solid parts. "I am a very gifted man and very confident in what I do every day," he told Tony Perez-Giese for the *Denver Westword* (May 29, 1997). Such self-assurance has helped Dwight to overcome the obstacles that have often faced artists interested in publicly commemorating subjects other than Caucasian males. According to Richard Halicks, writing for the *Atlanta Journal-Constitution* (May 26, 2002), "Dwight thinks and talks big, by turns strident and thoughtful." Dwight hopes that exposure to his work will prevent other African-American children from remaining ignorant about their heritage. Recalling his own youthful unawareness, he said in a speech at the unveiling of his memorial to Martin Luther King Jr., as quoted by Sandy Alexander in the *Baltimore Sun* (August 28, 2006), "There are a lot of Ed Dwights out there. They need this message."

The second of the four children and the only son of Edward J. Dwight Sr. and Georgia Baker Dwight, Edward J. Dwight Jr. was born in Kansas City, Kansas, on September 9, 1933 and grew up in the rural outskirts of that city. His father was a professional baseball player; he was often away from home, manning second base for the Kansas City Monarchs, a team in the Negro League. For that reason his mother, whose forebears included whites from Austria, was his primary caregiver. "My mother raised me to think of myself as a citizen of the entire universe, not a racial one," he told Karen Pride for the *Chicago Defender* (August 22, 2004). The family lived near Kansas City's Fairfax Airport, and Dwight's mother would often take him to watch planes take off and land. "My mother would tell me stories about where the planes went, and I was fascinated because after they took off, they always disappeared," he recalled to Pride. His mother encouraged his interest in art as well as in aircraft. When he was young she would read the text of newspaper cartoons aloud to him, and Dwight—who has said that he began to draw before he learned to walk—would then illustrate the stories himself, shading his sketches with cross-hatching. At 14 Dwight opened his own sign shop, creating church banners, ads, collages, and oil paintings for hundreds of customers. As part of an integration effort, he became the first black male student at Kansas City's Bishop Ward High School, a previously all-white Catholic school. When one of his teachers, a nun, entered his artwork in the annual Kansas Scholastic Art Competition, he won all three prizes. Thanks to that achievement, he won a scholarship to the Kansas City Art Institute, in Kansas City, Missouri, just across the Kansas border, but his father refused to let him attend. "'You are not going to be an artist. You are going to be an engineer,'" his father told him, as Dwight recalled to Alim. Dwight added that his father was "a macho man."

In 1953 Dwight joined the U.S. Air Force. After basic training and pilot training, Dwight became a military pilot, flying more than 2,000 hours in high-performance jets such as B-57s. He did so despite his being three-quarters of an inch below the then-minimum height requirement for pilots (five feet four inches). "Every night I was stretched out, and two guys pulled my legs to make me taller," he recalled to Michael Neill for *People* (May 25, 1987). "I didn't grow a goddamn inch." Nonetheless, Dwight's drive and determination led his superiors to allow him to continue up the ranks. In 1961 Dwight earned a degree in aeronautical engineering from Arizona State University–Tempe. That year, while serving as a captain at Travis Air Force Base, in California, Dwight received a letter bearing the signature of President John F. Kennedy and inviting him to apply to test-pilot school as an astronaut. As the first black astronaut trainee, Dwight was thrown into the international media spotlight, with his image appearing on the covers of *Ebony*, *Jet*, and *Sepia* magazines. He studied at the Experimental Test Pilot School and completed the Aerospace Research Pilot Course, but he was not selected to be an astronaut. After that rejection—which he has attributed to the abandonment of efforts to diversify the National Aeronautics and Space Administration (NASA) following Kennedy's assassination—Dwight sent a 15-page, single-spaced letter to officials in Washington, D.C., describing the racism he had experienced during training. He told Alim that he had never dealt with discrimination before he entered the space program and that he was shocked by what he felt was NASA's bias against him as an African-American. "I didn't even know I was black," he explained to Alim. "I knew black folks had some problems, and I didn't know what they were. I went to white schools and colleges and I lived in a white universe. It wasn't until I got to the space program that I found out how it was to be treated as a black man." In *Yeager: An Autobiography* (1986), Chuck Yeager, the first commandant of the United States Air Force Aerospace Research Pilot School, dismissed Dwight's claims. "Ed Dwight was an average pilot with an average academic background," Yeager wrote, as quoted by Perez-Giese. "He wasn't a bad pilot, but he wasn't exceptionally talented, either. He worked hard . . . but he just couldn't hack it." In *The Right Stuff* (1979), about the U.S. space program, Tom Wolfe offered a different take on what had happened. In his view, Dwight may not have had "the right stuff" to succeed as an astronaut, but as an unwitting subject in an experiment in diversity, he had been treated unfairly. "He was being set up for a fall because the chances of NASA accepting him as an astronaut appeared remote in any event," Wolfe wrote, as quoted by Perez-Giese. Out of frustration, his letter to Washington having elicited little attention, Dwight held a press conference at the Naval Ordnance Test Station in China Lake, California, in which he accused NASA and the federal government of racism. "I was just a guinea pig," he later reflected to Doug MacCash for the New Orleans, Louisiana, *Times-Picayune* (November 12, 2002). "I was on Kennedy's agenda. I was like a P.R. stunt. I was a pawn." Dwight soon received orders assigning him to West

Germany, considered a very undesirable post at the time; when he refused them, he entered into a prolonged dispute with the air force that ended with his resignation, in 1966.

Dwight next held a series of jobs, including one with the IBM Corp. and another as the manager of a chain of barbecue restaurants. He also worked as a real-estate and construction entrepreneur in Denver, Colorado; as the builder of condominiums there, he became a millionaire by the early 1970s. Then, in the middle of that decade, a housing-market recession caused him to lose much of his property. Meanwhile, while creating paintings to decorate model units in the condominiums, he experienced a reawakening of his passion for art. The paintings were popular with interior decorators and architects, and Dwight realized that making a career as an artist was a realistic possibility for him.

Dwight's first commercial artistic project was a 1974 commission to sculpt a bust of George Brown, Colorado's first African-American lieutenant governor. The following year he was offered a job by the Colorado Centennial Commission to create a series of sculptures with the title *Black Frontier Spirit in the American West*. His 30 bronze works depict the often-overlooked contribution of African-Americans in the settling of the West. For Dwight, working on the project was eye-opening. "There were black cowboys, black pioneers, black jockeys," he told Michael Neill. "I had never heard of this before." The completed series was exhibited throughout the United States.

Dwight received a master of fine arts degree from the University of Denver in 1977. In the vast workshop he opened around that time, the Ed Dwight Studios, he created his next large series, *Jazz: An American Art Form*, which illuminated the history of jazz through more than 70 bronze sculptures of such jazz greats as Miles Davis, Charlie Parker, Dizzie Gillespie, Louis Armstrong, and Ella Fitzgerald. With the jazz series, one of his best-known works, Dwight began to experiment with the concept of negative space. Positive space is that filled by the sculpture itself; negative space is the empty space around or between parts of the sculpture. Dwight designed the jazz luminaries so that the negative space of each piece seemed to have an energy of its own. "Though based in realism, Dwight's new gallery works take dramatic compositional liberties while depicting well-known and obscure jazz musicians," as MacCash wrote. "He often removes the legs, arms and lower torsos of his figures, to focus attention on the faces and hands, and to cause them to seem to float weightlessly in space." Part of the series was displayed at the Smithsonian Institution, in Washington, D.C.

As he established himself as one of the nation's foremost contemporary sculptors, Dwight found himself the artist of choice in projects involving African-American subjects, a long-neglected area in sculpture. "I have 12 huge memorials in the house right now, 'cause there's nobody else to do

'em," Dwight told Richard Halicks in 2002. Earlier, in the late 1990s, Dwight came to national attention with two prominent commissions. The first, a monument dedicated to the international underground-railroad movement, was completed in 2001. Dwight originally envisioned the monument—which stands in Detroit, Michigan, and Windsor, Ontario, Canada—as an arc that would span the river separating the two cities. When he visited the site, however, he realized that he would not be able to build such a structure. Instead, he fashioned a two-piece sculpture: on the Detroit side, a 42-foot-high monument called *Gateway to Freedom*, which shows a group of slaves about to be ushered to freedom in Canada, some looking back at the U.S. and others looking ahead, across the river; on the Windsor side, the 22-foot-high *Tower of Freedom*, which depicts the provider of a sanctuary on the underground railroad greeting a slave family. Writing for the *Baltimore Afro-American* (November 9, 2001), Vicki Lee described *Gateway to Freedom*, which had been selected from more than 100 other proposals, as "a true masterpiece that embodies the spirit of the Underground Railroad, its conductors and passengers." The following year Dwight unveiled his 26-foot-tall monument to the civil rights leader Martin Luther King Jr. in Denver. The bust of King measures nine feet eight inches, with smaller busts of other important U.S. and international civil rights figures—among them Rosa Parks, Sojourner Truth, and Mahatma Gandhi—surrounding King's figure, and quotes from King carved into the sides of the monument's base. The sculpture, like all of Dwight's work, is a literal representation of the subject. Dwight told Mary Voelz Chandler for the *Rocky Mountain News* (June 8, 2002) that he bristles at the idea of making an abstract sculpture of anyone or anything who represents his heritage. "When white people glorified themselves, they used figurative art," he explained. "When black people came along and want to do that, they say, 'Make it abstract.' You can't abstract history." Also in 2002 Dwight unveiled a memorial in Baltimore, Maryland, which commemorates the slave Kunta Kinte, who arrived in Baltimore from Africa, and Kinte's descendant Alex Haley, who wrote about Kinte's struggle for freedom in his book *Roots: The Saga of an American Family* (1976). Leonard Blackshear, the head of the Kunta Kinte–Alex Haley Foundation, which commissioned the piece, praised Dwight's depiction of Haley reading to a group of schoolchildren. "Ed Dwight expressed understanding of the individual heritage stories, but he also underlines the importance of adults sharing stories so they will not become rootless," Blackshear told Jamie Stiehm for the *Baltimore Sun* (May 15, 2005). "African-Americans are beginning to see the importance of memorializing their history, because it is American history."

Dwight has been working for several years on the Black Revolutionary War Patriots Memorial, which was to have been located between the Lincoln Memorial and the Washington Monument in Washington, D.C. In honoring the 5,000 free and enslaved black soldiers who served on the side of the colonists in the Revolutionary War, the memorial would have been the only one on the Washington Mall devoted specifically to African-Americans. Dwight's design calls for 63 figures occupying a space 90 feet long, with heights ranging from 30 inches to more than seven feet high. After securing the last vacant spot for a memorial on the Mall, the Black Patriots Foundation, the organizer for the memorial, was unable to raise enough funds to build Dwight's sculpture, and its claim expired. "The politics of the memorials has gotten outrageous," Dwight told MacCash. "I do mostly memorials to black people, but memorials to black folks don't warrant the same money as memorials to white people. If it's a white memorial and you ask for $20 million, it's fine. If it's a black memorial, they say, 'What are you going to do with $20 million?' The cost of marble and bronze isn't color coded." The location of the memorial has yet to be determined.

Among Dwight's recent projects is a monument called alternately the *Tower of Reconciliation* or the *John Hope Franklin Greenwood Tower of Reconciliation*, the latter title bearing the names of an eminent contemporary black historian and a once-prominent black neighborhood in Tulsa, Oklahoma. Destined for a site in Tulsa, the tower will commemorate the race riots that decimated Greenwood and left dozens of blacks dead in 1921. The 27-foot monument is designed to evoke the concepts of diversity and partnership, with the word "reconciliation" featured across the top of the tower. "The good news is reconciliation," Dwight told Judy Robinson for the *Oklahoman* (September 24, 2006). "It's not what you did, it's how you recover from it."

Dwight lives in Denver, which honored him with one of the 2002 Mayor's Awards for Excellence in the Arts. He has five children and has been married several times.

—C.S.

Suggested Reading: Ed Dwight's Web site; (New Orleans, Louisiana) *Times-Picayune* Living p1+ Nov. 12, 2002; *People* p115 May 25, 1987; *Sacramento (California) Bee* E p1+ Apr. 11, 2003

Selected Works: *Black Frontier Spirit in the American West*, 1975; *Jazz: An American Art Form*, 1977; *Gateway to Freedom*, 2001; *Tower of Freedom*, 2001; *Martin Luther King Jr. Monument*, 2002; *Kunta Kinte/Alex Haley Memorial*, 2002

Earnhardt, Dale Jr.

Oct. 10, 1974– Race-car driver

Address: Club E Jr., P.O. Box 5190, Concord, NC 28027

"I know when I go out there, I could die," the race-car driver Dale Earnhardt Jr. said in 2002, as quoted by Pam Lambert, Johnny Dodd, and other reporters in *People* (August 2, 2004). "If I quit driving race cars because of that, I wouldn't be living." Those words reflect the driver's understanding of the risks involved in racing at speeds upwards of 200 miles per hour—an understanding that deepened when his father, Dale Earnhardt Sr., died in a crash in 2001. Known as "Junior," "The Dominator," and "Little E," Dale Earnhardt Jr. is a third-generation NASCAR (National Association of Stock Car Racing) driver, and for over a decade after he started racing, at 17, his father's storied career overshadowed his own accomplishments. In recent years, however, the younger Earnhardt has developed a celebrity status of his own. While NASCAR's most prestigious championship—the Nextel Cup—has so far eluded Earnhardt, his statistics have grown more and more impressive, to include many wins and top-10, top-five, and top-three finishes. He has taken his father's place as the most visible NASCAR driver, with dozens of commercial appearances and other endorsements, the publica-

Doug Benc/Getty Images

tion of his memoir, *Driver #8* (2002), bit roles in movies including Pixar's animated hit *Cars* (2005), music-video appearances, and many awards. "Junior" has become the face of NASCAR, which, after years of regional popularity, has become—behind football—the second-most-watched sport in the United States.

Ralph Dale Earnhardt Jr. was born in Concord, North Carolina, on October 10, 1974 to Dale Earnhardt Sr. and his second wife, Brenda. When he was three his parents divorced, and afterward Dale Jr., his half-brother, Kerry, and sister, Kelley, lived with Brenda. Three years later the house where they were living caught fire, and the children's mother sent them to live with their father. There they were exposed to racing from two older generations of enthusiasts. Their grandfather, Ralph Lee Earnhardt, had begun racing on dirt tracks and became known for his skills as a driver when he won the 1956 NASCAR Sportsman Championship. His best-remembered contribution to the sport, however, was his innovation in the garage. His profile on the Stock Car Hall of Fame Web site states, "Ralph Earnhardt was the first car builder/driver to understand and use tire stagger [different-size tires to improve handling], developed the capability to adjust the amount of bite in his race cars as well as standardizing crash bars on the driver side door." Ralph Earnhardt discouraged Dale Earnhardt Sr. from racing, but soon the young man dropped out of high school to pursue his dream. Dale Sr. became one of the most successful NASCAR drivers ever, with 76 wins and seven championships—tying Richard Petty for most championships. Though observers have recognized similarities between the abilities of Dale Earnhardt Jr. and his father, they have pointed to contrasting qualities in the men themselves. "They both live in the fast lane, but in Dale Earnhardt Jr.'s case, it was the metaphor that defined him," Paola Boivin wrote for the *Arizona Republic* (November 2, 2000) before the elder Earnhardt's death. "Like many fathers and sons, the similarities seem to end at the cut of the jaw. Senior's words are measured. Junior's flow easily and with less calculation. Senior likes the sunrise. Junior often misses it. And, yes, senior is a little bit country and junior is more than a little bit rock and roll." One difference between the two has to do with their sport's increase in popularity and the resulting need for the young generation of drivers to adopt more restrained driving styles. Dale Earnhardt Sr., nicknamed "The Intimidator," drove aggressively, sometimes intentionally bumping or spinning-out other drivers. Now that NASCAR fines drivers for such aggressiveness, Dale Earnhardt Jr.'s driving is more calculated.

The sport of stock-car racing developed in the southern U.S. during the first half of the 20th century. Many of the drivers were bootleggers who had modified their cars to be faster and more maneuverable than other vehicles, particularly the police cars that chased them during their attempted moonshine runs. Early stock-car races were loosely organized and plagued by corrupt promoters, who would often abscond with the proceeds and prize money before races had ended. William France Sr., deciding that the sport's fan base would increase with the creation of a formal sanctioning organization, formed NASCAR, which held its first event in Daytona Beach, Florida, on February 15, 1948.

Stock-car racing has undergone many changes since then. Before NASCAR was set up, races in Daytona took place half on the highway and half on sand; as the sport developed, half-mile and one-mile oval tracks were built. Currently NASCAR events are held on superspeedways (tracks that are over one mile long), built with high banks. (The longest, at 2.66 miles, is Talladega, in Alabama.) Due to the high rate of accidents and possibility of fatalities, safety measures have been implemented. Originally the cars remained stock (that is, they retained their original manufacturer specifications), but for the sake of safety as well as performance, the modern-day "stock" cars bear only a surface resemblance to ordinary vehicles. Their engines are extremely powerful, with 750 horsepower, and the cars' insides are fortified with roll cages and safety bars; some tracks require that cars have restrictor plates, which limit speed. Building and maintaining the precision of today's race cars requires teams of engineers, mechanics, and designers.

Today NASCAR hosts many events worldwide, the most popular and profitable of which are the races in the Busch Series (akin to the triple-A leagues of professional baseball), the more prestigious Nextel Cup (formerly Winston Cup) Series, and the Craftsman Truck Series. Each series operates on a system of points, awarded to drivers over the course of the season. First-place drivers receive the most points (180 in the 2006 season), with progressively fewer points given to racers who place farther back. Drivers also score an additional five points in a race if they lead for at least one lap, and still more points if they lead for the greatest number of laps. Since it is impossible for a driver to win without having led for at least one lap during the race, the leader receives a minimum of 185 points. Points are awarded to the driver who starts the race; a driver who is injured after the first lap or unable to compete for the entire race may be replaced and receive the points that his relief driver earned. The current point system, aside from a few later alterations, was established in 1975, after NASCAR had tried dozens of others.

When Dale Earnhardt Jr. was 17, he and Kerry sold their go-kart in order to buy a 1978 Chevy Monte Carlo from a junkyard. Dale Sr. did not oppose his namesake's racing career, but, following Ralph Lee Earnhardt's example, he did not support it financially, at least in the beginning. That choice forced Dale Jr. and his brother to restore the Monte Carlo on their own, which in turn helped Dale Jr. gain an understanding of how his race car performed, and of how minuscule variations in engine performance and handling could affect the outcome of a race; that knowledge was crucial to his development as a racer. During his first years of racing, he honed his abilities in the Street Stock (a local competition sometimes sponsored by NASCAR) and later in races in NASCAR's Late

Model Stock Car divisions, at many tracks in the Southeast. Concurrently, he attended a community college in North Carolina and earned a two-year automotive degree, thus enabling him to begin working as a mechanic at his father's Chevy dealership—where, his Web site claims, he was the fastest oil changer.

In 1996 Earnhardt made 53 starts in the Late Model Stock Car division, earned eight pole positions, or poles (the pole is the foremost position on the starting grid, awarded to the fastest qualifier), and won two races to finish second in points for the season. His success demonstrated that he was ready to advance to NASCAR's Busch Grand Nationals. He decided to run a partial schedule in 1997, and in his first Busch Series race, at Myrtle Beach, South Carolina, he finished 14th. In the next year he began competing full-time. He drove the No. 3 ACDelco Monte Carlo for the racing team Dale Earnhardt Inc. in his first race, the NAPA 300, at Daytona International Speedway. In that contest his car flipped end over end, but it landed on its wheels, and he walked away, shaken but uninjured.

Earnhardt Jr.'s first win came on April 4, 1998 at the Texas Motor Speedway. He won six more races that season, earning enough points to claim the Busch Series—and to become the first third-generation driver to win a NASCAR championship. He repeated that feat the next year, even though his first win eluded him until his 15th race. On July 3 Earnhardt was involved in a crash during practice in Milwaukee, Wisconsin, and his backup driver, Ron Hornaday, drove the No. 3 car in the qualifying round. Still sore, Earnhardt returned to the driver's seat and mustered a third-place finish from a 15th-place starting position. Overall Earnhardt won six races in 1999, and his Busch Series earnings were a record-setting $1,680,598. After two successful seasons that garnered him two championships and more than $3 million, he decided to advance to the Winston Cup circuit full-time in 2000.

Earnhardt's rookie season in the Winston Cup series saw him move into a new car (No. 8) sponsored by Budweiser. He set records at tracks in Charlotte, North Carolina, and Michigan and won the Winston All-Star Race, the first time a rookie had done so. With race victories in his 12th and 16th career starts in the Winston Cup Series, he tied Davey Allison and Jimmie Johnson for the earliest multi-race wins in Cup history. Leading up to the season, Earnhardt was considered the favorite to win the Raybestos Rookie of the Year Award, but his friend and rival Matt Kenseth outraced him at the traditional, season-opening Daytona 500, often called the "Great American Race," and Earnhardt trailed Kenseth in points throughout the season, losing by 42 and coming in second among rookies. Also during Earnhardt's rookie year, at the Pepsi 400 at Michigan International Speedway, Dale Earnhardt Sr. raced against his two sons. (Dale Sr. finished eighth, Dale Jr. and Kerry 35th and 43d,

respectively.) That occasion marked only the second time in NASCAR history that a driver and his sons had competed in the same race. (On the first occasion Lee Petty raced against his sons Richard and Maurice.)

Earnhardt's sophomore season began with tragedy. On February 18, 2001, at the Daytona 500 season opener, the Dale Earnhardt Inc. drivers Michael Waltrip, Dale Earnhardt Jr., and Dale Earnhardt Sr. were in first, second, and third place, respectively, when, on the last turn of the last lap, Dale Sr. careened into the outer wall after another driver bumped him. Doctors reported that he died instantly from head and neck trauma. His death affected the NASCAR community immensely. Days after the funeral, Dale Earnhardt Jr. told reporters, as quoted by *People* (March 12, 2001), "I miss my father, and I've cried for him. I just try to . . . remember that he's in a better place." A week later he returned to the driver's seat and was involved in an accident that was described in the *People* article as "frighteningly reminiscent of the crash that killed his father."

The sentimental favorite when he returned to Daytona on July 7, 2001, for the first time since his father's crash, Earnhardt did not disappoint. He was in command of the race for most of the laps, when, with 17 laps to go, a 12-car pileup sent several vehicles to the garage. Because of the timing of the pileup, Earnhardt was stuck on the track while other drivers were able to make their pit stops. When he finally emerged from the pit, in sixth place, his chances of winning seemed slim. According to Mark Bechtel, writing for *Sports Illustrated* (December 3, 2001), Earnhardt's crew chief and uncle, Tony Eury Sr., said in an interview during the race that Earnhardt simply did not have time left to take first place. But within two laps Earnhardt made a move on the leader, Johnny Benson, in the same short stretch of track between turns three and four where his father had been killed five months earlier. With Waltrip's help in drafting (which occurs when two drivers take advantage of wind and aerodynamics to help each other move faster), Earnhardt won an emotional victory. As he crossed the finish line, according to the Web site dalejrpitstop.com, he told his crew over the radio, "Y'all know who that's for, guys." Earnhardt finished the 2001 season eighth in points for the year, with three victories (at Dover, Talladega, and Dayton), two Bud Pole Awards (monetary awards given by Anheuser Busch for each pole position won during point races, which also qualifies the driver to compete in the following year's season-opening all-star race, the Bud Shootout), and winnings of nearly $6 million.

During the 2002 season Earnhardt won at Talladega again and had multiple top-10 and top-five finishes. Nevertheless, he finished the season in 11th place. He nonetheless told Joel Poiley and Ed Duarte for *Sports Illustrated for Kids* (February 2003), "We grew as a team. I don't see why we can't string together that sort of consistency all year."

Along with racing, Earnhardt had time to publish a book, *Driver #8*, written with Jade Gurss, about his rookie season. He also signed endorsement deals with companies including Wrangler and Drakkar Noir, and made other commercial appearances for Budweiser, NAPA Auto Parts, Dominos's Pizza, Gillette, and Enterprise Rent-A-Car.

Returning for the next year's opener, Earnhardt tied the record for the most wins in a single Daytona Speedweek, with three: the Budweiser Shootout, one of the Twin-125-mile races for the Daytona 500, and a Busch Series race. His win at Talladega set a record for most consecutive victories there (four); his overall statistics, except for total laps led, were the highest of his career. He finished third overall in points in 2003, earned nearly $7 million, and had 10 top-three finishes as well as 13 top-five and 21 top-10 showings; in four races he led by the most laps. At the end of the season, he was awarded the National Motorsports Press Association's Most Popular Driver Award, receiving 1.3 million votes from NASCAR fans—more votes than were received by the other top 10 candidates combined.

The beginning of the 2004 season was also the start of NASCAR sponsorship by the cellular-phone company Nextel; the Winston Cup was rechristened the Nextel Cup. That year also saw the inaugural play-off series, the Chase for the Cup (more popularly known as the Chase), in which the top 10 racers compete during the last 10 races for the championship. Earnhardt began the season, on February 15, 2004, with his first Daytona 500 win. He had not only succeeded on the track where his father had lost his life, but won the race six years to the day after Dale Sr. had achieved his only win at the Daytona 500—the one victory that eluded him until late in his career. Dale Jr. again won one of the Twin-125 qualifying races for the Daytona 500, and with wins at Atlanta, Richmond, Bristol, Talladega, and Phoenix, he ended his season with the greatest number of single-season victories of his career. He also set career bests in top-three finishes (13), top-five finishes (16), and laps led (1,133) and tied a career-best record in top-10 finishes (21). He was again presented with the Most Popular Driver Award.

Many Winston/Nextel Cup drivers compete periodically in the Busch Series, whose races, run the day before the more elite division races, allow drivers to acclimate themselves to track conditions and evaluate the conditions of their cars. Earnhardt is no exception, and having achieved three Busch Series wins in as many starts in 2003, in 2004 he accomplished two "weekend sweeps," twice winning a Busch Series and a Cup Series race in the same weekend. As co-owner, with his stepmother, Teresa, of the Chance2 team, Earnhardt shared a NASCAR title in the Busch Series, thanks to the efforts of the driver Martin Truex Jr. Earnhardt finished the 2004 season with his second consecutive top-five finish, placing fifth overall for the season—an impressive feat, considering that on July

18, during a non-points contest at the Infineon Raceway in Sonoma, California, his canary-yellow Corvette spun out on the first turn, crashed into the wall, and burst into flame. He walked away from the accident badly shaken but with only second-degree burns.

The 2005 season proved to be one of change and disappointment for Earnhardt. His Budweiser-sponsored team finished 19th overall, and his statistics were down, with only one victory (in Chicago), three top-three finishes, seven in the top five, and 13 in the top 10. His team went through three different crew chiefs, finally settling on his cousin, Tony Eury Jr. The season was not without its triumphs, however. Earnhardt won the Most Popular Driver Award for the third straight year, becoming only the fourth driver since 1956 to have done so, and he earned the MBNA Mid-Race Leader Award, the Mobile 1 Command Performance Driver of the Race Award, and the WIX Filters Lap Leader Award in the Bass Pro Shops/MBNA 500 at Atlanta Motor Speedway. Also, his Busch Series team won its second consecutive championship. After that season Earnhardt announced that he would start his own company, J. R. Motorsports, with a driver who would compete in the Busch Series the next year. The Chance2 team has since disbanded.

The Budweiser team entered 2006 with their worst season to date behind them and with a renewed sense of purpose. Earnhardt and Eury stated, according to many sources, that while they had had problems communicating following a stressful 2004 season, they had learned to put their differences aside and focus on the future. That attitude seemed to benefit them, as Earnhardt recorded a win at the Crown Royal 400 in Richmond, Virginia, and 18 top-15 finishes over the season, which put him as high as third place in points, and no lower than 11th, leading up to the Chase. With a third-place finish at the Sharpie 500 at Bristol Motor Speedway, in Tennessee, and a second-place showing the following week at the Sony HD 500 at the California Speedway, Earnhardt emerged as a contender for the title.

Late in the race at Talledega, on October 8, 2006, Earnhardt was in first place and seemed about to win for the fifth time. Then Brian Vickers attempted to bump-draft his teammate Jimmie Johnson past Earnhardt in the final lap. (In bump-drafting, a driver uses drafting and slight bumping to propel the car ahead of him.) But the bump was too aggressive, and Johnson spun out of control, causing Earnhardt to spin as well. Vickers went on to win the race, while Earnhardt and Johnson finished 23d and 24th, respectively. Two weeks later Earnhardt spun out again, at the Subway 500, which caused him to drop to 22d place in the race. Next he managed a sixth-place finish at the Dickies 500 at the Texas Motor Speedway, while he was afflicted by strep throat and sore muscles. With two races left, Earnhardt was in third place in points behind the leader, Jimmie Johnson, and Matt Kenseth. The following week, at the Checker Auto Parts 500 in

Phoenix, due to spectacular races by Johnson (the eventual Chase winner) and others in contention, Earnhardt dropped to fifth place, his final standing for the season.

Early in the 2007 Nextel Cup season, Earnhardt finished second in the Gatorade Duel 1 and 32d in the Daytona 500. He finished seventh in the Food City 500, fifth in Goody's Cool Orange 500, and seventh in Aaron's 499. Later in the season he ended up fourth in the Lenox Industrial Tools 300, second in the Pennsylvania 500, and third in the Dodge Dealers 400. He had seven finishes in the top five and 12 in the top 10 as of the Bank of America 500 in October, in which he ended the course in 19th place.

In May 2007 NASCAR fined Eury $100,000 and suspended him for six races after illegal rear wing mounts were discovered on Earnhardt's car. In addition, Earnhardt's team was docked 100 championship points, which caused Earnhardt to drop from 12th to 14th place in the standings. Eury told David Newton for espn.com (May 19, 2007) that the illegal brackets were "a part that got put on there that shouldn't have. We've done a lot of off-season testing for NASCAR. There's been three different styles of brackets on there and it just happened to be one of those old-style brackets."

Shortly before that incident, Earnhardt announced his controversial decision to leave Dale Earnhardt Inc. after his contract for the season expired. In a news conference attended by Viv Bernstein for the *New York Times* (May 11, 2007), Earnhardt said, "At 32 years of age, the same as my father was when he made his final and most important decision, it is time for me to compete on a consistent basis and contend for championships now." Bernstein wrote that although Earnhardt was not the first NASCAR driver to become a free agent, "it is rare for a driver of Earnhardt's stature, at the height of his career and popularity, to make himself available to other teams." Earnhardt later picked up a contract to drive the No. 5 car for Hendrick Motorsports in 2008.

Dale Earnhardt Jr. is single. He lives in Mooresville, North Carolina, where he enjoys relaxing and drinking beer with his friends.

—F.C.

Suggested Reading: Dale Earnhardt Jr. Web site; *People* p56 Mar. 12, 2001, p62 Aug. 2, 2004; *Sports Illustrated* p34 Dec. 3, 2001; *Sports Illustrated for Kids* p48 Feb. 2003; Earnhardt, Dale Jr., and Jade Gurss. *Driver #8*, 2002

Elfman, Danny

May 29, 1953– Musician; composer for film

Address: c/o Kraft-Engel Management, 15233 Ventura Blvd., Suite 200, Sherman Oaks, CA 91403

"The nicest thing about going into film composing from rock & roll," Danny Elfman said to Jeff Gordinier for *Entertainment Weekly* (March 13, 1998), was that "I went from being an elder statesman in one profession to a young pup in the next." Elfman first achieved fame as the singer for the rock band Oingo Boingo, whose albums include *Only a Lad* (1981) and *Dead Man's Party* (1985). It was at the urging of the filmmaker Tim Burton that Elfman began composing for the screen; in Elfman, Burton had found a kindred soul, whose understanding of the director's darkly humorous vision enabled him to create music that captured the mood of Burton's movies. Since the pair's first collaboration, on *Pee-wee's Big Adventure* (1985), Elfman has scored each of Burton's films (with the exception of the 1994 release *Ed Wood*). "I found I was always on a tightrope in Tim's movies between the quirky and the spooky and the sweet and the energized and the on-the-money and the off-centre," Elfman told Jay Stone for the Victoria, British Columbia, *Times Colonist* (July 19, 2005). "Finding the correct tone is so crucial." Some of the best-known films on which Elfman and Burton have worked in-

Donald Weber/Getty Images

clude *Beetle Juice* (1988), *Batman* (1989), *Edward Scissorhands* (1990), *The Nightmare Before Christmas* (1993), *Big Fish* (2003), and the 2005 releases *Charlie and the Chocolate Factory* and *Corpse Bride*. Elfman's other screen work includes the scores for the movies *Dick Tracy* (1990), *To Die For* (1995), *Mission: Impossible* (1996), *Planet of the*

Apes (2001), *Spider-Man* (2002) and its 2004 sequel, and *Nacho Libre* (2006), as well as compositions for more than 100 other movies and TV shows, among them—perhaps most famously—the theme song for the animated television series *The Simpsons*, which was adapted for the silver screen in 2007. His music for the hit show *Desperate Housewives* won an Emmy Award in 2005. "The name—Elf-man—conjures up the image of a miniature person, with twinkling eyes, busy hands, a quick smile and a rather mischievous nature," Stephen Williams wrote for *Newsday* (December 22, 1996). "Danny Elfman is all of this, and it explains in part why he does what he does, which is write eclectic music for eclectic movies."

Daniel Robert Elfman was born on May 29, 1953 in Los Angeles, California, to two schoolteachers, Milton and Clare Elfman—the latter of whom also penned young-adult novels under the name Blossom Elfman. He was raised in the Crenshaw district of Los Angeles with his older brother, Richard, nicknamed Rick. (On one occasion, bored with repeating his life's story, Elfman claimed falsely that he was born in Amarillo, Texas, and that his father was an air-force officer.) As a youngster Elfman was fascinated with films, particularly those in the horror and science-fiction genres, and he papered his bedroom walls with pictures torn from his favorite magazine, *Famous Monsters of Filmland.* He also developed an affinity for film scores. "Most people probably never will notice film music: It's just a bunch of noise," Elfman said to Stephen Williams. "But I noticed. . . . If the movie had the names [of the composers] Ray Harryhausen or Bernard Herrmann [in the credits], I was in for an extra treat." Despite his appreciation for music, Elfman performed poorly in his music lessons, telling Rick Clark for *Mix* (May 2001), "I'm really bad at one-on-one. I'm much better in front of a thousand people." In high school, bespectacled and inept at sports, Elfman "was the little weird-looking albino kid that couldn't see anything in the sun," as he recalled to Clark. "When they did team sports, I was as blind as a mole in the light." A "pretty bitter kid, a nerd, at that age," as he admitted to Clark, Elfman felt out of place among most of his male classmates—who seemed to him "stupid and proud of it"—and much preferred the company of girls. "I had some friends who were boys, but they were misfits like myself," he said to Clark. "They were eccentrics."

To his parents' disappointment, Elfman left high school several months early in order to travel. (He had enough credits to graduate and later had his diploma sent to him.) He also began to teach himself to play the violin, choosing that instrument in part for its portability. In 1971 Elfman left for France, where his brother, Richard, was working with a musical-theater troupe called Le Grand Magic Circus. He spent nearly a year touring with the group as a violin player. According to John M. Glionna, writing for the *Los Angeles Times Magazine* (April 18, 1999), in an article appearing on Elfman's Web site, during those years Elfman also spent long periods traveling alone in West Africa, where he was often ill. "It was cleansing," he recalled to Glionna. "I spent months in quiet observance. I was like a ghost." Meanwhile, Richard Elfman had returned to Los Angeles to found a music/drama/improvisation troupe in the style of Le Grand Magic Circus, called the Mystic Knights of the Oingo Boingo. (They were once described as performing "dark, surrealistic cabaret," Danny Elfman told Richard Harrington, as quoted on *washingtonpost.com* [June 10, 1990].) When his younger brother arrived back home in California (with hepatitis), Richard Elfman promptly recruited him to become the troupe's music director.

Over the next eight years, Danny Elfman learned—mainly on his own—to play an assortment of instruments, including the trombone and percussion instruments, particularly enjoying the latter; he and one of the other troupe members, Leon Schneiderman, even built their own percussion instruments, based on those Elfman had encountered in Africa. (He also became one of the group's two fire-breathers, on one occasion accidentally igniting an audience member's hairsprayed Afro; his brother extinguished the flames.) The group's musical sound was based in part on early jazz, an influence that reflected what Elfman described to Clark as his decade-long refusal to listen to contemporary music. As musical director of the Mystic Knights, Elfman taught the other members of the troupe their parts by singing or humming his original tunes to them; as his musical creations became more elaborate, Elfman realized that reading and writing music had become a necessity. He taught himself composition by transcribing pieces by Duke Ellington, Django Reinhardt, and Cab Calloway. Moreover, Elfman learned to dream up or listen to snippets of music and remember them long enough to write down the notes, a vital skill in both transcription and composition. The final piece Elfman wrote for the Mystic Knights before the troupe disbanded was an ambitious work entitled "The Oingo Boingo Piano Concerto, Number $1\frac{1}{2}$."

Richard Elfman, wanting to create a record of the troupe's act, decided to direct a film showcasing Oingo Boingo's antics, with Danny Elfman providing the musical score. The movie, *Forbidden Zone*, details the bizarre adventures of a family who stumble through a portal in their basement into the Sixth Dimension, the realm of a diminutive king, played by Hervé Villechaize (best known for his work on the TV show *Fantasy Island*), and his jealous queen, portrayed by the B-movie actress Susan Tyrrell. Satan, played by Danny Elfman, sings Cab Calloway numbers, and underwear-clad actors parade around in blackface. The low-budget, determinedly silly film was so politically incorrect that some college theaters where it was shown in 1980 received arson threats. It has since grown in popularity on the midnight-movie circuit. Joyce Slaton, writing for the San Francisco, California,

SF Weekly (August 25, 2004), called *Forbidden Zone* a "loopy masterpiece" with a "delectably freaky soundtrack."

Upon the dissolution of the Mystic Knights of the Oingo Boingo, Elfman and several other members—Schneiderman, Steve Bartek, Kerry Hatch, John "Vatos" Hernandez, Sam Phipps, and Dale Turner—dropped part of the group's name, as well as its theatrical component, to form the band Oingo Boingo. A horn-heavy African musical style called Highlife became the model for their sound, and their live performances earned a reputation for being very high-energy. Their annual Halloween shows were favorites for both audiences and the band members, who included, in addition to Elfman and the other former Mystic Knights, John Avila, Richard Gibbs, Warren Fitzgerald, and a rotating group of other musicians. Oingo Boingo's early albums included *Only a Lad* (1981), *Nothing to Fear* (1982), *Good for Your Soul* (1983), and *Dead Man's Party* (1985). The band amassed a strong following on the West Coast, and they gained fans across the country with the release of their hit single, "Weird Science," the theme song of the 1985 film of the same title.

One of Oingo Boingo's fans was a young film director named Tim Burton, who approached Elfman about scoring an upcoming film about a character named Pee-wee Herman (the childlike persona of the actor and writer Paul Reubens). Though Elfman had scored only *Forbidden Zone* and was reluctant to accept Burton's offer, the director expressed such confidence in Elfman that the latter signed on as composer for the film, *Pee-wee's Big Adventure*. The movie was well-received and marked the beginning of a close and continuing collaboration between the pair. Before Burton and Elfman had a chance to work together again, though, Elfman was kept busy with other projects. He composed the main themes for the TV shows *Pee-wee's Playhouse* and *Sledge Hammer!* (both in 1986) and music for the films *Wisdom* (1986), *Summer School* (1987), and *Midnight Run*, *Big Top Pee-wee*, *Hot to Trot*, *Face Like a Frog*, and *Scrooged* (all 1988). He also worked with Oingo Boingo to release the albums *BOI-NGO* (1987) and *Boingo Alive* (1988). Discussing the differences between playing in a band and composing for film and TV, Elfman told Ron Givens for *Entertainment Weekly* (February 23, 1990), "You can't let song consciousness direct what you write for film. You have to resist the temptation to simplify things to verse-bridge-chorus." Elfman learned to match his scores to the onscreen action. "If a character lifts his arm and swings a knife at another guy, which kicks at the first guy and sends him crashing through a door, I want the music to reflect each of those four actions," he explained to Ron Givens.

Elfman told Rob Lowman for the *Daily News of Los Angeles* (August 5, 2001) that if a film or TV show is "very anything, it's likely that I can find some musical angle to grab onto." "That means very quirky, very silly, very dark, very dramatic, very stupid," he explained. Once Elfman agrees to write a score, he begins a lengthy ritual of sorts. "My process is to procrastinate as long as possible," Elfman explained to Kathy Cano Murillo for the Phoenix *Arizona Republic* (July 14, 2005). "And then, when I can't possibly procrastinate any longer, I lock myself away and get really depressed. I get miserable at the fact that I have no life. I always feel like saying, 'This is hopeless! I can't come up with anything!' And then finally, I quit [complaining] and get to work." But first he throws himself a party. "When I'm about to do a score," he told Rob Lowman, "I have a little going-away party, just like I'm going to jail. It's like I've been busted, had the arraignment and I have to show up and turn myself in. I'll say goodbye to everyone and then lock myself up." That is only a slight exaggeration: he works at home on a film score for 12 to 18 hours a day until his task is complete—usually after six to nine weeks—declining all invitations during the process. Elfman accomplishes much of his work at night. "I've got vampire's blood," he said to John M. Glionna. "Sunlight makes me ill and lethargic." First, he creates themes for each character. "I can't start writing the score until I have all of my themes completely laid out," he told Rick Clark. "I have to know what they are and how they are going to work and how they interrelate. . . . Once I have all of those elements together, there is no method anymore. I just dive into the first cue. I go as close to chronologically as I possibly can. I don't plan or think about where the music is going to go. It really is extremely unmethodical. I tend to let the music carry itself, and I become very often surprised by it. I never question it."

Burton and Elfman next collaborated on the films *Beetle Juice* (1988), *Batman* (1989), and *Edward Scissorhands* (1990). The two men, each of whom had grown up feeling like an outsider, shared a dark sense of humor and found that they worked well together. While Elfman's relationship with Burton flourished, the composer learned to his dismay about rumors that others had written his music. "For a while everybody who worked for me was getting credit for my music. That hurt," he told John M. Glionna. In addition, upon the premiere of *Batman*, Elfman was unhappy to discover that Warner Bros. Records had released a Prince album entitled *Batman: Motion Picture Soundtrack* (prior to releasing Elfman's soundtrack album, which was not completed until later), despite the fact that only six minutes of Prince's music was featured in the film. Newspapers and magazines frequently attributed the entire score to Prince. "None of this is Prince's fault," Elfman conceded to Dennis Hunt for the *Los Angeles Times* (June 27, 1989). "People heard Prince was writing songs for the movie and assumed he was doing the score. But the score is all that music that underscores the action. I did that. . . . I just spent three months, working day and night on this score. I'm proud of it. I want people to realize that *I* wrote it." That desire was fulfilled when Elfman won a 1989 Grammy Award for best instrumental composition, and a Grammy nomination for best score, for the theme from *Batman*.

In 1989 the cartoonist Matt Groening asked Elfman to write the theme song for Groening's animated television series *The Simpsons*. Elfman perused some of Groening's character sketches, found that his and the animator's ideas for a main theme were compatible—they agreed that something retro would be appropriate—and agreed to work on the project. *The Simpsons* premiered in 1989 and has been running ever since, beginning every episode with Elfman's theme. "That which I'm probably most famous for took me all of one day of work. There's some weird irony there," Elfman commented to Jay Stone. "There's so many projects where I've slaved literally 18 hours a day for three months only to have the [movie] disappear in one weekend. And this thing I worked—okay, maybe two days, but that's it—of my life, and it's following me around like my most known piece of work." During those years Elfman also wrote the themes for the TV shows *Tales from the Crypt* (1989), *The Flash* (1990), and *Batman Returns* and *Family Dog* (both 1992), as well as scores for the films *Nightbreed*, *Dick Tracy*, *Darkman* (all 1990), *Article 99* (1992), and *Sommersby* (1993). His albums with Oingo Boingo from that period include *Skeletons in the Closet: The Best of Oingo Boingo* (1989) and *Best O'Boingo* (1991).

In 1993 Elfman and Burton joined forces again to create an unusual movie: *The Nightmare Before Christmas*, an animated musical whose main character, Jack Skellington, the skeletal king of Halloweentown, discovers Christmas Town and decides to take over the duties of Santa Claus. "I realized that I was writing a lot from my own character," Elfman told Richard Zoglin for *Time* (October 11, 1993). "I went to Tim and said, 'I'm not the best singer alive by a long shot, but no one's going to sing Jack Skellington better than I am.' And he agreed." (The actor Chris Sarandon provided Jack's speaking voice.) While composing the *Nightmare* score, Elfman relied not only on Burton's advice but on that of his younger daughter, Mali, then nine, as well. He wanted to make sure that the songs were enjoyable and catchy, and so, as Elfman told Richard Zoglin, "until Mali signed off on it, nothing was approved." The resulting score—and film—were roundly praised. "In *Nightmare Before Christmas*, Elfman's witty, melodically intricate songs drive the action forward as surely as does the animation," Zoglin wrote. The film is arguably the most popular collaboration between Elfman and Burton to date. (After its completion the two men had a falling-out and did not speak to each other for nearly two years. Neither has publicly discussed the source of their disagreement.)

In 1994 Elfman's band changed its name from Oingo Boingo to simply Boingo. In the following year the group disbanded. "Nobody looks at a rock band as a lifelong career, except the Rolling Stones, maybe," Elfman pointed out to Mike Boehm during

an interview for the *Los Angeles Times* (October 25, 1990). "You know it's going to end." Oingo Boingo's final performance took place on Halloween night 1995, at the Universal Amphitheatre in Universal City, California, and was recorded as a live concert album, entitled *Farewell: Live from the Universal Amphitheatre* (1996). Tickets to the group's final four concerts sold out in less than an hour.

Free to concentrate on composing for the screen, Elfman took on projects including the 1995 movies *Dolores Claiborne*, *To Die For*, and *Dead Presidents* and the 1996 films *Freeway*, *Mission: Impossible*, *The Frighteners*, *Extreme Measures*, and another Burton project, *Mars Attacks!*. He worked on three 1997 movies: the drama *Good Will Hunting* and the comedies *Flubber* and *Men in Black*. Although he was initially reluctant to work on the lighthearted *Flubber*, preferring to focus on creating dramatic scores, Elfman told Don Jeffrey for *Billboard* (December 6, 1997), "There are times when I'm doing a really silly piece that I have to reluctantly admit to myself that I do it well. I don't want to be the king of wacky, but I do wacky very well." Elfman earned two Academy Award nominations in 1998, for best musical or comedy score (*Men in Black*) and best dramatic score (*Good Will Hunting*).

Also in 1998 Elfman again collaborated with Gus Van Sant, who had directed *Good Will Hunting*, on a remake of Alfred Hitchcock's classic horror film *Psycho*. In accepting that assignment Elfman took on the daunting job of adapting the original film's score, composed by Bernard Herrmann. When Jon Burlingame asked him in an interview for *Daily Variety* (October 21, 1998) about his approach to reworking the music, Elfman said that Herrmann's score is "sacred territory. There's no way I'm going to pollute it by trying to make it more modern or pumping it up with drums or anything else." Instead, he continued, "I'm going to attempt to do as respectful a recreation as I can, acknowledging the fact that it is a different movie and no scene is exactly the same length as the original." Other movies for which he wrote the scores during that period include *A Simple Plan* and *A Civil Action* (both 1998); *Instinct*, *Anywhere But Here*, and another Burton film, *Sleepy Hollow* (all 1999); *Proof of Life* and *The Family Man* (both 2000); *Spy Kids*, *Mazer World*, and the Burton remake of *Planet of the Apes* (all 2001); and *Spider-Man*, *Men in Black II*, and *Red Dragon* (all 2002). Also in 2002 he contributed music to the film version of *Chicago*, filling in any gaps left by the original score, by John Kander and Fred Ebb. That year he received the Richard Kirk Award for outstanding career achievement at the BMI Film and Television Awards. In 2003 Elfman composed music for *Hulk* and earned an Oscar nomination for his score for *Big Fish*, another collaboration with Burton. In the Charlottetown, Prince Edward Island, *Guardian* (March 5, 2004), Doug Gallant called the *Big Fish* score "a wondrous, fanciful and richly imaginative thing, artfully conceived and handsomely executed by a composer who, like Burton, has a gift for capturing minute detail."

Elfman next scored *Spider-Man 2* (2004) and provided the theme songs for the television shows *Desperate Housewives* (2004) and *Point Pleasant* (2005). His music for *Desperate Housewives* brought Elfman his first Emmy Award. He then rejoined Burton for two films released in 2005: *Charlie and the Chocolate Factory*, based on Roald Dahl's classic children's novel, and *Corpse Bride*, a story created by Burton in the vein of *The Nightmare Before Christmas*. In creating songs for the diminutive characters called Oompa Loompas in *Charlie and the Chocolate Factory*, Elfman took an approach different from that used in *Willy Wonka & the Chocolate Factory*, the 1971 film version of Dahl's book. Whereas the songs in that movie all had the same melody but different lyrics, Elfman—at Burton's suggestion—followed the example of Bollywood musicals, using a different genre of music for each of the songs. Thus, when the Oompa Loompas sing to the spoiled Veruca Salt, the music is reminiscent of 1960s folk rock; the video-game junkie Mike Teavee merits a hair-metal song; and the downfall of the obnoxious Violet Beauregarde is set to 1970s-style funk. Elfman recorded multiple tracks of his own voice to provide the voices of the Oompa Loompas. "Recording the songs, there were moments when it was hard to control myself, I was having such a good time," Elfman told Jay Stone. "I would have to stop because I was laughing and screwing up takes."

In February 2005 Elfman's first orchestral work for the concert stage, the 40-minute *Serenada Schizophrana*, premiered at Carnegie Hall, in New York City. Prior to that event, he had never been to Carnegie Hall, "and it was incredibly intimidating," as he told Mac Randall for the *New York Observer* (March 7, 2005). "I felt like a little kid in the playground of the big boys. I just thought, '. . . These walls are used to some serious [music], and they're going to hear my notes bouncing around and simply *reject* them." Those fears notwithstanding, his composition struck Mac Randall as being "imbued with a winning, what-the-hell spirit that left one hoping for a repeat performance." In 2006 Sony BMG Masterworks released a recording of *Serenada Schizophrana*.

Elfman's recent projects include the music for the 2006 Imax film *Deep Sea 3D*. Elfman's "mystical sounds serve up just the right atmosphere for this almost complete immersive experience," Laura Kern wrote for the *New York Times* (March 3, 2006, on-line). Later in the year Elfman collaborated with Erik Sanko on the music for Sanko's *The Fortune Teller*; that dark-themed puppet show, performed at the Here Arts Center, in New York City, is "a morality fable for grown-ups," as Anne Midgette described it in the *New York Times* (October 30, 2006, on-line). Elfman provided the score for the film *Charlotte's Web*, which is based on E. B. White's classic children's book and opened during the 2006 Christmas season. The *New York Times* (December 15, 2006) film critic A. O. Scott wrote that Elfman's music is "perfectly adequate if not terribly imaginative [and] plays under the action loudly and virtually without interruption, robbing the picture of a sense of rustic tranquility that would ground its antic flights"; he also described it as the film's "only serious flaw." In 2007 Elfman contributed the soundtracks to *The Kingdom* and *Meet The Robinsons*. His original music was to accompany *The Sixth Element*, directed by his brother, Richard, and *Hellboy 2: The Golden Army*, both set to be released in 2008. He was also composing the score for *Ripley's Believe It or Not!*, scheduled to reach theaters in 2009.

Elfman married the actress Bridget Fonda in November 2003. The couple's son, Oliver, was born in January 2005. Elfman has two daughters, Lola and Mali, from a previous marriage. Despite Elfman's penchant for the macabre (he collects such items as shrunken heads, sinister-looking dolls and ventriloquists' dummies, and drums made from skulls), he is "just a sweet kid with a streak of dark humor," as his mother told John M. Glionna, as well as a devoted parent. Elfman's quirky sense of humor is merely an expression of his creativity, his brother told Glionna: "He's the nice old lady who writes wicked mystery novels, not the village ax murderer." In 2007 Elfman received an honorary doctorate from the North Carolina School of the Arts, where he spoke at the commencement ceremony.

—K.J.E.

Suggested Reading: *Daily News of Los Angeles* L p11 Aug. 5, 2001; *Entertainment* p56+ Feb.23, 1990; Internet Movie Database; *Los Angeles Times Magazine* p10 Apr. 18, 1999; *Mix* p5 May 2001; *Newsday* C p23 Dec. 22, 1996; *Talk of the Nation* Apr. 6, 1999

Selected Recordings: with Oingo Boingo—*Only a Lad*, 1981; *Nothing to Fear*, 1982; *Good for Your Soul*, 1983; *Dead Man's Party*, 1985; *BOI-NGO*, 1987; *Boingo Alive*, 1988; *Skeletons in the Closet: The Best of Oingo Boingo*, 1989; *Best O'Boingo*, 1991; *Farewell: Live From the Universal Amphitheatre*, 1996; *Dark at the End of the Tunnel*, 1998; *Anthology*, 1999; *20th Century Masters: The Millennium Collection: The Best of Oingo Boingo*, 2002

Selected Film Scores: *Forbidden Zone*, 1980; *Pee-wee's Big Adventure*, 1985; *Wisdom*, 1986; *Summer School*, 1987; *Beetle Juice*, 1988; *Midnight Run*, 1988; *Big Top Pee-wee*, 1988; *Hot to Trot*, 1988; *Face Like a Frog*, 1988; *Scrooged*, 1988; *Batman*, 1989; *Nightbreed*, 1990; *Dick Tracy*, 1990; *Darkman*, 1990; *Edward Scissorhands*, 1990; *Article 99*, 1992; *Batman Returns*, 1992; *Sommersby*, 1993; *The Nightmare Before Christmas*, 1993; *Black Beauty*, 1994; *Dolores Claiborne*, 1995; *To Die For*, 1995; *Dead*

Presidents, 1995; *Freeway*, 1996; *Mission: Impossible*, 1996; *The Frighteners*, 1996; *Extreme Measures*, 1996; *Mars Attacks!*, 1996; *Men in Black*, 1997; *Flubber*, 1997; *Good Will Hunting*, 1997; *A Simple Plan*, 1998; *A Civil Action*, 1998; *Instinct*, 1999; *Sleepy Hollow*, 1999; *Proof of Life*, 2000; *The Family Man*, 2000; *Spy Kids*, 2001; *Mazer World*, 2001; *Planet of the Apes*, 2001; *Spider-Man*, 2002; *Men in Black II*, 2002; *Red Dragon*, 2002; *Chicago*, 2002; *Hulk*, 2003; *Big Fish*, 2003; *Spider-Man 2*, 2004; *Charlie and the Chocolate Factory*, 2005; *Corpse Bride*, 2005; *Charlotte's Web*, 2006; *Meet the Robinsons*, 2007; *The Kingdom*, 2007

Selected Television Scores: *Sledge Hammer!*, 1986; *Tales from the Crypt*, 1989; *Beetlejuice*, 1989; *The Simpsons*, 1989; *The Flash*, 1990; *Family Dog*, 1992; *Batman*, 1992; *Weird Science*, 1994; *Perversions of Science*, 1997; *Dilbert*, 1999; *Desperate Housewives*, 2004; *Point Pleasant*, 2005

Jonathan Ernst/Getty Images

Ellison, Keith

Aug. 4, 1963– U.S. representative from Minnesota (Democrat)

Address: 1130 Longworth House Office Bldg., Washington, DC 20515

On November 7, 2006 Keith Ellison became not only the first African-American elected to the U.S. House of Representatives from Minnesota but the first Muslim to be elected to Congress in the history

of the United States. While Ellison has said that his intention is to represent his entire Minnesota constituency rather than merely becoming a spokesman for Islam among the nation's lawmakers, he will likely find it difficult to separate himself from his faith in the eyes of the public. Religion has become an increasingly polarizing political issue in the United States in recent years, particularly since the September 11, 2001 terrorist attacks in New York and Washington, D.C., carried out by members of the Islamic extremist group Al Qaeda, and the subsequent launch of the "war on terror"; Ellison's candidacy, emerging in the context of that war—the rhetoric surrounding which has frequently equated Islam with terrorism—provoked a great deal of interest and controversy around the country. After Ellison's election, which was a front-page news item in many majority-Muslim countries, Nihad Awad, executive director of the Council on American-Islamic Relations (CAIR), told Rochelle Olson for the Minneapolis *Star Tribune* (November 13, 2006), "By default [Ellison] will become a national symbol in the Muslim community and a voice heard around the world." Agha Saeed, chairman of the California-based American Muslim Taskforce, said to Noam N. Levey for the *Los Angeles Times* (October 20, 2006) that Ellison's election is a "huge victory for both Muslim Americans and America," adding that it "has eradicated two stereotypes: one against Muslims, that they cannot work and succeed in a democratic setup, and the other against the United States, that it is not a tolerant society." As a Muslim legislator in the United States—which John Zogby of the polling firm Zogby International described to Tim Jones for the *Chicago Tribune* (June 29, 2006) as "a nation that, by and large, doesn't understand Islam"—Ellison will have an opportunity to advocate for American Muslims, who as a group have been widely vilified since the 2001 attacks. Ellison, while not wanting to limit himself to that role, understands that his religion will make him an influential voice in Congress, and believes that he will be able to help educate lawmakers who might hold views toward Islam grounded in ignorance or intolerance. "I see my faith as something that builds bridges—doesn't build walls. I mean, for example, if somebody got up on the House floor and said something misinformed or even bigoted about Islam, of course I would stand up and correct the record and put forth the truth. But that's not something only I would need to do. Anybody could do that if they studied the subject matter," Ellison explained in an interview with Farai Chideya for National Public Radio (November 20, 2006). Ellison, who has been appointed to the House Financial Services and Judiciary Committees, has ambitious legislative goals, specifically concerning the Iraq War and the protection of civil rights. He told Chideya, "I want to join with other members of Congress to say . . . this policy [regarding Iraq] not only is destructive to the lives of our soldiers, destructive to the lives of Iraqis but is actually having a corrosive effect on civil and human rights inside of the United States. Stuff like the Military Commissions Act, which deprives detainees [of] the right to challenge their detention. Stuff like domestic spying. These things are horrible . . . and they're not in the best tradition of this country. And I'm going to join with other members of Congress of any party, I don't even care, who believed that, you know, we should face the future bravely and not give in to fear because there are some bad people out there who are trying to get us."

The third of five sons, Keith Maurice Ellison was born on August 4, 1963 to Clida and Leonard Ellison. The family resided in Detroit, Michigan; Ellison's father was a psychiatrist, his mother a social worker. At an early age Ellison was inspired by stories of his mother's father, a former activist with the National Association for the Advancement of Colored People (NAACP), who had organized black voters in Louisiana during the 1950s—provoking anger on the part of some of the whites in the community. When Ellison's mother was a child, her family "would receive threats and had crosses burned on their front lawn," as Ellison told Chideya, "and it really was a topic that made a great impression on me." Issues of civil rights and justice were common subjects of dinner-table discussions in Ellison's youth. As a consequence, he told Chideya, "it really wasn't that unusual for me to gravitate toward political activism, trying to make a change, trying to include more people, make our society live up to the ideals that are stated in our Declaration of Independence and Constitution." Ellison's brothers—of whom three became lawyers, one a minister—were politically active as well, but Keith stood out. "He had a real sense of righteousness and justice," Ellison's brother Brian told Kathleen Gray for the *Detroit Free Press* (September 17, 2006), adding that Keith's passion sometimes led to confrontations, "maybe even [to] getting into a fistfight every once in a while" during elementary school. Ellison attended Hampton (now Barbara Jordan) Elementary before enrolling at the University of Detroit High School, where he was active in sports and the student senate. Ellison has credited his high-school football coach, Lou Offer, with helping him learn to avoid violent confrontations. "He was one of the people who helped me find a sense of purpose in my life," Ellison said of Offer to Kathleen Gray.

After high school Ellison enrolled at Wayne State University, in Detroit, where he studied economics, graduating with a bachelor's degree in 1987. At 19 Ellison, frustrated with social injustice and racism, converted to Islam, saying to Alan Cooperman for the *Washington Post* (September 11, 2006) about his conversion that it "had a political angle to it, a reaction against status quo politics." In 1987 Ellison moved to Minneapolis to attend the University of Minnesota Law School. Because he was one of only three black students in his class of 265, Ellison's awareness of his minority status increased, as did his political activism. He

was instrumental in bringing controversial African-American speakers, such as Kwame Ture, the former Black Panther once known as Stokely Carmichael, to campus to lecture. Ellison also wrote about his political frustrations in the school press and in other local newspapers, sometimes under the name Keith E. Hakim or Keith X. Ellison. His first editorial, published in the Minneapolis *Star Tribune* in 1988, raised concerns about racist and anti-Semitic graffiti on a pedestrian bridge near the university. In other articles Ellison discussed more controversial topics, such as reparations for descendants of slaves and the effects of affirmative action, sometimes drawing resentment from other students. His writings were later publicly scrutinized during his campaigns for elective office.

After graduating from law school, Ellison was hired as an attorney by the firm Lindquist & Vennum, in Minneapolis, where he worked for three years. He served as the executive director of the Legal Rights Center in Minneapolis before entering private practice in that city with the law firm Hassan & Reed Ltd.; there, he specialized in trial litigation, focusing on such issues as civil rights, employment, environmental justice, and indigent defense law. He was also an active community member, volunteering his time as host of a public-affairs radio program and as a youth track coach for several city organizations. Ellison was also directly involved in organizing citizens to address the issue of police-community relations, an effort that resulted in the establishment of the Minneapolis Police–Civilian Review Board in the early 1990s. He was active and vocal with regard to other issues as well, helping locally in 1995 to organize the Million Man March, the large gathering of black men in Washington, D.C., that was spearheaded nationally by the Nation of Islam leader Louis Farrakhan. He wrote editorials on such topics as the political implications of the highly publicized police beating of a black man, Rodney King, and contributed a piece in defense of the Symbionese Liberation Army member Kathleen Soliah. Ellison was eventually drawn toward politics, a transition he has described as a natural one for a concerned citizen and parent. He explained to Tom Lonergan for the *Session Weekly–Minnesota House of Representatives* (January 24, 2003) that he chose to become involved in politics instead of "sitting at home thinking about safe neighborhoods, community economic development, better schools and not doing anything about it."

In 2002 Ellison was elected to the Minnesota House of Representatives, representing District 58B, one of the most culturally, economically, and demographically diverse regions in the state. During his first term Ellison was appointed to the Governmental Operations and Veterans Affairs Policy Committee, the Judiciary Policy and Finance Committee, and the Local Government & Metropolitan Affairs Committee. He was reelected in 2004, carrying 84 percent of the vote, and served during his second term on the Civil Law and Elections Committee and the Public Safety Policy and Finance Committee. While a state representative Ellison developed a reputation as an effective lawmaker and was recognized for his ability to push progressive legislation through a largely conservative House of Representatives. Among other causes, Ellison advocated for non-prison alternatives to punishment and rehabilitation of nonviolent offenders; suffrage for paroled felons; public-school reform; and the opportunity for same-sex domestic partners of state employees to be included in state benefits programs. Ellison also argued that a proposed bill that defined marriage as "only the union of one man to one woman" was unconstitutional. In his time as a state representative, Ellison played an essential role in the creation of an organization called the Environmental Justice Advocates of Minnesota, which worked to combat the damaging effects of lead, mercury, and pesticides, which had long contributed to the health problems of Minneapolis children—specifically, a high incidence of asthma. That group worked toward the conversion of a north Minneapolis coal plant into a natural-gas facility.

In 2006 Ellison campaigned for a seat in the U.S. House of Representatives from Minnesota's Fifth District. That district, one of eight in the state, includes not only the 58B District of the Minnesota legislature but also upscale sections of downtown Minneapolis and several affluent suburbs. Ellison presented himself as a progressive candidate in the tradition of a late U.S. senator from Minnesota, Paul Wellstone; his campaign platform, which included providing universal health care, raising the minimum wage, and withdrawing troops from Iraq, jibed well with the opinions of voters in a generally liberal district. Ellison did not highlight his potential to be the first Muslim U.S. congressman and rarely discussed his religion unless asked to do so by interviewers, who in many cases found his Islamic faith to be among his most noteworthy attributes. "I'm proud to be a Muslim. But I'm not running as a Muslim candidate," Ellison explained to Alan Cooperman. "I'm running as a candidate who believes in peace and bringing the troops out of Iraq now. I'm running as a candidate who believes in universal, single-payer health care coverage and an increase in the minimum wage." After earning the endorsement of the Minnesota-based Democratic-Farmer-Labor Party—affiliated with the national Democratic Party—Ellison cruised to victory in the Democratic primary and was generally acknowledged as the favorite to win the congressional election, as the district had last elected a Republican in 1962.

Still, for voters in the Fifth District, which includes Muslim as well as Jewish communities, Ellison's Sunni Muslim religion and his past affiliation with the Nation of Islam created considerable controversy during the campaign. While a law student at the University of Minnesota, Ellison had written in defense of the Chicago-based Nation of Islam and its leader, Farrakhan, who has been ac-

cused of anti-Semitism. Republicans attacked Ellison for receiving campaign contributions from, and appearing at fundraisers with, leaders of the Council on American-Islamic Relations, a group that some—including Democratic U.S. senator Charles Schumer of New York—had previously accused of supporting Hamas before that Palestinian group was designated by the United States as a terrorist organization. In addition, Ellison came under fire for his defense, during his time as an attorney, of gang members charged with committing violent crimes; he also took heat for a quote he gave to the Minneapolis *Star Tribune* (May 1, 1992), in which he stated, with regard to the acquittals of policemen involved in the Rodney King beating, "Black people do not live under a democracy. You don't have an obligation to obey a government that considers you to be less than human." Conservatives used those past actions and statements to depict Ellison as a divisive, anti-Semitic radical who could not represent the best interests of the Fifth District. Alan Fine, Ellison's Republican opponent, launched a salvo on the day following the primaries. "I'm extremely concerned about Keith Ellison. . . . He is the follower of a known racist, Louis Farrakhan, who promoted division between the people of our nation. . . . I'm personally offended as a Jew that we have a candidate like this running for U.S. Congress," Fine said, as reported by Rochelle Olson for the Minneapolis *Star Tribune* (September 14, 2006).

Ellison's supporters were quick to counter what they saw as hypocritical and baseless attacks. The Minneapolis attorney Jordan Kushner, who had studied with Ellison at the University of Minnesota, publicly came to the candidate's defense, stating that Ellison's actions during his time in law school were being misrepresented. "There were things [Ellison] admired about the Nation of Islam," Kushner, who is Jewish, said to Aron Kahn for the St. Paul, Minnesota, *Pioneer Press* (October 31, 2006), "with the emphasis about black people having self-reliance, but it had nothing to do with anti-Semitism. He understood the connection between racism and anti-Semitism." In response to concerns by Jewish members of the Democratic-Farmer-Labor Party about his association with the Nation of Islam, Farrakhan, and others who had previously made anti-Semitic or anti-homosexual remarks, Ellison wrote a public letter addressed to the Jewish Community Relations Council. As quoted by Josh Gerstrin for the *New York Sun* (September 5, 2006), Ellison wrote that he "did not adequately scrutinize the positions and statements" of the Nation of Islam and its leaders. "They were and are anti-Semitic, and I should have come to that conclusion earlier than I did. I regret that I didn't. But at no time did I ever share their hateful views or repeat or approve their hateful statements directed at Jews, gays, or any other group," Ellison added. The letter assuaged the concerns of many voters, but others remained skeptical about Ellison's past. Ellison eventually received the endorsement of the *American Jewish World*, Minneapolis's foremost Jewish newspaper. Ira Forman, the executive director of the National Jewish Democratic Council (NJDC), posted a press release on the organization's official Web site on September 21, 2006, describing Fine's comments as intolerant and xenophobic. "Republicans can't beat Keith Ellison on the merits of their policy positions. So instead, they appear to be using his religion as a weapon to question his patriotism . . . ," Forman wrote. "Keith has recognized his past mistakes and renounced his brief association with the Nation of Islam and has condemned the anti-Semitic statements and beliefs of Louis Farrakhan and [his fellow Nation of Islam official] Khalid Muhammed." The press release put the NJDC at the forefront of Ellison's defense. Although Ellison received endorsements from many groups, a number of high-ranking Democratic candidates were conspicuously absent from his support base, avoiding Ellison because of the controversy surrounding his campaign.

Throughout the campaign Ellison tried to sidestep the personal attacks against him, arguing that the candidates owed it to their constituents to focus on the issues rather deriding one another. "I am the only person to say we must boldly and unapologetically affirm our progressive values by making peace the guiding principle of our nation, assert the right of labor to strengthen, and demand universal, single-payer health care," Ellison said when asked to differentiate his platform from those of his opponents, according to Aron Kahn of the St. Paul *Pioneer Press* (October 16, 2006). Despite Republicans' efforts to derail his campaign and a lack of support from local Democratic politicians, Ellison won the election over Fine, Tammy Lee of the Independence Party, and the Green Party nominee, Jay Pond. While Ellison's progressive political positions won support in the generally liberal district, political analysts and community organizers attributed his success in both the primary and general elections to a strong turnout from African-American Muslim and particularly immigrant Muslim voters—a rapidly growing constituency in Minnesota and one that includes many who voted in 2006 for the first time. Ellison told Neil Macfarquhar for the *New York Times* (October 8, 2006, on-line) that being the first Muslim and first African-American from Minnesota to win a seat in Congress "holds no magic for me," but he acknowledged the importance of his role in energizing black Muslim and immigrant voters, an effort he described to Macfarquhar as "build[ing] political power." He added, "They can't ignore us anymore when we show up to vote."

Ellison chose to take his oath of office with his hand on the Koran rather than the Bible, a decision that sparked further controversy and exposed the negative attitudes of a number of prominent figures toward Islam. In Townhall.com (November 28, 2006), Dennis Prager, a popular radio host and columnist, contended that Ellison's decision "under-mine[d] American civilization" and was "an act of hubris that perfectly exemplifies multiculturalist activism." Arguing that "when all elected officials take their oaths of office with their hands on the very same book, they all affirm that some unifying value system underlies American civilization," Prager concluded with the assertion that by taking the oath on the Koran, "[Ellison] will be doing more damage to the unity of America and to the value system that has formed this country than the terrorists of 9-11." Virgil Goode, a U.S. representative from Virginia, was also against Ellison's decision; he wrote in a December 7, 2006 letter to one of his constituents, who shared it with the Charlottesville, Virginia, publication *C-Ville* (December 19, 2006, on-line): "I do not subscribe to using the Koran in any way. The Muslim Representative from Minnesota was elected by the voters of that district and if American citizens don't wake up and adopt the Virgil Goode position on immigration there will likely be many more Muslims elected to office and demanding the use of the Koran. . . . I fear that in the next century we will have many more Muslims in the United States if we do not adopt the strict immigration policies that I believe are necessary to preserve the values and beliefs traditional to the United States of America." Goode's comments provoked an outpouring of support for Ellison by other members of the U.S. House of Representatives, among them Jim Moran of Virginia, Bill Pascrell of New Jersey, Michael M. Honda of California, and Tom Tancredo of Colorado. In a letter published on his official Web site and addressed to Goode, Pascrell stated that he was "greatly disappointed and in fact startled by your recent constituent letter." Pascrell also expressed alarm that Congressman Goode had "wrongfully equat[ed] the issue of immigration with a fear of Muslim integration in our society," and added that "promoting a fear and disrespect of Muslims is . . . wrongheaded." In taking his oath, administered by House Speaker Nancy Pelosi, Ellison used a copy of an English translation of the Koran, published in 1750, that was once owned by President Thomas Jefferson. Amy Argetsinger and Roxanne Roberts, writing for the *Washington Post* (January 3, 2007), called that choice "a savvy bit of political symbolism," referring to the "all-American" nature of the text. An Ellison spokesman, Rick Jauert, told Argetsinger and Roberts, "Keith is paying respect not only to the founding fathers' belief in religious freedom but the Constitution itself."

As the first-ever Muslim congressman, Ellison will likely have an important voice in congressional debate with regard to both initiatives in the Middle East and Muslims living in the United States. The freshman representative hopes that his election will influence the estimated five million to six million Muslims residing in the United States to become more active participants in the electoral process. The number of Muslim political candidates nationwide dropped from more than 700 in 2000 to just 70 in 2002, which in turn left the American Muslim population feeling disempowered. Abdisalam Adam, the director of a Somali cultural center in Minneapolis, who helped organize volunteers to recruit Muslim voters for the 2006 elections, believes that Muslims were more motivated to vote that year because there was a candidate who promoted a positive image of Islam. "They were resistant to voting [before] because a lot of them thought it wouldn't make a difference," Adam explained to Neil Macfarquhar. That view is shared by Parvez Ahmed, chairman of the Council on American-Islamic Relations. Ahmed said in reference to Ellison's candidacy, prior to the election, "Every other community wants someone from their community to be part of the mosaic that represents the country. [Ellison] would be a voice for the people who don't have representation," as reported by Frederic J. Frommer for the Associated Press Worldstream (September 22, 2006).

In May 2007 Ellison joined the Speaker of the House, Nancy Pelosi, and other Democrats in voting against H.R. 2206, which provided additional military funds for the war in Iraq but did not specify timetables for withdrawals of U.S. troops. The bill passed, 280–142. In the same year Ellison spent a weekend in Iraq with five other freshman representatives. There, he met with two Muslim sheiks who told him that the tenets of Al Qaeda misrepresented the principles of Islam. According to an Associated Press report published in *USA Today* (on-line), Ellison said that the sheiks explained to him "what I can possibly do to work with them to give a clearer, more accurate picture of what Islam is all about."

Ellison was described by Aron Kahn in the St. Paul *Pioneer Press* (October 16, 2006) as "a cross between a Gospel preacher and the silver-tongued political orators of the past." He is married to his high-school sweetheart, the former Kim Brookins, a high-school math teacher. The couple have four children. Ellison divides his time between his Washington, D.C., office and his home in Minneapolis.

—N.W.M.

Suggested Reading: *Detroit Free Press* p1 Sep. 17, 2006; *Los Angeles Times* A p14 Oct. 20, 2006; *New York Sun* p1 Sep. 5, 2006; (Minneapolis) *Star Tribune* B p1 June 28, 2006, A p1 Sep. 14, 2006, A p1 Nov. 13, 2006; *Washington Post* A p3 Sep. 11, 2006

Emanuel, Kerry A.

Apr. 21, 1955– Meteorologist; educator; writer

Address: MIT, Dept. of Earth, Atmospheric, and Planetary Sciences, Rm. 54-1620, 77 Massachusetts Ave., Cambridge, MA 02139-4301

During the last week of August 2005, a huge hurricane of near-record-breaking power slammed into the United States along the north-central coast of the Gulf of Mexico, bringing torrential rains and fierce winds to a 90,000-square-foot area encompassing parts of several southern states. Among the places hardest hit by the storm, named Katrina, was the city of New Orleans, Louisiana, where breaches in the levees along Lake Pontchartrain led to floods that left 80 percent of the city under water; more than a thousand people were killed, and many thousands were left homeless. An uncannily accurate description of what happened in New Orleans appears in a book that was published less than two months before Katrina began to form, on August 23, over the Bahamas: *Divine Wind: The History and Science of Hurricanes*, by Kerry A. Emanuel, a professor of meteorology at the Massachusetts Institute of Technology. On August 4, 2005, less than four weeks before the deadly storm reached its peak strength, the British journal *Nature* published an article in which Emanuel reported that in recent decades both the intensities and the lifetimes of tropical cyclones (which, like "typhoons," is another name for hurricanes) had in-

Donna Coveney, courtesy of the MIT News Office

creased significantly. That phenomenon, Emanuel wrote, "is highly correlated with tropical sea surface temperature, reflecting well-documented climate signals"—one of them being global warming. "My results suggest that future warming may lead to an upward trend in tropical cyclone destructive potential, and—taking into account an increasing coastal population—a substantial increase in hurricane-related losses in the twenty-first century." Although, for years, many scientists in addition to Emanuel had warned of the dangers that unusually forceful hurricanes posed to New Orleans, Emanuel's prescience regarding the events in that city, along with his timely words concerning the link between global warming and hurricane intensity, made him a highly sought-after hurricane expert during and after Katrina's devastating rampage, and he was interviewed and quoted widely by the media. In its May 8, 2006 issue, *Time* magazine named him one of the "100 people who shape our world." Earlier, the American Meteorological Society honored him with its Meisinger Award, in 1986, for his work on atmospheric motions; in 1992 the organization presented him—along with Richard Rotunno, a senior scientist at the National Center for Atmospheric Research—with its Banner I. Miller Award, for their paper on the relationship between sea-surface temperature and the inner dynamics of hurricanes, which the society deemed to be an "outstanding contribution to the science of hurricane and tropical-weather forecasting." In addition to *Divine Wind*, Emanuel's professional writings include some 120 journal articles and book chapters and the book *Atmospheric Convection*, published by Oxford University Press in 1994. With three others, he co-edited *Tropical Cyclone Disasters*, published by the Peking Press, also in 1994.

The second of three brothers, Kerry Andrew Emanuel was born in Cincinnati, Ohio, on April 21, 1955 to Albert Emanuel II and Marny Catherine (Schonegevel) Emanuel. His mother was a former flight instructor and homemaker, and his father was an aircraft mechanic. During his childhood his family moved several times, setting up house in Pennsylvania, Maine, and Florida as well as Ohio. The few hurricanes the Emanuels experienced while they lived in Florida made an indelible impression on young Kerry. Early on, the subjects of climate and weather interested him more than any others. In school, Emanuel told *Current Biography*, he was "pretty much a straight arrow." He attended the Massachusetts Institute of Technology (MIT), in Cambridge, Massachusetts, where he earned an S.B. degree (equivalent to a B.S.) in earth and planetary sciences in 1976 and a Ph.D. in meteorology only two years later. From 1978 to 1981 Emanuel taught as a member of the Department of Atmospheric and Oceanic Sciences at the University of California at Los Angeles (UCLA). Concurrently, in 1979, he held a postdoctoral fellowship at the Cooperative Institute for Mesoscale Meteorological Studies at the University of Oklahoma at Norman. (Mesoscale meteorology is the study of thunderstorms and other weather systems that extend anywhere from about 10 miles to about 600 miles.) In 1981 he returned to MIT, as an assistant professor in the Center for Meteorology and Physical Oceanography, which is associated with the Department of Earth, Atmospheric, and Planetary Sciences; he

was promoted to associate professor in 1983 and to full professor in 1987. He directed the center from 1989 to 1997.

Emanuel began his research on hurricanes in the early 1980s, after he was assigned to teach a course in tropical meteorology. While he was preparing his notes for the class, as he recalled to Claudia Dreifus for the *New York Times* (January 10, 2006), "I realized I didn't understand what I'd been taught on the subject. As with many things, you think you understand something until you try to teach it. After some reading, I realized that the reigning theory [of hurricane formation] had to be wrong." A hurricane forms when water vapor evaporates from the ocean and later condenses as a ring of tall thunderstorm clouds surrounding the eye of the storm. The accepted theory of how hurricanes develop, known as conditional instability of the second kind, as Emanuel told Dreifus, "held that the main thing that drives a hurricane is just ingestion of enormous quantities of water vapor from the atmospheric environment"; thus, it would depend on a "magical grouping" of winds and clouds. But the predictions that Emanuel derived from the theory were false, he discovered. "So it became a very big intellectual challenge to me. The more I got into it, the more interesting it became." Emanuel amended the theory of hurricane development in a way that accounted for the connection that exists between hurricane circulation and evaporation from the surface of the sea.

Hurricanes gather strength from the heat energy in tropical oceans. Warmer ocean waters evaporate more quickly than cooler ones and have been linked to hurricanes that are more powerful and travel faster than others. In a paper for *Nature* (April 2, 1987) entitled "The Dependence of Hurricane Intensity on Climate," Emanuel suggested that global warming, which causes the surface water of oceans to get warmer, could lead to an increase in hurricane strength. In preparing his paper, Emanuel assumed that if the quantity of carbon dioxide (one of the so-called greenhouse gases) in the atmosphere doubles by sometime in the 21st century, the temperature of the surface waters of the oceans in tropical regions will rise by about two to three degrees Centigrade, or four to five degrees Fahrenheit, and, in turn, "the maximum possible intensity for hurricanes could rise 40 percent to 50 percent generally and 60 percent in the Gulf of Mexico," as Malcolm Ritter wrote for the Associated Press (April 1, 1987), paraphrasing Emanuel's findings. But the assumption regarding the relationship between carbon-dioxide increase and water-temperature increase could prove to be unfounded, as Emanuel told Ritter. Indeed, until recently Emanuel believed that nobody had found any evidence that hurricanes were growing more intense; as Claudia Dreifus wrote, he remained a "cautious centrist on questions of global warming and hurricane ferocity," often asserting that "no firm link had been established between warming and the intensity and frequency of hurricanes." In an interview with Jules Crittenden for the *Boston Herald* (November 29, 1998), for example, Emanuel suggested that, even if projections of global warming were accurate, no evidence pointing to the increasing intensity of hurricanes would be findable until the last quarter of the 21st century. "In the Atlantic, natural variability is what we need to worry about right now," he said, referring to an apparent 20-year cycle of waxing and waning of hurricane strength, known as the Atlantic multidecadal oscillation.

Then, in the early 2000s, while conducting research on El Niño (an irregularly occurring current of unusually warm water in the Pacific Ocean) and other phenomena related to climate oscillations, Emanuel unintentionally discovered that hurricanes in the North Atlantic and western North Pacific had increased in overall power by roughly 60 percent since the 1970s. Until then, he told Dreifus, he and others had predicted that "if you warmed the tropical oceans by a degree Centigrade, you should see something on the order of a 5 percent increase in the wind speed during hurricanes. We've seen a larger increase, more like 10 percent, for an ocean temperature increase of only one-half degree Centigrade"—a trend closely correlated with the increase in ocean and air temperatures due to global warming. Emanuel acknowledged the existence of that correlation in his August 4, 2005 *Nature* paper, thus indicating how much his thinking about hurricane intensities had changed by that time.

Critics of Emanuel's *Nature* paper, which drew upon data from some 4,800 hurricanes, charged that he had left out measurements of storms in the 1950s and 1960s because they were inconsistent with his findings, and thus that he had based his conclusions on incomplete historical data. "His conclusions are contingent on a very large bias removal that is as large or larger than the global warming signal itself," Christopher Landsea, a researcher at the federal National Oceanic and Atmospheric Administration (NOAA) in Miami, Florida, told Joseph B. Verrengia for the Associated Press (August 1, 2005). Landsea, along with two others who disagreed with Emanuel—the Colorado State University meteorologist William Gray and Max Mayfield, the director of the National Hurricane Center—blamed the rise in hurricane intensity since the 1970s on the Atlantic multidecadal oscillation. "That cycle," according to Gray, "caused 11 major hurricanes to hit Florida's peninsula from 1933 to 1965," as Robert P. King wrote for the *Palm Beach (Florida) Post* (October 8, 2005). "In contrast, just one major hurricane—Andrew in 1992—struck during the lull that followed for the next three decades." Mayfield insisted before a U.S. Senate Committee that increased hurricane activity was due to the natural cycle and not to global warming. Emanuel responded to criticisms of his paper by reaffirming his stance. "I maintain that current levels of tropical storminess are unprecedented in the historical record and that a global-

warming signal is now emerging in records of hurricane activity," he wrote in a letter to *Nature* (December 29, 2005), as quoted by Mark Schleifstein in the New Orleans *Times-Picayune* (July 9, 2006, on-line). Less than six months later, Emanuel told Marc Airhart for *Earth and Sky* (June 14, 2006, on-line), "I think the idea that [the increase in hurricane intensity is] part of a natural cycle is dead."

Much of the media coverage of Emanuel's work during and after the Katrina disaster oversimplified his findings. In particular, news stories often failed to mention that his data came from records of hurricanes that had remained over the ocean as well as the much smaller number that had made landfall. Moreover, reporters neglected to remind the public that no conclusion about the connection between global warming and hurricane intensity can be derived from measurements of a single storm or even from a fraction of all hurricanes—although, as Jeffrey Kluger pointed out in *Time* (May 8, 2006), it was not surprising that journalists reporting on the events in New Orleans did just that. "It's easy to argue about the hypothetical causes and effects of global warming," Kluger wrote. "It's a lot harder for any serious disagreement to continue when extreme weather is demolishing a major city." "If you consider hurricanes over their entire life and not just when they make landfall, you really do see an upward trend in the power of hurricanes, not in their frequency but in the magnitude of the wind speed and also in their duration," Emanuel told Alex Chadwick for the National Public Radio program *Day to Day* (September 6, 2005). "But you really can't see such tendencies in landfalling storms in the U.S. simply because their numbers are so small. . . . It's impossible statistically to detect any kind of meaningful trend in that."

Emanuel's book *Divine Wind: The History and Science of Hurricanes*, which was published on July 1, 2005, was judged by most reviewers to be well-written, beautifully illustrated (with images of works of art as well as photos of storms), and suitable for lay readers as well as scientists. "Connoisseurs of natural disasters will devour [the book], but I hope it finds its way into numerous school libraries, too," Karen R. Long wrote for the Cleveland, Ohio, *Plain Dealer* (September 11, 2005). "The author's gifts as a science teacher combine with a cultivated taste in folklore, literature and art." She also wrote, in mentioning Emanuel's description of the hypothetical sequence of events if a Category 5 hurricane—such as Katrina proved to be—were to hit New Orleans: "The only thing [Emanuel] left out . . . is the likelihood of a loose barge crashing into the levee." In a review for *Weatherwise* (July/August 2006, on-line), Jeffrey B. Halverson wrote, "Those who have been touched by the awesome power of hurricanes, are curious about storms' long association with world culture, or just plain confused by what is being presented on the evening news will benefit from reading *Divine Wind*." When Dreifus asked Emanuel how he felt about the timing of the book's publication, he said, "Not terribly good. If one is just interested in sales, I suppose it was fortuitous. But I was trying to convey a sense of hurricanes as not just things of scientific interest, but as beautiful. A leopard is a very beautiful animal. But if you took it out of its cage, it would go for your jugular. Anyone can understand that neither a leopard nor a hurricane is a willful killer."

A decade earlier, in a paper for the *Journal of Geophysical Research* (July 20, 1995) co-written by Richard Rotunno and three others, Emanuel wrote about the types of hurricanes that would form if an asteroid were to hit a body of warm, tropical waters on Earth, or in the event of "shallow-sea volcanism, or, possibly, by overturning of superheated brine pools formed by underwater volcanic activity." The computer simulations that he and his colleagues devised indicated that the resultant groups of storms, dubbed "hypercanes," could produce winds of up to 90 percent the speed of sound. (The speed of sound varies with the type of medium through which the sound is moving—for example, air or water—and the temperature of the medium. Under "standard" conditions at sea level, the speed of sound is about 761 miles per hour.) Moreover, unlike normal hurricanes, hypercanes could drastically affect the climate of the entire planet. "[Emanuel's] model predicts that a hypercane would form in about a day if an area of water only 50 kilometers [about 31 miles] in diameter is heated to a temperature of 50 degrees C [122 degrees Fahrenheit]," Jeff Hecht wrote for *New Scientist* (February 4, 1995). "He calculates that such a hot spot could be formed if an object larger than 10 kilometers in diameter [about six miles] crashed into a shallow sea." In addition to intense winds, the hurricane could have an eye with atmospheric pressure less than a third the normal level. Air at such low pressure would act like a vacuum, pulling dust and water vapor up into the stratosphere, where it could remain for years. Moreover, as Hecht reported, "The Sun's ultraviolet radiation would act on stratospheric water droplets to form hydroxyl radicals. Together with chlorine from saltwater thrown up by the hypercane these radicals could destroy vast quantities of stratospheric ozone. UV radiation would then reach the Earth's surface unhindered, killing organisms on land and in the upper layers of the ocean." Emanuel believes that hypercanes could have contributed to the extinction of the dinosaurs.

In his most recent book, *What We Know About Climate Change* (2007), Emanuel continued to warn of the potential dangers of global warming as it relates to intensified hurricane activity. He offered a scientific explanation of global warming and discussed the media's influence on the public's understanding of it. In an assessment for nybooks.com (October 11, 2007), Bill McKibben wrote, "In an epic feat of concision, [Emanuel] manages in eighty-five very small pages to explain the state of the science of climate change, conclud-

ing on the optimistic note that 'the extremists [who deprecate the threat of climate change] are being exposed and relegated to the sidelines, and when the media stop amplifying their views, their political counterparts will have nothing left to stand on.'"

When Marc Airhart asked Emanuel if his new role of public hurricane expert had changed his life, the scientist answered, "It has. A lot of people write to me or phone me. They're all completely well-meaning people and they're curious about nature. It's frustrating, because I'd dearly like to be able to talk to each of these people and answer their emails, and it's become humanly impossible for me to do that. So it's forced me to make judgment calls. On the one hand, I want to use the opportunity to convey to the public my understanding of the problem. That's very much a part of the duty, perhaps even a moral obligation, of a scientist. But on the other hand, I want to get back to the work, to the research and the teaching. It's hard to know where to strike that balance under circumstances like this."

Emanuel lives in Lexington, Massachusetts, with his wife, Susan Boyd-Bowman, whom he married in 1990, and their son, David Tristan Emanuel.

—M.B.

Suggested Reading: *Earth and Sky* (on-line) Jan. 20, 2006, June 14, 2006; Kerry A. Emanuel's MIT home page (on-line); *New York Times* F p2 Jan. 10, 2006; *Time* p92 May 8, 2006; Rittner, Don. *A to Z of Scientists in Weather and Climate*, 2003

Selected Books: *Atmospheric Convection*, 1994; *Divine Wind: The History and Science of Hurricanes*, 2005; *What We Know About Climate Change*, 2007; as co-editor—*Tropical Cyclone Disasters*, 1994

Fallon, William J.

Dec. 30, 1944– Commander of the U.S. Central Command

Address: U.S. Central Command, 7115 S. Boundary Blvd., MacDill AFB, FL 33621-5101

On March 16, 2007 William J. Fallon, a four-star admiral in the United States Navy, became the commander of the United States Central Command—CentCom, as it is known familiarly—with responsibility for the entire U.S military in the Middle East, Central Asia, and East Africa. When Fallon assumed his new position, U.S. troops were involved in two distinct campaigns, in Iraq and Afghanistan, and in the estimation of many military historians, Iraq was on the cusp of civil war. "The situation in Iraq is critical and time is of the es-

William J. Fallon

U.S. Navy/Getty Images

sence," Fallon said at his swearing-in ceremony, as quoted by William R. Levesque in the *St. Petersburg (Florida) Times* (March 17, 2007). At his confirmation hearing before the Senate Armed Services Committee, as reported by Peter Spiegel for the *Los Angeles Times* (January 31, 2007), Fallon said, "Going back to 2003, we had hundreds of good ideas of things that we would like to see in Iraq that are more reflective of the kind of society and process that we enjoy here. We probably erred in our assessment of the ability of these people [Iraqis] to take on all these tasks at the same time." "Maybe we ought to redefine the goals here a bit and do something that's more realistic in terms of getting some progress and then maybe take on the other things later," he also said at the hearing, as reported by Carl Hulse and others for the *New York Times* (January 31, 2007). U.S. army general David H. Petraeus, the commander of multinational forces in Iraq, reports to Fallon.

Fallon began his military service as a bombardier/navigator in 1967, during the Vietnam War. In 24 years as a pilot, he logged 4,800 flight hours and landed on aircraft carriers 1,300 times. During the next decade and a half, he served as a commander both in the Persian Gulf War, in 1991, and during NATO intervention in the Bosnian civil war, in what had been Yugoslavia, in 1995. He next served as deputy commander in chief and chief of staff of the U.S. Atlantic Fleet (1996–97); commander of the Norfolk, Virginia–based Second Fleet (1997–2000); vice chief of naval operations, U.S. Navy (2000–03); commander of the U.S. Fleet Forces Command and U.S. Atlantic Fleet (2003–05); and commander of the U.S. Pacific Command (2005–07). He was selected to head CentCom as much for

his diplomatic credentials as his military expertise. Fallon, who holds a master's degree in international studies, is said to be "confident but not imperious, . . . combin[ing] a tough, unvarnished style with a light touch and a keen interest in other cultures," as Ann Scott Tyson wrote for the *Washington Post* (January 14, 2007). According to Tyson, Defense Secretary Robert M. Gates has described Fallon as "one of the best strategic thinkers in uniform today" and said that "his reputation for innovation is without peer."

William Joseph Fallon was born to Catholic parents on December 30, 1944 in East Orange, New Jersey. As the oldest of nine siblings, he had many duties from an early age. His younger brother Joseph told Joseph A. Gambardello for the *Philadelphia (Pennsylvania) Inquirer* (April 6, 2004), "Everybody looked up to Billy. He was a very strong leader. . . . Billy has never had a gray area. He's always black and white. Decisive." Fallon's father worked for the U.S. Postal Service as a mail carrier, and young Billy's first job was delivering newspapers alongside him. "Expectations were that you take advantage of what you had and get to work. Having an opportunity to do a variety of things . . . to get a little money to go to school and do other things . . . was good exposure as to how life really is on a working level. . . . You don't take things for granted," Fallon told Edward Colimore for the *Philadelphia Inquirer* (February 19, 2007). When he was 12 the family moved to Merchantville, New Jersey, a suburb of Camden (across the Delaware River from Philadelphia). Fallon attended Camden Catholic High School, where he was a member of the track team; after school he worked part-time at a supermarket. After he graduated from high school, in 1963, Fallon accepted a navy ROTC (Reserve Officers Training Corps) scholarship and enrolled at Villanova University, in Philadelphia. During summers Fallon had night jobs at the Campell Soup Co. factory in Camden; he unloaded boxcars and worked on assembly lines. He earned a B.A. degree in 1967.

That same year Fallon received his commission through the ROTC, and upon completion of flight training, in December 1967, he was designated a naval flight officer. He was then sent to Vietnam, where he co-piloted an all-weather carrier-based bomber. Fallon enjoyed that experience far more than he had anticipated. "I thought I would go in and just do some time," he told Gambardello. "When I came back [from Vietnam], I had a really interesting [navy] job and then another. . . . It was pretty challenging, and I thought, 'I'll do this,' and ended up staying for a few years. Then I had an opportunity to change to a different airplane, and that was interesting, so I thought I'd do that. So through a combination of very interesting work, challenging assignments and great people . . . I ended up staying in." During his 24 years as a navy pilot, Fallon served on five aircraft carriers in the Atlantic, Pacific, and Indian Oceans and the Mediterranean Sea. He earned the Defense Distinguished Service

Medal and seven other navy awards as well as various unit and campaign decorations.

In the 1991 Persian Gulf War, Fallon commanded Carrier Air Wing (CAW) Eight, which consists of 10 squadrons and, at that time, 2,400 sailors. CAW Eight was deployed in the Arabian Gulf during Operation Desert Storm, in which the U.S. and its allies ousted Iraqi troops from Kuwait. Between January 16 and February 28, 1991, when the war ended, the sailors conducted more than 4,300 missions. Four years later Fallon led the navy's battle group, which included the *U.S.S. Theodore Roosevelt*, in Operation Deliberate Force—NATO's first military action, which aimed to destroy Serbian strongholds in Bosnia and bring the warring factions (Bosnians and Croats as well as Serbs) to the peace table. Navy secretary John Dalton said that the 680 combat missions flown by the *Theodore Roosevelt*'s 70 planes played a crucial role in creating "an atmosphere of peace that has eluded Bosnia for years," as Jack Dorsey reported for the *Virginian-Pilot* (September 22, 1995). As a commander of coalition forces, Fallon learned important lessons about working with allies, especially the need for each nation's military leaders to recognize the capabilities of other countries' forces. During the next few years, Fallon oversaw training exercises for U.S. and foreign sailors and took part in "peace games," simulations of potential real-world events, whose goal was to maintain peace in a fractious region and avoid killing and destruction.

Fallon was named deputy commander in chief and chief of staff of the U.S. Atlantic Fleet in 1996 and then became commander of the Norfolk, Virginia–based Second Fleet in late 1997. In the latter position Fallon again directed the training of sailors, a task that had become difficult because of shortages of both materiel and manpower. He was especially hampered by the closure of the navy's live-fire range on the island of Vieques, in Puerto Rico, which naval officers have described as the only place in the Atlantic on American soil where sailors and Marines could practice amphibious landings while under fire. He arranged practice exercises at a firing range in Scotland but "felt badly about going over there and telling them, 'We can't do it in our country. Do you mind if we come over to your country to do it?'," as he told Dave Mayfield for the *Virginian-Pilot* (December 13, 1999).

In 2000 Fallon was promoted to vice chief of naval operations. He became a four-star admiral and relocated to the Pentagon, in Washington, D.C. In his new position he attracted international attention after an American submarine, the *U.S.S. Greeneville*, crashed into a Japanese fishing boat, the *Ehime Maru*, on February 9, 2001; the boat sank, and nine people died. Seven months earlier, the alleged molestation of a young girl by a U.S. Marine on the Japanese island of Okinawa, where thousands of American troops were stationed, had severely strained relations between Japan and the U.S. With tensions between the two nations worsening following the *Ehime Maru* accident, President George W. Bush selected Fallon to meet with Japanese leaders and the families of the victims. Koichi Yamamoto, a member of the Japanese Parliament, told Doug Struck for the *Washington Post* (March 2, 2001) that Fallon was "dealing with the situation in a very Japanese manner, considering Japanese sentiment. I think this will be a very strong turning point." Admiral Dennis Blair, who then headed the Pacific Command, told Susan Taylor Martin years later for the *St. Petersburg (Florida) Times* (January 14, 2007) that Fallon "wasn't terribly familiar with Japan at the time but he did a marvelous job handling a ticklish diplomatic situation."

In 2003 Fallon took over the navy's U.S. Fleet Forces Command and the U.S. Atlantic Fleet. He held that position until early 2005, when then–Defense Secretary Donald H. Rumsfeld named him head of the U.S. Pacific Command (PacCom). Based in Camp H.M. Smith, Hawaii, PacCom directs 300,000 troops and is responsible for activities in 43 countries spanning more than 100 million square miles in the Pacific Ocean and East Asia. That area includes two of the world's most serious potential hotspots—the Korean Peninsula and the Taiwan Strait. Fallon assumed control of PacCom when the command was overseeing military relief efforts for victims of the tsunami that devastated parts of Indonesia, Thailand, India, Sri Lanka and other countries in December 2004. With many Bush administration Cabinet members and other officials occupied with conflicts in the Middle East, Fallon became a de facto ambassador-at-large to countries on the Pacific Rim. Bates Gill, a China expert at the Center for Strategic and International Studies, told Susan Taylor Martin, "His main task was trying to create an atmosphere of mutual interests and reassurance." Fallon has said that China's size and the growth of its military, economy, and regional influence made rapport with that nation a priority in network-building efforts. The 2001 collision between a U.S. spy plane and a Chinese fighter jet had soured relations between the two countries' militaries, and Fallon tried to improve matters through visits with Chinese leaders and mutual-benefit military exercises with the Chinese navy. He gained a reputation for engaging with occasionally antagonistic governments, at times defying the Bush administration in doing so. In light of the expansion of China's military and the shrinking of the U.S. Pacific fleet from 350 ships in 2000 to about 100 in 2005, Fallon thought that the U.S. must combine diplomacy with undersea superiority. Although he often disagreed with Washington, Fallon was highly regarded within the Pentagon for his willingness to speak his mind and for his openness with subordinates.

In March 2007 Fallon succeeded army general John P. Abizaid as commander of the U.S. Central Command. Based at MacDill Air Force Base, in Tampa, Florida, CentCom is the headquarters for all U.S. military operations in the Middle East, Central Asia, and East Africa. Fallon is the first

FALLON

navy officer to lead CentCom since its inception, in 1983. Although threats in the region have usually been land-based, military leaders believed that Fallon was well-suited for the job, because of his diplomatic and strategic skills and because the U.S. had recently dispatched two carrier strike groups (including two aircraft carriers and other ships) to the Persian Gulf for the first time since 2003. "The reality is, if you look at the CentCom area of responsibility, there's a lot of water there," Defense Secretary Robert M. Gates told reporters, as quoted by Ann Scott Tyson and Glenn Kessler in the *Washington Post* (January 31, 2007). "And as you look at the range of options available to the United States, . . . it makes sense to me . . . for Admiral Fallon to have the job." Among those who disapproved of Fallon's appointment was an unnamed, retired Marine general, who told Sally B. Donnelly and Douglas Waller for *Time* (January 9, 2007), "To put in a naval aviator without any command combat experience is like putting a baseball coach in to run the offense in the Super Bowl."

In early 2007 the Bush administration decided to increase the number of troops in Iraq by some 20,000. General Abizaid was against that troop escalation, because he believed that it pushed the responsibility of security further from Iraqi law-enforcement officers. He believed that diplomatic, economic, and political pressures are more effective than military power in wars such as the one in Iraq—but that in any case, the Iraq conflict could last as long as 11 years. "The biggest problem we've got is lack of patience," Abizaid told David Ignatius for the *Washington Post* (March 16, 2007). "When we take upon ourselves the task of rebuilding shattered societies, we need not to be in a hurry. We need to be patient, but our patience is limited. That makes it difficult to accomplish our purposes." Fallon, by contrast, has described himself as "not a particularly patient man," according to Tyson and Kessler, and he has removed the term "long war" from the CentCom lexicon of words that can be used to describe the Iraq war in press releases and media statements. He also approved the so-called troop surge. "One of the reasons I have been selected is because I will be coming at [the war] from a different perspective," he told Edward Colimore. "I like to ask questions, and I'm naturally skeptical about what I hear."

Unlike Abizaid, Fallon will not focus on the day-to-day operations of combat, leaving those responsibilities to army lieutenant general David H. Petraeus, who became the commander of multinational forces in Iraq in January 2007. Instead, Fallon will concentrate on diplomacy. Stephen R. Pietropaoli, a retired rear admiral who now serves as executive director of the Navy League, an advocacy group, told Thom Shanker for the *New York Times* (January 8, 2007), "Admiral Fallon will have very experienced commanders in charge of operations in Afghanistan, Iraq, the Horn of Africa. But the Central Command commander needs to be above that, looking at how to enhance America's

influence throughout his area of responsibility and how to truly work hand in glove with the Department of State to enhance America's image and influence and prestige in that part of the world." "The extent [to which] we can understand better the thoughts and actions of others reduces substantially, in my experience, the danger of miscalculation, and so I strongly endorse that approach," Fallon said at his confirmation hearing, as reported by Peter Spiegel.

In a March 27, 2007 interview with Kyra Phillips for CNN, Fallon stressed that security in Iraq is unquestionably the biggest challenge for the nascent government and the U.S.-led troops and the biggest concern of the Iraqi people. "They want more security. They want to get out on the streets and do things," Fallon told Phillips. He added that Iraqis themselves needed to participate more in public affairs if peace is to return; they have to "do everything they can to help us identify those who don't abide by rules of justice," he explained. Others believe that the Iraqi government must bring about a political reconciliation between opposing factions before stability is possible. Former Democratic congressman Lee H. Hamilton of Indiana, who co-authored *The Iraq Study Group Report* (2006), told the Senate Foreign Relations Committee that making the security of Baghdad a precondition for other goals is a mistake. "You've got to deal with these problems comprehensively, and if you're focused solely on questions of security, you're not going to get there," Hamilton said, as quoted by Spiegel. "Because you can not isolate that security from the other aspects."

"There were a couple of times during the years when I wondered what I was doing—like spending a year away from home in the Indian Ocean. But, frankly, it has been fantastic," Fallon told Gambardello. With his wife, the former Mary Trapp, Fallon has four children, two of whom have served in the navy. Fallon is a world-history buff and an avid jogger and has recently taken up surfing.

—N.W.M.

Suggested Reading: *New York Times* A p6 Jan. 19, 2005, A p8 Jan. 8, 2007, A p1+ Jan. 31, 2007; *Philadelphia Inquirer* A p3 Feb. 16, 2007, B p1+ Feb. 19, 2007; *St. Petersburg (Florida) Times* A p1 Jan. 14, 2007, A p11 Mar. 17, 2007; *Time* (online) Jan. 9, 2007; U.S. Department of Defense Web site; *Washington Post* A p12 Jan. 14, 2007, p11 Jan. 31, 2007, A p21 Mar. 16, 2007

Jodi Hilton/Getty Images

Faust, Drew Gilpin

Sep. 18, 1947— President of Harvard University; historian

Address: Office of the President, Harvard University, Massachusetts Hall, Cambridge, MA 02138

On July 1, 2007 the historian Drew Gilpin Faust became the first woman to hold the post of president of Harvard University in the school's 371-year history, thus attaining what many consider to be the most prestigious post in academia in the United States. "I've spent a lot of time thinking about the past, and about how it shapes the future," Faust said five months earlier, when Harvard announced her appointment, as quoted by the *Harvard University Gazette* (February 11, 2007). "No university in the country, perhaps the world, has as remarkable a past as Harvard's. And our shared enterprise is to make Harvard's future even more remarkable than its past." Defying what was traditionally expected of a young woman from an affluent southern family in the 1970s, Faust earned a doctorate in American civilization and became a college teacher. During her 25 years as a faculty member at the University of Pennsylvania, she published five books on topics connected to the American Civil War, the last of which—*Mothers of Invention: Women of the Slaveholding South in the American Civil War*—became a *New York Times* best-seller and won several honors. In 2001 Faust was appointed dean of the Radcliffe Institute for Advanced Study, a newly created division of Harvard, in Cambridge, Massachusetts; she succeeded in transforming Radcliffe into an internationally renowned academic

center. That accomplishment and her "talent for stimulating people to do their best work, both individually and together," as James R. Houghton—a member of the Harvard Corp. and the chair of the Harvard presidential search committee—phrased it to the *Gazette*, made her a leading candidate to succeed Lawrence H. Summers, who had stepped down from the university's top post in 2006. Harvard, the oldest institution of higher learning in the U.S., is the fourth of the eight Ivy League universities to select a woman as president. Faust has acknowledged that her appointment is significant in women's struggle for equality in the workplace, but she has also said, as quoted by the Associated Press (February 12, 2007), "I'm not the woman president of Harvard. I'm the president of Harvard." The first president of Harvard since 1672 to hold neither an undergraduate nor a graduate degree from the university, Faust will be responsible for a number of recently launched projects, among them the overhaul of Harvard's undergraduate curriculum and the construction of a state-of-the-art science center in which stem-cell research will be conducted.

Catharine Drew Gilpin Faust was born on September 18, 1947 in New York City to the former Catharine Mellick and McGhee Tyson Gilpin, who owned several farms in the Shenandoah Valley and raised Thoroughbred horses. She has always been called by her middle name (and was nicknamed Drewdie as a youngster). Along with her older brother, McGhee Tyson Gilpin Jr. (called Tyson), and her two younger brothers, Donald and Lawrence, Faust grew up in Clarke County, Virginia, in a privileged household and a community ruled by rigid racial segregation. "I lived in a world where social arrangements were taken for granted and assumed to be timeless," she wrote for *Harvard Magazine* (May/June 2003). "A child's obligation was to learn these usages, not to question them. The complexities of racial deportment were of a piece with learning manners and etiquette more generally." Faust attended the Blue Ridge Country Day School, an all-white private school her family helped to found in Millwood, Virginia. When she was nine she had a conversation with the family's black handyman and driver that inspired her to send a letter to President Dwight D. Eisenhower in which she argued fervently for desegregation. Gender was also a defining aspect of Faust's upbringing; her mother repeatedly told her, "It's a man's world, sweetie, and the sooner you learn that the better off you'll be," as Faust recalled to Sara Rimer for the *New York Times* (February 12, 2007).

While Faust lived up to some of what was expected of a southern girl—she raised a beef cow, joined the Brownies, and took dancing lessons—she also resisted some of the traditional female activities of her time. She refused, for example, to become a debutante, a prelude, it was assumed, to marriage with a rich man and full-time homemaking. As a student at Concord Academy, a prep school in Massachusetts, Faust "took off on her own track . . . ," as her older brother, Tyson, now a lawyer, recalled to Rimer. "I think she read the scene pretty well. She was ambitious. She wanted to accomplish stuff." After she graduated from Concord, in 1964, she enrolled at Bryn Mawr College, a women's school in Pennsylvania. (Her father, two uncles, a great-uncle, and two of her three brothers attended Princeton University, but the college did not admit women until 1969.) Mary Maples Dunn, who, as acting dean, preceded Faust at the Radcliffe Institute, told Rimer that when Faust was an undergraduate, women's colleges "tended to give these young women a very good sense of themselves and encouraged them to develop their own ideas and to express themselves confidently. It was an invaluable experience in a world in which women were second-class citizens." Faust earned a B.A. degree in history magna cum laude from Bryn Mawr in 1968. That year she married Stephen Faust, a medical-school student at the University of Pennsylvania (Penn); soon after her graduation, she, too, enrolled at Penn, to pursue graduate degrees.

Faust earned a master's degree, in 1971, and a Ph.D. degree, in 1975, in American civilization at Penn. In 1976 she was appointed an assistant professor in Penn's Department of American Civilization; that year she also got divorced. In 1977 Faust's Ph.D. dissertation was published as the book *A Sacred Circle: The Dilemma of the Intellectual in the Old South, 1840-1860*. In 1980 she was promoted to associate professor at Penn. Two years later she published the books *The Creation of Confederate Nationalism: Ideology and Identity in the Civil War South* and *James Henry Hammond and the Old South: A Design for Mastery*. She was honored for distinguished teaching in 1982 and 1996. She became a full professor in 1984 and was named the Stanley I. Sheerr professor of history in 1988. From 1989 to 2000 she held the position of Annenberg professor of history. Her fourth book, *Southern Stories: Slaveholders in Peace and War*, appeared in 1992.

Faust's fifth book, *Mothers of Invention: Women of the Slaveholding South in the American Civil War* (1996) won the 1996 Avery O. Craven Award from the Organization of American Historians for the best book on the Civil War and the 1997 Francis Parkman Prize from the Society of American Historians for the best nonfiction book on an American theme. During the historian Sheldon Hackney's interview with Faust, recorded by Ellen Marsh for *Humanities* (July/August 1997), Hackney—at the time the chairman of the National Endowment for the Humanities—described the work as "a book about very large ideas and large implications," adding, "yet those ideas and implications don't intrude; it is the very interesting lives and words of real people that drive a reader along from chapter to chapter"; he praised *Mothers of Invention* as displaying "craftsmanship in the historical profession at its highest." In discussing the impact that southern women had on the outcome of the Civil War,

Faust examined two issues with which she had struggled since her youth—race relations and gender inequalities. "I guess I've been studying unpleasant people or politically incorrect people for my whole academic career," she told Hackney. "My feeling is that it's very important to understand how individuals in the past rationalized lives that we might find unthinkable, because we have our own set of rationalizations that make us blind to injustices in our own society." She also told Hackney that in some ways historians are like novelists, because both have a responsibility to address the complexities of the individuals in their accounts. "I also think that history should not simply be celebration of people in the past, even simply celebration of groups who've been neglected in the historical records. It is important to celebrate people but not to do so uncritically," she said. "They're not heroes and heroines. They're combinations of heroism and villainy."

While at the University of Pennsylvania, Faust increasingly took on administrative duties. From 1988 to 1990 she chaired the President's Committee on University Life, which focused on such campus issues as diversity, the relationships among faculty, students, and staff, and Penn's interactions with surrounding communities. From 1993 to 1994 Faust was a member of the university's presidential search committee, and she chaired the presidential inaugural committee in 1994. She chaired the Department of American Civilization for five years and directed Penn's Women's Studies Program from 1996 to 2000.

On January 1, 2001, after an eight-month search and evaluations of more than 80 candidates, Faust was named dean of the Radcliffe Institute for Advanced Study, a new academic center created out of Radcliffe College, formerly a women's college associated with Harvard University. (Harvard and Radcliffe stopped issuing separate degrees in 1977; on October 1, 1999 they officially merged, and all undergraduates became students of Harvard College.) Upon her appointment, Neil L. Rudenstine, then the president of Harvard, welcomed Faust as an innovator. "Drew Faust is a person and a scholar of unusual depth and range," he told a *Harvard University Gazette* (April 6, 2000) reporter. "Faust has the clarity of mind, the commitment, and the leadership qualities essential to the successful launching of this new venture—particularly within an institution as complex as Harvard." Faust's second husband, Charles E. Rosenberg, whom she had married in 1980, secured a tenured position in Harvard's Department of the History of Science. (Faust and Rosenberg had rejected offers of tenured positions at Harvard in 1989, citing in part the hassle of moving. The opportunity for Faust at the Radcliffe Institute, they felt, was too attractive to turn down.)

As dean, Faust oversaw the final steps of Radcliffe's transformation into a highly respected scholarly institute, one that currently receives about 800 applications a year for 45 to 50 fellowships. In recognition of its roots in the all-female Radcliffe College, she made sure that the institute maintained a commitment to the study of women, gender, and society. Faust also had to tackle the details of running a multimillion-dollar organization. Soon after she became dean, budget cuts forced her to reduce significantly the number of the institute's administrative positions. She also began aggressive fund-raising efforts and an extensive renovation of the campus. Within the greater community of Harvard University, she served on the Harvard Committee on the Status of Women from 2001 to 2006, and in 2004 she was a member of the Allston Task Force on Undergraduate Life. In 2002 she was a top candidate for dean of Harvard's faculty of arts and sciences, a post ultimately filled by the historian William C. Kirby. Three years later, as reported by Claire M. Guehenno for the *Harvard Crimson* (January 12, 2007, on-line), Lawrence H. Summers, then Harvard's president, tried without success to recruit Faust to replace Kirby. In 2003 Faust removed her name from a list of candidates being considered for the presidency of the University of Pennsylvania, and she later did so in connection with the top post at the University of Chicago.

In January 2005, at the National Bureau of Economics Research Conference on Diversifying the Science & Engineering Workforce, Summers made a comment that many interpreted as implying that women might be innately less talented at math and science than men. Later that year, amid a storm of controversy surrounding his remark, Summers created two task forces at Harvard, one whose aim was to increase the number of women on the faculty and the other regarding women in science and engineering, both of which were overseen by Faust. Still, Summers could not recover from the damage caused by his comment, and on February 21, 2006 he announced his intention to retire the following June; Derek Bok, Harvard's president from 1971 to 1991, agreed to serve as interim president for one year beginning on July 1, 2006, while the university searched for a new president.

On February 11, 2007 Faust was named the 28th president of Harvard. "This is a great day, and a historic day, for Harvard," James R. Houghton, a senior member of the Harvard Corp. and the chair of the presidential search committee, said in his announcement, according to a Harvard press release. "Drew Faust is an inspiring and accomplished leader, a superb scholar, a dedicated teacher, and a wonderful human being. She combines a powerful, broad-ranging intellect with a demonstrated capacity for strong leadership." In choosing Faust, the search committee consulted more than 150 people via e-mail messages and face-to-face interviews to determine whether she was qualified to make the move from overseeing the Radcliffe Institute (which has 87 employees and a $17 million annual budget) to presiding over all divisions of Harvard University (which has 24,000 employees with a $3 billion annual budget). Faust's appointment was approved by Harvard's two governing

boards—the Harvard Corp. and the board of overseers. "Drew wears her extraordinary accomplishments lightly," Houghton said. "Her many admirers know her as both collaborative and decisive, both open-minded and tough-minded, both eloquent and understated, both mindful of tradition and effective in leading innovation." Faust's official inauguration took place on October 12, 2007 at Harvard's Tercentenary Theatre.

Harvard is now the fourth of the eight Ivy League universities to appoint a female president; the presidents of the others—Amy Gutmann of the University of Pennsylvania, Shirley M. Tilghman at Princeton, and Ruth J. Simmons at Brown—all publicly declined consideration for the Harvard presidency. While the appointment of a new Harvard president is always newsworthy, Faust's appointment as the first female president became a media sensation. "Harvard is making a statement at a critical time when we are seeing student bodies that are well over 50 percent women," Claire van Ummersen, the director of the Office of Women in Higher Education at the American Council on Education, told Valerie Strauss and Susan Kinzie for the *Washington Post* (February 10, 2007). "We see women faculty increasing in number, and the place where we have lagged most is in research institutions having women at the executive level. Hopefully, [Faust's appointment] will have some influence on boards of trustees or overseers of other institutions." Some detractors speculated that the choice of Faust rested more on her gender than her qualifications, but everyone involved with the decision to choose Faust denied that suggestion. "All the reports have been 'gender, gender, gender,' and I'm thinking to myself 'isn't that funny? That has not been something we've talked about at all,'" Robert Reischauer, a member of the Harvard Corp., told Jesse Harland Alderman for the Associated Press (February 12, 2007). Faust herself said, as quoted by Richard C. Paddock in the *Los Angeles Times* (February 12, 2007), "Young women have come up to me and said this is really an inspiration. So I think it would be wrong not to acknowledge that this has tremendous symbolic importance. It's not about me Drew Faust. It's about a particular moment at an unparalleled institution and we need to acknowledge that."

Faust is a trustee of the Andrew W. Mellon Foundation, the National Humanities Center, and Bryn Mawr College, where she chaired the trustee committee on student life from 1998 to 2003. She serves on the educational advisory board of the Guggenheim Foundation. She was the vice president of the American Historical Association (1992–96); president of the Southern Historical Association (1999–2000); and an executive board member of both the Organization of American Historians and the Society of American Historians (1999–2002). She was a member of the jury for the Pulitzer Prize in history in 1986, 1990, and 2004; in the last year she chaired that jury. She is also an elected member of the American Academy of Arts and Sciences, the American Philosophical Society, and the Society of American Historians. In 2007 *Time* magazine included her on its list of the world's 100 most influential people.

The five-foot 11-inch Faust and her husband, Charles E. Rosenberg, live in Cambridge. Rosenberg, a leading historian of American medicine, is a professor of the history of science and also the Ernest E. Monrad professor in the social sciences at Harvard. From her union with Rosenberg, Faust has one daughter, Jessica Rosenberg, who graduated summa cum laude from Harvard in 2004 and now works as a fact-checker for the *New Yorker*. She also has one stepdaughter, Leah Rosenberg, a specialist in Caribbean literature who teaches at the University of Florida at Gainesville.

—C.S.

Suggested Reading: *Boston Globe* (on-line) Feb. 25, 2007; *Harvard Crimson* (on-line) Feb. 12, 2007; *Harvard University Gazette* (on-line) Apr. 6, 2000, Feb. 11, 2007; *New York Times* A p1+ Feb. 10, 2007, A p1+ Feb. 12, 2007; *USA Today* (on-line) Feb. 11, 2007

Selected Books: *A Sacred Circle: The Dilemma of the Intellectual in the Old South, 1840-1860*, 1977; *The Creation of Confederate Nationalism: Ideology and Identity in the Civil War South*, 1982; *James Henry Hammond and the Old South: A Design for Mastery*, 1982; *Southern Stories: Slaveholders in Peace and War*, 1992; *Mothers of Invention: Women of the Slaveholding South in the American Civil War*, 1996

Tim Sloan/AFP/Getty Images

Fenty, Adrian M.

Dec. 7, 1970– Mayor of Washington, D.C.

Address: Office of the Mayor, 1350 Pennsylvania Ave., N.W., Washington, DC 20004

Adrian Fenty's successful 2006 bid to become, at 36, the youngest-ever mayor of Washington, D.C., produced both excitement and uncertainty in the nation's capital. Fenty, a second-term City Council member representing Ward 4, which includes much of Northwest Washington, had previously shown himself to be a dedicated public servant, unusually attuned to individual citizens' needs—

from those that surfaced during PTA meetings to those arising from conditions of trees or curbs on specific streets. He nonetheless remained a polarizing figure, initially receiving no endorsements in the mayoral race from his fellow City Council members, who complained that he was primarily an attention-seeker and was not sufficiently involved in the larger decision-making process of the city government. Fenty did indeed attract media attention, with his highly visible, marathon campaigning sessions, in which he went door-to-door through much of the city to meet voters. He presented as his true aim, however, that of tackling problems in Washington that had not been solved during the otherwise largely successful tenure of his predecessor, Mayor Anthony Williams. A two-term mayor who declined to seek a third term, Williams was credited with straightening out the city's finances and with helping Washington to develop an attractive real-estate market. Fenty, for his part, vowed to address issues including education and crime, placing particular emphasis on school reform. In the *Philadelphia Inquirer* (September 10, 2006), Steve Goldstein wrote that the 2006 mayoral election represented "a referendum on the city's rapid gentrification" under Mayor Williams, "a rising tide that did not lift all boats, leaving many of the poorest residents high and dry."

Fenty's chief opponent for the Democratic nomination—and thus, in that mostly Democratic city, for the mayoralty—was a 26-year political veteran, City Council chair Linda W. Cropp. "The difference between the two is that she [Cropp] might try to keep the machinery of government well oiled; Adrian might be inclined to scrap it and try some new ideas," the deputy editor of the *Washington Post*'s editorial page, Colbert King, told Goldstein. The framing of the election as a choice between a safe, predictable veteran and a fresh, energetic newcomer was common in press coverage of the race. The *Post*'s endorsement of Fenty for mayor, on September 5, 2006, proclaimed, "He offers a vision of the city that challenges the best in people." Fenty was sworn in as mayor on January 2, 2007.

Adrian M. Fenty was born on December 7, 1970 in Washington, D.C., the second of the three sons of Phillip Fenty, an African-American, and Jan Fenty, who is white. He was raised in a row house in the working-class neighborhood of Mount Pleasant. His parents, whom Fenty described to Jura Koncius for the *Washington Post* (August 3, 2006) as "former hippies," were active in the civil rights movement; they had moved to Washington from Buffalo in 1968. When Fenty was a small boy, his father—an artist whose work adorned their house—stayed at home with the three boys while Jan Fenty taught school. By the time the boys were in their teens, their parents had opened an athletic-shoe store, Fleet Feet, in the Adams Morgan neighborhood of Washington, and Fenty and his brothers helped out at the store when they were not in school. Fenty attended Wilson Senior High, a public school, before completing his secondary education at the private Mackin Catholic High School. He told Vanessa Williams for the *Washington Post* (August 31, 2006) that he became interested in the process of lawmaking during an 11th-grade civics class. According to Williams, Fenty decided to become a lawyer so that he could "help shape public policy behind the scenes."

At Oberlin College, in Oberlin, Ohio, Fenty was a member of the basketball, cross-country, and track teams. During his college years he served as an intern for U.S. senator Howard Metzenbaum of Ohio; Washington, D.C., congressional delegate Eleanor Holmes Norton; and U.S. representative Joseph P. Kennedy of Massachusetts, all Democrats. Fenty earned a B.A. degree in English and economics from Oberlin in 1992, then studied law at Howard University, in Washington, receiving his J.D. degree in 1996. He met his wife, the former Michelle Cross, at Howard. The two were married in 1997 and settled in Crestwood, a neighborhood in northwest Washington. Fenty began attending meetings of his neighborhood association, which fueled his interest in elective office. He volunteered for the unsuccessful mayoral campaign of former City Council member Kevin Chavous and later served as counsel for the City Council's Committee on Education, Libraries and Recreation, which Chavous chaired. Fenty's first forays into local politics were as commissioner and treasurer of ANC (Advisory Neighborhood Commission) 4C— one of 37 such commissions in the city—and as president of the 16th Street Neighborhood Civic Association. Michelle Fenty told Williams that her husband did not carefully plan but, rather, fell into his political career. "I saw that [politics] was what gave him passion," she said. "He was the happiest when he was on the ANC. He would come home very excited about having talked to all these people and how he was going to help them with their problems."

During that time Fenty also practiced law, serving on probate cases for two law firms and acting as a victims' advocate with the Crime Victims Compensation Program of the D.C. Superior Court. His opponent in the 2006 mayoral race, Linda Cropp, would cite several of those cases in accusing Fenty of incompetence. In the most widely reported episode, Fenty was assigned by the court in 1999 to handle the affairs of an elderly man, William Hardy Sr., who was suffering from dementia and whose relatives were suspected of stealing his money. In the year that Fenty was responsible for the case, $22,500 vanished from Hardy's credit-union account. A judge wrote that Fenty's conduct was "either incompetent or negligent or both." Fenty, the court found, had not stolen from Hardy but had made errors in filing documents and overseeing the elderly man's finances that allowed Hardy's relatives to exploit him. The Office of the Bar Counsel informally admonished Fenty, who repaid $15,000 to Hardy's estate. Though he refused to go into detail when speaking to Williams about the incident, Fenty said, "I learned you have to cross every 't' and dot every 'i,' because one little thing can lead to a big problem."

Fenty was elected to the City Council of the District of Columbia in 2000, defeating the four-term incumbent Charlene Drew Jarvis for the Ward 4 seat and becoming, at 29, the council's youngest member up to that time. Fenty won the election through a relentless campaign of direct contact with voters, which included going door-to-door and listening to individual constituents' complaints. During his one-and-a-half terms on the 12-member council—he was reelected in 2004—Fenty continually addressed individuals' needs. Michael Grunwald suggested in the *Washington Post* (September 10, 2006) that as a City Council member, Fenty had relatively little involvement in the policy-making that led to various overall improvements in the city under Mayor Anthony Williams, such as stabilized finances and a revitalized downtown area. Instead, Fenty focused on such direct actions as getting trees pruned, attending PTA meetings, and "answering e-mail on his omnipresent BlackBerry," as Grunwald wrote. Fenty was chairman of the council's Committee on Human Services, which oversees the city's Department of Youth Rehabilitation Services, Child and Family Services Administration, Department of Human Services, and Office of Aging. During his tenure Ward 4 saw the opening of a number of restaurants and other businesses and the building of new housing units. Fenty opposed Mayor Williams's ultimately successful efforts to close the city's only public hospital, D.C. General. He also opposed public funding for a baseball stadium in the city, on the grounds that the project (which was later approved) would reap few benefits for taxpayers. In 2003 Fenty helped introduce legislation to ban smoking in almost all indoor workplaces, including bars and restaurants.

In 2005, in what was perhaps his most notable move as a council member, Fenty boldly proposed a $1 billion capital-improvement program for the city's ailing public schools, to be financed with proceeds from the local lottery. After persuading two colleagues to introduce the bill with him and five others to sign on as co-sponsors, Fenty began seeking media coverage for the plan. Other council members balked at Fenty's plan, particularly its reliance on lottery revenue, which they felt was untenable. Jack Evans, the chairman of the council's Finance Committee, told Grunwald, "Adrian's plan was absolutely absurd. The financing was hopeless—and the financing was the whole point." But with parents and educators passionately seeking improvements for the schools, Fenty's bill later passed unanimously—though not before Kathy Patterson, the council member who chaired the Education Committee, had changed the funding source to business taxes and Evans had altered the plan to call for $3 billion spent over 15 years on school construction and renovation. Those changes notwithstanding, Fenty's supporters cited the bill's passage as proof of his ability to get results.

In 2005 Fenty announced his mayoral candidacy. He embarked on an aggressive campaign that included eight- to 10-hour days of walking door-to-door, even in harsh weather, and personally asking residents for their votes. "Never has the District seen such intense hand-to-hand contact between a mayoral candidate and the electorate," Williams wrote, citing the candidate's claim that his volunteers had visited every house in Washington and that Fenty had been to more than half of those homes himself. After a July poll showed Fenty leading his opponents, Cropp stepped up her campaign efforts, which came to include negative ads about Fenty. One ad called Fenty "reckless" for voting against a limit on spending by the D.C. government, while another claimed that Fenty's vote against a crime bill "puts our safety at risk." Cropp also pointed to Fenty's mishandling of William Hardy's estate and of another probate case from which Fenty was dismissed; one ad stated that Fenty had "turned his back on the elderly." The ads were not enough to stop Fenty, who won the Democratic primary with an estimated 57 percent of the vote, while Cropp captured 31 percent. As Washington, D.C., is predominantly Democratic, Fenty easily prevailed in the general election on November 7, 2006, receiving 90 percent of the vote. The *Washington Post*'s endorsement of Fenty for mayor applauded his efforts toward improving schools: "At a time when most politicians were thinking small or not at all about the city's dilapidated school buildings, Mr. Fenty drew public attention to the problem with some well-timed media events. With the public mobilized, he introduced legislation with a price tag that prompted his colleagues to scoff. But his perseverance caused his detractors to sign on to the idea and find a way to finance the long-needed changes. Show-

manship? We call that leadership." The editorial added that Fenty had "worked hard and without much fanfare to bring positive changes to juvenile justice" and that his "oversight of the agency charged with caring for people with mental retardation has kept public focus on a long-neglected agency."

Fenty, who was sworn into office on January 2, 2007, is the youngest mayor in the city's history and its sixth elected mayor since the establishment of home rule in the district, in 1975. (Prior to that, D.C. was governed by a board of commissioners appointed by the president.) In filling his administration's top Cabinet posts, he chose officials from the Williams administration as well as members of his own campaign staff. His initial priorities as mayor included winning control of the city's school board, so that it would function as a mayoral advisory panel, arguing that he cannot otherwise achieve his goal of improving the city's schools. In its current configuration, the board consists of five elected members and four appointed by the mayor. Fenty's plan echoed New York City mayor Michael Bloomberg's successful 2002 takeover of that city's schools. Although Fenty had voted against a similar move by his predecessor, Williams, he claimed to have been persuaded, both by the apparent success of Bloomberg's model and by the continued poor performance of D.C. schools, to reverse his stance. In June 2007 Fenty fired the school superintendent, Clifford B. Janey, for acting too slowly to bring about reform; he chose as Janey's successor Michelle A. Rhee, a former teacher and the founder and president of the New York City–based New Teacher Project, a nonprofit organization that helps school districts to recruit and train new teachers. Taking another cue from Bloomberg, Fenty remade the mayor's office into a large, open work space called "the bullpen," with Fenty himself sitting in the center of the room. The new mayor dismissed the idea that his aides might feel intimidated by his constant presence. "People will stay more focused," he told David Nakamura for the *Washington Post* (December 3, 2006). "And they have their BlackBerrys if they want to do a personal message with no one seeing them."

Fenty said to Jura Koncius that in his personal life, "the big three for me are work, family and working out." He and his wife, who practices international business law, have twin boys, Matthew and Andrew, born in 2000. Fenty told Koncius that he enjoys swimming and playing football and basketball with his sons. Fenty also participates in triathlons, sometimes with his father, who is now in his mid-60s.

—M.B.

Suggested Reading: District of Columbia: Mayor's Office Web site; *Philadelphia Inquirer* A p2 Sep. 10, 2006; *Washington Post* C p1+ Aug. 31, 2006, B p1+ Sep. 10, 2006, C p5 Dec. 3, 2006, B p1+ Dec. 8, 2006

Evan Agostini/Getty Images

Ferrera, America

Apr. 18, 1984– Actress

Address: c/o Endeavor Agency, 9601 Wilshire Blvd., 10th Fl., Beverly Hills, CA 90212

With her role as Betty Suarez on the hit ABC television show *Ugly Betty*, the actress America Ferrera has helped to redefine beauty in an industry in which waistline measurements often matter more than talent. Prior to her work on the show, Ferrera, as a curvaceous Latina woman, struggled to find acceptance in the Hollywood community; although she knew from an early age that she wanted to pursue acting, she found few parts intended for actresses of her ethnicity and body type and few casting directors willing to look beyond those factors. Those early struggles have frequently found parallels in the lives of the characters Ferrera has since portrayed on screen. Her first feature film, *Real Women Have Curves* (2002), brought Ferrera a Special Jury Award for acting at the Sundance Film Festival. Her next major role, in *The Sisterhood of the Traveling Pants* (2005), was another that echoed her real life; her portrayal of Carmen, a daughter of divorced parents who yearns to be accepted by her father, earned praise from critics who were surprised to find a performance of such depth in what promised to be a superficial teenage drama. As the title character of the comedy *Ugly Betty*, Ferrera—and her refreshing take on beauty and celebrity—has begun to garner national attention. "I'm not a model. I never wanted to be a model. I never wanted to do ads for Neutrogena. That's not what I set out in my life to do," Ferrera told Rick Bentley for the *Fresno (California) Bee* (Au-

gust 20, 2006). "I set out to tell stories. I set out to represent real people. And to me, Betty is the most beautiful opportunity that's ever come across my path to represent a whole generation of young women who don't recognize themselves in anything they're watching." In her first season of portraying the lovable, braces-clad Betty, Ferrera won a Golden Globe Award, an Emmy Award, and a Screen Actors Guild Award for best actress in a comedy, honors that affirmed her belief that there is a place in film for actors of diverse appearances. As she told Doug Elfman for the *Chicago Sun-Times* (November 2, 2006), "I can't go out there and save the world, but if I can look at the child next to me and make them feel alive and like they are not invisible for a second, that feels like a real reward."

The youngest of six sisters, America Georgina Ferrera was born on April 18, 1984 in Los Angeles, California. Her parents, who are both Honduran, divorced when she was young; her mother, whose name is also America, raised the children. "The way my mother raised me and the values she instilled in me allowed me to be persistent," Ferrera told Claudia Puig for *USA Today* (October 18, 2002). "She taught me you can be whatever you want, no matter what people say." Ferrera, who grew up in a predominantly Jewish neighborhood of the Los Angeles suburb Woodland Hills, has said that her ethnicity was never an issue for her until she ventured into Hollywood for auditions. "Then people saw me as Latina," she recalled to Loren King for the *Boston Globe* (November 10, 2002). "The label was instant." Ferrera started acting at age eight, when she was cast in a junior-high-school production of *Romeo and Juliet*. From then on she was determined to become an actress, despite receiving little encouragement. "It was like saying I wanted to go to the moon," she told Puig. "People would say, 'What are you talking about? You don't look like anything special.'" At 16 Ferrera signed with a small talent agency, working as a waitress to pay for her first acting classes and taking the bus to her first auditions because her mother would not drive her. After she proved to her mother that she was serious about acting, however, the elder America began to drive her daughter to the auditions. Ferrera auditioned for a full year without a single callback, a reaction she attributed to her relatively large physical stature. "I went through a lot of self-doubt," Ferrera told Elizabeth Weitzman for *Interview* (October 1, 2002). "I never turned on the TV and saw a Latina woman with an average body and I thought, I'll never be a Charlie's Angel, because I can't fit into size zero leather pants." Meanwhile, Ferrera attended El Camino Real High School in Woodland Hills, where her interactions with other students did little to help her self-esteem. She found the process of auditioning, however, to be even worse in that regard. "I didn't even know I was fat until I started acting," she said, as quoted by Bentley.

Ferrera's figure, though, would be the key to her breakout role in HBO Films' *Real Women Have Curves*. (Earlier in 2002 she had appeared as a cheerleader in the Disney Channel's original movie *Gotta Kick It Up.*) Playing Ana Garcia, the daughter of an immigrant family who is torn between accepting a scholarship to an Ivy League school and working for the family business, Ferrera was the movie's emotional anchor, representing both the literal and metaphorical curves women face in life. "America came in for seven callbacks. It was such an important role; we knew the movie depended on that," the film's director, Patricia Cardoso, told King. "She's one of the smartest people I've ever met. The crew often forgot she was only 17." Originally intended to be aired solely on HBO, the film received such an overwhelmingly positive reaction after its premiere at the Sundance Film Festival that HBO Films decided to distribute it nationwide. The premiere was the first occasion on which Ferrera saw the movie—indeed, the first on which she saw herself on a movie screen. She left Sundance with a Special Jury Award for acting, which she shared with her co-star, Lupe Ontiveros; she was also subsequently nominated for an Independent Spirit Award. "I got so lucky," Ferrera told Dixie Reid for the *Sacramento (California) Bee* (June 1, 2005) about the role. "But it was not easy. It was hard. It was my first movie, my second project ever, and I had to be in every single frame. And then I had to confront all these things that are very relevant to my life, the whole image thing." Regarding the "image thing," Ferrera said that her character, Ana, was an ideal role model—both for her audience and herself. "I really liked playing this girl because she's so confident," Ferrera told Cindy Pearlman for the *Chicago Sun-Times* (October 25, 2002). "I think her confidence is actually contagious. It's so important to show young girls that you have to be strong to survive in this world." Most important, Ferrera said, was the movie's message: "You leave this movie feeling happy about who you are," she told Weitzman. "And that's something we're all hungry for."

After filming *Real Women* during her senior year of high school, Ferrera, like her character Ana, faced a choice—in Ferrera's case, whether to go to college or pursue her acting career. After graduating first in her high-school class, Ferrera decided to defer for a year from the University of Southern California (USC), where she planned to major in international relations, "because I wanted my life outside of acting to be, you know, a life," as she explained to Cindy Pearlman for the *Chicago Sun-Times* (May 29, 2005). Instead, she took a role in *The Sisterhood of the Traveling Pants*, a movie in which four teenage girls share one pair of jeans, sending them back and forth, during a summer when they are separated from one another. Based on a popular series of books by Ann Brashares, the film seemed at first to Ferrera to be light fare. "That script just sat on my desk for months," the actress told Bob Strauss for the *Daily News of Los Angeles*

(May 29, 2005). "My agent was like, 'Have you read it? Have you read it?' I'm like, 'I'll get to it,' and I finally did, begrudgingly so. But halfway through, I thought, 'Wow, this is great.'" The film, which deals with issues ranging from first love to the death of a loved one, appealed to Ferrera in large part because of the complexity of her character, Carmen—the half-Latina daughter of divorced parents who goes to visit her father for a summer and feels left out of his all-white family. A daughter of divorced parents herself, Ferrera said that she could identify with Carmen's struggle. "I wouldn't say my acting in this movie just comes from my life," she told Pearlman, "but I didn't have to stretch too far for the feelings of being isolated, abandoned and out of place." While she co-starred with other up-and-coming actresses, Alexis Bledel and Amber Tamblyn, Ferrera's scenes—helped by a story line considerably more compelling than those of the other actresses' characters—stole the movie. "Ferrera is the star of this show, no doubt about that," Allison Benedikt wrote for the *Chicago Tribune* (June 1, 2005). Many critics, like Ferrera, found the movie to be far more poignant than they had expected.

Later in 2005, while pursuing her degree at USC, Ferrera appeared in a variety of smaller projects. In *Lords of Dogtown*, a dramatized history of competitive skateboarding, she played the small role of Thunder Monkey. She also returned to Sundance for the premiere of *How the Garcia Girls Spent Their Summer*, which garnered her a Movieline Breakthrough of the Year award. In December of that year, Ferrera appeared in the Off-Broadway play *Dog Sees God: Confessions of a Teenage Blockhead*. She also became a spokeswoman for the Dove Campaign for Real Beauty, a series of advertisements for the cosmetics company that featured people without model-like figures. She told Jessie Milligan for the *Fort Worth (Texas) Star-Telegram* (May 31, 2005) that the ads were especially useful for giving young women a better standard of beauty than that usually proferred by the media. "I hope young girls understand the manufactured images around them," Ferrera said, commenting on typical advertisements featuring stick-thin models. "It's those people's job to look like that."

By taking the title role of Betty Suarez in the 2006 breakout hit television show *Ugly Betty*, Ferrera made it her job not to project a typical image of female stardom. Based on the hit *telenovela* (Spanish soap opera) *Yo Soy Betty, la Fea*—which translates as "I am Betty, the Ugly"—the show follows Betty's trials and tribulations as the ugly duckling at a high-profile New York fashion magazine. The distinctly unglamorous role appealed to Ferrera instantly, as she told Mike Parker for the *Sunday Express* (January 7, 2007). "As soon as [executive producer] Salma [Hayek] showed me the script, I knew it mirrored some of the insecurities I had—and still have. There's a vulnerable nakedness to Betty. She's an awkward young woman determined to succeed in a world which seems as though it has been specifically designed for hip people only. I think audiences look at her and say, 'I can recognize my own clumsiness, my own awkwardness, my own insecurity there.' There are times you feel sexy and confident and there are times you feel like Betty." More than 14 million viewers tuned in to watch the show, making it the number-one new TV program in the U.S. Though *Ugly Betty* has a mostly female audience, its viewers are of diverse ethnicities and ages; it is among the top 20 shows among the highly sought-after 18-to-49-year-old demographic, as well as among the top 20 shows with viewers who earn an annual salary of $100,000 or more. Among Latinos, *Ugly Betty* is the highest-rated new English-language show in terms of total number of viewers, as well as the number-one show with viewers between the ages of 18 and 49. Much of the show's appeal is attributed to Ferrera's endearing portrayal of Betty. "Ferrera's performances are small wonders to behold," Tim Goodman wrote for the *San Francisco Chronicle* (September 27, 2006).

Ugly Betty was nominated for a 2007 Golden Globe Award for best comedy, and Ferrera won the award for best performance by an actress in a television series—musical or comedy. In her acceptance speech, Ferrera said that she was grateful for the opportunity to present a body image on television more realistic, and therefore encouraging, than those she grew up watching. As quoted by Susan Abram in the *Daily News of Los Angeles* (January 22, 2007), she said, "It's such an honor to play a role that I hear from young girls on a daily basis how it makes them feel worthy and lovable and that they have more to offer the world than they thought." Responding to Ferrera's earning the Golden Globe Award, the Democratic U.S. congresswoman Hilda L. Solis of California made a statement on the floor of the House of Representatives, as quoted by *US Fed News* (January 17, 2007): "Madame Speaker, I rise today to congratulate America Ferrera for winning the Golden Globe for best actress in a comedy for her work in the ABC show *Ugly Betty*. . . . Through her work, Ms. Ferrera is breaking down barriers for Latinos in prime-time television. I commend America and everyone involved in *Ugly Betty* for helping to break down stereotypes and provide a role model for young Latinas." Ferrera agrees that the role—which requires her to don braces, bright red glasses, and a disheveled, frizzy wig—is about redefining standards of beauty for the public, and she said that it has also helped her to create a new understanding of beauty for herself. She told Bentley that she never feels "more confident, more beautiful and more pretty on the inside" than when she portrays Betty. "I wish that one day, as America, I can feel the way that I feel when I'm Betty. When I'm Betty, there's a light that shines from the inside and it's so wonderful to be her." Ferrera also won a Screen Actors Guild Award and an Emmy Award for outstanding performance by a lead actress in a comedy series

for her work on *Ugly Betty*. The second season of *Ugly Betty* began in September 2007.

Ferrera recently starred in and executive-produced the short film *Muertas*, directed by her boyfriend, the filmmaker and fellow USC student Ryan Piers Williams. She starred in and executive-produced the bilingual independent film *Towards Darkness*, released in 2007; the movie is based on the 2004 short film *Darkness Minus 12*, which Ferrera appeared in as well. Also due in 2007 is *Boy, Immigrant*, which features Ferrera in a Spanish-speaking role. As of January 2007, Ferrera had one semester of course work left to complete her degree.

—C.S.

Suggested Reading: *Fresno (California) Bee* L p1+ Aug. 20, 2006; *Sacramento (California) Bee* E p1+ June 1, 2005

Selected Films: *Real Women Have Curves*, 2002; *The Sisterhood of the Traveling Pants*, 2005

Selected Television Shows: *Ugly Betty*, 2006—

Gates, Robert M.

NOTE: An earlier article about Robert M. Gates appeared in *Current Biography* in 1992.

Sep. 25, 1943– U.S. Secretary of Defense

Address: Office of the Secretary of Defense, 1000 Defense Pentagon, Washington, DC 20301

Robert M. Gates "is not a man who reveals himself," Paul Burka wrote for *Texas Monthly* (November 2006). "He's all business, a man under total self-control. He doesn't fidget. He isn't a backslapper. He doesn't make small talk. He doesn't boast; neither does he engage in false modesty. He is a motivator, not a cheerleader. He is always polite. He wears an air of authority as if it were tailored by Brooks Brothers. He answers questions fully but volunteers little. Most of his laughter comes from a finely developed sense of irony. I would back him to the hilt in a no-limit poker game." Gates has in a sense been backed in such a "game" by President George W. Bush, who appointed him secretary of defense in late 2006, thereby making him one of the most important participants in the high-stakes military operations the U.S. has undertaken in the Middle East in recent years. A career intelligence analyst, Gates served as the 15th director of the Central Intelligence Agency (CIA) from 1991 to 1993 and then spent a number of years in academia, becoming, in 2002, Texas A&M University's 22d president, a position he held until being sworn in as the U.S.'s 22d secretary of defense. Despite an intense love for his work at A&M and an

Monica King, Department of Defense/Getty Images
Robert M. Gates

aversion to returning to Washington, D.C., Gates—who was one of the most popular presidents in A&M's history—accepted Bush's nomination, citing a sense of duty. At an on-campus farewell rally, Gates told the A&M student body, as Matthew Watkins reported for the Bryan, Texas, *Eagle* (December 8, 2006, on-line), "A little less than a month ago, I was worried about beating the hell out of Nebraska. Now, I am worried about beating the hell out of Al Qaeda. I can't tell you how much you all mean to me and how big a part of my life you have become, and I will miss you forever."

Robert Michael Gates was born on September 25, 1943 in Wichita, Kansas. His father sold wholesale auto parts for a living. Raised in a middle-class section of Wichita, Gates was, by all accounts, a model child—a straight-A student and an Eagle Scout. A voracious reader, he tutored underprivileged children in his spare time and took part in activities sponsored by local religious youth groups. After graduating from high school, Gates enrolled at the College of William and Mary, in Williamsburg, Virginia, as a premedical student, but he soon switched his major to history, concentrating in Western Europe. During his college days he worked part-time as a school-bus driver and developed the custom of teaching his riders German and Russian words and phrases. William and Mary granted Gates a B.A. degree with honors in 1965, also naming him the graduate "who has made the greatest contribution to his fellow man," as Dan Goodgame reported for *Time* (May 27, 1991). Gates went on to obtain an M.A. degree in history from Indiana University's Institute on Soviet and East European Studies—now called the Russian and East European Institute—in 1966. While studying

at Indiana, Gates was invited by a CIA recruiter to come to Washington, D.C., for an interview. Although he later admitted that he accepted the invitation only for the free trip to Washington, when the agency offered him a position as an analyst, he accepted it. Working for the CIA did not exempt Gates from the draft, and he served in Vietnam from 1967 to 1969 as a commissioned officer in the Strategic Air Command before entering the CIA full-time.

After returning from Vietnam Gates became an intelligence analyst specializing in Soviet affairs and impressed his superiors with his ability to peruse enormous amounts of information quickly and to produce crisply written, coherent reports. In 1971 he was rewarded for his outstanding work with an assignment on the CIA's support staff at the initial negotiations between the United States and the Soviet Union on reducing strategic arms. Although he appeared to be on the fast track at the CIA, Gates was still considering a career as a history professor, and in his off-hours he studied for a doctorate in Russian and Soviet history at Georgetown University, in Washington, D.C. He even refused a CIA offer to finance his studies because he "didn't want to feel obligated to stay," as Goodgame reported, in case an attractive teaching position opened up. Gates received his Ph.D. from Georgetown in 1974, having submitted a 290-page dissertation on Soviet assessments of China that later became known as an authoritative text on Sino-Soviet relations.

That year Gates was assigned to the staff of the National Security Council, where he remained for the next five years, serving under Presidents Richard Nixon, Gerald R. Ford, and Jimmy Carter. By 1979 he longed to return to the CIA, confiding to colleagues that his ambition was to someday be director of the agency. In January 1980 he was reassigned to the CIA as national intelligence officer for the Soviet Union and executive assistant to the director, Stansfield Turner. In 1980 Carter lost the presidency to Ronald Reagan, who appointed a new CIA director, William J. Casey. Casey soon became a mentor for Gates, and promoted him to deputy director for intelligence in January 1982, passing over about 60 other senior-level candidates. In September 1983 Casey appointed Gates to the concurrent position of chairman of the National Intelligence Council, with responsibility for overseeing the preparation of all intelligence estimates. Part of the reason Gates was able to rise to the top of the CIA so quickly was his expertise on the Soviet Union, which was the main focus of United States intelligence efforts in the Cold War–driven 1980s. Even after Mikhail Gorbachev's rise to power in the Soviet Union in 1985 and his introduction of glasnost, a policy of openness, shortly after that, Gates remained a strict cold warrior.

When Gates was promoted to deputy director of central intelligence, on April 18, 1986, succeeding the retiring John McMahon in the agency's number-two position, he received his first exposure to the operations side of espionage. Exactly eight months later, he was named acting director while Casey underwent surgery for the removal of a brain tumor. Casey resigned his post on January 29, 1987, and four days later Reagan nominated Gates to be his successor in what was expected to be a straightforward appointment. Evidence began to surface, however, that Gates had possibly been involved in the Iran-Contra affair—the administration's sale of arms to Iran, with funds illegally directed to anti-Communist rebels in Nicaragua. Republican senator William S. Cohen of Maine interrogated Gates at his confirmation hearing, accusing him of knowing more about the arms sales than he had admitted and describing him as "an ambitious young man, type-A personality, climbing the ladder of success," as Dusko Doder and Walter Pincus reported for the *Washington Post* (February 18, 1987). "You basically didn't want to rock the boat. You were not prepared to lay your career on the line over a matter you did not create. You didn't want to know about it." Gates conceded that he had not done enough to keep Congress fully informed of the administration's activities, but he refuted the charge that he had hesitated to step forward out of fear for his career. "Sycophants can only rise to a certain level," he responded in a rare show of emotion, Stephen Engelberg reported for the *New York Times* (February 19, 1987). "There is an ample supply of them in this town, and they only go so far. Senior officials understand that the most dangerous thing in the world is a yes man, and the people I have worked for felt the candor with which I apprised them was a valuable asset." With his chances for confirmation fading quickly, Gates withdrew his nomination on March 2, 1987. A day later Reagan nominated William H. Webster to be director of central intelligence; Webster was confirmed by the Senate on May 19. At Reagan's request Gates stayed on as deputy director of the agency. When Brent Scowcroft, Gates's former boss in the Ford administration, was named national security adviser by President-elect George H. W. Bush in December 1988, he arranged for Gates's appointment as his deputy.

On May 14, 1991 Gates got a rare second chance at his dream job when Bush named him to succeed as director of central intelligence William H. Webster, who was retiring. Although the Iran-Contra affair no longer dominated the headlines, Gates's peripheral role in it still posed a potential obstacle to his confirmation. He was also widely criticized for being too slow to anticipate the collapse of the Soviet Union. Gates's case was further weakened when Congressman Dave McCurdy of Oklahoma, the chairman of the House Intelligence Committee, recommended, on October 2, that Gates withdraw his nomination. Nevertheless, two weeks later, the committee, after hearing statements from members both in support of and in opposition to Gates, voted 11 to four to recommend his confirmation to the full Senate. On November 5 the Senate voted, 64 to 31, to confirm Gates, as 22 Democrats joined all 42

Republicans present in supporting him. Seven days later Gates was sworn in as the nation's 15th director of central intelligence. (At 48 he was the youngest person ever to assume that prestigious position, and he was the first CIA director to have risen through the agency's analytical branch, where raw intelligence is studied and interpreted, as distinct from the operational branch, which is responsible for the collection of intelligence.) Gates subsequently redirected the CIA's resources away from monitoring the former Soviet Union toward checking the spread of nuclear weapons in the Third World and combating the international drug trade.

Gates retired from the CIA on January 20, 1993. For the next several years he worked as a traveling academic, evaluating theses for the International Studies Program at the University of Washington and lecturing at a number of schools, including Harvard, Yale, Georgetown, and the College of William and Mary. He also published numerous articles on government and foreign policy and was a frequent contributor to the *New York Times*'s op-ed page. In 1996 Gates published a memoir of his time at the CIA, titled *From the Shadows: The Ultimate Insider's Story of Five Presidents and How They Won the Cold War*, to largely positive reviews. While its title seemed to promise a scandalous account, the book proved to be an analysis of policy—and a response to the longstanding criticisms of Gates's tough stance on the Soviet Union—rather than a confessional tell-all.

In 1999 Gates was appointed interim dean of the George Bush School of Government and Public Service at Texas A&M. Though he was initially reluctant to leave his home in Seattle, Washington, he and his wife began spending more and more time on the A&M campus. On August 1, 2002 Gates was appointed the university's 22d president. He explained his decision to take the post to the Associated Press (May 11, 2002): "If I could do one more public service, I should. And I couldn't think of a better place to do it than Texas A&M." During his tenure as president, Gates made marked progress in the school's "Vision 2020" plan, which seeks to turn A&M into one of the country's top 10 public universities by the year 2020.

Throughout his time at Texas A&M, Gates maintained a connection with national politics as a frequent guest on political talk shows. On the afternoon of the September 11, 2001 attacks on the World Trade Center, Gates defended the U.S. intelligence community to Paula Zahn for CNN News (September 11, 2001). "I think we have to bear in mind, even against the background of this catastrophe today, that the FBI and CIA have thwarted some very major terrorist operations against [the] United States in recent years," he said. "So they have had some very important successes and saved a lot of lives." In the years that followed, as the U.S. began its invasion of Iraq, Gates continued to appear frequently on the news-analysis circuit. He also began getting involved with Washington politics again. In January 2004 he co-chaired a Council on Foreign Relations task force on U.S. involvement in Iran, a country with which the United States had not had diplomatic relations since 1979. The task force urged the U.S. to pursue diplomacy over force on the issue of Iran's nuclear weapons, suggesting that Iran be allowed to develop its nuclear program in exchange for committing to use that resource solely for peaceful ends. "Washington should approach Iran with a readiness to explore areas of common interests, while continuing to contest objectionable policies," the task force's July 2004 report stated, according to the *Mideast Files* (on-line). In a press statement, Gates elaborated on the report, again urging diplomatic engagement as the more efficient means to a peaceful end. "It is not in our interest for Iran to have nuclear weapons," he said, as cited by National Public Radio (NPR, November 8, 2006). "It is not in our interest for Iran to oppose the new governments in Afghanistan and Iraq. And if we can engage them and try and bring some progress in those areas, then our interests have been served and that's what it's all about."

In 2005 President George W. Bush offered Gates the newly created post of United States director of national intelligence (DNI). Despite a reluctance to return to Washington, D.C., Gates initially decided to accept the position, feeling that it was his duty to serve the U.S. in a time of war. He scheduled a press conference to announce his decision and wrote an e-mail message to the Texas A&M student body expressing his sadness over leaving the school. Then Gates changed his mind, electing to stay at A&M—both because of how much he felt he could accomplish at the university and how little he felt he could accomplish as director of national intelligence. Even though he remained in Texas, Gates stayed active in the political sphere, and in 2006 Congress appointed him a member of the Iraq Study Group, also called the Baker-Hamilton Commission, a bipartisan panel formed to assess the situation in Iraq and make specific policy recommendations.

On November 8, 2006, one day after the Democrats succeeded in winning a majority in the House of Representatives and the Senate, Secretary of Defense Donald Rumsfeld resigned, and Bush nominated Gates to become the next defense secretary. Most pundits praised Gates's nomination, calling him the "anti-Rumsfeld," because it was widely believed that he would be more pragmatic and more cautious than Rumsfeld regarding military interventions; more apt to hold officials responsible for military disasters, such as the torture of prisoners at Abu Ghraib prison, in Iraq; more realistic regarding events in Iraq and other troublespots; and not defensive, prickly, or confrontational in his dealings with the media or Congress. Gates won even greater approval for the honesty he displayed in his Senate confirmation hearing a few weeks later. When asked by Senator Carl Levin, a Democrat from Michigan, if he believed the United

States was winning the war in Iraq, Gates responded with a simple "No, sir." His answer immediately became such big news that he felt the need to clarify his words a few hours later, saying instead, "We are not winning, but we are not losing." When asked if he thought it had been a good idea to invade Iraq, he answered, "I think it's too soon to tell," adding, "I suspect, in hindsight, some of the folks in the administration probably would not make the same decisions that they made." Despite such unexpectedly candid answers, Gates still underwent intense scrutiny from senators concerned that he would simply become a mouthpiece for the administration. Gates strongly asserted that he would act independently. "I am not giving up the presidency of Texas A&M, the job that I probably enjoyed more than any that I've ever had, making considerable personal financial sacrifice, and frankly, going through this process, to come back to Washington to be a bump on a log," Gates told Senator Edward M. Kennedy, as quoted on CNN's *The Situation Room* (December 5, 2006). He further stated, "If I am confirmed, I'll be independent. I intend to draw my own conclusions and I'll make my recommendations. . . . I can assure you that I don't owe anybody anything."

The 23 members of the Armed Services Committee voted unanimously to confirm Gates, and he was sworn in as the United States' 22d secretary of defense on December 18, 2006. During his speech at the swearing-in ceremony, Gates gave a measured analysis of the war in Iraq, refraining from making any concrete statements about plans for the future. "All of us want to find a way to bring America's sons and daughters home again," he said, as quoted by *The World Today* (December 19, 2006), an ABC Australia program. "But as the President has made clear, we simply cannot afford to fail in the Middle East. Failure in Iraq at this juncture would be a calamity that would haunt our nation, impair our credibility and endanger Americans for decades to come." That same day the Pentagon released its quarterly report on the situation in Iraq, which Jim Miklaszewski described for NBC News (December 18, 2006) as "its most devastating report yet." The report stated that the past three months had seen the highest number of attacks by Iraqi insurgents on record, with both American and Iraqi casualties on the rise. Some questioned whether Gates was the right person to handle the situation. "If you're expecting revolution inside the Defense Department, don't hold your breath," Guy Raz reported from the Pentagon on the day of the confirmation for NPR (December 18, 2006). "Robert Gates might very well personify the word technocrat. He's neither sassy like his predecessor, nor is he ideological." Mel Goodman, a colleague of Gates's from the CIA and a longstanding critic of Gates's Soviet policy, told Raz, "He knows who his master is. And he knows who will advance him or who could hurt him. And so he is a windsock." A month earlier, however, when Gates's nomination was first announced, Vago Muradian, the editor of

Defence News (November 10, 2006), told David Mark for ABC News that it was just that kind of insider knowledge that would help Gates to effect change within the Washington system. "With Gates you're getting a completely different kind of an individual who has very strong bipartisan credentials," Muradian said. "Someone who has a reputation for being able to listen. He is somebody who's really been associated with the levers and wheels of power at a very senior level. So he's somebody who's familiar with how this system works and how to get things done."

On December 21, 2006, three days after being sworn in, Gates went to Iraq to talk to the commanders and troops on the ground. At the beginning of 2007, he recommended increasing the U.S. Army's strength in Iraq by 65,000 troops; he has since overseen the addition of some 30,000 soldiers. In February of that year, Gates announced the firings of the secretary of the army, Francis J. Harvey, and the army's surgeon general, Kevin C. Kiley, following the disclosure in a series of *Washington Post* articles of inadequate medical care, instances of outright neglect, nearly impossible-to-negotiate red tape, and crumbling facilities at the Walter Reed Army Medical Center, in the nation's capital, where many servicemen and -women wounded in Iraq or Afghanistan were brought for treatment. In March 2007, reversing one of Rumsfeld's policies, he met with the directors of U.S. intelligence agencies with the goal of easing tensions between the intelligence community and the Pentagon. His recommendation that month that the detention center at Guantánamo Bay, Cuba, be closed was batted down by Vice President Dick Cheney and President Bush's former chief political strategist, Karl Rove.

In an effort to maintain adequate numbers of troops in Iraq and Afghanistan, Gates announced in April 2007 that the tours of duty for most active army units would increase from 12 to 15 months and that soldiers would remain at home for one year between tours. "This policy is a difficult but necessary interim step," he said at a news conference, as quoted by David S. Cloud in the *New York Times* (April 12, 2007). "Our forces are stretched, there's no question about that." The following September Gates spoke before the Senate Appropriations Committee regarding the continued involvement of the U.S. in Iraq, suggesting that in the future American forces there would consist of five combat brigades serving as a "long-term presence." "When I speak of a long-term presence, I'm thinking of a very modest U.S. presence with no permanent bases, where we can continue to go after Al Qaeda in Iraq and help the Iraqi forces," he said, according to David S. Cloud in the *New York Times* (September 27, 2007). He also said that, besides the many billions of dollars needed for other war-related expenses, the Pentagon wanted $11 billion for 15,000 additional heavily armored vehicles, to protect American troops from the increasingly sophisticated roadside bombs planted by insurgents

in Iraq. Gates has said that he writes personal letters of condolence to the families of all Americans killed in service in there.

Gates has been married for more than 40 years to the former Rebecca Wilkie, whom he met at Indiana University when they were dormitory counselors chaperoning a hayride together. They have two adult children, Eleanor and Bradley. Among the awards Gates has received are the Presidential Citizens Medal, the Intelligence Medal of Merit, and the Arthur S. Flemming Award, which is presented annually to the 10 most outstanding federal employees. In addition, Gates is a two-time recipient of the National Intelligence Distinguished Service Medal and a three-time recipient of the CIA's highest award, the Distinguished Intelligence Medal.

—C.S.

Suggested Reading: *Los Angeles Times* E p1 June 25, 1996, A p1 Dec. 4, 2006; *Texas Monthly* p154+ Nov. 2006; *Time* p18 Sep. 23, 1991

Selected Books: *From the Shadows: The Ultimate Insider's Story of Five Presidents and How They Won the Cold War*, 1996

George, Susan

June 29, 1934– Social scientist; activist; writer

Address: Transnational Institute, P.O. Box 14656, 1001 LD Amsterdam, Netherlands

When the political scientist Susan George accepted an honorary doctorate from the Universidad Nacional de Educación a Distancia, in Madrid, Spain, on April 25, 2007, she was characteristically forthright about her disdain for the political establishment, saying, as quoted on the Transnational Institute (TNI) Web site, "I believe that the forces of wealth, power and control are invariably at the root of any problem of social and political economy. The job of the responsible social scientist is first to uncover these forces, second to write about them clearly, without jargon, in order to give ordinary people the right tools for action; and finally—recognising that scholarly neutrality is an illusion—to take an advocacy position in favour of the disadvantaged, the underdogs, the victims of injustice. This is what I think the tools of scholarship are for and this is how I have tried in my own work to use them." Throughout her career, George has been a strident antiwar activist as well as a powerful voice against acts of corporate greed. At a time when women were not often allowed places of power in any organizational hierarchy, George established herself as a leader in the antihunger movement and legitimized her scholarship in the eyes of skeptics by obtaining an advanced degree

Joel Sage/AFP/Getty Images

Susan George

for the culture, language, and people of France. As a teenager she chose to attend Smith College, in Northampton, Massachusetts, specifically in order to participate in the junior-year-abroad program in France. In Paris during the 1954-55 academic year, she took courses at Sciences Po, a school specializing in social sciences. During that time, at the age of 20, she met a successful French lawyer, Charles-Henry George. In 1956, after obtaining her B.A. degree in government studies and French, she married George, 12 years her senior; she made France her permanent residence that year, but she did not obtain French citizenship until 1994. She told *Current Biography* that in her early years in France she felt homesick "for my women friends, probably, but not for America, per se. I'd made my choice." The couple soon started a family. Once her three children were in school full-time, George attended the Sorbonne, obtaining the French equivalent of a bachelor's degree in philosophy in 1967.

George became a political activist in response to France's war in Algeria and U.S. involvement in Vietnam. She told *Current Biography*, "Vietnam broke my loyal little still-American heart. The atrocities, the [U.S.] government's lies, the betrayal of the country's ideals, all this cried out for justice." In 1967 George joined the Paris-American Committee to Stop War. In 1969 she became the assistant to the director of a nongovernmental organization (NGO), the American Centre for Students and Artists, for which she frequently organized antiwar events. (Her activities did not escape the attention of the FBI or the CIA; years later, taking advantage of the Freedom of Information Act, she discovered hundreds of pages of information about herself that had been obtained through surveillance.)

George told *Current Biography* that the Vietnam War "was this sort of gateway to understanding what America could be, which is to say something quite negative, which I had not understood at all when I lived there. I had accepted the usual propaganda." In 1971 she began working with the Front Solidarité Indochine, a group that organized antiwar lectures and protests in France. Her participation in their activities forced her to overcome her fear of public speaking. She also began volunteering as a translator for American, Cambodian, and Laotian antiwar activists. When the Paris-American Committee to Stop War was forcibly dismantled by the French government (which, according to George, acted at the request of the U.S. government), George collaborated with the directors of the Institute for Policy Studies in Washington, D.C., to form a new NGO devoted to social justice—the Transnational Institute, which opened its doors in Amsterdam, the Netherlands, in 1973. George remains a fellow at TNI and also serves as its board chair.

After the Chilean president Salvador Allende was overthrown in a U.S.-backed coup in September 1973, George helped Chilean political refugees to settle in France. In 1974 she enrolled in a doctor-

from the Sorbonne as well as a doctorate from the University of Paris, in her adopted country of France. The author of 10 books, including *How the Other Half Dies: The Real Reasons for World Hunger*, *Ill Fares the Land*, and *The Debt Boomerang*, George is regarded as a preeminent political and economic thinker and activist for human rights.

George was born Susan Vance Akers on June 29, 1934 in Akron, Ohio. She was the only child of Edith and Walter Akers, Episcopalians whose families had been in America for many generations; George's ancestors arrived in Massachusetts in 1632. George's father was an insurance broker, and her mother was a homemaker and a member of the Junior League. Though born during the Great Depression, George was raised in a privileged environment; she had a nursemaid and took dance classes, music lessons, and, at a YMCA, swimming lessons. After attending a public, co-educational primary school, she went on to enroll at all-girls private preparatory academy. She told *Current Biography* that single-sex schooling "made me not a feminist. It was normal that women do whatever anybody did. Women were the sports experts. Women were the brains. You weren't in competition with men. You weren't expected to shut up— on the contrary! Even in my era, I never felt that I was particularly put down as a woman ever." George's father encouraged all her interests, including those outside the realm of traditional femininity, such as science and baseball. When Walter Akers went to serve in World War II, his daughter assisted in planting a victory garden.

As a young student, George was a voracious reader and always ranked first in her class. Around the age of 12, she began to develop a strong passion al program in political science at the School of Higher Social Science Studies at the University of Paris, completing her degree in 1978 and receiving highest honors. Meanwhile, in 1974 she traveled to the World Food Conference in Rome, Italy, where she was enraged by the corporate agribusiness representatives who dominated the proceedings. The World Food Conference was organized by the U.N. Food and Agriculture Organization (FAO), an agency designed to lead international efforts against famine and malnutrition; the two largest delegations at the conference were those of the United States and the agriculture industry. George felt that the FAO gave too much power to transnational agribusiness corporations. She told *Current Biography*, "This event was a turning point for me. . . . I was incensed at the level of official cant and the politics played with millions of hungry people's lives." She added that at the conference, "no one who counted took the real reasons for hunger—power and control in the wrong hands—into account."

In 1976 Penguin published George's first book, *How the Other Half Dies: The Real Reasons for World Hunger*. According to the Web site of the Transnational Institute, "Hunger is not a scourge but a scandal. This is the premise of Susan George's classic study of world hunger. Contrary to popular opinion, malnutrition and starvation are not the result of over-population, of poor climate or lack of cultivatable land. The reason why hunger exists on such a vast scale is because world food supplies are controlled by the rich and powerful for the wealthy consumer. . . . Working with local elites, protected by the powerful West, the United States paves the way and is gradually imposing its control over the whole planet. . . . The book's relevance, its ability to shock and its power to enrage have in no measure [diminished]." George told *Current Biography* that the book "launched" her when she was 42. "Everyone has the right to one enormous stroke of luck in life and this was mine. I've never looked back." *How the Other Half Dies* was a critical and financial success. William Diebold Jr. wrote for *Foreign Affairs* (January 1978) that the book was "a lively analysis. . . . The prescription is for change."

Thirty years after the book was published, George remained deeply concerned with issues of famine and food distribution. She attended the Table of Free Voices conference, held in Berlin, Germany, in September 2006 and organized by Dropping Knowledge, a German nonprofit organization dedicated to the promotion of international dialogue, art, and culture; as quoted on the TNI Web site, she said at the conference, "We . . . produce enough food for everyone, but most of this production is in places where people are not going hungry; and where people are going hungry, very often their farmers have been ruined by cheap imports coming from the rich countries. This has happened massively in Mexico. So, there are many more poor Mexicans than there were and many have lost their

farms and these people cannot compete. Thai rice farmers have lost their land; Filipino rice farmers have lost their land."

George published her 1978 doctoral dissertation, *Les Stratèges de la faim* (Strategists of Hunger), in Switzerland in 1982. In the following year she published *Food for Beginners*, illustrated by Nigel Paige. She played an active role in organizing the World Food Assembly, a meeting held in Rome, Italy, in 1984 for the purpose of fighting famine and seeking social justice and composed of representatives of nongovernmental organizations from the Northern and Southern Hemispheres. George's book *A Fate Worse Than Debt* appeared in 1987. In her address to the executive committee of the World Alliance of the Young Men's Christian Association (YMCA) in Geneva, Switzerland, on June 19, 1999, George said about her reasons for writing the book, "We identified the fact that debt [owed to wealthy lending nations by poor countries] was the biggest new contributing factor to world hunger. That is why, having worked on world hunger and with a lot of NGOs, I got involved in studying debt. I tried to make a clear explanation of how it was contributing to economic injustice, and the very real effects on human beings: hunger, misery, a much worse life for women in particular, increased crime, riots, conflict, ecological destruction. Debt was involved in all of these issues." In "Rethinking Debt," a paper presented at the nongovernmental organization (NGO) conference North-South Roundtable on Moving Africa into the 21st Century, held in Johannesburg, South Africa, in October 1995, George wrote, "Debt lies at the nexus of a strategic, worldwide reconfiguration of power. . . . It has accelerated transfers of wealth from the poor to the rich both within and between countries. . . . It has downgraded and diminished the importance of the State and the ability of governments to govern; as well as the overall influence and negotiating capacity of the 'third world.' . . . The creditors may not be open to moral arguments, but if Africans speak with one voice, they may, perhaps, convince them that their interest lies in severing the debt noose." At the time of the book's publication, as George told the executive committee of the World Alliance of the YMCA, further explaining her impetus for writing it, "there were . . . a good many campaigns and lots of NGOs . . . interested in this issue, but it was clear that we weren't getting any involvement from the top people, from either governments, or the World Bank and the International Monetary Fund."

In 1990 George published *Ill Fares the Land*. From that year until 1995, she served on the board of the environmental conservation group Greenpeace International and of Greenpeace France. She particularly admired the organization's ability to mobilize its many regional branches to focus on protesting one major issue at a time. In an interview with Caspar Henderson for the Web site OpenDemocracy.org (October 13, 2004), George said, "Greenpeace was quite successful with such campaigns. All its offices across the world would suspend their particular activities and join together."

The Debt Boomerang, George's 1992 volume, continued her analysis of the inequalities between the wealthier nations of the Northern Hemisphere and the poorer countries of the Southern Hemisphere. She told the executive committee of the World Alliance of the YMCA that she wrote the book "with the idea that if the suffering in the South was not enough to move the powers, perhaps it would help if it was explained that the debt was not just a problem for the South, but that in fact it was a boomerang and it was coming back and affecting the rich countries in a great many ways." In *Faith and Credit: the World Bank's Secular Empire* (1994), which she wrote with the anthropologist Fabrizio Sabelli, George expounded her beliefs regarding the negative impact of the World Bank on the worldwide poverty and hunger crisis. The World Bank, founded in July 1944 at the United Nations Monetary and Financial Conference at Bretton Woods, New Hampshire, consists of five organizations responsible for providing funds and advice to countries in order to promote economic development and eliminate poverty. Supporters of the organization argue that the World Bank conducts ethical and transparent business with countries in need of help. Critics, including George, contend that the World Bank is a corrupt institution that provides insufficient assistance to poorer countries. According to the Bretton Woods Project Web site, "With the World Bank, there are concerns about the types of development projects funded. . . Many infrastructural projects financed by the World Bank Group have social and environmental implications for the populations in the affected areas and criticism has centred around the ethical issues of funding such projects. For example, World Bank-funded construction of hydroelectric dams in various countries have resulted in the displacement of indigenous peoples of the area. There are also concerns that the World Bank working in partnership with the private sector may undermine the role of the state as the primary provider of essential goods and services, such as healthcare and education, resulting in the shortfall of such services in countries badly in need of them." George said at the Table of Free Voices conference, "Our wealth does not depend on the Third World being poor, but we have organized everything in the North so that the Third World does remain poor. If the Third World were less poor, we would be selling them more, and we would in fact be richer."

La Suisse aux enchères (whose title translates roughly as "Switzerland Auctioned Off"), another collaboration with Sabelli, appeared in Switzerland in 1997. Two years later George published *The Lugano Report: On Preserving Capitalism in the 21st Century.* The book is a fictional report issued by a group of imaginary pro-capitalist, pro-

globalization experts who raise the question of how to preserve capitalism forever. George explained at the Table of Free Voices conference that the book contains a scenario in which "I imagine that there is a report to be directed to Master of the Universe types who are asking pretty much that kind of question. How can we continue with this economic system without having total collapse? What must we do to make this continue to work? And the answer which is given unfortunately by this group of experts which I have invented . . . is, well, you cannot do it with eight billion people on earth as there are going to be in 2020. That's tomorrow in historical terms. So, the long emergency has already started. And, if we try to manage the world as we are doing now with eight billion people on earth, everything is going to collapse."

From 1999 to 2006 George served as vice president of the Association for Taxation of Financial Transactions to Aid Citizens (ATTAC France). During that period she also participated in the Helsinki Process, which she described to *Current Biography* as "a group established by the governments of Finland and Tanzania, with many other governments now acting as 'Friends' of the Process, trying to deal with the problems of globalization." She grew increasingly critical of the World Trade Organization (WTO) in the weeks before its 1999 meeting in Seattle, Washington. The World Trade Organization is responsible for negotiating and implementing new international trade agreements as well as enforcing member countries' adherence to those agreements. Its governing body, the Ministerial Conference, meets every two years. The WTO's advocates argue that the organization is an important intermediary between countries and is a positive force for financial growth in all nations. Detractors such as George argue that the WTO is biased in favor of wealthy countries and multinational corporations and that it harms smaller, less powerful countries. Critics see the WTO as a major force for globalization, the process by which corporations are allowed increasing flexibility with regard to global expansion as well as financial, environmental, and labor practices. The Seattle meeting of the Ministerial Conference of the WTO was disrupted by mass protests on the part of antiglobalization groups. George wrote for the London *Guardian* (November 24, 1999), "Without warning, the WTO has created an international court of 'justice' that is making law and establishing case law in which existing national laws are all 'barriers' to trade, and is sweeping aside all environmental, social or public health concerns." George wrote for *Le Monde diplomatique* (January 2000), "The civic movement's success in Seattle is a mystery only to those who had no part in it. . . . Trade must have no place in areas such as health, education and culture in the broadest sense of the term." George published *Remettre l'OMC a sa Place (Put the WTO in Its Place)* in 2001 and, the next year, *Pour ou Contre la Mondialisation Liberale*, consisting of a debate with Martin Wolf of the *Financial Times.* Offering a critical take on George's work, Mark O'Brien wrote for *International Socialism* (Spring 2000), "The weakness of George's analysis of the economic roots of the crisis of world capitalism leads directly to an uncertainty as to who her audience actually is. Often her writings read as an appeal to opinion formers and practitioners within government or development circles. . . . Her proposals border on an almost utopian belief in the humanitarian good sense of some elements within capitalist governments. . . . There is no sense in George's writings of the revolutionary potential of the working classes of the Third World and of the West."

George's book *Another World Is Possible If . . .* came out in 2004. She told Henderson, "This is at the heart of my book's argument—that Europeans must lead the world. My experience is that there are many people outside the movement who sense that there are a lot of things wrong with the world, but who are hesitant or unclear about what they are able to do. Here, my central argument is that, faced with an America that is going to be immovable . . . Europe has to lead the change. . . . So my plea to Europeans is to recognize who they are, what their achievements have been for the interests of the poor and working people over the last hundred years and say that a welfare model is possible for the entire world—and that it's up to us in Europe to make that happen."

In 2004 George half-heartedly supported the candidacy of U.S. senator John Kerry, Democrat of Massachusetts, for president. While she had canvassed for Kerry in Pennsylvania, she wrote for OpenDemocracy.org (November 3, 2004), "we all thought [Kerry] had a very good chance, even though everyone admitted it was hard to get really enthusiastic about him. . . . The man isn't the most charismatic ever to walk the earth. But at least he's not a proto-fascist or a go-it-aloner, and that's what we seem—apart from a last-minute miracle—to be stuck with now. With four years clear ahead of him and no re-election to worry about, I fear Bush and the ghastly neo-con/neo-liberals around him will now go on the rampage. They can continue with impunity their attacks on the Constitution and on hard-won freedoms; while profound economic inequalities and religious obscurantism spread throughout the country."

George published *Nou, Peuples d'Europe (We, the Peoples of Europe)* in 2005. She received an honorary doctorate in civil law from the University of Newcastle-upon-Tyne in January 2007, and in March of that year, the International Studies Association presented her with its first award for Outstanding Public Scholar at its congress in Chicago, Illinois. Also in 2007 she received an honorary doctorate in political science and sociology from the Universidad Nacional de Educación a Distancia, in Madrid. As of May 2007 George had written and was awaiting the publication of "Culture in Chains: How the Religious and Secular Right Captured America." Publishers in Spain, Brazil, and

France swiftly acquired the book. Her work has been translated into French, German, Spanish, Italian, Portuguese, four Scandinavian languages, Estonian, Japanese, Korean, Bengali, and Thai.

In 2002 George's husband, Charles-Henry George, died at their country home in France. She has three adult children—Valerie, Michel, and Stephanie—and is a grandmother. George told *Current Biography*, "Either we achieve together a new level of human emancipation, and do so in a way that preserves the earth, or we shall leave behind us the worst future for our children that capitalism and nature can deal them. No one knows in which direction the balance will tip nor does anyone know which actions, which writings, which alliances may achieve the critical mass that leads us one way or another, backwards or forwards. I am acutely conscious of the precariousness of our moment and my four much-loved grandchildren give me added resolve to address it."

—S.J.D.

Suggested Reading: (London) *Guardian* (on-line) Nov. 24, 1999; OpenDemocracy.org; Transnational Institute Web site

Selected Books: *How the Other Half Dies: The Real Reasons for World Hunger*, 1976; *Les Stratèges de la faim*, 1982; *Food for Beginners*, 1983; *A Fate Worse Than Debt*, 1987; *Ill Fares the Land*, 1990; *The Debt Boomerang*, 1992; *Faith and Credit: the World Bank's Secular Empire*, 1994; *La Suisse aux enchères*, 1997; *The Lugano Report: On Preserving Capitalism in the 21st Century*, 1999; *Remettre l'OMC a sa place*, 2001; *Another World Is Possible If . . .*, 2004; *Nou, Peuples d'Europe*, 2005

Gomes, Marcelo

(GO-mehz, mahr-SEH-lo)

1979– Ballet dancer

Address: c/o American Ballet Theatre, 890 Broadway, New York, NY 10003

A principal dancer with the New York City–based American Ballet Theatre (ABT), Marcelo Gomes has been hailed for his dramatic interpretation of ballet classics. "Where Gomes distinguishes himself from his exceptional peers is in his acting—not only with his face but his whole body," Apollinaire Scherr wrote for *Newsday* (June 12, 2005). "He joins an actor's acute sense of gesture and timing to a classically pure line and a modern dancer's feel for the gravity and texture of the movement. He combines physical amplitude with emotional clarity." Gomes has credited his success in such parts as Prince Siegfried in *Swan Lake* and Albrecht in *Giselle* to his ability to completely inhabit the char-

Rosalie O'Connor, courtesy of ABT

Marcelo Gomes

acters. "When I'm interpreting a role, that pirouette or jump matters, of course, but I'm someone else. I'm deep into the story and I'm not just doing an acrobatic trick," he told Astrida Woods for *Dance Magazine* (May 1, 2006).

Marcelo Gomes was born in 1979 to Haroldo Gomes, a lawyer, and Maze Mourao, a journalist, in Manaus, Brazil. He was raised in Rio de Janeiro. He has a brother, now a comedy writer, and a sister, now a television journalist. Gomes began studying musical theater as a five-year-old. "My sister was the dancer," he told Paula Durbin for *Américas* (September 1, 2003), "and one day I was waiting for her to finish class. In the same building there was a musical theater class and I went to check it out. I thought I could do it, and I did, even though I had come in the middle. Then I went to my parents and said I wanted to go back, and they said absolutely. I was already dancing around the house anyway, and my mother wanted to get me in a better space—before I broke something."

When Gomes was eight years old, Helena Lobato, a renowned Brazilian ballerina, saw him in a student production and invited him to take a ballet class with her. Gomes was instantly enthralled. "I found it so interesting, how [Lobato] worked with me, and all the steps. She would take me to her house and show me ballet videos, and I started to want to become what I was seeing. After a year with her, I decided to concentrate on ballet, and dropped the other [dance] classes," he told Mary Cargill in an interview for the Ballet Alert Web site (2003). His schedule was grueling. "I went to school in the morning," Gomes explained to Durbin. "I would eat my lunch from a box in the car, change out of my Catholic school uniform, go to ballet class, do my homework so I would do well on the tests—and I was exhausted at night."

After a few years of study at Lobato's school, Gomes joined a new dance studio run by Dalal Achcar, a former manager of the ballet company at Brazil's Teatro Municipal (Municipal Theater). There, he helped a fellow student make an audition tape for the Harid Conservatory, in Boca Raton, Florida. "It turned out Harid wasn't interested in her, but they wanted to know who I was," Gomes told Cargill. "I was only twelve, so I had to wait a year [before enrolling]." At 13 Gomes left Brazil—over the objections of Teatro Municipal administrators—to attend the conservatory. "In Brazil they really don't support dance that much, but once there is someone good, they want to keep them there," he explained to Cargill. "It's just like a soccer player, they don't want them to go play in Spain. So everyone wanted me to stay, but I really wanted to go, to open up my horizons." Gomes, then the only male student at his studio in Brazil, particularly welcomed the chance to study with other boys and to learn English. (English-speaking interviewers often comment on his fluency.)

Harid, founded in 1987, had gained, in its short history, a reputation for the quality and comprehensiveness of its program. "It was really a joy to go there," Gomes told Cargill. "We all took piano, and music theory, and singing. And dance history and art history. These came after ballet class, so we were all very tired! But it was very interesting to me, because I wanted to learn [everything] about the ballets." When he was 16 years old, the conservatory's instructors, most of whom were French, encouraged him to enter the prestigious Prix de Lausanne dance competition, in Switzerland. During the competition he performed a solo number by the choreographer Mark Godden and a piece from *The Nutcracker*. Gomes won the Hope Prize and was awarded a full-year scholarship to the Paris Opera Ballet School. "I wanted to go there because of the great tradition and training," he told Jennifer Dunning for the *New York Times* (June 23, 2000). He joked, "[When I went] I learned French a little bit and ate some cheese."

Before traveling to France, Gomes completed his final semester at the Harid Conservatory, graduating in 1996. He then returned to Brazil for a summer vacation. Coincidentally, ABT was performing there and Gomes, reasoning that it would be a good way to see the shows from the best vantage point, applied for work as a supernumerary (or extra). Once he had gotten that job, he inquired about taking a class with the dancers but was told by David Richardson, the assistant director, that it would be against ABT policy. Richardson relented after Gomes assured him that he was not seeking to join the dance troupe; scheduled to head to the Paris Opera Ballet School right after the summer, he wanted only to experience a single class with a company he admired. At the end of that class, Richardson was so impressed by the young dancer that he offered him an ABT contract. Gomes was wildly excited but, on the advice of his level-headed parents, turned down the offer in order to study in France.

Gomes attended the Paris Opera Ballet School, in Nanterre, a university town near Paris, for a year. "I had the passion, and I think [my instructors] saw the talent, but they wanted to refine everything," he explained to Woods. "At the beginning I was very resistant. I said to myself, 'What is there to revise?' But I quieted down my passion and just concentrated on my technique. Everything had to be precise and nothing tacky like sky-high extensions for boys. And when a foot left the floor it had better be pointed." Although he found the atmosphere of the school more restrictive than that of the conservatory in Florida, he credits his excellent technique, in large part, to his time there. "You definitely come out a French product," he told Durbin. "I was fortunate to be there; not many foreigners get that chance."

In 1997, after his year in France, Gomes approached ABT again. Administrators there remembered him and immediately offered him a contract to join the corps de ballet. (The corps refers to the dancers in a ballet company who perform as a group and have no solo parts.) Gomes remained in the corps for three years. "I wouldn't give up the corps experience for anything," he told Durbin. "In ABT you really feed off the other dancers. It's a very healthy environment. No one is alike, so there isn't a lot of rivalry." He was particularly happy to work with Julio Bocca, a famed principal dancer at ABT: Bocca is originally from Argentina and has been an inspiration to a number of Latin American dancers.

While in the corps, Gomes occasionally took on larger parts, filling in for injured dancers, and in 2000 he was promoted to soloist. Two years later he was named one of the company's principal dancers. He found the variety of roles he was cast in exhilarating. "You can be doing *Giselle* one day and the next you can be working with a choreographer who wants you rolling on the ground. It's such a marvelous [repertory], from *Swan Lake* to Paul Taylor [a modern choreographer]," he told Durbin. "I didn't know I could move as a modern dancer . . . but ABT has awakened another side of me."

While he enjoys performing modern choreography, Gomes has become perhaps most identified with a number of dramatic male roles that include Romeo, in *Romeo and Juliet*; Prince Siegfried and the dark sorcerer von Rothbart, both in *Swan Lake*; Albrecht, in *Giselle*; the title role in *Othello*; and the prince in *Cinderella*. Reviews of his performances in such roles are almost universally glowing. Of a 2002 performance of *Giselle*, for example, Theodore Bale wrote for the *Boston Herald* (November 15, 2002), "Last night's performance of *Giselle* by American Ballet Theatre at the Wang Theatre should have been called *Albrecht* instead, since principal dancer Marcelo Gomes gave such a gripping interpretation of the role that he domi-

nated both acts of this much-loved ballet." Apollinaire Scherr wrote of another of Gomes's signature performances, "In *Swan Lake*, when Prince Siegfried's mother tells him to hurry up and choose a wife, he responds with a private, melancholy solo. Many danseurs [male ballet dancers] don't tell you much when they move slowly. They look stiff and awkward. When Gomes performs this dance, the leg he stretches behind him is so full of yearning that we know how lonely his mother's demand has made him feel." Scherr also applauded Gomes's willingness to play not only noble, romantic roles but to portray villains as well.

Gomes discussed some of his favorite roles with Cargill: "Albrecht is a wonderful role, by far my favorite. There are so many angles to it, and it seems to fit my technique and personality," he said. "And I love Romeo." He is also fond of appearing in *Fancy Free*—a popular modern piece by the choreographer Jerome Robbins, in which he dances the role of a sailor on shore leave.

Gomes is considered one of the strongest partners a ballerina could hope for. "I actually started partnering very early, in Brazil, when I could barely lift, so I have been trying to put girls on their feet for a very long time," he told Cargill. "When I got to ABT, I really developed a joy in presenting the ballerina. . . . I really like to look into someone's eyes and feel like you are making a connection. That's really much more exciting to me than seven thousand pirouettes." Gomes has been partnered with several ABT ballerinas; his work with the Argentinean dancer Paloma Herrera is considered by critics and fans to be of particular note.

The 2007 season was a busy one for Gomes. As of October he had appeared in ABT productions of *Swan Lake*, *Othello*, *Fancy Free*, *Romeo and Juliet*, *The Sleeping Beauty*, *Manon*, *Cinderella*, *From Here On Out*, *The Leaves Are Fading*, *Sinatra Suite*, *Symphonie Concertante* (a 1947 ballet choreographed by George Balanchine and set to Mozart's Sinfonia Concertante in E-flat major for violin and viola), and *C. to the C.* (or "Close to the Chuck," a production of new works from the choreographer Jorma Elo, in collaboration with the composer Philip Glass and the painter Chuck Close).

Gomes surprised some ballet fans when he appeared on the cover of the gay-themed magazine the *Advocate* (February 4, 2003). In that issue he discussed his homosexuality, telling the interviewer, Joseph Carman, that he had known about his sexual orientation since his early teens and that his family, which included a beloved gay uncle, had always been supportive. He admitted, however, that things had not always been easy for him in his native country. "I had a really hard time dancing in Brazil because I was male," he told Carman. "But I think it is getting better. I've gotten a lot more recognition at home." (Gomes has been awarded the Order of Rio Branco by the Brazilian government, for his accomplishments in the field of dance.)

Gomes lives in New York City and in his free time enjoys Broadway shows, movies, and the city's many restaurants. He has stated that he may retire to Brazil one day. He hopes to purchase a beach house there and teach, choreograph, or direct his own troupe.

—B.M.

Suggested Reading: *Advocate* Feb. 4, 2003; American Ballet Theater Web site; *Américas* p48+ Sep. 1, 2003; Ballet Alert Web site; *Dance Magazine* p52 May 1, 2006; (New York) *Newsday* D p15 Oct. 21, 2001; *New York Times* E p5 Nov. 3, 1998, E p1 June 23, 2000

Jochen Luebke/AFP/Getty Images

Gondry, Michel

(mee-shell)

May 8, 1963– Filmmaker

Address: c/o Creative Artsists Agency, 2000 Ave. of the Stars, Los Angeles, CA 90067

"For me, when you produce art, you're trying to be in touch with who you were as a child, that purity of happiness," the filmmaker Michel Gondry told Margy Rochlin for the *New York Times* (April 7, 2002). Known for his whimsical concepts and arresting visual effects, Gondry has demonstrated his trademark style (several publications describe his work as "Gondrian") in a number of artistic mediums. He first gained widespread attention with a music video for the Icelandic singer Björk, in 1993, and has since worked with a wide variety of popu-

lar musicians—from the indie rocker Beck to the Australian pop star Kylie Minogue. At the same time Gondry also established a reputation as an innovative director of commercials; "Drugstore," his 1994 television spot for Levi's jeans, is listed in the *Guinness Book of World Records* as the most highly awarded commercial of all time. Though he got off to a shaky start in feature films, with the flop *Human Nature* (2001), Gondry has now solidified his niche—as the director of quirky, fantastical stories of romantic longing—with the films *Eternal Sunshine of the Spotless Mind* (2004) and *The Science of Sleep* (2006).

While Gondry's films capture a sense of childlike wonder, they also exhibit both intellectual and technical sophistication. "Crammed with fairytale images mined from dreams and childhood memories, the playfully faux-naif tone of Gondry's work often belies its stunning originality and technical complexity," Stephen Dalton wrote for the London *Times* (June 22, 2006). Chris Vognar, writing for the *Dallas Morning News* (September 29, 2006), described the director as "a contradictory conjurer, an alchemist whose interests and skills would seem to clash at every turn. He's among the most inventive filmmakers around, but he proudly employs low-tech methods and technology. His stories are willfully bizarre and brainy, but they're also achingly romantic fables that could come only from one who believes in true love." Gondry's unique vision is a large part of his appeal: he is as frequently described as a magician as he is a director—one who can take the often clichéd and overdone subject of true love and give it a new sheen. "I always thought of Michel as part illusionist and part film-maker," Gondry's friend and fellow music-video director Chris Cunningham told Dalton. "When I watch his videos I always feel like a seven-year-old being shown a trick."

Michel Gondry was born on May 8, 1963 in Versailles, France, where he grew up in a middle-class, creatively inclined family. Gondry's grandfather, Constant Martin, invented the clavioline, a forerunner of the analog synthesizer; Gondry's father was a musician and a computer programmer, and his mother was an accomplished pianist. The director's one sibling, his older brother, Olivier, also followed a creative path; he has designed special-effects software and directs television commercials and music videos. When the brothers were children, their father gave Michel a drum kit and Olivier a bass guitar, with which they formed their own punk band. Around age 12 Gondry also became particularly interested in photography—a hobby that served as an outlet for his frustrations over unrequited or problematic love. "I was hiding from reality," Gondry told Lynn Hirschberg for the *New York Times Magazine* (September 17, 2006). "I took pictures of one girl over and over. I was not even dating her, although I wished I was dating her. She ended up dating my older brother." Given that he is often described as "childlike," it is not surprising that the adult Gondry bears significant similarities to his childhood self. "As a kid, Michel was the same as he is today: losing things, angry not to find them, anxious at night," Olivier Gondry wrote for *Creative Review* (October 1, 2004). "But when he was interested in something, he did it with lots of energy: drawing, photography, drums."

Gondry put that considerable energy to work when he left Versailles for art school in Paris. He thought of himself as an aspiring painter and illustrator while also studying weaving and tapestry. He disliked, however, the institutionalization of the creative process, which often forced him to tailor his vision to fit those of his instructors. "My final project was cheesy," he told Hirschberg wryly. "Books becoming birds, which was something I knew they would like." At 22 Gondry took a job with a company that printed calendars. Bored by his tedious work, he bought a 16 mm camera at a flea market and began to make short films. He was also drumming in a band, Oui Oui, and produced the band's videos—often animated works of detailed fantasy sequences. Film soon became his primary passion, overtaking the musical pursuit that was its initial inspiration. "As a film-maker I am using 200 times more brain cells than as a drummer," he told Dalton.

In 1993 Björk, who is known for her eccentric musical and personal styles, saw one of Gondry's videos for Oui Oui on television. Attracted to his quirky sensibility, she hired him to direct a video for her song "Human Behaviour." The video, which featured Björk being chased and ultimately devoured by a giant teddy bear, caught the attention of a fellow video auteur, Spike Jonze, who would later prove instrumental in Gondry's transition to the big screen. In 1994 Gondry moved to London, England, where he worked for the advertising agency Partizan. He directed a slew of extremely successful advertising campaigns, most notably for Nike, Air France, and the Gap. In addition to "Drugstore," Gondry directed the "Mermaids" and "Swap" ads for Levi's jeans, as well as the famous "Bellybutton" (2001) commercial, which featured various girls' belly buttons singing Diana Ross's hit song "I'm Coming Out." Another of Gondry's standout commercials is "Smarienburg" (sometimes spelled "Smarienberg"), a 1997 spot for Smirnoff vodka, which pioneered the frozen-in-time technique that was later made famous by the blockbuster feature *The Matrix* (1999). Despite his success, Gondry told Hirschberg, he was restless. "London is the Hollywood of advertising," he said. "But advertising is dangerous for a director: the point of view in a commercial has to be expressed in 20 seconds, which is too simplistic for any other form. And the money is too good in commercials—you are always in luxury. I always knew that it wouldn't be wise to get used to those conditions."

Gondry continued directing music videos, working with such artists as Sinéad O'Connor, the Black Crowes, Massive Attack, and the Rolling Stones. His 1996 video for Cibo Matto's "Sugar Water" remains one of his most acclaimed works; using a split screen, it simultaneously follows the bandmates Yuka Honda and Miho Hatori—one woman moving forward through her day, while the other moves backward. He was also still directing many of Björk's videos—following "Human Behaviour" with "Isobel" and "Army of Me" in 1995; "Hyperballad" in 1996; and "Jóga" and "Bachelorette" in 1997. His successful collaborations with Björk encouraged him to try feature films. "When I was making commercials and videos in London, it was not in my mind that I would ever do a film in my life," Gondry recalled to Hirschberg. "But then we screened the Björk videos in a theater, and I realized how magical it was to see the work big."

In 1997 Gondry moved to the U.S. and settled in Los Angeles, California, where he wrote a script for an adaptation of the classic radio show *The Green Hornet* with Edward Neumeier, who had written the screenplays for *RoboCop* (1987) and *Starship Troopers* (1997). (The studio shelved the project after the writers had worked on it for two years.) Gondry also directed videos for Beck's "Dead Weight"—in which the sock-footed singer follows the path of his shoes, which walk on their own in front of him—and the Foo Fighters' "Everlong," which culminates with the lead singer, Dave Grohl, growing a pair of monstrous hands to defend his wife from a nightmare she is having. In 1998 Gondry released his first short film, *La Lettre* ("The Letter"), about a young boy's unrequited love.

By the time Gondry shot his first feature-length film, *Human Nature* (2001), he had become a critics' darling for his effective use of flights of fancy to convey earthly emotions. The movie—which follows a love triangle involving a controlling scientist (Tim Robbins), a woman covered in hair (Patricia Arquette), and the ape-man they try to civilize (Rhys Ifans)—was based on a script by Charlie Kaufman, who is often celebrated for his quirky, cerebral concepts. In 1999 Jonze, who had been working on *Being John Malkovich* with Kaufman, introduced him to Gondry. Upon meeting the screenwriter, Gondry proposed an idea for a movie that came from one his friends, the French artist Pierre Bismuth. Gondry suggested that he and Kaufman develop the idea—that of erasing the memory of a former lover from one's mind—into a feature-length film. The film would eventually become *Eternal Sunshine of the Spotless Mind* (2004), but Kaufman had to finish *Being John Malkovich* before he could begin writing the new script. In the meantime he gave Gondry—who was impatient to begin working on feature-length pictures—the script for *Human Nature*, which bombed both commercially and critically. Afterward, Gondry was discouraged almost to the point of artistic paralysis.

Gondry was at an all-time low in 2001 after the trying experience of directing the video for Radiohead's "Knives Out," which featured a plot that was even more autobiographical than his usual storylines; the lead singer, Thom Yorke, played Gondry in a story about one of Gondry's past girlfriends, who developed leukemia. Though Gondry considered "Knives Out" one of his best videos, he and the band parted on bad terms. "It really makes me cry to think about it," Gondry told Donald Clarke for the *Irish Times* (May 1, 2004). "Suddenly he [Yorke] decided he didn't like it. And, number two, he said: 'Why do I have to pay for Michel Gondry's therapy?' He then refused to let me put it on my own DVD." Then, in 2002, Gondry began what would become one of his most successful collaborations. For the video of "Fell in Love with a Girl," the White Stripes' 2002 breakout hit, Gondry painstakingly re-created the bandmates Meg and Jack White as Lego figures. With the success of that video, "I found I could be creative again," Gondry told Mottram. He went on to direct the band's videos for "Dead Leaves and the Dirty Ground" in 2002, "The Hardest Button to Button" in 2003, and "The Denial Twist" in 2005. In 2003 Palm Pictures collected a number of Gondry's most outstanding music videos for the DVD *Director's Series, Vol. 3—The Work of Michel Gondry*.

Gondry's return to music videos reinvigorated his creativity in time for him to film *Eternal Sunshine of the Spotless Mind*, which was released in 2004. His most successful film to date, *Eternal Sunshine* was received with unequivocally positive critical reviews, which credited Gondry with not only creating a visual masterpiece but also eliciting surprisingly powerful performances from the film's leads, Jim Carrey and Kate Winslet. One of Gondry's favorite directorial techniques was to leave the camera rolling continuously, leaving the actors unsure of whether or not they needed to be in character. The spontaneity of Gondry's style often led to confusion on the set but also a greater feeling of authenticity—for which Gondry happily sacrificed perfect consistency. "It's good, because life is so complex and unpredictable and nonjustified than the story that you generally show in a movie," he told Cassie Carpenter for BPI Entertainment News Wire (March 31, 2004). "Sometimes the character is a little bit out of character, because sometimes we are out of character." In an interview with Carpenter, Kaufman, himself given to idiosyncratic touches, praised Gondry's unusual approach to directing: "Michel allowed stuff to happen in a very organic way. What I like about Michel is that he's got this technical brilliance, and yet there's this human stuff going on. That's a really unusual combination." That combination did not go unnoticed by critics. "Gondry's virtuosity lifts the film far past science fiction into cinematic efflorescence," Stanley Kauffmann wrote for the *New Republic* (April 5, 2004). "He shows us, more seductively than other directors have done, how freehand use of film can capture the flashes in our minds that slip between words." The film received numerous awards, and in 2005 Kaufman, Gondry, and Bismuth shared the Academy Award for best

original screenplay. But while Gondry and Bismuth received credit for their contribution to the core idea of the film, it was Kaufman who gained widespread notice for his execution of the script, overshadowing the attention Gondry received for his directorial prowess—which the director reportedly took as a small but nonetheless hurtful slight.

By the time *Eternal Sunshine* premiered, Gondry already had a new project in the works—a film titled *The Science of Sleep*—which he wrote and was slated to direct. First, though, he took a pause from the love stories that were becoming his niche for a surprising side project, that of documenting the efforts of the comedian Dave Chappelle to put together a free concert in New York City featuring such artists as Kanye West, the Fugees, Mos Def, Talib Kweli, and the Roots. For *Dave Chappelle's Block Party* (2005), Gondry followed the concert from its conception to its execution on September 18, 2004. At Gondry's insistence, the concert took place in Bedford-Stuyvesant, a once notoriously disadvantaged neighborhood in the borough of Brooklyn, rather than in Manhattan's Central Park. "I said we should bring it to people for whom it means more," he told Jen Chaney for the *Washington Post* (March 3, 2006, on-line). Gondry also pushed for Chappelle to release the film in theaters, instead of having it go straight to DVD, so as to let audience members experience the film as if they, too, were at the concert. In an effort to further replicate the feel of a concert, Gondry gave up his usual special effects, knowing that they would only distract from the live performances. "All the concert films that have made it down to history were shot in a simple way . . . ," he explained to Chaney. "Otherwise they would distance you from experiencing the concert." Though the film seemed an unusual choice following *Eternal Sunshine*, it was in many ways a natural extension of Gondry's work in music videos. "It's very good to keep in touch with music," Gondry told Chaney. "It's moving faster than the film world. It's more in touch with reality." He later made more elaborate—and more typically "Gondrian"—videos for two of *Block Party*'s featured artists. In 2005 he directed a Christmas-themed video for the hip-hop star Kanye West's "Heard 'Em Say"; in 2006 he filmed the video for the Roots frontman Cody ChesnuTT's "King of the Game," which featured Gondry's animated drawings.

In the months before *Block Party*'s release, Gondry screened *The Science of Sleep* (which he had been filming almost simultaneously) at the Sundance Film Festival, setting off a bidding war for distribution rights, which were eventually won by Warner Independent Pictures for $6 million. Written and directed by Gondry, the autobiographical film centers on the character Stephane (Gael García Bernal), who has difficulty distinguishing his dreams from reality. Stephane falls in love with his neighbor, Stephanie (Charlotte Gainsbourg), who shares his eccentric, artistic nature; it is precisely their similarities, however, that end up driving the two apart, as Stephanie finds she would rather be with someone a little more grounded than Stephane. "I think dreams and real life are more interesting as inspirations than the movies themselves, because they are about us," Gondry explained to Carpenter.

Reactions to Gondry's first attempt at both writing and directing were mixed; while *The Science of Sleep*, like *Eternal Sunshine*, boasted a rich visual style, many reviewers felt that the script suffered without Kaufman's craftsmanship. "Other than being called childlike, the criticism that I most often receive is that I can't really tell a story. That while I have a strong sense of the visual, my narrative skills are weak," Gondry told Hirschberg before the film was released, anticipating the potential response. "I would like to think, instead, that my movies are more like real life. In a relationship, so much goes unsaid, but that doesn't mean the emotion is not felt. In my films, I want to show all the abstract ways that people can affect us when we are in love."

For the most part, critics seemed to appreciate the idea and effort behind the film, even while pointing out its sometimes flawed execution. "*The Science of Sleep*, Michel Gondry's beguiling new film, is so profoundly idiosyncratic, and so confident in its oddity, that any attempt to describe it is bound to be misleading . . . ," A. O. Scott wrote for the *New York Times* (September 22, 2006). "But its fugitive, ephemeral quality is part of its point: dreams, after all, are hard to remember, and perhaps don't hold the meanings they seem to. Without them, though, our minds would be emptier and our lives much smaller. So while *The Science of Sleep* may not, in the end, be terribly deep, it is undoubtedly—and deeply—refreshing." Gondry concurrently put on a show of props from the film and mementos of his failed relationships, called *The Science of Sleep: an exhibition of sculpture and creepy pathological little gifts*, at the Jeffrey Deitch Gallery, in Manhattan. While appreciating the public's interest in his props (which for *The Science of Sleep*, as for the video "Everlong," included a pair of giant hands), Gondry told Dalton that he wanted people to see beyond their fantastical nature. "I hope I am not only a technician," he said. "I always visualize the way I shoot on a horizontal axis, not looking down on people. What interests me most is to find a sort of intimacy, to converse with the people I shoot, to make them equal with the audience and the audience equal with them."

Gondry continues to direct music videos. In 2006 he reunited with Beck for "Cell Phone's Dead," and in 2007 he directed the video for the Paul McCartney single "Dance Tonight," featuring the actress Natalie Portman. His next film, again written by Kaufman, "Be Kind Rewind," stars Jack Black as a junkyard worker whose brain becomes magnetized and destroys the merchandise in his friend's video store. "Be Kind Rewind" is due for release in early 2008.

Gondry served as an artist in residence at the Massachusetts Institute of Technology in 2005 and 2006. He lives in Manhattan's East Village with his teenage son.

—C.S.

Suggested Reading: BPI Entertainment News Wire Mar. 31, 2004; *Interview* p118+ Sep. 1, 2006; (London) *Independent* p9 June 30, 2006; (London) *Times* Features p18 June 22, 2006; *New York Times Magazine* p54+ Sep. 17, 2006

Selected Films: *Human Nature*, 2001; *Eternal Sunshine of the Spotless Mind*, 2004; *Dave Chappelle's Block Party*, 2005; *The Science of Sleep*, 2006

Courtesy of Alison Gopnik

Gopnik, Alison

June 16, 1955– Psychologist; author; educator

Address: Dept. of Psychology, University of California at Berkeley, 3317 Tolman, Berkeley, CA 94720

"It is remarkable how much little children know and how much they learn in a short time. If you combine the psychological and neurological evidence, it is hard to avoid concluding that babies are just plain smarter than we are, at least if being smart means being able to learn something new." Those observations appear in the book *The Scientist in the Crib: Minds, Brains, and How Children Learn* (1999), co-written by Alison Gopnik, a pioneer in the field of cognitive psychology and a professor at the University of California at Berkeley (UC-Berkeley), and Andrew N. Meltzoff and Patricia K. Kuhl, co-directors of the University of Washington Institute for Learning and Brain Sciences. During the past three decades, Gopnik has made fundamental discoveries about the way infants' thinking processes develop and change as they compile a rapidly expanding body of knowledge about their worlds. Babies, Gopnik told an interviewer for *New Scientist* (May 17, 2003), "have ideas about other human beings, about objects and about the world—right from the time they are born. And these are fairly complex ideas, not just reflexes or responses to sensations." Starting at birth, according to Gopnik's "theory theory," developed in collaboration with Meltzoff and Henry M. Wellman, "children develop and change intuitive theories of the world in much the way that scientists do," as she put it on the Web site of the Institute of Human Development at UC-Berkeley. Thus, from the moment of birth, "extremely powerful learning capacities of several different kinds are . . . in place," as Gopnik explained to the *New Scientist* reporter. "Newborn babies have an initial 'theory' about the world and [have] the inferential learning capacities to revise, change and rework those initial ideas on the evidence they experience from the very beginning of their lives. Those capacities are much more powerful than can be explained by traditional ideas about learning: they involve much more than association and conditioning. Thanks to ideas from developmental psychology, computing and cognitive science, we are just starting to explain what those inferential learning mechanisms might be like."

Gopnik has been a faculty member of the Department of Psychology at UC-Berkeley since 1988. Earlier, among other institutions, she taught at the University of London, in England, and the University of Toronto, in Canada. Her extensive list of publications, the earliest of which appeared in 1981, includes chapters in such books as *Developing Theories of Mind*, *Chomsky and His Critics*, and *Explanation and Cognition*. Her articles have appeared in such professional journals as the *Journal of Child Language*, *Child Development*, *Psychological Review*, *Developmental Psychology*, *Behavioral and Brain Sciences*, and *Philosophy of Science*. She has also written for the *New York Times*, the *New York Review of Books*, and the *Times Literary Supplement*. With Meltzoff, whose expertise is cognition, personality, and brain development in young children, Gopnik wrote the book *Words, Thoughts, and Theories* (1998). In 2000 *The Scientist in the Crib* was reissued in paperback with the subtitle *What Early Learning Tells Us About the Mind*; in the British edition, the title was changed to *How Babies Think*. Gopnik's forthcoming book is entitled *How Children Change the World*.

The first of the six children of Irwin and Myrna Gopnik, Alison Gopnik was born on June 16, 1955 in Philadelphia, Pennsylvania, when her parents were both graduate students. One of her brothers, Adam Gopnik, writes essays and art criticism for the *New Yorker*; another, Blake Gopnik, is an art critic for the *Washington Post*. During Alison Gopnik's childhood her family moved to Montreal, Canada, where both of her parents joined the faculty of McGill University—her mother as a professor of linguistics and her father as a professor of English; Irwin Gopnik also served as the school's dean of students. Myrna Gopnik founded the Cognitive Sciences Group at McGill and became well-known in her field for her work on the genetic basis for a speech disorder known as dysphasia. Together, Myrna and Irwin Gopnik edited the book *From Models to Modules* (1986), which contains papers presented at workshops held at McGill on such topics as language acquisition and development, language comprehension, and scientific reasoning and problem solving.

After her high-school graduation, in 1970, Alison Gopnik entered McGill University. The school was "a wonderful place to be" at that time, she told Simon Hanson in 2000 for *Brain Connection* (online), in part because although the term "cognitive science" had not yet been coined, "that was what they were teaching at McGill. I got a wonderful education there." In a conversation with Katherine MacKlem for the Canadian magazine *Maclean's* (March 27, 2006), Gopnik recalled that during her freshman year, as an experiment, McGill began to discourage the use of the lecture system, in which, often, little or no interaction occurs between instructors and students. In the introductory linguistics course in which Gopnik enrolled at McGill in 1970, students were given "files that covered modules of learning," listing material that they were expected to read by themselves. The students could then gain a better or broader understanding of what they had learned by going to a designated campus lounge, where a faculty member or a graduate student connected with the course was always present. The lounge "became a hangout," as Gopnik told MacKlem; "students would talk to each other, faculty would talk to the students. It was enormously sensible and very successful. For the students, it was challenging to be in a situation in which we couldn't say to ourselves, 'I've learned something, because I went and sat in the lecture room.' We had to have actually learned something."

Although there is some dispute as to precisely when the first university came into existence, such schools certainly originated centuries before the printing press was invented, in the mid-1400s; since books were extremely scarce before then, the only way to impart information to large groups of students was by having a knowledgeable person lecture to them. However, as Gopnik explained to MacKlem, "the way people learn best is by effectively interacting with their environment." Ideally, in every field of discipline, a student would undergo a "guided apprenticeship," which would resemble training in a sport or craft or the playing of a musical instrument, in which an expert continually observes performance and assesses it; in addition, the student would have a laboratory and a library to "hang out in," as Gopnik put it, and then have a site where he or she could talk to peers or others about the subject. "People—including young children—seem to be designed to want to explore and experiment and interact with the things around them," Gopnik explained. "That kind of teaching is much closer to the natural way we learn." The lecture system, she said, "is, literally, a medieval form of learning."

Gopnik earned a B.A. degree in philosophy and psychology, with great distinction, in 1975. She next enrolled at Oxford University, in England. Having recognized there, as she told Hanson, that "the philosophical questions I was interested in were ones that you could answer empirically," she planned to continue to study both psychology and philosophy. She recalled to Hanson that as a first-year graduate student, she found herself spending her time with "two communities of people," one of which consisted of philosophy students and professors, the other of wives and babies of Oxford students and faculty. (Gopnik herself gave birth to her first and second sons during her graduate-school years.) In her interview with Hanson, she described one of those two communities as "a group of completely determined, disinterested, seekers of truth who spent all their waking hours trying to figure out deep important problems about the world" and the other as "these egocentric narcissistic characters who constantly demanded attention and care-taking. And, of course, the first group are the babies and the second group are the philosophers. So I decided if I was going to spend the rest of my life with a group of people, I would rather spend it with the babies than the philosophers."

For her doctoral research, Gopnik spent two years studying nine British babies, beginning when each was a year-and-a-half old. In particular, she recorded every word spoken by each child, except for common nouns and proper nouns. Referring to the renowned linguist Noam Chomsky, she told Hanson, "When I started out at Oxford I was an absolute rabid Chomskian of the most aggressive sort." She was "pretty much convinced," she said, that, as Chomsky theorized, all children are born with an innate knowledge of the universal grammar that is common to all languages. The question of how people gain language and other knowledge has engaged philosophers for thousands of years. According to one school of thought, the minds of newborns are "blank slates," completely empty of knowledge until exposed to it through experience or other outside mechanisms. Another school holds that all knowledge is inborn, placed there by a higher power or acquired during evolution or by chance, and that it becomes conscious with the proper stimulation. Chomsky, as Gopnik wrote in an essay for the book *Chomsky and His Critics* (2003), as reprinted on the Web site of the Institute of Human Development at UC-Berkeley, "made

two very important contributions to this debate. The first was to cast it as an empirical, scientific, psychological question, rather than simply as a philosophical question. . . . The second . . . was to present a particular, rationalist hypothesis, the innateness hypothesis, as the empirical answer to the problem of knowledge." According to that thesis, in Gopnik's words, "Human minds are highly constrained innately. We can only formulate a very small set of possible representations and rules. Information from the outside world may trigger the development of those representations, and may narrow the set of possibilities even further by processes like parameter-setting, but the constraints remain unchanged throughout life. Representations and rules are not inferred or derived from the input."

Gopnik's observations of the nine babies as they gained competence in language, as she told Hanson, led her to reject Chomsky's theory as a faulty explanation "of what was going on." Instead, her thinking moved in the direction taken by the 20th-century philosophers Willard Quine and Rudolf Carnap, who, as she summarized their ideas for Hanson, maintained that "the way science works is that we never start from scratch, we always have some sort of theory about what the world is like. But we also have enormous degrees of freedom in terms of how we can modify and revise and change our theories in the light of new evidence." Babies, too, she came to believe, "are born with innate theories about how the world works," and thus their brains at birth are not "blank slates." However, unlike the way they are portrayed in the "Chomskian picture," as she explained to Hanson, babies "can and do revise pretty much anything in those theories in fundamental ways as they interact with the world and get more information and knowledge." As humans approach adulthood, she said, we lose the enormous mental flexibility that we had in our early years, but we gain something that is also invaluable: the ability to apply automatically and efficiently what we have learned.

Gopnik earned a Ph.D. in experimental psychology from Oxford in 1980. During the 1980–81 academic year, she worked as a lecturer in the Department of Applied Linguistics at Birkbeck College, a division of the University of London; she also taught courses offered by the Department of Design Research at the Royal College of Art, in London. In 1981, having won a postdoctoral fellowship from the Social Sciences and Engineering Research Council of Canada, she joined the Department of Applied Psychology at the Ontario Institute for Studies in Education, in Canada, where she remained until 1983. Concurrently, in 1982–83, she lectured in linguistics at Scarborough College, a part of the University of Toronto. That college promoted her to assistant professor in the Departments of Psychology and Linguistics in 1983. Also in 1983 she won a three-year research grant from the Natural Sciences and Engineering Research Council (NSERC) of Canada, and the following year she won an additional three-year NSERC grant; since then her work has also been supported by various U.S. foundations and government agencies, including the National Science Foundation. As a member of the faculty of UC-Berkeley's Department of Psychology, she has held the positions of assistant professor (1988–91), associate professor (1991–96), and, since 1996, professor in the Department of Psychology.

In the 1990s, in one illustration of how babies' understanding of other people changes with time, Gopnik and a graduate student of hers, Betty M. Repacholi, devised an experiment centering on food preferences. In the experiment, Repacholi offered a succession of 14-month-olds a choice of raw broccoli florets or Goldfish crackers. Invariably, each baby chose the latter. In the baby's presence, Repacholi then tasted each food, displaying expressions of disgust and unhappiness while chewing one and expressions of delight and happiness with the other. When Repacholi then asked the baby for something to eat and held out her hand, each child would offer a cracker, not only after the researcher had indicated that she liked the crackers but also after she had shown an aversion to the crackers and a fancy for the broccoli; the baby evidently assumed, egocentrically, that the other person must share his or her preference. When exposed to the same experimental situation at 18 months, the babies would offer Repacholi the broccoli after she had expressed her dislike of Goldfish crackers but fondness for broccoli; the babies thus indicated that they now understood that others may like something that they themselves dislike. "These data constitute the first empirical evidence that 18-month-olds are able to engage in some form of desire reasoning," Gopnik and Repacholi wrote in the abstract of their article "Early Understanding of Desires," published in Developmental Psychology (January 1997). "Children not only inferred that another person held a desire, but also recognized how desires are related to emotions and understood something about the subjectivity of these desires."

In another experiment carried out under Gopnik's direction at UC-Berkeley, children ages two to four played with a machine-like toy consisting of "different combinations of gears and switches that make other gears go," as Gopnik wrote for the New York Times Education Life Supplement (January 16, 2005), and they also watched adults manipulate the same toy. Nearly all of the children quickly figured out which gears and switches did what, thus demonstrating a sophisticated understanding of cause-and-effect relationships—an ability that the 20th-century psychologist Jean Piaget, a pioneer in the study of cognitive development in children, and many of his successors maintained was absent in preschoolers.

Researchers have shown that in a typical three-year-old's brain, the number of synapses, or connections, per neuron (brain cell) greatly surpasses the number in adults, indicating that a child's brain is far more active than an adult's. "Human children in the first three years of life are consumed by a desire to explore and experiment with objects," Gopnik and her co-authors wrote in The Scientist in the Crib. "They are like scientists. The crib, the house and the backyard are excellent laboratories." Gopnik told Patricia McBroom for a UC-Berkeley news release (August 10, 1999, on-line) that toddlers "think, draw conclusions, make predictions, look for explanations and even do experiments." Their fierce desire to learn about the world, Gopnik believes, triggers the willful disobedience commonly associated with the "terrible twos," a developmental stage that often begins when a child is about two years old. "Toddlers are systematically testing the dimensions on which their desires and the desires of others may be in conflict," according to The Scientist in the Crib. Gopnik said to Malcolm Gladwell for the New Yorker (January 10, 2000), "They may stare gravely at you while they head for a forbidden object, because your reaction is the really interesting thing. The child is a budding psychologist. We parents are the laboratory rats."

Gopnik has drawn comparisons between imaginative play and the scientific method and has suggested that the history of humans' discoveries, inventions, and alterations of the environment are inseparable from both. In her essay "The Real Reason Children Love Fantasy," for example, published in Slate (December 20, 2005, on-line), she wrote that "theorizing and fantasizing have a lot in common." "A theory, in science or in everyday life," she continued, "doesn't just describe one particular way the world happens to be at the moment. Instead, having a theory tells you about the ways the world could have been in the past or might be in the future. What's more, a theory can tell you that some of those ways the world can be are more likely than others. A theory lays out a map of possible worlds and tells you how probable each possibility is. And a theory provides a kind of logic for getting to conclusions from premises—if the theory is correct, and if you accept certain premises, then certain conclusions and not others will follow. . . . This is why theories are so profoundly powerful and adaptive. A theory not only explains the world we see, it lets us imagine other worlds, and, even more significantly, lets us act to create those worlds. Developing everyday theories, like scientific theories, has allowed human beings to change the world. . . . The uniquely human evolutionary gift is to combine imagination and logic to articulate possible worlds and then make them real. . . . A human being who learns about the real world is also simultaneously learning about all the possible worlds that stem from that world." At the annual convention of the Association for Psychological Science (APS) in 2006, which focused on the brain as a flexible "learning machine" that can "change throughout life," Gopnik gave a talk titled "The Logic of Imagination: How Children Change the World." In it she said that thanks to both inborn assumptions about the world and the ability to "very rapidly use data to learn," children can "imagine new things in the world, and they can use that new information to do new things in the world"—in other words, "change the world." "Everything [made by humans] in the environment we live in now was completely imaginary at one point in time," she noted. "The deepest part of our human nature is that we are trying to escape human nature." In summarizing Gopnik's talk for the APS publication *Observer* (August 2006, on-line), Leah Nelson wrote that young children's "ability to reshape their assumptions according to reality and then reshape reality based on their imaginings reflects the course of human evolution as a whole. It is the capacity for plasticity that makes it possible for children to learn and for the species to evolve, build, change, and grow."

Gopnik's many years of research have led her to suggest that for babies, such nonnatural stimulants as flashcards and Baby Einstein audiotapes are of dubious value; much more worthwhile, she believes, is prolonged daily interaction between a baby and a devoted caregiver, involving such activities as speech, play, and naturally occurring demonstrations of basic skills—the sorts of interactions that have become far too scarce in the lives of many children, whose caregivers have little time to spend with them one on one or, in some cases, little inclination to do so. Gopnik has also sharply criticized the recent, renewed emphasis on rote learning in many schools, a consequence of the passage of the No Child Left Behind Act, signed into law by President George W. Bush in January 2002. In an attempt to make primary and secondary schools more accountable for the academic performance of students, the law requires state departments of education to rely on standardized-test results, which forces teachers to spend what Gopnik and other critics consider an inordinate amount of time preparing students for such tests, which ignore creative thinking. "From a developmental point of view, this is the worst thing that we could imagine . . . ," Gopnik said to Nancy Cook for *Instructor* (March 2006). "At the very least, we need to persuade the authorities that testing for children's conceptual understanding and inductive reasoning is more effective than testing for information retention."

Among many other professional activities, Gopnik has served as treasurer of the International Association for the Study of Child Language (1984–87), president of the Society for Philosophy and Psychology (1994–95), associate editor of the *British Journal of Developmental Psychology* (1993–95) and *Child Development* (1997–2000), a reviewer of research-grant applications, and guest lecturer at universities and other institutions. In the late 1970s she married George Lewinski, an instructor of radio reporting at UC-Berkeley's Graduate School of Journalism and a senior producer of *Pacific Time*, a program on the public radio station KQED; earlier, Lewinski spent 10 years as the for-

eign editor of the public-radio program *Marketplace*. Gopnik has three sons—Alexei, Nicholas, and Andres Gopnik-Lewinski.

—D.F.

Suggested Reading: BrainConnection.com, 2000; Institute of Human Development at UC-Berkeley Web site; *Instructor* p23+ Mar. 2006; *Maclean's* p38+ Mar. 27, 2006; *New York Times* Education Life Supplement p26 Jan. 16, 2005; *New Yorker* p80+ Jan. 10, 2000; *Slate* (on-line) Nov. 16, 2005, Dec. 20, 2005

Selected Books: *Words, Thoughts, and Theories* (with Andrew N. Meltzoff), 1997; *The Scientist in the Crib: Minds, Brains, and How Children Learn* (with Meltzoff and Patricia Kuhl), 1999

Donna Coveney, courtesy of MIT

Guarente, Leonard P.

(gwar-EN-tee)

June 6, 1952– Molecular geneticist; educator

Address: MIT Dept. of Biology, 31 Ames St., 68-280, Cambridge, MA 02139

Laboratory rats and mice fed very low-calorie but nutritious diets often live as much as 50 percent longer than their weightier peers in research labs and remain vigorous and healthy well into their old age. Scientists have recorded examples of similarly lengthened life spans among worms, spiders, fish, monkeys, dogs, and other animals whose diets contain far fewer calories than those of control groups. What accounts for such significant differences in life span? The work of the molecular geneticist Leonard P. Guarente has provided some answers. Guarente, who has held the title Novartis professor of biology at the Massachusetts Institute of Technology (MIT), in Cambridge, since 2000, has investigated the processes of aging since 1991, and he was among the first to do so from the perspective of the molecular components and inner workings of the cell. He and his co-workers made the pathbreaking discovery that a family of genes known by the acronym SIR (silent information regulator), or SIRT in humans, affect longevity. When caloric intake is severely restricted, such genes produce enzymes known as sirtuins (the name is derived from the gene SIR2, also spelled sir2). Writing for the *New York Times* (November 17, 2006), Nicholas Wade, who has followed Guarente's scientific progress since 1998, explained that according to the theory Guarente has helped to develop, "sirtuins sense the level of energy expenditure in living cells and switch the body's resources from reproduction to tissue maintenance when food is low." From the standpoint of evolution, the main function of every animal is to reproduce; during periods of food scarcity, the likelihood of producing healthy babies that would themselves reach adulthood (and get the opportunity to reproduce) is greatly diminished. Temporary suspension of the ability to reproduce (that is, postponement of breeding) thus makes sense, as it would enable cells to concentrate on survival (tissue maintenance) until food became more abundant. "There are people out there claiming science will allow people to live thousands of years," Guarente said to David Rotman for *Technology Review* (December/January 2005). "I tend to believe that is a lot of bunk. But the opportunity we do have is nothing to sneeze at. I think it is the major opportunity that Mother Nature has given us to intervene in the aging process. And by intervene I mean not just to promote longevity but to fight diseases." Guarente, who has taught at MIT since 1981, explained to Rotman, "The big idea here is that there is a close connection between aging itself and diseases of aging," among them cancer, heart disease, diabetes, and senile dementia and other degenerative diseases of the brain—"really major diseases," in Guarente's words. Thus, if a drug could delay aging by triggering the activation of the SIRT genes, and do so by a chemical process normally triggered by caloric restriction, "diseases of aging would also be forestalled." Such a drug, as David Stipp wrote for the *Wall Street Journal* (October 30, 2006), would be tantamount to a "gerontological grail or a crucial part of it." Guarente (writing as Lenny Guarente) described his research in *Ageless Quest: One Scientist's Search for Genes that Prolong Youth* (2003), a scientific memoir. In 2000, with the geneticist Cynthia Kenyon of the University of California at San Francisco and the virologist Cindy Bayley, a founder of DeCode Genetics, Guarente launched the company Elixir Pharmaceuticals,

whose mission, according to its Web site, is to develop drugs "that slow aging, reduce the disease and disability that accompany aging, and extend youthful health, vigor and productivity."

The son of Leonard Guarente and his wife, Norma, Leonard P. Guarente was born on June 6, 1952 in Chelsea, Massachusetts, and grew up in Revere, near Boston, Massachusetts. His grandparents were Italian immigrants. As a child he was "precocious by local standards," as he wrote in *Ageless Quest*. In high school Guarente was drawn more toward physics and chemistry than biology, a science that seemed to him to be "purely descriptive," as Wade wrote for the *New York Times* (September 26, 2000). What he heard about recent discoveries in molecular biology during his freshman year at MIT (1970–71) contributed to his decision to major in biology; he earned a B.S. degree in that subject in 1974. He then enrolled at Harvard University, also in Cambridge, where he conducted research in molecular genetics under the supervision of Jon Beckwith, a pioneer in developing techniques for isolating and cloning genes. Guarente received a Ph.D. from Harvard in 1978. His dissertation was entitled "Genetics of Transcription Termination"—transcription being the process in which cells make copies of the genes on their chromosomes.

For three years beginning in 1978, as the Jane Coffin Childs Postdoctoral Fellow at Harvard, Guarente worked under Mark Ptashne, a molecular biologist who specialized then, as now, in the actions of genetic switches, which activate and deactivate genes. In 1981 Guarente joined MIT's faculty as an assistant professor of biology; he became an associate professor in 1985 and a professor in 1991. During those years he headed a laboratory that concentrated on gene transcription. He also began to consider other areas of research, among them memory and learning, involving "some riskier subject, one where if he could make any headway at all he would have an impact," as Wade put it (September 26, 2000). He chose to study aging because, as he explained to Wade for the same article, he would have few competitors in that field, "partly because it's less clear what to do."

Although at that time little was known about molecular and genetic mechanisms of aging, scientists had established decades earlier that most rats whose diets have adequate nutrition but few calories live longer than rats that consume more calories. Prolonged life spans had also been recorded in other species fed extremely low-calorie diets. It thus seemed possible that caloric restriction would have a similar effect on humans. Currently in the U.S., the average woman consumes more than 1,800 calories a day, and the average man, more than 2,600. With very few exceptions, people unused to a drastically smaller caloric intake—say, 40 percent lower—cannot tolerate such diets; they suffer not only from fierce hunger pangs but from irritability, decreased sex drive, and an inability to concentrate or stay warm. (Countless people in many countries have no choice but to subsist on such diets, but since they suffer from insufficient nutrition as well, their potential life spans are shortened rather than lengthened.) Before Guarente began his studies, researchers had attributed longevity induced by caloric reduction to a genetic "starvation response," in which cells stop growing and reproducing in order to conserve energy. The energy instead goes to "cellular systems that limit damage from harmful 'free radical' molecules and other toxins produced as metabolic byproducts," as David Stipp wrote for the *Wall Street Journal* (October 30, 2006). Such damage, according to that theory, is what ages the cell. A crude analogy to negative effects of metabolism might be made with motor oil in a car, which, in addition to its other functions, acts as a detergent, keeping the moving parts clean. With use, the oil gets increasingly dirty, and its efficiency as a detergent diminishes; the dirtier it is, the less effectively it cleans. In time, it becomes useless, and may cause the engine to seize, or "die."

To find genes that control aging and get results as quickly as possible, Guarente had to study organisms with extremely short life spans. Mice did not qualify, as they live two to two and a half years, on average. Guarente chose to work with yeast, of which about 1,500 species have been identified (a small fraction of the number believed to exist); classified as fungi, yeast are eukaryotes—one-celled microorganisms with nuclei. Guarente told Rotman, "The question we wanted to answer was, Do yeast cells age? And if they do, are there one or a small number of genes that are particularly important in dictating the life span of these cells?" He added, "For four or five years we published nothing because we were just banging away at the problem." In 1995 two of Guarente's graduate students—Brian Kennedy (now at the University of Washington) and Nicanor Austriaco (now at Providence College)—found a species of yeast that lived longer than others. (Yeast reproduce asexually, by budding. When the parent—the so-called mother cell—undergoes division, it produces a bud, a smaller, so-called daughter cell, which separates from the mother cell. The life span of the mother cell is defined as the number of daughter cells that it produces.) Its longevity, Kennedy and Austriaco discovered, was due to the activity of a set of genes—the silent information regulator or SIR genes—that repressed the activity of other genes, by producing proteins that traveled to the tips of the yeast cell's chromosomes.

The SIR2 gene is crucial in that process. "We found that the sir-2 gene determines the life span of both yeast cells and roundworms," Guarente wrote for the *Scientist* (April 26, 2004). "In both organisms, if we add an extra copy of this gene, the life span is extended. Conversely, if we delete sir-2, life span is shortened." SIR2 was also shown to promote longevity in fruit flies. In a further discovery, David Sinclair, an Australian postdoctoral student in Guarente's lab, found evidence that as yeast cells age, their "machinery for copying chromosomes"—a process necessary for growth and reproduction—"runs amok," as Stipp put it, which leads to the cells' deaths. Armed with that knowledge, Guarente determined that SIR2 activation depends on the level in the cell of a particular chemical, which in turn reflects whether the cell's metabolism—the performance of its myriad functions—is proceeding at a normal rate or at a reduced rate because of insufficient nutrients, which usually would also indicate a reduced number of calories, or caloric restriction. As Wade explained in the *Times* (November 7, 2006), Guarente "proposed that sir-2 and its counterpart genes in animals were the mediators of caloric restriction: the genes sense when the body is running low on nutrients and direct a wide range of metabolic adjustments, from preserving tissues to burning off fat reserves." Mammals, Guarente found, possess the gene SIRT1, which corresponds to SIR2 in yeast. SIRT1 "makes a protein that Drs. Guarente and Sinclair believe triggers the slowed-aging mode in mammals when calorie intake is low," as Stipp wrote. Guarente believes that a cell's longevity under conditions of caloric restrictions depends not on the reduced production of harmful byproducts of metabolism, as the "starvation response" theory maintained, but on the deployment of SIRT1 and its protein—as well as six close relatives of SIRT1 and their proteins, which Guarente and his team later identified. The seven SIRTs would presumably be a key in the creation of a drug that fooled cells into operating as if they were grappling with caloric restriction.

Another promising development was the news—reported by Sinclair, after he had formed his own lab—that resveratrol, a plant compound present in red wine, had been found to activate the SIRT genes in worms and flies. Earlier studies had indicated that resveratrol lowers the probability that an organism will develop cancer, heart disease, and other maladies that accompany aging—"just what a substance that slows aging should do," as Stipp pointed out. When Sinclair and his team conducted the same experiments with SIR2 eliminated, the life spans of the worms and flies were not extended. "Sir2 is the key," Guarente told William Hathaway for the *Hartford (Connecticut) Courant* (July 14, 2004). "All roads go through Sir2." Moreover, he said to Hathaway, another substance or substances, yet to be identified, may prove to be better than resveratrol at activating SIR2.

In a review of *Ageless Quest* for *Science* (February 28, 2003), Daniel Promislow of the University of Georgia summarized Guarente's findings and also challenged his conclusions. "The real star of Guarente's narrative is . . . Sir2 . . . ," Promislow wrote. "Guarente argues that this single gene may . . . be a universal regulator of aging. He knows that a reader like me (an evolutionary biologist interested in aging) will question such a claim. Evolutionary theories of aging rest on the recognition that the strength of selection against deleterious genes declines as we age. As a result, natural selection is unable to remove a potentially very large number of deleterious alleles [different versions of a gene] that increase mortality rates late in life. Therefore, evolutionary models suggest that there should be a very large number of genes involved in the aging process. Guarente argues, however, that evolution may favor a single gene such as SIR2 if it enables an organism to survive hard times, albeit without reproducing. Given that just one gene can influence so many age-related processes, Guarente goes on to argue that, counter to evolutionary predictions, 'the causes of aging must not be infinitely complex and varied.' I applaud Guarente's attempts to reconcile the molecular aim of understanding how we age with the evolutionary aim of understanding why we age. . . . Nonetheless, I remain unconvinced that an understanding of how laboratory organisms slow aging during stressful times will necessarily tell us much about how organisms age in natural populations." Promislow noted that Guarente possesses "boundless enthusiasm" for his work and that "his excitement about his discoveries is tempered with a refreshing modesty. He spends far more time giving credit to his students and post-docs than to his own role in the discoveries he describes here. His book thus becomes more than simply a story about the genetics of aging: it also informs us about the mechanisms by which scientific discovery occurs."

In 2007 Guarente and his postdoctoral associate Nicholas A. Bishop found what they believed to be a connection between calorie-related longevity and the endocrine system of a species of worm: in *Nature* (May 31, 2007), they reported that after two particular neurons in the heads of the worms were removed, caloric restriction no longer affected longevity. In an article by Deborah Halber for MIT's Web page (June 18, 2007), Guarente was quoted as saying, "We suspect that the two neurons sense dietary restriction and secrete a hormone that increases metabolism—and life span—in the animal."

Guarente has published more than 150 journal articles. He has served on the editorial boards of several professional publications, among them the *Journal of Anti-Aging Medicine, Trends in Genetics, Experimental Gerontology*, and *Developmental Cell*. He served as associate editor of *Nucleic Acids Research* (1983–88) and of *Molecular and Cellular Biology*. He is a member of the scientific advisory boards of the National Institutes of Health (NIH), the Buck Center for Research in Aging, and the Maximum Life Foundation. His honors include a Presidential Young Investigator Award from the National Science Foundation (1984–89) and the Thomas D. and Virginia W. Cabot Career Development Professorship (1989–92).

When Guarente's four-year marriage to Barbara Weiffenbach, a geneticist, ended in divorce, in 1985, he won joint custody of their son, Jeffrey, who is now in his mid-20s.

—M.B.

Suggested Reading: MIT Dept. of Biology Web site; *Nature* p255 Nov. 9, 2000, p227 Mar. 8, 2001; *New York Times* F p2 Feb. 22, 2000, F p1+ Sep. 26, 2000, A1+ Nov. 2, 2006, F p1+ Nov. 7, 2006, A p20 Nov. 17, 2006; *St. Louis Post-Dispatch* A p1 July 18, 2004; *Science* Issue p1181 Feb.18, 2000, p1319+ Feb. 28, 2003; *Scientific American* p12+ June 2004; *Scientist* p34 Apr. 26, 2004; *Technology Review p38+* Dec. 2005–Jan. 2006; *U.S. News & World Report* p63 Dec. 25, 2000–Jan. 1, 2001

Selected Books: *Ageless Quest*, 2003

Courtesy of Gary Gygax

Gygax, Gary

(GUY-gaks)

July 27, 1938– Game designer; co-creator of Dungeons & Dragons; writer; entrepreneur

Address: c/o Author Mail, Troll Lord Games, P.O. Box 251171, Little Rock, AR 72225

Games, according to Gary Gygax, who has designed them, are "an interesting diversion from everyday life. Games give you a chance to excel, and if you're playing in good company, you don't even mind if you lose because you had the enjoyment of the company during the course of the game." Gygax, who made that observation during an interview with Allen Rausch for PC.GameSpy.com (August 16, 2004), is a creator of the immensely popular—and, for a while, highly controversial—roleplaying game *Dungeons & Dragons*. Inspired by war-strategy games and the many fantasy novels Gygax has read since childhood, *Dungeons & Dragons* differs from children's usual make-believe (when they play house or cops and robbers, for example) in that each participant takes on the role of a specific character in ongoing stories, most involving military-like campaigns, searches for treasure, and hazards that must be avoided or overcome, with complex rules guiding the action. A "dungeon master" or "game master" interprets those rules, which describe the characters' powers, the equipment each character should have, ways in which the characters interact, and many other aspects of the game. Unlike board games, card games, athletic contests, and games of chance, *Dungeons & Dragons* produces neither winners nor losers. Materials required to play are the *Dungeons & Dragons* rule books, sheets of paper on which the characters' traits are listed, pencils, and dice. *Dungeons & Dragons* is acknowledged as the first role-playing game of modern times and as the precursor to the flourishing industry built on multiuser, online role-playing games. The influence of *Dungeons & Dragons* on popular culture has been vast. As Malcolm Kelly wrote for the Canadian newspaper the *National Post* (August 24, 2005), "You can arguably trace so many movies, television shows, arcade, console, PC and board games, collectible figures, miniatures, toys, books, magazines and yes, even perhaps the adventures of Harry Potter, to January, 1974, when *Dungeons & Dragons* first hit the market in a box filled with three books, a unique set of dice and a lot of imagination."

Since 1985, when Gygax ended his association—not amicably—with Tactical Studies Rules (TSR), the company that he had co-founded to market *Dungeons & Dragons*, he has invented, alone or with others, additional role-playing games. Among them are *Dangerous Journeys* and *Lejendary Adventures*, table-top battle games, board games, and a three-layered form of chess. He has also written two series of fantasy novels, known as the *Greyhawk Adventures* and *Gord the Rogue Adventures*; many short stories; and a series of reference books, collectively called *Gygaxian Fantasy Worlds*, which offer instructions on how to create such worlds with the goal of constructing role-playing games. In his conversation with Allen Rausch, Gygax said, "I do stuff that I like. The books I write because I want to read them, the games because I want to play them, and stories I tell because I find them exciting personally. When you finish one you feel great." He also said, "I would like the world to remember me as the guy who really enjoyed playing games and sharing his knowledge and his fun pastimes with everybody else."

The son of Ernest Gygax and his wife, Ernest Gary Gygax was born on July 27, 1938 in Chicago, Illinois, where he grew up. (In some credits his name appears as E. Gary Gygax.) His father had immigrated to the U.S. from Switzerland or Germany, according to various sources; there is also disagreement about his mother's origins, some sources reporting that she was a native-born American and others that she was a German immigrant. Gygax began playing card games at age five and chess at age six. In his youth he enjoyed reading science-fiction and fantasy novels, including works by Jack Vance, Ray Bradbury, and Robert E. Howard. He has also named the fantasy writers L. Sprague DeCamp, Michael Moorcock, Roger Zelazny, H. P. Lovecraft, and Fritz Lieber among his major influences. According to a profile of him on the BBC Web site, he dropped out of high school and spent just over a year at the University of Minnesota.

In about 1966, while working as an insurance underwriter in Lake Geneva, Wisconsin, Gygax helped to set up the International Federation of Wargamers (IFW). In "wargaming," which began as a military training tool, possibly in early–19th-century Prussia, players use maps and figurines to enact battles, with outcomes decided by the rolling of dice. Members of the IFW met regularly in Gygax's and other members' houses. Before it disbanded, in 1974, the group had between 600 and 700 members, mostly in the U.S. Midwest. Many IFW members formed branches, to enable them to focus on games specific to their particular interests. Gygax, a medieval-history enthusiast, launched the Castle and Crusade Society; its members played Dark Ages–themed variants of war games, with rules linked to their figurines' possessions (horses or shields, for example). When Castle and Crusade players started to grow bored, Gygax and his friend Jeff Perrin added such features as wizards who had the power to throw fireballs. Those changes proved popular, and the game, called *Chainmail*, attracted many players, as well as the attention of Don Lowry, the owner of a mail-order business called Lowry's Hobbies. At about that time Lowry had launched a publishing imprint, Guidon Games, with the idea of offering a book series about wargaming with miniatures, and he recruited Gygax as an editor. In 1971 Guidon Games published Gygax and Perrin's manual *Chainmail: Rules for Medieval Miniatures*. That same year Guidon published rules for a naval simulation called *Don't Give Up the Ship!*, developed by Gygax and Dave Arneson, an IFW member whom Gygax had met at the 1970 GenCon gathering. Gygax had organized the first GenCon—or Geneva Convention, as it is formally known—in 1968; held at his home in Lake Geneva, it attracted about 100 gamers that year. The annual GenCon is currently among the world's major role-playing-game forums. Its conclaves take place at sites in Anaheim, California; Indianapolis, Indiana; Barcelona, Spain; Paris, France; and the United Kingdom. About 25,000 people attended the Indianapolis convention in 2006.

At GenCon 1971 Arneson introduced a gaming scenario in which each figurine represented one person rather than the traditional 20. According to Rausch in a five-part history of *Dungeons & Dragons* for PC.GameSpy.com (August 16–20, 2004), "While there had always been an element of 'role-playing' in wargames, the feeling of really 'being' a medieval warrior in Arneson's game was almost unprecedented." Encouraged by the enthusiastic response of gamers, Arneson and Gygax created additional fantasy scenarios, while adhering to the original *Chainmail* rulebook. Greyhawk, a mystical world of Gygax's invention, would endure as the setting for *Dungeons & Dragons*. Over the next two or three years, both Gygax and Arneson made further adjustments to what came to be known as the Fantasy Game. Arneson abandoned the *Chainmail* guidelines and introduced more elaborate settings, such as underground sites with dragons and treasures, while Gygax drew up new rules for the game, borrowing thematic elements wholesale from fantasy writers; among them was the Vancian magic system (named for Jack Vance), also known as "fire and forget," in which, as Gygax explained to Rausch, "the energy you draw when you memorize the spell energizes your brain. When you speak the words, the energy drains from your mind." Gygax also started using a 20-sided die (the Platonic solid known as an icosahedron), which he had seen advertised in a school-supply catalog. One day, while listening to him and Arneson speaking about dragons while they were occupied in Gygax's basement, Gygax's wife suggested that they call their game *Dungeons & Dragons*.

In 1973, after trying unsuccessfully to interest publishers in *Dungeons & Dragons* (among them Avalon Hill, which produced many war games and board games and rejected *Dungeons & Dragons* on the grounds that there was no clear way for players to win), Gygax and a longtime friend of his, Don Kaye, decided to publish the game themselves. With that end in mind, they formed the company Tactical Studies Rules (TSR, named after another gaming group Gygax had co-founded, with Kaye, Mike Reese and Leon Tucke—the Lake Geneva Tactical Studies Associaton). Another game enthusiast, Brian Blume, contributed most of the company's start-up funds. In January 1974 TSR placed *Dungeons & Dragons* on the market, and within 10 months, 1,000 copies had been purchased—a large number by wargaming-industry standards. The next thousand copies sold out in three months. In the next few years, spurred largely by word of mouth, nationwide sales steadily increased. Gygax would get phone calls, sometimes in the middle of the night, from players who had questions about rules. "*Dungeons & Dragons* was exposing thousands of people to the joys of gaming, fantasy, [and] history, and was creating new social networks around the hobby shops that sold the products," Rausch wrote. In 1977 TSR published a second version of *Dungeons & Dragons*, with far more complex rules; it became known as *Advanced Dungeons & Dragons*. During an interview with Harvey Smith for *Game Developer* (November 2002), Gygax said, "I do not, and I stress not, believe that the RPG [role-playing game] is 'storytelling' in the way that is usually presented. If there is a story to be told, it comes from the interaction of all partici-

pants, not merely the Game Master—who should not be a storyteller, but a narrator and co-player. The players are not acting out roles designed for them by the GM, they are acting in character to create the story, and the tale is told as the game unfolds, and as directed by their actions, with random factors that even the GM can't predict altering the course of things. Storytelling is what novelists, screenwriters, and playwrights do. It has little or no connection to the RPG, which differs in all aspects from the entertainment forms such authors create for."

By 1978 *Dungeons & Dragons* had become extremely popular among college students and teenagers. One day during the next year, James Dallas Egbert, a troubled Michigan State University student, disappeared in the steam tunnels under the school's campus. A rumor began circulating that just before he vanished, he had been playing *Dungeons & Dragons*. Egbert's disappearance triggered a wave of negative publicity surrounding *Dungeons & Dragons*. (In truth, Egbert had entered the tunnels determined to commit suicide. When his attempt failed, he hid at a friend's home for a month. He later left Michigan and in 1980 died of a self-inflicted gunshot wound.) In 1981, three years before the truth about Egbert's fate became public, Rona Jaffe published a roman à clef, called *Mazes and Monsters*, about the Egbert case; a cautionary novel about the supposed evils of RPGs, *Mazes and Monsters* was made into a television film starring Tom Hanks in 1981. During the next few years, Christian fundamentalist groups and coalitions of parents across the U.S. blamed the suicides of several teenagers on the alleged destructive effects of *Dungeons & Dragons*. Some condemned *Dungeons & Dragons* as having harmful spiritual and psychological effects and for promoting satanism, witchcraft, and other objectionable beliefs and practices. In Connecticut, for example, a spokesman for a group calling itself the Christian Information Council charged, "Playing these games can desensitize players to murder, suicide, rape, torture, robbery, the occult or any other immoral or illegal act," as quoted by James Brooke in the *New York Times* (August 22, 1985). Many reporters in the print and broadcast media presented stories concerning *Dungeons & Dragons* and its critics in a sensationalistic manner and likened players of the game to followers of a cult. In the opinions of many *Dungeons & Dragons* aficionados, Ed Bradley egregiously emulated such journalists when he interviewed Gygax for the CBS-TV news magazine *60 Minutes* in the mid-1980s. Gygax told Rausch, "In many ways I still resent the wretched yellow journalism that was clearly evident in [the media's] treatment of the game—*60 Minutes* in particular. I've never watched that show after Ed Bradley's interview with me because they rearranged my answers. When I sent some copies of letters from mothers of those two children who had committed suicide who said the game had nothing to do with it, they refused to do a retraction or even mention it on air." Gygax told Rausch that he had received deaths threats over the phone and in the mail. "I was a little nervous. I had a bodyguard for a while," he said. Although many observers noted that passionate *Dungeons & Dragons* players often immersed themselves thoroughly in the worlds created during games, no scientific studies ever found evidence of a link between *Dungeons & Dragons* and suicide or any other seriously antisocial behaviors. Ironically, the controversy surrounding the game helped greatly to boost its sales. In 1981 TSR, which then employed some 300 people, boasted gross earnings of $16.5 million, with $4.25 million in profits. In addition to glossy *Dungeons & Dragons* manuals, merchandise included beach balls, toys, and a book series launched as part of a campaign to educate parents and teachers about the game as a means of strengthening reading, mathematical, social, and imaginative skills.

Meanwhile, despite its success, TSR was beset by internal woes: Arneson left the company after a falling-out with Gygax over credit for the game's creation (a dispute that was settled out of court), and after Kaye's death, in 1975, contractual disputes with Kaye's wife forced Gygax to incorporate and rename the company TSR Hobbies Inc. In doing so Gygax—who, according to most accounts, lacked business savvy—overextended himself financially, and he could afford to retain only a minority share of TSR Hobbies. Brian Blume and Kevin Blume (variously identified as Brian's brother or father) gained majority control, with Brian as chief executive officer (CEO), and Gygax had limited say in the company's direction. In 1982, when the Blumes suggested that he develop *Dungeons & Dragons* products for television and film, Gygax moved to California; there, he set up a new company, called Dungeons & Dragons Entertainment, with himself as president but with the Blumes in control. "It took a long time and a lot of hard work to get to be recognized [on the West Coast] as someone who was for real and not just a civilian, shall we say, in entertainment," he recalled to Rausch. His efforts bore fruit when he negotiated with CBS the licensing of a *Dungeons & Dragons* cartoon spin-off. Co-produced by Marvel Productions and TSR, the *Dungeons & Dragons* cartoon series aired for three seasons beginning in 1983. According to Edward Power, writing for the *Irish Times* (December 16, 2000), "Despite its twee execution, the show exuded an otherworldliness approaching the haunting grandeur of Gygax's original vision."

While Gygax was in California, TSR's financial health deteriorated. Large sums were spent on company cars and frivolous office items, and according to Rausch, "nepotism under the Blumes' administration was rampant, with estimates that at least 90 relatives of the family had somehow ended up on the company payroll." When Gygax returned to Lake Geneva, as he told Rausch, "the bank was foreclosing and we were a million and a half [dollars] in debt." Gygax advised TSR's board of direc-

tors to remove Brian Blume as CEO, among other measures. His recommendations proved effective, but, not surprisingly, they angered the Blume family. In response, the Blumes then sold their shares in TSR to Lorraine Williams, a TSR board member who had inherited the rights to the *Buck Rogers* franchise. Gygax had little faith in Williams's potential as a manager for TSR (her disdain for TSR's audience of gamers had been widely noted), and he tried in vain, through legal means, to prevent her from gaining control of the company. At the end of 1985, he sold his remaining interest in TSR. (In 1997, with TSR deep in debt, Williams sold the company to the games publisher Wizards of the Coast.)

The year 1985 also saw the publication of *Saga of Old City*, the first of Gygax's two Greyhawk novels to bear the TSR imprint; the second, *Artifact of Evil*, followed a year later. The main character in both novels is Gord the Rogue, whose further adventures Gygax described in five additional novels, published in 1987 and 1988 by New Infinities Productions. In the early 1990s, after several years' preparation, Gygax and Dave Newton published the first installment of a new role-playing game, *Dangerous Journeys*, which came with an extremely complicated set of rules. Charging that the game bore too close a resemblance to *Dungeons & Dragons*, TSR sued Gygax for copyright infringement. Although Gygax contended that the accusation lacked merit, he agreed to settle the case by selling the rights to *Dangerous Journeys* to TSR, which agreed to pay his legal costs. His next role-playing game, created partly in collaboration with Chris Clark, is *Lejendary Adventures*. "Rules light and skill-bundle based," as Gygax described it to Rausch, the series was launched in 1999, with *Lejendary Rules for All Players*. As of early 2007, the series included two additional rule books, three "world setting" or "campaign world" source books, half a dozen adventure scenarios, and several boxed sets with "expansions." Gygax's publications also include *Role-Playing Mastery* (1987) and the reference manuals in his series Gygaxian Fantasy Worlds, which he described to Rausch as "generic books on how to construct a fantasy world"; the five volumes published since 2003 include *Gary Gygax's Nation Builder* and *Gary Gygax's Extraordinary Book of Names*.

Gygax had no direct involvement with the production of the film *Dungeons & Dragons* (2001), which was widely panned. In 2006 he lent his voice to Dungeons & Dragons Online, produced by Turbine Inc. Designed to replicate "that classic, sitting-around-the-kitchen-table Dungeons & Dragons experience," as Turbine's head, Jeff Anderson, told Seth Schiesel for the *New York Times* (February 27, 2006), that on-line game allows players to speak to one another via microphones on their computers, and a 20-sided die is displayed on screen. Contrasting the traditional Dungeons & Dragons with the Internet version, Gygax said to Schiesel, "The analogy I make is that pen-and-paper role-playing is live theater and computer games are television. People want the convenience and instant gratification of turning on the TV rather than . . . going out to see a live play. In some way, the computer is a more immediately accessible way to play games."

After he suffered a minor stroke and heart attack in 2004, Gygax quit his 50-year smoking habit and cut down on his workload. In 2006 he revealed on dragonsfoot.org that he had an inoperable, potentially fatal abdominal aortic aneurysm. (As of late 2007 he had provided no further information about the state of his health.) His first marriage, which ended in divorce, produced two sons and three daughters (Ernest Jr., Mary Elise, Heidi Jo, Cindy Lee, and Lucion Paul). A grandfather of seven, Gygax lives in Lake Geneva with his second wife, the former Gail Carpenter, whom he married in 1987;

the couple have one son, Alexander Hugh Hamilton. Gygax's personal library holds thousands of books (both fiction and nonfiction), magazines, and maps. His leisure activities include reading and fishing.

—M.B.

Suggested Reading: BBC Web site Feb. 25, 2002; GameSpy PC Web site, Aug. 16–20, 2004; *New York Times* E p1+, Feb. 27, 2006

Selected Gaming Manuals: *Chainmail*, 1971; *Dungeons & Dragons*, 1974; *Advanced Dungeons & Dragons Players Handbook*, 1977; *Dangerous Journeys*, 1992; *Lejendary Adventures*, 1999

Selected Fantasy Novels: *Saga of Old City*, 1985; *Artifact of Evil*, 1986; *Sea of Death*, 1987

Eric Richmond, courtesy of Angela Hewitt

Hewitt, Angela

July 26, 1958– Classical pianist

Address: c/o Seldy Cramer Artists, 3436 Springhill Rd., LaFayette, CA 94549

"What draws the listener to Angela Hewitt . . . has to do with contact," the music critic Bernard Holland wrote in a review of a concert by the pianist for the *New York Times* (February 17, 2007). "Most piano performances arrive in translation: the inner musician making a decision, then issuing a command that makes its way through the body onto the keyboard and into the ear. The process alters the

results. Ms. Hewitt is one of those rare musicians who seem to get something into their heads and hearts and find it at their fingertips instantaneously. To fuel this leap must require a fund of psychic energy beyond the average capacity. Good musicians are good athletes, not in the muscular sense but in the staying power of their imaginations. This pianist's resolve to imbue every musical moment with an unrelenting sense of theater would exhaust most of us in 10 minutes." A child prodigy, the Canadian-born Hewitt made her orchestral debut with the Ottawa Civic Symphony at the age of 10, in 1968. She captured the top prize in eight international piano competitions, the first when she was 17; the last, at the International Bach Piano Competition, in Toronto in 1985, earned her the opportunity to make her first recording, for Deutsche Grammophon. She made her New York City debut in 1984, at Alice Tully Hall, and her London, England, debut the next year, at Wigmore Hall. She has since performed in many other prestigious concert halls, both in solo recitals and alongside many highly regarded orchestras, among them the Japan, Cleveland, and BBC Philharmonic Orchestras and the Montreal, Toronto, Vancouver, Bournemouth, Philadelphia, San Francisco, and Baltimore Symphony Orchestras. She has toured extensively worldwide, in North America, Europe, the Middle East, Asia, and Australia; as a member of a six-member pianists' collective called Piano Six, she has also given many recitals in remote areas of Canada, for schoolchildren and others who had seldom if ever heard classical music. Currently, she maintains a schedule of about 100 concert dates each year. A recital of hers in London in 2003 inspired the music critic Paul Driver to write for the London *Sunday Times* (September 21, 2003) that Hewitt "is one of the reliably mesmerising musicians of the day. . . . She seems to me the complete performer, gifted not only with fingers that imprint each note with a svelte newness and a mind that is not deflected by such precision work from calmly surmising the larger structure, but also with the ability to convey a spiritual seriousness that nonetheless does not exclude an utter charm."

Hewitt's repertoire includes several hundred solo piano pieces and works for piano and orchestra—many hundreds of pages of music that she has memorized. They include music by composers from the Baroque period, which extended from the last decades of the 16th century to the middle of the 18th (among them François Couperin, Domenico Scarlatti, Jean-Philippe Rameau, and George Frideric Handel); the latter half of the 18th century and the 19th (among them Haydn, Mozart, Beethoven, Schubert, Schumann, Chopin, Brahms, Grieg, Mendelssohn, Liszt, Mussorgsky, and Chabrier); and the 20th century (among them de Falla, Ravel, Prokofiev, Rachmaninoff, Honegger, Barber, Copland, and Messiaen, and six contemporary Canadian composers who wrote works especially for her). In the classical-music world, she is widely considered the foremost living interpreter of the works of Bach. In a project that began in 1994 and continued for 11 years, she recorded, on 18 CDs, all of Bach's major keyboard compositions, among them the Well-Tempered Clavier (Books I and II), the Goldberg Variations, the Two- and Three-Part Inventions, the Partitas, the French Suites, the English Suites, the Toccatas, the Italian Concerto, the Keyboard Concertos, the Brandenburg Concerto no. 5, and the Triple Concerto in A minor; a scholar of music as well, she wrote the liner notes for all of those CDs (as well as her other albums). "This series is one of the record glories of our age," a London Sunday Times (January 21, 2001) reviewer enthused, after writing that "Hewitt's playing radiates joy, wit and profound understanding of the composer's keyboard style." Hewitt has also recorded all the solo piano music of Ravel and all of Chopin's nocturnes as well as albums devoted to music by Couperin, Beethoven, Messiaen, Chabrier, and Granados. "I like playing a wide variety of stuff," she told Richard Todd for the Ottawa Citizen (November 28, 1996), "but, to tell the truth, when I'm playing Bach, and that's the hardest to do well, I ask myself, 'Why do I ever play anything else when I could be playing this?'"

In 2006 Hewitt was named the Artist of the Year by Gramophone magazine. Each of her two albums of Bach's Keyboard Concertos (2005) was named the Recording of the Month by Gramophone; others among her recordings were named the Gramophone Editor's Choice, including the disc containing three Beethoven sonatas (2006), or Gramophone Critics' Choice, among them her rendering of Bach's Well-Tempered Clavier, Book I (1998). That recording was also named the BBC Music Magazine Best Album of the Year and won a 1999 Juno Award (equivalent to a Grammy) as best classical album, from the Canadian Academy of Recording Arts and Sciences. Hewitt won another Juno Award in 2002, for her album of Bach arrangements—transcriptions of works that Bach wrote for

other instruments, orchestra, or voice. Hewitt was named an Officer of the Order of Canada in 2000 and received the first annual BBC Radio 3 Listeners' Award/Royal Philharmonic Society Award in 2003. In a ceremony at Buckingham Palace, in London, on March 1, 2007, Queen Elizabeth II presented her with the Order of the British Empire.

The second of the two children and only daughter of Geoffrey and Marion Hewitt, Angela Hewitt was born on July 26, 1958 in Ottawa, Ontario, Canada. Her father, a native of England, gained some renown as the organist and choirmaster at the Christ Church Cathedral in Ottawa from 1931 to 1980; her mother was a high-school teacher of English and music. "My mother used to tie me into my playpen and I'd spend hours undoing the knots," Hewitt told Geoffrey Norris for the London Daily Telegraph (November 3, 2003), after noting that she has "always liked to unravel complicated things." Her parents played a vital role in shaping her musical development. On Sundays beginning early in her childhood, Hewitt would listen to her father play the organ in church. He "always performed Bach with great colour and drama, and the right sense of timing . . . ," as she recalled to Linda Scales for the University of Ottawa magazine Tabaret (Fall 2005, on-line). "My father was a perfectionist and I think he passed that onto me." As a toddler Hewitt played a toy piano; when she was three she began to study piano and classical ballet. "I was always responding to music by dancing around the room," she told Geoffrey Norris. Her pianistic gifts were apparent immediately. "My mother saw that I easily picked out tunes on the piano and had a really good ear," Hewitt told a writer for the Toronto Star (April 11, 2002). Her parents, who were her first music teachers, introduced her to the keyboard compositions of Bach "right away," as she told Norris. "Bach is the basis of all technique . . . ," she told Arthur Kaptainis for the Montreal Gazette (March 11, 1998). "For fingering, for articulation, for phrasing, for the acquisition of a beautiful singing tone." Hewitt was strongly influenced by the idiosyncratic recordings of the Canadian pianist Glenn Gould (1932–82), whose prodigious technique and many personal eccentricities were legendary. When she listened to Gould's radical interpretations of Bach's Inventions and other pieces, as she recalled to Norris, she would think, "That piece should surely go slowly. Why's he playing it so fast?" or "That piece is obviously a fast one. Why's he playing it so slowly?" "I knew from the beginning that there was something a bit strange in his character that meant that we could listen to him but would never imitate him," she said. During her youth Hewitt also took violin lessons (for 10 years), played the recorder, and sang in her father's choir.

Hewitt gave her first public performance at age four, at the Christ Church Cathedral. At five she won her first piano competition, in Rimouski, Quebec. The next year she won a scholarship to the Royal Conservatory of Music in Toronto, where she studied for nine years. She made her first appearance with an orchestra—the Ottawa Civic Symphony (now the Ottawa Symphony)—in 1968. At 15 Hewitt entered the University of Ottawa as a "special student." Her piano teacher there was Jean-Paul Sevilla, whom she described to Linda Scales as "fabulous from the first lesson. I never met anyone who taught like him. He just gave it his all; such joie de vivre!" Under Sevilla's tutelage Hewitt expanded her musical repertoire, studying, in addition to compositions by Bach, pieces by the 19th–20th-century French composers Paul Dukas, Maurice Ravel, and Olivier Messiaen. Sevilla taught her "more than just the piano," she said to Bob Clark for the *Calgary Herald* (February 9, 2002). "During his summer courses at Aix-en-Provence [in France] we'd have lessons every day, go to all the concerts and then go to the beach on weekends. So he made us enjoy life, too." In 1975 she won a top prize in a Bach competition held in Washington, D.C., and the Chopin Young Pianists' Competition, held in Buffalo, New York; she took the first prize in a Bach competition held in Leipzig, in what was then East Germany, in 1976, and a Schumann competition, in Zwickau, also in East Germany, in 1977. That year, at age 18, Hewitt graduated from the University of Ottawa with a bachelor's degree in music. The following year she moved to Paris, France. Also in 1978 she was victorious in the piano category in the Gian Battista Viotti Competition, in Italy, and in the piano competition of the CBC Talent Festival; in 1979 and 1980 she captured first prize at the Casadesus piano competition in Cleveland, Ohio, and the Dino Ciani Competition held at La Scala, in Milan, Italy, respectively. At around that time, having decided to focus on solo piano performance, she regretfully gave up her ballet training. Her ballet studies, she told a writer for the *Toronto Star* (April 11, 2002), had helped her to become disciplined. In addition, as a dancer, she said, "you learned stage presence and it even helps with how to play the piano, using your whole body rather than playing from the shoulders."

At her New York City debut, in 1984 at Alice Tully Hall, Hewitt played Ravel's *Tombeau de Couperin*, Bach's Toccata in C minor, Brahms's Piano Sonata no. 3, and, in a world premiere, Fantasia on a Theme of Robert Schumann, by the Canadian composer Steven Gellman. In 1985 she achieved a professional breakthrough, by winning the first prize at the International Bach Piano Competition, in Toronto, in a contest against 32 other pianists, whittled down from 166 applicants. (Olivier Messiaen was among the judges, and Hewitt played one of his pieces during the competition.) Hewitt's performance earned her a recording contract with the Deutsche Grammophon label and 20 concert engagements in Canada and Europe. Also in 1985 Hewitt moved to London and made her debut in that city, at Wigmore Hall. Her first recording, for Deutsche Grammophon, which went on sale in 1986, offered renditions of Bach's

Italian Concerto in F major, Toccata in C minor, Four Duets (two-part inventions), and the English Suite no. 6 in D minor. Though it was well received, Deutsche Grammophon executives decided that Bach piano recordings would never sell well, and Hewitt's album remained her only recording until the early 1990s, when, after years of concertizing worldwide, Hewitt devised an ambitious undertaking: to record all of Bach's major works written for keyboard. The existence of highly regarded recordings of the same music made earlier by two famous interpreters of Bach—Gould and the American pianist Rosalyn Tureck—did not give her pause. "I thought there was room for another . . . ," she told Bob Clark for the *Calgary Herald* (February 9, 2002). "I'm very different from both [Tureck and Gould]. I just felt I had my own way and that people were eager to hear it." For Hewitt, the primary challenge that the project presented lay in the preparation rather than the recording process itself. "Playing, for example, his preludes and fugues, you've got four or five voices going at once, each of which has to be as clearly defined as the other and perfectly balanced," she told David Prince for the *Santa Fe New Mexican* (September 23, 2005). "Also, there is the musical knowledge you need to play Bach because, of course, in his time, nothing was written in the score. . . . You have the odd indication of tempo but hardly at all in all of his keyboard output. You have to know what the dances of the time were like, their characteristics, so as to play and apply those to the music. And often it's not written that such-and-such dance is a minuet or a gigue or a bourrée—you have to recognize it just from the music." Commenting on the technical complexity of Bach's music, she said, "From memory, it's the hardest music you can play. You put one finger wrong and you're off, and it's very hard to improvise a Bach fugue. It takes enormous concentration. It takes a lot of preparation before you can even play it the way you can sort of muff your way through a Beethoven sonata. In Bach, there's no place to hide." After an extensive search for the most suitable instrument, Hewitt and her producer, Otto Ernst Wohlert, chose a Steinway piano on which the great 20th-century German pianist Wilhelm Kempff made many recordings.

"Bach wrote most of his music for pedagogical purposes, and there is a progression to be followed if you want to understand them correctly," Hewitt wrote in an article for the *Ottawa Citizen* (September 6, 2004). She began her recording project with the Fantasia in C Minor and Two-Part Inventions (1994). Next came Six Partitas (1997); The Well-Tempered Clavier, Book I (1998) and Book II (1999); and 48 preludes and fugues—"the Everest of the piano repertoire," in Hewitt's words. During five days in 2000, the year that marked the 250th anniversary of Bach's death, Hewitt recorded his Goldberg Variations at the Henry Wood Hall, in London, a famous rehearsal and recording studio, in what she judged to be "the best performance I had given in 24 years," as she wrote for the *Ottawa Citizen*. Hewitt completed her Bach project in 2005. Bearing the Hyperion label, the Bach cycle was universally hailed by classical-music aficionados and critics. Richard Todd, writing for the *Ottawa Citizen* (October 7, 2003), called it one of the most "distinguished achievements in the history of recording." According to Vivien Schweitzer, writing for the *New York Times* (February 14, 2007), "The greatest compliment for Ms. Hewitt came from her father, who after listening to one of her recordings, said, 'I didn't hear you. I only heard Bach.'"

Hewitt's recent albums include a 2002 two-disc recording of solo piano compositions by Ravel, whose music she has described as "dance inspired," according to Steve Mazey in the *Ottawa Citizen* (April 27, 2002); a 2005 album containing Chopin's 21 nocturnes and four impromptus; three volumes (2003–05) of Couperin's piano pieces; and a disc (2006) with 18 of Chabrier's 26 solo piano pieces. Her renditions of Bach's three sonatas for viola de gamba, recorded with the cellist Daniel Mueller-Schott and released in 2007, was named *Gramophone*'s Editor's Choice in October of that year.

After Hewitt repeatedly noticed, while giving master classes, that "students (and their teachers) often seem to have so little idea how to study Bach," as Vivien Schweitzer reported, Hewitt made a DVD in which she talked about and demonstrated her approach to Bach's keyboard music, stressing, as Schweitzer wrote, "that you must adhere to period conventions." The DVD arrived in stores in September 2007. That month Hewitt embarked on an international tour, during which she performed the Well-Tempered Clavier in its entirety at venues including the Royal Festival Hall, in London, and Carnegie Hall, in New York City.

In addition to her other honors, Hewitt was named Artist of the Year by the Canadian Music Council in 1986, and she received the National Arts Centre Award from the Governor General of Canada in 2000. Hewitt maintains homes in Ottawa, London, and near the city of Perugia, in Umbria, Italy, in a house that overlooks Lake Trasimeno. In July 2005 Hewitt, who is fluent in Italian, launched the Trasimeno Music Festival, an annual, weeklong event in Italy, in which she and guest musicians perform alone, in chamber ensembles, or with an orchestra assembled just for the festival. "Of course, I am international," Hewitt told Arthur Kaptainis for the Montreal *Gazette* (March 11, 1998). "Especially considering where I live and how much I travel. But deep down, I am Canadian."

—D.J.K.

Suggested Reading: Angela Hewitt's Web site; *Birmingham Post* p13 Jan. 24, 2001; *Calgary Herald* Arts and Style p8 Feb. 9, 2002; *Canadian Encyclopedia* (on-line); Hyperion Records Web site; (London) *Daily Telegraph* p17 Nov. 3, 2003;

Ottawa Citizen C p7 Nov. 28, 1996, C p1+ Sep. 6, 2004; *Santa Fe New Mexican* Pasatiempo p44 May 11, 2001, p32 Sep. 23, 2005; (University of Ottawa) *Tabaret* (on-line) Fall 2005; *Weekend Australian* B p16 Feb. 26, 2005

Selected Recordings: Bach: Fantasia in C minor; Two-Part Inventions; Three-Part Inventions; Chromatic Fantasia & Fugue, 1994; Bach: The Six Partitas, 1997; Bach: The Well-Tempered Clavier, Book I, 1998; Bach: The Well-Tempered Clavier, Book II, 1999; Bach: The Keyboard Concertos I, 2005; Bach: The Keyboard Concertos II, 2005; Bach Gamba Sonatas (with Daniel Mueller-Schott), 2007

Frederick M. Brown/Getty Images

Hickey, Dave

Dec. 5, 1940– Cultural critic; educator; writer; curator of exhibitions

Address: UNLV English Dept., Box 455011, Las Vegas, NV 89154-5011

"I know how to look and I remember what I see," the cultural critic Dave Hickey wrote in 2000 for the Web site of the arts organization SITE Santa Fe, whose 2001 biennial exhibition he organized. "I have seen a lot of art and my enthusiasms are catholic. . . . I believe that one's aim, when working as a curator in a public space, is to *create* art lovers, not to impress one's fellow professionals with expertise." Labeled "the philosopher king of American art criticism" by the *New Yorker* art critic Peter Schjeldahl, Hickey is among the most revered and influential figures in that field—and also one of the most outspoken and controversial. Hickey has advised museumgoers, for instance, to look attentively at paintings or sculptures but to ignore the little signs posted next to them, because he believes that information about what the artists felt or intended during the act of creation, or what others believe is the "meaning" of their work, is immaterial. "I care about what the art *does*," he told Michael Hall for *Texas Monthly* (February 2000). "I'm interested in consequences." In an interview for *Art Press* (June 2000), Hickey told Eleanor Heartney, "Public museums in my view should provide citizens with a refuge from commerce, fashion, relevance, and education." In another example of his unorthodox views, he said to Hall, "There's no difference between the highest art and the lowest art, except for the audience it appeals to."

Hickey has taught graduate courses in creative writing at the University of Nevada at Las Vegas (UNLV) since 2001; currently, he is the Schaeffer Professor of Modern Letters there. During the preceding decade, he was a professor of art theory and criticism at UNLV. Earlier, after he dropped out of graduate school, in the 1960s, midway through his work toward a doctoral degree, he held a series of nonteaching jobs, among them art-gallery manager, magazine editor, freelance writer, songwriter, and performer. Articles by Hickey have appeared in many publications, among them *Art News*, *Art in America*, *ArtForum*, *Interview*, *Harper's Magazine*, *Vanity Fair*, *Rolling Stone*, the *New York Times*, and the *Los Angeles Times*. His book *The Invisible Dragon: Four Essays on Beauty* (1993) catalyzed "the much heralded 'return' to beauty in art making and art criticism," as Grant H. Kester wrote for *Art Journal* (Spring 1997); his second nonfiction collection, *Air Guitar: Essays on Art and Democracy* (1997), was described by Deborah Solomon, writing for the *New York Times Magazine* (January 24, 1999), as "an elegant, lushly personal volume that gives equal attention to Renaissance portraits and female professional wrestling." "It's a breath of smoke-filled air," Solomon continued. "Instead of issuing lofty judgments, Hickey gives over to a nostalgic affection for the whole messy, pell-mell lot that is American culture, from the lyrics of Johnny Mercer songs to the television lawyer Perry Mason to—of course—Norman Rockwell, whose work, Hickey writes, shares with the fiction of Charles Dickens 'a luminous devotion to the possibility of domestic kindness and social accord.'"

In 2001 the MacArthur Foundation awarded Hickey one of its $500,000 fellowships, commonly referred to as "genius" grants. Hickey, the foundation declared on its Web site at the time, "reveals entirely original perspectives on contemporary art in essays that engage academic and general audiences equally. He conveys his interpretations and analyses, based on an encyclopedic knowledge of art history, through commonly shared experiences and metaphors. The accessibility of his writing in no way diminishes his intellectual influence;

scholars have formally debated the merits of his sometimes quite contrarian arguments. His free-spirited and occasionally irreverent musings reflect his passion for the wonders of artistic expression and his disdain for those who obscure it. . . . Writing with grace, precision, and humor, and absent of any pretension, Hickey invites his readers to experience art on its own terms. . . . His wisdom and unusual viewpoints provide fresh and provocative counterpoints to the traditional world of art criticism."

David C. Hickey was born on December 5, 1940 in Fort Worth, Texas, and grew up in a dozen places in Texas and California. His mother, who reportedly had Marxist leanings, taught economics at Texas Christian University, in Fort Worth, and ran the family's flower shop. As quoted by Jed Perl in the New *Republic* (September 24, 2001), Hickey has described his mother as "serious, high-strung, and fiercely ironic, like [the actress] Joan Crawford, always bustling around: painting bad paintings in the back bedroom and reading books while she cooked dinner." His father worked for General Motors—his job involved setting up distribution warehouses—and, avocationally, played jazz saxophone and clarinet. As an eight-year-old, Hickey witnessed a "Texas jam session that included his father, his father's redneck buddy, a Latino bongo player, two black beboppers, and a Jewish neighbor who had fled the Nazis," as Michael Hall wrote for *Texas Monthly* (February 2000). "I kept that musical afternoon as a talisman of memory," Hickey recalled in *Air Guitar*. "I handled it carefully, so as not to knock the edges off, keeping it as plain and unembellished as I could, so I could test the world against it, because it was the best, concrete emblem I had of America as a successful society and remains so." When Hickey was 11 his father committed suicide.

After he completed high school, at 15, Hickey entered Southern Methodist University (SMU), in Dallas, Texas, where he studied engineering. He changed his major to English when, after three years at SMU, he transferred to Texas Christian University. His extracurricular activities included writing short stories and editing articles for the campus literary and humor magazines. He earned a B.A. degree in 1961. In 1963 he earned a master's degree in linguistics from the University of Texas at Austin. He remained in graduate school to pursue a doctorate until he realized that the "optimal positive outcome" of his getting a Ph.D. degree—"a little job at a big university in a place where it snows—and a six-year battle for tenure," as he wrote in an essay in *Air Guitar*—held no appeal for him. "What I was doing was telling myself that I was a serious graduate student and what I was really doing was not being drafted," he recalled to Todd S. Purdum for the *New York Times* (September 4, 1999). "The day that I turned 26 and was ineligible for the draft, I was totally amazed at the way my enthusiasm for an academic career seemed to dissolve." By that time Hickey had married and become friendly with several local artists.

Earlier, in 1964, Hickey had visited Europe and New York City, where his interest in painting strengthened through his exposure to the work of artists including Andy Warhol, Edward Ruscha, and Roy Lichtenstein. In 1967, with a loan of $10,000, he and his first wife, Mary Jane Taylor, rented the ground floor of an old private house in Austin and converted it into an art gallery. Calling it a Clean, Well-Lighted Place (the title of a short story by Ernest Hemingway), Hickey and his wife opened the gallery with an exhibition of works by the cartoonist Jim Franklin. In time Hickey promoted the work of many other area artists at his gallery—Barry Buxkamper, George Green, Luis Jimenez, Peter Plagens, Juergan Strunck, Willard Midgett, and, after moving the gallery to another site, in 1969, Harry Geffert, Jim Schinder, and Richard Mock, to name some. According to Kendall Curlee, writing for the *Handbook of Texas Online*, the gallery "remained distinct from Austin's counterculture by advocating a pop sensibility reminiscent of Andy Warhol's Factory studio in New York City." In 1970 Hickey organized what Curlee described as "perhaps [his] most successful" exhibition in Austin; called South Texas Sweet Funk, it was mounted at St. Edward's University. While in Austin Hickey also wrote songs, played in rock bands, and experimented with drugs.

In 1971 Hickey moved with his wife to New York City, where he became the director of the Reese Palley Gallery, in the SoHo district. He soon started socializing with Andy Warhol and the artists and others who had gravitated toward Warhol. For one year Hickey worked as an editor for *Art in America*. Afterward, as a freelance writer, he wrote about rock and roll and country music for *Rolling Stone,* the *Village Voice,* and *Country Music*; he was among the writers who chronicled the burgeoning punk scene at the music club CBGB's, in New York City. In the late 1970s Hickey moved to Nashville, Tennessee, to work as a staff songwriter for Glaser Publications. Sometimes, he sang in public.

During the 1980s Hickey contributed essays to the book *Works of Edward Ruscha* (1982); two books about the artwork of Terry Allen—*Rooms and Stories* (1983) and *Terry Allen's "Ohio"* (1986); and *Pasadena Armory Show, 1989* (1989). His collection *Prior Convictions: Stories from the Sixties (Southwest Life and Letters)*, written in the 1960s, was published by Southern Methodist University Press in 1989. Hickey later wrote stories illustrated by John DeFazio for the 88-page graphic novel *Stardumb* (1999); published by Artspace Books, in San Francisco, the book pokes fun at real and imagined art-world figures.

In 1987, "faced with the unavailability of health insurance," as he wrote in *Air Guitar,* Hickey took the first of a series of teaching jobs at the college level. In 1992 he joined the faculty of the Art Department of the University of Nevada at Las Vegas, as a teacher of art criticism and theory. Prominent in his theory of art is his conviction that, in his words,

"Nothing redeems but beauty." As Michael Hall wrote, "While many modernists celebrate form and concept, Hickey seeks out the beautiful—and finds it where another finds banality (Norman Rockwell), phoniness (Liberace), or sordid pornography (Robert Mapplethorpe)." "I characterize visual beauty reflexively as the involuntary positive responses to an arrangement of the visible world," Hickey told Eleanor Heartney. "Visual beauty in art may be construed as an involuntary, positive response to an artificial stimulus. Every time we have such a response, we learn something about the extent to which our own idea of beauty dissents from the culture's idea of 'the beautiful.' Further, since the attribute of beauty elicits the involuntary approval of secular citizens, it may be construed as an instrument of real political power—all the more so since beautiful objects create constituencies around them and represent for us, not who we are, but what we want. In a free society, the question of what a constituency of citizens wants, what it lacks, is always in some sense political. Understanding this you will understand that I never intended to propose beauty as the end of art, but as its beginning—as the first condition of art's political independence and the primary occasion for writing about it."

Hickey's book *The Invisible Dragon: Four Essays on Beauty* was published by Art Issues Press/Foundation for Advanced Critical Studies in 1993. In its 64 pages of wide-ranging discussions about the nature and meaning of beauty in art in late-20th-century America, Hickey considered the artwork of Warhol, the photographer Robert Mapplethorpe, the illustrator Norman Rockwell, and the Italian painters Raphael and Caravaggio as well as the sonnets of Shakespeare; he also explored the ideas of other thinkers, among them theories of the French philosopher and historian Michel Foucault, which Hickey had chosen, along with ideas of another French philosopher, Jacques Derrida, as the subject of his never-completed Ph.D. dissertation. He argued against the prevailing view that art appreciation is inextricably linked with "sophistication, taste and learning—the property of the learned elite, the rich and famous," according to a writer for *Publishers Weekly* (1994, on-line), and he attacked public institutions—museums, universities, government agencies, and foundations, among others—"that in his eyes seek to turn art into a social good," as Christopher Knight wrote for *Art Journal* (Fall 1996). According to Eleanor Heartney, *The Invisible Dragon* won for Hickey "legions of followers and the disdain of more conventionally-minded readers." The book earned the College Art Association's 1994 Frank Jewett Mather Award for distinction in art criticism.

Air Guitar: Essays on Art and Democracy, published three years later, contains a mixture of narrative, memoir, and commentary. An examination of the effects of 20th-century highbrow and lowbrow art on the U.S., it ranges in subject matter from such musicians or music groups as Hank Williams, Chet Baker, and the Rolling Stones to the wrestler Lady Godiva, the TV series *Perry Mason*, Julius Erving's remarkable basket during the 1980 National Basketball Association Finals, and Las Vegas celebrities including Siegfried and Roy. "Obliged to theorize his impolite tastes, judgments, and ideas, Hickey lays his prejudices a little barer than altogether becomes them," the music journalist Robert Christgau wrote for the *Los Angeles Times Book Review* (October 17, 1997). "Even caught in that old trap, however, he's as good as it gets, starting with his prose. Although his diction is often highfalutin . . . , his rhythms aren't, and he's more than fluent in colloquial English—I mean, the guy can flat-out write." In a reference to the title of Hickey's collection, Margaret Juhae Lee, in a review for the *Nation* (December 1, 1997), wrote, "Hickey describes his chosen profession as 'the weakest thing you can do in writing. It is the written equivalent of air guitar—flurries of silent, sympathetic gestures with nothing at their heart but the memory of the music.' But however derivative criticism might be, Hickey creates music of his own with the style of a good short-fiction writer and the insights of a first-rate thinker. Like the 'cool economy and intellectual athletics' of Chet Baker's slightly off-key yet sensuous crooning, Hickey's musings point the way to 'a new ethos of living in the world.'" "What a treasure!" Sarah Vowell wrote for *Salon* (October 17, 1997, on-line). "The world is crammed with pages of cultural criticism that give us facts and thoughts and opinions and insights, but this book delivers love: love for the country, love for what its citizens can do."

Hickey has organized exhibitions for several museums and universities. In 2000 he accepted an invitation from the nonprofit arts organization SITE Santa Fe to curate its fourth biennial exhibition, which he named Beau Monde: Toward a Redeemed Cosmopolitanism. The exhibition ran for six months, beginning in mid-2001. In the blurb for the SITE Santa Fe Web site that he prepared before it opened, Hickey wrote, "I began the project without any preconceived notion of what a beau monde, or a 'beautiful world,' might be, only with a confirmed confidence that most artists have their own ideas about it—their own vision of how a beau monde might look—and that this vision is somehow embodied in their work. My task in mounting this exhibition will be to create" an environment "in which works of art from around the world, experienced in relation to one another, . . . will invest the elusive idea of a beau monde with new specificity and complexity, new meaning and resonance. The exhibition will come first, in other words. Meanings will arise as a consequence, since what I have in mind is not an ideological point that I wish to prove, but an exhibition that I want to *see*, and hope that others might, as well." His selections for the show, he continued, would be "singular works of art, which . . . celebrate the global field of overlapping and interfused idiomatic expression—the virtuoso accommodation of one cultural

idiom to another that constitutes the very definition of cosmopolitanism." The works, he wrote, would represent artists "from as many generations as possible, working in a variety of modern and postmodern styles . . . to reflect the actual circumstances of day-to-day contemporary art-making." The show revealed Hickey's "trademark passions," as Katy Siegel wrote in an article about the show for *ArtForum* (May 2001): "cool classics" (works by Ellsworth Kelly, Jo Baer, Bridget Riley, and Ed Ruscha, for example), "upbeat California color" (Ken Price and Jorge Pardo), "sex & drugs and rock 'n' roll" (Kenneth Anger, Jeff Burton, Stephen Prina), "and the just plain eccentric" (Darryl Montana). Beau Monde was widely praised and was named best show, alternative space, 2001–02, by the Association of International Critics of Art. By most accounts, the exhibit achieved what Hickey hoped it would. In a representative review, Deborah Rindge wrote for *Art Papers* (November/December 2001), "On the whole, 'Beau Monde' is a delightful dim sum. Unlike exhaustive biennials elsewhere, the viewer departs stimulated and refreshed, inspired to learn more and return again."

In September 2001 Hickey learned from the chairman of the UNLV Art Department that "the prevailing opinion in the department was that I 'would be happier' in another department or another school or another university," as he wrote in a letter to the *Chronicle of Higher Education* (April 26, 2003). (His letter was sent in response to an earlier article about the problems he and his second wife, the art historian Libby Lumpkin, who was also teaching at UNLV, were having there.) Soon afterward Hickey joined the UNLV English Department. On the department's Web site in mid-2007, his specialty was listed as creative writing, including fiction, intellectual journalism and cultural criticism, and nonfiction and the essay. In an interview for the *Las Vegas Sun* (September 28, 2007), Kristen Peterson asked Hickey if he was "sad about not teaching art." Hickey replied, "Damn right. At this time in my life, it is what I was born to do." Peterson's article also discussed the then-upcoming art show Las Vegas Diaspora: The Emergence of Contemporary Art from the Neon Homeland; organized by Hickey and held from September 30 to December 30, 2007 at the Las Vegas Art Museum, it featured works by two dozen artists who had studied with Hickey from 1990 to 2001. "What I wanted to prove [with the show] is that intellectual capital is real capital . . . ," Hickey told Peterson. "It pays off. That's why I'm doing this. If you take it seriously, people take it seriously. This is what the real thing looks like."

Hickey has been a visiting professor at other schools, among them the University of Texas at Austin; the Graduate School of Design at Harvard University; the University of California at Santa Barbara; and the Otis Parsons Institute, in Los Angeles. In the past decade he has written or co-written many monographs (some for exhibition catalogs) on contemporary artists, among them Peter Alexander, Terry Allen, Anthony Caro, Vija Celmins, Gajiin Fujita, Sol Lewitt, Helen Lundeberg, Lari Pittman, Robert Rauschenberg, Gerhard Richter, Susan Rothenberg, and Richard Serra; the fashion designer Todd Oldham; and the photographers Jeff Burton and Michael Childers. Hickey appeared in Ric Burns's four-hour documentary *Andy Warhol*, which aired on PBS television stations in 2006. According to the *Time Out NY* writer Tom Beer, as quoted on filmforum.org, his commentary was "virtuosic." Hickey's two-volume work *Feint of Heart: Essays on Individual Artists* is scheduled to be published in 2008 by the University of Chicago Press.

After attending a lecture by Hickey, Thomas McGovern wrote for *Afterimage* (November/December 2003) that Hickey's "slightly grumpy demeanor and ruffled appearance belie an infectious charm that easily overpowered the audience." Readily available sources do not indicate how his first marriage ended. Hickey and Libby

Lumpkin have lived in Las Vegas since the early 1990s. Lumpkin teaches at California State University at Long Beach and directs the Museum Studies Program there. She was the founding curator of the Bellagio Gallery of Fine Arts, in Las Vegas, and directs the Las Vegas Art Museum. She is the author of *Deep Design: Nine Little Art Histories* (1999).

—F.C.

Suggested Reading: *Art in America* p35 Nov. 1994, p122 Nov. 1, 2001; *Art Journal* p20+ Spring 1997; *Art Press* p45+ June 2000; *New York Times* (on-line) B p7 Sep. 4, 1999, II p31 July 8, 2001; *New Yorker* p82+ Aug. 13, 2001; *Salon* (on-line) Oct. 17, 1997; *Texas Monthly* p60+ Feb. 2000; Thirteen/WNET Online Pressroom

Selected Books: nonfiction—*The Invisible Dragon: Four Essays on Beauty*, 1993; *Air Guitar: Essays on Art and Democracy*, 1997; fiction—*Prior Convictions*, 1989; *Stardumb*, 1999

Higgins, Jack

Aug. 19, 1954– Editorial cartoonist

Address: Chicago Sun-Times, *350 N. Orleans, Chicago, IL 60654*

If one of Jack Higgins's editorial cartoons "offends [people] or makes them angry, it makes the cartoon memorable and it will make them think about it," as Higgins told Mike Moore for the *Quill* (June 1989). "As long as they remember it, I think I've had an impact on their thinking." Higgins's illustrated comments on and impressions of events and issues in Chicago, Illinois, his hometown, and elsewhere in the United States and beyond its borders have appeared since 1980 in the *Chicago Sun-Times*. His work, which skewers office-holders and -seekers from all parts of the political spectrum, is disseminated by Universal Press Syndicate to publications including *U.S. News & World Report*; the *Jewish World Review*; *Slate*; the *Washington Post* (on-line); *Buffalo (New York) News*; the *Modesto (California) Bee*; the *Indianapolis (Indiana) Business Journal*; the Glens Falls, New York, *Post-Star*; the Tokyo, Japan, *Seikei Jippon*; and the *Korea Herald*; it has also been reprinted in the *New York Times*, the *Washington Times*, *Newsweek*, *Salon.com*, and the *National Review*. "I can vent my anger through my drawings and have an effect where I can belittle the pompous guy by shrinking him to a size that makes him more manageable," Higgins has said, as quoted by Brenda Warner Rotzoll in the *Chicago Sun-Times* (April 14, 1999). But his favorites among his cartoons depict "good guys," according to Rotzoll, such as Joseph Cardinal Bernardin and the sportscaster Harry Caray,

Jim Frost, courtesy of Universal Press Syndicate

whom he memorialized after their deaths. Higgins's many honors include the 1989 Pulitzer Prize for editorial cartooning. In May 2007, in recognition of his work on the subject of political corruption, Higgins won top honors for editorial cartooning at the Herman Kogan Media Awards ceremony, hosted by the Chicago Bar Association.

A member of a large Irish-American, Roman Catholic family, John J. Higgins was born on August 19, 1954 in Chicago, to Maurice James Higgins and the former Helen Marie Egan. His maternal grandfather, John Egan, was Chicago's chief of detectives in the 1920s, during the Prohibition era; his father was a police captain in the same city. In an interview with Bob Herguth for the *Chicago Sun-Times* (September 15, 1996), Higgins described his mother (who is deceased) as "the artist in the family." He also told Herguth that his six siblings earned degrees from such prestigious schools as Harvard University, Cambridge University, the London School of Economics, the University of Virginia School of Law, and the University of Chicago Graduate School of Business; two of his brothers and sisters are scientists and another two are lawyers. Higgins, who remains a practicing Roman Catholic, attended St. Ignatius College Preparatory School, a Jesuit institution in Chicago that is known for its high academic standards; its mission includes "promot[ing] social justice for the greater glory of God," according to its Web site. After he graduated from high school, Higgins attended another Jesuit school—the College of the Holy Cross, in Worcester, Massachusetts. While on the staff of the campus literary magazine, he drew portraits of the former U.S. president John F. Kennedy; some of those drawings were later acquired for the permanent collection of the John F. Kennedy Presidential Library and Museum, in Boston. Higgins earned a B.A. degree in economics in 1976.

Higgins spent the next two years working with the Jesuit Volunteer Corps (JVC), whose members help people in need in the U.S. and overseas (among them, those who are homeless and unemployed, refugees, victims of AIDS, the elderly, abused women and children, and the mentally ill or physically handicapped). As explained on its Web site, the JVC emphasizes four values that "provide the cornerstone for living out a commitment to faith and justice": social justice, simple living, community, and spirituality. From 1978 to 1981 Higgins served as the editorial cartoonist for the *Daily Northwestern*, the campus newspaper of Northwestern University, in Evanston, Illinois. He was paid $5 for each of the four or five cartoons he produced weekly; he supplemented his income from the newspaper by bartending and loading trucks. The *Daily Northwestern* was where the journalist Bob Greene "first saw Higgins' cartoons, and was knocked out by them," as Greene wrote in a column for the *Chicago Tribune* (August 24, 1980). After describing Higgins as "already brilliant at what he does," Greene quoted from a letter in which Norman A. Cherniss, the executive editor of the Riverside, California, *Press-Enterprise*, told Higgins, "for whatever encouragement or consolation this may afford you," that although he had not won the award for editorial cartoonist that year, his cartoons were among the small number of those that Cherniss and other members of the Pulitzer Prize jury had considered most worthy of the prize. From 1980 to 1984 Higgins worked for the *Chicago Sun-Times* as a freelance editorial cartoonist. In 1984 he became a full-time *Chicago Sun-Times* employee. His job has occasionally taken him over-

seas, to Cuba, Hungary, Ireland, and—before its dismantling—the Soviet Union.

According to an article in the *St. Louis Post-Dispatch* (March 31, 1989) about the 1989 Pulitzer Prize winners, Higgins took courses in fine art at the College of the Holy Cross; most other sources, however, characterize him as a self-taught illustrator. In describing his workday routine to Bob Herguth in 1996, he said that he arose at 4:00 a.m. because his "thinking is really sharp" in the hours before dawn. In addition, being awake so early "gives me the same sort of feelings I had when I was a little kid and I was a paperboy: that you're up before everybody else; you've got a jump on the world." Before arriving at his office, between 8:15 a.m. and 9:00 a.m., he absorbed as much news as possible and jotted down ideas. "I think it's important to use everything there is out there at your disposal . . . reading, listening to the radio, watching television, talking to people. . . . It's important to free yourself to look at things in a different way," he said. He also declared, "The name of the game for cartooning is preparation." He told Mike Moore that he particularly enjoyed "the reading and thinking part" of his craft. "It's what takes the most labor," he added. "And that's what people respond to anyway. The drawing is very nice, but a good drawing is never going to carry a bad idea. Just like purple prose does not make a good editorial." He also told Moore, "I try to put in the cartoon the very picture I have in my mind's eye. I try to go with what my immediate reaction is once I've digested all the details. I try to be honest about it."

The first of Higgins's many professional honors came in 1984, when he won the Peter Lisagor Award (named for a renowned *Chicago Daily News* reporter and bureau chief), given by the Chicago Headline Club to recognize outstanding work by Chicago-area journalists. (Higgins won the Lisagor Award 10 additional times: in 1987, 1991, 1994, every year from 1996 through 2001, and 2003.) In 1988 he won both the first prize in the International Salon of Cartoons, in Montreal, Canada, and the Society of Professional Journalists' Sigma Delta Chi Award (also called the Distinguished Service Award); he won the latter in 1998 as well. In 1989 he won the Pulitzer Prize for editorial cartooning, three years after being named a finalist for that honor. The subject of one of the cartoons that captured the Pulitzer for him was Dan Quayle, at that time the U.S. vice president under President George H. W. Bush. During the Vietnam War Quayle had joined the Indiana National Guard, by his own admission as way of avoiding a two-year commitment to active duty overseas. Moreover, he gained acceptance in the guard not through normal channels but thanks to the clout of his father (a Republican newspaper publisher), the intercession of a former major general in the guard, and the willingness of another officer to bypass the unit's commanding officer. As a U.S. senator, Quayle had angered active and former soldiers by sponsoring legislation calling for the imposition of a tax on disability payments to veterans. In Higgins's cartoon Quayle, an avid golfer, is shown holding a set of golf clubs while standing on the side of a road on which Vietnamese children are fleeing aerial bombardments of napalm. Quayle is asking, "Mind if I play through?"

Northern Illinois University named Higgins the Illinois Journalist of the Year in 1996, and he earned an Illinois Press Association Award in 1997. He took top honors in the 1998 Fischetti Editorial Cartoon Competition, sponsored by Columbia College in Chicago and named for a Pulitzer Prize–winning *Chicago Daily News* and *Chicago Sun-Times* editorial cartoonist. Higgins's winning cartoon in the Fischetti contest showed a statue standing midway between the Washington Monument and the Lincoln Memorial, in Washington, D.C., in which, in poses like those of the lovers in Auguste Rodin's famous sculpture *The Kiss*, President Bill Clinton embraces Monica Lewinsky, a one-time White House intern with whom Clinton had an extramarital sexual encounter. (The affair led to Clinton's impeachment; he was later acquitted by the U.S. Senate.) The statue is identified as the Clinton Memorial.

"There can be a very fine line between what is truly slicing right to the heart of any issue and going overboard," Higgins said to Mike Moore. "I have to just settle with the feeling that not everybody has the same standard for what is tasteful, and I just have to go with my own feeling that this is the best interpretation that I have." Among the most controversial of Higgins's cartoons are those that express his opposition to abortion. One such cartoon was published in 2004, after a California judge ruled unconstitutional the federal law banning certain types of abortions (colloquially known as "partial-birth abortions"). The cartoon depicts a statue of a pregnant Lady Justice thrusting a sword (labeled "partial birth ruling") into her swollen belly. Others of Higgins's cartoons have sparked accusations that he harbors anti-Muslim prejudice. In a letter published in the *Sun-Times* on September 26, 2006, Ahmed Rehab, the executive director of the Chicago chapter of the Council on American-Islamic Relations (CAIR), condemned as an "impudent display of reductionism" a cartoon, published six days earlier, in which Higgins had commented on an uproar among members of the Islamic community. The uproar concerned a lecture in which, on September 12, 2006, the Roman Catholic supreme pontiff, Pope Benedict XVI, had quoted lines from a 14th-century book in which a Byzantine emperor called the Prophet Muhammad's teachings "evil and inhuman, such as his command to spread by the sword the faith he preached." Although the words were not the pope's, many Islamic leaders and others condemned him for giving voice to a description that they considered highly insulting and a mischaracterization of Islam. In Higgins's cartoon, Muhammad, wearing an expression of rage and brandishing an upraised sword, screams to the pope, "Islam

violent?! How dare you!!!"; the pope, referring to the mountain of skulls behind Muhammad and to the proverb "If the mountain won't come to Muhammad, Muhammad must go to the mountain," is saying calmly, "Well . . . the mountain came with Muhammad." Rehab's letter of protest notwithstanding, Higgins produced another, two-paneled cartoon, published in the *Sun-Times* on October 1, 2006, in which, in the first panel, an Arab man insists that Islam means "peace," while a second Arab maintains that it means "submission"; in the second panel, the two men face an immense manmade explosion, and one says to the other, "I wonder how many lives were lost in the translation." That cartoon led Ahmed Rehab, in a message posted on the CAIR Chicago Web site, to label Higgins a "bigot" and to write, "Higgins' cartoons are classic examples of a logical fallacy that is all-too-common in post 9/11 America. Rather than direct his anger at terrorists and violent radicals, . . . he projects his wrath unto Islam and Muslims."

Higgins aroused much anger among *Sun-Times* readers with another cartoon, published in early June 2006, which shows several corpses, one with the word "Haditha" printed on its back, and beside them the words "We will be greeted as liberators"—a prediction uttered by Vice President Richard B. ("Dick") Cheney in 2003, three days before U.S. troops invaded Iraq. Haditha is an Iraqi village where, on November 19, 2005, members of the U.S. Marine Corps allegedly murdered 24 unarmed Iraqi civilians, among them at least 10 women and children and an elderly man in a wheelchair, after a roadside bomb killed a marine from the accused men's company. Higgins had based his drawing on a photo (originally published in the London *Guardian*) posted on the Web site of MSN-BC/*Newsweek* near an image of a *Newsweek* cover bearing the headline "The Haditha Question," and he had mistakenly assumed that the photo showed victims of the Haditha massacre; in reality, the photo showed Shiite fishermen and Iraqi national guards who had been murdered by people identified as Iraqi insurgents. That mistake, combined with reports that the U.S. soldiers had acted in self-defense, caused anger among many who saw Higgins's cartoon. On June 8, 2006, after the *Sun-Times* received vehement complaints from readers, the newspaper apologized in print for its "egregious error" in fact-checking. "Jack Higgins and the *Sun-Times* deeply regret the mistake and apologize to the U.S. servicemen, especially those in the Marine Corps, and to our readers who were understandably offended by this cartoon," the apology stated. (In December 2006, in an ironic twist, U.S. military prosecutors announced that four marines associated with the Haditha killings had been charged with murder, and four Marine Corps officers had been charged with "dereliction of duty and failure to ensure that accurate information about the killings was delivered up the Marine Corps' chain of command," as Paul von Zielbauer and Carolyn Marshall wrote for the December 2, 2006 edition of the *New York Times*.)

In a cartoon published in the latter half of 2006, Higgins showed President George W. Bush speaking at that year's convention of the NAACP, having previously rejected—five years in a row—the organization's invitations to address its annual meeting. The cartoon shows Bush holding a basketball; referring to the National Collegiate Athletic Association, the man seated to Bush's left is saying to the person next to him, "Yes, this is truly a first. He wants us to sign his NCAA basketball." A second cartoon poked fun at the Democratic U.S. senators Hillary Rodham Clinton of New York and Barack Obama of Illinois, both of whom were considering a run for the presidency in 2008. Referring to Clinton's book *It Takes a Village*, Obama's book *The Audacity of Hope*, and the latter's middle name, Higgins depicted people lined up to get Clinton's signature on a book called "It Takes a Hussein to Tick Off My Campaign" and Obama's on a volume entitled "The Politics of Book." "And on page 383 you'll learn that I, too, have black roots," Clinton is saying; Obama, sitting a few feet away, is saying, "Who knew but her hairdresser?" In a third cartoon Higgins commented on the proposal by the new majority leader of the House, Democratic representative Steny Hoyer of Maryland, that, most weeks, members of Congress devote more time to their duties in the nation's capital than in their own districts. The drawing shows a family of seven at the breakfast table; the father, reading the newspaper, is saying, "Some congressman wants the House to spend 5 workdays a week in D.C. instead of 3!," and the mother, feeding the youngest of her five children, responds, "That spending part scares me." The subject of a fourth cartoon is the board of commissioners of Cook County, Illinois. In March 2006, a week before that year's primary election, John Stroger, the board's president, was incapacitated by a stroke, and the name of his son, Todd Stroger, replaced his on the ballot. Todd Stroger won the primary and, in November, was elected president; he was sworn into office on December 4, 2006. Meanwhile, Bobbie Steele, a longtime board member, had been named John Stroger's temporary successor as president. Steele won reelection in November, but she was still the nominal president of the board when, shortly after Election Day, she announced that she was retiring. Since she still held the title of president, she retired with a far larger pension than she would have had she remained a commissioner. (In addition, the board approved the appointment of her son Robert to succeed her.) Higgins's cartoon shows five Christmas stocking hanging from the mantel of a fireplace. The toe of the middle one, which bears the name "Bobbie Steele," has torn from the pressure of all the cash that has been stuffed into the stocking; bills pouring from the hole are landing atop a growing pile of cash. Next to the mound of money is a message that reads, "Merry Christmas! From your friends at the Cook County Board."

In addition to his other honors, Higgins was a finalist for the 2000 and 2004 Scripps-Howard Award in editorial cartooning. He won the Chicago Bar Association's Herman Kogan Media Award for best editorial cartooning in 1993, 1995, and 2007. Higgins has appeared as a guest on such television programs as *Good Morning America*, *The Today Show*, *CNN Headline News*, *NBC Nightly News with Tom Brokaw*, and broadcasts of the Chicago affiliates of NBC, PBS, and CBS. In 1997 he married the former Mary Elizabeth Irving; the couple have five children. Higgins's avocational interests include painting and bicycling.

—D.F.

Suggested Reading: American Universal Press Syndicate Web site; *Chicago Sun-Times* p14 Sep. 15, 1996, p4 Apr. 14, 1999; *Quill* p24+ June 1989

Koichi Kamashida/Getty Images

Howard, Ryan

Nov. 19, 1979– Baseball player

Address: Philadelphia Phillies, Citizens Bank Park, One Citizens Bank Way, Philadelphia, PA 19148

Ryan Howard, the first baseman for the Philadelphia Phillies of Major League Baseball (MLB), won the National League's 2006 Most Valuable Player Award and that year's Hank Aaron Award as the league's top slugger. A left-hander who combines prodigious power with an ability to send the ball to any part of the field, Howard has established himself as one of the sport's most capable home-run hitters, producing 58 in 2006—his first full season in the majors. "Besides being superstrong, Ryan is fearless at bat," the Baseball Hall of Fame inductee Mike Schmidt told Dave Kindred for the *Sporting News* (October 6, 2006). "I have a high regard for today's athlete, and he's an example of that regard. He has a wonderful temperament. He's a smart young man who's able to adapt, as we see when he's using the entire ballpark. He's a great example of how hitting has evolved into an art where even power hitters can spray the ball." With the number of African-American players declining in Major League Baseball, and with the sport plagued by allegations of steroid abuse and resulting congressional inquiries, Howard's presence has bolstered MLB's image in terms of both diversity and respectability. Lee Jenkins, writing for the *New York Times* (June 30, 2005), described Howard as the ideal star for baseball, which "has long been looking for the kind of power hitter who can take pitches and hit to the opposite field, who has been to college and been seasoned in the minor leagues, who can prove to young African-American athletes that basketball and football are not the only marquee options." In Philadelphia, one of the last National League teams to sign a black baseball player, Howard—one of three African-American position players on the current team—has "completely transformed" fans' attitudes, Rob Holiday, assistant director of scouting for the Phillies, told Derrick Goold for the *St. Louis Post-Dispatch* (September 29, 2006). "What we have here is, we are witnessing a superstar in the making. He has galvanized this city like it hasn't been before."

Ryan James Howard was born on November 19, 1979 to Cheryl and Ron Howard and grew up in the suburbs of St. Louis, Missouri. He has an older brother, Chris; an older sister, Roni Karen; and a fraternal twin brother, Corey. Ryan, who is six foot four inches tall, is the shortest of the brothers. Howard's parents were both born in Birmingham, Alabama, and were active in civil rights demonstrations in the 1960s. Their experiences led them to adopt the attitude that any achievement was possible, which they instilled in their children. "Don't focus on the blockers, on the challenges, if you have a chance to be what you want to be, be the best, be the pinnacle," Ron Howard told his children, according to Derrick Goold, writing for the *St. Louis Post-Dispatch* (January 15, 2006). "The door opens a little bit, you push it all the way open." Chris Howard told Goold for the same article that their father "prepared us for the world, telling us, 'I will not allow you to be mediocre.' The pressure we had in our home to succeed in our father's eyes, nothing can match that. Not the corporate world, not Major League Baseball. Nothing." Ryan's mother, now retired, worked in marketing, and his father is an engineer and a manager at IBM. Howard's upbringing combined "old-time Southern values" and "middle-class aspiration," as Michael Sokolove put it in the *New York Times* (March 4, 2007). "All our kids were taught to say

'Yes, sir,' 'Yes, ma'am' and so on," Ron Howard told Sokolove. "We valued hard work and taught them: believe in oneself, believe in each other and believe in the Almighty." Howard told Rich Hofmann for the *Philadelphia Daily News* (August 27, 2006) that he learned from his mother "common sense, being courteous," and that from his father he got his "aggressiveness, that fire to want to be the best."

Howard's parents insisted that their children develop well-rounded interests. Ron Howard urged his children, who were athletic, to find interests outside sports as well, "to give them an appreciation for the fact that you have people in the world that do different things," as he said to Hofmann. Accordingly, Howard, who competed in both high-school and American Legion baseball as well as basketball, football, and soccer, also played trombone in Lafayette High School's marching band. "Football and the marching band are pretty mutually exclusive for most people, but he wanted to do both," Phil Milligan, the Lafayette band director during Howard's years there, told Hofmann. He added that Howard "could communicate well with his peers and with adults. He could carry on a conversation with an adult—not sounding like a high school kid. But I'd see him in situations with the other kids and see how he could have fun too."

Baseball became Ryan's primary sport as he progressed through high school. (His mother had decided that football was too dangerous.) With the help of a batting cage his father installed in the basement of their home, he developed into a good but not outstanding player at Lafayette, earning all-conference honors but just honorable mention in the all-metro selections. He nonetheless believed that someday he could play professional baseball. He began to think seriously about that goal during a game in high school, at which a number of professional scouts were present to see another player on Ryan's team. During the game Ryan hit a home run, which "put me on the scout map," as he recalled to Hofmann. In Ryan's senior year he set school records in home runs for a season (eight) and a career (17). A number of four-year universities showed interest in him, but some were farther from his home than he wanted to go, and he rejected others because they placed limits on playing time for freshmen. Howard considered playing at a junior college or trying to get drafted by a professional baseball team. Then, late in the summer following his high-school graduation, he received an offer to play for Keith Guttin, who coached at Southwest Missouri State (now Missouri State) University, in Springfield. Guttin, a friend of Howard's high-school coach, could not offer Howard a scholarship but guaranteed that he could earn playing time his freshman year—and that if he was successful, he would get a scholarship in each of the following three years. "College was important for me," Ryan told Rich Hofmann. "My parents are both very big on education, so there was that. But college allowed me to mature, not only as a baseball player but also as a person. I was glad I went to college. Without the maturity I gained, I don't think I'd be the player that I am today."

Howard easily earned the first-base position at Southwest Missouri State (SMS) and earned Missouri Valley Conference Freshman of the Year honors on the strength of his .355 batting average, 19 home runs, and 66 runs batted in (RBIs). After a similarly successful sophomore campaign, Howard won a position on the U.S. Junior National Team, which had been represented in the past by many players currently in the major leagues. Playing on the international stage also introduced Howard to many professional scouts, some of whom came to regard the slugger highly. Howard had a disappointing junior season, however, batting a comparatively low .271, and though his SMS career statistics brought him impressive rankings of fifth all-time in home runs (50) and sixth in RBIs (183) at the school, his draft prospects suffered. The beneficiaries of that perceived decline in value were the Philadelphia Phillies, who drafted Howard in the fifth round. "I think where we [drafted] him, we thought he was a very good gamble," Mike Arbuckle, the Phillies' assistant general manager, told a reporter for the Philadelphia Inquirer (July 8, 2002). "There was nothing physically wrong. It just looked like he was [trying too hard]. This kid is kind of a perfectionist." Howard left college after his junior season, three semesters shy of graduating with a degree in communications; he promised his parents that he would eventually complete his eduation.

Howard made his professional debut in the summer of 2001 for the Batavia, New York, Muckdogs of the New York–Pennsylvania League. The following year he played for the Class A Lakewood, New Jersey, BlueClaws, leading all Phillies minor-leaguers in home runs, with 19, and making the South Atlantic League All-Star team. He still holds the BlueClaws' single-season RBI record, with 87. Howard had one glaring deficiency, however—strikeouts (he had 145 in 135 games in 2002)—and also needed improvement at first base. Although the strikeouts soured Howard's reputation among some talent evaluators, the BlueClaws' manager, Jeff Manto, believed that Howard's approach to hitting and his work ethic would help him overcome that shortcoming. "The strikeouts don't even bother me . . . ," Manto told the reporter for the Philadelphia Inquirer. "He has a good idea of the strike zone. He'll take curveballs and he's not afraid of lefthanders. His defense has gotten better." Manto also said, "This guy really believes in himself. . . . He's a flat-out joy to work with. He doesn't even know how to really hit yet and he's already hitting well. It will be exciting to watch him as he gets more repetitions and learns more and more about how to hit." Howard wanted to prove wrong the scouts who thought that he would not succeed as a major-league player. "A lot of people, I think gave up on me after my junior year [at SMS]," Howard told Derrick Goold for the January 15, 2006 St. Lou-

is Post-Dispatch article. "My first year in pro ball was all about me getting myself back on that track, just because a lot of people I felt backed off. It bothered me. I knew what I was capable of doing, and those first two years were about showing that." In 2003 Howard was promoted to the single-A Clearwater, Florida, team, on which he hit .304 with 23 home runs and 82 RBIs and earned the Florida State League's most-valuable-player honors. He was also invited to participate in the 2003 Futures All-Star Game, which pits the best American-born minor-league prospects against those from other nations. As part of the MLB All-Star weekend, that event allows up-and-coming players to meet current big-league stars.

Prior to the 2003 season, the Phillies signed the first baseman Jim Thome to a six-year contract, the most lucrative in franchise history. With Thome entrenched at first base, Howard's chances of rising soon to the majors seemed slim. Unlike many players in his position, though, Howard was not in a rush to get to the big leagues; he was content to work on his deficiencies and wait for an opportunity to arise. "You've got to . . . make sure you're ready when you get [to the majors]," Howard told Scott Puryear for the Springfield (Missouri) News-Leader (July 1, 2003), "so when you do get there, you don't have to come back down."

Howard was invited to Major League Spring Training in 2004. Although his fellow left-hander Thome was blocking his path to earning a place on the team, Howard used the experience to learn as much from Thome as he could during his few weeks with the major-league team. Thome, for his part, was committed to helping Howard become a better player. Once the regular season began, Howard was assigned to the double-A Reading, Pennsylvania, Phillies, for whom he hit .297 with 37 home runs—breaking the team's single-season home-run record—and 102 RBIs, thereby establishing himself solidly as a top major-league prospect. He was promoted to the triple-A team in Scranton/Wilkes-Barre, Pennsylvania, for 29 games before reaching the majors in September, when MLB teams expand their rosters. The Scranton/Wilkes-Barre manager, Gene Lamont, was impressed by Howard's power, telling Lee Jenkins for the New York Times (June 30, 2005), "I've managed in the minor leagues a long time, and Ryan is the best power hitter I've ever had." Howard concluded the 2004 season in the Arizona Fall League, playing for the Phoenix Desert Dogs. The young slugger's combined statistics for the four leagues in which he played that season were a .298 batting average, 50 home runs, and 160 RBIs. Howard won the Paul Owens Award as the Phillies' top minor-league position player, and USA Today Sports Weekly named him the minor-league player of the year for 2004. Because Thome continued to play well at the major-league level, many believed that the Phillies would do well to trade Howard, both to help the current Phillies team, because they could trade him for a good player at another position, and to give Howard, who had little left to prove in the minor leagues, an opportunity to fulfill his dream of playing in the major leagues. But while the Phillies did not have an opening for Howard at the major-league level, they did not want to see him develop into a superstar for another MLB team; and though Howard wanted to play in the major leagues, he had also grown attached to the Phillies organization. During his stint with the Arizona Fall League, as a way of gaining other opportunities to enter the majors, Howard tried a different position—left field. Though he possessed surprising speed for a 260-pound player, his performance in the outfield was not impressive, and it became obvious that his path to the majors would be as a first baseman.

Howard performed well at the following year's spring training, but the Phillies decided that it would be better for him to play every day for the triple-A Scranton/Wilkes-Barre team than to serve sporadically as Thome's backup. Howard was frustrated by that decision, and his agent asked the team to consider trading him, since, at 25, he was getting old to be a rookie. The Phillies did not want to do so. Then, early in the 2005 season, Thome was slowed by injuries, and in May he was placed on the disabled list. As a result Howard was promoted to the majors, where he struggled, with a .214 batting average and just one home run in 28 at-bats. When Thome was ready to play, Howard was again assigned to triple-A ball, becoming one of the top players in the Eastern League. In July 2005 Thome was again stricken by injuries, and Howard was given another opportunity with the Phillies; this time he outperformed expectations, batting .288 with 22 home runs and 63 RBIs in 88 games. Howard proved able to perform well under pressure, often hitting the winning home run in close games, and was particularly vital to the team in the season's final month, when he was instrumental in leading the Phillies to within one game of a play-off berth. Howard hit 10 home runs in September, leading the majors in that category for the month. His performance brought Howard praise on a national scale—as well as the National League Rookie of the Year Award. He also gained immense popularity among fans in Philadelphia, a city notorious for its brutal treatment of black baseball players. Jackie Robinson, the first black MLB player, famously wrote that he came to associate Philadelphia with the Deep South because of the way he was received there as a visiting player. Before Howard, the Phillies had had only one African-American superstar, Dick Allen—who was reduced to wearing a batting helmet when he took the field at home games because fans threw batteries, fruit, and refuse at him. Howard, by contrast, was beloved by fans, and his success and acceptance went a long way toward changing the image of the franchise.

Howard's surge in production and popularity with the fans gave the Phillies little choice but to trade either him or Thome. In the off-season the team's general manager, Pat Gillick, traded Thome to the Chicago White Sox of the American League in exchange for Aaron Rowand and two minor-league pitchers. Howard was officially installed as the permanent first baseman of the Phillies. He rose to that responsibility in a sensational 2006 season, in which he won the National League Most Valuable Player Award and earned his first All-Star selection. That year Howard batted .313 and hit 58 home runs, a single-season total exceeded by only five men in baseball history—Barry Bonds, Mark McGwire, Sammy Sosa, Roger Maris, and Babe Ruth. Howard also knocked in a major-league-leading 149 RBIs, including 42 in August, the highest number by a player in a single month in 34 years. He was only the second player in MLB history (the first was Cal Ripkin Jr.) to win the Rookie of the Year Award and Most Valuable Player Award in back-to-back seasons, obliterating the notion of a sophomore slump. Howard also won the Home Run Derby at the 2006 All-Star competition. As the season progressed, Howard's home-run production was limited by opposing managers, who were so wary of his power that he was intentionally walked 37 times, the second-highest number of intentional walks received by a batter in the major leagues that season. In the Phillies' last 21 games, Howard walked 28 times and hit only two home runs. For the second consecutive year, he kept the Phillies in contention for postseason play, but they lost their bid for the play-offs in the last week of the regular season. Howard continued to perform his best in the most pressured circumstances, with 28 of his home runs either tying a game or putting the Phillies ahead. Howard's achievements rank among the best ever for a second-year player; no sophomore has ever hit as many home runs, and only Joe DiMaggio had more RBIs: 167 in 1937.

On June 27, 2007 Howard set a record by hitting 100 home runs faster than any other player, achieving the milestone in 325 games. (It took the previous record holder, Ralph Kiner, 385 games.) Howard finished the 2007 season with a .268 batting average, hitting 47 home runs, driving in 136 runs, and helping the Phillies win the National League East division and earn their first play-off berth since 1993. On a negative note, he struck out 199 times, setting a new MLB single-season record. In the National League Division Series against the Colorado Rockies, Howard batted .250 and hit one home run. The Rockies swept the Phillies in the best-of-five series.

Michael Sokolove described Howard as being "big all over. He has biceps that it would take two large hands to fully encircle, thick-muscled forearms and—more noticeable in the locker room than on the field, where he wears a baggy uniform top—a surprisingly ample midsection. Howard is Ruthian, only bigger. Even his round, expressive face—quick to break into a smile, more open and inviting than the typical impassive countenance of the big-time pro athlete—seems extra large."

Howard lives in Philadelphia.

—N.W.M.

Suggested Reading: (Allentown, Pennsylvania) *Morning Call* C p12 Mar. 14, 2004, C p1 Nov. 8, 2005; *New York Times* D p1 June 30, 2005, VI p42 Mar. 4, 2007; *Philadelphia Inquirer* F p2 July 8, 2002, D p19 Sep. 25, 2005; *Philadelphia Tribune* C p1 Sep. 29, 2006; *Springfield (Missouri) News-Leader* D p1 July 1, 2003; *St. Louis Post-Dispatch* D p10 Jan. 15, 2006; *USA Today* C p1 Sep. 13, 2006

Mark Mainz/Getty Images for DPA

Howard, Terrence

Mar. 11, 1969– Actor

Address: c/o Flavor Unit Management, 155 Morgan St., Jersey City, NJ 07302

After Terrence Howard's highly lauded portrayal of Cameron, an emasculated television director, in Paul Haggis's film *Crash*, and his Oscar-nominated depiction of DJay, a pimp turned rapper, in Craig Brewer's *Hustle & Flow*, both released in 2005, "people went from calling me 'that actor' to 'Terrence Howard' to 'Mr. Howard.'" In the 12 years before he made that remark, during an interview with Neil Drumming for *Entertainment Weekly* (March 23, 2007), Howard had failed to make much of a mark in Hollywood. He had, however, appeared in three dozen feature films; another handful of made-for-television movies, among them *Muhammad Ali: King of the World*, in which he played the title role; and episodes of a bevy of TV series, in-cluding *Family Matters*, *Picket Fences*, *NYPD Blue*, and the sitcom *Sparks*, in which he had a leading role. Moreover, he had received an impressive number of positive reviews for his work, in motion pictures including *Mr. Holland's Opus*, *The Best Man*, and *Hart's War*, and several industry awards. His distinctive qualities as an actor, aside from his unusual hazel eyes, include the ability to convey a mixture of emotions all at once. Paul Haggis, for instance, told Carrie Rickey for the *Philadelphia Inquirer* (July 17, 2005) that during some scenes in *Crash*, Howard was "both admirably strong and completely defenseless—in the same moment." In another example, in a review of *Hustle & Flow* for the *Washington Post* (July 22, 2005), Ann Hornaday wrote that as DJay, Howard "simultaneously radiates a hypnotic blend of determination, danger and soul." "There's little doubt that Howard is the archetypal driven character-actor," Phil Hoad wrote for the London *Independent* (November 18, 2005); "hence the constant expansive, conflicted performances that transcend whatever labels are slapped on them." Most recently Howard appeared in Richard Shepard's *The Hunting Party*, Neil Jordan's *The Brave One*, and Kirsten Sheriden's *August Rush*, all released in 2007. *The Perfect Holiday*, scheduled to arrive in theaters in December 2007, stars Howard alongside Queen Latifah, Morris Chestnut, and others in what comingsoon.net described as "the first African American ensemble comedy for the Christmas season."

The second of the four sons of Tyrone Howard and Anita Howard, Terrence Dashon Howard was born on March 11, 1969 in Chicago, Illinois. He has often used his full name professionally. From his parents' other marriages, he has seven half-brothers and -sisters. His father, a sometime insurance agent and building contractor, and his mother are of mixed white and black parentage. One of his uncles is the blues guitarist Nathan Hawkins. Soon after Terrence's birth the Howards moved to Cleveland, Ohio. In December 1971 Howard witnessed his father fatally stab a man during an altercation in a department store, where the man, his family, and the Howards had been waiting in line for a visit with a Santa Claus. Accounts of what triggered the tragedy, among them the recollections of members of both families, differ markedly. The killing made headlines, and in 1972 Howard's father was convicted of manslaughter; after serving less than a year in prison, he was freed on parole. After his incarceration his wife and children moved into a Cleveland housing project and went on welfare. A few years later Howard's parents divorced. Howard and his brothers were forbidden to play with the tough kids in their neighborhood, and largely for that reason, he has said, they stayed out of trouble. Some summers Howard lived with his father in Los Angeles.

Howard's great-grandmother Minnie Gentry was a singer and actress whose credits included roles on Broadway, Off-Broadway, television, and the silver screen. During his childhood and youth,

Terrence sometimes spent summer vacations with her in Manhattan and would attend rehearsals with her; as time passed he began to memorize her lines and those of others. He told Cherie Saunders for the *Jacksonville (Florida) Free Press* (March 6, 2002) that one day when he was 15, he watched her in a one-woman play: "She walked out on stage with nothing but a chair. She sat down and opened up this imaginary bag, and had an imaginary cigarette sitting on an imaginary table, and started picking imaginary string beans and talking about having to commit her son into a mental hospital. . . . I was spellbound." He added, "I knew at that moment, that I wanted to have that ability." During his teens, according to the Cincinnati, Ohio, *Call and Post* (September 5, 1996), Howard appeared in *A Raisin in the Sun* and other productions mounted at the Karamu House Performing Arts Center, in Cleveland. When he was 16 he moved with his father and siblings into a ramshackle house in that city. To earn money for his family, Howard sometimes played hooky and did odd jobs, including shoveling snow for neighbors. During that period he spent time with a local pimp, a friend of his father's nicknamed Tweety Bird. "Tweety would come in my room and say, 'Stop crying. . . . You gotta be a man.' I know it sounds strange," Howard recalled to Cindy Pearlman for the *Chicago Sun-Times* (July 17, 2005), "but he was a mentor in a way."

Howard has said that his high-school grade-point average was far below the norm and that he gained acceptance to Pratt Institute, a college in the New York City borough of Brooklyn, and scholarship aid through false pretenses. Some reports state that he had declared himself to be independent of his parents by then. As an undergraduate he persuaded the casting director of *The Cosby Show* to give him a chance to audition. After his second audition he was given a role, but the scenes in which he appeared were cut. "I was angry," he recalled to Lynn Hirschberg. "I banged on Cosby's dressing-room door, and amazingly, he answered. I told him, 'I'm a man just like you.' He didn't like it, and the casting agent never took my calls again." He added, "That's the mold for the rest of my professional life. I say the hell with it, and I suffer the consequences." He earned a B.S. degree in chemical engineering from Pratt. Earlier, in 1989, he had married Lori McComas.

Thanks to his efforts to "mak[e] friends in the business," as he put it to the film critic Carrie Rickey, in 1992 Howard won the part of Jackie, the oldest member of the legendary singing group the Jackson 5, in the Emmy Award–winning ABC miniseries *The Jacksons: An American Dream* (1992). He next appeared in small roles in the Hollywood comedy *Who's The Man* (1993) and in a few episodes of several television series. In 1995, he told Lynn Hirschberg, he moved to Los Angeles and then "worked regularly." That year Howard appeared in the small parts of Cowboy, a sadistic Vietnam War veteran, in Albert and Allen Hughes's film *Dead Presidents*, and Louis, a student whose athletic talents dwarf his musical aptitude, in Stephen Herek's *Mr. Holland's Opus.* In the UPN television network sitcom *Sparks*, which aired from mid-1996 to early 1998, he performed the role of Greg Sparks, an attorney in a law firm whose other partners are his father and two siblings (James Avery, Miguel A. Nunez Jr., and Robin Givens, respectively). Nonetheless, according to Stephen Galloway in the *Hollywood Reporter* (December 12, 2005), in 1997 Howard "nearly abandoned Hollywood in despair, moving to Philadelphia and taking a job as a carpet cleaner for $7.50 an hour."

"Before I got *The Best Man*," Howard told Hirschberg, "I was ready to quit the business. I was minutes away from suicide. My wife had left me. And she had good reason." As Quentin in Malcolm D. Lee's *The Best Man* (1999), made with an ensemble cast including Taye Diggs, Morris Chestnut, and Nia Long, "Terrence Howard doesn't miss a thing as a guitar-playing truth-teller," Bob Graham wrote for the *San Francisco Chronicle* (March 3, 2000), in one of many admiring reviews of both the film and its actors. Speaking of his role, Howard—an accomplished, self-taught guitarist and pianist—told Walter Dawkins for *Savoymag.com* (April 2002), "Most of the time we all like to be truthful, but it's hard to deal with the consequences of being brutally honest. My character in *The Best Man* always said what he felt, and I actually learned a lot from him." For his depiction of Quentin, Howard was nominated for Independent Spirit and Chicago Film Critics Association Awards for best supporting male actor and most promising actor, respectively, and he won an Image Award from the NAACP (National Association for the Advancement of Colored People) as outstanding supporting actor in a motion picture. In 2000 he portrayed the boxer Cassius Clay (before he changed his name) in the ABC made-for-television movie *Muhammad Ali: King of the World* (based on a biography by David Remnick) and a murderous escapee from prison in Martin Lawrence's film *Big Momma's House* (2000). In a representative, lukewarm assessment of the latter movie, Elvis Mitchell wrote for the *New York Times* (June 2, 2000), "Flittering on the periphery is Mr. Howard, who acts as if he is in a substantial movie, which makes a difference. With his movie-star concentration, in his few scenes he gives *Big Momma's House* weight."

In an assessment of Howard's work in the widely panned *Glitter* (2001), starring Mariah Carey, Paul Clinton wrote for CNN.com (September 25, 2001) that the actor had "once again turn[ed] in a believable, strong performance" as "an underhanded record producer who takes advantage of the talents of others." Also in 2001 Howard appeared in the HBO film *Boycott*, as the civil rights leader Ralph Abernathy, and in *Angel Eyes*, starring Jennifer Lopez. For his work in the latter, he received a Black Reel Award, in the supporting-actor category, from the Foundation for the Advancement of

African-Americans in Film. In the World War II drama *Hart's War* (2002), directed by Gregory Hoblit, Howard portrayed Lincoln Scott, a fictional member of the famous Tuskegee Airmen fighter pilots, who is accused of murdering a racist American sergeant while in a German prisoner-of-war camp. In a review for the *Chicago Sun-Times* (February 15, 2002) of the picture, which also starred Bruce Willis and Colin Farrell, Roger Ebert wrote, *"Hart's War* would be just another military courtroom drama if it were not for the work by Terrence Howard," and in *Rolling Stone* (March 14, 2002), Peter Travers declared Howard's portrayal of Scott to be "outstanding." Howard played the guitarist Gossie McKee in the highly acclaimed motion picture *Ray* (2004), about the legendary singer/songwriter Ray Charles (Jamie Foxx, in an Academy Award–winning performance).

In what might be considered a breakthrough performance, in terms of the amount of attention it attracted, Howard portrayed Cameron, an outwardly successful television director, in *Crash*, which was shown in 2004 at the Toronto Film Festival and was released internationally in the late spring of 2005. Written and directed by Paul Haggis and set in contemporary Los Angeles, *Crash* offers overlapping stories dealing with race, class, and crime as it follows a diverse group of characters, played by an ensemble cast (Don Cheadle, Brendan Fraser, Sandra Bullock, Ryan Philippe, Chris "Ludacris" Smith, Michael Peña, and Jennifer Esposito, among others). When a white police officer (Matt Dillon) molests Cameron's wife (Thandie Newton) during an arrest, Cameron is too fearful to attempt to protect her, and afterward he is forced to question his image of himself and his assumptions about his role as a black man in a white-dominated world. "Cameron had made so many compromises in his life leading up to that moment, that he'd long since lost his self-confidence, because he didn't have anything true to draw on," Howard said in an interview with Kam Williams for the African American Literature Book Club Web site. "So, I think it's just something that naturally occurs when you're in a place of conflict with self and dignity." "If an actor is talented . . . , then it is very difficult to tell where the man starts and the actor begins," Haggis told Carrie Rickey. "Terrence opens his eyes and lets you right into his soul." For his depiction of Cameron, Howard won an NAACP Image Award and a Screen Actors Guild Award.

Howard accepted the role of DJay, the character he brought to life in *Hustle & Flow*, after turning it down twice. "I was afraid that instead of trying to kill a stereotype, they were trying to propagate a stereotype," he told Phil Hoad. "Blaxploitation, glorification of pimps, glorification of the gangsta life. I didn't want to participate in anything like that." DJay is a small-time Memphis, Tennessee, pimp who is experiencing a midlife crisis when he learns that a rap superstar (played by Ludacris) who had his beginnings in Memphis is returning to the city; eager to earn more money and move out of the slums, DJay makes an all-out effort to break into the music industry as a rapper. To prepare for the role, over a two-year period Howard interviewed more than 75 prostitutes, spent a month living in a bordello, talked to 120 pimps, and lived with some of them briefly as well; he also watched many pornographic movies. "The thing about it was how do you make an unlikable person, an anti-hero, into a hero of a human spirit," he said to Janice Rhoshalle Littlejohn for the Associated Press (July 18, 2005). "Because that's the true hero of this movie, the human spirit and its resilience and determination to do more and more." "The complexity—one might less charitably say the incoherence—of DJay's character requires a lot from an actor, and Mr. Brewer's good fortune in casting Mr. Howard can hardly be overstated," A. O. Scott wrote in a review of the movie for the *New York Times* (July 22, 2005). The *Los Angeles Times* (July 22, 2005) reviewer, Kevin Thomas, wrote, *"Hustle & Flow* places Howard front and center as a man with little education but much street wisdom. . . . DJay seems a world apart from Howard's sophisticated, uptight Hollywood director in *Crash*, but Howard makes them equally indelible." Howard won the Audience Award at the 2005 Sundance Film Festival and the Los Angeles Film Critics Association's New Generation Award for his performance, and he also earned Academy Award and Golden Globe Award nominations in the best-actor category. His other screen credits in 2005 include his roles in Mark Brown's *The Salon*, John Singleton's *Four Brothers*, and Jim Sheridan's *Get Rich or Die Tryin'*. He also appeared in the ABC made-for-TV drama *Their Eyes Were Watching God*, whose screenplay, by Suzan-Lori Parks, was based on the same-titled novel by Zora Neale Hurston, and the HBO Films production of *Lackawanna Blues*, directed by George C. Wolfe from Ruben Santiago-Hudson's teleplay.

Craig Brewer told Donna Freydkin for *USA Today* (February 22, 2006) that in conversation, Howard often quickly shifts from talking about "the crunk to the cosmic." The actor, who swam 150 to 200 laps a day to prepare for his portrayal of the real-life inner-city swimming coach Jim Ellis in the film *Pride*—Ellis himself helped Howard improve his technique—has said that every morning he does hundreds of push-ups and sit-ups and runs three miles on his treadmill. Howard lives in a suburb of Philadelphia, Pennsylvania, near the house where his daughters (Aubrey and Heavenly) and son (Hunter) live with their mother, Lori McCommas. Howard and McCommas divorced and then, in 2005, remarried; currently, they are separated. Howard owns a contracting business and has restored what he has described as "historical houses." He currently hosts the Public Broadcasting System weekly series *Independent Lens*, about independent films.

—D.F.

Suggested Reading: Associated Press Worldstream July 14, 2005; *Chicago Sun-Times Sunday Showcase* p8 July 17, 2005; *Entertainment Weekly* p19+ Mar. 23, 2007; *Fresh Air* (transcript) Jan. 20, 2006; imdb.com; (London) *Independent* p14 Nov. 18, 2005; Mahogany Cafe Web site; *New York Times* VI p38 Feb. 8, 2001; Newhouse News Service July 13, 2005; *Philadelphia Inquirer* H p1+ July 17, 2005; *USA Today* B p8 Feb. 22, 2006

Selected Television Shows: *Street Legal*, 1989; *Tall Hopes*, 1993; *Living Single*, 1994; *Coach*, 1994; *Family Matters*, 1994; *Picket Fences*, 1994; *Sparks*, 1996–98; *NYPD Blue,* 1998–99; *Soul Food*, 2002–03

Selected Films: *The Jacksons: An American Dream*, 1992; *Who's the Man?*, 1993; *Mr. Holland's Opus*, 1995; *Shadow-Ops*, 1995; *Lotto Land*, 1995; *Dead Presidents*, 1995; *The O.J. Simpson Story*, 1995; *Sunset Park*, 1996; *Spark*, 1998; *The Players Club*, 1998; *The Best Man*, 1999; *King of the World*, 2000; *Big Momma's House*, 2000; *Love Beat the Hell Outta Me*, 2000; *Investigating Sex*, 2001; *Boycott*, 2001; *Angel Eyes*, 2001; *Glitter*, 2001; *Hart's War*, 2002; *Biker Boyz*, 2003; *Crash*, 2004; *Ray*, 2004; *The Salon*, 2005; *Hustle & Flow*, 2005; *Lackawanna Blues*, 2005; *Four Brothers*, 2005; *Get Rich or Die Tryin'*, 2005; *Their Eyes Were Watching God*, 2005; *Idlewild*, 2006; *Pride*, 2007; *The Hunting Party*, 2007; *The Brave One*, 2007; *August Rush*, 2007

Andy Lyons/Getty Images

Howland, Ben

May 28, 1957– Men's head basketball coach of the UCLA Bruins

Address: UCLA Athletic Dept., J.D. Morgan Center, P.O. Box 24044, Los Angeles, CA 90024

"When you think of college athletics, there's Notre Dame football and UCLA basketball. That's always the way it's been." Ben Howland made that remark to Gerry Dulac for the *Pittsburgh (Pennsylvania) Post-Gazette* (February 11, 2004) during his first season as the head coach of the Bruins, the men's basketball team at UCLA—the University of California at Los Angeles—a job that he had dreamed

of filling for much of his life. Although he had excelled as a player in his high school and college, Howland "wasn't good enough" to play with the Bruins, as he told Dulac. "But the opportunity to coach here is even better," he said. "You know, as a player you only get to stay for four years. I hope to stay a lot longer than that." Except for one year in the beginning of his professional life, Howland has always earned his living as an assistant or head coach, and he has distinguished himself with his uncommon skill at transforming losing teams into winners. He accomplished that feat as the head coach at Northern Arizona University, for five years beginning in 1994, and at the University of Pittsburgh for four. When he arrived at UCLA, in April 2003, the Bruins had just ended their first losing season since 1948, with their worst record since 1942. Howland is the eighth person to serve as UCLA's men's basketball coach since the retirement of the legendary John R. Wooden, who guided the squad from 1948 through 1975. During Wooden's 27 seasons there, UCLA won 10 National Collegiate Athletic Association (NCAA) championships, lost no games in four seasons, and from 1971 to 1974 won 88 consecutive games—a record that remains unbroken. Commenting on the pressure on him to succeed at UCLA, Howland said to John Blanchette for the Spokane, Washington, *Spokesman Review* (January 7, 2004, on-line), "Fear of failure is a driving motivation, but I heard it said once that if you're afraid to fail, you'll never experience success. It's a job that comes with high expectations and I understand that, but I'm not going to be afraid of that, either." In Howland's first season with the Bruins, the team won 11 games and lost 17; since then, the team has accrued win–loss records during the regular season of 18–11, 27–6, and 26–5, and in both 2006 and 2007, UCLA made appearances at the Final Four of the NCAA championships. Jerry Pimm, whom Howland served as an assistant for 12 years when Pimm was head coach of the men's basketball team at the University of California at Santa Barbara, told Todd Harmonson for the *Orange County (California) Register* (March 20, 2006) that Howland is "an intense, passionate, dogmatic worker. He's got great energy. He's got great passion for the game. He prepares for every detail. It definitely was easy to see that he would make a great coach."

One of the four children of Bob Howland, a Presbyterian minister, and Mary Howland, a college English teacher, Ben Howland was born on May 28, 1957 in Lebanon, Oregon. His siblings are all teachers. As an adult Howland described his father (who died in 2003) as his best friend. Howland grew up in Goleta, California, a suburb of Santa Barbara. As a youngster he was an avid fan of the UCLA Bruins and would watch broadcasts of Bruins games on television. UCLA had won a record 10 NCAA championships in the 1960s and 1970s and captured seven consecutive (1967–73) national titles under John R. Wooden. With such players as the future NBA stars Kareem Abdul-Jabbar, Bill Walton, and Lucius Allen, UCLA had set the gold standard in college basketball with its precision offense, sound discipline, and impeccable teamwork. Howland himself began to hone his playing skills in summer pickup games at the Goleta Boys Club. To some extent his scrappiness and tenacity made up for what he lacked in athletic talent.

Howland attended Dos Pueblos High School, in Santa Barbara, before transferring to Cerritos High School, in Los Angeles, after his father accepted a post at a church in nearby Norwalk. At Cerritos Howland became a standout defender and long-range shooter, earning two Suburban League Most Valuable Player honors. He also won All-California Interscholastic Federation honors twice. He spent two years at Santa Barbara City College, serving as team captain and guard for the men's basketball team, the Vaqueros, and then completed his junior and senior years at Weber State University, in Ogden, Utah. As a guard for the Weber State Wildcats, he led the Wildcats to two Big Sky conference championships and consecutive berths in the NCAA Tournament and was named the team's Most Valuable Defensive Player after the 1978–79 and 1979–80 seasons. At Weber, according to Pete Thamel in the *New York Times* (March 4, 2007), "Howland had a reputation for nervous excitability—he typically vomited 10 minutes before every game." Howland graduated from college in 1979 with a B.A. degree in physical education. In 1980 he played with a professional basketball team in Uruguay. Back in the U.S., in 1981 he entered Gonzaga University, in Spokane, Washington, where he earned an M.S. degree in administration and physical education. Concurrently, and continuing into 1982, he served as a graduate assistant to Jay Hillock, the head coach of the Bulldogs, the Gonzaga men's basketball team.

In 1982 Howland joined the staff of the University of California at Santa Barbara (UCSB) as an assistant to the men's basketball team's head coach, a position filled the next year by Jerry Pimm. During his 12 years in that post, Howland was credited with nurturing the future NBA players Brian Shaw and Connor Henry. Between 1987 and 1994 he helped lead UCSB's Gauchos to five postseason appearances. Though he remained behind the scenes, his reputation as a program builder, astute recruiter, and developer of talent became widely known. In 1994 he left UCSB to join Northern Arizona University (NAU), in Flagstaff, as the coach of its men's basketball team, the Lumberjacks. The team had had four straight losing seasons, resulting in a record of 34–76 and a ranking of 280 out of 290 Division I-A programs. Howland regarded the job as being "one of the worst" in the whole country, as he told Bill Modoono for *Pitt Magazine* (Winter 2003), but also a great opportunity. "I got a one-year contract for $60,000 a year, and I couldn't wait to sign up," he told Jim Derry for the New Orleans, Louisiana, *Times-Picayune* (March 31, 2006).

Having made recruitment his top priority, Howland adopted the motto "Recruit to shoot" and set about luring athletes with superior shooting skills. He then fashioned an offensive scheme that was so effective that the Lumberjacks soon topped most other college teams in shooting accuracy. In three of Howland's five years as coach, the Lumberjacks led the nation in three-point shooting percentage, and in 1998–99 they became the only team in NCAA history to lead the nation in both field-goal percentage and three-point field-goal percentage in the same season. Beginning in 1996, in Howland's third season as head coach, NAU won at least 20 games in three consecutive seasons, gained two Big Sky conference titles, and made two appearances in postseason play: in the National Invitation Tournament, in 1997, and, for the first time, the NCAA Tournament, in 1998. Although, in the latter contest, the Lumberjacks fell to the Cincinnati Bearcats in the first round, their performance attracted national attention. In 1997 Howland was named Big Sky Conference Coach of the Year. He remained at NAU for one more season.

After Ralph Willard, the men's coach of the University of Pittsburgh Panthers, announced that he would retire at the end of the 1999 season (which Pitt finished with a 14–16 record), Steve Pederson, the school's athletic director, interviewed Howland for the job. "It was like I knew exactly what he was trying to do and he knew exactly what I was trying to do," Pederson said to Bob Smizik for the *Pittsburgh Post-Gazette* (February 24, 2002, online). Referring to Howland's accomplishments at NAU, Pederson told Bill Modoono, "He had already done this once. There's something to be said for being through this before and succeeding." Howland assumed the head-coach position at Pitt on March 8, 1999, inheriting what Pederson described to Smizik as a program in "bad, bad shape." Again focusing on recruitment, at Pitt—which belonged to a conference known for its gritty, punishing games—Howland sought disciplined, physical players who would create a bruising defense. "If you look at all sports, whether you're talking about the Pittsburgh Steelers or the New England Patriots or baseball, it all starts and ends with defense," Howland told David Wharton for the *Los Angeles Times* (March 31, 2006). "You need to play defense to have a chance to win championships." He also dismissed players for disciplinary reasons. "You've got to get good kids," he told Bill Modoono. "No kid's perfect, no kid's not going to make mistakes. But if you have really good kids and you put them around other good kids, the peer group determines a lot." In 1999–2000, Howland's first season with the Panthers, the team won 13 games and lost 15; in the next season they advanced to the second round of the National Invitation Tournament. In 2001–02, led by the All-American junior point guard Brandin Knight, Pitt won 29 games—a school record—and lost only six to capture the Big East regular-season title, the team's first such title in 14 years. They then advanced to the "Sweet 16" (a contest among the top 16 teams in the 64-team NCAA Men's Division I Basketball Championship), which they lost to the Kent State University Golden Flashes, 78–73. Howland was named the Naismith College Coach of the Year by the Atlanta Tipoff Club's board of selectors (made up of eminent basketball journalists, coaches, and administrators), and he was chosen as the National Coach of the Year by the Associated Press, *ESPN Magazine*, the U.S. Basketball Writers Association, and the *Sporting News*. In addition, he won three Big East Coach of the Year honors. In 2002–03 Pitt finished the season with 28 wins and five losses, gaining another Big East conference title and "Sweet 16" appearance, where they lost to the Marquette University Golden Eagles, 77–74. Speaking of Howland, Barry Rohrssen, who joined Pitt as an assistant coach in 1999, told Gerry Dulac, "Every game for four years, before we walked out on the court, I never felt we would lose a game with him. He had such a thorough understanding of the opponent. The first time I watched tape with him, he took something from the tape I had never seen before. He was a master of being able to do that. It would be like giving someone a brush and can of paint and giving Michelangelo a brush and a can of paint and tell them to go paint a ceiling. You're going to see two different things. Ben sees a whole different game."

In March 2003, after the Bruins ended the season with a record of 10–19, UCLA fired the team's head coach, Steve Lavin, and rumors grew that Howland was eyeing the vacancy. The following month UCLA's athletic director, Dan Guerrero, hired Howland to fill the position. During Lavin's seven years as head coach, UCLA had amassed a record of 145–78; the Bruins had won at least 20 games every season except the last, and they had reached the Sweet 16 of the NCAA tournaments five times in six years (a feat matched by only one other college coach, Mike Krzyzewski of Duke University). Nevertheless, attendance at Bruins games had steadily decreased as fan dissatisfaction grew, with criticism that the team was unpredictable and

inconsistent and made up of undisciplined underachievers. Gerry Dulac, writing in early 2004, described the team as "shockingly devoid of skill" and as "soft and non-aggressive," while the former Bruins coach John Wooden told Dulac that he did not think that the players were "the type of material [Howland] works with best. He wants a more physical team. Every place he's been, when he gets his material, he does a good job."

Howland set about creating a team that embodied the "spirit of what [Wooden] is all about, which is teamwork, which is unselfish play, which is team defense, which is giving yourself up for your teammates," as he recalled to Ed Graney for SignOnSanDiego.com (March 31, 2006). Although his first season at UCLA ended with an 11–17 record, observers noted improvements in defense and signs of greater intensity and cohesion among the players. He acquired for the Bruins two star high-school players from Southern California—Jordan Farmar and Arron Afflalo. "All he did was talk about defense," Farmar told a writer for *USA Today* (April 3, 2006). "There's no big secret to this . . . ," Howland explained to Malcolm Moran for *USA Today* (April 4, 2006). "The best players in the world are players that play both ends of the floor, starting with Michael Jordan. . . . It's not a hard sell because all players want to be great. Be like Mike." Remaining true to form, Howland also emphasized the importance of executing every move meticulously. During practices, according to Bruins players, as Marc Carig reported for the *Washington Post* (March 24, 2007), "it's not uncommon to run plays over and over again, until [they are] completed with precision." "Just when we're doing walk-throughs, [Howland] wants everybody to be in the precise spots," the guard and forward Josh Shipp told Carig. "I mean, we try to shortcut things just to save time. He stops us and points it out and says we need [to] get in the right spots. That's how precise it is." The point guard Darren Collison told Pete Thamel that each practice session is "exactly like a class." Howland also stresses to the team the importance of pride in the UCLA basketball tradition. "They need to understand this is a unique fraternity and it is truly an honor to be part of it," he told Ed Graney. Howland told Thamel that every week he devotes about 15 to 20 hours to studying videos of games; after one of the Bruins' losses in 2005–06, Thamel reported, he watched the video of the game nine times, and after another defeat, he watched the video of the game three times that same night.

The Bruins finished the 2004–05 season with 18 wins and 11 losses and made their first NCAA Tournament appearance since 2002; there, they lost to the Texas Tech Raiders in the first round. In 2005–06, after a loss to the University of Southern California Trojans, the Bruins won 12 games in a row, finishing with a conference record of 14–4 (giving them a rank of seven nationally) and winning the Pacific 10 (Pac-10) regular-season and end-of-season tournament titles. After securing the number-two seed in the Oakland regional bracket of the NCAA Tournament, the Bruins advanced past the Gonzaga Bulldogs, the University of Memphis Tigers, and the Louisiana State University Tigers, averaging 56.2 points per game, before losing to the number-one–ranked University of Florida Gators, 73–57, in the National Championship game. Howland's achievements that year earned him more than half a dozen honors, among them the Jim Phelan Award as National Coach of the Year and selection as Conference Coach of the Year by CBSSportsline.com, SI [Sports Illustrated].com, and CollegeInsider.com.

In November 2006, in the preseason Maui Invitational, a tournament hosted by Chaminade University of Honolulu, in Hawaii, the Bruins captured the championship by defeating the Chaminade, University of Kentucky, and Georgia Tech teams. The Bruins were also victorious at the John R. Wooden Classic, in December, vanquishing Texas A&M, 65–62. The Bruins started their 2006–07 campaign with 13 wins and no losses, and that winter an Associated Press poll ranked the team number one for six weeks in succession. UCLA was seeded second in the Pac-10 going into the 2007 NCAA Tournament, where the team lost to the Florida Gators, 76–66, in the national semifinals, held on March 31.

In 2007 Howland signed a seven-year contract with UCLA at a base salary of $1.5 million annually, with potential yearly additions of up to a half-million dollars. He told Diane Pucin for the *Los Angeles Times* (October 4, 2007), "I'm very lucky. I've got my dream job . . . and I know how lucky and blessed I am."

According to Thamel, Howland is "an ever-revving engine of obsessive energy." He and his wife, the former Kim Zahnow, have two children—Meredith and Adam, both of whom are college students. In his leisure time Howland enjoys fly-fishing.

—D.J.K.

Suggested Reading: *New York Times* (on-line) Mar. 4, 2007; *Orange County (California) Register* (on-line) Mar. 30, 2006; *Pitt Magazine* (on-line) Winter 2003; *Pittsburgh Post-Gazette* (on-line) Feb. 24, 2002, Feb. 11, 2004; UCLA Bruins Web site; *UCLA Magazine* (on-line) Summer 2003; *USA Today* (on-line) Apr. 4, 2006; *Washington Post* E p10 Mar. 24, 2007

Hudson, Jennifer

Sep. 12, 1981– Singer; actress

Address: c/o William Morris Agency, 1325 Ave. of the Americas, New York, NY 10019

Since 2002, when the televised singing contest *American Idol* began airing on the Fox network, the winners of the competition have gone on to varying degrees of success, with some selling millions of albums and earning multiple music-industry awards. Even the runners-up have achieved a considerable measure of acclaim, perhaps none more so than Jennifer Hudson, who competed in 2004, during the third season of Fox's ratings juggernaut. Hudson, whose gospel-tinged, five-octave performances made her a formidable contender, finished the competition in a dismal seventh place, sparking rumors of racism and vote tampering. She was vindicated, however, when she earned a Golden Globe Award, a Screen Actors Guild Award, and an Academy Award for her portrayal of Effie White, a talented but troubled singer in a 1960s-era Motown-style girl group, in the long-awaited film version of *Dreamgirls* (2006). (The stage version of *Dreamgirls*, starring Jennifer Holliday as White, ran on Broadway in the early 1980s.) To get the role, Hudson beat out almost 800 other women who had also auditioned, including, ironically, Fantasia Barrino, the season-three *American Idol* winner.

Roberto Schmidt/AFP/Getty Images

Jennifer Kate Hudson was born on September 12, 1981. Accounts of her youth vary, with some sources stating that she was raised, along with her older brother, Jason, and her older sister, Julia, by a single mother. It is unclear how long her mother, Darnell Hudson, who worked as a secretary, remained single. She eventually married Samuel

Simpson, a bus driver, and some sources make reference to Hudson's having either two stepsiblings or two half-siblings.

Hudson grew up in Englewood, a predominately black neighborhood on the South Side of Chicago, Illinois. She told Nick Curtis for the London *Evening Standard* (January 25, 2007), "It was a decent neighborhood. We were poor but we weren't that poor. . . . We had everything we needed." Hudson modeled for a Sears catalog as a five-year-old and, thanks to Darnell's belief that her children should be exposed to enriching extracurricular activities, also took ballet lessons as a child.

The family belonged to the Pleasant Gift Missionary Baptist Church, and Hudson attended twice a week—on Sundays for worship and Tuesdays to practice for the choir, which she joined at age seven. "Church is where I'm from," she told Dave Hoekstra for the *Chicago Sun-Times* (December 17, 2006). "It will always be my favorite place to sing."

In her teens Hudson also began performing in such secular venues as local talent shows, community musicals, and wedding receptions. She attended Dunbar Vocational Career Academy, which had previously produced such performers as Cleotha and Pervis Staples of the Staple Singers and Lou Rawls. There, she impressed the school's music faculty and was voted most talented female musician by her peers. "She exuded confidence," her former choral director, Richard Nunley, told *Us Weekly* (March 5, 2007). "She always told me she'd be as successful as [the singer] Whitney Houston."

Hudson's grandmother died in 1998, and the following year, shortly after Hudson's graduation from Dunbar, Samuel Simpson succumbed to cancer. While the deaths of two beloved relatives in so short a period proved wrenching for Hudson, she took great consolation in her faith. Determined to continue her education, she briefly attended Langston University, in Langston, Oklahoma, but was unhappy at being so far from her remaining family members. She then transferred to Kennedy-King College, one of the institutions in Chicago's City Colleges system. While studying music at Kennedy-King, in 2001 Hudson earned a singing part in a local production of *Big River*, a musical based on Mark Twain's 1884 novel *The Adventures of Huckleberry Finn*. "Quite honestly I will never forget Jennifer Hudson coming in and singing for us," Rick Boynton, the show's artistic director, told Mark Caro for the *Chicago Tribune* (December 18, 2006). "She just came into the room and opened her mouth, and it was something I had never heard [before]. It was incredible."

In the fall of 2002, after *Big River* closed, Hudson, confident that she could earn a living by singing, auditioned for the chance to perform on a Disney cruise ship. In February 2003 she began appearing in the shipboard production *Hercules: The Musical* as the head muse, Calliope. Despite her attachment to her family and her hometown, she told Caro, "From the moment I stepped on that ship, I

was like, I will never be at home for good ever again."

Although she was invited to renew her contract with Disney, Hudson decided instead to audition for the third season of *American Idol*, a show that had proven exceedingly popular and that had launched the careers of its first two winners, Kelly Clarkson and Ruben Studdard, as well as that of Studdard's close season-two runner-up, Clay Aiken.

On the show the contestants' singing is critiqued—sometimes harshly—by the judges: Simon Cowell, Paula Abdul, and Randy Jackson. The judges are advised by a series of celebrity guest judges, who included, during season three, the pop stars Barry Manilow and Elton John. At the end of each weekly telecast, viewers are invited to vote for their favorites by calling in or sending text messages; the contestant with the fewest votes in a given week is eliminated and does not compete the following week. During the early rounds of the competition, Hudson sang such popular numbers as "Baby I Love You," an Aretha Franklin number, and "I Have Nothing," originally performed by Whitney Houston. She was sometimes compared to those two stars by the judges, who generally praised Hudson's vocal abilities—if not some of her more outlandish costume choices. (One pink dress, made for her by a friend, an aspiring designer, was widely described in the tabloid press as "cringe-inducing.")

Hudson, while inarguably one of the most talented competitors, was voted off the show in seventh place. Cowell, Abdul, and Jackson expressed shock at that outcome—Jackson, for example, described it as "insane," according to Sarah Rodman in an article for the *Boston Herald* (April 27, 2004). Various theories explaining her ouster were put forth by journalists, music-industry figures, and distressed fans. A phone outage in Hudson's native Chicago, which prevented many of her supporters from voting, was blamed by some, while others suggested that because Hudson was so good, many of her fans thought their votes would be superfluous.

Hudson's competitors on *American Idol* included LaToya London and Fantasia Barrino, two black women with gospel-inspired singing styles; Hudson, London, and Barrino were often referred to collectively by the judges and the show's host, Ryan Seacrest, as "the three divas." Some felt that the three singers had ended up splitting the vote—to the detriment of each. (Barrino and London were also in the bottom three the week Hudson was eliminated.)

Elton John, who had been deeply impressed by Hudson's rendition of his song "Circle of Life" when he served as a celebrity judge, described the viewers' decision as racially motivated. Many immediately disputed that conjecture, since Ruben Studdard, the previous season's winner, was black, and George Huff, a charismatic black competitor, had fared well that week. Later, Barrino was named the season-three victor.

The Fox network received so many angry phone calls and letters regarding Hudson's loss that the *American Idol* producers released a statement confirming that the decision had been based solely on viewer voting. Hudson expressed her view that fans of the show ignored singing skill when deciding their favorites. "If we're going to base [the contest] on talent, I know I was robbed," she told Janet Zimmerman for the *Riverside (California) Press Enterprise* (April 27, 2004). "I think people need to reconsider and think what this competition is supposed to be, rather than what such-and-such is wearing." Otherwise, she responded philosophically to being eliminated in what was then the closest vote in the show's history. "It was meant to be and that's fine with me," she explained to Zimmerman. "It was God's will." Similarly, she told Faridul Anwar Farinordin for the Malaysia *New Straits Times* (December 11, 2004), "I'm thankful for being in the final round and I respect the voters' choice. What's important is that the show has opened new doors for me to pursue my career in music." Hudson also defended her fellow contestant John Stevens, a young, white singer whom many voters believed should have been dismissed instead of her. "[Stevens] deserves to be there as much as me and anybody else," Hudson told Zimmerman. "He has fans just like we do and obviously they're voting." (Stevens was voted off the show the week after Hudson.)

After *American Idol* Hudson was inundated with invitations to perform. Rather than jumping into an ill-conceived project—a pitfall that she believed some of her *American Idol* predecessors had encountered—Hudson carefully considered her options. She was first obliged to participate in the 50-date *American Idol: Season Three* tour, in the summer of 2004, which featured the top 10 contestants of the show. Hudson followed up that group tour by performing concerts around the Midwest and singing at a charity event on Broadway, at which she was introduced to theater executives who urged her to consider moving to New York to pursue a stage career.

Hollywood, however, beckoned; Hudson, after a grueling series of auditions, earned the part of Effie White in the film *Dreamgirls*, which premiered on December 4, 2006 and was released nationwide on Christmas Day of that year. "Effie is such a hugely complex role," the director and writer Bill Condon told Susan Wloszczyna for *USA Today* (November 17, 2005). "She is at once exasperating and heartbreaking. Jennifer emerged as the person who captured both sides."

The Dreamettes, the fictional singers featured in *Dreamgirls*, were loosely patterned on the phenomenally popular Motown trio known as the Supremes, and Effie was based in part on the late Florence Ballard, who had been marginalized by the thinner, lighter-skinned singer Diana Ross. "I've had a similar journey as Effie," Hudson told Hoekstra. "Me being a part of *Idol*, her being part of the group. I was kicked off the talent show. She was [originally] the lead singer of the group and [was] kicked off to the background. We both go through our journeys, trying to hold on to our dream and achieve our goal. We have hardships but we prevail at the end."

When the stage version of *Dreamgirls* appeared on Broadway, playing the role of White made Jennifer Holliday a star and earned her a Tony Award. Holliday's rendition of the show-stopping song "And I Am Telling You I'm Not Going" became legendary among theater aficionados. Hudson, who had grown up idolizing Holliday, described the part to Wloszczyna as "the ultimate, the greatest role in theater history." The movie also starred Beyoncé Knowles, Anika Noni Rose, Jamie Foxx, and Eddie Murphy. At the start of *Dreamgirls*, Effie White is the confident lead singer of an aspiring girl group. At a talent show they impress an ambitious salesman, Curtis Taylor Jr., played by Foxx, who becomes their manager (and White's boyfriend). The group soon secures a spot singing back-up for James "Thunder" Early, played by Murphy. In an effort to improve the group's appeal to white audiences, Taylor makes the slimmer, lighter-skinned Deena Jones (Knowles) the lead singer, sending Hudson's character into a self-destructive tailspin. As she is forced from the group, White sings the powerful anthem "And I Am Telling You I'm Not Going." Hudson had first heard the song as a 12-year-old and had occasionally performed it at talent shows. She was initially intimidated at the thought of following in Holliday's footsteps, but she told Joey Guerra for the *Houston Chronicle* (December 21, 2006), "The first thing I had to do was just realize the character is Effie White and not Jennifer Holliday. Just like [Holliday] put her stamp on it and created her own Effie White, I have to put my Jennifer Hudson mark on it and show why I'm here."

Hudson's work in the film was almost universally acclaimed. It was reported that film audiences across the country were on their feet screaming and applauding during the scene in which Hudson sings "And I Am Telling You I'm Not Going." The *Los Angeles Times* reporter Tom O'Neil wrote on his newspaper-sponsored Web log that Hudson "not only owns the movie, she rides it like a rocket to instant stardom." A. O. Scott wrote for the *New York Times* (December 15, 2006, on-line), "The dramatic and musical peak of *Dreamgirls*—the showstopper, the main reason to see the movie—comes around midpoint, when Jennifer Hudson, playing Effie White, sings 'And I Am Telling You I'm Not Going.' That song has been this musical's calling card since the first Broadway production 25 years ago, but to see Ms. Hudson tear into it on screen nonetheless brings the goose-bumped thrill of witnessing something new, even historic." Scott continued, "It's not often you go to the movies and see a big-boned, sexually assertive, self-confident black woman—not played for laughs or impersonated by a male comedian in drag—holding the middle of the screen. And when was the last time you saw a first-time film actress upstage an Oscar winner [Foxx], a pop diva [Knowles] and a movie star [Murphy] of long standing? Ms. Hudson is not going anywhere. She has arrived." (Scott was alluding to the fact that Hudson, already more curvaceous than the typical actress, had gained an additional 20 pounds to play the role.) For *Variety* (November 30, 2006, on-line), David Rooney wrote, "The emotional intensity [of the film] is immediately pushed several notches higher with Hudson's raw, devastating delivery of 'And I Am Telling You I'm Not Going.' The anthem of proud desperation is forever linked to Jennifer Holliday's defining original interpretation but Hudson makes it her own, singing it on a bare stage backed by mirrors. . . . An *American Idol* finalist without prior screen experience, Hudson comes fully-formed to film."

For her work in *Dreamgirls*, Hudson earned awards in the category of best supporting actress from the African-American Film Critics Association and the Screen Actors Guild. In addition, she took home both a Golden Globe and an Academy Award for best supporting actress. At the Academy Awards ceremony, Hudson joined her co-stars Knowles and Rose for a medley of songs from the movie.

During the awards season, the press widely reported on Hudson's fashion choices, and most observers agreed that Hudson, who had accepted the help of several designers and stylists, including André Leon Talley, an editor at large for the American edition of *Vogue*, had the potential to become a style icon and an inspiration for other full-figured women. Hudson appeared on the cover of the March 2007 edition of *Vogue*, becoming one of only a handful of African-American women whose images have graced the front of that magazine. Anna Wintour, the magazine's famed editor, wrote in her column that month, "[Hudson's] happiness in her own skin is something we can draw strength from. The question of body image is a current one, and I can't think of a more compelling and beautiful argument for the proposition that great fashion looks great on women of all sizes than the sight of Hudson in a Vera Wang [designer] dress on the red carpet."

Despite such adulation, Hudson does have detractors. She was widely quoted as referring to *American Idol* as a "stepping stone," raising the ire of Simon Cowell, who deemed her ungrateful for the opportunities the show had brought her. Additionally, some journalists questioned what they saw as her intolerance of homosexuality; after a flood of such criticism, she wrote on her Web site, "In a recent interview, I was asked how I reconciled being a Christian with performing at events for my gay fans. I find it upsetting that some folks equate being a Christian with being intolerant of gay people. That may, unfortunately, be true for some, but it is not true for me. I have talked often of my love and support of the gay community. I have said again and again that it was the gay com-munity that supported me long before and long after *American Idol*, and kept me working and motivated. It is the gay community that celebrated my voice and my size and my personality long before *Dreamgirls*. Yes, I was raised Baptist. Yes, I was taught that the Bible has certain views on homosexuality. The Bible also teaches us not to judge."

In late 2006 Hudson signed a recording contract with Arista Records, and she is currently working on an album scheduled for release in 2008. She was to appear in two upcoming films. The first, "Winged Creatures," based on a novel of the same name by Roy Freirich, is about a group of strangers who form unique relationships after surviving a random shooting at a Los Angeles diner. That film also stars Kate Beckinsale and Dakota Fanning. In the second motion picture, "Sex and the City: The Movie," Hudson was cast with Sarah Jessica Parker, Kim Cattrell, Cynthia Nixon, Kristin Davis, and others associated with the hit HBO comedy series *Sex and the City*. Hudson was to play Louise, the assistant to Parker's character, Carrie Bradshaw. In June 2007 Hudson was one of 115 actors, filmmakers, studio executives, and others invited to join the Academy of Motion Picture Arts and Sciences, which manages the Oscar-selection system each year.

Hudson, who currently lives in the Hyde Park neighborhood of Chicago, has hinted jokingly that if her film and music career does not work out, her love of drawing may lead her to become a tattoo artist.

—N.W.M.

Suggested Reading: *American Idol* Web site; *Chicago Sun-Times* D p1 Dec. 17, 2006; *Chicago Tribune* Dec. 18, 2006, p6 Feb. 28, 2007; *Jet* p54 Dec. 25, 2006–Jan. 1, 2007; (London) *Evening Standard* A p32 Jan. 25, 2007; (Malaysia) *New Straits Times* p3 Dec. 11, 2004; *New York Times* (on-line) Dec. 15, 2006; *USA Today* D p1 Nov. 17, 2005

Selected Films: *Dreamgirls*, 2006

Hunter, Charlie

May 23, 1967– Jazz guitarist

Address: c/o Leslie DeHaven Spire Artist Management, 5290 College Ave., Oakland, CA 94618

Over the past several decades, musical genres and subgenres have increased seemingly exponentially, and the work of numerous musicians has reflected the influences of those new forms, singly or in combination. As to be expected with any type of experimentation, there have been grand failures and spectacular successes. Responsible for some of

Michael Weintrob, courtesy of charliehunter.com

Charlie Hunter

the latter is the jazz guitarist Charlie Hunter. In his late teens Hunter discovered the music of jazz greats including Charlie Parker, John Coltrane, and Thelonious Monk; afterward he began composing songs that used jazz as a foundation while mirroring the various other musical styles he had absorbed—sounds that ranged from Motown, soul, funk, and gospel to reggae, punk, and rockabilly. Playing unique music on his custom-made eight-string guitar, Hunter started leading groups whose fans were as varied as the influences on his style. Since the appearance of his first album, *The Charlie Hunter Trio*, in 1994, Hunter has released or contributed to dozens of records, the size and memberships of his ensembles changing with almost each one, in keeping with his constant striving for innovation.

Charlie Hunter was born on May 23, 1967 in Providence, Rhode Island, where he lived with his mother and sister. When he was four years old, after his mother had transformed a school bus into a mobile home, the trio set out on a four-year exploration of the United States. Ultimately, his mother decided to settle in Berkeley, California, where she found work as a luthier—a builder and repairer of stringed instruments. "That's how I got my start in playing music, just being surrounded by musicians all the time," Hunter told Chris Kelsey for *Onstage* (January 2001). At first he was interested in playing the drums, but after neighbors complained about the noise, he turned to the guitar.

During Hunter's teen years, in the 1980s, the San Francisco Bay Area was a hotbed of musical activity. Hunter told Jesse Hamlin for the *San Francisco Chronicle* (October 16, 1994) that where he grew up, "there were actual Jamaicans playing reggae,

people playing funk, people playing jazz, real blues and country musicians, actual Africans playing African music. I had the opportunity to delve into all these different kinds of music. I'd get really into one thing, have a nervous reaction to it and go onto the next, as if they were incompatible. The reality is that all music is convergent. My focus is the jazz idiom. That's where I take off from. But I listen to everything and cop whatever I can." Listening to his AM radio, Hunter also knew the popular songs of the day.

Meanwhile, Hunter—like other future music stars, including Kirk Hammett of the band Metallica and David Bryson of Counting Crows—had the good fortune to study with Joe Satriani before that master guitarist gained fame. As a high-school student, Hunter began playing rock and blues in gigs around the Bay Area. Then, at 18, at the suggestion of friends, he began exploring jazz. He told Kelsey, "I heard [the guitarist] Charlie Christian, and my ears were really ready for that. It blew me away and I understood it, and from there I got into the whole bebop thing." Describing his self-education in jazz, he added, "I did it chronologically. I figured out the Charlie Christian stuff and some Tony Grimes solos. From there I went on to learning a few Lester Young things, Coleman Hawkins solos, and then Charlie Parker and on to Coltrane. After that, I got into jazz guitar players like Joe Pass and Wes Montgomery."

At Berkeley High School, renowned for its music program, Hunter struggled, as the traditional environment there clashed with his improvisational style. For a brief period after high school, he studied music theory at a community college, with similar results. He moved to New York City for a short time, then decided to visit a friend in Europe and sharpen his skills by busking on the streets. "I'd play for 12 hours a day . . . ," Hunter recalled to Munson Kyle for the *Des Moines (Iowa) Register* (April 29, 1999). "It's not about introspection. . . . It taught the value of having a show, trying to play for people as opposed to making the people feel like what you're doing is a private thing you're allowing them the privilege of watching." For a few years he returned to Europe each summer.

At one point Hunter decided to play backup for singers, since they drew larger crowds than instrumentalists; that, in turn, led him to add a stronger bass line to his sound. In 1992 Hunter approached a Bay Area luthier, Ralph Novak, about creating a variation on the traditional eight-string guitar. The result was a guitar whose top five strings were tuned to A, D, G, B, and E, while the bottom three were tuned to E, A, and D, like those found on a bass. The most innovative features of the design, now patented by Novak, were the fanned frets: on a normal guitar the frets are perpendicular to the neck, but on Novak and Hunter's creation, the frets fan out, thus allowing for a greater depth of tone. Since then the two have continued to modify Novak's design. Hunter commented to Jeff Niesel for the *Dallas (Texas) Observer* (August 31, 2000) about playing his new instrument, "It's so difficult, I can't even explain it. Imagine pushing a van up the hill with the brake on, and there's a time constraint, and you have to push it with a certain rhythm. While juggling. I'm not interested in just being another guitar player. There's millions of them, so what's the point? What service would I be providing? I'm glad they're doing it, but it's not the road for me, and I'm glad to be doing something different." Fellow musicians have often marveled at Hunter's ability to play bass lines while soloing. Hunter's new instrument would allow him to emulate his jazz-organ heroes, Larry Young and Jimmy Smith, who were able to provide bass lines while performing solos.

In the 1990s Hunter became a prominent figure in a new jazz-fusion scene in the Bay Area, to which critics attached such labels as "hip-hop jazz," "grunge jazz," "avant-rock jazz," "punk-jazz," and, most popularly, "acid jazz." The last-named term soon became an umbrella description for any instrumental music that had jazz riffs but could not be classified as traditional jazz. From the beginning Hunter resisted such labels—he jokingly referred to his sound as "antacid jazz"—while defending the music itself, which he described to Hamlin as being "a lot of fun." Hunter wanted his style to be accessible to his and subsequent generations whose members might not be familiar with many classic jazz tunes. "We know the lineage of jazz, and we're completely in debt to it. We've built the foundation of our music on John Coltrane, on Charlie Parker, on Art Tatum and Thelonious Monk, all the way back through Louis Armstrong and Jelly Roll Morton to the turn of the century," Hunter told Bill Kohlhaase for the *Los Angeles Times* (May 5, 1996). "We want people to know that this is the music that means the most to us. But we also want our audience to know that we're from the twenty something generation, that we share the same experiences as a lot of people our age. That's what we want to communicate; that's what inspires us."

For a time Hunter performed in a duo with Michael Franti, a local poet and rapper. When Franti formed the Disposable Heroes of Hiphoprisy, a politically minded hip-hop group, he asked Hunter to join him on tour. After that ended, Hunter decided that performing before large crowds was not conducive to his musical intentions, and he returned to the Bay Area to participate in a more intimate jazz scene. He soon started the Charlie Hunter Trio with the tenor saxophonist Dave Ellis, an old schoolmate of his, and Jay Lane, the original drummer for Primus. After a series of gigs around the Bay Area, they secured a weekly Tuesday-night engagement at the Elbo Room in San Francisco. As they played together more regularly, the group began to develop their signature sound, and soon Les Claypool, the bass player and leader of Primus, asked them to record an album for his label, Prawn Song. In 1994 the Charlie Hunter Trio released their eponymous first album, recorded on an eight-track tape for $100.

The shows at the Elbo Room and another venue, the Up and Down Club, grew in popularity as word spread about the musical amalgamation driven by an eight-string guitar. The trio also attracted the attention of Blue Note Records, whose president, Bruce Lundvall, recognizing their crossover appeal, offered them a contract in 1994. In the following year they released their first major-label record, *Bing, Bing, Bing!* Hunter stated for his Web site, "I think our music is an alternative to the suit-and-tie club that says you have to be well-to-do and super-intellectual to understand jazz music. We don't have that attitude." *Bing, Bing, Bing!* sold more than 50,000 copies in its first year, a significant figure for a jazz recording. The record drew a positive response from fans and most critics.

Meanwhile, Hunter also worked on his other project, T. J. Kirk. (That group had originally called itself James T. Kirk, the name of the iconic lead character of the first *Star Trek* TV series, played by William Shatner; in the group's case, "James" was inspired by the soul legend James Brown, "T" by Thelonious Monk, and "Kirk" by the jazz multi-instrumentalist Rahsaan Roland Kirk. The name change came about after *Star Trek* representatives threatened a lawsuit.) The band was made up of Hunter, the drummer Scott Amendola, and two more guitarists, John Schott and Will Bernard. They focused solely on the work of the three musicians who made up their namesake, often deconstructing the songs, sometimes melding them. T. J. Kirk was signed by Warner Bros. and released two albums: a self-titled debut (1994) and *If Four Was One* (1996). They reunited in 2003 and released a live album, *Talking Only Makes It Worse*, in 2005.

Soon after the release of the Charlie Hunter Trio's major-label debut, Jay Lane left the group in order to play more rock-oriented music, and Hunter brought in Amendola from T. J. Kirk. Then, having grown weary of the limitations of the trio, Hunter added an alto saxophonist—an old friend from his days of busking in Europe, Calder Spanier. The quartet released the Blue Note album *Ready, Set . . . Shango!* The word "shango," an invention of Hunter's, was inspired by—and meant to confuse—critics who constantly sought to label his work. "It's a total gag," Hunter commented to Jesse Hamlin for the *San Francisco Chronicle* (June 2, 1996). "We invented a new trend to hoodwink the public and give the press something to hang onto."

Hunter's musical interests, like the personnel of his albums and bands, continued to change. A few months after the release of *Shango!*, Dave Ellis left the group to pursue a solo career, and Hunter brought in the tenor-sax player Kenny Brooks from a local Bay Area hip-hop jazz outfit, Alphabet Soup. Meanwhile, Blue Note asked the new version of the Charlie Hunter Quartet to participate in their Cover Series, comprising fresh takes on other artists' music. The result was *Natty Dread* (1997), a new version of the classic, same-titled 1974 reggae album by Bob Marley. The new record received universal praise. "Hunter is the perfect musician for the project [*Natty Dread*] because his musical reach is as expansive as his talent," Michael Point wrote for the *Austin (Texas) American-Statesman* (June 7, 1997). "He's equally at home in a neo-bop jazz mode as he is when locking into the backsliding reggae riddim, and everything he plays is infused with a modern rock attitude." Numerous observers have credited Hunter's rise in popularity to the success of that third Blue Note release.

More innovations followed. "I had worked with horns so long I felt it was time for a change," Hunter told Jay Miller for the Quincy, Massachusetts, *Patriot Ledger* (April 2, 1998). "I've been able to see and hear a lot of different stuff, and I found myself really getting into bands like Dave Holland's, with Steve Nelson on [vibraphones]. And of course I loved the older stuff with vibes, like Cal Tjader, Bobby Hutcherson and Milt Jackson." Hunter formed Pound for Pound, with Amendola on drums, John Santos—the leader of the Machete Ensemble—on other percussion, and Stefon Harris on vibraphone. The new group released *Return of the Candyman*, another departure from Hunter's previous sound. "The philosophy of this whole record is kind of inspired by a hip-hop record," Hunter revealed to Kenn Rodriguez for the *Albuquerque (New Mexico) Journal* (May 15, 1998). "I was inspired by the way hip hop-guys like Tribe Called Quest and Wu-Tang make records. They kinda make these whole theatre pieces with little snippets interspersed here and there. I didn't want [this record] to be just a jazz record. I wanted it to be people with jazz sensibilities trying to make an organic hip-hop record."

Return of the Candyman received mixed reviews. "The varied directions Hunter moves in are what makes *Return of the Candyman* the deep-grooved, rhythmic treat that it is," Kevin Rodriguez wrote. "Using the new line-up and his guitar . . . Hunter is free to make the aural experimentation and shortened songwriting that make the 12-song CD the tasty treat it is, from the funky, odd-timed workout 'Enter the Dragon' to the catchy, soulful 'Pound for Pound' to Hunter's smooth take on Steve Miller's cheese-pop classic 'Fly Like an Eagle.'" Kevin Le Gendre, while praising Hunter's abilities, was less favorably impressed by *Candyman*, writing for the *Journal* (April 3, 1998), "Hunter's playing is superlative—the guy can get lowdown and dirty with the best of 'em but he's let down by the material and production. The basic approach to *Candyman* is very much 'heads down, groove hard' which is all well and good but the problem is that the very fine playing is undercut by the lack of edge in the arrangements."

In late 1997, shortly after the release of *Candyman*, Hunter decided that after more than 20 years in the Bay Area, he needed a change of locale. He felt that New York City was the logical place to move, because the caliber and number of musicians there would offer him a new challenge. Continuing to play with the members of Pound for Pound after the move involved increasingly difficult coast-to-coast travel, so Hunter adjusted the band's roster. "I'm playing with these two badass New York guys," Hunter told Adam Levy for *Guitar Player* (August 1998). "Willard Dyson on drums and Monte Croft on vibes [who toured with Hunter after the release of *Candyman*]. . . . It's atrocious how much better they are than I am. They destroy me every single night, but it's great. They're seasoned New York jazz professionals, they're great musicians, and they're men, not kids. . . . Playing with guys like this is how you grow."

For the next couple of years, Hunter toured extensively, performing with Pound for Pound and in some impromptu ensembles. Then, in 1999, he relaxed his touring schedule in order to work with just one other person, the drummer Leon Parker. "I ran into Leon on the street one day. We talked for quite a while about music in general and then what I had in mind," Hunter stated for his Web site. "He wasn't very familiar with my albums, which was a good thing because we developed a style of playing together that wasn't built on preconceived notions." Later that year the two released the album *Duo*. A reviewer for *Guitar Player* (June 1, 1999) praised the record: "Charlie Hunter's penchant for exploring fresh jazz territory reaches a climax on his fifth release *Duo*. . . . Hunter improvises with uncanny skill—his silky guitar melodies and fat, groovatious bass lines ebb and flow harmoniously, yet remain completely independent. Quite a feat, indeed! Always the pioneer, what Hunter brings to the table this time around is perhaps his most challenging and inspiring album to date." The two-person live performances received similar praise, even after Parker's former roommate and fellow drummer, Adam Cruz, replaced him on the road.

In 2000 Hunter released two albums: *Charlie Hunter* and *Charlie Hunter: Solo Eight-String Guitar*. On the former he worked with Parker again, rounding out the album's personnel with Peter Apfelbaum on tenor saxophone, Josh Roseman on trombone, Stephen Chopek on drums, and Robert Perkins on other percussion. For his next album Hunter decided to include vocalists. While he had worked with singers during his summers in Europe and in a few early gigs in the Bay Area, he found recording with vocalists to be a new experience. Hunter told Andrew Gilbert for the *San Jose (California) Mercury News* (December 14, 2001), "On instrumental things, you have a lot more leeway as far as where the improvisations can go. With singers, you're trying to make three-and four-minute tunes that really work, and you have to come up with arrangements that support the singing, that tie the vocals and the band together." The release, *Songs from the Analog Playground* (2001), included work by the rapper Mos Def, a then-obscure Norah Jones, the jazz crooner Kurt Elling, and Theryl "Houseman" de Clouet, from the New Orleans funk outfit Galactic; those performers were backed up by Hunter's relatively new quartet, with Chopek returning to play drums alongside Chris

Lovejoy on other percussion and John Ellis on tenor saxophone. Numerous critics found the album's songs to be innovative and stimulating, especially those on which Jones performed.

Analog Playground was Hunter's last release of new material on Blue Note Records, as he felt that the label's corporate mission was not a good match with his music. He next signed with a small New York label, Rope-A-Dope Records. In mid-2003 Hunter and Rope-A-Dope released *Right Now Move*, for which Hunter performed with a quintet. "This time I wanted to put together a quintet with a nutty horn section," Hunter remarked to Jay Miller for the *Patriot Ledger* (February 21, 2003). "We have Derek Phillips on drums, Curtis Fowlkes on trombone, John Ellis on tenor sax, and Gregoire Maret on chromatic harmonica. . . . It's been great writing music for this band, this revolving cast of characters." The release received universally good reviews.

Concurrently, Hunter worked on a number of other projects, most notably performing as part of Garage a Trois, whose other members were the drummer Stanton Moore, the vibraphonist/percussionist Mike Dillon, and the saxophonist Skerik. "My thing is always about trying to find the middle ground, that balance between the intellectual and the visceral, and I just feel like New Orleans is what that's about . . . ," Hunter said to Richard Harrington for the *Washington Post* (May 30, 2003). "Stanton is from New Orleans, and he just has that New Orleans feel in everything he plays, whether it's a Brazilian groove, jazz or a shuffle. We just put the group together for fun and played one time at the New Orleans Jazz and Heritage Fest. It was so much fun we decided to keep doing it." Garage a Trois has released three albums: *Mysteryfunk* (1999), *Emphasizer* (2003), and a movie soundtrack, *Outre Mer* (2005). Also, Hunter released two albums, *Longitude* and *Latitude*, with another group, Groundtruther, with Bobby Previte on drums and electronics and DJ Login on turntables.

Ellis and Phillips stayed with Hunter for the releases *Friends Seen and Unseen* (2004) and *Copperopolis* (2006), the latter of which, with its rock influence, marked an even further departure from Hunter's previous recordings. "For the new trio, I wanted to write tunes that weren't as jazzy," Hunter said to Andrew Gilbert for the *San Diego Union-Tribune* (December 7, 2006). "I write these tunes and they're melodic and there's counter melodies, but the player is free to do them when he wants. It's a much looser kind of approach. Improvisation isn't always one person taking a solo while the others are comping behind him. A lot of the time we're trying to improvise as a group." "Hunter is never predictable, and even in his most rock-influenced moments on *Copperopolis*, he avoids recycling tired rock riffs. His ability to play bass and guitar lines simultaneously is just short of amazing, suggesting a fluency approaching Stevie Ray Vaughn levels. 'Cueball Bobbin,' a killer track that opens

the disc, rocks out the most, but as Hunter and company move through the material, their approach changes," Tim Blangger observed for the Pennsylvania *Morning Call* (June 10, 2006). "By the time the musicians arrive at the Thelonious Monk tune, 'Think Of One,' they are playing ephemeral, intriguing stuff, a sea change from 'Cueball.'" As of early 2007, Hunter was playing with a trio that was completed by Erik Deutsch on keyboard and Simon Lott on drums. In the summer of 2007, the trio released *Mistico*, another album that defies categorization.

Charlie Hunter lives in New Jersey with his wife and two children.

—F.C.

Suggested Reading:*Austin American-Statesman* D p7 Apr. 10, 1999, E p9 June 7, 1997; *Boston Globe* D p13 Oct. 26, 2001; Charliehunter.com; *Dallas Observer* Aug. 31, 2000; *Guitar Player* p88 Aug. 1998, p132 June 1, 1999; *Los Angeles Times* p46 Feb. 2, 2003; *Oregonian* p8 June 16, 1995; (Quincy, Massachusetts) *Patriot Ledger* p26 Apr. 2, 1998, p17 Feb. 21, 2003; *San Francisco Chronicle* p35 Oct. 16, 1994, p31 June 2, 1996; *San Jose (California) Mercury News* p26 Dec. 14, 2001; *Washington Post* N p11 Aug. 11, 1995, T p6 May 30, 2003

Selected Recordings: *Charlie Hunter Trio* 1994; *Bing, Bing, Bing!* 1995; *Ready, Set . . . Shango!* 1996; *Natty Dread* 1997; *Return of the Candyman* 1998; *Duo*, 1999; *Charlie Hunter*, 2000; *Solo Eight-String Guitar* 2000; *Songs from the Analog Playground*, 2001, *Right Now Move*, 2003; *Come in Red Dog, This is Tango Leader*, 2003; *Friends Seen and Unseen*, 2004, *Steady Groovin'* , 2005; *Earth Tones*, 2005; *Copperopolis*, 2006. With T.J. Kirk—*T. J. Kirk*, 1994; *If Four Was One*, 1996; *Talking Only Makes it Worse*, 2005; With Garage a Trois— *Mysteryfunk*, 1999; *Emphasizer*, 2003; *Outre Mer*, 2005. With Groundtruther—*Latitude*, 2004; *Longitude*, 2005

Iyengar, B. K. S.

Dec. 14, 1918– Yogi

Address: RIMYI, 1107 B/1 Hare Krishna Mandir Rd., Model Colony, Shivaji Nagar, Pune–411 015, Maharashtra, India

The yoga guru B. K. S. Iyengar was born in a small Indian village during the 1918 influenza pandemic and subsequently fell victim to malaria and tuberculosis. Doctors did not expect him to live past the age of 20. But Iyengar, who turned 89 in 2007, made a dramatic recovery, one he attributes to the physical and spiritual healing powers of the yogic

John Freeman, courtesy of DK Publishing

B. K. S. Iyengar

practice he began when he was 15. Iyengar—whom the BBC has called "the Michelangelo of yoga"— went on to become one of the most famous yogis in the world, widely credited with bringing the approximately 3,000-year-old practice to the West. Described by Stacy Stukin for the *Los Angeles Times* (October 10, 2005) as a man with "wild eyebrows, infectious charisma and notoriety for a ferocious teaching style that includes whacks on the head and slaps on the bum," Iyengar developed his own style of yoga, known for its emphasis on precision and alignment and its use of props such as blocks and ropes to make the yoga positions easier to attain. Iyengar yoga, as the practice is called, now has approximately four million practitioners around the world and is taught at 534 institutes. Over the course of his almost 75 years of practice, Iyengar has given an estimated 10,000 lecture/demonstrations and authored 18 books. Speaking to Iyengar during the guru's most recent visit to the United States, the Reverend Thomas J. Mikelson, a Harvard Divinity School professor, praised his wide-reaching influence. "Because of you, our breath is stronger. Our posture is straighter," Mikelson said, as quoted by Elizabeth Gudrais in the *Providence (Rhode Island) Journal* (October 13, 2005). "We dance more lightly on the earth." The yogi has become such an institution that the word "Iyengar" was recently added to the *Oxford English Dictionary*. "Iyengar means yoga," he told Amy Waldman for the *New York Times* (December 14, 2002). "Yoga means Iyengar. They are synonymous terms."

Yoga, one of the six schools of Hindu philosophy, combines meditation with physical poses— which can range in difficulty from a simple lunge

to an elaborate headstand—as a way of achieving mental clarity, self-knowledge, and eventual enlightenment. Iyengar told Waldman that the practice also gives him "emotional stability" and "spiritual delight." "I can remain thoughtfully thoughtless," Iyengar explained to Waldman. "It is not an empty mind." Today, more than 17 million Americans regularly practice yoga, making it a multibillion-dollar-per-year industry. As yoga has grown in popularity it has also, perhaps inevitably, undergone some distortion. And while Iyengar is consistently praised for bringing yoga to the West, he is also often criticized for his emphasis on physicality and accused of competitiveness with other forms of yoga and other gurus. Iyengar dismisses such criticisms, asserting that his spiritual connection to yoga has freed him from such earthly concerns. "I have not been to school or college. I had no teacher to guide me. Yet I've written books and addressed universities. Is that not enlightenment?" Iyengar told Suma Varughese for *Life Positive* (February 1999). "Yoga gave me the ability to see my body as my small self, and my soul as my infinite self." Speaking with Charlie Rose on *The Charlie Rose Show* (October 14, 2005), Iyengar again attributed the positive developments in his life to his practice. Helping others discover the benefits of yoga—which he credits with saving his life—is his driving purpose, he said. He explained to Rose, "From the years I started yoga up until now, I have lived a contented, happy, healthy life, physically, mentally, intellectually and spiritually."

The 13th child of a poor family, Bellur Krishnamachar Sundararaja Iyengar was born on December 14, 1918, in the village of Bellur, in the Indian state of Karnataka. Iyengar's early life was difficult. The influenza pandemic left both him and his mother sick and weak; his father, Sri Krishnamachar, a schoolteacher, died when Iyengar was nine. Afterward Iyengar left Bellur to live with one of his brothers in Bangalore. Throughout his childhood and adolescence, he was plagued by malaria, tuberculosis, and typhoid fever. "I was an anti-advertisement for yoga," he told Colleen O'Connor for the *Denver Post* (October 9, 2005), adding that he twice considered committing suicide to escape the physical pain of his day-to-day existence. At 15 Iyengar went to live with a sister and her husband, Sri Tirumalai Krishnamacharya, on his brother-in-law's invitation. There, he began to learn yoga under Krishnamacharya's strict instruction. Practicing for 10 hours each day, Iyengar tolerated his teacher's frequent abuse for the sake of improvement. As Iyengar's yogic practice improved, so did his health—a confluence of events he believed was not coincidental. "Health is a dynamic endeavor that requires tremendous intellectual attention," he reflected to Stukin. "You can't walk into the pharmaceutical shop and buy health. It has to be earned with persistence and sweat." Many of Krishnamacharya's other students were scared off by his harsh teaching style; the day before an important demonstration, Krishnamacharya's favorite student ran away, and Iyengar filled in, performing flawlessly.

Iyengar's formal education ended when, at about age 16, he failed his matriculation exam in English by three points. With few other skills, he continued pursuing yoga, in the hope of making a living. Nearly recovered from his illnesses, in 1937 he moved to the city of Pune, in the Indian state of Maharashtra, to teach yoga. But finding students was not always easy, and he often spent days wandering from village to village to teach, sometimes living on just rice and water. "I had tenacity," he told Waldman. "That is a fact." In 1943 his brothers introduced him to a woman named Ramamani, and though he was reluctant to get married, because he felt he could not support a family, he married her that year. He trained Ramamani in the basic yoga poses so that she could supervise him, helping him to perfect his practice. In 1948 Swami Sivananda, the Indian spiritual leader and founder of the Divine Life Society, conferred the title "Yoga Raja" on Iyengar, but despite his success within the practice, the couple lived in poverty for the first several years of their marriage. Still, Iyengar persisted in his attempts to spread the practice of yoga. "Yoga saved me," he explained to Rose. "And I took it as a . . . mission to serve other people who may be suffering like me."

After years of anonymity, Iyengar suddenly rose to fame in 1952, when he took a trip often credited with first exposing the West to the practice of yoga. While still a struggling yogi in India, he was summoned to Bombay for what was supposed to be a five-minute interview with the famous violinist Yehudi Menuhin. Iyengar reluctantly took the seven-hour train ride to the city; the seven a.m. meeting turned into a three-and-a-half-hour yoga session, and Menuhin was instantly taken with yoga. Menuhin arranged for Iyengar to travel to England, France, Switzerland, and other Western European countries to teach. In 1956 the Standard Oil heiress Rebekah Harkness invited Iyengar to travel to the United States, where he was shocked by American life and its incompatibility with the teachings of yoga. "I saw Americans were interested in the three W's—wealth, women and wine," he recalled to O'Connor. "I was taken aback to see how the way of life here conflicted with my own country. I thought twice about coming back." He continued to tour, primarily in Western Europe. Largely through Iyengar's efforts, yoga was increasingly seen as a legitimate practice, as perhaps best indicated by Iyengar's teaching the 85-year-old queen mother of Belgium in 1958 to stand on her head. In 1962 Iyengar's guru, Krishnamacharya, gave him a gold medal inscribed with the words *Yoganga Sikshaka Chakravarti*, which translate as "king among yoga teachers."

Iyengar cemented yoga's influence in the West—as well as his own fame—with his 1966 book, *Light on Yoga*, an illustrated guide to more than 200 *asanas*, or poses. Now translated into 19 languages, the book has sold more than three million copies. Iyengar told Varughese that he knew from the start that he could reach the largest number of people with an illustrated book. One day, he recalled, he saw a book on yoga whose drawings of poses were incorrect. "I decided: 'Here I will hit . . . ,'" he told Varughese. "I decided to show alignment of body, mind and intelligence." The thoroughness and clarity of *Light on Yoga* made it an instant classic—it is often described as "the Bible of yoga"—and made yoga a well-known option among those seeking both physical training and spiritual healing. "*Light on Yoga* is the yoga canon of this century," Joseph S. Alter, the author of *Yoga in Modern India: The Body Between Science and Philosophy*, told Stukin. "It is the most detailed, systematic and precise book out there about yoga [poses and techniques]."

With the success of *Light on Yoga*, Iyengar was able to realize his goal of opening his own yoga studio, the foundation for which was laid on January 26, 1973. Soon afterward, his wife died suddenly, and when the building was dedicated, on January 19, 1975, Iyengar named it the Ramamani Iyengar Memorial Yoga Institute (RIMYI). The institute currently has a three-year waiting list for international students; to attend, an applicant must have eight years of training from an Iyengar school. In 1981 Iyengar published *Light on Pranayama*, a guide to breathing patterns. Three years later he officially retired from teaching yoga, though he continued to publish books and lead special courses. In 1988 he published *The Tree of Yoga*, which compares the eight strains of yoga to the growth of a tree from a seed. A collection of essays on aspects of yoga, the book urges readers to maintain a distinction between their mental and physical properties. "When my body is tired, I say my body is tired," Iyengar wrote, as quoted by Sonja Carberry in *Investor's Business Daily* (January 4, 2007). "I never say I am tired." He also emphasized the utmost importance of self-control and willpower. "So the mind is the maker and the mind is the destroyer. On one side the mind is making you and on the other side it is destroying you. You must tell the destructive side of the mind to keep quiet— then you will learn," he wrote. In 1993 Iyengar published *The Art of Yoga*, a photograph-heavy volume examining the details of each move. He taught an 800-student workshop for a week in Pune to celebrate his 80th birthday, in 1998. The next year he published *Light on Astanga Yoga*, explaining a type of yoga that, according to Iyengar, concerns both the microcosm of man and the macrocosm of the universe. In 2000 he again led a special yoga course, this time for senior Iyengar teachers from 40 countries. Iyengar's book *Yoga: The Path to Holistic Health* appeared in 2001; Susan Salter Reynolds described it for the *Los Angeles Times* (August 5, 2001) as having a "unique look, marrying very clear photos, bright colors and a lot of white space with Iyengar's clear-minded descriptions of the asanas or positions of yoga." She added that the volume is, "essentially, a coffee table book," calling it "completely unintimidating, very Western-looking, very non-mysterious," the last a quality that she felt "has pros and cons"—as it puts an emphasis on the accessibility of a physical understanding of yoga, rather than on the more difficult spiritual underpinnings of the practice. Iyengar, who is frequently criticized for his focus on the physical, defended his method to Kim Lawton for *Religion & Ethics NewsWeekly* (August 4, 2006): "Can a musician play the violin without body?" he asked. "Then you say, 'He played beautifully. It was spiritual.' How can you say spiritual when he has used his body, holding the instrument? So we are also using the body as an instrument to tune the inner mind and the consciousness."

For his role in bringing yoga to the West, *Time* named Iyengar one of its "100 Most Influential People of 2004." Even at an advanced age, Iyengar maintained a reputation for being a demanding teacher, whose predilection for hitting his students until they achieved the correct position led to the joke that his initials—B.K.S.—actually stand for "beat, kick, slap." "People brand me as a tough teacher," he told Tom Dunkel for the *Baltimore Sun* (October 14, 2005). "Unfortunately, this is a wrong word. I am an 'intense' teacher. A tough teacher has a quality of roughness, and an intense teacher has the qualities of keenness, softness, smoothness and rhythm." In 2004 the journalist and yoga practitioner Elizabeth Kadetsky published her memoir, *First There Is a Mountain: A Yoga Romance*, which contains a controversial profile of Iyengar. Kadetsky told Stukin that she set out to show him as "a fascinating, complicated genius with all the convoluted character particularities any genius has"; those "particularities" included a decided competitiveness between Iyengar and teachers of other forms of yoga.

In 2005 Iyengar published his most recent book, *Light on Life*, which he promoted with a five-city U.S. tour—his last U.S. visit, he said. Since he retired, Iyengar has continued to practice yoga privately between five and six hours a day. "I can't say, 'I'm old, so I don't want to do it,'" he explained to Waldman. "The escapism of other people, I don't want." In 2005, at age 86, he told Dunkel that he was still able to do the majority of the yoga poses he could do in his youth, but emphasized that the focus of his practice is the present and his present capabilities. "What I do today is important, and I do not brood about my past practices," he said. "But what I do at this age, I do it to the maximum. I do not make any concessions, but I work harder with the wisdom that I gained."

Iyengar lives in Pune. He holds honorary doctorates from the University of Pennsylvania and the University of Mysore and has won state and national awards in India. He also oversees a charitable foundation working to alleviate poverty in his home village of Bellur.

Iyengar did not remarry after Ramamani's death. From their marriage he has five daughters—Geeta, Vinita, Suchita, Sunita, and Savita—and one son,

Prashant. Both Geeta and Prashant—who were instructed by their father and mother—teach at RIMYI. Iyengar explained to Stukin the significance of that legacy: "I have to give them the secrets so they can help humanity and carry on."

—C.S.

Suggested Reading: *Baltimore Sun* D p4 Oct. 14, 2005; bksiyengar.com; *Denver Post* L p1 Oct. 9, 2005; *Los Angeles Times* F p1 Oct. 10, 2005; *Life Positive* (on-line) Feb. 1999; *New York Times* A p4 Dec. 14, 2002

Selected Books: *Light on Yoga*, 1966; *Light on Pranayama*, 1981; *The Tree of Yoga*, 1988; *The Art of Yoga*, 1993; *Light on Astanga Yoga*, 1999; *Yoga: The Path to Holistic Health*, 2001; *Light on Life*, 2005

Chung Sung-Jun/Getty Images

Jacobs, Paul E.

Oct. 30, 1962– Telecommunications executive

Address: Qualcomm, 5775 Morehouse Dr., San Diego, CA 92121

In 2005 Paul E. Jacobs became the CEO of Qualcomm, the company his father, Irwin Jacobs, had founded two decades earlier. Upon taking the reins of the firm, which is at the forefront of Code Division Multiple Access (CDMA) technology for wireless voice and data products, the younger Jacobs came under intense scrutiny. "If the company is successful under me, it's because I'm carrying on what Irwin put into place," he told David Whelan for *Forbes* (November 28, 2005). "If there's a glitch, it's because I'm his dumb kid." While it may be possible to characterize the new CEO as a kid (at age 42, he was considered young to be placed at the helm of a Fortune 500 company), it is unlikely that anyone would ever call him dumb: Jacobs has a doctoral degree in electrical engineering and holds more than 30 patents in the area of wireless technology. "I firmly believe the wireless Internet is going to have a bigger impact on the world than the wired Internet," Jacobs told Julie Schlosser for *Fortune* (April 18, 2005). "In a lot of the world people don't have PCs [personal computers] or wired connections. Their only connection to the Internet will be through their phone. As you fold all these technologies into the phone, it will become the main personal device that people use."

Paul Eric Jacobs, the third of four sons, was born on October 30, 1962 in Cambridge, Massachusetts, to Irwin M. and Joan Jacobs. His father was an electrical engineer and a professor at the Massachusetts Institute of Technology. When Paul was four years old, the family moved from Massachusetts to Southern California, and his father took a job in one of the engineering departments at the University of California–San Diego. Paul Jacobs, a *Star Trek* enthusiast, shared his father's scientific bent. While growing up he "discussed antennas and data transmission rates with his father the way many of his friends and their fathers talked balls and strikes," as Matt Richtel wrote for the *New York Times* (April 14, 2003, on-line). (Jacobs did have some interest in sports, however; he and his brothers were avid basketball players and sometimes broke bones during their spirited competitions on the court.)

While Jacobs was in high school, he spent his summer vacations working in the drafting department of his father's first company, Linkabit, a defense contractor that the elder Jacobs had founded in the late 1960s, and that designed software for satellites. The father and son "would talk about all the angles sitting at dinner, driving everyone else crazy," as he told Richtel. At La Jolla High School, Jacobs showed an early knack for entrepreneurial ventures, teaming with his friend Jeff Belk, who later joined Qualcomm, to form J&B Enterprises; the two friends sold skateboards to fellow students—using some of their profits to obtain the best boards for themselves.

In 1984 Jacobs graduated from the University of California–Berkeley, with a B.S. degree in electrical engineering. He continued at the school and earned a master's degree, in 1986, and a doctoral degree, in 1989. (His dissertation was on the subject of robotic path planning.) Jacobs was a popular figure around the Berkeley campus during his years there; he once started an intramural volleyball team—primarily to meet women. From that point of view, the undertaking was a success: he met his future wife, Stacy, as a result. A skilled networker, he often helped his friends secure jobs at Qualcomm, which his father had founded in 1985.

(Qualcomm's earliest consumer products were Eudora, an e-mail program, and OmniTRACS, a satellite-communications technology that enabled companies to track freight.) Besides his prowess in the social arena, Jacobs was considered a stellar student. A former professor of his, John Canny, told Jennifer Davies for the *San Diego Union-Tribune* (November 4, 2001), "Paul has all the attributes of a great researcher. Most importantly, he is a prolific generator of ideas. He backs this up with patience and attention to detail." Upon completing his Ph.D. program, Jacobs moved to Toulouse, France, for postdoctoral work at a robotics laboratory. He returned to California in 1990 and joined Qualcomm as a full-time development engineer. (As he had done at Linkabit, Jacobs had worked at the company during school breaks, designing chips and assembling circuit boards.) His mother made it clear to him that she was not happy about his career choice; she had expected him to become a professor. "I just wasn't that excited by the idea of doing research and then presenting a paper," Jacobs told Davies. "I really like the idea of building products, getting things out there that everyone can use." Jacobs's brother Jeff started at the company on the same day, in the finance department; he is now the company's president of global development.

As often happens in the private sector, other Qualcomm workers complained that Jacobs owed his job entirely to nepotism. "People thought Irwin did the homework for him at night and gave him the answers," Allen Salmasi, Jacobs's first boss at Qualcomm, told Whelan. Jacobs worked hard, however, and his colleagues quickly began to acknowledge him as a valuable member of the team. Whelan wrote, "[Jacobs] soon came to be regarded as a brilliant and intense competitor, much like his father but marked by a macho, I'll-show-you attitude of someone who has something to prove." Jacobs developed many of the patents he now holds during those early years at Qualcomm, when his work focused on speech-coding technology for cell phones. Once, when his father demanded that he design a speech synthesizer (called a vocoder) of low quality in order to preserve valuable radio-wave spectrum, Jacobs, without the consent of his supervisors, covertly developed a high-quality product that offered improved voice clarity; with that invention, the company entered lucrative Asian markets, in which such clarity is especially prized.

CDMA, which enables more subscribers of a cell-phone network to make connections simultaneously than would otherwise be possible, remains among the most profitable of Qualcomm's technologies. By 1995 the potential of CDMA had become obvious to those at Qualcomm, but finding a manufacturer willing to distribute CDMA–based cell phones proved to be difficult. Most mobile-phone manufacturers at the time were basing their products on Global System for Mobile (GSM), then the industry standard. In order to prove the superiority of their new technology, Qualcomm joined with the Sony Corp. to create a new handset-manufacturing business that would build mobile phones based on CDMA. Jacobs was appointed vice president and general manager of the fledgling concern; at the time he was 33 years old. He was pleased with the promotion yet occasionally awed by the added responsibility of his new position. "I could come in on any given day and be presented with a problem that could cost the company . . . $100 million," he told Davies. There were many such problems: manufacturing bugs were frequently discovered in Qualcomm's early phone models, and on one occasion Jacobs shut the factory down. "We had two products come out that had very bad quality," he told Davies. Greg Heinzinger, who is now a vice president at Qualcomm, recalled to Davies, "We stopped building phones for basically three months while we fixed our problems. It cost a lot of money in the short run. But we got respect from our customers."

As the market for CDMA technology increased, revenue from Qualcomm mobile phones soared, reaching a peak of nearly $1.5 billion in 1999. Still, Jacobs was unable to turn a profit, and the handset division was deemed unsuccessful. (Most observers blame Jacobs's insistence on manufacturing in La Jolla rather than in a cheaper labor market.) In 2000 Qualcomm sold the handset business to Kyocera of Japan for $242 million, recouping most of the firm's losses, and in 2001 Jacobs was appointed group president of Qualcomm Wireless & Internet (QWI). By that time Qualcomm had proven the viability of CDMA, which it began licensing to other manufacturers for use in their mobile phones.

While group president of QWI, Jacobs initiated many innovative programs. One of his most substantial contributions to the company's fortunes was the development of the software and the business plan for BREW (Binary Runtime Environment for Wireless). BREW is a software application that allowed users to download and run small programs for playing games, sending messages, and sharing photos on mobile handsets. It is now used by more than 50 carriers and almost that many phone manufacturers. Jacobs had less success with other ideas, however. Wingcast, his attempt to partner with Ford to put a wireless communications system in certain automobile models, lost $25 million. Digital Cinema, his venture to transmit film digitally instead of using movie reels, had a similar fate, as did a planned project with Microsoft. Jacobs, Whelan wrote, "racked up a reputation for combining high intelligence with a low success rate for business decisions." Nevertheless, Qualcomm insiders quietly acknowledged that Jacobs was the likely successor to his father.

In June 2005 Qualcomm celebrated its 20th anniversary with a massive party held at Qualcomm Stadium, home of the San Diego Chargers football team. (In 1997 the company had donated $18 million to the city for use in renovating the ve-

nue, in exchange for naming rights.) By July 2005, when Jacobs officially took over as CEO of Qualcomm, the company had 9,000 employees and was earning nearly $6 billion in annual revenues. Some within the industry believed that Jacobs lacked the requisite experience and business acumen to run a company that size, but because the decision of the board of directors was perceived as a foregone conclusion, no serious candidates—internally or externally—emerged to challenge Jacobs. The board dismissed accusations of nepotism, assuring stockholders that there had indeed been a formal search process and that Jacobs had been the strongest candidate.When Qualcomm's board announced the appointment, its director Marc Stern explained the choice to Bruce Bigelow for the *San Diego Union-Tribune* (March 9, 2005): "The perfect CEO would have a technical background. We thought that was important. We wanted someone experienced in the industry. We wanted someone, who if we could find them, had been at Qualcomm for a long time and who was part of the unique culture at Qualcomm." Jan Dehesh, a former Qualcomm executive, told Bigelow, "You can be assured that Paul has been groomed in every way for this position. He started at the bottom, and he's worked in engineering in numerous places. So he's seen all levels. He's worked at all levels. I think he is respected internally because he is a Ph.D., and Qualcomm is an engineering company."

Because a large percentage of Qualcomm's revenues came from licensed technologies, and the wireless telecommunications business was booming, Jacobs stepped into a position in which simply maintaining the status quo would mean financial success for the company. (Qualcomm receives royalties estimated at 5 percent of the sales price of wireless handsets using its chips or CDMA technology.) At the end of the 2005 fiscal year, Qualcomm had $2.1 billion in net revenues—a 25 percent increase from the previous year—but Jacobs was not content to see the company compete in a quickly developing field by relying on existing technologies. One of his first actions as CEO was to increase Qualcomm's $1 billion annual research and development budget by 40 percent, in an effort to develop lower-cost phones, new wireless technology, and integrated circuit products. Qualcomm-designed chips and technologies were used in the majority of cell phones in the U.S. and a growing number in Europe, particularly in high-end cell phones, but Jacobs saw a greater potential in developing markets. "The next 1 billion subscribers will come from markets with low per capita GDP [gross domestic product]," Jacobs told Mike Allen for the *San Diego Business Journal* (July 25, 2005). Jacobs also expanded OmniTRACS, with an eye toward increased homeland security, establishing initiatives to track hazardous materials and implementing technology that would allow emergency personnel to be contacted instantly in the event of an accident.

As CEO Jacobs orchestrated the purchase of Flarion Technologies, a wireless technology company that specialized in transmitting large amounts of data to mobile devices, and in 2006 Qualcomm introduced MediaFLO, a technology designed to reduce significantly the cost of delivering multimedia content to mobile handsets. (Jacobs has pointed out that mobile handsets will be an effective way of delivering vital information to subscribers in the event of a natural disaster or war.) Also in 2006 Jacobs, after earlier failing to do so, reached an agreement with Microsoft to create Windows-based phones. Industry observers have noted that Microsoft brings credibility to Qualcomm's attempt to extend beyond CDMA and that the agreement positions Qualcomm to be a potential leader in the emerging mobile-content industry. Jacobs tries always to keep his father's vision in mind. "The transition from Irwin Jacobs to me went smoothly because I was not looking to change the entire direction of the company," he told a reporter for *Business 2.0*, posted on CNN.com. "I wanted to push even harder toward what he started: turning the phone into much more than a device for making calls."

The still-athletic Jacobs once swung down more than 30 feet from the rafters of an auditorium in a ninja costume during a company meeting. (He had arranged for an ambulance to park outside the building in case the stunt failed.) He and his wife, Stacy, live in Southern California with their three children. The couple recently endowed an engineering chair at the University of California, Berkeley. Jacobs serves on several boards, including those of San Diego's Museum of Contemporary Art, the Salk Institute for Biological Studies, and the Jacobs School of Engineering—an institution named after his father at the University of California–San Diego. He enjoys downhill skiing in Colorado and loves to eat the French dishes that Stacy learned to prepare while they were living in France. He carries two cell phones, one of which is said to be a Motorola prototype.

—N.W.M.

Suggested Reading: *BusinessWeek* p2 May 23, 2005; *Forbes* p130 Nov. 28, 2005; *Fortune* p45 Apr. 18, 2005; *Network World* Feb. 5, 2001; *New York Times* C p1 Apr. 14, 2003; *San Diego Business Journal* p1 June 27, 2005, p4 July 25, 2005; *San Diego Union-Tribune* H p1 Nov. 4, 2001, (on-line) Mar. 9, 2005, Aug. 12, 2005

John, Daymond

Feb. 3, 1969– Fashion designer

Address: c/o W & W Public Relations Inc., 476 Union Ave., Second Fl., Middlesex, NJ 08846

In the 1990s the apparel company FUBU emerged as a standard-bearer for urban fashion. The company's signature bright colors and logo—the letters "FUBU" in a modern font—won over a broad array of devotees, from African-American youth in the New York City borough of Queens, where the brand was born, to teenagers in South Korea. In just a few years, FUBU's founder, Daymond John-Aurum, commonly known as Daymond John, went from waiting tables at a Red Lobster restaurant to overseeing a company worth hundreds of millions of dollars. While his three closest friends have played a large part in FUBU's success since its earliest days, it was John's vision that catapulted FUBU from a cramped workshop in his mother's basement in Hollis, Queens, to its current headquarters, on the 66th floor of the Empire State Building, in Manhattan. FUBU has 60 stores around the world, and its clothing is carried in a variety of outlets and department stores, most notably Macy's. According to the FUBU Web site, FUBU is sold in 17 countries on six continents. The line sells particularly well overseas, especially in France and South Korea.

David Klein/Getty Images

Daymond John was born in the New York City borough of Brooklyn on February 3, 1969 to Margot John, an African-American, and Garfield John, an immigrant from Trinidad. Margot John had competed in the first Miss Black America pageant and in the Miss New York pageant; she was also one of

JOHN

the first black women to work as a hostess at the Playboy Club in New York. Daymond John has recalled that his mother kept on their kitchen wall a two-foot-long can opener emblazoned with the words "Think Big." She taught her son to cook his own meals and sew his own clothing. Her sewing lessons were to have a great influence on her son's future career.

John's family moved to Farmers Boulevard in the borough of Queens when he was a child. When John was 10 his father moved out, and his mother filed for divorce. Soon, Margot and Daymond John were living on food stamps and struggling from month to month to pay the bills. At 12 John chose to stop speaking to his father, and he has not gone back on that decision since. After his father left, John's mother worked two jobs—or three, during particularly tough times—in order to support herself and her son. John told *People* (March 17, 1997), "I owe my success to my mom, who instilled in me the fact that I could do anything I wanted to do."

John was entrepreneurial from a very early age. At the private, Catholic St. Gerard Magellan School, he picked up or stole all the pencils he could find, shaved the yellow paint off the sides with a pen knife, put his own designs on them, and sold them for a quarter each. He rebuilt old bicycles salvaged from the trash with the assistance of his mother's boyfriend, Steve, who replaced Garfield John as the boy's father figure. When he was 12 his mother gave him a supply of condoms to take with him to YMCA summer camp for his own use; John sold the condoms to other campers. When he was 14 he became a junior counselor at the same camp, hustling campers and fellow counselors at pool for money. According to his memoir, *Display of Power: How FUBU Changed a World of Fashion, Branding and Lifestyle* (2007, co-written by Daniel Paisner), John used the money—despite minimum-age requirements—to buy cigarettes and beer in the nearest town, returning to camp to sell the items at a high markup. He also sold marijuana that he had brought with him from Queens. He told Mitchell S. Jackson for *Smooth* magazine (March 2007), "Not that I'm trying to portray myself as a big drug dealer, but I was trying to scramble for a nickel and a dime one way or another." He made approximately $1,800 on top of his $200 camp salary.

When John entered high school, his mother took out an $80,000 mortgage on their house so that she could stop working and keep a close eye on him. She also sent him away each summer, for trips to visit family and friends in California, Hawaii, Bermuda, Canada, and Trinidad so that he could witness ways of life different from that in his tough neighborhood and stay out of trouble. During the school year he had jobs at fast-food restaurants or retail stores. He also became acquainted with the future rap star LL Cool J, then known as James Todd Smith III, whose assistance would be as important to John's success as his mother's sewing lessons.

After he graduated from high school, John's mother took a full-time job at American Airlines, and the family no longer needed to depend on food stamps. John started a commuter van service in South Jamaica, Queens, and became a waiter at a Red Lobster restaurant. He told Danielle Stolich for the *Source* (March 2007), "At 20, I was very confused and felt it was time to be a man. You have this idea of 'making it' but when you fall short of that you tend to go towards making quick, easy money. No matter who you are, it's never easy money; it's just borrowed time you're on. Watching a lot of my friends die or go to jail made me feel that I could end up that way too. I then decided to do something that was fulfilling, not just in a monetary aspect but that I wouldn't have to watch my back."

In 1992 John saw a music video starring the pioneering hip-hop group De La Soul and noticed that one of the group members wore a tie-top hat. He embarked on a day-long quest to find a similar hat. In *Display of Power*, as quoted by *King-Mag.com* (February 8, 2007), John wrote, "This was really the first time I was consciously aware of the subliminal power of music videos as a marketing tool, and I was a textbook case. . . . And when I finally found [a hat like the one in the video], I was disappointed. They were charging like thirty dollars for it, and the thing was so poorly constructed it looked like it wouldn't last but a week . . . and soon as I got home with the thing I got out my mother's sewing machine and started sewing a couple knock-offs. . . . Soon, a couple friends wanted to know if I could make a hat for them, so I turned out a few more."

John began making hats in his mother's basement to sell at concerts and neighborhood festivals. He told *People* (March 17, 1997) about a day he spent at a Queens shopping mall, where he and a friend "sold about $800 worth of hats, and I was hooked." While keeping his full-time job at Red Lobster, he set out to build a fashion business on the side. He told *People*, "I would get up at 8, go buy fabrics, make some hats until 2 p.m., call stores or go try and sell them until 4 or 5 o'clock, go to work the dinner shift, get home about 12 and make hats until around 5 in the morning." He recruited his childhood friends Alexander Martin, Carl Brown, and Keith Perrin to work with him. Brown had a job loading and unloading trucks; Perrin worked as an apartment-building supervisor; and Martin, a Gulf War veteran, was attending the Fashion Institute of Technology, in the borough of Manhattan. Martin frequently consulted his professors for advice on how to expand the friends' business. John said on the program *CNN Movers with Jan Hopkins* (January 8, 2000) that Martin "definitely [had] a vision for fashion. We had a hunger for money. So you know, that put it together."

John, Martin, Brown, and Perrin chose as the name of the business the acronym FUBU (For Us, By Us), which referred to their identities as friends and as young African-American men. John told Tavis Smiley for National Public Radio (October 21, 2002), "We were frustrated because around 1990 . . . a lot of articles came out where designers were saying that they didn't make things cut for black people, they didn't sell boots to black people because we were all drug dealers and none of their money came from us . . . we were saying, you know, 'We know [black people are] starting all the trends. When is anybody going to acknowledge it, or is it that, you know, we're just like a sickness or a disease that nobody wants to acknowledge?'"

Within half a year FUBU sold $10,000 worth of hats. John and his partners used the profits to start a line of shirts. Soon the company fell victim to its own success: by the end of 1993, FUBU had received $60,000 worth of orders but lacked the funds for material to fill them. Meanwhile, the urban sportswear market was exploding, with the multimillionaire fashion designers Tommy Hilfiger and Ralph Lauren attracting scores of young black male customers—exactly the demographic that FUBU wished to court. Recognizing that he could not match the other designers' advertising power, John embarked on an innovative grassroots marketing campaign, offering free merchandise to rappers and singers if they agreed to wear the apparel in their music videos. He said on CNN Movers with Jan Hopkins, "It was persistence, because I went to video sets where I got doors slammed in my face. Stylists would not talk to me, or the artist would say, wait here, I'm going to wear it. I wait there for 12 hours and then they don't wear it, and they tell me, go home."

John approached his childhood acquaintance LL Cool J about wearing FUBU hats in his videos. Reluctant initially, the rapper began to do so, and eventually other celebrities, including the singer Mariah Carey and the actor and rapper Will Smith, did the same. In 1994 Team FUBU, as John and his partners called themselves, traveled to Las Vegas, Nevada, to attend the MAGIC trade show, the world's largest industry event for designers, textile manufacturers, and corporate buyers. Unable to pay for a booth at the convention, the young men rented a hotel room and invited people to view the new, expanded FUBU line of apparel. They garnered $400,000 worth of clothing orders—a triumph that, ironically, only added to their troubles, multiplying the number of orders they could not afford to fill. John approached several banks for funding and was turned down by all of them. He told Charles Molineaux on the TV program CNN Business Unusual (May 30, 1998), "I decided, 'It's either do or die right now, and we need the capital, and nobody else really cares about what we're doing or actually believes in us.'"

Guided by those realizations, John, along with his mother, took out a $100,000 mortgage on his mother's home. Margot John moved out, and Perrin, Brown, and Martin moved in. John bought 10 sewing machines and hired four professional sewers. Still unable to keep up with the mounting orders, Team FUBU grew despondent and, according to John, nearly gave up, until his mother urged them to seek outside financing once again. Without her son's knowledge, Margot John placed a classified ad in the New York Times. Daymond John wrote in Display of Power, "The ad said something like, 'One million dollars in orders, need financing.' And we got a couple dozen calls on it." Finally, in 1995 the South Korea–based electronics manufacturer Samsung Corp. agreed to invest $2 million in FUBU through its U.S. branch, Samsung America. The corporate backing lent Team FUBU the credibility they needed to attract the interest of major department-store chains.

In 1996 FUBU became the first design company owned by African-Americans to have its own display window in Macy's flagship store in Manhattan. That same year LL Cool J became the company's first paid spokesman. He famously wore a FUBU cap in a commercial for The GAP clothing company. As a result of those developments and support from other corners, "you couldn't turn on the TV without seeing" FUBU clothing, as John told Smiley. "So it was like an explosion onto the scene. And that kicked open a lot of doors where a lot of these huge retailers started buying our product. . . . The younger African-Americans were feeling, 'These brothers look like me and they understand me. Whether I want to support them or not, I can't resist. These guys live like me.' And as in anything in this country, African-Americans set the trends for a lot of things, and after that everything else fell into place." John noted to Smiley that FUBU's "first huge markets" were in Japan and Seattle, Washington, "where there are very few African-Americans. But, you know, those were niche markets."

In 1997 sales of FUBU apparel reached $70 million. Team FUBU created the FUBU Foundation, which they endow with $1 million annually; the foundation contributes money to food drives, organizations for the homeless, and other projects and groups. In 1998 FUBU grew into a $200 million empire thanks to expanded distribution in the retail chains Nordstrom, Foot Locker, and Champs and in thousands of independent shops and boutiques. With FUBU's success came complaints that its clothes cost too much. According to Diane Seo, writing for the Los Angeles Times (July 8, 1998), John argued that FUBU products were less expensive than those bearing the Tommy Hilfiger or Polo labels, "with quality that is just as high." John said to Seo, "The assumption is because we're black designers, we shouldn't sell expensive clothes." Also as a result of dramatically widened distribution, FUBU reached a new market: white suburban teenagers. Some critics felt that white teenagers' wearing FUBU fashions weakened the brand's street credibility as a homegrown African-American clothing line. John told Ryon Horne for the Atlanta Journal-Constitution (October 22, 2000), "To be real with you, it has never been just for African-Americans. . . . We won't deny that blacks are the majority who buy it, and it's energized by blacks. But it's here for everyone to enjoy."

FUBU's ubiquity in malls across the nation also meant that the line was subject to wider scrutiny by the American public. In several well-publicized instances, public schools banned students from wearing the brand on the grounds that it had become associated with gangs and crime. John told Horne, "We know they did this to Tommy [Hilfiger], and they did it to Starter, saying it was gang-related. They're always going to pick on somebody, but we understand that our label is not created out of hate. Clothes don't hurt anyone. We're just trying to make it hot for everyone."

In 1999 FUBU joined with the National Basketball Association to create a line of sports apparel called FUBU NBA. The next year Team FUBU founded FB Entertainment, a company designed to create and produce entertainment in various media. FB Entertainment soon signed a development deal with Artists Television Group (ATG) that enabled Team FUBU members to serve as executive producers on any entertainment properties acquired through the partnership. The following year FB Entertainment released an album, *FB Entertainment Presents the Good Life*, with tracks by various artists. The album spawned a radio hit, "Fatty Girl," featuring the rappers Keith Murray, Ludacris, and LL Cool J. In February 2001 Senator Hillary Rodham Clinton of New York honored John for his charitable efforts in New York City. That year *Crain's New York* ranked FUBU second on its list of the top minority-owned companies in New York City. By 2002 more than 5,000 retail stores in 26 countries carried FUBU clothing, which now included suits, children's wear, a women's line, loungewear, accessories, shoes, watches, bedding and bath items, clothes for infants, a "plus-size" women's clothing line, and a fragrance, Plush.

In February 2005 LL Cool J filed suit with the New York County Supreme Court claiming that Team FUBU had failed to compensate him adequately for endorsing the clothing line. (Easily accessible sources do not yield information on the status of the lawsuit.) The lawsuit came on the heels of a period in which FUBU had seen its popularity decline in the United States, while remaining strong overseas. FUBU also saw part of its market share eaten away by competing urban streetwear lines including the Sean John line, started by the rapper, actor, and producer Sean "P. Diddy" Combs; the rapper Jay-Z's Rocawear line; and the hip-hop mogul Russell Simmons's Phat Farm label.

In the fall of 2005, the FUBU Foundation donated $1 million in clothing to victims of Hurricane Katrina in Baton Rouge, Louisiana. John, Perrin, the talk-show host Montel Williams, and members of the nonprofit Christian relief and development group World Vision Inc. traveled to the city to distribute the clothing.

Over the years John and Team FUBU have received many awards, among them, in 1999, the Congressional Achievement Award for Entrepreneurship, the New York African American Business Award for Outstanding Business Achievement, *Brandweek*'s Marketer of the Year Award, the NAACP Entrepreneurs of the Year Award, a Citation of Honor from the Borough of Queens in the City of New York, and the *Essence* Award, the last marking the first time that *Essence* presented its highest honor to a company; in 2000, the Black Alumni of Pratt Creative Spirit Award; in 2001, the *Source* Foundation's Hip Hop Cares Award; and in 2003, Ernst & Young's New York Entrepreneur of the Year Award.

In 2007 John published *Display of Power: How FUBU Changed a World of Fashion, Branding and Lifestyle*. He became the first-ever retailer to sell a book at the MAGIC apparel convention in Las Vegas. A reviewer for *Publishers Weekly* (January 29, 2007, on-line) called the book "informative and well written . . . this is a worthwhile read for aspiring businessmen, fashionistas and laymen alike." John told Claire Sulmers for *King-Mag.com* (February 8, 2007) that he decided to write the book because "the corporate world thinks that people like us [African-Americans] are just hanging out, smoking weed, [wearing] baggy pants, and drinking Cristal. I want them to understand that we are strategic thinkers, there's a method to our madness, and that our market is a strong, educated and disciplined market in some regards." In 2006 FUBU opened its 60th store, in Beijing, China.

John serves as CEO of FUBU and of an independent marketing company, Stealth Branding Group, through which he engages in work as a motivational speaker, marketing and corporate consultant, and life coach. He also oversees the FUBU brands Coogi, Heatherette, Kappa USA, Drunkn Munky, and Ether. He has two daughters, Destiny and Yasmeen, with his ex-wife, Maria. He resides in New York City. When asked by Jackson, "What do you want your peers to say about you?" John responded, "He was morally correct. He was always straight up with you, whether he liked you or not. And he uplifted a lot of young people and helped better our culture."

—S.J.D.

Suggested Reading: *Atlanta Journal-Constitution* Dixie Living p8M Oct. 22, 2000; *Chicago Tribune* C p1 June 20, 1999; *People* p62 Mar. 17, 1997; *Upscale* p102 Mar. 2007

Selected Books: *Display of Power: How FUBU Changed a World of Fashion, Branding and Lifestyle* (with Daniel Paisner), 2007

Ronald Martinez/Getty Images

Johnson, Avery

Mar. 25, 1965– Basketball coach

Address: Dallas Mavericks, The Pavilion, 2909 Taylor St., Dallas, TX 75226

Avery Johnson has made a name for himself in the National Basketball Association (NBA) by proving his doubters wrong. Considered to be undersized for an NBA player, at five feet 11 inches tall, Johnson joined the Seattle Supersonics in 1988 after being passed over earlier that year for the NBA draft. In 16 seasons in the league, he became a career journeyman, calling six cities home over the years and playing in more than 1,000 regular-season games, making him only the second NBA player under six feet to pass that mark. As a player he will always be most celebrated for sinking a jump shot in the waning seconds of Game Five of the 1999 NBA finals, clinching the San Antonio Spurs' championship victory over the New York Knicks and quieting the many coaches, players, and fans who, at every point in his playing career, had questioned Johnson's ability to make such medium-range field-goal attempts. By the end of his first full season as head coach of the Dallas Mavericks, in 2006, Johnson had helped squash the team's reputation for having a superior offense but a weak defense: he led the Mavericks to a 60–22 regular-season record, which matched a franchise high for wins in one season. In postseason play Johnson directed the team to basketball's most coveted stage, the NBA finals, a level the franchise had never reached since it joined the league for the 1980–81 season. Although Dallas lost the series to the Miami Heat, most observers judged the Mavericks'

2005–06 season, buoyed by their new defensive skills, to be a significant step forward, and in April 2006 Johnson was named the NBA's coach of the year. In just over one season as an NBA head coach, Johnson had reached the 50-win mark faster than any other coach and earned the best record for a starting coach in the first 82 games of his career.

Known as the "Little General" even before he officially became a coach, Johnson is considered a hard-driving motivator, and his players welcome his instruction. "If there was a wall there and Avery said to go through it, if he's telling me to do it, in my mind I'm thinking there is a soft spot in there somewhere because everything he's told me up to this point has been real and has helped me," Jerry Stackhouse, a vital reserve on the Mavericks' roster, told Michael Lee for the *Washington Post* (June 11, 2006). Johnson is likewise regarded as genuinely kindhearted by fellow coaches and former teammates alike. "He's such a fun-loving, good guy," one of Johnson's teammates from his days with the Spurs, Tim Duncan, told Oscar Dixon for *USA Today* (February 19, 2006, on-line). "He's one of the greatest in the NBA, period. I don't think you can find anyone who would say a bad word about him. You love to root for people like that."

The ninth of 10 children and the youngest of six sons, Avery Johnson was born on March 25, 1965 in New Orleans, Louisiana, to Jim and Inez Johnson. His father, a carpenter, strongly shaped Johnson's work ethic. "I look up to my father because every time I went to sleep, he was up," Johnson told John Peoples for the *Seattle Times* (October 23, 1990). "Whenever I woke up, he was already up. My dad never set bad examples for me. He was always working. That's the kind of person I wanted to be. A hard-working person." Raised in the Lafitte housing projects, in the neighborhood known as Tremé, near the city's French Quarter, Johnson was shielded from the area's rougher elements by his parents, and those close to him at the time describe Johnson as an energetic and ebullient young person. "He always seemed to be the smallest person in the room," Andrea Johnson, Avery's younger sister, said to Barry Horn for the *Dallas Morning News* (May 7, 2006). "But he always had the biggest heart. Everyone could see that."

Media profiles of Johnson often portray his emergence as a reliable NBA performer as a "small miracle." Beginning in high school and carrying over to each subsequent stage of his playing career, Johnson's athletic abilities were routinely questioned because of his small stature. As a senior on the basketball team at St. Augustine High School, Johnson never even reached five and a half feet in height, and he spent virtually the entire regular season on the bench. "I was the 14th man on a 14-member team," he recalled to Lars Anderson for *Sports Illustrated* (July 7, 1999), adding: "I was the backup to the backup's backup." In postseason play in 1983, however, the team lost its starting point guard, and Johnson stepped in, contributing to his high school's win at the Louisiana state championships.

On the heels of his postseason work, Johnson received an offer to play basketball for New Mexico Junior College, in Hobbs. Taking his only opportunity for a scholarship, Johnson spent one season in New Mexico before transferring to Cameron University, in Lawton, Oklahoma. His play improved during his one season in Oklahoma, leading to his recruitment and subsequent signing with Southern University, in Baton Rouge, Louisiana, in 1985. National Collegiate Athletic Association (NCAA) rules governing transfer students stipulated that Johnson was not allowed to play right away at Southern University, so he officially joined the team the next year, at the beginning of the 1986–87 season. Johnson proved to be an "impact player" for Southern, leading all NCAA Division I players in assists, with an average of 10.7. In the 1987–88 season, his senior year, he surpassed his own record, averaging 13.3 assists for the season and claiming the NCAA Division I record for the highest single-season assists average. He also holds the NCAA Division I record for the highest career-assists average (12) and is tied with two other players for the record for assists in a single game, having made 22 for Southern against Texas Southern on January 25, 1988. In addition to the leadership qualities he exhibited on the court, Johnson helped his teammates stay out of trouble in their off hours as well. "AJ kept all the kids straight," Ben Jobe, Johnson's coach in Baton Rouge, told Anderson, referring to Johnson by his other nickname. "When I had AJ, we never had guys breaking into Coke machines, breaking curfew. AJ is what you need if you want a guy who has character."

Johnson graduated from Southern University with a bachelor's degree in 1988. Though ignored in the June NBA draft that year, he was determined to have a professional basketball career and passed a summer season in Florida with the Palm Beach Stingrays, a short-lived franchise in the developmental U.S. Basketball League. "I just wasn't ready to stop playing," he told Phil Taylor for *Sports Illustrated* (June 14, 1999). "If I wasn't good enough to be a pro, so be it, but I was going to find out for myself." Johnson also had what he described to Chad Bonham for the magazine *Breakaway* (online) as "a Plan B": earning a master's degree from Tulane University, in New Orleans. "I think the pressure of making it [into the NBA] wasn't on me as great as some other players that had no other options," Johnson told Bonham. "I was going to do something special in life and I wanted to play in the NBA. I had a backup plan but I went full speed ahead."

On August 2, 1988 the Seattle Supersonics signed Johnson to a free-agent contract, and over the next two seasons, he played in 96 games for the franchise, making 10 starts, all of them in his second season. The Supersonics traded him to the Denver Nuggets for a second-round draft choice on October 24, 1990. On December 23, 1990, after appearing in 21 games for the Nuggets, Johnson was informed by the team's then-coach, Paul West-

head, that effective the following day he would be cut from the roster. Less than a month later, the San Antonio Spurs signed him. Although his playing time and points-per-game average increased in San Antonio, Johnson was deemed expendable, and in December 1991 the Spurs waived him. After signing on with the Houston Rockets, in January 1992, Johnson finished the season there but was not re-signed. Instead, he went back to the Spurs for the 1992–93 season and then joined the Golden State Warriors at the beginning of the following fall. He appeared in all 82 regular-season games that year for the Warriors, averaging 10.9 points and 5.3 assists per game.

In the summer of 1994, Johnson, having spent time with five teams in six seasons, signed with the Spurs for a third—and final—time, and he remained in San Antonio through the end of the 2000–01 season. Regarding the difficulty he encountered in remaining with one franchise for an extended period, the devoutly Christian Johnson told Anderson, "When those things happen, the human part of you sometimes gets you discouraged. But then your faith kicks in and says to keep on going." One of the aspects of Johnson's game that especially concerned NBA team executives and decision-makers was the lack of "touch" he showed when shooting the ball, particularly his failure to convert some jump shots into field goals. "We all made the same mistake with Johnson, the same mistake we make all the time in the NBA. Instead of seeing what he was, we were worried about what he wasn't," Bernie Bickerstaff, a former Denver Nuggets coach, told Mark Kiszla for the *Denver Post* (April 30, 1995). "The rap on him was always, 'Johnson doesn't have a jumper.' But some guys are born to have a basketball in their hands."

In the 1994–95 season, Johnson enjoyed career high averages of 13.4 points and 8.2 assists per game and started in all 82 of the Spurs' regular-season games. His 670 assists were the fourth-highest total in the NBA that season; in the 1995–96 season, his 789 assists placed him second in the league. As Phil Taylor observed, "What no one seemed to notice was that Johnson had been quietly but steadily getting better." Indeed, Johnson's scoring average increased in each of his first seven seasons in the NBA. His shooting percentage also improved steadily. Of particular value to Gregg Popovich, who took over as the Spurs' head coach in 1996, was the sense that, with Johnson running the team as its point guard, the Spurs in many ways had a coach on the court. "Avery is kind of like the head of a snake," Popovich said to Anderson. "No Avery, no team. He's got a heart bigger than the Alamodome. His work ethic is scary, and he's personable enough to be a leader. When a guy has all those elements, that's who you want to work with."

Johnson worked both on and off the court to secure the 1999 NBA championship for the Spurs. He served as a role model for the team's emerging star center, Tim Duncan, and also forged a close-knit relationship with David Robinson, another center and, like Johnson, a born-again Christian. The three were instrumental in leading the Spurs through the play-offs, past the Minnesota Timberwolves, the Los Angeles Lakers, the Portland Trailblazers, and, finally, the Knicks. Yet it was Johnson's final jump shot that gave the Spurs the game-winning points. "For all those years, to have people tell him you're no good, you can't do this, to the way they didn't even guard him when he played—and then to have him make the championship shot in '99, now to be the coach," Bill Walton, an NBA analyst and former player, told Oscar Dixon. "And the way he does it with such class and humility, with such dignity and pride, he is a fantastic human being." Johnson finished his tenure with San Antonio at the end of the 2000–01 season, rounding out his time there with 4,474 assists, the most in the franchise's history. In the summer of 2001, he signed a free-agent contract with the Denver Nuggets, valued at some $14.4 million over three years. The Nuggets traded him, in 2002, in a seven-player deal to the Mavericks. The following year the Mavericks moved Johnson to the Warriors in a trade involving nine players.

Although Johnson rejoined the Mavericks in September 2004, Don Nelson, the Mavericks' head coach since 1997, and Mark Cuban, the Mavericks' owner, persuaded Johnson to end his playing career and join the team's coaching staff. (Johnson finished his career with an average of 8.4 points, 5.5 assists, 1.7 rebounds, and 25.3 minutes per game. He also had an impressive 3.34 assist-to-turnover ratio.) The understanding was that Nelson would groom Johnson to succeed him as head coach. Within months Johnson was organizing the team's practices, and when Nelson needed a replacement midway through the season, Johnson took over the interim duties. Then, on March 19, 2005, with 18 games remaining in the season, Nelson permanently handed over the reins to Johnson. The team responded positively to their new head coach, winning all but two of their remaining contests.

In recent years the franchise, which included a core of such versatile young players as the German-born forward Dirk Nowitzki, the guard Jason Terry, and the swingman Josh Howard, had earned a reputation for having an impressive offense that was often undercut by a weak defense. Johnson set about changing that perception in the short time he was at the helm at the end of the 2005–06 season, and in the first round of play-offs, the Mavericks dispatched the Houston Rockets in seven games, before being eliminated by the Phoenix Suns in six. Before the start of the 2005–06 NBA season, Johnson continued to emphasize to his players the value of slowing down opponents, and during the regular season the team reached previously unattained heights, holding the opposition to an average of 93.1 points per game, a record for the franchise. Michael Finley, currently of the San Antonio Spurs and a guard with the Mavericks from 1997 to 2005, told Sean Deveney for *Sporting News*

(May 6, 2005), "Getting more physical, pushing people first instead of letting other people push. [Johnson] is trying to get us to take on that mentality." The Mavericks finished with a 60–22 record, tying a franchise mark that was set in the 2002–03 season under Nelson. In February 2006, with the Mavericks commanding the conference's best record at that point in the season, Johnson was tapped to coach the Western Conference All-Star Team. The Spurs later edged the Mavericks out of their topmost position, and the Mavericks entered the play-offs as their conference's fourth seed, despite having the second-best record in the West.

Heavily favored in the first round of the 2006 NBA play-offs, the Mavericks quickly dispatched their opponents, the Memphis Grizzlies, in the first four of the series' seven games. That victory set up a much-anticipated showdown between the Mavericks and Johnson's former team—and the reigning 2005 NBA champs—the Spurs. After the teams split the first two games in San Antonio, the Mavericks, using their quickness and scoring depth, came away with victories on their home court in the third and fourth games, to take a commanding 3–1 lead. The series then shifted back to San Antonio, where the Spurs won Game Five by a single point. The day after that pivotal game, the NBA suspended the Mavericks' Jason Terry from the next game, which was to be played in Dallas, after footage from the game revealed that Terry, in the final moments of Game Five, had punched the Spurs' Michael Finley. Without Terry in the line-up, the Mavericks lost to the Spurs in the next game by five points, setting up a decisive final game in San Antonio. Billed as an epic clash of two of the NBA's best teams, the taut, seesaw affair went into overtime, during which the Mavericks scored their way to a 119–111 win.

In the Western Conference finals, the Mavericks faced the NBA's highest-scoring team, the Phoenix Suns, known for their uptempo style of play and led by the point guard Steve Nash, the NBA's most valuable player in 2004–05 and 2005–06. After losing the first game in the series, the Mavericks rebounded to win four of the next five games, taking the best-of-seven series and advancing to the NBA finals to face the Miami Heat, another team that, like the Mavericks, had never before reached that last stage of postseason play.

The 2006 NBA championships featured a mix of vibrant young stars and veterans, exemplified by the Heat's exceptionally talented third-year guard Dwyane Wade and aging superstar center Shaquille O'Neal. The teams were closely matched, but one notable difference between them was in the levels of experience of their respective head coaches. One of the NBA's most successful coaches, the Heat's Pat Riley had led the Los Angeles Lakers to four championships in the 1980s and later took the Knicks to the 1994 NBA finals. Despite Riley's greater experience, Johnson led the Mavericks past the Heat for the first two games of the series, both played in Dallas; so impressive, in fact, were the

Mavericks' two series-opening victories that many sportswriters dismissed the possibility of a turnaround. In Game Three, however, the Mavericks raced to a commanding second-half lead only to watch Miami erase a 13-point deficit in the fourth quarter and win the game, 98–96. When the series was later tied at two games each, Johnson moved his players from a luxurious hotel in downtown Miami to a more modest spot some 45 minutes away. He had hoped that the change of scenery would break what he referred to as his team's "vacation mentality" and also unify his players, who were ordered to share rooms rather than take private rooms. In Game Five Wade commanded the court, shooting 43 points to lead the Heat to a 101–100 victory, Miami defeated Dallas 95–92 to take Game Six—and win its first championship. After beginning the 2006–07 season with four losses, the Mavericks won 50 of the next 55 games, and Johnson set a record as the coach who reached 100 wins fastest. The regular season ended with the Mavericks posting the sixth-best record, 67–15, in NBA history. As the number-one seed in the Western Conference and with the league's best record, they were heavily favored to win the NBA Championship. Nevertheless, they did not make it past the first round. In one of the NBA's greatest upsets, the Mavericks were defeated by the number-eight Golden State Warriors, who were coached by Don Nelson.

Johnson prepares his team relentlessly, both in practice and in the film room. Before most Mavericks' practices Johnson devises a script aimed at smoothing over a particular aspect of the team's execution. "Avery is very organized," Shawn Bradley, who played for the Mavericks through the end of the 2004–05 season, told Deveney. "He has a good grasp on what he wants, he has a good idea of the structure he wants." Johnson, known for speaking in a high-pitched Louisiana accent, does not hesitate to pull a player from a game if he is ignoring defensive responsibility or is not hustling, and the coach is not shy about making disparaging remarks about players to the press. Riley told Michael Lee: "I used to hear him [as a player] when I coached against him, he would be barking . . . those high-pitched orders telling everybody where to go and admonishing David Robinson and Tim Duncan and they would say, 'Yes, sir.' It's great to see a young coach come along that has gained in a short period of time the ultimate respect of his players." Describing his coaching philosophy to Bonham, Johnson said, "You want to be a man of integrity and you want the players to know that you care about them. Whether they still like you or not is a whole other deal."

Johnson lives in Houston, Texas, with his wife, Cassandra (Merricks) Johnson, whom he married in 1991; they have two children, Christianne and Avery Jr. Johnson reportedly reads the Bible every day. "I take [being a role model] very seriously because I'm trying to be an example as a Christian, as a man," he told Chad Bonham. "I've got a lot of

people who are looking up to me." When Hurricane Katrina battered New Orleans, in late August 2005, Johnson and his wife transformed their Houston home into a refuge for family members and others who had fled the city; they also organized a charity basketball game in Houston that raised more than $1 million to help victims of the disaster. Johnson hired Bernard Griffith, his high-school coach, as a Mavericks' assistant coach after St. Augustine High School was devastated by the hurricane. Johnson told Barry Horn: "I know I will be judged ultimately not for what I did as the Dallas Mavericks' basketball coach, but I will be judged for what I did in times of need by others." His avocational interests include golfing and tennis. At the end of 1997–98 regular-season play, Johnson received the NBA's Sportsmanship Award.

—D.F.

Suggested Reading: *Breakaway* (on-line); *Dallas Morning News* (on-line) May 7, 2006; NBA Web site; *Sporting News* p14+ May 6, 2005; *Sports Illustrated* p48+ June 14, 1999, p44+ July 7, 1999; *USA Today* (on-line) Feb. 19, 2006; *Washington Post* E p1 June 11, 2006

Johnson, Sheila Crump

Jan. 25, 1949– Co-founder of Black Entertainment Television; co-owner and president of the Washington Mystics

Address: Salamander Hospitality, 100 W. Washington St., Middleburg, VA 20118

"I always had a drive in me that desired to be the best that I could be," Sheila Crump Johnson said at a college commencement address a few years ago, as quoted by Karen W. Arenson in the *New York Times* (May 8, 2003). In 1979 Johnson and Robert L. Johnson, whom she had married 10 years earlier, founded Black Entertainment Television (BET), the first cable network to offer programming created specifically by and for African-Americans. A dozen years later BET Holdings Inc., which the Johnsons had set up as BET's parent company, became the first African-American–controlled firm to be listed on the New York Stock Exchange. By that time BET had grown into one of the main sources of news and entertainment for nearly 30 million subscribers throughout the United States, and Sheila Johnson was working as BET's executive vice president of corporate affairs. She held that post until 1999, when, after years of discord between the Johnsons regarding the network's programming, Robert Johnson fired her. In 2000 Viacom Inc. acquired BET Holdings in a stock deal valued at $3 billion, and two years later, when the Johnsons' marriage ended in divorce, Sheila Johnson became the nation's first black female billionaire.

Bryan Bedder/Getty Images

Sheila Crump Johnson

Sheila Johnson is an accomplished violinist and trained music educator, and during the first half of her marriage to Robert Johnson, she taught music in schools in the Washington, D.C., metropolitan area; she also formed an orchestra for young violinists and other players of stringed instruments. As a cultural representative of the United States Information Agency in the Middle East for five years in the 1980s, she helped Jordan establish a national music conservatory and was honored by King Hussein, the country's monarch, for her efforts. Since 1989, when she set up the Sheila C. Johnson Foundation, she has been a major benefactor of schools, her biggest monetary gift so far being a donation of $7 million to the Parsons School of Design, in New York City. A resident of Virginia since 2002, she has become a community leader in Washington, D.C., and its environs. Johnson is a co-owner of the Washington Mystics, who belong to the Women's National Basketball Association (WNBA), and she holds the titles of team president, managing partner, and governor. "I'm a firm believer in not looking back," Johnson told Dionne Walker for the Associated Press (January 8, 2006). "I've been through a lot of fire and still come out alive."

The elder of two siblings, Johnson was born Sheila Crump on January 25, 1949 in McKeesport, Pennsylvania. She has one brother. At that time her father was one of fewer than a dozen African-American neurosurgeons in the U.S.; her mother was a homemaker. Because her father "could not practice in white hospitals," as Johnson told Kristen A. Nelson for the *Washingtonian* (November 2003), the family relocated often as he was transferred to a series of veterans' hospitals. After some years the Crumps settled in Maywood, a suburb of

Chicago, Illinois. By her own account, Johnson had a privileged upbringing—a rarity among African-Americans during the 1950s and 1960s—but she was not unaware of racism. Once, she recalled to Walker, a friend's father referred to her as a "blackie." Her own father, an amateur pianist, instilled in her a passion for classical music. At the age of five, Johnson began studying the violin. She attended the Irving Elementary School and Proviso East High School, both in Maywood. In high school Johnson served as the student orchestra's concert-mistress (traditionally, a post held by the first, or lead, violinist), and she was elected class vice president and captain of the cheerleading squad. To ensure that the cheerleaders learned their routines without the distraction of boyfriends, she would lock the doors of their room during practice sessions. She also chaired an Illinois state youth orchestra.

Johnson attended the University of Illinois School of Music at Urbana-Champaign on a scholarship. There, she studied under Paul Rolland, a renowned violin teacher, and took classes in performance, conducting, and music education. She became the school's first African-American cheerleader and a member of the Mortar Board, a women's honor society. In 1969 she married Robert L. Johnson, who had graduated from the university the previous year. After she earned a bachelor's degree, in music performance and education, in 1970, she moved with her husband to Princeton, New Jersey, where Robert Johnson earned a master's degree in international affairs from Princeton University in 1972. They then set up house in Washington D.C., where Sheila Johnson worked briefly as a research analyst for U.S. senator Jacob K. Javits of New York.

In 1973 Johnson began teaching music at several local schools, among them the Sidwell Friends School, the Lab School of Washington, and the Levine School of Music. Johnson also gave private violin lessons, and in 1975 she formed a touring, 140-member orchestra called Youth Strings in Action. (She described her teaching methods, which were based on Paul Rolland's, in a manual called *Youth Strings in Action*.) Queen Noor of Jordan attended one of the group's performances, and later, at her invitation, the ensemble performed at the Jerash Festival of Culture and Arts, in Jordan. That event led to Johnson's appointment as the United States Information Agency cultural liaison in the Middle East. In that position she had a major role in the establishment of Jordan's national conservatory of music. For her contributions to the country's educational system, Johnson was awarded Jordan's highest civilian honor.

Earlier, one day in 1979, while Robert Johnson was working as a lobbyist for the National Cable Television Association, he had met a businessman who expressed the desire to create a television network that would cater to the interests and needs of the elderly. The Johnsons had often bemoaned the absence of "the black perspective" or black voices on the major TV networks, as Sheila Johnson told Michael Shelden for the London *Daily Telegraph* (October 11, 2004), and during Robert Johnson's conversation with the businessman, the idea of setting up a network for African-Americans came to him. Using some of their savings along with loans and lines of credit totaling $500,000, the Johnsons launched BET in 1980. "I worked hard for him," Sheila Johnson said of her husband to Shelden. "I loved him, I adored him, I was proud of him. And I put 100 percent into helping him build up the network and his public image." In 1989 BET entered the publishing business, with the debut of *Emerge*, a news and general-interest magazine aimed at black readers; the magazine *YSB* (Young Sisters and Brothers) followed in 1991. BET also bought Arabesque Books, which publishes black-themed romance novels, and *Heart and Soul* magazine, possibly the first health-and-fitness magazine for black women in the U.S.

By 1990 Sheila Johnson had stopped teaching and was serving BET full-time as executive vice president of corporate affairs, becoming the "conscience" of the company, as she told Ann Gerhart for the *Washington Post* (May 26, 2002). In an effort to counteract the influence of the music videos carried by BET, which increasingly emphasized materialistic lifestyles, sex, and sexist references to women, Johnson had pushed for socially conscious programming. Toward that end she had overseen the creation of *Teen Summit*, which was launched in 1989 and featured young people discussing such issues as drugs use, the spread of AIDS, and teen pregnancy. She and her husband "bickered constantly over programming," as she told Shelden. "I wanted us to cover news and important social issues, especially for our young audiences. Unfortunately, those kind of shows don't bring in the ratings." She also told Shelden about BET, "It's now just a black MTV, really. But it all comes down to economics. You can't fight that. It just wasn't profitable to do more serious things, and my husband moved the business in a different direction." Even more destructive to the couple's relationship were Robert Johnson's dalliances with other women. In 1999 Robert Johnson, who then held the titles of chairman, president, and CEO of BET Holdings, fired Sheila Johnson, ending their two-decade-long business partnership. The following year the media conglomerate Viacom Inc. acquired BET for $3 billion. In 2002 the Johnsons divorced; the couple split their assets, and Sheila Johnson and her former husband became billionaires.

During that period Sheila Johnson purchased a $7 million, 350-acre property outside Middleburg, Virginia, a Washington, D.C., suburb, and converted part of it into a horse ranch that she named Salamander Farm. (According to myth, salamanders can emerge from fire unscathed.) She set up a company called Salamander Hospitality and, in Middleburg in 2004, opened a take-out gourmet-foods shop, the Market Salamander. Overcoming objec-

tions from some people in the community, who opposed bringing more foot and vehicular traffic to Middleburg, she obtained approval to construct a vacation facility, the Salamander Inn and Spa, on her land; it is scheduled to open in 2008.

Johnson has also continued to devote herself to philanthropic activities, underwriting fund-raising events on behalf of the Loudoun (County) Hospital Center's health vans, which service low-income residents of the area, and the Piedmont Environmental Council's conservation programs. She has donated millions of dollars to the United Negro College Fund and educational institutions including, in addition to the Parsons School of Design (a division of the New School), the Hill School, a Middleburg private school (which is now the site of the Sheila C. Johnson Performing Arts Center); the Curry School of Education at the University of Virginia; Bennett College for Women, in Greensboro, North Carolina; Howard University, in Washington, D.C.; and the State University of New York (SUNY) at Morrisville. "I studied wealthy people—this was before I had money—and saw the confidence in their kids because the world is their oyster," she explained to Nicole Lewis for the *Chronicle of Philanthropy* (June 12, 2006). "We need to give all . . . kids that same kind of entitlement. They may not have monetary entitlement, but let them feel entitled, because that is the only way they are going to grow socially and morally, and that is really the reason I give money away." SUNY-Morrisville houses the Sheila Crump Johnson Institute, which awards scholarships and fellowships and aims to build character and leadership skills among college students and promote diversity. "In educating young people, it is imperative to address the whole person," Johnson told a writer for *Black Issues in Higher Education* (November 21, 2002). "Focusing on character and leadership in addition to academics will serve to prepare students well for their roles as employees, employers, parents and leaders."

In May 2005 Johnson acquired a partnership in Lincoln Holdings LLC, a sports and entertainment company co-founded by Theodore J. "Ted" Leonsis, a vice chairman of America Online Inc. Lincoln Holdings owns the Washington Mystics and the Washington Capitals, a team in the National Hockey League, among other companies and properties. Johnson is the first African-American female owner of a professional sports franchise. "She's making history," Donna Lopiano said to Miki Turner for ESPN.com (February 22, 2007). "Unless your team was in the family and your father died and left it to you, you didn't get to be an owner. She's the first generation of women, who in their own right . . . are team owners and who are going to shape a franchise in their own image as opposed to letting the guys do it." As team president, Johnson has promised to do everything possible to reverse the decline in attendance at Mystics games and those of other WNBA teams. "We have a long climb on our hands as far as the perception and value of women in the sports world," she said to Mark Berman for the *Roanoke* (*Virginia*) *Times* (August 9, 2005). "It's still very much a male-dominated arena. We as women have got to start being a lot more aggressive as far as marketing ourselves and getting ourselves out there so that the general public can see us as the athletes that we are and really show that we can be valued just as much as any of these NBA [National Basketball Association] players or any of these other male sports teams." "To have someone like [Johnson], someone who has been so successful at whatever she's done, come in and say she believes in us and she still loves us like that, it was special . . . ," the Mystics' point guard Temeka Johnson said to Ivan Carter for the *Washington Post* (August 26, 2005). "I think it gives us motivation to go out there and perform because we want to make her look good." The Mystics finished the 2005 season with a 16–18 record. Their 18 wins and 16 losses the next season earned them a berth in the play-offs, where they lost to the Connecticut Sun in the first round.

Johnson has served as the president of the Washington International Horse Show and is currently the chair of its board of directors. She is a member of the boards of trustees of the United States Equestrian Team, the American Horse Show Association, the Pennsylvania National Horse Show, and the Equestrian Alliance; a member of the Community and Friends Board of the Kentucky Center for the Performing Arts; co-chair of Carnegie Hall's Educational Advisory Council; and a member of the national advisory board of the Salvation Army. In news releases her name appears as Dr. Sheila C. Johnson, in recognition of her two honorary doctoral degrees, from SUNY-Middleton and Bennett College. Her photographs, mostly landscapes, have been exhibited at the Byrne Gallery, in Middleburg, and have been used in some of her fundraising efforts. In 2006 Sheila Johnson was named Woman of the Year by Women in Sports and Events, and in 2007 she was honored by the Jackie Robinson Foundation for her "commitment to social progress."

When Lynn Norment interviewed her for *Ebony* (September 2003), Johnson owned 18 show horses. She also owns a horse farm in Wellington, Florida. Johnson's children from her marriage to Robert L. Johnson are a daughter, Paige, a champion equestrian, who is now 21, and a son, Brett, 17. In 2005 about 700 people attended her wedding to William T. Newman, the Arlington County Circuit Court chief judge. "Money can be a blessing or a curse," she told Ann Gerhart. "I have seen money destroy people, athletes and entertainers who really came up from nothing and used their money for all the wrong reasons, whether it went up their nose or into 50 cars or spent on houses that even 5,000 people can't begin to live in. In the end, it means nothing. They got what they wanted, but they lost what they had, and that is their soul."

—D.J.K.

Suggested Reading: *Chronicle of Philanthropy* (on-line) June 12, 2006; *Ebony* p167 Sep. 2003; *Essence* p144 May 2005; (London) *Daily Telegraph* p15 Oct. 11, 2004; *New York Times* B p1+ May 8, 2003; *VirginiaBusiness.com* June 2005; *Washington Post* F p1+ May 26, 2002; *Washingtonian* p72+ Nov. 2003

Courtesy of Borders

Jones, George L.

Oct. 25, 1950– President and CEO of Borders Group Inc.

Address: Borders Group Inc., 100 Phoenix Drive, Ann Arbor, MI 48108

"I'm very competitive, and if I wasn't gunning for No.1, I shouldn't be here," George L. Jones, the chief executive officer and president of the Borders Group Inc. since July 2006, told Sheena Harrison for *Crain's Detroit Business* (September 25, 2006). Borders is the second-largest bookstore chain in the United States, after Barnes & Noble. "What we want to do," Jones said to Harrison, "is create something that's powerful enough that a good number of customers would drive past the competitor's store to get to ours." Jones began his retail career when he was fresh out of college, in one of a series of jobs with department-store chains based in Tennessee, Arkansas, and Arizona. In 1985 he joined Target Stores, in Minneapolis, Minnesota, as vice president of the ready-to-wear division; later, he was promoted to senior vice president of merchandising and then executive vice president of operations, overseeing the management of more than 450 stores nationwide. After half a dozen years with Target, Jones headed another retail chain, Rose's Stores Inc., headquartered in Henderson, North Carolina, from 1991 to 1994. He next joined Warner Brothers (WB) Consumer Products, a division of the Time Warner Entertainment Company, where he served as president of worldwide licensing and retail merchandising (1994–2001); he also managed five additional divisions. While with WB he acquired the film rights to J. K. Rowling's immensely popular fantasy novel *Harry Potter and the Sorcerer's Stone* and negotiated highly profitable licensing deals for Harry Potter–related products. From 2001 to 2005 he held the positions of president and CEO of the Saks Department Store Group, a Birmingham, Alabama–based chain of some 250 department stores (not including those bearing the Saks Fifth Avenue name). Jones is "a solid, professional merchant," Ken Gassman, a retail analyst at Davenport & Co., told Ted Pratt for the *Birmingham (Alabama) News* (January 30, 2001). "He's a good mix of merchandiser and administrator." In a press release (July 13, 2006, online) distributed by the executive search firm Korn/Ferry International that announced his appointment to Borders, Jones was quoted as saying, "For many years, I have been a devoted Borders customer, enjoying countless hours in the stores. I am passionate about books, music and movies and truly honored to lead this fine company."

George L. Jones was born on October 25, 1950 in Little Rock, Arkansas, to George L. Jones Sr. and the former Gwendolyn Grissom. He attended Henderson State College, in Arkadelphia, Arkansas, where he majored in both marketing and economics. He also played guitar for a rhythm-and-blues band called Merging Traffic; he harbored aspirations of making music his career until he realized that he was "a mediocre guitar player who doesn't sing very well or write very well," as he told Ted Pratt for the *Birmingham News* (May 6, 2001). Jones earned B.A. and B.S. degrees in 1972 and then, after declining invitations to enter the management-trainee programs of Procter & Gamble and Merrill Lynch & Co., became an executive trainee with Gus Mayer, a Memphis, Tennessee–based department-store chain. "People on campus asked me how could I have turned down those other two primo offers to take [Mayer's]," Jones told Pratt. "I said this is what I thought I would like to do. If I wasn't going to be doing music, I was going to be doing something that I liked." After three years with Gus Mayer, Jones took jobs with a series of other department-store chains: Gold's, based in Little Rock, where he served as general manager (1975–78); Dillard's, also headquartered in Little Rock, where he worked first as a buyer (1978–80) and then as the manager of divisional merchandise (1980–82); and Diamond's, based in Phoenix, Arizona, where his title was manager of general merchandise (1982–84). Jones next moved to Minneapolis and joined Target Stores (then a division of the Dayton Hudson Corp.) as the vice president of

ready-to-wear apparel (1985–86); he was promoted to senior vice president of merchandising (1986–87) and then executive vice president of operations (1988–91), which placed him over 90,000 employees in 450 stores that generated annual sales exceeding $9 billion. As executive vice president Jones played a key role in differentiating the Target brand from its rivals Wal-Mart and Kmart, by promoting a more upscale look in Target stores. As David Moin wrote for the Harrisonburg, Virginia, *Daily News-Record* (March 15, 1989), Target stores were considered "the best-looking of the three discounters, [with] more expensive fixturing, including color graphics and carpeting to complement the better apparel, wider aisles and a brighter appearance." Concurrently, from 1987–88, while he was with Target, Jones served as the chairman and CEO of Monica Scott Inc., a chain of specialty stores.

In 1991 Jones left Target to become the president and chief executive officer of Rose's Stores Inc., a struggling Henderson, North Carolina–based retail chain, which had experienced a $23 million loss on $1.4 billion in revenues during the fiscal year prior to Jones's arrival. Ken Gassman told Kelly Greene for the *Charlotte (North Carolina) Business Journal* (September 5, 1994) that Jones took on the challenge that Rose's presented because "he knew he'd never have the opportunity to be president at Target." The first nonmember of the Rose family to run the chain in its 76-year history, Jones "kept Rose's from falling apart," as Gassman told Ted Pratt (May 6, 2001). Over the next three years, Jones steered Rose's through bankruptcy reorganization and led it to profitability. He also helped the retailer withstand the growing competition from Wal-Mart stores in the Henderson area. In mid-1994 Jones asserted, "Rose's is at the highest point it's seen in several years in terms of optimistic outlook for the company," according to a *Greensboro (North Carolina) News & Record* (August 19, 1994) reporter.

Soon afterward Jones left Rose's to join Warner Brothers (WB) Consumer Products, a division of the Time Warner Entertainment Co., as president of worldwide licensing and retail merchandising. He also managed WB worldwide publishing, Kids WB Music, WB Interactive Entertainment, WB Sports, and the WB Studio Stores. Among his chief responsibilities at WB, Jones oversaw a vast archive of WB brands, logos, and characters for such film and television franchises as Looney Tunes, Batman, and Superman, for all of which there were more than 3,700 active licensees. In 1998, in one of his more noteworthy achievements, Jones revived public interest in the Scooby-Doo franchise—connected with one of the longest-running animated series in television history and featuring the talking Great Dane Scooby-Doo and his friends. He did so by licensing the Scooby-Doo brand to Equity Marketing Inc., a global marketing-services company, for the production and distribution of Scooby Doo–related figurines and other toys. "We thought of it as an unmined gem," Jones told Laura Petrecca for *Advertising Age* (February 14, 2000). "We really stepped back and looked at the opportunity to build Scooby-Doo as a brand." In 1999 Jones acquired the film rights to the first of J. K. Rowling's series of fantasy novels—*Harry Potter and the Philosopher's Stone* (1997), retitled *Harry Potter and the Sorcerer's Stone* for the U.S. market. "I acted like I had read the book," Jones confessed to Betsy Butgereit for the *Birmingham News* (November 17, 2001). "[Rowling] knew I hadn't. She gave me a copy of the book. I read it and later loved it." Jones championed Rowling's involvement in the early phases of film production (with Jones's support, for example, Rowling created mock-ups for the book's characters). He also spearheaded the merchandising effort for Harry Potter products, orchestrating some four dozen licensing deals with manufacturers, among them the toy company Mattel Inc. and the pharmaceutical-products company Johnson & Johnson. In November 2001 the film adaptation of *Harry Potter and the Sorcerer's Stone* opened in more than 5,000 theaters nationwide, and it went on to earn gross sales worldwide of nearly $1 billion, making it the fourth-highest-grossing film of all time. During Jones's eight-year tenure at WB Consumer Products, the annual retail sales of the licensing division increased to $7 billion, second in revenues only to those of the Walt Disney Co. (which grossed $13 billion).

In March 2001 Jones returned to the retail sector, succeeding Robert Mosco as chief executive officer of the regional department-stores division of the Birmingham, Alabama–based Saks Department Store Group (SDSG). SDSG was then operating about 250 stores in 24 states, bearing the names Parisian, Proffitt's, McRae's, Younkers, Herberger's Carson Pirit Scott, Bergner's, and Boston Store. (Fred Wilson, the CEO of SDSG's umbrella company, Saks Inc., was in charge of the Saks Fifth Avenue chain.) At that time SDSG had begun to see stagnant sales, a situation that many observers traced to the mid-1990s consolidation that had tied the upscale Saks Fifth Avenue stores with regional department stores, creating a "fashion misstep" through attempts to "blend two widely different merchandising cultures," according to Doris Hajewski in the *Milwaukee (Wisconsin) Journal Sentinel* (April 8, 2001). The task of stimulating sales and increasing profits, as Jones saw it, did "not require a massive overhaul. This is not turnaround. This is an opportunity. There is a difference," as he told Pratt for the *Birmingham News* (May 6, 2001). Jones told David Moin for *Women's Wear Daily* (May 2, 2001), "Customers have a loyalty to brands carried only in department stores in cosmetics, home and apparel, and we have terrific real estate. Saks Inc. has 28 million square feet of department store space. We're in the right malls, we have favorable long-term leases and good real estate. . . . We ought to be able to sell a heck of a lot of something. We can have very meaningful growth by improving productivity in existing stores." "Department

stores are built around brand-consciousness, and the vast majority of sales come from branded vendor goods, not private-label merchandise," Jones told Matthew Haeberle for *Chain Store Age* (October 2002). Ultimately, he said to Jean E. Palmieri for the Harrisonburg, Virginia, *Daily News-Record* (February 11, 2002), "it comes down to product, price and service" as well as "picking certain categories of merchandise to build dominance in."

Jones identified "differentiated merchandise" as the key to sparking SDSG's financial renewal, as he told a writer for the *Birmingham Business Journal* (October 4, 2002). He told Palmieri, "I don't think I'm the only one recognizing this problem, but there's just way too much sameness. . . . Right now, if you plop customers into our stores or most of our competitors', there's so much sameness in terms of the offerings, the ambience, the service experience—everything. They're not distinguishable enough." In one of his early initiatives at SDSG, Jones revitalized the Parisian specialty stores, capitalizing on the chain's history, decor, and upscale fashions to "achieve something very special," as he told David Moin for *WWD* (May 2, 2001)."Parisian is an institution in Birmingham. There are beautiful stores in Birmingham and Charleston [South Carolina], and in a number of other cities too. It feels like a better department store. . . . The key part of the strategy is to return that specialty feeling to Parisian." Jones enhanced the consumer experience at SDSG stores by increasing sales staff, making shopping carts available, and offering gift-wrapping services during holiday periods. "Everything he says is customer-driven, and that's different from what department store executives talked about in the past," Robert Robicheaux, a retailing professor at the University of Alabama, told the *Birmingham Business Journal* reporter. "Gift wrap stations and shopping carts are designed to appeal to customers. It doesn't make vendors feel better, but it draws customers into the store." Jones also secured partnerships with WB Consumer Products and the Cartoon Network to create special areas in the children's sections of 31 department stores with merchandise related to Scooby-Doo and the Powerpuff Girls. In other partnerships, he set aside spaces in SDSG stores to display products from Smith & Hawken, an upscale lawn-and-garden retailer; the outdoor and athletic apparel company Roots Canada Ltd.; and Ruff Hewn apparel, accessories, and home products. On another front, Jones tried to revive sales by introducing technological features and amenities in stores; additions to a Younkers store in Des Moines, Iowa, for example, included a wine bar, a spa, and outdoor lighting displays. Under Jones's leadership, SDSG posted $58.5 million in operating income (income before deductions of interest payments and taxes), up from $55.4 million the previous year.

In July 2005 Saks Inc. sold the Proffitt's and McRae's chains to Belk Inc. and revealed plans to divest itself of all of its regional stores except those in the Parisian chain. Meanwhile, in August 2005

Jones had announced his resignation, effective on September 30 of that year. "For the middle market, he made some good choices," one of his colleagues told David Moin for *WWD* (August 25, 2005). "But there was never enough money to advertise and market the products."

In July 2006, after a six-month search, the Borders Group Inc. chose Jones to succeed Greg Josefowicz as the firm's president and CEO. (The chairman's post was filled by Larry Pollock, a member of the Borders board of directors.) Borders began as a single bookstore, opened by two brothers, Tom and Louis Borders, in Ann Arbor, Michigan, in 1971. In 1992 the Kmart Corp., which earlier had acquired Waldenbooks and Brentano's, bought Borders, at that time consisting of 21 large stores in the Midwest and Northeast. In 1995, by means of a stock buyout, Borders and Waldenbrooks formed their own corporation, called the Borders-Walden Group, which was renamed Borders Group Inc. three years later. In 2001 Borders agreed to use the services of the Internet bookseller Amazon.com for Internet sales of books listed on the Borders and Waldenbooks Web sites. In 2004 Borders signed a contract with Seattle's Best Coffee, a subsidiary of the Starbucks Corp., stipulating that that coffee would be served in cafés in all Borders superstores. That same year the Borders Group gained a controlling interest in Paperchase Products Ltd., a British chain specializing in stationery, gift wrap, and greeting cards; Paperchase products are sold in special sections of all British Borders superstores and a small number of Borders superstores in the U.S. Currently, there are about 1,300 Borders and Waldenbooks outlets in the U.S. (including three in Puerto Rico, one of which is the highest-grossing Borders superstore on U.S. territory) and overseas (in Ireland, England, New Zealand, Australia, Malaysia, and Singapore).

Earlier, during the 2005 fiscal year (which ended on January 28, 2006), Borders's profits had dropped 23 percent, and sales had trailed those of Barnes & Noble, its chief rival, by nearly $1 billion. Jones vowed to revive the bookseller by "differentiating" Borders's products and consumer experiences from those of its rivals. "If we think of ourselves as more than just selling books or music or movies but as being a provider of information and entertainment, then there are a lot of things we can do," he told Greta Guest, who interviewed him for the *Detroit Free Press* (July 20, 2006). "I have a ton of ideas of things I can do with the relationships I built over those years in Hollywood that I think I can tap into that could help differentiate us as a company and make us stand out." In a gesture of solidarity with Borders's 35,000-employee workforce, Jones promised not to cut jobs. "I don't think the answer to Borders becoming an even better company lies in the new guy coming in and taking out tons of expenses," he told Guest. "I think our road to greatness comes more from increasing sales and a more compelling offering for our customers. That's what it's all about." One of Jones's

early goals was to persuade browsers to spend more money per visit. "Our customers on average spend a lot longer in a store than what I've been used to . . . they like our stores; they're staying there, but they're not spending as much as they could," he told Motoko Rich for the *New York Times* (July 19, 2006).

Jones served for two years (1999–2001) on the board of directors of Liz Claiborne Inc. He has one daughter, Keeshan, from his first marriage (1972–78), to Marion A. Hartwick, which ended in divorce. He and his second wife, Judy M. Cowan, whom he married in 1988, have two sons, Dylan and Bailey.

—D.J.K.

Suggested Reading: *Crain's Detroit Business* p3 Sep. 25, 2006; *Detroit Free Press* p1 July 20, 2006; (Harrisonburg, Virginia) *Daily News Record* p56 Feb. 11, 2002; *New York Times* E p3 July 19, 2006; *Women's Wear Daily* p6 May 2, 2001

Christian Steiner, courtesy of Leila Josefowicz

Josefowicz, Leila

(Joe-SEF-oh-wits, LAY-la)

Oct. 20, 1977– Violinist

Address: c/o Linda Marder, CM Artists New York, 127 W. 96th St., Rm. 13B, New York, NY 10025

Leila Josefowicz, Lynne Walker observed for the London *Independent* (April 19, 2005), "is a gifted communicator, a musician with no airs or graces" who seems to be, Walker went on to write, "unfazed by the media spotlight" that often surrounds her. A child prodigy, Josefowicz began performing regularly at the age of 10, and since she released her first CD, *Tchaikovsky: Violin Concerto in D/Sibelius: Violin Concerto in D*, at 17, she has performed with many of the world's most prestigious orchestras—the Boston and Chicago Symphonies, the Cleveland and Philadelphia Orchestras, and the London Philharmonic, among others—and collaborated with several leading modern composers, including John Adams and Mark Grey. Having successfully made the transition from prodigy to adult performer, Josefowicz has taken control of her career, avoiding the safety of building her repertoire around old masters and actively seeking to play the work of her contemporaries. "It's very, very exciting, working with composers and being part of the creative process. That's another thing that I find inspiring—that you can share ideas, share what the strong points are of my playing, and they can cater to the way I play, as opposed to just being handed the score," Josefowicz told Rebecca C. Howard for the Salt Lake City *Desert Morning News* (February 25, 2007). Howard went on to report, "Josefowicz said that she wants to be a messenger to new composers that there is a performer who is willing to give their music the same attention, study and performance they would a piece by Bach."

Leila Bronia Josefowicz was born outside Toronto in Mississauga, Ontario, on October 20, 1977 to Wendy and Jack Josefowicz. Her mother is a former geneticist, and her father is a physicist and university professor. When Leila was three her family moved to a suburb north of Los Angeles, California, and she took up the violin, learning to play through the Suzuki method, an approach to teaching children to play instruments based on the way parents teach them language. "I didn't want to practice much," she told *People* (March 7, 1988). "I was only a baby, and you know how babies are." Two years later, while her father was vacuuming, Josefowicz's parents discovered that she had perfect pitch. "Out of the blue she said, 'Daddy, that's F sharp!'" her father recalled to R. Daniel Foster for the *Los Angeles Times* (March 25, 1988). "I said, 'What's F sharp?' and she said, 'The vacuum!'" Foster went on to note that Josefowicz's father "later tested his daughter by playing on the piano random notes that she identified perfectly." Thereafter, practicing ceased to be optional for Josefowicz, and at the age of eight, she began studying with Robert Lipsett, one of the most respected violin teachers on the West Coast. "He really taught me a lot about the technique of the instrument, how to practice, what to practice, ways that you can practice things, and it really did me a lot of good," she told Peter Wynne for the Bergen County, New Jersey, *Record* (May 1, 1998). She also earned her first professional credit when she was eight, playing the German composer Max Bruch's Violin Concerto no. 1 with a local orchestra.

Despite the fact that her talent set her apart from other children, Josefowicz was sent to public schools, "because my parents thought it would be better for my social life," she explained to Andrew Palmer for *Strings* (May/June 2000, on-line). The school accommodated her need to focus on the violin, arranging with her parents for her to study core subjects during free periods so that she could leave school by 1:30 each day and go to lessons or practice at home. When she was 10 Josefowicz's career began in earnest: she was featured on NBC's television tribute to the comedian Bob Hope, an event that marked the opening of the Bob Hope Cultural Center, in Palm Desert, California. Lucille Ball introduced Josefowicz's segment, during which the young violinist performed the Polish composer Henri Wieniawski's Scherzo-Tarantelle. "I was in amazing company and received an enormous amount of media coverage. But I didn't have any idea at the time just what it all meant," she told Palmer. The appearance led to a contract with the talent agency and production company IMG Management, and she began performing at Hollywood parties, in serious concerts, and on television programs such as the *Smothers Brothers Comedy Hour*.

When Josefowicz was 13, her family moved to Philadelphia, Pennsylvania, so that she could attend the Curtis Institute of Music, one of the most prestigious music schools in the world. She took classes there part-time for several years, studying under the renowned violinists Jascha Brodsky and Jaime Laredo, before entering the bachelor-of-music program full-time. All the while she continued performing in concerts, and at the age of 16, she made her debut at New York City's Carnegie Hall, accompanied by the Academy of St. Martin in the Fields chamber orchestra. Shortly thereafter, having signed a five-year contract with the prestigious record label Philips Classics, she recorded her first CD, playing concertos by Tchaikovsky and Sibelius, again with the Academy of St. Martin in the Fields orchestra. Released in 1995, the CD was well received. Scott Duncan wrote for the *Orange County Register* (August 27, 1995): "Josefowicz plays with a musical maturity and an individuality of expression that escapes most of the current crop of violin prodigies." The following year, Josefowicz released her second disc, *Solo* (1996), tackling "a collection of unaccompanied works that make sustained demands and require coloristic breadth and flexibility," Allan Kozinn observed for the *New York Times* (November 7, 1996). "In her gripping account of the Bartok Sonata, for example, she produces an acidic sound that serves this tempestuous score well; yet she also captures the warm, deep hues of Ysaye's Third and Fourth Sonatas. Kreisler's 'Recitativo and Scherzo-Caprice,' Paganini's variations on a Paisiello aria and Ernst's sizzling 'Grand Caprice,' based on Schubert's 'Erlkonig,' offer opportunities for unalloyed virtuosity, and in these Ms. Josefowicz's musicality is as dazzling as her technique."

After graduating from Curtis, in 1997, Josefowicz moved to New York City and released *Bohemian Rhapsodies*, a collection of violin pieces, and *Violin for Anne Rice* to honor Rice's novel *Violin* (1997), a book for which Josefowicz was reportedly the inspiration. "I'm nearly 20 and people don't talk about me as a cute little prodigy any more. They listen differently now, to an adult performer, and I like that," she told Joanna Pitman for the London *Times* (May 24, 1997). The following year she released *For the End of Time* (1998), a recording on which she was accompanied by the pianist John Novacek, with whom she has worked throughout her adult career. She also became one of the faces for Chanel's Allure perfume campaign. "They wanted faces, not models," she told Rita Zekas for the *Toronto Star* (April 1, 2006). "There was me, a sculptor and a women's rights activist from Kenya."

In 2000 she released *Mendelssohn & Glazunov: Violin Concertos* and *Americana*. For the latter CD Josefowicz turned to composers who are taken less seriously than figures such as Tchaikovsky, Brahms, and Beethoven, performing pieces by Stephen Foster, Scott Joplin, and George Gershwin, among others. She wanted, she told Ellen Pfeifer for the *Boston Globe* (November 8, 2000), "to let the emotions fly. We wanted to forget about tradition and start from scratch, from our hearts and souls." She added that those composers' music "came from the gut. If you listen from that point of view, then probably this music is the deepest you can get. After all, music from the dawn of time has always been intended to sort of celebrate our emotions." The following year, further exploring her interest in newer music, Josefowicz released a CD that featured the music of the 20th-century composer Sergei Prokofiev as well as that of Tchaikovsky, called *Prokofiev: Violin Concertos 1 & 2. Tchaikovsky: Serenade Melancholique.* "Leila has a great interest in learning new music, and this has added depth to everything she plays," the conductor with the Rochester Philharmonic Orchestra, Christopher Seaman, remarked to John Pitcher for the *Rochester (New York) Democrat and Chronicle* (November 14, 2001) about Josefowicz's progression from child prodigy to adult performer. "The public can be very fickle when it comes to former prodigies, but Leila is a probing interpreter, so I think her career is going to last."

Josefowicz continued to show interest in exploring new music, particularly the work of the California-based minimalist composer John Adams, and for a while she "made a mini-career of interpreting" his work, as David Mermelstein observed for the *New York Times* (May 29, 2005). In January 2002 she played Adams's Violin Concerto with the BBC Symphony for a televised concert at the John Adams Festival. Conducted by Adams, the performance was taken on tour to Paris, France, and Brussels, Belgium. In the following few years, Josefowicz stayed focused on Adams, releasing *John Adams: Tromba Lontana; Violin Concerto; The Wound-Dresser* in 2003 and *John Adams: Road Movies* in 2004 and developing a personal relationship with him. "I'm in awe of the fact that he's a living composer and I have a friendship with him—and we can talk about stuff like the Supremes or Cream or *The Simpsons*. I'd dreamed from a very young age of having this kind of relationship with a living composer, rather than just being in awe of dead composers' work," Josefowicz told the London *Guardian* (July 22, 2002). Other contemporary composers Josefowicz has worked with include Oliver Knussen, John Harbison, Esa-Pekka Salonen, and John Zorn. "I don't know about everyone else, but I am so bored with CDs where the same repertoire is repeated again and again," she told Peter Culshaw for the London *Daily Telegraph* (April 5, 2005), adding, "Most people haven't realized just how lyrical so much of this new music is."

For her next recording, a self-titled two-CD set that was released in 2005, Josefowicz, showing the freedom that her success had brought her, performed a mixture of old and new music, playing pieces by Brahms, Beethoven, and Ravel and contemporary works by Esa-Pekka Salonen and Mark Grey. (One piece, San Andreas Suite, was written by Grey specifically for Josefowicz.) "It can be so refreshing when a musician abandons the record industry's penchant for completism and puts together a disc that presents a number of different works and composers as if it were a live recital," Matthew Rye wrote for the London *Daily Telegraph* (May 14, 2005). "And that is the case with Leila Josefowicz's latest release, a studio recording of repertoire that she has indeed played regularly in concert with pianist John Novacek." Other critics were also impressed. Mark Stryker, writing for the *Detroit Free Press* (June 14, 2005), argued that the collection illustrated "the maturation of [a] former prodigy" and went on to note that "rather than fall prey to Great Masterpiece Syndrome, [Josefowicz is] applying her virtuosity, expressive musicianship and hot-and-sweet style to a striking range."

Josefowicz's next release, in 2006, was a live performance of the Russian composer Dmitri Shostakovich's Violin Concerto no. 1, recorded with the City of Birmingham Symphony Orchestra. She told Christopher Blank for the Memphis, Tennessee, *Commercial Appeal* (September 15, 2006) that she chose the piece, which Terry Grimley described for the *Birmingham Post* (May 16, 2006) as "great but grim," because it spoke to the trials of her personal life: "Sometimes there is that challenge to stay afloat in life. And that's my concept of the violin concerto. When you take into consideration what Shostakovich went through when he wrote it, if your own life has been roses, you're going to miss the message." (Shostakovich, who was born in 1906 and died in 1975, was denounced multiple times by the Soviet leader Joseph Stalin's regime and forced to write in a less avant-garde, more accessible style. Many of his pieces were banned by the government, and he hid some of his more personal compositions. He joined the Communist Party in 1960, a move some viewed as "selling out," according to Blank, who also observed: "Many musicologists divide his vast musical output into two categories: that written to glorify the regime, and a number of darker pieces said to be encoded with dissident messages.") His Violin Concerto no. 1 is "more than a violin concerto, it's a kind of a confession. It's more than just music because what he was writing about at the time was really about life. He was really restricted in those years and this concerto was 'anti-people' music. I think all the pent-up emotion he felt at that time was put into this piece," Josefowicz said.

Josefowicz has one son, Lukas, from her marriage at 21 to the conductor Kristjan Järvi, which ended in divorce. Difficulties such as her divorce, she believes, have given her music a sense of perspective. "There's not a single day that I regret anything [that has] happened with me, and the more that you live, the more there is to play about; it's very simple. So I have a lot to play about these days," she told Eugenia Zukerman on CBS's program *Sunday Morning* (August 10, 2003, on-line).

—M.B.

Suggested Reading: (London) *Guardian*, G2 p10, July 22, 2002; (London) *Independent* Apr. 19, 2005; *New York Times* II p32 May 29, 2005; *Toronto Star* M p3, Apr. 1, 2006; *Strings* (on-line) May/June 2000

Selected Albums: *Tchaikovsky: Violin Concerto in D/Sibelius: Violin Concerto in D*, 1995; *Solo*, 1996; *Bohemian Rhapsodies*, 1997; *Violin for Anne Rice*, 1997; *For the End of Time*, 1998; *Mendelssohn & Glazunov: Violin Concertos*, 2000; *Americana*, 2000; *Prokofiev: Violin Concertos 1 & 2. Tchaikovsky: Serenade Melancholique*, 2001; *John Adams: Tromba Lontana; Violin Concerto; The Wound-Dresser*, 2003; *John Adams: Road Movies*, 2004; *Leila Josefowicz*, 2005; *Shostakovich: Violin Concerto No. 1 in A minor, Op. 99 & Violin Sonata, Op. 134*, 2006

July, Miranda

Feb. 15, 1974– Writer; filmmaker; performance artist; musician

Address: P.O. Box 26596, Los Angeles, CA 90026

Miranda July's quirky style of narrative and signature themes, developed over the past decade, have infused her performance pieces, feature-film work, video art, Internet projects, and even seven-inch recordings. Indeed, despite the multitude of forms her work has taken, some things about July's projects—which have been called both self-consciously adorable and borderline creepy—are remarkably the same. As she explained to Rachel Kushner for *Bomb* magazine (Summer 2005), "I was (and am) interested in seeing different kinds of people together, unusual pairs in terms of age and gender and race." Kushner summed up the predominating themes in July's work as "people hoping for miraculous events to intervene in their lives, children cultivating their own private and idiosyncratic longings, everyone improvising ways to communicate with one another." July's recent endeavors, the feature film *Me and You and Everyone We Know* (2005) and a collection of short stories called *No One Belongs Here More Than You* (2007), have significantly expanded her audience and celebrity.

Miranda July was born Miranda Grossinger on February 15, 1974 in Barre, Vermont, and raised in Berkeley, California. She has an older brother, Robin Grossinger, a biologist with the San Francisco Estuary Institute. Her parents, Lindy Hough and Richard Grossinger, are the founders and publish-

Pascal Le Segretain/Getty Images

ers of North Atlantic Books, whose mission, according to its Web site, is to "develop new ideas, nurture practical education, spread timeless wisdom, and help turn destructive energies into positive forces." Books published by the company include *Healing with Whole Foods* and *Your Inner Physician and You*. In an interview with Kimberly Cutter for *New York Magazine* (May 21, 2007), July recalled that during her childhood, her parents talked with her about their personal—even marital—problems. "I wasn't neglected at all," she told Cutter, "but my parents didn't have the best boundaries in the world." She added that her parents' openness contributed to her own "desire to be the one who understands." The environment proved to be a nurturing one for the young girl's talents. At age seven she began recording herself holding one end of a conversation and then playing it back, so she could "chat with herself," as Karen Durbin reported for the *New York Times* (June 19, 2005). A precocious and creative teen, she created, with a friend, a "girlzine" called "Snarla," in which she wrote about her experiences. That activity generated a character called July, whose name she adopted as her own—marking the first of many instances of self-reinvention in her career. She began writing plays and staging them at the 924 Gilman Street Project, also known as the Alternative Music Foundation, an all-ages club in North Berkeley.

July attended the University of California at Santa Cruz, where she studied film. She dropped out at age 20, disenchanted with a course that was "all guys" and in which "every project had a gun or a dog in it," as she told Durbin. Within a year she was living in Portland, Oregon, where she fell in with a group of musicians called the CeBe Barnes Band. She contributed vocals to a seven-inch punk record called *The CeBe Barnes Band*, released on the Horse Kitty label. Next, she collaborated with a band called the Need, providing vocals for a second seven-inch record, *Margie Ruskie Stops Time* (1996), released on the Kill Rock Stars label. At music venues she was paired with alternative-rock acts, among them Sleater-Kinney, Chicks on Speed, and Dub Narcotic.

In 1996 July also began making short videos and creating performance pieces, quickly gaining attention and funding. Within a year she had received grants from organizations including the Andrea Frank Foundation, Art Bridge Association, and the Regional Arts and Culture Council. The character-oriented performances July produced during that period, including *Atlanta* (1996), *The Amateurist* (1998), and *Love Diamond* (1998–2000), often involved her playing many or all of the roles (she portrayed, for example, both a woman and the woman's mother); the works also featured slide and video projection and music. Her videos were screened in a wide variety of venues, among them the Chicago Underground Film Festival, the Whitney Museum of Art, in New York, and the Barbara Gross Gallery in Munich, Germany. As a result of that exposure, July won additional awards and grants as well as guest-artist positions at the University of California, Swarthmore College, and Bryn Mawr College.

As July continued to portray characters in her films, videos, and performance pieces, her roster of characters grew. In *Nests of Tens*, for example, a teenage boy performs an elaborate cleaning ritual on a baby in an empty house, creating an atmosphere that is at once nonsexual and unnerving. The notions of striking juxtapositions and of disparate but functioning communities are present in other projects, such as *Learning to Love You More* (begun in 2002), in which July and a fellow artist, Harrell Fletcher, brought together segments of the public through art assignments, whose results are shared via the Internet. Assignments range from finding art in the everyday ("Draw a constellation from someone's freckles"), to pursuing meaningful experiences ("Spend time with a dying person"), to creating self-reflective art ("Make a Learning to Love You More assignment"). Other, more performance-oriented works, including *How I Learned to Draw* (2002–04) as well as *Things We Don't Understand and Definitely Are Not Going To Talk About* (2006–), also rely in part on viewer participation. In *Draw*, the collective title for July's performances from 2002 to 2004, she chose by intuition the audience members who could potentially be good friends with each other, then introduced them to one another before casting them, on the spot, in roles in her live performances. *How I Learned to Draw*, like *Learning to Love You More*, was—according to July's Web site—"primarily concerned with drawing attention to the present moment."

July next explored the world of narrative film. *Me and You and Everyone We Know* (2005) is a visually lush, 90-minute work described on its Web site, meandyoumovie.com, as "a poetic and penetrating observation of how people struggle to connect with one another in an isolating and contemporary world." The film centers on Christine (played by July), a struggling video artist who sets her sights on Richard (John Hawkes), a recently divorced shoe salesman. The story includes other unusual matchups: a gallery director and a seven-year-old who are in contact through the Internet and a teenage boy and younger girl who lie on the carpet of the girl's bedroom, talking about her fantasies of marriage. The soundtrack, created by Michael Andrews, full of "winsome beep-and-buzz keyboards" (according to the Summer 2005 edition of *Sight and Sound*), underscores the melodic dissonance of the central, interrelated characters. Some felt that July had shied away from the reality of her awkward cinematic couplings once their humorous or startling effects had been achieved. Many others, however, celebrated July's first feature film, which won the Originality of Vision award at the Sundance Film Festival, the Camera d'Or prize at the Cannes Film Festival, and an Independent Spirit Award nomination. In the *New York Times* (June 17, 2005), A. O. Scott declared, "I like [the film] very much, and I hope you will, too."

July has attributed her forays into fiction to encouragement from the fiction writer and essayist Rick Moody. In 2003 her stories had begun to appear in journals including the prestigious *Paris Review* as well as the *Harvard Review* and *Tin House*. In those stories July continued to explore unsettling sexual dynamics and atypical pairings in intimate situations. Some of the pieces, among them

"Making Love in 2003," were collected for the 2007 volume *No One Belongs Here More Than You.* Discussing the book with August Brown for the *Los Angeles Times* (May 6, 2007), July explained that the year-long press tour for her first film had left her exhausted, self-conscious, and strapped for funds. "I was trying to pull myself together creatively . . . ," she recalled. "I was very broke. I thought, 'Well, if I can finish this book and write a bunch more stories, I bet I can sell it now that I have a little bit of an audience.' I was happy to have something to do, a task at hand." July described the writing process to Kimberly Cutter as being difficult, explaining that she forced herself to continue even though "everything I wrote seemed terrible." She also said, "The stories aren't technically autobiographical, but in an emotional sense, they are."

Some critics heralded the collection as marking a new phase in July's work, a more mature period that would see her refrain from what her detractors saw as posturing—or, as Cutter phrased it, "serv-[ing] up preciousness in place of thoughtfulness, trafficking in . . . faux-earnest indulgences." The book's effervescent tales feature sexual idiosyncrasy (stemming in part, once again, from unlikely, uncomfortable pairings) as well as a wide variety of odd subjects and details, including a little dog named Potato, earthquake awareness, and Prince William of Great Britain. Such seemingly random references, which become entrances into her characters' complicated emotional lives, are a signature part of July's creative voice, regardless of medium. The uniformity of her narrative voice, in fact, is perhaps the most frequently cited aspect of *No One Belongs Here More Than You.* Josh Lacey wrote for the London *Guardian* (June 30, 2007), "Whether the narrators are men or women, young or old, gay or straight, they all tend to speak in a very similar tone." Lacey also called the book's 16 stories "blisteringly good." David Wiegand, reviewing the collection for the *San Francisco Chronicle* (June 28, 2007), agreed, exclaiming, "July's stories startle us at every turn . . . sometimes by passages of impossibly lush eloquence that rise from their postminimal settings like great adagios, and very often, by their sheer inventiveness."

Though the critical and commercial success of her more recent projects, her most mainstream works to date, has attracted the attention of dealmakers in the entertainment industry, July has chosen to stick to her own—not necessarily mainstream—agenda. As she told the *New York Sun* (February 27, 2007), her response to "brand new fancy movie agents" attempting to capitalize on her newfound celebrity and success was, "Oh, by the way, just don't even talk to me for a year because you're not going to care what I'm doing." While working on the screenplay for her next feature film, July has also devoted time to playing the typewriter in a Los Angeles, California, band, hiking in the Hollywood Hills with her boyfriend, and working on smaller-scale projects, such as an art book related to the *Learning to Love You More* Web

site. Discussing future projects, July said to Rachel Kushner, "I have a gigantic plan . . . and it involves performance, and fiction, and radio, and the [World Wide Web], and TV and features that are both 'conventional' and totally not. And when I am done with my plan, when I am very old, hopefully there will be a little more space for people living with profound doubt to tell their stories in all different mediums. Also Hollywood won't be so sexist. . . . But one thing at a time."

July lives in Los Angeles with her boyfriend, the graphic artist and film director Mike Mills, whose recent releases include *Thumbsucker* (2005).

—J.W.

Suggested Reading:*Artweek* p26+ Oct. 2003; *Bomb* p62+ Summer 2005; *Los Angeles Times* E p10 June 19, 2005; *New York Sun* Arts and Letters p11 Feb. 27, 2007; *New York Times* II p13 June 19, 2005

Selected Books: *No One Belongs Here More Than You,* 2007

Selected Films: *Me and You and Everyone We Know,* 2005

Kagan, Elena

Apr. 28, 1960– Dean of Harvard Law School

Address: Harvard Law School, 1563 Massachusetts Ave., Cambridge, MA 02138

In 2003, 50 years after the graduation of Harvard Law School's first class to include women, Elena Kagan was appointed the school's first female dean. "For many of our women graduates, this was a not very hospitable place for many years," Kagan, who earned a law degree at Harvard in 1986, told Beth Potier for the *Harvard University Gazette* (September 16, 2004). One example of the ways in which female students were made to feel unwanted was a 1960s tradition called Ladies' Day; while at all other times, certain professors refused to call on any of their few female students, who sat scattered among their male classmates, on that day the women were forced to sit together and submit to a barrage of questions from the professors and male students. "For those graduates, it does have real meaning that the place is being led by a woman," Kagan continued. "In the wider world, it does send a message that Harvard Law School is today a very inclusive institution, and I think that's a great message to send." Kagan held the title Charles Hamilton Houston professor of law at Harvard when she was appointed dean. In that post, among other measures, Kagan has increased the diversity of the law school's faculty and taken steps to strengthen its curriculum, in an effort to keep Harvard at the

Courtesy of Harvard Law School

Elena Kagan

forefront of legal education, and she has made the nonacademic needs of students one of her priorities. Kagan taught at the University of Chicago Law School before she joined the faculty of Harvard. She also has experience in government, having worked with President Bill Clinton at the White House. "There are some people who are good at the big visions of the future . . . and there are other people who are better at the here and now, have incredible interpersonal skills, and can really make the moment much better than it was," Carol Steiker, a Harvard law professor who attended law school with Kagan, told Potier. "[Kagan] really can do both."

Elena Kagan was born on April 28, 1960 in New York City. Her mother, an elementary-school teacher, and her father, a lawyer, were both the first in their families to attend college. Kagan graduated from Hunter College High School, in Manhattan, in 1977 and then entered Princeton University, in New Jersey, where she received a B.A. degree in history summa cum laude. For the next two years, she studied at Worcester College, a division of Oxford University, in England, as Princeton's Daniel M. Sachs graduating fellow. After she earned an M. Phil. (master's of philosophy) degree at Oxford, she enrolled at Harvard Law School, in Cambridge, Massachusetts. "I think I was one of these students who go to law school for all the wrong reasons, because they can't figure out exactly what else they want to do . . . ," she told Andrea Sachs for *Ms.* (Summer 2003). "Once I arrived, I actually loved it right away, and I really felt as if I had found something I was good at." Kagan served as supervising editor of the *Harvard Law Review*. She earned a J.D. degree magna cum laude in 1986. From 1986 to

1987 Kagan worked as a law clerk for Judge Abner Mikva on the U.S. Court of Appeals for the District of Columbia Circuit. Next, until 1988, she clerked for U.S. Supreme Court justice Thurgood Marshall. In 1989 Kagan left the public sector to become an associate at the Washington, D.C., law firm Williams & Connolly, where she worked until 1991. In that year she accepted an appointment as an assistant professor at the University of Chicago School of Law, in Illinois. In the summer of 1993, she acted as special counsel to the U.S. Senate Judiciary Committee during the confirmation hearings of Ruth Bader Ginsburg for a seat on the Supreme Court. That year the University of Chicago's Law Student Association honored her with its Graduating Students' Award for Teaching Excellence. She became a tenured professor at the school in 1995.

During a leave of absence from the university in 1995 and 1996, Kagan served as associate counsel to President Bill Clinton, and in 1997 she became deputy assistant to the president for domestic policy and deputy director of the Domestic Policy Council. She played an important role in the executive branch's formation and implementation of both law and policy in areas ranging from education and crime to public health. Kagan was especially forceful in pursuing anti-tobacco legislation, helping to craft a comprehensive tobacco bill, sponsored by Senator John S. McCain of Arizona, which failed to gain passage. "The issues were fascinating," she recalled to Sachs. "Anyone who works at the White House will tell you it's great fun." Kagan became known as a feminist and a powerful advocate for progressive politics and also gained a reputation for being brusque and impatient in her negotiations. (At Harvard, however, she is regarded as a conciliatory figure.) "Kagan uses knowledge as a weapon, absorbing thousands of pages of legal and policy minutiae and then deploying information to beat down opposing arguments," Dana Milbank wrote for the *New Republic* (May 18, 1998), in an article headlined "Wonderwonk." A person who had opposed Kagan in negotiations regarding tobacco legislation told Milbank, "I don't want to tell you that she rolled me, but she was coming at me so hard. She reminds me of Bobby Knight's old [University of Indiana basketball] teams that used to wear you down with defense." In 1999 Clinton nominated Kagan for a seat on the U.S. Court of Appeals for the District of Columbia Circuit, widely considered the second-most-powerful court in the country after the U.S. Supreme Court. The Republican-led Senate Judiciary Committee refused to bring her nomination forward for a hearing; when Congress adjourned in the fall of 2000, her nomination expired, after being held in committee for 18 months.

In 1999 Kagan left government service to teach at Harvard Law School as a visiting professor; she became a professor of law at Harvard in 2001. The subjects of her courses included constitutional law, civil procedure, and administrative law—the last topic being her specialty. "Presidential Administration," a 140-page article by her that appeared in the *Harvard Law Review* (June 2001), was named the top scholarly article of the year by the American Bar Association's Section on Administrative Law and Regulatory Practice; Kagan is currently expanding the piece into a book to be published by Harvard University Press.

On April 3, 2003 Kagan was named the 11th dean of Harvard Law School, becoming the first female dean in the school's history. "I think it is a milestone, a great thing that shows how far Harvard has come and how far the legal profession has come, in terms of women's position," she told Sachs. Lawrence H. Summers, then the president of Harvard University, praised Kagan's ability to understand both the intellectual and practical aspects of law, which would help her make the curriculum of Harvard Law School more relevant to contemporary society. Kagan "understands both academia and legal practice, and has excelled in both domains," Summers said, as quoted by the *Harvard University Gazette* (April 10, 2003). "At a time when legal education faces intriguing questions, and when the legal profession confronts profound changes, I have every confidence that her talents will advance Harvard Law School's vitality as a place of learning, and carry forward its leadership role in the world of law." Kagan's predecessor, Robert C. Clark, who had been dean for over a decade and had earned praise for his handling of the school's notoriously fractious faculty, indicated that Kagan, too, would prove adept in dealing with differences among the staff. In the months leading up to her assumption of the deanship, on July 1, 2003, Kagan displayed the skill at consensus building for which she would become known, meeting individually with all 81 members of the law-school faculty, in part to hear their concerns about the school.

As dean, Kagan immediately began to make small improvements that, for her, symbolized an increased emphasis on student satisfaction and community, and she made moves to signal the kind of leader she would be at a school that consistently ranks behind the other top law schools in terms of students' quality of life. She ordered renovations of two areas: Pound Hall, where free coffee was added to its amenities, and the patios outside Harness Commons; she also made minor improvements to Hemenway Gym and initiated the construction of an outdoor skating rink. "You have to keep your eye on both balls, the long-term and the short-term," she told Beth Potier. "We are what we are because of the students who come here and what they go on to do in their lives. We should communicate that to them in everything that we do."

One month before Kagan took over from Clark, Harvard Law School had launched a $400 million capital campaign, the largest fundraising effort ever by a law school. Scheduled to end in 2008, the campaign will raise money primarily for building and renovations and—of greater importance, in Kagan's view—more endowed professorships and in-

creased financial support for students. Many members of the faculty have commended her emphasis on recruiting a greater number of teachers and a more diverse staff (in terms of gender, race, ethnicity, and political views); between the time of her appointment and March 2006, the school had made approximately 20 offers, including several to political conservatives. "As many quality appointments as we can make, that's how many we should make," she said to Potier. "The thing that will most change Harvard Law School over the next 10 years is the quality of the faculty. . . . That's what makes a school." Kagan also said that the money would allow Harvard to be more generous in forgiving the debts of students who choose jobs in the public sector rather than the more lucrative positions available in private firms. At present only 6 to 10 percent of Harvard Law School graduates begin their professional lives in government or with nonprofit organizations. "Our students ought to say, 'How can I take all this experience and knowledge that I have about legal rules and institutions and find a way to give back to the public?'" she told Kathryn Beaumont for *Princeton Alumni Weekly* (December 17, 2003).

In 2003 Kagan initiated the first wholesale review of the Harvard Law School curriculum since it was introduced by Dean Christopher Langdell in the 1870s and became the model for most law schools in the U.S. (Her immediate predecessor and others before him had made relatively minor changes.) "It really is time to say, 'Is that really what students should be taking? Are they learning the set of competencies that they need to master in order to go out and be a great lawyer in today's world? How has the world changed in the last 100 and some years?" Kagan said to Potier. After three years of study, the eight-person curricular-review committee proposed that Harvard overhaul the first-year curriculum to focus more on complex problem-solving, international law, and modern law-making by government bodies and administrative agencies. In a 2006 vote in which approximately 70 percent of the faculty participated, the committee's recommendations were unanimously approved. "If we do our jobs well in this area, we'll be creating a law school curriculum not just for Harvard but for legal education in general," Kagan told Potier in the middle of the process. "It's the great fun of this job, but it's also the great responsibility of it."

Dean Kagan has dealt with several controversies both within Harvard and within the greater academic community. She was mildly criticized for the way she handled a plagiarism incident in 2004, in which two top Harvard law professors publicly acknowledged that they had misused sources, albeit, as they insisted, unintentionally. The same misuse—whether accidental or intentional—would have meant a severe reprimand and even expulsion for an undergraduate or graduate student, but the professors were allowed to remain on the faculty. Another controversy stemmed from the

Pentagon's policy of "Don't ask, don't tell," which prohibits admitted homosexuals from membership in any branch of the armed services, and a 1994 federal law known as the Solomon Amendment, which allows the secretary of defense to deny federal funding to universities that prevent on-campus military recruitment. Harvard—along with a number of other prominent law schools, among them Yale, the top-ranked law school in the country—banned Pentagon representatives from activities on campus, because they judged the military's "Don't ask, don't tell" policy to be in violation of the school's guidelines of nondiscrimination for on-campus recruiters. According to the *Weekly Standard* (October 3, 2005), Kagan called the military's discriminatory practice "repugnant" and a "moral injustice of the first order." In 2004 the U.S. Third Circuit Court of Appeals upheld universities' rights to prohibit military recruitment on their property, and in November of that year, Harvard announced that it would limit such activity. But Kagan had to reverse that decision in October 2005, when the Defense Department threatened to take away the University's federal funding despite the Third Circuit Court's ruling. Most of the law school's teachers and students supported Kagan's decision, as Harvard University stood to lose approximately $400 million to $500 million a year, or 15 percent of its annual budget, if it defied the Pentagon. In an e-mail message sent to Harvard Law School students and faculty, quoted by the *Weekly Standard*, Kagan told them "how much I regret making this exception" to the school's nondiscrimination policy, which banned recruiters who refused to consider openly homosexual candidates. On March 6, 2006 the U.S. Supreme Court upheld the Solomon Amendment in a unanimous decision, leaving Harvard with little choice other than to continue to allow military recruitment on campus.

When Summers announced in 2006 that he was stepping down from the presidency of Harvard, Kagan was named a top contender for the position, with many newspapers calling her the favorite candidate. The search committee chose instead another woman, Drew Gilpin Faust, the head of Harvard's Radcliffe Institute. After news of Faust's appointment became public, Harvard Law School students and faculty organized a party in Kagan's honor. "Sometimes you win by losing," she said to the party crowd, as Kevin Zhou reported for the *Harvard Crimson* (February 14, 2007). "All of you have made me feel like a real winner today. This really is a great place."

One year into her deanship, Kagan said that her gender had played little, if any, role in her day-to-day activities. "It's not something I think about on a daily basis, and it's something that in many ways has seemed remarkably not relevant in the job," she told Potier. Kagan has often been mentioned as a possible future appointee to the U.S. Supreme Court. She lives in Cambridge, near the Harvard campus.

—C.S.

Suggested Reading: *Harvard Law Review* p947+ Feb. 2006; *Harvard Magazine* (on-line) July-Aug. 2003; *Harvard University Gazette* (on-line) Apr. 10, 2003, Sep. 16, 2004; *Ms.* (on-line) Summer 2003; *New Republic* p19+ May 18, 1998

Kagan, Frederick W.

Mar. 26, 1970– Military historian; writer

Address: American Enterprise Institute, 1150 17th St., N.W., Washington, DC 20036

"Few neoconservatives can claim to have had as much influence on the course of the Iraq war as the trio of scholars in the Kagan family," Sarah Baxter wrote for the London *Sunday Times* (January 14, 2007). The youngest of the three is Frederick W. Kagan, a military historian and resident scholar in defense and security-policy studies at the American Enterprise Institute for Public Policy Research (AEI), in Washington, D.C. Kagan is a widely published expert on military affairs. His early work centered on Soviet and Russian military history; in recent years he has focused on Iraq, Afghanistan, U.S. defense policy, and international terrorism. He is the primary author of "Choosing Victory: A Plan for Success in Iraq," a study that has been described as the blueprint for President George W. Bush's current policy regarding the war in Iraq. In a summary of "Choosing Victory" posted on the AEI Web site (December 14, 2006), Kagan wrote, a few months before the war entered its fifth year, "Victory in Iraq is still possible at an acceptable level of effort. We must adopt a new approach to the war and implement it quickly and decisively." Kagan has frequently offered his views on the Iraq war on television—on CNN and such PBS programs as *Frontline* and *NewsHour with Jim Lehrer*—and on the National Public Radio (NPR) program *Weekend Edition*. He is a regular contributor to the *Weekly Standard*, a leading conservative/neoconservative magazine, and his writings have also appeared in *Foreign Affairs, Policy Review*, the *Washington Post*, the *Los Angeles Times*, and the *Wall Street Journal*. He is the author of several books, among them *While America Sleeps: Self-Delusion, Military Weakness, and the Threat to Peace Today* (2000), written with his father, Donald Kagan, and *The End of the Old Order: Napoleon and Europe, 1801–1805* (2006). With Robin Higham, a former editor of the journal *Military Affairs*, Kagan edited *Military History of Tsarist Russia* (2002) and *The Military History of the Soviet*

Chip Somodevilla/Getty Images

Frederick W. Kagan

Union (2002). Kagan, who taught history for a decade at the U.S. Military Academy at West Point, New York, is reportedly pleased to have had the opportunity to use his scholarship to serve his country. "Fred has always been a devout patriot, just more than the average patriotic American," his father told Michael Rothfeld for *Newsday* (January 11, 2007).

The younger of the two sons of Donald Kagan and Myrna Dabrusky, Frederick Walter Kagan was born on March 26, 1970 in Highland Falls, New York, a village adjacent to West Point. His father, who is of Jewish descent, emigrated from Lithuania to the United States as a child, in 1934. Currently the Sterling professor of classics and history at Yale University, Donald Kagan is an expert on the Peloponnesian War (431–404 B.C.), fought between the ancient Greek city-states Athens and Sparta and their respective allies. According to a brief biography of him on the Yale Web site, he "has applied his extensive knowledge of classical history to understand contemporary diplomacy and international relations"; he won a National Humanities Medal in 2003 and has written, co-written, or edited many books. A leftist during his youth, he began to embrace conservative principles during the Vietnam War. Frederick Kagan's brother, Robert (born in 1958), worked in the U.S. State Department from 1984 to 1988, during the second term of President Ronald Reagan; among other jobs, he served as a speechwriter for Secretary of State George P. Shultz. Currently, Robert Kagan writes a monthly column on world affairs for the *Washington Post* and contributes articles regularly to the *Weekly Standard* and the *New Republic*. His wife, Victoria Nuland, has been the

U.S. permanent representative, or ambassador, to NATO since 2005. In 1997, with William Kristol, a founder of the *Weekly Standard*, Robert Kagan set up the Project for the New American Century (PNAC), a neoconservative think tank. The PNAC's stated goal is to promote U.S. leadership globally. (Critics have alleged that its real mission is to advance and maintain U.S. dominance over world affairs through military might.) Donald Kagan is among the signers of the PNAC's "Statement of Principles," and Frederick Kagan has been a member of many PNAC study groups. In 1998 the PNAC sent an open letter to President Bill Clinton that strongly recommended the use of American diplomatic, political, and military power to oust Saddam Hussein, who was then the president of Iraq.

Frederick Kagan graduated from Yale University, in New Haven, Connecticut, in 1991, with a bachelor's degree in Soviet and East European studies. He remained at Yale to complete a Ph.D. degree in Russian and Soviet military history, in 1995. From 1995 through 2005 Kagan taught history at the U.S. Military Academy at West Point. He earned an Excellence in Teaching Award there in 1997.

Kagan's first book, *The Military Reforms of Nicholas I: The Origins of the Modern Russian Army*, was published in 1999. In his second, *While America Sleeps: Self-Delusion, Military Weakness, and the Threat to Peace Today* (2000), Kagan and his father attempted to refute the idea that the U.S. was invulnerable to foreign attack. The Kagans argued that the federal government—which was then spending more on arms than the governments of the 13 next-biggest militaries combined—needed to increase its defense budget by at least 25 percent to fulfill its global responsibilities and to avoid capitulation to a foreign power, as had been the fate of Austria, Poland, the Netherlands, and other European nations during Adolf Hitler's rule of Germany (1933–45). In a review of *While America Sleeps* for the *Bulletin of the Atomic Scientists* (March/April 2001), the University of Chicago historian Bruce Cumings wrote, "The storm has been gathering for a decade, according to the Kagans, but in 1991 we failed to comprehend that we were at a critical turning point. . . . It would indeed be one of the great ironies of modern times if 1991— the year the United States emerged from the Cold War as the only remaining superpower . . . —was really the beginning of the end of American dominance. But the United States can save itself, say the authors, if it spends more on defense and acquires loads of new weapons. This last message, which dominates the latter third of the book, seems to have been perfectly timed for the 2000 presidential campaign. . . . There is one good thing about *While America Sleeps*: No one who reads it is going to run out and buy a flak jacket, teach kindergartners to 'duck and cover,' or restock a backyard bombshelter. This is a book to assign to students who want to know what professors mean when they say 'a little history is a bad thing.'" The editors of *Orbis* (March 22, 2001), published by the Foreign Policy Research Institute, remarked in their review of the book: "In sum, [the Kagans] boldly affirm the Clinton administration's rhetoric about America's responsibility to be the world's policeman, but offer no recommendations about where, when, and why U.S. forces ought to be deployed, or what force structures and weapons are likely to be needed in case one or two regional wars erupt." Referring to the Kagans' assertion that Britain's failure to maintain military superiority during the 1920s left that nation ill-prepared for the threat posed by Germany during the ensuing decade, the *Orbis* editors continued, "Their only remedy to our putative 'British disease' is to spend more money. But on what, and for what?" Although *While America Sleeps* received mixed reviews when it was published—because of its highly academic style as well as its controversial subject matter—the Kagans' thesis gained greater recognition, and the book a wider audience, following the September 11, 2001 terrorist attacks on the U.S.

In an article published in *Policy Review* in September 2003, less than six months after Baghdad, Iraq's capital, fell to U.S. troops, Kagan criticized U.S. strategies with regard to Iraq and Afghanistan and found fault in particular with the civilian head of the U.S. military at that time—Secretary of Defense Donald Rumsfeld. "The U.S. has been far less successful in winning the peace than it was in winning the war," Kagan wrote. He tried to show the ways in which the military's increasing reliance on technology and decreasing use of ground troops was unwise. Kagan maintained that although technological advances had enabled the U.S. military to suffer fewer casualties while killing greater numbers of insurgents and other enemies, the extended occupation of Iraq required far more than gadgetry and sophisticated computer systems. He expanded that thesis in his book *Finding the Target: The Transformation of American Military Policy* (2006). That volume discusses in depth the widely repeated neoconservative belief that the military's troubles in the era of the Bush administration and the Iraq war are due in part to the attempted wholesale shift toward high-tech weaponry—an effort spearheaded by Rumsfeld. In an assessment of *Finding the Target* for the *New York Times Book Review* (December 17, 2006), Barry Gewen wrote that Kagan "is concerned with distinguishing genuine transformations from false ones. In *Finding the Target* he argues that what the Rumsfeld Pentagon has proclaimed as a technological revolution in military affairs is no such thing, and that this fundamental misconception has produced the debacle that is the Iraq War." Gewen also wrote, "Kagan contends that . . . by concentrating on raw power, especially air power, to the exclusion of politics and culture, the Bush administration has courted disaster and defeat in a region [the Middle East] it never took the trouble to understand." Kagan also judged to be wrongheaded the insistence of Rumsfeld and senior military figures

on "a rapid handover of security responsibilities to Iraqis" as well as on "a relatively light military footprint," as Spencer Ackerman wrote for the *American Prospect Online* (December 15, 2006). The military historian and classicist Victor Davis Hanson wrote for *Commentary* (December 2006) that Kagan's "bipartisan indictment fingers two primary culprits: Bill Clinton, who dismantled crucial elements of the cold-war military establishment, and George W. Bush, who, not understanding the larger political purposes of war, has lacked the necessary vision to reap the advantage of our vast conventional power. . . . 'War is not just about killing people and blowing things up,' he writes. 'It is purposeful violence to achieve a political goal.'"

In early 2006, as criticism of the war in Iraq mounted, Congress named nine prominent former government figures and one businessman (five Democrats and five Republicans) to a newly formed Iraq Study Group (ISG) and charged them with suggesting alternatives to the Bush administration's "stay-the-course" policy in Iraq. Headed by former secretary of state James A. Baker III and former Indiana congressman Lee Hamilton, the ISG determined that the military situations in Iraq and Afghanistan were worse than Pentagon officials had reported. *The Iraq Study Group Report: The Way Forward—A New Approach*, released in December 2006, contains 79 recommendations. Among other proposals, the ISG suggested that the U.S. meet with representatives of Iraq's neighbors, including Syria and Iran, in order to ease tensions in the region. The group also called for a short-term increase in U.S. troops, who would concentrate on training Iraqi soldiers to prepare them for the withdrawal of American soldiers. After the report became public, the White House announced that the administration would also consider recommendations from other sources, among them the Pentagon, the U.S. State Department, and the National Security Council.

Earlier, in June 2006, at a meeting with President Bush and Pentagon officials, Kagan had pushed for a different strategy for Iraq. He said that the achievement of stability in Iraq required more-aggressive military activities. According to Sarah Baxter, at the meeting Donald Rumsfeld was unimpressed by Kagan's ideas, but Kagan later got an enthusiastic response from the president, who reportedly said, "Wow, you mean we can still win this war?," and encouraged Kagan to continue studying the matter. In late 2006 AEI announced the creation of its own Iraq Planning Group, which was referred to as the "Real Iraq Study Group" by Mark Benjamin of *Salon* and other political commentators to indicate that AEI, rather than ISG, had the President's ear. The group was led by Kagan and a retired U.S. general, John "Jack" Keane, and also included about a dozen other AEI scholars as well as several other retired army officers. Some observers believed that the group's sole purpose was to negate the influence of the Iraq Study Group and to offer an aggressive alternative to what many expected the ISG's recommendations would be. With much fanfare, including speeches by Senators John S. McCain of Arizona and Joseph Lieberman of Connecticut, AEI made public its report, *Choosing Victory: A Plan for Success in Iraq*, in January 2007. Among other proposals, *Choosing Victory* recommended shifting the focus from training Iraqi soldiers to using U.S. troops to secure the Iraqi population and contain the escalating violence. That change required the deployment of additional U.S. combat troops to Iraq as soon as possible, to clear the most violent neighborhoods (mainly in Baghdad) not only of insurgents but also a large percentage of the ordinary population; destroy guns and other weapons that people might have been hoarding; and then allow people to reenter their neighborhoods slowly, through checkpoints where they would be screened. The AEI report also called for increasing the money allocated for reconstruction and mobilizing American and other military-materiel industries to "provide replacement equipment" for troops. *Choosing Victory* insisted that not only was a military victory possible, it was a necessary precondition for the return of stability to the region.

Choosing Victory received staunch support from Kagan's AEI colleagues and resonated with people who disparagingly labeled the ISG's report a recipe for surrender. In an article for *Time* (January 15, 2007), William Kristol, the editor of the *Weekly Standard*, referring to General John P. Abizaid, the former head of U.S. Central Command, and General George W. Casey, the former commander of coalition forces in Iraq, wrote that Kagan's plan "reverses the debilitating Rumsfeld-Abizaid-Casey emphasis on a 'light footprint' for the U.S. military and on drawing down American troops as soon as possible." Kristol praised the methodology of Kagan's analyses, remarking that Kagan "follows classic counterinsurgency doctrine by sending enough troops to . . . the center of gravity of the conflict."

Some Pentagon officials saw little difference between Kagan's plan and Operation Forward Together, which the U.S. had launched with high expectations in July 2006. That campaign, which had increased the troop presence in Baghdad, had backfired, and violence had increased to record levels. President Bush argued that Operation Forward Together "failed for two reasons," as quoted by David Wood in the *Baltimore (Maryland) Sun* (January 11, 2007): "There were not enough Iraqi and American troops to secure neighborhoods that had been cleared of terrorists and insurgents. And there were too many restrictions on the troops we have." The Bush administration hoped that by including Kagan's proposals in future strategy considerations, such failures would be avoided in the future.

Many left-leaning pundits hailed the results of the November 2006 elections—which would return control of the House of Representatives and the Senate to the Democrats the following Janu-

ary—and the release of *The Iraq Study Group Report* as harbingers of change in the military strategy in Iraq, which was growing increasingly unpopular among the public. However, such change has not occurred. Paul Campos, a professor of law at the University of Colorado, wrote for the *Rocky Mountain News* (December 19, 2006) that the strategy in Iraq, which was seen by many to be failing, had been strongly influenced by Kagan and other neoconservatives, and he expressed frustration at the Bush administration's decision to continue to rely on the ideas of groups such as AEI. "The chief architects of the Iraq war have suffered no punishment whatsoever for plunging the nation in the biggest foreign policy disaster in our history," Campos wrote, yet "people like [Frederick] Kagan still control our Iraq strategy." Critics of the AEI report also included military officers who had served in Iraq. Among them was James Pasquarette, an infantry commander, who told Spencer Ackerman, "It is beyond military means to fix the issues in Iraq right now. Most everybody agrees there is not a military solution." General George Casey told a reporter for the *New York Times* (January 2, 2007), "The longer we in the U.S. forces continue to bear the main burden of Iraq's security, it lengthens the time that the government of Iraq has to take the hard decisions about reconciliation and dealing with the militias. And the other thing is that they can continue to blame us for all of Iraq's problems." In an article for the *Booman Tribune* (December 16, 2006, on-line), which on its home page calls itself "a stalwart friend of children, but a nocturnal terror for corrupt politicians, lazy reporters, and hypocritical Republican operatives," a retired navy commander, Jeff Huber, wrote, "Fred Kagan has lost all credibility as an honest broker of military thought and scholarship. He's become a compliant tool of the neoconservative cabal headed by his brother Bob Kagan and Bill Kristol, whose objective is to commit America to expanding its conventional military forces to engage in an eternal state of warfare against a marginally definable 'enemy' that has no army, air force or navy."

Although Kagan suggested that the number of U.S. combat troops in Iraq be increased by 50,000, with a similar number of support troops, Bush proposed an increase of just over 20,000. Kagan has said that the effectiveness of the so-called surge in troop strength will not be evident for at least 18 months and that the public must be patient. "We have to be prepared for a bloody year because the enemy will fight us . . . ," Kagan warned, as reported by David Wood for the *Baltimore Sun* (January 11, 2007). "It will take us all of 2007 to get Baghdad under control."

Kagan lives near Washington, D.C.

—N.W.M.

Suggested Reading: *American Prospect Online* Dec. 15, 2006; *Baltimore Sun* A p1+ Jan. 11, 2007; *Booman Tribune (on-*line) Dec. 16, 2006; (London) *Sunday Times* p21 Jan. 14, 2007;

Newsday (on-line) Jan. 11, 2007; *Rocky Mountain News* (on-line) Dec. 19, 2006

Selected Books: *The Military Reforms of Nicholas I: The Origins of the Modern Russian Army*, 1999; *While America Sleeps: Self-Delusion, Military Weakness, and the Threat to Peace Today* (with Donald Kagan), 2000; *Finding the Target: The Transformation of American Military Policy*, 2006

Alex Wong/Getty Images

Kempthorne, Dirk

Oct. 29, 1951– U.S. Secretary of the Interior; former U.S. senator; former governor of Idaho (Republican)

Address: U.S. Interior Dept., Mail Stop 7229, Washington, DC 20240

As secretary of the United States Department of the Interior, Dirk Kempthorne has authority over more than 500 million acres (781,000 square miles) of federally owned land—about 20 percent of all the land in the U.S. His department employs about 57,000 people, and its budget totals about $10.8 billion. His domain includes the National Park Service, which oversees 58 national parks and 333 other entities, among them national monuments, seashores, and heritage trails; the Fish and Wildlife Service, whose responsibilities include enforcement of the Endangered Species Act and the management of more than 500 national wildlife refuges; the Bureau of Indian Affairs, which provides health, education, and other services to

about two million American Indians and oversees the conservation and development of natural resources on 56 million acres (87,500 square miles) of Indian lands; the Bureau of Reclamation, which manages more than 800 dams, reservoirs, and other facilities that provide water to millions of individuals and farms; the U.S. Geological Survey, a purely scientific agency whose workers study the nation's natural resources (and natural hazards, such as earthquakes) and carry out research in biology, geography, geology, and hydrology; the Minerals Management Service; and several other divisions.

Kempthorne, a Republican, is the 48th person to head the department since its formation, in 1849, and like all but a few of his predecessors in the past century, he is closely identified with a state west of the Mississippi River—in his case, Idaho. A native of California, Kempthorne has lived primarily in Idaho since he entered college, in 1971. He began his political life in that state in 1981, as the manager of an unsuccessful gubernatorial campaign. In 1986 he was elected mayor of Boise, Idaho's capital and largest city, and he won reelection four years later. He spent one term as a U.S. senator and then, in 1998, captured the governorship of Idaho. He was serving his second term as governor when, on March 16, 2006, President George W. Bush nominated him to replace Secretary of the Interior Gale A. Norton, who had announced that she was stepping down. Alluding to Kempthorne's steadfast advocacy of states' rights, Bush said, according to a White House press release (March 16, 2006), "Dirk understands that those who live closest to the land know how to manage it best, and he will work closely with state and local leaders to ensure wise stewardship of our resources." While mining-industry spokespeople and other business representatives lauded Bush's choice of Kempthorne for the Interior Department post, environmental and conservation organizations condemned it. On May 26, 2006, after a vote of 85–8 to limit debate on the nomination, the Senate approved it by a voice vote, and on June 7, 2006, Kempthorne was sworn in. Among other actions in his less than 11 months as head of the Interior Department, he persuaded President Bush to earmark $10 billion for improvements in national parks over the next 10 years, according to Sheryl Gay Stolbert and Felicity Barringer in the *New York Times* (February 8, 2007). He has also approved the sales of leases for offshore oil and gas development in 48 million acres along the coasts of Alaska, the Gulf of Mexico, and Virginia that were previously protected from such activity; has proposed permitting as many as 720 snowmobiles in Yellowstone National Park every day; and has authorized the Fish and Wildlife Service to propose regulatory changes that would significantly diminish the powers of federal wildlife-protection agencies.

The youngest of three brothers, Dirk Arthur Kempthorne was born to James Henry "Jim" Kempthorne and the former Maxine Jesse Gustason on October 29, 1951 in San Diego, California. In his early years his family lived in Spokane, Washington. When he was in the fourth grade, he moved with his family to San Bernardino, California, where his father had purchased a hospital-supply business, American Surgical Corp. (Kempthorne's brothers, Mark and James, currently run the company.) In 1970 Kempthorne won election as president of the senior class at San Gorgonio High School, in San Bernardino. The following year he enrolled at the University of Idaho in Moscow, with the intention of preparing for a career in medicine; he later changed his major to political science. In college he served as student-body president in his senior year. He earned a B.S. degree in 1975.

After his graduation Kempthorne spent three years as an assistant to Gordon Trombley, the executive director of Idaho's Department of Lands. In 1978 he entered the private sector, becoming the executive vice president of, and a lobbyist for, the Idaho Home Builders Association. He left that job in 1981 to manage the unsuccessful campaign of Idaho's lieutenant governor, Phil Batt, to win election as the state's governor the following year. (Batt succeeded in a later quest for the governorship, in 1994.) In 1982 Kempthorne worked as a broker for Swanson Investments before becoming the Idaho public-affairs manager for the FMC Corp., a Philadelphia, Pennsylvania–based chemical company that specializes in products for industry and agriculture. During his three years with FMC, he helped set up an office for the company in downtown Boise, where he lived with his wife (they had married in 1977) and their two young children. "We had a wonderful community," he said to Betsy Z. Russell for the Spokane, Washington, *Spokesman Review* (October 20, 1998), "but . . . for too many years it wasn't reaching its potential." One problem was that indecision on the part of Boise city officials and lawmakers had led to the demolition of a sizeable part of the downtown area to make way for a shopping center that was never built. In 1985 Kempthorne ran successfully for mayor of Boise on a platform of reviving the city's downtown. Several sources indicate that on the issue of downtown development, Kempthorne delivered results simply by demanding that representatives of all the interested parties, including City Council members, remain in City Hall on a particular day until a decision on the shopping center was made. Shortly thereafter work began on the construction of the Centre on the Grove, which includes a public plaza and several restaurants and other businesses. "The first key was building relationships, not bricks and mortar, because that town was divided," Kempthorne said to Russell. In 1989 Kempthorne won reelection unopposed. As mayor he also held the posts of first vice president of the Association of Idaho Cities (1990–93); chairman of the U.S. Conference of Mayors standing committee on energy and environment (1991–93); and secretary of the National Conference of Republican Mayors and Municipal Elected Officials (1991–93).

In 1992 Kempthorne made a bid for the seat in the U.S. Senate held by the conservative Republican Steve D. Symms, who had announced his retirement. Kempthorne won the Republican primary with 57 percent of the vote. In the general election he faced Idaho's three-term Democratic congressman Richard Stallings. Although Kempthorne was an elected politician, during the campaign he emphasized that, unlike Stallings, he was not a Washington "insider" and was thus untainted by the dishonesty which he indicated was so prevalent in the nation's capital. He often mentioned that Stallings had written eight checks when he had insufficient funds in his House of Representatives bank account. (Amid mounting public pressure, the House bank had been shut down permanently in 1991.) Kempthorne's platform emphasized the importance of balancing the federal budget. On Election Day he earned 57 percent of the 478,500 votes cast.

In the U.S. Senate Kempthorne emerged early on as a champion of states' rights, as defined by the Tenth Amendment to the Constitution: "The powers not delegated to the United States by the Constitution, nor prohibited by it to the States, are reserved for the States respectively, or to the people." According to *Politics in America 1996*, Kempthorne's voting record during the the 103d Congress reflected his belief that "when it comes to government's exercise of power, the further away from Idaho that decisions are made, the more likely they are to be suspect." He was one of 10 Republican senators who voted against the North American Free Trade Agreement (NAFTA), in 1993, and one of 11 to vote against the General Agreement on Tariffs and Trade (GATT), in 1994; the latter was the precursor of the World Trade Organization, established in 1995, which sets rules for international trade and settles trade disputes between member states. In debate on the floor of the Senate regarding GATT, he said on November 20, 1993, according to the *Congressional Record*, "The United States should seriously reconsider any agreement which gives up sovereignty to any multinational group that will place the needs of international trade over the interests of the American people." Kempthorne attempted without success to seek an exemption from the National Voter Registration Act of 1993 for states in which at least 75 percent of eligible voters had already registered. Also during the 103d Congress, he introduced legislation aimed at blocking so-called unfunded mandates—requirements that the federal government imposes on state or local governments without providing the money necessary to fulfill them. The measure failed to pass; its opponents included Democrats who contended that such mandates (which include, for example, provisions in the Americans with Disabilities Act) aim to protect the public in various ways and safeguard civil rights. On the first day of the 104th Congress, Kempthorne introduced a similar bill, called the Unfunded Mandates Reform Act; it became law in 1995, after the Republicans gained control of both the House and the Senate for the first time since 1952.

Regarding other measures, in 1993 Kempthorne voted yes on a bill designed to bar higher grazing fees on public land, and no on bills to allow federal funds to be used for some abortions, ban some types of semiautomatic assault weapons, and impose a five-day waiting period for handgun purchases. In 1994 he voted against a bill that would have increased funding for research in renewable-energy sources and against a measure that called for safeguarding access to abortion clinics, and the following year he voted for a constitutional amendment prohibiting the desecration of the American flag. In 1996 he voted for bills that limited punitive damages in product-liability lawsuits and exempted small business from paying the minimum wage, and the next year he voted against approval of the Chemical Weapons Convention, a treaty that prohibits the production, stockpiling ,and use of chemical weapons. As the chairman of the Senate Subcommittee on Fisheries, Wildlife, and Drinking Water beginning in 1995, Kempthorne sponsored a short-lived bill to scale back provisions of the Endangered Species Act. He also failed in an attempt to set limits on fines imposed on companies found guilty of polluting rivers and streams with hazardous wastes. Twice, he voted for bills that would have opened up the Arctic National Wildlife Refuge to oil drilling. The League of Conservation Voters gave Kempthorne a near-zero rating for five of his six years in Washington—that is, with only one exception, he had voted against legislation that the league supported and voted for legislation that the organization opposed. In one typical year, 1995, two politically left-wing groups, Americans for Democratic Action and the AFL-CIO (American Federation of Labor–Congress of Industrial Organizations), gave Kempthorne zero ratings, while two politically right-wing groups, the Institute for Cooperative Capitalism and the American Conservative Union, rated him at 100 percent and 96 percent, respectively.

In October 1997, after Phil Batt made public his decision not to seek reelection as Idaho's governor, Kempthorne announced that he would run for the governorship instead of a second term in the Senate. He immediately became the front-runner, and on Election Day 1998 he won in a landslide, capturing 68 percent of the vote; his Democratic challenger, Robert Huntley, a lawyer and former Idaho Supreme Court judge, captured 29 percent. In 2002 Kempthorne ran against the Democrat Jerry Brady, a lawyer and newspaper publisher, and won reelection with 56 percent of the vote. As governor, in early January 2000, Kempthorne tried to block the Clinton administration's attempts to reintroduce up to 25 grizzly bears into the Bitterroot wilderness over a five-year period. (The plan was later withdrawn by Interior Secretary Norton.) In 2005 Kempthorne negotiated an agreement with the Nez Perce Tribe concerning claims to the waters of the Snake River, which stem from an 1855 treaty. The

compromise—"one of Kempthorne's biggest accomplishments as governor," according to a University of Idaho Web site—was the culmination of "a decade of talks that resolved the tribe's water rights, protected Idaho water rights and put in place rules and projects to protect endangered salmon and steelhead habitat." The following year the governor and Secretary Norton signed a so-called memorandum agreement whereby Idaho gained a greater role in managing gray wolves within state boundaries. Also in 2006 Kempthorne approved the proposed opening of a gravel mine in Idaho's Eagle Island State Park.

On March 16, 2006, when Norton announced that she was leaving the Interior Department, President Bush nominated Kempthorne to succeed her. His selection pleased industry groups and their supporters in western states. Kempthorne "has the unique advantage of having one foot in Washington and one foot in the West and that is extraordinarily important," Jim Sims, a longtime lobbyist for extractive industries and the head of both the Western Business Roundtable and the Partnership for the West, said to Robert Gehrke for the *Salt Lake (Utah) Tribune* (March 17, 2006). "We want to have a Westerner, but we also want someone who understands the ways of Washington. He knows them both, and I think it makes him uniquely qualified to do the job." By contrast, the nomination of Kempthorne appalled environmentalists and their backers. "In his last campaign as governor," according to an editorial in the *Boston Globe* entitled "America the Bulldozed," as quoted by Gregory Hahn in the *Idaho Statesman* (March 21, 2006), "Kempthorne received a larger percentage of his campaign contributions from the timber, mining, and energy industries than any other Western gubernatorial candidate. . . . Within a Republican Party that has long abandoned the conversation ethic that Theodore Roosevelt embodied, Kempthorne seems at home." Philip E. Clapp, the president of the National Environmental Trust, told Michael Janofsky for the *New York Times* (April 9, 2006), "[Kempthorne] represents a continuation of five years of an administration policy of exploiting public lands for oil and gas development and other resource extraction. President Bush could not have named a Western governor more in line with this administration." "President Bush nominated someone who has consistently opposed protecting public health and public lands," Carl Pope, the executive director of the Sierra Club, told Janofsky. "American families deserve an interior secretary who actually values our national heritage. America deserves someone who will promote safe energy policies that protect sensitive lands and wildlife habitat, instead of giving over our public lands to developers and the oil and gas companies." There were no reports of surprise, however, when the Senate approved the nomination of Kempthorne; as Troy Maben of the Associated Press noted, in an article published by *USA Today* (March 17, 2006), "The Senate rarely turns down one of its former members for the Cabinet."

Among the Interior Department proposals that have come to light since Kempthorne's arrival that have most alarmed environmentalists are those designed to seriously weaken the Endangered Species Act. As Rebecca Clarren reported in *Salon.com* (March 27, 2007), which obtained a copy of a 117-page draft intended for circulation only within the Fish and Wildlife Service, proposed changes to the act would limit the number of species that could be listed as endangered and would prohibit from inclusion on the list any species unlikely to become extinct in 20 years or 10 generations, with the agency deciding which time frame to consider. (The act currently refers to a time frame of "the foreseeable future"—"a species-specific timeframe that can stretch up to 300 years," as Clarren wrote.) In addition, the proposed plans would change the defined geographic range of any endangered species to the current range, ignoring the fact that great reductions in a species' historical range because of development or other human activities are responsible for the animal's precarious hold on survival and hampering the government's ability to foster its recovery in the wild. "Perhaps the most significant proposed change," Clarren wrote, "gives state governors the opportunity and funding to take over virtually every aspect of the act from the federal government. This includes not only the right to create species-recovery plans and the power to veto the reintroduction of endangered species within state boundaries, but even the authority to determine what plants and animals get protection." Large portions of the proposal's text were lifted from legislation that Kempthorne and other Republicans had sponsored in the Senate and that had failed to win passage. "The proposed changes fundamentally gut the intent of the Endangered Species Act," Jan Hasselman, an attorney with Earthjustice, an environmental law firm, told Clarren. "This is a no-holds-barred end run around one of America's most popular environmental protections. If these regulations stand up, the act will no longer provide a safety net for animals and plants on the brink of extinction." Bob Halleck, an endangered-species specialist who worked with the Fish and Wildlife Service for 34 years before his retirement, told Clarren, "If states are involved, the act would only get minimally enforced. States are, if anything, closer to special economic interests. They're more manipulated. The states have not demonstrated the will or interest in upholding the act. It's why we created a federal law in the first place."

Kempthorne has often been described as a master of conciliation. Roger Singer, a onetime director of the Idaho chapter of the Sierra Club, said to Tomas Alex Tizon for the *Los Angeles Times* (March 19, 2006), "[Kempthorne's] charisma carries him a long way. Even when we were at odds, he was very quick to approach our group with a smile and a handshake." According to Betsy Russell, "Kempthorne's critics say he relies on personal charm and vague generalities to win political success." Kemp-

thorne and his wife, the former Patricia Jean Merrill, have two adult children, Heather and Jeffrey.
—D.F.

Suggested Reading: *Idaho Falls Post Register* A p1+ Oct. 16, 1998; *Los Angeles Times* A p18 Mar. 19, 2006; *New York Times* A p16 Mar. 17, 2006; *Salon.com* Mar. 27, 2007; (Spokane, Washington) *Spokesman Review* D p1+ Oct. 20, 1998; U.S. Department of the Interior Web site; *Who's Who in America, 2006*

Scott Cunningham/Getty Images

Kovalchuk, Ilya

(KOVE-al-chook, EEL-yah)

Apr. 15, 1983– Hockey player

Address: Atlanta Thrashers, Centennial Tower, 101 Marietta St., N.W., Suite 1900, Atlanta, GA 30303

On June 23, 2001 the Atlanta Thrashers named the heralded Ilya Kovalchuk as the first overall selection in the National Hockey League (NHL) draft, making him the first Russian-born player ever to be the number-one pick. Kovalchuk has since lived up to his widely touted potential, leading the NHL in goals scored in his third NHL season and delivering the fledgling Thrashers franchise to the brink of play-off contention. Though on occasion the young forward has been criticized for lapses in concentration on defense, Atlanta's head coach, Bob Hartley, told Steve Hummer for the *Atlanta Journal-Constitution* (December 25, 2005) that Kovalchuk has the makings of an all-around player: "He obviously relies on his shot a lot, but there's other parts of his game he's very good at. With a little experience, he's going to have more than one pitch in his arsenal. . . . I'm trying to make him combine speed, responsibility on the ice and his goal-scoring touch." Responding to criticism that he lets his emotions get the better of him after scoring goals—as well as at other times—Kovalchuk has cited his passionate nature as a factor in his success. "I'm an emotional player and hockey is an exciting sport . . . ," he said to Shawn P. Roarke for NHL.com (March 17, 2004). "If you score a goal, that's the most exciting moment in your night. You should show some excitement." Kovalchuk's ability to score led Roarke to compare him to one of hockey's greatest luminaries: "Like [Wayne] Gretzky, Kovalchuk's offensive brilliance comes naturally. Sometimes, it appears that he is barely working at being the best player on the ice."

Ilya Kovalchuk was born on April 15, 1983 in Tver, Russia, near the confluence of the Volga and Tvertsa rivers, some 150 miles north of Moscow. His father, Valeri, had played for the national basketball team of what was then the Soviet Union; he later operated a sporting-goods store in Tver. He died in 2005. Kovalchuk's mother, Luba, is a dentist and an administrator at a health clinic. A precociously skilled athlete, Kovalchuk played a number of sports as a boy, including basketball, soccer, and street hockey, always finding the last-named most enjoyable and best suited to his abilities. Seeing the boy's strong interest in the sport, Kovalchuk's father showed him a video of the Russian hockey player Valeri Kharlamov, who led the Soviet Union's team to gold medals at the 1972 and 1976 Olympic Games and was considered to be one of the best players in the world. The young Kovalchuk quickly adopted Kharlamov—who died in a car accident in 1981—as an idol. He told Robert Picarello for NHL.com (March 17, 2004), "I never saw him play live, but . . . We would watch tapes of his games for hours together. He was really unbelievable to watch." In honor of him, Kovalchuk wears Kharlamov's uniform number, 17.

Early on, as he competed in hockey championship games in his home town and in Russia's Northeast League, Kovalchuk did not imagine a future as a professional hockey player in North America. "I never had aspirations as a child to play in the NHL," he explained through an interpreter to Gare Joyce for the Ottawa Citizen (June 23, 2001). "I didn't even know what the draft was or what the NHL was until I was 15." It was then that Kovalchuk went to Moscow to play for Spartak, a professional team. Kovalchuk's height (he stood over six feet tall), manual dexterity, skating ability, and strength were uncommon for players his age. Throughout his pre-NHL hockey career, Kovalchuk exhibited both extraordinary skill on the ice and a mercurial personality. He first played in North America when, at 15, he competed in a junior tournament in Ontario, Canada. His outstand-

ing play in that event caught the attention of North American hockey scouts. Later, as part of a team of under-17 Russians in international competition, Kovalchuk demonstrated his unpredictability by purposely crashing into the Canadian team's bench and afterward cross-checking its goaltender, which resulted in a brawl involving many players. At the 1999 Canada Challenge Cup, another international, under-17 competition, Kovalchuk scored 14 points in just six games, leading Russia to a gold medal. Apparently Kovalchuk's skills overshadowed his volatility in the minds of NHL officials, who, in the lead-up to the 2001–02 NHL draft, saw him as the best prospective player "since at least Eric Lindros and maybe since Mario Lemieux," as Gare Joyce reported.

That year the Atlanta Thrashers, who had joined the NHL in 1999, were given the first selection in the draft. The team's general manager, Don Waddell, narrowed the choice to two players, Kovalchuk and the similarly touted, Canadian-born Jason Spezza. Talking with a reporter for the Ontario Windsor Star (April 25, 2001), Waddell expressed the view that prevailed among scouts and team executives: "Offensively, [Spezza] is a very creative player who knows how to dish the puck off and has great instincts. Kovalchuk is a much more individual player. He does a lot by himself, maybe to a fault. He's got the best individual skills in the draft, no doubt about it." On June 23, 2001 the Thrashers signed Kovalchuk to a three-year contract valued at approximately $3.5 million.

Prior to the start of the 2001–02 season, the Thrashers were faced with a difficult decision regarding Kovalchuk's future. There was widespread concern in the organization that he was not ready to handle the physical demands of an 82-game NHL season. The team ultimately decided to acquaint him with league play by sending him to a rookie tournament in Traverse City, Michigan, held in the summer of 2001, before allowing him to start his NHL career that year. In addition to Kovalchuk, the Thrashers had selected another much-talked-about player, Dany Heatley, with the second overall pick in the 2001 draft. Many sportswriters and Thrashers fans saw Kovalchuk and Heatley as potential saviors of the team, which had not qualified for the play-offs in its brief existence. At the 2001 Rookie Evaluation Tournament, in early September 2001, Heatley outperformed Kovalchuk, scoring six goals and making four assists in four games; Kovalchuk tallied one goal and two assists during that time. The pair led the Thrashers to a bronze medal, along the way forming a close relationship in time for the start of the 2001–02 NHL season.

Kovalchuk brought to the NHL the mix of skill and feistiness he had demonstrated elsewhere. In a preseason game against the New York Islanders, he was at the center of a tussle between the two teams' players. During a regular-season game against the Los Angeles Kings, after allowing the Kings to score twice, Kovalchuk was benched by the Thrashers' coach, Curt Fraser. While praising the forward for his goal-scoring ability, sportswriters began to criticize Kovalchuk for what they perceived to be a lack of focus on defense. "There's a clear line of demarcation in Kovalchuk's game between hockey with the puck and hockey without the puck," Michael Farber wrote for *Sports Illustrated* (November 12, 2001). "He's as possessive of the puck as a coach potato is of the remote, passing it only with an air of regret. . . . When Kovalchuk doesn't have the puck and doesn't think he can get it, he lacks urgency on the offensive end and sloughs off his defensive duties, like a teenager who can't see the point in making his bed."

Kovalchuk's offensive abilities, though, were rarely questioned. In the NHL's YoungStars Game, held over the league's midseason break, he scored six goals and was named most valuable player. He finished the 2001–02 season with 29 goals, leading all NHL rookies, and 22 assists, but with a low "plus/minus" rating of negative 19. (A player's plus/minus rating refers to the number of goals scored by his team when he is on the ice, minus those scored against the team.) Kovalchuk finished second to his teammate Heatley in the voting for the Calder Memorial Trophy, awarded annually to the NHL's best rookie of the year. (Heatley and Kovalchuk became the league's first teammates to place first and second, respectively, in rookie ranking since the New York Rangers' Brian Leetch and Tony Granato did so in the 1988–89 season.) Despite Kovalchuk and Heatley's individual achievements, the Thrashers finished the 2001–02 season with the lowest point total in the NHL. When the NHL halted its regular season for two weeks in February 2002 to allow its marquee players to participate in the Olympic Games in Salt Lake City, Utah, Kovalchuk played for the Russian team. In six games he scored one goal and made two assists. The Russian team defeated Belarus by a score of 7–2 to win the bronze medal in the competition.

During the 2002–03 NHL regular season, Kovalchuk continued to play steadily on offense and poorly on defense. At mid-season he was selected to play in his first NHL All-Star Game. Meanwhile, the Thrashers, who had hoped to make significant progress in the standings that season, fell short of their goal. In January 2003 Bob Hartley took over as the team's head coach and set about remaking the Thrashers, stressing the importance of defense and paying close attention in particular to Kovalchuk's progress. The Thrashers' assistant coach Steve Weeks told Picarello that Kovalchuk made improvements on defense under Hartley's tutelage: "Bob has really worked a lot with him and he's very receptive to every thing that Bob shows him. He's shown him lots of video and we're working on his defensive side of the game. . . . And I think he takes pride in now being able to be put in that position. He really has shown us that he wants to work on improving his defensive side of the game, as well as his offensive side." Kovalchuk finished the season with 38 goals and 29 assists. He also, how-

ever, had a negative 24 plus/minus rating, which, some argued, was more emblematic than his point total of his contribution to the young franchise.

Tragedy befell the Thrashers in the fall of 2003, when Dan Snyder, a forward on the team, died from injuries he received in a car accident in Atlanta on September 29. Heatley, who was driving the car at the time of the accident, sustained a broken jaw and tore ligaments in his right knee. Snyder's death cast a shadow of grief over the team. Entering the 2003–04 regular season without the injured Heatley, who did not return to the lineup until the end of January, Kovalchuk became the team's de facto leader. Hartley had increased Kovalchuk's time on the ice: he gave the forward a role on the team's penalty-killing unit, made up of players other than goalies who try to prevent the opposing team's "power-play" unit from scoring; he also used Kovalchuk on lines to generate pressure on offense when needed. (A "line" refers to a unit of three forwards who play together throughout a game.) That season Kovalchuk became the fifth-youngest player in league history to score 100 career goals. He was also selected to start in the 2004 NHL All-Star Game. In a vote taken among 30 NHL players (one per NHL team) by *Hockey News* during the 2003–04 season, Kovalchuk was named the league's most exciting player. He scored 41 goals, tying him with Jarome Iginla of the Calgary Flames and Rick Nash of the Columbus Blue Jackets for the league high; along with Iginla and Nash, Kovalchuk was named the winner of the Maurice "Rocket" Richard Trophy, awarded annually to the player who leads the NHL in goals scored. Kovalchuk set a career high in total points in the 2003–04 season, with 87, and brought his plus/minus rating to negative 10. Speaking to Mike Heika for the *Dallas Morning News* (January 11, 2004), Waddell said about Kovalchuk, "He is just so much more mature this year. I could tell when he came back to the team after spending the summer in Russia, that he had done some growing up. First, because you could tell he had really dedicated himself to working out and was in the best condition he had ever been in. Second, you could just see the maturity in his face, in his manners." Although the Thrashers—for a fifth straight season—fell short of qualifying for the play-offs, the team ended the year with a franchise-record 78 points. In the summer of 2004, Kovalchuk represented Russia at the World Cup of Hockey, helping the team to a surprise victory in its first game against the U.S. team. The U.S. team later eliminated Russia from competition, before the medal round.

With the 2004–05 NHL season canceled by a 301-day lockout, Kovalchuk returned to his native country to play in the Russian Super League with the Kazan Ak-Bars. According to John Manasso, writing for the *Atlanta Journal-Constitution* (December 12, 2004), Kovalchuk received a reported $3 million to play for Kazan. In 53 games he scored 19 goals and made 23 assists. Due to clashes with the team's coaching staff, he did not enjoy his stay with the team. In October 2005, after missing the first few games of the new NHL season and threatening to remain in Russia due to stalled contract negotiations with the Thrashers, Kovalchuk signed a five-year contract with the team valued at more than $30 million. He thus became one of the highest-paid players in the NHL. With the Thrashers' having traded Heatley prior to the start of the 2005–06 season to the Ottawa Senators in exchange for the forward Marian Hossa and the defenseman Scott de Vries, Kovalchuk was again thrust into a leadership role. He rose to the challenge, ending the season with 52 goals and 46 assists in 78 games and a negative six plus/minus rating. With 41 wins and 33 losses, the Thrashers also enjoyed a successful season. Along the way there were flashes of Kovalchuk's earlier style of behavior: he was suspended for one game in late December 2005 after he threw a broken hockey stick into the stands, and in April 2006 he was fined $2,500 after an altercation with the Ottawa Senators player Chris Neil.

Kovalchuk had a strong 2006–07 season. He brought his plus/minus rating down to a career best of negative two, and with 42 goals and 34 assists in 82 games, he helped the Thrashers reach the Stanley Cup play-offs for the first time. There, the New York Rangers defeated them in the first round. As of October 2007, with the 2007–08 season just underway, Kovalchuk had made three goals and one assist in five games.

Recognized as one of the NHL's most prolific goal scorers, Kovalchuk told Shawn P. Roarke that his method for slipping the puck past a goalie is instinctive. "When you go in on the goalie, you just try to beat him somewhere," he said. "For me, it's just instinct when you see the goalie. I don't have any idea in my head. You should just wait and see what the goalie shows you and then try to use that." Kovalchuk's celebratory antics following goals, while angering some opposing players and coaches, have impressed many sportswriters. "Kovalchuk erupts in a paroxysm of joy, fist pumping, grin lopsided," Michael Farber wrote for Sports Illustrated (November 17, 2003). "In formal interviews he is stiff and programmed and says all the right things, but on the ice his body language is far more quotable." Paul Newberry, commenting for the Associated Press (January 9, 2006) on the perceived stodginess of the NHL, also praised the fiery Kovalchuk: "His knee-sliding, fist-pumping celebrations put an exciting face on a league that had turned boring and stale before its crippling lockout." Echoing a popular reaction to Kovalchuk's antics, his teammate Slava Kozlov told Farber, "I have never seen anything like him in my life. Sometimes I have to tell him he didn't just win the Stanley Cup."

Kovalchuk and Nicol Ambrazaitis, a Russian-born pop singer, have a daughter, Carolina, born in 2005. The three live in Atlanta. Kovalchuk is active in charitable work involving childhood cancer programs in the Atlanta area. "I like kids," he told

Steve Hummer. "I think that's a big part of your life. You have to share with kids. When I was young and some guys like famous basketball players or hockey players came and visit[ed] you and talk[ed] to you, it was really cool. I remember that and want to do the same."

—D.F.

Suggested Reading: *Atlanta Journal-Constitution* F p1 Dec. 25, 2005; NHL.com Mar. 17, 2004; *Ottawa Citizen* F p1 June 23, 2001; *Sports Illustrated* p56+ Nov. 12, 2001, p72+ Nov. 17, 2003; *Toronto Sun* S p6 June 2, 2001

Mandel Ngan/AFP/Getty Images

Krupp, Fred

Mar. 21, 1954– President of Environmental Defense; lawyer

Address: c/o Environmental Defense, 257 Park Ave. S., New York, NY 10010

"The strategy of the early environmental movement, according to some, could be boiled down to three words: 'mandate, regulate, litigate,'" Fred Krupp wrote for *PERC Reports* (March 2007, online), a publication of the think tank Property and Environment Research Center. As the head, since 1984, of Environmental Defense (formerly known as the Environmental Defense Fund), one of the leading nonprofit environmental-advocacy groups in the United States, Krupp has adopted a different strategy for achieving a healthier environment— one that relies on collaboration with businesses rather than confrontation and antagonism and that emphasizes the bottom line rather than humanitarian concerns. Persuading corporations that "going green" can be profitable has proven successful for both Krupp and Environmental Defense and the environmental movement as a whole. In the nearly quarter-century since he took the reins at Environmental Defense, its annual budget has risen from $3 million to more than $70 million, its full-time staff has grown from 50 to more than 300, and its membership has increased from 40,000 to more than 500,000. Founded in 1967, Environmental Defense "has carved out a space that no one else has, dancing with companies, while groups like Greenpeace tend to dance on companies," Kert Davies, Greenpeace's U.S. climate-campaign coordinator, told David Wessel for the *Wall Street Journal* (March 1, 2007). Under Krupp's direction Environmental Defense has guided corporations including McDonald's, FedEx, and the Texas energy company TXU to become more environmentally responsible; it has also played a key role in the passage of environmental legislation at the federal and state levels and in the formulation of several international environmental treaties. Recently, the organization opened two new offices: one in Beijing, China, and the other in Bentonville, Arkansas, where it will be working with Wal-Mart on the chain's environmental policies. Krupp told *Current Biography* that Environmental Defense is striving to make use of the media attention that now surrounds environmentalism, as well as the public's growing awareness of environmental problems, in pushing for new laws and rules aimed at safeguarding the environment. "I think it's great that the public and the media are focusing on environmental things," he told *Current Biography*, "but the spotlight comes and goes quickly in our society. So what we're focused on is taking this moment and turning it into as much tangible benefit as we can."

The youngest of three brothers, Fred Krupp was born on March 21, 1954 in Mineola, on Long Island, New York, to Rosalind (Mehr) Krupp, a high-school history teacher, and Arthur Krupp, a small-business owner. Krupp's brothers, Jan, a retired physician, and Bart, are the owners of Krupp Brothers Estates, which maintains vineyards and produces several wines. Krupp grew up in Verona, a town in northeastern New Jersey. His interest in environmentalism was sparked when, as a child, he visited the park across the street from his house and found frogs and fish belly-up in the lake, the victims of a chemical spill. At Verona High School Krupp excelled in biology. He was a member of the Model U.N. Team, and during his junior year, he helped to organize an Earth Day celebration that featured seminars and classes in environmental subjects. After he graduated from high school, in 1971, Krupp enrolled at Yale University, in New Haven, Connecticut, where he entered what was known as the combined-science program; required to choose two sciences as majors, he picked political science and biology. He wrote his senior thesis on the lack of political action regarding pollution in New Haven's harbor, on Long Island Sound. One year he served as president of the Yale Political Union. Acting on the advice of his mentor, the chemical-engineering professor Charles A. Walker, who chaired the Committee on the Combined Sciences Major, he decided to apply to law school. "The only reason I went to law school was because of my interest in environmental law," he told *Current Biography*. Walker gave Krupp the book *Defending the Environment: A Strategy for Citizen Action*, by Joseph Sax, a professor at the University of Michigan Law School. The book reinforced Krupp's interest, and after a year at the University of Virginia Law School, he transferred to the law school of the University of Michigan to study with Sax. In the summer of 1977, Krupp interned at Environmental Defense's Washington, D.C., office; in the fall of that year, he interned at the Natural Resources Defense Council in New York City. Krupp graduated from law school in 1978.

That same year he moved to Connecticut and co-founded the private law firm Albis & Krupp; he also helped to set up the Connecticut Fund for the Environment (CFE), splitting his time evenly between the two. CFE, for which Krupp served as general counsel, rose to prominence almost immediately, in connection with a case of contaminated drinking-water wells in Southington, Connecticut; CFE's actions led in 1979 to a new state policy requiring that residents be notified when a well is or is discovered to be contaminated. The next year CFE won a $1.5 million lawsuit against the Upjohn Corp., which had discharged toxic chemicals into the Quinnipiac River alongside North Haven, Connecticut. In both the Southington and North Haven cases, CFE was one of the first groups to publicize the threat of toxicity in the water supply—an important example of the direct impact on communities of environmental degradation. In 1983 Krupp's law partner decided to relocate, and the practice broke up. The following year Krupp joined the law firm of Cooper, Whitney & Cochran, which then changed its name to Cooper, Whitney, Cochran & Krupp.

Within a few months Krupp was offered the position of executive director—later termed president—of what was then called the Environmental Defense Fund. He accepted the post without hesitation. The group's first major accomplishment with Krupp as its head was its work (most of it before his arrival) leading to a 1985 decision by the federal Environmental Protection Agency (EPA) to phase lead out of gasoline. In 1987 Environmental Defense was among the principal groups advising the U.S. government on the Montreal Protocol, an international agreement to eliminate a number of substances that had been shown to be factors in the depletion of Earth's ozone layer. The Clean Air Act of 1990, which Krupp helped to negotiate, was the first clear example of his pragmatic environmental philosophy. The legislation, one in a series of amendments to the Clean Air Act of 1963, required power plants east of the Mississippi River to reduce their sulfur dioxide emissions (which cause acid rain) by 50 percent, so as to lower emissions from 20 million tons of sulfur dioxide to no more than 10 million tons per year. It embraced, as proposed by Krupp and Environmental Defense, a "cap-and-trade" system, in which plants that cut their sulfur emissions by more than the required 50 percent could earn credits that they could then sell to plants that were not able to cut their emissions to the required levels. Krupp described the plan to *Current Biography* as "the first major example of it being in the company's interest to do more than the law required," thereby creating a profit motive— rather than just a humanitarian motive—for companies to improve their environmental policies. Some environmentalists disagreed with that strategy, and though it has been widely praised retrospectively, it was sharply criticized at the time. Krupp told William H. Miller for *Industry Week* (August 15, 1994) that he was confident about the benefits of working with businesses rather than against them. "Any novel, creative idea will encounter initial doubts . . . ," he said. "But more and more people in the movement are seeing that there is power in these ideas—that they get results. And more and more of them are willing to abandon the outdated yardstick that the more a law or regulation hurts business, the better it is for the environment."

While on a family outing to McDonald's (he had married in 1982), Krupp took note of the polystyrene clamshells holding the Happy Meals he had bought for his sons, and he saw another opportunity to cooperate with big business. Instead of starting litigation, he sent suggestions for more environmentally sound practices to Edward H. Rensi, then the president of McDonald's U.S.A. The company—which had already shortened its straws and repackaged its orange juice in attempts to be more environmentally friendly—entered into an unusual partnership with Environmental Defense, with Krupp's group insisting that it would accept no money (even for travel expenses) from McDonald's and that McDonald's was forbidden to use the organization's name in any marketing or advertising material. As a whole, only about 2 percent of the garbage produced annually in the U.S. came from the fast-food industry, but Krupp saw McDonald's as a symbol of the corporate world's disregard for the environment. "My idea was that if McDonald's made major changes they could help set a new environmental ethic of what is acceptable and what isn't," he explained to Connie Koenenn for the *Los Angeles Times* (November 12, 1990). "The polystyrene clamshell is an icon, a symbol of unnecessary form of waste. I think the fact that McDonald's has put an end to it really could mark the turning of the tide on our throwaway society." At the time McDonald's served approximately 22 million meals a day at 11,200 restaurants worldwide, and the announcement that they would use paper-based wraps instead of polystyrene containers made front-page news across the country. Environmental

Defense also advised the restaurant chain on other environmentally beneficial practices, which Krupp said he hoped would set an example for the rest of the country's businesses. "Imagine, a fast-food chain composting!" Krupp said to Susan Reed for *People* (April 13, 1991). "It proves that McDonald's recognizes the future is green. Now all we have to do is help convince the rest of corporate America."

During the next decade Environmental Defense advised a number of corporations on improving their environmental standards and played a key role in several environmental conferences. In 1994 Environmental Defense helped General Motors with its "Cash for Clunkers" program, aimed at removing old cars, which tend to add more pollutants to the air than newer ones, from the roads. In 1997 Krupp and his staff advised President Bill Clinton as White House staff drafted the U.S. proposal for the Kyoto Conference, an international conference on climate change. (Clinton signed the resulting Kyoto Protocol, in which nations pledged to reduce carbon emissions, but it was never ratified by the United States Senate; President George W. Bush has expressed his opposition to the treaty. The United States and Australia are the only two industrialized nations that have not agreed to the treaty.)

As the issue of environmental protection, and especially global warming, became more prominent, Environmental Defense found itself with some unexpected, high-profile partners: in 2000 it joined with companies including British Petroleum (BP), DuPont, and Shell International to form the Partnership for Climate Action, in which the firms agreed to markedly reduce their greenhouse-gas emissions. In 2002 Environmental Defense helped to get passed a California law requiring automobile manufacturers to cut carbon-dioxide emissions from cars and light trucks by the 2008 model year. Congress did not pass the Environmental Defense–backed 2003 McCain-Lieberman Climate Stewardship Act to reduce carbon-dioxide emissions, but Krupp applauded the effort as an important first step in achieving such national legislation. "The history of environmental laws shows we gain momentum when these issues leave the back rooms for the sunshine of recorded votes," he told AScribe Newswire (October 30, 2003). He also said, "When the history books are written, today's vote will mark the first chapter in getting climate legislation through Congress." Environmental Defense also worked with FedEx in introducing new hybrid-electric delivery trucks that reduced particulate pollution by 96 percent and increased fuel economy by 57 percent; the trucks debuted in 2004 in Sacramento, California; Tampa, Florida; Washington, D.C., and New York City. In another noteworthy victory, in 2005, the EPA introduced the Clean Air Interstate Rule (CAIR), which tightened the Clean Air Act's guidelines by requiring an additional 70 percent cut in sulfur-dioxide emissions in 28 eastern states, bringing the level of annual emissions down to approximately three million tons. Environmental Defense was an official co-sponsor of AB32, the California Global Warming Solutions Act of 2006, which was signed into law in September. The goal of the legislation is the reduction of greenhouse-gas emissions in California by 25 percent by 2020.

At the beginning of 2007, Krupp led Environmental Defense in developing two prominent business partnerships. His meetings with General Electric's head, Jeffrey Immelt, and the World Resources Institute's president, Jonathan Lash, led to the unveiling, on January 10, of the U.S. Climate Action Partnership (USCAP). USCAP—which includes such companies as Alcoa, BP America, Caterpillar, and DuPont, and nongovernmental organizations, among them the Pew Center on Global Climate Change and the Natural Resources Defense Council—is modeling its guidelines on those of Environmental Defense's 1990 cap-and-trade strategy, calling for 10 to 30 percent reductions in carbon-dioxide emissions within 15 years and 60 to 80 percent reductions by 2050. "This is a game changer for action on global warming," Krupp told the Environment News Service (January 22, 2007). "These negotiations weren't easy—we all had strong points of view on the specifics—yet there was a real sense that we were doing something that could be historic." "Environmentalists have been criticized for not having priorities," he said to Bill Slocum for *Greenwich* (May 2007). "Everything is important. But if we don't solve global warming, it affects everything else."

In February the equity firms Kohlberg Kravis Roberts & Co. and Texas Pacific Group turned to Krupp after they announced that they had bought the Texas energy company TXU Corp. for $45 billion, the largest buyout in history. In an effort to make sure Texas officials would accept the buyout, the terms of the deal had specified that before the purchase would become final, the buyers would have to seek ways to make TXU more environmentally sound; to that end, the equity firms told Krupp that their purchase would be contingent upon his approval of the proposed steps. Before the buyout, TXU had planned to build 11 new coal plants, which would have emitted an estimated 78 million tons of additional carbon dioxide into the atmosphere; by the end of negotiations with Environmental Defense, the buyers had agreed to build only three plants. Krupp told Steve Inskeep for the National Public Radio program *Morning Edition* (February 27, 2007, on-line) that the agreement indicated an attitude shift on the part of big business: "I think it clearly means that the world is changing, and there is an awareness that we're moving into a carbon-constrained world." William Reilly, a senior adviser at Texas Pacific, agreed with Krupp. "We all swim in the same culture," Reilly told John Carey for *BusinessWeek* (March 12, 2007), "and the culture is going green." The deal—and the extensive press coverage it received—also offered another sign of the

changing relationship between corporations and environmentalists and a new awareness among the former that being considered "green" has become increasingly important financially. "We have come to an intersection between business trends and environmental realities that can work to the benefit of both," Krupp wrote in an op-ed piece for the *Miami (Florida) Herald* (March 19, 2007). "And there's more to come: The precedent-setting events of the last few weeks are evidence of a rapidly changing global economy." He continued: "It's clear we have reached a point that no major business can ignore the impact of its decisions on our climate. CEOs who disregard the effect of the carbon emissions from their operations will find themselves targeted not only by environmental advocates and regulators, but eager investors as well. Like any other management weakness, it will put a financial bulls'-eye on a company's back."

Krupp is a member of the board of the Environmental Professional Interest Council at Harvard University's John F. Kennedy School of Government and of the Leadership Council of the Yale School of Forestry, where a fellowship has been established in his honor. He received the Keystone Center's Leadership in Environment Award in 1999 and the Champion Award from the Women's Council on Energy and the Environment in 2002.

Krupp lives in New Canaan, Connecticut, with his wife, Laurie Devitt, a nutritionist with a special interest in public-health issues. He and his wife enjoy rowboating. The couple have three children: Alexander and Zachary, who are undergraduates, and Jackson, a high-school student.

—C.S.

Suggested Reading: Environmental Defense Web site; *Greenwich* p114+ May 2007; *Industry Week* p93 Aug. 15, 1994; *People* p61+ Apr. 15, 1991; *Who's Who in America*, 2007

Kummant, Alexander

Aug. 27, 1960– President and chief executive officer of Amtrak

Address: Amtrak, 60 Massachusetts Ave. N.E., Washington, DC 20002-4225

"Even today, I believe that the operations of a railroad represents some of the most engrossing and challenging opportunities in terms of a professional career. Therefore, the opportunity to join Amtrak is more than just another job to me, it is a chance to get back into an industry that has kept its hold on me and to advance something I believe in—passenger railroading." Alexander Kummant, the president and chief executive officer of Amtrak, made those statements on September 28, 2006, during his maiden appearance before the

Alex Wong/Getty

Alexander Kummant

U.S. House of Representatives Subcommittee on Railroads, as reported by the Federal News Service in *US Fed News* (September 28, 2006). Kummant spoke to the legislators 16 days after he assumed his post as the head of Amtrak—formally, the National Railroad Passenger Corp., a quasi-governmental entity that took over operation of the nation's intercity passenger trains in 1971. In the 16 years preceding his arrival there, the 46-year-old Kummant held jobs with a series of at least eight private companies. For about four years beginning in 1999, he worked in executive positions with the Union Pacific Railroad. He has earned the nickname "Steamroller," a reference both to the construction machinery and other large equipment that some of his employers manufactured and to his reputation as an uncompromising labor negotiator.

The National Railroad Passenger Corp. (Amtrak) was created by an act of Congress in 1970, following the initiation of bankruptcy proceedings by several major passenger-carrying rail companies, notably Penn Central, and many years of decreasing ridership and increasing deficits throughout the passenger-train industry. The legislation, known as the Rail Passenger Service Act, called for the government subsidization and oversight of intercity passenger trains. Private rail companies were invited to join the system, and 20 of the 26 eligible carriers did so. On its official start date, May 1, 1971, Amtrak offered service on roughly half of the total miles of track in use, with the remaining track set aside for the more profitable carriage of freight. Almost all members of Congress thought that Amtrak would require government subsidies only temporarily, with some believing that passen-

ger rail travel would become obsolete as the popularity of auto travel grew, and others convinced that Amtrak, unburdened by competition, would become a self-sufficient corporation. Thus, from its inception, Amtrak was in the impossible position of trying to become a profitable commercial enterprise despite the steady decline in demand and Congress's disinclination to invest in the corporation as a system of transport. Some viewed the creation of Amtrak as a "last hurrah" for the passenger-rail industry, which had seen both track mileage and ridership shrink during the previous 100 years. In 2006 Amtrak operated its trains over 22,000 miles of track, most of it owned by freight-hauling railroad companies, and carried 25.3 million passengers—the latter being the highest number since 1970. By contrast, in 1917 the privately owned railroad companies in the U.S. operated passenger trains over 245,000 miles of track, more than 10 times as many; railroads carried nearly 95 percent of intercity travelers, in peak years serving nearly 800 million people. Unlike the Interstate Highway System and the commercial aviation industry, which enjoy permanent subsidies through the Highway Trust Fund and the Airport and Airway Trust Fund, respectively, and also benefit from user fees and fuel taxes, Amtrak is forced to lobby Congress each year for the allotment of funds to keep passenger trains in operation. Compounding Amtrak's problems are the powerful lobbies that represent petroleum, trucking, and automobile interests. As a result Amtrak's federal subsidies are minuscule compared with those enjoyed by air- and highway-transport systems: according to reports by the *New York Times* and the *Washington Post*, between the years 1971 and 2002, the latter received a total of $1.89 trillion in government subsidies, while Amtrak—which serves more than 500 communities in 46 states—received less than 2 percent of that amount, or $30 billion. Although Congress designed Amtrak to be self-sufficient or even profitable, during its 35-year history, the corporation has never posted an operating profit. In almost all other countries in both the developed and the developing world, governments have for most of the past 100 years owned and operated passenger railroads, just as they have built and maintained highways, as public necessities, with no thought of profit; attempts at privatization in Great Britain, which started during Prime Minister Margaret Thatcher's term in office, have led to service and maintenance problems on a par with Amtrak's, while government-owned railroads throughout the rest of Europe offer service at levels that the United States has never approached.

Kummnant was chosen to head Amtrak by its board of directors, all of whom were nominated by President George W. Bush. His selection, which did not require confirmation by the U.S. Senate (board members do have to go through that process), aroused much criticism among those who favor greater reliance on and expansion of passenger rail service. Those critics argued that Kummant's skimpy experience in the railroad industry, none of it involving passengers, left him ill-equipped to manage Amtrak, which is deeply in debt and plagued by deteriorating infrastructure and other serious troubles. (With few exceptions, members of Amtrak's board have lacked experience in railroad management.) Kummant's critics also maintained that none of his previous jobs had provided him with the insight, shrewdness, and skills necessary in dealing with politicians and lobbying members of Congress, and thus he was not equipped to carry out one of his most important tasks as head of Amtrak: promoting the corporation to members of Congress, who decide how much money the federal government will allocate for Amtrak, and persuading the legislators of the importance of meeting Amtrak's short-term and long-term goals. Kummant's detractors attributed his appointment to his generosity as a Republican donor and the paucity of qualified candidates willing to head the beleaguered corporation, and they warned that the board's choice showed that its members actually wanted to downsize Amtrak or privatize it entirely, as do Senator John S. McCain of Arizona, one of Amtrak's most outspoken critics, and a sizable number of other members of Congress.

Although, when questioned by members of the House Subcommittee on Railroads last September, Kummant offered no concrete suggestions for tackling Amtrak's many problems, he presented himself as a zealous supporter of passenger rail transport. "I believe we are at a pivotal point in the history of passenger rail service," he said, as quoted by the US Fed News reporter. "I am committed to operating a national system of trains. I believe long-distance trains are an important part of the nation's transportation network, and I believe that it is our challenge to run them in the most efficient and effective way." He also said, "At a time of high oil prices, growing highway and airport congestion and record freight volumes, problems which beset and constrain our transportation system, we should be embracing rail and developing it as quickly and as responsibly as we can."

Alexander Karl Kummant, the youngest of three children of Austrian immigrants, was born on August 27, 1960 in Lorain, Ohio, and raised in nearby Amherst, a few miles from Lake Erie. His brother, Peter, is a physician; his sister, Inge, is a teacher. His father worked first as an engineer and then as an engineering manager at U.S. Steel Lorain Works. During his childhood Kummant spoke only German at home, and he took Suzuki-method violin lessons at the music conservatory at Oberlin College. After he graduated from the Marion L. Steele High School, in Amherst, he enrolled at Case Western Reserve University, in Cleveland, Ohio, where he majored in mechanical engineering. During summers he worked at the Lake Terminal Railroad, which has served the Lorain Works for over a century; in one of his jobs there, he wielded a sledgehammer as a member of a track crew. Gregory Meyer, writing for Crain's Chicago Business (June 1, 2005, on-line), remarked that as a young adult, Kummant developed an "emotional tie to big stuff in industrial settings." Kummant earned a B.A. degree in mechanical engineering from Case Western Reserve in 1982. He received an M.S. degree in manufacturing engineering from Carnegie Mellon University, in Pittsburgh, Pennsylvania, in 1986, and an M.B.A. from Stanford University's Graduate School of Business, in California, in 1990.

In the early 1990s Kummant worked in the solar-energy unit of Standard Oil of Ohio, now British Petroleum. Next, he created software for an artificial-intelligence firm in Pittsburgh. He then spent two years as a business analyst with the Timken Co., in Canton, Ohio. Timken is a major manufacturer of tapered roller bearings (including those for railroad applications) and specialty steels. Kummant left Timken to join the Emerson Electric Co., in St. Louis, Missouri, which manufactures such products as electric motors, instruments for climate control, and professional tools. At Emerson he worked as the personal assistant of the company's then–vice president, Ivor J. "Ike" Evans, before being promoted to president of an Emerson division, in Cincinnati, Ohio, called Sweco, which manufactures customized equipment for non–oil-related industrial separation processes. "I grew up at Emerson," Kummant told Bette Pearce for the Elyria, Ohio, Chronicle-Telegram (September 6, 2006). "That's where I got the financial and strategic training that I come with in my tool kit to this day." Kummant left Emerson Electric in 1998 to become president of Filtran, a division of the SPX Corp. that manufactures automobile transmission filters; he held that position until September 1999.

Kummant left SPX thanks to an unexpected phone call he received during the summer of 1999 from Ike Evans, who in 1998 had been named president and chief operating officer of the Union Pacific Railroad Co. (UP), headquartered in Omaha, Nebraska. With the words "How'd you like to run a $4 billion business?," as Kummant recalled to Bette Pearce, Evans offered him the position of UP's vice president and general manager of industrial products—that is, the division of UP responsible for the transport from point of origin of such items as lumber, cement, paper, appliances and other consumer goods, and trash and other waste products, a function that generates approximately a fifth of UP's income. (Other UP divisions direct the transport of chemicals, coal, new cars and trucks, containers bound for ships, and containers and truck trailers for domestic destinations, the last of which is called "intermodal" business.) "So, I went," Kummant told Pearce. Kummant had impressed Evans, as the latter told Gregory Meyer, as having "an intellectual curiosity. He wants to understand how things work." Kummant was soon promoted to vice president of UP's central operating region in Kansas City, where he oversaw the performance of the intermodal and automotive divisions as well as nearly 6,000 transportation employees who supported an 8,000-mile rail network. According to an Amtrak press release (August 29, 2006, on-line), Kummant was credited for gains that UP made in customer service, on-time delivery of products, and both financial and operational performance. While testifying before the House Subcommittee on Railroads, Kummant asserted that his years with UP had left him with "an indelible and abiding interest in the railroad industry," as reported by the *US Fed News* writer.

In 2003 Kummant, turning to advantage his fluency in German, left the Union Pacific Railroad to become president of Bomag, a manufacturer of heavy industrial equipment, based in Boppard, Germany. After just over a year there, citing "personal reasons," as reported by a writer for *World Highways* (January 2005), he resigned from Bomag and returned to the United States. In 2005 he was hired by the Japanese company Komatsu Corp. to fill the post of executive vice president and chief marketing officer at the firm's U.S. headquarters, in Rolling Meadows, Illinois. Komatsu, best known in North America for its huge mining and quarrying machinery, is the world's second-largest supplier of construction equipment. Kummant spearheaded a marketing campaign designed to promote in the U.S. Komatsu's new offerings—smaller bulldozers, excavators, and other equipment with relatively low horsepower, for personal use—a scheme that was moderately successful despite strong competition from Deere & Co. (also called John Deere).

On August 29, 2006 Amtrak's board of directors announced that Kummant had been selected as its next CEO and president and would assume those positions two weeks later. Kummant replaced David Hughes, Amtrak's chief engineer, who had served as Amtrak's head on an interim basis after the ouster of David L. Gunn, in November 2005. When Kummant joined Amtrak, the organization was struggling with both external and internal problems, as it has for much of its existence. In 2005 Amtrak had accumulated over $550 million in operating losses, according to the Associated Press, adding to its total debt of over $3.5 billion. The growing debt had led to increasingly limited maintenance, which in turn had led to a rash of technical failures. A discovery of faulty brakes on some of Amtrak's train cars resulted in the suspension of high-speed Acela Express service in April 2005 and an investigation by the federal Government Accountability Office concerning the way the corporation monitored performance and managed its finances. The technical troubles continued into 2006, when several power failures along the Northeast Corridor, Amtrak's busiest route, caused significant delays, the worst of which lasted for over three hours and provided a stark example of the railroad's deteriorating infrastructure. Another ongoing problem involved failures in labor negotiations, which had left some of Amtrak's unions, representing more than two-thirds of its 19,000 employees, without new contracts for nearly a de-

cade; according to Frank N. Wilner, writing for the *Journal of Transportation Law, Logistics & Policy* (September 2006), existing Amtrak labor contracts are "inflexible." In addition, Amtrak has had great difficulty in attracting skilled workers in several busy locations, notably in New York City and on the West Coast, primarily because the wages being offered are not competitive. Moreover, as Wilner wrote, obtaining sufficient funds merely to operate the trains daily requires "24/7 cadging on Capitol Hill."

Fund-raising has become more difficult recently, because since 2003 President Bush has tried to eliminate federal support of Amtrak. Pia Sarkar, writing for the *San Francisco Chronicle* (February 25, 2005), reported that Bush's proposed 2004 budget allocated just $800 million for Amtrak, $1 billion less than Amtrak's request; Congress raised the allocation to $1.2 billion. In the *Washington Post* (June 30, 2005), Shailagh Murray explained that President Bush's proposed 2006 allocation was zero dollars (again voted down by Congress), further evidence of an executive approach that favors the elimination of Amtrak as a monolithic passenger-rail service and the privatization of the industry, with only the Northeast Corridor, Amtrak's most-successful route, remaining in public custody. Some members of Congress support those measures, while others have maintained that elimination of Amtrak subsidies would lead to the immediate bankruptcy of the corporation. According to some observers, the vehemence with which David L. Gunn opposed the privatization of passenger-rail service led to his ouster. Referring to the splitting-off of the Northeast Corridor, Representative John Mica, a Florida Republican, told a reporter for the Associated Press (November 9, 2005), "David Gunn bucked that idea, so that was the straw that broke the camel's back. He's a very capable operational manager, but he wasn't willing to go along with the dramatic changes that need to be made." Gunn's firing provoked some controversy in Congress, because of his perceived success in leading Amtrak; many observers believe that the Amtrak board of directors searched for a replacement who would be more amenable to the Bush administration's long-term goals, rather than one capable of strengthening Amtrak. As reported by the Associated Press (November 9, 2005), Democratic senator Charles E. Schumer of New York called Gunn's removal "a crushing blow to Amtrak's hopes for success and reform."

Few people qualified to succeed Gunn expressed interest in applying for the top position at Amtrak, despite the board of directors' decision to raise the CEO's annual salary from $300,000 to $400,000. Kummant was one of the small number of potential candidates who seemed to be undaunted by the prospect of heading the floundering organization. "An old professor once told me, it's the hard things that are worth doing. This [Amtrak] matters, and I'm excited to be a part of it," he told Bette Pearce. After the Amtrak board announced his selection, according to the Associated Press (August 29, 2006, on-line), Senator Schumer said, "It's good they finally appointed someone, but given [the Bush] administration's record on Amtrak, we need to know whether he was brought in to build up Amtrak or tear it down." An unnamed freight-railroad insider who had worked with Kummant at Union Pacific told Frank N. Wilmer, "If you backed [Kummant] into a corner and demanded he tell you everything he knows about railroads, he wouldn't be talking more than a couple of minutes." There is no shortage of people willing to offer the new president and CEO advice. An Amtrak worker whom Jim Wrinn interviewed for *Trains* magazine (December 2006) suggested that Kummant ride the trains and converse with passengers and employees about their experiences. "First-hand data beats statistical assumptions hands down," the man said. "Even the lowly redcap who totes bags gets to understand why people use the train, what they want, and most of all, what they expect. Involve these people in making your decisions."

Kummant has been forthright about the limitations of his experience with passenger rail. Paul Dyson, the president of the Rail Passenger Associa-

tion of California, wrote in an article for the group's Web site (October 18, 2006) that Kummant "doesn't seem daunted by the challenges" facing him and "has the attitude of any good executive taking the helm of a corporation; that it's his job to grow the business and improve the bottom line." Dyson also wrote that he and Kummant agreed that the issue of passenger-rail service "is on the public agenda as it has not been for many years."

Kummant currently lives in Washington, D.C., with his wife, Kathleen Regan Kummant, a former senior executive with the Burlington Northern Santa Fe Railway. The couple enjoy outdoor activities.

—N.W.M.

Suggested Reading: Amtrak.com; Associated Press (on-line) Aug. 29, 2006; *Crain's Chicago Business* (on-line) June 1, 2005; (Elyria, Ohio) *Chronicle-Telegram* p1+ Sep. 6, 2006; *Journal of Transportation Law, Logistics & Policy* (on-line) Sep. 2006; *National Journal's CongressDaily* Transportation Section Sep. 28, 2006; *US Fed News* Sep. 28, 2006

Kushner, Jared

1981– Newspaper publisher; real-estate developer

Address: New York Observer, *915 Broadway, New York, NY 10010*

When the then-25-year-old New Jersey native Jared Kushner bought the *New York Observer* for $10 million in July 2006, he ignited a media frenzy. By acquiring the financially struggling, salmon-colored weekly paper from its founding owner, Arthur L. Carter, Kushner became the youngest owner of a major media property in New York City, inviting comparisons to the legendary tycoon William Randolph Hearst. Though the *Observer* has a relatively modest circulation of 50,000, it is renowned for its influence among the elite political and business leaders of Manhattan. Among other changes, Kushner has made some alterations to the paper's physical format and devoted increased space to its coverage of real estate, one of his wealthy family's greatest passions. By purchasing the *Observer*, Kushner assumed the leadership of a paper that, like other New York City media outlets, had devoted considerable attention to the legal and financial troubles of his father, Charles Kushner, a prominent real-estate developer— troubles that involved a sex scandal and an investigation by federal authorities. While the younger Kushner has made efforts to distance himself publicly from his father with regard to those matters,

Peter Kramer/Getty Images

in December 2006 he acted as proxy for his father's corporation, Kushner Companies, in a record-setting, $1.8 billion purchase of the 41-story building at 666 Fifth Avenue in Manhattan. In interviews Jared Kushner has been reserved about revealing plans for the *Observer*'s future; still, his

March 2007 purchase of PoliticsNJ.com indicates a strong interest in Web-based news media.

Jared Kushner was born in 1981 in New Jersey to Charles and Seyrl Kushner. His siblings are Dara, 27 as of 2007; Nicole, 24; and Joshua, 21. The patriarch of the Kushner family was Jared's grandfather, Joseph, a Holocaust survivor who married in Russia, emigrated from there in 1949, became a construction worker and father, and joined the group of immigrant Jewish families known as the Holocaust builders—who settled in northern New Jersey and launched extraordinarily successful building and real-estate ventures. The group includes, in addition to the Kushners, the Wilf, Rosen, Zuckerman, and Pantirer families. Like the other families in that small subculture, the Kushners have long been involved in philanthropic activities, donating money to Jewish causes in the U.S. and Israel, building schools, and engaging in a variety of other charitable endeavors. Charles Kushner funded the building of the Joseph Kushner Hebrew Academy, a school in Livingston, New Jersey, for students in pre-kindergarten through eighth grade, and the Rae Kushner Yeshiva High School, named in honor of his mother. Both are Modern Orthodox Jewish institutions that combine religious and secular study.

While Joseph Kushner amassed a fortune over the years, it was Charles Kushner who developed the family business, Kushner Companies, into the powerhouse it is today. Charles Kushner attained his bachelor's degree at New York University (NYU) in 1976. In 1979 he earned a law degree from Hofstra University and an M.B.A. degree from NYU. In Jared's early years, his father was a lawyer at the firm Brach, Eichler, Rosenberg, Silver, Bernstein, Hammer, and Gladstone, in Roseland, New Jersey. When Jared was four his father joined Kushner Companies. Jared told Geoffrey Gray for *New York* magazine (August 14, 2006), "Growing up, around the dinner table my father and I didn't talk sports. We talked business. He took me to job sites when I was four years old. . . . Sundays my friends would go to football games with their dads. I'd go look at new property to buy."

Kushner attended the Frisch School, a private, co-ed Orthodox Jewish yeshiva high school in Paramus, New Jersey. Controversy surrounds his admission to Harvard University, in Cambridge, Massachusetts, in 1999. Alex Beam reported for the *Boston Globe* (September 4, 2006) that when Jared was applying to colleges, his father pledged $2.5 million to Harvard. According to Beam, in *The Price of Admission: How America's Ruling Class Buys Its Way into Elite Colleges—and Who Gets Left Outside the Gates*, by the *Wall Street Journal* deputy bureau chief Dan Golden, an official at the Frisch School was quoted as saying, "There was no way anybody in . . . the school thought [Kushner] would on the merits get into Harvard. His GPA did not warrant it, his SAT scores did not warrant it. We thought, for sure, there was no way this was going to happen." A Kushner family spokesman,

Howard Rubenstein, told the New York *Daily News* (August 23, 2006), "Jared is a very unusual and talented man. He graduated Harvard with honors, proving that they were correct in admitting him." Harvard's dean of admissions, William Fitzsimmons, according to Beam, issued a statement declaring that "all students admitted to Harvard are fully qualified to be here."

At Harvard, Kushner became the chairperson of Chabad House, a social, educational, and recreational Jewish community organization. Also during his college years, he raised capital from his parents and family friends to form Somerville Building Associates, a division of Kushner Companies, through which he purchased nine buildings in Somerville, Massachusetts, near Cambridge. He told Gabrielle Birkner for the *New York Sun* (August 4, 2006, on-line), "I'd be in class, and get a call that a toilet broke, and have to get a contractor over there. . . . We did significant upgrades, putting in new kitchen countertops, new floors, and better lighting. These were very neglected buildings, and we turned them into places that people could go home, and be proud of." In 2000 he purchased a residential building for approximately $2.3 million. He renovated the building and sold its 16 condominium homes for $4.3 million two years later. He gave credit to his father for advising him, telling Birkner, "I had a very convenient expert at my disposal." While at Harvard Kushner made sizable monetary contributions to the Democratic Party. After graduating, in 2003, he joined Kushner Companies, a $1 billion umbrella organization encompassing a vast array of real-estate and business holdings spread over nine states. He also entered the four-year, combined J.D./M.B.A. program at his father's alma mater, NYU.

By that point Charles Kushner had become known as a major financial supporter of James McGreevey's successful 2001 campaign for the governorship of New Jersey. As Governor McGreevey named him to head the Port Authority of New Jersey, despite the fact that the elder Kushner had held neither a political office nor a security post. Charles Kushner resigned the post to avoid questions from William Gormley, head of the New Jersey State Senate Judiciary Committee, about potential conflicts of interest. In 2004 Charles Kushner found himself at the center of a full-blown scandal, when he was accused of retaliating against a federal witness and filing false tax returns and campaign-finance reports. While the latter two charges attracted ample notice in the media, the most sensational details emerged from the first charge. The United States attorney's office had approached Charles Kushner's sister, Esther, and her husband to cooperate with a campaign-finance investigation. In retaliation, Charles Kushner paid a prostitute $10,000 to lure his sister's husband, William Schulder, to a motel room at the Red Bull Inn in Bridgewater, New Jersey, while arranging for the tryst to be videotaped via a hidden camera; the tape was later sent to Esther Schulder on the day of a family party. She reported the incident, and on August 19, 2004 Charles Kushner pleaded guilty to 18 counts of tax evasion, witness tampering, and illegal campaign donations. He later served a year in prison.

The scandal surrounding the elder Kushner's activities was mentioned in nearly every article about Jared Kushner's $10 million purchase of the *New York Observer* in July 2006. According to Katharine Q. Seelye, writing for the *New York Times* (July 31, 2006), "Mr. Kushner said that he bought the newspaper because it was a marquee property in the media capital of the world, and that the opportunity to buy a newspaper did not come around very often. . . . He also said the *Observer* was a good brand that could one day make a lot of money, though it now loses about $2 million a year." In an interview with David Carr for the *New York Times* (July 31, 2006), Kushner said, "As far as this transaction goes, it is about me. It is not about my father."

The bulk of most articles about Kushner's purchase of the *Observer* had to do with his relative youth. Patrick Phillips noted for the Web site *I Want Media* (August 7, 2006), "At age 25, he is perhaps the most high-profile young U.S. newspaper owner since William Randolph Hearst, at age 23, became proprietor of his first newspaper back in 1887." Kushner told Phillips, "As I have said before, age is just a convenient barometer that people use to compare someone to their peers at a given point in their life. Being young, I am not bound by conventional wisdom and, in this changing industry, I have the ability to see media for what it is becoming without having an emotional attachment to what it once was. . . . I believe that when it comes to the news, my generation has shorter attentions spans and greater expectations."

Other media coverage of the purchase focused on Kushner's lack of experience in journalism. By his own admission, he had been an *Observer* reader for only a few years. Kushner told Birkner that he began reading the *Observer* during college on the short shuttle flights between New York and Boston, adding, "So many media properties are owned by big companies, and they either have a liberal bias or a conservative bias, but the *Observer* praises the good and goes after the bad. It's about getting the truth."

The London *Guardian* (August 1, 2006) reported that Kushner sent the *Observer* staff an e-mail message reading, "At 25 and with only non-publishing-related business experience, I am now equipped with two of the finest tools a publisher could ever have: this fine staff and the inquisitive energy to tackle convention." As a writer for the London *Independent* (August 1, 2006) put it, the *Observer*'s relatively modest circulation—about 50,000—"belies its importance in New York," as the paper "has long been a must-read for members of New York's social, media, literary and political circles." Carr described the paper as "a small but mighty piece of Manhattan media . . . a paper that

has long preoccupied wagging tongues in New York because of the youthful insouciance of its writers." Kushner told Carr, "The truth of the matter is that I would have loved this chance to come along in a few years, but that's not how life works. Life brings opportunities as they occur, and this is one I could not pass up. . . . This is a phenomenal brand, with an elite readership and one of the best editors there is."

Kushner was referring to Peter W. Kaplan, who joined the paper in 1994 and has earned a reputation as a top-notch editor and mentor to the *Observer*'s staff members; drawing comparisons to characters in J. K. Rowling's Harry Potter novels, Carr described Kaplan as "Professor Dumbledore to the paper's young editorial wizards." Kaplan told Carr, "When he [Kushner] said he would not interfere in the editorial process, I believed him. . . . The way the world is working, I find that I have as much to learn from 25-year-olds as they do from me. . . . He exists in the world that is about to be, and that seems worth trading for my information about the world as it has been."

In December 2006 Kushner made a successful bid for the 41-story building at 666 Fifth Avenue in Manhattan, purchasing it on behalf of the Kushner Companies for $1.8 billion and setting a record for the highest price ever paid for a building. According to the Web site of Tishman Speyer, the company that previously owned the building, it was erected in 1957 and comprises about 1.5 million square feet. Kushner paid approximately $1,200 per square foot for 666 Fifth Avenue, which houses the National Basketball Association (NBA) store and the Noguchi Museum, among other commercial tenants. He told the *New York Times* (December 7, 2006), "This is a major acquisition for our company. We are upping our presence in Manhattan. It's a logical expansion for us."

In February 2007 a redesigned *New York Observer* debuted on newsstands. The most obvious change was the addition of an outside four-page wrap containing headlines, photos, a small version of the paper's illustrated logo, and an advertisement. In addition, the back page covered real estate, breaking with the city tabloids' tradition of devoting the back page to sports stories. Peter Kaplan, referring to the 1969 film starring Paul Newman and Robert Redford, told Keith J. Kelly for the *New York Post* (February 12, 2007), "There's definitely a Butch Cassidy and Sundance Kid thing going on here, and that's fine"— which Kelly interpreted to mean that Kaplan and Kushner "have similar goals but different styles." According to Katharine Seelye, Kushner told Kaplan that he had "three objectives" for the paper: "to market the brand name of the *Observer*; to build its Internet traffic; and to provide resources for more news beats" in order to create "a stronger paper with more constituencies and more advertising."

In March 2007 Kushner's newly formed Observer Media Group purchased PoliticsNJ.com, a popular Web site run by an anonymous figure who uses the pseudonym Wally Edge (a nod to the former New Jersey governor Walter Evans Edge, who served in that post during both world wars). According to John Holl, writing for the *New York Times* (March 11, 2007), Kushner said that he bought the site because "it's become a place for people to break news and because it's independent."

When Phillips asked Kushner what he saw himself doing at 35 or 45, Kushner replied, "Life is very interesting and it takes us all on many unexpected paths. The truth is, if you told me that at 25 I would own a premier New York newspaper and be actively purchasing real estate while completing a JD/MBA, I wouldn't have believed you. At 35, 45?

Your guess is as good as mine. Whatever I am doing, I hope to be having as much fun as I am now."

—S.J.D.

Suggested Reading: *Bergen County (New Jersey) Record* (on-line) June 16, 2002; *Harvard Crimson* (on-line) Aug. 4, 2006; *I Want Media* (on-line) Aug. 7, 2006; (London) *Guardian* p15 Aug. 1, 2006; *New York* (on-line) Sep. 20, 2004; *New York Post* p31 Feb. 12, 2007; *New York Sun* (on-line) Aug. 4, 2006; *New York Times* C p1 July 31, 2006, New Jersey edition XIV p2 Mar. 11, 2007, (on-line) July 31, 2006; *Slate* (on-line) Aug. 1, 2006

Courtesy of Ann Huntress Lamont

Lamont, Ann Huntress

Oct. 1956– Venture capitalist

Address: c/o Oak Investment Partners, One Gorham Island, Westport, CT 06880

Ann Huntress Lamont never got to rip open the presents she received as a child. Instead, she and her five siblings were told to unwrap the paper carefully so it could be reused. Now Lamont, whom Alison Leigh Cowan described in the *New York Times* (October 16, 2006) as "one of the most successful women ever in the lofty realm of venture capital," can afford to buy all the wrapping paper she wants. Lamont is currently one of four managing partners of Oak Investment Partners, a leader in its field. Venture-capital firms such as

Oak typically finance new, growing, or struggling businesses in investments that are too risky for standard public-investment markets or other forms of private investing, such as bank loans; such high-risk deals usually either reward the investor with exponential returns or fail completely. Oak was founded in 1978 with $25 million in funds; in 2006, the company boasted $8.4 billion in holdings. A specialist in the especially risky fields of biotechnology and financial-services information technology, Lamont has spearheaded some of Oak's most successful ventures, including investments in the pharmaceutical company Cephalon and the hospice provider Odyssey Healthcare. Companies count on Lamont for her "money, market intelligence and moxie," Cowan wrote. But even while serving as a role model for women in finance and proudly investing in companies run by women, Lamont prefers to leave the spotlight to her husband, Ned Lamont, who mounted an ultimately unsuccessful run for the United States Senate in 2006. Her reticence has hardly had a negative effect on her career; rather, her thoughtful nature has proven to be a distinct advantage, and her ability to listen and willingness to work behind the scenes are two of her most valuable traits in the demanding field of venture capital. "We're not the heroes," Lamont explained to Cowan. "We're here to support the entrepreneurs."

The youngest of six children, Lamont was born Ann Greenlee Huntress in October 1956 in Whitefish Bay, Wisconsin. Lamont's father, Carroll Benton Huntress Jr., was president of Huntress Realty in Milwaukee. Lamont "grew up in a big family with a small budget—and one Coke a week," as her husband's campaign literature read, according to Cowan. The family was very money-conscious; in addition to reusing wrapping paper, the family would "wash Glad bags 10 times," Lamont told Cowan. In 1975 Lamont entered Stanford University, in California, where she earned a B.A. degree in political science. During her junior year, while she was studying in England, she received a call from home saying that her father was sick and could not work and that the family would not be able to afford her next quarter's tuition—approximately $1,500. Instead of taking her out of school, Lamont's parents decided to cash in a life-insurance policy so that she could return to Stanford in the fall and graduate with her class. (While Lamont participated in her class's graduation ceremony in 1979, she did not officially receive her degree for another 10 years, having failed to turn in a paper in the spring of her senior year.)

After graduation Lamont moved to San Francisco, California, where she worked briefly as a paralegal before taking a position as a research associate at Hambrecht & Quist Capital Management, a pioneer in the venture-capital field. While Lamont was with Hambrecht & Quist, the firm helped many future top-performing companies to go public—that is, to open to public investment. Those companies included U.S. Surgical, which produces medical devices; Genentech, a pharmaceutical developer; and Apple Computer (now Apple Inc.).

In 1982 Michael Levinthal, a friend of Lamont's from Stanford, introduced her to the venture capitalist Ed Glassmeyer. Glassmeyer "was obviously taken by her," Levinthal recalled to Cowan; he soon offered Lamont a job at Oak Investment Partners, a new private equity firm he had co-founded. When Lamont began work at Oak's Westport, Connecticut, office, the company was only four years old, begun with a capital base of $25 million. From the start, Lamont focused her investments in health care and biotechnology, a particularly risky investment option. "Investors in biotech have the potential to reap tremendous rewards, but at the same time, the risk can be enormous—sometimes in the same stock," Marc Lichtenfield wrote for the financial Web site TheStreet.com (July 27, 2006). Emerging biotechnology companies normally have an extremely difficult time raising initial funds, even from habitual risk-taking investors such as venture capitalists. Claire Philpott, a biotechnology attorney for Lane Powell PC, told MedAd News (July 1, 2005, on-line), "[Venture capitalists] don't like to dabble in biotech and life sciences. . . . It's such a long runway to cash revenue coming from paying customers. The turnaround time can be a decade." But when biotechnology investments pay off, they do so extraordinarily well. According to Barath Shankar, a research analyst for the pharmaceutical and biotechnology consulting firm Frost & Sullivan, also interviewed by MedAd News, an investment of $1,000 in any of the top 10 biotechnology companies in 1994 would be worth $240,000 today.

In the late 1980s Lamont initiated one of Oak's most successful investments, in the pharmaceutical company Cephalon, which produces the sleep-disorder drug Provigil, the anticonvulsant Gabitril, and the analgesic Actiq. In 2004 the company's revenues exceeded $1 billion. In the mid-1990s Lamont also led Oak's investment in Odyssey Healthcare, a hospice operator. Odyssey began in 1996

with two operating locations; in 2006 it had more than 85 locations across the country and was one of the larger hospice providers in the U.S. Both investments have had returns of 10-fold or higher. Lamont's more recent investments have been focused primarily in the biotechnology sector, in companies such as Athenahealth, American Esoterics, CareMedic, Harbor Payments, Health Dialog, iHealth Technologies, NetSpend, United BioSource, and Vesta. In 2006 Lamont became one of four managing partners of Oak Investments. That same year Oak finished raising a $2.56 billion fund—the largest venture fund ever among any firm. Every year or two, Oak raises a new fund for that year's investment portfolio; the $2.56 billion fund, which is the company's 12th, represents capital that Oak designated for new investments in the 2006 portfolio. The size of a fund can be seen as one measure of investor confidence in a venture-capital firm, with higher investment indicating higher confidence. Oak already has $8.4 billion from previous funds invested in more than 320 companies.

Like all high-risk investors, Lamont has also had her share of failures. Lamont led Oak's investment in BMJ Medical Management Inc., which went into sharp decline after its initial public offering (IPO) on February 4, 1998. The company ended up filing for bankruptcy in December of the same year. In a class-action lawsuit filed on February 2, 1999, disgruntled shareholders sued Lamont, among a number of other parties instrumental in BMJ's development, for securities fraud, accusing her of withholding information about BMJ's management practices and business prospects that would have been valuable in deciding whether or not to invest in the stock. Lamont and the other defendants agreed on a multimillion-dollar settlement, and Lamont resigned from BMJ's board of directors on June 4, 1999.

In September 2000 Oak became the lead investor in a new on-line and cash gift-certificate company called Flooz.com, based on the record of the company's chief executive officer (CEO), Robert Levitan, who had co-founded the successful women's Web site iVillage. Flooz.com was an example of a new kind of venture-capital market, driven by Internet start-up companies that no longer required 40-page business plans to raise initial funds. "The competitive profile changes daily for these kinds of startups, and so a business plan becomes outdated very fast," Lamont explained to Katherine Goncharoff for the financial newspaper Daily Deal (February 15, 2000), citing as an example Oak's investment in a European e-commerce site, OneSwoop.com, which was also made without the normal lengthy written proposal. "Funding without a formal plan is becoming more of a norm," she continued, adding that venture capitalists were far more willing to "make a leap of faith" when it came to investments in Internet companies proposed by trusted entrepreneurs. Oak's leap of faith in Flooz.com, however, was followed by a fall, as the new company folded shortly after its inception.

Asked by Cowan in 2006 to talk about some of her past underperforming investments, Lamont responded only by saying, "Who wants to talk about their failures?" Lamont's peers and partners have cited such reserve as one of her greatest professional attributes. "She's wise and practical and doesn't talk when it's not important and does talk when it is," Jonathan Bush, CEO of the Oak-backed healthcare company Athenahealth Inc., told Cowan. Lamont's friends agree with the description of the businesswoman as a realist. Elena Phleger, a friend of Lamont's from Stanford, said about her former classmate to Cowan, "If you were on a range of idealism versus pragmatism, her needle would be a little more over on the pragmatic side."

On the more idealistic side is Lamont's husband, the politician and businessman Edward Miner ("Ned") Lamont Jr. The pair met shortly after Ann Lamont—then Ann Huntress—moved to Connecticut; they were married in 1983, at Ned Lamont's family home on Long Island, New York. (Their wedding reception was catered by Martha Stewart, a then-unknown culinary talent Ann Lamont had met at a gym.) In 1984 Ned founded Lamont Digital Systems, a small telecommunications network. In 1990 he ran unsuccessfully for a Connecticut State Senate seat, and in 2006 he launched a run for the United States Senate against the incumbent Democrat Joe Lieberman. Ned Lamont surprised many pundits by winning the primary in August, but he ultimately lost the seat to Lieberman, who ran as an independent in the general election. The race focused a great deal of scrutiny on the Lamont family, particularly its finances. While Ned Lamont came from more privileged circumstances than his wife (Harvard University's Lamont Library is named after his great-grandfather, Thomas W. Lamont, who made a fortune at J. P. Morgan & Co.), reports published during the campaign indicated that Ann Lamont contributed considerably more than her husband to the family's income. The *New York Times* estimated the Lamont family's assets at between $90 million and $332 million, further stating that $54 million to $193 million of that total came from Ann Lamont's work at Oak Investment Partners. Lamont has never publicly disclosed her annual income, but competitors calculate that she takes home an annual salary of at least $15 million. Some of that money has gone to political causes—for example, Lamont contributed $2,000 each to the Democratic presidential candidates Howard Dean and John Kerry in 2003, according to opensecrets.com, a Web site that monitors political donations. By September 30, 2006, less than two months before the general election, two-thirds of Ned Lamont's campaign money, totaling approximately $8.7 million, had come from the couple themselves.

In addition to contributing financially to the campaign, Ann Lamont worked behind the scenes, organizing her husband's schedule and networking with her contacts from the business world. The Lamonts' daughter Emily described her mother to Cowan as the "campaign's master secretary and policy adviser." Still, Lamont told Cowan—who described Lamont as she appeared in her husband's campaign material as "the petite, well-dressed blonde at the rim of the frame"—that she preferred to stay out of the limelight. "I don't have any desire to be public or famous," she said. Both Lamont and her husband denied that her history in finance could adversely affect his political aspirations. "She's hardly a lobbyist or anything like that," Ned told Cowan. "She's a woman who has had a wonderful career."

Lamont lives with her husband in Greenwich, Connecticut. The couple have three children: Emily, who is a freshman at Harvard; Lindsay; and Teddy.

—C.S.

Suggested Reading: *New York Times* B p1 Oct. 16, 2006; Oak Investment Partners Web site

Courtesy of Robert J. Lang

Lang, Robert J.

May 4, 1961– Physicist; engineer; origami artist

Address: c/o Alice and Klaus Peters Publishers, 888 Worcester St., Suite 230, Wellesley, MA 02482

When Robert J. Lang quit engineering to pursue his other passion—origami, the Japanese art of paper folding—as a full-time career, he had written more than 80 technical papers and held 46 patents on lasers and other optoelectronics (devices for emitting, modulating, transmitting, and sensing light).

Now one of the premier origami artists in the world, Lang has created more than 480 designs and expanded the field both artistically and scientifically, finding practical applications for origami in fields ranging from medical technology to space exploration. Lang—whom Susan Orlean described for the *New Yorker* (February 19, 2007) as "composed, moderate, painstaking"—has been practicing origami since he was six years old, when a teacher gave him an instruction book to keep him from getting bored during math class. "The thing that got me hooked on origami all those years ago was the 'something for nothing' aspect," he told Chad Berndston for the South Boston, Massachusetts, *Patriot Ledger* (November 8, 2004). "The wonder of the things we can make has grown enormously." Among Lang's greatest artistic achievements is a full-size cuckoo clock, though in general he is best known for his figures that represent the natural world. Lang's shapes, which range from a simple banana slug to a koi fish complete with scales, can require more than 300 folds; he is among an elite group of artists whose creations defy the normal scale of difficulty in origami, prompting the creation of the new "super-complex" category. "I've always loved problem-solving—it's part of being a scientist and an engineer," he told Berndston. "Coming up with a design is just another form of that, and while it's fun to fold an origami figure, it's also fun to solve the puzzle of how you create a new figure." That problem-solving also extends to the scientific realm, in which Lang's knowledge of origami has contributed to many advances, including ways to fold tricky items such as a heart stent, an airbag, and a telescope lens. Lang told Orlean that the field of origami is advancing rapidly, with almost limitless potential for both artistry and practical applications. "It's like math," he said. "It's just out there waiting to be discovered. The exciting stuff is the stuff where you don't even know how to begin."

Robert James Lang was born on May 4, 1961 in Dayton, Ohio, to Carolyn Lang, a secretary and homemaker, and Jim Lang, who worked for the Airtemp division of the Chrysler Corp. Lang has one older brother, Greg, who is a professor of horticulture at Michigan State University, in East Lansing; his younger sister, Marla, is a commercial interior designer. The family moved frequently when Lang was young but settled in Atlanta, Georgia, by the time he was 10. Lang was always a "super-duper math whiz," his father told Orlean, recalling that his son often read the recreational math column in *Scientific American*. Lang became interested in origami at age six, when an elementary-school teacher gave him a book about origami to keep him entertained during math class. Those two interests—math and origami—persisted throughout the family's many relocations, with Lang creating his own origami figures from an early age. "I sought out all the books I could from the local library, and there weren't that many, and if I wanted to make an animal I couldn't find in the book, I wanted to try to make it up," he told Berndston. "All the people in the books had, so why couldn't I?" In high school Lang joined the school math team, which placed in state and regional competitions.

After graduating from high school, in 1978, Lang enrolled at the California Institute of Technology (Caltech), in Pasadena. "Caltech was very hard, very intense," he told Orlean. "So I did more origami. It was a release from the pressure of school." The mathematical work involved in origami "revs your brain up into high gear," he explained to *Current Biography*, adding that the increased stimulation spilled over into other intellectual areas. "Origami was just a way of exercising your brain in a different direction from quantum mechanics," he said. Although he began to pursue origami seriously during that time, developing his own designs for a Pegasus, a parrot, a crab, and a squirrel, he kept his hobby largely to himself. "I guess I thought it was a kid's pastime that I hadn't grown out of," he told Orlean. "I was a little embarrassed about it." In 1982 Lang graduated from Caltech with a degree in electrical engineering and a growing stock of original origami designs. After earning a master's degree in electrical engineering at Stanford University, in Palo Alto, California, Lang returned to Caltech to pursue a Ph.D. in applied physics. While working on his dissertation, "Semiconductor Lasers: New Geometries and Spectral Properties," Lang created more than 50 origami designs, including those for a hermit crab, an ant, a skunk, and a mouse stuck in a mousetrap. From the beginning Lang's figures displayed not only sophisticated artistry but also striking realism. "They were dense and crisp and precise but also full of character: his mouse conveys something fundamentally mouse-ish, his ant has an essential ant-ness," Orlean wrote. For several months after receiving his Ph.D., in 1986, Lang stayed at Caltech to finish his research; he then traveled to Germany for a 10-month postdoctoral program, studying semiconductor lasers. While in Germany, Lang also created an origami version of the traditional Black Forest cuckoo clock; described as a "tour de force" by Constance Ashmore Fairchild, writing for *Library Journal* (February 15, 2004), the figure took him three months to design and six hours to build.

After completing his postdoctoral studies, Lang returned to Pasadena to work at the National Aeronautics and Space Administration (NASA) Jet Propulsion Laboratory, where he focused on optoelectronics. That same year, 1988, Lang also published his first collection of origami designs, *The Complete Book of Origami: Step-by-Step Instructions in Over 1000 Diagrams*. He followed that effort with *Origami Zoo: An Amazing Collection of Folded Paper Animals* (1990), written with Stephen Weiss, and *Origami Sea Life* (1990), co-written by John Montroll. In 1992 he published his fourth book, *Origami Animals*, and became the first Westerner ever invited to address the annual meeting of the Nippon Origami Association, in Japan. Meanwhile, Lang continued to work as an engineer, beginning a stint at Spectra Diode Labs, in San Jose, California, in 1992.

In the early 1990s Lang began to integrate mathematics and origami, developing a computer program named Origami Simulation that allowed the user to fold a sheet of paper on screen. When not working on such projects as fiber-optic networks for space satellites or the patenting of self-collimated resonator lasers, Lang continued to pursue origami with an increasing number of side projects. In 1995 he published *Origami Insects and Their Kin: Step-by-Step Instructions in Over 1500 Diagrams*, a collection of designs for 20 complex insect figures, and in 1997 he published *Origami in Action: Paper Toys That Fly, Flap, Gobble, and Inflate*, a book of his collected designs for beginners. In 1999 Lang was commissioned to create four works for the Downtown Transit Mall in Santa Monica, California. He made four animals representative of the area's fauna—a tree frog, a sea urchin, a dragonfly, and a garibaldi (a species of fish)—which were then cast in bronze and used to adorn drinking fountains around the city. Lang's creations received the Southern California American Public Works Association's award for streets and transportation project of the year in 2002, and in 2005 Lang was commissioned to create two more figures, a sea turtle and a flying fish.

Around that time Lang began to think seriously about quitting his job as an engineer and pursuing origami full-time. Besides his work on the Santa Monica project, he had been a consultant for companies or government agencies that applied origami techniques in various ways. The Lawrence Livermore National Laboratory, for example, hired him to devise a way of folding a telescope that was to be sent into space. Lang calculated that from those kinds of consulting jobs, as well as his artistic commissions, he could make a living out of paper folding. In addition to those projects, Lang wanted to create a different kind of origami book. "Most origami books at the time were collections of recipes for specific origami figures, but what I wanted to do was to teach people how to come up with their own recipes," he explained to *Current Biography*. That book, though, would require his full attention, he realized. The idea for the book came to him around the time of the dot-com bust, during which the company for which he was then working, JDS Uniphase (which makes equipment used to build fiber-optic-telecom, data, and cable-television networks), lost a large portion of its business. By then Lang was in a managerial position at the company; with the bust, his duties largely changed from overseeing research and development to dealing with pay cuts and plant closings. "Laying people off was a lot less fun than inventing things," he told Orlean. "There were plenty of people doing lasers. The things I could do in origami—if I didn't do them, they wouldn't get done. Deciding to leave was a convergence of what I wanted to do plus what was happening at my company." By

the time he left JDS Uniphase, in 2002, Lang had written more than 80 technical papers and held 46 patents on lasers and optoelectronics. Although he admitted to *Current Biography* that the idea of leaving a successful career in engineering for one in origami "sounds pretty crazy," he said that he was confident in his decision: "Sometimes, you know the crazy thing is the right thing to do. It was one of those few times when I knew it was the right decision."

The following year Lang published *Origami Design Secrets: Mathematical Methods for an Ancient Art* (2003)—which he refers to on his Web site as his "magnum opus"; he also published *Origami Insects II* (2003), a collection of 18 new insect designs. That same year he was featured in the Origami Masterworks exhibit at the Mingei International Museum, in San Diego, California. The exhibit, which included a six-foot-tall heron that Lang had folded, was originally supposed to run for six months, but it proved so popular that it was extended first by six months and then by an additional eight. Lang's pieces have also been featured in a number of commercial venues: he created a menagerie of toilet-paper origami animals as part of a commercial for the fabric deodorizer Febreze; a life-size model of Drew Carey for *The Drew Carey Show*; and airplane seats for the cover of an aircraft-seating magazine. He worked a week of 14-hour days to supervise the folding of hundreds of origami figures for a 2006 commercial for the Mitsubishi Endeavor, in which the car is driven through a world composed entirely of origami. Most recently, he completed a series of figures for a McDonald's commercial; the human figures, who wear such accessories as gold chains and Kangol hats, are folded from what appears to be McDonald's cheeseburger wrappers (actually origami paper printed with the McDonald's pattern).

Lang is constantly breaking ground in the area of practical applications of origami—specifically, fitting large items into small spaces. Among his designs are a pouch for medical instruments that can be opened without any unsterile surface touching a sterile one; a cell-phone antenna that fits inside the body of the phone; a heart implant that is folded into a tube for implantation, then unfurled when in place; and a computer model that simulates the folding and deployment of airbags.

Lang has also continued to develop two computer programs that allow for the mapping of complicated figures. TreeMaker, a program he began working on in the late 1980s and first released in 1994, can describe in mathematical terms any origami figure that can be represented by a stick-figure drawing—for example, an insect or a human, but not a cloud—and produce a replica of the creases necessary to fold the figure. Although some criticize the program as a perversion of the origami tradition, Lang said that he firmly believes that using a computer is an obvious step in the evolution of origami. "If people object to using computers to create origami, do they also object to using brushes to create a painting?" he said to *Current Biography*. Lang rarely uses TreeMaker in his work. When he created the program, he needed it specifically to make such complex features as deer's antlers and insects' legs. In general, however, he sees Tree-Maker as a learning tool; by writing the program, he said, he gained valuable insight into the design process, which he could then translate into his more intuitive work. That intuitive work, he said, is what makes for the most amazing origami. "The computer is a tool. It's efficient for laying down a pattern or framework," he told Bennett Daviss for *New Scientist* (January 18, 2003). "But human skill will always be needed to implement the design. It's the person that makes the difference between creating something awkward and lifeless or something elegant and beautiful." TreeMaker is now on its fifth version; because it is freely distributed on Lang's Web site, he does not know exactly how many people have downloaded it, but he has estimated that a couple of hundred people do so every year.

While TreeMaker creates a pattern of creases, it cannot calculate the sequence in which the creases should be folded. To solve that problem, Lang created a different program, ReferenceFinder (currently in its fourth incarnation), which is also available for free download on his Web site. ReferenceFinder helps the origami artist find the most efficient folding pattern for a given crease; however, with upwards of 200 creases per figure, it is still inefficient to run ReferenceFinder on every crease. The artist must decide on his or her own which creases would be best to run through the program.

In his willingness to share origami designs and design strategy, Lang co-founded the Origami Design Challenge at OrigamiUSA's annual convention. Conceived by Lang and a friend, the origami expert Satoshi Kamiya, the informal event involves no judges or winners—just the exchange of ideas. All of the contributors create the same general shape, but with different designs and, ultimately, different results. In 2004 Lang and Kamiya both brought versions of an origami beetle to the convention. The next year they announced that they would make hermit crabs, along with the eight other artists who had entered the challenge. In 2006 the ever-growing group made sailing ships. "It is a pleasant and remarkable situation, this mixture of sharing and competition that has remained nicely balanced for many years. Yes, we're all trying to outdo each other, but we're also 'giving away the store,' so to speak, by showing each other how our latest invention is constructed . . . ," Lang wrote for his Web site. "By this means, the entire art is advanced." In 2007 the competition centered on a complete plant—roots were optional, but the plant had to have a stem. The emphasis remained on the community of origami and on the personal challenge of pushing to do one's best, even without prizes. "The purpose of a design challenge is not rooted in some award, the joy of getting a bit of ribbon stuck onto one's effort," Lang wrote for his Web site. "The purpose of a design challenge is in the process, that it provides a spur and a goad to try something new and different. And the only opinion that matters is one's own. (Well, and maybe the opinions of other origami composers.)"

Lang recently completed a life-size flying pteranodon for a permanent installation at the Redpath Museum at McGill University, in Montreal, Canada. He is one of the few Western columnists for *Origami Tanteidan Magazine*, the journal of the Japan Origami Academic Society. In January 2007 Lang was named editor in chief of the *Journal of Quantum Electronics*, published by the Institute of Electrical and Electronic Engineers. He has also consulted for Cypress Semiconductor for several years.

Lang lives in Alamo, California, with his wife, Diane, whom he met at Caltech as an undergraduate when they were both in a campus production of *The Music Man*. They have one teenage son, Peter.

—C.S.

Suggested Reading: *Boston Globe* (on-line) Nov. 11, 2004; *Discover* (on-line) July 29, 2006; *New Yorker* (on-line) Feb. 19, 2007; *Patriot Ledger* (on-line) Nov. 8, 2004; Robert Lang's Web site

Selected Books: *The Complete Book of Origami: Step-by-Step Instructions in Over 1000 Diagrams*, 1988; *Origami Zoo: An Amazing Collection of Folded Paper Animals* (with Stephen Weiss), 1990; *Origami Sea Life* (with John Montroll), 1990; *Origami Animals*, 1992; *Origami Insects and Their Kin: Step-by-Step Instructions in Over 1500 Diagrams*, 1995; *Origami in Action: Paper Toys That Fly, Flap, Gobble, and Inflate*, 1997; *Origami Insects II*, 2003; *Origami Design Secrets: Mathematical Methods for an Ancient Art*, 2003

Lanier, Cathy L.

(luh-NEER)

July 22, 1967– Chief of the Metropolitan Police Department of the District of Columbia

Address: Metropolitan Police Dept. Headquarters, 300 Indiana Ave., N.W., Washington, DC 20001

On January 2, 2007 Cathy L. Lanier assumed the position of acting chief of police and chief executive officer of the Metropolitan Police Department of the District of Columbia (MPDC), one of the most high-profile, demanding jobs in law enforcement. The D.C. City Council confirmed her appointment as chief of police and CEO in March. Lanier leads a 3,800-member uniformed force whose responsibilities include fighting crime in the Washington, D.C., metropolitan area, coordinating presidential

Mannie Garcia/AFP/Getty Images

Cathy L. Lanier

motorcades, protecting dignitaries, and maintaining order at such events as parades, protest marches, and state funerals. Lanier began her career in the MPDC as a foot-patrol officer in 1990 and earned a series of promotions with unusual rapidity. For eight months before she became the acting head of the MPDC, she occupied the top position at the city's Office of Homeland Security and Counter-Terrorism, where she functioned within the inner circle of her predecessor as police chief, Charles H. Ramsey. Lanier is the first woman to serve as chief of police permanently in the nation's capital (Sonya Procter served as interim chief before Charles H. Ramsey's tenure); currently, she is one of a half-dozen women to supervise a police department in a major U.S. city. At a press conference held in early January 2007, Lanier said, as quoted by Allison Klein in the *Washington Post* (January 6, 2007), "Our overriding goal is to reduce crime and the fear of crime in every neighborhood." "When I stand in the mirror, I see somebody who is compassionate but with a strong desire to help people do what's right, to help maintain that line between right and wrong," Lanier told Courtland Milloy for the *Washington Post* (December 6, 2006, on-line). "Sometimes, it's a balancing act. I feel just as compassionate when I see someone involved in criminal activity. Something caused that person to be in an environment that contributed to the criminal behavior. I feel sorry and empathetic, even though what they are doing is wrong. We have to get them off the streets, but I have to keep the compassion because that's what keeps us from policing in a way we shouldn't."

Cathy Lynn Lanier was born on July 22, 1967 and, along with her two brothers, was raised by her mother in a modest neighborhood in Tuxedo, Maryland. Her father, who did not live with the family, was deputy chief of the Prince George's County, Maryland, fire department before his retirement. Lanier has said that her youth was spent as "one of the boys," and that at times she literally took her share of punches from her brothers; one brother is now a captain in the Prince George's County fire department, and the other is a detective in the Greenbelt, Maryland, police department. When Lanier was in ninth grade, she gave birth to a baby boy and dropped out of school. At 15 she married the child's father; their union ended after two years. Inspired by her mother, who had held several jobs while her children were growing up, Lanier earned a high-school equivalency diploma and worked as a print-shop assistant and as a canopy and awning saleswoman. When she was about 20, following what had become a family tradition of public service, Lanier entered the police academy and recognized immediately that she had found her calling.

Lanier began active duty with the Metropolitan Police Department of Washington, D.C., in 1990, during a time when the MPDC was struggling to field a full complement of officers. Between the years 1988 and 1990, because of escalating crime rates in the city, department officials had been under heavy pressure to hire and train hundreds of new officers, and they had cut corners in conducting background checks and in training recruits. Those shortcuts later haunted them, as dozens of fledgling officers began to be prosecuted on criminal charges or disciplined for other serious offenses. In that environment, Lanier stood out for her exemplary behavior, and she moved quickly up the law-enforcement ladder. After serving as a uniformed patrol officer in the Fourth District in the northeastern part of the capital, she advanced to the rank of sergeant, in 1994, and was assigned to the Sixth District, in the city's southeastern quadrant. In 1996 she was promoted to lieutenant and returned to the Fourth District as patrol supervisor. As a member of the department's reorganization team, known as G21, she helped develop the district's community-policing model.

In 1996 Lanier and a female sergeant, Lena Johnson, brought charges against the city for alleged sexual harassment on the part of some of MPDC employees. The previous year, *Washington Post* investigative reporters had found evidence that sexual harassment was widespread in the Police Department; dozens of police officers and administrators had acknowledged or complained that women in the department were often subjected to physical and verbal harassment. Along with many of their female colleagues, Lanier and Johnson shared a belief that MPDC officials did not regard sexual harassment as a serious problem and that they rarely enforced sexual-harassment regulations or followed up on complaints. Lanier and

Johnson brought a lawsuit against the city, stating that the department showed indifference to their right to work in an atmosphere free of sexual harassment. The lawsuit was settled out of court, and the two officers were awarded $75,000 each. In addition, as their lawyer explained to Martin Weil for the *Washington Post* (January 8, 1997), the Police Department agreed to provide additional training concerning sexual harassment to all its employees and resolved to make clear to all of them that such behavior would not be tolerated.

In January 1999 Lanier was promoted to captain and assigned again to the Sixth District, where she served as assistant district commander. Later that year she again rose in the department, gaining the title of inspector; she was placed in charge of the Major Narcotics Branch and the Gang Crime and Vehicular Homicide Units in the Special Services Bureau.

In 2000 Lanier was promoted to commander in charge of the Fourth District, perhaps the most diverse and populous of the city's seven police districts. The district was the only one in the city in which crime rates had increased during 1999; moreover, four of the officers on duty there had been arrested for criminal charges ranging from burglary to armed robbery. Many of the district's problems were attributed to a lack of leadership and excessive turnover among those in command of law enforcement; prior to Lanier's becoming commander in charge, the Fourth District had had three commanders in succession in two years. In her new post Lanier was credited with introducing "precision control teams," whereby, based on data analyses indicating in which places and at what times criminals were most apt to strike, extra officers were stationed in crime hotspots. With additional officers assigned preemptively to Fourth District neighborhoods that were potentially at risk, the number of crimes in those parts of the city dropped. As paraphrased by David Nakamura and Allison Klein in the *Washington Post* (November 21, 2006), Leopold Wilburn, a social activist who lived in the district, said that Lanier "developed a reputation as someone willing to listen to residents and incorporate their ideas." Wilburn and others thus distinguished her from her predecessors, whom they criticized as merely uniformed bureaucrats who had no concern with the well-being of district residents.

In 2002 Lanier was again promoted, to commanding officer of the MPDC's Special Operations Division (SOD), where she managed the Emergency Response Team; Aviation and Harbor Units; Horse Mounted and Canine Units; Special Events/Dignitary Protection Branch; and Civil Disturbance Units. During her tenure as SOD commander, Lanier set up the Police Department's Homeland-Security/Counter Terrorism Branch and created a department-wide chemical, biological, and radiological response unit known as the Special Threat Action Team. Lanier also spearheaded a campaign to enlist Washington, D.C.–

area businesses to help law-enforcement agencies. As part of a renewed terrorism-prevention initiative, the MPDC set up a dedicated telephone line that businesses could use to report suspicious purchases, requests, or activities. Lanier told reporters that the police were particularly interested in places where boats were sold or serviced, marinas, parking garages, and special-events sites.

In April 2006 Lanier was named the commanding officer of the Office of Homeland Security & Counter-Terrorism (OHSCT), an arm of the office of the chief of police. As head of OHSCT Lanier played a major role in developing and implementing counterterrorism strategies for all units within the MPDC. Among the many colleagues impressed by her management skills and leadership abilities were Joseph Persichini Jr., assistant director of the Washington Field Office of the FBI, who told Allison Klein and Sara Horowitz for the *Washington Post* (November 21, 2006), "Cathy just epitomizes the collaborative spirit."

Meanwhile, Lanier had been continuing her education, and by her own account, the degrees that she earned while working full-time and raising her son are a source of great personal pride. Lanier received a bachelor's degree in criminal-justice studies from the University of the District of Columbia, bachelor's and master's degrees in management from Johns Hopkins University, in Baltimore, Maryland, and a master's degree in national security studies from the Naval Postgraduate School (NPS) in Monterey, California. Her NPS thesis was titled "Preventing Terror Attacks in the Homeland: A New Mission for State and Local Police." She also graduated from the FBI's National Academy, the Federal Drug Enforcement Agency's Drug Unit Commanders Academy, and took courses at the John F. Kennedy School of Government at Harvard University. In addition, she is certified at the technician level in Hazardous Materials Operations.

After Adrian Fenty won the Washington mayoral election, in November 2006, he announced that he was nominating Lanier for the position of police chief, to replace Charles H. Ramsey, who would step down at the end of the year. During his mayoral campaign Fenty had criticized Ramsey, echoing the complaints of many Washingtonians, especially those living in the city's poorest neighborhoods, that he had focused too much on federal security issues and too little on street crime. Lanier has said that Fenty's decision to nominate her took her completely by surprise; rank-and-file officers were "stunned" by Fenty's choice, as Officer Kristopher Baumann, the chairman of the MPDC police union, told Nakamura and Klein. The union's leaders, who had feuded with Ramsey, had hoped that Fenty would select someone with an independent point of view, preferably a person from outside the department, and certainly not a protégé of Ramsey's, as Lanier had been; indeed, Ramsey had been responsible for many of Lanier's promotions. Phil Mendelson, the chairman of the Judiciary Committee of the Council of the District of Columbia (whose members are elected by city residents), approved of Fenty's choice but said that he would have preferred a broader search for a successor to Ramsey, who had been selected in 1998 from more than 50 applicants nationwide; but Mendelson also noted to Nakamura and Klein that "hiring from within means it's more likely that changes will be in line with current improvements rather than just doing things differently, which is more likely with an outsider." During a November 20, 2006 press conference, as reported by Gary Emerling for the *Washington Post* (November 21, 2006), Fenty defended his decision, saying, "We needed someone who knows the department, someone who knows community policing, someone who knows how to protect the interests in the District of Columbia, which are unique to this city. There's only one person who I would recommend for this position, and that's Cathy Lanier." He also said, according to Nakamura and Klein, "It's indisputable that the police department [under Ramsey] has made objective improvement[s], but it's always appropriate to bring in someone who has a new set of eyes and brings new ways to attack the problems. Cathy Lanier will do that without losing the good initiatives of Chief Ramsey." In addition, he said, as quoted by the Associated Press (November 20, 2006), that Lanier "has superbly served the residents of the District of Columbia for nearly two decades and brings a unique understanding of both the importance of community policing and the expertise in homeland security that the top law enforcement officer of the nation's capital must possess."

Although crime rates decreased during the eight years that Ramsey was chief, the department's performance was a source of concern for voters in 2006 elections, in part because the police were still dogged by the reputation they got in the 1990s, when officers were criticized for using excessive force, botching investigations, and engaging in criminal activity. "It does not matter what the crime statistics are if people feel afraid," Lanier explained at a news conference, as reported by Nakamura and Klein. Lanier believes that making the force more efficient will be more effective than increasing its size, as some have suggested. (Still, according to Allison Klein's January 6, 2007 *Washington Post* article, the department plans to hire 100 new officers.) Lanier has said repeatedly that she does not anticipate making any drastic changes. To increase the visibility of the MPDC, she plans to make foot and bicycle patrols more common than assignments of officers in storefronts and substations. She has said that she will retain a controversial Ramsey initiative requiring patrol cars in certain areas to flash their white lights at all times to announce their presence; though some residents find that measure intrusive, and it limits the MPDC's ability to make covert arrests, Lanier believes that it deters potential criminals from acting. She has also started to alter the top-down prob-

lem-solving structure on which the MPDC has relied, on the grounds that it is not fruitful and hurts officers' morale. In one change, she has given more authority to commanders and beat officers to customize crime-fighting programs and to include community members in decision-making. "With community policing, there is not one template you can implement across the city," Lanier said in an interview with Allison Klein for the *Washington Post* (November 27, 2006). "Every neighborhood is different." She also plans to sponsor research at local universities to investigate past and potential effects of police procedures. "I want us to be innovative," she told Klein. "I want us to change the way we do this to mirror a successful business." She has also expressed her determination to make MPDC changes and protocols known to the public.

In another effort to increase efficiency, Lanier has ordered investigations of the use of omnidirectional microphones, which other cities use to pinpoint the location of gunfire. The so-called "shot spotters" pick up the distinctive sound of gunfire and transmit radio signals to police, thus drastically reducing response time. Lanier also intends to maintain a system, introduced by Ramsey, that relies on cameras at fixed locations to create records of cars whose drivers break traffic laws. By identifying such drivers, the system potentially could serve as a deterrent to speeding or going through red lights. The automated system has enabled the Police Department to issue more tickets and has generated more than $38 million in fines since 1999, but it has not yet had a measurable effect on the number of traffic fatalities. Lanier also applauded recently passed legislation that will permit Washington's police chief to have neighborhood surveillance cameras installed. The cameras would be placed in high-risk areas and not monitored in real time; rather, recorded images would be reviewed only after a crime was reported in the area. Lanier has called the cameras a "very good use of technology," according to Matthew Cella in the *Washington Times* (December 6, 2006).

Lanier is aware of the difficulties she may face as a white chief of police in a city that has a history of racial polarization and whose population of more than a half-million people is about 60 percent black. "I've been feeling a bit frustrated, because I thought more people would be interested in the new police chief's policies and crime-fighting strategies than in her race and hairstyle," she told Courtland Milloy. Referring to her race, she told Klein and Horowitz, "If people get to know you, I think it's not a big deal. If I treat everybody the way a chief should treat them, there won't be a problem."

Lanier, whose annual salary is $175,000, lives in a house on six acres in Anne Arundel County, Maryland, with her son, her mother, and her boyfriend, an MPDC police sergeant. As of early 2007 she was house-hunting, because, as Washington's police chief, she is required to live within city limits. According to many sources in the fall of 2007, the Fox network was planning to create a TV series about her life.

—N.W.M.

Suggested Reading: Associated Press Nov. 21, 2006, (on-line) Nov. 20, 2006, Dec. 8, 2006; *Washington Post* B p1+ Aug. 28, 2000, A p1+ Nov. 21, 2006, A p1+ Nov. 27, 2006, B p1+ Dec. 6, 2006, B p1+ Jan. 6, 2007; *Washington Times* A p1+ Dec. 1, 2006, A p1+ Nov. 21, 2006, B p1+ Nov. 21, 2006

Courtesy of the office of Tom Lantos

Lantos, Tom

Feb. 1, 1928– U.S. representative from California (Democrat)

Address: 2413 Rayburn House Office Bldg., Washington, DC 20515

"I'm only at the midpoint of my political career," the 79-year-old U.S. congressman Tom Lantos told Edward Epstein for the *San Francisco Chronicle* (January 1, 2007). A Democrat from California, Lantos—the only Holocaust survivor ever to hold a seat in the U.S. Congress—is currently serving his 14th term in the House of Representatives. He is a former professor of economics whose political career included only senior-advisory roles for various members of the U.S. Senate, until he became the only Democrat in the 1980 congressional elections to beat an incumbent Republican who was not facing indictment; he thus claimed the seat representing California's 11th Congressional District, encompassing southwest San Francisco County

and northern San Mateo County. Lantos's first year in Congress was marked by open hostility from a Republican-dominated Senate after Ronald Reagan's landslide victory in the 1980 presidential race. Since then, the Hungarian-born Lantos has won respect for his strong advocacy of human rights and careful handling of foreign affairs. Lantos, the current chairman of the House Committee on Foreign Affairs, on which he has served for 26 years, has also furthered his presence on the world stage as the founder of the Congressional Human Rights Caucus. Domestically, Lantos has backed liberal causes, supporting, for example, the rights of gays to marry and the use of marijuana for medical purposes, and he is strongly pro-choice. Although the congressman has recently received a wave a criticism for changing his stance on the Iraq war (he initially voted to authorize the war and now stands adamantly against it), Lantos is widely respected on both sides of the political fence and has continued to dominate general elections, receiving an average of about 75 percent of the vote. Lantos is "the last lion," Representative Adam Schiff, a fellow California Democrat, said to Epstein. "That's in the sense that he brings historical understanding, has earned immense respect, and has a level of gravitas second to none."

The only child of Pal Lantos, a banker, and Anna Lantos, a high-school English teacher, Thomas Peter Lantos was born on February 1, 1928 in Budapest, Hungary. He came from a Jewish family with a tradition of teaching: one of his uncles was a professor at the University of Budapest, and his grandmother was a former principal of a local gymnasium (high school). Although most of the Jews in Hungary, including Lantos's family, were assimilated and deeply patriotic, the end of World War I brought new restrictions upon Hungarian Jews, which included the passing of a law in 1923 that prohibited the percentage of Jews entering universities from exceeding the proportion of them in the overall Hungarian population. In 1933, when Lantos was five years old, Adolf Hitler came to power in Germany, increasing the anti-Semitic sentiment in the region. A Nazi movement had begun within Hungary, and Lantos and his friends feared the Hungarian Nazis' emblem, the arrow cross, even more than the swastika. Walking to and from school, Lantos often saw fellow Jews being attacked and beaten. Lantos, a voracious reader even as a young boy, has said that one of his most vivid childhood memories is of buying his first newspaper in 1938, when he was 10 years old; walking home from school, he read the headline "Hitler Marches into Austria." In James Moll's Academy Award–winning 1998 documentary, *The Last Days*, in which Lantos was one of five Holocaust survivors featured, he recalled, as quoted on his official Web site, "I sensed that this moment, this event would have a tremendous impact on the lives of Hungarian Jews, my family and myself."

When Hitler invaded the Soviet Union, in the summer of 1941, he demanded that both Hungary and Romania provide troops to fight alongside the Germans against the Soviets. Both countries responded eagerly, largely for the sake of acquiring territory in the Carpathian Basin (Hitler had divided the area known as Transylvania between Hungary and Romania in 1940; the area had been Hungarian prior to World War I, but Romania had taken all of it by war's end). Hungarian Jews, forbidden to serve in the army, were forced to do menial and dangerous work on the Soviet front, which included walking through minefields to clear the way for troops. All the young men in Lantos's extended family were made to perform such tasks, and all of them perished, as he recalled in *The Last Days*: Back in Hungary, many Jews were forced out of their jobs and businesses. On March 19, 1944, when Lantos was 16, German troops occupied Hungary. Afterward, it became mandatory for every Jew to wear a yellow Star of David.

While most Hungarian Jews outside Budapest were sent to the infamous concentration camp at Auschwitz, many Jewish young men in the capital city were dispatched to forced-labor camps. Lantos was sent to a camp in Szob, a small village about 40 miles north of Budapest. His parents were later deported from Budapest; his father survived the war, but Lantos never found out what happened to his mother. On one occasion Lantos escaped from the work camp but was caught and severely beaten. His second attempt succeeded: he made contact with the Hungarian Underground, led by Raoul Wallenberg, which provided escapees with food, shelter, medical supplies, and fake passports. Staying in what was called a safe house, Lantos found himself among more than 50 people who shared a room that would normally have been occupied by four or five. Lantos, whose blond hair and blue eyes allowed him to pass for an Aryan, was sent around Budapest in a military cadet's uniform to deliver bread, medicine, and other supplies to various safe houses. Despite his looks, he was continually at risk of being discovered by German or Hungarian Nazi officers, who often identified Jewish men by ordering them to lower their pants (only Jews were circumcised) and shot them to death on the spot—the fate of some of Lantos's friends. Lantos recounted in the documentary, "There was one occasion when the people in the protected house next to the one I was living in were ordered by a group of Nazi military or police—Hungarian or German—down to the Danube. They were machine-gunned or shot one by one and their bodies pushed into the river. It was as simple as that. The 'protected' house only provided protection when the good Lord and good fortune were with you."

On May 8, 1945, with the German surrender to Allied forces, World War II officially ended in Europe, and Hungary became a Communist satellite state of the Soviet Union. In the fall of 1946, Lantos began studies at the University of Budapest. He intended to study medicine, until, as he recalled to

Jon Marmor for the *University of Washington Alumni Magazine* (September 1999, on-line), "they brought in the first corpse, and I was through with medical school." Then, in the summer of 1947, he was awarded a Hillel Foundation scholarship to study in the United States, based on an essay he had written about U.S. president Franklin D. Roosevelt.

Recalling his arrival at the University of Washington, in Seattle, Lantos said to Marmor, "Here I was, coming out of the Holocaust, starvation, poverty, persecution, the worst horror of mankind, and I had landed in this bucolic setting. People were friendly and wonderful, there was all the food I could eat. I couldn't believe my eyes." He worked part-time jobs to support himself and to send chocolate and other items to friends and family in Hungary. He even persuaded officials at the university to hire him to teach Hungarian, which he began doing at 19. (At the time the school was one of only two universities in the nation to offer instruction in Hungarian.) Lantos received his bachelor's degree in 1949 and master's degree in 1950 from the University of Washington—both in economics. In June 1950 he married his childhood sweetheart and fellow Holocaust survivor Annette Tillemann (a cousin of the actresses Eva and Zsa Zsa Gabor). The couple moved to the San Francisco Bay Area, where Lantos pursued graduate studies at the University of California, Berkeley. Three years later he received his doctorate in economics and began teaching the subject at San Francisco State University, where he would remain for the next 30 years.

While teaching, Lantos chaired the Millbrae, California, board of education; developed his own public-television program on international affairs; served as an economic consultant to a number of businesses; and was actively involved in politics—his real love. In 1978 he took a year's leave of absence from San Francisco State to work as a foreign-policy adviser to Democratic senator Joseph Biden of Delaware. Then, on November 18, 1978, California's 11th Congressional District representative, the Democrat Leo Ryan, was killed at an airstrip in Guyana; he had gone there in search of former constituents who had moved to Jonestown—the site of the camp founded by the cult leader Jim Jones, who later died amidst the murders and suicides of more than 900 of his followers. In the 1980 race for the congressional seat, after running unopposed in the Democratic primary, the inexperienced Lantos defied odds to defeat the incumbent Republican, William Royer, who had won the special election after Ryan's death. Lantos won his seat with the lowest plurality of any member of Congress elected that year, winning 46 percent to Royer's 43 percent. He was sworn in on January 5, 1981.

One of Lantos's first acts as a congressman was to initiate legislation to make Raoul Wallenberg an honorary citizen of the United States. Once President Reagan signed the legislation, in October 1981, Wallenberg became only the second foreigner ever to receive the honor. (British prime minister Winston Churchill was the first.) In 1983 Lantos and the Republican John Edward Porter of Illinois founded the Congressional Human Rights Caucus. Over the years, the group has become the leading voice in Congress on human-rights issues. The group's activities have included speaking out for Christians seeking to practice their faith in Saudi Arabia and Sudan, fighting for Tibetans' right to retain their culture and religion, and advocating for other oppressed minorities worldwide. In 1987 the caucus became the first official U.S. entity to host the Dalai Lama, when the spiritual leader proposed a "Five Point Peace Plan" to Congress. During much of the 1980s, Lantos helped lead the Human Rights Caucus in expressing opposition to Communist regimes as well as other dictatorships. For example, in 1988 he called for economic sanctions against Iraq in response to that country's gassing of the Kurds. In 1990, as communism was facing its demise (Germany reunified in October 1990, and the Soviet Union collapsed in December 1991), he became the first U.S. official since 1946 to visit Albania. He sponsored the first U.S. aid to the newly democratic countries of Eastern Europe and became a strong advocate for NATO expansion.

Long an outspoken opponent of political fraud and of the misuse of campaign funds, Lantos explained to Edvins Beitiks for the *San Francisco Examiner* (June 1, 2000), "I'm one of those in Congress who thinks campaign fund-raising is getting out of hand. I favor shortening campaigns, both presidential and congressional." In 1989 and 1990 he conducted hearings to investigate allegations of misconduct on the part of HUD (the Department of Housing and Urban Development) secretary Samuel Pierce. In 1991 Lantos became the center of controversy himself, during the buildup to the Persian Gulf War, which he strongly supported. That U.S.-led war followed Iraq's invasion of neighboring Kuwait; the Human Rights Caucus had hosted a number of hearings at which a Kuwaiti woman identified only as Nurse Nayirah brought to light the atrocities committed by Iraqi soldiers. Support in Congress for the invasion of Iraq increased as a result of her testimony. After the war it was found that Nurse Nayirah was in fact the 15-year-old daughter of the Kuwaiti ambassador to the United States—one of the perpetrators of a hoax contrived by a public-relations firm on behalf of the Kuwaiti government to generate U.S. support for an invasion. It was also revealed that the firm, Hill & Knowlton, had provided free office space to the Congressional Human Rights Foundation, an affiliate of the Human Rights Caucus. Lantos had been reported as saying that Nayirah's last name must remain classified, or her family in Kuwait might face reprisals from Iraqi occupiers. With many believing that he was a participant in the hoax, Lantos continues to receive criticism for the episode.

After the 1992 general election, in which he won 69 percent of the vote, Lantos took the seat representing California's 12th Congressional District.

(He had made the move from the 11th district due to redistricting that followed the U.S. census of 1990.) For much of the 1990s, Lantos continued to champion human-rights issues, with many of the conflicts on which he focused mirroring his own experiences in the Holocaust. That was particularly true of the war in the former Yugoslavia, waged from 1992 to 1995, in which Bosnian Serbs carried out a campaign of so-called ethnic cleansing against that country's ethnic Serbs and Croats (most of whom were Muslims). Lantos advocated a more active American role in Bosnia and in other parts of the former Yugoslavia. He sharply criticized China for its human-rights violations and opposed the normalizing of U.S. trade relations with China. Over the years he had also been quick to criticize what he perceived as anti-Semitic behavior. For example, in 1996, after the controversial Nation of Islam leader Louis Farrakhan made a number of anti-Semitic remarks and met with the leaders of Libya, Iran, and Iraq in what the press called a "thugfest tour," Lantos helped introduce a resolution to censure Farrakhan. Lantos's action brought disapproval from members of the Congressional Black Caucus, but he did not retreat from his position.

At the outset of the new millennium, Lantos continued supporting sanctions against Iraq, which had been imposed in the aftermath of the Persian Gulf War; Democrats in the House remained divided over the issue, with many arguing that sanctions were contributing unduly to poverty and disease in Iraq. Lantos and fellow pro-sanction representatives, however, maintained that Iraq's leader, Saddam Hussein, was withholding available food and medicine as a means of garnering sympathy and ending sanctions. Lantos also cited Iraq's anti-Jewish, anti-Israel, and anti-Western policies as a justification for sanctions. His stance on China remained firm: he sponsored a resolution in September 2000 urging (unsuccessfully) that Beijing not be selected as the site of the 2008 Olympics. Lantos came out against U.S. participation in the United Nations conference on racism in Durban, South Africa, arguing that it would perpetuate anti-Semitism. As quoted in the *Almanac of American Politics*, Lantos called the conference "another forum for Israel-bashing and for the most extreme form of antisemitism to gain global notoriety." In particular, he felt that the conference had strayed away from its ostensible purpose—that of addressing past and present racial discrimination on a global level—by singling out Israel for its alleged persecution of the Palestinians in the occupied regions. In April 2002 Lantos and Majority Whip Tom DeLay co-sponsored a resolution backing Israel's military response to Palestinian suicide attacks on Israeli civilians; the measure passed by a vote of 352–21 in May of that year. Lantos also worked with the former House International Relations Committee chairman, Henry Hyde, to fight AIDS around the world, directing $1.3 billion toward that purpose in December 2001 and, in May

2003, $3 billion of the $15 billion pledged by President George W. Bush. Lantos's other acts included a meeting with Muammar Al-Qaddafi in January 2004, after which Lantos announced that the Libyan leader had renounced all forms of mass destruction. Lantos was also among the first members of Congress to visit the country since the 1960s. In October 2004 he persuaded Congress to pass a bill that suspended aid to Ethiopia and Eritrea until they settled their border dispute. Although Eritrea had gained independence from Ethiopia in 1993, after a 30-year guerrilla war, no border was agreed upon, and a full-scale war between the two countries took place from 1998 to 2000, claiming tens of thousands of lives. Even after a peace agreement was reached, in 2000, the two countries remained in conflict.

On April 28, 2006 Lantos and four other members of Congress were arrested after blocking the entrance to the Sudanese Embassy in Washington, D.C. Their action was a protest against the Sudanese government's sponsorship of genocide against non-Arab citizens in the region of Darfur, where an estimated 200,000 to 450,000 people have perished. Lantos said, as quoted by Jim Doyle in the *San Francisco Chronicle* (April 28, 2006), "We have been calling on the civilized world to stand up and to say, 'Enough.' The slaughter of the people of Darfur must end." The Bush administration denounced a trip that Lantos made with House Speaker Nancy Pelosi, Democrat of California, to Syria, in an attempt to improve relations with the country. Since 2003 U.S.-Syrian relations have been marked by open hostility, especially regarding U.S. foreign policy in the Middle East. The U.S., for its part, has accused Syria of allowing terrorists safe passage into neighboring Iraq and has criticized its involvement in Lebanese politics. Many political observers called the Pelosi-Lantos visit ill-timed, arguing that it allowed Syria to exploit the lack of unified resolve in Washington over the issue of Iraq. As quoted in a transcript from *Lou Dobbs Tonight* (April 12, 2007), Lantos called the administration's intense criticism of the visit "particularly pathetic," noting that Republican colleagues had joined Lantos and Pelosi on their Damascus trip and adding: "So if this is not hypocrisy, I don't know what is." In addition, Lantos has received a firestorm of criticism from many of his House peers for doing an about-face on the current war in Iraq, four years after he voted to authorize the war. He claimed that his initial support for the war was based on the intelligence available at the time, which indicated that Saddam Hussein had obtained weapons of mass destruction. After learning that the intelligence was false, he changed his stance. About his current stance, Lantos explained to Edward Carpenter for the *San Francisco Examiner* (March 19, 2007), "The dream of erecting a prosperous and peaceful democracy in Iraq won't happen in my lifetime or yours." He added, "You can't unscramble an omelet." Lantos, along with House Speaker Pelosi and other members of Con-

gress, drafted a bill that would have funded overseas military operations ($124 billion in emergency spending and an estimated $100 billion to continue the wars in Iraq and Afghanistan), with the proviso that the president would begin withdrawing troops from Iraq as early as July 2007. Bush vetoed the bill. Lantos has denounced that veto and continues to advocate withdrawal of troops from Iraq.

Lantos has a head of white hair that "belies a mind filled with intellectual firecrackers," as described by Edvins Beitiks, and he speaks with what Edward Epstein called "a charmingly accented English that younger generations on Capitol Hill swear sounds like Count von Count on *Sesame Street*." He maintains his youthful vigor by swimming each morning. Lantos and his wife have two grown daughters, Annette and Katrina, and 17 grandchildren. The congressman speaks five languages and dedicates six hours daily to reading books and magazines. "Really the only reason I wouldn't enjoy dropping dead tomorrow is because there's still so many books I want to read," Lantos told Janine Zacharia for the *Jewish Bulletin News* (April 20, 2001). A secular Jew, Lantos is nonetheless deeply proud of his heritage; his office is filled with lithographs of scenes from Jerusalem and colorful Israeli-made pottery. Since January 2007 Lantos has been hard at work in his new role as chairman of the House Committee on Foreign Affairs. His main areas of focus include the ongoing Darfur conflict, the war on terrorism, and the nation's policy on combating AIDS in Africa. Lantos said to Epstein: "In a sense my whole life has been a preparation for this job."

—C.C.

Suggested Reading: *San Francisco Chronicle* D p1 Oct. 13, 2002, A p13 Jan.1, 2007; *San Francisco Examiner* B p1 June 1, 2000; Tom Lantos Web site; *University of Washington Alumni Magazine* (on-line) Sep. 1999; U.S. House of Representatives Web site; *Almanac of American Politics, 2006*

Lanzone, Jim

1971– CEO of Ask.com

Address: Ask.com, 555 12th St., Suite 500, Oakland, CA 94607

"We are like a cockroach—for a long time, with a sub-par product, we survived," Jim Lanzone, the chief executive officer of Ask.com, told Richard Waters for the London *Financial Times* (August 1, 2006). "We're still in the game." The "sub-par" product to which he referred was Ask.com's earlier incarnation, the search engine AskJeeves.com. Lanzone joined Ask Jeeves Inc. in 2001, when it ac-

Courtesy of Ask.com

Jim Lanzone

quired the assets of eTour, the company he had co-founded several years earlier. Launched in 1997 by David Warthen and Garrett Gruener, AskJeeves.com took the name of a character created by the 20th-century British comic writer P. G. Wodehouse: the supremely efficient, seemingly omniscient valet Jeeves. Unlike other search engines, AskJeeves.com "encouraged users to type in questions rather than simply entering keywords," as Verne Kopytoff explained in the *San Francisco Chronicle* (July 19, 2004). AskJeeves, as Lanzone told Kate Bulkley for the London *Guardian* (October 5, 2006), was "editorial based, with editors literally coming up with answers and creating a 'technology' that would match those answers to certain questions." The downside was that "frustratingly, [the user] would also get back a list of more questions." Thus, as Lanzone put it to Bulkley, AskJeeves "over-promised and under-delivered," while its rivals "weren't promising anything and [were] over-delivering." The solution to that problem came shortly after Lanzone's arrival at Ask Jeeves, when the firm acquired an innovative new search system called Teoma. In 2005 AskJeeves itself was acquired by the Internet conglomerate IAC/InteractiveCorp.; it was rechristened Ask.com in 2006. Although, in terms of market share, it is well behind Google, Yahoo!, and MSN (the Microsoft Network), Ask.com is currently the nation's fastest-growing search engine, and as Lanzone told Justin Ewers for *U.S. News & World Report* (November 20, 2006), it is "the seventh-largest Web property . . . , ahead of Amazon and the *New York Times*." "We have over 25 million people a month in the U.S. and 40 million worldwide using Ask," he said. In a re-

view of Ask.com for *PC Magazine* (December 26, 2006), Davis D. Janowski wrote, "Jeeves has retired, but his employer's search service looks better than ever. . . . Extras such as the Smart Answers feature, which tries to place related and authoritative results above other search returns, put Ask ahead of rivals for anyone looking for answers to specific questions or doing research. Smart Answers content often meshed well with what I was looking for. And a useful binocular view produces a pop-up preview of a results page before you go to it. A notable new mapping feature lets you easily generate either walking or driving directions—a capability unique among the Web search/mapping players. And the well-organized image search does a good job of associating similar images, sometimes providing a wider range of results on its first few pages than Google. There's a lot more to discover on Ask.com, and the new format is worth a look."

James Lanzone was born in California in 1971 to Robert J. Lanzone, a lawyer, and Barbara Lanzone, a teacher. He grew up in San Carlos, California, a few miles from San Francisco Bay, where he attended St. Charles Elementary School, a Catholic parish school. In 1985 he enrolled at Junipero Serra High School, a boys-only Catholic school in nearby San Mateo, where his mother was then teaching English. He was a member of the school basketball team and, in his senior year, served as editor of the *Friar*, the student newspaper. In a piece written for an article in the Serra publication *Traditions* (Summer 2006, on-line), he stated, "The real world is very competitive, and Serra taught me how to compete, in sports and academics. That's carried through to running a business, where winning usually depends more on hard work and team work than just being the smartest guy in the room." After his graduation, in 1989, Lanzone enrolled at the University of California at Los Angeles (UCLA), where he received a B.A. degree. He then entered a dual-degree program, in law and business, at Emory University, in Atlanta, Georgia. As a graduate student he developed an interest in Internet technologies and startup ventures. While working toward his M.B.A. and J.D. degrees, which he earned in 1998, Lanzone worked briefly in product marketing and management for KnowX.com (a division of the Thomson Corp.), an Internet service that specialized in searches of public records.

In 1997 Lanzone teamed up with his Emory business-school classmate Roger Barnette to set up an innovative Web-browsing guide called ProLaunch, with the help of a $100,000 investment from a third party. Adopting the slogan "Surf without searching," ProLaunch—which subsequently adopted another name, eTour—gathered information about the interests and preferences of frequent Internet browsers (Web surfers) and used that data to direct them to other creative, quirky Web sites in such categories as sports, entertainment, and shopping. ETour quickly gained a reputation as a very useful virtual tour guide of the Web. Within a few years Lanzone and his partner had raised over $40 million in venture capital and expanded their staff to nearly 150 employees. As eTour's president and chief marketing officer, Lanzone acquired revenue-generating ads placed by the Ralston Purina Co., Mercedes-Benz, and General Electric, among other corporate clients. ETour was named the Most Addictive Web Site of 1999 by the *Industry Standard*, an on-line news magazine, and in 2000 it was recognized as both the "coolest site" in the Web Tool category, at the Fifth Annual Cool Site of the Year Awards ceremony, and the Useful Best of Breed, by *Entertainment Weekly*. That year eTour had more than 2.5 million registered users and attracted an average of 15,000 new registrants every day. But in the wake of the dramatic collapse of the dot-com industry, eTour's fortunes soon took a sharp turn for the worse. With revenues shrinking, eTour was forced to lay off many workers, and Barnette resigned as chief executive officer. Lanzone tried in vain to revive the company by selling its proprietary search technology to other Web sites. In May 2001 the Emeryville, California–based Ask Jeeves Inc. acquired eTour's assets, among them what Tiffany Kary, writing for CNET News.com (May 22, 2001), described as "a proprietary direct e-mail marketing technology with 2.2 million newsletter subscribers" and "a strong advertiser base." A few months later Lanzone became Ask Jeeves's vice president of product management.

In the fall of 2001, in an attempt to improve AskJeeves.com, Ask Jeeves Inc. purchased, for $4.4 million, the New Jersey–based company Teoma Technologies and its unique Internet search software. Teoma was the creation of half a dozen computer scientists, among them Apostolos Gerasoulis. (Gerasoulis served as a vice president of research and development for AskJeeves in 2001–02, during a leave of absence from Rutgers University, where he was a professor of computer science.) Teoma began as a research project that compared the contents of two technical papers, published in 1998, that offered contrasting approaches to Web searches. One paper, "The Anatomy of a Large-Scale Hypertextual Web Search Engine," written by Larry Page and Sergey Brin, Stanford University graduate students who later founded Google, argued that the best search results could be obtained by tabulating links to the most popular Web sites. Their PageRank algorithm, according to a writer for the *Economist* (June 17, 2006), "treated the links to web pages as votes conferring authority, just as the best academic papers tend to get the most citations in other research." The second paper, "Authoritative Sources in a Hyperlinked Environment," written by the IBM researcher Jon Kleinberg, proposed that more-focused and accurate search results would be obtained through a Web site analysis based on concepts, rather than the frequency of "hits." Its premise was that regarding Web sites, popularity among the general public did not necessarily correlate with correctness, but popularity among experts did. Though many considered

Kleinberg's "concept-grouping" method the superior algorithm, it was heavily dependent on computing power, which significantly slowed the search process and thus made it impractical for the average user. Gerasoulis and his colleagues theorized that if the algorithm were modified to permit slightly less accuracy, Kleinberg's search process would be much speedier. "If you made [Web results] 95% accurate instead of 100% percent, it was feasible to get results in less than a second," he told Kevin Maney for *USA Today* (October 4, 2006). With alterations to Kleinberg's methods, Gerasoulis and his team created Teoma. As Kaizad Gotla, an Internet analyst with Nielsen/NetRatings, told Chris Gaither for the *Houston Chronicle* (December 25, 2004), "While Google, Yahoo, and MSN give you the most popular pages, Ask Jeeves gives you the most credible ones."

Armed with Teoma technology, AskJeeves formed several partnerships to bolster its position in the increasingly crowded and swiftly evolving search-engine market. In 2002 the company negotiated a deal that permitted Google to place sponsored links valued at $100 million on the Ask framework. Two years later Lanzone, who by then had become AskJeeves's senior vice president of search properties, signed an agreement whereby CitySearch, a specialized local-search database, agreed to license its local dining and merchant information in exchange for its share of advertising revenue. "It's our technology and their data," Lanzone told Pete Barlas for *Investor's Business Daily* (September 21, 2004). "They, for example, have eight years of restaurant reviews." Also in 2004 AskJeeves introduced a personalized search service called MyJeeves, which allowed users to store Web pages and mark them with personalized notes. Chris Sherman, an expert on search engines who heads the consulting firm Searchwise, told Gaither that although AskJeeves had a "very small share" of the market, "a very dedicated group of people" was using it.

In 2005 the Internet conglomerate IAC/InteractiveCorp., headed by the media mogul Barry Diller, acquired Ask Jeeves Inc. for $1.85 billion, making it a featured component of IAC's newly branded venture IAC Search & Media. In early 2006 AskJeeves changed its name to Ask.com. "We were dealing with a 10-year-old brand with Jeeves that was closely identified with the dot-com boom," Lanzone told Justin Ewers. "The brand had baggage in terms of being known for having a poor product in the late '90s [and] as a pure Q&A site," he said, characterizing the rechristening as "a way to take the shackles off." Soon afterward, following the departure of Steve Berkowitz, the CEO of IAC Search & Media, Lanzone was promoted to chief executive of Ask.com. Among his first actions, he oversaw a redesign of Ask.com's home page; upon opening Ask.com, the viewer would now see, prominently displayed, a so-called palette of search tools. "We have some great tools, and we wanted to move them more up-front for the user," Lanzone told Gord Hotchkiss for *MediaPost Publications* (May 18, 2006, on-line). "We didn't want to hide them with tabs, which no one clicks on. With the palette, it's right there, waiting for them." Ask.com also introduced a feature called "zoom," which enables users to expand or narrow their searches and, as the Ask.com site explains, offers "related names"—"a list of names that are conceptually tied to topic options within the 'Narrow Your Search' and 'Expand Your Search' lists."

Lanzone has said that he wants Ask.com to grow gradually. "We don't want to climb Everest right now," he told Hotchkiss. "We're not planning on knocking out Google. Our goal is to take our 20 million users, who are currently using us twice a month, and bump that up to four times a month. That doubles our market share." During an interview with the blogwriter John Battelle for battellemedia.com, Lanzone said, "Remember that a 1 point gain in market share for Ask (from 6% to 7% share) is a 15% increase in share of queries. The way our business works, that's also likely a 15% increase in share of revenue. So just one point of share has an incredible impact on our business growth, and I think people forget that because they're comparing us to Google, rather than to our own growth curve." "It's not a zero-sum game," he added. He told Kate Bulkley, "[Search] is still the number one need, it's the doorway. We are going to build great doorways, not destinations. The product roadmap for us is to be able to find stuff that you're looking for faster, whether it's content, commerce or community. Our first job is to become a preferred primary search engine."

In the fall of 2006, Ask.com began to embrace some of IAC's 60 e-commerce assets, among them Ticketmaster and evite.com, an on-line invitation service (for parties and other events). In December 2006 Ask.com introduced AskCity, which offers maps and information on merchants, restaurants, and entertainment listings in several dozen localities. "There's no one single feature that catapults [AskCity] to the top, but instead the totality of features," Greg Sterling, an analyst for Sterling Market Intelligence, told Jefferson Graham for *USA Today* (December 4, 2006). "It takes local search to another level because it packages data and features together in a very user-friendly way."

In 2006 and 2007 Lanzone was a featured speaker at the Search Engine Strategies Conference and Expo, held in Milan, Italy. His wife, Shannon, a fellow graduate of the Emory University School of Law, worked as a district attorney before becoming a homemaker. The couple live in Alamo, in the San Francisco Bay Area, with their son, Asher, and two daughters, Devin and Reese.

—D.J.K.

Suggested Reading: *Economist* p74 June 17, 2006; *Goizueta Magazine* (on-line) Spring 2000; John Battelle's Searchblog (on-line) Apr. 18, 2006; Junipero Serra High School *Traditions* (on-line) Summer 2006; (London) *Financial Times* p8 Aug. 1, 2006; (London) *Guardian* Technology p5 Oct. 5, 2006; *MediaPost Publications* (on-line) May 18, 2006; *New York Times* C p1+ Dec. 4, 2006; News.com May 2, 2006; *sfgate.com* July 19, 2004; *U.S. News & World Report* Nov. 12, 2006; *USA Today* B p3 Oct. 4, 2006

Courtesy of Hubert Laws

Laws, Hubert Jr.

Nov. 10, 1939– Flutist

Address: c/o Scepterstein Records, 444 S. Flower St., Suite 1800, Los Angeles, CA 90071

"It is like speaking two languages, really—knowing two cultures. I don't want to belabor the point, but it just doesn't make much of a difference to me, playing classical music or jazz," the internationally renowned and multifaceted jazz flutist Hubert Laws Jr. told Bob Karlovits for the *Pittsburgh Press* (January 17, 1991). Over the past 40 years, Laws has explored both forms—releasing albums of straight-ahead jazz or of jazz interpretations of classical music—while also mastering pop, funk, and rhythm and blues. Described by Jon Pareles, writing for the *New York Times* (August 3, 1989), as "the leading jazz flutist of his generation" and as having "technique to spare," Laws has enjoyed popular as well as critical success: for 10 years in a row he was voted the best living American jazz flutist by the readers of *Down Beat* magazine. Upon graduating from the esteemed Juilliard School of Music, Laws recorded as a solo artist before serving as a session musician for legends as varied as Miles

Davis, Herbie Hancock, Paul McCartney, Aretha Franklin, Roberta Flack, and Leonard Bernstein, among many others. In addition, Laws, who has been nominated for Grammy Awards on three occasions, has appeared with the New York Philharmonic under Zubin Mehta; the symphony orchestras of Los Angeles, Dallas, Chicago, Cleveland, Amsterdam, Japan, Detroit; and the Stanford String Quartet. With a discography comprising 20 albums, Laws has also lent his musical talents to a variety of other projects, which include music for the bittersweet film comedy *California Suite* and scores for several other films, among them *The Wiz* and *The Color Purple.* "Most of Laws' writing has been in the jazz vernacular with strong emphasis on beautiful melodic structure, though always with the goal of emotional interaction and communication with the listener," Lauren McMinn wrote for the *Juilliard Journal* (February 2004, on-line). "For Laws, the flute is his 'voice,' and when playing with others he listens closely to 'what the other instruments have to say.'"

The second of eight children, Hubert Laws Jr. was born in the Studewood section of Houston, Texas, on November 10, 1939, into a Baptist family. His musical education came from a variety of sources, including a honky-tonk saloon, Miss Mary's Place, directly across the street from his home. At Miss Mary's, which hosted a diverse mix of live musical acts, a very young Laws often watched his grandfather perform on harmonica and his mother, Miola, play gospel music on the piano. Laws himself took up the piano when he was six years old. In elementary school he learned to play the mellophone, clarinet, and alto saxophone, and he performed with rhythm-and-blues bands at neighborhood dances in his early teens. When he entered Phillis Wheatley High School, in the early 1950s, he was exposed to jazz through the influence of his band director, Sammy Harris. Listening to the likes of Gil Evans, John Coltrane, and Miles Davis, the young musician developed an affinity for the improvisation allowed jazz musicians. Then, during his senior year, after learning that his high-school band needed a flute player, Laws gave up the other instruments and volunteered to become the band's regular flutist. He recalled to Rick Nowlin for the *Pittsburgh Post-Gazette* (December 6, 2000), "I was called to play a flute solo during the *William Tell Overture.* There's a slow movement that starts out called 'Dawn,' with [what sounded like] bird calls and stuff like that. It was a horrible rendition, and I'm glad it wasn't recorded." Laws took private flute lessons from a teacher named Clement Barone, who contributed to his understanding of classical music. He built up experience and confidence through an early solo performance with the Houston Youth Symphony and regular gigs with a Houston-area jazz group known by names including the Swingsters, the Modern Jazz Sextet, the Night Hawks, and the Crusaders.

After high school Hubert enrolled at Texas Southern University, in Houston, where he studied music for two years before going with the Crusaders—as they were known then—to Los Angeles, California, where they tried to broaden their audience. Between gigs, Laws took classes at the Los Angeles State College of Applied Arts and Sciences. He then auditioned for a chance to attend the Curtis School of Music, in Philadelphia, Pennsylvania, but was rejected. Undaunted, he next auditioned for the world-renowned Juilliard School of Music, in New York City, and was accepted there in 1960. While a scholarship covered his tuition, he met his other expenses via music performances. Speaking to a reporter for *Houston Newspages* (May 14, 1990), as quoted on his Web site, Laws recalled that in the fall of 1960, he was "down to my last fifty bucks and wondering what to do" when he received an offer to play at Sugar Ray's Lounge, in the Harlem section of the city. He added, "I haven't looked back since." Laws studied music every day, under the guidance of Julius Baker, one of the foremost American orchestral flute players of his time, then spent his nights gigging around the city. As his musical ability grew, so did his popularity, and before long he was playing with the likes of the acclaimed jazz percussionist Mongo Santamaria; the Lloyd Price Big Band; John Lewis of the Modern Jazz Quartet; and the Berkshire Festival Orchestra at Tanglewood, Massachusetts, the summer home of the Boston Symphony Orchestra.

Upon graduating from Juilliard, in 1964, with a bachelor of music degree, Laws began recording as a bandleader for Atlantic records, releasing the albums *The Laws of Jazz* (1964), *Flute By-Laws* (1965), and *Laws' Cause* (1969). *The Laws of Jazz,* which featured the future Grammy Award–winner Chick Corea, was well-received for its straight-ahead jazz tunes, with highlights that included "Miss Thing," "Bessie's Blues," and "Bimbe Blue." Each album was marked by a strong Latin sound, due in part to the influence on Laws of Santamaria's Afro-Cuban rhythms. During those years Laws also developed a reputation as a ubiquitous session player, recording with Santamaria, Clark Terry, Benny Golson, Jim Hall, and fellow flutist James Moody. In addition, he was a frequent guest performer on albums by artists including the husband/wife rhythm-and-blues duo Ashford and Simpson, the jazz trumpeter Chet Baker, and the multifaceted guitarist George Benson. On the subject of such diverse collaborations, Laws explained to the writer for *Houston Newspages,* "There are only a few openings nationwide with the symphony orchestras. You have to be practical." Despite the scarcity of such openings, in 1968 Laws became a member of the Metropolitan Opera orchestra, where he would remain officially until 1973. He kept up his guest work during that period, as heard on the title track of Quincy Jones's highly acclaimed, star-studded 1969 album *Walking in Space.* Laws later collaborated with the impresario on *Body Heat* (1974), a soul record that included work by artists as varied as Herbie Hancock and Wah Wah Watson. Jones opened doors for Laws to work with still other artists, and the flutist found himself teaming with Aretha Franklin, Roberta Flack, Bob James, Paul Simon, and Carly Simon. "I was first call on a lot of that, especially with Quincy," Laws recounted to Rick Nowlin, adding, "Anytime he had something, he called me."

During the 1970s Laws reached his full artistic maturity, releasing a handful of innovative jazz albums under Creed Taylor's CTI label while working with the New York Philharmonic from 1971 to 1974. Since his launch of CTI, a subsidiary of A&M Records, in 1968, Taylor had been looking for a standout title in the then-new jazz-fusion genre, which the label would soon come to typify. In 1970 he realized that goal with the release of Laws's *Crying Song*. For that record Taylor had originally booked the noted jazz saxophonist Stanley Turrentine, who became unavailable at the last minute; Taylor then contacted Laws. *Crying Song* featured Laws's cover of the Beatles' "Let It Be," recorded before the Beatles' version was even released on what would be the group's 12th and final studio album. (Taylor had won the admiration of Paul McCartney, who sent the producer a demo of the soon-to-be-classic song.) *Crying Song* garnered praise for Laws's flute work, which helped initiate an entirely new sound for the instrument in the decade to come. A reviewer for *Dusty Groove America* (on-line) noted that the album was "a landmark record" and "a sublime exploration of sound and space—very different than Laws' 60s Latin sides for Atlantic, and handled in a baroque mode that has his flute drifting over a mixture of organ, piano, and rhythms augmented with strings—easy and jazzy in the same moment." Later that year Laws released his second CTI effort, *Afro-Classic*, which was also considered groundbreaking for its melding of jazz, classical, and pop-music forms. The album included covers of James Taylor's hit "Fire and Rain," two pieces by Bach, "Theme from Love Story," by Francis Lai, and a Mozart flute sonata. Thom Jurek wrote for the All Music Guide Web site, "It was *Afro-Classic* that established a new role for the flute in contemporary jazz."

For Laws *Crying Song* paved the way for more musical exploration, and in 1971 he released *Rite of Spring*, on which he recorded his interpretations of four classical-music pieces. In addition to his rendition of Stravinsky's masterpiece on the title cut, the album included takes on Debussy's "Syrinx," Fauré's "Pavane," and two movements of Bach's Brandenburg Concerto no. 3. With that admixture of classical music and jazz, Laws further expanded the boundaries of the latter genre. Reviewing the album upon its re-release in 2002, Jules Epstein noted for *Jazzmatazz* (February 2002, on-line), "*Rite of Spring* is a compelling event even thirty years after its original issue. It is not a pop recapitulation of classical music, but a portrayal of classical music that hews to the original and then

remakes it without losing the composer's intent/essence." Thom Jurek, writing for the All Music Guide, disagreed, calling most of the recording "stiff, rigid, oddly intoned, and lackluster" and adding that the album was "a brave but ultimately failed experiment." Most critics, however, have ranked the album as an important work in the annals of jazz history. "The jazz brings a certain freedom to the classical," Laws explained to Mark Kanny for the *Pittsburgh Post-Gazette* (January 19, 1991). "The composer may have had definite ideas in mind, but, as a composer myself, I realize that maybe he could be liberal about how his pieces should be played. Many times composers realize that what's been written can be enhanced by the players."

While recording albums under the CTI label, Laws continued doing session work and making records under different labels, going back to Atlantic to record *Wild Flower* in 1972. Craig Jolley, writing for *All About Jazz* (on-line), called that album "the best flute record I know of" and applauded its intricate ensemble work. Laws released four more records for CTI over the course of the decade: the flute-heavy *Morning Star* (1972); the live album *At Carnegie Hall* (1973); the more commercial *Chicago Theme* (1975); and most notably, *In the Beginning* (1974). The last-named record is widely considered to be Laws's masterpiece, integrating 1970s-style funk elements into his classically oriented jazz and including work by the guitarist Gene Bertoncini, the bassist Ron Carter, the drummer Steve Gadd, three string performers, and Laws's brother Ronnie on tenor saxophone. Scott Yanow declared for the All Music Guide that the recording is "one of the most rewarding of Hubert Laws' career."

After CTI went bankrupt, in 1978, Laws moved to Columbia Records to record four albums in the latter half of the 1970s—including *Romeo and Juliet* (1976); *Land of Passion* (1979), an R&B-inflected album that, like other, similar records he released around that time, was generally thought to be unsuccessful; and the better-received soundtrack to the film comedy *How to Beat the High Cost of Living* (1980). In that period he also contributed to soundtracks for the films *California Suite* and *The Wiz*. In 1980 Laws released the aptly titled *Family*, which featured the work of his brothers and sisters (who have established themselves in the music world as well), including his brother Ronnie on saxophone and his siblings Johnnie, Eloise, and Debra on vocals. The versatile flutist gained residency at the Atlantic Center for the Arts, based in New Smyrna Beach, Florida, in 1983, the same year he performed with the Los Angeles Chamber Orchestra for the Montreux Festival in Switzerland.

While playing live in a number of venues, including the Playboy Jazz Festival in Los Angeles and the Cultural Center of the Philippines in Manila, Laws recorded only one more album in the 1980s (*Make It Last*, in 1983). While his absence from the studio was in part a response to the critical lambasting he had received for several of his records in the preceding years, Laws was also beginning to raise a family, and he decided to put music on hold for an indefinite period. Except for work on the soundtracks of *The Color Purple* (1985), which was produced by Quincy Jones, and the made-for-television film *Spot Marks the X* (1986), Laws stayed out of the musical limelight for about five years. As he explained to Kanny, "I've had a career, but I've never experienced anything like having children. Although it's a lot of work, a lot of dedication, it is really the most important thing. Life is about life, and things about things. Music is a thing, although it's an excellent gift to have and to appreciate."

With the dawn of a new decade, the flutist reappeared on the music scene, with the release of *My Time Will Come* (1990), on the Music Masters label. In addition to standout solo performances by Laws himself, the album featured remarkable work by the pianist John Beasley. Critics regarded the record as a return to form for Laws. The following year he joined the opera singers Kathleen Battle and Jessye Norman as a guest player on the recording *Spirituals in Concert*. Then, in 1994, he released his second effort under the Music Masters label, *Storm Then the Calm*, which featured two interpretations of Kurt Weill and Ira Gershwin's "My Ship." After touring extensively for much of the 1990s, Laws recorded a tribute album to the jazz pianist and popular-music legend Nat King Cole, entitled *Hubert Laws Remembers the Unforgettable Nat King Cole*, (1998), under RKO Records. Receiving much critical acclaim at the time of its release, it featured renditions of such Cole classics as "Tenderly," "Unforgettable," and "Mona Lisa." Laws also released a solo album, *I Love My Daddy*, in 1998 under Columbia.

In 2000 Hubert released an eclectic greatest-hits album, *The Best of Hubert Laws*, made up of recordings from 1970 to 1975 and featuring adventurous interpretations of John Coltrane's "Moment's Notice," Maria Muldaur's "Midnight at the Oasis," and Stravinsky's *Rite of Spring*. Laws returned to his Latin roots in the fall of 2002 with *Baila Cinderella*, released under his own Scepterstein label. An homage of sorts to one of his early collaborators, Mongo Santamaria, the album was a "throw back to those years when Laws was heavy into the Latin sway," as noted by Nelson Rodriguez for *Latin Beat* (August 1, 2002). He next collaborated with musicians who included the pianist Dave Budway, the guitarist Evan Marks, the bassist John Leftwich, and the drummer Ralph Penland for *Moondance* (2004), which recalled the smooth soul-jazz he had recorded with CTI in the 1970s. The record's standout songs included a version of a Van Morrison tune (the title track), the piccolo-driven "Summer of '75," and the dreamy "Bloodshot"; in addition, Herbie Hancock played acoustic piano on the midtempo number "Nighttime Daydream." John Kelman, in a review for *All About*

Jazz (on-line), called the record "a step above most smooth jazz recordings" despite being "a little too conservative for a capable artist who has always seemed to represent more about potential and less about realization." In 2005 Laws honored Bach in a tribute album.

Although the flutist has been criticized for hewing to commercial trends for much of the latter half of his career, his legacy of innovation remains. Thom Jurek, acknowledging that Herbie Mann "may have been the first" to gain attention as a jazz flutist, explained, "Laws explored jazz and all the sound worlds that informed it—especially in the electric domain—with the kind of grace and innovative vision that made him a mainstay." In 2007 the Mosaic Contemporary label re-released Laws's *Afro-Classic*.

A self-described health freak, Laws stays in shape by playing tennis. He lives with his wife in Los Angeles.

—C.C.

Suggested Reading: *All About Jazz* (on-line); All Music Guide Web site; Hubert Laws Web site; *Juilliard Journal* Feb. 2004; *New York Times* C p13 Aug. 3, 1989; *Pittsburgh Post-Gazette* C p2 Dec. 6, 2000; *Pittsburgh Press* Music Jan. 17, 1991; Berendt, Joachim. *The Jazz Book: From Ragtime to Fusion and Beyond*, 1992

Selected Recordings: *The Laws of Jazz*, 1964; *Flute By-Laws*, 1965; *Laws' Cause*, 1969; *Crying Song*, 1970; *Afro Classic*, 1970; *Rite of Spring*, 1971; *Wild Flower*, 1972; *Morning Star*, 1972; *At Carnegie Hall*, 1973; *In the Beginning*, 1974; *Chicago Theme*, 1975; *Romeo and Juliet*, 1976; *The San Francisco Concert* (live), 1977; *Say It With Silence*, 1978; *Land of Passion*, 1979; *Family*, 1980; *Make It Last*, 1983; *My Time Will Come*, 1990; *Storm Then the Calm*, 1994; *Hubert Laws Remembers the Unforgettable Nat King Cole*, 1998; *I Love My Daddy*, 1998; *The Best of Hubert Laws*, 2000; *Baila Cinderella*, 2002; *Moondance*, 2004; *Hubert Laws: Plays Bach*, 2005; *Afro Classic* (re-release), 2007; film scores—*California Suite*, 1978; *How to Beat the High Cost of Living*, 1980

Legend, John

Dec. 28, 1978– Singer; songwriter; pianist

Address: c/o Columbia Records, Sony BMG Entertainment, 550 Madison Ave., New York, NY 10022

At a time when R&B and hip-hop songs are dominated by the themes of money and sexual conquest, John Legend stands out as a singer-songwriter whose music is focused more on love and commit-

John Legend

Scott Gries/Getty Images

ment than on lust and one-night stands, characterized more by melody than by thumping beat. "It's frustrating to realize that in so much R&B these days, the songwriting just doesn't measure up," Legend told Jim Farber for the *Ventura County (California) Star* (November 16, 2006). "I can't listen to it." As sales of his records suggest, however, plenty of people are able—and willing—to listen to Legend. His 2004 debut album, *Get Lifted*, sold close to three million copies worldwide and garnered three Grammy Awards, and his 2006 follow-up, *Once Again*, was also wildly acclaimed. On both records Legend eschewed dominating trends in contemporary music, instead pursuing his own brand of piano-driven, emotion-laden songs that otherwise defied easy categorization. "I think the most important thing is that I'm making music that the people enjoy," Legend told Farai Chideya for the National Public Radio program *News & Notes* (November 20, 2006). Alicia Keys, who collaborated with Legend early in his career, attributed his success to his willingness to be different from—and perhaps more emotionally honest than—many of his peers. In an interview published in the *Manila Times* (February 3, 2006), Keys, herself a nine-time Grammy Award–winner, described her former touring mate: "He's special. . . . There's nothing more special than to see an artist playing his own music. I think a lot of people are seeking it out—the truth of it."

The singer was born John Stephens on December 28, 1978 in Springfield, Ohio, the son of Ronald Stephens, a factory worker, and Phyllis Stephens, a seamstress. The second-oldest of four children, Legend grew up with his sister and two brothers in a working-class neighborhood. His entire family was involved in the local Pentecostal church—his grandfather was the minister, his grandmother the organist, his mother the choir director, and his father a drummer for the band—and gospel became an important early influence on Legend. After begging to begin piano lessons at age four, Legend quickly joined his family on the church stage, singing in the choir at age six and writing arrangements for the 30-member adult group when he was only 11. "I don't know if you believe in destiny, but John seemed favored from the beginning . . . ," Legend's father told John Soeder for Newhouse News Service (July 26, 2005). "He always put his whole heart into singing." When he was 11 Legend also began entertaining at weddings, earning up to $100 at each ceremony for performing songs such as Stevie Wonder's "Ribbon in the Sky."

In 1989 Legend's parents divorced; they would reunite 12 years later. Legend has often credited their relationship with sparking his interest in the complexities of love and commitment, which have become the primary focus of his work. Home-schooled off and on by his mother through junior high school, Legend had skipped two grades by the time he entered Springfield North High School. Only 12 years old when he entered his freshman year, he soon earned the nickname "Doogie," as in Doogie Howser, M.D., the title character of a TV sitcom about a boy physician. "My saving grace was that I could sing," Legend told Margeaux Watson for *Entertainment Weekly* (November 10, 2006). "I killed [at] all the talent shows, but I was still a nerd." But his combination of brains and talent paid off; when Legend graduated, at 16, he was not only his class's salutatorian but also prom king and student-body president.

Legend turned down both Harvard and Georgetown Universities to attend the University of Pennsylvania (Penn) in Philadelphia, where he performed for one year with the school's nationally acclaimed a capella group Counterparts. Majoring in English with an emphasis on African-American literature, Legend spent 20 hours per week in a work-study job to help pay his tuition. On Sundays he drove to Scranton, where he worked in a musical capacity at the Bethel African Methodist Episcopalian Church, putting his salary from the church toward his schooling as well. From 1995 (his freshman year at Penn) to 2004, Legend served variously as the church's pianist, its choir director, and, ultimately, the head of its music department, leaving his post only upon the release of his first album. Meanwhile, in 1998, Legend had met the singer Lauryn Hill through a mutual friend. At the friend's urging, Legend played the piano in a private performance for Hill, who then asked him to accompany her on "Everything Is Everything," one of the hit singles from her mulitple-Grammy-Award–winning album *The Miseducation of Lauryn Hill*. Legend subsequently auditioned for a place in Hill's band but was rejected. After graduating magna cum laude from the University of Pennsylvania, in 1999, at the age of 20, Legend moved to New York City, where he was an associate consultant with the prestigious Boston Consulting Group for three years.

It was in New York that Legend—still John Stephens at the time—got his big break, thanks to an up-and-coming producer and rapper named Kanye West. Devon Harris, West's cousin and Legend's former Penn classmate, sensing that both West and Legend were bound for stardom, pushed for the two to meet. After much prodding, West agreed to attend one of Legend's solo nightclub shows and, impressed by what he saw, entered into what is often described in the press as a mentor-protégé relationship with Legend. Legend—the supposed protégé—has taken issue with that description. "I guess the media needed a way to explain who I was," he told Tamara Conniff for Billboard Magazine (August 26, 2006). "It's funny, though, because Kanye and I started at the same time. It was never a student and teacher relationship. We were always collaborators." Whatever the terminology used to describe the pair, the partnership clearly paid off for Legend. Over the next few years, Legend was featured as both a vocalist and a pianist on a number of hip-hop and R&B hits, including tracks by Jay-Z, Janet Jackson, the Black Eyed Peas, Talib Kweli, and Keys, many of which were produced by West. Legend also contributed significantly to West's 2004 smash hit, College Dropout. "I didn't look at it as starting as a session musician and then doing my own thing," Legend told James Wigney for the Townsville (Australia) Bulletin (November 3, 2006). "I was always doing my own thing—I just wasn't famous for it yet."

In the midst of his rising visibility, Legend acquired his new name. In 2002 the Chicago, Illinois–based poet John ("J") Ivey began calling the singer "Legend" because of his stylistic similarities with legendary soul artists, such as Marvin Gaye and Stevie Wonder. The nickname quickly caught on, and Legend adopted it permanently in the hope that it would serve as a self-fulfilling prophecy. "The nickname kind of grew, and it got to the point where more people were knowing me by that name than by my own name," he recalled to Bill Harris for the Toronto Sun (October 24, 2006). "And then I'm deciding, do I actually want to take this on as a stage name? It's kind of presumptuous and I know people are going to hate on me if I do that. But eventually I said, you know what? It's going to make a bit of a statement. It announces its arrival beforehand. And then I'm going to have to live up to it."

In 2004 Legend became the first artist signed to West's production company, KonMan Entertainment, and the first artist to release an album on West's Columbia-distributed label, GOOD (Get Out Our Dreams) Records, distributed by Columbia. With West serving as executive producer, Legend's 2004 debut, Get Lifted—released on December 28, his 26th birthday—landed at the number-one spot on the first Billboard R&B album chart of 2005, selling more than 115,000 copies in its first week

alone. It entered the Billboard Top 200 chart at number seven and jumped to number four the following week. The record was a critical as well as a popular success, considered a standout achievement in a genre that had come to be defined by themes of obtaining wealth and sex. "With its old-school emphasis on live instrumentation, lushly crafted melodies and lyrics that were more about romance than sexual conquests, Get Lifted seemed like a breath of fresh air on an R&B scene dominated by stale synthesized sounds and raunchy, pandering seductions," Jim DeRogatis wrote for the Chicago Sun-Times (November 5, 2006). In the New York Times, Kelefa Sanneh described Legend as "a lovely crooner" and his songs as "strikingly handsome" (January 3, 2005). Even without significant radio play, the album sold 1.8 million copies in the U.S., and another one million copies overseas. The record was certified gold and platinum (indicating sales of half a million and a million, respectively) on February 10, 2005, less than three months after its release.

The album's standout track, a ballad titled "Ordinary People," featured only Legend's voice and minimal piano accompaniment. Directly inspired by his parents' breakup and reunion, the song describes the confusion that comes with falling deeply in love and the necessity of beginning a relationship slowly to make it last. On the strength of "Ordinary People," Legend was nominated for eight Grammy Awards, including those for song of the year, best new artist, best R&B song, best R&B album, and best male R&B vocal performance. Only two other artists received as many nominations that year; one of them was West, for his second album, Late Registration—which featured Legend on the Grammy-nominated track "They Say." Legend took home three Grammys, for best new artist, best R&B album, and best R&B male vocal performance. In addition, Get Lifted earned Legend four Vibe Award nominations, two Brit Award nominations, and two Soul Train Awards.

Legend released his second album, Once Again, on October 24, 2006. The record's style was as difficult to categorize as its predecessor's, incorporating the influences of artists as varied as the hip-hop duo Outkast, the Beatles, the rock musician Jeff Buckley, and the "indie" star Sufjan Stevens. "I refuse to be pigeonholed in terms of what music I can and can't play," Legend told Farber. "All music is available to me. My only responsibility is to do it right." The album debuted at number three on the Billboard charts and garnered almost unanimously positive reviews, with critics pointing to Legend's development as an artist. "Once Again . . . paints a more complete portrait of Legend than did its predecessor, and it rides a more relaxed, vintage-feeling vibe," Adam Graham wrote for the Detroit News (November 8, 2006). Farber also noted Legend's evolution: "If his first album stood out by defying R&B clichés, this time he broadened the palette to sometimes push beyond that genre entirely." In the Washington Post (October 24, 2006),

J. Freedom du Lac lauded Legend for his growing immunity to contemporary trends, writing that *Once Again* "is among the genre's most audacious artistic statements of 2006."

That audacity is just what Legend had in mind, he told Farber. "Millions of people hate what's on the radio right now," he said. "I also hate what's on the radio right now. So I've put my bet on being different." But not all critics viewed Legend as a breath of fresh air. Writing for *Daily Variety* (November 20, 2006), Jeff Miller described Legend's oeuvre as a "brand of half-soulful, half-schticky R&B." And in an otherwise favorable review of one of Legend's live shows, Jim Harrington, writing for *Inside Bay Area* (November 21, 2006), expressed the opinion that Legend has "the looks, the moves, and the voice. . . . What he doesn't have, at least as of yet, are many memorable songs."

Legend currently lives in New York. In 2005 he made his acting debut in the film *Loverboy*, directed by Kevin Bacon. He also appeared as himself in the 2005 movie *Dave Chappelle's Block Party*, alongside his former and current collaborators Hill, Kweli, and West. Musically, he is constantly widening his scope, contributing to new albums by artists as diverse as Tony Bennett and Jay-Z. Still, Legend remains faithful to his roots in soul—maintaining, for example, his admiration for the arguable king of soul, Stevie Wonder, with whom he has appeared onstage multiple times. In 2005 Legend covered Wonder's song "Don't You Worry 'Bout a Thing" for the film *Hitch*, starring Will Smith, and he played Wonder himself on an episode of the NBC drama *American Dreams*. But Legend dismisses comparisons between him and Wonder or soul greats of the past, insisting that he has not yet lived up to his name. "It's an honor to hear those kinds of comparisons, and I'm absolutely flattered, but I don't let it go to my head too much," Legend told DeRogatis. "I know that my career can't be compared to Stevie's anytime soon. . . . I have a lot of dues to pay before I can really be compared to Stevie or Marvin."

—C.S.

Suggested Reading: *Jet* p60+ Nov. 6, 2006; National Public Radio's *News & Notes* (on-line) Nov. 20, 2006; *People* p109 Nov. 6, 2006; *Washington Post* C p1 Feb. 9, 2006

Selected Recordings: *Get Lifted*, 2004; *Once Again*, 2006

Lewis, Ray

May 15, 1975– Football player

Address: The Ray Lewis Foundation, P.O. Box 342, Owings Mills, MD 21117

Ray Lewis, now in his 12th season as a linebacker for the Baltimore Ravens, is one of the most dominating defensive players in the National Football League (NFL), known for his ferocious tackling, seemingly limitless energy, superior speed, and unfailing work ethic. Over the past decade Lewis has led a Ravens defensive unit that perennially ranks as one of the best in the league and that has set several single-season records. Along the way Lewis has won numerous accolades, among them the NFL Defensive Player of the Year Award for the 2000 and 2004 seasons and, in 2001, the Super Bowl XXXV Most Valuable Player (MVP) Award, presented after he led the Ravens to their first championship. Lewis has led the NFL in tackles during four seasons and has made eight Pro Bowl appearances, including play in five consecutive games (1997–2001). His coaches have praised his tenacity, through which he inspires his teammates. "The players who've left [Baltimore] aren't as successful as they were here," the Ravens' owner, Steve Bisciotti, told Peter King for *Sports Illustrated* (September 1, 2003). "I think Ray gets the people around him to play 30 percent better than they are." Lewis's former teammate Corey Fuller agreed, telling King, "Ray plays so hard that all these play-

Brian Bahr/Getty Images

ers on defense don't want to let him down." Once widely considered too small to make a mark in professional football, Lewis has since been described as one of the toughest players in the NFL and has often played while injured. As reported by Paul Attner for the *Sporting News* (October 27, 2003), the former New Orleans Saints general manager

Randy Mueller believes that Lewis is unique in today's NFL and is comparable only to past NFL legends. "There have been tough guys who have played before, but they haven't been the athlete he is or produced like he has," Mueller declared. "He wants to break someone in half each time he hits them; he has no fear for his body. He has the explosion of [Ray] Nitschke and the instincts of [Dick] Butkus but the speed and natural talents that separate him from everyone else. They are on top, and he is right there with them. It's hard to conceive anyone else is tougher." Lewis's exemplary career and Hall-of-Fame-worthy statistics reflect his desire to be the best football player in the history of the NFL. "I already believe that I am the best linebacker in the game," Lewis told Mike Preston for the *Baltimore Sun* (September 8, 2005). "Now, I have to show one more thing—that I am the most dominating, influential person in the game and the best football player to ever put on a pair of cleats."

Lewis, who spends as much time preparing for games as his coaches do, enjoys a level of autonomy with the Ravens that is rare in the NFL. He is allowed to change up to 10 plays per game before the ball is snapped, as he anticipates particular offensive formations that the coaching staff might not have predicted. "He is as close to a true defensive quarterback as anyone I've ever coached," the former Ravens defensive coordinator Mike Nolan remarked to Jamison Hensley for the *Baltimore Sun* (October 3, 2004). Nolan told Brian Costello for the *New York Post* (September 12, 2004), "I have no reservations about saying he's the best defensive player ever to play the game."

Ray Anthony Lewis Jr. was born on May 15, 1975 in Bartow, Florida, midway between Orlando and Tampa. His mother was in her teens when Lewis was born, and his father left the family before Lewis had developed any memory of him. (Lewis and his father reunited briefly while Lewis was in college but quickly fell out of contact again.) Growing up, Lewis helped his mother, who remained single and often had to work up to three jobs to support her family, by cooking dinner and putting his four younger siblings to bed. Lewis's grandfather, with whom he occasionally lived, was an early mentor. "My grandfather was my father," Lewis told Randall Mell for the Fort Lauderdale, Florida, *Sun-Sentinel* (January 22, 1996). "He showed me the love of a father. . . . My grandfather's the biggest reason I'm not on a corner selling drugs or robbing banks or doing crazy things." Lewis found other role models in his neighborhood, many of them older boys. One of them, Raymond King, four years Lewis's senior and also fatherless, introduced him to weightlifting and otherwise kept him out of trouble after school.

Lewis attended Kathleen Senior High School, in Lakeland, Florida, where he excelled at both wrestling and football. He eclipsed nearly every wrestling record at the school and became a state champion in his senior year. He showed even more promise as a football player. Starring on both offense and defense, Lewis played linebacker and tailback as well as contributing on special teams as a part-time returner of kick-offs and punts. In one game he made an 85-yard punt return for a game-winning touchdown, and he made an 81-yard rush for a touchdown in another. His high-school coach, Ernest Joe, described Lewis as having been "quick as a hiccup," according to Susan Miller Degnan, writing for the *Miami Herald* (May 8, 2006). "He went sideline to sideline in an instant. Ray had an air about him that said, 'I'm the best, and I'm going to show you why.'" Although he showed great potential as an athlete, most recruiters in the National Collegiate Athletic Association (NCAA) lost interest in him after he failed four times to reach a 700 on the Scholastic Aptitude Test—the minimum for eligibility to play on an NCAA team. Only two local universities, Florida State and the University of Miami, maintained an interest in Lewis. Once he achieved a higher score on the test, each school offered him a scholarship. He chose the University of Miami.

That year, 1993, Lewis joined the school's football team, the Hurricanes, which was widely regarded as one of the best NCAA Division I teams in the country—a perennial contender for the national championship. Lewis, at six feet one inch tall and just over 200 pounds, was undersized for a collegiate linebacker, particularly at Miami, which in recent years had sent three players at that position—Jesse Armstead, Michael Barrow, and Darrin Smith—to the NFL. Midway through his freshman year, Lewis was elevated to a starting position and was overwhelmed at first by the responsibility. "He was wild-eyed, no hair on his head, a skinny little-old thing; barely 205 pounds," the Hurricanes' All-American defensive lineman Warren Sapp recalled to Rick Stroud for the *St. Petersburg Times* (December 29, 2001). "He stepped into the huddle, and [the coaches] gave him the call. And he's like, 'Uh, uh, uh.' I had to stop him. I said, 'Wait, wait, wait! Stop this. You are the middle backer. This is your huddle. Take control, and let's roll.' It's the last time I ever had to say something like that." Sapp's swift intervention brought about a turning point for Lewis, who in his first game as a starter recorded 17 tackles, leading the team in that category. He came to embrace his role as the emotional leader of a defense known as much for their persistent "trash talk" as they were for their aggressive play. Lewis rarely failed to back up his talk with excellent performances; at the same time he was so impulsive that coaches prohibited him from attending most media events, because of what he might say.

In his sophomore year Lewis made 152 tackles, 92 of them unassisted, leading a defense rated at the end of the season as the best overall in college football. The Hurricanes advanced to the national championship game, which they lost to Nebraska in the Orange Bowl by a score of 24–17. For his performance during the 1994 season, Lewis was named by the Associated Press as a third-team All-American.

Heading into the 1995 season, Lewis was included on almost every preseason All-American list and was chosen as the Big East Conference's preseason Defensive Player of the Year. He also emerged as a leading contender for the Butkus Award, presented annually to college football's best linebacker. With many defensive standouts from the 1994 team having left, Lewis was the undisputed leader of a young and inexperienced defense, and many critics predicted failure. But Lewis had his finest season up to that time, recording 160 tackles. His 95 unassisted tackles in the 1995 season were a Miami record. He was named a first-team All-American and was voted the Big East's Defensive Player of the Year. Lewis was the runner-up for the Butkus Award, which went to Kevin Hardy of the University of Illinois. (Lewis was the only junior in consideration for the honor.)

Despite the success that Lewis found on the football field at the University of Miami, off-field incidents began to weigh on the young star. Several of his friends, including Raymond King and Lewis's college roommate, Marlin Barnes, were murdered while Lewis was at Miami. Lewis had his own legal trouble: he was twice accused of assault, although he was never formally charged. During the 1995 season Lewis also became a father for the first time. Tatyana McCall, Lewis's girlfriend and the mother of Ray Lewis III, was a classmate of Lewis's at Miami and an international-finance and marketing major. When she became pregnant, McCall tried to distance herself from Lewis, but he was determined to help raise his son. "I looked at myself last summer, and I said, you have a child now," Lewis explained to Randall Mell. "A lot of fathers abandon their children these days, let the mother do what they want to do. That's never going to happen with me. That's a promise I made to myself, that I would always take care of my child no matter what." Lewis and McCall later moved into an apartment together, taking classes on alternating days after the baby was born so that one of them would always be at home with their son. Lewis has said that the experience of raising his child, more than any other, helped him mature into an adult.

At the end of his junior season, Lewis declared himself eligible for the 1995 NFL draft, leaving Miami with a record of 408 career tackles. Although he was considered a strong NFL prospect, questions regarding his size and problems away from the field dampened enthusiasm about him; in the end he was selected by the Baltimore Ravens as the 26th pick in the first round. At 20 years of age, he was the youngest player ever selected in the NFL draft's first round. After signing a contract for $4 million per year, he bought his mother a house in Randallstown, Maryland, near his own new home.

Lewis's rookie season, 1996, was also the inaugural season of the Baltimore Ravens. The franchise had moved to Maryland from Cleveland, Ohio, as a result of then-owner Art Modell's growing financial disputes with that city. The organization needed players to energize its new fan base and endear the team to the city, and thus had high expectations for the rookies and other young players. The Ravens' other first-round pick that year, Jonathan Ogden, was immediately named the starting left guard, while Lewis was placed behind the 10-year veteran Pepper Johnson at the middle-linebacker position. His mobility and strength—he weighed in now at nearly 240 pounds—helped him perform well even against the larger NFL players. Surprising some sportswriters, just before the start of the 1996 season, the Ravens released Johnson and announced that Lewis was the starting middle linebacker. In his first professional start, Lewis recorded nine tackles and an interception, earning the NFL's Defensive Player of the Week honors. By the conclusion of his rookie year, Lewis had accumulated 110 tackles, which led the team, and had earned *USA Today* All-Rookie honors. Despite the efforts of Lewis, Ogden, and the star quarterback Vinny Testaverde, the Ravens finished the season with four wins and 12 losses.

Lewis was determined to make an even larger impact on the NFL during the 1997 season. "You have a choice—either you're going to be an average player in the NFL or one of the great ones," Lewis said to John Eisenberg for the *Baltimore Sun* (November 16, 1997). "Either you just play and pick up your paycheck every Monday, or you become known as a great football player. I want that." He increased his already intensive workout routine and developed a reputation for being one of the most well-prepared players in the league. "The big change for me [from 1996] is studying and focusing," Lewis said to Eisenberg. "I like to go home, sit downstairs by myself and just study film alone. You can read things when you're alone. You can just focus on the field and learn the formations. And then I see the formations on Sunday and I know what's coming. It's easy." The results of Lewis's approach were not lost on his coaches. The defensive coordinator Marvin Lewis remarked to Eisenberg, "Ray did a good job last year, but this year he has a much better understanding of the different offenses he is facing every week, and what his role is in stopping them." Marvin Lewis also told Eisenberg, "Ray is also more prepared physically. A lot of first-year players need that first off-season to develop after they get here [to the NFL] and realize how tough and physical it is. Ray was one of the guys who was here early every morning and every day during the off-season." Lewis was also becoming a leader on a team filled with young would-be stars. As the middle linebacker, he was responsible for calling defensive plays and ensuring that his teammates were in the proper positions. At the same time he led by example, and his energy and effort were contagious. His former teammate Jamie Sharper said to Jamison Hensley about Lewis's influence on the team: "The way he played, if you missed a tackle and he just looked at you, you said to yourself, 'I've got to make that next tackle.' I don't think he had to verbally say anything. His play on the field made everyone else raise their game." Lewis channeled his energy to great effect during the 1997 season, recording 183 tackles, 155 of them unassisted—both figures topping the league. Although Baltimore won only six games, Lewis was selected as a backup for his first of five consecutive Pro Bowl games.

By the beginning of the 1998 season, Lewis, as the anchor of a terrific defense, had earned a reputation as one of the best defensive players in the league. Opposing coaches were forced to alter their offensive game plans in an effort to help their players avoid Lewis. That season Lewis logged 118 tackles, 99 unassisted, though he missed two games due to injuries. As a team the Ravens did not improve, winning only six games. Brian Billick replaced Ted Marchibroda as head coach. In 1999 Billick led the team to modest improvement, winning eight games and losing eight. Lewis again led the league in tackles, with 167, 131 unassisted, and was invited to his third straight Pro Bowl game.

After the 1999 season, following a Super Bowl party on January 31, 2000, Lewis was at the scene of an altercation outside an Atlanta, Georgia, nightclub that resulted in the stabbing deaths of two men. Lewis and his entourage fled the scene in Lewis's limousine but later turned themselves in to investigators. The athlete and two of his associates were charged with murder and aggravated assault. During the 15 days he spent in an Atlanta prison awaiting trial, Lewis insisted that he was innocent and that he was a victim of circumstance—and of his own celebrity. "The truth is this is not about those two kids who are dead," Lewis said during a pre–Super Bowl interview nearly 13 months later, as reported by Jim Slater for the Agence France Presse (January 23, 2001). "It's about me being Ray Lewis. It was about 'getting' Ray Lewis." In June 2000 Lewis pleaded guilty to obstruction of justice, a misdemeanor, in order to have the more serious charges dropped. He also agreed to testify against the other two defendants, who were ultimately acquitted. There was little evidence that linked Lewis directly with the murders, and he was sentenced to 12 months' probation. The families of the two victims brought civil suits against Lewis, which he settled out of court. Some sportswriters argued for Lewis's suspension from the league. He was eventually fined $250,000, one of the largest fines ever levied by the NFL against a player, for "conduct detrimental to the game." Lewis also lost all of his endorsement contracts and became something of a pariah around the league. It was not until 2003 that he again won contracts for product endorsements.

The incident affected Lewis greatly. He became deeply religious and cut ties with many of his friends. Lewis later explained to Susan Miller Degnan for the *Miami Herald* (May 8, 2006), "The first thing that changes when you choose God is your crowd. You don't get along with your crowd. Because now I don't drink no more, I don't go to clubs no more, I don't hang out no more." Ryan McNeil, a friend of Lewis's and a former University of Mi-

ami player, told Degnan, "Since the incident [Lewis has] been a lot more reserved, more selective in what he does and who he does it with and where he goes. He learned you can't keep doing the same thing, make the same mistakes, go to the same places and hang out with the same crowd. He has done a 180—inward and outward." Lewis also began devoting much of his spare time to charity work, in particular to the Ray Lewis Foundation, whose mission is to provide personal and economic support to disadvantaged youth.

Lewis returned to the Ravens for the 2000 season with a renewed desire to win—as well as a chip on his shoulder, born of his belief that there was a universal misconception about his character. Building on the previous year's momentum, the team finished the season with a 12–4 record. While the veteran quarterbacks Tony Banks and Trent Dilfer and the rookie sensation Jamal Lewis were critical to that success, the Ravens' defense became the hallmark of the team; some writers argued that it was the greatest defensive squad ever assembled. That season the Ravens' defense broke two notable NFL records, both previously held by the 1985 Chicago Bears: they held opposing teams to a total of 165 points, eclipsing the Bears' standard of 198, and limited opposing teams to 970 yards rushing, well below the previous mark of 1,319. They also posted four shutouts, just one shy of the NFL record. Lewis's squad was so effective that they propelled the Ravens to three victories during a five-game stretch in which the offense failed to score a single touchdown. Lewis, with 137 tackles, was named the NFL's Defensive Player of the Year; the Ravens' defensive tackle Sam Adams and defensive back Rod Woodson were named to the Pro Bowl along with Lewis, who celebrated his fourth selection. The Ravens earned the AFC wild-card berth in the play-offs, making their first postseason appearance since they relocated to Baltimore. Their defense dominated the first game, leading the team to a 21–3 victory. In their next contest they defeated top-seeded Tennessee, 24–10, with Lewis providing a decisive interception. They followed that success by winning the American Football Conference (AFC) championship game, 16–3, earning their first and only trip to the Super Bowl, where they would meet the New York Giants, who possessed one of the hottest offenses in the NFL. In a matchup of contrasting styles, the Ravens' defense neutralized the offensive finesse of the Giants, forcing five turnovers en route to a 34–7 victory. The Ravens became only the third wild-card team to win a Super Bowl. Following the game, Lewis was honored with the Most Valuable Player trophy. He is only the second player in NFL history to win the Defensive Player of the Year Award and a Super Bowl MVP trophy in the same season.

In 2001 Lewis again led the NFL in tackles, with 161, and was honored with his fifth straight invitation to the Pro Bowl. The Ravens lost in the second round of the play-offs, after posting a 10–6 record during the regular season. Afterward, for financial reasons, the Ravens organization decided to rebuild the team, releasing or trading many of its best players. The team started the 2002 season with the youngest players in the league, including 19 rookies. Nevertheless, the general manager, Ozzie Newsome, was determined to keep Lewis, signing him to a seven-year contract worth $50 million, which made him one of the league's highest-paid defensive players. For the Ravens Lewis was valuable not only for his work as a defensive player but also for his role as a mentor and leader of the players around him. Lewis embraced the responsibility of teaching the younger players. "In 2000 we had Hall of Famers," he told Peter King. "What can I tell Rod Woodson? But now we have a bunch of young guys who want to be great. I stress learning from film, doing the extra things. At the end of practice I say, 'If you stop your preparation here, you lose. We lose.'" A shoulder injury limited Lewis to five games in 2002, and the team struggled to a 7–9 record. Despite having missed games, Lewis finished fifth on the team in tackles, with 57.

In 2003 some doubted that Lewis could return to form after having missed so much of the previous season. A number of sportswriters surmised that years of brutal treatment had taken its toll on a body that was small by the standards of NFL linebackers. But as it turned out, the time off revitalized Lewis. "They say the ultimate prize is a Super Bowl Ring. I have that. They say the ultimate prize is an MVP award. I have that," Lewis explained to David Ginsburg for the Associated Press (August 21, 2003). "I don't care about none of that. I care about being the most dominant player in this business. I'm trying to be the greatest ever." In 2003, one of his finest seasons, he posted 161 tackles and had a career-high six interceptions. At the conclusion of the season, he was voted the NFL's Most Dominant Player by head coaches and CBS SportsLine. He won his second Associated Press Defensive Player of the Year Award, earning 43 of 50 first-place votes. (Only Lawrence Taylor, formerly of the New York Giants, has won the award three times; several players have won it twice.) Paul Attner wrote about Lewis: "When the NFL's toughest man tackles a running back, he never tries to duck his head. He wants to look him square in the eyes; he wants to see the results of the pain and intimidation he is inflicting. . . . 'I read body language,' he says. 'I know when it is over, when I have won, when I am in control, when that guy won't want to come back for any more.'"

In 2004 Lewis excelled again, posting 146 tackles. The Ravens, however, managed only a 7–9 record. The 2005 season brought further frustration for Lewis; beset again by various injuries—including one to a hamstring, which required surgery—he played in only six games, recording 46 tackles. At the end of the season, there were reports that Lewis was unhappy with the direction in which the organization was headed. Again, many predicted that Lewis would never return to the level of ability he had formerly displayed; they also

argued that his lucrative contract was prohibitive to overall team success, preventing the team from acquiring other top players, and some suggested that the Ravens should trade Lewis, or that the athlete should retire. Lewis countered with typical defiance. "I don't want to be a GM [general manager]. I don't want to be a coach," Lewis said, as reported by Mike Preston for the Baltimore Sun (October 22, 2005). "I'm going to be a player again and end up being the Most Valuable Player, not just on defense, but for the entire league." Lewis was outspoken about his distaste for Baltimore's defensive philosophy, which had shifted in recent years to a team-oriented approach that Lewis felt downplayed his relevance and limited his personal production. While he insisted that he would not demand to be traded, he often hinted at the opposite. "Baltimore is my city . . . ," Lewis told Jamison Hensley for the Baltimore Sun (April 22, 2006). "But at the same time, it's just like another businessman or businesswoman in America. What's better for me? Because if I'm not being used right, you might as well let me go."

In part to help Lewis, the Ravens acquired Haloti Ngata, a 340-pound defensive tackle, in the 2006 NFL draft. The team's coaches believed that Ngata's size would overwhelm opponents and force them to commit multiple players to stopping him, allowing Lewis more freedom and maneuverability. Heading into the 2006 season, the Ravens hired a new defensive coordinator, Rex Ryan, who changed their defensive strategy to a formation known as the 46. In that format Lewis returned to his prominence as the central playmaker, and the defensive tackles were responsible for opening up lanes through which Lewis and other linebackers could attack the ball. The Ravens finished the 2006 regular season with a franchise-best record of 13 wins and three losses and were granted a bye for the first round of the play-offs. They lost their first game, 15–6, to that year's eventual Super Bowl champions, the Indianapolis Colts; thanks in part to the Lewis-led defense, there were no touchdowns scored throughout the entire game. Lewis ended the season with 164 tackles, five sacks, and two interceptions; he was named to his eighth Pro Bowl team, but due to a hand injury, he bowed out, allowing his teammate Bart Scott to play in his first Pro Bowl.

In total, by the beginning of the 2007 season, Lewis had amassed 1,838 tackles, 1,259 of them unassisted, nine forced fumbles, 80 passes defended, 80.5 tackles for loss, 28 sacks, 12 fumble recoveries, and 23 interceptions in 148 games. As of mid-October 2007, in his 12th season with the Ravens, he had made 45 tackles, 32 of them unassisted.

Lewis is very active in community service, particularly in the Baltimore area. Each year he hosts a charitable back-to-school event for Baltimore children, a holiday gift drive, and a Thanksgiving turkey benefit. He also hosts annual bowling events, which draw teammates and other celebrities, in an effort to raise money for community projects in Baltimore. Lewis tries to separate his persona as a football player from his service efforts, never wearing his uniform and rarely signing autographs at charity events. In 2004 Lewis was one of 32 finalists for the Walter Payton Man of the Year Award, given annually by the NFL to a player to recognize community service as well as athletic excellence. In 2006 Lewis contributed his efforts to the Sports for Life program of the Veterans for America Foundation (formerly the Vietnam Veterans of America Foundation), which uses sports as a means of rehabilitating and empowering landmine survivors and other victims of conflict around the world—particularly children. "Sport has always played an important role in my life, and this is something that I want to share with the next generation. My work with kids around the country has taught me that organized sporting activities can help kids feel good about themselves, it can help them assimilate into society, teach confidence

and self-reliance," Lewis stated in a press release issued by the foundation.

Lewis is single and has homes in Baltimore; Highland Beach, Florida; and Orlando, Florida. He has four sons and two daughters and spends the off-season with all of his children in Florida. In 2006 Lewis was inducted into the Miami University Hall of Fame, an honor he has called one of the highlights of his career. His hobbies include fishing and bowling.

—N.W.M.

Suggested Reading: Associated Press Sep. 11, 1998; *Baltimore Sun* C p1 Nov. 16, 1997, D p1 Dec. 10, 1997, D p1 Oct. 3, 2004, F p1 Oct. 21, 2005, C p1 Apr. 22, 2006; *Miami Herald* May 8, 2006; *New York Post* p56 Sep. 12, 2004; *Sporting News* p24 Oct. 27, 2003; *Sports Illustrated* p134 Sep. 1, 2003

Courtesy of Georgia Tech

Marcus, Bernie

May 12, 1929– Co-founder of Home Depot; philanthropist

Address: Marcus Foundation, 2455 Paces Ferry Rd., S.E., Atlanta, GA 30339-4024

As the co-founder of Home Depot Inc., the largest chain of its kind in the United States, Bernie Marcus can trace his success to his getting fired from a company called Handy Dan Home Improvement in 1978, when he was 49 and already had years of

experience in the retail industry, many of them as an executive. The next year, along with Arthur Blank, who had also lost his job with Handy Dan, Marcus opened the first three Home Depot stores in Atlanta, Georgia. In unadorned quarters that resembled warehouses rather than retail outlets, with many sealed but empty cartons scattered about to give customers an impression of abundant stock, the men began to sell lumber and other building materials; electrical, plumbing, and kitchen equipment and supplies; hardware; and paint, flooring, and wallpaper. In the years to come, they added such seasonal items as snow shovels, plants, and lawn fertilizers. "The concept was far from a safe bet," Megan McRainey wrote for the *Atlanta Business Chronicle* (May 3, 2002). "The idea, a home improvement warehouse, was a new one. And Atlanta shoppers in the 1970s were unaccustomed to such a specialized store." While Blank served as chief operating officer and focused on matters such as time management, Marcus—who has been widely described as a charismatic visionary—concentrated on building employee morale and customer satisfaction, developing Home Depot's reputation for vast inventories, low prices, and exemplary service. Two other men played key roles in the fledgling company: Patrick Farrah, a master of merchandising, and Ronald Brill, an expert in financial management. By 1986 Home Depot had opened a total of 60 stores, in many additional locations, and the company's annual sales had climbed to more than $1 billion. By 2002, when Marcus retired as chairman and CEO, positions he had held for nearly a quarter-century, Home Depot's annual sales exceeded $58 billion; the figure for fiscal year 2006 was $81.5 billion. Currently, Home Depot employs close to 350,000 people and operates more than 2,000 stores, with at least one in each of the 50 states, the District of

Columbia, Puerto Rico, the U.S. Virgin Islands, every Canadian province, Mexico, and China.

"There's great satisfaction in building a business and making money, but there's also great satisfaction in doing something and knowing how good you're making people feel," Marcus told Wendy Bowman Littler for the *Atlanta Business Chronicle* (September 17, 2004). "Whether saving a life or just helping someone along, part of my job is to convince people to try it and experience the feeling." During the years that Marcus was an almost daily presence at Home Depot outlets, he encouraged workers to donate their energy and time to community projects, such as building houses as volunteers for the nonprofit group Habitat for Humanity. Since the late 1980s Marcus—who became a billionaire at Home Depot and who remains the corporation's largest stockholder—has given more than $650 million to various organizations and institutions, much of it through the Marcus Foundation, which he set up with his wife in 1988. The Georgia Aquarium, in Atlanta, which opened in 2005, owes its existence to his gift of $250 million to the city. In *BusinessWeek*'s 2006 list of the 50 most generous philanthropists in the United States, he ranked 25th. Marcus has earned many honors, both locally, in Georgia, and nationally, but, perhaps in an example of his stated desire to focus on others rather than himself, he listed only one of them—a 2006 Golden Plate Award from the Academy of Achievement—in his citation for *Who's Who in America, 2007*.

Bernard Marcus was born on May 12, 1929 in Newark, New Jersey, where he and his three siblings grew up in a tenement. His father, a cabinetmaker, and mother were Jewish immigrants who met in the U.S. after fleeing persecution in Russia; in their home in the U.S., they followed many of the tenets of Orthodox Judaism. "My mother used to call [the U.S.] the golden land in Yiddish," Marcus told Jim Tharpe for the *Atlanta Journal-Constitution* (May 29, 2005). "We had cockroaches. We had mice. But this was heaven to them compared to what they came from." Although his father worked extremely long hours, he earned barely enough to support the family. Young Bernie would sometimes "try to help him build these things, and he would take out every nail I put in," as Marcus told Tharpe. "My father was a perfectionist, and I couldn't satisfy him." Beginning at an early age, Marcus hung around with gangs of black youths in his gritty section of Newark: "A lot of the guys that I ran with are dead," he said, as quoted by Littler. "One of them went to the electric chair . . . he killed somebody." According to Littler, Marcus's parents moved from that neighborhood when the boy was 12, because it was getting too rough. At 13 he started working at various odd jobs; during high school they included soda jerk and, during summers, busboy. Despite the family's financial struggles, Marcus's mother taught him the importance of giving. "When I was a boy, I donated nickels to help plant trees in Israel," he told

Littler. "That's what my mother taught me; that you have to give back. I couldn't understand why I was doing it. This was my ice cream money that I was giving away. But, she said, 'You have to help people who are less fortunate; this is what we do.' It is a concept in Judaism called *tzedaka*, which means 'to give back.' I honestly believe that when you give, you get back in spades. And, if you don't get it back in financial reward, you get it back in satisfaction. You don't have to have a lot of money to do these things. You can give of your own soul. You can give of your own time."

After his high-school graduation, Marcus entered a pre-med program at Rutgers, New Jersey's state university. During his college years, by his own account, he often cut classes to sell freezers to homeowners, and in the summers he sometimes entertained as a stand-up comedian in Catskill Mountains hotels, in New York State. Various sources have reported that he abandoned hopes of becoming a psychiatrist after learning that Harvard Medical School maintained an ethnic quota system, and that as a Jew, "he would have to bribe a medical school administrator in order to gain admission," according to Marcus's profile in the *New Georgia Encyclopedia* (November 17, 2005, on-line). Lacking the thousands of dollars supposedly required for such a bribe—or, according to some sources, having insufficient funds to attend any medical school—he got work in a pharmacy after he earned a B.S. degree, in 1954. As a drugstore salesman, he discovered that he loved dealing with customers. His fondness and aptitude for sales soon led to progressively higher-ranking jobs at Two Guys (later renamed Vornado's), which sold goods ranging from appliances to lawn furniture; when he left, in 1968, after more than a dozen years there, he held the title of vice president. He next served for two years as president and chief operating officer of Odell, a company that manufactured shoe polish and other consumer products. In 1970 he joined Daylin Inc., where he directed a division that oversaw 34 discount stores. In 1972 Daylin placed him in charge of its Handy Dan Home Improvement stores; he held the title of president and later became the chairman of Handy Dan's board of directors. At Handy Dan he worked closely with Arthur Blank, the firm's chief financial officer, and helped to expand the chain significantly. He also learned a lot about the equipment, supplies, and skills needed for home-improvement projects. In the mid-1970s the Brand Names Foundation named Handy Dan the Home Center of the Year.

In 1978 Sanford Sigiloff, Daylin's CEO, abruptly fired Marcus, Arthur Blank, and a third Handy Dan executive, Ronald Brill. In their book, *Built from Scratch: How a Couple of Regular Guys Grew the Home Depot from Nothing to $30 Billion* (1999), written with Bob Andelman, Marcus and Blank maintained that the reasons for their dismissals were purely personal. Chris Roush, who looked into the matter for his book *Inside Home Depot: How One Company Revolutionized an Industry*

Through the Relentless Pursuit of Growth (1999), came to the same conclusion. Earlier, Marcus had confided to Kenneth G. Langone, an investment banker who had had dealings with Handy Dan, that he dreamed of launching his own home-improvement business, in which he would buy merchandise directly from manufacturers and stock it in huge, warehouse-like buildings; the bare-bones settings, he believed, would give customers the accurate impression that prices would be lower than elsewhere. Within days of Marcus's ouster, Langone remarked to Marcus that he was now free to go into business for himself. With $2 million that Langone raised from a group of investors, and a $3.5 million loan from a West Coast bank that had worked with Marcus when he represented Handy Dan, Marcus and Blank set about starting up their company. (They had hoped to have a far larger sum to start off with, but a deal that Langone had tried to negotiate with the real-estate and investment-company mogul Ross Perot fell through.) Marcus took the positions of chairman and chief executive officer, and Blank, the title of president. The partners benefited from the merchandising expertise of Patrick Farrah, whom they recruited after learning that a similar home-improvement warehouse that Farrah had recently opened in Los Angeles, California, was failing—not because of any inadequacies on Farrah's part but because the business "lacked adequate financial controls," as the economist Richard E. Hattwick wrote in a history of Home Depot for the Web site of the American National Business Hall of Fame. Heeding Marcus and Blank's advice, Farrah closed his store and joined Home Depot. In time, according to Hattwick, Farrah "may have been a stronger motivational force among the rank and file than were either Blank or Marcus." Ronald Brill, too, came on board, as comptroller.

Serendipitously, at around the time that Marcus and Blank decided to base their operations in Atlanta, four Treasure Island stores in the Atlanta area became vacant. The men negotiated leases for those spaces, and the first three Home Depots opened there, in 1979. In its first year the company earned $7 million in sales, for an overall loss of about $1 million. "We sweated bullets" in the beginning, Langone told Roush. "It didn't take off right away. Bernie and Arthur used to call me and say, 'We're in trouble.'" Determined to succeed, Marcus resorted to such measures as having his three children distribute $1 bills to prospective customers in Home Depot parking lots, and sending workers to other stores to buy products sought by customers who failed to find them in Home Depot. The fourth Home Depot store opened in 1980. That year total sales reached $22 million and profits totaled $856,000. "Bernie, he would say things in terms of the stock, in terms of the size of the company, the size of the industry, the size of the market, that had no foundation whatsoever," Blank recalled to Tharpe. "But half the time half of what he said ended up becoming reality."

In 1981 Home Depot made an initial public stock offering of 750,000 shares at $12 apiece. "An investor who bought 1,000 shares at that price could have cashed them out 19 years later for about $15.6 million," Tharpe noted. Also that year Home Depot opened four stores in Florida, attracting huge crowds with greatly discounted prices on ceiling fans. By the end of 1983, the 19 Home Depot outlets then in existence produced total revenues of $250 million; in 1984 another 31 stores opened. That year Home Depot stock began selling on the New York Stock Exchange. A $250 million loan from Security Pacific National Bank in 1985 enabled the chain to add another 50 stores, at sites in Texas, California, and Louisiana. Within a year, with 10 more stores, the company's sales had exceeded $1 billion. Home Depot's expansion into the Northeast in the late 1980s led to a surge in sales and profits. "The stores we opened there did many, many times higher volume than even we were accustomed to . . . ," Marcus and Blank recalled in their book. "In the South, we would sell 60 electrical receptacles and then order 72 more. In the Northeast we needed a thousand of the same item. So then we went back to the vendors and said, 'We will no longer buy these in 48-packs. . . . We want you to bundle up a thousand of them at a time." Among the new stores was Home Depot's first supersize outlet, covering 140,000 square feet—currently, the standard floor space. Aiding the chain's expansion were Marcus and Blank's purchases of related businesses, such as Georgia Lighting, and wholesale distributors. Home Depot opened its 500th store in 1997; the 1,000th opened in 2000, and the 2,000th, in 2005.

Earlier, in 2002, having reached the mandatory retirement age of 72, Marcus relinquished his titles to Robert Nardelli. (Frank Blake succeeded Nardelli after the latter resigned, under pressure from shareholders, in early 2007.) Meanwhile, in the 1980s, he had begun to involve himself in philanthropic activities. According to *BusinessWeek*'s list of the most generous U.S. philanthropists in 2006, he has given to charities a total of $650 million, or 34 percent of his net worth; between 2002 and 2005 he gave or pledged $317 million. His beneficiaries have included Autism Speaks, which supports research into the causes and possible cures for autism; the Centers for Disease Control (CDC) Foundation, for a state-of-the-art bioterrorism unit at the CDC's headquarters, in Atlanta; a nanotechnology research facility at Georgia Tech University; the National Holocaust Museum; and the Shepherd Center, which aids disabled and severely injured people. With funds totaling more than $70 million, he and his wife established and have helped to maintain the Marcus Institute, in Atlanta; the institute, which is associated with the Emory University Medical School, in Atlanta, and the Kennedy Krieger Institute, in Baltimore, Maryland, has served more than 30,000 children and adolescents suffering from neurological and behavioral disorders, learning disabilities, and other developmental problems. In 1991 Marcus helped to found the Israel Democracy Institute, a nonpartisan think tank based in Israel, to promote and defend democracy in that country. Marcus's gift, through his foundation, of more than $250 million made possible the construction of the Georgia Aquarium, in Atlanta; containing more water and housing more aquatic and marine animals than any other aquarium in the world, the facility opened to the public in 2005. According to the Association of Fundraising Professionals, Marcus "personally solicits major donors for gifts, resulting in six-figure contributions for the organizations he supports."

A member of the Jewish Republican Coalition, Marcus contributed nearly $1.3 million to Republican candidates between 1998 and 2005, according to Jim Tharpe in the *Atlanta Journal-Constitution* (June 6, 2005). "Generally, I'm a supporter of the free enterprise system," he told Tharpe. "I believe the Republicans better respond to that. Creating jobs is more important than giving people a handout. There's a big difference between the Republican Party and the Democratic Party on that issue. The free enterprise system has allowed me to become what I am."

Home Depot won the Governor's Council on Developmental Disabilities Award for the State of Georgia in 1997 and the Gold Award of Honor for Employer of the Year from the National Business and Disability Council in 2000. In 1998 Marcus was named Georgia Philanthropist of the Year. His other honors include, in 2006, the National Marine Sanctuary Foundation Stewardship Award, a Golden Plate Award from the Academy of Achieve-

ment, and a "Friends of Georgia's Children" Award from the Georgia Parents-Teachers Association. In 2007 he earned the America's Democratic Legacy Award from the Anti-Defamation League and the Paschal Murray Award for his outstanding philanthropical activities from the Association of Fundraising Professionals. Also that year Boys & Girls Clubs of Metro Atlanta named Marcus and his wife, Billi, among Atlanta's Hometown Heroes.

When Marcus met his wife, she was raising an adolescent son. He has three children from an earlier union. In his spare time he enjoys playing golf and reading.

—M.B.

Suggested Reading: American National Business Hall of Fame Web site; *Atlanta Business Chronicle* A p25 May 3, 2002, p4+ Sep. 17, 2004; *Atlanta Journal-Constitution* G p1+ Jan. 12, 1997, E p1+ Nov. 17, 1998, H p1+ July 30, 2000, A p1+ June 6, 2005, (on-line) May 29, 2005; Jewish Virtual Library Web site; *New Georgia Encyclopedia* (on-line); Marcus, Bernie, Arthur Blank, and Bob Andelman. *Built from Scratch: How a Couple of Regular Guys Grew The Home Depot from Nothing to $30 Billion*, 1999; Roush, Chris. *Inside Home Depot: How One Company Revolutionized an Industry Through the Relentless Pursuit of Growth*, 1999

Selected Books: *Built from Scratch: How a Couple of Regular Guys Grew the Home Depot from Nothing to $30 Billion* (with Arthur Blank and Bob Andelman), 1999

Matisyahu

(MAH-tiss-YAH-hoo)

June 30, 1979– Reggae singer/songwriter

Address: c/o Or Music, 37 W. 17th St., Suite 5W, New York, NY 10011

"In my music, I'm really not trying to preach to people, or trying to tell people how they should lead their lives," the reggae/rap singer/songwriter Matisyahu told David Prince for the *Santa Fe New Mexican* (September 23, 2005). "It's really more of a reflection on my own life, and what are the lessons that I've come to . . . and then just putting them in the music." A dreadlocked Deadhead (as fans of the Grateful Dead are known) and nonpracticing Jew as a young teenager, Matisyahu floundered spiritually and dropped out of high school before embracing the branch of Orthodox Judaism known as Chabad-Lubavitch Hasidism, when he was in his early 20s. Channeling his newfound faith into reggae and hip-hop–inspired songs, he

made his first studio album, *Shake off the Dust . . . Arise*, in 2004. His next recording, *Live at Stubb's* (2005), reached number one on the *Billboard* reggae charts and sold more than 500,000 copies. In the past three years, although his religion forbids him to perform during the Jewish sabbath, thus prohibiting Friday-night or Saturday-matinee gigs, and although his apparel is limited to the staid garb dictated by Chabad-Lubavitch tradition, he has secured hundreds of concert dates every year at clubs, festivals, and elsewhere, and he regularly sells out 2,000–3,000-seat halls. The style and melodies in his music, he told Diane Cardwell for the *New York Times* (December 11, 2004), do not resemble those categorized as Jewish, but his work "is filled with images of Judaism. I created my own internal feelings about what it meant to be Jewish and connected it to reggae music." "Matisyahu sings music that is open, rangy, catchy, novel, and compulsively appealing enough that any listener can take from it the sound and feel of a certain kind of freedom—a licentiousness of the spirit . . . ," Devin McKinney wrote for the liberal publication *American Prospect* (May 3, 2006, on-line). Ma-

Matisyahu

Mark Mainz/Getty Images

tisyahu, McKinney continued, "incarnates" Chabad-Lubavitch's "18th-century comprehension of song as religious rapture and its emphasis on joy expressed through wild dance, free gesticulation, the open throat." He also wrote, "Matisyahu and his three-man band, Roots Tonic, combine the joyous leap of reggae with the spatial expanse of dub and the aggression of rap. The pieces come together, and the whole hurtles itself outward in multiple directions." "I'm just trying to put my music out there," Matisyahu told Nekesa Mumbi Moody for the Associated Press (April 19, 2005), "and at the end of the day, I hope people take away from it what I took away from music growing up, that it gave me a sense of strength and hope and peace, and stability and inspiration." Matisyahu's gold-certified CD *Youth* (2006) was nominated for a 2007 Grammy Award as best reggae album. In mid-2007 Matisyahu revealed his intention to affiliate himself with a branch of Hasidism outside the Lubavitch movement.

Matisyahu ("Matis" to his friends) was born Matthew Paul Miller on June 30, 1979 in West Chester, Pennsylvania, to Robert Miller and Rochelle Lieber-Miller, both social workers. Shortly after his birth Matisyahu's family moved to Berkeley, California, where they lived until 1983, when they settled in White Plains, New York, about 25 miles northeast of New York City. Some sources have described his parents as nonobservant Jews; others have reported that they are adherents of Reconstructionism, the most recent of the four branches of contemporary organized Judaism (the others being Orthodox, Conservative, and Reform Judaism). According to the Web site of the Jewish Reconstructionist Federation, Reconstructionist

Judaism "integrates a deep respect for traditional Judaism with the insights and ideas of contemporary social, intellectual and spiritual life" and emphasizes "respect for such core values as democratic process, pluralism, and accessibility." Its followers "continue to turn to Jewish law for guidance, if not always for governance. We recognize that in the contemporary world, individuals and communities make their own choices with regard to religious practice and ritual observance." As a youngster Matisyahu enjoyed playing ice hockey. Neither school nor religion interested him. He hated attending Hebrew lessons after his regular schoolday and was so disruptive at Hebrew school that he was almost expelled. His troublesome behavior continued into junior high and high school, as did his conflicts with his parents. Meanwhile, by the age of 14, he had become an ardent fan of the band the Grateful Dead and wore his hair in dreadlocks. He often sang and became "the guy that made the beats, like did the beats with my mouth" (known as beatboxing), as he told Anthony Mason for the TV series *CBS Sunday Morning* (March 26, 2006, on-line). He recalled to Robin Eggar for the London *Sunday Times* (January 22, 2006), "I loved the Allman Brothers, the Grateful Dead, reggae bands like Israel Vibration and Steel Pulse, dancehall singers Sizzla and Buju Banton. Then I got into hip-hop and groups like Outkast and the Roots. Bob Marley's music gripped me. His lyrics fitted in terms of my life. There were references to the Old Testament, to overcoming obstacles and the system. That was where I found a lot of strength in those years." During his junior year of high school, after he caused a fire that badly damaged the chemistry classroom, Matisyahu went camping by himself in the Rocky Mountains of Colorado. There, he began to reevaluate his life. "I think I was a typical teen," he told T'cha Dunlevy for the Montreal, Canada, *Gazette* (January 18, 2005), "trying to find a place, and to [figure out] what's truthful and real in the world. A lot of times, you feel like you're not in control of situations, you're at the whim of the system. It rubs you the wrong way." "As a kid you're just born into a certain system, into a certain place," he commented to Anthony Mason. "And you're just expected to go along with that. . . . What if it doesn't work? What if you feel it's not right? What if you feel it's not true?" In the wilderness, isolated from society, Matisyahu felt the presence of God.

Soon afterward Matisyahu took a trip to Israel, where he was struck by the way Jewish culture and religion seemed to imbue every aspect of the lives of Orthodox Jews, especially followers of Hasidism. Hasidic Judaism came into being in the 18th century in what is now the Ukraine, through the teachings of a mystical rabbi known as the Baal Shem Tov. The Baal Shem Tov maintained that everything in the universe is a manifestation of God—"God is all and all is God"—and that the most important goal in worshipping God is the achievement of a feeling of oneness with Him. He also emphasized the importance of finding joy in daily life and worshipping God exuberantly, which would please God, and avoiding asceticism, which would not. While in Israel Matisyahu felt his "dormant Jewish identity stirred into consciousness," as he wrote for his Web site. He told Dunleavy, "I felt a connection to Judaism that seemed real. The Hasidim seemed real, devoted. . . .When I saw the Hasidim in Israel, there was something very true about it." Chabad-Lubavitch is one of more than a dozen Hasidic sects (which are considered ultra-Orthodox). Starting when they turn 13, Lubavitch males wear dark suits (usually black), tieless white shirts, yarmulkes (skullcaps), and, out of doors, black felt fedoras. They keep their hair (and sideburns) short and never shave.

Back in the U.S., Matisyahu chafed at the restrictions imposed upon him at school and at home. (Now, as a fully observant Jew, he must obey God's 613 commandments, as conveyed in the Hebrew Bible, among them such "positive" commandments as "Love God and fear Him" and "Circumcize all males on the eighth day after their birth" and such "negative" commandments as "Do not testify falsely" and "Do not embarrass others.") At 17 he left home and school to follow the jam band Phish on one of their national tours. After a few months of being on the road and experimenting with illegal drugs, Matisyahu ran out of money and returned home, feeling "burnt out," according to his Web biography. At his parents' insistence, he enrolled in a wilderness-therapy program for teenagers in Oregon. The program allowed Matisyahu to cultivate his musical talents, and he began to study reggae and hip-hop and to develop his own hip-hop–infused reggae sound. He thrived on the attention he received rapping, singing, and beatboxing before an audience at the weekly open-mike event.

After he completed the program, through which he earned a high-school diploma, Matisyahu remained in Oregon for another two years, working at a ski resort and performing in coffeehouses with Soul for I, a band he had put together. In 1998, in part because he had started taking drugs again and had resolved to stop, he returned to New York. In addition to taking classes in the New School's Arts in Context program, he performed at the Nuyorican Poets Cafe's open mikes. His sets comprised his own songs, whose themes echoed those of Bob Marley, a follower of the Rastafarian religion. "It was how I expressed myself," Matisyahu told Joan Anderman for the Boston Globe (June 20, 2004). "I just felt that music. Lots of reggae artists are called conscious and the words are about Jah, but they're talking about God. . . . I was able to find my culture and identity in Judaism and hold onto the truth in this music." Spiritually, he was "looking for something more" during that period, as he told Teresa Wiltz for the Washington Post (February 19, 2006). "I was looking for a way to stay clean, I was looking for a way to fill the gap or hole in my life . . . to glue all the pieces of my life together in one common focus." He found some of what he was seeking at Congregation Kehilath Jacob, called the Carlebach Shul (for its founder, Shlomo Carlebach), a synagogue on the Upper West Side of New York City known for its "hippie-friendly vibe and exuberant singing," according to Matisyahu's Web biography. At around that time, by chance, while walking in a New York City park, Matisyahu met a Lubavitch rabbi, Dov Yonah Korn. A formerly secular Jew who had met his wife at a Grateful Dead concert, Korn spoke to him about the benefits of returning to one's Jewish roots and embracing the Chabad-Lubavitch way of life. To gain an understanding of what that would entail, Matisyahu boarded with the rabbi's family for several months. He then enrolled at a yeshiva (a religious school for Jewish males) in the Crown Heights section of Brooklyn, where many Lubavitcher Hasidim live. Abandoning his music, he immersed himself for most of the next year in prayer, study, and quiet reflection. In 2001 he officially changed his given name to Matisyahu ("Matthew" in Hebrew).

While in the yeshiva Matisyahu wrote more than 20 songs. He left the school with the determination to celebrate his spirituality by performing his own brand of reggae music. "The rabbis at first were like, 'You're in yeshiva—why would you want to go to these clubs and go to these bars and go back to this lifestyle that you used to be a part of?'" as he told Nekesa Mumbi Moody. He gained their approval of his plans after he performed for a group of young Hasidic boys at a local community center. "I closed my eyes and sang the song, and afterwards I looked up, the two rabbis from the yeshiva were right next to me, and I looked up at them and they like had huge smiles," Matisyahu told Moody. "Ever since then, they got it, and the whole community is totally supportive." With the guitarist Aaron Dugan, the bassist Josh Werner, and the drummer Jonah David, all New School classmates of his, Matisyahu formed the band Roots Tonic and began to perform more widely in public. He was soon picked up by JDub Records—a relatively little-known New York label whose goal is to introduce young Jewish artists to mainstream audiences.

Matisyahu's first album, Shake Off the Dust . . . Arise, was released in October 2004. In a review of it for the Denver Post (January 23, 2005), Elana Ashanti Jefferson wrote, "This artist's versatile, studied delivery coupled with hip-hop and dub production results in one of the more appealing reggae CDs in years." Matisyahu's video for the disc's track "King Without a Crown" aired on MTVU (a version of MTV that targets university students), and Matisyahu quickly attracted a cult following, as students voted on-line to place the video in the number-one spot on MTV's countdown show The Dean's List. Shake Off the Dust . . . Arise spent nine weeks on Billboard's top-reggae-albums list and was a crossover hit as well, reaching number seven on Billboard's modern-rock chart. Matisyahu's music " is just connecting at a moment where eclecticism is prized more than ever," Ross Martin, MTVU's head of programming, told Wiltz. "His message is one of unification. . . . It's broad enough that people from all walks of life can connect." Concurrently, Matisyahu's performances at clubs and festivals nationwide, as well as appearances on *Jimmy Kimmel Live* and *Last Call with Carson Daly*, in 2004, attracted much notice. He has since been a guest on programs including *The Tonight Show with Jay Leno*, *Late Night with Conan O'Brien*, *Late Show with David Letterman*, and the BBC's *Later . . . with Jools Holland*.

Whereas *Shake Off the Dust . . . Arise* sold only 20,000 copies (it is no longer available), Matisyahu's second album, *Live at Stubb's*—a recording of a performance of the songs on *Shake Off the Dust . . . Arise* at a club in Austin, Texas—sold upwards of half a million copies after it was issued in 2005 by Epic Records, a division of Sony BMG. It also earned much critical acclaim. In an assessment for the *Boston Globe* (May 13, 2005), for example, Renee Graham wrote, "Matisyahu brings a generous spirituality to his brand of reggae, something that has been lacking as the music has been overwhelmed by sexually explicit and sometimes hateful lyrics. . . . He can rip with the kind of supple dancehall-style delivery designed to get crowds on their feet." Graham added, "Rather than a punch line or a sendup, Matisyahu proves himself as a fine new artist whose music revives the righteousness and uplift of heartfelt reggae music." In the *Edmonton (Alberta, Canada) Journal* (December 3, 2005), Sandra Sperounes called Matisyahu's performance on the album "passionate, propulsive, and soulful." *Live at Stubb's* remained on *Billboard*'s reggae charts for months, peaking at number one.

Matisyahu's voice, according to Devin McKinney, is "deep-throated" and "rich" and like "a living thing, a wild, charismatic entity excited by the world and by itself as a force in the world." "Matisyahu allows himself no great range of vocal subtlety—his goal is exhortation, not reflection, statement, not nuance. But his tones can soar and succor like those of a Southern soul man, and in stray stanzas . . . he evinces some of Bob Marley's warmth," McKinney wrote. In *La Scena Musicale* (May 3, 2006, on-line), Norman Lebrecht took note of Matisyahu's "sweet high-baritone voice and a crisp elocution that ensures no word gets missed." Tom Breihan, however, in writing for *Pitchfork Media* (January 10, 2007, on-line) about Matisyahu's seven-track CD *No Place to Be*, released at the end of 2006, compared Matisyahu's voice unfavorably to that of the reggae singer Barrington Levy, describing it as "a flat, weedy simulation of Barrington Levy's honeyed scatter-croon. He floats between singing and chatting without ever mastering either, and there's precious little vigor or conviction in his washed-out tenor." After attending a performance by Matisyahu at the 25th Ragga Muffins Festival, in Long Beach, California, Richard

Cromelin wrote for the *Los Angeles Times* (February 21, 2006), "Any sense of novelty suggested by his thick beard and black Hasidic garb was quickly dissipated by the force of his music and his presence. . . . The tall singer covered the stage in long strides, and sometimes in huge, high hops that got the capacity crowd roaring. . . . He trusted his music to form the link with his listeners, and the no-nonsense earnestness of his manner demanded attention and respect."

In 2006 Matisyahu teamed up with the band P.O.D., whose music has been categorized as Christian rock, to record two tracks on their album *Testify*. He worked with the renowned producer Bill Laswell, whose many credits include albums by Herbie Hancock, Bootsie Collins, and Mick Jagger, on his next album, *Youth* (2006). According to Richard Cromelin, the album "doesn't lock on one sound, instead moving smoothly from classic-sounding roots-reggae to rapid-fire dancehall to American hip-hop. It's the perfect platform for Matisyahu's plunge into the big time—diverse and entertaining enough to make curious listeners comfortable, but uncompromised in theme and music." In a critique for the London *Guardian* (May 5, 2006, on-line), Caroline Sullivan wrote that Matisyahu "applies his reedy toasting style to fiery promises of redemption and grim predictions of hellfire" and concluded that the album was "more invigorating than you would believe." By contrast, Kelefa Sanneh, a reviewer for the *New York Times* (March 8, 2006), deemed the record "dull" and found little to enjoy in a sold-out Matisyahu performance at the Hammerstein Ballroom in New York City; but Sanneh acknowledged that among those in the audience, "no one seemed disappointed."

In mid-2007 Matisyahu told an interviewer for the *Miami (Florida) New Times* (July 17, 2007, on-line) that he no longer felt attached to the Lubavitch community and was planning to expose himself to other forms of Judaism. Later in the year, as Yair Ettinger reported for the Israeli newspaper *Haaretz* (October 12, 2007, on-line), Matisyahu, while maintaining the importance of "connect[ing] to a universal message," visited synagogues in Israel maintained by members of the branch of Hasidim associated with the 18th-century Rabbi Nachman of Bratslav.

Matisyahu lives in Crown Heights with his wife, the former Tahlia Silverman, whom he met while she was a film student at New York University. The couple, who married in 2004, have two sons.

—I.C.

Suggested Reading: (Albany, New York) *Times Union* A p1+ Oct. 12, 2005; (Allentown, Pennsylvania) *Morning Call* E p17 Dec. 22, 2005; *American Prospect* (on-line) May 3, 2006; Associated Press State & Local Wire Apr. 19, 2005; *Billboard* (on-line) Mar. 5, 2006; *Boston Globe* N p2 June 20, 2004; *Canadian Jewish News* p41 Feb. 10, 2005; (London) *Sunday Times* p27 Jan. 22, 2006; Matismusic.com; (Montreal)

Gazette D p5 Jan. 18, 2005; *New York Times* p8 May 15, 2005, E p1+ Mar. 8, 2006; *Washington Post* N p4 Feb. 19, 2006

Selected Recordings: *Shake off the Dust . . . Arise*, 2004; *Live at Stubb's*, 2005; *Youth*, 2006

Elsa/Getty Images

Matsuzaka, Daisuke

(mat-soo-ZAH-kah, DICE-kay)

Sep. 13, 1980– Baseball player

Address: Boston Red Sox, Fenway Park, 4 Yawkey Way, Boston, MA 02215

Although the 2007 season was the first in Major League Baseball (MLB) for the Japanese-born Daisuke Matsuzaka, the term "rookie" was not an entirely appropriate one for the stocky, right-handed pitcher. Matsuzaka first gained a following in his native country as a teenager, when he led his team to victory in the national high-school baseball tournament; he then signed with the Seibu Lions of Japan's Nippon Professional Baseball League (NPB). In eight seasons with the Lions, he enjoyed celebrity on a level perhaps unprecedented for an athlete in Japan, with roaring crowds filling stadiums mainly to see him pitch. When Matsuzaka signed with the Boston Red Sox, in late 2006, he instantly became MLB's most heralded new player in many seasons. Predictions varied as to how well Matsuzaka would fare on the mound in the U.S. Though some Japanese pitchers, such as Hideo Nomo, Kazuhiro Sasaki, and Takashi Saito, have enjoyed successful initial seasons in MLB, others have failed spectacularly, and nearly all of them have come to the United States after enduring years of unregulated pitch counts that often leave them injury-prone as they age. Some observers noted that batters in the U.S. are stronger on average than those in Japan and would present a particular challenge to Matsuzaka, while others predicted that the intense emotions of rival fans would come as a shock to the pitcher, who was accustomed to adoring crowds in Japan. Still others, however, felt that Matsuzaka came to the U.S. well prepared for what he would face, in terms of both his attitude and his pitching arsenal—which in Japan consisted of a 96-mile-per-hour fastball, a cut fastball, a curve, a changeup-like *shuuto*, three sliders, and a mysterious, double-spin "gyroball," which broke toward and then away from right-handed batters. Before the 2007 season Tadahito Iguchi, a onetime baseball star in Japan who has played in the U.S. since 2005, said that while he and Matsuzaka would face each other as opponents, he would root for Matsuzaka's success—and anticipated that most other Japanese players in MLB would, too. Iguchi told Adam Rubin for the New York *Daily News* (November 8, 2006) about Matsuzaka, "This is one of our best pitchers, and we want him to be, and we need him to be, one of the best pitchers in the States, too." After some ups and downs in his rookie season, Matsuzaka started the postseason—in which the Red Sox were pitted against the Cleveland Indians—in a slump, then recorded a win in Game Seven of the division championship, helping the Red Sox reach the World Series. When he took the mound for Game Three of the series, he became the first Japanese pitcher to start a World Series game. After nearly six innings of strong pitching and two RBIs (a rare statistic for a pitcher in the World Series), Matsuzaka recorded his second postseason win. In the next game the Red Sox finished their sweep of the Colorado Rockies, to win their second World Series championship in four years.

Daisuke Matsuzaka was born on September 13, 1980 in Higashi Tsugaru-gu, in the Japanese province of Aomori. During the time that Matsuzaka's mother was pregnant with him, Daisuke Araki, then a high-school freshman, captivated the nation by leading the Waseda Jitsugyo High School team to the championship game of Japan's Koshien Tournament; Matsuzaka's mother named her baby boy after the young pitcher. After showing great promise as a pitcher during his youth, Matsuzaka himself became a national hero during the Koshien Tournament in his final year of high school. (Koshien elicits the type of national fervor that "March Madness," the men's basketball tournament organized by the National Collegiate Athletic Association, generates in the United States; the series draws sell-out crowds and the largest TV audience of any sporting event in Japan.) Matsuzaka, Yokohama High School's then-skinny,17-year-old ace, gave a dazzling performance during the 1998 tournament. Yokohama cruised through the first two rounds, and Matsuzaka threw a shutout in round three to advance the team to the quarterfinals. The next day Matsuzaka again went the distance, this time needing 250 pitches to earn the victory in a game that lasted 17 innings, nearly twice the usual nine. In the semifinals the following day, he played left field with his right arm wrapped in layers of bandages, both to protect it and to allow it to recover from the previous day's pitching; then, in the eighth inning, his manager summoned him back to the mound for the final two innings of the game—which ended in a come-from-behind victory. Matsuzaka cemented his legend the next day in the championship game against Kyoto Seisho High School, in which he threw a no-hitter—pitching nine innings without allowing a single hit—a feat that had not been accomplished in the championship game at Koshien since 1939. "I went into the game thinking I didn't want to give up any runs but I didn't mean to pitch a no-hitter," the surprised teenager told Koichi Nakagawa for the Asahi News Service (August 24, 1998). "Nobody will ever forget what Daisuke did," the baseball writer Keizo Konishi said, as reported by Tim Larimer for *Time* magazine (September 11, 2000). Following his achievement at Koshien, Matsuzaka led Japan to the World Amateur Championship title, earning the Most Valuable Player award for his effort, and completed his final year of high school without recording a single loss.

After graduating from high school, Matsuzaka announced that he would pursue a career in Japan's Nippon Professional Baseball League. Unlike in the United States, where many players have been drafted by professional baseball teams straight out of high school, a 17-year-old pro in Japan was a rarity. In December 1998 the Seibu Lions selected Matsuzaka first overall in the draft and signed him to a contract for 13 million yen per year and a 50-million-yen signing bonus, a total value of over $500,000. Matsuzaka was given the number 18, which in Japan is typically reserved for an ace pitching prospect. Shintaro Kano, writing for the Asahi News Service (April 8, 1999), compared the Japanese media's anticipation of Matsuzaka's professional career to a "stallion broke out of its corral." In the time between Matsuzaka's signing with Seibu and his first start as a rookie, the following April, Kano wrote, "there hasn't been a day . . . that his name hasn't been mentioned in the press." Matsuzaka did not disappoint during his eagerly awaited rookie campaign. He received a standing ovation upon entering the game that saw his first professional start, and a second roar of applause from the still-standing, sell-out crowd followed his strikeout of the first batter. The remainder of the year brought more of the same. Matsuzaka finished the season with a league-high 16 wins against five losses and an earned-run average (ERA) of 2.60, good enough to earn Rookie of the Year honors in the Pacific League. He also earned a Golden Glove for his fielding skills and made the Best Nine team

as the top pitcher in his circuit. He was elected to the All-Star team, receiving the most votes of any pitcher, and struck out five batters in the All-Star Game.

In the 2000 season Matsuzaka, the ace of the Seibu Lions, became the first teenager in 15 years to start on opening day. Although he still dominated at times, completing the season with 144 strikeouts and winning 14 games, his ERA rose to 3.97 as hitters began to adjust to his unusual delivery and an overreliance on his finest pitch, the fastball. At midseason Matsuzaka had a 5–5 record and a decidedly mediocre 4.19 ERA, and some writers speculated that the young pitcher's success would prove to be a flash in the pan. Noting the inconsistency of his pitching motion (most successful pitchers repeat the exact same motion every time they throw a particular kind of pitch), many observers felt that Matsuzaka was not practicing sufficiently, which they blamed on his fast-paced lifestyle—an outgrowth of his celebrity. Matsuzaka was reprimanded by the Seibu Lions several times for his actions off the field, which included late-night partying and one instance of driving without a license. The Seibu Lions, embarrassed by their star player's attempt to cover up his antics, briefly suspended him from the organization. Some team officials blamed the Lions for giving their star special treatment and effectively spoiling him. Matsuzaka's high-school coach, Motonori Watanabe, told Hideko Matsuhisa and Katsutoshi Hashimoto for the *Mainichi Daily News* (July 8, 2000) that he had never doubted Matsuzaka's ability and described the young pitcher's indiscretions as evidence of immaturity that would dissipate over time. "I'm not worried," Watanabe said. "What he's going through now is a natural part of being a professional baseball player." True to his former coach's expectations, Matsuzaka rebounded during the season's second half, notching nine wins and only two losses in the remainder of the year and earning his second Best Nine placement.

Following the 2000 season Matsuzaka joined other Japanese players, both professional and amateur, in representing Japan at the Olympic Games in Sydney, Australia. Among the Japanese fans who went to Sydney were more than 80 Matsuzaka devotees who traveled in a special tour arranged by the pitching ace's fan club. One member of the group, Naomi Odagiri, skipped her university examinations to attend the games. "I know I will pay for it later, but watching him on the mound at the Olympics is very important, in my opinion," she explained to Jun Saito for the Asahi News Service (September 26, 2000). "I want to see him strike out as many powerful hitters as possible." Matsuzaka did not fare well, however, losing games to South Korea and to the United States. Against the U.S. Matsuzaka pitched 10 innings in an eventual 4–2 loss. He nonetheless impressed the U.S. players and their manager, Tommy Lasorda. "He pitched a heck of a ball game," Lasorda said, according to Saito. "We knew he was going to be tough, and we knew we were going to be in for a battle."

In his third professional season, Matsuzaka pitched a league-high 240 innings and built a 15-win, 15-loss record; he allowed 27 home runs, more than in his two previous seasons combined. He led the league in both wins and losses and worked hard to develop his secondary pitches, which had remained unrefined. During the 2001 season his cut fastball—slower than a traditional fastball, but with greater movement—became a reliable "out pitch." Batters could make contact with the pitch, but not solidly, and the weakly hit balls made for easy outs. Kazuhiro Wada, a teammate of Matsuzaka's, explained to Jim Allen for the *Daily Yomiuri* (November 16, 2006) that by using the cut fastball the pitcher sacrificed some of his strikeout potential—but that, on the positive side, the alternative pitch helped him stay on the mound longer, as evidenced by his league-leading 12 complete games. At the end of the season, Matsuzaka earned his third straight Best Nine commendation and won the Sawamura Award as the best pitcher in Japan.

In 2002 Matsuzaka's effectiveness and playing time were limited for much of the season by an elbow injury. Many scouts saw him as a victim of his own ability and of his manager's desire to coach every game as if it were the team's last, which made Matsuzaka a constant presence on the mound. A typical major-league pitcher throws between 100 and 120 pitches in a game, but even in his teens Matsuzaka had been throwing 150-pitch games routinely. As the Lions' most effective pitcher, he had often been left in games until he was totally exhausted, far past the limit of what is healthy for a teenage pitcher. One writer, in an article for the *Yomiuri Shimbin* (May 20, 1999), explained that in Japan a team's standing is placed above the health of the players: "Fans and baseball people instinctively know that Matsuzaka's arm will be sacrificed for the glory of baseball. Matsuzaka likely won't be a great pitcher for long, so they need to celebrate him while he lasts and then wait for the next hero to come along." Isao Ojimi, a former professional Japanese player, agreed, telling Tim Larimer, "I worry about [Matsuzaka's] future because he throws a lot compared to American pitchers and even other Japanese pitchers. Managers in Japan aren't worried about their players' futures, they only care about winning today. . . . He needs rest."

In 2003 Matsuzaka seemed to have recovered fully from his injuries, pitching to a record of 16–7 while his 2.83 ERA and 215 strikeouts paced the league. He had similar success in 2004, winning 10 games with a league-low 2.90 ERA. The Seibu Lions won the Pacific League title and advanced to the Japan Series, in which, despite a below-average performance from Matsuzaka, they were able to capture their first title in 14 years. Following the 2004 season, Matsuzaka again represented Japan in the Olympics, in Athens, Greece, where he became the first Japanese pitcher to throw a 100-mile-per-hour pitch. He excelled in both of his starts, shutting out Cuba through eight innings for a victory and earning a hard-luck 1–0 loss against Australia when his offensive support vanished. Overall, the Japanese team met expectations, winning the bronze medal at the Games.

In 2004 Matsuzaka remained by far the most popular baseball player in Japan, having reached heights of celebrity that were unusual for an athlete in that culture. Everywhere he went he was surrounded by adoring fans, and because of his many product endorsements, his face was among the most recognizable in Japan. The 35,000-seat Seibu Stadium was generally full during the games in which he pitched—and half-empty for those in which he was not slated to appear. When the team went on the road, the home teams, too, could expect better-than-usual turnouts for games. Younger players and fans admired Matsuzaka's bravado and red-dyed hair. "He says brave things, like how he will strike out batters, but then he backs it up," a 21-year-old fan told Larimer. "That's exciting." Unlike those of American sports stars, Matsuzaka's personal life was not chronicled on a daily basis, and his fame was largely confined to his exploits on the field. Still, some details of his lifestyle in Japan were well-noted, in articles mentioning, for example, his expensive Tokyo apartment and his collection of cars, which includes a $130,000 Mercedes G-Class.

Matsuzaka thrilled fans again in the 2005 season, though he received little offensive support, leading to a 14–13 record despite a 2.30 ERA, the best of his career up to that time. He totaled 226 strikeouts, which led the league, and completed 15 of his 28 starts, with three shutouts. During the season he reached the 1,000-strikeout milestone, becoming the fifth-fastest Nippon Professional Baseball pitcher ever to do so, and won another Golden Glove.

Following that season Matsuzaka asked to be released from his contract and to be allowed to play for Major League Baseball. MLB teams had expressed an interest in the pitcher, and Matsuzaka feared that if he played to the final year of his contract, 2008, he might get hurt and lose the opportunity to play in the United States, which had been his lifelong goal. During the process of posting a player for consideration by MLB, the U.S. teams bid for the right to negotiate with the Japanese player, and the player's team has the option to accept or reject the highest bid. If a contract agreement is reached, the player's former team receives the amount of the bid, in exchange for the contractual rights to the player. Several Japanese players had transferred to MLB previously, with Ichiro Suzuki bringing in a then-record posting bid of $13.25 million. Although the Seibu Lions were in need of the funds that could be obtained by posting Matsuzaka, he was their best player and the primary draw for fans; the team decided to keep him against his wishes but agreed to post him the following year if he performed well enough to bring a large bid from a U.S. team.

Prior to the 2006 Nippon season, Matsuzaka again led the Japanese team on the international stage, this time in the inaugural World Baseball Classic, a 16-nation tournament. While Japan's other starting pitchers collectively accumulated a 2–3 record, Matsuzaka went 3–0 with a 1.38 ERA and was named the tournament's MVP after beating Cuba in the final. He followed that dominating performance with another stellar season in the Pacific League, going 17–5 while pitching 200 strikeouts and 14 complete games and establishing a career-best 2.13 ERA. At the end of the season, Seibu agreed to post him, with the expectation that bids would likely be in excess of $30 million. Indeed, the top bid, offered by the Boston Red Sox, was $51.1 million (6.1 billion yen), which exceeded the second-highest figure by over $12 million and represented, according to Tom Singer, writing for MLB.com (December 14, 2006), "approximately *triple* the Lions' total payroll for the 2006 season." The Lions accepted the bid, and after a lengthy negotiation process, Matsuzaka inked a contract with the Red Sox worth $52 million over six seasons. He finished his eight-season career in NPB with totals of 108 wins, 60 losses, 1,355 strikeouts, an overall ERA of 2.95, and six Golden Gloves.

The benchmark for pitching success by a Japanese player in the U.S. is that of Hideo Nomo, who achieved a 123–109 record in the major leagues. Nomo and Matsuzaka had comparable success in Japan, but Nomo suffered from an even more burdensome workload, and by some accounts his health was already in decline when he moved to the U.S. Hideki Irabu, another highly touted Japanese pitcher, was a disappointment for the New York Yankees because he was injury-prone and could not control his weight or his pitches. While those pitchers enjoyed celebrity similar to Matsuzaka's upon arriving in the United States, most observers feel that Matsuzaka has greater ability than his predecessors, as well as a greater diversity of pitches, both of which, they feel, should ease his transition to his new league. Still, some have questioned whether Matsuzaka will be able to adapt to the pressure of pitching amid the intense, decades-old Boston Red Sox–New York Yankees rivalry, which Irabu ultimately proved unable to handle. Lou Merloni, a former infielder who spent time playing in both Boston and Japan, has predicted that the emotions surrounding the Red Sox–Yankees games might surprise Matsuzaka. "Games [in Japan] get pretty intense, but it's a friendly intense," he explained to Jeff Horrigan for the *Boston Herald* (December 29, 2006). "There's no hatred like you can feel over here." The pressure that Matsuzaka is to face will likely include being booed and having his failures celebrated by American sportswriters—a notoriously cynical lot—up and down the East Coast. Most Japanese sportswriters, though, believe that such treatment will not rattle the young pitcher. "He knows how to deal with pressure," the Japanese writer Hideki Okuda told John Powers for the *Boston Globe* (December 15,

2006). "He pitched in the World Baseball Classic. He pitched in the Olympic Games twice. He helped win the championship for Seibu. He knows how to handle it."

In his first major-league start, on April 5, 2007, Matsuzaka faced the Kansas City Royals; after pitching seven innings with 1.29 ERA, including 10 strikeouts, he recorded his first win in MLB. In May he pitched his first complete game in MLB, in a 7–1 win over the Detroit Tigers; against the New York Yankees, he recorded one win and one loss during the regular season. At one point he recorded wins for four games in a row, and a month before the completion of the regular season, he broke the Red Sox's record for most strikeouts by a rookie. When the regular season ended, his record stood at 15 wins and 12 losses, and the Red Sox were the American League East champions. The team went on to sweep the Los Angeles Angels of Anaheim in the American League Division Series. During that series Matsuzaka started an MLB play-off game for the first time; his performance was mediocre, and he was removed during the fifth inning. In the conference play-offs, against the Cleveland Indians, Matsuzaka returned to the mound in Game Three, in which he again pitched poorly and was taken out of the game before the end of the fifth inning; with that game he recorded his first play-off loss, because he was pulled after passing the 100-pitch mark. Down three games to one, the Red Sox made a comeback and forced a seventh game, which Matsuzaka began by retiring the first eight batters. He pitched five solid innings, allowing only two runs, thereby helping the Red Sox to win, 11–2, and move on to the World Series, against the Colorado Rockies.

In Game One of the 2007 World Series, the Red Sox, playing in their home stadium, defeated the Rockies 13–1; in the next, they squeaked by, 2–1. The series moved to Colorado for the next two games. In Game Three Matsuzaka became the first Japanese pitcher to start in a world championship; he allowed two runs and three hits in five and a third innings, and with his first major-league hit, a single, he drove in two runs. The next day the Red Sox beat the Rockies, 4–3, for a four-game sweep of the series.

The sportswriter Wayne Graczyk described Matsuzaka to John Powers as "friendly, outgoing, polite, confident, a little cocky." Matsuzaka and his wife, Tomoyo Shibata, a former television announcer, have a daughter. The pitcher's main interest beyond baseball is golf; he reportedly boasts an impressive 300-yard drive.

—N.W.M.

Suggested Reading: Asahi News Service Nov. 24, 1998, Sep. 26, 2000; *Boston Globe* A p1 Dec. 15, 2006; *Boston Herald* p58 Dec. 29, 2006; *Mainichi Daily News* p1 July 8, 2000; (New York) *Daily News* p102 Nov. 5, 2006; *New York Times* D p1 Dec. 15, 2006; *Time* p44 Sep. 11, 2000

Elsa/Getty Images

Mauer, Joe

Apr. 19, 1983– Baseball player

Address: Metrodome, 34 Kirby Puckett Pl., Minneapolis, MN 55415

In 2006 Joe Mauer of the Minnesota Twins became the third catcher in history to record the highest batting average in all of Major League Baseball (MLB) and the first to do so in the American League. At 23 years of age, he was also the youngest batting champion since Alex Rodriguez earned that distinction in 1996. Mauer relies on a simple, swift, compact swing that sends line drives to all parts of the field and that produced only one strikeout in his entire high-school career. According to Daniel Paulling, writing for the Web site At Home Plate (July 12, 2004), the Baseball Hall of Fame inductee Paul Molitor said that Mauer possesses "one of the best swings" he has ever seen. Others have compared Mauer's hitting technique to that of Ted Williams, widely considered one of the best hitters in MLB history, and have suggested that Mauer—given his age and rare ability—could become one of the greatest catchers ever to play the game. "We've tried to downplay expectations, but he's a phenomenon," the Twins' manager, Ron Gardenhire, told Jim Souhan for the Minneapolis, Minnesota, *Star Tribune* (April 4, 2004). Veteran teammates are equally impressed with Mauer. "That's a rare guy right there," the center fielder Torii Hunter told Souhan during Mauer's rookie year, in 2004. "He's 20, but he's 20 going on 40. To take pitches like he does, to throw out people the way he does, to call games like he does, and to do it all with that personality and character, that's

special." Commenting on Mauer's demeanor, Hunter added, "He got me a drink of water the other day. I'm like, 'What? A first-round draft pick getting me water?' Most of those guys have too much testosterone and ego to do that." Despite the predictions of greatness, the *Sports Illustrated* cover articles about him, his batting title, and a new, $33 million contract—the second-largest in Twins history—Mauer has remained humble. "The thing you hear all the time is what a great kid he is," Mauer's mother told Dean Spiros for the *Star Tribune* (April 6, 2004). "As a parent, regardless of how he plays baseball, you think about what kind of person he is. As parents, that's what we're most proud of." "I don't think his parents would let him change the way he carries himself, which for him has always been as a true professional," Mauer's friend Tony Leseman told Ray Richardson for the *St. Paul (Minnesota) Pioneer Press* (July 9, 2006). "I still see him as a regular Joe, as a friend . . . not as a huge superstar. He comes from a special family that raised him right."

The youngest of three sons, Joseph Patrick Mauer was born on April 19, 1983 in St. Paul, Minnesota, into a close-knit family with a passion for sports—baseball in particular. Mauer's great-grandparents emigrated in 1900 from Austria to Minnesota, where their four sons became local baseball stars at Cretin High School (now Cretin-Derham Hall High School), in St. Paul; each later played for a living, with Mauer's grandfather Jake sustaining the longest professional career—28 days. The following generation, which included Joe's father, Jake Jr., consisted of 12 boys, all multi-sport high-school stars in Minnesota. As their playing days ended, they took up the coaching of the next generation. Mauer's father and mother, Teresa Tierney Mauer, herself a three-sport athlete at St. Paul Central High School, coached many of their sons' teams. "Joe's got [athletic] genes coming at him from both sides," Ken Mauer, Joe's great-uncle, told Roman Augustoviz for the *Star Tribune* (August 30, 2000). "That makes him doubly tough. . . . The youngest one always has the privilege of learning from the other ones in the family, and that Joe is a freak in the same way Michael Jordan and Mark McGwire are freaks." As a child Mauer tagged along with his brothers, Jake III and Billy, whose athletic feats he tried to emulate. He first stepped into a batting cage at the age of two and took to it right away. As a four-year-old Mauer was banned from the tee-ball leagues at the local playground because he hit the ball so hard that other parents worried for their own children's safety; by the time he was eight, he was holding his own against overhand pitching from his brothers and father; and at 10 he was banned from a league for 12-year-olds after he pitched a no-hitter. In fifth grade Mauer started on the eighth-grade basketball team alongside Billy, and he filled in on his brothers' baseball teams when they needed an extra player. Mauer's parents believed that the competition he faced when playing with older boys was good for his development. "We figured if somebody hit a ball at him too hard he could always get out of the way . . . ," Mauer's father told Augustoviz. "In youth sports, sometimes parents hold their kids back. We didn't think it was good for Joe to dominate at his age group." The three brothers played highly competitive but friendly games of stickball in their backyard, a tradition that lasted until they were in their 20s. "They [played with] some trucks growing up," Teresa Mauer told a writer for the *St. Paul Pioneer Press* (April 4, 2004). "But mostly it was baseballs, footballs, basketballs. . . . We had a lot of broken glass." To keep his sons busy with something other than video games during the bitter Minnesota winters, Mauer's father built and installed in the garage a hitting device—consisting of a V-shaped chute made of plastic piping and attached to a pole, whose base was a coffee can filled with cement. The Mauer boys fed wiffle balls into one end of the chute, moved into hitting position as the balls rolled through the piping, and hit them into a tarpaulin. The drill helped them to develop quick, compact swings and good eye-hand coordination. It also allowed them to take thousands of swings without having to venture outside during the winter or find other boys to play with. (After Joe Mauer became a professional baseball player, his father refined the device and began selling it in sporting-goods stores.)

Mauer's brothers both excelled at baseball at Cretin-Derham Hall High School. Jake III went on to star as a second baseman at the University of St. Thomas, a Division III national baseball power in Minnesota, and Billy was a pitcher for North Hennepin Community College. Joe Mauer proved a more versatile athlete than either of his brothers, performing well in baseball, basketball, and football. In basketball, playing shooting guard, he averaged 20 points per game in his junior season at Cretin-Derham and was voted the most valuable player in the St. Paul City Conference; he was selected as an all-state performer in his junior and senior years. Mauer was even more of a standout on the football team, starting at quarterback in his junior and senior seasons and becoming one of the best players in the history of the school. His record over two seasons as a starter was 25–2. In his junior season Mauer led the team to its Minnesota Class-A state championship victory. Although the team fell one win short of repeating that feat during his senior season, Mauer compiled impressive statistics, including 3,022 passing yards and 41 touchdowns—both school records, according to the *Minnesota Football Record Book*. Regarded as one of the top quarterback prospects in the nation, in 2000 Mauer was named the *USA Today* top offensive player in football; Metro Player of the Year; Minnesota Player of the Year (by the Associated Press); athlete of the fall season (by the *Pioneer Press*); and the Gatorade national player of the year. Mauer was recruited by some of the best college-football programs in the nation, including those at Florida State University, the University of

Arizona, the University of Miami, and the University of Minnesota, which offered him a scholarship for both football and baseball. Nonetheless, Mauer's closest supporters believed that his future lay in baseball. Jake Mauer said that while he believed his grandson could be a collegiate star in any of the three sports he had played, he had pushed Mauer to pursue baseball, because it was the family's tradition. "I've told him when he grows up, I want to sit in a box seat at Yankee Stadium and watch him play," Jake Mauer told Augustoviz. "That's the only desire I have in my life. That's where he belongs."

In baseball Mauer showed promise as an infielder before moving to his current position, catcher, in high school. In his sophomore season he hit .576 with 28 runs batted in (RBIs) and won All-Metro honors. The following season he hit .542 with 31 RBIs. In those two seasons he led the team to records of 24–3 and 27–2, respectively. In his junior year he excelled in both hitting and pitching, building a 4–0 record and a 1.27 earned-run average as a starter and striking out 50 opponents in 33 innings with his 89-mile-per-hour fastball. Following his senior year, in which he hit .605 with 15 home runs and 53 RBIs while leading Cretin-Derham to the Class 3-A championship, Mauer was rated the seventh-best high-school baseball player in the United States by *Baseball America*. He became the first athlete ever to be named player of the year in two sports, football and baseball, by *USA Today*. Additionally, from 1998 to 2000 Mauer played on the U.S. Junior National Team, earning a spot as a backup before becoming one of the team's stars in his final year. In the summer of 2000, at the World Juniors Tournament in Panama, he earned most-valuable-player (MVP) honors after leading the entire tournament in hitting with a .559 average and 15 RBIs, which raised his profile further among the nation's scouts. Teresa Mauer told Jim Wells for the *St. Paul Pioneer Press* (November 30, 2000) that her son was at times uncomfortable with his local celebrity. "I think he's a little embarrassed by it all," she said. "He knows that he's playing a team sport and that if it wasn't for his [blockers] he wouldn't get all that passing yardage, and if someone wasn't setting screens he wouldn't score all those points. And baseball is every bit a team sport, too." A good student as well as all-around athlete, Mauer maintained a 3.26 grade-point average in high school. He was a member of Choice Group, an organization of student-athletes who pledged to remain drug-free and traveled to local schools to talk about the dangers of drug use, whether for athletic enhancement or recreation.

Although Mauer had signed a letter of intent to play football at Florida State University, the Minnesota Twins of Major League Baseball selected Mauer with the first overall pick in the June 2001 amateur players' draft, marking the first time in modern history that a Minnesotan had been taken first overall in any professional sports draft; Mauer also became the first catcher selected number-one overall since B. J. Surhoff, in 1985. As a left-handed power-hitting catcher, Mauer was a rarity who filled a need in the Twins organization, and as a local talent he seemed likely to draw fans. In July 2001 Mauer signed his first professional contract, which included a $5.15 million signing bonus—the largest that the Twins had ever offered, and the second-largest in MLB history. The Twins also selected Mauer's brother Jake as an infielder with the 667th overall selection.

With their All-Star catcher A. J. Pierzynski entrenched in his position at the major-league level, the Twins were able to let Mauer develop in the minors. Mauer began his professional career in the summer of 2001 in Tennessee, playing for the Elizabethton Twins of the rookie Appalachian League. His brother Jake was assigned to the same team, and they lived together with three other teammates. In 32 games Mauer managed a .400 average with 14 RBIs and impressed his teammates and coaches with his keen batting eye, which led to only 10 strikeouts against 19 walks. In 2002 he played for the Quad City River Bandits of the Class-A Midwest League, for which he batted .302 in 110 games, with four home runs, and again amassed more walks than strikeouts; he was named the top overall prospect in the Midwest League at the conclusion of the season. In the spring of 2003, Mauer was assigned to Fort Myers of the Florida State League, where he was reunited with Jake. After 62 games Mauer was promoted to the Class-AA New Britain Rock Cats of the Eastern League. He continued to impress, batting .341 with four home runs in 73 games. Overall during the 2003 season, Mauer hit over .335 at each stop and compiled five home runs and 85 RBIs. He was chosen as Minor League Player of the Year by *Baseball America* and named by that publication as the top prospect for 2004.

Although Mauer's hitting and defensive skills, including his above-average throwing arm, gave him the tools to succeed in the major leagues, he needed to develop his talents in the other aspects of being a catcher—which most consider the hardest position in baseball to master. In particular, he had to become adept at calling pitches, or telling pitchers which pitches to throw; controlling base runners (that is, keeping opposing players from stealing bases); and observing the tendencies of both his team's pitching staff and opposing hitters. In 2002 and 2003 Mauer was invited to attend spring training with the Twins' major-league team; he was paired with the veteran catcher Tom Prince to learn the minutiae of his position. As well as learning about handling a pitching staff, Mauer gained an appreciation for the importance of each pitch and became a thoughtful signal-caller. Mauer also impressed the major-league veterans with his hitting, compiling a .400 average during spring training in 2003. Overall during his minor-league career, Mauer hit .330 in 277 games, while showing an innate ability to learn the tendencies of new

pitchers and new hitters at his various minor-league posts. Mauer's experience as a quarterback helped him to digest information quickly, made him comfortable with split-second decisions on the field, and helped develop his considerable arm strength.

In November 2003 the Twins traded Pierzynski to the San Francisco Giants. Many saw the transaction as a way of allowing Mauer to play at the major-league level, despite his being only 20 years old. After another strong showing in spring training, Mauer earned the starting position. Observers immediately began drawing comparisons between Mauer and the Hall of Fame catcher Johnny Bench, who won rookie-of-the-year honors as a 20-year-old with the Cincinnati Reds in 1960. A rookie starting catcher is rare in the major leagues; in the previous 40 years, only four other 20-year-olds had become everyday catchers: Bench, Ivan Rodriguez, Butch Wynegar, and Bob Didier. "[Catcher is] the toughest position to break in at," the Los Angeles Angels manager and former Los Angeles Dodgers catcher Mike Scioscia told Jim Souhan. "You have to know so much. The 140 pitches you call will have more chance of deciding the game than anything else you do, even if you hit two home runs." According to Scioscia, a catcher needs to play in about 500 games before having the experience necessary to play every day at the major-league level. "Catching is a total feel thing," Scioscia told Souhan. "It's not a push-button operation. It's the last thing that really develops in a catcher, and it's a constant state of evolution, because you're always working with new pitchers against different hitters. . . . What wins games at the major league level is calling a good game. There's no substitute for experience."

An opening-night crowd of 49,584 cheered Mauer on as he made two hits and drew two walks in his MLB debut: a 2004 game against the Cleveland Indians, whom the Twins defeated. In the second game of his rookie season, while sliding to recover a pop foul, Mauer sustained a knee injury—a distressing development for a catcher, who spends most of the game crouched behind home plate. After undergoing out-patient surgery to repair the damage, he recovered quickly; he appeared in a few minor-league games, to regain his batting timing and test his knees and stamina, then returned to the Twins, having missed eight weeks of play. After 33 more games, because of continued pain and swelling in his knee, he was placed on the disabled list for the remainder of the season. In his 35 MLB games, Mauer had offered a glimpse of his potential, batting .308 with six home runs and 17 RBIs.

Mauer returned for the 2005 season intent on relieving concerns that his injured knee might force a position change to first or third base, as had been the case with many catchers. He was solid, if unspectacular, in his second season, batting .294 with nine home runs and 55 RBIs. Most importantly, he was consistently healthy, appearing in 131 games.

His .372 on-base percentage led all Twins regulars, and he spent 108 games batting in the third spot in the lineup. The Twins, however, stumbled to a 83–79 record, finishing third in their division.

The 2006 season was a stellar one for Mauer, as he became the first catcher ever to lead the American League in batting average. He demonstrated competence rare for one so young; since the Hall of Famer Al Kaline won the batting title in 1955, at the age of 20, only five other players had won a batting title before the age of 24. (Mauer was 23.) When asked how he had developed from a good hitter into one of the game's elite players, Mauer responded to La Velle E. Neal III for the *Star Tribune* (July 11, 2006), "I have been more patient. I'm trying to hit pitches that I can handle. . . . Just trying to put together more quality at-bats." Mauer finished the season batting .347, after spending much of the summer chasing the .400 mark, which had not been eclipsed since 1941. Hitting .388 at the time of the All-Star break, Mauer made his first All-star team. He finished sixth in the MVP race, won by his teammate Justin Morneau. The Twins overcame the Detroit Tigers to win the American League Central Division in the regular season's final weekend. In the first round of the play-offs, the Twins were defeated by the Oakland Athletics. In early May 2007 Mauer strained a quadriceps muscle and missed 30 games. He ended the season with a .293 average in 109 games, with seven home runs and 60 RBIs. The Twins, meanwhile, finished the season with a losing record, 79–83.

Mauer's talent, likability, and good looks have opened up marketing opportunities for the Twins. During its 2006 games the organization held numerous promotional events centered on the catcher, including Joe Mauer Bobble-head Doll Day, Joe Mauer Autographed Bat Day, and Joe Mauer Sideburns Day—on which fans received synthetic sideburns to match those that Mauer grew during the season. "You put the name 'Mauer' or Joe's No. 7 on any item and it sells," Matt Noll, the Twins' merchandise director, said in a press interview, as reported by Paul Levy for the *Star Tribune* (June 29, 2006). Following that season Mauer signed a $33 million, four-year contract with the Twins, the second-biggest guaranteed contract in franchise history. He is currently the only Twin locked into contract through 2010, when the team is scheduled to open its new stadium.

Mauer divides him time between his homes in Minnesota and Fort Myers, Florida. His hobbies include playing golf, video games, and pool.

—N.W.M.

Suggested Reading: (Fort Myers, Florida) *News-Press* C p1 Apr. 2, 2003; (Minneapolis, Minnesota) *Star Tribune* S p3 Aug. 30, 2000, C p11 Dec. 8, 2000, C p9 Mar. 21, 2004, T p4 Apr. 4, 2004, A p1 Apr. 6, 2004, A p1 June 29, 2006, A p1 Oct. 3, 2006; *New York Times* A p5 Apr. 4, 2004; *St. Paul (Minnesota) Pioneer Press* A p1 May 27, 1999, G p4 Nov. 30, 2000, A p1 June 6, 2001, A p1 July 23, 2001, A p1 Nov. 15, 2003, D p1 Feb. 28, 2004, A p1 Feb. 18, 2005

McClurkin, Donnie

Nov. 9, 1959– Gospel singer; minister

Address: Sierra Management, 1035 Bates Court, Hendersonville, TN 37075

"Entertainment is not my goal," the gospel singer, songwriter, and Pentecostal minister Donnie McClurkin wrote for his Web site. Rather, his aim as a performer is that "God be pleased and someone who hears experiences Jesus in a greater way." That objective notwithstanding, sales of McClurkin's albums have eclipsed those of many other gospel singers, and his skills and appeal as an entertainer have earned him two Grammy Awards—for best contemporary soul gospel album (in 2003), for *Donnie McClurkin . . . Again*, and best traditional soul gospel album (in 2005), for *Psalms, Hymns, & Spiritual Songs*. In a review of a multi-artist concert presented at the Theater at Madison Square Garden, in New York City, in 2006, the music critic Jon Pareles wrote for the *New York Times* (September 15, 2006), "Mr. McClurkin has one of the strongest and most supple voices of his generation of gospel singers. He uses the velvety baritone

croon of an R&B ballad singer, rising to an almost operatic falsetto; he can be tenderly imploring or commanding. At times his singing suggests Al Green and Mr. Green's inspiration, the Rev. Claude Jeter. Mr. McClurkin can pepper a song with rhythmic syllables or sustain a long, arching phrase. His set reached back to old-fashioned gospel and up to a dance hall, and he also drew a doctrinal line, singing 'You are the only living God: not Buddha, not Krishna, not Muhammed.'" In the sermons McClurkin has given as the pastor of the Perfecting Faith Church in Freeport, New York, and in many interviews, as well as in his songs, his memoir, *Eternal Victim, Eternal Victor*, and the documentary *The Donnie McClurkin Story: From Darkness to Light*, he has talked about or alluded to his family's struggles with substance abuse and violence, his being raped by relatives when he was eight and 13 years old, his struggles with his sexuality, and his fathering a child out of wedlock. "My battle with loneliness is my greatest battle and wanting, in fact, to be 'normal,'" he told Shirley Henderson for *Ebony* (October 2005). McClurkin has performed on Broadway, at the White House, and for the Democratic and Republican National Conventions in 1992 and 2004 respectively. With the gospel super-

Donnie McClurkin

stars Kirk Franklin and Yolanda Adams, he was a
headliner during the 2002–03 Hopeville Tour. In
2004 he was inducted into the International Gospel
Music Hall of Fame and Museum, in Detroit, Michigan. "Singing is secondary to me," he told Kelly
L. Carter for the *Detroit Free Press* (October 26,
2004). "It really is. I'm a pastor of a church and
that's the primary thing."

Among the oldest of the 10 children of Frances
and Donald McClurkin Sr., Donald McClurkin Jr.
was born on November 9, 1959 (some sources say
1961) and raised in Amityville, New York, on Long
Island. Music was always prominent in his life; he
hummed in tune before he learned to talk, and he
and his siblings sometimes sang for their parents
and neighbors. The lives of the McClurkins took a
tragic turn when, one day when he was eight, his
two-year-old brother got killed by a car on their
street. Donnie, who had been been told to watch
the toddler, witnessed the accident, and he felt
devastated, holding himself responsible for the
tragedy. Compounding his misery, on the day of
the funeral, a maternal great-uncle of his raped
him. McClurkin told no one about the rape, in large
part, he has since said, because he did not understand what had happened. His great-uncle "went
on to habitually molest McClurkin and two of his
sisters," as Celia C. Peters wrote in a review of
From Darkness to Light for afro-netizon.com (February 3, 2005). His brother's death led to, or exacerbated, his parents' substance abuse and violent
quarreling. McClurkin tried to act as peacemaker
between his mother and father; he has recalled hiding knives so that his parents would not stab each
other during arguments. He himself became increasingly withdrawn and burdened with feelings

of shame. At the family church he found some degree of comfort: the church became "my world, a
place where I felt at peace and felt like I belonged,"
he told Glenn Jeffers for *Ebony* (August 2001). "The
only way my mother could punish me was saying
I couldn't go to church," McClurkin told Brian Mc-
Collum for the *Detroit Free Press* (March 28, 1997).
"That's the only reason I would cry." One day during the summer before his 10th birthday, he was
"saved" and dedicated himself to God.

One of McClurkin's aunts was a backup singer
with the influential gospel singer Andraé Crouch
and his group, the Disciples. At a performance by
the Disciples that McClurkin attended when he
was 11, he and Crouch were introduced. Crouch
encouraged him both musically and spiritually,
and in letters that he wrote to the boy, he would
suggest Bible passages to read and advise using
music as a release from inner turmoil. McClurkin
taught himself how to play the piano and began to
sing more in church. "I was the guy that was scared
of crowds, that was inferior," he told Kim Lawton
for *Religion & Ethics Newsweekly* (March 3, 2006,
on-line). "I had such an inferiority complex. And
the only way that I could really depict any feelings
or any emotions was through music." His problems
with his self-image increased when, at age 13, he
was raped by a son of his abusive great-uncle.

Also at 13 McClurkin joined the choir of the
Kings Temple Church of God in Christ, in Amityville. "I remember running home and saying, 'Ma,
I joined the choir,'" McClurkin told Lynette Hol-
loway for *Essence* (May 2003). "She said: 'Why did
you do that? You can't sing.' That hurt my heart.
But my family's always been frank. I couldn't sing
a lick, but it was a matter of getting comfortable
with my voice." By the time he was 14, McClurkin
had become the pianist for the church's youth
choir, in which his sisters were standouts. Along
with four sisters and four friends, he formed a
group called the McClurkin Singers. "What I
couldn't verbalize, I could express musically
. . . ," McClurkin said, according to Jeffers.
"When you sang, you left everything. You entered
a place that was literally divine." The McClurkin
Singers performed in prisons and some of New
York City's poorest, most dangerous neighborhoods. In the mid-1970s the group brought in new
members and renamed themselves the New York
Restoration Choir. In 1975 they recorded *I See a
World* for the roots-oriented Savoy label. Two
songs from *I See a World*—"Speak to My Heart"
and "Prayer"—became hits for McClurkin during
his subsequent solo career.

Meanwhile, inspired by Crouch's counseling of
troubled youths, McClurkin had become a street
evangelist in and around Amityville and in New
York City. In 1983 he attended a religion-oriented
seminar hosted by the minister and gospel singer
Marvin Winans. Four years later he was cast as a
choir member in the Broadway musical *Don't Get
God Started*, for which Marvin Winans wrote the
music and lyrics and Ron Winans created the mu-

sical and vocal arrangements. The show ran for about 10 weeks in 1987–88.

In 1989 McClurkin moved to Detroit, Michigan, to become an assistant to Marvin Winans, the leader of that city's 2,000-member Perfecting Faith Church. Soon afterward he was diagnosed with leukemia. Doctors suggested immediate treatment, but McClurkin decided to postpone chemotherapy. After a month, during which he prayed steadily, he felt better, and he returned to his doctor prepared to turn down treatment. An examination revealed that the cancer was in remission and nearly undetectable. McClurkin has since revealed that the prospect of trying to conquer the disease without medical help frightened him, but that he felt that he had to turn to God. "I tell people to believe that God will save you," he said, as reported by Jeffers, "[and] I had to turn around and practice the very thing that I preached."

As a representative of Marvin Winans's church and a leader of Winans-affiliated choirs, McClurkin performed at churches and gospel venues around the country, and his reputation grew. He performed at the White House during the presidencies of George H. W. Bush and Bill Clinton, toured internationally, lent his background vocals to several Winans recordings, and spent some of his free time writing his own music. His exhausting schedule led to his suffering a nervous breakdown during one tour. "I told God, 'Why can't I just be normal with a wife and kids and cat and white picket fence? This is not what I signed up for.' I wanted to know, 'Where is mine?'" After he had reflected and prayed, McClurkin said to Henderson, "God told me, 'I never promised you that you would not feel the burden of ministry.'" His breakdown inspired him to write "Stand," which became one of his signature songs.

During that period McClurkin developed a friendship with Demetrus Alexander (now Alexander-Stewart). After she became an executive with Warner Alliance, she helped him secure a recording contract with that label. In October 1996 McClurkin released his self-titled debut album, which included "Stand," "Speak to My Heart," "Just a Little Talk with Jesus," "Jesus, the Mention of Your Name," and five additional songs. Most reviewers praised the album, as did the critic for the *Tennessee Tribune* (October 30, 1996), who wrote, "The nine tracks on *Donnie McClurkin* . . . [contain] an amazing range of musical and spiritual expression, as well as a stellar list of guests and producers . . . who added to the album's power, joy and reverence." Around that time Oprah Winfrey promoted *Donnie McClurkin* on her television talk show. "You've heard me talk about Donnie McClurkin before," she told her viewers, as McClurkin recalled to Kim Lawton. "This is a voice that you've got to reckon with, and this ['Stand'] is my favorite song." Within two weeks of Winfrey's recommendation, sales of "Stand" had surpassed half a million copies. The album, too, gained gold status, and it earned a Grammy Award nomination.

With his sisters Olivia and Cheryl McClurkin, Andrea McClurkin-Mellini, and Tanya McClurkin-Bulgin and several other female singers, McClurkin next recorded *The McClurkin Project* (1999), for the Gospo Centric label. "Family is sometimes more than blood," McClurkin told a reporter for the *New Pittsburgh Courier* (December 11, 1999) during a conversation about *The McClurkin Project*. "We have been working together for 20 years, my blood sisters and my sisters who are just like blood sisters. It's great to finally share with the world what we have experienced for the past 20 years." The album demonstrated McClurkin's songwriting and arranging abilities and featured his vocals on four tracks. It debuted at number 12 on the gospel charts and earned critical and popular success, securing for McClurkin a 2000 Detroit Music Award and two Stellar Gospel Music Awards. The *New Pittsburgh Courier* writer described the album as "characterized by the use of classic melodies, rhythmic hooks, compelling and inspiring lyrics and complex harmonies."

McClurkin's 2000 album, *Live in London and More*, was recorded in part in 1999 at Fairfield Halls, in London, England. Among other tracks, it included the songs "We Fall Down," "That's What I Believe," "I Trust You, Lord," "Lord, I Lift Your Name on High," "Caribbean Medley," and the duet "Who Would've Thought," sung with Marvin Winans. The single "We Fall Down" remained on the gospel charts for 40 weeks and also climbed near the tops of *Billboard*'s R&B charts, while the album sold more than two million copies and remained on the *Billboard* charts for 126 weeks. "I don't know if anyone can really be prepared for something like that . . . ," McClurkin told Kelley L. Carter for the *Detroit Free Press* (October 26, 2004). "It's amazing how one CD, one successful CD, can thrust you into such a whirlwind of acclaim. The task is to keep your balance and not to change. That's been the greatest task. I'm surrounded with people who help me achieve that."

Soon after his ordination as a pastor, in mid-2001, McClurkin became the spiritual leader of the Perfecting Faith Church, a Pentecostal house of worship, that he set up at the site of an abandoned supermarket in Freeport, New York. His work there, he told a *Jet* (June 25, 2001) interviewer, "is the greatest joy I have ever known. I never thought I would love this like I do, because ministry means people." He added, "The vision for the church is to heal those that have been broken in life and in the church. To introduce people to the living Saviour. To move on from religious tradition, to a relationship with God. To raise people from being obedient followers, to becoming powerful leaders to whatever capacity they have ability." The congregation of the church currently numbers about 1,000, and the services there, according to Kim Lawton, are "exuberant and interactive. Church members are likely to be dancing in the aisles, speaking in tongues or lying on the floor, overcome by the Holy Spirit." During the summer months

McClurkin also conducts outdoor services in a strip-mall parking lot near his church, with the goal of attracting the unchurched or lapsed Christians who might hesitate to enter a church but might be drawn to the singing that dominates the outdoor services. He also hopes to build a congregation that is racially integrated. "I set out to reflect God . . . ," he told Katti Gray for Newsday (August 26, 2004). "[People] made the black church, the white church, the Asian church, the Hispanic church. That's never been God and never will be."

McClurkin has attributed his success as a minister to his openness about what he has called his sins, among them his out-of-wedlock sexual activities, both homosexual and heterosexual. He has traced his leanings toward homosexuality, which he has called a "curse," to his having been raped in childhood; he has also said that during his teens, his feminine mannerisms and speech embarrassed him, and that older female members of his church helped him learn to control them. The hypocrisy of many church leaders "angers me in a way, because the bottom line is, if you mess up, just say, 'I messed up.' Don't cover it up . . . ," he said to Kim Lawton. "If you're a preacher and a pastor or a minister and you mess up, just come clean." Writing his memoir, Eternal Victim, Eternal Victor (2001), required the painful process of revisiting his childhood traumas, but "it also gave closure and resolution to a lot of things, and I was able to deal with a lot of taboo issues, like sexuality and my struggle with bisexuality and how God helped me find myself, find who I really am," McClurkin said, according to Nekesa Mumbi Moody of the Associated Press (April 13, 2005). "The man—not the bisexual, the homosexual, the man that I am, that's made for one woman." "My desires were toward men, and I had to fight those things because I knew that it wasn't what we were taught in church was right," McClurkin told Lawton. Through Bible study and intense prayer, McClurkin has said, he turned away from homosexuality. "God gave me the wherewithal to get out of that and to find out who I really am and, consequently, that's how the change took place. . . . God walked me through it, " he told Lawton.

Eternal Victim, Eternal Victor and the documentary The Donnie McClurkin Story: From Darkness to Light (2004) were greeted with warm praise from those who found McClurkin's story forthright, inspiring, and moving; they sparked fierce criticism from those who construed his message as homophobic and dishonest. McClurkin has defended himself against accusations of homophobia by arguing that he is merely trying to help people who have decided for themselves that they do not want to live as gays or lesbians. "If [homosexuality is] your desire, I'm not looking to change you, but there is a contingent of people who are miserable, who want out, who are hard-pressed and committing suicide. To them, I offer my testimony . . . ," McClurkin told Jeffers. "My thing is not about hatred . . . ," he continued. "God loves everybody. He doesn't condone everything."

Earlier, the Grammy Award–winning Donnie McClurkin . . . Again (2003) had debuted at the top of the gospel charts and at number 12 on the Billboard R&B charts. Yolanda Adams joined McClurkin in the duet "The Prayer," one of the 11 tracks on the recording. "His new album . . . is just as wonderful as his Live in London," Lynn Norment wrote for Ebony (April 2003). "McClurkin's dynamic, unique sound and wonderful vocals continue to minister to the hearts of listeners." McClurkin's second Grammy Award winner, Psalms, Hymns & Spiritual Songs (2005), debuted at number one on the gospel charts and number five on the R&B charts. In an assessment of it for Billboard (April 9, 2005), Gordon Ely wrote, "McClurkin returns facing great expectations, and he doesn't disappoint. . . . He is clearly making music for the flock—albeit with a lush pop veneer and otherworldly lead and ensemble vocals that should please non-churchgoing folk as well. The 15 songs draw significantly on praise and worship standards, revamped with a gospel/R&B flavor that lends them new life and excitement ('Agnus Dei,' 'Draw Me Close'). McClurkin takes things home in grand fashion on two traditional foot-stompers ('I Love to Praise Him' and 'I Love Jesus') and wraps it dueting with Kirk Franklin on the cool, retro soul of 'Ooh Child.' McClurkin's focus on who he is and what he does only gets tighter and more exhilarating each time out." Following the release of Psalms, Hymns & Spiritual Songs, McClurkin was named best gospel artist at the BET (Black Entertainment Television) Awards ceremony. In early 2007 he was named a "Gospel Giant" by the Trumpet Award Foundation, which is supported by Turner Broadcasting.

In September 2007 Verity Records released The Essential Donnie McClurkin, a two-disc collection of the singer's best-known material. The following month McClurkin joined "Embrace the Change," a three-date gospel concert tour inspired by the presidential campaign of the Democratic U.S. senator Barack Obama of Illinois. The concert series was scheduled to take place in South Carolina, where Obama was trailing his fellow Democratic presidential hopeful Hillary Rodham Clinton in opinion polls, and demonstrate "how Barack Obama's family values and faith have shaped his leadership and commitment to bringing all people together around his movement for fundamental change," according to the States News Service (October 15, 2007). Some political pundits and members of the lesbian, gay, bisexual, and transgender (LGBT) community chided Obama for aligning himself with McClurkin, who some see as an anti-gay bigot. "I have consistently spoken directly to African-American religious leaders about the need to overcome the homophobia that persists in some parts our community so that we can confront issues like HIV/AIDS and broaden the reach of equal rights in this country," Obama said, according to the Associated Press (October 23, 2007). "I strongly believe that African Americans and the LGBT community must stand together in the fight for equal rights. And so I strongly disagree with Reverend McClurkin's views and will continue to fight for these rights as president of the United States to ensure that America is a country that spreads tolerance instead of division."

In addition to performing on such television programs as the *Arsenio Hall Show* and *Oprah*, McClurkin has appeared in several feature films, among them *The Fighting Temptations* (2003), *The Gospel* (2005), and *Diary of a Mad Black Woman* (2005). He contributed to the soundtracks of *The Prince of Egypt* (1998) and *The Ladykillers* (2004). He hosts a nationally syndicated radio show and has co-hosted the Stellar Gospel Music Awards ceremony several times.

McClurkin has one son, born in 2000, and one daughter, the latter of whom he adopted when she was 10; she is now in her 20s and lives in London, England. "God has been so great to me . . . ," he told Henderson in 2005. "The one thing missing is a wife and family." In his leisure time he enjoys watching cartoons, old movies, and sitcoms from the 1960s and 1970s.

—N.W.M.

Suggested Reading: *Detroit Free Press* G p1 Oct. 1, 2000, C p1 Oct. 26, 2004; *Ebony* p110 Aug 2001, p140 Oct. 2005; *Jet* p18 June 25, 2001, p54 Jan. 22, 2007; *New Pittsburgh Courier* p4 Dec. 11, 1999; *Newsday* B p2 Aug. 26, 2004; *Religion & Ethics Newsweekly* (on-line) Mar. 3, 2006

Selected Recordings: *Donnie McClurkin*, 1996; *Live in London and More*, 2000; *'Tis So Sweet*, 2000; *Donnie McClurkin . . . Again*, 2003; *Psalms, Hymns, & Spiritual Songs*, 2005; *The Essential Donnie McClurkin*, 2007

Selected Books: *Eternal Victim, Eternal Victor*, 2001

Selected Films: *The Donnie McClurkin Story: From Darkness to Light*, 2004

McConnell, Mike

July 26, 1943– U.S. director of national intelligence

Address: Office of the Director of National Intelligence, Washington, DC 20511

On February 20, 2007 John M. ("Mike") McConnell was sworn in as the director of national intelligence, charged with overseeing the 16 agencies that comprise the intelligence community of the United States government. Succeeding John Negroponte, McConnell is the second national director since the position was created, in 2004, on the recommendation of the National Commission on Terrorist Attacks Upon the United States—better known as the 9/11 Commission—which investigated intelligence failures surrounding the September 11, 2001 terrorist attacks. In his announcement of McConnell's nomination, as quoted in a White House press release on January 5, 2007, President George W. Bush lauded McConnell, a former vice admiral and career intelligence officer in the U.S. Navy, for demonstrating "the experience, the intellect, and the character to succeed in this position," and highlighted McConnell's track record of "ensuring that our military forces had the intelligence they need to fight and win wars." In accepting the nomination, McConnell vowed, as part of the global war on terror, to implement "better sharing of information" across the various intelligence agencies while improving "security processes" and ensuring "deeper penetration of our targets to provide the needed information for tactical, operational, and strategic decision-making."

Jim Watson/AFP/Getty Images

McConnell's 40-year career in intelligence began in the 1960s and includes distinguished tours as a naval intelligence officer in both Vietnam and Japan. Known for his integrity, work ethic, and keen insight into the rapid developments of global intelligence, McConnell quickly advanced through the military ranks, serving in the early 1990s as the joint intelligence officer for General Colin L. Powell, then the chairman of the Joint Chiefs of Staff, and Richard B. ("Dick") Cheney, then the secretary of defense, during Operation Desert Storm in the

Persian Gulf. From 1992 to 1996 McConnell was director of the National Security Agency (NSA) under President Bill Clinton, guiding the agency during pivotal, geopolitical shifts in the aftermath of the Cold War. In the dawn of the age of information technology and cellular communications, he made information security a priority for the NSA. Under McConnell's leadership, the organization was also credited with providing vital intelligence relating to the Bosnian conflict. Following his tenure at the NSA, McConnell spent 10 years as senior vice president at Booz Allen Hamilton Inc., a strategy consulting firm, leading its efforts in developing cutting-edge intelligence and information operations for both the private financial and government sectors. In that role McConnell became a prominent—albeit controversial—advocate for increased public-private partnership with regard to intelligence exchange and information security.

McConnell has been described by colleagues as a "soft-style gentleman," as Ben Szobody wrote for the South Carolina *Greenville News* (January 7, 2007), leading some to wonder, in the wake of his nomination as director of national intelligence, whether his gentle and courteous temperament was appropriate for such a post. Mark M. Lowenthal, a former staff director for the U.S. House Intelligence Committee, dismissed such concerns, telling Scott Shane for the *New York Times* (January 5, 2007), "[McConnell's] quiet manner and his lovely South Carolina accent belie it, but I have no doubt he can be forceful when necessary."

John Michael McConnell was born on July 26, 1943 in Greenville, South Carolina. His father, Harold E. "Mack" McConnell, worked in the shipping business, his mother, the former Dorothy Beatrice Cassell, in the garment industry. As a teenager McConnell attended the local Wade Hampton High School, from which he graduated in 1962. He next attended North Greenville College (renamed North Greenville University in 2005), for the first two years of college, becoming student-body president while working his way through school. Nicknamed "Dobie" by his fellow students, as Ben Szobody noted, McConnell is remembered by classmates for his quiet temperament, which perhaps masked his growing military ambition. McConnell finished his collegiate studies at Furman University, also located in Greenville, in 1966, graduating with a bachelor's degree in economics. He then joined the U.S. Navy and was commissioned as a line officer. Beginning in 1967 he served a tour in Vietnam as a member of the navy task force aboard the USS *Colleton* in the Mekong Delta, and from 1968 to 1970 he was stationed in Japan as a counterintelligence analyst for the Naval Investigative Service. Among his other naval assignments during the 1970s, McConnell served as commander of the Middle East Force in the Persian Gulf from 1974 to 1976 and as an intelligence officer for the Fleet Ocean Surveillance Information Facility in Spain, from 1976 to 1979. McConnell's building a career as a naval intelligence officer, which encompassed nearly 25

years, surprised his family and friends—particularly his father, who initially suspected that "Mike was just going to go ahead and get his [military] obligation over with," as he put it, according to Szobody.

In the mid-1980s McConnell worked as an intelligence officer of the Chief Pacific Fleet in Honolulu, Hawaii, and of the Seventh Fleet Western Pacific, before serving as executive assistant to the director of naval intelligence, in Washington, D.C. He earned a master's degree in public administration from George Washington University and a master's degree from the National Defense University, both in 1986, as well as a Ph.D. degree from the National Defense Intelligence College in 1992. In 1991 McConnell was chosen to be the director for joint staff intelligence, or J-2, for General Colin L. Powell, then the chairman of the Joint Chiefs of Staff, and Dick Cheney, then the secretary of defense, during Operation Desert Storm—the U.S.-led military campaign to liberate Kuwait from Iraqi invaders. McConnell conducted daily briefings for Powell and Cheney. At first "he didn't really know a lot of the Army-speak," Mark Gerencser, a senior vice president and director of Booz Allen's global government business, told Ben Szobody. "He immediately learned, studied it real hard, was honest with Powell and then rose to be one of his best advisers." McConnell also teamed with Lieutenant General Thomas W. Kelly, director of operations for the Joint Chiefs of Staff, to deliver daily reports on troop movements and aerial assaults for the news media. In his press briefings McConnell was admired for "distill[ing] complex ideas into easily understood terms," as Siobhan Gorman noted in the *Baltimore Sun* (January 6, 2007). According to Melissa Healy, writing for the *Los Angeles Times* (January 29, 1991), the press corps came to dub McConnell and Kelly's news briefings as the "Tom and Mike Hour." One journalist, as Healy reported, labeled the pair the "Huntley and Brinkley of the Pentagon's briefers [a reference to the longtime newscasters Chet Huntley and David Brinkley of the *Huntley-Brinkley Report*], complementing each other's talents and providing a calm but frank picture of the unfolding Persian Gulf War." "Against Kelly's bluff loquacity," Healy observed, "McConnell is the picture of a military intelligence analyst—meticulous, detail-oriented and scrupulously organized." Bill Smullen, a former aide to Powell, characterized McConnell as "measured, methodical, and detailed," according to Scott Shane, while U.S. senator Arlen Specter of Pennsylvania, as quoted by Globalsecurity.org, assessed McConnell's Gulf War service as "instrumental in saving U.S. and coalition lives" and in "bringing about a quick and decisive victory for allied forces."

In 1992 McConnell was promoted to vice admiral and appointed the head of the National Security Agency (NSA), reportedly the largest intelligence-gathering agency in the world. Assessing the role of the NSA, McConnell noted, as quoted by Scott

Shane and Tom Bowman in the *Austin-American Statesman* (January 7, 1996), "There is not a single event that the U.S. worries about in a foreign policy or foreign military context that NSA does not make a very direct contribution to." McConnell's four-year tenure, which coincided roughly with President Bill Clinton's first term, began during a pivotal juncture in the geopolitical landscape. With the dissolution of the Soviet Union, in December 1991, and the resulting end of the Cold War, McConnell redirected the NSA's attention toward emerging Internet technologies and cellular communications, whose growing importance revealed vulnerabilities within the agency's intelligence-gathering operations. He lobbied for information assurance (IA) and information defense, helping initiate an encryption technology that protected sensitive electronic transmissions across the Internet from enemy saboteurs. As Matthew M. Aid, an NSA historian, told Scott Shane in 2007, "[McConnell] begged and borrowed and took money from research and development to pay for operations." Under McConnell's watch the NSA was also credited with gathering vital intelligence relating to the violent ethnic clashes among Bosnian Muslims, Serbs, and Croats in the former Yugoslavia. McConnell drew criticism for permitting Congress to slash the NSA's budget in the mid-1990s; that reduction, though, resulted in the streamlining of top-level staff and reallocation of responsibility that enabled him to manage "in a more effective way, with oversight and accountability," as he explained to Siobhan Gorman. By the end of his tenure, in 1996, McConnell had received more praise than criticism for his leadership. William P. Crowell, McConnell's deputy at the NSA, told the *New York Times*, as quoted by a writer for the *BBC News* (January 5, 2007, on-line), that McConnell was a "consummate professional," while another colleague, Ronald D. Lee, characterized him as "an exceptionally gifted leader who was completely devoted to the rule of law and the Constitution." Senator Specter lauded McConnell for "his candor and openness with the Congress," as quoted by Globalsecurity.org.

In the spring of 1996, McConnell officially retired from military service and became a senior vice president at the McLean, Virginia–based Booz Allen Hamilton Inc., one of the world's leading strategy consulting firms. In recent years Booz Allen, a noted supplier of intelligence contracting for the U.S. government, particularly the NSA, had sparked a growing trend in government circles toward the outsourcing of intelligence initiatives to private firms. (John Gannon, a former CIA official, characterized Booz Allen as having probably "the biggest chunk of recent former CIA people of any of the corporations," as Siobhan Gorman noted.) McConnell spearheaded Booz Allen's programs in information security for the private finance and banking sectors. He oversaw the firm's support of the Presidential Commission on Critical Infrastructure Protection (PCCIP) and the Presidential Decision Directive 63 on Critical Infrastructure Protec-

tion, initiatives established by President Bill Clinton in 1997 to protect critical infrastructures in the private sector from computer sabotage. Addressing business leaders at the LOMA (formerly, Life Office Management Association) Systems Forum, a preeminent financial-services technology conference, McConnell observed, as quoted by *Business Wire* (April 11, 2002), "Business security is a key aspect of homeland defense. Security planning needs to be incorporated across an entire organization to reduce risks in operations, personnel and financial areas, as well as information systems, through a single, integrated strategy." He further lobbied for more "public-private partnership." McConnell also led Booz Allen's support of national defense clients, such as the U.S. Navy, the Defense Information Systems Agency, and the NSA. Commenting on the vulnerabilities of the federal security branches, McConnell told Charles Smith for *Insight on the News* (December 1, 1997), "Our biggest problem is how do we tell if we are under IW [information warfare] attack. It is difficult to determine if an incident is merely a software error, a teenage vandal intent on causing trouble, a criminal, a terrorist cell or another country actually carrying out an attack." With increasing threats to information security, McConnell also helped launch Booz Allen's "Intelligence to Operations" campaign, which helped the firm identify internal weaknesses and improve upon its own intelligence support for clients. Under McConnell's leadership, Booz Allen accumulated $1.59 billion in government contracts in 2006.

McConnell's 10-year tenure at the firm saw some controversy. From 1997 to 2002 McConnell helped Booz Allen secure $63 million in government contracts for the "Total Information Awareness" (TIA) program, a data-mining project launched by John M. Poindexter, a former national security adviser under President Ronald Reagan; the TIA program enabled the government to track potential terrorist activities through a unified systems search of government databases, private financial data, and personal records. Writing for *Salon.com* (January 8, 2007), Tim Shorrock described the TIA as a "warrantless surveillance of the telephone calls and e-mails of American citizens," and as Michael Hirsh and Mark Hosenball reported for *Newsweek* (January 4, 2007, on-line), the American Civil Liberties Union (ACLU) called TIA an "Orwellian program"—a reference to the novelist and essayist George Orwell, who wrote about threats to free society. Congressional lawmakers, too, questioned the TIA's observance of privacy laws. Raising eyebrows as well was McConnell's association with Poindexter, who was indicted during the 1980s for his role during the Iran-Contra affair, a political scandal involving the U.S. government's illegal sale of arms to Iran—with profits going to support the Contras, an anti-Communist militia in Nicaragua. Congress banned the TIA program in 2003. Many, though, continued to object to Booz Allen's close ties with the U.S. government. In June

2006 it was publicly revealed that the government was inspecting financial transactions of the Society for Worldwide Interbank Financial Telecommunication (SWIFT)—with Booz Allen hired to ensure that the process was handled fairly; the ACLU questioned whether Booz Allen was sufficiently objective for that task. Reports also surfaced that two Booz Allen infrastructure-service projects for the NSA, dubbed Groundbreaker and Trailblazer, had ended in failure. Despite the controversies, McConnell's tenure at Booz Allen garnered the admiration of his peers. Mark Gerencser described McConnel as a "futurist," as paraphrased by Szobody—"one of the best I've ever seen," Gerencser added.

On January 5, 2007 President George W. Bush nominated McConnell to succeed John Negroponte as the nation's second national director of intelligence—or "intelligence czar"—a position that was established in 2004 for oversight of 16 agencies of the intelligence community. Negroponte, whose tenure lasted 20 months (he has been appointed deputy to Secretary of State Condoleezza Rice), predicted that McConnell, with "wise stewardship and success," would "continue to drive forward the reforms we have initiated," as Katherine Shrader reported for SignOnSanDiego.com (January 5, 2007)—reforms aimed at unifying the intelligence networks. For his part, McConnell stated that his 10 years at Booz Allen had helped prepare him for his new post, by allowing him "to stay focused on national security and intelligence communities as a strategist and as a consultant. Therefore, in many respects, I never left," as quoted by Mark Mazzetti and David E. Sanger for the *New York Times* (January 5, 2007, on-line). Some lawmakers, however, including California Democratic congresswoman Jane Harman, expressed reservations concerning McConnell, who, along with General Michael V. Hayden, the recently appointed head of the CIA, "may complete the military takeover of all the civilian intelligence agencies," in her words, as Gorman reported in the *Baltimore Sun* (January 5, 2007). Such objections notwithstanding, the Senate confirmed the appointment of McConnell, who was sworn in on February 20, 2007.

In April 2007, two months after taking office, McConnell unveiled a "100-day plan" to improve national intelligence. His goals included hiring more immigrants and children of immigrants, decreasing the time it takes for candidates to undergo security checks, and establishing stronger ties with foreign intelligence groups.

The following August McConnell was among those who successfully urged Congress to amend the Foreign Intelligence Surveillance Act (FISA) so as to grant the government permission to eavesdrop on international telephone calls made from or received in the U.S., provided overseas parties are the primary subjects of the surveillance. Under the law—which is effective for six months, and which McConnell has said he wants to make permanent—intelligence officials still need to secure warrants from secret courts in order to listen in on conversations of U.S. residents or citizens. Some Democrats and legal observers have expressed concern about the newly revised FISA, suggesting that the law might give the government authority to seize business records and physical property in the U.S., so long as it is done under the guise of targeting a foreign suspect.

In September 2007 McConnell said that fewer than 100 Americans have had their phones tapped as a result of conversations with foreign terror suspects. (He declined, however, to elaborate on what period of time that figure covered.) He added that no Americans had been spied on without court orders and insisted that no warrantless tapping of Americans had occurred since at least as far back as February 2007, when he became director of national intelligence. In addition to arguing that the FISA amendments should be made permanent, McConnell proposed a measure that would extend retroactive legal immunity to telecommunications firms who cooperated with the NSA's programs prior to FISA's passage. The next month McConnell made public a "500-day plan" intended to build on six key areas outlined in the "100-day plan," including "creating a culture of collaboration," "accelerating information sharing," and "clarifying and aligning . . . authorities" of the director of national intelligence, as quoted in *Washington Technology* (October 12, 2007).

McConnell has received numerous honors, including three Bronze Stars and the Meritorious Service Medal with two Gold Stars from the secretary of the navy. In 2002 McConnell was named one of the top 25 most influential consultants by *Consulting* magazine. In 2004 he joined the board of directors of CompuDyne Corp., an industry leader in information security technologies for the public sector. McConnell is married to Terry McConnell, a homemaker, with whom he has two children and two stepchildren. He also has two children from a previous marriage.

—D.J.K.

Suggested Reading: *Baltimore Sun* A p3 Jan. 6, 2007; *Greenville (South Carolina) News* A p1 Jan. 7, 2007; *Los Angeles Times* p2 Jan. 29, 1991; *New York Times* A p3 Jan. 5, 2007; *Newsweek* (on-line) Jan. 4, 2007; *Salon.com* Jan. 8, 2007

Courtesy of John McNeil

McNeil, John

Mar. 23, 1948– Jazz trumpeter; writer; educator

Address: 500 Second St., No. 2, Brooklyn, NY 11215-2503

Writing about the jazz trumpeter John McNeil for the *New York Times* (February 15, 2007), Ben Ratliff remarked that McNeil, a "kind of trickster figure," is the stylistic scion of a trumpet lineage that traces its roots to Freddie Hubbard and Thad Jones, "with a little of Blue Mitchell's dark, warm sound, and Lester Bowie's imagination in free improvising." McNeil is frequently hailed by colleagues and music journalists as one of the most talented musicians in the business. Renowned for his ability to fuse classical harmony with bebop and free jazz, he is also acclaimed for his mastery of difficult meter and complex arrangements; he tours with several bands and is in demand as a producer, arranger, writer, composer, and educator. Since his days as part of the underground jazz scene that flourished in New York City's Greenwich Village in the 1970s, McNeil's career and professional reputation have grown enormously. To the evident disappointment of critics including Ratliff—who called McNeil "one of the best improvisers working in jazz" while referring to the "rather questionable choices" of nominees for 2007 Grammy Awards in the jazz category—McNeil has never gained entree to prominent awards ceremonies or enjoyed mainstream success. Yet he commands enormous respect among both academics and ordinary jazz fans, a feat that is doubly impressive given the physical hardship he has had to overcome.

John McNeil was born on March 23, 1948 in Yreka (pronounced "why-REE-kuh"), California, near the Oregon border. His father owned a grocery store in the town. His sister, Rory McNeil, currently the mayor of Yreka, "wields absolute power over all Yrekans," McNeil said to *Current Biography*. In the late 1950s McNeil saw the legendary trumpeter Louis Armstrong on Milton Berle's television show and developed a desire to master the trumpet himself. But beginning in childhood, he struggled with the neuromuscular disorder Charcot-Marie-Tooth disease, an illness he inherited from his father (who did not display signs of the disorder until he was in his 70s). Charcot-Marie-Tooth disease affects the nerves and muscles in the extremities of the body; though it rarely has an impact on the facial musculature, McNeil's face, as well as his tongue and diaphragm, bear the effects of the disorder. McNeil laughed when he told Ben Ratliff, "So, basically, I have the big three for trumpet playing." McNeil wore braces from his legs to his neck from age seven through 16, when he underwent operations that eliminated the need for them. When he was in high school, he underwent diagnostic tests at the Mayo Clinic and was told that he should not attempt to build a career as a musician, advice that he ignored.

When he was in grade school, McNeil taught himself to play the trumpet and read music. He told Frank Tafuri for the Omnitone Web site (January 2006) that he "used to copy Chet Baker a bit" when he started out. By the time he graduated from high school, in 1966, he had already begun playing professionally. He enrolled as a trumpet major at the University of Portland, in Oregon, where an instructor revamped his technique, eliminating "many of the bad habits acquired from being self-taught," as McNeil told *Current Biography*. McNeil graduated with a degree in trumpet performance and then studied the instrument briefly at the University of Miami. Afterward, he launched his professional career in earnest, playing as many gigs as he could. At one point, when a gig required it, he learned to play the alto saxophone. During a December 2006 interview with the Swedish Web site *Jazz pa svenska*, McNeil recalled, "I played alto sax at a dude ranch, which is a ranch where people from the city can go and pretend they are cowboys. It was a terrible band, I was a terrible saxophonist and the whole experience was like being trapped in a Salvador Dali painting."

In the mid-1970s McNeil left the West Coast for New York. There, he occasionally played trumpet with the Thad Jones/Mel Lewis Orchestra and the Gerry Mulligan Concert Jazz Band. He began leading his own groups at venues including the famed Greenwich Village jazz club Boomer's; his sidemen included the pianists Mulgrew Miller and Hal Galper, the bassist Rufus Reid, and the saxophonist Bill Evans. In the late 1970s McNeil joined the Horace Silver Quintet, touring Europe and North America. At around the same time, he signed with the Danish label SteepleChase as a solo artist. He made nine recordings for the label, among them *Embarkation* (1978), *Faun* (1979), *Look to the Sky* (1979), and *Clean Sweep* (1981), with musicians such as David Liebman on tenor sax, soprano sax, and flute; Richie Beirach on piano; Buster Williams on bass; Billy Hart on drums; and Joanne Brackeen on piano. *Look to the Sky* in particular stands as a perennial favorite among trumpet players, since it features McNeil's collaboration with his fellow trumpeter Tom Harrell. The year after that album was released, McNeil began teaching occasional clinics at the prestigious New England Conservatory of Music. His former students include the successful jazz trumpeter Dave Douglas.

In 1982 McNeil's physical condition took a turn for the worse. After completing work on *I've Got the World on a String* (1983) and having a particularly bad day in 1983 while recording the live album *Things We Did Last Summer*, he abruptly stopped recording; he did not release another solo album for 13 years, due primarily to Charcot-Marie-Tooth disease. He began to experience unexpected bouts of bodily weakness and a loss of motor control, which sometimes made it impossible to play. For a time he kept up a regular performance schedule, but the difficulty of predicting how well he would be able to play eventually made that impractical. He told Ratliff, "Then I just stopped everything. The irregularity was maddening. I began to think I didn't have any talent. It does strange things to your confidence. You don't have to fail absolutely to have no confidence; you just have to fail every so often." He focused once again on revamping his technique, developing a method of balancing the muscles in his face in order to maintain sufficient compression in his lips. He also underwent surgery to have his spine reconstructed.

In 1989 McNeil increased his duties at the New England Conservatory of Music, taking on a weekly music-theory class that he still teaches. According to McNeil's faculty biography on the conservatory's Web site, "He has a reputation for encouraging his students to establish an emotional connection to their playing, and to develop a strong personal style." In an interview with Craig Jolley for the Web site *All About Jazz* (May 19, 2005), McNeil said, "Students get from me in the classroom what they would get playing in a band. I'm not big on theory for theory's sake. I teach students how to play better, how to put things together. . . . I'm also kind of a brass troubleshooter. I had a lot of trouble learning to play the trumpet, a lot of problem-solving experience, so I became a good brass teacher. There's a whole range of people that call me up for lessons from time to time, which is ironic considering I've been known more as a creative trumpet player than technician." In 1993 Gerard & Sarzin Publishing Co. brought out McNeil's two-volume treatise *The Art of Jazz Trumpet*, a comprehensive study of modern jazz trumpet playing. Six years later the company published an updated edition of the work, combined into a single volume

and augmented by a CD. The book includes a brief history of McNeil's own experience with the jazz trumpet, a selected discography, and extensive analysis of valve technique, phrasing, alternate fingerings, and articulation. It also includes practice exercises to develop rhythmic diversity, finger coordination, and jazz articulation. In the introduction, McNeil wrote, "I remember how abysmally long it took me to learn to play jazz on the trumpet, and I would hate to see anybody else have to spend the same amount of time. . . . Jazz is, however, an expression of life, and life can be untidy. If a player is operating at the far frontiers of his or her ability, pushing the envelope so to speak, it seems to me that a certain amount of failure is inevitable. Maybe even desirable." Early in the book, McNeil acknowledged one of his heroes, the alto saxophonist and bebop pioneer Charlie Parker, as "the fountainhead of contemporary jazz."

By 1996 McNeil's playing was reliable enough for him to return to the recording studio. He released *Hip Deep*, a collaboration with the clarinetist and saxophonist Kenny Berger, on Brownstone Records; the album also featured John Mosca on trombone, Dean Johnson on bass, and Steve Johns on drums. *Brooklyn Ritual* (1998), another collaboration with Berger, released on the Synergy label, also included the work of Mosca and Johns. In 1997, after *Brooklyn Ritual* was recorded but before it was released, Charcot-Marie-Tooth disease once again threatened McNeil's career. He temporarily lost the ability to extend the fingers in his right hand—which he used to play. He had two trumpets made for the left hand, and over the next couple of years he taught himself to play them. Having made that transition, he recorded the album *Fortuity*, released in 2001 on his old label, SteepleChase. *Fortuity* featured Allan Chase on alto saxophone and baritone saxophone, Eric Thompson on drums, Kate Vincent on viola, and Derek Olphy on flute. Eventually, McNeil regained the use of his right hand and returned to his normal way of playing. He was recently fitted for a set of sterling-silver finger braces that give him stability and allow for greater flexibility in his fingers, thus vastly improving his valve technique. He has once again become a consistent performer on the New York jazz scene.

In 2001 International Production Group released an instructional video called *John McNeil's Jazz Series*, in two volumes. According to *Music Educators Journal* (January 2001), McNeil "introduces viewers to major scales and modes, minor (major seventh) scales, basic concepts of chords and scales, scale construction, tetrachords, and the advantages of being able to sing jazz and blues scales in order to recognize and play them on an instrument." Those videos were re-released on DVD in 2007.

In 2003 McNeil signed with a small label, Omnitone, and released *This Way Out*, a record that included Gorka Benitez on tenor saxophone, Giulia Valle on bass, and Joe Smith on drums. The album, which McNeil recorded in Barcelona, Spain, exhibits clear Spanish influences. He originally composed the music in preparation for a three-week tour in Spain with Benitez; the tour was so successful that McNeil booked a studio at its conclusion and spent two days recording an album with Benitez and others. McNeil told a reporter for *Jazz pa svenska*, "Spanish music tends to have a high emotional content. If you're into self-expression and speaking the truth about who you are (as I am) it's a natural fit. There's a lot of room in there to laugh and cry." David Adler wrote for *Jazz Times* (January/February 2004) about the album, "McNeil's writing is enormously sophisticated and a bit warped . . . full of conceptual surprises."

In 2004 Omnitone released *Sleep Won't Come*, with McNeil on trumpet, Jeff Jenkins on piano and prepared piano, and Kent McLagan on bass. The album was inspired by McNeil's frequent bouts with insomnia, for which he takes the prescription sleeping medication Ambien. The band that played on the album was jokingly called Insomnia. Jay Collins wrote for the Web site *One Final Note* (December 22, 2004, on-line), "What emerges is a slightly bi-polar program of haunting reveries, mixed in with some arousing, energized performances that demonstrate the breadth of McNeil's goal and his trio's talents. . . . While the musicians are top-flight and McNeil proves that he deserves more ink, taken as a whole, this can be a disjointing listen, as several of the pieces prove to be mere mood-setters or unresolved sketches. . . . However, when one keeps McNeil's purpose in mind [capturing 'the scenes that went through your head when you are laying in the dark staring at nothing'], this diverse range of compositional moods and terrains proves worthwhile." Mark Keresman, a contributing writer for *Jazz Review* (on-line), remarked on the record's "concise, witty tunes."

The year 2004 also saw the publication of McNeil and Laurie Frink's *Flexus* (published by OmniTone Books), which addressed the physical demands of trumpet improvisation. The jacket blurb states that "the physical act of playing needs to be a conditioned reflex." In 2006 Omnitone released *East Coast Cool*, whose title alludes to the West Coast—or "cool"—school of jazz dating back to the 1950s; the record includes the work of Allan Chase on baritone saxophone, John Hebert on bass, and Matt Wilson on drums. Writing for *Dusted* (January 3, 2006, on-line), Derek Taylor opined, "Temperature tags have long since fallen out of fashion as codifiers for coastal jazz differences. But damn if trumpeter John McNeil hasn't struck pay dirt, intended incongruities aside, with *East Coast Cool*. . . . The tunes, all but three written by McNeil, delight in subtle and mischievous upendings of expectation. But it's all done with a close attention to tunefulness and it often takes a careful ear to fully discern just how subversive the band's being with both its arrangements and improvisations." Troy Collins, a contributor to *All About Jazz*, wrote, "Enjoyably accessible yet intriguingly innovative, McNeil and his quartet have taken [Gerry] Mulligan and [Chet] Baker's piano-less quartet inspired music and drawn an overt parallel to Ornette Coleman's piano-less quartet innovations of the same time period [the 1950s], building a conceptual link between the two." Chuck Graham wrote for the *Tucson (Arizona) Citizen* (March 9, 2006) about the record, "The artistic effect is a little like seeing an impressionist painter's version of DaVinci's *The Last Supper*."

In his interview with Craig Jolley, McNeil said, "I tend to write arrangements with improvisation integrated into the composition instead of head-improv-head. There's nothing wrong with that; it's just boring if you do it on every tune. These days, when it's time to write, something clicks, and I can usually just do it . . . if I were going to give advice to anyone about how to write I'd say, 'Don't fall in love with what you write.'" McNeil told Frank Tafuri, "To be a jazz musician, you have to be a 'professional listener'. . . . There's basically no kind of music on this planet that I don't hear on a semi-regular basis. And New York's a great place for listening."

McNeil recently helped put together My Band Foot Foot, in order to cover the music of the 1960s teenage girl group The Shaggs, a campy favorite of a number of New York City underground musicians. McNeil told Jolley, "It's the best or the worst thing you've ever heard. They didn't know anything about music. The drummer was inept—sometimes she'd be playing in two different tempos at once; and their melodies were unstructured. There's a cult following—people know the lyrics. We're doing largely instrumental versions. It's trumpet, trombone, squeezebox, violin, guitar, bass and drums, and we all sing a little."

McNeil's latest regular gig is a standing Sunday-night date in a small back room at Biscuit, a barbecue restaurant in the Brooklyn, New York, neighborhood of Park Slope. With the noted tenor saxophonist Bill McHenry, he co-leads a quartet there that plays mainly pieces from the 1950s by Dizzy Gillespie, Wilbur Harden, Gerry Mulligan, and Russ Freeman. (McNeil's group played at the same site when it was a jazz restaurant called Night & Day.) Ratliff wrote of the quartet's performances, "The gig has become one of the best regular jazz events in the city," and he called McNeil "one of the best improvisers working in jazz." The McNeil/McHenry Quartet earned stellar reviews for their performances at the Village Vanguard in August 2007.

McNeil is married to a professional trombonist, Lolly Bienenfeld.

—S.J.D.

Suggested Reading: *Dusted* (on-line) Jan. 3, 2006; New England Conservatory of Music Web site; *New York Times* (on-line) Feb. 15, 2007

Selected Recordings: *Embarkation*, 1978; *Faun*, 1979; *Look to the Sky*, 1979; *The Glass Room*, 1979; *Clean Sweep*, 1981; *Things We Did Last Summer*, 1983; *I've Got the World on a String*, 1983; *Hip Deep*, 1996; *Brooklyn Ritual*, 1998; *Fortuity*, 2001; *This Way Out*, 2003; *Sleep Won't Come*, 2004; *East Coast Cool*, 2006

Selected Videos: *John McNeil's Jazz Series, Vol. One*, 2001

Selected Books: *The Art of Jazz Trumpet, Vols. One and Two*, 1993; *Flexus* (with Laurie Frink), 2004

Michael Weschler Photography, courtesy of Union Square Hospitality Group

Meyer, Danny

Mar. 14, 1958– Restaurateur

Address: Union Square Hospitality Group, 24 Union Sq. E., New York, NY 10003

Over two decades ago, at the age of 27, the New York City restaurateur and philanthropist Danny Meyer became a novice entrepreneur as the owner of the Union Square Cafe, in a then-downtrodden neighborhood near New York University. Today he is credited with almost single-handedly revitalizing the Union Square area and transforming it into an upscale neighborhood. Meyer founded and owns the Union Square Hospitality Group (USHG), which operates five of the most critically acclaimed fine dining establishments in New York: Gramercy Tavern, Eleven Madison Park, Tabla,

and Blue Smoke and Jazz Standard as well as the Union Square Cafe. Meyer and USHG operate Hudson Yards Catering and all three restaurants housed in the Museum of Modern Art: Terrace 5, Café 2, and the Modern. He also owns Shake Shack, a wildly popular fast-food outlet in Madison Square Park that donates part of its profits to the Madison Square Park Conservancy. Meyer is well-known for his charitable work with local and national organizations that fight hunger, and he has long won praise for the hospitality shown to patrons of his restaurants. He told Julie Schlosser for *Fortune* (July 24, 2006), "Once a month I meet with every employee who's been hired in the previous four weeks. We have over 1,000 employees right now. And we spend a lot of time talking about the power of hospitality."

Daniel Harris Meyer was born on March 14, 1958 in St. Louis, Missouri, to Morton L. Meyer and Roxanne Harris Frank. He has at least one sibling—a brother, Thomas. His maternal grandfather, Irving B. Harris, an entrepreneur and philanthropist, founded the Toni Home Permanent Co., the Pittway Corp. (a manufacturer of burglar and fire alarms), and other highly successful businesses, and he financed the creation of the Yale Child Study Center, the Erickson Institute for Advanced Studies in Child Development, the University of Chicago's Graduate School of Public Policy Studies, and the Ounce of Prevention Fund, among other educational, child-welfare, and cultural endeavors. Meyer's father owned a travel, hospitality, and real-estate company. He became a representative of a French firm that grew into the Relais & Chateaux chain of luxury restaurants and hotels, and for a time he operated the Seven Gables Inn in St. Louis. According to the USHG Web site, Meyer's family "relished great food, cooking, get-togethers, travel and hospitality." Both his parents loved French culture and cuisine, and as a youngster Danny took French-language lessons. He often accompanied his father on business trips to Europe. He told Julie Schlosser that his father "founded some exciting companies" but "expanded far too quickly and didn't surround himself with the kind of people who could compensate for his weaknesses." "I watched him go bankrupt on two different occasions," Meyer said. "That has colored the way I view growth. It was almost a decade before I could even get comfortable with the idea of a second restaurant."

Meyer attended the John Burroughs School, a college-preparatory junior high and high school in St. Louis, and then Trinity College, in Hartford, Connecticut. During his undergraduate years he worked summers for his father as a tour guide in Rome, Italy. After he graduated, with a bachelor's degree in political science, he moved to Chicago, Illinois, to work as the Cook County field director for the unsuccessful 1980 presidential campaign of Republican congressman John B. Anderson of Illinois, who ran as an independent. He then worked as a salesperson for several years before moving to

New York. He spent much of 1984 as an assistant manager at Pesca, an Italian seafood restaurant in the Flatiron District. He next studied cooking as an apprentice in Italy and Bordeaux, France. In both countries he "learned a lot about shopping for food" as well, as he told an interviewer for the Web site of the Institute of Culinary Education (ICE) in 2003.

In 1985, at the age of 27, Meyer opened his first restaurant, the Union Square Cafe. He told Robert Levin for the *New York Enterprise Report* (August 16, 2006), "I just had to give birth to this business. It was bubbling inside me; it was a passion that just had to happen." He chose the then-scruffy Union Square site, which is bounded by 17th Street on the north side and 14th Street on the south, in large part because of the Greenmarket Farmers Market located there; four days a week, proprietors of small farms come to Union Square to sell their produce, which includes a far greater variety of items than is offered in stores. According to the restaurant critic Frank Bruni, writing 20 years later for the *New York Times* (October 12, 2005), Meyer was then "relatively inexperienced" but also "wildly optimistic" when, disregarding the many people who disparaged his plan as "foolhardy," he opened his "unusual restaurant in a Manhattan neighborhood not then associated with fine dining." "The neighborhood wasn't the only wild card," Bruni continued. "This restaurateur had decided to wed serious food to mirthful, big-hearted service, to make diners feel that in going out they were coming home. He had also decided to jettison ethnic boundaries, emphasizing Italian but inviting French and even Asian into the mix." The Union Square Cafe was an instant success, immediately earning three stars out of four from the *New York Times*. Later, in the Zagat Survey, which rates restaurants, Union Square Cafe was voted the most popular restaurant in New York an unprecedented seven times (1996–2002). In 1992 the café won the prestigious James Beard Award for Excellence in Service and Hospitality. Meyer told Levin, "Excellence is how well something works technically. Hospitality is how well the people who are using that product feel while they're using it. They're very different things, but both matter." Robin Landis of Ridgewood, New Jersey, echoed the sentiments of many of the café's patrons when she wrote in a letter to the *New York Times* (September 24, 2006) that 15 years earlier, when she worked near the café and sometimes ate there, "Meyer was usually up front greeting the line of waiting patrons. Scruffy and jeans-clad though we were, he treated us like favored guests and as though our business really mattered to him. He was so gracious that to this day, I still have warm feelings for the restaurant. And the food is fabulous." Meyer has often been credited for almost single-handedly rejuvenating the Union Square area through his activism and commitment to neighborhood improvement projects.

In 1994 Meyer opened his second restaurant, the Gramercy Tavern, in collaboration with the chef Tom Colicchio. The week that it began operating, its image appeared on the cover of *New York* magazine. Gramercy Tavern quickly earned three stars from the *New York Times,* and it took first place in the Zagat Survey's list of New York City's most popular restaurants in 2003, 2005 and 2006. (In 2007 it fell to second place, with the Union Square Cafe having become most popular.) In mid-2007 the tavern charged $36 for a three-course lunch, $55 for a five-course lunch, and $76 for a three-course dinner. It also offered so-called tasting menus, in which, for either $82 or $98, diners received small portions of nine dishes. Adam Platt, who reviewed the restaurant after Michael Anthony took over as chef, wrote for *New York* (April 23, 2007) that the menu is filled with "subtle, slightly bucolic creations like lightly smoked lobster (decked with seasonal springtime ramps), crispy poached barnyard chicken, and delicious soups made with parsnips and strips of bacon or chunks of creamy heirloom cauliflower." Platt's smoked-trout appetizer "melted, in a most pleasing way, into a bed of crunchy pickled onions and sunchoke puree"; the braised lamb shoulder, he reported, "comes wrapped in a tight little roll, which breaks open over a bed of Swiss chard when you crack it with your fork." "The star of the show . . . ," he wrote, "is the bread pudding, which is flavored with rich deposits of chocolate and served with candied cherries and a spoonful of barely melting anise ice cream."

In 1998 Meyer formed the Union Square Hospitality Group as an umbrella company for his businesses. That same year he opened Eleven Madison Park in a historic skyscraper facing the long-neglected Madison Square Park. "Social historians will be fascinated by Eleven Madison Park, a conscious homage to the area's past," the restaurant critic Ruth Reichl wrote for the *New York Times* (January 27, 1999). "The enormous painting on the back wall is a misty remembrance of the park at the turn of the century, and the menu is a thoughtful return to Continental cuisine." Reichl had mixed feelings about the cuisine, awarding the restaurant only two stars, but she praised the staff as unusually warm and friendly and noted that "the place has been packed since it opened three months ago." Five years later Eleven Madison Park won the James Beard Award for Best Service in America. Also in 1998 Meyer opened Tabla, next door to Eleven Madison Park. Offering the chef Floyd Cardoz's new Indian cuisine, Tabla immediately garnered three stars from Ruth Reichl in the *New York Times* (February 24, 1999). It was soon voted the top Indian restaurant in New York by the Zagat Survey, the Web site CitySearch, and the magazine *Time Out New York.* In the same neighborhood in 2004, Meyer opened Shake Shack, as part of a $10 million fundraising effort to improve Madison Square Park. A portion of every purchase at Shake Shack is given to the Madison Square Park Conservancy. Shake Shack, which sells hot dogs, hamburgers, fries, frozen custard, thick milkshakes, lemonade, iced tea, beer, and wine, quickly became a popular lunchtime destination for local office workers, who sometimes wait in line for an hour or more before being served. Would-be customers can check the length of the line in real time via the Internet.

In 2002 Meyer judged the 14th Annual Jack Daniel's Barbeque Championship in Lynchburg, Tennessee. In March of that year, he opened a pit-barbeque and jazz restaurant called Blue Smoke and Jazz Standard. The eatery won the 2003 CitySearch Awards for best barbecue and best jazz club in New York City and was featured in *New York*'s "Where to Eat Now" issue in 2004. At Blue Note and Jazz Standard, as a way of keeping children occupied and inspiring them to behave properly during their meals, they are given a chance to decorate their own cookies before the meals begin. Each child's particular cookie is served to him or her after the main course is eaten. "That's hospitality, not service . . . ," Meyer told Joe Yonan for the *Washington Post* (February 21, 2007), adding, "All people are kids. They want to be delighted, and they want to know you did something for them."

In the winter of 2004–05, after a restoration and expansion project, the Museum of Modern Art reopened in Manhattan with three new restaurants owned and managed by USHG: Terrace 5 and its twin, Café 2, and the Modern, a fine-dining restaurant, which was named best new restaurant of 2005 by the James Beard Foundation. USHG also caters events at the museum. In 2005 USHG added a division called Hudson Yards Catering, located in a former warehouse on 28th Street on Manhattan's West Side. The ground floor was converted into an event space, and kitchens were installed on the upper floors.

With the award-winning chef Michael Romano, who became the Union Square Cafe's chef in 1988 and Meyer's business partner in 1993, Meyer wrote *Union Square Cafe Cookbook: 160 Favorite Recipes from New York's Acclaimed Restaurant* (1994) and *Second Helpings from Union Square Cafe* (2001). The former earned the Julia Child Award from the International Association of Culinary Professionals (IACP) for best new cookbook by a first-time author. Meyer's third book, *Setting the Table: The Transforming Power of Hospitality in Business*, was published in 2006.

Meyer told R. W. Apple Jr. for the *New York Times* (February 2, 2005) that Jean-Claude Vrinat, the owner of the acclaimed restaurant Taillevent, in Paris, is his role model. "He is the first, best and most persevering hospitalitarian I have ever met," Meyer said. "From him I learned that luxury and kindness need not mean pomposity. At Taillevent, they have fun taking service seriously." In an interview with Linda Tischler for *Fast Company* (September 2006), Meyer listed the characteristics he looks for in potential workers: "The first is a natural warmth and optimism. I either feel that from a

person, or not. The second is intelligence and curiosity, and it doesn't have to be about the restaurant business. I love when I can converse with people about theater, art, books, or sports. The third is work ethic. You'd be surprised at how many people show up late for an interview, or don't shave. The fourth is empathy. I like to ask how their previous employer felt when they gave notice, and gauge their response. And the fifth is a combination of integrity and self-awareness. I want somebody who's thoughtful about who they are and where things fit into their lives. If they're not accountable to themselves, it's unlikely they'll be accountable to the people they're working with."

In the early 1990s Meyer testified at a U.S. Department of Agriculture hearing about school lunches. He told Marian Burros for the *New York Times* (December 8, 1993), "By buying from the Greenmarkets, we have forced the traditional sources of food distribution to offer safer, fresher food. The Government as a purchaser has so much more power than we do. If it can come up with a coherent kind of diet objectives for schools, because it is shelling out all that cash, it could change the way food is produced. If the Government doesn't care if apples have little holes in them, the producers will say, 'Fine, we won't spray them.'"

Meyer currently serves on the executive boards of Share Our Strength, an organization whose aim is to eliminate hunger among children in the U.S., and City Harvest, which collects unused food from such sources as hotels, restaurants, and corporate cafeterias in New York City and delivers it to community food programs in the city's five boroughs. He is on the executive committees of NYC & Co., the city's official tourism and marketing agency, and the Madison Square Park Conservancy and is the co-chair of the Union Square Partnership. He is a frequent guest at *Food & Wine*'s annual Aspen Classic and has been a guest speaker for the Culinary Institute of America, Cornell University, and the National Restaurant Association, among other institutions or organizations.

In 1996 Meyer won the IACP Restaurateur of the Year Award and the James Beard Humanitarian of the Year Award for charitable work and service to the community. The next year he earned the New York City Partnership and Chamber of Commerce Annual Small-Business Award "for his success in the restaurant world as well as his work to improve the Union Square neighborhood and for the campaign against hunger," as Lisa W. Foderaro reported for the *New York Times* (May 2, 1997).

R. W. Apple Jr. described Meyer as "tall, lean and soft-spoken" and as unusually self-effacing. With the former Audrey Heffernan, a one-time actress whom he married in 1988, Meyer has two daughters and two sons: Hallie, Gretchen, Charles, and Peyton. The family live in New York. Meyer told the ICE interviewer, "My wife and I usually eat what's in season. We belong to a community-supported agricultural farm. We pick up different organic vegetables once a week at an Upper West

Side church. Since I'm not home a lot and my wife doesn't cook, I tend to make soups, stews, pastas and things I know she can reheat during the week. When I am home, I keep it simple and fun. . . . If we have friends over, I like to serve cheeses, bread, dips and simple food so I can spend as much time as possible with my guests."

—S.J.D.

Suggested Reading:CBS News (on-line) Jan. 26, 2003; Fast Company p29+ Sep. 2006; Fortune p42 July 24, 2006; Forward.com Nov. 17, 2006; Inc.com July 2006; Institute of Culinary Education Web site; New York Enterprise Report (on-line) Aug.16, 2006; New York Times F p1+ Feb. 2, 2005; Union Square Hospitality Group Web site; Washington Post F p1+ Feb. 21, 2007

Selected Books: Union Square Cafe Cookbook (with Michael Romano), 1994; Second Helpings from Union Square Cafe (with Michael Romano), 2001; Setting the Table: The Transforming Power of Hospitality in Business, 2006

Mitchell, Jerry

1960– Choreographer; theater director

Address: c/o McDonald/Selznick Associates, 140 Broadway, 46th Fl., New York, NY 10005

In early 2004 a theater fan seeking tickets for a show on Broadway could have chosen to see a revival of the musical *Gypsy*; the long-running hit *Hairspray*; or *Never Gonna Dance*, an old-fashioned yarn about a vaudeville hoofer who comes to New York City to earn cash. Those productions all featured dance numbers by Jerry Mitchell, one of the only choreographers ever to have three Broadway musicals running simultaneously. He repeated that feat in 2005, with simultaneous runs of *Hairspray*, *La Cage Aux Folles*, and *Dirty Rotten Scoundrels*. "I love Broadway!" Mitchell exclaimed in his acceptance speech for the 2005 Tony Award for best choreography in a musical, as quoted by Christine Cox in the *South Bend (Indiana) Tribune* (July 17, 2005). (That year he had been nominated for his work on both *La Cage Aux Folles* and *Dirty Rotten Scoundrels* and won for the former.) Mitchell himself was a successful Broadway dancer before he became a choreographer and—more recently—a director. "I have exacting standards," he told Jesse Green for the *New York Times* (April 15, 2007), "and unlike most dancers always knew what everyone else was supposed to be doing. I'm mathematical. I can't spell my own name, but I can see where everyone is now and where they will be a moment later. I was always outside the box."

Mitchell's career has included work on several Broadway adaptations of hit films—*Hairspray*, *Never Gonna Dance*, *Dirty Rotten Scoundrels*, and *The Full Monty*, among others. Such adaptations are easy prey for critics, who sometimes automatically dismiss a show as either too similar to or too different from the original version. Mitchell, however, has won wide praise for his ability to navigate those pitfalls successfully. *Legally Blonde*, which premiered in 2007, is his first show as both director and choreographer. "The thing that I love most about what I do is I get a group of people together into one place and they're transported into a place outside their daily lives," he told Cox. "It's not always a happy place. . . . But the stories I'm interested in are stories that give people hope. I think, in general, it's what theater does the best."

Born in 1960, Jerry Mitchell grew up in Paw Paw, Michigan, a farming town with a population of approximately 3,500. His parents, Gene and Katie Mitchell, owned and operated a Paw Paw restaurant named Gene's Friendly Place. Mitchell has two older brothers: Gary, a firefighter, and Rick, the athletic director for Paw Paw High School, the Mitchell brothers' alma mater. Mitchell has remained exceptionally close to his family, and his parents have attended many of his awards ceremonies. They have been accepting of his homosexuality, which he revealed to them when he was 30. "My parents and my brothers have always been there for me. Always," he told Cox. "In this business, I've met a lot of people who don't have that support." Rather than finding the town's small size stifling, Mitchell has said that Paw Paw's intimacy made for an especially supportive atmosphere. "Living in Paw Paw and growing up there I was sort of free to do whatever I wanted to do and that was a great thing for me as a kid," he told Pam Gehl for the *Kalamazoo (Michigan) Gazette* (June 20, 2005). From a young age, Mitchell was interested in musicals. "I *knew* I was going to be in this business," he recalled to Cox. "I think I knew since I was five years old. I don't know how I knew. I didn't see a Broadway show until I was 17." When Mitchell was eight, the Paw Paw Village Players, the local theater troupe, cast him in a production of *The Music Man*. Mitchell has dated his awareness of his homosexuality to around that time, although he had girlfriends as a teenager.

Mitchell focused on such sports as football, basketball, and track until, at age 15, he was sidelined after breaking his collarbone in a bicycle accident. He began taking jazz and tap lessons, despite initial reluctance, to keep his legs in shape. "I was a little afraid, as most boys are," he explained to a reporter for *American Theatre* (October 2004), "but once I was there, you couldn't get me out." Mitchell's first instructor, Cindy Meeth of Paw Paw's Meeth Dance Studio, offered him free dance lessons and paid him to teach younger students as an incentive to keep him dancing. After his collarbone healed, Mitchell returned to athletics; in addition, he frequently choreographed routines for the school's

Paul Hawthorne/Getty Images

Jerry Mitchell

band and pompom and cheerleading squads and also choreographed several school plays, including a production of *Grease*. The summer after his junior year in high school, Mitchell was accepted as an apprentice at the Hope Summer Repertory Theatre, in Holland, Michigan. During his senior year he auditioned to replace an injured dancer in a touring show of *West Side Story*; though the show interrupted his studies, both his parents and his school principal allowed him to leave for the six-month, 42-state tour. Despite that absence—which required him to give up the post of class president and also to miss the basketball season—Mitchell graduated with his class, in 1978, and he won a conference championship for the high jump, a track event. That fall he enrolled at Webster University, in St. Louis, Missouri, which had awarded him a scholarship. There, he studied ballet and earned membership in the Actors' Equity Association, a professional group. He also began receiving his first residual checks, for dancing in an advertisement for the soft drink Dr. Pepper.

Mitchell's schooling was interrupted when, on a spring-break trip to New York City in 1980, he accompanied two female friends to an open audition for Agnes de Mille's production of the musical *Brigadoon*. Neither of Mitchell's friends made the cut, but de Mille was impressed with Mitchell's height (six feet, four inches) and offered him a role. Webster officials allowed Mitchell to earn academic credit for his performance, and he planned on returning to school after the show closed. Instead, he immediately got another part, as a dancer in the musical version of *Woman of the Year*, which was followed by a part in the film version of the musical *The Best Little Whorehouse in Texas*. Mitchell

never returned to Webster, instead pursuing a career as a dancer. As he won parts in the choruses of numerous shows, Mitchell became more and more interested in being behind the scenes, designing the dance moves rather than performing them. "It was an amazing time," he recalled to Judith Newmark for the *St. Louis Post-Dispatch* (June 5, 2005). "I'm big and strong. I can lift girls. I could always get a job. But when I was in my 20s, I realized that choreography was more creative. My favorite place to be is in the rehearsal hall with really talented people." In 1989 Mitchell worked as an assistant to the choreographer for *Jerome Robbins' Broadway*, thus beginning his transition to a career out of the spotlight. He returned to it as a scantily clad dancer in the 1991 hit *The Will Rogers Follies*. The role led to a larger mission. "When I was dancing naked in *The Will Rogers Follies*, somebody said, 'Why don't you dance naked and make money for a cause?'" he explained to Valerie Gladstone for the Newark, New Jersey, *Star-Ledger* (October 19, 2000). Inspired, Mitchell created the Broadway Bares event, benefiting the organization Broadway Cares/Equity Fights AIDS. In the first Broadway Bares, in 1992, Mitchell danced at the gay bar Splash, in New York City. That event raised $8,000. Mitchell continued to organize the event until 2002. (The latest Broadway Bares, in 2007, collected $650,000; the total raised in 15 years is more than $3 million.)

Meanwhile, Mitchell had begun to work steadily as an associate choreographer on several large shows, among them the 1994 Broadway production of *Grease*, and as a full choreographer on smaller shows including *Seconds Out* (1993), *Follies* (1998), and *Jekyll and Hyde* (1999). In 1999 Mitchell also choreographed the well-received Broadway revival of *You're a Good Man, Charlie Brown*.

Mitchell's experience with Broadway Bares proved useful in 2000, when he choreographed the high-profile musical version of the hit 1997 film *The Full Monty*. The story follows a group of unemployed steelworkers, who, out of financial desperation, form a striptease act. One of the men needs the money to pay child support and salvage his relationship with his son. "*The Full Monty* is not about six guys who take their clothes off," Mitchell said to John Moore for the *Denver (Colorado) Post* (October 18, 2002). "It's about a father and how far he would go for the love of his son." The characters do not know how to dance, so Mitchell's choreography emphasized their endearing awkwardness, especially evident when they finally bare all. The show became a critical hit and earned more than $50 million during its two-year run. As a choreographer Mitchell "knows how to be riotous as well as raunchy," a reviewer wrote for the *Toronto (Canada) Star* (December 5, 2000). "This is obviously the guy to take on when you want to take it off." Mitchell earned nominations for a Tony Award and a Drama Desk Award for best choreography for his work on *The Full Monty*.

Mitchell next choreographed a revival of *The Rocky Horror Show*, the musical that inspired the cult movie *The Rocky Horror Picture Show*. The revival opened on Broadway later in 2000 to widely varying reviews. "Mitchell's choreography is generally uninspired and wan," Jacques le Sourd wrote for the Westchester County, New York, *Journal News* (November 16, 2000). The *Toronto Star* (December 3, 2000) reviewer, however, praised the choreographer: "Mitchell's choreography can be campy, klutzy, or erotic as the moment demands." Mitchell was nominated for a Drama Desk Award for his work for *Rocky Horror*. The show—which critics generally considered fun but unimpressive, lacking much of the shock value and spark of the original—ran until January 2002.

In 2002 Mitchell choreographed *Hairspray*, a musical based on a 1988 film by John Waters. Set in 1962, the story follows an overweight teenage girl who wins a place on a popular dance show and uses her newfound fame to promote racial integration. Mitchell told interviewers that he did not seek work on musicals based on films but nonetheless saw them as a natural choice for producers and audience members. "It's certainly not my choosing that our last two projects have been film adaptations, but I can't say I'm surprised by it," Mitchell told Moore. "When people find a story they like, they enjoy seeing it told in different ways." Still, Mitchell said, he was careful not to follow each movie too closely. "I had seen [the film] *Hairspray* when it first came out," he explained to Sylviane Gold for *Dance* (November 2002, on-line). "And when I was offered the musical, I watched the movie once—the same thing I did with *The Full Monty*. Then I never went back. You could fall into a real pit if you watch it too much, because in a movie, the camera tells an audience where to look. Onstage, your dance has to tell 2,500 heads where to look." Although Mitchell emphasized that he was not trying to replicate the film *Hairspray* but rather to use it as a jumping-off point, comparisons with the original were inevitable—and often unfavorable. "Choreographer Jerry Mitchell manages to capture the essence of teen dance in the 1960s, but fans of John Waters' 1988 film version are likely to miss the sexiness of the film's footwork," Jeffrey Eric Jenkins wrote for the *Seattle (Washington) Post-Intelligencer* (August 27, 2002). Other critics applauded both the musical and Mitchell's choreography, with Sylviane Gold describing the 1960s-style steps as "frisky dance numbers that look dead-on accurate but somehow new." The musical immediately recouped the producers' approximately $10.5 million investment, with advance-ticket sales totaling $15 million by opening night. Mitchell was nominated in the category of best choreography for an Outer Critics Circle Award, an Astaire Award, a Drama Desk Award, and a Tony Award. The show won the 2003 Tony Award for best musical, and as of mid-October 2007, it was still playing on Broadway.

Mitchell next worked on a new production of *Gypsy*, a now-iconic story of an overbearing stage mother that had already been adapted many times for stage and screen. His version starred the actress Bernadette Peters as the mother—the role made famous on Broadway by Ethel Merman—and ran from May 2003 to May 2004. He took on an even more intimidating adaptation late in 2003, when he premiered *Never Gonna Dance*, a stage version of the 1936 film *Swing Time*, which starred the dance team of Fred Astaire and Ginger Rogers. "Mitchell's choreography is the backbone of the show," Charles Isherwood wrote for *Variety* (December 8, 2003). For his work on *Never Gonna Dance*, which had only a short run, from December 2003 to February 2004, Mitchell was nominated for Drama Desk and Tony Awards.

For the 2004 revival of *La Cage Aux Folles*, Mitchell again worked with a previously known production—not a movie this time but a Broadway show that had debuted in 1983. The story is about a gay couple, Georges and the flamboyant Albin; when Georges's son brings home his fiancée and her conservative parents, humorous antics follow. Although the story line was considered progressive in the early 1980s, earning the original musical six Tony Awards, many critics pointed out that the show had lost much of its surprise by 2004. Nevertheless, Mitchell's choreography was widely praised. In a review for *USA Today* (December 10, 2004), Elysa Gardner called it "exhilarating," and Frederick Winship, writing for United Press International (January 3, 2005), described it as having "the energy and humor of the opulent burlesques that are endangered species all over the world today except in Paris." For his choreography, Mitchell won a Drama Desk Award, an Outer Critics Circle Award, and a Tony Award. (Because of quirks in the awards cycle, Mitchell was nominated for the Tony for both *La Cage Aux Folles* and his subsequent musical, *Dirty Rotten Scoundrels*.) "Awards are strange anyway because I don't know how you compare one type of dancing to another type of dancing or one type of actor to another type of actor," he told Gehl. "I know it sounds [like a] cliché, but to be included in the community and be honored with a nomination is award enough. I've been nominated [for a Drama Desk Award] five times and I won this time but I truly believe I won for all the times I've been nominated."

The other musical for which Mitchell had been nominated, *Dirty Rotten Scoundrels*, made its Broadway debut in 2005. Based on the 1988 film of the same name, which concerns a competition between two low-level con men, the musical was a moderate success, running until September 2006. "Although there are few full-blown dance sequences, Jerry Mitchell's sprightly choreography is first rate," F. Kathleen Foley wrote for the *Los Angeles Times* (August 18, 2006). In addition to his Tony nomination, *Dirty Rotten Scoundrels* earned Mitchell a Drama Desk Award nomination for best choreography.

With *Legally Blonde*, which premiered on April 29, 2007, Mitchell made the transition from choreographer to choreographer-director. "For me it was a natural step," he told Cox. "You start out as a dancer; you're working with these choreographers and you're watching them and you become their assistants. I'm ready now to be in charge of the entire project." Based on the 2001 hit film of the same name, *Legally Blonde* follows a sorority girl named Elle Woods to Harvard Law School, where, after various difficulties, she realizes that she is exceedingly bright as well as beautiful. Though executives at MGM, the film studio, were hesitant to entrust their $13 million investment to the untried Mitchell, the producers recognized his enthusiasm for the project and his deep understanding of the story. "The condescension in the culture toward male dancers is extreme. Just as it is to[ward] supposedly dumb blondes like Elle Woods," Mitchell said to Jesse Green. "Which is why *Legally Blonde* was clearly the right story for me to tell my first time as a director. Elle exists in the space between feminism and [the pop star] Britney Spears, and speaks directly to the problem of girls who dumb themselves down to be attractive to boys. Girls still need to be told it's O.K. to be beautiful and smart. Or more importantly, it's O.K. to be smart."

The show has garnered 10 Drama Desk Award nominations, including those for outstanding musical, outstanding director, and outstanding choreographer. In the *San Francisco Chronicle* (February 8, 2007), Robert Hurwitt praised the "knock-'em-dead dance numbers" and added that Mitchell has "given *Blonde* a remarkably fluid, cinematographic incarnation that succeeds in making the musical look not only larger than life but bigger than film." Among reviewers who felt less enthusiastic was Clive Barnes, who wrote for the *New York Post* (April 30, 2007), "Jerry Mitchell, making his debut as a full-scaled Broadway director, gives the story a staging that moves from the frenetic to the frantic, and his choreography is what paint-by-numbers is to portraiture. That said, his dances certainly have a slick snap, crackle and pop." Linda Winer, in a lukewarm assessment for *Newsday* (April 30, 2007, on-line), wrote, "With *Legally Blonde*, his directing debut, [Mitchell] takes the logical well-worn step from moving bodies to energizing the total vision. Everything gets moved—except, you know, your heart."

Mitchell will choreograph a musical adaptation of the 2002 film *Catch Me If You Can*; the stage version is set to debut in 2008. He is also helping David Rockwell, a set designer with whom he has often collaborated, to design the new JetBlue Airways terminal at John F. Kennedy International Airport, in New York City; he was hired to choreograph, in effect, a smooth flow of people through the structure.

Mitchell has choreographed dance sequences for a number of movies, among them *Scent of a Woman* (1992), *Jeffrey* (1995), *In & Out* (1997), *The Object of My Affection* (1998), and *Hedwig and the*

Angry Inch (2001). He was nominated for an Emmy Award in 2000 for choreographing an episode of the television sitcom *The Drew Carey Show*.

In 2005 Mitchell was presented with an honorary diploma from Webster University. He lives in New York City with his partner, Eric Sherr, an actor.

—C.S.

Suggested Reading: *American Theatre* p160 Oct. 2004; *Dance* p80+ Apr. 2007, (on-line) Nov. 2002; *Denver (Colorado) Post* FF p1+ Oct. 18, 2002; *Kalamazoo (Michigan) Gazette* A p5 June 20, 2005; *New York Times* II p10 Nov. 30, 2003, II p1 Apr. 15, 2007; *Newsday* (on-line) Apr. 30, 2007; *San Francisco Chronicle* E p1 Feb. 8, 2007; *Seattle Post-Intelligencer* D p1 Aug. 27, 2002; *South Bend (Indiana) Tribune* F p1 July 17, 2005; *St. Louis Post-Dispatch* F p5 June 5, 2005; (Westchester County, New York) *Journal News* E p1 Nov. 16, 2000

Selected Musicals: as performer—*Brigadoon*, 1980–81; *Woman of the Year*, 1981; *The Will Rogers Follies*, 1991–93; as assistant to the choreographer—*Jerome Robbins' Broadway*, 1989–90; as associate choreographer—*Grease*, 1994–98; as choreographer—*Seconds Out*, 1993; *Follies*, 1998; *Jeykll and Hyde*, 1999; *You're a Good Man, Charlie Brown*, 1999; *The Rocky Horror Show*, 2000; *Hairspray*, 2002; *Gypsy*, 2003–04; *Never Gonna Dance*, 2003; *La Cage Aux Folles*, 2004; *Dirty Rotten Scoundrels*, 2005; as choreographer and director—*Legally Blonde: The Musical*, 2007

Selected Television Shows: as choreographer—*The Drew Carey Show*, 2000

Selected Films: as performer—*The Best Little Whorehouse in Texas*, 1982; as choreographer: *Scent of a Woman*, 1992; *Jeffrey*, 1995; *In & Out*, 1997; *The Object of My Affection*, 1998; *Hedwig and the Angry Inch*, 2001

Monte, Elisa

(MOHN-tay, eh-LEE-sah)

May 23, 1946– Dancer; choreographer

Address: Elisa Monte Dance, 481 Eighth Ave., Suite 543, New York, NY 10001

The dancer and choreographer Elisa Monte founded her company, Elisa Monte Dance, in 1981, with the "conviction of bridging cultural barriers through the universal language of dance," according to the company's Web site. Almost three decades later, Elisa Monte Dance has toured more than 45 nations, the particularly active nature of their

Roy Volkmann

Elisa Monte

dancing helping them to accomplish their long-time mission. "We're known for being physical. We're known for being muscular, we're known for being sensual, we're known for sort of having an intelligence of the body. Glorifying the body as a message and as a tool," Monte explained to Ellen Dunkel for the Bergen County, New Jersey, *Record* (June 4, 1999). "And that's one of the reasons we've been successful in so many milieus, because you didn't need any words to interpret what we were doing." As a young woman, after years of classical training, Monte left ballet for modern dance, becoming a principal dancer of the Martha Graham Dance Company. She remained with that company for eight years before forming her own, dancing with many others along the way. Her choreography, informed by her own sensibilities and her varied training, is eclectic but always suggestive of a driving force behind the moves. "Whether an Elisa Monte dance lurches in fast-forward or lingers on a juncture for precarious poses, it quickens the pulse," Guillermo Perez wrote for *Dance Magazine* (July 1, 2006). "The rush seems full of ritualistic purpose, and stationary figures loom with totemic magic." While critics universally admire the company's sheer physicality, they are more divided on the merits of Monte's choreography. "Though sleekly assured in its dancing, the Elisa Monte Dance Company lacks individuality in its dances," Molly McQuade wrote for *Dance Magazine* (July 1, 2006). "The company seems to depend on eclecticism, but also carries it as a sort of burden." Monte, for her part, has said that she could not work in any other way. "Which is better: to speak seven languages, but with an accent, or only one language perfectly?" she asked Jack Anderson for the *New York Times* (May 2, 1982). For Monte, the answer has long been clear—to risk sacrificing perfect fluency for the sake of variation and diversity. As she told Anderson, "To move in just one way is to lock myself in a kind of prison I don't want to be in."

Elisa Monte was born on May 23, 1946 in the New York City borough of Brooklyn to Anthony Montemarano, a bookkeeper, and Elisa Montemarano. Both Monte and her older sister, Barbara, who is a personal fitness trainer, shortened their surname to "Monte." From the age of six, Monte would accompany her older sister to her ballet lessons; Monte began taking lessons herself at age nine. "I just always loved to dance," she told *Current Biography*. "I was hooked from the beginning." When she was 10 she began taking ballet lessons with Vladimir Dokoudovsky, a renowned ballet dancer who had recently retired. At 11, Monte made her professional debut in a revival of the musical *Carousel* at New York's City Center. For high school she attended New York City's Professional Children's School, founded for young people with professional careers in the performing arts; she simultaneously attended the School of American Ballet. After graduation, however, Monte realized that she was not interested in pursuing ballet professionally. "Although I loved the technique, whenever it became time to look for a company to perform, I realized I wasn't really enthralled with the ballet repertory," she explained to *Current Biography*. Unsure what she wanted to do next, Monte went abroad for a year, to study at the American College in Paris, France. Back in the U.S., she enrolled at St. John's University, in New York City, to study psychology.

After a year at St. John's, Monte decided that she wanted to return to dance—but modern dance, not ballet. She began studies with the Pearl Lang Dance Theater, a modern-dance group that at one point boasted Madonna as a member, and subsequently appeared with the Lar Lubovitch Dance Company. In 1974 Monte joined the prestigious Martha Graham Dance Company, one of the most influential troupes in the world of modern dance. As a principal dancer Monte appeared in numerous Graham classics, including *Seraphic Dialogue*, *Clytemnestra*, and *Appalachian Spring*, as well as in the premiere of *O Thou Desire Who Art About to Sing* in 1977. Beginning in 1975, Monte also worked with the Marcus Schulkind Dance Company for such shows as *The Fred and Barbara Section*, *Ladies' Night Out*, *Circular Ruins*, and *Affetuoso*, first as the assistant artistic director, then as co–artistic director, and finally as co-director. Monte has long believed that a dancer should be capable of working with a variety of choreographers and companies, describing the ideal dancer to Dunkel as being "without borders" and "neutral." Monte herself exemplified that philosophy: in addition to her work with Graham and Schulkind, she became involved with the Pilobolus Dance Theatre through a lucky coincidence in 1977, when she was renting space to the 5 by 2 Dance Company. Moses Pendleton, a member of Pilobolus, was choreographing a work for 5 by 2; Monte told Pendleton that she greatly admired Pilobolus, and he invited her to join the company for the 1977–78 season. As all works for Pilobolus are devised collectively by members of the company, Monte became responsible for a work of her own, *Molly's Not Dead* (1978). While Pilobolus was her best-known side project, Monte also danced with the Mary Anthony Dance Theatre, Ballet Etudes, and the Morse Donaldson Dance Company. The year 1977 was an important one for Monte in other ways: that was when she met David Brown, a new dancer for Graham. The two were instantly drawn to each other, and in 1979 Monte asked Brown to be her partner in her first choreographed piece as a director. Created for a Graham workshop, the duet—*Treading*—centered on a story about sea creatures, with corresponding amphibious movements. The couple moved in together soon afterward and were married a few years later.

Even before marriage, the couple cemented their partnership with the founding of the Elisa Monte Dance Company, in 1981. With Monte as the choreographer and Brown as artistic director, the company aimed to promote diversity—not only by varying the ethnicities of the featured dancers, but also by encouraging multidisciplinary collaboration and educational efforts. The company's three goals, as listed on its Web site, are to "train and maintain a select group of professional dancers of multi-ethnic origin," to "commission work from distinguished artists in other disciplines for collaborative projects," and to "educate individuals in the art of movement, and audiences in the appreciation of live dance performance." The following year Monte and the company got their first break when Monte met the modern-dance legend Alvin Ailey at a theater; Ailey told Monte that he had heard about *Treading* and asked to see it performed. Soon, the Alvin Ailey Dance Theater itself began performing *Treading*, a glowing endorsement of a new choreographer's talents. Based on the success of *Treading*, Ailey commissioned a second piece from Monte, which she titled *Pigs and Fishes*. "To me, pigs and fishes symbolize some of the basic things of life," she explained somewhat obliquely to Anderson, adding that a friend of hers, who grew up on a farm, had found the title "perfectly clear because, if you live on a farm, pigs and fishes are all you may need." The dance debuted at City Center later in 1982, displaying the kind of physicality that would become Monte's trademark. "*Pigs and Fishes* is a dance of great, almost violent energy, and it is rare that women dancers embody this," Maggie Lewis wrote for the *Christian Science Monitor* (August 23, 1982), pinpointing one of Monte's areas of interest: emphasizing the power of women. "They danced well, with convincing, but not threatening, strength." In 1982 the Elisa Monte Dance Company was named best company at the International Dance Festival of Paris. Monte premiered a number of dances during the compa-

ny's first decade, including *Dreamtime* (1986), based on Australian Aboriginal rituals, and *Audentity* (1987), created soon after the birth of Monte and Brown's daughter, Elia. After *Diamond Song* (1993), Monte co-choreographed a piece with Brown, *Vejle/Border Crossing*, a duet for two men set to the music of Puccini. In reviews of those pieces, critics continued to praise the dancers' extraordinary physical presence. "They exude power, dynamism and commitment, throwing themselves into all of Monte's choreographic patterns with genuine intensity," R. M. Campbell wrote in a review of a Monte tour for the *Seattle Post-Intelligencer* (March 31, 1990). "Arms slice the air like cleavers, while whole bodies are thrown into swings with the centrifugal force of cars turning corners at high speed." But while critics lauded Monte for choreography that took full advantage of the high skill of her dancers, they also often criticized her for relying too heavily upon the dances' sheer physical impact. "The pace and stupendous variety of movements [demand] so much attention that you want to cry, 'Stop! I can't take it all in!'" Margaret Putnam wrote for the *Dallas Morning News* (May 1, 1995). Also, the order of the individual dances within the overall performance was sometimes criticized as incoherent. "Even a powerfully innovative, beautifully presented series of steps adds up to very little if it isn't shaped both as a dance and as one of a group of dances forming the beginning, the middle and the end of an evening's performance," Janice Berman wrote for *Newsday* (February 11, 1993). In 1994 Monte and Brown co-choreographed *Absolute Rule*, which examined the sexual power dynamic of male-female relationships.

Monte and Brown teamed up again to choreograph *Feu Follet* (1995), a two-act production, celebrating Cajun culture, that became one of the company's best-known works. Loosely based on Henry Wadsworth Longfellow's poem "Evangeline," the dance unfolds in three parts, successively set in France, Nova Scotia, and Louisiana. Examining how a culture and a community survive being displaced, *Feu Follet* draws heavily on traditional Cajun dance, which Monte and Brown researched extensively before choreographing the work. "When touring Louisiana, I realized this is one of the few dance cultures that America has. There are not many cities or people or communities that you meet where dance is very much the basis of part of their social life," Monte told Theodore P. Mahne for the New Orleans, Louisiana, *Times-Picayune* (September 21, 1995). Monte told Mahne that she was originally intrigued by the integral nature of dance in Cajun society: "It's often basic forces of life that hold a community together. [The Acadians] are one of our few cultures that keeps dance as an important aspect to who they are. So I'm very drawn to it. I want to know why. I want to find out more about it." Monte acknowledged that she was an outsider to the culture and did not presume that she would be able to understand its complexities fully. "It's really us looking at this culture and illuminating it from our perspective, which is the only way we can," she told Mahne. "In the program notes we say we're not trying to out-Cajun the Cajuns because we would fail instantly." Commissioned by the Performing Arts School of Acadiana, the performances were sponsored primarily by the Louisiana division of the National Endowment for the Arts (NEA), a federally funded program constantly in danger of being cut. Monte argued that her project was proof that the NEA is a necessary organization, pointing to the NEA's unique record of funding projects that might not otherwise be considered commercially viable and adding that the loss of the NEA would be debilitating for the advancement of culture in America. "Here I am doing a piece saying that the essence to life is music and dance and keeping yourself connected in that way to stay alive and interested and honest and true and responsive . . . ," she told Mahne. "If [the NEA opponents] would look at some of the very old cultures that have lasted for thousands of years through many hardships, they would find that the strength of the culture and the society was through their artistic endeavors." The year 1997 saw the premiere of *Volkmann Suite*, a piece inspired by the work of the dance company's photographer, Roy Volkmann, and the interplay between his work and Monte's—between the art of still photography and the movement of dance.

When the Elisa Monte Dance Company was founded, Monte was choreographing almost all of the dances, with Brown serving as artistic director; by 1998 Brown and Monte were evenly splitting choreography duties, prompting Monte to change the company's name that year to Monte/Brown Dance. Monte told Dunkel that she saw the change as a "natural evolution." "For me, my work and my personal life are one thing," she said. "It's not two separate compartments to me at all. The art I do as a dancer-choreographer has always been who I am, and who I'm married to is who I am, and my child is who I am. So for me, it's all one picture." Monte/Brown Dance premiered a number of Monte's works, including *Amor Fati* (1999), *Day's Residue* (2000), and *Shattered* (2000), which was especially praised—as many of Monte's works had been—for its marked physicality: "The action, as clusters of dancers spread out and then paired up, could look like stormy discharges: whirls, jittery footwork, big leaps," Guillermo Perez wrote.

Monte and Brown divorced in 2002, and the company returned to Monte's sole control and to its original name. In the years that followed, Monte choreographed two "high-concept" works, *Shekhina* (2004) and *Via Sacra* (2005). *Shekhina* was commissioned by the actor and photographer Leonard Nimoy. According to *kabbalah* (Jewish mysticism), the shekhina is the feminine aspect of the divinity, symbolizing creativity and wisdom. In 2002 Nimoy had published a controversial book of his photographic representations of the shekhina; for her dance, which was inspired by

those images, Monte incorporated Nimoy's photographs into the staging. Dance, she told Julia Goldman for the *Jewish Week* (February 6, 2004), was the perfect medium for the message of the shekhina. "Dance is a feminine art. It deals with things that can't be spoken. It's not about explaining what you see, but about looking at your reaction to it." She also said that her dance was designed to emphasize the empowering nature of the shekhina. "It's for us girls to . . . realize what is lacking [in the world]," she told Goldman. "We need to get on the stick and take our place in running the world, so it becomes more balanced."

The next year Monte took on her most ambitious project to date with the three-act *Via Sacra*. Begun in 2001 as a reflection on personal grief, the piece changed its focus after that year's terrorist attacks to a meditation on universal loss. Named after a temple-lined street in ancient Rome, the dance featured three distinct acts, originally staged as separate pieces with their own titles: "The Way It Was (Lost Things)," "The Way It Is (Psyche's Journey)," and "The Way It Should Be (Light Lies)." Though critics expressed appreciation for the efforts behind the work, they commented less favorably on its execution. "*Via Sacra*, though deeply felt, was not fully convincing," Jack Anderson wrote for the *New York Times* (February 4, 2005). "The finale resembled a thematically appropriate contrivance, rather than a carefully motivated resolution. The scenes of mourning looked repetitive, as if Ms. Monte had stretched her choreographic phrases to excessive length. Each act might have greater impact if presented as a separate item on a program with other dances in totally different moods." Other works in 2005 included *A Woman's Way (To Nancy, with Love from Tom)*, a piece that was commissioned by a man for his wife's birthday, a sponsorship that represented a new way for permanently underfunded arts initiatives to stay afloat financially. "You have to find creative ways to get people to support your work," Monte explained to Julie Bloom for the *New York Sun* (January 31, 2005). "Gifts like this are wonderful—they allow me to do my work, and support my company and the dancers."

Elisa Monte Dance celebrated its 25th anniversary in 2006 with the premiere of *Hardwood*, at the Joyce Theater in New York City. In 2007 the company toured Italy and Germany, then returned to New York City in October for revivals of *Treading*, *Pigs and Fishes*, and *Hardwood*, among other works.

Monte's company is based in New York City, where Monte lives. She has served as choreographer-in-residence at Robert Redford's Sundance Institute; Southern Methodist University in Dallas, Texas; New York University's Tisch School of the Arts; Philadanco; and the Alvin Ailey American Dance Center.

—C.S.

Suggested Reading: (Bergen County, New Jersey) *Record* p26 June 4, 1999; Elisa Monte Dance Web site; *New York Times* E p1+ Sep. 21, 2006; *Village Voice* (on-line) Sep. 26, 2006

Selected Works: *Molly's Not Dead*, 1978; *Treading*, 1979; *Pigs and Fishes*, 1982; *Dreamtime*, 1986; *Audentity*, 1987; *Diamond Song*, 1993; *Vejle/Border Crossing* (with David Brown), 1994; *Absolute Rule* (with David Brown) 1994; *Feu Follet* (with David Brown) 1995; *Volkmann Suite*, 1997; *Amor Fati*, 1999; *Day's Residue*, 2000; *Shattered*, 2000; *Shekhina*, 2004; *Via Sacra*, 2005; *A Woman's Way (To Nancy, with Love from Tom)*, 2005

Uli Weber, courtesy of ICM Artists

Montero, Gabriela

May 10, 1970– Classical pianist

Address: c/o Biglife Management, 67–69 Chalton St., London, England NW1 1HY

"Improvisation used to be an integral part of performing [classical music]. Mozart, Beethoven and Liszt were all virtuoso improvisers whose concerts often included ad-lib fantasies and spontaneous variations on themes called out by adoring audiences," Vivien Schweitzer wrote for the *New York Times* (September 25, 2006, on-line). "But in the 20th century, apart from the chance music of composers like John Cage, Karlheinz Stockhausen, Gyorgy Ligeti and Pierre Boulez, which includes improvisatory elements, it was largely a lost, or at least ignored art in classical music, practiced by or-

ganists but few others." Gabriela Montero, a Venezuelan pianist, is currently one of the rare classically trained artists known for her ability to improvise—a talent often in evidence in jazz venues but very rarely in symphony halls. "I was always an improviser since I was a child. It was a most natural way for me to express myself with music," Montero told Robert Siegel for the National Public Radio show *All Things Considered* (September 18, 2006, on-line). Schweitzer reported that at one of Montero's performances, an audience member requested that she play the song "I Will Survive." Montero, Schweitzer wrote, "[picked] out the first bars of Gloria Gaynor's disco hit and feminist anthem on the piano. Then she took it for a fantastic ride, threading the melody through an improvisation that dazzlingly (if improbably) morphed from Baroque counterpoint through jazzy syncopation to Mozartean Classicism." Similarly, Jeremy Eichler wrote in a review of a Montero concert for the *Boston Globe* (May 1, 2007, on-line), "The most fun was when someone near the front row shouted for 'La Cucaracha.' Montero said 'That's a great one!' and then promptly took this humble folk song about a cockroach on a grand stroll, splicing it into music that resembled Bach's 'Goldberg Variations,' dropping it by a tango club, schooling it in ragtime, and on and on."

Gabriela Montero was born on May 10, 1970 in Caracas, Venezuela, into a family that was not particularly musical. When she was seven months old, her grandmother gave her a two-octave toy piano for Christmas. "They put this piano in my crib and it became my favorite toy," Montero told Siegel. "And because my mom sang to me every night like most South American mothers, I started to pick out the melodies and play them." By the time she was about 18 months old, Montero had begun playing with both hands. "At first my parents were stunned," she told Siegel, "and then they just started to tell everybody in the neighborhood. Nobody believed them. They thought they'd gone mad." Montero soon began improvising on songs she had learned by ear. "It was like playing games and it was absolutely the most normal thing for me," she explained to Siegel. "I used to do a lot of improvisations in D minor and A minor." She received her first real piano, an upright model, when she was three. When she was four she began studying with Lyl Tiempo, a local teacher who encouraged Montero's natural talent for improvisation. Tiempo introduced Montero to the renowned Argentinean concert pianist Martha Argerich, who had herself been a child prodigy.

Montero gave her first public recital at the age of five, and at eight she made her concert debut with the Simón Bolívar National Youth Orchestra of Venezuela. Shortly thereafter the government of Venezuela offered her a scholarship to study music in the U.S. Her parents were willing to relocate for the sake of her studies, and they settled in Miami, Florida. Montero took classes with such teachers as Rosalina Sackstein and Edna Golansky but became unenthusiastic about playing after one of her instructors discouraged her from improvising. "She told me [my improvising] was not serious, nothing very special. She said there was only one pianist I should listen to, and try to play like, and that was Claudio Arrau. It went completely against my spirit," Montero told Peter Aspden for the *Financial Times* (March 11, 2006). (Montero, who has related the tale to many journalists, has never revealed who gave her that advice; some reporters have suggested that it must have been Sackstein, who once studied under Arrau.)

Montero stopped improvising and, as Aspden wrote, "submitted to the strictures of a proper classical-music training." She found herself deeply unhappy. "I felt this sense of panic," she told Aspden. "I would cry on my way to the lessons." Still, she got much positive feedback for her playing. In 1983 she won the American Music Scholarship Association (AMSA) World Piano Competition for Young Artists, and the next year she claimed the top prize at the Music Teachers National Association's (MTNA) Baldwin Keyboard Competition. In 1987 she triumphed at the Palm Beach Invitational International Piano Competition. By the age of 18, however, Montero had decided to stop playing altogether. She spent the next two years traveling, first to Caracas, then in the U.S., and later in Canada and Europe. (She recently estimated that she has moved more than 30 times.) "You have to live life. You can't be stuck in a practice room," she told Siegel. "If you haven't lived through . . . major changes and even crisis and . . . joys and disappointments, you don't have a story to tell."

In 1990, ending her absence from the piano, Montero moved to London, England, to attend the Royal Academy of Music. Studying under the renowned teacher Hamish Milne, she felt her passion for playing classical music revive. "Hamish really inspired me, and he gave me a completely different focus on music than I'd previously had," she told *BBC Music Magazine* (August 2005, online). Montero also took lessons from Andrzej Esterházy and participated in master classes with the classical pianists András Schiff and Tamás Vásáry. While at the academy she won the Christian Carpenter Prize and the Anna Instone Memorial Award. She graduated from the Royal Academy of Music with honors in 1993.

In March 1995 Montero was among 14 native-born or naturalized American pianists to participate in the National Chopin Competition, which has been held every five years (since 1975) in Miami; the top four contestants are awarded cash prizes, concert appearances at venues throughout the world, and a chance to represent the country at the International Chopin Competition. Montero finished in fourth place and was awarded a $3,500 cash prize. In October 1995 she competed in the International Chopin Competition, which is held every five years, in Warsaw, Poland. Montero's international career was launched following her third-place victory in Poland, behind Philippe Giusiano

of France and Alexei Sultanov of Russia. (The men shared second place; no first-place winner was chosen that year by the notoriously exacting judges.) Montero's bronze-medal win included a cash prize of $15,000.

After the competition Montero embarked on a concert tour of Japan and Taiwan with the Warsaw Philharmonic Orchestra and its conductor, Kazimierz Kord. She also performed at the International Chopin Festival (1996), in Poland; the inaugural Miami International Festival of Discovery (1998), in Florida; the Lachine Festival (1999), in Montreal, Quebec (as part of an international tribute to commemorate the 150th anniversary of Chopin's death); and the Old First Church Concert (2000), in San Francisco, California. In a review of the last-named concert for the *San Francisco Classical Voice* (February 25, 2000, on-line), John McCarthy wrote, "Several of the [Chopin pieces played] are so familiar that even the most casual listener can whistle the tunes. [But] Montero's refreshing spirit breathed life into a repertoire that is often trivialized by novelty and cliché." During that period Montero also recorded two discs for the newly established Palexa Records: *Gabriela Montero: En concert à Montréal* (1998), a live recording, and *Frédéric Chopin: Oeuvres pour piano* (1999).

Despite such successes, Montero continued to harbor mixed feelings regarding a career in music. Twice divorced and the mother of two children, she periodically stopped playing. "A life in music takes such commitment," she told Stuart Isacoff for *Playbill Arts* (March 21, 2006, on-line). "It's especially tough when you are a single mom, like me." In 2001 she paid a visit to Martha Argerich, who was playing a concert in Montreal. Like Montero, Argerich had also raised children as a single mother and endured self-imposed periods when she never played the piano. "I wanted to talk to her about being a mother, being a woman, being an artist. You know, I was still very confused," Montero told Morley Safer for the CBS television show *60 Minutes* (December 3, 2006). After Argerich's concert she and Montero visited a local barroom with a piano, where Montero reluctantly gave an impromptu—and career-affirming—performance. "[Argerich] asked to hear me [play]," Montero told Isacoff. "I said, 'No, let's just have coffee.' But she insisted. . . . I ran through some standard repertoire and also improvised. Her enthusiasm and encouragement were unbelievable. Something in that moment transformed my life."

Argerich, whom many consider one of the most accomplished pianists in the world, was fiercely supportive of Montero. She convinced the younger pianist that it was possible to combine a music career with motherhood and that her skill for improvisation was a valuable asset. In November 2001, at Argerich's invitation, Montero performed at the annual Martha Argerich Music Festival, in Buenos Aires, Argentina. She also performed with Argerich at the 2002 Lugano Festival, which is part of the Progetto Martha Argerich (Martha Argerich

Project), a chamber-music festival held annually in Lugano, Switzerland.

In February 2004 Montero was named a rising star by the French music publication *Le Monde de la Musique*. Later that year she signed with a major record label, EMI Classics. *Gabriela Montero: Chopin, Falla, Ginastera, Granados, Liszt, Rachmaninov, Scriabin*, her first recording for the label, was released in 2005. It consists of two discs, one of which is devoted to her improvisations. "The main attraction here is the second half of the two-disc set . . . on which Montero takes off on 12 short improvisations on specific pieces—including two of the compositions on the first half—and on generic styles," Richard S. Ginell wrote for the *Los Angeles Times* (October 9, 2005). "Hers is the rare and welcome case where a musician's natural impulse to invent was not stifled by pedantic teachers." John von Rhein wrote for the *Chicago Tribune* (November 4, 2005), "The evidence of this debut album suggests she is a formidable talent very much in the Argerich mold. . . . Which is not to say she [merely] copies her famous mentor: There is individuality aplenty here, too, and a willingness to take risks that puts her in a special class of ascending pianists."

In March 2006 Montero was invited to play with the New York Philharmonic, under the famed conductor Lorin Maazel. Anthony Tommasini wrote of that concert for the *New York Times* (March 24, 2006, on-line), "Ms. Montero's playing had everything: crackling rhythmic brio, subtle shadings, steely power in climactic moments, soulful lyricism in the ruminative passages and, best of all, unsentimental expressivity. That she is also a tall, dark, and lovely young woman can only help her career." Jay Nordlinger, in a review for the *New York Sun* (March 24, 2006), called her debut with the Philharmonic "most impressive" and continued, "You could tell there was something good about her when she played her opening octaves: solidly, confidently, into the keys. In fact, everything about this pianist would prove confident. She played with extraordinary rhythmic assurance. . . . Her musicality could be seen in her phrasing (natural and shrewd). She played with a combination of solidity and fluidity—an exceptional combination to have. And her technique? So assured as to be demonic."

Montero's second album on the EMI Classics label was recorded at the legendary Abbey Road Studios, in London. *Bach and Beyond*, inspired by 12 of the composer Johann Sebastian Bach's most celebrated works, was released in September 2006 to glowing reviews. John Terauds, for example, wrote for the *Toronto Star* (December 28, 2006), "Montero brings a contemporary twist to the music that may get a new generation of listeners interested in Baroque-era masterpieces." Immediately after that album reached stores, Montero embarked on a U.S. tour, performing at venues considered unconventional for a classical artist, including the Black Orchid, a nightclub in Chicago, Illinois, and

Joe's Pub, a live-music club in New York City. "I'm sure if Mozart were here today, he'd be visiting all the jazz bars in New York, eager to learn new harmonies," Montero told Howard Kissel for the New York *Daily News* (September 10, 2006).

Montero has designed a popular format for her performances. During the first half of each, she plays classical pieces as they were originally written; the second half features improvisations—often spontaneous variations on songs or themes called out by the audience. "Ninety-eight percent of the people who listen to me improvise love it—something real is happening, and they're a part of it . . . ," she told Kissel. "Why do the 2 [percent]—the intellectuals, the critics—disagree? One reason is this sense that the work of the great composers came out of suffering. With improvisation, there's no suffering. It's about joy, about freedom. I think critics prefer the idea of suffering." She concluded, "Even when I'm not improvising I'm conscious that the better we integrate the celebratory and emotional aspects, the more the public will see that classical music is as exciting, as passionate, as engrossing as other types of music." On her album *Baroque* (2007), Montero gave her renditions of classic Baroque pieces, among them improvisations on Johann Pachelbel's famous Canon in D major. In 2007 she also began to offer live improvisations on the Internet, available for downloading from her Web site.

Gabriela Montero lives in the Park Slope section of Brooklyn, New York, with her two daughters.

—B.M.

Suggested Reading: *60 Minutes* (on-line) Dec. 3, 2006; *All Things Considered* (on-line) Sep. 18, 2006; *BBC Music Magazine* (on-line) Aug. 2005; *Boston Globe* (on-line) May 1, 2007; *Chicago Tribune* C p23 Nov. 4, 2005; *Financial Times* p46 Mar. 11, 2006; *Los Angeles Times* E p42 Oct. 9, 2005; (New York) *Daily News* p12 Sep. 10, 2006; *New York Sun* p15 Mar. 24, 2006; *New York Times* E p5 Sep. 25, 2006; *Playbill Arts* (on-line) Mar. 21, 2006; *San Francisco Classical Voice* (on-line) Feb. 25, 2000; *Toronto Star* G p11 Dec. 28, 2006

Selected Recordings: *Gabiela Montero: En concert à Montréal*, 1998; *Frédéric Chopin: Oeuvres pour piano*, 1999; *Gabiela Montero: Chopin, Falla, Ginastera, Granados, Liszt, Rachmaninov, Scriabin*, 2005; *Bach and Beyond*, 2006; *Baroque*, 2007

Michael Buckner/Getty Images

Morgan, Tracy

Nov. 10, 1968– Actor; comedian

Address: c/o Gersh Agency, 232 N. Canon Dr., Beverly Hills, CA 90210

"I try to keep the 'fun' in funny," the comedian Tracy Morgan joked to Jae-Ha Kim for the *Chicago Sun-Times* (November 7, 2003). "When you take the 'fun' out, you just have 'ny,' and I never want to be 'ny.'" Known for the dead-on impressions and zany character sketches he performed for seven years on the comedy-variety show *Saturday Night Live* (*SNL*), Morgan is currently winning praise in a (somewhat) more sedate role as the demanding comic actor Tracy Jordan on NBC's hit comedy *30 Rock*. His character's diva-like turns aside, the premise of the show has a firm basis in reality: executive-produced by *SNL* creator Lorne Michaels, created by—and starring—the former *SNL* head writer Tina Fey, *30 Rock* clearly draws on the shared experiences of Morgan, Fey, and Michaels on the esteemed late-night television show filmed before a live audience. Morgan's career, in fact, has largely involved performing before live crowds. After getting his start at Harlem's Uptown Comedy Club, Morgan began appearing regularly on the HBO channel's *Def Comedy Jam*. In the mid-1990s he parlayed one of his stand-up characters into a recurring role on the TV sitcom *Martin*. But even with his current success in prime-time television, with *30 Rock*, Morgan remains best-known for his work on *Saturday Night Live*, on which he portrayed everyone from the real-life figures Maya Angelou and Mike Tyson to his beloved fictional creations Astronaut Jones and the nature guide Brian Fellow.

Tracy Morgan was born on November 10, 1968 in the New York City borough of the Bronx and grew up in Brooklyn. He was still a small child when his father, a musician who performed stand-up comedy while serving in the U.S. Army in Vietnam, first encouraged him to develop his comic streak, instructing the boy in the art of "joning"—or trading insults. "One day he sat me on his lap and made me jones on somebody, and that was my very first joke," Morgan recalled to Bruce Fretts for *Entertainment Weekly* (December 5, 2003). Morgan's parents separated when he was six, his father leaving Morgan's mother and her five children. "One of the reasons why I got so funny is because, out of all my siblings, I think I took it the hardest," Morgan explained to Frazier Moore for the Associated Press (December 11, 2003). "My sense of humor was a defense mechanism." In interviews Morgan has often described his tendency to joke as a defense against various difficulties in his life—most notably his parents' separation and his brother's cerebral palsy. "[Comedy] became my defense mechanism and when I got older, it became my craft," Morgan reflected to Erika Gonzalez for the *Rocky Mountain News* (March 2, 2005). He also told Gonzalez, "I've been around it my whole life. I don't know anything else."

While Morgan was still in high school, his girlfriend, Sabina, became pregnant with their first child. Four credits short of graduating from DeWitt Clinton High School, in the Bronx, Morgan dropped out to try to support his new family through a variety of jobs; those included some of the illegal activities so prevalent in the Brooklyn housing project where he grew up. "I did some things I'm not proud of. I tried my little hand at drug dealing, but that wasn't me," he told Fretts. After a few years of struggling to support Sabina and their child, Morgan went out with his friends one night to the Uptown Comedy Club, in the Harlem section of New York City. "I saw people doing stand-up and I just thought, 'I can do that,'" he recalled to Gonzalez. Morgan returned to the club for a stand-up comedy workshop; four months later he appeared as a featured act on *Uptown Comedy Club*, a 1992 nationally syndicated television show inspired by the club. Morgan "could've wound up like a lot of other people—in jail or dead," the television producer David M. Israel told Fretts. "Comedy was his saving grace." That same year Morgan became a regular on HBO's *Def Comedy Jam*, where he met Martin Lawrence, a successful comedian who would become instrumental in Morgan's career. "He was the one that actually taught me the business," Morgan told Gonzalez of Lawrence. "He told me about the right business choices to make to keep yourself around in the game." In 1994 Lawrence cast Morgan in a recurring role on Lawrence's television show *Martin*; he appeared in six episodes as Hustleman, a character he had first introduced during his days of performing in Harlem. In 1996 Morgan made his film debut, playing a bartender in the Lawrence vehicle *A Thin Line Between Love and Hate*.

Most importantly, though, Lawrence introduced Morgan to Lorne Michaels, the creator and producer of *Saturday Night Live*, a long-running comedy-variety television show that has become an institution of late-night television. The show is responsible for launching the careers of famous comic actors including Bill Murray, Mike Myers, Adam Sandler, David Spade, Chris Rock, and Eddie Murphy. The success of the African-Americans Rock and Murphy aside, *Saturday Night Live* has been frequently criticized for a lack of diversity in its cast, a complaint voiced by Morgan. "It's a white program," Morgan told Jim Carnes for the *Sacramento Bee* (July 22, 2005). "It is what it is. It's been that way for 30 years." Those sentiments notwithstanding, Morgan joined the cast of the show in 1996. He attributed the program's eventual embrace of diversity to changes in the nation itself: "Look at society today," he told Carnes. "Hip-hop is at the top of the charts. [The show] had no choice but to change. Times are changing." Appearing mostly in minor parts at the beginning of his tenure on *Saturday Night Live*, Morgan had become a featured star by the end of his time on the program, known for over-the-top sketches in which he played such characters as Brian Fellow, the practically illiterate host of the fake documentary-style television show *Brian Fellow's Safari Planet*. Other notable characters portrayed by Morgan included Astronaut Jones, a space explorer who romanced female aliens; Bronx superintendent Dominican Lou; and Woodrow the Homeless Guy, who, in a particularly memorable sketch, attempted to woo guest star Britney Spears. Morgan was also famous for his pitch-perfect impressions of a wide range of real-life figures, including Aretha Franklin, Harry Belafonte, Maya Angelou, Samuel L. Jackson, Mike Tyson, and Star Jones. "I learned how to be patient," he told Fretts of his gradual rise in status on the program, a process that has often frustrated other cast members. "And when my shot came, I took full advantage of it." In 2004 *Saturday Night Live* aired the compilation installment "The Best of Tracy Morgan," an honor few cast members receive. "That was monumental for me and my career because that means I'm in the books," Morgan told Kim. "I'm grateful for that." During his time at *SNL*, Morgan also made several film appearances, most notably in *30 Years to Life* (2001), *Jay and Silent Bob Strike Back* (2001), and *Head of State* (2003). In 2002 he began a recurring role as the voice of the character Spoonie Love on *Crank Yankers*, broadcast on Comedy Central.

After seven years of playing wacky characters on *SNL*, Morgan left the ensemble show to play a character who more closely resembled himself. On *The Tracy Morgan Show*, which premiered on NBC in 2003, Morgan played Tracy Mitchell, a Brooklyn mechanic and family man. "I've played outrageous characters my whole career," Morgan told Fretts. "People don't know this part of me." Many critics questioned Morgan's ability to move from being part of an ensemble to headlining his own televi-

sion show, as few *SNL* alumni had successfully made the transition from characterizations of ridiculous figures to sincere portrayals of three-dimensional people. "*SNL* hasn't had a ton of success with crossovers to sitcom stars," Israel, who served as the executive producer of Morgan's show, told Fretts. "But people are going to be surprised by Tracy's warmth and depth." Morgan was confident in his own abilities as a leading man, especially since he would be playing a character in which he felt personally invested. "This character is close to me," he told Fretts. "The only difference is in real life, it takes more than 22 minutes to solve problems." Critics, however, overwhelmingly panned *The Tracy Morgan Show*. In a review for the *Boston Globe* (December 2, 2003), Matthew Gilbert wrote that the show fell short of Morgan's goal of presenting an old-fashioned family program. "The former *Saturday Night Live* comic brings his overstimulated-child shtick to series TV," Gilbert wrote. "Playing the immature father of two boys . . . Morgan spends the half-hour mugging and yelling his way through adolescent mishaps and juvenile one-liners." The show in general, Gilbert wrote, "is familiar, harmless, and loud. It represents yet another mediocre American family comedy with predictable gags and cute kids." The show was canceled after one season, leaving Morgan ambivalent about a career in television. "I'm proud of what we did on my show, but it came about at a time when reality TV was all that was making it. It's like they put television on autopilot," he told Carnes. "I don't know about doing more television. Maybe in the future, we'll try again. But once you've done *Saturday Night Live*, that's basically the top ticket, you know?"

For the next two years, Morgan focused on creating a new persona—not that of a wacky *SNL*-style comic actor or a wholesome father but, rather, an adult with a mature sense of humor. "I've rededicated myself to stand-up. That's what I'm focused on. That's the foundation of my career," he told Carnes. Touring the country, Morgan took on a style of humor that his fans, who knew him for playing such harmless characters as the animal lover Brian Fellow, may not have been expecting. "My stand-up is adult-rated. . . . I'm an adult, I'm 35 years old, I've lived some life and I just want to talk about it," he told Mark McGuire for the Albany, New York, *Times Union* (March 25, 2004). "It's not always politically correct, but it is going to show the adult side of me." Touring relentlessly, Morgan was quick to assert that he did not consider himself to be on the level of his idols in comedy, who included Bill Cosby and Chris Rock—at least not yet. He told McGuire, "I don't consider myself a comedian yet. You have to be doing this at least 20 years, 22 years. I'm just a stand-up." Meanwhile, Morgan continued to appear in the occasional film, such as *The Longest Yard* (2005) and *Little Man* (2006).

Morgan made his way back to the small screen in 2006, with a co-starring role in the NBC hit comedy *30 Rock*. Created by—and starring—Morgan's *SNL* co-star Tina Fey and executive-produced by *SNL*'s creator, Lorne Michaels, *30 Rock* is a situation comedy focusing on the lives of several characters working at NBC's headquarters, 30 Rockefeller Plaza, in New York. Fey plays the head writer of a comedy-variety show much like *Saturday Night Live*; Alec Baldwin appears as an NBC executive; and Morgan plays the temperamental star of the show-within-a-show. "I'm just playing an unstable comedian," he told R. D. Heldenfels for the *Akron (Ohio) Beacon Journal* (June 4, 2006) of the part. "I could be playing me." Although Baldwin's performance garnered the most critical raves, Morgan received his share of praise. "*30 Rock* is amusing enough before Morgan makes his entrance, but it's much funnier after his arrival," Rob Owen wrote for the *Pittsburgh Post-Gazette* (October 8, 2006). Critics especially pointed to Morgan's deft negotiation of the show's tricky racial humor. "*SN-Ler* Tracy Morgan does a Martin Lawrence/Tracy Morgan parody: the out-of-control black man," Ken Tucker wrote for *Entertainment Weekly* (October 11, 2006). "He'd be insufferable were he not so funny, and so willing to make potentially racist setups occasionally pay off with lovable harmlessness." Despite being critically well-received, the show got off to a rocky start with viewers. NBC stuck by the show, however, moving it from its original Wednesday night position to a Thursday slot, attempting to reestablish the network's two-hour block of comedy on that night, once touted as "Must See TV." The show made "best of 2006" lists in *Entertainment Weekly*, the *New York Daily News*, and *Los Angeles Weekly*, with other publications giving it consistently good reviews. On December 1, 2006 NBC announced that it would commit to a full season of the show; the contract was renewed for the 2007–08 season. In 2008 Morgan is also set to appear in the TV comedies *Deep in the Valley* and *First Sunday*.

Morgan and his wife, Sabina, live in New York City; they have three sons, Tracy, Malcolm, and Gitrid. "If I had my way, I wouldn't want any of my kids to follow me into show business," Morgan told Kim. "It's rough." On December 2, 2005 Morgan was arrested in Hollywood, California, on a charge of impaired driving. He pleaded no contest to that misdemeanor charge and was sentenced to 36 months' probation, a $390 fine, and mandatory attendance of an alcohol-education program. On November 28, 2006 he was arrested in New York City on charges of driving while intoxicated. After pleading guilty to that charge, in February 2007, Morgan—who had violated the probation imposed after the Los Angeles sentencing—was ordered to wear for 90 days a Secure Continuous Remote Alcohol Monitoring (SCRAM) device, which detects alcohol vapors through the skin. The following September Morgan was ordered to wear the device for another 80 days, after he admitted to having consumed alcohol the previous month. "I'm not a goody goody," he told Gonzalez in March 2005 (before either arrest) in response to reports in the press about his frequent partying. "I'm a stand-up. I like to have fun."

—C.S.

Suggested Reading: *Albany (New York) Times Union* Preview p20 Mar. 25, 2004; *Chicago Sun-Times* Weekend Plus p3 Nov. 7, 2003; *Entertainment Weekly* p57 Dec. 5, 2003; *Rocky Mountain News* D p8 Mar. 2, 2005; *Sacramento (California) Bee* p39 July 22, 2005

Selected Television Shows: *Def Comedy Jam*, 1992; *Martin*, 1994–96; *Saturday Night Live*, 1996–2003; *The Tracy Morgan Show*, 2003; *30 Rock*, 2006–

Selected Films: *A Thin Line Between Love and Hate*, 1996; *Half Baked*, 1998; *30 Years to Life*, 2001; *Jay and Silent Bob Strike Back*, 2001; *Head of State*, 2003; *The Longest Yard*, 2005; *Little Man*, 2006

Moulitsas Zúniga, Markos ("Kos")

(moo-LEE-tsahs ZOO-nee-gah, MAR-kohs)

Sep. 11, 1971– Blogger; social activist; writer

Address: Daily Kos, P.O. Box 3327, Berkeley, CA 94703

For four days in June 2006, a group of highly important figures in the Democratic Party gathered at a convention in Las Vegas, Nevada, to meet with a group of their most influential constituents. Harry Reid, then the U.S. Senate minority leader, and Mark Warner, a former governor of Virginia and potential presidential candidate, were the first to confirm their presence on the list of attendees, and other big names soon followed. General Wesley Clark, a former—and possibly future—presidential candidate, Iowa governor and potential presidential candidate Tom Vilsack, U.S. senator Barbara Boxer of California, New Mexico governor Bill Richardson, and Howard Dean, a former presidential candidate and currently the Democratic National Committee chairman, were all in attendance. The politicians had not come to meet with a labor union, environmental group, or other traditionally influential segment of voters. They were in Las Vegas to meet 900 left-wing bloggers, all of whom had descended on the city at the urging of one man, Markos Moulitsas Zúniga, the creator of the most widely read political blog in the country, Daily Kos. Currently boasting up to 600,000 Internet visits per day, Daily Kos is at the forefront of a movement to reorganize the Democratic Party, and politics in general, by moving a measure of

Markos ("Kos") Moulitsas Zúniga

power away from the seat of national government, in Washington, D.C., and spreading it across the country through the Web. "The whole phenomenon has overturned the traditional understanding of how groups organize themselves to affect politicians," Ryan Lizza wrote for the *New Republic* (June 26, 2006). As the de facto leader of this phenomenon, christened the "netroots movement," Moulitsas has risen to a position of enormous political influence in just a few years—using only a computer. In its current form, Daily Kos, an interactive Web site, allows anyone with Internet access to post a "diary" on the site; readers rate the diaries, and those with the highest recommendations appear most prominently. Daily Kos bloggers who support particular politicians can reach up to 600,000 people per day with their endorsements, making it worth the Democrats' while to put in personal appearances at conventions such as the one in Las Vegas. While other left-wing political blogs also hold sway, Daily Kos is by far the most influential in the netroots movement. "I don't have any illusions that I'm a great writer," Moulitsas said to *Current Biography*, explaining his success. "The skill that I do have is being able to organize communities, and that's why Daily Kos has crushed any other political blog out there."

Blogs—short for "Web logs"—are a relatively new medium. The veteran journalist Mickey Kaus is widely credited with inventing the blog in 1999, when he began a political diary posted on the on-line magazine *Slate*. The form soon took off, with people creating blogs on topics from politics to home improvement to motherhood. Blogs and bloggers are part of a culture separate from journalism or other forms of more traditional media: the

language is more casual, the effects are more immediate, and, most importantly in the political realm, the blogger is not expected to conform to standards of objectivity. As a leader in that increasingly influential field, Moulitsas has gained legions of followers as well as his share of critics. He is known for a polarizing personality that has made him a multitude of enemies among both Republicans and the mainstream media. In an article for the *New York Times* (September 26, 2004), Matthew Klam described Moulitsas as "cruel and superior," and while Benjamin Wallace-Wells noted in the *Washington Monthly* (January-February 2006) that Moulitsas is "extremely smart," he also went on to call the blogger "intense and high-strung" as well as "irascible, self-contradictory, often petty, always difficult." Those within the blog world itself, however, tend to speak favorably of Moulitsas. "Kos is the platonic ideal of a blogger; he posts all the time, he interacts with his readers," Ana Marie Cox, formerly a political blogger, told Klam. Alex S. Jones, director of Harvard University's Shorenstein Center on the Press, Politics, and Public Policy, expressed a theory about the level of examination now leveled at Moulitsas, one that has little to do with his personality and everything to do with the revolutionary changes in blogging over the past couple of years. "The blogosphere has always been mainly about scrutinizing everybody else and expressing violent opinions about them," Jones told Michael Grynbaum for the *Boston Globe* (July 6, 2006). "Kos is a very powerful blog, so in that sense it's taken on the vulnerability of one of the [political] leaders."

Markos Moulitsas Zúniga was born September 11, 1971 in Chicago, Illinois, to Markos Moulitsas, an ethnic Greek, and Maria Zúniga, who came from El Salvador. (In keeping with Spanish custom, his first name is followed by his father's surname—by which Moulitsas is known—and then his mother's surname.) His father was a furniture salesman, his mother a secretary. Moulitsas has a younger brother, Alexander, who is a graphic designer. In 1975, the year Alexander was born, the family moved to El Salvador during that country's brutal civil war, in which anti-Communist government forces had the backing of the United States. Living in an environment where gunshots and explosions were everyday occurrences deeply affected Moulitsas's views on war—and on recent U.S. policy regarding armed conflict. In the U.S., "war is a video game," he told Kara Platoni for the *East Bay Express* (December 15, 2004). "I've seen firsthand the ravages of war and the hatred, and just the notion that politics can be a life or death issue." In 1980, when Moulitsas was nine years old, his parents received an envelope containing photographs of him and his brother boarding a bus to school, a threatening gesture from the rebel troops who wanted to use the Moulitsases' house as headquarters. The family left El Salvador soon afterward and returned to the Chicago area, this time to Schaumburg, a suburb of the city.

After nine years of speaking mostly Spanish, and five years in a war-torn country, Moulitsas found the transition to life in the U.S. to be difficult. For the first two years after his family's return, Moulitsas attended a bilingual program at Schaumburg Elementary School. In fourth grade he switched to an all-English curriculum at another school, Thomas Dooley. He described his time there—and, subsequently, at Robert Frost Junior High School and Schaumburg High School—to *Current Biography*: "What was tough for me, of course, was I had the funny accent, and I looked younger [than] my age." Those years, he added, were "pretty miserable." While in high school Moulitsas began taking piano lessons; playing the piano became a passion that provided an escape from the challenges of school and led him to consider a career as a professional musician. His ambitions were not limited to music, though. "I wanted to be everything when I grew up," he told *Current Biography*. "I wanted to be president of the United States."

In 1989, when he was 17 years old and weighed 118 pounds, Moulitsas joined the U.S. Army, an experience he has cited as the turning point in his life. "I would not be the person I am today without my military service," he told Tim Russert in an interview for CNBC News (June 3, 2006, on-line). "I'm extremely proud of it." He said to Platoni, "It was the Army, basically, that gave me the cocky arrogance I carry these days." For Moulitsas, who came from a lower-middle-class family, entering the military seemed a good way to obtain a college education. In addition, Moulitsas, who planned to run for elective office in the future, felt that military service would benefit him in the long term. "I thought if I was ever in a position to send people to war, it would be hypocritical for me to do so if I myself had not served in the army," he told *Current Biography*. During basic training in Oklahoma, Moulitsas managed—despite his considerably smaller build—to finish with the lead group in a grueling, 16-mile road march, the first in a series of confidence-building experiences he underwent in the army. He spent most of his service as a fire-direction specialist for a missile unit in the small town of Bamburg, Germany. After the Persian Gulf War of 1991 was launched, Moulitsas's unit was scheduled to be deployed to Saudi Arabia. The war ended, however, before they could be called into action. Moulitsas returned to the U.S. with a newfound confidence, the nickname "Kos," and, perhaps most importantly, a radically altered set of political beliefs. When Moulitsas entered the army, he had been a fervent Republican, largely because of the Republican president Ronald Reagan's support for the Salvadoran government. "I didn't know any better," he told *Current Biography*. But the communal nature of his experiences in the army made him think differently about what he described as the Republicans' "selfish" approach to government. In 1992, while still casting a vote for the Republican candidate—George H. W. Bush that year—in the presidential race, he voted for Democrats in many statewide races. "It was hard for me to make a transition because I spent all my formative years as a Republican, and a pretty hardcore one," he told *Current Biography*. "It's always difficult when you believe in something so long, to admit to yourself that you were wrong." By 1996, however, Moulitsas had become what he called a "straight ticket Democrat," completely embracing a liberal agenda.

Upon his return to the U.S., in 1992, Moulitsas enrolled at Northern Illinois University, in DeKalb, where he planned to major in music, with the hope of making a living composing film scores. His focus changed after he read a negative column about Mexican-American students in the school newspaper, the *Northern Star*. Moulitsas felt the need to write a column of his own in response; a few semesters later, he not only had a regular column but was also the editor in chief of the paper, while also freelancing for the *Chicago Tribune*. Under his direction, the *Northern Star* became one of the first college newspapers to be posted on the Internet, in 1995, in the very earliest days of the Web. "It's always been a point of pride of mine, that I'm always on the cutting edge of technology everywhere I go," he told *Current Biography*. He dropped his music major and graduated in 1996 with two degrees—one in philosophy, the other in political science and journalism. Also in 1996, several years before the term "blog" was coined, Moulitsas started the Hispanic-Latino News Service, a Web site to which he devoted three hours each day, sifting through and uploading news stories from around the U.S. and entering all the programming code manually.

In the fall of that year, Moulitsas entered the Boston University School of Law, a move that surprised many who knew him well. "I wanted a way to kill three years of my life in a respectable fashion," he told Platoni, adding, "I knew within thirty minutes that it wasn't for me." Rather than focusing his energy on his schoolwork, Moulitsas spent the three years mainly as an activist, working as a legislative aide for the Massachusetts state legislator David Magnani and helping the Massachusetts Association of Hispanic Attorneys with their efforts to organize independent Latino grocers. The association named him law student of the year in 1998. During that period he also served as a quality-assurance tester for a number of software firms, work that helped him remain afloat financially and stay abreast of the continuing innovations in computer technology.

After completing his law degree, in 1999, Moulitsas was offered a job by the Latino Web site PicoSito.com and moved to San Francisco, California, in the midst of the "dot-com" boom, to join the new company. PicoSito soon went out of business, but Moulitsas managed to get a job at a Web-development company across the hall. His work there allowed him to stay aware of the latest technology. He has also credited the company with teaching him how to create a distinct product brand, one of Daily Kos's greatest strengths.

The 2002 midterm elections, in which Republicans expanded their control of the House of Representatives and regained control of the Senate, were demoralizing for the Democratic Party and for Democratic supporters including Moulitsas. Moulitsas had been reading and occasionally posting entries on the political blog MyDD.com, founded in 2001. ("MDD"originally stood for "My Due Diligence"; the site was renamed "My Direct Democracy" in 2006.) Inspired by MyDD.com and its founder, Jerome Armstrong, in 2002 Moulitsas created his own blog, calling it Daily Kos, after his army nickname. "When I started, I had no illusions that anyone would ever read it," he recalled to *Current Biography*, explaining that he created the blog as simply a means of venting his feelings about the election results and the state of the Democratic Party. The blog immediately began attracting a readership that extended beyond his family and friends, the only people Moulitsas had expected to be interested in it. Soon after Daily Kos's launch, Joe Trippi, the campaign manager for the 2004 presidential candidate Howard Dean, recruited Moulitsas and Armstrong as technology advisers to the Dean campaign. The pair formed a consulting firm, Armstrong-Zúniga, suggesting such then-radical ideas as using Web sites for fund-raising and enlisting the activist site MeetUp.com to organize Dean supporters in their respective locales. Armstrong stopped blogging for the duration of the campaign, moving to Dean's headquarters in Burlington, Vermont. Moulitsas continued blogging, disclosing his work as a consultant to Dean on Daily Kos the day after the deal was made. He would be criticized often for endorsing Dean while receiving a salary from the campaign, but ultimately, because of his full disclosure, his reputation did not suffer serious damage. Dean dropped out of the race on February 18, 2004; John Kerry later became the Democratic presidential nominee.

As the 2004 election drew closer, Daily Kos grew more and more popular, and Moulitsas's passionate, often harshly worded postings came under greater scrutiny. In April 2004 Moulitsas posted a controversial statement about the killings of four private military contractors in Fallujah, Iraq. He wrote, "I feel nothing over the death of mercenaries. They aren't in Iraq because of orders, or because they are trying to help the people make Iraq a better place. They are there to wage war for profit. Screw them." The immediate reaction to his posting was decidedly negative, with Kerry's official Web site removing its link to Daily Kos. Moulitsas later apologized, explaining that he was angry that the contractors' deaths had received much more media attention than the deaths of five marines on the same day. Still, he was not wholly repentant, defending his actions to Martin Bashir for ABC's *Nightline* (July 24, 2006, on-line). "The blogs are a raw, emotional medium . . . ," he said. "They're not measured conversation. They're not edited. They're raw."

Whether despite or because of that episode, readership of Daily Kos continued to grow. Moulitsas used the site's increasing popularity to start a fund-raising campaign for 15 Democratic candidates for various offices around the country, those he had identified as being most in need of funding in the 2004 elections. Readers donated approximately $500,000 to Moulitsas's picks, often giving money to candidates who were not even running for office in the donors' home states. All 15 candidates lost their races, much to the delight of Moulitsas's growing number of critics. Moulitsas, however, said that he still considered the effort a success, as he and his readers had forced several incumbent Republican candidates to spend their time and money campaigning for their previously safe seats, instead of traveling the country to stump for other candidates. The Daily Kos's fund-raising campaign also was one of the earliest examples of a movement christened "netroots," driven by an increasingly recognized group of on-line Democratic activists. By rallying his readers around specific candidates, Moulitsas nationalized what would have been, in many cases, races of purely local interest.

With the Democrats' widespread defeat in 2004, most notably Kerry's loss to the incumbent George W. Bush, Moulitsas furthered his efforts to mobilize the party. He and Armstrong wrote a book, published in 2006 as *Crashing the Gate: Netroots, Grassroots, and the Rise of People-Powered Politics*. "This book was really written for those of us— and there's a lot of us—who really thought John Kerry was going to win the election . . . ," Moulitsas told Russert. "When election night came and went, we lost the election, we decided to set out and find out why we lost and what we could do to change that in the future." The "gate" of the title refers to Washington, D.C., and what Armstrong and Moulitsas see as the insularity of national politics—a quality they believe can be eliminated, at least partially, through the Internet. "What we're saying is that people now are empowered by technology to take an active role in their government, take an active role in the media and not let D.C. dictate what happens and what doesn't happen in this country anymore," he told Russert. In an assessment for the *New York Times Book Review* (March 26, 2006), Peter Beinart called the book "persuasive" and an "insightful guide to how the Democratic Party can retake power." Lee Drutman similarly praised the book in the *Los Angeles Times* (May 30, 2006). "*Crashing the Gate* is brash and infuriating, as it should be . . . ," she wrote. "It commands attention."

Moulitsas commanded even more attention through the convention he organized in June of that year. Dubbed "Yearly Kos," the conference drew more than 1,000 attendees: 900 bloggers (calling themselves "Kossacks"), 100 reporters covering the conference, and a dozen politicians trying to win the bloggers' support. Widely heralded in news reports as a turning point for the netroots movement, the conference demonstrated a new level of power and influence on the part of the bloggers. As Ronald Brownstein observed in the *Los Angeles Times* (June 11, 2006), the Yearly Kos "may have marked a milestone in the evolution of the online liberal community from scruffy insurgents to an institutionalized force within the Democratic Party." Lizza viewed the scene differently, noting the $50,000 party thrown by former governor Warner, the open-bar party at the Hard Rock Casino hosted by General Clark, and the breakfast function organized by Governor Richardson. "Las Vegas could be the beginning of a new era of blogger influence and authority," Lizza wrote. "Or it might just be the weekend they all sold out." For his part, Moulitsas assured the bloggers that they still represented a movement separate from the political establishment. In his keynote address at the convention, he asserted the need for bloggers and other ordinary citizens to take action. "The media elite has failed us; the political elite, both parties, has failed us—Republicans have failed us because they can't govern; Democrats have failed us because they can't get elected. So now it's our turn," he said, as quoted by Brownstein. "We have arrived," he added, as quoted by the *National Review* (July 5, 2006). "There's no doubt we're turning the political world upside down."

Indeed, the netroots movement wielded considerably more power in the 2006 mid-term elections than it had only two years earlier. Moulitsas's endorsement on Daily Kos was a major factor in Ned Lamont's primary victory over the incumbent Democratic U.S. senator Joseph Lieberman of Connecticut. (Lieberman went on to run as an Independent and defeat Lamont in the general election, thanks to the large numbers of Republicans who voted for him.) As in the 2004 elections, Moulitsas picked a roster of candidates to support on-line. This time, a number of them—most notably the U.S. Senate candidates Jon Tester of Montana and Jim Webb of Virginia—won, helping to give control of both the Senate and the House of Representatives to the Democrats for the first time in 12 years. Regarding those results, Moulitsas told *Current Biography*, "I'm focused, really, on building a long-term movement. So I don't get too disappointed about losing . . . and I don't get too excited about winning." He said that he is looking ahead to the elections of 2016, the year he predicts the Democrats will be competitive with the Republicans in terms of party infrastructure.

Along with the increased influence and popularity of his site has come an increased scrutiny of Moulitsas himself. Although he fully disclosed his work for Dean, Moulitsas consulted in 2004 for a number of other political candidates whose names he refused to reveal, leading many news outlets to speculate that he was being paid to endorse certain candidates on his blog. "While the Daily Kos is a community site, it is hardly a democracy," Brian Reich wrote for the Web site Personal Democracy Forum, as quoted by Platoni. "Make no mistake, it

is Kos' world, and his readers are all just playing into it." Others continue to criticize Moulitsas for the tone of his blog. "The liberal blogosphere are a group of people who feel incredibly disenfranchised," Franklin Foer, the editor of the *New Republic,* told Grynbaum. "They feel their country's been hijacked and they're essentially powerless and the only way to stop it is to scream as loudly as you can." Moulitsas is not particularly bothered by his critics. "Clearly, I make a living throwing stones, so I'm going to take some incoming," he told *Current Biography*. He also sees little need to defend himself against criticism of his use of Daily Kos to endorse candidates. "My site is my site," he told Platoni. "You can start your own site. That's the whole point: Anybody can do this."

Moulitsas is currently at work on his second book, tentatively titled "The Libertarian Democrat." He is also working on a redesign of the Daily Kos site that would allow for considerably more traffic; that project is slated for completion in 2008. In 2004 Daily Kos launched dKospedia.com, an encyclopedia of more than 7,000 political articles written and compiled by members of the Daily Kos community. In January 2005 Moulitsas began to post SB Nation, a network of sports blogs. Both dKospedia.com and SB Nation are active and expanding.

Moulitsas lives in Berkeley, California, with his wife, Elisa Batista, a former reporter for *Wired News*, and their son, Aristotle, who is three years old, and daughter, Elisa, born in April 2007. In 2003 Moulitsas devoted an additional blog, fishyshark.com, to the travails of fatherhood, and Batista now contributes to mothertalkers.com, a blog about parenting.

—C.S.

Suggested Reading: *Newsweek* p34+ July 3, 2006; *New York Review of Books* (on-line) Apr. 27, 2006; *New York Times* IV p12 June 25, 2006; *San Francisco Chronicle* A p1+ Apr. 5, 2006; *Washington Monthly* p18+ Jan./Feb. 2006

Selected Books: *Crashing the Gate: Netroots, Grassroots, and the Rise of People-Powered Politics,* 2006

Nakamura, Dan

1967(?)– Music producer

Address: c/o Riverhead Books, 375 Hudson St., #4079, New York, NY 10014

"There are no rock stars among music producers, but Nakamura comes closer than anyone," Jane Ganahl, a *San Francisco Chronicle* (November 29, 2004) columnist, wrote of Dan Nakamura, who is an arranger, mixer, studio engineer, and composer

Scott Gries/Getty Images

Dan "the Automator" Nakamura

as well as a producer and has often appeared on stage with one or another of his many collaborators. Nicknamed "the Automator" in the mid-1980s for reasons that he no longer remembers, Nakamura "has so many identities, bands, and projects, it's difficult to keep them straight," as Christopher Muther wrote for the *Boston Globe* (January 11, 2002). Nakamura's name is listed in the credits of dozens of albums that together have sold many millions of copies. Among the numerous individuals and groups with whom he has worked are the rappers Kool Keith Thornton, Del tha Funkee Homosapien, Prodigy, Prince Paul, and Zack de la Rocha; the reggae musician Ziggy Marley; the punk rocker Daryl Palumbo; the hip-hop/trip-hop artist DJ Krush; the rock groups Stereolab, Depeche Mode, Cheap Trick, Jon Spencer Blues Explosion, Little Barrie, Head Automatica, and Primal Scream; the funk and jazz group Galactic; the turntable musician Kid Koala; and the hard-to-categorize Beck. His "lack of fussiness in the studio," as Christopher Muther wrote, accounts in part for his unusual productivity. "I don't sit there for three weeks at the mixing board debating whether the hi-hat is the right level," Nakamura said to Muther, referring to the set of cymbals that is typically part of a drum kit. According to Marc Weingarten, writing for the *Los Angeles Times* (February 17, 2002), "Dan the Automator is dance music's great alchemist of the moment. A prolific idea man who can weave social criticism into party-time hip-hop or make non-ironic love songs coexist with sharp-tongued humor, Nakamura is one of the leaders of the current alternative rap movement, a subgenre in which craven materialism and casual sexism are ditched in favor of playful exper-

imentation." Many of the recordings that Nakamura has produced display what Neva Chonin described in the *San Francisco Chronicle* (November 20, 2001) as "a signature production style of dense, muscled beats and elaborately layered instrumentation incorporating everything from old-school hip-hop to classical compositions."

"I tend to be really disappointed by records with only one or two good songs or eight different producers and no continuity through the album," Nakamura told James Rotondi for *Remix* (March 2001). "When I set out to do an album, I want to anchor it to something so you can listen from beginning to end and really enjoy the whole thing." The release of Kool Keith's album *Dr. Octagonecologyst* (1996) gave Nakamura's career a substantial boost, as did the album he made with the hip-hop artist Prince Paul, *So . . . How's Your Girl?* (1999), for which the two formed a duo called the Handsome Boy Modeling School. Nakamura's biggest commercial success to date is *Gorillaz* (2001), which he made with the singer/songwriter Damon Albarn and the comic-book artist Jamie Hewlett. Featuring a fictional band of stylized cartoon apes called the Gorillaz, the album has sold upwards of five million copies, and it earned nominations for both a Grammy Award and, in Britain, a Mercury Music Prize.

Dan Nakamura was born in the latter half of the 1960s in San Francisco, California, where he grew up. (No easily accessible source mentions his date of birth, and published accounts are inconsistent regarding his age.) His father was a civil engineer for the city and county of San Francisco; his mother was an educator. His only sibling, a brother, holds a doctorate in cell biology. When Nakamura was three years old, his parents arranged for him to begin studying the violin, with a teacher who used the Suzuki method of instruction. "I had a somewhat acrimonious relationship with classical music," he told Rotondi, "because I had to practice a lot when I didn't really want to." He continued to study the violin seriously for the next dozen years, even though sometimes, because his skin was so dry, as he told Jane Ganahl, the tips of his fingers would bleed during practice. By his own account, he occasionally gave recitals and played with orchestras. "I was by no means a prodigy, but I was good for my age," he told Rotondi. In grade school, he recalled to Muther, he was "really fascinated by hip-hop, pop and Top 40 music. I was much more inspired by Michael Jackson than Beethoven." He told Andrew Weiner for *Slate* (March 18, 2002, on-line) that his musical direction changed when he heard "Rapper's Delight" (1979), by the trio the Sugarhill Gang—"the song that served as the gateway into hip hop for everyone around Nakamura's age," as Zac Crain put it in an article for the *Dallas (Texas) Observer* (November 11, 1999).

Nakamura attended Lick-Wilmerding High School, in San Francisco, a private, nonprofit college-preparatory day school. During his years there his appetite for hip-hop music increased, and he often listened to the San Francisco State University radio station KPOO, the only station in the area that broadcast hip-hop then. He also began to collect recordings by such early hip-hop standouts as Doug E. Fresh, UTFO, and Whodini and, later, Run-DMC and LL Cool J. For some time he aspired to become a professional hip-hop disc jockey. "I didn't know what a producer did," he told Jane Ganahl. "I did know from the beginning that I didn't want to be in a band, or be a singer or guitar player." But he always felt "curious about how music is made. I would hear songs and listen closely and think, 'That's not a natural drum sound,' or 'I wonder how they got that tone.'" In his teens Nakamura taught himself how to program a drum machine. He also became proficient at the technique called scratch, or scratching, invented by the hip-hop disc jockey Grand Wizard Theodore, in which the person spinning discs—the turntablist, in hip-hop parlance—moves a vinyl record tiny distances as it revolves, without lifting the phonograph needle from the grooves (or permitting it to leave the grooves), and thus changes the sound of the recording to create new music. "I thought I was going to be a really good DJ-editor-remixer guy or something . . . ," Nakamura told Crain. "But when I was coming up, becoming a good DJ, it was the same period when Q-Bert, Mix Master Mike, all these other people were coming up in my neighborhood." The "other people" included D-Styles, Yogafrog, and Shortkut, all of whom, along with Q-Bert and Mix Master Mike, became known collectively as the Invisibl Skratch Piklz and built reputations as superlative turntablists. Nakamura realized, as he told Crain, that his skills would never equal those of Q-Bert, who was several years his junior. "At some point, Q-Bert really inspired me not to DJ . . . ," he said to Crain. "It was inspiration by discouragement."

As a teenager Nakamura secured gigs as a disc jockey at parties and weddings, and for a while during the mid-1980s, he served in that role at KPOO. After he completed high school, he enrolled at San Francisco State University, where he studied industrial and graphic design and earned a B.A. degree in 1990. A few years earlier he had begun producing music—"some remixes and stuff," as he told Bevan Jee for an undated interview for Bomb Hip Hop Magazine (on-line)—for Depeche Mode and Herbie Hancock, among others. His first single to bear his own name, "Music to Be Murdered By," was released on the HomeBass label in 1988 and sold about 9,000 copies. "It was my coming of age or sound at the time . . . ," he recalled to Jee. "That kind of sound was what I was into. . . . If you listen carefully you can hear shades of Octagon in there, maybe in its infancy." "Octagon" refers to one of the personas adopted by Kool Keith Thornton—that of Dr. Octagon, a sex-obsessed, demented extraterrestrial gynecologist.

Kool Keith's first album, Dr. Octagonecologyst, was released in the U.S. by Bulk Recordings and the British label Mo' Wax in 1996 and by Dream-Works the next year. It was enhanced by Q-Bert's innovative scratching and became "an underground sensation, as Nakamura's dirty, arty beats saw and raised Thornton's wacked-out sensibility," in Crain's words. Nakamura's "rhythm tracks weren't really revolutionary," Andrew Weiner wrote of the album; "they were built around syncopated drum rhythms lifted from the same funk and break-beat records that DJs had been sampling for years. But the bass lines loped and brooded through a drowsy and discreetly menacing noir atmosphere that owed much to the trip-hop stylings of contemporary acts like Portishead. At the same time, the Automator was incorporating other influences from outside the rap world, such as those permeating more avant-garde electronica." Dr. Octagonecologyst, along with a second disc (released at the same time), called The Instrumentalyst: Octagon Beats; the album DJ Shadow's Endtroducing . . . (1996), which Nakamura worked on; and Nakamura's solo EP, the six-track A Better Tomorrow, which appeared at about the same time, brought Nakamura much attention and offers for many remixing and production jobs. When I Was Born for the 7th Time (1997), which he produced for the Anglo-Indian indie band Cornershop, reached number one on British charts. Others with whom he worked included the Jon Spencer Blues Explosion, which, according to the Matador Records Web site, took "cues from rock, punk, r&b, garage, hardcore, and hip hop idioms, while transcending the limitations of each." Nakamura produced Anandji and Kalyanji Shah's Bombay the Hard Way: Guns, Cars & Sitars (1997), which contained beats by DJ Shadow and which, according to John Ballon, a reviewer for musthear.com, was "a potent cross-pollination of Secret-Agent-Man guitar themes, Blaxploitation grooves, jazzy horn and flute riffs, hip-hop beats and loops, and traditional Indian instrumentation."

Kool Keith's decision against promoting Dr. Octagonecologyst on tour or engaging in other collaborations with Nakamura (for personal reasons; the two parted amicably) enabled Nakamura to devote more of his working time to rock bands, whom he found were "more amenable [than hip-hop artists] to trying new things, working with new sounds," as Crain wrote. "They're like, 'Let's see how far we can take it. Let's try this. Let's try that,'" Nakamura said to Crain. "To me, that just makes it a lot more fun. The truth of the matter is, I love making hip-hop records. I would make them all the time. But there isn't a lot of bands willing to go that route, so I find myself making more alternative records." James Rotondi's 2001 article for Remix describes in detail some of the equipment and techniques Nakamura has used in making recordings.

In 1999 Nakamura and the former De La Soul producer and hip-hop artist Prince Paul, dubbing themselves Nathaniel Merriweather and Chest

Rockwell, respectively, formed a duo called Handsome Boy Modeling School. That name and the concept for their recording *So . . . How's Your Girl?* were inspired by an episode in Chris Elliott's TV comedy series *Get a Life* (1990–92). Contributors to the album included Mike D, Miho Hatori of Cibo Matto, Sean Lennon, Money Mark, DJ Shadow, Alec Empire, Josh Haden of Spain, Roison Murphy of Moloko, and Father Guido Sarducci (Don Novello). Nakamura told Maximillian Mark Medina for the Asian-American magazine *Yolk* (September 30, 2001) that he and Prince Paul "had a really good time" making the album. "All the guests on that record were friends. We didn't talk to any labels or managers . . . we just had our phone books. . . . It was the first time I ever made a record just strictly with people I purely enjoy, because that's what I want to do. I've been trying to carry that philosophy since that time." *So . . . How's Your Girl?* "is a beautiful garbage heap of 40 years of music," Zac Crain wrote, "piled high with everything from old-school hip-hop (the duo liberally samples from Paul's former band, Stetsasonic) and blaxploitation horns ('Holy Calamity Bear Witness II,' easily the best of a good bunch) to gauzy trip-hop (the lush 'The Truth') and prolonged bursts of static. . . . Like most of the projects Prince Paul and Nakamura have worked on, it's hard to take in all at once. . . . More than anything else, it's a tribute to the early days of hip-hop, when there were no record deals, only mix tapes made by DJs." Pharrell Williams, Julee Cruise, Jamie Callum, John Oates, Chino Moreno, RZA, Cat Power, the rock band Mars Volta, and the comic actor Tim Meadows, among others, collaborated with Nakamura and Prince Paul on Handsome Boy Modeling School's second album, *White People* (2004). Nakamura described *White People* to Jane Ganahl as "a cultural satire of sorts." "I think music in general is pretty humorless," he said to Ganahl. "People can sing about being in love, being in lust, happy, sad, angry—so why isn't it OK to sing about being silly? The thing about Handsome Boy is that it's not just about being funny, but it's a commentary on hip-hop, on people taking on drug dealer names." "Humor is a good way to get into people's heads," he told Marc Weingarten.

Also in 1999 Nakamura and the music-publishing veteran Erik Gilbert co-founded 75 Ark Entertainment and launched a new label, 75 Ark, which remained in operation for only a few years. Nakamura told Richard Harrington for the *Washington Post* (January 19, 2001), "There has always been, and is even more so today, a need for an outlet for records that are not on the major label level. There's a lot of great records out there that are only meant to sell 10,000 to 15,000 copies, or maybe even 100,000. . . . But to a major label, those numbers are unacceptable. . . . We're trying to create a situation where it's 'in-between,' with relatively decent distribution and some press and some publicity but without the expectation of selling 600,000 copies, much less a million, for it to be deemed successful or worthwhile."

On *Deltron 3030* (2000), which bears the 75 Ark label, three characters hurtle through space in the year 3030: Deltron Zero, portrayed by Del tha Funkee Homosapien; the Cantankerous Captain Aptos (Nakamura); and Skiznod the Boy Wonder (Kid Koala). Other contributors to the album included Prince Paul, Brandon Arnovick, and Damon Albarn. "I'm not a particularly avid science-fiction fan—I don't follow it closely—but the future is interesting to me," Nakamura told Richard Harrington. "Setting 'the story' in the future allows us liberties to talk about what we think is going to happen based on what's going on today; it gives us a more creative edge." "The tracks address such familiar targets as multinational corporations, media monopolies, invasive technology and rampant consumerism," Harrington wrote, "suggesting that even a millennium from now, the more things change, the more they remain the same." Although Nakamura assured Harrington that "we're making records because we enjoy making music, and only secondarily doing a message," he also remarked, "Not only is nothing going to change, but people really have to be a little more cognizant about what's going on today with companies like CNN, who are telling us what the news is all over the world based on what they feel the news is." (On *Deltron 3030*, "The News" is a subsidiary of Microsoft.)

In 2001, having concluded that no "great love records" had appeared in the past 25 years, Nakamura produced the album *Nathaniel Merriweather Presents Lovage: Music to Make Love to Your Old Lady By*. In addition to Merriweather (Nakamura), the group Lovage includes Mike Patton, from the hard-rock band Faith No More; Jennifer Charles of the pop group Elysian Fields; and Kid Koala. Others heard on the album are Damon Albarn, the former lead singer of the British rock band the Blur; Maseo, from the hip-hop group De La Soul; and the DJ Afrika Bambaataa. Neva Chonin wrote, "Lovage mixes hilariously eclectic samples and Nakamura's equally diverse instrumental arrangements—violin, guitar, Melotron and everything between—into a Serge Gainsbourg-inspired traipse through the twin arts of looking good and making love."

Together with Damon Albarn and Jamie Hewlett, best known as the creator of the cult comic *Tank Girl*, Nakamura invented the virtual band Gorillaz, whose members are animated characters named 2-D, Murdoc, Russel, and Noodle. Those who lent their voices to *Gorillaz* (2001) included Ibrahim Ferrer, of the band Buena Vista Social Club, Haruka Kuroda, and Chris Frantz and Tina Weymouth, from the band Tom Tom Club (and formerly of the Talking Heads). Writing for the *Seattle (Washington) Post-Intelligencer* (March 1, 2002), Gene Stout described *Gorillaz* as "a blend of hip-hop, pop, rock, electronica and dub music augmented by a fascinating mix of sound effects and distorted instruments." The Gorillaz's single "Clint Eastwood" (whose lyrics make no mention of that actor), performed by Del tha Funkee Homo-sapien, became a major hit, and several other sin-gles from the album—"19-2000," "Tomorrow Com-es Today," and "Rock the House"—also sold very well, especially in Great Britain. Nakamura has not worked on subsequent Gorillaz albums.

In 2006 Nakamura wrote 12 compositions for the video game NBA 2K7. The soundtrack, which features Mos Def, E-40, Fabulous, Ghost Face, Rhymefest, and A Tribe Called Quest, among oth-ers, was released in the same year. Beginning in late 2006 hip-hop compositions by Nakamura, commissioned by Adidas, accompanied Internet ads for National Basketball Association–connected models of Adidas's "Superstar" athletic shoes. That year Nakamura also teamed up with Russell Simins, the drummer for the Jon Spencer Blues Ex-plosion, to record the 12-track album *Men Without Pants*, scheduled for release by Expansion Team Records in early 2008.

The six-foot two-inch Nakamura, who is unmar-ried, was described by Marc Weingarten as "as easy going as they come"; his characteristics include "gentle zaniness," according to Jane Ganahl. The basement of his home, in the Bernal Heights sec-tion of San Francisco, contains a recording studio, called the Glue Factory. Socializing with his many friends seems to be Nakamura's main recreational activity.

—M.B.

Suggested Reading: *Remix* p3+ Mar. 2001; *San Francisco Chronicle* D p1+ Nov. 29, 2004; *Slate.com* Mar. 18, 2002; *Washington Post* Weekend p6 Jan. 19, 2001

Selected Recordings: *Dr. Octagonecologyst*, 1996; *So . . . How's Your Girl?*, 1999; *Deltron 3030*, 2000; *Gorillaz*, 2001; *Nathaniel Merriweather Presents Lovage: Music to Make Love to Your Old Lady By*, 2001; *White People*, 2004

Jed Jacobsohn/Getty Images

Nelson, Don

May 15, 1940– Basketball coach

Address: Golden State Warriors, 1011 Broadway, Oakland, CA 94607

With more than 1,200 victories to his credit, Don Nelson is the second-winningest coach in the his-tory of the National Basketball Association (NBA), surpassed only by the Hall of Famer Lenny Wilkens. On August 30, 2006 Nelson—who led an all-star squad known as Dream Team II to a gold medal at the 1994 World Championships—was named the head coach of the Golden State War-riors, an Oakland, California-based franchise; that season marked Nelson's 43d in the NBA as, vari-ously, a player, coach, general manager, or consul-tant. Nelson has coached NBA teams in Wisconsin, California, New York, and Texas, and he is one of only two coaches in history to earn NBA Coach of the Year honors three times. (The other is Pat Ri-ley.) During the 1996–97 season, which marked the 50th anniversary of the NBA's founding, Nelson was named by fans as one of the top 10 basketball coaches of all time.

Don Arvid Nelson, the only son of Agnes and Arvid Nelson, was born on May 15, 1940 in Muske-gon, Michigan. His parents were Swedish immi-grants who struggled to earn a living as farmers. Nelson had a solitary childhood: he attended a one-room schoolhouse with only seven other stu-dents and lived at least three miles from his nearest friend. His father made him his first basketball hoop, fashioned from an old bicycle tire, which he attached to the chicken coop. Nelson's usual play-mates were his dog, Pal, and a crippled pig named Butchie whom he nursed back to health. When he was about eight years old, Nelson returned from school to discover that his father had been forced to sell Butchie for slaughter—an act that gave him his first sense of his family's financial straits.

When Nelson was 12 his parents, after years of hardship, sold the farm and moved to Rock Island, Illinois, where his father found work at a farm-implement factory. Agnes Nelson devoted much of her time to volunteering at the Rock Island Rescue Mission, a homeless shelter. Nelson, an enthusias-tic athlete, welcomed the opportunity to play orga-nized sports in Rock Island, trying football, basketball, and track. In his second year of high school, he settled on basketball. "The basketball coach took an interest in me, told me I had a chance to make the varsity [team] my sophomore year. I was [six feet five inches]. So I came out early and left the football team," Nelson told Roy S. Johnson for the *New York Times* (May 9, 1983).

Nelson attended the University of Iowa, in Iowa City, majoring in physical education and becoming a standout basketball player—one of the best in the program's history—as well as participating on the track team. In his junior season Nelson led the basketball team to an 18–6 record and a final national ranking of eighth and was named to the National Collegiate Athletic Association (NCAA) All-American team. Nelson left Iowa after three years with career averages of 21.1 points and 10.9 rebounds per game.

Nelson was a third-round draft selection of the Chicago Zephyrs, a struggling NBA franchise now known as the Washington Wizards. An unexceptional player on a poorly performing team, he averaged 6.8 points per game and appeared in 72 contests. After one season his contract rights were sold to the Los Angeles Lakers; he suffered through two unproductive seasons with the Lakers before being waived.

Returning to the Quad Cities area of Iowa, Nelson found a job as a roofer and began reevaluating his dream of playing professional basketball. During the following NBA season, 1965–66, the Boston Celtics called to offer him a tryout, because the team had sustained injuries and needed to hire an additional player; Nelson had a successful audition and earned a spot. "He was just an average player with limited skills," a former Celtics assistant coach, John Killilea, told Johnson. "But he was smart enough to drift in the Celtic break to a place where he could score. He manufactured that into a long and productive career."

Nelson was not as physically gifted as many of his NBA counterparts and was forced to learn how to exploit his opponents' mistakes to his advantage. While never a star player, Nelson complemented such team members as Bill Russell, John Havlicek, Paul Silas, and Tommy Heinsohn. In Nelson's best season, 1969–70, he averaged 15.4 points and 7.3 rebounds a game, both career highs. During Nelson's tenure with the team, the Celtics enjoyed great success, winning the NBA championship in 1966, 1968, 1974, and 1976. Nelson played outstandingly on at least one occasion, when he sank the winning jump shot in the closing seconds of the 1969 championship game to lead the Celtics past the Lakers for the title. After the 1976 championship season, however, the Celtics decided to part ways with Nelson, and he retired. During his 14 years in the NBA, Nelson had amassed more than 10,000 points, and during one stretch he appeared in 465 consecutive games. Known as one of the NBA's best-ever "sixth-men" (that is, a team's top substitute player), Nelson had his number—19—retired by the Celtics in 1978.

Though his playing days were behind him, Nelson wanted to remain active in the NBA. After taking an unsuccessful turn at officiating, Nelson received an unexpected opportunity when Wayne Embry, a former teammate who had become the general manager of the Milwaukee Bucks, offered him a position as an assistant coach for the 1976–77 NBA season. Larry Costello, the head coach of the Bucks, needed a young former player to act as a liaison between himself and his players, and Nelson took the job, believing that it could be the first step in a coaching career. "I was lucky," Nelson told Johnson. "I wanted to get into coaching, but didn't know how. Once I was here [in Milwaukee], I figured [I would] stay here two years, then move on to be an assistant somewhere else for a year or so before I try to get a head coaching job." Just 18 games into the season, however, Nelson's timetable changed when Costello resigned and Embry promoted Nelson to head coach, despite Nelson's protestations that he was not ready to take on the responsibility.

In Nelson's rookie season as head coach of the Bucks, the team continued to struggle, and he was ejected from four games for bad behavior, gaining a reputation for belligerence in the process. During one ejection, in Philadelphia, Pennsylvania, Nelson took off his suit coat and threw it onto the court as he exited the arena. When the Bucks next played in Philadelphia, the home team sponsored a coat-throwing contest, which Nelson claimed to find hilarious.

Nelson often became physically ill and slept poorly after his team lost. He had little time to spend with his family, which now included four children. "During those early years, we never saw him," Nelson's son Donnie (also called Donn) once remarked, as reported by Kevin Lyons for the St. Paul, Minnesota, *Pioneer Press* (January 6, 2002). "He came to maybe one or two of my high school games a year. It was the most stressed I'd ever seen him. It completely consumed him. It was about surviving. He felt like he was a step away from going back to roofing in Iowa, and so he did what he needed to do to stay in the league." In his first season as head coach, the Bucks finished with a record of 30 wins and 52 losses—putting them in last place in the Midwest Division. In his second year, however, Nelson led the Bucks to a 44–38 season, putting them second in the Midwest Division and earning the team a berth in the play-offs. They missed the play-offs the following season, but from 1981 to 1987 (his final seven seasons in Milwaukee), Nelson led the team to more than 50 victories and a play-off spot each year.

In Milwaukee Nelson earned a reputation for being an innovator, and he popularized several strategies that are now commonplace in the NBA. One of those innovations was the concept of a "point forward," a forward who sets up the offense, a function that was traditionally that of the point guard. (He first used the player Paul Pressey in the new position.) Nelson later made the seven-foot-tall Caldwell Jones a "point center," which forced the opposing team to bring its biggest player away from the basket to defend Jones. Those types of maneuvers shattered NBA conventions and helped Nelson's team members make up for their physical shortcomings—as Nelson himself had once done as a player.

Nelson explained that his basic strategy was to put his five best players on the court, regardless of their size, and devise ways to help them compete successfully against typically bigger opponents. That approach often led to a fast-paced, high-scoring style of play, which came to be described as "Nellie Ball." Nelson also institutionalized the concept of the "double team," which had previously been used only as a gimmicky defense for the NBA's most spectacular post players, including Kareem Abdul-Jabbar and Wilt Chamberlain. Nelson turned that strategy into a basic defensive principle, routinely sending two defenders to opposing players who received the ball near the basket and rotating the other players to the closest threats. By popularizing that strategy Nelson became, as Mark Heisler wrote for the *Los Angeles Times* (May 8, 1991), "the father of modern NBA defense."

For his surprising success in Milwaukee, Nelson was given the NBA Coach of the Year trophy twice during his tenure with the Bucks, in 1983 and 1985. Referring to the latter season, in which the Bucks won 59 games and the Central Division title, Pat Williams, then the general manager of the Philadelphia 76ers, explained to Chris Dufresne for the *Los Angeles Times* (May 6, 1985), "He's taken a club that was supposed to be in a rebuilding year, meshed two all-stars with a bunch of overachievers, unwanted and fringe players. This was supposed to be a concession year and then, my God, they have the third-best record in the NBA. It's really one of the most remarkable stories of the last decade." Donnie Nelson has described his father's ingenuity as a necessity. "Early in his career he did conventional things and was losing," the younger Nelson explained to David Dupree for *USA Today* (March 11, 1992). "He finally said, 'I'm going to do things my way and if I go down, I'll go down swinging.'"

Nelson's creative strategies, work ethic, and preference for rumpled suits, sneakers, and garish neckties made him a cult hero in Milwaukee, and he remains one of the most revered coaches in Wisconsin. Jon McGlocklin, a former Bucks player, described Nelson to Dufresne as "the type of guy that could put on a $1,000 suit and look like he'd just been in a fight. He's a no nonsense guy, definitely not a hair-spray and have-your-suit-made-at-the-tailor guy. He's almost a loner, yet he likes to sit at the bar and shoot the breeze." Nelson chose to forgo a signed contract, instead negotiating his compensation each year in a bar and settling it with a handshake—a practice that frustrated other coaches and league officials but endeared him to Midwestern fans, who saw him as one of their own. Nelson also organized Nellie's Farm Fund, through

which he raised more than $500,000 for struggling farmers; as part of the fundraiser, Nelson rode a tractor for 250 miles through Wisconsin.

Despite Nelson's success as a coach and the adoration of both players and fans, his relationship with Howard Kohl, who purchased the Bucks in 1985, was strained, in part because of Nelson's desire for complete control over personnel decisions. While that had worked well with the previous owners, Kohl wanted to limit Nelson's influence. After the 1986–87 season, in which the Bucks finished 50–32 and won six play-off games, Nelson resigned as a result of his power struggle with Kohl. He finished his career as coach of the Bucks with a 540–344 record, seven 50-win seasons, and 37 play-off wins, but without an NBA championship.

Nelson next took a job in the front office of the Golden State Warriors, as an executive vice president; he also purchased 10 percent of the team. Though hired to acquire players for the new head coach, George Karl, Nelson was installed as head coach after only one season, when the Warriors fired Karl. Now exercising complete control over personnel, Nelson began to display his unconventional thinking: although the team needed a center, he used first-round draft choices to select the guards Mitch Richmond, in 1988, and Tim Hardaway, in 1989, to pair with his young perimeter star Chris Mullin. Nelson started the three together and ignited a new incarnation of Nellie Ball, which helped the Warriors become one of the highest-scoring, most exciting teams in the league. Nelson's three stars were referred to as "Run-TMC" (a play on the name of the popular hip-hop group Run-D.M.C.), and Nelson used the players' speed and shooting ability to counteract their size disadvantages. Using a fast-paced, high-scoring offense, in 1992 the Warriors won 55 games, and Nelson was named NBA Coach of the Year for a then-unprecedented third time. Nelson was fast becoming one of the most popular coaches in the league, renowned for his ability to relate to groups of players with diverse backgrounds and persuade them to prize the success of the team over individual statistics and traditional roles. Nelson had a particularly strong relationship with Mullin. (Nelson was the first to suggest that the young player get help for his alcoholism, and Mullin eventually made a recovery.)

At the same time, Nelson was a controversial figure within the NBA. Some observers saw only Nelson's flexibility, charisma, fairness, loyalty, and compassion for those players he liked; others saw an egocentric tyrant. Nelson told Heisler for an article in the *Los Angeles Times* (April 27, 1989), "If ego means that I want credit given to me, that's not me. . . . If ego means that it must be done my way, then I've got a big ego. Because basketball-wise, it's got to be done my way." Despite the differing perceptions, Nelson became the face of the Warriors, and as in Milwaukee, he was one of the few coaches in the NBA who outshone his superstar players. (Adding to his mystique, in 1991, Nelson married his second wife, Joy Wolfgram, at center court.)

During the 1993 draft the Warriors traded for the rights to Chris Webber, the number-one draft pick and the top forward prospect in the country. Webber represented a unique challenge for Nelson; the precocious player had immense talent but objected to Nelson's loud and often blunt style of instruction, and the two feuded openly. By the end of the season—in which the team advanced to the playoffs with a 50–32 record but was defeated in the first round—they were not speaking. The conflict polarized players and fans, and many believed that a large part of the problem was Nelson's powerful role as both general manager and coach, which left those who disagreed with him with no outlet for their concerns.

Nelson was successful in trading Webber to Washington midway through the 1995 season, but the repercussions devastated the franchise. The players, who had once been devoted to Nelson, mutinied; they saw the trading of Webber, the team's best player, as a sign that Nelson was giving up on the players who remained. The team went into a tailspin following Webber's departure, losing 12 of 13 games. In open rebellion, players wrote Webber's number on their shoes. Adding to his difficulties, Nelson contracted viral pneumonia, which hospitalized him for five games. In February, with the team suffering a 14–31 record, Nelson resigned. He took responsibility for the team's failures but was hurt by judgments on the part of some observers that he was past his prime, had lost control of the franchise, and was unable to communicate with modern players. "The only thing that bothered me about the Webber thing was how quickly people seemed to believe all the bad stuff," Nelson told Diane Pucin for the *Philadelphia Inquirer* (November 1, 1995). "That's the only thing that hurt. We all get fired. We all lose jobs. That's our business. But to see how fast your reputation can go. . . ." Nelson left the team following the All-Star break in February and went to Hawaiian island of Maui to regain his health.

Nelson's retirement did not last long. Despite the Golden State fiasco, he was still considered by many to be a top coach, and during the summer of 1995, he was offered a contract to coach the New York Knicks. The Knicks were a veteran team of older players, which Nelson believed would make for an experience different from that of coaching the young roster at Golden State. The Knicks, for their part, needed a veteran coach to usher the team to a championship, and Nelson wanted a chance to prove that he was not a "dinosaur," as some sportswriters had labeled him. The previous coach of the Knicks, Pat Riley, had been a demanding taskmaster who drove the team through three-hour practices and concentrated on a bruising, defensive style of play. Nelson tried to model himself as the anti-Riley—he yelled less than he had previously and limited practices to 90 minutes, in part to avoid injuring the team's older players. Nelson soon discovered, however, that his new approach was not working. As Nelson fine-tuned the Knicks

lineup, the players started to complain. The Knicks' captain, Patrick Ewing, was especially vocal, because Nelson had decided to run plays through other players rather than focus the offense entirely around Ewing. "I thought change would be good for this team," Nelson said at the time, as reported by Jackie MacMullan for *Sports Illustrated* (March 18, 1996), "but looking back, it was a bad fit. I'm kind of a creative coach, and this is an uncreative team." The same players who had once complained about Riley's discipline now accused Nelson of being too casual. The team's results were good—they quickly tallied an 18–6 record and were 34–25 by midseason—but it was clear that the players were not responding to Nelson, who was fired in March 1996 and succeeded by Jeff Van Gundy, a longtime Knicks assistant. Nelson again took responsibility for his ouster, telling reporters that he would return to Maui to reflect and regroup. "I plan on taking a good look at myself, without blaming anyone else, and trying to figure out why I've failed twice," Nelson said, as reported by MacMullan.

Again, Nelson's retirement was short. Though he enjoyed living in Maui and had begun to develop a real-estate career there, his ties to professional basketball remained strong. On February 7, 1997 he was hired as the general manager of the Dallas Mavericks, at that time one of the worst teams in the league. Many NBA executives believed that hiring Nelson was a mistake; his reputation as both a coach and talent evaluator had been diminished by his disastrous exits from the Knicks and the Warriors. Nelson had nonetheless coaxed impressive results out of mediocre teams at several points in his career, and Dallas viewed the hiring as a calculated risk.

Nelson made his presence known immediately, cutting one player in his first 10 days and trading away six more, including the top four scorers on the team. Despite those changes the Mavericks did not improve immediately, and in December of the following season, with the team still struggling, Nelson fired the head coach, Jim Cleamons, and assumed the role himself. When Nelson failed to lead the team to success, despite his unique offensive and defensive strategies, again many in the NBA wondered whether his best years were behind him. Some speculated that Nelson was chiefly interested in rebuilding his reputation as an innovator and that he placed victory second to creativity. "Nellie always goes for the home run," one NBA executive told Phil Taylor for *Sports Illustrated* (April 26, 1999). "Many times when you don't hit the home run, you swing and miss." Nelson responded to such criticism with typical self-assuredness. "I try a lot of different techniques that are unorthodox," he told Taylor. "They don't always work, but very often they do. There are a lot of times when something we do might look strange at first glance, but there's a well-thought-out reason behind it. I'm not going to stop doing things that I think can help us win just because they seem unusual or just because I get lambasted for it from time to time."

Nelson finished the 1997–98 season with a 16–50 record, as the Mavericks continued to be one of the worst teams in the league. During the 1998 draft Nelson orchestrated two controversial draft-day trades to bring Dirk Nowitzki and Steve Nash to Dallas. Nowitzki, a rookie, was an unproven and little-known German player, and Nash, while talented, had been used primarily as a substitute for his previous team. Nelson, however, valued both players for their versatility and potential. Nowitzki in many ways was the quintessential Nellie Ball player: he stood seven feet tall and could make three-point shots and play three positions. Nowitzki was not, however, the instant success that Nelson had predicted, and the team struggled for the next two seasons. Nelson's strategies remained unorthodox, but his coaching style had changed. "Back in the Bucks days, [he] was the super-duper taskmaster," his son Donnie said, as reported by Lyons. "Now he's more at peace with who he is and where he is in his career. He doesn't need to prove a point or to create an identity."

In 2001 Nelson's player-development efforts were rewarded. Nowitzki, having blossomed into one of the premier players in the league, joined with Nash and Michael Finley to form a high-scoring nucleus, making Dallas a league leader in points scored. The 2000–01 season ended with the Mavericks reaching the play-offs for the first time since 1990. (They lost in the second round.) In 2001–02 the Mavericks won 57 games but again were defeated in the second round of the play-offs. The team peaked in 2002–03, when they won 60 games, which tied them for most wins in the league, and advanced to the Western Conference Finals—only the second time in franchise history that the team had made it that far.

During the 2003–04 season the Mavericks again enjoyed some success, but with just 18 games remaining in the season, Nelson resigned as head coach during a practice, handing the reins to his hand-picked successor, the assistant coach Avery Johnson. Drained from coaching and confident that the team was responding well to Johnson, Nelson remained with the team only as a behind-the-scenes consultant. He was rarely asked for advice, however, and his relationship with the new owner, Mark Cuban, soon soured. Eventually he felt so marginalized that he once again retired to Maui. He left the Mavericks having guided them to 329 wins, a franchise record, and four consecutive play-off appearances. (Medical problems were also a source of trouble for Nelson during his final years in Dallas. He had recovered fully from prostate cancer in 2001 but had suffered through shoulder surgery and his wife's bout with breast cancer during the 2004–05 season.)

Nelson found time for several other interests after leaving the Mavericks. He golfed frequently, returned to the real-estate career he had begun in Maui, acted in a failed television pilot about a professional basketball team, and started a restaurant in the Dallas area. Then, in the summer of 2006, he was approached by Chris Mullin, now the executive vice president of basketball operations for the Warriors. The team had struggled since Nelson resigned in 1995, going through eight coaches since then and never once making the play-offs. Nelson—unsure about returning to the Warriors, whose youth and inexperience made them resemble the franchise as it was during his first tenure—required some convincing to begin coaching again. The presence of Mullin, who also worked to restore good relationships between Nelson and the Warriors' owners, reassured him. "He's comfortable here because I really am something of a son to him," Mullin told Mark Emmons for the San Jose Mercury News (November 1, 2006). "I sure know he's been a father figure for me." Nelson signed a three-year contract with the Warriors. Despite Nelson's relationship with Mullin, many NBA observers were surprised that Nelson would give up his life in Maui for the frustrations of rebuilding an ailing team. "I would understand that thinking if I were going to die at 69," Nelson, who was 66 at the time, explained to Emmons. "But I don't plan on dying in three years. I'm going to have time to spend in Maui. Besides, retirement isn't everything it's all cooked up to be."

Nelson entered the 2006–07 season with a career regular-season coaching record of 1,190–880, putting him one spot behind Lenny Wilkens (1,323) on the list of all-time coaching wins. The Warriors got off to a mediocre start in 2006–07, but Nelson, after admitting that his initial evaluations of the players were not entirely accurate, challenged his players to improve, and they responded. He was pleasantly surprised by some of the younger players. "It's easier coaching veterans than kids, but it's more rewarding coaching young kids and watching them develop," he told Art Garcia for the Fort Worth Star-Telegram (November 6, 2006). The Warriors finished the season with a 42–40 record and earned their first play-off berth since 1994. The team defeated Dallas in the first round before losing to the Utah Jazz in the Western Conference semifinals.

Nelson reached his 1,200th win with an at-home game on December 9, 2006; he celebrated with a single cigar and one beer—all his health allows. His team lost the following night, however, and he suffered another sleepless night. "Not to be able to enjoy [1,200 wins] for a few days is the nature of the business we're in," Nelson told Liz Robbins for the New York Times (December 17, 2006). "It was history, see you later, probably as it should be." Although Nelson has yet to win an NBA championship, he has said that doing so is not his primary goal; he is more focused on seeing his current team play more consistently. Even a slight improvement in the Warriors' performance could mean that at the end of his current contract, Nelson would surpass Wilkens to become the winningest coach in NBA history.

Before the start of the 2007–08 season, Nelson renegotiated his contract with the Warriors. While his annual salary for that season and the next jumped from $3.1 million to $5.1 million, the Warriors were given the option of letting him go before his final season.

During the off-season Nelson and his wife, Joy, live in Maui. The couple have five children. Their son son Donnie is president of basketball operations for the Dallas Mavericks.

—N.W.M.

Suggested Reading: *Dallas Morning News* B p16 Nov. 25, 2002; *Hartford Courant* C p1 Nov. 2, 1995; *Los Angeles Times* Sports p10 May 6, 1985, C p1 May 8, 1991; *New York Times* C p6 May 9, 1983, VIII p2 Dec. 17, 2006; *Philadelphia Inquirer* C p1 Nov. 1, 1995; *Sporting News* p24 Feb. 6, 1989; *Sports Illustrated* p38 Jan. 16, 1995; (St. Paul, Minnesota) *Pioneer Press* C p8 Jan. 6, 2002; *USA Today* C p1 Mar. 11, 1992

Bryan Bedder/Getty Images

Norman, Christina

July 30, 1963– President of MTV

Address: MTV, 1515 Broadway, New York, NY 10036

"You wouldn't want to stand next to me if I were singing," Christina Norman, the president of MTV, said during an interview with *Music Trades* (March 1, 2004). She went on, however, to explain the importance of music in her life, saying that it "is linked to every memory I have." As the person responsible for some of the most successful programming in the history of the music-video cable channel MTV and its sister channel, VH1, Norman

has ensured that a new generation will link pop culture, particularly music, with its own memories. Norman, who grew up without cable in the working-class South Bronx neighborhood of New York City, began her television career with a low-level job at a commercial production company in Boston, Massachusetts. She later worked for MTV on a freelance basis before joining the network full-time, in 1991; her rise up the company's ranks culminated in her appointment to its top post in 2005. As president of MTV, Norman is one of the leading corporate executives of color in the United States.

Christina Norman was born on July 30, 1963 and grew up in a South Bronx neighborhood whose population reflected her own Puerto Rican and African-American heritage. Norman has credited her mother, who worked as an administrative assistant, with being the first to teach her about corporate etiquette. She told Rachel Landy for *CosmoGIRL!* (June 1, 2006), "I learned how to carry myself in a corporate setting. For example, you were not mean to my mother on the phone. If you were, you didn't get to talk to her boss." Norman's father was a passionate music aficionado who would spend hours listening to jazz and classical records. Though they were not wealthy, Norman's parents purchased a piano for the home and paid for lessons for her and her brother.

Norman attended Boston University, where she majored in film production. After college she worked for a small production company that made commercials. Her specialty was the tabletop shot, the static image of the product in the commercial. Advertisers and producers consider the tabletop shot the least creative part of an ad, and Norman found the job to be quite dull.

Norman next moved back to New York to pursue other production work on a freelance basis. In the late 1980s she interviewed unsuccessfully for a full-time position with MTV; over the next few years, though, she worked as a freelance production staff member on two MTV shows. In 1991 the cable channel hired her as the production manager for its promotional spots. Her first major success at the network came in 1993, when she designed promotional spots for the cartoon program *Beavis and Butthead* before its MTV premiere. *Beavis and Butthead*, created by the animator Mike Judge and focusing on two mischievous teenage boys, frequently featured scatological humor and mockery of old MTV videos. The show became a huge hit, running from 1993 to 1997 and spawning successful marketing tie-ins, among them toys, apparel, videos, and books. Norman rose steadily through the company's ranks in the 1990s and was eventually promoted to senior vice president for marketing, advertising, and on-air promotion. In 2002, after 11 years at MTV, she put together the successful marketing campaign for *The Osbournes*, a reality television series centering on the adventures of the musician Ozzy Osbourne and his unruly family. In its first season, fueled by publicity largely engineered by Norman, the show reportedly scored the highest ratings of any television program in MTV history. The show aired until 2005.

MTV's sister network, VH1, floundered at the turn of the 21st century. Founded in 1985—four years after MTV—in the wake of MTV's early success with teenagers, VH1 was designed to attract older viewers with music videos by more-established adult-contemporary and pop artists. That strategy was highly successful during the latter half of the 1980s and throughout the 1990s. Television critics and industry watchers attributed VH1's sudden downturn at the end of 2000 to a lack of new programming; by 2002 the network lagged far behind MTV in terms of prime-time ratings. Judy McGrath, the CEO of MTV Networks, tapped Norman to revive VH1, hiring her as the channel's first-ever general manager. McGrath had high praise for Norman's ability to lead writers and other creative workers in a positive direction, telling Elizabeth MacBride for *Crain's New York Business* (January 27, 2003), "When kids are kicking the backseat in the car, you need someone who can drive." Norman told P. Llanor Alleyne for *Broadcasting & Cable* (June 16, 2003), "I hadn't really thought of going for [the job], but . . . I always wanted to run something someday or have a different kind of responsibility here." McGrath told Alleyne, "When I thought about who would be the best person to take VH1 to the next place by setting a high bar creatively, I thought of Christina." In 2002 *Ebony* named Norman one of its "Top 10 African-Americans in Television."

After consulting with fellow executives, Norman decided to remake's VH1's identity through an overhaul of its approaches to advertising and programming. She pioneered the use of Pop Art–influenced on-air graphics. (Pop Art, which emerged in the 1950s, flouted tradition by relying on symbols of popular entertainment and culture, rather than religion or nature, for inspiration. Notable practitioners of Pop Art include Jasper Johns and Andy Warhol.) Norman also encouraged VH1 staff members to take creative risks, advising them to pitch show ideas that might have been rejected under the leadership of VH1's previous president, John Sykes. She told Megan Larson for *Media Week* (March 24, 2003), "Morale was really down. Everyone was waiting around for permission, but . . . it's all about generating ideas. The staff needed to be unstocked and freed." She told Richard Linnett for *Advertising Age* (September 29, 2003), "From day one, we've been making sure VH1 is returned to its former glory. Viewership was going down, and people viewed us [as] a kind of dry music-history channel." Linnett wrote that Norman worked to make the channel "younger, more exciting and sexy." In addition, Norman emphasized her commitment to VH1's Save the Music campaign, a series of public-service announcements and charity concerts to raise funds for public-school music programs. She told Mark McEwen for the *Early Show* (June 10, 2002, on-line), "Music education isn't just important to VH1. It should be important to everyone. Studies have shown that music education builds brainpower. We feel that restoring music programs in public schools across the country is helping kids do better in school."

Less than a year after Norman's arrival, VH1 launched the pop-culture nostalgia program *I Love the '80s*, which spawned spin-offs in *I Love the '70s* and *I Love the '90s*. Featuring clips from old television shows and music performances combined with commentary from comedians and former pop stars, the series quickly attracted attention from viewers and television critics alike. Another show, *Bands Reunited*, featured aging rock stars coming together with their former band mates for documentary-style interviews. *Best Week Ever* featured comedians' often critical commentary about pop-culture events of the past week. Norman summed up her new programming strategy by telling Larson, "It's all stuff you can use to get into a conversation at a cocktail party. The collective memory of the last 35 years is mine to play with. How cool is that?"

Along with a string of hits, Norman had a few notable misses, including *Rock Behind Bars*, a series showcasing bands composed of prison inmates. The show prompted some objections from crime victims' families and others, including the Fox News pundit Bill O'Reilly, and was soon canceled. Well-publicized plans for a reality show documenting the new marriage of the singer Liza Minnelli and David Gest fell apart after the relationship grew troubled. Overall, however, both the industry and the press praised Norman's new approach. In January 2003 *Crain's New York Business* named her one of its Top 40 Under 40 businesspeople in New York City. Also in 2003 *Hollywood Reporter* named her one of its Power 100 Women in Entertainment. In January 2004 McGrath promoted Norman to president of VH1. That year, Norman led the network to its highest viewership levels ever. She oversaw a complete overhaul of the network's on-air look, extending the Pop Art–influenced sensibility to set design and other visual elements.

In 2005 McGrath named Norman president of MTV. In that post she oversees the network's business development, research, marketing, communications, finance, and human-resources areas. She is also responsible for the strategic direction of MTV2, which runs more music videos than MTV and is seen in almost 55 million homes; mtvU, the channel's college service; MTV Tr3s, a channel for young Hispanic-Americans; and MTV Desi, MTV Chi, and MTVK—channels for South Asian, Chinese, and Korean music, respectively—that were unsuccessful on television and now exist only on the Web. Norman also oversees the digital-cable networks MTV Hits and MTV Jams as well as MTV.com and MTV Overdrive, a broadband Internet video-on-demand service. As of August 2006, MTV Networks owned more than 50 channels, broadcast in 28 languages in 168 countries. MTV programming reached more than 442 million households worldwide, including more than 88 million households in the United States. Norman told Michael Paoletta for *Billboard* (August 27, 2005), "Reaching out to multicultural audiences, I believe, will be a hallmark of the Christina Norman era."

In 2005 *Ebony* honored Norman with its Entertainment Marketing Award at the Sixth Annual Outstanding Women in Marketing and Communication Luncheon at the Hilton New York & Towers in Manhattan. Also in 2005 *Fortune* named her to its Diversity List of the most powerful businesspeople of color in corporate America.

In 2006 Norman introduced a major organizational restructuring plan for MTV. The new plan called for the company to be divided into two "ecosystems." One ecosystem was devoted to short-form content for television as well as on-line formats and wireless devices. The other focused on long-form content for television, with such reality series as *The Hills*. Also in 2006 *Cableworld* named her one of cable's most powerful women.

In April of that year, Norman announced the implementation of Break the Addiction, an initiative to encourage young people to fight global warming by using less oil. In a speech before the National Press Club in Washington, D.C., on April 27, Norman said, as quoted by the Federal News Service (April 27, 2006), "At MTV, we have been pulling out the latent activist inside of our audience since we blasted onto the scene 25 years ago. . . . The spirit of rebellion is part of our rock and roll DNA. . . . Every generation of young people has chafed against the world they've inherited. . . . It's our mission at MTV and our privilege to focus that revolutionary energy and to build tomorrow's leaders. Now, we do it all through a three-step mantra: engage, educate and empower. Engage young people on the issues they care about. Educate them about those issues. And empower them to take action that's going to make a difference."

That November the *New York Post* named Norman one of its Top 25 New York Latino Movers and Shakers. Norman told Krista Garcia and Sandra Guzman for the *Post* (November 8, 2006), "Women rock cable. It's an environment where creativity and hard work are rewarded." In interviews she has often emphasized MTV executives' efforts to engage their audience in face-to-face interactions in order to do market research. Norman told Neda Ulaby for the National Public Radio program *Morning Edition* (August 1, 2006), "I was in a Dunkin' Donuts in Brooklyn a couple of weeks ago, and these two girls are sitting there listening to Christina Aguilera's new song on their cell phone. And I accosted them and wanted to know like, did you download the video? Where did you get this content? . . . You know, we spend a lot of time talking to young people on-line, in person—it's what we do. It's . . . our mission." In 2007 MTV continued to claim the lion's share of the teen viewership, its ratings barely dented by Fuse or others among the newer networks.

Norman resides in Brooklyn, New York, with her husband and two daughters.

—S.J.D.

Suggested Reading: *Advertising Age* S p26 Sep. 29, 2003; *Billboard* Sep. 2, 2006; *Broadcasting & Cable* p42 June 16, 2002; *CosmoGIRL!* p122 June 1, 2006; *New York Post* p52 Nov. 8, 2006

Chip Somodevilla/Getty Images

Norquist, Grover

Oct. 19, 1956– Conservative activist

Address: Americans for Tax Reform, Suite 200, 1920 L St., N.W., Washington, DC 29936

Grover Norquist "just may be the most influential Washingtonian most people have never heard of," Susan Page wrote for *USA Today* (June 1, 2001). In 1985, while Norquist was working as a speechwriter for the U.S. Chamber of Commerce during the administration of the Republican Ronald Reagan, the president asked him to form an ad-hoc committee to generate support for what became the Tax Reform Act of 1986. The committee, Americans for Tax Reform (ATR), with Norquist as president, went on to become a permanent fixture in the nation's capital and played a vital role in the passage of sweeping tax cuts under President George W. Bush. Another prominent Washington entity begun by Norquist is the Wednesday Meeting, a weekly gathering of politicians, strategists, businesspeople, and lobbyists dedicated to advancing a national conservative agenda. (Similar meetings are being held in 40 states.) Speaking with John Aloysius Farrell for an article in the *Boston Globe* (April 17, 2002), the combative Norquist described his followers as the "leave-us-alone coalition" and explained their desires. "Taxpayers: Don't raise my taxes. Property owners: Don't mess with my property. Home-schoolers: I just want to educate my kids. Gun owners: Don't take my guns away. Traditional-values conservatives—Orthodox Jews, Roman Catholics, Muslims, Evangelicals: I just want to raise my kids in my faith. Each of the groups is there on the issue that brings them to politics, which is that they want to be left alone." In keeping with his belief in a very limited federal government—he has often been quoted as saying that he wants to reduce government "to the size where we can drown it in the bathtub"—Norquist told Michael Scherer for *Mother Jones* (January 1, 2004), "My ideal citizen is the self-employed, homeschooling, IRA-owning guy with a concealed-carry [gun] permit. Because that person doesn't need the . . . government for anything."

Of Swedish descent, Grover Glenn Norquist was born on October 19, 1956, the first of the four children of Warren Elliott and Carol (Lutz) Norquist. He grew up in Weston, Massachusetts, one of the wealthiest suburbs in the Boston area. His father was a vice president at Polaroid and a former engineer; his mother was a former schoolteacher who later became the town's tax assessor. From the time that he was very young, Norquist's parents taught him to live according to three principles: order, self-reliance, and individual responsibility. They also made their political views known to him: often, after church on Sunday, Norquist's father treated him and his three younger siblings to ice-cream cones; he would then take bites out of the cones, playfully blaming each bite on a different tax levied by the government. Norquist's own political leanings began to show as early as the sixth grade, when he argued with classmates over the Vietnam War, which he apparently supported; he has recalled debating with a fellow student who tried to convince him that the Republican Richard Nixon was a fascist and that Alger Hiss—a former State Department official whom Nixon, as a U.S. congressman, had played a major role in getting convicted on perjury charges related to alleged Communist activity—was innocent. At 11, at a sale at the public library in Weston, he picked up anti-Communist literature including *Masters of Deceit*, by the longtime FBI director J. Edgar Hoover, and *Witness*, by Hiss's accuser, Whittaker Chambers. Norquist's conservative ideology has its roots in the anti-Communist stance he adopted before his views on domestic policy were formed. When Norquist was 12 he volunteered for Nixon's successful 1968 presidential campaign. A short time later his ideas on tax reform began to take shape, when he formulated a "no new taxes" ideal for the Republican Party.

During his teenage years in Weston, in the early 1970s, Norquist wore his hair long, listened to rock music, played soccer, and learned how to shoot firearms at the target range in the family basement. He attended the prestigious Weston High School, where he focused more on academics and on studying politics than on dating. A standout student, he was listed in his senior-class yearbook as being "most intelligent," "most likely to succeed," "most studious," "most responsible," and "most ambitious." While other students quoted figures ranging from the philosopher Socrates to the singer Joni Mitchell under their yearbook photos, Norquist, as noted in Nina J. Easton's book *Gang of Five*, wrote his own text: "A dictatorship is like a machine with a warranty—it works well for a while. A democracy has no guarantees and as such needs to be constantly maintained, nurtured, even pampered, lest the people allow her to rust and begin to cast covetous glances at her more expedient rival."

In 1974 Norquist enrolled at Harvard University, in Cambridge, Massachusetts. One of few vocal conservative students on campus, he has said that he flourished in that atmosphere according to what he calls the "Boy Named Sue" theory—a reference to the Johnny Cash song in which the protagonist is given a girl's name by his departing father in order to force him to fight and learn to survive. Norquist recalled to John Aloysius Farrell for the *Boston Globe* (April 17, 2002) that the experience of being a conservative among liberal students (whom he called "Bolsheviks") "toughened you up. It made you think. It also convinced me that it all mattered: Those guys at Harvard were going to go out and run the country. We were cooked if some of us didn't get active . . . too." He attracted attention at the school as the co-publisher of a libertarian paper called the *Harvard Chronicle* and also wrote for the business section of the *Harvard Crimson*. He graduated in 1978 with a B.A. degree in economics.

The mid-1970s had seen, in some circles, an antitax movement spurred by high inflation, rising unemployment, and "bracket creep," or the placement of wages and salaries into higher income-tax brackets even as inflation caused workers' buying power to decrease. The movement culminated in the June 6, 1978 passage of California's Proposition 13, which slashed property taxes by an average of 57 percent, limited property-tax rates to one percent of market value, and outlawed any future tax increases that were not approved by a two-thirds majority in the state legislature. Proposition 13 created a domino effect, with other states passing similar measures in what has often been referred to collectively as a "modern Boston tea party." Norquist joined the movement, working briefly for the National Taxpayers Union (NTU) in Washington, D.C., and then—after earning an M.B.A. degree from Harvard—returning to Washington to become executive director of both the NTU and the organization National College Republicans. Those positions helped him to make vital contacts with rising stars of a new generation of right-wing conservative activists. He held both jobs until 1983, when he started working as an economist and as the chief speechwriter for the U.S. Chamber of Commerce. Then, in 1985, at the request of President Ronald Reagan, Norquist established an ad hoc group called Americans for Tax Reform, to help build grassroots support for Reagan's Tax Reform Act of 1986. The legislation simplified the income-tax code, broadened the tax base, and eliminated many tax shelters; it also marked the first time in history that the top tax rate was lowered and the bottom rate was increased simultaneously. Despite approving of the tax cuts, many conservatives were initially skeptical of the legislation, fearing that a double cross lay among the elimination of tax credits, breaks, and shelters. "They said, 'We're going to get rid of these credits and deductions, we're going to broaden the base and then they're going to come back and raise the [tax] rates again, and we won't even have the deductions and credits anymore,'" Norquist recalled to Nicholas Confessore for the *New York Times* (January 16, 2005). "At which point, I said, 'Well, what if we made it difficult for them to raise rates?'" Acting on the same "no new taxes" philosophy he had formed as a teenager, in 1985 Norquist circulated among members of the U.S. Congress a document that became known as the Taxpayer Protection Pledge (or simply the Pledge)—a promise never to vote to raise tax rates—which was signed by more than 100 members of Congress. (In 1988 the Republican presidential candidate George H. W. Bush used the very words "no new taxes" in making a campaign pledge, one he broke while in office.) Not long after the Tax Reform Act became law, Norquist took ATR private and began serving as its president.

During the latter half of the 1980s, Norquist took a hiatus from tax reform to work as an overseas liaison for the government in support of anti-Soviet guerrilla armies, deemed "freedom fighters." He visited the war zones of Pakistan, Afghanistan, and Angola and worked as a lobbyist alongside supporters of the Nicaraguan Contra rebels and other Reagan-backed insurgent groups. He rallied support for such anti-Communist groups as Mozambique's RENAMO and Jonas Savimbi's UNITA in Angola, both of which were backed by South Africa's apartheid regime. From 1985 to 1988 he also served as Savimbi's economic adviser; he was registered with the United States Department of Justice during that time as a foreign agent of Angola.

In the early 1990s Norquist began working closely with the Republican congressman Newt Gingrich of Georgia to make Americans for Tax Reform into a major force in the antitax movement. With the election of the Democratic president Bill Clinton in 1992, Norquist set out to instill an antitax mindset in politicians around the country, reemphasizing opposition to taxes as one of the central tenets of American conservatism; in the process he became a leader of conservatism's center-right. In 1993, in response to President Clinton's proposal for a government-run health-care system, Norquist launched the now-famous Wednesday Meeting, an invitation-only, weekly gathering of conservatives in his Washington office for the purpose of coordinating activities and strategy. Beginning with a dozen or so attendees, the Wednesday Meeting had grown to an average of about 45 a year later, with participants including representatives of the National Rifle Association, the Christian Coalition, and the Heritage Foundation. An early sign of the meetings' importance—and Norquist's power—emerged in 1994: Republicans, led by Gingrich, the new Speaker of the House, gained the majority of seats in the House of Representatives and the Senate for the first time in 40 years, in a victory attributed largely to Gingrich's "Contract with America." Co-authored by Norquist and other conservatives, the so-called contract detailed legislation that Republicans would introduce if their party gained control of Congress, including bills aimed at reforming the welfare system, requiring a three-fifths majority in both houses of Congress to raise taxes, passing a balanced-budget amendment, and setting congressional term limits.

Norquist used the Republicans' newfound power to expand Americans for Tax Reform through networking, direct-mail fund-raising, and pursuit of corporate backing; currently, the organization boasts an annual budget of approximately $7 million. He also helmed each Wednesday Meeting with a "big-tent" approach, deemphasizing such social issues as gay rights and abortion—which tend to divide conservatives—and placing a strong emphasis on tax cuts, tort reform, and the rollback of federal business regulations. That strategy helped to draw the support of major corporations including Microsoft, Pfizer, AOL Time Warner, UPS, and Philip Morris. While some conservatives maintained that catering to corporate interests would result in too many compromises of core conservative principles, Norquist insisted that his organization's alliance with corporations would benefit the Republican Party. For example, the promise of tort reform attracted millions of campaign dollars from corporations and undermined the clout of trial lawyers, who constituted an important segment of the Democratic support base; also, the anticipation of tax cuts for rich investors led them to give more money for Republican campaigns. In addition, the privatization of Social Security, a goal of conservatives, would greatly benefit Wall Street brokers, who were strong Republican allies and generous campaign contributors.

Norquist broadened his "leave-us-alone" coalition through alliances with a number of religious groups, among them evangelical Protestants, Mormons, conservative Catholics, and Orthodox Jews. In the mid-1990s he drew criticism when he cast his eyes on the American Muslim community, whose support he saw as necessary for the conservative movement. Many on the right condemned Norquist's efforts to make allies of such groups as the Council of American-Islamic Relations (CAIR), citing its members' failure to oppose the terrorist activities of Hamas and Hezbollah. Norquist viewed his pursuit of Muslim support as part of a larger purpose: defeating the Democrats. He told a gathering of *National Journal* reporters and editors, as quoted by Paul Starobin in that publication (November 19, 2005), "The point of being an American is that you are for individual liberty and freedom and the Constitution. It doesn't matter, frankly, what language Mom speaks, or what religion you are."

In 1997 Norquist and the lawyer David Safavian founded a lobbying firm, the Merritt Group, which was later renamed Janus-Merritt Strategies. (The firm was sold in 2002 to the Virginia-based Williams Mullen Strategies.) Emphasizing free markets and seeking to reduce the size of the federal government, Merritt represented businesses including BP America (the U.S. division of British Petroleum), Seagram, Universal Studios, and a wide range of Mexican industrial groups. In the area of gaming interests, the firm, together with the lobbyist Jack Abramoff, advocated for Native American tribes such as the Saginaw Chippewa and the Viejas Band of Kumeyaay Indians. The firm became known for its controversial clients, such as Pascal Lissouba, the corrupt former president of the Republic of the Congo, and Abdurahman Alamoudi, the founder of the American Muslim Council, who was an outspoken supporter of Hamas and Hezbollah. In 1998 Norquist co-founded the Islamic Free Market Institute with the Washington lobbyist and libertarian Khaled Saffuri, who had numerous contacts in the U.S. Muslim community. The institute sought to inspire and facilitate the development of economically conservative grassroots Muslim movements. Alamoudi devoted tens of thousand of dollars to the group before being convicted, in July 2004, of tax and immigration violations and illegal dealings with Libya; he was sentenced to 23 years in prison, having confessed to a role in an assassination plot targeting Saudi Arabia's crown prince. Right-wing critics attacked Norquist's alliance with the Muslim community as being a hindrance to the conservative movement and a threat to the safety of the American public. In a December 2003 article for *Front-PageMag.com*, Frank J. Gaffney Jr., a Norquist nemesis and a former assistant secretary of defense in the Reagan administration, wrote, "Grover Norquist's efforts to legitimate and open important doors for pro-Islamist organizations in this country must be brought to an immediate halt." Norquist has refused to talk about Alamoudi for the record, and his partner, Saffuri, has claimed that he was deceived by Alamoudi and had no prior knowledge of his criminal activities.

Meanwhile, Norquist had been a major force in George W. Bush's first presidential campaign. In November 1998 he met with Bush and his top political aide, Karl Rove (later his deputy chief of staff at the White House), in Austin, Texas. Impressed with Bush's stances on tax cuts, school choice, tort reform, pension reform, and other subjects, Norquist decided that Bush was the best hope for the

Republican Party in the 2000 presidential election. He started rallying support for Bush in Washington, helping to bring the majority of conservatives there into Bush's camp. He was also responsible for organizing the conservative counterattack against Bush's main Republican competitor, U.S. senator John McCain of Arizona. In early 2000, after McCain defeated Bush in the New Hampshire primary, Norquist led a crusade against the senator and his policies. He helped develop TV spots that assailed McCain's campaign-finance proposals as being in opposition to First Amendment rights and that showed an image of McCain's face being morphed into Clinton's. Bush went on to win the next 11 of 16 primaries and clinched the Republican nomination easily. Robert Dreyfuss wrote for the *Nation* (May 14, 2001, on-line), "To a significant degree, George W. Bush owes his election to Norquist." After Bush was elected, in November 2000, Norquist became the "field marshal," as some called him, of Bush's $1.3 trillion tax-cut package, known as the Economic Growth and Tax Relief Reconciliation Act of 2001. To win bipartisan support for the legislation, he put pressure on congressional Democrats by coordinating a campaign to get state legislatures to pass resolutions of support; he also organized 17 conservative groups under the umbrella of the American Conservative Union to champion Bush's plan. When passed, in June 2001, the bill became the third-largest tax cut since World War II.

Norquist supervised Bush's second tax cut, the Jobs and Growth Tax Relief Reconciliation Act of 2003, which accelerated the tax-rate cuts that were enacted in 2001 and temporarily reduced the tax rate on capital gains and dividends to 15 percent. The cuts were controversial, with some calling them bad economic policy and noting that they favored the wealthy and other special-interest groups. Bush's supporters asserted that the cuts fostered job growth and increased the pace of economic recovery from the recession caused by the terrorist attacks of September 11, 2001. The Congressional Budget Office estimated that the tax cuts would increase budget deficits by $60 billion in 2003 and by $340 billion by 2008. Detractors have noted that increased deficits will leave the U.S. more indebted to other nations in the years to come, reduce the resources necessary to invest in the future of the country, and pass on debt to future generations.

In October 2003 Norquist found himself in the midst of more controversy when, during an interview with Terry Gross for National Public Radio, he compared the estate tax to the Holocaust. (He later apologized for the comparison.) Meanwhile, he was active in Bush's 2004 reelection campaign. After Bush's victory, Norquist's candor was on full display. He told the *Washington Post*, as quoted in its November 4, 2004 edition, "Once the [Democratic] minority of [the] House and Senate are comfortable in their minority status, they will have no problem socializing with the Republicans. Any farmer will tell you that certain animals run around and are unpleasant, but when they've been fixed, then they are happy and sedate." In 2005 and 2006 Norquist's Americans for Tax Reform helped pass two more Bush tax bills, which extended through 2010 the rates on capital gains and dividends that had been enacted in 2003, raised the exemption levels for the Alternative Minimum Tax, and enacted new tax incentives designed to persuade individuals to save more money for retirement.

In 2006 Norquist's ties to the lobbyist Jack Abramoff, who had been sentenced to more than five years in prison after being convicted of fraud, conspiracy, and tax evasion, became a focus of media attention—as did the indictment of Norquist's former partner at Janus-Merritt Strategies, David Safavian, on charges of making false statements and obstructing investigations into his dealings with Abramoff. In June of that year, an investigative report on Abramoff's lobbying was released by the Senate Indian Affairs Committee, chaired by Norquist's longtime adversary John McCain. The report implicated Americans for Tax Reform in a money-laundering scheme. ATR was labeled a cash "conduit" for financing Abramoff's clients in other grassroots lobbying campaigns; Abramoff, it was determined, had been instructing his gambling clients, many of them Native Americans whom he had misled, to write checks to ATR, which passed them on to other conservative organizations, sometimes after keeping a percentage. As a result, Norquist faced possible indictment for violating the provisions of his organization's tax-exempt status. The potential charges against him included lobbying for companies without reporting that activity as a business expense and introducing Abramoff's clients to important Washington officials, among them Karl Rove, in exchange for donations to ATR. Norquist maintained his innocence, explaining to Rachel Van Dongen for *Congressional Quarterly Weekly* (November 3, 2006), "There are no tax implications at all." The Norquist-McCain feud turned public, as noted by Ryan Lizza for the *New Republic* (March 20–27, 2006), when Norquist called the Arizona senator a "nut job" and a "gun-grabbing, tax-increasing Bolshevik." McCain's chief of staff countered Norquist by saying that "most Reagan revolutionaries came to Washington to do something more patriotic than rip off Indian tribes." While Norquist's reputation suffered, he was not indicted.

Norquist has expressed optimism about a Republican presidential and congressional win in 2008. In the meantime, he has urged his conservative peers not to work toward accomplishing anything in the 110th, Democratic-controlled Congress. At a March 2007 Conservative Political Action Conference, as quoted on a transcript posted on the Think Progress Web site (March 2, 2007), he said, "Get married, develop a hobby, learn to belly dance, learn to golf—you know, we got two years free, but we gotta spend time and effort playing defense here. Our job is to say 'no, no, no, no' for two

years." Norquist has remained steadfast in his support for the war in Iraq but has acknowledged its detrimental effect on other national matters, explaining to Ronald Kessler for the News Max Web site (July 26, 2007), "You have an unease among a lot of non-political people, but the real cost of Iraq is not even so much that unease as the drowning out of other issues. We can't run against the Democrats—calling them the party that wants to raise taxes—if the president can only talk about Iraq."

Norquist remains an influential figure in Washington circles as the head of ATR; his long-term goals include cutting the cost of government in half over the coming decades, converting Social Security and public-pension programs into systems of private investment accounts, and replacing affirmative action with "color-blind" policies. He explained to Susan Page, "As long as the Christians don't steal anyone's guns, the anti-tax activists don't violate anyone's property rights, the property owners don't interfere with the home-schoolers, the home-schoolers don't want to regulate the small businessmen and the gun owners agree not to throw condoms at the Christians' kids, then we can all work together."

Norquist "is often described as an eccentric," Laura Blumenfeld wrote for the *Washington Post* (January 12, 2004), before his marriage. "For a bedside table, Norquist uses a giant green canister for Kraft parmesan cheese. He displays what he hopes will be the world's largest collection of airsickness bags. At staff meetings, employees say, he holds court while variously sitting on a giant red plastic ball, eating tuna from a can, rubbing his feet against a massager and sniffing hand lotion as he kneads it into his fingers. He excuses himself to go to the 'ladies room.' His manner is charming, though bitterness creeps into his voice when he talks about classmates at Harvard." Norquist currently serves on the board of directors of the National Rifle Association and the American Conservative Union and is a contributing editor at the *American Spectator* magazine, for which he writes a monthly column. He is also a member of the Council on Foreign Relations and the chairman emeritus of the Islamic Institute. In 1995 he authored the book *Rock the House*, which gives an in-depth insider's account of the Republican takeover of Congress in 1994. Norquist exercises 40 minutes daily, enjoys reading murder mysteries, and occasionally listens to literary works on audiotape. He and his wife, Samah Alrayyes, whom he married in April 2005, reside in Washington, D.C. "From the moment [Norquist] gets up to the moment he gets to bed, he thinks, 'How am I going to hurt the other team?'" Stephen Moore, the president of the antitax group Club for Growth, explained to Scherer. "One time I was telling Grover about this woman I met. Most guys would say, 'Oh, is she really good-looking?' or something like that. Grover said, 'Is she good on guns?' He was being totally serious."

—C.C.

Suggested Reading: *Boston Globe* F p1+ Apr. 17, 2002; *Mother Jones* p42+ Jan. 1, 2004; *Nation* (on-line) May 14, 2001; *National Journal* (on-line) Nov. 19, 2005; *New Republic* p9+ Mar. 27, 2006; *New York Times* p35 Jan. 16, 2005; *Slate* (on-line) July 7, 2003; *USA Today* A p13+ June 1, 2001; *Washington Post* A p1+ Jan. 12, 2004; Easton, Nina J. *Gang of Five: Leaders at the Center of the Conservative Crusade*, 2000

Selected Books: *Rock the House*, 1995

Doug Benc/Getty Images

Ouma, Kassim

Dec. 12, 1978– Boxer

Address: Golden Boy Promotions, 626 Wilshire Blvd., Suite 350, Los Angeles, CA 90017

Many have predicted that the Ugandan-born boxer Kassim "The Dream" Ouma will be one of the sport's next international superstars. Russell Peltz, one of his promoters, has noted that Ouma's friendly and engaging demeanor outside the ring belies a ruthlessness inside it. "As you see [Ouma] flashing, grinning, combing his hair, he looks like a little teddy bear that you'd like to kiss, cuddle and hold and put to sleep at night," Peltz told reporters for the Ugandan publication *New Vision* (July 14, 2005). "But I can assure you that once the bell rings, he'll cut your heart out." Ouma comes from a Ugandan boxing tradition whose golden age, which produced such legendary fighters as Ayub Kalule, John Mugabi, and Cornelius Boza Edwards, coincided with the violent regime of Ugandan president Idi Amin. Ouma himself, growing up in the midst of Uganda's civil war, endured a horrifyingly violent childhood that included 10 years of forced military service before he defected to the United States to pursue a professional boxing career. His handlers have said on many occasions that Ouma will not—or cannot—speak much about his childhood experiences, and that questions about it have sometimes sent him spiraling into depression and insomnia. He has compiled an impressive 25–3–1 record with 15 knockouts during a professional career that has been marked by others' recognition of his astonishing potential as well as periods of seeming indifference and lapses in concentration on Ouma's part. Though he continues to struggle with his past and suffers from symptoms said to be consistent with post-traumatic stress disorder, his supporters believe that as a boxing talent he may have few equals. Oscar De La Hoya, himself once regarded as one of the world's best boxers and currently one of Ouma's promoters, described the southpaw as "exciting, talented, charismatic," and "capable of becoming the next world superstar," according to Daniel K. Kalinaki, writing for *New Vision* (July 15, 2005). In 2005 De La Hoya predicted that Ouma had at least five more peak years in competitive boxing and remarked to Kalinaki: "They call him the Dream because he has big dreams of becoming a world champion, and he has the ability to achieve that."

The seventh of 13 children, Kassim Ouma was born on December 12, 1978 near Kampala, Uganda. His parents were farmers. In 1979 that East African nation was thrown into political turmoil and civil war following the ouster of Idi Amin, who had led the country since the military takeover he spearheaded in 1971. As a child Ouma was sent to a boarding school in Kiboga, Uganda. In 1984 Ouma and many of his elementary-school classmates were kidnapped by the National Resistance Army (NRA) of Yoweri Museveni, one of the largest rebel armies fighting to overthrow the regime of Milton Obote, who had become president in 1980, following a bitterly disputed election. Ouma and his classmates were trained to be soldiers, or *kadogos*, and joined as many as 3,000 child-soldiers who were forced to fight for the NRA during the insurrection. As a six-year-old Ouma was ordered to shoot a classmate who was crying uncontrollably, and was told that refusal to do so would mean his own death. "Other incidents are just as traumatising," Tom Moran, Ouma's current manager, told Owen Slot for the London *Times* (December 7, 2006). "One of the worst he remembers is, 6 or 7 years old, sitting on a pile of bodies. One of the bodies was one of his friends. And Kassim was just casually smoking a cigarette. The things he describes—people chopping ears off, people chopping limbs off—were not witnessed from a distance. And some of these things he was forced to do himself." Ouma has said that while he has been able to forget some of the incidents, many others haunt him. "The first time I shot, I was not as big as a gun," Ouma recalled to Ron Borges for the *Boston Globe* (June 15, 2004). "I fell right to the ground. I had to learn not to fall so I put a stone behind my foot. I figured it out. If you didn't, you died. I became a guerrilla. A soldier for my country. A corporal. Nobody can mess with that. I was mean. . . . I seen so many people blown up. Women. Children. You do things or you die. So much stuff went on. It wasn't until I was 10 that I began to understand." In 1986 the NRA displaced Obote and installed Museveni as president. The violence in Uganda did not stop, however, as other groups, finding Museveni's regime to be as oppressive as its predecessor, opposed the new government. Ouma, along with other kadogos from the NRA, joined the Ugandan Army. "We were just growing up, but we had guns," Ouma said during an undated interview that appears on the official Web site of Canadastar Boxing Inc. "You try to escape, but you cannot. They put me in jail and took me back. They roughed me up, took my pants off and whipped me. After that, they took me to war again. It is a time of my life that I do not want to remember." In a conversation with reporters following a U.N. Security Council briefing on the subject, as reported by the *Los Angeles Times* (April 15, 2004), a U.N. emergency relief coordinator, Jan Egeland, described the abduction, enslavement, torture, and conscription of children—an estimated 10,000 were abducted in 2004 alone—as "the world's most neglected humanitarian crisis." Although Ouma suffers from what appears to be post-traumatic stress disorder, with symptoms including recurring nightmares that sometimes leave him barely able to sleep for days at a time, he says that he is not resentful about his conscription into the NRA or the Ugandan Army. "I was fighting but I didn't know what I was doing," Ouma explained to Borges. "I don't like what happened to me, but I don't blame the government for what happened. It was bad I got picked, but it was good for my country. I helped to free my people. Child soldiers were the freedom fighters."

In his early teens Ouma joined the Ugandan Army's martial-arts team. (Representing Uganda in sports competitions was one of the only ways for a soldier to escape combat duty.) Boxing had the highest profile of any sport in Uganda—had, indeed become the de facto national sport in the 1970s—and Ouma, excited by the opportunity to travel, soon switched to it. He boxed locally in Kampala before being promoted to the national team, which traveled to tournaments all over Africa. In 1996, despite his success against Uganda's lightweight champion, Ouma was passed over for the Olympic team because of his relative lack of experience. By November 1997 he had become a three-time Uganda national champion and the East African regional amateur champion, compiling a 60–3 record. He was recognized as one of the finest boxers in the country and earned the distinction of Ugandan Sportsman of the Year. In 1998 he qualified for the World Military Games, in San Antonio,

Texas. Uganda could not afford to send a team to the tournament but nonetheless issued him a travel visa. Ouma raised money for his plane ticket by going door-to-door in search of sponsors. He secured a passage to the United States but did not intend to compete in the tournament; instead, he used the opportunity to defect.

When his plane to San Antonio stopped for a layover in Washington, D.C., Ouma deboarded. He spoke little English and had lost the contact information for the one person he knew who lived in the United States. He nonetheless believed that he could make a life for himself as a boxer. After a period of confusion and homelessness, Ouma got a job delivering flyers for a pizza restaurant. At the end of each day, he washed trays at the restaurant and ate scraps of food left by customers. After several months of working at that and other jobs, Ouma found work in a boxing gym as a sparring partner for professional fighters. Although for his opponents those sparring matches were only practice, Ouma treated them like real fights, in an effort to impress the trainers. He caught a break when, before an amateur fight in Norfolk, Virginia, one of the contestants could not make weight, and Ouma was selected to fill in. He had not prepared for the fight or trained properly for several months, but he jumped at the opportunity. "I was like this is my life right here, so I got to—it's my time to shine," Ouma told Johnny Dwyer for the *Village Voice* (June 10, 2003). During the match, which Ouma won, he caught the eye of the legendary trainer Lou Duva, who offered him a temporary job in Florida as a sparring partner for Pernell Whitaker. Duva also recommended Ouma to Jimmy Rowan, a boxing manager. "I just thought he had something special," Rowan said, as reported by Todd Traub for the *Arkansas Democrat-Gazette* (December 7, 2006). "He's got great looks, great smile, great story. And your heart sort of went out to him because of his story and I took him on." Ouma was initially trained by Rowan, Johnny Bumphus, the former heavyweight champion Tim Witherspoon, and Fred Muteweta. Witherspoon told Don Steinberg for the *Philadelphia Inquirer* (August 4, 2006) that Ouma showed promise immediately but was at times overwhelmed by his emotions, even as he tried to suppress his memories.

In July 1998, in his first professional fight, Ouma knocked out Napoleon Middlebrooks in the first round. In an effort to win political asylum in the United States, Ouma married an American woman and established a home in West Palm Beach, Florida. Although the relationship dissolved in less than a year, Ouma was successful in earning permanent residency in the United States. He continued to fight locally, becoming Florida's 154-pound champion by defeating Victor Ramos in January 1999. By 2000 Ouma had entered the national boxing scene in the 154-pound weight class, also referred to as the light-middleweight or junior-middleweight class. He developed a reputation as a well-conditioned boxer who made up for his relative lack of power with an extraordinary drive, overwhelming opponents with an aggressive style and the sheer number of punches he threw. In a 2001 victory over Verno Phillips, Ouma set a world record for most punches thrown in a 10-round fight (1,331) and most connections (460), according to Compubox, a boxing-statistics service whose data go back to the mid-1980s.

Following that fight Ouma's plan to return to his native country was crushed, as Museveni labeled him a deserter of the army and a traitor to Uganda—charges punishable by death. At around that time Ouma's father was beaten to death by soldiers, in retaliation, Ouma believes, to the boxer's defection. Ouma was unsuccessful at negotiating through political channels in the United States for a way to return to Uganda to see his family. He had left two young children and a wife there; three of his brothers have been killed in the continuing unrest, and his immediate family includes 23 children whose parents are missing or dead. Ouma did not earn much money during his first few years in the U.S., but he was nonetheless able to send enough back to his family to put three of his siblings through college. Well aware that his family's struggles are not unique, he has said that he would like to start a foundation for African orphans—but also that African governments are so corrupt that most donations do not reach the people in need. Ouma has hoped for years that he will be able to bring some of his family to the United States. "I miss them so much," he told Carlos Arias for the *Orange County (California) Register* (July 12, 2005). "I want to bring them over here. Life is so good here."

In 2002 Ouma saw his profile in international boxing circles reach a new level. In May he stopped Jason Papillion in eight rounds to win the U.S. Boxing Association (USBA) light-middleweight crown; with that victory he became a genuine contender for more prestigious belts. In October Ouma defended his USBA title with an 11th-round technical knockout (TKO) of Darrell Woods. (A TKO occurs when a boxer is declared unable to continue fighting.) The outcome was changed to a no decision after Ouma tested positive for marijuana following the fight. Also as a result of the drug test, he lost his title, and his International Boxing Federation (IBF) ranking slipped from fourth to ninth. In December 2002 Ouma suffered a major setback when he was shot by a fellow restaurant worker following an argument. "I spent 12 years in the army and I never got shot," Ouma said, as reported by Traub. "If I can survive a bullet, boxing cannot scare me. Nobody can scare me." After a successful operation, which removed portions of his small intestine, and a three-month recovery, Ouma returned to the gym. He won his next bout, against the renowned body-puncher Angel Hernandez, in May 2003.

In October 2004 Ouma entered the most important fight of his professional career up to that point, again battling Verno Phillips, this time for the IBF junior-middleweight title. Ouma outlasted Phillips, winning a unanimous decision after a bruising 12 rounds. He successfully defended his world title against the highly acclaimed challenger Kofi Jantuh in January 2005 and appeared to be settling in for a long run as champion. In his second defense, however, he lost his belt to Roman Karmazin in a 12-round bout in Las Vegas, Nevada. Some speculated that Ouma, who went into that match as a better than four-to-one favorite, had taken too cavalier an approach to the older, more experienced Karmazin. "I think Kassim thought he was Superman," Peltz said at the time, as reported by Bernard Fernandez for the ESPN Web site (December 7, 2006). "I think he had questionable out-of-the-ring activities in the weeks leading up to the Karmazin fight. He had 25 people in his hotel room every night. He was staying out late. I tried telling myself that it'd be all right. . . . But 30 seconds into the first round, I could tell that Kassim wasn't himself." Those close to Ouma said that the fighter was worried about his family at the time, particularly after his failed attempt to arrange a trip to the United States for his grandmother, and that he had surrounded himself with friends to dull the pain. "Kassim doesn't want to make excuses, so I won't make excuses for him," Tom Moran told reporters, according to Fernandez. "Karmazin beat him on that particular night, all right? But Roman Karmazin did not beat the best Kassim Ouma. Not even close. Put it this way: Kassim's body was in Las Vegas, but his mind was in Africa."

The surprising loss to Karmazin affected Ouma greatly, making him determined to perform well in future bouts. He followed the loss with four straight victories. One of those, an eight-round TKO of Francisco Antonio Mora, earned Ouma the World Boxing Organization (WBO) light-middleweight title. The last of the four fights was against the previously undefeated Sechew Powell—another junior-middleweight fighter who appeared to be on the rise to stardom—at Madison Square Garden, in New York City. Ouma, employing his usual tactic of overwhelming his opponent with the quantity of his jabs, landed an average of 38 punches per round over the course of the fight and averaged 46 connections in the final four rounds.

By defeating Powell, Ouma earned an opportunity to fight Jermain Taylor, the World Boxing Council (WBC) and WBO champion in the 160-pound, or middleweight, class. Taylor was one of the country's most popular boxers, with a flawless record and, at six feet one inch, towered over the five-foot seven-inch Ouma. Ouma called the match the "biggest fight of my life," as reported by James Bakama for *New Vision* (December 9, 2006). The fight drew more than 10,000 fans to Alltel Arena, in Little Rock, Arkansas, Taylor's hometown. Pundits believed that Ouma was too small to hurt Taylor, and many predicted that the fight would end with an early-round knockout. An 8-to-1 underdog, Ouma made it through all 12 rounds. Taylor

PÄÄBO

won a unanimous decision on points, however, and by nearly all accounts was in command for the entire fight. Despite his loss, Ouma's performance against the bigger fighter impressed many, and Ouma was upbeat after the bout, requesting a rematch minutes after the conclusion. He has said that he would like another chance at the middleweight title and would also seek to regain his IBF light-middleweight crown, which is currently held by Cory Spinks.

In November 2006, just before his match with Taylor, Ouma got engaged to the Miami, Florida–based, Uganda-born singer Juliana Kanyomozi. The following month Ouma was reunited with his nine-year-old son Umar, whom he had not seen since he left Uganda, eight years earlier. In April 2007 Ouma was pardoned by the Ugandan government and returned to his native country for a one-week holiday. While there he met with family and friends as well as government and army officials. Ouma also traveled to northern Uganda to visit refugee camps for people displaced by his country's conflict, and he made appearances at several charity events for child laborers and kadogos. He was accompanied by an HBO film crew making a documentary about his return to Africa.

Although he is not outspoken about politics, Ouma has made several efforts to raise awareness of African issues. He has established a nonprofit organization, Natabonic, which provides aid—in particular, potable water—to disadvantaged populations in Africa. "As one person you can only do so much, but as God blessed me with a chance in America then I want to give back to my people in Africa," Ouma said for his official Web site. "Even if it is just raising awareness and making connections between people, I want people to know why we need clean water. When I was a child soldier we would drink anything we had to. It's not just an African problem. Lots of poor people can't find clean water. . . . Everybody can contribute." Ouma is also working with the nongovernmental organization Athletes for Africa and its GuluWalk campaign to raise awareness about kadogos—as well as about children who commute nightly to shelters to avoid capture and forced service in the Ugandan and rebel armies. "Those kids are innocent and deserve to live a better life. . . . We all have a role to play in the future of these kids," Ouma told reporters for the Ugandan *Daily Monitor* (August 3, 2006). Ouma has raised controversy by promoting Oxfam and GuluWalk on his boxing trunks and robe; traditionally, boxers do not promote products or companies on their clothing.

Ouma and Kanyomozi live in Florida. The couple hope to marry in Uganda in the presence of their families. In addition to his two children in Uganda, Ouma has a son, Oundo, by an American woman. Ouma hopes to retire with a reputation as the greatest-ever African boxer, then pursue a career in Hollywood.

—N.W.M.

Suggested Reading: *Arkansas Democrat-Gazette* Sports Dec. 7, 2006; *Boston Globe* C p1 June 15, 2004; ESPN (on-line) Dec. 7, 2006; (London) *Times* p94 Dec. 7, 2006; (New York) *Daily News* p78 Dec. 11, 2006; *Orange County (California) Register* Sports July 12, 2005; (Passaic County, New Jersey) *Herald News* D p1 Aug. 5, 2006; *Philadelphia Inquirer* A p1 Aug. 4, 2006; (Uganda) *New Vision* July 15, 2005, Dec. 9, 2006

Bela Dornon, courtesy of MPI-EVA

Pääbo, Svante

(PAH-boh, s-VANT-ah)

Apr. 20, 1955– Molecular biologist; paleogeneticist

Address: Max Planck Institute for Evolutionary Anthropology, Deutscher Platz 6, 04103 Leipzig, Germany

"I'm driven by curiosity, by asking the questions, where do we come from, and what were the important events in our history that made us who we are," the molecular biologist Svante Pääbo told Steve Olson for *Smithsonian* (October 2006, on-line). "I'm driven by exactly the same thing that makes an archaeologist go to Africa to look for the bones of our ancestors." But rather than exploring the past through the excavation of archaeological ruins or fossilized remains, Pääbo uses segments of ancient DNA strands to map the key genetic changes that made humans who we are today. "Studying DNA is exciting to me, I think, because, in a way, it is like making an archaeological exca-

PÄÄBO

vation," he said in an interview for "Family That Walks on All Fours," a November 14, 2006 installment of the PBS program *Nova*. "But you don't do it in a cave somewhere, you do it in our genes. And you find out things about our ancestors that we cannot find out any other way—that the bones and the stones will not tell us."

Considered the founder of paleogenetics—the name given to the use of genetics to study ancient populations—Pääbo is making rapid strides in answering the question that has perplexed humanity for ages: what differentiates humans from other primates? "Svante is going to be the first anthropologist to win a Nobel Prize," Richard Klein, a paleoanthropologist at Stanford University, in California, told Nancy Shute for *U.S. News & World Report* (January 20, 2003, on-line). "He just comes out with one paper after another that seems to be a breakthrough in human evolution." Nonetheless, Pääbo has remained modest about the scope of his work. "It is a delusion to think that genomics in isolation will ever tell us what it means to be human," he told Laurent Belsie for the *Christian Science Monitor* (February 14, 2001). "The history of our genes is but one aspect of our history, and there are many other histories that are even more important."

An only child, Svante Pääbo was born on April 20, 1955 in Stockholm, Sweden. His mother, Karin Pääbo, was a food chemist, and his father, Sune Bergström, was a biochemist. Even as a child Pääbo was interested in ancient civilizations, and when he was 13 years old, his mother finally granted his most fervent wish: a trip to Egypt. "It was absolutely fascinating," Pääbo told Olson. "We went to the pyramids, to Karnak and the Valley of the Kings. The soil was full of artifacts." In 1975 Pääbo enrolled in Sweden's Uppsala University. He intended to study Egyptology but was disappointed by the program's emphasis on such desk work as memorizing hieroglyphic verb forms rather than performing archaeological fieldwork. "It was not at all what I wanted to do," he told Olson. Instead, Pääbo switched to studying medicine and molecular immunology, and in 1981 he became a full-time Ph.D. student in the Department of Cell Research at Uppsala.

But even as he pursued other areas of study, Pääbo remained interested in his first love, Egypt. "I knew about these thousands of mummies that were around in museums, so I started to experiment with extracting DNA," he told Olson. With the help of his former Egyptology professors, Pääbo obtained skin and bone samples from 23 mummies, and—while still a graduate student—worked in secret at night and on weekends, worried about the consequences of his actions for his academic career if he was found out. Ultimately, he extracted a short segment of DNA from a 2,400-year-old mummy of an infant boy, becoming the first scientist to isolate ancient human DNA. Pääbo sent the resulting paper to *Nature*, one of the world's foremost scientific journals, which published the landmark study as its cover story.

Pääbo also sent the results to Allan Wilson, a molecular biologist at the University of California at Berkeley, who was famous for first suggesting that a comparative analysis of mitochondrial DNA could be used to determine the relationships of different species to one another. Wilson, assuming that someone who had managed such an achievement as Pääbo's must be a full-fledged professor, responded by asking to spend his sabbatical at Pääbo's lab. Pääbo wrote back, telling Wilson that he was still a graduate student and asking if he could work in Wilson's lab instead. After receiving his Ph.D. in molecular immunology from Uppsala University, in 1986, Pääbo conducted postdoctoral research at the Institute for Molecular Biology at the University of Zürich, in Switzerland. He also worked briefly for the Imperial Cancer Research Fund, in London, England, before joining Wilson at Berkeley, in 1987, to continue his postdoctoral studies. In Wilson's lab, Pääbo focused on developing new ways to extract DNA from such extinct organisms as a flightless bird called a moa and marsupial wolves. (Michael Crichton credited the group and its groundbreaking work for inspiring his best-selling 1990 novel, *Jurassic Park*.) It was at Wilson's lab that Pääbo became familiar with polymerase chain reaction (PCR), a recently invented method for rapidly replicating multiple strands of a DNA sequence. PCR could turn a minuscule amount of DNA into an amount large enough to study; it turned out to be the key to allowing scientists to analyze—and not just extract—ancient DNA.

In 1990 Pääbo was appointed to his first academic post, becoming a full professor of general biology at Ludwig-Maximilians-Universität München, in Germany, where he continued to study the DNA of such ancient animals and plants as mammoths, European cave bears, and maize. Pääbo was also part of the team that analyzed the corpse of a man who had died around 3300 B.C. and had been preserved in an Alpine glacier on the Italian-Austrian border. The team confirmed that "Otzi," as they named the ice man, was indeed an ancient human and not the product of a hoax. The analysis of such old samples was especially impressive given the formidable obstacles in obtaining ancient DNA. Shortly after the death of an organism, the nucleic acid that comprises its DNA begins to degrade rapidly. It is possible, however, to extract segments of DNA from a specimen that is thousands of years old, particularly when it has been preserved in stable and cold conditions in caves or in the permafrost. Even if a scientist is able to locate a well-preserved specimen, he or she must contend with the problem of contamination. The modern humans who handle specimens leave traces of their own DNA, which is extremely difficult to discern from that of their ancient counterparts.

As the analysis of ancient DNA grew more commonplace, Pääbo gained a reputation as not only one of the technique's pioneers but also one of its most reliable practitioners and stalwart defenders. At a conference on ancient DNA at the University of Oxford, in England, Pääbo urged accountability for testing results, according to Nigel Williams for *Science* (August 18, 1995): "The field has established itself and shown that you can go back in time and gather data on molecular evolution," Pääbo said. But, he warned his colleagues, "if the field is to become fully respectable it is vital to ensure the reproducibility of results."

In the mid-1990s Pääbo began making significant strides in what would become his greatest project to date, mapping Neanderthal (*Homo neanderthalensis*) DNA. Neanderthals—human ancestors whose remains, dating from roughly 30,000 to 200,000 years ago, have been found in Europe, northern Africa, and western Asia— coexisted with modern humans (*Homo sapiens*) for tens of thousands of years. Scientists have long debated what role Neanderthals played in the evolution of modern humans. Most anthropologists currently support the Out-of-Africa theory, which contends that modern humans originated in Africa, spreading out over the globe and gradually forcing Neanderthals into extinction. Another camp, made of up those who support the Multiregional theory of human development, proposes that Neanderthals and modern humans interbred, which would mean that Neanderthals did not die out but rather were subsumed into the modern human species.

Pääbo's own research into that debate provided significant evidence to bolster the Out-of-Africa position, when, in 1997 (some sources state 1996), a team of American and German scientists that he led became the first to extract mitochondrial DNA from Neanderthal remains. (Mitochondrial DNA is more abundant and consequently easier to extract than nuclear DNA. For example, the typical human cell contains 500 to 1,000 copies of mitochondrial DNA and only two copies of nuclear DNA. Mitochondrial DNA, however, contains DNA only from the mother's side.) Using a bone fragment from the Neanderthal specimen that was found in Neandertal, Germany, in 1856, the region that gave its name to the group of hominids, Pääbo and his team were able to extract and analyze one sequence of Neanderthal DNA. That one sequence differed drastically from the same stretch of DNA in a modern human, suggesting that Neanderthals and modern humans were in fact two separate species that had diverged approximately 600,000 years ago (some sources state 500,000 or 550,000) with little or no interbreeding. "It's a fantastic achievement," Christopher Stringer, a leading proponent of the Out-of-Africa theory, told Curt Suplee for the *Austin (Texas) American-Statesman* (July 11, 1997). "In terms of our knowledge of human origins, it's as big as the Mars landing." Even the most forceful supporters of Multiregionalism took notice, influenced by Pääbo's impeccable research record. Milford Wolpoff, a harsh critic of the Out-of-Africa theory, was quoted by Suplee as calling Pääbo's re-

sults "exciting." Wolpoff continued, "If anybody could do this beyond criticism, it's Svante Pääbo and his laboratory."

While continuing his work on Neanderthal DNA, Pääbo has also been involved in a number of other important projects. In 2001 Pääbo and his colleagues published a study that was intended as a response to Edward Hooper's hypothesis— detailed in *The River: A Journey to the Source of HIV and AIDS* (1999)—that researchers had accidentally sparked the AIDS epidemic by using HIV–infected chimp kidneys to manufacture experimental polio vaccines that were distributed in Africa during the 1950s. Pääbo and his fellow researchers tested samples of the polio vaccine for traces of the HIV virus or chimpanzee DNA, finding neither. "I feel confident that we have done everything we can to detect chimp DNA in this sample, so as far as I can see there is not much more one can presently do in order to clarify the situation further," Pääbo told Raja Mishra for the *Boston Globe* (April 26, 2001).

Pääbo's work, however, continued to focus primarily on discerning what separates humans from other primates. Describing his research, he told *Current Biography*, "We work on understanding various aspects of what makes humans unique from a genetic perspective, for example by studying gene expression in various tissues in humans and apes." Apes—and specifically chimpanzees— constitute the best point of comparison because they are our closest living relations. Modern humans and chimpanzees have evolved separately since they split from a common ancestor between five and seven million years ago. Still, the two species have 98.7 percent of their genes in common. "I'm still sort of taken aback by how similar humans and chimps are," Pääbo told Malcolm Ritter for the Associated Press (August 31, 2005). "I'm still amazed, when I see how special humans are and how we have taken over this planet, that we don't find stronger evidence for a huge difference in our genomes." Human and chimpanzee genomes may differ slightly, but, according to a paper by Pääbo published in *Science* in 2002, many of the genes that the species share operate differently in human brains from the way they function in chimpanzee brains. Pääbo's findings potentially explain why the two species have such different mental capacities. Though Pääbo insisted that the results were not absolutely conclusive, they did single out the brain as a specific focal point for human evolution.

In 1997 Pääbo and three other collaborators were invited to start a new institute on human evolution, the Leipzig-based Max Planck Institute for Evolutionary Anthropology, which was generously funded by the German government. Pääbo's co-directors were a linguist, a comparative psychologist, and a specialist in wild chimpanzees, and the combination of specialties complemented the interdisciplinary nature of his own pursuits. Inspired by a 2001 finding that linked a mutation in the gene *FOXP2* to human speaking disorders, Pääbo began comparing the gene in humans and other primates. His team's findings, published in the August 22, 2002 issue of *Nature*, confirmed that the *FOXP2* gene carries mutations unique to modern humans. Those differences became widely established among humans within about the last 200,000 years, and while not directly responsible for the emergence of speech, the gene probably allowed our ancestors to speak more clearly. "We had communication of a sort, and then this change happened and allowed the carriers to articulate much better," Pääbo explained to Alex Dominguez for the Associated Press (August 14, 2002). "This may have been the time we arrived at truly modern, articulate language." That ability to communicate, Pääbo told Dominguez, may have been the key to the survival and eventual dominance of modern humans, giving those who carried changes in the gene an advantage in hunting, for example. Still, not all the mysteries of the *FOXP2* gene were resolved, and Pääbo rejected the hypothesis that the gene alone allows for speech. "People might say if we put this in a chimpanzee, it could talk," he told Dominguez. "I don't think that is the case, speech is more complex than that."

In 2006 Pääbo and his team announced that, using a novel method, they had extracted the first sample of nuclear DNA from Neanderthal remains. Later that year, in November, they published their findings—analysis of one million units of Neanderthal DNA—in *Nature*. Pääbo's team released its findings simultaneously with another team, led by Edward Rubin of the Lawrence Berkeley National Laboratory, in California, which had independently analyzed 62,250 units of DNA from Pääbo's sample and published the results in *Science*. Accounting for acceptable margins of error, the two teams agreed that Neanderthals and modern humans share 99.5 percent of their DNA, making Neanderthals modern man's closest genetic relation. While the .5 percent discrepancy seemed to further bolster the Out-of-Africa position, neither team was willing to entirely dismiss the possibility that humans and Neanderthals interbred—at least until more of the Neanderthal genome can be sequenced. Pääbo announced plans to have a draft of the full genome—a total of 3.2 billion units—ready in two years. "The next big step is the retrieval of sequences of entire genomes of extinct creatures," he told *Current Biography*. "And that revolution is about to happen as we speak."

A foreign member of the United States' National Academy of Sciences and other academies, Pääbo has received many awards and honors, including the Prix Louis-Jeantet de Médecine, the Ernst Schering Prize, and the Max Delbrück Medal. In 2007 *Time* magazine named him among the 100 men and women "whose power, talent or moral example is transforming the world."

Pääbo, who was described by Michael Dumiak in *Archaeology* (November/December 2006) as "a bristly browed Swede with a penchant for wearing

sandals and goofy socks," lives in Leipzig, Germany, with his partner, Linda Vigilant, and the couple's son, Rune Vigilant.

—C.S.

Suggested Reading: *Archaeology* p22+ Nov./Dec. 2006; *Discover* (on-line) Dec. 2006; Max Planck Institute for Evolutionary Anthropology Web site; *Smithsonian* (on-line) Oct. 2006; *U.S. News & World Report* (on-line) Jan. 20, 2003

Courtesy of the Office of the Governor of Massachusetts

Patrick, Deval

July 31, 1956– Governor of Massachusetts (Democrat)

Address: State House, Office of the Governor, Rm. 360, Boston, MA 02133

Describing Deval Patrick during his campaign to become the governor of Massachusetts, Jon Keller wrote for *Boston Magazine* (May 2006): "With his flawless diction, restrained tone, and flat Midwestern accent, Patrick is a soothing study in sincerity. He does not play pretend by mimicking the evangelical passion of the pulpit or the rostrum-pounding rhetorical heat of the pol on the make. He's a calm, Ivy League lawyer, artfully leading the jury to its inevitable endorsement of his argument. . . . The image projected is of intelligence, poise, and, above all, thoughtfulness, a trait emphasized by his habit of cocking his head to one side and looking off to a brighter horizon as he reaches for a particularly profound expression: 'I am so in my soul convinced the same old thing isn't gonna work.'" As Patrick vowed to revitalize the local economy, schools, and health-care system—specifically, for low-income communities—his message resonated with voters, and he twice won their endorsement: in September 2006 he upset Tom Reilly, the Massachusetts attorney general, and Chris Gabrieli, a former nominee for lieutenant governor, to win the Democratic gubernatorial nomination, and in November of that year, he beat the Republican Kerry Healey to become, in 2007, Massachusetts's first African-American governor—and the second African-American governor since Reconstruction.

Deval Laurdine Patrick was born on July 31, 1956 to Laurdine "Pat" Patrick, a noted baritone saxophonist, and Emily Patrick, a mail sorter for the U.S. Postal Service. He grew up on South Wabash Avenue in the gritty South Side section of Chicago, Illinois. When Patrick was around four years old, his father abruptly left the family to perform in New York City with the cosmic-jazz legend Sun Ra, and his ensemble, the Arkestra, leaving his mother to raise him and his older sister, Rhonda, alone. Emily Patrick made ends meet through odd jobs and welfare assistance, moving with her children back and forth between a cramped basement apartment and her parents' home, near the infamous Robert Taylor public-housing development. The bleak atmosphere of poverty and violence notwithstanding, the Patricks remained a remarkably close-knit family and "a pillar of the community," as their former neighbor Sondra Brigandi recalled to Scott Helman for the *Boston Globe* (May 24, 2006, on-line). As a young child, Patrick, under his family's guidance, resisted the threat and lure of neighborhood gangs by simply "run[ning] from them," as his sister told Wil Haygood for the *Washington Post* (October 25, 2006). "That—him running—gave us a sign that he was not going to surrender or concede to the gangs." Patrick was gifted academically, impressing teachers with his discipline and poise. "What they would have said in those days is that he had good home training," Darla Weissenberg, Patrick's seventh-grade English and social-studies teacher, told Helman. "He just knew how to talk to people, look people in the eye."

When Patrick was in seventh grade, Weissenberg recommended him for the New York–based A Better Chance, a program committed to "recruiting, identifying, and developing leaders among young people of color," as stated on its Web site, by sending talented, underprivileged youth to the nation's finest independent and college preparatory schools. Patrick, who graduated first in his eighth-grade class, was selected by the program and received a full scholarship to the prestigious Milton Academy, a private boarding and day school, founded in 1798, in Milton, Massachusetts. Patrick's transition to life at Milton was not entirely smooth. In a speech given to the National Association of Minority Media Executives (NAMME), as quoted by the *Chicago Tribune* (June 22, 1994),

Patrick recalled making an early faux pas that reflected his socioeconomic background: "We had a dress code then: Boys wore jackets and ties to classes. Now, a jacket on the South Side of Chicago is a 'windbreaker.' So when the clothing list arrived at home, explaining the dress code, my family splurged on a new windbreaker. That first day of classes, when all the other boys were donning their blue blazers and tweed coats, there was I in my windbreaker. I had a lot to learn indeed." Soon, however, Patrick adapted to the social mores of the Milton Academy—"the jackets, the rep ties, indeed the whole line of Brooks Brothers merchandise," as he said in his NAMME speech—while distinguishing himself as a promising student and campus leader. "He wasn't an athlete, he wasn't Phi Beta Kappa, he wasn't lead singer in a group," Will Speers, a classmate of Patrick's at Milton, said to Glen Johnson for the Associated Press (August 25, 2006). "He was just a person who was more mature than most of us."

As one of the few African-American students on campus, Patrick tried to bridge the cultural divide between the black and white students, being "a great friend to a wide variety of people even though he didn't have a niche on campus in traditional ways," as Speers recalled to Johnson. Helman noted that as a result, some African-American students called him "'Oreo'—black on the outside, white on the inside." More positively, Matthew A. Peckham, a Milton classmate, described Patrick to Helman as a "moderator and peacemaker," and George Chase, another classmate, remembered Patrick as having been able to explain to different factions of students the views of others, putting in reasonable terms "what the more extreme kids were voicing. And he was able to articulate that in a way that was non threatening and intellectually engaging." Patrick graduated from the Milton Academy in 1974, having gained an appreciation for education as "more than accumulated information and prestige, but instead, to borrow from [the American poet] Robert Frost, as 'learning to listen to anything, without losing your temper or your self-confidence,'" as he explained in his speech for NAMME. That fall Patrick entered Harvard College, in Cambridge, Massachusetts, on a full scholarship; he majored in English and American literature, developing a particular liking for the work of Mark Twain.

After graduating from Harvard with honors, in 1978, Patrick received a Michael Clark Rockefeller Traveling Fellowship to spend the next year studying and traveling in Africa. Among other ventures, he worked on a United Nations developmental project in the Sudan. "It was as remote a place as you can imagine—five days across the Nubian Desert to get there—no phone, no mail service for months. I was out of touch," Patrick recalled to Natalie Jacobson, a reporter for Boston's NewsCenter 5, as posted on BostonChannel.com (November 3, 2006). "I think I came away from that feeling incredibly strong. There is a resilience and a self-confidence, I think, that comes from that that makes it so much easier for me to think about new things, about taking on new challenges and not feeling that they are beyond my capacity."

In the fall of 1979, Patrick began his studies at Harvard Law School, where he quickly distinguished himself as a compelling orator, winning the "best oral advocate" award at Harvard's Ames Moot Court finals, in which competing teams of students argued cases before a Supreme Court justice. Patrick also headed the Harvard Legal Aid Bureau, the oldest student-run legal-services office in the U.S., which provided free legal counsel to low-income residents in the Boston area. He graduated with honors from Harvard Law School in 1982 and secured a coveted clerkship with the federal judge Stephen Reinhardt of the U.S. Court of Appeals, Ninth Circuit, in Los Angeles, California. The following year Patrick moved to New York City, where he worked for the Legal Defense Fund of the National Association for the Advancement of Colored People (NAACP). In that capacity, he was involved in a series of racially charged capital-punishment cases in the southern U.S. "I've gone to prisons to tell clients their appeals have been successful," he said to Wil Haygood for the Boston Globe in 1993. "And I've gone to prisons to tell clients we lost, and goodbye, because they were within hours of execution." In one case, McCleskey vs. Kemp (1987), which involved the death-penalty appeal of Warren McCleskey, an African-American man accused of murdering a white police officer, Patrick argued—unsuccessfully—before the U.S. Supreme Court that racial bias had played a factor in the disproportionately high number of blacks sentenced to death, and that McClesky's conviction was therefore unconstitutional. While with the NAACP Patrick won a case involving African-Americans in Selma, Alabama, who were accused of voter-registration fraud. In another case Patrick prevailed against the state of Arkansas—whose governor at the time, Bill Clinton, went on to become president—over state violations of the Voting Rights Act with regard to voter registration. In 1986 Patrick joined the Boston law firm Hill & Barlow; he became a partner at the firm in 1990. He also continued to take on pro bono cases, defending local low-income homeowners, mostly elderly African-American women, who had been pressured by BayBank (now called BankBoston) into signing for high-interest home-improvement loans. As a result of Patrick's negotiated settlement, BayBank agreed to devote $11 million to low-interest housing loans for low-income communities.

In February 1994 President Clinton nominated Patrick for the post of assistant attorney general for civil rights at the U.S. Department of Justice. Confirmed by the U.S. Senate in March of that year, Patrick vowed to "restore the great moral imperative" of civil rights, according to Jill Lawrence, writing for the Chicago Sun-Times (June 26, 1994). Upon his appointment, Patrick launched a campaign to investigate incidents of racial discrimination, including the racist treatment of black customers by the Denny's restaurant chain, racially motivated burnings of churches in the South, and discrimination against residents of low-income neighborhoods by banks and insurance companies. Patrick's aggressive initiatives—along with his staunch advocacy of affirmative-action policies in higher education and in the workplace—drew criticism from some conservative policymakers, who accused him of pushing "quotas and race-based preferences," as William L. Clay noted in About . . . Time Magazine (December 31, 1994). One columnist for the Washington Times, as quoted by Scott Helman in the Boston Globe (May 24, 2006), went as far as to call Patrick "the grand autocrat of affirmative action." Patrick fired back at his critics, clarifying his views during a conversation with Ana Pugo for the Boston Globe (May 8, 1994): "Nobody is really talking about quotas as an appropriate remedy in almost any kind of case. Affirmative action is a different thing from quotas. The Supreme Court has said that affirmative action, in certain limited circumstances and crafted in a certain kind of way, is an appropriate response to the solving of a problem." He added, "We have people in this country who cannot get jobs, who cannot get adequate education—because of race, disability, gender or some other immutable characteristic. They cannot enjoy the same fullness of American citizenship as a white citizen. If you appeal to the American citizenry on that level, and you show them how that is happening, then they understand."

One notable case during Patrick's tenure with the Justice Department—in which the school board of Piscataway, New Jersey, retained a black teacher rather than her equally qualified white counterpart, for the expressed purpose of implementing racial diversity in the workplace—sparked furious debate among policymakers for its implications for future hiring practices. Clint Bolick, vice president of the conservative Institute for Justice, accused the Justice Department of "playing the numbers game in civil rights," as quoted in Business Week (December 12, 1994). Patrick, who spearheaded the case, insisted that "Piscataway is not a quota case," and he took the criticism of the Justice Department's actions in stride. "Being a lightning rod takes getting used to," he admitted to Business Week. "If I walked on water, certain of my critics would still say that Patrick can't swim." As for the primary impetus behind his tireless campaign for civil rights, Patrick, as Jon Keller reported, referred to his own experience with racial prejudice. "I have sat in the Oval Office and counseled a president of the United States," he said, "and then had trouble hailing a cab when the meeting was over."

In 1997 Patrick returned to private practice, this time at Day, Berry, & Howard, in Milton, Massachusetts. He continued to engage in civil rights advocacy, seeking in one case to reform the hiring practices of private corporations. Patrick supervised a seven-member task force charged with ensuring that Texaco comply with a 1996 settlement mandating the promotion of qualified minority employees in the company. In late 1998, in what Scott Helman called "the first of several instances in which Patrick . . . went to work for the accused," Patrick joined Texaco as vice president and general counsel. "I've worked with a lot of corporations that are trying in good faith not to turn into what they think Texaco once was," Patrick told Ross Kerber for the *Boston Globe* (December 16, 1998), referring to Texaco's reputation for not hiring or promoting minorities. "But few of those companies have made the kind of progress that Texaco has made. I'm not saying that Texaco is the promised land. But they've taken this crisis as a platform for change." In the approximately two years that he worked at Texaco, Patrick fended off charges relating to the company's record of pollution and contamination of the rainforests of Ecuador, which were blamed for thousands of deaths among native residents (a result of decisions made at the company before Patrick's arrival). For his part, Patrick successfully lobbied to have the legal suits against Texaco tried in the Ecuadorian courts, rather than the U.S. courts, which might well have posed a tougher challenge for the company. Most of Patrick's time at Texaco was spent in preparation for its merger with the Chevron Corp., in 2001.

That year Patrick joined the Atlanta, Georgia–based beverage giant Coca-Cola, as vice president and chief legal counsel. His nearly four-year tenure there was defined by the controversy surrounding widely reported labor violations at Coca-Cola bottling plants in Colombia, South America—specifically, allegations that the company was guilty of negligence while workers were physically abused and in some cases killed by Colombian paramilitary groups. "Deval Patrick got paid a lot of money to help cover up Coca-Cola's misdeeds and crimes and help keep his mouth shut," Ray Rogers, a veteran labor-union organizer and human-rights activist, said to Frank Phillips for the *Boston Globe* (February 8, 2005, on-line). Others, such as Andrew Hanson, an environmental lawyer, and Anna Waring, a former classmate of Patrick's at the Milton Academy, defended Patrick's record and praised his ability to temper corporate mission with the pursuit of justice. "What [Patrick] effectively did was to deny responsibility on behalf of the company and then offer to do a fact-finding mission, which by any measure was a relatively progressive way to respond," Hanson remarked to Phillips. Waring noted to Jon Keller, "The law wasn't a game for [Patrick]. It really was about making somebody whole or trying to correct the system." Patrick has characterized his role at Coca-Cola as a delicate balancing act between preserving corporate interest and advocating corporate responsibility. "It's unnecessary to separate those two," he insisted to Phillips. "It's the duty of the general counsel to protect the interest of the shareholders. I do not think that requires or has ever required I leave my conscience at the door." In the

spring of 2004, in the face of intensifying criticism, Patrick resigned from Coca-Cola and joined the board of ACC Capital Holdings, the parent company of the California-based mortgage lender Ameriquest, which in recent times had endured accusations of predatory lending practices. (In January 2006, for example, Ameriquest had agreed to a $325 million settlement with 49 states for its questionable lending activities in low-income areas.) Patrick helped consolidate Ameriquest's decentralized operations and restore, to some degree, its sullied reputation. "I've fixed hard problems of all kinds, civil rights and business problems," he told Brian C. Mooney for the *Boston Globe* (August 13, 2006, on-line). "It's the stuff I like to do, and I'm good at it."

In 2005, after eight years in the private sector, Patrick set his sights on public office, announcing his candidacy for the governorship of Massachusetts. "The leadership vacuum is huge," Patrick told Scott Helman. "And frankly only the governor gets to set the agenda." With the incumbent Republican governor, Mitt Romney, deciding to forego a reelection campaign in favor of a 2008 presidential run, Patrick joined one of the more wide-open gubernatorial races in recent state history. He was considered a dark horse in a contest that also included the Democratic candidates Tom Reilly, the state attorney general, and Chris Gabrieli, a former nominee for lieutenant governor. Nonetheless, armed with optimism, a distinguished track record of civil rights advocacy, and an inspiring life story, Patrick wooed low- and middle-income voters across the state. "Sometimes I look at Massachusetts and all the people who took a chance on a runny-nosed kid from Chicago, and who exposed him to all the opportunities it had, and I think: If they can do that for me, how come we can't do that for all the kids?" he said, as Haygood reported in 2006. In September of that year, Patrick captured the Democratic Party's gubernatorial nomination, with 58 percent of the vote.

Patrick next faced the incumbent Republican lieutenant governor, Kerry Healey, who was attempting to make history as the state's first female governor. Running on a platform of traditional liberal values, Patrick opposed the reduction of state taxes and promised, instead, to reinvigorate the Massachusetts economy with a series of state-funded initiatives aimed at renewing dilapidated urban centers and improving the mass-transit network. He expressed adamant support for the legalization of same-sex marriage and stem-cell research, positions opposed by Healey and Governor Romney, and promised to work for better education and health care for the state's poorer communities. In addition, Patrick made a concerted effort to appeal to "all kinds of people from all corners of the commonwealth," not just African-Americans, as he told Susan Page for *USA Today* (November 1, 2006). In an attempt to erode Patrick's increasing popularity, Healey attacked what some perceived as his soft stance on crime, by sponsoring ads that focused on Patrick's advocacy of Benjamin LaGuer, an African-American man convicted of the 1983 rape of a Massachusetts woman. (Patrick, who wrote letters on behalf of LaGuer to the state parole board, later withdrew his support for the convicted man after a 2002 DNA test confirmed LaGuer's guilt.) Healey's tactics, however, had little effect. In November 2006 Patrick defeated Healey by a 21-percentage-point margin, to become the first African-American governor of Massachusetts and the second black person elected governor since Reconstruction, in the 19th century. "It's a profound thing to be witness to and a central part of this historic moment," Patrick said just hours after his victory, as quoted by Andrew Ryan for the *Boston Globe* (November 8, 2006). "If people around the country are looking at Massachusetts and thinking about Massachusetts differently than they have in the past, then good for us." Patrick was sworn in as the 71st governor of Massachusetts on January 4, 2007.

The first months of Patrick's governorship were marred by public-relations missteps, such as his trading the previous governor's state-funded Ford for a Cadillac that cost twice as much to rent. In an article for the *Boston Globe* (February 21, 2007), Frank Phillips and Andrea Estes reported that Patrick had also spent around $10,000 on new drapes as part of a $27,387 office makeover. Later, Phillips and Estes wrote, Patrick "changed his mind after a weekend spent struggling with the state's dismal finances and the budget cuts he has asked his agency leaders to make," and he announced that he would contribute half the money required to lease the Cadillac and reimburse the state for the cost of the drapes. "I realize I cannot in good conscience ask the agencies to make those choices without being willing to make them myself," Patrick said in an official statement, as quoted in the *Globe*. Nonetheless, an unnamed administration source told the *Globe* writers that the Cadillac lease, the costly furniture, and the hiring of an aide for his wife at a salary of $72,000 a year "constituted a building public relations crisis."

At a September 11 memorial service in 2007, as Matt Viser reported for the *Boston Globe* (September 14, 2007), Patrick said that the terrorist attacks had indicated "the failure of human beings to understand each other and to learn to love each other. It seems to me that lesson [of] that morning is something that we must carry with us every day." According to Viser, state Republicans "seized on his comments as implying the terrorist attacks could have been prevented." A few days later Patrick responded publicly, saying on the *Eagan & Braude* show on WTKK Radio, as quoted by Viser, "Let me be clear: I don't think America bears any fault for the attack on us in 9/11, and I don't think that any of the family members with whom I spoke that day heard it or saw it that way."

Patrick has continued his efforts to stay connected to the voters, most significantly by hosting a radio program on which he takes calls from the public. "We ran a campaign—and we talked about it on your show—that was very much about asking people who had checked out to check back in," he said on the show, CNN.com (February 20, 2007) reported. "'And it was a strategy to win. But I also think that asking all those people to check in, we have to keep faith in them. We have to continue to have a way to talk directly to me, for me to hear their ideas, to get their advice.'" Also in 2007 Patrick began pushing a proposal to open three resort casinos in Massachusetts to create additional jobs, increase economic activity, and generate revenue for the state.

Patrick serves on the board of directors of Coca-Cola Enterprises, Reebok International, and A Better Chance, and on the board of overseers of Harvard University. He is the recipient of honorary law degrees from Morris Brown College, Curry College, and the District of Columbia School of Law. He has taught law at Stanford and Harvard universities. Patrick and his wife, Diane, a labor and employment lawyer, have two daughters, Sarah and Katherine, and live in Milton, Massachusetts.

—D.J.K.

Suggested Reading: Associated Press Aug. 25, 2006; *Boston Globe* p63 Sep. 23, 1993, A p1 May 24, 2006, A p1 Aug. 13, 2006; *Boston Magazine* (on-line) May 2006; *Chicago Tribune* N p23 June 22, 1994; *Washington Post* C p1 Oct. 25, 2006

Perkins, Elizabeth

Nov. 18, 1960– Actress

Address: c/o Gersch Agency, 232 N. Canon Dr., Beverly Hills, CA 90210

At first glance Elizabeth Perkins's career appears not to have fulfilled certain expectations held by a Hollywood actress. Perkins, now 46, has never attained superstar status. Apart from her current, acclaimed work in the role of a narcissistic neighbor on the Showtime network's comedic drama *Weeds*, Perkins is probably best known for her portrayal of a marketing executive with a heart of gold in *Big* (1988). In more recent years, at the expense of sounding disgruntled, she has criticized the lack of good roles available to women in Hollywood. However, a look at Perkins's earliest comments on the subject reveals that she was always uncomfortable with the Hollywood mainstream—even as she was receiving top billing in high-grossing films—and that her career has taken essentially the course she predicted. "Box office potential isn't that important to me," she told Ian Spelling for the *Chicago Sun-Times* (April 4, 1993), shortly before she appeared in two of the most lucrative films of her career, *The Flintstones* and *Miracle on 34th Street*. Roles in big-budget movies, she continued, are

Kevin Winter/Getty Images

Elizabeth Perkins

"more about being a persona than an actor. Every now and then I'll try to do a commercial picture—something commercial but good—just to keep me visible, but I find it very stifling." Instead, Perkins has acted in a wide variety of film, television, and theater roles, avoiding being typecast by intentionally playing different characters back-to-back. "I don't aspire to greatness," she told Michael J. Bandler in a February 14, 1993 interview for the *Chicago Tribune*. "At least, my definition of greatness has been redefined. I've lowered my sights. I used to look at Bette Davis and say, 'That's greatness.' But that doesn't exist anymore. When I was in my early 20s, Sally Field was doing *Places in the Heart*. Meryl Streep was in *Silkwood*. Jane Fonda had just done *The China Syndrome*. What I aspired to existed. . . . Hollywood was in a different place than it is now. Today it's making cartoon movies about cartoon characters." Though her frustration with the film industry has grown as she has aged and fewer and fewer roles are available to her, she may have finally achieved on the small screen the combination of popular and critical success that has proved elusive in the past. Receiving a great deal of critical praise for her performance in *Weeds*, Perkins "has brought to life the most deliciously vile character since the puppy-skinning Cruella De Vil," according to Marisa Guthrie, writing for for the New York *Daily News* (August 21, 2006).

The daughter of James Perkins, a writer and businessman, and Jo Williams, a drug-treatment counselor and concert pianist, Elizabeth Ann Perkins was born on November 18, 1960 in the New York City borough of Queens. (The Greek surname of Perkins's paternal grandparents is Pisperikos;

they anglicized their name when they moved to the U.S.) Perkins's parents divorced when she was three. She spent her childhood going back and forth between her father's New York City apartment and a 600-acre farm in Vermont, where her mother and stepfather lived and where Perkins spent most of her time between the ages of nine and 15, along with her two sisters. "I lived way out in the middle of nowhere," she told Bandler. "We got on the bus at a quarter of 7 to be at school 25 miles away at 8:30. I spent an enormous amount of time—6 years—alone." That, she told Kirk Honeycutt for the *Los Angeles Times* (March 14, 1990), "played an enormous part in my becoming an actress. Any child that isolated will develop an overactive imagination. I used to be absolutely fascinated when I was around people." Perkins played the tiger in her junior-high-school production of the folktale *The Tiger and the Brahmin*. Acting in that role "gave me such a feeling of satisfaction, of purpose, that it felt right even at that age," she told Luaine Lee for the *Oregonian* (August 16, 1991).

Admittedly a hell-raiser in her youth, Perkins has said that she experimented with drugs in her teens. For her secondary education, she was sent to a boarding school, from which she was expelled—just two months shy of her graduation—for cutting classes and being generally insubordinate, as she told Bandler. She then went to live with her father, who had recently relocated to Chicago, Illinois. Perkins finished high school there at Robert A. Waller (now Lincoln Park) High School. She originally considered becoming a veterinarian. "I love animals and animal behavior," she told Lee. However, "when I got to be about 18 I realized I loved human behavior and that became my impetus to go into acting because it's basically the study of human behavior. It became for me my creative release and I can't ever imagine not doing it."

Perkins attended the prestigious Theatre School (originally founded as the Goodman School of Drama) at DePaul University, in Chicago, and after graduating with her B.F.A. degree in theater, in 1981, she spent three years working as a professional stage actress in Chicago, before moving to New York City. "I just packed up my cat and my trunk and drove to New York City on a whim one day," she told Leslie Bennetts for the *New York Times* (July 25, 1986). "I was never so scared in my life. I had $500 in my pocket, no place to live, no job and no real prospects." Within two months Perkins landed a role in Neil Simon's play *Brighton Beach Memoirs* on Broadway. She subsequently performed in various roles at the Ensemble Studio Theatre, Playwrights Horizons, and New York City's annual Shakespeare festival organized by the Public Theater. In 1986 she made her feature-film debut in *About Last Night . . .*, a screen adaptation of the David Mamet play *Sexual Perversity in Chicago*, about the city's singles scene. Perkins portrayed a caustic, unstylish roommate of Demi Moore's character in the film, which also starred Rob Lowe. "While many critics stood in line to pan the film and its brat-pack stars, most raved about the brash newcomer's aggressive performance," Steve Weinstein wrote for the Los Angeles Times (July 25, 1988), referring to Perkins. Other, less memorable films followed, including From the Hip (1987), in which Perkins was cast as the girlfriend of an attorney played by Judd Nelson, and Sweet Hearts Dance (1988), a movie about the adult lives of high-school sweethearts, which also starred Don Johnson, Jeff Daniels, and Susan Sarandon.

In 1988 Perkins appeared in the role for which she has become best known: that of a slightly uptight marketing executive in Big. Directed by Penny Marshall, the film tells the story of a 12-year-old boy who makes a wish to be "big" and wakes up the next day in the body of an adult (played by Tom Hanks). He lands a job at a New York City toy company, where Perkins's character works; they forge a tentative and unusual relationship, in which "the repressed, yuppie career woman . . . discovers the little kid inside herself as she seduces Tom Hanks' boy-man," Weinstein wrote. The film was a popular and critical success. "I was fortunate enough at 24 to get my first movie audition and get the part and my name was above the title," Perkins told Maggie Wicks for the Auckland, New Zealand, Sunday Star-Times (August 13, 2006). "I was born under a lucky star."

Following Big Perkins took off work for 18 months. She told Lee, "I went to Europe, lived in this funky house up in the Hollywood hills and had dinner parties, bought myself a convertible and moved to Los Angeles. My life was not about work. It was not about responsibility, about doing the right thing and being at the right places. It felt great." In the early 1990s Perkins appeared in such films as Love at Large (1990), described by Honeycutt as "a stylized meditation on romance set in a mythic urban landscape"; Avalon (1990), a well-received drama, written and directed by Barry Levinson, about multiple generations of a Jewish family in the U.S.; He Said, She Said (1991), with Kevin Bacon, which told a single story from both the male and female characters' perspectives; and The Doctor (1991), in which Perkins portrayed a cancer patient giving advice to a physician, played by William Hurt, who learns he has cancer.

In 1993 Perkins made her television debut in For Their Own Good, an ABC movie based on the true story of several women who underwent sterilization in order to retain their jobs at a chemical plant. (Some companies in the late 1970s and early 1980s implemented "fetal protection policies," which forced women of childbearing age who worked around dangerous chemicals to leave their jobs or agree to sterilization. A Supreme Court ruling in 1991 effectively outlawed such policies.) In the film Perkins played Sally Wheeler, a paint-factory worker and mother in a small Texas town, whose company enforces just such a policy. The actress explained to Bandler that her shift toward television reflected the superior roles she felt were offered there as opposed to film: "I read the script [of

For Their Own Good] and thought it was important. And for this particular story, television is by far the best medium, because millions are going to see it." In the 1990s Perkins also appeared in the television movies Rescuers: Stories of Courage: Two Women (1997) and Cloned (1997) and the miniseries From the Earth to the Moon (1998).

In 1994 Perkins starred in two of her most commercially successful films to date: The Flintstones, in which she portrayed the classic cartoon cavewoman, Wilma, the wife of Fred Flintstone (John Goodman); and a remake of the 1947 holiday classic Miracle on 34th Street, for which she was cast in the role originally played by Maureen O'Hara. Though The Flintstones was a box-office success—it has grossed more than $350 million worldwide since it was released—it was almost universally panned in the press. The remake of Miracle on 34th Street fared slightly better with critics, receiving mixed reviews.

Perkins worked only part-time in the late 1990s, taking time off to raise her daughter, but she still fit in a number of projects, appearing in such films as Lesser Prophets (1997), I'm Losing You (1998), and Crazy in Alabama (1999). In 2000 Perkins starred in her first television series, the NBC sitcom Battery Park, about a group of policeman in that section of New York City. "It's the first time in a long time that somebody came to me with a great women's role and said, You know, I wrote this for you," Perkins said in an interview broadcast on Fox News Channel's The Edge with Paula Zahn (April 10, 2000). In the show Perkins played the precinct leader, Captain Madeleine Dunleavy. "Starting out in theater in Chicago, my greatest experience was acting in ensembles," she told Steve Hedgpeth for the Newhouse News Service (March 17, 2000). "And doing this series is kind of like working in theater, doing a one-act play every week." Furthermore, Perkins, who was then 39, felt privileged to have gotten the role. "I'm just lucky to be working," she told Hedgpeth. "You hit 35 and all of a sudden you're too old to play opposite guys like Sean Penn or Kevin Bacon in films. You're thinking, 'I acted with you guys before; how can I be too old for you now?'" When Battery Park was canceled after just one season, Perkins continued working in film, appearing in 28 Days (2000), with Sandra Bullock; Cats & Dogs (2001), opposite Jeff Goldblum; The Ring Two (2005), alongside Naomi Watts; and Must Love Dogs (2005), with her longtime friend Diane Lane, among other projects. She also acted in a number of made-for-television movies, including What Girls Learn (2001), What Leonard Comes Home To (2002), Speak (2004), and Hercules (2005).

Weeds, which began running in 2005, stars Mary-Louise Parker as the widowed suburban mother Nancy Botwin, who begins selling marijuana in order to maintain her comfortable lifestyle after her husband's death. Perkins plays Botwin's neighbor, Celia Hodes, a housewife who was described by Marisa Guthrie as "the high priestess of narcissism." Hodes is overly concerned with having the right house, neighborhood, hairdresser, and clothes: "She's sort of based on the great American suburban lie: If you can keep the grass green, keep the rabbits at bay and maintain a perfect-looking existence, everything on the inside will fix itself," Perkins told Eirik Knutzen for the Copley News Service (August 25, 2006). "She's the most politically incorrect person in town and at home she is a nightmare," she told Maggie Wicks. "It is a pleasure to play someone so unheroic." For her performance as Celia, Perkins was nominated for a Satellite Award in 2005 and 2006 and for a Golden Globe and an Emmy Award in 2006 and 2007.

In addition to live-action films, Perkins has lent her voice to such animated productions as the highly popular film *Finding Nemo* (2003) and, from 2002 to 2004, the long-running television series *King of the Hill*. Perkins's first marriage, to the actor Terry Kinney, lasted from the time she was 22 until she was 27. She lives in California's San Fernando Valley with Hannah, 14, her daughter from an earlier relationship with the writer-director Maurice Phillips, and three stepsons, the children of the cinematographer Julio Macat, whom she married in 2000.

—M.B.

Suggested Reading: *Chicago Sun-Times* p14 Apr. 4, 1993; *Daily News* p35 Aug. 21, 2006; *New York Times* C p21 July 25, 1986, II p2 Oct. 9, 2005

Selected Television Shows: *For Their Own Good*, 1993; *Cloned*, 1997; *Rescuers: Stories of Courage: Two Women*, 1997; *From the Earth to the Moon*, 1998; *Battery Park*, 2000; *If These Walls Could Talk 2*, 2000; *What Girls Learn*, 2001; *My Sister's Keeper*, 2002; *What Leonard Comes Home To*, 2002; *King of the Hill*, 2002–2004; *Speak*, 2004; *Hercules*, 2005; *Weeds*, 2005–

Selected Films: *About Last Night . . .*, 1986; *From the Hip*, 1987; *Big*, 1988; *Sweet Hearts Dance*, 1988; *Avalon*, 1990; *Enid is Sleeping*, 1990; *Love at Large*, 1990; *The Doctor*, 1991; *He Said, She Said*, 1991; *Indian Summer*, 1993; *The Flintstones*, 1994; *Miracle on 34th Street*, 1994; *Moonlight and Valentino*, 1995; *Lesser Prophets*, 1997; *I'm Losing You*, 1998; *Crazy in Alabama*, 1999; *28 Days*, 2000; *Cats & Dogs*, 2001; *Finding Nemo*, 2003; *Gilded Stones*, 2004; *Jiminy Glick in Lalawood*, 2004; *Fierce People*, 2005; *Kids in America*, 2005; *Must Love Dogs*, 2005; *The Ring Two*, 2005; *The Thing about My Folks*, 2005

Petraeus, David H.

(peh-TRAY-us)

Nov. 7, 1952– U.S. Army general; commander of multinational forces in Iraq

Address: The Pentagon, Washington, DC 20310

The commander of multinational forces in Iraq, General David H. Petraeus, "is one of the most fascinating people in the United States Army," Julian E. Barnes wrote for *U.S. News & World Report* (October 31, 2005). Petraeus boasts an unusual mix of military and academic accomplishments, of physical prowess and analytical skill; a graduate of the U.S. Military Academy at West Point, the four-star general holds a Ph.D. in international relations from Princeton University, emblematic of the intellectual approach to military missions that has led him to be called, as Barnes wrote, "the military's warrior-scholar." In January 2007 President George W. Bush chose Petraeus to succeed George W. Casey in Iraq. Petraeus assumed command of the approximately 132,000 U.S. troops on the ground there, at a time when support for the war among the American public had decreased sharply—in the face of continued instability in that occupied country and the deaths of more than 3,000 U.S. soldiers over four years and an estimated 34,000 Iraqi civilians in 2006 alone. In earlier assignments in Iraq, from 2003 to 2005, Petraeus was charged with lead-

Chris Hondros/Getty Images

ing the 101st Airborne Division's invasion, establishing order in the city of Mosul and its surrounding province and training Iraqi army and police forces; he brought to all of those missions the thoughtfulness, intense drive, ambition, and competitiveness for which he is known. Unanimously confirmed in his new post by the U.S. Senate on January 26, Petraeus took on his new duties amid ever-increasing doubt that the war can be won. During his confirmation hearings, while calling conditions in Iraq "dire," Petraeus urged patience and dedication. "The way ahead will be neither quick nor easy, and undoubtedly there will be tough days," he said, as quoted by Ann Scott Tyson in the *Washington Post* (January 24, 2007). "We face a determined, adaptable, barbaric enemy. He will try to wait us out. Any such endeavor is a test of wills, and there are no guarantees."

David Howell Petraeus was born on November 7, 1952 in Cornwall, New York, to Dutch-American parents, Sixtus and Miriam (Howell) Petraeus. Petraeus's father was a sea captain who served on one of the "Liberty" ships, merchant vessels that delivered supplies to the Allies during World War II; he immigrated to the United States from the Netherlands after his service in the war. At Cornwall Central High School, Petraeus served as president of the ski club, played striker on the school's 1969 championship soccer team, and was a National Honor Society Scholar. After graduating from high school, in 1970, Petraeus entered the United States Military Academy at West Point, in New York State, graduating 10th in his class in 1974. "A striver to the max, Dave was always 'going for it' in sports, academics, leadership, and even his social life," according to a description of him in the 1974 West Point yearbook, quoted by Rick Atkinson in the *Washington Post* (January 7, 2007).

Petraeus was commissioned as an infantry officer in 1974 and assigned the following year as a platoon leader with the 509th Airborne Infantry Battalion in Vicenza, Italy. Having attained the rank of first lieutenant, Petraeus served briefly as assistant operations officer for the 2nd Brigade, 24th Infantry Division (Mechanized), at Fort Stewart, Georgia. In 1979, when he was promoted to captain, he was given command of Company A, 2nd Battalion, 19th Infantry Regiment (Mechanized), in the same division. Two years later Petraeus became aide-de-camp to the 24th Infantry Division's commanding general, the first of many aide positions that would lead his detractors to call him a "professional son."

To complement his army training, Petraeus felt it important to cultivate his intellectual understanding of the world in which the army functioned. To that end he returned to West Point for further schooling, receiving the General George C. Marshall Award as the top graduate of the U.S. Army Command and General Staff College Class of 1983. He then attended Princeton University's Woodrow Wilson School of Public and International Affairs, in Princeton, New Jersey, where he earned a master of public administration (M.P.A.) degree in 1985 and a Ph.D. in international relations in 1987. His Ph.D. dissertation, titled "The American Military and the Lessons of Vietnam," examined the U.S. military's failings in the Viet-

nam War and the implications of that defeat for future warfare. His interactions with scholars at Princeton affected him profoundly. "The truth is not found in any one school of thought, and arguably it's found in discussion among them," he told Barnes. "This is a flexibility of mind that really helps you when you are in ambiguous, tough situations." From 1985 to 1987 Petraeus was an assistant professor of international relations at the U.S. Military Academy. He has often said that he considers his time in graduate school to be one of the most valuable experiences of his career and a major influence on the scholarly way he approaches military challenges. "You know, we in the Army, we have to admit, that we're living sometimes a sort of a grindstone cloister existence . . . ," he told Ullrich Fichtner for *Spiegel* (December 18, 2006, online). "So we have to try to raise, as one of my colleagues once put it, our sights beyond the maximum effective range of an M-16 rifle. Graduate school and other experiences that get us out of our intellectual comfort zone help us do just that."

From 1987 to 1988 Petraeus served as the military assistant to General John Galvin, the Supreme Allied Commander in Europe. From 1988 to 1989 he was the operations officer to 2d Battalion, 30th Infantry (Mechanized) and its 1st Brigade, both in the 3rd Infantry Division (Mechanized). Next, he served as assistant executive officer to U.S. Army chief of staff general Carl Vuono in Washington, D.C. Promoted to the rank of lieutenant colonel, Petraeus moved to Fort Campbell, Kentucky, to take command of the 101st Airborne Division's 3rd Battalion, 187th Regiment. There, in 1991, Petraeus was shot in the chest when a soldier tripped during a live-fire exercise, accidentally discharging his M-16 rifle. Petraeus was rushed to Vanderbilt University Medical Center, in Nashville, Tennessee, where he was operated on by the future U.S. senator (and onetime Senate majority leader) Bill Frist. Petraeus underwent five hours of surgery and the removal of part of his lung before returning to Fort Campbell. From 1993 to 1994 he served as the director of plans, training, and mobilization for the 101st Airborne Division (Air Assault).

In 1994 Petraeus enrolled at Georgetown University, in Washington, D.C., on a fellowship. His studies were cut short when he was assigned as the chief of staff to the United Nations command in Haiti during Operation Uphold Democracy, the planned invasion of that country to reinstall its democratically elected leader, Jean-Bertrand Aristide, following a coup; the threatened invasion turned into a peacekeeping mission after the coup's leader, General Raoul Cédras, stepped down. That mission was Petraeus's first—albeit brief—actual military operation. He returned from Haiti to command the 1st Brigade, 82d Airborne Division, centering on the 504th Parachute Infantry Regiment. The brigade's training, at Fort Polk's Joint Readiness Training Center, was described in Tom Clancy's military novel *Airborne*. In another aide position, from 1997 to 1999 Petraeus acted as executive assistant to the director of the Joint Staff and then to the chairman of the Joint Chiefs of Staff, General Henry Shelton. In 1999, having been promoted to brigadier general, Petraeus was deployed to Kuwait as assistant division commander of operations, again with the 82d Airborne Division. His time in Kuwait—part of Operation Desert Spring, which placed troops in Kuwait on a rotating basis during the decade after the 1991 Gulf War—was Petraeus's second experience in the field; during that time he briefly served as acting commanding general. From Kuwait, Petraeus became chief of staff of XVIII Airborne Corps, at Fort Bragg, North Carolina. There, he sustained his second major injury, a broken pelvis, when his parachute collapsed in midair during a training jump. Petraeus's third overseas assignment came in 2001, as part of Operation Joint Forge, a 10-month tour in Bosnia-Herzegovina, during which he served as assistant chief of staff for operations of the NATO Stabilization Force. He also served as deputy commander of the U.S. Joint Interagency Counter-Terrorism Task Force, a unit created after the September 11, 2001 terrorist attacks to give U.S. forces in Bosnia counterterrorism training.

The United States invasion of Iraq officially began on March 20, 2003. (It was undertaken for the stated purpose of ridding Iraq of so-called weapons of mass destruction, none of which have been found there.) By then a major general, Petraeus entered his first combat zone, commanding the 101st Airborne Division during Operation Iraqi Freedom, the drive to Baghdad. As chronicled by the Washington Post reporter Rick Atkinson in his book In the Company of Soldiers, Petraeus led his troops through the battles of Karbala, Hilla, and Najaf. Atkinson, who was embedded with the 101st throughout the siege, reported Petraeus's reaction after a particularly sobering attack on U.S. troops by Iraqis in March; according to Atkinson, Petraeus said to the reporter, "Tell me how this ends," words that would become the general's mantra for the whole of the campaign and that Atkinson interpreted as signaling an acknowledgement—which the general made long before others in the military or the government did—that the U.S. involvement in Iraq would not be short-lived.

On April 11, 2003, two days after the fall of Baghdad, the northern city of Mosul also fell. Located in Nineveh Province, Mosul is Iraq's third-largest city, housing more than 10 percent of the Iraqi population. In the days after the Baathist forces deserted Mosul, Kurdish fighters took over, but after failing to quell the looting and violence, they agreed to hand the city over to the U.S. military. On April 22, 2003 Petraeus and the 101st Airborne occupied the city, a strategic location in the war and one that, despite the ethnic conflict there between Kurds and Arabs, the U.S. believed it could secure. From the start, Petraeus emphasized the importance of Iraqi involvement in the efforts to rebuild the country following the invasion, both

for the sake of gaining the Iraqis' trust and to help them feel more invested in their new state. He also emphasized his troops' role as representatives of their country, posting signs in their tents that read, "What have you done to win Iraqi hearts and minds today?" To fund the rebuilding efforts, Petraeus received $57 million, which struck many as a surprisingly large sum, from the Commanders' Emergency Response Program (CERP)—an arm of the U.S. military that gives discretionary funds to commanders to use for reconstruction. "This guy, he has a capacity to blow through bureaucracy that not many guys do," Major General Paul Eaton told Rod Nordland for Newsweek (July 5, 2004, online), explaining Petraeus's ability to raise such impressive funding. "He doesn't understand the nature of a wall; he'll either go through it or over it or around it." During his tenure in Mosul, Petraeus oversaw approximately 5,000 rebuilding projects in the city, varying from necessary improvements in infrastructure to morale-building entertainment ventures. Petraeus told Martin Smith for the PBS program Frontline (November 23, 2003), "We're not over here working our fingers to the bone, fighting and dying, with the idea that this task is beyond us. We are over here with the idea that it can be accomplished—that we have made incredible progress . . . and that what we have to do is continue to prevail and to persist and to work very, very hard at this."

As the 101st established a tenuous peace, Petraeus prepared for the challenge of implementing a new system of government in Mosul and the rest of Nineveh Province. "You have to remember that, not only did the Iraqis not understand democracy and the philosophy, if you will, of democracy, because they haven't been allowed [under the deposed leader Saddam Hussein] to even discuss these things . . . ," he told Smith. "They certainly don't know in particular what shape and size and form democracy should take for Iraq, either at the national or the local or regional level. And that's what they're working out." Petraeus wanted to get Iraqis involved in the government and police force as early into the occupation as possible, especially since the low levels of employment in other parts of Iraq were among the major causes of unrest. "The sooner you get an Iraqi face on things, the better off you are," Petraeus told Smith. On May 5, 2003 the 101st oversaw elections in Nineveh Province to elect a government council, which would in turn elect the province governor. Despite the considerable ethnic tensions in the area, the elections proceeded peacefully, and the new government took control in relative stability. For the remainder of Petraeus's tenure as leader of the occupation in Mosul, the area remained secure; the troops of the 101st Airborne returned to the U.S. in February 2004. Petraeus had laudatory words for his troops, telling Wolf Blitzer for CNN's Late Edition with Wolf Blitzer (May 17, 2004), "They're the new greatest generation of Americans and every American should be proud of what they accomplished during their time in Iraq." His assessment of their experience in Iraq, however, was more measured, given the deaths of more than 60 soldiers during the mission of the 101st Airborne. "It's been a long, tough year, and I am older in more ways than just age," he said upon the troops' return to the U.S., as quoted by Atkinson in 2007. After the 101st pulled out, Mosul descended into sectarian violence between the Kurds and the Sunni Arabs—a development for which some blamed Petraeus, alleging that he implemented many short-term solutions without creating a long-term vision for the city.

In June 2004 Petraeus returned to Iraq with the rank of lieutenant general and a new assignment, as commander of the Multi-National Security Transition Command–Iraq (MNSTC-I), responsible for training the new Iraqi army and security forces. Upon his appointment Petraeus emphasized the need to build the Iraqi army's confidence. "We need to have what we sometimes call tactical patience . . . ," he explained to Melissa Block for the National Public Radio program *All Things Considered* (May 20, 2004). "I think we have to be very careful not to overaccelerate this and actually rush to failure. We have to be careful that we don't ask more of these forces than they are ready to deliver. We need to be careful about not putting them in situations where they really will be challenged and we may set them up for failure instead of success." Assessments of Petraeus's command were mixed. Though he oversaw massive expansion of Iraq's army and police force, those continued to experience many problems, including a high incidence of desertion and tension between units. Four months after assuming command of MNSTC-I, and a year and a half after he first went to Iraq, Petraeus wrote a piece for the *Washington Post* (September 26, 2004) detailing his feelings about the struggle to secure the country. "Helping organize, train and equip nearly a quarter-million of Iraq's security forces is a daunting task," he wrote. "Doing so in the middle of a tough insurgency increases the challenge enormously, making the mission akin to repairing an aircraft while in flight—and while being shot at. Now, however, 18 months after entering Iraq, I see tangible progress." Again, Petraeus urged patience and dedication: "There will be more tough times, frustration and disappointment along the way. . . . It will not be easy, but few worthwhile things are."

During his second tour in Iraq, Petraeus focused on modifying the training of Iraqis, in order to improve the skills of the officers rather than simply increasing the number of soldiers. He told Barnes that "the key ingredient" to success in Iraq "has become Iraqi leadership." The January 2005 elections in that country were important to Petraeus's overall Iraq strategy, both in terms of creating an Iraqi government and proving that the army and police force had the capability to ensure that government's survival. Protected by the members of the police force trained by Petraeus, several of whom

sacrificed their lives over the course of the day to thwart suicide bombers, Iraqis went to the polls to vote for a Transitional National Assembly, which would be responsible for drafting a new constitution. That September Petraeus handed over his command to Lieutenant General Martin Dempsey.

In October, back in the United States, Petraeus assumed command of Fort Leavenworth, Kansas, and the U.S. Army Combined Arms Center (CAC) based there. While at Fort Leavenworth, Petraeus oversaw the 1st Infantry Division's efforts to revamp the training of advisory teams that were to be deployed to Iraqi military and police units. He also co-authored, with Marine lieutenant general James F. Amos, the U.S. Army's new official counterinsurgency manual, titled *Field Manual 3-24*. The army's first counterinsurgency manual in 20 years, and the first for the Marine Corps in 25 years, the manual was created to address the issues surrounding a new kind of insurgency, of the sort that was being carried out by groups of Iraqis and undermining U.S. efforts to stabilize the country. Petraeus told Fichtner, "Counterinsurgency operations are war at the graduate level, they're thinking-man's warfare." The manual outlined many beliefs that Petraeus had acted upon in Iraq, primarily the view that "soldiers and Marines are expected to be nation builders as well as warriors," as he and Amos wrote in the foreword. The manual also asserted one of Petraeus's most deeply held beliefs: that the local population must be protected from insurgent violence, even at the expense of counterinsurgency personnel. As he had demonstrated in Iraq, stabilizing the local infrastructure reduced threats from insurgents by taking away support they received from discontented local Iraqis. Still, Petraeus and Amos recognized that a U.S. victory against the insurgents would hinge on support and cooperation not only from Iraqis but also from the American people. "Most enemies either do not try to defeat the United States with conventional operations or do not limit themselves to purely military means," Petraeus and Amos wrote in the manual's introduction. "They know that they cannot compete with U.S. forces on those terms. Instead, they try to exhaust U.S. national will, aiming to win by undermining and outlasting public support."

By January 2007, when President George W. Bush announced that he had chosen Petraeus as the new commanding general of Multi-National Force–Iraq (MNF-I), the American public's support for the war had almost run out; the number of U.S. troops killed in Iraq had reached 3,000, and frustration with the situation there was seen as having been a major factor in the outcome of the 2006 midterm elections, which gave Democrats control of Congress. Poised to succeed General George W. Casey Jr., whose 2006 plan for reducing troops in Iraq had failed, Petraeus stood to inherit a military command in a country with escalating sectarian violence. Also in January Bush announced his plan to deploy 21,500 more troops to secure Baghdad. "Bush and his senior advisers have been wrong so many times on Iraq that the public no longer trusts them to frame a successful strategy," David Ignatius wrote in an op-ed piece for the *Washington Post* (January 24, 2007, on-line). "So now the public face of the war passes to a bright, ambitious general. It is an intensely political role, and it puts Petraeus in a hot seat that many military officers try to avoid." On January 22 Petraeus submitted written testimony to the Senate Armed Services Committee, in which he outlined a number of the errors he thought the U.S. government had made in Iraq, including inadequate planning of the occupation; failure to recognize the emergence of the insurgency; insufficient numbers of troops; and a mishandling of the election. During his January 23 hearing with the Senate Armed Services Committee, he called the situation in Iraq "dire." The next day, during further testimony before the Senate, Petraeus—who had been characterized up until then as politically neutral—surprised some when he argued against a possible Democrat-led Senate resolution against the troop surge. Some senators were skeptical about both the surge and Petraeus, whose support of the troop increase seemed to conflict with the guidelines of his counterinsurgency manual; according to the ratios in the manual, a total of 120,000 troops would be needed to secure Baghdad, a number that would not nearly be reached with the 21,500 additional troops whose deployment Bush proposed and Petraeus publicly supported. "It appears, also, General, that the strategy that is being put forth here inspires skepticism for good reason," Hillary Rodham Clinton, a Democrat from New York, said during the hearing, according to the Associated Press. "This escalation, despite the rhetoric about other goals, places primary emphasis on American military involvement, not Iraqi institutions. The manual makes clear the interconnections of political and military progress [and] that one cannot be achieved without the other." Petraeus noted that 325,000 Iraqis had been trained, though he added, "They are not all reliable." Despite senators' doubts about the plan for Iraq, Petraeus was confirmed in a unanimous vote on January 27.

On September 10, 2007 Petraeus appeared before the Senate Foreign Relations Committee and Armed Services Committee to report on the situation in Iraq. He advised against the major troop reductions urged by some Democrats. Referring to a Defense Intelligence Agency report issued a month earlier, he said that he agreed that a "rapid withdrawal would result in the further release of the strong centrifugal forces in Iraq and produce a number of dangerous results." He also said that military objectives were being met and that he had recommended to President Bush the withdrawal by the summer of 2008 of the roughly 30,000 additional troops sent to Iraq after January 2007, with about 130,000 troops remaining there.

Not surprisingly, opinions on Petraeus's testimony were mixed, with most—but not all—Republicans in Congress expressing their satisfaction with it and nearly all Democrats dismissing much of what he had said as part of a disinformation campaign orchestrated by the White House. Adding to the heat of the public debate about the merits of Petraeus's statistics and predictions was a full-page advertisement placed in the *New York Times* by the liberal activist group MoveOn.org. Appearing on the day that Petraeus spoke to the committee members, the ad accused the general of "cooking the books for the White House" and charged that although Petraeus had claimed that violence in Iraq had decreased, the Pentagon's "bizarre formula for keeping tabs on violence" left many violent incidents, along with numbers of Iraqis wounded and killed, uncounted. What sparked by far the biggest outcry was not the text of the ad but its headline, which read "General Petraeus or General Betray Us?" That ad hominem attack drew condemnation from both supporters and opponents of the Bush administration's policy in Iraq. The House and Senate passed resolutions condemning the ad.

Predictions are divided as to whether Petraeus can succeed in stabilizing Iraq. Even some of his supporters doubt that anyone can significantly improve conditions in what many view as a quagmire. "Petraeus is being given a losing hand . . . ," the retired army general Barry R. McCaffrey told Atkinson. "The war is unmistakably going in the wrong direction. The only good news in all this is that Petraeus is so incredibly intelligent and creative." For his part, Petraeus—who has said that he does not vote so as to maintain his political neutrality—asserts that his job is not to make policy, but to implement it. "I truly think that the Army is best served when its leaders adopt a professional approach that includes, of course, the principle of civilian control of the military," he told Fichtner. "This is a hugely important principle. Our elected officials determine the objectives, and soldiers figure out the resources required and the risks involved."

In his 2004 interview with Nordland, Petraeus's outlook about Iraq's future was positive. "There are limits to what you can do," he said. "There are limits, but actually, damn few." In his 2007 Senate confirmation hearing, Petraeus spoke with a decidedly different tone. "Many of the e-mails I've received in recent weeks have had as their subject line 'Congratulations—I think,'" he said, as quoted by Tyson. "I know how heavy a rucksack I will have to shoulder in Iraq."

Petraeus, who is a compact five feet nine inches and 155 pounds, is known to challenge soldiers half his age to push-up contests and mile-long races—and win. Two months after graduating from West Point, he married Holly Knowlton, the daughter of army general William A. Knowlton, who was then the superintendent of the academy. The couple have two grown children.

—C.S.

Suggested Reading: *Frontline* (on-line) Nov. 23, 2003; *New York Times* A p1+ Jan. 6, 2007; *Newsweek* (on-line) July 5, 2004; *Spiegel* (on-line) Dec. 18, 2006; *U.S. News & World Report* (on-line) Oct. 31, 2005; *Wall Street Journal* A p1+ Nov. 3, 2003; *Washington Post* (on-line) Jan. 7, 2007; *Weekly Standard* (on-line) Jan. 29, 2007

Courtesy of michaelpollan.com

Pollan, Michael

Feb. 6, 1955– Journalist; writer; editor; educator

Address: Graduate School of Journalism, 121 North Gate Hall #5860, University of California, Berkeley, CA 94720

Michael Pollan has described himself as a nature writer who does not enjoy camping in the great outdoors. "There are a lot of common threads through my books," Pollan told Dave Weich for Powells.com (May 11, 2006). "In retrospect, they're all about nature. They're all about our relationship to the natural world, but I look to nature closer to home. . . . I like finding nature where we don't usually look for it. We usually look for it in the wilderness and the woods, but of course it's all around us. I find that's the unplowed ground in American writing about nature, the places where nature and culture cannot help but engage and change one another." In his four best-known books—*Second Nature: A Gardener's Education*, *A Place of My Own: The Education of an Amateur Builder*, *The Botany of Desire: A Plant's-Eye View of the World*, and *The Omnivore's Dilemma: A Natural History of Four Meals*—Pollan has focused on the importance of

people's connections to their natural surroundings, enriching and enlivening his discussions with accounts of his own experiences as a backyard gardener, neophyte carpenter, and enthusiastic, informed eater. For example, for *The Omnivore's Dilemma*—which vividly describes the principal means of production of the foods Americans eat and the implications of each process for the individual, society, and the environment—Pollan not only took on the role of researcher and investigative reporter but also grew, foraged for, or hunted and butchered all the ingredients for a meal that he prepared himself. A best-seller, *The Omnivore's Dilemma* won several book awards and was chosen as one of the 10 best books of 2006 by the *New York Times*, the *Washington Post*, and the *Boston Globe*, and it reinforced Pollan's reputation as an expert and a leader in the movement for what has become known as socially responsible eating.

Pollan, who began his career in journalism before he entered college, served as an editor at *Harper's Magazine* from 1983 until 2003, and since 1995 he has been a contributing writer at the *New York Times Magazine*. Articles by him have been included in many anthologies, among them *The Best American Essays* (1990 and 2003 editions), *The Norton Anthology of Nature Writing* (2001), *The New Humanities Reader* (2005), and *American Food Writing* (2007). His skill in cultivating the "unplowed ground" in literary territory linked with such earlier writers as Henry David Thoreau (author of *Walden*), Upton Sinclair (*The Jungle*), Rachel Carson (*Silent Spring*), and Frances Moore Lappé (*Diet for a Small Planet*) has earned him such honors as the John Burroughs Prize for best natural history essay, in 1997; the Reuters–World Conservation Union Global Award for excellence in environmental journalism, in 2000; the Genesis Award from the Humane Society of the United States, in 2002; and the James Beard Award for best writing on food, in 2007. In *Newsday* (April 30, 2006), Josh Ozersky described Pollan as "a botany writer of such unparalleled imaginative power that he makes plants seem human—all too human"; Jim Downing, writing for the *Sacramento (California) Bee* (November 26, 2006), called him "the nation's most articulate champion of alternative food systems." "The culture wants to have a conversation on these issues," Pollan told Downing. "You have to speak while it's listening." In 2003 Pollan was named the Knight professor of journalism at the Graduate School of Journalism of the University of California at Berkeley, where he directs the Knight Program in Science and Environmental Journalism.

One of the four children of Stephen Pollan and Corky Pollan, Michael Pollan was born on February 6, 1955 and grew up in a suburban town on Long Island, New York. He has three sisters; one of them is the actress Tracy Pollan, who is married to the actor Michael J. Fox. His father is an attorney, life coach, financial consultant, and the author or co-author of many books, among them *It's All in*

Your Head: Thinking Your Way to Happiness, *Lifescripts: What to Say to Get What You Want in Life's Toughest Situations*, and *Die Broke: A Radical Four-Part Financial Plan*. His mother wrote the "Best Bets" column and cover articles for *New York* magazine for 17 years; currently, she is the style director for *Gourmet*. When Pollan was 10, his father, who hated lawns, gave the boy permission to plant what Pollan described in *The Omnivore's Dilemma* as a "farm" in the family's yard. "The mysteries of germination and flowering and fruiting engaged me from an early age," he recalled in that book, "and the fact that by planting and working an ordinary patch of dirt you could in a few months' time harvest things of taste and value was, for me, nature's most enduring astonishment. It still is."

In the summer of 1973, the year he graduated from high school, Pollan worked as a reporter for the *Vineyard (Massachusetts) Gazette*. He attended Bennington College, in Vermont, where he majored in English; he spent one undergraduate year studying English literature at Oxford University, in England. For three summers beginning in 1974, he worked at the *Village Voice*, in New York City, as an assistant editor. After his graduation, in 1977, Pollan was hired as an assistant editor at the short-lived alternative newspaper *Politicks & Other Human Interests*, which folded in 1978. That year he worked as an associate producer for *A House Divided*, a syndicated TV documentary about the U.S. House of Representatives. In 1980 Pollan helped to produce *Straight Talk*, a daily public-affairs talk show. Next, in 1981, supported by a school fellowship, he earned a master's degree in English from Columbia University, in New York City. From 1981 to 1983 he was a senior editor at *Channels*, a nonprofit magazine covering telecommunications.

In 1983 Pollan joined the staff of *Harper's* as a senior editor; two years later he was promoted to executive editor, in charge of the editorial staff and budget and other aspects of the magazine's daily management. *Harper's* won six National Magazine Awards while Pollan was executive editor. "I got my training as a journalist, in large part, at *Harper's* . . . ," Pollan told Russell Schoch for *California Monthly* (December 2004, on-line), the alumni magazine of the University of California at Berkeley. "The editor, Lewis Lapham, insisted that the writers of our big pieces put in a paragraph somewhere that sort of declares where they're coming from—why they cared about a subject, and where they were standing." Lapham did so, Pollan continued, "because he thought that writers hid behind the convention of the third-person omniscient objective journalist, which allowed them to write a very slanted article, all the while pretending that they were absolutely disinterested. He felt that writing, finally, is an individual talking; we shouldn't forget that there is a man or woman behind these sentences, and we should know where he or she is coming from. I find a lot of truth in

that." He also said, "I think perfect objectivity is an unrealistic goal; fairness, however, is not. Fairness forces you—even when you're writing a piece highly critical of, say, genetically modified food, as I have done—to make sure you represent the other side as extensively and as accurately as you possibly can. . . . In my writing I've always been interested in finding places to stand, and I've found it very useful to have a direct experience of what I'm writing about. For example, when I bought a steer as part of writing about the cattle industry, the fact that I owned a steer forced me to give more credence to and to be more fair to points of view I disagreed with. I was able to understand the logic of why you would give a hormone implant to a steer: There is essentially no way you could make money in the system if you didn't do that."

In 1995 Pollan reduced his duties at *Harper's*, serving as a contributing editor until 2003. Meanwhile, in 1995 he became a contributing writer for the *New York Times Magazine*, a position he still holds. His many articles for the magazine have included "The Pot Proposition: Living with Medical Marijuana" (July 27, 1997); "A Very Fine Line" (September 12, 1999), about shifting views regarding certain drugs and their legality; "Produce Politics" (January 14, 2001), about the introduction of "eco labels" on supermarket products, in which Pollan wrote, "Food that comes with a story—whether it's organic, fairly traded, humanely grown, sustainably caught or whatever—represents a not-so-implicit challenge to every other product in the supermarket that dares not narrate its path from farm to table"; "Power Steer" (March 31, 2002), for which he bought a steer and then traveled to Kansas, where the animal was being raised, "to find out how a modern, industrial steak is produced in America these days, from insemination to slaughter"; "The (Agri)Cultural Contradictions of Obesity" (October 12, 2003), in which he linked the rising incidence of obesity in the U.S. to the overabundance of corn and the ubiquity of such corn-derived products as fructose, a consequence of federal subsidies to corn growers; "Our National Eating Disorder" (October 17, 2004), about dietary fads in the U.S.—"how little it takes to set off . . . nutritional swings in America; a scientific study, a new government guideline, a lone crackpot with a medical degree can alter this nation's diet overnight"—and the difficulty many Americans have in deciding what to eat in a time when there are thousands of choices in any supermarket; "The Vegetable-Industrial Complex" (October 15, 2006), in which he stated, "These days, the way we farm and the way we process our food, both of which have been industrialized and centralized over the last few decades, are endangering our health"; and "Unhappy Meals" (January 28, 2007), which began, "Eat food. Not too much. Mostly plants. That, more or less, is the short answer to the supposedly incredibly complicated and confusing question of what we humans should eat in order to be maximally healthy." Working concurrently, from 1998 to 1999, as a *New York Times Magazine* contributing editor, Pollan assisted with six special issues marking the coming of the 21st century. He also oversaw the production of the issue (December 5, 1999) about the *New York Times* time capsule, which was the most successful issue in the magazine's history.

Earlier, with Lewis Lapham and Eric Etheridge, Pollan compiled *The Harper's Index Book* (1987), a compendium of statistics from the magazine's "Harper's Index" column, in such categories as social studies, history, economics, communications, and science. With his father and Mark Levine, Pollan wrote *Field Guide to Home Buying in America* (1988). His next book, *Second Nature: A Gardener's Education* (1991), about his efforts to cultivate a garden in the rocky five acres surrounding his suburban Connecticut home, was named one of the 75 best gardening books of the century by the American Horticultural Society. In a representative assessment for the *EPA Journal* (March/April 1991), published by the U.S. Environmental Protection Agency, Douglas Lea wrote, "*Second Nature* artfully dodges the snares that typically plague books on gardening and nature. Loaded with how-to information, it nevertheless avoids becoming an arid recitation of familiar facts and data. Committed to a high standard of environmental citizenship, it avoids preaching. . . . And, written by a real writer, it avoids rhapsodizing about nature. . . . To his everlasting credit, Pollan uses the deceptively simple device of a garden book to reinvigorate conversations about our environment, about our places and our surroundings . . . [and] ties down-to-earth gardening to larger, more global concerns. In the end, he succeeds magnificently." In *Newsweek* (April 29, 1991), Malcolm Jones Jr. wrote that Pollan had "written a book about gardening that even nongardeners might want to read." Although Jones complained that "for long stretches in this book Pollan is so sober and fair-minded you just want to slug him," he acknowledged, "When he's critiquing our relationship to nature, Pollan is uncommonly sensible." A decade later Mark Tredinnick, writing for the *Canberra (Australia) Times* (November 3, 2001), praised *Second Nature* as "full of humour and shapely prose" and wrote that the book revealed Pollan to be "one of the best essayists and prose stylists around."

In *A Place of My Own: The Education of an Amateur Builder* (1997), Pollan related the process of building in his backyard a shack to be used as a writing studio. "I'd be a lesser person if I hadn't had that experience," he said to Karol Menzie for the *Baltimore (Maryland) Sun* (August 24, 1997) about the project, which took far longer and proved to be far more costly than he had anticipated. Reviewers' reactions to the book were mixed. Among those who expressed disappointment was Jonathan Yardley, who wrote for the *Washington Post* (April 9, 1997), "Pollan could not resist the temptation to intellectualize. Though he does not completely scant his education as a carpenter, it plays second fiddle to his somewhat gassy ruminations on the deeper meaning of it all. . . . Though *A Place of My Own* has its charms, they are fewer than one hopes for and expects." By contrast, Verlyn Klinkenborg wrote for the *New York Times Book Review* (March 16, 1997), "One of the things that make Mr. Pollan such an attractive writer is the modest way he presents his discoveries. . . . The role he assigns himself here isn't that of buffoon, though slapstick dogs an amateur carpenter, or that of sage, though sagacity abounds in this book. Mr. Pollan takes the role of the self: deliberative, half-amused and tolerant."

In *The Botany of Desire: A Plant's-Eye View of the World* (2001), Pollan wrote about people's desire for sweetness (in apples), beauty (in tulips), intoxication (from marijuana, derived from the cannabis plant), and control (as exemplified by genetically modified potatoes that become "perfect" french fries)—to examine how humans and plants have interacted throughout history. "In a common schoolbook image of evolution, all forms of life are represented by the forking branches of a vast tree," Christopher Hewat noted in a review of *The Botany of Desire* for the *Wilson Quarterly* (Summer 2001). "This scheme positions man and his fellow mammals far from their green cousins, the elms, algaes, and artichokes. Pollan . . . shows how the evolutionary branches of man and plant have come to be intertwined, with complicated consequences for each. In a meditation by turns poetic, historical, and scientific, he traces the reciprocal strategies of the cultivator and the cultivated. If man has moved nature by domesticating certain plants, so nature has moved man, first by stimulating his desires, and then by evolving to gratify them." "It's an absorbing subject, and Pollan brings a clutch of quirky talents to the task of exploring it," Burkhard Bilger wrote for the *New York Times Book Review* (June 3, 2001). "He has a wide-ranging intellect, an eager grasp of evolutionary biology and a subversive streak that helps him root out some wonderfully counterintuitive points. His prose both shimmers and snaps." Bilger went on to complain, though, that *The Botany of Desire* "can be a maddening book. Pollan . . . doesn't just walk us through this material, he swoons and pirouettes his way through it, scattering ideas like so many seeds . . . True, circling the same ground sometimes leads him to startling new ideas, but more often he simply overburdens his subjects." *The Botany of Desire* was named the best book of the year by Amazon.com and the American Booksellers Association.

After the publication of *The Botany of Desire*, Pollan's writings focused increasingly on responsible eating. Responsible eating, in his view, is a subjective term. Primarily, people who are responsible eaters make it their business to be aware of where their food comes from, be it a small, local farm, a huge farm owned by corporation, a farm on which produce or cattle are raised organically, or one that employs conventional means (with heavy use of fertilizers and pesticides for plants, or, in the case of animals, with manufactured foods, vitamins, and other products that such animals do not normally consume). Responsible eaters then use that information in choosing the foods that they buy. Pollan also began to investigate in depth the political and economic ramifications of the U.S. government's agriculture policies and consumers' attitudes about food. In his view, one of the biggest problems regarding food in the U.S. is the overproduction of corn, which damages the environment by impeding crop diversity and causing pollution from fertilizer runoff; threatens consumer health; and requires tremendous consumption of oil, which in turn has made the U.S. dependent on oil from the Middle East and elsewhere. ("It takes a half gallon of fossil fuel to produce a bush of corn," Pollan told Russell Schoch.) "The great lesson of ecology is that everything is connected. And it's true. So next time you're reaching for that cheap food, you might ask, is it really so cheap?" Pollan said on the PBS series *Frontline* (April 18, 2002, on-line). He told Schoch, "We're paying for a 99-cent burger in our health-care bills, in our environmental cleanup bills, in our military budget, and in the disappearance of the family farm. So it really isn't cheap at all."

"When you can eat just about anything nature has to offer, deciding what you should eat will inevitably stir anxiety," Pollan wrote in his most recent book, *The Omnivore's Dilemma: A Natural History of Four Meals* (2006). That decision is the omnivore's dilemma, one that has only grown more complicated in recent years as the variety of foods has increased manyfold and food has become an increasingly globalized commodity. "Is knowledge about our food a burden or a pleasure? A lot of people don't want to know where their 99-cent hamburger comes from, in the same way that people don't want to know how their sausage is made," Pollan told Weich. "There are people happy to eat in ignorance. Ignorance is bliss, but it's a very fleeting bliss, an empty pleasure, I think, compared to eating in full knowledge of what is involved." For *The Omnivore's Dilemma*, Pollan investigated four channels through which food arrives in stores. In the first section of the book, which discusses foods produced by corporate farms and factories, Pollan examined the American overreliance on corn. In the second, which focuses on organic food produced by corporate farms, he argued that the activities of grocery chains such as Whole Foods are not as good for the environment as they might seem; for example, most of Whole Foods' produce comes from large farms in California and has to be shipped across the country, with considerable environmental costs. In the third section of *The Omnivore's Dilemma*, Pollan described the work of a farmer who practiced sustainable farming (the aims of which include environmental conservation and equitable labor conditions). For the fourth section Pollan cooked a meal made entirely from products he himself grew or killed. (The main dish was meat from a feral pig.) "Perhaps that's what the perfect meal is: one that's been fully paid for, that leaves no debts outstanding," Pollan wrote of that meal, in a piece adapted from the book for the *New York Times Magazine* (March 26, 2006). "This is almost impossible ever to do, which is why, real as it was, there was nothing very realistic about this meal. Yet as a sometimes thing, as a kind of ritual, a meal that is eaten in full consciousness of what it took to make is worth preparing every now and again, if only as a way to remind us of the true cost of our food, and that, no matter what we eat, we eat by the grace not of industry but of nature."

The Omnivore's Dilemma won the California Book Award and the Northern California Book Award and was a finalist for the National Book Critics Circle Award. "Michael Pollan has perfected a tone—one of gleeful irony and barely suppressed outrage—and a way of inserting himself into a narrative so that a subject comes alive through what he's feeling and thinking," Patric Kuh wrote in an assessment of the book for the *Los Angeles Times* (April 9, 2006). "He is a master at drawing back to reveal the greater issues." David Kamp, in a critique for the *New York Times Book Review* (April 23, 2006), wrote that Pollan's "supermeticulous reporting is the book's strength—you're not likely to get a better explanation of exactly where your food comes from." "If I have any caveats about *The Omnivore's Dilemma*," Kamp added, "it's Pollan's tendency to be too nice. . . . Likewise, I wish Pollan would stick his neck out and be more prescriptive about how we might realistically address our national eating disorder." Pollan, however, has often expressed his reluctance to tell people how to eat. Instead, he advocates making informed decisions about food purchases. "I think the key is to have a lot of transparency in the food system," he told Downing, "so people can see the implications of their choices—and then make choices that are consistent with their own ethics." He said to Terry Gross for the National Public Radio program *Fresh Air* (April 11, 2006, on-line), "I don't think you can call yourself an environmentalist if you're thoughtless about your eating. It's too important a relationship to the rest of the world."

Pollan lives in Berkeley, California, with his wife, the painter Judith Belzer, and their son, Isaac. He and his family eat mainly locally grown food; sometimes, though, he shops at Whole Foods and eats a meal at McDonald's.

—C.S.

Suggested Reading: *Baltimore (Maryland) Sun* L p1 Aug. 24, 1997; *California Monthly* (Dec. 2004, on-line); *Fresh Air* (on-line) June 7, 2002, Apr. 11, 2006; Michael Pollan's Web site; *San Francisco Chronicle Magazine* p10 May 2, 2004; powells.com May 11, 2006; *Sacramento (California) Bee* D p1+ Nov. 26, 2006; truthdig.com Apr. 11, 2006

Selected Books: *The Harper's Index Book* (with Lewis H. Lapham and Eric Etheridge), 1987; *Field Guide to Home Buying in America* (with Stephen M. Pollan and Mark Levine), 1988; *Second Nature: A Gardener's Education*, 1991; *A Place of My Own: The Education of an Amateur Builder*, 1997; *The Botany of Desire: A Plant's-Eye View of the World*, 2001; *The Omnivore's Dilemma: A Natural History of Four Meals*, 2006

Matthew Stockman/Getty Images

Prado, Edgar

June 12, 1967– Jockey

Address: c/o The Jockeys Guild, P.O. Box 150, Monrovia, CA 91017

Only a few strides into the 2006 Preakness Stakes, the Kentucky Derby–winning racehorse and Triple Crown hopeful Barbaro took a high-speed stumble, breaking his right hind leg in several places. During his undefeated career, Barbaro had risen to hero status, providing a rallying point for a beleaguered America much like the famed racehorses Seabiscuit and Secretariat. The Preakness injury, however, not only ended Barbaro's hopes of being the first Triple Crown winner since 1978, but also threatened to end his life, with only the quick thinking of the jockey Edgar Prado, who pulled the horse up immediately, giving Barbaro any chance of survival. Though Barbaro had to be euthanized a little over six months later for complications related to surgery, the horse's story—from a dominating victory to heartbreaking injury to miraculous recovery to slowly degenerating condition—had

made Barbaro and his jockey two of the most celebrated figures to come out of horseracing in years. Prado, one of the preeminent jockeys in the horseracing world, began riding horses in his native Peru, leaving for the United States in 1986 after having become the top Peruvian jockey. By the mid-1990s he had established himself in the Maryland racing world, leading the nation in victories for three consecutive years, with 536 wins in 1997, 470 wins in 1998, and 402 wins in 1999. In 2002, three years after he moved to New York, Prado won the Belmont Stakes, following up that victory with another Belmont win in 2004 as well as two Breeders' Cup wins in 2005 and one in 2006—a year he finished second in the nation in purse earnings, with $19,765,013. Never one to dwell on either his victories or his defeats, Prado said in 2004—when he had not yet won a Breeders' Cup (an event composed of a series of races), despite having competed in 33 races—that he had no regrets. "I only look forward. I cannot start over," he told Jennie Rees for the Louisville, Kentucky, *Courier Journal* (October 26, 2004). "I have to concentrate on what I want to do today. Tomorrow is another day." He voiced a similar sentiment after Barbaro's Derby win, expressing the optimism he would maintain throughout the horse's ultimately failed recovery. "I always think positive. I always try to do something in a better way," he told Tom Pedulla for *USA Today* (May 16, 2006). "Even if you achieve something, you can't be standing in one place."

Prado "tries to correct himself; he wants to be perfect," his wife, Liliana, told Mike Klingaman for the *Baltimore Sun* (December 22, 1998) upon Prado's winning 1,000 races in only two years, a rare feat. "He always says, 'I should have done this,' or 'I shouldn't have done that.' He wants to be the best." Steve Rushing, Prado's agent from 1988 to 1999, told Pedulla that Prado's understanding of horses gives him a distinct advantage over other jockeys. "You can't teach them to communicate with a horse. Some people have it; some people don't," he said. "Edgar definitely, definitely has it." Horseracing is "a game of mistakes," Prado said to Pedulla. "Sometimes you have a fraction of a second to make a decision. If you second-guess yourself that you think you might make a mistake, you might as well stay in the jockeys room."

The 10th of 11 children and the youngest of eight boys, Edgar Prado was born on June 12, 1967 in Lima, Peru. His father, Jose, had wanted to be a jockey, but because he could not keep his weight down, he became a trainer instead. Jose Prado hoped that one of his sons would become a jockey; two of Edgar's brothers became involved in horseracing—Jorge, a former jockey, is now a trainer in Maryland, and Anibal is a jockey at Philadelphia Park. Edgar Prado was exposed to the profession at an early age, mucking out stables beginning when he was five. With money tight—all 13 members of the family lived in a one-bedroom, one-bathroom apartment—the Prados relied heavily on Anibal's early winnings as a jockey for financial support.

400   CURRENT BIOGRAPHY YEARBOOK 2007

"When I first started riding, I would watch everything he would do," Prado recalled to Bill Finley for the *New York Times* (May 10, 2006). "He was my idol, not just as a rider, but as a brother and a person." When he was seven Prado began selling fruit on the street to bring in extra income. He remained involved with horses, however, beginning to exercise them at 14 and to race at 15. He came in last in his first race; with his future as a jockey uncertain, he continued to attend high school faithfully, with plans to become a lawyer. Prado won his first race in October 1983 on the mount Tatin, starting what would become an extremely successful career in Peru. During his two years of riding there, he became the top jockey in the country, leading him to try his luck in the United States.

At 17 Prado made a house payment for the family before taking $3,000 of his savings with him to Miami, Florida, becoming the first member of his family to go to the U.S. Once there, he spent nearly all of the money on lawyers' fees in an attempt to obtain a work visa. Finding little paid work, he exercised horses for free at the Calder Race Course, in Miami, in the mornings. He soon ran out of money altogether, calling a brother to ask for $500 and promising that if that money ran out, too, he would return to Peru. Despite the many setbacks he faced, Prado persisted, largely thanks to the encouragement from his family, particularly his mother, Zenaida. "I knew maybe two people here. I didn't speak English. I didn't know how to drive. But I had my goals and dreams," he recalled to Pedulla. His first win as a jockey in the U.S. came on June 1, 1986 at the Calder Race Course, on a horse named Single Love. Subsequent successes gave him the money to bring three of his siblings to the United States. In 1988 he married a woman named Liliana, the daughter of a track veterinarian he had met while competing in Peru.

In 1989 Prado moved to Maryland to race, beginning a period that would establish him as a top-level jockey in a race-course circuit that was larger than Florida's but still much smaller than that in New York, the biggest horseracing center in the U.S. His first victory at Laurel was on a long shot, Long Allure, who broke from the pack to win by four lengths in a move that would become a kind of Prado trademark. He became known among the other jockeys for an abrasive, competitive personality that often resulted in physical fights away from the racetrack. "I was kind of reckless then," Prado recalled to Mike Klingaman. "Sometimes, I would just push my way through other horses. Now, I make sure no one will get hurt. At first, I tried too hard to win, and to prove to myself that I could ride. I changed gradually. When you win, you ride with a more cool head." Meanwhile, he was involved in numerous accidents on the track. In 1991 he was thrown from his horse and rushed to the hospital for X-rays, returning to Pimlico in time for his last race of the day. In 1993 he somersaulted forward from his horse; the accident was so severe that the horse broke a leg, but Prado simply

changed his silks and went on to win three races that day. Two years later Prado suffered his biggest setback up to that time, when a filly named Machinegungirl crumpled during a race, slamming Prado to the ground, an accident that broke his back, pelvis, and collarbone. Prado could not race for three and a half months, during which he rode a mechanical horse at home as rehabilitation.

In those years Prado slowly became the top jockey in Maryland and gained attention elsewhere, leading the U.S. in victories for three consecutive years and winning the 1994 Young Jockeys World Championship at Japan's Nakayama Race Course. In 1997 he had 536 wins, making him the fourth rider to win 500 races in a single year; he had 470 wins in 1998 and 402 in 1999. Prado and his wife bought a five-and-a-half-acre farm in Howard County, Maryland, that they named Leariva Farm, after a favorite mount of Prado's. Decorated with two iron statues of jockeys at the door, the farm was home to several old track ponies Prado had rescued from the usual, bleak lot of such animals.

In 1999 Prado got his chance to prove himself in New York, when the jockey Richard Migliore, who regularly rode for the trainer John Kimmel, was injured, and Kimmel needed a new rider. For Prado, accepting the job meant leaving the place where he had established himself. The decision was a hard one for Prado, whose family was living happily on the farm and whose agent, Steve Rushing, was also content in Maryland. But he decided to move, signing with a new representative, Bob Frieze. The move quickly paid off: Prado won 36 races at the 1999 Saratoga meet, second only to the jockey Jerry Bailey. But even as Prado won more and more races, victories in the biggest contests—the Kentucky Derby, Belmont Stakes, Preakness Stakes, and Breeders' Cup—continued to evade him. In 2002 Prado rode Harlan's Holiday—the favorite to win—in the Kentucky Derby, and, anticipating his first major victory, brought his mother to the track. Instead, Harlan's Holiday finished in a disappointing seventh place. Before the race, Prado had expressed his usual attitude, telling Tom Keyser for the *Baltimore Sun* (May 1, 2002), "I've got lots more goals to achieve. Every day you come in here you want to win a race. Yesterday is history, and tomorrow is a mystery. You live in today trying to achieve as much as you can." While the loss was demoralizing, Prado scored an enormous victory just a few weeks later at the Belmont Stakes, where he and his mount, Sarava, beat War Emblem, a contender for the Triple Crown—the seldom-achieved combined wins in the Kentucky Derby, Belmont Stakes, and Preakness Stakes. At odds of 70¼ to one, Sarava was the longest shot ever at the Belmont Stakes to win, a victory credited largely to Prado's skillful maneuvering.

In March 2004 Prado won the 5,000th race of his career, riding Wynn Dot Comma in the Swale Stakes, at Gulfstream Park, in Florida. Three months later, again at Belmont Stakes, Prado defeated another Triple Crown contender, Smarty

Jones, who had captured much of the country's attention and affection. Prado and his mount, Birdstone, closed Smarty Jones's four-length lead to win by a length. "I'm very sorry that happened, but I had to do my job," Prado told Joe Drape for the *New York Times* (June 6, 2004), explaining that he had been rooting for Smarty Jones to win and secure the Triple Crown. "I'm happy and sad—sad because I was looking forward to a Triple Crown. This sport needs heroes." Prado had ridden Birdstone only after that horse ran poorly with another jockey, who switched to a different mount for the Derby. Birdstone then missed the Bluegrass, came in eighth in the Derby, and missed the Preakness. Prado stuck with him, though, through the victory at Belmont. "Maybe you can ride for 'now,' but I don't do that," Prado told Rees, explaining his reluctance to abandon a mount. "In this business you lose more than you win. But when you win, you want to do it the right way. . . . It's important that you're happy and other people are happy for you." In 2005 Prado won two Breeders' Cup races, riding Juvenile Fillies and Sprint; the following year he won the Breeders' Cup Distaff. He continued giving most of the credit for his success to the horses themselves. "I feel very happy and very proud of myself," he told Rees. "It took a lot of hard work and a lot of good horses to take me there. You cannot go to the Indy 500 riding a Honda. In order to show you can ride, you have to have the ammunition to do it."

With Barbaro, Prado got the ammunition he had long sought. Despite a reported falling-out in 2004 with Barbaro's trainer, Michael Matz, when Prado chose another horse over Matz's Kitchen Kirs in the Arlington Million, Prado was chosen to ride the powerful colt in the Tropical Park Derby, Holy Bull Stakes, and Florida Derby, winning all three races. On May 6, 2006 Barbaro and Prado won the 132d Kentucky Derby, six and a half lengths ahead of the second-place finisher, in the largest margin of victory since the Triple Crown winner Assault won by eight lengths in 1946. Barbaro's enormous victory made him a national hero, as it seemed he would become the first Triple Crown winner since Affirmed was crowned in 1978. Prado said that the country was rallying around the horse, not him, to win the Triple Crown. "It would help everyone in racing because we need a hero," Prado told Richard Rosenblatt for the Associated Press (May 15, 2006). "And Barbaro would be the hero. I'm just the jockey." In the race, Barbaro, the Kentucky-bred son of Dynaformer, had stumbled a bit coming out of the gate, but he soon burst out of the pack, with little urging from Prado—who did not use a whip. "If he's running real hard, why should he be punished?" Prado explained to Pedulla. "I'm a horse lover more than anything else." Although jockeys typically try not to get attached to their mounts, both because of the high number of accidents on the track and because of the potential need to switch to a different mount at any time, Prado felt an unusual bond with Barbaro. "It was like love at

first sight," he told Hal Habib for the *Palm Beach (Florida) Post* (July 16, 2006). And while Prado typically refuses to dwell on the past or look very far ahead, his success with Barbaro prompted him, for once, to anticipate future victory.

On May 20, 2006, to the shock and sadness of racing fans and casual watchers alike, Barbaro fell early on in the Preakness, not only dashing hopes of a Triple Crown victory but putting his very survival into question. After a false start, Barbaro was reloaded into his gate; once the race began, he took a bad step after just a few strides, resulting in multiple fractures in his right hind leg. Prado's quick action in pulling Barbaro to a stop was widely credited with saving the colt's life at the time. While many feared the horse would be put down immediately, he was instead taken to the University of Pennsylvania's New Bolton Center, where he was given a 50-50 chance of survival, odds that worsened in the following months. Still, Prado remained optimistic. "As long as he's alive, there's hope," he told Habib. "It only takes maybe 1 percent to make the difference. I hope that 1 percent shows up. They say he has a 20 percent chance to survive. Why not give him that 20 percent chance? Why take it away from him?" Prado, who had long wanted to finance a monument at Laurel for the thoroughbreds that had been put down as a result of racing accidents, was deeply affected by Barbaro's accident. In 1998 he had described the bond between horse and rider to Klingaman: "The horse is your partner, your only friend in the race. People fall in love with these horses. To see one put down drives you crazy." Though he went back to riding immediately after Barbaro's accident, he told Sherry Ross for the New York *Daily News* (May 31, 2006) that returning to the racecourse was very difficult—but preferable to "staying home and doing nothing and doing too much thinking." Barbaro's accident came five months after Prado's mother, Zenaida, died of breast cancer; unable to obtain a new visa, she could not visit the United States, and Prado was unable to see her before her death. "This year has been a roller coaster for me," Prado told Habib. If anything, Prado added, the accident only deepened his relationship with Barbaro; the jockey visited his injured mount several times at the hospital. Still, he asserted that if there ever came a day when the pain was too great for the horse to endure, he would support euthanizing Barbaro. On January 29, 2007 Barbaro was euthanized at the New Bolton Center after a case of laminitis—an often fatal hoof disease—proved uncurable. Months before Barbaro's euthanasia, but months after his accident, Prado mourned the horse's potential. "Even though everybody says he won very convincingly, the Derby, nobody even saw his best yet," Prado told Habib. "Nobody saw what he could have done, what he could have been. Unfortunately, we won't. We can use only our imagination." Prado finished 18th in the 2007 Kentucky Derby, riding Scat Daddy; on May 18, 2007 he won the Black-Eyed Susan Stakes atop Panty Raid. As of the beginning of October 2007, according to the National Thoroughbred Racing Association (on-line), he ranked fourth in the U.S. in earnings so far that year, with $12,314,024, and had won 181 of the 979 races in which he had participated.

Prado and his wife, Liliana, have a daughter, Patricia, and two sons, Edgar Jr. and Luis. Prado won the National All-Star Jockey Championship in both 2000 and 2003 and was the recipient of the Four-stardave Award for Special Achievement, awarded at Saratoga by the New York Turf Writers Association, in both 2002 and 2005. In 2003 he became the 54th recipient of the George Woolf Memorial Award. Following his work with Barbaro in 2006, Prado was presented with the Mike Venezia Award, given to those "who exemplify extraordinary sportsmanship and citizenship" and named for the jockey Mike Venezia, who was killed in a 1988 accident at Belmont Park. Prado also received the ESPY Award and the Eclipse Award for outstanding jockey in 2006. Prado is a longtime supporter of Anna's House, a day-care center for the children of backstretch workers at Belmont Park.

—C.S.

Suggested Reading: *Baltimore Sun* D p1 Dec. 22, 1998; *Courier Journal* C p1 Oct. 26, 2004; *USA Today* (on-line) May 16, 2006; *Washington Post* B p1 Aug. 12, 1992

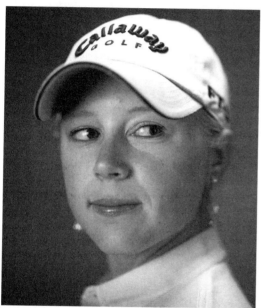

Robert Laberge/Getty Images

Pressel, Morgan

May 23, 1988– Professional golfer

Address: c/o LPGA, 100 International Golf Dr., Daytona Beach, FL 32124-1092

"I love to compete. I love the search for perfection. I'm constantly refining things, trying to be as perfect a player as I can be," the golfer Morgan Pressel told Dave Kindred for *Golf Digest* (February 1, 2006). Mentored and coached since the age of eight by her maternal grandfather, Herbert ("Herb") Krickstein, Pressel scored less than 80 on a nine-hole course when she was nine years old and broke 70 at 11. She was 12 when she qualified for the 2001 U.S. Women's Open, thus becoming the youngest female golfer ever to do so. (That record was broken in 2007 by Alexis Thompson.) During the next several years, Pressel won 11 American Junior Golf Association (AJGA) titles, among them—in the space of a single year—all five invitational events for which she was eligible. She was named a Rolex Junior All-American five times and selected for the All-American first team three times (in 2003, 2004, and 2005). A dominant secondary-school athlete, Pressel won three straight Florida State High School 1A titles (2003–05). In 2005 the AJGA named her the Girls Rolex Junior Player of the Year. Outstanding academically, Pressel turned down a golf scholarship offered by Duke University when—having had one of the most successful careers among American junior-level golfers—she decided to turn pro rather than attend college. She made her debut as a professional on February 16, 2006, a few months before both her high-school graduation and (thanks to a waiver of the age rule by the Ladies Professional Golf Association, or LPGA) her 18th birthday. During her rookie season she finished in the top 10 in nine of the 31 events in which she participated.

On April 1, 2007, at 18 years of age, Pressel won the Kraft Nabisco Tournament, making her the youngest golfer to date to capture a major LPGA title. That week, in the Rolex Women's World Golf Rankings, Pressel reached fourth place; as of October 1, 2007 she was in ninth place on that list, which is updated weekly. In other Rolex statistics compiled for the first nine months of 2007, Pressel had finished in the top 10 in eight of 20 events; made a hole in one; driven balls an average distance of 244.7 yards (about 32 yards fewer than the average of Karin Sjodin, the top woman in that category, and about 50 fewer than that of the top male, Tiger Woods); scored below par in 34 rounds, placing her sixth in the world in that category (Lorena Ochoa was first, with 51); and earned more than $900,000.

The five-foot five-inch Pressel has been described as tough-minded, exceptionally focused, fearless, fiercely competitive, outspoken, opinionated, and exuberant, with nerves of steel and a "blond-haired, fresh-faced, all-American look," as Dave Hyde wrote for the *Fort Lauderdale (Florida) Sun-Sentinel* (November 27, 2005). In mid-2005, when Carlos Monarrez interviewed her for the *Detroit (Michigan) Free Press* (July 6, 2005), Pressel had hung on her closet door a sign that read "Winning isn't a life or death situation. It's more important than that." "What I like best about her game is her consistency and the fact she doesn't appear to have any weaknesses," Herb Krickstein told Ryan O'Halloran for the *Newport News (Virginia) Daily Press* (May 4, 2005). Pressel told Hyde, "I want to be the best. No.1, Hall of Fame—all of it."

The first of the three children of Michael "Mike" J. Pressel and Kathryn "Kathy" Krickstein Pressel, both real-estate brokers, Morgan Lee Pressel was born in Tampa, Florida, on May 23, 1988 and grew up in Boca Raton, on the east coast of Florida. Earlier, her father had played ice hockey; her mother was a tennis champion at the University of Michigan during the 1970s and later taught tennis for two decades. Herb Krickstein, Pressel's maternal grandfather, played tennis, golf, and baseball as a young man and once was invited to try out for the Detroit Tigers, a Major League Baseball team. In 1963, at age 16, Morgan's uncle Aaron Krickstein became the youngest player ever to win an Association of Tennis Professionals (ATP) tournament; he was top-ranked in tennis (rising to sixth in the world) until injuries forced him to give up that sport, in the early 1970s. Morgan Pressel seemed destined for a tennis career until her grandfather noticed that although she displayed excellent hand-eye coordination, she was relatively slow on her feet. As an alternative, when she was eight, he introduced her to golf. At age nine she began getting weekly golf lessons with Martin Hall, a former European Tour professional whose wife, Lisa Hackney Hall, is a former member of the LPGA Tour. (As of May 2007 he was still her teacher.) Before long Pressel was accompanying her grandfather during his Sunday golf outings with his friends at the St. Andrews Country Club in Boca Raton. Soon, she was winning most of the rounds, and Krickstein took on the role of her coach. He gave himself a crash course in every aspect of the game, and after each day that Morgan played, he would critique her performance at every hole, thus helping her to get "a real feel for course management," as he told Charlie Nobles for the *New York Times* (May 29, 2001).

Pressel attended the Banyan Creek Elementary School, in Delray Beach, near Boca Raton, and the Omni Middle School, in Boca Raton. On May 14, 2001, after shooting a 70 to lead the field at a U.S. Women's Open qualifier, the 12-year-old Pressel, then a seventh-grader, became the youngest person ever to proceed past the qualifying events for that competition; afterward, she missed the final cut before the last round. (Beverly Klass competed in the Women's Open when she was only 10, in 1967, but that was nine years before the introduction of qualifying events.) The success of a preteenager led the LPGA to change the rules (by increasing the number of holes) so as to increase the difficulty of qualifying. In 2002 Pressel, who is Jewish, entered the St. Andrew's School, a nonsectarian, private high school associated with the Episcopal Church. That year she again made headlines, with her performance at the Ione D. Jones/Doherty Women's Amateur Championship, held at the Coral Ridge Country Club, in Fort Lauderdale, Florida. There, after trailing by five shots with six holes remaining, she birdied three holes (that is, hitting one below par for each) before sinking a 35-yard chip (a type of stroke) to eagle (hit two strokes below par) the final hole and advance to the finals. Although she lost the championship, to Aimee Cho, her success in reaching the finals greatly boosted her confidence, and she began to earn a reputation as a strong finisher. In 2002 she played with the triumphant U.S. team at the Ping Junior Solheim Cup, in which top American and top European golfers ages 13 through 17 compete every other year. Pressel failed to qualify for the 2002 U.S. Women's Open. According to Krickstein, that defeat may have been "the best thing to happen to her," as he told Craig Dolch for the Cox News Service (May 2, 2007, online). "You need to get knocked on your butt once in a while."

In September 2003 Pressel's mother died of breast cancer, at age 43. Afterward Pressel's relationship with her father soured, and she moved in with her maternal grandparents, Herb and Evelyn Krickstein, who lived 10 minutes from her childhood home. (Her sister, Madison, and brother, Mitchell, remained with their father; both siblings are now playing in junior amateur golf tournaments. Currently, Pressel and her father are said to have an amicable but cool relationship.) After a hiatus of six weeks following her mother's death, during which she withdrew from the Junior Solheim Cup, Pressel resumed competitive play. Krickstein, a retired pathologist, and his wife accompanied her on tours. During summers her grandparents took her to Grosse Pointe, Michigan, where they had raised their children, so that she could practice her sport in a different environment. Golf is an expensive pursuit at top amateur levels; Krickstein has estimated that within a few years, he spent $400,000 on Morgan's lessons, travel, housing, equipment, and tournament fees.

Meanwhile, in 2003–04, during her junior year at St. Andrew's School, in Boca Raton, Pressel earned a 3.9 grade-point average while taking several advanced-placement courses. Her favorite subjects were science and math; on the math portion of the Scholastic Aptitude Test (SAT), she reportedly scored 790 out of a possible 800. Unable to attend classes during the weeks (sometimes as many as 10 a year) when she played in amateur or junior tournaments, she would get her assignments by fax or e-mail and study on the road. As a member of her high-school golf team, she helped to coach her teammates and to lead them to three straight Florida state high-school titles. She is said to have displayed unfailing good nature in obliging opposing players and spectators who wanted her autograph or who asked to have their pictures taken with her at high-school competitions.

In June 2003, about two months after the beginning of that year's golf season, Pressel won the AJGA Buick Junior Open, presented by *Golfweek*, and a few days later, she won the AJGA Toldo Group Eastern Canadian Junior. After making the cut at the 2003 U.S. Women's Open, also in June, she finished 52d, with a total score of 304 (one 70 and three consecutive 78s), 20 over par. The following month the 15-year-old Pressel defeated 13-year-old Michelle Wie in the third round of the United States Girls' Junior Championship. In the same year Pressel won the Florida Junior Golf Association Tournament, setting a University of Florida course record of 64. For her accomplishments that year, she was crowned the Florida high-school individual champion and was selected as an AJGA first team All-American. She was also named the *South Florida Sun-Sentinel* high-school golfer of the year.

In June 2004 Pressel defeated Lisa Ferrero, a University of Texas senior and the 2000 U.S. Girls' Junior Champion, to become the youngest winner in the history of the North and South Women's Amateur Championship, a century-old, invitational event held in Pinehurst, North Carolina. (Invitational events are those in which participants are selected on the strength of their performance in national amateur championships and overall records.) Pressel clinched that match, in which the lead changed hands nine times, with a five-foot putt on the 36th hole. She was caddied by the celebrated, then–71-year-old Willie McRae, who had also served as her caddy three years earlier. "She's improved a whole lot," McRae told Charlie Bergmann for the North Carolina *Pilot* (June 30, 2004, on-line). "Chipping and putting, she's got all the shots. She hits them all better now. She's got a better attitude. She's a real nice girl." In July 2004 Pressel captured her seventh AJGA victory, at the Valero Texas Open Junior Shootout, in San Antonio, Texas, with a tournament total of four-under-par 212. Her margin of victory was 16 strokes, thus tying the record for that event. Also in July she won the Rolex Tournament of Champions—one of the principal competitions on the AJGA circuit; the following November she won the Polo Golf Junior Classic. She again became the Florida State Champion, winning the decisive tournament by 15 strokes, setting records with her single-round (62) and two-round (128) scores, the latter of which broke the previous low-score record (set by Beth Bauer in 1998) by nine strokes. She was the runner-up at the Junior Orange Bowl International and was again selected for the first team All-American. At the 2004 Canon Cup, she and her partner, her fellow Floridian Brittany Lincicome, triumphed over Amanda Blumenherst and Paula Creamer.

In January 2005 Pressel became the number-one–ranked golfer in the AJGA, after defeating the U.S. Girls' Junior Champion, Julieta Granada, in the final of the Harder Hall Invitational in Sebring, Florida. She earned AJGA victories at three additional invitational events—the Rolex Girls Junior Championship, the McDonald's Betsy Rawls Girls Championship (in which she had a hole in one on the third hole and won by an 11-shot margin), and the Thunderbird Invitational Junior. She also won the U.S. Women's Amateur and earned a second-place finish at the North and South Women's Amateur Golf Championship. At the U.S. Women's Open Pressel was tied for first place with Karen Stupples at the 72d, final hole when another competitor, Birdie Kim, made what was universally viewed as a highly improbable bunker shot and finished the match with a two-stroke lead over Pressel, who tied with Stupples for second place. When Pressel saw Kim's ball roll onto the green, she placed her hands on her head in an expression of disbelief and later wept, a reaction that sparked criticism from those who regarded her as a spoiled teenager or sore loser. (After that incident negative and positive comments about Pressel flooded Internet blogs.) In each of seven 2005 LPGA Tour events, Pressel finished 25th (in a tie) or better against professional golfers. Also in 2005 she helped lead the U.S. team to victory in the Junior Solheim Cup and placed fifth in the State Farm Classic, in which only one other amateur participated. In August, surmounting persistent, intense heat and humidity, she captured the U.S. Women's Amateur Championship, a week-long tournament held in a suburb of Atlanta, Georgia. "She is the best junior golfer I've ever seen," Steve Ethun, the director of communications of the AJGA, told Emily J. Minor for the *Palm Beach (Florida) Post* (August 14, 2005).

Pressel won a golf scholarship to Duke University, in Durham, North Carolina, a school whose women's golf team won the National Athletic Collegiate Association (NCAA) championship in 2005, 2006, and 2007. Her success at the U.S. Open, however, led her to abandon her plans of entering college and to pursue tennis full-time as a professional. "A few LPGA players told me they didn't think college golf would help my game," she told E. M. Swift and Jim Suttie for *Sports Illustrated* (August 8, 2005). "I'm ready to go out and make a difference." Traditionally, LPGA Tour members must be at least 18, but individuals can petition for a waiver of that rule. When Pressel did so, the organization's commissioner at that time, Ty Votaw, told her that she would be permitted to attend the LPGA's qualifying school after she graduated from high school but could not become a full professional until her 18th birthday, nearly a year later. Before then, he said, she would be allowed to participate in up to six LPGA events, but any money she earned would be considered unofficial, and she would not earn points toward any LPGA awards or season-ending play-offs or other similar events.

Later in 2005, a new LPGA commissioner, Carolyn Bivens, overturned Votaw's ruling, and Pressel was given full membership for the entire 2006 season. "Morgan is going to bring a passion, an excitement, an interest level" to women's professional golf, Bivens said, according to Don Markus, writing for the *Baltimore Sun* (February 16, 2006). "You're not going to see a lot of political correctness. Morgan is going to tell you how she feels about things. She wears her feelings on her sleeve. She's highly competitive. She's ready to take on the world." "I want to make a splash," Pressel told E. M. Swift and Jim Suttie. "My ultimate goal is to be Number 1 in the world and to make it to the Hall of Fame. I want to bring more money and attention to the LPGA. There's a younger generation coming along that has the potential to do that, and some interesting rivalries developing."

Pressel made her professional debut at the SBS Open at Turtle Bay, in Hawaii, on February 16, 2006, finishing in a tie for fifth place. In all, Pressel competed in 23 tournaments in her inaugural season, making the cut in 21 of them. She did not win any events but finished in the top 10 in nine tournaments, including a season-best third-place finish at Longs Drug Challenge in September. She earned nearly $500,000 in prize money that year. On April 1, 2007, for the first time, she won an LPGA event—the Kraft Nabisco. At 18 years, 10 months, and nine days of age, Pressel became the youngest player—by over a year—in the organization's 58-year history to win one of its major tournaments. She shot the only bogey-free round on the event's final day, helping her to overcome a four-shot deficit to capture a one-stroke victory over three players, who tied for second place. Also in 2007 she placed second in the Jamie Farr Owens Corning Classic and tied for third place in the Fields Open, Hawaii; fourth place in the SBS Open, Turtle Bay; eighth place in the Wegmans LPGA; ninth place in the State Farm Classic; and 10th place in the U.S. Open and the Michelob Ultra Open. On September 16, 2007, thanks in part to Pressel's upset victory over Annika Sorenstam of Sweden, the world's third-ranking player at that time, the U.S. team won the Solheim Cup. Like Pressel, the other members of the Solheim team—Juli Inkster, Paula Creamer, Nicole Castrale, Laura Diaz, Natalie Gulbis, Pat Hurst, Cristie Kerr, Brittany Lincicome, Stacy Prammanasudh, Angela Stanford, and Sherri Steinhauer—are among the world's 50 top female golfers, according to the Rolex Women's World Golf Rankings.

Represented by IMG, a management agency, Pressel has signed endorsement contracts with Callaway Golf, the Gemesis Diamond Co., Audemars Piguet, and Ralph Lauren. In 2006 she won the Nancy Lopez Award, sponsored by Florida's Natural Charity Championship, and the CoURagE Award, from Birdies for Breast Cancer. Her recreational interests include taking photographs, listening to music, and watching ice hockey. Pressel, who has described herself as being "politically incorrect," lives with her grandparents in a gated community in Boca Raton.

—N.W.M.

Suggested Reading:ajga.org; (Fort Lauderdale, Florida) *Sun Sentinel* A p1 Nov. 27, 2005; *Golf World* p24+ Feb. 3, 2006; *Jewish Exponent* (on-line) Oct. 4, 2007; lpga.com; *Miami (Florida) Herald* D p1+ Mar. 22, 2005; morganpressel.org; (Newport News, Virginia) *Daily Press* SS p8+ May 4, 2005; *Palm Beach (Florida) Post* D p1+ Aug. 14, 2005; (Palm Springs, California) *Desert Sun* C p1 Apr. 2, 2007; *Sports Illustrated* p52+ Aug. 8, 2005; *USA Today* C p3 May 16, 2001, (on-line) Apr. 10, 2007

Mark Wilson/Getty Images

Prince, Charles O. III

Jan. 13, 1950– Former chief executive officer and chairman of Citigroup Inc.

Address: c/o Council on Foreign Relations, 58 E. 68th St., New York, NY 10021

From January 2004 to November 2007, Charles O. Prince III served as the chief executive officer of Citigroup, a company that is "likened by some to the Roman Empire, by others to that misunderstood giant of sci-fi films, Godzilla," according to Marcia Vickers, writing for *Fortune* (March 6, 2006). Offering such services as consumer financing, stock brokerage, insurance underwriting, and investment banking, among others, Citigroup manages more than $1 trillion in custodial accounts and employs about 300,000 persons, in more than

100 countries worldwide. In selecting Prince as his replacement, Sanford I. Weill, the founder and then–CEO of Citigroup, chose a trusted confidant and longtime adviser who had been with the company in its numerous incarnations, dating back to 1979, when it was known as the Commercial Credit Co.

Those who expected Prince to follow closely in Weill's footsteps—including the former CEO himself—were surprised: Prince tried to shift the company's focus away from quarterly profits to the long-term economic interests of the institution. In addition, after having inherited a series of ethical scandals, Prince cleaned house, instituting new ethical standards and dismissing many of Weill's old allies from the management team. Howard K. Mason, a senior financial analyst at Sanford Bernstein & Company, told Mara Der Hovanesian for *BusinessWeek* (February 20, 2006), "Chuck Prince has extended accountability from numbers to behavior." Despite the praise he garnered for emphasizing ethical business practices, Prince did not match the high levels of profitability achieved by his predecessor; the summer of 2007 brought news of mortgage and credit-card crises, exposing some shortfalls in Citigroup's risk-management procedures and leading to a disappointing performance in the third quarter of the year. In early November, following a $5.9 billion write-down—or deliberate devaluing—of the company's assets to reflect market value, Prince announced his resignation as Citigroup's CEO.

Charles O. ("Chuck") Prince III was born on January 13, 1950 in Lynwood, California, which is near the city of Los Angeles. His mother was a homemaker; his father was a construction worker who later assumed a union leadership position. Prince was raised just a few miles from the Disneyland theme park, in Anaheim. As a teenager he played the trumpet and wanted to become a professional musician. He attended the University of Southern California (USC), in Los Angeles, receiving his bachelor's degree in 1971. In 1975, after graduating with a law degree and a master's degree in international relations from USC, he accepted a position as an attorney for the United States Steel Corporation, in Pittsburgh, Pennsylvania. In 1979 he became the general counsel for the Commercial Credit Company, a struggling consumer-loan company, in Baltimore, Maryland. While working there he continued his education at Georgetown University, in Washington, D.C., earning his master of laws degree from that institution in 1983.

In 1986 the former president of the credit-card company American Express, Sanford I. Weill, who had $7 million of his own money invested in the Commercial Credit Company, took over as CEO. Weill began buying out ailing firms and vigorously slashing costs in the new, single company. In 1987 he acquired Gulf Insurance. The next year he paid $1.5 billion for Primerica Corp., the parent company of Smith Barney and the A. L. Williams insurance company, and renamed his expanded corporation Primerica Financial Services. In 1989 he acquired Drexel Burnham Lambert's retail brokerage outlets. Then, in 1992, he paid $722 million to buy a 27 percent share of Travelers Insurance, which had fallen on hard times because of poor real-estate investments. In 1993 Weill acquired Shearson Lehman from American Express for $1.2 billion. By the end of the year, he had completely taken over the Travelers Corp. in a $4 billion stock deal and officially begun calling his corporation Travelers Group Inc. In 1996 he added to his holdings, at a cost of $4 billion, the property-and-casualty operations of Aetna Life & Casualty.

Throughout that period of remarkable activity, Prince served as a trusted adviser to Weill. Prince, who established a reputation as a jack-of-all-trades, wrote many of the CEO's speeches, emceed Weill's elaborate birthday celebrations, and negotiated many of the company's acquisitions. In 1983 Prince was promoted to senior vice president (also maintaining his duties as general counsel), and in 1996 he assumed the position of executive vice president. Known as a reliable troubleshooter, Prince advanced that reputation two years later, when he met with regulators and members of the U.S. Congress to smooth the way for the acquisition by Travelers Group of the banking giant Citicorp—the largest supplier of credit cards and the parent company of Citibank, which at the time was the second-largest bank in the U.S. Valued at $76 billion, the merger was the biggest in corporate history, dwarfing the previous record, the $37.4 billion union of MCI and WorldCom, announced just five months earlier. The thinking behind the Citicorp merger was that by combining a bank and insurance business under one brand, the company would become akin to a financial supermarket, with the capacity to offer customers an unparalleled array of financial services. The deal was considered historic in part because, prior to it, banks and insurance underwriters had been kept separate by the Glass-Steagall Act, passed during the Great Depression. At a public hearing in June 1998, Prince assured members of Congress, as quoted by Ian Watson for *Scotland on Sunday* (July 20, 2003): "We will treat each individual's information with the same high privacy protection that each of us wants for our own personal data, yours and mine. Our policies and procedures will be fully consistent with the caution expressed by regulators." The merger was completed on October 8, 1998, creating Citigroup, the largest financial-services company in the U.S. (Though the Glass-Steagall Act was still in place at the time, the company was allowed to operate during a legally mandated two-to-five-year grace period—but before that time expired, the act was repealed by Congress in 1999.)

Prince was made chief administrative officer of Citigroup, the new entity, in early 2000. He was promoted again the following year to chief operating officer. Beginning in 2001 Citigroup found itself at the center of an extensive conflict-of-interest scandal that tarnished several Wall Street firms. The following September Weill sought to restore credibility of Salomon Smith Barney, Citigroup's retail brokerage and stock-research unit, by appointing Prince as its chief executive. The highly publicized ethical scandals resulted in several months of bad publicity and a noticeable decline in Citigroup's stock; the company was fined millions of dollars in federal and local charges for helping the energy company Enron hide its debt and inflate its cash flow. Eliot Spitzer, then the New York State attorney general, was also investigating the Salomon Smith Barney stock analyst Jack Grubman, who had arranged to give certain companies a "buy" rating, a designation that amounted to a recommendation, with the understanding that those companies would conduct investment-banking business with Citigroup. Again demonstrating his mettle as a negotiator, Prince was instrumental in reaching a June 2003 settlement with securities regulators, in which Citigroup was slapped with approximately $400 million in penalties. According to Brooke A. Masters, writing for the *Washington Post* (July 17, 2003), Prince impressed "regulators and legislators with his ability to get to the bottom of issues and willingness to institute reforms." Spitzer praised Prince for his role in negotiating the settlement, telling Der Hovanesian, "He was willing to step back and figure out the strategic impact of the settlement on the business rather than focus on the complaint itself. He confronted the tough issues and acted more like a CEO than a general counsel."

Weill personally chose Prince, in July 2003, to replace him as the head of Citigroup. That news caused Citigroup's shares to fall 3 percent. Industry observers immediately took note of the comparative inexperience that Prince, a career attorney, brought to the running of a financial institution as far-reaching as Citigroup, when compared with that of the magnetic Weill. "It's like they took the lawyer for an NFL team," a source identified as an "industry insider" told Vickers, "and made him the quarterback overnight." That assessment notwithstanding, Prince remained supremely confident that he could steer Citigroup in the right direction. "My job is not, and has not been for a very long time, to be the lawyer," he said to Watson. "My job has been to run the business, to focus on growing our market share, to putting in the right levels of accountability for results, to call on customers. And that's what I have been focused on, and what I'm going to continue to focus on." Though he turned his position as CEO over to Prince, Weill remained the chairman of the board. (On April 18, 2006 Prince assumed that position as well.)

When Prince began investigating the business practices of Citigroup's various departments, shortly after assuming his position as CEO, he discovered lax ethical standards throughout the company. The new CEO spent the early part of his tenure dealing with the fallout as more ethical scandals emerged. In early August 2004 traders in Citi-

group's London offices sold billions of dollars in European government bonds only to purchase a portion of them back at lower prices within half an hour, netting as much as $24 million. "Citi's actions weren't illegal," Mara Der Hovanesian, Paula Dwyer, and Stanley Reed wrote for *Business Week* (October 4, 2004, on-line), "but broke an unwritten understanding not to whipsaw markets or take advantage of the thin summer trading. When a rival trader called to ask what was up, the Citi crew laughed and hung up. No one is laughing now, least of all Charles O. 'Chuck' Prince III. . . . He has been telling his 275,000 troops worldwide in a welter of visits and messages that he doesn't want any more bad publicity." The following month, however, the company made headlines again, when authorities in Japan ordered the closure of Citigroup's private banking operations in that country for violations that included money laundering and selling risky services to consumers.

To counter those lapses Prince introduced a plan to monitor and promote good behavior among the employees. He also encouraged Citigroup's staff to embrace its corporate history, distributing videos and books designed to "unify" the culture. "Chuck is trying to introduce a change of culture rather than reinforce a long-held one, and that's . . . difficult," William C. Weldon, the CEO of Johnson & Johnson, told Der Hovanesian. "It's one thing to talk, it's another to go out there and make sure it's reinforced and people understand you're serious. That's what [he] has to do." On Prince's watch Citigroup has endured a management shake-up as well. Several of Weill's former top lieutenants were either fired or chose to leave of their own accord, including Robert Willumstad, Marge Magner, Thomas Jones, Peter K. Scaturro, and Deryck Maughan. Prince has replaced them with a younger team, including Sallie Krawcheck, Citigroup's chief financial officer; Todd Thompson, the CEO of Smith Barney; Ajay Banga, head of the company's international consumer business; and Steven J. Freiberg, CEO of the Global Consumer Group for North America.

Citigroup's shares have remained more or less stationary since Prince's assumption of the post of CEO, in January 2004. In December 2005 Citigroup announced its intention to add 70 to 100 domestic bank branches, another 200 consumer finance centers, and an additional 400 branches in such fast-growing foreign markets as Brazil, India, and Russia. One of Prince's stated goals is to oversee the expansion of the financial institution's consumer businesses into all 100 countries where Citigroup currently operates. "We're not going to do big, complicated deals," Prince said to Eric Dash for the *New York Times* (December 17, 2005). "We are going to do string-the-pearls, extend-the-franchise type of deals."

Nonetheless, investors and analysts worried that Prince's costly plans for expansion will interfere with his ability to live up to the lofty expectations—in terms of profitability—set by his predecessor. On November 28, 2006 Citigroup's main rival, Bank of America, surpassed it in market size and was able to claim the title of world's largest bank. Analysts blamed Prince and Krawcheck for the dismal performance of Citigroup's consumer-finance, banking, and credit-card operations, which have not measured up to those of their U.S. competitors. Rumors abounded that Prince and Krawcheck might be replaced and that Citigroup might be broken up into different businesses.

On December 14, 2006 Prince named the Citigroup executive Robert Druskin—a longtime friend of Prince's who was known to have strong management and expense-cutting skills—as the firm's new chief operating officer. Prince announced that Druskin would be responsible for cutting operational costs, a step that was designed to yield long-term benefits and help create a "leaner, thinner Citigroup," in his words, as quoted by Dash in the *New York Times* (December 15, 2007). In February 2007 Prince named Gary L. Crittenden, formerly the chief financial officer at American Express, to the same post at Citigroup. Although the hiring of Crittenden was reportedly intended to attract investors, many experts predicted that the move was not likely to stimulate growth anytime soon. In April 2007 Prince announced plans to lay off or reassign more than 26,000 Citigroup workers, 8 percent of the company's 327,000 employees worldwide. The reorganization was part of broad cost-cutting and streamlining efforts led by Druskin, who had reviewed the company's costs and found, as he told Dash for the *New York Times* (April 12, 2007), that "in many instances, we had simply too many layers." Prince argued that the savings would eventually enable the company to "grow organically" and that shrinking the company's bureaucracy would make Citigroup "more nimble."

In mid-July 2007 Citigroup posted its second consecutive strong quarter, with an 18 percent increase in income, marking the two best quarters since Prince had became chief executive. That relative success was soon followed by the collapse of credit markets during the same summer, which hurt all banks. In August 2007 the price of Citigroup's shares were only 2 percent higher than they had been four years earlier, while those of Bank of America and JPMorgan Chase had increased more than 23 percent in the same period. In an attempt to reassure investors, Prince said, "I think our performance is going to last much longer than the market turbulence does," according to the *New York Times* (August 3, 2007). On October 7, 2007 the *Times* quoted several financial experts and Citigroup employees who blamed Prince for Citigroup's problems, complaining that he had altered Citigroup's long-held strategy of acquisition-driven growth, "bled reserves to generate positive earnings power," and failed to keep qualified people in the right positions or to "win over Wall Street." Later in October Prince announced several major changes to both Citigroup's organization and management, among them the combination of its investment-banking and alternative-investment units under one group, called the institutional client group, headed by Vikram S. Pandit, who had joined the company a few months before.

On October 15, 2007 Citigroup reported that the company had experienced a 57 percent drop in third-quarter profits—with shares falling $1.63, to $46.24, slightly lower than their value four years earlier—and admitted that its risk-management models had not functioned properly during the summer credit crisis. Early in the following month, on the heels of Citigroup's $5.9 billion write-down, Prince announced at an emergency meeting of the company's board of directors that he would resign his post. Days later, in a statement quoted by the *New York Times* (November 5, 2007, on-line), Prince said, "We have made strong progress in our strategy for building for the future, evidenced in the momentum we have achieved in most of our businesses. Nevertheless, it is my judgment that given the size of the recent losses in our mortgage-backed securities business, the only honorable course for me to take as Chief Executive Officer is to step down. . . . It has been my privilege to lead this powerful diversified financial services company for the past four years and to be affiliated with the directors, shareholders and employees of Citi and its predecessor companies for the past 29 years."

Prince has served on the boards of the United Negro College Fund and the New York Urban League. An active member of the Council on Foreign Relations, Prince sits on the board of directors of Johnson & Johnson and serves as a trustee for the Juilliard School and Columbia University's Teachers College, both in New York City. Vickers described Prince as possessing a "linebacker-esque frame," having "a reputation for being folksy at some times and bristly at others," and being "generally adverse to introspection." He has two adult children from his first marriage, which ended in divorce. In September 2003 he married Margaret L. Wolff, a partner in the law firm Skadden, Arps, Slate, Meagher & Flom.

—D.F.

Suggested Reading: *BusinessWeek* p74+ Feb. 20, 2006; *Fortune* p132+ Mar. 6, 2006; *New York Times* III p2 Sep. 29, 2002, (on-line) October 15, 2007; *Scotland on Sunday* p6 July 20, 2003

Donald Denton, courtesy of Steven Barclay Agency

Rakoff, David

(RAY-kof)

1964(?)– Writer; humorist; social critic; actor; radio personality

Address: c/o Steven Barclay Agency, 12 Western Ave., Petaluma, CA 94952

Shortly after he completed his undergraduate education, in the late 1980s, the humorist, essayist, social critic, and actor David Rakoff took a temporary job that required him to pose as Sigmund Freud, the creator of psychoanalysis, in a window of the upscale New York City department store Barneys during the Christmas season. Uncomfortable with sitting by himself in a replica of Freud's office for hours at a stretch every Saturday and Sunday for a month in full view of pedestrians, Rakoff started inviting friends of his to join him, one at a time, by appointment. While passersby looked on, seeing the lips of the "analyst" and his "analysand" move but hearing nothing through the thick plate glass, Rakoff and one friend or another would engage in semi-serious discussions. That experience became the subject of "Christmas Freud" (1996), the first of Rakoff's audio essays for the National Public Radio (NPR) series *This American Life.* Fifteen more have followed—the most recent, "What I Learned from Television," aired in March 2007; meanwhile, dozens of his articles have been published in such periodicals as *GQ, Outside,* and the *New York Times Magazine.* In those pieces Rakoff has used self-deprecating humor and what Joel Hanofsky, writing for the Montreal, Canada, *Gazette* (July 21, 2001), described as a "refreshing blend of light-

hearted sarcasm and cranky sentiment" to reflect upon events in his life, both ordinary and peculiar, and offer his takes on contemporary American society. In deciding which subjects he will write about, he told Nina Willdorf for *Columbia College Today* (September 2001, on-line), "There's the question, 'Is this going to afford me some fodder for wisecracks?' And then, 'Is it going to afford me some fodder for larger, non-wisecracky stuff?'" Rakoff's friend David Sedaris, a comic writer and actor who also contributes to *This American Life,* said to an interviewer for the Toronto (Canada) *Star* (October 23, 2005) that Rakoff "has a fierce intelligence and is incredibly sophisticated and he's got a tape recorder in his head." Sedaris told Barbara Hoffman for the *New York Post* (June 4, 2001) that Rakoff is "the funniest man I know." Revised versions of Rakoff's essays have appeared in his two books, *Fraud* and *Don't Get Too Comfortable: The Indignities of Coach Class, The Torments of Low Thread Count, The Never-Ending Quest for Artisanal Olive Oil, and Other First World Problems.*

The youngest of three children, David Rakoff was born in about 1964 in Montreal, Canada, and raised in a Jewish household in Toronto. His father, Vivian Rakoff, is a high-profile Toronto psychiatrist; a college professor, essayist, playwright, and occasional poet as well, for 10 years he directed the Clarke Institute of Psychiatry, in Toronto. Rakoff's mother, Gina Shochat-Rakoff, is a physician and psychotherapist. His brother, Simon, is a stand-up comedian; his sister, Ruth, is a family-conflict mediator. As a child, Rakoff enjoyed painting, drawing, acting, and dancing as well as writing. "A certain kind of verbal fleet-footedness was always a high priority in my life," he told Peter Terzian for *Newsday* (May 13, 2001). Rakoff attended Forest Hill Collegiate Institute, a Toronto public high school known for its academic rigor. After his graduation from Forest Hill, in 1982, he enrolled at Columbia University, in New York City, where he majored in East Asian studies and became fluent in Japanese. He also participated in stage productions mounted by student groups of Columbia and its sister school, Barnard College. After he earned a bachelor's degree, in 1986, he moved to Tokyo, Japan, to work as a translator for a publisher of art books. Four months later he was diagnosed with Hodgkin's lymphoma, a type of cancer (also known as Hodgkin's disease), and he returned to Toronto, where he underwent chemotherapy and radiation therapy and became skeletally thin. In a conversation with Terry Gross for the NPR program *Fresh Air* (May 14, 2001, on-line), he described himself as being "adept" at handling his illness and treatments. "I was iron-fisted and funny and bright and kind of adamantine in this impermeable way. So to the world at large, I think I manifested as being eminently humorous and terrifically stoic. Internally, I was similarly so," he said. "I was . . . never bored with myself . . . I simply had something to think about all the time. . . . But in terms of the larger questions of possible mortality or illness or whatever . . . they didn't bubble to the surface. My pond, such as it was, was iced over very efficiently." While facing the possibility of succumbing to the disease, Rakoff began to place less importance on his material desires and to view other aspects of his life from a new perspective. "Like many children of privilege, I was raised to believe that a certain sense of entitlement was completely justified in my life, and I conducted myself accordingly, like many people do," he explained to Simon Houpt for the Toronto *Globe and Mail* (May 12, 2001). "And then I got sick."

Rakoff's cancer went into apparently complete remission in a year and a half—a relatively short time. (For that reason Rakoff has often referred to himself not as a cancer survivor but as a cancer tourist.) He then moved back to New York City, where for years he worked as an editorial assistant at various publishing houses, primarily HarperCollins. Although he had regained health physically, he felt emotionally numb and was hesitant to pursue more-fulfilling opportunities, preferring instead to be "quiet and small and not tempt fate," as he recalled to Houpt. He also felt frustrated by his seeming inability to act upon his desire to write. In an interview with Dave Weich for Powells.com (April 25, 2002), he said, "I was terrified that [my writing] would suck, so I didn't write. . . . One of the big things that I really worried about was how would I ever sound like I do when I speak? Then of course you start and you can't help it. It becomes an inexorable, horrible mask you can't take off. I would *love* to sound like someone else at this point."

One day in 1993 Rakoff heard David Sedaris reading one of his essays on *This American Life* on NPR. The material struck Rakoff as hilarious, and he wrote to Sedaris at NPR to tell him so. The men discovered that they lived on the same street, and Rakoff soon became friends with Sedaris and his sister Amy, a comedian and storyteller. The Sedaris siblings found that Rakoff's dry wit complemented their goofy, provocative senses of humor and gifts for satire. In 1994 Rakoff directed the Sedaris's play *Stitches*, which was produced at La MaMa Experimental Theater Club, in New York. The play is about a young woman whose face is disfigured in a waterskiing accident. She goes on to star in her own soap opera, setting off a fashion trend among her many fans, who undergo plastic surgery to aquire the same mangled look. "In *Stitches*, the corrosively funny, if overextended, comedy by . . . David and Amy Sedaris . . . irony doesn't take the form of a wink but of a steady, wide-eyed gaze that flattens everything to the absurd dimensions of a macabre animated cartoon," Ben Brantley wrote in a review of *Stitches* for the *New York Times* (January 11, 1994), adding that Rakoff had brought the writers' unusual voices "into cleanly focused life." In 1995 Rakoff appeared on stage in the Sedarises' play *One Woman*

Shoe, which, in a critique for *Newsday* (January 24, 1995), Jan Stuart called "easily more satisfying and consistently performed than the woefully erratic *Stitches*." Stuart praised Rakoff's acting, noting that he exuded "the quirky appeal of a tall, dark David Hyde Pierce." Rakoff told Christina Nunez for the *Hartford (Connecticut) Courant* (May 20, 2001) that he enjoyed performing, because it gave him a cover for his extreme shyness. In 1997 he appeared in the Sedarises' dark comedy *The Little Frieda Mysteries*, and in 2001 he earned glowing reviews for his performance in their play *The Book of Liz*, about a woman who leaves the weird religious order that she had joined years earlier. In *Strangers with Candy* (2005), written by Amy Sedaris, Stephen Colbert, and Paul Dinello, Rakoff was cast as Boswell, who—like James Boswell, who recorded the words and activities of Samuel Johnson in the 1700s—serves as an amanuensis, in this case to a high-school science teacher (played by Matthew Broderick).

Meanwhile, at David Sedaris's urging, Rakoff had begun to contribute to *This American Life*, which in each hour-long installment offers nonfiction journalism, essays, memoirs, and short fiction by several contributors—"little movies for the radio," in the words of its producer and host, Ira Glass. "Christmas Freud," Rakoff's first piece for *This American Life*, aired in December 1996; afterward, Rakoff joined the show's stable of contributors. According to a writer for *Publishers Weekly* (December 5, 2005), Rakoff's "understated, suave delivery has endeared him to throngs of public-radio fans, and it's an excellent foil for setting up his frequently stinging brand of ridicule." In his December 18, 1998 essay for an installment entitled "What You Lookin' At?," Rakoff talked about his visit to "a place where everyone seems to be looking at him, a place where no one follows the customs people follow back home in New York City, a place called . . . New Hampshire," as it was described on the show's Web site; for "Welcome to America" (March 19, 1999), he observed several Austrians hired to teach math and science in New York City public schools and discovered that they had "started to see things about this country that few Americans ever get to see"; for "Urban Nature," he traveled to Reykjavík, Iceland, where "the government is careful not to disturb certain boulders when it builds roads because some people believe that invisible 'hidden people'—like elves—live at those sites"; "Office Politics" (March 15, 2002), a segment read before a live audience at Town Hall in New York City, was about "what happens when you call yourself an editorial assistant but the editor you're assisting calls you a secretary"; and for "What I Learned from Television" (March 16, 2007), Rakoff, who stopped watching TV as an undergraduate, tried to watch 29 hours' worth of programs in one week—as many as the average American views. Rakoff is the first and thus far only person to guest-host the program; standing in for Ira Glass on August 24, 2003, he talked about the day during his childhood that "he realized that he would inevitably be viewed a certain way by his classmates, no matter what he did or said," as paraphrased on thisamericanlife.org.

Earlier, in 1998, Rakoff had left his job in publishing to pursue freelance writing full-time. Among the dozens of articles by him that have appeared in popular magazines are "Chewing Your Way to Mental Health" (*GQ*, May 1999), a series of letters supposedly written to the maker of a real snack—St. John's Wort Tortilla Chips—touted as an antidote to depression; "Let the Games Begin," about the instant popularity of the Sega Dreamcast, a video-game console, and "Better Late Than Never," an interview with a navy seaman wrongfully convicted of mutiny in 1945 (both for the *New York Times Magazine*, October 24, 1999 and January 9, 2000, respectively); "Land of Rising Fun" (*Condé Nast Traveler*, June 2000), about Tokyo, Japan, as a destination for tourists; "An American in Paris" (*Harper's Bazaar*, October 2000), in which Rakoff offered his impressions of Paris fashion shows; "Teaching Yourself New Tricks" (*Sports Illustrated Woman*, March/April 2002), about fencing lessons Rakoff took with the former Olympic competitor Sharon Monplaisir; "Isle of Joy" (*House & Garden*, July 2003), in which he wrote about his love for summertime New York City; and "Some Pig" (*Gourmet*, August 2006), in which he revealed that he rarely feels more Jewish than just before he takes a bite of pork, a food forbidden to observant Jews, who follow a complicated set of dietary laws.

Rakoff's first book, *Fraud* (2001), is a collection of expanded versions of some of his articles and radio essays. The title refers to his feeling that professionally as well as personally, he is often a fraud. In an assignment for *Outside*, for example, which required him to go on a hike—his first ever—he pretended to be a person who likes the outdoors. In the book's final essay, "I Used to Bank Here, but That Was Long, Long Ago," he described his search in Toronto hospitals and clinics for the sperm he had had frozen before undergoing chemotherapy. His quest led him to reflect on his year of treatment, a depressing and frightening period during which he presented himself to others as happy and calm. According to various critics, his account, which in less capable hands might have come across as maudlin and sentimental, skillfully blends comedy and deep feeling. Some reviewers also mentioned their pleasure in reading essays in which benign mockery and genuine compassion intermix. As Houpt wrote of *Fraud*, Rakoff "brings a blithely alienated approach to each of [his] subjects, and delights in finding the bizarre in the everyday. . . . Yet [he] also has a deep capacity for understanding and sympathy, which is on full display in his droll new collection of personal stories." In a review that echoed several others' reservations, Charles Russell wrote for the *Calgary (Alberta, Canada) Herald* (June 23, 2001), "Rakoff is obviously extremely intelligent and a remarkably original, talented and wickedly funny writer, but his perception is so overwhelmingly cynical and pessimistic that his writing, like irritating relatives, can be taken only in short visits."

Rakoff's second book, *Don't Get Too Comfortable: The Indignities of Coach Class, The Torments of Low Thread Count, The Never-Ending Quest for Artisanal Olive Oil, and Other First World Problems*, was published in 2005. The book's essays include "What Is the Sound of One Hand Shopping," which describes Rakoff's incredulous reaction to a much-glorified organic dinner at which dessert consisted of a single Medjool date (a fruit originally from Morocco that was served only to royalty and dignitaries) and a perfect tangerine. *Don't Get Too Comfortable* skewers the culture embraced by some upper-middle-class Americans, who, in Rakoff's view, had confused consumerism with moral values. But while expressing his scorn for those who, when drinking fine Scotch whiskey, reject local-tap-water ice cubes in favor of ice cubes made of water from the Scottish Highlands, Rakoff admitted that he was not immune to such luxury items; as evidence, he cited the French sea salt and extra-virgin olive oil in his kitchen cabinet. *Don't Get Too Comfortable* received uniformly positive reviews, with most critics noting Rakoff's incisive wit and the restraint he displayed in reserving his most biting commentary for the greatest offenders while exhibiting a great deal of compassion toward the average Joe. "He's funny, he's smart, and not merely does he not suffer fools gladly, he doesn't suffer them at all . . . ," Jonathan Yardley wrote for the *Miami (Florida) Herald* (October 30, 2005). "The pleasures of reading what results when an exceedingly sharp pen encounters an exceedingly inviting target are not to be denied, and Rakoff offers many such delights in these pages. He also, by no means incidentally, has a humane view of human society at its most ordinary and unpretentious. But the bloated wallets and bloated egos are his subjects here, and he deflates them with precision and self-evident satisfaction."

In a recent article for the *New York Times Travel Magazine* (May 20, 2007), Rakoff wrote about his one-week stay at the John C. Campbell Folk School, in Brasstown, North Carolina. He chose to study basket-weaving, which he found not only "rocks" but is also exceedingly "soothing." At the final show of the students' work, he wrote, "we are all so proud of one another. It is astonishing what people have managed to accomplish in six days." "There is a certain magic" to the school, he wrote, and while weaving several baskets, he discovered a "spiritual alchemy that takes place in that time out of time when one is engaged in making something. There is not sleep enough in the world that is nearly so restorative. . . . The week I spent there is about as close as it gets to my idea of paradise."

Rakoff performed in the short film *Bad Bosses Go to Hell* (1997) and had a brief part in the feature-length movie *Capote* (2005). He has made several appearances on Comedy Central's fake-news TV program *The Daily Show with Jon Stewart*. A resident of the Union Square section of Manhattan, Rakoff has held dual U.S.–Canadian citizenship since 2003.

—C.S.

Suggested Reading: *Columbia College Today* (online) Sep. 2001; *Hartford (Connecticut) Courant* Arts G p2 May 20, 2001; Langfield Entertainment *Newsletter* (on-line) Oct. 23, 2005; *Newsday* B p11 May 13, 2001; powells.com Apr. 25, 2002; *Salon.com* June 11, 2001; (Toronto, Canada) *Globe and Mail* D p2 May 12, 2001, R p3 Oct. 22, 2005; *Toronto (Canada) Star* (on-line) Oct. 23, 2005

Selected Books: *Fraud*, 2001; *Don't Get Too Comfortable: The Indignities of Coach Class, The Torments of Low Thread Count, The Never-Ending Quest for Artisanal Olive Oil, and Other First World Problems*, 2005

Bard Martin, courtesy of Random House

Redlener, Irwin

(RED-leener)

Aug. 12, 1944– Pediatrician; children's advocate; organization official; educator

Address: Children's Health Fund, 215 W. 125th St., Suite 301, New York, NY 10027

"There is a very strong connection between poverty and ill health. So like it or not, doctors, or at least organized medicine, have to be players in the larger arena," the pediatrician and child advocate Ir-

win Redlener told Richard C. Firstman for *Newsday Magazine* (January 13, 1991). A blend of "kindly family doctor, political animal, and aggressive entrepreneur," as Polly LaBarre described him in *Fast Company* (April 2002, on-line), Redlener told LaBarre, "For me, it's never been just a question of providing health services to children in need. It's about using health care as a lever to address the global needs of the most disadvantaged kids. For these children, health care is a foot in the door to the future. If we give them a shot at being happy and healthy while they're young, we give them the opportunity to realize their potential as adults." For much of his professional life, the 63-year-old Redlener has devoted himself to the well-being of poor, underserved, and medically neglected children in the United States and overseas. As a worker with VISTA (Volunteers in Service to America) in the early 1970s, he provided hands-on care to children in a poverty-stricken county of Arkansas. In the mid-1980s, while with the private group USA for Africa, Hands Across America, he ministered to similarly needy children in Ethiopia, the Sudan, and other African nations. The Children's Health Fund (CHF), which he co-founded in 1987 with his wife, Karen B. Redlener, and the singer/songwriter Paul Simon, has become the biggest health-care system for homeless children in the U.S. Irwin Redlener was a driving force behind the construction of the state-of-the-art Children's Hospital at Montefiore Medical Center, in the New York City borough of the Bronx; he also served as the first president of that hospital, which opened in October 2001 and provides medical care without cost. He has been the director of the National Center for Disaster Preparedness at Columbia University since 2003 and an associate dean for public-health advocacy and disaster preparedness and professor of clinical public health and pediatrics at Columbia's Mailman School of Public Health since 2006. "We can in fact do things better than we have in the past," Redlener told a reporter for the *Newark (New Jersey) Star Ledger* (July 27, 2007), referring to the fact that in the U.S., approximately 20 million children lack adequate health care. "These problems are not intractable. They can be solved. They can be dealt with. It's our obligation to make sure that whatever we have to put in place to make it happen, actually happens."

Irwin Elliott Redlener was born to Jewish parents on August 12, 1944 in the New York City borough of Brooklyn. He has at least one sibling—a younger brother, Neil B. Redlener, who is a psychiatrist and staff member of the Mailman Psychological Counseling Center. In an interview with Robin Finn for the *New York Times* (March 4, 2003), Irwin Redlener described his father, a child psychologist, and mother, a schoolteacher, as "more or less activist parents who expected their kids to be involved in issues of the day and take their share of social responsibility." When he was a little boy, Redlener's fondness for expressing his opinions led his mother to call him Doc. According to Finn,

Redlener applied for admission to the U.S. Military Academy at West Point but was turned down. Instead, he attended Hofstra University, in Hempstead, Long Island, New York, where he earned a B.A. degree in 1964. He then enrolled at the University of Miami School of Medicine, in Florida. After he received an M.D. degree, in 1969, he trained in pediatrics, with a specialty in pediatric cardiology, at the University of Miami–Jackson Memorial Hospital; Babies Hospital at Columbia-Presbyterian Medical Center, in New York City; and the University of Colorado Medical Center at Denver. By the time he completed his residency, he had married and become a father. That marriage ended in divorce.

While he was still in Denver, a recruitment poster that Redlener happened to see spurred him to join VISTA, a domestic version of the Peace Corps that is now part of the AmeriCorps program. (The poster, which now hangs on a wall in Redlener's CHF office, read "Doctors: join now! . . . Sign up for a year of tough practice in the other America. If you're not part of the solution, you're part of the problem.") Under VISTA's auspices, from 1971 to 1973 Redlener directed a health clinic in rural eastern Arkansas, in what was the state's poorest county and the sixth-poorest in the U.S. A fellow VISTA volunteer, Karen Blomberg, became his second wife.

After he completed his VISTA service, Redlener established a private pediatric practice in Utica, a city in central New York State. In 1976 he helped victims of a devastating earthquake in Guatemala. Ten years later he left his medical practice to become the medical director and director of grants for the USA for Africa Foundation, bankrolled by United Support of Artists for Africa (USA for Africa), a charitable organization made up of 45 prominent musicians, among them Michael Jackson, Lionel Richie, Kenny Rogers, Harry Belafonte, and Paul Simon. Through sales of the recording of the song "We Are the World," USA for Africa raised several million dollars to aid famine-stricken Africans; eventually, the total collected topped $50 million. (Critics of USA for Africa charged that portions of the money it had collected had ended up in the pockets of corrupt government officials in various African countries.) During his two years with USA for Africa, Redlener visited parts of the Sudan, Ethiopia, and other African nations where medical care was nonexistent and people lived at subsistence levels.

Redlener and Simon became friends and discovered that they shared a desire to fight hunger not only in Africa but in the United States. Together they toured what Redlener called the "invisible" New York City and its "underbelly": homeless shelters and neglected hotels that housed homeless welfare recipients. Among the many disturbing sights that greeted Redlener and Simon, they were particularly horrified by conditions at the Martinique, a welfare hotel in midtown Manhattan that was infested with roaches and rats, housed many crack addicts, and provided its residents with hot-plates but no stoves, refrigerators, or food-storage cabinets. Redlener told Polly LaBarre, "There were a thousand children and their parents in that building. It was total chaos. The elevators were broken, there were drug deals going on, and there were about 80 kids waiting outside the dining room for the one meal they'd get that day. Even though I had already been very immersed in the problems of underserved children, I was stunned. And Paul Simon was absolutely speechless. The question after the visit was, 'What can we do?'"

In 1987 Redlener, his wife, and Simon founded the nonprofit organization Children's Health Fund, with the goal of bringing medical services to homeless children and families. They envisioned a fleet of mobile medical units that would make stops at homeless shelters and welfare hotels. For a cost of $80,000, Simon purchased a 30-foot van and had it outfitted with two examination rooms, medical equipment, a tiny diagnostic laboratory, and a waiting area. To raise more money, he tapped musicians including Bruce Springsteen, Billy Joel, and James Taylor to perform at a benefit concert for CHF at Madison Square Garden, in Manhattan. The concert netted $400,000, which enabled CHF to purchase more mobile medical units. Additional funds came from the city and federal governments, wealthy donors, and New York Hospital–Cornell Medical Center, which also contributed office space and staff. In its first year of operation, CHF served 3,000 children, nearly half of whom, CHF physicians discovered, had not received some or any of the inoculations routinely given to nearly all babies and toddlers in the U.S. and required for entrance into public schools. Moreover, the majority of the children suffered from such acute or chronic illnesses as ear infections; hearing loss; pneumonia, asthma, or other respiratory ailments; stomach disorders; lead poisoning; heart murmurs; anemia; or malnutrition. Many of them had multiple, interlinked disorders. For example, as Redlener explained to Howard Kurtz for the Washington Post (March 21, 1989), "We saw a lot of kids who had chronic untreated ear infections, leading to hearing loss, leading to speech problems and problems at school." Further compounding the difficult task of treating the children, many mothers failed to keep their children's follow-up appointments at New York Hospital, mainly for logistical reasons. Redlener solved that problem by having the hospital's car service pick up patients and their families free of charge. As of mid-2007 CHF, which is headquartered in New York City, was serving 150,000 disadvantaged children each year in 21 rural and urban communities in 13 states and Washington, D.C. The newest mobile medical unit, which cost $250,000, will serve residents of Newark and Elizabeth, New Jersey, cities in which one-third of the children live in families whose incomes are below the federal poverty level.

Earlier, in 1993, early in the first term of President Bill Clinton, Redlener served as a member of the White House's Task Force on National Health-Care Reform. Headed by then–First Lady Hillary Rodham Clinton, the temporary team produced a complicated plan for an expensive health-care system designed to meet the needs of all Americans. The proposal succumbed under a barrage of fierce criticism from members of the U.S. Senate and House of Representatives. In 2000, on another matter involving the Clinton administration, Redlener was named the government's chief medical adviser in the highly controversial, highly publicized case of Elián González, a six-year-old Cuban boy who was rescued from the ocean off the Florida coast in November 1999, after his mother drowned while fleeing Cuba by boat along with other would-be refugees to the U.S. The boy's father, who had remained in Cuba, asked the U.S. to return Elián to him, while Elián's relatives in Miami insisted that the boy be allowed to stay with them. Thousands of Cubans who had previously taken refuge in Florida, to escape the rule of the Cuban dictator Fidel Castro, supported the boy's Miami relatives, arguing that in the U.S., Elián would have all the benefits of those growing up in a democracy, while sending him back to Cuba was tantamount to condemning him to a life of oppression. As reported by Rick Bragg for the *New York Times* (April 19, 2000), a group of mental-health experts, chosen by Redlener and representatives of the U.S. Immigration and Naturalization Service, spoke to Elián's great-uncle in Miami; afterward, Redlener advised the then–U.S. attorney general, Janet Reno, that Elián was being "horrendously exploited" in the "bizarre and destructive" environment that prevailed in his relatives' home and that his behavior as seen on a video taped by his relatives resembled that of someone being held hostage. Redlener expressed that view in several TV interviews, thereby inciting the anger of supporters of Elián's U.S. relatives, who pointed out that Redlener had never met or talked to the child. The Supreme Court refused to consider an appeal by Elián's relatives to keep him in the U.S., and at the end of June 2000, the boy's father took him back to Cuba.

Earlier, in 1996, Spencer Foreman, the president of Montefiore Medical Center, in the Bronx, tapped Redlener to lead the development of a new facility for children. "The problem with most children's hospitals is that they are passive," Redlener told Polly LaBarre. "They are high quality. They are filled with the best doctors. But their function is to wait until kids get sick and get referred in. I wanted to establish a much more dynamic relationship between a children's hospital and the community." He also said, "We wanted to recast the idea of what could be achieved in a children's hospital. We decided to change the expectation of what happens during treatment and recovery. Our mission was to provide excellent health care and a total environment that ignites the imagination of children. Hospitals are about healing. This one is about changing lives." Thanks to multimillion-dollar donations, aggressive fundraising, and the input and advice of such eminent scientists as the paleontologist, evolutionary biologist, and science historian Stephen Jay Gould; Daniel S. Goldin, a former head of the National Aeronautics and Space Administration (NASA); and Neil Tyson, director of the Hayden Planetarium at the American Museum of Natural History, Redlener's vision became a reality. Now in its seventh year of operation, the children's hospital is part of a network of 30 city health facilities, which, as LaBarre wrote, includes "the largest school-based health program in the country, a cutting-edge neonatal intensive-care unit, the city's leading child-protection program, and a fleet of mobile medical units." In addition, Redlener incorporated into the hospital's design elements that reflected the conviction of his friend Carl Sagan, an astronomer and famous popularizer of astronomy, that "the process of finding out where you fit into the universe and the inspiration that comes from learning something about your world can be a gateway to a whole set of possibilities for children who have otherwise been contained in a very limited worldview." To provide such a gateway, the hospital houses a science museum, a high-tech classroom, a discovery center, and an ultramodern playground.

After the terrorist attacks on New York City and Washington, D.C., on September 11, 2001, Redlener became active in disaster-preparedness research and training. In December 2001, with George Fotlin, the head of the Center for Pediatric Emergency Medicine at New York University Medical Center, he set up the New York City Task Force on Pediatric Disaster Preparedness. Also in 2001 he helped to organize the American Academy of Pediatrics Task Force on Terrorism. Both groups have worked to establish specific provisions for children's physical and mental health in emergency terrorist-response plans.

In 2003 Redlener left his job at the Children's Hospital at Montefiore Medical Center and joined the Mailman School of Public Health, at Columbia University, as the associate dean for public-health advocacy and disaster preparedness. He also became the first director of the new National Center for Disaster Preparedness, based at Mailman. In a Mailman press release (April 28, 2003, on-line), Redlener stated, "These are extraordinary times for public health. Clearly we need to make sure that the country is optimally prepared for disasters in general and for the terrible potential of more terrorism. The new Center will be a resource on many critical aspects of preparedness for the region and the nation. The other challenge we face is to make sure that we stay focused on the traditional public health agenda, including access to health care for everyone, preventing tobacco-related illness, dealing with global concerns of HIV/AIDS, environmental hazards, and other problems."

In an interview for *All Things Considered* on National Public Radio (January 4, 2005, on-line), Redlener told Michele Norris, "In my experience in large disaster situations, it's almost impossible to be totally efficient. You may have hundreds of organizations and thousands of people who are coming in an area to help, so coordinating them can be a difficult task. There are formulas for getting a basic initial handle on how much of particular items you'll need . . . So the number of water-purification tablets or the number of blankets or emergency tents as shelters would be determined . . . Very shortly thereafter we really do have the need to make sure that . . . children have things to play with and distract them; that there is sufficient clothing for people." In August 2005 Hurricane Katrina caused devastating floods in New Orleans, Louisiana, and in other parts of the American South. CHF responded by sending some of its mobile medical units to the affected area. In the first month after the storm, Redlener traveled to flood-devastated regions three times to monitor the work of CHF staff members and assist in the delivery of services.

Redlener's book, *Americans at Risk: Why We Are Not Prepared for Megadisasters and What We Can Do Now* (2006), contains a highly critical account of the response to the Hurricane Katrina disaster of the Federal Emergency Management Agency (FEMA), along with descriptions of five potential calamitous events, among them an avian-flu pandemic and an accidental release of chemicals in the "tornado belt" of the Midwest. As Redlener defined it, a megadisaster is "a catastrophic, high-consequence event that overwhelms or threatens to overwhelm local and regional response capacity, and is caused by a natural phenomenon, massive infrastructure failure, industrial accident, or malevolent intention." In a review of the book for *Civil Engineering* (November 2006), Ray Bert wrote, "The objective of *Americans at Risk* is not to instill fear but rather to educate everyone from policy makers to the person on the street that, the Department of Homeland Security notwithstanding, there is still much that needs to be done and much that needs to be fixed" to prepare adequately for the worst. "Throwing money at the problem, which this country has most assuredly done, is inadequate when the money is going to fund scattershot ideas divorced from a central plan. Redlener spends the second half of the book explaining the barriers to becoming truly prepared—poor leadership and accountability, lack of attention to detail, and the difficulty of convincing the American public of the importance of preparedness—as well as describing his own prescriptions for making us safer." Bert concluded, "Compelling, detailed, and quite possibly a book that could keep you up nights, *Americans at Risk* is at times a devastating critique of how far we have not come in recent years, despite all the rhetoric, tax dollars, and 'lessons learned.'"

Redlener's wife, Karen B. Redlener, is the executive director and vice president for New York City operations at the Children's Health Fund. She also serves as the executive director of Community Pediatric Programs at Montefiore Medical Center. From his first marriage, Redlener has one son, David; another son, Jason, died in a snowboarding accident in 1999. From his current marriage he has a son, Michael, and a daughter, Stephanie. Irwin and Karen Redlener live in New Rochelle, New York.

—S.J.D.

Suggested Reading: *Fast Company* (on-line) Apr. 2002; *New York Times* G p1 Nov. 29, 2001; *Newsday Magazine* p12 Jan. 13, 1991; *Washington Post* A p3 Mar. 21, 1989

Selected Books: *Americans at Risk: Why We Are Not Prepared for Megadisasters and What We Can Do Now*, 2006

Jorge Uzon/AFP/Getty Images

Reyes, Silvestre

(RAY-ez, sil-VES-tray)

Nov. 10, 1944– U.S. representative from Texas (Democrat)

Address: 2433 Rayburn House Office Bldg., Washington, DC 20515-4316

In January 2007 U.S. representative Silvestre Reyes, a Democrat from Texas, became chairman of the House Intelligence Committee. In that post,

Reyes, currently serving his sixth term in Congress, leads the committee in drafting laws, authorizing funding, and providing congressional oversight for all 16 U.S. spy agencies, including the Central Intelligence Agency and the National Security Agency. Prior to serving in Congress, Reyes worked for 26 years as an officer of the Border Patrol, heading the agency's El Paso, Texas, arm for two years and establishing himself as an ambitious and creative policy maker. In the U.S. House of Representatives, in addition to his work with the Intelligence Committee, he has served on the Armed Services Committee and the Veterans' Affairs Committee and as chairman of the House Hispanic Caucus. In his tenure as Intelligence Committee chairman, Reyes has overseen the passage of several pieces of legislation pertaining to the spy agencies and has also led investigations into potentially improper or illegal activities within the organizations under his committee's jurisdiction.

The eldest of 10 children, Silvestre "Silver" Reyes was born on November 10, 1944 to farmers in the community of Canutillo, Texas, five miles north of El Paso. His grandparents had immigrated to the United States early in the 20th century to escape the violence of the Mexican Revolution, and as a sixth-grader Reyes's father began working full-time on the family's farm. "It was an environment of very hard work," Reyes recalled about his own childhood, as reported by Frank Davies for the *Miami (Florida) Herald* (June 13, 2001). "Some might have called our circumstances austere or poor, but we did not feel that way. We worked hard, but had everything we needed." Reyes attended Canutillo High School, where he played fullback on the football team. Following his graduation, in 1964, he began attending the University of Texas on a debate scholarship. After just one year there, Reyes withdrew to work on the family farm, which was struggling at the time. The following year he enrolled at Texas Western College, now the University of Texas–El Paso, but again was forced to postpone his studies in order to work full-time. In 1966 Reyes was drafted into the U.S. Army. He served in Vietnam as a helicopter crew chief, earning the Purple Heart after sustaining a wound during a combat tour that lasted a little over a year. Following the death of his father, he received a hardship discharge from service abroad and concluded his tenure with the army in the United States.

During his final weeks in the army, Reyes, with an eye toward the future, took several civil-service exams. The first federal agency to reply to his queries was the U.S. Border Patrol of the Immigration and Naturalization Service (INS), with which he took a position in 1969. His first assignment was as an inspector in Del Rio, Texas, a job he held until 1974, when he was transferred to El Paso; he was eventually promoted to supervisor there. While working in El Paso, Reyes found time to return to his studies, earning an associate's degree in criminal justice from El Paso Community College in 1976. In 1978 Reyes took a break from policing the

border to study at the Federal Law Enforcement Training Center in Glynco, Georgia. He then returned to the Border Patrol, and in 1983 he was named assistant commissioner of the Dallas Regional Office. In 1984 he again transferred, this time to McAllen, Texas, where he became the first Hispanic in the agency's history to become head of a sector. In July 1993 he was reassigned to El Paso as chief, a position he held until his retirement from INS, in November 1995.

During the time that he led the Border Patrol in El Paso, Reyes became a national figure for spearheading an unconventional and controversial system. The border separating El Paso from Juarez, Mexico, had been one of the most-trafficked border spots in the United States. Although estimates vary greatly, the number of people crossing illegally every day in 1993 was reported to be as high as 10,000. Traditionally, the policy of the Border Patrol was to apprehend foreign nationals after they had crossed into the U.S.; Congress used the numbers of arrests in the various sectors as a guide for allocating manpower and funding along the border. Reyes recognized several problems with that approach with regard to conditions in El Paso. As the number of agents there increased, so did the number of arrests, as there were far more offenders than arresting officers. In addition, Reyes's sector bore the costs of transporting large numbers of illegal workers and immigrants back to Mexico, only to have many of them return to Texas the following day. Furthermore, his officers had difficulty in distinguishing between Mexicans and Mexican-Americans, which led to improper arrests and the harassment and detention of U.S. citizens thought to be Mexican nationals living or working illegally in El Paso. To combat those problems, Reyes placed all of his officers on, rather than near, the border, to prevent anyone from crossing except through official ports of entry. By making it more difficult for illegal workers and immigrants to cross into the United States, Reyes was able to eliminate many of the problems created by the existing strategy. He called the initiative Operation Blockade. Referring to illegal workers and immigrants, Reyes told Rene Romo for the *Albuquerque (New Mexico) Journal* (November 29, 1995), "If you don't arrest them, you don't have to detain them, you don't have to process them, you don't have to feed them, you don't have to house them and you don't have to transport them." At first Operation Blockade—later changed to the more politically palatable "Operation Hold the Line"— was unpopular among federal officials. The Mexican government was outraged at what they saw as blatant xenophobia on the part of the U.S.; members of the INS and other government officials, meanwhile, disapproved of Reyes's 24-hour surveillance scheme because it ran against time-tested protocols, called for a larger budget to cover overtime pay and technology, and decreased the number of arrests, which remained Washington's chief measure of effectiveness.

In the first week after the initiative was adopted, there was a measurable reduction in the number of people in El Paso; merchants complained that they had fewer customers, and employers complained that employees were not showing up for work. Along with what Reyes described to Thaddeus Herrick, reporting for the *Houston Chronicle* (October 1, 1995), as "glue sniffers, pickpockets and prostitutes," there were evidently a large number of Mexicans who commuted to El Paso daily to work and shop. Those problems were alleviated in the following weeks as some workers, who had once found it easy to cross illegally, gained daily work permits, and others found places outside Reyes's sector to cross the border. Crime rates in El Paso plummeted following the shift in border enforcement, and Reyes became a national celebrity in part because of the audacity of his initiative. In general the citizens of El Paso were pleased with the changes, and as Joel Brinkley reported for the *New York Times* (September 14, 1994), public-opinion polls indicated an 80 to 95 percent approval rating for the plan. "We've made a dramatic impact on the quality of life of El Paso," Reyes said to Helen Thorpe for *Texas Monthly* (November 1995). "We've cleared the beggars and windshield washers from the intersections. Vehicle thefts are down, home burglaries are down, assaults are down." Operation Hold the Line also reduced the number of alleged abuses by border agents, which had peaked in the early 1990s to "an average of 15 to 25 a week," as Reyes estimated to Thorpe, and had culminated in a 1992 lawsuit in which a federal judge found that agents routinely violated the constitutional rights of U.S. citizens.

Such statistics did not convince everyone. Many argued that the effectiveness of the strategy was impossible to quantify and that the findings about its effects were misleading. A 1994 study by the University of Texas's Population Research Center suggested that many of the people prevented from crossing the border illegally were not immigrants but commuters with day jobs in the United States; after Operation Hold the Line was implemented, some of the commuters began to live illegally in El Paso, to avoid the daunting task of crossing the border daily. With a diminished INS presence away from the border, living illegally in El Paso became a common means of avoiding arrest. Reyes's policy also shifted the location of the most frequent crossings to areas outside the city boundaries, which were largely devoid of law-enforcement representatives. In 1995, to augment his officers' efforts in Operation Hold the Line, Reyes installed a 1.3-mile-long chain-link fence in the Sunland Park neighborhood of El Paso, where the Mexican *colonia* of Anapra abuts El Paso and where cultures and economies spill across the border in both directions. Thorpe suggested that residents of Mexico likened the fence to the Berlin Wall. Suzan Kern, president of the El Paso–based Border Rights Coalition, told Rene Romo that Operation Hold the Line worsened El Paso's relationship with Juarez,

by severing the once-fluid border and separating the populations. "Operation Hold the Line has done much more to increase those [racial] divisions than to heal them, and that's unfortunate," Kern said. Romo paraphrased Bonnie Escobar, leadership director of the Mexican-American Legal Defense and Educational Fund, as saying that she was "concerned that Hold the Line took the focus away from poverty as a root cause of illegal immigration while it emphasized stopping the illegals." Many Mexican-Americans saw irony in the fact that Reyes, himself a Mexican-American, had won fame by cracking down on impoverished Mexicans while employing "rhetoric that fans fears about job security and crime," according to Thorpe. Juan Sybert-Coronado, a teacher at Bowie High in El Paso, told Thorpe: "This is one of the ugliest things Reyes has done. He's not only divided El Paso and Juarez, he's divided Chicanos and Mexicans. He's made Mexican Americans forget where they came from."

After a difficult battle with officials in Washington, Reyes was able to arrange for additional funding to make Operation Hold the Line a permanent fixture in El Paso. By the 1995 political-campaign season, Reyes's strategy had been embraced by those who favored a hard-line response to immigration, and presidential and congressional hopefuls sought photo opportunities and speaking engagements with Reyes to show their commitment to his philosophy. Additionally, Operation Hold the Line forced a dialogue between the INS and Congress about finding indicators besides arrests for measuring policy effectiveness.

Reyes retired from the INS in 1995 with the intention of challenging incumbent U.S. representative Ron Coleman of Texas's 16th District in the Democratic primary election; Reyes remained a candidate after Coleman, later in the year, announced that he would not seek reelection. Reyes, who had developed significant name recognition and political capital with Operation Hold the Line, told the media that he decided to run because he was frustrated with the congressional representation of El Paso. "When I found out that the INS was going to start a new Border Patrol Training Academy, I recommended El Paso and Fort Bliss [a military base in El Paso] because I thought that this was a very good opportunity to bring the Border Patrol back to the border . . . ," Reyes later told Mike Juarez for *Hispanic* (July 31, 1996). "I was unable to generate any support from the local congressional office, so that frustration of not being able to get that support gave me reason to think somebody needs to run, and maybe I ought to consider it." Furthermore, Reyes believed that as a legislator he could continue to be an asset to El Paso with regard to border issues and that his experience in the field would make him a more successful advocate than his predecessor. Among the changes that Reyes wanted to enact were the consolidation of, or greater cooperation among, the U.S. Border Patrol, INS inspectors, the Customs Service, parts of the U.S.

Department of Agriculture, and the U.S. Coast Guard, so that each agency could better enforce laws while facilitating trade between the U.S. and Mexico. Reyes also wanted to make consistent the rules for ports of entry into the United States; many checkpoints operated under individual protocols, which frustrated and confused travelers and officers alike. In addition, Reyes advocated training the Border Patrol in the areas of civil rights, human rights, and the specific needs of border communities as well as in law-enforcement techniques.

Reyes's support from city officials and voters cut across party lines. Although his platform called for promoting education, high-tech jobs, highway development, and cuts in the capital-gains tax, the immigration issue remained his area of expertise and his strongest political asset. "I think my career in the Border Patrol was an excellent basis for [serving in Congress]," Reyes told David LaGesse for the *Dallas Morning News* (July 6, 1997). "Being a Border Patrol agent on the border can be controversial—it can be a tough job if people don't understand what it is you're doing, why you're doing it and why it's important. So I did a lot of things with schools, with community groups, and put a human face on the agency so people wouldn't look at the Border Patrol as an invading army but as part of the community. From that perspective, for those 12 or 13 years, I did a lot of things that I think helped me transition into a political career." During the rally at which he announced his candidacy, Reyes said that he was frustrated by El Paso's reliance on a "minimum wage economy," according to United Press International (December 1, 1995). "It is time to work to insure that a strong and vibrant business community provides the impetus for a long-term and diverse economic base for El Paso that provides not only jobs, but jobs that require unique and technically challenging skills that pay accordingly," Reyes said. An important aspect of Reyes's strategy in that regard was to combine the cutting-edge technology in use at Fort Bliss with resources at local universities to provide job training for students.

Reyes won the Democratic primary with a slim 51 percent of the vote but coasted through the general election against the Republican candidate, Rick Ledesma, and Carl Proffer, an Independent. (El Paso had not elected a Republican in any county-wide election since 1984.) In his first term Reyes had a long list of goals but decided to focus primarily on just a few: strengthening education, veterans' programs, and national security and cementing his reputation in Congress as a border expert. Ignoring the usual protocol, which keeps freshmen representatives on the sidelines, Reyes was outspoken, particularly on border issues. He has said that his lack of experience, which made him feel unencumbered by the traditional hierarchies, worked to his benefit. He fought against a proposal that would sanction Mexico for its drug policies and also opposed a proposal to place 10,000 troops on the U.S.-Mexico border to combat drug traffic and

illegal immigration. Because of his years with the Border Patrol, he was not ignored.

At the same time, because of his prior experience in—and outspoken approach to—border issues, Reyes had to work hard to avoid being pigeonholed as a border expert exclusively. One way that he did so was to concentrate on another sector of policy important to his constituents—the military. Fort Bliss is a key military base, and a large number of veterans make their homes in and around El Paso. In 1999 Reyes, a member of the House Veterans' Benefits Subcommittee, drew on his experience in Vietnam to advocate for further research into the effects of Agent Orange and for veterans' programs to address the causes of Gulf War Syndrome and provide diagnosis and treatment. Reyes was also a vocal opponent of the 2003 U.S. invasion of Iraq, whose leader, Saddam Hussein, was said to have acquired so-called weapons of mass destruction; in making the case for the invasion, the George W. Bush administration had strongly suggested a link between Hussein and the September 11, 2001 terrorist attacks on the U.S. "Thirty-five years ago, I found myself half a world away in a place called Vietnam," Reyes said, as reported by Juan Gonzalez for the New York *Daily News* (October 15, 2002). "Mothers and fathers and veterans come to me and tell me, 'Please, do not let us get back into a war without exhausting all other avenues.'" Reyes also said, "As a member of the Committee on Intelligence, I have asked consistently the question . . . what is the connection between 9/11 and Iraq and Saddam Hussein? None. What is the connection between Iraq and Saddam Hussein and Al Qaeda? Very little, if any. As to weapons of mass destruction . . . there is a lot of speculation." Reyes, the chairman of the Hispanic Caucus since 2000, organized opposition to the invasion, and eventually the Hispanic Caucus voted unanimously against it. In a 2006 interview Reyes spoke about his frustration with what he described as "intelligence [that] was cherry-picked and manipulated" to justify the Iraq invasion. His view gained popularity, as policies regarding the invasion and subsequent occupation of Iraq have since been widely criticized and emerged as a primary concern of voters during congressional elections in 2006. Although Reyes spoke out initially against the invasion of Iraq, he has since called for increasing the number of troops in both Iraq and Afghanistan, to provide stability in the two countries.

In late 2006, following elections that gave Democrats control of Congress, the incoming House Speaker, Nancy Pelosi, appointed Reyes chairman of the House Intelligence Committee, passing over two representatives with greater seniority. Pelosi issued a statement after Reyes's appointment praising him for "impeccable national security credentials," as reported by Greg Simmons for the Web site of Fox News (December 1, 2006). "When tough questions are required, whether they relate to intelligence shortcomings before the 9/11 attacks or the war in Iraq, or to the quality of intelligence on Iran or North Korea, he does not hesitate to ask them," Pelosi added. Reyes took over the House Intelligence Committee at a pivotal time, as the Democrats attempted to shape the U.S. course in Iraq and Afghanistan and examine the constitutionality of domestic-surveillance programs and other national-security directives. In an interview with Katherine Shrader for the Associated Press (December 1, 2006), Reyes said that he wanted to study the present state of U.S. intelligence, specifically changes made following the Iraq invasion regarding "human intelligence," or traditional spying, versus electronic surveillance. Reyes, who enjoys some bipartisan support despite having voted primarily along party lines during his five previous terms in office, was viewed by some pundits as a good choice to unite the Intelligence Committee, which has been beset by partisan infighting.

Reyes soon weathered criticism focusing on his qualifications for the key congressional post. Jeff Stein, writing for *Congressional Quarterly* (December 8, 2006), reported shortly after Reyes took over as House Intelligence chairman that the congressman had not been able to distinguish between Sunni Muslims and Shi'ite Muslims. Talking to Stein, Reyes also incorrectly described the terrorist network Al Qaeda as "predominantly Shi'ite" (it is a Sunni organization) and seemed confused when asked about the Islamic militant group Hezbollah. Stein's article drew considerable attention from the news media; the late-night TV talk-show host Jay Leno joked in response to the story, "Apparently, the term 'intelligence committee' is just a suggestion." Stein noted a week later for *Congressional Quarterly* (December 15, 2006), "Reyes's evident ignorance about Islamic terrorists is common among members of the intelligence oversight committees and rampant in the ranks of new recruits to the spy agencies themselves." Reyes, Stein noted, merely "had the misfortune to be . . . Pelosi's awkward choice to head the House Intelligence Committee." Despite that inauspicious beginning, Reyes has proven to be a capable facilitator. Under his watch the committee has investigated the Federal Bureau of Investigation's use of national security letters, or subpoenas used to obtain data relating to individuals; the U.S. intelligence services in Iraq; and the Executive Warrantless Surveillance Program. Reyes has also overseen the passage of the Foreign Intelligence Surveillance Act, which sets guidelines for requesting authorization of electronic surveillance or physical searches, and the Intelligence Authorization Act, authorizing appropriations for fiscal year 2008 for intelligence activities.

Reyes divides his time between Washington, D.C., and El Paso. He lives with his wife, Carolina; the couple have three children and three grandchildren. Reyes's hobbies include woodcarving, reading, and drawing.

—N.W.M.

Suggested Reading: Associated Press Dec. 1, 2006, Dec. 29, 2006; *Congressional Quarterly* (on-line) Dec. 8, 2006, Dec. 15, 2006, Dec. 18, 2006; *Dallas Morning News* J p1 July 6, 1997; Fox News (on-line) Dec. 1, 2006; *Miami Herald* July 13, 2001; *New York Times* A p1+ Sep. 14, 1994

Sarah Huff, courtesy of University of Tennessee College of Law

Reynolds, Glenn Harlan

Aug. 27, 1960– Law professor; blogger

Address: University of Tennessee College of Law, 1505 W. Cumberland Ave., Knoxville, TN 37996

Called the "king of the bloggers" and the "blogfather," among other labels, Glenn Harlan Reynolds, the Beauchamp Brogan distinguished professor of law at the University of Tennessee, describes himself on his Web site as a "libertarian transhumanist." Reynolds is widely known for spearheading the "warblog" movement on InstaPundit, the Web log, or blog, that he began running in August 2001 and that has since earned the name "the Grand Central Station of Bloggerville." Reynolds's blog came to prominence following the terrorist attacks on the U.S. on September 11, 2001, when the public was hungry for commentary on the event. He has since discussed other matters of great interest, including national politics and developments in Iraq. He has also used his blog to comment about his favorite band, Creedence Clearwater Revival. "The site is universal: it's about anything and everything," Joshua Micah Marshall, who runs the blog Talking Points Memo, told Noah Shachtman for the *New York Times* (January 16, 2003). "And [Reynolds] is so prolific that reading his site is a great way to get an entree into what's going on in the media. It's like he's showing you around the Web." InstaPundit is now consistently ranked among the 100 most-visited blogs on the Internet.

Reynolds's work in academia focuses on space law and the Second Amendment to the U.S. Constitution. Since his status in the blogosphere has grown, he has become a commentator on the new media and other technologies that are helping to transform the world. He is the author of *An Army of Davids: How Markets and Technology Empower Ordinary People to Beat Big Media, Big Government, and Other Goliaths* (2006), which examines the intersection between technology and individual liberty. While Reynolds believes that the new media have the power to change society, his main motivation for blogging is that he thinks it is fun, especially when compared with writing an article for a law journal. "The essence of blogging is that it's done in real time and you can revise it in real time," he explained to Jonathan Weisberg for the *Yale Law Review* (Summer 2003). "It's as close to a seamless experience of having thoughts in your head appear in front of people as has been made possible so far." "The Internet's just a big playground for guys like me," he told Shachtman. "I've got all these ideas, and now there's a way to act on them."

Glenn Harlan Reynolds was born on August 27, 1960 in Birmingham, Alabama, to Charles Harlan Reynolds, a professor in the Religious Studies Department at the University of Tennessee, and Glenda Lorraine Childress, a librarian. He has at least one sibling, a brother. Reynolds grew up largely in Knoxville, Tennessee, and became a voracious learner when he was very young. "I literally read the encyclopedia when I was a kid," he told Jeffrey Knight for the *American Lawyer* (September 12, 2002). "I'm a geek. I'm a dweeb. I'm not ashamed of it." Reynolds graduated from the University of Tennessee with a B.A. degree in 1982 and then entered the Yale University Law School, where he co-founded the Law and Technology Association. After earning a J.D. degree, in 1985, he became a law clerk for the U.S. Court of Appeals in Nashville, Tennessee. In 1986 he moved to Washington, D.C., and became an associate with the firm Dewey, Ballantine, Bushby, Palmer and Wood. His specialty was the growing field of space law. In 1989 he published *Outer Space: Problems of Law and Policy*, a textbook he wrote with Robert P. Merges. Explaining his interest in the field to Dean Calbreath for the *Washington Business Journal* (December 19, 1988), Reynolds said, "It's a wide open area, which can be particularly exciting for a young lawyer, since if you make a good argument in a case, you can sometimes end up making law."

Reynolds returned to the University of Tennessee in 1989 to teach law and work as a scholar. He also remained active outside academia. In 1994 he

was given a one-year appointment as the chair of the executive committee of the National Space Society, for which he had served on the White House Advisory Committee in 1992. In 1997, with Peter W. Morgan, he published *The Appearance of Impropriety: How the Ethics Wars Have Undermined American Government, Business, and Society*. In that book Reynolds and Morgan argued that the value of true ethical behavior has diminished in the U.S., because people are being rewarded for the appearance of such behavior rather than its reality. Reviewing the book for the *Dallas (Texas) Morning News* (November 2, 1997), Philip Seib wrote, "A true understanding of ethics requires careful thought, not reliance on slogans and self-serving rhetoric. By pointing out this need for intellectual sophistication, *The Appearance of Impropriety* . . . serves an important purpose."

A prolific writer for law journals, Reynolds began posting his opinions on blogs in 2001, contributing to the Fray—the readers' forum for the online magazine *Slate*—for which he wrote under several pseudonyms, among them AGAndroid. Reynolds's posts soon caught the attention of readers, who were impressed by their diverse subject matter, strong opinions, and frequency. Buoyed by his reception on the Fray, Reynolds began his own blog, called InstaPundit, in August 2001. "Part of a law professor's job description is 'public service and education.' I'm supposed to write op-eds, talk to community groups and alumni, etc," he explained on his Web site. "InstaPundit is just that sort of thing writ large." The site originally covered all sorts of topics, from gun control to nanotechnology to Hollywood blockbusters. Within the first few weeks, Reynolds noticed that his blog had had 600 individual visitors, far more than he had expected. On September 10, 2001 some 1,600 readers visited it to read Reynolds's opinions about certain tax cuts. The next day—the day of the terrorist attacks—Reynolds's site had almost three times as much traffic. Amidst the chaotic footage of the attacks and the confused reportage in the mainstream news media, Reynolds posted 34 pieces, offering facts and assessing the situation with what proved to be great foresight. One post, for example, bore the headline "George Bush Is Now the Most Powerful Person in the World," and another warned about "hysterical overreaction against American Muslims and Arab-Americans." After the attacks InstaPundit's popularity continued to increase, with readers drawn to Reynolds's measured perspective and dedicated posting. "What surprised me was that it seemed to mean a lot to people who were reading it," Reynolds told Weisberg. "I got a lot of very emotional email from people thanking me for making sense of [the terrorist attacks], saying that they couldn't stand sitting there and watching CNN and seeing them run the footage of the planes hitting the towers for the 900th time."

In the wake of the terrorist attacks and especially after the U.S. invasion of Iraq, in 2003, a new type of blogger appeared: the so-called warblogger. Before September 11, 2001 bloggers had been largely avoiding politics, concentrating instead on developments in technology or such personal matters as parenting, food, gardening, and crafts. The warblog, by contrast, consists of posts exclusively or almost exclusively about politics, often regarding the war on terror or the war in Iraq. Reynolds, who defended the war in Iraq, was among the most prominent warbloggers. "I really didn't intend to write so much about war and international relations and all that, because that was not such a big issue when I started," he told Weisberg. "And I have to say I regret the change in emphasis, even if it's getting me more page views. . . . I'd really rather be making fun of media coverage of shark attacks." Reynolds and other warbloggers take issue with that label, because it suggests a focus on the war rather than politics in general. Reynolds has written about political topics unrelated to the war on terror and the war in Iraq. In December 2002, for instance, Reynolds was among a small group of bloggers who called attention to comments made by Trent Lott, then the U.S. Senate minority leader, that suggested that Lott supported racial-segregation policies. Lott's statement—that America might be a better place if the segregationist Strom Thurmond, a longtime U.S. senator from South Carolina, had won his bid to become president in the late 1940s—had been overlooked by the mainstream press but was discussed on two blogs and was brought to Reynolds's attention. After several InstaPundit posts calling for Lott's resignation, the senator and his remark became a major subject of discussion in the wider blogosphere and then in the traditional news media. Lott was forced to step down from his post days before he was to become the Senate majority leader. For Reynolds, the Lott episode illustrated bloggers' ability to give ordinary individuals power. "The challenge for webloggers will be to keep it that way and avoid getting too full of themselves; the challenge for traditional journalism will be to emulate the weblog world's speed, openness, and lack of pretension," Reynolds wrote in a piece for the London *Guardian* (February 20, 2003), concluding, "Such characteristics are particularly valuable."

Reynolds's book *An Army of Davids: How Markets and Technology Empower Ordinary People to Beat Big Media, Big Government, and Other Goliaths* (2006) is an extended argument on the potential of technology to be used as an equalizing force in society. According to Reynolds, blogs are only the beginning. "Individuals are getting more and more powerful," he wrote in *An Army of Davids*, as quoted by Andrew Keen in the *Daily Standard* (March 17, 2006, on-line). "With the current rate of progress we're seeing in biotechnology, nanotechnology, artificial intelligence, and other technologies, it seems likely that individuals will one day—and one day soon—possess powers once thought available only to nation-states, superheroes or gods." Those powers, in Reynolds's view, will help ordinary people take greater control of their lives, as they will use technology not only to give themselves a voice in political debates, as they do while blogging, but also to brew their own beer, create better garage-band music, custom-build children's toys, and more. "The central point of the book is the power of fun," Reynolds told Christine Rosen for the *New Republic* (June 26, 2006).

An Army of Davids was widely criticized for what were seen as its exaggerated argument and uninspired prose style: it was, nonetheless, viewed as an important introduction to blogs as a genre. "This tome won't be remembered for its lapidary prose or polemical genius. But, in its way, the book is a defining work of an era," Rosen wrote. She went on to call into question Reynolds's attitude toward blogs' superiority to the mainstream press, observing that "as the ideology's core assumptions and convictions are laid bare, the idiocies and dangers of this triumphalism become all too apparent." Rosen concluded on a positive note, however: "You have to admire [Reynolds's] argumentative boldness. He has taken figures who have been historic punch lines—the dilettante, the hack—and turned them into civilizational saviors. It's a brave new world." Reviewers also complained that Reynolds had not made his blog-writing—frequently one- or two-word comments accompanied by a link to an article—digestible in book form. "*An Army of Davids* has all the virtues and failings that you'd expect in a blogger's book: You get a personable introduction to the author and his obsessions, but the whole is less than the sum of its parts," Scott Rosenberg wrote for *Salon.com* (March 29, 2006). "To the limited extent that this scattershot approach succeeds, it's because the book resembles Mr. Reynolds' blog: cheery, brief, optimistic, opinionated, idiosyncratic," Chris Suellentrop wrote for the New York *Observer* (April 3, 2006). "Unfortunately, [the book] . . . often resembles Mr. Reynolds' blog: condescending, slight, triumphalist, data-free, idiosyncratic."

For his part, Reynolds told Kent Allen for *U.S. News & World Report* (April 2, 2006), "People oversell the power of blogs and alternative media. They don't yet have a lot of power, but they do have a fair amount of influence. They have the ability to get things into the national conversation that would otherwise be left out. That's a big change from just a little while ago, when a small set of gatekeepers controlled it all." Still, Reynolds believes that blogs will become as ubiquitous as newspapers, or—as the newspaper business shrinks—electricity. "Someone will soon announce that blogs are 'over,' but weblogging will continue at a higher rate than it's going on now," he wrote for his Web site. "It will just have become part of normal life. We don't hear much about the 'electric light revolution' anymore, but that doesn't mean we've all returned to candles."

From 2002 to 2006, in addition to maintaining InstaPundit, Reynolds wrote for www.glennreynolds.com, a blog sponsored by MSNBC. He has been a frequent contributor to Comment Is Free, a blog run by the London *Guardian*, and is a supervising executive editor at Pajamas Media. In 1991 he received the Harold C. Warner Outstanding Faculty Scholarship Award, and in 1998 he earned the W. Allen Separk Outstanding Faculty Scholarship Award. He plays in several bands, including Mobius Dick, the Nebraska Guitar Militia, and Defenders of the Faith, and with his brother he runs a small record company, WonderDog Records. Reynolds is married to Helen Smith, a forensic psychologist. The couple host a weekly podcast called *The Glenn and Helen Show*, which is available on the InstaPundit Web site.

They have one daughter.

—C.S.

Suggested Reading: InstaPundit Web site; *New Republic* p14 June 26, 2006; *New York Times* G p5 Jan. 16, 2003; *Yale Law Review* p48+ Summer 2003

Selected Books: *Outer Space: Problems of Law and Policy* (with Robert P. Merges), 1989; *The Appearance of Impropriety: How the Ethics Wars Have Undermined American Government, Business, and Society* (with Peter W. Morgan), 1997; *An Army of Davids: How Markets and Technology Empower Ordinary People to Beat Big Media, Big Government, and Other Goliaths*, 2006

Evan Agostini/Getty Images

Richards, Cecile

July 15, 1957– President of Planned Parenthood Federation of America

Address: Planned Parenthood Federation of America, 434 W. 33d St., New York, NY 10001

In a climate in which the issue of health care has grown increasingly politicized, the traditionally nonpartisan organization Planned Parenthood Federation of America (PPFA) is becoming more politicized as well. The organization's decision in February 2006 to turn for leadership to Cecile Richards—the first PPFA president since its founding, in 1916, whose background is not in health care

but in politics—is the foremost indicator of that shift. A daughter of the late Ann Richards, a governor of Texas and two-term state treasurer, she has been involved in politics and organizing for much of her life. As a college student and for years afterward, she coordinated grassroots efforts ranging from helping to unionize janitors in Los Angeles, California, to mobilizing hotel workers in New Orleans, Louisiana. After she returned to her native Texas, she formed the Texas Freedom Network, a group dedicated to monitoring and combating the expanding influence of conservative Christians on Texas school boards. After pro-choice work with the Turner Foundation and a stint as deputy chief of staff for Democratic U.S. congresswoman Nancy Pelosi of California (currently the Speaker of the House), Richards became president of America Votes, a coalition of Democratic interest groups. During her time with America Votes, she was often praised for her persistence and diplomacy in bringing together disparate groups. Her supporters have noted that such characteristics and skills will serve her well as she tries to reenergize the pro-choice movement, which has lost much of its urgency in the decades since the U.S. Supreme Court's decision in *Roe v. Wade* (1973), which ruled as unconstitutional most state and federal laws that outlawed or restricted abortions. "For today's increasingly antichoice, burned-out climate, Richards is just what Planned Parenthood's legendary founder, Margaret Sanger, might have ordered: quietly confident, friendly, and genuine," Jennifer Baumgardner wrote for the *Nation* (November 13, 2006). "Cecile has 'it' the way some people just have it," Jatrice Martel Gaiter, the head of Planned Parenthood Metropolitan Washington, told Baumgardner. "'It' being charm, class, beauty, brains, and being tough as nails." In light of her political pedigree and extensive experience, Richards has often been asked to run for elective office, but she has turned down all entreaties, preferring to remain in the more hands-on role of an organizer. "I love organizing," she told Dave McNeely for the *Austin (Texas) American-Statesman* (July 15, 1998). "I love building something where there was nothing, giving people an opportunity to do something for themselves—particularly women." Richards told Robin Finn for the *New York Times* (March 11, 2006) that her job at Planned Parenthood is perfect for her at this stage of her career. "I've had the luxury all my life of having jobs where I got to feel like I was making an enormous difference in the lives of working people, and coming to Planned Parenthood is like coming full circle. I'm serving the women who grew up in the same families I was organizing. It feels totally right."

The first of the two daughters and two sons of David Richards and Ann Richards (the former Dorothy Ann Willis), Cecile Richards was born on July 15, 1957 in Waco, Texas. Her father was a labor and civil rights attorney; at the time of her birth and for more than a dozen years afterward, her mother was a homemaker. During Richards's early years, in Dallas, both of her parents were active in Democratic politics in Texas. "I grew up in a very political family," she told S. C. Gwynne for *Texas Monthly* (August 2004). "Other families did bowling. We did politics." "Our four kids grew up in an atmosphere where you could not eat on the dining room table because it was always full of political mailings," Ann Richards, who died in 2006, told Gwynne. "When they were really small, they could fold letters and stuff them into envelopes and seal them. As they progressed in their abilities, they learned how to put a stamp on them and sort them out by precinct." The first dance Richards attended, when she was nine, was the kickoff for a protest march on the state capitol, in Austin, by Chicano farmworkers. When Richards was 10 she started a recycling campaign in her household. One day when she was 12, she wore a black armband to school to protest the Vietnam War and was sent home. In 1969 the Richardses moved to Austin. Two years later Cecile became the first female page in the Texas State Senate. In 1972, while attending Saint Stephen's Episcopal School, a private Austin high school, she worked on the successful campaign for a seat in the state House of Representatives of Sarah Weddington, one of the attorneys who, in 1971 and 1972, represented "Jane Roe" (the pro-abortion side) in arguments before the U.S. Supreme Court in the case of *Roe v. Wade*. (Ann Richards managed Weddington's campaign and became her administrative assistant.)

After Richards graduated from high school, in 1975, she enrolled at Brown University, in Providence, Rhode Island, where she majored in history. As an undergraduate she actively supported a janitors' movement for better working conditions on campus. She earned a bachelor's degree from Brown in 1980. Richards told Diane Jennings for the *Dallas Morning News* (March 12, 2006) that her sense of duty contributed to her choice of career. "I had lived a very privileged life. I had an education that very few, very few people are so fortunate

to get, and what was I going to give back?" After her graduation Richards became involved in various movements across the country; she organized garment workers in the Rio Grande Valley, nursing-home employees in East Texas (an area encompassing all or parts of 49 counties), janitors in Los Angeles, and hotel workers in New Orleans, Louisiana. In New Orleans she met her future husband, Kirk Adams, who was also a labor organizer. The couple married in 1982.

In 1990, Richards and Adams moved with their first child, a daughter, to Austin to help with Ann Richards's campaign for Texas governor. By that point Ann's political career was moving at full steam. The elder Richards endured a brutal campaign, which included frequent references to her former (and admitted) problems with alcoholism and unfounded allegations of drug problems. She narrowly won the race, becoming the first female governor of Texas to be elected in her own right. (The previous female governor, Miriam A. "Ma" Ferguson, had run for office and served as a proxy for her husband, James E. "Pa" Ferguson, who had been impeached and removed from the governorship.) In 1994 Richards helped with her mother's reelection campaign, this time against the Republican George W. Bush. Ann suffered a surprising defeat, losing to Bush by 7 percentage points. Although the loss was a blow for the Richards family, in some ways it helped Cecile. "I think my mom's loss was a liberating thing," Richards told Nancy Kruh for the *Dallas Morning News* (July 5, 1996). "I was no longer the governor's daughter." Nevertheless, Richards was deeply disturbed and angered by the smear campaigns against her mother—which included suggestions that her mother promoted homosexuality and was possibly a lesbian herself. "The whole tone and feeling about politics had changed, just in four years," she recalled to Kruh. "I was really alarmed by the whole dynamic of politics. I was really concerned that people were feeling very hateful. They were on a mission to eradicate these 'godless, anti-family officials' they thought were ruining the country."

Rather than blaming Republicans for the poisoning of the political atmosphere, Richards took a nonpartisan stance, focusing her energy on the increasing power of conservative Christian groups in Texas. In 1995 she founded the Texas Freedom Network, a nonprofit, nonpartisan group that, according to its Web site, "advances a mainstream agenda of religious freedom and individual liberties to counter the religious right"; currently, its membership includes more than 26,000 members of the clergy and community leaders. Richards formed the alliance in response to what she and many others saw as a movement by conservative Christian groups to win seats on local Texas school boards, where they could push for changes in school curriculums to mirror their personal beliefs, particularly in connection with school prayer and the controversial topics of evolution and creationism. "Regardless of party or background, people are not comfortable with extremists taking over, whether in the schools or in their political party or in running government," Richards told Sue Anne Pressley for the *Washington Post* (November 7, 1995). "They [the Christian right] definitely have a right to be involved and I applaud their efforts . . . . Our concern is when folks with a fairly extreme ideology want to run everything and there's no room for people who look at things differently." In deciding to establish the organization, Richards was inspired by the example of her mother; as she told Kruh, "One thing my mom would always say to us is, 'What's the worst that could possibly happen?' I decided the worst thing is I could wake up when I was 70 and say, 'I wish I'd done that.' And that would be worse than any failure." In the early days of the network, Richards could afford to pay only herself and one full-time assistant, because she depended entirely on donations for funding; the rest of the work was handled by a band of devoted volunteers. The response of many sectors of the public to news of the group's formation was "amazing," as she recalled to Pressley. "The interesting thing to me is the diversity of folks. I was thinking this would only appeal to people who are very political. But what I'm finding are PTA [Parent-Teacher Association] moms, people who have served on school boards, people who have been run out of their own churches. When you get right down to it, the question is, is the mainstream finally going to organize?" Members of the religious right, not surprisingly, reacted negatively to the alliance's activities. "I think, by and large, they simply follow us around," Wyatt Roberts, the executive director of the Texas chapter of the conservative Christian group the American Family Association, told Sue Anne Pressley. "From what I can tell, they have no agenda other than to oppose conservative Christians. I think it goes deeper, though. I think there's a sincere dislike for Christians. I think it's religious bigotry."

To counter such claims, and to promote a more mainstream version of Christianity throughout the state by involving religious leaders in speaking out against aspects of conservative Christian movements, in 1996 Richards formed the Texas Faith Network, as an arm of the Texas Freedom Network (which already had religious leaders among its members). Richards, who was raised a Unitarian and had embraced Methodism as an adult, has said that her difficulties with politically and socially conservative Christians helped her to clarify her own religious beliefs. "I've said to people on the right, I have to thank them for getting me back to my religious faith," she told Kruh. "The Methodist church, besides my family, has been the single most important support this year." Jim Rigby, a Presbyterian minister and an early member of the Texas Freedom Network, praised Richards for her balanced approach to their work. "Her genes should be donkeylike, but she doesn't want to be a talking head for the Democrats," he told Kruh. "The issues are much deeper than that. The princi-

ples that animate her activities belong to both parties." Richards told Kruh, "I've made the best friends and best enemies in the past year." She also said, "I don't seek controversy, but we all have an obligation to stand up for what we believe in, no matter the consequences. That sounds so heroic, but that's the way I was brought up."

In 1998 Bill White, the chairman of the Texas state Democratic Party, announced that he would not run for another term. Richards, who by then had three children, was the party favorite for the position, but she decided not to run. "For the first time, we really faced what being a full-time party chair would require and the sacrifices it would mean for us as a family," she told Ken Herman for the *Austin American-Statesman* (April 29, 1998). That year Richards's husband accepted the position of chief organizer of the AFL-CIO (the American Federation of Labor and Congress of Industrial Organizations), an association of national and international labor unions, and the family moved to Washington, D.C. There, Richards became involved in a variety of causes. She served as an AFL-CIO organizing director before working with the Turner Foundation (which makes grants in the areas of environmental conservation and population control), designing and directing a pro-choice project. She also created and served as president of Pro-Choice Vote, the largest 527 political committee active in the 2000 election season. (Such organizations, named for the section of the federal tax code that regulates them, are permitted to raise unlimited amounts of money as long as they do not use the funds to actively support or oppose specific candidates.) In 2002 Richards became deputy chief of staff for Congresswoman Nancy Pelosi, shortly after Pelosi's colleagues elected her the minority whip of the House. During the first year of her 18-month stint as Pelosi's aide, Pelosi won election as House minority leader.

Federal campaign-finance reform measures in 2002 led to Richards's next job: president of America Votes, a Washington-based coalition of unions and liberal interest groups, founded in mid-2003, which was allowed to receive unlimited donations as long as it did not communicate directly with, or run advertisements for or against, specific candidates; it could, however, run ads about specific issues, which would imply which candidates the organization supported or opposed. Conservatives vehemently criticized America Votes, and some, among them Richard Poe, a senior fellow at the Center for the Study of Population Culture, a conservative think tank, questioned the coalition's legality. "The organization she ran was nothing more than a way to circumvent the campaign-finance laws against groups that illegally coordinate with a political party," Poe told Michael Anft for the *Chronicle of Philanthropy* (March 23, 2006). America Votes raised more than $350 million in 2003-04, most of which was spent to register voters in localities where the majority of residents were believed to be sympathetic to the Democratic Party platform. The party has historically been plagued by factionalism, which has caused many people to regard it as little more than a collection of strident special-interest groups; America Votes was an effort to coordinate Democrats' efforts in pursuit of the greater goal of electing a Democratic president. Although the 2004 Democratic presidential candidate, Senator John Kerry of Massachusetts, lost his bid for the White House, Richards considered America Votes to be a success. "I think it really grew into a much stronger coalition just because folks realized the benefit of people joining hands and working together from the labor movement, the environmental movement, women's movement, civil rights movement," she told Robert Siegel for National Public Radio's Election Day news special (November 2, 2004). "And what we saw today was just an unbelievable coming together of this coalition across the country from Pennsylvania to Florida."

On February 15, 2006 Richards succeeded the interim president of PPFA, Karen Pearl, who had replaced Gloria Feldt, Planned Parenthood's head from 1996 to 2005. PPFA is the nation's largest provider of sexual and reproductive health care; it operates 860 clinics, with at least one health center or affiliate health center in each state. Beyond their common mission, the clinics have little holding them together. "We are a federation of separate and distinct entities trying to knit ourselves into a movement," PPFA's chief executive officer, Sarah Stoesz, told Baumgardner. "Before Cecile, we didn't have a chance. Now we do." Richards's background in political organizing rather than health care has been regarded, both positively and negatively, as evidence of the increasing politicization of PPFA. In 2004, while Feldt was still its president, PPFA endorsed a presidential candidate (John Kerry) for the first time in its history. "We have the potential to swing the vote in 2006, 2008, and 2010, and that's a lot of power," Richards told Baumgardner. "The question is, What are we going to do with it? And the answer is, We're going to use it. . . . Planned Parenthood is going to become more political so that healthcare can become less politicized."

Weeks after Richards assumed the presidency of PPFA, South Dakota's governor signed into law a bill banning abortion under all circumstances except cases in which the life of a pregnant woman was endangered, making it the most far-reaching ban on abortion to be signed into law since Roe v. Wade legalized abortion in 1973. "Who knew it would actually happen?" Richards told Robin Finn. "I guess it's what I bargained for in general when I took this job. They're kind of going for broke to see if they can undo Roe." South Dakota voters rejected the new law, but it was a narrow victory for the pro-choice camp, and one that rested largely on the failure of the law to make exemptions for victims of rape or incest. The court also backed the rights of anti-abortion demonstrators to protest at abortion clinics, overturning a previous injunction by the Seventh U.S. Circuit Court of Appeals. Richards believes that the challenge presented in South Dakota is in some ways a necessary catalyst for a generation of women who grew up taking for granted the Roe v. Wade ruling and their right to undergo abortions. "I think it's going to be extremely hard for the average American to realize now that these people are talking about criminalizing abortion," she said to Finn. "Maybe it will be a bit of a wake-up call to everybody else in this country—is this a right that women have, or is this a right that politicians can take away?"

Meanwhile, the U.S. Supreme Court heard a case, called Gonzales v. Carhart, about the consitutionality of a federal ban on late-term abortion, the Partial Birth Abortion Act of 2003, which was struck down by judges in California, Nebraska, and New York. On April 18, 2007, in a five-to-four decision, the Supreme Court upheld the consitutionality of the ban, marking the first time the justices banned a specific abortion procedure and the first time since Roe v. Wade that they approved a restriction on abortion that did not include an exception for the health of a woman. The majority decision was written by Justice Anthony Kennedy, who was joined by Justices Antonin Scalia and Clarence Thomas, as well as Bush's appointees, Chief Justice John G. Roberts and Justice Samuel A. Alito. In a blog that appeared in the Huffington Post (April 18, 2007, on-line) under the headline "A Dark Day for Women's Health and Safety," Richards called the decision "devastating." "The court told women that, with their health at risk during a pregnancy, deciding what to do is no longer up to them and their doctors," she wrote. "The Bush Supreme Court has let politicians come barging into that most personal of decisions." Richards also noted that Justice Ruth Bader Ginsberg, one of the four justices who opposed the majority's decision and the court's only woman, wrote in her dissenting opinion, "For the first time since Roe, the Court blesses a prohibition with no exception protecting a woman's health." Many joined Richards in interpreting the decision as representative of an ideological shift within the Supreme Court on the subject of abortion, especially since, in 2000, in Stenberg v. Carhart, the Court had rejected a Nebraska law banning late-term abortion for the very reason that it lacked an exception to preserve the woman's health.

Richards has been quick to point out that PPFA's primary focus is not abortion; more than 90 percent of the organization's services are not abortion-related. With an annual budget of $800 million, PPFA puts much of its resources into providing birth-control information and materials, giving Pap tests and pregnancy tests, and testing for sexually transmitted infections. According to PPFA, more than 600,000 unwanted pregnancies were prevented each year by the organization's clinics through birth-control services. "No one does more to reduce the need for abortions in this country than Planned Parenthood," Richards told

Finn. "I would welcome legislators, including those from South Dakota, to work with us on family planning instead of focusing on making doctors and women criminals." Still, with two new appointees on the U.S. Supreme Court who are expected to be more sympathetic to pro-life arguments, and with pro-life advocates becoming increasingly vocal—and increasingly critical of Planned Parenthood—Richards is ready for a struggle. "I've never taken an easy job, I don't think. I can't remember one," she told Diane Jennings. She continued, "When [Planned Parenthood] turn[s] 100 in ten years, I want women and families to be able to access safe, affordable community-based health care in every state in this country. If I can

do that I will feel like we—as my mom would say—we carried a bear over a mountain."

Richards lives in New York City with her husband, Kirk Adams, who is now chief of staff of the Service Employees International Union, the largest union in the U.S., and their three children: Lily, a college student, and Hannah and Daniel, teenage twins.

—C.S.

Suggested Reading: *Dallas Morning News* C p1 July 5, 1996, A p1 Mar. 12, 2006; *Nation* (online) Nov. 13, 2006; Planned Parenthood Federation of America Web site; *Texas Monthly* p112 Aug. 2004; *Washington Post* C p1 Mar. 25, 2006

Chip Somodevilla/Getty Images for Meet the Press

Ricks, Thomas E.

Sept. 25, 1955– Journalist; novelist; nonfiction writer

Address: Washington Post, *1150 15th St., N.W., Washington, DC 20071*

Thomas E. Ricks, a journalist who has covered the United States military and its civilian Pentagon support staff for many years, believes that the war in Iraq launched by the U.S. in 2003 has forced his colleagues to "reconsider how they thought about war," as he put it in an interview for the PBS television program *Frontline* (February 26, 2004, online). "There's almost this attitude among some journalists that war is something that occurs in the

field, and you can sit [in] the stands. It's not. Sure, it might be like a football stadium, but you have troops rumbling all over that stadium. You have [ammunition] being shot in every direction, missiles going off. There is no safe place in the stadium. I don't think it's reasonable to expect that there be a safe place in the stadium." During the same interview he said, "One of the most striking stories of the war that I can remember is, Bill Branigin of the *Washington Post* witnessed an exchange in which an American officer was chewing out some of his troops for killing a family of Iraqis. . . . He was saying, 'If you fired warning shots earlier, you wouldn't have had to shoot at their car. But you waited and waited. Then you had to shoot at their car, and it turned out to be an Iraqi family that was scared and trying to run away, and they zoomed right into your checkpoint.' He said, 'You just got this family killed because you guys didn't shoot fast enough.'" Referring to the practice of having journalists travel with U.S. military units during armed conflicts, he added, "It actually was a great example of why embedding reporters was a good thing. You don't get that sort of story sitting hundreds of miles away. You only get it if you're out there, listening to officers talk to troops, and seeing what's happening on the battlefield."

Ricks himself has often reported from war zones. For 17 years beginning in 1982, while serving in a series of capacities at the *Wall Street Journal*, he sent dispatches from scenes of fighting in places including Somalia, Bosnia, Afghanistan, and the Persian Gulf states, among them Iraq, Iran, Kuwait, and Saudi Arabia. In 2000 he moved to the *Washington Post*, where he was given the title of military correspondent. Since then he has taken a half-dozen trips to areas in turmoil in Iraq. Ricks has won two Pulitzer Prizes—in 2000, while he was with the *Wall Street Journal*, and in 2002, as a *Washington Post* reporter. He has written a widely praised novel, *A Soldier's Duty*, and two well-received books of nonfiction—*Making the Corps*, about the training and indoctrination of Marine recruits, and *Fiasco: The American Military Adventure in Iraq*, about the current Iraq war.

Thomas Edwin ("Tom") Ricks was born on September 25, 1955 in Beverly, Massachusetts, one of the three sons and three daughters of David F. Ricks and Anne (Russell) Ricks. His father was a psychology professor who taught in colleges in Ohio, Massachusetts, New York City, and—for two years (1969–71)—Kabul, the capital of Afghanistan. While the teenage Tom Ricks lived in Kabul, as he recalled to Lauren Jenkins for the National Public Radio (NPR) program *Talk of the Nation* (January 9, 2007), he "was very conscious . . . that guerrilla warfare is the Afghan national sport." Ricks attended Yale University, in New Haven, Connecticut, where he earned a B.A. degree in 1977. From that year until 1979, he taught literature at Lingnan College, in Hong Kong (part of the British Commonwealth at that time). After he returned to the U.S., he worked as an assistant editor at the *Wilson Quarterly*, published by the nonpartisan Woodrow Wilson International Center for Scholars, in Washington, D.C. In 1982 he joined the staff of the *Wall Street Journal* (*WSJ*), serving successively as a Miami, Florida– and Atlanta, Georgia–based reporter (1982–86); deputy chief of the Miami bureau (1986); a Washington, D.C.–based reporter (1987–89); and features editor (1989–92). At various times during those years, he reported on activities of the U.S. military in Somalia, Korea, Kosovo (in Serbia), Bosnia, Macedonia, the Persian Gulf, Haiti, Turkey, and Afghanistan. In 1992 he became the paper's Pentagon reporter.

In an article for the *WSJ* (July 27, 1995) entitled "'New' Marines Illustrate Growing Gap Between Military and Society," Ricks wrote that in Marine Corps boot camp, new recruits develop such admirable qualities as courage, selflessness, self-discipline, perseverance, and the desire to do their best. The particular methods used to inculcate those traits, he wrote, also foster in them disdain for American society and feelings of alienation from the civilian world. In his view, the Marine Corps had created a subculture that had set it apart from other branches of the military and led it to resist adaptation to changes in society. Moreover, he cautioned, at a time when those threatening the well-being of the U.S. were increasingly scattered and splintered, the Marines' feelings of moral superiority over those in other branches of the military and civilians, along with their belief that they were uniquely qualified to detect threats to the nation's well-being, might lead the Marine Corps to "blur the line between foreign and domestic enemies." Ricks made that warning in his first book, *Making the Corps* (1997), which expanded on his *WSJ* article. The idea for *Making the Corps* grew out of Ricks's impressions of Marines during the early 1990s in Somalia and other trouble spots, where he was struck by their fierce loyalty to one another and their sense of fellowship. In large part the book is a record of his observations of the 63 recruits in one platoon whom he followed during

their 11 weeks of basic training at the Parris Island, South Carolina, boot camp in 1995 and for a year afterward. *Making the Corps* also contains an account of Ricks's attempt to discover what distinguished the Marine Corps from the army, navy, and air force and what made being a Marine a matter of identity rather than occupation. While some reviewers thought that, Ricks's fears notwithstanding, there was little or no chance that the Marine Corps would pose a danger to the nation, *Making the Corps* received universal praise.

In 2000 the *Wall Street Journal*, along with a team of its reporters who included Ricks, won a Pulitzer Prize for national reporting for "The Price of Power," a 1999 series on the financial and personnel priorities of the Pentagon and other branches of the U.S. military in the years following the end of the Cold War, in 1991. The judges cited the series for its "revealing stories that question U.S. defense spending and military deployment in the post-Cold War era and offer alternatives for the future," according to the Pulitzer's Web site. Also in 2000 Ricks left the *Wall Street Journal* to become a military correspondent for the *Washington Post*.

Ricks's novel *A Soldier's Duty* was published the following year. Set in 2004, the plot revolves around the dilemmas several members of the military face when they are sent by an unpopular president on a disastrous mission in Afghanistan. Writing for the *Los Angeles Times* (June 10, 2001), Tony Perry called the book a "briskly paced, engrossing tale." In the *Chicago Tribune* (October 14, 2001), Mark Luce described the plot as "gripping and timely," adding, "Ricks writes with military precision, ably capturing the acronym-laced Pentagon and its snake-pit politics." Despite "a few flat moments and a couple of boilerplate plot twists," Luce wrote, "overall *A Soldier's Duty* does what it is supposed to do: thrill and entertain while giving readers a fascinating glimpse inside a culture shrouded in secrecy."

As the administration of President George W. Bush began to set in motion its plans for invading Iraq, Ricks's opinion as an expert on the U.S. military became high in demand in the broadcast media. Many interviewers remarked on his prescience, in *A Soldier's Duty*, in foreseeing the military's conflict in being ordered to a war that many of its members did not fully support. "Right argument, wrong country," Ricks said to Barbara Bogaev for the NPR program *Fresh Air* (August 7, 2002, on-line). "In the novel, I looked at the US military trying to resist intervening in Afghanistan. As it turned out, [in real life] they were actually quite happy to invade Afghanistan. But the argument that I had in *A Soldier's Duty* you're now seeing play out over Iraq, where you have an administration very eager, apparently, to go into a country and the US military saying, 'Hold on. Time out. Let's really talk this through. What does this entail? What are the consequences both for us as an institution and for the nation? And bottom line, we're not going anywhere unless we see the American people behind us.'" In 2002 Ricks and colleagues of his at the *Washington Post* won a Pulitzer Prize for national reporting, for their "comprehensive coverage of America's war on terrorism, which regularly brought forth new information together with skilled analysis of unfolding developments."

Since the United States invaded Iraq, in March 2003, Ricks has traveled there repeatedly to cover the war and its consequences. During one of those trips, the convoy with which he was traveling in the city of Najaf, about 100 miles south of Baghdad, was bombed and machine-gunned. The title for his next book, *Fiasco: The American Military Adventure in Iraq* (2006), came to him after that brush with death. *Fiasco* is a critique of the handling of the war by the officials in the federal government and the military, from its inception to early 2006. "When I first started working on it, a lot of people said, 'Why are you calling it that?'" Ricks recalled to Steve Koepp and Mark Thompson for *Time* (December 25, 2006). "By the time my book came out, nobody said that to me." In *Fiasco*, Ricks stated his opinion of the war in Iraq bluntly: "The US-led invasion was launched recklessly with a flawed plan for war and a worse approach to occupation. Spooked by its own false conclusions about the threat, the Bush administration hurried its diplomacy, short-circuited its war planning and assembled an agonizingly incompetent occupation," he wrote. He told the *Frontline* interviewer in 2004, "This war was conceived of as a decapitation war, where really they defined the center of gravity, in Clausewitzian terms, as Baghdad"—a reference to Carl von Clausewitz, an early-19th-century Prussian army officer and military theoretician. "Going in and toppling the regime, for them, equaled victory. Now what we saw in fact was, when you chopped off the head, Iraq became like a chicken running around with its head cut off, in fact in some ways harder to deal with, harder to catch. They really had not anticipated that, I think." Ricks told Terry Gross for *Fresh Air* (July 25, 2006, online) that his longtime career as a Pentagon reporter and his personal ties to many in the military did not prepare him for some of the discoveries he made while working on the book. "I like and admire people in the military. I spend a lot of time around them. I enjoy them," he said. "And as I did my research and as I read these tens of thousands of pages of documents, patterns began to emerge that were very disturbing to me. It was a little bit like having a photograph develop in front of your eyes, one of those old Polaroids or something, and you expect it'll be a photograph of your daughter's birthday party or something, and instead, as the photograph develops, you see an ax murderer standing in the background."

Ricks wrote the book, as he revealed during a live chat on the *Washington Post* Web site (July 24, 2006), "because I want to win in Iraq. I don't know a lot of officers who think the current posture is sustainable, especially as the chaos continues in Baghdad. But I still think it is possible to win in Iraq, if we get better at recognizing mistakes and adjust better and faster." He also said, "I think we could win in the sense of prevailing. But it would not look like victories in some other wars. In this war, for example, it would be a victory if, say, a leading insurgent agreed to put down his weapon and become, say, minister of agriculture." "What I tried to do in the book is summarize the views of hundreds of soldiers I interviewed, as well as facts I found in 37,000 pages of documents I read," Ricks explained in the same chat. (Those documents included uncensored e-mail messages and letters written by American troops and others with first-hand experience of the war.) "There is a ton of information out there. Is it the final word? No. But it does tell you a lot that isn't broadly understood yet about this war." In addition, he said, "I'd say the book argues that you don't get a mess as big as Iraq from the failings of one or two men, such as President Bush and Defense Secretary Rumsfeld. Rather, I think there was a systemic failure. Sure, the Bush Administration made mistakes, and failed especially to recognize the nature of the conflict in which it was engaged (which, as Clausewitz says, is the key task of the supreme leader). But I would say the military establishment bears much of the blame, especially for the flawed occupation. In addition, the media and the intelligence community made mistakes. Finally, I think that Congress was asleep at the wheel. That's crucial. Congressional hearings provide oversight and accountability and (when done well) pump information into the American system. In other wars, you had hawks and doves. In this war you had the silence of the lambs."

Not surprisingly, given its controversial subject, the book met with polarized reactions, with virtually all of those on the left of the political spectrum expressing their admiration and agreement and most of those on the right voicing their vehement objections, with some in the latter group accusing Ricks of being unpatriotic. Ricks responded to that charge by maintaining that, on the contrary, he had criticized the way the war had been launched and was being handled because of his love for the U.S. and his fervent hope for a good outcome. Those who lauded *Fiasco* included military personnel. Ricks told Larry Kudlow for the CNBC program *Kudlow & Company* (August 21, 2006), "I've been keeping track of it. So far, it's running about 12 to one from officers in Iraq, in support of this book, saying, 'Thank you for finally saying publicly what we've been saying privately.'" *Fiasco* was a finalist for the 2007 Pulitzer Prize for general nonfiction, and it won the *Washington Monthly*'s annual political-book award. "When future historians want to know what went wrong in the first years of America's occupation of Iraq, they will doubtlessly turn to Tom Ricks's *Fiasco*. . . . And when journalism professors assign books of great war reporting to their students, we hope Ricks's book will be one of them . . . ," the *Washington Monthly* (March 2007) declared in announcing the award. "Ricks's writing is clear, measured, and free from bombast—and will, without a doubt, inspire outrage in any reader who cares about America."

Ricks has been married to Mary Catherine Giblin since 1981. The couple live in Silver Spring, Maryland, and have one daughter.

—C.S.

Suggested Reading: *Editor & Publisher* (on-line) Apr. 17, 2000; *Frontline* (on-line) Jan. 28, 2004, June 29, 2004, Sep. 28, 2004; *Washington Post* (on-line) July 24, 2006

Selected Books: *Making the Corps*, 1997; *A Soldier's Duty*, 2001; *Fiasco: The American Military Adventure in Iraq*, 2006

Alexander Heimann/Getty Images

Rihanna

(REE-anna)

Feb. 20, 1988– Singer

Address: c/o Def Jam Recordings, 825 Eighth Ave., New York, NY 10019

Def Jam Recordings head Shawn Carter, better known as the rapper Jay-Z, reportedly gave Rihanna two choices after hearing her audition for the label in early 2005. Def Jam executives "locked me into the office—till 3am," the Barbados-born singer told Sylvia Patterson for the London *Observer* (August 26, 2007). "And Jay-Z said, 'There's only two ways out. Out the door after you sign this deal. Or through this window.' And we were on the 29th

floor." Rihanna, just 16 at the time, chose the former, launching a career that as of 2007 has yielded three hit albums, two number-one singles on *Billboard*'s Hot 100 chart, and a host of awards, including Monster Single of the Year and Video of the Year honors, both for the smash "Umbrella," at the 2007 MTV Video Music Awards. The singer has built a reputation for recording summer hits, including "Pon de Replay" and "SOS." "The 19-year-old ingenue, who butterflied her way from Bajan dancehall queen to American pop princess in a few short years, has executed a genre-swapping crossover move as smooth as her elastic-limbed choreography," Shanel Odum wrote for *Vibe* (July 2007), adding that the singer "seductively straddles the line between doe-eyed sweetheart and sassy sex kitten."

The oldest of three children, Robyn Rihanna Fenty was born on February 20, 1988 in Saint Michael, Barbados. Her father, Ronald, is a native of that Caribbean island; her mother, Monica, is Guyanese. Throughout Rihanna's childhood her father struggled with addictions to alcohol and crack cocaine, leaving her mother to care for her and her two brothers, Rorrey and Rajad, while working accounting jobs. Ronald's substance-abuse problems led to frequent arguments with Monica. As she watched her parents fight, Rihanna internalized her feelings and kept mostly to herself. Around the time that she turned eight, she began having bad headaches, and for years doctors were unable to figure out their cause. "They even thought it was a tumor, because it was that intense," Rihanna told Margeaux Watson for *Entertainment Weekly* (June 29, 2007). The headaches stopped when she was 14, after her parents divorced. Rihanna stayed with her mother and has remained in touch her father, who eventually overcame his addictions. "Everybody has something that makes them stronger in their life," she told Georgina Dickinson for the English publication *News of the World* (September 2, 2007). "My childhood experiences helped to make me a stronger person and a stronger woman. That is very necessary in this industry and in this career. I need to be strong and I need to be very responsible."

Rihanna told Derek Paiva for the *Honolulu Advertiser* (September 15, 2006) that she "always sang" while growing up, "but no one ever was really pushing me to do it." As a child she listened to a mix of Caribbean music—her mother would often play reggae records around the house—and American hip-hop and R&B. In interviews she has cited Whitney Houston and Mariah Carey as major influences on her style. Despite her interest in singing, she was an introvert and a tomboy. Adding further to her feelings of isolation, her schoolmates teased her for her light skin color. "I had to develop a thick skin because they would call me white," she told Watson. By her early teens she had overcome her shyness enough to start a singing group with two female classmates. In 2004, the same year Rihanna won her school's beauty pageant, the trio landed an audition with Evan Rogers, one-half of Syndicated Rhythm Productions, the producing/songwriting team behind hits for musical acts including 'N Sync and Christina Aguilera. The audition came about after Rogers's wife, a native of Barbados, heard about Rihanna while she and her husband were vacationing there. "The minute Rihanna walked into the room, it was like the other two girls didn't exist," Rogers told Watson, recalling the audition he conducted in his hotel room. "She carried herself like a star even when she was 15." Rihanna sang "Emotion," a song by the popular American group Destiny's Child, and though Rogers thought that her voice was rough, he decided to fly the singer to New York to record a demo.

Rihanna and her mother spent the next year flying back and forth between Barbados and Rogers's home in Stamford, Connecticut. After Rihanna turned 16, she moved in with Rogers and his wife, finishing her high-school coursework with the help of tutors. By January 2005 Rogers had produced a four-song demo recording, which he began sending to record labels. The first to respond was Def Jam Recordings, and Rihanna was invited to audition for the company's newly named CEO and president, Shawn ("Jay-Z") Carter. "I had butterflies," she told Patterson. "I'm sitting across from Jay-Z. Like, Jay-Zee. I was star-struck." She sang three songs, including "Pon de Replay," which Rogers co-wrote. Jay-Z was impressed with what he heard. "After my audition, he clapped and said: 'OK, at Def Jam we don't sign songs, we sign artists and we want you,'" she told Nui Te Koha for the Australian Sunday Sun Herald (July 8, 2007). Rihanna has claimed that Jay-Z kept her locked in an office for some 12 hours, until she signed with Def Jam.

On August 30, 2005 the label released Rihanna's debut album, Music of the Sun. The album's first single, "Pon de Replay," reached number two on the Billboard Hot 100 chart, and many critics called it the song of the summer. "An inspired mix of Jamaican reggae and American R&B, 'Pon de Replay' is the ideal single for a late summer heat-wave," Adrian Thrills wrote for the London Daily Mail (September 2, 2005). "One of the catchiest songs to come out of the Caribbean in years, it also acts as the perfect primer for Rihanna's first album." Though the single was well received, critics were not as enthusiastic about the album as a whole. "A hard beat and a soft voice: it's a reliable formula, and on her debut album, Music of the Sun, Rihanna spends 25 minutes sticking to it . . . ," Kelefa Sanneh wrote for the New York Times (September 5, 2005). "Just one problem: this CD is twice that long, and Rihanna sounds a bit stranded when she doesn't have a beat to ride." Despite such criticism, the album reached number 10 on the Billboard 200 chart. The second single, "If It's Lovin' that You Want," was less successful, peaking at number 36 on the Hot 100.

As the teenage Rihanna adjusted to life in the public eye, she thanked her mother for helping her to develop a mature outlook. "I know a lot for my age," she told Amina Taylor for the London Guardian (November 25, 2005). "My mom raised me to be a child and know my place but also to think like a woman. She never held back from me in terms of being too young to know certain things, so fortunately I am very mature for my age. In this business you have to work with the things that get thrown your way, the good, the bad and the ugly." The "ugly" included losing friends. "When I signed my recording deal, a few fake friends and I parted ways," she told Taylor. "I gained some who wanted to get close to me because of the deal, so they had to go as well."

In April 2006, eight months after releasing her debut, Rihanna returned with A Girl Like Me. Among the new musical styles the singer explored on that album was 1980s pop, echoed in her song "SOS," which was built around a sample from Soft Cell's 1981 hit "Tainted Love" and reached number one on the Billboard Hot 100 chart. Critics again praised Rihanna for recording the "song of the summer," and the sportswear company Nike decided to use "SOS" in one of its promotions, making Rihanna the first non-athlete to endorse the brand. "SOS" also reached number one on Billboard's Pop and Hot Dance Airplay charts and made top 10 lists in Europe. "Unfaithful," the album's second single, reached number six on the Billboard Hot 100. "We Ride" failed to make the Hot 100 but climbed to number one on the Hot Dance Club Play chart.

As with Rihanna's first album, many critics found A Girl Like Me to be a spotty collection. Writing for the New York Times (April 24, 2006), Sanneh found that despite the standout "SOS," "this scattershot album is full of duds." Barry Walters, reviewing the album for Rolling Stone (May 26, 2006), agreed, though he saw the singer's second album as an improvement over her first. The album reached number five on the Billboard 200. Rihanna was nominated for two awards—Best New Artist in a Video and Viewers' Choice—at the 2006 MTV Video Music Awards, held on August 31.

Rihanna soon had to contend with rumors that she and Jay-Z were romantically involved and that she was in the midst of a feud with Jay-Z's girlfriend, the former Destiny's Child lead singer and top-selling solo artist Beyonce Knowles. Rihanna denied the rumors. Even as they persisted, critics continued to compare the two female artists, with some calling Rihanna the "Bajan Beyonce." ("Bajan" is another term for "Barbadian.")

As Rihanna prepared to record her next album, Good Girl Gone Bad, she decided to distance herself from the image of her that Def Jam had attempted to project. "I got really rebellious," she told Watson. "I was being forced into a particular innocent image and I had to break away from it." On a superficial level, that meant cutting and dyeing her hair and trading her long brown locks for a jet-black "shiny new power-bob haircut," as Craig McLean wrote for the London *Daily Telegraph* (May 31, 2007). Rihanna told McLean, "Now I'm on a mission and I have a vision. The haircut is very liberating. The title [of her second album] *Good Girl Gone Bad* symbolises that. It symbolises freedom."

For the third summer in a row, Rihanna released what many called the song of the season, as "Umbrella," the first single from *Good Girl Gone Bad*, topped the *Billboard* Hot 100 chart for seven weeks in June and July. It also reached number one on *Billboard*'s Hot Dance Club Play, Hot Digital, and Pop 100 charts. In the United Kingdom the song held the top spot for 10 weeks, besting Whitney Houston's record for most weeks at number one for a female artist. Rihanna said that she knew "Umbrella" would be a hit as soon as she heard it, and she urged the song's producers, who initially were not sure who they wanted to record it, to choose her. "I said: 'Listen, Umbrella is my song!'" she told Matt Glass for the British newspaper *Daily Star* (July 18, 2007), recalling the night she met one of the producers. "He must've thought I was really pushy and laughed it off. But I turned his face back to my own: 'No, I'm serious—I need Umbrella.' Two days later, we found out the song was mine." On "Umbrella" Rihanna had help from Jay-Z, who agreed to rap in the song's introduction. Other high-profile guest artists who collaborated on *Good Girl Gone Bad* included the solo star and former 'N Sync singer Justin Timberlake, who wrote and sang background vocals for the song "Rehab." Further ensuring the song's success, Rihanna—long known for her beauty—filmed a portion of the video naked but for the silver paint covering her body.

The much-in-demand producer Timbaland oversaw the recording of three songs, and the singer and songwriter Ne-Yo penned "Hate That I Love You" and "Question Existing," a song about the downside of pop stardom. "Ne-Yo just knew how to say exactly what I feel . . . ," Rihanna told Patterson. "With success has come a lotta great stuff, but there's cons, too. Who to trust is a huge one." Rihanna told Sanchez her star status made it hard for her to date: "Every time I meet someone now, I always keep my guard up," she said. "I guess that can get in the way sometimes. It's like a reflex action."

Good Girl Gone Bad met with mostly favorable reviews. "All other contenders may want to consider finding a beach towel to throw in: Rihanna has got the summer locked up," Sarah Rodman wrote for the *Boston Globe* (June 12, 2007). In his review for the *New York Times* (June 4, 2007), Sanneh wrote that the album "should secure [Rihanna's] place on pop music's A-list. She has an instantly recognizable voice (giddy enough for teen-pop, plaintive enough for R&B), great taste in beats. . . . This CD sounds as if it were scientifically engineered to deliver hits." Tom Breihan, writing for the popular on-line music Web site Pitchfork.com (June 15, 2007), criticized Rihanna

for failing to reflect enough of her personality in her songs—a criticism echoed by other writers. "The chief characteristic of Rihanna's voice, after all, is a sort of knife-edged emptiness, a mechanistic precision that rarely makes room for actual feelings to bulldoze their way through," Breihan wrote. Still, he praised the album for its diverse mixture of sounds, writing, "*Good Girl Gone Bad* makes for an unexpectedly varied and satisfying listen." The album reached number two on the *Billboard* 200. Its second single, "Shut Up and Drive," which samples another 1980s song, New Order's "Blue Monday," peaked at number 15 on the Hot 100 chart.

On June 8, 2007 Gillette, manufacturer of a women's razor, gave Rihanna its 2007 Celebrity Legs of a Goddess award. The company also insured the star's famously shapely legs for $1 million. The next month Rihanna performed in Tokyo, Japan, as part of Live Earth, a worldwide series of concerts meant to raise awareness of climate change. At the 2007 MTV Video Music Awards, held in Las Vegas, Nevada, on September 9, Rihanna—in addition to performing—took home Monster Single of the Year and Video of the Year honors, both for "Umbrella." Later that month she received three nominations for the MTV Europe Video Music Awards, among them solo artist of the year.

Rihanna lives in Los Angeles, California.

—K.P.

Suggested Reading: (Australia) *Sunday Sun Herald* E p5 July 8, 2007; *Entertainment Weekly* p 80 June 29, 2007; *Honolulu Advertiser* T p14 Sept. 15, 2006; (London) *Daily Mail* p53 Sept. 2, 2005; (London) *Daily Telegraph* p34 May 31, 2007; (London) *Guardian* p9 Nov. 25, 2005; (London) *Observer* p14 Aug. 26, 2007; (London) *Times* p16 Sept. 2, 2005; *People* p49 Aug. 29, 2005

Selected Recordings: *Music of the Sun*, 2005; *A Girl Like Me*, 2006; *Good Girl Gone Bad*, 2007

Risen, James

(RYE-zen)

Apr. 27, 1955– Journalist; author

Address: New York Times, Washington Bureau, 1627 I St., N.W., Washington, DC 20006

"Everybody who knows me well knows I'm an aggressive reporter," James Risen, an investigative correspondent for the *New York Times*, told Lucinda Fleeson for the *American Journalism Review* (November 2000). "My biggest sin is that I want to be on page one. You get on page one by investigative reporting, and what I investigate is the admin-

James Risen

Alex Wong/Getty Images for Meet the Press

istration. . . . The only thing I've been in my entire life is a reporter. Everyone always thought I was a good reporter. All I want to do is come out of this with people thinking: 'He's a good reporter.'" Risen uttered those words while discussing one of his most famous—or notorious—investigations: that of the case involving the Taiwanese-born Wen Ho Lee, a naturalized American citizen, who spent nine months in prison in 1999–2000 on charges that turned out to have no basis in fact. Lee was accused of having conveyed to China, while working at the Los Alamos National Laboratory, secret information that enabled China to make great strides in its development of nuclear missiles. In that matter, Risen found himself subjected to intense criticism for having relied too heavily on information from government sources that proved to be inaccurate or false; New York Times editors, however, publicly expressed their belief that he and other Times reporters had carried out their jobs properly.

Risen was among the large team of New York Times reporters who covered the September 11, 2001 terrorist attacks on the U.S. and wrote about the events of that day, the victims, and the repercussions of the attacks, both locally and globally; their work earned the Times a 2002 Pulitzer Prize for public service. He was both praised and condemned for his revelations in the New York Times, beginning on December 16, 2005, that within months of the 2001 attacks, the National Security Agency, with the secret authorization of President George W. Bush, had begun eavesdropping on the telephone calls and e-mail messages of unknown numbers of Americans and others "to search for evidence of terrorist activity" but "without the court-approved warrants ordinarily required for domestic spying," as Risen and his colleague Eric Lichtblau wrote. While their detractors claimed that Risen and Lichtblau's disclosures aided those planning terrorist acts, the men shared a 2006 Pulitzer Prize for national reporting for their "carefully sourced stories," which, as the Pulitzer judges stated, "stirred a national debate on the boundary line between fighting terrorism and protecting civil liberty." Much of the information printed in the New York Times about the government's electronic-spying activities came from Risen's book State of War: The Secret History of the CIA and the Bush Administration (2006). "Risen has produced some of this era's best journalism on the Central Intelligence Agency and the dysfunctional relationship between the White House and the U.S. spy community," Tim Rutten wrote in a review of State of War for the Los Angeles Times (January 20, 2006).

Risen is also the co-author of the books Wrath of Angels: The American Abortion War and The Main Enemy: The Inside Story of the CIA's Final Showdown with the KGB. Before his arrival at the New York Times, he worked for three years for the Detroit Free Press and then for 14 years for the Los Angeles Times. At a meeting of the Council on Foreign Relations on February 2, 2006, as recorded by the Federal News Service, Dana Priest, a Pulitzer Prize–winning national-security correspondent for the Washington Post, said that Risen is "renowned among reporters as being never among reporters. Whenever there are news conferences or big events . . . Jim is always working in the background somewhere, which always bothers us, because we can't keep track of him."

The son of a U.S. Postal Service middle manager, James Risen was born on April 27, 1955 in Cincinnati, Ohio, and raised in Bethesda, Maryland. Readily available sources reveal nothing else about his early years. He earned a B.A. degree in history from Brown University, in Providence, Rhode Island, in 1977 and an M.S. degree in journalism from Northwestern University, in Evanston, Illinois, in 1978. In the latter year Risen got a job at the Journal Gazette in Fort Wayne, Indiana. He later joined the Miami (Florida) Herald, and then, in 1981, the Detroit (Michigan) Free Press. In 1984 the Los Angeles Times hired him as its Detroit bureau chief, and he began to report on the auto industry and labor. In 1990 he moved to the Los Angeles Times's Washington, D.C., bureau and became that newspaper's chief economics correspondent. Soon afterward Tom Wicker based one of his New York Times "In the Nation" op-ed columns (January 5, 1991) on a Los Angeles Times article (December 29, 1990) in which Risen reported that three of President George H. W. Bush's top aides had gutted an Energy Department plan, 18 months in the making, to promote energy conservation—information previously unknown to Wicker or the public. In 1995 the Los Angeles Times named Risen a national-security and intelligence reporter. Along with his colleague Doyle McManus, Risen again scooped other U.S. newspapers with a report (April 5, 1996) revealing that President Bill Clinton, flouting both a United Nations embargo and expressed administration policy, had secretly approved covert shipment of arms from Iran to Bosnia in 1994. With those articles and his other intelligence reporting, Risen attracted much favorable attention among those in the news media, and in one week in 1998, he received job offers from both the *Washington Post* and the *New York Times*. He chose to become an investigative correspondent for the latter. "The main attraction to me at the *New York Times* was visibility and impact—the same reasons everybody else goes there," he told Lucinda Fleeson.

During Risen's first year with the *New York Times*, his articles (a few written with other reporters) bore such titles as "U.S. May Have Helped India Hide Its Nuclear Activity" (May 25, 1998); "Iraq Is Smuggling Oil to the Turks Under Gaze of U.S." (June 19, 1998); "U.S. Details 6 Neutral Countries' Role in Aiding Nazis" (June 21, 1998); "C.I.A. Says It Used Nicaraguan Rebels Accused of Drug Tie" (July 17, 1998); "U.S. Directs International Drive on Bin Laden Networks" (September 25, 1998); "U.S. Stands Firm in Calling For U.N. Inspections in Iraq" (December 24, 1998); and "C.I.A. Sees a North Korean Missile Threat" (February 3, 1999).

During that period Risen completed his first book, *Wrath of Angels: The American Abortion War* (1998), co-written by the *Kansas City Star* reporter Judy L. Thomas. The book provides a history of the antiabortion movement in the U.S. following the Supreme Court's decision in *Roe v. Wade* (1973), which ruled unconstitutional most legislation that banned abortions. "The Supreme Court likes to have the last word; on abortion, it instead had the first," they wrote in the book. But the court's ruling "settled nothing; it set in motion a soul-searching, endless national argument over life and death, men and women—and God." "*Wrath of Angels* is far and away the most thorough and knowledgeable history of anti-abortion activism after *Roe*," David J. Garrow wrote for the *New York Times Book Review* (January 25, 1998). In the *Women's Review of Books* (June 1998), Celia Morris described the book as "a remarkable achievement, demonstrating how *Roe* mobilized a wholly new element in American politics—Evangelical Protestants and the Radical Right—and led to a political realignment that has profoundly reshaped the political calculus." In a review for the *Nieman Reports* (Spring 1998), Jan Collins described the book as "a compelling account" and wrote, "Based on hundreds of hours of taped interviews, personal documents and video tapes, *Wrath of Angels* gives the definitive explanation of why the movement ultimately descended into murderous violence."

On March 6, 1999 the *New York Times* published an unusually long, front-page article headlined "Breach at Los Alamos: A Special Report: China Stole Nuclear Secrets For Bombs, U.S. Aides Say," written by Risen and the veteran investigative reporter Jeff Gerth. "Working with nuclear se-

crets stolen from an American Government laboratory," the article began, "China has made a leap in the development of nuclear weapons: the miniaturization of its bombs, according to Administration officials. . . . The espionage is believed to have occurred in the mid-1980s, officials said. But it was not detected until 1995, when Americans analyzing Chinese nuclear test results found similarities to America's most advanced miniature warhead, the W-88." In 1996, the article continued, government investigators had focused on a man whom they suspected of transferring the secrets to China; in the weeks leading up to the publication of Risen and Gerth's article, the man had been identified as a Chinese-American computer scientist working at Los Alamos National Laboratory, in New Mexico. Two days after the article appeared, the suspect, identified as Wen Ho Lee, was fired. On December 10, 1999, after the U.S. government accused him of being a spy, Lee was imprisoned; he spent the next nine months in solitary confinement, sometimes in shackles, in a windowless cell—treatment usually reserved for the most dangerous criminals. During that time Risen wrote nearly 50 additional articles about the case.

Then, on September 13, 2000, in a scathing rebuke to federal prosecutors, Judge James A. Parker, who was handling the case, asserted that Lee had been imprisoned without cause and on the basis of evidence that had no foundation in fact. On the same day Lee gained his freedom, after agreeing to plead guilty to a single count (that of improperly collecting and keeping national-security data) among the 59 counts with which he had been charged. On September 26, 2000, in a note to readers that appeared on the editorial page, the *New York Times* expressed regret about its presentation of Lee's experience. There were "some things we wish we had done differently in the course of coverage to give Dr. Lee the full benefit of the doubt," the editors wrote. They also declared, "Nothing in this experience undermines our faith in any of our reporters, who remained persistent and fair-minded in their newsgathering in the face of some fierce attacks." The federal government and five U.S. newspapers later paid Lee a total of $1.6 million in damages for their roles in his ordeal. "I think I acted responsibly . . . ," Risen told Lucinda Fleeson. "At every step we reported to the best of our ability. You lay out all the facts we had at the time in front of most good reporters, and I contend that they would have [written] more or less the same story." Risen also told Fleeson, "I didn't foresee the political explosion. We wrote this piece, and the whole world exploded. Now I understand what it's like to be in the middle of a media circus . . . I can understand why people don't like reporters. It's been a learning experience. A humbling experience. It makes you realize the responsibility you have when reporting."

In 2000 Risen took a four-month leave from the *Times* to work on a book about the CIA and the KGB (the Soviet Union's secret police and intelligence service) in the late 1980s—a subject that he had covered while working for the *Los Angeles Times*. *The Main Enemy: The Inside Story of the CIA's Final Showdown with the KGB* (2003) was written with Milton Bearden, a former chief of the CIA's Soviet Division, who retired in 1994. *The Main Enemy* provides a "fascinating look at two wars—the external one between the Soviet and American spies, and the internal one between the old-line and the new-school CIA bureaucrats," James Bamford wrote for the *New York Times* (July 4, 2003). In a review for the *Los Angeles Times* (June 1, 2003), David Wise described the book as "a fast-paced page turner, a richly woven tapestry of the spy wars between Moscow and Washington in the fading twilight of the Cold War." Wise added, "The real value of *The Main Enemy* is that it assembles in one place all the interlocking cases of the period. . . . The result is an essential guide to the endgame of the Cold War, a sort of espionage Michelin with a lot of three-star stopping places along the way."

On December 16, 2005, in a widely quoted and reprinted *New York Times* article titled "Bush Lets U.S. Spy on Callers Without Courts," Risen and Eric Lichtblau wrote that, within months of the September 11, 2001 terrorist attacks, under White House pressure and a secret executive order signed in 2002 by President Bush, the National Security Agency (NSA) had been conducting taps of telephone calls and e-mail messages sent or received by people within the U.S. "without the court-approved warrants ordinarily approved for domestic spying." Risen and Lichtblau based their article on material in Risen's book *State of War: The Secret History of the CIA and the Bush Administration*, which had not yet been published; the information in the book had come from "nearly a dozen current and former officials, who were granted anonymity because of the classified nature of the program," as Risen and Lichtblau wrote (without mentioning the book). "The previously undisclosed decision to permit some eavesdropping inside the country without court approval was a major shift in American intelligence-gathering practices," they wrote, "particularly for the National Security Agency, whose mission is to spy on communications abroad. As a result, some officials familiar with the continuing operation have questioned whether the surveillance has stretched, if not crossed, constitutional limits on legal searches." "This is really a seachange," a former senior official who specialized in national-security law told Risen and Lichtblau. "It's almost a mainstay of this country that the N.S.A. only does foreign searches." The article explained that although the USA Patriot Act, which became law in October 2001, eased some restrictions on intelligence-gathering within the U.S., law-enforcement and intelligence officials were still required to seek a warrant "every time they want to eavesdrop within the United States," as stipulated by the Foreign Intelligence Surveillance Act (FISA) of 1978. "The Bush ad-

ministration views the operation as necessary so that the agency can move quickly to monitor communications that may disclose threats to the United States," Risen and Lichtblau wrote, paraphrasing Risen's anonymous sources. "Defenders of the program say it has been a critical tool in helping disrupt terrorist plots and prevent attacks inside the United States."

On the same day that Risen and Lichtblau's article appeared, the *Times* published a statement by the newspaper's executive editor, Bill Keller, revealing that Risen had obtained the information in the article a year earlier, and that at that time the *Times* had spoken to officials in the Bush administration about the possibility of publishing it. The officials had "argued strongly that writing about this eavesdropping program would give terrorists clues about the vulnerability of their communications and would deprive the government of an effective tool for the protection of the country's security," Keller wrote, and the *Times* decided against publication. The decision to proceed a year later, albeit with "a number of technical details" withheld, Keller explained, came after the *Times* obtained additional information about "the concerns and misgivings that had been expressed [by various unnamed sources and others within the government] during the life of the program" and after Keller and others at the *Times* "satisfied ourselves that we could write about this program . . . in a way that would not expose any intelligence-gathering methods or capabilities that are not already on the public record." On December 17 President Bush confirmed the *Times* report and defended the NSA's actions as vital for the nation's security.

In addition to winning the Pulitzer Prize for their reporting, Risen and Lichtblau were nominated for a Michael Kelly Award, named for the first U.S. journalist to die in the current Iraq war and bestowed by Atlantic Media (which publishes the *Atlantic Monthly*, *National Journal*, and *Government Executive*, among other periodicals). The Kelly Award citation read, "By exposing the National Security Agency's domestic wiretaps, Risen and Lichtblau brought an issue into public view that goes to the very heart of our democracy: whether the chief executive is accountable to the laws of the land—or is a law unto himself."

Risen's book *State of War: The Secret History of the CIA and the Bush Administration* appeared in bookstores in early January 2006. Like the December 16, 2005 *New York Times* article, it aroused strong feelings among those who denounced the federal eavesdropping program, the Iraq war, and other activities of the Bush administration and those who supported them. The former group argued, for example, that the administration had seriously undermined many of the nation's bedrock principles, such as the ban, in the Fourth Amendment to the Constitution, on unreasonable searches and seizures. The latter accused the *Times* of treason, for divulging government secrets during wartime and thereby jeopardizing the safety of both the U.S. and its allies. Admirers of the book included Spencer Ackerman, who, in a review for *Washington Monthly* (March 2006), wrote that it contained "a wealth of information and insight into how the intelligence community has been pushed by the Bush administration—and in many cases, willingly jumped—into its own shameful acts," and Romesh Ratsenar, who, in an asssessment for *Time* (January 9, 2006), described *State of War* as "a brisk, if dispiriting, chronicle of how, since 9/11, the 'most covert tools of national-security policy have been misused.'" Lawrence D. Freedman gave *State of War* a mixed review, writing for *Foreign Affairs* (May/June 2006), "Risen has written a short and at times disjointed book packed with startling stories, a number of which appear to be true. It reflects the view that the intelligence community's mission was undermined by Bill Clinton's indifference, a readiness to sacrifice deep research to superficial reportage, a failure to acquire reliable agents in key countries, former Director of Central Intelligence George Tenet's desire to stay too close to the Bush administration, and, finally, the collapse of standards and safeguards in the readiness to facilitate torture and domestic spying. Risen provides new examples of the shoddiness of the analytic work on Iraq and its interaction with the administration's erroneous rationale and botched occupation. There is also some intriguing material on Iran and Saudi Arabia, the veracity of which is hard to determine. This is the sort of book that focuses on the 'secret history' without bothering to explain the known history, that would provide context, and Risen is so enamored with anonymous sources from the intelligence community that he does not acknowledge those who have already written well on these topics or consider how their evidence fits with his." The book's detractors included Gabriel Schoenfeld, a senior editor for *Commentary*, who wrote for the March 2006 issue of that magazine, "The real question is . . . not whether secrets were revealed but whether, under the espionage statutes, the elements of a criminal act were in place. . . . What the *New York Times*"—and, by extension, Risen—"has done is nothing less than to compromise the centerpiece of our defensive efforts in the war on terrorism. If information about the NSA program had been quietly conveyed to an al-Qaeda operative on a microdot, or on paper with invisible ink, there can be no doubt that the episode would have been treated by the government as a cut-and-dried case of espionage."

In addition to articles about the government's domestic-eavesdropping activities, Risen's work for the *New York Times* in recent months has included a report about a surge in Afghanistan in the growing of poppies, the source of the drug opium. "Poppy growing is endemic in the countryside, and Afghanistan now produces 92 percent of the world's opium," Risen wrote in his story "Poppy Fields Are Now a Front Line in Afghanistan War"

(May 16, 2007). He also wrote, "It is a measure of this country's virulent opium trade, which has helped revive the Taliban while corroding the credibility of the Afghan government, that American officials hope that Afghanistan's drug problem will someday be only as bad as that of Colombia." Until recently, he reported, the CIA, military leaders, and Department of Defense officials, among them former secretary of defense Donald H. Rumsfeld, minimized the importance of dealing with the opium industry and "played down or dismissed growing signs that drug money was being funneled to the Taliban." Specialists from the U.S. Drug Enforcement Administration (DEA) are currently attempting to build what Risen described as "an elite Afghan drug strike force," but their recruits "lack even basic law enforcement skills." "It's Narcotics 101," Vincent Balbo, the DEA's chief in Kabul, Afghanistan, told Risen.

In a *Times* article (May 19, 2007) written with John M. Broder, Risen reported that the death toll among civilian contractors in Iraq had reached 917 in the slightly more than four years since the U.S. launched the war there, with upwards of 12,000 injured during fighting or in non-battle-related incidents. Moreover, since the beginning of 2007, the number killed or injured among the 126,000 civilian contractors currently working in Iraq has increased at an unprecedented rate. "The numbers, which have not been previously reported, disclose the extent to which contractors—Americans, Iraqis and workers from more than three dozen other countries—are largely hidden casualties of the war, and now are facing increased risks alongside American soldiers and marines as President Bush's plan to increase troop levels in Baghdad takes hold," Broder and Risen wrote. In an article dated July 5, 2007, Risen reported on the plight of civilians who return from their stints in Iraq with combat-related mental-health problems. Unlike members of the military, "the private workers are largely left on their own to find care, and their problems often go ignored or are inadequately treated," he wrote.

In an article dated October 4, 2007, Risen, along with the *Times* reporters Scott Shane and David Johnston, reported that in February 2005, shortly after Justice Department officials declared that torture was "abhorrent," they secretly issued an endorsement of the Central Intelligence Agency's harshest interrogation techniques, including painful physical and psychological tactics. Risen wrote, "The classified opinions, never previously disclosed, are a hidden legacy of President Bush's second term and [Attorney General Alberto] Gonzales's tenure at the Justice Department, where he moved quickly to align it with the White House after a 2004 rebellion by staff lawyers that had thrown policies on surveillance and detention into turmoil."

Risen lives in a Washington, D.C., suburb in Maryland with his wife, Penny, a former newspaper editor. The couple have three sons—Thomas,

William, and Daniel—who in 2007 ranged in age from mid-20s to mid-teens.

—D.F.

Suggested Reading: *American Journalism Review* p28+ Nov. 2000; Federal News Service Feb. 2, 2006; *Fresh Air* (on-line) Jan. 23, 2006

Selected Books: *Wrath of Angels: The American Abortion War* (with Judy L. Thomas), 1998; *The Main Enemy: The Inside Story of the CIA's Final Showdown with the KGB* (with Milton Bearden), 2004; *State of War: The Secret History of the CIA and the Bush Administration*, 2006

Clifford Robinson, courtesy of Macmillan Publishers

Robinson, Peter

Mar. 17, 1950– Crime writer

Address: c/o Dominick Abel Literary Agency, 146 W. 82d St., #1B, New York, NY 10024

If you have not yet read the mystery-suspense novels of Peter Robinson, the horror and fantasy writer Stephen King advised in his first column for *Entertainment Weekly* (February 1, 2007, on-line), "you have some catching up to do." Robinson's crime novels, whose main character is Inspector Alan Banks, "are, simply put, the best series now on the market," King declared earlier in a back-cover blurb for one of them. "In fact, this may be the best series of British novels since the novels of Patrick O'Brian. Try one and tell me I'm wrong." The 57-year-old Robinson, a native of England who has spent most of the past quarter-century in Canada,

is the best-selling author of 16 books featuring Inspector Banks, who works in a town in rural Yorkshire, England. Banks "came partially from me and from a lot of mystery books I read," Robinson told Lori Littleton for the St. Catharines, Ontario, *Standard* (May 4, 2006). "He evolved [into] a detective more interested in people and psychology than forensic clues." "He's an Everyman character, he's not really a super sleuth like Sherlock Holmes, or Poirot; he's an ordinary guy," Robinson told a reporter for the *Guelph (Ontario, Canada) Mercury* (April 8, 2004). "I think a lot of people, when they're reading the books, can relate to him and a lot of things that happen in his life: his failed marriage, his failed affairs, whatever successes that he may have had—I can't actually think of those, except at his job." Robinson has said that most of the e-mail messages he has received from readers have dwelled not on the plots of his books but on Banks: his emotional life; his experiences on and off the job; his relationships with colleagues and family members; his eclectic musical tastes; and his fondness for bitter (a type of beer), malt whiskey, and wine. "My readers tell me that they love Banks's humanity and fragility, and that he has become very real to them," Robinson told Stephen Clare for the *Halifax (Nova Scotia) Daily News* (June 4, 2006). "That might go against the Hollywood stereotypes of the modern-day super detective, but it seems to have struck a chord with audiences."

Robinson's first Inspector Banks mystery to be published, the critically acclaimed *Gallows View*, appeared in England in 1987 and in the U.S. in 1990; the most recent book in the series, *Piece of My Heart*, arrived in stores in 2006. Robinson's bibliography also includes two books of poems; the novels *No Cure for Love* (1995) and *First Cut* (2004; published earlier in Great Britain with the title *Caedmon's Song*); and the short-story collection *Not Safe After Dark* (1998). His short stories, some of them prize winners, have also been included in *Ellery Queen's Mystery Magazine* and compilations such as *The Year's Best Mystery and Suspense Stories, 1992*. Robinson has won a bevy of literary prizes, among them several Arthur Ellis Awards, from the Crime Writers of Canada, and a Dagger in the Library Award, through which the organization Crime Writers of America acknowledges the body of work of "the author of crime fiction whose work is currently giving the greatest enjoyment to readers."

Peter Elliot Robinson was born on March 17, 1950 in Castleford, Yorkshire, England, to Clifford Robinson, a photographer, and Miriam (Jarvis) Robinson, a homemaker. He began writing and illustrating stories as a preschooler, inspired by tales that his mother read to him. When he got older he read Arthur Conan Doyle's Sherlock Holmes stories and books by Enid Blyton (the author of a dozen series, among them the Famous Five). During his adolescence and teens, Robinson grew deeply interested in rock music and, by his own account, became "a bit of a rebel." He sang, wrote songs, and played guitar in a band called Jimson Weed. After he graduated from West Leeds Boys' High, he attended the University of Leeds, in West Yorkshire, where he earned a B.A. degree with honors in 1974. Drawn by a course taught by the American writer Joyce Carol Oates, he next entered a graduate program in English at the University of Windsor, in Ontario, Canada. Robinson has credited Oates with helping him to take himself seriously as a writer. After he received an M.A. degree, in 1975, he returned to England, where he spent several years trying in vain to find work as a teacher. He then returned to Canada, where part-time teaching jobs were abundant, and enrolled in the doctoral program in English at York University, in Toronto. Suffering from homesickness, he returned to England during school holidays. He earned his Ph.D. degree in 1983; his dissertation was about the sense of place in 20th-century British poetry. Earlier, Gabbro Press, in Toronto, had published two collections of his poetry: *With Equal Eye* (1979) and *Nosferatu* (1982). (The books were never copyrighted in the U.S.; used copies are exceedingly scarce and cost upwards of $195.) Robinson told Sandra Martin for the Toronto *Globe and Mail* (October 17, 2001), "A lot of the images and impulses from my poetry have gone into the novels."

With the assumption that he would devote his professional life to writing poetry and teaching, Robinson began working on mystery novels as a diversion. During his visits to England, his father, a voracious reader, had introduced him to books by such mystery writers as Raymond Chandler, Georges Simenon, Agatha Christie, Ross Macdonald, and Dashiell Hammett; he also read crime novels by Nicolas Freeling and the team of Maj Sjowall and Per Wahloo. He began to think that he was capable of producing stories as good as or even better than some of those writers' works. His first three efforts did not interest any publishers. "They just didn't work," he told Martin, "probably because they were far too close to me. It wasn't until I started writing about what I cared about and what I could imagine—even though I had never been in the police—that I was able to create Banks, a character who isn't just an obvious extension of me." The idea of Banks began to take shape around that time. As revealed here and there in the series, Banks's childhood and youth were similar to Robinson's. Banks does not resemble his creator physically, however, and, unlike Robinson, instead of attending college after he completed high school, he joined the military and then the police. In writing his second Banks book and its successors, the author resolved to avoid what he saw as a flaw in some classic mystery series: the failure of their recurring characters—Christie's Hercule Poirot and Chandler's Philip Marlowe, for example—to change emotionally or even age from one story to the next. "I wanted a detective who did get old, who did go through crises," he explained to Mel Gussow for the *New York Times* (July 15, 2003). "The idea was not to come up with a fully formed

character right from the start but to have somebody who is a little mysterious."

When he wrote the first Banks book, *A Dedicated Man*, Robinson did not have an agent; instead, he sent his manuscript unsolicited to publishing houses. *A Dedicated Man* drew interest from Viking in Canada, and the firm acquired it along with Robinson's second book, *Gallows View*. Viking editors altered the chronology in them, in order to publish *Gallows View* first, "because it would make a more sensational debut," as Robinson explained to Anne Denoon for *Books in Canada* (March 1994). "It had more sex and violence in it," he added. In Canada *Gallows View* appeared in hardback in 1987 and in paperback the next year; in the U.S. the hardback and paperback editions were published in 1990 and 1991, respectively.

At the beginning of the series, Inspector Alan Banks, seeking a less stressful environment, has left his job in London for one in the ficticious town of Eastvale, population 14,000, in the imaginary Swainsdale area of Yorkshire. Since Banks often works long, irregular hours, he appreciates as well as respects the desire of his wife, Sandra, for a degree of independence; after more than a dozen years with her and the births of two children, he still considers Sandra uncommonly attractive, and he regards his marriage as good. *Gallows View* presents Banks's introduction to the Eastvale Criminal Investigation Department, his boss, Superintendent Gristhorpe, and others among his colleagues. Eastvale, a popular tourist destination, has its share of crime, as Banks quickly learns, and in *Gallows View* he is soon tracking down a peeping tom; those responsible for a series of burglaries, one of which leads to rape; and the murderer of an old woman. In attempting to understand the behavior of the peeping tom, Banks consults a psychologist and finds himself increasingly attracted to her. *Gallows View* received enthusiastic reviews. In a representative assessment, Marilyn Stasio wrote for the *New York Times* (December 30, 1990) that Robinson was "an expert plotter with an eye for telling detail," and she described the book as "extremely well-fashioned." *Gallows View* was short-listed for the John Creasey Memorial Award, bestowed by the Crime Writers' Association of Great Britain for best first crime novel, and for the Crime Writers of Canada Award, also for best first novel.

In *A Dedicated Man* (1988; U.S. edition, 1991), Banks must apprehend the person who bludgeoned to death a highly respected historian and archaeologist and left the man's body half buried in a field. The victim in *The Hanging Valley* (1989, 1992) is a British-born resident of Canada, whose decomposing corpse is discovered by a tourist in the lush valley in which he had been hiking. *The Hanging Valley* earned Robinson his first Arthur Ellis Award. It was followed by the Ellis Award–winning *Past Reason Hated* (1991, 1993); *Wednesday's Child* (1992, 1995), which was nominated for an Edgar Award (formally, Edgar Allan Poe Award) by the Mystery Writers of America; *Final Account* (1994, 1995; published in Great Britain as *Dry Bones That Dream*), which won an Author's Award from the Foundation for the Advancement of Canadian Letters; and *Innocent Graves* (1996), winner of an Ellis Award and nominated for a Hammett Award by the International Association of Crime Writers in honor of "literary excellence in the field of crime writing."

The plot of *Blood at the Root* (1997; called *Dead Right* in Great Britain) hinges in part on enmity between neo-Nazis and other white-supremacy groups, on one side, and Pakistani immigrants and their offspring, on the other—a phenomenon that has often led to violence in England and other parts of Europe in recent years. The inspirations for many of Robinson's other books, too, have been real-life crimes, especially those that are not "all neatly solved and wrapped up," as the author explained to an interviewer for bookreporter.com (February 2005, on-line). "I like newspaper stories that are incomplete, that give me room to imagine the rest . . . ," he told the interviewer. "That's why so many of my stories revolve around human psychology, around why someone commits a certain crime, or series of crimes. I don't profess to know the answers, but I like to explore the possibilities." Robinson told Michelle Griffin for the Melbourne, Australia, *Age* (July 27, 2003), "I never know where I'm going with a story. Plotting is the hard thing. What I love is writing about people, finding out what they'll do, how they feel. How a crime was carried out—I find that very difficult and not that interesting." He said to Mike Gillespie for the *Ottawa Citizen* (April 11, 2004) that with each new book, he starts "by examining [the victims'] lives and sense of place." Often, until he is almost finished writing, he himself does not know the identity of the guilty person. Then, "when . . . one of the characters has presented himself as the obvious killer, I go back and plant little clues," as he explained to an interviewer for *ylife* (June 2006, on-line), a York University newsletter. "I use psychology and character, things [the culprit] says or doesn't say. That's done in the revision stage. I'm following my instinct when I'm writing."

Robinson set his 10th Inspector Banks book, *In a Dry Season* (1999), in both the present, when the skeleton of a murdered women is discovered in a drained Yorkshire reservoir, and the World War II years, when the killing took place. Banks, whose wife has left him, is feeling depressed and is drinking heavily. Against departmental rules, he begins a romantic relationship with Annie Cabbot, a new member of the Eastvale police force who is grappling with her own inner demons. Part of the novel is a first-person account by a woman who became friendly with the victim in the 1940s. In a review of *In a Day Season* for the *Boston Globe* (June 14, 1999), John Koch described Robinson as an "able plotter and smooth stylist" and a "gifted creator of fully fleshed and vividly present characters." Koch added that Robinson's "rather daring approach to

the genre has the effect both of deepening the form and intensifying the anguish and excitement we expect from good suspense fiction." The *New York Times* named *In a Dry Season* a notable book of 1999, and the novel won an Anthony Award from the Bouchercon World Mystery Convention; a Barry Award, whose winners are chosen by representatives of the periodicals *Mystery News* and *Deadly Pleasures*; a Martin Beck Award, from the Swedish Academy of Crime Writers; and the Grand Prix de Littérature Policière (2001), a French prize that recognizes the year's best international crime novel. It was also nominated for an Edgar Award.

For the plot of the 12th book in the series, *Aftermath* (2001), which followed the multi-prize-winning *Cold Is the Grave* (2000), Robinson researched cases of real couples who killed for sexual pleasure. What he learned sometimes kept him awake at night. "The problems simply don't go away when the criminals are caught and sentenced," he explained to Jamie Portman for the St. Johns, Newfoundland, *Telegram* (December 2, 2001); "they actually ruin more lives than those of the immediate victims." "*Aftermath* depends more on psychological suspense and fear than gratuitous violence," Oline H. Cogdill wrote in an assessment of the book for the Fort Lauderdale, Florida, *Sun-Sentinel* (December 14, 2001). "While Robinson is careful not to make *Aftermath* a sociological study, he explores the cycle of domestic abuse better than novels that are soapboxes in disguise." Robinson's next book, *Close to Home* (2003; published in Great Britain as *The Summer That Never Was*), finds Banks investigating both the abduction of a rock star's teenage son and the unsolved murder, in 1965, of a childhood friend of Banks. "Like Dennis Lehane's *Mystic River*, which it resembles in ambition and in pointed contrasts between past and present, *Close to Home* applies a full career's worth of investigative hindsight to re-examining events gone by . . . ," Janet Maslin wrote for the *New York Times* (February 20, 2003). "As it assesses ways the world has changed since 1965, . . . [the novel] takes on a mature, substantial aspect that is especially welcome in police procedural fiction. . . . Mr. Robinson, like his hero, understands the deeply mixed emotions that accompany a return to the past."

Number 14 in the Banks series, *Playing with Fire* (2004), was nominated for both a Macavity Award, by members of Mystery Readers International, and a Dashiell Hammett Award, by the North American branch of the International Association of Crime Writers. In that book, in addition to attempting to catch the person who set two fires that left three people dead, Banks is suffering misery and jealousy, provoked by his learning that Sandra, now his ex-wife, has had a baby with her new, younger husband and that Annie Cabbot, who had ended their relationship, has embarked on an affair with another man. In identifying the murderer, Banks almost loses his own life. Banks is dealt another blow in *Strange Affair* (2005), when he loses his only sibling, Roy, to murder. In the course of his sleuthing, he begins to regret that he and his brother had so little contact after each left home, but he also wins the grudging respect of his father, who never approved of his choice of profession.

Robinson—who in 1970 attended the celebrated Live at Leeds concert given by the rock group the Who—divided his next book, *Piece of My Heart* (2006), into alternating tales. One involves Detective Inspector Stanley Chadwick, a tough, hidebound veteran of World War II, who is probing the murder of a young woman during an outdoor rock festival in 1969. The other involves Banks, whose quarry is the killer of a music journalist. At the time of his death, the journalist had been on the trail of members of a rock group who had performed at that 1969 festival; the man turns out to have been the illegitimate son of the woman murdered there. Some months before the publication of *Piece of My Heart*, Robinson suffered a mild heart attack and went through a period of anxiety and depression. Banks, however, is more emotionally stable in the story than he had been in some of its predecessors. "I thought he needed some time and a place to heal," Robinson told Nick Miliokas for the Regina, Saskatchewan, *Leader-Post* (May 27, 2006), referring to Banks's brush with death in *Playing with Fire* and the loss of his brother in *Strange Affair*. "I felt I owed him that much."

In Robinson's most recent mystery, *Friend of the Devil* (2007), Banks is working with Annie Cabbot to solve the possibly connected murders of two women, a quadripalegic and a young college student. In a review for BookLoons On-line, Hilary Williamson wrote, "Peter Robinson masterfully moves his detectives, through the maze of his mystery, and the turmoil in their personal lives, to a cathartic ending. *Friend of the Devil* is a must read for series fans and for anyone who enjoys an intelligent, well-written procedural."

Robinson, whose Yorkshire accent is still strong, has been married since 1993 to Sheila Halladay, a lawyer and member of the Ontario Energy Board. With Halladay, to whom he has dedicated nearly all his books, he lives in the Beaches section of Toronto. The couple also have a summer home in northern Ontario, and every year Robinson spends a few weeks in Yorkshire. Robinson writes for five or six hours daily in his study at home. He told Lori Littleton, "I always have to try and find new things about [Banks]. I have to dig deeper and it gets more difficult." Robinson's avocational interests include attending concerts, traveling, reading, swimming, and relaxing in pubs with friends. He has taught writing at the University of Toronto's School of Continuing Studies for many years.

—N.W.M.

Suggested Reading: *Books in Canada* p23 Mar. 1994; *Edmonton Journal* E p13 Oct. 29, 2000; *New York Times* E p5 July 15, 2003; *Ottawa Citizen* B p4 Nov. 27, 1994, C p11 Sep. 24, 2000, C p3 May 28, 2006; *(St. Catherines, Ontario)*

Standard B p1+ May 4, 2006; (Toronto, Canada) *Globe and Mail* R p3 Oct. 17, 2001

Selected Books: novels—*Gallows View*, 1987; *A Dedicated Man*, 1988; *A Necessary End*, 1989; *The Hanging Valley*, 1989; *Caedmon's Song*, 1990; *Past Reason Hated*, 1991; *Wednesday's Child*, 1992; *Final Account*, 1994; *No Cure for Love*, 1995; *Innocent Graves*, 1996; *Dead Right*, 1997; *In a Dry Season*, 1999; *Cold Is the Grave*, 2000; *Aftermath*, 2001; *The Summer That Never Was*, 2003; *Playing with Fire*, 2004; *Strange Affair*, 2005; *Piece of My Heart*, 2006; *Friend of the Devil*, 2007; poetry—*With Equal Eye: Poems 1976–79, 1979*; *Nosferatu*, 1982

Courtesy of Lauren Havens

Rockwell, Llewellyn H. Jr.

July 1, 1944– Political commentator; educator

Address: Ludwig von Mises Institute, 518 W. Magnolia Ave., Auburn, AL 36832-4528

"I believe in civilization and oppose its enemy, the state. I believe in liberty, and oppose its enemy, the state," Llewellyn H. Rockwell Jr. told Marina Galisova during an interview for the Slovak magazine *Os* (October 9, 2001), as posted on his heavily trafficked Web site, LewRockwell.com. "I see no conflict between these two positions. It is possible to be a bourgeois radical, even a revolutionary aristocrat. The *Magna Carta* and the American Revolution were brought about by such people." A former book editor, magazine editor, and congressional aide, Rockwell is an adherent of the philosophy known as libertarianism (but he does not support the Libertarian Party or any other political party). He has often described himself as a "paleolibertarian"; referring to the British historian John Dahlberg-Acton (1834–1902), he has said, as quoted on his Web site, "Paleolibertarianism holds with Lord Acton that liberty is the highest political end of man, and that all forms of government intervention—economic, cultural, social, international—amount to an attack on prosperity, morals, and bourgeois civilization itself, and thus must be opposed at all levels and without compromise. It is 'paleo' because of its genesis in the work of Murray N. Rothbard and his predecessors . . . and the entire interwar Old Right [during the years between World Wars I and II] that opposed the New Deal and favored the Old Republic of property rights, freedom of association, and radical political decentralization. Just as important, paleolibertarianism pre-dates the politicization of libertarianism that began in the 1980s, when large institutions moved to Washington and began to use the language of liberty as part of a grab bag of 'policy options.' Instead of principle, the neo-libertarians give us political alliances; instead of intellectually robust ideas, they give us marketable platitudes. What's more, paleolibertarianism distinguishes itself from left-libertarianism because it has made its peace with religion as the bedrock of liberty, property, and the natural order."

The prefix "paleo" is derived from a Greek word meaning "ancient" or "remote in time," but the economists whose thoughts have most powerfully influenced Rockwell lived during the 19th and/or 20th centuries. Prominent among them are Carl Menger (1840–1921), who is considered the founder of the Austrian school (also known as the Vienna or psychological school) of economics; Ludwig von Mises (pronounced "MEE-zez," 1881–1973); Henry Hazlitt (1894–1993); Friedrich Hayek (1899–1992); and Murray N. Rothbard (1926–95). The basic tenets of paleolibertarianism are that economic principles and theories can be deduced only from correct axioms of human action, which in turn are derived from analyses of "the *individual*, on the acting individual as he makes his choices on the basis of his preferences and values in the real world," as Rothbard wrote in 1973 in an essay about von Mises that was posted on the Web site of the Libertarian Press. "Starting from the individual," Rothbard continued, von Mises and other economists identified with the Austrian school "were able to ground their analysis of economic activity and production in the values and desires of the individual *consumers*. Each consumer operated from his own chosen scale of preferences and values; and it was these values that interacted and combined to form the consumer demands which form the basis and the direction for all productive activity. Grounding their analysis in the individual as he faces the real world, the Austrians saw that productive activity was based on the expectations of serving the demands of consumers." In the eco-

nomic sphere, paleolibertarians value personal freedom and free markets unimpeded by government controls of any sort above all else. In an essay that appeared in *Policy* (Spring 2001, on-line), a publication of the Centre for Independent Studies in Australia, Gerard Radnitzky, professor emeritus of the philosophy of science at the University of Trier, Germany, wrote that Mises "defined the state as a territorial monopolist with powers to coerce. For him, the only role of government is the provision of security and protection of life, body and property. Anything beyond that is evil. . . . Collectivism has become a demon that has instigated wars and robbed generations of young people of their best years. . . . Mises also recognized that the nationalisation of monetary systems enabled the state to wage war to an extent and with a cruelty which were unprecedented." In a speech entitled "The War the Government Cannot Win," presented at the Wisconsin Forum on May 1, 2007 and posted on the Web site mises.org, Rockwell said, "There are some things that a state just cannot do, no matter how much power it accumulates or employs. I'm sorry to tell this to the American Left, but the war on warm weather [global warming] is not going to be any more successful than any other of these wars [the war on drugs or poverty, for example]. And I'm sorry to tell this to the American Right, but there is no way that the American government can kill every person on the planet who resents U.S. imperialism. The attempt to do so will generate more, not less terrorism." Paleolibertarians reject what they describe as the mathematization of economics (as practiced by the economists Paul Samuelson, Kenneth Arrow, W. Stanley Jevons, Gérard Debreu, Léon Walras, Irving Fisher, Gary Becker, and Robert Lucas, among others) as unsuitable for the study of human action.

The doctrine of paleolibertarianism has relatively few adherents. Rockwell acknowledged as much in his introduction to the text of a speech, posted on mises.org, that he gave at a rally held in September 2005 in Birmingham, Alabama, sponsored by the Alabama Peace and Justice Coalition, to protest the war launched by the U.S. in Iraq in 2003. "As you might guess," Rockwell wrote, "the program [at the rally] was dominated by leftists who rightly oppose the war but want big government to run the economy. I accepted [the invitation to speak] for the same reason I would accept an engagement to speak against taxes even if sponsored by a right-wing group that also favored the war and militarism. The opportunity to make a difference in favor of freedom should not be passed up, even if one's associates have a mixed-up ideology. After all, most ideologies these days are mixed up, and have been for the better part of a century. Those who want free markets domestically typically want central planning and socialism when it comes to war and peace, while those who see the merit of diplomacy and minding one's own business in foreign policy can't reconcile themselves to capitalism as the only economic system that lets people alone to live happy, prosperous lives." Rockwell ended his speech by exhorting the audience to "believe in peace. Proclaim peace. Stand up to the state. Be a dissident. Tell what is true. And do not fear the emperor-pirates. They, after all, fear you. For you help tilt the balance of history against their barbarism, and in favor of peace and freedom."

In 1982 Rockwell founded the Ludwig von Mises Institute, in Auburn, Alabama, and he has served as its president ever since. According to its Web site, the institute supports research and publishes works "in defense of" the Austrian school of economics and related subjects; it "is not a 'think tank' in the conventional sense, because it serves no political party, offers no revolving door for public officials, nor seeks to embroil itself in the pseudo-sciences of social and economic management." Its current publications include the *Quarterly Journal of Austrian Economics*, the *Journal of Libertarian Studies*, the *Mises Review* (which contains reviews of books on economics, politics, philosophy, and law), the *Free Market* (a monthly newsletter), and the *Austrian Economics Newsletter* (a quarterly). In addition to articles for those periodicals, Rockwell has written for such magazines or journals as the *National Review, Forbes, Policy Review*, the *Mid-Atlantic Journal of Business*, and *Far Eastern Policy Review*. He is the author of *Speaking of Liberty* (2003) and has edited or co-edited the books *The Gold Standard: Perspectives in the Austrian School* (1985); *Man, Economy, and Liberty: Essays in Honor of Murray N. Rothbard* (1988); *The Free Market Reader: Essays in the Economics of Liberty* (1988); *The Economics of Liberty* (1990); *Why Austrian Economics Matters* (1992); and *Irrepressible Rothbard: The Rothbard-Rockwell Report: Essays of Murray N. Rothbard* (2000). Rockwell is the vice president of the Center for Libertarian Studies, in Burlingame, California.

Llewellyn Harrison Rockwell Jr. was born into a Roman Catholic family in Boston, Massachusetts, on July 1, 1944. While growing up he often discussed politics with his father, whom he has described as a "Taft Republican," referring to Robert Taft of Ohio, a staunch opponent of Democratic president Franklin D. Roosevelt's New Deal and of the military draft, which had been reinstated in 1940. As a young student Rockwell argued with his teachers about topics about which he felt strongly; for example, he would express his opposition to the New Deal, introduced in the 1930s during the Roosevelt administration, and his belief that the U.S. was wrong to participate in World War II. He was particularly critical of the hunt for Soviet sympathizers within the U.S. government during the 1950s, instigated by the Republican U.S. senator Joseph R. McCarthy of Wisconsin. Rockwell told Brian Doherty for the now-defunct Web site SpintechMag.com (May 12, 1999), as posted on LewRockwell.com, "I told them that [McCarthy] should have been attacking the U.S. government all along, because it was the real threat to our liberties. That drove my teachers crazy. None of them

would be surprised that I grew up to be a full-time gadfly against the conventional wisdom." When Rockwell turned 12, in 1956, a friend of his father's gave him a copy of *Economics in One Lesson* (1946), by the libertarian philosopher, economist, and journalist Henry Hazlitt. In the book's preface, Hazlitt wrote, "The whole of economics can be reduced to a single lesson, and that lesson can be reduced to a single sentence. *The art of economics consists in looking not merely at the immediate but at the longer effects of any act or policy; it consists in tracing the consequences of that policy not merely for one group but for all groups.*" Rockwell told Doherty, "That book taught me how to think in economic terms, and I have been reading in economics ever since, with a special appreciation for the old French liberal school and the modern Austrians from Menger to Rothbard."

During high school Rockwell was a voracious reader; in college he majored in English. (Easily accessible sources do not reveal which school he attended or whether he earned a degree.) As an undergraduate he became fascinated by British writers' attacks against the existence of the state, German writers' commentary on property rights, and American writers' praise of liberty. He was captivated by the works of the Roman statesman, lawyer, political theorist, and philosopher Cicero (106–43 B.C.), in particular by Cicero's "love of liberty and the old republic; his celebration of natural elites and opposition to egalitarianism; and, most of all, his fighting, indefatigable spirit," as he told Doherty. He was also drawn to the later writings of the Roman historian Tacitus, who lived during the first and second centuries A.D.

In 1965, after he left college, Rockwell began working for Neil McCaffrey, who—within months of his founding the Conservative Book Club, in 1964—had launched Arlington House, with the goal of publishing literature that espoused conservative ideas. McCaffrey assigned Rockwell the task of producing new editions of three books by Ludwig von Mises: *Omnipotent Government: The Rise of the Total State and Total War* and *Bureaucracy* (both published in 1944) and *Theory and History: An Intepretation of Social and Economic Evolution* (1957). Rockwell told Doherty, "Reading these books, I became a thoroughgoing Misesian. I was so thrilled to meet him at dinner in 1968. He was already in serious decline, but it was still wonderful."

The worldview and most of the political ideas that Rockwell was embracing agreed with neither mainstream Republican nor Democratic thought. He leaned toward the Republicans when it came to the supremacy of capitalism but found himself sympathizing with Democrats who opposed the Vietnam War (though not with the hippie counterculture associated with many war protesters). He strongly opposed the 1964 Civil Rights Act on ideological grounds, telling Doherty that it was "a statist, centralizing measure that fundamentally attacked the rights of property and empowered the state as mind reader: to judge not only our actions, but our motives, and to criminalize them." He felt disdain for the civil rights leader Martin Luther King Jr. until King began to speak out against the Vietnam War. In 1964 he favored the Republican candidate for president, Senator Barry M. Goldwater of Arizona. In 1968 he worked briefly for the Democratic candidate, Senator Eugene McCarthy of Minnesota. Rockwell was deeply troubled by the domestic and foreign policies of President Richard M. Nixon, a Republican, who occupied the White House from 1969 until his resignation, in 1974. "Affirmative action, the EPA [Environmental Protection Agency] . . . massive inflation, welfarist ideology, huge deficits, price controls, and a host of other D.C. monstrosities were Nixon creations—not to mention the bloodiest years of the war . . . ," Rockwell said to Doherty. "Nixon, Kissinger and the rest have blood on their hands."

In the late 1960s Rockwell got a job at Hillsdale College, in Hillsdale, Michigan, whose faculty and student body were and are among the most politically conservative in the nation. (In 2006 the company Princeton Review ranked its students first in that category.) Rockwell's responsibilities involved public relations, fund-raising efforts, and arranging a speakers' series, and he helped to start the Hillsdale College Press. Several volumes of Champions of Freedom: The Ludwig von Mises Lecture Series were published during his time with the press.

In 1975 Rockwell met Murray Rothbard, a student of von Mises's and his most vocal advocate. Rothbard was then a professor at the Polytechnic Institute of Brooklyn, New York (now called Polytechnic University) and the editor of Libertarian Forum. (He began publishing the Journal of Libertarian Studies two years later.) Rothbard, who labeled himself an anarcho-capitalist, held that the free market was superior to any government, even in maintaining law and order domestically and securing the safety of the nation against foreign invaders. "It was clear to me at the time that Murray Rothbard was Mises's successor, and I followed his writing carefully . . . ," Rockwell told Doherty. "Like all the other living intellectuals I respected, he was on the margins, laboring at a fraction of the salary he deserved, and excluded from conventional outlets of academic and political opinion. I cannot remember the day that I finally came around to the position that the state is unnecessary and destructive by its nature . . . but I do know that it was Rothbard who finally convinced me to take this last step." Rothbard was a highly controversial figure, and Rockwell failed in his attempts to persuade Hillsdale College to invite him to speak at the school.

After Rockwell left Hillsdale, in the late 1970s, he became the editor of Private Practice, "a journal of socioeconomic medicine," as he described it to Doherty. "I worked to integrate the work of the Austrians and apply it to health economics and government intervention in that industry," he told

Doherty. "It proved to be a fruitful mix, and in my mind demonstrated the possibilities of using the Austrian tradition to explain the way the world works in a very practical way." Rockwell next became an aide to Congressman Ron Paul, a Republican who represented Texas's 22d District in 1976 (when he won a mid-term election to fill a seat that had been vacated) and from 1979 to 1985. (Since 1997 Paul has represented Texas's 14th District.) Rockwell joined Paul's staff during the congressman's first full term in office. Paul, who ran for president as the Libertarian candidate in 1988 (and has announced his candidacy for the same post as a Republican in the 2008 general election), has steadfastly condemned the federal government as a force for harm nationally and internationally, called for abolition of the federal income tax, and insisted that only Congress can declare war. "We never saw his office as a conventionally political one," Rockwell told Doherty. "It was a bully pulpit to get the message out. We sent out hundreds of thousands of tracts on freedom, inserted amazing articles in the Congressional Record, and drafted libertarian legislation as an educational effort. As for his voting record, Ron had a clear standard: if it meant stealing people's money, he was against it. If it gave people back the liberty and property the government had taken, he was for it." Rockwell supported the nomination of Patrick Buchanan as the Republican candidate for the presidency in 1992, until he decided that Buchanan's views were unacceptably nationalistic.

Earlier, in 1982, Rockwell had founded the Ludwig von Mises Institute; Rothbard served as founding vice president and head of academic affairs, and Mises's widow, Margit, assisted in various capacities. Their mission was to introduce Mises's teachings into academia and popular culture and create a formal and academically respected setting in which students could undertake research in Austrian economics. "Idealism is what stirs the young heart, and the only idealism that seemed to be available to students in those days was from the left," Rockwell told Doherty. He told Marina Galisova, "I also had my private goal of providing a megaphone for Rothbard and the Rothbardians, some institutionalized means for them to reach students and gain a voice. We were doing all of this within the first year, even though we had no financial backing to speak of." Since its inception, the institute has been funded almost entirely by donations from individuals. It has generated hundreds of scholarly papers and popular articles and hosted hundreds of conferences and seminars. Its library contains 24,000 volumes, and its Web site reportedly gets 3.5 million hits annually.

Since the terrorist attacks of September 11, 2001, Rockwell has often lectured and written about what he sees as the reasons behind them and the futility of the United States' efforts to create a peaceful democracy in Iraq and to combat terrorism there and elsewhere. He believes that if pilots had had the right to carry guns before September

11, the attacks might never have occurred. In his talk "The War the Government Cannot Win," he wrote, "The war on terror can only be considered a failure from the point of view of the stated aims. It is not a failure for those who directly benefit from the increased funding and power." The September 11 attacks provided "a pretext for war preparedness and war itself that rivaled the old communist threat. . . . No expense is spared on arms escalation. . . . What is missing in the war on terror is the essential means to cause the war to yield beneficial results. Of all the billions of potential terrorists out there, and the infinite possibilities of how, when, and where they will strike, there is no way the state can possibly stop them, even if it had the incentive to do so." Rockwell also said, "We should not ask government to win a war on terror, end poverty, make everyone healthy and literate, provide for us when we are old, or anything else. Nothing the government does takes place without a greater cost than benefit to society. Knowing this, we can still be good citizens. We can be good par-

ents, teachers, workers, entrepreneurs, church members, students, and contributors to society in a million different ways. This is far more important to the future of liberty than anything else we do. We must regain our confidence in our capacity for self-governance."

According to his entry in *Who's Who in America, 2006*, Rockwell has one daughter, Alexandra.
—S.J.D.

Suggested Reading: *Calgary (Alberta, Canada) Herald* Observer—Religion p8 Oct. 5, 2002; Frontpagemag.com Mar. 12, 2002; LewRockwell.com; Mises.org; *Orange County (California) Register* Commentary Dec. 12, 2004; pbs.org/now Mar. 7, 2003

Selected Books: *Speaking of Liberty*, 2003; as editor or co-editor—*The Gold Standard: Perspectives in the Austrian School*, 1985; *The Economics of Liberty*, 1990; *Why Austrian Economics Matters*, 1992

Rosenfeld, Irene B.

May 3, 1953– Chairwoman and chief executive officer of Kraft Foods

Address: Kraft Foods Global Inc., Three Lakes Dr., Northfield, IL 60093

On June 26, 2006 Irene B. Rosenfeld was appointed chief executive officer (CEO) of Kraft Foods Inc., a $34 billion enterprise, thus making it the largest company in the world to be headed by a woman. Nine months later Rosenfeld became the chairwoman of the firm as well. Headquartered in Northfield, Illinois, a suburb of Chicago, Kraft is the largest packaged-food company in the United States and the second-largest in the world, behind the Swiss company Nestlé; it owns some of the most recognizable brands in the U.S., among them Post, Nabisco, Maxwell House, Sanka, Kool-Aid, Tang, Velveeta, Jell-O, Planters, Oreo, and Oscar Mayer. Rosenfeld joined Kraft in the 1980s, after completing a Ph.D. in marketing. In the years that followed, she rose through the company's ranks, holding such titles as executive vice president and general manager of the beverages division and president of Kraft Foods Canada. During that time she developed a reputation as an innovator and clever marketer. In 2003, after she had served for two years as president of Kraft Foods North America, dissatisfaction with the management of the company led her to quit. She spent two years as the chair and CEO of Frito-Lay Inc. before returning to Kraft as its top officer.

One of the world's most powerful businesswomen, according to *Fortune*, Rosenfeld, now 54, is a "no-nonsense problem-solver with an almost laser-

Courtesy of Kraft Foods Inc.

like focus on improving business," as Robert A. Eckert, a former Kraft executive, told Patricia Sellers for that magazine (October 16, 2006). Tierney Remick of the executive search firm Korn/Ferry International told Susan Chandler for the *Chicago Tribune* (June 27, 2006), "She brings a great balance of strategy and execution, and she truly understands the organization—where it has come from and where it needs to go. The credibility she has with the employee population, combined with her knowledge of the business and its challenges, will translate into a very fast start." Jean Spence, Kraft's executive vice president of global technology and quality, told Chandler that Rosenfeld "is really courageous and willing to speak up for what needs to be done. She is one of the smartest people I have ever worked with in business." In recent years Kraft has been plagued by serious problems, some of which have also affected other companies in the food industry, such as the rapidly rising costs of raw materials and energy. One of Rosenfeld's primary goals is to make Kraft "bolder, more agile, more creative and more focused," according to Robert Manor, writing for the *Chicago Tribune* (September 12, 2006). "I think there's an optimistic feeling at the company," Jean Spence told Adrienne Carter for *BusinessWeek* (June 26, 2006, online). "Her focus has always been on growth—growth through innovation."

A native of Long Island, New York, Irene B. Rosenfeld was born on May 3, 1953 in the New York City borough of Brooklyn. She attended Cornell University, in Ithaca, New York, graduating with a B.A. degree in psychology in 1975. She stayed on at Cornell to earn both an M.S. degree in business, in 1977, and a Ph.D. in marketing and statistics, in 1980. In 1979, while pursuing her doctorate, Rosenfeld took a job with Dancer Fitzgerald Sample Advertising (now Saatchi and Saatchi). In 1981 she joined the General Foods Corp. as an associate market-research manager. In 1989 the Philip Morris Companies (now the Altria Group Inc.), which owned both General Foods and Kraft Foods, merged those two companies, and she became an employee of Kraft.

Early in her career with General Foods and Kraft Foods, Rosenfeld served as product manager for Country Time Lemonade. She rose on the corporate ladder to become the head of Kraft's beverage division in 1991. In that post, in which she oversaw such brands as Kool-Aid, Tang, and Maxwell House, Rosenfeld handled Kraft's acquisition of the distribution rights in North America for Capri-Sun juice drinks, which are produced by a German company. She transformed what was then a regional product in the United States into a nationally recognized brand that filled a significant void in Kraft's portfolio. Rosenfeld's success in the beverage division led to a promotion to general manager of desserts and snacks in 1994.

In 1996 Rosenfeld was named president of Kraft's Canadian operations, a position in which she earned praise for her innovations. In one example, Rosenfeld mailed free copies of a magazine of recipes and cooking tips to one million households in Canada. The stratagem sparked increased sales for the Kraft products featured in the recipes. Its success prompted the mailing of similar material to an additional 12 million households in the United States as well as Canada. In 2000, while retaining her duties in Canada, Rosenfeld was named a Kraft Foods group vice president and president of operations, technology, and procurement. In 2001 her responsibilities grew to include the management of Kraft's information services and its activities in Mexico and Puerto Rico. Among her many accomplishments during that period, Rosenfeld led the highly successful $19 billion integration of Nabisco into the Kraft portfolio after Nabisco was acquired by Philip Morris in 2000. In 2001 Rosenfeld served on the senior executive team that handled Kraft's initial public offering in the stock market, which brought the company a profit of $9 billion.

In 2002 Rosenfeld was promoted again, this time to president of Kraft Foods North America, by far the company's largest division, with five operating groups and 15 divisions. In July 2003, with Kraft struggling to maintain its stock price, Rosenfeld unexpectedly resigned, stating, according to Susan Chandler in the *Chicago Tribune* (June 27, 2006), that she had grown frustrated by the slow decision-making of Kraft's co-CEOs, Betsy Holden and Roger Deromedi. By then Rosenfeld was seen by many as one of the stars in the company, and some analysts thought that Kraft should have tried harder to retain her. "I felt at the time that the wrong person [left], that it should have been Betsy," John McMillan, a senior food industry analyst with the Prudential Equity Group, a Wall Street investment firm, said, as quoted by Chandler. He added that in 2005, when Holden resigned, "people realized how badly Irene was missed."

Rosenfeld was offered a slew of jobs after she left Kraft, and for over a year she considered her options. She turned down several CEO positions, heeding the advice of her onetime boss, James M. Kilts, a longtime Kraft executive, who told her, "Always go with the super company. Don't get caught up in the title," as Kilts recalled to Patricia Sellers for *Fortune* (October 16, 2006). In 2004 Rosenfeld accepted the position of chair and CEO of the $10 billion Frito-Lay division of PepsiCo Inc. Frito-Lay is composed of two main businesses, Salty Snacks and Convenience Foods, and features brands such as Lay's, Doritos, Fritos, Cheetos, Rold Gold, Tostitos, and Quaker. During her less than two years with Frito-Lay, Rosenfeld directed the addition of healthier snacks to the firm's product lines. Sales of such snacks increased by double digits in 2005, while sales of the company's traditional products grew by single-digit figures. Under the Quaker label Frito-Lay introduced a 90-calorie chewy granola bar—30 percent fewer calories than the original bar—and acquired Stacy's Pita Chips, adding to the company's appeal to increasingly nutrition-conscious consumers. In March 2006, making good on a promise for continuous innovation, Rosenfeld announced the debut of 100-calorie miniature versions of Frito-Lay's popular Doritos and Cheetos snacks. In an attempt to satisfy increasing consumer demand for spicy foods, Frito-Lay also began to offer new lines of snacks known as Lay's Sensations and Tostitos Sensations, flavored by, for example, "lime and cracked black pepper" and "sweet chili and sour cream." Overall, Frito-Lay's net revenues rose 8 percent in 2005,

Rosenfeld's first full year with the company, while operating profits (defined by investorwords.com as "a measure of a company's earning power from ongoing operations, equal to earnings before deduction of interest payments and income taxes") climbed 5.5 percent, to $2.5 billion.

In June 2006 Rosenfeld abruptly resigned from Frito-Lay to assume the CEO position at Kraft Foods. According to Lorene Yue in *Crain's Chicago Business* (June 29, 2006, on-line), she was given a base salary of $1.3 million, guaranteed bonuses of $1.95 million and $3.2 million in 2006, and 387,230 shares of Kraft stock (equivalent to $12 million, based on the then-current stock price) as a signing bonus. Rosenfeld has said that her experiences at Frito-Lay and, by extension, PepsiCo—where she "learned the value of a relentless focus on growth," as she told Sellers—made her a stronger leader and better prepared her to manage Kraft Foods. When Rosenfeld took over the reins at Kraft, the company was suffering financially. Its stock price had not grown since its IPO, and its profits had stagnated, in part because of fierce global competition and rising commodities prices. The former CEO, Roger Deromedi, who had run the company as its sole CEO since 2003, had begun to cut costs aggressively with the goal of increasing Kraft's profits. Rosenfeld has continued those cost-cutting measures, and by the time the company finishes the gradual restructuring that Deromedi started, the company will have eliminated 14,000 jobs and closed nearly 40 factories around the world. Deromedi had also shed the company of such barely profitable products as Altoids and Milk-Bones and developed several new items, the most successful being the South Beach Diet brand of frozen foods, which recorded more than $170 million in sales in its first year (2005–06). "I feel very good about a lot of things that have happened," Rosenfeld told John Schmeltzer for the *Chicago Tribune* (October 24, 2006). "The company is in much better shape than it was two years ago." On the other hand, Deromedi had been criticized for not using that additional capital to buy new businesses or to develop more new products. Many industry observers believed that Kraft needed a change in leadership and a more visionary business plan. "[Rosenfeld is] not a bureaucrat, and she will shake the place up," Barbara Pickens, the founder and president of the executive search firm Pickens & Co., told Stephanie Thompson for *Advertising Age* (July 3, 2006). Rosenfeld, Pickens continued, is "made of different material than a lot of people at Kraft—the overanalytical, super-playing-it-safe types. She is a tiger, she really is."

While Deromedi had favored a top-down leadership approach, Rosenfeld believed that empowering regional directors would necessarily give them a greater understanding of consumer preferences in their markets. She therefore spent the first 100 days on the job traveling to the company's business centers and factories around the world, meeting not only with Kraft staff but also with retailers,

their employees, and their customers, in order to discern their interests and motivations. Rosenfeld learned that, too often, Kraft had relied on decision-making from those at its center of operations, in Northfield, Illinois, and often launched products globally without assessing the strength of particular brands or the prospects for particular products in individual markets. Rosenfeld said that those discussions reinforced her conviction that much decision-making should be in the hands of "the people closest to our consumers, customers and markets," as quoted by Robert Manor in the *Chicago Tribune* (September 12, 2006). Some analysts have expressed skepticism about that philosophy, on the grounds that Kraft's more-general business concerns may get short shrift. "More autonomy can create more chaos, less focus on brands," Laura Reis, the president of the marketing firm Reis & Reis, told Sonia Reyes for *Brandweek* (September 18, 2006). "It's like each military general following his own orders. This is not going to solve the problem of companies like Kraft relying on line extensions [that is, applying an existing brand name or image to new products] rather then trying to build new brands. I mean, how many Jell-O and Philadelphia Cream Cheese extensions can consumers take?"

Most business analysts agree that Rosenfeld's task of increasing profitability and growth will be difficult. They have pointed to Kraft's reliance on middle-of-the-road customers who view many food-staple brands as interchangeable and are just as likely to purchase house brands at Wal-Mart, Target, or Costco as Kraft products. At the same time, Kraft must contend with the tendency of growing numbers of consumers to seek high-end, organically produced, or more nutritious or healthful items. The rising costs of raw materials, packaging, and energy present additional problems. Between 2003 and 2005 the amount that Kraft paid for raw materials increased by $1.7 billion. Robert Campagnino of the Prudential Equity Group wrote in a note to investors, as reported by Dave Carpenter for the Associated Press (June 26, 2006), "Kraft decided to switch jockeys. . . . Ultimately the horse matters, and unless new CEO Irene Rosenfeld can push commodity prices lower . . . Kraft is still, in our view, a somewhat troubled company."

In early 2007 the Altria Group (formerly Philip Morris), Kraft's parent company for years, announced the imminent spin-off of Kraft. In March of that year, Altria distributed 89 percent of Kraft's stock to shareholders, and Kraft was rendered an independent company. Subsequently, Louis Camilleri, the CEO of Altria, stepped down as the chairman of Kraft's board of directors, and Rosenfeld succeeded him in that post. Analysts predicted that the spin-off would bring Rosenfeld more freedom for innovation and possibly more challenges.

Rosenfeld has two grown children, both now in their 20s, and keeps a kosher home. She earned a Masters in Excellence Award from the Center for

Jewish Living in 2005 and has been elected to the YWCA Academy of Women Achievers. She has served on the boards of Cornell University, the Steppenwolf Theatre Company, in Chicago, and AutoNation Inc., and has also held leadership roles with the Grocery Manufacturers Association.

—N.W.M.

Suggested Reading: *Advertising Age* p3 July 3, 2006; *BusinessWeek* (on-line) June 26, 2006, Feb. 1, 2007; *Chicago Tribune* C p1+ June 27, 2006, Business Sep. 12, 2006, Oct. 24, 2006; *Crain's Chicago Business* p39+ Aug. 7, 2006; *Fortune* p134+ Oct. 16, 2006; *Who's Who in America, 2007*

Courtesy of Alex Ross

Ross, Alex

Jan. 22, 1970– Comic-book artist

Address: c/o Pantheon Publicity, 1745 Broadway, New York, NY 10019

"I'm a bona fide Superman nut," the comic-book artist Alex Ross told Russell Lissau for the *Chicago Daily Herald* (April 2, 1998). Coming from a painter who has spent most of his life portraying Superman and other costumed superheroes—revolutionizing the art of comics illustration along the way—that assertion is, if anything, an understatement. *Marvels* (1994), Ross's first book for a major comics publisher (Marvel Comics), introduced his unique style of superhero portraiture to the public. He became an instant star within the industry for his realistic representations of long-

established Marvel heroes from Spider-Man to Captain America, renderings that emphasize the characters' humanity as well as their special powers. Ross "has administered a superpowered transfusion to the medium," a "radiation blast of thrills, chills and amazingly photo-realistic artwork," Sam Weller wrote for the *Chicago Tribune* (July 13, 1999), noting the realistic details of Ross's work, which include scars, bruises, zippers in costumes, and circles under eyes. "Take one look at Ross' Superman or Batman or Spiderman and one would swear these mythical pop-culture heroes really do walk our streets and soar in our skies." With *Kingdom Come* (1996), Ross again garnered scores of positive reviews, winning a place in the pantheon of great comic-book illustrators; that position was confirmed in 2004 with *Mythology: The DC Comics of Alex Ross*, a collection of his work for DC Comics. "There are a couple of artists at his level of popularity," the graphic artist Chip Kidd, who designed and wrote the text for *Mythology*, told Frank DeCaro for the *New York Times* (October 30, 2003). "But there are very few who fit the bill of comic book artist as rock star, and Alex is definitely one of them."

Ross, though, has said that he does not illustrate comics as a way of attaining celebrity. For him, despite a surge of interest in graphic novels in recent years, comics represent an underappreciated art form, a state of affairs he bemoaned during a conversation with Jon Bigness for the *Chicago Tribune* (July 19, 1998): "Ninety-nine percent of people in America have no conception of what a comic book is like these days." In his conversation with Lissau, Ross described comics as a storytelling medium on a par with books and film: "They have a great life to them, and a valid way of communicating thoughts and images in a way that's truly their own." Even more than increasing the visibility of the form, Ross concerns himself with perpetuating the positive messages contained in the stories of his favorite characters. "Ultimately superheroes were created as not just entertainment icons, but as metaphors for virtuous thought," he explained to Robert Wilonsky for *SF Weekly* (June 14, 2000). "The entire concept of the superhero is an altruistic act, so, therefore, there's a philosophy behind that that is generally lost on modern society. Are these comics going to be part of rekindling a little bit of that? I can only pray so, but you never know if that is going to be the case." Ross's belief in the transformative power of comics has driven much of his career. "A lot of what's made me successful to a strong degree in this business is that it's obvious I'm a fiend for this stuff," Ross told Wilonsky. "I've been willing to say, look, this stuff is pure to me. It's important to me. Superman or any of these icons have intrinsic value other than the fact [that] they're nostalgic for me. I think that they have a use to the world—period."

The youngest of four children, Nelson Alexander Ross was born on January 22, 1970 in Portland, Oregon, and grew up primarily in Lubbock, Texas.

His mother, Lynette C. Ross, was a fashion illustrator who created paper-doll books; his father, Clark Norman Ross, was a minister of the United Church of Christ. Ross demonstrated his artistic proclivities early on, when, at the age of three, he drew a picture based on a television commercial he had just seen. He discovered superheroes while watching the children's television program *The Electric Company*, which sometimes featured live-action Spider-Man skits. His devotion to superheroes formed at that point, as he recalled for his Web site: "I just fell in love with the notion that there were colorful characters like this, performing good, sometimes fantastic deeds. I guess I knew this was what I wanted to do. I wanted to bring these characters to life." From the start, Ross was interested in realistic portrayals of the human—and superhuman—condition; as a result, the cartoonists who served as his role models were those known for their naturalistic style, among them Neal Adams, George Perez, and Bernie Wrightson. An equally important influence was the school of artists who straddled the line between painting and illustration, including the painters Andrew Loomis, J. C. Leyendecker, and—most prominently—Norman Rockwell. Ross also found inspiration outside the traditional bounds of art. In particular, he has said that the cover artwork for *Queen II* (the second album by his favorite band, Queen) stimulated his imagination. The style of the illustration, which showed a group of figures with partially shadowed faces against a black background, was echoed in his subsequent work. Unlike many of his peers, Ross continued reading comics throughout his adolescence, an interest he has credited with giving his life stability. "High school can be a chaotic time," he is quoted as saying on his Web site. "Through my art and through what these characters represented, I found a sense of order that I wanted to apply to my life. It's not that I wasn't interested in dating or socializing. It's just that part of me didn't want to let go of the colorful characters I'd loved for so long."

After graduating from high school, Ross enrolled at the American Academy of Art in Chicago, Illinois. (His mother had graduated from the school in 1948.) There, he learned a variety of painting techniques and familiarized himself with the human form. Meanwhile, his interest in comics continued. While the academy did not offer classes in comic-book illustration, he found his time there to be very beneficial, as it gave him the necessary tools to create his signature style. After graduating, in 1989, Ross began working as a storyboard artist with the Leo Burnett advertisement agency in Chicago, another experience he has credited with helping him to perfect his realistic portrayal of the human form. Meanwhile, Ross was also working on his first graphic novel, *Terminator: The Burning Earth* (1990), based on the popular *Terminator* movie series. Created with the writer Ron Fortier for the now-defunct Now Comics, *Terminator* was illustrated in the traditional comic-book style, with line drawings and borders. It was only in 1993 that Ross got his first assignment to paint a superhero, for the cover of a Superman novel.

The breakout success of Ross's next project, the four-issue limited series *Marvels* (1994), which used paintings for internal as well as cover art, demonstrated the commercial appeal of Ross's style and instantly made him one of the most prominent figures in the business. The series came about after Ross's work on *Terminator* caught the eye of the writer Kurt Busiek, who was also struggling for recognition in the industry. Busiek approached Ross with the idea of teaming up; the pair pitched the idea of telling the history of superheroes through the eyes of an ordinary person, examining how the fantastic interacts with the everyday in the world of comics. Marvel Comics—second only to DC Comics in sales—accepted the pitch, giving the two a wide repertoire of characters from which to draw. The *Marvels* series, which chronicled the life of a New York photojournalist and featured classic Marvel characters such as Spider-Man, Captain America, the Silver Surfer, and the members of the Fantastic Four and the X-Men, sold hundreds of thousands of copies and helped to revive a flagging industry. Critics widely praised *Marvels* for elevating the comic form, taking plot and character development seriously, engaging with wider thematic issues, and—most of all—presenting a breathtakingly original aesthetic vision of the superhero world. In a preview of the series, Mike Sangiacomo, writing for the *Cleveland Plain Dealer* (April 29, 1993), predicted that Ross's would be the next big name in comics. "There's a richness and a detail in his work that's missing from most comics," Sangiacomo wrote. "He paints scenes that ring true. Giant-Man would have looked that way to a person on the ground. The Green Goblin's mask would look like a mask, as it does in Ross' work. And people look like people, not comic book characters." Ross and Busiek also won acclaim for daring to engage with the psychological and metaphysical aspects of superhero identity, creating a story of literary worth rather than pure entertainment. Robert Wilonsky described *Marvels* as "a comic book that read like a novel and looked like a movie." In their next series, *Astro City*, first published in 1995, Ross and Busiek—with the addition of penciller Brent Anderson—continued exploring the question of how ordinary people would react to the fantastic world of superheroes. Because his intricate painting is so time-consuming, Ross began to scale back on his work; for *Astro City* he painted the issues' covers and contributed to the general look of the series but did not paint the individual pages.

For his 1996 book, *Kingdom Come*, for DC Comics, Ross returned to the painstaking painting of each page, an effort that cemented his place as a superstar within the comic-book industry. Working with the writer Mark Waid to develop one of his own ideas, Ross again engaged the dichotomy between superheroes and mere mortals. This time, however, the plot was set in the future—when, with today's superheroes in retirement, their descendants abuse their super-powers and let the world slip into chaos. Though the story is populated with characters from Superman to Wonder Woman, the main character is again an ordinary human, the minister Norman McCay, who has been given the duty of assessing the superhero civil war to decide who will be at fault for the coming Armageddon. Ross gave his main character the profession—and part of the name—of his own father, thereby placing Clark Norman Ross in the world of the fantastic. "It was essentially my driving inspiration to create a comic series that he was the lead character in, interacting with all these classic superheroes," Ross told Lissau. "I thought it would be so cool to see my dad standing there with Superman." Using his father as a model helped Ross emphasize the blurring of the line between superheroes and ordinary humans; to Ross, his father was, in a sense, a superhero—a mortal who nonetheless embodied the best qualities Ross saw in comic-book heroes. "There was a positive effect to being around him, and his actions tied into what the superhero comics were teaching me," Ross said, describing his father on his Web site. "Superheroes aren't heroes because they're strong; they're heroes because they perform acts that look beyond themselves." *Kingdom Come*, which Ross has identified as the project he most enjoyed, won the Will Eisner Award—considered the Oscar of the comics industry—in 1997. "It is, hands down and feet on the floor, one of the best modern comic tales ever made," Jarvis Slacks wrote for the Wilmington, North Carolina, *Star News* (July 7, 2005), describing Ross's artwork as "amazing page for page, panel for panel." The book remains Ross's most widely acclaimed work and was reissued as an oversized hardcover—*Absolute Kingdom Come*—in 2006. Looking back on the book's history, Steve Raiteri, writing for *Library Journal Reviews* (November 15, 2006), called it "one of the finest and most celebrated superhero graphic novels," adding that "Ross's extraordinary painted artwork is masterful, realistic, and beautiful; and the story has resonance both biblical and mystical."

Ross followed the success of *Kingdom Come* with the 1999 graphic novel *Uncle Sam*, a dark portrayal of American history whose down-and-out title character is present at pivotal events, from the Revolutionary War to a 1930s labor protest to the 1963 assassination of President John F. Kennedy. "This truly subversive graphic novel, more explicitly radical than anything else from DC Comics in recent memory, almost makes up for years of muscular patriotism and jingoistic violence that have long defined most of the company's product[s]," Steve Darnall wrote for *Kirkus Reviews* (February 15, 1999). Despite critical praise, the book did not fare well commercially, selling a comparatively modest 20,000 copies. Still, Ross has said that *Uncle Sam* is the project of which he is most proud.

After that foray into political storytelling, Ross returned to the world of superheroes, creating a six-issue series to commemorate the 60th anniversary of DC Comics. Each of the first four issues of the series focused on a different superhero. The first, *Superman: Peace on Earth*, saw the Man of Steel trying to fight world hunger, ultimately learning that even a superhero cannot solve such a large problem on his own. That work won the 1998 National Cartoonists Society Book Award. The next three books followed a similar format: in *Batman: War on Crime*, the Caped Crusader goes on a mission to break up street gangs and drug labs; in *Shazam!: Power of Hope*, Captain Marvel visits a children's hospital; and in *Wonder Woman: Spirit of Truth*, the original feminist superhero has adventures around the world—including a stint as a veiled woman in Islamic society—in glimpses into the travails of womanhood. The fifth and sixth books in the series focused on the Justice League of America (made up of Superman, Batman, Wonder Woman, and others). The fifth book, *JLA: Secret Origins*, explores the beginnings of the Justice League; the sixth and final book in the series, *JLA: Liberty and Justice*, takes the story into the future, in which the heroes must battle a mysterious alien virus. The entire series, which was printed issue-by-issue from 1998 to 2003, was well received both critically and commercially. Ross donated the original artwork for *Batman* to be auctioned to benefit the John A. Reisenbach School in the Harlem section of New York City; the original artwork for *Shazam!* was also auctioned, to benefit the Make-a-Wish Foundation.

While finishing work on the 60th-anniversary series for DC, Ross also began a trilogy for Marvel—*Earth X*, *Universe X*, and *Paradise X*—which brought together dozens of characters in an epic that spanned time and space. In a first for Ross's career, the work disappointed fans and was almost universally panned by critics. Ross painted only the covers of the issues; though he collaborated with the writer Jim Krueger on the story line, he did not contribute at all to the internal artwork. Without Ross's lavish illustrations, problems with the plot development became apparent, and the series was widely criticized for weaving a confusing narrative that required previous knowledge of the Marvel characters.

For the next several years, as graphic novels gained more attention in the media, Ross completed a series of smaller, though more mainstream, projects. In the fall of 2001, he painted four interrelated covers for *TV Guide*, featuring characters from the television show *Smallville*, which followed Clark Kent's development into Superman. Ross also designed and sculpted a series of busts based on characters from *Earth X*, bringing his focus on realism to a three-dimensional medium. Later that year, after the September 11 terrorist attacks, Ross illustrated the cover of *9-11: The World's Finest Comic Book Writers and Artists Tell Stories to Remember*, the sales of which benefited the families of those killed during the catastrophe. The original of his cover art, which included portraits of paramedics, police officers, and firefighters, was hung in the Library of Congress. In 2004 Ross designed the opening credits for the film *Spider-Man 2*, in which he told the story from the first Spider-Man movie in 20 paintings.

By 2004 Ross had amassed a wide-ranging body of work, which was collected that year in *Mythology: The DC Comics of Alex Ross*, written and designed by the graphic artist and comics buff Chip Kidd. The lavish coffee-table book included an introduction by the movie director M. Night Shyamalan and a short biography of Ross, written by Kidd. Ross's illustrations made up the bulk of the volume, with work ranging from early sketches to excerpts of his creations for DC Comics. In the book Kidd described Ross's appeal, as quoted by L. D. Meagher for CNN (December 11, 2003, on-line): "What makes Ross's approach unique to Superman and the other DC characters is twofold. First, on the page, we simply weren't used to seeing them this way. Second, it wasn't just that we saw them differently, it was as if we were allowed to really see them for the first time. The effect was like finally meeting someone you'd only ever heard about." In August 2005 Ross began work on the 12-issue limited series *Justice* for DC Comics. The series reunites the team from the *Earth X* trilogy, with writing by Krueger and Ross and illustrations by Ross and Doug Braithwaite. In typical Ross fashion, *Justice* tackles a complex story line rather than telling a simple good-versus-bad tale. The members of the Justice League of America once again fight their enemies (Lex Luthor and the Riddler, among others), but this time the enemies are not mere personifications of evil. The villains have banded together after experiencing a shared vision of the Apocalypse, which they believe will be brought about by humans' over-reliance on superheroes; they want to defeat the Justice League in order to force humans to fend for themselves, avoiding the planet's destruction. The last installment of the series appeared in June 2007.

Ross lives in Wilmette, Illinois, a suburb of Chicago. He met his wife, T.J., in 1999 at the Superman Celebration, a four-day festival held annually in Metropolis, Illinois.

—C.S.

Suggested Reading: alexrossart.com; *Chicago Tribune* C p1 July 13, 1999; *New York Times* F p1 Oct. 30, 2003; *Seattle Times* E p1 Jan. 13, 2004; *Washington Post* C p1 Nov. 28, 2003

Selected Books: *Marvels*, 1994; *Kingdom Come*, 1996; *Superman: Peace on Earth*, 1998; *Uncle Sam*, 1999; *Batman: War on Crime*, 1999; *Shazam!: Power of Hope*, 2000; *Wonder Woman: Spirit of Truth*, 2001; *JLA: Secret Origins*, 2002; *JLA: Liberty and Justice*, 2003; *Mythology: The DC Comics of Alex Ross*, 2004

Frazer Harrison/Getty Images

Rubin, Rick

Mar. 10, 1963– Music producer

Address: Columbia Records, Sony BMG Music Entertainment, 550 Madison Ave., New York, NY 10022

"Rubin is the musical equivalent of a great, modern chef—not only able to make magic with any given set of ingredients, but bold enough to mix styles and cultural origins in ways that enhance each element without betraying its authenticity," Andrew Gumbel wrote for the London *Independent* (February 13, 2007), in describing the music producer Rick Rubin. From producing now-classic rap albums in the 1980s, including LL Cool J's *Radio* and the Beastie Boys' *Licensed to Ill*, to overseeing the making of such landmark rock albums as Slayer's *Reign in Blood* and the Red Hot Chili Peppers' *Blood Sugar Sex Magik*, to reviving the careers of the musical icons Johnny Cash, Donovan, and Neil Diamond, Rubin has redefined musical production over the last quarter-century, amassing a discography of more than 90 albums whose combined sales exceed 100 million. Since he began running the legendary Def Jam label out of his college dorm room in the 1980s, with his then-partner Russell Simmons, Rubin has won a reputation as a visionary among producers, offering advice on every aspect of an album, from its music to its cover art. "I'm just trying to make my favorite music. That's how I work; I just do things based on the way they feel to me. I want to be touched by the music I'm making. Luckily, other people have shared that response to my work over the years," Rubin explained to J. Freedom du Lac for the *Washington*

Post (January 15, 2006). He added, "I don't even know what a traditional producer is or does. I feel like the job is like being a coach, building good work habits and building trust. . . . My goal is to just get out of the way and let the people I'm working with be their best."

While most producers begin their careers as studio technicians, Rubin "came up as a fan," as he told Josh Tyrangiel for *Time* (February 19, 2007). Much of Rubin's success lies in his practice of stripping songs of such common production elements as backup vocals and string sections, in order to focus on the essence of the material. David Hajdu noted for the *New Republic* (May 29, 2006), "His primary concerns as a producer are composition and performance, and his main objective is to capture the sound of people in the act of music-making. He thinks of recording as [Thomas] Edison did, as the documentation of an art made by others rather than as a creative act in itself." His expertise brought him "best producer of the year" honors at the 2007 Grammy Awards, in recognition of his work on the Red Hot Chili Peppers' *Stadium Arcadium*, the Dixie Chicks' *Taking the Long Way*, and Justin Timberlake's *FutureSex/LoveSounds*, among a host of other records. Daron Malakian, the principal songwriter for System of a Down, told du Lac that Rubin might be described best as a "song doctor," adding, "If you play something for him, it's like going in for a checkup. He's like, 'Here, take a couple of these vitamins and see how you feel.' And the songs always feel better after his suggestions. And so do you." The comedian Chris Rock, a friend of Rubin's, said to Josh Tyrangiel, "Most producers have their own sound, and they lease it out to different people, but we know it's still their record. The records you make with Rick are your records. He makes it his job to squeeze the best out of you—and not leave any fingerprints." In 2007 Rubin's musical expertise was tapped by Columbia Records: since May he has been Columbia's co-head, with Steve Barnett, working to help the label adjust to changing times. As part of an agreement with Columbia, Rubin will continue to produce music with artists who have not signed with that record label.

The only son of Mickey and Linda Rubin, Frederick Jay Rubin was born on March 10, 1963 in the upper-middle-class area of Lido Beach, in Hempstead, on Long Island, New York. His father worked in the wholesale shoe business; both of his parents hoped that he would pursue a career in medicine or law. Rubin wanted early on to become a magician, spending hours at a time perfecting tricks in front of a mirror. During his teenage years his interests shifted to music, and he began teaching himself to play guitar. Soon afterward he formed a punk band called the Pricks. Meanwhile, he listened to music by artists ranging from James Brown, the Beatles, and Led Zeppelin to punk acts including Black Flag and the Germs. "Typically, people learn about music from older brothers and sisters, and I didn't have that, which forced me to create my own taste and really know what I like," Rubin recalled to Maureen Droney in an interview for *Mix* (October 2000).

In 1980, during his senior year at the racially mixed Long Beach High School, Rick developed an affinity for a newly emerging musical style called rap. He began frequenting record stores in New York City's East Village, purchasing the latest rap singles and mingling with young people in the city, who exposed him to still more cutting-edge music. In his senior year Rubin started Def Jam Records, using the school's four-track recorder to create his own hip-hop samples and beats. (The slang phrase *def jam* was used in the hip-hop community to describe the ideal musical sound.)

In 1981 Rubin enrolled at New York University (NYU), intending to major in philosophy before going on to law school. He later changed his focus to film and video. During his freshman year he formed another punk band, Hose, with his friends Joel Horne (on bass) and Rick Rosen (on vocals); Mike Espindle later replaced Rosen. In 1982, in Rubin's dorm room, Hose recorded an EP, which would become the first official release under the Def Jam label. Rubin managed to secure a gig for Hose at the New York club CBGB's. It was there that he struck up a friendship with three Jewish punk rockers then in their mid-teens: Adam Yauch, Mike Diamond, and Adam Horovitz, who went on to form the rap trio Beastie Boys. For a while, Rubin was the fourth member of the group, acting as the band's official deejay, under the name DJ Double R. During one of his weekly stops at another club, Negril, Rubin met DJ Jazzy Jay, a member of Afrika Bambaataa's group Universal Zulu Nation. After listening to a number of beats that Rubin had programmed on his drum machine, Jazzy Jay offered to help Rubin, introducing him to one of Rubin's favorite hip-hop groups at the time, the Treacherous Three—Kool Moe Dee, Special K, and DJ Easy Lee.

The Treacherous Three were known as the first hip-hop group to integrate rap and rock, using guitars to accent rap vocals on the song "Body Rock." Rubin, too, was interested in blending those genres, along with scratches from turntables. Due to contract obligations with another independent label, Special K offered to have his brother, T. La Rock, work in his place with Rubin and Jazzy Jay in using a deejay and drum machine as the central elements of a track. In December 1983 Rubin, T. La Rock, Horovitz, and Horovitz's best friend, Dave Skilken, recorded in Jazzy Jay's apartment a single entitled "It's Yours"—mixed and mastered at a cost of $5,000, supplied by Rubin's parents. The release of the 1984 musical film *Beat Street*, whose cast included Jazzy Jay, drew much attention to the rapper, which in turn led "It's Yours" to be played on radio stations across the country. In August 1984 Jazzy Jay introduced Rubin to a fast-talking rap promoter and producer named Russell Simmons. Simmons had risen to prominence as the head of his own hip-hop–based management company,

Rush Productions, which represented popular acts such as Run D.M.C. As noted by Stacy Gueraseva in the book *Def Jam, Inc.* (2005), when Jazzy Jay told Simmons that Rubin had produced "It's Yours," he responded, "I can't believe you made that record and you're white! 'Cause that's the blackest hip-hop record that's ever been!"

With Simmons's help, and more financial assistance from his parents, Rubin was able to get Def Jam Records—still headquartered in his dorm room—off the ground. After discovering a 16-year-old rapper named James Todd Smith III, who was going by the name LL Cool J, Rubin invited him to his dorm to rap over several beats that he had produced. The resulting single, "I Need a Beat," cost around $400 to produce and sold 120,000 copies, eventually attracting the attention of major record labels.

Rubin graduated from NYU with a degree in film and video in 1985. In November of that year, LL Cool J's album *Radio* was released. The first popular rap album to use traditional song structures, *Radio* received much critical acclaim. At his own request, Rubin was given a "reduced by" credit on the record rather than the usual "produced by" designation. In 1986 Rubin's vision of fusing rap and rock became a reality when he persuaded Run D.M.C. to collaborate with Aerosmith for a cover of the rock group's 1975 classic "Walk This Way." The video for the song became the first rap video ever played in heavy rotation on MTV. The song was featured on Run D.M.C.'s 1986 triple-platinum breakthrough album, *Raising Hell*, which was co-produced by Rubin.

With Rubin at the helm, Def Jam inked a lucrative distribution deal with Columbia Records and produced the Beastie Boys' debut album, *Licensed to Ill*, the first hip-hop album to win mainstream popularity and the first to reach the top spot on the *Billboard* Hot 100 chart. Part of the group's appeal was attributed to Rubin's use of hard-rock samples with the rappers' freestyle rhymes. Rubin also designed the album's controversial cover, which showed an airplane crashing into a mountain. He next produced Slayer's equally controversial third album, *Reign in Blood*. Rubin eliminated the thrash-metal group's complex song structures in favor of shorter, faster-paced songs with clearer production elements; that approach became known as the "Rubin touch." Slayer's vocalist and bassist, Tom Araya, recalled to Gueraseva, "He took our sound and kind of fine-tuned it: that Slayer sound that we could never capture in the studio. We kinda realized, 'Oh my God, this guy, he's got the touch of gold.'" Whereas the *Village Voice* had called Rubin "the king of rap" several years earlier, his association with Slayer—whom rumors had linked with devil worship—led the publication to label him "Satan's record producer." With subject matter including concentration-camp torture, *Reign in Blood* caused an uproar. Defending the record in an interview for the *Los Angeles Times* (April 16, 1989), Rubin said to Robert Hilburn,

"Who said rock n' roll was supposed to be nice? Rock n' roll is about going against the rules." In 1987 Rubin produced the rap group Public Enemy's classic first album, *Yo! Bum Rush the Show*, and helped produce and assemble the first-ever rap-rock soundtrack, for the film *Less Than Zero*. Then, in the midst of the controversy surrounding Slayer and power struggles within Def Jam, Rubin decided to part ways with the company he helped found. He ended his partnership with Simmons amicably, deeming their friendship more important than their business arrangement.

In 1988 Rubin launched his own label, Def American Records, moved to Los Angeles, California, and concentrated for a time on his first love: hard rock. Over the next three years, he produced more Slayer albums, including *South of Heaven* and *Decade of Aggression*, and records by other against-the-grain acts, among them Danzig, Masters of Reality, and Wolfsbane. He even added comedy to his repertoire, producing an album for the profane comic Andrew Dice Clay. In 1990, while doubling as a freelance producer for major record companies, Rubin got the opportunity to produce the Red Hot Chili Peppers' next album under the Warner Bros. label. Over a six-month period, Rubin worked with the band through an extensive brainstorming, songwriting, and rehearsal process that would result in some of the group's best work. During that period he came across a poem by the group's singer, Anthony Kiedis, entitled "Under the Bridge." Although Kiedis was reluctant at first to make the poem into a song, Rubin persuaded him to present it to the band. Then, after feeling dissatisfied with the atmosphere in the recording studio, Rubin came across an empty mansion in Los Angeles's Laurel Canyon, once owned by the escape artist Harry Houdini and later inhabited by such luminaries as Rudolph Valentino, the Beatles, and Jimi Hendrix, and moved the band into the house to live in seclusion for a month. (Only the drummer, Chad Smith, refused to stay there, believing that the house was haunted.) On September 24, 1991 *Blood Sugar Sex Magik* was released to unanimous critical acclaim. Its first single, the ultra-funky "Give It Away," won a Grammy Award in 1992 for best hard-rock song, and "Under the Bridge" went on to reach number two on the *Billboard* charts. *Blood Sugar Sex Magik* is widely considered to be one of the seminal rock albums of the 1990s.

In the early 1990s Rubin was one of rock's busiest producers-for-hire, working with Tom Petty and the Heartbreakers to produce the album *Wildflowers* and producing a solo effort by Mick Jagger, *Wandering Spirit*, among other projects. Meanwhile, in 1993, after Rubin came across the word "def" in a dictionary, he not only dropped it from the name of his label, feeling that it had become overused—he conducted a funeral ceremony for it, complete with coffin and grave. The label became known simply as American Recordings. With the name change came a desire to work with different kinds of artists, which resulted in his "American Series" albums with the country-music legend Johnny Cash. For several weeks in the autumn of 1993, under minimal instruction from Rubin, Cash recorded the solo tracks for the *American Recordings* album in his living room, accompanying himself on guitar. Describing their first sessions together, David Kamp wrote for *Vanity Fair* (October 2004), "Rubin sat in his living room like the musicologist Alan Lomax on a Mississippi porch, listening and recording intently while a gnarled, authentic article of Americana banged away at his repertoire." The album immediately brought Cash renewed mainstream popularity. *Rolling Stone* gave a five-star rating to *American Recordings*, which went on to win a Grammy Award for best contemporary folk-song album.

During the same period, and through much of the decade, Rubin continued producing albums for Slayer *(Divine Intervention)*, Danzig *(Danzig IV)*, and the Red Hot Chili Peppers (*Californication*), in addition to recordings of the heavy-metal icons AC/DC *(Ballbreaker)* and the pop veteran Donovan *(Sutras)*. Each of his successful albums with those groups resulted from a long, often tedious production process. Rubin had Donovan, for example, write an abundance of new material; the singer arrived at the studio with more than 100 songs. Referring to *Sutras*, which was several years in the making, Rubin explained to Craig Rosen for *Billboard* (August 31, 1996), "Artists that have made lots of records get into a very specific habit. They make a record, go on the road, and record again whether they are prepared to make a record or not, because that's the cycle. In the case of grown-up artists, which I like to call them, it's not easy to try to break that cycle. They should spend as much time as it takes to write, like they did on their first album, and not rush into making an album." Through hard work, Rubin was able to help veteran artists break out of their comfort zones. *Sutras* proved to be a hit and had drawn more media attention to the American Recordings label by the time Rubin's second album with Cash, *Unchained*, appeared in 1996. Backed on the record by Tom Petty and the Heartbreakers, Cash, at Rubin's urging, focused less on original material than on covers of songs whose styles were not normally associated with the country icon, among them Soundgarden's "Rusty Cage." Cash "thought I was insane," Rubin recalled to Kamp, when he first had the singer listen to the Soundgarden version of the song. Rubin's radical vision paid off, and the album took home a Grammy Award for best country album that year—despite being all but ignored by the country-music community.

Rubin collaborated with the art-metal group System of a Down on their eponymous debut album, in 1998, and on their 2001 follow-up, *Toxicity*. The latter debuted at number one on the *Billboard* chart, and the magazine *Spin* named it the number-one record of the year. Keith Harris, in an album review for *Rolling Stone* (September 27, 2001), praised Rubin's production, remarking that it allowed the music to insist "on forward motion without trapping itself in a thrashy lock-step rut." In 2000 Cash released his third American Series record with Rubin, *American III: Solitary Man*, which featured covers such as Tom Petty's "I Won't Back Down," U2's "One," and Neil Diamond's "Solitary Man." Cash won another Grammy for the Neil Diamond cover, taking home the award for best song by a male country singer. In 2002 came Cash and Rubin's fourth collaboration, *American IV: The Man Comes Around*, which became Cash's first gold record in more than 30 years and represented even more radical departures for the singer, including covers of Depeche Mode's "Personal Jesus" and Nine Inch Nails' "Hurt." *American IV* was the last collaboration between Rubin and Cash, who remained close friends until Cash's death, on September 12, 2003. Two more Rubin/Cash albums were released posthumously: *Unearthed* (2003), a boxed set featuring outtakes and alternative versions of songs, and *A Hundred Miles* (2006).

In the new millennium Rubin has continued to collaborate with recording artists in a wide range of genres, working on the rapper Jay Z's song "99 Problems" for *The Black Album* (2003), the metal group Slipknot's 2004 record *Vol. 3 (The Subliminal Verses)* (2004), and the Colombian pop artist Shakira's *Fijacion Oral Vol. 1* and its English-language follow-up, *Oral Fixation Vol. 2*, both of which won numerous awards. Rubin's second most unlikely collaboration—after his partnership with Cash—came when he worked with the pop star Neil Diamond. Rubin helped Diamond to think of himself once more as a singer/songwriter, having him use his own early albums as a springboard to new material and even persuading him to play guitar again—which the artist had not done since the 1960s. Diamond's *12 Songs* (2005) became his most successful and critically acclaimed studio album in years, debuting at number four on the *Billboard* album chart. Rubin's influence was also in evidence during the subsequent tour for the album, as Diamond used tougher-sounding background arrangements for some of his classic songs. Diamond told Edna Gundersen for *USA Today* (July 7, 2006), "With Rick, I found the right path. He picked up on the vibe of acoustic guitar and understatement, something I haven't done in years and wasn't able to replicate until this album."

Rubin's success has not been founded on technical mastery; he does not read music, write lyrics, or know how to use a standard mixing board. As reflected in his accomplishments with Cash, Diamond, and other artists, Rubin's gift has been in his ability to put the musicians he works with—veterans and newcomers alike—at ease while guiding them toward their full creative potential, through hard work and patience. "I try to get them in the mind-set that they're not writing music for an album," he explained to Josh Tyrangiel. "They're writing music because they're writers and that's what they do." As a result, many of Rubin's projects take years to complete, which is why he often finds himself working on several projects at once. Because he grants almost full autonomy to the artists, frequent collaborators have described his studio atmosphere as a "real democracy." Rubin said to Tyrangiel, "In the old days, when I'd hear something that's not working, I'd say, 'O.K., this is how we're going to fix it.' Now I ask, 'How do we fix it?' And nine times out of 10, what they come up with is as good as or better than how I would've done it."

In 2006 Rubin was greatly in demand as a producer, overseeing the recording of albums for Slayer (*Christ Illusion*), the Red Hot Chili Peppers (*Stadium Arcadium*), and the Dixie Chicks (*Taking the Long Way*). He did additional work on Justin Timberlake's multiplatinum *FutureSex/LoveSounds*, working on the track "(Another Song) All Over Again," and produced U2/Green Day's cover of the Skids' song "The Saints Are Coming." Tyrangiel noted, "It's clear [Rubin's] aesthetic range is essentially limitless." Rubin was connected with 15 artists and recordings nominated for 2007 Grammy Awards; Rubin himself, who had been nominated for "producer of the year" on three previous occasions, took home his first Grammy in that category.

In May 2007 Rubin's career took a turn that surprised many observers, when he accepted an offer from Steve Barnett, the head of Columbia Records, to join him as co-head of the label. Barnett hoped that Rubin would provide fresh ideas for saving the record-label industry, in which the most successful CDs were selling 30 percent fewer copies than their counterparts in 2006. Rubin agreed with stipulations: that he not have to travel, wear suits, or maintain a desk or phone at any corporate office. He also strongly suggested that Columbia become the first major record company to "go green" and end the practice of packing its CDs in plastic cases. Columbia's willingness to accommodate Rubin led him to feel that he could be effective in his new post. "I felt like I could be a force for good," Rubin told Lauryn Hirschberg for the *New York Times Magazine* (September 2, 2007). "In the past, I've tried to protect artists from the [Columbia] label, and now my job would also be to protect the label from itself. So many of the decisions at these companies are not about the music. They are short-sighted and desperate. For so long, the record industry had control. But now that monopoly has ended, they don't know what to do. I thought it would be an interesting challenge." In his new job Rubin must seek out fresh talent rather than concentrate on reinvigorating the careers of established artists. His major challenge, though, is one that faces not only Columbia but the entire industry: adjusting belatedly to an age when increasing numbers of people download music illegally, no longer listen to music on the radio, and learn about music primarily through word of mouth. Rubin has noted that for 50 years, record labels sold music through such channels as Tower Records and other major retail chains, MTV, and *Rolling Stone* and other large-circulation music magazines. Although Columbia has made some changes—creating a promotion division at Columbia that sells music directly to TV and a "word of mouth" department that spreads buzz through chat rooms—Rubin believes that such minor gestures may merely make Columbia the "best dinosaur" and that the time has come for more drastic action. Along with others in the industry, he has suggested the use of a subscription-based model, whereby subscribers would pay a monthly fee to gain access to music from a virtual library. That approach would require cooperation among record companies, and many, including Barnett, view it as risky. Rubin, however, sees no alternative. "Either all the record companies will get together or the industry will fall apart and someone like Microsoft will come in and buy one of the companies at wholesale and do what needs to be done," he told Hirschberg. He added, "The existing people will either get smart, which is a question mark. Or new people will understand what a resource the music business is and change it without us. I don't want to watch that happen."

An adherent of yoga and Zen Buddhism, Rubin shares his recently restored 1923 English Tudor–style mansion, perched above Los Angeles's Sunset Strip, with his girlfriend. "Physically, he is little short of arresting—a big man, with a yawning pot belly and a beard so wide and long it could be its own ecosystem," Andrew Gumbel wrote. Rubin does not drink alcohol and, surprisingly for someone in his line of work, has never tried drugs. The film actor Owen Wilson, a longtime friend of Rubin's, said to Edna Gundersen about the producer, "We just have a good time laughing. He has a funny take on stuff. A lot of lines in my movies came directly from Rick." J. Freedom du Lac reported that Rubin often reads and meditates at home. "It's a big theme in my life, learning about myself and being a better person," Rubin told du Lac. "I'm a work in progress; I have revelations every day."

—C.C.

Suggested Reading: *Billboard* Nov. 5, 2005, Aug. 31, 1996; (London) *Independent* World p26 Feb. 13, 2007; *Los Angeles Times* p65 Apr. 16, 1989; *Mix* (on-line) Oct. 2000; MTV Web site; *New Republic* p25+ May 29, 2006; *New York Times* E p1 Feb. 5, 2007; *New York Times Magazine* p28+ Sep. 2, 2007; *Time* p62+ Feb. 19, 2007; *USA Today* E p1+ July 7, 2006; *Vanity Fair* p200+ Oct. 2004; *Washington Post* N p1+ Jan. 15, 2006; Guerseva, Stacy. *Def Jam, Inc.*, 2005

Courtesy of Bahman Maghsoudlou/IFVC
Andrew Sarris (right) with the Iranian director Amir Naderi in 1978

Sarris, Andrew

Oct. 31, 1928– Film critic, theorist, and historian

Address: School of the Arts, Columbia University, 513 Dodge Hall, 2960 Broadway, New York, NY 10027

In the lexicon of contemporary film criticism, the French term *auteur*—meaning "author" or "originator"—is typically used to suggest that "the director [is] a movie's dominant artistic force, that in his or her work one could detect an individual signature, a coherent pattern of themes, visual styles and personal meaning," as Patrick Z. McGavin wrote for the *Chicago Tribune* (May 11, 2001). That idea first emerged in the 1950s, in the French journal *Cahiers du Cinéma,* as a somewhat loosely defined way of thinking about film. Advanced tentatively by the journal's co-founder, the critic André Bazin, the auteur theory was formulated most explicitly in the 1954 *Cahiers* essay "Une certaine tendance du cinéma français" ("A Certain Tendency in French Cinema") by François Truffaut, then a young critic and Bazin's protégé and later one of the most acclaimed directors of the French New Wave. Yet for most American cineasts, auteurism coalesced into a working framework for film criticism in the 1960s, only once Andrew Sarris, then an upstart movie reviewer for the New York City newspaper the *Village Voice*, penned his famous essay "Notes on the Auteur Theory" for the avantgarde magazine *Film Culture*. In 1968 Sarris further detailed his views in the landmark text *The American Cinema: Directors and Directions, 1929–1968*,

which almost single-handedly made auteur theory the dominant mode of American film criticism and, with its three-tiered categorization of directors and their oeuvres, radically challenged the existing critical hierarchy. "I didn't set out on a crusade," Sarris explained to Robert W. Welkos for the *Los Angeles Times* (June 30, 1996). "I wasn't interested in pushing one craft over another. I argued that many of the American directors who had been underrated were just as good as the art-house directors from abroad and that the best American films are generally genre films." Nonetheless, Sarris's auteur theory sparked a maelstrom of controversy, most notably inciting the outrage of the acclaimed *New Yorker* film critic Pauline Kael, who emerged as Sarris's formidable foil. "For anyone into film criticism during that era [the 1960s and 1970s], which in retrospect looks like *the* era for film criticism, they were the twin titans," Godfrey Cheshire wrote for the North Carolina *Independent Weekly* (September 12, 2001, on-line). Despite its early and often vociferous critics, *The American Cinema* has endured to become a classic of contemporary film theory. "I'm still reading it [today]," Michael Barker, one of the co-presidents of Sony Picture Classics, told McGavin. "The book gave me the context to really appreciate film. . . . That book is the cornerstone of the art house business—that filmmakers have a specific vision, that you trust in certain directors."

Sarris's distinguished career in film criticism, which has spanned more than 50 years, began at *Film Culture*, but to many of his fans, he is most closely associated with the *Village Voice*, for which he served as the primary film critic from 1960 to 1989. Since he left the *Voice*, he has written film reviews for another New York City paper, the *New York Observer*. Sarris's published works include such auteur studies as *The Films of Josef von Sternberg* (1966) and *The John Ford Movie Mystery* (1976) as well as film surveys including *Confessions of a Cultist: On the Cinema, 1955–1969* (1970), *The Primal Screen: Essays on Film and Related Subjects* (1973), and *Politics and Cinema* (1978). Sarris was a finalist for a Pulitzer Prize in criticism in 2000. In 2001 the film critic Emanuel Levy edited the book *Citizen Sarris, American Film Critic: Essays in Honor of Andrew Sarris,* which highlighted Sarris's boundless passion for the cinema. Sarris told Keith Uhlich for the Senses of Cinema Web site that "movies will never die and for an interesting reason. It's something Bazin sort of indicated and something that I've always felt— movies are not entirely an art form. . . . There's a lot of art in film but it's not entirely art. A lot of it is just reality and consequently the reality is always changing."

Andrew George Sarris was born on October 31, 1928 in Brooklyn, New York, to George Andrew and Themis (Katavolos) Sarris, both of Greek descent. Sarris's father had a prosperous real-estate business, and his financial success allowed Sarris, the elder of two boys, to live his first few years in luxury. According to a story often told in Sarris's family, his first experience with the movies began by chance at the local theater. "One day my mother was pushing me in a standing stroller and we were passing a theater," Sarris told Uhlich. "I jumped out of the stroller and rushed into the theater. My mother ran in to get me, but when she tried to get me out of the theater, I began raising hell. I was screaming! The manager came over and said he'd let us both sit there without paying if my mother could keep me quiet. And boy did that movie keep me quiet!" Sarris became a frequent moviegoer, but, as he added to Uhlich, "The movies were not my whole life." Radio, particularly the compressed renderings of Broadway shows and Hollywood hits on *Lux Radio Theater*, also left a lasting impression on the boy.

The Great Depression dramatically affected Sarris's family in the early 1930s, and the lavish lifestyle young Andrew had enjoyed in his first few years came to an end. "We were never poor," he told Uhlich. "We were always broke. We didn't have any money. My father didn't work, but my mother was some sort of a genius. A dollar a day and she could feed all four of us." The family's fortunes had reversed again by 1946, when Sarris entered Columbia University, in New York City, as one of only a few dozen civilian students in what was otherwise a class weighted heavily toward veterans returning from World War II. During his time there his interest in cinema deepened—partially the result, once again, of chance. During his sophomore or junior year, Sarris was coming out of a screening of the 1941 film *That Hamilton Woman* when he was hit by a truck. Forced to use crutches for roughly the next year, Sarris let his schoolwork slide and devoted himself to watching films.

Sarris earned his bachelor's degree in 1951 and joined the army signal corps the following year. During his off-duty hours, he watched "three movies a week on the army post for free," he told David Walsh for the World Socialist Web Site (July 1, 1998). "I had a huge backlog of movie memories that I had no idea what to do with." (Sarris, who grew up in a staunchly Republican home, found his political views shifting to the left during his college years, and by all accounts he remains a moderate liberal on many issues; in the interview Walsh noted that he and Sarris "don't see eye to eye on political issues.") When Sarris completed his military service, in 1954, he enrolled in a course taught by the filmmaker Roger Tilton at Teachers College, Columbia University. The course, he told Walsh, "dealt mostly with sociological subjects and television, which was just starting up. It was one of the first in the US. Very solid, instructive course. For the first time I started to think systematically about movies." The course also introduced Sarris to Jonas Mekas, the pioneering American avant-garde filmmaker and theorist, who had recently launched the journal *Film Culture*. Mekas agreed to publish film reviews by Sarris in exchange for editorial help on the magazine.

Sarris's first review appeared in 1955, in the journal's second issue, and concerned the 1954 film *The Country Girl*. It was "a real pan," he told a fellow film critic, Richard Schickel, in an interview for *DGA Monthly* (March 2001, on-line), the magazine of the Directors' Guild of America, "and I learned something from reading it. It looked so brutal. It looked like an act of homicide. . . . I realized for the first time how powerful print is and to see the difference between what you say in a coffee house and what you say [in a publication]." Sarris told Uhlich that becoming a film critic also eventually meant cultivating a "visual sense," adding: "In the beginning, it didn't matter because like most people I *looked* at movies, I didn't *see* them."

While writing periodic pieces for *Film Culture*, Sarris also worked, beginning in 1955, as a story analyst and occasional screenwriter for Twentieth Century–Fox; later he took a position with the U.S. Census Bureau. In 1960 he became a guest reviewer for the *Village Voice*, assuming the spot Mekas had briefly relinquished to finish editing the film *Guns of the Trees* (1964). Sarris's first *Voice* review argued for the merits of the Alfred Hitchcock film *Psycho* (1960) and celebrated Hitchcock as "a major avant-garde artist," as he told Uhlich. "Everybody knew what Hitchcock did. Most people liked him, but didn't take him seriously." The review drew strong criticism—which impressed the paper's editors, who invited Sarris to write additional columns.

In 1961, grieving over the accidental death of his younger brother the year before, Sarris sojourned in Paris, France, and immersed himself in French film culture. He became acquainted with many of the figures tied to *Cahiers du Cinéma*, including Bazin and Truffaut, as well as the directors Jean-Luc Godard and Eric Rohmer, and grew intrigued by auteurism as an approach to analyzing films. Part of what drew Sarris to that way of thinking was that it downplayed the sociological or political aspects of movies in favor of subtexts. In his interview with Schickel, Sarris defined the subtext as what lies underneath the surface of a film—"sometimes very much underneath, sometimes very little. But the subtext . . . is very difficult to ascertain unless you're aware of the previous works [by the filmmaker]. Auteurism concentrates on the stylistic differences between [filmmakers]—the stylistic and thematic differences [that implicitly state] how they feel about characters." In 1962, after his return to New York and to his post at the *Village Voice*, Sarris published his famous essay "Notes on the Auteur Theory," which applied the auteur framework to the analysis of American cinema and daringly argued for the artistic integrity of many American genre films. "Notes" ignited a heated debate among film professionals, spurring Kael to offer, in spring 1963, a rebuttal entitled "Circles and Squares: Joys and Sarris," which was published in *Film Quarterly*. "With her trademark slash-and-burn brio, Kael likened auteurists in general, and Sarris in particular, to children 'who prefer simple action films and westerns and horror films to works that make demands on their understanding,'" as Thomas Doherty wrote for the *Chronicle of Higher Education* (March 30, 2001). "Kael also tagged Sarris as a 'list queen,' which was viewed by indignant Sarrisites as a jibe at his masculinity. . . . Sarris responded to the 'wench' in a 1970 essay in *Film Comment*, calling Kael 'more an entertainer than an enlightener' whose 'critical apparatus has more in common with a wind machine than a searchlight.'" Recalling the intensity of the debate about his article, Sarris told Schickel: "I was making $20 a column and I was a menace to western civilization as we knew it. It got a little objectionable. There were different layers of people attacking me. There were the people who said, 'Aw, you're just full of crap—this is nothing.' And there were people who said, 'Yeah, you have a point, but you stole it all from the French.' So I was either an idiot or a plagiarist. I couldn't win." Like some of Sarris's fellow critics, screenwriters took umbrage at what they considered to be Sarris's claim that the director was the sole source of a film's creative identity—or at least at the effect that that idea has had on the collaborative process in Hollywood. "The theory was that the director has the most to do—not everything; I never said everything—but the most to do with a movie," Sarris told Welkos. The article, furthermore, "was . . . a way of grouping the history of cinema. I am a film historian. What better way to organize them than by what the directors do."

After several years of refining his theories, Sarris published *The American Cinema: Directors and Directions, 1929–1968*, which attempted to show, Sarris told McGavin, "that there was considerable artistry in the studio cinema. I could only have written *The American Cinema* when I wrote it. It was a spasm, a polemical state." The first comprehensive guide to Hollywood moviemaking ever published, *The American Cinema* distilled the essence of Sarris's auteurist sentiments. The book, Doherty wrote, "was a mind-boggling , eye-opening appreciation of the maligned art of Hollywood cinema—as well as a fearless foray into canon formation." Sarris classified—presumptuously, in the view of many of his critics—a range of noted American film auteurs into 11 categories, including the exalted "Pantheon," the mediocre "Less than Meets the Eye," and the negligible "Strained Seriousness." He drew praise and ire for celebrating the artistry of such filmmakers as Hitchcock, John Ford, and Buster Keaton, while denigrating, among others, the widely acclaimed oeuvre of the Galician-born American director Billy Wilder and the director and actor John Huston. The film critic Rober Ebert told Doherty that Sarris's volume proved groundbreaking because "someone had the [nerve] to make a list so others could fight over it." To another film critic, Dave Kehr, Sarris's compact profiles were, he told McGavin, "a list of exotic destinations in a travel office window, places I hoped to visit some day but that for now were re-

mote and inaccessible." Sarris's book fanned the fires of his rivalry with Kael, and the two remained inextricably linked in the minds of many film fans up until Kael's retirement from the *New Yorker*, in 1991. Assessing what he judged to be "the consensus opinion among film scholars" about the different contributions of Sarris and Kael, Doherty wrote that "while Kael had a better eye for the jugular, Sarris had a better eye for cinema; while Kael made you want to read more Kael, Sarris made you want to see more movies; while Kael's compendium *5001 Nights at the Movies* [1982] is useful, Sarris's *The American Cinema* remains essential."

During the 1970s and 1980s, Sarris published several additional volumes of film criticism, and for all but a year of those two decades he continued to write weekly film reviews for the *Village Voice*, ending his tenure in 1989, when he joined the *New York Observer* as its chief film critic. In 1998, on the 30th anniversary of the appearance of *The American Cinema*, Sarris published *"You Ain't Heard Nothin' Yet": The American Talking Film, History and Memory, 1927–1949*. Sarris's widely anticipated follow-up was also partially, as Mark Shaiman noted for the *Journal of Popular Film and Television* (Winter 2002), "a mea culpa for some of his statements from *The American Cinema*." Regarding his early rejection of Billy Wilder, for example, Sarris conceded that "I have grossly underrated [him], perhaps more than any other director," as quoted by Shaiman. The primary subject of the book, however, is the first two decades in the history of talking pictures. (The title is a reference to the entertainer Al Jolson's first words in what is generally identified as the first "talkie," the 1927 film *The Jazz Singer*.) Calling *"You Ain't Heard Nothin' Yet"* "a warmer, less polemical work than *The American Cinema*," Charles Matthews wrote for the *Washington Post Book World* (May 17, 1998): "Sarris acutely observes of Wilder that 'his apparent cynicism was the only way he could make his raging romanticism palatable.' In a way this could be said of Sarris: His advocacy—he refers to himself as 'a practicing polemicist'—of the auteur theory was the only way he could make his own romanticism palatable. For the auteur theory itself is romantic in essence. It puts the emphasis on the director's personal vision rather than on his skill as a movie-maker, valuing sincerity over technical competence, just as the Romantic poets valued true feeling over true wit."

In addition to his work as a critic, Sarris edited, between 1965 and 1967, the English-language version of *Cahiers du Cinéma*. In 1982 he was made an officer of the French Ordre des Arts et Lettres (Order of Arts and Letters). A founding member and former chair of the National Society of Film Critics, Sarris began his teaching career in 1966, at the School of Visual Arts, in New York City. After a two-year stint, starting in 1967, at New York University, he moved to Columbia Univeristy's School of the Arts; he continues to teach at Columbia, which also awarded him an M.A. degree in 1998.

In the spring of 2001, Columbia's School of the Arts presented Sarris with the inaugural Andrew Sarris Award "for his outstanding contributions as a teacher and critic," according to the Columbia University *Record* (March 29, 2001, on-line). Also in 2001 the film critic and scholar Emmanuel Levy published *Citizen Sarris, American Film Critic*, a collection of essays by noted film professionals about Sarris's contributions to cinema. The inspiration behind *Citizen Sarris*, as Levy explained to Patrick Z. McGavin, was to "reassess auteurism and to reaffirm my feelings that Andrew Sarris is the most influential critic in American history. I'm not saying the best, but the most influential." In one of the book's touching tributes, as quoted by Ulrika Brand on the Columbia University News Web site, the legendary filmmaker Martin Scorsese described Sarris as "one of the most fundamental and valued teachers. His writings led me to see the genius in American movies at a time when the cinema was considered a mindless form of entertainment, worthy of serious attention only if it came from Europe or Asia."

Commenting on the nature of film education, Sarris told Uhlich that "there are two stages with film and TV and everything. The first stage is the way you see it, be it half-drunk in a bar or at home with family or friends. You're seeing something always. Once you've seen something, some of it sticks and it takes on a different dimension in your mind. That's the second stage. For about a century now we've been looking at movies and I think some things stick and some things don't and that's what's interesting. That's why I love teaching kids and showing them these old classics and seeing the things that work with them."

Sarris married the film critic, essayist, and scholar Molly Haskell in 1969. She wrote extensively about their relationship—especially after Sarris almost died, in 1984, from an encephalitic viral infection—in her book *Love and Other Infectious Diseases* (1990). The couple live on East 88th Street, in the New York City borough of Manhattan, just behind the famed Guggenheim Museum.

—D.J.K.

Suggested Reading: *Chicago Tribune* Movies p7 May 11, 2001; *Chronicle of Higher Education* B p17 Mar. 30, 2001; *DGA Monthly* (on-line) Mar. 2001; *Los Angeles Times* p25 June 30, 1996; Senses of Cinema Web site; *Washington Post Book World* p4 May 17, 1998; World Socialist Web Site

Selected Books: *The Films of Josef von Sternberg*, 1966; *The American Cinema: Directors and Directions, 1929–1968*, 1968; *Confessions of a Cultist: On the Cinema, 1955–1969*, 1970; *The Primal Screen: Essays on Film and Related Subjects*, 1973; *The John Ford Movie Mystery*, 1976; *Politics and Cinema*, 1978; *"You Ain't Heard Nothin' Yet": The American Talking Film, History and Memory, 1927–1949*, 1998; as editor—*Interviews with Film Directors*, 1967; *The St. James Film Directors Encyclopedia*, 1998

Schwartz, Gil

May 12, 1951– Communications executive; humor columnist; writer

Address: CBS Television, 51 W. 52d St., New York, NY 10019

"I think that Schwartz is necessary to Bing and Bing is necessary to Schwartz. We feed off each other," Gil Schwartz, the CBS Corp.'s executive vice president for communications, told David Bauder for the Associated Press (July 12, 2006, on-line). Schwartz, whose title makes him CBS's chief spokesperson, is also known as Stanley Bing, the pseudonym he assumed when he began writing a column for *Esquire*, in 1985. Four years earlier he had taken a job as a public-affairs associate for the TelePrompTer Corp.; he became a communications executive at CBS in 1996, after a series of promotions that took place following TelePrompTer's acquisition by Westinghouse Broadcasting (Group W) and the latter's merger with CBS. Since 1989, when his first book appeared, Schwartz—as Bing—has published two novels, *Lloyd: What Happened* and *You Look Nice Today*, and eight volumes that,

with tools ranging from razor-sharp, acerbic wit to gentle satire, poke fun at the corporate world and its denizens, among them *Biz Words: Power Talk for Fun and Profit*; *Crazy Bosses: Spotting Them, Serving Them, Surviving Them* (and an updated version); *What Would Machiavelli Do? The Ends Justify the Meanness*; *Throwing the Elephant: Zen and the Art of Managing Up*; and *Rome, Inc.: The Rise and Fall of the First Multinational Corporation*. "I don't know if I'd have gone this route if I hadn't started out as a mole within the corporate government, but once Bing popped out he sort of had a life of his own that was a nice addition to my own . . . ," Schwartz told Dorian Benkoil for mediabistro.com (March 22, 2006). "They say you're supposed to write about what you know. . . . I write about organizations and how they work on people. I write about festering, bleeding, suffering humanity, put to work in stultifying social structures that attempt to squeeze the life out of them and almost never succeed. I write about madness and struggle and triumph in a constricted, formalistic environment that brings both the best and worst out of people." He told Melissa Thomas for the *New York Sun* (July 8, 2004) that he would last "about a month if I was a full-time

Gil Schwartz

writer. I like being on the inside, being part of something." Since 1995, when he left *Esquire*, Schwartz, as Bing, has written two dozen columns a year for *Fortune*; most of them are currently posted on his blog, stanleybing.com, which he launched in 2007. Under his real name he wrote a column for *Seventeen* (in the guise of a 17-year-old boy) from 1984 to 1990, and since 1993 he has produced a column for *Men's Health*. He has also written articles for publications including *Mademoiselle*, *Working Woman*, *New York*, and *PC Computing*.

Gil D. Schwartz was born on May 12, 1951 in Illinois. His father was a social worker who studied group dynamics—a subject in which Schwartz, too, has become a specialist of sorts, at least regarding groups in the world of business. Schwartz's family moved from Highland Park, Illinois, to New Rochelle, a suburb of New York City, when he was 11. He attended Brandeis University, in Waltham, Massachusetts, where he earned a B.A. degree in theater arts and English. In the half-dozen years following his graduation, he worked as a humor writer for the *Boston Phoenix* (a weekly alternative newspaper that focuses on the arts and entertainment) and as a theater-company manager, among other jobs. At age 28 Schwartz moved to New York, with the expectation, as he told Jack Myers for mediavillage.com (March 15, 2004), that with his "rugged good looks and on-screen charisma," he would be cast in leading-man roles on the stage or in TV shows filmed in the city. Instead, he said, he found himself playing such parts as the "slow witted henchman, criminal, and bad guy." Schwartz told Bauder that he earned a part on the soap opera *As the World Turns* because "they were looking for someone who looked like he would take a bribe."

Schwartz next turned to writing plays. Two of them—*Ferocious Kisses* and *Love As We Know It*—were mounted Off-Broadway and directed by Josh Mostel (a son of the comic actor Zero Mostel). In a review of *Ferocious Kisses* for the New York *Daily News* (February 3, 1982), Don Nelson described it as "a farcy parody that burlesques show-big sleaze to make its point." "Schwartz' ear is acute," Nelson continued. "He skillfully reproduces the jargon and kissy-poo bogus affection that passes for communication within the scurrying maze of devious managers, pettifogging press agents and scheming hangers-on that populate the theatrical world." Stanley Bing was a character in *Love As We Know It*, about which Edith Oliver wrote for the *New Yorker* (November 11, 1985), "As is true with many humorists of limited experience, Mr. Schwartz's effort to be funny occasionally shows, thereby, of course, killing his joke. More often than not, though, the effect is carefree, sly, and original; there are many more hits than misses."

Years before, in 1981, to support his writing, Schwartz had found work as an associate in the public-relations department of the TelePrompter Corp., which was then among the largest cable-systems operators in the U.S. His responsibilities included speechwriting. Through what Bauder labeled "a Byzantine series of corporate acquisitions," Schwartz's job led directly to his current position: shortly after his arrival the Westinghouse Broadcasting Co., also known as Group W, acquired TelePrompter, and Schwartz became the company's manager of public relations. He was named director of communications for Group W Cable in 1984, and he retained that title after the company abandoned the cable format two years later. When Group W merged with CBS, in 1996, Schwartz was made CBS Television's senior vice president for communications.

Concurrently, in February 1985, *Esquire* published the first of Schwartz's essays on corporate strategies for men in their 30s, "How to Draw the Line," in which he offered advice about preserving one's personal life while progressing professionally. He conceived of the column, called "Executive Summary," and the Bing character in collaboration with David Blum, an *Esquire* editor. "I wanted to express what it's like to work for a living," he said to Thomas. He told Dorian Benkoil, "Inside every suit, there's a human being. When I was a kid, I always loved stuff about guys with secret identities. Zorro in particular. Big nerd by day. Guy in a silky black cape at night, flying through windows, saving people, being sort of dangerous and legendary. This was as close as I could get to that." The column changed over the years in ways that reflected Schwartz's corporate ascent. He told Benkoil facetiously that when he began writing it, "I was younger, and didn't understand at the time how splendid senior management generally is."

Bing's first book, *Biz Words: Power Talk for Fun and Profit* (1989), an amalgam of humor and advice for those aspiring to climb the corporate ladder, contains a glossary of terms commonly used in business circles, along with their "true" definitions according to Bing. "It will come as no surprise to anyone who has read Bing's monthly . . . column . . . that each *Biz Words* definition is at once hilarious but dead-serious," J. Michael Kelly wrote for the Syracuse, New York, *Post-Standard* (June 4, 1989). *Crazy Bosses: Spotting Them, Serving Them, Surviving Them* (1992), Bing's next book, catalogues the types of neuroses that supposedly afflict employers and suggests ways for workers to deal with them. Types of crazy bosses, as Bing pigeonholed them, include the bully, the narcissist, the paranoid boss, the "bureaucrazy" boss (a mixture of wimp and fascist), and the disaster hunter— "the shared terminal stage of all four types," as Alan Farnham wrote in a review of *Crazy Bosses* for *Fortune* (May 4, 1992), as posted on CNN-money.com. "Since craziness has become pandemic (and thus inescapable)," Farnham continued, "Bing recommends sane employees give up all hope of escaping crazy bosses and concentrate instead on learning how to manage them. With a little cleverness, he says, and a great deal of care, the rational underling can topple his crazy boss without himself getting crushed in the process. To that end, Bing provides advice specific for each type of boss. . . . This book's tips on office politics ring true. Where crazy bosses are concerned, Bing is bang-on." The updated edition of *Crazy Bosses* appeared in 2007.

Bing's last column for *Esquire* appeared in that magazine's July 1995 issue; his first for *Fortune* was published in its August 7, 1995 edition. Five months later Bing's identity was revealed in the *New York Times* (January 8, 1996) by Mark Landler, in a piece about a feature article entitled "The Smartest and Dumbest Moves of 1995" in *Fortune*. In his introduction to that article, Bing had poked fun at the Walt Disney Co. for what he described as its "colonization" of ABC, CBS's chief rival. Bing's words were generally seen as a "backhanded salute" to the competition, Landler wrote. "Now that he is chief spokesman for CBS, Mr. Schwartz might find it harder to keep the opinionated Mr. Bing in the shadows," he continued, noting that in 1992, while promoting *Crazy Bosses*, Schwartz had appeared on *Good Morning America* "without a disguise, but as Mr. Bing." At that time, however, "despite appearing on national television, Mr. Schwartz was able to maintain a low profile as Stanley Bing, in part because of Group W's rather nondescript image in the broadcast industry." Schwartz told Benkoil, "I'd been outed internally a while before, so very few insiders were shocked, maybe that made things easier." Since he was exposed as Bing, Schwartz has often said that his dual identity is the worst-kept secret in publishing. David Blum, who was then a *New York Times Magazine* contributing editor, told Landler that the distinctly different contributions to society of Bing and Schwartz "could be one of the great synergies of modern times. It's pretty much unheard of for the top P.R. guy at a major American corporation to write a humor column." Discussing the potential for a conflict of interest to compromise the work of Schwartz or Schwartz as Bing, Howard Stringer, the former president of the CBS Broadcast Group, told Landler, "Given that Andy Rooney has a column in which he routinely ridicules the network, and that David Letterman does it on his show, I think it's in the grandest tradition of CBS."

Bing's first novel, *Lloyd: What Happened: A Novel of Business*, appeared in 1998. It follows an ambitious executive and the changes he undergoes while carrying out layoffs deemed necessary for an anticipated merger. Schwartz told Jennifer Nix for *Daily Variety* (March 16, 1998) that Lloyd is "a decent enough guy, who doesn't have the greatest hairline, who's a little chunky and who makes well into the mid-six figures, but who sees through the corporate crap when he isn't closing his eyes." The book contains 80 satirical pie charts and graphs, with such titles as "Percent of Lloyd's Bosses Displaying Insane Behavior" and "The Battle for Lloyd's Soul." The inclusion of a 5,000-word excerpt of the novel in *Fortune* (May 11, 1998) marked the first time any fiction had appeared in that magazine since 1947. In an undated review for mindjack.com, J. M. Frank wrote, "Writers, as a general rule, don't live the same kinds of lives that most of the rest of us do. This causes an excess in novels of protagonists who are either writers or artists and a noticeable lack of stories involving the types of jobs and lives many of us have. . . . *Lloyd: What Happened* is one of the rare novels that actually focuses on the real life trials and tribulations of many people: life in the modern corporate workplace. Stanley Bing's main goal here is social satire. You will not be moved to tears by this book, nor discover deep insights into the nature of our modern world. But you will be entertained, and you will laugh. . . . The author . . . has a keen eye for the small hypocrisies in human behavior. The sense of realism and believable characters makes this satire work." In a less enthusiastic review for the *New York Times* (May 28, 1998), Joe Queenan complained that the book was much too long and that there were not enough funny scenes. "In the end," he wrote, "*Lloyd: What Happened* may try to do in prose what *Dilbert* does in pictures. Unfortunately, as is often the case, a picture is worth a thousand words. Especially a thousand of these words."

In the last seven years, in addition to his new edition of *Crazy Bosses*, Bing has published seven books. His *What Would Machiavelli Do? The Ends Justify the Meanness* (2000) is "a satirical manual on how to become mean in order to get to the top," according to Claire Atkinson, writing for *PR Week* (June 24, 2002). *Throwing the Elephant: Zen and the Art of Managing Up* (2002) offers advice on how to do well with "elephant" bosses. Schwartz told Peter Johnson for *USA Today* (March 19, 2002) that *Throwing the Elephant* advises workers to view themselves as having "incredible minimal importance. You are tiny. You have no significance. If you just do your job and abandon hope, you have much more power and much more access to happiness. It's people who try to be as big and as important as the elephant who suffer miserably." *The Big Bing: Black Holes of Time Management, Gaseous Executive Bodies, Exploding Careers, and Other Theories on the Origins of the Business Universe* (2003) is a collection of Bing's *Esquire* and *Fortune* columns. In *Sun Tzu Was a Sissy: Conquer Your Enemies, Promote Your Friends, and Wage the Real Art of War* (2004), Bing "assails the ancient Chinese war philosopher, a favorite of vicious bosses, and offers what he calls a handy guide to making war in the workplace," as Thomas wrote. *100 Bull[expletive] Jobs . . . and How to Get Them* (2006) offers Bing's mathematical formula for finding the "BS Quotient" of a variety of jobs, including wine-industry professional, pet psychic, life coach, consultant, executive vice president—new media, and "writer of this book." In *Rome, Inc.: The Rise and Fall of the First Multinational Corporation* (2006), as William Grimes wrote for the *New York Times* (March 18, 2006), Schwartz "simply reverses a common metaphor, the business as an empire, and looks at the Roman empire as a multinational corporation, with a business model, a coherent management structure and greedy executives." "Mr. Bing, on occasion, plays fast and loose with facts. . . . But on the main questions, Mr. Bing proves to be a keen analyst," and "the funny parts . . . are very funny."

In *You Look Nice Today* (2003), Bing's second novel, a secretary brings a sexual harassment lawsuit against her boss, a corporate executive, after he attempts to have her transferred out of his department. A large portion of the book is dedicated to footnoted transcripts from the harassment trial. David Exum, in a critique posted on bookreporter.com, wrote, "Although *You Look Nice Today* is purely fictional, it does a triumphant job in detailing the conclusion of corporate excess in America at the end of the 1990s," and he expressed the opinion that "the trial itself is possibly Bing at his best." An anonymous reviewer for the *New Yorker* (September 8, 2003), by contrast, wrote, "Unfortunately, the courtroom animates Bing's comic gift less effectively than the daily grind of the office and the soul-smothering masquerade of being a company man." Ron Charles, the reviewer for the *Christian Science Monitor* (September 4, 2003), noted that *You Look Nice Today* "does nothing to disturb those pernicious stereotypes" according to which women who file complaints about "boorish advances, off-color jokes, and crude bargains for promotion" are "bad team players, humorless shrews, or fragile hysterics who misinterpret the most harmless remarks. . . . But it's very funny." "What a wonderful novel to argue about and chuckle over," Charles wrote. "If there are any truly integrated book clubs in America—not just by race, but by gender and class—here's a title for discussion that will delay dessert."

In 2004 Schwartz was named executive vice president of the newly created CBS Communications Group, responsible for public relations, media relations, and corporate and internal communications for all the divisions directed by Leslie Moonves, the president and chief executive officer of the CBS Corp., among them CBS Television, UPN, Paramount TV, Infinity Radio, and Viacom Outdoor. "Gil is clearly a great consigliere," Moonves said, as quoted by Pamela McClintock in *Daily Variety* (November 5, 2004). "He's a great adviser, not only on press issues, but on issues that go across the company." When Benkoil asked Schwartz how he succeeds in balancing the seemingly contradictory pursuits of business humorist and corporate spokesman, Schwartz said, "I really see no reason to comment on that at this time." In the same month Schwartz amused participants at CBS's annual affiliates meeting, held that year in Las Vegas, Nevada, when, in the guise of the late singer Johnny Cash, he sang songs about CBS and the television industry, written by himself. Anybody who has attended those meetings in recent years, Michele Greppi wrote for *Television Week* (June 5, 2006), knows that "Schwartz's portion of the program is a must-see laff riot, an annual look at the network business as only he could see it or say it." In one song, "Wholesome Prison Blues" (set to the tune of Cash's "Folsom Prison Blues"), Schwartz lamented, "When I was just a baby, my mama told me, 'Tex / You can program violence, just never program sex.' / So we stuck to rotting corpses, on shows like *CSI* / But when I think of nipple jewelry / I hang my head and cry."

"It's almost impossible to direct conversation with the highly entertaining Schwartz," Claire Atkinson wrote for *PR Week* (June 24, 2002). "He is, after all, a master of manipulation." Schwartz lived in New Rochelle, New York, while his children, Nina and Will, were growing up. He currently maintains homes in Manhattan and Mill Valley, California, where he lives with his wife, Laura Svienty, a writer. Svienty founded the Web site PhilanthroFlash and contributes regularly to *Benefit*, a "lifestyle of giving" magazine.

—M.B.

Suggested Reading: Associated Press (on-line) July 12, 2006; CBS Corp. Web site; mediabistro.com Mar. 22, 2006; *New York Sun* p13 July 8, 2004; *New York Times* p33 Jan. 8, 1996; *PR Week* p17 June 24, 2002

Selected Books: *Biz Words*, 1989; *Crazy Bosses*, 1992; *Lloyd—What Happened*, 1998; *What Would Machiavelli Do?*, 2000; *Throwing the Elephant*, 2002; *The Big Bing*, 2003; *You Look Nice Today*, 2003; *Sun Tzu was a Sissy*, 2004; *100 Bulls*** Jobs . . . and How to Get Them*, 2006; *Rome, Inc.*, 2006

Scorsese, Martin

NOTE: An earlier article on Martin Scorsese appeared in *Current Biography* in 1979.

(skor-SAY-zee)

Nov. 17. 1942– Filmmaker

Address: c/o All-American Speakers Bureau, 4717 Knights Arm Dr., Durham, NC 27707

"Could you double-check the envelope?" Those words were spoken before a national television audience on February 25, 2007 by Martin Scorsese, as he accepted the Academy Award for best director for his film *The Departed*. Scorsese's quip was an allusion to his five previous Oscar nominations in that category, none of which had brought him the award; that scenario had long puzzled those who call Scorsese the greatest filmmaker of his generation, one that includes Francis Ford Coppola, George Lucas, and Steven Spielberg—each of whom helped to revolutionize American cinema in the 1970s. Scorsese's work has often been lauded for its innovative style, characterized by his signature tracking shots, his use of slow motion and voiceover narration, and his unusual approach to narrative, with segments from the middle of the story sometimes opening the film. He is also noted for the weighty, often disturbing themes he has explored; the characters in Scorsese's films—many of them Italian-American—struggle with issues of guilt, redemption, and personal honor while reflecting the corrupting influence of violence and greed in modern American society. Though most of his movies have not been box-office smashes, a number of them, most notably *Taxi Driver* (1976), *Raging Bull* (1980), and *GoodFellas* (1990), are considered to be among the finest works in American film. Long an outsider to the Hollywood system, Scorsese once asked rhetorically, as quoted on the Internet Movie Database (imdb.com), "What does it take to be a filmmaker in Hollywood? . . . I still wonder what it takes to be a professional or even an artist in Hollywood. How do you survive the constant tug of war between personal expression and commercial imperatives? What is the price you pay to work in Hollywood? Do you end up with a split personality? Do you make one movie for them, one for yourself?"

The son of Italian-Americans of Sicilian descent, Martin Luciano Scorsese was born on November 17, 1942 in Flushing, in the New York City borough of Queens. His parents, Charles and Catherine (Cappa) Scorsese, had recently moved from their native Little Italy, in the borough of Manhattan; for financial reasons they returned there when Martin was eight. Remaining in Little Italy until the age of 24, Scorsese came to know thoroughly the flavor and rhythm of life in that confined Italian-American community.

Poor health, specifically asthma, prevented Scorsese from joining his older brother, Fred, and other neighborhood boys in sports, street fights, and work at odd jobs during the summer. In Little Italy his frailty made him an outsider, a role he was to examine repeatedly in his films. To relieve his loneliness and idleness, his father took him to the movies. Afterward the boy would sketch scenes of his own on drawing pads. "There's a great similarity in the way I look at reality and the things I saw in the musicals and the dark 'noir' films of the '40s," he told David Sterritt for the *Christian Science Monitor* (May 1, 1978). "My reality and film reality are interchangeable. They blend."

Raised a Roman Catholic, Scorsese attended a Catholic grade school and at 14, with the intention of becoming a priest, enrolled in a junior seminary on the city's Upper West Side. On being expelled at the end of the year—"for roughhousing during prayers," according to one account—he transferred to Cardinal Hayes High School, in the Bronx. He did not abandon the idea of renewing his study for the priesthood until he found in filmmaking what he has called his "true vocation." "My whole life has been movies and religion. That's it. Nothing else," Scorsese once said, as quoted on imdb.com. In several interviews he disclosed that he stopped attending Mass after he heard a priest endorse the Vietnam War as a holy cause. Though he now describes himself as a lapsed Catholic, he still considers himself to be a member of that faith, and many critics have noted strains of Catholic sensibility in his work.

After he failed the examination for Fordham College's divinity program, Scorsese entered New York University (NYU), planning to major in English. But after discovering the film department at the university's School of the Arts, he devoted himself to the fundamentals of filmmaking and was soon turning out films that won awards from the Edward L. Kingsley Foundation, the Screen Producers Guild, and the Brown University Film Festival. He learned of the auteur theory—that a film ideally realized the director's individual vision—which had been developed by the French film theorist Andre Bazin; that discovery convinced Scorsese that, although he had been taught that American films were far inferior to their European counterparts, he did not have to reject the American films he had loved as a child, perhaps because many of them represented the auteur theory in action. While studying to obtain his B.S. degree in film communications, in 1964 and his M.A. degree, in 1966, he taught in NYU's film department as an assistant instructor from 1963 to 1966. He returned to the NYU faculty in 1968 and taught film until 1970.

Among Scorsese's award-winning student films were "What's a Girl Like You Doing in a Place Like This?" (1963) and "It's Not Just You, Murray" (1964). His fascination with violence emerged particularly in the blood-drenched, six-minute color film "The Big Shave" (1967–68), described by its

Kevin Winter/Getty Images

Martin Scorsese accepts the Oscar for best director for The Departed *during the 79th Annual Academy Awards ceremony*

sponsor, Belgian Cinematheque, as a "brief American nightmare." In 1968, while still an instructor at NYU, Scorsese wrote and directed his first feature film, *Who's That Knocking at My Door?*, about the struggle of a young Italian, J.R., to reconcile his rigid Catholic sexual mores with the actualities of Little Italy. The film introduced Harvey Keitel, an actor who became part of an informal Scorsese ensemble. To attract a distributor for his low-budget production, Scorsese was forced to add an explicit, though psychologically dubious, sex scene, but the film attracted considerable critical interest. While some reviewers agreed with William Wolf of *Cue* (August 19, 1972), who thought it "a sophomoric cinematic exercise," others praised the film's vividness and authenticity of feeling.

A later movie on which Scorsese worked while at NYU, *Street Scenes* (1970), documents an anti–Vietnam War demonstration in New York City. He was associated, as supervising editor and assistant director, with another documentary, *Woodstock* (1970), an account of the gathering in 1969 of a half-million rock-music fans in the Catskills, which was directed by Michael Wadleigh, the photographer of *Who's That Knocking at My Door?* Somewhat reminiscent of *Woodstock*, *Medicine Boy Caravan* (1971), of which Scorsese was associate producer, chronicles a cross-country bus junket of music-loving, long-haired San Franciscans. He also did some editing on the music documentary *Elvis on Tour* (1973). His other early work included making television commercials in England in 1968 and editing news footage for CBS.

In 1972 the B-movie producer Roger Corman hired Scorsese to direct his low-budget film *Boxcar Bertha*, based on the story of an unhappy vagrant young woman during the Depression. A reviewer for *Variety* (May 3, 1972) summed up that potboiler with the verdict: "Whatever its intentions, *Boxcar Bertha* is not much more than an excuse to slaughter a lot of people." However, Arthur Winsten pointed out in the *New York Post* (August 17, 1972) that Scorsese "is very strong with the crucifixion that does place this picture off by itself."

Admonished by the movie director John Cassavetes about wasting his time and talents on *Boxcar Bertha*, Scorsese resolved to pursue his own film ideas. In 1973 he filmed *Mean Streets*, based on a script he had written with Mardik Martin seven years earlier about the relationship between a small-time hood, Charlie, and his reckless friend Johnny Boy, both of whom are caught up in the criminal world of Little Italy. Torn between loyalty to his friend and the desire to get ahead in the Mafia, Charlie sacrifices his epileptic girlfriend and Johnny Boy. Scorsese appears in a cameo role as the gunman who shoots Johnny Boy and the girlfriend. He adopted Cassavetes's improvisational techniques to direct Harvey Keitel as Charlie and the then-unknown Robert De Niro, who also grew up in Little Italy, as Johnny Boy.

Mean Streets won widespread acclaim upon its showing at the 1973 New York Film Festival. In a long, laudatory review for the *New Yorker* (October 8, 1973), Pauline Kael called it "a true original of our period, a triumph of personal filmmaking. . . . What Scorsese, who is thirty, has done with the experience of growing up in New York's Little Italy

2007 CURRENT BIOGRAPHY YEARBOOK 463

has a thicker-textured rot and violence than we have ever had in an American movie." Martin Knelman described the film for the Toronto, Canada, *Globe and Mail* (December 28, 1973) as "a brutally unforgettable street drama about a kind of life that is not at all remote or exotic, but it has the imagination and the spell of a visionary work."

Too grim for many moviegoers, *Mean Streets* was not a box-office success. The film did, however, earn Scorsese studio sponsorship and funding for his next movie, *Alice Doesn't Live Here Anymore* (1974). A strong departure from his previous work, the film was based on Robert Getchell's television screenplay about a mediocre singer who seeks a career in the music world after she is suddenly widowed. Ellen Burstyn, who owned the film property and gave an Oscar-winning performance as Alice, was acknowledged to have contributed substantially to the shaping of the film, as was Scorsese's then-girlfriend, Sandy Weintraub, its associate producer. But the hand-held camera sequences, the homage to *The Wizard of Oz* in the opening of the film, the violent interlude with Alice's sadistic lover, and the pivotal role of friendship in the story all reflect Scorsese's directorial vision.

Overall critical response to *Alice* was mixed. Several reviewers agreed with Steven Farber of the *New York Times* (March 30, 1975), who wrote, "Although dressed up to look modern, *Alice* is just another Technicolor advertisement for cotton candy romance." Several rejected the happy ending as "wrongheaded," but Diane Jacobs, in *Hollywood Renaissance* (1977), saw it as appropriate to "a transcendent comedy." The film confirmed her view that "Scorsese's study of Middle Americans today concentrates on their humor, their tenacity, their ability to help each other survive and, just maybe, ameliorate." Ordinary filmgoers embraced the movie, which was a solid box-office hit, making Scorsese a "bankable" director.

During 1973 Scorsese had also made a 45-minute documentary of an after-dinner conversation with his parents. His affectionate portrait of them is realized through family reminiscences and a scene showing his mother making spaghetti sauce. *Italianamerican* received a standing ovation when it was premiered at the 1974 New York Film Festival. It was later shown on public television as part of a PBS series, *Storm of Strangers*. (His parents would go on to make cameo appearances in a number of his films. Most notably, his mother portrayed the mother of the Joe Pesci character in *GoodFellas*.)

Scorsese took a huge commercial risk with his next film, *Taxi Driver* (1976), about an ex-Marine cabbie who, pushed to the edge of insanity by loneliness and rejection, attempts to "cleanse" himself and New York City in an orgiastic massacre. Much critical controversy surrounded the bloody climax of the film, in which the taxi driver (played by De Niro) murders the pimp, the customer, and intruders in the room of a teenage prostitute he is trying

to reform. Although the color of that sequence was desaturated to avoid an X rating, reviewers in general were unnerved by Scorsese's depiction of such butchery; several considered it an amoral glorification of violence. Diane Jacobs commented, "A pictorial affection for violent death gets out of control and dulls the impact of a still extraordinarily forceful psychological study." Audiences, however, on the whole seconded the approval of David Sterritt, who in the *Christian Science Monitor* (February 19, 1976) called *Taxi Driver* "the nastiest masterpiece in years," and Pauline Kael, who contended in the *New Yorker* (February 9, 1976), "No other film has ever dramatized urban indifference so powerfully." Abroad, *Taxi Driver* won the Golden Palm grand prize at the Cannes Film Festival in 1976.

Venturing into an entirely different genre for his next film, Scorsese set out to create a lavish, 1940s-style Hollywood musical, replete with flashy production numbers and a romantic story line about two ambitious musicians. During the filming of *New York, New York* (1977), however, Scorsese grew more interested in exploring the troubled relationship between the musicians, played by Liza Minnelli and Robert De Niro, than in making a Hollywood extravaganza. Through lengthy sessions of improvisation recorded on videotape, Scorsese and his actors rewrote the script to focus on the conflict between career and love that keeps the couple apart. "My light frothy musical turned out to be my most personal film," Scorsese said in an interview for *Newsweek* (May 16, 1977). The $8.7 million film impaired Scorsese's reputation with most critics. In a review for the *Wall Street Journal* (July 18, 1977), Joy Gould Boyum lamented, "Still another gifted young filmmaker has succumbed to that current pandemic of the movie world, cloying and crippling nostalgia."

While still at work on *New York, New York*, Scorsese took time out to direct *The Last Waltz* (1978), a documentary tribute to the rock group called the Band on the occasion of its "last" concert on Thanksgiving Day, 1976. "The coverage is nearly perfect and puts to shame all those murky rock movies of the past," Chris Hodenfield wrote for *Rolling Stone* (June 1, 1978), an assessment shared by a host of critics. Some reviewers found fault with Scorsese's interrupting the concert footage with interviews of the musicians, which the director himself reportedly included only grudgingly, but the movie fared well at the box office.

In 1978 Scorsese was hospitalized, suffering from asthma and chronic fatigue brought on by overwork and drug abuse. After doctors told him that his lifestyle would soon lead to his death, Scorsese, on De Niro's advice, decided to overcome his drug habit by devoting himself wholly to the making of what he believed would be his final film. Using all he had learned, he adopted what he has called a "kamikaze" approach to filmmaking. "My thinking at the time," he told Hal Hinson for the *Washington Post* (November 24, 1991), "was just pull out all the stops and then find a new career." Though the film proved to be a box-office failure, it was not only a personal triumph for Scorsese but, arguably, his masterpiece.

Raging Bull (1980) depicts the real-life story of the boxer Jake La Motta, who worked his way up from the tough streets of his Italian neighborhood in the Bronx to become middleweight champion, only to suffer a drastic decline that left him out of shape, destitute, alienated from his family, and eking out a living as a stand-up comedian in dive bars. As played by De Niro—who, during the course of filming, changed himself physically to portray the boxer as both chiseled champion and overweight has-been—La Motta is a thuggish man whose behavior is not fully explained by either his background or his environment. Critics admired Scorsese's deft direction, in particular his ability to present an absorbing protagonist who is not at all sympathetic. In a review for the *New York Times* (November 14, 1980), Vincent Canby declared: "Though it's a movie full of anger and nonstop physical violence, the effect of *Raging Bull* is lyrical. To witness Jake's fury is to swing through the upper atmosphere of the emotions. It's breathtaking and a little scary. This has to do both with Mr. De Niro's performance and with the film's literary and visual style." *Raging Bull*, Canby added, displays "an effortlessness that is as rewarding as it is rare in films." Commenting on the film 20 years later for the *Village Voice* (August 2–8, 2000), Amy Taubin noted, "In almost all of Scorsese's other movies, there are moments when you sense the dilemma of a director pulled between the desire to make art and the need to be a success (enough of a success to be allowed to make more movies). Even when the films are great, there are compromised moments. But from the first shot in *Raging Bull* of a nearly disembodied Robert De Niro, alone in the ring, jogging in slo-mo, his face obscured by the hood of his robe, like a monk in [Roberto] Rossellini's *The Little Flowers of St. Francis*, you know that for Scorsese, this is the big one, the title fight, and it's only art that's at stake. The sense of risk is palpable and the payoff is exhilarating. There's not a single pulled or wasted punch. The film is a perfect match of form and content." For *Raging Bull*, Scorsese earned his first Academy Award nomination and won a National Society of Film Critics Award for best director.

For *The King of Comedy* (1983), Scorsese again teamed with De Niro to depict an unstable loner, this time in the form of Rupert Pupkin—the obsessed fan of a television talk-show host named Jerry Langford, who is portrayed by Jerry Lewis. Vincent Canby, writing for the *New York Times* (February 18, 1983), noted that *The King of Comedy* is "very funny, and it ends on a high note that was, for me, both a total surprise and completely satisfying. Yet it's also bristly, sometimes manic to the edge of lunacy and, along the way, terrifying. It's not an absolute joy by a long shot but, in the way of a film that uses all of its talents to their fullest, it's exhilarating." Though many reviewers, like Canby, felt ambivalent about the film upon its release, *The King of Comedy* has since gone on to enjoy a cult status among film fans, who see it as a prescient study of fame-obsessed contemporary culture.

During the early 1980s Scorsese found himself at a crossroads as a filmmaker. Though he wanted to continue making the kinds of personal films he had long been attracted to, he also knew that the film industry had become far more market-driven than in years past. Since the late 1960s he had wanted to make a film version of *The Last Temptation of Christ*, a 1951 novel by Nikos Kazantzakis. In 1983 he began working with Paramount Pictures on the film version, with Aidan Quinn cast as Jesus and Sting as Pontius Pilate. However, the studio, bowing to pressure from conservative Christians who feared that Scorsese's film would depict Christ as a sensualist, canceled the project. Bitter at the way he had been treated by the Hollywood system, Scorsese put his efforts into an independent film, *After Hours* (1985), which had a comparatively low budget of $3.5 million.

Shot on location in New York, the dark comedy *After Hours* follows the nightmarish misadventures of a computer programmer, Paul, played by Griffin Dunne, after he meets a neurotic young woman, played by Rosanna Arquette, in a coffee shop. *After Hours* generally met with praise. Roger Ebert remarked in the *Chicago Sun-Times* (October 11, 1985): "*After Hours* is a brilliant film, one of the year's best. It is also a most curious film. It comes after Scorsese's *The King of Comedy*, a film I thought was fascinating but unsuccessful, and continues Scorsese's attempt to combine comedy and satire with unrelenting pressure and a sense of all-pervading paranoia. This time he succeeds." On the other hand, in his review for the *New York Times* (September 13, 1985), Vincent Canby wrote: "*After Hours* is, at best, an entertaining tease, with individually arresting sequences that are well acted by Mr. Dunne and the others, but which leave you feeling somewhat conned. There is no satisfying resolution to the tension, as effectively built up here as it was in *King of Comedy*, *Raging Bull* and *Taxi Driver*." Later that year, Scorsese's work on the film earned him the best-director award at the Cannes Film Festival, in France.

In order to prove that he could make a commercial picture, Scorsese agreed to helm *The Color of Money* (1986), a sequel to *The Hustler*, the highly regarded 1961 film by Robert Rossen that starred Paul Newman as the young pool hustler Fast Eddie Felson. In *The Color of Money*, Newman reprised the role; now a middle-aged liquor salesman living in Chicago, Illinois, Eddie meets a young pool shark, played by Tom Cruise, and sees in him a means of redeeming his own life and his love of the game. A critical and commercial success, the film earned Newman an Oscar for best actor. It also enabled Scorsese to persuade executives at Universal Pictures to finance his film of *The Last Temptation of Christ*, which was released in 1988—though not without difficulties along the way. The studio allotted the biblical epic a budget of only $6.5 million, a far cry from the $15 million he was granted for *The Color of Money*. In addition, when conservative Christians learned that the film was being made, Universal Pictures executives found themselves targets of demonstrations and threats of a boycott, as a result of which the film gained a considerable reputation even before it debuted. In it, Jesus (portrayed by Willem Defoe) is more man than God, longing to be relieved of his burden as the world's savior, even imagining, while dying on the cross, a life spent with Mary Magdalene. For an article in *People* (August 8, 1988), Scorsese explained to David Grogan, "I dreamed for a while that the church and clergy would like the film, and that it would stimulate positive dialogue. What I've tried to create is a Jesus who, in a sense, is just like any other guy in the street. In his struggle to reach God . . . he reflects all our struggles. I thought it would give us all hope."

Scorsese was again nominated for an Academy Award for best director, but his controversial film divided not only the public but critics as well. Hal Hinson, writing for the *Washington Post* (August 12, 1988), called it "a probing, unflinching film. And Scorsese's motive here is to stimulate and provoke, not to sensationalize. The director's failure, though, comes at the most basic level. In spite of all he accomplishes, he is unable to bring Jesus close to us." The *New York Times* (August 12, 1988) critic Janet Maslin remarked, "What emerges most memorably is [the film's] sense of absolute conviction, never more palpable than in the final fantasy sequence that removes Jesus from the cross and creates for him the life of an ordinary man. Though this episode lasts longer than it should and is allowed to wander far afield, it finally has the mightily affirmative, truly visceral impact for which the whole film clearly strives. Anyone who questions the sincerity or seriousness of what Mr. Scorsese has attempted need only see the film to lay those doubts to rest."

After collaborating with Francis Ford Coppola and Woody Allen on *New York Stories* (1989), for which each director filmed a segment, Scorsese began work on *GoodFellas* (1990), which would be ranked alongside *Taxi Driver* and *Raging Bull* as one of his great achievements and would reestablish his reputation as one of the preeminent directors of his generation. The film, adapted from Nicholas Pileggi's book *Wiseguy*, also brought Scorsese back to the kind of gritty crime drama that had first earned him respect, telling the story of the real-life gangster Henry Hill (played by Ray Liotta); the film tracks the decline of organized crime as seen through Hill's eyes, from the moment he becomes enraptured with it as a boy in the 1950s to his entry into the Federal Witness Protection Program in the late 1970s. For *GoodFellas* Scorsese re-teamed with Robert De Niro and Joe Pesci, who had first worked together under his direction in *Raging Bull*.

In addition to receiving some of the best reviews of his career for *GoodFellas*, Scorsese won best-director awards from the National Society of Film Critics, the New York Film Critics Circle, and the Los Angeles Film Critics Association, as well as an Academy Award nomination for best director. In the *Chicago Sun-Times* (September 2, 1990), Roger Ebert proclaimed: "Most films, even great ones, evaporate like mist once you've returned to the real world; they leave memories behind, but their reality fades fairly quickly. Not this film, which shows America's finest filmmaker at the peak of his form. No finer film has ever been made about organized crime—not even *The Godfather,* although the two works are not really comparable." Desson Howe of the *Washington Post* (September 21, 1990) called *GoodFellas* "an incredible, relentless experience about the singleminded pursuit of crime. Suddenly Scorsese, who with Francis Ford Coppola, Robert Altman, George Lucas, Steven Spielberg and Brian De Palma led the 'significant directors' pack in the 1970s, stakes the first authoritative claim of the '90s."

Scorsese's next film, *Cape Fear* (1991), a remake of a 1962 thriller starring Robert Mitchum and Gregory Peck, found De Niro portraying a psychotic, recently released convict who stalks his lawyer, played by Nick Nolte. A commercial hit, the film earned $80 million in the United States alone. While that mainstream thriller represented an unexpected departure for Scorsese, his admirers were even more surprised by his next film, *The Age of Innocence* (1993). Based on the 1920 novel of the same name by Edith Wharton, set in New York's high society of the 1870s, the movie depicts a man's struggles against the confines of his class after he falls in love with the scandal-plagued cousin of the woman he is planning to marry. Starring Daniel Day-Lewis, Michelle Pfeiffer, and Winona Ryder, the film earned five Academy Award nominations, including one for Scorsese for best adapted screenplay, and won an Oscar for costume design. Rita Kempley of the *Washington Post* (September 17, 1993) declared: "Like *Raging Bull*, *GoodFellas* and other Martin Scorsese films, *The Age of Innocence* is about the tyranny of the culture over the individual and the rites that preserve the tribe, be it the Mafia or a coterie of 19th-century snobs. Perhaps it shouldn't come as such a grand surprise that he is as deft at exploring the nuances of Edwardian manners as he is the laws of modern-day machismo."

Scorsese returned to crime drama with his next film, *Casino* (1995), which teamed De Niro, Pesci, and Sharon Stone in a story about mob involvement in the gambling world of Las Vegas, Nevada, in the 1960s and 1970s. While Stone won praise—and an Academy Award nomination for best actress—for her work in the film, De Niro and Pesci were widely criticized by reviewers for repeating, almost parodying, their earlier performances; Scorsese himself was taken to task for employing techniques similar to those that had inspired admiration in *GoodFellas*.

Casino's reception notwithstanding, in October 1996 the American Film Institute (AFI) announced that Scorsese would be the recipient of its 1997 Lifetime Achievement Award for his contributions to cinema. The honor was seen by many as compensation for Scorsese's having never won an Academy Award, despite his direction of four Oscar-winning performances: Ellen Burstyn's in *Alice Doesn't Live Here Anymore*, De Niro's in *Raging Bull*, Newman's in *The Color of Money*, and Joe Pesci's in *GoodFellas*.

Scorsese's next film, *Kundun* (1997), examines the life of the 14th Dalai Lama, who as a young man endured the invasion of Tibet by Chinese armed forces and was forced into exile in India. In addition to changing his focus from Western to Eastern religion, Scorsese also abandoned his typical dramatic flourishes for a more meditative approach, which used colorful visuals to accentuate moods and left many of his fans, as well as critics, puzzled. In a review for *New York* (January 5, 1998), David Denby declared that, "lovely as it is, *Kundun* is of very little dramatic interest—it's an extremely beautiful, boring movie. . . . Approaching an alien tradition, Scorsese is entirely respectful, and the respectfulness dulls out the movie." Scorsese directed and narrated the 1999 documentary *My Voyage to Italy*, in which he discussed the Italian films that he had enjoyed in his youth and that had influenced his own work. The four-hour documentary focused extensively on the films of masters including Roberto Rossellini, Vittorio De Sica, Luchino Visconti, Michelangelo Antonioni, and Federico Fellini.

With the black comedy *Bringing Out the Dead* (1999), set in the early 1990s, Scorsese returned to the gritty underside of New York City that he had depicted in *Taxi Driver*. He focused this time on a paramedic, portrayed by Nicolas Cage, who has spent a few too many nights working the graveyard shift in Hell's Kitchen—where the frequency of unnatural death causes him to see the ghosts of patients. Though many critics found much to like about the film and Cage's performance, a number agreed with William Arnold, who wrote for the *Seattle Post-Intelligencer* (October 22, 1999), "Scorsese's legion of admirers will find pockets of brilliance, and the movie has a certain morbid fascination, but it has no real bite, and finally seems so contrived and pointless it borders on being out-and-out exploitation."

With *Gangs of New York* (2002), Scorsese simultaneously took on the most lavish film project of his career (with a budget estimated at $100 million) and saw the fruition of an idea he had had for 25 years. In July 1977, on the heels of his successes with *Alice Doesn't Live Here Anymore* and *Taxi Driver*, Scorsese had placed a two-page ad in *Variety* indicating that his next project would be a film adaptation of Herbert Asbury's *The Gangs of New York* (1927), a survey of New York gangs of the previous century. With the box-office failures of such personal big-budget projects as

Coppola's *Apocalypse Now* (1979) and Michael Cimino's *Heaven's Gate* (1980), however, studio executives reined in their maverick young directors and exerted more control over their projects. One casualty of the executives' new assertiveness was Scorsese's adaptation of Asbury's book. "It was the end of the power of the director," Scorsese recalled to Chris Nashawaty for *Entertainment Weekly* (August 23, 2002). "It was the end of making films that were big and provocative. There was just no way *Gangs of New York* could get made after that."

A quarter-century later, with the backing of Harvey Weinstein, co-founder of Miramax Films, Scorsese was able to make the movie. In *Gangs of New York*, Leonardo DiCaprio played Amsterdam Vallon, who as a young boy sees his father (Liam Neeson), the head of an Irish-immigrant gang, killed by his nativist rival Bill "The Butcher" Cutting (Daniel Day-Lewis). Years later Amsterdam sets out to avenge the killing. The film, set against the backdrop of the approaching American Civil War, received multiple Academy Award nominations, including a fourth best-director nomination for Scorsese. Though *Gangs of New York* was widely regarded as a good film, many agreed with Mick LaSalle, who wrote for the *San Francisco Chronicle* (July 4, 2003, on-line), "Scorsese takes us to a New York we never knew existed and shows us so much we can almost smell it. He also never bores us, and in a 166-minute movie, that's not a small thing, either. Yet for all the epic size and epic investment, *Gangs of New York* lacks the one quality that might have tipped it into greatness—an epic grandeur. Though big in size, *Gangs* isn't big in ideas. The lavish setting lends color to what turns out to be a simple story."

With *The Aviator* (2004), Scorsese combined the lavishness of *Gangs of New York* with the psychological approach to portraying a real-life figure he had used in *GoodFellas* to tell the story of Howard Hughes—the multimillionaire film producer and aviation pioneer who is perhaps best known today for his eccentricities. The film, which starred DiCaprio as Hughes, Cate Blanchett as Katharine Hepburn, and Kate Beckinsale as Ava Gardner, tracked Hughes's rise and decline while evoking the glamour of golden-age Hollywood. The film received mostly favorable reviews. Writing for *Variety* (November 29–December 2, 2004), Todd McCarthy cheered: "An enormously entertaining slice of biographical drama, *The Aviator* flies like one of Howard Hughes' record-setting speed airplanes. While it doesn't dig deeply into the psychology of one of the most famous industrialists and behavioral oddballs of the 20th century, Martin Scorsese's most pleasurable narrative feature in many a year is both extravagant and disciplined, grandly conceived and packed with minutiae." The movie earned 11 Academy Award nominations, including those for best picture, best director, best actor, best supporting actress (Blanchett, who took home the award), and best supporting actor (Alan Alda, as a senator engaged in a feud with Hughes). The best-director award went to Clint Eastwood for *Million Dollar Baby*, underscoring the irony that Scorsese—often called the greatest living American director—had yet to win an Oscar.

After directing *No Direction Home* (2005), a documentary about the early days of the singer Bob Dylan's career, Scorsese returned to the crime genre with *The Departed* (2006). Unlike his previous crime films, *The Departed* is set not in New York but in Boston, Massachusetts; inspired by *Infernal Affairs*, a well-regarded police drama made in Hong Kong, the film focuses on the infiltration of the Irish mob into the police department. In it DiCaprio played Billy Costigan, a police officer working undercover as an underling of Jack Nicholson's character, the mobster Frank Costello. Costigan must uncover the mole (Matt Damon) whom Costello has placed in the police department while keeping his own identity from being discovered. Critics hailed *The Departed* as Scorsese's triumphant return to the crime drama. For *Newsweek* (October 9, 2006), David Ansen wrote: "Martin Scorsese's profanely funny, savagely entertaining *The Departed* is both a return to the underworld turf he's explored in such classics as *Mean Streets* and *GoodFellas* and a departure. What's new is that he's hitched his swirling, white-hot style to the speeding wagon of narrative. For all his brilliance, storytelling has never been his forte or his first concern. Here he has the devilishly convoluted plot of the terrific 2002 Hong Kong cop thriller *Infernal Affairs* to work from, and it's a rich gift. . . . *The Departed* is Scorsese's most purely enjoyable movie in years." *The Departed* went on to win four Academy Awards, including those for best motion picture and best director—rectifying what many saw as the academy's greatest oversight in recent memory.

Scorsese's next project, expected to be released in 2008, was "Shine a Light," a documentary about the Rolling Stones, focusing on two concerts the group gave at the Beacon Theater in New York City in October and November 2006, during their tour for their 2005 album, *A Bigger Bang*. The movie will offer historical and contemporary behind-the-scenes footage and interviews. Other films directed by Scorsese that were in production in 2007 included "The Rise of Theodore Roosevelt," based on a book by Edmund Morris and starring Leonardo DiCaprio as the president during his formative years; a film about George Harrison of the Beatles; and "Silence," about two Jesuit priests in 17th-century Japan.

Since July 1999 Scorsese has been married to Helen Morris, with whom he has one daughter. His four previous marriages ended in divorce. He has one daughter from his marriage to Laraine Brennan and another from his union with Julia Cameron. He has also been married to Isabella Rossellini and Barbara De Fina.

—C.M.

Suggested Reading: *Chicago Sun-Times* (on-line) Oct. 11, 1985, Oct. 17, 1986, Sep. 2, 1990, Dec. 20, 2002; *Entertainment Weekly* p23+ Aug. 23–30, 2002; *Newsweek* p65 Oct. 9, 2006; *New York Times* II p17+ Dec. 16, 1973, II p1+ Mar. 30, 1975, (on-line) Nov. 14, 1980, Feb. 18, 1983, Sep. 13, 1985, Aug. 12, 1988, Sep. 12, 1993; *People* p40+ Aug. 8, 1988; *Premiere* p60+ Nov. 1991; *Rolling Stone* p58+ Nov. 1, 1990; *San Francisco Chronicle* (on-line) Nov. 22, 1995, July 4, 2003; *Time* p150 Dec. 20, 2004; *Washington Post* (on-line) Oct. 17, 1986, Aug. 12, 1988, Sep. 21, 1990, Sep. 17, 1993

Selected Films: *Mean Streets*, 1973; *Alice Doesn't Live Here Anymore*, 1974; *Taxi Driver*, 1976; *New York, New York*, 1977; *The Last Waltz*, 1978; *Raging Bull*, 1980; *The King of Comedy*, 1983; *After Hours*, 1985; *The Color of Money*, 1986; *The Last Temptation of Christ*, 1988; *Goodfellas*, 1990; *Cape Fear*, 1991; *The Age of Innocence*, 1993; *Casino*, 1995; *Kundun*, 1997; *Bringing Out the Dead*, 1999; *My Voyage to Italy*, 1999; *Gangs of New York*, 2002; *The Aviator*, 2004; *No Direction Home: Bob Dylan*, 2005; *The Departed*, 2006

Sean Paul

Jan. 8, 1973– Jamaican dancehall reggae artist

Address: VP Records, 89-05 138th St., Jamaica, NY 11435

"Music is the voice of the Jamaican people,"' the dancehall-reggae singer/songwriter Sean Paul told Steve Garbarino for the *New York Times* (May 30, 2004). "We think about it hour to hour, year to year. The speed of it changes, the voice changes. But it always depends on what is happening in our society." In the United States, the 34-year-old Sean Paul is the best-known performer of dancehall, a genre that originated in Jamaica, his native land, around the time of his birth. Dancehall mixes elements of rap and reggae; the singers, known as deejays or sing-jays, vocalize over a digitized bass-and-drum background, sometimes incorporating the melodies of others' earlier songs. After describing Sean Paul as "reggae's biggest success" since Bob Marley, Kelefa Sanneh, a pop-music critic for the *New York Times* (March 25, 2006), wrote that he "makes hits by making only minimal changes to the genre's standard operating procedure. He slides cool, tuneful rhymes over sharp dancehall beats. . . . What's most exciting about Sean Paul is his example: he has helped prove that the old model of crossing over is outdated. You don't need to overhaul your sound or hire an American star; all you need is a great beat and an infectious hook." *Dutty Rock* (2002), the second of the three albums

Vince Bucci/Getty Images

Sean Paul

could afford luxuries like running water, people who could afford a car. It's not ghetto, but not American luxury by any means." With his very mixed genetic heritage, Sean Paul is typical of many Jamaicans, whose country's motto is "Out of many, one people." Both of his parents are native-born Jamaicans. Some of his father's forebears came to Jamaica from Africa; others were Sephardic Jews from Portugal who settled on the island in the 17th century. Sean Paul's mother is descended from immigrants from China and England. Sean Paul's skin tone is unusual among Jamaicans, and it led his childhood friends to refer to him as "copper-color Chiney bwoy," according to the Web site dancehallminded.com.

Sean Paul's father, a businessman, and his mother, a professional artist, were champion swimmers, his father in long-distance swimming and his mother in the butterfly stroke. His father also excelled at water polo; in recent years he has coached the national Jamaican water-polo team, and currently he is the vice president of the Amateur Swimming Association of Jamaica. In a conversation with Ian Burrell for the London *Independent* (September 2, 2005, on-line), Sean Paul described his father as a "hustler." "He came from a good family but didn't do a lot of schooling," he said. "We had to go and get him and pick him up from the ghettos where he would be burning a chalice [marijuana pipe] with his friends. That kind of stuff happened regularly when I was a kid." When Sean Paul was 13 years old, his father was convicted of illegal narcotics trafficking and sentenced to prison; he spent the next six years behind bars. In his father's absence, Sean Paul has told interviewers, his mother provided comforting nurturance and firm discipline. His relationship with his father since the latter's release from prison, he told an interviewer for the "dot rap magazine" *Murder Dog* (June 2003, on-line), is "all good"; according to other reports, the two have only occasional contact.

During his early years Sean Paul attended the Hillel Academy, a nonsectarian, multicultural private school founded by Kingston's Jewish community. As a teenager he transferred to Wolmer's Boys' School, a sports-oriented high school near downtown Kingston, where many of his classmates were economically disadvantaged and teased him about his middle-class lifestyle; some bullied him. He had little interest in academics and "wasn't a great student," as he told the *Murder Dog* interviewer. Starting at about 14 he became active in competitive swimming. Honing his skills in freestyle swimming and the backstroke, he joined the Jamaican national swim team, which participated in contests internationally as well as in Jamaica. He also joined the Jamaican national water-polo team. Swimming, he told Ian Burrell, "taught me a lot of discipline. Exercise does a lot for the mind. Knowing that my father and mother were champions meant that I had a lot to look up to, to try and be a champion for Jamaica for myself. I'm

that Sean Paul has released since 2000, has sold some six million copies worldwide; it won a Grammy Award as best reggae album in 2003 and earned Sean Paul a bevy of other honors, including the MTV Europe Award for best new act of the year. His single "Temperature," from *The Trinity* (2005), his third album, claimed the top spot on the *Billboard* Hot 100 singles chart in early 2006. "I try to write familiar songs, songs people can listen to in clubs," Sean Paul said to reporters for *Teen People* (March 1, 2003). "I try to keep it on an international vibe so all people can feel my music."

The singer was born Sean Paul Henriques to Garth and Frances ("Fran") Henriques on January 8, 1973 in Kingston, the capital of Jamaica, a small island nation less than 100 miles south of Cuba in the Caribbean Sea. (Some sources, among them the Library of Congress, have erroneously listed "Paul" as the singer's surname.) He and his younger brother, Jason "Jigzag" Henriques, were raised in Norbrook, a relatively well-to-do, uptown section of Kingston. In Jamaica Sean Paul is known as an "uptown" deejay, thus distinguishing him from most other dancehall artists, who grew up in impoverished neighborhoods. In recent years the incomes of at least one-sixth of Jamaica's population of 2.75 million have remained below the poverty level, with economic deprivation particularly severe in rural areas. In parts of Kingston and other cities, gang violence connected with the drug trade is common; the high level of violent crime has also been linked to the activities of the island's major political parties and their deeply entrenched patronage systems. Sean Paul explained to Joseph Patel for the *Boston Globe* (November 22, 2002) that neighborhoods like Norbrook are for "people who still a swimmer and the swim team are my closest friends."

After he completed high school, Sean Paul attended the College of Arts, Science, and Technology (also called the University of Technology, Jamaica), where he studied hotel management and took classes in cooking. After two years he dropped out. He then worked briefly as a bank teller. He has recalled how impressed he was by a customer who deposited several million dollars during a single week. "It made me realize how much money was out there in the world," he said to Alona Wartofsky, who interviewed him for the *Washington Post* (September 13, 2000), "and [that] I should go out and get some of it." With the idea that he might accomplish that goal as a professional musician, in about 1994 Sean Paul began to spend much of his time writing songs.

Music, Sean Paul has said, has always been a big part of his life. His mother often played recorded music at home—he remembers in particular hearing songs by the Beatles—and as a Jamaican, as he told the *Murder Dog* interviewer, he would hear reggae music "all over the place, everywhere." Reggae originated in the 1960s in Jamaican shantytowns, providing an outlet for some of the many poverty-stricken residents who despaired of improving their lot in life. Associated with such performers as Bob Marley and the Wailers, Peter Tosh (one of the Wailers), Jimmy Cliff, and Desmond Dekker, reggae often focused on calls for social and political justice and other public issues. Dancehall reggae, or simply dancehall, came into being in the 1970s and took hold in Jamaica in the 1980s, when the digital revolution blossomed; it is distinguished from reggae by the bawdiness ("slackness," in Jamaican slang) of the lyrics and the presence in every song of an aggressive *riddim* (a Jamaican slang term for "rhythm"), a digitized bass and drum background whose beats are significantly faster than those of reggae. "The rhythm isn't merely a pattern of beats, it's an electronic composition—add some singing or shouting and your song is done," Kelefa Sanneh wrote for the *New York Times* (March 9, 2003, on-line). (There are dozens of riddims, with new ones being created each year. Each riddim has a name, such as Sleng Teng, Playground, Space Invaders, Ching Chong, Bookshelf, Bada Bada, Diwali, and Jonkanoo; often, the name is derived from the first song that used it.) Other characteristics of dancehall are singsong intonations and the use of a patois that is often unintelligible to non-Jamaicans. Dancehall rapping is called "toasting."

During Sean Paul's childhood his mother arranged for him to take piano lessons, but he disliked them and soon discontinued them. When he entered his teens, his mother, at his request, bought him an inexpensive electronic keyboard, which he used to create simple riddims. By that time he had become an ardent fan of dancehall and of such dancehall stars as Super Cat, Shabba Ranks, Major Worries, Papa San, and Lt. Stitchie; he also found

hip-hop music from the U.S. to his liking. He enjoyed helping one of his aunts in her "sound-system" business, called Sparkles Disco. The proprietors of such enterprises, which sprang up in Jamaica during the 1950s, travel with generators, records or CD players, and large speakers and provide music for street parties that they have organized. Attendees, sometimes numbering in the thousands, pay for admission and food and drinks. A sound system's major draw is brand-new music. Sean Paul sometimes performed his own songs at his aunt's street parties.

In the early 1990s Sean Paul tried without success to form a business relationship with one or another experienced record producer. "No producer at the time would look at me as that kind of DJ," he recalled to Alona Wartofsky. "They said, 'No one's gonna hear that from you because you don't come from the ghetto, you don't really know these experiences, and because of your class and complexion. Your image is just different. . . . It's not marketable from you at this time.'" A turning point came in about 1993, when his father introduced him to a longtime acquaintance of his, Stephen "Cat" Coore, a founding member of the popular Jamaican reggae group Third World. Impressed by Sean Paul's musical talents, Coore arranged for him to record demos in the producer Rupert Bent's small music studio, which Third World used. Sean Paul soon gained access to other studios as well, and he started to become a familiar figure among Jamaican musicians. To make himself known among the public, he began making dub plates—one-off vinyl records—for sound systems in addition to his aunt's, among them Stone Love, Renaissance, and Coppershot, the last-named being that of his brother. (Jigzag Henriques has been involved in the making of all of Sean Paul's recordings.) By 1996, Sean Paul told the *Murder Dog* interviewer, "everybody was trying to get dubs from me." That year, with the producer Jeremy Harding, whom he had met in 1995, he recorded "Baby Girl (Don't Cry)," using Harding's Fearless riddim; it received wide radio play in Jamaica and became his first hit there (but is not included on any of Sean Paul's albums). During that period he became associated with the Dutty Cup Crew ("dutty" being slang for "dirty"), a group of aspiring deejays including Don Yute, Mossy Kid, Looga Man, Kid Kurupt, Chicken, Daddigon, and Froggy. (The names of some of them appear with alternate spellings on various Web sites.)

During the next few years, in addition to performing occasionally with the Dutty Cup Crew, Sean Paul recorded several singles that enjoyed great popularity in Jamaica: "Infiltrate," made with Jeremy Harding's Playground/Zim Zimma riddim, and "Hackle Mi," also produced by Harding; "Nah Get No Bly (One More Try)," with Donovan Germain as producer; and "Excite Me" and "Deport Them," with Tony Kelly as producer. "Deport Them," made with Kelly's Bookshelf riddim, was aired by radio stations in Miami, Florida, and New York City as well as Jamaica. The reggae specialist

Derek A. Bardowell wrote for the *Voice* (September 9, 2002) that at that time in his career, Sean Paul sounded like one of the originators of dancehall—Super Cat, with "words crawling out of his mouth as if they'd endured piercing heat for some hours but delivered with the intensity of someone slightly irritated"—and like "a vexed weed head," or a person who smokes a lot of marijuana (as does Sean Paul). With the dancehall artist Mr. Vegas and the rapper DMX, Sean Paul recorded the song "Here Comes the Boom" (also called "Top Shotta" or "Top Shotter") for the soundtrack of the director Hype Williams's debut feature film, *Bell*y (1998), starring DMX. Also with Mr. Vegas, he recorded the crossover hit "Hot Gal Today," made with the producers Steely and Clevie's Street Sweeper riddim, which in 1999 reached the top of the reggae charts in Jamaica and hit the number-six spot on *Billboard*'s Top Rap Singles chart. Both "Hot Gal Today" and "Deport Them" appeared in the Top 100 on *Billboard*'s R&B Singles chart, the former at number 66 and the latter at 85.

In June 2000 Sean Paul performed at Summer Jam, an annual outdoor concert sponsored by the New York City radio station WQHT (known as Hot 97 FM); other entertainers at the event included Jay-Z, Dr. Dre, Snoop Dogg, Eminem, and Aaliyah. His appearance at the concert followed by a few months the release of his debut album, *Stage One*, which became a big seller in Jamaica. Although *Stage One* sold poorly in the U.S., *Billboard* named it the number-four reggae album of the year, while ranking Sean Paul third among reggae artists of 2000. In a review of *Stage One* for the All Music Guide Web site, Rosalind Cummings-Yeates wrote, "Since [Sean Paul] possesses neither an unusual voice nor outstanding skill, this CD can become rather tiresome after awhile. . . . Still, there are some enjoyable tunes here." Alona Wartofsky credited part of Sean Paul's appeal to "the way he rides the beats." "Dancehall artists chant their lyrics over spare, percussive rhythm tracks," she explained, "and their gift for filling the space is as important as a rapper's talent for lyrical flow. Sean Paul's vocal style is reminiscent of vintage dancehall star Supercat, the words coming flat and fast." Wartofsky also wrote, "The 17 songs and eight skits and interludes . . . suggest that Sean Paul is preoccupied with women: getting them to look right, getting them to act right, getting them into bed right, then getting rid of them." Noting that two of the tracks, "Next Generation" and "You Must Lose," deal with the issues of poverty and violence, she wrote, "These tracks suggest that perhaps Sean Paul, like so many dancehall stars before him, may find that his passions shift as his career develops." Sean Paul told Cary Darling for the *Miami Herald* (June 9, 2000), "That's my image, to be the player. But I'm trying to bring it forward with more conscious vibes."

With *Dutty Rock* (2002), made in collaboration with the producers Tony Touch, Rahzel, the Neptunes, and others, Sean Paul achieved great commercial success in the U.S. and Europe as well as in Jamaica. One of the disc's tracks, "Get Busy," was certified gold by the Australian Recording Industry Association and rose to the top spot on the *Billboard* Hot 100 chart. A second single, "Gimme the Light," which features catchy instrumentals created by the Miami-based producer Troyton Rami, reached number seven on the same chart. The popularity of "Gimme the Light" was attributed in part to its video, which celebrated popular Jamaican dance moves and enjoyed regular play on MTV. "Gimme the Light" refers to a potent form of hydroponic marijuana known as "dro" in American slang and contains the phrase "pass the dro." Speaking to Rashaun Hall for *Billboard* (November 23, 2002), Sean Paul explained that, with words as well as music, he consciously tried to lure Americans into singing along with "Gimme the Light": "I've had a few other hits . . . and I noticed that people liked the songs but they couldn't understand certain things I was saying. Since I wanted to cross over into the hip-hop world, I figured I should start writing songs that hip-hop heads would be able to pick up easier. That's why 'Gimme the Light' is so successful. It has a good melody, it's on a straight dancehall riddim, and people can identify with the words." Another single from *Dutty Rock*, "Baby Boy," for which Sean Paul collaborated with the American R&B singer and megastar Beyoncé Knowles, spent nine weeks at number one on the *Billboard* Hot 100 chart in the summer of 2003. "*Dutty Rock* is almost revolutionary," Tim Sendra wrote for the All Music Guide Web site, in one of many favorable reviews of the album, in which he also described it as "infectious," "bursting with hooks and filled with energy," and "easy to dance to." Sean Paul "has a good ear for melody and his flat, distinctive voice is perfect for his sing-jay style." In 2003 *Dutty Rock* earned the Grammy and the *Source* magazine awards for best reggae album, and Sean Paul was named MTV Europe's best new artist.

Sean Paul's third and most recent album, *The Trinity* (2005), was three years in the making and was recorded entirely in Jamaica, using Jamaican artists. "I felt a sense of responsibility to give people a great record and also give a chance to younger people back home," Sean Paul said to Mark Edward Nero for the *San Diego (California) Union-Tribune* (December 2, 2005). "So I went back there to do the album." *The Trinity* earned mixed reviews. Tim Sendra, for example, wrote that the preponderance of the album's tracks are "hypersexualized, tough, and semi-raw" and that "each song relies on standard synth sounds and straightforward beats and there are precious few surprises on the record, sound-wise." He continued, "[Sean Paul's] vocals are strong enough but, overall, lack the freshness and vigor of those on *Dutty Rock*." Such lukewarm assessments notwithstanding, "Temperature," a dance anthem and the second single to be released from the record (the first single was "We Be Burnin'"), became very popular, reaching number one on the *Billboard* Hot 100 chart.

Sean Paul's solo performances or collaborations with other artists are included on dozens of albums in addition to his own. Among them are *Platinum Jam '98*, *DJ's Choice* (2000), *Reggae Gold 2000*, *Ultimate Dancehall Mix*, Vol. 1 (2000), Michael Knott's *Things I've Done, Things to Come* (2000), *Riddim Ryders*, Vol. 1 (2001), Kardinal Offishall's *Quest for Fire: Firestarter*, Vol. 1 (2001), and Choobakka's *My Time* (2002). Feature-film soundtracks to which he has contributed include *Shark's Tale* and *Chasing Liberty* (both 2004) and *Step Up* (2006). Sean Paul has also made many appearances on TV, on such programs as *The Tonight Show with Jay Leno*, *Late Night with Conan O'Brien*, *Live with Regis and Kathie Lee*, *It's Showtime at the Apollo*, and at the opening ceremonies of the 2007 Cricket World Cup.

In September 2006 Sean Paul began recording a new album. In light of the deaths of two of his friends from violence in Jamaica, many of its songs will address more serious issues than his earlier

songs. "The content is just a little different than what people expect from me," he told MTV News (January 23, 2007, on-line). "[On] one or two of the songs . . . it's not about partying, it's not about ladies; it's about the kids with the guns in the streets. It's more reality."

Sean Paul lives in a suburb of Kingston with his mother, grandmother, and brother. He donated $1 million to help victims of Hurricane Ivan, which caused widespread devastation in Jamaica in 2004.

—D.F.

Suggested Reading: All Music Guide Web site; *Boston Globe* C p14 Nov. 22, 2002; dancehallminded.com; DancehallReggae.com; (London) *Independent* (on-line) Sep. 2, 2005; *Jamaica Gleaner* (on-line) Dec. 18, 2003; Sean Paul's Web site; *Washington Post* G p1+ Nov. 24, 2002

Selected Recordings: *Stage One*, 2000; *Dutty Rock*, 2002; *The Trinity*, 2005

Sheehan, Cindy

July 10, 1957– Political activist; writer

Address: Gold Star Families for Peace, 2010 Linden Ave., Venice, CA 90291

Cindy Sheehan is a political activist and writer whom some credit with reviving protest against the Iraq war. Her most highly publicized activity took place in 2005, when she camped out near President George W. Bush's Crawford, Texas, home, demanding to speak with him about the loss of her son, U.S. Army specialist Casey Sheehan, who was killed in Iraq in 2004. Her son's death contributed to Sheehan's transformation from a politically inactive mother and office worker into one of the antiwar movement's most visible exponents. Sheehan has accused President Bush of deceiving the American public during the buildup to the U.S.-led war in Iraq, which was launched in March 2003—18 months after the terrorist attacks on the U.S.—ostensibly to rid Iraq of so-called weapons of mass destruction. No such weapons were found there, and many, including Sheehan, have charged that the Bush administration knowingly rushed to war on the basis of faulty intelligence and that it implied connections between Iraq and the 2001 attacks in order to justify the war. "Before Casey was killed, I thought that one person couldn't make a difference," Sheehan explained to Deanne Stillman for *Rolling Stone* (December 15, 2005, on-line). "Millions protested against the invasion [of Iraq] in 2003, but it didn't do any good. Then, after Casey was killed, my daughter Carly read me a poem she wrote. It moved me to action. I thought,

Gabriel Bouys/AFP/Getty Images

'If one person can't make a difference, at least I'm gonna go to my grave trying.'" Through her actions and often-incendiary words—she has labeled Bush a terrorist and demanded his impeachment, likened the Iraq war to genocide, and publicly clashed with the parents of other soldiers who have died in the Iraq war, parents who continue to support the war and the president—Sheehan has become a lightning rod for controversy, reflected in the wide variety of ways she is portrayed in the media and particularly in the sphere of Web logs. To some, Sheehan is an inspiring figure with the courage to stand up to the president of the United States. To others, she is at best a tool of wealthy radicals who exploit her sympathetic story for their own political ends or, at worst, an anti-American, publicity-seeking narcissist, an abettor of terrorism, or an anti-Semite—the last charge stemming from her comments on the Israeli-Palestinian conflict. Sheehan has written numerous articles published on Web sites including Common Dreams, Truth Out, Daily Kos, and the Huffington Post, as well as on the Web sites of the filmmaker Michael Moore and the political commentator Lew Rockwell. She has also published three books: *Not One More Mother's Child* (2005), an account of her first year of activism; *Dear President Bush* (2005), a collection of writings and speeches; and the memoir *Peace Mom: A Mother's Journey through Heartache to Activism* (2006). In August 2007 Sheehan announced her candidacy for the seat in the House of Representatives currently held by the House Speaker, the Democrat Nancy Pelosi, who represents California's Eighth Congressional District. She has attributed her decision to oppose Pelosi to the failure of the Democrats in Congress to take steps to impeach President Bush or end the war in Iraq.

Sheehan was born Cindy Lee Miller on July 10, 1957. She grew up in Bellflower, California, a small suburb of Los Angeles. She has said that as a child she was shy and introverted and had few friends. Her family life, by her account, was dysfunctional; her father was an alcoholic and her mother was physically abusive to Cindy and her sister, Dede. Sheehan, the only member of her family who belonged to the local church, found solace there and enjoyed both the stability of the church community and the feeling of independence that came with attending services.

Cindy's future husband, Patrick Sheehan, attended high school in nearby Norwalk, California. The two met and started dating when Cindy was 16 and were married on April 30, 1977; they moved into a small home in Norwalk. Patrick worked as a hardware-store sales representative in California and Nevada, while Cindy had a job as a loan adjuster for the Security Pacific National Bank. She left that position in 1979, prior to the birth of her first child, Casey Austin, in order to raise her family. The couple had three other children in the next six years: Carly, Andy, and Jane. When Casey was 14 the family moved to Vacaville, a town in northern California, and Sheehan, who had converted to Catholicism after her marriage, served in Vacaville as a youth minister at St. Mary's Church. (Sheehan has since left the church because of the historical role organized religion has had in global conflicts and what she sees as the inaction of religious leaders with regard to the antiwar movement in the United States.) Sheehan later took a position with Napa Valley Health and Human Services.

Casey Sheehan joined the U.S. Army with an eye toward earning money for college while serving as a chaplain. Instead, he was assigned as a Humvee mechanic, and in early 2004 he was deployed to Iraq. On April 4, after less than a month there, Casey was killed in an ambush near Sadr City while attempting to rescue wounded soldiers. On June 17, 2004 the Sheehans, along with 17 other families who had lost children in the Iraq war, were invited to meet with President Bush at a military base near Seattle, Washington. Although Cindy Sheehan and her family were upset by the war and questioned its purpose (Carly had begun to write poetry about the conflict), they decided to approach the meeting as Casey would have wanted them to and refrained from venting their frustration at President Bush. The president initially seemed to make a positive impression on the family, who praised him for coming to the meeting without political motivation. Sheehan told David Henson for the Vacaville *Reporter* (June 24, 2004, on-line) that she was affected by President Bush's apparent sympathy for their loss and his being a "man of faith." The most comforting and satisfying part of the experience for the Sheehans was the chance to meet with other families of soldiers who had been killed—to share their grief with those families and engage in mutual support. Referring to that, Sheehan told Henson, "That was the gift the president gave us, the gift of happiness, of being together." In an interview a year later with Wolf Blitzer for CNN (August 7, 2005), however, Sheehan accused the president of having been callous during the interview. "We wanted to use the time for him to know that he killed an indispensable part of our family and humanity," she said. "And we wanted him to look at the pictures of Casey. He wouldn't look at the pictures of Casey. He didn't even know Casey's name. He came in the room and the very first thing he said is, 'So who are we honoring here?'. . . . Every time we tried to talk about Casey and how much we missed him, he would change the subject. And he acted like it was a party." According to Greg Szymanski, writing for the *LewisNews* (July 5, 2005, on-line), Sheehan recalled her meeting with Bush as "one of the most disgusting experiences I ever had."

Sheehan held herself partially responsible for his son's death, feeling that she had not done enough to dissuade him from joining the army. Partly for that reason she suffered from depression and stress, which caused her to miss work. In July 2004 she was fired from her job. That year Sheehan, who had until then been a nominal Democrat and would not have described herself as politically active, began speaking out against the war in Iraq. In October 2004 she appeared on nationally broadcast television spots sponsored by the political action committee Real Voices. In one, according to Michelle Goldberg, writing for *Salon* (October 1, 2004, on-line), Sheehan was filmed addressing the president with the words, "I imagined it would hurt if one of my kids was killed, but I never thought it would hurt this bad, especially someone so honest and brave as Casey, my son. When you haven't been honest with us, when you and your advisors rushed us into this war. How do you think we felt when we heard the Senate report that said there was no link between Iraq and 9/11?" Sheehan told Goldberg that by speaking out against President Bush, she was able to assuage some of the sense of helplessness she felt about her son's death. "I need to speak out for what I think is right, and I have this chance right now because people want to listen to me," she said. "If I didn't do that, I wouldn't be able to get up in the morning or face a new day." She went on to refer to the 2000 presidential election, which was so close that votes were recounted in Florida—until the U.S. Supreme Court halted that process, effectively declaring Bush the winner. "My biggest regret in my entire life is that when Bush was selected as president by the Supreme Court that I didn't go out and say, 'No, this is B.S., we can't stop this election until we count every single vote.' I just regret it so much. I don't know if I did something more maybe my son would still be alive." Reportedly, Sheehan, along with a number of others who had lost family members during the Iraq war, was approached by the Democrat John Kerry's presidential campaign staff about appearing in additional television broadcasts against the war. As Sheehan became more involved in the antiwar cause, she alienated nearly all of her friends, who for the most part supported Bush in the 2004 election, as well as her husband's family, who were mostly conservative Republicans. Her television spots spawned hate mail and angry telephone calls, and some derided her as a traitor to the United States. Referring to those who wanted to silence her, Sheehan told Goldberg, "I think those people are traitors, because my son and millions of brave Americans before him have died for my right to speak out against the government." Using the insurance money that she received after her son's death, Sheehan spent the rest of 2004 traveling around the United States to speak out against the war.

During the January 2005 presidential inauguration of George W. Bush, Sheehan protested in Washington, D.C. She spoke at the opening of Eyes Wide Open: the Human Cost of War, a traveling exhibition, sponsored by the American Friends Service Committee, that featured the combat boots of slain military personnel and otherwise honored U.S. soldiers and Iraqi civilians who had been hurt or killed in wartime. Sheehan later became one of the nine founders of a group called Gold Star Families for Peace. Inspired by the name of the organization American Gold Star Mothers, and by the U.S. military tradition of presenting gold stars to the mothers of soldiers killed in combat, Sheehan and others sought to extend similar recognition to all family members of deceased soldiers and to work toward the prevention of warfare. Through her appearances in television broadcasts and her attendance at numerous antiwar protests after her son's

death, Sheehan became the group's spokesperson and most visible member.

Sheehan appeared at many more antiwar functions in 2005. One appearance of hers that drew particular criticism was at a San Francisco State University forum in support of the civil rights lawyer Lynne Stewart, who in February of that year was found guilty of giving support to terrorists. In a widely quoted speech, Sheehan took aim at the American public-school system for what she saw as its incorrect and politically motivated interpretation of U.S. history; attacked President Bush; and otherwise engaged in what her detractors would later describe as anti-Americanism. In one of the most controversial and widely quoted parts of her speech, Sheehan, while discussing the deaths of soldiers in the Iraq war, stated: "This country [the U.S.] is not worth dying for."

Sheehan's continued political activism strained her personal life considerably. While her sister, Dede, and daughter Carly publicly supported her, few others of her acquaintances did. Her husband's family wrote opinion pieces denouncing Sheehan's views, and Patrick Sheehan himself disapproved of his wife's activities; the couple separated in June 2005 and divorced in August of that year. Cindy Sheehan has said that her conflict with her husband grew from the difference between their ways of handling grief. While Cindy Sheehan found comfort in making public appearances and statements, her husband grieved privately. As for his feelings about his wife's activism, Patrick Sheehan told Jill Smolowe for People (August 29, 2005) that "Casey's life isn't being honored" by it. "I'd like you to know that Casey was proud to be a soldier." In the same interview, he said, "My kids and I feel like we've had two losses: Casey, and now our wife and mother. The kids are angry and lonely for her. . . . I don't think she's done the best for the family. When we see Cindy talking about Casey, we all relive the loss."

Sheehan's most widely publicized action came in August 2005, when she camped roughly three miles from the home of President Bush, in Crawford, Texas, and announced that she would remain there until he spoke with her about the Iraq war. Sheehan called for the immediate removal of U.S. troops from Iraq and railed against Bush for misleading Americans during the buildup to the war. The president, who spent most of August in Crawford, refused to meet with her, on the grounds that he had already done so. He publicly stated his sympathy for Sheehan's loss but argued that removing troops from Iraq would be a mistake. Bush sent National Security Adviser Stephen Hadley, Deputy Chief of Staff Joe Hagan, and other top White House aides to meet with Sheehan, but she continued to demand to meet with the president himself. Sheehan explained during her interview with Wolf Blitzer that she had brought her protest to Crawford because she took offense at comments the president had been making in regard to the U.S. soldiers who had been killed. "He said that the families can rest assured that their children died for a noble cause. And he also said that we have to honor the sacrifices of the fallen soldiers by continuing the mission in Iraq," Sheehan told Blitzer. "And I have said this so many times: I do not want him to use my son's name to continue the killing. . . . Why would I want one more mother, either Iraqi or American, to go through what I'm going through?"

Sheehan began her vigil, which ultimately lasted 26 days, in the company of four supporters. Later, Gold Star Families for Peace sponsored a TV spot featuring Sheehan, which was broadcast in the Texas towns of Waco and Crawford, and further publicized her demands to meet with the president. The group also conducted a march to a police station just outside the perimeter of Bush's ranch to deliver letters written by activists to First Lady Laura Bush; the letters appealed to her as a mother to support their antiwar cause. To many opponents of the Iraq war, Sheehan's personal tragedy granted her an unassailable moral authority, and she was quickly embraced as an icon of the antiwar movement. Hundreds soon joined her at her campsite, not only to protest the war but to speak out on issues ranging from women's rights to U.S. support of Israel. Sheehan's campground, which became known in the media as "Camp Casey," drew up to 1,000 visitors each day, including members of Congress and prominent actors and musicians. The activity there—one of the biggest news stories of the summer of 2005—attracted a huge media contingent that documented the daily goings-on, which in turn prompted as much controversy and counter-demonstration as support. A counter-protest organized by the Dallas, Texas–based talk-show host Darrell Ankarlo took place at the Yellow Rose gift shop, a few hundred yards from Camp Casey, and at times drew as much local support as Sheehan's group.

Sheehan's critics included Robert L. Jamieson Jr., who wrote for the Seattle Post-Intelligencer (August 13, 2005), "That Sheehan would allow her private grief to be plied for a public stunt seems unfathomable even if her underlying message about unnecessary blood being shed by American soldiers hits the mark." Cathy Young, writing for the Boston Globe (August 22, 2005, on-line), compared Sheehan's political relevance to that of Terri Schiavo, the St. Petersburg, Florida, woman whose death—following years spent on life support—was preceded by a highly publicized and politicized legal battle between her husband, who sought to remove life support, and her parents, who opposed the move. "The Sheehan circus has a lot in common with the Schiavo circus, none of it good," Young wrote. "Both stories represent a triumph—on different sides of the political divide—of emotion- and sentiment-driven politics. Schiavo's parents could go off on crazy, paranoid, vitriolic rants, and enjoy a certain immunity by virtue of their unthinkable tragedy. The same is true of Sheehan. Sheehan's grief entitles her to sympathy. . . . But

her loss does not give her, as New York Times columnist Maureen Dowd [August 10, 2005] has claimed, an 'absolute' moral authority—any more than it would if her reaction to her son's death was to demand a U.S. nuclear strike against the [Iraqi] insurgents." In the activist's defense, the columnist Frank Rich of the New York Times (August 21, 2005) argued that what he deemed the smearing of Sheehan was similar to previous attacks against opponents of Bush's policies, such as the former government official Richard Clarke. Many believed strongly in Sheehan's protest and in her right to be critical of the government and President Bush but felt that her message was being undermined, and her credibility compromised, by the various activists and groups who had aligned themselves with her.

Sheehan's protest ended in late August, when Hurricane Katrina caused flooding that devastated much of New Orleans, Louisiana, and its surrounding areas and prompted President Bush to leave Crawford. Sheehan left as well, but not before declaring her intention to return each time Bush went to Texas on vacation. "I look back on it, and I am very, very, very grateful he did not meet with me, because we have sparked and galvanized the peace movement. If he'd met with me, then I would have gone home, and it would have ended there," Sheehan told Angela K. Brown for the Associated Press (August 31, 2005). Following her stay in Crawford, Sheehan wrote articles for various on-line sites, restating her antiwar position, denying what she termed inaccurate rumors about her, and attempting to maintain the momentum that her vigil had brought to the antiwar movement. In those articles Sheehan argued that President Bush had falsified information during the buildup to the Iraq war and that he continued to fabricate reasons for maintaining a U.S. military presence in Iraq. She contended that he had made the U.S. less safe by sending personnel and equipment to Iraq, thereby leaving vulnerable regions of the country ill-prepared to cope with disaster, and she called for the impeachment of the president. In September 2005 Gold Star Families for Peace teamed with Iraq Veterans Against the War, Military Families Speak Out, and Veterans for Peace, among other groups, to organize the Bring Them Home Now Tour—a traveling antiwar protest that began in Crawford and crossed the United States to raise awareness about the war in Iraq. Sheehan spoke at many rallies along the way, and the tour culminated in a September 24 protest in Washington, D.C. Sheehan returned to Crawford when Bush vacationed there during Thanksgiving.

Sheehan used her celebrity in an attempt to persuade government officials to seek an end to the Iraq war. In the fall of 2005, she met with U.S. senator John McCain of Arizona, and on a separate occasion she urged Arizona governor Janet Napolitano to withdraw Arizona National Guard troops from Iraq. In October 2005 Sheehan tried unsuccessfully to earn an audience with California governor Arnold Schwarzenegger; she wanted to ask him to limit the number of California National Guardsmen made available for duty in Iraq. At the time 16,000 of the roughly 20,000 National Guardsmen of California were in Iraq, Sheehan argued, reducing the manpower that would be available to Californians in the event of a natural disaster, such as an earthquake or flood.

In late 2005 Sheehan traveled to London, England, where she addressed the International Peace Conference, sponsored by the Stop the War Coalition and held at the Royal Horticultural Hall. In London she attended the premiere of a play by the Nobel Prize winner Dario Fo, *Peace Mom*, which was inspired by her story. She also participated in a series of interviews with the London *Guardian* newspaper and BBC Radio. Traveling to Ireland, she met with that country's foreign-affairs minister, Dermot Ahern, to discuss the policy of allowing U.S. warplanes to refuel at airbases in Ireland. In January 2006 Sheehan made headlines when she traveled to Venezuela—whose government, headed by Hugo Chavez, has had strained relations with the U.S.—to attend the Caracas World Social Forum, which drew more than 10,000 antiglobalization activists. Her trip was financed by Venezuela's foreign ministry, a fact that, together with Sheehan's speech at the event, generated controversy in the United States. (According to Jan James, writing for the Associated Press [January 24, 2006], Sheehan said, "We really need to stop the imperialist tendencies of countries like the United States and Great Britain.") In May 2006 Sheehan spoke at a rally in Melbourne, Australia, to call for the release of David Hicks, an Australian citizen who had been detained without trial for over five years at Guantánamo Bay, in Cuba, as a terror suspect. (Hicks was freed in April 2007, after pleading guilty to one relatively minor charge.)

Sheehan maintained her activism in the United States as well. On January 31, 2006 she gained notice when she was arrested at the U.S. Capitol during President Bush's State of the Union address, for wearing a T-Shirt that read "2,245 Dead. How Many More?"—a reference to the number of U.S. soldiers who had died in Iraq up to that point. (The dress code for the State of the Union address prohibits the wearing of clothing containing type of any kind, and at least one other person, the wife of Republican representative Bill Young of Florida, was also told to leave the premises; her shirt read, "Support Our Troops.") Sheehan was arrested again, in New York on March 7, 2006, for obstructing entry to the office of the U.S. Mission to the United Nations while participating in a protest with Iraqi-American women against the Iraq war. She participated in a wider antiwar protest in New York on April 9, 2006.

Sheehan also continued to contribute pieces to blogs and other Web sites, urging readers to get involved in the antiwar movement and defending herself and the movement against attacks from the political right. In an article published on the Web site Common Dreams (April 7, 2006), Sheehan wrote about her frustration over conservatives' predictions of the demise of the antiwar movement and over what she saw as a complacent, easily manipulated U.S. citizenry. She argued that although many people shared her belief that the Iraq war was a misbegotten and failed enterprise, few were willing to speak out against it, or make sacrifices, as she had done, to achieve the goal of ending the conflict. "Some, like Casey and almost 2400 other Americans and their families give all, while some, like the people of Iraq, have everything stolen from them by unlawful war; some, like myself, give a lot; some give some, by writing letters, attending an occasional vigil or march; but the majority of Americans give nothing—except an occasional vote, which we all know counts practically for nothing with our electoral process being so corrupted and almost rendered meaningless . . . ," she wrote. "The challenge of the peace movement, now that we have identified the problem so well, and have the vast majority of Americans on our side, is to convince each and every last American that he/she has a very intimate and personal stake in what we are allowing our government to do in Iraq and the world."

In July 2006 Sheehan invited further controversy by meeting again with Venezuelan president Chavez and suggesting that he was a better leader than President Bush. She also purchased five acres of land in Crawford, with some of the insurance money she received after her son was killed. She announced that she would return to Crawford in August, when President Bush went on vacation, and that this time she would go on a hunger strike until the U.S. troops returned home. Soon after that announcement, on July 6, 2006, Sheehan appeared on MSNBC's program *Hardball*, whose guest host, Norah O'Donnell, expressed her suspicion that Sheehan's planned hunger strike was "just more of a publicity stunt" and questioned whether her politics truly reflected the beliefs of the American people or were in fact "extremist." O'Donnell also referred to Sheehan's connection with the "socialist dictator Hugo Chavez." The MSNBC interview brought Sheehan a great deal of hate mail. She responded with an article published on the Web site TruthOut.org (July 18, 2006), in which she defended herself against charges of anti-Americanism while repeating her assertion that Chavez is a better leader than Bush. Pointing out that Chavez is a democratically elected president, having carried 60 percent of his country's vote in 2004, and referring to Bush's actions as a presidential candidate and president, Sheehan wrote: "From stealing two elections and saying and acting like you [Bush] have a mandate to destroy the world; to circumventing Congress at every turn with 'signing statements' and just not telling them things; to wiretapping Americans without proper warrants; to reading our emails and looking at bank records without warrants; to illegally detaining people and torturing them; to insisting on staying a course in Iraq that is killing nearly more innocent people per month than were killed in our country on 9/11; to authorizing the leak of covert agents' names; to selling our democracy to the highest bidders, such as [federal lobbyist] Jack Abramoff; to appointing avowed [United Nations] hater John Bolton to the UN in a recess appointment because he [Bush] knew that a normal confirmation process would fail; to allowing the neo-cons to take over our foreign policy to the detriment of our nation; to etc., etc.—I ask Norah O'Donnell and MSNBC, who is the dictator here? George or Hugo?" She added, "I didn't say that I would rather live in Venezuela. I am an American, and I love my country which I believe is on a distinctly disordered course right now."

In 2006 Melanie Morgan and Catherine Moy published the book *American Mourning: The Intimate Story of Two Families Joined by War, Torn by Beliefs.* That controversial work, which chronicles both Sheehan's story and that of the family of another soldier who was killed in Iraq, attacked Sheehan on a personal level, describing her as a philanderer and as having ties to the Ku Klux Klan in addition to Chavez. Alan Colmes of the television program *Hannity & Colmes* described the book as "disgusting" and the authors' attack on Sheehan as "despicable." In September of that year, Sheehan published her memoir, *Peace Mom: A Mother's Journey through Heartache to Activism.* The book polarized opinions, as had most of her public activity. *Peace Mom* recounts Sheehan's experience of losing a son, her struggle to recover from the loss, and her transformation into an antiwar activist. Included in the book is criticism not only of President Bush but of John Kerry, John McCain, and Democratic U.S. senator Hillary Rodham Clinton of New York, among others. In the book's foreword, Sheehan described writing the memoir as one of the hardest things she had ever done, as it forced her to relive Casey's death daily; she also found, however, that the process was cathartic in the end. The foreword includes this passage: "This book is a story of one mom's journey from being a 'normal' mom to one who went to the seat of power and challenged the king and triumphed and who meets and is lauded by heads of state and also vilified and hated by other heads of state and much of the American media. This book is a story of one mom's journey from believing that her son was a 'war hero' to believing that her son died as a victim of the war machine. This is a book of one mom's journey from ignorance of history (even though, ironically, she majored in history) to being an active participant in making history and having an effect on social change. This is a book of one mom's journey from trusting her leaders even when they so brazenly take our country to bogus war, to one of pacifism and nonviolence at all costs."

In December 2006 Sheehan participated in a forum on impeachment at Fordham University with Carolyn Ho, the mother of Ehren Watada, a commissioned army officer who refused to go to Iraq. The next month she traveled to Cuba, where she called for the closing of the U.S. military prison in Guantánamo Bay. On May 4, 2007 Sheehan spoke at Kent State University, at an event commemorating the anniversary of the shootings in 1970 of four Kent State students by members of the Ohio National Guard during a Vietnam War protest on the school's campus.

That month Sheehan announced that she was abandoning the antiwar movement, because she had become disillusioned with the stubborn resistance to change that, in her view, characterizes the American system of government. In July 2007, however, she again spoke out publicly, after President Bush commuted the prison sentence of Lewis "Scooter" Libby, a former aide to Vice President Richard B. "Dick" Cheney. (Libby had been convicted of lying and obstructing justice in an investigation into the leak of a CIA officer's identity.) Sheehan also stated publicly that if, by July 23, 2007, Congress did not take action toward impeaching President Bush, she would run as an Independent for the seat in the House held by Nancy Pelosi, the House Speaker, who represents California's Eighth Congressional District. Sheehan told a reporter for the Associated Press (July 8, 2007), "Democrats and Americans feel betrayed by the Democratic leadership. We hired them to bring an end to the war." On August 9, 2007, in light of Congress's inaction regarding the president's impeachment, Sheehan announced her candidacy for Pelosi's seat, offering a platform that focused on universal health care, affordable college tuition, and higher ethical standards in government. Although she had no campaign funds, she insisted that she would not accept contributions from corporations. On September 10, 2007 Sheehan, along with nine others, was arrested for shouting outside a Senate hearing room in which General David H. Petraeus, the commander of the multinational force in Iraq, and Ryan C. Crocker, the U.S. ambassador to Iraq, were to testify about the war.

—N.W.M.

Suggested Reading: *Boston Globe* A p11 Aug. 22, 2005; *Detroit News* A p11 Aug. 19, 2005; *New York Times* IV p11 Aug. 21, 2005; *People* p86 Aug. 29, 2005; *Rolling Stone* (on-line) Aug. 25, 2005; *Salon* (on-line) Oct. 1, 2004; *Seattle Post-Intelligencer* B p1 Aug. 13, 2005; *Time* Aug. 15, 2005; (Vacaville, California) *Reporter* June 24, 2004

Selected Books: *Not One More Mother's Child*, 2005; *Dear President Bush*, 2005; *Peace Mom: A Mother's Journey through Heartache to Activism*, 2006

Shins

Music group

Mercer, James
Dec. 26, 1970– Songwriter; guitarist

Crandall, Martin
Apr. 20, 1975– Keyboardist; guitarist

Hernandez, Dave
Sep. 22, 1970– Bass guitarist

Sandoval, Jesse
Nov. 15, 1974– Drummer

Johnson, Eric
June 7, 1976– Keyboardist; guitarist

Address: Sub Pop Records, P.O. Box 20367, Seattle, WA 98102

In the 2004 film *Garden State*, directed by and starring Zach Braff, the character played by Natalie Portman says to the Braff character, "You gotta hear this one song—it'll change your life." She was referring to "New Slang," by a then-underground indie-rock band known as the Shins. The film, produced for a modest $2.5 million, went on to gross more than $26 million, and the songs in it, hand-picked by Braff, won a Grammy Award for best compilation soundtrack for a motion picture. Those developments propelled the relatively unknown group of Portland, Oregon–based musicians to mainstream stardom and helped their 2001 debut album, *Oh, Inverted World*, to achieve gold-record status, with sales increasing by approximately 400 percent. Since then the band has sold upwards of a million copies of its first two albums combined and debuted at number two (eventually reaching number one) on the *Billboard* 200 album chart with its third record, *Wincing the Night Away*, which sold 118,000 copies in its first week. The group, which performed for nearly a decade under a succession of names before becoming known as the Shins, is led by James Mercer. A songwriter and guitarist, Mercer "acquits himself quite well with a pen, and never allows his words to detract from (or often even draw attention from) the music," according to Josh Love, writing for *Stylus Magazine* (October 12, 2003, on-line); he was described as "one of indie-rock's most wordy and elliptical lyricists," by Kitty Empire, writing for the London *Observer* (April 1, 2007). The innovative quintet includes the keyboardist and sometime guitarist/bassist Martin Crandall, the bassist/guitarist Dave Hernandez, the drummer Jesse Sandoval, and the recently added multi-instrumentalist Eric Johnson, formerly of the Seattle, Washington–based group the Fruit Bats. The Shins have managed to transcend indie-pop clichés (such as cheesy keyboard passages and asinine lyrics) with innovative musical arrangements, complemented by Mercer's lyrical poetry. "Songwriting is really a weird process for me," Mercer explained to Jenny Eliscu for *Rolling Stone* (February 8, 2007). "It's almost as though you start fishing out into nothingness and there's these beautiful things out there that have yet to be realized. And it has to do with the math of the relationship between the actual notes and the harmonies and the chords. It's like you're putting your hand in a blind hole and feeling around, and once in a while you can grab onto something and keep it."

A son of Jim Mercer, a lieutenant colonel in the U.S. Air Force, and Alice Mercer, James Russell Mercer was born on December 26, 1970 in Honolulu, Hawaii. Due to their father's occupation, Mercer and his younger sister, Bonnie, had a peripatetic lifestyle, moving from city to city and country to country, which later contributed to the sophisticated and anecdotal nature of Mercer's lyrics. Early on in his childhood, Mercer's family traveled around the U.S. in a motor home, making stops in Utah, Kansas, and Alabama, before heading to Europe. They lived in Germany for a year before Mercer's father was transferred to Greece. At that point his mother decided to take him and his sister back to the United States, where they settled in Albuquerque, New Mexico, for several years. Back in the States, as Mercer recalled to Eliscu, "I didn't fit in. Kids were drinking and smoking pot and having sex. The social dynamic was much more mature than I was ready for at eleven. I became depressed for months. My dad and mom are both farm people and were not versed in child psychology. I remember that as being the end of my childhood." He went on to attend high school in England, spending a good deal of time on a Suffolk air-force base, where he began to develop an affinity for music. He listened to the likes of the Smiths, the Cure, the Beach Boys, and the Jesus and Mary Chain, and was greatly influenced by the group Pink Floyd's masterpiece, *Dark Side of the Moon*.

After returning to Albuquerque to attend college, Mercer picked up his first guitar (he had no formal training in music) and joined the local music scene—defined by hard punk acts such as Cracks in the Sidewalk, Big Damn Crazy Weight, and Elephant. His future band mates Martin Crandall, born on April 20, 1975, and Jesse Sandoval, born on November 15, 1974, were still in high school when they first met Mercer and his friend Neil Langford, a bassist, through other musicians. Mercer, who had played in such local groups as Orange Little Cousins, Subculture, and Blue Roof Diner, soon joined Langford, Crandall, and Sandoval in forming a lo-fi rock group called Flake. ("Lo-fi" is a subgenre of indie rock; the term refers to the use of low-fidelity recording methods, which produces more "authentic" sound. Many lo-fi artists use inexpensive cassette tape recorders in producing their music.) The "power punk pop" ensemble, as Mercer described them in an interview with *Ear Shot Magazine* (November 10, 2004, on-line), renamed themselves Flake Music after another Seat-

Four of the Shins (l. to r.): D. Hernandez, J. Mercer, J. Sandoval, M. Crandall. Photo: Courtesy of Sub Pop Records

The Shins

tle-based group, also called Flake, threatened to sue them. Flake Music soon made a name for themselves with their frenetic, counterpoint guitars, mathematically calculated keyboard passages, and sometimes rambling fuzz-pop style. Over the next eight years, they released a number of records, including their 1993 debut, a seven-inch single on Resin Records called "Mieke"; a 10-inch EP under Spork Science Project, in 1995, that included the songs "Pull Out of Your Head Size," "Dying Lack of Spit," "Tott," "Nuevo," and "Dilly Dally"; another seven-inch single in 1996, under Headhunter/Cargo; and, with the band Scared of Chaka, a split seven-inch single on 702/Science Project that contained the songs "Submarines" and "The Shins." In 1997 Flake Music released their only full-length album, *When You Land Here, It's Time to Return*, on Omnibus Records, which was well received despite minimal exposure outside college radio stations.

As early as 1996, Mercer—a self-described "control freak"—began to stray from Flake Music to begin work on a side project, which would result in the formation of the Shins. The band's name was based on both the Flake Music song of the same name and a fictional family in the Broadway show *The Music Man*, which was a favorite of Mercer's father. Because Neil Langford had gotten a job at about that time that involved piloting a corporate-owned hot-air balloon around the country, which forced him to be away from the band for long periods, the Shins started off as a duo, with Mercer on vocals and guitar and Sandoval on drums. Developing an affection for the "feel-good" retro-pop sound that harked back to the 1960s, as exempli-

fied by such Beatles-inspired bands as Apples in Stereo and the Olivia Tremor Control, Mercer and Sandoval started playing together live, opening for acts including the American Analog Set and Cibo Matto. Speaking with Lindsey Byrnes for *Thrasher Magazine* (April 2004), Sandoval recalled, "We realized that we wanted to expand to a fuller sound on stage so we asked Dave [Hernandez, from the band Scared of Shaka] to play bass. Then we realized that we wanted keys, so we asked Marty [Crandall] to play keyboards." Later they added the drummer Ron Skrasek, with whom they had previously collaborated. Shortly thereafter, due to Scared of Chaka's heavy touring schedule, both Hernandez and Skrasek were forced to leave the band, reopening the bassist slot for Langford. Thus, for the most part, the members of Flake Music became the Shins.

In 1998 the Shins released a seven-inch single under Omnibus entitled "Nature Bears a Vacuum." (By 1999 Flake Music had run its course; as Mercer explained to Eliscu, "I was so sick of trying to pretend to be punk rock.") In 2000 the group released another seven-inch single, "When I Goose-Step." With those two records the band received some critical acclaim and found themselves touring with the indie favorites Califone and Modest Mouse as a supporting act. At a show in San Francisco, California, during the tour with Modest Mouse, the Sub Pop Records founder, Jonathan Poneman, was so impressed by the group that he signed them to a contract. The contract came as a relief for Mercer, who had had minimal financial success with Flake Music and had been living on credit cards for some time. "I had a conversation with my parents where I said, 'Look I'm going to make this one last push at music,'" he recalled to Eliscu. "I told them, 'If this doesn't work, I'll go back to school.'"

In 2001 the Shins debuted their single "New Slang" under Sub Pop, followed by the release of their first album, *Oh, Inverted World*. Drawing comparisons to other groups of the genre, such as Apples in Stereo and Modest Mouse, critics almost unanimously hailed the album as a triumphant return to a style of rock from an earlier era, when the Beatles and the Beach Boys reigned supreme. In a review for *Pop Matters* (November 10, 2001, online), Paul Bruno wrote that the album "is filled with musical allusions that will probably go over the heads of many backpack-and-thick-rimmed-glasses wearing listeners: lots of Brian Wilson–like vocal lines, [Roger] McGuinnesque jangley guitar, some [Syd] Barrett-oid psych here and there," adding that "musically and lyrically, all the emotions are bubbling just beneath the surface but obvious to anyone who is paying attention." Critics noted the melancholic feel of such songs as "Caring Is Creepy," "The Past and Pending," and "Girl on the Wing," with their dreamy vocals and strummed guitar licks interspersed with space-like synthesizer sounds. "Weird Days" drew fond comparisons to the sun-induced rhythms of the Beach Boys, and other songs won praise for their complexity, evident in Kinks-like songs such as "Know Your Onion!" The album's centerpiece, "New Slang," was praised across the board; Eliscu noted for *Rolling Stone* (August 16, 2001) that "the most affecting song is 'New Slang,' a shuffling folk ballad with a spaghetti-western feel and a somber melody," while Bruno declared that it had "instant classic status written all over it."

Around that time Langford decided to pursue his air-balloon work exclusively, paving the way for Dave Hernandez (born on September 22, 1970) to rejoin the band. Soon after that, Mercer persuaded his Albuquerque-born bandmates to relocate to Portland, Oregon, which was home to such notable indie acts as the Decemberists and Sleater-Kinney. Martin Crandall noted to Douglas Wolk, writing for *Billboard* (February 3, 2007), "Albuquerque's nice, but there's not much going on musically, unless you want to watch some ska bands."

The Shins had established a fan base in indie circles by the time their second album, *Chutes Too Narrow*, was released, on October 21, 2003. Produced by Phil Ek, the album featured cleaner production work than did *Oh, Inverted World*, and garnered even more praise as a result. Robert Christgau, writing for *Rolling Stone* (January 25, 2007), recalled *Chutes* as being "one of the deftest, subtlest and just plain loveliest guitar-rock albums of the decade." While many had seen the Shins' first album as a flash-in-the-pan fluke, *Chutes Too Narrow* converted skeptics. Mike Baker, in a review for *Splendid Magazine* (October 27, 2003, on-line), commented, "The Shins' second effort sparkles with a clarity that was not always evident on their debut and energizes with a spark and an enthusiasm that previously seemed forced." The poetic nature of Mercer's songwriting was most apparent on tracks such as "Mine's Not a High Horse," whose words include, "After that confrontation you left me wringing my cold hands," and "Kissing the Lipless," among whose lyrics is the line, "I want to bury in the yard / the grey remains of a friendship scarred." Marked by an anxious New Wave spirit and a stronger emphasis on guitars, the songs "Saint Simon" (featuring violin work by Annemarie Ruljancich), "So Says I," and "Those to Come" were considered standouts, as Baker remarked: "There is an album's worth of well written and ably conceived pop tunes, each of which capture the spirit of *Oh, Inverted World*'s few truly inspiring songs." The album went on to win a Grammy nomination for best recording package and has sold nearly 400,000 copies to date.

Despite having firmly established themselves in the indie-rock world with their first two albums, the Shins were still relative unknowns on the mainstream music scene. Then, in 2004, Zach Braff's independent film *Garden State* featured two songs from the band's debut album, "Caring Is Creepy" and "New Slang." The film's endorsement helped quadruple sales of *Oh, Inverted World* and made the Shins known to millions of filmgoers. Three years later, on January 23, 2007, the band re-

leased its much-anticipated follow-up album, *Wincing the Night Away*, to equally favorable reviews and a number-two spot on the *Billboard* charts. A play on the name of a Sam Cooke song, "Twistin' the Night Away," the album's title referred to Mercer's woes as an insomniac. Mercer had brought other personal issues to his songwriting process for the new album, after finding himself alienated from old friends due to his success, trying to overcome a painful breakup with his girlfriend, and receiving death threats from crack-dealing former neighbors. "It started feeling like a David Lynch movie, where it's a normal scene and there's this latent dread and you don't know why," Mercer recalled to Brian Hiatt for *Rolling Stone* (November 30, 2006). "When we were mixing the record, I would say, 'More ghosts on the chorus.'" Considered the Shins' most experimental work to date, using elements ranging from hip-hop loops to psychedelic, ukulele-based Hawaiian folk meanderings, *Wincing the Night Away* included "Phantom Limb," the album's first single, which was followed by "Australia," "Sleeping Lessons," and "Spilt Needles." Jonathan Cohen wrote for *Billboard* (January 27, 2007), "*Wincing the Night Away* might actually be their best yet, a quietly ambitious effort that nudges the Shins' trademark indie pop into unexpected new directions. There's a drum machine beat, loping bass groove, strings and even flute on 'Red Rabbits,' ghostly reverb and noises on 'Black Wave,' and 'Spilt Needles' drops the jangle in favor of a dark melody and surreal lyrics."

While their music falls into a category—indie rock—whose name derives from the fact that many of its artists fail to be signed to major record labels, the Shins have almost singlehandedly catapulted indie rock into the mainstream. In addition to *Garden State*, "New Slang" has been used in commercials for McDonald's, Guinness, and other brands as well as on television shows, among them *Scrubs*, *Buffy the Vampire Slayer*, and *The Sopranos*. A handful of the group's other singles, including "Gone for Good," "Caring Is Creepy," "Pink Bullets," and "Phantom Limb," have been used in films including *In Good Company* and *Wicker Park* and in a variety of television shows, such as *Ed*, *One Tree Hill*, and *The O.C.* Although fans may interpret that widespread media exposure as evidence of "selling out," Mercer has defended the Shins' decision to license their material. "All this licensing and these different ways of exposing people to your music, it's just a way to compete with these big labels. The infrastructure that something like Warner Brothers or Sony has, they really can literally shove stuff down people's throats," Mercer said to Wince Charming, in an interview for *Time Off* (January 2007, on-line). When they prepared to launch *Wincing the Night Away*, the Sub Pop label had to use unorthodox marketing methods, reaching younger fans through Web-based vehicles such as MySpace (the band currently has more than 154,000 "friends" listed on its MySpace page) and prospective older fans through sales at the java behemoth Starbucks. *Wincing* sold 118,000 copies in the first week after its release.

On January 2, 2007, in an interview with Matt LeMay for the indie music Web site pitchfork-media.com, Mercer announced that the multi-instrumentalist Eric Johnson (born on June 7, 1976), from the group Fruit Bats, had officially joined the Shins. Johnson had played with the group on its most recent tour, performing on guitar, keyboards, slide guitar, and even maracas. Mercer has insisted in interviews on his desire to collaborate with new musicians continually. On January 13, 2007 the Shins' celebrity status was highlighted by their appearance on *Saturday Night Live* with the actor Jake Gyllenhaal; they performed "Phantom Limb" and "New Slang." Discussing honors and distinctions he would like to see his band attain, Mercer told Douglas Wolk, "There's always the cover of *Rolling Stone*. Or having a video on MTV that they're actually playing and not just at 3:30 in the morning."

The Shins began touring for *Wincing the Night Away* in February 2007, taking a break of several months the following spring and summer when Mercer's wife, the journalist Marisa Kula, gave birth to the couple's first child. (Mercer met Kula in April 2006, when she interviewed the Shins for an article she was writing.) The band resumed their tour in the fall.

The members of the Shins reside in Portland's more bohemian-friendly regions. Mercer lives in a former 1920s-era speakeasy, once occupied by one of Portland's indie legends, the late singer-songwriter Elliott Smith. Crandall lives in another storied Portland dwelling, the Alfred J. Armstrong House—which is listed in the National Register of Historic Places. In their spare time, the band members enjoy surfing, riding motocross, and playing video games.

—C.C.

Suggested Reading: *Albuquerque (New Mexico) Journal* Venue p18 Apr. 6, 2007; *Billboard* p28+ Feb. 3, 2007; (London) *Observer* p21 Apr. 1, 2007; *Rolling Stone* p22 Nov. 30, 2006, p71+ Jan. 25, 2007, p53+ Feb. 8, 2007; *Thrasher* (on-line) Apr. 2004; *Time Off* (on-line) Jan. 2007

Selected Recordings: *Oh, Inverted World*, 2001; *Chutes Too Narrow*, 2003; *Wincing the Night Away*, 2007

Shubin, Neil

Dec. 22, 1960– Evolutionary biologist; paleontologist

Address: University of Chicago, Dept. of Organismal Biology and Anatomy, Culver 108, University of Chicago, 5801 S. Ellis, Chicago, IL 60637

"The world is filled with puzzles, all kinds of interesting questions, and it's our challenge to figure them out," the paleontologist and evolutionary biologist Neil Shubin told Elizabeth Vargas for the ABC-TV program *World News Tonight* (April 7, 2006, on-line). "It's not just like this static file cabinet of things that human beings know. It's ever expanding." Shubin made those remarks one day after the announcement by him and his research team of their discovery of a fossil with features of both fish and tetrapods—the generic term for any vertebrates that have two sets of limbs. Christened "*Tiktaalik roseae*" and referred to whimsically as a fishapod, the fossil was found in the Canadian Arctic, about 600 miles from the North Pole, in rock roughly 375 million years old, and it made its public debut in an article in the journal *Nature* (April 6, 2006). In another article in the same issue of *Nature*, the paleontologists Erik Ahlberg, of Uppsala University, in Sweden, and Jennifer A. Clack, of the University of Cambridge, in England, wrote that *Tiktaalik* is undoubtedly an intermediate "link between fishes and land vertebrates," and

as such it "might in time become as much an evolutionary icon as the proto-bird Archaeopteryx"—a link between dinosaurs (and their reptilian descendants) and birds. "The fishapod appears to be a crucial link in the long chain that over time led to amphibians, reptiles, dinosaurs, birds and mammals," J. Madeleine Nash wrote for *Time* (April 10, 2006, on-line), noting that *Tiktaalik* "has become scientists' Exhibit A in their long-running debate with creationists and other antievolutionists who have been using the lack of such missing-link organisms to argue that Darwin's theory [of evolution] is wrong." Shubin told Elizabeth Vargas that *Tiktaalik* "opens a remarkable window on one of the major events in the history of life on Earth. We are dealing with the transformation from life in water to life on land. Those animals that took the first steps on land are the animals that evolved limbs." He also said to her, "The transition from life in water to life on land is a piece of our own past. We are uncovering our own past." In addition to shedding light on the water-land transition, Shubin's discoveries have shaped ideas about such topics as the origins of mammals and the ancestries of frogs, turtles, salamanders, and flying reptiles. According to a biography of him on Edge.org, Shubin is considered "one of the major forces behind a new evolutionary synthesis of expeditionary paleontology, developmental genetics, and genomics."

Shubin has chaired the University of Chicago's Department of Organismal Biology and Anatomy since 2000, when he joined the school's faculty as a professor. (Organismal biology focuses on indi-

John Weinstein, courtesy of the Field Museum

Neil Shubin

vidual parts of organisms and the relationships of those parts, as well as on the organism as a whole.) In 2006 he was appointed associate dean for organismal and evolutionary biology at the university and also provost of the Field Museum (formerly, the Field Museum of Natural History), in Chicago, a major research facility in the areas of evolutionary biology and paleontology. For 11 years beginning in 1989, he taught at the University of Pennsylvania. He is a research associate of the American Museum of Natural History, in New York, and the Academy of Natural Sciences of Philadelphia, in Pennsylvania. He has led fossil-hunting expeditions in the continental United States, Africa, Asia, and Greenland as well as Canada. Shubin's main research interest is the emergence of limbs in the evolution of life forms. In his essay "The 'Great' Transition," in the book *Intelligent Thought: Science Versus the Intelligent Design Movement*, edited by John Brockman, Shubin noted, "True limbs are not seen in any living fish." He specializes in fossils that date from two of the most important geologic periods in evolution: the Devonian period, lasting from about 410 million to about 356 million years ago, which is also known as the Age of Fishes, during which the first amphibians appeared; and the Triassic, which extended from 230 million to 190 million years ago, in which the earliest dinosaurs appeared. "These periods . . . witness the origin of both new ecosystems and new anatomical designs," Shubin wrote in a statement for the Web site of the University of Chicago's Division of the Biological Sciences. Regarding his research interests, he wrote, "I seek to understand the mechanisms behind the evolutionary origin of new anatomical features and faunas. The philoso-

phy that underlies all of my empirical work is derived from the conviction that progress in the study of evolutionary biology results from linking research across diverse temporal, phylogenetic, and structural scales"—that is, those measuring the passage of time, changes through time in organisms that are related genetically, and changes through time in particular structures of organisms. In addition to *Tiktaalik*, Shubin's most important discoveries include those of the first known frog (found in 1982); a huge collection of fossils some 200 million years old (1984); the remains of one of the earliest animals to walk on land (1995); and the 375-million-year-old fossil of a creature that had fingers (1997).

One of the two children of Seymour Shubin, a novelist, and Gloria Shubin, Neil H. Shubin was born on December 22, 1960 and grew up outside Philadelphia. His sister, Jennifer Shubin Levine, is a homemaker and former assistant district attorney for Philadelphia. As an undergraduate at Columbia University, in New York City, he often visited the American Museum of Natural History, which houses more than a million fossils and currently displays more than 500 of them. During his college years he became increasingly intrigued with the process of evolution. "I was interested in the big steps, the big jumps," he told Vargas. "How did fish evolve? How did things evolve to walk on land? How did birds evolve to fly?" After he earned a bachelor's degree, in 1982, he enrolled at Harvard University, in Cambridge, Massachusetts, to pursue a doctorate in organismic and evolutionary biology. While at Harvard Shubin won the Harvard-Danforth Award for Excellence in Teaching and a Biology Undergraduate Teaching Fellowship. He earned a Ph.D. in 1987. His dissertation was entitled "The Morphogenesis and Origin of the Skeletal Pattern of the Tetrapod Limb."

Earlier, during the summer of 1984, Shubin and Paul E. Olsen, who was then an assistant professor of geology at Columbia University's Lamont-Doherty Earth Observatory, searched for fossils along the north shore of the Minas Basin, an arm of the Bay of Fundy, between northwestern Nova Scotia and New Brunswick, in Canada. Their research site, near Parrsboro, Nova Scotia, lay near the northernmost portion of what geologists call the Newark Supergroup, a noncontinuous assemblage of extremely thick sedimentary deposits laid down 225 million to 175 million years ago, between the late Triassic and early Jurassic periods; it extends along the east coast of the U.S. as far south as South Carolina. Shubin was looking for fossils from about 200 million years ago, when, as the fossil record shows, almost half of all existing life forms disappeared; afterward, dinosaurs began to dominate Earth, and the first mammals appeared. The Bay of Fundy has the world's highest tides, and one day, when the tide forced Shubin and Olsen to continue their searching some distance from the rocky shoreline, Shubin "noticed a glint in the rock," as Hans Durstling reported for the *Toronto (Ontario, Canada) Star* (August 21, 1988). The "glint" was a bone embedded in a deposit that turned out to contain one of the richest conglomerations of fossils in North America—more than 100,000 fossilized bones or pieces of bone. The next year Shubin and Olsen arranged to have several tons of the rock shipped to Harvard's Museum of Comparative Zoology, where the fossils were found to include 13 skulls and jaws of cat-size, mammal-like reptiles known as trithelodonts; 50 skulls of crocodilian creatures; remains of a 12-foot-long dinosaur; and bones of ancient turtles and the prehistoric lizard sphenodonid. The fossils offered new clues about the extinction event that occurred between the Triassic and the Jurassic periods and about mammalian evolution.

"You know, you think of paleontologists working in exotic environments like the deserts or the Arctic," Shubin told Richard Harris for the National Public Radio program *All Things Considered* (April 1, 2004). "And . . . the reason why paleontologists go to those places is because rocks are exposed to the surface." Some of Shubin's discoveries, however, have occurred in such prosaic locations as rock exposed by the Pennsylvania Department of Transportation during road construction. In 1994 Shubin and the paleontologist Ted Daeschler (a former student of Shubin's who now heads a laboratory at the Academy of Natural Sciences of Philadelphia) reported in the journal *Science* their discovery of a shoulder bone and parts of a skull of a 365-million-year-old fossilized amphibian in north-central Pennsylvania. It was the oldest fossil of its kind ever found in North America and the second-oldest such fossil to be unearthed anywhere. The shoulder bone, as Shubin

told Paul Recer for the Associated Press (July 28, 1994), "has struts and beams going across it which suggest it once had extensive musculature"—muscles that could have supported the animal while it moved about on land. *Hynerpeton bassetti*, as the creature was named, seemed better suited for land locomotion than other known early amphibians. "Our conception of early tetrapod evolution is really changing," Daeschler said, as quoted by John Noble Wilford in the *New York Times* (August 2, 1994). "We can see that at this point in time, there was a diversity of the types of animals experimenting in ways to adapt to living on land."

In 1995, in sandstone deposited during the Devonian period and uncovered by the Pennsylvania Department of Transportation, Shubin and Daeschler found the fossilized remains of a fish with a wrist-like joint and eight finger-like bones inside its front fins. The presence of fossilized scales in the same rock established that the creature was a fish, not an amphibian. The evidence of "fingers" contradicted prevailing evolutionary theories, which held that fingers first appeared in land-dwelling vertebrates. Furthermore, "while most fish use their front fins for steering, Daeschler and Shubin's fish seems to have appropriated them for a new use—locomotion," as the science reporter Faye Flam wrote for the *Philadelphia Inquirer* (January 8, 1998). The fish, Shubin and Daeschler speculated, probably used the finger-like structures to help move its large body along the muddy bottoms of swamps.

In the April 2, 2004 issue of *Science*, Shubin and Daeschler reported finding the oldest known fossil of an arm bone. Dug up in 1993 in the Red Hills, 200 miles north of Philadelphia, in land that had been excavated to make way for a highway, the 365-million-year-old fossil was not closely examined until 2001. A bone from an upper arm, it was a few inches long and thinner than a pencil and came from a creature that Shubin described as "a mosaic of primitive fish and derived amphibian," according to Dave Newbart in the *Chicago Sun-Times* (April 2, 2004). The fossil served as evidence that "the role of the limb in propping the body arose first in fish fins, not tetrapod limbs," as Shubin and Daeschler asserted in their *Science* article. The ancient animal "would have been good at doing push-ups," Shubin said, as quoted by Faye Flam in the *Philadelphia Inquirer* (April 2, 2004). "What we're discovering," he told Richard Harris, "is that evolution, at this stage, is not a simple ladder of progress, you know, from fish to land. What we're finding, as we sample in rocks of this age, is a great diversity, a great menagerie of the earliest known limbed creatures. There are all kinds of different types."

Earlier, in 1982, Shubin and a Harvard colleague, the zoologist and vertebrate paleontologist Farish A. Jenkins Jr. (Shubin's graduate-school adviser), had found in a layer of Jurassic-era rocks in an Arizonan desert a scattering of 190-million-year-old bone fragments. When he and Jenkins examined the fragments closely—a job that occupied them on and off for years—they determined that the bones were those of a frog—the earliest known frog. After the additional years required to arrange the fragments into a skeleton, Shubin and Jenkins described the five-centimeter-long animal, named *Prosalirus bitis*, in *Nature* (September 7, 1995). With hind limbs that were longer than its forelimbs and a distinctive joint that made its pelvis unusually flexible, the creature "was clearly a good jumper," as Shubin told Beth Silver for the *Los Angeles Times* (October 15, 1995). Referring to the fossil of a frog ancestor (but not a true frog) millions of years older than *Prosalirus bitis* that had been found in Madagascar, Jeff Hecht wrote for *New Scientist* (September 16, 1995), "Paleontologists can now trace the evolution of the frog body plan back 190 million years, narrowing the gap between [the Madagascar specimen] and modern frogs and toads." The discovery of *Prosalirus bitis* provided evidence of frogs' resilience in the face of severe climate change, such as the enormous changes in the atmosphere that, according to one widely held theory, followed the collision of a huge asteroid with Earth about 65 million years ago and led to the extinction of the dinosaurs and many other animal species as well as plants. "Yet for some reason [frogs are] not able to cope with what's happening today," Shubin told Silver, alluding to the plummeting populations of dozens of frog species, and apparent disappearance of others, in recent decades.

The discovery by Shubin and Daeschler's team of *Tiktaalik* in the Canadian Arctic was not a "fluke," as Laura Helmuth put it for *Smithsonian* (June 2004). As Shubin explained to her, "We were actually looking for a fossil like this. By looking at maps and geological publications, we saw that the rocks were of the right age and the right type—they were formed in ancient stream environments. Another thing that's special about the Arctic is the rocks are at the surface. They're not hidden under plants or buildings or miniature golf courses." In July 2004 the researchers found three well-preserved, fossilized *Tiktaalik* specimens, ranging in length from four to nine feet, in sediments that, 375 million years ago, were streambeds straddling the equator. Once the fossils were dug out, they were sent to a lab, where technicians meticulously removed excess rock from the bone. "It took a long time for us to figure out really the extent of what we had," Shubin told Nelson Wyatt for the *Canadian Press* (April 5, 2006). The creature had a broad skull, a flexible neck, and eyes on top of its head (as are crocodiles'). Its large ribcage indicated that it may have had lungs. Within its pectoral fins were "the beginnings of a tetrapod hand, complete with a primitive version of a wrist and five finger-like bones,"as J. Madeleine Nash wrote. The scientists theorized, according to John Noble Wilford in the *New York Times* (April 6, 2006), that "in all likelihood, . . . *Tiktaalik* flexed its proto-limbs mainly on the floor of streams and might have pulled itself up on the shore for brief stretches." In his essay "The 'Great' Transition," Shubin wrote that *Tiktaalik* was among a series of discoveries that have complicated the designations of "fish" and "tetrapod." "Our earlier definition of tetrapods distinguished them from fish by their possession of limbs," he explained. "In what group, then, do we put our fish with wrists?" The fishapod's features suggested that "the fish-to-tetrapod transition likely happened not in creatures that were adapting to land but in creatures living in water. Moreover, everything special about tetrapods—limbs, digits, ribs, neck, the lot—might well have evolved in water, not on land," Shubin wrote. Nash noted, "*Tiktaalik roseae* . . . falls anatomically between the lobe-finned fish *Panderichthys*, found in Latvia in the 1920s, and primitive tetrapods like *Acanthostega*, whose full fossil was recovered in Greenland not quite two decades ago. Together, these fossils have overturned the old picture of the fish-tetrapod transition, which conjured up the image of creatures like the modern lungfish crawling out of water onto land."

Shubin has written a book, *Your Inner Fish: A Journey into the 3.5-Billion-Year History of the Human Body*, to be published by Random House in early 2008. The book traces the evolution of human organs and diseases back millions of years, to such creatures as worms and fish. According to the Random House Web site, "By examining fossils and DNA, Shubin shows us that our hands actually resemble fish fins, our head is organized like that of a long-extinct jawless fish, and major parts of our genome look and function like those of worms and bacteria."

Shubin's honors include fellowships from the National Science Association of the University of Pennsylvania, the Miller Research Institute of the University of California at Berkeley, and the John Simon Guggenheim Memorial Foundation. He and his wife, Michele Seidl, married in the early 1990s. Seidl, a geologist by training, is currently a senior research-project manager in the office of the dean of the University of Chicago's Division of the Biological Sciences. The couple live in Chicago with their two young children, Nathaniel and Hannah, both of whom were adopted from Korea.

—M.B.

Suggested Reading: ABCNews.com Apr. 7, 2006; *All Things Considered* (on-line) Apr. 1, 2004; *Chicago Sun-Times* p4 Apr. 2, 2004; *Columbia* p20+ Oct. 1986; Edge.org 2006; *Los Angeles Times* A p13 Oct. 15, 1995; *New Scientist* p20 Sep. 16, 1995; *New York Times*, C p3 Sep. 30, 1986, C p7 Aug. 2, 1994, A p1+ Apr. 6, 2006; *Philadelphia Inquirer* A p1+ Jan. 8, 1998, A p1+ Apr. 2, 2004; *Smithsonian* p36 June 2006; *Time* (on-line) Apr. 10, 2006; *Toronto Star* A p14 Aug. 28, 1988, A p3 Jan. 30, 1986; University of Chicago Division of Biological Sciences Web site; University of Chicago News Office (on-line) May 26, 2006

Courtesy of American Program Bureau

Silva, Daniel

Dec. 19, 1960– Writer

*Address: c/o Marilyn Ducksworth/Putnam
Publishers, 375 Hudson St., New York, NY 10014*

"I think people are . . . intrigued by the notion that there's a secret world inhabited by people who don't play by the same rules as you and I do and aren't bound by the same laws and morals," the novelist Daniel Silva told Karin Carlin for the *Pittsburgh Post-Gazette* (March 26, 1998). Silva has portrayed such worlds, to the delight of fans of the spy genre, in novels including *The Unlikely Spy* (1996), *The Kill Artist* (2000), *The Prince of Fire* (2005), *The Messenger* (2006), and *The Secret Servant* (2007)—books that have made Silva's name a frequent presence on best-seller lists and drawn comparisons to such masters of the thriller as John Le Carré and Tom Clancy. A onetime journalist and former producer of CNN's Washington, D.C.–based public-affairs programs, Silva left that news network in 1997 to focus on writing full-time. Regarding his unconventional career path, he told Scott Simon for National Public Radio (April 17, 2004), "I think that subconsciously I chose journalism because I thought it would be good preparation and good practice in the art of storytelling and it would give me a life that I could draw from later, and that proved to be the case." Asked how his extensive background in reporting facts had affected his efforts to weave fiction, he told Simon, "I don't have a problem slipping through that doorway between fact and fantasy. I like a very strong factual underpinning of my story, but I have a very fertile imagination."

Daniel Silva was born on December 19, 1960 in Michigan to Richard and Carol Ann (Koerber) Silva and grew up in Merced, California. In his youth he read the thriller novels belonging to his parents, particularly the works of Le Carré, Len Deighton, Jack Higgins, Frederick Forsyth, and Alistair MacLean, as a way to escape the frequent boredom that he said characterized his youth. Silva told Paul D. Colford for the *Los Angeles Times* (April 2, 1998) that in the worlds evoked in those books, "anything is possible and betrayal is common." In 1984, while he was pursuing a graduate degree in international relations at San Francisco State University, the news organization United Press International (UPI) hired him on a freelance basis to cover that year's Democratic National Convention, held in San Francisco. A week later UPI offered him a full-time job, and Silva left graduate school to work for the organization. He was based in San Francisco for a year before UPI transferred him to the foreign desk of its Washington, D.C., bureau, where he remained for two years. In 1987 UPI promoted him to Middle East correspondent. Based in Cairo, Egypt, he reported on a number of regional disputes. While there Silva met his future wife, Jamie Gangel, a correspondent for NBC's program *Today*, when both were covering the eight-year Iran-Iraq war that had begun in 1980. The couple married in 1988, after which Silva returned to Washington and took a job at CNN. He initially worked in the station's newsroom, producing such programs as *Prime News*, *The World Today*, and *Inside Politics*. In 1993 he moved to the talk-show unit, producing shows including *Evans and Novak*, *Crossfire*, *The Capital Gang*, and *Inside Politics Weekend*.

Soon after taking his position in CNN's talk-show division, Silva began writing his first novel, which would be published in late 1996 as *The Unlikely Spy*. He told Carlin, "I had moved up the management food chain at CNN and wasn't doing any writing anymore, and it left this big hole. I was a print journalist before CNN. I needed to write something, so I started working on this in my spare time." Silva said that in order to complete the book, he rose each morning at 4:45 and worked on it for two to three hours before driving to the CNN offices. He found fiction writing to be a welcome diversion from the seriousness of the material he was covering in Washington. He told Linda Wertheimer for National Public Radio (January 9, 1997): "I deal with the news of this town for 14 hours a day at CNN. And it was a wonderful place to go for two hours each morning. Great fantasy. Great escape. And it was tremendous fun."

In *The Unlikely Spy*, set in Britain during World War II, Catherine Blake, a seductive German operative, discovers secrets about Allied plans to invade Normandy. The British prime minister, Winston Churchill, dispatches a history professor, Alfred Vicary, to make sure that Blake's and other German spies' knowledge do not get back to Germany. "[The Normandy invasion] was the climactic battle of the war, and everyone understood that that was going to be the case," Silva told Wertheimer, discussing his choice of the book's theme. "You know, Hitler understood that the war would be won or lost in the beaches of France. And so did the Allies. And it was the climactic point of the war." The novel became a best-seller. Assessing it for the *New York Times* (January 8, 1997, on-line), Richard Bernstein wrote that despite its shortcomings, which included writing that "never rises above the workmanlike" and "too many predictable spy genre scenes," *The Unlikely Spy* is "a high-grade yarn. Mr. Silva's cast of secondary characters is especially strong, and he has a knack for allowing the unforeseen, the accidental, the all-too-human to intrude, pushing the plot in an unexpected direction. We know, of course, who won World War II, and that gives us a clue about the outcome of this story, but the route to that outcome is filled with the kind of dark and twisting passages that keep fans of spy thrillers guessing as they eagerly turn the pages."

Silva's first novel also stirred controversy, when the prominent British spy novelist Ken Follett accused Silva of taking the idea for *The Unlikely Spy* from Follett's 1978 runaway best-seller *Eye of the Needle*. As reported by Lawrence Donegan in the London *Guardian* (September 16, 1996), Follett said, "I was asked to give the publishers [of Silva's novel] a quote about the book. I did. I've told them *The Unlikely Spy* is the best book I have ever written." Silva expressed admiration for Follett's works but denied the charge of literary theft.

In 1997 Silva left CNN and focused on producing novels at the rate his publishers expected—approximately one per year. He told Carlin that the decision to leave journalism "was something I agonized over. I very much wanted to continue to do both. They were a nice complement to each other. I could have a foot in the real world and a few hours in my study doing whatever I wanted on my computer screen." Realizing, however, that to maintain both jobs would mean he was either "going to be a lousy TV producer, a lousy writer or a lousy father," as he said to Carlin, Silva became a "stay-at-home-Dad/spy-novelist kind of guy," as Lisa Frydman described him for the *Chicago Sun-Times* (February 26, 2004). "Picture car pools and capers, play dates and Pentagon files," Frydman added.

Silva had already begun writing his second novel, *The Mark of the Assassin* (1998), by the time *The Unlikely Spy* was published. The second book follows the CIA officer Michael Osbourne as he pursues the assassin Jean-Paul Delaroche, a former KGB operative codenamed "October," who helped shoot down a (fictional) TransAtlantic Airlines flight departing New York's Kennedy Airport. The incident is believed to have been the work of Islamic militants acting alone, but Osbourne discovers that a more mysterious international ring of politicians and criminals, known as "The Society," was behind it. Osbourne has a personal vendetta against October, who murdered Osbourne's lover in London, England, 20 years earlier. While researching the book, Silva, already a self-described intelligence buff, spent time with CIA members at their workplace. He told Matt Lauer during an interview on *Today* (March 11, 1998, on-line), "I was the proverbial kid in the candy shop and got to go inside the counterterrorism center and see what it looks like and talk to these people about how they do their jobs, and go have lunch with them and let them throw a few bones across the table. It was . . . fascinating." Silva also told Lauer, "One thing I decided very early on was that I did not want to get painted into a corner as [a] writer only of . . . historical fiction. And I thought it was better to just make the break now. Get it over with, jump to contemporary." Although it quickly became a national best-seller, *Mark of the Assassin* received lukewarm reviews, with some critics finding it to be derivative ("The trouble with this would-be spy thriller is that it wasn't so much written as assembled from clichés and left-over spare parts," David Nicholson declared in the March 24, 1998 edition of the *Washington Post*) and others, insensitive ("Silva irked me early on with his use of an airline disaster, obviously drawn from the real-life tragedy of TWA Flight 800," Bill Nichols wrote for the April 2, 1998 issue of *USA Today*).

Both Osbourne and October were brought back for *The Marching Season* (1999), named for the traditional parades in Northern Ireland that celebrate Protestant rule and are often characterized by violence between Protestants and Catholics. In the story, a group of Protestant terrorists, the Ulster Volunteer Brigade, intent on blocking the Irish peace process, coordinate simultaneous bombings in London; Dublin, Ireland; and Belfast, Northern Ireland. Osbourne is summoned from retirement to protect his father-in-law, Douglas Cannon, the U.S. ambassador to Great Britain, who is being targeted by the Brigade. Meanwhile, October has been hired by The Society—the shadowy group from *The Mark of the Assassin*, now intent on exploiting the Irish "troubles" for political and financial gains—to murder Cannon. To research the book, Silva walked through some of the most dangerous streets in Belfast. He found a stark contrast between the city's tense atmosphere and the surrounding natural beauty, saying, as quoted by Julie E. Washington in the Cleveland *Plain Dealer* (March 24, 1999), that Northern Ireland was "the most terrifying, violent society I've ever been in. The air crackles with tension."

As with its predecessors, *The Marching Season* brought brisk sales and mixed reviews. "Most thriller authors can only hope that the reader will keep turning the pages so quickly in their fast-paced and breathtaking novels that they won't notice how vapid and one-dimensional their characters are," Nancy Connors wrote for the *Plain Dealer* (March 28, 1999). "Unfortunately, all of the above applies to *The Marching Season*. . . . But despite its linguistic howlers, literary pretensions and characters that practically wear signs reading 'evil,' 'good' and 'evil with an explanation,' the book isn't completely awful. Reading it is kind of like eating that third slice of cake: you know it's doing you no good, and that you'll feel kind of empty and sick afterward, but you do it anyhow." For *USA Today* (March 26, 1999), Ann Prichard wrote that *The Marching Season* is "a readable Tom Clancy-esque thriller that makes up in action what it lacks in satisfying prose."

The Kill Artist (2000) introduced the character who would be the focus of each of Silva's five subsequent works: the Israeli art restorer and former assassin Gabriel Allon. Silva conceived of the character in what was, as he told Adam Dunn for *Publishers Weekly* (April 1, 2002), "one of those thunderbolt moments," basing him in part on the real-life art restorer David Bull. Silva said to Dunn that Allon is "a reluctant destroyer," adding, "I wanted to show what this kind of work does to people. It's awful work, and it leaves scars." In *The Kill Artist* Allon is called into action by Ari Shamron, the head of an Israeli intelligence agency called "The Office," to hunt down a Palestinian assassin named Tariq, who was behind a terrorist attack that killed some of Allon's family. (Shamron is based on the Israeli leader Ariel Sharon, the agency on the Israeli military intelligence network Mossad.) Allon is summoned out of retirement again in Silva's next book, *The English Assassin* (2002); he is sent by Shamron to meet with a financier, Rolfe, in Switzerland—where he finds him murdered. Like other Swiss bankers, Rolfe had helped to finance the Third Reich; he was in possession of a trove of French art looted by the Nazis, and knowing that he was dying, he sought to return the artworks to their rightful places. A group of Rolfe's fellow bankers try to stop that from occurring, and Allon, with the help of Rolfe's daughter, must fulfill Rolfe's mission in spite of opposition from some of Switzerland's most powerful men. "Daniel Silva is going to move into the upper echelons of spy and adventure novelists," John D. Gates wrote for the *Winston-Salem Journal* (March 24, 2002), in a review of *The English Assassin*. "His touch is surer. His plots are more subtle and tense. His characters are more compelling. . . . [*The English Assassin*] may just well boost Silva into the top ranks of the spy novelists."

In *The Confessor*, Silva's sixth novel, published in 2003, Allon is called upon to avenge the death of his friend Benjamin Stern, a researcher who was about to publish evidence of the Catholic Church's complicity in the Holocaust. A mysterious Vatican brotherhood called Crux Vera ordered Stern's murder. The story's themes have personal relevance for Silva, who grew up in a Catholic home but converted to Judaism as an adult. *The Confessor* was followed by *A Death in Vienna* (2004), the last in Silva's trilogy of novels concerning the Holocaust. In it, Allon tries to bring to justice former war criminals who have escaped punishment. One of Allon's friends, Eli Lavon, who works toward restitu-

tion for Holocaust victims, dies when his office is bombed—apparently the work of Islamic terrorists. When it is revealed that a former Nazi war criminal whom Lavon was pursuing is behind the bombing, Allon picks up the investigation where his friend left off. Silva's next novel, *The Prince of Fire* (2005), deals with the Arab-Israeli conflict. In that book Allon seeks vengeance against a terrorist who works under the Palestinian leader Yasir Arafat and was responsible 10 years earlier for the death of Allon's infant son and the mental and physical scarring of his wife (as mentioned in *A Death in Vienna*); the terrorist is now a suspect in a bombing in Rome. "Though he handles them better than most espionage writers, Silva is not above dishing up some of the hoariest cliches of the genre . . . ," Richard Lipez wrote for the *Washington Post* (April 24, 2005, on-line). "But thriller readers are used to it and easily forgive such excesses in the hands of a writer otherwise as talented and intelligent as Daniel Silva."

The Messenger (2006), finds Allon and Sarah Bancroft, a beautiful American art expert, attempting to infiltrate a Saudi terrorist network that is planning an attack on the Vatican. "Unlike other thriller writers who rely on tricks and seemingly endless (and ultimately unrealistic) twists for effect," Ron Terpening wrote for *Library Journal* (July 2006), "Silva builds suspense through realistic threats, harrowing situations, and gripping action." Silva's most recent novel, *The Secret Servant* (2007), follows Allon to Amsterdam, where he is summoned to sort through the archives of a Dutch terrorism analyst who has recently been murdered. On what first appears to be a routine mission, Allon discovers an elaborate Islamic conspiracy expected to target the middle of London. Like Silva's other novels, *The Secret Servant* received mixed reviews. A critic for *Publishers Weekly* (May 21, 2007, on-line) raved, "Bestseller Silva's superlative seventh novel to feature Gabriel Allon, the legendary but wayward son of Israeli Intelligence, puts Silva squarely atop the spy thriller heap." Similarly, Claire E. White, in an assessment for the *Internet Writing Journal* (August 2007), declared that with *The Secret Servant*, Silva had reached "a new high. . . . The plotting is airtight, the suspense is breathtaking and the characters are memorable. With some very welcome—and unexpected—touches of humor near the end of the book, *The Secret Servant* sets the standard for the modern spy thriller." Others criticized the book for what they viewed as an oversimplified portrayal of political scenarios. In *Entertainment Weekly* (July 20, 2007, on-line), Jennifer Armstrong called the work "stiff" and "didactic," writing, "The rise of Islamic terrorism is good news for no one but, perhaps, authors of espionage fiction. So far, however, they haven't figured out how to handle this rich, sad material. . . . [*The Secret Servant*] is unswervingly pro-Israel, shrill about the threat of Muslim immigration to Europe, and contemptuous of 'quisling' liberals. This is the stuff of fiery editorials, but heavy-handed novels." Silva told Allen Apell for *Publishers Weekly* (June 4, 2007, on-line) that the novel reflects his concerns about the growing population of radical Muslims in Europe. "In many ways the European Islamists are more violent, more toxic than they are in Cairo," he said. "There are radical mosques and terrorist recruiters all across Europe. The European security services are doing the best they can, but I wouldn't be surprised if the next time we're hit by al-Qaeda, the people who do it are carrying European passports." Silva also told Apell that he is interested in the increasingly centralized and authoritarian nature of Russia's government and that the subject of a future book of his may be "a new Cold War that might be looming."

In his spare time Silva enjoys competitive bicycling. He has described himself as "a passionate [Oakland] Raiders fan"—a result of the time he spent in the San Francisco Bay Area as a fledgling journalist. He lives in Washington, D.C., with his wife and their twins, Lily and Nicholas.

—M.B.

Suggested Reading: *Chicago Sun-Times* Features p54 Feb. 26, 2004; *Pittsburgh Post-Gazette* G p1 Mar. 26, 1998; *Publishers Weekly* p46 Apr. 1, 2002

Selected Books: *The Unlikely Spy*, 1996; *The Mark of the Assassin*, 1998; *The Marching Season*, 1999; *The Kill Artist*, 2000; *The English Assassin*, 2002; *The Confessor*, 2003; *A Death in Vienna*, 2004; *Prince of Fire*, 2005; *The Messenger*, 2006; *The Secret Servant*, 2007

Chip Somodevilla/Getty Images

Sinegal, James D.

(sin-uh-GAHL)

Jan. 1, 1936– President and CEO of Costco

Address: Costco Wholesale Corp., P.O. Box 34331, Seattle, WA 98124

James D. Sinegal, the co-founder, president, and CEO of Costco Wholesale Corp., the world's most successful warehouse retail operation, has for the past six years turned down raises and occasionally even bonuses in an effort to keep his salary within the same realm as that of the company's lowest-paid employee. Admittedly, with an annual salary of $411,688 in 2006, plus 2.4 million shares of Costco stock, worth about $1.3 billion, Sinegal is no pauper. But in an era in which CEOs' salaries are typically in the millions of dollars (the top-10 highest-paid CEOs earned more than $30 million each in 2006), Sinegal's take-home pay seems modest, especially for the CEO of a company as successful as Costco. (In June 2007 Ellen Simon reported for the Associated Press reported that Sinegal was the lowest-paid CEO among the 368 examined by the Securities and Exchange Commission that year.) When Costco was founded, in 1983, it represented a new kind of discount store, based on the "warehouse model" pioneered by Sinegal's mentor, Price Club founder Sol Price. Costco, which in the beginning mostly sold groceries in bulk, now sells items ranging from big-screen television sets to grandfather clocks to designer clothes. Often praised as the "anti-Wal-Mart," Costco is known for valuing its customers and employees above its profit margin, which—though shareholders' occasional grumbling might suggest the opposite—has remained healthy. Costco, which had $101 million in annual sales in 1984, ended the 2006 fiscal year with sales totaling $58.96 billion. Now employing around 118,800 workers and boasting profits of $1.1 billion in 2006, Costco is one of the largest companies in the U.S. Still, in a 2005 presentation for local business leaders in Bend, Oregon, Sinegal said about Costco, as reported by Chuck Chiang for the *Bulletin* (November 18, 2005), "We like to think of ourselves as a small company that's hands-on." Sinegal is nothing if not hands-on, traveling 200 days out of the year in an attempt to visit each Costco outlet twice annually. "Retail is detail," he told Julie Schmit for *USA Today* (September 24, 2004, on-line). "Show me a big-picture guy, and I'll show you a guy who's out of the picture." That devotion to every aspect of his business has led Sinegal to win numerous accolades for his management prowess; he was named one of *Business Week*'s best managers of 2002 and one of *Time*'s top 100 "People Who Shape Our World" in 2006. "Sinegal manages to be demanding without being intimidating," John Helyar wrote for *Fortune* (November 24, 2003). Helyar also wrote, "He's got energy that leaves people half his age floundering in his wake." And yet, Helyar continued, even as Sinegal heads one of the only large retailers that has managed to compete successfully with the mega-conglomerate superstores, "he seems more like a twinkle-eyed grandfather (which he is, eight times over) than a killer retailer." For his part, Sinegal sees the key to Costco's success as being simple. "This is not a tricky business," he explained to Mark Veverka for *Barron's* (May 12, 2003). "We just try to sell high-quality merchandise at a cost lower than everybody else."

The company's enormous success is predicated, perhaps paradoxically, on a particularly bare-bones business strategy. A typical Costco store has no signs marking the aisles and no shopping bags in the checkout lines. While the company has a partnership with American Express, the cashiers do not accept Visa or Mastercard (to save on service charges), and the stores rely primarily on natural light (to save on electricity). Other than direct-mail campaigns, the chain does not advertise. No salespeople walk the floors, except in the stores' electronics sections. Unlike such superstores as Wal-Mart or Kmart, which can carry more than 100,000 products, a Costco outlet stocks approximately 4,000 items at any given time, both in an effort to offer only products of greatest value to customers and to defray shipping and stocking costs for the company. "Costco's business plan is elegantly simple—and simply elegant," Veverka wrote of what is known in the industry as the "Costco site-maximization strategy." But what has truly distinguished Costco from its rivals is its focus on an elegantly simple customer base. Warehouse operations, such as Costco and its rivals Sam's Club and BJ's, are open only to members; annual membership fees for Costco range from $45 to $100, depending on added perks. And while the discounted prices and bulk quantities they offer might indicate otherwise, warehouse clubs actually attract the largest proportion of affluent shoppers of all U.S. retail channels—according to A. C. Nielsen, about 54 percent of the stores' traffic. The average annual salary of a Costco member is $95,333, as reported by Helyar. (A 2005 *New York Times* article placed it at $74,000 but also noted that 31 percent of members earn over $100,000.) The retail consultant Michael Silverstein described the typical Costco shopper to Helyar as one who wants to "trade up" to top-of-the-line brand names when it comes to luxury goods such as watches and golf clubs but seeks to "trade down" to discounted basic goods such as paper towels and

detergent. Costco, more than Sam's Club or BJ's, fulfills those desires. In 2003 Costco was the country's biggest seller of both fine wines ($600 million worth) and rotisserie chickens (55,000 per day). In 2002 the chain sold approximately 60,000 carats of diamonds and 45 million hot dogs. "It's the ultimate concept in trading up and trading down," Silverstein told Helyar. "It's a brilliant innovation for the new luxury."

James D. Sinegal was born on January 1, 1936 in Pittsburgh, Pennsylvania. His father was a coal miner and steelworker until he broke his back; afterward he started a small business. Sinegal has cited the less-than-privileged circumstances of his childhood as a major factor in the way he now runs his business, as they inspired his efforts to give employees fair salaries and benefits. In 1951, when Sinegal was 15, the family moved to San Diego, California, where Sinegal graduated from high school in 1953. He then enrolled at San Diego Junior College (now San Diego City College), from which he received an associate's degree in 1955. That year he began attending San Diego State University as a premedical student.

In 1954, while he was still at San Diego Junior College, Sinegal took a part-time job with Fed-Mart, a discount department store that had been opened that same year by Sol Price, who would later be known as the pioneer of the warehouse-store retail model. Price—who had graduated from San Diego State University—became a mentor to Sinegal, who is often referred to by the press as Price's "surrogate son." Starting in an entry-level position at Fed-Mart and working his way up, Sinegal eventually became the company's executive vice president of merchandising and operations. He has implemented a similar policy of internal promotion at Costco. "If somebody came to us and said he just got a master's in business at Harvard, we would say fine, would you like to start pushing carts?" he explained to Nina Shapiro for *Seattle Weekly* (December 15, 2004, on-line). "That's how I started in this business—tying mattresses on tops of cars." Price's influence on Sinegal's later vision for Costco was significant in other ways as well. Posted on Sinegal's office bulletin board is a memo from Price, dated August 8, 1967; according to Shapiro, it reads, "Although we are all interested in margin, it must never be done at the expense of our philosophy."

In 1975 Fed-Mart was sold to the German retail operation Hugo Mann, and Price was ousted from the company. The following year, Price opened Price Club—the first warehouse club, with an annual membership fee of $25. Sinegal followed his mentor to Price Club, where he became executive vice president by the end of the decade. Originally conceived as a discount office-supply store for small businesses, Price Club almost failed in its first few years, before deciding to expand its offerings and attract a wider customer base. In 1977 the company had one warehouse with annual sales of $13 million; in 1982 it had 10 warehouses with annual sales of $366 million. Concurrently, Sinegal also briefly held positions as vice president of merchandising for Builders Emporium, a chain of home-improvement stores, and as president of his own company, Sinegal/Chamberlin & Associates, a wholesale food distributor.

In 1983 the entrepreneur Jeff Brotman recruited Sinegal to be his partner in a new warehouse-club venture. Brotman and Sinegal opened the first Costco in a warehouse in Seattle, Washington, purposely targeting urban shoppers. That same year Sam Walton, the founder of Wal-Mart, opened the first Sam's Club, which is also a warehouse operation inspired by Price's example and which is Costco's biggest rival. But while Sam's Club boasts the distinct advantage of Wal-Mart's buying power, its affiliation with the megastore has made it difficult for Sam's Club to craft a distinct identity. "The biggest thing with Sam's was that it didn't have a free hand to compete with Wal-Mart," Price told Helyar. "There was this fundamental thing where they didn't want to kill Wal-Mart." Price explained to Helyar that the other shortcoming of Sam's Club was that it did not pursue the "higher class" of customer to whom Costco catered. To keep its discerning shoppers happy and stay one step ahead of Sam's Club, Costco continually introduced new offerings. In 1986 Costco began selling fresh meat and produce; Sam's Club began selling fresh groceries three years later. In 1995 Costco added gas pumps to many of its locations, adding to its ability to provide "one-stop shopping"; Sam's Club followed suit in 1997. Also in 1995 Costco started its own line of clothes, Kirkland Signature; Sam's Club introduced its own line, Member's Mark, in 1998. "Pity poor Wal-Mart . . . ," Helyar wrote. "In this one niche, it's run up against a company that shows you can't discount some old business verities: The nimble first mover can outrun the powerful colossus; the innovator can stay a jump ahead of the imitator; the quality of leadership can trump the quantity of resources."

The one rough patch in the company's history came in 1993, when Costco bought Price Club, creating the company PriceCostco Inc. As Helyar wrote, "what appeared to be a harmonic convergence of protégé and mentor instead became a troubled marriage," as Sinegal and Price's son, Robert, had difficulty in sharing leadership duties. Eight months after the merger, Costco created a separate company called Price Enterprises, led by Robert Price, which eventually evolved into PriceSmart and now operates warehouse clubs overseas. In 1997 Sinegal's company restored the name Costco Wholesale Corp. Still, there were no hard feelings between mentor and protégé. "Jim has done a pretty damned remarkable job," Sol Price told Helyar. "He puts a great emphasis on quality and has moved into the food business and other new lines. We [the Prices] were very good at creating, but Jim was very good at developing."

By having each Costco outlet stock, for example, a $14.99 seven-pound chocolate cake a couple of aisles away from a $300 cashmere coat or a $3,000 plasma-screen television, Sinegal has created stores where people do not come just for everyday items. "Our customers don't drive 15 miles to save on a jar of peanut butter," he told Helyar. "They come for the treasure hunt." Markups of products at Costco are capped at 14 percent, except for its premium Kirkland brand, which is capped at 15 percent; Wal-Mart's markup is closer to 20 percent, while department stores can increase items' prices by up to 50 percent. Costco also gives blanket permission for returns on all items except computers—a customer does not need a receipt, there are no questions asked, and there is no time limit. "I'm a big admirer of Wal-Mart, but I admire Costco more," Charles Munger, Warren Buffett's business partner at Berkshire Hathaway and a Costco board member, told Schmit. "Virtually none of the sins of modern capitalism are at Costco." The company is widely lauded for its employee benefits, highly unusual in an industry known for paying minimum wage and offering minimal health-care coverage. At Costco workers earn an average of $17 per hour, reportedly the best salary in the retail industry. The vast majority of employees are eligible for health-care benefits, for which they pay only 9 percent of the cost. (The average retail employee would have to pay a prohibitive 23 percent of his or her insurance coverage, a reason why so few workers at other retail outlets have health insurance.) While those policies stem partly from a generous company philosophy, they are also effective for Costco's bottom line. Happier employees, Sinegal claims, are more productive employees. "Paying good wages is not in opposition to good productivity," he told Nanette Byrnes for Business Week (September 23, 2002). "If you hire good people, give them good jobs, and pay them good wages, generally something good is going to happen." For Costco, good wages have led to low employee turnover—under 17 percent, or one-third of the industry average. Satisfying employees may also lead to minimal "shrinkage," retail lingo for employee theft; at Costco, as Helyar reported, the rate of such activity is 13 percent of the industry average.

Not everyone, however, agrees that such treatment of workers is good for the bottom line. The Deutsche Bank analyst Bill Dreher told Stanley Holmes and Wendy Zellner for Business Week (April 12, 2004), "At Costco, it's better to be an employee or a customer than a shareholder." Many shareholders contend that if Costco were to lower wages and raise health-care prices to meet the industry averages, the company would be even more profitable—and that its stock price would go even higher. But Sinegal—who owns 2.4 million shares of Costco stock with an option for an additional 1.2 million—has rejected that view. "We think when you take care of your customer and your employees, your shareholders are going to be rewarded in the long run," he told Helyar. "And I'm one of them [the shareholders]; I care about the stock price. But we're not going to do something for the sake of one quarter that's going to destroy the fabric of our company and what we stand for." Costco stock reached a then–all-time high in March 2000, at $60 a share, setting off a wave of speculation about whether the company could keep up its high stock value. "Costco is still unique, the best in its class," the PaineWebber Inc. analyst Jeffrey Edelman wrote, arguing that the stock was a safe investment, as quoted in the business journal *MMR* (June 26, 2000). "It sets the standards for the industry, continues to gain market share and has significant expansion opportunities."

It was precisely that expansion, however, that later brought the stock prices down. In the years after 2000, the company opened a larger number of stores than in the past, and more of them in new markets—a more expensive proposition than expanding where there are already outlets. Because Costco does not advertise in ways other than direct mail, building a new store's ideal customer base and reaching peak profit potential may take as long as five years—which made the expansion efforts between 2000 and 2003 a good long-term investment but not one that pleased shareholders in the short-term. In May 2003 Costco shares were trading at approximately $35 each. By July 2007 the company had slightly surpassed 2000 levels, hitting a high of $60.31 per share. Again, analysts disagreed about whether the company's stock-market success would be sustainable. "I'm not disputing that Costco is a great company," the HSBC analyst Mark Husson told Nat Worden for the finance Web site TheStreet.com (March 14, 2006). "I just think the stock has gotten too expensive considering the risks that it's facing." But Husson was one of only two analysts (out of 24 on Wall Street) who held a negative rating on the stock. The Morningstar analyst Anthony Chukumba told Worden that he expected even more growth from Costco. "Costco's stock is starting to get pricey, but I think it definitely deserves a premium over Wal-Mart since it's one of the few retailers out there that competes head-on with them and, quite frankly, beats the pants off them. They're incredible merchants. Their customer service is pretty much the best out there in all of retail. They treat their employees better. They pay them more. Their benefits are better, and the company still has room to grow both at home and abroad." Costco opened 20 new stores in 2004 and 16 in 2005 and plans to open 35 more in fiscal year 2007. "We've been a growth company since our inception," Sinegal told Worden. Still, he added that he was reluctant to make any concrete statements about the future. "The way we view things at the moment, we think it's possible that we could double the size of our company in the next 10 years, but that's obviously easier to say than to do," Sinegal said. "That plan could be altered by a lot of different things. We can't account for floods, wars, depressions and everything else that could happen." In 2007 Costco was number 15 on *Fortune* maga-

zine's list of the most-admired companies in the world and number 18 on its list of most-admired companies in the United States.

Sinegal lives in the Seattle area. He received an honorary degree from Seattle University in 2003 and another from the University of Notre Dame in 2004. He is especially active in promoting education, serving on the founding board of the Zion Preparatory Academy (**a** Seattle private school for underprivileged youth), on the national board of Communities in Schools, on the board of United Way of King County, and as a member and former chair of the Seattle University Board of Trustees. In 2000 Sinegal and Brotman created the Costco Scholarship Fund, which helps qualified minority students attend Seattle University and the University of Washington. In 2006 Sinegal was a recipient of the American Association of Community College's outstanding alumni award for his success at Costco and his philanthropic work. Sinegal has also been actively involved in politics, endorsing the Democratic candidate John Kerry for president in 2004 and donating more than $400,000 to Democratic candidates and liberal interest groups. Both Sinegal's son and brother-in-law are employed by Costco.

—C.S.

Suggested Reading: *Fortune* p158 Nov. 24, 2003; *New York Times* Business p1+ July 17, 2005; *Seattle Weekly* (on-line) Dec. 15, 2004; *USA Today* B p1+ Sep. 24, 2004

Sklansky, David

Dec. 22, 1947– Gambler; writer

Address: c/o Two Plus Two Publishing, 226 Garfield Dr., Henderson, NV 89014

Recent years have seen a surge of interest in the game of poker, particularly the variety known as Texas Hold 'Em. Televised poker tournaments on ESPN and the Travel Channel have brought the game new followers, and on-line gambling forums are now frequented by a younger and more diverse set of players than make up the traditional casino crowd. "It's estimated several million new players have begun to play, both in person and on the Internet," Howard Schwartz, a director of the Gambler's Book Club, a publisher of books on gaming, told John Grochowski for the *Chicago Sun-Times* (May 7, 2004). David Sklansky, a professional poker player and author, has been in an excellent position to benefit from poker's newfound popularity. An expert on Hold 'Em since the 1970s, Sklansky is the author of *Hold 'Em Poker*, the 1976 work that is still considered the definitive book on the subject. As sole author or co-author with his publishing partner, Mason Malmuth, Sklansky has pro-

David Sklansky

Courtesy of Two Plus Two

duced more than a dozen books on gambling, including *Getting the Best of It* (1982), *Theory of Poker* (1983), *Fighting Fuzzy Thinking in Poker, Gaming and Life* (1997), and *Small Stakes Hold 'Em: Winning Big with Expert Play* (2004). He has served as a consultant to casinos; developed Internet gaming sites and electronic gaming devices; produced instructional videos, including *Sklansky: The Video* (1994); and written for various gaming publications. With Malmuth, Sklansky launched the gaming publishing company Two Plus Two, in 1989. The authors' books explain ways to profit from gambling in a practical, logical manner. "Winning at gambling isn't about discovering some earth-shattering secret," Sklansky told Michael Konik for *Cigar Aficionado* (May/June 1998). "It's about finding a whole bunch of small edges. We've uncovered all the edges."

Describing himself as the possessor of a "mega IQ," Sklansky has attributed his poker prowess to an extensive knowledge of mathematical probability. "First and foremost, in terms of statistics and odds or hand data, David is the authority," Mike Sexton, a leading professional poker player and a host of the Travel Channel program *World Poker Tour*, told Marc Schwarz for the Passaic County, New Jersey, *Herald News* (July 12, 2005). "Every player I know, if they have a question about the math they go to David. And you take what he says as gospel." Sklansky told Schwarz, "I came from a different side of town than the typical professional poker player when I first came to Vegas. I was academic oriented." Indeed, Sklansky's books have ushered in an approach to poker based less on instinct than on theory—an approach preferred among the younger generation of players. According to Schwarz, "What Sklansky did with *Hold 'Em Poker* . . . was bring a new perspective to a game that until recently was considered a back-room game played by hustlers and low-lifes."

David Bruce Sklansky was born on December 22, 1947 in Teaneck, New Jersey, to Irving and Mae Sklansky. His father was a mathematics and computer professor at Columbia University, in New York City. Sklansky was immersed in mathematical concepts from an early age; according to Schwarz, his father "began teaching him calculus at the dining room table by the sixth grade." Irving Sklansky told Schwarz, "I was constantly working with him with math. My wife didn't like it. She wanted to raise my Jewish son to be a doctor." Perhaps owing to that training, at age 12 Sklansky scored an 800, the highest possible score, on the math portion of the Scholastic Aptitude Test (SAT). Sklansky attended Teaneck High School, graduating in 1966. He had played poker recreationally during high school; he took a more serious interest in the game while attending the Wharton School of Business at the University of Pennsylvania, in Philadelphia. There, along with some of his classmates, he analyzed the game in great detail. "The thing that distinguished [those college poker sessions] from any other poker game I played in," he told Schwarz, "is that even though it was for fairly serious money, after each hand we'd discuss what the person should have done and it made everyone think a lot about poker."

Unhappy in the academic world, Sklansky dropped out of the Wharton School after a year. He returned to Teaneck, where he briefly pursued a career as an actuary. "I hated it," he told Schwarz of his stint at the actuarial consulting firm Kwasha Lipton Group, in Fort Lee, New Jersey. "The only notable thing when I worked there was that was when calculators were first invented. . . . They were fairly expensive and fairly big, the size of an adding machine. But Kwasha Lipton was able to afford them for their people. I used them to figure out the odds on draw poker. So when I left there I was armed with all the information I needed to play." Unfulfilled by his work as an actuary, and realizing that "he didn't want to wear a tie," as his father told Schwarz, Sklansky set out to become a professional gambler, arriving in Las Vegas, Nevada, in the early 1970s. There, he earned a reputation as not only a good player but a theorist of the game. As a result he was approached by the Gambler's Book Club about writing a volume on his favorite version of poker, high-low split. Instead, Sklansky offered to write about a poker variation he had recently encountered, Texas Hold 'Em—which, according to Schwarz, was then played in only two casinos. (Soon afterward it became the most popular game in Las Vegas; it is now played to decide the winner of the annual World Series of Poker.) Sklansky told Schwarz, "I had a feeling Hold 'em would become big and I said to them I'd rather write a book on Hold 'em even though I barely played it because I had a feeling I could write a pretty good book."

In Texas Hold 'Em each player is dealt two cards face down ("hole cards"), while three "community" cards are placed face down in the center of the table. After the opening round of betting, the three community cards are turned face up (in what is called the "flop"), followed by another round of betting. Next, a fourth community card is turned face up (in what is called the "turn"). Players make a third round of bets, before a fifth card is turned face up (the "river"). Each player then attempts to construct the best five-card hand, using his or her hole cards and the community cards. Any player may use both, one, or neither of the hole cards, and any or all of the community cards.

Sklansky's *Hold 'Em Poker* (1976), the first book ever written on the game, explains how it is played, discusses the importance of the first two cards dealt, and shows how to read other players' "tells," or body language indicating their reactions to their hands. It also provides a system for ranking hands, listing them in order from strongest to weakest. "Beginners should latch on to *Hold 'Em Poker* before sitting down at their first tables," Scott Jacobson wrote for the *Kansas City Star* (July 17, 2004). "With plenty of graphics and hypothetical situations, Sklansky walks you through the deal, the strategy and finally the probabilities, all in a fairly conversational tone." The book has been updated several times to stay current with changes in the game's rules and theories. Howard Schwartz told Grochowski, "It remains the book that created millions of players and revealed material only the pros knew in the early days." Sklansky told Marc Schwarz, "I'm sure my book had something to do with the expansion of Hold 'em. There's a lot of people who became much more comfortable playing it once they were able to read about some of the basics." In *Theory of Poker* (1983), Sklansky recommended maximizing one's "positive expectation," or long-term profits, rather than trying to win dramatic individual hands.

Sklansky and Mason Malmuth began their collaboration in 1984, when Sklansky, by then a recognized poker expert, gave Malmuth lessons in playing Hold 'Em. Malmuth, who was working as a probability theory specialist for Northrop Corp., an airline manufacturer, "wanted to not have a job," as he told Konik; he had decided to explore gambling as an alternative to conventional employment. Sklansky tutored Malmuth at the Bicycle Club card room, in Los Angeles, revealing to Malmuth "what were then little-known secrets that give the accomplished player a demonstrable edge," as Konik wrote. Based on Sklansky's teaching, Malmuth compiled an extensive set of written notes, which the two published in 1988 as the book *Hold 'Em Poker for Advanced Players*. Sklansky and Malmuth then decided to form the company 2+2=4 (or simply Two Plus Two), its name a reference to the pair's use of mathematics in gambling; the company began publishing books by Sklansky, Malmuth, or both. For the books on which they collaborate, as Konik reported, Sklansky has been re-

sponsible for as much as 70 percent of the ideas presented, while Malmuth has taken on a similar share of the writing, elucidating sometimes complex concepts. Two Plus Two titles also include *Fighting Fuzzy Thinking in Poker, Gaming and Life* (1997), a collection of essays Sklansky had published in magazines devoted to gambling; some of the pieces are specifically about poker, while others tackle such subjects as discipline and will power. In 1997 Sklansky and Malmuth published *Gambling for a Living (How to Make $100,000 a Year)*. "Although the title sounds reminiscent of a late-night infomercial," Konik wrote, "the book is the straight dope. Instead of ridiculous theories, the authors advance irrefutable facts, showing which casino games are beatable, which are not, and why. They are realists, not fabulists. Their prose does not shimmer with the gloss of fantasy; it's dry, clear and honest. And it's true." Among the other Two Plus Two volumes are *Sklansky Talks Blackjack* (1999), *Tournament Poker for Advanced Players* (2002), and *No Limit Hold 'Em Theory and Practice* (2006), by Sklansky and Ed Miller. Sklansky announced on his Web site that on December 1, 2007, *Tournament Poker for Advanced Players: Expanded Edition* was to be published; the updated edition was to include more than 100 additional pages devoted to no-limit hold 'em tournaments. The Two Plus Two Web site, which features forums on poker, has in recent years become a "virtual clubhouse for bright twentysomething players," Daniel G. Habib wrote for *Sports Illustrated* (May 30, 2005).

In 1999 Sklansky was asked to join the scientific advisory board of Infectech Inc., a Pennsylvania-based biotechnology company (which in 2005 changed its name to Nanologix Inc.) specializing in high-speed testing to identify deadly bacteria in hospital patients. The company developed detection methods for bacteria such as Pseudomonas, a leading cause of death in cancer patients, and MAI, the chief bacterial infection of AIDS patients. Sklansky was recruited for his knowledge of mathematical probabilities. As Sklansky explained to a writer for *PR Newswire* (April 28, 1999): "There are situations that come up in medicine where once the information is gathered and the probability assessments are made, it is no longer a question for a doctor. It is now a question for a gambler." Mitchell Felder, a co-founder of the company, said to the reporter, "[Sklansky is] quite brilliant at understanding concepts of probability. . . . A lot of what he understands is very apropos to business concepts. For those reasons alone, he's a great asset." Sklansky said to *PR Newswire*, "I'm excited about the fact that I've been recognized finally by a mainstream organization who has acknowledged that in spite of the lack of a formal education I could be valuable. I'm very happy that this has happened."

In June 2007 Sklansky attempted to test his math and probability skills by reviving a controversial wager that he had made in 2003 regarding the intel-

2007 CURRENT BIOGRAPHY YEARBOOK   493

ligence of conservative "exclusionary" Christians. Addressing Christians who believed both that Jesus Christ was resurrected from the dead and that any person who did not hold that belief would go to hell after death, he challenged them to join him in taking the standardized SAT and GRE tests in half the normally allotted time and get scores higher than his. Sklansky wagered $50,000 and asked that any challenger confirm that he or she held those two beliefs by taking a polygraph test. On his Two Plus Two Internet magazine, twoplustwo.com (June2007), Sklansky used statistics to calculate that there were about 2,000 Christians in the United States who might be able to top his scores, assuming that Christians' intelligence quotients were distributed along the I.Q. bell curve the way other people's were. "But," Sklansky wrote, "I'm betting fifty grand they are not [able to attain scores higher than mine]. Their beliefs make them relatively stupid (or uninterested in learning). Or only relatively stupid people can come to such beliefs. One or the other. That is my contention. And this challenge might help demonstrate that." Sklansky sparked much criticism from those who said that his challenge was insulting and demonstrated his egotism. Among those critics was the record holder for most money won on the television quiz show *Jeopardy*, Ken Jennings, a member of the Church of Latter Day Saints, who wrote for his blog, as quoted by Erin Warner on pokerlistings.com (June 23, 2007), "Maybe this kind of bluster is expected in the poker world, but here in the real world, it makes you sound like an arrogant jackass." (Jennings's religious beliefs ruled out the possibility of his engaging in a wager such as Sklansky's.) Sklansky predicted that most Christian mathematicians would turn down the challenge not because they feared losing the competition, but because they would fail the polygraph test. Readily available sources do not reveal whether anyone took up Sklansky's challenge.

Sklansky has won three events at the World Series of Poker (WSOP), which is held annually in Las Vegas and draws thousands of participants. In 1982 he won two bracelets, in the $800 Mixed Doubles and $1,000 Draw Hi categories; the following year he won another, in the $1,000 Limit Omaha Hi category. He was the victor at the Poker by the Book invitational event of the World Poker Tour in 2004. As of 2006 he had won over $900,000 in broadcast live tournament events. In the first six months of 2007, he won $73,139.

Konik wrote that Sklansky is "prone to grandiloquent pronouncements and a conviction in his infallibility that might seem arrogant in anyone less bright." Sklansky said to Schwarz that the fame he has gained through gambling and writing feels "weird actually. It's not so much being recognized, but being stared at. It's a funny feeling. In fact during the World Series of Poker I get asked almost 10 times a day to sign an autograph." Sklansky has a son, Matthew, and lives in Henderson, Nevada. Discussing his parents' initial reaction to his be-

coming a professional gambler, Sklansky told Schwarz, "They were appalled. They've certainly come around now. Though I think my mother would still rather I was working at an office as an assistant manager."

—M.B.

Suggested Reading: *Chicago Sun-Times* p17 May 7, 2004; *Cigar Aficionado* (on-line) May/June 1998; *Kansas City Star* E p2 July 17, 2004; (Passaic County, New Jersey) *Herald News* C p4 July 12, 2005

Selected Books: *Hold 'Em Poker*, 1976; *Getting the Best of It*, 1982; *Theory of Poker*, 1983; *Hold 'Em Poker for Advanced Players*, 1988; *Fighting Fuzzy Thinking in Poker, Gaming and Life*, 1997; *Gambling for a Living (How to Make $100,000 a Year)* (with Mason Malmuth), 1997; *Sklansky Talks Blackjack*, 1999; *Tournament Poker for Advanced Players*, 2002; *Small Stakes Hold 'Em: Winning Big with Expert Play*, 2004; *No Limit Hold 'Em Theory and Practice*, 2006; *Tournament Poker for Advanced Players: Expanded Edition*, 2007

Smith, Lovie

May 8, 1958– Football coach

Address: Chicago Bears, Conway Park, 1000 Football Dr., Lake Forest, IL 60045

The popular image of a football coach is of a person who motivates players by screaming and swearing. Lovie Smith, head coach of the Chicago Bears of the National Football League (NFL), stands in contrast to that model. "When he's ticked off, he'll say, 'Jiminy,'" the coach's wife, MaryAnne Smith, told Jarrett Bell for *USA Today* (December 28, 2006). "Now, if you get a 'Jiminy Christmas' out of him, he is really frustrated and disgusted." The absence of swearing does not seem to have hampered Smith's coaching ability. On January 21, 2007 Smith's Bears defeated the New Orleans Saints to advance to the Super Bowl, making Smith the first African-American coach to achieve that feat—just hours before Tony Dungy, head coach of the Indianapolis Colts, became the second black coach to do so. Although Indianapolis emerged victorious, defeating Chicago 29–17, the season was a successful one for the Bears, marking the first time in 21 seasons that the team had appeared in the Super Bowl and bringing to mind the halcyon days of "Iron" Mike Ditka's dominant Bears of the mid-1980s. Smith, who was named the 13th head coach of Chicago's storied franchise on January 15, 2004, set a team record for fastest progress toward a National Football Conference (NFC) championship, winning back-to-back titles in 2005 and 2006; in 2005

Jonathan Daniel/Getty Images

Lovie Smith

he also set a Bears record for victories by a sopho-more coach, with 11. Prior to joining the NFL, Smith worked his way through the ranks of colle-giate coaching, serving as a linebackers' coach for the University of Tulsa, the University of Wiscon-sin, Arizona State University, and the University of Kentucky and as a defensive backs' coach for the University of Tennessee and Ohio State Universi-ty. In 1996 Dungy hired him to become the line-backers' coach for the Tampa Bay Buccaneers of the NFL, for which the two men formed an innova-tive defensive strategy known as the Tampa 2, helping to transform one of the weakest defenses in the league into a juggernaut. Following Dungy's departure from the Buccaneers, in 2001, Smith signed on as defensive coordinator for the St. Louis Rams, a post he held for three seasons. In 2005 he was awarded "Coach of the Year" honors after turning a moribund Bears team into NFC titlehold-ers. Smith's coaching has been defined by a father-ly loyalty and a calm, low-key style. Sean Gregory, writing for *Time* (October 23, 2006), noted that during the years Smith worked under other coach-es, he had the greatest respect for those who felt that "screaming was for guys that didn't have any-thing to say." Similarly, Smith told Kevin Chappell for *Ebony* (December 2004), "Yelling and scream-ing, that's one of the most overrated [coaching] ideas out there. . . . What I've found is that if you tell guys what to do . . . they will do it. You don't have to belittle them, threaten them. I simply tell them what I want done. If they can't do it, there are other guys waiting for the chance to do it."

The third of five children, Lovie Lee Smith was born on May 8, 1958 in Gladewater, Texas, 100 miles east of Dallas, to Thurman and Mae Smith, who were devout Christians. (In choosing his name before his birth, Smith's parents—who were cer-tain they were going to have a daughter, having had two sons—settled on the nickname of the boy's great-aunt Lavana.) Smith grew up in the East Tex-as farming town of Big Sandy, whose population was 300. As a fifth-grader, displaying an ambition rare in his impoverished surroundings, Smith re-portedly declared to his entire class that he was go-ing to be a football coach when he grew up. Smith's father was an alcoholic who had trouble holding down jobs; his mother, a factory worker, barely made enough money to sustain the household. They nonetheless taught the boy to work hard, lead a disciplined life, and maintain a strong sense of faith. From an early age the good-natured and soft-spoken boy had various jobs, doing construction work, picking berries, and loading watermelons. As his older brothers moved away, and his father's alcoholism led to his being hospitalized much of the time, Smith took on more responsibility at home. His mother recalled to Jaime Aron for the Associated Press (January 28, 2007), "Everything just kind of fell on him. That made him grow up."

Inspired by the Dallas Cowboys, Smith played defense for the Big Sandy High School Wildcats, winning all-state honors for three consecutive years. His hard-hitting style and intensity on the playing field won the admiration of his teammates. Smith also excelled in the classroom; he was a member of the National Honor Society and was voted by his classmates (33 in total) as "Most Like-ly to Succeed." Attending the University of Tulsa on a football scholarship, Smith played linebacker and safety and went on to become a two-time All-American and a three-time All-Missouri Confer-ence defensive back. While in college Smith re-ceived a call from his father, who announced that he had given up alcohol for good. Smith said to Jar-rett Bell, "We dealt with alcoholism my whole life. Family never leaves family. That's where I got that from and my mother could have left my father many times, but she didn't. She stayed there." His father remained sober for the next 20 years, until his death, in 1996, from emphysema.

Meanwhile, given his success at Tulsa, Smith had hopes of playing for the NFL. A series of inju-ries in his senior year ruined his chances of doing so; he tried out for several NFL teams and was giv-en serious consideration by the Atlanta Falcons but never made the final cut. After graduating from the University of Tulsa in 1979, with a bachelor's degree, Smith went back to his hometown to take a coaching job with his high school's junior-varsity football team. He also taught history at the school. As a coach he led his squad of seventh- and eighth-graders to a perfect season, in addition to helping out the varsity team in his spare time. In 1981 Smith took a job as head coach of Tulsa's Cascia Hall Prep School, and from 1983 to 1986 he coached linebackers at the University of Tulsa. He served the same function at the University of Wis-consin, beginning in 1987, and then at Arizona State University, from 1988 to 1991.

Smith had just begun coaching at Arizona State when one of the defining events in his life occurred. One day, while he was checking filters in his family's pool, his son Matthew, who had come up behind him without his noticing, fell into the water. Unable to swim, Smith initially felt helpless; soon he yelled for his wife and jumped into the pool after his son. Shortly after his wife performed CPR on Matthew, the boy regained consciousness. Since that incident, Smith has felt the need to give people—particularly his players—second chances after they make mistakes. "I was no kind of hero at all," Smith said to Jarrett Bell. "I let my guard down and let [Matthew] down. . . . That's why you always have to pay attention to the smallest details."

Smith served as the linebackers' coach at the University of Kentucky in 1992, then moved to the University of Tennessee to work as a defensive backs' coach from 1993 to 1994. He held the same title in 1995 at Ohio State University. In 1996 Smith was hired by Tony Dungy to become linebackers' coach for the Tampa Bay Buccaneers of the NFL, for whom Dungy had just taken on the position of head coach. Dungy would become Smith's good friend and mentor. "Right away I knew Tony was a special guy and it was good to see someone with such a great reputation who had the same basic philosophies I have on life and football. I think in this profession, you want the good guys to win, and I knew that Tony was one of the good guys right away; I felt blessed to be on his staff," Smith recalled to Melody K. Hoffman and Kevin Chappell for *Jet* (February 19, 2007). Prior to the two men's arrival, Tampa's defense had not ranked above 20th in the league in four seasons, and the team as a whole was among the worst in the NFL. With Dungy, Smith, and the team's new defensive coordinator, Monte Kiffin, in place, the Buccaneers underwent a metamorphosis. The three coaches devised a blitzkrieg-like defensive strategy that became known as the Tampa 2, inspired by the Pittsburgh Steelers' defense of the 1970s. A variation of the Cover 2 formation, which requires zone coverage rather than man-to-man defense, the Tampa 2 calls for four linemen, three linebackers, two cornerbacks, and two safeties and relies heavily on aggressiveness, speed, and simplicity; the strategy is also characterized by gang tackles and a hard-hitting secondary unit, which often leads to turnovers. By 1998 Tampa's defense ranked second in the league, and during their five seasons under Smith's tutelage, the Buccaneers' defenses allowed fewer than 300 points each year. A number of Smith's players went to the Pro Bowl; he helped to develop Derrick Brooks and Hardy Nickerson into two of the best linebackers in the NFL and John Lynch into a powerful free safety.

Although the Buccaneers made it to the postseason four times under Dungy, the team's management fired him in 2001, due to their repeated losses in the play-offs. Smith left at the same time and became the St. Louis Rams' defensive coordinator

that year. The season before Smith arrived, St. Louis's defense was ranked 23d in the NFL and allowed more than 29 points per game. In his first season he turned their defense into a powerhouse, helping them to reach the Super Bowl and to allow fewer points and yards per game than they had the previous year. Smith orchestrated a Ram defense that posted shutouts in 2001 and 2003 and helped the team rank among the top 10 in nearly every defensive category in the league. In 2003 Smith served as the Rams' assistant head coach as well as defensive coordinator.

On January 15, 2004 the Chicago Bears hired Smith, giving him a four-year contract worth $1.35 million per year. In the wake of the Bears' dismal 7–9 record in the 2003 season, Smith went to Chicago with the intention of creating a team that would compete in the Super Bowl. Fostering an aggressive style among his players, Smith helped Chicago's defense improve from 22d in the league in 2003 to 13th in 2004. The team as a whole struggled in his first season, finishing with a record of 5–11, due to a series of injuries. Then, in 2005, Smith's Bears made a dramatic turnaround. After winning only one of their first four contests, due to a poor passing game, the team compiled an 11–5 record, becoming only the 20th team in the league's history to reach the play-offs after starting the season at 1–3. The Bears used a solid running game and strong defense to win eight consecutive games during the regular season, Chicago's longest streak since Mike Ditka's 1985 Super Bowl–winning team. The Bears' hopes of appearing in the Super Bowl in the 2005 season were shattered by the Carolina Panthers, who upset the Bears, 29–21, in postseason play. In Smith's first two seasons in Chicago, his defense allowed an average of only 16.7 points per game and 56 total touchdowns; it had the lowest opponent-passer rating, opponent third-down percentage, fourth-down conversion percentage, and opponent red-zone touchdown percentage in the league. The Bears' worst-to-first improvement led the Associated Press to name Smith the NFL Coach of the Year.

The Bears opened their 2006 season with a 26–0 shutout of the Green Bay Packers. The rivalry between the two teams was one of the most bitter in all of sports; after the Bears shut out the Packers on October 17, 1991, Green Bay went on to win 22 of the next 31 games against Chicago. The Bears' 2006 season opener thus indicated a shift in power in the division. Smith's team won their next six games; following a loss to the Miami Dolphins, they won six of their last eight games of the season to capture their second consecutive NFC North Division title. On January 14, 2007 the Bears squared off on their home turf, Soldier Field, against the Seattle Seahawks; rebounding from his dismal late-season performance against the Packers, the Bears' quarterback Rex Grossman led his team to a dramatic 27–24 win in overtime, and Chicago advanced to the NFC Championship game, against the New Orleans Saints. With snow falling on Soldier Field, the Saints acquired more offensive yards than their opponents, but Chicago forced four turnovers, which helped secure their first Super Bowl berth in 21 seasons—and made Smith the first African-American head coach ever to reach that position. Just hours later, Tony Dungy led his Indianapolis Colts to victory over the New England Patriots, becoming the second African-American coach to reach the Super Bowl.

Given the dearth of black head coaches in the NFL, many saw the 2007 Super Bowl matchup as football's equivalent of Jackie Robinson's breaking the baseball color barrier in 1947. U.S. senator Barack Obama of Illinois, a Democratic presidential hopeful and longtime Bears fan, said to Fran Spielman for the *Chicago Sun-Times* (January 23, 2007), "Obviously, to see two African-American coaches go to the Super Bowl when it's been historically difficult for black coaches to break in to the NFL is terrific. But what makes it even better is that they're both men of humility. . . . They never trash-talk. They're not yellers and screamers on the sidelines. They're just a couple of class individuals, and you can tell the loyalty and affection their players have for them. So it's a wonderful story—not just for African-Americans, but for all Americans to see men like that who are good fathers, who are good leaders, who do things the right way [and] succeed. That's a good lesson for all of us."

Super Bowl XLI started well for the Bears: their receiver Devin Hester returned the opening kickoff 92 yards for a touchdown, and on the ensuing Colts possession, the Bears' Chris Harris intercepted a pass from Peyton Manning. By halftime, however, Chicago had lost momentum and was trailing Indianapolis 16–14. In the second half Manning and the Colts kept control of the game; Rex Grossman threw two costly interceptions in the fourth quarter, ruining a last-chance Bears rally, and the Colts won, 29–17. Manning was named the game's Most Valuable Player, and Dungy became the first black head coach ever to win a Super Bowl. Commenting on Dungy's landmark victory, Smith told Jeff Zillgitt, writing for *USA Today* (February 5, 2007), "If someone had to win besides us, I'm glad it's Tony. . . . We are going to continue to take steps in building our program. This is our third year, and I felt like we took a big step. Hopefully next season we can take one more step and finish the job." Even after the Super Bowl, Smith remained the lowest-paid coach in the league—until the Bears organization granted him a new, four-year contract worth $22 million.

Lovie Smith abstains from drinking, smoking, swearing, and—to the dismay of his wife of 26 years, MaryAnne—dancing. He even skipped the ceremonial slow dance at their wedding. "I've told him that it's the one thing in life that we've got to do, but he won't budge . . . ," MaryAnne Smith said to Jarrett Bell in 2006. "He doesn't do anything a little bit. He goes all the way." The couple have three sons: Miles, who plays high-school football; Mikal, a University of Arizona alumnus, who

coaches defensive backs at International University; and Matthew, who played basketball in high school and is now a pre-med student at Northwestern University. Smith also has twin grandsons, Malachi and Noah. He enjoys listening to music, especially funk classics, including songs by Parliament Funkadelic, on his iPod.

Because his mother's blindness is caused in part by type-2 diabetes, and both his brother Will and sister, Sandra, are diabetic, Smith supports the American Diabetes Association (ADA). He donates 10 tickets for every Bears home game to children suffering from the disease and participates in ADA-sponsored events, such as the Tour de Cure Bike Ride and the ADA Care to Cure Gala. In addition, with his wife, he co-chairs the Lovie Smith and MaryAnne Smith Foundation, which gives eligible high-school students from low socioeconomic backgrounds the opportunity to attend college.
—C.C.

Suggested Reading: *Baptist Press* (on-line) Jan. 30, 2007; Chicago Bears Web Site; *Chicago Sun-Times* Sports p109 Mar. 2, 2007; *Ebony* (on-line) Dec. 2004; *Sports Illustrated* p88 Oct. 22, 2001; *Time* p76 Oct. 23, 2006; *USA Today* C p1+ Dec. 28, 2006, A p1+ Feb. 2, 2007, C p7 Feb. 5, 2007

Solomon, Phil

Jan. 3, 1954– Filmmaker; educator

Address: Dept. of Film Studies, Macky 119, University of Colorado, Boulder, CO 80309

"I muck film up, often with chemical treatments, so that the image is not so easily read . . . ," the filmmaker Phil Solomon told Josh McDaniel for *EMedia: The Digital Studio Magazine* (September 2003). "Yet the treatments I perform are, I hope, expressive, and not just a decorative gesture. I try to make the emulsion itself have as much expression as anything else. That's been the challenge of my work, to make the look of the film expressive of what I'm saying." An associate professor of film studies at the University of Colorado at Boulder for the past 16 years, Solomon began experimenting with emulsion-covered celluloid film as a college student, in the mid-1970s. He shot what is considered his first professional film, *The Passage of the Bride*, in 1978. The 20 films he has made since then have been shown in solo or group exhibitions in all of the foremost venues for experimental film in the United States and Europe, and he has won many honors, awards, and grants for his work. Yet among American moviegoers, Solomon and his films remain largely unknown. "Mr. Solomon's stunningly beautiful films have an emotional power that might well attract more viewers, if not for the maddening divisions that find a few rarefied films clas-

Courtesy of Phil Solomon

Phil Solomon

me the optical printer was a way of re-seeing the world two-dimensionally, with another layer of aesthetic distance," he told Scott MacDonald for the book *A Critical Cinema 5: Interviews with Independent Filmmakers* (2006). "There's something about the process of rephotography at the frame level that's very in tune with my personality; it has to do with a kind of artistic introversion, and with the idea of working with a secret magic machine." In an article for *Music Works* (Summer 1995, online), a Canadian quarterly, the great experimental filmmaker Stan Brakhage—whose name is closely linked with Solomon's—described the results of Solomon's physical or chemical alterations as "transformative mulch" and "aesthetic compost." "Solomon disintegrates the entire pictorial 'fabric' . . . of old movies in various states of emulsion rot," Brakhage explained. "He utilizes the organic mold and dry crack patterns, the natural decay of the footage, until the original subject matter, its anima, crawls with the textural 'maggots' of its own chemical decomposition and dissolves in a beautiful display of multi-faceted light."

In a conversation with an interviewer for *Cinemad* (December 2006, on-line), Solomon said that in the late 1970s, when he began to envision himself in the "historical trajectory of art-making, rather than only considering the Hollywood industrial model of making films," he "no longer thought about making 'avant-garde' films, or 'radical cinema,' or 'underground' cinema. . . . I simply thought about making films along the same lines of the individual artisan tradition in the other kindred arts of painting, poetry, photography and music. Individual, rather than collaborative filmmaking. Economy of gesture—retaining only the essential images. An emphasis on poetic form, including visual rhymes, metaphor, ellipsis, and ambiguity—reading between the lines, so to speak, and therefore reading between elliptical juxtapositions of non-linear, non-narrative sequenced shots, and so on. I find the analogy of most narrative film as akin to popular literature to be a useful one. My films seem much closer in their temperament, ideas and tendencies to the form and content of certain—somewhat hermetic—poets like Emily Dickinson, John Ashbery, Wallace Stevens, and Jorie Graham. Or textural narrative painters like Albert Pinkham Ryder, Francis Bacon, and Anselm Kiefer. Or the polyphonic re-imagined, and re-remembered aural American narratives of [the 20th-century composer] Charles Ives. Or the ambiguous, lush, and mysterious ambient landscapes in the organic electronic music of Brian Eno." Solomon told Scott MacDonald, "It is absolutely essential to me that my work somehow comes out of my life experience," but that the viewer need not know anything about him in order to relate to the work; as he explained, "The premise of all my work is that there *is* a private core of references but *also*, I hope, enough emotional truth so that the meaning will emerge even if you don't know the biographical data."

sified (read: ghettoized) as art, while the vast majority are relegated to the commercial trough . . . ," the film critic Manohla Dargis, who is among the most enthusiastic of Solomon's admirers, wrote for the *New York Times* (November 18, 2005). "Although part of a long avant-garde tradition, Mr. Solomon makes films that look like no others I've seen. The conceit of the filmmaker as auteur has rarely been more appropriate or defensible." "The wow factor of Mr. Solomon's finest films can be as difficult to convey as the deep feeling they instill in the viewer," Dargis continued. "One of the pleasures of this sort of work is how it can loosen the grip that narrative traditionally has on the medium, inspiring different ways of seeing and feeling. . . . Created in the shadow of the mainstream, films like these underscore the stultifying sameness of most movies, an industrial uniformity that reminds me of a film project [the German playwright and theater director] Bertolt Brecht conjured up . . . titled 'Boy Meets Girl, So What.' The liberating effect of Mr. Solomon's work suggests a rather different realm: Film Meets Vision, Rejoice!"

The method Solomon has adopted to create his films is extraordinarily painstaking: like the process used in traditional cel animation for most of the 20th century, it involves the manipulation of each individual frame of film. Solomon uses film that he has shot himself and, to a greater extent, frames gleaned from what is called found footage— old movies made by others, often people whose identities are no longer known. He works with chemicals and a device called an optical printer, or step printer, which makes films of previously created films—a process called rephotography. "For

The son of Samuel David Solomon and the former Ruth Ann Rozencrantz, Philip Stewart Solomon was born in the borough of Manhattan, in New York City, on January 3, 1954. With his older sister, he spent his first few years in Queens, another of the city's boroughs; then, in 1959, the family moved to Monsey, New York, a short distance north of the city. Solomon's father worked as a butcher until he and his wife became the co-owners of a car-rental agency. Solomon told MacDonald that his father made home movies of the family with an 8mm camera, and his projection of them, on a Bell & Howell machine, "always seemed so special to me. It wasn't like today with videocassettes where kids can pop the films into the VCR themselves. My father had to get out the whole apparatus, set up the screen; it was a rare and exciting event." As a child Solomon "was drawn to the idea of making tiny worlds," as he recalled to Scott MacDonald. "I played with super-hero models and created little movie sets in the landscapes of my bed." Solomon has traced many of his artistic impulses to such play, as well as to observations and impressions dating from his early years. His father, hoping that the boy would become a physician, gave him microscopes and chemistry sets and books about the history of medicine. His fascination when he watched the movements of one-celled animals in his microscope "inadvertently led to, or at least fed, my love of peering down the 'corridor' of the optical printer," Solomon said to MacDonald. He also enjoyed reading comic books and drawing. In junior high school he won a school art competition with his caricatures of teachers.

By his own account, Solomon was also "a child of television," perhaps a member of "the first or second generation to be so hooked," as he said to the *Cinemad* interviewer; his favorite TV programs included Saturday-afternoon horror and science-fiction films, *The Twilight Zone*, *Star Trek*, and *The Ed Sullivan Show*. By the time he was 14, he had begun making 8mm films, most of which parodied movies or TV programs. In high school Solomon often traveled to New York City to see motion pictures by such European directors as Federico Fellini, Ingmar Bergman, and Michelangelo Antonioni and by American directors including Francis Ford Coppola, Bob Rafelson, and Martin Scorsese. He also admired the work of the filmmakers Buster Keaton, Charlie Chaplin, and Orson Welles and loved movies from what he considers the golden era of cinema in the U.S.—the 1940s to early 1970s. "I think there is something in my work that very much references these films, which remain so vivid in my consciousness, my daydreams and—most unfortunately—my romantic ideals," he remarked to the *Cinemad* interviewer.

After he completed high school, Solomon enrolled at Harpur College, a division of the State University of New York (SUNY) at Binghamton, with the intention of becoming a veterinarian. He switched his major from pre-med to film after taking a course in cinema taught by Ken Jacobs, a noted maker of experimental films and the co-founder of the college's film program. At the first lecture Jacobs showed *The Flicker* (1965), a film consisting of totally white and totally black screens alternating with increasing rapidity. That work and the other avant-garde films that Jacobs showed left Solomon feeling "perplexed, but mostly frustrated and suspicious," as he told the *Cinemad* interviewer, because he "didn't know how to consider the screen as a formal rectangle with two-dimensional spatial tensions, rather than as a window to a daydream. I didn't have an informed understanding of what we might call, for want of a better term, the 'aesthetic' experience, as opposed to the semi-hypnotic trance state induced by the lull of complex identification cues that literally entrances us when we experience narrative film. . . . It took me some time to realize that the condition of watching most narrative films was actually antithetical to experiencing the contemplation of form, which in my mind is the essence of artistic apperception." Jacobs and his SUNY colleagues taught filmmaking as an art rather than a craft and emphasized visual aesthetics over narrative. Gradually, Solomon recalled to MacDonald, "as I was becoming more disenchanted with the soulless studies of pre-med science and math, I found myself, much to my parents' dismay, completely committed to this exciting and weird little scene of poetic filmmaking, mostly because of the passion and intelligence of the teachers I had the good fortune to engage with. I am an artist of film *because* of the academy [that is, college], not despite it."

While Solomon was an undergraduate, Stan Brakhage visited SUNY-Binghamton to show and discuss his work, which (like Solomon's) has been described as an effort to translate poetry to the medium of cinema; few of his films have narratives, most are silent, and a central theme of many is the process of seeing. Brakhage's movies influenced Solomon so powerfully that for years after he saw some of them (Brakhage, who died in 2003, made about 400), he had difficulty in separating his ideas and his approach to filmmaking from Brakhage's; as he told MacDonald, much of his early work, in the latter half of the 1970s, was "immature in form and derivative, particularly in still trying to come to terms with Brakhage." He overcame his difficulties through rephotography with an optical printer. The experimental filmmakers Peter Kubelka, who taught at SUNY-Binghamton as a visiting professor, and Saul Levine, with whom Solomon studied production at SUNY, also strongly affected his ideas. "What I learned from Saul . . . was to appreciate the beauty of the mundane," he told MacDonald.

Solomon's senior thesis at SUNY, a film entitled *Night Light* (1975), showed clouds moving in front of the moon, images of children playing with flashlights, lightning storms, and nighttime bombing scenes shot by others during wartime. Solomon described *Night Light* to the *Cinemad* interviewer as "a rather unformed but beautiful film. Really like a sketch," and he told MacDonald that he considers it his first "fully realized" film. Greeted with enthusiasm by SUNY teachers and students, it later served as the basis for his highly praised film *Nocturne* (1980), a product of several years' work. (He revised *Nocturne* in 1989.) Inserting found footage into his films, he told *Cinemad*, "seemed to broaden the scope of my own material. In lieu of actors, found footage gave me allegorical images to work with that could speak to what I thought were larger concerns than just a formal assembly of my technical experiments. I'm very taken with that idea, to using found footage as something that is archeologically 'true.'"

After he earned a B.A. degree, with honors, in 1975, Solomon moved to Irondequoit, New York, on Lake Ontario, where he lived in a small house in the woods with a longtime school friend, Wrick Wolff (now a composer, performer, and audio engineer). The pair worked as waiters and spent their free time making movies on 8mm and 16mm film; "investigat[ing] ecstatic and illuminating drug usage," as Solomon put it to *Current Biography*; and listening to music, particularly to compositions by Brian Wilson, Charles Ives, Brian Eno, and progressive rock bands. To prepare himself for a teaching career in the arts—and also to "prolong adolescence" as much as possible, as he told *Current Biography*—Solomon taught himself art history and also sneaked into the prestigious Eastman School of Music, in nearby Rochester, to learn to read musical scores.

In 1978 Solomon began teaching night classes in filmmaking and cinema aesthetics and analysis at the Massachusetts College of Art, in Boston. He also entered a graduate program at that school, where he made the film *The Passage of the Bride* (1978). For *Passage*, he manipulated a single 100-foot roll of home-movie footage that showed a wedding held in the 1920s or 1930s (its date is uncertain) and the newly married couple on their honeymoon. Solomon told MacDonald, "I became utterly fascinated with the moment [in the reel] when the woman runs across the lawn, and I kept watching the roll over and over again, and finally put it on the printer and started to work with it. I did everything I could to it: I bi-packed it with a variety of elemental images, I slowed it down, sped it up, I went in close, I re-photographed several generations." (In bipacking, two rolls of film pass through a camera simultaneously.) Writing for the *Village Voice* (May 23, 1989), Manohla Dargis described *The Passage of the Bride* as "hypnotic, dreamy. Solomon compulsively repeats recognizable images until they melt like distilled essences of the originals." Dargis also wrote, "Solomon's work—some of the best of contemporary experimental film—is difficult. Its optical and moral density eludes language, as if the films, which are often dark and cracked, were a palimpsest of obscured meaning." *The Passage of the Bride* earned Solomon first prize at the 1979 New England Student Film Festival, and it was nominated for an Academy Award as best student film of the year in the category of experimental works.

Solomon earned a master of fine arts (M.F.A.) degree from the Massachusetts College of Art in 1980. He served as a teaching assistant at Harvard University, in Cambridge, Massachusetts, from 1979 to 1981 and won that school's Distinction in Teaching Award in 1981. Concurrently with his other activities, for about 10 years he worked as a film projectionist in an 11-auditorium theater in Boston.

In the early 1980s Solomon began to use the T/I button ("T" for "time exposure," "I" for "instantaneous") on his Bolex movie camera. "I started to do these time exposures quite accidentally," he recalled to the *Cinemad* interviewer, "not quite knowing what I was doing. I got back this roll of film shot at night, with about a second of footage that looked like it was the middle of the afternoon. That just floored me. It opened up new possibilities for experimentation and then expression. That's the way my work often evolves. I'll bump into a technique and then find a way to use the technique expressively, essentially."

Solomon told *Current Biography* that until his professional "coming-out party," in 1980, at the Collective for Living Cinema in New York, arranged by a former SUNY-Binghamton classmate of his, he showed his work only to close friends. Even after that event he rarely exhibited his films in public. Among the few that were so exhibited was *What's Out Tonight Is Lost* (1983), which—in a departure from the sharp cuts and contrasts of some of his earlier work—reflects his use of smoother editing techniques and a greater number of parallel images. Solomon told MacDonald, "I wanted to soften the juxtapositions of images and became very intrigued by dissolves; and since then, almost all my work has been involved with trying to find new ways to have one image placed meaningfully next to another." Since 1988, thanks in part to his befriending of show organizers in some major galleries in New York City, Boston, and San Francisco, California, Solomon's films have appeared before audiences regularly in solo and group exhibitions. (He did not aggressively promote himself, however, until he needed an impressive résumé to gain employment in a college or university.)

In his film *The Secret Garden* (1988), Solomon combined footage of water out-of-doors and sections of *The Wizard of Oz* to evoke the human expulsion from the Garden of Eden. That work won an honorable mention at the 1988 Black Maria Film and Video Festival, held at New Jersey City University. (Through the years Solomon has won five first prizes at that festival.) *Remains to Be Seen* and *The Exquisite Hour*, both produced in 1989, dealt with his father's death and the impending death of his mother, who was terminally ill. Those films include video and audio recordings that Solomon had made of his parents while they were hospitalized. *Remains to Be Seen* and *The Exquisite Hour* were among the *Village Voice*'s top 10 films of 1989, and in *Sight and Sound* magazine (December 1992), Stan Brakhage included *Remains to Be Seen* among the top 10 films of all time. *Remains to Be Seen* also won first prize, experimental category, at the 1990 Oberhausen International Short Film Festival, in Germany. Solomon revised *Remains to Be Seen* and *The Exquisite Hour* in 1994, and the next year the latter won the Marvin Felheim Award (first prize, experimental category) at the Ann Arbor Film Festival and the Judge's Award at the Onion City Film Festival, held in Chicago, Illinois. Also in 1995 Solomon made *The Snowman*, which he has described as "a meditation on burial, decay, and memory" and "a belated Kaddish" (in Judaism, the mourner's prayer) for his father. *The Snowman* earned the Jurors' Award (first prize) at the Black Maria Film Festival and was named one of the top 10 films of 1995 in *Film Comment*'s critics' poll.

The deaths of Solomon's parents and the departure from Boston of many of his friends left Solomon "mentally freed," in his words, to move to other parts of the country. In 1990 he served as a visiting artist at both the San Francisco Art Institute and San Francisco State University, in California. The following year he secured a teaching position at the University of Colorado at Boulder. He applied for the job partly so that he could become better acquainted with Brakhage, who was on the school's faculty. "I never could have anticipated what was to come—that [Brakhage] would own all of my work, write about it, that we would make films together, that he would be my best friend in Boulder," Solomon told *Current Biography*. He and Brakhage collaborated on four films: *Elementary Phrases* (1994), *Concrescence* (1996), *Alternating Currents* (1999–2002), and *Seasons . . .* (2002). To create *Seasons*, Brakhage etched Japanese-style patterns onto film using dental tools and also applied paint, after which Solomon manipulated each image with an optical printer. Since Brakhage's death, Solomon has continued to promote his work, in part through the college courses that he teaches. Currently, he is working on a book-length compilation derived from Brakhage's Sunday salons, to be titled *A Snail's Trail in the Moonlight: Conversations with Brakhage*.

At the University of Colorado at Boulder, Solomon told *Cinemad*, he has complete creative freedom both as a teacher and a filmmaker, and he has received "generous" funding. The school's film library contains an abundance of movies on celluloid as well as on DVD and video. Solomon has said that without the many grants the university has awarded him, he would not have been able to make his films. He has also received grants from the National Endowment for the Arts (in 1983 and 1991), the Massachusetts Council on the Arts (1983), and the Colorado Council on the Arts (1997).

In what he described to *Cinemad* as a "very wonderful experience," in 2002 Solomon worked in Hollywood for a few days on a credit sequence for the movie *The Mothman Prophecies* (2002), directed by Mark Pellington. Although his suggestions for the sequence were not used, mostly for financial reasons, and the job exhausted him, he learned a great deal about the Hollywood film industry through his conversations with Pellington and the preproduction crew, design and special-effects team, and cinematographer (Fred Murphy). "I gained a little insight into that world," he told the *Cinemad* interviewer, "and was definitely reassured that I wasn't cut out for it, both temperamentally and physically." He said to Scott MacDonald, "As a filmmaker, I've always identified much more with the experience of the single artist painting or writing a poem or composing music out of some private personal necessity, rather than the collaborative nature of the industrial model of making films."

In 1999 Solomon began making the as-yet-unfinished *The Twilight Psalms: A Cine-Poem for the Twentieth Century*, seven short works that he has characterized as "a series of painterly audio/visual tone poems." Each film focuses on an individual's experience of an important 20th-century event and has the title of an episode of *The Twilight Zone*. (Solomon has dedicated his series to *The Twilight Zone*'s creator, Rod Serling.) In an on-line blurb for the 37th New York Film Festival, held in 1999, Solomon described *Twilight Psalm I: The Lateness of the Hour* as "a deep blue overture to the series. Breathing in the cool night airs, breathing out a children's song; then whispering a prayer for a night of easeful sleep." In a review of *Twilight Psalm II: Walking Distance* for the *New York Times* (October 9, 1999), Stephen Holden wrote, "Solomon's supremely lyrical *Psalm* imagines a movie extracted from a rusted medieval film can left over from the Bronze Age. What unfolds on the screen suggests an ancient abstract painting encrusted with rust and sand behind which human faces half-form and disappear, suggesting eons of time and civilizations rising and falling. As the film's hues metamorphose in tandem with a shifting abstract soundtrack, *Psalm* evokes not only rust and sand but fire, wind and oceans as well, a never-ending cycle of creation and destruction." *Psalm III: Night of the Meek*, according to Solomon, is a *kindertotenlied* (a song about the deaths of children) "in black and silver on a night of gods and monsters." He told *Current Biography* that *Psalm IV: On Thursday We Leave for Home* is, "in a way, [about] 'the greatest generation'—about my father returning home from WWII, raising a family in the American suburbs, growing old, moving to Florida and dying . . .—the second half of the last century." *Psalm II* won the Douglas Wandrei Award for best lighting design at the 2000 Ann Arbor (Michigan) Film Festival and second prize at the 2001 Art Cité International Film Festival, held in Windsor, Ontario, Canada.

Solomon's *Innocence and Despair* (2002) is one of about 30 short works made by documentary and experimental filmmakers as part of Underground Zero, a collaborative project organized soon after the September 11, 2001 terrorist attacks. Solomon has described his five-minute contribution as "an underwater lullaby for my hometown, in another time, an engulfed cathedral of innocence and loss." Between 2005 and 2007 he made three films that made use of the video and computer game *Grand Theft Auto: San Andreas*, developed by Rockstar Games. Set in a fictionalized version of California, the game allows players to navigate the digital environment and interact with computer-generated characters and vehicles. For his so-called San Andreas trilogy, Solomon used that interactive platform to create the films *Untitled (for David Gatten)*, made with the experimental filmmaker Mark LaPore; *Faultline*; and *Rehearsals for Retirement*, in each of which he controlled the actions of the game's character. (David Gatten was a friend of Solomon and LaPore; LaPore died in September 2007, shortly after the completion of *Untitled*.) In a *Cinema Scope* (number 30) article posted on Michael Sicinski's Web site, academichack.com, Sicinski noted that ignoring the game's narrative structure had made it possible for Solomon to explore the limits of the game's elements and "their ability to generate mood and meaning in relative isolation." *Untitled* and *Rehearsals for Retirement* were shown at the 14th annual Chicago Underground Film Festival in August 2007.

Solomon recently completed *American Falls*, a six-channel digital installation that will debut at the Corcoran Gallery, in Washington, D.C., in 2008. Inspirations for the installation included Frederick Church's painting *Niagara Falls* (1857); murals by Diego Rivera and other artists employed during the 1930s by the federal Works Progress Administration (WPA, later renamed Work Projects Administration); war memorials in the nation's capital; the 1967 *Star Trek* episode "The City on the Edge of Forever"; and 20th-century newsreels. In a University of Colorado news release (August 30, 2007, online), Solomon was quoted as saying that *American Falls* reflects both his "great hope, stemming from a lifelong love for this American experiment of ours that seemed so vivid to me during my television-infused childhood" and his deep concern for the "present and future directions" of the U.S. The project won the 2007 Thatcher Hoffman Smith Creativity in Motion Prize, awarded every two years by the University of Oklahoma's College of Arts and Sciences to a work in any field of creativity.

In 2001 Solomon won the Marinus Smith Teaching Award from the Parents Association of the University of Colorado at Boulder. He lives in Broomfield, Colorado, midway between Boulder and Denver.

—M.B.

Suggested Reading: Canyon Cinema Web site; channel.creative-capitol.org/-resumes/solomon.pdf; *Cinemad* (on-line) Dec. 2006; *EMedia* (on-line) Sep. 2003; *Music Works* (on-line) Summer 1995; *New York Times* E p3 Nov. 18, 2005; MacDonald, Scott. *A Critical Cinema 5: Interviews with Independent Filmmakers*, 2006

Selected Films: *The Passage of the Bride*, 1978; *As If We*, 1979–80; *Nocturne*, 1980, revised 1989; *What's Out Tonight Is Lost*, 1983; *The Secret Garden*, 1988; *Remains to Be Seen*, 1989, revised 1994; *The Exquisite Hour*, 1989, revised 1994; *Clepsydra*, 1992; *The Snowman*, 1995; *BiTemporal Vision: The Sea* (with Ken Jacobs), 1995; *Yes, I Said Yes, I Will, Yes*, 1999; *Twilight Psalms—I: The Lateness of the Hour, II: Walking Distance, III: Night of the Meek, IV: On Thursday We Leave for Home*, 1999– ; *Innocence and Despair*, 2002; with Stan Brakhage—*Elementary Phrases*, 1994; *Concrescence*, 1996; *Alternating Currents*, 1999–2002; *Seasons . . .* , 2002; *Untitled (for David Gatten)* (made with Mark LaPore), *Faultline*, *Rehearsals for Retirement*, 2005–07

Spade, Kate

1962– Fashion designer; author

Address: Kate Spade LLC, 48 W. 25th St., New York, NY 10010

The fashion designer Kate Spade, who is largely credited with revolutionizing the handbag market, carries a straw tote bag with her everywhere, even during winters in New York. She loves green so much that she considers it a neutral color. She sees nothing amiss in wearing raspberry satin shoes with a white wedding gown—and, accordingly, includes such shoes in her wedding collection. At five feet two inches, she refers to herself as "fun-sized," according to the *Fast Company* (March 2005) writer Linda Tischler, who described the designer as being "stylish without the intimidating edge of New York fashionistas"—a quality that Tom Julian, a trend analyst for Fallon Worldwide, pinpointed as the key to Spade's success: "There is some psyche that Kate Spade is able to tap into and capitalize on," Julian told Stephanie Thompson for *Advertising Age* (April 12, 2004). "Not trendy and fashionista, but rather the purity factor of a Midwesterner turned New Yorker." After six years of climbing the editorial ladder at the now-defunct fashion magazine *Mademoiselle*, Spade—who had moved to New York from her native Kansas City, Missouri—left the world of photo shoots and sample closets in 1993 to start a business with her then-boyfriend and now husband, Andy.

Evan Agostini/Getty Images for TFF
Kate Spade

Spade began with six simple designs of the kinds of handbags she herself wanted but could not find. Within a few years, she, Andy, and two of their friends and primary investors had built Kate Spade LLC into a multimillion-dollar company, and in 1999 the four partners sold 56 percent of the company to the Neiman Marcus Group for $33.6 million. After the sale the company grew overextended, its very popularity and cachet bringing about its downfall, through an inundation of counterfeiters on the one hand and licensing agreements on the other. Still, Spade continued to be lauded for her quirky, eye-catching designs, winning awards from such prominent organizations as the Council of Fashion Designers of America (CFDA). In November 2006 Liz Claiborne Inc.—a company many analysts feel is more in tune with Kate Spade's interests than Neiman Marcus—announced that it had purchased Kate Spade LLC for $124 million, leading industry observers to predict a comeback for the brand. In mid-2007 Kate and Andy Spade left the company, citing their desire to explore other interests.

"Kate is without a doubt a style icon," Robert Burke, vice president and senior fashion designer of the department store Bergdorf Goodman, told Sophia Chabbott for *Women's Wear Daily* (July 25, 2005). "She's always stayed true to her design aesthetic. She represents a modern feminine sensibility. There's always going to be a customer that embraces color and whimsy." Color and whimsy are, indeed, two key elements of Spade's very distinctive style. "The Spade look is not retro exactly," Julia Reed wrote for *Vogue* (August 2004), "but it is definitely evocative of a now-vanquished suburban America . . . the lost paradise of patio theme

parties and Country Squire station wagons, of lazy backyard cookouts and moms who smoked Salems and carried wicker handbags." Kate Spade—the brand—directly reflects the sophisticated yet down-to-earth personality of Kate Spade, the designer. "Kate has a dry wit, an Irish girl's raucous laugh, and a soft spot in her heart for her spoiled Maltese, Henry," Tischler wrote. The bright palette of her company's accessories stems directly from Spade's wardrobe tastes, which she described to Samantha Critchell for the Associated Press (June 14, 2004): "I realized pretty early on that jeans don't look good on me. . . . For better or worse, I can't do trends. I have a basic look, no muted or tough colors, and then I work hard to give it a lift." That "lift"—provided by the handbag or shoe that makes an outfit stand out—is Spade's focus. Instinctive desire for fashion objects—rather than the mindless following of trends—is what Spade seeks to encourage. "Dress for yourself," she told Jackie White for the *Kansas City Star* (November 25, 2006). "It's so much more fun."

Spade was born Katherine Noel Brosnahan in Kansas City in 1962, the fifth of six children in an Irish-Catholic family. Her mother was a homemaker; her father ran a construction company. Spade has cited her midwestern upbringing as the primary influence on her fashion philosophy. In the Midwest "you have to have [an item of clothing] because you like it, not because you're supposed to have it," she told Critchell. Her first purse—a pink velvet bag with a chain handle—came with a pink dress her mother gave her. Spade remembers her childhood as one spent in a constant attempt to distinguish herself from her two sisters, which involved asking her mother to drive her to thrift shops so she could look for outfits with the bright colors she preferred even then. Spade has named her mother as one of her greatest fashion role models, because of both her taste and her simple approach to dressing up. "I thought she dressed beautifully and she also really . . . loved it . . . ," Spade told Willow Bay for CNNfn (November 9, 2002). "I remembered kind of watching and thinking I can't wait until I can do that. I want to paint my nails. I want to wear lipstick." Spade entered college at the University of Kansas, then transferred, along with her good friend Elyce Arons, to Arizona State University (ASU), where she majored in broadcast journalism. While in school she worked at Johns and Co., a traditional clothing store, where she soon began dating her fellow salesclerk Andy Spade.

After graduating, in 1985, Spade spent the summer backpacking alone through Europe, then moved to Manhattan, in New York City. Living with four other women in a two-bedroom, one-bathroom apartment in the Hell's Kitchen section, Spade began working as a temp at the fashion magazine *Mademoiselle*. That assignment led to a position as an editorial assistant, for which she earned an annual salary of $14,500. Meanwhile, Andy Spade was still in Arizona, running a company he had started while at ASU—which was named one of the state's top 10 new companies in 1987. As successful as he was, Andy missed Kate and decided to sell the company and head to New York himself, taking a job there at the advertising firm Bozell & Jacobs. By the time she was 28, Kate held the enviable position of senior fashion editor at *Mademoiselle*, covering accessories. Her job—though by no means lucrative—provided a forum for her to experiment with and refine her taste, an experience that would help her immensely as a designer. "I became a little more confident with what I did and did not like," she told Sonya Colberg for *Tulsa World* (January 15, 1998) of her time as an editor. Still, Kate felt that something was missing from her life—and from her wardrobe. Having received promotions at the magazine, "I wasn't sure the next step [at *Mademoiselle*] was one I wanted to make," as she explained to Ellyn Spragins for *Fortune Small Business* (September 2003).

Spade and her boyfriend began to discuss the idea of starting a business of their own, possibly an advertising agency, which would play to Andy's strengths. They soon realized that because Andy made considerably more money at his job than Kate made at hers, the best plan would be for Andy to keep his position and finance a company run mostly by Kate. It was Andy who suggested that Kate start her own line of handbags—accessories that had been a source of frustration during her time at *Mademoiselle*, where she had been disappointed by the selection of handbags available for photo shoots and often chose not to include them at all. "I was looking for something that could be less serious. More personal," she told Suzanne C. Ryan for the *Boston Globe* (July 14, 1999). "I also wanted timelessness." In addition, she sought handbags that were both functional and fashionable, a combination she felt designers were not considering. Betting that other women felt the same way, Andy and Kate both cashed out their 401(k) accounts, and their friends Arons and Pamela Bell signed on as principal investors in their new company. In 1992 Kate quit her job to design and launch the line, a process she found to be easier than she had expected. "I sat down with some tracing paper, and I knew immediately what the shape should be—a very simple square," Spade told Spragins. "At the time no one was doing anything that clean. The shape gave me a real flexible canvas for applying all the ideas I had for a lot of colors, patterns, and fabrics."

The first bag Spade designed was made of burlap, with a fringe of raffia—the only materials the pair could afford. For the company's first show, Spade designed six bags, some of which, including the now-iconic square bag, remain in her collection today. For their first show, in 1993, "Kate Spade," the name that Andy had suggested for their products, was printed in white type on small black labels and sewn into the linings of the bags. Though they sold a few bags to the upscale clothing and accessories store Barneys, they did not

make up the costs of the show, and Kate began to get discouraged. Andy pressed on, however, convincing her that the name recognition commanded by Barneys was worth their investment. The night before their second show, Kate suddenly decided to move the "Kate Spade" logo to the outsides of the bags, to give the eye something on which to focus; she stayed up all night to remove the labels from the insides and resew them on the outsides. Her work paid off: though the handbags' sales again failed to cover the cost of a booth, this time the fledgling company got orders from the luxury department stores Fred Segal and Charivari as well as Barneys, and soon received mentions in the high-end fashion magazines *Vogue* and *Elle*. In 1996 (two years after Kate and Andy married) the Council of Fashion Designers of America named Kate America's New Fashion Talent in Accessories. That year Andy quit his advertising job and joined Kate Spade full-time, as CEO. The company also opened its first stand-alone store, in the Soho area of New York City. In 1998 a second store opened in Boston, Massachusetts; that year Kate was named Accessory Designer of the Year by the CFDA. She expanded the line beyond handbags, into the unexpected area of stationery.

The next year saw a windfall for the pair, when they—along with their partners, Arons and Bell—sold 56 percent of the business to Neiman Marcus for $33.6 million. In that unusual deal, Kate Spade LLC became a subsidiary of Neiman Marcus, with the four original partners retaining 44 percent of the company's stock. The deal, while a great financial gain for Kate and Andy, signaled the beginning of a decline for the brand, which began to stray further from its core products—handbags—and its core customers, the affluent, fun-loving women Kate had so purposefully pursued in the early days of the company. In 1999 Estée Lauder Inc. announced that it had signed a licensing agreement to create a Kate Spade Beauty line. Kate and Andy also launched Jack Spade, a corresponding men's line, as well as a small collection of women's shoes. Also in 1999 one of Kate Spade's main contractors, Veje Leather, became involved in an intense battle over unionization efforts by its workers. Spade tried to distance herself from the controversy, but the company still received a great deal of negative publicity over charges of patronizing sweatshop labor—a rare practice in a market as high-end as that in which Kate Spade operated. The following year, Kate Spade opened stores in Chicago, Illinois; San Francisco, California; Greenwich, Connecticut; and Manhasset, New York. Meanwhile, its Soho store was picketed by about 60 protestors—members of Local 2325 and their supporters—who alleged that KC Accessories, another manufacturing firm whose primary business was Kate Spade products, also had unfair work practices and had attempted to prevent unionizing.

The year 2001 saw the greatest challenge the company had faced yet, as the brand, along with considerably more upscale labels such as Gucci and Chanel, became one of the most popular targets for counterfeiters. While big-name designers can devote enormous resources to quelling counterfeiting and maintaining their brand integrity, Kate Spade was unable to control the lucrative business, which was quickly chipping away at the cachet of a Kate Spade purse. "It saturates the market," Arons, who was in charge of the company's anti-counterfeiting efforts, told Margaret Webb Pressler for the *Washington Post* (July 28, 2002) of the problems caused by the illegal trade. "If you're riding a train in the morning and 25 people around you are carrying those counterfeit bags, you may not want one anymore." At one point the company's executives estimated that for every true Kate Spade bag sold through a legitimate retailer, a fake bag was sold on the street. Over the course of a couple of years, Kate Spade bags went from being highly coveted items to being—or seeming to be— common objects.

Meanwhile, Kate Spade LLC continued to expand, trying to make a name for itself not only as a handbag line but as a lifestyle brand. In 2002 Kate appeared as herself on an episode of the NBC sitcom *Just Shoot Me*, starring her brother-in-law, the comic actor David Spade, to promote her new beauty line. In 2003 Delta Airlines hired Kate Spade to design the flight attendants' uniforms for their new discount airline, Song. The following year saw Kate Spade expand even further and, according to some critics, go even further off track. In a three-book deal with the publishing house Simon & Schuster, Kate wrote the guides *Occasions*, *Manners*, and *Style*, manuals on party throwing, etiquette, and fashion, respectively. "The books are not a dictatorial 'How To' thing, but more lighthearted suggestions and observations," she told Susanne Hiller for the Canadian *National Post* (March 20, 2004). "There are things in terms of entertaining, little reminders. It's not about being fussy and pretentious, because having manners means being respectful and inclusive." Also in 2004 Kate—alongside other fashion designers, among them Giorgio Armani—was the model for a limited-edition Barbie doll, dressed in a pink, three-quarter-length trench coat, matching Kate Spade sandals, and grass-green pants. The doll even featured Kate's signature flip hairstyle and carried a wicker basket from the designer's latest handbag collection. In October of that year, the British band Beaumont released the album *Kate Spade Music*, which features eight tracks and was sold exclusively in Kate Spade stores. And in yet another realm of design, Spade's home collection won three awards in 2004: *House Beautiful*'s Giants of Design Award for Tastemaker, *Bon Appetit*'s American Food and Entertaining Award for Designer of the Year, and *Elle's Decor*'s International Design Award for Bedding.

That year was not only one of expansion for the Kate Spade brand, but also one of reassessment. "It's a great time for us, to make it to this point in time and see the growth, and get ready to take it to the next level . . . ," Andy said to Marc Karimzadeh for *Women's Wear Daily* (August 16, 2004). He continued, "I feel like there's now a world of Kate Spade, it's really become a brand. It still has a lot of potential for growth." To allow for that growth, though, many analysts felt that Kate Spade needed a new person at the helm, and Andy—who had taken on the CEO post reluctantly to begin with—announced late in the year that the company would begin looking for his replacement. In May 2005 Neiman Marcus was sold for $5.1 billion to Texas Pacific Group and Warburg Pincus LLC, two equity firms. Many observers expected the new owners to put Kate Spade up for auction; where the company landed next would be pivotal in determining the future of the brand. "After 10 years, Kate and Andy are at a point where they're poised to grow exponentially," CFDA's executive director, Peter Arnold, told Tischler. "But they need to loosen up a little bit on their control of the brand and push the envelope in terms of appealing to a broader customer base. That's the inevitable tension that all designers have: How do I stay true to me and yet grow the business?"

On November 8, 2006 Liz Claiborne Inc. announced that it had purchased Kate Spade LLC for $124 million. In another unusual deal, Neiman Marcus bought out the Kate Spade partners for $59 million to allow the deal to go through, leaving Kate and Andy Spade and their two original investors with no shares in the company. Liz Claiborne's president, Trudy Sullivan, said that she had been eyeing Kate Spade for several years and was happy with the deal: "Kate Spade is an iconic American brand with the potential for broad lifestyle offerings," she wrote in an e-mail message to Eric Newman for *Footwear News* (November 13, 2006). "At this point, it is premature to speculate into what categories those extensions may be, but certainly fragrance, jewelry and apparel are viable possibilities." Kate Spade earned approximately $84 million in revenues for the fiscal year ending July 30, 2006. The company has 19 Kate Spade retail stores worldwide, as well as four Kate Spade outlets and one Jack Spade specialty store. In the next few years, Liz Claiborne plans to refocus the brand on its core categories and expand Kate Spade's retail business significantly, aiming for 200 stores worldwide.

In July 2007 Kate and Andy Spade announced that they would not remain with the company after their service agreements expired, preferring to stay on as board members only. According to *Fashion Wire Daily* (July 27, 2007, on-line), the Spades issued the following statement: "This new situation offers us the perfect opportunity to work closely with Bill"—William L. McComb, the Liz Claiborne company's chief executive officer—"on the transition, to explore some of our other areas of interest, travel and spend time with our two and a half year old daughter." In November 2007 Liz Claiborne appointed Deborah Lloyd as co-president and creative director of Kate Spade.

Kate and Andy Spade were married in 1994, the year after they founded their company. They work on different floors in the Kate Spade headquarters, in Manhattan; by all accounts, they maintain the rare combination of a happy marriage and productive business partnership. Their daughter, Frances Beatrix Spade, was born in 2005.

—C.S.

Suggested Reading: *Boston Globe* F p1 July 14, 1999; *Fast Company* p44 Mar. 2005; *New York Times* (on-line) Mar. 12, 1999; *Oregonian* L p11 Apr. 13, 2003; *Vogue* p200 Aug. 2004

Selected Books: *Occasions*, 2004; *Manners*, 2004; *Style*, 2004

Brad Barket/Getty Images

Spektor, Regina

Feb. 18, 1980– Singer; songwriter

Address: c/o Ron Shapiro Management, 135 W. 26th St., Suite 4A, New York, NY 10001

"If I wasn't gonna be a musician, I'd probably be an actor . . . ," Regina Spektor told Michael Dwyer for the *Age* (December 8, 2006). "I love roles and I love portraying people." Indeed, it is through her idiosyncratic third-person character studies, set against a blend of classical piano, folk, jazz, and punk-rock rhythms, that Spektor—a 27-year-old, Soviet-born, Bronx-bred singer-songwriter—has established herself as the queen of the so-called anti-folk scene of the Lower East Side, the famed mecca for emerging talent in New York City.

Though her broad vocal range and charismatic stage presence have called to mind the modern folk-rock chanteuses Tori Amos, Ani DiFranco, Fiona Apple, and Joni Mitchell, Spektor has departed from their confessional song styles to spin tales comparable in their detachment to the narrative conventions of film and short fiction. Spektor's musical style, which has been described variously as quirky, discordant, melodic, angry, and poetic, has wowed audiences and left critics scrambling for adjectives. Writing for *Blender* (December 2004), Pauline O'Connor called Spektor's music "a weirdly ancient-sounding mash-up of pre-rock and art-school piano delivered in a voice that swoops from whisper to moan and back again," while JR Griffin, in the *Alternative Press* (August 2006), likened her to "that crazy girlfriend you just know is a heap of trouble, but even still, she's so hard to resist." Mainstream record executives, who overlooked Spektor during her days as a fixture in the college and local indie-music scene, have also come to regard her as a "genius" and a "culture-changing artist," as Susan Visakowitz noted in *Billboard* (January 13, 2007).

Spektor has recorded five albums, three of them produced and released independently. While *11:11* (2001) and *Songs* (2002) established Spektor in the indie-music world, her third album, *Soviet Kitsch*, released in 2004, broadened her appeal to the mainstream audience. Described as "beautifully strange" by Jonathan Durbin, writing for *Paper Magazine* (April 2004), *Soviet Kitsch* drew the attention of Julian Casablancas, lead singer of the esteemed modern rock band the Strokes, who in 2003 invited Spektor to perform as the opening act for the group's North American tour. Their high-profile collaboration later spawned the popular duet "Post Modern Girls & Old Fashion Men" and landed Spektor a coveted recording deal with Sire Records, which reissued *Soviet Kitsch* in 2004 to critical acclaim. The noted singles "Ode to Divorce," "Chemo Limo," and "Your Honor" from *Soviet Kitsch* confirmed Spektor's talents as a genre-hopping musical wordsmith. In June 2006 Spektor released *Begin to Hope*, her first original recording for the Sire label. In her review of *Begin to Hope* for *Rolling Stone* (June 29, 2006), Jenny Eliscu praised Spektor's "gorgeous, fluttery voice, her burgeoning writer chops and her God-given quirks," while Amanda Petrusich, in *Paste* (June/July 2006), pronounced Spektor's latest offering to be "as elegant as it is addictive."

One of the two children of Jewish parents, Regina Spektor was born on February 18, 1980 in Moscow, Russia, in what was then the Soviet Union. Her father, a photographer and violinist, and her mother, a teacher of music history, encouraged her early interest in music. At the age of six, Spektor began her training on piano. She has cited a range of famed classical composers, including Tchaikovsky, Mozart, and Chopin, as influences. "For me it was all classical music," she told Shane Roeschlein for Themusicedge.com (March 25,

2005). "We had records, went to concerts, ballets and operas. There were also these bards that were writing simple songs musically but deep and beautiful and poetic lyrics." Spektor's father also exposed her to an eclectic mix of European and British pop music, frequently playing tapes with songs by such British rock legends as the Beatles, Queen, and Moody Blues. The Beatles' songs were "the first . . . pop music I knew growing up in Russia . . . ," Spektor wrote in a piece for *Harp Magazine* (July/August 2006, on-line). "I learned all the songs phonetically even though I couldn't understand a word." In addition to their shared enthusiasm for music, the Spektor family—which included Regina's younger brother, Bear—felt a bond because of their Jewish identity, having withstood a wave of anti-Semitism that spread throughout the Soviet Union in the 1970s and 1980s. "The fact that I'm Jewish is definitely one of the most important, defining things in my life," Spektor told Mark Huntley for the *New York Sun* (April 21, 2005). "Not necessarily the religion, but the ethnicity. I was aware of it when I was very young—having certain customs in the family, always knowing in Russia that I was different."

In 1989, with the advent of *perestroika*, the political and economic reform movement initiated by then-Soviet premier Mikhail Gorbachev, Spektor's family fled Russia under new laws permitting mass emigration. After spending several months in refugee camps in Italy and Austria, they arrived in New York City, in August 1989, settling in the borough of the Bronx. Spektor, then nine, wished to resume her piano playing, but with no access to a piano (the family's Petrof piano was left behind in Russia) and little money for lessons, she resorted to "practicing on window sills and tables," as she told Anthony Mason for CBSnews.com (January 21, 2007). She was later able to practice on a piano discovered in the basement of a local synagogue. Matters improved again after Spektor's father met Samuel Marder, a concert violinist, on the subway. Marder's wife, Sonia Vargas, a professor at the Manhattan School of Music, later met Spektor and offered to give her free lessons; that arrangement lasted until Spektor turned 17. "In a lot of ways, [my family] had failed in the American sense of owning this or owning that, but we have been overly successful in terms of education," Spektor said to Jon Caramanica for *New York Magazine* (June 12, 2006). "We've always had educators come into our lives when we needed them."

In her teens Spektor attended the Frisch Yeshiva High School, in Paramus, New Jersey, then transferred to Fair Lawn High School, in Fair Lawn, New Jersey. Meanwhile, as her music lessons continued, she grew frustrated by what seemed to be the limits of her ability on piano. "Playing piano is almost like being an athlete," she explained to Caramanica. "The art happens amidst routine. For me, it was always a real struggle. I wasn't consistent enough to make that my art." Spektor instead found her creative freedom in songwriting and, lat-

er, singing, inspired in part by peers who heard her sing her own songs during a summer sojourn in Israel and encouraged her to continue doing so. "[Singing and songwriting] had never occurred to me," Spektor admitted, as quoted by a writer for the EMI Music Publishing Web site. "To me, the mentality was you sit at the piano and play Bach or Mozart or Chopin. You didn't ever improvise, so the idea of writing my own music was an intimidating one." Spektor soon ended her classical training and began to compose original a capella songs, slowly blending them into her piano performance. She found the transition from classical music to be difficult at first. As she told Caramanica, "It was very painful to be so crude. You go from being at a certain level to being an Oompa-Loompa person. You don't have the dexterity." Caramanica reported, "Having not been raised on pop music, she also didn't have the traditional songwriting reference points, or boundaries, all of which proved to be a boon. Her songs quickly grew florid and intricate, her lyrics teeming with oddball characters that she didn't discover and inhabit so much as cut from whole cloth."

At the renowned Conservatory of Music at Purchase College, a division of the State University of New York (SUNY–Purchase), Spektor majored in studio composition and completed her studies in three years. During that time she put on live shows for the Purchase community. With her quirky, folksy, piano-driven pop beginning to generate positive buzz, Spektor teamed with the jazz bassist Chris Kuffner in early 2001 to record her first, independently produced album, *11:11*, which had a modest printing of 1,000 copies but sparked local fanfare. After her graduation, in 2001, Spektor returned to New York City and began to perform in such venues as the Knitting Factory, the Sidewalk Café, and the Living Room in the East Village and Lower East Side, home to a thriving musical subgenre known as anti-folk; that performance style combined the sparse acoustic sounds of 1960s American folk music with the raw energy of 1970s punk rock and ironic, stream-of-consciousness lyrics. "I don't think [anti-folk is] necessarily a sound of music, or a type of music," Spektor explained to Noel Murray for avclub.com (June 21, 2006). "It's more like an attitude. People with acoustic instruments, playing songs and singing in their own voice. Not in a really stylized way, but kind of conversational." Spektor quickly emerged as a fixture in the anti-folk scene, drawing a devoted local audience with songs in which she strived for "really intelligent lyrics" and "a punk attitude," as she put it in an interview with Jeff Guinn for the *Fort Worth Star Telegram* (April 18, 2004). In early 2002 Spektor released her second album, entitled simply *Songs*, which veered from the jazzy sounds of *11:11* to reveal "a more intrepid spirit: revisionist stories about Samson and Delilah, Oedipus Rex, and more, delivered in an extraordinarily powerful voice with a slight pinch, giving it a naïve edge," Jon Caramanica wrote. "It's fabulist cabaret as incisive emotional therapy." *Songs* showcased Spektor's powerful vocals and versatility, proving her to be an "Old World soul in a New World reality," in the view of George Varga, writing for the Copley News Service (November 17, 2006). Spektor told Varga, "You feel this [old] world, in which your parents, grandparents and childhood reside. You also have all the literature and art that comes with that, and the language. Then, you have the new world, which is very modern and is sort of your future, and you are always trying to keep the two connected. So, it's kind of like making these little sutures to keep the two worlds together."

Songs emerged as a bona fide hit among many of New York City's music fans and made converts of contemporaries including the acclaimed singer-songwriter David Poe and Allan Bezzozo, the drummer for the alternative rock group They Might Be Giants. "I never had enough money to do a big run so I'd do 200 at a time, sell them out, and then make more," Spektor told the writer for the EMI Publishing Web site. One of Spektor's spunky performances impressed Gordon Raphael, then the record producer for the popular garage-rock band the Strokes. Raphael wrote for a British music Web site, as quoted by Caramanica, "[Spektor is] a revelation . . . one of the purest musical offerings I've ever seen, certainly among the most brilliant." At Raphael's urging, Spektor recorded "Poor Little Rich Boy," a hit on the local club circuit; on that song she played piano with one hand while striking a drum with the other, creating an unusual, frenetic melody. That single was included on Spektor's third album, *Soviet Kitsch* (2004), which revealed the variety of influences on the songwriter, ranging from the jazz singer Billie Holiday to the Icelandic rock artist Björk. It also featured contributions from highly regarded New York City musicians, including the guitarist Oren Bloedow, the bassist Graham Maby, and the cellist Jane Scarpantoni. Commenting on the album, Spektor told the writer for the EMI Publishing Web site, "I don't have an overall sound. I tend to think of each song as its own little world, so one can be a complete punk song, while another could be a chamber ensemble with strings." *Soviet Kitsch* attracted a strong cult following, with songs that featured memorable characters, imaginative, wry narratives, and quirky wordplay, closer in form to short stories and films than to conventional pop songs. "I'm much more attracted to fiction and novels and movies—things that are less autobiographical and more mythological," Spektor told Kristyn Pomranz for the St. Louis, Missouri, *Riverfront Times* (November 8, 2006). "I guess they're not fantasies that are made up altogether but observations. Characters that I've seen or glimpsed." Spektor's interest in "character exploration," as she put it for Ernest Jasmin in the Tacoma, Washington, *News Tribune* (April 8, 2005), also rendered the songs "personal, because they're rooted in real emotions."

As *Soviet Kitsch* had confirmed Spektor's status in the anti-folk movement, her subsequent stint on the Strokes' North American "Room on Fire" tour, in 2003, made her known her to a mainstream audience. Invited by Julian Casablancas, the lead singer of the Strokes, to open for the band, Spektor—who was still not signed to a record label—paid her own expenses to perform with musicians she admired. "[The Strokes] were the closest I had heard rock come to classical," she told Nick Catucci for the *Village Voice* (June 26, 2006). "Their music is extraordinarily orderly and composed. It's almost like Mozart." On the tour Spektor's ironic, reflective numbers proved to be an odd contrast to the gritty songs of the band—and drew mixed responses from fans. "I got tougher toward the end of the tour," she told Jeff Gunin for the *Fort Worth (Texas) Star Telegram* (April 18, 2004), "but a couple of nights, I ran offstage when I was done playing so nobody would see me cry." Still, Spektor's work impressed Casablancas, who asked her to record a song with the band, "Post Modern Girls & Old Fashion Men," featured on the Strokes' sophomore album, *Room on Fire* (2003). In the wake of Spektor's tour and collaboration with the Strokes, major record labels took notice of her. Sire Records, owned by the Warner Music Group, signed Spektor to her first professional recording contract. Sire reissued *Soviet Kitsch* in 2004, through the mass distribution network of Warner Bros. Records. On Spektor's initiative, Sire also mounted an "old-school, word-of-mouth" sales campaign sustained by "hard work and belief," as the label's president, Michael Goldstone, told Susan Visakowitz for *Billboard* (January 13, 2007). The re-release of *Soviet Kitsch* received enthusiastic reviews from critics. Writing for the *Bangor (Maine) Daily News* (April 2, 2005), Dale McGarrigle praised Spektor for "straddl[ing] the line between confessional angst and funny, observational songwriting. Spektor's primary strength is her expressive, elastic voice." In the *Lancaster (Pennsylvania) New Era* (April 14, 2005), Judy Jarvis hailed one of Spektor's musical signatures—the ability to "meld her voice to fit the tone of her song" and create "separate and unique worlds with each track."

In 2006 Sire Records issued Spektor's second major-label release, *Mary Ann Meets the Gravediggers and Other Short Stories*, a compilation album of older tracks that served as an introductory offering for the European market. In June of that year, Spektor released her first new album under the Sire label, *Begin to Hope*, recorded the previous summer under the direction of David Kahne, the Grammy Award–winning producer of records by Paul McCartney and Tony Bennett. Though Spektor remained wary of the "big machine" aspect of a major record label, as quoted by Bob Gendron for the *Chicago Tribune* (April 21, 2006), she reveled in the luxury of bigger budgets and flexible studio time afforded a label signee. "My other records I had to speed-record," she said to Michael Dwyer.

"You know, you have a couple of days and no budget and no players and then you get three string players and you have four hours with them. This record, I had more of a chance to really learn about sounds and arranging." *Begin to Hope* marked a departure for Spektor, incorporating a wider mix of electronic instrumentation and natural percussion for more "radio-ready pop, if indeed radio were ready for Spektor's whimsy and warmth," Jon Caramanica wrote. At its core, though, *Begin to Hope* was quintessential Spektor, weaving the raw and the tender into sometimes fantastical narratives that some took as evidence of a range of colorful experiences on the singer's part. Spektor dismissed speculation that she had "lived" the tales in her songs, insisting on her role as a storyteller. Discussing the album's personal, introspective feel, Spektor chalked it up to "becoming less of a narrator and more of a character. . . . I was always used to observing and writing third-person narrative stories about things I was seeing. Then, as time went on, I started placing myself in these scenes, more like an actor," as she told Stirling. While songs including "Lady," an ode to Billie Holiday; "Samson," about the Old Testament figure with Herculean strength; and "Summer in the City," a tale of bizarre discovery on New York's Delancey Street, garnered critical praise for their eclecticism, innovation, and quirky insight, it was the single "Fidelity," a "sweet, reflective love song," as described by Andrzej Lukowski for the London *Evening Standard* (February 16, 2007), that propelled Spektor's album into mainstream popularity. The song's music video netted 200,000 hits over two days on the popular video-sharing Web site YouTube and went on to be included in the VH1 cable channel's "You Oughtta Know: Artists on the Rise" video series. In December 2006 *Begin to Hope* reached the number-one spot on the Apple Computer iTunes alternative-album chart in the United States. Two months later Sire released an EP, called *Live in California 2006*, containing two songs from *Begin to Hope* and another two from *Soviet Kitsch*.

Spektor lives in New York City. "New York feeds me creatively," she told Imogen Tilden for the London *Guardian* (June 23, 2006). "A lot of my inspiration comes from walking in the streets. It's a kind of country of its own. This is the place that makes me feel more at home than anywhere else on the planet."

—D.J.K.

Suggested Reading: *Billboard* Jan. 13, 2007; EMI Music Publishing Web site; (London) *Guardian* Film and Music p3 June 23, 2006; Musicedge.com Mar. 25, 2005; *New York Sun* p20 Apr. 21, 2005; (St. Louis, Missouri) *Riverfront Times* Music Nov. 8, 2006; (Tacoma, Washington) *News Tribune* F p7 Apr. 8, 2005; Womanrock.com

Selected Recordings: *11:11*, 2001; *Songs*, 2002; *Soviet Kitsch*, 2004; *Mary Ann Meets the Gravediggers and Other Short Stories*, 2006; *Begin to Hope*, 2006

St. Louis, Martin

(sahn loo-EE, mar-TAN)

June 18, 1975– Hockey player

Address: Tampa Bay Lightning, St. Pete Times Forum, 401 Channelside Dr., Tampa, FL 33602

Most National Hockey League (NHL) players today are over six feet tall, so Martin St. Louis, at several inches shy of that mark, is comparatively small. Despite his physical stature, which has caused some sports observers to question his suitability to play the game professionally, in 2004 the Tampa Bay Lightning right wing became the first NHL team member in over a decade to win the coveted Art Ross Trophy, Hart Trophy, and Stanley Cup all in the same season. "His long suit is his passion. Small players have to have some special attribute that makes them stand out. He's got great acceleration and hockey sense," Scotty Bowman, a highly regarded former coach, told Michael Farber for *Sports Illustrated* (March 8, 2004). "Very few shifts go by without something happening when he's out there."

Martin St. Louis was born on June 18, 1975 in Laval, Quebec, a suburb of Montreal, Canada. His father, Normand, had been one of 14 brothers. Normand worked at his father's lumber mill in his youth and later became a postman, a job he kept for three decades; he took on additional work as a handyman when St. Louis and his sister, Isabelle, were growing up. "He would work 16-, 17-hour days," St. Louis told Scott Carter for the *Tampa (Florida) Tribune* (December 13, 2003). "I didn't see him much. The time I saw him was during hockey games or practice. I think I definitely inherited his work ethic. He is stubborn that way. He doesn't give up. . . . To me, that's the only way."

St. Louis was an enthusiastic hockey player as a child. He practiced on an outdoor rink a few hundred yards from the family's home, often sporting a wool hat with a bright pom-pom on top, so that his mother, France, could keep an eye on him from the kitchen window. Each year, when the weather became warmer, St. Louis played street hockey and also enjoyed soccer and gymnastics.

Bruce Bennett/Getty Images

Martin St. Louis

In Laval and its surrounding areas, the sport of hockey is followed closely and admired greatly. Many people who live in Laval cheer for the Montreal Canadiens, whose stellar championship record is often compared to that of the New York Yankees baseball team. Since they joined the NHL, in 1917, the Canadiens have won 23 Stanley Cup Championships, far more than any of the NHL's other franchises. St. Louis particularly identified with the Canadiens player Mats Näslund, a Swedish-born forward who played with the team from 1982 until 1990. Näslund, at five feet seven inches tall, possessed terrific agility, which compensated for his size. "He was my idol," St. Louis told Tom Worgo for *Hockey Digest* (February 2003, on-line). "I thought him being a small player in the NHL was so cool. I kind of associated myself with him because I was always the smallest player on my team as well."

Doubts about St. Louis's ability to handle the physical nature of the sport began to emerge when he reached the bantam level, the first rung of organized hockey in which body checking is permitted. (Body checking is the practice of using a hip or shoulder to knock an opponent into the boards or onto the ice.) St. Louis, confounding expectations, flourished at the bantam level. He demonstrated a readiness to enter the area of the hockey rink referred to as the corner boards—where rough-and-tumble play is common—that is with him still. Scott Carter observed that while playing in a summer league in Quebec at the age of 15, St. Louis "was skating circles around the other players, outworking players nearly double his size." His performance caught the eye of Mike Gilligan, then the hockey coach at the University of Vermont, in Bur-

lington. In the fall of 1993, despite his not being a fluent English speaker, St. Louis entered the school along with his childhood companion Eric Perrin. The two played together for four years at college, forming an impressive scoring tandem and being dubbed the "French Connection." (Over the years, as their sons developed impressive professional careers, Normand and his wife, France St. Louis, have remained good friends with Perrin's parents back in Laval; the two couples eat dinner together weekly and celebrate their wedding anniversaries together.)

Competing in the Eastern College Athletic Conference (ECAC) as a freshman during the 1993–94 season, St. Louis led the University of Vermont Catamounts in overall scoring, with 51 points, and was later named to the ECAC All-Rookie Team. In his sophomore year St. Louis earned ECAC player-of-the-year honors, leading the team in points for a second season, with 23 goals and 48 assists. (In hockey, the total number of points earned is tabulated by adding goals and assists.) St. Louis's efforts on the ice as a sophomore earned him national recognition; he was voted a first-team All-American and named a finalist for the Hobey Baker Award, an annual prize given to the top college ice-hockey player.

As a junior St. Louis guided the Catamounts to a record of 27–7–4 (the best in the school's history to that point) and a berth in the year-ending National Collegiate Athletic Association (NCAA) tournament. The Catamounts advanced as far as the semifinals—known as the Frozen Four. (The University of Michigan ultimately won the championship, defeating Colorado College in overtime by a score of 3–2.) That season St. Louis was named a Hobey Baker Award finalist for the second consecutive season and tied with Perrin for most points scored, at 85. In December 1996, as a senior, with a goal scored against Providence College, St. Louis became the Catamounts' all-time leading scorer, surpassing a record that had been held by Tim O'Connell for over two decades. That year the Catamounts were ranked number one in the NCAA hockey standings for a brief period, marking the first such occasion in school history. St. Louis, a Hobey Baker Award finalist for his third consecutive year, finished his college career with a total of 91 goals and 176 assists, four points short of eclipsing Lance Nethery's all-time ECAC record.

Despite his prowess as an amateur, St. Louis was not drafted after graduation by an NHL club. (Scouts had joked that he looked more like a newspaper boy than a professional athlete.) He signed instead with the Cleveland Lumberjacks, a franchise of the International Hockey League. During the 1997–98 season with the Lumberjacks, St. Louis tallied 50 points in 56 games. Midway through his season, on February 19, 1998, the Calgary Flames, an NHL team, signed him to a free-agent contract and placed him with their American Hockey League (AHL) affiliate in St. John, New Brunswick, Canada. That season St. Louis scored

15 goals and collected 11 assists in 25 games as a member of the St. John Flames. He also helped the team advance to the championship round of the AHL play-offs, where the Philadelphia Phantoms (the affiliate of the NHL Flyers) defeated the Flames in six games.

St. Louis began the next season with St. John but was promoted midway through the season to the Calgary Flames' roster. He made his NHL debut on October 9, 1998, playing against the San Jose Sharks at a match held in Japan. Brian Sutter, the head coach, and the general manager, Al Coates, optimistically tapped St. Louis for the team's checking line, which is frequently assigned to defend the opposition's best offensive players. The assignment was not a good fit for St. Louis, who in 13 games scored only one goal and one assist and was sent back to St. John to finish the season. Returning to the less demanding ranks of the AHL, St. Louis led the Flames' affiliate with 28 goals and 62 points. After starting the 1999–2000 season with St. John, he was once again called to Calgary, on November 11, 1999. St. Louis showed more confidence during his second NHL stint. His first multi-point game came just weeks after his return to Calgary, in a match against the New Jersey Devils. In the 56 games he played with Calgary during the 1999–2000 season, he scored three goals and recorded 15 assists. His improvement was insufficient, however, and the Flames chose not to sign him again at the end of the season. "I'm not mad at the way things worked out," St. Louis later told John Kreiser for *Hockey Digest* (July–August 2004, on-line). "It was probably the best thing for my career."

In July 2000 St. Louis found a new home when the Tampa Bay Lightning signed him to a two-year contract valued at $540,000, slightly more than the league's minimum salary. ("Little did Lightning [general manager] Rick Dudley know it at the time, but he had just happened upon the biggest bargain in the league," an article posted on JockBio.com stated.) Since they joined the NHL, in 1992, as an expansion team, the Tampa Bay Lightning had been hampered by gross mismanagement and an inexperienced roster. The Lightning became the first NHL team to lose 50 games in each of three consecutive seasons (from 1997 to 2000). The team had qualified for the play-offs only once during the 1990s and had missed the post-season for four consecutive seasons prior to St. Louis's arrival. While the purchase of the team by a successful entrepreneur named Bill Davidson in the spring of 1999 had ushered in new hope for the faltering franchise, expectations for the Lightning were not high at the start of the 2000–01 season. St. Louis's first with the team, which included such yet-unproved NHL players as Fredrik Modin, Vincent Lecavalier, and Brad Richards. Playing a career-high 78 games that season, St. Louis, who was given increased opportunity to play offense, recorded 18 goals and 22 assists. More than three-quarters of his points were generated after December 1, once he had gotten ac-

climated to the style of Steve Ludzik, the head coach.

The Lightning's 24 wins during the 2000–01 season marked a slight improvement from the previous year, but looking for more dramatic gains, Davidson hired John Tortorella to replace Ludzik prior to the start of the 2001–02 season. The Lightning also acquired the goaltender Nikolai Khabibulin from the Phoenix Coyotes to fortify its defense. With those new hires, the team entered the 2001–02 season expecting to make significant gains in the standings. Team management also expected St. Louis himself to mature that season, and he was promoted to one of the team's scoring lines. During the first part of the season, however, St. Louis suffered a concussion and an injury to his heel that caused him to miss three games. After his recovery, he resumed playing and was soon leading the team in scoring, with 33 points in 48 games. Then, on January 23, 2002, St. Louis broke his right fibula, causing him to miss over two months of the season. He returned to the Lightning's lineup in April, but by then the team's play-off chances had dissipated.

St. Louis told Carter, "Breaking my leg was definitely a jab to my confidence. I really worked hard that [following] summer because I wanted to pick it back up where I left off. I didn't want to take two steps back, I wanted to take another step forward." His determination paid off, and during the 2002–03 NHL season, St. Louis emerged as one of the sport's most exciting players. On January 30, 2003 he recorded his first career hat trick (three goals scored in one game) in a home contest against the Carolina Hurricanes. By the end of the season, he had established several career highs, with 82 games played, 33 goals, and 37 assists. He was selected for the first time, as a representative of the Eastern Conference, to play in the 2003 NHL All-Star Game, as a reserve. Hockey enthusiasts were beginning to take notice of St. Louis. "You have to like the guy," Bruce Cassidy, the coach of a rival team, told Worgo. "He's fun to watch, exciting and flying around. He's got a lot of heart. He loves the game and plays hard." The Lightning's other players were also maturing, and that season the team captured the Southeast divisional championship, the franchise's first-ever divisional title. Facing the Washington Capitals in the first round of the Stanley Cup play-offs, the Lightning won four consecutive games and captured the best-of-seven series. During those four matches St. Louis scored five goals, including three game-winning goals. Michael Farber remarked that for St. Louis, "the 2003 playoffs were a professional growth spurt." (The New Jersey Devils ultimately took home that year's Stanley Cup.)

The Lightning finished the 2003–04 NHL regular season with 106 points and the best record in the Eastern Conference. (Perrin had joined the team late that season, much to the delight of fans in Laval, who were thrilled to have two home-grown players to cheer on.) St. Louis's own numbers soared to previously unseen heights—38 goals and 56 assists in 82 games—and he was elected to start in the 2004 NHL All-Star Game. (St. Louis's 94 points were the most scored by any player in the NHL that season.) He was also named the NHL Player of the Month in January 2004 and February 2004, thus becoming the first player to win the award in consecutive months since the hockey legend Wayne Gretzky did so during the 1986–87 season. Many sportswriters credited St. Louis directly for the Lightning's achievements, and he took home several honors at the end of the season, including the Hart Trophy, given to the NHL's most valuable player, as selected by the Professional Hockey Writers Association; the Art Ross Trophy, presented to the league's top regular-season scorer; and the Lester B. Pearson Award for most valuable player, as voted by the members of the National Hockey League Players Association. *Hockey Digest* also named him the 2003–04 Player of the Year.

Seeded first in the Eastern Conference, the Lightning began the 2003–04 play-offs with five wins against the New York Islanders, then moved on to defeat the Canadiens in a four-game sweep. During those nine games St. Louis scored five goals and seven assists. The Lightning next outlasted the Philadelphia Flyers in seven games. Making their first Stanley Cup finals appearance, the Lightning took on the Calgary Flames, St. Louis's former club. (It was apparent to most observers by then that the Flames had made a serious mistake in letting St. Louis go.) St. Louis's goal in the second overtime of Game Six sent the series back to Tampa Bay for a deciding Game Seven, which the Lightning won by a score of 2–1 to earn their first Stanley Cup championship. St. Louis thus became the first player since 1987, when Gretzky managed the feat, to bring home a Stanley Cup, Art Ross Trophy, and Hart Trophy, all in a single season.

Representing Canada at the 2004 World Cup of Hockey, St. Louis contributed to the team's first-place finish, and with the 2004–05 NHL season canceled due to a 301-day lockout, he next played in Switzerland for HC Lausanne, a franchise in the Swiss national league. After the NHL dispute was settled, in August 2005 St. Louis signed a six-year contract with the Lightning valued at more than $31 million. Jay Feaster, the Lightning's general manager, told a reporter for ESPN.com (August 25, 2005), "I've said it many times in the past and I continue to maintain that Martin St. Louis is the heart and soul of our hockey team. Dating all the way back to the summer of 2004, there was never a moment when we were not firmly committed as an organization to getting Marty signed long term." Despite such hype St. Louis's record for the 2005–06 season disappointed expectations; playing 80 games, he scored 31 goals and 30 assists. In the 2006–07 season St. Louis bounced back, with a personal NHL high of 102 points, 43 goals, and 59 assists. In one particularly exciting match held against the Carolina Hurricanes in October 2006, St. Louis broke his own team record for three fastest goals—completing a hat trick in a span of only six minutes and 17 seconds.

St. Louis played as part of Team Canada during the 2006 Winter Olympics, held in Turin, Italy. Canada made it only to the quarterfinals, where they were trounced by Russia, 2–0. Sweden ultimately took home the gold medal in what has been widely characterized as a lackluster tournament. For the 2007–08 season, St. Louis was named alternate captain while Tim Taylor, the regular captain, underwent hip surgery.

According to the Lightning's official Web site, Martin St. Louis is five feet nine inches tall and weighs 185 pounds. He "is more likely closer to 5-7 and 175," according to Kreiser. He is sometimes met with taunts about his height from opposing players or their fans, but he typically shrugs them off. During the off-season St. Louis lives in Burlington, Vermont. On June 13, 2004 his wife, Heather, whom he met while attending the University of Vermont, gave birth to the couple's first child, Ryan. "My life changed a lot," he told Carter regarding his adjustment to fatherhood. "It's a learning process every day. It's a challenge, but a fun one."

St. Louis's Tampa Bay jersey features the number 26, in honor of Näslund, his boyhood idol, who wore the same number for the Canadiens. St. Louis is now providing a similarly admirable figure for young hockey fans, particularly in Laval, where he is a local hero.

—D.F.

Suggested Reading: ESPN.com Aug. 25, 2005; *Hockey Digest* (on-line) Feb. 2003, July–Aug. 2004; JockBio.com; *New York Times* D p1 June 8, 2004; *Sports Illustrated* p62+ Mar. 8, 2004; Tampa Bay Lightning Web site; *Tampa (Florida) Tribune* Sports p1 Dec. 13, 2003, p1 Apr. 27, 2004

Steitz, Joan A.

(stites)

Jan. 26, 1941– Biochemist; educator

Address: Yale University, Dept. of Molecular Biophysics & Biochemistry, 333 Cedar St., P.O. Box 208024, New Haven, CT 06520-8024

"A personal romance"—that is how Joan A. Steitz has described her relationship with ribonucleic acid (RNA), a component of cells that plays a crucial role in the construction of proteins, which are required for the execution of all the basic biological processes of the human body and from which muscle, nerves, blood vessels, bone, and everything else in the body is made. Steitz, a biochemist, has been studying RNA since the early 1960s, and her work has remained at the forefront of RNA research for many years. She is best known for discovering in the cell nucleus particles identified as small nu-

Courtesy of Joan A. Steitz

Joan A. Steitz

clear ribonucleoproteins—snRNPs, pronounced "snurps," consisting of RNA plus a protein—and for illuminating the function of snRNPs in the synthesis of a form of RNA known as messenger RNA, or mRNA. In particular, she discovered that snRNPs handle a step in that synthesis called splicing. Steitz's work has huge ramifications for medical science, not least because defects in the splicing process may account for 10 to 15 percent of all genetic diseases. Colleagues of Steitz's as well as other interested observers have predicted that her discoveries will lead to new ways of diagnosing and treating autoimmune diseases (in which the immune system, which is designed to protect an organism against disease and infection, mistakenly attacks the organism itself) and other disorders.

Steitz holds the title Sterling professor of molecular biophysics and biochemistry at the Yale University School of Medicine—Yale's highest academic rank—and heads a laboratory at the Howard Hughes Medical Institute (HHMI) at Yale's Boyer Center for Molecular Medicine. John Dirks, a professor of medicine at the University of Toronto and the president of the Gairdner Foundation, told Elaine Carey for the *Toronto (Ontario) Star* (April 3, 2006) that Steitz is "one of the most distinguished molecular biologists of her time and has been an outstanding role model to scientists and students everywhere." She is also a "tireless promoter of women in science," as the biochemist Christine Guthrie described her in an interview for the *ASCB (American Society for Cell Biology) Newsletter* (June 2006), and she "has made it a priority" to give up-and-coming female scientists "something she didn't have: a female network within the system," as Margaret N. Woodbury

wrote for the *HHMI Bulletin* (February 2006). In 2006, in recognition of her extraordinary contributions to biomedical science, Steitz won a Gairdner Foundation International Award and the National Cancer Institute's Rosalind E. Franklin Award for Women in Science—two of the several dozen honors she has received. Among the others are the Eli Lilly Award in Biological Chemistry (1976), the National Medal of Science (1986), the Weizmann Women in Science Award (1994), the UNESCO-L'Oréal Award for Women in Science (2001), and 11 honorary doctorates.

The daughter of Glenn D. and Elaine (Magnusson) Argetsinger, both schoolteachers, Steitz was born Joan Elaine Argetsinger on January 26, 1941 in Minneapolis, Minnesota. She showed an early inclination toward science at a time when very few women had made careers in that field, and her teachers and family encouraged her to pursue that interest. After her graduation from a girls-only high school, Steitz attended Antioch College, in Yellow Springs, Ohio, where her chemistry classmates included the future evolutionary biologist and essayist Stephen Jay Gould and the future biochemist and textbook author Judith G. Voet. Antioch's acclaimed science program included three-month "co-ops" each year, in which students worked in research labs around the country. During one of her co-ops, Steitz worked in the laboratory of Alex Rich at the Massachusetts Institute of Technology (MIT), where she was introduced to the emerging science of molecular biology. A second co-op brought her to the Max Planck Institute, in Germany. Although Steitz's fascination with science increased during her undergraduate years, she was unsure about committing herself to the extremely long hours and weekends that laboratory research invariably demanded. Furthermore, the career prospects for a female researcher seemed virtually nonexistent; she herself knew no female senior scientists or full professors. "I decided that my best future course was to attend medical school. I had known several women physicians, so this seemed a reasonable choice," Steitz wrote for the Web site Agora: For Women in Science (April 6 , 2006). Steitz gained acceptance to Harvard Medical School, in Cambridge, Massachusetts, and planned to begin her studies there in the fall of 1963, a few months after she earned a B.S. degree.

During the summer of 1963, Steitz engaged in research in the University of Minnesota laboratory of the embryologist Joseph Gall, who gave her a project to work on—not with other people, as had always happened in the past, but independently. Her subject was *Tetrahymena pyriformis*, a one-celled protozoan that has two nuclei and is covered with hundreds of cilia (hairlike structures used in feeding, swimming, and other activities) and that, like the fruit fly, has been the focus of hundreds of scientific investigations. Gall asked Steitz to determine whether *Tetrahymena*'s cilia contain nucleic acid—a task that relied on the recent finding that mitochondria possess their own complement of

DNA. (Mitochondria are among the organelles of cells. The other organelles in cells—each of which has a specific function and may be considered somewhat analogous to organs of a body—include the nucleus, ribosomes, the nucleolus, Golgi apparati, and centrioles.) Steitz told Elaine Carey, "All of a sudden I got completely turned on. I decided even if I wasn't ever going to be able to do this like all the men professors I'd known, that this was what I wanted to do, pursue science. It really, really got me and I couldn't believe how much fun it was making discoveries." Recognizing her aptitude, Gall urged Steitz to transfer from Harvard's medical school to the university's new graduate program in biochemistry and molecular biology (BMB). One faculty member in the program was James D. Watson, a friend of Gall's, who, in 1962, along with Francis Crick and Maurice Wilkins, had won the Nobel Prize for Physiology or Medicine for their discovery of the molecular structure of DNA. With Watson's help, Steitz was admitted into the program. "As [Steitz has] become more and more famous, it's been gratifying to think that I had a small part in influencing her," Gall told the ASCB interviewer. "She just had that summer in my lab. Still, my guess is that she would have gone into research, no matter what."

In graduate school Steitz had no female professors; she was the only woman in her BMB class of 10 at Harvard and the first female graduate student in Watson's lab. Under Watson's direction Steitz began to study RNA structure and function in bacteriophages (viruses, also known as phages, that are without nuclei and that infect bacteria). Seeking an adviser who would oversee her doctoral research, she approached a "famous, well-respected, and now deceased" male scientist, as she described the man—whom she declined to name—to Margaret Woodbury. The scientist said he would not work with her, on the grounds that she was a woman. Steitz recalled to Woodbury that she ran from the room and burst into tears, but that afterward she came to regard the experience as extraordinarily fortunate: Watson became her Ph.D. adviser, and their professional relationship strengthened into a lifetime bond. "He was an excellent mentor and very supportive of my work," Steitz said of Watson in an undated interview posted on the HHMI Web site. "He was truly an inspiration and taught me to focus on the important questions in science." For her Ph.D. thesis Steitz examined in vitro (that is, in test tubes) a bacteriophage known as R17 and shed light on how protein and nucleic-acid components of viruses come together. While at Harvard she met Thomas A. Steitz, a microbiologist and X-ray crystallographer; the two married in 1966. In 1967 Joan Steitz earned her Ph.D. degree.

That year the Steitzes moved to Cambridge, England, where Joan Steitz, as a National Science Foundation and later Jane Coffin Childs Memorial Fund postdoctoral fellow, joined Francis Crick and the molecular biologist Sydney Brenner (winner of a Nobel Prize in 2002) at the Medical Research Council Laboratory of Molecular Biology. There, working with bacteriophages, Steitz investigated the exact point (the so-called start point) on a strand of messenger RNA on which a ribosome binds and the manufacture of protein begins. Messenger RNA is one of several types of RNA synthesized within the cell in the process known as transcription, which is guided by the genetic information, or codes, in DNA. In her first independent discovery, Steitz located three start points on bacteriophage mRNA. As the sole author, she described her discovery in "Polypetide Chain Initiation: Nucleotide Sequences of the Three Ribosomal Binding Sites in Bacteriophage R17 RNA," published in the December 6 , 1969 issue of Nature.

Back in the U.S. in 1970, Steitz embarked on a lecture tour and was surprised to find that many universities were interested in hiring her. A profusion of job offers came her way in part because of the attention that her Nature paper had attracted. Another cause of the interest in her was that in recent years, American universities had begun to add increasing numbers of women to their math and science faculties, in response to growing pressure from within and outside academia. That same year Steitz accepted a position as an assistant professor at Yale University, in New Haven, Connecticut; her husband also joined the Yale faculty. "I was exceedingly nervous about accepting a 'real job' because I knew I had not prepared myself to be a faculty member in the same way that my male colleagues had," Steitz wrote in an article for the Agora: For Women in Science Web site (April 6, 2006). At Yale Steitz continued her work on bacteriophage RNA binding sites before shifting her focus to eukaryotic cells (which house genetic information within a membrane-bound nucleus). Her paper "How Ribosomes Select Initiator Regions in mRNA: Base Pair Formation Between the 3' Terminus of 16 S rRNA and the mRNA During Initiation of Protein Synthesis in Escherichia coli," co-written by Karen Jakes and published in PNAS (Proceedings of the National Academy of Sciences of the United States, December 1, 1975), explains how ribosomes identify the start site on a strand of mRNA. Steitz regards that discovery as a highlight of her career.

The work for which Steitz is most famous, however, was performed later in the 1970s and is described in another seminal paper: "Are snRNPs Involved in Splicing?," published in Nature (January 10 , 1980), which she wrote with four others. That work made use of the discovery (also in the late 1970s, by scientists at MIT and Cold Spring Harbor Laboratory, in New York, among other facilities) that the DNA in eukaryotic cells contains combinations of two types of sequences, known as exons and introns, that alternate within a gene. Exons code for the synthesis of proteins; that is, they contain the information necessary for its construction. Introns do not code for proteins; indeed, they are referred to as "nonsense segments" of DNA or "junk" DNA. (Steitz later found, however, that on occasion an intron includes a small nucleolar RNA found in a snRNP. Those molecules chemically modify ribosomal RNA and are essential to its function.) The process of creating proteins starts with the synthesis of what is called pre-mRNA, which contains both introns and exons. Messenger RNA, created from pre-mRNA in a later phase of the process, contains only exons. Nobody yet knew the mechanism by which the introns are removed from the pre-mRNA. Steitz discovered, first, that antibodies from patients suffering from the autoimmune disease lupus reacted with previously unknown particles—the snRNPs. That observation led to her hypothesis that snRNPS, operating within the nucleus, are part of what has been named the spliceosome—the complex of molecules that removes the introns from pre-mRNA and splices together the remaining exons to form messenger RNA. "We did the first experiments that showed they were, in fact, involved in splicing," as Steitz told Woodbury. "[Steitz's] insight was a true inspiration," according to Susan Berget of the Baylor College of Medicine, as quoted in the *ASCB Newsletter*. "Her hypothesis set the field ahead by light years and heralded the avalanche of small RNAs that have since been discovered to play a role in multiple steps in RNA biosynthesis." Steitz is currently studying viral snRNPS as well as other effects of splicing on RNA in its activities later in the process of protein synthesis. She and her colleagues are also investigating types of snRNPS that are involved in excising a rare class of introns. Medical scientists have translated her findings into clinical uses that Steitz regards as, in her words, "absolutely amazing." One team, for example, found a way to use aberrant splicing to prevent the effects of muscular dystrophy in dogs. "Basically, they designed a snRNP to undo the drastic consequences of a mutation. I think that is just extremely cool," Steitz told Woodbury.

Steitz directs the work of two dozen people in her lab, among them seven graduate and undergraduate students and, in the summer, high-school students. "Part of the reason Yale is so great is that it has such fabulous undergraduates. Getting them into your lab is such a joy," she told the ASCB interviewer. Steitz makes sure that, in addition to group investigations, each person conducts his or her own project, "even if it's very simple, to get them hooked on how much fun it is," as she told Carey. "It's very valuable for the future and for getting women into science," she noted. At Yale, and particularly since she became a department head, she has seen firsthand the many ways in which scientists' careers can be affected by subjective decisions on the parts of their colleagues and others, regarding matters ranging from the question of who deserves extra laboratory space, a personal secretary, or research assistants, to whom should be granted a trip to a major conference, where presenting a paper confers at least some degree of prominence and offers the possibility of making useful

contacts, to who merits tenure. Steitz found that women were rarely the beneficiaries of such decisions. "Unless you really know what's going on inside the department, it all looks perfectly reasonable," Steitz told Kate Zernike for the *New York Times* (April 8 , 2001). "If a woman is a star there aren't that many problems. If she is as good as the rest of the men, it's really pretty awful. A woman is expected to be twice as good for half [the pay]." Steitz wrote for the Agora web site, "Even today, I find from conversations with young women that they are frightened by the prospects of what lies ahead because so few women seem to have 'made it' in academic science without encountering difficulties [because of their gender]. We cannot expect to capture the interest and talents of girls and women for the scientific enterprise unless they can view their own participation as possible. . . . Our challenge now is to devise more effective practices in our universities and other research venues for capturing and advancing women in the scientific hierarchy."

Woodbury described Steitz as having "a particular smile that flickers beneath her rosy, yet elegant cheekbones when she is talking about or with her students. It's something her students notice and appreciate. The smile plays there as a message of encouragement, endorsing their right to think aloud even as they sometimes fumble with their biological formulations." Steitz told Woodbury, "Almost every time I lecture at another university, someone comes up to me and says, 'I took your biochemistry course back in 19 xx, and it was terrific.' What more can one wish for?" Steitz's husband is a Sterling professor of molecular biophysics, biochemistry, and chemistry at Yale. Steitz told an HHMI interviewer that having a spouse who can empathize with "the pressures and joys of a career in academic science makes it all possible." The couple have one son, Jon, who played minor-league baseball for a few years after earning a bachelor's degree from Yale and is currently attending Yale Law School.

—N.W.M.

Suggested Reading: Agora: For Women in Science Web site Apr. 6, 2006; *ASCM (American Society for Cell Biology) Newsletter* p18+ June 2006; HHMI.org; *Howard Hughes Medical Institute Bulletin* p21+ Feb. 2006; *M2 Presswire* (on-line) May 21, 2002; *New York Times* Education Life Supplement p34 Apr. 8, 2001; *Toronto (Ontario) Star* (on-line) Apr. 3, 2006; *Who's Who in America, 2006*

Michal Daniel, courtesy of the Public Theater

Stew

Aug. 16, 1961– Musician; songwriter

Address: 19 W. 44th St., Suite 1410, New York, NY 10036

"We have these fans who think it's wrong that we're not more famous," the rock musician Stew explained to Deborah Sontag for the *New York Times* (May 21, 2007), referring to himself and his partner, Heidi Rodewald. "But we know that fame just isn't the judge of quality, except in America. Only in America do they go: 'You've made six records? You're making a play? But I've never heard of you.'" Stew's musical, *Passing Strange*, which debuted in October 2006 at the Berkeley Repertory Theater, in California, and had a successful limited engagement at the Public Theater in New York in the spring of 2007, has helped to grant his fans' wishes, winning acclaim and followers for its innovative and experimental approach to musical theater. *Passing Strange*, performed by an all-black cast with Stew as the guitar-playing onstage narrator, uses rock to tell the story of a character called Youth—whose travels from California to Europe, search for identity, and adventures with sex and drugs draw on Stew's own past. Prior to *Passing Strange*, Stew served as the frontman for the band the Negro Problem, which released the critically acclaimed albums *Post Minstrel Syndrome* (1997), *Joys & Concerns* (1999), and *Welcome Black* (2002); his albums with Rodewald are *Guest Host* (2000), *The Naked Dutch Painter . . . and Other Songs* (2002), and *Something Deeper Than These Changes* (2003). Stew's category-resistant songs often contain social commentary, while their melo-dies have inspired comparisons to 1960s pop; his influences include a wide variety of acts, from R&B artists to the principal figures of the British Invasion.

Stew was born Mark Stewart on August 16, 1961 in the middle-class Fairfax District of Los Angeles, California, a neighborhood he described to David Ng for the *Village Voice* (May 2, 2007) as "a black-Jewish-Mexican-Asian bubble of liberalism." Early on his family exposed him to a wide variety of music; his sisters and cousins eagerly awaited new albums by artists and groups ranging from the Beatles to James Brown. That eclecticism influenced Stew's own tastes and would inform his work as a musician. When he was eight years old, he started taking piano lessons; he took up the guitar at 12. He recalled to Gary Shipes for the *Stuart (Florida) News/Port St. Lucie News* (December 19, 1997), "I remember being at my cousin's house when I was really little and being faced with this terrible dilemma. James Brown was on TV at the same time as The Beatles' cartoon. We didn't know what to do, so we had to jump between the two. That's still my musical philosophy in a nutshell." In addition to musicians, Stew's role models included comedians; he grew up idolizing such stand-up comics as Richard Pryor and Lenny Bruce (influences that would later be exemplified in his lyrics).

Stew has recalled that while there was pressure from African-American students in the schools he attended to listen only to R&B and other black music, he enjoyed music that included punk, hard rock, progressive rock, and New Wave. "In my junior high school," he said to Jim DeRogatis for the *Chicago Sun-Times* (August 2, 2002), Stew and his friends "used to have to get protection from guys on the football team because the hardcore guys in school would beat us up if they heard us listening to, like, the Who." Stew has taken exception to what he sees as the different standards applied to black and white musicians and music fans, telling Gilbert Garcia for the *Phoenix (Arizona) New Times* (October 22, 1998), "It's okay for skinny English white guys to try to [appropriate the] blues, and it's okay for skinny New York white guys like David Byrne to try to pretend they're African, but I'm playing so-called 'white music'? . . . Paul Simon can find some Brazilian or African music history, but if you're black, you're supposed to do what your neighborhood's doing. Well, my neighborhood wasn't that boring." In his teens, in the mid-1970s, Stew sang gospel music in a choir in a Baptist church in Los Angeles, played the guitar and piano in a number of garage bands, and made his first recording with a band called the Animated. Also during his teenage years, Stew began immersing himself in art history. He started reading about Dadaist performance art and Viennese Actionism (a brief movement in 20th-century art that surfaced in the 1960s). The concept of melding performance art and music soon became his passion.

After attending Fairfax High School for a year and a half, Stew went on to graduate from Hamilton High School in 1979. He enrolled at Los Angeles City College several times for the sole purpose of having access to film equipment; he never graduated. Feeling constricted by middle-class life in Los Angeles, the musician relocated to New York City before he was 20. There, he performed with what he has described as a "found-object all-percussion performance combo" as well as with a more conventional R&B/pop band. (The drum set Stew used in the "found-object all-percussion performance combo" consisted of discarded objects he found on the street on the way to his gigs.) At 21 he began traveling in Europe, settling in the early 1980s in Berlin, Germany, where he fell in with artists in an underground bohemian scene. For a number of years, he traveled extensively around the continent with a collective whose members performed a hybrid of musical theater and performance art. Stew's exposure during those years to German cabaret and to the works of the German playwright Bertolt Brecht and the Belgian singer-songwriter Jacques Brel had a significant impact on his life and art; the lyrics in his subsequent work, packed with cultural allusions and quotations, reflect those influences. In Europe Stew met his first wife, to whom he was married for 12 years and with whom he fathered a daughter.

Stew next returned to his work with more conventional bands—and to Los Angeles, where an indie-rock scene was thriving. In the early 1990s he performed with a series of bands, including ImPOPisation, Crazy Sound All Stars, and Popular Front, before teaming up with the drummer Charles Pagano in an experimental group affiliated with a local art gallery. Although the group's sound—characterized by heavy use of tape loops and improvisation—appealed to him, he found that the verse-chorus-verse format of his lyrics were at odds with the group's avant-garde style. He explained to Garcia, "I was pretty much closeted about being a pop songwriter. It's almost exactly as if you were a gay person wanting to come out in front of all these straight people, and you didn't want to freak them out too much. So you dropped little hints here and there. Every couple of songs I showed the band, it would get a little more melodic." After the departure of the group's original bassist/guitarist, Stew stayed on with the band, which came to be known as the Negro Problem. The group's other musicians—all of them white—included Pagano, the keyboardist/accordionist Jill Meschke Blair, the bassist Gwynne Kahn (who had formerly been in the band Pandoras), and an auxiliary member, the multi-instrumentalist Probyn Gregory, who also played with the Wondermints. In late 1995 they released a collection of singles (including an innovative cover of Richard Harris's "MacArthur Park" and a multi-part pop operetta entitled "Miss Jones") in a limited-edition boxed set. Then, after Blair filled in as keyboardist for the British band Elastica's lucrative U.S. tour, she re-turned to the Negro Problem with enough money to buy an eight-track recorder, which the group used to record their first album, *Post Minstrel Syndrome.*

Made for the modest sum of $900, *Post Minstrel Syndrome* was distributed nationally, due almost solely to the critical acclaim it received. (The band's name, a phrase first used by whites in the Reconstruction era who were wary of integration, was also an attention-grabber; as Gilbert Garcia wrote, "Not since the . . . heyday of the Dead Kennedys has an American band managed to make people squirm so readily at the mere mention of its moniker.") "We just thought it was hilarious," Stew said to Gary Shipes about the band's name. "Though there is a serious side to it, because I'm a black person making this music, we're always going to run into the race issue. And as a band, we always thought of some record executive wringing his hands and saying, 'God, they could be so massive if it wasn't for the Negro problem.'" The group sought to challenge the idea of the divide between so-called "white" and "black" music, categories that had no place for an otherwise white band that was fronted by an African-American—and that counted among its influences artists as far-ranging as Sly Stone, George Clinton, Stephen Sondheim, and Burt Bacharach. Critics lauded *Post Minstrel Syndrome*'s sophisticated blend of pop melodies, pun-happy lyrics, and psychedelic touches reminiscent of Jimi Hendrix and the Chambers Brothers. Shipes wrote that *Post Minstrel Syndrome* "delivers delectable melodies tinted with timely racial views that swing between satire and despondency," adding that it was "simply the best album of 1997." Stew told Shipes about the work, "I wanted to make an album that sounded like some curio recorded in 1968, some dusty jewel box you'd find in an attic." The album included five hidden tracks, featuring three solo acoustic performances by Stew that hinted at the introspective sound of his future solo efforts.

Following the departures of Blair and Kahn, Stew quickly added the former Wednesday Week musician Heidi Rodewald, with whom he became romantically involved, as both bassist and keyboardist. Since 1997 Rodewald has served as co-writer, arranger, and producer of songs by Stew and the Negro Problem. In 1999 the Negro Problem released their follow-up album, *Joys & Concerns*, which included work by guest musicians Probyn Gregory and Lisa Jenio. A much darker, melancholic work than their debut, the album was inspired by Stew's personal troubles, among them the breakup of his 12-year marriage and his hand-to-mouth existence as a musician living on the earnings from relatively obscure albums. "I was very depressed back then," he recalled to Sara Scribner for the *Phoenix New Times* (September 28, 2000). "The hard part was not being with my kid." He added, however, "I wasn't depressed at all making this record. It was a very happy experience." Like their debut, the band's sophomore effort garnered unanimous praise from critics. Matthew Greenwald, in a review for the All Music Guide Web site, called the album "easily one of the finest power pop records of 1999," adding that it created a "post-psychedelic LA feel that is infectious." The glowing feedback was not enough, however, to bring the group financial stability or keep its members from seeking more lucrative projects. Pagano's departure from the group, in late 1999, marked the beginning of the Negro Problem's dissolution (though he continued to appear with them occasionally). Stew, for his part, was now free to experiment with songwriting for solo acoustic guitar.

Stew realized that desire in 2000, with the release of Guest Host, a record that received "album of the year" honors from Entertainment Weekly. He attributed much of the success of Guest Host to his relationship with Rodewald, who co-produced the album. Stew told Scribner, "She really helped me in knowing when to stop. With Negro Problem, I would say, 'One more triangle overdub!' Those guys wouldn't tell me to stop. If I said, 'Hey, dude, I'm hearing fuzz accordion and bagpipes,' they'd be like, 'Okay, dude, I think I know a bagpipe player!' She'd stop it right there." Sean Westergaard, writing for All Music Guide, called the album a "sunny pop masterpiece" and praised in particular Stew's lyrics and gift for storytelling. A song called "The Stepford Lives," whose title is a play on that of the film The Stepford Wives, was considered a highlight of the album, with lines such as, "A husband named 'honey' with too much money / He's sort of a jerk he told her not to work." The song "Rehab" includes the lines, "When she got out of rehab for the very first time / she was very very very very very very very very very optimistic very very very very very very very very very very very very optimistic"; as the song's last verse begins, the character enters rehab for the 22d time.

In 2002 Entertainment Weekly picked as "album of the year" Stew's next solo record, The Naked Dutch Painter . . . and Other Songs, which was recorded during live sessions at the Knitting Factory in Los Angeles and enhanced with overdubbing in a studio. Matthew Greenwald wrote about Stew and the album, "Filled with kaleidoscopic originality and an iconoclastic point of view, he remains one of the finest songwriters to come out of Los Angeles in decades, and this, his sophomore solo album, underlines the fact. One of Stew's greatest strengths is not just his melodic sensibility, but his ability to use lyrics as musical phrases." Songs such as "Single Woman Sitting" and "Giselle" were particularly noted for their formally elegant narrative structures; their subject matter ranges from sex and drugs to rock music to race. The latter song, about an intellectual young woman who carries a switchblade and takes acid, has lyrics that include: "Her cat has a personal chef / Her dog wears a dead-mink sweater / Her rabbit won't pose for Hef / She wears leather / whatever / the weather / Giselle is the cross and the nails and the crown and the thieves / She howls at the street

lights and dances whenever she pleases." (A number of Stew's songs have centered on such unconventional, defiant women.) "The Negro Problem is like having a party, and the solo records are like writing a letter," Stew explained to Erin Aubry Kaplan for LA Weekly (April 12, 2002). "I wouldn't tell the Naked Dutch Painter story at a party, but I would tell it in a letter."

In late 2002 Stew returned to the studio to record Welcome Black, a Negro Problem album whose personnel consisted of only Stew and Rodewald, playing different instruments under the pseudonyms Vox Marshall, Sigfried Gretsch, Ennio Lessaconi, and Eddie Munch. The following year brought Stew's third solo effort, Something Deeper Than These Changes. Matt Cibula, in a review of that record for Pop Matters (November 13, 2003, on-line), wrote that Stew was "the best songwriter in the United States," adding, "It's the most melodic set of songs he's ever done, but it's also more overtly folky than any of his other records, too: hushed, soft, minimal."

In 2004 Stew put his two main projects—his solo work and work with the Negro Problem—on hold and began touring the country with Rodewald to appear in various versions of a cabaret called Travelogue, with many of the shows at Joe's Pub in New York City, a 180-seat performance space connected with the Public Theater. Like his previous live acts, Stew's cabaret was complete with storytelling and humor between songs. The move into the theater realm came about when the Public's proprietors sought to turn the music fans who patronized Joe's Pub into theatergoers; having observed the theatrical elements in Stew's rock shows, Bill Bragin, the director of Joe's Pub, suggested that the musician could help achieve the theater's goal. A meeting with the Public's then-dramaturge, Rebecca Rugg, left Stew feeling reluctant, as he recalled to Mike Boehm for the Los Angeles Times (October 22, 2006): "I said, 'Becca, I don't want to do theater, because I don't know anything about doing theater.'" After Rugg introduced Stew to the theater director Annie Dorsen, who challenged him and Rodewald to create a story that would be told through rock music, the musician was persuaded. Over the next two years, Dorsen, Stew, and Rodewald transformed Travelogue into Passing Strange, a semi-autobiographical odyssey that follows a character named Youth from middle-class Los Angeles to Europe and back. "Passing Strange is more like a rock concert than a musical," Stew told David Ng. "When people hear the album for this, I don't want them to think, 'Wow, that's a great show-tunes album.' I want them to think that it's a great rock album, period."

When the rock musical opened at the Berkeley Repertory Theater, in Berkeley, California, in October 2006, many critics complained that the nearly three-hour production was episodic and unfocused. Stew and his collaborators largely rewrote the show in the months leading up to its New York debut. Passing Strange opened at the Public in May

2007 to mixed-to-good reviews. The actors in the show's all-black cast played multiple roles; Stew narrated the different stages of Youth's life, as the character tries to "find" himself and make connections with those around him. Charles Isherwood, in a review for the *New York Times* (May 15, 2007), wrote, "Bald and big-bellied, with a neat goatee and quirky eyeglasses, [Stew] has an air more professorial than swoon-inducing. . . . But Professor Stew can also play a mean guitar, and when necessary, he strides the stage like an evangelical preacher, or a preening rocker, to whip the audience into a froth. Part concert, with Stew leading an onstage band; part book musical with a full (and terrific) cast, *Passing Strange* defies generic categories. . . . Because Stew's aesthetic and moral awakening takes place against a shifting backdrop, no other characters stick around long enough to claim a full role in the proceedings, despite perfectly pitched comic performances from the whole cast. The spectacle of watching a young man try on various emotional and artistic attitudes will strike happy chords in the hearts of ex-dreamers of youthful dreams, but colder eyes may see it as an extended exercise in musical navel-gazing." Isherwood also, however, wrote that the show was "full of heart." Mark Blankenship, writing for *Variety* (May 14, 2007), called Stew "a cerebral writer" and noted that the arguments he makes in his lyrics reveal "a humanity that makes them just as accessible as drama as they are as social analysis." Stew considers the innovative play to be just an extension of his music, admitting to David Ng, "I'm not a playwright, and I'm comfortable with that. . . . We don't think theater is some sort of pinnacle. We've been invited to this big party, and the truth is that we're really here to take the sandwiches."

Stew is an insatiable reader who claims to make a beeline for the bookshelves of any house he enters. Despite critical acclaim, sales of his albums average around 3,350 copies; to date, he has drawn his largest audience with "Gary's Song," which he wrote for a 2005 episode of the TV cartoon *SpongeBob SquarePants*. Stew is the subject of a documentary entitled *What's the Problem?*, directed by Jeffrey Winograd and tentatively scheduled for release in 2007.

—C.C.

Suggested Reading: All Music Guide (on-line); *Los Angeles Times* F p2 Sep. 22, 1997, E p34 Oct. 22, 2006; *New York Times* E p1 May 21, 2007; *Phoenix (Arizona) New Times* Music Sep. 28, 2000; Stew's Web Site; *Stuart (Florida) News/Port Lucie News* D p1 Dec. 19, 1997; *Village Voice* p65 Sep. 17, 2002, May 2, 2007

Selected Recordings: as leader of the Negro Problem—*Post Minstrel Syndrome*, 1997; *Joys & Concerns*, 1999; *Welcome Black*, 2002; as solo artist—*Guest Host*, 2000; *The Naked Dutch Painter . . . and Other Songs*, 2002; *Something Deeper Than These Changes*, 2003

Selected Theatrical Works: *Passing Strange*, 2006

Michael Lavine, courtesy of Workman Publishing

Stoller, Debbie

(STOH-luhr)

Nov. 3, 1962– Co-founder and editor of Bust; *writer*

Address: Bust *Magazine, 78 Fifth Ave., Fifth Fl., New York, NY 10011*

When the editor, author, knitter, and feminist Debbie Stoller founded the magazine *Bust*, in 1993, she needed to get something—so to speak—off her chest. Having recently earned a Ph.D. in social psychology, with a dissertation on the media's attitude toward women, she had become increasingly aware of the effect that a magazine can have on the public's perception of gender—and increasingly frustrated that she could not find a magazine that embodied her brand of feminism. So Stoller decided to create her own, one that would embrace the values that she could not find represented on newsstands. "I knew I wanted to make some media that would influence women in a more positive way, and I felt like it was really important that we figure out new lives for women, and bust stereotypes, and talk honestly about the things we're insecure about, and be really loud and boisterous about sex," Stoller recalled to Daphne Gordon for the *Toronto Star* (June 5, 2002). As the editor in chief and co-founder of *Bust*—subtitled *The Magazine for Women with Something to Get Off Their Chests*—Stoller has reinvented the idea of the women's magazine and, in doing so, introduced a new, subversive perspective on feminism. The magazine is frequently identified with third-wave feminism, a controversial movement that began in the early 1990s as a response to the second-wave feminism of the 1960s, 1970s, and 1980s, which is credited with making large advances in many areas, specifically abortion rights, co-education, and workplace discrimination. (First-wave feminism, of the late 19th and early 20th centuries, relates largely to the struggle for women's suffrage.) Third-wave feminists often consider second-wave feminism an essentialist philosophy, criticizing it for assuming a universal female identity; instead, third-wave feminism strives to focus on the individual. "The way women are presented in popular culture is really influential," Stoller told Gordon. "*Bust* is completely intended to change the way people think about women, and the way people think about feminism and the way women think about themselves." Along with her work at *Bust*, Stoller is the author of the popular *Stitch 'n Bitch* series of knitting guides, bringing her same subversive, feminist slant to the craft. With three books so far—*Stitch 'n Bitch: The Knitter's Handbook*, *Stitch 'n Bitch Nation*, and *Stitch 'n Bitch Crochet: The Happy Hooker*—the series has played a leading role in the resurgence of knitting as a hobby, showing women that knitting can be a hip thing to do rather than merely the so-called "women's work" it is often derogatorily perceived to be. "In the past couple years, I've definitely seen knitting go from something that was pretty embarrassing to something that people are proud of," Stoller told *Library Journal* (September 1, 2003). "I don't care what anyone says. That has to be good for feminism." Between *Bust*'s circulation of 100,000 and the best-selling *Stitch 'n Bitch* books, Stoller's message—that feminism, ultimately, is about a woman's right to simply be herself—has helped to redefine feminism for a generation of women. "I feel like we've had an influence on young women in the past 10 years," Stoller said about *Bust* to Zoe Williams for the London *Guardian* (January 8, 2005). "It's not enormous, but among these young women, who talk to other young women, we've created a space for people to think about feminism and what's possible in feminism."

Deborah Susan Stoller was born on November 3, 1962 in the New York City borough of Brooklyn. Her father, Bernard, was a radio operator for the Merchant Marine; her mother, Johanna, who had emigrated from Holland, was a homemaker. Stoller has one younger brother, Peter, who is a graphic designer. Growing up in housing projects in the Canarsie section of Brooklyn, where she attended elementary school at P.S. 272, Stoller realized early on that her mother's position as an unemployed woman came with certain limitations. Still, Johanna Stoller's attitude toward her role taught her daughter a lesson in feminism. "I felt like my mother definitely had a lot less opportunities than my father, but I realized that she really took a lot of pride in being a homemaker," Stoller told *Current Biography*. Stoller attributed that pride to a cultural difference she observed during summer trips to visit family in Holland. There, she found, house-

work—cleaning, cooking, sewing—is appreciated for the labor and skill it requires, while in America the same chores, and the role of the homemaker who performs them, are often denigrated. "As a culture we didn't respect that role at all," Stoller explained to *Current Biography*. "And other cultures where the role really was respected, women really seemed to be valued as well." When Stoller was 11 the family moved to Spring Valley, a suburb of New York City. She spent one year at North Main Street School before going on to Kakiat Junior High School and then Spring Valley Senior High, where she sewed all the costumes for the school plays. During high school Stoller also became increasingly attuned to feminism—an interest, as she only half-jokingly told *Current Biography*, that she credited to "being smart and aware." After graduating she enrolled at the State University of New York (SUNY) at Binghamtom, the only school that she could afford, as she had to pay for her education herself and did not qualify for financial aid. Having entered SUNY with one year of course credits from high school, Stoller graduated in two and a half years, with a major in psychology and a minor in computer science; she had also taken a number of classes in dance and women's studies. After college she spent six months in Holland, working at a research institute in Utrecht.

When she returned to the U.S., Stoller enrolled in the graduate program at Yale University, in New Haven, Connecticut, planning to earn a Ph.D. in psychobiology. Because she had graduated from SUNY so early, Stoller was only 20 when she arrived at Yale. "So I was still pretty young and still pretty dumb," she recalled to *Current Biography*. For the next two and a half years, while focusing primarily on the concrete science of psychobiology, she also took a wide range of classes to fill what she felt were the gaps in her education. She found the new academic focus on film theory and women's studies particularly exciting, but she eventually realized that she would not be able to incorporate those areas of study into her lab work. Unsure if she even wanted to spend her days in a laboratory, Stoller decided to switch her doctoral focus to social psychology. "I wasn't going to be able to hack the lifestyle," she told Marcy Smith Rice for the Raleigh, North Carolina, *News & Observer* (March 25, 2006). "I changed the focus to psychology of women instead of the psychology of leeches." Although Yale did not yet have an official women's studies department, Stoller managed to fashion a women's studies niche within the broader scope of social psychology, applying her science background to clinical research of the new feminist ideas she was encountering. She received her Ph.D. in 1988. In conducting research for her dissertation, which concerned images of women in the media, she presented male and female test subjects with advertisements representing men or women as sexual objects and then observed the power dynamics of the test subjects' subsequent interactions with one another. The results of Stoller's study were inconclusive; a number of similar studies have been done since.

After earning her doctorate, Stoller returned to New York City. Rather than remaining in academia, she wanted to apply her theories about women in the media to the improvement of women's everyday experiences with television, advertisements, and other influential forms of communication. "I did not really know what to do with myself," she recalled to *Current Biography*. "I knew I wanted to try to help make some better media for women." She went to work for the television network MTV, thinking that it might be a place from which she could effect change. Too timid to emphasize her doctorate in trying to get a job, she entered MTV's typing pool, starting a series of extended temp jobs at the network that included a stint as a production assistant on one of its first *Sex in the 90s* specials. Having gained some notice at MTV, Stoller moved to Nickelodeon, one of its sister companies, where she worked first in the marketing-services division, then as a producer, and finally as a multimedia producer, charged with designing the network's first Web site. "That was fun, but it wasn't relating to anything else," she told *Current Biography*. "I was trying to figure out how I could, you know, possibly ever have the influence I wanted to have. But I had to pay my rent." Sitting in the office one day in 1992, Stoller read *Sassy*, a magazine for teenage girls, whose message of empowerment impressed her. Though she was much older than the magazine's target readers, Stoller thought that *Sassy* presented an interesting and positive media image for women—one that she wanted to replicate for her age bracket. "I felt like there were so many things for my generation to figure out that we could use something that would be encouraging," Stoller told *Current Biography*.

A year later Stoller and her former Nickelodeon co-worker Marcelle Karp founded *Bust*, subtitled *The Magazine for Women with Something to Get Off Their Chests*. Besides the obvious anatomic connection, Stoller thought the word "bust" carried symbolic power, which she explained to *Current Biography*: "It's kind of sexy and it's kind of aggressive, kind of like busting out or busting stereotypes." Working on the magazine while holding down their full-time jobs, Stoller and Karp put together the first issue by photocopying and stapling pages on the sly at the Nickelodeon offices. "It was exciting to us that we made something," Stoller told *Current Biography*. "Instead of just talking about making something, we actually made it." Published in July 1993, the magazine's first run of 500 copies, priced at one dollar each, sold out, prompting a second 500-copy run. For the second issue, Stoller and Karp secured an art director, Laurie Henzel, and a small distributor, who advised them to upgrade to newsprint for the 3,000-copy order. For the next six years, while maintaining their other jobs, Stoller, Karp, and Henzel continued to produce *Bust*, which grew a little bit bigger and a bit more professional in appearance with

each issue. They earned no money from *Bust*'s sales, since all the profits went into producing the next issue. During the late 1990s Stoller also wrote a biweekly column for the Canadian digital magazine *Shift*. The column, "The XX Files," examined the interplay between gender and the Internet.

By 1999, when Stoller and Karp published *The Bust Guide to the New Girl Order*, the magazine's circulation had risen to 32,000. An anthology of work from the first six years of *Bust*, *The Bust Guide* contains 69 essays, with such titles as "Sex and the Thinking Girl" and "Men Are from Uranus," organized in eight sections, ranging from "Girlhood" to "Young Motherhood." In the introduction to the book, as quoted by Laura Compton in the *San Francisco Chronicle* (October 3, 1999), Stoller and Karp explained the theory behind *Bust*. "In *Bust*, we've captured the voice of a brave new girl," the editors wrote, "one that is raw and real, straightforward and sarcastic, smart and silly, and liberally sprinkled with references to our own Girl Culture—that shared set of female experiences that includes . . . sexism and shoplifting, *Vogue* and vaginas." Compton praised the honesty of the writing collected in *The Bust Guide*. "*Bust*'s allure has always been its candor and fresh first-person writing," she wrote. "Reading these pieces—on subjects ranging from cheerleading tryouts to abortion, lesbian motherhood to teenybopper obsessions—is like eavesdropping at the beauty parlor or reading an older sister's diary." Some reviewers, however, argued that the book's spirit of freedom went too far in some directions; specifically, they objected to anonymous submissions and to a lack of careful editing—which was presumably meant to ensure the writers' freedom but which critics thought tended, like the anonymous submissions, to undermine the collection's seriousness. "There is plenty to entertain in this meaty collection, and it's a fun read for women of any age," Ameland Copeland wrote for the *Women's Review of Books* (November 1, 1999). "But if you're looking for more—enlightenment, salvation or even just a new literary best friend—perhaps *The Bust Guide to the New Girl Order* is best left to the combat boots and Hello Kitty barrettes set." Compton, however, defended the book's place in contemporary feminism, noting only that it is not a perfect representation of the magazine. "If *The Bust Guide* has a flaw, it's that it loses some of its subversiveness in book form. Although some illustrations are reproduced, much of the retro clip art and typography that give the zine its flavor is missing, most likely due to copyright issues," she wrote. "Still, *The Bust Guide* goes where too many so-called feminist authors fear to tread, embodying the convictions and contradictions of '90s feminism without apology. For that, it deserves a place on best-seller lists as well as women's studies programs."

Shortly after getting the book deal, Stoller had left Nickelodeon, though she still worked for the network on freelance projects. With the book's publication, and the resulting press coverage of

Bust, MTV asked Stoller and Karp to put together a pilot of a television show. They created a series of *Sesame Street*–like skits about women's issues, but the show was not picked up. In 2000 Stoller and Karp sold *Bust* to the dot-com company Razorfish, in a deal they hoped would allow them to work on the magazine full-time. From 2000 to 2001 *Bust* appeared in four glossy issues, and a September 10, 2001 article in the *New York Times* Business section described it as being at the forefront of the new zine economy. But the September 11 terrorist attacks, combined with the continuing failure of the dot-com industry, forced Razorfish to declare bankruptcy. (It has since re-formed, as Avenue A./Razorfish Inc.) To regain control of *Bust*, then a Razorfish property, Stoller and Henzel had to raise the money to buy back the magazine. (Karp had left *Bust* earlier in 2001.) "It was a difficult time to be engaged in something so stressful," Stoller recalled to *Current Biography*. "Everyone was heartbroken and depressed and scared." She and Henzel put out word that *Bust* was in danger, and within two months they had raised $40,000. Readers re-subscribed in advance, fans sent cash, a group of girls in Toronto, Canada, held a bake-sale fund-raiser, and some of Stoller's friends put on a musical benefit that alone raised $10,000. Stoller and Henzel raised enough money to buy the magazine, and they remain its sole owners today.

Meanwhile, as *Bust* was gaining prominence in the late 1990s, Stoller had begun making another contribution to the feminist dialogue, reclaiming the seemingly outdated hobby of knitting for the modern woman (and man). On the *Bust Guide* book tour in 1999, Stoller—who is afraid of flying—took a train all over the country. To keep herself occupied, she picked up an abandoned project, which was to knit one sleeve of a sweater. By the end of the tour, the sweater was finished, and Stoller was hooked. She began knitting in earnest and soon established the first "Stitch 'n Bitch" network in New York City, a social group that is dedicated to knitting and whose name dates at least as far back as the 1950s. She began writing about the group in *Bust*, which already ran articles on crafts regularly, and the idea began to spread to other cities around the country, becoming part of a growing national knitting craze. Soon, Workman Publishing approached Stoller about writing her own knitting book. The result, *Stitch 'n Bitch: The Knitter's Handbook*, was published in 2003. Featuring such patterns as the "Coney Island Fireworks Scarf" and the "Queen of Hearts Bikini," the book revamped knitting for a younger generation of women. "This is not your same old knitting tutorial," Denise Gamino wrote for the *Austin (Texas) American-Statesman* (November 11, 2003). "It's a witty and charming companion for anyone interested in how two sticks and a piece of string can clothe—or decorate—the world." The book's more outlandish patterns aside, Stoller told *Current Biography* that she thought *Stitch 'n Bitch* was a success because it was, at bottom, a very practical guide to the ba-

sics of knitting. "I spent a lot of time writing the instructions for that book. I was mostly a self-taught knitter too and I knew what kind of things made me bang my head against the wall," she said. "I happen to love to teach and I wanted to make the instructions painfully clear."

With 400,000 copies in print, *Stitch 'n Bitch: The Knitter's Handbook* started a veritable movement. Stoller followed that book up with *Stitch 'n Bitch Nation* (2004) and *Stitch 'n Bitch Crochet: The Happy Hooker* (2006). *Stitch 'n Bitch Nation* includes instructions for more complicated knitting techniques as well as 50 new patterns, such as "Spiderweb Capelet" and "Roller Girl Legwarmers." The "sequel" to *Stitch 'n Bitch* "is a bit like the follow-up to many great movies: it draws you in, but doesn't pack anywhere near the punch of the first one, probably because the first one set the bar so high," a reviewer wrote for *Publishers Weekly* (October 25, 2004). *Stitch n' Bitch Crochet* updated crocheting in the same way that the first *Stitch n' Bitch* book modernized knitting, through funky designs and an irreverent writing style. "A seamless treat for madames and misters alike, this nifty new guide in the best-selling series lets home couturiers crochet their way to funky chic, with needles 'n puns galore," according to CNN.com (March 27, 2006).

When *Stitch 'n Bitch* was first published, many people were confused by the idea of a feminist like Stoller picking up knitting needles. Stoller, however, asserted that there was no inherent contradiction between being a feminist and knitting. Feminism, she said, does not have to mean a refutation of traditionally female pursuits; instead, it should allow women to embrace those previously stigmatized hobbies—or any other hobby—freely. "Among a certain group of younger knitters there is a bit of a political aspect to proudly brandishing the knitting needles," she explained to Neda Ulaby for the National Public Radio program *All Things Considered* (January 15, 2002). Stoller—who comes from a long line of knitters—also pointed out that learning the craft shows contemporary women (and men) how difficult knitting can be. "Knitting is a little bit harder I think than most people realize. And that's one of the great things," she told Kathleen Hays, Valerie Morris, and Gerri Willis for the CNNfN program *The Flipside* (February 4, 2004). "Because I think when you start to learn it, you really do gain this newfound respect for all the people who did it before you. Because you realize it takes skill." Stitch 'n Bitch groups have been formed in almost every state in the U.S., as well as in many foreign countries. Explaining the appeal of knitting and crocheting to Julie Anderson for the *Omaha (Nebraska) World-Herald* (April 20, 2006), Stoller emphasized that ultimately the Stitch 'n Bitch groups are not about feminism, or even, truly, about knitting. "I think people, women especially, have been hungry to have something in their lives but losing weight, getting fit and chasing a man," Stoller said. "And it's great for socializing in a casual, simple way. It's never really about making the thing. It's really more about the pleasure that's involved in doing it and in learning a new skill. . . . It's just so relaxing and delicious."

Stoller continues in her role as editor in chief of *Bust*. Her most recent book, *Son of Stitch 'n Bitch: 45 Projects to Knit and Crochet for Men*, was published in November 2007. She lives in New York City.

—C.S.

Suggested Reading: (London) *Guardian* p27 Jan. 8, 2005; (Minneapolis, Minnesota) *Star Tribune* E p1 Dec. 10, 1994; *Toronto Star* F p8 June 5, 2002

Selected Books: *Stitch 'n Bitch: The Knitter's Handbook*, 2003; *Stitch 'n Bitch Nation*, 2004; *Stitch 'n Bitch Crochet: The Happy Hooker*, 2006; *Stitch 'n Bitch: 45 Projects to Knit and Crochet for Men*, 2007; as co-editor—*The Bust Guide to the New Girl Order*, 1999

Karen Bleier/AFP/Getty Images

Storch, Gerald L.

Oct. 31, 1956– Chairman and chief executive officer of Toys "R" Us

Address: Toys "R" Us, 1 Geoffery Way, Wayne, NJ 07470-2035

Gerald L. Storch assumed the post of chairman of the board and chief executive officer of Toys "R" Us on February 7, 2006, four months after he abruptly left his post as vice chairman of the Target Corp. During his 12 years with Target, that compa-

ny—along with Wal-Mart—pushed Toys "R" Us from first place to a not-very-close second among retailers of playthings in the U.S. "Pound for pound, Target does the best job in toys. If you were going to take an executive from a rival, you would take from Target," the toy-industry analyst Sean P. McGowan of the financial-services company Harris Nesbitt told Michael Barbaro and Andrew Ross Sorkin for the *New York Times* (February 7, 2006). Toys "R" Us chose Storch after a nearly one-year search for a successor to John H. Eyler Jr., who had stepped down as chairman and CEO after the firm was sold, in July 2005, to an investment group consisting of affiliates of Bain Capital Partners LLC, Kohlberg Kravis, Roberts & Co., and Vornado Realty Trust. Despite fierce competition from Wal-Mart and Target and the decline in toy sales in recent years (partly because of the growing popularity of electronic games), Storch has said that to a large extent the troubles besetting Toys "R" Us were self-inflicted. "In every segment of retail, there are dedicated specialty retailers that are succeeding against Wal-Mart and Target," he told Michael Barbaro for the *New York Times* (November 19, 2006). "The model is out there. Best Buy is clearly thriving. Walgreen's is the leader in pharmacy. Bed Bath & Beyond does very well in the home segment. What they all do is become the authority." Storch, who holds graduate degrees in both law and business, began his professional life at McKinsey & Co., a consulting firm that advises businesses on ways to function more effectively and increase profits. He spent 12 years with McKinsey before joining Target, in 1993, when the chain was among the retail-store holdings of the Dayton-Hudson Corp. (renamed Target in 2000), the corporate umbrella for hundreds of stores. During his tenure the company's total revenues rose from $21.3 billion, in 1994, to $52.6 billion, in 2005. Storch, Michael Barbaro observed, "is clearly more comfortable crunching numbers and fine-tuning store operations than he is around toys." But, he also wrote, "such analytical steeliness may be just the medicine that Toys 'R' Us needs to survive."

Gerald L. Storch was born on October 31, 1956 and grew up in Jacksonville, Florida. Easily accessible sources contain no information about his parents, childhood, or any other aspect of his personal life aside from his higher education. Storch attended Harvard University, in Cambridge, Masschusetts, where he was editor in chief of a short-lived campus magazine called *Harvard Response*. He earned a B.A. degree with honors in 1977 and then enrolled in Harvard's dual-degree graduate program in law and business. He received an M.B.A. degree with honors in 1981 and a J.D. degree magna cum laude in 1982. In the latter year he joined the Boston office of McKinsey & Co., a New York City–based management consulting firm, where he specialized in retail-sector matters and consumer and financial services. Storch later worked in other branches and became a partner of the firm during his 12 years with McKinsey.

In 1993 Storch joined the Dayton-Hudson Corp., in Minneapolis, Minnesota, with the title of senior vice president of strategic planning. The fourth-largest retailer in the U.S. at that time, Dayton-Hudson owned 834 general-merchandise retail stores in 33 states, including two discount chains—Target and Mervyn's—and the more upscale chains Dayton's, Hudson's, and Marshall Field's. Among Storch's priorities was the revival of Mervyn's nearly 300 stores, many of which were struggling to remain competitive with such rivals as Kohl's, Sears, J.C. Penney, and Montgomery Ward (the last of which closed its doors in 2001 and now sells only through its catalogs and the Internet). In a failed marketing campaign undertaken before his arrival, Mervyn's had tried to promote trendier clothing labels at the expense of traditional brands. Storch steered Mervyn's back to "more middle-of-the-road approaches" to fashion, as Sally Apgar and Kristin Tillotson reported in the Minneapolis, Minnesota, Star Tribune (July 20, 1995), focusing on such clothing labels as Levi's, Lee, and Dockers and on well-known home-appliance brands. "Our customers want things that are fun and cool but not too crazy," Storch told Apgar for the Star Tribune (July 23, 1995). "We had gone too far before. The customer voted." He added that less familiar private labels "are still a key strategic advantage that will positively differentiate us from the competition." Over the next few years, Storch's remedial actions produced mediocre results.

In 1996, prompted by the success of Target stores, which in 1995 had accounted for two-thirds of Dayton-Hudson's revenues, Storch and Robert J. "Bob" Ulrich, who had become Dayton-Hudson's chairman and chief executive officer in 1994, launched what they termed the Targetization of all the firm's stores. Until then each Dayton-Hudson chain had operated its business independently. As Apgar wrote for the Star Tribune (March 1, 1993), "It was unheard of for a [Hudson's, Dayton's, or Marshall Field's] department store buyer who'd been to New York City on a buying trip to share his or her fashion list with a buyer at Target . . . or Mervyn's. . . . But now hip tips are swapped along with negotiating points to use on certain manufacturers." Storch told Apgar, "If some of the excitement level at Target is transferred to the other operating companies, that's great. If some of the urgency transfers, that's great. If some of the culture transfers, that's great." He also said, "More and more American corporations are coming to the same conclusion that you simply can't afford to operate in a Balkanized fashion. That's why we believe in the power of one." (Like "Targetization," "power of one" became a Dayton-Hudson mantra.)

Also in 1996 Dayton-Hudson began offering a Target credit card—called a guest card or red card and now known as a REDcard—to attract more customers. "We viewed this from the beginning as much more important [than] a branding matter," Storch told a reporter for MMR (Mass Market Retailers, December 14, 1998). "We viewed it as part of a loyalty program as well." Kenneth B. Woodrow, then Dayton-Hudson's president, told the MMR writer that the card gave the company "a platform from which to communicate with a guest [that is, customer] on a one-to-one basis that we've never had before. We know who that guest is for the first time, and we know what she's buying. We can wrap services around the card that we can't offer in the stores themselves, so it gives us a way to intensify our relationship with the guest." At the end of 1997, Dayton-Hudson reported $751 million in profits, a 62 percent increase from the previous year. By the end of the next year, 11 million REDcards were in the hands of consumers.

In 1999 Storch became president of credit and new business at Dayton-Hudson. In that position he oversaw the development and expansion of SuperTargets, combination grocery stores/discount superstores that contained Starbucks cafés and offered Archer Farms (Target's label) foods. "We're working to convey the atmosphere of an upscale grocer . . . ," Storch told Jim McCartney for the Saint Paul, Minnesota, Pioneer Press (October 6, 1999). "We want to bring fashion to food." In 2001 Storch was promoted to vice chairman of what had been renamed the Target Corp. His responsibilities included financial services and new businesses for the Target, Mervyn's, and Marshall Field's stores. In an interview with a writer for MMR (March 19, 2001), he reiterated his belief that Target's success lay in enhancing its brand, which "stands for being cool and hip and hot, and for providing value as well." "We had three strategic choices," he told a writer for the Economist (May 5, 2001). "To specialise, to become the low-cost producer or to differentiate ourselves. . . . Target chose differentiation—by repositioning itself as a branded designer chain, but priced for the masses." Storch saw no future in Web-based retailing. As he told Bob Keefe for the Austin (Texas) American-Statesman (April 15, 2001), "The bottom line is that the stupid era of the Internet is over. It's not as big as television. It's not as big as print, and it's still got a long way to go before it's a viable way to do business." In Storch's view, the Internet served mainly as a means of "communicating with your customer," in his words.

Among other initiatives that Storch directed, Target introduced a program called Take Charge of Education, whereby 1 percent of the sum that enrollees spent in credit-card purchases was donated to schools that program participants chose from a list compiled by Target. Target also joined with Visa to launch the Target Visa card nationwide. In late 2001 Storch and Jeff Bezos, the CEO of Amazon.com, one of the world's largest Internet retailers, signed a five-year contract that called for Amazon to integrate Target.com product offerings and order fulfillment with its own; in exchange, Target agreed to pay Amazon an annual service fee and share a fixed portion of the profits that accrued from Web transactions. Target's alliance with Amazon was another way "to reach an addition[al] stream of customers on the Internet," according to Storch, as quoted by the *Alameda (California) Times-Star* (November 6, 2001). By the end of 2002, Target posted overall sales of nearly $40 billion; in 2003 the amount was $43.9 billion. At that point Target surpassed Kmart to become the second-biggest discount retailer in the U.S., behind Wal-Mart. The knowledge that the figure of $43.9 billion was precisely the amount that Wal-Mart had amassed in sales in 1992 led Storch to tell Julie Schlosser for CNNMoney.com (October 18, 2004), "This is uncanny. You could say, 'We're ten years behind.' Or you could say, 'Wow, we're the same size as the world's largest company was ten years ago!'" According to Schlosser, Target may have had "only a fifth of the sales and profits of Wal-Mart, but [it] reels them in with ten times the panache." Schlosser also wrote that, by offering affordable clothing by such couture designers as Isaac Mizrahi and Mossimo Giannulli, Target had emerged as "the king of cheap chic." In 2003, according to the *New York Times* (October 5, 2005), Storch's earnings amounted to $1.8 million, with bonuses and options constituting 45 percent. In 2004, according to the same *Times* article, the total was $2.17 million.

One day in October 2005, Storch suddenly handed in his resignation, for reasons that neither he nor Target publicly revealed. The following February Toys "R" Us announced the appointment of Storch as the company's new chairman and CEO. Founded by Charles Lazarus, Toys "R" Us began in 1948 as a Washington, D.C., store called Children's Bargain Town, which sold furniture for babies and children. In response to public requests, Lazarus added toys to his stock, and in the late 1950s, he redesigned his store as a supermarket, in which customers could pick out items themselves. His second store opened with the name Toys "R" Us (with a backward R—a stylistic choice that drew criticism from parents and teachers). The company went public in 1978. With the opening of its first Babies "R" Us store, in 1996, the firm separated most of its items for infants (ranging from pacifiers, nursing bottles, and onesies to strollers and cribs) from products for older children. Because the average buyer of baby merchandise shops for such goods considerably more often than the average person shops for toys, impulse purchases of toys (for older children in tow, for example) in the Toys "R" Us stores began to drop significantly. Toys "R" Us branches grew shabby, and marketing efforts, such as the placement of circulars in newspapers, grew lackadaisical, further eroding customer interest. Competition from Wal-Mart and Target compounded the problem of steadily shrinking sales. In July 2005 Toys "R" Us was sold, and the company reverted to private ownership. John H. Eyler Jr. handed in his resignation, and Richard L. Markee, the head of Babies "R" Us, took over as interim CEO. In January 2006 Toys "R" Us closed dozens of its stores and cut 3,000

jobs, reducing its work force by 11 percent of the total.

When Storch assumed the top spot at Toys "R" Us, in February 2006, according to Michael Barbaro, "he found an undisciplined company that he believed blamed others for its problems rather than facing its own mistakes. He also found a corporate culture wedded to impulsive strategic forays rather than hard data." Storch told Barbaro, "Toys 'R' Us had fallen into the pattern of being a follower, not a leader. Instead of buying product that is hot, we need to make products hot. We need to be like a fashion house." Determined to end what he has termed "victim thinking," Storch adopted the slogan "Playing to win" and ordered the words affixed to employees' ID badges. He dismissed more than half of the company's senior executives, replacing some of them with people recruited from Best Buy and Home Depot, and created a new position, director of trends, to make sure that Toys "R" Us became aware of all the latest crazes early on. He impressed upon store managers the importance of having knowledgeable salespeople on staff. "When a customer comes in our store, our people can tell them what's a great toy for a 10-year-old boy for their birthday, because all we do is toys," he explained to Jeffrey Gold for the Associated Press, as reported in the *Canadian Press* (July 3, 2006). "When you go to a large, multi-product discount chain, you'll be lucky to find someone who can point you to the toy department, or will even take you there, much less answer specific questions." Storch also instituted monthly conference calls that are mandatory for selected managers—including some from branches in the 33 countries overseas in which Toys "R" Us has stores. He ordered renovations of the dowdiest stores, increased signage at all locations, and demanded more-aggressive marketing campaigns, including the publication of better-designed, more-attractive advertising supplements. He has also placed some Babies "R" Us and Toys "R" Us branches under one roof and has plans to unite others. In time for the 2006 Christmas season, he negotiated contracts for 70 exclusive products, among them the Thomas Ultimate Train Set, the Lego Star Wars X-Wing Fighter, and the Girlfriendz line of Bratz dolls. According to a posting on CNNMoney.com in April 2007, Toys "R" Us held the 202d spot (up from 208 the previous year) in the Fortune 500 ranking of the largest corporations in the U.S.; the most recent information for quarterly financial results indicated that the company had increased its revenues by 8.3 percent over those of the equivalent quarter in 2005.

"It is not only the future of Toys 'R' Us that is at stake here," Michael Barbaro warned. "Major toy makers say that their profitability depends on its survival. If Toys 'R' Us fails, everyone from industry conglomerates like Hasbro and Mattel to scrappy innovative upstarts like Wild Planet and Zizzle say they will be at the mercy of the penny-pinching merchants at Wal-Mart and Target." "The reality,"

Neil B. Friedman, the president of Mattel Brands, told Barbaro, "is that it's not healthy for this industry to not have a healthy Toys 'R' Us."

—D.J.K.

Suggested Reading: Bloomberg.co.uk Dec. 29, 2006; *Business Wire* Mar. 1, 1993, Feb. 7, 2006; CNNMoney.com Oct. 18, 2004; (Minneapolis, Minnesota) *Star Tribune* D p1+ Mar. 12, 1996, D p1 June 20, 2001; *New York Post* p35 Nov. 6, 2006; *New York Times* C p1+ Feb. 7, 2006, III p1+ Nov. 19, 2006; Toys "R" Us Web site

Strokes

Music group

Casablancas, Julian
Aug. 23, 1978– Singer; songwriter

Fraiture, Nikolai
Nov. 13, 1978– Bassist

Hammond, Albert Jr.
Apr. 9, 1979– Guitarist

Moretti, Fabrizio
June 2, 1980– Drummer

Valensi, Nick
Jan. 16, 1981– Guitarist

Address: Nasty Little Man Publicity, 110 Greene St., #605, New York, NY 10012

Released in October 2001, the Strokes' debut album, *Is This It*, went far toward changing the face of mainstream rock music, ushering in a new sound and a wave of garage bands heavily inspired by late-1970s underground rock. "On Jan. 1, 2001 rap-metal was in its death throes and angst-metal in its unfortunate life throes," Mark Lepage wrote for the *Toronto (Canada) Star* (October 12, 2003), describing the setting from which the Strokes emerged. "There was Eminem, Britney [Spears] and Jay-Z, Creed, Kid Rock and Matchbox 20. Into this came the dirty Converse sneakers and artfully trashed jackets of a crew of thrift-shop mods. The sound was a lean shot of contradictions: slacker-passionate, retro-neo, vocal lines descended from Italian crooners, a lean white-kid beat taken from the skinny-tie bands. The attack was indie, but the melodic sense classicist and irresistibly rock 'n' roll." "Fans and detractors alike heard and saw [the Strokes] as part of a movement; retro-rock was exploding, and this tidy, brilliant band seemed like the fuse," Kelefa Sanneh wrote for the *New York Times* (March 3, 2006). Hailing from New York City, the Strokes have often been compared to groups associated with the Manhattan under-ground of earlier decades, among them the Velvet Underground (the band in which the rocker Lou Reed got his start), Television, and the Talking Heads. Writing for the London *Guardian* (February 6, 2001), Betty Clarke characterized the Strokes' music as "Chuck Berry to a Velvet Underground backing track, a simple and blistering formula that finishes abruptly after all of three minutes." The Strokes' guitarist Nick Valensi told Jay McInerney for *New York* (January 16, 2006), "The reason people liked the first record, maybe, was because it was kind of New Wave, kind of retro, and no one was doing that music then—the Ramones, Talking Heads, Blondie, the Cars. That music never went out of style, but no one was playing it. We were filling some kind of void in music."

The members of the Strokes—the lead singer, Julian Casablancas; the bassist, Nikolai Fraiture; Nick Valensi and his fellow guitarist Albert Hammond Jr.; and the drummer Fabrizio Moretti—became celebrities almost immediately after *Is This It* reached stores, with the media focusing as much on their personal styles and love lives as on their music. "The Strokes were so hip it hurt," Craig MacLean wrote for the London *Independent* (November 26, 2005), describing the band's arrival on the music scene as having been "a fashion moment rather than a proper rock event." In the *Weekend Australian* (August 25, 2001), Iain Shedden, writing shortly before the release of the group's debut album in the U.S., expressed the view that the Strokes were "arguably the most exciting band to come out of the US since Nirvana. They may not be as innovative or, in time, influential, but they have that special intangible something that makes you want to bounce off the walls when you hear them, just as the Velvets sometimes do." Wary of collapsing under the weight of the hype surrounding *Is This It*, the Strokes quickly produced a follow-up album, *Room on Fire* (2003), which was widely panned for resembling its predecessor too closely. By contrast, their next recording, *First Impressions of Earth* (2006), elicited favorable reviews.

The Strokes' vocalist, Julian Casablancas, was born on August 23, 1978 in New York City, to John Casablancas, the founder of the Elite modeling agency, and Jeanette Christjansen, the winner of the 1965 Miss Denmark title. After his parents divorced, when Casablancas was a child, he lived with his mother, who remarried. He has credited his stepfather, Sam Adoquei, a painter from Ghana, with beginning his education in music. "Every night he'd talk to me about artists and what made great artists great," Casablancas told Iain Shedden. "He was the best teacher I ever had. Then I'd just go play guitar for hours and think I sucked and I had to get better." Casablancas, according to Ted Kessler in the London *Observer* (December 16, 2001), was "a disruptive, unruly presence" in school. When he was in his teens, his father enrolled him at the Institute Le Rosey, an international, bilingual boarding school in Switzerland. Dur-

The Strokes (left to right): Nick Valensi, Fabrizio Moretti, Albert Hammond Jr., Julian Casablancas, Nikolai Fraiture

ing his six months there, his stepfather sent him a tape of songs by the rock group the Doors. After listening to it repeatedly, he told Kessler, "it all fell into place. Sounds kind of corny, I realise, but I knew then how music was built." Also while at the school, Casablancas befriended Albert Hammond Jr., the school's only other American student, who was born on April 9, 1979 in Los Angeles, California. Hammond's father, Albert Hammond Sr., is a singer and songwriter; he is the co-writer of "It Never Rains in Southern California" and "To All the Girls I've Loved Before," the latter of which became a hit for Willie Nelson and Julio Iglesias, singing as a duo, and for several other performers. After Casablancas returned to New York, he and Hammond lost touch.

Casablancas then entered the Dwight School, a private high school on New York's Upper West Side, where he met Nick Valensi (born on January 16, 1981 in New York City) and Fabrizio Moretti (born on June 2, 1980 in Rio de Janeiro, Brazil). The three of them, along with Nikolai Fraiture (born on November 13, 1978 in New York City), a friend of Casablancas's since kindergarten, formed a rock band. Shortly afterward, by chance, Casablancas was reunited with Hammond, who was studying filmmaking at New York University. Hammond soon joined the group, and the quintet christened themselves the Strokes. The band rented a small rehearsal studio, where they practiced for several years, often becoming frustrated with their slow progress. "We didn't know what we were doing," Casablancas told John Robinson for the London *Guardian* (June 28, 2001). "It sounded so bad, I remember us talking about what we wanted to do

with it, and it was like, 'Throw it in the garbage.'" "We were searching for a sound for a long time and didn't know what it would end up being," Casablancas recalled to Richard Harrington for the *Washington Post* (October 26, 2001). "Anytime I would hear a song or a band, I would try to understand what their weak points were, as well as what their strong points were, and then absorb as much as I could and learn from their mistakes." Eager to learn more about music composition, Casablancas began taking classes at Five Towns College, in Dix Hills, on Long Island, New York, whose specialties include music and the performing arts. "I don't really believe that if you study the rules, it makes you uncreative," he told Harrington. "I think a lot of people study the rules too much and then don't know how to be creative. I just want us to learn the basic rules to help me figure out other songs and make me know more what I'm doing."

When the Strokes gained confidence in the quality of their music, they started to perform at local clubs. At one of them, the Mercury Lounge, on Manhattan's Lower East Side, they caught the attention of Ryan Gentles, the club's booking agent. Gentles quit his job and became the band's manager, and, using his industry connections, he got the Strokes work as the opening act for such established bands as Guided by Voices and the Doves. Gentles played the group's three-song demo for Geoff Travis, the founder of Rough Trade Records, who quickly signed the group to his label. "After about 15 seconds, I agreed to release it," Travis told Ted Kessler. "What I heard in The Strokes were the song-writing skills of a first-class writer and music that is a distillation of primal rock 'n' roll mixed

2007 CURRENT BIOGRAPHY YEARBOOK   527

with the sophistication of today's society. The primitive in the sophisticated, to paraphrase [the filmmaker] Jean Renoir. It also has an unmacho quality that embodies grace and love, and it touches me."

Soon afterward, the members of the Strokes—who at the time were either students or workers in non-music-related jobs—embarked on a concert tour of England. "That's when our lives changed," as Casablancas told Neala Johnson for the Melbourne, Australia, *Herald Sun* (July 12, 2001). In addition to receiving rave reviews, the Strokes found themselves deluged by publicity and the focus of exaggerated claims made by writers for the British music press. "It never seemed like we had articles just saying we were a great band and people should check us out; from the get-go, it was 'This band is soooo hyped,'" as Casablancas told Sharon O'Connell for *Time Out* (August 29, 2001). "There was never any actual hype, there was just talk about the hype!" "We are not here to save rock 'n' roll! . . . ," Casablancas also said to O'Connell. "We're not going to change your life, and the way everyone is idealising our arrival on the scene is ridiculous. Look, the bottom line is the music. That's it. Simple." The fever surrounding the Strokes in England soon spread to the United States, where the band's debut album, *Is This It*, was released in the fall of 2001 with great fanfare. "The Strokes are a body shot to popular music," Vaughn Watson wrote for the *Providence (Rhode Island) Journal-Bulletin* (September 27, 2001). "They make thoughtful and irreverent pop. Nearly every song on *Is This It* has a memorable hook, and the band unashamedly has a blast with all of it."

The hype surrounding the Strokes sparked a negative backlash from fans and critics who had wearied of hearing about the group. "That the Strokes are getting media attention should not, on its face, be the reason to love or hate the band," Jennifer Maerz wrote for *Salon.com* (November 28, 2001). "But even music purists have a tough time closing their eyes to hype, and the Strokes themselves are not blameless in creating an image for themselves. Singer Julian Casablancas is not only a noncommittal, take 'em or leave 'em slacker in his lyrics, he also plays at being combative during the band's live act." "Casablancas half-sang, half-sneered his way through *Is This It*, as if he could hardly be bothered to talk to you, wouldn't even deign to look at you," Laura Barton later wrote for the London *Guardian* (November 25, 2005). "They sounded so cool, they looked so cool, they were so very, very cool." The Strokes also inspired a wave of similarly minded groups. Craig McLean wrote for the London *Daily Telegraph* (January 12, 2006), "Without the Strokes' model of a groovy gang playing snappy guitar music, Franz Ferdinand, Kaiser Chiefs and Arctic Monkeys wouldn't exist."

The Strokes' sophomore effort, *Room on Fire* (2003), struck most reviewers as "a pretty straightforward re-run of their all-conquering, if strangely flimsy, debut *Is This It*," as Ben Thompson wrote

for the London *Observer* (September 21, 2003). "There are the same number of songs (11), the same producer . . . the same short, sharp songs of vaguely personalized alienation and breezy emotional underkill. In fact, clocking in at a terse 33 minutes, *Room on Fire* manages to be a full three minutes pithier than its famously compact predecessor." "The Strokes . . . have been hailed as potential saviors (rather than imitators) of rock 'n' roll," Craig Semon wrote for the *Sunday Telegram* (November 2, 2003), a central Massachusetts newspaper. "Don't believe it. The so-called stroke of genius of a bunch of twentysomethings delving deep into the legacy of the NYC underground sounds somewhat generic and less exuberant on the second go-around. With lyrics and licks sounding virtually interchangeable from song to song, there is little that leaves a lasting impression here." "We felt we needed more material out there just to catch up with the attention we had been getting," Nick Valensi later told Neala Johnson for the *Herald Sun* (December 20, 2005). "But [*Room on Fire*] suffered from that. When I listen to that record now, I feel that if I'd had more time to really think about the songs and the guitar parts, and if the band had had more time to focus on the production, it would have been a lot more interesting. And that's a shame." The group's live performances at the time, however, were well-received. "Casablancas and his bandmates proceeded to destroy any lingering skepticism about their garage-rock credibility," Christopher Blagg wrote for the *Boston Herald* (May 17, 2004), after attending a Strokes concert. "Their balance of punk attitude and melodic hook-drenched songwriting was evident with the slamming guitar crunch of 'Trying My Luck' and the sneering barbs of 'The Way It Is.'"

After touring to promote *Room on Fire*, the Strokes disappeared briefly from the public spotlight, concentrating instead on their personal lives. In February 2005 Casablancas married Juliet Joslin, the Strokes' assistant manager; in that or the previous year (sources do not agree), Nikolai Fraiture had fathered a child with his wife, Ilona. In 2006 the band released a third album, *First Impressions of Earth*, a collection of songs that was seen as a departure from their previous material. "Musically, their characteristic leanness has filled out a little, the sound is less immediate, more labyrinthine, less recognizably Strokesian," Laura Barton wrote. "It is perhaps more of a cerebral album, after the vigorous physicality of *Is This It* and *Room on Fire*, and, as a result, it hits your brain before your belly." "There's some kind of distance from the past records," Casablancas told Steve Hochman for the *Los Angeles Times* (January 1, 2006). "We don't want to do the same thing. The second record musically was different, but the production was the same and people swept the music under the rug." Jay McInerney wrote, "By almost any measure," *First Impressions of Earth* is "their best album. The propulsive rhythmic energy and the instant melodic appeal of the best songs provide a taut counterpoint to the wounded sneer of Casablancas's lyrics, which are as disillusioned, doomy, and sarcastic as ever."

On their tour in support of *First Impressions of Earth*, the Strokes earned favorable reviews. Ryan White wrote for the *Oregonian* (April 4, 2006), "Casablancas has rediscovered his performer's mojo in a serious way. . . . Much like on their new record, the Strokes seemed focused on where they want to go, not where they've been." The Strokes' tour ended in October 2006. That month Albert Hammond released his first solo album, *Yours to Keep*. In September 2007 he reported on MySpace.com that he

planned to release another solo disk. He and the other members of the Strokes also planned to record their fourth album in 2008.

—R.E.

Suggested Reading: *Chicago Tribune* C p3 Oct. 17, 2003; (London) *Guardian* p16 Feb. 6, 2001; (Melbourne, Australia) *Herald Sun* p40 July 12, 2001; *New York* p16+ Jan. 16, 2006; *Time Out* p19 Aug. 29, 2001

Selected Recordings: *Is This It*, 2001; *Room on Fire*, 2003; *First Impressions of Earth*, 2006

Reed Hutchinson, courtesy of UCLA

Tao, Terence

July 17, 1975– Mathematician; educator

Address: Department of Mathematics, UCLA, Los Angeles, CA 90095-1596

"You just put your head down and you solve your problems," the mathematician Terence Tao told Sabra Lane during an interview for ABC News (September 28, 2006, on-line). Tao's rare ability to tackle immensely difficult mathematical problems—including one whose solution eluded the greatest mathematical minds for more than 2,000 years—has made him, at the age of 32, a towering figure in his discipline. Unlike Andrew Wiles and others in his profession who devote themselves to solving a single problem (albeit one that has confounded their peers), Tao, a professor at the University of California–Los Angeles (UCLA), has ven-

tured into an array of mathematical fields and has made remarkable contributions in several. In August 2006 the International Mathematical Union (IMU) awarded him a Fields Medal; considered the discipline's highest honor, the medal is often referred to as the Nobel Prize for mathematics. Tao is the first Australian to win the Fields Medal, which is awarded every four years to mathematicians under the age of 40, and he is among the youngest ever to do so. In a press release (November 27, 2006, on-line), the IMU described Tao as "a supreme problem-solver whose spectacular work has had an impact across several mathematical areas. He combines sheer technical power, an otherworldly ingenuity for hitting upon new ideas, and a startlingly natural point of view that leaves other mathematicians wondering, 'Why didn't anyone see that before?'"

Tao's specialties include real-variable harmonic analysis, the analysis of nonlinear partial differential equations, number theory, ergodic theory, combinatorics, representation theory, and the structures of honeycombs, among other topics. He views the breadth of his research as a natural result of problem solving. "I work in a number of areas, but I don't view them as being disconnected," he explained during an interview posted on the Web site of the Clay Mathematics Institute (September 2003). "I tend to view mathematics as a unified subject and am particularly happy when I get the opportunity to work on a project that involves several fields at once." "My research I do now, five years ago I wouldn't have had a clue that this is what I'd be doing," he told Sabra Lane. "You solve a problem and it leads naturally to two new problems that you didn't know before, and you follow your research organically and then all the other stuff, the recognition stuff happens by itself." Tao has published more than 80 papers, many of them written with others, and four books. "Terry is like Mozart; mathematics just flows out of him," John B. Garnett, a professor of mathematics at UCLA, told a reporter for *UCLA News* (April 16, 2007, on-line). "Mathematicians with Terry's talent appear only once in a generation. He's an incredible talent and probably the best mathematician in the world right now."

TAO

The oldest of three boys, Terence Chi-Shen Tao was born on July 17, 1975 in Adelaide, in the Australian state of South Australia, to Grace and Billy Tao. His brother Trevor, who is autistic and a musical savant, has a doctorate in math and works for the Defense Science and Technology Organisation, a division of Australia's Defense Department. His brother Nigel is a computer engineer for Google Australia. Tao's father is a pediatrician; his mother taught high-school mathematics in Hong Kong (now part of China) before the couple moved to Australia, in 1972. Tao's unusual intelligence became apparent when he was a toddler. By the time he was two, he had taught himself to read, using toy blocks imprinted with numbers and letters, which his parents had bought for him; he had also taught other children how to count. At four he could multiply two two-digit numbers in his head. "Ever since I can remember, I have enjoyed mathematics; I recall being fascinated by numbers even at age three, and viewed their manipulation as a kind of game," he said during the Clay Institute interview. His parents were surprised by his abilities and believed that Tao had taught himself primarily by watching the television program *Sesame Street.* "We gave him lots of toys, but he didn't like cars or trains. He loved to play with alphabets and numbers, so we kept on going according to his wishes," his mother told a reporter for the *Sydney (Australia) Morning Herald* (August 25, 2006). When his parents discovered that he could read, they bought and borrowed many books for him.

When he was three, Tao's parents enrolled him in a private school in a class with five-year-olds. They removed him six weeks later, when it became apparent that he was not socially prepared to spend that much time in a classroom with older children, and that the teacher was unable to teach a student like him. Tao's parents view that episode as crucially important in his development, because it showed them that the pace of his education hinged as much on his emotional and social maturity as on his academic abilities. They also decided that not only must his school have a good reputation and a principal who supported suitable education for the gifted, but also that the teacher who would work daily with their son had to be flexible and able to cope with an extremely steep learning curve. Tao's parents decided to get more involved in teaching their son at home.

Between the ages of three and a half and five, Tao attended a kindergarten with children his age. At home, he voraciously read math textbooks and completed nearly the whole elementary-school math curriculum. His mother has said that he did not like to be told what to do in the subject, choosing instead to work problems out by himself. Tao's parents worked hard to instill a love for the intellectual process in their son. "All along, we tend to emphasize the joy of learning," Billy Tao told Kenneth Chang for the *New York Times* (March 13, 2007). "The fun is doing something, not winning something." During that period the Taos joined the South Australian Association for Gifted and Talented Children, a group of teachers and parents who held weekend seminars and workshops and provided a setting for the children to interact with one another. Even within that setting Tao joined students two or three years his senior. Although he did not meet any young people whose prodigious math abilities matched his own, he played with other children who shared his hunger for information, ability to assimilate abstract concepts, and delight in creative exploration.

At five Tao entered a public school. Because Australian school systems, by and large, do not have lesson plans or other provisions for exceptionally gifted students (Tao's estimated I.Q.—220—is exceedingly rare), his teachers and school administrators, in collaboration with his parents, drew up a program for him built around his specific needs. While Tao accelerated through several grades in math and science, he remained close to his age group in other subjects. In English, for example, he felt confused by the flexibility inherent in essay writing. "I never really got the hang of that," he told Chang. "These very vague, undefined questions. I always liked situations where there were very clear rules of what to do." In response to a writing assignment that called for him to describe what was going on at home, Tao made detailed lists of the contents of every room in his house.

By the time he was six, Tao had taught himself the computer programming language BASIC, and by eight he had produced a BASIC program to calculate perfect numbers. (A perfect number is half the sum of all of its positive divisors. For example, the positive divisors of the perfect number 6 are 1, 2, 3, and 6; 6 is half of $1 + 2 + 3 + 6$, which equals 12.) When he was seven, Tao began to attend math classes at the local high school while spending the rest of the school day with his peers. He was reportedly friendly and well-adjusted and displayed no conceit about his extensive gifts. For his part, Tao has explained that because he had nobody with whom to compare himself, his situation felt natural. At eight, Tao gained international notice when he achieved the highest score ever for someone his age in the math portion of the Scholastic Aptitude Test (SAT, the standardized test used by colleges in the admission process)—760 out of a possible 800, or better than those achieved by 99 percent of college-bound high-school seniors. As an elementary-school pupil, Tao also excelled in high-school math competitions. Although he failed to make the Australian national team as a nine-year-old, he became a strong contender at the International Mathematical Olympiad, regarded as the pinnacle of math excellence for high-school students. In competitions involving two four-hour exams that tested problem-solving skills, he won a bronze medal in 1986, a silver medal in 1987, and a gold medal in 1988, at age 13. By that time, as he told the Clay Mathematics Institute interviewer, he had "started to realize that mathematics is not just about symbolic manipulation, but has useful things to say about the real world; then, of course, I enjoyed it even more."

Aware that later in life many former child prodigies suffer socially and academically, Tao's father felt reluctant to have his son complete high school and college too quickly. "To get a degree at a young age, to be a record-breaker, means nothing," Billy Tao told Chang. "I had a pyramid model of knowledge, that is, a very broad base and then the pyramid can go higher. If you just very quickly move up like a column, then you're more likely to wobble at the top and then collapse." Rather than having him emulate Jay Lu, who graduated with a bachelor's degree in math from Boise State University in 1982 at age 12, Tao's parents saw to it that, beginning just before his 10th birthday, he split his time between Blackwood High School and Flinders University, both in Adelaide. When he was 14 Tao began attending classes at Flinders full-time; as before, his parents worked with administrators and professors in formulating a program for him. He studied under Garth Gaudry, an internationally known mathematician with expertise in harmonic analysis and functional analysis. He completed his undergraduate education in two years, earning a B.S. degree with honors in mathematics in 1991. The following year Tao earned an M.S. degree in math from Flinders; his thesis was titled "Convolution Operators Generated by Right-Monogenic and Harmonic Kernels." Gaudry told Stephen Cauchi for the Australian publication the *Age* (August 23, 2006, on-line), "Even at that age, he exhibited stunning insight and creativity. Discovering new mathematics was such an enjoyable adventure for Terry. To be Terry's teacher was, for me, the privilege of a lifetime." The year 1992 also saw the publication of Tao's first book, *Solving Mathematical Problems: A Personal Perspective*. Reprinted by Oxford University Press in 2006, the book contains Olympiad-level math problems, which typically have simple constructions but extremely complex solutions.

In 1993 Tao moved to the United States to pursue his Ph.D. at Princeton University, in New Jersey, under the multi–award-winning mathematician Elias M. Stein, whose specialty is harmonic analysis. At Princeton Tao felt for the first time that he was among his peers in math. Although he was the youngest student in his classes, he was not the smartest in every area of math all the time. As a child, as he told Chang, he had had "this vague idea that what mathematicians did was that, some authority, someone gave them problems to solve and they just sort of solved them," a process he compared to "a sprint." At Princeton he developed a more mature attitude toward math, beyond problem sets, exams, and competitions, and discovered, according to Chang, that "math research is more like a marathon." He graduated from Princeton in June 1996; his dissertation was titled "Three Regularity Results in Harmonic Analysis."

In 1996 Tao joined the Mathematics Department at UCLA as a Hendrick assistant professor. He divided his time between California and Australia before becoming a permanent resident of the U.S., where he now lives full-time. (He has retained his Australian citizenship.) He became a full professor in 2000. Between 1996 and 2000 Tao published more than a dozen articles in various publications, including *Proceedings of the American Mathematical Society*, the *Journal of Mathematical Physics*, the *Indiana University Mathematics Journal*, *Geometric and Functional Analysis*, *Mathematical Research Letters*, and the *Annals of Mathematics*, the last-named published by Princeton and the Institute for Advanced Study, also in Princeton, New Jersey.

One of Tao's most important discoveries to date is in the field of prime numbers (numbers that are divisible, without any remainders, by only themselves and one, such as 2, 3, 5, 7, 13, and 17). Intuitively, one might think that large numbers must have divisors in addition to themselves and one; in fact, however, the number of prime numbers is infinite, as the Greek mathematician Euclid proved around 300 B.C. The numbers 151,121; 68,718,952,447; and 953,467,954,114,363, for example, are prime. The study of prime numbers used to be considered one of the most esoteric fields of mathematics. Currently, prime numbers are used to encode electronic data, such as the details of an ATM transaction, for transmission along telephone lines or other unsecure channels. Euclid believed that there are an infinite number of "twin primes"—that is, prime numbers separated by 2, such as 3 and 5 or 11 and 13—but he was unable to prove that conjecture, and before 2004 no one else had provided a proof. Tao and Ben Green, a professor of mathematics at the University of Bristol in England, devised that proof. They also tackled another question—whether prime numbers exist randomly or if patterns exist in their sequences—and they proved (in 48 pages of labyrinthine mathematics) that it is always possible to find, somewhere in the sequence of integers, a progression of any length of equally spaced prime numbers. For example, the difference between the prime numbers 3 and 7 is four, and that between the next two primes, 7 and 11, is also four; 3, 7, and 11 thus represent a progression of three equally spaced prime numbers. The differences between pairs of the following 10 prime numbers—199; 409; 619; 829; 1,039; 1,249; 1,459; 1,669; 1,879; 2,089—is 210. According to *UCLA News* (January 11, 2007), "Tao and Green's discovery reveals that somewhere in the prime numbers there is a progression of length 100, and length 1000, and every other finite length, and that there are an infinite number of such progressions in the primes."

Tao has also worked widely in harmonic analysis, an advanced form of calculus that borrows equations from physics. In that field he is well known for his work on the Kakeya conjecture, a series of five problems; his contributions include a

50-page proof in which he and two colleagues obtained the most precise known estimate for the size of a particular three-dimensional geometric shape. Another interest of Tao's involves wave maps, a topic connected with Einstein's general theory of relativity. Tao has also expanded the understanding of nonlinear Schrödinger equations, which are used, for example, to describe the behavior of light in an optical cable. In collaboration with Allen Knutson, Tao solved Horn's conjecture, which is of interest to mathematicians studying representational theory. "The way he crosses areas would be like the best heart surgeon also being exceptional in brain surgery," Tony F. Chan, a professor of computational and applied mathematics at UCLA, told a *Sydney Morning Herald* (August 26, 2006) reporter. According to that reporter, the International Mathematics Union described Tao's "beautiful work" on Horn's conjecture as "akin to a leading English language novelist suddenly producing the definitive Russian novel."

"Mathematicians often work on pure problems that may not have applications for 20 years—and then a physicist or computer scientist or engineer has a real-life problem that requires the solution of a mathematical problem, and finds that someone already solved it 20 years ago," Tao said during an interview posted on the UCLA Web site (November 9, 2005). One area of his research—compressed sensing—may have major ramifications for military surveillance and other digital transmissions. With Emmanuel Candes, a professor of applied and computational mathematics at the California Institute of Technology, Tao is working on a way to record digital information using less computer power than is currently necessary. By means of powerful algorithms, Tao has shown that it is possible to reconstruct digital information even when large portions of the original recordings are missing. With tools from geometry, statistics, and calculus, Tao and Candes proved that they could reconstruct garbled messages—a discovery that has applications for government-surveillance wiretappers or code-breakers and those trying to comprehend a jumbled cell-phone signal or an incomplete MRI or CAT scan. According to a writer for *Popular Science* (September 2006), "The work is quintessential Tao: a breakthrough in a new field that requires a mastery of techniques from across the mathematical spectrum."

Tao hopes to increase general interest in mathematics and to help people without an extensive math background to be able to think mathematically. He has occasionally lectured on those goals and has discussed the ways in which basic math skills can help in activities such as computing one's income tax. "It's not magic," he told Lane. "Using mathematics, you can see where all of science comes from, a lot of technology. And it's really empowering. You realize that the world [is not] this incomprehensible scary place, it's actually just built out of very simple, logical ideas." "One of the problems is that mathematics, in order to get to the good

stuff you have to start with a lot of drills, a lot of menial work," he said to Lane. "It's like if you want to be a good pianist, you have to do a lot of scales and a lot of practice, and a lot of that is kind of boring, it's work. But you need to do that before you can really be very expressive and really play beautiful music. You have to go through that phase of practice and drill. And unfortunately the high school and primary school math education system . . . well there's a lot of that." "It's not about being smart or even fast," Tao said during the interview published on the UCLA Web site. "It's like climbing a cliff; if you're very strong and quick and have a lot of rope, it helps, but you need to devise a good route to get up there. Doing calculations quickly and knowing a lot of facts are like a rock climber with strength, quickness and good tools; you still need a plan—that's the hard part—and you have to see the bigger picture."

From 1992 through 2000 Tao was supported by grants or fellowships from organizations including the Australian-American Fulbright Commission, the Sloan Foundation, and the National Science Foundation. He taught at the University of New South Wales, in Sydney, during two six-month visits in 1999, and at the Australian National University, in Canberra, during two six-month visits in 2001 and 2003, respectively. In addition to *Solving Mathematical Problems*, he has written a two-volume introduction to analysis, both published in India in 2006, and, also in 2006, the books *Nonlinear Dispersive Equations: Local and Global Analysis* and, with Van Vu, *Additive Combinatorics*. In the same year, besides the Fields Medal, Tao won a $500,000 MacArthur Fellowship, commonly called the "genius grant." His earlier honors include the Salem Prize (2000); the Bocher Memorial Prize (2002), from the American Mathematical Society; the Clay Research Award (2003), from the Clay Mathematical Institute; the Levi L. Conant Award (2004), from the American Mathematical Society; the Robert Sorgenfrey Distinguished Teaching Award (2005), from UCLA; the Australian Mathematical Society Medal (2005); and the SASTRA Ramanujan Prize (2006), from the Shanmugha Arts, Science, Technology, and Research Academy, in India. In January 2007 UCLA appointed him to the James and Carol Collins Chair in the College of Letters and Sciences. In May of that year, he was named a fellow of the Royal Society, the national academy of science of Great Britain and its commonwealth of nations.

Tao is married to Laura Kim, an engineer at NASA's Jet Propulsion Laboratory, at the California Institute of Technology. The couple live in Southern California with their son, William Kwang-Hee Tao, who was born in 2002.

—N.W.M.

Suggested Reading: ABC News (online) Sep. 28, 2006; *Australian Mathematical Society Gazette* Supplement (on-line) Aug. 2006; Clay Mathematics Institute Web site (Sep. 2003); *Daily*

Princetonian (on-line) May 19, 2006, Aug. 22, 2006; *New York Times* F p1+ Mar. 13, 2007; *Seed Magazine* (on-line) Sep. 22, 2006; *Sydney (Australia) Morning Herald* (on-line) Aug. 25, 2006; UCLA Department of Mathematics Web site; *UCLA News* (on-line) Nov. 9, 2005, Jan. 11, 2007; *Who's Who in America, 2007*

Selected Books: *Solving Mathematical Problems: A Personal Perspective*, 1992, 2006; *Additive Combinatorics* (with Van Vu), 2006; *Analysis Vol. I*, 2006; *Analysis Vol. II*, 2006; *Nonlinear Dispersive Equations: Local and Global Analysis*, 2006

Denis Finnin/AMNH

Tattersall, Ian

May 10, 1945– Paleoanthropologist; museum curator

Address: American Museum of Natural History, Central Park W. at 79th St., New York, NY 10024–5192

Ian Tattersall, the curator of biological anthropology in the Division of Anthropology of the American Museum of Natural History, in New York City, differs from many of his colleagues by suggesting that as many as 20, not only six or seven, different species of hominids are represented in the present-day fossil record. "This notion of human evolution as being a linear trudge from primitivism to perfection is totally wrong," he told Amy Otchet for the *UNESCO Courier* (December 1, 2000). "I came to paleoanthropology from the study of lemurs [mon-key-like primates] in Madagascar where you have a huge diversity of animals. You cannot help asking, 'How did these creatures become so diverse?' Yet this question is not asked in paleoanthropology because there is only one species of humans today. Somehow we believe it is normal and natural for us to be alone in the world. Yet in fact, if you look at the fossil record, you find that this is totally unusual—this may be the first time that we have ever had just one species of humans in the world." With his colleague Jeffrey H. Schwartz, Tattersall recently published the most complete compendium documenting and analyzing the major specimens of the hominid fossil record. In addition to his contributions to academia, Tattersall has published several nonfiction books for general readers. Gilbert Taylor, writing for *Booklist* (February 1, 1998), described Tattersall as "perhaps the best popular expositor of paleoanthropology."

Ian Michael Tattersall was born in Paignton, Devon, England, on May 10, 1945 and raised in East Africa. He returned to England to pursue his bachelor's and master's degrees, studying archaeology and anthropology at the University of Cambridge. In 1967 he immigrated to the U.S. and enrolled at Yale University, in New Haven, Connecticut. After he earned a Ph.D. in geology and geophysics, in 1971, he moved to New York City to teach at the New School for Social Research and the Lehman College of the City University of New York (CUNY). That same year he was also hired as an assistant curator at the American Museum of Natural History (AMNH), a position he held until 1976, when he became an associate curator. In 1981 he was promoted to head of the biological anthropology section. He currently serves on the faculty of CUNY's Graduate Center.

During the 1970s Tattersall published several scholarly works on lemurs—a group of primates that were once widespread but are now found, in the wild, only on the island of Madagascar, off the eastern coast of Africa. Although they are all from the same superfamily (*Lemuroidea*), the estimated 30 to 35 extant species of lemurs vary widely in body size and habitat. "The lemurs of Madagascar have always been a fascination of mine . . . ," Tattersall said in an interview posted on the AMNH Web site. "Why they're really important, in a scientific sense, is that they're a whole parallel world; they're a separate independent radiation of primates that show exactly how primates can exploit their basic primate potential to do many many different things. And they give us a new perspective on ourselves, on our own evolutionary group, by making this comparison." Tattersall's book *Primates of Madagascar* (1982) was described by a reviewer for *Library Journal* (May 15, 1982) as "likely to be the definitive work on its subject."

That same year Tattersall, collaborating with the noted American paleontologist Niles Eldredge, published *The Myths of Human Evolution*, in which they attempted to introduce the general public to contemporary evolutionary theory. While the scientific community is nearly unanimous in its acceptance of Charles Darwin's assertion that all species have diverged from common ancestors through the process of natural selection, many now question whether evolution occurred at the gradual pace that Darwin first suggested. In 1972 Eldredge and the famed naturalist Stephen Jay Gould proposed the theory of punctuated equilibrium, which posits that the characteristics of organisms remain the same before undergoing short periods of rapid change. Describing *The Myths of Human Evolution* as a "lightweight polemic in favour of a 'punctuationist' view of human evolution," J. R. Durant, writing for the London *Times Literary Supplement* (February 18, 1983), complained that "the 'myths' referred to in the title are many and varied, since the authors consign to this category virtually any idea on the subject of evolution with which they happen to disagree." The book, Durant concluded, "contributes more or less nothing of any consequence to the current debate about the pattern and process of evolution, be it organic, human, social, or whatever. . . . [The authors] have produced yet another popular work that will merely add to the confusion of those interested lay people who turn to it for guidance through the maze of contemporary arguments about evolution." Offering a different view was the critic for *Choice* (February 1983), who, while agreeing that "the authors spend an inordinate effort" offering evidence to support their favored approach to evolution, nonetheless described the book as "a fine introduction to the current facts and theories of human evolution."

In 1993 Tattersall presided over the opening of the Hall of Human Biology and Evolution at the AMNH, which had taken nearly a decade to plan and construct. Writing for the *New York Times* (April 23, 1993), Malcolm W. Browne praised the exhibit, which had replaced the museum's old Hall of Human Biology, for its combination of "spectacular dioramas with models, animated displays and lucid explanations"; he predicted that it would "become one of the most popular museum exhibitions New York City has seen." The first exhibit in the new hall was a diorama showing a family of skeletons gathered in a typical American living room. While the rest of the family watched television, the father relaxed in his easy chair, reading a copy of *The Human Odyssey: Four Million Years of Human Evolution*, written by Tattersall to coincide with the exhibition's unveiling. The book became one of the all-time best-sellers in the museum shop, with nearly 1,000 copies sold within the first month. *The Human Odyssey* "is sure to be the general-readership book on human evolution for the 1990s," E. Delson wrote for *Choice* (September 1993). "Drawing heavily on exquisite graphics prepared for the exhibit (two glorious Jay Matternes murals, site photographs, and dioramas, as well as numerous photos of the included fossil casts), Tattersall has produced a lucid and literate guide to the whole range of human biological history."

In *The Fossil Trail: How We Know What We Think We Know About Human Evolution* (1995), Tattersall traced the development of differing theories of evolutionary biology. According to Linda Gamlin, reviewing the book for *New Scientist* (April 8, 1995), Tattersall "simultaneously handles half-a-dozen different themes," tracing the development of the field from the 19th century onward. "It is a complex mix," Gamlin wrote, "which also zigzags geographically from the rock art of Lascaux in France to the caves of South Africa, from the river valleys of Indonesia to Olduvai Gorge in Tanzania. . . . The task of organising such complex material into a narrative account would have defeated most writers, but Tattersall has mastered it with remarkable skill. The result is a smoothly flowing and wonderfully readable book that grips the attention without oversimplifying the arguments." In contrast, Christopher Dornan wrote for the Toronto, Canada, *Globe and Mail* (April 20, 1995) that Tattersall's treatment of evolution "makes its subject boring beyond belief. There's nothing wrong with the factual content. It may be plodding, but it's all here, the full closet of famous skeletons—from Java Man to the Taung Child, from Turkana Boy through Lucy to the 'First Family.' The problem is that the author . . . cannot tell a story to save his life."

Tattersall examined the evolutionary milestones that define our species in *Becoming Human: Evolution and Human Uniqueness* (1998). Beginning roughly five million years ago, with the emergence of australopithecine—small-brained hominids that were no more adept at tool use than other great apes—Tattersall attempted to parse the evolutionary pressures that transformed our ancestors into thinkers capable of producing such sophisticated paintings as those found in Lascaux. "Tattersall believes humanity was achieved in a quantum leap," Robert J. Richards wrote for the *New York Times Book Review* (April 26, 1998). "After consideration of anatomical and artifactual evidence, he is reluctant even to admit that the Neanderthals had language and the kind of symbolic understanding that would mark them close cognitive cousins to their contemporaries, the cave-painting Homo sapiens. This quantum evolutionary theory seems more a conclusion derived from deep cultural belief than from strong evidence or convincing hypothesis."

Though Richards acknowledged that Tattersall had provided an "an interesting, if unorthodox, theoretical support for his belief," the complaint that the book's content is skewed by the author's endorsement of punctuated equilibrium prompted a reply by Niles Eldredge in the May 17, 1998 issue of the *New York Times Book Review*: "Though Richards pronounces the 'anchoring evidence' to be 'relatively light,' the truth is that the fossil record of hominid evolution over the past four million years is remarkably dense—the outcome of especially intense collecting over the past 40 years. Tattersall has seen more hominid fossils than anyone else. That he has concluded that the patterns of hominid evolution are really no different from patterns in the evolutionary history of all other life-forms for at least the past 535 million years should by now come as no surprise. Patterns of species stability interrupted by relatively quick intervals of change (the whole triggered by ecosystem-wide extinction and subsequent speciation events) are well established as the norm rather than the exception in the history of life." Despite the scholarly controversy over Tattersall's stance, the book proved accessible to lay audiences, prompting David Perlman to write for the *San Francisco Chronicle* (May 10, 1998), "There is no more literate anthropologist writing on human evolution today than Ian Tattersall. . . . His important new book, *Becoming Human*, is at once absorbing in its details, provocative in its thoughtful speculations and delightfully informal in its style."

In his next book for a general readership, *The Last Neanderthal: The Rise, Success, and Curious Extinction of Our Closest Human Relatives* (1999), Tattersall attempted to present a coherent overview of the debate surrounding one of the most perplexing and controversial questions in paleoanthropology: what happened to the Neanderthals? While the book clearly outlines the two competing answers to that question—multiregionalism, which suggests that Neanderthals interbred with early humans, and the Out of Africa hypothesis, which argues that they were replaced by humans—most reviewers noted that Tattersall clearly favored the latter. In a review for the *American Anthropologist* (September 2002), Trenton W. Holliday wrote, "Writing books for a popular audience cannot be easy—yet Tattersall has done an admirable job of weaving a narrative of the Neanderthals that is readily accessible to nonspecialists."

Working with Jeffrey H. Schwartz, Tattersall published *Extinct Humans* in 2000. In that book he broadened the scope of his study to include many other extinct species of hominids in an effort to trace human evolution in a way that explained humans' development as not following a single line but, rather, as resembling a tree with myriad branches—some dying out rapidly and others flourishing. In a review for *Booklist* (December 1, 2000), Gilbert Taylor wrote, "Tattersall has few peers in popular paleoanthropological writing," describing *Extinct Humans* as a "superior overview."

In 2002 Tattersall published *The Monkey in the Mirror: Essays on the Science of What Makes Us Human.* In eight essays Tattersall tackled such topics as the scientific process, the origins of modern humans, and humans' relationship to Neanderthals. The dual aims of the book, according to Alan Bilsborough, who reviewed it for the *Times Higher Education Supplement* (December 6, 2002), "are to summarise our understanding of human evolutionary diversity and to review the means whereby we reach that understanding." The book, Bilsborough concluded, "is vigorously and authoritative-

ly written, and Tattersall has an enviable gift for explaining complex ideas clearly and vividly. "

From about 1998 to 2005, Tattersall and Schwartz were involved in an ambitious project to analyze and photograph as much of the hominid fossil record as possible. "I realized that we had, in the course of doing research on Neanderthals, accumulated a lot of descriptions of fossil hominids that we'd made according to a very consistent protocol, and in such a way that all these descriptions could be compared directly with each other. And we realized that we had the basic element here of a resource that really wasn't available to the paleoanthropological profession," Tattersall said, according to the interview posted on the AMNH Web site. "Virtually all known human fossils have been described in the literature but they've been described by different people in different times and in different ways, and usually using a sort of comparative schema which made it very, very difficult for you to use one description in the record from one source with a description that's gained from another source. So we decided to try to see nearly all the fossils, or all of the hominid fossils that we could get access to, and describe them all according to this single protocol that we developed." The most recent edition of the four-volume set *Human Fossil Record* was published in 2005, but given that paleoanthropologists are constantly making new discoveries, Tattersall has said that he regards the series as a work in progress.

In 2007 Tattersall and his colleagues unveiled the Hall of Human Origins (which replaced the Hall of Human Biology and Evolution) at the AMNH. The new displays, which incorporate the most recent discoveries in molecular biology, include interactive multimedia elements. In a review for CNET News (March 16, 2007, on-line), Caroline McCarthy reported, "Where the old Hall of Human Biology and Evolution had once been an austere set of skeleton casts and dioramas depicting Neanderthals who looked like they'd stepped out of Geico Auto Insurance's 'So Easy, A Caveman Can Do It' ad campaign, the refurbished Hall of Human Origins is a multimedia wonderland. The old dioramas are still intact, but the surrounding explanations and diagrams have been replaced with more information, better graphics, and often video or interactive touch-screen displays."

In addition to his books for adults, Tattersall has written two children's books, *Primates: Lemurs, Monkeys, and You* (1994) and *Bones, Brains and DNA: The Human Genome and Human Evolution* (2007). He lives in New York City.

—N.W.M.

Suggested Reading: *Chronicle of Higher Education* A p18 Sep. 8, 2000; *Newsday* A p29 Jan. 21, 2003; *New York Times* F p1 Dec. 31, 2002; *Pittsburgh Post-Gazette* A p8 Oct. 7, 1996; *Science* p1500 Dec. 19, 1986, p1666 Mar. 31, 1989, p1464 Aug. 30, 2002; *Unesco Courier* (on-line) Dec. 2000

Selected Books: *Man's Ancestors: An Introduction to Primate and Human Evolution*, 1970; *Primates of Madagascar*, 1982; *The Myths of Human Evolution* (with Niles Eldredge), 1982; *The Human Odyssey: Four Million Years of Human Evolution*, 1993; *The Fossil Trail: How We Know What We Think We Know About Human Evolution*, 1995; *Becoming Human: Evolution and Human Uniqueness*, 1998; *The Last Neanderthal: The Rise, Success, and Mysterious Extinction of Our Closest Human Relatives*, 1999; *The Monkey in the Mirror: Essays on the Science of What Makes Us Human*, 2002; *Human Origins: What Bones and Genomes Tell Us About Ourselves* (with Rob Desalle), 2007; with Jeffrey H. Schwartz—*Extinct Humans*, 2000; *The Human Fossil Record: Volume 1, Terminology and Craniodental Morphology of Genus Homo*, 2002; *The Human Fossil Record: Volume 2, Craniodental Morphology of Genus Homo (Africa and Asia)*, 2003; *The Human Fossil Record: Volume 3, Brain Endocasts—The Paleoneurological Evidence*, 2004; *The Human Fossil Record, Volume 4, Craniodental Morphology of Early Hominids (Genera Australopithecus, Paranthropus, Orrorin), and Overview*, 2005; for children—*Primates: Lemurs, Monkeys, and You*, 1994; *Bones, Brains, and DNA: The Human Genome and Human Evolution*, 2007

Nick Laham/Getty Images

Taurasi, Diana

(tore-AH-see)

June 11, 1982– Basketball player

Address: Phoenix Mercury, 201 E. Jefferson St., Phoenix, AZ 85004

Diana Taurasi, the star player of the Phoenix Mercury of the Women's National Basketball Association (WNBA), has been called one of the greatest female basketball players of all time—a designation that puts her in a class with the legends Nancy Lieberman, Cheryl Miller, Lisa Leslie, Sheryl Swoopes, and Chamique Holdsclaw. "Perhaps Taurasi's greatest attribute is that she has so many attributes. Shooting, passing, ability in the clutch, she has mastered them all," Jeff Goldberg wrote for the *Chicago Tribune* (April 3, 2004). The six-foot-one-inch guard has played effectively at four positions—point guard, shooting guard, small forward, and power forward—while her charisma has helped revive a WNBA program that has often struggled for mainstream relevance. Bringing to the game a joie de vivre in the tradition of such past male stars as Larry Bird and Magic Johnson, Taurasi is often at her best in—and seems to relish—nail-biting situations. Frank Deford wrote for *Sports Illustrated* (November 24, 2003) that Taurasi "sees things on the court that God hasn't arranged for other people to pick out."

Taurasi attended the University of Connecticut (UConn), a women's college basketball juggernaut, from 2000 to 2004, leading the Huskies to three consecutive NCAA (National Collegiate Athletic Association) championships and, in her sophomore year, to a perfect 39–0 record. In 2004 she became the youngest player to earn a spot on the U.S. women's basketball team at the Summer Olympics, in Athens, Greece, and aided the squad in capturing the gold medal. The number-one overall pick in the WNBA draft that year, Taurasi took home Rookie of the Year honors after averaging 17 points, 4.4 rebounds, and 3.9 assists per game for the Mercury. After missing the play-offs in each of her first three seasons with the team, Taurasi led the Mercury to their first WNBA title on September 16, 2007, when they defeated the Detroit Shock (the league's defending champions), 108–92; she thus became just the sixth player ever to win an NCAA title, an Olympic gold medal, and a WNBA championship. Since she joined the WNBA, the superstar has broken its records for points in a season (741), points in a game (47), and average number of points per game (25.3). "Is she one of the best players ever to play this game? Absolutely," the Seattle Storm coach Anne Donovan told Goldberg about Taurasi. "I can't remember anybody shooting the ball as well as Diana has. Just a pure shooter with tremendous range that has showed such poise in clutch situations."

The younger daughter of Mario Taurasi, a builder of aircraft parts, and Liliana Taurasi, a waitress, Diana Lurena Taurasi was born on June 11, 1982 in Glendale, California, and raised in Chino, a suburb of Los Angeles. Both of her parents were from Argentina; her father had moved there from Italy when he was seven. Her father had been a professional soccer goalie for a local league in Argentina and emphasized the sport above others during Taurasi's youth. While Taurasi played on a number of soccer teams as a girl, which helped her to develop footwork skills, it was at basketball that she truly shone, beginning with organized play in the fourth grade; she also played past sunset every day at home, using the hoop in her family's driveway. Her parents instilled in her and her sister, Jessika, the idea that playing sports should be enjoyable above all else, a notion currently reflected in Diana Taurasi's blithe attitude on the court. By the time she was 12 years old, standing at five feet 11 inches, many coaches in the Southern California basketball circuit had come to consider her a prodigy. When she was 11 her family moved to Argentina, where they stayed for close to a year before a traumatic experience led them back to Chino: one evening three men robbed the family in their home at gunpoint.

In her teens back in California, Taurasi sought challenges on the basketball court beyond what she had faced. She frequently traveled to Venice Beach and to the Morgan Center, an athletic arena at the University of California at Los Angeles (UCLA), to play pickup games with men. Those games led her to develop a rough and aggressive playing style, which separated her from most other female athletes. "The best players in the world are men," Taurasi said to Aimee Berg for *Sports Illustrated for Kids* (June 2005). "So why wouldn't you want to play like them?" She established herself as the best player in her junior high school. Guy Haarlammert, her coach in the Amateur Athletic Union (AAU), which included players aged 10 to 18, campaigned for her to play for an AAU all-star squad called SoCal Women's Basketball. In doing so, Taurasi won national attention. In the summer between her eighth- and ninth-grade years, the SoCal team won tournaments all over the country as well as the national championship for their age group.

Taurasi was a dominant player throughout her years at Don Lugo High School. During her junior year she had a five-game streak of making the winning shot in the final minute of play. By the time she was a senior, she had become the most sought-after female player in the country, amassing a stunning 3,047 points in four years and taking home the coveted Naismith Prep Player of the Year Award. Taurasi initially intended to enroll at UCLA, but Geno Auriemma, the legendary coach at the University of Connecticut, in Storrs, lured her to that school to play for the Huskies. On the subject of her choice, Diana explained to Frank Deford, "I know this will irritate a lot of coaches, so I never said it then, but I wanted to play for a man. Anyway, Geno was different from all the other coaches. He'd tell me things that were real. And 99 percent of it was true."

At first, Taurasi—whose manner bordered on cockiness at times—butted heads with Auriemma, whose team had won the NCAA championship the year before, and who wanted Taurasi to understand that his other players were her equals or betters. At the outset, Auriemma reportedly told Taurasi every day in practice that she was "uncoachable" and "undisciplined." "Every practice was a dogfight," Taurasi explained to Kevin Conley for the *New Yorker* (March 8, 2004). "Coming in, you're like, Wow. You're used to playing jayvee teams in high school, and now you're playing against the best players in the country." Auriemma revealed to Deford that Taurasi's bravado frequently masked insecurity: "[Taurasi] will say, 'I don't care what anyone thinks of me.' That's her style. That's what she says, and that's her strength, but sometimes your greatest [strength] is your greatest weakness, and I knew there were times when [Taurasi] was dying inside." Her ability was put to the test when the team's two top scorers, Shea Ralph and Svetlana Abrosimova, were sidelined with injuries early in Taurasi's freshman season. She filled in at both starting point guard and shooting guard, so successfully that UConn made the NCAA tournament in March 2001 and Taurasi became the only freshman ever to be named Most Outstanding Player of the NCAA East regional division. Her team progressed to the Final Four, where they faced Notre Dame. The most important game of Taurasi's basketball career up until then proved to be a humbling experience for her: she missed all but one of 15 shots before fouling out. Notre Dame capitalized on Taurasi's shooting slump and won easily, 90–75. Recalling that Taurasi burst into tears on the bench, Auriemma said to Conley, "I remember just sitting in front of her saying, . . . 'Yeah, you're the reason we lost, but you know what? You're the reason we're here. So relax, man! It works both ways.'" He added that she spent the next week practicing in the UConn gym, "just killing people. Making every shot, destroying everybody on the floor."

Taurasi went on to have a stellar sophomore season, as a member of what was arguably the greatest women's college basketball team ever assembled. The Huskies, who also included Sue Bird, Swin Cash, Asjha Jones, and Tamika Williams (all of whom would be among the first six players drafted by the WNBA later that year) were 39–0 for the season, trampling opposing teams with the combination of Bird at point guard and Taurasi at shooting guard. The team's first true challenge of the year came when they faced their bitter rivals, the number-two–seeded University of Tennessee Lady Volunteers, in January 2002. The Huskies rose to the occasion, with Taurasi scoring a career-high 32 points and helping her team to defeat the Lady Vols, 86–72. The team went into the 2002 NCAA tournament undefeated and advanced to the title game, against the University of Oklahoma Sooners. The Huskies led for most of the game, but with less than two minutes remaining, the Sooners threatened to make a comeback. With Sooners defenders in her face, Taurasi made an extremely tough shot in the paint, then converted a free-throw opportunity into a three-point play, sealing the Huskies' victory, 82–70. By season's end Taurasi had an average of 14.5 points (eighth in the league), 5.3 assists (sixth in the league), and 2.36 three-point field goals (fifth in the league) per game. She also led her team in assists on 17 occasions and in blocks 12 times.

Taurasi was the unquestioned leader and star of the Huskies during her junior and senior seasons (2003–04 and 2004–05, respectively). With the departure of the four star seniors, Taurasi both carried the team and tried, by instilling confidence in the other players, to avoid the necessity of doing so. Despite Taurasi's chronic ankle and back injuries, caused in part by double- and triple-teaming by opposing players, the Huskies extended their winning streak from the previous season to 70 (the longest in women's Division I history) by winning their first 31 games. They lost to Villanova, 52–48, in the Big East Conference tournament, which also ended UConn's nine-year tournament-title streak in the Big East conference. Taurasi, who ranked among the top 10 players in the nation in nearly every major offensive and defensive category, nonetheless felt that she was not playing at the level required by her team. On the subject of the loss to Villanova, a game in which she scored 13 points, Taurasi told Kelli Anderson for *Sports Illustrated* (April 17, 2003), "It made me look in the mirror and say, 'You need to step up.' That game I let my teammates down, my coaches down, and from then on I just wanted to do everything I could." Her determination to "step up" resulted in 663 points for the season (third-most in UConn's history), 54 points in that year's Final Four (the fourth-highest two-game total in NCAA women's-basketball history), and an average of 26.2 points per game in six NCAA tournament games. She also led the Huskies in scoring (with an average of 17.9 points per game), rebounding (6.1 per game), assists (4.4 per game), blocks (1.2 per game), free-throw percentage (.815), and minutes per game (31.9). Facing the University of Tennessee in the 2003 NCAA Championship game, Taurasi scored 28 points, including a pair of crucial free throws with 20 seconds left in the game, to lead the Huskies to a hard-fought 73–68 victory—UConn's third national title in four years. Taurasi's dominance garnered her the Naismith Player of the Year and Big East Player of the Year awards.

In her senior year Taurasi led her team to their third straight NCAA Championship, helping once again to defeat Tennessee, 70–61. That season the versatile guard became the first Huskies player ever to achieve more than 2,000 points, 600 rebounds, and 600 assists over a career, breaking UConn records for assists and three-pointers. She

was again named Naismith Player of the Year and Big East Player of the Year. She graduated from UConn with a degree in sociology.

Many considered Taurasi's career at UConn to have been one of the finest in the history of women's college basketball, which in turn led to her being the hottest prospect in WNBA history. The Phoenix Mercury, who had secured a number-one bid in the draft lottery after amassing a WNBA-worst 8–26 record for the 2003 season, considered Taurasi a potential savior of their franchise and one who might increase ticket sales, given her fame around the country. The team thus made Taurasi the number-one overall pick in the 2004 WNBA draft. Practically overnight, merchandise sales for the Mercury rose by 87 percent, and traffic on the team's Web site increased by 200 percent, making it the most popular site among WNBA teams. Taurasi's jersey became the number-two seller behind that of Lisa Leslie (probably the best-known WNBA player to date). At the time the 22-year-old was preparing to compete in the 2004 Summer Olympic Games, in Athens, as the youngest member of the U.S. women's basketball team.

In her WNBA debut, a 72–66 loss to the Sacramento Monarchs, Taurasi led all scorers with 22 points and made three assists, three rebounds, and three blocks. She then became the first WNBA player in history to score 20 or more points in each of her first three games, averaging 20.8 points over her first four contests. In her 23 games before the WNBA suspended play during the Olympics, Taurasi led all rookies in scoring, with an average of 17.7 points per game, and averaged 4.1 rebounds, 3.8 assists, and 1.3 steals per game. In Athens, playing alongside stars she had idolized while growing up—including Dawn Staley, Lisa Leslie, and Sheryl Swoopes—she scored 13 points in a game against Japan and went on to average 8.5 points per contest, helping the U.S. to defeat Australia, 74–63, and take home the gold medal. Returning to the WNBA, Taurasi closed out her rookie season with per-game averages of 17 points, 4.4 rebounds, and 3.9 assists—good enough to earn her Rookie of the Year honors and a spot on the All-WNBA first team. The Mercury failed to make the play-offs, but the season was regarded as successful overall, with the team managing a 17–17 record—a significant improvement over the previous year.

Taurasi's second season with the Mercury was similarly successful. She became the fifth player in the franchise's history to score over 1,000 points and only the second player to reach that mark in her first two seasons. In August 2005, in a game against Houston, she came close to a triple-double, finishing the game with 27 points, nine rebounds, and eight assists. (There have been only four triple-doubles in the history of the WNBA.) Another highlight included scoring a career-best 31 points against the Seattle Storm in the season finale. The Mercury finished the year with one fewer win than the previous season, missing the play-offs for the second year in a row. Given the comparatively low salaries of WNBA players (an average of about $53,000 per year, compared with $4 million for NBA athletes), Taurasi, like many of her colleagues, traveled overseas to play in a professional Russian league in the winter prior to the 2006 WNBA season.

When the coach Paul Westhead, a veteran of the NBA, took over the Mercury in time for that season, Taurasi returned to Phoenix with hopes of making the play-offs. She thrived amid the fast-paced, energetic play Westhead demanded, averaging 25.3 points per game—breaking the record of 23.1, set by Katie Smith. In her 26th game (a regular season includes 34), she also broke Jennifer Gillom's mark for points scored in a season, finishing with 741 in total. In addition, Taurasi led her team in assists (an average of 4.2 per game) and managed to cut her turnovers in half from the previous year. Her most spectacular night came in August 2006, when she broke the record for points made in a game, scoring 47 against the Houston Comets in a dramatic 111–110 triple-overtime victory—the highest-scoring game in the league's history. Despite winning their last seven games for an 18–16 record, the Mercury again fell short of a play-off berth. Taurasi said to a writer for *Arizona Central* (August 14, 2006, on-line), "Everyone is happy that we're not in it. I mean who really wants to play against us. Think about it, I wouldn't want to play against us." In 2006 Taurasi was named a WNBA All-Decade Team honorable mention—a remarkable feat, considering that she had completed only her third year in the league.

After getting off to a slow start in the 2007 season, with a 7–7 record, the Mercury went on to win 16 of their last 20 games, led by the one-two punch of Taurasi and the star point guard Cappie Pondexter—and entered the play-offs with the best record in the Western Conference. Taurasi helped her team eliminate the Seattle Storm in the first round and the San Antonio Silver Stars in the second. Despite Phoenix's dominant play late in the season and into the play-offs, the team entered the WNBA Finals as a heavy underdog, facing the defending champion Detroit Shock. After the teams split the first two games in Detroit, the Mercury suffered a disappointing loss at home in Game Three, 88–83. For Game Four, the team barely escaped elimination when they defeated the Shock in the final seconds, 77–76. Then, on September 16, 2007, the Mercury upset the Shock in the fifth game, 108–92, and won the championship. Taurasi scored 17 points and grabbed a game-high seven rebounds.

Frank Deford noted that the six-foot-one-inch, 170-pound Taurasi—known to friends and family as "D"—"actually looks very much like that other inscrutable Italian lady, Mona Lisa." The energetic Taurasi, who has trouble sitting still for extended periods, reportedly dislikes watching movies and claims to have read only one book from cover to cover: *Practical Modern Basketball*, by the former UCLA coach John Wooden. In her spare time she

enjoys playing cards and video games and spending time with her family, with whom she speaks Spanish. The WNBA great Dawn Staley said to Marcia C. Smith for the *Orange County (California) Register* (August 1, 2004) about Taurasi, "Of all the young players in the past 10 years whom people described as a prototype superstar, she is the one who has lived up to every bit of her reputation."

—C.C.

Suggested Reading: *Chicago Tribune* C p6 Apr. 3, 2004; Diana Taurasi's official Web site; *Los Angeles Times* D p1 Mar. 20, 2004; *New Yorker* p42+ Mar. 8, 2004; *Newsday* D p24 Mar. 15, 2004; *Orange County (California) Register* Sports Aug. 1, 2004; *San Antonio (Texas) Express-News* C p1 July 30, 2004; *Sports Illustrated* p52+ Apr. 17, 2003, p124+ Nov. 24, 2003; *Sports Illustrated for Kids* p22+ June, 2005; WNBA Web site

Jonathan Daniel/Getty Images

Thome, Jim

(TOH-mee)

Aug. 27, 1970– Baseball player

Address: Chicago White Sox, 333 W. 35th St., Chicago, IL 60616

Hitting a home run, a feat that requires a combination of eye-hand coordination, proper timing, and strength, is one of the most celebrated achievements in sports, as suggested by the seemingly endless list of slang terms for "home run": big fly, bomb, dinger, homer, jack, tater, moonshot, gopher ball, long ball, clout, and blast, to name just a few. Barry Bonds, Josh Gibson, and Sadaharu Oh, the career home-run record holders of Major League Baseball (MLB), the Negro League in the United States, and Japan's Nippon Professional League, respectively, occupy hallowed places in sports. For many, the six-foot three-inch Jim Thome, the designated hitter and sometime first baseman of MLB's Chicago White Sox, has evoked thoughts of those greats; a rare slugger who combines unusual patience in the batter's box with immense strength, he has proven to be one of the most efficient home-run hitters of all time. After an unproductive 2005 season—his 11th full season in the big leagues—which was cut short by back trouble and elbow surgery, Thome rebounded in 2006, earning the American League Comeback Player of the Year Award and reasserting himself as one of the sport's most feared left-handed power hitters. On September 16, 2007, with his customary short swing, Thome hit his 500th career home run, becoming the 23d player in baseball history to accomplish that feat. His rate of one home run per every 13.5 at bats is even more impressive, good for fourth-best in the history of the majors, behind only Mark McGwire, Babe Ruth, and Barry Bonds. During the 2002 season Thome hit a home run in each of seven consecutive games, a streak bested by only three MLB players, past or present. Despite his remarkable record, Thome has insisted that he does not try to hit home runs—that he merely tries to make contact with the ball. "I try to go out and hit .300. . . . You can't try to hit homers. If you have a good swing, you'll get your homers," Thome told Edward de la Fuente for the Wilmington, Delaware, *News Journal* (March 31, 2003). After even his most impressive home runs, Thome does not stand at home plate to bask in his achievement, as many players do, before running the bases; instead he immediately circles the bases at a brisk clip, with his head down. "My dad always told me not to show a lot of emotion, and the last thing I'd ever want to do was show somebody up," Thome told Terry Pluto for the *Akron (Ohio) Beacon Journal* (September 25, 2001). "That's not how I was taught to play the game."

As that comment may suggest, Thome is known in baseball circles as much for his charitable nature as for his prodigious power. "I've never heard one person say they don't like Jimmy," the radio broadcaster Tom Hamilton told Terry Pluto. "During the games, everyone who reaches first base talks to him. And Jimmy signs as many autographs as anyone on the team. He hasn't changed a bit over the years." Mike Nadel, writing for the Copley News Service (February 21, 2006), described Thome as "equal parts Babe Ruth and Dudley Do-Right, . . . a massive man with a huge home-run swing and a heart the size of Illinois." At a time when professional athletics are increasingly plagued by controversy over issues ranging from players' contracts to performance-enhancing drugs, many see Thome as an example of what is right in sports.

The youngest of five children (his twin sister, Jenny, is two minutes his senior), James Howard Thome was born to Joyce and Chuck Thome Jr. in Peoria, Illinois, on August 27, 1970. His father, an auto worker at Caterpillar Industries Inc., was a legend in the local fast-pitch softball leagues. Thome and his siblings continued a family tradition of excelling in sports that went back at least to Chuck Thome Sr., who played professional baseball in the now-defunct Three-I League in the Midwest. Chuck Sr., Chuck Jr., Art Thome, and Carolyn Thome Hart (the latter two are an aunt and uncle of Thome's) were elected to the Greater Peoria Sports Hall of Fame in 1982. (Carolyn had been inducted into the National Softball Hall of Fame in 1966.) Thome's old-fashioned habit of wearing his uniform pants extremely high, to expose a great deal of sock, is an homage to his grandfather and father; he began that practice soon after his grandfather died. "He never got to see me play in the big leagues," Thome said, as reported by Don Bostrom for the Allentown, Pennsylvania, *Morning Call* (March 30, 2003). "My dad showed me old photographs of him and that's how he wore his uniform when he played. . . . I do it out of respect to him and my family."

Thome's first childhood dream was to be a professional baseball player, and he looked forward to the family's annual trips to Wrigley Field to watch the Chicago Cubs of MLB's National League. Thome also spent his childhood admiring the accomplishments of his older brothers, Chuck III and Randy—his seniors by 14 and 12 years, respectively—who in high school excelled in both basketball and baseball and by most accounts were even more athletically gifted than Jim. As a youngster Thome tried to imitate his brothers, and Joyce Thome has recalled Jim's asking her how much milk his brothers drank when they were his age, so that he could follow suit. Thome first played baseball with his father, during evening sessions at a run-down public tennis court near the family's house. At Limestone High School in Bartonville, a Peoria suburb, Thome shone in basketball, emerging as a contender for the state scoring title in his senior year, but baseball remained his passion. "Jim's two older brothers were bigger, stronger and had more ability than him," Thome's father told Paul Hoynes for the *Cleveland Plain Dealer* (August 27, 1995). "But they didn't want it like Jimmy did. When the high school season was over and the summer leagues ended, . . . Jimmy would drive around town with a bucket of balls in the back seat until he found a couple of kids to play with."

While Thome was a strong baseball player in high school, he was often overshadowed by the legacies of his older brothers and even by players on his own team. He hoped to be drafted by a professional team following his graduation, but many scouts thought that the then–175-pound shortstop was too small to succeed as a pro, despite his quick feet and hands. Unable to generate much interest from four-year college-baseball programs, either,

Thome enrolled at Illinois Central Junior College, in Peoria, where he played both basketball and baseball. (At least one team offered to sign Thome as a free agent during the summer before he began studying at Illinois Central, but he declined, choosing instead to try his luck in the following year's draft.) During his freshman year Thome earned All-American honors in baseball and began to draw some interest from scouts. Tom Couston, a Midwest-area scout for MLB's Cleveland Indians who had scouted Thome's brothers years earlier (but did not recommend that they be drafted), came across Thome almost accidentally: while attending an Illinois Central game to see a highly regarded player on the opposing team, Couston was more impressed by Thome than by the other player. "Every ball he hit was a rocket," Couston said to Hoynes about Thome. "His swinging was so quick and powerful that I was surprised he didn't kill somebody." Prior to the 1989 MLB amateur players' draft, the Minnesota Twins and the Cincinnati Reds brought in Thome for tryouts; in the end, though, through Couston's recommendation, he was selected by the Indians in the 13th round of the 1989 draft—331st overall—and signed a contract for $15,000 per year.

Thome began his professional career in the Indians' Rookie League Gulf Team, where, with a .237 batting average and no home runs, he did not immediately impress. At the end of his first spring training, in 1990, he failed to make the cut for any of the Indians' minor-league teams and had his training extended. He then met Charlie Manuel, a minor-league hitting instructor at the time. Manuel had been assigned to mentor a highly touted Indians prospect, and Thome began tagging along to their instructional sessions to glean all that he could. Manuel told Paul Hoynes that Thome and the other player "used to hit together when I worked out with them. I must have worked with [the other prospect] for two weeks, talking to him about hitting, about where to put your feet and hands, but he didn't get it. . . . In those two weeks, Thome started hanging out rockets all over the place. I said to myself, 'Maybe I better start paying attention to this guy.'" Manuel and Thome developed a personal relationship during that spring that lasted for years. Manuel saw that while Thome had uncommonly good eye-hand coordination and reflexes, his technique, both offensive and defensive, was very poor. For example, Thome lacked the skill to hit the ball into right field, instead sending it to the left with only moderate power. In order to increase Thome's hitting power, Manuel started him on a weight-training program and opened his stance at the plate so that his body was twisted, allowing him more time and space to hit the ball with authority to right field. For the final alteration Thome and Manuel were indebted to a team screening of the 1984 film *The Natural*. In it, Robert Redford, playing the role of a mysterious slugger, begins each trip to home plate by waving his bat horizontally toward center field. Thome decid-

ed to do the same during batting practice that evening and discovered that it relaxed him, improved his balance, and made his swing more consistent. Thome eventually earned a spot as a third baseman in the Class A Appalachian League. Showing improvement immediately, he was promoted to the stronger Class A Carolina League. Overall during the 1990 season, Thome managed a .340 average and, of perhaps greater interest to management, generated 16 home runs and 50 runs batted in (RBIs).

Thome began the 1991 season at Cleveland's Canton-Akron double-A affiliate, for which he hit .337 with 45 RBIs in 84 games. He was promoted to triple-A ball in Colorado Springs, Colorado, and, later that season, to the major leagues for 27 games. Thome, then 20 years old, fared well in his first big-league appearances, earning a .255 batting average but with only one home run. In 1992 he spent time with both the double-A Canton-Akron team and the triple-A squad in Colorado Springs, where he was reunited with Manuel, who was a triple-A manager until he became the Indians' hitting coach, in 1994. During the 1992 season Thome was again impressive in the minor leagues and was sent to the majors, this time for 40 games. He appeared overmatched, however, batting just .205 and striking out 34 times in 117 at bats. In 1993, following a stellar performance against major-league pitchers during spring training, he was again assigned to triple-A ball, with the Charlotte, South Carolina, Knights—which came as a let-down for Thome, who had hoped to begin the year in the major leagues with Cleveland. Manuel believed that Thome would benefit from the additional experience of playing every day in triple-A instead of competing with the third baseman Alvaro Espinoza for playing time on the major-league team. "[Thome is] a natural hitter. He's shown me things with the bat that you just don't coach," Manuel told Ray Stein for the *Columbus (Ohio) Dispatch* (July 25, 1993). "He does have some holes, though. Pitchers can still get him out. . . . Defensively, he still makes mistakes," Manuel continued. "If [the Indians] called today and said they wanted to bring him up, I'd say, 'He's ready. He's a premier hitter but I promise you, he's going to make some mistakes in the field.' . . . Because of that, I think he should spend every day here he can. The longer he stays here, the better." Triple-A pitching, however, did not pose much of a challenge for the promising slugger, who by then had filled out to 220 pounds. By mid-season Thome was leading the International League in batting average (.341) and RBIs (89) and had hit 21 home runs, second-best in the league. With 47 games left in the 1993 major-league season, Thome was promoted to the Indians. He acquitted himself well in his third call-up, hitting .266 with seven home runs while displaying a keen batting eye that enabled him to nearly triple his base-on-balls total; he also saw his strike-out rate reduced from the previous year. The Indians, however, finished the season in last place in the American League East Division.

In 1994, after decades of struggle, the Indians began to see their fortunes turn. They had opened a new stadium, Jacobs Field, and the promise shown by the younger players, including Thome, rejuvenated the fan base. Thome began the season as the Indians' regular third baseman and displayed the ability that would later make him a star. When a players' strike ended the season, on August 12, Thome had played in 98 of the team's 113 games and earned a .268 batting average with 20 home runs and 52 RBIs—though he remained challenged defensively, committing 15 errors. In 1995 the Indians, with a lineup buoyed by Carlos Baerga, Manny Ramirez, Albert Belle, and Thome, finished with 100 wins, 44 loses, and a berth in the playoffs. After defeating the Boston Red Sox and the Seattle Mariners during the American League playoffs, the Indians advanced for the first time since 1954 to the World Series, where they met the Atlanta Braves. Although the Braves defeated them, the season was a huge success for the Cleveland franchise. Thome proved to be an effective complement to the team's established stars, hitting a career-high .314 for the season.

Thome started the 1996 season strongly. Midway through the season he approached the general manager, John Hart, to discuss moving up in the batting order to replace Carlos Baerga, who had been traded. Thome had to that point struggled against left-handed pitching, and occasionally other batters substituted for him. Still, Mike Hargrove, the Indians' manager, was inspired by Thome's recent boost in confidence and believed that the normally soft-spoken Thome would not have made the suggestion unless he was prepared to handle the responsibility that the switch would bring. "Jimmy has quietly had almost an MVP year," Hargrove said, according to Terry Pluto in the *Akron Beacon Journal* (October 1, 1996). "He is such a great kid. He doesn't shoot off his mouth. He has made himself into a solid third baseman, when some people were wondering if he'd ever he able to play there in the big leagues. He has become a smart hitter. I love having Jim Thome on my team." Positioned third in the lineup following the All-Star break, Thome responded in superior fashion, showing unprecedented ability against left-handed pitchers, against whom he hit .300 for the remainder of the season. The switch also placed Thome in a leadership position on the team. The Indians were a strong team during the 1996 season, winning 99 games and making it to the first round of the play-offs, where they lost to the Baltimore Orioles. Thome finished the season with career highs in games played (151), at bats (505), hits (157), home runs (38), RBIs (116), and walks (123), while putting together a .311 batting average.

Prior to the 1997 season, Cleveland made a trade to acquire Matt Williams, a strong-hitting veteran third baseman, which forced Thome to switch to first base. Although Thome preferred to remain at third, he understood that by gaining Williams the Indians became a better team, and he endorsed the move. "You come right down to it, I work for the Indians," Thome told Terry Pluto for the *Akron Beacon Journal* (February 23, 1997). "It's not for me to say where I should play. It's for [management] to decide what is best for the team." Thome made a smooth transition to first base, where his size and agility were strong assets, and made only 10 errors, seven fewer than the year before. He also maintained solid hitting through the position change, getting 40 home runs along with 102 RBIs and a .286 average. Thome was selected to play in his first All-Star Game, and at the conclusion of the season, he led the major leagues in walks, a testament to his patience at the plate. Cleveland won the regular-season Central Division title for the third consecutive year. In the first round of the play-offs, the Indians beat the New York Yankees, the 1996 champions, before beating Baltimore to advance to the World Series. The Indians blew a late lead and lost the decisive seventh game against the Florida Marlins in 11 innings. For Thome, who had hit two home runs during the series, the 1997 defeat was harder to accept than the loss in 1995.

By the 1998 season Thome had become one of the senior members of the team and a quiet leader through his example of hard work and diligence. When asked by Sheldon Ocker for the *Akron Beacon Journal* (March 1, 1998) about his individual goals prior to the 1998 season, Thome focused instead on the goals of the team. "Honestly, I would pass up all the individual stuff to get the [World Series] ring," he said. "Individual accomplishments are nice. And when you do good things individually, you help the team. But the ultimate is winning the World Series. If I'm a guy who hits 40 home runs with 100 RBI and our team wins the World Series, that's great. If I hit 50 homers and drive in 150 runs and we don't win the Series, that's not so great. People might not believe it, but it's the truth." In an effort to keep his teammates focused on winning the World Series, Thome printed T-shirts that read, "It doesn't mean a thing 'til we get the ring," and handed them out during a practice. Batting alongside Manny Ramirez, Thome was elected to his second consecutive All-Star Game, thanks to a .326 batting average, 23 home runs, and 73 RBIs. His season was derailed in August, when he was hit by a pitch and suffered a broken hand, an injury that placed him on the disabled list for six weeks. Thome was not able to return to form after the injury, and he managed just seven more home runs and a .221 batting average through the rest of the season. The Indians won 89 games to lead the Central Division but were defeated by the New York Yankees in the play-offs.

In 1999 Thome increased his home-run total to 33 and gained an odd distinction, leading MLB in both walks (127) and strikeouts (171). Ironically, both figures were attributed to Thome's patience at the plate: by refusing to swing at borderline pitches and waiting for those he deemed to be sure strikes, Thome was vulnerable to called third strikes. Led by Thome, Manny Ramirez, David Justice, and

Robbie Alomar, the Indians were considered one of the top teams in the league—notwithstanding that year's postseason, when they experienced one of the more spectacular collapses in MLB history. Leading the Boston Red Sox two games to none in the best-of-five divisional play-off round, the Indians went on to lose the next three games and the series. The Indians began the 2000 season poorly, and although they rebounded in the season's second half, they could not overtake the Chicago White Sox, and finished second in the Central Division championship. Thome finished among the league leaders in home runs (37), walks (118), and strikeouts (171).

By the 2001 season Thome had become the face of the Cleveland Indians and the most recognizable athlete on any of Cleveland's professional sports teams. (The only other batter remaining from the 1993 Indians team was Kenny Lofton, whose time with the team had been interrupted by a stint with the Atlanta Braves.) Thome responded well to the spotlight, posting the best season of his career to that point. He set career highs in home runs, with 49, and RBIs, with 124—both statistics in the top five in MLB. The Indians won the Central Division title but again fell in the first play-off round, this time to Seattle. Thome had another superlative season in 2002, hitting for a .304 average while amassing totals of 52 home runs and 118 RBIs. The 2002 season also marked the expiration of Thome's contract with Cleveland. Although the Indians attempted to retain his services, Thome signed a six-year, $85 million contract with the Philadelphia Phillies, who offered more money than the Indians and, in Thome's estimation, stood a better chance of winning the World Series in 2003.

Thome made an instant impact on the Phillies, both on the field and in the locker room, his veteran's presence lending a sense of stability to a team of mostly young players. As the team's highest-paid player, he was expected to be a leader and to perform at an All-Star level. He also became a focal point for the media, which took pressure off the younger star players. Thome found that the Phillies were as unified as the Indians had been when he first came up to the major leagues. "The thing I see here is each guy truly rooting for each other, like we did in Cleveland. It's not two guys here, two guys there. The guys pull for everybody," Thome said, as reported by Edward de la Fuente for the Wilmington, Delaware, *News Journal* (March 31, 2003). During his first two seasons with the Phillies, Thome did not disappoint, ringing up 89 home runs and 236 RBIs combined over the two seasons. In 2004 he was selected for the All-Star Game, his first in the National League.

Thome did not enjoy similar success in 2005. He played in only 59 games, as back trouble and a sore elbow, which eventually needed surgery, kept him sidelined for most of the season. While he was playing, Thome hit only seven home runs with a .207 batting average. In his absence the Phillies placed at first base the emerging star Ryan Howard,

who went on to earn the National League Rookie of the Year Award. Many local sportswriters believed that Thome would struggle to complete the final three years of his contract, and that the Phillies should attempt to trade him. The presence of Howard enabled the team to do just that, a move that "I think . . . really hurt him . . . ," Charlie Manuel, who had become the Phillies' manager prior to the 2005 season, told Jayson Stark for ESPN (April 27, 2006, on-line). "He'd never say anything about that at all. But it hurt him." Thome went to the Chicago White Sox, as part of a trade that turned out to have many positive ramifications for him. Playing in Chicago, he could be closer to his childhood home, in Peoria, at a time when his father was struggling with the death of Thome's mother from lung cancer, in 2005. Thome told Jayson Stark, "What this has done, coming back to Chicago, is that it's really revitalized [my father]. . . . And more than anything else, that's why it makes me so happy to be here." Another result of the move was that, by returning to the American League, Thome would be able to play at the designated-hitter position, which many believed would help extend his career by keeping him from the rigors of playing defense. Finally, the White Sox were the defending World Series champions, and Thome thought that as a member of the team, he had a good chance at a World Series win. He worked hard during the off-season, to defy claims that his career was over, earn the respect of his new teammates, and prove to himself that he was able to compete at an elite level.

Thome got off to a fast start in 2006, becoming the first White Sox player to hit 10 home runs in the month of April. "Baseball can be very humbling, and I had that experience a year ago," he told Stark. "And that's the reason I'm having so much fun—because I was hurt. And I understand now it's not going to last forever. So I'm going to cherish every time I step on the field, because you never know when it's going to end." On May 6, 2006 Thome hit his 443d career home run, passing his childhood hero Dave Kingman as the all-time leader in home runs hit by an Illinois native, and May 24 was declared Jim Thome Day statewide. Thome finished the season with terrific statistics that included 42 home runs, third-most in the American League, and he earned a position on the All-Star team. He was named the American League Comeback Player of the Year at the conclusion of the season.

Coming into the 2007 season, Thome was 28 homers shy of the 500-home-run mark. He reached that number on September 16, 2007— "Jim Thome Bobblehead Day"—in a contest with the Los Angeles Angels that took place at the White Sox's home stadium, U.S. Cellular Field. The teams were tied, 7–7, in the bottom of the ninth inning when Thome came up to the plate; in his previous 11 at-bats, including four that day, he had struck out. Facing the Angels' pitcher Dustin Moseley, with his count at three balls and two strikes, he hit a two-run home run—the 500th homer of his career. He became the 23d player in MLB history to accomplish that feat and, along with Alex Rodriguez and Frank Thomas, the third that year; he was the first ever to do so with a walk-off home run. He ended the season with a career total of 507 career homers, thus surpassing Eddie Murray's 504 and climbing to 22d place on the list of home-run leaders. In the 130 games he played in 2007, he batted .275 with 96 RBIs.

Through annual golf tournaments and other functions, Thome has raised over $1 million for the Children's Hospital of Illinois in Peoria, whose patients he regularly visits. Thome was honored with the Roberto Clemente Award for Sportsmanship and Community Involvement in 2002, and in 2005 he was selected by the *Sporting News* as baseball's "No. 1 Good Guy" and received the Lou Gehrig Award for character and integrity both on and off the field. Thome pays for the college tuition of his

nieces and nephews and feels a special connection with a nephew who was paralyzed in a pool accident.

Thome's main avocational interest is bowhunting deer. He reportedly has 15 deer heads on the walls of his hunting lodge; his wife, the former Andrea Pacione, does not allow them in the family's home. The couple have one daughter.

—N.W.M.

Suggested Reading: *Akron Beacon Journal* C p1 Mar. 1, 1998, C p1 Sep. 25, 2001; *Chicago Sun Times* p102 Jan. 20, 2006; *Chicago Tribune* C p1 Feb. 17, 2006; (Cleveland) *Plain Dealer* D p12 Aug. 27, 1995, S p2 Oct. 1, 1996, D p1 Oct. 28, 1997; *Columbus (Ohio) Dispatch* D p1 July 25, 1993; Copley News Service Feb. 21, 2006; *Philadelphia Daily News* B p12 Mar. 31, 2003; *Sports Illustrated* p72 Apr. 3, 2006

Streeter Lecka/Getty Images

Thompson, John III

Mar. 12, 1966– College basketball coach

Address: McDonough Gym, Athletic Dept., Georgetown University, Washington, DC 20057

When John Thompson III coached the Georgetown University Hoyas men's basketball team to the NCAA (National Collegiate Athletic Association) Final Four in 2007, he became not only the team's first coach to accomplish that feat in 22 years but part of the first father-and-son duo in NCAA histo-

ry to do so: it was Thompson's father, the Hall of Fame coach John Thompson Jr., who took the Hoyas to the Final Four in 1985. Incorporating elements of his father's style—in particular, an aggressive, some would say menacing, defense—along with the focus on offense of another mentor, the Hall of Fame Princeton University coach Pete Carril, Thompson has gained national attention for his intellectual approach to the game. Before he was named the 17th head coach of men's basketball in Georgetown history, in 2004, Thompson—nicknamed JT3—served from 1995 to 2000 as an assistant coach of his alma mater's team, the Princeton University Tigers, under Carril and his successor, Bill Carmody. As that team's head coach beginning in 2000, Thompson guided Princeton to three Ivy League Championships, two NCAA tournaments, and a National Invitation Tournament (NIT) appearance. In contrast to his physically imposing (six-foot 10-inch), outspoken, and controversial father, Thompson is known as a low-key avoider of the limelight whose accomplishments on the basketball court speak for themselves. His younger brother, Ronny, the head coach of men's basketball at Ball State University, explained to Eric Brady for *USA Today* (March 29, 2007) about Thompson, "He's a lot like Mom in that he doesn't outwardly show things. He has Dad's temper. . . . But John doesn't show it (publicly). Dad doesn't hide it. You always know what he's thinking." When it was announced that Thompson would become coach of the Hoyas, he spoke at a press conference about the large shadow, literal and figurative, cast by his father. "I am John Thompson's son," he said, as Julie Wood wrote for the *Hoya* (April 30, 2004). "I've been John Thompson's son for 38 years. And I'm pretty comfortable being John Thompson's son. No one's going to put more pressure on me than myself." Thompson was named a finalist for the Naismith Coach of the Year award in his first and third seasons with the Hoyas and earned the Black Coaches Association's Fritz Pollard Male Coach of the Year Award in his second season.

The oldest of the three children of Gwendolyn and John Thompson Jr., John ("Little John") Thompson III was born on March 12, 1966 in Washington, D.C. His father had been a star basketball player at Providence College and had had a brief professional career with the Boston Celtics before achieving his greatest fame as coach of the Hoyas, becoming, in 1984, the first black coach to win a NCAA Division I championship. In addition, he was a vocal—often controversial—proponent of racial equality in collegiate sports. Ronny Thompson said to Jim Benson, writing for the Bloomington, Illinois, *Pantagraph* (February 17, 2007), "My brother and I have always been 'Coach Thompson's sons.' It's something we've always had to deal with. It's a little second nature now." He told Jason Whitlock for the *Kansas City Star* (March 31, 2007), "My father would be mad if we tried to do everything the way he did it. He always wanted us to think for ourselves and make our own decisions."

Spending much of his childhood on the Georgetown University campus, Thompson grew up around basketball players, including the future NBA stars Patrick Ewing and Eric Augustus ("Sleepy") Floyd. Like his siblings, who also included his sister, Tiffany, he came to view basketball less as a sport than as a way of life. He sometimes tagged along with his father to the annual national coaches' convention, meeting and having dinner with such Hall of Fame coaches as Winston-Salem State University's Clarence ("Big House") Gaines and Temple University's John Chaney. Thompson said to Matt Golden, writing for *Princeton Alumni Weekly* (November 22, 2000), "The average fan would naturally remember the year that [Georgetown] won the national championship or the years that they lost in the finals, but for me, it was just the day-to-day duties of my father's job that made an impression. It doesn't end when you leave the office. You get home and there is film to be watched or there are calls to be made. It's a never-ending process." From his father, other coaches, and the players surrounding him, Thompson learned lessons in playing basketball and in standing up for himself on and off the court.

Thompson attended Gonzaga College High School, a Jesuit, all-boys institution in Washington, from 1980 to 1984. He excelled there at both academics and basketball, and as a senior he was named first-team all-metro by the *Washington Post*. Highly sought-after by colleges, Thompson decided to attend Princeton University, in Princeton, New Jersey, after meeting with the school's legendary coach, Pete Carril, during a visit to the campus. "I sat [in Jadwin Gymnasium] and coach Carril reminded me a lot of my dad," Thompson told Golden. "As a high school senior, you go

through the whole recruiting process and everyone is telling you that you're great. But we sat there and coach Carril was telling me what I needed to work on, that I needed to get better, and that if I didn't, I was going to be a [junior varsity] player. I just knew that I would learn more here from a basketball point of view."

Playing forward for the Tigers, Thompson thrived under Carril's direction. He also learned from Carril the fundamentals of what would become his own chief coaching strategy, the Princeton Offense—in which four perimeter players move, passing and weaving, around the team's center. Innumerable picks, rolls, and cutting schemes follow from that strategy, whose purpose is to eat up as much time as possible on the 35-second shot clock (thereby limiting opponents' possessions) while setting up the best possible shots. As a player Thompson made 358 assists during his four years with the Tigers, with 103 assists and just 34 turnovers during his senior year alone, good for a ranking of third all-time on Princeton's list of assist leaders. He served as a co-captain on the 1988 team and shared the B. F. Bunn trophy that year as one of Princeton's most valuable players.

After graduating, in 1988, with a degree in political science, Thompson put basketball aside for several years to concentrate on succeeding in the business world, working for the Ford Motor Co. in the dealer-development program. "I was foolish initially," he told Golden. "You go through a school like this, and you truly have unlimited options once you graduate. I almost felt obligated to try different things even though, in my heart, I think I always knew coaching is what I wanted to do." Eventually Carril persuaded Thompson during a telephone conversation to pursue his passion for coaching, to the initial dismay of Thompson's father, who had provided "Little John" with an Ivy League education in part so that he would have career options beyond basketball. Thompson, however, followed his desire.

Thompson began his coaching career in 1995, as a volunteer assistant coach on Carril's staff at his alma mater, where he worked long hours without pay. When Carril retired, the following year, his longtime assistant coach Bill Carmody stepped in as his successor. Carmody named Thompson as his number-two assistant, a post he held for several seasons before the team's number-one assistant coach, Joe Scott, got the head-coaching job with the U.S. Air Force Academy. Thompson became Carmody's number-one assistant and then, when Carmody moved to Northwestern University, took over as the Tigers' head coach. In his years as an assistant coach, Princeton had made five consecutive postseason appearances; Princeton's director of athletics, Gary Walters, called the decision to name Thompson as head coach "a no-brainer." Assembling a staff that included a former high-school teammate, Robert Burke, and two former Princeton players, Thompson created a familial atmosphere in which his players could communicate easily with the coaching staff. Thompson explained to Joseph White for the Associated Press (March 5, 2007) about his coaching mentality, "In the Ivy League, every game is a playoff game. . . . In that environment, you do learn that every game is urgent. If you beat Penn on Tuesday and lose to Dartmouth on Saturday, you have one loss in the league and that could end up costing you the league [title]." That approach paid off: as head coach he compiled a 68–42 record, guiding the team to three Ivy League Championships, two NCAA tournaments, and an NIT appearance.

While Thompson enjoyed success at Princeton, officials at Georgetown sought his help in reviving their men's basketball program, which had faltered in the years since the elder Thompson resigned from the team, in 1999. Coach Craig Esherick was fired in 2004, after the Hoyas went 13–15 and missed postseason play for the first time in 31 seasons. In April 2004, not long after Princeton lost to Texas in the first round of that year's NCAA tournament, it was announced that Thompson would be the Hoyas' next head coach. He restored order almost immediately, improving the Hoyas' record to 19–13 in his first season. That success was attributed largely to his introduction of the Princeton Offense, combined with an aggressive defense—a Hoyas trademark established by his father. In the Washington Post (March 23, 2006, on-line), Mike Wise described Thompson's variation on Carril's strategies as being the Princeton Offense "on steroids," adding, "It is the most aesthetically [appealing] offense in the pro and college game today, and it is dissecting very good teams." Wise wrote about the cohesiveness of the Hoyas' players under Thompson, "In an increasingly I-gotta-get-mine, sneaker-deal world, they bought into a system of five teammates playing as one." While the Big East Conference—of which Georgetown is a part—had been known over the years for its prolific scorers, such as Chris Mullen of St. John's University, Carmelo Anthony of Syracuse, and Georgetown's Allen Iverson, Thompson's team flourished with a passing game. During the 2004–05 season, the Hoyas advanced to the quarterfinals of the NIT. Other highlights during the season included a 66–64 victory over Villanova, which spoiled that team's 25th-anniversary celebration of its NCAA championship win—in a game against Georgetown that ended with the same score. Thompson also became one of the finalists for the Naismith Coach of the Year award and produced a Big East Rookie of the Year in the forward Jeff Green.

At the conclusion of the 2005–06 season, Thompson's Hoyas had an astonishing 23–10 record. In Thompson's fifth trip to the postseason in six years as a head coach, his newly invigorated team made it to the Sweet 16. One of the highlights of the season occurred on January 21, 2006, when Thompson's unranked team upset the number-one-ranked Duke University, 87–84, marking the first time the team had defeated a number-one-

ranked team since 1985, when the elder Thompson led the Hoyas to victory over St. John's. Several nights after the Duke game, Thompson got his 100th win as a head coach, when the Hoyas beat Notre Dame, 85–82, in a dramatic double-overtime finish. They entered the 2006 NCAA Men's Division I tournament as the seventh seed. After a first-round victory against Northern Iowa, they took on second-seeded Ohio State, upsetting the Big 10 champions, 70–52. Georgetown's sophomore star center, Roy Hibbert, dominated the game with 20 points, 14 rebounds, and three blocked shots, while three of his teammates also scored in the double digits. "It was indicative of how our team played all year," Thompson told Camille Powell for the Washington Post (March 20, 2006, on-line) after the game. "For us to win, everyone has to help, from me on down." In their first regional semifinal game since 2001, the Hoyas lost 57–53 to the University of Florida Gators, who went on to win the national championship that year. The Hoyas were the only team to hold the Gators to a victory under 10 points that season, as well as the only team to lead Florida in the second half of a game. Thompson was the recipient of the Black Coaches Association's Fritz Pollard Male Coach of the Year Award.

Thompson's 2006–07 season was defined by adversity, drama, and success. Added to the ongoing pressure of coaching was the stress of his wife's two-year battle with breast cancer, about which he had said little publicly since his arrival at Georgetown. Every day Thompson showed up at his office at seven a.m., went to the hospital at nine, ran workouts beginning at noon and practice starting at four, and cared for his three children, all under nine years old, in the evening. Monica Thompson recalled to Andy Katz for ESPN (March 25, 2007, on-line) that her husband "was at every single chemo treatment." "She's enabled me to balance, and that's the truth . . . ," Thompson told Katz about his wife. "She's allowed me to do my job and fortunately we've been doing OK." Indeed, after starting the 2006–07 season with four wins and three losses, the Hoyas ended with a record of 30–7, winning both the Big East regular-season and tournament crowns for the first time since 1989. In one memorable game, in November, Georgetown played Ball State University, coached by Thompson's brother, Ronny, with whom he is very close. Speaking of that contest, which the Hoyas won, 69–54, Ronny Thompson—who had played for Georgetown under his father—recalled to Jim Benson, "It was probably the most emotionally draining game I've ever been part of playing against my brother, my alma mater, and back in Washington." As the tournament play got underway, Ronny Thompson rooted for his brother, telling Erik Brady, "I'm his biggest fan. I just don't tell him enough."

Georgetown entered the 2007 NCAA tournament as the "son of" team, as Thompson called them: in addition to his being the son of a famous former coach, one of his players, Patrick Ewing Jr., is the son of another Georgetown legend, and the guard Jeremiah Rivers is the son of the Boston Celtics coach and former player Doc Rivers. In the first round the Hoyas routed a team from Tennessee, the 15th-seeded Belmont University Bruins, 80–55. After a hard-fought victory against Boston College in the second round, the Hoyas advanced to the Sweet 16, narrowly beating Vanderbilt, 66–65, with a game-winning shot by Jeff Green. Two days later the team made the Final Four, when Georgetown defeated the University of North Carolina in overtime, 96–84. The Tar Heels had held a 10-point lead with seven minutes remaining but missed nine of their last 10 shots in regulation play. Georgetown's guard Jonathan Wallace made a three-pointer with only 31 seconds remaining to bring the score to a tie. Then, in overtime, while the Tar Heels missed their first 12 shots, the Hoyas secured a victory, scoring 14 points. All five Georgetown starters finished in double figures, led by Green's 22 points. With that win Thompson joined his father as the only father-and-son duo ever to reach a Final Four berth. After the game the elder Thompson explained to William Rhoden for the *New York Times* (March 26, 2007), "I told people before, all that old stuff about 'Do you miss coaching?' No, I don't miss it. I'm lucky to have been able to experience my child and that's far more important than me getting another spittoon, getting another ring. This is the greatest thing that can happen for you." Though the Hoyas lost to Ohio State,

67–60, in the next round of play, John Thompson III had led the Hoyas to their first Final Four in 22 years. He was again a finalist for the Naismith Men's College Coach of the Year honor.

John Thompson III is six feet four inches tall and is known for his "puppy-dog" eyes and placid demeanor. He and his wife, Monica, whose cancer is now in remission, live in Washington with their three children: Morgan, John Wallace, and Matthew. A superstitious man, Thompson has a good-luck routine: before a game his secretary must be the one to hand him the Georgetown pin he will wear on his lapel; before boarding the bus to the basketball arena, he has to drink yellow Gatorade; during a game he draws X's and O's with a blue marker ("The managers learn that quickly," Thompson told Joseph White. "I don't want black. I don't want green"); and he knocks on wood when answering questions from reporters. In late September 2007 Thompson signed a six-year contract extension with Georgetown.

—C.C.

Suggested Reading: Associated Press Mar. 5, 2007; (Bloomington, Illinois) *Pantagraph* B p1 Feb. 17, 2007; Georgetown University Web site; *Kansas City Star* D p1 Mar. 31, 2007; *New York Times* D p1 Mar. 30, 2007; Princeton University Web site; *Time* p111 Apr. 9, 2007; *Washington Post* A p17 Mar. 31, 2007

Trethewey, Natasha

1966– Poet

Address: N209 Callaway Center, Creative Writing Program, Emory University, 537 Kilgo Circle, Atlanta, GA 30322

The Pulitzer Prize–winning poet Natasha Trethewey commented to Kathy Janich for the *Atlanta Journal–Constitution* (September 15, 2002), "I think perhaps if you're an African-American writer, you always have a love-hate relationship with the South. And I love it, but I know it has secrets that need to be uncovered." Some of the secrets that Trethewey has unearthed in her volumes of poetry—*Domestic Work* (2000), *Bellocq's Ophelia* (2002), and *Native Guard* (2006)—are the injuries done to black working women in her grandmother's time; life among prostitutes in early-20th-century New Orleans, Louisiana; the story of a black regiment in the Union Army whose history was largely erased; and the life story of her mother, who was forbidden by race laws to marry Trethewey's white father—and who was murdered by her second ex-husband. In an interview with Deborah Solomon for the *New York Times Magazine* (May 13, 2007), Trethewey said, "I've been inter-

ested in historical erasure and historical amnesia for a long time, those things that get left out of the record. . . . For the sake of sanity, there is a lot of necessary forgetting. But the trick is to balance forgetting with necessary remembering, to avoid historical amnesia." A master of form, Trethewey has placed her images in ghazals, pantoums, sonnets, and other restrictive styles of verse, creating what Donna Seaman, writing for *Booklist* (February 1, 2006), called "exacting and resonant poetry" that "is rooted in the shadow side of American history."

Natasha Trethewey was born in Gulfport, Mississippi, in 1966, the daughter of Gwendolyn Ann Turnbough Trethewey, a social worker, who was African-American, and Eric Trethewey, a poet and college professor. (Her parents' marriage violated antimiscegenation laws then in place in the state; in one poem Trethewey refers to their having wed in Ohio.) When Trethewey was a child, she was "acutely aware of people staring" at her because of her mixed racial heritage, as she revealed to Deborah Solomon. "I have been asked all my life, What are you?" Trethewey also told Solomon that in the late 1960s the Ku Klux Klan burned a cross in her family's yard.

Trethewey's parents divorced before she started grade school. She moved with her mother to Decatur, Georgia, near Atlanta; in the summers she

Jon Rou, courtesy of Houghton Mifflin

Natasha Trethewey

before being hired to teach creative writing at Emory University, in Atlanta, in 2001.

Many of the poems in Trethewey's first collection, *Domestic Work* (2000), are portraits of black workers and families in the American South in the first half of the 20th century, before the civil rights era. Trethewey drew on the jobs her African-American grandmother held in Gulfport, as a domestic worker, elevator operator, beautician, factory employee, and seamstress. Other glimpses of Trethewey's own family are offered in the poem "Early Evening, Frankfort, Kentucky," quoted in part by Kelly Ellis in *Black Issues Book Review* (November/December 2000, on-line); in it, the poet's "mother, who will not reach/forty-one, steps into the middle/of a field; lies down among clover/and sweet grass, right here, right now— /dead center of her life." Trethewey "brilliantly discusses family not for its extremes or its small hurts, but rather for the small intimacies that symbolize larger sufferings of history, both personal and public . . . ," Kevin Young observed for *Ploughshares* (Winter 2001). "The contradictions of stillness and motion are what Trethewey's poems seek to capture, questioning whether we can ever nail down (or up) a moment, a life, or history—particularly that belonging to women." The *Publishers Weekly* (August 14, 2000) reviewer noted, "The sonnets, triplets and flush-left free verse [Trethewey] employs give the work an understated distance, and Trethewey's relatively spare language allows the characters, from factory and dock workers to homemakers, to take on fluid present-tense movement. . . . Trethewey's work follows in the wake of history and memory, tracing their combined effect on her speaker and subjects, and working to recover and preserve vitally local histories." The prominent poet Rita Dove selected Trethewey's book for the Cave Canem Poetry Prize, established to recognize the "best collection of poems submitted by a previously unpublished African American poet." *Domestic Work* also won the 2001 Lillian Smith Book Award, given in recognition of work that exposes racial and social inequality in the American South.

Trethewey's second book of poetry, *Bellocq's Ophelia* (2002), was inspired by E. J. Bellocq's photographs of prostitutes in Storyville, the red-light district in New Orleans, at the beginning of the 20th century. A fictionalized prostitute, an octoroon named Ophelia, serves as the protagonist of Trethewey's volume, which is divided into three sections—the first two composed of Ophelia's letters to a friend, the third made up of sonnets. "Each poem offers one still image, which when seen in a series chronicles Ophelia's reconciliation of her divided worlds of parentage . . . and womanhood," Courtney Dodson noted for the New Orleans *Times-Picayune* (May 26, 2005). "With Trethewey's masterfully light touch, these images are coaxed forth, like the slow development of a face under a blur of water. The images we're left with are as difficult as they are resonant." For Adrian

stayed with her father in New Orleans and with her grandmother in Mississippi. "I loved being my mother's only child for a while," Trethewey told Solomon. (She later had a stepbrother, Joel.) It was Trethewey's father who first encouraged her interest in writing, advising her to write poems when she grew bored during car trips. "He used to say that it is a problem if you don't have inner resources," she recalled to Solomon. Eric Trethewey was also a tough critic of his daughter's work; Natasha Trethewey recalled to Mike Hudson for the *Roanoke (Virginia) Times* (October 3, 2001) that the first time she showed him one of her poems, he "ripped it to shreds." While she found his response discouraging at first, she later came to view it as evidence that he took her writing seriously, as Hudson noted. Trethewey graduated from Redan High School, in Stone Mountain, Georgia, where she was editor of the yearbook. She next enrolled at the University of Georgia at Athens.

During Trethewey's freshman year of college, when she was 19, her mother was murdered by her second ex-husband. "To try to grapple with that huge loss, I turned to poetry, to try to make sense of the world and me in it," Trethewey said to a writer for *Emory Magazine* (Winter 2002, on-line). She received a B.A. degree in English and creative writing in 1989, then earned an M.A. degree in the same subjects at Hollins University, in Roanoke, where her father taught. She also received an M.F.A. degree from the University of Massachusetts in 1995.

Apart from a year or so spent as a welfare caseworker in Augusta, Georgia, Trethewey has earned her living teaching and writing poetry. She taught creative writing at Auburn University, in Alabama,

Oktenberg, writing for the *Women's Review of Books* (October 2003), "Trethewey's language throughout is calm, fluid, one line moving into the next as a fish moves through water, language borne in its natural element." Oktenberg added, "In all, the book is finely crafted, elegantly played out— but not finished! It ends rather suddenly. . . . But what better compliment could be given a book than that it's too short?"

As Trethewey revealed to Pam Firmin for the *Biloxi (Mississippi) Sun Herald* (April 19, 2007), much of her third poetry collection, *Native Guard* (2006), had its origin in a conversation she had in a restaurant with her grandmother. Trethewey told Firmin that "a woman, a white woman, was eavesdropping on our conversation," which involved, among other subjects, Ship Island, off the coast of Mississippi—where Trethewey had often had picnics on Independence Day. The woman "stopped at our table and said, 'I think there's something else you need to know about Ship Island,'" Trethewey recalled. "She told me about the black soldiers who were stationed on that island [during the Civil War], and that they guarded Confederate soldiers." There is no monument to those soldiers, and most people, including Trethewey herself, previously knew nothing of them. *Native Guard*'s 10-sonnet title poem is narrated by a former slave who guards Confederate soldiers imprisoned in the Union fort on Ship Island. Another poem in the collection focuses on Trethewey's mother, to whom the volume is dedicated. The poems' lines "have a stately, chiming perfection . . ," Darryl Lorenzo Wellington wrote for the *Washington Post* (April 16, 2006). "Trethewey has a gift for squeezing the contradictions of the South into very tightly controlled lines. A certain staid, formal approach is both her strength and the only possible grounds I have to criticize her poetry. *Native Guard* is a small book, containing mostly short poems, a few of which read like exercises. When poets find their voices, form and content intermesh seamlessly. One can still see Trethewey's technique and feel the influence of poetry workshops. One feels a bit let down when a poem sets up an interesting emotional crisis, then resolves it almost too quickly. One feels at times as though her poems are succinct for the sake of making them work, rather than fulfilling either the poet's memory of her experience or the reader's heightened expectations. . . . Though this is her third book, Trethewey is still perfecting her voice and may have only scratched the surface of her remarkable talent." Other reviewers, by contrast, had unqualified praise for Trethewey's collection. Writing for *Magill Book Reviews* (on-line), Kevin Boyle declared *Native Guard* to be "a monumental success," adding, "On every level, from the formal assuredness of the verse to the regions of history her poetry is able to inhabit, Trethewey proves why she is one of the best young contemporary American poets." In 2007 Trethewey was awarded the Pulitzer Prize for poetry for *Native Guard*.

Trethewey has been a finalist for the Academy of American Poets James Laughlin and Lenore Marshall Prizes. She has received the Pushcart Prize as well as fellowships from the Guggenheim Foundation, the Rockefeller Foundation, and the Bunting Fellowship Program of the Radcliffe Institute for Advanced Study at Harvard University. Trethewey teaches at Emory University and lives in Decatur with her husband, Brett Gadsden, an assistant professor of African-American studies at Emory.

—S.Y.

Suggested Reading: *Atlanta Journal-Constitution* L p8 Sep. 15, 2002; *Black Issues Book Review* (on-line) Apr. 2006; *Boston Globe* D p4 July 7, 2002; (New Orleans) *Times-Picayune* B p5 May 26, 2002; *New York Times Magazine* (on-line) May 13, 2007; *Ploughshares* (on-line) Winter 2001; *Publishers Weekly* (on-line) Aug. 14, 2000; *Women's Review of Books* p20+ Oct. 2003

Selected Books: *Domestic Work*, 2000; *Bellocq's Ophelia*, 2002; *Native Guard*, 2006

Tufte, Edward R.

(TUF-tee)

Mar. 14, 1942– Information-graphics designer and analyst; writer; teacher; business owner

Address: Graphics Press, P.O. Box 430, Cheshire, CT 06410

"Good design is a lot like clear thinking made visible. Bad design is stupidity made visible," Edward Tufte told Sheri Rosen for *Communication World* (April 1, 2000). An analytical or data designer, artist, statistician, political scientist, writer, and educator, Tufte has said that his mission is to teach people how to communicate ideas truthfully, concisely, clearly, and persuasively in visual displays—charts, graphs, diagrams, maps, and arrangements of text, among others. In his own work, he told Michael Shermer for *Scientific American* (April 2005), he aims for "simple design [and] intense content." Tufte's skills "seem uniquely suited to the moment: he knows how to turn seas of information into navigable—even scenic— waterways," Deborah Shapley wrote for the *New York Times* (March 30, 1998), in an article in which she described Tufte as "one of the information age's admired prophets." In his books *The Visual Display of Quantitative Information* (1983), *Envisioning Information* (1990), *Visual Explanations* (1997), and *Beautiful Evidence* (2006)— which, in total, have sold more than 1.4 million copies and earned more than two dozen awards— Tufte has emphasized the idea, in his words, that "clarity and excellence in thinking is very much

Robert Del Tredici, courtesy of Edward Tufte

Edward R. Tufte

like clarity and excellence in the display of data. When principles of design replicate principles of thought, the act of arranging information becomes an act of insight." "At its heart, my work is about how to think clearly and deeply, using evidence . . . ," Tufte told Charlotte Thralls and Mark Zachry for *Technical Communication Quarterly* (Autumn 2004). "In writing about the display of evidence and presentations of evidence, I am also writing about how to reach credible conclusions. Entangled in that is a strong ethical component," which has led him to discuss "the lie factor in graphics" and "encourag[e] the mass media to stop lying about data. When you say that graphics lie, that means you believe that there are truths, or things that are a lot closer to the truth than what is being said in the lying graphics. I am certainly not an intellectual relativist, nor a moral relativist. I hope that I am generous and tolerant, but certainly on the intellectual side I think that there are discoverable truths, and some things that are closer approximations to the truth than others." In an article for *Salon.com* (March 10, 1997), Scott Rosenberg wrote, "Grasping our world demands grasping numbers—and trusting that we have grasped them correctly. Under these circumstances, Tufte's work becomes a friendly compass in an informational wilderness—and when necessary, a machete to chop through thickets of disinformation." "Tufte takes dull data and turns it into magical and meaningful pictures," Paul May wrote for the London *Guardian* (November 8, 2004). "Forget those clunky bars and pizza slices you were taught in school. Tufte produces such inventive and even decorative graphs it's enough to have you weeping over your squared paper. And each one helps us

understand the world a bit better, or alerts us to the crimes that can be committed when the people with the numbers seek to confuse the have-nots."

As an example of successful design, Tufte has cited the street map on which the 19th-century British surgeon John Snow recorded deaths from the 1854 cholera epidemic in London. On his map, Snow marked each death with a dash adjacent to the building in which the victim had lived. An inordinately high number of deaths clustered around the intersection of Broad and Cambridge Streets, the site of a pump used by thousands of people; the water from that pump came from the Thames at a point where the river had far more sewage than at the other locations where water was pumped for Londoners. From his current study and previous ones, Snow had concluded that the source of cholera was contaminated water and not bad air, as was then universally assumed. With his map as evidence, he persuaded London officials to remove the handle of the Broad/Cambridge Streets pump, and soon afterward, the epidemic ceased. Another of Tufte's examples of an eminently useful graphic design is the thematic map made by the 19th-century French engineer Charles Joseph Minard to show the catastrophic troop loss suffered by Napoleon's army during the so-called Russian campaign of 1812. In June of that year, 450,000–500,000 soldiers led by Napoleon invaded Russia; about two-thirds of them perished before they reached Moscow, and by the time the army had completed its retreat, in December, it numbered only about 10,000 men. In what Tufte, on his Web site, called "probably the best statistical graphic ever drawn," Minard used five variables (troop strength, location, direction, date, and air temperature) to show on a single page the correlation between the weather—blazingly hot in the summer and bitterly cold in the winter, which arrived early in Russia in 1812—and the number of fatalities among the troops. A third of Tufte's examples is the chart constructed by defense lawyers for use during the trial of the accused racketeer and Mafia kingpin John Gotti in 1987. The chart listed the seven main witnesses for the prosection and 69 crimes, including kidnapping, extortion, sales of illicit drugs, and the pistol-whipping of a priest. Boldface crosses indicated the crimes for which those witnesses had been found guilty in the past. With its profusion of crosses, the chart cleverly raised the jury's suspicions about the wisdom of trusting the testimony of those witnesses; it was the only piece of evidence that the jury asked to see during their deliberations, which ended with Gotti's acquittal.

Among examples of misleading graphic designs, Tufte has cited Colin L. Powell's PowerPoint presentation made on February 5, 2003 to the United Nations General Assembly, in which the then–U.S. secretary of state, perhaps unwittingly, used misinformation and half-truths to argue that Iraq possessed weapons of mass destruction. Made by Microsoft, PowerPoint is a software program that enables users to create overhead transparencies for presentations. In an essay called "The Cognitive Style of PowerPoint" (published as a booklet in March 2003 by Tufte's company, Graphics Press), Tufte argued that PowerPoint presentations do not convey information clearly, require oversimplification, and hinder the ability of audience members to detect relationships between the serially proffered images and/or ideas. In such presentations, according to Tufte, marketing and the wielding of power often take precedence over candor and the provision of useful evidence, and to the extent that PowerPoint facilitates deception, obfuscation, and confusion, it is unethical. "In my work, there is an effort to raise standards—by admiring excellence, saying that there are things that are good and there are things that are bad, so get out and tell the world about it," he told Thralls and Zachry.

In connection with the dangers of badly executed visual displays, Tufte has also discussed the disaster in which seven American astronauts died when the space shuttle *Challenger* fell apart a little over a minute after its launch, on January 28, 1986. For years before that tragedy, engineers at the National Aeronautics and Space Administration (NASA) had known about problems with small but vital rubber rings, called O-rings, used in the construction of the shuttle's booster rockets; specifically, they knew that the capacity of O-rings to function properly diminished with decreasing air temperature. On the morning of January 28, the temperature was 28 degrees Fahrenheit, and NASA engineers warned their managers of the dangers of a launch in such cold weather. But, Tufte has maintained, the crucial information about the potential O-ring failure was buried among a lot of other data in 13 charts, and the managers failed to grasp the magnitude or imminence of the danger. That failure, in his view, compounded by pressures within and outside NASA to carry out the launch (which had already been delayed half a dozen times), led directly to the catastrophe. (In 1996 several engineers who worked on the *Challenger*, among them Wade Robison and Roger Boisjoly, refuted Tufte's analysis. An updated version of their account was published in *Science and Engineering Ethics* in January 2002.) As reported by John Schwartz in the *New York Times* (September 28, 2003), Tufte has also linked a faulty PowerPoint presentation to the fiery destruction of the space shuttle *Columbia* during its return to Earth in January 2002.

Tufte taught at Princeton University from 1967 to 1977 and at Yale University for the next 20 years. The sales of his books, along with the fees he charges for the one-day workshops on the principles of successful design that he gives about 25 times a year, have made him a multimillionaire. As a consultant, he has worked for print and television news organizations, corporations, and a range of government agencies, among them the U.S. Census Bureau, the Centers for Disease Control and Prevention, the National Science Foundation, and NASA. For Bose, a firm that produces audio equip-

ment, Tufte designed a poster that can be used anywhere in the world: without text, it explains step-by-step how to set up a complicated audio system. "The idea of trying to create things that last—forever knowledge—has guided my work for a long time now," Tufte told Thralls and Zachry. According to Christopher Reynolds, writing for the *Los Angeles Times* (November 14, 2002), Tufte has been "credited with doing for graphic communication what William Strunk Jr. and E. B. White did for grammar in *The Elements of Style*." In *Presentations Magazine* (March 2004), Tad Simons wrote of Tufte, "No one knows more about effective data design, and no one in the field is more respected."

Edward Rolf Tufte was born in Kansas City, Missouri, on March 14, 1942 to Edward E. Tufte and Virginia James Tufte. When he was in his early teens, the Tuftes moved to Southern California. There, his father became head of the Beverly Hills Public Works Department; his mother, who had worked as a journalist, became a professor of English at the University of Southern California. As a youngster, as Tufte recalled to Fran Smith for *Stanford Magazine* (March/April 2007), "I thought I was one of the smartest people around." When he entered Beverly Hills High School, he was taken aback to discover, as he told Smith, that "20 people around me were smarter than I was." After he graduated from high school, in 1960, Tufte attended Stanford University, in Palo Alto, California. He told Smith that as an undergraduate, he was influenced and inspired intellectually and professionally by three Stanford professors: the statistician Lincoln Moses and the political scientists Richard Brody and Raymond Wolfinger, all of whom showed him "how successful scholars lived," as he recalled to Smith. "I wanted to get done with school as quickly as possible and become a professor," he said. "I realized the academic world is a more humane and ethical place with better values than most of the world. . . . It's also much more tolerant of idiosyncrasy and independence. I've always been contemptuous of authority. There aren't better places than the university to do that and get away with it." Wolfinger and his wife, Barbara, found Tufte's seriousness, curiosity, and enthusiasm for faculty dinners remarkable. "Most undergraduates had no interest in us at all," Barbara Wolfinger told Smith. "Most were only interested in mating. Ed was different. There are very few truly unusual people one meets in life. Ed was certainly one of them." Richard Brody told Smith that Tufte "was always trying to devise user-friendly approaches to statistics that non-specialists like me could use."

Tufte majored in statistics at Stanford and earned both a B.S. degree, in 1963, and an M.S. degree, in 1964, in that subject. He then enrolled at Yale University, in New Haven, Connecticut, to pursue a doctorate in political science. "I was always interested in politics, and I was always interested in numbers, and my statistical work was in epidemiology, which is people and surveys and detective work and somewhat quantitative . . . ," he told Dan Doernberg, who combined two interviews with Tufte, conducted in 1994 and 1997, for *Computer Literacy Bookshops* (on-line). "I don't think I was mathematically smart enough to make any kind of mathematical contributions to statistics. Ironically, I've come this indirect route, made the visual contributions. . . . I cared a lot about political issues. But they lack, notoriously lack, in the aesthetic." Tufte received a Ph.D. from Yale in 1968. The day after he completed his dissertation, titled "The Civil Rights Movement and Its Opposition," he took up painting as a hobby.

For a decade beginning in 1967, Tufte taught courses in public policy as a member of the Politics and Public Affairs Department at Princeton University, in New Jersey. During that time he edited the book *Quantitative Analysis of Social Problems* (1970) and wrote *Data Analysis for Politics and Policy* (1974). He also wrote or co-wrote articles for professional journals, among them "Improving Data Analysis in Political Science," for *World Politics* (July 1969); "Relationship between Seats and Votes in Two-Party Systems," for the *American Political Science Review* (June 1973); "Are There Bellwether Electoral Districts?," for *Public Opinion Quarterly* (Spring 1975); and "Electronic Calculators and Data Analysis," an assessment of four calculators, for the *American Journal of Political Science* (November 1975). With his Yale adviser, the political scientist Robert Dahl, Tufte wrote the book *Size and Democracy* (1973), in which they offered evidence for their contention that small, local governments, "by virtue of their greater accessibility and understandability, . . . nurture participation and heighten the citizen's sense of effectiveness." In larger political jurisdictions, they found, members of the public are less inclined to participate actively in government. According to Tufte and Dahl, as paraphrased by Frank Denton for the Web site of the American Association of Newspaper Editors (July 20, 1999), bigger governments "may be necessary to handle larger needs (defense, highways, universities, welfare systems)," but "they also seem to contribute to feelings of political powerlessness among people."

In 1975 Tufte began writing *The Visual Display of Quantitative Information*, which grew out of notes he had prepared for one of his courses. He completed the book in 1982, five years after he had left Princeton to teach at Yale. Adamant that the appearance of the book reflect the principles he had articulated in the text, he looked in vain for a publisher who would accede to his precise specifications—heavyweight paper, high-resolution images, and notes at the foot of the page rather than in an appendix—and his insistence that the retail price be moderate. "Publishers seemed appalled at the prospect that an author might govern the design," he told Dan Doernberg. Tufte decided to publish the book himself, with the help of the highly regarded book designer Howard Gralla. Unlike many others in his field, Gralla "was willing to

work with [a] difficult author who was filled with all sorts of opinions about design," as Tufte recalled to Doernberg, and the two "spent the summer in [Gralla's] studio laying out the book, page by page." "It turned out that all self-publishing required was a really good book designer, some money, and a large garage. . . . My view on self-publishing was to go all out, to make the best and most elegant and wonderful book possible, without compromise. Otherwise, why do it? If I wanted to mess it up, I could have gone to a real publisher." Published by Tufte's newly set up company, Graphics Press, *The Visual Display of Quantitative Information* (1983) was instantly hailed as a classic of graphic design. In what Tufte described to Doernberg as a "dreamlike" result, thousands of orders poured in, and Tufte, who had taken a second mortgage on his home, earned enough from the sales to pay it off in full in just six months. The second edition of the book (2001) has been translated into half a dozen languages.

In *The Visual Display of Quantitative Information*, Tufte analyzed such displays of data as railroad schedules, balance sheets, and weather summaries and offered rules for presenting numerical data in a graphically arresting manner. "*Visual Display* is startling in its originality, eclecticism, and cost-is-no-object presentation. It stood in the same relation to its predecessors as did *Star Wars* to earlier science-fiction movies," Ray Duncan wrote for the *Electronic Review of Computer Books* (February 24, 1997). Interest in the book has remained strong; at one point in 1997, 14 years after its first appearance, it ranked eighth on the best-seller list of Amazon.com. Tufte worked on his next book, *Envisioning Information* (1990), for seven years. His focus in that volume is the representation of reality, through such means as maps, charts, diagrams, graphs, tables, photographs, pop-ups, guides, and courtroom exhibits. In one example, Tufte compared a 1937 train schedule from Java, an Indonesian island, with a schedule for trains running in the northeastern corridor of the United States. The first presents more than 10 types of information on a page and, in Tufte's view, is the product of rare ingenuity in graphic design. The American timetable, by contrast, barely fulfilled its purpose and reflected bureaucratic muddleheadedness.

Visual Explanations: Images and Quantities, Evidence and Narrative, which appeared seven years after its predecessor, reached seventh place on Amazon.com's best-seller list. In that book Tufte analyzed images that illustrate dynamic processes and function as explanatory narratives, such as the maps constructed by John Snow and Charles Joseph Minard. In a chapter co-authored by a professional magician, Jamy Ian Swiss, Tufte discussed sleight of hand and other conjurors' tricks to explain what *not* to do if one's goal is to tell the truth. "To create illusions is to engage in disinformation design, to corrupt optical information, to deceive the audience," they wrote. Cullen Murphy wrote in a review of the book for *Slate* (May 22, 1997, on-line), "What one does not expect in a book of this kind—a book that is technical even as it is beautiful—is that the author will be not just fastidious but also an evocative and wonderfully quirky writer. Tufte is all of these." Tufte's most recent book, *Beautiful Evidence* (2006), like his other books on information design, is lavishly illustrated. Tufte told Charlotte Thralls and Mark Zachry that *Beautiful Evidence* "follows a growing concern in my work: assessing the quality of evidence and of finding out the truth." In the same interview he said, "I also want to move the practices of analytical design far away from the practices of propaganda, marketing, graphic design, and commercial art."

Earlier, in the 1990s, Tufte began to host one-day workshops, "Presenting Data and Information," at sites nationwide. The seminar is a crash course in designing, constructing, and evaluating effective presentations, and it draws accountants, engineers, marketers, personal-computer chart makers, and people in many other occupations. As quoted by Michael Shermer, Tufte offers six principles of design: "(1) documenting the sources and characteristics of the data, (2) insistently enforcing appropriate comparisons, (3) demonstrating mechanisms of cause and effect, (4) expressing those mechanisms quantitatively, (5) recognizing the inherently multivariate nature of analytic problems, (6) inspecting and evaluating alternative explanations," or, briefly stated, "Information displays should be documentary, comparative, causal and explanatory, quantified, multivariate, exploratory, skeptical." At his lectures Tufte has noted that in our daily lives we are surrounded by poorly displayed data, ranging from annual reports that portray years of rising revenues without making adjustments for inflation to the U.S. surgeon general's warning on cigarette packages, whose nondescript appearance weakens its message, to Web sites whose advertising banners and flashy graphics reduce the force of the information the users seek. Eager to get feedback from interested outsiders, he maintains an open forum on his Web site, in which he has posted drafts of chapters of his books and complicated problems that he is working on. He has also dispensed advice and criticism. "Sometimes the contributors are disappointed," Nicolas Bissantz, the managing director of a German software firm, told Fran Smith. "They'll post an idea and he has three or four points of criticism, and they're devastated. They want to defend their concept, but it's ridiculous—he just demolishes the idea. It's worthwhile to just sit back and say, 'Thank you, Master.'"

Writing for *Fortune* (October 27, 1997), Michael H. Martin described Tufte as "a lanky, precise man who dresses a bit better than most academics." Tufte lives, and runs Graphics Press, in Cheshire, Connecticut, with his wife, the graphic designer Inge Druckrey. He was the president of the Cheshire Neighborhood Association from 1984 to 1987.

Since the late 1990s he has created large metal sculptures; those and other works of his have been exhibited in museums and gallery shows. Seven schools, among them the Cooper Union, the Minneapolis College of Art, and the University of the Arts, have awarded him honorary doctoral degrees.
—N.W.M.

Suggested Reading: *Austin (Texas) American-Statesman* E p1 Jan. 18, 2000; *Computer Literacy Bookshops* (on-line); Edward Tufte Web site; *Forbes* p121 May 18, 1987; *Fortune* p273+ Oct. 27, 1997; *Los Angeles Times* p12 Nov. 14, 2002; *New York* p125+ June 18, 2007; *New York Times* D p8 Mar. 30, 1998; NPR (on-line) *Weekend Edition Sunday* Aug. 20, 2006; *Salon.com* Mar. 1997; *Scientific American* p38 Apr. 2005; *Stanford Magazine* (on-line) Mar./Apr. 2007; *Technical Communication Quarterly* p447+ Autumn 2004

Selected Books: *Size and Democracy* (with Robert Dahl), 1973; *Data Analysis for Politics and Policy*, 1974; *The Visual Display of Quantitative Information*, 1983; *Envisioning Information*, 1990; *Visual Explanations: Images and Quantities, Evidence and Narrative*, 1997; *Beautiful Evidence*, 2006; as editor—*Quantitative Analysis of Social Problems*, 1970

Underwood, Carrie

Mar. 10, 1983– Singer

Address: c/o Grabow & Associates, 4219 Creekmeadow Dr ., Dallas, TX 75287; c/o Headline Entertainment, 7655 N. San Fernando Rd., Burbank, CA 91505

Since she won the *American Idol IV* competition, on May 25, 2005, Carrie Underwood has become one of country music's biggest stars. Underwood's debut album, *Some Hearts*, which was released half a year after her success on *American Idol* and contains the hit single "Jesus, Take the Wheel," earned positive critical notices, was the top-selling album in any genre in 2006, and as of mid-October 2007, had sold more than six million copies. After picking up multiple honors at the awards shows hosted respectively by Country Music Television, the Academy of Country Music, and the Country Music Association, Underwood won five prizes at the December 4, 2006 *Billboard* Music Awards ceremony: album of the year, female *Billboard* 200 artist of the year, country album of the year, new country artist of the year, and female country artist of the year. Then, on February 11, 2007, she received the Grammy Awards for best new artist and, for "Jesus, Take the Wheel," best female country vocal performance. Described by a reporter for

Carrie Underwood

Ethan Miller/Getty Images

parents listened to recordings by the Beatles and the Bee Gees, and her sisters enjoyed rock, but of all of them, only Carrie was musically inclined. Her first public singing experiences came at the First Free Will Baptist Church in Checotah, whose day camp she attended during summer vacations. Underwood's vocal talents were apparent to her teachers, and she earned roles in every musical production at her elementary school. In fourth grade she gave her first solo performance, as a character called Mother Nature. As she got older she began singing in talent contests, both locally and regionally; she won a few but, more often, came in second or third. For some years, beginning when she was in seventh grade, according to Chad Previch and Carrie Coppernoll in the *Oklahoman* (May 27, 2005), her school's choir teacher gave her instruction in breath control and in approaches to different musical styles. She reportedly never took singing lessons from any other professional.

While attending Checotah High School, Underwood performed at county fairs and parties, occasionally backed by a country-style band. When she was 15 a talent scout brought her to Music Row in Nashville, Tennessee, in hopes of securing a recording contract for her. A deal the scout was negotiating with Capitol Records fell through when the company underwent a change in management. Afterward, Underwood put her musical ambitions on hold and concentrated her efforts on her academic pursuits. "I had reached a point in my life where I had to be practical and prepare for my future in the 'real world,'" she explained on her Web site. She graduated second in her class and made a speech at the graduation ceremony.

In the fall of 2001, Underwood enrolled at Northeastern State University (NSU), in Tahlequah, Oklahoma, one hour away from Checotah. She majored in mass communication, with a focus on broadcast journalism. "I definitely wanted to do something in news, whether it was in front of the camera or behind the camera," she told Tracey Smith for *CBSNews* (August 16, 2006). By her own account, she was very shy when she entered college; she has credited the members of the sorority she joined, Sigma Sigma Sigma, with helping her gain self-confidence and become more extroverted. Through the sorority Underwood became involved in community service, volunteering at a hospice and at a veterinary clinic; she also sang at sorority events. In addition, she worked at the campus television station and wrote for the student newspaper. During summer vacations in 2003 and 2004, she sang, danced, and performed comedy routines in Tahlequah's Downtown Country Show, a Branson-style musical revue, which, she has said, prepared her more than anything else for her current career. C. H. Parker, the show's artistic director, remembers Underwood as an egoless team player. "She has a good heart, and she knows the meaning of the word 'ensemble,'" he told David Zizzo for the *Oklahoman* (May 23, 2005). "In a room full of people, she wouldn't be one you would hear a lot

Rhapsody.com as having "all the makings of classic ballad belter, with an extremely powerful voice and a gift for emotiveness," Underwood has performed at the White House and at the All-Star Games of Major League Baseball and the National Basketball Association and has appeared as a guest and performer on such television shows as *Today*, *Good Morning America*, *The Tonight Show*, *Late Show with David Letterman*, and *Oprah*. She has said that keeping true to herself, despite her fame, is a priority for her. Questioned during an on-line interview for the *Washington Post* (January 20, 2006) about pressure to conform to a certain industry image, she said, "I made it quite clear in the beginning who I am and everybody knows how important it is to stay that way, so nobody has ever tried to get me to change." Underwood is a spokeswoman for Skechers Footwear, and she has signed a contract with the Hershey Co. to sing jingles on television advertisements for several of the firm's products.

The youngest of the three daughters of Stephen Underwood, a retired paper-mill worker, and Carole Underwood, an elementary-school teacher, Carrie Marie Underwood was born on March 10, 1983 in Muskogee, Oklahoma, the town made famous by Merle Haggard in the song "Okie from Muskogee." She grew up on her family's ranch (which her father now operates as a hobby) in nearby Checotah, Oklahoma, a village of 3,500. Her sisters are nine and 12 years her senior. On her Web site, Underwood described her childhood as "very happy" and as "full of the wonderful simple things that children love to do. . . . I enjoyed things like playing on dirt roads, climbing trees, catching little woodland creatures and, of course, singing." Her out of." Suzanne Myers, an NSU professor, told Zizzo, "She's not the life of the party. She's just very sweet."

In the fall of her senior year, Underwood, encouraged by friends and family, decided to try out for a place on *American Idol*, a talent contest that airs on the Fox network. At the regional auditions in St. Louis, Missouri, she impressed the show's judges (Paula Abdul, Simon Cowell, and Randy Jackson) with her a cappella rendition of Bonnie Raitt's "I Can't Make You Love Me." Chosen to compete in the second round, she dropped out of NSU, one semester shy of graduation. (She returned in 2006 and graduated magna cum laude.) At the next audition, held in Hollywood, California, Underwood sang "Young Hearts (Run Free)," by Candi Staton, and "Independence Day," by Martina McBride, and became one of the 30 finalists who would compete on television.

American Idol, which premiered in 2002, is based on a weekly British TV program in which contestants sing and are critiqued—often cruelly—by three judges. Each week viewers call in to the program to vote for their favorite among that installment's performers. The American version of the show, which attracted 33.5 million viewers in its fourth season, has become one of the most-publicized talent contests in the world; in the U.S. in 2005, *American Idol* was ranked number one in the Nielsen ratings. Throughout the competition Underwood relied on songs with which she was most familiar—such country songs as "Trouble," by Elvis Presley, "When God Fearin' Women Get the Blues," by Martina McBride, and "Sin Wagon," by the Dixie Chicks, among others. Underwood also displayed ability in pop and rock, singing "Could've Been," by Tiffany, "Crying," by Roy Orbison, and "Alone," by the rock band Heart. During the *American Idol* competition, fans never voted Underwood into the "bottom three," and thus she was never a candidate for dismissal. (Among all other *Idol* hopefuls, only Kelly Clarkson and Clay Aiken, the winner and runner-up of seasons one and two, respectively, achieved that distinction.) After her performance of "Alone," Simon Cowell made the often-quoted remark, "Carrie, you're not just the girl to beat, you're the person to beat. I will make a prediction, not only will you win this show, but you will sell more records than any other previous *Idol*." On the last night of the program, on May 24, 2005, Underwood was pitted against Bo Bice. Her performance of "Angels Brought Me Here," a song written by Guy Sebastian for *Australian Idol*, received a standing ovation from Randy Jackson. Although Underwood's presentations struck some observers as stiff and emotionless, she defeated Bice in a three-part finale, during which each sang "Inside Your Heaven," written expressly for the show.

The first country-oriented winner of *American Idol*, Underwood earned a lucrative recording contract with the Nashville-based Arista Records, as well as a 2005 Ford Mustang convertible and the use of a private jet for a year. "Inside Your Heaven" was released as a single on June 14, 2005; it sold 170,000 copies during its first week in stores and became the first country song since 2000 to debut at number one on the all-genre *Billboard* Hot 100 chart. (On the *Billboard* country chart, it reached no higher than 59. According to Keith Groller, writing for the Allentown, Pennsylvania, daily *Morning Call* [August 12, 2006], "Inside Your Heaven" "wasn't really a country song.") The recording earned Underwood three *Billboard* Music Awards in 2005, for top-selling Hot 100 song of the year, top-selling country single of the year, and country singles sales artist of the year. In an interview with Tina Potterf for the *Seattle Times* (August 17, 2005), Underwood described the months following her *Idol* win, which included a national tour with 10 *American Idol* finalists to promote the album *American Idol 4: Showstoppers*, as "crazy." "Everything has been a complete whirlwind, and I'm just trying to keep my head on straight," she said to Potterf. "It's important to keep in touch with people who knew me before, and I talk to my mom every day."

Some previous *Idol* winners and runners-up have recorded stylistically diverse albums, in attempts to appeal to the public's various musical preferences. Underwood, by contrast, has refused to veer from the pop-country genre. Simon Fuller, one of *Idol*'s creators, who also serves as president of its production and management company, 19 Entertainment, told Brad Schmitt for the *Tennessean* (June 9, 2005), "I see a huge opportunity right now for the right country artist to break into the whole world, never mind mainstream America, but the whole world. I think the right person is Carrie. She's adorable [and] talented." Underwood told Sarah Rodman for the *Boston Globe* (July 14, 2006), "I definitely made it clear [to 19 Entertainment] what I wanted to do and where I wanted to go." For her first album, she hired the producer Dann Huff, who had worked with Faith Hill, and some Nashville-based writers and musicians. "We were really smart about it," Underwood said to Rodman. "I knew what I wanted to be. It's a good time for females in country music. I think there's not enough, and it's always nice to be a minority like that." Underwood's debut album, *Some Hearts*, was released on November 15, 2005; selling 314,000 copies in its first week, it debuted at number one on the *Billboard* Top Country Albums chart—the highest ranking for a country artist's debut album in more than a dozen years. Despite its being available for under two months, *Some Hearts* was the top-selling female country album of 2005. As of December 2006 *Some Hearts* had sold upwards of four million copies. Jennifer O. Cuaycong, who reviewed the disc for the Philippine newspaper *BusinessWorld* (June 16, 2006), wrote, "Underwood has obviously grown in the interim between her *American Idol* victory and her debut as [a] professional recording artist. What was once a 'pitchy' and sometimes unsure talent has metamorphosed into a genuine vocalist with masterful grace and controlled strength." Cuaycong also wrote, "Her voice is soulful, her feelings heartfelt. The power in her vocals displays maturity beyond her years." Some of the album's success has been attributed to that of its first single, "Jesus, Take the Wheel," which remained at number one on *Billboard*'s Hot Country Songs charts for a record six straight weeks.

From April to October 2006, Underwood maintained a busy touring schedule, sometimes performing with the country stars Kenny Chesney and Brad Paisley. "When you're a warm-up act, you know your place," she told Keith Groller. "You basically do your 25 minutes and get off the stage. Being the headliner is different and it's an awesome feeling to know that all of those people paid their money to come see you. Everybody is hanging on your every word." In response to the occasional criticism that onstage she lacks vibrancy, she told Sarah Rodman, "I honestly don't consider myself to be a great stage performer. I'm a singer, that's what I do. If I were going to see me in concert, I would like to be able to sit and listen and hear me hit all the right notes, not see me jumping around stage and flying through the air and being crazy." Ann Wilson, a member of Heart, who performed a duet of "Alone" with Underwood for VH1's *Decades of Rock Live* series, told Rodman that at first Underwood struck her as having a "smooth and very manicured kind of modern day Motown charm school presence about her. . . . The talk backstage was 'Oh my God, who is this girl? She's really young, is she going to be able to pull it off?' Of course later when she came to actually perform, she just came out of her skin, she was just really great and confident and took it big."

On December 7, 2006 Underwood and *Some Hearts* received four Grammy Award nominations, for best new artist, best female country vocal performance, best country song, and song of the year. She won the first two awards, the second for "Jesus, Take the Wheel." After the awards ceremony she said, as quoted by Christopher Rocchio on the Reality TV World Web site (February 12, 2007), "I think tonight proved that *American Idol* can transcend the talent show stereotype that it has." The singer made many high-profile appearances in 2007, among them a guest spot on the TV show *Saturday Night Live* on March 24, 2007.

In October 2007 Underwood released her second album, *Carnival Ride*. Its first single, "So Small," reached the Top 10 on the *Billboard* singles charts. In a review of *Carnival Ride* for the *New York Times* (October 22, 2007), Kelefa Sanneh wrote, "On her new album, . . . Underwood has done something clever: She resisted the urge to de-Carrie Underwood herself. This CD isn't full of rootsy, old-fashioned songs straining for NPR credibility. It's not a mad dash into the dance-pop mainstream. It's not an unvarnished collection of ostentatiously personal confessions. Instead it's a straight-up Carrie Underwood album, and a very good one, with a handful of romps and laments that exist mainly to set the stage for the big-voiced, '80s-influenced, Southern-accented power ballads she sings so well. Much more than any of her fellow *American Idol* winners (and more than the losers too) she has become a mainstream pop star without much departing from that show's musical formula. When she rears back and lets the high notes fly, she still sounds as if she were out to impress the judges." After expressing disappointment with some of the tracks on the album, Sanneh added, "She's not wrong . . . to believe that one of her high notes is enough to make everything else seem inconsequential." In *Newsday* (October 23, 2007), Glenn Gamboa wrote that *Carnival Ride* "goes down extraordinarily easy—lots of lush, inspirational ballads that make the most of [Underwood's] gorgeous voice and a handful of rock-tinged up-tempo numbers about getting out of town or following your dreams, where she channels the Dixie Chicks, without all that, you know, messy political stuff." *Carnival Ride* "sticks incredibly close to the formula of *Some Hearts*," Gamboa continued, and for that reason "starts to pick up an assembly-line feel that is only staved off by Underwood's standout delivery." He concluded that Underwood is "trying to be a singer, not a personality—kind of refreshing, in a time when private lives so often triumph over public work. But as nice as *Carnival Ride* has turned out, Underwood will simply be going around in circles until she invests a little more of herself into the process."

Underwood has served as a fund-raiser for the Humane Society, often donating clothing worn at her concerts for the organization's auctions. Regarding her success, she told Sarah Rodman, "I definitely know I'm very lucky and I know that it doesn't happen like this for everybody. But I try to live in the moment as much as I possibly can. . . . I definitely keep my fingers crossed that everything I do turns out that well, but if not I've had a really awesome time and I've loved every second of it." Underwood recently bought a house outside Nashville, where she lives with three dogs and two cats.

—N.W.M.

Suggested Reading:(Allentown, Pennsylvania) *Morning Call* D p1 Aug. 12, 2006; *Boston Globe* D p1+ July 14, 2006; *BusinessWorld* S p3 June 16, 2006; *Oklahoman* A p1 May 27, 2005; *Palm Beach (Florida) Post* E p1 May 3, 2006; *Seattle (Washington) Times* H p21 Aug. 17, 2005; *Tennessean* A p1+ June 9, 2005, D p5 June 4, 2006

Selected Recording: *Some Hearts*, 2005; *Carnival Ride*, 2007

Frederick M. Brown/Getty Images

Villaraigosa, Antonio

(vee-yah-rye-GO-sah, an-TOH-nee-oh)

Jan. 23, 1953– Mayor of Los Angeles (Democrat)

Address: Office of the Mayor, 200 N. Spring St., Rm. 303, Los Angeles, CA 90012

When Antonio Villaraigosa was sworn in as Los Angeles's 41st mayor, on July 1, 2005, he became the first Latino to hold the office since 1872, a milestone for a city that is now almost 50 percent Latino. "I don't want to be known as the Latino mayor," Villaraigosa, a Democrat, told Farai Chideya for the National Public Radio show *News & Notes with Ed Gordon* (May 19, 2005, on-line). "I want to be known as the mayor who happens to be Latino who made a difference. I ran to make a difference." After six years in the California State Assembly (including two years as speaker), one unsuccessful mayoral run, and two years on the Los Angeles City Council, Villaraigosa took on the highest post in the city in which he has spent his entire life. During his childhood, adolescence, and young adulthood—which, until a laser procedure a few years ago, was represented by tattoos reading "Born to Raise Hell" and "Tony [heart] Arlene"—he endured the presence of an abusive father, his father's abandonment of the family, surgery to remove a tumor on his spine, a hiatus from high school, excessive consumption of alcohol, the births of two children out of wedlock, and other experiences that might seem to preclude a political career. Villaraigosa has made his youthful mistakes an important aspect of his electoral campaigns, because they have made him someone with whom many others

can easily relate, while at the same time providing evidence of his firsthand understanding of many of the problems plaguing the city and of his unique position in attempting to tackle them. "Antonio has a real human story, and this makes him someone we can truly touch, feel, and connect with," Martin Ludlow, a former top aide to Villaraigosa, told an interviewer for *U.S. News & World Report* (October 31, 2005), which named the mayor one of the nation's best leaders. Villaraigosa sees his success as emblematic of the American dream, proof that hard work and perseverance will be rewarded. "I'm a guy who has fallen down my whole life," he told the *U.S. News* reporter, "but I've gotten up and wiped the blood off my knees every time." "Do you know what it is to grow up under the circumstances I did and to have a job like this?" he asked Rick Orlov rhetorically for the *Daily News of Los Angeles* (July 2, 2006). "I wake up every morning grateful and blessed to have this job." Villaraigosa—whom Jennifer Warren described for the *Los Angeles Times Magazine* (August 2, 1998) as "impetuous, charming, and unusually frank"—told Chideya, "I say to people that Los Angeles is a city of America's hope and its promise. It's a city where we come from every corner of the earth here to make the American dream happen. It's a place where we come from every part of the United States to remake ourselves and to, you know, find our destiny, if you will. And I'm excited about Los Angeles because I believe in her. I believe in her destiny."

The oldest of three children, Villaraigosa was born Antonio Ramon Villar Jr. in East Los Angeles on January 23, 1953. He has two sisters, Deborah and Mary Lou. His father, Antonio Ramon Villar Sr., was a Mexican immigrant whose jobs included butcher and cab driver. Villaraigosa has often described his father as an abusive alcoholic, allegations that Villar Sr. has denied. When Villaraigosa was five years old, his father left the family. Villaraigosa's mother, Natalia, who worked for the California Department of Transportation, later remarried and gave birth to another son, Robert Delgado. In their two-bedroom house in the City Terrace neighborhood of East Los Angeles, the family maintained a modest standard of living. To help make ends meet, Villaraigosa shined shoes and sold newspapers beginning at the age of seven. He attended the private, Catholic, all-boys Cathedral High School. During his sophomore year Villaraigosa was suddenly struck with partial paralysis, caused by a benign tumor in his spinal column; after surgery, part of the tumor remained embedded in his spine. Following three weeks in the hospital, he returned to school, where, although he could walk again, he was no longer able to play football or run track. He quickly became frustrated and lost interest in his studies; his grade-point average dropped to 1.4 out of a possible four. The next year, in 1969, he got into a fight while watching a student football game; that incident, compounded by his failing grades, led Cathedral to expel him. Villaraigosa's expulsion was a blow to his mother, whom he has consistently named as his major inspiration. Still, she continued to encourage her son, and in a letter to him she wrote, "I just want you to know I haven't given up on you," as quoted by Warren. He enrolled at the public Roosevelt High School and was placed in remedial classes, where he grew "alienated, mad at the world," as he put it to Warren, and then dropped out of school altogether. During the next several months, he got tattooed and spent his time wandering around his neighborhood, getting into fights. At the urging of his mother, he returned to Roosevelt, taking night classes and graduating the year in which he would have completed his education had he remained at Cathedral.

Villaraigosa then enrolled at East Los Angeles College, a two-year facility, and later transferred to the University of California at Los Angeles (UCLA), where he earned a B.A. degree in history in 1977. Earlier, at 21, he had fathered a child with a woman he had known for a matter of weeks. On his 24th birthday he was arrested for fighting in a Los Angeles restaurant; at his trial he insisted that he had been defending his mother and a sister following inappropriate comments, and the jury voted for acquittal. At 25 Villaraigosa fathered his second child with a different woman. In 1985 he graduated from the unaccredited People's College of Law in Los Angeles; he failed the California bar exam four times, however, meaning that technically he cannot practice law. Also in 1985, at a conference on immigrant rights, he met Corina Raigosa, a public-school teacher. When they married, in 1987, they combined their surnames into one—Villaraigosa. Villaraigosa has said that he suggested the merger, believing it to be an important, progressive step in marriage. Meanwhile, he had begun working as an investigator for the federal Equal Employment Opportunity Commission, where his co-workers elected him union steward. He next got a job as a field representative and organizer for United Teachers Los Angeles and played an important role in that union's 1989 strike. In 1991 the Los Angeles County supervisor, Gloria Molina, appointed Villaraigosa to a seat on the city's Metropolitan Transportation Authority, where he acted as an advocate for bus riders, opposing fare increases, fighting for better security, and trying to eliminate graffiti.

In 1994 Villaraigosa ran for a vacated seat in the California State Assembly. Although his opponent made public the details of his arrest of 17 years earlier, Villaraigosa won the election to represent California's 45th District, a diverse area encompassing the communities of Mount Washington, Boyle Heights, Silver Lake, and Hollywood. One day after the election, his wife filed for divorce, on the grounds that he had been engaging in an extramarital affair. The scandal caused Villaraigosa to lose some of his political allies, including Molina. (The couple reconciled two years later.) During his first few years as an assemblyman, Villaraigosa spon-

sored almost three dozen bills, but with only moderate success. Many of his higher-profile proposals—among them those that would have allowed terminally ill convicts to be released into their families' care, required trigger locks on firearms, reintroduced food stamps for legal immigrants (under federal welfare reform, they had been eliminated)—failed to garner support. One of his best-known bills, which made it legal for women to breast-feed in public, passed after a second attempt. In 1996 Cruz Bustamante, California's first Latino speaker of the Assembly, appointed Villaraigosa majority leader. The following year Villaraigosa sponsored a bill creating the Healthy Families Program, to provide health insurance to 250,000 children from families categorized as "working poor." The bill passed and was signed into law by Governor Pete Wilson, thus ushering in the largest new medical program in the state of California since Congress launched Medicaid (called Medi-Cal in California), in 1965. That achievement was clouded by accusations from Assemblywoman Martha Escutia that Villaraigosa's bill was more or less a copy of a health-care bill that she had introduced earlier. Villaraigosa denied Escutia's claim and noted that he had unsuccessfully sponsored a bill in 1996 that sought universal health care for all children under the age of 18.

In 1998, after four years in politics, Villaraigosa became the speaker of the 80-member Assembly. California's strict term limits prevented his predecessor, Bustamante, from running again, but rumors circulated that Villaraigosa had forced Bustamante out months before Bustamante wanted to leave. Villaraigosa assumed the position in January 1998, at the beginning of his final term as an assemblyman. "Am I prepared?" he said to Warren. "Absolutely not. But we live in the era of term limits, where all of us are amateurs. The fact is, I got the job. And in the land of the blind, the one-eyed man is king." Villaraigosa suffered an embarrassing defeat later in 1998, when a bill he sponsored that would have outlawed discrimination against gay high-school students failed to pass because moderates within his own party refused to support it. That same year he enjoyed one of his biggest successes: the signing into law of the Leroy F. Greene School Facilities Act—a $9.2 billion school bond bill that had failed twice before Villaraigosa brokered a compromise with key Republicans in the Assembly. During his years in the Assembly, and especially his years as speaker, Villaraigosa became known for both his willingness and his ability to cooperate with Republicans. "I'm very much somebody who understands that at the end of the day, you've got to move the ball a little bit forward," he told Ray Suarez for National Public Radio's *Talk of the Nation* (March 11, 1998). "It's not enough to grandstand and protect, you know, your ideological, philosophical spheres of influence and the like, you have to move that ball, and you have to fix problems." To "move the ball," Villaraigosa explained to Suarez, he does his best to see all

VILLARAIGOSA

sides of an issue: "You know, I'm a grandpa and have four kids and I can tell you the older you get, the grayer you see the world. There is always room for honest differences of opinion."

In 1999 Villaraigosa was instrumental in winning the passage of a law banning the manufacture, import, and sale of assault weapons; his critics were quick to point out that while Villaraigosa handled the bill on the Assembly floor, state senator Don Perata had done much of the work behind the scenes. That year Villaraigosa joined Assemblyman Fred Keeley to sponsor a $2 billion bond issue for state parks, a greater sum for bonds than ever before for any purpose in California. Keeley had been responsible for much of the legwork for the bill, while Villaraigosa had introduced a new emphasis on urban beautification, including at least $90 million for land along the Los Angeles River. Looking back on Villaraigosa's record as speaker, the veteran journalist Rone Tempest, who was based for decades in Sacramento, the California state capital, wrote for the *Los Angeles Times* (May 24, 2001), "A lackluster detail man by his own admission, he was forced by his weaknesses in the mechanics of policy to lean heavily on a strong staff as well as on intellectually gifted colleagues who didn't always agree with him."

As was expected, after Villaraigosa's last term in the Assembly ended, he entered the race for mayor of Los Angeles. In that city's nonpartisan mayoral race, the candidates run in a general election; the top two vote-getters in that contest, regardless of party affiliation, then compete in a run-off. Villaraigosa won the general election in April with 30 percent of the vote; his closest competitor, James K. Hahn, got 25 percent. In the following months Villaraigosa and Hahn campaigned intensely, often attacking each other. Especially damaging to Villaraigosa was the revelation that while he was an assemblyman, he had written a letter to President Bill Clinton on behalf of Carlos Vignali, who had then served less than half of a 15-year prison sentence after being convicted on federal charges of drug trafficking. At the request of Vignali's father, a friend of his, Villaraigosa, reportedly without seeking more information about Vignali's sentence, had protested it as an unjustifiably harsh punishment. Just before Clinton left office, he commuted Vignali's sentence. In the June run-off, Hahn captured 56 percent of the vote to win the mayorship. Supporters of Villaraigosa noted that, despite his defeat, the race had helped him to gain national exposure. "People all over the country now know the name Antonio Villaraigosa," Tony McAuliffe, then the chairman of the Democratic National Committee, told Michelle DeArmond for the Associated Press (June 9, 2001). An exhausted Villaraigosa announced that he would be taking some time off from politics. "I put everything I had into this race," he told DeArmond. "I don't have anything left, frankly, at least on the short term." Immediately after Election Day, Villaraigosa underwent two operations: one on his vocal cords

and the other on his spine, where his tumor had started to enlarge. Within a few months he was appointed a distinguished fellow at UCLA and at the University of Southern California, where he co-authored the policy blueprint "After Sprawl," which addressed the myriad problems facing urban centers.

In the 2003 election for members of the Los Angeles City Council, Villaraigosa defeated the incumbent, Nick Pacheco, for the seat representing the 14th District. While in that post Villaraigosa did not push through any major laws, serving instead mainly as a negotiator. He helped secure $800 million in federal funding for the extension of the Los Angeles County rail system into East Los Angeles, and he played a key role in settling the city's 2003 transit strike. He also focused on the larger political arena. In 2003–04 he was the national co-chairman of the Democratic U.S. senator John Kerry's presidential bid. The following year Villaraigosa announced that he would again run for mayor of Los Angeles. While many residents welcomed him as a candidate, in the belief that he would bring much-needed energy to the mayoralty, others complained that he was breaking his promise to remain on the City Council for his full four-year term. Some among the latter group attempted without success to mount a recall election, to oust him from his council seat.

The rematch between Villaraigosa and Hahn (who emerged in first and second place, respectively, in the March 8, 2005 general election) brought some of Villaraigosa's faults to the fore. "His volcanic reactions to Hahn's attacks are beginning to reveal what political insiders have known for years: The former Assembly speaker can be thin-skinned, easily angered and even vindictive," Gregory Rodriguez wrote in his May 2, 2005 *Los Angeles Times* column. "Although great politicians learn to distinguish between what is political and what is personal, Villaraigosa has not. He can try to hide this side of his personality, as he has erased his tattoo, but, so far, he can't make it go away." Despite such criticism and Hahn's solid achievements, in the run-off election, held on May 17, 2005, Villaraigosa got 58.7 percent of the vote to Hahn's 41.3 percent. "In large measure, Mr. Villaraigosa's electoral success . . . is the product of his ability to talk," John M. Broder wrote for the *New York Times* (May 30, 2005). "His landslide victory in the May 17 election transcended the lines of race, class, ethnicity and geography that make Los Angeles less a city than a collection of enclaves. It was Mr. Villaraigosa's ability to keep talking across all of Los Angeles's divisions that enabled him to put together a coalition that defeated Mayor James K. Hahn by a stunning 17-point margin. . . . His evident earnestness, contrasted with Mr. Hahn's detachment and seeming lack of passion, apparently was just what residents of this city were eager to hear. His election coincided with the release of the film *Crash*, which depicts Los Angeles as a seething hell of racial fear, and his

2007 CURRENT BIOGRAPHY YEARBOOK 559

message of hope seemed a welcome tonic." After he won the election, Villaraigosa said, as quoted by Michael Finnegan and Mark Barabak in the *Los Angeles Times* (May 18, 2005), "It doesn't matter whether you grew up on the Eastside or the Westside, whether you're from South Los Angeles or Sylmar. It doesn't matter whether you go to work in a fancy car or on a bus, or whether you worship in a cathedral or a synagogue or a mosque. We are all Angelenos, and we all have a difference to make." As Los Angeles' first Latino mayor since 1872, Villaraigosa also emphasized that while his heritage was important to him, he did not want it to be the defining characteristic of his mayorship. "I'm an American of Mexican descent, and I'm proud of that," he said, as quoted by John M. Broder in the *New York Times* (May 19, 2005). "But I intend to be the mayor of all of Los Angeles. As the mayor of the most diverse city in the world, that's the only way it can work."

In one of his first moves after being sworn into office as mayor, on July 1, 2005, Villaraigosa banned construction during rush hours on major streets. He has since embarked on several ambitious projects, most notably an overhaul of the city's school system. During his first year in office, he tried to shift control of the schools from the Los Angeles United School District (LAUSD) to the mayor's office; in the end, he settled for a compromise that allows him to hire the superintendent and also oversee the three lowest-performing high schools and their feeder campuses. The new arrangement, which went into effect in September 2006, has been a source of much contention, with the LAUSD school board claiming in a lawsuit that it violates the state constitution. Villaraigosa also made crime prevention a priority, pledging to add 1,000 police officers to the Los Angeles Police Department by 2010, which would bring the total number of police officers to more than 10,000 for the first time. (Citywide violent crime went down by 14 percent in 2005 and by another 11 percent in the first six months of 2006.) In addition, Villaraigosa spearheaded several environmental initiatives, among them a new bus route and a project to plant one million trees. He has also said that he wants to increase the city's renewable energy to 20 percent of its total energy consumption by 2010.

During the summer of 2007, after Villaraigosa urged Los Angeles residents to decrease their use of water because of the severe drought that affected large parts of the American West, Duke Helfand reported in the *Los Angeles Times* (August 10, 2007) that the mayor and his family had used close to twice as much water in their home as had the average family. The mayor later attributed the excessive use to gophers that had been chewing holes through rubber pipes in his estate's lawn-sprinkler system. On another front, in efforts to make Los Angeles more of a national and global presence, Villaraigosa has been trying to bring the National Football League (NFL) back to the city and is promoting a bid for the 2016 Olympics.

Villaraigosa has often been described as seeking attention and celebrity to an extent perhaps unbecoming for the average politician but acceptable in the mayor of a city as star-driven as Los Angeles. "If Villaraigosa does nothing else in his first term, he will have at least given L.A. a mayor as colorful, as flashy and as able to play in the national big leagues as the City of Angels itself aspires to be. And that's something," Mariel Garza wrote for the *Daily News of Los Angeles* (June 25, 2006). In his *Los Angeles Times* (October 15, 2006) column, Gregory Rodriguez pointed out the ambiguities of Villaraigosa's personality: "It's impossible not to admire the mayor's extraordinary energy," he wrote, adding, "But his attendant braggadocio is both endearing and disturbing." Rodriguez continued, "Of course, a big ego isn't necessarily a bad thing in a politician. . . . But with Villaraigosa, as with every great politician, there's a fine line between the drive for personal glory and the desire to make the world a better place."

Given that term limits on statewide office in California require that the current governor, Arnold Schwarzenegger, step down in 2010, many suspect that Villaraigosa is primed to move on to bigger things. "He's earned our patience—up to a point—by working frantically and making us feel good. It's hard not to wonder, however, whether his ardor for this relationship ultimately will wane," Kevin Roderick wrote for the *Los Angeles Times Magazine* (December 1, 2006). "Although he calls being mayor of Los Angeles the best political job in the country, most who know Villaraigosa believe that a piece of his heart always belongs to the next office." Currently, Villaraigosa serves as one of four national co-chairmen of Hillary Rodham Clinton's presidential campaign.

On June 12, 2007 Villaraigosa and his wife filed for divorce, citing "irreconcilable differences." On July 3, 2007 Villaraigosa announced that he was romantically involved with the Spanish-language television reporter Mirthala Salinas. With his former wife, he has a son, Antonio Jr., and a daughter, Natalia Fe. His two older children are his daughters Marisela and Prisila. In May 2006 the mayor was named one of *People en Espanol*'s 50 Most Beautiful People.

—C.S.

Suggested Reading: *Hispanic* p24+ Aug. 2005; *LA Weekly* p32+ July 1, 2005; lacity.org; *Los Angeles Magazine* p132+ Dec. 1, 2006; *Los Angeles Times* A Part I p1+ Mar. 16, 2001, A Part I p1+ May 24, 2001, A p1 Feb. 8, 2005; *Los Angeles Times Magazine* p12+ Aug. 2, 1998; *U.S. News & World Report* (on-line) Oct. 31, 2005

Scott Gries/Getty Images for The Miami Project

Visser, Lesley

Sep. 11, 1953– Sportscaster

Address: CBS Sports, 524 W. 57th St., New York, NY 10019-2924

Lesley Visser has said that when she decided, at age 12, to become a sportswriter, "the job didn't exist" for women. "I wasn't at the dawn of women covering sports. But I made the breakfast," she joked to Sally Jenkins, who interviewed her for *Sports Illustrated* (June 17, 1991). Visser joined the sports department of the *Boston Globe* in 1974, while in college. Two years later she became the first female writer to cover a National Football League (NFL) team. For much of the past two decades, she has worked as an on-air reporter for CBS Sports; she has also appeared on sportscasts as a reporter for ESPN (1994–98) and ABC (1994–2000). During her years in print and broadcast journalism, she has reported on college football bowl games; National Collegiate Athletic Association (NCAA) men's Division I basketball tournaments (known as the Final Four); the World Series; Olympic Games; the U.S. Tennis Open; and the tennis competitions at Wimbledon, in England. Her career "firsts" include becoming, in 1992, the first woman to emcee a live network broadcast of the Lombardi Trophy presentation following the Super Bowl; the first woman to report from the sidelines during the telecast of a Super Bowl game; and, in 1998, the first woman assigned to ABC's *Monday Night Football* series. In 2006 she became the first woman to be honored by the Pro Football Hall of Fame, when she received the Pete Rozelle Radio-Television Award, for her "longtime exceptional contribu-

tions to radio and television in professional football." Reflecting on her experiences in a talk with Barbara Matson for the *Boston Globe* (August 4, 2006), Visser said, "My real core knowledge and my passion met opportunity. I wasn't pretending to love football, I really do love it. I've said it before: There are two kinds of women who do television sports"—those "who want to be on TV and end up in sports," and those, like herself, "who love sports and end up on TV."

Commenting on Visser's achievements, Bud Collins wrote for the *Miami (Florida) Herald* (August 13, 2006, on-line), "It took grit, patience, determination, diplomacy, [and] a sharp sense of humor to earn reportorial equality as barriers bent, then fell. She was a leader for women who loved sports and grew up wanting to write the scene." With regard to the hurdles Visser faced as a woman, the New York *Daily News* sports columnist Mike Lupica told Patrick Dorsey for the *South Florida Sun-Sentinel* (August 1, 2006), "I've never known her to be overwhelmed by anything. She just soldiered on with her talent and immense charm, and she acted like she'd been there before." The sports commentator and writer Christine Brennan told Barbara Matson, "There's no doubt that any of us [women] who appear in front of a camera have Lesley Visser to thank. She's remarkable. Let's face it, she knows as much about sports as anyone because she is so quick and so sharp and her ability to convey to the viewer is remarkable." Visser said to Sherry Ricchiardi for the *American Journalism Review* (December 2004/January 2005), "I wasn't a fraud, just a pretty face, not passionate or committed. I had to stand up for myself on many occasions. I also had good support." Referring to a major Allied offensive during World War II, she added, "You don't land on Normandy by yourself."

The younger of the two children of Max Visser, an engineer, and Mary (Coughlin) Visser, a high-school English teacher, Lesley Candace Visser was born on September 11, 1953 in Quincy, Massachusetts. Her father was a native of the Netherlands; the son of a Jewish physician, he was living in Amsterdam when German troops invaded Holland, in 1940. "I grew up appreciating the opportunities of freedom," Visser said to Tony DeFazio for *Pittsburgh Sports Report* (August 2004, on-line). During her childhood the Vissers moved several times, within the greater Boston, Massachusetts, metropolitan area, and Visser attended a series of schools. She has traced her appreciation of sports to her older brother, Chris J. Visser (a veterinarian), and her mother, who was a devotee of University of Notre Dame athletic teams and encouraged her dream of becoming a sports journalist.

Various articles about Visser relate that on one Halloween, she donned a Boston Celtics' jersey bearing the number 24, in homage to Sam Jones, one of her favorite basketball players, while her friends dressed as ballerinas or *Mary Poppins* characters. Her heroines included the tennis player Billie Jean King, whose defeat of Bobby Riggs in 1973 made an indelible impression on Visser. She also admired the track and field athlete Wilma Rudolph, and she followed the careers of both women as they broke gender barriers in their respective sports. The football player Tucker Frederickson, a star of the Auburn University team (he later played for the Giants), was also a favorite of hers, as were the Boston Red Sox, the Boston Celtics, the Green Bay Packers, and the football team of the University of California at Los Angeles (UCLA). Visser served as the captain of her high school's basketball and field-hockey teams and was named the school's best female athlete one year.

After her high-school graduation, Visser enrolled at Boston College, in Newton, Massachusetts, where she majored in English. She served as a cheerleader and worked at the campus newspaper. In her senior year she joined the sports department of the *Boston Globe* as an intern, on a grant from the Carnegie Foundation that was designed for women seeking jobs in fields dominated by men. After she earned a B.A. degree, cum laude, in 1975, the *Globe* hired her as a full-time reporter. For her early assignments, she covered high-school football games. "She was young, she was a good writer, and she obviously was someone who related to people," Vince Doria, at that time the *Globe's* assistant sports editor (he is currently the director of news at ESPN), told Patrick Dorsey. Doria added, "Her outgoing personality is probably the first thing you see. She connects with people very easily. . . .You could see that she was the kind of person that could move around as a reporter and make contacts, develop relationships." Visser told Rachel K. Sobel for *U.S. News & World Report* (September 17, 2001) that knowing sports trivia is not the most important qualification for a sports reporter. "It's more, do you know what you're looking at?" She has advised young women who want to learn about football "to watch the game with the sound turned down." Referring to a particular defensive tactic, she continued, "Do you see the safety blitz yourself? That to me is knowing the game." At the *Globe* Visser worked among such veteran sportswriters as Bud Collins, Will McDonough, Bob Ryan, Peter Gammons, and Leigh Montville.

In 1976 the *Globe* assigned Visser to an NFL beat—specifically, to cover the New England Patriots. At that time women were not allowed access to stadium press boxes, and there were no bathrooms for women in the press area. Furthermore, few NFL locker rooms were open to female visitors; as alternatives, Visser would conduct interviews with athletes and coaches in such settings as weight rooms and parking lots. "I was businesslike. I knew the questions I had to ask. Asked them and got out fast, appreciating that I was pioneering," she said to Collins, "but it was a class in humiliation to be out on the frontier, wading through insults and indignities as one of the female reporters handling the same assignments as men." Visser recalled to Sobel that on one chilly afternoon in the mid-1970s, when she approached the quarterback

Terry Bradshaw to ask him a few questions after a game, he took her note pad and, apparently assuming that she was a fan, autographed it and then walked away. (She ended up getting a quote from the "third-string tight end," she said.) On the occasion of the 1980 Cotton Bowl, Bill Yeoman, the coach of the University of Houston's team, "marchpushed me out of the locker room, even though it was against the rules," as Visser recalled to Bud Collins. "I was clearly accredited, and I was doing my job. He was yelling, 'I don't give a damn about the Equal Rights Amendment—get *ouuuut!'* I walked to the top of the stadium, sat down and cried my heart out. But I got over it." While she was with the *Globe*, Visser also covered college football games, the U.S. Open and Wimbledon tennis competitions, NCAA basketball contests, the World Series, the National Basketball Association (NBA) Finals, and some international events.

In 1982 CBS Sports hired Visser as a part-time features reporter. During her first year with CBS, Visser appeared tense and uncomfortable on the air and sometimes made embarrassing mistakes. In time—by following advice like that of the CBS news reporter Charles Osgood, who suggested that she try to emulate a duck gliding along on a placid lake while its feet paddle furiously beneath the surface, as she told John Scheibe for the *Los Angeles Times* (April 4, 1993)—she corrected those defects, and her personal magnetism, cheerfulness, and love of sports gained her increasing success. She became a regular on *The NFL Today*, with Greg Gumbel and Terry Bradshaw, and reported from the sidelines of Final Four college basketball tournaments, NBA games, the Winter Olympics, and the U.S. Open Tennis Championships, among other events. In 1989, for CBS News, she covered the fall of the Berlin Wall, in Germany, offering her opinion about the effects that a united Germany might have on sports.

On June 13, 1993, while jogging in New York City's Central Park, Visser stumbled and fell, severely injuring her pelvis, a hip, and her face. The accident kept her from working for approximately 10 weeks, during which she underwent several surgical operations. The next year she left CBS and joined ESPN and ABC Sports, for which she contributed to the coverage of Triple Crown horse races, Major League Baseball games, including the World Series, *ABC's Wide World of Sports*, the Special Olympics, and skiing competitions. Also in 1994 Visser drew some negative publicity, when she appeared in a TV ad that pitched Dexatrim, an over-the-counter diet pill. She agreed to serve as a spokesperson for the product, she told Alexander Wolff and Richard O'Brien for *Sports Illustrated* (November 14, 1994), because the pill contained vitamins as well as weight-loss ingredients. "As someone who has worked out all her life, I'm not advocating diet pills in place of eating well and exercising regularly," she said. Wolff and O'Brien pointed out that many male sportscasters had pitched products on TV "without attracting much comment." "But because Visser comes with a newspaper pedigree and does more than read scores on the air, we hold her to a higher standard," they wrote. Donna Lopiano, the chief executive officer of the Women's Sports Foundation, said to Wolff and O'Brien, "On the surface [objections to Visser's endorsement] might seem like a double standard applied to a female journalist. But the fact is, men aren't the ones suffering from drugs that perpetuate the aesthetic value of thinness."

In 1998 Visser became the first woman to report from the sidelines for *Monday Night Football*. According to many sports aficionados, she helped to establish the standard for such TV sideline reporting. By her own account, Visser was shocked when, before the 2000 football season began, Don Ohlmeyer, the executive producer of *Monday Night Football*, fired her and hired as her replacement the sports journalist Melissa Stark (who is 20 years younger than Visser). According to *Sports Illustrated* (August 2, 2000), Ohlmeyer said that he "wanted to go in another direction"; some media observers speculated that his intention was to attract a greater number of young male viewers.

In August 2000 Visser returned to CBS Sports. She currently serves as a lead reporter for CBS's coverage of the NFL; on Sundays she teams up with Phil Simms and Jim Nantz. She also contributes reports for CBS News and the HBO Sports program *Real Sports with Bryant Gumbel*.

Visser has received many honors recognizing her excellence in sports journalism. She was named the Outstanding Woman Sportswriter in America in 1983 and both the New England Newswoman of the Year and the WISE (Women in Sports and Events) Woman of the Year in 2002. She received the Women's Sports Foundation's Journalism Award in the network-television category in 1992; the first Association for Women in Sports Media (AWSM) Pioneer Award, in 1999; the Pop Warner Female Achievement Award (named for an early-20th-century American college football coach), in 2005; and the Gracie Allen Award from American Women in Radio & Television, in 2006. In 2005, along with the Boston Celtics basketball player Bob Cousy and the 1980 U.S. Olympic Hockey Team, she was inducted into the New England Sports Museum Hall of Fame. In 2004, a few weeks before the opening of the Olympic Games, in Athens, Greece, Visser carried the Olympic torch through New York City, an honor bestowed on her by the International Olympic Committee in recognition of her accomplishments as a "pioneer and standard-bearer."

Lesley Visser and the CBS sportscaster Dick Stockton married in 1983. The couple maintain homes in Boca Raton, Florida, and the New York City borough of Manhattan. They have no children. "I didn't want kids," Visser said to Jan Hoffman for the *New York Times* (January 28, 2004). "That was never a debate for me. I have six godchildren and I love 'em, love 'em, love 'em, but sports reporting means travel. I couldn't have had my career if I had

kids." According to her Web site, Visser has worked with such organizations as the V Foundation for Cancer Research, the United Way, the March of Dimes, the Hubbard House for Domestic Violence, the Bone Marrow Foundation, and the Cystic Fibrosis Foundation.

—D.F.

Suggested Reading: *Boston Globe* (on-line) Aug. 4, 2006; CBS Sportsline.com; *New York Times* B p2 Jan. 28, 2004; LesleyVisser.com; *Miami (Florida) Herald* Sports p10 Aug. 13, 2006; *New York Times* B p2 Jan. 28, 2004; *Pittsburgh Sports Report* (on-line) Aug. 2004; *South Florida Sun-Sentinel* Sports Aug. 1, 2006; *Sports Illustrated* p78+ June 17, 1991, p24 Aug. 21, 2000

Chris Jackson/Getty Images

Watson, Emily

Jan. 14, 1967– Actress

Address: c/o Screen Actors Guild, 5757 Wilshire Blvd., Los Angeles, CA 90036-3635

Since she was nominated for an Oscar, a Golden Globe Award, and a British Academy Award for her motion-picture debut, in the 1996 independent film *Breaking the Waves,* the British actress Emily Watson has chosen roles that are emotionally jarring and, above all, challenging. Sharon Waxman, writing for the *Washington Post* (January 17, 1999) and comparing Watson's career with those of better-known actresses of her generation, opined, "Few leap headfirst into the most complex, soul-baring, high-risk roles there are. Emily Watson did." In such films as *The Boxer* (1997), *Hilary and Jackie* (1998), and *Red Dragon* (2002), Watson has shown a knack for bringing to life, often with harrowing realism, the vulnerable, angst-ridden, and sexually frustrated characters she has portrayed. "It's the people she plays that you remember. She disappears into her roles," Richard E. Grant, who directed Watson in the 2005 film *Wah-Wah*, remarked to Stuart Husband for the London *Mail on Sunday* (November 21, 2005). "I don't think she's interested in stardom; that's why she chooses interesting projects and collaborators." Assessing Watson's career, which includes more than 20 screen credits on both sides of the Atlantic, Catherine Shoard, writing for the London *Telegraph* (May 3, 2006, on-line), observed: "Emily Watson is perhaps the most visionary—and uncompromising—actress of her generation, prepared to face down her demons in role after grueling role." Watson, however, has downplayed her versatility and risk-taking, telling Anwar Brett for the London *Times* (August 15, 1998), "Playing different roles gives you the chance to emotionally jump off the deep end in a way that would be very unhelpful in real life. But if you were to think of it as therapy then that would be wrong. My job is to tell a story and if that involves taking an emotional risk then I'm well prepared to do it, but I don't do it for the sake of it."

The daughter of an architect and an English teacher, Emily Watson was born on January 14, 1967 in Islington, a district in London, England. When she and her older sister, Harriet, were growing up, the family moved frequently, living in several different neighborhoods in London, including Acton, Brixton, Chiswick, Hammersmith, and Kew. Watson's parents strongly encouraged the intellectual development of their daughters, and she grew up a freethinker, though a fairly sheltered one. "I'm a soft-bellied liberal, me," she told Tim De Lisle for the London *Independent* (February 15, 1998). "A nice English middle-class girl. I've never had to make choices that were hard." Growing up without a television set, Watson was forced to rely on her own creative powers to entertain herself. She also read voraciously, reportedly completing the Russian novelist Leo Tolstoy's epic *War and Peace* by the time she was 11.

Although Watson admired the English actresses Juliet Stevenson, Miranda Richardson, and Claire Higgins, she did not aspire to a career in theater or film. "I didn't really have a dream," she told Jamie Portman for the *Ottawa Citizen* (January 4, 2002). "I was a contented child. I wanted to study literature when I grew up." After graduating from the St. James Independent School, a private all-girls institution noted for its progressiveness, Watson went on to study literature at the University of Bristol. There, she got her first acting experience, participating in the university's stage productions. She graduated with a B.A. degree in English in 1988, and at age 22 she decided to try acting as a career. She was twice rejected by the Drama Studio London before being admitted to its prestigious program—which also counts the Academy Award–winning actor Forest Whitaker among its alumni.

After graduating from the Drama Studio London, Watson secured a series of small theater roles. In 1991 she appeared in the one-act plays *School for Mothers* and *The Mistake* at the White Bear Theatre, in London. In 1992 and 1993 she worked as an understudy at the Royal Shakespeare Company in Stratford-upon-Avon. She appeared in the troupe's 1992 productions of *All's Well That Ends Well* and *The Taming of the Shrew*. She also played small roles at the West Yorkshire Playhouse, in Leeds, and the National Theatre, in London. In 1994 she appeared in the National Theatre's production of *The Children's Hour*, a 1934 play by the American writer Lillian Hellman. Watson's portrayal of Mary Tilford, a teenage girl who falsely claims that her two female teachers are secretly involved in an affair, won her local acclaim. Soon afterward, at the behest of her agent, she auditioned for a part in *Breaking the Waves*, which was to be the Danish filmmaker Lars von Trier's first English-language film. Despite having never appeared in a movie or television role before, Watson won the part of Bess McNeill, the film's protagonist. Von Trier remarked to Richard Mowe for *Scotland on Sunday* (August 11, 1996), "The instant she began screen testing—and it was a particularly difficult scene—I knew she was Bess." The role, nitially offered to the actress Helena Bonham Carter, who turned it down because it called for many nude scenes, represented a breakthrough for Watson, who has worked steadily since.

Set in the picturesque Scottish Highlands, *Breaking the Waves* tells the story of Bess's marriage to an oil-rig worker named Jan (Stellan Skarsgård)—a marriage that takes place over the objections of many members of the closed Calvinist world in which she was raised. After Jan is paralyzed in an accident and unable to make love, he persuades Bess that she can help him to recover by having sex with other men and describing the encounters to him. The film debuted at the 1996 Cannes Film Festival and was awarded the festival's Grand Jury Prize. Critics were particularly impressed by Watson's performance: in addition to taking home the European Movie Award for actress of the year, she won awards from the film critic associations in Los Angeles, London, and New York and earned nominations for an Academy Award, a Golden Globe Award, and the British Academy of Film and Television Arts (BAFTA) Award, all for best actress. "I still don't know how I did it," Watson told Stuart Husband. "It was my first movie, so to an extent I didn't know what I was doing, which helped hugely, I think. It brought on the most fantastic artistic adventure." Critics gushed about Watson's performance. "Nothing about *Breaking the Waves* is more fortuitous than the choice of Ms. Watson . . . who so fervently and glowingly embodies Bess," Janet Maslin wrote for the *New York Times* (October 4, 1996). "The role calls for a trusting, absolutely unguarded performance, and the film would have been destroyed by anything less. Ms. Watson creates Bess with a devastating immediacy, and she deeply rewards the camera's penetrating gaze."

In the following year, 1997, Watson appeared in a series of roles that highlighted her versatility. In the BBC production *The Mill on the Floss*, an adaptation of the 19th-century novel by George Eliot, she played Maggie Tulliver, a tomboyish young woman whose encounters with men lead to her humiliation. That same year she portrayed Marion, a faithful suburban housewife to Chris (played by Christian Bale), in *Metroland*, a screen adaptation of a 1980 Julian Barnes novel. Writing for the *Los Angeles Times* (April 8, 1999), Kevin Thomas noted that Watson's character at first appears to be only a minor figure in the film, yet "slowly but surely Marion emerges as a strong woman, smarter and more perceptive than her sweet-natured but essentially ordinary and conventional husband. You can see why Marion appealed to Watson; she is as cool and controlled as her two previous heroines were tempestuous. Yet such is the force of Watson's presence, here deliberately understated, that even when she is off-screen, sometimes for substantial lengths of time, her Marion is rightly the film's dominant figure."

In *The Boxer* Watson played Maggie, the former lover of Danny Flynn (Daniel Day-Lewis), a one-time champion boxer from Belfast who spends 14 years in prison for his slight involvement with the Irish Republican Army (IRA). Released from prison, Danny discovers that Maggie is now married to another IRA prisoner and the mother of a teenage son. Like many other critics, Roger Ebert of the *Chicago Sun-Times* (January 9, 1998) praised the acting in the film, especially "the delicacy of the relationship between Maggie and Danny." Ebert added: "Played by two actors who have obviously given a lot of thought to the characters, they know that love is not always the most important thing in the world, that grand gestures can be futile ones, that more important things are at stake than their own gratification, that perhaps in the times they live in romance is not possible. And yet they hunger. Day-Lewis and Watson . . . are smart actors playing smart people; when they make reckless gestures, it is from despair or nihilism, not stupidity."

Working with Day-Lewis, an actor famed for his labor-intensive preparation for each new role, inspired Watson to go to similar lengths for her next role, playing the renowned real-life English cellist Jacqueline du Pré, in the film *Hilary and Jackie*, directed by Anand Tucker. Based on the controversial book *A Genius in the Family* by Piers and Hilary du Pré—the brother and sister, respectively, of the cellist—the film portrayed the sisters' complex relationship, which was troubled by a rivalry over musical ability as well as for the affection of Hilary's husband. To re-create du Pré's cello performances, Watson brought a cello onto the set of *The Boxer* and spent hours each day practicing. Mean-

while, to depict accurately the cellist's slow decline—a result of multiple sclerosis—Watson consulted with medical experts and people suffering from the disease. Though booed at its opening at the Venice Film Festival, presumably because of its unsparing portrait of one of the most revered figures in English classical music, the film went on to achieve substantial critical acclaim, and Watson's performance was hailed as a tour de force. Stephen Holden of the *New York Times* (December 20, 1998, on-line) called the movie "one of the most insightful and wrenching portraits of the joys and tribulations of being a classical musician ever filmed," adding, "Watson infuses Jacqueline with the same incendiary emotionality that she brought to the role of an obsessively devoted young wife in *Breaking the Waves*. Saucer-eyed, with a sly duckbill smile, she radiates a wanton erotic willfulness that at moments borders on madness." While offering the film itself more qualified praise, Michael Atkinson wrote for the *Village Voice* (December 30, 1998–January 5, 1999, on-line) that Watson's performance "shakes the rafters. Her Jackie isn't just a disjointed talent, she's thorny, girlish, anarchic, given to mocking foreign languages right to natives' faces, and prone to self destructively leaving her priceless cello behind at airports. Watson is a mercurial presence with huge, nervous baby eyes, and when she cuts loose, an otherwise conventional film shudders with anxiety." Watson's performance earned her best-actress awards from the London Film Critics' Circle and the British Independent Film Awards, as well as nominations for an Academy Award, a Golden Globe Award, and a BAFTA Award.

Watson next appeared as part of a large ensemble in Tim Robbins's *Cradle Will Rock* (1999), a fictionalized account of Orson Welles's 1936 mounting of the Marc Blitzstein musical *The Cradle Will Rock*; the film received mixed reviews. *Angela's Ashes* (1999), based on the best-selling 1996 memoir by Frank McCourt, received a similar response, with many reviewers praising the film's careful recreation of Depression-era New York City and Limerick, Ireland, but commenting that the movie had divested McCourt's story of its humor. Watson's portrayal of McCourt's mother, Angela, was widely admired. "It is impossible to conceive of better casting of Angela," Roger Ebert wrote for the *Chicago Sun-Times* (January 21, 2000, on-line), adding that Angela, as portrayed by Watson, "has the kind of bitterness mixed with resignation that was forced on a woman in a country where marriage to a drunk was a life sentence, and it was a greater sin to desert him than to let him starve her children." Kenneth Turan, writing for the *Los Angeles Times* (December 24, 1999), also singled out Watson's performance as one of the movie's high points but observed: "While Watson as Angela is compelling as always, she's mainly called on to suffer and endure." In order to portray McCourt's chain-smoking mother, Watson herself began smoking.

As the title character in *Trixie* (2000), directed by Alan Rudolph, Watson showed she could handle comedy with the same aplomb she had brought to drama. In *The Luzhin Defence* (2000), the Dutch director Marleen Gorris's adaptation of Vladimir Nabokov's 1930 novel, Watson starred alongside the actor John Turturro, who played a Russian chess grand master named Alexander Luzhin; Luzhin falls in love with Watson's character, Natalia Karkhov. "The love story is touchingly and convincingly played by Mr. Turturro and Ms. Watson," A. O. Scott wrote for the *New York Times* (April 20, 2001, on-line). "Their odd, attractive faces and slightly nervous performing styles seem perfectly complementary, and their romance is a welcome respite from the usual mechanistic movie star courtship. Neither seems to possess an ounce of vanity." For her performance Watson received best-actress nominations from the London Film Critics' Circle Awards and the British Independent Film Awards.

Watson received critical praise for her interpretation of Elsie, the head housemaid and her master's mistress, in *Gosford Park* (2001), the director Robert Altman's study of the British class system of the 1930s. Written by Julian Fellowes, who won an Academy Award for best original screenplay, the film was praised particularly for its ensemble cast; Watson's performance was singled out for a best-actress nomination at the 2002 European Film Awards. Watson also earned plaudits for her work as the mysterious Lena Leonard, who falls in love with Barry Egan (Adam Sandler), in *Punch-Drunk Love* (2002), written and directed by Paul Thomas Anderson. Taken with both the film and Watson, A. O. Scott of the *New York Times* (October 5, 2002, on-line) wrote: "Ms. Watson, her blue eyes nearly as wide as the screen . . . has a smart, quiet oddness that plays beautifully off Mr. Sandler's somersaulting bipolarity. Lena may be a romantic convention rather than a fully conceived personality, but she is also the audience's surrogate: her love for Barry is the cue for our own, and Ms. Watson (who some of us are half in love with already) brings us to him in the palm of her hand."

In 2001 Watson turned down the title role in *Amélie* (also released as *Le Fabuleux destin d'Amélie Poulain*), directed by Jean-Pierre Jeunet, who had written the part with Watson in mind. ("Amélie" is the French version of "Emily.") The film became a major hits in France and the highest-grossing French-language film in U.S. history, making the actress Audrey Tautou, who played Amélie, an international star. "I don't regret saying no," Watson told Charlotte O'Sullivan for the London *Independent* (September 11, 2004). She added, "Anyway, it happens all the time—someone gives way, stands back, and a star is born. It happened to me with *Breaking the Waves*. It was going to be Helena Bonham Carter. . . . You step into somebody else's shoes, and hey presto!" (The French actress Audrey Tatou, who played Amélie, received rave reviews for her performance in the

film and has gone on to enjoy international stardom.)

Watson played Reba McClane, a young blind woman who develops a relationship with Francis Dolarhyde (Ralph Fiennes), a shy, slightly disfigured loner, in *Red Dragon* (2002), an adaptation of the Thomas Harris novel of the same name, a prequel to *The Silence of the Lambs* (1988). The film, directed by Brett Ratner, received generally negative reviews. To prepare for the role, Watkins studied briefly at the Royal National Institute for the Blind and spent time with an active young woman who was almost completely blind. Watson told Martyn Palmer, in an interview for *Unreel* (online), "What was very interesting for me was to try and express myself without using my eyes and to have on screen chemistry with somebody without ever making visual contact." Watson's next appearance on screen was in the box-office flop *Equilibrium* (2002), a dystopic science-fiction movie that was roundly mocked by critics.

In 2002 and 2003 Watson took lead roles in the Donmar Warehouse repertory productions of the Shakespeare comedy *Twelfth Night* and Anton Chekhov's tragicomedy *Uncle Vanya*. The two plays, both directed by Sam Mendes, opened in London in 2002 and then were mounted at the Brooklyn Academy of Music, in New York City, in 2003. Ben Brantley of the *New York Times* (January 21, 2003) praised the company's rendition of *Uncle Vanya*, with Watson in the role of Sonya, but found faults in its version of *Twelfth Night* and with Watson's performance as Viola: "Ms. Watson exudes a charming air of confident resourcefulness . . . [but] lacks that core of vulnerability that would make you root for her."

Though wary of biographical films after *Hilary and Jackie*, Watson returned to the genre in 2004 in the HBO movie *The Life and Death of Peter Sellers*, in which she portrayed Anne Howe, the first wife of the title character; she received a Golden Globe nomination for best supporting actress for her work. In 2005 Watson lent her voice to the character Victoria Everglot in the animated film *Corpse Bride*, co-directed by Tim Burton and Mike Johnson, and starred as Martha Stanley in the critically acclaimed Australian Western *The Proposition*, directed by John Hillcoat. Watson again ventured far from her native country, in terms of setting, for *Wah-Wah* (2005), a domestic drama set in the early 1960s in the small southern African nation of Swaziland. *Wah-Wah* ffeatured Watson as Ruby, the new American wife of Harry Compton (Gabriel Byrne), the father of the main character, Ralph (Nicholas Hoult). Roger Ebert argued in the *Chicago Sun-Times* (June 16, 2006, on-line), "The key performance in the movie is by Emily Watson, as a good and sensible woman who married too quickly to know what she was getting herself into. . . . She's the one who says the [British] locals speak 'snooty baby talk' that all sounds to her like 'Wah-wah-wah-wah-wah.' She gives her marriage a brave try but eventually it's toodle-oo."

Watson reunited with Julian Fellowes, the screenwriter of *Gosford Park*, for *Separate Lies* (2005), Fellowes's directorial debut, in which she portrayed Anne, the wife of a well-to-do lawyer, James Manning (Tom Wilkinson). After the Mannings's neighbor, Bill Bule (Rupert Everett), is implicated in a hit-and-run accident, Anne acknowledges that she is having an affair with Bill and claims that she was the driver of the car. "As Ms. Watson, who has always excelled at displaying a wide-eyed sneakiness, slowly peels away Anne's decorous defenses to reveal an unruly inner fire, James's lordly composure begins to crumble," Stephen Holden wrote for the *New York Times* (September 16, 2005). Holden added: "The richest scenes are the painful confrontations between James and Anne in which you feel the texture of a complicated marriage whose layers of love, affection, accommodation, disappointment and deception seep into one another so that nothing is easy or absolute."

In 2006 Watson appeared in *Crusade in Jeans*, an adaptation of the Dutch young-adult novel *Kruistocht in spijkerbroek* (1973), and *Miss Potter*, about the life of the children's author and illustrator Beatrix Potter. As Potter's sister-in-law, Millie Warne, Watson earned positive reviews in a film that critics generally found unimpressive. Calling *Miss Potter* "a Merchant Ivory film trapped in a Disney movie's body," Carina Chocano wrote for the *Los Angeles Times* (December 29, 2006), "Watson is funny and endearing as Millie, who immediately recognizes Beatrix as a kindred spirit unlike the other unmarried daughters in their circle, who 'sit around gossiping all day and unaccountably bursting into tears.'"

Most recently Watson appeared in the film *The Water Horse: Legend of the Deep* (2007), and she is slated to star in the movie "Fireflies in the Garden," scheduled for release in 2008.

Watson has been described variously as mercurial, playful, and pensive by journalists—all of whom have called her intelligent. She is "more elegant in person than you expect," according to Mark Morris. "The reason she is so effective on screen is that she acts with her face. Sure, she is no slouch at accents, but the expression comes from the corners of her mouth, her vast eyes." In 2005 she and her husband, the actor Jack Waters, became the parents of a daughter, Juliet, who was named for one of the title characters in the Shakespeare tragedy *Romeo and Juliet*. "I don't really regret not having Juliet earlier," she said to Catherine Shoard. "Sometimes I feel like it might have been physically easier at 22, but I've had a chance to build a wonderful career that's not going away. I feel satisfied, you know? I've had a crack at things. I've seen the world." Watson lives in London with her husband and daughter and is an avid fan of the northern London soccer team Arsenal.

—D.F.

Suggested Reading: (London) *Observer* p2 Aug. 13, 2000; (London) *Telegraph* (on-line) Mar 5, 2006, Jan. 19, 2003; (London) *Times* Features Aug. 15, 1998; *New York Times* C p1 Oct. 4, 1996

Selected Films: *Breaking the Waves*, 1996; *Metroland*, 1997; *The Mill on the Floss*, 1997; *The Boxer*, 1997; *Hilary and Jackie*, 1998; *Cradle Will Rock*, 1999; *Angela's Ashes*, 1999; *Trixie*, 2000; *The Luzhin Defence*, 2000; *Gosford Park*, 2001; *Punch-Drunk Love*, 2002; *Red Dragon*, 2002; *The Life and Death of Peter Sellers*, 2004; *Corpse Bride*, 2005; *Separate Lies*, 2005; *The Proposition*, 2005; *Wah-Wah*, 2005; *Crusade in Jeans*, 2006; *Miss Potter*, 2006; *The Water Horse: Legend of the Deep*, 2007

Selected Plays: *School for Mothers*, 1991; *The Mistake*, 1991; *The Taming of the Shrew*, 1992; *All's Well That Ends Well*, 1992; *The Children's Hour*, 1994; *Twelfth Night*, 2002; *Uncle Vanya*, 2002

Watts, Naomi

Sep. 28, 1968– Actress

Address: c/o Creative Artists Agency, 9830 Wilshire Blvd., Beverly Hills, CA 90212-1825

Naomi Watts appeared in more than 20 movies for television and the big screen before she gained widespread notice, in 2001, for her tour-de-force performance in David Lynch's surrealist film *Mulholland Drive*, in which she played two dissimilar characters. When asked to explain what it was about the then little-known actress that convinced him that she could tackle the dual role, Lynch told Scarlet Cheng for the *Los Angeles Times* (October 12, 2001), "I saw someone that I felt had a tremendous talent, and I saw someone who had a beautiful soul, an intelligence—possibilities for a lot of different roles, so it was a beautiful full package." Other directors who have worked with Watts, as well as many critics and other filmgoers, have also commented on the actress's versatility and chameleonlike abilities. In an interview with Stuart Husband for the London *Observer* (February 8, 2004), the director Alejandro González Iñárritu, for example, said, "She has the beautiful face of an innocent angel one moment, and the next moment she will have the face of the devil. It's like she has all these layers that she peels away." The commercial success of *The Ring* (2002), in which Watts portrayed a journalist determined to beat the clock to save herself and her son from a mysterious killer, reinforced her status as an A-list actress. Her performance opposite Sean Penn and Benicio Del Toro as a psychologically devastated woman, in

Vince Bucci/Getty Images

Naomi Watts

González Iñárritu's *21 Grams* (2003) earned her nominations for best actress from the Academy of Motion Picture Arts and Sciences (which awards the Oscars), the Screen Actors' Guild, and the British Academy of Film and Television Arts (BAFTA). She deftly handled a comedic role in David O. Russell's existential comedy *I [Heart] Huckabees* (2004), and her depiction of the love object of the humongous, hirsute title character in Peter Jackson's remake of *King Kong* (2005) earned many critical plaudits and favorable comparisons with the performance of Fay Wray, who starred in the original, classic 1933 version of the film. After seeing her in *King Kong*, the movie critic A. O. Scott wrote for the *New York Times* (December 13, 2005), "Watts incarnates the glamour and emotional directness of classical Hollywood." Her work in *The Painted Veil* (2006), which she also co-produced, inspired another reviewer for the *New York Times* (December 20, 2006), Manohla Dargis, to write that Watts's "remarkable talent helps keep movie faith and love alive, even in the tinniest, tiniest vehicles."

The younger of two siblings, Naomi Watts was born to Peter ("Puddy") Watts and Myfanwy ("Miv") Watts on September 28, 1968 in Shoreham, Kent, England. Her brother, Ben Watts, who is a year and a half her senior, is a well-known commercial photographer, specializing in fashion and celebrity shoots. Watts's father was a sound engineer and road manager for the popular rock group Pink Floyd, work that often kept him away from his family. Miv Watts was a professional actress before the births of her children. Later, she became a set dresser and costume designer for film and television; more recently, she established an interior-design business and opened two boutiques in England. As a small child, Watts watched her mother in the role of Eliza Doolittle in a local, amateur production of *My Fair Lady*. "I wanted to be up there playing with her in that world," she recalled to Ingrid Sischy for *Interview* (December 1, 2003). Seated in the first row of the theater, Naomi waved vigorously to get her mother's attention, and when her mother responded, only after initially staying in character and ignoring Naomi's waves, the little girl understood that the action on stage "was pretend. And that just seemed so fascinating to me; it was like a little secret that I was let in on, and it just transported me into that world of make-believe. Somehow I thought, That's what I'm going to do one day."

When Watts was four years old, her parents divorced; afterward, with her mother and brother, she lived for a few years with relatives of her mother's in Wales, where she learned to speak Welsh. During the next several years, the three sometimes lived with Miv's boyfriends in various parts of England, where Naomi was exposed to an array of regional British accents. After her mother married again (her second husband, like her first, worked in a band), Watts was sent to a boarding school. Meanwhile, in 1976, Peter Watts (who had also remarried) had died, reportedly from an overdose of heroin. At the time, Watts has told reporters, she got little help from her mother or anyone else in handling her feelings of "dislocation and apartness," as she described them to Stuart Husband. "When I was preparing for *21 Grams*, I spent countless hours reading about people and talking to people who had suffered a terrible loss, lost a loved one, lost children," she told Steven Kotler for *Variety* (February 9–15, 2004). "When I read all these books and heard all that talk, I realized the things these people were dealing with were things I've carried with me my whole life. It was startling. It was—wow—that's what's going on with me."

When she was 14 Watts left Great Britain with her mother (some of whose forebears were Australian) and brother and relocated to a suburb of Sydney, Australia. Although she had objected vehemently to being separated from her British friends, within six months of the move, Watts had settled in happily, not least because, at her insistence, her mother had enrolled her in acting classes. Soon afterward, through an audition for a modeling job, she met Nicole Kidman, who is close to her in age, and the two became fast friends. She made her debut on the silver screen in the little-noticed film *For Love Alone* (1986), playing the unnamed girlfriend of one of the characters.

The study of acting interested Watts far more than did academic subjects, and she left high school without graduating. At about age 18 she went to Japan in search of modeling work. Her experiences in Japan were depressing, as she recalled to Sischy: "I found it to be a real attack on the spirit, one that I wasn't prepared for. It was a very strange, disappointing time in my life." After about a year, convinced that she "didn't want to be in front of the camera ever again," as she told Sischy, Watts returned to Sydney, where she took a job in advertising, producing fashion shoots at a department store. She next was hired as an assistant fashion editor at a magazine called *Follow Me*, then left for a better-paying position, as fashion editor, at another magazine. One weekend, at the urging of a friend, she attended a drama workshop. "By the end of the weekend I realized I had been living a lie," she said to Sischy, "that this was my dream, and I was asking myself how I could walk away from something that truly excited me."

In 1989, at the premiere of the film *Dead Calm* (1989), which co-starred Kidman, Watts was introduced to the director John Duigan, who invited her to audition for a part in his upcoming film *Flirting*, a sequel to *The Year My Voice Broke* (1987). Watts won the small role of Janet Odgers in *Flirting* (1991), in which Kidman co-starred with Thandie Newton. Also in 1991 Watts appeared in two television miniseries: *Brides of Christ*, whose cast included Russell Crowe, and *Home and Away*. In 1992 Duigan tapped her for another brief role, in *Wide Saragasso Sea* (1993).

Watts then moved to Hollywood, where she spent the better part of the next decade acting on the big screen in mostly forgettable parts and on television in somewhat more memorable ones. (She became far better known for her friendship with Nicole Kidman than for her acting skills.) In *Tank Girl* (1995), the film adaptation of the British comic book of the same name, Watts played Jet Girl, "a scantily-clad survivor of a comet strike that wipes out mankind," in the words of a reporter for the London *Mail on Sunday* (February 2000). Although the film enjoyed a cult following, it was a failure at the box office. Watts followed *Tank Girl* with appearances in films including *Children of the Corn IV: The Gathering* (1996), *Persons Unknown* (1996), *Under the Lighthouse Dancing* (1997), and *Dangerous Beauty/Destiny of Her Own* (1998). Watts also lent her voice to a character in the box-office failure *Babe: Pig in the City* (1998). Her television roles during that period included parts in the Hallmark Hall of Fame production *Timepiece* (1996), with James Earl Jones and Ellen Burstyn; the CBS miniseries *The Hunt for the Unicorn Killer* (1999); and the two-part BBC period drama *The Wyvern Mystery* (2000), in which Watts starred opposite Derek Jacobi, Jack Davenport, and Iain Glen. During those years she found Kidman's success a source of both frustration and hope. As she told David Eimer for the London *Sunday Times* (January 19, 2003), "Sometimes it was like, 'Oh God, I wish I could get a role that good,' but the minute you let bitterness drive you, you're ruined. So I would turn it into: 'She did it, and she came from the same place as me, so maybe it'll happen to me as well.'" There were occasions, however, when Watts failed to squelch her feelings of resentment. For example, in her interview with *Daily Mail on Sunday* reporter, in 2000, she said, "I don't like L.A. at all. I don't like the fact that everyone in Hollywood is in the industry. You have to spend all day making an appointment to see someone, and then it takes an hour to get to the meeting, and an hour to get back, and the whole day's gone. It's not a real city like London or New York." She added, "And the people are phoney. Everyone is out for themselves. The friendships aren't real." In 2001, by contrast, in her conversation with Scarlet Cheng, she said, "There was a time I was very much blaming the way I felt on L.A. That it was a vacuum of creativity, of humor or anything organic, and I was really angry at the place. But then today I feel completely different—I love L.A.!"

Compounding Watts's disillusionment was ABC-TV executives' decision not to add to the network's lineup David Lynch's proposed series *Mulholland Drive*, in which Watts was to play a leading role, on the grounds that it was too avant-garde for American audiences. Scott Coffey, who appeared with Watts in *Tank Girl* and had worked on the series, told Steven Kotler that the show's cancellation led Watts to believe that her career in film would never take off (a fear that he felt with regard to his own career). "That was a really, really bad time . . . ," he said. "We thought we'd both be doing bad TV for the rest of our lives if we were lucky." (The story told in Coffey's short film *Ellie Parker*, made in about 2001 and starring Watts, mirrors to a great extent their experiences during that time.) Then, in 2001, the French producer Alain Sarde and the French-based production and distribution company StudioCanal provided the funding necessary to turn *Mulholland Drive* into a feature film. The picture was shown at the 2001 Cannes Film Festival, in France, where Lynch was a co-winner of the prize for best director, and it opened in the U.S. later that year. A surreal, ambiguous, and nonlinear take on the inner workings of the Hollywood film industry, *Mulholland Drive* became the subject of much discussion. In the film, Watts first appears as Betty Elms, an attractive aspiring actress, who has just come to Los Angeles from her native Ontario. Upon arriving at her aunt's supposedly vacant apartment, Betty discovers a woman identifying herself as Rita (played by Laura Harring), who is suffering from amnesia as a result of a car accident that occurred the night before. Initially, Betty and Rita work together to unravel the mystery surrounding Rita's presence in the aunt's apartment. Following a romantic encounter between Betty and Rita, the plot takes a bizarre twist: Watts now portrays an unhappy actress named Diane Selwyn, whose girlfriend Camilla (again, Laura Harring) had abandoned her in favor of a male film director (played by Justin Theroux), whom she has married. Todd McCarthy, writing for *Variety* (May 21–27, 2001), expressed the opinion that Watts's performance had given *Mulholland Drive* "its most unanticipated boost." "The . . . actress at first comes across as a one-dimensional goody-goody, so all of her character's progressions—to genuinely protective and reliable friend, to actress of unexpected intimacy and depth, to open and responsive lover—are surprising and gratifying," he wrote. "It's a stunning starring debut." Watts received several honors for her work in *Mulholland Drive*, among them "breakthrough-performance" awards from the National Board of Review and the New York Film Critics Online, the latter of which also named her runner-up for its best-actress award (won by Judi Dench); she also earned the awards for best supporting actress from the San Diego Film Critics Society and the Las Vegas Film Critics Society and a best-actress award from the Chicago Film Critics Association. Lynch, Watts told Stuart Husband, "made me believe in myself. I'd become a sort of diluted person in Los Angeles, trying to succeed in what seemed a horribly uncreative place, auditioning in front of people who didn't understand me for a role I didn't believe in for one second. You leave pieces of yourself everywhere until you feel like a shell, a hulk. David tapped into that. . . . He saw through all the skins I'd built around myself." He also taught her, she said, "that it was OK to embrace" the "dark" part of herself.

Watts appeared next as Rachel Keller in *The Ring* (2002), directed by Gore Verbinski, which marked the first time that a major Hollywood studio had tapped her for a starring role. In that remake of a hugely popular 1990s Japanese film called *Ringu*, directed by Hideo Nakata, Rachel sets out to investigate the agonizing deaths of her niece and several other teenagers one week after they watched a nightmarish video. "The camera loves [Watts]," William Arnold wrote in a review of *The Ring* for the *Seattle Post-Intelligencer* (October 18, 2002), "and she projects an intelligence, determination and resourcefulness that carry the movie nicely." Elvis Mitchell, the *New York Times* (October 18, 2002) reviewer, was less enthusiastic about Watts's performance, writing that although "initially . . . [she] does a fine job of communicating Rachel's off-putting toughness, . . . once it becomes clear that tight-jawed anxiety is surprisingly the only note on her piano, the movie feels numbed." Hideo Nakata directed Watts in *The Ring Two* (2005), which struck reviewers as almost completely illogical, even given the license usually afforded films in the genre. Nonetheless, the movie, like its predecessor, earned handsome profits.

Thanks to the first American *Ring*, Watts found herself much in demand as a leading actress. She received rave reviews for her potrayal of Christina Peck in Alejandro González Iñárritu's grief-filled *21 Grams*, whose title refers fancifully to the difference between a person's weight immediately before and after death, when the soul supposedly departs. Peck, a former addict, returns to drug use and becomes romantically involved with Paul, a mathematics professor (played by Sean Penn); earlier, in a transplant operation, Paul received the heart of Christina's husband, after a career criminal turned born-again Christian (Benicio del Toro) killed both her husband and her two daughters in a hit-and-run car crash. "Because Ms. Watts reinvents herself with each performance, it's easy to forget how brilliant she is. She has a boldness that comes from a lack of overemphasis," Elvis Mithcell wrote in a review of *21 Grams* for the *New York Times* (October 18, 2003).

In 2005 Watts landed the leading female part, that of Ann Darrow, an aspiring actress, in Peter Jackson's critically acclaimed remake of the 1933 epic film *King Kong*. "The fact that I get to work with Peter Jackson . . . and get to play Ann Darrow in one of the greatest love stories ever written— that's the kind of unbelievable part I used to dream about, it's the kind of part any actress dreams about," she said to Steven Kotler. Set in the Depression-era U.S., *King Kong* is about an ambitious producer (played by Jack Black), who travels with Ann, a screenwriter (Adrien Brody), and a film crew to the mysterious Skull Island to shoot a movie. On the island they discover an immense gorilla, King Kong, whom the island's inhabitants consider their god. Kong then falls in love with Ann. "Watts is absolutely fabulous—funny, sexy and moving," Peter Travers wrote in his highly enthusiastic review of *King Kong* for *Rolling Stone* (December 8, 2005, on-line). In a criqtue for the London *Independent* (January 27, 2006), Anthony Quinn wrote, "When [King Kong] gently picks up Ann in his mighty mitt and they stare at one another in close-up, we sense the oncoming tragedy of their requited but impossible love; the depth of feeling in Kong's regal gaze is beautifully matched by Ann's luminous compassion: is it loneliness she sees in those dark eyes? Watts hasn't been this affecting since her entranced ingenue in *Mulholland Drive*, and given that most of the time she's acting against technology, it's doubly impressive." "Watts expresses a range of emotion that Fay Wray, bless her heart, was never allowed in 1933," Roger Ebert wrote for the *Chicago Sun-Times* (December 13, 2005). "Never have damsels been in more distress, but Fay Wray mostly had to scream, while Watts looks into the gorilla's eyes and sees something beautiful there."

Watts and the actor Edward Norton strived for six years to bring a second adaptation of W. Somerset Maugham's novel *The Painted Veil* to the silver screen. (The first, starring Greta Garbo, Herbert Marshall, and George Brent, premiered in 1934.) Directed by Jon Curran from a screenplay by Ron Nyswaner, the 2006 retelling, set in the 1920s, co-starred Watts as Kitty, an aimless British woman whose mother pushes her into a marriage of convenience with an inhibited bacteriologist, Walter Fane (Norton). The couple move to Shanghai, where Kitty has a passionate affair with a British politician, a married lothario named Jack (Liev Schreiber). When Walter discovers Kitty's infidelity, he insists that she accompany him to a Chinese village in which an epidemic of cholera rages. Faced with the possibility of death, both Kitty and Walter undergo transformations, which in turn significantly change their relationship. In one of many admiring reviews of the film and its stars, Manohla Dargis wrote for the *New York Times* that Watts "risks our love and earns our awe, ensuring that we never lose sight of [Kitty] even when the film almost does."

In her latest film, *Eastern Promises* (2007), directed by David Cronenberg, Watts portrayed a Russian midwife working in a British hospital. The woman's attempts to unite an orphaned newborn with the child's Russian relatives leads her to become entangled with London's expatriate Russian underworld. In *Rolling Stone* (September 4, 2007), Peter Travers described Watts's work as "extraordinary"; in a review for the *Boston Globe* (September 14, 2007), Ty Burr wrote, "As the film's bruised innocent, Watts is very good, but *Eastern Promises* isn't about her so much as it's about the lengths men will go to plunder or protect." In a movie whose release was scheduled for early 2008, Watts was cast opposite Tim Roth in the director Michael Haneke's *Funny Games*, an English-language remake of one of Haneke's German-language films.

"I always have doubts about every film I take on," Watts told Jeanne Wolf for Wolf's column on movies.go.com in 2006. "I think it's fear. It's so weird, because I'm so convinced at the time that I can't do it, and I must get out of it. It's like clockwork. I do it with every project." Steven Kotler described the five-foot-five-inch, blue-eyed, blond Watts as "pretty and perky and polite." He added, "There is something slightly tomboyish about her and something slightly aristocratic at the same time." Watts lives in the Los Angeles area and maintains an apartment in New York City; in her spare time she enjoys doing yoga. In 2006 she signed a contract to appear in ads for the jewelry-maker David Yurman. She and the actor Liev Schreiber became the parents of a son, Alexander, in 2007. Recalling to Wolf her experiences with Schreiber on the set of *The Painted Veil*, she told Wolf that she had "never done a love scene before with someone with whom I'm involved. You suddenly get very aware of yourself and think, 'Oh, gosh, I've got to work extra hard here and make sure that you can't see traces of me coming through.' I don't want people to think this is how we do it when we're not acting."

—D.F.

Suggested Reading: Internet Movie Database; *Interview* p133+ Nov. 1, 2001, p162+ Dec. 1, 2003; (London) *Daily Mail on Sunday* p30 Feb. 20, 2000; (London) *Observer* p14 Feb. 8, 2004; *Los Angeles Times* Calendar p20 Oct. 12, 2001; *Variety* p15 May 21–27, 2001, p68+ Feb. 9–15, 2004

Selected Films: *Flirting*, 1991; *Wide Sargasso Sea*, 1993; *Tank Girl*, 1995; *Persons Unknown*, 1996; *A House Divided*, 1998; *Dangerous Beauty*, 1998; *Babe: Pig in the City*, 1998; *Strange Planet*, 1999; *Ellie Parker*, 2001; *Mulholland Dr.*, 2001; *The Ring*, 2002; *Ned Kelly*, 2003; *Le Divorce*,

2003; *21 Grams*, 2003; *I [Heart] Huckabees*, 2004; *The Ring Two*, 2005; *King Kong*, 2005; *Stay*, 2005; *The Painted Veil*, 2006; *Eastern Provinces*, 2007

Selected Television Series or Miniseries: *Home and Away*, 1991; *Brides of Christ*, 1991; *Timepiece*, 1996; *The Hunt for the Unicorn Killer*, 1999; *The Wyvern Mystery*, 200; *The Outsider*, 2001

Alex Wong/Getty Images for Meet the Press

Webb, Jim

NOTE: An earlier article about Jim Webb appeared in *Current Biography* in 1987.

Feb. 9, 1946– U.S. senator from Virginia (Democrat); former secretary of the U.S. Navy; novelist; journalist

Address: 144 Russell Senate Office Bldg., Washington, DC 20510

On Election Day in 2006 the Democrat Jim Webb, a highly decorated veteran of the Vietnam War, onetime official in the administration of President Ronald Reagan, former secretary of the U.S. Navy—and former Republican—unseated George Allen, a popular Republican incumbent who was widely viewed as a potential presidential candidate, for one of Virginia's seats in the U.S. Senate. Webb, who was sworn into office on January 4, 2007, shortly before his 61st birthday, is also a lawyer and former teacher who has written a well-regarded book of military science and several novels and won an Emmy Award for broadcast journalism. Webb identified himself as a Democrat until he attended law school, in the early 1970s. The attitude of many of his left-leaning classmates toward the Vietnam War and veterans of that war contributed to his decision to become a Republican. The war in Iraq, which he has never supported, and the economic policies of the administration of President George W. Bush, which he believes have favored the rich over the middle and lower classes to an extreme degree, drove him to turn away from the Republican Party and register as a Democrat. Webb strongly supports the right of individuals to bear arms and opposes the free-trade agreement negotiated under President Bill Clinton; on other key issues, among them abortion, he supports the positions of the Democratic Party. His status as a freshman senator notwithstanding, Webb's name recognition, combat experience, and straightfoward, sometimes blunt style of speaking led the Democrats to select Webb to present the party's rebuttal to President Bush's 2007 State of the Union address. Webb is a member of the Foreign Relations, Armed Services, and Veterans Affairs Committees, and in his first nine months in office, he introduced several bills on the floor of the Senate; the legislation addresses the redeployment of troops in Iraq, the awarding of contracts for private firms involved in the military activity in Iraq and Afghanistan, and the provision of educational benefits to veterans of "the 9/11 era," as he put it on his official Web site, that would resemble those provided under the G.I. Bill of 1944 for veterans of World War II.

James Henry Webb Jr. was born on February 9, 1946 in St. Joseph, Missouri, to James Henry Webb Sr. and Vera (Hodges) Webb. His father was a colonel in the U.S. Air Force and a bomber pilot during World War II; earlier, beginning with the American Revolution, members of the family fought in every war in which the U.S. engaged. Webb has likened his father to the title character in the novel and film *The Great Santini*, a military man whose aggressiveness gravely damages his relations with his wife and children. Webb has recalled that when he was five, he, his brother, and his two sisters had to stand at attention while his father conducted military-style inspections of their rooms. Sometimes James Sr. "would clench a fist and dare his son to strike it, taunting him to keep punching until the tears flowed," as Peter J. Boyer wrote for the *New Yorker* (October 30, 2006). In what Webb viewed as essential rights of passage, he learned from his father how to fight, hunt, and use a gun. Webb has owned guns since he was eight, as has his own son.

Like many other children in military families, Webb attended more than a dozen schools in the U.S. and England. After his graduation from high school, in Bellevue, Nebraska, he entered the University of Southern California, in Los Angeles, on a naval ROTC (Reserve Officers Training Corps) academic scholarship. A year later he transferred to the U.S. Naval Academy, in Annapolis, Maryland.

While there he became a member of the Brigade Honor Committee and was a finalist for brigade commander in his senior year. He also distinguished himself as a varsity boxer. On one occasion he lost the brigade boxing championship to Oliver North, a fellow classmate and future fellow aide to President Reagan. (Webb, North, and three other naval-academy graduates—U.S. senator John S. McCain and Reagan's national security advisers John Poindexter and Robert MacFarlane—are the subjects of Robert Timberg's 1995 book, *The Nightingale's Song*.) Webb was one of 18 graduates in the class of 1968 to receive letters of commendation from the academy's superintendent for outstanding leadership.

After he left the academy, Webb chose a commission with the Marine Corps. He attended the Basic School for Marine Corps officers, in Quantico, Virginia, graduating first in his class of 243. In 1969, as a rifle-platoon leader and company commander with the Fifth Marine Regiment, he spent nine months in Vietnam, gaining the rank of captain. During his tour in the Vietnam War, he saw considerable action in the An Hoa Basin and earned the Navy Cross, a Silver Star, two Bronze Stars, and two Purple Hearts. Complications arising from a severe shrapnel wound led to Webb's evacuation from the combat zone and, after he underwent surgery several times, a medical discharge. He then served as a platoon commander and as an instructor in tactics and weapons at the Marine Corps Officer Candidates School. Next, he joined the staff of the secretary of the navy.

Webb left military service in 1972 to pursue a degree in law at the Georgetown University Law Center, in Washington, D.C. While there he became involved in a study of U.S. military strategy in the Pacific. He traveled to Micronesia in 1972 and 1973 to conduct research for a territorial planning commission and presented his findings in a book, *Micronesia and the U.S. Pacific Strategy: A Blueprint for the 1980s* (1974). Webb supported the doctrine, held by the administration of President Richard Nixon, of providing a "nuclear shield" for the defense of U.S. allies, but he warned that heavy concentrations of American troops on the islands stretching from Guam to Tinian, in the Mariana Islands (part of Micronesia), could negatively affect the lives of the islanders and lead them to end their traditional acceptance of the goals of the U.S. military. Webb earned a J.D. degree in 1975, that year winning the Horan competition for excellence in legal writing.

Before he served in Vietnam, Webb had not had strong political feelings and had considered himself a nominal Democrat. At Georgetown he was distressed by some aspects of the leftist political culture that prevailed among the students. He came to believe that the Democratic Party had betrayed veterans and that many Democrats were benefiting from a politically manufactured misrepresentation of the Vietnam War. Webb thought that, as Peter Boyer wrote, during the 1960s the

WEBB

party had "sacrificed a broad populist tradition to the passions of the intemperate margins." He felt outraged by students who, although all males were required to register for the military draft when they reached the age of 18, had found ways to avoid military service and, while pursuing their education, had protested the war and seemed to regard their stance as that of genuine heroes. Webb was incensed when Jimmy Carter pardoned war resistors on the first day of his presidency, in 1977, and he condemned Carter's action as a "rank betrayal and an abuse of Presidential power," in Boyer's words.

Driven partly by such feelings, Webb wrote *Fields of Fire* (1978), which is now widely ranked among the finest and most realistic Vietnam War novels. The book, which contains scathing depictions of Ivy League graduates who manipulate the draft system to avoid service, focuses on U.S. soldiers in Vietnam, where the absence of a front (a specific line or zone separating allied and enemy armies, as existed during World Wars I and II) contributed to the moral ambiguity of the conflict. Almost all the sympathetic characters in *Fields of Fire* get killed, and both soldiers and civilians, American as well as Vietnamese, are portrayed as being trapped in an imbroglio beyond their control. More than a million copies of *Fields of Fire* were sold, and the book was nominated for a Pulitzer Prize.

During that period Webb taught literature and writing at the U.S. Naval Academy and served as the national co-chairman of a Vietnam veterans group that supported conservative political candidates, including President Gerald R. Ford. (Ford, a Republican who had been vice president under Nixon and assumed office when Nixon resigned, now sought to be elected in his own right.) Between 1977 and 1981 Webb worked for the House Committee on Veterans' Affairs as an assistant minority counsel and then as lead minority counsel. His public statements sometimes sparked controversy; on one occasion, for example, he charged that antiwar demonstrators had cost 10,000 Americans their lives during the Vietnam War. He resigned from the committee that sponsored the construction of the Vietnam Veterans Memorial in the nation's capital, because he objected to the selected design, which he predicted would become a "wailing wall for future antidraft and antinuclear demonstrators," as Robert Cross reported in the *Chicago Tribune* (March 10, 1987). Later, Webb pushed successfully for the addition to the memorial of a sculpture that included the figure of an African-American soldier. Among several op-ed pieces he wrote for periodicals was a piece for the *Washingtonian* (November 1979) titled "Women Can't Fight," in which he criticized Congress's decision to open the nation's military academies to women; the presence of women, he warned, would damage the effectiveness of those schools as producers of combat leaders.

Webb's second novel, *A Sense of Honor* (1981), is set at the U.S. Naval Academy in 1968 and sheds light on the regimented, difficult lives of midshipmen. During the next five years, sales of the book reached about 250,000. Peter Braestrup, in a review for the *American Spectator* (September 1981), noted the book's "special value as a timely, unfashionable reminder that schooling, testing, developing future military commanders is no ordinary educational task." At the naval academy *A Sense of Honor* was available only through special request, because, as the officer who had banned it from the academy's bookstore told a *New York Times* (February 28, 1981) reporter, "in the opinion of most people who read it, there's a large amount of vulgarity and a less-than-accurate picture of the officers, midshipmen, and faculty of the academy." An angry and offended Webb told *Publishers Weekly* (March 20, 1981), "I don't believe I have to create a fairy tale in order to show that I'm proud to have attended the naval academy. I think it's a disservice to the institution to try and paint [the school] like something out of a '30s movie called 'Men of Annapolis.'"

In 1981 Webb withdrew his name from a list of potential candidates to head the Veterans' Administration under President Ronald Reagan, choosing instead to devote himself to writing. His decision reflected, in part, his frustration with the legislative process and with the widely held attitude that government should solve societal problems, including those of veterans. "In writing, you can affect people's emotions and attitudes," he said to David Shribman for the *New York Times* (August 15, 1983), adding that he thought *Fields of Fire* "touches people more deeply than veterans' programs." He also remarked on the differences in the ways that literature and politics treat ethical questions. The characters he created, he told Shribman, "face situations where morality is not clearly defined. In Vietnam we faced them all the time. Throughout the past 25 years we've had these choices. But politics is the art of taking ambiguities and boiling them down simply enough so you can say 'yes' or 'no.' It is the opposite of writing. In writing you take these ambiguities and you expand them. You flesh them out. You deal with them." *A Country Such as This* (1983), Webb's next novel, follows three naval-academy roommates from 1951, their year of graduation, through the mid-1970s, and shows how their differing military experiences influence their lives and relationships. The novel received mixed reviews and fared poorly in the marketplace. During a brief foray into broadcast journalism, Webb earned an Emmy Award for his coverage for the TV program *The MacNeil/Lehrer NewsHour* of the 1983 bombing of a U.S. Marines barracks in Beirut, Lebanon, in which 241 servicemen were killed.

In February 1984 Webb accepted the newly created position of first assistant secretary of defense for reserve affairs in the Reagan administration. He created little controversy during his three years in

2007 CURRENT BIOGRAPHY YEARBOOK 573

the job and earned a Distinguished Public Service Medal for his efforts.

On February 18, 1987, after John F. Lehman Jr. declared his intention to resign as secretary of the navy, President Reagan nominated Webb to replace him. The Senate Armed Services Committee confirmed him unanimously, and the Senate approved his appointment by voice vote. The 41-year-old Webb was sworn in as the 66th secretary of the navy on April 10, 1987. He immediately assured the 500 highest-ranking officers that he would consult them on policy matters instead of relying solely or primarily on the advice of civilian leadership, as Lehman had tried to do. As navy secretary Webb's tasks included the creation of a plan for the United States' presence along the oil routes of the Persian Gulf, where an Iraqi attack on a navy ship in May 1987 resulted in the deaths of 37 U.S. sailors. He also worked on ways for the U.S. to stay competitive with the Soviet Union regarding submarines. After serving as navy secretary for less than a year, Webb resigned, on the grounds that he could not support proposed budget cuts that he believed were "motivated by other than military and strategic reasoning," as quoted by the New York Times (February 23, 1988). Some later reports suggested that his resignation stemmed from irreconcilable differences with Frank Carlucci, the secretary of defense.

Webb next wrote three novels: Something to Die For (1992), The Emperor's General (1999), and Lost Soldiers (2001). Something to Die For is a war novel cum political thriller about an American soldier fighting in a war that was launched to promote the political ambitions of a small group of Washington bureaucrats. The Emperor's General drew much praise for its vivid characterization of General Douglas MacArthur in the aftermath of World War II. In Insight on the News (July 19, 1999), for example, George Garrett described the novel as "a strongly plotted, cleanly told story." Webb's "history is authentic in detail and appropriately accurate in judgement," Garrett continued. "There is an earned sense of authority in the novel." Lost Soldiers, set in Vietnam at the turn of the 20th-21st centuries, recounts the efforts of an American Vietnam War veteran to locate former deserters. A story of Webb's was the basis for the film Rules of Engagement (2000), starring Tommy Lee Jones as a Marine lawyer hired to defend his former friend, a 30-year Marine Corps veteran, played by Samuel L. Jackson.

Webb's next book, Born Fighting: How the Scots-Irish Shaped America (2004), a work of nonfiction, discusses the history and political legacy of the often overlooked Scots-Irish subculture in the U.S. Descendants of clans in Northern Ireland—among them the ancestors of Andrew Jackson, the nation's seventh president—they migrated to North America in large numbers in the 17th and 18th centuries and settled in and near the Appalachians, from Pennsylvania in the north to Georgia in the south. According to Webb, in the 20th century the Scots-

Irish were cast aside by the Democratic Party, in the mistaken belief that doing so was necessary for electoral success, and disingenuously wooed by the Republicans. Although he suggested that some Republican strategists have appreciated the importance of southern white men as voters, other Republicans privately and publicly disdain them. In an opinion piece published in the Wall Street Journal (October 19, 2004), Webb argued that the the the Scots-Irish and African-Americans had been the victims of both major political parties' efforts to pit them against each other, despite their many shared fundamental values stemming from roots in the poverty-stricken South. Both groups, he added, suffered in modern times from the outsourcing of jobs and widespread problems with public education. "The greatest realignment in modern political history would take place rather quickly if the right national leader found a way to bring Scots-Irish and African Americans to the same table," he declared.

Webb has also contended that political attacks on veterans have been increasing since George W. Bush became president. In an op-ed piece for the New York Times (January 18, 2006), he wrote, "In recent years extremist Republican operatives have inverted a longstanding principle: that our combat veterans be accorded a place of honor in political circles. . . . The casting of suspicion and doubt about the actions of veterans who have run against President Bush or opposed his policies has been a constant theme of his career. This pattern of denigrating the service of those with whom they disagree risks cheapening the public's appreciation of what it means to serve, and in the long term may hurt the Republicans themselves." He mentioned Republican candidates' TV ads attacking such distinguished Vietnam veterans as former senator Max Cleland, Senator John F. Kerry, and Congressman John Murtha. "The political tactic of playing up the soldiers on the battlefield while tearing down the reputations of veterans who oppose them could eventually cost the Republicans dearly," Webb wrote. "It may be one reason that a preponderance of the Iraq war veterans who thus far have decided to run for office are doing so as Democrats. A young American now serving in Iraq might rightly wonder whether his or her service will be deliberately misconstrued 20 years from now, in the next rendition of politically motivated spinmeisters who never had the courage to step forward and put their own lives on the line."

In recent years Webb has criticized the doctrine of preemptive regime change in the Middle East and elsewhere, as well as other facets of the foreign policy of neoconservatives in the George W. Bush administration (among them Richard B. "Dick" Cheney, Donald Rumsfeld, and Paul D. Wolfowitz), and he has been an outspoken opponent of the U.S.-launched war in Iraq. In 1990, before the first Gulf War (during the administration of President George H. W. Bush), Webb had asserted at a Senate hearing that removing the regime of the

Iraqi dictator Saddam Hussein from power would destabilize the entire region, empower Iran, and do more harm than good to U.S. interests in the Middle East. Webb maintained that position throughout the 1990s and into the next millennium. In a prescient article published in the *New York Times* (March 30, 2003) 10 days after the U.S. invaded Iraq, he warned that a protracted guerrilla war was a more likely outcome of that military action than a swift and total victory. In an opinion piece published 11 months later in *USA Today* (February 18, 2004), Webb labeled the Iraq war "the greatest strategic blunder in modern memory." He argued that faulty planning had led the U.S. to attack "the wrong target" in the war on terror and that the U.S. military was ill-equipped for a lengthy occupation. President Bush, he continued, "decapitated the government of a country that was not directly threatening the United States and, in so doing, bogged down a huge percentage of our military in a region that never has known peace. . . . The reckless course that Bush and his advisors have set will affect the economic and military energy of our nation for decades. It is only the tactical competence of our military that, to this point, has protected him from the harsh judgment that he deserves." Webb favors removing American troops from Iraq and stationing them, in smaller numbers, in Jordan, Kuwait, and other nearby countries. He also advocates working diplomatically with nations including Iran and Syria to end the war and try to remove potential threats to peace.

Webb had endorsed Allen during the latter's campaign in 2000 for a seat in the U.S. Senate, because he believed that the former Virginia governor held a stronger position on national security than the Democratic incumbent, Chuck Robb, for whom Webb had voted in 1994. Webb met with Allen in both 2002 and 2003 to discuss his concerns about the Iraq war and a foreign policy that he described as "a complete failure," but Allen maintained his steadfast confidence in President Bush's policies. After coming to the conclusion that Virginians were not being well represented by a senator who was simply rubber-stamping the Bush administration's foreign policy, Webb decided to run for the Senate himself. He officially announced his candidacy on February 7, 2006. Months later, partly in response to a grass-roots Internet campaign urging him to do so, he announced his move to the Democratic Party. "I don't wake up in the morning wanting to be a U.S. senator," he told reporters, according to Michael D. Shear in the *Washington Post* (February 8, 2006). "I wake up every morning very concerned about the country."

On Primary Day, June 13, 2006, Webb defeated his only opponent, Harris Miller, a businessman, with 53.5 percent of the vote. In the months preceding the general election, in addition to reiterating his antiwar message, Webb talked about the widening gap between the very rich and everybody else in the U.S.—the "two Americas" theme emphasized by the Democrat John Edwards during his failed bid for the vice presidency, in 2004. On another domestic issue, immigration, Webb supported the construction of a fence along the U.S.–Mexico border and stricter enforcement of laws meant to stop corporate exploitation of illegal labor. He opposed NAFTA (the North American Free Trade Agreement), corporate outsourcing of jobs, and gun control, and backed civil unions for gay couples and abortion rights. His espousal of a mixture of liberal and conservative positions made him an unusual but strong candidate in Virginia, not least because Allen, a close Bush ally, represented the status quo. In 2006 Webb's son, Jimmy, was serving in Iraq as a Marine infantryman, and Webb wore a pair of his son's combat boots while campaigning, in a display of solidarity with him and other servicemen and -women. He also attended rallies in a camouflage-painted Jeep. "Jim Webb is George Allen's worst nightmare," the University of Virginia political analyst Larry J. Sabato told Sally B. Donnelly for *Time* (May 7, 2006): "a war hero and a Reagan appointee who holds moderate positions. Allen tries to project a Reagan aura, but Webb already has it."

Largely because of discrepancies in their campaign budgets and political experience—Allen had significantly more of both; indeed, Webb entered the race before he had raised any money or hired a staff—pundits gave Webb virtually no chance of unseating Allen. Moreover, Webb had no interest in the etiquette of campaign politics. As Bill Connelly Jr., a political-science professor at Washington and Lee University, in Virginia, said to Boyer after observing Webb at a rally, "He looks like somebody who's making his first serious run for public office. He doesn't ask for votes. . . . Part of George Allen's appeal is that he's this down-home country guy with cowboy boots, chewing tobacco, . . . a down-to-earth-guy. Retail politics matters, and Webb is not as good at it." Nevertheless, Webb attracted supporters among many conservative columnists, Vietnam War veterans, Hollywood figures, and working-class white southerners. He also had the support of the former Virginia governor Mark Warner, a moderate Democrat.

Turning to advantage his relationship with former president Reagan, Webb ran a TV ad that opened with footage of Reagan during his commencement address at the U.S. Naval Academy in 1985, when he spoke about Webb as an example of what academy graduates might accomplish. Allen, considering the use of that footage to be unfair, wrote a letter of protest to Webb, demanding that he stop running it. The controversy became a national news story, with Webb gaining greater exposure when portions of the ad were broadcast during evening news shows. Webb was also helped by the growth of suburbs of Washington, D.C., in northern Virginia, where many recent residents rejected Allen's conservative views. He was still trailing Allen in polls when, in mid-August 2006, at a campaign rally, Allen referred to a Virginia-born, student volunteer of Indian descent in Webb's camp as "Macaca," the name of a genus of monkeys, and then directed his audience to "give a welcome to Macaca here. Welcome to America and the real world of Virginia." A videotape of the incident was disseminated via the Internet, and though Allen apologized for the slur and insisted that he had not known the meaning of "macaca," his words received much negative attention in the media. By October 2006 Webb had climbed to within four percentage points of Allen in polls. He won the election, the following November 7, by less than 1 percent of the vote; the result was not made official until two days later. Thanks to his victory and that of Jon Tester of Montana in a similarly close contest, the Democrats regained control of the Senate.

A four-sentence conversation between Webb and President Bush that took place at a White House reception for newly elected members of the House and Senate in late November 2006 aroused a flurry of attention in the print and broadcast media. At that event Webb had chosen not to join those lining up to have their photos taken with President Bush. The president later approached him, and, knowing that Webb's son was then stationed in Iraq, asked Webb, "How's your boy?" "I'd like to get them out of Iraq, Mr. President," Webb responded, according to many sources. "That's not what I asked you," Bush retorted. "How's your boy?" "That's between me and my boy, Mr. President," Webb answered. Perhaps not surprisingly, supporters of the president accused Webb of behaving in a manner insulting to Bush, while critics of Bush accused the president of rudeness.

Webb was sworn into office on January 4, 2007. Reflecting his military and foreign-policy expertise, he was assigned to the Senate's committees on foreign relations; armed services; and veterans' affairs. He also joined 10 representatives and nine senators (eight Republicans and 11 Democrats) as a member of the Joint Economic Committee, which studies matters connected with the economy. During his first day in office, Webb introduced a bill titled the Post-9/11 Veterans Educational Assistance Act, which sought to expand benefits to military families. Later in January he was selected to present the televised, official Democratic response to President Bush's 2007 State of the Union address. Rather than read from a prepared rebuttal, Webb wrote his own remarks (which Democratic congressional leaders approved). "There are two areas where our respective parties have largely stood in contradiction . . . ," Webb said in his rebuttal. "The first relates to how we see the health of our economy—how we measure it, and how we ensure that its benefits are properly shared among all Americans. The second regards our foreign policy—how we might bring the war in Iraq to a proper conclusion that will also allow us to continue to fight the war against international terrorism, and to address other strategic concerns that our country faces around the world. When one looks at the health of our economy, it's almost as if we are living in two different countries. Some say that things

have never been better. The stock market is at an all-time high, and so are corporate profits. But these benefits are not being fairly shared. When I graduated from college, the average corporate CEO made 20 times what the average worker did; today, it's nearly 400 times. In other words, it takes the average worker more than a year to make the money that his or her boss makes in one day. Wages and salaries for our workers are at all-time lows as a percentage of national wealth, even though the productivity of American workers is the highest in the world. Medical costs have skyrocketed. College tuition rates are off the charts. Our manufacturing base is being dismantled and sent overseas. Good American jobs are being sent along with them. In short, the middle class of this country, our historic backbone and our best hope for a strong society in the future, is losing its place at the table. Our workers know this, through painful experience. Our white-collar professionals are beginning to understand it, as their jobs start disappearing also. And they expect, rightly, that in this age of globalization, their government has a duty to insist that their concerns be dealt with fairly in the international marketplace."

Regarding the war in Iraq, Webb said, "The President took us into this war recklessly. He disregarded warnings from the national security adviser during the first Gulf War, the chief of staff of the army, two former commanding generals of the Central Command, whose jurisdiction includes Iraq, the director of operations on the Joint Chiefs of Staff, and many, many others with great integrity and long experience in national security affairs. We are now, as a nation, held hostage to the predictable—and predicted—disarray that has followed. The war's costs to our nation have been staggering. Financially. The damage to our reputation around the world. The lost opportunities to defeat the forces of international terrorism. And especially the precious blood of our citizens who have stepped forward to serve. The majority of the nation no longer supports the way this war is being fought; nor does the majority of our military. We need a new direction. Not one step back from the war against international terrorism. Not a precipitous withdrawal that ignores the possibility of further chaos. But an immediate shift toward strong regionally-based diplomacy, a policy that takes our soldiers off the streets of Iraq's cities, and a formula that will in short order allow our combat forces to leave Iraq."

In March 2007 Webb introduced legislation that would prohibit the executive branch from using funds for military operations in Iran without congressional authorization. In a statement made in the Senate, as trascribed for the senator's Web site, he asserted that the goal of the bill was "to restore a proper balance between the executive and legislative branches when it comes to the commencement of military activities." "The major function of this legislation," Webb continued, "is to prevent this Administration from commencing unprovoked military activities against Iran without the approval of the Congress." In July 2007 Webb introduced an amendment to the National Defense Authorization Act that would require that troops be permitted to remain at home for periods at least as long as their previous tours of duty before being redeployed. He also led the way for a bill that sought to establish an independent, bipartisan commission on wartime contracting that would investigate contracting policies in Iraq and Afghanistan. On his U.S. Senate Web site, Webb suggested that the bill, while "significantly [increasing] transparency and accountability," could potentially save taxpayers billions of dollars. Webb has co-sponsored bills pertaining to stronger ethics rules, prescription-drug-pricing negotiations, the recommendations of the 9/11 Commission, stem-cell research, energy and global warning, college costs, and the rebuilding of the military.

Webb is married to the former Hong Le, a lawyer, who arrived in the U.S. from Vietnam as a child, in 1975; the couple's family includes Hong Le Webb's daughter, Emily, from an earlier marriage, who is in elementary school, and a baby, Georgia, who was born in December 2006. The family lives in Arlington, Virginia. Webb's first two marriages ended in divorce. From the first, to Barbara Samorajczk, Webb has one daughter, Amy; from the second, to Ann Krukar, he has, in addition to his son, James Robert Webb, two daughters, Sarah and Julia. Webb has traveled extensively, particularly in Asia, as a journalist, business consultant, humanitarian, and screenwriter. Fluent in Vietnamese, he has worked without pay for Vietnamese-American communities since the 1970s. To keep fit, he makes use of a heavy punching bag.

—N.W.M.

Suggested Reading: *National Review* (on-line) Feb. 13, 2006; *New Yorker* p42 Oct. 30, 2006; *New York Times* B p6 Aug. 15, 1983, A p1 Sep. 18, 2006; *Washington Post* B p5 Feb. 8, 2006, A p1 Nov. 29, 2006, B p1 Dec. 2, 2006

Selected Books: fiction—*Fields of Fire*, 1978; *A Sense of Honor*, 1981; *A Country Such as This*, 1983; *Something to Die For*, 1991; *The Emperor's General*, 1999; *Lost Soldiers*, 2001; nonfiction—*Born Fighting: How the Scots-Irish Shaped America*, 2004

Weis, Charlie

(whyss)

Mar. 30, 1956– Football coach

Address: Athletic Dept., University of Notre Dame, Notre Dame, IN 46556

In December 2004 Charlie Weis, who never played college or professional football, was named the head football coach at his alma mater, the University of Notre Dame. Weis began his coaching career at the high-school level before becoming the special-teams assistant coach for the New York Giants of the National Football League (NFL) in 1989. With the Giants and, later, the New York Jets and New England Patriots, Weis honed his skills under two of the modern era's most celebrated football coaches, Bill Parcells and Bill Belichick. As Belichick's offensive coordinator with the Patriots, Weis helped build the team into a contemporary dynasty, the winners of three Super Bowls over four seasons, from 2001 to 2004. At the helm of the legendary Notre Dame team, Weis led the Fighting Irish to winning seasons in 2005 and 2006.

Weis's trademark is his ability to make seamless adjustments as needed to his teams' game plans, basing changes on the capabilities of his players; he is equally adept at exploiting weaknesses in the opposition's defense through imaginative plays. Mark Bavaro, a Notre Dame graduate who went on to play for the Giants, said about Weis to Heather Van Hoegarden for the *Observer* (April 22, 2005),

Jonathan Ferrey/Getty Images

a Notre Dame publication: "He's a football geek. The guy loves football . . . and you really have to study the game. . . . That's what he thrives on, especially a guy like Charlie, for some reason, he has an affection for it. Most guys don't put that effort into it; they just try to get away with the bare minimum. He keeps delving deeper and deeper looking for different ways—he's never satisfied, that's for sure, he's always coming up with something."

The second of five children and the oldest of four boys, Charlie Weis was born on March 30, 1956 in Trenton, New Jersey, and raised primarily in nearby Middlesex. Weis's mother was a nurse; his father, an accountant, had briefly played minor-league baseball for the St. Louis Cardinals organization. Because the Weis children enjoyed Wiffle ball, a variant of baseball, the family constructed a playing field in their backyard. When Weis was growing up, his enthusiasm for playing sports, particularly baseball and football, exceeded his talents; as a senior in high school, for example, he was passed over for the starting center position on the football team. He was, however, the starting catcher for the Middlesex High School baseball team.

Weis was a fan of New York's professional sports teams, including the Giants (football), the Yankees (baseball), the Rangers (hockey), and the Knicks (basketball). Beginning when he was a boy, he listened to the radio sports broadcasts of the well-known commentators Marty Glickman and Marv Albert. As he grew older, he began to think that a career in sports broadcasting might suit him well.

Weis attended the University of Notre Dame, in Notre Dame, Indiana, near South Bend. Since childhood he had watched televised highlights of the games played by the school's storied football team, the Fighting Irish. As a student at Notre Dame in the mid- to late 1970s, Weiss befriended Terry Eurick, a running back on the football team. He also became an enthusiastic fan of many of the school's other sports teams. When the football team played a home game, he was known to arrive early, in time to see the players warm up. "He was always into sports, always analyzing games, always watching every play," Weis's college roommate, Jim Benenati, recalled to Heather Van Hoegarden. Weis's ambition eventually shifted from sportscasting to coaching.

In 1978 Weis earned his bachelor's degree in speech and drama from Notre Dame. The following year he responded to a newspaper job listing for an assistant freshman football coach and teacher at Boonton High School, in New Jersey. Weis filled the vacancy and began his coaching career. In 1980 he moved to Morristown High School, becoming the freshman football team's assistant coach under John Chironna. Chironna recognized Weis's sharp intellect and diligence; according to one source, Chironna often found Weis at the school well before 7:00 a.m., working on the team's game plan. When Chironna was named the school's athletic director, he promoted Weis to head coach of the junior-varsity football team and assistant coach of the varsity squad. In addition to his duties with the football teams, Weis coached lacrosse, fencing, and basketball, leading the basketball team to a county championship one year. "The kids loved him," Chironna told Pete Thamel for the *New York Times*

(December 19, 2004). "He'd tell them: 'I never played football. I was too fat and I wasn't good enough.' That's his personality." Thamel reported that while Weis was coaching at Morristown, he was offered a business opportunity that would have increased his salary threefold—but that he did not want to leave coaching.

Weis left Morristown in 1985, when he accepted a graduate-assistant position with the Fighting Gamecocks, the football team at the University of South Carolina. There, he worked under Heach Coach Joe Morrison, formerly a New York Giants player. During his four years at South Carolina, Weis earned a reputation for his strong work ethic and versatility, serving in a variety of roles, including coach of the team's defensive backs, linebackers, and defensive ends. In 1988, his final season at South Carolina, Weis was the team's assistant recruiting coordinator. "He was an extremely, extremely hard worker. He was like a sponge regarding everything with the program," the Gamecocks quarterback at the time, Todd Ellis, told Thamel. On the field, with a record of 8–4 in both 1987 and 1988, the Gamecocks qualified for play in the Gator Bowl and Liberty Bowl. Concurrent with his position on the football team, Weis worked toward earning his master's degree in education, which he obtained from the school in 1989.

In the winter of 1989, Morrison died of a heart attack. When his replacement chose not to retain any of Morrison's staff, Weis returned to New Jersey. He landed a job as the football coach at Franklin Township High School, his first head-coaching position. The school's successful football program—gutted by the graduation of several of its premier players and the defection of its coach, Len Rivers, to Montclair High School in New Jersey— was expected to begin a rebuilding process under Weis. Franklin Township's athletic director, Pat Dolan, a Notre Dame alumnus, had been impressed by Weis's ability to implement the "run 'n' shoot" offense, a pass-heavy, multiple-receiver formation that was gaining popularity at the time in the NFL. After hiring Joe Stinson—a finalist for the head-coach position himself—to coordinate the offense, Weis gained the trust of his players and led the team to a 10–1 record and a state championship, the school's second in three years. Many of Weis's players recalled later that his having them watch films of the team's previous games and opponents' earlier games contributed heavily to Franklin Township's success. In late 2004, when he was named Notre Dame's head coach, Weis told Avani Patel for the *Chicago Tribune* (December 26, 2004) regarding his year with the Franklin team, "Of all the jobs I have ever had, and maybe being a head coach at Notre Dame will compare to this, . . . it was the most rewarding. You're a coach, you're a counselor, you're a second father, you're a community leader."

While coaching the Franklin high-school team during the 1989 season, Weis began working part-time for the New York Giants of the NFL, analyzing opponents' game film and other tape. Then, in 1990, the Giants' head coach, Bill Parcells, hired Weis as a defensive and special-teams assistant coach. That year the Giants won Super Bowl XXV, defeating the Buffalo Bills by a score of 20–19 in what many regard as one of the most dramatic Super Bowl contests of all time. (Afterward, Parcells, citing health issues, retired from his position and was replaced by Ray Handley.) With the Giants Weis became known for, among other talents, his ability to evaluate players' skills; in particular, he wrote concise and insightful scouting reports. "Everyone, even Parcells, learned to take him very seriously," Tim Rooney, the Giants' director of personnel at the time, told Thamel. "Charlie was one of the most persistent and confident people, but not in a negative way. Some people may view it as arrogance, but he's been able to back it up." For the 1991 and 1992 seasons, Weis served as the Giants' running-backs coach.

Weis left the Giants in 1993, when he was hired as the tight-end coach by the New England Patriots, again serving under Parcells, who had come out of retirement to coach the team. The Patriots had fallen on hard times, with an unimpressive roster and, as a result, an apathetic fan base; the organization's executives hoped that the hiring of Parcells would reverse the team's fortunes. Over the course of Parcells's first three seasons in New England, the Patriots' roster steadily improved, through savvy draft picks who included the running back Curtis Martin from the University of Pittsburgh in 1995. Meanwhile, Weis contributed to the team through the development of several young players. In 1993 and 1994 he was the coach of the team's tight ends, presiding over the maturity of Ben Coats, who, in 1994, set a then–NFL record with 96 pass receptions in a single season. In 1995 Weis was the team's running-backs coach and was credited with helping to develop Martin, the winner of the NFL's Offensive Rookie of the Year Award, who had set franchise records with 1,487 rushing yards gaining and 14 rushing touchdowns. Prior to the 1996 season, Parcells hired Bill Belichick, a past member of his staff and the former head coach of the Cleveland Browns, as the Patriots' new defensive coordinator. By the start of the season, Parcells's and Weis's fourth full year together in New England, the team had been rebuilt and seemed poised to make a credible bid for a Super Bowl berth. Moved to the Patriots receivers' coach position that year, Weis coached a talented core of young receivers, among them the rookie Terry Glenn, who set an NFL rookie record with 90 catches. The Patriots finished the year with an 11–5 record and won the American Football Conference (AFC) championship, then lost Super Bowl XXXI to the Green Bay Packers, by a score of 35–21. Parcells left the Patriots after the 1996 season to fill the head-coaching vacancy with the New York Jets, another team that had fallen on hard times; Weis and Belichick went with him.

In his first year with the Jets, Weis was named the team's wide-receivers coach and given the duty of calling the team's offensive plays. That meant that Parcells—and the media—would hold Weis directly responsible if a given offensive play was unsuccessful. Weis flourished in the role. In 1997 the Jets finished with a 9–7 record, marking a vast improvement over their 1–15 record of 1996. The following year Weis was promoted to the position of offensive coordinator, retaining the duties of calling plays and coaching wide receivers. Finishing with a 12–4 record in 1998, the Jets went on to defeat the Jacksonville Jaguars in the divisional round of the AFC play-offs—the team's first home play-off game since 1985—by a score of 34–24. The Jets then lost the AFC championship game, 23–10, to the Denver Broncos, who went on to win the Super Bowl. Many attributed the Jets' success that season to Weis's offense, which scored 416 points over the course of the season, the second-highest total in franchise history. Both Keyshawn Johnson and Wayne Chrebet, the team's leading wide receivers, eclipsed the 1,000-receiving-yards benchmark for the year. In 1999, Weis's third and final season with the Jets, the team finished with an 8–8 record, after their veteran quarterback Vinny Testaverde suffered an Achilles heel injury in the first week of the season.

After Parcells resigned as the Jets' head coach, at the conclusion of that season, Weis went back to New England with Belichick, who had been named the head coach of the Patriots. Weis became the offensive coordinator, a position he would maintain for six seasons. In Belichick's first season as head coach, in 2000, the Patriots finished with a mediocre 5–11 record. Then, beginning in 2001 and extending to New England's 24–21 defeat of the Philadelphia Eagles in Super Bowl XXXIX, on February 6, 2005, Belichick and Weis, together with the Patriots' defensive coordinator, Romeo Crennel, oversaw one of the most successful four-year periods of any team in NFL history. The Patriots won three Super Bowls in four years, matching a record set by the Dallas Cowboys in the early and mid-1990s. On February 3, 2002 the Patriots defeated the St. Louis Rams, 20–17, in Super Bowl XXXVI, with a last-second, 48-yard field goal by the kicker Adam Vinatieri, to win their first-ever championship. With less than two minutes remaining in the game, Weis allowed the Patriots' second-year quarterback, Tom Brady, who had replaced the injured veteran Drew Bledsoe, to drive the team boldly down the field rather than play conservatively; that move, considered risky given Brady's relative inexperience, proved to be the right choice, as Brady was able to put Vinatieri within field-goal distance. The team missed the play-offs in the 2002 season, finishing with a 9–7 record. The following season the Patriots assured themselves of the home-field advantage throughout the AFC play-offs, posting an NFL-best 14–2 regular-season record. On February 1, 2004, with four seconds remaining in the game, Vinatieri kicked a 41-yard field goal, helping his team to defeat the Carolina Panthers, 32–29, in Super Bowl XXXVIII. Vinatieri's kick and Brady's sharp passing were the crucial elements of the Patriots' victory in that dramatic, high-scoring game. The team's triumph in Super Bowl XXXIX confirmed its status as a contemporary football dynasty. Before Weis's arrival at Notre Dame, many considered his finest achievement as a coach to be his development of Brady, who is counted among the NFL's biggest stars. Speaking to Karen Guregian for the *Boston Herald* (December 21, 2003) about Weis, Brady said, "I think he's probably the best coach I ever had. He's extremely hard-working, smart, he always puts us in a great position to do well."

Meanwhile, as he played a key role in the Patriots' success, Weis weathered personal and health difficulties. With his weight exceeding 300 pounds, he tried several weight-loss programs without success. Then, in the summer of 2002, he underwent gastric bypass surgery, which is meant to limit food consumption by shrinking the stomach. Complications from the procedure resulted in a month-long stay in the hospital, where Weis fell into a coma. According to several reports, on more than one occasion Weis's wife, Maura, had a priest administer last rites to Weis. After his recovery came reports that Weis had undergone the surgery in part to improve his appearance and thereby increase his chances of landing a head-coaching position in the NFL or the college ranks. An indignant Weis told Tim Layden for *Sports Illustrated* (April 25, 2005), "My father had a heart attack at 51 and died at 56—that's what scared me. Was I concerned with my appearance? Yeah, but I was also concerned with being a fat slob, dropping dead and leaving my wife with two kids, one with special needs." The operation left him with no feeling in the lower part of his right leg; he now walks with a pronounced limp. He recovered in time to rejoin the Patriots in August 2002, at the team's training camp. In December 2004 Weis filed a malpractice suit against the five Massachusetts General Hospital surgeons who performed the June 2002 procedure; in July 2007 a Boston jury decided in favor of the surgeons.

On December 12, 2004 Weis was named the 28th head football coach at Notre Dame, agreeing to a six-year contract. (He retained his position with the Patriots through the completion of the Super Bowl in February 2006.) Boasting more than 10 NCAA (National Collegiate Athletic Association) football championships, seven winners of the Heisman Trophy (awarded annually to college football's top player), and many famous head coaches, Notre Dame's football program is the most storied in the history of college football. Notre Dame had begun a nationwide search to replace Tyrone Willingham, who had been released on November 30 of that year after accumulating a three-year record of 21–15. In assuming his new post, Weis became the first Notre Dame graduate to be handed the reins of the school's football program

since Hugh Devore, a 1934 graduate who coached the team on an interim basis in 1963. At the press conference introducing him as the Fighting Irish's head coach, Weis said, as reported by Mike Dodd for *USA Today* (December 14, 2004), "I'm here because expectations weren't met. And my job here is to raise those expectations. You are what you are, folks, and right now you're a 6–5 football team. And guess what? That's just not good enough."

The Fighting Irish began the 2005 season with a pair of impressive road victories against the University of Pittsburgh Panthers and the University of Michigan Wolverines. After the first seven games of the season, with the team's record at 5–2, Notre Dame extended Weis's contract through 2015. The new contract made Weis college football's highest-paid coach. The team finished the year at 9–3, including a loss to the Ohio State University Buckeyes in the Fiesta Bowl, on January 2, 2006. The Fighting Irish's winning play continued in 2006, with a 10–2 regular-season record that included eight straight victories. They again failed in the championship series, losing to the Louisiana State University Tigers, 41–14, in the Allstate Sugar Bowl on January 3, 2007. The Fighting Irish's 2007 regular season got off to a rocky start, with four straight losses by late September. At a press conference on September 23, following the previous day's 31–14 loss to Michigan State, Weis spoke of his "reasons for optimism," explaining, as quoted on the Notre Dame Web site, "I think probably the thing that encouraged me the most of anything was how many people in the locker room after the game showed obvious emotion on the outcome of the game. It's probably the first time this year that I saw so many players that were moved by the game, and that is, more than anything else, the one thing that people don't get a chance to see, and it's probably the greatest reason for optimism—how much they really care." In mid-November the team's 2007 record was 1–9.

Weis met his wife, Maura, live with their children, Charles Joseph and Hannah Margaret, in Indiana, near the campus of Notre Dame. Hannah is autistic; in 2003 Charlie and Maura Weis launched Hannah and Friends, a nonprofit foundation that raises awareness of autism and provides assistance to families with children suffering from that disorder.

—D.F.

Suggested Reading: *Chicago Tribune* C p1 Dec. 26, 2004; *New York Times* VIII p1+ Dec. 19, 2004; *South Bend (Indiana) Tribune* W p1 Oct. 29, 2005; *Sports Illustrated* p52+ Apr. 25, 2005; University of Notre Dame *Observer* (on-line) Dec. 12, 2005; University of Notre Dame Official Athletic Web site

Evan Agostini/Getty Images for Tribeca Film Festival

Weisberg, Jacob

(WICE-berg)

Aug. 3, 1964– Editor; author

Address: Slate*, 251 W. 57th St., 19th Fl., New York, NY 10019*

"I think of what we do as a cross between the AP [the Associated Press] and the *New Yorker*," Jacob Weisberg, the editor in chief of the on-line magazine *Slate*, told Barbara Matusow for the *Washingtonian* (May 2000). "I can respond as fast as the AP, but I can be analytical, I can be discursive." Weisberg went on to note that people could read what he wrote almost as fast as he finished writing it. *Slate* uses tools unique to the World Wide Web, such as embedded links, podcasts, and Web logs, or blogs; known for its thoughtful content, the magazine has played an influential role in the development of on-line journalism, its editors and writers having learned early in the Internet revolution how to present material specifically for Internet readers. Most of its articles, for example, are under 1,000 words, so that they can be digested quickly, and most are accompanied by links to other pertinent stories or Web sites. *Slate* now draws around six million viewers a month (some of whom visit the site more than once) and has the distinction of being the first news-related Web site not serving as an adjunct to a traditional media source to earn a profit. (It first did so in 2003, a year after Weisberg took over the top editorial position.)

Weisberg, who writes "The Big Idea," a weekly *Slate* column about politics and current affairs that runs concurrently in the *Financial Times* (which is published in Great Britain), first established himself as a writer in traditional media. Before joining *Slate* as a political correspondent, in 1996, he was on the staff of the *New Republic* during the late 1980s and early 1990s and served as a contributing writer for *New York* and *Vanity Fair* and as a reporter for *Newsweek*. He continues to maintain a voice in traditional media, contributing articles to the *New Yorker*, the *Partisan Review, Esquire, GQ*, the *Washington Monthly*, the *New York Times*, the *Washington Post*, the London *Sunday Times*, and the *Observer*. He is also the author of several books, including *In Defense of Government* (1996) and *In an Uncertain World* (2003), which he coauthored with Robert E. Rubin, who served as the U.S. secretary of the treasury under President Bill Clinton. In addition, he is the editor of the popular Bushisms series, which contain books that quote President George H. W. Bush's and President George W. Bush's ungrammatical sentences to comic effect.

Jacob M. Weisberg, the older of two sons, was born on August 3, 1964 and raised in Chicago, Illinois. His mother, Lois Weisberg, is currently Chicago's commissioner of cultural affairs; she previously held various positions with a series of non-profit organizations. His father, Bernard Weisberg, was an attorney for the American Civil Liberties Union during the 1960s and a charter member of a group of reformers called the Lakefront Liberals, a political presence in Chicago during the 1960s and 1970s; from 1985 until his death in, 1994, he was a federal judge. Weisberg's brother, Joseph, is a writer; his novel *10th Grade* and a five-part series by him for *Salon* appeared in 2002. His father passionately loved books, and every night he would read to his sons stories by Charles Dickens and others. Bernard Weisberg believed that those sessions not only nurtured his sons' affinity for literature but also helped to unify his family, because everyone shared a core body of knowledge. Weisberg has recalled his childhood home as lively. His parents' home was a meeting place and de facto boarding house for various luminaries traveling through Chicago, among them Burgess Meredith, Ralph Ellison, Dizzy Gillespie, Allen Ginsberg, Arthur C. Clarke, and Tony Bennett. "As a child, I thought everyone had an Italian poet or Indian graduate student living in a spare bedroom," Weisberg told Ron Grossman for the *Chicago Tribune* (May 4, 2007). After he graduated from high school, Weisberg attended Yale University, in New Haven, Connecticut. There, in 1986, he received an invitation to join the exclusive Yale secret society Skull and Bones from one of its members, Senator John F. Kerry of Massachusetts. "I was writing about politics, so I thought maybe he was going to give me a scoop or something," Weisberg told Robin Abcarian for the *Los Angeles Times* (March 23, 2004). "I said, 'Sen. Kerry, as a liberal, how do you justify supporting this club that doesn't admit women?'" Weisberg then declined the invitation. After he earned a bachelor's degree at Yale, he won a

Rhodes scholarship and studied for a year at New College, a division of Oxford University, in England.

From 1989 through 1994 Weisberg worked at the *New Republic* in various capacities, including associate editor, managing editor, deputy editor, and senior editor. During those years he developed a critical, often acerbic writing style and came to be recognized as a protégé of the *New Republic*'s then-editor, Michael Kinsley, whose way of writing was similar. (The style, Matusow explained, works particularly well on the Web, where "iconoclasm is the preferred mode.") Weisberg began making a name for himself in wider media circles in 1991, provoking controversy with an editorial for the *New Republic* that was called "Houses of Ill Repute." In it he described the American book-publishing industry as morally and intellectually bankrupt, complaining that it was so profit-driven that editors frequently neglected the task of improving manuscripts in the rush to get them into print and thus sometimes allowed very obvious errors to be published. While agreeing that Weisberg had made some valid points, his critics took issue with his choice of a central target: Alice Mayhew, the editorial director at Simon & Schuster. Mayhew had a multitude of supporters, among them such authors as Taylor Branch, J. Anthony Lukas, Sally Quinn, Stephen Ambrose, and Charles Murray; their letters in her defense filled over five pages of the *New Republic* when they were printed. *Publishers Weekly* also joined the fray, defending Mayhew in its pages. Some journalists, however, supported Weisberg, arguing that his article, as well as the response from Mayhew's defenders, exposed the cronyism rampant in the publishing industry. Howard Kurtz, writing for the *Washington Post* (July 21, 1991), lauded Weisberg for attacking an industry that he claimed many journalists were reluctant to criticize for fear of losing potential book deals. Kurtz also praised the *New Republic* for running the editorial despite its reliance on book publishers' advertising dollars. Later that year Weisberg published a similarly brazen criticism of the *Washington Post*. (The *Post* purchased *Slate* in 2004.)

During that period Weisberg also launched his Bushisms series, which began by documenting the malapropisms of President George H. W. Bush. The first book, *Bushisms*, co-edited with Andrew Sullivan, was published in 1992; the focus of the series shifted to George W. Bush during the 2000 presidential campaign. The Bushisms series—now published by Simon & Schuster—includes such titles as *George W. Bushisms: The Slate Book of the Accidental Wit and Wisdom of Our 43rd President* (2001), *More George W. Bushisms: More of Slate's Accidental Wit and Wisdom of Our 43rd President* (2002), *Still More George W. Bushisms: Neither in French nor in English nor in Mexican* (with Al Franken, 2003), *The Deluxe Election Edition Bushisms: The First Term, in His Own Special Words* (with Molly Ivins, 2004), and *George W. Bushisms*

V: New Ways to Harm Our Country (with Calvin Trillin, 2005). The word "Bushism" is frequently used colloquially to refer to George W. Bush's verbal slipups.

Between 1994 and 1996 Weisberg wrote about politics for *Newsweek* and the column "National Interest" for the *New York Times*. In his first book, *In Defense of Government: The Fall and Rise of Public Trust* (1996), Weisberg examined the Republican sweep in the 1994 midterm congressional elections. He described that event as the end of the progressive era of big government and argued that the Democrats' defeat was a result of the public's loss of trust in the federal government's ability to ameliorate social problems. He traced that loss to such phenomena as economic anxiety, a decline in government accountability, grandiose unfulfilled promises, poorly implemented welfare programs, and disillusionment with the consequences of the 1964 Civil Rights Act. He predicted that a more moderate progressive agenda—one in which politicians worked to cut ineffective programs, made less-dramatic promises, and established an end-point for the growth of the federal government, among other actions—would flourish and help the government to be seen as supporting the American people. Phil Gardner, who reviewed *In Defense of Government* for *Policy Studies Journal* (Spring 1997), described Weisberg's conclusions as lacking "earth-shattering ideas" but expressed the view that the book was "helpful" and "worth reading." In a negative critique published in the *National Review* (June 1996), Paul Craig Roberts took issue with Weisberg's assertion that the government should be less transparent. ("Weisberg writes that if 'white bungalow dwellers don't know' that their tax dollars are being used to move black welfare recipients onto their block, 'they are less likely to object.'") Comparing Weisberg's book to John Kenneth Galbraith's *The Good Society* (1996), Roberts remarked: "Weisberg and Galbraith confirm what we already know about liberals. They take it for granted that only their ideas and agendas are legitimate. No one else has a moral leg to stand on. . . . Galbraith and Weisberg are so confident that their higher morality puts them above criticism that they openly show their contempt and disdain for the 70 percent of their fellow citizens who are so uncouth as to prefer less government. Democracy is acceptable to liberals only if it can be manipulated to produce the right results."

In the fall of 1996, Weisberg took a position as a political correspondent at *Slate*, which Michael Kinsley had launched earlier in the year. *Slate* was initially conceived as a weekly magazine with page numbers that would be assembled like a print weekly but posted on-line rather than shipped to magazine racks. Kinsley had hoped that avoiding the costs of printing and distribution would allow *Slate* to become profitable without relying on financial backers, who might attempt to direct its political or intellectual direction. At that time on-line media were in their infancy and considered little more than novelties. Weisberg, whose first responsibility was to cover the 1996 presidential campaign, was something of an oddity among journalists. "I was one of two Internet reporters covering the presidential campaign. The other was John Heilemann of HotWired.com," Weisberg recalled to Matusow. "The campaigns didn't even know where to put us on the plane. Should they seat us with the sound guys? Nobody was paying any attention to us." Weisberg wrote a column for *Slate* called "Strange Bedfellow" and was the originator of the magazine's "Ballot Box" column.

Weisberg remained with *Slate* after the election and returned to the campaign trail for the 2000 presidential election, making him the only full-time dot-com journalist at that point to have covered more than one election. *Slate* thus found itself at the vanguard of Internet journalism, and Weisberg and his colleagues played a prominent role in the development of the form that, with its real-time updates, is now a staple of political reporting. In 2000, however, no one knew if the effort would be sustainable. "This is the Wild West," Weisberg told Matusow at the time. "Which is part of the Net's appeal. Nobody has decided what political journalism is on the Web. For those of us who are doing it, it's an unusual opportunity to be able to invent journalism in a new medium. The last time that happened was with television. Before the '60 [presidential] campaign, television lacked credibility; afterward people started taking it seriously." Weisberg collected his on-line coverage of the 2000 presidential election for the e-book *The Road to Chadville*.

In 2002 Kinsley stepped down as *Slate*'s editor in chief, and after a brief stint as interim editor, Weisberg succeeded him. In Weisberg's first year in that position, *Slate* turned a profit, providing evidence that a serious-minded on-line political magazine could be financially viable. Weisberg attributed *Slate*'s success to improved marketing and aggressive content expansion. In 2003 the site added a regular television column, a music feature, and a travel section as well as increased coverage of technology, business, art, and architecture. In May 2003 *Slate* made deals to publish the comic strip *Doonesbury* and to co-produce a show on National Public Radio called *Day to Day*. "When we started up, we looked at [*Slate*] as a print publication, but it is much closer to a broadcast property," Jack Shafer, editor at large for *Slate*, told David Carr for the *New York Times* (April 28, 2003). "*Slate* is a media product that scales very inexpensively. The cost of adding readers in print—the printing, mailing and subscriber acquisition—makes it difficult to scale. *Slate* is much more like a television station or a radio station." In May 2003 Slate won a National Magazine Award for general excellence on-line.

In 2003 Weisberg published *In an Uncertain World: Tough Choices from Wall Street to Washington,* written with Robert E. Rubin. The book details Rubin's rise from New York City investment banker to head of the U.S. Department of the Treasury, where he worked with Alan Greenspan, the head of the Federal Reserve Board, and Lawrence Summers, who was the secretary of the treasury during the last year and a half of Bill Clinton's administration. That trio were dubbed the Committee to Save the World, and *Time* magazine named the economic policies that characterized the Clinton presidency Rubinomics. David Warsh, reviewing *In an Uncertain World* for the *New York Times* (November 30, 2003), called it a "gem of [a] book" but noted that it left out discussions of the primary criticism of Rubinomics—the Clinton administration's poor relationship with Russia.

Since 2003 Weisberg has continued to work for *Slate* and has also served as a political commentator on numerous radio and television shows. In May 2007 he moderated a debate about religion, held at the New York Public Library, in Manhattan, between the Reverend Al Sharpton and Christopher Hitchens, the author of *God Is Not Great*. The debate stirred much controversy regarding a remark made by Sharpton about Mormons and Mitt Romney, a Republican presidential candidate and former governor of Massachusetts, who is a Mormon. Weisberg is married to Deborah Needleman, the editor in chief of *Domino* magazine. The couple live with their son and daughter in a loft in the Tribeca neighborhood of New York City.

—N.W.M.

Suggested Reading: *Boston Globe* E p1 June 25, 2002; *National Review* p52 June 17, 1996; *New York Times* C p1 Feb. 14, 2000, C p1 Apr. 28, 2003, VII p10 Nov. 30, 2003; *Newsweek* p61 July 8, 1991; *Policy Studies Journal* p177 Spring 1997; *Washington Post* C p2 July 21, 1991; *Washingtonian* VIII p47 May 2000

Selected Books: as writer—*In Defense of Government: The Fall and Rise of Public Trust*, 1996; *The Road to Chadville*, 2000; *In an Uncertain World* (with Robert E. Rubin), 2003; as editor—*Bushisms* (with Andrew Sullivan), 1992; *Still More George W. Bushisms: Neither in French nor in English nor in Mexican* (with Al Franken), 2003; *The Deluxe Election Edition Bushisms: The First Term, in His Own Special Words* (with Molly Ivins), 2004; *George W. Bushisms V: New Ways to Harm Our Country* (with Calvin Trillin), 2005

Bruce Bennett, courtesy of the Houston Ballet

Welch, Stanton

Oct. 15, 1969– Artistic director of the Houston Ballet; dancer; choreographer

Address: Houston Ballet, 1921 W. Bell St., Houston, TX 77019

"Choreography was part of what I did as soon as I started dancing," Stanton Welch, the artistic director of the Houston Ballet since 2003, told Wayne Lee Gay for the *Fort Worth (Texas) Star-Telegram* (September 17, 2003). "Dancing and creating are part of the same thing to me." Welch, a native of Australia whose parents were both celebrated ballet dancers, began his training in classical ballet in the mid-1980s, at the relatively late age of 17. In 1989 he joined the Australian Ballet Company; he became a soloist there within a few years and a resident choreographer in 1995. He has also created dances on commission, or restaged dances, for troupes including the San Francisco Ballet, the Birmingham (England) Ballet, American Ballet Theatre, the Houston Ballet, the Royal Danish Ballet, the Singapore Dance Theatre, and the Moscow Dance Theatre. Since late 2001 he has held the position of artistic associate of BalletMet Columbus, in Ohio. Kevin McKenzie, a renowned dancer, choreographer, and longtime artistic director of the American Ballet Theatre, told Molly Glentzer for the *Houston (Texas) Chronicle* (February 9, 2003) that Welch is "steeped in ballet, has a fresh and energetic approach to the art form, and is an enormously inventive choreographer."

Welch's short pieces include *The Three of Us*, *Of Blessed Memory*, *Maninyas*, *Taiko*, *Powder*, *Onset*, *Ander*, *Indigo*, *Bruiser*, *Blindness*, *Bolero*,

Nosotros, and *Clear*; his full-length works include *Madame Butterfly*, *Cinderella*, *Don Quixote*, *The Sleeping Beauty*, *Tales of Texas*, and *Swan Lake*. "All of my ballets, even those that don't look like they do, have a plot," Welch told Rita Felciano for *Dance Magazine* (March 1, 1999). "Story comes foremost—above pretty feet, great lifts, everything," he told Molly Glentzer for the *Houston Chronicle* (September 15, 2002). Under Welch's guidance, staff members of the Houston Ballet's school, the Ben Stevenson Academy, search for potential dancers in Houston public schools, with the aim of nurturing home-grown talent for the troupe. Selected youngsters attend dance classes on scholarships. Welch hopes that someday, on international tours, the Houston Ballet will present only works that are "new and unique to us, with commissioned scores and design, with dancers from our school," as he told Glentzer (February 9, 2003). "And every other company is coveting those ballets."

The first of the two children of Garth Welch and Marilyn Jones, Stanton Welch was born on October 15, 1969 in Melbourne, Australia. His father and mother were stars of the Borovansky Australian Ballet Company before becoming principal dancers with its successor, the Australian Ballet Company, in its inaugural year (1962). His mother served as artistic director of the Australian Ballet from 1979 to 1981 and founded the Dancers Company for third-year students of the Australian Ballet School; she has since taught extensively outside Australia as well. Welch's father served as artistic director of the West Australian Ballet from 1980 to 1982; he, too, has taught widely, and he has choreographed many dances. "Mom has a beautiful line and incredible technique as a dancer, but I always thought of her as more of an actress than a dancer," Welch told Wayne Lee Gay. "My father gave me much of the same, and also instilled in me a great love of classical music and made me feel that classical music is very important." Welch's brother, Damien, has danced with the Australian Ballet since 1992 and as a principal there since 1998.

Stanton Welch made his dance debut as a preschooler, but for years afterward he had no desire to study dance. "I saw the world of dance from backstage, and what I saw was very destructive and traumatic," he told Barbara Zuck for the *Columbus (Ohio) Dispatch* (October 20, 2002). "It was about long rehearsals, bad reviews, injuries and visiting Mum in the hospital with a blown Achilles tendon." After Welch's parents retired from active performance, they moved with their sons to Sydney, Australia, where they opened the Marilyn Jones and Garth Welch School of Ballet. During his adolescence and early teens, Welch attended ballets as a spectator. "That's when I fell in love with the art form," he told Wayne Lee Gay. As a teenager he worked after school as a dresser at the Sydney Opera House. In 1986, at 17, Welch began taking classes at his parents' school. "I think it was a good thing that I became a dancer when I was an adult, because it became a very conscious, deliberate decision," he told Rick Nelson for the Minneapolis, Minnesota, *Star Tribune* (October 7, 2005). Welch showed unusual natural talent as a dancer, and within a year he had entered the prestigious San Francisco Ballet School, in California, on a scholarship. Helgi Tomasson, the artistic director of the school, invited him to join the San Francisco Ballet after one year of training. Instead, in 1989 he joined the Australian Ballet and soon became a principal there. Among his early roles were those of Des Grieux in Kenneth MacMillan's *Manon*; Lensky in John Cranko's *Eugene Onegin*; Alan Strang in Domy Reiter-Soffer's *Equus*; and Camille in Ronald Hynd's *The Merry Widow*.

Welch soon showed great promise as a choreographer as well. His first dance, *Hades*, earned praise from Maina Gielgud, the artistic director of the Australian Ballet at that time. In 1990 Welch choreographed *The Three of Us*, his first commissioned work for the Australian Ballet. The following year he created *Of Blessed Memory* (1991), for which he was voted best new choreographer by readers of the British magazine *Dance & Dancers* in 1992. Also in 1992 Welch received a Churchill Traveling Fellowship from the Winston Churchill Memorial Trust of Australia. The fellowship enabled him to serve an apprenticeship with the choreographer Jiri Kylian and study with two others, Lester Horton and Martha Graham, in New York City, where he was introduced to tap dancing and techniques connected with jazz and African dancing. He won the 1992 New South Wales (Australia) Young Achiever Award. In 1993 he choreographed *Before the Rain* for that year's Dancers Company tour.

For the Australian Ballet, Welch choreographed *Divergence* (1994), set to Bizet's *Suites L'Arlésienne*. Described as "sexy and naughty" by Natasha Gauthier in the *Ottawa Citizen* (May 4, 2006), "rivetingly physical and witty" and "full of playfully antagonistic minidramas" by Molly Glentzer (February 28, 2004), and "brilliantly inventive" with "fiendishly difficult things to dance" by Rita Felciano, *Divergence* features a "central figure that acts as catalyst," as Welch explained to Jean Battey Lewis for the *Washington Times* (October 9, 1994). "But everyone at some point is the person you're watching."

In 1995 Welch was named one of the Australian Ballet's resident choreographers. That same year he created his first full-length piece for the company, the ballet *Madame Butterfly*. Set in the 19th century and based on an opera by Giacomo Puccini, *Madame Butterfly* portrays a tragic love story about a Japanese geisha, Cio-Cio-San, and an American seaman, Lieutenant Pinkerton. In an effort to make the motivations of the characters more believable, Welch added scenes not found in Puccini's version. One of his signature works, Welch's *Madame Butterfly* is in the repertoires of companies including the Houston Ballet, the Atlanta Bal-

let, the Boston Ballet, the National Ballet of Canada, and the Singapore Dance Theater. Another work commissioned by the Australian Ballet, Welch's *Corroboree* (the name of an ancient Australian aboriginal ceremony), debuted at the 1995 United We Dance Festival in San Francisco. Welch choreographed *Many Colours Blue* (1995) for the Dancers Company tour and, on commission, *Maninyas* (1996) for the San Francisco Ballet. The year 1996 also marked the premiere of his dance *Red Earth*, created for and presented by the Australian Ballet.

In 1997, for his second full-length production for the Australian Ballet, Welch choreographed a work based on the tale of Cinderella, set to music by Sergei Prokofiev. Danced at its premiere by all 60 members of the company as well as Welch's mother and brother, Welch's *Cinderella* is "an innovative mixture of classical and contemporary choreography," Katrina Creer wrote for the Sydney *Sunday Telegraph* (March 16, 1997). "I don't find that I am restricted by classical ballet," Welch told Rita Felciano. "Just because you have pointe shoes on a woman doesn't limit your work. You can bring anything to classical ballet; it's completely, exhilaratingly free." In Welch's version, Cinderella is "no shrinking violet but a tough little cookie in a gamine haircut who gives as good as she gets, socking her stepsisters . . . when she can get away with it," according to Felciano, and Cinderella chooses to marry not Prince Charming—who is portrayed as fully human rather than as an idealized character—but one of his servants. "It really bothered me even as a child, the idea that this gorgeous, beautiful, rich person would come along and sweep you off your feet," Welch told Louise Nunn for the Adelaide, Australia, *Advertiser* (October 1, 1997). "I guess I was more interested in exploring the idea that one day your prince will come along but he may not be rich, or attractive . . . he might be short, or tall, or whatever. The important thing is that he is a prince to you."

During the next few years, Welch created *Powder* and *Onsket*, for the Birmingham Royal Ballet and the Danish Royal Ballet, respectively, in 1998, and *Indigo* (1999) and *Bruiser* (2000) for the Houston Ballet. In *Indigo*, which uses music by the Baroque composer Antonio Vivaldi, eight dancers offer a "kaleidoscope of classic movement, dance mannerism, emotion, and fleeting suggestions of relationships," all of which demonstrates Welch's "unerring command of a ballet's structure," according to Clive Barnes, writing for *Dance Magazine* (June 1, 1999). Also in 1999 Welch returned to the San Francisco Ballet to direct the premiere of *Taiko*, his second work for the company, and he reworked *Maninyas* for the Singapore Dance Theatre and *Of Blessed Memory* for the Colorado Ballet. He staged *A Time for Dance* for the Royal Ballet School in London, England, in 2000.

Welch's *Fingerprints* (2000; the name sometimes appears as *Finger Prints*) was the product of a rare joint commission by four regional ballet companies: the Tulsa Ballet Theater, in Oklahoma; the Cincinnati Ballet, in Ohio; the Fort Worth/Dallas Ballet, in Texas; and the Washington Ballet, in the nation's capital. *Fingerprints* offers Welch's take on an aspect of chaos theory popularly known as the butterfly effect, according to which a seemingly insignificant event, such as the flapping of a butterfly's wings, can lead to a major event, such as a tornado, in a far distant place. For *Fingerprints*, Welch used music from *Pieces of Africa*, a composition created by the members of the Kronos Quartet in collaboration with seven African composer/performers. In 2000 Welch made his debut in Moscow, Russia, with a new work called *Green*, created for the ballerina Nina Ananiashvili and principal dancers of the Bolshoi Ballet, and in Atlanta, Georgia, with another new dance, *The Garden of Mirth*, choreographed for the Atlanta Ballet.

Welch's *Clear*, set to concertos for violin and oboe by Bach, premiered during the American Ballet Theatre's 2001–02 season in New York City. "The choreography is explosive, fiercely danced" by seven men and a single ballerina, as Anna Kisselgoff wrote in a review for the *New York Times* (October 30, 2001). She continued, "*Clear* is a work that uses classical technique but not classical style. . . . It explores the academic dance idiom in depth. Mr. Welch knows how to play around with that idiom: *Clear* has a contemporary look but not the self-consciousness about the ballet vocabulary sometimes seen in . . . works by modern-dance choreographers. This naturalness extends to the way Mr. Welch has matched the ferocity of his fast footwork with the delicate sound of the violin and oboe in Bach. . . . Music and dance fused." Kisselgoff also wrote, "As a choreographer Mr. Welch, 32, is something of a chameleon. When the Australian Ballet introduced his work to Americans at the Kennedy Center in Washington in 1994, the roots of his British-derived classical training were obvious. But so was his rebellion against tradition. *Clear* is a variation on that theme; the early promise is being fulfilled."

Welch was one of four choreographers whom the American Ballet Theatre commissioned to create dances for *Within You Without You: A Tribute to George Harrison*, which premiered in 2002. Each of the six new works was set to a song written by Harrison, a member of the Beatles who died in 2001. Welch's contributions were *Something*, for a male dancer and a female who merely stands and watches, and *Isn't It a Pity?*, for 10 males and one ballerina. Also in 2002 the BalletMet Columbus, in Ohio, recruited Welch to serve as an artistic associate. *Don Quixote*, a full-length ballet that he created for that company, premiered in 2003. Based loosely on the classic novel by Miguel de Cervantes, the choreography incorporated "nonclassical movement and magical theatricality," according to Wilma Salisbury, writing for *Dance Magazine* (September 2003), and as a whole it "demonstrated [Welch's] ability to produce a small-scale story ballet with wit, energy, and audience appeal."

In July 2003 Welch succeeded Ben Stevenson as the artistic director of the Houston Ballet. With its 52-member troupe, state-of-the-art facilities, and operating budget of nearly $13 million, the Houston Ballet had by then joined the ranks of the nation's most revered companies. One of its chief distinctions, in Welch's view, was its imaginative revivals of classic story-ballets. "What makes [this company] different is that artistry is as important as technique," Welch told Wayne Lee Gay. "So often, one is sacrificed for the other." K.C. Patrick, the editor of *Dance Magazine*, echoing the sentiments of some other dance insiders, told Molly Glentzer (February 9, 2003), "[Welch is] versatile and anchored in the classics but has a vision, and he's willing to work with others, so it won't be a one-man show. But his youth does raise a few eyebrows." Cecil C. Conner Jr., the Houston Ballet's managing director, told Marene Gustin for *Dance International* (Winter 2004), "What Stanton brings to the company is a fresh eye to the creative process, both choreographically and for marketing."

Early on, in an effort to diversify the company, Welch rehired Barbara Bears, one of its former ballerinas, who had given birth in 2002. "Dancers who've had babies dance differently, with a different acting scope, a different approach," he explained to Glentzer (February 9, 2003). "I really want to make ballet grow up that way, so ladies know they can have babies and come back." Welch enlivened the company's training regimen by inviting former ballet dancers to teach master classes, and he hired Maina Gielgud, who most recently had been the artistic director of the Royal Danish Ballet, to serve as an artistic associate for two years. Welch told Glentzer (February 9, 2003) that "change needs to be gradual. Any sudden veer to the right or left throws off what you've already got on track. I'm going to build my artistic team and try to excite and encourage great dancers to come, but it will be very gradual. It hopefully will be something people will start to notice, but never be able to pinpoint. Then 10 years from now, they'll go, 'Wow.'"

The three acts of *Tales of Texas* (2004), Welch's first evening-length dance for the Houston Ballet (commissioned before he became its artistic director) are called "Big Sky," with music by Aaron Copland; "Cline Time," set to Patsy Cline songs; and "Pecos," about the mythical Pecos Bill, set to a commissioned score by Matthew Pierce. *Tales of Texas* explores "the idea of Texans as pioneers, journeying from a very civilized environment to this land that is harsh," as Welch explained to Ingrid Grobey for *Texas Monthly* (March 2004). "I wanted to illustrate how tremendously difficult it must have been for those people to find a way of learning to farm the land . . . and the complete cultural change that goes along with that struggle." "Choreographically this ballet is way Stanton," Lauren Anderson, a principal dancer with the Houston Ballet and a native Texan, told Christie Taylor for the *New York Times* (March 11, 2004).

"He's a hopeless romantic. In one way when it comes to his choreography, he doesn't have a heart because it's really hard. But when it comes to the story, his emotions run deep." Welch later choreographed *Bolero* and *Blindness* (both in 2004) and *Nosotros* (2005) for the Houston Ballet. "I am constantly amazed at the ebb and flow of where I am being led," he told Joseph Carman for *Playbill Arts* (March 7, 2007, on-line). "I am a big believer in instinctively knowing where the next piece needs to go. My ballets are all quite different. I like to go from rough dancing—rolling on the floor—to pure, classical pieces to story ballets." In the aftermath of Hurricane Katrina, which devastated large parts of several U.S. Gulf Coast states in the summer of 2005, the Houston Ballet offered free dance classes and performances to victims of the storm who had been relocated to the Houston area.

In the fall of 2005, Welch returned to Sydney to create a lavish rendition of *The Sleeping Beauty* for the Australian Ballet. The production required "258 costumes that took 30,000 work hours to create, plus another 18,000 hours for props and scenery," according to a writer for the *Age* (September 11, 2005, on-line), an Australian publication. Even more ambitious was his version of Tchaikovsky's *Swan Lake*, which premiered in Houston in 2006. To make *Swan Lake* relevant to contemporary audiences, Welch made changes to the story, "the most critical of them," as William Littler noted for the *Toronto (Ontario) Star* (March 11, 2006), "showing the prince falling in love not, as fairytale tradition dictates, with the feathered swan queen Odette but with the human princess she originally was." "There's not an ultimate version of *Swan Lake* that hangs in a museum and everyone comes to see," Welch told Molly Glentzer for the *Houston Chronicle* (February 19, 2006). "That's what makes it so exciting to work with today. It's absolutely limitless." Marene Gustin, in a review for the *Houston Press* (March 2, 2006), called Welch's *Swan Lake* "beautiful, contemporary, and dramatically interesting."

Welch choreographed three dances that were scheduled to have world premieres during the Houston Ballet's 2007–08 season: *The Four Seasons*, set to music by Antonio Vivaldi; a ballet set to George Gershwin's Piano Concerto in F; and *A Doll's House Story*, set to a composition for percussion ensemble by István Márta.

Openly gay, Welch lives with Gene Walsh, a retired New York City firefighter. Welch has helped his partner recover from a crippling stroke that he suffered several years ago.

—D.J.K.

Suggested Reading: *Age* (on-line) Sep. 11, 2005; *Australian* p12 Aug. 26, 2003; Australian Ballet Web site; BalletMet.org; *Columbus (Ohio) Dispatch* G p1+ Oct. 20, 2002; *Dance International* (on-line) Winter 2004; *Dance Magazine* p88+ Mar. 1, 1999, p78 June 1, 1999; Houston Ballet Web site; *Houston (Texas)*

Chronicle Zest p16 Sep. 15, 2002, p8+ Feb. 9, 2003; (Minneapolis, Minnesota) *Star Tribune* E p1+ Oct. 7, 2005; *Ottawa (Ontario) Citizen* F p1+ May 4, 2006; *Texas Monthly* p1+ Mar. 2004

Selected Ballets: as choreographer—*Hades*, 1989; *The Three of Us*, 1990; *Of Blessed Memory*, 1991; *Before the Rain*, 1993; *Divergence*, 1994; *Madame Butterfly*, 1995; *Corroboree*, 1995; *Many Colours Blue*, 1995; *Maninyas*, 1996, *Red Earth*, 1996; *Cinderella*, 1997; *Powder*, 1998; *Onsket*, 1998; *Indigo*, 1999; *Bruiser*, 2000; *A Time for Dance*, 2000; *Fingerprints*, 2000; *Green*, 2000; *The Garden of Mirth*, 2000; *Clear*, 2001; *Within You Without You: A Tribute to George Harrison*, 2002; *Don Quixote*, 2003; *Bolero*, 2004; *Blindness*, 2004; *Tales of Texas*, 2004; *Nosotros*, 2005; *The Sleeping Beauty*, 2005; *Swan Lake*, 2006; *The Four Seasons*, 2007

Courtesy of Fatal1ty

Wendel, Johnathan

Feb. 26, 1981– Cyberathlete

Address: c/o Auravision Inc., 4505 Las Virgenes Rd., Suite 207, Calabasas, CA 91302

The playing of video games, often called simply "gaming," is an area in which the U.S.—honorably or lamentably, depending on one's viewpoint—lags behind other parts of the world. In countries including South Korea, China, Russia, and Malaysia, gaming is an established industry, and "professional gamers are used to six-figure salaries and living like rock stars," as Tamara Chuang wrote for the *Orange County (California) Register* (April 17, 2006, on-line). In the past several years, gaming has made great strides toward being recognized as a professional sport in the U.S., but there are still only a handful of gamers, or "cyberathletes," successful enough to play video games for a living. The most prominent of them, and the one many hope will do much to boost the sport's national profile, is Johnathan Wendel, known within the gaming community by his screen name: Fatal1ty (pronounced "fatality"). His Web site boasts that Fatal1ty has "helped change the image of the video gamer into one of a well rounded, well spoken and dedicated professional." A professional gamer since 1999, Wendel is the first to win championships in five first-person shooter games (in which the player shares the point of view of the game's character): *Quake III, Alien vs. Predator 2, Unreal Tournament 2003* and *2004, Doom 3,* and *Painkiller.* He has taken home, by his estimation, over $300,000 in prize money.

Like other professional sports, gaming is run by several sanctioning bodies, or leagues. Gaming leagues earn proceeds in the same ways as more established sports leagues, albeit on a smaller scale: through sponsorships, player fees, spectator admission tickets, and television contracts. The most prominent of the gaming leagues, the Cyberathlete Professional League (CPL), founded in 1997, hosts competitions around the world. Beginning modestly, CPL has gone on to stage tournaments that "have become flashy, big-money affairs," as Jimmy Lee Shreeve wrote for the London *Independent* (March 1, 2006), and that award millions of dollars annually in prize money. The tournaments are played on super-charged personal computers, rather than arcade machines or gaming consoles such as Xbox or Playstation, and are sponsored mainly by technology companies such as Jitachi, Intel, and the processor manufacturer Nvidia. Wendel has become an icon on the gaming circuit, and advertisers recognize his appeal; computer companies sponsor Wendel heavily, paying the costs of his frequent international tournament appearances, and he has been featured on ESPN, USA Networks, the Discovery Channel, the CBS program *60 Minutes,* and MTV. He oversees his own brand of gaming products, in partnership with several makers of computer parts. Like others in the emerging gaming industry, he looks to more established sports, such as baseball and football—and to the extra-athletic endeavors of those sports' star athletes—for models on which to base his own career. "It's kind of like what Michael Jordan is to basketball," he told David Becker for CNET News.com (February 10, 2004). "My name's become kind of valuable, and I want to make sure that if it's on a product, it's really done to my specifications." "For the new millennium comes a new sportsman, the e-sportsman," Wendel's marketing adviser, Mark Walden of Auravision, a computer company that produces several Fatal1ty brand products, told Steve Kroft for *60 Minutes* (August 6, 2006). "So

he's the first cyberathlete, so to speak. You know, you look back . . . , and there had to be somebody at the turn of the century that played baseball. There had to be a Babe Ruth and a Ty Cobb. There has to be Johnathan Fatal1ty Wendel."

Johnathan Wendel was born on February 26, 1981 in Independence, Missouri. When he was five his father, who owned a billiards parlor and worked in a factory, gave him a Nintendo gaming system, on which he played his first video game, Ikari Warriors; he eventually collected around 120 games. "Gaming was just something I did with my friends," he told Kevin Raub for *American Way* magazine (May 15, 2006, on-line). "We had nothing else to do. We were bored half to death." Growing up, Wendel also played and excelled at numerous sports, including baseball, football, soccer, tennis, and pool. "Most top gamers were pretty good athletes in high school," Wendel told Becker. "It's a lot of the same skills. It's about being competitive and thinking fast and knowing how to win—it's not about sitting at a computer all day." He also became adept at playing some of the earliest electronic games. "I'm totally into arcade games and all that stuff," he told Becker. "I was a huge Mortal Kombat fan back in the day. I got so good, I could put one quarter in and play for two or three hours." When he was 13, Wendel's parents divorced, and he moved in with his mother, who works, like Wendel's stepfather, on a Ford Motor Co. assembly line. On several occasions while Wendel was growing up, his mother, worried that he was spending too much time playing games, kept him from competing in tournaments; when he was 13 she told him he could not enter the junior national pool tournament, and when he was in high school, she forbade him from entering a gaming tournament with a $10,000 grand prize. Wendel felt oppressed by his mother's rules. "I always thought I had the talent and skill to do whatever I wanted to do, but I was never given the shot to do what I wanted to do," he told Raub. "I realized I had to take things into my own hands and do it myself."

For Wendel, that meant moving into his father's basement after his 18th birthday. That arrangement proved similarly stifling, as his father also pressured him to concentrate less on games and more on work and school. (Wendel was then working part-time at a private golf course and studying at DeVry University, in Kansas City.) Wendel persuaded his father to make a deal: Wendel could compete in the 1999 Cyberathlete Professional League Frag 3 championships; if he took home any prize winnings, his father would allow him to continue gaming, and if not, Wendel would give up the pursuit altogether and attend school full-time. At the tournament Wendel came in third—and took home $4,000. His performance earned him an all-expenses-paid trip to represent the U.S. in the 2000 *Quake III* world championships, held in Sweden. There, he "dominated the whole thing," as he recalled to Raub, defeating a dozen of the world's top *Quake III* players. Shortly afterward he decided to pursue gaming as a profession. "So I'm sitting in my kitchen at home," he told Bobby White for the *Boston Globe* (January 23, 2005), "and I'm still going to school and everything, and I'm thinking, 'Man, like, if I really want to take advantage of this, I should probably quit school.'"

In 2000, his first year as a professional gamer, Wendel—then 19—made $100,000. Still, he recalled to Chuang, "I just felt like I wasn't being paid what I was worth. I saw a much bigger picture. Why don't I create my own brand and sell my own product?" That decision led to the creation, in 2002, of Fatal1ty Inc., a company that currently sells around a dozen gaming-related products. (At 15 Wendel had adopted the gaming screen name Fatal1ty, a reference to "fatality," a term for a form of killing in the computer game Mortal Kombat; the "1" is in honor of the T1 high-speed Internet connection that greatly improved his standing in worldwide competition.) The first item Wendel produced was a 14-by-17-inch mouse pad, which was bigger than many mouse pads then in use and which "improved my game," as Wendel noted to Chuang. When he called various companies to offer them the chance to market the product using his name, he discovered that many of the people he spoke to were familiar with his gaming alias. "Most people were like, 'Whoa. I'm talking to Fatal1ty? Is this really Fatal1ty? You don't have people doing this for you?'" he said to Chuang. In five months Wendel earned $50,000, investing some of the money in his company and using another portion to sponsor five players on the Fatal1ty gaming team, Inevitable Fate. Wendel originally distributed the mouse pads himself, mailing them from his local post office. "I loved the business side of it, but at the same time, I wanted to keep gaming and winning," he said to Chuang. He soon partnered with the California-based computer company Auravision—makers of an illuminated keyboard that is now a product in the Fatal1ty line—and turned over daily operations of Fatal1ty Inc. to them. He also formed deals with several other companies, which now produce other items in the Fatal1ty line. Wendel reportedly plans to market clothing, hats, and shoes in addition to gaming equipment. "I knew what my vision was at 22, to create my own brand," he told Chuang in 2006. "I envisioned all this would happen. Being only 25 now, my dreams have come true so quickly." Auravision's co-founder, Steve Gould, told Chuang, "Johnathan is the first name and face and still the only one to be put on a computer product. I compare him to the business model of [the famed skateboarder and businessman] Tony Hawk. If you ask who is the second skateboarder, nobody knows."

Wendel has competed on six continents in an estimated 40 countries. He follows a daily regimen of intensive video-game playing and running three to five miles. He also plays tennis often. Asked how he trains for tournaments, Wendel told Becker, "I get to the city a couple of weeks before the tournament . . . and basically all that time before

the event I'm training, practicing. I prepare myself just like a regular athlete would in a real sport—eight or 12 hours a day, every day." "I had three goals when I started this," he told Raub. "I wanted to travel overseas playing video games. I wanted to become the number one gamer in the world. And the third was when I became number one, I wouldn't become the stereotypical, arrogant jerk that you'd think number one would be. I was able to accomplish them all in about six months." Wendel lives in what Matt Sedensky described in the *Pittsburgh Post-Gazette* (November 21, 2005) as an "unremarkable suburban ranch" in Overland Park, Kansas, a home that "offers no glimpse of his executive-level salary." He spends most of his time traveling to compete and promote his products. The absence of such "glimpses" is perhaps due to the fact that "I don't really have time to indulge in anything," as Wendel told Sedensky. "I'm so dedicated and so determined to be the best I don't have time to indulge in other stuff."

Wendel has competed on six continents in an estimated 40 countries. He is known to follow a daily regimen that consists of intensive video-game playing and running three to five miles. He also plays tennis often. Asked how he trains for tournaments, Wendel told Becker, "I get to the city a couple of weeks before the tournament . . . and basically all that time before the event I'm training, practicing. I prepare myself just like a regular athlete would in a real sport—eight or 12 hours a day, every day." "I had three goals when I started this," he told Raub. "I wanted to travel overseas playing video games. I wanted to become the number one gamer in the world. And the third was when I became number one, I wouldn't become the stereotypical, arrogant jerk that you'd think number one would be. I was able to accomplish them all in about six months." Wendel lives in what Matt Sedensky described in the *Pittsburgh Post-Gazette* (November 21, 2005) as an "unremarkable suburban ranch" in Overland Park, Kansas, a home that "offers no glimpse of his executive-level salary." He spends most of his time traveling to compete and promote his products. The absence of such "glimpses" is perhaps due to the fact that "I don't really have time to indulge in anything," as Wendel told Sedensky. "I'm so dedicated and so determined to be the best I don't have time to indulge in other stuff." In August 2007 he was honored with the first Lifetime Achievement Award in the four-year history of electronic sports (commonly referred to as eSports). As of mid-October of that year, he was serving as the spokesperson of the Championship Gaming Series.

—M.B.

Suggested Reading: *American Way* (on-line) May 15, 2006; *Boston Globe* C p5 Jan. 23, 2005; *Los Angeles Times* Ap1 Nov. 19, 2005; *Orange County (California) Register* (on-line) Apr. 17, 2006

Wendrich, Willeke

(WEN-dreekh, WILL-eh-keh)

Sep. 13, 1961– Egyptologist; archaeologist; educator

Address: UCLA, Dept. of Near Eastern Languages and Cultures, 3235 Hershey Hall, Mail Code 151105, P.O. Box 951511, Los Angeles, CA 90095-1511

As an associate professor of Egyptian archaeology at the University of California at Los Angeles (UCLA), Willeke Wendrich focuses on both the physical remnants of cultures that vanished thousands of years ago and on state-of-the-art, up-to-the-minute computer technologies that enable her and many others in her field to disseminate descriptions of their discoveries far faster than has ever before been possible. Wendrich has participated in many archaeological excavations, sometimes as leader or co-leader, in el-Amarna, Qasr Ibrim, Abu Sh'ar, Hierakonpolis, Elephantine Island, Berenike, and the Giza Plateau, all in Egypt, as well as in Yemen and Turkey. She is also the editor in chief of a UCLA project whose goal is to make available on-line a peer-reviewed encyclopedia dedicated to all aspects of ancient Egypt. Scheduled to become available to the public in 2008 with, initially, about 600 articles, the *UCLA Encyclopedia of Egyptology*, to be known by the acronym *UEE*, will eventually contain around 4,000 entries, in both English and Arabic. On another front, Wendrich is the faculty director of UCLA's Digital Humanities Incubator Group, whose aim is to promote research projects in the humanities— the many pursuits (such as art, literature, linguistics, history, religion, philosophy, politics, and economics as well as archaeology) that illuminate the human condition and human relationships. Nowadays, Wendrich wrote in an e-mail message to *Current Biography*, people pay "too little attention" to the humanities, although the areas encompassed by that term include "the core activities . . . that enable human co-existence: communication, intercultural understanding and historical awareness." While engineering and the sciences "are of course important disciplines," she continued, "I feel that at present the contribution of the humanities is grossly underestimated. The underrating of the humanities is linked to the definition of 'value' as 'monetary value.' With the development of digital humanities we are exploring new avenues of communication: the Web is preeminently suited to support and stimulate the core tasks of the humanities. Sharing information, providing access through well-developed databases, and the use of new media are invigorating tools to include exponentially more people in the world's knowledge base." Wendrich is a faculty member of UCLA's Cotsen Institute of Archaeology. Concurrently, for four years beginning in 2000, when she

joined the Department of Near Eastern Languages and Cultures at UCLA, she held a postdoctoral fellowship from the Department of Archaeology at Leiden University, in the Netherlands.

The oldest of four siblings, Willemina ("Willeke") Zwanida Wendrich was born on September 13, 1961 in Haarlem, the Netherlands, and grew up in the seaside town of Zandvoort. ("Willeke" is a diminutive of "Willemina"; Wendrich prefers the former and has published under that name since 1999.) Her father, Hans Wendrich, worked as a police officer and later as the director of a community-housing corporation; her mother, Fransje Wendrich-Brouwer, taught vocational classes at the junior-high-school level for prospective waitresses, cooks' assistants, and shop assistants. Wendrich recalled to an interviewer for *Backdirt* (Fall/Winter 2001), a Cotsen Institute newsletter, "From a very young age, I felt attracted to history, in particular, Egyptian history. As a 5-year-old my favorite route was through 'the old streets' [of my town]. Egypt had a similar inexplicable attraction." During her high school years, she lived in Texel, an island off the northern coast of the Netherlands, where she met her future husband, Hans Barnard. In 1979 Wendrich enrolled at the University of Amsterdam. Concerned that specializing in a subject as "narrow" as Egyptology would leave her without prospects of employment, as she told the *Backdirt* interviewer, she majored in the history of religion. In addition to becoming proficient in three required languages—Latin, Greek, and Hebrew—she learned Egyptian hieroglyphs, for her own satisfaction. She also took courses in archaeology and the philosophy of science. At the suggestion of a friend, she embarked on a small project devoted to archaeological basketry. That unusual subject led to her acceptance as a member of what she described for *Backdirt* as "perhaps the most famous archaeological project in Egypt": the excavation at Amarna (in ancient times, Akhet-Aton, the capital during the reign of Pharaoh Achnaton), directed since the late 1970s by the British Egyptologist and archaeologist Barry Kemp, under the auspices of the Egypt Exploration Society. To prepare for her fieldwork at Amarna, conducted in 1987, she approached a half-dozen experts in such fields as fiber identification and conservation, whose generosity in sharing their knowledge with her struck her as "quite remarkable," as she put it to *Backdirt*. (She returned to Amarna twice, in 1989 and 1992.) At the University of Amsterdam, she earned a B.A. degree in 1986 and an M.A. in 1988, both in the history of religion.

In 1989 Wendrich embarked on doctoral work in archaeology and Egyptology at the CNWS (Centre of Non-Western Studies) Research School for Asian, African, and Amerindian Studies at Leiden University. She was "shocked," she told *Backdirt*, when her archaeology adviser judged the paper she had written for Kemp's *Amarna Reports* about her findings in Egypt to be "the work of a well-meaning amateur." Wendrich responded by studying even

Reed Hutchinson, courtesy of UCLA
Willeke Wendrich

more assiduously than she had in the past. One year later, the same adviser told her after attending a lecture she had given, "You have become an archaeologist"—"the best compliment he could give," as Wendrich told *Backdirt.* For her doctoral dissertation, Wendrich compared basketry produced more than 3,000 years ago with corresponding materials made at the same sites by contemporary Egyptians; she found many similarities in the ancient and recent items. A 60-minute video about present-day basket makers accompanied her text, entitled *The World According to Basketry: An Ethno-archaeological Interpretation of Basketry Production in Egypt.* Wendrich received her Ph.D. in 1999.

During the decade beginning in 1989, in addition to her graduate work, Wendrich planned and designed, by herself or with others, a number of museum exhibitions, among them one at the Netherlands-Flemish Institute in Cairo (NVIC, previously named the Netherlands Institute for Archaeology and Arabic Studies) and another at the visitors' center set up in connection with the Ottoman Fort preservation project in Quseir, on the Red Sea, in Egypt. She also co-organized several conferences, including two at the NVIC, and, from 1992 to 1996, served as a freelance course leader in Egyptology for the Leiden Institute for Cultural Studies. From 1995 to 1999, while stationed at the NVIC, she held the position of assistant professor of Egyptology as a member of the Leiden University faculty. Also, for eight years beginning in 1994, with permission from Egypt's Supreme Council on Antiquities, she co-directed, with Steven Sidebotham of the University of Delaware, excavations at Berenike.

Founded by the Egyptian king Ptolemy II in 275 B.C., Berenike was the most important seaport on the Red Sea coast until the sixth century A.D. In June 2002 Wendrich and Sidebotham reported in *Sahara*, an international journal published annually in Italy, that their team had unearthed extensive evidence suggesting that during the first and second centuries A.D. (the Early Roman period in Egypt), Berenike functioned as a "transfer port" for cargo from the Indian subcontinent and Arabia Felix (now Yemen) destined for Alexandria and Rome and other parts of Europe. The excavators unearthed a lot of black peppercorns, native to southern India, and teak, a hardwood indigenous to the Indian subcontinent, which was used in shipbuilding. "We talk about globalism today as if it were the latest thing, but trade was going on in antiquity at a scale and scope that is truly impressive," Wendrich told a writer for Ascribe Newswire (June 11, 2002). "These people were taking incredible risks with their lives and fortune to make money." The researchers also found evidence of trade between Berenike and places as far distant as the Indonesian island of Java and what is now Thailand. The maritime trade route may have rivaled the better-known Silk Road, a network of overland routes that was long believed to be the chief commercial route between China and Europe for thousands of years. "This turns around our way of viewing the world at the time," Wendrich said to Thomas H. Maugh II for the *Los Angeles Times* (June 12, 2002). "We are used to looking at it from the point of view of the Roman Empire, but clearly a lot of the initiative was on the Indian side. It was not a one-way trade initiated by Rome." "These findings go a long way toward improving our understanding of the way in which a whole range of exotic cargo moved into Europe during antiquity," Wendrich told the AScribe Newswire reporter. "When cost and political conflict prevented overland transport, ancient mariners took to the Red Sea, and the route between India and Egypt appears to have been even more productive than we ever thought."

Many of the present-day inhabitants of the area around ancient Berenike are members of the Ababda, a nomadic tribe. The preservation of the Ababda's cultural heritage is the focus of the Eastern Desert Antiquities Protection Project (financed by the Royal Netherlands Embassy in Cairo), which Wendrich headed from 1996 to 2002. Along with the architect and filmmaker Gabriel Mikhail, Wendrich designed a permanent exhibit devoted to Ababda culture at the Wadi el-Gemal National Park, in southeastern Egypt. The exhibit opened in December 2006.

Since 2003 Wendrich has been working in the Fayum Oasis (also spelled Fayoum or Fayyum), an agricultural region located about 60 miles southwest of Cairo; along with the archaeobotanist René Cappers, she serves as the co-director of a project of UCLA and the Rijksuniversiteit Groningen, in the Netherlands. The excavators discovered several grain-storage pits, lined with basketry and capped with lids made of a mixture of sand, shell fragments, salt, and water. The pits date from the Neolithic Period (the last era of the Stone Age, from about 5000 to about 4000 B.C.) and provided evidence of the earliest-known agricultural activities in Egypt. Wendrich and Cappers have also been examining ancient remnants of grain in several Greco-Roman agricultural villages, such as Karanis and Qarah el-Hamra, an ancient site that she discovered at Fayum in 2003. Those studies have shed light on the maintenance of political authority in the Mediterranean region during the Greco-Roman period (from about 300 B.C. to about 400 A.D.).

In 2006 UCLA announced its plans to offer online a new *Encyclopedia of Egyptology* (UEE), funded by a grant of $325,000 from the National Endowment for the Humanities. Wendrich, as editor in chief, and Jacco Dieleman, a UCLA associate professor of Near Eastern Languages and Cultures who will serve as editor, will work with an international team of Egyptologists in compiling some 600 entries to be made available to the public in 2008. The idea for the encyclopedia, which will be "dedicated to all aspects of ancient Egypt and its legacy," according to *UCLA News* (April 27, 2006, online), originated with Wendrich, who, like others in her field, had long lamented the presence on the Internet of too much inaccurate information about ancient Egypt and the lack of a single trustworthy repository of data. Every article posted in the *Encyclopedia of Egyptology* will be peer-reviewed, and none will ever be removed from the site, so that as "a beautiful side effect" of the new reference source, as Wendrich put it in an interview with Jennifer Howard for the *Chronicle of Higher Education* (May 5, 2006), "a history of the discipline" will be created, showing "the changing thoughts that people have on the subject, the changing angles." "We want to set the gold standard for reference materials about ancient Egypt, and we hope our standard won't be carved in stone," Wendrich declared, according to *UCLA News*. The UEE's Academic Editorial Committee consists of the world's top Egyptologists and Archaeologists, and the endeavor has been endorsed by the International Society of Egyptologists. When the *Encyclopedia of Egyptology* goes on-line, it will replace as the standard reference work the seven-volume *Lexikon der Ägyptologie* (1972), a German encyclopedia that is available only in print and was last updated about 20 years ago. The UEE "will allow users to combine data, images, interpretive articles and Virtual Reality 3-D computer models of monuments and to link information in ways otherwise not possible," Wendrich said, as quoted in *UCLA News*. All articles will be accessible free of charge, and the enhanced features will be available free to anyone with an Egyptian computer signature (IP, or Internet Protocol, address).

Wendrich currently devotes much of her energy to UCLA's Digital Humanities Incubator Group (UDHIG), which, among other activities, assists UCLA faculty members in preparing grant applications for digital humanities projects. Current projects, in addition to the *Encyclopedia of Egyptology*, include "Hypermedia Berlin," which, according to the UDHIG Web site, is "an interactive, web-based research platform and collaborative authoring environment for analyzing the cultural, architectural, and urban history of a city space"; a study of Danish folklore; creation of a Web repository of speech errors; an investigation into the history of dance; and a study called "The First Generation of British Industrialists: Scientific Culture and Civic Life, 1780–1832."

A permanent resident of the U.S., Wendrich lives with her husband, Hans Barnard, in Los Angeles, near the UCLA campus. Barnard worked as a physician until the end of 1994, when he moved with Wendrich to Egypt; afterward, as Wendrich told *Current Biography*, he gave up medicine "to dedicate himself to the much less lucrative but much more exciting profession of archaeology." Barnard is a research associate at the Cotsen Institute; his specialty is pottery made 1,300 to 1,500 years ago by inhabitants of the desert between the Red Sea and the Nile River. Wendrich's hobbies include horseback riding, in-line skating, and modern dance, the last of which, she told *Current Biography* in 2006, "is something I do too little of at the moment, but it is a great way to relax and counterbalance the cerebral activities I'm normally involved in."

—D.F.

Suggested Reading: AScribe Newswire (on-line) June 11, 2002, Apr. 27, 2006; *Backdirt* (on-line) Fall/Winter 2001; Cotsen Institute of Archaeology Web site; *New York Times* F p1+ July 9, 2002; UCLA Department of Near Eastern Languages and Cultures Web site; *UCLA News* (on-line) Apr. 27, 2006

Selected Books: *The World According to Basketry: An Ethno-archaeological Interpretation of Basketry Production in Egypt*, 1999; *Report of the Baynun Mapping Project, Yemen, 1998*, 1999; as editor—*Moving Matters: Ethnoarchaeology in the Near East*, 1998; *Berenike '98: Report of the 1998 Excavations at Berenike and the Survey of the Egyptian Eastern Desert, Including Excavations in Wadi Kalalat*, 1998

Kevin Winter/Getty Images

Wexler, Haskell

Feb. 6, 1922(?)– Cinematographer; filmmaker

Address: c/o Skouras Agency, 1149 Third St., Third Fl., Santa Monica, CA 90403

Haskell Wexler has been rivaled perhaps only by his friend Conrad L. Hall (who died in 2003) as America's most important and innovative cinematographer. He is certainly the most controversial: an outspoken and cantankerous ultra-liberal, he has been blacklisted by Hollywood; fired from movie sets by legendary directors including Francis Ford Coppola (during the shooting of *The Conversation*) and Milos Forman (*One Flew Over the Cuckoo's Nest*); gassed by police amid the filming of a landmark docudrama; subpoenaed by the FBI; and made the subject of scandalous behind-the-scenes stories from his numerous collaborators. (Giving a hint of the difficulty of working with him, he declared in the 2005 documentary *Tell Them Who You Are*, directed by his son Mark, "I don't think there's a movie I've been on that I didn't think I could direct better.") An extremely talented visual artist, Wexler has shot films as distinct from one another as they are from works of others, leading John Patterson, writing for the London *Guardian* (June 2, 2006), to call him "a Zelig of the post-second world war American left." Among his feature-film credits are such well-known movies as *Who's Afraid of Virginia Woolf?*; *America, America*; *In the Heat of the Night*; *The Thomas Crown Affair*; and *Matewan*. In addition, Wexler—a pioneer of the cinema verité style of documentary filmmaking—has directed works in that genre that include the films in his Bus series

and the 2006 work *Who Needs Sleep?* Amassing a catalogue of some 35 feature films, dozens of documentaries, and hundreds of commercials, Wexler has garnered five nominations for Academy Awards (winning two) and is one of a select group of cinematographers to receive a star on the Hollywood Walk of Fame. In 1993 he became the first active cinematographer ever to receive a Lifetime Achievement Award from the American Society of Cinematographers (ASC), and in 2007 he was honored with two more Lifetime Achievement Awards, from the Independent Documentary Association and the Society of Operating Cameramen, respectively. "Movies are a voyeuristic experience," he explained to Bob Fisher for *American Cinematographer* (February 1993). "You have to make the audience feel like they are peeking through a keyhole. I think of myself as the audience. Then I use light, framing and motion to create a focal point." He added, "Our job is full of compromises. You take thrusts into the future by experimenting. You hope they work. If they do, you soar. If they don't, you are miserable. The more experience you have, the more it should be possible for you to experiment. What I see and put on the screen is in a sense the sum of all I have learned from all of the people whom I have worked with throughout the years."

One of the four children of Simon and Lottie Wexler, Haskell Wexler was born on February 6, 1922 in Chicago, Illinois, to a well-to-do family. (Some sources list his year of birth as 1919 or 1926.) His father, one of the founders of Allied Radio (which would later become Radio Shack), frequently took his family on lavish vacations to Europe, where Haskell would use the family's 16mm Bell and Howell camera to shoot home movies. While still in grade school, he worked as an assistant to Mickey Pallas, a Chicago still-photographer who was affiliated with the trade-union movement and would later gain fame for his images of 1950s America. In eighth grade Wexler began taking pictures of striking unionists for the Newspaper Guild, for which he continued to work through high school. One of his most vivid memories from his time at the guild is of photographing striking meatpackers as they dangled scab workers by their feet from elevated trains. Those experiences influenced the pro-labor stance that would be expressed in Wexler's future films. Wexler himself, at the age of 17, organized a strike at his father's electronics factory.

After graduating from Francis Parker High School, in 1940, Wexler attended the University of California at Berkeley. He stayed there for less than a year before either dropping out (as many sources have it) or, according to Wexler, being asked to leave after agitating for the right of assembly for the American Students Union. In 1941, as the U.S. prepared to enter World War II, Wexler volunteered as a seaman in the Merchant Marine, where he briefly met fellow sailor Woody Guthrie (who later gained fame as a folk musician and became the subject of the film *Bound for Glory*, for which Wexler won an Oscar). In the Merchant Marine Wexler was an advocate for the desegregation of seamen. He also survived two torpedo attacks. On Friday, November 13, 1942, he was aboard the tanker *S.S. Excello* when it was torpedoed by a submarine and sank off the coast of South Africa in the shark-infested waters of the Indian Ocean. He spent 10 days on a lifeboat with nine other crew members before being rescued. "Up to that time, I thought I was immortal," Wexler recalled to Aljean Harmetz for the *New York Times* (March 25, 1990). After the war Wexler received the Silver Star and was promoted to the rank of second officer.

Upon returning to Chicago, in 1946, after his discharge, Wexler spent a few months working for his father in a stockroom at Allied Radio Co. He next decided to become a filmmaker, despite having no experience in the industry. His father helped him open up a film studio (formerly an armory) in Des Plaines, Illinois. Wexler shot industrial films at factories in the Midwest before the studio folded. Though it had failed financially (Wexler's father lost around a million dollars), the business served as an unofficial film school for Wexler. He later worked as a freelancer, joining the International Photographers Guild, in Chicago, in 1947. He started off as an assistant cameraman and worked his way up the technical ladder.

In the years that followed, unable to work in Hollywood because of the leftist political views he held during an era of anti-Communist witch hunts, Wexler got experience in hard news under the newsreel cameraman Tony Caputo; made campaign shorts with Carl Marzani for the Progressive Party presidential hopeful Henry Wallace in 1948; shot films for the United Electrical Workers Union; crafted documentaries for Encyclopedia Britannica Inc. (including the 1953 film *The Living City*, which won an Oscar); and contributed to Herbert Biberman's *Salt of the Earth*, a well-known documentary about a miners' strike in New Mexico in 1954. Wexler then became an apprentice of the esteemed cameraman James Wong Howe, arguably the most important cinematographer during the first half of the 20th century, as part of the second unit for the 1955 film *Picnic*. As posted on the International Cinematographers Guild Web site, Wexler recalled Howe's advice to him: "He said that if you can light with one light, light with one light. . . . Early on, he encouraged me to try to simplify lighting. . . . There's a window and a room and if you can light the whole room from the window you do it that way." That Hollywood experience landed him another camera-assistant position on the phenomenally popular television series *The Adventures of Ozzie & Harriet*. For the latter half of the 1950s, Wexler spent a great deal of time filming commercials for Kling Studios (later the Fred Niles Studios). It was during that time that he struck up a lasting friendship with his fellow cinematographer Conrad L. Hall. Together they formed Wexler-Hall, a television-commercial pro-

duction company, and made hundreds of commercials. In addition to being profitable, those projects further refined Wexler's style.

Between making commercials, Wexler shot various television programs and visually sophisticated docudramas under a number of pseudonyms, which included Mark Jeffrey and Phil Lewis. Wexler's innovative work on several films with Irvin Kershner, including *Stakeout on Dope Street* (1958), *Hoodlum Priest* (1961), and *A Face in the Rain* (1963), helped the cinematographer gain notice in Hollywood. In *A Face in the Rain*, for example, Wexler filmed a chase scene with a handheld camera while he was running down an alley—a shot that would subsequently be emulated in hundreds of movies. The stylized grittiness of *Hoodlum Priest*, filmed in St. Louis, Missouri, caught the eye of the Academy Award–winning filmmaker Elia Kazan (the director of the cinematic classics *On the Waterfront* and *A Streetcar Named Desire*, among other movies), who asked Wexler to be the cinematographer for *America, America*—a masterful coming-of-age story about Kazan's uncle Joe Kazan, which won the director an Oscar. Calling that film his "big break," Wexler said to Lewis Beale, as reprinted in the *Chicago Tribune* (April 28, 1988), "I think that was my best work. I didn't know so much [then], and at a certain level, ignorance allows you to take chances. And if you're lucky, those chances can just soar."

Wexler provided the cinematography for *The Best Man* (1964), starring Henry Fonda and adapted by Gore Vidal from his play of the same name. In the following year he made his first foray into directing as well as screenwriting, with *The Bus*. That documentary centered on the freedom riders, activists who worked to secure voting rights for African-Americans in the South. In 1966 he shot another feature film, *The Loved One*, adapted from Evelyn Waugh's satire about the funeral business. While in preparation for another collaboration with Kershner, on a film called *A Fine Madness*, Wexler was asked by the director Mike Nichols to shoot Nichols's first feature, *Who's Afraid of Virginia Woolf?* Again making use of a handheld camera, Wexler captured the intense emotions and instability of the film's sparring couple (played by Elizabeth Taylor and Richard Burton) through forceful camera movements. Wexler explained to Bob Fisher, "I read in Burton's book that he didn't want me to shoot *Virginia Woolf*. Because of my documentary background he was concerned that my lighting wouldn't be kind to his face which was kind of pock-marked. But Elizabeth went to bat for me." To create the unique look of the film, Wexler put every light on a dimmer and used very soft single-source bounce light from white umbrellas. The use of umbrellas, derived from still photography, created gorgeously vivid black and white images, much to Burton's liking. The film received Oscar nominations in every category for which it was eligible and claimed five awards, with Wexler taking the statuette for best black-and-white cinematography. (That category was eliminated after that year.)

Wexler's Oscar paved the way for work on other A-list films, among them *In the Heat of the Night* (1967) and *The Thomas Crown Affair* (1968), both directed by Norman Jewison. For the former, Wexler stretched silks over the tops of sets and aimed 10-Kelvin lights at their centers to enhance the juxtaposition of light and dark, visually augmenting the racial tension between Sidney Poitier's character, the big-city black detective Virgil Tibbs, and the white southern police chief Bill Gillespie, played by Rod Steiger. Wexler also used desaturated color film stock to produce a dull, almost unwelcoming, look, reflecting the feel of Tibbs's arrival in the South. By contrast, for *The Thomas Crown Affair*, Wexler used rich, vibrant colors to emphasize the Steve McQueen character's flamboyant lifestyle; for that film he also used other innovative visual techniques drawn from his documentary background. In one scene, for example, a character's face is shown through a series of empty phone booths, making it appear as if he were in a glass tunnel. For the climactic heist sequence, Wexler placed four hidden cameras on the exterior of a bank, which allowed the director to alternate among characters' viewpoints. The hidden cameras captured authentic reactions from bystanders outside, who thought the robbery was real—which led in turn to the arrival of gun-drawing police officers on the set, much to the amusement of the film crew.

Wexler took on the responsibilities of financier, director, writer, producer, and cameraman for his next film, *Medium Cool* (1969), made for $600,000. The movie, the story of a stubborn television photographer (played by Robert Forster) set against the backdrop of violent confrontations between police and protestors at the 1968 Democratic National Convention, was innovative in its insertion of fictional characters into actual—and dangerous—situations. Wexler, who was gassed by Chicago police during the filming, captured footage of officers assaulting students with billy clubs, among other real and disturbing events. The film's lead actors included Peter Boyle; the supporting "cast" was largely comprised of nonactors. The movie's receiving an X rating, which Wexler called a political move, led to an extremely limited distribution, but critics unanimously agreed that *Medium Cool* was a landmark film. Vincent Canby, in a review for the *New York Times* (August 28, 1969), noted the film's historical significance, writing, "*Medium Cool* . . . is an angry, technically brilliant movie . . . a film of tremendous visual impact, a kind of cinematic *Guernica* [the antiwar painting by Pablo Picasso], a picture of America in the process of exploding into fragmented bits of hostility, suspicion, fear and violence." Wexler recalled to Guy Flatley for the *New York Times* (September 7, 1969), "I was under surveillance for the entire seven weeks that I was in Chicago. By the police, the Army, and the Secret Service. As we made the movie, they made movies of us. I would look up from my camera and see a guy in the back seat of a police car taking pictures of us."

In the 1970s Wexler made well-received documentaries, including the Academy Award–winning *Interviews with My Lai Veterans* (1970). He also worked on some of the most acclaimed feature films of the decade, among them *American Graffiti*, *The Conversation*, *Bound for Glory*, *One Flew Over the Cuckoo's Nest*, and *Days of Heaven*. Although listed only as a "visual consultant" on *American Graffiti*, Wexler contributed significantly to the colorful, "jukebox" look of George Lucas's film, set in the early 1960s. After shooting the much-lauded, paranoia-evoking opening sequence of Francis Ford Coppola's *The Conversation*, Wexler was fired from the set, having butted heads with the equally headstrong director. Wexler's difficult nature was also said to be in evidence on the set of Milos Forman's *One Flew Over the Cuckoo's Nest*, another film from which the cinematographer was dismissed. Forman claimed that Wexler was undermining his direction of the actors. Wexler nonetheless shared an Oscar nomination with Bill Butler for the film's cinematography, through which bleak images emphasized the physical confinement and mental deterioration of the characters—patients in a psychiatric hospital.

In 1976 Wexler took home his second Oscar, for the Hal Ashby–directed film *Bound for Glory*, about the folk musician Woody Guthrie. In shooting the film Wexler became the first cinematographer to use a Steadicam image stabilizer for a tracking shot—a memorable one that follows Guthrie (played by John Carradine) from behind his shoulder as he walks through a crowd of migrant workers. Also notable was Wexler's juxtaposition of beautiful landscapes with images of Depression-era poverty. Wexler made a stir with his work on Emile de Antonio's 1976 documentary *Underground*, featuring surreptitiously filmed interviews with members of the Weather Underground—a radical offshoot of Students for a Democratic Society whose goal was to commit acts of domestic terrorism. The FBI brought Wexler in front of a federal grand jury and briefly subpoenaed the interview footage of the fugitives, who were all on the agency's Ten Most Wanted List at the time. In 1978 the cinematographer teamed up with Ashby again, for the Oscar-winning Vietnam War drama *Coming Home*. Wexler received an "additional photography" credit for Terrence Malick's *Days of Heaven* (1978), a credit that has sparked controversy ever since. Considered by some to be the most visually stunning film ever made, *Days of Heaven* was shot mostly at dusk and dawn, resulting in beautiful images that conveyed the loneliness and lushness of the wide-open Texas prairie. For those images, Néstor Almendros won that year's Oscar for best cinematography, despite Wexler's claims of once sitting in a theater with a stopwatch and proving that over half of the film's footage was shot by him.

Highlights of the cinematographer's work in the 1980s included two more Oscar nominations (for *Matewan* and *Blaze*); the making of another controversial feature film, *Latino;* and an "additional photographer" credit for Ridley Scott's visually surreal science-fiction triumph *Blade Runner. Latino* (1985), a narrative film written and directed by Wexler, examines U.S. foreign policy in Nicaragua, making use of a number of documentary-style visual techniques for effect in some scenes. Vincent Canby wrote in a review of *Latino* for the *New York Times* (February 28, 1986), "The passion is there, but it's subverted by the perfunctory nature of the fiction [Wexler] has concocted." Canby added that the movie's screenplay made only "minimal use of the freedom allowed by fiction to dramatize the contradictory nature of human behavior." In *Matewan* (1987), John Sayles's film about a labor-union organizer who discovers the mistreatment of workers by a mining company circa 1920, Wexler lit the miners' coal-blackened faces by bouncing light from graphite-flame lamps off reflective aluminum cards. For *Blaze* (1989), a Ron Shelton film about the latter years of the flamboyant Louisiana governor Earl Long (played by Paul Newman), Wexler gradually saturated the images with color, as a means of representing the progression of Long's love interest, a stripper (played by Lolita Davidovich), from seedy to more glamorous clubs. Among other films from that decade, Wexler contributed to Dennis Hopper's 1988 police/gang drama *Colors.*

In the early 1990s Wexler began to work on some lighter fare, reteaming with Norman Jewison on *Other People's Money* (1991) as well as doing the photography for Arthur Hiller's 1992 biographical film about Babe Ruth, *The Babe.* In the latter movie, Wexler's cinematography was praised for its depiction of baseball's seedier side, through the use of dark hues. After working on John Sayles's Irish fable *The Secret of Roan Inish* (1994), Wexler did notable work on the neo-noir 1996 film *Mulholland Falls.* While the movie, starring Nick Nolte, was almost universally panned, Wexler's cinematography was almost universally praised. Between feature films Wexler continued to make documentaries, including *Bus Rider's Union* (1999), the third installment of his ever-evolving Bus series, and *The Man on Lincoln's Nose,* the Oscar-winning documentary about the work of the renowned production designer Robert Boyle. In 2001 he scored an Emmy nomination for his sumptuous cinematography in Billy Crystal's made-for-TV film *61*,* and he collaborated with John Sayles for a fourth time in *Silver City* (2004), a socio-political thriller starring Chris Cooper and Richard Dreyfuss.

In *Tell Them Who You Are,* made by the documentary filmmaker Mark Wexler, Wexler's son from his second marriage, Wexler is shown criticizing his son for the way he sets up shots and refusing to sign a release form for the movie until it was completed and met with his approval. Featuring interviews with Michael Douglas, Milos Forman, Jane Fonda, Paul Newman, George Lucas, Elia Kazan, and other famous Hollywood figures with whom the cinematographer had collaborated, *Tell Them Who You Are* highlights Wexler's accomplishments and ability—as well as the ways in which his work has been hampered by his confrontational nature. Stephen Holden wrote in a review of the film for the *New York Times* (May 20, 2005), "Like an aged monarch who is not about to let go of life or to cede control, Mr. Wexler, fully aware that his son's portrait may be taken as the final word on his character and achievements, treats the work-in-progress as an embattled collaboration." Wexler won acclaim for his 2006 documentary *Who Needs Sleep?,* which tackled the long hours and sleep deprivation experienced by workers in Hollywood. In the following year he campaigned unsuccessfully to be president of the International Cinematographers Guild (ICG). Also in 2007 he directed *From Wharf Rats to Lords of the Docks,* about the life of the labor activist Harry Bridges.

Wexler's other children are Jeffrey S. "Jeff" Wexler, a sound mixer for more than 60 films, and Kathy. He is married to his third wife, the actress Rita Taggart, and is the step-uncle of the actress Daryl Hannah. Wexler remains active in his 80s; he is currently working on a documentary about the war correspondent Chris Hedges. In a recent survey fellow ICG members named him one of the 10 most influential cinematographers in film history. Wexler was quoted on the ICG Web site as saying, "I don't want to sound pompous but I do think that all of us have a limited time on this earth. To spend so much of our time on work which does not in some way express something positive, something we can be proud of, then we are living less than a full life."

—C.C.

Suggested Reading: *American Cinematographer* p44+ Feb. 1993; *Advertising Age* p10 Feb. 13, 1986; *Chicago Sun-Times* p11 May 8, 2005; *Film Quarterly* p3+ Spring 1968; International Cinematographers Guild Web site; (London) *Guardian* p10 June 2, 2006; *Los Angeles Times* E p4 May 13, 2005; *New York Times* E p10 May 20, 2005; *Orange County (California) Register* F p13 Feb. 5, 1995; *Progressive* Apr. 1998; *South Bend Tribune* D p4 Apr. 8, 2007; *Vancouver Sun* C p3 Jan. 25, 2006

Selected Films: feature films—*The Savage Eye,* 1960; *The Hoodlum Priest,* 1961; *A Face in the Rain,* 1963; *America, America,* 1963; *The Best Man,* 1964; *The Loved One,* 1966; *Who's Afraid of Virginia Woolf?,* 1966; *In the Heat of the Night,* 1967; *The Thomas Crown Affair,* 1968; *Medium Cool,* 1969; *American Graffiti,* 1973; *One Flew over the Cuckoo's Nest,* 1975; *Bound for Glory,* 1976; *Coming Home,* 1978; *Days of Heaven,* 1978; *Latino,* 1985; *Matewan,* 1987; *Colors,* 1988; *Blaze,* 1989; *The Babe,* 1992; *The Secret of Roan Inish,* 1994; *Mulholland Falls,* 1996; *61*,* 2001; *Silver City,* 2004; documentaries—*The Living City,* 1953; *The Bus,*

1965; *Interviews with My Lai Veterans*, 1970; *Brazil: A Report on Torture*, 1971; *Introduction to the Enemy*, 1974; *Underground*, 1976; *No Nukes*, 1980; *Richard Pryor: Live on the Sunset Strip*, 1982; *Bus II*, 1983; *Bus Rider's Union*, 1999; *Good Kurds, Bad Kurds: No Friends But the Mountains*, 2000; *The Man on Lincoln's Nose*, 2000; *Who Needs Sleep?*, 2006; *From Wharf Rats to Lords of the Docks*, 2007

Courtesy of Kehinde Wiley Studio

Wiley, Kehinde

(kuh-HIN-dee)

Feb. 28, 1977– Painter

Address: Deitch Projects, 76 Grand St., New York, NY 10013

Art should "show you something you've never seen before," the painter Kehinde Wiley told Matt Lauer during an interview for *NBC News* (May 22, 2006, on-line). "Art should take the familiar and represent it in such a way that it gives us hope, and . . . redeems the value of life itself." Wiley's specialty is portraiture; his subjects are young, urban, African-American men, dressed in everyday outfits familiar to contemporary Americans. What makes the men look unusual in Wiley's portraits are their heroic, even majestic, poses, which mimic those of men (or, occasionally, women) in well-known pictures painted centuries ago, and the settings in which Wiley places them: backgrounds covered with floral and other designs reminiscent of the 19th-century wallpapers and fabrics created

by the British artist William Morris, or filigrees patterned to resemble medieval Christian or Islamic scrollwork. His portraits are slightly larger than life-size, and he encloses them in elaborately carved, gilded frames of the kind fashioned 300 years ago, during the Rococo period in France. In a representative review of one of Wiley's solo shows, Margaret Hawkins wrote for the *Chicago Sun-Times* (September 22, 2006), "In one 10-foot canvas, the young man posed as a larger-than-life, modern-day St. Peter holds an enormous gold key that looks like a serious piece of bling. Here, Wiley has translated the keys to heaven into a comically huge gold ornament that might be a kind of stunt key to some jackpot. Or is the promise of heaven the jackpot? None of this would work if Wiley weren't such a surpassingly good painter. Larger-than-life portraiture usually falls flat, distorting and flattening figures so that they function as characters in some generalized mural-like concept at best. Not so with Wiley's figures, beautiful young men that they are, who are dazzlingly real as well as psychologically expressive. Their hip-hop style—huge white Nike trainers, glittery earrings, big white T-shirts, team jerseys and baseball caps—takes on a kind of seriousness simply because Wiley renders them with such respect. By inserting these uncharacteristic figures into art history, Wiley appropriates that history and makes the obvious but important assertion that context is all. Without representation, these men are invisible, but when presented with dignity and gravitas, they instantly take a place in our collective imagination."

In a conversation for *Interview* (October 1, 2005) with Thelma Golden, the chief curator and executive director of the Studio Museum in Harlem, Wiley characterized traditional portrait painting as "an enterprise about very powerful men." His own paintings, in his words, "quote historical sources and position young black men within that field of power." Most of Wiley's subjects have been young men who attracted his attention on the streets of the Harlem section of New York City or South Central Los Angeles, California: people who struck him as unusually self-possessed or appeared to him to be "alpha" males. Each person who agrees to sit for him decides on a pose by choosing a picture from among full-body portraits executed by such old masters as Titian, Rubens, Holbein, and Tiepolo. "In a sense, [the models] are performing a language of power that predates them," Wiley told Celia McGee for the New York *Daily News* (October 7, 2004), "occupying a field of power amplified by virtue of the absence of people like us from the Western canon of art." Wiley's paintings "make you rethink the old masters, as well as rethink our image of young black males in our culture," John Houston, an associate curator at the Columbus Museum of Art, in Ohio, told Paul Young for *Daily Variety* (June 2, 2006). Wiley told Sarah Lewis for *Art in America* (April 2005), "Black masculinity has been codified in a fixed way. I'm not trying to provide a direct corrective, but I am trying to point to a history of signs as they relate to black people in the media. . . . There is a certain desire in my work to tie the urban street and the way it's been depicted with elements that are not necessarily coded as masculine."

Wiley currently works in a studio in the borough of Brooklyn, in New York City, where, under his direction, assistants paint much or all of the backgrounds in his pictures. Since 2002, works by the 30-year-old artist have appeared in a dozen solo shows and two dozen group shows, in Canada, Austria, Poland, Italy, Belgium, the Czech Republic, and China as well as the United States. His paintings are in the permanent collections of seven museums, among them the Brooklyn Museum of Art, the Columbus (Ohio) Museum of Art, and the Studio Museum in Harlem, and in private collections including that of Russell Simmons, the founder of the hip-hop record label Def Jam. More than 70 articles about his life and work have appeared in the past half-dozen years in periodicals ranging from *Art News*, *Art in America*, *Art Forum*, the *International Review of African-American Art*, and artnet.com to the *New York Times*, the *Ottawa (Canada) Citizen*, *Essence*, *Vibe*, and the French magazine *Le Monde*.

Kehinde Wiley was born on February 28, 1977 and raised by his mother, Freddie Wiley, in the South Central neighborhood of Los Angeles. In the *New York Times* (December 19, 2004), Mia Fineman described his mother as a linguist. Wiley's father was a Nigerian architect who returned to Africa before Wiley's birth. His mother enrolled him and his six siblings (among them his twin brother) in art classes and encouraged them to experiment in the visual arts. At the age of 11, Wiley entered an art program that combined instruction with trips to local museums. At the Huntington Library, Art Collections, and Botanical Gardens, in San Marino, California, he was drawn to portraits of the 18th-century British painters Thomas Gainsborough and Joshua Reynolds. "They were so artificial and opulent," he told Mia Fineman. "There was this strange otherworldliness that, as a black kid from Los Angeles, I had no manageable way of digesting. But at the same time, there was this desire to somehow possess that or belong to that." Wiley reportedly displayed a talent for portraiture at an early age. His mother told Lauer, "He wanted just to know everything. There was just no stopping him. He could just reproduce almost anything that he saw, just drawing. And he delighted in doing so." Wiley attended the Los Angeles County School for the Arts, a specialized high school, where he impressed his teachers with his focus and dedication. "Kehinde came with a lot of talent, and I think what he had to do is convince himself . . . ," Joe Gatto, a former dean at the school, told Lauer. "He discovered very early what his potential was, and he just developed it." During his high-school years, Wiley won medals in several student art contests.

Wiley earned a bachelor's degree at the San Francisco Art Institute, in California, in 1999. He next entered the master's program in fine arts at Yale University, in New Haven, Connecticut. There, Wiley found himself contending with instructors who expected him to focus on the politics of black identity in his work. "There was this overwhelming sense of, 'O.K., Kehinde, where's your Negro statement?'" he recalled to Fineman. He responded by painting images of watermelons in the surrealist style of Magritte or de Chirico. Wiley keeps those paintings hidden in one of his closets. "While they're not some of the most sophisticated or beautiful paintings I've made,'" he said, "they're some of my favorites because they remind me of a point in my life that felt absolutely desperate and lost and powerless. I don't want to romanticize that too much, but it's interesting to look at."

In 2001, after he earned an M.F.A. from Yale, Wiley became the artist-in-residence at the Studio Museum in Harlem, on West 125th Street in Manhattan, where he lived in his studio. "I had my work there, a futon, and a television. It was just the most insane, overcrowded, intense moment, but it allowed me to engage in my work in a way I never had," he told Wendy Goodman for *New York* (May 1, 2006). He described the Studio Museum to Thelma Golden as "my saving grace, coming as I did out of the very sheltered community at Yale. The Studio Museum provided the perfect environment for me to delve into my work without the concerns of professors or academic expectations. There was a big weight lifted—I was free to create without having to think about a day job or a gig. That allowed me to . . . take risks that I wouldn't necessarily take. I had no idea that the Studio Museum was as prestigious as it is. I just assumed that I'd be doing a residency, and that it'd be a great chance to do more work. But when the exhibition occurred at the end of the year and all that attention started to come through, that's really what I think launched the beginnings of the career I'm starting to enjoy now."

Wiley spent some of his time observing the similarities and differences between the Harlem community and his Los Angeles neighborhood. "What defined that difference had to do with people in public space," he told Golden. "Los Angeles by and large is about people driving around in cars. New York is more pedestrian, and there was a vibrancy there that I found really interesting. The idea of walking down 125th Street has this runway element to it: there's a sort of pomp that surrounds it." In Harlem, he told Andre Banks for *ColorLines* (January 31, 2006), "in the space of five blocks you get the chance to shop, eat, peacock, parade and be seen. It's violent in the shocking immediacy of people's presence. For me, its incredibly engaging . . . something I wanted to somehow grapple with in my work." His desire to connect with the community and his interest in portraiture led him to search for subjects for his paintings among his new neighbors. He started by carrying around photos of his previous projects and showing them to young men in mostly unsuccessful attempts to persuade them to pose for him. He fared far better after he approached men with one or another attractive female assistant in tow and told the men that he would pay them for their time.

Another defining experience for Wiley during that period occurred when he came across a discarded police department "Wanted" poster bearing a picture of a black man. He tacked the poster to a wall of his studio and gazed at it often. "It changed my way of thinking about portraiture," he told Elizabeth Fitch for the *New York Amsterdam News* (July 21, 2004). "Those things had to do with people having a choice about portrayal; this thing had choices reduced down to a central thing. My decision was to run directly at this and create something redeeming. I ended up doing a whole series of mug shot portraits, with the aim to make it so beautiful so as to overcome the sad truth about young Black men in prison."

In 2001 Wiley's work was displayed publicly in his first professional group exhibition, at the Rush Arts Gallery, in New York City. The following year his paintings were included in four group shows, among them two at the Studio Museum and one in an Ottawa, Canada, gallery. Also in 2002 he had his first solo show, called Passing/Posing, at the Rhona Hoffman Gallery, in Chicago, Illinois. (That exhibition is not mentioned in lists of Wiley's exhibitions on his Web site or those of the galleries that represent him—the Hoffman Gallery; Roberts & Tilton, in Los Angeles; and Deitch Projects, in the Soho section of Manhattan. Those lists do include the Passing/Posing exhibition that was mounted at the Brooklyn Museum of Art in 2004–05.) As he created the works on view in Passing/Posing, Wiley told Andre Banks, his goals included an examination of whether black masculinity is "defined by hypersexuality, anti social behavior and a propensity towards sports, or is it something that is more authentic and elusive?" Most of the images in the show were based on centuries-old paintings of saints, prophets, or angels; a few related to secular paintings. In a review of Passing/Posing for the *Chicago Sun-Times* (December 27, 2002), Margaret Hawkins wrote, "There's a clash between the modern and the traditional going on here that is dissonant and unsettling. The neon colors of the men's sweatshirts are set against the somber jewel tones of the upholstery fabric. The hip-hop culture represented by the figures is exactly opposite the kind of stodgy, expensive interior that would find use for these fabrics. The spatial realism of the figure painting is flattened by the surrounding pattern. It's an uneasy mix Wiley has offered up and he lets it and us hang unresolved, not at war exactly but just uncomfortably side by side." In a critique of Passing/Posing when that show was mounted at the Brooklyn Museum of Art, Sarah Lewis noted in *Art in America* (April 2005) that "the self-mythologizing that undergirds hip-hop culture makes Wiley's mimicry of religious works apt."

Those less impressed by the show included Clare Henry, who wrote for the *Financial Times* (January 7, 2005), "Using . . . photos for reference, Wiley paints his picture, floating his figures on a sea of blue or orange, adding elaborate ornamental flat patterns to enhance and decorate this surrounding space. The results are brash, eyecatching and full of panache but his billboard technique, more appropriate to posters, T shirts and record sleeves, lacks technical and psychological depth."

Wiley was represented by a painting at the Prague Biennale 1, in the Czech Republic, and in group exhibits in galleries in New York and Glen Ellyn, Illinois, all in 2003. That year he also had two solo shows: Faux/Real, held at Deitch Projects, and Pictures at an Exhibition, mounted at Roberts & Tilton. Holly Myers, who assessed the latter for the *Los Angeles Times* (November 7, 2003), wrote that "the contrast between the realistically modeled figures and the two-dimensional backdrops produces a lively spatial ambiguity that Wiley exaggerates by occasionally pulling fragments of pattern across the body, as though in front of it. Shrewd combinations of deliciously vivid color . . . also stimulate productive tensions, making the work so vibrant in places that it's almost difficult to look at." Myers also described the subjects as having "an unusually stable sense of masculinity. Despite all the flowers and curlicues, the sensual color and compulsive ornamentation, there is a candid emphasis throughout on the particular presence, both physical and sociological, of the African American man. It's not an especially erotic appreciation, but it nonetheless encompasses the beauty of skin tone, musculature and posture. It lingers on the sensual qualities of clothing and respects its many layers of signification. And it recognizes the associations—positive and negative— that this body inspires."

Wiley took part in two solo and six group shows in 2004, and the following year, three solo and four group shows. His 2005 solo exhibition Rumors of War, at Deitch Projects, included paintings of men on horseback, based on traditional Western equestrian paintings that glorify military heroes— Jacques-Louis David's painting (1800–01) of Napoleon crossing the Alps, for example. To replicate the images, Wiley hired stuntmen and horses that had been trained for feature films. "Military portraiture is one of the most fascinating [genres] because male power is being aestheticized in a pure way," Wiley told Golden. "They don't play around; it gets to the point in the most obscene way. There's a type of heroicism there, undergirded by a kind of pathos; it's so self-conscious that it's pathetic in a way." Reviewing the exhibit for the *New York Times* (December 9, 2005), Holland Cotter remarked: "The transfer seems, at first, a little too straightforward, too obvious. But it has complications. People once excluded from Western art, or reduced to the role of servants, are now in command: Mr. Wiley has used old cultural tools to create a new rule. At the same time, these young aristocrats are presented in settings and poses traditionally associated with masculine dominance, updated with hip-hop attire. . . . On the whole, though, like any good historian, he balances contradictions where he finds them. And, like any good artist, he pushes the story ahead."

In 2006 Wiley's artwork was exhibited in seven solo or group shows at sites including galleries in Austria and Belgium, the Zacheta National Gallery of Art, in Poland, and the Whitney Museum, in New York. The paintings in his show The World Stage—China, which opened at the Kohler Arts Center, in Sheboygan, Wisconsin, in March 2007, depicted African-American men posed as figures in propaganda posters produced during the decade-long Chinese Cultural Revolution (1966–76). Wiley painted those pictures in a studio that he set up in China; he plans to open additional studios in Nigeria, India, Turkey, Colombia, Poland, and else-where, with the goal of blending incidents from the histories of those nations with the contemporary black experience.

Wiley lives in New York City with his two Italian greyhounds, Liza and Macy. His interests include cooking.

—N.W.M.

Suggested Reading: *Art in America* p120+ Apr. 2005; *Chicago Sun-Times* Weekend p48 Sep. 22, 2006; *Chicago Tribune* C p29 Sep. 15, 2006; *ColorLines* p57 Jan. 31, 2006; *Columbus (Ohio) Dispatch* G p4 Sep. 3, 2006; *Daily Variety* V p4 June 2, 2006; Deitch Projects Web site; *Interview* p158+ Oct. 2005; *Los Angeles Times* E p21 Nov. 7, 2003; *New York Amsterdam News* p21 July 21, 2004; (New York) *Daily News* p52 Oct. 7, 2004; *New York Times* p39 Dec. 19, 2004; *Vanity Fair* p342+ Dec. 2006

Williams, Preston Warren II

1939(?)– Presiding bishop of the Seventh District of the African Methodist Episcopal Church; former president of the Council of Bishops of the AME Church

Address: 110 Pisgah Church Rd., Columbia, SC 29203

For one year beginning on June 26, 2006, the Right Reverend Preston Warren Williams II served as the president of the worldwide Council of Bishops of the African Methodist Episcopal (AME) Church—the highest-ranking position in that Christian denomination. Williams became a bishop in 2000, after many years of service within the church and work in secular endeavors, in both private enterprise—he was the owner of an insurance company—and education. After his consecration as a bishop, he became the spiritual leader of the 17th Episcopal District, which encompasses seven countries in Africa. Currently, he is the presiding prelate of the Seventh Episcopal District, comprising South Carolina; it is the denomination's second-largest district, with 300,000 members. Bishop James Davis, spiritual leader of the AME Church in South Africa, said about Williams to Carolyn Click for the Columbia, South Carolina, newspaper the *State* (June 27, 2006), "I know him to be one of the most productive people on the bench, with little mouth and a lot of work."

Williams was the 119th person to become a bishop in the AME Church, which grew out of the Free African Society, a religiously oriented mutual-aid organization established in Philadelphia, Pennsylvania, in 1787, with the help of Quaker philanthropists. The founders of the society were several free black men, foremost among them Richard Allen (1760–1831), a former slave who, with the encouragement of his owner, had bought his freedom and that of his brothers when he was in his mid-20s, with money he had earned working on his own during the Revolutionary War. Although Allen and the other founders had become Methodist preachers, and many Methodists supported the emancipation of the slaves, the local, racially mixed Methodist church in Philadelphia, administered by whites, treated Allen and other blacks as inferiors. Blacks could conduct services, but only for other blacks and only at 5:00 a.m., for example; they were made to sit in a segregated section of the church; and they were denied burial in the church cemetery. As a result, in 1794 Allen and 10 other blacks opened the Bethel Church, in a former blacksmith shop in an increasingly black area of Philadelphia. As the historian James Henretta wrote in an essay for *Early America Review* (Spring 1997), posted on the Web site Archiving Early America, Allen's action "reflected a desire among African-Americans to control their religious lives, to have the power, for example, 'to call any brother that appears to us adequate to the task to preach or exhort as a local preacher, without the interference of the Conference'"—"Conference" referring to periodic official meetings of the national church administrators and elected representatives. In 1807, to distinguish Bethel from traditional Methodist churches, whose opposition to slavery had weakened, an "African Supplement" was added to the church's articles of confederation. In 1816 Bethel earned legal status as an independent church, and later that year Allen and the leaders of four other black Methodist congregations in the eastern U.S. established the African Methodist Episcopal Church as a new denomination—the first to be organized by blacks in the U.S. The AME Church now has more than 7,000 congregations in North and South America, Europe, Africa, and the Caribbean; its membership in the U.S. is about

Courtesy of the Seventh District, AME Church
Preston Warren Williams II

2.5 million, with another half million overseas. Its credo is "God our Father, Christ our Redeemer, and Man our Brother," and its activities emphasize the fight for social justice. According to AME church law, the president of the Council of Bishops may serve in that post for one year only. In June 2007 Bishop Wilfred Jacobus Messiah succeeded Williams as president.

Preston Warren Williams II was born in about 1939 in Willacoochee, a tiny town in Georgia about 45 miles from the Florida border. He attended the Christian-oriented Southeastern University, in Lakeland, Florida, where he earned a B.S. degree. He later earned a master of divinity degree from Turner Theological Seminary, which is associated with the AME Church and is a division of the Inter-denominational Theological Center, in Atlanta, Georgia. Williams received a doctoral degree in theology from the Wesley Theological Seminary at American University, in Washington, D.C., in 2000. His dissertation was entitled "Evangelism and Worship in the African Methodist Episcopal Church: From Modernity to Post-Modernity."

Earlier, Williams had served as the spiritual leader at a series of churches in Georgia. At Bethel AME Church and St. Mark AME Church, Williams increased membership and introduced more diverse community-outreach initiatives. At Trinity AME Church in Atlanta, he oversaw the purchase of a multimillion-dollar worship complex, which also included classroom space for the city's public schools. As senior pastor of Allen Temple AME Church in Atlanta, he oversaw the $22 million renovation of the church's 580-unit apartment complex, which provided affordable housing to families and senior citizens. For 16 years beginning in

1981, he was the pastor of the St. Paul AME Church, where his accomplishments include the building of a multimillion-dollar Family Life Center (for use by the community as well as church members), the purchase of a 33-unit apartment complex for homeless mothers and children, and expansion of the congregation's outreach ministries.

In 2000 Williams became an AME Church bishop and was assigned to the 17th Episcopal District, home to more than 1,000 AME congregations in the Democratic Republic of the Congo (also known as Congo, Congo-Kinshasa, and, formerly, Zaire), Zambia, Zimbabwe, Burundi, Rwanda, Malawi, and Tanzania. Focusing on evangelism, he saw AME membership in Africa increase from 152,000 to nearly 256,000 in 2004. Williams also worked on AIDS prevention programs, and with the help of his wife, he started projects to help people plant vegetable gardens and start their own businesses. Reflecting on his experiences, he told Christina Lee Knauss for the *State* (July 21, 2004), "Africa was one of the most blessed places I've been fortunate to serve. The people there are beautiful. But they need our help because they've been exploited. It was my happy privilege to help them while I was there, but they still have their work cut out for them." Currently, membership in the AME Church is rising faster in Africa than anywhere else.

In 2004 Williams returned to the United States to become the bishop of the Seventh Episcopal District (South Carolina), whose membership is surpassed only by that of the First District, which covers Delaware, the New England states, New Jersey, New York City and other parts of New York State, Philadelphia, and Bermuda. Charleston, South Carolina, is the AME Church's birthplace in the American South—the Mother Emmanuel AME Church was founded there in 1818; AME members from the southeastern U.S. look to South Carolina for direction and often visit the Seventh District as tourists. Williams's first action as bishop was to visit nearly all of the district's congregations, to emphasize the importance of involvement in community affairs. In July 2005 all AME churches in South Carolina joined with the state Department of Juvenile Justice to create a program that made neighborhood centers available for young people for recreational, mentoring, and tutoring (but not religious) purposes after school and during the summer. More than 27,000 teens were referred to the state's Juvenile Justice Department in 2005, and Williams hoped that the program might help reduce the number of repeat offenders. District AME churches also worked with the state Department of Social Services to establish a "foster parent" (not foster care) program and provide free lunch to underprivileged children when they were not in school. Williams's administrative duties included ordaining new ministers, assigning pastors to churches within the district, and ensuring that ministers were properly servicing their communities. "Nothing is done loosely in the Methodist church," Williams told Vanita Washington for the *Greenville (South Carolina) News* (October 6, 2005). "Everyone must answer to someone. The pastors have to give an account of the number of souls saved, members dying, social issues in their communities and how they have related to their community. Then the pastor is graded and the grade includes attitude and how well he gets along with the membership."

In June 2006 Williams became president of the AME Church's Council of Bishops. He succeeded Gregory Ingram of Texas, the 118th bishop. Williams said that his priorities included working toward social justice and expanding the influence of the AME Church abroad, with specific attention to strengthening ties with Africa. AME bishops overseas believe that most of the denomination's growth will occur in underdeveloped nations, where poverty, hunger, war, and AIDS cause untold suffering. During his inaugural speech at his investiture, Williams said, as reported by Carolyn Click for the *State* (July 1, 2006), "The African Methodist Episcopal Church has always stood at the forefront of liberation theology and remains faithfully committed to the core values upon which the institution was founded over two hundred years ago. Some of those fundamental principles are to feed the hungry, clothe the naked, and set free those who live within the confines of degradation, poverty and disease." He also said, "God is not calling us to merely add land and buildings to our Zion, but more importantly to bring more souls to Christ. AME Church growth must be about not only the mainstream, but also going into the hedges, hamlets, homeless shelters and harlot havens to proclaim a gospel that not only saves but liberates."

One of Williams's responsibilities was to ensure that the church leadership and body are inclusive of all groups and races. "Race relations here [in South Carolina] are tenuous at best," he told reporters at a Columbia, South Carolina, press conference, as reported by Tim Smith for the *Greenville News* (April 26, 2006). "We have a goodly number of whites in our church in South Carolina. They did not come, by and large, because of racial marriages. They appreciate the kind of ministry we are going towards. . . . Once you get beyond the ethnic groups and personalities, they are driven by the same urges or notions as any human being. They hurt. They cry. They have conflicts. They are without jobs. They are homeless. We have to get in there and try to work with them."

Williams expressed the hope that as president of the Council of Bishops, he would be influential in attracting attention to the problems of South Carolina communities. "South Carolina needs a new beginning," he said, as reported by Smith. "Government cannot do it itself. We must as citizens work together to bring about change there." Mark Sanford, South Carolina's governor, told Smith, "Every time we see each other, [Williams] literally grabs ahold of me and says, 'We need to do some-

thing more about health care in South Carolina.'" Getting more people to register to vote and to come to the polls on Election Day—and thus increase their power in the social and political spheres—was another of Williams's missions. Since presidents of the Council of Bishops may serve for one year only, in June 2007 Williams relinquished his post. His successor was Wilfred Jacobus Messiah, the bishop of the 20th Episcopal District, which encompasses Malawi and parts of Zimbabwe, in southeastern Africa.

For eight years Williams was the treasurer of the Sixth Episcopal District (Georgia). He served as a board member and comptroller of finance of Turner Theological Seminary, in Atlanta, Georgia, and a member of the General Assembly of the World Council of Churches. As a member of the Atlanta board of education, he held, successively or concurrently, the posts of president, vice president, chairman of the finance committee, and chairman of the superintendent search committee. For a while he served as Georgia's state director of communications in radio and television. As the longtime owner of an insurance company, he "partnered with Allied Health Agencies to provide financial support services for the communities in which he lived and worshipped," according to the Seventh Episcopal District's Web site. He sits on the governing board of Wesley Theological Seminary and is chairman of the board of Allen University, in Columbia, South Carolina.

Williams and his wife, the former Wilma Delores Webb, have one son and three daughters: Arnold Andre, a physicist; Wilma Priscilla, a chemist, and Stella Jacinta, a geologist, who are twins; and Prestina Delores, a television news anchor and reporter.

—N.W.M.

Suggested Reading: African Methodist Episcopal Church Web site; ame7.org; (Charleston, South Carolina) *Post and Courier* A p1 June 27, 2006; (Columbia, South Carolina) *State* B p1 July 21, 2004, A p1 Apr. 21, 2006, A p15 Apr. 21, 2006, B p1 June 27, 2006, B p3 July 1, 2006; *Greenville (South Carolina) News* B p13 Oct. 6, 2005, B p1 Apr. 26, 2006; *Jet* p40 May 15, 2006

Williams, Roy

Aug. 1, 1950– College basketball coach

Address: University of North Carolina Athletic Dept., P.O. Box 2126, Chapel Hill, NC 27514

In 2003 the men's college basketball coach Roy Williams made a difficult decision. Having served as head coach of the University of Kansas Jayhawks for 15 years, during which he had built the team into a perennial contender for the National Colle-

Streeter Lecka/Getty Images

Roy Williams

giate Athletic Association (NCAA) championship, he returned to the University of North Carolina— where he had last earned $2,700 per year as an assistant coach for the Tar Heels, working under his mentor, the legendary coach Dean Smith. In at least one respect, the move paid off: in the 2004–05 season, his second at the helm of the North Carolina team, Williams led the Tar Heels to the NCAA title, the prize that had eluded him in his years as the Jayhawks' coach. Under Williams the Tar Heels have been a constant presence in NCAA tournament play; in late 2006 Williams celebrated his 500th career victory. As a boy from a broken home, Williams had embraced basketball in part as an escape from his personal troubles and had found father figures in his coaches, who helped him to build self-confidence. As a coach himself, he is known for the admiration, loyalty, and sense of team spirit he inspires in his players. On April 1, 2007 Williams was elected to the Basketball Hall of Fame.

Roy Williams was born on August 1, 1950 in Spruce Pines, North Carolina, the second of the two children of Mack Clayton Williams, known as Babe, and Lallage Williams, whom family members called Mimmie. When Williams was eight years old, he and his family moved to the industrial town of Asheville, in the Blue Ridge Mountains of North Carolina. Williams's father was an abusive alcoholic during that time; to get Roy and his older sister, Frances, away from him, Roy's mother would sometimes take them to a local motel owned by a relative. One summer Roy, his sister, and their mother lived in a small motor home in a trailer park. Decades later, after Babe Williams had expressed remorse for the way he behaved during his

children's formative years, Roy Williams told William Nack for *Sports Illustrated* (March 10, 1997) that he was not angry at his father. "I think I'm mad at alcohol," he said. "I don't think it's my dad that did that."

In 1963 Williams's parents permanently separated. "It wasn't pleasant," Williams recalled to Nack. "Back then I didn't understand it, I didn't like it, but I didn't let it dominate my life." Williams and his mother and sister went to live in a small, two-bedroom, rented house in Biltmore, North Carolina. Mimmie Williams worked full-time in a factory. Because her salary was not enough to support herself and two children, she took additional work as a maid and laundress. Williams, who has often referred to his mother as a "hero" and an "angel" because of the sacrifices she made for him and his sister, said to Nack, "Some of my worst memories are coming home in sixth or seventh grade and finding her ironing. Ten cents for a shirt, 10 cents for a pair of pants. And this after she had worked all day. You don't think that was hard to see? I knew that a lot of moms didn't have to do that, and I didn't want to watch her, so I'd just leave." Over the years Williams became increasingly devoted to and protective of his mother, whom Nack described as a "strong, shy, humble" person. "He never spent a night away from home until high school," his sister told Nack. "He felt he needed to be there. He was like a protector to her." (Williams's mother died in 1992, his father in 2004.)

As difficult as they were in other ways as well, Williams's years in Biltmore, following a period of constant moving, gave him a sense of stability. He began to spend the bulk of his spare time shooting baskets by himself in the gymnasium of a school near his home; he used the gym as a refuge, a place where he could collect his thoughts. Because the school was locked after hours, he would get into the gym by climbing to the second floor and through a window. On one occasion a local police officer, who had frequently seen Williams climbing the walls, took him in a squad car to the school principal's house. Neither the police officer nor the principal—who helped Williams get his first coaching job after college—wanted to punish Williams; rather, the principal presented him with a key to the school, to prevent him from getting hurt while climbing to the gym.

Williams said to Dick Jerard for the *Philadelphia Daily News* (December 19, 1996) that baseball, not basketball, was his "real love" at first—and that only after signing up for basketball in eighth grade did he develop a passion for playing that sport with others. In his first game, he passed the ball three times to players who then missed shots. "The fourth time," he said, "I shot it and it went in. . . . After that, a lot of them went in and I just fell in love with it." While attending T. C. Roberson High School, in Asheville, where he played basketball, Williams befriended Buddy Baldwin, a graduate of the University of North Carolina and the coach of

Roberson's basketball team. Baldwin became a father figure to Williams. "He really was the first person to give me a great deal of confidence, to make me feel good about myself," Williams told Vahe Gregorian for the *St. Louis Post-Dispatch* (March 8, 1992). "All of a sudden I realized I can't be the only person he's doing it to. Think how good it would feel to be able to do that for people." By the time Williams was a senior in high school, Baldwin had convinced him that he should pursue a career in coaching. Coaching became "the most important thing in the world for me," Williams told Nack. "I woke up in the morning, and it was the first thing I thought about, and when I went to bed at night, it was the last thing I thought of."

Williams earned letters for both basketball and baseball in each of his four years at Roberson, won all-county and all-conference honors as a basketball player in his junior and senior seasons (1967 and 1968, respectively), and finished his career at Roberson as the school's all-time leading scorer in basketball. He received offers of athletic scholarships from several small colleges; an excellent student, he was also offered a full scholarship to study engineering at the Georgia Institute of Technology. He turned those schools down, however, in order to take Baldwin's advice, which was to attend the University of North Carolina at Chapel Hill. Baldwin had played for the legendary college basketball coach Dean Smith at North Carolina, on the reserve freshman team. "[Baldwin] had a great deal of respect for coach Smith so I started watching North Carolina basketball as a junior [in high school]," Williams told Dick Weiss for the *New York Daily News.*

At North Carolina, where he received a B.A. degree in education in 1972 and an M.A.T. (master of arts in teaching) degree in the following year, Williams competed for one season (1968–69) on the university's freshman team as a non-scholarship player, under the charge of Bill Guthridge, a longtime assistant to Smith. After his freshman year he was forced to leave the team in order to earn money to stay in school. Williams financed his education by taking out loans and by working several nights per week as an intramural softball umpire, rising to become, by his senior year, the supervisor of intramural officials at the school. He began to keep statistics for Smith at the home games of the basketball team, the Tar Heels; by the time he became a sophomore, he was allowed to attend the team's practices. Observing those practices "as if they were academic lectures," in Nack's words, Williams would sit high in the stands and take notes.

In 1973 Williams accepted a position as the basketball coach at Owen High School, in Swannanoa, North Carolina, 10 miles from Asheville. Meanwhile, he maintained his ties to Smith, refereeing at his summer basketball camp. At Owen, Williams imparted to his players the principles he had learned from Baldwin, seeking to foster self-confidence in them. He also coached golf and football at the school and served for two years as

Owen's athletic director. He quickly developed a reputation among his players as a sincere, nurturing coach. "He always made you feel like you were somebody," Bobby Stafford, a former player of Williams's at Owen, told Nack. "I don't care how much you had or who you were. He made you feel like you mattered."

In 1978 Smith offered Williams, who by that time was married with an infant son, a position as a part-time assistant coach at the University of North Carolina. Despite his wife's protests, Williams accepted the position, which paid him a sum of $2,700 a year. To earn extra money, for five years Williams also delivered videotapes of the basketball and football teams' games to TV stations in such locations as Asheville and Greensboro, North Carolina, driving 500 miles to do so—on his day off from coaching. In addition, during the off-season he worked as a traveling salesman, peddling calendars that featured pictures of North Carolina's basketball players. By 1987, his ninth and penultimate season as an assistant coach at North Carolina, he was earning an additional $30,000 annually as a salesman. Calling the sales job "the hardest thing I ever did in my life," Smith recalled to Nack, "I was the best calendar salesman in the country." The Tar Heels qualified for the NCAA Tournament in each of Williams's 10 seasons as an assistant coach with the team. In 1981 the team advanced to the championship game, which they lost to the Indiana Hoosiers, 63–50. The Tar Heels returned the following season to the finals, this time outscoring Georgetown, 63–62, to win the national championship. During his last two seasons as an assistant under Smith, Williams also served as the team's chief recruiter.

Receiving a recommendation from Smith, in July 1988 the University of Kansas's athletic director, Bob Frederick, hired Williams as head coach of the school's basketball team. Williams, then 37, inherited a team that was—for all its recent success—in disarray. A few months earlier the Jayhawks had won the national title, led by the head coach, Larry Brown, and the All-American forward Danny Manning. But neither Brown or Manning, who had been drafted by the National Basketball Association (NBA), was to return to Kansas, and to many the team's future seemed bleak, with an unknown coach—Williams—as the Jayhawks' leader. Making matters worse, the NCAA had suspended Kansas from postseason tournament play for Williams's first season, 1988–99, due to recruiting infractions incurred during Brown's five-year tenure. As a result the team became the first in college basketball history to be ineligible to defend its title.

Despite those daunting conditions, in his first season in Kansas, Williams guided the Jayhawks to a 19–12 record. Rumors began to circulate that other Division I schools with coaching vacancies, among them Ohio State University and the University of Kentucky, were pursuing him as a possible head coach; thus began the first of many such rounds of speculation during Williams's 15 years in Kansas. Williams soon released a statement declaring that his intentions were to remain with Kansas for the foreseeable future.

Again exceeding expectations, the Jayhawks finished the following season (1989–90) with a 30–5 record and a berth in the NCAA Tournament. For his team's performance on the court, Williams earned his first United States Basketball Writers Association National Coach of the Year honor and his first Associated Press (AP) Big XII Conference Coach of the Year honor. The team advanced as far as the second round in the NCAA Tournament, defeating Robert Morris College, 79–71, before losing to the University of California at Los Angeles (UCLA), 71–70. With a 22–8 record, the Jayhawks entered the 1991 NCAA Tournament as co-champions of the Big Eight Conference's regular season. The team won five consecutive NCAA Tournament games, upsetting such powerful teams as Indiana and Arkansas on its way to the Final Four. The only team that stood between Kansas and the championship game was the North Carolina Tar Heels.

The semifinal game between Smith's Tar Heels and the Jayhawks was a watershed moment in Williams's career—marking his first appearance in the Final Four and pitting him against his mentor. Entering the game, the more experienced Tar Heels were soundly favored, but the Jayhawks built a 10-point lead in the second half and held on for a 79–73 victory. Referring to the game in a conversation with Vahe Gregorian, Smith said about Williams, "What really bugs me is he runs our stuff better than we do." Kansas advanced to play Duke University in the national championship game, losing by a score of 72–65. Williams won the AP Coach of the Year Award in 1992. In the 1992–93 season, Kansas faced North Carolina in the Final Four again. This time Smith outmaneuvered his former pupil, and the Jayhawks lost, 76–68.

Williams guided the Jayhawks to the Final Four again in 2002 and 2003, his last season in Kansas. In 2002, after wins against Holy Cross, Stanford, Illinois, and Oregon in the Midwest regional conference, the number-one-seeded Jayhawks faced the University of Maryland Terrapins in the Final Four. Maryland overcame the Jayhawks' early 13–2 lead to win the game, 97–88. In the 2003 tournament successive victories against Utah State, Arizona State, Duke University, the University of Arizona, and Marquette University placed the Jayhawks in the national championship game against Syracuse University. As the higher-seeded team, Kansas was favored to win, but the team's inconsistent free-throw shooting, along with the Syracuse players' ability to make three-point baskets consistently, led to a 81–78 loss for the Jayhawks.

Although in the world of college basketball, he was "the winningest coach to never win" a national title, as several sportswriters put it, Williams compiled some highly impressive statistics as the head coach at Kansas. His teams were a model of consistency, especially at home, where their re-

cord over 15 seasons was 201–17, making for an astounding winning percentage of better than 92 percent; that included a 62-game winning streak over four seasons at home. Overall in Williams's tenure, the Jayhawks' record was 401–101. For a period of 145 consecutive weeks, from 1991 to 1999, the Jayhawks were ranked among the 25 top Division I teams in the country. In six of Williams's 15 seasons, the team held the number-one AP ranking for at least part of the regular season.

To his peers and players, Williams is known as an inspiring teacher but also as a no-nonsense disciplinarian—one given to kicking trash cans or throwing duffel bags when his players do not make sufficient effort. He is known, though, to be fair and compassionate. Bill Lyons wrote about Williams for the *Philadelphia Inquirer*, as quoted on hitrunscore.com, "He does not scream and snarl into the sweaty perplexed face of a 19-year-old who is doing the best he can." His players have rarely been suspended for academic shortcomings. On the court, his teams play in a style similar to that of Smith's teams, employing a high-pressure man-to-man defense, committing a minimal number of turnovers on offense, and outrunning opponents on the open floor to create a high number of field-goal opportunities. During his time in Kansas, Williams served on the NCAA basketball rules committee six times; in 2000–01 he was chairman of the committee. Several of his former staff members have gone on to become head coaches at the college level.

In 2003 Williams was offered the position of head coach of the University of North Carolina basketball team. Several years earlier Dean Smith had retired from the post, and the Tar Heels' most recent coach, Matt Doherty, had been forced to resign after leading the once-formidable team to 36 losses over two years. The choice Williams faced led to "seven days of self-torture," as a writer for *Sports Illustrated* (November 17, 2003) put it; he felt torn between remaining in Kansas, where he had enjoyed a great deal of success and earned a loyal following, and returning to the University of North Carolina, which he had long felt to be, in a sense, his true home. The determining factor in his decision was his dissatisfaction under Al Bohl, who had been athletic director at the University of Kansas since 2001. Williams accepted the offer from North Carolina, amid accusations of being a traitor. Some in Kansas began wearing T-shirts that read "Benedict Williams," a reference to Benedict Arnold, the American army general who became a traitor during the Revolutionary War. "Those BENEDICT WILLIAMS T-shirts, that hit me harder than anything has ever hit me," Williams told the *Sports Illustrated* writer.

Williams's transition to North Carolina was a successful one: in his first season as coach of the Tar Heels, in 2003–04, the team advanced to the second round of postseason play, in which they lost, 78–75, to the University of Texas Longhorns. The following season, in April 2005, the Tar Heels defeated the University of Illinois, 75–70, to capture the NCAA title—Williams's first championship win. Referring to Buddy Baldwin and Dean Smith, who were among the more than 47,000 in attendance on that occasion, Williams told reporters afterward, as quoted by Jeff Carlton in the Greensboro, North Carolina, *News & Record* (January 20, 2006, on-line), "I will never be as good as either of them. But I do try." In the 2005–06 season the Tar Heels again advanced to the second round of tournament play, losing to the George Mason University team by a score of 65–60. That season Williams was presented with the AP Coach of the Year Award, becoming only the second coach to win the honor at two schools and the seventh to win it more than once. Before the 2006–07 season, Brandan Wright, Ty Lawson, and Wayne Ellington joined the team. The three helped the Tar Heels win 25 games and lose only six during the regular season. After defeating the University of Southern California Trojans, 74–64, in the third round of tournament play, they advanced to the East Regional Final, where they lost to the Georgetown Hoyas in overtime, 96–84.

Williams has played an active role in basketball at the international level, with United States (USA) Basketball. In 1991, at the World University Games, serving as an assistant alongside the former NBA head coach P. J. Carlesimo, he helped lead Team USA to a 6–0 record and a gold medal. The following year he helped coach the United States Olympic Development Team, which consisted of eight college basketball stars, as it scrimmaged against the first USA Olympic Dream Team—a unit that featured such former NBA superstars as Michael Jordan, Earvin "Magic" Johnson, Larry Bird, Patrick Ewing, and Charles Barkley. Most recently he served at the 2004 Olympic Games, in Athens, Greece, as an assistant to Larry Brown for the USA Olympic Team, which included the current NBA stars Allen Iverson, Tim Duncan, LeBron James, and Amare Stoudemire. The team won a bronze medal.

Roy Williams met his wife, Wanda, during a freshman algebra course in high school. (The two did not begin dating until they were classmates once again, in college.) The couple have two children, Scott and Kimberly. "Roy is as good as it gets in a person," the basketball Hall of Fame player Jerry West was quoted as saying on the Tar Heels' official athletic Web site. "There's nothing deceptive about him. He is what he is—a wonderful person and a great coach. . . . If you go to his practices, you know why his teams are successful. His players play the right way. They're team-oriented. They play a fun way offensively. They're aggressive. He changes defenses. He does it all. He's just a wonderful coach."

—D.F.

Suggested Reading: *Philadelphia Daily News* p84 Dec. 19, 1996; *St. Louis Post-Dispatch* F p1 Mar. 8, 1992; *Sports Illustrated* p52+ Mar. 10, 1997, p76+ Nov. 17, 2003; University of North Carolina Official Athletic Web site

---

Wilmore, Larry

1961(?)– Television actor; scriptwriter; producer

Address: Comedy Central, 1775 Broadway, New York, NY 10019

"Comedy is in me and show business is how I get it out," the television writer, actor, comedian, and producer Larry Wilmore has said, according to Lorena Fernandez in the *Los Angeles Wave* (June 29, 2007, on-line). Wilmore "has a completely unique comic point of view . . . ," his friend and fellow writer and producer Peter B. Aronson told Felicia R. Lee for the *New York Times* (April 2, 2007). "It's smart and manages to be racially sensitive and completely mainstream at the same time." Wilmore's gifts for comedy and improvisation, powers of observation, and extensive knowledge of current events are currently displayed on *The Daily Show*, the faux-news program hosted by Jon Stewart, in which Wilmore poses as the senior black correspondent—a job title that comes with an invisible smirk, since he is the show's *only* black correspondent. Wilmore was an undergraduate when, in about 1980, he launched his career as a stand-up comedian. Foiled in his attempt to establish himself as an actor in feature films, he turned to writing for television. With the actor and comedian Eddie Murphy and the writer and producer Steve Tomkins, he created and co-wrote the animated TV sitcom *The PJs*; his work on that series, which aired for three seasons beginning in 1999, earned him an Emmy Award nomination. In 2002, as the creator and writer of *The Bernie Mac Show*, Wilmore became the first African-American to capture a solo Emmy Award for writing for a network program. More recently, in addition to his work on *The Daily Show*, Wilmore has written, acted in, and produced several episodes of NBC's series *The Office*, which parodies the work lives of nine-to-fivers in a typical contemporary American office. In 2006 he and 10 others shared two Emmy nominations for *The Office*, in the categories of best comedy series and best new series.

Larry Wilmore was born in about 1961 and grew up in Pomona, California, a suburb of Los Angeles. One of his brothers, Marc Wilmore, has co-written scripts for, and occasionally lent his voice to, the animated TV series *The Simpsons*. Wilmore's father and mother divorced when he was young, and he and his five siblings were raised by their moth-

Jon Kopaloff/Getty Images

Larry Wilmore

er. His father was a probation officer when he moved away (he later became a doctor), and the family struggled financially after his departure. "It's funny, it gives you an interesting perspective on life, too, when you really don't have any material goods, and you're not sure if you're going to be able to pay your light bill or your heat bill or all this stuff," Wilmore told Terry Gross, who interviewed him for the National Public Radio program *Fresh Air* (June 5, 2007, on-line). Nevertheless, he continued, he "always had a middle class sensibility" and believed that success is possible if one works hard enough. Once, when the roof of his family's house gave way during a heavy rain, he told his brother Marc, as he recalled to Gross, "I am not going to wind up like this, man." As a child, he also told Gross, he "used to have the *TV Guide* memorized. I could tell you what night everything was on." He enjoyed watching such comedians as Buster Keaton, the Marx Brothers, Richard Pryor, and Steve Martin, and his favorite programs included *Get Smart*, *All in the Family*, *Sanford and Son*, and *The Flip Wilson Show*. The last-named series, he has recalled, was the first to have a "black man with a TV show that was his own . . . ," as he told Gross. "In those days, that was unheard of. I think Diahann Carrol was the only other black person to have her own show as the lead. And Bill Cosby was on *I Spy*, but that was a little different, you know? Here, it was Flip Wilson's show, and he was just so funny to me. That was my first big influence." Wilmore attended the Catholic, all-male Damien High School, in La Verne, California, on a scholarship. He abandoned his plan of becoming an astronaut when his interest in theater blossomed. Following his graduation from high school, in 1979,

Wilmore attended California State Polytechnic University, in Pomona, where he studied theater. As an undergraduate he performed stand-up comedy, first on the street and then in local clubs. That experience led him to drop out of college, join the Actors' Equity Association (a trade union), and pursue a full-time career as a stand-up comic. He also dreamed of getting parts in Hollywood films.

In the 1980s Wilmore was seldom without work in clubs and other venues that hired stand-up comedians, but he had little success in Hollywood. He told Felicia R. Lee that the few directors who expressed interest in him usually wanted to cast him as a "fast-talking ex-con." He earned small parts in the movie *Good-bye Cruel World* and the TV series *The Facts of Life*, both in 1983, and had a recurring role on ABC-TV's *Sledge Hammer* (1986–88), a spoof of violent detective shows. In 1990 he made five appearances on the talent show *Star Search* and once hosted *An Evening at the Improv*, televised on the Entertainment Network from the Hollywood branch of a chain of comedy clubs.

Determined to remain in the entertainment industry, Wilmore began to try his hand at writing. He built an impressive résumé by writing for diverse TV programs, among them the short-lived late-night show *Into the Night with Rick Dees*; the sitcom *The Fresh Prince of Bel-Air*, starring Will Smith; *Def Comedy Jam*, a monthly showcase on HBO for black comedians; and the sketch-comedy series *In Living Color*, created by Keenan Ivory Wayans and starring Wayans and several of his siblings. Wilmore and his collaborators won a 1992 Emmy Award nomination for their work on *In Living Color*. He also wrote for *Sister Sister* and *The Jamie Foxx Show*.

In 1997 the actor Eddie Murphy tapped Wilmore to develop the animated sitcom that became *The PJs*. The series was created by a process called stop-motion animation, or claymation, with characters made not of clay but of foam. To show movement, each figure was photographed two dozen times for each second of tape, with each episode taking about two months to complete. A satire of African-American culture and that of the U.S. in general, the story was set in a decrepit inner-city public housing project and dealt with topics rarely touched upon in sitcoms: poverty, crime, police brutality, the unresponsiveness of the U.S. Department of Housing and Urban Development (HUD), and individuals' excessive use of alcohol and drugs. The characters included Thurgood Stubbs, a big-bellied, big-haired, cantankerous building superintendent, whose voice was that of Murphy; Stubbs's wife, a kind, reasonable woman with big buttocks; a crack user; a parole officer with a shady past; and a perpetually unhelpful HUD employee. Co-written by Steve Tompkins, the show premiered on the Fox network in January 1999. The first episode drew 22 million viewers, the second-largest premier in Fox history after *The Simpsons*, and during its first season an average of 11.4 million people tuned in to watch it.

In a review of *The PJs* for the Associated Press (January 11, 1999), Lynn Elber wrote, "The look is winsome, the tone breezy, the overall effect in keeping with Fox's tradition of cutting-edge animated comedy that began with *The Simpsons* and is followed up in *King of the Hill*." By contrast, Caryn James, a *New York Times* (January 8, 1999) critic, implied that *The PJs'* exaggerations were "nothing more than stereotypes." She also wrote, "There may have been potential here, but the first episode is deadening in its lame comedy and obvious reach for good lessons. . . . *The PJs* shows that animation can breed bad comedy just as easily as live action can." The filmmaker Spike Lee, according to Jeff Z. Klein, writing for the *New York Times* (August 27, 2000), complained that *The PJs* of "show[ed] no love for black people." "I'm not saying we're above being made fun of and stuff like that," he added, "but [*The PJs* is] really hateful, I think, toward black people, plain and simple." In response to Lee's comments, Wilmore told Rob Owen for the *Pittsburgh (Pennsylvania) Post-Gazette* (January 18, 1999), "You know, it's funny that as African-Americans, we fought for years to be treated as individuals. And then we put on a show [with characters] we hoped would be judged as individuals, and many African-Americans say, 'Well, how come you're representing the whole?' Who said we were doing that? When was there ever a thing in the script that said [the character Thurgood] represents all superintendents of projects? These people are individuals, just in the same way you wouldn't say *Seinfeld* represents all Jews." Wilmore also expressed the opinion that if the show had been a drama, the portrayals of *The PJs* characters would not have raised eyebrows. He told Scott D. Pierce for the Salt Lake City, Utah, *Deseret News* (February 1, 1999), "We don't always do the right thing or hit the right mark. And I think people have every right to their opinion. If they feel it's offensive, they're probably right that it offends them." But when such people behave as though they are expressing the opinions of all viewers rather than only themselves, Wilmore added, he and the show's other creators "take offense." In terms of ratings, *The PJs* was successful; the show and its creators also won an Emmy nomination in 1999 for outstanding animated program for shows of one hour or less. *The PJs* was not a favorite of Fox executives, however, because of its touchy subject matter and its high production costs. After two seasons the show moved to the WB network, where its run ended after a single season.

Wilmore was the creator of *The Bernie Mac Show*, which debuted on Fox in 2001. He also co-wrote and co-produced that sitcom, which starred Bernie Mac as a successful comedian whose life changes dramatically when he and his wife, who are childless, take into their home the son and two daughters of his sister, who is in a drug-rehabilitation program. The idea for the story grew out of a sketch that Wilmore had seen Mac perform during the actor's tour with the "Original Kings of Comedy" (recorded for the 2000 film with that name). "I wanted an emotionally involving situation," Wilmore told Manuel Mendoza for the *Dallas (Texas) Morning News* (November 14, 2001). "We'd feel sorry for those kids. We'd feel that, 'Boy, that's a big responsibility, and [Mac's] doing it for a good reason.' It doesn't seem like a sitcom, made-up situation. I thought Bernie's personality was big enough to carry it off, too." At first Mac felt reluctant to work in television, because he feared excessive censorship, but the deal Wilmore negotiated with Fox gave him an unusual amount of artistic freedom, and his scripts allowed Mac to retain his edgy, often politically incorrect sense of humor. "I just wanted to do something different in television," Wilmore explained to Lillian A. Jackson for *Electronic Media* (February 4, 2002). "And I was . . . frustrated with the form of the sitcom. A lot of them don't work because people are just so used to the form. It's hard to surprise [viewers] anymore, to really be funny in a different way." Wilmore borrowed ideas from reality television, one of the fastest-growing genres in TV at that time. "I thought the real entertainment value [of reality television] was the unpredictability . . . ," he told Jackson. "So I came up with this concept, this show: making it seem like we're eavesdropping on the situation, really using the camera as a storytelling device." To further that conceit, when alone Mac often spoke directly to the camera, in "confessional" scenes. "His lectures and soliloquies are actually expressions of his own deep affection and concern for the children, reminding us of what is truly important for families," as a writer put it on the Peabody Awards Web site (2001).

Taped without a laugh track or a studio audience, *The Bernie Mac Show* was shot in high-definition video on a colorful set. Hoping to appeal to diverse viewers, Wilmore focused on the difficulties of raising children—a problem common to all racial and ethnic groups and one that in the developed world periodically gives rise to theories of parenting that contradict earlier ones. Mac's character displayed an anachronistic approach to the task, often threatening his wards with physical violence. Wilmore explained to Gail Pennington for the *St. Louis (Missouri) Post-Dispatch* (November 13, 2001) that he tried "to deal with those two issues, old school vs. new school, and at the same time making it a fair fight. You know, giving good arguments for people today as well as good arguments for Bernie's point of view." He also said, "It really isn't so much a racial-cultural thing as a social-cultural issue, how society was a bit more authoritarian when we were kids. We are a little more lax today as parents." Wilmore won a 2002 Emmy Award for outstanding writing for a comedy series for the pilot of *The Bernie Mac Show*. The program was also recognized with a Humanitas Prize, an NAACP (National Association for the Advancement of Colored People) Image Award, and a Peabody Award, the last, according to the Peabody's Web site, for offering valuable insights "in a manner that makes us laugh aloud even when we are viewing alone."

In its second season *The Bernie Mac Show* aired at the same time as ABC's family comedy *My Wife and Kids*, and its ratings declined by 13 percent. Meanwhile, Wilmore and Fox executives had increasingly frequent differences of opinion regarding scripts and other aspects of the show, with some within the network charging that he did not pay sufficient attention to secondary story lines and that the inclusion of provocative dialogue might offend viewers. For his part Wilmore complained to various sources about Fox's handling of the show, which included pulling it from its Wednesday time slot during sweeps week and airing *American Idol* in its stead. In the middle of *The Bernie Mac Show*'s second season, Fox fired him.

Soon afterward, in April 2003, Wilmore signed a lucrative contract with NBC that called for him to develop new shows. The network rejected several of his ideas before approving the comedies *Whoopi*, starring Whoopi Goldberg, which lasted for two seasons (2003–04) and earned two Emmy nominations, and *Beverly Hills S.U.V.* (2004). He later acted as a consultant, producer, and writer for several episodes of the sitcom *The Office* and acted in two episodes in 2006.

In August 2006 Wilmore joined the cast of *The Daily Show*, which airs on Comedy Central. The show, hosted by Jon Stewart, includes a half-dozen other "commentators"; as the so-called senior black correspondent on the program, which spoofs nighttime TV news broadcasts, Wilmore supposedly reports from the field. "A lot of times when something happens in a black neighborhood, [networks] will send the one black correspondent to cover it. That was our satirical jumping off point," he told Lee. Wilmore, who writes some of his own material, believes that his presence as an African-American makes it possible for *The Daily Show* to satirize topics that would be off-limits to non-black "reporters." In one sketch, for example, Wilmore and the British comedian John Oliver interviewed New York City councilman Leroy Comrie and satirized Comrie's efforts to prohibit use of the "n-word" ("nigger"). In another sketch Wilmore poked fun at Black History Month, telling Stewart that it serves only to "mak[e] up for centuries of oppression with 28 days of trivia." He also said, "Jon, let's be honest, Black History Month is a drag, OK? White people have to pretend they care about black people, black people have to pretend they care about history, it's a lose-lose, OK?" Wilmore told Gross that rather than act, or pretend to act, as a representative of African-Americans, he regards his contribution to the show as the addition of a contrarian voice. "There were some ideas to make me maybe a black conservative," he said, "but I didn't want to be pigeonholed. . . . I thought it would be more fun to be contrary. . . . So whatever point you're going to take, I'm not going to take the opposite point, I'll just be contrary to you. . . .You're not sure where this person really

stands, and the ability to argue either side of the issue with as much passion, too, can frustrate people. And I think it's a fun place to do comedy from." Wilmore told Felicia R. Lee that he welcomes viewers' strongly negative or positive reactions to his character. "It's indifference that's the bad one," he said.

Wilmore lives in San Marino, California, outside Los Angeles, with his wife and their two children. He reads two or three newspapers a day and often goes on-line to keep up with current events.

—N.W.M.

Suggested Reading: *Daily Variety* p5 Apr. 1, 2003; *Electronic Media* p1+ Feb. 4, 2002; *Fresh Air* (on-line) June 5, 2007; imdb.com; *Los Angeles Wave* (on-line) June 29, 2007; *New York Times* II p21 Aug. 27, 2000, E p1+ Apr. 2, 2007; *Pittsburgh (Pennsylvania) Post-Gazette* D p6 Jan. 18, 1999; *St. Louis (Missouri) Post-Dispatch* F p1+ Nov. 13, 2001; *TV Week* (on-line) Sep. 16, 2007

Selected Television Shows: as writer—*Into the Night with Rick Dees*, 1990; *The Fresh Prince of Bel-Air*, 1990; *In Living Color*, 1990–92; *The PJs*, 1999–2000; *The Bernie Mac Show*, 2001–02; *Whoopi*, 2003–04; *Beverly Hills S.U.V.*, 2004; *The Office*, 2006; as actor—*Sledge Hammer*, 1986–88; *The Daily Show*, 2006–

Selected Films: as actor—*Goodbye Cruel World*, 1983

Woertz, Patricia A.

Mar. 17, 1953– CEO of the Archer Daniels Midland Co.

Address: Archer Daniels Midland, 4666 Faries Pkwy., P.O. Box 1470, Decatur, IL 62525

On May 1, 2006 Patricia A. Woertz succeeded G. Allen Andreas to become the eighth chief executive officer (CEO) in the 104-year history of the Illinois-based Archer Daniels Midland Co. (ADM), one of the world's largest agricultural processors and producers of biofuels. Woertz, who has a distinguished record of penetrating the so-called glass ceiling for female advancement in corporate America, has downplayed her reputation as a trailblazer, despite her appointment as ADM's first-ever female CEO. "I hope people will judge me by my performance . . . ," Woertz told Michael Kinsman for the Springfield, Illinois, *State Journal-Register* (July 2, 2006). "Obviously, I'm a woman, but I also am an executive [who] has developed skills through the years just like any other executive, male or female." Indeed, during her 30-year career in the petroleum industry, first at the Houston,

Courtesy of Archer Daniels Midland Company

Patricia A. Woertz

Texas-based Gulf Oil Corp. and later at the Chevron Corp., in San Francisco, California, Woertz's business acumen—far more than her status as a woman in a male-dominated field—accounted for her rise up the corporate ladder. Kenneth Derr, the CEO of the Chevron Corp. from 1989 to 1999, recalled the combination of focus and ambition Woertz demonstrated early in her career. "She told me she wanted to be chairman," Derr said to Jon Birger for *Fortune* (October 16, 2006). He added, however, "Some people spend more time worrying about the next job than doing the one they've got. That wasn't Pat."

Woertz began her career as a certified public accountant at the firm Ernst & Young. She joined the Gulf Oil Corp. in 1977, working in the finance, marketing, and strategic-planning departments. During the merger of Gulf Oil with the Standard Oil Co. of California, in the mid-1980s, Woertz succeeded in reducing costs at the new company, Chevron. In the late 1980s and 1990s, Woertz took on a variety of leadership roles at the firm. She was appointed president of Chevron Canada Ltd. in 1993, becoming the highest-ranking female executive of a Chevron subsidiary, then promoted to president of Chevron International Oil and vice president of Chevron U.S.A. Products. After the merger between Chevron and the oil company Texaco Inc., in 2001, Woertz became executive vice president for global downstream, charged with overseeing the company's worldwide chain of petroleum production, distribution, and marketing. In April 2006 Woertz accepted her current post, making ADM, for a brief time, the largest public company in the world to be headed by a woman. Her arrival at ADM was well-timed: after a stellar

fiscal year 2006, which saw the company earn $1.04 billion on revenues of $35.9 billion, the longtime agricultural processor diversified its manufacturing portfolio to include biofuels production. Increasing its research and development of agricultural-based fuels, such as ethanol, ADM—with the oil-industry veteran Woertz at the helm—stands poised to be a leader in the now lucrative alternative-energy industry. "She understands how to get the product from the processing plant to the consumer's gas tank," the analyst Gregory Warren of Morningstar Inc. said to Susan Diesenhouse and Michael Oneal for the *Chicago Tribune* (April 29, 2006). "ADM is betting the future on energy products." Woertz "is a proven executive with an exceptional blend of strategic, analytic, business and leadership skills," Andreas stated in a press release for the ADM Web site (April 28, 2006). "Her selection was endorsed unanimously by our Board of Directors, and we are confident that she is the ideal person to sustain ADM's strong performance and lead the Company into the next chapter of its history."

Patricia A. Woertz was born on March 17, 1953 in Pittsburgh, Pennsylvania, one of the two children of Chuck Woertz, the CEO of a large home-construction and development company in western Pennsylvania, and Vi Woertz, a school librarian. As a child Woertz spent summers taking unusual field trips with her family, which included her brother, Chuck Jr., visiting corporate offices and touring manufacturing plants. "My mother felt we'd be earning a living during our entire adult lives, and therefore believed we should spend summers in learning activities," Woertz said, as quoted by Ameet Sachdev and Mark Skertic for the *Chicago Tribune* (April 30, 2006). "Consequently, I got to see a plate glass factory in Pittsburgh, a U.S. Steel plant and how Heinz made ketchup." The Woertz family also made trips to local oil refineries and to the headquarters of Mellon Bank (now called the Mellon Financial Corp.). Woertz took a liking to the industrial environments that she visited. "Definitely there was a seed of inspiration sown there. I've always enjoyed seeing how things are made," she told Jon Birger for *Fortune* (October 16, 2006).

Woertz enrolled at Penn State University, in State College, Pennsylvania, where she earned a B.S. degree in accounting in 1974. That year she took her first job, as a certified public accountant for the Pittsburgh office of the global accounting firm Ernst & Young. Woertz was one of only two women in the class of 200 first-year recruits at the company. After a three-year stint at Ernst & Young, which counted the Houston-based Gulf Oil Corp. as one of its clients, Woertz, lured by the opportunity to work in the global-energy industry, joined Gulf Oil in 1977. Gulf, which had been embroiled in a political scandal in the mid-1970s involving illegal contributions to the reelection campaign of President Richard M. Nixon, took measures to revamp its internal auditing department. "Gulf was cleaning house, and I saw opportunities in the energy field," Woertz said to Michael Kinsman. At Gulf, Woertz had responsibilities in the areas of oil refining, marketing, strategic planning, and finance. In the early 1980s Gulf Oil resisted a corporate takeover from the chairman of Mesa Petroleum, T. Boone Pickens, who was known to "frighten a firm by first investing in it and then proclaiming that he could run the corporation, which invariably dwarfs Mesa in size, better than its current officers," as John Greenwald wrote for *Time* (March 4, 1985). Though Pickens's bid to take over Gulf Oil failed, the company succumbed in 1984 to a $13.4 billion merger with the Standard Oil Co. of California (Socal), one of the largest global-energy companies in the world. The merger, the largest corporate consolidation in history up to that time, raised concerns over potential antitrust violations at the Federal Trade Commission, which required Socal (known after the buyout as the Chevron Corp.) to sell off thousands of its holdings, including pipelines and gas stations. Woertz was assigned the task of overseeing the divestitures as well as reducing the overall debt. "It was a kind of turning point in my career," she told Jon Birger. "I learned about M&A [mergers and acquisitions] and how to value assets and work with investment bankers."

In 1987 Woertz, who was by then married with three young children, moved with her family to the Chevron headquarters, in San Francisco. There, she became the manager of strategic planning, overseeing the information-technology, refining, and marketing divisions. "I looked for and took the opportunities I could," she told Michael Kinsman. "The oil business was global and that gave me lots of opportunities." Her career advancement sometimes came at the expense of her family life. Noted for her intense work ethic, Woertz admitted to Susan Berfield for *BusinessWeek* (May 15, 2006) that "some people expressed surprise I had kids." She credited her husband, a logistics consultant, whom she later divorced, for putting her career ahead of his own. "At one point, we sort of said to each other, 'Gee, somebody's career is going to have to take priority,'" Woertz said to Jon Birger. Woertz was appointed president of Chevron Canada Ltd., a refining and marketing subsidiary, located in Vancouver, British Columbia, in 1993. Entrusted with overseeing 430 employees, a Canada-based refinery, 230 service stations, and annual revenues of $500 million, Woertz became the first female president of a Chevron subsidiary and the highest-ranking female executive in the company's 95-year history. "There is not a job I've held in my career that was held by a woman before me," Woertz said in a 2000 interview, as quoted by Sachdev and Skertic. In 1996 Woertz became president of Chevron International Oil and vice president of Chevron U.S.A. Products, assuming responsibility for the supply and distribution of the firm's petroleum products worldwide. She became president of Chevron U.S.A. Products in 1998.

In 2001 Woertz's career benefited from another historic corporate merger, this time Chevron's buyout of the American oil company Texaco Inc. The merger, which was valued at $35.2 billion, made the new ChevronTexaco the third-largest oil and gas producer in the United States. Woertz became executive vice president for global downstream, "which is essentially almost everything that happens to oil once we get it out of the ground," Woertz explained, as quoted in an on-line transcript of a speech she delivered for the Women in Leadership Conference at the Haas School of Business, at the University of California at Berkeley (October 26, 2002). As the highest-ranking female in the oil industry, Woertz managed business operations, spanning six continents, that included the running of more than 20 oil refineries and the marketing of the Chevron, Texaco, and Caltex brands at more than 25,000 retail outlets. She attributed her rise in leadership circles in part to her having served as president of both Chevron Canada and Chevron International Oil, which honed her global business acumen. "These assignments exposed me to different cultures and provided experience in the quite different dynamics of running international operations," she told the Haas audience. "They prepared me, as much as anything could, for expanding my responsibilities in 2001 from refining and marketing operations in one country only—the United States—to the responsibility I have today for operations in over 180 countries throughout the world."

In early 2002, not long after ChevronTexaco's formation, its downstream division suffered a setback, due to lower refining margins—resulting from sinking gas prices in a weak U.S. economy—as well as to operational inefficiencies; downstream revenues plummeted from $1.1 billion to only $43 million. For her part, Woertz, beginning in 2003, cut $500 million in costs by restructuring her upper-management team, reducing operating expenses, and negotiating favorable oil deals for her refineries. Her strategy "underscores the shadow side of creativity," she explained in a speech given in 2005 at the Wharton Business School, at the University of Pennsylvania, as quoted by Jon Birger. "Nothing is created without something being destroyed." Woertz also began to analyze the geographical regions that consistently saw the highest returns on investment, identifying Asia, Latin America, and the west coast of North America in particular as locations that rewarded the company's focus. "We asked what areas we would be investing in. We also found out which areas would be less likely to attract new capital. Europe was identified as an area that is non-strategic. Now we are studying these areas to see what our new ideas could be," she told Lucinda Kennedy for the London *Sunday Times* (August 22, 2004). Thanks to Woertz's efforts, ChevronTexaco's profit margin from international assets rose from 5 percent to 10 percent by the end of 2003.

In February 2006, after nearly three decades of service at Chevron, Woertz left the company, in part to seek a CEO position elsewhere. (As Jon Birger noted, the current Chevron CEO, David J. O'Reilly, at age 60, was "presumably several years from retirement.") Woertz's decision, one of the bolder moves in the modern corporate arena, was met with great enthusiasm by the executive search committee at the Decatur, Illinois–based Archer Daniels Midland Co., which had been scouting candidates to fill its top executive spot. Dubbed "the alpha male of agribusiness" by Susan Berfield, ADM is one of the world's largest processors of oilseeds and corn for the food industry. G. Allen Andreas had served as its CEO since 1997 and as chairman since 1999; his uncle and predecessor, Dwayne O. Andreas, had led the company's growth from a $450 million business in the early 1970s to a firm with revenues of $14 billion. G. Allen Andreas retained the chairmanship while Woertz took on the CEO post, which for a time made ADM the largest publicly traded company run by a woman. ADM's choice of Woertz, rather than a successor groomed within the company, came as a shock to many familiar with ADM's history. "By God, if you only knew the culture there," a former ADM manager told Jon Birger. "Bringing an outsider, a woman no less, into a company that's a bastion of lifers and good ol' boys—I can't tell you how huge a change that is." Andreas saw Woertz's selection as a sensible one. "We were looking for skills to manage the business. She's capable, knowledgeable, and had strong ethics," he told Susan Diesenhouse and Michael Oneal. Leonard Teitelbaum, an analyst with the financial firm Merrill Lynch & Co., suspected that for ADM, "it would be easier to teach an energy executive the agricultural side of the business, than an agricultural executive the energy side," as he put it, according to Sachdev and Skertic. Diesenhouse and Oneal framed Woertz's appointment differently: "She's a woman, she hails from Big Oil and she's not a member of the Andreas family. For all three reasons, [Woertz] is a trailblazer." On April 28, 2006 ADM officially named Woertz as CEO, the eighth in the company's 104-year-history. With her appointment Woertz became just the 10th woman ever to head a Fortune 500 company. Woertz herself continued to downplay her gender, preferring to highlight her corporate track record. "I'm fairly certain that Archer Daniels Midland didn't hire me because I'm a woman. I think my background and my performance mean more," she told Michael Kinsman.

Woertz's tenure began during a favorable period in ADM's history. From 2003 to 2005 the company saw an impressive 17 percent revenue growth and amassed $35.9 billion in total revenue, while developing a reputation as "one of Wall Street's hottest alternative-energy plays," in Birger's words. "Because the company is in good shape, the pressure is more intense on her than if she was inheriting a mess," the executive coach Debra Benton

pointed out to Del Jones for USA Today (May 1, 2006). "If she does well, at least for a while, people will say she inherited it. If she fails, they'll say women don't have the right stuff." "This isn't a turnaround situation, it's about growing for the future," Woertz said to the Associated Press, as quoted by Jones. She explained to Birger, "My objectives in my first 100 days have been to listen and learn and build trust. I've met with over 4,000 employees, been to 32 ADM locations. I want to get to a lot of people early on and find out what we do very well and where we can improve." From the outset Woertz touted the company's historically profitable food and feed businesses, which have included corn and oilseed processing, while strengthening ADM's commitment to renewable energy sources (or biofuels), such as ethanol, made from crops including corn and sugarcane. With hefty tariffs on fuel imports; with rapid strides in molecular science making it possible to create ethanol from sources other than corn kernels and sugarcane; and with ethanol's value soaring in the energy market, due in large part to federal subsidies (refiners of the substance receive a 51-cent federal tax credit for every gallon of gasoline into which ethanol is blended), some experts forecast a "transformation from a petroleum-based economy to a carbohydrate-based economy," as Mark Emalfarb, a biotechnology executive, told Diesenhouse and Oneal. Consequently, Woertz has positioned ADM at the forefront of the energy as well as the agricultural processing industry. In one notable move, Woertz recently instructed ADM's Washington, D.C., office to register as a political lobbyist, hoping to generate increased governmental support for ethanol production and usage. Woertz has urged ADM's research and development divisions to shift their investments from strictly corn-based ethanol to cellulosic ethanol, produced from grasses and agricultural waste; she has also outlined plans to allocate large portions of the company's $3 billion capital-improvement budget for the construction of a dozen new production plants worldwide, including locations in Cedar Rapids, Iowa, and Columbus, Nebraska. "I come from an industry that understands margins can be the jaws of life or the jaws of death," she said to Birger. "Any industry building capacity as rapidly as the ethanol industry has to ask itself whether margins are going to fluctuate. ADM's strength is we're building these big plants that are very cost-competitive."

Judy Olian, the former dean of the Smeal College of Business at Penn State University, commented on Woertz's management style, as quoted by Ameet Sachdev and Mark Skertic: "Pat is a straight-shooter. She doesn't like to waste time on things that people should have been prepared with. She expects you to have done your homework. She expects people to have in-depth knowledge of what they're responsible for. And she does her share of it. She asks questions and expects polished answers." Woertz serves on the boards of the American Petroleum Institute, the California

Chamber of Commerce, the University of San Diego, and the Smeal College of Business. She graduated from the International Executive Development Program at Columbia University, in New York City, in 1994, and received the Alumni Fellow Award from the Smeal College of Business in 2002. *Fortune* magazine ranked Woertz fourth on its list of the 50 Most Powerful Women in Business in 2006. Woertz, a divorced mother of three adult children, makes her home in San Francisco.

—D.J.K.

Suggested Reading: *Chicago Tribune* p1 Apr. 29, 2006, p1 June 14, 2006; *Fortune* p166 Oct. 16, 2006; (Springfield, Illinois) *State Journal-Register* p47 July 2, 2006

Stephen Shugerman/Getty Images for HRTS

Wong, Andrea

Aug. 18, 1966– Broadcasting executive

Address: Lifetime Television, 309 W. 49th St., New York, NY 10019

Known for the scope of her television experience and for her innovative programming choices, Andrea Wong was named president and chief executive officer of Lifetime Entertainment Services in April 2007. Co-owned by the Hearst Corp. and the Walt Disney Co., Lifetime offers televised movies, sitcoms, dramas, and other fare primarily geared toward women. Wong is in charge of programming, ad sales, marketing, and affiliate relations for Lifetime's three networks—Lifetime Television, Lifetime Movie, and Lifetime Real Women—as well as

Lifetime Digital (which appears on the Internet as LifetimeTV.com). When she started her job, Lifetime had been struggling for months with slumping ratings, shrinking revenues, strong competition from the Oxygen and WE (Women's Entertainment) Networks, and a breach-of-contract lawsuit brought by one of its distributors (EchoStar Communications Corp., the parent company of the Dish satellite service). She has professed to be unfazed by the task of reinvigorating the Lifetime brand. "Certainly there's a learning curve. There's always one the first time someone becomes a CEO," she told Michael Schneider for *Variety* (April 26, 2007, on-line). "But I have absolute confidence in my ability to learn, and I'm a quick study." Before she assumed her current post, Wong spent one year (1993–94) as a researcher with the ABC news show *PrimeTime Live* and then 13 years in a series of jobs with the ABC Television Network, the last three years as executive vice president for alternate programming, specials, and late-night shows. She was a prime mover in the launch on ABC of such popular and commercially lucrative programs as *The Bachelor, Extreme Makeover, Supernanny, Wife Swap,* and *Dancing with the Stars.* In announcing that the Disney–ABC Television Group had chosen her to head Lifetime, Anne Sweeney, the president of the group and the co-chair of Disney Media Networks, described Wong as "a straight shooter who is smart enough to know which challenges to undertake and fearless enough to see them through," according to a Disney–ABC Television Group press release (April 26, 2007, on-line). "She is also a true 'consumer-facing' executive, one who understands her audience and uses her experience to speak to them in compelling ways." Wong told Jon Lafayette for *Television Week* (April 30, 2007), "There is a huge upside opportunity to broaden and evolve the network to appeal to a whole group of women out there that are not viewers right now that we can capture." She also noted the "strong opportunity on the digital side to expand the brand beyond just television so that Lifetime is everywhere a woman could want it to be."

One of the five children of Manfred Wong, a schoolteacher, and Wanda Wong, a nurse, Andrea Lynn Wong was born on August 18, 1966. She has two brothers, Jeff and Greg, and two sisters, Lauri and Wendy. She and her siblings grew up in Sunnyvale, California, a suburb of San Jose. Her parents, as her mother told Gerrye Wong for *AsianWeek* (June 30, 2006, on-line), taught Wong and their other children "to respect elders, maintain a strong work ethic, the value of education, and the awareness and acceptance of diversity whether it be cultural, religious or physical." During the same interview, her mother said that Wong was a curious child with a knack for assimilating information and applying it to her life, and that as a teenager, "she never feared challenge and would always reach for goals, sometimes attaining them and other times failing but always learning from the experience." Wong attended the Massachusetts Institute of Technology (MIT), in Cambridge, Massachusetts, where she graduated with a B.S. degree in electrical engineering in 1988. But she did not feel "passion" for that discipline, as she told Gerrye Wong, and after she left MIT she spent a while "in constant evolution trying to find a satisfying career." In the early 1990s she entered the master's-degree program at the Stanford Graduate School of Business, in California. During one summer during that period, she worked at NBC. Her experience there inspired her to pursue a career as a television-news producer. After she earned an M.B.A., in 1993, she took a job as a researcher for the ABC news show *Primetime Live*. "I have to admit my MBA had exactly zero value to the people who hired me, but I was willing to start at the bottom to learn the business and told them so," she told Wong. "Looking back I feel that although not directly applicable, my MBA experience taught me skills I drew on later such as managing projects and more importantly, being a strong leader."

Through a series of promotions, Wong learned about television programming and other aspects of the business from various points of view. In June 1994 she was named executive assistant to the president of ABC Television. Seventeen months later she became executive assistant to the president of ABC Inc., a post in which she assisted in the launch of ABC's soap-opera cable network and channel. In September 1997 she was promoted to executive assistant to the president of ABC, with the title vice president. Wong moved to Los Angeles in 1998 to assume the position of vice president of alternative series and specials, and two years later she was made senior vice president, alternative series and specials.

In that position, in 1999, Wong launched a version of the British show *Who Wants to Be a Millionaire* in the United States. The same-named American edition of the quiz-style game show, originally hosted by Regis Philbin, offers contestants an opportunity to win large sums of cash—up to $1 million—for correctly answering a series of multiple-choice questions of increasing difficulty. The series became enormously popular. During its first season, and at its peak, it aired several times a week in prime time. The program spawned the spin-off *Super Millionaire* as well as a few ABC specials. In 2001 Wong helped to launch the U.S. version of *The Mole*, a reality show similar to the CBS hit *Survivor*, and she was involved in the development of its spin-off, *Celebrity Mole*. Her most notable achievement during that period was the development of *The Bachelor*, which debuted in 2002. That unscripted reality series features an elimination contest in which 25 women vie to be chosen by one unattached male, with marriage and cash as rewards. The show, currently in its 10th season, led to the spin-off series *The Bachelorette* and a special, *Trista and Ryan's Wedding*, that attracted nearly 26 million viewers in November 2004; it has also spawned over a dozen copycat shows around the world.

Also in 2002 Wong was prominent on the team that brought *Extreme Makeover* to ABC, first as a one-night special; that show's excellent ratings led ABC to expand the format into a full series. In *Extreme Makeover*, volunteers selected by program officials radically transformed their physical appearances through plastic surgery, cosmetic dentistry, new hairstyles, exercise, and wardrobe changes. The subjects' friends and relatives did not see them during their weeks-long metamorphoses and often expressed amazement or shock at the outcomes. Wong next helped develop the spin-off *Extreme Makeover: Home Edition*, which began airing in 2003. In that show, private houses, usually belonging to people deemed needy or deserving, undergo major alterations. *Home Edition* became more popular than the original series, which ended its run in July 2007, after a long period of sporadic airings during off-prime-time hours. *Home Edition* is now a fixture in the ratings top 10, has captured two Emmy Awards for best reality program (noncompetitive), and buoys ABC's Sunday-night lineup. In May 2004, in large part because of the success of the *Makeover* programs, Wong was promoted to ABC Entertainment's executive vice president of alternative programming, specials, and late-night programs.

Later that year Wong brought to the U.S. *Wife Swap*, in which two mothers traded families for a while. In 2005 she orchestrated the American premiere of *Supernanny*, a British show that featured the actress Jo Frost (in both the Great Britain and U.S. editions) as a brusque disciplinarian. In each episode Frost observes a family's seemingly ineffective approach to handling the challenges of child rearing and, using rigid, formulaic guidelines, advises the parents on how to handle what she views as deficiencies in their children's behavior. Both shows entered their third seasons in the fall of 2007. Wong was reportedly the sole executive to push for the move to ABC of another British hit, *Strictly Come Dancing*. The American version of that show, *Dancing with the Stars*, debuted to impressive ratings in June 2005 and remained one of ABC's most popular programs as it entered its fourth season, in 2007. An elimination-style reality show, *Dancing with the Stars* has couples (comprised of one celebrity and one professional ballroom dancer) compete in various genres of dance. Two original programs championed by Wong, *The Benefactor*, which featured the billionaire Mark Cuban, and *American Inventor*, met with a mixed reception from viewers. *The Benefactor* was canceled midway through its first season. *American Inventor* featured 12 contestants who, individually, had developed unique products and who vied for support from viewers, who selected a winner by voting over the phone. That program was relatively successful, and its second season began in the summer of 2007.

In many cases, critics did not share audiences' enthusiasm for the programs Wong championed. Alfie Kohn, for example, who reviewed *Super-*

nanny for the *Nation* (May 23, 2005), suggested that the methods used by Frost were detrimental to the development of the children and that "improvements" were more likely the result of careful editing than behavioral changes in the parents or children. Steve Barnes and others, writing for *Time* (December 22, 2003), who interviewed people who had participated in *Extreme Makeover*, found that many had had difficulty readjusting socially after their cosmetic surgeries; in some extreme cases, their children could not recognize them.

On other fronts, in 2004 Wong supported the inclusion in ABC's lineup of the *Nick and Jessica Variety Hour*, with Nick Lachey and Jessica Simpson; other specials with the same hosts aired during the next two years. In 2006, in an industry coup, Wong lured the Country Music Association Awards presentation from CBS to ABC. In the realm of late-night programming, she oversaw the addition to the lineup in 2003 of the talk show *Jimmy Kimmel Live.*

According to a profile of her on the Web site Goldsea, Wong began eyeing the top spot at Lifetime after being passed over for the position of president and general manager of the Learning Channel. Knowing that Lifetime's fortunes were sinking and that its president and CEO, Betty Cohen, had lost the confidence of Hearst and Disney, Wong openly lobbied for Cohen's job, according to an article dated April 26, 2007, written by the *Los Angeles Times* reporter Meg James, and posted on the Web site of the World Women's Forum. In late April 2007, a day after Cohen stepped down, Wong assumed her position. Her responsibilities include areas in which she has years of expertise, such as programming, as well as those in which she does not, including advertising sales and affiliate relations. Upon her arrival at Lifetime, Wong said that she would not immediately try to change programs for the upcoming year, among them three new dramas: *Army Wives, Side Order of Life,* and *State of Mind.* Her plans include efforts to expand the network's presence on the Web. She also intends to look for a signature program for Lifetime, possibly a reality series. "First and foremost, I want to get to know the team and get their perspective on what's working well, what the opportunities are and what we can work on as a team . . . ," Wong told Kimberly Nordyke and Nellie Andreeva for the *Hollywood Reporter* (April 27, 2007 on-line). "It's also about growing the brand, the opportunity to grow Lifetime and evolve it, to appeal to even more women and deepen our relationship [with our viewers]."

"In an industry largely populated with those who make everyday Casual Friday, Wong is a standout, often looking as if she has just stepped from the pages of *Vogue*," Deborah Starr Seibel noted for *Broadcasting & Cable* (August 30, 2004). Wong maintains a home in California but spends most of her time in New York, where Lifetime is headquartered. "I enjoy the opportunity to mentor people new to the business, and am proud that I am

able to be involved in community work," she told Gerrye Wong. "If you join the entertainment or television field, it can bring a lot of satisfaction and excitement, but demands a lot of dedication, sacrifice and disappointments along the way." Wong has served on the boards of Asians in the Arts, the Los Angeles Free Clinic, the Hollywood Radio and Television Society, the Academy of Television Arts & Sciences, the National Association of Television Program Executives, and the California Museum for History, Women, and the Arts. "The bottom line is that you want to be happy," Wong once told an ABC intern, as quoted by Deborah Starr Seibel. "You spend so many hours of your life working, you better like it." She also said, "Figure out what your passion is. And then be better than everybody else."

—N.W.M.

Suggested Reading: *Asian Week* (on-line) June 30, 2006; *Broadcasting & Cable* (on-line) Aug. 30, 2004, Jan. 22, 2007; disneyabctv.com; *Hollywood Reporter* (on-line) Apr. 27, 2007; *New York Times* C p5 Apr. 27, 2007; *Television Week* p3 Apr. 30, 2007

Yusuf, Hamza

1960– American Islamic leader

Address: Zaytuna Institute, 631 Jackson St., Hayward, CA 94544

"Violence is the last refuge of the incompetent, and I think that's really what we're dealing with here, incompetence," Hamza Yusuf told Linden MacIntyre during a September 2006 interview for the Public Broadcasting System television program *Frontline/World* (on-line). Yusuf, a prominent American Muslim spiritual leader and lecturer, was referring to the fighting that has taken the lives of untold thousands of people in the Middle East in the past six decades. He went on to say, "Both sides"—that is, Western governments and Israel, on one side, and Middle Eastern Muslim-led governments and political factions on the other—"have been incredibly ineffective at achieving their goals—at least their stated goals." A native of the United States whose father's surname was Hanson, Yusuf, who is in his late 40s, embraced Islam as a teenager; he later earned the title "sheikh," in recognition of his wisdom and knowledge, and he is now an imam, a leader of Muslim group prayers. Except for the 10 years (late 1970s to late 1980s) that he spent studying Islam in the Middle East and Africa, he has always lived in the U.S. Since the mid-1990s he has taught at the Zaytuna Institute and Academy, in Hayward, California, which he co-founded with Zaid Shakir, an influential American Islamic scholar; the facility is the first of its

Courtesy of the Zaytuna Institute

Hamza Yusuf

kind in the U.S. "It is our belief," the Zaytuna Web site states, "that Islam offers a cohesive understanding of the world" and that the practical application of Islam will enable its adherents "to cut through the illusion of contemporary nihilism and materialism." Yusuf has maintained that a widespread lack of religious knowledge among Muslims has led to narrow readings of texts used to justify extremism; for that reason, the primary aims of the Zaytuna Institute, according to its Web site, include the restoration of "broad-based pluralistic and true scholarship" to it "proper place as a first priority of Muslims." The institute calls, in other words, for a holistic approach to Islam that values the pursuit of knowledge over the strict interpretation of texts.

A frequent lecturer, Yusuf is fluent in Arabic; he "speaks to Americans as a Muslim, and to Muslims abroad as a member of that most powerful tribe on earth: Americans," as Carla Power wrote for *Newsweek* (August 19, 2002). He is regarded as one of the "leading intellectual lights for a new generation of American Muslims looking for homegrown leaders who can help them learn how to live their faith without succumbing to American materialism or Islamic extremism," as Laurie Goodstein wrote for the *New York Times* (June 18, 2006), and as "an antidote to traditional clerics cloaked in long robes and known for their stern warnings that Western life is incompatible with the teachings of the Koran," as Geneive Abdo wrote for the *Chicago Tribune* (September 6, 2004). Yusuf differs significantly from most other leaders of U.S. mosques, nearly all of whom were recruited from countries overseas and who, as Goodstein wrote, "cannot begin to speak to young American Muslims growing

up on hip-hop and in mixed-sex chat rooms." Yusuf, by contrast, as Goodstein noted, is "equally at home in Islamic tradition and modern American culture" and has strived to help second-generation American Muslims reconcile the opposing influences of their religion and American society.

Yusuf has also tried to change the negative attitudes many non-Islamic Americans harbor about Muslims. "People have to be exposed to Muslims, just experience Muslims; talk to them," he said to Linden MacIntyre. "Reach out, read about Islam, try to find out about it. There are 20,000 Muslim physicians in the United States, Americans putting their lives in the hands of Muslims every day. You're going under and the anesthesiologist is a Muslim, right? He's looking out for you. He doesn't want you to die in that operation because you're an infidel. He's doing his job. As is your pediatrician who's trying to heal your child. And the mechanic who's fixing your car? He's not putting a bomb in your car. It's Abdullah, the guy down at the Chevron station, right? . . . Muslims have been an almost entirely benevolent force in the 20th century. They did not wreak the havoc the Western powers wreaked on the world. They have not come anywhere near to the environmental degradation that we've done to the planet. So I think Muslims need to be seen in the proper light. They're mostly decent, hardworking people, people with deep family values, and they want to live in peace. My experience on this planet, almost 50 years, is that if you treat people with respect, they tend to treat you with respect." For some years, until the September 11, 2001 terrorist attacks on the U.S., Yusuf often criticized the "decadence, injustice and impoverished spirituality" of Western nations, as Jack O'Sullivan put it in the London *Guardian* (October 8, 2001), and he occasionally used blatantly anti-American rhetoric. "September 11 was a wake-up call to me," he told O'Sullivan. "I don't want to contribute to the hate in any shape or form. I now regret in the past being silent about what I have heard in the Islamic discourse and being part of that with my own anger." He has also rejected anti-Semitism and has "called others to reject it," as he told MacIntyre.

Yusuf derives a large part of his income from sales of his many videos, CDs, DVDs, and books, which bear such titles as *The Life of the Prophet Muhammad*; *The Love of the Prophet Muhammad*; *Prophet Muhammad: The Greatest Teacher*; *Religion, Violence & the Modern World*; *Building Bridges of Understanding*; and *The Seventeen Benefits of Tribulation*. Some of his publications carry the byline Hamza Yusuf Hanson. Yusuf has also translated works of prose and poetry written by others, among them Habib Ali al-Jifri's *Jihad: Its Significance and Understanding in Islam*, Sidi Ahmed Zarruq's *The Poor Man's Book of Assistance*, and Imam al-Mawlud's *Matharat al-Qulub*, which Yusuf entitled *Purification of the Heart: Signs, Symptoms, and Cures of the Spiritual Diseases of the Heart*. With John Taylor Gatto (an activist for school reform and opponent of compulsory schooling and a former New York City and New York State Teacher of the Year), he wrote and recorded *Educating Your Child in Modern Times: Raising an Intelligent, Sovereign, Ethical Human Being* (2004), and with Noah Feldman, a professor at the New York University School of Law, he wrote and recorded *Islam & Democracy: Is a Clash of Civilizations Inevitable?* (2004).

Hamza Yusuf was born Mark Hanson in 1960 in Walla Walla, Washington, and grew up in what Goodstein described as "a bohemian but affluent" section of Marin County, north of San Francisco. His father, a Roman Catholic, taught college courses in the humanities; his mother, whose religion was Greek Orthodox, also worked in academia. Yusuf was raised, as Power described it, "on a '70s diet of surfing and spiritual eclecticism." According to Richard Scheinin, writing for the *San Jose (California) Mercury News* (January 27, 1996), Yusuf's mother brought him to services held in synagogues, Buddhist sanghas (places where Buddhist monks and nuns stay), and Unitarian churches and to civil rights demonstrations. Yusuf was baptized into the Greek Orthodox Church and took Holy Communion on Sundays; he attended Catholic parochial schools. Scheinin wrote that Yusuf felt "uncomfortable with the notion of Jesus' divinity, and disturbed by the 'guilt and stigma' that he thought too common among Christian believers." Yusuf's sister converted to Judaism and married a Jewish man; she and her husband are raising their sons in the Jewish faith.

When Yusuf was 17 he was in a near-fatal car accident. The profound realization of his mortality led him to a serious study of the Koran (the Muslim bible) and the Hadith (the collected sayings of the prophet Muhammad and accounts of the traditions and customs of Muhammad and his followers). As Goodstein paraphrased his comments, Yusuf found that "the simplicity of 'no God but Allah' made far more sense to him than the Trinity, and he found the five daily prayers [traditional in Islam] a constant call to awe about everything from the sun to his capillaries." Yusuf formally converted to Islam soon afterward. He told Scheinin, "What struck me about Islam was that it confirmed all the traditions before it. . . . It says that Christianity and Judaism are true traditions from God." He also told Scheinin that Islam had "a type of universality," explaining, "The Muslims never persecuted other religions—there are a few periods, but it always was rejected by the teachings. Whereas with Christianity, it was justified through the teachings." Additionally, he told Scheinin, "You don't have genocide in the history of Islam. And it's not that they're better people. I think it's that they had this thing called the Sharia, or sacred law, that 'you can't do that!' In Arabic, the word for the Jew, the Christian, the fire worshiper is dhimmi. It means 'the protected.'"

After his conversion Yusuf spent a decade studying Islamic law and theology, as well as the Arabic language, with Muslim scholars in the Middle East and North Africa. He earned teaching licenses in the United Arab Emirates, Algeria, Morocco, and Mauritania (where he earned the honorific "sheikh" (also spelled "sheik" and "shaykh"), in recognition of his wisdom. (As the leader of a mosque, he later acquired the title "imam.") He then returned to the U.S., where he earned an associate's degree in nursing from Imperial Valley College, in Imperial, California, and a bachelor's degree in religious studies from San Jose State University, also in California. By the mid-1990s Yusuf had become a respected spiritual leader among many Muslims in California and had begun lecturing at Islamic conferences abroad. In an article highly critical of Yusuf published in the *Daily Standard* (January 24, 2005), the on-line sister publication of the conservative *Weekly Standard*, Stephen Schwartz wrote that in 1991, Yusuf delivered a speech entitled "Jihad Is the Only Way" to "a local group of the Islamic Circle of North America (ICNA), an arm of the Jama'at-I-Islami movement in Pakistan, which in turn is an al Qaeda ally." According to Goodstein, at times Yusuf's speeches contained "the kind of zealous rhetoric he now denounces." She cited as one example a talk in 1995 in which he said that Judaism is "a most racist religion" because one of its tenets is that "God has this bias to this small little tribe in the middle of the desert." Goodstein also reported that on September 9, 2001, two days before the terrorist attacks that destroyed the World Trade Center, in New York City, damaged the Pentagon, in Washington, D.C., and resulted in the deaths of nearly 3,000 people," Yusuf said that the U.S. "stands condemned" for its invasions of Muslim lands. "I was not raised as an anti-Semite . . . ," Yusuf told MacIntyre. "I was not raised with any prejudice at all. But I was infected when I lived in the Muslim world. . . . But I grew out of it and realized that not only does it have nothing to do with Islam, but it has nothing to do with my core values."

Yusuf later came to regard some of his public statements as extremist, especially after September 11, 2001. "When I started speaking in the early 90's, our discourse was not balanced," he said in a recent lecture, as quoted by Goodstein. "We were focused so often on what was negative about [the United States]. We ended up alienating some people. I've said some things about other religions that I regret now. I think they were incorrect." Carla Power wrote that after September 11, Yusuf "was quick to condemn the terrorists, not as a humanist but as a Muslim scholar. Under Muslim law, he pointed out, any Muslim with a U.S. passport or green card had signed a treaty, effectively, to obey American laws, making support for acts of violence on American soil unIslamic." Yusuf told O'Sullivan, "Many people in the west do not realise how oppressive some Muslim states are—both for men and for women. This is a cultural issue, not an Islamic one. I would rather live as a Muslim in the West than in most of the Muslim countries, because I think the way Muslims are allowed to live in the West is closer to the Muslim way. A lot of Muslim immigrants feel the same way, which is why they are here."

Yusuf was the sole Muslim among the six religious leaders invited to meet with President George W. Bush shortly after the September 11 attacks. As a press conference outside the White House, Yusuf said, as quoted by O'Sullivan, "Islam was hijacked on that September 11, 2001, on that plane as an innocent victim." His appearance with Bush helped to raise Yusuf's national profile, and among members of the media, as Goodstein noted, it earned him "a title other than sheik: 'adviser to the president.'" During their meeting Yusuf suggested to the president that the label "Operation Infinite Justice"—the name for the military campaign that was launched in Afghanistan in response to the terrorist actions—be changed, as "it would offend Muslims, who believe the only source of infinite justice is God," as Goodstein wrote. Bush reportedly explained that the Pentagon, which had come up with the name, had no theologians on staff. Subsequently the operation was renamed "Enduring Freedom." Except for that change, however, Bush "hasn't taken any of my advice," Yusuf told Goodstein. After his visit to the White House, Yusuf addressed religious leaders at the British House of Lords. O'Sullivan wrote that he was "fast becoming a world figure as Islam's most able theological critic of the suicide hijacking."

"Yusuf laments that many of the seminaries that once flourished in the Muslim world are now either gone or intellectually dead," Laurie Goodstein wrote. In part for that reason, in the mid-1990s he co-founded the Zaytuna Institute. The Zaytuna Institute and Academy, as it is now known, was built on land in Hayward, California, that was purchased several years later. The school aims "to train a new generation of imams and scholars who can reconcile Islam and American culture," in Goodstein's words. Its instructors teach a variation of classical Islam, "stripped of the cultural baggage and prejudices that have crept in over the centuries," in Power's words; its theology is neither conservative nor liberal. Zaytuna also offers classes in the Arabic language. "Our hope is to see the Muslims of the West, in particular, working towards the same goal," its Web site states.

Following the September 11, 2001 attacks, Yusuf found himself stopped and searched regularly at airports. In one instance a security worker examining the contents of his bag discovered atop his clothing a U.S. government brochure called "Who Becomes a Terrorist and Why" and a much-thumbed copy of the Koran. The worker "looked up at me with some fear," Yusuf recalled to Don Lattin for the *San Francisco Chronicle* (September 2, 2002). "Knowledge can be a dangerous thing," he commented. According to O'Sullivan, "Yusuf's language has a rare cultural fluency shifting easily between the Bible and the Koran, taking in, within a few breaths, Shakespeare, Thoreau, John Locke, Rousseau, Jesse James, Dirty Harry and even, at one point, the memoirs of General George Paton." Yusuf and his family live in Danville, a suburb of Oakland, California. His wife, Liliana, is Mexican-American and was raised Catholic; after meeting Yusuf, she converted to Islam. She home-schools the couple's five sons.

—M.B.

Suggested Reading: *Chicago Tribune* Metro p3 Sep. 6, 2004; (London) *Guardian* Features p4 Oct. 8, 2001; *New York Times* p1+ June 18, 2006; *Newsweek* p57 Aug. 19, 2002; PBS (on-line) *Frontline/World* Sep. 2006; *San Francisco Chronicle* A p3 Sep. 2, 2002; *San Jose (California) Mercury News* E p1+ Jan. 27, 1996; *Toronto Sun* p16 Jan. 16, 2004; *Washington Post* A p16 Oct. 2, 2001; Zaytuna Institute Web site

Selected Books: as translator—*The Burda of Al-Busiri*, 2002; *Purification of the Heart: Signs, Symptoms and Cures of the Spiritual Diseases of the Heart*, 2004; *The Creed of Imam al-Tahawi*, 2007

Selected DVDs: *Islam and Democracy: Is a Clash of Civilizations Inevitable?* (with Noah Feldman), 2004

Obituaries

Written by Kieran Dugan

ALTMAN, ROBERT Feb. 20, 1925–Nov. 20, 2006 Film and television director. Robert Altman was one of the most revered filmmakers of the latter half of the 20th century. He had been active in the entertainment industry for more than 20 years when he directed the film *MASH* (1970), his critical and commercial breakthrough. He would go on to direct another 33 feature films, receiving five Academy Award nominations for best director and a Lifetime Achievement Award from the academy in 2005. Known for his defiance of Hollywood conventions, Altman often employed ensemble casts, interweaving plot lines, and overlapping dialogue. He encouraged his casts to improvise much of their material, which made him extremely popular among actors. The son of a successful life-insurance salesman, Altman was raised in Kansas City, Missouri, where he attended Jesuit schools. He abandoned Catholicism around the time he joined the U.S. Army in 1943. Serving as a bomber pilot during World War II, he flew 46 missions over Borneo and the Dutch East Indies. After his discharge, in 1943, he found work with the Calvin Company, in Kansas City, creating industrial films for corporate clients. In 1957 he convinced United Artists to distribute *The Delinquents*, a low-budget teen drama that he had written, produced, and directed. It failed to generate much commercial or critical interest. After Altman's biographical documentary *The James Dean Story* (1957) received warm reviews, he was able to find work in television. Over the next decade he wrote, directed, and produced a myriad of television programs, including *Bonanza, Combat!*, and *Troubleshooters*. Altman's scripts for these shows often ran counter to the conventions of television, bringing him into conflict with network executives. He told Aljean Harmetz of the *New York Times Magazine* (June 20, 1971), "Because the star of *Combat*, Vic Morrow, couldn't be killed off, I'd take an actor, establish him as an important character in one segment, use him three or four times more, and then kill him early in the next script, offscreen, in a way that had nothing to do with the plot. That was unorthodox. It made them nervous. I used to get fired for it." Altman soon quit television to focus on feature filmmaking, starting with *Countdown* (1968), a dramatization of the first manned space flight to the moon. He followed that with *That Cold Day in the Park* (1969) and *Brewster McCloud* (1970), neither of which captured much attention. Then 20th Century Fox offered Altman the opportunity to direct *MASH*, the film version of Richard Hooker's novel about combat surgeons serving in the Korean War—a project that 15 other directors had reportedly turned down. Released during the increasingly unpopular Vietnam War, the dark comedy was well received by audiences and reviewers alike. It won a host of awards, garnering the grand prize at the 1970 Cannes Film Festival and five Academy Award nominations, in-

cluding best picture and best director. "*MASH* was a pretty good movie," Altman later said, according to Rick Lyman for the *New York Times* (November 21, 2006). "It wasn't what 20th Century-Fox thought it was going to be. They almost, when they saw it, cut all the blood out. I fought with my life for that. The picture speaks for itself. It became popular because of the timing. Consequently, it's considered important, but it's no better or more important than any of the other films I've made." Altman followed *MASH* with a series of films which deconstructed popular Hollywood genres, including *McCabe & Mrs. Miller* (1971), a Western about an ill-fated gambler and prostitute who co-own a brothel, and *The Long Goodbye* (1973), a modern take on the noir genre starring Elliott Gould as Philip Marlowe, Raymond Chandler's hard-boiled detective popularized on film by Humphrey Bogart in the 1940s. Both films initially received tepid responses from critics but were later reevaluated, receiving significant critical praise. *California Split* (1974) was the first film of Altman's to use the "Lion's Gate 8-Track Sound," an innovative system that allowed the director to record sound live from microphones planted on set or on location, eliminating a lot of cumbersome equipment as well as the necessity for postdubbing; he could also mix and unmix the sound at will. Altman received perhaps the best reviews of his career for *Nashville* (1975), an ambitious story that featured 24 different characters, set amid the background of a fictional presidential primary. According to Lyman, the *New Yorker* film critic Pauline Kael praised *Nashville* as "a radical, evolutionary leap. Altman has already accustomed us to actors who don't look as if they're acting; he's attuned us to the comic subtleties of a multiple-track sound system that makes the sound more live than it ever was before; and he's evolved an organic style of moviemaking that tells a story without the clanking of plot. Now he dissolves the frame, so that we feel the continuity between what's on the screen and life off-camera." Altman's popularity fell slightly following *Nashville*, when a series of his films, including *Buffalo Bill and the Indians, or Sitting Bull's History Lesson* (1976), *3 Women* (1977), and *Popeye* (1980) were disappointments both critically and commercially. When a studio refused to distribute a film directed by Altman's longtime assistant director, Alan Rudolph, Altman founded Lion's Gate, a film and television distribution company, which he then sold in 1981. He returned to prominence in the 1990s with *The Player* (1992)—which received three Academy Award nominations, including a nod for Altman's direction—and *Short Cuts* (1993), for which he received his fourth best-director nomination. In 2001 Altman made another critical comeback with *Gosford Park*, a murder mystery featuring an ensemble cast. It was nominated for seven Academy Awards, including best picture and best director. In 2005 Altman was diagnosed with cancer but continued filming the well-received *Prairie Home Companion* (2006), based on the long-running radio program hosted by Garrison Keeler. Altman died in Los Angeles at the age of 81 from complications of cancer; he was married three times and is survived by his wife, Kathryn Reed Altman, with whom he had two sons, Robert and Matthew. He had 12 grandchildren and five great-grandchildren. See *Current Biography* (1974).

Obituary *New York Times* A p1+ Nov. 22, 2006

ANDERSON, WILLIAM R. June 17, 1921–Feb. 25, 2007 United States Navy officer; Democratic congressman. As a navy officer, William Robert Anderson was best known as the captain from 1957 to 1959 of the USS *Nautilus,* the first nuclear-powered submarine. As a congressman, he represented Tennessee's Sixth Congressional District for four terms, from 1965 to 1973. After graduating from the U.S. Naval Academy, Anderson served in World War II aboard the submarines USS *Tarpon,* USS *Narwhal,* and USS *Trutta.* For his conduct in combat in the war, he received a Commendation with Ribbon and Combat V Medal and a Bronze Star. During the Korean War he was executive officer aboard the *Trutta* and commander of the USS *Wahoo.* In the summer of 1958, he captained the *Nautilus* 6,000 miles from Pearl Harbor to Great Britain, the first undersea voyage from the Pacific to the Atlantic in history. At the climax of that voyage, the *Nautilus* crossed 400 feet beneath the ice cap at the North Pole, another historic first. For that voyage, Anderson received the Legion of Merit. Immediately after he retired from the navy, in 1962, he ran unsuccessfully for governor of Tennessee. In the U.S. House of Representatives he criticized the U.S.'s pursuit of the war in Vietnam without a full national commitment to victory and what he perceived to be the Nixon administration's apparent willingness "to throw the Bill of Rights out the window." As a friend of the Catholic priests and antiwar activists Daniel and Philip Berrigan, he took the floor of the House of Representatives in December 1970 in defense of the Berrigan brothers and against what he termed the "McCarthyist" treatment of them by the FBI director, J. Edgar Hoover. His speech lost him much of his popularity in his constituency. He was narrowly defeated in his bid for a fifth term in 1972. With Clay Blair Jr., he wrote a book about his historic 1958 undersea voyage, *Nautilus 90 North* (1959). In the private sector, he and his wife, Pat, founded the Public Office Corp., a data management firm in Washington, D.C. He died in Leesburg, Virginia. His survivors included his wife, three sons, and a daughter. See *Current Biography* (1959).

Obituary *New York Times* C p13 Mar. 6, 2007

ANTONIONI, MICHELANGELO Sep. 29, 1912–July 30, 2007 Italian filmmaker. With his radically innovative techniques and themes, Michelangelo Antonioni helped to turn Italian cinema inward, away from social neorealism, and with his moody explorations of psychic ennui and spiritual and emotional alienation, he established a new filmic idiom. In his major films—many of which he co-wrote—Antonioni used opaque plotting, sparse action and dialogue, and

long, fluid camera takes to convey the "spiritual aridity" and "moral coldness" of his characters, most of whom are members of the leisure class whose lives lack meaning and who cannot communicate with each other; as he said, "They never come together, and they like it that way." Antonioni became an international art-house icon in the early 1960s with a trilogy of black-and-white films depicting existential malaise, the first and best known of which was *L'Avventura* (The Adventure), an ambiguous, unresolved mystery in which a man and woman become romantically involved while searching for the man's lover, who disappears during a yachting trip and is never found. Antonioni achieved popular box-office success internationally with the English-language color film *Blowup* (1966), about a hip London photographer who discovers in one of his photos evidence of a murder but is morally incapable of pursuing the matter. In presenting a special Academy Award for lifetime achievement to Antonioni in 1995, the actor Jack Nicholson observed that the filmmaker had "in the empty, silent spaces of the world . . . found metaphors that illuminate the silent places in our hearts." Antonioni himself once said, "If I hadn't become a director, I would have been an architect, or maybe a painter. In other words, I think I'm someone with things to show rather than things to say." Antonioni was born into an affluent family in Ferrara, in northern Italy, and reared in the puritanical Jansenist Catholic tradition of the region, which, coupled with a bourgeois family background that embarrassed him, had a major influence on the development of the dominant themes in his films. As a child he made puppets and sets for them, and as a teenager he began to paint in oils and experiment with a 16mm movie camera. He matriculated at the University of Bologna to major in liberal arts but followed a girlfriend into economics instead; he also co-founded a student theatrical company. After completing his university studies, he wrote film criticism for several publications and studied at the Experimental Cinematography Center in Rome. His earliest professional jobs were as a co-scenarist and assistant director. During World War II he made the short documentary *Gente del Po,* which was released after the war. He filmed several other documentaries before making his first feature film, *Cronaca di un amore* (*Chronicle of a Love,* 1950), in which an adulterous couple plan the murder of the woman's husband. His first critical and box-office success in Italy was his fifth feature, *Le Amiche* (*The Girlfriends,* 1955), about a group of rudderless middle-class women. The bleak *Il grido* (*The Cry,* 1957), about a despondent, unemployed factory worker, is the first instance of his practice of improvisation, of using screenplays as "sheets of notes for those, who, at the camera, . . . write the film themselves." "It's only when I hear dialogue from the actor's mouth itself that I realize whether the lines are correct or not," he once said. *L'Avventura,* which subverted prevailing cinematic conventions, was fully appreciated only over time. At the 1960 Cannes Film Festival, it was a *succès de scandale* as well as *d'estime,* winning a Special Jury Prize (the first of Antonioni's several honors at Cannes) but booed by many in attendance. Early European audiences tended to be confounded by *L'Avventura*'s slow tempo and other innovations, but the film went on attract crowds at art-house box offices internationally and to establish Antonioni as "a hero of the highbrows," as he is dubbed in *Halliwell's Film and Video Guide. L'Avventura* is commonly seen as the first in a trilogy also including *La Notte* (The Night, 1961) and *L'Eclisse* (The Elipse, 1962), the former about creative and marital disintegration in the lives of a Milanese novelist and his wife and the latter about a Roman stockbroker working in an environment in which greed contributes to "the eclipse of all feeling." In all three films, Monica Vitti, Antonioni's favorite actress, stands out as a positive character who retains some emotional warmth and sensitivity in the midst of people devoid of such qualities. The desolate universe charted in the trilogy was visited a final time by Antonioni in his first color film, *Il Deserto rosso* (The Red Desert, 1964), an expressionistic, somewhat Luddite depiction of a wife and mother (Vitti) pushed to the limits of her sanity while living amidst the smoke from a factory chimney. Under the aegis of the producer Carlo Ponti and Metro-Goldwyn-Mayer, Antonioni made *Blowup,* which became a cult favorite as well as a big popular hit; while sexually daring for its time, that film was essentially about the relativity of perception and the fallibility of memory. It won the Grand Prix at Cannes and was nominated for the Academy Awards for best director and best screenplay. Under his contract with Ponti and M-G-M, Antonioni made two more movies. One was his only American film, *Zabriskie Point* (1970), a widely panned fantasy about a rebellious young American man and woman who leave a society they view as over-civilized and escape into Death Valley. The other was the Hitchcock-like thriller *The Passenger* (1975), starring Jack Nicholson as a television reporter who becomes a gun runner in Africa. In China Antonioni shot the footage for the short documentary *Chung Kuo* (1972). He shot the feature *Il Mistero di Oberwald* (*The Mystery of Oberwald,* 1980)—an adaptation of Jean Cocteau's *L'Aigle a deux tetes*—in video and transferred it to film. He returned to more familiar ground with *Identificazione di una donna* (*Identification of a Woman,* 1982), about a filmmaker who fails in his relationships with two women and his pursuit of a screen project about the "ideal woman." In 1985 Antonioni suffered a stroke that left him barely able to move. Nevertheless, with some help from Wim Wenders, he made *Al di là delle nuvole* (*Beyond the Clouds,* 1995), aka *Par dela les nuages,* based on three stories in his fiction collection *Quel bowling sul Tevere* (1983; *That Bowling Alley on the Tiber,* 1985). His last screen work was the segment he contributed to the anthology film *Eros* (2004). The short documentary *Lo Squardo di Michelangelo* (*Michelangelo Eye to Eye*) was released in 2004. Following his marriage to and divorce from Letizia Balboni, Antonioni married Enrica Fico, 41 years his junior, who survived him. He died at his home in Rome. See *Current Biography* (1993).

Obituary *New York Times* A p1+ Aug. 1, 2007

APPLE, R. W. JR. Nov. 20, 1934–Oct. 4, 2006 Journalist. In his 43-year career with the *New York Times,* Raymond Walter ("Johnny") Apple Jr. distinguished himself as a colorful reporter, news analyst, associate editor, and peripatetic national and international correspondent and bureau chief. Apple wrote widely, on subjects ranging from war, politics, and other world affairs to travel, food, and wine. Born into a family that owned a chain of supermarkets in northern Ohio, Apple received his secondary education at Western Reserve Academy in Hudson, Ohio. After studying abortively at Princeton University and working briefly at the *Wall Street Journal,* he served in the U.S. Army for two years. Following his graduation from Columbia University with a B.A. degree in history, in 1961, he joined the NBC television network as a writer for NBC News. In 1963 he won an Emmy Award for his writing for NBC's nightly prime-time newscast, *The Huntley-Brinkley Report.* During the same year he joined the *New York Times* as a city room reporter, and in 1964 he became the newspaper's bureau chief in Albany, New York. He was bureau chief in South Vietnam from 1966 to 1968, when he won the George Polk and Overseas Press Club Awards for his Vietnam War reportage and commentary. In 1968 he contributed to the newspaper's coverage of the presidential campaigns of Richard M. Nixon and Hubert H. Humphrey, and he was subsequently chief of the *Times*'s bureaus in Lagos, Nigeria, and Nairobi, Kenya. As the paper's national political correspondent from 1970 to 1976, he covered numerous electoral campaigns, local and national, including Jimmy Carter's successful presidential run. He headed the *Times*'s London bureau from 1977 to 1985, with the exception of one year (1980–81) when he served as bureau chief in Moscow, in what was then the Soviet Union. As the paper's chief Washington correspondent, beginning in 1985, and later as deputy Washington editor, he was given free rein to write as he wished, about grand events such as the Persian Gulf war and the fall of successive Communist governments in Eastern Europe or, more personally, about travel and cuisine. In 1992 he was promoted to chief of the Washington bureau, a position he held until 1997. His last article in the *Times,* "The Global Gourmet," was published posthumously, on October 5, 2006. He published the books *Apple's Europe: An Uncommon Guide* (1986) and *Apple's America: The Discriminating Traveler's Guide to 40 Great Cities in the United States and Canada* (2005). After his divorce from his first wife, Edith Smith, Apple married Betsy Pinckney Brown, by whom he had a stepson and a stepdaughter. With his wife, he maintained homes in Washington, D.C., on a farm near Gettysburg, Pennsylvania, and in the Cotswolds, near Oxford, England. He died in Washington, D.C. See *Current Biography* (1993).

Obituary *New York Times* B p8 Oct. 5, 2006

ASTOR, BROOKE Mar. 30, 1902–Aug. 13, 2007 New York socialite and philanthropist. Brooke Astor (neé Roberta Brooke Russell), the heiress by marriage to the fortune accumulated by the fur trader, real-estate tycoon, and financier John Jacob Astor (1763–1848), was a grande dame in the *richesse oblige* tradition. Her favorite quotation was from Dolly Levi in Thornton Wilder's play *The Matchmaker:* "Money is like manure; it's not worth anything unless it's spread around." She acquired the name Astor from the third and last of her three marriages, to Vincent Astor, the eldest son of John Jacob Astor IV, the latter of whom perished in the sinking of the *Titanic* in 1912. When Vincent Astor—who sired no children—died, in 1959, he willed to Brooke Astor $2 million outright in addition to the income generated by approximately $60 million (the principal to be disposed of in her will) and control of a roughly similar amount in the form of the assets of the Vincent Astor Foundation, which he had founded for "the amelioration of human misery." Brooke Astor concentrated the foundation's largesse in New York City, where most of the Astor fortune had been acquired. The chief recipients of her generosity were several cultural institutions that she viewed as the city's "crown jewels," for some of which she was a trustee. Her first priority was the New York Public Library, which John Jacob Astor had co-founded. She made numerous grants to the library, rescuing it from severe financial crisis on at least one occasion and ultimately giving it a total of more than $25 million. Her runner-up favorite charity was probably the Metropolitan Museum of Art. Also high among her priorities were Rockefeller University, the Pierpont Morgan Library, and the Bronx Zoo (part of the Wildlife Conservation Society, originally named the New York Zoological Society), as well as such institutions and sites as Central Park, the New York Botanical Garden, and Cornell University Medical College. She contributed to the development of the Intrepid Sea-Air-Space Museum, the South Street Seaport, and the Bedford-Stuyvesant Restoration Corp.; the enhancement of the Apollo Theater, in Harlem; the rehabilitation of a row of houses on 130th Street in Harlem; programs in the barrios of East Harlem; the establishment of inner-city recreation areas; the preservation of low-rent beach-side bungalows; settlement houses; and many programs for the disadvantaged, including centers for pregnant young women and gang-prone urban youths. In addition, she funded a veterinary facility for pets of the elderly. The Vincent Astor Foundation's single project outside of New York City was Ferncliff, Vincent Astor's family estate in Rhinecliff, New York, which became the site of facilities for emotionally disturbed children and for senior citizens. Astor funded a total of some 3,000 causes. A hands-on benefactor, she gave no monies without first visiting the groups and projects asking for them, and she returned regularly to check on the results. In all of her visits to sites high and low, she was regal, finely coifed, attired in designer clothes and hats, and discretely jeweled, and she sometimes brought along one of her little pet dogs. Unlike most philanthropists, she finally drew upon the capital of her assets as well as the interest, so that most of the worth of the Vincent Astor Foundation was disbursed within her lifetime. By the time she liquefied the foundation's assets, in 1997, the disbursements totaled approximately $195 million. Relatively early in her career, she edited and wrote feature articles for *House and Garden* magazine, and she later contributed articles to *Vanity Fair*. She wrote two novels, *The Bluebird Is at Home* (1965) and *The Last Blossom on the Plum Tree* (1986), and two autobiographies, *Patchwork Child* (1962) and *Footprints* (1980). In 1998 she was awarded the Presidential Medal of Freedom. She had one child, a son, Anthony Dryden Kusar, from her first marriage, to J. Dry-

den Kusar, which ended in divorce in 1930. After her marriage to Charles H. Marshall, in 1932, Anthony changed his name to Anthony Dryden Marshall. Following Charles H. Marshall's death, in 1952, she married Vincent Astor, in 1953. In her final years she was under the guardianship of her son, until her grandson Philip Marshall filed a lawsuit in 2006 seriously challenging the quality of that guardianship. Pursuant to a settlement, Astor's close friend Annette de la Renta replaced Anthony Dryden Marshall as her guardian. In addition to her Park Avenue home in Manhattan, Astor maintained an estate called Holly Hill in Briarcliff Manor, New York. She died at Holly Hill, of pneumonia. See *Current Biography* (1987).

Obituary *New York Times* A p1+ Aug. 14, 2007

AUERBACH, ARNOLD Sep. 20, 1917–Oct. 28, 2006
Basketball coach; professional basketball-franchise executive. Arnold Jacob Auerbach, better known as Red, was the most accomplished pro basketball mentor of his time, best known for guiding the Boston Celtics to 16 National Basketball Association championships. First as coach and subsequently as general manager and president, he was associated with the Celtics for 57 years, beginning in 1950. A perfectionist with a fierce will to win, he described himself as "a dictator with compassion" in presiding over his teams, and his legendary eruptions of temper were the scourge of officials and opponents. He began his basketball career as a player in high school and junior college and at Georgetown University, where he led the team in scoring in his senior year. After coaching high school and U.S. Navy teams, he became the founding coach of the Washington, D.C., Capitols in 1946–47, when that team finished first in the Eastern Division of the Basketball Association of America, the predecessor of the NBA. During the 1949–50 season, when the NBA superseded the BAA, he became coach of the Tri-City (Illinois) Blackhawks. The Blackhawks' 28–29 record that season would be his only losing annual tally in his 19-year professional coaching career, during which he compiled a winning record unrivaled by any of his peers—938–479 (.662) in regular-season play and 99–69 (.589) in postseason games. He began his long association with the Boston Celtics as the coach of that team in 1950, when it was stagnating at the bottom of the NBA's Eastern Division. While gradually building the Celtics into a strong running team, he realized no play-off victories until 1956, when, by astute trading, he signed Bill Russell, the star center who proceeded during the following 10 seasons to captain the team to nine NBA championships. In 1966 Auerbach moved into the Celtics' front office and appointed Bill Russell player-coach. During the following 20 years, as the team's general manager (1966–84) and then as its president, Auerbach acquired such stellar players as Larry Bird, Robert Parrish, Danny Ainge, Dennis Johnson, and Bill Walton. During that period the Celtics won seven more NBA championships, in 1968, 1969, 1974, 1976, 1981, 1984, and 1986. In collaboration with professional writers, Auerbach published seven books about basketball and about his life and career, including *M.B.A: Management by Auerbach* (1991) and *Let Me*

Tell You a Story (2004). He died in Washington, D.C. He was predeceased by his wife, Dorothy (née Lewis) and survived by two daughters, a granddaughter, a great-grandson, and two great-granddaughters. See *Current Biography* (1969).

Obituary *New York Times* B p8 Oct. 29, 2006

BAHCALL, JOHN N. Dec. 30, 1934–Aug. 17, 2005 Astrophysicist; John N. Bahcall pioneered a new field in astrophysics with his studies of the subatomic particles known as neutrinos—the lightest known particle with mass, similar to the electron but electrically neutral. He provided the theoretical basis for the groundbreaking experimental work—conducted first by Raymond Davis and later by Masatoshi Koshiba—that demonstrated that the nuclear reactions that produce neutrinos also, in Bahcall's words, "cause the sun to shine," as quoted by Dennis Overbye for the *New York Times* (August 19, 2005). Bahcall was also a leading advocate of the Hubble Space Telescope, arguing first for its construction and later for its continued maintenance. Born in Shreveport, Louisiana, he was initially interested in becoming a rabbi, intending to study philosophy when he enrolled at Louisiana State University as an undergraduate. He soon decided to change his major to science and transferred to the University of California at Berkeley, from which he graduated with a bachelor's degree in physics, in 1956. The following year he received a master's degree from the University of Chicago. In 1961 he earned a Ph.D. in physics from Harvard University, in Cambridge, Massachusetts. Bahcall first became interested in the study of neutrinos while completing his postdoctoral work at Indiana University, in Bloomington. Lectures by Emil Kanapenski on the theory of weak nuclear interactions led him to read widely about beta decay, a process in which the weak nuclear force causes changes in nuclei, among them the emission of neutrinos. In 1962 Bahcall joined the staff of the Kellogg Radiation Laboratory, at the California Institute of Technology, in Pasadena, where he continued his work on weak interactions. About three years later Raymond Davis of the Brookhaven National Laboratory, on Long Island, New York, and the University of Pennsylvania, suggested using Bahcall's calculations on solar nuclear reactions to deduce the presence of neutrinos in the sun. Davis's idea bore fruit: it was proved that energy indistinguishable from stellar energy is produced in nuclear reactions. That finding ended a debate about nuclear reactions that had been ongoing since the mid-19th century. For 35 years, beginning in 1971, Bahcall served as a professor at the School of Natural Sciences at the Institute for Advanced Study, in Princeton, New Jersey. From 1973 to 1992 he served as an interdisciplinary scientist with the Hubble Space Telescope Working Group and was a principal lobbyist for the development of that telescope, which was launched into orbit in 1990. Shortly after the Space Shuttle *Columbia* disaster, in 2003, the NASA administrator Sean O'Keefe canceled further space-shuttle missions to refurbish the telescope; Bahcall publicly protested the decision. He published five books and more than 600 papers on dark matter, quasars, the reshift controversy, and other subjects in the field of astrophys-

ics. He received the NASA Distinguished Public Service Medal, the National Medal of Science, and the Gold Medal of the Royal Astronomical Society, among numerous other awards. He served as the president of the American Astronomical Society from 1990 to 1992. Bahcall is survived by his wife, Neta; sons, Safi and Dan; daughter, Orli; and brother, Robert. See *Current Biography* (2000).

Obituary *New York Times* C p14 Aug. 19, 2005

BAMPTON, ROSE Nov. 28, 1907–Aug. 21, 2007 Opera singer. Rose Bampton, a vocalist celebrated for her musicality and versatility, was one of the last surviving veterans of the regime of the general manager Giulio Gatti-Casazza at New York's Metropolitan Opera during the Depression era of the 1930s, when, as E. Paul Driscoll wrote for *Opera News,* she "established a distinctive and distinguished career, anchored by her rigorous interpretative standards and unfailingly honest musicianship . . . abetted by her tall, slim figure, graceful deportment, and genial stage presence." Bampton, who ranged in her roles from mezzo and coloratura soprano to contralto, made her professional debut as Siébel in Gounod's *Faust* with the New York Chautauqua Opera in 1929. After three years with the Philadelphia Opera Company, she debuted at the Metropolitan Opera as Laura in *La Gioconda,* in 1932. In the same year she sang the role of the Wood Dove in Arnold Schoenberg's *Gurre-Lieder,* conducted by Leopold Stokowski. (Schoenberg called her voice "a miracle.") During her 18 years with the Met, her roles included Amneris in *Aïda,* Leonora in *Il Trovatore,* Donna Anna in *Don Giovanni,* Sieglinde in *Die Walküre,* Elsa in *Lohengrin,* Elisabeth in *Tannhaüser,* and Kundry in *Parsifal.* Away from the Met, she performed with the Chicago Opera and the San Francisco Opera and gave concerts in other U.S. venues, and she toured England, Scandinavia, Central Europe, Brazil, and Argentina. In 1944 she sang Leonore in the conductor Arturo Toscanini's broadcast of Beethoven's opera *Fidelio* on the NBC radio network. (The recording of that performance is available on CD, along with others of her recordings.) After leaving the Metropolitan Opera, in 1950, Bampton concentrated on concerts, recitals, and television appearances. Following her retirement as a performer, in 1963, she taught at the Juilliard School. She and her husband, the conductor and pianist Wilfrid Pelletier (who died in 1982), had no children. She died in Bryn Mawr, Pennsylvania. See *Current Biography* (1940).

Obituary *New York Times* C p13 Aug. 23, 2007

BANCROFT, ANNE Sep. 17, 1931–June 6, 2005 Actress; a spirited stage, film, and television performer; had a rare "combination of brains, humor, frankness, and sense" as well as a beauty that was "constantly shifting with her roles," as the director Mike Nichols said, and a husky voice that could, in the words of Tom Vallance of the London *Independent,* "convey either vulnerability or grit"; is most indelibly engraved in the popular memory as Mrs. Robinson, the seducer of her daughter's boyfriend (Dustin Hoffman), in the satirical film *The Graduate* (1967), which brought her one of her five Oscar nominations; on Broadway, won the 1958 Tony Award for outstanding featured dramatic actress for her creation of the role of Gittel Mosca, a quirky Greenwich Village beatnik from the Bronx, in *Two for the Seesaw*, and the 1960 Tony Award for best dramatic actress for her creation of the role of Annie Sullivan, the tutor who tames the intractable blind and mute 10-year-old Helen Keller, in *The Miracle Worker*; won the Academy Award for best actress for her reprise of the latter role in the film of *The Miracle Worker* (1962); was born Anna Maria Italiano to Italian immigrants in the Bronx; after graduating from high school, in 1947, studied at the American Academy of Dramatic Arts in Manhattan; under the name Anne Marno, acted professionally on TV during the early stage of that medium's so-called Golden Age of live network drama; made her TV debut on the dramatic anthology *Studio One* and later had roles in productions on such drama showcases as *Kraft Television Theatre* and *Playhouse 90* and episodes of the series *Danger* and *Climax!*, among other programs; changed her name to Anne Bancroft under studio pressure when she went to Hollywood; made her movie debut as Lyn Lesley, the hotel lounge singer who is the girlfriend of the hero (Richard Widmark), in *Don't Bother to Knock* (1952); over the next several years, accrued 14 more film credits, usually secondary roles in low-grade flicks, among which a notable exception was the film noir *Nightfall* (1957), in which she was cast as Marie Gardner, the woman who befriends the protagonist (Aldo Ray), a man falsely accused of murder who is on the run from both police and the actual killers; meanwhile, more than a year earlier, unhappy with the progress of her movie career, returned to New York City and studied under Herbert Berghof at the Actors Studio while resuming her TV work and preparing for her appearances on Broadway; after returning to the big screen, drew best-actress Oscar nominations for her roles as Jo Armitage, a mother of eight with an unfaithful husband, in *The Pumpkin Eater* (1964), as the veteran ballerina Emma Jacklin in *The Turning Point* (1977), and as Mother Superior Miriam Ruth, in *Agnes of God* (1985); had a total of some 57 feature-film roles, including those of Jenny Churchill in *Young Winston* (1972), Mrs. Kendall in *The Elephant Man* (1980), Helene Hanff in *84 Charing Cross Road* (1987), Ma in *Torch Song Trilogy* (1988), and the Contessa in *The Roman Spring of Mrs. Stone* (2003); co-starred with her second husband, the comedy writer, producer, and actor Mel Brooks, in *To Be or Not to Be* (1983); starred on Broadway in *Mother Courage* (1963), *Golda* (1977), and *Duet for One* (1981); at Lincoln Center, was seen in *The Little Foxes* (1967) and *A Cry of Players* (1968); was nominated for Emmy Awards for her work in the TV films *Mrs. Cage* (1992) and *Oldest Living Confederate Widow Tells All* (1994); starred in several TV series, including *Freddie and Max* (1990) and *The Mother* (1994); won an Emmy Award in the musical/variety category for her performance in *Annie, the Women in the Life of a Man* in 1970 and another Emmy for outstanding supporting actress in a miniseries for her role in *Deep in My Heart* in 1999; died in Manhattan; was survived by Mel Brooks and their son, Maximilian. See *Current Biography* (1960).

Obituary *New York Times* A p17 June 7, 2005

BARRE, RAYMOND Apr. 12, 1924–Aug. 25, 2007 French economist and statesman. Raymond Barre, regarded by many of his peers in academe as France's top economist, scaled the heights of governmental service despite his relative freedom from personal political ambition. A technocratic center-right independent with somewhat flexible ad-hoc party affiliations, he reached his peak in government as prime minister of France from 1976 to 1981 in the centrist coalition administration of President Valéry Giscard d'Estaing. Giscard d'Estaing had been elected in 1974 as the candidate of the national Federation of Independent Republicans, a party he described as "liberal, centrist, and pro-European." Following the dissolution of that party, Giscard d'Estaing founded the center-right Union for French Democracy in 1978. In the prime ministry, Barre succeeded Jacques Chirac, who resigned because of disagreements with Giscard d'Estaing on issues including the administration's approach to the political left. (Chirac favored confrontation, while Giscard d'Estaing wanted to win the cooperation of moderate Socialists.) In recruiting Barre, Giscard d'Estaing sought to stabilize his precarious centrist coalition. He also saw in Barre "the public figure most likely to solve" France's dire economic problems at that time—a combination of recession and inflation, the worst such national crisis in 30 years—and thus to diminish popular grievances that were fueling the mounting electoral success of a Communist-Socialist alliance. During the first two years of his prime ministry, Barre also served as minister of economics and finance (1976–78). The national economic austerity program he introduced—including a sound money policy, selective price and wage controls and decontrols, and higher taxation (except for the value-added tax on goods and services)—was relatively successful, but it failed to stem the growth in the rate of unemployment, making it vulnerable to attack from the right by Chirac and his neo-Gaullists and from the left by François Mitterrand and his Socialists. In the 1981 presidential race, Mitterrand defeated Giscard d'Estaing. After receiving his doctorate in law and economics at the University of Paris, in 1950, Barre taught successively at the University of Tunis, in Tunisia, and the University of Caen, in France, before becoming a professor at the Institute of Political Sciences in Paris and the faculty of law and economic sciences at the University of Paris. His most enduring affiliation was with the Institute of Political Sciences, where, after a long leave of absence, he ended his academic career (1982–94). He ventured into government service when President Charles de Gaulle's Fifth Republic was established, serving as chief adviser to the minister of industry from 1959 to 1962. From 1967 to 1972 he was France's chief representative at meetings of the European Economic Community—also known as the Common Market—in Brussels, Belgium, where he began helping to shape the economic policies of the future European Union; he continued doing so subsequently as the EU's vice president in charge of economic and financial affairs. He was France's minister of foreign trade from January 1976 until he became prime minister, the following August. In 1978, with the backing of Giscard d'Estaing's Union for French Democracy, he was elected to represent the

Rhone department in the National Assembly, where he remained a deputy until 2002. He ran for the presidency of France, unsuccessfully, in 1988, and he was mayor of Lyon from 1995 to 2001. He published several books, including the classic textbook *Économie politique* (eighth edition, 1969), *Une Politique pour l'avenir* (1981), and *Reflexions pour demain* (1984). He died at Val de Grace hospital in Paris. His survivors included his wife, Eva (née Hegedug), and two sons. See *Current Biography* (1977).

Obituary *New York Times* Aug. 27, 2007

BAUDRILLARD, JEAN July 29, 1929–Mar. 6, 2007 French cultural theorist and philosopher. The insightful and provocative postmodern social theorist Jean Baudrillard was a self-described "intellectual outlaw" who pioneered the concept of virtual reality in bringing an extraordinarily original perspective to the analysis of contemporary Western culture. Although dismissed by some critics as an "obscurantist" dispenser of a "politically useful aesthetics of gibberish," Baudrillard was more widely recognized as "the Marshall McLuhan of the cyber culture," a brilliant and insightful contributor to an understanding of the effects of new forms of communication on society. In his intellectual odyssey Baudrillard was influenced in stages by Marxism, Freudianism, structuralism, and semiotics, but he finally rejected the premises of logic and rationality in those systems of thought and arrived at his own bleak view of the "post-industrial" consumerist Western world as one in which there has been a hopelessly catastrophic "collapse of the real" under the weight of "hyperreality," of media-driven signs that are simulations of reality. After successfully defending his thesis in sociology at the University of Paris in 1966, Baudrillard joined the faculty of the university's branch in Nanterre, where he taught until 1987. His first two books, written in the late 1960s, were influenced by Marxism and structural linguistics. In his third book, *Pour une critique de l'économie politique du signe* (1972; *For a Critique of the Economy of the Sign*, 1981), he both employed and criticized semiotic theory. While remaining on the left in politics, he definitively broke from Marxism with his book *Le miroir de la production* (1973; *The Mirror of Production*, 1975). He expanded his critique of modernist theories, including Marxism and psychoanalysis, in *De la seduction* (1979; *Seduction*, 1990). In that book he asserted that seduction by appearances trumps economic laws and the processes of the unconscious mind in the shaping of personal and social reality. He further developed his idea that in today's society the "real" has lost its primary significance in his next book, *Simulacres et simulation* (1981; *Simulacra and Simulation*, 1983). In that book he referred to the make-believe world of California's Disneyland amusement park as a distraction from the fact that the surrounding American society itself is also a simulation of reality, one that is hyperreal. Beginning in 1980 Baudrillard traveled extensively in the United States, which he viewed as "the ultimate postmodern culture." The reflections inspired by those travels make up the contents of his book *Amérique* (1986; *America,* 1988) and the first of the five volumes of his aphoristic journal published in transla-

tion as *Cool Memories* between 1988 and 2005. In his book *Illusion de la fin* (1989; *The Illusion of the End*, 1994), he wrote: "The acceleration of modernity, of technology, events and media, of all exchanges—economic, political, sexual—has propelled us to 'escape velocity,' with the result that we have flown free of the referential sphere of the real and of history." He published more than a score of books of theory, including those translated as *The Vital Illusion* (2000) and *Impossible Exchange* (2001). His ideas were the inspiration for the Wachowski brothers' popular motion picture *The Matrix* (1999), its two sequels, and its video-game spin-offs. (Baudrillard himself rejected any connections between his theories and *The Matrix*.) Baudrillard was married twice and had two children. He died in Paris. See *Current Biography* (1993).

Obituary *New York Times* C p11 Mar. 7, 2007

BERG, PATRICIA JANE Feb. 13, 1918–Sep. 10, 2006 Golfer. Patty Berg, a founder of the Ladies Professional Golf Association, stood beside Babe Didrikson Zaharias as one of the first two great pioneers in women's golf in the United States. During the 1940s and 1950s, Berg won a record 15 major professional women's championships—the Women's Open, the Titleholders seven times, and the Western Open seven times. Counting the professional titles she won before the LPGA tour was founded in 1950, she registered 60 overall pro victories, placing her fourth in the all-time pro women's rankings. Berg began competing in amateur golf in her native Minneapolis in 1933, when she was 14. As an amateur, she won 29 tournaments, including the U.S. Amateur title in 1938, when the Associated Press named her woman athlete of the year. (The AP would so honor her twice again, in 1943 and 1955.) She turned professional in 1940, when she was a student at the University of Minnesota. Because there were only three money-making events in women's pro golf at that time, she gladly accepted sponsorship by the Wilson Sporting Goods Co., which began manufacturing a line of Patty Berg golf clubs and subsidizing her golf clinics and exhibitions. After winning the Western Women's Open, in 1941, she suffered a severe knee injury in an automobile accident and was sidelined for more than a year. After recuperating, she won the Western Open again and the All-American at Tam O'Shanter, both in 1943. Later in 1943 she enlisted for wartime stateside clerical service as an officer in the U.S. Marine Corps Women's Reserve. After her service in World War II, she returned to the pro links and won the 1946 Women's Open. In 1948 she joined with 12 other female golfers in forming the Ladies Professional Golf Association, which was officially chartered in 1950. She served as the first president of the LPGA, until 1952. She won the Vare Trophy for lowest round on the professional tour in 1953, 1955, and 1956 and was the leading money winner on the tour in 1954, 1955, and 1957. Between 1948 and 1962 she had one of the most impressive runs in the history of professional golf, winning 44 titles, including nine majors. After retiring from competition, she continued working under the auspices of the Wilson Sporting Goods Co., traveling about the U.S. mentoring young golfers, conducting clinics, exhibiting her golfing skills in the "Patty Berg Show," and generally promoting the game of golf. Her many honors included induction into the LPGA Hall of Fame and the LPGA's establishment of the Patty Berg Award for outstanding contributions to women's golf. Berg died at Hope Hospice in Fort Myers, Georgia. See *Current Biography* (1940).

Obituary *New York Times* B p6 Sep. 11, 2006

BERGMAN, INGMAR July 14, 1918–July 30, 2007 Film, stage, and television director; scriptwriter. The Swedish filmmaker Ingmar Bergman was, as the critic Philip Bradshaw wrote, "the great gaunt magus of European art-house cinema." In his films Bergman created lonely characters in search of love and metaphysical meaning in a universe in which suffering and mortality are certain and God is inexplicably silent. The movie scholar Leonard Quest—who has criticized Bergman's "sometimes unremitting sense of life as a vale of tears"—wrote for *Cineaste* (September 22, 2004): "There is no other director who can convey the heart of his characters' psyches and souls as profoundly and as intensely as Bergman. He's the most personal and honest of filmmakers—a man whose work is a direct expression of his guilt, dreams, frustrations, and confusions." Starting in the 1940s Bergman directed 44 films, most in black and white and most of which he wrote. His films were nominated for a dozen Academy Awards; he won three for best foreign film, for *The Virgin Spring* (1960), *Through a Glass Darkly* (1961), and *Fanny and Alexander* (1982), the last of which (a thinly veiled evocation of his tormented early years) was also honored with Oscars for cinematography, set/art direction, and costume design. His oeuvre was achieved in collaboration with a stable of actors, outstanding among them Max von Sydow, Liv Ullmann, Ingrid Thulin, Bibi Andersson, Erland Josephson, Gunnar Björnstrand, and Harriet Andersson. He also worked closely with the cinematographers Sven Nykvist and Gunnar Fischer. Ernst Ingmar Bergman traced to his childhood the real-life demons that drove him into a world of fantasy and inspired his art. His father, a high-placed Lutheran clergyman (the pastor to the Swedish royal family), was a strict disciplinarian, as he recalled in his autobiography *Laterna Magica* (1987; *The Magic Lantern*, 2007), whose title refers to a treasured childhood possession of his, the precursor of the slide projector. His parents endured a loveless marriage, and Bergman credited them with creating "a world for me to revolt against." After dropping out of college, Bergman became a gofer at the Royal Opera House in Stockholm. In 1944 he began directing plays at the Helsingborg City Theatre. He later became director at other theaters, including the Royal Dramatic Theatre in Stockholm, where he worked on and off into his old age, becoming best known for his staging of dramas by August Strindberg. Meanwhile, he had been writing scripts at Svensk Filmindustri, Sweden's largest film-production company, since 1943 and directing his own screenplays since 1949. In his development as an auteur, he was influenced by the films of the German expressionists, the French surrealists, and the Italian neorealists as well as by Strindberg's plays. As a writer/director he spent six years making

10 films in relative obscurity before *Smiles of a Summer Night* (1955) brought him international attention and the first of his several Cannes Film Festival awards. A rare deviation from his more typical darker work, that film is a relatively lighthearted romance. In the austere medieval morality drama *The Seventh Seal* (1957), a bleak meditation on death, a knight (Max von Sydow) returns from the Crusades to find the black plague decimating his homeland. Two of the most haunting scenes in cinema history open and close the film: in the beginning, Death personified confronts the knight on a beach, and the two start to play a game of chess; in the finale, the scythe-wielding, black-shrouded Death figure is seen leading a dancing parade of religious fanatics and other travelers to their deaths. The film brought Bergman international cult status. Dream and reality converge in the perception of the protagonist of *Wild Strawberries* (1957), an elderly professor "cut off from all human emotion" (as Bergman described himself) who reflects back on his flawed life. *The Virgin Spring* (1960), about a brutal rape set in medieval times, was followed by *Through a Glass Darkly* (1961), about a young woman's descent into madness and its effect on her family. In *Winter Light* (1962) a village pastor's crisis of faith contributes to the suicide of a despondent parishioner. Later in the 1960s Bergman made, among other films, *The Silence*, which deals with unconventional sexuality; the strong anti-war statement *Shame*; and *Persona*, a Jungian study of womanhood and identity. Beginning with the six-part miniseries *Scenes from a Marriage* (1973)—later released as a feature film—Bergman increasingly turned to TV as his medium of choice. His *Magic Flute*, an experimental production of Mozart's opera, aired on Swedish TV in 1975. After a tax dispute with the Swedish government in 1976, Bergman lived in self-exile in Germany for several years, until the conflict ended. Back in Sweden, he made *Fanny and Alexander*, a 312-minute, four-part TV production that was made into a 188-minute film. For two decades thereafter he concentrated exclusively on work for TV, theater, and opera. In 2003 he emerged from his cinematic retirement with *Saraband* (2003), a film about a couple who psychologically injure each other and their children. In 1990 he published a second memoir, translated as *Images in Film* (1994). Bergman was married five times and had many affairs. He had nine children whom he acknowledged to be his own, including the film directors Daniel Bergman and Eva Bergman. He died at home on the Swedish island of Fårö, his main residence since 1966. See *Current Biography* (1981).

Obituary *New York Times* A p1+ July 30, 2007

BOTHA, P. W. Jan. 12, 1916–Oct. 31, 2006 White South African political leader who served as prime minister (1978–84) and president (1984–87) of his native land. Pieter Willem Botha was known among his compatriots as "die Groot Krokodil" ("the Old Crocodile" in Afrikaans, one of the two official languages of South Africa), a reference to his pugnacity, cantankerousness, hot temper, finger-wagging, and overbearing, fearsome manner as well as for his "ability to charm, outwit and crush his opponents," as Joseph R. Gregory wrote for the *New York Times*

(November 1, 2006). Botha was the last head of South Africa to enforce apartheid ("apartness" in Afrikaans), a system that, through a series of laws passed in the 1950s, institutionalized the racial segregation of the nation's white minority (which comprised 8 percent of the population) and the nonwhite majority and maintained the brutal repression of the latter. In a widely quoted statement released shortly after Botha's death, the black South African political leader Nelson Mandela, who spent more than 10 of his 27 years in prison during Botha's rule and later, in 1994, won election as the nation's first post-apartheid president, noted that while Botha was a symbol of apartheid and South Africa's "horribly divided past," "we also remember him for the steps he took to pave the way towards the eventual peacefully negotiated settlement in our country." Botha was born into an Afrikaner family in what was then known as the Orange Free State, a South African province. He grew up on his father's farm, where he "came to know black people very well . . . ," as he said in an interview for the book *Move Your Shadow: Black and White* (1985), by the *New York Times* reporter Joseph Lelyveld. "I was taught by my father to be strict with them, but just." As a teenager he joined the right-wing National Party. His desire to become active in the party's activities led him to drop out of college, in 1935. In 1946, after a decade as a full-time party organizer in Cape Province and elsewhere, he was appointed the party's public-information officer and also first secretary of the National Youth League. He won election to the House of Assembly (now called the National Assembly), one part of the bicameral national Parliament, as a representative of the city of George, Cape Province, in 1948, a seat he held for the remainder of his years in public life. He served as chief secretary of the National Party in the Cape Province from 1948 to 1958. In the latter year Prime Minister Hendryk F. Verwoerd appointed him deputy minister of the interior. He joined the Cabinet when Verwoerd named him minister of colored affairs and minister of community development and housing, in 1961; he earned the additional post of minister of public works in 1964. In 1966 he became minister of defense; he continued to serve in that position after Verwoerd's assassination, later that year, and the ascension of John Vorster as prime minister. In late 1966 he was elected leader of the National Party in the Cape Province. In 1975 he became leader of the House of Assembly. After Vorster resigned, in 1978, because of poor health, a National Party caucus selected Botha to succeed him. By that time apartheid had been in force for a quarter of a century; the terrible oppression of black South Africans had led to the country's expulsion from the United Nations, in 1974, and the imposition of a weapons embargo, in 1977. Botha made some attempts to improve conditions for nonwhites (people of mixed race and ethnic Indians living in South Africa), by granting them limited political rights, and smaller efforts to help blacks—for example, by approving the formation of multiracial regional advisory commissions to advise his administration on problems encountered by blacks in urban areas. Toward the end of his time as president, he corresponded with the imprisoned Mandela and met with him for secret talks in the presidential residence, but he refused to

free him. "I told him to renounce violence, which he did not do. He kept himself in jail at that stage," he said, according to Alex Duval Smith in the London *Independent* (Novemer 1, 2006). Botha firmly opposed giving blacks any political power and strenuously fought opponents of apartheid, prominent among them members of the African National Congress (ANC), which was outlawed during Botha's tenure. (The ban was lifted in 1990 by Botha's successor, F. W. de Klerk; a national referendum ended apartheid two years later.) As revealed in testimony before the Truth and Reconciliation Commission, set up in 1995 under Nelson Mandela, the State Security Council, which Botha founded in 1972 and chaired, "carried out a program to murder anti-apartheid activitists," as Joseph R. Gregory reported, not only within South Africa but in neighboring countries to which some ANC members had fled; sites in Angola, Botswana, Lesotho, Mozambique, Zambia, and Zimbabwe were attacked by South African ground and air forces. In South Africa, according to Gregory, "Actions by the country's security forces and police during Mr. Botha's years in power . . . killed 4,000 people; as many as 50,000 others were held without trial." As condemnation of apartheid increased outside South Africa, a grassroots campaign began in the U.S. to pressure state governments and managers of public pension systems, college endowment funds, and money-market and other interest-generating funds to divest themselves of stock in companies doing business with or in South Africa. The harmful effects of the divestment campaign on South Africa's economy led Botha to harden his stance. "The Old Crocodile was obsessed with looking tough and in control," Hendrick Jacobus Coetsee, one of his aides, told Gregory. "He never wanted to show any sign of weakness." In early 1989, within weeks of suffering a stroke, he resigned his position as National Party head. He stepped down as president the following August, at the urging of de Klerk, the new party leader, and other Cabinet ministers. He refused to answer a summons to attend a 1997 hearing of the Truth and Reconciliation Commission; his conviction, for contempt of the law, and 12-month prison sentence were overturned on appeal. In its final report, however, the commission stated, as Alex Duval Smith wrote, that he had been "directly accountable for the 1987 bombing of the ANC's London headquarters" and had "ordered the 1988 bombing of a Johannesburg building that was housing an anti-apartheid group." As far as is known, Botha never expressed any regrets for his actions. "I have nothing to apologize for," he said, as quoted by Gregory, after receiving the commission's summons. "I will never ask for amnesty. Not now, not tomorrow, not after tomorrow." After Botha's death, Mosima Gabrial ("Tokyo") Sexwale, an anti-apartheid activist and ANC member who spent 22 years in prison and then, during Mandela's administration, became premier of the South African province of Gauteng, said, as quoted by BBC News (November 1, 2006, online), "We should not forget the kind of regime he represented, he was ruthless, he was brutal, he was a leader of apartheid during the harshest years of that regime, the sad truth is that he is leaving with many secrets which he should have revealed perhaps during the time of the Truth and Reconciliation Commission." Botha died at his home, along the southern shore of the Cape of Good Hope. His first marriage, to the former Anna Elizabeth ("Elize") Roussouw, ended with the death of his wife, in 1997. His survivors included his second wife, the former Barbara Robertson; two sons, Pieter Willem and Roussouw; three daughters, Elanza, Amelia, and Rozanne; and a number of grandchildren. See *Current Biography* (1979).

Obituary *New York Times* B p9 Nov. 1, 2006

BRADLEY, ED June 22, 1941–Nov. 9, 2006 Newscaster; journalist. One of the most familiar faces in broadcast journalism, Ed Bradley worked for CBS news for almost 40 years, reporting on such events as the Vietnam War and the 1976 presidential elections before joining the staff of the network's most prestigious newsmagazine, *60 Minutes*, in 1981. The first African-American at CBS to serve as a White House correspondent and a Sunday-night anchor, he was described by Patricia Sullivan, writing for the *Washington Post* (November 10, 2006), as "a suave and streetwise reporter considered one of the best interviewers on television." Bradley, whose parents separated soon after his birth, was raised in Philadelphia, Pennsylvania, where he attended Roman Catholic parochial schools. He entered Cheyney State College, in Pennsylvania, as an education major but became interested in broadcasting after befriending Georgie Woods, a disc jockey at WDAS-FM, a local Philadelphia radio station. One night, while Bradley was visiting him at the station, Woods allowed Bradley to announce part of the evening's news; the experience inspired Bradley to pursue broadcasting as a career. He graduated from Cheyney in 1964 and took a job as a sixth-grade teacher, but he continued to work unpaid for WDAS as a newscaster and the host of an evening jazz show. Bradley's thorough coverage of local race riots later led the station's management to give him a paying job. He continued to split his time between teaching and working as a disc jockey and newscaster until 1967, when he landed a job with WCBS, in New York. After spending more than three years there, Bradley grew frustrated with the fast-paced, competitive environment and quit his job, moving to Paris, where he dabbled in poetry and supported himself doing voice-overs for commercials. In 1971 he began working as a stringer for the CBS bureau in Paris, and the following year he returned to New York. Shortly after his return, the network shipped him off to Saigon (now Ho Chi Minh City) to cover the Vietnam War. He was wounded by mortar fire in Cambodia but escaped serious injury. He returned to the U.S. in 1974 to work as a general assignment reporter for CBS's Washington, D.C., bureau, but he volunteered to return to Vietnam the following year to cover the fall of Saigon to North Vietnamese troops. After he returned to the U.S., he was assigned to cover the presidential campaign of Jimmy Carter, and after Carter's victory he was appointed one of CBS's three White House correspondents. Around that time he also worked as the anchorman of CBS's *Sunday Night News* program, becoming the only African-American anchorman in network news at the time. Bored with covering White House press conferences, he signed on as a

principal correspondent for *CBS Reports*. For that program, he produced such award-winning documentary segments as "The Boat People" (1979) and "Blacks in America: With All Deliberate Speed" (1979). In 1981 he was named as a replacement for Dan Rather on the newsmagazine *60 Minutes*, one of the most-watched news programs on the air since its inception, in 1968. Bradley's work for the show included memorable celebrity interviews with the likes of Lena Horne, Robin Williams, and Michael Jackson. He also interviewed notable criminals, including the convicted killer Jack Henry Abbott and Timothy McVeigh, the latter of whom was executed in 2001 for carrying out the bombing of a federal building in Oklahoma City. Bradley received many honors for his work, including the George Foster Peabody Award and 19 Emmys, one of which was awarded in 2003 for lifetime achievement. Bradley was a fan of jazz music and hosted the weekly radio broadcast *Jazz at Lincoln Center Radio* until shortly before his death, at the age of 65, from complications of leukemia. He was survived by his wife, Patricia Blanchet; the couple had no children. See *Current Biography* (1988).

Obituary *New York Times* A p1 Nov. 10, 2006

BROWN, JAMES May 3, 1933(?)–Dec. 25, 2006 Singer; dancer; band leader; songwriter. The pompadoured "Godfather of Soul," the legendary James Brown was a colossus among the American musical showmen of his time—and perhaps, as he was often called, "the hardest-working man in show business." With the innovative chord changes and progressions in his music, his distinctive voice, and his shifting, sliding, flashing "good foot" performances—electric combinations of studied theatrical perfectionism and ecstatic improvisation—Brown was a pervasive force in the popular music of the second half of the 20th century, with an influence evident in the work of artists ranging from Mick Jagger and the white glitter rockers to Prince, Michael Jackson, and a host of rap musicians. As his friend the Reverend Al Sharpton said, he was "an American original" who "made soul an international music genre." "Without Brown, R&B might never have become soul, and funk might never have been invented," James McNair wrote for the London *Independent* (July 2, 2004). "Where black pride is concerned, moreover, Brown pioneered the soundtrack." Brenda Dixon Gottschild, the author of *Waltzing in the Dark: African American Vaudeville and Race Politics in the Swing Era*, has pointed out that Brown was "a wellspring of inspiration for artists and amateurs not only on the dance floor and the popular stage but also in the clubs of the hip-hop generation and the concert performance venues of postmodern dance." Brown left a discography of more than 50 bestselling albums and more than 100 singles, which began registering on the R&B charts in the mid-1950s. His debut on the pop charts came in 1963 with *The James Brown Show Live at the Apollo*, which was on *Billboard*'s pop album chart for 63 weeks, peaking in the top five. In 1965 his signature singles "I Got You (I Feel Good)" and "Papa's Got a Brand New Bag" reached the pop Top 10. The latter brought him the first of his three Grammy Awards; the second was for

"Living in America," the theme song from the film *Rocky IV* (1985), and the third was a Lifetime Achievement Award (1992). His classic singles range from "Say It Loud, I'm Black and I'm Proud," "I Don't Want Nobody to Give Me Nothing (Open Up the Door, I'll Get It by Myself)," and "Don't Be a Dropout" to "It's Too Funky in Here," "Hot Pants," and "Sex Machine." Brown was born on May 3 sometime between 1928 and 1933 into a broken family living in a one-room shanty in rural Barnwell, South Carolina. He grew up there and in hardscrabble ghetto streets across the state line in Augusta, Georgia, where he learned "the value of moving fast and hitting hard," survival skills that he would translate into his performance art, as Gottschild observed. "Brown cut his eye teeth on swing," Gottschild wrote for *Dance Magazine* (August 1, 2000), on the music of such "dancing bandleaders" as Louis Jordan and Cab Calloway, along with gospel, jazz, and blues influences. (Later, he would be influenced by such contemporaries as Ray Charles and Little Richard.) A seventh-grade dropout in trouble with the law, Brown spent three and one-half years in a reform school in Georgia. Early on, he learned to play harmonica, drums, piano, organ, and guitar. In 1953 he joined the Gospel Starlighters, a vocal group founded by Bobby Byrd that soon turned from gospel to R&B and changed its name to the Famous Flames. Fronting that group, Brown developed a highly theatrical show, in which he wore makeup and glittery, unusually cut suits. "Using his feet as percussion instruments," as Gottschild observed, he made rhythm "his basic strength" and "danced faster—and harder—than . . . anyone had ever seen before. Even standing in place, he worked his feet . . . to accompany the beats in his deceptively simple music." His first R&B hit was the ballad "Please Please Please" (1956), the tearful performance of which would be the closing ritual of his show for many years. His "Try Me" was the best-selling R&B single of 1958. Such hits as "Think," "Night Train" and "Out of Sight" followed in the early 1960s. His later recordings included such singles as "Cold Sweat" (1967), "Funky Drummer" (1970), and "Get on the Good Foot" (1972) and such albums as *The Payback* (which went gold in 1974) and *The Original Disco Man* (1979). Meanwhile, his strenuous touring itinerary, having long since expanded beyond the Southern chitlin circuit, included such venues as the Apollo Theater, Madison Square Garden, and sites in Great Britain and Africa. He had cameo roles in several films, including that of the preacher Cleophus Jones in the dancing-in-church scene in *The Blues Brothers* (1980). In 1986 he was a charter inductee into the Rock and Roll Hall of Fame. After a series of arrests on various charges, and leading police on a long high-speed car chase, he served 15 months in prison and 10 months in work release between late 1988 and early 1991. He championed black self-reliance and economic free enterprise and devoted time and money to a "Stay in School" program he initiated. Every year (including 2006, on the Friday before his death) he participated in a Christmas toys-for-children charity in Augusta. With Bruce Tucker, he wrote the autobiography *James Brown: The Godfather of Soul* (1986), and with Marc Eliot, the memoir *I Feel Good* (2005). He died of a heart attack in At-

lanta. His survivors included his fourth wife, Tomi Raye Hynie (though the legality of their marriage has been questioned), and at least six children. His oldest son, Teddy, predeceased him. See *Current Biography* (1992).

Obituary *New York Times* A p1+ Dec. 26, 2006

BROYHILL, JOEL T. Nov. 4, 1919–Sep. 24, 2006 U.S. congressman. Joel Thomas Broyhill represented Virginia's Tenth Congressional District (which is just across the Potomac River from Washington, D.C.) in Congress from 1953 to 1975. As a conservative Republican he was generally in support of less government, lower taxes, and less federal spending, with some exceptions in the areas of his priorities, which included more federal jobs for his constituents, increased pay and benefits and better working conditions for such government employees as postal workers, improved trans-Potomac infrastructure for commuters, and federal aid to local schools. For many of his years in Congress, he wielded influence as a member of the House Post Office and Civil Service and District of Columbia Committees. He sponsored legislation authorizing construction of the Roosevelt and Woodrow Wilson Bridges across the Potomac, the addition of a second span to the Fourteenth Street Bridge, and the widening of the Shirley Highway. He clashed with District of Columbia leaders on such issues as D.C. home rule, which he adamantly opposed. He was also steadfast in his opposition to civil rights legislation, anti-poverty programs, and federally subsidized open housing in the suburban municipalities surrounding Washington, D.C. As a U.S. Army captain in World War II, he was captured by the Germans during the Battle of the Bulge and spent about six months in a prisoner-of-war camp before escaping. Following the war he became a partner in his father's building and real-estate firm, M. T. Broyhill & Sons, in northern Virginia. He returned to that business after leaving Congress. He also served as the manager of John W. Warner's successful first campaign for the U.S. Senate, in 1978. Broyhill died at his home in Arlington, Virginia. He was predeceased by his first wife, Jane Marshall Bragg, and survived by his second wife, Suzanne M. Broyhill, three daughters, a stepdaughter, four grandchildren, and three great-grandchildren. See *Current Biography* (1974).

Obituary *New York Times* A p29 Oct. 4, 2006

BUCHWALD, ART Oct. 20, 1925–Jan. 17, 2007 Writer. With his sharp but good-natured eye for the absurd in high places, the comic newspaper columnist Art Buchwald—perhaps most aptly described as "a Will Rogers with chutzpah"—earned the distinction of being the most widely published American journalistic humorist of the second half of the 20th century. His columns, which first appeared in the Paris-based European edition of the *New York Herald Tribune* (the forerunner of the *International Herald Tribune*) later ran in the *Washington Post* and were syndicated to 500 or more newspapers. He published more than 30 books, most of which were collections of his previously published newspaper columns. The nature of his wit—and its political and social targets—is implicit in such titles as *How Much Is*

That in Dollars? (1961), I Chose Capitol Punishment (1963), . . . And Then I Told the President (1965), The Establishment Is Alive and Well in Washington (1969), I Never Danced at the White House (1973), "I Am Not a Crook" (1974), Washington Is Leaking (1976), Down the Seine and Up the Potomac with Art Buchwald (1977), The Buchwald Stops Here (1978), While Reagan Slept (1983), You Can Fool All of the People All of the Time (1985), I Think I Don't Remember (1987), and Beating Around the Bush (2005). In addition to his collections of columns, his books included the novels A Gift from the Boys (1958), The Bollo Caper (1974), and Irving's Delight (1975), the Broadway play Sheep on the Runway (1970), the memoir I'll Always Have Paris (1996), and Stella in Heaven: Almost a Novel (2000). Arthur Buchwald was born in Mount Vernon, New York, to Jewish parents who had immigrated from Austria-Hungary. After his mother was institutionalized with a mental illness and the family business (curtain and drape manufacturing) failed, his father placed him—along with at least one of his three sisters—in a succession of foster and foundling homes, including Manhattan's Hebrew Orphan Asylum. After he dropped out of high school, he joined the U.S. Marines and began his journalistic career editing his outfit's newspaper on the Pacific atoll of Eniwetok during World War II. After the war, as a beneficiary of the G.I. Bill, he took liberal arts courses at the University of Southern California at Los Angeles, where he was managing editor of the Wampus, the campus humor magazine. In 1948 he used a G.I. bonus check to buy a one-way ticket to Paris, France, where he found a livelihood first as a stringer for the American show-business newspaper Variety and then, beginning in 1949, as a restaurant and entertainment columnist and interviewer of celebrities for the European edition of the New York Herald Tribune. His first column was titled "Paris After Dark." A second column, "Mostly About People," was added in 1951. Increasingly, the columns manifested Buchwald's antic bent. Beginning in 1952 the columns were published on both sides of the Atlantic. In the New York edition of the Herald Tribune, they appeared under the titles "Europe's Lighter Side" and "Art Buchwald in Paris." With his wife and three adopted children, Buchwald returned to the United States and settled in Washington, D.C., in the early 1960s. In 1967 he began writing a column for the Washington Post in which he satirized, spoofed, and otherwise treated humorously a wide range of subjects, including the minor foibles and the major follies of Washington politicians and bureaucrats, among other people of power, fame, or riches. During the 1970s his column appeared three times weekly in some 400 newspapers in the United States and some 100 more in other countries. (Among newspaper humorists, his closest rival for readership was his friend Russell Baker.) In 1982 he received a Pulitzer Prize for outstanding commentary. His column was syndicated by the Los Angeles Times Syndicate until 2000 and thereafter by Tribune Media Services. Suffering kidney failure, he checked himself into a Washington, D.C., hospice in February 2006 and, refusing dialysis, prepared for death. During the following several months he wrote the reflections on life and death comprising the book Too Soon to Say Goodbye (2006). After spending the summer of 2006 at his vacation cottage, in Tisbury, on Martha's Vineyard, Massachusetts, he retuned to Washington, D.C., where he died at the home of his son, Joel. His other survivors included his daughters, Connie and Jennifer, and five grandchildren. His wife, Ann McCarry Buchwald, predeceased him. His sense of humor never left him. By prearrangement, immediately after his death he appeared in a video on the New York Times Web site announcing, "Hi, I'm Art Buchwald and I just died." See Current Biography (1960).

Obituary New York Times A p1+ Jan. 19, 2007

CAMPBELL, BEBE MOORE Feb. 18, 1950–Nov. 27, 2006 Novelist; social critic; journalist. Through her novels, nonfiction books, and magazine articles, Bebe Moore Campbell examined gender conflict and race relations in contemporary American society, with particular emphasis on the challenges that African-Americans face as they strive for upward mobility. "I wanted to give racism a face," she said, referring to her first novel, Your Blues Ain't Like Mine (1992), as quoted by Margalit Fox for the New York Times (November 28, 2006). "African-Americans know about racism, but I don't think we really know the causes. I decided it's first of all a family problem." Described by Donna Seaman for Booklist (June 1–15, 1994) as "a keen and candid social critic, and a masterful storyteller," Campbell often appeared in the media to discuss race relations and was a frequent commentator on the National Public Radio program Morning Edition. Campbell's parents, Doris and George Moore, divorced when she was young, and during her childhood she lived with her mother, aunt, and maternal grandmother in Philadelphia. She spent the summer months in North Carolina with her father and later chronicled those visits in the memoir Sweet Summer: Growing Up With and Without My Dad (1989). After earning a B.S. in education from the University of Pittsburgh, she worked as a schoolteacher in Atlanta, Georgia, and later in Washington, D.C. In the mid-1970s, after the birth of her daughter, Maia, she began writing for newspapers and magazines, including the Washington Post, Publishers Weekly, Black Enterprise, and Ebony. In 1980 she received a grant from the National Endowment for the Arts to adapt a nonfiction account of her youth, Old Lady Shoes, into a short story. She later converted that piece into an award-winning radio play of the same title. In 1986 Campbell published her first book, Successful Women, Angry Men: Backlash in the Two-Career Marriage, which examined the stress placed upon upper-middle-class households in which both the husband and wife work. Your Blues Ain't Like Mine was published six years later and features a story inspired by the murder of Emmett Till, a black youth from Chicago who, while visiting Mississippi in the summer of 1955, was killed by white men for whistling at a white woman. In School Library Journal (January 1993), Judy Sokoll wrote that the book "exposes family, race, and class divisions in America from the 1950s to the present, and the rich characterization explores the base, the noble, and the ordinary in all of us." In Campbell's next novel, Brothers and Sisters (1994), she described the interracial friendship between co-workers at a bank. Campbell described the book to Pamela Newkirk in the *New York Times* (November 15, 1995) as her "attempt to bridge a racial gap. That's the story that never gets told: how many of us [blacks and whites] really like each other, really respect each other." Campbell's later novels included *Singing in the Comeback Choir* (1998), about a talk-show producer who returns to the neighborhood where she was raised to spend time with her ailing grandmother; *What You Owe Me* (2001), about the friendship between an African-American and a Jewish woman; and *72 Hour Hold* (2005), about bipolar disorder. Campbell is also the author of two children's books, *Sometimes My Mommy Gets Angry* (2003) and *Stompin' at the Savoy* (2006). She died from complications of brain cancer and is survived by her second husband, Ellis Gordon Jr.; her mother, Doris Moore; her daughter from her first marriage, Maia Campbell; her stepson, Ellis Gordon III; and her two grandchildren. See *Current Biography* (2000).

Obituary *New York Times* A p21 Nov. 28, 2006

CAREY, ERNESTINE GILBRETH Apr. 5, 1908–Nov. 4, 2006 Author; retail executive. With her younger brother Frank B. Gilbreth, Ernestine Gilbreth Carey wrote the best-selling creative memoir *Cheaper by the Dozen* (1949), a fictionalized recounting of their and their 10 siblings' childhoods in a household ordered in strict accordance with the time-and-motion principles of their eccentric efficiency-expert father and quietly monitored by their mother, an industrial psychologist and engineer who was the father's partner in the family's management-consulting firm. That lighthearted autobiographical novel was made into the feature film *Cheaper by the Dozen* (1950), starring Clifton Webb and Myrna Loy as the Gilbreth parents and Jeanne Crain as Ann, the eldest Gilbreth daughter. In a sequel to the book, *Belles on Their Toes* (1950), Gilbreth and Carey told of the family's adventures after their mother took direct control of the ménage following the death of their father, in 1924. The 1952 motion-picture adaptation of *Belles on Their Toes* again starred Myrna Loy as the widow and Jeanne Crain as Ann. (Steve Martin and Bonnie Hunt played the leads in a loose remake of *Cheaper by the Dozen*, released in 2003. *Cheaper by the Dozen 2*, an even looser screen sequel, with Martin and Hunt again starring, was released in 2005.) After receiving a B.A. degree in English at Smith College in 1929, Ernestine Gilbreth, as she was then known, became a buyer with R. H. Macy & Co. in New York City, and she was subsequently a buyer for several other department stores, for a total of the better part of 20 years. In addition to the two books written with her brother Frank, she wrote *Jumping Jupiter* (1952), which was adapted into the stage comedy *Buy Jupiter!* by William Davidson, *Rings Around Us* (1956), consisting of reminiscences of her married life, and *Giddy Moment* (1958). Carey lived in Reedley, California, and died at St. Agnes Medical Center in Fresno, California. She was predeceased by her husband, Charles E. Carey. Her survivors included a son, a daughter, six grandchildren, and five great-grandchildren. See *Current Biography* (1949).

Obituary *New York Times* B p9 Nov. 6, 2006

CLAIBORNE, LIZ Mar. 31, 1929–June 26, 2007 Fashion designer and business executive. One of the most successful American womenswear designers in the waning decades of the 20th century, Liz Claiborne, as Elaine Woo observed in an obituary for the *Los Angeles Times*, "built a global empire by taking career women out of 'uptight' suits and offering them a wide range of affordable, feminine, and colorful separates that were stylish without being trendy." For just over 25 years beginning in 1950, Claiborne worked for other designers and clothing manufacturers. As a working mother at a time when more and more women were entering into and rising in the commercial and professional workforces, she became increasingly aware that the male-dominated fashion industry was ignoring an unfilled niche in the market for feminine career clothes, where the basic pattern was dull imitation of the male business suit. In January 1976, with several partners, including her second husband, the textile-industry executive Arthur Ortenberg, she founded Liz Claiborne Inc., a fashion house dedicated to filling that niche. Elaine Woo quoted Ilse Metchek, executive director of the California Fashion Association: "At that point you looked like either a hippie or . . . [the actress] Donna Reed. She filled that hole. The whole concept of sportswear as career clothing is her legacy." "The concept," Claiborne explained in an interview for *Women's Wear Daily* in 2006, "was to dress the American working woman [not] in that little navy blue suit with a tie [but] in sportier clothes and colors," separates that could be variously combined to make attractive outfits. In addition, her intention was to make her clothes easily available to the busy working-woman shopper at relatively moderate prices—to "bring good taste to a mass level." Her first collection, in the fall of 1976, included pants, pleated skirts, ponchos, and cowl-neck sweaters that she described as "business-like but not too pinstripe, more casual, more imaginative." An immediate success, Liz Claiborne Inc. had sales of $23 million by 1978, and it entered *Fortune* magazine's list of America's 500 largest companies in 1986. Over the years the company diversified, adding divisions for dresses, shoes, jeans, accessories, fragrances, and menswear. When Claiborne retired from active management of the company, at the end of the 1980s, it was the largest women's-apparel maker in the U.S., with $1.4 billion in sales. In retirement she, with her husband, concentrated on the work of the Liz Claiborne and Art Ortenberg Foundation, which has spent millions of dollars supporting environmental-conservation projects throughout the world. She and Ortenberg maintained homes in Manhattan, on Fire Island, and on a ranch in Montana. She died at New York-Presbyterian Hospital in Manhattan, of complications from abdominal cancer. Her survivors included Alexander, a son from her first marriage (to Ben Schultz), Arthur Ortenberg, and two stepchildren. See *Current Biography* (1989).

Obituary *New York Times* C p16 June 28, 2007

COMDEN, BETTY May 3, 1917–Nov. 23, 2006 Songwriter; screenwriter; playwright. Along with her collaborator Adolph Green, Betty Comden was one of the most successful songwriters in popular-music history, with a body of work that was revered by the public and critics for its wit, intelligence, and humor. The duo of Comden and Green wrote the lyrics and librettos for some of the most beloved musicals on Broadway, including *On the Town* (1944), *Wonderful Town* (1953), *Peter Pan* (1954), *Bells Are Ringing* (1956), and *Applause* (1970). They were also accomplished screenwriters, penning such classics as *Singin' in the Rain* (1952) and *The Band Wagon* (1953). Born and raised in Brooklyn, New York, Comden (who changed her surname from Cohen when she began her stage career) studied drama at New York University, graduating in 1938. While trying to establish a career, she was introduced to another frustrated actor, Adolph Green, by a mutual friend. The pair, along with the actors Judy Holliday, Alvin Hammer, and John Frank, formed a cabaret troupe known as the Revuers, which performed weekly shows at the Village Vanguard nightclub in New York City's Greenwich Village. The group was frequently joined onstage by the pianist Leonard Bernstein, who would later become a legendary conductor and composer. The Revuers were wildly successful and were soon booked for shows throughout New York City, including performances that were broadcast on the radio. The team thought they were on their way to establishing themselves in Hollywood when they were invited to appear in *Greenwich Village* (1944), which starred Dom Ameche and Carmen Miranda—but most of the troupe's scenes ended up on the cutting-room floor. When Comden and Green returned to New York, Bernstein employed them to write the book and lyrics for the Broadway version of *Fancy Free*, a ballet that he had been working on with the choreographer Jerome Robbins. The resulting show, *On the Town*, which told the story of three sailors on shore leave in New York City, was a major success on Broadway. Comden and Green also wrote the screenplay for the film version, which starred Frank Sinatra and Gene Kelly. The writing duo worked with Kelly on several projects, the most famous of which is perhaps *Singin' in the Rain*. In 1953 Comden and Green won their first Tony Award, for *Wonderful Town*. They were nominated 11 more times, taking home six statuettes for their contributions to *Hallelujah, Baby!* (1967), *Applause* (1970), *On the Twentieth Century* (1978), and *The Will Rogers Follies* (1991). In 1958 Comden and Green starred in *A Party With Betty Comden and Adolph Green*, performing material from their various works. The revue had a successful run on Broadway and later went on a national tour. After seeing the 1977 Broadway revival of the show, Clive Barnes wrote for the *New York Times* (February 11, 1977), "As writers, the two of them [Comden and Green] are unusually gifted. They have a manic dexterity with words, a gift for rhyme and an ear for reason. As performers they have this dazzling charm, which makes them the kind of people you would really like to invite into your home." Green and Comden continued their partnership until Green's death in 2002. Comden, who died of heart failure, is predeceased by her husband, Steven Kyle, and their son, Alan, who died in 1990 from complications of a drug addiction. Comden is survived by her daughter, Susanna Kyle. See *Current Biography* (1945) and *American Songwriters* (1987).

Obituary *New York Times* A p33 Nov. 24, 2006

CRANE, EVA June 12, 1912–Sep. 6, 2007 British authority on bees; author. As a scholar, editor, and world-traveling researcher and writer, Eva Crane (née Widdowson) vastly broadened, disseminated, and organized knowledge about bees, beekeeping, and honey-hunting past and present; she contributed to a greater appreciation of the vital ecological role of bees and the nutritional value of honey; and she rallied beekeepers and bee enthusiasts throughout the world to form an information-sharing community. Her books include world pollination and honey-source directories; a beekeeping dictionary (which she edited) and a bibliography; books on honey, the archaeology of beekeeping, and tropical apiculture; and the encyclopedic tomes *Bees and Beekeeping* (1990) and *The World History of Beekeeping and Honey Hunting* (1999). Crane, who held advanced degrees in nuclear physics and quantum mechanics, was a university lecturer in physics and mathematics for a decade before she was serendipitously introduced to apiculture and apiology. The occasion was her wedding to James Alfred Crane, in 1942, when, because of the exigencies of World War II, sugar was rationed in Britain and one of her wedding gifts was a honey-producing beehive. Plunging into her second vocation, she began to read her way voraciously through the existing literature in the field and joined a local beekeeping organization. Subsequently she became the secretary of the British Beekeepers Association, and in 1949 she founded the Bee Research Association, renamed the International Bee Research Association in 1976. She edited the association's *Journal of Apicultural Research* from 1962 to 1982. In support of the association, she established the Eva Crane Trust, dedicated to advancing the science of apiculture through the publication of books and the promotion of apicultural libraries and museums of historical beekeeping artifacts throughout the world. She edited the journal *Bee World* from 1949 to 1984 and the database *Apicultural Abstracts* from 1950 to 1984. Collecting and filing papers and periodicals devoted to apiology and apiculture, she compiled an archive of 60,000 items that is housed in the National Library of Wales at Aberystwyth. In her field research she traveled in more than 60 countries over a period of several decades. She chronicled her travels in her book *Making a Bee-line* (2003). Crane's husband died in 1978. She died in Slough, England. See *Current Biography* (1993).

Obituary *New York Times* I p34 Sep. 16, 2007

CRESPIN, REGINE Feb. 23, 1927–July 5, 2007 French opera singer. The soprano—and later mezzo and dramatic soprano—Régine Crespin was a magnetic lyrical artist, with a stage presence as assured and commanding as her voice was big, warm, and clearly projected. Comfortable in German and Italian as well as French opera, she was internationally admired for her luxurious delivery of a repertoire that included Sieglinde and Brünnhilde, among other roles in the works of Richard Wagner; Verdi's Desdemona and Leonora; Richard Strauss's Marschallin; Carl Maria von Weber's Reiza; Giacomo Puccini's Tosca; Charles Gounod's Marguerite; Jules Massenet's Salomé and Charlotte; Gabriel Fauré's Pénélope; Hector Berlioz's Cassandra and Dido; and Georges Bizet's Carmen. Crespin made her operatic debut in Mulhouse, France, in 1950, singing Elsa in Wagner's *Lohengrin*. Later in the same year, she again sang Elsa at her debut at the Paris Opera, where she continued to perform more or less continuously until the late 1950s and occasionally thereafter. Backstage at the Paris Opera after one performance in the mid-1950s, the French composer Francis Poulenc introduced himself to her and told her of his plan to set to music *Les Dialogues des Carmélites*, Georges Bernanos's drama about a group of nuns martyred during the French Revolution. She doubted the feasibility of that plan until Poulenc played for her some of the music he was composing for the opera, including that for the role he then envisioned for her: Madame Lidoine, the second and younger of the two prioresses in the story. (He felt that her voice was not yet deep enough for the role of the older prioress, Madame de Croissy.) Crespin sang Madame Lidoine in the premiere of the French version of *Les Dialogues des Carmélites* at the Paris Opera, in June 1957. (The opera had first been performed in an Italian version at La Scala in January 1957.) She made her debut at the Bayreuth Festival as Kundry in Wagner's *Parsifal* in 1958, at La Scala as Pizzetti's Phaedra in 1959, at the Berlin State Opera as the Marschallin in *Der Rosenkavalier* in 1960, and at Covent Garden as Marschallin in 1961. In October 1962 she made her American debut, singing the title role in *Tosca* with the Chicago Lyric Opera. Again singing Marschallin, she debuted at the Metropolitan Opera House in New York City in November 1962. She sang with the Met every year thereafter until the early 1970s, when she suffered a vocal crisis along with a nervous breakdown. Retreating from the operatic stage, she returned to vocal studies under a new teacher, Rudolf Bautz, in Cologne, Germany, an experience that led her to drop roles no longer suitable for her voice, including Tosca, Elsa, and all the Verdi heroines, and to begin to sing mezzo roles—as a soprano. After an absence of two years from opera, she began her comeback singing the title role in *Carmen*—a part she had sung in concert but never before on the operatic stage—with the Opéra national du Rhin in Strasbourg. When she returned to the Met as Carmen in October 1975, the critic Speight Jenkins observed that her voice had regained its "good health" and that "her sexiness engulfed everyone in the audience capable of comprehending it." In February 1977, 20 years after her creation of the role of the second, younger prioress in the French version of *Les Dialogues des Carmélites*, she sang the role of the first, older prioress, Madame de Croissy, in the Met's first English-language production of that opera. Never having sung on stage in English before, and being the only foreigner in the cast, she approached the role with trepidation, but critics rated her diction the clearest of any cast member's and lauded her performance. One of her last operatic performances was as the Countess in Tchaikovsky's *Queen of Spades* at the Paris Opera in 1989. She also enjoyed successful careers as a recitalist, a guest soloist with symphony orchestras, a recording artist, and a teacher of master classes at the Paris Conservatory and elsewhere. Crespin was married to the French writer and professor of German literature Lou

Bruder from 1962 until they divorced, in 1969. They had no children. Crespin's autobiography, *La Vie et l'amour d'une femme* (1982) was updated and translated as *On Stage, Off Stage* (1997). She died in Paris. See *Current Biography* (1979).

Obituary *New York Times* B p7 July 6, 2007

DOUGLAS, MIKE Aug. 11, 1925–Aug. 11, 2006 Television personality; singer. Genial Mike Douglas, who began his career as a pop and big-band singer, became a television trailblazer in the early 1960s as the host of *The Mike Douglas Show*. That 90-minute program was the first nationally syndicated first-run music/talk/variety show to establish itself successfully in a daily afternoon time slot, opening the way for similar daytime shows hosted by others, from Merv Griffin (1962–86) to Rosie O'Donnell (1996–2003). *The Mike Douglas Show* ran for 21 years (1961–82) and a total of some 6,000 programs. It was the first such daytime show to win an Emmy Award, in 1967, and it went on to receive a total of five Emmys. At the height of its popularity, in the late 1960s and early 1970s, it attracted an audience estimated at 650,000 in more than 200 markets across the United States. In that period of great cultural turbulence and change, Douglas charmed his traditionalist viewers (including a large contingent of housewives) with his easygoing and affable persona and offered them a comfortable, old-fashioned entertainment refuge, away from national and world troubles and political and social strife and controversy. The gentle and friendly tone of each show was set at its beginning, when Douglas sang a romantic ballad, a pop standard, or his signature "Hi, Neighbor." (His recording of one song, "The Men in My Little Girl's Life," made the pop charts.) The tone was maintained in his rapport with his guests, whom he tried, as he said, to make "look as good as I possibly could." The thousands of guests who appeared on the show over the years ranged from musicians (among them Ray Charles, Johnny Cash, Roger Miller, Barbra Streisand, the Beach Boys, the Cowsills, Little Richard, Frank Sinatra, the Rolling Stones, and Liberace) and comedians (such as Totie Fields, Bob Hope, Richard Pryor, Henry Morgan, Bill Cosby, Jay Leno, and George Carlin) to such notable figures as Ralph Nader, Malcolm X, Robert Frost, Bobby Seale, Truman Capote, Mother Teresa, a juvenile Tiger Woods, and seven former, incumbent, or future U.S. presidents. John Lennon and Yoko Ono were among his occasional guest co-hosts. *The Mike Douglas Show* was commonly categorized as a talk show, but Douglas himself viewed it as "really a music show, with a whole lot of talk and laughter in between numbers." Douglas was born Michael Delaney Dowd Jr. in Chicago, Illinois. He began his career as a child singer on radio station WLS in Chicago. His first adult job was that of the singing master of ceremonies on a Great Lakes cruise ship, and his second, that of staff singer at radio station WKY in Oklahoma City, Oklahoma. He began studying real estate at Oklahoma City University but decided to concentrate on a career in entertainment while he was serving in the U.S. Navy stateside during World War II. After his discharge from the navy, he moved to Los Angeles, where he sang in several supper clubs and on various radio programs heard all along the West Coast. He thus came to the attention of Kay Kyser, "the Old Perfesser," a comedy-oriented big-band leader who had been conducting a novelty musical-quiz contest on radio and on the road since the 1930s. (It was at Kayser's suggestion that he changed his last name to Douglas.) When Kayser took his "Kollege of Musical Knowledge" to network television (NBC, December 1949–December 1950), Douglas was a featured singer on the show. With Kayser he recorded hit covers of several songs, including "Old Lamplighter," "Ole Buttermilk Sky," and "Coffee Time." During the same period he provided the voice of Prince Charming in the animated Disney feature film *Cinderella* (1950). After briefly pursuing a solo singing career, he returned to Chicago in 1953 and joined the staff of WGN, comprising the radio station and television station owned by the *Chicago Tribune* newspaper. His chores at WGN over the next several years included the hosting of a radio program called *Hi, Ladies* and regular appearances on a television variety show called *Club 60*. The latter show was directed by Forrest (Woody) Fraser, who subsequently went to work for television station KYW, the Cleveland affiliate of the Westinghouse Broadcasting Co. (later renamed Group W Broadcasting). Douglas was reconsidering a career in real estate when Woody Fraser invited him to audition for master of ceremonies of an afternoon variety show at KYW, which he did successfully. *The Mike Douglas Show*, launched in 1961, was at first broadcast only locally in Cleveland; its syndication in other markets began in 1963. It was broadcast live until 1965, when a remark violating FCC standards of good taste uttered by Douglas's guest Zsa Zsa Gabor prompted Group W Broadcasting to switch to prerecorded tape. By 1967 *The Mike Douglas Show* was the most popular national program on daytime television. It originated from Philadelphia from 1965 to 1978, when the operation moved to Los Angeles. In 1980 Group W Broadcasting dropped the series and hired John Davidson to fill the same time spot. Douglas found another distributor, and his show remained in syndication under his control for two years. In its final months, in 1982, it ran on the newly founded CNN cable network with the new name *The Mike Douglas Entertainment Hour*. Among the albums recorded by Douglas were *The Mike Douglas Christmas Album* (1979) and *You Don't Have to Be Irish* (1995); his 1966 album, *The Men in My Little Girl's Life*, which was reissued on audio CD in 1995; his CDs *A Rare Treasure of Memorable Music* and *Love Songs*, released in 1997 and 2004, respectively; and his single "Happy Birthday Jesus," released in 2005. Douglas published two books of memoirs: *Mike Douglas: My Story* (1978) and *I'll Be Right Back: Memories of TV's Greatest Talk Show* (1999). The latter was co-written by Tom Kelly. Douglas died in a hospital in Palm Beach Gardens, Florida. His survivors included his wife, Genevieve, three daughters, and several grandchildren and great-grandchildren. See *Current Biography* (1968).

Obituary *New York Times* A p13 Aug. 12, 2006

DRINAN, ROBERT F. Nov. 15, 1920–Jan. 28, 2007 Jesuit priest; lawyer; legal scholar; professor of law; author; United States Democratic representative from Massachusetts (1971–81). Throughout his long and multifaceted career in religion, law, and politics and on the printed page, the Reverend Robert Frederick Drinan was unwavering in his dedication to a progressive advocacy of social and economic justice. With his outspoken views supporting human rights in areas ranging from war and peace and U.S. foreign policy to affirmative action and abortion, he drew praise in many quarters and criticism in others, sometimes including his own church. He was the first Roman Catholic priest to be a voting member of Congress. Drinan, an early critic of the American military expedition in Vietnam, was motivated to enter electoral politics—against the wishes of the superior general of the Society of Jesus, Father Pedro Arrupe, according to some sources—when he visited South Vietnam in 1969 and discovered that, contrary to U.S. State Department reports, the already large number of political prisoners there was increasing rapidly. Running on an antiwar platform, he was first elected to Congress from Massachusetts's Third Congressional District in 1970. (In his four subsequent terms in the House of Representatives he represented Massachusetts's Fourth Congressional District.) In Congress he served on the Internal Security and Government Operations Committees, among others. As a member of the Committee on the Judiciary and chairman of the Judiciary Subcommittee on Criminal Justice, he was concerned with questions relating to the Watergate scandal and the possible impeachment of President Richard M. Nixon. He was the first congressman to file a motion for Nixon's impeachment, in 1973, on grounds related not to Watergate but to the Nixon administration's undeclared extension of the Vietnam War into Cambodia. "Can we impeach a president for concealing a burglary," he asked, "but not for concealing a massive bombing?" Two decades later, at the invitation of Congress, he testified against the impeachment of President Bill Clinton, saying that the sex-and-perjury charges against Clinton did not in his opinion rise to the category of official high crimes and misdemeanors. During his tenure in Congress, as before and after, Drinan consistently tried to apply, as he said, "the Second Vatican Council's linking of faith and justice." Edward Markey, a fellow congressman from Massachusetts and a fellow Catholic, saw him as "the conscience of the Congress," a man who "lived the Beatitudes." But some more traditional Catholics disagreed with Markey, objecting in particular to Drinan's consistent support of abortion rights. That support was at first "moderate" (as progressives tended to describe it), favoring unrestricted abortion only during the first few months of pregnancy, but "pro-life" Catholics did not view it as such. Eventually, 15 years after leaving Congress, Drinan shocked even many liberal Catholics when he defended President Bill Clinton's veto of a bill passed by Congress outlawing so-called partial-birth abortion, an end-of-term "dilation and extraction" procedure they regarded as extremely brutal as well as gratuitous. Drinan subsequently withdrew that defense, explaining that he had "misunderstood" the nature of the procedure. Before, during, and after his tenure in Congress, Drinan traveled on human rights missions to more than a dozen countries around the world. Obeying a Vatican directive barring Catholic priests from candidacy in electoral politics, Drinan did not seek reelection to Congress in 1980. Before entering Congress he had been dean of the Boston College Law School. After leaving Congress he taught classes on legal ethics, international human rights, constitutional law, and civil liberties at Georgetown University, in Washington, D.C.; lectured elsewhere; wrote a regular column for the *National Catholic Reporter* newspaper; and contributed to other publications. In his lectures and opinion pieces, he editorialized on current issues, including same-sex-union adoptions, gun control, and prisoner rights (including voting rights for felons), which he supported, and the death penalty, which he opposed. In a number of the pieces he wrote in the wake of September 11, 2001, he condemned "new, radical, and dangerous" American policies, including the war in Iraq. He published more than a dozen books, including *Democracy, Dissent and Disorder: The Issues and the Law* (1969), *Honor the Promise: America's Commitment to Israel* (1977), *God and Caesar on the Potomac: A Pilgrimage of Conscience* (1985), *Stories from the American Soul: A Reader in Ethics* and *American Policy for the 1990s* (1990), and volumes relating religion and the law to public policy and war and peace. He founded the Lawyers Alliance for Nuclear Arms Control and the National Interreligious Task Force on Soviet Jewry and served a term as president of Americans for Democratic Action and board chairmanships or similar positions with the American Civil Liberties Union (ACLU) and the NAACP (National Association for the Advancement of Colored People) Legal Defense Fund, among other liberal and progressive organizations. In 2004 he received the American Bar Association's ABA Medal for "exceptionally distinguished service to the cause of American jurisprudence." He died in Washington, D.C. See *Current Biography* (1971).

Obituary *New York Times* A p17 Jan. 30, 2007

DUNN, JENNIFER July 29, 1921–Sep. 5, 2007 Republican U.S. congresswoman. Jennifer Dunn (née Blackburn) represented Washington State's Eighth Congressional District from 1993 to 2005. She was a trailblazer for women in her leadership roles in the Washington State Republican Party and in the House of Representatives, where she served on the Ways and Means Committee and was vice chairperson of the Committee on Homeland Security. She was the first woman to serve on the Senate/House Joint Economic Committee. An avowed libertarian, she championed reform of the tax code and welfare system and was concerned with technology issues. She sponsored the Amber Alert legislation, aimed at facilitating the search for missing children, and backed bills promoting small and women-owned businesses. She was pro-choice but against government subsidization or other involvement in abortion-related activities except in cases of rape or incest or to save the mother's life; in the instance of a minor seeking an abortion, she favored parental notification. Representative Jim McDermott, a liberal Democrat from Seattle who served with her on the Ways and Means

Committee, said that she was able to rise above political partisanship and to "think about what was best for the state of Washington." Dunn, who earned a B.A. in English literature from Stanford University, was an IBM systems engineer before she entered politics. She chaired the Republican Party in Washington State from 1980 until 1992. After deciding against running for reelection to Congress in 2004, she worked briefly for DLA Piper, a Washington, D.C., law and lobbying firm. After a battle with cancer, she died of a pulmonary embolism at her home in Alexandria, Virginia. Her survivors included her second husband, two sons, and a stepson. See *Current Biography* (1999).

Obituary *New York Times* B p6 Sep. 6, 2007

EAGLETON, THOMAS F. Sep. 4, 1929–Mar. 4, 2007 Democratic politician from Missouri; lawyer. After holding a succession of increasingly powerful elective posts in his home state, Thomas Francis Eagleton was for 18 years a pivotal legislator in the United States Senate on a range of issues relating to war, peace, health care, education, the environment, and other matters. He is remembered in games of trivia not for his positive accomplishments but for a blemish on his career dating to 1972, when he became the first and only vice-presidential nominee in American history to withdraw from that candidacy. After serving in the U.S. Navy, Eagleton earned degrees in liberal arts as well as law, joined his father's law firm in St. Louis, and entered politics. He was elected circuit attorney of St. Louis in 1945, attorney general of Missouri in 1960, and lieutenant governor of Missouri in 1964. Running for the U.S. Senate in 1968, he called for additional federal funds for education and housing, expanded East–West trade, strong gun-control legislation, and an unconditional halt to the bombing of North Vietnam. Elected to the Senate in November 1968, Eagleton was scheduled to succeed Senator Edward V. Long in the upper house of Congress in January 1969, but, in order to give Eagleton a beginning edge in seniority, Long resigned on December 27, 1968. Appointed by Missouri governor Warren E. Hearns, Eagleton immediately took office as Long's successor. In the Senate he strongly asserted the constitutional authority of Congress to challenge the White House's prosecution of the war in Southeast Asia. He was an original sponsor of the War Powers Resolution and the chief sponsor of the amendment to a defense appropriations bill that cut off funding for the bombing of Cambodia and effectively ended the Vietnam War. He was also prominently instrumental in the Senate's passage of the Clean Air Act of 1970, the Clear Water Act of 1972, the Individuals with Disabilities Act, and the bills that created the Educational Opportunity Grants (better known as the Pell Grants) and the National Institute on Aging. On July 13, 1972 Democratic presidential candidate George McGovern, who was campaigning on an antiwar platform, chose Eagleton as his running mate in part because Eagleton was a pro-life Roman Catholic and would balance the ticket. Shortly thereafter Eagleton's political enemies made public the facts that during the 1960s he had been hospitalized three times for nervous exhaustion and had received electroshock therapy for depression—a devastating political revelation in that era. After 18 days, Eagleton withdrew as the vice-presidential candidate. At the polls in 1974 and 1980, Missouri voters reelected Eagleton to second and third six-year terms in the Senate. He did not seek reelection 1986. Upon leaving the Senate, in 1987, he joined the faculty of Washington University in St. Louis, where he was a professor of public affairs and political science until 2000. He later taught a course called "The Presidency and the Constitution" at the Saint Louis University School of Law. He wrote the books *War and Presidential Power: A Chronicle of Congressional Surrender* (1974) and *Issues in Business and Government* (1991). With William Kottmeyer he co-wrote the secondary-school textbook *Our Constitution and What It Means* (1987). He died at St. Mary's Hospital in Richmond Heights, Missouri, of heart, respiratory, and other problems. His survivors included his wife, Barbara, two children, and three grandchildren. See *Current Biography* (1973).

Obituary *New York Times* B p7 Mar. 5, 2007

ECEVIT, BÜLENT May 28, 1925–Nov. 5, 2006 Turkish prime minister; journalist; translator. The former Turkish prime minister Bülent Ecevit was known as a leftist who was deeply concerned with the poor and founded various social programs aimed at protecting the Turkish working class. He became a national hero in 1974 when he ordered military intervention on the island of Cyprus, where a Greek-backed right-wing militia had organized a military coup to overthrow the island nation's democratically elected government. Ecevit was born in Istanbul. His father, Fahri Ecevit, was a professor of medicine and Turkish parliamentarian; his mother, Nazli, was a painter and art teacher. In 1944 Ecevit earned his bachelor's degree in English from the American-sponsored Robert College, in Istanbul. From 1944 to 1946, while pursuing a graduate degree in English literature at Ankara University, Ecevit worked for the Turkish government's press and publicity department. In 1946 he moved to England, where he studied art history and Sanskrit at the University of London, also working for the press attaché's office in the Turkish embassy. In 1950 he returned to Turkey and joined the Republican People's Party (RPP), working for the group's newspaper, *Ulus*, initially as an art critic and later as the managing editor. After serving for two years in the Turkish army, Ecevit traveled to the U.S. in 1954. He served as a guest writer at North Carolina's *Winston-Salem Journal*. On his last day, January 9, 1955, the newspaper published a front-page article in which Ecevit wrote, as quoted by Steven Kinzer for the *New York Times* (November 6, 2006), that he found it strange that the U.S. would claim to fight oppression in the world while white Americans were "guilty of refusing to drink from the same fountain as the man who has fought on the same front for the same cause; guilty of refusing to travel on the same coach or seat as the man who has been working with equal ardor for a common community; guilty of refusing to pray to God side by side with the man who believes in the same prophet's teaching." While in the U.S. he had continued to contribute articles to the Ankara-based newspaper *Halkçi*, and from 1956 to 1961 he worked

as a political columnist for *Ulus*. In 1957 Ecevit was awarded a fellowship at Harvard University, in Cambridge, Massachusetts. That year he was also elected a deputy in the Turkish Parliament, becoming its youngest member at that time. In 1960 he was elected to an assembly to draft a new Turkish constitution, and from 1961 to 1965 he served as the minister of labor in the several government coalitions headed by his political mentor, Ismet Inönü. Ecevit was re-elected in 1965, this time as a representative for Zonguldak. The following year he became the secretary general of the RPP—the organization's second-highest position. By 1972 the relationship between Ecevit and Inönü had become strained over the party's decision to support the military-appointed government of Nihat Erim; Ecevit resigned from his post as secretary general in protest. He later forced Inönü to resign his seat as the party chairman, thus replacing his former mentor. In 1973 the military ended its reign and called for general elections; the RPP made significant gains in those elections, and in January 1974 Ecevit formed a ruling coalition with the Islamic, traditionalist National Salvation Party (NSP) and became the prime minister of Turkey. As prime minister, Ecevit raised the nation's minimum wage, increased the salaries of civil servants, and abolished Turkey's ban on opium production. Later that year the historically tense relationship between Greece and Turkey was inflamed when the Cypriot national guard, at the instigation of the Greek military regime, staged a coup in Cyprus. On July 20 Ecevit ordered Turkish forces to invade the island, causing the collapse of both the Greek and Cypriot military regimes. In the aftermath of the incident, Ecevit was hailed by his countrymen as a national hero; he nonetheless resigned as prime minister shortly thereafter amid tensions with his conservative coalition partners. During the tumultuous era from November 1974 to March 1999, the Turkish Parliament formed 16 different coalition governments—one lasting only three months. Ecevit served his second term as prime minister from June 1977 to January 1978 and his third term from January 1978 to November 1979. The military staged a coup on September 12, 1980, in which Ecevit and other political leaders were arrested. He was released from jail shortly afterward but banned from political activity. Ecevit returned to politics in 1987, taking control of the Democratic Left Party, which had been formed by his wife, the former Rahsan Aral, in his absence. In 1995 Ecevit asked his supporters, according to Kinzer, to "make me prime minister once more before I die." Ecevit realized this goal in 1998, serving a final term in which he opened Turkey up to many pro-Western economic reforms, allying the country with the U.S. and maintaining its status as a member of NATO. In addition to his work in the political arena, Ecevit wrote poetry and translated T. S. Eliot's *The Cocktail Party* and some of the works of Ezra Pound. He had no children and is survived by his wife. See *Current Biography* (1975).

Obituary *New York Times* B p9 Nov 6, 2006

ELLIS, ALBERT Sep. 27, 1913–July 24, 2007 American psychologist; educator. Albert Ellis was the creator of one of the most popular and successful forms of psychotherapy, the procedure he called rational emotive behavior therapy, in which cognitive philosophy is combined with emotive techniques in changing mental attitudes and effecting behavioral changes. That adaptation of the psychoanalyst's "talking cure"—along with work done independently by Aaron T. Beck—laid the ground for the cognitive-behavioral procedures used by one in four mental-health professionals in North America today. In a 1983 survey of clinical psychologists, Ellis was ranked in influence above Sigmund Freud, the founder of psychoanalysis. Freud believed that the source of neuroses could be found in unconscious mental/emotional mechanisms rooted in the stages of childhood psychosexual development and in early parental influence; in Freudian psychoanalysis, the clinician painstakingly guides his patient into protracted monologues in search of the unconscious mechanisms. Ellis rejected that procedure as unnecessarily lengthy and basically misdirected. "Infantile sexuality in my view is very rarely related to emotional disturbance," he explained. "As I see it, psychoanalysis gives clients a cop-out. They don't have to change their ways or their philosophies; they get to talk about themselves for ten years, blaming their parents and waiting for magic-bullet insights." He viewed neurosis as "a high-class name for whining" and said that "if humans would stop their whining, then they could start winning." His "practical, action-oriented approach" in psychotherapy was a new formulation of the first-century Stoic philosopher Epictetus' dictum, "What disturbs people's minds is not events but their judgments on events." A secular humanist, he believed that human beings have an innate aspiration to happiness, but that they also have "a talent for crooked thinking" that is inimical to that aspiration; in addition, however, they have "great self-changing and self-actualizing powers." In his form of talk therapy, he helped clients to improve their lives by confronting their problems immediately, day-to-day, controlling their irrational and self-defeating thoughts and feelings and changing their behaviors. His fundamental tenet was this: "People can live the most self-fulfilling . . . lives by disciplining their thinking." Early in his career he drew criticism from many of his colleagues with his promotion of what he called the "sex revolution" and his pioneering work in sex therapy and marriage counseling, which was widely considered shockingly unorthodox at the time. Throughout his career he was notorious for his irreverence in communicating his ideas and his frequent use of obscenities in speaking extemporaneously. He received a bachelor's degree in business administration at City College in New York City in 1934, and he later earned a Ph.D. degree in psychology at Columbia University and underwent psychoanalytical training under Richard Hulbeck. Initially aspiring to a literary career, he first tried his hand at fiction and as a young man also wrote a number of nonfiction manuscripts on sex, love, and marriage; only one of his works from that early period was published, appearing decades later as *The Case for Sexual Liberty* (1965). Through his extensive reading, he had become, as he said, "something of a walking encyclopedia of erotic fiction and nonfiction" whose advice was sought by friends at first and subsequently by clients, even before he became credentialed in psychology. He began

practicing professionally as a psychotherapist in 1943. Over the following dozen years, he increasingly departed from the Freudian model, doing more of his own talking than condoned in classical psychoanalysis and becoming "a much more eclectic, exhortive-persuasive, activity-directing kind of therapist," goading his patients to mental and behavioral change. Beginning in 1950 he adopted the innovative practice of treating both members of a couple at the same time in the same room. In approaching problems of a nonsexual nature, he remained a neoanalyst, influenced by Alfred Adler, Karen Horney, and Harry Stack Sullivan as well as Epictetus and others. In 1956 he publicly announced his new system of "rational-emotive therapy," which he renamed rational emotive behavior therapy, or REBT, 38 years later. To help his clients respond immediately and positively to their problems, he came up with what he called the ABC's of REBT: A is the (outside) activating event; B is one's belief about such an event, and C is the emotional consequence. The main point of REBT is that B, not A, leads to C. In 1959 Ellis founded in Manhattan the Institute for Rational-Emotive Therapy (originally called the Institute for Rational Living). He was executive director of that nonprofit clinical and educational facility until 1989 and president thereafter. He published scores of books, among them *How to Live with a Neurotic* (1957), *The Art and Science of Love* (1960), *The Road to Tolerance : The Philosophy of Rational Emotive Behavior Therapy* (2006), and guides to rational living, successful marriage, child rearing, overcoming procrastination, and refusing "to make yourself miserable about anything." Following his first two marriages (which ended in annulment and divorce, respectively), he lived from 1966 to 2003 with Janet L. Wolfe, a colleague at his institute. He died of kidney and heart failure in his Manhattan apartment, above the offices of his institute. His survivors included his third wife, Debbie Joffee-Ellis, another colleague. See *Current Biography* (1994).

Obituary *New York Times* A p1+ July 25, 2007

FALLACI, ORIANA June 29, 1930–Sep. 15, 2006 Italian journalist; writer; "the tigress of the typewriter"; "citizen of the world"; "prophet of decline." The bold, fiercely impassioned, and provocative international correspondent Oriana Fallaci was arguably the most renowned and the most controversial European journalist of modern times. Her fame was based primarily on her coverage of wars and other international events and in even larger measure on her aggressive and extraordinarily penetrating interviews with world leaders. A self-described antifascist and anti-clerical atheist, she early on began writing against fundamentalism of all sorts and abuses of power (always her chief target always, along with threats to freedom) wherever she found them, including Italy's ostensibly democratic parties as well as its Communist Party. Although she had differences with some feminist and other liberal and progressive factions on issues such as abortion on demand (which she opposed), she was generally considered an icon of the radical left for four decades—until the last five years of her life, when, acting, she believed, like Cassandra warning Trojans of the Trojan Horse, she published several books raising the alarm over what she regarded as the slow submission of the Judeo-Christian West to conquest by immigrant Muslin "hordes." While those angry works drew death threats from Islamists and allegations of "Islamophobia" from critics in and outside the world of Islam, they also brought Fallaci her widest readership and such praise as that accorded her by the conservative American pundit Michelle Malkin, who wrote, "Her books, her life, her rage and her reason serve as fiery inspirations in an era of flinching dhimmitude" ("dhimmitude" usually referring to the condition of a non-Muslim who lives in a country governed according to the laws of Islam). Born to working-class socialist parents in Florence, Italy, and growing up under the fascist dictatorship of Benito Mussolini, Fallaci was imbued in childhood, as she said, with "the cult for freedom which permeates all my writings and which makes up the leitmotif of all my books." Her sense of mission, based on the view that "disobedience toward the oppressive" was "the only way to use the miracle of having been born," was reinforced by her experience as a juvenile courier and lookout for her father and others who were fighting in the underground Italian Resistance against the Nazi occupiers of Florence and its environs during World War II. In 1950 she joined the staff of a Florentine daily newspaper, soon graduating from the local police beat to roving coverage of national and European events and celebrities, ranging from royal weddings to interviews with entertainers and prominent literati. In 1954 she began her long tenure as an international correspondent with the glossy Italian weekly magazine *Europeo.* (Her reportage also appeared later in such Italian publications as *Epoca* and in translation in publications including *La Gazeta Ilustrada*, *Stern*, *Life*, *Look*, and the *New Republic.* Her writings were translated into more than a score of languages.) Her topics as a foreign correspondent included Hollywood, the situations of women in various countries, and the American space program. Her reports on those subjects were collected, respectively, in the books *I sette peccati di Hollywood* (1958) and the volumes translated as *The Useless Sex* (1961; translation, 1964), and *If the Sun Dies* (1965; translation, 1966). As a war correspondent, she reported from Vietnam, the Middle East, India and Pakistan, and the sites of South American insurrections. Her book translated as *Nothing, and So Be It* (1969; translation, 1972) included, in addition to Vietnam War reportage, an account of her experiences at the Olympic Games in Mexico City in 1968, when she was caught in the middle of a brutal Mexican police crackdown on a student/worker demonstration and was seriously wounded by three gunshots. The petite and glamorous Fallaci realized her greatest triumphs by beguiling world movers and shakers—chiefly males, among them Henry Kissinger, the Shah of Iran, Ayatollah Khomeini, Yasir Arafat, Archbishop Makarios, Zulfikar Ali Bhutto, and Muammar Al-Qaddafi—into submitting to interviews and then overwhelming them with "brilliantly incisive [lines] of interrogation" that reduced them "to human size" and made other interviewers look like wielders of powder puffs, as Christopher Hitchens observed in *Vanity Fair* (December 2005). Many of her interviews were collected in the volumes translated as *The Egoists* (1965; translation, 1968) and *Interview with History* (1974; translation, 1976). Her radical credentials were augmented by her great romantic liaison with the Greek freedom fighter Alekos Panagoulis from 1973 until his death in a suspicious auto accident in 1976. Her loss of his child in a miscarriage inspired her novel translated as *Letter to a Child Never Born* (1975; translation, 1976); her novel *Un uomo* (1979; translated as *A Man*, 1980) was a tribute to Panagoulis. Her novel *Insciallah* (1992; translated as *Inshallah*, 1992) was inspired by her experiences while embedded with an international military force in civil-war–torn Beirut, Lebanon, in 1983, when Muslim suicide bombers made their first attacks against Western interests, killing hundreds, mostly U.S. Marines. After covering the Persian Gulf War in 1991, she began a long battle with cancer and retreated into a decade of media silence during which she lived alternately at her home in Florence, Italy, and in her brownstone in Manhattan. She was in the brownstone when, on September 11, 2001, a terrorist attack leveled the World Trade Center. That event immediately prompted her to put aside a novel she had been writing and, "out of duty toward my culture" and her "duty toward the freedom fighter" in her, to plunge furiously and single-mindedly into polemicism against what she viewed as the emergence of a new equivalent of "Nazi fascism"—a militant and fundamentalist Islam on the march toward the conquest of Western civilization, the vanguard of which was the growing restive immigrant Muslim population in Western Europe ("Eurabia"). As with Nazi fascism, she believed that "no compromise is possible" with hegemonic-minded, intolerant "Islamofacism," and that "those who do not understand this simple reality are feeding the suicide of the West." Her first diatribe on the subject was an article that filled four full pages of the Milan, Italy, daily newspaper *Corriere della Sera* on September 29, 2001. She expanded that article into the best-selling book *La rabbia e l'orgoglio* (2001), which she herself translated into English under the title *The Rage and the Pride* (2001). She pursued the same subject further in another best-selling book, *La forza della ragione* (2004), which was translated as *The Force of Reason* (2005) and in an interview with herself. The latter was published, along with an essay on the "European Apocalypse," in the book *Oriana Fallaci intervista sé stessa; L'Apocalisse* (2004), which has not yet been translated. Responding to a lawsuit launched by an extremist Muslim of Scots origin named Adel Smith, an Italian judge ordered her to stand trial for "defaming Islam," but the case never came to trial. Ironically, in her last days the anticlerical Fallaci found a "soul mate" in Pope Benedict XVI, whom she called by his pre-papal name, Ratzinger. During the summer of 2006, she returned to Florence, Italy, where she died in a private hospital. See *Current Biography* (1977).

Obituary New Yorjk Times B p8 Sep. 16, 2006

FALWELL, JERRY Aug. 11, 1933–May 15, 2007 Baptist clergyman. Jerry Falwell, a televangelist who felt called by God "to confront the culture," was the co-founder (in 1979) of the Moral Majority and the president of that conservative political coalition during most of its 10-year existence. As the most visible figure in the emergence of a mainstream political force that became known as the religious right, Falwell was a lightning rod in the cultural storms of his time, demonized on the left and drawing scathing attacks from liberals, feminists, civil-libertarians, and gay activists. He was also at times the target of protests by fellow Christian fundamentalists less ecumenical than he. Falwell, a native of Lynchburg, Virginia, became a born-again Christian in 1952. He originally belonged to the Baptist Bible Fellowship International and later changed his affiliation to the Southern Baptist Convention. After graduating from the Baptist Bible College in Springfield, Missouri, in 1956, he returned to Lynchburg and founded the Thomas Road Baptist Church there. As senior pastor, he oversaw the growth of that congregation into a megachurch, with 24,000 parishioners and several affiliated ministries, including an educational system comprising the kindergarten–12th grade Liberty Christian Academy and Liberty University, both situated on the 5,000-acre Liberty Mountain campus in Lynchburg, and the *Old-Time Gospel Hour*, televised from the church's sanctuary nationally and overseas every Sunday; total annual revenues from all the Falwell ministries grew to more than $200 million. Originally, Falwell, like many if not most Baptists at the time, eschewed political activism, because he "never thought the government would go so far afield . . . never thought courts would go so nuts to the left." During the 1970s he began to think that they had, and early in 1979 Paul M. Weyrich, the Melkite Catholic co-founder of the Heritage Foundation and founder of the Free Congress Foundation, suggested to him the feasibility of creating a political "moral majority" by bringing together "morally conservative" Americans from diverse groups and backgrounds—mostly religious, but not necessarily excluding even atheists—who were in agreement on some or all of such issues as a strong American military and opposition to abortion-on-demand, pornography, the validation of homosexuality, and bans on school prayer no matter how much they otherwise differed in their views on the Bible and theology. With the tutelage of the conservative direct-mail fund-raiser Richard Viguerie and the help of Howard Philips, the Jewish organizer of the Conservative Caucus, and others, Falwell in June 1979 founded the Moral Majority Inc., a "pro-life, pro-[patriarchal] family, pro-Israel, and pro-strong national defense organization," dedicated to reversing "the politicization of immorality in our society" through political lobbying, voter education, endorsement of candidates, and legal aid. With his associates, Falwell not only rallied politically dormant Baptists and other fundamentalist and evangelical Protestants into registering and voting in elections; he forged many of them into an alliance with traditionalist Catholics and some Orthodox Jews, and into that religious and socially conservative mix he added large numbers of military and fiscal conservatives. With a membership of 6.5 million at one point, the Moral Majority became a constituency of "new right" Republican Party candidates and helped to elect President Ronald Reagan in 1980 and reelect him in 1984 and to send numerous legislators to

Washington during the 1980s. Some of the Moral Majority's membership overlapped with that of James Dobson's Focus on the Family movement, and much of the membership morphed into the political constituency of Pat Robertson, the Baptist televangelist who sought the Republican nomination for president unsuccessfully in 1988 and launched the Christian Coalition in 1989. Falwell stepped down as president of the Moral Majority Inc. in 1987 and disbanded the organization two years later. He published 14 books, including two autobiographies: *Strength for the Journey* (1987), written with Mel White, and *Falwell* (1997). Some 200 homosexual Christians led by Mel White were the guests in a "reconciliation" service conducted by Falwell at his Thomas Road Baptist Road in October 1999. Falwell issued an apology of sorts after saying in September 2001 that "the pagans [and] all of [those] who have tried to secularize America helped" to bring on the terrorist attacks on the World Trade Center by contributing to America's loss of divine protection. Abe Forman, national director of the Anti-Defamation League, said of Falwell, "While he was a passionate fundamentalist, he was also a pragmatist. He knew when to back off." The pornographic-magazine publisher Larry Flynt, who had been sued by Falwell, said he later "became good friends" with him and "always appreciated his sincerity." Mel White mourned Falwell's death while being "glad his voice is silent." Apparently suffering an attack of cardiac arrhythmia, Falwell collapsed in his office at Liberty University and was subsequently pronounced dead at Lynchburg General Hospital. His survivors included his wife, Macel (née Pate), his daughter, Jeannie Falwell Savas, a surgeon, his son Jerry Jr., Liberty University's general counsel, and his son Jonathan, the executive pastor of Thomas Road Baptist Church. See *Current Biography* (1981).

Obituary *New York Times* A p1+ May 16, 2007

FERRÉ, GIANFRANCO Aug. 15, 1944–June 17, 2007 Couturier; "the architect of Italian fashion." With his signature ready-to-wear clothing lines as well as his luxurious custom collections, the grand couturier Gianfranco Ferré helped to confirm Milan's place alongside Paris as a capital in the international fashion industry; as a custom designer of glamorous women's clothes, he attracted a roster of celebrities including Paloma Picasso, Sophia Loren, Princess Diana of Wales, Princess Michael of Kent, Marie-Hélène de Rothschild, Elizabeth Taylor, Julia Roberts, Barbra Streisand, Oprah Winfrey, and the wives of two French presidents. Basic to Ferré's style was a sharply tailored silhouette—most apparent in his white blouses and elegant suits for businesswomen—consisting of simple sculpted shapes and clearly defined lines punctuated (most flamboyantly in his evening gowns) by such exuberant flourishes as ruffles, bows, sashes, and strongly stated collars and cuffs. He rendered his haute couture in rich fabrics and with embroidery; in his collections he often combined gray and beige tones with two or more primary colors. His designs reflected a variety of cultural influences, including his sojourns in China, Japan, and, especially, India, and his wide-ranging passion for art, from baroque and neoclassical to futuristic.

In his craftsmanship and his attention to form, structure, and proportion, he was strongly influenced by his early training as an architect at the Politecnio di Milano institute. After earning his degree in architecture, in the late 1960s, he worked first in interior design and then as a designer of accessories for several established fashion houses. In 1974 he began designing dresses for the Bolognese garment manufacturer Franco Mattioli, and four years later, with Mattioli as his business partner, he founded his own label, Gianfranco Ferré SpA. His first collection was of women's casual and sports clothes, and all of his early collections were of women's ready-to-wear. He added accessories and men's ready-to-wear collections during the 1980s, and he presented his first couture collection in 1986. A stir was created in the international fashion industry when he became artistic director of the French fashion house Christian Dior in Paris in 1989. (French fashion designers had tended to regard their Italian counterparts as "excessive.") For seven years he divided his attention between Dior and his own label, commuting between Paris and Milan in his private plane. He left Christian Dior late in 1996, after supervising the preparation of Dior's spring 1997 collection. In December 2000 he and Mattioli agreed to sell Gianfranco Ferré SpA to Gruppo Tonino Parna, the parent company of the Italian fashion group IT Holding. The sale was completed in January 2001. Ferré remained creative director of Gianfranco Ferré SpA. At the time of his death, he had already overseen the preparation of his house's spring 2007 menswear collection and its September 2007 couture collection. After suffering a massive brain hemorrhage, he died at San Raffaele Hospital in Milan. See *Current Biography* (1991).

Obituary *New York Times* A p17 June 18, 2007

FORD, GERALD R. July 14, 1913–Dec. 26, 2006
Thirty-eighth president of the United States (1974–77); "the accidental president." In the wake of the great constitutional and political crisis known as Watergate, Gerald R. Ford was thrust into the presidency as a decent, calm, and conciliatory figure who had been elected neither to the presidency nor the vice presidency—a unique occurrence in White House history. Ford was a Republican laissez-faire centrist from Grand Rapids, Michigan, who had spent a quarter of a century in Congress, where he was minority leader of the House of Representatives for eight years and earned a reputation on both sides of the political aisle for hard work, honesty, and unpretentious, self-effacing integrity. His unsought ascent to the presidency began in October 1973, when Spiro T. Agnew, President Richard M. Nixon's vice president, resigned under a cloud of uncontested charges of fiscal malfeasance dating back to his years as governor of Maryland and earlier. On the recommendation of congressional leaders, President Nixon chose Ford to replace Agnew, and Ford was sworn in as vice president in December 1973. Meanwhile, Nixon himself was increasingly beset with disclosures of his administration's culpability in the so-called Watergate scandal, a political conspiracy that began with a bungled espionage burglary of the Democratic National Committee headquarters in the Watergate building complex in Washington, D.C.,

during the Nixon reelection campaign of 1972 and included the Nixon White House's subsequent cover-up activities. Faced with imminent impeachment, Nixon became the first U.S. president to resign from office, which he did at noon on August 9, 1974. Ford was sworn in as president moments later. "My fellow Americans, our long national nightmare is over," he declared in an inaugural address broadcast on radio and television. "Our Constitution works. Our great republic is a government of laws and not of men. Here, the people rule." He brought to the Oval Office a spirit of openness and goodwill, and his presence there generated among the American citizenry a restoration of confidence in the national leadership and the basic institutions of government—temporarily, at least. His popularity suddenly plummeted on September 8, 1974, when he issued a proclamation granting Richard Nixon "a full, free, and absolute pardon . . . for all offenses against the United States which he has committed or may have taken part in" during his tenure as president. Ford began to regain some of his popularity with two actions the following spring: his swift military response to the seizure of the American ship *Mayaguez* by Khmer Rouge naval forces off the coast of Cambodia, and his handling of the evacuation from Saigon, South Vietnam, of several thousand South Vietnamese allies and their children as well as Americans when that city was about to fall to North Vietnamese military forces. (One of his few legislative successes with a heavily Democratic Congress was his subsequent request for the allocation of almost $500 million for the resettlement of 140,000 refugees from Indochina.) During successive trips to California in September 1975, Ford was the target of foiled assassination attempts by two gun-toting women (Lynette "Squeaky" Fromme on the first occasion and Sara Jane Moore on the second). In approaching the challenges facing him as president, he was, as he had described himself in Congress, "a moderate in domestic affairs, a conservative in fiscal affairs, and a dyed-in-the-wool internationalist in foreign affairs." As in Congress, while consistently open to appropriations for maintenance of a strong military establishment and for aid to countries aligned with the United States, he was just as consistently wary of possibly "wasteful" liberal social legislation that would increase the federal budget deficit. During his first 14 months in office, he vetoed 39 nonmilitary measures. (A quarter of the vetoes were overridden by Congress.) In confronting national economic problems—first inflation, then recession, and chronic energy shortages—he sought long-range solutions that would limit federal spending and reduce government intervention in the economy. In foreign affairs he carried forward the Nixon administration's policy of détente vis-à-vis the Soviet Union and pursuit of peace in the Middle East; signed the Helsinki Accords; and began negotiating the ceding of the Panama Canal to Panama. In the presidential elections of 1976, he defeated the conservative insurgent (and future president) Ronald Reagan in the Republican primaries but lost the general election to the Democratic candidate, Jimmy Carter. In his televised debates with Carter, he was hurt by his inept and widely misunderstood assertion that "there is no Soviet domination of Eastern Europe." Ford was christened Leslie Lynch King Jr. following his birth in Omaha, Nebraska. After the divorce of his parents and his mother's remarriage (in 1916), he was raised in Grand Rapids, Michigan, by his mother and step-father, Gerald Rudolff Ford (the proprietor of a paint company) and renamed Gerald Rudolff Ford Jr. He changed his name legally to Gerald Rudolph Ford in 1935 (and preferred to be called Jerry Ford). He was a star center and linebacker in football at South High School in Grand Rapids and at the University of Michigan, where he received a B.A. degree in economics and political science in 1935. While employed as a boxing coach and assistant football coach at Yale University, he worked his way to the reception of a law degree there, in 1941. As a decorated officer with the U.S. Navy during World War II, he attained the rank of lieutenant commander. Before and after the war, he practiced law in Grand Rapids, where he became active in Republican Party politics. In 1948 he was elected to the first of 12 terms as the representative from Michigan's Fifth Congressional District in the U.S. Congress. In 1965 his fellow Republicans in the House of Representatives elected him minority leader. After serving as a member of the Warren Commission investigating the assassination of President John F. Kennedy, he wrote (with John R. Stiles) *Portrait of the Assassin* (1965). Later he wrote the autobiography *A Time to Heal* (1980). Ford died at his home in Rancho Mirage, California. He had lived longer than any other American president, a month longer than Ronald Reagan, who had also died at age 93. He was survived by his wife, Elizabeth ("Betty") Ford, three sons, and a daughter. Ford was an Episcopalian and a Freemason (Master Mason, 32d degree). See *Current Biography* (1975).

Obituary *New York Times* A p1+ Dec. 28, 2006

FORD, GLENN May 1, 1916–Aug. 30, 2006 Actor. As the actor/critic Jon Ted Wynne has pointed out, Glenn Ford was an underappreciated Hollywood performer, whose "flawless ability to be truthful and real in front of a camera" was never honored with an Academy Award nomination, much less a win. "Ford's biggest drawback towards critical and mass appreciation for his outstanding talent was his inherent ability to make acting look easy." In a related vein, the screen historian David Thomson has observed that Ford, with his "sympathetic good looks" and "generally likable" screen presence, "managed to make genial, relaxed sincerity interesting." Ford, a non-Method actor of the "just do it" school and a flexible master of facial expression and physical gesture, applied himself in a workmanlike manner to a variety of roles in a number of genres, from dramas, melodramas, and films noir to romantic comedies and action pictures, especially Westerns. He reached the height of his half-century career in the 1950s, in such roles as Dave Bannion, the gang-busting police detective in *The Big Heat* (1953), Jeff Warren, who falls in love with the Gloria Grahame character and thus becomes involved with murder in *Human Desire* (1954), and Richard Dadier, the New York City public-high-school teacher coping with harrowing disciplinary problems in *The Blackboard Jungle* (1955). Of Welsh descent, Ford was born Gwyllyn Ford in Quebec, Canada. He was raised in Ste.-

Christine, Portneuf County, Quebec, and in Santa Monica, California. At the insistence of his father, he early on learned a range of manual skills—including mechanics, carpentry, electrical wiring, and plumbing—that, as he said, "tided me over during the years I was trying to crash the theater." As a teenager he did manual stage work at the Wilshire Theater in Santa Monica. After graduation from high school, he played bit parts in Wilshire Theater productions while serving as the theater's stage manager, and he found more substantial roles with little-theater groups. He began accruing movie credits in 1937. He had top billing for the first time as the title character in *The Adventures of Martin Eden* (1942). He co-starred with Pat O'Brien in *Flight Lieutenant* (1942), with Randolph Scott and Claire Trevor in one of his early Westerns, *The Desperadoes* (1943), and with Edward G. Robinson in the World War II morale booster *Destroyer* (1943). After wartime service in the U.S. Marine Corps (1942–45), he was top-billed opposite Bette Davis in the tear-jerker *A Stolen Life* (1946), and he established himself as an actor of considerable range with his against-type performance as Johnny Farrell, the ruthless male protagonist in *Gilda* (1946), a character involved in intense emotional chemistry with the title character (Rita Hayworth), the sultry wife of his employer. While panned by many critics, *Gilda* was a blockbuster box-office hit and a personal favorite of Ford's. In the bio-pic *Gallant Journey* (1946), Ford played the little-known flight pioneer John J. Montgomery. He was subsequently cast as Mike Lambert, the protagonist in the angst-laden film noir *Framed* (1947), and, in a change of pace, as Doug Andrews, the bus-driver protagonist (opposite Evelyn Keyes) in the romantic comedy *The Mating of Millie* (1948). In the unusual Western *The Man from Colorado* (1948), he starred as a brutal territorial judge, and he co-starred with Ida Lupino in the Western *Lust for Gold* (1949), based on an Arizona legend. In *The Doctor and the Girl* (1949), he was cast in the title role of the aloof young physician whose heart is won by a young woman played by Janet Leigh. He starred as the mountain climber Martin Ordway in *The White Tower* (1950), as Gil Kyle in *The Redhead and the Cowboy* (1951), and as John Stroud in *The Man from the Alamo* (1953). He made a total of more than 80 feature films, including *Heaven with a Barbed Wire Fence* (1939), *Texas* (1941), *So Ends Our Night* (1941), *Go West, Young Lady* (1941), *Ransom!* (1956), *The Fastest Gun Alive* (1956), *The Teahouse of the August Moon* (1956), *Cimarron* (1960), *Pocketful of Miracles* (1961), *The Courtship of Eddie's Father* (1963), *Smith!* (1969), *Santee* (1973), *Superman* (1978), *The Visitor* (1979), and *Border Shootout* (1990). He also made more than a dozen movies for television, and he starred as Sam Cade, the sheriff in in the TV series *Cade's County* (CBS, 1971–72), and as the Reverend Tom Holvak, the Depression-era southern preacher in the brief series *The Family Holvak* (NBC, 1975). Peter Ford, his son from his first marriage, also had a role in *Cade's County*. In 1978 Glenn Ford was inducted into the Hall of Fame of Great Western Performers in Oklahoma City. Ford was married to and divorced from the dancer/actress Eleanor Powell (1943–59), the opera singer/actress Kathryn Hays (1966–68), the model Cynthia Howard

(1977–84), and his personal nurse, Jeanne Baus (1993–94). He died at his home in Beverly Hills, California. See *Current Biography* (1959).

Obituary *New York Times* C p11 Aug. 31, 2006

FRANCA, CELIA June 25, 1921–Feb. 19, 2007 British-born Canadian ballet dancer, choreographer, and director. Celia Franca was the founder of the National Ballet of Canada, of which she was artistic director for 24 years. Franca joined the Ballet Rambert in London when she was 15. She danced with several other London companies before moving in 1941 to the Sadler's Wells Ballet (now the Royal Ballet) for six years and then to the Metropolitan Ballet as soloist and ballet mistress. With Sadler's Wells she choreographed the ballet *Khadra* (to music by Sibelius), and with the Metropolitan Ballet, she choreographed the ballets *Eve of St. Agnes* and *Dance of Salome*. As a guest artist with the Ballet Rambert in 1950, she choreographed *Lament* (to music by Beethoven). In 1951 she immigrated to Canada, and in November of that year, in Toronto, she led the initial performance of what became the National Ballet of Canada. In 1959 she retired as a principal dancer, but she continued to perform occasionally for many years. Also in 1959 she co-founded Canada's National Ballet School. As artistic director, she led the National Ballet of Canada on tours of Canada, the United States, Mexico, Japan, and countries in Europe. Among the works she choreographed for the troupe were her versions of *The Nutcracker* (1964) and *Cinderella* (1968). In 1972 she reluctantly agreed to an expensive Rudolf Nureyev production of *Sleeping Beauty* by the company—a production that found its way across North America to the Metropolitan Opera House in New York City and won a CBC television award. She retired as artistic director in 1974, but when her personally chosen successor, David Haber, was dismissed after less than a year, she returned to guide the company until Alexander Grant took over as director, in 1976. Under Grant, she returned regularly for a number of years as a guest dancer and as the supervisor of the Christmas production of *The Nutcracker*. She later helped to found the Theatre Ballet of Canada. After two marriages and divorces, Franca married James Morton, who predeceased her. She died in Ottawa, Canada. See *Current Biography* (1956).

Obituary *New York Times* A p21 Feb. 22, 2007

FRIEDMAN, MILTON July 31, 1912–Nov. 16, 2006 Economist; Nobel Prize winner. Milton Friedman, described by Holocomb B. Noble, writing for the *New York Times* (November 17, 2006), as "the grandmaster of free-market economic theory," was one of the most influential economists of the 20th century. His ideas fueled the rise of what became known as the Chicago School of economics, a conservative movement based at the University of Chicago, where he taught for many years. In 1976 Friedman received the Nobel Prize in economics, "for his achievements in the fields of consumption analysis, monetary history and theory and for his demonstration of the complexity of stabilization policy," according to the Noble Foundation's Web site. "Among economic scholars, Milton Friedman had no peer," Ben Bernanke, who was appointed chairman of the Federal Reserve in 2006, told Holocomb B. Noble. "The direct and indirect influences of his thinking on contemporary monetary economics would be difficult to overstate." The youngest son of Eastern European immigrants, Friedman was born in Brooklyn, New York. Shortly after his birth the family moved to Rahway, New Jersey, where they operated a small retail store. In 1932 Friedman earned a B.A. degree from Rutgers University, with the equivalent of a double major in mathematics and economics. He then earned an M.A. from the University of Chicago. In 1937 he accepted a position at the National Bureau of Economic Research (NBER), working with Simon Kuznets on *Incomes from Independent Professional Practices*. That research served as the foundation for Friedman's doctoral thesis, for which Columbia University awarded him a Ph.D. in 1946. In a trend seen throughout the rest of his career, *Incomes* proved controversial—it accused the medical profession of monopolistic practices—and was not published until after World War II, though it had been completed in 1940. During the war Friedman worked on tax policy at the U.S. Treasury Department and on military statistical problems at Columbia University. He taught economics at the University of Minnesota from 1945 to 1946. He then returned to the University of Chicago as an assistant professor of economics. In 1950 Friedman visited Paris as a consultant to the Marshall Plan, created by George C. Marshall to help rebuild Western Europe's fragmented postwar economies. In that capacity Friedman became a forceful advocate of floating exchange rates and predicted that the fixed-exchange-rate system of currencies established at the 1944 Bretton Woods Conference would eventually collapse, as it did in the early 1970s. Building on his earlier work with Kuznets, Friedman, in collaboration with the economists Dorothy Brady, Margaret Reid, and Rose Director (whom he had married in 1938), formulated and empirically tested his "permanent income hypothesis" of consumption. In his book *A Theory of the Consumption Function*, published in 1957, Friedman argued that John Maynard Keynes's concept of consumption function, which relates current consumption to current income, was misleading. Instead, he maintained that consumers do not base their consumption decisions, except transitory ones, on current income but on their expected long-run, or "permanent," income. Important advances in econometrics during the 1960s and 1970s owe much to the statistical methods Friedman used for estimating permanent income. In *A Monetary History of the United States, 1867– 1960* (1963), Friedman and the economic historian Anna J. Schwartz documented the pervasive role of changes in the nation's money supply on its inflationary episodes, laying much of the blame for the Great Depression on the Federal Reserve for failing to keep an adequate level of liquidity in the U.S. banking system. By the late 1960s Friedman was arguing against the predominant, Keynesian notion of a stable trade-off between the rate of inflation and unemployment; his assertion was later confirmed by the "stagflation" of the 1970s, which was characterized by both high unemployment and persistent inflation. In the 1980s Friedman's suggestions for controlling monetary supply by regulating interest rates were put into practice by the governments of the U.S. president Ronald Reagan and the British prime minister Margaret Thatcher. His popular book *Free to Choose*, published in 1980, became the title for his television series on economics and social questions. In the mid-1980s, after Friedman failed to correctly predict what would happen as a result of specific increases in the money supply, the general enthusiasm for his theories waned. Conservatives, however, continued to regard him as a guiding light; his free-market ideals and belief in governmental nonintervention remained influential throughout the fall of the Soviet Union and the privatization of Eastern European enterprises. Though he retired from teaching in 1977, Friedman continued to publish scholarly articles and books. In 1998 he and his wife (writing under her married name, Rose D. Friedman) published *Two Lucky People: Memoirs*. He died in San Francisco, California. In addition to his wife, Friedman was survived by a son, David, and a daughter, Janet Martel, as well as four grandchildren and three great-grandchildren. See *Current Biography* (1969), *Nobel Prize Winners* (1987).

Obituary *New York Times* A p1 Nov. 17, 2006

GALBRAITH, JOHN KENNETH Oct. 15, 1908–Apr. 29, 2006 Canadian-born American economist. John Kenneth Galbraith was as conspicuous a figure in economics as he was in physique—a lanky six feet eight inches tall. Influenced by Thorstein Veblen and John Maynard Keynes, Galbraith was generally pigeonholed as a liberal, but he was sui generis, an unorthodox progressive practitioner of economics who dissented from "the conventional wisdom" (a term he is believed to have coined), especially regarding production and consumption. As a Harvard University professor, an adviser to Democratic U.S. presidents and other party leaders, a U.S. diplomat, and above all a prolific and popular author who explained economics in a highly readable style, he had a long-term influence on economic thought and policy during the century of the U.S.'s rise to world hegemony. One of his special interests was the economic problems of developing nations. In their obituary of him for the *New York Times*, Holcomb B. Noble and Douglas Martin wrote that Galbraith "treated economics as an aspect of society and culture rather than as an arcane discipline of numbers" and strove "to change the very texture of the national conversation about power and its nature in the modern world by explaining how the planning of giant corporations superseded market mechanisms." In the *Dictionary of the Social Sciences* (Oxford University Press, 2002), Craig Calhoun pointed out that Galbraith's "contribution to economics was to attract attention to the role that government can play in modern industrial society by empowering the powerless and by balancing the provision of public goods against the excesses of self-interested behavior." The most important of Galbraith's books (many if not most of which were written more for the educated general reader than for his academic peers) were those making up his seminal trilogy on economic theory: *American Capitalism: The Concept of Countervailing Power* (1952; revised 1956), *The Affluent Society*

(1959), and *The New Industrial State* (1967). In the first of those books he debunked prevalent theories about oligopoly and monopoly, proposing that in the American free-market economy, powerful corporate and other entities tend to counterbalance, creating stability; for example, the forces driving prices down, such as giant chain and discount stores, and those driving prices up, such as organized labor, together result in an equilibrium. (He subsequently modified that view.) In *The Affluent Society*, the most widely read of his books, he criticized corporate advertising's creation of artificial consumer demands and the resulting overproduction of consumer goods. He called for a reprioritizing in favor of the public-service sector, with less spent on the accumulation of material possessions and more on the quality of life. In *The New Industrial State*, he scrutinized the roles of industry, the state, and the individual in an economy in which power had shifted to the "techno-structure" of modern corporations. He argued that despite the power shift, in some areas in the economy, such as housing and transportation, private business may not be as effective as government-financed public projects. Reviewing *The New Industrial State* in the *New York Review of Books*, Robert L. Heilbroner described Galbraith as "an economist who seeks to infuse economics with a social relevance" in ways considered heretical to many of his peers, especially the more conservative; but even those peers could not but admire his "aphoristic, terse, above all mocking" literary style. Galbraith was born and grew up on his father's farm near Iona Station, Ontario, Canada. After receiving a B.S. degree in animal husbandry at the University of Toronto, in 1931, he earned M.S. (1933) and Ph.D. (1934) degrees in agricultural economics at the University of California at Berkeley. Between 1934 and 1940 he taught successively at Harvard and Princeton universities. As a research fellow at Cambridge University, in England, in the late 1930s, he was imbued with the work of John Maynard Keynes. In Washington, D.C., during World War II, he held a succession of government positions, including deputy administrator in charge of the price division in the Office of Price Administration. After the war he directed the Office of Economic Security Policy at the U.S. Department of State. He returned to Harvard as a professor of economics in 1949. Meanwhile, he had become involved in Democratic Party politics as, in his words, an "independent operator at the guerrilla level." He was a speechwriter for and policy adviser to Adlai E. Stevenson, the unsuccessful Democratic candidate for president in 1952 and 1956, and to John F. Kennedy, the party's successful presidential candidate in 1960. Appointed by President Kennedy, he served as U.S. ambassador to India from 1961 to 1963. After returning to Harvard University in 1963, he spent some of his time advising President Lyndon B. Johnson in the conception of the Great Society program, but he broke with Johnson on the issue of the Vietnam War and was a supporter of Eugene McCarthy, the antiwar Democratic presidential candidate in 1968. He published more than 30 books, among them *A Theory of Price Control* (1952), *The Great Crash, 1929* (1955), *Economics and the Public Purpose* (1973), *The Good Society* (1996), *The Economics of Innocent Fraud* (2004), *The Galbraith*

Reader (1977), *The Essential Galbraith* (2001), and several memoirs, including *The Scotch* (1964) and *Ambassador's Journal* (1969). He also wrote about the art of India, which he collected. In addition to his nonfiction, he wrote three satirical novels based on his experiences in government and academia. For British television in 1977, he wrote and narrated a 13-part survey of modern economic history titled *The Age of Uncertainty*. He retired from his chair as Paul M. Warburg Professor of Economics at Harvard University in 1975. Galbraith, who maintained a home near the university in Cambridge, Massachusetts, and another on an "unfarmed farm" near Newfane, Vermont, died in a hospital in Cambridge. His son James K. Galbraith is also a noted economist. His survivors included his wife, Catherine, three sons, and six grandchildren. See *Current Biography* (1975).

Obituary *New York Times* I p1+ Apr. 30, 2006

GRIFFIN, MERV July 6, 1925–Aug. 12, 2007 Television personality; producer; entrepreneur. A former big-band crooner and a popular eponymous TV talk-show host, the genial Merv Griffin moved into high gear as a packager of television game shows, including the two most successful such programs still in syndication in 2007: *Jeopardy*, which is ranked the number-one quiz show of all time by GSN, the premier television network for games, and *Wheel of Fortune*, the highest Nielsen-rated daily syndicated series and longest-running syndicated game program in television history. Griffin's income from television and from his Griffin Group business holdings, including real estate, gave him an estimated worth of $1.6 billion at the time of his death. Originally aspiring to a career in music, at 19 Griffin applied for a job as staff pianist at radio station KFRC in San Francisco, but the station instead hired him as a singer. In 1948 he left KFRC to become the featured male singer with Freddy Martin and his orchestra. With Martin's big band he made several popular recordings, including the novelty number "I've Got a Lovely Bunch of Coconuts," which went to number one on the charts, selling three million copies, in 1950. His first appearances on television were on *The Freddy Martin Show* on the NBC network in 1951. Through the instrumentality of the movie star Doris Day, he was signed to a motion-picture contract with Warner Bros. in 1952. He was cast in eight Warner films, usually in minor parts. His only starring assignment was the non-singing role of Buddy Nash opposite Kathryn Grayson in the musical *So This Is Love* (1953). Moving to New York City in 1954, he made his stage debut as Woody Mahoney in a revival of the musical *Finian's Rainbow* at City Center and began a busy schedule as both guest and host on network radio and television. In 1954 he headlined a summer-replacement musical program on the CBS television network, and the following year he hosted *Look Up and Live*, a CBS Sunday morning show using music in its exploration of religious themes. In 1957 and 1958 he headlined a musical show on ABC radio. For three years (1958–61) he hosted the television game show *Play Your Hunch*, which was aired by all three networks in succession. On the NBC network in 1960–61, he hosted *Saturday Prom*, a weekly dance-

music show for teenagers. He substituted for Jack Paar on NBC television's late-night crown-jewel talk/variety program, *The Tonight Show*, twice, in January and again in February 1962. After Paar left *The Tonight Show*, in April 1962, Griffin was one of the succession of guest hosts who filled the gap before Johnny Carson took over as Paar's successor, six months later. The first incarnation of Griffin's own talk show, *The Merv Griffin Show*, was an afternoon version of *The Tonight Show* that ran weekdays on NBC in 1962–63; the second was syndicated by Westinghouse Broadcasting—on weekday afternoons in most markets—from 1965 to 1969; the third was a late-night production that ran on CBS in competition with *The Tonight Show* from 1969 to 1972; the fourth was syndicated by Metromedia from 1972 to 1986. The initial effort of Griffin's own production company was the daytime game show *Word for Word*, hosted by him on NBC in 1963–64. The trivia show *Jeopardy!*, in which the contestants are given the answers and win by producing the questions, originally had a daily daytime run on NBC from 1964 to 1975 and subsequently ran in syndication as well as, briefly, on the NBC and ABC networks; the current syndicated version, hosted by Alex Trebek since 1984, began its 24th season in September 2007. The premise of *Wheel of Fortune* is a variation of the children's game called Hangman; the contestants vie to solve a word puzzle by correctly guessing missing letters. That show was originally broadcast on NBC from 1975 to 1989 and subsequently ran for several years successively on CBS and again on NBC. The syndicated version hosted by Pat Sajak (with the assistance of Vanna White) since 1983 has been renewed to run through the 2011–2012 television season in the United States; worldwide, it is syndicated in 54 countries and seen by 100 million viewers per week. Griffin wrote the theme music for both *Jeopardy* and *Wheel of Fortune*. His other creations include the *Dance Fever* series and *Merv Griffin's Crosswords*. The latter game show began syndication in September 2007. While retaining multiple executive-producer titles and royalty rights, Griffin sold his production company, Merv Griffin Enterprises, to Coca-Cola's Columbia Pictures Television, now owned by Sony Pictures Entertainment, for $250 million in 1986. He used much of the income from that sale to acquire a score of hotels, gambling casinos, and resort properties in the United States and abroad, most of which he eventually sold at a profit. He also bought and sold 17 radio stations, owned a stable of race horses, including the prize-winning colt Stevie Wonderboy, and founded Teleview Racing Patrol, a closed-circuit track and off-track broadcast system. In addition, he had a winery on his ranch on California's Monterey Peninsula. He donated property he owned in Arizona and California, which was worth millions of dollars, to Childhelp USA to facilitate the housing and treatment of severely abused children. With Peter Barsocchini he wrote the books *Merv: An Autobiography* (1980) and *From Where I Sit: Merv Griffin's Book of People* (1982). In 1983 he published a second autobiography, *Merv: Making the Good Life Last*. From his marriage to Julann Elizabeth Wright, Griffin had a son, Anthony. Griffin was guarded about his private life. After he and his wife divorced, in 1973, his companionship with the actress Eva Gabor was publicized. A close friend of Ronald and Nancy Reagan's, he kept in constant touch with Mrs. Reagan during the former president's final years and after his death. He or his shows won a number of Emmy Awards, and in 2005 he received a daytime Emmy for lifetime achievement. Scores of Griffin's interviews with celebrities during his years as host of *The Merv Griffin Show* have been released on two sets of DVDs. Griffin died in Cedars-Sinai Medical Center in Los Angeles, of prostate cancer. His survivors included his son and two grandchildren. See *Current Biography* (1967).

HADLEY, JERRY June 16, 1952–July 18, 2007 Opera singer and recitalist. The repertoire of the agile and adventurous world-class lyric tenor Jerry Hadley encompassed classical and romantic operatic roles and works by George Gershwin, Bertolt Brecht, Leonard Bernstein, Paul McCartney, and other 20th-century and contemporary composers. He performed in the world's leading opera houses, ranging from the San Francisco Opera and the Metropolitan Opera in New York City—where he created the title role in John Harbison's *The Great Gatsby*—to the Royal Opera in Covent Garden, London, the Deutsche Oper in Berlin, and La Scala in Milan. "Jerry's singing would make you cry, and his jokes would make you laugh uncontrollably," the tenor Richard Leech told Chris Pasles for the *Los Angeles Times* (July 19, 2007). "He was always there for his fellow singers, 100 percent, and, in an era of competition and vain rivalry, chose the other road, making those of us in his club of tenors feel like brothers." After earning a master's degree in music at the University of Illinois, in 1977, Hadley taught voice and diction at Mount Holyoke College, in Massachusetts, and at the University of Connecticut. He began his operatic career with regional troupes, including a company in Sarasota, Florida, with which he sang Lyonel in a production of *Martha*. Beginning in 1979 he was associated for several years with the New York City Opera, appearing in such roles as Lord Arturo in *Lucia di Lammamoor*, Gaston in *La Traviata*, Fenton in *Falstaff*, and Count Almaviva in *The Barber of Seville*. In the early 1980s he made a number of appearances with the Washington (D.C.) Opera, singing such roles as Stravinsky's Tom Rakewell and Tchaikovsky's Eugene Onegin; his ventures abroad included a series of appearances with the Vienna (Austria) Staatsoper in 1982, singing Nemorino in *L'Elisir d'Amore*, Pinkerton in *Madame Butterfly*, and the Italian Singer in *Der Rosenkavalier*. In the mid-1980s his singing career was seriously threatened by a painful condition known as TMJ syndrome, caused by tension in or faulty articulation of the temporomandibular joint in his jaw, traced to a birth injury. For half a year, he retreated into therapy, under the guidance of his voice teacher, Thomas LoMonaco, and a TMJ syndrome specialist, Harold Gelb. In 1985–86 he returned to a full schedule, the highlight of which was his performance as Lord Percy in a televised production of *Anna Bolena*. The following season he sang Verdi's Rodolfo, Massenet's Werther, and Gounod's Faust with the New York City Opera. In the late 1980s he made debuts with the Lyric Opera of Chicago, the Teatro Comunale in Florence, Italy, and the

State Opera in Hamburg, Germany. At the Metropolitan Opera he made his first appearance as an emergency replacement in the role of Des Grieux in Massenet's *Manon* in 1987 and his official debut as Don Ottavio in *Don Giovanni* in 1990. In subsequent appearances at the Met, he sang the roles of the Duke in *Rigoletto* and Tamino in *The Magic Flute*. He preferred the ambience of recital halls to that of the operatic stage because of the "more personal contact with the audience . . . the direct style of communication." With his wife, Cheryll Drake Hadley, accompanying him on the piano, he sang a recital repertoire that included Brahms's Daumer settings, Vaughn Williams's "Songs of Travel," and Benjamin Britten's "Seven Sonnets of Michelangelo." His extensive discography ranged from Beethoven's Ninth Symphony and Mozart's Requiem to recordings of Gershwin's *Porgy and Bess*, Leos Janacek's opera *Jenufa* (which won a Grammy), Leonard Bernstein's *Candide*, and Paul McCartney's autobiographical *Liverpool Oratorio*. With Hadley singing the title role, Bernstein conducted the London Symphony Orchestra in the concert recording of *Candide*. Hadley had created the role of Shanty, the protagonist in *Liverpool Oratio*, singing that role in the oratorio's world premiere at the Liverpool Anglican Cathedral in 1990. In 1996 Hadley commissioned Daniel Steven Crafts to set a number of poems by Carl Sandburg to music. The result was *The Song and the Slogan*, which won an Emmy Award when performed on PBS television. In addition to his vocal problems caused by TMJ syndrome, Hadley was beset with financial difficulties and severe bouts of depression. In an apparent suicide attempt, he shot himself in the head with an air rifle on July 10, 2007, causing severe brain damage. He died at St. Francis Hospital in Poughkeepsie, New York, eight days later. His survivors included two sons from his marriage, which ended in divorce. See *Current Biography* (1991).

Obituary *New York Times* B p7 July 19, 2007

HALBERSTAM, DAVID Apr. 10, 1934–Apr. 23, 2007 Writer. The Pulitzer Prize–winning journalist and best-selling author David Halberstam combined diligence in investigative reporting with a storyteller's narrative skill in writing books devoted to contemporary history and popular culture, on topics ranging from war and politics to sports. Halberstam began laying his claim to fame, and to journalistic integrity, with his enterprising work as a war correspondent in Vietnam in the early 1960s and reporting that effectively countered the sanguine White House–Pentagon–State Department line regarding the then-nascent U.S. military incursion there. In his most provocative book, *The Best and the Brightest* (1972), he indicted McGeorge Bundy and Robert S. McNamara, et al, the elite team of gifted men in the Kennedy and Johnson presidential administrations ("victims of their own brilliance, of hubris, and of the Cold War mentality," in his words) who, paradoxically, crafted the unwinnable war in Vietnam, "the worst tragedy to befall this country since the Civil War." Three decades later he negatively assessed the handling of foreign-policy challenges by the presidential administrations of Bill Clinton and George H. W. Bush in *War in a Time of Peace* (2001), another tour de force in storytelling. In *The Powers That Be* (1979), he traced the transformation of modern corporate media—beginning with President Franklin D. Roosevelt's "fireside chats" on radio and culminating with the resignation of President Richard M. Nixon under the cloud of the newspaper-sparked Watergate scandal—from simple chroniclers of news to potent shapers of public opinion, policy, and events. He did so by focusing on CBS News as a power in radio and television, on *Time* magazine, and on the *Washington Post* and *Los Angeles Times* newspapers as well as on people involved in those four enterprises. In breaks from his heavy—albeit highly readable—books with political and social themes, Halberstam wrote seven books on sports that were lighter in mood but whose subjects tended to serve as mirrors of what was happening in the wider world. Save for one book on the professional football coach Bill Belichick and another on an Olympic rowing team, those books are about pro baseball and basketball teams and players: *The Breaks of the Game* (1981), *Summer of '49* (1989), *October 1964* (1994), *Playing for Keeps* (1999), and *The Teammates* (2003). After graduating from Harvard University, Halberstam moved south to work as a reporter with the *Daily Times Leader* in West Point, Mississippi (1955–56) and the *Nashville Tennessean* (1956–60). He joined the Washington, D.C., bureau of the *New York Times* in 1960; the following year the *Times* sent him to the Congo to cover the war of independence there; and in September 1962 the newspaper, at his request, assigned him to South Vietnam. Not satisfied with the official reports handed out to members of the press in downtown Saigon, he ventured out into the civil war–torn countryside, gathering firsthand the ingredients for the realism that informed the bottom-up stories he sent to New York. Those dispatches, prophetic of the disaster that the U.S. military expedition in Vietnam would become, embarrassed President John F. Kennedy, who personally complained to the publisher of the *New York Times*, to no avail. In recognition of his war reportage, Halberstam received the George Polk Memorial Award in 1963 and shared the Pulitzer Prize for international reporting with Malcolm W. Browne of the Associated Press in 1964. He published *The Making of a Quagmire: America and Vietnam During the Kennedy Era* in 1965. In the mid-1960s he was posted successively to Warsaw, to Paris, and to the *Times*'s metropolitan staff in New York City. While in Poland he married the actress Elzbieta Czyzewska. (They divorced in 1977, and he married Jean Sandness Butler in 1979.) In 1967 he resigned from the *New York Times* and became a contributing editor of *Harper's* magazine. He published *The Unfinished Odyssey of Robert Kennedy* in 1968 and *Ho*, a slim study of the Communist Vietnamese leader Ho Chi Minh, in 1971. In *The Reckoning* (1986) he examined the automobile industry and the decline of Detroit in its competition with Japan, and he offered a rather pessimistic preview of America's future in *The Next Century* (1991). In *The Fifties* (1993) he revisited the politics, public personalities, and defining events of the 1950s. In *The Children* (1999) he wrote about the civil rights movement of the late 1950s and early 1960s by focusing on the lives of eight black college students he had met in

Nashville when he was a young reporter covering the lunch-counter sit-ins there. The title of *Firehouse* (2002) was a reference to Engine 40, Ladder 35, the fire station in the Manhattan neighborhood in which he lived; in that book he recounted the lives of the 13 firefighters from the station who responded to the terrorist attacks on the World Trade Center on September 11, 2001 and of the deaths of all but one of them that day. In addition to his books of nonfiction, he wrote two novels: *The Noblest Roman* (1961), about bootlegging and political corruption in a rural town in the Deep South, and *One Very Hot Day* (1968), set in wartime Vietnam. At the time of his death, his 21st and last book, on the Korean war, was being readied for publication. He died of blunt-force trauma in a fiery traffic accident in Menlo Park, California, when the automobile in which he was the front-seat passenger was broadsided (on the passenger side) by another car and slammed into a third vehicle. He was survived by his wife, Jean, and their daughter, Julia. See *Current Biography* (1973).

Obituary *New York Times* C p13 Apr. 24, 2007

HARRIS, MARK Nov. 19, 1922–May 29, 2007 Author. Mark Harris wrote a dozen novels on serious themes, often tempered by his characteristic and abiding sense of humor. His protagonists are essentially self-portraits, "about one man trying to come to terms with his society . . . without losing his own identity or integrity," as he explained in 1972. "I am spiritually at the center of my novels . . . , disguised as poet or baseball player or professor or historian. I am always a minority person in some sense, either because I am fictionally left-handed or, most recently [in *The Goy*, 1970], gentile in a Jewish milieu." Harris wrote his first novel, *Trumpet to the World* (1946), from the perspective of a young black man in the Deep South who marries a well-to-do white woman. His best-known books are four novels narrated by Henry W. Wiggen, the star pitcher of the New York Mammoths, a fictionalized version of the New York Yankees. The tetralogy begins with *The Southpaw* (1953). The most celebrated of the four books is the second, *Bang the Drum Slowly* (1956), a touching and finally lachrymose account of Wiggen's relationship with the Mammoths' catcher, Bruce Pearson, a socially slow country bumpkin; his teammates, including Wiggen, disdain and deride him until Wiggen learns that Pearson is terminally ill with Hodgkin's disease and proceeds, with compassionate discretion, to rally the team to the catcher's support. (*Bang the Drum Slowly* was adapted into a teleplay broadcast as part of the *U.S. Steel Hour* dramatic anthology series on the CBS network in 1956; it was made into a theatrical motion picture—with scenario by Harris—released in 1973.) The third novel in the tetralogy is *A Ticket for a Seamstitch* (1957); the fourth is *It Looked Like for Ever* (1979), in which the now 39-year-old Wiggen loses his fastball. Harris's other novels include *Something About a Soldier* (1957), *Wake Up, Stupid* (1959), *Killing Everybody* (1983), *Lying in Bed* (1984), *Speed* (1990), and *The Tale Maker* (1994). *City of Discontent: An Interpretative Biography of Vachel Lindsay* (1952) is classified by some as a novel and by others as nonfiction. In 1999 Harris published the collection of short stories

The Self-Made Brain Surgeon. His play Friedman & Son was produced in San Francisco in 1962, and his teleplay The Man That Corrupted Hadleyburg, an adaptation of a Mark Twain story, was broadcast in the U.S. in 1980 and in the United Kingdom in 1983. His books of nonfiction include Mark the Glove Boy, or The Last Days of Richard Nixon (1964), his partly autobiographical reportage on the 1962 California gubernatorial race; the journal Twentyone Twice (1966); the autobiography Best Father Ever Invented (1976); Saul Bellow (1980); and Diamond: Baseball Writings (1994). Harris was born Mark Harris Finkelstein and later changed his name legally. He held advanced degrees in English and American studies and worked as a journalist before becoming a professor of English and creative writing at a succession of universities. He lived in Goleta, California, and died in Cottage Hospital in Santa Barbara, California. His survivors included his wife, Josephine (née Horen), a daughter, two sons, and three grandchildren. See Current Biography (1959).

Obituary New York Times C p10 June 2, 2007

HART, KITTY CARLISLE Sep. 3, 1910–Apr. 17, 2007 Stage and screen actress and singer; television quiz-show panelist; arts administrator and promoter. Following her careers on stage, in motion pictures, and on TV, Hart, the widow of the playwright-director Moss Hart, chaired the New York State Council on the Arts, from 1976 to 1996. Subsequently, well into her 90s, she pursued a fourth career, as a cabaret and concert singer. Born in New Orleans, Louisiana, to parents of German-Jewish descent, Hart was originally named Catherine Conn. (She chose "Kitty Carlisle" as her stage name.) After the death of her father, a physician, when she was 10, her mother took her to Europe, where she attended private schools in Switzerland, made her society debut in Rome, and studied acting under Charles Dullin in Paris and at the Royal Academy of Dramatic Art in London. Returning to the United States in the late 1930s, she made her stage debut as Rita Ferguson with the touring company of the hit Broadway operetta Rio Rita. On Broadway she was cast as Prince Orlofsky in the musical Champagne, Sec (1933–34), a light adaptation of Die Fledermaus. She made her screen debut as the female lead in the musical comedy Murder at the Vanities (1934); was cast opposite Bing Crosby in the musical farce She Loves Me Not (1934); played the second lead in the romantic musical Here Is My Heart (1934); as the ingénue, joined the Marx Brothers in A Night at the Opera (1935); and later starred in the musical film Larceny with Music (1943). Back on Broadway she starred in the operettas White Horse Inn (1936–37) and Three Waltzes (1937–38), was cast as Pamela Gibson in the musical comedy Walk with Music (1940), sang Lucretia in the chamber opera The Rape of Lucretia (1948–49), and played Alice Walters in the farce Anniversary Waltz (1954). Meanwhile, during the late 1930s and early 1940s, she played the regional and summer-theater circuits. Between stage engagements she sang in supper clubs. In the early 1950s she became increasingly familiar to television viewers as a guest celebrity panelist on the quiz shows Who Said That? (NBC/ABC) and I've Got a Secret (CBS). She

became a national celebrity beginning in the mid-1950s as a regular member of the panel of celebrities on To Tell the Truth, a CBS network program in which the panelists tried to discern which of several guests, each professing to be the same person, was telling the truth. She remained with that program, with some interruptions, after it went into syndication (1966–77). In 1967 she sang Prince Orlofsky in Die Fledermaus at the Metropolitan Opera several times. As chair of the New York State Council on the Arts, she effectively lobbied for public and private support of artists, especially small performing and musical-arts groups. Later, as a singer, she gave her last public performance in a concert in October 2006. Hart's voice may be heard in recordings of the operettas The Merry Widow, Desert Song, and Roberta, originally released in the 1940s and 1950s as 78 rpm records, which were remastered and released as CDs on the Decca Broadway label in 2002. Hart was married to Moss Hart from 1946 until his death, in 1961. She died at her home in Manhattan of congestive heart failure resulting from pneumonia. She was survived by a son and a daughter. See Current Biography (1982).

Obituary New York Times C p13 Apr. 19, 2007

HERBERT, DON July 10, 1917–June 12, 2007 Television personality; science popularizer. A huge number of people in the scientific and medical professions in the United States and Canada have traced the origins of their vocational aspirations to their viewing of Donald Jeffrey Herbert's television shows, which introduced general science to preteenage children in an entertaining way. In 1951 Herbert, then employed at WMBQ-TV, the NBC television network's outlet in Chicago, created Watch Mr. Wizard. That half-hour weekly program, originally produced live (first in Chicago and later in New York) and in black and white, ran continuously on the NBC network for 14 years (March 1951–July 1965). Each week, accompanied on camera by one or two juvenile guests ready to register amazement, Herbert conducted simple but exciting laboratory experiments to explain the principles behind natural phenomena, "what goes on in the world—why the wind blows, what makes a cake rise, how water comes out of a kitchen tap." As much as possible, he used common household items in his experiments—a recycled mayonnaise jar as a beaker or as the casing for a rocket, for example—and he encouraged his young viewers to try the experiments at home. At the height of its popularity, Watch Mr. Wizard had an audience estimated at more than five million, inspired the formation of thousands of Mr. Wizard Science Clubs, and was the recipient of a Peabody Award. In 1971 the program was reincarnated as Mr. Wizard, produced in Ottawa, Canada. Over a period of one year beginning in September 1971, 26 installments of Mr. Wizard were televised on Canada's CBC network as well as on NBC in the U.S. In a third, faster-paced incarnation, the show became Mr. Wizard's World, produced in Calgary, Canada. That series was televised on Nickelodeon, the U.S. children's cable network, between January 1983 and January 1991. Herbert subsequently developed Teacher to Teacher with Mr. Wizard, a 15-minute series on which he introduced elementary-school science teachers and their projects. That series ran on Nickelodeon in 1994. Reruns of some of Herbert's TV shows have been carried on PBS stations and on digital cable's Science Channel. In addition to his work on television, Herbert produced science films for junior and senior high schools, and he published several books, among them *Mr. Wizard's 400 Experiments in Science* (1967). Herbert, who was born Donald Herbert Kemske, was initially an actor. After majoring in general science and English at La Crosse (Wisconsin) State Teacher's College, he worked in summer stock. During World War II he was a U.S. Army Air Corps combat pilot in Europe. His early work in broadcasting in Chicago was on radio, as an actor in such adventure series as *Jack Armstrong* and *Tom Mix* and as a writer of scripts. Married twice, Herbert was survived by his second wife, Norma (nee Kasell), and six children and stepchildren. He died of multiple myeloma at his home in Bel Canyon, Los Angeles County, California. See *Current Biography* (1956).

Obituary *New York Times* B p9 June 13, 2007

HILL, ANDREW June 20, 1931–Apr. 20, 2007 Modernist jazz musician. During his half-century career—which included teaching and band leading—the modally and tonally eclectic pianist and composer Andrew Hill was for too long under-appreciated for the originality with which he bridged the gap between bop and newer experiments in jazz. As one of Blue Note Records' "in and out" players in the 1960s, Hill was, as Phil Freeman observed in the *Village Voice* (April 30, 2007), "equally comfortable with freedom, complexity, and the deceptively simple joys of hard bop. His compositions were frequently tricky, almost to the point of dissonance, but 'Pumpkin,' 'Refuge,' 'Black Fire,' and many more have melodies and a swinging energy that's impossible to shake loose once you hear them." Hill's introduction to the piano was via an old pianola his parents owned when he was a child in Chicago. Hill told Phil Johnson for the London *Independent* (April 25, 2007, on-line) that he taught himself to play by stopping the pianola roll and putting his fingers in the keys that remained depressed. "He didn't realize that some of the performances were for four hands rather than two, which may account for his unusually chromatic style," Johnson commented. Hill later acquired an accordion, which he would play for money on the streets of Chicago's South Side. There he came to the attention of the jazz musicians Earl "Fatha" Hines and Bill Russo, who encouraged him, and the classical German composer Paul Hindemith, who was teaching nearby and gave him tips about music theory and asymmetrical as well as symmetrical composition. Growing up in Chicago, Hill was influenced by Afro-Cuban musicians he knew and by the advanced harmony he heard on movie soundtracks and the jazz and pop hits and other music he heard on the radio. In the early 1950s he performed with local rhythm-and-blues bands and with Charlie Parker and other visiting jazz musicians at the Graystone Ballroom in Chicago. His first recordings were on Chicago labels, as a sideman beginning in 1954 and as leader and instrumentalist in a chiefly vocal session with the Debonairs (Ping Records,

1956). His generally recognized "debut" album, the trio session *So In Love* (Warwick Records), was cut and released in 1959 (not 1955, as some sources state). His big break came when he toured as the singer Dinah Washington's accompanist in 1961. After a stint with Rahsaan Roland Kirk's band in Los Angeles, he settled in New York City, where he was a mentor to such younger musicians as Herbie Hancock, Chick Corea, and Keith Jarrett. In 1963 he signed with Blue Note Records, whose founder, Alfred Lion, viewed him as "the next Thelonious Monk." In his liner notes for Hill's first Blue Note album, *Black Fire* (1963), the writer A. B. Spellman cooperated with Hill in launching the myth that Hill had been born in Haiti. "I lied . . . and A. B. Spellman helped me plot the crime," Hill confessed to Phil Johnson. "It helped me get gigs on the college circuit. . . . People looked at jazz music as exotic, and pretending you came from Haiti helped." Blue Note Records subsequently released Hill's albums *Smoke Stack* (1963) and *Judgement* (1964). His most celebrated Blue Note album was *Point of Departure* (1964), a model combination of artful composition and improvised performance. *Andrew!* was released later in 1964 and *One for One* in 1965. Among his band members on his first six classic albums with Blue Note were Kenny Dorham, Joe Henderson, Bobby Hutcherson, Richard Davis, Joe Chambers, Freddie Hubbard, and Tony Williams. His next few Blue Note albums included *Compulsion!* (1965), *Grass Roots* (1968), *Dance with Death* (1968), and *Lift Every Voice* (1969). At Blue Note he was also the pianist on albums with Johnny Woods, Sam Rivers, Hank Mobley, and others. For two decades beginning in 1970, while recording for the Freedom/Arista and Soul Notes labels, he was generally out of public sight, occupied with teaching at Colgate University, in Hamilton, New York (1970–72), in public schools and prisons in California, and finally at Portland State University in Oregon. With his first wife, the organist LaVerne Gillette Hill (who died in 1989), he performed in the Smithsonian Institution's touring program for several years. After marrying his second wife, Joanne Robinson Hill, he returned with her in the mid-1990s to the greater New York City area and resumed his jazz career, more as a concert performer than a recording artist, although he had already begun recording again with Blue Note, cutting the CDs *Eternal Spirit* (1989) and *But Not Farewell* (1991). He also recorded on the Palmetto label. With his Point of Departure Sextet he recorded the album *Dusk* (Palmetto, 2000), which brought him a streak of adulatory attention. With a big band he had formed, he recorded *A Beautiful Day* (Palmetto, 2002) live at the Birdland jazz nightclub in Manhattan. A 1969 Blue Note session of his, *Passing Ships*, was released for the first time in 2003, and his acclaimed new Blue Note CD *Time Lines* was released in 2006. During the first years of the 21st century, he was honored with Denmark's JazzPar Prize and numerous awards from *Down Beat*, *Playboy*, and *Jazz Times* magazines, and the Jazz Journalists Association. Mosaic Records began remastering his recordings, releasing the seven-CD boxed set *The Complete Andrew Hill Blue Note Sessions 1963-66*, the three-CD boxed set *Andrew Hill Solo*, including 25 previously unreleased Blue Note tracks from 1967–70, and the three-CD boxed set *Andrew Hill Solo*, comprising Fantasy sessions from 1978. During the early 2000s Hill toured Great Britain and other western European countries with his Anglo-American Big Band. He played his final concert at Trinity Church in Manhattan in March 2007. He died of lung cancer at his home in Jersey City, New Jersey, at the age of 75, six years older than he had pretended to be during most of his career. His wife, Joanne, survived him. See *Current Biography* (2004).

Obituary *New York Times* C p10 Apr. 21, 2007

HILL, ARTHUR Aug. 1, 1922–Oct. 22, 2006 Canadian-born actor of stage, screen, and television. With instinct and subtle intelligence, during his four-decade career Arthur Edward Spence Hill projected a dependable, disciplined, and stoic persona in authoritative interpretations of dozens of varied roles, ranging from his creation on Broadway of George, the browbeaten academic husband opposite Uta Hagen in *Who's Afraid of Virginia Woolf?*—which brought him the Tony and New York Drama Critics Awards for best actor of the 1962–63 season—to such feature-film credits as Sam Bonner, the protective husband of the Jane Fonda character in *In the Cool of the Day* (1963), Neil Stanton, the inattentive psychiatrist husband of the Jean Seberg character in *Moment to Moment* (1965), Albert Graves, the duplicitous attorney in *Harper* (1966), and Jeremy Stone, the scientist investigating a lethal virus from outer space in *The Andromeda Strain* (1971). On television he guest-acted on numerous dramatic shows and realized his greatest popularity starring as the compassionate small-town defense attorney in the popular ABC series *Owen Marshall, Counsellor at Law* (1971–74). After serving as a mechanic with the Royal Canadian Air Force during World War II, Hill received a pre-law B.A. degree at the University of British Columbia but quit his pursuit of a law degree to concentrate on acting with the University Players Club. In 1948 he and his first wife, the actress Peggy Hassard Hill, moved to London, England, where he worked on BBC Radio before moving to roles on BBC Television and in motion pictures and theater. His British screen credits between 1949 and 1955 included featured roles in the director Val Guest's *Miss Pilgrim's Progress*, *The Body Said No!*, *Mister Drake's Duck*, and *Life with the Lyons*. Among his London stage credits were Finch in *Home of the Brave* (1948), Tommy Turner in *The Male Animal* (1949), Hector Malone in *Man and Superman* (1951), and Paul Unger in *The Country Girl* (1952). In the West End in 1954, he starred with Ruth Gordon in *The Matchmaker*. In 1955 Gordon and he (in the Cornelius Hackl role) moved with the production to the United States, where *The Matchmaker* ran for more than a year on Broadway and then enjoyed a successful national tour. In *Look Homeward, Angel* (1957–59), another Broadway hit, Hill touchingly created the role of the dying older brother. Following supporting parts in *The Gang's All Here* (1959–60) and *All the Way Home* (1960), he created the role of Jay Follett, the young father whose demise in an auto accident haunts the play *A Death in the Family* (1960–61). Following the sensational 664-performance run of *Who's Afraid of Virginia Woolf?* (1962–64), he co-

starred with Barbara Cook in the musical *Something More!* (1964) and with Ingrid Bergman in Eugene O'Neill's drama *More Stately Mansions* (1967). Between engagements on the New York stage, he was cast on American network television in teleplays on such live-drama showcases as *Armstrong Circle Theatre*, *Studio One*, *The U.S. Steel Hour*, and *Hallmark Hall of Fame* and in filmed episodes of such series as *Alfred Hitchcock Presents*, *The Defenders*, *Ben Casey*, *Mission: Impossible*, *The Untouchables*, *The F.B.I.*, *The Fugitive*, *Marcus Welby, M.D.*, and *The Nurses*. Outstanding among his made-for-TV film roles were those of John Gunther in the poignant drama *Death Be Not Proud* (1975) and Judge Horton in *Judge Horton and the Scottsboro Boys* (1976). He made his American feature-film debut as Tomaselli in *The Young Doctors* (1961). His subsequent screen credits included Grainger in *The Ugly American* (1961), Marshal Shelby in *The Chairman* (1969), Cap Collis in *The Killer Elite* (1975), Dr. Duffy in *Futureworld* (1976), the tough U.S. medical corps colonel in *A Bridge Too Far* (1977), Richard King in *A Little Romance* (1979), Brewer in *The Amateur* (1981), and Caleb Grainger in *One Magic Christmas* (1985). His final acting credits were in episodes of the television series *Columbo* and *Murder, She Wrote* in 1990. After suffering for years from Alzheimer's disease, he died in an assisted-living facility in Pacific Palisades, California. He was predeceased by his first wife, Peggy Hassard Hill, and his daughter, Jennifer. His survivors included his second wife, Anne-Sophie Taraba Hill, his son, Douglas, a stepdaughter, and a stepgranddaughter. See *Current Biography* (1977).

Obituary *New York Times* B p11 Oct. 27, 2006

HUSSEIN, SADDAM Apr. 28, 1937–Dec. 30, 2006 President of Iraq (1979–2003); vice president of Iraq (1969–79). Saddam Hussein, who began establishing his brutal dictatorship de jure in Iraq in 1969, was the most hated Arab leader of his time. While he was admired by some Middle Eastern leaders for his defiance of the West, he was more feared by his own people than any other head of state in that region. As the Iraqi expatriate Kanan Makiya (aka Samir al-Khali) wrote in later editions of his 1989 book, *The Republic of Fear*, Hussein's regime amounted to "a chamber of horrors . . . that not even the most morbid imagination could have dreamed up." He was merciless in ordering the torture and summary executions of political dissidents and in his mass-punishment responses to plots or perceived plots to assassinate him and to rebelliousness on the part of such ethnic and religious populations within Iraq as the Shi'a Muslims, the Kurds, and the ethnic Turks. Hussein, who was born into the Sunni branch of Islam, began his political career as a student in Baghdad in 1959, when he joined the pan-Arab nationalist and socialist Baath Party. In a coup by Iraqi army officers in 1958, King Faisal II was overthrown and General Abdul Karim Kassem assumed power. With nine other young Baathists, Hussein took part in a failed U.S.-backed plot to assassinate Kassem in 1959. Sentenced to death, he escaped via Syria to Egypt. When Kassem's administration was toppled, in 1963, Hussein returned to Baghdad, where he was imprisoned by the new regime for several years beginning in 1964. Meanwhile, he rose to the position of Baath Party secretary. In that post, he was instrumental in organizing a party militia, which was indispensable in the party's seizure of power in a bloodless coup led by Ahmed Hassan al-Bakr, in 1968. After Bakr assumed the presidency, he chose Hussein as his vice president and deputy chairman of the Revolutionary Command Council (the Cabinet). Hussein began making himself the prime mover in the government, behind the scenes and then more overtly, as Bakr's health failed. He laid the foundation for his rule-by-terror with the public hanging in 1969 of some 17 people accused of spying for Israel. Hundreds of arrests, imprisonments, and executions of suspected subversives would take place during the following decades. Citing his poor health, Bakr relinquished the presidency to Hussein in 1979. Hussein consolidated his dictatorship with a monstrous party purge in which 500 or more Baathists died, according to Kanan Makiya. His dictatorial excesses aside, as head of state, prime minister, chairman of the Revolutionary Command Council, commander of the Iraqi armed forces, and secretary general of the Baath Party, Hussein pursued a secular course of socialism and modernization. While maintaining a ruthlessly repressive regime, fostering a cult of personality, and spending lavishly on his private palaces, for some time he also used Iraq's great petroleum-based wealth to lift the Iraqi masses out of poverty and significantly raise the national standard of living. He oversaw the building of housing projects as well as high-rise business buildings, set up a generous welfare system, and made free medical care and higher education widely available. In addition, relatively speaking, under his regime women enjoyed a greater freedom of dress and movement and more educational and career opportunities (as long as they did not challenge the regime) than in Muslim countries where strict Sharia law prevailed. But his positive domestic programs were in time undercut by the disastrous effects of his aspiration for geopolitical hegemony through conquest in the Middle East. His invasion of Iran in 1980 resulted in the costly Iran-Iraq War (1980–88), which ended in a stalemate, and his occupation of Kuwait in 1990 provoked the first Gulf War (1991), which he lost to the United Nations/U.S. forces. He later provoked the U.N. to impose sanctions on Iraq and sparked the wrath of neoconservatives in the U.S. White House with his failure to live up to the terms of the Gulf War cease-fire and his shiftiness in cooperating with U.N. inspectors investigating his possible possession of "weapons of mass destruction." His government collapsed when a U.S.-led coalition of military forces invaded Iraq in the spring of 2003. On July 22, 2003 U.S. forces tracked down his sons Uday and Qusay to a safe house in Mosul, Iraq, and killed them. Hussein remained in hiding for eight months. On December 13, 2003 U.S. Special Operations Forces ferreted him out of a hole-in-the ground hiding place in Ad-Dawr, Iraq, near his birthplace. On June 30, 2004 he and 11 of his senior Baathist associates were booked to stand trial for war crimes, crimes against humanity, and genocide. On November 5, 2006 an Iraqi special tribunal sentenced Hussein to death for his role in crimes committed against Shi'a Muslims in Dujail,

Iraq, in 1982, when he was the target of an assassination attempt there. The charges included the killings of 148 people, the illegal arrests of 399 others, and the torture of women and children. The verdict and sentencing were upheld by Iraq's Supreme Court of Appeals on December 26, 2006. Four days later Hussein was executed by hanging. In retrospect, many observers credited Hussein's savage administration with imposing and maintaining law (of sorts) and order on a population composed of several fractious ethnic and religious elements, including Shiite Muslims (55 percent of the population) and dominated by Sunni Muslims (20 percent of the population). See *Current Biography* (1981) and *Current Biography International Yearbook* (2002).

Obituary *New York Times* A p1+ Dec. 30, 2006

HUTTON, BETTY Feb. 26, 1921–Mar. 11, 2007 Singer and actress. The supercharged "blonde bombshell" Betty Hutton burst to prominence on the musical stage when she was 19 and subsequently enjoyed a dozen years of stardom in motion pictures, from the early 1940s into the 1950s. One of her proudest achievements was her portrayal of the main character, Trudy Kockenlocker, a promiscuous and pregnant wartime USO dancer who does not know which serviceman has fathered her child, in *The Miracle of Morgan's Creek* (1944), a daffy comedy, daring for its time, written and directed by Preston Sturges. Her electric combination of singing and acting was most famously demonstrated in her boisterous portrayal of Annie Oakley in the 1950 screen adaptation of the musical comedy *Annie Get Your Gun*. Dropping out of school in Detroit, Michigan, Hutton (born Elizabeth June Thornburg) began her professional career as a teenager, singing solo in clubs and with bands, eventually with the Vincent Lopez orchestra. Following appearances in several short musical films, she was cast on Broadway as a featured performer in the revue *Two for the Show* (February–May 1940), most prominently as the jitterbug dancer in the number "The Jitter Dance," and later as Flossie in the original cast of the musical comedy *Panama Hattie*, which began a 14-month run in October 1940. Both *Two for the Show* and *Panama Hattie* were produced by B. G. "Buddy" DeSylva, who signed her to a movie contract when he became executive producer at Paramount Pictures. Her first feature-film roles were those of Bubbles Hennessy (singing "Murder She Says") in the musical *Happy Go Lucky* (1942) and Bessie Dale (singing "Arthur Murray Taught Me Dancing in a Hurry") in *The Fleet's In* (1942). As Polly Judson, she headed a cast of studio luminaries in the musical farce *Star Spangled Rhythm* (1942). She was cast as the female lead opposite the comedian Bob Hope in the wartime musical *Let's Face It* (1943) and as the female leads (twin sisters) opposite the crooner Bing Crosby in another wartime musical, *Here Come the Waves* (1944). As Bobby Angel in the musical *As the Angels Sing* (1944), she was cast as a member of a sisters singing group (similar to the Andrews Sisters) exploited by a band leader in the course of their rise to fame. She played the real-life Prohibition-era nightclub performer Texas Guinan in *Incendiary Blonde* (1945) and the silent-movie actress Pearl White in another biopic, *The Perils of Pauline* (1947). Her other starring credits in the middle and late 1940s included Judy Peabody, the nightclub hat-check girl in *The Stork Club* (1945), Peggy Harper in the murder mystery *Cross My Heart* (1946), the romantic dreamer Georgina Allerton in the light comedy *Dream Girl* (1948), and Eleanor Collier in *Red, Hot and Blue* (1949). She co-starred with Fred Astaire in the musical *Let's Dance* (1950), played the singer Blossom Seeley in the biopic *Somebody Loves Me* (1952), and shone as the trapeze artist Holly in the star-studded circus movie *The Greatest Show on Earth* (1952). She left Paramount in a contract dispute in 1952 and did not make another movie until *Spring Reunion* (United Artists, 1957), in which she and Dana Andrews co-starred as former college sweethearts whose romance is rekindled when they meet again at their 15th class reunion. She returned to occasional work in nightclubs; attempted a transition to television by starring in the musical-comedy production *Satins and Spurs* (NBC, September 12, 1954) and the situation comedy *The Betty Hutton Show* (CBS, 1959–60); and on Broadway replaced Carol Burnett in the musical *Fade Out, Fade In* for one week in 1965. Following a suicide attempt in 1972, she was rescued from addiction to sleeping pills; she converted to Catholicism under the tutelage of Father Peter Maguire and became the housekeeper at St. Anthony's Church rectory in Portsmouth, Rhode Island. In 1981 she returned to Broadway for two weeks as Miss Hannigan in the hit musical *Annie*. After earning a master's degree in liberal arts at Salve Regina College (now a university) in Newport, Rhode Island, in 1986, she taught classes for aspiring actors there and at Emerson College, in Boston. Her singing has been recorded on Living Era, Jasmine, and other labels. Hutton was married and divorced four times and had three daughters. She died of complications from colon cancer at her home in Palm Springs, California. See *Current Biography* (1950).

Obituary *New York Times* A p21 Mar. 14, 2007

IRWIN, STEVE Feb. 22, 1962–Sep. 4, 2006 Australian naturalist, conservationist, and television personality. Stephen Robert Irwin's familiarity with wildlife and passionate concern for its preservation were combined with an extraordinary flair for fast-paced and daring showmanship. He first exhibited that flair with his near-manic death-defying stunts (while exclaiming such catchwords as "Crickey!") during crocodile-feeding time at the Australia Zoo—a facility that he inherited from his parents—and he became known internationally through the autobiographical *The Crocodile Hunter: The Birthday Present Was a Python and Other Adventures* (1997), which he wrote with his wife, Terri; through his appearances on major American television talk shows, on which he presented clips of himself wrestling with crocodiles and boa constrictors and handling other dangerous animals, including venomous snakes; and above all through his own TV series, *The Crocodile Hunter*, which was syndicated in some 100 countries. (A number of installments were yet to be aired at the time of his death, from puncture by a stingray; the accident occurred while he was filming on location.) Irwin, who was born in Victoria,

Australia, was eight years old when he moved with his parents to Beerwah, on what is known as Australia's Sunshine Coast, where they established the Australia Zoo, first known as the Queensland Reptile and Fauna Park. As a boy he traveled the Australian outback with his father, procuring crocodiles, snakes, lizards, and other animals for the zoo's collection, and helped his mother raise orphan joey kangaroos and wallabies and rehabilitate injured birds and other fauna. He was also involved with his father in the Australian government's East Coast Crocodile Management Program, trapping and relocating crocodiles to prevent their being slaughtered by fearful locals in populated areas. In 1991 his parents retired and turned control of the Australia Zoo over to him. That same year he met Terri Raines, an American conservationist especially devoted to the preservation of predatory mammals. In 1992 he and Raines were married, and she became his partner in the management of the zoo and his other projects, including his television documentaries, in which she was a supporting on-screen presence and/or off-screen commentator. Under their direction the zoo grew from four to 16 acres and the wildlife population rose to approximately 550. The first hour-long documentary in the series *The Crocodile Hunter*, consisting of footage of the couple's crocodile-hunting expeditions while on their honeymoon, was televised on Australia's Channel 10 in 1992. The series (originally numbering 10 episodes) was subsequently syndicated to other countries, including the United States, where it became one of the earliest and most highly rated programs on Animal Planet, an offshoot of the Discovery Channel on cable television, beginning in 1996. On the motion-picture screen, Irwin had a cameo role in *Dr. Doolittle 2* (2001), and he and his wife co-starred in *The Crocodile Hunter: Collision Course* (2002), a feature film in which they try to save a crocodile from poachers, realizing only belatedly that the croc swallowed an American spy satellite that had fallen to Earth and that the "poachers" are actually CIA agents trying to retrieve the intelligence drone. Irwin died of cardiac arrest when he was struck in the chest by the barb of a stingray; the accident occurred while he was filming a segment for a television documentary in the Great Barrier Reef off the Low Isles near Port Douglas in Queensland, Australia. (The documentary, *Ocean's Deadliest*, was to be completed for broadcast in 2007. At the same time Discovery Communications channels worldwide were in the process of televising *New Breed Vets*, consisting of six hour-long episodes in which Irwin is seen interviewing veterinarians in a number of countries involved in advances in animal health science; also airing internationally were several additional episodes of *The Crocodile Hunter* and two seasons of *The Crocodile Hunter's Croc Files*, a children's program hosted by Irwin and his wife and involving their daughter, Bindi Sue, who turned eight in 2006.) In addition to his wife and daughter, Irwin was survived by his son, Robert, whose third birthday was in December 2006. Animal Planet aired a 15-hour marathon of Irwin's programs on September 17 and September 18, 2006. Irwin's father declined the offer of a state funeral for his son, but many Australian and international dignitaries and celebrities attended a memorial service in the Crocoseum, a 5,500-seat stadium at the Australia Zoo. The service was televised live on Animal Planet in the United States on September 19, 2006 and carried worldwide by Discovery Communications affiliates. See *Current Biography* (2000).

Obituary *New York Times* C p13 Sep. 5, 2006

IVINS, MOLLY Aug. 30, 1944–Jan. 31, 2007 Journalist; opinion columnist; political humorist; best-selling author. Molly Tyler Ivins was a sassy political agitator with a joyful motto: "Raise hell and have fun." A native of Texas who lived there most of her life, she described herself as "a little-'d' democrat, a populist, maybe even a left-wing Libertarian." "There's nothing you can do about being born liberal," she once wrote. "Fish gotta swim, hearts gotta bleed." The favorite targets of her sharp, folksy wit were Republicans, especially President George W. Bush (with whom she attended high school and whom she dubbed "Shrub" and "Dubya") and the war in Iraq launched in 2003, but she did not spare "calculating, equivocating, triangulating, straddling, hair-splitting" Democrats, including President Bill Clinton and U.S. senator Hillary Rodham Clinton of New York. Ivins was born in Monterey, California, and grew up in Houston, Texas. She earned a B.A. degree in history at Smith College, in Northampton, Massachusetts, and an M.A. degree in journalism at Columbia University, in New York City. Her first jobs as a journalist were with the *Houston Chronicle* and the *Minneapolis Tribune* (now the *Star Tribune*). As co-editor of the independent biweekly magazine the *Texas Observer* for six years (1970–76), she covered the state legislature in Austin, Texas, regaling her readers with unvarnished accounts of the good-old-boy antics of the legislators and verbatim quotations of their often foul language, with bad grammar unrectified. In 1976 she joined the staff of the *New York Times,* where she remained for five years, doing stints covering New York City Hall, the New York State Capitol in Albany, and the Rocky Mountain beat out of the *Times*'s Denver bureau. She was, as she said, "miserable" at the *Times,* "a great newspaper" but "also No Fun." She was particularly unhappy that the color of her unique down-home prose was constantly turned to gray by the *Time*'s editors. The executive editor at that time, A. M. Rosenthal, for his part, did not feel that she "showed due respect and reverence to the great dignity" of the newspaper. In 1982 she returned to Texas as a columnist for the *Dallas Times-Herald* newspaper, which offered her absolute freedom in expressing her opinions. After the *Times-Herald* folded, she moved with her column to the Fort Worth *Star-Telegram*, in 1992. Nine years later she went independent and signed with Creators Syndicate, which distributed her column twice weekly to between 300 and 400 newspapers. In a eulogy, her Creators Syndicate editor, Anthony Zurcher, said: "One of my most important jobs was to tell her newspaper clients that, yes, Molly meant to write it that way. We called her linguistic peculiarities 'Molly-isms.' Administration officials were 'Bushies,' government was in fact spelled 'guvment,' business was 'bidness,' and if someone was 'madder than a peach orchard boar,' well, he was quite mad indeed." Regarding one Tex-

as Republican congressman, Ivins quipped, "If his IQ slips any lower we'll have to water him twice a day." She was also a freelance contributor to the *Progressive*, among other publications, and an occasional commentator on National Public Radio and the CBS television program *60 Minutes*. In an article for the March 2006 issue of the *Progressive*, she wrote: "I can't see a damn soul in D.C. except Russ Feingold who is even worth considering for President." Her last Creators Syndicate column was "Stand Up Against the Surge [in Iraq]," published on January 11, 2007. She published four collections of her columns and other essays: *Molly Ivins Can't Say That, Can She?* (1991), *Nothin' But Good Times Ahead* (1993), *You Got to Dance with Them What Brung You: Politics in the Clinton Years (1998),* and *Who Let the Dogs In?: Incredible Political Animals I Have Known* (2004). With Lou Dubose, she wrote the books *Shrub: The Short But Happy Political Life of George W. Bush* (2000) and *Bushwhacked: Life in George W. Bush's America (2003)*. At the time of her death, she was collaborating on a third book with Dubose. Ivins never married. After battling breast cancer for six years, she died at her home, in Austin. See *Current Biography* (2000).

Obituary *New York Times* B p7 Feb. 1, 2007

JACKSON, MICHAEL May 7, 1942–Aug. 29, 2007 Writer; beer connoisseur. The best-selling author Michael Jackson, "the maven of malt," was arguably the world's most knowledgeable beer expert and certainly the preeminent authority on the subject writing in English. He was "the Linnaeus of the new generation of brewers, classifying myriad styles by species and genus and educating people about the culture and history of brewing regions," as he was described in *Modern Brewery Age* (December 13, 1999). A veteran journalist, he published more than a dozen books, which sold millions of copies in more than 15 languages. Touring the world in pursuit of brewing excellence beyond bland mainstream lagers, he contributed singularly to the popularization of a host of unique obscure beers and ales, including oatmeal stouts, the Lambic beers of Belgium, and India Pale Ale. Beginning in the late 1970s, when there were 40 U.S. breweries, he helped spur the growth of the country's microbrewery movement. By the end of the century, there were 1,440 American breweries, 1,390 of which were small, independent craft brewhouses. A native of Yorkshire, England, Jackson dropped out of school when he was 16 to venture into journalism. He worked for many years as a newspaper reporter on Fleet Street, chiefly with the London *Daily Mail,* and subsequently as a current-events commentator on television as well. He also wrote several United Kingdom tourist guides for American Express. In the early 1970s he began covering food and drink, and he soon focused on beer, inspired in part by the work of the wine journalist Hugh Johnson. He later explained: "Beer is by far the more extensively consumed [alcoholic drink] but less adequately honored [than wine]. In a small way, I want to put right that injustice." His first book (written with input from Frank Smyth) was *The English Pub: A Unique Social Phenomenon* (1976). The following year he published *The World Guide to*

Beer: The Brewing Styles, the Brands, the Countries. He later wrote, among other books, The New World Guide to Beer (1988), The Great Beers of Belgium: A Complete Guide and Celebration of a Unique Culture (1992), and Michael Jackson's Beer Companion: The World's Great Beer Styles, Gastronomy, and Traditions (1997). In addition to his writings on beer and ale, he published several books on the world's whiskeys, including single-malt scotch, and guides for bartenders and cocktail-party hosts. As the host of the six-part BBC/Discovery Channel television documentary The Beer Hunter (1990), he took viewers on tours of breweries and pubs in Great Britain, Belgium, and the Netherlands; the U.S. Videos from that documentary became available on CDs in 1996. Jackson was a food-section columnist for the London Independent newspaper and a contributor to Food & Wine and other periodicals. Until Parkinson's disease crippled him too badly, he toured Europe and the U.S. regularly, interviewing brewmasters and barley and malt growers, holding sold-out beer, ale, and whiskey tastings, conducting seminars, giving speeches, and making guest appearances on television. Following the death of his wife, Maggie Jackson, in about 1980, he formed a second life partnership, with Paddy Cunningham. He died of a heart attack at his home in west London. His survivors included Paddy Cunningham, her son, Sam Hopkins, whom he had helped raise, and two grandchildren. See Current Biography (2005).

Obituary New York Times B p5 Sep. 3, 2007

JOHNSON, CLAUDIA ALTA Dec. 22, 1912–July 11, 2007 First Lady of the United States (1963–69). Lady Bird (as she was called from infancy) was the widow of President Lyndon Baines Johnson (popularly nicknamed LBJ) and, in her own right, was a prominent environmentalist, champion of the preservation of native American flora, and promoter of urban and roadside scenic enhancement. Lady Bird was "the brains and money of this family," as President Johnson said; the late presidential chronicler Hugh Sidey found that she was "as close to being a Godly creature as that anguished realm [national politics] ever produced." With her business savvy, genteel disposition, and unfailing moral support, Lady Bird Johnson was indispensable in her rough-hewn and volatile husband's rise to power, as long-suffering as she was devotedly helpful. The suffering she long endured with loving forbearance was described in Time magazine's on-line obituary of her (July 11, 2007) as "the outrageous and roguish behavior of her husband," documented in "tape recordings and extensive scholarship, including a volume by LBJ biographer Robert Caro, which detailed Johnson's philandering and mean and humiliating outbursts in front of others against her ideas and lifestyle, even down to how she fixed her hair and the shoes she wore." In the New York Times (July 12, 2007) obituary, Enid Nemy quoted Bonnie Angelo, a reporter who covered Lady Bird for Time: "She took a lot from him, but she always said, 'Lyndon is larger than life,' and she took him with equanimity. She was the eye of the hurricane, the calm center of the maelstrom that was Lyndon Johnson." The Time obituary summed up her relationship with LBJ: "She

found a natural force, understood that, and guided it to the top. Otherwise she might have been a forgotten housewife in clunky shoes and he just another eccentric and embarrassing politician in [a] mohair suit . . . marching into oblivion." LBJ's entry into electoral politics was financed by money that Lady Bird borrowed against a family inheritance. She subsequently invested that inheritance in KTBC, a small, debt-ridden Austin radio station, which grew into a major Texas radio-and-television corporation, the foundation of the Johnson partnership's fortune. After earning a degree in journalism at the University of Texas at Austin, Lady Bird married LBJ in San Antonio, Texas, in 1934, when he was an administrative assistant to U.S. representative Richard M. Kleberg. In a special election in Texas's 10th Congressional District in 1937, LBJ was elected to fill the seat vacated by the death of U.S. representative James P. Buchanan. He was reelected to full terms in the U.S. House of Representatives in 1938, 1940, 1942, 1944, and 1946. He subsequently served two terms in the U.S. Senate, beginning in 1949, and he was majority leader in the Senate from 1955 through 1960. All along, Lady Bird was quietly working with diligence at his side, and following his nomination as vice president on John F. Kennedy's presidential ticket in 1960, she began doing so publicly; participating in the Democratic presidential campaign that year, she traveled 35,000 miles, stumping through 11 states, chiefly in the South and usually alone. She thus helped the Kennedy/Johnson ticket to carry seven Southern states in its victory at the polls in November 1960. In the role of "second lady" during LBJ's vice presidency (1961–63), she made 47 trips across the United States and visited 33 foreign countries. After he became president, following the assassination of John F. Kennedy, in November 1963, she lent vocal support to his Great Society policies—including those concerned with civil rights, Medicare, urban development, the "war on poverty," and, especially, federal aid for schools and the preschool Head Start program—and she played a prominent role in his winning election to a full term as president by an overwhelming margin over the Republican Barry Goldwater in 1964. She became best known for what the press described as her "beautifying" projects. With her husband's help she successfully lobbied Congress for passage of the $320 million Highway Beautification Act of 1965, which called for the removal of billboards, the screening of junkyards, and the planting of trees and plants, chiefly wildflowers, along interstate highways. She also raised hundreds of thousands of dollars for her Society for a More Beautiful Capital, which planted millions of flowers throughout the District of Columbia and inspired similar projects in other municipalities. As protests against the war in Vietnam grew, President Johnson's popularity diminished accordingly, leading him to decide against seeking reelection in 1968. When the Republican Richard Nixon succeeded LBJ in the White House, in January 1969, the Johnsons retired to the LBJ Ranch in Stonewall, Texas (now a National Historic Site) and worked at establishing the Lyndon Baines Johnson Library and Museum, which opened on the University of Texas campus at Austin in 1971. Meanwhile, in honor of Lady Bird's campaign to beautify

Washington, Columbia Island on the D.C. side of the Potomac River had been renamed Lady Bird Johnson Park, in 1968. Following LBJ's death, in 1973, 17 acres in the park were set aside for the Lyndon Baines Johnson Memorial Grove. Lady Bird Johnson was also involved in a beautification project in Austin, Texas, where she maintained a second residence. She published *A White House Diary* in 1970, and the documentary film *The First Lady: A Portrait of Lady Bird Johnson* was released in 1981. Near Austin in 1982 she co-founded what has been incorporated into the University of Texas at Austin as the Lady Bird Johnson Wildflower Center. She received both the Presidential Medal of Honor and the Congressional Gold Medal. A stroke in 1993 left her legally blind, and she had difficulty speaking following a second stroke, in 2002. She died of respiratory failure at her home in Austin. Her survivors included her older daughter, Lynda Bird, the wife of the former U.S. senator Charles S. Robb of Virginia; her other daughter, Luci Baines, whose second husband, Ian Turpin, a banker, is president of the Johnson family business, the $150 million LBJ Holding Co.; seven grandchildren; a step-grandchild; and 10 great-grandchildren. See *Current Biography* (1964).

Obituary *New York Times* A p1+ July 12, 2007

KAISER, PHILIP M. July 12, 1913–May 24, 2007 United States government official; diplomat; New York state official; educator. Philip Mayer Kaiser began his career as an economic analyst in the Federal Reserve System (1939–42). During World War II he was chief of planning with the U.S. Foreign Economic Administration. He joined the Department of Labor as an executive assistant concerned with international affairs in 1946 and was director of the department's office of international affairs from 1947 to 1949 and assistant secretary of labor for international affairs from 1949 to 1953. He was U.S. ambassador to Senegal and Mauritania, simultaneously, from 1961 to 1964 and deputy chief of mission at the U.S. Embassy in London from 1964 to 1969. He subsequently served as U.S. ambassador to Hungary (1977–80) and Austria (1980–81). In stints away from federal-government service, he was a special assistant to Governor W. Averell Harriman of New York (1955–56), a professor of international relations at American University (1959–61), and chairman and managing director of *Encyclopedia Britannica* (1969–75). He was also a member of the board of directors of Guinness Mahon Ltd. (1975–77). Kaiser died of pneumonia at Sibley Memorial Hospital in Washington, D.C. His survivors included his wife, Hannah (nee Greeley), three sons, and four grandchildren. See *Current Biography* (1949).

Obituary *New York Times* B p7 May 25, 2007

KAPUŚCIŃSKI, RYSZARD May 4, 1932–Jan. 23, 2007 Polish writer; journalist. Kapuściński was Poland's first internationally celebrated foreign correspondent. Over a period of more than three decades, he covered social and political unrest— including 27 coups and revolutions—in developing countries in Africa, Latin America, and the Middle and Far East. He did so at repeated risk to his own life and on a shoestring budget, which forced him to live frugally,

close to the indigenous people, and thus helped him to chronicle the hard facts of the often turbulent decolonization of the Third World with telling empathy. The cables he sent back to Poland were crisp, clipped models of economy and objectivity in news reportage. By contrast, some of the books he based on his experiences were literary works of art with fantastic elements reminiscent of the magical realism of the novelist Gabriel García Márquez. The book that made him famous internationally was *Cesarz* (1978), translated as *The Emperor: Downfall of an Autocrat* (1983), an impressionistic and mordantly humorous account of the last years of Emperor Haile Selassie of Ethiopia based on the author's interviews with the old emperor's courtiers. Polish readers understood that book to be a veiled allegorical reference to the repressive and sterile Communist regime they were living under at that time. Another symbol of state authoritarianism was the subject of Kapuściński's second book to be translated into English, *Szachinszach* (1982; *Shah of Shahs*, 1985), about Shah Mohammed Reza Pahlavi of Iran and the revolution that replaced his rule with another repressive government, the religious dictatorship of the Ayatollah Khomeini. Again, Poles read that book as a metaphor relevant to their own condition, as Kapuściniski had intended. As a youth, Kapuściński was a member of the Polish Communist Party, which was routine. Following his receipt of an M.A. degree in history at the University of Warsaw, in 1955, he joined the staff of the Polish youth magazine *Sztandar Mlodych*. After he achieved a succès de scandale with a series of reports on exploitative working conditions at Nowa Huta, a vaunted steel factory in southern Poland, the magazine sent him on assignment to India at his request. He subsequently made his first trip to Africa as a correspondent for the weekly *Polityka*. In 1962 he began a 10-year association with the impecunious Polish Press Agency (Polska Aghencja Prasowa) as its solitary international correspondent, and he continued to rove the Third World as a freelance journalist (1972–74) and as a correspondent for the cultural weekly *Kultura* (1974–81), and he subsequently reported from Afghanistan and elsewhere under various auspices. During the 1980s he was closely but unofficially involved with Solidarity, the revolutionary labor movement that brought about the downfall of the Communist regime in Poland. He published more than a dozen books, including *Wojna futbolowa* (1979; The Soccer War, 1971), about explosive civil strife in Latin America, *Imperium* (1993; translated under the same title, 1995), about his travels through the former Soviet Union, and a series of collections of essays under the title *Lapidarium*, issued during the 1990s. Kapuściński and his wife, Alicja (neé Mielczarek), had one daughter. He died in Warsaw, Poland. See *Current Biography* (1992).

Obituary *New York Times* C p14 Jan. 24, 2007

KIRKPATRICK, JEANE Nov. 19, 1926–Dec. 7, 2006 Political scientist; political polemicist; diplomat; professor emeritus, Georgetown University. The neoconservative luminary Jeane J. Kirkpatrick (née Jordan) was arguably President Ronald Reagan's closest and most influential foreign-policy adviser and, as the first American woman to serve as ambassador to the United Nations (1981–85), the truest exponent of Reaganism in international debate. After earning an M.A. degree in political science at Columbia University, doing postgraduate work at the University of Paris, and marrying Evron M. Kirkpatrick, a fellow political scientist, Jeane Kirkpatrick conducted academic research part-time while delaying her full-time academic career for a few years to minister to the needs of her growing family. She taught political science at Trinity College in Washington, D.C., from 1962 to 1967, when she became associate professor of political science at Georgetown University, also in Washington. She earned a doctorate in comparative politics at Columbia University in 1968, was promoted to full professor at Georgetown in 1973, and became a resident scholar at the American Enterprise Institute for Public Policy, a conservative Washington think tank, in 1977. Meanwhile, she was writing prolifically and had been spurred to political activism by her disaffection with the rise of the counterculture and antiwar movements in the 1960s. At that time she was a self-described "Humphrey–Jackson Democrat" and "AFL-CIO Democrat," was generally liberal on domestic issues, prolabor, and in favor of social-welfare programs. As such, she then regarded the Republicans as so preoccupied with private concerns, such as profits and taxes, that they failed to articulate "any conclusive vision of the common good." On the other hand, she held some traditionalist cultural values, and on foreign-policy issues, she was a Cold War hawk. Thus, in 1972 she opposed the McGovern-for-President movement in the Democratic Party, viewing it as a "dovish" and unrealistically utopian embodiment of the counterculture and antiwar movements. She joined with other like-minded Democrats—most of them writers and scholars who would become known as neoconservatives—to form the Coalition for a Democratic Majority, dedicated to reclaiming the Democratic Party from the "antiwar, antigrowth, antibusiness, and antilabor activists." In 1976 she helped found another vanguard neoconservative group, the Committee on the Present Danger, aimed at making Americans "aware of the growth of Soviet military power and the risks posed by the SALT II treaty." She supported Jimmy Carter's successful candidacy for the presidency in 1976 but subsequently grew increasingly critical of President Carter's foreign policy. In the November 1979 issue of *Commentary* magazine, she published "Dictatorships and Double Standards," the article that brought her to the attention of Ronald Reagan. In that article she denounced the Carter administration's policy of undermining pro-American right-wing autocracies in the world, especially in Central and South America, while ignoring or treating benignly pro-Soviet dictatorships that were, she asserted, more totalitarian in their suppression of human rights, less efficient economically, and less likely to evolve into democracies. As the U.S. permanent representative to the U.N. beginning with the inauguration of President Reagan in January 1981, Kirkpatrick had Cabinet rank and was a member of Reagan's National Security Planning Group, where she argued for the invasion of Grenada and the support of such groups as the Contras in Nicaragua and the anti-

Soviet rebels in Afghanistan. She participated in the Iran-Contra affair and the discussions leading to the withdrawal of the U.S. military presence from Lebanon following the Jihadist suicide massacre of 250 Marines in their barracks in Beirut in October 1983. In her most shining moment on the floor of the U.N., she read the roster of names of those being held as political prisoners in the Soviet Union, an act that made her "name known in every cell in the Gulag," as Andrei Sakharov reported. As she had promised, she served at the U.N. only through President Reagan's first term in the White House, resigning in the spring of 1985. Later in the same year, she changed her political party registration from Democrat to Republican. She continued to serve as an informal adviser to President Reagan during his second term. In 1986 she returned to Georgetown University, where she remained a professor until 2002. In 1990 she became president of the Helen Dwight Reid Educational Foundation. Among the books she published are *The Strategy of Deception: A Study in World-Wide Communist Tactics* (1963), *A Study of Peronist Argentina* (1971), *Political Woman* (1974), *The Withering Away of the Totalitarian State—and Other Surprises* (1990), and the essay collections *Human Rights and American Foreign Policy* (1982) and *Dictatorships and Double Standards* (1982). She was a senior fellow at the American Enterprise Institute until her death. She died of congestive heart failure at her home in Bethesda, Maryland. She was predeceased by her husband, Evron (better known as Kirk), and her son Douglas. Her survivors included her sons John Evron and Stuart Alan. See *Current Biography* (1981).

Obituary *New York Times* A p1+ Dec. 9, 2006

KLEPPE, THOMAS S. July 1, 1919–Mar. 2, 2007 U.S. government official. Thomas Savig Kleppe was a two-term Republican representative from North Dakota's Second Congressional District (1967–71), and he later served as administrator of the federal Small Business Administration (1971–75) under presidents Richard M. Nixon and Gerald R. Ford and as secretary of the interior (1975–77) in President Ford's Cabinet. In Congress Kleppe usually voted with the conservative coalition; at the Small Business Administration, he was credited with raising to 80 percent the contracts awarded to minority businesses and raising the number of banks accepting SBA business loans from 8 percent of the national total of banks to 70 percent; as secretary of the interior, he promoted a cautious development of the country's natural resources. Kleppe was a warrant officer in the U.S. Army during World War II. After the war he joined the Gold Seal Co.—a small concern founded by a family friend to manufacture the product Glass Wax (and, later, such products as Mr. Bubble and Snowy Bleach); he worked his way up from bookkeeper to president (1958–64). From 1964 to 1966 he was a vice president and director of Dain, Kalmar & Quail, a Minneapolis-based investment-banking firm. Meanwhile his career in elective politics had begun when he was elected to a four-year term as mayor of Bismarck, North Dakota, in 1950. He was an unsuccessful candidate for the U.S. Senate twice, in 1964 and 1970. After the death of his first wife, Frieda, Kleppe married Glendora Loew Gompf, a widow, who survived him. His other survivors included a son and daughter from his first marriage, a daughter and stepdaughter from his second marriage, 11 grandchildren, and four great-grandchildren. He died at his home in Bethesda, Maryland. See *Current Biography* (1976).

Obituary *New York Times* C p10 Mar. 10, 2007

KOLLEK, TEDDY May 27, 1911–Jan. 1, 2007 Legendary six-term mayor of Jerusalem, Israel (1965–93). With his down-to-earth charisma and his pragmatic and energetic hands-on stewardship, Theodor Kollek, universally known as Teddy, presided over the reunification of Israel's capital city, developed it into a modern-day metropolis, and fostered coexistence among its diverse populations. Kollek "strove to improve the lives of all the residents of Jerusalem and saw each of them—Jewish, Muslim, or Christian—as a partner in making Jerusalem a beacon of hope," as Ruth Chesin, president of the Jerusalem Foundation, observed in a eulogy. The Jerusalem Foundation was established by Kollek for the purpose of raising funds for the city's development. A pioneer Labor Zionist and an aide to David Ben-Gurion, he had participated in the founding of Israel and the formation of its foreign-intelligence service. Born in Budapest, Hungary, and raised in Vienna, Austria, he embraced Zionist goals at an early age. After immigrating to what was then British-controlled Palestine, in the mid-1930s, he honed his leadership skills in a kibbutz and joined the left-wing Mapai, or Workers Party, the forerunner of Israel's Labor Party. In the late 1930s he began working with the Haganah, the paramilitary arm of the Mapai that would, along with the Palmach, evolve into the post-independence Israeli Defense Forces. In contrast to the Irgun, the paramilitary arm of the center-right Herut Party, the Haganah often worked in cooperation with the British in its efforts to rescue Jews in Europe and the Middle East and to establish a Jewish homeland in Palestine. After the outbreak of World War II, Kollek went to London and joined the political department of the Jewish Agency, the embryo of the Israeli government-in-making, headed by the Mapai/Haganah leader David Ben-Gurion, who would become modern Israel's first prime minister. Later in the war, stationed in Istanbul, Turkey, Kollek was a liaison between Allied intelligence personnel and Jewish underground groups in Europe and the Near East. After the war he facilitated the settlement of thousands of displaced European Jews in Palestine. In 1947 he traveled to the United States to oversee the surreptitious acquisition of arms and planes for the Haganah. After the establishment of the state of Israel, in 1948, he remained in Washington, D.C., first as a liaison of the Israeli Foreign Ministry with the U.S. Central Intelligence Agency and subsequently as Israeli ambassador (1951–52). In 1952 he was summoned to Jerusalem to become director general of Prime Minister Ben-Gurion's office, a position he held until his election as mayor of Jerusalem in 1965. As mayor he initially had jurisdiction only over Jewish West Jerusalem, where he "signaled his ambitions . . . by founding the Israel Museum," as an anonymous obituary writer observed in the American edition of the *Economist* (January 13, 2007). "But history dropped an opportunity in his lap. After Israel captured [Jordanian] east Jerusalem . . . in the 1967 war, he had another vision: he would reunite the divided city into a multicultural 'mosaic,' like the Vienna of his youth. . . . His excellent relations with the local mukhtars and his emphasis on 'pluralism' put him well to the left of most of his Jewish voters. Nonetheless, they five times elected him." (Residents of East Jerusalem did not have citizenship, and Arabs with citizenship persistently boycotted the polls.) In reuniting the city Kollek rebuilt its infrastructure (including the Jewish Quarter in East Jerusalem's Old City), provided it with parks and promenades, planted trees and gardens, and constructed civic, community, cultural, and recreational centers, including the Teddy Stadium, the Biblical Zoo, the Cinematheque, the Kahn Theater, and the Jerusalem Theater. He did so chiefly with money he raised abroad through his Jerusalem Foundation. In his early years as mayor, he made daily inspection tours of the city on foot and without bodyguards; in later years he was chauffeured through the city streets early every morning as he noted potholes to be filled, trash bins to be emptied, and whatever else needed to be done. Beginning with the first intifada, in 1987, repercussions of the Palestinian uprising affected civil harmony in Jerusalem. While not as severe as in Romallah or Gaza, outbreaks of violence in Arab sections of the city caused changes in patterns of living, discouraged tourism (the city's chief industry), and set in motion a tide of emigration from the city. In the mayoral election of 1993, Kollek was defeated by Ehud Olmert, a member of the Likud, Israel's leading conservative party. (In 2006, after two terms as mayor, Olmert was elected prime minister of Israel.) After stepping down as mayor, Kollek concentrated on his fund-raising work with the Jerusalem Foundation. When a Hamas terrorist cell was discovered in Jerusalem in August 2002, he concluded that Israel could no longer control East Jerusalem and, in a change of heart, called for a division of the city. Palestinians should be given control over some neighborhoods, including disputed holy sites in the Old City, he explained, because "you can't achieve calm if you don't give them part of what they want and can control." Kollek died in the Hod Yerushalayim retirement home in the Kiryat Yovel neighborhood of Jerusalem. He was survived by his wife, Tamar (nee Schwartz), his son, Amos, his daughter, Osnat, and five grandchildren. See *Current Biography* (1993).

Obituary *New York Times* A p18 Jan. 3, 2007

KUHN, BOWIE Oct. 28, 1926–Mar. 15, 2007 Lawyer; sports administrator. Bowie Kent Kuhn was commissioner of Major League Baseball from February 1969 through September 1984. As a member of the New York law firm of Willkie, Farr & Gallagher in the 1950s and 1960s, Kuhn served as legal counsel for a number of major-league teams, and in 1968 he represented the National League club owners in their negotiations with the Major League Players Association, which was threatening to strike if its pension demands were not met. The owners of the 20 major-league franchises unanimously elected him commissioner of baseball following the termination of those negotiations, and he was elected to a second term following the 1975 season. During his tenure as commissioner, the number of major-league teams expanded to 26, and there was a huge rise in both attendance at games and the market value of franchises. Television revenues soared when, chiefly thanks to him, the staging of the World Series was changed from afternoons to evenings, to coincide with prime-time TV broadcasting slots. Kuhn suspended a number of players for involvement with drugs or gambling, and he sometimes ruled against owners. For example, at one point he suspended George Steinbrenner, the owner of the New York Yankees, for 15 months for making illegal political contributions, and he fined or reprimanded Charles O. Finley, the owner of the Oakland Athletics, several times. He dealt with several strikes called by the Major League Players Association and with the dispute over the "reserve clause," the paragraph in every major-league player's contract allowing the team's owners automatically to renew the contract. Traditionally, the clause was invoked indefinitely by owners, keeping players in virtual indentured servitude, to be kept, sold, traded, or released at the will of the owners. Kuhn sided with the owners on that issue. When the outfielder Curt Flood was traded by St. Louis to Philadelphia following the 1969 season, he asked Kuhn to intervene and declare him a free agent. Kuhn declined, and Flood launched a legal suit, which progressed to the U.S. Supreme Court, which ruled against Flood in 1972. Two years later, when there was a similar contract dispute between the pitcher Catfish Hunter and Charles O. Finley, an independent arbitrator ruled in Hunter's favor. A federal judge ruled in favor of free agency in a contract dispute in February 1976, and later that year free agency was locked into the collective-bargaining agreement reached between owners and players. Following the 1982 season, Kuhn failed to win enough owner support in his bid for a third seven-year term, to begin in 1983, but he remained in office during the search for his successor. He left office on October 1, 1984, when Peter Ueberroth replaced him. He returned to the law firm of Willkie, Farr & Gallagher and became president of the Kent Group, a business, sports, and financial consulting firm. In January 1988 he and Harvey Myerson formed the New York law firm of Myerson & Kuhn; they filed for bankruptcy in December 1989. Kuhn then moved from New York to Florida. In his last years he was a member of the boards of directors of Domino's Pizza and the Ave Maria Foundation and chairman of the board of Ave Maria Mutual Funds. He died in a hospital in Ponte Vedra Beach, Florida, of complications from pneumonia. His survivors included his wife, Luisa, a son, a daughter, and two stepsons. See *Current Biography* (1970).

Obituary *New York Times* C p10 Mar. 16, 2007

L'ENGLE, MADELEINE Nov. 29, 1918–Sep. 6, 2007
Author. Madeleine L'Engle (née Camp) was a prolific writer with a wide-ranging oeuvre that included four collections of poetry, some plays, four memoirs, several books of essays on religious themes and the arts, including the writing life and mythmaking, and, most prominently, more than a score of novels, a number of which are in the fantasy or science-fiction genres. Although she insisted that she never wrote for or with "any age group in mind," L'Engle is commonly remembered as the author of children's and young-adult fiction. She is most celebrated for the classic *A Wrinkle in Time* (1962), an adventure story in cosmic spiritual warfare that won the American Library Association's Newbery Medal for best American children's book in 1963, has sold more than eight million copies through 69 printings, and is widely ranked in its genre with C. S. Lewis's *Chronicles of Narnia*. The protagonist is Meg Murry (one of the author's several fictional alter egos), a 12-year-old who, motivated by love and accompanied by her telepathic younger brother, Charles, and her friend Calvin O'Keefe, embarks on a magical, sometimes harrowing intergalactic journey. Assisted by three stellar guides, she and her companions pass through the fourth-dimension gateway called the tesseract—the wrinkle in time—and thence proceed through time as well as space to rescue her physicist father, who is captive on Camazotz, a populated distant planet where society is controlled by a dark spiritual entity, a demonic, disembodied brain. By her own account, only after *A Wrinkle in Time* was written did she understand the meanings of parts of it. In an interview for the *National Catholic Reporter* in 1986, she said that the novel reflected the actual "modern world in which children know about brainwashing and the corruption of evil"; that it was "based on Einstein's theory of relativity and Planck's quantum theory"; and that it was "good solid science but also good solid theology." Meg Murry's adventures were continued in four sequels to *A Wrinkle in Time*. In a spin-off series, beginning with *The Arm of the Starfish* (1965), Meg and Calvin O'Keefe are married and the parents of a new generation of adventurers. The O'Keefe family novels are for the most part romantic suspense stories set in exotic places in the real world. Madeleine L'Engle Camp was born in Manhattan and grew up there, in Western Europe, and in South Carolina. She was seminally influenced by the fairy tales and fantasy novels of George MacDonald. After earning a B.A. degree in English at Smith College, she worked in theater in New York City while writing stories. She dropped her original surname when she began publishing some of the stories in small-circulation magazines. In 1945 she published her first book, *The Small Rain*, a poignant semiautobiographical novel about the coming of age of the character Katherine Forrester in a boarding school in Switzerland, in France, and back in her native New York City. Thirty-seven years later, again semiautobiographically, L'Engle updated Katherine's life through middle age in the sequel *A Severed Wasp*. Following *Ilsa* (1946), an adult novel about the travail of a woman who marries into a traditional southern family, she took a lighthearted approach to boarding-school life in her first so-called children's novel, *And Both Were Young* (1949). She created a teenage protagonist facing imminent adulthood with bewilderment in *Camilla Dickinson* (1951) and took that character into later life in *A Live Coal in the Sea* (1996). After a publishing hiatus of nine years, she introduced another young heroine, Vicky Austin, in *Meet the Austins* (1960), the first of five generally re-

alistic and upbeat novels about a close-knit and loving family. In 1972 she published *A Circle of Quiet*, her first book of nonfiction and the first of her memoirs. For many years she lived alternately in Goshen, Connecticut, and Manhattan, where she was a volunteer librarian and the writer-in-residence at the Episcopal Cathedral of St. John the Divine. As a Christian, she found it difficult to understand the vehement attacks launched against *A Wrinkle in Time* by fundamentalist adherents of her own faith who perceived it to be a pernicious mixture of mythology and the occult with Christian theology. For a number of years, *Wrinkle* was the most banned book in the United States. It was adapted into a made-for-television movie, first broadcast on the ABC network in 2004. L'Engle died in a nursing home in Litchfield, Connecticut. She was predeceased by her husband, the actor Hugh Franklin, and by her son, Bion, and survived by her daughters, Josephine and Maria (whom she and her husband had adopted after the deaths of Maria's parents), five grandchildren, and five great-grandchildren. See *Current Biography* (1997).

Obituary *New York Times* A p13 Sep. 8, 2007

LAINE, FRANKIE Mar. 30, 1913–Feb. 6, 2007 Singer. An energetic live performer and a best-selling recording artist, Frankie Laine was one of the most popular American pop singers in the pre–rock-and-roll era, and his career remained robust through seven decades. Among his multitude of hit singles (on many of which he was co-lyricist), he is probably most closely identified with the songs "Mule Train" and "Rawhide," the theme tune sung by him on the CBS television Western series of the same name (1955–66). Moviegoers have heard his voice on numerous soundtracks, including those of the mock Western *Blazing Saddles* (1974) and the straight Westerns *Man Without a Star* (1955), *3:10 to Yuma* (1957), and *Gunfight at the OK Corral* (1957). As a recording artist, he sold more than 100 million records. The oldest of eight children of Sicilian immigrants, Laine was born Francesco Paolo LoVecchio in Chicago, Illinois. Relatively early in his career, he changed not only his name but his vocal style—from smooth balladeering to distinctive dramatic phrasing. Using his voice, as he said, "like a horn," he concentrated on "the pulse, the beat," not singing a note directly but "bending" it, stressing the rhythmic downbeat. After performing with Freddy Carlone's band in Cleveland, he moved to Los Angeles, where he earned money singing in the background of motion pictures and occasionally performed gratis at Billy Berg's, a club on Sunset Boulevard and Vine Street in Hollywood. It was at Billy Berg's in 1946 that his big break came, when the composer Hoagy Carmichael discovered him. Soon he was in demand at Las Vegas hotels and other choice rooms on the nightclub circuit and under contract to Mercury Records. His first Mercury release was also his first Gold Record, "That's My Desire," which almost immediately reached the number-one spot on the R&B charts—as a result of which he was at first assumed to be black—and gradually climbed up the mainstream pop charts. In a poll of radio disk jockeys in October 1947, "That's My Desire" ranked number

three among their favorites, and Laine's subsequent single "Black and Blue" ranked number 15. His early recordings at Mercury were done with bands conducted by Carl Fischer—with whom he wrote "We'll Be Together Again"—and with several jazz musicians. He found an ideal collaborator in the band leader Mitch Miller, who took charge of artists and repertory at Mercury in 1948. The first Laine/Miller collaboration, "That Lucky Old Sun," Laine's fifth gold record, was the number-one song on the pop charts until it was surpassed by their second, "Mule Train," which sold 1.4 million copies. Other Laine/Miller hits on the Mercury label included "Shine," which sold 1.1 million copies, and "Sunny Side of the Street," which sold almost a million. Miller moved to Columbia Records in 1950, and Laine joined him there in 1951. Under his contract with Columbia, Laine was the highest-paid recording artist in the industry until Elvis Presley signed a more lucrative contract with RCA, in 1956. In the early 1950s Laine dominated the pop charts with such singles as "Jezebel," "Rose, Rose, I Love You," "I Believe," "Jealousy," "Hey Joe," and his covers of "High Noon," "Cool Water," and "Your Cheatin' Heart." His other hits during that period included "The Girl in the Woods," "When You're in Love," "Granada," "Someday," "A Woman in Love," and "Moonlight Gambler." As a member of duets, he had hits with singers including Patti Page, Doris Day, and, above all, Jo Stafford, with whom he recorded many chart-toppers, including "Way Down Yonder in New Orleans" and "Hey, Good Lookin'." During 12 years with Columbia, he had a total of 39 hit singles, many of which were included in his *Greatest Hits* album (1957). He later recorded *Jazz Spectacular*, *Rockin'*, and *Hell Bent for Leather*, among other LPs. His last Columbia album, *Wanderlust*, included the cut "De Glory Road," a personal favorite of his. Between 1949 and 1956 Laine was cast as himself singing in seven motion-picture musicals, including *Sunny Side of the Street* (1951) and *Meet Me in Las Vegas* (1956). On television he was a guest singer on many variety shows, a singer or actor in episodes of a number of dramatic series and sitcoms, and the host of several summertime replacement variety programs, including *Frankie Laine Time* (CBS, 1955–56) and the *Frankie Laine Show* (syndicated, 1957). After he left Columbia Records, he signed with Capital Records, in 1963. With ABC Records beginning in the late 1960s, he made the charts with singles including "I'll Take Care of Your Cares," "Making Memories," and "Lord You Gave Me a Mountain." Following a brief stint at Amos Records, he founded his own label, Score Records. Among his last albums were *Wheels of a Dream* (1998), *Old Man Jazz* (2002), and *The Nashville Connection* (2004). His greatest recordings have been reissued on many compact disks, among them the three-CD set *That's My Desire*. With Joseph F. Laredo, he wrote the autobiography *That Lucky Old Son* (1993). Laine was active in civil rights and children's charities. He was married to Nan Grey from 1950 until her death, in 1993, and to Marcie Ann Kline from 1999 until his death. He died of heart failure in San Diego, California. His survivors included his stepdaughters Jan Steiger and Pam Donner, the children of his first wife from a previous marriage. See *Current Biography* (1956).

Obituary *New York Times* A p17 Feb. 7, 2007

LEDERLE, JOHN May 26, 1912–Feb. 13, 2007 Educator; lawyer. The high point of John William Lederle's career was his 10-year (1960–70) presidency of the University of Massachusetts, that school's period of greatest growth, from a small rural land-grant institution to a world-class research university. Lederle, who had degrees in political science and law, worked during the first two decades of his career in a wide variety of positions, from member of a Detroit law firm and congressional consultant to assistant professor at Brown University and organizer and director of the Institute of Public Administration at the University of the Philippines. At the University of Michigan, his alma mater, he was a professor of political science for many years and served in several administrative posts, including director of the university's Institute of Public Administration (1950–60). Leaving Michigan, he assumed the presidency of the University of Massachusetts at Amherst in September 1960. During his tenure as president of UMass—as it is familiarly known—he obtained unprecedented state funding and federal research dollars for the state university, and its budget grew by 700 percent. The university's offering of academic programs was greatly expanded, especially at the graduate level; the student body (numbering less than 6,000 when he arrived) tripled; the number of faculty increased from 366 to 1,157; and faculty salaries rose, doubling in the advanced academic programs. The erection of approximately 50 major buildings was completed or begun on the Amherst campus, including those housing the Research Computing Center, the Radio Astronomy Observatory, the Polymer Research Institute, the Water Resources Research Center, the Labor Relations Research Center, a graduate research tower, and a new library (to accommodate a quadrupling of the number of book acquisitions). A public radio station and a university press were established. In addition, the university system was expanded beyond the flagship campus in Amherst to include a Boston campus and a medical school in Worcester. After his retirement as president of UMass, in 1970, Lederle remained on the faculty as Joseph B. Ely professor of government until 1982. The Lederle Graduate Research Center, on the Amherst campus, was named in his honor in 1983. In retirement, he lived in Naples, Florida, where he died of heart failure at Naples Community Hospital. He was survived by his wife, Angie Lederle, a daughter, a son, and a grandson. See *Current Biography* (1961).

Obituary *New York Times* A p21 Feb. 22, 2007

LEVERT, GERALD July 13, 1966–Nov. 10, 2006 Rhythm-and-blues singer, songwriter, and producer. Gerald Levert, one of R&B's most popular vocalists for a score of years beginning in the mid-1980s, delivered his soulful songs in a powerful baritone voice, ranging from gruff and sultry to fiery in tone. With his rendition of such romantic ballads as "Made to Love Ya," "Baby I'm Ready," "That's What Love Is," "Already Missing You," and "My Forever Love," he especially appealed to a strong following of female fans, who nicknamed him "G-Bear" and to whom he would toss teddy bears (moist with his own perspiration, à la Elvis Presley) during his live performances. Born in Philadelphia, Pennsylvania, he was the second of four children of Eddie Levert, the founder and frontman of the Cleveland-based soul vocal trio the O'Jays. While still a teenager he teamed up with his younger brother Sean and his friend Marc Gordon (with whom he co-wrote many of his songs) to form the trio LeVert and record *I Get Hot* (1985). Among the cuts on that album was "I'm Still," which he co-wrote with his father. The LeVert trio's second album, *Bloodline* (1986), spun off the hit single "(Pop, Pop, Pop, Pop) Goes My Mind." That song, the first of the trio's recordings to saturate the urban radio airwaves, reached number one on *Billboard*'s R&B charts. LeVert's third album, *The Big Throwdown* (1987), went gold, with more than $1 million in sales and more than 500,000 copies sold, and it spawned several Top 10 singles, including "Casanova" (written by the Calloway brothers), which crossed over to the pop charts. The trio's gold disc *Just Coolin'* (1988) included the number-one R&B track "Addicted to You," which Levert co-wrote with his father. With *Rope a Dope Style* (1990), the trio again went gold and realized a number-one R&B single with "Baby I'm Ready." In the early 1990s Levert recorded two hit singles—"I Swear" and "I'd Give Anything"—written by the pop composer/producer David Foster. The second of the two went platinum, with sales of two million copies. Levert and his father recorded the number-one R&B single "Baby Hold On to Me" in 1992 and the album *Father and Son* in 1995. With *For Real Tho'* (1993) the LeVert trio yet again went gold. The trio's seventh and last album, *The Whole Scenario*, released in 1997, was a blend of pop, hip-hop, and traditional soul and had contributions from several rap artists. With Keith Sweat and Johnny Gill, Gerald Levert recorded the albums *Levert.Sweat.Gill* (1997)—a platinum crossover work that included the track "My Body"—and *LSG2* (2003). Over the years he performed from time to time alongside such artists as Barry White, R. Kelly, Patti LaBelle, Kelly Price, and the Rude Boys. He also did much songwriting and producing for others, including LaBelle, Anita Baker, the O'Jays, and Teddy Pendergrass, and he co-founded the Travel Production Co. Inc., located in Cleveland Heights, Ohio. (As of late 2006 Andy Gibson remained in charge of the company as well as its companion R&B Foundation.) Most of the songs on Levert's first solo album, *Private Line* (1991), were written in collaboration with Edwin "Tony" Nicholas. That record went platinum and reached number one on the R&B charts, as did the title track, a dance number. Five of his subsequent solo albums—*Groove On* (1995), *Love and Consequences* (1998), *G* (1999), *Gerald's World* (2001), and *The G Spot* (2002)—all reached number two in the R&B listings, and several crossed over into the Top 10 on the pop charts. *Stroke of Genius* (2003) reached number one in the R&B listings and number six on the pop charts. *Do I Speak for the World* (2004) reached number seven on the R&B charts. *Voices* was released in 2005, and Levert's final solo CD was scheduled for release early in 2007. At the time of his death, Levert had been working on a book with his father, in collaboration with Lyah LaFlore, and on a reality television show in which he and 12 of his female fans were in a weight-loss competition. He died in his sleep, apparently of a heart attack, at his home in Newbury, a neighborhood bordering Cleveland Heights. He was pronounced dead at Geauga Community Hospital in suburban Cleveland. His survivors included several children (as many as five, according to some sources). See *Current Biography* (2003).

Obituary *New York Times* C p10 Nov. 11, 2006

LEWITT, SOL Sep. 9, 1928–Apr. 8, 2007 Sculptor and graphic artist. With the seemingly simple geometry of his posters, pen-and-ink and other graphics on paper, books of photographs, and especially his brightly colored wall paintings (which he called drawings) and the sculptures he called "structures," Sol LeWitt bridged the gap between the minimalist movement in art, in which he was initially involved, and conceptualism, in which he was a pioneer. As Michael Kimmelman, a *New York Times* art critic, observed, LeWitt "reduced art to a few of the most basic shapes (quadrilaterals, spheres, triangles), colors (red, yellow, blue, black), and types of lines, and organized them by guidelines he felt in the end free to bend." In *Art forum* (April 1967), LeWitt published the manifesto "Paragraphs on Conceptual Art," in which he stressed the importance of the initial idea and the planning behind his art and the "perfunctory" nature of its execution. To him, the idea and the planning were equivalent to simple directions that could be carried out just as well by others—as they sometimes were. For example, none of the wall drawings included in a four-decade LeWitt retrospective at the San Francisco Museum of Modern Art in 2000 were executed by LeWitt himself. He also engaged in what he viewed as interdisciplinary "collaboration," famously with musicians and dancers and less so with authors. LeWitt was educated at Syracuse University (B.F.A. degree, 1949) and the Cartoonists and Illustrators School (now the School of Visual Arts) in Manhattan. Early in his career, in the 1950s, he worked briefly as a designer at *Seventeen* magazine, a graphic artist in I. M. Pei's architectural firm, and a receptionist and information clerk at the Museum of Modern Art in New York City. Russian constructivism was one of the formative influences on his art. With other minimalists—although the term had not yet been invented—he revolted against the "mushiness"—psychologically charged drippings and brushwork and gestural forms of abstract expressionism—that had gained mainstream dominance in the 1950s. In contrast, he sought to create simple, impersonal forms. Inspired by Eadweard Muybridge's frame-by-frame, instantaneous, sequential photographs of animals and humans in motion, he began creating series of sequential, angled drawings, prints, and photographs before turning his mind and hand in 1962 to sequential three-dimensional "structures," including geometric reliefs and box forms, often in repetition. Thenceforth sequence or seriality, implying the passage of time or the progress of narrative, would be one of his major fascinations, along with transformation and permutation. His six-foot-square steel "Modular Cube" (1965–66) set the pattern for his later structures. One of his most important works is *Variations of Incomplete Open Cubes* (1974), a serial assemblage of 122 variations on cubic form intended to involve the

spectator in the task of mentally completing the series. From the cube shape he went on to create freestanding modular pieces, including such large outdoor structures as those installed in Dag Hammarskjold Plaza at the United Nations in Manhattan in 1976. Meanwhile, his massive and "jazzy" (as Michael Kimmelman described them) wall drawings—rendered directly on walls at first in pencil, crayon, colored pencil, and ink washes and finally in acrylic paint—evolved from straight and parallel lines to configurations of squares, arcs, triangles, and circles. In keeping with his concept of the artist as "a thinker and originator of ideas rather than a craftsman," he provided schematic drawings and notes that contributed to the composition and performances of aleatory and serial music by Philip Glass and Steve Reich and the performance art of Laurie Anderson. He also collaborated with the choreographer/dancer Lucinda Childs, creating the rectilinear (black grid on white floor cloth) décor for her performance of her *Dance* (with music by Philip Glass), presented at the Brooklyn Academy of Music in November 1979. An unusual reprise of that event took place at the Kitchen performance center in Manhattan in April 2002. In an assessment for the *Dance Insider* (April 25, 2002, on-line), Chris Dohse wrote, "Lucinda Childs inhabits the immaculate geometry of Sol LeWitt's 1979 film *Dance* like an angel dancing on the head of a pin . . . Childs also ghosts herself, dancing live behind the scrim upon which LeWitt's film is projected. Her repetitive skips, steps and small jetes done in the now . . . correspond nonchalantly to filmed cadences and parabolas." Childs also credited LeWitt as collaborator when she performed her dance *Mayday* in Milan, Italy, in June 1989. LeWitt was one of the founders of Printed Matter, an organization devoted to the dissemination of artists' books at reasonable prices. He himself published 64 books and booklets, including the volumes *Photogrids* (1977), a collection of his photographs of sewer covers and other examples of urban geometry; *Brick Wall* (1977), a collection of hundreds of close-up photographs of a wall under changing atmospheric conditions; and *Autobiography* (1980), a 1,116-photo inventory of every nook and cranny of his Manhattan loft. Most of the other publications are slim booklets limited to photos of specific works, such as *Six Geometric Figures and All Their Combinations* (1980). LeWitt died in New York City. He was survived by his wife, Carol, and two daughters. Following his death, the Museum of Contemporary Art in Chicago ran an exhibition "in memoriam" that included his series *Suite of 16 in Color*. See *Current Biography* (1986).

Obituary *New York Times* A p15 Apr. 9, 2007

LUSTIGER, JEAN-MARIE Sep. 17, 1926–Aug. 5, 2007 Jewish-born French Roman Catholic prelate; archbishop emeritus of Paris (1981–2005); a member of the Vatican's College of Cardinals. Cardinal Lustiger, a protégé of and adviser to Pope John Paul II, was a staunch defender of Catholic doctrinal orthodoxy and traditional values against the tides of liberalism, relativism, materialism, and secularism, which had reduced the number of practicing Catholics in France (once "the eldest daughter of the

Church") to less than 5 percent of the population. Like John Paul II, Lustiger combined his conservatism in matters of faith and morals with ecumenical openness, seeking dialogue with other faiths, including Islam, condemning anti-Semitism, and promoting reconciliation with Judaism. Lustiger, who was fluent in Yiddish, was born in Paris to Jewish shopkeepers who had emigrated from Poland. He was the paternal grandson of a Silesian rabbi—after whom he was named Aaron—but his parents were nonpracticing Jews. The process of his religious conversion—or "crystallization," as he viewed it—began when he came across a Christian Bible in 1937, when he was 10. In the spring of 1940, on the eve of the German occupation of Paris, his parents sent him to live with a Catholic family in Orleans, 80 miles south of Paris, where he was baptized in August 1940, adding the name Jean-Marie to his given name. Seeing Christianity as "the fruit of Judaism," he felt not that he was denying his Jewish identity but rather that he was becoming "a fulfilled Jew" with "a dual affiliation." His father managed to escape the Nazi pogrom in France by going underground, but in 1942 his mother was sent to the Auschwitz-Birkenau complex of concentration/extermination camps near the town of Auschwitz, Germany (which had been the Polish town of Oswieçim before German annexation), where she was put to death in 1943. Lustiger graduated from the University of Paris with a degree in literature in 1946. He began his studies for the priesthood at the Carmelite seminary in Paris in 1946 and later earned degrees in philosophy and theology at the Catholic Institute of Paris. After his ordination to the priesthood, in 1954, he was assigned to the University of Paris as chaplain (1954–59) and subsequently for 10 years as director of the Richelieu Center, a campus Catholic facility devoted to training chaplains for universities and other schools throughout France. From 1969 to 1979 he was vicar in the parish of Sainte Jeanne de Chantal in Paris. Pope John Paul II appointed him bishop of Orléans in 1979 and promoted him to archbishop of Paris in 1981. His status as head of France's principal archdiocese was enhanced when the pope named him a cardinal, a "prince of the church," in 1983. To the Paris archdiocese he attracted an increased number of applicants for the priesthood, and he tightened the orthodoxy of their training as seminarians. Always intent on giving the church a voice in the public forum, he established a Catholic radio station and television station. Outside of the Paris archdiocese, his power was limited by failure of his fellow French bishops to elect him to head their national conference, but he nevertheless played successful leadership roles in opposing the French government's plan to secularize Catholic schools and in forcing the resignation of Bishop Jacques Gaillot of Evreux in accordance with the wishes of the Vatican. He was one of the few French bishops who refused to defend the French church's modernized catechism *Pierres Vivantes* (Living Stones) when it was attacked by Pope John Paul II's guardian of doctrinal orthodoxy, Joseph Cardinal Ratzinger (who would become Pope Benedict XVI) in 1983. Lustiger was made a member of the Académie Française in 1995. His books include those published in translation as *The Mass* (1987) and *First Steps in Prayer* (1987); *Le Choix de*

Dieu (1987), a book of conversations, translated by Rebecca Howell Balinski as *Choosing God, Chosen by God* (1991); and *La Promesse* (The Promise), a collection of meditations, published in 2002. Lustiger retired as archbishop of Paris in 2005. He died of cancer at a medical center in Paris. As he planned, his funeral at Notre Dame Cathedral in Paris included two rites. Outside the cathedral, before the Catholic service inside, his cousin Jonas Moses Lustiger placed earth from Israel on his coffin, and another cousin, Arno Lustiger, recited Kaddish. During a visit to Australia in 2001, Lustiger was quoted in the Australian press as saying, "I was born Jewish, and so I remain, even if that is unacceptable to many. For me, the vocation of Israel is bringing light to the goyim. That is my hope, and I believe that Christianity is the means for achieving it." In writing his own epitaph, he echoed that statement, saying that he had remained Jewish "as did the Apostles." See *Current Biography* (1984).

Obituary *New York Times* B p7 Aug. 6, 2007

MAHFOUZ, NAGUIB Dec. 11, 1911–Aug. 30, 2006 Egyptian author. The novelist and short-story writer Naguib Mahfouz (spelled Najib Mafuz in Arabic) was an ecumenical, humane, truth-pursuing observer of the life around him, a writer worthy of the soubriquets "the Dickens of the Cairo cafés," "the Balzac of Egypt," and "the Naipaul of the Nile." Early in his career Mahfouz applied his talents as a novelist to ancient Egyptian history, but his reputation rests chiefly on his subsequent works—especially the masterpiece known as the Cairo Trilogy—in which he chronicled with rich and vivid detail the tumultuous development of his country during the 20th century and the lives of a range of middle- and lower-class characters in teeming Cairo trying to cope with social modernization and ambivalence between traditional Arab/Islamic values and the lure of Western lifestyles. Long regionally regarded as the preeminent Arabic novelist of his time, Mahouz finally gained international recognition when he received the Nobel Prize in literature, in 1988. In awarding the prize to Mahfouz—the first Arabic writer to be so honored—the Swedish Academy cited him for having formed "through works rich in nuance—now clear-sightedly realistic, now evocatively ambiguous . . . an Arabian narrative art that applies to all mankind." In his presentation speech for the prize, Sture Allen pointed out that the excellence of Mahfouz's fiction was "the result of a synthesis of classical Arabic tradition, European inspiration, and personal artistry." Mahfouz himself said that when he decided to become a writer he "sat down to study literature systematically, century by century." Open to Western as well as Arabic and other Eastern literary traditions, he read widely in several languages, proceeding, as he said, from the classics of Russian, French, and British realistic and naturalistic fiction to "such recent new departures as the expressionism of Kafka, the stream-of-consciousness realism of Joyce, and the annihilation of time in Proust." The major formative influences on his thought included the Fabian socialism of the Egyptian intellectual Salama Musa and the philosophy of Sufism. Mahfouz grew up in the Gamilya, the picturesque medieval quarter of

Cairo where much of his fiction is set. After earning a degree in philosophy at the University of Cairo (then called King Fuad I University), in the early 1930s, he supported himself in part with steady incomes he earned as secretary at the university (briefly), as a journalist, and as a civil servant. In 1939 he entered the Egyptian government bureaucracy, and he remained employed there for more than 30 years in successive influential positions in ministries and agencies concerned with religion and culture, including Islamic mortmain, the cinema, and art. In the mid-1930s he began writing short stories in a style influenced in part by de Maupassant and Chekhov, among others. Those stories anticipated his longer works of fiction in their combination of surface detail and psychological depth. In 1938 his first collection of short stories was published under the title *Hams al-junun* (translated as *The Whisper of Madness*, 1973). His three earliest published novels, beginning with *Abath al-Agdar* (1939), were historical romances set in the time of the pharaohs. With those works behind him, he proceeded on a new course with a series of six novels of modern social-political-cultural-psychological realism leading up to his monumental Cairo Trilogy. Of those six novels only one has been translated into English: *Zugag al-Midaqq* (1947; *Midaq Alley*, 1977). The first volume in the Cairo Trilogy, *Bayn al Qasrayn*, was published serially between 1954 and 1956 and was translated as *Palace Walk* (1989); the second, *Qasr al-Shawq* (1957), was translated as *Palace of Desire* (1991); and the third, *Al-Sukkariyah* (1957), was translated as *Sugar Street* (1992). The trilogy focuses on the lives of the Cairo patriarch Al-Sayyid Ahmad Abd al-Jawad and three generations of his family over a period of more than three decades, from World War I to the 1950s. Mahfouz departed from modern realism in his next novel, *Awlad Haritna* (1959; translated as *Children of Gebelawi* in 1981 and as *Children of the Alley* in 1995), a quasi-biblical allegory in which he portrayed Muhammad as an all-too-human womanizer, a characterization judged blasphemous by Islamic fundamentalists. That book was banned by governments throughout the Arab/Muslim world, and it reportedly provoked a fatwa (call for assassination) by Sheikh Abdul-Rahman (the blind cleric accused of being the mastermind behind the first attack on the World Trade Center, in 1993). During the 1960s and early 1970s, Mahfouz turned to existentialist themes in such novels as *Al-Liss Wa-al-Kilab* (1961, *The Thief and the Dogs*, 1984), *Al-Tariq* (1964, *The Search*, 1991), *Miramar* (1967; translated under same title, 1978), and *Al Maraya* (1971; *Mirrors*, 1999). During the 1980s he published, among other books of fiction, *Layali alf Laylah* (1981; *Arabian Nights and Days*, 1995) and *Rihlat ibn Fattumah* (1983; *The Journey of the Fattouma*, 1992). In 1994 he published *Asdaa Al-Sira Al-Dhatiyya* (1994; *Echoes of an Autobiography*, 1997). Meanwhile he had further offended militant Islamists with his support of Egyptian president Anwar Sadat's signing of a peace treaty (the Camp David Accords) with Israel in 1978. One day in 1994, on a street near his home in Cairo, he was the victim of an attempted assassination, suffering several near-fatal knife wounds. He never fully recovered from the effects of the assault, one of which was the incapacitation of his writing

hand. Debilitated by aging as well, he confined his writing in his last years chiefly to brief vignettes, such as the supernatural fantasies he contributed to an Egyptian women's magazine between 2000 and 2003. *Dreams*, a translated collection of those pieces, was published by the American University in Cairo Press in 2005. In addition to his novels (totaling more than 30) and shorter fiction (some 350 pieces, collected in 13 volumes), Mahfouz worte 30 screenplays and five stage plays. The novelist seldom left Cairo, where he and his wife, Attiyat-Allah, raised two daughters. He died in Cairo. See *Current Biography* (1989).

Obituary *New York Times* A p23 Aug. 31, 2006

MALONEY, WALTER E. May 5, 1911–June 14, 1999 Marine association president; lawyer. Maloney, a maritime lawyer, was the chief attorney of the American Merchant Marine Institute (AMMI) from 1942 to 1952; he then served as the organization's president and chairman of the board. Maloney earned his bachelor's degree from Lafayette College, Easton, Pennsylvania, in 1933, and graduated from the Columbia University School of Law, in New York City, in 1936. From 1939 to 1941 he served as the assistant corporation counsel for New York City. Maloney took a two-year hiatus from the AMMI to serve as a lieutenant in the U.S. Coast Guard Reserve during the final years of World War II. After the war he accepted a position with Burns, Currie & Rich, the Wall Street firm that handled legal work for the AMMI. As the organization's chief legal representative, Maloney negotiated collective bargaining agreements with maritime labor unions. In 1952 Maloney was unanimously elected the president of the AMMI, which represented 70 percent of the U.S.'s private shipping industry at that time. His tenure with the AMMI ended in 1955. In 1961 he became a partner at the maritime law firm of Bigham, Englar, Jones & Houston; he later became a senior partner and retired from the firm in 1981. Maloney's first wife, the former Mary Reynolds, died in 1955. He is survived by his second wife, Hilda, eight sons, three daughters, 43 grandchildren, and 19 great-grandchildren. See *Current Biography* (1952).

Obituary *New York Times* I p39 June 20, 1999

MARCEAU, MARCEL Mar. 22, 1923–Sep. 22, 2007 French mime. As a solo performer and as the leader of a mimodramatic troupe, Marcel Marceau entertained international audiences for more than half a century and repopularized the ancient "art of expressing feelings by attitudes," as he described pantomime. With his supple, seemingly gravity-defying body movements, precise hand gestures, and pliant face, Marceau wordlessly conveyed a comprehensive range of emotions through the attitudes of a gallery of personae, including his signature alter ego, Bip, a daydreaming clown with face painted white who wore a shabby striped French sailor's shirt and a battered black top hat surmounted by an artificial red flower. As Bip Marceau was sometimes woebegone but always open to wonder and joy as well as sadness, and he engaged in such adventures as hunting butterflies with an imaginary net and taming invisible lions. His other characters included an irritable head waiter, an insane sculptor, a matador, a dictator, a ballet dancer, and an elderly woman who wordlessly gossiped as she knitted. He cast himself as judge, prosecutor and defendant in a sketch titled "The Tribunal" and as a number of passersby in "The Park." His other sketches included "The Cage," "Walking Against the Wind" (which inspired the pop-music performer Michael Jackson's "Moonwalk" routine), "The Mask Maker," and "Creation," his version of Genesis. In "Youth, Maturity, Old Age, and Death," he transformed himself from embryo to corpse in four minutes. Part of Marceau's legacy is L'École Internationale de Minodrame Marcel Marceau, the school for mimes that he founded in Paris in 1978. Marcel Marceau, originally named Marcel Mangel, was born into a Jewish family in Strasbourg, France. Unlike his father, who died in the Nazi concentration camp at Auschwitz, Marcel escaped the Holocaust, joining the French Resistance against the Nazi occupation of France and serving in the French army after the liberation of the country. (The rest of his family had escaped to Belgium.) He began performing pantomime publicly as a member of an army entertainment unit. In Paris after World War II, he studied *mime corporeal*—the grammar of pantomimic facial and body control—under Étienne Decroux, the mentor of the actor Jean-Louis Barrault. One of Marceau's inspirations was Barrault's whiteface portrayal of Pierrot, the naïve and melancholy classic mime clown, in the motion picture *Les Enfants de Paradis* (1945). Also influential were the silent film comedies of Buster Keaton, Harry Langdon, Stan Laurel, and, above all, Charlie Chaplin. In Paris in 1946 Marceau first won recognition playing the classic mime character Harlequin with Barrault's acting company and presenting an original mimodrama of his own at the Théâtre Sarah Bernhardt. In 1947 he began performing solo at a tiny Montparnasse cabaret called the Théâtre de Poche. A year later he formed his own troupe and proceeded to present at various venues in Paris classic mimodramas as well as such original productions as a mime adaptation of Gogol's story "The Overcoat." He disbanded that troupe in the mid-1960s and formed a new company, La Nouvelle Compagnie de Mimodrame, three decades later. His popularity in France did not for many years begin to approach his success abroad, beginning with Israel, Italy, Britain, and the Scandinavian countries in the early 1950s, later including Germany, Australia, and Japan (where he was extraordinarily esteemed), and ultimately totaling more than five dozen countries. The turning point on his route to international stardom was the phenomenal success of his first U.S. tour, a one-man venture in 1955 and 1956 that included a two-week engagement on Broadway, a longer engagement in Los Angeles attended by a number of Hollywood luminaries, including the Marx Brothers, and the first of his many appearances on television. For his performance on a prime-time NBC network variety show, he won the Emmy Award for best specialty act in 1956. He thereafter returned to the U.S. every year or two through 2004. In his later American tours, he brought with him La Nouvelle Compagnie de Mimodrame, presenting with that troupe a show about two hours long that included such ensemble theater pieces as "The Masquerade Ball," the touching story of an ugly girl wearing a beautiful mask, a gift from a mysterious stranger. In *Daily Variety* (September 22, 2004), Frank L. Rizzo described that piece as a "sublime blending of music, motion, and drama . . . a mime marvel [that] predicts the future of the art form." Before retiring, in 2005, Marceau staged a very successful full-company production titled *Les Contes Fantastiques* in Paris. Marceau made cameo appearances in several motion pictures, among them *Silent Movie* (1976). He was named a chevalier of the French Legion of Honor in 1970. He wrote and illustrated several books, including *The Story of Bip* (Harper & Row) and two books for very young children. Married three times, he had four children. After retiring from the stage, he lived primarily in his home in Cahors, France. According to most news reports and published obituaries, he died in Paris. He was buried in Père Lachaise Cemetery, in Paris. See *Current Biography* (1957).

Obituary *New York Times* B p8 Sep. 24, 2007

MARLETTE, DOUG Dec. 6, 1949–July 10, 2007 Cartoonist; writer. The internationally syndicated cartoonist Doug Marlette viewed his irreverent and often controversial craft as "the acid test of the First Amendment" and himself as an "equal-opportunity offender" in wielding the fearsome power of his incisive wit. He spared no quarter in selecting the targets of his ridicule, public figures in whom he discerned pomposity, duplicity, self-righteousness, or absurd foibles, including "true believers of every stripe." In politics he most famously skewered the likes of the right-wing Republican senator Jesse Helms of North Carolina, but he also memorably drew such cartoons as "The Clinton Monument," a picture of a gigantic trouser zipper inspired by the philandering of the Democratic president Bill Clinton. Early in his 35-year career, Marlette incited the wrath of Christian fundamentalists by attacking Jim and Tammy Faye Bakker's "televangelism scam" and Jerry Falwell's television ministry. He later outraged Catholics by lampooning Pope John Paul II, and Jews by criticizing Israel, and he often poked fun at the mainstream Protestant denominations, including his own Presbyterian faith. He tapped into what he described as "a new level of hate and violence" in December 2002, when he drew a cartoon showing a jihadist at the wheel of a Ryder truck toting a nuclear warhead. It was captioned, "What would Muhammad drive?" When the cartoon appeared in the on-line edition of the *Tallahassee Democrat* newspaper (then his home base), it drew more than 20,000 e-mail hate messages, many of which threatened mutilation or death. With that experience behind him, Marlette later staunchly defended the Danish newspaper *Jyllands-Posten,* which commissioned drawings of Muhammad by a dozen artists in 2005 and became the target of a fatwa as a result. A self-described "Southern Baptist Marine Corps brat," Marlette was born in Greensboro, North Carolina, and grew up there and in a succession of other southern towns and cities where his father was posted. After studying philosophy at Florida State University, he joined the staff of the *Charlotte Observer*, in Charlotte, North Carolina, where he was the editorial cartoonist for 15 years (1972–87). He was subsequently on the staffs of the

Atlanta Journal-Constitution (1987–89), Newsday (1989-2001), and the Tallahassee Democrat (2002–06). At the time of his death, he was on the staff of the Tulsa World. In addition to his editorial cartoons, Marlette drew (beginning in 1980) Kudzu, a syndicated satirical comic strip influenced in part by Al Capp's Lil' Abner and Johnny Hart's The Wizard of Id and B.C. but rooted in Marlette's own experience. The strip, set in fictional Bypass, North Carolina, had a cast of characters including the eponymous young protagonist (representing Marlette), the unholy Baptist preacher Will B. Dunn, and Uncle Dub, "the classic good ol' boy." In collaboration with the folk-music group the Red Clay Ramblers, Marlette created the stage adaptation Kudzu: A Southern Musical (1998). He published a score of collections of his editorial cartoons and comic strips, with such titles as Faux Bubba: Bill and Hillary Go to Washington and A Town So Backwards Even the Episcopalians Handle Snakes. In addition, he wrote a book about cartooning, In Your Face (1991), and he published two novels. The first novel was The Bridge (2001), a thinly veiled account of life in Hillsborough, North Carolina, including his own somewhat dysfunctional family's history. That book angered a number of Hillsborough citizens (including some writers) who felt that Marlette had caricatured them. The Southeast Booksellers Association named The Bridge the year's best book of fiction, and BookSense, the on-line arm of the American Booksellers Association's Book Sense program, named it one of the best books of the previous five years. The protagonist of Marlette's second novel, Magic Time (2006), is Carter Ransom, a New York newspaper columnist shocked by the bombing of a Manhattan art museum and sent back in memory to his youth in Mississippi and specifically to the Freedom Summer of 1964. "Through Ransom's eyes," the syndicated columnist Kathleen Parker observed, "we see the affinity between those who murdered civil rights workers and those who blow up art museums. Or fly airplanes into buildings. Fueled by resentment, both wrap themselves in a mantle of religion." Among the causes Marlette was known to champion was opposition to the death penalty. He taught in the schools of journalism at the University of North Carolina and the University of Oklahoma. He won every major award in editorial cartooning, including the Pulitzer Prize, in 1988. With his wife, Melinda (nee Hartley), Marlette lived in both Hillsborough, North Carolina, and Tulsa, Oklahoma. He died in a single-vehicle accident on rain-slicked U.S. highway 78 en route from the airport in Memphis, Tennessee, to Oxford, Mississippi, where students at Oxford High School were preparing a production of Kudzu: A Southern Musical, to be presented at the Edinburgh Fringe Festival in Scotland in August 2007. The passenger in a pickup truck driven by John P. Davenport, the Oxford High School theater director, he was killed instantly when the truck hydroplaned off the road and struck a tree. Marlette was survived by his wife and their adult son, Jackson. Posthumously, at the funeral service held for him, he received North Carolina's highest civilian award, presented by the state's governor, Michael F. Easley. See Current Biography (2002).

Obituary New York Times C p11 July 11, 2007

MATHIAS, ROBERT BRUCE Nov. 17, 1930–Sep. 2, 2006 Legendary track and field champion; actor; U.S. congressman. Bob Mathias was a "one-man track team, capable of winning the majority of U.S. track meets single-handed," as a Time magazine cover story put it in 1952. In the Olympic Games in Helsinki that year, Mathias won his second consecutive Olympic gold medal in the decathlon, becoming the first athlete to win back-to-back Olympic championships in that event. (He had won the first at the 1948 Olympic Games, in London.) After retiring from amateur athletic competition, when he was 21, he acted on television and in four motion pictures (It Happened in Athens, China Doll, Theseus and The Minotaur, and The Bob Mathias Story, in the last of which he played himself), and he later pursued a career in politics. A conservative Republican, he represented the Fresno area in California's northern San Joaquin Valley in the U.S. House of Representatives for four terms, from 1967 to 1975. It was as a high school athlete in Tulare, California, that he began competing in track and field, ultimately specializing in the decathlon, which consists of 10 events for one prize: four track events (the 100-, 200-, and 1,500-meter races and the 110-meter hurdles) and six field events (javelin, discus, shot put, pole vault, high jump, and broad jump). In high school he excelled as an all-state basketball player and as a running back in football. He also starred as a fullback at Stanford University, where he earned a degree in physical education before serving as an officer in the U.S. Marine Corps for two years. He qualified for the 1948 U.S. Olympic team by winning the Amateur Athletic Union decathlon championship earlier that year. He won the AAU championship in 1949, 1950, and 1952 as well. In the 1952 Olympics he set a world record of 7,887 points in the decathlon. His margin of victory—more than 900 points—was the largest in Olympic decathlon history. By the time he retired from amateur competition, following the 1952 Olympics, he had won all of the decathlons he had entered (between nine and 11, according to differing counts) and set three world records. After leaving Congress he was a consultant to the President's Council on Physical Fitness and a fund-raiser for the U.S. Olympic Committee. From 1977 to 1983 he was director of the U.S. Olympic Training Center in Colorado Springs, Colorado. He was a charter inductee into the National Track and Field Hall of Fame, in 1974, and the U.S. Olympic Hall of Fame, in 1983. Following his divorce from his first wife, Melba, he married Gwen Haven Alexander. Mathias died of lung cancer in a hospital in Fresno, California. His survivors included his wife, four daughters, a son, and 10 grandchildren. See Current Biography (1952).

Obituary New York Times B p6 Sep. 4, 2006

MCCOLOUGH, C. PETER Aug. 1, 1922–Dec. 13, 2006 Corporation executive. Charles Peter McColough's chief claim to fame was his leadership of the Xerox Corp. (originally the Haloid Co.), whose name in the public mind remains synonymous with photocopying machines but which McColough greatly expanded and diversified. "In the late 1960s Peter McColough redefined our company," Jacob E. ("Jack") Goldman, Xerox's one-time chief scientist, once pointed out. "It's the old question of whether you consider yourself as providing a function or a product. We're not a copier-maker. We're an information company that got into the business via copiers." After earning an M.B.A. degree at Harvard University's Graduate School of Business Administration and serving as vice president in charge of sales at the Lehigh Navigation Coal Sales Co., McColough joined the Haloid Co., a pioneer in electrophotographic technology, in 1954. The term "xerography" (from the Greek words for "dry" and "writing") was coined at Haloid. Haloid began manufacturing and marketing Xerox copying machines—the earliest of which were relatively crude—in 1949, and its owners changed its corporate name to Xerox Inc. 12 years later. Rising up through Xerox's sales and marketing ranks, McColough was named executive vice president in charge of operations in 1963; he subsequently became president (1966–71), chief executive officer (1968–82), and chairman of the board of directors (1971–85). During the 1960s Xerox acquired Ginn and Co., a textbook-publishing firm, and Scientific Data Systems, which became Xerox Data Systems. "Our objective in acquiring SDS was to offer broader-based information systems," McColough explained. "We feel that to really seize the opportunities around the world for supplying information, we had to broaden out from graphics." He continued to diversify with the acquisition of Diablo Systems, a producer of peripheral computer equipment, in 1972, and later in the 1970s, he took Xerox into the word-processing field. As an adjunct to Xerox, he founded the Palo Alto Research Center for developing commercial products in the field of personal computers. Under him, Xerox's revenues grew to more than $7 billion a year and its annual profits to approximately $600 million. McColough's activities and interests outside Xerox were numerous. He was on the boards of trustees of the New York Stock Exchange and many other institutions, including several banks, served a term as chairman of United Way of America, was treasurer of the Democratic National Committee from 1974 to 1976, and was involved with the Council on Foreign Relations. Most importantly, perhaps, he funded the C. Peter McColough Roundtable Series on International Economics. He died of cardiac arrest in Rye Brook, New York. Two of his five children predeceased him. His survivors included his wife, Mary Virginia (née White), two sons, a daughter, and seven grandchildren. See *Current Biography* (1981).

Obituary *New York Times* B p7 Dec. 18, 2006

MCNAIR, BARBARA Mar. 4, 1934–Feb. 4, 2007
Singer; actress; television personality. The famously glamorous Barbara McNair, who began her career at the dawn of the modern civil rights movement, cut a wide swath as an African-American show-business trailblazer. In the mid-1950s, following her debut as a cabaret singer at the Village Vanguard jazz nightclub, in Manhattan's Greenwich Village, McNair won a competition on Arthur Godfrey's television series *Talent Scouts* and sang on Godfrey's radio show. After an engagement at the Purple Onion, a Manhattan room showcasing new talent, she moved upward in the club circuit, into such venues as the

Copacabana and the Plaza Hotel's Persian Room in New York City, the Eden Roc in Miami Beach, the Coconut Grove in Los Angeles, and major hotels in Las Vegas. Discovered by the producer Richard Kollmar, she was cast in a supporting role in the Broadway musical *The Body Beautiful* in 1958. She toured with Nat King Cole in the musical *I'm with You* in 1961. Two years later she replaced Diahann Carroll as the feminine lead in the hit Broadway musical play *No Strings*, and in 1973 she starred in a revival of the musical *Pajama Game*. On network television beginning in the late 1950s, she was a guest singer on many variety shows, including those hosted by Jack Paar, Garry Moore, Ed Sullivan, Flip Wilson, and Johnny Carson. She herself hosted several television specials as well as *The Barbara McNair Show*, a talk-and-music program with many A-list guests that was syndicated during the 1969–70 television season. Between the mid-1960s and the mid-1980s, she was cast in a score of straight dramatic roles in episodes of television series, including *Dr. Kildare*, *I Spy*, *Mission: Impossible*, *Vega$*, and *The Mod Squad*, and she played Donna Travers in the TV movie *The Lonely Profession* (1969). On the motion-picture screen, she made her debut with a singing performance in *Spencer's Mountain* (1963) and subsequently starred as the nightclub singer Lily in *If He Hollers, Let Him Go* (1968), as Rita in the surreal sex mystery *Paroxismus* (aka *Venus in Furs*, 1969), as Ahn Dessie in the Mafioso melodrama *Stiletto* (1969), as Sister Irene Hawkins (opposite Elvis Presley) in *Change of Habit* (1969), and as Valerie Tibbs (opposite Sidney Poitier) in *They Call Me MISTER Tibbs* (1970) and its sequel, *The Organization* (1971). Her last roles were those of the English teacher in the TV movie *Fatal Charm* (1990) and Grace in the feature film *Neon Signs* (1999). She continued to tour occasionally as a singer until mid-2006. The *New York Times* music critic John S. Wilson once described her as "a gorgeous-looking woman with a warm, easy, communicative personality and a voice that can range from softly intense ballads to the edges of gospel, to crisp and rhythmic comedy or to a saloon singer's belt." In the course of her career, McNair recorded on the Coral, Signature, Motown, and Warner Bros. labels. Among her biggest hits were the singles "Bobby," "For Once in My Life," "You Could Never Love Him," "You're Gonna Love My Baby," "What a Day," "Talking in My Sleep," and "Face to Face with Love." Her mid-1960s albums *Livin' End* and *I Enjoy Being a Girl* were remastered as CDs and released by Collectables Records in 2006. Remastered versions of her late-1960s LPs *Here I Am* and *The Real Barbara McNair* are included in the CD boxed set *Motown: The Ultimate Collection* (2006). With Stephen Lewis, she wrote *The Complete Book of Beauty for the Black Woman* (1972). Following two earlier marriages (and divorces), McNair married Rick Manzie, who was alleged by some sources to have had underworld connections and was murdered by an unknown gunman in 1976. She died of throat cancer. Her fourth husband, Charles Blecka, survived her. See *Current Biography* (1971).

Obituary *New York Times* D p8 Feb. 6, 2007

MENOTTI, GIAN CARLO July 7, 1911–Feb 1, 2007
Opera composer; lyricist; director. Gian Carlo Menotti, a theatrically oriented musician widely viewed as a latter-day Puccini, was the most prolific and accessible opera composer/lyricist of his time. An immigrant from Italy, Menotti came to prominence in the United States with the Broadway success in 1947 of his macabre chamber opera *The Medium*, about a fraudulent clairvoyant who succeeds in invoking a more harrowing manifestation than she had bargained for. He soon reinforced his position as a crossover giant in classical music with many other productions, including several additional Broadway shows and a classic Christmas television opera. The Broadway productions included two that won Pulitzer Prizes: *The Consul* (1950), a grim political opera, and *The Saint of Bleecker Street* (1954–55), an opera about a saintly stigmatic visionary in Manhattan's Little Italy and her unbelieving brother. The television opera, *Amahl and the Night Visitors*, a one-act work, is the touching story of a crippled boy miraculously healed after he offers his crutches to the Three Wise Men as a gift for the Infant Jesus. First produced on the NBC television network on December 24, 1951, it became a perennial holiday presentation on that network. After serial and aleatory music came into vogue in the 1960s, Menotti refused to join in what called the "fashionable dissonance" and continued to work in a melodious, tonal vein dismissed as "passé," "light," and "frothy" by some academics but which remained theatrically effective. He wrote his own librettos, provided his own orchestration, and as often as possible directed the productions of his operas, which totaled 23. In 1958, in collaboration with Thomas Schippers, Menotti founded the Festival of Two Worlds in Spoleto, Italy. In 1977 he founded an American counterpart of that festival in Charlotte, South Carolina. Menotti was introduced to music by his mother, Ines Pellini Menotti, a pianist and a friend of Carla De Martini, the wife of Arturo Toscanini. He studied at the Verdi Conservatory in Milan, and then, in 1927, accompanied by his mother and armed with a letter of recommendation from Carla De Martini, he immigrated to the United States to study composition under Rosario Scalero at the Curtis Institute of Music in Philadelphia. At the institute, he began his life partnership with the composer Samuel Barber, a fellow student. That personal and musical partnership lasted until Barber's death, in 1981. Menotti's first mature work was the one-act opera buffa *Amelia al Ballo*, which he himself translated into English as *Amelia Goes to the Ball*. It had its world premiere at the Philadelphia Academy of Music in 1937 and was first performed at the Metropolitan Opera in New York City in 1938. On commission from the NBC network, Menotti composed the radio opera *The Old Maid and the Thief* (1939), which was later adapted for the stage (1941). Following the disappointing reception of the premiere of his opera *The Island God*, staged by Lothar Walterstein at the Metropolitan Opera in 1942, he made it his usual practice to direct the premieres of his works himself. Following the run of *The Medium* on Broadway—on a bill with his comic one-act curtain-raising musical revue sketch *The Telephone*—in 1947, it was staged in London and Paris, then adapted into a theatrical feature film directed by Menotti

and released in 1951. Menotti's opera *Maria Golovin* ran on Broadway for only four days in 1958. In 1963 NBC televised his mini-opera *Labyrinth*. His 1963 three-act comic opera *L'Ultimo Selvaggio* was translated into French as *Le Dernier Sauvage* and into English as *The Last Savage*. He wrote a number of children's operas, including *Help, Help, The Globolinks!*, which was first produced in 1968. The most confessional of his works is the play *The Leper* (1970), an ambivalent polemic urging toleration of sexual deviance only as long as it does not threaten the social order. His opera *The Most Important Man* was premiered by the New York City Opera in 1971. His first attempt at an historical work of grand opera was *La Loca*, about Queen Juana la Loca (Joan the Mad) of Spain. Its first performance was by the San Diego Opera in 1979. Menotti later composed the operas *The Wedding* (1988) and *The Singing Child* (1993). In addition to operas, he composed, among other works, concert and chamber pieces and *The Halcyon*, a symphony, and he wrote librettos and incidental music for works by others. Menotti died at Princess Grace Hospital in the principality of Monaco. He was survived by a son, Francis Phelan (also known as Chip Menotti), whom the composer adopted in 1974, when Phelan was a young man, and for whom Menotti's chamber opera *Chip and His Dog* (1978) was named. See *Current Biography* (1979).

Obituary *New York Times* C p11 Feb. 2, 2007

MESSMER, PIERRE Mar. 20, 1916–Aug. 29, 2007
French statesman. Pierre August Joseph Messmer was a lifelong loyal Gaullist, best known for his tenure in France's Fifth Republic as a prime minister as well as for his colonial and defense portfolios. After earning a doctorate in law in addition to academic credentials for colonial service, Messmer fought as a Foreign Legion paratroop officer in General Charles de Gaulle's Free French forces during World War II. As a colonial administrator in the Far East after the war, he had the task of trying to deal with Ho Chi Minh and the Viet Minh forces, who would ultimately succeed in winning the independence of North Vietnam (the Socialist Republic of Vietnam). Recalled to Paris, he was chief administrator of the ministry of France d'Outre-Mer (France Overseas) in 1951 and 1952. He subsequently helped to ease the transformation of France's African colonies into independent republics in a succession of positions: governor of Mauritania (1952), governor of Ivory Coast (1954–56), high commissioner of Cameroon (1956–58), high commissioner of French Equatorial Africa (1958), and high commissioner of French West Africa (1958–59). In 1959 he was employed briefly in the private sector by Baron Guy de Rothschild, leader of the French branch of the Rothschild banking dynasty. In December 1959 President de Gaulle sent Messmer in a military capacity (as a lieutenant colonel in the army reserve) to Algeria, where Arab nationalists were waging a guerrilla war for independence and French settlers were opposing de Gaulle's plan to concede self-determination to the nationalists. In January 1960 the opposition of the French settlers erupted into an insurrection that had the support of many French military officers and civilian officials, extending even into the government

of the Fifth Republic, which had been founded with de Gaulle as its first president in 1959. Acting swiftly to rid his government of dissident and ineffective elements, de Gaulle ordered a shake-up of the cabinet headed by Prime Minister Michel Debré in January 1960. Among the cabinet changes was the appointment of Messmer as minister of the armed forces. In that position he responded to an abortive coup led by four French generals in Algeria; several hundred French army officers were arrested and a number of elite regiments were dissolved or "modified." Messmer barely escaped an assassination attempt in 1962, when peace was negotiated with the nationalists and the French withdrawal from Algeria began. After the resolution of the Algerian crisis, he concentrated on reorganizing the French armed forces, implementing de Gaulle's policies of professionalizing the army and developing nuclear forces. De Gaulle resigned the presidency in 1969 and died the following year. Quitting his cabinet post in 1969, Messmer set up the Présence et Action du Gaullism, a group dedicated to carrying forward de Gaulle's ideas and ideals, including opposition to a federal Europe. Under Georges Pompidou—who succeeded to the presidency of the Fifth Republic in 1969—Messmer was minister of France d'Outre-Mer (1971–72) and prime minister (1972–74). Messmer represented Sarrebourg in the French National Assembly from 1968 to 1988. In 1992 he published his autobiography, *Après tant de batailles* (After So Many Battles). In 1999 he was inducted into the Académie Française. After the death of his first wife, Gilberte (née Duprez), he married Christiane Terrail in 1999, when both were 83 years old. He died in Paris, leaving behind his wife. He had no children. See *Current Biography* (1963).

Obituary *New York Times* A p13 Sep. 1, 2007

MILLER, G. WILLIAM May 9, 1925–Mar. 19, 2006 Corporate executive; investment banker; lawyer; U.S. government official. George William Miller was chairman of the board of governors of the Federal Reserve banking system and secretary of the treasury in the administration of President Jimmy Carter. Before going to Washington, Miller guided Textron Inc. through the initial stage of its diversification and growth into one of the largest Fortune 500 multi-industry-cum-finance companies, a $10 billion conglomerate employing more than 43,000 people in 40 countries. After serving in the U.S. Coast Guard and earning degrees in marine engineering and law, Miller joined the Wall Street law firm of Cravath, Swaine & Moore in 1952. In the course of his legal work, he represented Textron Inc., then a relatively small Rhode Island textile manufacturing company, in a proxy battle. Victory in that battle enabled the company to begin to diversify beyond the textile field. In 1956 Miller joined Textron as an executive assistant secretary charged with overseeing acquisitions. He became a vice president and treasurer of the company in 1957 and president in 1960. (In the latter year Textron acquired Bell Aerospace, including Bell Helicopter, the world's leading manufacturer of commercial and military helicopters, and it would later acquire Cessna Aircraft. In addition to aircraft, the conglomerate manufactures weapons, tools, machinery, plastic tanks, electrical instru-

ments, surveillance systems, armored vehicles, and golf and industrial carts and other off-road vehicles, among other products. It also provides after-market and financial services.) Miller became chief executive officer of Textron in 1968. During his tenure at the conglomerate, he took time out to serve on a presidential committee on equal employment opportunity during the Kennedy and Johnson administrations, and he chaired Businessmen for Humphrey-Muskie in the Democratic presidential campaign of 1968. He was also a director of the Federal Reserve Bank of Boston. At Textron, he was chairman of the board as well as CEO from 1974 until President Carter named him chairman of the board of governors of the Federal Reserve System, America's quasi-governmental, multi-bank approximation of a central bank. When he became chairman of the Federal Reserve, in March 1978, the national economy was suffering from what was called "stagflation," a combination of stagnant economic growth (manifested in unemployment) and rising inflation. During his 17 months as chairman of the Fed, he made what his critics regarded as the mistake of not seeing inflation as a greater danger than unemployment and fighting it decisively. Giving equal attention to both problems, he was cautious in using an increase in interest rates as a deflationary lever, while the rate of inflation continued rising. The national Consumer Price Index rose from 4.8 percent when President Carter took office in 1977 to 12 percent in 1980, when the soaring inflation rate contributed to Ronald Reagan's victory over Carter in that year's presidential election. Miller served as secretary of the treasury in President Carter's Cabinet from August 6, 1979 until the end of the Carter administration, on January 20, 1981. After leaving government he held many corporate directorships, and from 1990 to 1992 he was chairman and chief executive of Federated Stores Inc. He died at his home in Washington, D.C. His wife, Ariadna, survived him. See *Current Biography* (1978).

Obituary *New York Times* A p21 Mar. 20, 2006

MIRVISH, EDWIN July 24, 1914–July 11, 2007 Canadian business entrepreneur; theatrical impresario; philanthropist. In addition to being a pioneer among North American discount retailers, Edwin Mirvish was the revitalizer of the theatrical scene in Toronto, Canada, and the financial savior of the legendary Old Vic Theatre in London, England. Mirvish was born in the United States and originally had the given name Yehuda. In 1923, when he was in fourth grade, his parents moved with him and his brother, Robert, to Toronto, where his father opened a grocery store on Dundas Street West in the city's Jewish quarter. When he was 15 his father died, and he dropped out of school to help run the family store. From 1938 through 1940 he was a merchandising manager with the Power Supermarkets chain in Canada. While in that position he, with his wife Alice (nee Maklin), opened a dress shop on Market Street in Toronto, first called the Sport Bar and then Anne & Eddy's. Early in 1941 he left Power Supermarkets to concentrate on his own business, which he expanded in 1948 into Honest Ed's Famous Bargain House. Occupying a full block on Markham Street, that emporium was billed as "the world's biggest discount department store." In his no-frills store, Mirvish sold goods—displayed on orange crates—he had acquired from fire and bankruptcy sales and in odd lots from wholesale jobbers, offering the items at low prices and attracting customers with "door-crasher" opening specials and below-cost "loss-leaders" (a now common merchandising gimmick he claimed to have invented) and by engaging in publicity stunts—riding an elephant, displaying other zoo animals, and presenting round-the-clock dance marathons. On his birthday each year, he hosted a street party in front of his store at which the public enjoyed free food, entertainment, and children's rides. When he gave away thousands of pounds of turkeys each Christmas, people queued up for hours outside the store. In the late 1950s he added a pioneering cut-rate pharmacy to the store's departments. During the same period he began buying up houses and other buildings in the area comprising Markham, Bloor, and Bathhurst Streets. He leased or rented many of the premises to local artists and crafts people, who set up studios, galleries, and boutiques, turning the area into what is now known as Mirvish Village. He first ventured into theatrical investment in 1962, when he saved Toronto's Royal Alexandra Theatre from demolition by buying it for approximately $215,000 (Canadian dollars); he subsequently spent another $489,000 restoring that theater to its original Edwardian splendor. It opened in 1963, with a staging of *Never Too Late,* the first of a number of productions Mirvish produced himself. He acquired additional property in the King Street area, where the Royal Alexandra Theatre is located, and opened several restaurants there. In 1982 he bought the Old Vic for £550,000 (approximately one million dollars), and he subsequently spent £2.5 million refurbishing and restoring the structure, London's oldest producing theater. With his son, David (to whom he turned over management of the family's theaters and its production company in 1987), he spent $22 million building the Princess of Wales Theatre in Toronto. That structure, the largest new theater in North America and the first free-standing privately financed theater to be built in Canada, opened in 1993. At the Old Vic over the years, the Mirvishes produced revivals of *Kiss Me Kate* and *Henry IV,* among other productions. In Canada they produced revivals including the musicals *Chicago* and *Miss Saigon.* They presented a Stratford Festival version of *The Mikado* on Broadway as well as in London. In 1998 the Mirvishes sold the Old Vic to Sally Greene's Old Vic Theatre Trust. In Canada in 2001 Mirvish Enterprises took over the management of the Pantages Theatre Company, renamed the building the Canon Theatre, and sent that troupe on tour with a production of *Saturday Night Fever.* Mirvish published the autobiography *Honest Ed Mirvish* in 1993. He was an officer of the Order of Canada and commander of the Order of the British Empire. He died at St. Michael's Hospital in Toronto. His survivors included his wife, Anne, his son, David, and his sister, Lorraine. See *Current Biography* (1989).

Obituary *New York Times* C p10 July 13, 2007

MIYAZAWA, KIICHI Oct. 8, 1919–June 28, 2007 Japanese politician and statesman. As noted in the *Daily Yomiuri,* Japan's largest-circulation newspaper, Kiichi Miyazawa was "the embodiment of postwar Japanese politics." David McNeill elaborated on that point in his obituary for the London *Independent:* "Miyazawa's career spanned the great arc of Japan's phenomenal rise to economic superpower status, and the slow decline that set in during his final years. As minister for trade, finance, and foreign affairs, and in 1991–93 as prime minister, Miyazawa played a defining role in both eras." The scion of a family of prominent politicians, Miyazawa attended Tokyo University before going to work in the foreign ministry in Tokyo in 1942. He remained in that ministry as private secretary to the foreign minister during the American occupation of Japan following World War II. From 1953 to 1965 Miyazawa served in the House of Councilors, the upper chamber of the Diet, the Japanese Parliament. In 1967 he won his first election to the House of Representatives, the Diet's more powerful, lower chamber. In the cabinet he held in succession the portfolios of minister of international trade and industry (1970–71), foreign minister (1974–76), finance minister (1986–88), and deputy prime minister (1987–88). Over the course of those years, he became the leader of a large faction in the long-dominant Liberal Democratic Party, and in 1991 he was elected party leader. As prime minister, from 1991 to 1993, he took several reconciliatory steps in relation to other Asian countries, including opening the Japanese rice market to cheaper imports and making Japan's first official acknowledgment of its guilt in the sex enslavement of Korean and other Asian females as "comfort women" for its expeditionary military forces in the late 1930s and during World War II. Although he was a staunch supporter of Article Nine in his country's current (post–World War II) constitution—the article banning the threat or use of offensive military force as an instrument of international policy—he approved the passage of legislation enabling him to send a self-defense force on a "peacekeeping" mission to Cambodia. His fluency in English contributed to his success as prime minister in negotiating a major trade agreement with the United States in 1993. (To most Americans he was known chiefly, if not solely, for hosting a 1992 state dinner in Tokyo, at which a suddenly ill President George H. W. Bush vomited in his lap.) As prime minister Miyazawa introduced banking reforms calculated to deal with a looming national economic malaise, but the malaise ensued despite the reforms. In the summer of 1993, failing to offset allegations of corruption with promised political reforms, his government lost a parliamentary vote of confidence, and in the subsequent national election, the Liberal Democrats lost their majority in the House of Representatives for the first time since 1955. On August 9, 1993 Miyazawa was succeeded in office by Morihiro Hosokawa of the Japan New Party, and the Liberal Democrats remained out of power until January 1996. Returning to the cabinet as finance minister (1998–2001), Miyazawa helped to alleviate an Asian economic crisis by persuading the countries affected to participate in a system of bilateral currency swaps. He retired from the House of Representatives in 2003. Miyazawa and his wife,

Yoko (who survived him), had a son, Hiro, and a daughter, Keiko. He died at his home in Tokyo. See *Current Biography* (1992).

Obituary *New York Times* A p27 June 29, 2007

MOFFO, ANNA June 27, 1932(?)–Mar. 9, 2006 Opera singer. The American coloratura soprano Anna Moffo was gifted with statuesque beauty, a voice modest in size but warm and pure in tone, and a dramatic ability of wide range, best manifested in such roles as Violetta in Verdi's *La Traviata* and Mimi in Puccini's *La Bohème*. The credibility of her acting was enhanced by the way she "approached the psychology of [all of her] parts conscientiously and thoughtfully," as the opera critic John Steane observed, as quoted by Vivien Schweitzer in *PlaybillArts* (March 13, 2006). She sang Violetta a total of more than 900 times in opera houses across Europe and the United State. Eighty of those performances were with the Metropolitan Opera in New York City, her American base for 17 years. Her next-most-performed role was Lucia in Donizetti's *Lucia di Lammermoor*, which she sang a total of some 500 times. Also outstanding among her interpretations was that of Amina in Bellini's *La Sonnambula*, Nannetta in Verdi's *Falstaff*, Nedda in Leoncavallo's *I Pagliacci*, and Liù in Puccini's *Turandot*. Her entire repertoire comprised scores of roles, including Philine in Thomas's *Mignon*, Susanna in Mozart's *Le nozze di Figaro*, Marguerite in Gounod's *Faust*, Gilda in Verdi's *Rigoletto*, Adina in Donizetti's *L'Elisir d'Amore*, the four heroines in Offenbach's *The Tales of Hoffmann*, Mélisande in Debussy's *Pélleas and Mélisande*, Pamina in Mozart's *The Magic Flute*, Rosina in Rossini's *The Barber of Seville*, Rosalinde in Strauss's *Die Fledermaus*, Lauretta in Puccini's *Gianni Schicchi*, Zerlina in Mozart's *Don Giovanni*, Maria in Donizetti's *The Daughter of the Regiment*, Elvira in Bellini's *I Puritani*, Fiora in Montemezzi's *L'Amore dei Tre Re*, and the title roles in Offenbach's *La Perichole* and Massenet's *Manon*. In addition to her stage performances, she pursued careers as a recitalist and recording artist, and in Italy—where she began her operatic career and enjoyed superstar status—she was cast in nonoperatic roles in a number of feature films (including the prize-winning *Una storia d'amore*, in which she created a succès de scandale by appearing nude in one scene) and hosted her own television show from 1960 to 1973. The daughter of Italian-American parents, Moffo studied under Eufemia Giannini-Gregory at the Curtis Institute of Music, in Philadelphia, and under Luigi Ricci and Mercedes Llopart at the Santa Cecilia Academy in Rome. She made her professional debut singing Norina in Donizetti's *Don Pasquale* at the Spoleto Festival in 1955. The following year she sang the title role in an Italian television production of Puccini's *Madama Butterfly*, which was directed by Mario Lanfranchi, who became her manager and first husband. Following that production she was in demand at La Scala in Milan and other Italian operatic houses, and before long she was filling engagements in opera houses across Europe, from the Vienna State Opera to Covent Garden in London. During the first four years of her career, Lanfranchi pushed her to sing an average of 12 new major roles a year, an exhausting regimen that took a toll on her spirit (and ultimately on her voice as well). "I was working too hard and traveling too much," she later recalled. "I got mixed up in TV, films, things like that. Psychologically, I was miserable." She made her American debut singing Mimi with the Lyric Opera of Chicago in 1957. With the Chicago company later in the same season, she sang Philine and Nannetta. In 1960 she sang Mimi in her debut with the San Francisco Opera. She began her long tenure at the Metropolitan Opera singing Violetta in 1959. Her other roles at the Met in addition to Lucia and Mimi included Nannetta, Marguerite, Nedda, Adina, Gilda, Liù, Mélisande, Pamina, Rosina, Rosalinde, La Perichole, Lucia, and Manon. In the late 1960s she began having problems with her voice, and in 1974 she suffered a complete vocal collapse. By that time she had given 220 performances in 18 operas at the Met. After a two-year absence, she returned to the operatic stage in 1976. She gave her last operatic performance at the Met on March 15, 1976, singing Violetta. Meanwhile, she retrained her voice, which had thickened and lost some vibrato, and adopted a revised repertoire, which included Leonora in *Il Trovatore* and Lina in *Stiffelio*, both by Verdi. In 1972 Moffo and Lanfranchi divorced, and two years later she married Robert W. Sarnoff, then the board chairman and CEO of the RCA Corp. Sarnoff died in 1997. After battling breast cancer for 10 years, Moffo died of a stroke, at New York–Presbyterian Hospital, in New York City. Her survivors included three stepdaughters. See *Current Biography* (1961).

Obituary *New York Times* C p14 Mar. 11, 2006

MOORE, THOMAS W. Sep. 17, 1918–Mar. 31, 2007 Television executive; former president of the ABC television network; award-winning producer. After serving as a U.S. Navy aviator during World War II, Thomas Waldrop Moore sold radio advertising at a Columbia Broadcasting System radio station in Los Angeles. He joined the CBS television network as an account executive in 1952 and was soon promoted to general film sales manager. The American Broadcasting Co.'s television network hired him as vice president in charge of sales in 1957, promoted him to vice president in charge of programming in 1958, and to president in 1962. At the beginning of his presidential tenure, ABC was lagging far behind the CBS and National Broadcasting Co. television networks in ratings and volume of business, in part because ABC's original programming was limited chiefly to a few hours of largely grade-B action and adventure shows per week. As president, Moore expanded ABC's original programming, improved its quality, and widened its demographic appeal, especially in the 18-to-35-year-old age range. Among other innovations, he launched ABC's first sports department and hired Roone Arledge to head it. He left ABC in 1968, and two years later he founded the television production company Tomorrow Entertainment Inc. with the financial backing of the General Electric Corp. (According to the Horatio Alger Association's biography of Moore, in the meantime he had founded Ticketron, the computerized ticket-selling company that was later absorbed by Ticketmaster.) Tomorrow Entertainment won its first Emmy Award (in the category of outstanding single drama program) for the TV movie *A War of Children,* about the sectarian strife in Ulster, Northern Ireland, originally televised on CBS during the 1972–73 season. The company subsequently produced the TV movie *The Autobiography of Miss Jane Pittman,* an adaptation of Ernest J. Gaines's novel about a black woman born into slavery in the South who lives to play a part in the early days of the modern civil rights movement. Televised on CBS in January 1974, the movie won nine Emmys, including one for its star, Cicely Tyson, who aged (with the help of make-up) from 19 to 110 in the course of the filming. *I Know Why the Caged Bird Sings,* the company's TV-movie adaptation of Maya Angelou's memoir of her childhood, was first televised on CBS in 1979. Tomorrow Entertainment won a Peabody Award for its program *Judge Horton and the Scottsboro Boys* in 1976. Among the outstanding series the company produced was the weekly hour-long prime-time documentary show *Lifeline,* in each installment of which the cameras were trained on a physician or surgeon going about his work. Televised on NBC for 17 weeks early in the 1978–79 season, *Lifeline* brought an Emmy Award to its executive producers, Moore and Robert Fuisz. Moore was executive producer of *The Body Human,* a medical series exploring the interior of the body that ran on CBS and brought Moore won four Emmys between 1978 and 1983. He was a leader in the founding of the Naval Aviation Museum in Pensacola, Florida. According to the Horatio Alger Association biography, he and his wife owned and operated a cattle ranch and vineyard—the grapes from which were sold to the Robert Mondavi Winery—in St. Helena, California. Moore died near his home in Palm Springs, California. His survivors included his wife, the former Claire Stirrat, a son, a daughter, four grandchildren, and two great-grandchildren. See *Current Biography* (1967).

Obituary *New York Times* A p13 Apr. 4, 2007

MURRAY, ELIZABETH 1940–Aug. 12, 2007 Artist. Best known for her energetic, vibrantly colored, and intricately shaped and layered multi-canvas compositions, Elizabeth Murray was a major postminimalist force in New York–based painting beginning in the late 1970s, following the decline of abstract expressionism. She was an innovator who, in the words of the critic Stephen Westfall, "synthesized the many forms of modernist painting while at the same time developing and expanding imagistic themes of private domestic anxiety and pleasure." In *Art in America* (January 1, 2006), Westfall wrote: "No painter in the last fifty years besides Stella and Rauschenberg has so stretched our notion of what the outline and surface of a painting might look like, and none has done so while remaining as committed to integrating a descriptive, expressionist imagery with abstract form-giving." As Deborah Solomon observed in the *New York Times Magazine* (March 31, 1991), Murray's work recapitulated "cubism's splintered planes, fauvism's jazzy colors, surrealism's droopy biomorphic shapes, the heroic scale of abstract expressionism." After graduating from the School of the Art Institute of Chicago and earning a master's degree in fine art at Mills College, in Oakland, California, Murray moved to the East Coast, fi-

nally settling in New York City. She was inspired to initiate what became a new style in painting when, in the late 1970s, she "spotted some small canvases lying around her New York studio," as Peter Plagens wrote for *Newsweek* (October 31, 2005). She told Plagens: "I just screwed them together in a jumbled way and started painting on them. Then a studio assistant showed me how to stabilize them with aluminum bars in the back." In the early 1980s, as Plagens added, she "'went baroque, stretching canvases over jigsaw-puzzle forms made from plywood." She also executed smaller works, some on paper, from paintings to pencil and ink drawings and lithographs. Reviewing an exhibition of a group of her small paper pieces under glass at PaceWildenstein, her Manhattan gallery, David Frankel wrote for *Art forum* (June 22, 2002): "Much has been said of Murray's sense of fun and of her Pop-ish affection for the treatments of form seen in comics and cartoons. But comics use pratfalls for comedy, and these paintings are full, if not of anxiety, at least of vertiginous precariousness." Robert Storr, the dean of the Yale University School of Art and the curator of a major retrospective of Murray's work at the Museum of Modern Art in Manhattan (October 2005–January 2006), observed on National Public Radio on the occasion of the retrospective: "There's a great deal of pain and a great deal of tragedy and a great deal of anger in her work. So she expresses that anger and that pain in forms that seem kind of comfortable"—including such elements of everyday life and domesticity as kitchen tables, coffee cups, shoes, and canine pets. "You can get close to them. And then when you really get close to them you realize that they can bite." Murray's works are in the permanent collections of many American museums, and two large mosaic murals by her adorn walls in the New York City subway system, at the 59th Street and Lexington Avenue station in Manhattan and the 23rd Street and Ely Avenue station in Queens. She received a MacArthur Foundation "genius" award in 1999. Following her divorce from her first husband, Don Sunseri, Murray married the poet Bob Holman, in 1973. In addition to her residence in Manhattan, she maintained a home in Washington County, New York. She died at her Washington County home, of complications from lung cancer. Her survivors included her husband; a son, Dakota Sunseri, from her first marriage; two daughters, Sophia Murray Holman and Daisy Murray Holman, from her second marriage; and two grandchildren. See *Current Biography* (1995).

Obituary *New York Times* B p6 Aug. 13, 2007

NELSON, BYRON Feb. 4, 1912–Sep. 26, 2006 American golfer; philanthropist. John Byron Nelson Jr., a man of courtly demeanor who was affectionately nicknamed "Lord Byron," not only established himself as a legendary champion during his relatively brief career on the Professional Golf Association tour, but he maintained a lifelong supportive relationship with the tour, its younger players, and related charities. That relationship confirmed his reputation as pro golf's "first gentleman," a role model in sportsmanship and benevolence and a goodwill ambassador for the game. Between 1935 and 1946 Nelson won 51 events on the PGA tour. He reached his peak as a player in 1944 and 1945, when he won 31 of the 54 events in which he competed and was the leading moneymaker on the tour. In 1945 he realized the best single season in the history of pro golf, capturing 18 tour titles, including 11 in a row, two records that have never been surpassed. His 1945 stroke average of 68.33 over 120 rounds stood as a record for 55 years, until Tiger Woods broke it, in 2000. His record of 113 consecutive cuts (roughly meaning paychecks received for event finishes) was also recently surpassed by Woods, but Nelson's record for consecutive top-20 finishes—also 113—remains unbroken. Standing six feet one inch tall, holding his arms close to his body, and using a grip modeled after that of Harry Vardon, Nelson was credited with introducing the long and fluid swing suitable for the modern metal golf club. (Clubs had previously been made of wood.) As a child in Fort Worth, Texas, Nelson barely survived typhoid fever, which left him with an inability to sire children and a blood disorder that would exempt him from military service during World War II. He was introduced to golf as a 12-year-old caddie in Fort Worth, and he turned professional in 1932, when the Great Depression was at its worst and jobs were scarce; golf was his activity of choice, in any event. Between 1933 and 1944 he was employed, successively, as the pro at clubs in Texarkana, Texas; Ridgewood, New Jersey; Reading, Pennsylvania; and Toledo, Ohio. He began gathering PGA tour victories in 1935, and he won the Masters, the first of his five major championships, in 1937. His subsequent major victories were in the 1939 U.S. Open, the 1940 PGA Championship, the 1942 Masters, and the 1945 PGA Championship. After he won the Chicago Victory National Open (his 51st tour victory), in 1946, he retired from full-time competition, having achieved his goal of earning enough money to buy and stock a farm in Roanoke, Texas. For a few years he returned periodically to competition, and in 1951 he won the Bing Crosby Pro-Am. That victory brought his career wins to 52, the sixth-ranking total in PGA history. Outside of the PGA tour he won 14 events. He was a member of the U.S. Ryder Cup teams in 1937 and 1947, and he was nonplaying captain of the team in 1965. After his retirement from competitive golf, he took time off from his farming to provide golf commentary on television and to mentor such younger golfers as Tom Watson and Ken Venturi and encourage a host of others, including Tiger Woods. After the Dallas Open stop on the PGA tour was renamed the EDS Byron Nelson Championship, in 1968, he devoted much time and energy to promoting that event, all net proceeds of which benefit the Salesmanship Youth and Family Centers, a nonprofit agency that offers education and mental-health services for children and families in the greater Dallas area. Since its inception the EDS Byron Nelson Championship has raised $82 million for charity. Nelson published the books *Winning Gold* (1946) and *How I Played the Game* (1992). In the new epilogue for an edition of the latter published in 2005, he stressed his strong religious faith. (He was a member of the Richland Hills Church of Christ.) Nelson was married to Louise (Shofner) Nelson from 1935 until her death, in 1985. His second wife, Peggy (Simmons) Nelson, whom he married in 1987, survives him. He died on his farm in Roanoke, Texas.

The honors bestowed on him included induction into the World Golf Hall of Fame, in 1974, and the Congressional Gold Medal, which he received posthumously, on October 16, 2006. See *Current Biography* (1945).

Obituary *New York Times* C p14 Sep. 27, 2006

NYKVIST, SVEN Dec. 3, 1922–Sep. 20, 2006 Swedish cinematographer. Sven Vilhem Nykvist, a deft master of low-tech light and composition, is regarded by many to have been the most gifted lensman in 20th-century filmmaking. Building on a Swedish cinematographic tradition established by Julius Jaenzen, Gunnar Fischer, and others, Nykvist helped to bring to the international motion-picture screen a new modernist standard in photography, simple and austere but intense, preferably using available light and marked by subtle gradations in luminescence. He is best known for his score of collaborations (in a filmography exceeding 120 feature films) with the Swedish director Ingmar Bergman. "Nykvist managed to capture every psychological nuance of [Bergman's] work on a visual plane," Nathan Southern observed in All Movie Guide (on-line), "something that has rarely been accomplished before or since in a director-cinematographer relationship." In an obituary of Nykvist for the *New York Times*, Stephen Holden wrote: "In his films, especially those with Mr. Bergman, light assumed a metaphysical dimension that went beyond mood. It distilled and deepened the feelings of torment and spiritual separation that afflicted Bergman characters. But in scenes of tranquility filmed outdoors, the light might evoke glimpses of transcendence." As Bergman himself said, he and Nykvist shared the views that "the camera is an incredible instrument for registering the human soul as reflected in the human face" and that "a picture shouldn't look lit." "We are both utterly captivated by the problems of light," Bergman wrote in his autobiography, *The Magic Lantern* (1988), "the gentle, dangerous, dreamlike, living, dead, clear, misty, hot, violent, bare, sudden, dark, springlike, falling, straight, slanting, sensual, subtle, limited, poisonous, calming, pale light. Light." Nykvist was a hands-on cinematographer, not only directing photography but also operating the camera (except when he was working in Hollywood, where union division-of-labor rules forbade him from handling the lens). Nykvist began his career in cinematography as a camera assistant at Sandrew Film and Theater, a combination production-distribution company in Stockholm, in the early 1940s, and he became a principal cinematographer there in 1945. On leave from Sandrew, he visited the Belgian Congo, where his parents were nonconformist Christian missionaries and where he made two documentaries, one about a witch doctor and the other about Albert Schweitzer. During a decade and a half at Sandrew, he photographed approximately 40 feature films. In his first collaboration with Ingmar Bergman, he photographed the interior scenes for *Gycklarnas afton* (*Sawdust and Tinsel*, aka *The Naked Night*, 1953); Hilding Bladh shot the exterior scenes. When Bergman became independent of the Sandrew company, in 1959, he recruited Nykvist to photograph the black-and-white film *The Virgin Spring* (1960; originally titled *Jungfrukällan*), which won the Academy Award for best foreign film in 1961. The following year Nykvist succeeded Gunnar Fischer as Bergman's cinematographer of choice, making his debut as such with the black-and-white film released with subtitles under the English title *Through a Glass Darkly* (1961). Over the following 23 years, he photographed 19 more Bergman films (several of them for television), including the color picture released with subtitles under the English title *Cries and Whispers* (1972), which won the Oscar for best cinematography in 1973. His other collaborations with Bergman included the black-and-white films *Winter Light* (1963), *The Silence* (1963), *Persona* (1966), *Hour of the Wolf* (1968), and *Shame* (1968) and the color pictures *All These Women* (1964), *The Passion of Anna* (1969), *Scenes from a Marriage* (1972), and *Autumn Sonata* (1978). Another of their color collaborations, *Fanny and Alexander* (1982), won four Oscars, including one for cinematography. Nykvist photographed *The Serpent's Egg* (Bergman's only English-language film) alternately in black and white and color, and he opened *From the Life of the Marionettes* (1980) with a blood-red murder scene and shot the rest in black and white. After Bergman retired, Nykvist photographed Woody Allen's films *Another Woman* (1988), *Crimes and Misdemeanors* (1989), and *Celebrity* (1998) and Allen's segment ("Oedipus Wrecks") in the three-part film *New York Stories* (1989). He was nominated for a third Oscar for cinematography for the director Philip Kaufman's *The Unbearable Lightness of Being* (1988). Other directors with whom he briefly collaborated included Roman Polanski, Nora Ephron, Liv Ullmann, Alan J. Pakula, Louis Malle, Paul Mazursky, John Huston, Bob Fosse, Norman Jewison, Andrei Tarkovsky, Lasse Hallström, Peter Brook, Bob Rafelson, and Volker Schlöndorff. He himself directed as well as photographed the feature films *Gorilla* (1956), *Lianbron* (*The Vine Bridge*, 1965), and *The Ox* (aka *Oxen*, 1991). *The Ox* was nominated for the Oscar for best foreign film of the year. Nykvist's son, Carl-Gustaf Nykvist, directed *Light Keeps Me Company* (2000), a documentary about his father. Nykvist was predeceased by another son (a suicide) and by the mother of his sons, Ulrika ("Ulla") Soderlind (from whom he was divorced). His survivors included his son Carl-Gustaf, a daughter-in-law, Helena Berlin, and two grandchildren. He died in a nursing home in Stockholm, Sweden. See *Current Biography* (1989).

Obituary *New York Times* B p6 Sep. 21, 2006

O'DAY, ANITA Oct. 18, 1919–Nov. 23, 2006 Singer; "the Jezebel of jazz." The sultry-voiced Anita O'Day was a prime originator of the "cool school" of female vocalism in the big-band/swing scene of the 1940s and one of the most durable of the great jazz singers to emerge from that era. As a white singer she enjoyed a rare respect among her black counterparts. Even Betty Carter, whose standard for accepting non-black performers into the pantheon of jazz is almost impossibly high, once said, "I can't think of any white girl singer who has her own style, except perhaps Anita O'Day." O'Day's husky legato style—marked by a vulnerable crack in her voice—was in-

deed unique, in part because a botched childhood tonsillectomy left her without a uvula and therefore without a vibrato, the ability to sustain notes. "The dynamic range of her voice may be smaller than any other jazz singer's except Blossom Dearie's," the critic Charles Michener observed, "but her flexibility with it allows her to scat, slide, and skitter through a song the way a cat laps up milk." The name O'Day was a stage pseudonym. She was born Anita Belle Colton in Chicago, Illinois, into a broken home. A high-school dropout, she began singing publicly as a teenager, while participating in the brutal Depression-era endurance contests known as dance marathons and walkathons. At 17 she became a singer in a burlesque show in the Vanity Fair nightclub in the Uptown section of Chicago. A short time later she was hired by another Uptown club, the Planet Mars, where she made the acquaintance of the hipster humorist Lord Buckley, who influenced the development of her hip sense of humor and mannerisms. Subsequently, she was booked into the Off-Beat jazz club in downtown Chicago. She was discovered there by the drummer Gene Krupa, who hired her in 1941 to sing with his big band. Teamed with the trumpeter/singer Roy Eldridge, she sang "Let Me Off Uptown," which became the Krupa band's biggest hit and her first million-selling single. She and Eldridge also made the charts with "Thanks for the Boogie Ride" and "That's What You Think." *Down Beat* named her "New Star of the Year" in 1941, and the following year the magazine ranked her one of the top-five female singers in the country, alongside Helen O'Connell, Billie Holiday, Helen Forrest, and Dinah Shore. With the Krupa band in the mid-1940s, she scored hit singles with "Boogie Blue" and "Opus One." During an interlude when Krupa was jailed for possession of marijuana, she sang with the band of Stan Kenton, giving Kenton his first million-selling hit, "And Her Tears Flowed Like Wine." She also sang briefly with Woody Herman. Following a nervous breakdown in 1946, she embarked on her solo career, performing in clubs from Los Angeles to New York City. Convicted of possession of marijuana in 1947, she served 90 days in prison. After her release, she moved back to Chicago and sang in jazz clubs there, including her own Hi Note (which she opened in partnership with her second husband, Carl Hoff, and Marty Dennenberg). In 1950 she made her first appearance at the Apollo Theater in Harlem, New York City. In 1952 she was introduced to heroin by her long-time collaborator John Poole, the drummer in the trio that often backed her. Convicted of possession of heroin, she was again imprisoned, from September 1953 to February 1954. In the late 1940s she recorded such singles as "Key Largo," "Hi Ho Trailus Boot Whip," and "How High the Moon," many of them on small labels. Her career was abetted by Norman Granz, who began reissuing her Mercury recordings on his jazz label, Clef, in 1952. Among those sides were several collaborations with Roy Eldridge, including "Lover Come Back to Me" with "Rock 'n' Roll Blues," and "Lullaby of the Leaves" with "Love for Sale." In 1956 she became a charter recording artist on Granz's Verve label. Over a period of six years, she recorded on Verve such singles as "Just One of Those Things," "Slaughter on Tenth Avenue," "We'll Be Together Again," "I'll See You in

My Dreams," "Let's Face the Music and Dance," "Sing Sing Sing," "Honeysuckle Rose," and "Pick Yourself Up." Among her 17 Verve albums were *Anita, Make Mine Blues*, and *Anita O'Day Swings Cole Porter*. On her recordings she was accompanied by Oscar Peterson, Stan Getz, Andre Previn, and Buddy Di Meoa, among others. At jazz festivals and in concerts, she collaborated with musicians including Dave Brubeck, Count Basie, Louis Armstrong, and Lionel Hampton, She won the appreciation of a widened audience both in the United States and abroad when part of her performance at the 1958 Newport Jazz Festival was included in the documentary film *Jazz on a Summer's Day* (1959). She toured Sweden and Germany (with the Benny Goodman Orchestra) in 1959, Britain in 1961, and Japan several times beginning in 1964. A near-fatal overdose in 1966 motivated her to overcome her addiction to heroin, but she remained a heavy alcohol drinker for many years. Her career slumped with the arrival of the rock-and-roll boom in the 1960s, then enjoyed a revival beginning in the late 1970s, and she continued performing in clubs on and off for more than two decades. Her autobiography, *High Times, Hard Times* (1981), was as-told-to George Eells. The two marriages into which she entered when she was very young, to Don Carter and Carl Hoff, ended, respectively, in annulment and divorce. The documentary film *Anita O'Day: Life of a Jazz Singer*, directed by Robbie Cavolina, her manager, and Ian McCrudden, is scheduled for release in 2007. O'Day died in Los Angeles. See *Current Biography* (1990).

Obituary *New York Times* A p33 Nov. 24, 2006

OGILVIE, ELISABETH May 20, 1917–Sep. 9, 2007 Writer. Elisabeth May Ogilvie wrote 45 colorful books of fiction, including 31 adult novels and 14 novels for young adults or children. Most of the stories were set on the Maine coast or on islands off that coast; some were set in Nova Scotia or Scotland. Ogilvie was born to parents of Scots descent in Boston, Massachusetts, and she grew up in Dorchester and Quincy, Massachusetts. Her only college credit was an extension course, "Writing for Publication." Beginning in childhood, she spent summer vacations on the Maine coast, and she moved there permanently in the mid-1940s. In her first novel, *High Tide at Noon* (1944), she created the Bennetts, a lobster-trapping family living and working on Bennett's Island, a fictional setting bearing some resemblance to craggy Criehaven Island, 25 miles off the Maine coast. She carried the Bennett family saga forward through successive generations in eight subsequent novels: *Storm Tide* (1945), *The Ebbing Tide* (1947), *The Dawning of the Day* (1954), *The Seasons Hereafter* (1966), *Strawberries in the Sea* (1973), *An Answer in the Tide* (1978), *Summer of the Osprey* (1987), and *The Day Before Winter* (1997). She created another saga in her Jennie Glenroy trilogy—comprising the novels *Jennie About to Be* (1984), *The World of Jennie G.* (1986), and *Jennie Glenroy* (1993)—covering 18 years in the life of the protagonist, a native of the Scottish highlands who immigrates to the Maine coast in the 19th century. Among other Ogilvie novels set on Maine coast islands are the Brontë-like story *Rowan Head* (1949) and *Image of a Lover* (1974),

which begins with merriment and ends in murder. Her novel *When the Music Stopped* (1989) is a murder mystery with a stunning conclusion. *The Dreaming Swimmer* (1976) is a suspenseful romance novel. Among her other novels are *No Evil Angel* (1956), *The Witch Door* (1959), *Call Home the Heart* (1962), *There May Be Heaven* (1964), *The Face of Innocence* (1970), *Where the Lost Aprils Are* (1975), *The Devil in Tartan* (1980), *The Silent Ones* (1981), and *The Road to Nowhere* (1983). Among her novels for younger readers are the romances *Blueberry Summer* (1956), *How Wide the Heart* (1959), and *Beautiful Girl* (1980). Her autobiography, *My World Is an Island*, first published in 1950, was updated in 1990. For more than half a century, beginning in the mid-1940s, Ogilvie lived with her friend Dorothy Simpson, who was also an author, on a 33-acre farm they owned on Gay's Island in the mouth of the St. George River, off Pleasant Point, Maine. Ogilvie moved to Cushing, on the mainland of Maine, in 2001, three years after the death of Simpson. She died in Cushing. See *Current Biography* (1951).

Obituary *New York Times* D p8 Sep. 14, 2006

OLITSKI, JULES Mar. 27, 1922–Feb. 4, 2007 Ukrainian-born American artist. With his voluptuous mirage-like color-field paintings, Jules Olitski (born Jevel Demikovsky) was a central figure in the second generation of American abstract artists, the "post-painterly abstractionists" (as the critic Clement Greenberg dubbed them) whose works were minimal departures from the first-wave abstract expressionism most famously exemplified by Jackson Pollock's splash-and-drip "action" canvases. "Olitski . . . was a lovely man and a beautiful painter, celebrated as a hero of American modernism from around 1960 to the beginning of the 1970s," Tim Hilton wrote in an obituary for the London *Guardian* (February 13, 2007). "But his reputation sank at the time of his first major retrospective, at the Boston Museum of Fine Arts in 1973, and it will be for future historians to decide whether he was a victim of the rise of conceptual art." After his father was executed by the Bolsheviks, Olitski, with his mother and grandmother, escaped from Ukraine and the Soviet Union and settled in the United States when he was less than two years old. He was trained in art at Pratt Institute, in Brooklyn, the National Academy of Design, in New York City, and New York University. In the canvases he painted in the 1940s, he was strongly influenced by fauvism. In his first solo show, in Paris, France, in 1950, he exhibited impastos reminiscent of the work of Jean Fautrier. Throughout the 1950s, while teaching art at a succession of American universities, he worked more heavily in impasto, kneading plaster with paint to produce nonobjective canvases that were really bas-reliefs with spatial illusions. In the early and middle 1960s—when he headed the Art Department at Bennington College, in Vermont—he changed his technique radically, breaking from brush strokes and impasto and applying stains and dyes (directly or with sponges) as well as acrylics (with a spray gun) to unprimed canvases, creating paintings layered with bright misty hues, nontactile and relatively flat but suggesting depth as well as surface. At a competition at the Corcoran Gallery of

Art, in Washington, D.C., in 1967, he won first prize with *Pink Alert*, a large spray painting in shades of peach, green, mauve, and pink, with strands of similar colors running along three sides. In addition to painting, in the late 1960s he began creating a significant body of large-scale sculpture, at first in painted metal. In 1973 he began to use the weathering steel alloy Cor-Ten, which gave a monochromatic sheen to his outdoor sculptures, such as *King Kong* (on the grounds of Middlebury College, in Vermont). Meanwhile, coincidentally with the ascendancy of Pop Art and full-blown Minimalism over abstraction, he went retro in his painting technique, abandoning the spray gun and using household mops and brushes and the like in executing more textured canvases, such as *Fertile Crescent Flesh-Six* (1975). Over the years his paintings—some adorning the walls of airports and the atria of banks—grew ever larger. *Beauty of Lauren* (1975), for example, is 60 square feet. He stored many of his paintings in the vault of a former bank building he owned in Brooklyn, where his daughter Lauren Olitski Poster (from his second marriage) catalogued them. Throughout his career, while abstractionist in his painting and sculpture, he was always figurative in his drawings of nudes and other subjects from life. In his later years he concentrated on monotype prints and on landscape paintings, many inspired by sunrises and sunsets he witnessed at his homes in Meredith, New Hampshire, and Islamorada, Florida. His paintings are in the permanent collections of the Museum of Modern Art, the Metropolitan Museum of Art, and the Guggenheim Museum, all in New York, and other venues. He and his work were the subject of Kenworth Moffett's book *Jules Olitski* (1981) and catalogues published by the Boston Museum of Fine Arts (1973) and the Sallander-O'Reilly Galleries in Beverly Hils, California (1990). Olitski's first two marriages ended in divorce. He died at Memorial Sloan-Kettering Cancer Center in New York City. His survivors included his third wife, Joan Kristina (nee Fourgis) Olitski, his daughters Eve (from his first marriage) and Lauren, a stepdaughter, Natasha, and five grandchildren. See *Current Biography* (1969).

Obituary *New York Times* B p7 Feb. 5, 2007

PALANCE, JACK Feb. 18, 1919–Nov. 10, 2006 Actor. Jack Palance brought to his character portrayals the assets of a chiseled and craggy Slavic face, a lanky and gaunt physique, and a deep and musical but gravelly voice. In the fifth decade of his Hollywood career, in 1992, on the occasion of his third Academy Award nomination, Palance finally won an Oscar, for his self-parodying performance as Curly Washburn, the wise old rancher in the comic Western *City Slickers* (1991). That supporting role was against type for Palance, who until then had been chiefly identified with his intense portrayal of heavies, beginning with Blackie, the infected murderer whom public-health and police authorities in New Orleans are racing to find in order to prevent a bubonic-plague epidemic, in the director Elia Kazan's *Panic in the Streets* (1950). Palance's first Oscar nomination was for his third screen role, that of Lester Blaine, the unscrupulous, opportunistic actor who romantically pursues a playwright/heiress (Joan

Crawford) for ulterior reasons and plots her murder after marrying her, in the thriller *Sudden Fear* (1952); his second was for his portrayal of Jack Wilson, the sadistic hired gun in the classic Western *Shane* (1953). Palance had begun his career as an actor in the legitimate theater, where Elia Kazan discovered him, and he accumulated many acting credits on television, the most memorable of which was his Emmy Award–winning performance as Harlan ("Mountain") McClintock, the pathetic broken-down prize fighter in the teleplay *Requiem for a Heavyweight*, broadcast live in the CBS dramatic anthology series *Playhouse 90* in 1956. A son of Ukrainian immigrants, Palance (who pronounced his name with the accent on the first syllable) was born Volodymyr Palahnuik in the Lattimer Mines section of Hazle Township, Pennsylvania, where his father was a coal miner, as he himself was briefly in his late teens. On a football scholarship he attended the University of North Carolina for two years. He subsequently had a brief career as a professional prize fighter. Following military service in World War II, he matriculated at Stanford University, intending to major in journalism but instead becoming more involved in the university's dramatic club. Leaving Stanford without a degree in 1946, he traveled east and began seeking his theatrical fortune in New York City. His breakthrough came during the 1947–48 theatrical season, when he replaced an ailing Marlon Brando in the original Broadway production of *A Streetcar Named Desire*, directed by Elia Kazan. (If legend is correct, Brando's "ailment" was a broken nose, suffered when he and Palance traded friendly punches in a workout in the theater's boiler room.) Kazan subsequently provided Palance with his debut film role, in *Panic in the Streets*. After his second screen role, that of Pigeon Lane, a member of a squadron of U.S. Marines fighting in the Pacific in World War II, in *Halls of Montezuma* (1950), Palance shuttled to New York to play the Russian commissar Gletkin in the original Broadway production of *Darkness at Noon* (January–June 1951). Aside from a subsequent tour in the play *Dark of the Moon* and some performances at the American Shakespeare Festival in Stratford, Connecticut, he thereafter concentrated on his film career. He appeared in a total of more than 70 roles in feature films, including Toriano, the renegade Apache, in *Arrowhead* (1953), Slade, the lodger assumed to be a serial killer, in *Man in the Attic* (1953), Atilla the Hun, in *Sign of the Pagan* (1954), Simon the Magician, the fictional rival to Jesus, in *The Silver Chalice* (1954), Charles Castle in *The Big Knife* (1955), Lieutenant Joe Costa in *Attack!* (1956), Jesus Raza in *The Professionals* (1966), Parson Josiah Galt in *The Desperados* (1969), Tursen in *The Horsemen* (1971), Hellman in *Oklahoma Crude* (1973), Boss Morono in *The Four Deuces* (1976), Jim Buck in *Portrait of a Hitman* (1977), Wade in *The One Man Jury* (1978), Lawrence G. Murphy in *Young Guns* (1988), Beelzebub in *The Incredible Adventures of Marco Polo* (1998), and Long John Silver in *Treasure Island* (1999). He had starring or featured roles in more than a score of movies made in Europe, including Ogatai, the son of Genghis Khan, in *I Mongoli* (*The Mongols*, 1961), Torvald in *Barabbas* (1962), Jeremy Prokosch, the vulgar Hollywood producer, in Jean-Luc Godard's *Le Mépris* (*Contempt*, 1963), and Ricciolo in the superior spaghetti Western *Il Mercenario* (*A Professional Gun*, 1968). Because his Curly Washburn character had died in *City Slickers*, a twin brother, Duke Washburn, was created for Palance to play in *City Slickers II: The Legend of Curly's Gold* (1994). Among his appearances on television outside of his many dramatic performances were those as host of *Ripley's Believe It or Not*, an hour-long weekly "reality show" that ran on the NBC network from 1982 to 1986. His hobby was painting and drawing, and he illustrated his book of poetry *Forest of Love* (1996). Palance was married to and divorced from Virginia Baker and Elaine Rogers, successively. He was predeceased by a son, from his first marriage, and survived by two daughters, also from his first marriage. He died at his home in Montecito, California. See *Current Biography* (1992).

Obituary *New York Times* C p10 Nov. 11, 2006

PALEY, GRACE Dec. 11, 1922–Aug. 22, 2007 Short-story writer; poet; activist. As a lifelong political and social activist, Grace Paley (née Goodside) was a self-described "somewhat combative pacifist and cooperative anarchist," involved in numerous social-justice causes, including feminist, civil rights, and antinuclear campaigns and the antiwar movement, from Vietnam to Iraq. Her radical activist commitments were reflected—especially through the recurring character of Faith Darwin, her fictional alter ego—in her tragicomic short stories about daily lives, chiefly those of struggling wives and mothers and other women in New York City. Those finely crafted vignettes also manifested her ear for the cadences of speech in the city, beginning with the Yiddish spoken by her parents—Isaac and Manya Gutseit (anglicized as Goodside), socialists who had emigrated from the Ukraine—and including the vernacular spoken in the streets of the east Bronx, where she grew up, and Greenwich Village, where she lived as an adult. In her writing of fiction she was most influenced by the work of Isaac Babel. Her short stories were collected in the volumes *The Little Disturbances of Man* (1959), *Enormous Changes at the Last Minute* (1974), and *Later the Same Day* (1985); those collections were brought together in one volume, *The Collected Stories of Grace Paley* (1994). Among her other books are the poetry collections *Leaning Forward* (1985), *New and Collected Poems* (1991), and *Begin Again* (2000) and the volume of essays *Just As I Thought* (1998). Vera B. Williams illustrated Paley's book of poems and short fiction *Long Walks and Intimate Talks* (1991). Over the years Paley taught at a number of colleges and universities, among them Sarah Lawrence College and the City College of New York. Her honors included a Guggenheim fellowship, a National Endowment of the Arts Award for lifetime contribution to literature, the first New York State Writer citation, and designation as poet laureate of Vermont. She acquired the name Paley from her first marriage, to Jess Paley, a film cameraman. After her divorce from Paley, she married the playwright Robert Nichols, with whom she co-authored the collection of stories and poems *Here and Somewhere Else* (2007). In addition to her apartment in Greenwich Village, she had a home in Thetford Hill, Vermont, where she died, of compli-

cations from breast cancer. She was survived by her husband, Robert Nichols, a son, Dan, and a daughter, Nora, from her first marriage, and three grandchildren. See *Current Biography* (1986).

Obituary *New York Times* B p7 Aug. 24, 2007

PANOFSKY, WOLFGANG K. H. Apr. 24, 1919–Sep. 24, 2007 German-born American physicist; arms-control and peace advocate. As a pioneering particle physicist, Wolfgang Kurt Hermann "Pief" Panofsky's crowning achievement was the founding, in 1961, and 23-year direction of the Stanford Linear Accelerator Center (SLAC), a U.S. Department of Energy national laboratory operated by Stanford University in Menlo Park, California, adjacent to Stanford's campus in Palo Alto. Panofsky co-designed and oversaw the construction of a 10,000-foot-long ultra-high-speed accelerator at SLAC in the early 1960s, and he later introduced two particle colliders. He directed research at the center that significantly contributed to the so-called Standard Model, the most advanced current theory in physics explaining the subatomic chemical/nuclear building blocks of matter, the quarks and leptons, and the forces that influence them. The results of that research included the first observations of the tau lepton, the J/psi particle, and up-and-down quarks, discoveries that brought Nobel Prizes to three of Panofsky's colleagues. At the same time Panofsky, who had long been having second thoughts about his involvement in the invention of the atomic bomb, was pursuing a parallel career fueled by his deep concerns as an ethical and socially responsible scientist. At Stanford he co-created an undergraduate course called International Security in a Changing World (originally titled Arms Control and Disarmament), a political-science class that led to the establishment of Stanford's Center for International Security and Cooperation. The same ethical and social concerns informed Panofsky's relations with the U.S. government, beginning in the 1950s—when he advised the State Department about the feasibility of monitoring the radioactive fallout from nuclear-bomb testing in the atmosphere, which was then being conducted by the Soviet Union—and continuing through his positions as a science adviser to several U.S. presidential administrations (1961–64, 1965–73, and 1978–80). His efforts helped bring about the treaties banning atmospheric nuclear testing (1963) and limiting antiballistic missiles (1972). He criticized the Reagan administration's proposed "Star Wars" defensive missile shield in 1983, and to the end of his life, he was tireless in promoting close collaboration and information exchange with scientists and academics in other countries, notably China and the nations of the former Soviet Union. Panofsky was born into an academic Jewish family in Berlin, Germany. With his family he emigrated from Germany to the United States after Hitler issued his first anti-Jewish decrees, in 1934. The family settled in Princeton, New Jersey, where his father, the art historian Erwin Panofsky, joined the faculty of the Institute for Advanced Study; meanwhile, Pief, as he was nicknamed, then 15, matriculated at Princeton University. After earning a B.S. degree in physics at Princeton and a doctorate in physics at the California Institute of Technology, he briefly directed a scientific research and development project at Cal Tech. As a consultant with the Manhattan Project in Los Alamos, New Mexico, during the last three years of World War II (1943–45), he helped to design instruments that measured the yield of the first atomic bombs when they were test-exploded in July 1945. At the University of California at Berkeley after the war—first as a staff physicist in the university's radiation laboratory and later with the title of associate professor—he, with others, succeeded in isolating a neutral pi meson, a type of the subatomic particle called the pion. He joined the faculty of Stanford University as a full professor of physics in 1951; he became the director of the university's high-energy physics laboratory in 1953 and of the Stanford Linear Accelerator Center in 1961. After resigning as director of SLAC in 1984, he continued teaching at Stanford until 1989, and he maintained his campus office thereafter. Panofsky was the author of the book *Particles and Policy* (1994) and the co-author of *Classical Electricity and Magnetism* (hardcover, 1955; paperback, 2005) and *Panofsky on Physics, Politics, and Peace: Pief Remembers* (2007). He died of a heart attack in Mountain View, near Los Altos, California. His survivors included his wife, the former Adele Dumond, three sons, two daughters, nine grandchildren, and two great-grandchildren. In his obituary in the *Washington Post*, Martin Weil quoted Panofsky's daughter Carol as affirming that her father "really believed in disarming the world" and furthering "pure science for the sake of pure science." See *Current Biography* (1970).

Obituary *New York Times* Sep. 28, 2007

PATTERSON, FLOYD Jan. 4, 1935–May 11, 2006 Prize fighter; world heavyweight boxing champion (1956–59, 1960–62). Patterson won pugilism's most coveted title when he was 21 years old, younger than any of his predecessors, and he set another precedent when he regained the championship after having lost it. On the negative side, he set a record of sorts by being floored 17 times in 13 championship bouts. "They said I was the fighter who got knocked down the most," he remarked after his retirement, "but I also got up the most." Finally, his personality, sensitive and gentlemanly, set him apart from most of his peers in a brutal sport. Even at six feet and 185 pounds, he was undersized as heavyweights go, but he compensated with speed of fist and foot. Born in a cabin in Waco, North Carolina, and reared in the black Bedford-Stuyvesant ghetto of Brooklyn, in New York City, he found in boxing an escape route from poverty and juvenile delinquency. At age 14 he began working out at the Gramercy Gym, operated on Manhattan's Lower East Side by Constantine "Cus" D'Amato, who became his manager. (D'Amato later managed Mike Tyson as well.) Patterson entered the New York Golden Gloves competition in 1950; he won the Golden Gloves open middleweight title the following year. In three years as an amateur, he won 40 fights, 37 of them by knockout, and lost four. He captured nine titles, including the 1952 Olympic middleweight championship, before turning professional in September 1952. As a pro, he competed as a middleweight and light-heavyweight before entering the heavyweight division. Out of his

first 31 pro fights, he lost only one, to Joey Maxim in a highly disputed decision in June 1954. In his 32d bout, on November 30, 1956, he captured the heavyweight championship by knocking out Archie Moore in the fifth round. Over the following 16 months, he successfully defended his heavyweight title four times before losing to Ingemar Johansson on June 26, 1959, when the referee stopped the fight in the third round after Patterson had been floored seven times. He regained the championship in a rematch with Johansson on June 20, 1960, when he knocked Johansson out in the fifth round with one of the most powerful left hooks in boxing history. (Having done so, he surprised the crowd by hastening to help the fallen Swede back to his corner.) In a third encounter with Johansson, on March 13, 1961, he again won by a knockout, in the sixth round. On September 25, 1962 Sonny Liston took the title from Patterson by a knockout in the first round. In a rematch with Liston the following year, Patterson was again knocked out in the first round. After Muhammad Ali wrested the heavyweight title from Liston, Patterson challenged Ali, on November 22, 1965; Ali pummeled him brutally for 12 rounds and won by a technical knockout. When Ali was stripped of his title for refusing to submit to military conscription, in 1967, the World Boxing Association staged a tournament to decide a new champion, during which Jimmy Ellis won a 15-round referee's decision over Patterson. In the last fight of his career, on September 20, 1972, Patterson challenged Ali for the North American Boxing Federation heavyweight title and lost by a technical knockout in the seventh round. Patterson's totals in 20 years as a professional were 55 victories, eight losses, and one draw. He retired to New Paltz, New York, where he devoted himself to farming and running an amateur boxing club. One of the young neophytes he trained in his New Paltz gym was an orphaned boy named Tracy Harris, whom he adopted. Tracy, who won the World Boxing Council super featherweight championship in 1992, later became estranged from his stepfather. Patterson was a member of the New York State Athletic Commission from 1977 to 1984, and he chaired the commission from 1995 to 1998. He died on his farm in New Paltz. Not counting Tracy Harris Patterson, his survivors included his third wife, Janet, four daughters, two sons, and eight grandchildren. See *Current Biography* (1960).

Obituary *New York Times* A p2 May 12, 2006

PAVAROTTI, LUCIANO Oct. 12, 1935–Sep. 6, 2007 Italian opera singer. Luciano Pavarotti was among the most popular lyric tenors of his time. A hefty and charismatic presence on the operatic and recital stages, he won not only the esteem of operagoers but the hearts and imaginations of the masses, to a degree reminiscent of Enrico Caruso. Combining emotional depth with power and quality, he made the rafters ring with his clarion flights through the high C's without ever losing his perfect pitch and purity of tone and articulation. "His phrasing was stylish, his diction impeccable, and he could infuse a simple love song or a complicated aria with exquisite tenderness . . . ," Elizabeth Forbes wrote for the London *Independent* (September 7, 2007). "As his voice matured, it gained in warmth and colour, as well as strength, without losing the flexibility that enabled him to sing the bel-canto roles of Bellini and Donizetti [and] in particular Elvino in *La Sonnambula*, Arturo in *I Puritani*, Edgardo in *Lucia di Lammermoor*, and Fernando in *La Favorita*." Pavarotti's repertoire also included Tonio in *La Fille du Régiment*, Riccardo in *Un Ballo in Maschera*, Idamante in *Idomeneo*, Canio in *Pagliacci*, Radames in *Aïda*, Cavaradossi in *Tosca*, and the title role in Verdi's *Otello*. Pavarotti made his professional debut in Reggio Emilia, Italy, in 1961. Two years later he began his international career, with performances in London, Dublin, Amsterdam, Zurich, and Vienna; he later made his debuts at the Rome Opera and at La Scala, in Milan, Italy. He began a long association with Joan Sutherland with his U.S. debut, in Miami, Florida, in 1966, in which he sang Edgardo opposite Sutherland as Lucia. Two years later he made his debut at the Metropolitan Opera in New York City, as Rodolfo in *La Bohème*. During his years with the Met, he gave 379 performances, including 357 in fully staged productions. During the latter years of his career, when he had added excessive weight to his five-foot nine-inch frame and when his recital venues had become larger, he was, in Forbes's words, "a giant, both literally and figuratively, who sang in football stadiums, sports arenas and open-air theatres . . . one who turned a Puccini aria into a pop number and whose trademark was the large white handkerchief, clutched in his left hand, with which he frequently mopped his brow." With Plácido Domingo and José Carreras, he made world concert tours as a member of the Three Tenors. That trio's first recording, *Carreras, Domingo, Pavarotti*, is the most commercially successful classical album of all time. In a series of charity concerts called "Pavarotti and Friends," he performed with the Spice Girls, Elton John, Sting, and other pop-music stars. As a recording artist he had, in the opinion of the soprano Renee Fleming, "the most perfect technique in the history of recorded music," and his sales of more than 100 million records were extraordinary for a classical singer. Being a natural "by ear" singer more than he was a reader of music, as he grew older he found it increasingly difficult to memorize new roles. He gave his last performance with the Royal Opera in London in January 2002 and with the Met in March 2004 (his last stage appearance). With William Wright, he wrote two autobiographies, both in English: *Pavarotti: My Own Story* (1981) and *Pavarotti: My World* (1995). He died of pancreatic cancer at his home in his native Modena, Italy. His survivors included three daughters from his first marriage, one daughter from his second, and one granddaughter. See *Current Biography* (1973).

Obituary *New York Times* B p7 Sep. 7, 2007

PINOCHET, AUGUSTO Nov. 25, 1915–Dec. 10, 2006 Chilean dictator. After graduating from the Escuela Militar in Santiago in 1936, Augusto Pinochet rose up the ranks of the Chilean army to become a general in the late 1960s and commander in chief of the army under President Salvador Allende, a Marxist who was democratically elected in 1970. On September 11, 1973 Pinochet participated in a bloody coup that toppled the Allende government and resulted in Allende's death in the bombed ruins of the presidential palace. Following the coup Pinochet became chairman of a four-man ruling junta, and in June 1974 he assumed the presidency of Chile. As president, following the advice of a group of free-market economists, he led the country into a two-decade period of sustained economic growth. At the same time he oversaw the execution or "disappearance" of more than 3,000 persons who were perceived to be enemies of his regime and the torture or exile of tens of thousands more. In 1990, after promulgating a constitution guaranteeing what he viewed as a "protected democracy," he resigned the presidency, but he remained commander in chief of the army. As such, for eight years he exerted influence as a gray eminence behind the successive elected, ostensibly centrist and center-left governments of Patricio Aylwin, Eduardo Frei Ruiz-Tagle, and Ricardo Lagos. In March 1998 he resigned as army commander in chief and was named a senator for life. In the autumn of 1998, he went to London, England, for a back operation, evidently not realizing how vulnerable he was to prosecution by international jurists. On October 10, 1998 the Spanish magistrate Baltasar Garzón issued a warrant for his arrest for the kidnapping, torture, and death of Spanish citizens during his years as president of Chile and for his extradition for trial in Madrid. Six days later Pinochet was arrested while he was recuperating at a London clinic. After 16 months of legal wrangling, a medical panel on March 2, 2000 decided that his health did not allow him to stand trial. The following day he was flown back to Chile, where the legal wrangling continued and he was eventually placed under house arrest. He died in Santiago, Chile. His survivors included his wife, Lucia (nee Hiriart Rodriguez), and their two sons and three daughters. See *Current Biography* (1974).

Obituary *New York Times* A p1+ Dec. 11, 2006

POSTON, TOM Oct. 17, 1921–Apr. 30, 2007 Stage, screen, and television actor. Tom Poston, a tall performer with a long, pale face and a droll manner, was best known for the good-natured but befuddled comic characters he created on television. Beginning in December 1956 he was for several years one of the resident eccentrics on the NBC weekly comedy/variety program *The Steve Allen Show*, playing a dazed Everyman unable to remember even his name in mock street interviews. For that role he won an Emmy Award in 1959. Outstanding among his many later television "goof-up" roles, as he called them, was that of George Utley, the kindly but incompetent handyman who appeared in 184 episodes (1982–90) of the CBS show *Newhart*, the second of Bob Newhart's situation comedies. Thomas Poston began his career as a child acrobat. After serving as a decorated U.S. Army Air Corps pilot in combat in World War II, he studied acting in New York City and performed with stock companies in Delaware. On Broadway he made his debut as the replacement for Jose Ferrer in *Cyrano de Bergerac* in 1947; he subsequently replaced Orson Bean in *Will Success Spoil Rock Hunter?*, in 1955, and Peter Ustinov in *Romanoff and Juliet*, in 1958. During the 1958–59 Broadway season he created the role of Miles Pringle in the comedy *Drink to Me Only*; in 1959–60 he had star billing in the farce *Golden Fleecing*; and in 1960–61 he played the title role in the musical *The Conquering Hero*. His subsequent Broadway credits included the roles of Alan Baker in *Come Blow Your Horn* (1960), Bob McKellaway in *Mary, Mary* (1962), Walter London in *But Seriously . . .* (1969), Billy Boylan in *Forty Carats* (1970), and Prologus and Pseudolus in *A Funny Thing Happened on the Way to the Forum* (1972). Away from Broadway he played in stock-company and touring stage productions until the mid-1970s. Meanwhile, since 1950 he had been playing roles on network television, at first in dramatic series and in teleplays on such showcases as *Studio One* and *Hallmark Hall of Fame*. He had also briefly hosted a TV game show, and for 10 years beginning in the mid-1950s, he was a frequent celebrity panelist on the quiz show *To Tell the Truth*. It was the understated ad-libbing ability he displayed as host of the live two-and-a-half-hour daily daytime variety show *Entertainment* in 1955 that caught the attention of Steve Allen. In addition to his roles on *The Steve Allen Show* and *Newhart*, he played comic characters on two episodes (1956–57) of the situation comedy *The Phil Silvers Show* (CBS), seven episodes (1978–80) of *Mork & Mindy* (ABC), and four episodes (1992–93) of *Bob* (CBS), Bob Newhart's third sitcom. Among his numerous later television credits was the character Floyd Norton in 23 episodes (1995–98) of the sitcom *Grace Under Fire* (ABC). Not counting his five made-for-TV movie roles, he had a dozen motion-picture credits, including the starring roles in the quirky comedy *Zatz!* (1962) and the comic thriller *The Old Dark House* (1963). Following his divorce from his first wife, Jean Sullivan, Poston married, divorced, and remarried Kay Hudson, who died in 1998. His survivors included his third wife, the actress Susanne Pleshette, whom he married in 2001, a daughter from his first marriage, and a daughter and son from his second marriage. Poston died at his home in Los Angeles. See *Current Biography* (1961).

Obituary *New York Times* C p17 May 2, 2007

RICHARDS, ANN Sep. 1, 1933–Sep. 13, 2006 Forty-fifth governor of Texas (1991–95). Ann Richards was the second female governor of the Lone Star state, the first being Miriam Amanda ("Ma") Ferguson (1925–27, 1933–35). The silver-haired, bouffant-coiffed Richards was a progressive Democrat with a sassy and flamboyant persona, a quick wit, unfailing high spirits, and a commanding albeit homespun speaking style. Avoiding adversarial politics, she disarmed her opponents with humor, using laughter, as she said, "to open doors and bring down walls." Richards's maiden name was Dorothy Ann Willis. As a high-school student in Waco, Texas, she was known for the plainspoken directness that would serve her so well on the political podium, as she recalled in her autobiography, *Straight from the Heart* (1989): "I only knew how to go straight to the heart of a thing. I said what I was thinking." After earning a B.A. degree in speech and government at Baylor University and a certificate in teaching at the University of Texas at Austin, she taught government and history at a junior high school in Austin for

two years (1955–57). Even while raising her four children, beginning in the 1950s, she was involved in politics, partly as the wife of David Richards, a lawyer and a Democratic precinct chairman, and, more importantly, out of her own spirit of activism in the causes of civil rights and economic justice. Early on, she helped found North Dallas Democratic Women, an organization devoted to increasing the strength of women in the party, and became a volunteer in many political campaigns. In 1972 she managed the successful campaign for election to the Texas state legislature of Sarah Weddington, the chief lawyer in the abortion-rights case *Roe v. Wade*. In 1976 she was elected a commissioner of Travis County, Texas. During six years in that position, she not only excelled in supervising road maintenance (the most important commissioner's job up to that time) but created agencies—including a rape crisis center, a center for battered women, and a program for families with Down syndrome children—that collectively became the inspiration for and nucleus of a panoply of Travis County human-service offerings. She was elected Texas state treasurer in 1982 and reelected in 1986. During her eight years in that job, she was credited with modernizing the state's treasury. She moved into the national spotlight with her keynote address at the 1988 Democratic National Convention, which included her memorable quip about George H. W. Bush (the Republican candidate, who would win election that year as the 41st president of the United States): "Poor George, he can't help it—he was born with a silver shoe in his mouth." Also noteworthy was her remark during the same speech in which, alluding to the capabilities of women and men and referring to a famous dance team, she said, "Ginger Rogers did everything Fred Astaire did. She just did it backwards and in high heels." As governor of Texas, she attempted to make government regulatory agencies more business friendly and thereby initiated programs that reversed an economic slump the state had been in since the mid-1980s. Stressing efficiency and ethics, she authorized comprehensive audits of every agency in the state bureaucracy, which resulted in savings of $6 billion. In reforming the state's corrections system, she reduced the rate at which violent offenders were released, increased space to accommodate a rising penal population, and introduced substance-abuse programs in prisons. Regarding gun control, she supported proposals to reduce the sale of automatic and semi-automatic assault firearms and "cop-killer" bullets. In education, she attempted a redistribution of funding across school districts, from rich to poor, and instituted "site-based management" in an effort to decentralize control over school districts and college and university campuses. In a related action, she oversaw the institution of a state lottery promoted as a potential source of supplementary funding for education. She also signed into law an amendment to the Texas Financial Responsibility Law that essentially stressed the requirement that a motorist must have a valid auto-insurance policy. Perhaps above all, she contributed to diversification, bringing more women and members of minority groups into state government. In 1994 she lost the Texas gubernatorial election to George W. Bush, the son of President George H. W. Bush and himself the future 43d president of the United States. An addiction to the smoking of tobacco probably contributed to the lines in Richards's face, and the alcoholism that gripped her for many years certainly contributed to her divorce from David Richards, in 1984. When she died, at her home in Austin, Texas, her daughters, Cecile and Ellen, and her sons, Daniel and Clark, were at her side. She was also survived by eight grandchildren. Her daughter Cecile Richards is currently the president of the Planned Parenthood Federation of America and the Planned Parenthood Action Fund. See *Current Biography* (1991).

Obituary *New York Times* D p8 Sep. 14, 2006

RICHARDS, LLOYD June 29, 1919–June 29, 2006 Theatrical director; actor; dramaturge; educator. Although Lloyd George Richards's great influence in American theater—including his pioneering contributions to regional theater and his nurturing of successive generations of diverse dramatic talent—transcended ethnicity, he was perhaps best known as Broadway's first director of color and as the groundbreaking directorial collaborator with the black playwrights Lorraine Hansberry and August Wilson. Richards made theatrical history in 1959 as the director of the premiere of Hansberry's *A Raisin in the Sun*, the first serious drama about the African-American experience (as well as the first play by a black woman) to be produced on the Great White Way, and he later mentored much of the Broadway career of Wilson, the dramatic chronicler of life in Pittsburgh's Hill District. Wilson was among the playwrights Richards discovered at the Eugene O'Neill Center in Waterford, Connecticut, where he was artistic director of the National Playwrights Conference (1969–99). Among his other protégés there were the playwrights Wendy Wasserstein, John Guare, and David Henry Hwang. As dean of the School of Drama at Yale University and artistic director of the Yale Repertory Theatre (1979–91), he cultivated the works of the white South African playwright Athol Fugard, among others. Richards also taught acting for many years at Hunter College, New York University, the National Theater Institute, and his Manhattan studio. One of five children, Richards was born to Jamaican immigrants in Toronto, Canada. His family immigrated to the U.S. when he was four years old. He was raised in Detroit, Michigan, under difficult conditions but with "a lot of pride," as he recalled to N. Graham Nesmith for the *African American Review* (September 22, 2005). His father, a master carpenter and a supporter of Marcus Garvey, the leader of the Back-to-Africa movement, died when Lloyd was nine; his mother became blind when he was 13. His older brother Allan assumed the mantle of head of the household and found a job. Lloyd Richards worked at odd jobs after school, and later, as a young adult, he became the chief support of his mother. "I connected to theatre in intermediate school when we studied Shakespeare . . . ," he told N. Graham Nesmith. "Some of us were called up to recite in front of the class. . . . That experience of using language, beautiful language that affected people [gave me] the same sense I felt when I read lessons as a vestryman [in the local Episcopal church]." After graduating from high school, Richards enrolled at Wayne State University (then Wayne University), in Detroit. He intended to study pre-law, but his attraction to theater arts prevailed. His education was interrupted by World War II. Drafted into the U.S. Army midway through the war, he volunteered for pilot training in the Army Air Corps. At first certified as a bombardier, he received radio training before his orders were changed and he was sent to the Tuskegee Institute (now Tuskegee University), in Alabama. There, he trained as one of the so-called Tuskegee Airmen, the famous group of black fighter pilots who flew during World War II as the 99th Pursuit Squadron, later incorporated into the 332d Fighter Group. He was still at Tuskegee when the war ended, in 1945. He returned to Detroit and resumed his studies at Wayne State while earning a living as a social worker. With 19 others at the school, he formed a dramatic troupe first called These Twenty People and then The Actors Company. He worked at the school radio station and later as an announcer and disc jockey for the Detroit radio station WJLB. In 1947 he moved to New York City, where over the next few years, into the 1950s, he studied at the Paul Mann Actors Workshop and occasionally played character roles in Equity Library Theatre and Off-Broadway productions and on radio and TV. On Broadway he played Oz in *Freight* in 1950 and Perry Hall in *Egghead* in 1957. Meanwhile, he was acquiring a reputation as a teacher and director. From 1952 to 1962 he taught and served as assistant director at the Paul Mann Actors Workshop; he was resident director of the Great Lakes Drama Festival in 1954 and of the Northland Playhouse, in Detroit, from 1955 to 1958. He became the director of *A Raisin in the Sun* thanks to the actor Sidney Poitier, a former Paul Mann student. Poitier—chosen to play the male lead in Hansberry's drama—showed Richards the script and introduced him to Hansberry and the producer Philip Rose late in 1957. Investors were reluctant to back the play, and the financing for it accumulated piecemeal over many months. Rehearsals began in December 1958, and the play had tryouts in three cities before opening on March 11, 1959 on Broadway, where it ran for 530 performances. Richards later directed the Broadway premieres of August Wilson's plays *Ma Rainey's Black Bottom* (1984–85), *Fences* (1987–88), *Joe Turner's Come and Gone* (1988), *The Piano Lesson* (1990–91), *Two Trains Running* (1992), and *Seven Guitars* (1996). As director of *Fences*, Richards won a Tony Award, and James Earl Jones won the best-actor Tony for his performance in that play. Richards's other Broadway credits included the directing of the original productions of *The Long Dream* (1960), *The Moon Besieged* (1962), *I Had a Ball* (1964–65), *The Yearling* (1965), *Paul Robeson* (1978), *A Lesson from Aloes* (1980–81), *"Master Harold" . . . and the Boys* (1982–83), *A Walk in the Woods* (1988), *The Cemetary Club* (1990), and revivals of *Blood Knot* (1985–86), *Long Day's Journey into Night* (1988), and *Ah, Wilderness!* (1988). On TV, he directed an episode of *Roots: The Next Generation* in 1979 and an adaptation of *The Piano Lesson* in 1995, among other productions. He died in Manhattan and was survived by his wife, the actress Barbara Davenport, and two sons. See *Current Biography* (1987).

Obituary *New York Times* C p10 July 1, 2006

RIZZUTO, PHIL Sep. 25, 1918–Aug. 13, 2007 Professional baseball player; sports broadcaster. With the New York Yankees between 1941 and 1956, the scrappy little shortstop Phil "Scooter" Rizzuto was a sparkplug complementing the vaunted slugging of such teammates as Joe DiMaggio and Mickey Mantle in the winning of 11 American League pennants and seven World Series. In addition to his surehanded and nimble fielding—which was often acrobatic, including diving catches—the five-foot-six right-hander was offensively a superb "small ball" clutch hitter whose fortes included strategic sacrifice bunting and swift running of the bases. After his retirement as a player, he was for 40 years a popular radio and television broadcaster of Yankee games, his Brooklyn-accented commentary punctuated with such expressions as "Holy cow!" and "You huckleberry!" Philip Francis Rizzuto began playing in the New York minor-league farm system in 1937. He moved up to the majors in 1941, when he had a batting average of .307 and a fielding average of .957 and led the American League in double plays. In 1942 he batted .284, fielded .962, and led the league in putouts as well as double plays. Wartime service in the U.S. Navy kept him out of pro baseball for three seasons, until 1946. In 1947 he had a .969 fielding average, a new record for Yankee shortstops, and he bettered that record to .973 the following year. In 1949 he led league shortstops in fielding with a .971 percentage. At that time he was moved into the leadoff position in the New York lineup. The Baseball Writers of America voted him the league's Most Valuable Player in 1950, when he batted .324, had 200 hits (including 50 for extra bases and home runs), scored 125 runs, and made 288 straight plays at shortstop without an error. A memorable demonstration of his complementary role in the Yankees' offense took place on September 17, 1951 during a game against the Cleveland Indians that decided the American League championship. The decisive moment occurred in the bottom of the ninth inning, when Joe DiMaggio began his sprint home from third base just as the Cleveland pitcher Bob Lemon was throwing to Rizzuto at the plate a pitch that was deliberately high, to make a bunt difficult. With both feet off the ground, Rizzuto overcame the difficulty and squeeze-bunted the ball toward first base, enabling DiMaggio to score and clinch the pennant. During his 13 years in Yankee pinstripes, Rizzuto's career average at the plate was .273; he had 1,588 career hits, including 239 doubles, 62 triples, and 38 home runs; his career on-base percentage was .351; he stole 149 bases, scored 877 runs, and drove in 563. In the field his career percentage was .968, second in history only to Lou Boudreau's .973 among American League shortstops; his career total of 1,217 double plays was second only to Luke Appling's 1,424 among league shortstops. He was on five American League All-Star teams, and he established World Series records for most games played, putouts, double plays, and assists as a shortstop. He was released as a player by the Yankees in August 1956. At the beginning of the following season, he became one of the announcers of Yankee games on radio station WPIX and television station WPIX-TV in New York City. He remained in that broadcasting post for 40 years, until 1996. The Yankees retired his uniform

number—10—in 1985. He was inducted into the Baseball Hall of Fame in 1994. In retirement, he owned and operated the Rizzuto-Berra Bowling Lanes in Clifton, New Jersey, in partnership with Yogi Berra. Through his acquaintance with a blind boy named Ed Lucas, he became a supporter of St. Joseph's School for the Blind in Newark, New Jersey, which Lucas attended. In addition to his personal donations, he raised more than $2 million for the school by organizing celebrity golf tournaments. He published a collection of verse, *O Holy Cow!* (1993), and with Al Silverman he wrote the book *The "Miracle" New York Yankees* (1962). Suffering from muscular atrophy, among other ailments, he spent the last months of his life at Green Hill, an assisted-living facility in West Orange, New Jersey, where he died. The immediate cause of death was pneumonia. His survivors included his wife, Cora Anne (nee Ellenborn), three daughters, a son, and two granddaughters. See *Current Biography* (1950).

Obituary *New York Times* A p1+ Aug. 15, 2007

ROACH, MAX Jan. 10, 1924–Aug. 16, 2007 Jazz percussionist, composer, bandleader, and educator; "the Duke Ellington of the drums." Max Roach is generally acknowledged to have been the world's greatest bop drummer. No modern master of the jazz drums of any school has been more influential than he in defining the role, extending the reach, and fulfilling the potential of his drum kit, which he called his "multiple percussion unit." In an article about jazz for the *New York Times* (July 31, 1988), the trumpeter Wynton Marsalis wrote of Roach, "All great instrumentalists have a superior quality of sound, and his is one of the marvels of contemporary music. . . . The roundness and nobility of sound on the drums and the clarity and precision of the cymbals distinguishes Max Roach as a peerless master." Early in his career, in the 1940s and early 1950s, Roach participated in the bebop revolution, in which black musicians unhappy with the elaborately scored and arranged music of the swing era's big bands formed small, more improvisational ensembles in which they explored faster tempos, overlapping harmonies, altered chords, and chord substitutions. During that revolution Roach personified the gravitation of the drummer away from mere time-keeping, and he soon became recognized as that new phenomenon among jazz drummers, a virtuoso. Throughout his career of more than half a century, he continued to seek new challenges not only inside jazz but also outside, including collaborations with the Boston Symphony Orchestra, the Alvin Ailey Dance Company, the rapper Fab Five Freddie, such avant-garde musicians as the pianist Cecil Taylor and the saxophonist Anthony Braxton, the playwright/actor Sam Shepard, and the writers Amiri Baraka and Toni Morrison (in spoken-word concerts). His work as an educator included a full-time professorship at the University of Massachusetts at Amherst from 1973 to 1979 and a subsequent summer-session adjunct professorship at that university. No black jazz musician of his time was more forthright and fearless in his advocacy of civil rights and racial equality. Maxwell Lemuel Roach, who was largely self-taught in music, was born in Newland,

North Carolina, and grew up in the Bedford-Stuyvesant section of Brooklyn, New York City. His first break as a working musician came when, while still in his teens, he sat in on the drums for an ailing Sonny Greer with the Duke Ellington orchestra for three nights at the Paramount Theater in Manhattan. Beginning in the early and mid-1940s, he performed at other Manhattan venues—including clubs in Greenwich Village, on 52d Street, and in Harlem (especially Minton's Playhouse)—and in recording studios with the older bop musicians Dizzy Gillespie, Thelonious Monk, and Charlie Parker. He later worked as well with such bop musicians as J. J. Johnson and Dexter Gordon and recorded with Miles Davis, Bud Powell, and Sonny Rollins. The pianists and horn players in bop quartets, quintets, and sextets—all of which usually included a throbbing string bass—enjoyed a kind of free-flowing musical intercommunication impossible in the big bands, and the pianist, no longer required to mark rhythm four times per measure, had the opportunity to join in. No one—not even Kenny Clarke, the undisputed founder of bop drumming—exploited that opportunity more fully than Roach. While maintaining the rhythmic pulse in legato patterns on the ride cymbal, he produced a wash of sound for the ensemble and performed a contrapuntal function similar to that of the pianist; using various components of the drum kit, including the bass and snare drums and the crash cymbal, he achieved what he called "melodic drumming," setting up "lyrical patterns in rhythm which give indications of the structure of the song you're playing." He explored such time signatures as 3/4 and 5/4 and the superimposition of 6/4 on 4/4. As a critic observed on one occasion, he "plays in front of and behind the beat, stops and starts the pulse unexpectedly, and plays melodic variations that counterpoint the quick changes voiced by [the] saxophonist," and another noted that he was capable of drumming even "in waltz time." One of the high points in his career in his own view was his formation in partnership with the stellar young trumpeter Clifford Brown in 1954 of the Roach-Brown Quintet, which proceeded to record several seminal hard-bop albums. Emotionally devastated when Brown was killed in an automobile accident, in 1956, Roach descended into a state of alcoholic depression for several years. In collaboration with the lyricist Oscar Brown Jr., he composed "The Freedom Now Suite," included in his protest jazz album *We Insist!* (1960), a landmark musical contribution to the civil rights movement. The vocalist on that LP was Abbey Lincoln, who would become his second wife (1962–70). In 1970 he formed M'Boom, an ensemble with eight players and a variety of percussion instruments. Between the late 1970s and 2000, he led a succession of ensembles, including quartets, one of which, in the mid-1980s, joined in performance with a string quartet led by his daughter, Maxine, a violist. He also participated in duets and gave solo performances. The pianist Marian McPartland once remarked that he was the only musician she had ever seen "perform a concert entirely of drum solos." In 1988 he received a MacArthur fellowship, the so-called "genius" grant, and in 1995 he was inducted into the Grammy Hall of Fame. In 2002 he made the last of his many recordings, with the trumpeter Clark Terry.

He was married and divorced three times and had two common-law relationships. Diagnosed with hydrocephalus in 2004, he spent the final years of his life in an assisted-living facility in Brooklyn. He died at a hospital in Manhattan. His survivors included two sons, Daryl and Raoul, and three daughters, Maxine, Ayodele, and Dara. See *Current Biography* (1986).

Obituary *New York Times* A p1+ Aug. 17, 2007

ROBINSON, EDDIE Feb. 12, 1919–Apr. 3, 2007 Football coach at Grambling State University (1941–97), in Louisiana. Beginning against odds in the Jim Crow era, Eddie Robinson built the Grambling Tigers from an obscure, traditionally black-college team into a Southwestern Athletic Conference (SWAC) and National Collegiate Athletic Asociation Division I powerhouse. In the process he had 45 winning seasons and set collegiate records for games coached (588) and for number of years coaching at one college (57, counting two early seasons when the Tigers were inactive). Twenty of his players won All-American honors, four were inducted into the College Football Hall of Fame, and a record 210 became pros in the National Football League. In 1985 Robinson surpassed Paul "Bear" Bryant's record for games won (323) to become the winningest coach in college-football history, and in 1995 he became the first to reach the 400 mark. His final record of 409 victories (with 165 losses and 15 ties) was broken in 2003 by John Gagliardi at St. John's University in Minnesota, whose career record at the end of the 2006 season stood unbroken at 443–120–11. With Richard Lapchick, Robinson wrote the autobiography *Never Before, Never Again* (1999). Aaron S. Lee compiled the volume *Quotable Eddie Robinson* (2003), comprising 408 quotations about football, life, and success by and about Robinson. Eddie (not Edward) Gay Robinson was born to a sharecropper father and a domestic-worker mother in Jackson, Louisiana. He starred in various backfield positions in football at Leland College in Baker, Louisiana, where he earned a B.A. degree in 1940. He then joined the faculty of Grambling State University, then known as Grambling State College. (It was previously called the Louisiana Negro Normal and Industrial Institute and had been founded as the Colored Industrial and Agricultural School, in 1901.) Robinson immediately began reorganizing and developing the school's nondescript, small-town athletic program and football team. He did so virtually single-handedly at first, with some volunteer help from the school's night watchman. (For reasons connected with World War II, there was no football at Grambling between 1943 and 1945. During those seasons Robinson coached the football team at Grambling High School, winning a championship.) In 1949 one of Robinson's protégés, Paul "Tank" Younger, became the first player from a traditionally black college to sign with a National Football League team. Robinson subsequently sent 209 more players to the NFL. Seven were first-round draft choices. (A number of other Grambling players went to the Canadian Football League and the now-defunct U.S. Football League.) In 1954 he earned an M.S. degree from the University of Iowa. The following year, with a 10–0 record, Grambling claimed the first of nine NCAA Division 1-AA National Black College Championships under Robinson. In 1959 the Grambling Tigers were admitted into the Southwestern Athletic Conference. The next year Robinson guided them to the first of 17 SWAC championships or co-championships. One of Robinson's outstanding protégés was Doug Williams, the first black quarterback to be named a Superbowl Most Valuable Player. Succeeding Robinson as coach at Grambling in 1998, Williams coached the team for six seasons, during which the Tigers won three straight NCAA Division 1-AA National Black College and SWAC championships. Robinson "wasn't just about football," Williams said in a press interview after Robinson's death. "He was about human beings. . . . The work Coach has done is not so much about the football field and the number of players he put in the NFL. It's about the people he didn't send to the NFL." A positive thinker who was happy to "be an American," in his words, Robinson said that he tried to teach his players to eschew attitudes of victimhood and to concentrate on the opportunities to be found if you "understand the system" and "aren't lazy." Eighty percent of the 4,000 players he coached received college degrees. He was inducted into the College Football Hall of Fame in 1997. Among his other honors were five honorary degrees, coaching awards named for him by the Football Writers Association of America and Street & Smith Publications, and the football stadium named for him at Grambling State University. Following his death, from complications of Alzheimer's disease, at Lincoln General Hospital in Ruston, Louisiana, Robinson's body lay in state in the Capitol Rotunda in Baton Rouge, Louisiana, on April 9, 2007. He was survived by his wife of 64 years, Doris, a son, a daughter, five grandchildren, and, according to most sources, nine great-grandchildren. See *Current Biography* (1988).

Obituary *New York Times* B p7 Apr. 5, 2007

RODDICK, ANITA Oct. 23, 1942–Sep. 10, 2007 British businesswoman and social activist; "the queen of green." Anita Roddick (née Perilli) was the founder of the Body Shop chain of stores, which offer eco-friendly cosmetics and toiletries, manufactured without cruelty to animals, to many millions of customers worldwide. As such, Roddick was not only one of Britain's most successful retailers but also a foremost pioneer in turning the once fringe ideals of entrepreneurial social conscience and ethical consumerism into mainstream corporate concerns. As envisioned by Anita Roddick, the Body Shop was dedicated to "using our stores and our products to help communicate human rights" and to pursue "social and environmental change." The chief source of the original knowledge she brought to the founding of the Body Shop was her international traveling as a young adult, when, in such places as Tahiti, the New Hebrides, New Caledonia, and the Australian outback, she noted the efficacy of the beauty rituals of indigenous women using freely available natural ingredients such as cocoa butter and tea-tree oil. Such ingredients from renewable sources, along with vitamins, became the core components of the products she created with the assis-

tance of an herbalist. Unlike traditional cosmetic manufacturers, she tried to offer women not over-priced chemical creations promising unattainable glamour but, essentially, a line of relatively affordable creams, shampoos, and other products designed to "cleanse, polish, and protect the skin and hair." (She would later add a great variety of other items, including makeup and bath items and fragrances.) In addition, she was able to boast that none of her products had been tested on animals. Having been taught by her mother to recycle everything possible—and originally experiencing a shortage of the plastic bottles in which she sold her wares—she first ventured into environmental activism on a small scale by offering to refill bottles brought back by customers. She opened her first Body Shop in Brighton, England, in the spring of 1976 and her second in Chichester, England, the following September. Her husband, Gordon Roddick, joined her in the business, as CEO, in 1977. The couple began franchising in 1978, and within 30 years there were more than 2,000 Body Shop stores in 51 markets across 12 international time zones. In 1984 the company went public. In the mid-1980s the Body Shop became the first cosmetics company to establish a direct business relationship with suppliers of cocoa butter and other natural ingredients through a program called Community Trade (originally "Trade Not Aid"). Community Trade began with one supplier in India and in time provided essential income to 15,000 people across the globe, from Brazil to Zambia. Anita Roddick brought the Body Shop's clout to the aid of Nigerians seeking justice against Shell Oil in 1993. In stepping down as managing director of the Body Shop, in 1998, and as co-chair, in 2002, she freed herself to work more fully in her many causes and charities. Those included Amnesty International, Greenpeace, Human Rights Watch, the Nuclear Age Peace Foundation, the Hepatitis C Trust, Friends of the Earth, the National Coalition to Free the Angola 3; she also supported organizations or projects promoting the development of alternative energy or the protection of battered women or fighting slave-labor sweatshops in Bangladesh or capital punishment anywhere. She founded Anita Roddick Publications, published the autobiography *Business as Usual* (2000), and edited *Take It Personally* (2001), a book attacking globalization and the World Trade Organization. She also founded the organization Children on the Edge, to help children in distress or at risk internationally, and Body & Soul, to help families living with or affected by HIV or AIDS, and she co-founded the magazine the *Big Issue,* produced and sold by homeless people. Queen Elizabeth II made her a Dame of the British Empire in 2003. The Body Shop was sold to the L'Oréal Group in 2006. Dame Anita Roddick, who suffered from hepatitis C, died in St. Richard's Hospital in Chichester, England, after suffering a major brain hemorrhage. Her survivors included her husband and her two daughters, Samantha and Justine. See *Current Biography* (1992).

Obituary *New York Times* C p11 Sep. 12, 2000

ROSENTHAL, JOE Oct. 9, 1911–Aug. 20, 2006 Photographer. In February 1945, during World War II, the Associated Press cameraman Joe Rosenthal took a photograph of five U.S. Marines and a U.S. Navy corpsman raising a giant American flag atop Mount Suribachi on Iwo Jima, a volcanic island 600 nautical miles south of Tokyo. That dramatic documentation of the first American foothold within Japanese homeland jurisdiction gave a tremendous boost to U.S. home-front morale and remains one of the most recognizable images in American history. During 1945 it was seen on several million posters promoting a Treasury Department war-bond campaign, was selected as the design for a commemorative postage stamp, and brought Rosenthal a Pulitzer Prize; later, it was replicated in the gigantic bronze sculpture that is the central feature of the Marine Corps Memorial near Arlington National Cemetery; and over the years it has been reproduced countless times in newspapers, magazines, books, and films. Rosenthal began his career as a photojournalist in San Francisco in the early 1930s. In 1936 he went to work for Wide World Photos, and he became an Associated Press photographer when the A.P. acquired Wide World, in August 1941. Because of his poor eyesight he was rejected for military service after the U.S. entered World War II, in December 1941, but in August 1943 he was allowed to enlist as a warrant officer in the U.S. Maritime Service. In that post he photographed convoy activity across the Atlantic and in ports in the United Kingdom and North Africa. Rejoining the A.P. as an accredited war photographer in the Pacific in March 1944, he covered the U.S. invasions of New Guinea, Hollandia, Guam, Peleliu, and Angaur before accompanying one of the early waves of Marines landing at Iwo Jima on February 19, 1945. (The island was small but strategic for supporting planned flights of American long-range B-29 bombers and the option of an invasion of Japan.) The celebrated event photographed by Rosenthal four days later was the second American flag-raising on Iwo Jima, but it was not posed, a common misconception notwithstanding. (The first took place at a lower height and with a smaller flag.) The event was far from marking the climax or denouement of one the hardest-fought and costliest campaigns in the history of the Marines. The U.S. victory did not come until March 19, 1945, and the concluding operations lasted seven more days. Rosenthal also photographed action in several carrier bombing missions, including that which contributed to the U.S. conquest of the Japanese island of Okinawa in the last major battle (March–June 1945) of World War II, which was also the largest sea-air-land battle in world history. After the war he joined the staff of the *San Francisco Chronicle* as a general-assignment photographer. He remained with the *Chronicle* for 35 years. Rosenthal's marriage to the former Dorothy Lee Walch ended in divorce. He died in an assisted-living facility in Novato, California. His survivors included a daughter, a son, two grandchildren, and four great-grandchildren. See *Current Biography* (1945).

Obituary *New York Times* C p11 Aug. 22, 2006

ROSTROPOVICH, MSTISLAV Mar. 27, 1927–Apr. 27, 2007 Russian musician. Born in Baku, Azerbaijan, in the Soviet Union, the cellist, pianist, and conductor Mstislav Leopoldovich Rostropovich was in-

ternationally celebrated not only for his musicianship but also for his brave advocacy of civil rights and artistic freedom in his native land. Rostropovich made his debut as a cellist in 1940. He taught at the Moscow Conservatory beginning in 1953, and then at the Leningrad Conservatory and the Cuban National Conservatory until he left the Soviet Union, in 1976—the year before he became the music director and conductor of the National Symphony in Washington, D.C. With his wife, the operatic soprano Galina Vishnevskaya (whom he often accompanied in concerts and recitals), he lived thereafter in the West as an expatriate until 1990, when the Soviet Union was in the process of dissolving. A global commuter, he continued leading the National Symphony until 1994, building it into a world-class orchestra. As a conductor, he was at his best with Russian works, including those of his modernist mentors, Shostakovich and Prokofiev. As a virtuoso cellist who ranked with Pablo Casals, he ranged in his repertoire from Bach's suites for unaccompanied cello to scores of works written for him by composers including Shostakovich, Benjamin Britten, and Leonard Bernstein. At the cello and piano, as in his conducting, he combined technical command with the emotional intensity he called "heart." A jet-setting guest conductor, recitalist, and master-class teacher, he earned many honors, in the Soviet Union, Europe, and the West. He died in Moscow of cancer. His survivors included his wife and their two daughters. See *Current Biography* (1988).

Obituary *New York Times* A p1+ Apr. 28, 2007

ROTHSCHILD, BARON GUY DE May 21, 1909–June 12, 2007 International banker and financier. Baron Guy Édouard Alphonse de Rothschild was a senior scion of the French branch of the House of Rothschild, the complex European banking dynasty that originated in Germany in the early 19th century and was subsequently elevated to nobility by Austrian and British governments. In Paris in the mid-1930s, Baron Guy de Rothschild joined the family firm of MM. de Rothschild Frères—the largest private investment bank in France, headed by his father, Baron Édouard Alphonse de Rothschild—and became involved in running various companies controlled by the bank, including at that time the Chemin de Fer du Nord, the major French railroad. (The physical assets of the railroad were subsequently nationalized but its corporate apparatus remained under Rothschild control, becoming the Compagnie du Nord, a vast holding company with far-flung interests in shipping, mining, oil, and chemicals.) Early in World War II, Rothschild's parents and other relatives fled to the United States; he himself, as a French cavalry officer, was evacuated at Dunkirk during the German invasion of France in the spring of 1940. Staying only briefly in England, he returned to Paris, where he watched helplessly as the Nazis took over his family's houses and other properties, forced the sale of Rothschild-owned stocks on a depressed market, and confiscated the vast Rothschild art collection. Attempting to keep a semblance of MM. de Rothschild Frères in operation, he moved the bank's offices from Paris to the Auvergne region in the south of France, where it withered under the oppressive jurisdiction of the collaborationist and fiercely anti-Semitic Vichy government of Marshal Pétain. After a Pétain government decree stripped him of his French citizenship, he traveled to Lisbon, Portugal, and flew from there to the U.S. in October 1941. During a period of a year and several months, he reassembled those Rothschild assets over which he was able to exercise control from New York. In 1943 he crossed the Atlantic again, joining General Charles de Gaulle's Free French Forces in London. In the rank of captain, he carried out several special missions for de Gaulle and served as adjutant to the general's military governor in Paris following the liberation of the French capital, in 1944. In the postwar years, at first as de facto head of the French Rothschilds, he reestablished MM. de Rothschild Frères in Paris, opened new branches throughout France, and expanded the bank's operations internationally. (For many years he shared control of the family's interests with two cousins.) With the death of his father, in 1949, he became de jure president of MM. Rothschild Frères and director general of the Compagnie du Nord. The best known of his protégés among his employees was Georges Pompidou, who went on to become president of France (1969–74). In 1967 Rothschild reorganized the family holdings and transformed the private investment bank MM. Rothschild Frères into the Banque Rothschild S.A., an incorporated commercial bank. With the baron as its president, Banque Rothschild was grouped with other Rothschild interests under the aegis of an expanded Compagnie du Nord. The other interests included the international mining company Société de Penarroya, the world's largest producer of lead and a major producer of other metals. Rothschild remained president of Banque Rothschild until 1978. In the early 1980s, to his shock and horror, the bank was nationalized by President François Mitterrand's Socialist-Communist coalition government and renamed the Compagnie Européenne de Banque. During the 1980s his son David (from his first marriage, to Alix Schey de Koromia) built a new Paris banking entity, the Rothschild & Cie Banque. In 2003 David became head of Group Rothschild, a merger of the French and English Rothschild banking networks. Following the dissolution of his first marriage, Baron Guy de Rothschild married Marie-Hélène de Zuylen de Nyevelt van de Haar. With her, he hosted famous high-society galas at his mansion in Paris and his chateau northeast of the city. He was also celebrated for his Thoroughbred racehorses and his prowess at golf, and he shared in his family's renown for its Bordeau wines. For a number of years, in the position of president of France's Jewish Consistory, he was the leading spokesman for the country's Jews. He also chaired France's United Jewish Social Fund for many years. His book of memoirs *Contre Bonne Fortune* (1983) was translated as *The Whims of Fortune* (1985). In 2002 he published a revision of his memoirs, *Surprises de la Fortune*. He died in Paris. He was predeceased by his second wife and survived by his two sons, David and Édouard, the latter from his second marriage. See *Current Biography* (1973).

Obituary *New York Times* A p29 June 14, 2007

RUBIN, WILLIAM S. Aug. 11, 1927–Jan. 22, 2006

Art historian; curator. As the director of the Department of Painting and Sculpture at New York City's Museum of Modern Art (MoMA) during the 1970s and 1980s, William S. Rubin was key in defining the character of the collection and exhibitions of one of the world's preeminent museums. According to Roberta Smith, the art critic for the *New York Times* (January 24, 2006), "Rubin's painstakingly worked-out presentations" recounted a "version of modernism with a clarity and level of detail that many curators still consider unmatched." Born in Brooklyn and raised in the Bronx, he was the eldest of three sons of immigrant parents. His father, Mack Rubin, began his career in America by selling textiles from a pushcart and ended up owning several factories. While attending the progressive Fieldstone School, Rubin became close with one of his teachers, Victor D'Amico, who was also the director of education at MoMA. Rubin spent most of his free time at the museum, assisting D'Amico with various projects. After serving with the U.S. Army in postwar Italy, he returned to New York City and earned a bachelor's degree in Italian language and literature from Columbia University, in 1949. Hoping to become an orchestra conductor, he studied musicology briefly at the University of Paris; he was discouraged from continuing further. With the intention of studying history, he returned to Columbia, but switched to art history after taking a class with the 20th-century art historian Meyer Schapiro. Rubin earned an M.A., in 1952, and a doctorate, in 1959. He taught undergraduate courses in art history at Sarah Lawrence College for 15 years, beginning in 1952, and he concurrently taught at the City University of New York, beginning in 1954. At the invitation of Alfred H. Barr Jr., the founding director of MoMA, he joined the museum's staff as a curator in 1967, resigning both of his tenured professorships to do so. He became chief curator in the museum's Department of Painting and Sculpture, in 1969, and director of the department, in 1973. During his tenure he expanded the museum's collection of Abstract Expressionism, purchasing pieces by Jackson Pollock and Barnett Newman. Perhaps Rubin's greatest acquisition was Pablo Picasso's *Guitar*, a metal-construction sculpture from 1912–13; the curator visited the artist at his home, in Nice, France, to offer one of the museum's paintings by Paul Cézanne in exchange for the sculpture. Picasso donated *Guitar* and refused to take the painting as payment. Picasso and Rubin became good friends, which led the artist to donate several more of his works to MoMA. Rubin "was known for his indefatigable energy wooing collectors and negotiating with dealers once he had zeroed in on art that he felt the Modern should own," Smith wrote. In addition, Rubin donated pieces—including David Smith's seminal sculpture *Australia*—from his own private collection. In 1980 he mounted Picasso: A Retrospective, filling the entire gallery with Picasso's work. The exhibition included about 1,000 pieces in every medium and represented every period of the artist's career. About 300 of those works had never been viewed in the U.S., and 30 had never been publicly exhibited anywhere. When the Picasso exhibition ended, MoMA closed its doors for a four-year renovation. The redesigned gallery spaces, which forced visitors to view the collection in a particular order, were cited by some as evidence of Rubin's dogmatic approach to art. He and his colleagues faced even more criticism for the show that marked the museum's reopening, "Primitivism" in Twentieth Century Art: Affinity of the Tribal and Modern. The exhibition, which illustrated the influence of African, Oceanic, Native American, and Inuit art on modern artists, was criticized for weighing its thesis—displayed on extensive labels—with innumerable subtleties. In addition, the art historian Thomas McEvilley attacked Rubin's overall conception in a polemic published in *Artforum*, lamenting that the tribal objects were presented as mere archetypes of modernism. Rubin fired off a long rebuttal. He later summed up his philosophy, telling Calvin Tomkins for the *New Yorker* (November 4, 1985), "The notion that you can look at a work of art as pure form strikes me as idiocy. If a work comes at you, it comes with everything it's got, all at once. You can't not be aware of the psychological, or the poetic, or all its other aspects, and you can't separate them from the structural aspects of the work." Though Rubin stepped down from his position at MoMA, in 1988, accepting the title of director emeritus, he mounted several more exhibitions. Over the course of his career he wrote and edited numerous volumes on art history, and from 1959 to 1964 he served as the American editor of *Art International*. Rubin maintained residences in Manhattan and Pound Ridge, New York, where he died at the age of 78. He is survived by his fourth wife, Phyllis Hattis; their daughter, Beata; and his brothers, Richard and Lawrence. See *Current Biography* (1986).

Obituary *New York Times* B p7 Jan. 24, 2006

RUSSELL, ANNA Dec. 27, 1911–Oct. 18, 2006 Concert comedienne; musical satirist. For the thousands of people who attended her performances, the antic humor of Anna Russell was a refreshing antidote to pomposity in the world of "serious" music. Academically trained in voice and several instruments and professionally grounded in straight concertizing, Russell brought the strength of insider erudition and authenticity to her irreverent spoofs of a range of musical repertories, especially the operatic. The best known of the parodies she wrote and performed were her hilarious analyses of Wagner's operatic *Ring* cycle and the operettas of Gilbert and Sullivan; but she also did send-ups of German lieder, oratorios, salon and flamenco music, torch and folk singing, and concert pianism, among other types of music. An accident she suffered as a teenager, in which a hockey puck slammed into her nose, "ruined [her] acoustic" and left her with what she described as an "idiosyncratic voice," a loud "yodel" that was "heartbreaking" but, ultimately, "a godsend for comedy." Anna Claudia Russell-Brown was born to a Canadian mother and a British father who was in the military. While some British sources claim that she was born in London, England, almost certainly she was born in London, Ontario, Canada, and, from the age of six months, raised in England, with sojourns on the European continent. After studying voice, piano, theory, harmony, and cello at the Royal College of Music in London, she gave folksong recitals on BBC Radio and traveled the United Kingdom with an opera company. When she was in her late 20s, she returned to Canada, where she sang English music-hall songs on a Toronto radio station and continued to pursue a serious concert career before deciding that her forte was lampoonery. Her first lampoons were presented in Christmas charity concerts with the Toronto Symphony Orchestra. When she made her New York City debut, with the first of several presentations of her one-woman comic show, at Town Hall in 1948, a New York critic noted her "skillful mimicry of the affectations and mannerisms of lieder singers, fading operatic artists, and pianists of varying types." In the early 1950s she began appearing on U.S. television and in such venues as Carnegie Hall, and she recorded the best-selling albums *Anna Russell Sings?* and *Anna Russell Sings Again! Again?*. Over the following years she was constantly on tour, playing to full houses across the United States, Canada, Australia, and Great Britain. Some of her appearances were with major orchestras and with the San Francisco Opera, New York City Opera, and Canadian Opera companies. Between 1953 and 1960 she took her one-woman show to Broadway several times, in productions titled *Anna Russell's Little Show* and *All by Myself*. In the late 1960s she announced her retirement, but, in imitation of some of the aging prima donnas she mocked, she continued giving "farewell" concerts into the 1980s. Russell was twice married and twice divorced. Albums she originally recorded on the Columbia label—including *The Anna Russell Album*, *Anna Russell at the Sydney Opera House*, and *The Guide to Concert Audiences*—have been reissued as Sony CDs. Her videos include *Anna Russell—the Clown Princess of Comedy* and *The (First) Anna Russell Farewell Special*, taped in 1985. Her first book was *The Power of Being a Positive Stinker* (1955). *The Anna Russell Songbook* (1958) included "How to Write Your Own Gilbert and Sullivan Opera" and "A Square Talk on Popular Music." The title of her autobiography, *I'm Not Making This Up, You Know!* (1985), was the catchphrase in her analysis of the *Ring* cycle. Russell's adopted daughter, Dierdre Prussak, an Australian health and beauty columnist and television personality, wrote the tour memoir *Anna in a Thousand Cities*. After living for many years in Unionville, Ontario, Canada, Russell moved in her old age to Australia to live with her adopted daughter. She died in Batemans Bay, New South Wales, Australia. See *Current Biography* (1954).

Obituary *New York Times* A p21 Oct. 20, 2006

SCHIRRA, WALTER M. May 12, 1923–May 3, 2007 United States Navy captain; astronaut. Wally Schirra, a Korean War air combat veteran and a navy test pilot, was one of the original seven astronauts chosen by the National Aeronautics and Space Administration in 1959, and he was the only astronaut to fly in each of the three NASA programs—Project Mercury, Project Gemini, and Project Apollo—that culminated in the sending of six manned spacecraft to the moon and back. His special responsibility in Project Mercury was the development of environmental-control and life-support systems for the optimum safety and comfort of the astronauts in flight, an assignment that included the testing of their pressurized suits. In his first NASA flight, on October 3, 1962, he piloted the Mercury space capsule *Sigma 7* through six orbits of Earth. During the fourth orbit he demonstrated an ability to operate the craft free of ground control and thus to conserve fuel, an important consideration in determining the feasibility of longer space flights. In his second flight he was command pilot of *Gemini 6* (officially, *Gemini VI-A*) in 16 orbits of Earth on December 15 and 16, 1966. The chief purpose of the *Gemini 6* mission was a (non-docking) rendezvous with the already orbiting spaceship *Gemini 7*. Schirra and his co-pilot, Thomas P. Stafford, accomplished that task—the first rendezvous of two manned space vehicles—during the fourth orbit of the flight, maneuvering *Gemini 6* into a position within six to 10 feet of *Gemini 7* and subsequently into a wider formation with the other craft; the two spaceships flew in formation for six hours. NASA's third program, Project Apollo, was designed for the purpose of landing astronauts on the moon and returning them safely to Earth. That program began in tragedy in January 1967, when three astronauts died in a launch-pad fire in the command module of *Apollo 1*. During the following months the *Apollo* command module was extensively redesigned to prevent the risk of such a conflagration occurring again, and the new design was incorporated into the construction of *Apollo 7*. That spacecraft, command-piloted by Schirra and crewed by Donn F. Eisele and Walter Cunningham, lifted off on October 11, 1968 and splashed down on October 22, 1968; during their 11 days in orbit, Schirra and his crew successfully tested the space-worthiness of the new command module along with that of the service module, including the service propulsion system that would ultimately be used in placing an *Apollo* vehicle in and out of lunar orbit. (The only moon-mission item not included in *Apollo 7* was the lunar landing module.) From orbit, Schirra, Eisele, and Cunningham beamed 10-minute daily television shows back to Earth, unprecedented transmissions for which they received an Emmy Award. (Their flight prepared the way for the first manned orbits of the moon, by the crew of *Apollo 8* in December 1968 and *Apollo 10* in May 1969. Following the successful testing in Earth orbit of the lunar module by the crew of *Apollo 9*, Neil Armstrong, the commander of *Apollo 11*, became the first man to land on the moon, in July 1969; during the following three and a half years, NASA accomplished five additional lunar landings.) By the time he retired from NASA, in 1969, Schirra had logged 4,577 hours in flight time, 295 of them in space. After his retirement he briefly served as president of Regency Investors Inc., a Denver-based leasing and finance company, and he was subsequently CEO and chair of Ecco Corp., an environmental-control company. He sat on the boards of numerous other companies, and with other surviving Mercury astronauts, he founded the Mercury Seven Foundation, a nonprofit scholarship fund for promising young students in science and technology. As a navy test pilot before joining NASA, Schirra contributed to the development of the Sidewinder air-to-air missile. With Ed Buckbee, he wrote about himself and his fellow astronauts in the book *The Real Space Cowboys* (1971). In *The Right Stuff*

(1983), the motion-picture adaptation of Tom Wolfe's book about the astronauts, Schirra was played by Lance Henriksen. Mark Harmon portrayed him in the television miniseries *From the Earth to the Moon* (HBO, 1998). Beginning in 1984 Schirra lived in the San Diego suburb of Rancho Santa Fe, California. He died in Scripps Green Hospital in La Jolla, California, of a heart attack. His survivors included his wife, Josephine, and a son and a daughter. See *Current Biography* (1966).

Obituary *New York Times* B p7 May 4, 2007

SCHLESINGER, ARTHUR M. JR. Oct. 15, 1917–Feb. 28, 2007 Historian; liberal Democratic theorist and activist. Arthur M. Schlesinger Jr. was an unusual combination of eminent scholar and controversial public thinker, a self-described "unrepentant and unreconstructed liberal and New Dealer" who rejected both far-right and radical-left positions in politics. He is probably best known to the general public for his close association with John F. and Robert F. Kennedy and such books as his memoir/chronicle *A Thousand Days: John F. Kennedy in the White House,* which won a Pulitzer Prize and a National Book Award in 1965, and *Robert Kennedy and His Times* (1979), which also won a National Book Award. In the scholarly community and among educated readers, he drew initial and sustained attention with his seminal work *The Age of Jackson* (1945), which brought him the first of his two Pulitzer Prizes. In that book he departed from the previously prevailing view of the first progressive presidential administration as a simple egalitarian product of westward expansion and frontier innocence. Instead, he offered a class-based interpretation, picturing Jackson as a great proactive populist—not unlike Franklin D. Roosevelt, in his view—who boldly assumed an expansion of executive power in response to a restive back-East urban labor movement demanding presidential protection from uncontrolled business interests. In his next book, *The Vital Center: The Politics of Freedom* (1949), Schlesinger advocated an anti-Communist foreign policy and a centered domestic policy, wary of unregulated capitalism on the one hand and the far-left fellow-traveling of Henry Wallace and his ilk on the other. Between 1957 and 1960 he published his highly sympathetic trilogy The Age of Roosevelt: *The Crisis of the Old Order, 1919-1933, The Coming of the New Deal 1933-1935,* and *The Politics of Upheaval, 1935-1936.* The elder of two sons of the historian Arthur Meier Schlesinger and Elizabeth (Bancroft) Schlesinger, he was named Arthur Bancroft Schlesinger at birth but changed his name to Arthur Meier Schlesinger Jr. when he was a teenager. At Harvard University, where his father was a professor, he received a B.A. degree in history (his only degree) in 1938, and he was subsequently a member of the Society of Fellows at Harvard for three years. His honors thesis at Harvard became his first book, *Orestes A. Brownson: A Pilgrim's Progress* (1939). During World War II he was a writer with the Office of War Information in Washington, D.C., and with the Office of Strategic Services reports boards in London and Paris. He began teaching at Harvard in 1946, was a full professor there from 1954 to 1961, and was a professor at the

City University of New York from 1966 to 1994. He participated in the founding of Americans for Democratic Action in 1947 and subsequently served for many years as national vice chairman of that liberal pressure group. He was a speechwriter in the unsuccessful presidential campaigns of the Democratic candidate Adlai Stevenson in 1952 and 1956 and the successful presidential campaign of the Democratic candidate John F. Kennedy in 1960. He became President Kennedy's special assistant for Latin American affairs in January 1961, and he remained in the White House for two months under President Lyndon B. Johnson following the assassination of President Kennedy, in November 1963. Resuming his Democratic speechwriting, he worked for Robert F. Kennedy's 1968 presidential campaign, which ended with Kennedy's assassination, and for George S. McGovern in his unsuccessful presidential campaign in 1972, and he was active in Edward M. Kennedy's unsuccessful bid for the Democratic presidential nomination in 1980. Viewing Democratic president Jimmy Carter as too conservative, he did not support Carter in either of his presidential campaigns. In *The Imperial Presidency* (1973), he argued for the impeachment of Republican president Richard M. Nixon (which appeared imminent until Nixon agreed to resign as president). A quarter-century later he railed loudly against the prosecution in the impeachment of Democratic president Bill Clinton. He published more than a score of books, including *The Politics of Hope* (1963), *The Bitter Heritage: Vietnam and American Democracy* (1967), and *The Crisis of Confidence: Ideas, Power, and Violence in America* (1969). In his book *The Cycles of American History* (1986), he pursued the theory that political conservatism and "heroic" liberalism enjoy popularity or dominance alternately, generation after generation. Beginning in the 1980s he became concerned with the rise of multiculturalism in the United States and the increasing refusal of ethnic groups to assimilate in the American melting pot. That was the subject of his book *The Disuniting of America: Reflections on a Multicultural Society* (1991). In 2000 he published the memoir *A Life in the Twentieth Century: Innocent Beginnings, 1917–1950*. In his last book, *War and the American Presidency* (2004), he attacked the administration of President George W. Bush, describing the war in Iraq as "a ghastly mess" and challenging the curbs on civil liberties imposed domestically as well as abroad under the Patriot Act in the war on terror. Schlesinger was married to and divorced from Marian Cannon before marrying Alexandra Emmet in 1971. He was predeceased by his daughter Katharine from his first marriage; he was survived by both his wives, his sons Stephen and Andrew and daughter Christina from his first marriage, and his son Robert and his stepson Peter Allan from his second marriage. Schlesinger's journals from 1952 to 2000, edited by Stephen and Andrew, were published in 2007. Schlesinger died at Downtown Hospital in Manhattan after suffering a heart attack while he was dining out with family members. See *Current Biography* (1979).

Obituary *New York Times* A p2 Mar. 1, 2007

SEMBÈNE, OUSMANE Jan. 1, 1923–June 9(?), 2007
Senegalese author and auteur. As a gifted novelist and as the acknowledged father of sub-Saharan cinema, Ousmane Sembène contributed mightily to the cultural awakening of postcolonial black Africa, especially that of his native region, formerly known as French West Africa, and most particularly that of his native country, Senegal, which won its independence from France in 1960. He was the polar opposite of his illustrious compatriot Léopold Senghor, the "Westernized" poet who served as independent Senegal's first president. In his dual craft, Sembène was radically subversive, a Marxist—as well as a Muslim turned atheist—with a satirical sense of humor, who aimed his barbs at a range of social, political, and religious targets and who was as uncompromising in calling attention to the faults in the post-independence establishment in Senegal as he had been in attacking its racist and economically parasitical colonial predecessor. Individual corruption aside, the basic fault that he perceived in the new order was the carrying forward of old colonial attitudes and a continued relationship with Western capitalism and dependence on Western aid, including agricultural support. He viewed that continuation, profitable to an elite, as inimical to indigenous economic self-realization and frustrating to the aspirations of Senegal's ordinary, decent people. His intention as a filmmaker, he once explained, was "to talk to my people, my county" because "Africa needs to see its own reflection." His most famous feature film is *Xala* (1974), his adaptation of his 1973 novel of the same title, a scathing farce lampooning a group of venal businessmen who assume power in a newly independent black African state, one of whom buys a third wife, only to find himself cursed with impotence. The film *Xala* was heavily censored by the Senghor government, and Sembène's film *Ceddo* (1977), dealing with African cooperation in the slave trade, was banned for some time. Sembène was a cofounder of the monthly magazine *Kaddu*, the world's first publication in Wolof, the language most widely spoken in Senegal. Born into a fisherman's family in Ziguinchor in southern Senegal, Sembène was largely self-taught. Shortly after the outbreak of World War II, in 1939, he was conscripted into the French colonial army, and he subsequently served with the Free French Forces. After the war he returned to Dakar, Senegal, where he helped to organize the 1947–48 Dakar-Niger railroad strike, an experience that would inspire his novel *Les Bouts de bois de Dieu* (1960; *God's Bits of Wood*, 1970). When the strike was over, he moved to Marseilles, France, where he became a stevedore and a member of the Communist Party and began to publish poetry and short stories. What he experienced as a dock worker— including racism—became grist for his first novel, *Le Docker noir* (1956; *The Black Docker,* 1987). In his second novel, *O Pays, mon beau peuple!* (1957), he told the story of the opposition encountered by Oumar, a young Senegalese man who returns from Europe with a white wife and unwanted ideas for modernizing his country's agricultural practices. Sembène subsequently published, among other novels and novellas, *L'Harmattan* (1964), a fictional retelling of the politics involved in the 1958 referendum (opposed by Senghor) calling for Senegal's complete break

with France; *Le Mandat* (1966; *The Money Order*, 1972), a Kafkaesque tragicomedy about a naïve Muslim man driven to ruin trying to cash a money order in the corrupt postcolonial financial system; *Xala* (1973; published in English translation under the same title, 1976); and *Le Dernier de l'empire* (1981), a satirical roman à clef covering the history of postcolonial Senegal. Meanwhile Sembène, who was writing his short stories, novels, and novellas in French, turned to filmmaking as a way of reaching and raising the consciousness of his compatriots, few of whom knew French and most of whom were illiterate or without access to books. After spending the year 1962 studying filmmaking at the Gorki Studios in Moscow, he returned to West Africa, filmed a short documentary commissioned by the government of Mali, and then made *Borom Sarret* (1963), a short pseudo-documentary in the neorealist tradition of *The Bicycle Thief* purporting to chronicle a day in the life of a Senegalese cart driver who suffers not only the theft of his cart (crucial to his livelihood) by a petty criminal but his general impoverishment in a system dominated by a new moneyed class. His next film was another short, *Niaye* (1964), the adaptation of a short story of his about incest in a noble village family, symptomatic of the decay of traditional moral values. Another short story was the basis for his first full-length feature film, *La Noire de . . .* (*Black Girl*, 1965), the protagonist of which is Diouana, a young Senegalese woman who travels to France as a nanny with a white family; homesick and lonely, and treated shabbily by the family, she commits suicide. Sembène adapted his novella *Le Mandat* into *Mandabi* (1968), his second feature film and the first of his many films in the Wolof language. His film *Taaw* (1971) was followed by *E Mitai* (1971). The latter, regarded by some as his masterpiece, is a bitter film based on the Diola tribe's resistance to the French conscription of their men and the confiscation of their rice during World War II; it was suppressed in France for five years. *Camp de Thiaroye* (1987) is a fictional treatment of the racism experienced by Senegalese veterans of World War II in a French "transit" camp on their way home from Europe. The premise of Sembène's satirical film *Guelwaar* (1992) is the mistaken burial of a Catholic corpse in a Muslim cemetery. In his eighth feature, the comedy *Faat-Kine* (1999), Sembène told the politically powerful story of a single mother in Dakar, Senegal. In his final feature film, *Moolade*, which won him the last of his several Cannes Festival awards, he attacked the brutal practice of female genital mutilation called clitoridectomy. Sembène, who was married twice, had three sons (two, according to one source). He died in Dakar, Senegal. See *Current Biography* (1994).

Obituary *New York Times* B p7 June 11, 2007

SERVAN-SCHREIBER, JEAN-JACQUES Feb. 13, 1924–Nov. 7, 2006 Journalist; politician. The author of *Le défi americain* (*The American Challenge*, 1967), one of the most influential books in European economics, Jean-Jacque Servan-Schreiber succeeded in both journalism and politics, founding the newspaper *L'Express* and serving in the French National Assembly. Servan-Schreiber was a descendant of an influential family: his grandfather, Joseph Schreiber, was a political secretary to the unifier of Germany, Otto von Bismark; his father, Emile, co-founded *Les Echos*, the first French newspaper to specialize in economic and financial news. When the Nazis invaded France in 1940, Servan-Schreiber and his family, who were of Jewish heritage (though practicing Catholics), fled to Spain. From there Servan-Schreiber traveled to the U.S., where he trained as a fighter pilot for the Free French. After the war he returned to France, where he received a degree in engineering from the Ecole Polytechnique, in Palaiseau. In 1947 he became a political writer for the prestigious French newspaper *Le Monde*. He also served as the European correspondent for *Reporter* and a foreign-affairs writer for *Paris-Presse*. In 1953 Servan-Schreiber, along with his friend Françoise Giroud, founded *L'Express*, a magazine modeled after the American periodical *Time*. Three years later Servan-Schreiber was drafted into the French military to serve in its colonial war against Algeria, for which he earned a medal of valor from the French army. Upon returning from active duty, he wrote the book *Lieutenant en Algerie* (*Lieutenant in Algeria*, 1957), which criticized France's colonial practices and accused its forces of committing acts of torture. In response to the book's publication, Servan-Schreiber was indicted on charges of lowering the morale of French soldiers, though the charges were later dropped. In 1964 he founded the weekly periodical *L'Expansion*, and three years later published his most noted work, *The American Challenge*, which immediately became a best-seller upon its publication in France. He published several other books, including *Le Reveil de la France, mai-juin* (*The Spirit of May*, 1968) and *Le défi mondial* (*The World Challenge*, 1980). Servan-Schreiber served as the deputy from Lorraine, Nancy, to the French National Assembly, beginning in 1970, and was elected the president of the Radical Socialist Party, in 1971. He was also appointed to serve as the minister of reforms by President Valery Giscard d'Estaing, but he resigned after only 12 days to protest France's testing of nuclear weapons. In the mid-1980s Servan-Schreiber moved to the U.S., where he taught at Carnegie Mellon University, in Pittsburgh, Pennsylvania. He later returned to France, continuing to write and exert his influence on politics from behind the scenes. He died in Fécamp, France, due to complications from bronchitis. He is survived by his second wife, the former Sabine Becq de Fouquières; his four sons, David, Emile, Franklin, and Edouard; and his two grandchildren. See *Current Biography* (1955).

Obituary *New York Times* C p16 Nov. 8, 2006

SHELDON, SIDNEY Feb. 11, 1917–Jan. 30, 2007 American writer. In the course of his long and varied career, Sidney Sheldon achieved extraordinary success as a screenwriter, a Broadway playwright, a television writer, and finally and most spectacularly as the author of racy and fast-paced novels of suspense. According to the *Guinness Book of World Records*, his books have been translated into more languages than those of any other novelist, with total sales of approximately 300 million copies in 180 countries. Sheldon (born Sidney Schechtel) began collaborating on screenplays in 1941, had his first solo screen credit with *She's in the Army* (1942), won an Academy Award for best original screenplay for *The Bachelor and the Bobby-Soxer* (1947), co-wrote the script for the musical *Easter Parade* (1948), adapted the book of the musical *Annie Get Your Gun* for the screen (1950), reworked an old libretto for the musical *Nancy Goes to Rio* (1950), co-wrote the story for the musical *Rich, Young, and Pretty* (1951) and the script for *Dream Wife* (1953), and wrote the screenplay for the comedy/mystery *Remains to be Seen* (1953). His subsequent motion-picture credits included the screenplays for *You're Never Too Young* (1955), *The Birds and the Bees* (1955), and *Jumbo* (1962). He directed the film *Dream Wife*, produced, directed, and co-wrote *The Buster Keaton Story* (1957), and co-wrote *All in a Night's Work* (1961). He began his career in New York City, where he first tried his hand at songwriting on Tin Pan Alley, unsuccessfully, in the 1930s. On Broadway he collaborated on the book for a revival of the operetta *The Merry Widow* (1943) and co-wrote the musical comedy *Jackpot* (1944) and the musical fantasy *Dream with Music* (1944). He also co-wrote the wartime Broadway comedy *Alice in Arms*, a flop. Returning to Broadway more than a decade later, he collaborated on the book for the musical *Redhead* (1959)—for which he shared a Tony Award—and wrote the comedy *Roman Candle* (1960). Moving on to television, he joined the writing staff of the ABC network's situation comedy *The Patty Duke Show*, for which he wrote 13 episodes in the 1964–65 season. On the NBC network he created *I Dream of Jeannie* in September 1965 and was executive producer and chief writer of that sitcom until it went into syndication at the end of 1970. His sitcom *Nancy* had an aborted run on NBC early in the 1970–71 television season. He later wrote episodes of the ABC adventure series *Hart to Hart*, beginning in 1979, and the scripts for a number of TV movies, several of which were spin-offs of *Hart to Hart*. His first novel was *The Naked Face* (1970), a psychological thriller about a psychoanalyst who learns that he has been targeted for murder. His second was *The Other Side of Midnight* (1974), a triangular love story involving a a rags-to-riches Parisienne, her American lover, and her jealous and vengeful tycoon husband. That novel was on the *New York Times* best-seller list for 53 weeks, a record at that time. It was followed by *Stranger in the Mirror* (1976), a sensational account of the career of a Los Angeles–based comedian, and *Bloodline* (1977), a story of intrigue and murder in the international pharmaceutical industry. (*The Other Side of Midnight* and *Bloodline* were made into motion pictures, in 1977 and 1978, respectively.) Sheldon published a total of 18 novels, including *Rage of Angels* (1980), *Master of the Game* (1983), *If Tomorrow Comes* (1985), *Windmills of the Gods* (1987), *The Sands of Time* (1988), *The Doomsday Conspiracy* (1991), and *The Stars Shine Down* (1992). His memoir, *The Other Side of Me*, was published in 2005. Following a brief early marriage, Sheldon married the former actress Jorja Curtright, who died in 1985. He was survived by his third wife, the former child actress Alexandra Kostoff, and by the actress and screenwriter Mary Sheldon, his daughter from his second marriage. He died in Rancho Mirage, California, of complications of pneumonia. See *Current Biography* (1980).

Obituary *New York Times* B p8 Feb. 1, 2007

SILLS, BEVERLY May 25, 1929–July 2, 2007 Opera singer; arts administrator; "the people's soprano." Known for her vibrant personality, soaring, silver-toned voice, and dramatic flair, the Brooklyn-born coloratura soprano Beverly Sills (née Belle Silverman) rose to fame during a quarter-century (1955–80) as a diva with the New York City Opera. She was subsequently accomplished as general director of that company and chairwoman of Lincoln Center for the Performing Arts—the largest such arts complex in the world—and the Metropolitan Opera. The tall, red-haired Sills was a trailblazing American original, an unpretentious and buoyant home-grown prodigy in a traditionally highbrow "grand" branch of the performing arts in which European training and orientation had long been de rigueur. "As her operatic success mounted," Liz Giegerich observed for *VOA News* (July 6, 2007, on-line), "Beverly Sills accomplished the seemingly impossible: demystifying the world of opera for average Americans." In an obituary for the Bergen County, New Jersey, *Record*, Jeffrey Page wrote: "Sills was the popular face of opera in the Sixties and Seventies. . . . From her, the words of opera were almost unreal in their shimmering purity." A personal favorite among her more than 80 roles was that of Baby Doe in the 1958 New York premiere of Douglas Moore's opera *The Ballad of Baby Doe* (1956), a quintessentially American, historically based work—set in Colorado and Washington, D.C.—about a romantic triangle, frontier silver mining, and populist politics in the 1880s and 1890s. In her most celebrated performance, she combined stunning vocal acrobatics with the creation of a complex queenly character as Cleopatra in *Giulio Cesare in Egitto* (*Julius Caesar in Egypt*) in 1966. She regarded as "the greatest artistic challenge and the finest achievement" of her career her bel canto performances as the Tudor queens in Donizetti's *Maria Stuarda*, *Anna Bolena*, and *Roberto Devereux* in the early 1970s. Nicknamed "Bubbles" from infancy, Sills was an effervescent child performer—another Shirley Temple, in her mother's eyes—who studied voice under Estelle Liebling and sang on radio programs (including the network show *Major Bowes' Original Amateur Hour,* on which she won first place) and in one or two short Twentieth Century-Fox films. In the years following her graduation from the Professional Children's School, in Manhattan, in 1945, she toured the United States with companies presenting operettas and operas and made a minor appearance with the Philadelphia Civic Grand Opera (1947) and several appearances with the San Francisco Opera (beginning in 1953). In October 1955 she began her long association with the New York City Opera with her performance as Rosalinde in *Die Fledermaus*. Among her other early roles with the company were Violetta in *La Traviata*, Pamira in *The Siege of Corinth*, Philine in Thomas'a *Mignon*, Madame Goldentrill in Mozart's *The Impressario*, the Prima Donna in Weisgal's *Six Characters in Search of an Author*, and Milly Theale in Douglas Moore's *The Wings of the Dove*. In the early 1960s she took time off from her career to concentrate on caring for her two recently born children: her daughter, who is congenitally deaf, and her son, who is severely mentally impaired. On her return to the New York City Opera, in October 1965, she sang all three of the heroines in Offenbach's *The Tales of Hoffmann*. Over the following decade and a half, she expanded her repertory to include such roles as Violetta in *La Traviata*, Gilda in *Rigoletto*, the title role in *Thais*, a Mozart cycle, and Massenet's Manon, Rameau's Aricie, and Donizetti's Lucretia, Marie, and Lucia. As her voice (originally lyric coloratura soprano) changed, so did her choice of roles. During her years with the New York City Opera, she also performed many times with the Opera Company of Boston, headed by her friend Sarah Caldwell, and beginning in 1969 she performed abroad on several occasions, at La Scala in Milan, the San Carlo in Naples, Covent Garden in London, and the Vienna State Opera. Beginning with a performance as Pamira in April 1975, she sang with the Metropolitan Opera Company several times. With the San Diego Opera in 1979, she created the role of Joanna in Menotti's *La Loca*, which she reprised in her farewell performance at the New York City Opera in October 1980. In addition to her work on the operatic stage, she was a recitalist and a soloist with major orchestras. She also often appeared on television, and it was especially as a host and guest on network TV variety programs that she, with her spontaneity, warm and joyful personality, and self-denigrating sense of humor, won a wider popular following. (She received an Emmy Award in the category of outstanding classical music in 1975.) Ten months before her retirement as a performer at the New York City Opera, she became the general director of the company. During her nine-year tenure (1979–88) in that position, she added a variety of new operas to the company's repertory, and she introduced the practice of supplying English subtitles (on the backs of seats) during foreign-language productions. She was also a prodigious fund-raiser, as she continued to be when chairing the boards of Lincoln Center (1994–2002) and the Metropolitan Opera (2002–05) and in her work for the March of Dimes and the Multiple Sclerosis Society. Her dedication to the work with charities was inspired by her experience coping with the birth defects suffered by her son and daughter and, more recently, her daughter's contracting of multiple sclerosis. Her many honors included two Grammy Awards, the Medal of Freedom, and induction into the National Women's Hall of Fame. Sills wrote two autobiographies—*Bubbles: A Self-Portrait* (1976) and *Beverly: An Autobiography* (1987)—and left a rich legacy of recordings. She died at her home in Manhattan. Her survivors included her daughter, Meredith (nicknamed Muffy), her son, Peter Jr., and three stepdaughters. Her husband, Peter Greenough, predeceased her. See *Current Biography* (1969).

Obituary *New York Times* B p6 July 3, 2007

SMATHERS, GEORGE A. Nov. 14, 1913–Jan. 20, 2007 New Jersey–born southern politician; lawyer; Democratic United States representative from Florida's Fourth Congressional District for two terms, from 1947 to 1951, and a U.S. senator from Florida for three, from 1951 to 1969. After earning a law degree from the University of Florida, in 1938, George Armistead Smathers worked as an assistant U.S. attorney in Miami, Florida, from 1940 to 1942. For three years during World War II, he served in the U.S. Marine Corps. In the House he served on the Foreign Affairs and House Administration Committees. As a senator he supported voting rights for African-Americans but fought other civil rights measures, voting against the Civil Rights Act of 1964. He condemned as a "clear abuse of judicial power" the 1954 Supreme Court decision in *Brown v. Board of Education*, which ruled school segregation to be unconstitutional. He advocated expansion of free trade with Latin America and voted for the legislation that created Medicare, the Small Business Administration, and Everglades National Park. He was an outspoken supporter of the Vietnam War as vital in the battle to contain Communism. After leaving elective office he resumed the practice of law in Washington, D.C., and Miami and earned millions of dollars as a lobbyist and entrepreneur. He was the subject of Brian Lewis Crispel's study *Testing the Limits: George Armistead Smathers and Cold War America* (1999). After his divorce from his first wife, Rosemary Townley, Smathers married Carolyn Hyder. He died in Miami. His survivors included his second wife, his two sons, and three grandchildren. See *Current Biography* (1954).

Obituary *New York Times* B p8 Jan. 21, 2007

SMUIN, MICHAEL Oct. 13, 1938–Apr. 24, 2007 Ballet dancer, choreographer, director, and producer. Michael Smuin was a consummate showman, demonstrating theatrical flair both with his mercurial stage presence as a performer early in his career and with the eclectic choreography in which he tried to give "the idiom of classical dance an American accent" by infusing ballet "with the rhythm, speed, and syncopation of American popular culture." Smuin was a demi-caractère dancer with the San Francisco Ballet from 1957 to 1962. He and his wife, the ballerina Paula Tracy, put together a "disguised ballet" specialty act that they performed on television and in nightclubs and cabarets for several years, until 1966, when Smuin joined the American Ballet Theatre as a dancer and occasional choreographer. He returned to the San Francisco Ballet as artistic co-director (with Lew Christensen) and choreographer in 1973, when the company was artistically moribund and nearly bankrupt. Within five years he had helped to restore to the San Francisco Ballet the luster befitting America's oldest classical-ballet troupe. He remained with the company for 12 years, leaving in 1985 following a dispute with the business side of the management. In 1994 he founded his own company, the Smuin Ballet. His choreographic works—some 30 or more—range from the Shakespearean adaptations *Romeo and Juliet* and *The Tempest* to *Bluegrass/Slyde* and *Stabat Mater* (his homage to the firefighters and others who perished in the World Trade Center on September 11, 2001). In addition to his work with ballet companies—including the Pacific Northwest Ballet and the Dance Theater of Harlem—he was creatively involved in a number of multimedia productions, including circuses and motion pictures. On television he received an Emmy Award for *A Song for Dead Robbers* (music by Charles Fox), an American Indian dance drama presented on the PBS network in its *Great Performances: Dance in America* series. On Broadway, he was nominated for a Tony Award in 1981 for his choreographing and staging of the musical *Sophisticated Ladies*, based on the music of Duke Ellinngton, and he won a Tony in 1988 for his choreography for a revival of *Anything Goes*. Smuin and Paula Tracy divorced in 2000. His survivors included his son, Shane. He died in San Francisco after suffering a heart attack. See *Current Biography* (1984).

Obituary *New York Times* A p25 Apr. 25, 2007

SNYDER, TOM May 12, 1936–July 29, 2007 Broadcast journalist; radio and television personality. Idiosyncratic Tom Snyder, who thought of television as "picture radio" and of himself as a topical "storyteller," was, amidst the ascendancy of "narrowcasters," "a true American broadcaster, a rare thing," as Peter Lassally, his last executive producer at the CBS network, observed. "He made the camera disappear," Lassally explained. "He was talking directly to the viewer." The NBC executive Robert E. Mulholland said of Snyder: "I have never seen a person read the news with such excitement and clarity. He read as if he were talking to you." Snyder's greatest accomplishment was his inauguration of network television's late-late-night talk show, bringing compelling television to a time slot previously filled with old movies or dead air. That post-midnight slot might more properly be called early-early-tomorrow, and in fact Snyder's breakthrough program was called *Tomorrow*, which he introduced on NBC in 1973 as the follow-up to *The Tonight Show*. He was, as Tim Cuprisin of the Milwaukee *Journal Sentinel* has noted, "a breath of fresh air: quirky, opinionated, but always interested in the opinions of his interview subjects." Two decades later he became the host of CBS's entry into late-late-night talk programming, *The Late Late Show with Tom Snyder*. He began developing his improvisational style and ad-libbing ability as a local radio news reporter while he was a pre-medical student at Marquette University, in Milwaukee. After dropping out of his pre-med studies to pursue a career in broadcast journalism full-time, he soon moved from radio into television, and he found increasingly responsible posts with stations in a succession of cities, from Kalamazoo, Michigan, to Atlanta, Georgia. He anchored the evening news at station KYW-TV in Philadelphia in the late 1960s and at the NBC affiliate KNBC-TV in Los Angeles beginning in 1970. The NBC network launched the hour-long (1:00 a.m. to 2:00 a.m.) *Tomorrow* show in October 1973. The program originated out of Burbank, California, until December 1974, when it moved to New York City. Except for a two-year period back in Burbank (1977–79), Snyder hosted the show out of Manhattan for the duration of its run. A chain smoker, he appeared on screen exuding clouds of cigarette smoke, adding to the program's air of informality. He opened the show with a monologue and with his catchphrase exhortation, "Fire up a colortini, sit back, relax, and watch the pictures, now, as they fly through the air." He spent most of the rest of the show in what he described as "slice-of-life conversation" with his guest or guests, who ranged from rock musicians— including John Lennon, the group U2, and many Punk and New Wave rockers—to such public figures as the U.S. vice president Spiro Agnew, the filmmaker Alfred Hitchcock, the novelist and philosopher Ayn Rand, the science-fiction writer Harlan Ellison, the actor Marlon Brando, the labor leader Jimmy Hoffa, the radio and TV shock jock Howard Stern, and the murderer and cult leader Charles Manson. (Snyder traveled to the California Medical Facility to interview Manson.) As an interviewer he was often digressive, and some critics thought he was ego-driven. He interspersed the hour with tangential off-the-cuff witticisms (some in the form of banter with his unseen crew) and the signature sound of his hearty laugh. (That laugh and others among his distinctive characteristics were captured and caricatured in a parody by Dan Aykroyd that became one of the most popular skits on the NBC comedy/variety show *Saturday Night Live* in the late 1970s.) *Tomorrow* had no studio audience; Snyder's basic rapport was with the viewer at home, and he clashed with Fred Silverman and his other bosses in the NBC front office when their tinkering hurt that rapport. The tinkering, which began in the autumn of 1980, took the form of expanding *Tomorrow* into a 90-minute bicoastal talk/variety show with a live audience—what Snyder described, disapprovingly, as "a three-ring circus." In January 1981 the program was retitled *Tomorrow Coast to Coast,* and the Hollywood gossip columnist Rona Barrett, based in Los Angeles, served (with equal billing) as Snyder's West Coast co-host for several months thereafter. "We were a successful show right up until then," Snyder later commented. "We could have gone on forever . . . just delivering good solid basic journalism." Early in 1982 *Tomorrow Coast to Coast* was cancelled and replaced by *Late Night with David Letterman.* For the next several years, Snyder, who had been doing other network and local news stints during *Tomorrow*'s run, concentrated on local television news anchoring in New York City. In 1985 he moved to Los Angeles, where he briefly hosted a local afternoon television talk show before launching, on the ABC radio network, *The Tom Snyder Show*, a three-hour program devoted to chatting with celebrities and other journalists and taking telephone calls from fans, who sometimes included such well-known people as his television peers Ted Koppel, David Letterman, and Sherman Hemsley. After that show went off the air, in 1992, he hosted a talk show on the CNBC cable network for two years. Meanwhile, in 1993 David Letterman moved to the CBS network to compete with NBC's *Tonight Show* as the host of *The Late Show with David Letterman*. Through Letterman's instrumentality, CBS signed Snyder to follow Letterman's late show with the hour-long (12:30 a.m–1:30 a.m.) *The Late Late Show with Tom Snyder*, a program similar in format to *Tomorrow* that ran from 1995 to 1998. Snyder's marriage to Mary Ann Bendel ended in divorce in 1975. He died in San Francisco, of complications from leukemia. His survivors included his companion, Pamela Burke, a daughter (by Mary Ann), and two grandchildren. See *Current Biography* (1980).

Obituary *New York Times* B p9 July 31, 2007

SPARK, MURIEL Feb. 1, 1918–Apr. 13, 2006 Scottish-born postmodernist author. Dame Spark (née Camberg) was originally and at heart a poet but is best known for her fiction—which she viewed as "an easier way to write poetry"—and especially for her novel *The Prime of Miss Jean Brodie*. Her novels (most of which are slim novellas), along with her short stories, were nourished by her harvest of observations as a real-life people watcher (and listener) and by such autobiographical grist as an early nervous breakdown, the craft of novel writing itself, and her religious conversions, to Anglicanism in 1953 and Roman Catholicism in 1954. The conversions were "high-church" intellectual experiences in large measure inspired by the example of the 19th-century Catholic converts Gerard Manley Hopkins, the poet, and John Henry Cardinal Newman, the churchman, theologian, and author of the autobiography *Apologia Pro Via Sua*. In her novels Spark dealt with the dark themes of sin, madness, the absurdities of life, and death, and she did so with a light touch and a detached and acerbic wit. In the denouements of her stories, her often heartless characters, caught in situations of moral ambiguity, typically expose their inner mischief with sudden illuminating phrases or gestures. Her claim to a secure niche in English literature was established with her creation of the enigmatic, splendidly sinister title character of *The Prime of Miss Jean Brodie* (1961), a charismatic teacher in an Edinburgh girls school in the 1930s who is devoted to cultivating in her students—"la crème de la crème"—and especially in her favorite among them (Sandy Stranger, who ultimately betrays her) a high romantic and artistic sensibility that is fascist in its social and political ramifications. The popularity that *The Prime of Miss Jean Brodie* achieved as a novel was compounded by the success of its stage, film, and television adaptations. Dame Spark was born Muriel Sarah Camberg in Edinburgh to a Jewish father and a Presbyterian mother. When she was 19 she met and married a man she hardly knew, a "mad" (according to her) teacher named Sydney Oswald Spark, whom she accompanied to Southern Rhodesia (later Zimbabwe), where she lived unhappily for seven years before obtaining a divorce and returning to Great Britain. In London she was secretary of the Poetry Society and editor of its publication *Poetry Review* from 1947 to 1949. Over the next several years, she concentrated on her poetry and on scholarly and critical writing and editing, publishing editions of the letters of the Brontë sisters and studies of John Masefield and Mary Shelley. With Derek Stanford, she edited *Tribute to Wordsworth* (1950), *Letters of John Henry Newman* (1957), and *Emily Brontë: Her Life and Work* (1960). Meanwhile, her publication of fiction had begun with a short story that won a contest sponsored by the London *Observer* newspaper in 1951. As an aspiring novelist she was supported by a stipend (the equivalent of $40 a month) from the older novelist (and fellow Catholic convert) Graham Greene, with the curious, apparently facetious proviso that she not pray for him. Her first novel was *The Comforters* (1957), a bizarre experimental work (based very loosely on the Book of Job) in which the heroine undergoes a series of hallucinations and the fear that she is a character in a novel. Among her immediately

subsequent novels were *Memento Mori* (1959), a macabre comedy about octogenarians harassed by an anonymous telephone caller reminding them of their imminent deaths, *The Ballad of Peckham Rye* (1960), in which a demonic Scotsman charms his way into a suburban London community and creates havoc there, *The Bachelors* (1961), in which a London spiritualist medium is on trial for fraud, and *The Girls of Slender Means* (1963). The last-mentioned novel, set in a genteel hostel for girls in bomb-devastated London circa 1945, was written in a mock elegiac style echoing that of Gerard Manley Hopkins in "The Wreck of the Deutschland," his epic poem about five nuns who drowned at sea when fleeing anti-Catholic legislation in Germany in 1875. Spark's only long novel was *The Mandelbaum Gate* (1965), set in a Jerusalem reflecting spiritual fragmentation. One of the central characters is Barbara Vaughn, a Roman Catholic pilgrim of Jewish descent. Many of Spark's characters are mentally or emotionally troubled or deranged, including the woman seeking a man to murder her in *The Driver's Seat* (1970) and the female protagonist whose shadow falls in the wrong direction in *The Hothouse by the East River* (1973). Among the most amusing of Spark's later novels is *Loitering with Intent* (1981), a Booker Prize nominee. In that sparkling mystery/entertainment, set in London in 1949, Fleur Talbot, a struggling but blithe-spirited young writer, to support herself while working on a novel, takes a job as a secretary/editor with an association devoted to helping its old VIP members write their memoirs. As the story proceeds, art begins to dictate reality; the lives of the association members conform increasingly to those of characters in Fleur's novel, as if she is inventing the real-life memoir-writers. Spark published a total of 24 novels, including *Reality and Dreams* (1996), *Aiding and Abetting* (2000), and *The Finishing School* (2004). *All the Stories of Muriel Spark* was published in 2001 and *All the Poems of Muriel Spark* in 2004. Her autobiography, *Curriculum Vitae*, was published in 1992. Spark was made a Dame of the British Empire in 1993. Subsidized by the *New Yorker* magazine, where *The Prime of Miss Jean Brodie* had first appeared, she lived in New York City for several years beginning in 1962. In the late 1960s she moved to Italy, where she lived in Rome before settling in Civitella della Chiana, near Florence. She lived in that ancient Tuscan village for almost 30 years, until her death, with her platonic friend and secretary Penelope Jardine. She died in a hospital in Florence. Her survivors included her estranged son, the painter Samuel Robin Spark, the only offspring from her marriage, who had been raised by her parents. See *Current Biography* (1975).

Obituary *New York Times* A p32 Apr. 16, 2006

STANTON, FRANK Mar. 20, 1908–Dec. 24, 2006 Broadcast executive. Through his work in master-building the Columbia Broadcasting System between the 1930s and the 1970s, Frank Stanton contributed mightily to the general development of network radio and television in the United States and especially to the establishment of the credibility of television as a serious public-spirited information medium. He was also widely admired for his championship of broadcast journalism's First Amendment rights and its inclusion under the shield law that protects print journalists from government intrusion. Originally as a psychologist specializing in audience research and subsequently as a top executive with CBS Inc. for 35 years, Stanton—in a strained but nonetheless effective collaboration with CBS's founder and chairman, William S. Paley—guided the growth of CBS from a relatively small chain of radio stations into a communications empire, the crown jewel of which was CBS Television. After receiving a master's degree in psychology at Ohio State University in 1932, Stanton taught there while earning his doctorate. In his graduate work he specialized in the psychology of mass communication, and in his doctoral dissertation he presented a "plan for studying radio listening behavior." At that time he invented a small recording device—the forerunner of the A. C. Nielsen Audimeter—which when installed in radio receivers logged the listening habits of audiences. Several years later he co-invented the Stanton-Lazarsfeld Program Analyzer, an electronic system (still in use) for measuring the reactions of selected studio audiences to radio and television programs and motion pictures. He joined the staff of the Columbia Broadcasting System's research department in New York City in 1935 and became director of the department in 1938. He was promoted to vice president and general manager of CBS in 1945 and president in 1946. Although he made some contributions to entertainment programming (the domain of the less technologically savvy William F. Paley), Stanton's specific responsibilities were the hands-on running of the company and the development of its several divisions. His special focus was on the CBS News division, to which he recruited a roster of stellar personnel, including the broadcaster Edward R. Murrow. He launched the pioneering high-quality public-affairs series *See It Now* (1951–58), hosted by Murrow, followed in 1959 by *CBS Reports*, a series of documentary specials. Both series included some programs innovative in their exposure of the negative side of the federal government and national politics. (*CBS Reports* ran intermittently into the 1990s.) In 1959 he helped to persuade the Federal Communications Commission to suspend Section 315 (requiring "equal time" for all political candidates in broadcasts) of the Federal Communications Act of 1934, making possible the televised debate between presidential candidates John F. Kennedy and Richard M. Nixon in 1960. One of the controversial documentaries in the *CBS Reports* series was "The Selling of the Pentagon" in 1971. When subpoenaed by a congressional committee to turn over notes and outtakes from that program, Stanton refused. The committee cited him for contempt, but the full House of Representatives rejected the citation, narrowly. In addition to radio and television operations, Stanton oversaw CBS Laboratories and CBS investments in Columbia Records, the Holt, Rinehart and Winston publishing company, Creative Playthings, and, for a time, the New York Yankees baseball team. After he stepped down from the presidency of CBS, in 1971, he served as vice chairman until 1973. Meanwhile, he had chaired the Rand Corp. from 1961 to 1967. He remained a CBS director and consultant until 1987. From 1973 to 1979 he

chaired the American Red Cross, and from 1978 to 1984, he was an overseer of Harvard University. Among his many honors were three Peabody Awards. He died at his home in Boston, Massachusetts. His wife, Ruth Stanton (nee Stephenson), predeceased him. He had no close family survivors. See *Current Biography* (1965).

Obituary *New York Times* A p1+ Dec. 26, 2006

STARR, CHAUNCEY Apr. 14, 1912–Apr. 17, 2007 Physicist; founder and president emeritus of the Electric Power Research Institute, a nonprofit utility consortium devoted to public-interest research in energy and the environment. Chauncey Starr, who contributed to the U.S.'s wartime development of the atomic bomb, later devoted his energies to the peacetime applications of nuclear energy, including electrification and heating; advocacy for those applications; and nuclear-risk assessment. Originally a specialist in the physics of metals under extreme temperatures and high pressures, Starr moved from research at Harvard University and the Massachusetts Institute of Technology into the federal government's top-secret Manhattan Project during World War II. With the North American Aviation Co. in the late 1940s and early 1950s, he directed the design and construction of a model for a relatively small (garage-size, eight-megawatt) nuclear reactor for the production of steam and electricity. (That model failed to become the reactor of choice in American industry.) He was subsequently a vice president of the Rockwell International Corp., where he was concerned with the development of nuclear propulsion for rockets, ramjets, and miniaturized nuclear reactors for use in space. During the 1950s and 1960s, he noted with satisfaction that the nuclear generation of energy was doubling in the United States every 10 years. Nuclear power aside, he evangelized for electrification itself, pointing out, for example, that as a means of producing electricity, the wood burned in an open fire was 98 percent less efficient than wood burned in a boiler. In arguing for the greater use of nuclear power, he tried to dispel what he considered popular misconceptions of the risk posed by nuclear reactors and to put the risk factor in perspective. The ratio of nuclear risks balanced against social benefits, he argued, was far more acceptable than, say, the "voluntary" risks assumed by nicotine addicts or athletes in contact sports. From 1967 to 1963 he was dean of the School of Engineering and Applied Science at the University of California, Los Angeles. In 1972 he founded the Electric Power Research Institute in Palo Alto, California, in which he was fully active until the day before his death. He died at his home in Atherton, California. His survivors included his wife, Doris, a daughter, a son, and five grandchildren. See *Current Biography* (1954).

Obituary *New York Times* C p12 Apr. 19, 2007

STEWART, THOMAS Aug. 29, 1928–Sep. 24, 2006 Opera singer. The American bass-baritone Thomas Stewart, a man of commanding presence both physically and vocally, was one of the foremost Heldenbaritones of his time. While impressive in such roles as Hans Sachs in *Die Meistersinger von Nurnberg*, Balstroe in *Peter Grimes*, Orestes in *Elektra*, and Jochanaan in *Salome*, he was best known as a Wagnerian specialist, particularly renowned for his Zeus-like performances as Wotan in the *Ring* cycle. On the opera stage, in recitals, and on recordings he often performed in partnership with his wife, the soprano Evelyn Lear, and with her he taught master classes in the Emerging Singers Program of the Wagner Society in Washington, D.C. Early in life Stewart aspired toward careers in both singing and electrical engineering. His initial major at Baylor University in the mid-1940s was electronics, but when he returned to the university after service in the U.S. Air Force, he changed his major to music. After receiving his B.A. degree in music at Baylor, in 1953, he studied voice at the Juilliard School of Music in New York City. It was there that he met Evelyn Kwartin Lear, a fellow student, whom he married in 1955. At Juilliard he made his operatic debut as La Roche in a school production (and the U.S. premiere) of Richard Strauss's *Capriccio*, and he subsequently made his professional debut with the Chicago Lyric Opera as Raimondo in *Lucia di Lammermoor*. In 1957 he and Lear traveled on Fulbright scholarships to Berlin, Germany, where both joined the Deutsche Oper (then called the Städische Oper). With the Berlin company until 1964, Stewart mastered major roles in the standard repertory, beginning with Escamillo in Bizet's *Carmen* and including Don Giovanni, the Flying Dutchman in Wagner's *Der Fliegende Holländer*, Iago in *Otello*, Golaud in *Pelléas et Mélisande*, and Doctor Falke in *Die Fledermaus*; in addition, he created the role of William in Boris Blacher's *Rosamunde Floris* and the title role in Milhaud's *L'Orestie d'Eschyle*. At the Bayreuth Festival between 1960 and 1972, he performed numerous Wagnerian roles, including the Flying Dutchman, Wolfram in *Tannhäuser*, Donner in *Das Rheingold*, and Amfortas in *Parsifal*. His success at Bayreuth led to engagements in major opera houses across Europe, from Covent Garden in London to the Vienna State Opera. In the United States in 1966, he began his association with the San Francisco Opera with a performance as Prince Yeletsky in Tchaikovsky's *Queen of Spades*. During the same year he made his debut at the Metropolitan Opera in New York City, as Ford in *Falstaff*. Returning to the Met regularly over the following 13 years, he became familiar to audiences there in such Wagnerian roles as the Flying Dutchman, Amfortas, the Wanderer in *Siegfried*, Gunther in *Götterdämmerung*, Kurwenal in *Tristan und Isolde*, and especially Wotan in *Das Rheingold* and *Die Walküre*; outside of the Wagnerian repertory, his roles included Count Almaviva in *The Marriage of Figaro*, Amonasro in *Aïda*, and, most often, the four villains in Offenbach's *Les Contes d'Hoffmann*. During the 1971–72 season at the Met, he and his wife performed together in *The Marriage of Figaro*, *Falstaff*, and *Don Giovanni*. In a final return to the Met, in 1993, he sang the role of the Speaker in Mozart's *The Magic Flute*. Among the many operatic performances by Stewart that can be heard on Deutsche Grammophon recordings are his portrayals of Wotan, the Wanderer, Amfortas, Gunther, and Hans Sachs. Stewart died suddenly while playing golf in Rockville, Maryland. He was survived by his wife, a stepson, and a stepdaughter. See *Current Biography* (1974).

Obituary *New York Times* C p14 Sep. 26, 2006

STOLZ, MARY Mar. 24, 1920–Dec. 15, 2006 Author. Mary Stolz (née Slattery) wrote warm and insightful juvenile fiction for readers ranging from beginners to young adults. Particularly impressive are her trail-blazing, sensitive coming-of-age portrayals, in which the relation of often painful experiences, sometimes family-related, is usually relieved by a sense of humor. The Boston-born and New York City–bred Stolz, who majored in English at Columbia University, had written verse, essays, and stories from her earliest days as a schoolgirl, but she postponed her professional career for many years while attending to housekeeping and raising her son, William. She began a long association with Harper & Brothers (now HarperCollins Publishers) when Ursula Nordstrom, Harper's estimable children's book editor, accepted the manuscript of her first published novel, *To Tell Your Love* (1950), about a teenage girl coping with the breakup of her first romantic relationship. That book was followed by *The Organdy Cupcakes* (1951), about three student nurses in a New York hospital, and *The Seagulls Woke Me* (1951), the story of a sheltered 16-year-old girl's first summer away from home. Also written for adolescent girls are Stolz's novels *Ready or Not* (1953), *And Love Replied* (1958), *Some Merry-Go-Round Music* (1959), and *Leap Before You Look* (1972). She won a Child Study Book Award with her time-travel fantasy *Cat in a Mirror* (1953) and a Boys' Club Junior Book Award for *The Bully of Barkham Street* (1963). *The Edge of Next Year* (1974) was a finalist for the National Book Award. Two of her books for younger readers, *Belling the Tiger* (1961) and *The Noonday Friends* (1965), were runners-up for the Newbery Award. In *Ivy Larkin* (1986), set in New York City during the Great Depression of the 1930s, the protagonist is a 14-year-old girl from a struggling family—her father has lost his job—who feels miserably out of place as a scholarship student in an elite private school and finds refuge in the school library. Stolz's historical fiction includes *Zelmet, The Stone Carver: A Tale of Ancient Egypt* (1996) and *A Ballad of the Civil War* (1997). Her novel *Truth and Consequence* (1953) is for adult readers. She published a total of 61 books, including *The Leftover Elf* (1952), *Emmett's Pig* (1959), *A Dog on Barkham Street* (1960), *The Beautiful Friend and Other Stories* (1960), *The Story of a Singular Hen and Her Peculiar Children* (1969), *Go and Catch a Flying Fish* (1979), *What Time of Night Is It?* (1981), *King Emmett the Second* (1991), *Cezanne Pinto: A Memoir* (1994), and *Stealing Home* (1997). After her divorce from her first husband, Stanley Burr Stolz, she married Thomas C. Jaleski, who died in 2001. She died at her home in Longboat Key, Florida. Her survivors included her son, William, a stepson, Eugene Jaleski, five grandchildren, and three great-grandchildren. See *Current Biography* (1953).

Obituary *New York Times* B p8 Jan. 22, 2007

STROESSNER, ALFREDO Nov. 3, 1912–Aug. 16, 2006 President of Paraguay (1954–89); commander in chief of the Paraguayan armed forces (1951–54). Alfredo Stroessner Matiauda, a neo-Fascist, was Latin America's longest-ruling dictator in the 20th century until his endurance record was exceeded by his opposite leftist number, Fidel Castro, the Communist president and prime minister of Cuba. Stroessner rightly boasted first of bringing "peace and tranquility" to his country after decades of instability in Paraguayan politics and then of spurring economic progress. His underlying achievement of "order" came at a price, in part from the imposition of a cult of personality but in far greater measure from an adroit combination of patronage, fraud, and harsh repression enforced by fearsome security forces. The son of a German immigrant father, Hugo Stroessner, and a wealthy indigenous Paraguayan mother, Heriberta Matiauda, Stroessner joined the Paraguayan army when he was 17 and rose through the ranks to become a brigadier general in 1949 and commander in chief of the armed forces in 1951. He assumed the presidency of Paraguay in August 1954, three months after the beginning of a complex military coup engineered by him. Behind a democratic façade, he maintained an intermittent state of siege in which constitutional guarantees in Paraguay were suspended for 34 and a half years. He did so with the support of the military and especially that of the Partido Colorado, a multi-class political party that assured his victory in a succession of presidential elections widely thought to be rigged. For many years he also had the support of the United States, which viewed him as a Cold War ally because he wrapped his violations of human rights in Paraguay in the cloak of anti-Communism and because he was a robust participant in Operation Cobra, a joint intelligence plan to thwart Marxist and other leftist activism in South America's Southern Cone (chiefly comprising Paraguay, Uruguay, Chile, and Argentina). Among the charges brought against his authoritarian and corrupt regime was the harboring of a number of Nazi war criminals (including Josef Mengele) among the 200,000 Germans who had immigrated to Paraguay in the years following World War II. Stroessner also gave asylum to deposed fellow Latin American dictators, including Anastasio Somoza of Nicaragua. On the positive side, he was credited with building schools and filtration stations, with infrastructural improvements, especially in the highway system, and with the sale of tracts of farmland to military veterans for a nominal price. His greatest achievements were his economic policies, as a result of which between 1953 and the mid-1970s Paraguayan per capita income increased by one-third and export sales increased nine times. In the mid-1970s he initiated the construction of the Itaipú Dam on the Paranas River, financed with billions of dollars from Brazil, which in return was given a reduced rate in purchasing electricity therefrom. At the time the project was completed, in the mid-1980s, Itaipú was the largest hydroelectric power plant in the world. Although Paraguay received only 2 percent of the energy and 15 percent of the contracts, the export sales of electricity from the plant further contributed to Paraguay's rate of economic growth, the highest in Latin America at the time. Following his ouster in a military coup d'état in February 1989, Stroessner received political asylum in Brazil, where he lived in exile for the rest of his life. After surgery for a hernia in the summer of 2006, he suffered pneumonia, with lung complications. He died of a stroke, in Brasília, Brazil. See *Current Biography* (1981).

Obituary *New York Times* B p7 Aug. 17, 2006

STYRON, WILLIAM June 11, 1925–Nov. 1, 2006

Novelist. "The catastrophic propensity on the part of human beings to attempt to dominate one another" was the constant theme of William Clark Styron Jr., a southern-born writer whose intense awareness of human evil—including racism and genocide—was balanced with a belief in redemption. As the critic Alan Cheuse, one of his protégés, has observed, Styron was "a writer with a deep conscience and a broad grasp of human character and history . . . who dared to take on . . . dangerous subjects that some of the commissars of literature declared out of bounds for him." That naysaying notwithstanding, Styron earned secure status as a preeminent figure in American letters in the second half of the 20th century, acclaimed for his rich (sometimes even ornate) classical style and densely textured language, consonant with the complexity of his subject matter, and for a narrative drive missing in many of the postmodern generation of novelists following his own. Styron began "groping for enlightenment" and trying to exorcise unfathomable guilt as a boy growing up in the Tidewater region of Virginia, the grandson of a slave owner. He arrived on the literary scene with éclat with his brilliant first novel, *Lie Down in Darkness* (1951), about the moral decay of an old Tidewater family and the "genteel" pressures that drive Peyton Loftis, the daughter in the family, to flee to a bohemian life in New York City (where Styron himself had been working as an editor for several years), where she commits suicide. The final events in Peyton's life occur simultaneously with the atomic bombings of Hiroshima and Nagasaki, in Japan, which provide the menacing macrocosmic overtone for the novel's microcosmic angst and sense of doom. An incident Styron experienced during a stint in the U.S. Marine Corps at Camp Lejeune, in North Carolina, inspired his novella *The Long March* (1953). During a grand European tour (1952–54), he helped to found the *Paris Review* and gathered some of the grist for his novel *Set This House on Fire* (1960), a sprawling tragicomedy about degenerate American expatriates in Italy and the regeneration of one of them. Styron spent two decades preparing to write and five years researching and composing *The Confessions of Nat Turner* (1967), the fictional memoirs of the house slave turned rebel who led the bloody, brutally crushed slave insurrection in Southampton, Virginia, in 1831. That novel was a runaway best-seller, and it won several prizes, including the Pulitzer; it also drew sustained critical flak from black intellectuals angry at a 20th-century white man (especially one with roots in the old racist South) presuming to enter into and speak from the mind of a 19th-century African-American slave. Styron wrote the play *In the Clap Shack* (1973) and co-wrote the scenario for the made-for-television film *A Death in Canaan* (1976), the true story of a Connecticut city rallying to the support of a teenager accused of murdering his mother. Styron undertook his fourth novel, *Sophie's Choice* (1979), with the encouragement of the German-Jewish political theorist Hannah Arendt, who warned him, however, that he would be accused by some of "poaching on their turf." Set circa the late 1940s, *Sophie's Choice* is a story in which a young southern writer in a Brooklyn boardinghouse meets Sophie Zawistowska, a Polish

Catholic refugee secretly haunted by a "guilt past bearing" dating from her experiences in the Nazi concentration camp at Auschwitz, where she had been forced to choose which one of her two children would be allowed to live. (The inspiration for the character came from the background of a displaced woman from Poland whom Styron himself had met in a Brooklyn boardinghouse and an incident related by Olga Lengyel in her Auschwitz memoir, *Five Chimneys*, that led him to realize how refined was the cruelty of a totalitarian system "that could force a mother to become her child's murderer.") *Sophie's Choice* was a best-seller and won a National Book Award in 1980, and the 1982 screen adaptation of the book was nominated for several Oscars; Meryl Streep won the Academy Award for best actress for her portrayal of the title character. The critical response to *Sophie's Choice* was not entirely positive; among the negative assessments was the charge that Styron's limited, gentile's perspective obscured the fact that the primary purpose of the Nazi Holocaust was the total extermination of Jews. When the Auschwitz Jewish Center bestowed its Witness to Justice Award on Styron, in December 2002, he accepted it as "a kind of vindication" and "a kind of solid validation of what [he had] tried to do as a novelist." The Modern Library and the Radcliffe Publishing Course have chosen *Sophie's Choice* as one of the 100 best novels written in English in the 20th century. Styron's slim volume *Darkness Visible: A Mirror for Madness* (1990; originally published as an essay in *Vanity Fair* magazine in December 1989) is a harrowing memoir about his struggle with near-suicidal clinical depression. In *A Tidewater Morning* (1993), Styron told—in the voice of a boy growing up in Tidewater—three semiautobiographical tales concerned with mortality, including one about his mother's death. One story from that book, "Shadrach," set in 1935, was adapted into a feature film (1998) directed by his daughter Susanna. Essays by Styron were collected in *The Quiet Dust* (1982), and numerous uncollected essays by him appeared in various publications during the 1980s and 1990s. In a paper published in the *Southern Literary Review* (March 22, 1998), Rhoda Sirlin stressed the point that in Styron's nonfiction pieces, as in his fiction, he was a politically engaged writer who not only concerned himself with "the sinister forces in history and modern life which threaten us all" but provided "a kind of artistic redemption to help us conquer fear" and "transcend despair." His long-awaited Korean War novel, *The Way of the Warrior*, was published in 1996. Styron maintained homes in Roxbury, Connecticut, and on Martha's Vineyard, Massachusetts. He died of pneumonia in Martha's Vineyard Hospital. His survivors included his wife, Rose (née Burgunder), three daughters, a son, and eight grandchildren. See *Current Biography* (1986).

Obituary *New York Times* B p9 Nov. 2, 2006

SWEARINGEN, JOHN Sep. 7, 1918–Sep. 14, 2007 Corporation executive. John Eldred Swearingen was the most prominent American oil-industry leader of his time, known among his corporate peers for his acumen, strength of will, and aggressiveness in building the Standard Oil Co. of Indiana from an in-efficient, ragtag cluster of scattered second-rate petroleum enterprises—midwestern fragments from the U.S. Supreme Court's breakup of John D. Rockefeller's oil monopoly—into a robust global conglomerate. He was visible to a wider public as the head of the American Petroleum Institute, a position in which he served as the spokesman for the oil industry during the energy crisis of the late 1970s, and he later played a key role in the Federal Deposit Insurance Corp.'s rescue of the Continental Illinois National Bank and Trust Co. from bankruptcy—the largest bank resolution in United States history. Credentialed in chemical engineering, Swearingen rose up through the research, manufacturing, and management ranks at the Standard Oil Co. of Indiana to become president in 1958, chief executive officer in 1960, and chairman of the board five years later. Developing an organization of managers and personnel to assist him in the task, he proceeded to consolidate and streamline the company's corporate structure and operations; improve research and development programs; coordinate marketing, sales, and accounting practices; introduce labor-saving refinery technology and other cost-cutting innovations; expand domestic and foreign exploration, drilling, and refining of oil and production of natural gas; and increase chemical operations. At his behest the company acquired such subsidiary holdings as service stations, 700 of them in Italy. By the time he relinquished the helm of the company, at the mandatory retirement age of 65, in 1983, annual sales had risen to $29.8 billion, net income to $1.8 billion, and net assets to $245.8 billion. The value of the firm's stock placed it sixth among America's largest corporations, after Exxon, IBM, General Motors, General Electric, and Eastman Kodak. Meanwhile the company was undergoing a succession of identity changes. In the 1970s it changed its logo at gas stations in the United States to Amoco (the acronym for American Oil Co., long the company's major production branch), and in the mid-1980s Amoco replaced Standard Oil of Indiana as the company name. In 1998 Amoco merged with the petrochemical giant British Petroleum America to become BP Amoco (aka BP PLC in the stock market), the world's third-largest integrated oil company. BP Amoco grew bigger with the acquisition of the American Richfield Co., known by the acronym ARCO, in 2000. After leaving the oil industry, Swearingen was asked by the Federal Deposit Insurance Corp. to assist in the rescue of the troubled Continental Illinois National Bank and Trust Co., which the FDIC had taken over. Responding to that request, he became chairman and chief executive officer of the Continental Illinois Corp., the bank's parent company, in 1984. In tandem with William S. Ogden, the new chairman and CEO of the bank itself, he succeeded in returning Continental Illinois to solvency in short order. He retired from his executive positons at Continental Illinois in 1987 and from the board of directors in 1989. He subsequently wrote the autobiography *Think Ahead* (2004). Falling ill with pneumonia while visiting relatives in Birmingham, Alabama, he died at Brookwood Medical Center in Birmingham. His survivors included his wife, Bonnie, two daughters from an earlier marriage, seven grandchildren, and four great-grandchildren. See *Current Biography* (1979).

Obituary *New York Times* B p6 Sep. 18, 2007

TAUFA'AHAU, TUPOU IV July 4, 1918–Sep. 10, 2006 King of Tonga (1965–2006) As ruler of the last Polynesian kingdom in the Southwest Pacific, an archipelago of 150 islands with a total population of approximately 90,000, King Tupou negotiated his country's independence from Great Britain, and with his younger brother Prince Fatafehi—who as prime minister shared power with him—began to modernize Tonga and its government. The eldest son of Queen Salote Tupou III, Tupou IV was educated at Newington College and Sydney University in Australia. Under his mother, he served successively in the Tonga government as minister of education (1943–44), minister of health (1944–49), and prime minister (1949–65). He succeeded to the throne upon the death of his mother, in 1965, when Tonga was still a protectorate within the British Commonwealth. Among his accomplishments as king was his loss of 154 pounds—bringing his weight down to 300 pounds and setting a royal example for a diet and exercise regime among Tonga's generally overweight population. Another achievement was a bizarre change he made in international time zoning. Decreeing that the 180th meridian of longitude, which passes through the Fiji island of Taveuni, 400 miles west of Tonga, be moved (on the Tonga version of the world map) eastward so as to place Tonga in the Western Hemisphere, he enabled Tongans to say that they are 13 hours ahead of Greenwich Mean Time instead of 11 hours behind it. "It was always a satisfaction to the King," Kenneth Bain wrote for the London *Independent* (December 29, 2006), "that his people were the first in the world to greet the new day." King Tupou died in a hospital in Auckland, New Zealand. He was succeeded by his eldest son, who now reigns as King George Tupou V. See *Current Biography* (1968).

Obituary *New York Times* B p6 Sep. 11, 2006

TETLEY, GLEN Feb. 3, 1926–Jan. 26, 2007 Ballet dancer; choreographer; director. Glenford Andrew Tetley Jr. was not the only pioneering 20th-century ballet master to infuse elements of the idiom of modern dance into the discipline of classical ballet, but he was among the boldest. In the intense hybrid strain of kinetic dance that he created, the exploration of the dynamics of human movement and what he called the "journey into the psyche" did not primarily serve to enhance narrative. Rather, they often tended to displace plot and character development—a drastic innovation that found readier acceptance abroad than in his native country, the U.S., where he began his career. He was a late starter in doing so, having turned to dance while earning a B.S. degree. He was associated for five years (1946–51) with Hanya Holm and her School of Contemporary Dance as a dancer and production assistant. In that association he garnered credits in several Broadway musicals, including *Kiss Me Kate*. He also studied under Margaret Craske, Anthony Tudor, and Charles Weidman. During the 1950s and early 1960s, he danced in the companies of Doria Humphrey, John Butler, Martha Graham, Robert Joffrey, Jerome Robbins, José Limon, and Pearl Lang, and he was a principal dancer with the American Ballet Theatre. In 1961–62 he stopped dancing for a year to concen-

trate on his choreography. Gathering a small group of dancers, he presented the first all-Tetley program at New York City's Fashion Institute of Technology in May 1962. The highlight of that program was his ballet *Pierrot Lunaire*, which brought him to the attention of European ballet companies. While continuing to choreograph for his own company (until 1969), he began working with the Netherlands Dance Theatre, in 1964, and with the Ballet Rambert, in 1967. He was co-director of the Netherlands Dance Theatre from 1969 to 1971 and artistic director of the Stuttgart Ballet from 1974 to 1976. During the 1970s and early 1980s, he also choreographed works given their premieres by the Hamburg State Opera, the Munich Ballet, the Paris Opera, the Royal Danish Ballet, the Royal Ballet, the London Festival Ballet, and the Australian Ballet. As an artistic associate with the National Ballet of Canada (1986–89), he created the ballets *Alice*, *La Ronde*, and *Tagore* (1989). The Canadian company also premiered his dance *Oracle* (1994). His works have also been danced by the Houston Ballet, the English National Ballet, the Norwegian National Ballet, and the Dance Theater of Harlem. He created a total of 68 ballets, including *Voluntaries*, *Rite of Spring*, *Daphnis and Chloe*, *Sphinx*, *The Anatomy Lesson*, *Sargasso*, *Field Mass*, *Mythical Hunters*, *Mutations*, *Embrace Tiger*, *Field Flowers*, *The Game of Noah*, and *Freefall*. His *Lux in Tenebris* was premiered by the Houston Ballet in 1999. He choreographed to music by composers including Gubaidulina, Poulenc, Stravinsky, Landowsky, Schubel, Sobotnik, and Stockhausen. The movement in his ballets reflected his interest in t'ai chi chuan, the stylized Chinese meditative exercise/martial art. Tetley is the subject of Michael Blackwood's documentary film *Glen Tetley: Pierrot's Tower*, first shown on American and European television in 1995. Tetley died of melanoma in West Palm Beach, Florida. He was predeceased by Scott Douglas, his life partner from 1954 to 1996, and survived by his partner Raffiele Ravaioli. See *Current Biography* (1973).

Obituary *New York Times* B p8 Jan. 30, 2007

TOLEDANO, RALPH DE Aug. 17, 1916–Feb. 3, 2007 Writer. The political pundit and cultural critic Ralph de Toledano described himself as "a nonconformist conservative with general (though often critical) Republican sympathies." Toledano was in the vanguard of what Kenneth R. Weinstein labeled in *Azure* magazine (Autumn 1999, on-line) "the rise of the Judeo-Cons," the influential movement of some American Jewish intellectuals from the political left to the right during the second half of the 20th century, culminating in what has come to be called neo-conservatism. Toledano's political migration took place between the late 1930s and early 1950s, a time when, in the words of his friend Hugh C. Newton, a veteran Washington, D.C., communications executive, the term "'Jewish conservative' was truly an oxymoron." In the mid-1950s Toledano was one of the seven Jewish luminaries who assisted the Catholic intellectual William F. Buckley Jr. in founding the *National Review*, described by Weinstein as the journal of opinion "that laid the foundation for an intellectually respectable American conservatism by providing a platform that forged the now familiar front uniting anti-Communists, economic liberals, and cultural traditionalists." Weinstein described the *National Review* seven as "Jewish ex-student radicals who sought to defend the individual against the state, whether from the full-fledged totalitarianism of Soviet Communism or from the soft despotism they saw as endemic to the welfare state." With *National Review*, Toledano was a contributing editor, a Washington-based political columnist from 1956 to 1960, and a contributor of music criticism as well as occasional political and social commentary thereafter. For some years beginning in 1960, he wrote a Washington column that was distributed by King Features Syndicate, and in his later years, he was a regular contributor to the journal of opinion *Insight on the News*. He published two novels and two collections of poetry in addition to a score of books on political subjects, including the classic best-seller *Seeds of Treason: The True Story of the Chambers-Hiss Tragedy*, written with Victor Lasky and first published in 1950; *Notes from the Underground: The Whittaker Chambers–Ralph de Toledano Letters 1949–1960* (1997), and two books about President Richard M. Nixon, published in 1956 and 1960, respectively, when Nixon was vice president. A nonpracticing Jew who traced his ancestry to a line of Spanish Sephardic rabbis, Toledano was born in Tangier, Morocco, to parents who were journalists of American citizenry. With his parents and siblings, he immigrated to the United States when he was five years old. As an undergraduate in literature and philosophy at Columbia University, he distinguished himself as an editor of and contributor to campus literary publications. In campus politics he was a socialist who had Communist friends. After receiving a B.A. degree, in 1938, he held several editorial positions, including that of managing editor of the liberal journal of opinion *New Leader*. One of the mileposts on his migration from left to right was his disgust at the Hitler-Stalin pact of 1939. Following service in the U.S. Army during World War II, he worked briefly as the publicity director of the International Ladies Garment Works Union and then, in 1946, began a 12-year stint with *Newsweek*. His conversion to conservatism was definitively clinched by the case of Alger Hiss. As an associate editor assigned to *Newsweek*'s "subversive beat," he covered the confrontation between Hiss, a former U.S. State Department diplomatic aide, and the self-confessed, former Communist underground organizer and information conduit Whittaker Chambers. In hearings conducted by a congressional subcommittee headed by Richard M. Nixon (then a representative from California) in 1948, Chambers testified that Hiss had conspired closely with him in a Washington, D.C., Communist cell between 1934 and 1938 and had passed on secret State Department documents to him in 1937 and 1938. Hiss, who denied the charges, was tried for perjury, found guilty in 1950, and served 44 months in prison. Nixon prominently referenced his part in the conviction of Hiss in his vice-presidential campaign in 1952, when Dwight D. Eisenhower (with Nixon as his running mate) was elected president of the United States. Toledano's coverage of the Chambers–Hiss affair occasioned the beginning of a close association with Nixon and an enduring friendship with Chambers. In *Spies, Dupes and Diplomats* (1952), Toledano tried to explain how not only spies but some misguided American liberals in and out of government were serving the Soviet goal of world conquest. His next book was the novel *Day of Reckoning* (1955), about an American newspaperman's hunt for a murderous Communist. For *Newsweek* during the 1950s, he covered the Democratic as well as the Republican presidential campaigns and events in Washington, including those in the Eisenhower White House. Nixon wrote the foreword to Toledano's autobiographical book *Lament for a Generation* (1960), in which Toledano recounted his intellectual/political passage from liberalism to conservatism and from agnosticism to a religious faith just short of a conversion to Catholicism. He subsequently wrote *The Winning Side: The Case for Goldwater Republicanism* (1963); *R.F.K.: The Man Who Would Be President* (1967); *America, I Love You* (1968); *J. Edgar Hoover: The Man and His Time* (1974); *Little Cesar*, about Cesar Chavez (1971); *Let Our Cities Burn* (1975, later retitled *The Municipal Doomsday Machine*); *Hit and Run: The Rise—and Fall?—of Ralph Nader* (1977); *The Greatest Plot in History*, about the Soviet theft of American atomic-bomb information (1977); and *Cry Havoc: The Great American Bring-down and How It Happened* (2006). He ghost-wrote W. Mark Felt's memoir *The FBI Pyramid: From the Inside* (1979), and he edited the anthology *Frontiers of Jazz* (1962). After his divorce from the former Nora Romaine, he married Eunice Godbold, who died in 1999. He died of cancer in Suburban Hospital in Bethesda, Maryland. His survivors included his sons, Paul and James, from his first marriage. See *Current Biography* (1962).

Obituary *New York Times* D p8 Feb. 6, 2007

TROYAT, HENRI Nov. 1, 1911–Mar. 4, 2007 Russian-born French writer; a member of the Académie Française since 1959. Troyat was one of the most prolific, popular, and prize-honored French authors of his time. His first books were short psychological novels sometimes compared to those of François Mauriac and Georges Simenon. Later he drew heavily on his Russian-émigré heritage in writing seven multi-novel cycles, set chiefly in Russia or France. He also wrote novellas, short stories, literary and historical biographies, travel accounts, the play *Sébastian* (1946), theater criticism, and essays. All of his writing was done in a clear, accessible style. Henri Troyat was the pseudonym of Lev Aslanovitch Tarassoff, who fled Russia with his father, mother, and siblings at the time of the Bolshevik Revolution, when he was six years old. The family arrived in Paris in 1920. Troyat began writing in French in childhood, and he published the first of his early psychological novels, *Faux Jour* (False Light), a study of a father-son relationship, in 1934, shortly after he earned a law degree and about the time he obtained a civil-service position in the budget department of the Prefecture of the Seine, a job he held until 1942. Later in 1934 he published his second novel, *Le Vivier* (The Fish Pond), a study of manners centered on a domineering provincial dowager. His third novel, *Grandeur nature* (1936, translated as *One Minus Two*, 1938), was another study of a father-son relationship—a troubled one, in a theatrical milieu. *La Clef de voute* (The Keystone, 1937) was followed by his sexually explicit fifth novel, *L'Araigne* (1938; translated as *The Web*, 1984), which won the Prix Goncourt, France's highest literary award. During the Nazi occupation of France, Troyat published only three novellas and the novel *Le Mort saisit le vif* (1942), an eerie story inspired by the notebooks of a childhood friend of his, who served in the military during the early days of World War II. Next he embarked on the first of his multivolume series of historical novels. Drawing on the wealth of stories his parents and their friends had told him, in addition to his own memories, he wrote a trilogy that recounted the saga of a fictional White Russian family, the Danovs, from prerevolutionary Russia through the revolution and civil war and into exile: *Tant que la terre durera* (1947; translated as *My Father's House*, 1951), *Le Sac et la cendre* (1948; translated as *The Red and the White*, 1956), and *Étrangers sur la terre* (1950; translated as *Strangers on Earth*, 1958). An even greater effort went into the five-volume series with the general title *Les Semailles et les moisons* (The Seed and the Fruit, 1953–58), an epic fictional narrative covering the history of France from pre–World War I to 1944. He later wrote the five-volume cycle *La Lumière des justes* (The Light of the Just, 1959–63), the three-volume *Les Eyglétière* (The Eygletiere Family, 1965–67), the trilogy *Les Hértiers de l'avenir* (The Inheritors of the Future, 1968–70), and the trilogy *Le Moscovite* (1974–76). The seventh and last of his fictional cycles was the three-volume *Viou*. The publication of the last volume in that trilogy in 1980 brought the total number of his cycle volumes to 25. Meanwhile, Troyat had returned to single-volume fiction with such novels as *La Tête sur les epaules* (Head on His Shoulders, 1951), about a youth who discovers that his father is a murderer, and *La Neige en deuil* (1952; translated as *The Mountain*, 1953). (*The Mountain* was made into a 1956 feature film with same title.) Troyat's first literary biography was *Dostoievski* (1940; translated as *Firebrand: The Life of Dostoyevski*, 1946). It was followed by *Pouchkine* (1950; translated as *Pushkin*, 1950), *L'Étrange destin de Lermontov* (The Strange Fate of Lermontov, 1952), *Tolstoi* (1965; translated as *Tolstoy*, 1967), and *Gogol* (1971; translated as *Divided Soul: The Life of Gogol*, 1973). He also wrote literary biographies of de Maupassant, Zola, Verlaine, Baudelaire, Chekhov, Turgenev, Gorky, and Flaubert and historical biographies of Peter the Great, Catherine the Great, Czar Alexander I, Czar Alexander II, Rasputin, and Ivan the Terrible. He published a volume of memoirs, *Un si long chemin* (Such a Long Road, 1976), and his novel *Aliocha* (1991), the story of an immigrant boy growing up in Paris, was virtually autobiographical. In total, his books, including collections of short fiction, numbered more than 100. Married twice, Troyat was survived by a son, a stepdaughter, three grandchildren, and six great-grandchildren. He died in Paris. See *Current Biography* (1992).

Obituary *New York Times* C p13 Mar. 6, 2007

VALENTI, JACK Sep. 5, 1921–Apr. 26, 2007 U.S presidential aide; movie trade-organization executive. Jack Joseph Valenti, the first member of President Lyndon B. Johnson's White House staff, served as Johnson's most devoted factotum from 1963 until 1966, when he began his 38-year term as president of the Motion Picture Association of America, representing most of the major Hollywood companies in seeking federal legislation favorable to the industry, avoiding or handling censorship, fighting piracy of intellectual property, enforcing trade agreements with foreign countries, and generally promoting Hollywood's image and products. Diminutive in stature, dapper in dress, eloquent (and often grandiloquent) in speech, and, above all, congenial, Valenti was an effective spokesman and lobbyist for the MPAA. Aside from the winning impact of his personal presence, his best-known achievement was the creation of the modern movie rating system, which freed filmmakers from the puritanical Hays Production Code and allows them to explore more realistic and commercially successful themes. Lesser known but just as impressive was his success for many years, by various interventions, in keeping the Federal Communications Commission from striking down the protectionist rules that kept the three broadcasting networks from sharing in the rerun profits enjoyed by the Hollywood production companies. After serving as a decorated U.S. Air Corps bomber pilot in World War II, the Houston, Texas–born Valenti received a B.A. degree in business at the University of Houston and an MBA degree at Harvard University and headed the advertising and promotion department at the Humble Oil and Refining Co. in Houston. In 1952 he left Humble and co-founded the Houston advertising agency Weekley and Valenti. He met his fellow Texan Lyndon B. Johnson in 1956, when Johnson was a U.S. senator, and he worked for Johnson in the latter's unsuccessful bid for the presidential nomination at the 1960 Democratic National Convention, which nominated John F. Kennedy for president, with Johnson as his vice-presidential running mate. In the subsequent presidential campaign, Valenti's agency handled the advertising for the successful Kennedy-Johnson slate in Texas. Valenti was in the presidential motorcade when President Kennedy was fatally shot at Dealey Plaza in Dallas, Texas, on November 22, 1963. Following the assassination, he helped to arrange the impromptu inauguration of Johnson as president at the Dallas Airport, then flew to Washington at Johnson's side. In the White House, he was President Johnson's constant troubleshooter, expediter, and confidant, with the successive titles of special consultant and special assistant. There were also reports that he was the favorite whipping boy of Johnson, a notoriously bad-tempered taskmaster. In an effort to rebut those reports, in 1965 Valenti gave a speech containing such egregiously fulsome praise of President Johnson that it became an international joke. When he assumed the presidency of the Motion Picture Association of America, in 1966, Valenti's first task was to replace Hollywood's outdated Hays Production Code, a form of self-censorship installed in the early 1930s as a means of warding off censorship by federal legislators and local review boards. He found that the code's puritanical prohibitions against explicit sex (including "lustful kissing"), violence, and profanity were incompatible with the more liberal standards of the 1960s, preventing the MPAA from giving its imprimatur to American films whose realism echoed that of European films. In its place, he oversaw the creation of a ratings system giving advance cautionary warnings about the contents of films and thus making it easier, for example, for parents to decide which films they might allow their children to see. "I believe that every director, studio has the right to make the movies they want to make," he explained, "[and] everybody else has a right not to watch." The ratings system, installed in 1968 and later revised, has four classifications: G (for general audiences), PG (parental guidance suggested), PG-13 (parents strongly cautioned), R (restricted), and NC-17 (no one 17 or under admitted). The system is operated by the MPAA in conjunction with the National Association of Theater Owners, and the rating for each film is decided upon by a board of parents. Valenti was later involved in the creation of the similar television ratings system established in connection with the content-blocking V-chip. Toward the end of his tenure as president of the MPAA, he was concerned with the digital hard-goods counterfeiting of motion pictures from DVDs, VHS tapes, and optical discs as well as piracy from the Internet, which was costing the motion-picture industry $3.5 billion each year. In the anti-piracy cause, on Valenti's recommendation, in September 2003 the major Hollywood studios announced a ban on screeners, the DVDs and videotapes traditionally mailed (in the hundreds of thousands) to every group of Academy Awards voters in the U.S. and abroad to assure their seeing the films to be voted on. The ban, met with much anger in the cinema world, especially among independent filmmakers, was modified the following month and lifted by a federal judge in December 2003. Valenti retired as president of the MPAA in September 2004. He published five books: a guide to oratory, a collection of essays, a political novel, a book about President Johnson, and his memoirs, *This Time, This Place* (2007). He died at his home in Washington, D.C., of after-effects of a stroke. His survivors included his wife, Mary Margaret Valenti, a son, two daughters, and two grandchildren. See *Current Biography* (1968).

Obituary *New York Times* C p10 Apr. 27, 2007

VAN ALLEN, JAMES A. Sep. 7, 1914–Aug. 9, 2006 American astrophysicist; professor emeritus of physics, University of Iowa. The pioneering space scientist James Alfred Van Allen began doing seminal high-altitude rocket research in the mid-1940s, and beginning in the late 1950s, he was responsible for the scientific instrumentation on the first American artificial satellites and interplanetary spacecraft—more than 20 missions in all—that contributed to human knowledge of such phenomena throughout the solar system as magnetospheres, cosmic plasmas, solar X-ray emission, solar wind, and radio waves. Van Allen is probably best known to the lay public as the namesake of the Van Allen Belts, comprising an Earth-encircling zone of intense radiation that he and his team discovered. After earning a Ph.D. degree in nuclear physics at the University of Iowa in 1939, he became a fellow in the Department of Terrestrial Magnetism of the Carnegie Institution of Washington, where, as he recounted in an autobiographical article for the *Annual Review of Earth and Planetary Sciences* (1990), his "interest in low energy nuclear physics dwindled" and he "resolved to make geomagnetism, cosmic rays, and solar-terrestrial physics my fields of research—at some unspecified future date." At the Carnegie Institution he concentrated on the development of a rugged vacuum tube until the summer of 1940, when he joined a team of scientists involved in a U.S. defense-related project: the development of radio proximity fuzes (devices that set off the explosive charges of bombs or shells when they reach within specific distances of their targets) to eliminate the range error of time-fuzed shells fired from antiaircraft guns. With that team, he moved to the Applied Physics Laboratory of Johns Hopkins University early in 1942, just after the entry of the U.S. into World War II. In November 1942 he was commissioned a U.S. Naval Reserve line officer and sent to field test and perfect the use of the fuzes with the navy's Pacific Fleet. When World War II ended, he returned to the Applied Physics Laboratory at Johns Hopkins and headed high-altitude research there, supervising tests of captured German V-2 rockets and developing the small Aerobee rocket for use in probing the upper atmosphere. He remained at Johns Hopkins until 1951, when he became a professor and head of the Department of Physics at the University of Iowa. In 1952 he resumed his high-altitude research with the help of several of his graduate students at Iowa and the sponsorship of the Office of Naval Research—support that he would continue to enjoy during the rest of his career. To place his testing instruments higher into the atmosphere than had ever been done before and to do so on a modest budget, he invented a balloon-rocket combination called the "rockoon," which he launched from locations in the Arctic, at the equator, and elsewhere on a series of occasions between 1952 and 1957. Meanwhile, beginning in January 1956, he headed a panel of scientists in developing proposals for the launch of a scientific satellite as part of a research program during the International Geophysical Year of 1957–58. At Iowa he supervised the final design of the satellite (including a micrometeorite detector and cosmic-ray recording equipment). Following the Soviet Union's successful launch in October 1957 of *Sputnik*, the first artificial satellite, the launching of the Van Allen team's *Explorer 1* satellite was authorized by the U.S. Army. (The National Aeronautics and Space Administration did not come into existence until October 1958.) *Explorer 1* was launched into Earth's orbit on a Jupiter C missile in January 1958. It and *Explorer 3* (launched the following March) provided data enabling Van Allen to announce the first major scientific discovery of the space age: the existence a band of radioactively charged particles trapped by Earth's magnetic field. The *Pioneer 3* satellite, launched in December 1958, revealed that there were in fact at least two Van Allen Radiation Belts encircling Earth. Van Allen was subsequently responsible for the scientific instruments on additional NASA projects, including sounding rockets, the satellite *Hawkeye 1*, and interplanetary space probes (including the *Mari-*

ner and *Voyager* programs and the *Galileo* space-craft) to the planets Venus, Mars, Jupiter, Saturn, Uranus, and Neptune. He retired as professor and head of the Physics Department at the University of Iowa in 1985. With his wife, Abigail, he had two sons and three daughters. He died in Iowa City, Iowa. See *Current Biography* (1959).

Obituary *New York Times* C p14 Aug. 10, 2006

VARNAY, ASTRID Apr. 25, 1918–Sep. 4, 2006 Swedish-American opera singer. The dramatic soprano Astrid Ibolyka Varnay, an alluring natural actress especially renowned for her Wagnerian portrayals, brought an intense and exciting presence to the international operatic stage. She was born in Stockholm, Sweden, to parents of Hungarian descent; both were eminently involved in opera, her mother as a coloratura soprano and her father as a tenor and later a stage director. Her father died soon after the family immigrated to the United States via South America in 1923, and she was raised by her mother in Manhattan and Brooklyn in New York City and in Jersey City, New Jersey. At first aspiring to become a concert pianist, she did not begin to train her voice and study opera until she was 20, at first under her mother's tutelage and subsequently under that of Hermann O. Weigert, the assistant conductor at the Metropolitan Opera and her future husband. (They were married in 1944.) She made her debut at the Met substituting for a suddenly indisposed Lotte Lehmann in the role of Sieglinde in a production of *Die Walküre* that was broadcast nationally on radio on December 6, 1941; a week later, again on short notice, she substituted for Helen Traubel in the same opera, as Brünnhilde. In January 1942 she sang Elsa in *Lohengrin* and Elisabeth in *Tannhäuser*, and, again filling in for Traubel, she sang Isolde in *Tristan und Isolde* in February 1945. During 14 consecutive seasons at the Met, she became the only soprano to have sung all 11 of the soprano roles and all three of the major contralto roles in the Wagnerian repertory at a major opera house. Outside of that repertory, she created the part of Telea in Menotti's *Island God*, sang various soprano leads in Italian operas (including Amelia in *Simon Boccanegra* and Santuzza in *Cavalleria Rusticana*), and was the leading Strauss soprano at the Met, outstanding in the title roles in *Elektra* and *Salome*. Meanwhile, she was also performing at other opera houses, in San Francisco, Chicago, Mexico City, Rio de Janeiro, London, and Florence, Italy. After Rudolph Bing became general manager of the Met, in 1950, differences with him led her increasingly to concentrate on her career in Europe. Beginning in 1951 she performed at the Bayreuth Festival every year for 17 years, singing such Wagnerian roles as Isolde, Ortrud, Kundry in *Parsifal*, and Senta in *Der Fliegende Hollander* and alternating with Martha Moedl in the roles of Brünnhilde and Sieglinde. After leaving the Met, in 1956, she became a frequent performer at the Paris Opera, La Scala in Milan, and companies in Munich, Berlin, Vienna, Hamburg, and Stuttgart. At Stuttgart in 1959 she created Jocasta in Carl Orff's *Oedipus Rex*. When her voice changed in the late 1960s, she moved to mezzo roles, including Clytemnestra in *Elektra* and Herodias in *Salome*. Her best mezzo-soprano portrayal

was Kostelnička in Janacek's *Jenufa*, which she first performed at Covent Garden in London in 1969 and reprised in a return to the Met in 1974. Five years later at the Met, she sang Leokadja Begbick in the first English production of Kurt Weill and Bertolt Brecht's *Aufstieg und Fall der stadt Mahagonny* (*The Rise and Fall of the City of Mahagonny*). She retired in 1985, following performances as the old Countess in Tchaikovsky's *Queen of Spades* at Marseilles and the Wardrobe Mistress in Berg's *Lulu* at the Bavarian State Opera in Munich. At the time of her retirement, she had already begun teaching at schools in Munich and Dusseldorf. With Donald Arthur, she wrote the autobiography *Hab mir's gelobt* (1997), which was translated as *Fifty-five Years in Five Acts* (2000). The intensity of her live performances comes through only partially on the audio recordings of those events, such as a recently released disc on the Testament label that includes her portrayal of Brünnhilde at Bayreuth in 1955. She died of a pericardial infection in Munich, Germany. Her husband, Hermann O. Weigert, predeceased her. See *Current Biography* (1951).

Obituary *New York Times* D p6 Sep. 6, 2006

VONNEGUT, KURT Nov. 11, 1922–Apr. 11, 2007 Writer. Kurt Vonnegut wrote antic fantasies in which his absurdist perspective on the human condition and his pessimism regarding the future of the human race are relieved by social satire, ironic gallows humor, and elements of science fiction, including alternate universes, time travel, and other departures from linear experience. Vonnegut's darkly comic jeremiads and prophecies of doom relating to mankind's follies and horrors in the 20th century—including genocide, racism, environmental pollution, the dehumanizing effects of run-amuck science and technology, and total warfare heedless of "collateral damage"—won him a large following, especially among socially and politically disenchanted or alienated young-adult readers. He struck an especially responsive chord in the youthful counterculture with the sixth of his 14 novels, the classic anti-war book *Slaughterhouse-Five* (1969), about the 1945 Allied firebombing of Dresden, Germany, "the largest single massacre in European history." That story was quasi-autobiographical. Vonnegut's pursuit of a B.S. degree at Cornell University was cut short by his enlistment in the U.S. Army after the U.S. entered World War II. As an infantryman during the Battle of the Bulge, in 1944, he was captured by the Germans and placed in a prisoner-of-war facility in Dresden. "I was a prisoner in a meat locker under a slaughterhouse when the worst of the firestorm was going on," he recounted. "After that I worked as a miner of corpses, breaking into cellars where over a hundred thousand Hansels and Gretels were baked like gingerbread men." Vonnegut began publishing short stories while working as a General Electric Co. publicist (1947–50). He essentially mocked G.E. in his first novel, *Player Piano* (1952), about an automated future world where the protagonist leads a Luddite-style revolution. *The Sirens of Titan* (1959) is a parodic science-fiction–like novel involving the Church of God of the Utterly Indifferent. *Mother Night* (1961), a novel of moral ambiguity, is about an

American writer whose propaganda broadcasts for the Third Reich in Germany contain coded messages for the Allies. (Like *Slaughterhouse-Five*, that novel was made into a movie.) The protagonist of *Cat's Cradle* (1963) is a convert to Bokononism (a religion of "harmless untruths") who witnesses the destruction of Earth by a substance called Ice-9; that of *God Bless You, Mr. Rosewater* (1965) is a philanthropist who preaches kindness as the only panacea for the world's problems. The message of *Jailbird* (1979) is that America's political plutocracy and capitalist economy make the practice of Christian altruism impossible. *Galapagos* (1985) targets a host of political, social, and economic evils. *Hocus Pocus* (1990) is about the possible dire results of environmental, economic, and societal trends in the U.S. In *Timequake* (1999) humans are forced to relive the 1990s with no chance of altering events, with the result that people forget how to think for themselves. Vonnegut also published three collections of short stories; five collections of essays, including the autobiographical *Palm Sunday* (1981) and *Fates Worse Than Death* (1992); the children's Christmas story *Moon Star* (1980); and the 1970 Off-Broadway play *Happy Birthday, Wanda June*. After his divorce from his first wife, Vonnegut married the photographer Jill Krementz. He was survived by Krementz, their adopted daughter, two daughters and a son from his first marriage, and three adopted nephews, the orphaned offspring of his sister. He died in Manhattan, after suffering irreversible brain damage in a fall. See *Current Biography* (1991).

Obituary *New York Times* A p1+ Apr. 12, 2007

WALDHEIM, KURT Dec. 21, 1918–June 14, 2007 Austrian statesman. As a member of the conservative People's Party, Kurt Josef Waldheim was the first non-Socialist in Austria's post–World War II history to serve as president of his country, a largely ceremonial post. (Executive power is wielded by the prime minister.) Waldheim, a career diplomat and former secretary-general of the United Nations, was elected president in 1986 amid bitter controversy over his service in the German Wehrmacht during the war and his selective memory regarding that service. The Wehrmacht, which comprised the traditional German armed forces, is not to be confused with the Waffen SS, the elite combat arm of the Nazi Party, which was specifically dedicated to the military enforcement of the party's genocidal policies. But the Wehrmacht was not free of guilt in Nazi war crimes, and Waldheim was at the very least a cog in the wheel of the machinery of the "cleansing operations" that took place in the Balkans and Greece during the war. Waldheim was 19 years old when, on March 12, 1938, a vanguard of German troops invaded Austria, followed by a motorcade bearing Adolf Hitler himself. The following day Hitler's desired *Anschluss Osterreichs* was officially realized, annexing Austria into Greater Germany. Like other young Austrian men, Waldheim became subject to German military conscription. Shortly after the outbreak of World War II, in 1939, he was drafted into the *heer*, the army branch of the Wehrmacht, at the rank of lieutenant. Sent to the Eastern front in the spring of 1941, he suffered an ankle wound the fol-

lowing December. According to his memoir, *Glaspalast der Weltpolitik* (1985, translated as *In the Eye of the Storm*,1986), that wound ended his military service; he recalled only returning to Vienna to complete his studies for his doctorate in law, leaving the impression that he remained in civilian status in the Austrian capital until war's end. While denying any responsibility for war crimes, he rectified his public recollection after investigations conducted by the World Jewish Congress and others—including Professor Robert Edwin Herzstein of the University of North Carolina—brought to public light long available but somehow ignored evidence of his complete wartime activity, including witnesses, photographs, and medals, such as a commendation from the Nazi puppet government in Croatia. In fact, he returned to military duty in the spring of 1942 as an intelligence, administrative, and liaison officer in Yugoslavia, where he remained—except for a period of duty in Greece—until the end of the war, serving on the staffs, successively, of General Friedrich Stahl and General Alexander Löhr. General Löhr's German Army Group E was especially ruthless in its repression of and reprisal campaigns against Yugoslav partisans and civilians, in which numerous villages were razed and untold thousands of men, women, and children were massacred. In addition, captured Allied commandoes were routinely executed, and some 40,000 Jews from Salonika, Greece, were deported to the Auschwitz death camp. (Only an estimated 10,000 of those Jews survived.) Löhr was executed as a war criminal in 1947. Waldheim's initials were on much of the paperwork relating to the atrocities, but he described his role as only that of "a clerk and an interpreter." Professor Herzstein wrote: "Waldheim did not in fact order, incite, or personally commit what is commonly called a war crime. But [his] significant roles in military units that unquestionably committed war crimes makes him at the very least morally complicit in those crimes." Waldheim entered the Austrian foreign service soon after the end of World War II, in 1945. His succession of assignments included first secretary at the Austrian Embassy in Paris (1948–51), minister plenipotentiary (1956–58) and ambassador (1958–60) to Canada, observer (1955–56) and representative (1964–68) at the United Nations, and several staff positions in the foreign ministry in Vienna. He was foreign minister from 1968 to 1970, when he again became permanent representative to the United Nations. He served two five-year terms as secretary-general of the U.N. (January 1972–December 1981). In the voting in the Security Council in 1981, the United States, the Soviet Union, and the United Kingdom supported his bid for a third term as secretary-general, but China vetoed it. After leaving the U.N., he was a guest professor of diplomacy at Georgetown University (1982–84) in Washington, D.C. His successful run for the presidency of Austria in 1986 was his second campaign for the post; he had run unsuccessfully in 1971, when the Socialist Party was in the ascendancy. During his six-year term as president (1986–92), he was persona non grata in most Western countries, including the United States, where the Justice Department put him on its immigration agents' "watch list" in 1987. His state visits were perforce limited to a very few countries, including Germany and several

Arab and Communist states, and to the Vatican. Waldheim died in Vienna. He was survived by his wife, a son, and two daughters. See *Current Biography* (1987).

Obituary *New York Times* B p7 June 15, 2007

WALSH, BILL Nov. 30, 1931–July 30, 2007 College and professional football coach. William ("Bill") Walsh, nicknamed "the Genius," was one of American football's great offensive innovators in the second half of the 20th century. Walsh originated such practices as the laminating of carefully scripted play sheets, now commonly seen in the hands of coaches on sidelines, and he is best known as the father of the so-called West Coast offense, a pass-oriented strategy that he introduced at a time when the conventional wisdom was to make passing attacks secondary elements in a running game. "[From] his meticulously crafted and cerebral practice regimens . . . to his daring personnel decisions and his visionary offensive schemes, he created an enduring model," Michael Silver wrote for *Sports Illustrated* (March 2007). "Today the West Coast, with its reliance on short passes, precisely timed routes, and progressively planned progressions, is the NFL's preeminent scheme. But in the early 1980s it merely drove opposing coaches nuts." Walsh's most vaunted tenure as a head coach was with the previously lowly San Francisco 49ers, whom he built into the top franchise in the National Football League in the 1980s. He had what seemed to be a preternatural eye for spotting potential talent, and as a pro coach he was extraordinarily successful in manipulating the college draft to his advantage. He was the mentor of the Hall of Fame quarterbacks Steve Young, Joe Montana, and Dan Fouts and of the All-Pro quarterback Ken Anderson. His influence throughout college and professional football proliferated through the legion of former assistants of his who moved on to head-coaching positions elsewhere. In 1987 he created the Minority Coaching Fellowship, which facilitated the rise of such talents as Tyrone Willingham and Marvin Lewis in a traditionally white-dominated profession. As a young man Walsh played quarterback at San Mateo (California) Junior College for two years before transferring in the early 1950s to San Jose State University, where he played wide receiver while earning bachelor's and master's degrees in physical education. He began his coaching career at Washington Union High School in Fremont, California (1957–59) and moved up to college coaching as an assistant at the University of California at Berkeley (1960–65). He entered the professional ranks as an offensive backfield coach with the Oakland Raiders of the now defunct American Football League in 1966. The following year he coached the San Jose Apaches of the short-lived Continental Football League. In 1968 he joined the coaching staff of the AFL's Cincinnati Bengals, and he soon became that team's offensive coordinator. The genesis of the West Coast offense occurred in Cincinnati in 1970, as Walsh recounted in an interview for *Football Digest*: "We couldn't control the football with the run; [other] teams were just too strong. So it had to be the forward pass, and obviously it had to be a high-percentage, short, controlled passing game. So

through a series of formation-changing and timed passes . . . using all eligible receivers . . . we were able to put together an offense." After leaving the Bengals at the end of the 1976 season following a bitter dispute with head coach Paul Brown, he spent one season as offensive coach with the San Diego Chargers and two seasons as head coach at Stanford University before moving into the National Football League as head coach of the San Francisco 49ers in 1979. Under Walsh, the 49ers rose from the basement of the NFL to win the National Football Conference's Western Division title in 1981 and to follow that triumph up immediately with the NFC title and then with victory in the Super Bowl in January 1982. During his 10 seasons coaching the 49ers, the team won five more NFC Western Division championships, followed by NFC titles in 1984 and 1988 and Super Bowl victories in January 1985 and January 1989. His record with the 49ers was 102 wins, 63 losses, and one tie, including postseason games. From 1989 through 1991 he appeared on national television as an analyst and color commentator in broadcasts of football games on the NBC network. He was inducted into the Pro Football Hall of Fame in 1993. Back with the Stanford Cardinals, he was head coach from 1992 through 1994. His totals at Stanford, including two seasons in the late 1970s, were 34 wins, 24 losses, and one tie. In 1994 he was instrumental in the establishment of the World League of American Football, and he helped to manage that organization, which later became known as NFL Europe. Returning to the 49ers, he served as general manager of the San Francisco team from 1999 until 2001. He subsequently contributed to programs in the development of business-management skills for sports executives at Stanford and helped to strengthen the athletics programs at San Jose State University. In collaboration with others, he wrote the books *Building a Champion: On Football and the Making of the 49ers* (1990), *Bill Walsh: Finding the Winning Edge* (1997), and *The Business of Sports: Cases and Text on Strategy and Management* (2005). Walsh died of leukemia at his home in Woodside, California. He was predeceased by his son Steve and survived by his wife, Geri, his daughter, Elizabeth, and his son Craig. See *Current Biography* (1989).

Obituary *New York Times* B p9 July 31, 2007

WASHBURN, BRADFORD June 7, 1910–Jan. 10, 2007 Explorer; mountaineer; photographer; mapmaker; museum director. Bradford Washburn was the world's foremost authority on the mountains of Alaska and the Yukon and a superb, innovative photographer and cartographer of numerous peaks there, in New Hampshire's White Mountains, and in the French Alps as well as of the heights and depths of Arizona's Grand Canyon. He was also, peripherally, an expert on glaciers, cold-climate equipment, and the nature, prevention, and treatment of frostbite. From 1939 to 1980 he was the director of the Boston Museum of Science (originally named the New England Museum of Natural History). By the time he graduated from prep school and matriculated at Harvard University, he was already a seasoned mountaineer and the author of two books, one about his experiences climbing the Alps and the other a climbers' guide to the White Mountains, both illustrated with his own photography. As an undergraduate at Harvard, he began exploring the mountains in Alaska's Coast Range. After receiving a B.A. degree at Harvard, in 1933, he taught in Harvard's Institute of Geographical Exploration while earning a graduate degree there. Leading the National Geographic Society's Yukon Expedition across the Saint Elias Range from Canada to Alaska in 1935, he discovered the then-unnamed Mount Kennedy. Under the auspices of the National Geographic Society the following year, he undertook the first aerial photographic expedition over Alaska's Mount McKinley, the highest peak in North America. Subsequently in Alaska he made the first ascents of Mount Sanford and Mount Marcus Baker and conducted aerial surveys of thousands of square miles of previously unmapped territory in the Saint Elias Range. Also in Alaska, he and Robert Bates made the first ascent of Mount Lucania and he and his wife, Barbara Teel Polk Washburn, made the first ascents of Mount Bertha and Mount Hayes. His wife accompanied him on a number of other expeditions, including his fourth ascent of Mount McKinley, in 1947. In 1960 he completed a detailed map of Mount McKinley based on his fieldwork as a climber and the aerial surveys he had made there. During the 1970s he and a cartographical team from the National Geographic Society used helicopters, lasers, and reflecting prisms in photographing and measuring all aspects of the Grand Canyon in creating a map of the site unprecedented in its authentic detail. In the late 1980s, using global-positioning devices, he completed his definitive map of Mount Everest. In remeasuring the world's tallest peak, he concluded that its altitude was 29,035 feet, seven feet higher than previously recorded. Among the books he published that are illustrated with his own photography are *Bradford on Mount Fairweather* (1930), several about Mount McKinley, and *Washburn: Extraordianry Adventures of a Young Mountaineer* (2004). With Donald Smith he wrote *On High: The Adventures of Legendary Mountaineer, Photographer, and Scientist Brad Washburn* (2002), and with Lew Freedman he wrote *Bradford Washburn: An Extraordinary Life* (2005). He died at his home in Lexington, Massachusetts. His survivors included his wife, Barbara, and two daughters. See *Current Biography* (1966).

Obituary *New York Times* B p8 Jan. 16. 2007

WEIZSÄCKER, CARL F. VON June 28, 1912–Apr. 28, 2007 German theoretical physicist; philosopher of science. Carl Friedrich Freiherr von Weizsäcker, the co-discoverer of the hydrogen-to-helium cycle in astrophysics, was the last surviving member of the team of physicists who tried unsuccessfully to develop an atomic bomb for Nazi Germany during World War II. During the decades following the war, he was a leading peace activist and promoter of peace research. As a philosopher seeking to unify all aspects of physics into a holistic system, he was influenced by Hindu mysticism as well as his own Christian faith. With Pandit Gopi Krishna he founded a research foundation "for Western science and Eastern wisdom." He also founded the Max Planck Institute for Social Sciences (originally called the Max Planck

Institute for Research into Conditions of Life in the Scientific-Technological World), a think tank devoted to fostering ethics and responsibility in science and studying such related matters as the peaceful pursuit of social and economic justice. Weizsacker was the son of the German diplomat Ernst von Weiszäcker, the grandson of the Württemberg political leader Carl von Weiszäcker, and the great-grandson of the prominent Protestant theologian Heinrich von Weiszäcker. His uncle Viktor von Weizsäcker is widely credited with having founded psychosomatic medicine; his brother, Richard Weizsäcker, was president of the Federal Republic of Germany from 1984 to 1994; and his son-in-law, Konrad Raiser, is a prominent ecumenical Christian theologian. In physics, he was a protégé of Werner Heisenberg, Niels Bohr, and Friedrich Hund. After earning his doctorate at the University of Leipzig, in 1933, he pursued research and/or taught successively at the Kaiser Wilhelm Institute in Berlin, the University of Berlin, and the University of Strasbourg. In 1937 he published the so-called Weizsacker formula for measuring the energy content of the atomic nucleus, a formula useful in calculating geological time. In 1938 he and Hans Bethe, working independently, arrived at what is known as the Bethe-Weizsacker explanation of the carbon-nitrogen-oxygen cycle as the energy-making process powering the stars (a theory confirmed when the first hydrogen bomb was exploded 14 years later). Building on the work of Pierre Laplace, Weiszäcker also developed a model for the development of the planets and the evolution of the solar system. In 1940 he joined the German atomic-bomb project, headed by Werner Heisenberg. He later claimed that Germany failed to build the bomb during World War II not because he and his colleagues lacked knowhow but because they did not want to succeed in their task. In 1944 he published a new version of the nebular hypothesis explaining the discrepancy between the comparatively low angular momentum of the sun and the high angular momentum of the outer planets. After World War II, in 1946, be became director of the Department of Theoretical Physics at the Max Planck Institute for Physics in Göttingen. While he did not advocate unilateral Western nuclear disarmament, in 1957 he joined 17 other prominent German physicists in issuing a manifesto promising they would not be involved in any way with atomic weapons and protesting the proposal that the West German army be equipped with tactical nuclear weapons. Two years later he co-founded the Association of German Scientists, in part as a platform for warning of the dangers of nuclear war. From 1957 to 1969 he was professor of philosophy at the University of Hamburg. He directed the Max Planck Institute for Social Sciences in Starnberg, Germany, from 1970 until 1980, and he was active in the institute for many years thereafter. His books include those translated into English as *The History of Nature* (1949), *The World View of Physics* (1952), *The Rise of Modern Physics* (1957), *The Relevance of Science: Creation and Cosmogony* (1964), *The Politics of Peril: Economics, Society, and the Prevention of War* (1978), *The Unity of Nature* (1980), *The Ambivalence of Progress: Essays on Historical Anthropology* (1988), and *The Structure of Physics* (2006). He wrote the introduction—comprising half the book—to Gopi Krishna's book *The Biological Basis of Religion and Genius* (1971). Weizsacker died in Söcking, near Starnberg. His survivors included his wife, Gundalena (née Wile), three sons, and a daughter. See *Current Biography* (1985).

Obituary *New York Times* C p17 May 2, 2007

WOOLDRIDGE, DEAN E. May 30, 1913–Sep. 20, 2006 Physicist; electronics engineer. While Dean Everett Wooldridge was lettered in theoretical physics, he achieved his international reputation in the practical application of electronics to high technology, including long-range missiles. After earning his doctorate in physics at the California Institute of Technology in 1936, Wooldridge joined Bell Telephone Laboratories, where he became an expert in the theory of magnetism underlying modern electronics. Under U.S. Army auspices during World War II, he supervised Bell's creation of a computerized fire-control system—the precursor of missile-control systems—enabling fighter planes to be precise in targeting. After the war he joined Simon Ramo (who had been a classmate of his) in the electronics division of the Hughes Aircraft Co., where they directed for the U.S. Air Force the development of airborne radar and computers, which became standard equipment for first-line interceptors and other planes. They also supervised the development of the Falcon air-to-air guided missile for tracking and destroying enemy planes. Their work transformed Hughes from a relatively minor aircraft company into the largest contributor of electronic equipment and guided missiles to the U.S.'s Cold War defense strategy. In 1953 Ramo and Wooldridge left Hughes Aircraft and, with the financial assistance of Thompson Products Inc., founded the Ramo-Wooldridge Corp., where their chief products at first were parts for Hughes's Falcon missile. When President Dwight D. Eisenhower assigned the nation's highest priority to the U.S. Air Force's Intercontinental Ballistic Missile program in 1955, the Ramo-Wooldridge Corp. was awarded the prime ICBM contract for overall systems engineering and technical direction. During the following several years, the Ramo-Wooldridge Corp. executed the systems engineering of the Atlas, Titan, and Minuteman ICBMs and the intermediate-range ballistic missile Thor, and it became the first corporation to build and launch a spacecraft, *Pioneer I*. A later Ramo-Wooldridge spacecraft, *Pioneer 10*, was the first to leave the solar system and transmit data back from Jupiter, Saturn, and beyond. In 1958 the Ramo-Woolbridge Corp. merged with Thompson Products Inc. to become TRW Inc., one of the world's leading high-technology companies. In 2002 TRW Inc. merged into the Northrop Grumman Corp., making the new firm second only to the Lockheed Martin Corp. among military contractors in the United States. Wooldridge was president of TRW Inc. until 1962. During his retirement he ventured into two new fields of scientific inquiry, neurology and microbiology, and wrote the books *The Machinery of the Brain* (1963), *The Machinery of Life* (1966), *Mechanical Man: The Physical Basis of Intelligent Life* (1968), and *Sensory Processing in the Brain* (1979). Wooldridge died in Santa Barbara, California. He

was predeceased by his wife, Helene (née Detweiler), and survived by two sons, a daughter, and three grandchildren. See *Current Biography* (1958).

Obituary *New York Times* C p10 Sep. 23, 2006

WYMAN, JANE Jan. 4, 1917–Sep. 10, 2007 Actress. Academy Award– and Golden Globe Award–winner Jane Wyman was, as Elizabeth Blair of National Public Radio News observed in a eulogy, "that rare Hollywood actress who could do a little bit of everything, and did, from the wisecracking sidekick to the tragic romantic lead" in addition to roles that gave her "a chance to sing on screen." The actress herself summed up her career in a newspaper interview in 1981: "I've been through four different cycles in pictures: the brassy blonde, then came the musicals, the high dramas, then the inauguration of television." In addition to her claim to fame as an actress, Wyman had the distinction of being the only ex-wife of a U.S. president—Ronald Reagan, the only divorcé ever to reach the Oval Office. Born Sarah Jane Mayfield, she underwent several name changes, once to Jane Fulks, which included the surname of her foster parents, and another time to Jane Durrell, the name she assumed as a teenage radio singer. According to Edmund Morris, the biographer of President Reagan, Wyman or Weyman was the surname of her first husband. As a contract player at Warner Bros. under the old studio system, Wyman was, with some notable exceptions, typecast in some 40 pictures over the period of a decade before she drew special attention from critics, with her performance as Helen St. James, the patient girlfriend of the alcoholic protagonist (Ray Milland) in *The Lost Weekend* (1946). She received the first of her four Academy Award nominations for her performance in *The Yearling* (1946) as Orry Baxter, the stern pioneering mother in the Florida scrublands who drives her son to kill his beloved pet deer, which had been eating the struggling family's crops. She won an Oscar as well as a Golden Globe for her portrayal of Belinda McDonald, the deaf-mute rape victim in *Johnny Belinda* (1948). In that concentrated speechless performance, as the film critic David Thomson noted, she succeeded in communicating the horror happening in "this girl's soul . . . naked through the eyes." Subsequently, she played the crippled Laura in *The Glass Menagerie* (1950) and Eve Gill in Alfred Hitchcock's thriller *Stage Fright* (1950); won the Golden Globe Award for best actress for her performance as Louise Mason, the self-sacrificing governess of other people's progeny in *The Blue Veil* (1951); sang the hit song "In the Cool, Cool, Cool of the Evening" with Bing Crosby in *Here Comes the Groom* (1952); and was reunited with Crosby in the musical *Just for You* (1952) and with Ray Milland in the musical *Let's Do It Again* (1952). "She could sing and dance with the best of them," Milland said, "and her comedy timing was top-notch." Following her performance as Selina De-Jong in *So Big* (1953), she starred in the melodramas *Magnificent Obsession* (1954), *Lucy Gallant* (1955), *All That Heaven Allows* (1955), and *Miracle in the Rain* (1956). Her rare subsequent Hollywood credits included the supporting part of Aunt Polly in the sentimental picture *Pollyanna* (1960) and a co-starring role with Bob Hope and Jackie Gleason in the comedy *How to Commit Marriage* (1969). Making the transition to television, in 1955 she became the co-producer and host of *Fireside Theatre*, an NBC weekly program of half-hour filmed dramas, in many of which she starred. She introduced and acted in that dramatic showcase (which was retitled *Jane Wyman Presents the Fireside Theatre* in 1956) through 1958. She also had many credits in other television dramatic anthologies and series. In her most important TV role, she starred as Angela Channing, the strong-willed Napa Valley vineyard owner, a power-hungry and ruthless schemer, in the popular CBS prime-time soap opera *Falcon Crest,* an hour-long show broadcast weekly from December 1981 to May 1990. In 1984 she won a best-actress Golden Globe for her performance as Angela Channing. The number of Wyman's marriages and divorces—whether four or five of each—is in dispute. In 1940 she married Ronald Reagan, then a fellow contract player at Warner Bros.; they had co-starred in the films *Brother Rat* (1938) and *Brother Rat and a Baby* (1940). She and the future president divorced in 1948. She died in her sleep of natural causes at her home in Rancho Mirage on the outskirts of Palm Springs, California. She was predeceased by her daughters Christine Reagan (who lived less than a day) and Maureen Reagan. Her survivors included her adopted son, Michael Reagan, and two grandchildren. See *Current Biography* (1949).

Obituary *New York Times* B p5 Sep. 11, 2007

YELTSIN, BORIS Feb. 1, 1931–Apr. 23, 2007 Russian politician and statesman; the father of contemporary Russian democracy. Boris Nikolayevich Yeltsin was a central figure in the dissolution of the Soviet Union and of the Communist Party of the Soviet Union (CPSU) and the first directly elected president of the Russian Federation (1991–99), the largest and most dominant of the remnants of the 15 states that had comprised the empire known as the Union of Soviet Socialist Republics. Yeltsin was born in the village of Butka in the Talitsky district of Sverdlovsk Oblast in European Russia. Trained at a polytechnic institute, he worked for 13 years (1955–68) as a civil engineer. He joined the Communist Party in 1961, became a full-time party worker in 1968, and seven years later was appointed first secretary of the party committee in charge of regional development in Sverdlovsk. In 1985 Mikhail Gorbachev, the new secretary general of the CPSU, appointed him first secretary of the Moscow city party committee, a position comparable to that of a mayor and including membership in the Politburo, the CPSU's executive committee and chief policy-making body. Two years later, when he criticized the slow pace of Gorbachev's policies of *glasnost* ("openness," in the sense of greater social and political freedoms, including speech) and *perestroika* (the "restructuring" of the stagnant Soviet economy, away from central control and planning and toward privatization), Gorbachev dismissed him from that post and from the Politburo. The fundamental difference between the two men was that Gorbachev intended to preserve the Soviet Union and the CPSU while modernizing and liberalizing them, whereas Yeltsin's thrust was more radical. Subsequently, Yeltsin's political fortunes rose

as he gained the support of a widening pro-democracy constituency, while those of Gorbachev declined. One of the reforms included by Gorbachev in *glasnost* made possible the replacing of entrenched elites with popularly elected candidates. Running for a Moscow citywide seat in a revamped legislature, the Congress of People's Deputies, in March 1989, Yeltsin won 90 percent of the vote. In July 1990 he quit the Communist Party, and in June 1991 he won 57 percent of the popular vote in the first democratic presidential elections, defeating Gorbachev's choice, Nikolai Ryzhkov. When hard-line Communist holdovers attempted a coup d'état in August 1991, Yeltsin dramatically faced them down, standing atop an armored T-72 personnel carrier outside the Parliament building in Moscow. He later overcame an effort by hard-liners to impeach him. In December 1991 he signed the document marking the end of the Soviet Union, and in 1993 he won the approval of a new constitution allowing for a super-presidency. While successful in destroying the old Soviet regime and in restoring freedom of speech and religion to Russia, he experienced great difficulty in trying to introduce a market economy, and the terribly costly war in Chechnya (a republic that sought independence but that Yeltsin considered an integral part of Russia), beginning in 1994, was an enervating distraction, as were Yeltsin's personal health problems, exacerbated by his notorious alcoholism. Corruption became rife, and the economy fell to the mercy of unscrupulous busnessmen, many from the underworld. In a national television broadcast on December 31, 1999, Yeltsin gave his resignation speech, apologizing for his mistakes and failures and announcing that Vladimir V. Putin, a former KGB colonel who had been heading the Federal Security Service, would immediately succeed him. Unlike Yeltsin, the autocratic Putin proceeded to concentrate power in an authoritarian central government and tighten political, social, and economic controls. Yeltsin died of heart failure in a hospital in Moscow. He was survived by his wife, Naina, two daughters, and three grandchildren. See *Current Biography* (1989).

Obituary *New York Times* A p1+ Apr. 24, 2007

ZAHIR SHAH, MOHAMMED Oct. 30, 1914–July 23, 2007 Last King of Afghanistan (1933–73). Mohammed Zahir Shah was a descendant of Ahmad Shah Durrani, who founded the Pashtun dynasty and the modern state of Afghanistan in 1747. Zahir ascended the throne when his father, King Nadir, was assassinated, in November 1933. His four-decade reign marked the longest period of stability in Afghan history. He quietly made some effort to liberalize his traditionalist Islamic country—proposing, for example, freedom of the press and the legalization of political parties—to virtually no avail. He did succeed in changing Afghanistan from an absolute to a constitutional monarchy, with a constitution giving women the right to attend school, work outside the home, and vote and mandating primary education for all children. Taking a neutral position in the Cold War—as he had during World War II—he won aid from both the United States and the Soviet Union. The United States funded irrigation projects, for example; the Soviets provided the Afghans with fighter jets; and both countries built airfields in Afghanistan. In 1973, while Zahir was at a health spa in southern Italy, Sadar Mohammed Daoud Khan, a relative of his who had felt slighted, staged a successful bloodless palace coup in Kabul and declared a republic, with himself as president, thus ending the 300-year Pashtun monarchy. Zahir spent the next three decades living reclusively in suburban Rome, where he survived an assassination attempt by a Muslim fanatic in 1991. Meanwhile, back in Kabul, the fundamentalist Islamic militia called the Taliban seized power in 1996. Following the overthrow of the Taliban regime in December 2001 by an American-backed coalition of Afghan forces, a new democratic Afghan Interim Authority was set up, with Hamid Karzai as president. At the invitation of Hamid Karzai, Zahir returned to Afghanistan, where he was officially welcomed home as "the father of the nation." See Current Biography (1956).

Obituary New York Times B p7 July 24, 2007

ZINDEL, PAUL Mar. 15, 1936–Mar. 27, 2003 Playwright; young-adult author. Paul Zindel was best known as the author of the semiautobiographical play The Effect of Gamma Rays on Man-in-the-Moon Marigolds, for which he won an Obie in 1970 and a Pulitzer Prize in 1971. The story of two daughters who are taught to fear the outside world by their domineering mother, the play was drawn from Zindel's own experience growing up in Staten Island, New York. "Our home was a house of fear," he said, according to James Barron for the New York Times (March 29, 2003). "Mother never trusted anybody, and ours wasn't the kind of house someone could get into by knocking on the front door. A knock at the front door would send mother, sister and me running to a window to peak out." After Zindel's father, a New York City policeman, abandoned the family, his mother struggled to support him and his sister, taking in terminally ill borders and working variously as a caterer, a breeder of collie dogs, a shipyard laborer, a hatcheck girl, and a hot-dog vendor. Zindel began writing in high school, and one of his plays won a contest sponsored by the American Cancer Society. Nevertheless, he majored in chemistry while attending Wagner College, in Staten Island. He earned his B.S. in 1958 and his M.S. in 1959. Zindel then became a high-school chemistry teacher, working on his plays in his spare time. After several unsuccessful Off-Broadway stagings, Zindel wrote The Effects of Gamma Rays on Man-in-the-Moon Marigolds. It opened in Houston, Texas, in 1965, and then moved Off-Broadway in 1970 and on to Broadway in 1971, where it ran for 819 performances. Zindel also wrote the screenplay for a film adaptation, which was directed by Paul Newman and starred Joanne Woodward. None of Zindel's subsequent plays—And Miss Reardon Drinks a Little (1971), The Secret Affairs of Mildred Wild (1973), Let Me Hear You Whisper (1973), and The Ladies Should Be in Bed (1973)— achieved the success of his first. Meanwhile, Zindel started writing novels for teenage audiences, beginning with The Pigman (1968), which told the story of two adolescents who befriend and then exploit an older man. "Few books that have been written for young people are as cruelly truthful about the human condition," a reviewer wrote for the Horn Book (February 1969). "Fewer still accord the elderly such serious consideration or perceive that what we term senility may be a symbolic return to youthful honesty and idealism." More than 20 novels for young adults followed. While some adults objected to the bizarre situations and repulsive parents that Zindel depicted, teenagers delighted in them, making many of his novels best-sellers. Zindel died from cancer in 2003; he was survived by his ex-wife, the novelist Bonnie Hildebrand; his children, Lizabeth and David; and his sister, Betty Hagen. See Current Biography (1973), World Authors 1970–1975 (1980).

Obituary New York Times A p 9 Mar. 29, 2003

CLASSIFICATION BY PROFESSION—2007

ACTIVISM
Blum, William
Carter, Majora
Davis, Evelyn Y.
George, Susan
Krupp, Fred
Moulitsas Zúniga, Markos ("Kos")
Ouma, Kassim
Richards, Cecile
Rockwell, Llewellyn H. Jr.
Sheehan, Cindy
Williams, Preston Warren II

ANTHROPOLOGY
Pääbo, Svante
Tattersall, Ian

ARCHAEOLOGY
Pääbo, Svante
Wendrich, Willeke

ART
Abel, Jessica
Aitken, Doug
Carter, Matthew
Dwight, Ed
Gondry, Michel
Hickey, Dave
Higgins, Jack
July, Miranda
Lang, Robert J.
Ross, Alex
Tufte, Edward R.
Wiley, Kehinde

ASTRONAUTICS
Dwight, Ed

BUSINESS
Agatston, Arthur
Anderson, Tom and DeWolfe, Christopher
Athey, Susan
Burns, Ursula M.
Carter, Matthew
Chen, Steve; Hurley, Chad; and Karim, Jawed

Davis, Evelyn Y.
Guarente, Leonard P.
Gygax, Gary
Jacobs, Paul E.
John, Daymond
Johnson, Sheila Crump
Jones, George L.
Kempthorne, Dirk
Kummant, Alexander
Kushner, Jared
Lamont, Ann Huntress
Lanzone, Jim
Marcus, Bernie
Meyer, Danny
Norman, Christina
Prince, Charles O. III
Rosenfeld, Irene B.
Rubin, Rick
Schwartz, Gil
Sinegal, James D.
Storch, Gerald L.
Tufte, Edward R.
Wendel, Johnathan
Williams, Preston Warren II
Woertz, Patricia A.

COMPUTERS
Anderson, Tom and DeWolfe, Christopher
Beck, Kent
Chen, Steve; Hurley, Chad; and Karim, Jawed
Lang, Robert J.

DANCE
Gomes, Marcelo
Mitchell, Jerry
Monte, Elisa
Welch, Stanton

ECONOMICS
Athey, Susan
Lantos, Tom
Rockwell, Llewellyn H. Jr.

EDUCATION
Abel, Jessica
Acocella, Joan

Ajami, Fouad
Alterman, Eric
Ames, Jonathan
Anderson, Winston A.
Athey, Susan
Bawer, Bruce
Borowitz, Andy
Coleman, Mary Sue
Dallek, Robert
Damasio, Antonio R.
Dodge, Charles
Emanuel, Kerry A.
Faust, Drew Gilpin
Gates, Robert M.
Gopnik, Alison
Guarente, Leonard P.
Hickey, Dave
Iyengar, B. K. S.
Johnson, Sheila Crump
Kagan, Elena
Kagan, Frederick W.
Lantos, Tom
McNeil, John
Pollan, Michael
Redlener, Irwin
Reynolds, Glenn Harlan
Robinson, Peter
Rockwell, Llewellyn H. Jr.
Sarris, Andrew
Shubin, Neil
Solomon, Phil
Steitz, Joan A.
Tao, Terence
Trethewey, Natasha
Tufte, Edward R.
Webb, Jim
Wendrich, Willeke
Williams, Preston Warren II
Yusuf, Hamza

FASHION
Banks, Tyra
John, Daymond
Spade, Kate

FILM
Banks, Tyra

Borowitz, Andy
Carell, Steve
Craig, Daniel
Elfman, Danny
Ferrera, America
Gondry, Michel
Howard, Terrence
Hudson, Jennifer
July, Miranda
McClurkin, Donnie
Mitchell, Jerry
Morgan, Tracy
Perkins, Elizabeth
Rakoff, David
Sarris, Andrew
Scorsese, Martin
Solomon, Phil
Watson, Emily
Watts, Naomi
Wexler, Haskell
Wilmore, Larry

FINANCE
Davis, Evelyn Y.
Lamont, Ann Huntress
Prince, Charles O. III

GOVERNMENT AND
    POLITICS
Addington, David S.
Ajami, Fouad
Baker, James A. 3d
Booker, Cory
Crocker, Ryan
Ellison, Keith
Fallon, William J.
Fenty, Adrian M.
Gates, Robert M.
Kagan, Elena
Kagan, Frederick W.
Kempthorne, Dirk
Kummant, Alexander
Lantos, Tom
McConnell, Mike
Moulitsas Zúniga, Markos
    ("Kos")
Norquist, Grover
Patrick, Deval
Reyes, Silvestre
Richards, Cecile
Rockwell, Llewellyn H. Jr.
Villaraigosa, Antonio
Webb, Jim

HISTORY
Anderson, Winston A.
Dallek, Robert

JOURNALISM
Acocella, Joan
Alterman, Eric
Bawer, Bruce
Blitzer, Wolf
Blum, William
Cohen, Richard
Deutsch, Linda
Higgins, Jack
Moulitsas Zúniga, Markos
    ("Kos")
Pollan, Michael
Rakoff, David
Ricks, Thomas E.
Risen, James
Schwartz, Gil
Silva, Daniel
Stoller, Debbie
Visser, Lesley
Webb, Jim
Weisberg, Jacob

LAW
Addington, David S.
Baker, James A. 3d
Booker, Cory
Ellison, Keith
Fenty, Adrian M.
Kagan, Elena
Krupp, Fred
Patrick, Deval
Reynolds, Glenn Harlan

LAW ENFORCEMENT
Coleman, Ronnie
Lanier, Cathy L.
Reyes, Silvestre

LITERATURE
Abel, Jessica
Ames, Jonathan
Atkinson, Kate
Bawer, Bruce
Borowitz, Andy
Desai, Kiran
Gygax, Gary
Hickey, Dave
Ricks, Thomas E.
Robinson, Peter
Schwartz, Gil

Silva, Daniel
Trethewey, Natasha
Webb, Jim

MATHEMATICS
Tao, Terence

MEDICINE
Agatston, Arthur
Anderson, Winston A.
Damasio, Antonio R.
Redlener, Irwin

MILITARY
Dwight, Ed
Fallon, William J.
Gates, Robert M.
McConnell, Mike
Ouma, Kassim
Petraeus, David H.
Webb, Jim

MUSIC
Barber, Patricia
Cat Power
Chung, Kyung-Wha
Decemberists
Dodge, Charles
Elfman, Danny
Gondry, Michel
Hewitt, Angela
Hudson, Jennifer
Hunter, Charlie
Johnson, Sheila Crump
Josefowicz, Leila
July, Miranda
Laws, Hubert Jr.
Legend, John
Matisyahu
McClurkin, Donnie
McNeil, John
Montero, Gabriela
Nakamura, Dan
Rihanna
Rubin, Rick
Sean Paul
Shins
Spektor, Regina
Stew
Strokes
Underwood, Carrie

Gondry, Michel
Howard, Terrence
Hudson, Jennifer
Johnson, Sheila Crump
Mitchell, Jerry
Morgan, Tracy
Norman, Christina
Perkins, Elizabeth
Schwartz, Gil
Underwood, Carrie

Visser, Lesley
Watts, Naomi
Wilmore, Larry
Wong, Andrea

THEATER
Bergeron, Tom
Carell, Steve
Craig, Daniel
Ferrera, America

Howard, Terrence
Mitchell, Jerry
Morgan, Tracy
Perkins, Elizabeth
Rakoff, David
Stew
Watson, Emily
Wilmore, Larry

CUMULATED INDEX 2001–2007

This is the index to the January 2001–November 2007 issues. It also lists obituaries that appear only in this yearbook. For the index to the 1940–2005 biographies, see Current Biography Cumulated Index 1940–2005.

Bannister, Constance obit
Yrbk 2005
Bánzer Suárez, Hugo obit
Yrbk 2002
Barber, Patricia Sep 2007
Barber, Ronde see Barber,
Tiki and Barber, Ronde
Barber, Tiki see Barber, Tiki
and Barber, Ronde
Barber, Tiki and Barber,
Ronde Oct 2003
Barbieri, Fedora obit Aug
2003
Barker, Travis see blink-182
Barnard, Christiaan N. obit
Nov 2001
Barnes, Brenda May 2006
Barnett, Etta Moten Feb 2002
Barney, Matthew Aug 2003
Barnouw, Erik obit Oct 2001
Barre, Raymond obit Yrbk
2007
Barris, Chuck Mar 2005
Barsamian, David Mar 2007
Bartiromo, Maria Nov 2003
Bartlett, Bruce Jun 2006
Barton, Jacqueline K. Sep
2006
Barzel, Rainer obit Yrbk 2006
Bassler, Bonnie Apr 2003
Bateman, Jason Oct 2005
Bates, Alan obit Yrbk 2004
Baudrillard, Jean obit Yrbk
2007
Bawer, Bruce Jul 2007
Beach, Edward obit May 2003
Beame, Abraham D. obit Apr
2001
Beane, Billy Jul 2005
Bebey, Francis obit Sep 2001
Beck, Kent Jan 2007
Beckinsale, Kate Aug 2001
Beckman, Arnold O. Jan 2002
obit Yrbk 2004
Bedford, Sybille obit Yrbk
2006
Beehler, Bruce Aug 2006
Beene, Geoffrey obit Mar
2005
Beers, Rand Oct 2004
Behar, Ruth May 2005
Behe, Michael J. Feb 2006
Bel Geddes, Barbara obit Yrbk
2005
Belaúnde Terry, Fernando
obit Yrbk 2002
Belcher, Angela Jul 2006
Belichick, Bill Sep 2002
Bell, James A. Jul 2006
Bellow, Saul obit Aug 2005
Benchley, Peter obit Jun 2006
Benedict XVI Sep 2005
Bennett, Lerone Jr. Jan 2001

Bennington, Chester see
Linkin Park
Bentsen, Lloyd obit Oct 2006
Benyus, Janine M. Mar 2006
Benzer, Seymour May 2001
Berg, Patricia Jane obit Yrbk
2007
Berg, Patty see Berg, Patricia
Jane
Bergeron, Tom Oct 2007
Bergman, Ingmar obit Sep
2007
Berio, Luciano obit Yrbk 2003
Berle, Milton obit Yrbk 2002
Berlin, Steve see Los Lobos
Berlitz, Charles obit Yrbk
2004
Berman, Lazar obit Yrbk 2005
Bernanke, Ben S. Mar 2006
Bernhard Leopold, consort of
Juliana, Queen of the
Netherlands obit Mar 2005
Bernstein, Elmer Jun 2003
Berrigan, Philip obit Mar
2003
Berryman, Guy see Coldplay
Berton, Pierre obit Yrbk 2005
Bertozzi, Carolyn R. Jul 2003
Bethe, Hans obit Aug 2005
Bethune, Gordon M. Jun 2001
Bettis, Jerome Aug 2006
Bible, Geoffrey C. Feb 2002
Big Boi see OutKast
Bilandic, Michael A. obit Apr
2002
Biller, Moe obit Yrbk 2004
Bing, Stanley see Schwartz,
Gil
Birendra Bir Bikram Shah
Dev, King of Nepal obit Sep
2001
Bishop, Eric see Foxx, Jamie
Bittman, Mark Feb 2005
Björk Jul 2001
Black Eyed Peas Oct 2006
Black, Jack Feb 2002
Blackburn, Elizabeth H. Jul
2001
Blades, Joan see Blades, Joan
and Boyd, Wes
Blades, Joan and Boyd, Wes
Aug 2004
Blaine, David Apr 2001
Blake, James Mar 2006
Blakemore, Michael May
2001
Blanco, Kathleen Jun 2004
Blass, Bill obit Nov 2002
Blind Boys of Alabama Oct
2001
blink-182 Aug 2002
Blitzer, Wolf Feb 2007

Block, Herbert L. obit Jan
2002
Bloomberg, Michael R. Mar
2002
Blount, Winton Malcolm obit
Jan 2003
Blum, William May 2007
Blur Nov 2003
Blythe, Stephanie Aug 2004
Bocelli, Andrea Jan 2002
Boehner, John Apr 2006
Boland, Edward P. obit Feb
2002
Bolten, Joshua Jul 2006
Bolton, John R. Feb 2006
Bond, Julian Jul 2001
Bontecou, Lee Mar 2004
Booker, Cory Feb 2007
Boorstin, Daniel J. obit Yrbk
2004
Borge, Victor obit Mar 2001
Borodina, Olga Feb 2002
Borowitz, Andy Jul 2007
Borst, Lyle B. obit Yrbk 2002
Bosch, Juan obit Feb 2002
Bosselaar, Laure-Anne Sep
2006
Botha, P. W. obit Yrbk 2007
Boudreau, Lou obit Oct 2001
Boulud, Daniel Jan 2005
Bourdain, Anthony Jan 2006
Bourdon, Rob see Linkin Park
Bowden, Mark Jan 2002
Boyd, John W. Feb 2001
Boyd, Wes see Blades, Joan
and Boyd, Wes
Bracken, Eddie obit Feb 2003
Bradley, Ed obit Yrbk 2007
Brady, Tom Aug 2004
Bragg, Rick Apr 2002
Branch, Michelle May 2005
Brando, Marlon obit Yrbk
2004
Bravo, Rose Marie Jun 2004
Brazile, Donna Mar 2006
Breathitt, Edward T. obit Sep
2004
Breen, Edward D. Jul 2004
Brenly, Bob Apr 2002
Brewer, Roy M. obit Yrbk
2006
Brier, Bob Sep 2002
Brier, Robert see Brier, Bob
Brin, Sergey and Page, Larry
Oct 2001
Brinkley, David obit Sep 2003
Brodeur, Martin Nov 2002
Brody, Adrien Jul 2003
Broeg, Bob May 2002
Brokaw, Tom Nov 2002
Bronson, Charles obit Mar
2004
Brooks & Dunn Sep 2004

Brooks, David Apr 2004
Brooks, Donald obit Yrbk 2005
Brooks, Geraldine Aug 2006
Brooks, Gwendolyn obit Feb 2001
Brooks, Kix see Brooks & Dunn
Brooks, Vincent Jun 2003
Brower, David obit Feb 2001
Brown, Aaron Mar 2003
Brown, Charles L. obit Sep 2004
Brown, Claude obit Apr 2002
Brown, Dan May 2004
Brown, Dee obit Mar 2003
Brown, J. Carter obit Yrbk 2002
Brown, James obit Mar 2007
Brown, Jesse obit Yrbk 2002
Brown, Junior Nov 2004
Brown, Kwame Feb 2002
Brown, Lee P. Sep 2002
Brown, Robert McAfee obit Nov 2001
Brown, Ronald K. May 2002
Brown, Troy Oct 2007
Browning, John obit Jun 2003
Broyhill, Joel T. obit Feb 2007
Brueggemann, Ingar Nov 2001
Brumel, Valery obit Jun 2003
Brunson, Doyle Sep 2007
Bryant, C. Farris obit Yrbk 2002
Brynner, Rock Mar 2005
Bryson, David see Counting Crows
Buchanan, Laura see King, Florence
Buchholz, Horst obit Aug 2003
Buchwald, Art obit May 2007
Buckingham, Marcus Aug 2006
Buckland, Jon see Coldplay
Buckley, Priscilla L. Apr 2002
Budge, Hamer H. obit Yrbk 2003
Bujones, Fernando obit Yrbk 2006
Bundy, William P. obit Feb 2001
Bunim, Mary-Ellis obit Yrbk 2004 see Bunim, Mary-Ellis, and Murray, Jonathan
Bunim, Mary-Ellis, and Murray, Jonathan May 2002
Burford, Anne Gorsuch see Gorsuch, Anne
Burgess, Carter L. obit Yrbk 2002
Burnett, Mark May 2001
Burns, Ursula M. Oct 2007

Burroughs, Augusten Apr 2004
Burrows, James Oct 2006
Burrows, Stephen Nov 2003
Burstyn, Mike May 2005
Burtt, Ben May 2003
Bush, George W. Aug 2001
Bush, Laura Jun 2001
Bushnell, Candace Nov 2003
Busiek, Kurt Sep 2005
Butcher, Susan obit Yrbk 2006
Butler, R. Paul see Marcy, Geoffrey W., and Butler, R. Paul
Buttons, Red obit Yrbk 2006

Caballero, Linda see La India
Cactus Jack see Foley, Mick
Calderón, Sila M. Nov 2001
Caldwell, Sarah obit Yrbk 2006
Callaghan, James obit Yrbk 2005
Calle, Sophie May 2001
Camp, John see Sandford, John
Campbell, Bebe Moore obit Yrbk 2007
Campbell, Viv see Def Leppard
Canada, Geoffrey Feb 2005
Canin, Ethan Aug 2001
Cannon, Howard W. obit Yrbk 2002
Cantwell, Maria Feb 2005
Canty, Brendan see Fugazi
Capa, Cornell Jul 2005
Capriati, Jennifer Nov 2001
Caras, Roger A. obit Jul 2001
Card, Andrew H. Jr. Nov 2003
Carell, Steve Feb 2007
Carell, Steven see Carell, Steve
Carey, Ernestine Gilbreth obit Yrbk 2007
Carlson, Margaret Nov 2003
Carmines, Al obit Yrbk 2005
Carmona, Richard Jan 2003
Carney, Art obit Yrbk 2004
Carone, Nicholas see Carone, Nicolas
Carone, Nicolas Jul 2006
Carroll-Abbing, J. Patrick obit Nov 2001
Carroll, Vinnette obit Feb 2003
Carson, Anne May 2006
Carson, Johnny obit Jul 2005
Carter, Benny obit Oct 2003
Carter, Jimmy see Blind Boys of Alabama
Carter, Majora Oct 2007

Carter, Matthew Oct 2007
Carter, Regina Oct 2003
Carter, Shawn see Jay-Z
Carter, Vince Apr 2002
Cartier-Bresson, Henri obit Yrbk 2004
Cary, Frank T. obit May 2006
Casablancas, Julian see Strokes
Casey, George W. Jr. Mar 2006
Cash, Johnny obit Jan 2004
Cassini, Oleg obit Yrbk 2006
Castle, Barbara obit Yrbk 2002
Castro, Fidel Jun 2001
Cat Power Oct 2007
Cattrall, Kim Jan 2003
Cavanagh, Tom Jun 2003
Cavanna, Betty obit Oct 2001
Cave, Nick Jun 2005
Cedric the Entertainer Feb 2004
Cela, Camilo José obit Apr 2002
Celmins, Vija Jan 2005
Chaban-Delmas, Jacques obit Feb 2001
Chafee, Lincoln Jan 2004
Chaikin, Joseph obit Yrbk 2003
Chamberlain, Owen obit Jul 2006
Champion, Will see Coldplay
Chandler, Otis obit Yrbk 2006
Chandrasekhar, Sripati obit Sep 2001
Chao, Elaine L. May 2001
Chapman, Duane Mar 2005
Chapman, Steven Curtis Oct 2004
Chappelle, Dave Jun 2004
Charles, Eugenia obit Yrbk 2006
Charles, Michael Ray Oct 2005
Charles, Ray obit Yrbk 2004
Chase, Alison Becker Nov 2006
Chase, David Mar 2001
Chauncey, Henry obit Mar 2003
Cheeks, Maurice Feb 2004
Chen, Steve see Chen, Steve; Hurley, Chad; and Karim, Jawed
Chen, Steve; Hurley, Chad; and Karim, Jawed Jan 2007
Cheney, Richard B. Jan 2002
Chertoff, Michael Oct 2005
Chesney, Kenny May 2004
Chiang Kai-shek, Mme. see Chiang Mei-Ling

Chiang Mei-Ling obit Mar 2004
Chieftains Mar 2004
Child, Julia obit Nov 2004
Chillida, Eduardo obit Yrbk 2002
Chisholm, Shirley obit Apr 2005
Chung, Kyung-Wha Feb 2007
Churchland, Patricia S. May 2003
Claiborne, Liz obit Yrbk 2007
Claremont, Chris Sep 2003
Clark, Kenneth B. obit Sep 2005
Clarke, Richard May 2006
Clarkson, Kelly Sep 2006
Clarkson, Patricia Aug 2005
Clemens, Roger Aug 2003
Click and Clack, the Tappet Brothers see Magliozzi, Tom and Ray
Clinton, Hillary Rodham Jan 2002
Clooney, Rosemary obit Nov 2002
Clowes, Daniel Jan 2002
Clyburn, James E. Oct 2001
Coburn, James obit Feb 2003
Coca, Imogene obit Sep 2001
Cochran, Johnnie L. Jr. obit Oct 2005
Cochran, Thad Apr 2002
Coddington, Grace Apr 2005
Coffin, William Sloane obit Yrbk 2006
Cohen, Richard Nov 2007
Cohen, Rob Nov 2002
Cohen, Sasha Feb 2006
Cohn, Linda Aug 2002
Colbert, Edwin H. obit Feb 2002
Colbert, Gregory Sep 2005
Colbert, Stephen Nov 2006
Coldplay May 2004
Coleman, Cy obit Feb 2005
Coleman, Mary Sue Feb 2007
Coleman, Norman Sep 2004
Coleman, Ronnie Feb 2007
Coleman, Steve Jul 2004
Collen, Phil see Def Leppard
Collier, Sophia Jul 2002
Collins, Jim Aug 2003
Collins, Patricia Hill Mar 2003
Columbus, Chris Nov 2001
Comden, Betty obit Yrbk 2007
Cometbus, Aaron Mar 2005
Como, Perry obit Jul 2001
Conable, Barber B. obit Sep 2004
Conlee, Jenny see Decemberists

Conneff, Kevin see Chieftains
Connelly, Jennifer Jun 2002
Conner, Nadine obit Aug 2003
Connor, John T. obit Feb 2001
Conway, Gerry see Fairport Convention
Conway, John Horton Sep 2003
Cook, Richard W. Jul 2003
Cooke, Alistair obit Oct 2004
Coontz, Stephanie Jul 2003
Cooper, Anderson Jun 2006
Cooper, Chris Jul 2004
Coppola, Sofia Nov 2003
Corbijn, Anton Jun 2006
Corelli, Franco obit Mar 2004
Corzine, Jon Aug 2006
Coulter, Ann Sep 2003
Counsell, Craig Sep 2002
Counting Crows Mar 2003
Cowher, Bill Nov 2006
Cox, Archibald obit Yrbk 2004
Cox, Lynne Sep 2004
Coyne, Wayne see Flaming Lips
Craig, Daniel Apr 2007
Crain, Jeanne obit Sep 2004
Crandall, Martin see Shins
Crane, Eva obit Yrbk 2007
Cranston, Alan obit Mar 2001
Creed May 2002
Creeley, Robert obit Yrbk 2005
Crespin, Regine obit Yrbk 2007
Crick, Francis obit Yrbk 2004
Crittenden, Danielle Jul 2003
Crocker, Ryan Oct 2007
Cromwell, James Aug 2005
Cronyn, Hume obit Yrbk 2003
Croom, Sylvester Jr. Aug 2004
Crosby, John obit Yrbk 2003
Crossfield, A. Scott obit Yrbk 2006
Cruz, Celia obit Nov 2003
Cruz, Penelope Jul 2001
Cuban, Mark Mar 2001
Culpepper, Daunte Sep 2007
Cummings, Elijah E. Feb 2004
Cunhal, Álvaro obit Yrbk 2005
Currie, Nancy June 2002
Curry, Ann Jun 2004

Dacre of Glanton, Baron see Trevor-Roper, H. R.
Daddy G see Massive Attack
Daft, Douglas N. May 2001
Dallek, Robert Sep 2007
Daly, Maureen obit Yrbk 2006

Damasio, Antonio R. Oct 2007
Dan the Automator see Nakamura, Dan
Dancer, Stanley obit Yrbk 2005
D'Angelo May 2001
Dangerfield, Rodney obit Feb 2005
Darling, Sharon May 2003
Davidson, Gordon Apr 2005
Davidson, Richard J. Aug 2004
Davis, Benjamin O. Jr. obit Yrbk 2002
Davis, Evelyn Y. Oct 2007
Davis, Glenn obit Yrbk 2005
Davis-Kimball, Jeannine Feb 2006
Davis, Nathanael V. obit Yrbk 2005
Davis, Ossie obit Yrbk 2005
Davis, Shani May 2006
Davis, Wade Jan 2003
Dawdy, Shannon Lee Apr 2006
de Branges, Louis Nov 2005
de Hartog, Jan obit Jan 2003
De Jong, Dola obit Sep 2004
de la Rúa, Fernando Apr 2001
de Meuron, Pierre see Herzog, Jacques, and de Meuron, Pierre
De Sapio, Carmine obit Yrbk 2004
De Valois, Ninette obit Aug 2001
de Varona, Donna Aug 2003
de Waal, Frans Mar 2006
Deakins, Roger May 2001
Dean, Howard Oct 2002
DeBusschere, Dave obit Yrbk 2003
DeCarlo, Dan Aug 2001 obit Mar 2002
Decemberists Aug 2007
Deep Throat see Felt, W. Mark
Def Leppard Jan 2003
Del Toro, Benicio Sep 2001
Delilah Apr 2005
Dellinger, David obit Yrbk 2004
DeLonge, Tom see blink-182
DeLorean, John Z. obit Yrbk 2005
Deloria, Vine Jr. obit Yrbk 2006
Delson, Brad see Linkin Park
DeMarcus, Jay see Rascal Flatts
DeMille, Nelson Oct 2002

Densen-Gerber, Judianne obit Jul 2003

Derrida, Jacques obit Mar 2005

Desai, Kiran Jan 2007

Destiny's Child Aug 2001

Deutsch, Linda Apr 2007

DeWolfe, Christopher see Anderson, Tom and DeWolfe, Christopher

Diamond, David obit Yrbk 2005

Diaz, Cameron Apr 2005

Dickerson, Debra Apr 2004

Dickinson, Amy Apr 2004

Diebold, John obit Yrbk 2006

Dillon, C. Douglas obit May 2003

Dimon, James Jun 2004

Dionne, E. J. Jr. May 2006

Dirnt, Mike see Green Day

Djerassi, Carl Oct 2001

Djukanovic, Milo Aug 2001

DMX Aug 2003

Dobbs, Lou Nov 2006

Dodge, Charles Aug 2007

Domini, Amy Nov 2005

Donald, Arnold W. Nov 2005

Donaldson, William Jun 2003

D'Onofrio, Vincent May 2004

Donovan, Billy Feb 2007

Donovan, Carrie obit Feb 2002

Donovan, Landon Jun 2006

Doubilet, David Mar 2003

Doudna, Jennifer Feb 2005

Douglas, Ashanti see Ashanti

Douglas, Dave Mar 2006

Douglas, Jerry Aug 2004

Douglas, John E. Jul 2001

Douglas, Mike obit Yrbk 2007

Drake, James Jul 2005

Drinan, Robert F. obit Yrbk 2007

Drozd, Steven see Flaming Lips

Drucker, Eugene see Emerson String Quartet

Drucker, Peter F. obit Apr 2006

Duany, Andrés see Duany, Andrés and Plater-Zyberk, Elizabeth

Duany, Andrés and Plater-Zyberk, Elizabeth Jan 2006

Dude Love see Foley, Mick

Duesberg, Peter H. Jun 2004

Duff, Hilary Feb 2006

Dugan, Alan obit Oct 2004

Duke, Annie Aug 2006

Dungy, Tony Aug 2007

Dunham, Katherine obit Yrbk 2006

Dunlop, John T. obit Sep 2004

Dunn, Jennifer obit Nov 2007

Dunn, Ronnie see Brooks & Dunn

Dunne, John Gregory obit Yrbk 2004

Dunst, Kirsten Oct 2001

Durbin, Richard J. Aug 2006

Duritz, Adam see Counting Crows

Dutton, Lawrence see Emerson String Quartet

Dwight, Ed Jul 2007

Dworkin, Andrea obit Yrbk 2005

Eagleton, Thomas F. obit Yrbk 2007

Earnhardt, Dale Jr. Jan 2007

Eban, Abba obit Mar 2003

Eberhart, Richard obit Yrbk 2005

Ebsen, Buddy obit Yrbk 2003

Ecevit, Bülent obit Yrbk 2007

Eckert, Robert A. Mar 2003

Eddins, William Feb 2002

Edwards, Bob Sep 2001

Edwards, John R. Oct 2004

Edwards, Ralph obit Yrbk 2006

Egan, Edward M. Jul 2001

Egan, Jennifer Mar 2002

Eggleston, William Feb 2002

Ehlers, Vernon J. Jan 2005

Eiko see Eiko and Koma

Eiko and Koma May 2003

Eisner, Will obit May 2005

Elfman, Danny Jan 2007

Elgin, Suzette Haden Aug 2006

Elizabeth, Queen Mother of Great Britain obit Jun 2002

Elling, Kurt Jan 2005

Elliott, Joe see Def Leppard

Elliott, Sean Apr 2001

Ellis, Albert obit Yrbk 2007

Ellison, Keith Apr 2007

Emanuel, Kerry A. Jan 2007

Emerson String Quartet Jul 2002

Eminem Jan 2001

Engibous, Thomas J. Oct 2003

Ensler, Eve Aug 2002

Epstein, Samuel S. Aug 2001

Epstein, Theo May 2004

Ericsson-Jackson, Aprille J. Mar 2001

Estenssoro, Victor Paz see Paz Estenssoro, Victor

Etherington, Edwin D. obit Apr 2001

Eugenides, Jeffrey Oct 2003

Eustis, Oskar Oct 2002

Eustis, Paul Jefferson see Eustis, Oskar

Evanovich, Janet Apr 2001

Evans, Dale obit Apr 2001

Evans, Donald L. Nov 2001

Eve Jul 2003

Everett, Percival L. Sep 2004

Everett, Rupert Jan 2005

Exon, J. James obit Yrbk 2005

Eyadéma, Etienne Gnassingbé Apr 2002 obit Yrbk 2005

Eyre, Chris May 2003

Eytan, Walter obit Oct 2001

Faber, Sandra Apr 2002

Fadiman, Anne Aug 2005

Fagles, Robert Apr 2006

Fahd, King of Saudi Arabia obit Yrbk 2005

Fahd, Prince of Saudi Arabia see Fahd, King of Saudi Arabia

Fairclough, Ellen obit Yrbk 2005

Fairport Convention Sep 2005

Falco, Edie Mar 2006

Fallaci, Oriana obit Yrbk 2007

Fallon, Jimmy Jul 2002

Fallon, William J. Jul 2007

Falls, Robert Jan 2004

Falwell, Jerry obit Aug 2007

Fangmeier, Stefen Aug 2004

Farhi, Nicole Nov 2001

Farmer, Paul Feb 2004

Farmer-Paellmann, Deadria Mar 2004

Farrell, Dave see Linkin Park

Farrell, Eileen obit Jun 2002

Farrelly, Bobby see Farrelly, Peter and Bobby

Farrelly, Peter and Bobby Sep 2001

Fast, Howard obit Jul 2003

Fatal1ty see Wendel, Johnathan

Fattah, Chaka Sep 2003

Faulk, Marshall Jan 2003

Faust, Drew Gilpin Jul 2007

Fausto-Sterling, Anne Sep 2005

Fawcett, Joy May 2004

Fay, J. Michael Sep 2001

Fay, Martin see Chieftains

Feifel, Herman obit Yrbk 2005

Felt, W. Mark Sep 2005

Fenty, Adrian M. Mar 2007

Fenty, Robyn Rihanna see Rihanna

Fergie see Black Eyed Peas

Ferguson, Maynard obit Yrbk 2006

Ferguson, Stacy *see* Black Eyed Peas
Ferré, Gianfranco obit Yrbk 2007
Ferré, Luis A. obit Mar 2004
Ferrell, Will Feb 2003
Ferrer, Rafael Jul 2001
Ferrera, America Sep 2007
Ferris, Timothy Jan 2001
Fey, Tina Apr 2002
Fiedler, Leslie A. obit Yrbk 2003
Fields, Mark Apr 2005
Finch, Caleb E. Sep 2004
Finch, Jennie Oct 2004
Finckel, David *see* Emerson String Quartet
Firth, Colin Mar 2004
Fishman, Jon *see* Phish
Fitzgerald, Geraldine obit Yrbk 2005
Fitzgerald, Patrick J. Jan 2006
Flagg, Fannie Nov 2006
Flaming Lips Oct 2002
Flanagan, Tommy obit Mar 2002
Fletcher, Arthur obit Yrbk 2005
Flowers, Vonetta May 2006
Foer, Jonathan Safran Sep 2002
Foley, Mick Sep 2001
Folon, Jean-Michel obit Yrbk 2006
Foner, Eric Aug 2004
Fong, Hiram L. obit Yrbk 2004
Fong-Torres, Ben Aug 2001
Foote, Shelby obit Yrbk 2005
Ford, Gerald R. obit Feb 2007
Ford, Glenn obit Yrbk 2007
Forrest, Vernon Jul 2002
Forsberg, Peter Nov 2005
Forsee, Gary D. Oct 2005
Forsythe, William Feb 2003
Fortey, Richard Sep 2005
Foss, Joseph Jacob obit Yrbk 2003
Fossett, J. Stephen *see* Fossett, Steve
Fossett, Steve Apr 2005
Fountain, Clarence *see* Blind Boys of Alabama
Fowles, John obit Apr 2006
Fox Quesada, Vicente May 2001
Foxx, Jamie May 2005
Fraiture, Nikolai *see* Strokes
Franca, Celia obit Yrbk 2007
Franciosa, Anthony obit Yrbk 2006
Franciosa, Tony *see* Franciosa, Anthony

Francis, Arlene obit Sep 2001
Francisco, Don Feb 2001
Franco, Julio Sep 2006
Frank, Reuven obit Yrbk 2006
Frankenheimer, John obit Oct 2002
Franklin, Shirley C. Aug 2002
Franks, Tommy R. Jan 2002
Franzen, Jonathan Sep 2003
Fraser, Brendan Feb 2001
Fredericks, Henry St. Clair *see* Mahal, Taj
Freed, James Ingo obit Yrbk 2006
Freeman, Lucy obit Yrbk 2005
Freeman, Orville L. obit Yrbk 2003
Freston, Tom Aug 2003
Friedan, Betty obit May 2006
Friedlander, Lee May 2006
Friedman, Jane Mar 2001
Friedman, Milton obit Yrbk 2007
Frist, Bill Nov 2002
Froese, Edgar *see* Tangerine Dream
Froese, Jerome *see* Tangerine Dream
Frum, David Jun 2004
Fry, Christopher obit Yrbk 2005
Fu, Ping Oct 2006
Fugazi Mar 2002
Fukuyama, Francis Jun 2001
Funk, Chris *see* Decemberists

Gades, Antonio obit Yrbk 2004
Gagne, Eric Jun 2004
Gaines, Donna Jun 2006
Galbraith, James K. Feb 2006
Galbraith, John Kenneth obit Yrbk 2007
Galinsky, Ellen Oct 2003
Galloway, Joseph L. Sep 2003
Galtieri, Leopoldo obit Yrbk 2003
Gandy, Kim Oct 2001
Garcia, Sergio Mar 2001
Gardner, John W. obit May 2002
Gardner, Rulon Nov 2004
Garfield, Henry *see* Rollins, Henry
Garofalo, Janeane Mar 2005
Garrels, Anne Mar 2004
Garrison, Deborah Jan 2001
Gary, Willie E. Apr 2001
Garza, Ed Jun 2002
Garzón, Baltasar Mar 2001
Gaskin, Ina May May 2001
Gates, Melinda Feb 2004

Gates, Robert M. May 2007
Gaubatz, Lynn Feb 2001
Gawande, Atul Mar 2005
Gayle, Helene Jan 2002
Gebel-Williams, Gunther obit Oct 2001
Geis, Bernard obit Mar 2001
Gelb, Leslie H. Jan 2003
Gennaro, Peter obit Feb 2001
George, Susan Jul 2007
Gerberding, Julie Louise Sep 2004
Gerbner, George obit Yrbk 2006
Germond, Jack W. Jul 2005
Gerson, Michael Feb 2002
Giamatti, Paul Sep 2005
Giannulli, Mossimo Feb 2003
Gibson, Althea obit Feb 2004
Gibson, Charles Sep 2002
Gibson, Mel Aug 2003
Gierek, Edward obit Oct 2001
Gilbreth, Frank B. Jr. obit Jul 2001
Gillingham, Charles *see* Counting Crows
Gillis, John *see* White Stripes
Gilmore, James S. III Jun 2001
Ginzberg, Eli obit Yrbk 2003
Giroud, Françoise obit Jul 2003
Giulini, Carlo Maria obit Yrbk 2005
Gladwell, Malcolm Jun 2005
Glass, H. Bentley obit Yrbk 2005
Glavine, Tom Oct 2006
Goff, M. Lee Jun 2001
Gold, Thomas obit Yrbk 2004
Goldberg, Bill Apr 2001
Golden, Thelma Sep 2001
Goldman-Rakic, Patricia Feb 2003
Goldovsky, Boris obit Aug 2001
Goldsman, Akiva Sep 2004
Goldsmith, Jerry May 2001 obit Nov 2004
Goldstine, Herman Heine obit Yrbk 2004
Golub, Leon obit Yrbk 2004
Gomes, Marcelo May 2007
Gomez, Jaime *see* Black Eyed Peas
Gondry, Michel May 2007
Gonzales, Alberto R. Apr 2002
Gonzalez, Henry obit Feb 2001
Good, Mary L. Sep 2001
Good, Robert A. obit Yrbk 2003

Goodpaster, Andrew J. obit
Yrbk 2005
Googoosh May 2001
Gopnik, Adam Apr 2005
Gopnik, Alison Jan 2007
Gordon, Bruce S. Oct 2005
Gordon, Cyrus H. obit Aug
2001
Gordon, Ed Jul 2005
Gordon, Edmund W. Jun 2003
Gordon, Mike see Phish
Gorman, R. C. Jan 2001
Gorsuch, Anne obit Yrbk
2004
Gorton, John Grey obit Yrbk
2002
Gottlieb, Melvin B. obit Mar
2001
Gould, Stephen Jay obit Aug
2002
Gourdji, Françoise see
Giroud, Françoise
Gowdy, Curt obit Yrbk 2006
Gowers, Timothy Jan 2001
Gowers, William Timothy see
Gowers, Timothy
Graham, Franklin May 2002
Graham, Katharine obit Oct
2001
Graham, Susan Oct 2005
Graham, Winston obit Yrbk
2003
Granholm, Jennifer M. Oct
2003
Grasso, Richard Oct 2002
Graves, Florence George May
2005
Graves, Morris obit Sep 2001
Gray, L. Patrick obit Yrbk
2005
Gray, Spalding obit Yrbk
2004
Greco, José obit Mar 2001
Green, Adolph obit Mar 2003
Green, Darrell Jan 2001
Green Day Aug 2005
Green, Tom Oct 2003
Greenberg, Jack M. Nov 2001
Greene, Wallace M. obit Aug
2003
Greenstein, Jesse L. obit Yrbk
2003
Greenwood, Colin see
Radiohead
Greenwood, Jonny see
Radiohead
Gregory, Frederick D. Oct
2005
Gregory, Wilton D. Mar 2002
Griffin, Merv obit Yrbk 2007
Griffin, Michael Aug 2005
Griffiths, Martha W. obit Yrbk
2003

Grigg, John obit Apr 2002
Grohl, Dave May 2002
Groopman, Jerome E. Oct
2004
Grossman, Edith Mar 2006
Gruber, Ruth Jun 2001
Gruber, Samuel H. Aug 2004
Grubin, David Aug 2002
Guarente, Leonard P. May
2007
Gudmundsdottir, Björk see
Björk
Guerard, Albert J. obit Mar
2001
Guerrero, Vladimir Jun 2006
Guillen, Ozzie May 2006
Guillermoprieto, Alma Sep
2004
Guinier, Lani Jan 2004
Gunn, Thom obit Yrbk 2004
Gupta, Sanjay Aug 2006
Gursky, Andreas Jul 2001
Gygax, Gary Mar 2007

Haas, Jonathan Jun 2003
Hacker see Hackett, Buddy
Hackett, Buddy obit Oct 2003
Hadley, Jerry obit Yrbk 2007
Hadley, Stephen Nov 2006
Hagel, Chuck Aug 2004
Hagen, Uta obit Yrbk 2004
Haggis, Paul Aug 2006
Hahn, Hilary Sep 2002
Hahn, Joseph see Linkin Park
Hailey, Arthur obit Yrbk 2005
Hailsham of St. Marylebone,
Quintin Hogg obit Feb 2002
Hair, Jay D. obit Jan 2003
Halaby, Najeeb E. obit Yrbk
2003
Halasz, Laszlo obit Feb 2002
Halberstam, David obit Jul
2007
Hall, Conrad L. obit May
2003
Hall, Deidre Nov 2002
Hall, Gus obit Jan 2001
Hall, Richard Melville see
Moby
Hall, Steffie see Evanovich,
Janet
Hall, Tex G. May 2005
Hallaren, Mary A. obit Yrbk
2005
Hallström, Lasse Feb 2005
Hamilton, Laird Aug 2005
Hamilton, Tom see
Aerosmith
Hamm, Morgan see Hamm,
Paul and Morgan
Hamm, Paul see Hamm, Paul
and Morgan

Hamm, Paul and Morgan Nov
2004
Hammer, Bonnie Apr 2006
Hammon, Becky Jan 2003
Hammond, Albert Jr. see
Strokes
Hammond, Caleb D. Jr. obit
Yrbk 2006
Hammons, David May 2006
Hampton, Lionel obit Yrbk
2002
Hancock, Graham Feb 2005
Hancock, Trenton Doyle Apr
2006
Hanna, William obit Sep 2001
Hannity, Sean Apr 2005
Hansen, Liane May 2003
Hanson, Mark see Yusuf,
Hamza
Harcourt, Nic Oct 2005
Harden, Marcia Gay Sep 2001
Hardin, Garrett obit Apr 2004
Hargis, Billy James obit Yrbk
2005
Hargrove, Marion obit Yrbk
2004
Harjo, Joy Aug 2001
Harper, Ben Jan 2004
Harrer, Heinrich obit Yrbk
2006
Harris, Eva Mar 2004
Harris, Mark obit Yrbk 2007
Harris, Richard obit Yrbk
2003
Harrison, George obit Mar
2002
Harrison, Marvin Aug 2001
Harrison, William B. Jr. Mar
2002
Hart, Kitty Carlisle obit Yrbk
2007
Hartke, Vance obit Yrbk 2003
Hartmann, Heidi I. Apr 2003
Hashimoto, Ryutaro obit Yrbk
2006
Haskins, Caryl P. obit Feb
2002
Hass, Robert Feb 2001
Hassenfeld, Alan G. Jul 2003
Hastings, Reed Mar 2006
Hauerwas, Stanley Jun 2003
Haughey, Charles obit Yrbk
2006
Hawkinson, Tim Aug 2005
Hax, Carolyn Nov 2002
Hayden, Melissa obit Yrbk
2006
Hayden, Michael V. Nov 2006
Hayes, Bob obit Jan 2003
Hayes, Edward May 2006
Haynes, Cornell Jr. see Nelly
Haynes, Todd Jul 2003
Haysbert, Dennis Nov 2006

Headley, Elizabeth *see* Cavanna, Betty

Heath, Edward obit Yrbk 2005

Heath, James R. Oct 2003

Hecht, Anthony obit Yrbk 2005

Heckart, Eileen obit Mar 2002

Heilbroner, Robert L. obit Yrbk 2005

Heilbrun, Carolyn G. obit Feb 2004

Heiskell, Andrew obit Yrbk 2003

Held, Al obit Yrbk 2005

Helms, Richard obit Yrbk 2003

Henderson, Donald A. Mar 2002

Henderson, Hazel Nov 2003

Henderson, Joe obit Oct 2001

Henderson, Skitch obit Apr 2006

Hendrickson, Sue Oct 2001

Henriques, Sean Paul *see* Sean Paul

Henry, Brad Jan 2005

Henry, John W. May 2005

Hepburn, Katharine obit Nov 2003

Herbert, Don obit Yrbk 2007

Herblock *see* Block, Herbert L.

Hernandez, Dave *see* Shins

Herndon, J. Marvin Nov 2003

Herring, Pendleton obit Yrbk 2004

Herring Wonder *see* Ames, Jonathan

Hersch, Fred Apr 2006

Hertzberg, Arthur obit Yrbk 2006

Herzog, Jacques *see* Herzog, Jacques, and de Meuron, Pierre

Herzog, Jacques, and de Meuron, Pierre Jun 2002

Hewitt, Angela Apr 2007

Hewitt, Lleyton Oct 2002

Hewlett, Sylvia Ann Sep 2002

Heyerdahl, Thor obit Yrbk 2002

Heym, Stefan obit Mar 2002

Heymann, David L. Jul 2004

Hickey, Dave Sep 2007

Hicks, Louise Day obit Jun 2004

Hidalgo, David *see* Los Lobos

Higgins, Chester Jr. Jun 2002

Higgins, Jack Feb 2007

Hildegarde obit Yrbk 2005

Hill, Andrew Apr 2004 obit Yrbk 2007

Hill, Arthur obit Yrbk 2007

Hill, Dulé Jul 2003

Hill, Faith Mar 2001

Hill, George Roy obit Jun 2003

Hill, Grant Jan 2002

Hill, Herbert obit Yrbk 2004

Hillenburg, Stephen Apr 2003

Hiller, Stanley obit Yrbk 2006

Hiller, Wendy obit Yrbk 2003

Hines, Gregory obit Yrbk 2003

Hines, Jerome obit Jun 2003

Hinojosa, Maria Feb 2001

Hirschfeld, Al obit Jul 2003

Hobson, Mellody Aug 2005

Hobson Pilot, Ann May 2003

Hoffman, Philip Seymour May 2001

Hogg, Quintin *see* Hailsham of St. Marylebone, Quintin Hogg

Holden, Betsy Jul 2003

Holdsclaw, Chamique Feb 2006

Holl, Steven Jul 2004

Holland, Dave Mar 2003

Hollander, Robert B. Sep 2006

Holm, Ian Mar 2002

Hondros, Chris Nov 2004

Hong, Hei-Kyung Nov 2003

Hooker, John Lee obit Sep 2001

Hope, Bob obit Yrbk 2003

Hopkins, Bernard Apr 2002

Hopkins, Nancy May 2002

Hoppus, Mark *see* blink-182

Horwich, Frances obit Oct 2001

Hounsfield, Godfrey obit Yrbk 2004

Hounsou, Djimon Aug 2004

Houston, Allan Nov 2003

Houston, James A. obit Yrbk 2005

Howard, Ryan Jul 2007

Howard, Terrence Jun 2007

Howard, Tim Sep 2005

Howe, Harold II obit Yrbk 2003

Howland, Ben Jun 2007

Hoyer, Steny H. Mar 2004

Hoyle, Fred obit Jan 2002

Hrawi, Elias obit Yrbk 2006

Huckabee, Mike Nov 2005

Hudson, Jennifer May 2007

Hughes, Barnard obit Yrbk 2006

Hughes, Karen Oct 2001

Hugo, Chad *see* Neptunes

Hull, Jane Dee Feb 2002

Hunt Lieberson, Lorraine Jul 2004 obit Yrbk 2006

Hunt, Swanee Mar 2006

Hunter, Charlie Nov 2007

Hunter, Evan obit Yrbk 2005

Hunter, Kermit obit Sep 2001

Hunter, Kim obit Yrbk 2002

Hurley, Chad *see* Chen, Steve; Hurley, Chad; and Karim, Jawed

Hussein, Saddam obit Apr 2007

Hutton, Betty obit Yrbk 2007

Iakovos, Archbishop obit Yrbk 2005

Ifill, Gwen Sep 2005

Ilitch, Michael Feb 2005

Illich, Ivan obit Yrbk 2003

Immelt, Jeffrey R. Feb 2004

India.Arie Feb 2002

Inkster, Juli Sep 2002

Irwin, Steve obit Yrbk 2007

Isbin, Sharon Aug 2003

Istomin, Eugene obit Feb 2004

Ive, Jonathan Oct 2006

Ivins, Michael *see* Flaming Lips

Ivins, Molly obit Yrbk 2007

Iyengar, B. K. S. Jun 2007

Izetbegovic, Alija obit Jun 2004

Ja Rule Jul 2002

Jackman, Hugh Oct 2003

Jackson, Alan Apr 2004

Jackson, Hal Oct 2002

Jackson, Lauren Jun 2003

Jackson, Maynard H. Jr. obit Yrbk 2003

Jackson, Michael Aug 2005 obit Yrbk 2007

Jackson, Peter Jan 2002

Jackson, Thomas Penfield Jun 2001

Jacobs, Jane obit Yrbk 2006

Jacobs, Paul E. Feb 2007

Jagger, Janine Apr 2004

Jakes, T.D. Jun 2001

James, Alex *see* Blur

James, Bill Jun 2004

James, Edgerrin Jan 2002

James, LeBron Nov 2005

Janeway, Elizabeth obit Yrbk 2005

Jarecki, Eugene May 2006

Jarring, Gunnar obit Yrbk 2002

Jarvis, Erich D. May 2003

Jay-Z Aug 2002

Jeffers, Eve Jihan *see* Eve

Jefferts Schori, Katharine Sep 2006
Jeffery, Vonetta *see* Flowers, Vonetta
Jeffords, James Sep 2001
Jenkins, Jerry B. *see* LaHaye, Tim and Jenkins, Jerry B.
Jenkins, Roy obit Yrbk 2003
Jennings, Peter obit Sep 2005
Jennings, Waylon obit Apr 2002
Jensen, Oliver O obit Yrbk 2005
Jet *see* Urquidez, Benny
Jimenez, Marcos Perez *see* Pérez Jiménez, Marcos
Jin, Deborah Apr 2004
Jobert, Michel obit Yrbk 2002
Johannesen, Grant obit Yrbk 2005
Johansson, Scarlett Mar 2005
John, Daymond Aug 2007
John Paul II obit Jun 2005
Johnson, Avery Jan 2007
Johnson, Brian *see* AC/DC
Johnson, Claudia Alta obit Oct 2007
Johnson, Eddie Bernice Jul 2001
Johnson, Elizabeth A. Nov 2002
Johnson, Eric *see* Shins
Johnson, John H. obit Yrbk 2005
Johnson, Lady Bird *see* Johnson, Claudia Alta
Johnson, Philip obit Sep 2005
Johnson, Sheila Crump Jun 2007
Jones, Bobby Jun 2002
Jones, Chipper May 2001
Jones, Chuck obit May 2002
Jones, Edward P. Mar 2004
Jones, Elaine Jun 2004
Jones, George L. Apr 2007
Jones, Larry Wayne Jr. *see* Jones, Chipper
Jones, Norah May 2003
Jones, Sarah Jul 2005
Jones, Scott Jan 2006
Jonze, Spike Apr 2003
Josefowicz, Leila May 2007
Joyner, Tom Sep 2002
Judd, Jackie Sep 2002
Judd, Jacqueline Dee *see* Judd, Jackie
Judson, Olivia Jan 2004
Juliana Queen of the Netherlands obit Yrbk 2004
July, Miranda Nov 2007

Kabila, Joseph Sep 2001
Kael, Pauline obit Nov 2001

Kagan, Elena Jun 2007
Kagan, Frederick W. Jul 2007
Kainen, Jacob obit Aug 2001
Kaiser, Philip M. obit Yrbk 2007
Kamen, Dean Nov 2002
Kane, Joseph Nathan obit Nov 2002
Kani, John Jun 2001
Kann, Peter R. Mar 2003
Kaptur, Marcy Jan 2003
Kapuściński, Ryszard obit Yrbk 2007
Karbo, Karen May 2001
Karim, Jawed *see* Chen, Steve; Hurley, Chad; and Karim, Jawed
Karle, Isabella Jan 2003
Karon, Jan Mar 2003
Karpinski, Janis Apr 2006
Karsh, Yousuf obit Nov 2002
Karzai, Hamid May 2002
Kase, Toshikazu obit Yrbk 2004
Kass, Leon R. Aug 2002
Katsav, Moshe Feb 2001
Katz, Jackson Jul 2004
Kaufman, Charlie Jul 2005
Kavafian, Ani Oct 2006
Kazan, Elia obit Yrbk 2004
Kcho Aug 2001
Keane, Sean *see* Chieftains
Keegan, Robert Jan 2004
Keener, Catherine Oct 2002
Keeshan, Bob obit Yrbk 2004
Keith, Toby Oct 2004
Kelleher, Herb Jan 2001
Keller, Bill Oct 2003
Keller, Marthe Jul 2004
Keller, Thomas Jun 2004
Kelman, Charles obit Yrbk 2004
Kempthorne, Dirk Jun 2007
Kennan, George F. obit Yrbk 2005
Kennedy, Randall Aug 2002
Kennedy, Robert F. Jr. May 2004
Kent, Jeff May 2003
Kentridge, William Oct 2001
Kenyon, Cynthia Jan 2005
Kepes, György obit Mar 2002
Kerr, Clark obit May 2004
Kerr, Jean obit May 2003
Kerr, Mrs. Walter F *see* Kerr, Jean
Kerry, John Sep 2004
Kesey, Ken obit Feb 2002
Ketcham, Hank obit Sep 2001
Keys, Ancel obit Yrbk 2005
Keys, Charlene *see* Tweet
Khalilzad, Zalmay Aug 2006
Kid Rock Oct 2001

Kidd, Chip Jul 2005
Kidd, Jason May 2002
Kiessling, Laura Aug 2003
Kilbourne, Jean May 2004
Kilpatrick, Kwame M. Apr 2004
Kim, Jim Yong Nov 2006
King, Alan obit Yrbk 2004
King, Coretta Scott obit Apr 2006
King, Florence Apr 2006
Kirkpatrick, Jeane obit Yrbk 2007
Kittikachorn, Thanom obit Yrbk 2004
Klaus, Josef obit Oct 2001
Kleiber, Carlos obit Yrbk 2004
Klein, Naomi Aug 2003
Klein, William Mar 2004
Kleppe, Thomas S. obit Yrbk 2007
Klinkenborg, Verlyn Jul 2006
Knievel, Robbie Mar 2005
Knipfel, Jim Mar 2005
Knoll, Andrew H. Apr 2006
Knowles, Beyoncé *see* Destiny's Child
Koch, Kenneth obit Yrbk 2002
Koff, Clea Nov 2004
Koh, Jennifer Sep 2006
Koizumi, Junichiro Jan 2002
Kolar, Jiri obit Yrbk 2002
Kollek, Teddy obit Yrbk 2007
Koma *see* Eiko and Koma
Konaré, Alpha Oumar Oct 2001
Koner, Pauline obit Apr 2001
Kopp, Wendy Mar 2003
Kos *see* Moulitsas Zúniga, Markos ("Kos")
Kostunica, Vojislav Jan 2001
Kott, Jan obit Mar 2002
Kournikova, Anna Jan 2002
Kovalchuk, Ilya Mar 2007
Kramer, Joey *see* Aerosmith
Kramer, Stanley obit May 2001
Krause, David W. Feb 2002
Krawcheck, Sallie Mar 2006
Kreutzberger, Mario *see* Francisco, Don
Kripke, Saul Oct 2004
Kristof, Nicholas D. Feb 2006
Krugman, Paul Aug 2001
Krupp, Fred Sep 2007
Kübler-Ross, Elisabeth obit Yrbk 2004
Kuhn, Bowie obit Yrbk 2007
Kummant, Alexander Jan 2007
Kunitz, Stanley obit Aug 2006
Kushner, Jared Jun 2007

Kushner, Tony Jul 2002
Kusturica, Emir Nov 2005
Kyprianou, Spyros obit May 2002

La India May 2002
La Montagne, Margaret see Spellings, Margaret
La Russa, Tony Jul 2003
Labov, William Mar 2006
Lacy, Dan obit Nov 2001
LaDuke, Winona Jan 2003
LaFontaine, Don Sep 2004
Lagardère, Jean-Luc obit Aug 2003
LaHaye, Tim see LaHaye, Tim and Jenkins, Jerry B.
LaHaye, Tim and Jenkins, Jerry B. Jun 2003
Laimbeer, Bill Jan 2006
Laine, Frankie obit Yrbk 2007
Laker, Freddie obit Yrbk 2006
Lally, Joe see Fugazi
Lamont, Ann Huntress Feb 2007
Lampert, Edward S. Sep 2005
Landers, Ann obit Nov 2002
Lang, Robert J. Jul 2007
Lange, David obit Yrbk 2005
Langevin, Jim Aug 2005
Lanier, Cathy L. Mar 2007
Lantos, Tom Jul 2007
Lanzone, Jim May 2007
Lapidus, Morris obit Apr 2001
Lapp, Ralph E. obit Feb 2005
Lara, Brian Feb 2001
Lardner, Ring Jr. obit Feb 2001
Laredo, Ruth obit Yrbk 2005
Lassaw, Ibram obit Yrbk 2004
Lauder, Estée obit Yrbk 2004
Lavigne, Avril Apr 2003
Law, Ty Oct 2002
Lawal, Kase L. Nov 2006
Laws, Hubert Jr. Jul 2007
Lax, Peter D. Oct 2005
Le Clercq, Tanaquil obit Mar 2001
Leakey, Meave Jun 2002
Lederer, Esther Pauline see Landers, Ann
Lederle, John obit Yrbk 2007
Ledger, Heath Jun 2006
Lee, Andrea Sep 2003
Lee, Barbara Jun 2004
Lee, Debra L. Jun 2006
Lee, Geddy see Rush
Lee, Jeanette Oct 2002
Lee, Mrs. John G. see Lee, Percy Maxim
Lee, Peggy obit May 2002

Lee, Percy Maxim obit Jan 2003
Lee, Richard C. obit Jun 2003
LeFrak, Samuel J. obit Yrbk 2003
Legend, John Feb 2007
Lehane, Dennis Oct 2005
Leiter, Al Aug 2002
Lelyveld, Joseph Nov 2005
Lem, Stanislaw obit Yrbk 2006
Lemmon, Jack obit Oct 2001
L'Engle, Madeleine obit Yrbk 2007
Leo, John Sep 2006
Leon, Kenny Nov 2005
Leonard see Hackett, Buddy
Leone, Giovanni obit Feb 2002
Leslie, Chris see Fairport Convention
LeSueur, Larry obit Jun 2003
Lethem, Jonathan Mar 2006
Letterman, David Oct 2002
Levert, Gerald Oct 2003 obit Yrbk 2007
Levin, Carl May 2004
Levine, Mel Nov 2005
LeVox, Gary see Rascal Flatts
Levy, Eugene Jan 2002
Lewis, Ananda Jun 2005
Lewis, David Levering May 2001
Lewis, David S. Jr. obit Yrbk 2004
Lewis, Dorothy Otnow May 2006
Lewis, Flora obit Yrbk 2002
Lewis, John obit Jun 2001
Lewis, Kenneth Apr 2004
Lewis, Marvin Nov 2004
Lewis, Ray Jan 2007
Lewitt, Sol obit Yrbk 2007
Li, Jet Jun 2001
Li Lian Jie see Li, Jet
Libeskind, Daniel Jun 2003
Lifeson, Alex see Rush
Lilly, John C. obit Feb 2002
Lilly, Kristine Apr 2004
Lima do Amor, Sisleide see Sissi
Lincoln, Abbey Sep 2002
Lincoln, Blanche Lambert Mar 2002
Lindbergh, Anne Morrow obit Apr 2001
Lindgren, Astrid obit Apr 2002
Lindo, Delroy Mar 2001
Lindsay, John V. obit Mar 2001
Ling, James J. obit Yrbk 2005
Lingle, Linda Jun 2003

Link, O. Winston obit Apr 2001
Linkin Park Mar 2002
Linowitz, Sol M. obit Yrbk 2005
Lipinski, Anne Marie Jul 2004
Lippold, Richard obit Yrbk 2002
Little Steven see Van Zandt, Steven
Liu, Lucy Oct 2003
Lloyd, Charles Apr 2002
Locke, Gary Apr 2003
Logan, Lara Jul 2006
Lohan, Lindsay Nov 2005
Lomax, Alan obit Oct 2002
London, Julie obit Feb 2001
Long, Russell B. obit Yrbk 2003
Long, William Ivey Mar 2004
Lopez, Al obit Yrbk 2006
López Portillo, José obit Yrbk 2004
Lord, Walter obit Yrbk 2002
Los Lobos Oct 2005
Loudon, Dorothy obit Yrbk 2004
Love, John A. obit Apr 2002
Lowell, Mike Sep 2003
Lozano, Conrad see Los Lobos
Lucas, George May 2002
Luckovich, Mike Jan 2005
Ludacris Jun 2004
Ludlum, Robert obit Jul 2001
Ludwig, Ken May 2004
Luke, Delilah Rene see Delilah
Lumet, Sidney Jun 2005
Luns, Joseph M. A. H. obit Yrbk 2002
Lupica, Mike Mar 2001
Lustiger, Jean-Marie obit Yrbk 2007
Lyng, Richard E. obit Jun 2003
Lynne, Shelby Jul 2001

Mac, Bernie Jun 2002
Machado, Alexis Leyva see Kcho
MacKaye, Ian see Fugazi
MacKenzie, Gisele obit Jul 2004
MacMitchell, Leslie obit Yrbk 2006
Maddox, Lester obit Yrbk 2003
Madsen, Michael Apr 2004
Magliozzi, Ray see Magliozzi, Tom and Ray
Magliozzi, Tom see Magliozzi, Tom and Ray

Magliozzi, Tom and Ray Jun 2006
Magloire, Paul E. obit Nov 2001
Maguire, Tobey Sep 2002
Mahal, Taj Nov 2001
Mahfouz, Naguib obit Yrbk 2007
Maki, Fumihiko Jul 2001
Malina, Joshua Apr 2004
Malley, Matt see Counting Crows
Maloney, Carolyn B. Apr 2001
Maloney, Walter E. obit Yrbk 2007
Manchester, William obit Yrbk 2004
Mankind see Foley, Mick
Mankoff, Robert May 2005
Mann, Emily Jun 2002
Mansfield, Michael J. see Mansfield, Mike
Mansfield, Mike obit Jan 2002
Marceau, Marcel obit Yrbk 2007
Marcinko, Richard Mar 2001
Marcus, Bernie Aug 2007
Marcus, George E. Mar 2006
Marcus, Stanley obit Apr 2002
Marcy, Geoffrey W. see Marcy, Geoffrey W., and Butler, R. Paul
Marcy, Geoffrey W., and Butler, R. Paul Nov 2002
Margaret, Princess of Great Britain obit May 2002
Markova, Alicia obit Yrbk 2005
Marks, Leonard H. obit Yrbk 2006
Marlette, Doug Jul 2002 obit Yrbk 2007
Marshall, Burke obit Yrbk 2003
Marshall, Chan see Cat Power
Marshall, Charlyn see Cat Power
Marshall, Rob Jun 2003
Martin, A. J. P. see Martin, Archer
Martin, Agnes obit Apr 2005
Martin, Archer obit Yrbk 2002
Martin, Chris see Coldplay
Martin, George R. R. Jan 2004
Martin, James S. Jr. obit Yrbk 2002
Martin, Jesse L. Jul 2006
Martin, Kenyon Jan 2005
Martin, Kevin J. Aug 2005

Martin, Mark Mar 2001
Martinez, Pedro Jun 2001
Martinez, Rueben Jun 2005
Martinez, Vilma Jul 2004
Martz, Judy Mar 2005
Mary Kay see Ash, Mary Kay
Massive Attack Jun 2004
Masters, William H. obit May 2001
Mathers, Marshall see Eminem
Mathias, Bob see Mathias, Robert Bruce
Mathias, Robert Bruce obit Yrbk 2007
Matisyahu Mar 2007
Matsui, Connie L. Aug 2002
Matsui, Robert T. obit Apr 2005
Matsuzaka, Daisuke Apr 2007
Matta obit Yrbk 2003
Mauch, Gene obit Yrbk 2005
Mauer, Joe Aug 2007
Mauldin, Bill obit Jul 2003
Mauldin, William Henry see Mauldin, Bill
Mayne, Thom Oct 2005
Mayr, Ernst obit May 2005
Mays, L. Lowry Aug 2003
Mayweather, Floyd Oct 2004
McBride, Martina Mar 2004
McCain, John S. Mar 2006
McCambridge, Mercedes obit Yrbk 2004
McCann, Renetta May 2005
McCarthy, Eugene J. obit Mar 2006
McCaw, Craig Sep 2001
McCloskey, Robert obit Yrbk 2003
McClurkin, Donnie Apr 2007
McColough, C. Peter obit Yrbk 2007
McConnell, John M. see McConnell, Mike
McConnell, Mike Apr 2007
McConnell, Page see Phish
McCracken, Craig Feb 2004
McCrary, Tex obit Yrbk 2003
McCurry, Steve Nov 2005
McDonald, Gabrielle Kirk Oct 2001
McDonough, William Jul 2006
McGhee, George Crews obit Yrbk 2005
McGrady, Tracy Feb 2003
McGrath, Judy Feb 2005
McGraw, Eloise Jarvis obit Mar 2001
McGraw, Phillip Jun 2002
McGraw, Tim Sep 2002

McGreal, Elizabeth see Yates, Elizabeth
McGruder, Aaron Sep 2001
McGuire, Dorothy obit Nov 2001
McIntire, Carl obit Jun 2002
McIntosh, Millicent Carey obit Mar 2001
McKeon, Jack Apr 2004
McKinney, Robert obit Yrbk 2001
McLaughlin, John Feb 2004
McLean, Jackie Mar 2001 obit Nov 2006
McLean, John Lenwood see McLean, Jackie
McLurkin, James Sep 2005
McMath, Sid obit Jan 2004
McNabb, Donovan Jan 2004
McNair, Barbara obit Yrbk 2007
McNair, Steve Jan 2005
McNally, Andrew 3d obit Feb 2002
McNeil, John Jun 2007
McQueen, Alexander Feb 2002
McWhirter, Norris D. obit Yrbk 2004
McWhorter, John H. Feb 2003
Meat Loaf Nov 2006
Mechem, Edwin L. obit Yrbk 2003
Meier, Deborah May 2006
Meiselas, Susan Feb 2005
Meloy, Colin see Decemberists
Mendes, Sam Oct 2002
Menken, Alan Jan 2001
Menotti, Gian Carlo obit Yrbk 2007
Mercer, James see Shins
Merchant, Ismail obit Yrbk 2005
Merchant, Natalie Jan 2003
Meron, Theodor Mar 2005
Merrifield, R. Bruce obit Yrbk 2006
Merrill, Robert obit Feb 2005
Merton, Robert K. obit Yrbk 2003
Messick, Dale obit Yrbk 2005
Messier, Jean-Marie May 2002
Messing, Debra Aug 2002
Messmer, Pierre obit Yrbk 2007
Meta, Ilir Feb 2002
Meyer, Cord Jr. obit Aug 2001
Meyer, Danny Jul 2007
Meyer, Edgar Jun 2002
Meyers, Nancy Feb 2002
Michel, Sia Sep 2003
Mickelson, Phil Mar 2002

Middelhoff, Thomas Feb 2001
Miller, Ann obit Yrbk 2004
Miller, Arthur obit Jul 2005
Miller, G. William obit Yrbk 2007
Miller, J. Irwin obit Yrbk 2004
Miller, Jason obit Yrbk 2001
Miller, John Aug 2003
Miller, Judith Jan 2006
Miller, Marcus Feb 2006
Miller, Matthew *see* Matisyahu
Miller, Neal obit Jun 2002
Millionaire, Tony Jul 2005
Millman, Dan Aug 2002
Mills, John obit Yrbk 2005
Milosevic, Slobodan obit Yrbk 2006
Milosz, Czeslaw obit Yrbk 2004
Mink, Patsy T. obit Jan 2003
Minner, Ruth Ann Aug 2001
Mirabal, Robert Aug 2002
Mirvish, Edwin obit Yrbk 2007
Mitchell, Dean Aug 2002
Mitchell, Jerry Oct 2007
Mitchell, Pat Aug 2005
Mitha, Tehreema May 2004
Miyazaki, Hayao Apr 2001
Miyazawa, Kiichi obit Yrbk 2007
Moby Apr 2001
Moen, John *see* Decemberists
Moffo, Anna obit Yrbk 2007
Mohammed, W. Deen Jan 2004
Mohammed Zahir Shah *see* Zahir Shah, Mohammed
Moiseiwitsch, Tanya obit Jul 2003
Molina, Alfred Feb 2004
Molloy, Matt *see* Chieftains
Moloney, Paddy *see* Chieftains
Monk, T. S. Feb 2002
Monseu, Stephanie *see* Nelson, Keith and Monseu, Stephanie
Monte, Elisa Jun 2007
Montero, Gabriela Jul 2007
Montresor, Beni obit Feb 2002
Moore, Ann Aug 2003
Moore, Dudley obit Yrbk 2002
Moore, Elisabeth Luce obit Yrbk 2002
Moore, Gordon E. Apr 2002
Moore, Paul Jr. obit Yrbk 2003

Moore, Thomas W. obit Yrbk 2007
Moorer, Thomas H. obit Yrbk 2004
Morella, Constance A. Feb 2001
Moretti, Fabrizio *see* Strokes
Morgan, Tracy Mar 2007
Morial, Marc Jan 2002
Morris, Butch Jul 2005
Morris, Errol Feb 2001
Morris, James T. Mar 2005
Morris, Lawrence *see* Morris, Butch
Morrison, Philip obit Aug 2005
Mortensen, Viggo Jun 2004
Mos Def Apr 2005
Moseka, Aminata *see* Lincoln, Abbey
Moses, Bob *see* Moses, Robert P.
Moses, Robert P. Apr 2002
Mosley, Sugar Shane Jan 2001
Mosley, Timothy *see* Timbaland
Moss, Adam Mar 2004
Moss, Frank E. obit Jun 2003
Moss, Randy Jan 2006
Moten, Etta *see* Barnett, Etta Moten
Motley, Constance Baker obit Feb 2006
Moulitsas Zúniga, Markos ("Kos") Mar 2007
Moynihan, Daniel Patrick obit Yrbk 2003
Muhammad, Warith Deen *see* Mohammed, W. Deen
Mulcahy, Anne M. Nov 2002
Murkowski, Frank H. Jul 2003
Murphy, Mark Sep 2004
Murphy, Thomas obit Yrbk 2006
Murray, Bill Sep 2004
Murray, Donald M. Jul 2006
Murray, Elizabeth obit Yrbk 2007
Murray, Jonathan *see* Bunim, Mary-Ellis, and Murray, Jonathan
Murray, Ty May 2002
Musharraf, Pervaiz *see* Musharraf, Pervez
Musharraf, Pervez Mar 2001
Musk, Elon Oct 2006
Mydans, Carl M. obit Yrbk 2004
Mydans, Shelley Smith obit Aug 2002
Myers, Joel N. Apr 2005
Myers, Richard B. Apr 2002

Nabrit, Samuel M. obit Yrbk 2004
Nachtigall, Paul E. Jan 2006
Nagin, C. Ray Jan 2006
Najimy, Kathy Oct 2002
Nakamura, Dan May 2007
Napolitano, Janet Oct 2004
Narayan, R. K. obit Jul 2001
Nash, Steve Mar 2003
Nason, John W. obit Feb 2002
Nasser, Jacques Apr 2001
Nathan, Robert R. obit Nov 2001
Navratilova, Martina Feb 2004
Ne Win obit Yrbk 2003
Neals, Otto Feb 2003
Neeleman, David Sep 2003
Negroponte, John Apr 2003
Nehru, B. K. obit Feb 2002
Nelly Oct 2002
Nelson, Byron obit Yrbk 2007
Nelson, Don May 2007
Nelson, Gaylord obit Yrbk 2005
Nelson, Keith *see* Nelson, Keith and Monseu, Stephanie
Nelson, Keith and Monseu, Stephanie Jun 2005
Nelson, Marilyn Carlson Oct 2004
Nelson, Stanley May 2005
Neptunes May 2004
Neustadt, Richard E. obit Yrbk 2004
Newman, Arnold obit Yrbk 2006
Newman, J. Wilson obit Yrbk 2003
Newmark, Craig Jun 2005
Newsom, Lee Ann Oct 2004
Newton, Helmut obit Yrbk 2004
Nguyen Van Thieu *see* Thieu, Nguyen Van
Nicol, Simon *see* Fairport Convention
Nikolayev, Andrian obit Yrbk 2004
Nilsson, Birgit obit Sep 2006
Nitze, Paul H. obit Mar 2005
Nixon, Agnes Apr 2001
Nofziger, Lyn obit Yrbk 2006
Nooyi, Indra K. Nov 2006
Norman, Christina Nov 2007
Norquist, Grover Oct 2007
Norton, Andre obit Yrbk 2005
Norton, Gale A. Jun 2001
Nottage, Lynn Nov 2004
Novacek, Michael J. Sep 2002
Nowitzki, Dirk Jun 2002
Nozick, Robert obit Apr 2002

Nugent, Ted Apr 2005
Nykvist, Sven obit Yrbk 2007

Obama, Barack Jul 2005
Obote, Milton obit Yrbk 2006
O'Brien, Ed see Radiohead
O'Connor, Carroll obit Sep 2001
O'Connor, Donald obit Apr 2004
O'Day, Anita obit Jan 2007
Ogilvie, Elisabeth obit Yrbk 2007
O'Hair, Madalyn Murray obit Jun 2001
Ohno, Apolo Anton Feb 2006
O'Keefe, Sean Jan 2003
Okrent, Daniel Nov 2004
Olin, Lena Jun 2003
Olitski, Jules obit Yrbk 2007
Ollila, Jorma Aug 2002
Olopade, Olufunmilayo Sep 2006
O'Malley, Sean Patrick Jan 2004
O'Neal, Jermaine Jun 2004
O'Neal, Stanley May 2003
O'Neill, Paul H. Jul 2001
Oppenheim, Chad Sep 2006
Orbach, Jerry obit Apr 2005
O'Reilly, Bill Oct 2003
Orlean, Susan Jun 2003
Orman, Suze May 2003
Ortiz, David Aug 2005
Ortner, Sherry B. Nov 2002
Osawa, Sandra Sunrising Jan 2001
Osborne, Barrie M. Feb 2005
Osbourne, Sharon Jan 2001
Osteen, Joel Jan 2006
Oudolf, Piet Apr 2003
Ouma, Kassim Jun 2007
OutKast Apr 2004
Oz, Mehmet C. Apr 2003

Pääbo, Svante Feb 2007
Paar, Jack obit Yrbk 2004
Pace, Peter Jun 2006
Page, Clarence Jan 2003
Page, Larry see Brin, Sergey, and Page, Larry
Paige, Roderick R. Jul 2001
Paik, Nam June obit Yrbk 2006
Palance, Jack obit Feb 2007
Paley, Grace obit Yrbk 2007
Palmeiro, Rafael Aug 2001
Palmer, Violet Nov 2006
Paltrow, Gwyneth Jan 2005
Panofsky, Wolfgang K. H. obit Yrbk 2007
Park, Linda Sue Jun 2002

Park, Rosemary obit Yrbk 2004
Parker, Mary-Louise Apr 2006
Parker, Robert M. May 2005
Parks, Gordon obit Jun 2006
Parks, Rosa obit Jan 2006
Parsons, Richard D. Apr 2003
Pascal, Amy Mar 2002
Patchett, Ann Apr 2003
Patrick, Danica Oct 2005
Patrick, Deval May 2007
Patterson, Floyd obit Yrbk 2007
Patty, Sandi Feb 2004
Pau, Peter Feb 2002
Paulson, Henry M. Jr. Sep 2002
Pavarotti, Luciano obit Nov 2007
Payne, Alexander Feb 2003
Paz Estenssoro, Victor obit Sep 2001
Peart, Neil see Rush
Peck, Gregory obit Sep 2003
Peck, M. Scott obit Yrbk 2005
Pegg, Dave see Fairport Convention
Pekar, Harvey Jan 2004
Pelikan, Jaroslav obit Yrbk 2006
Pelosi, Nancy Feb 2003
Pelzer, Dave Mar 2002
Pennington, Ty Feb 2006
Perdue, Frank obit Oct 2005
Pérez Jiménez, Marcos obit Feb 2002
Pérez, Louie see Los Lobos
Perkins, Charles obit Feb 2001
Perkins, Elizabeth Jan 2007
Perle, Richard Jul 2003
Perry, Joe see Aerosmith
Perry, Tyler Jun 2005
Person, Houston Jun 2003
Perutz, Max obit Apr 2002
Petersen, Wolfgang Jul 2001
Peterson, Martha obit Yrbk 2006
Petraeus, David H. Apr 2007
Pettibon, Raymond Apr 2005
Pevear, Richard see Pevear, Richard and Volokhonsky, Larissa
Pevear, Richard and Volokhonsky, Larissa Jun 2006
Peyroux, Madeleine Nov 2005
Phelps, Michael Aug 2004
Phillips, Sam Apr 2001
Phillips, Scott see Creed
Phillips, William obit Yrbk 2002
Phish Jul 2003

Phoenix see Linkin Park
Piano, Renzo Apr 2001
Picciotto, Guy see Fugazi
Pickering, William H. obit Yrbk 2004
Piel, Gerard obit Feb 2005
Pierce, David Hyde Apr 2001
Pierce, John Robinson obit Jun 2002
Pierce, Paul Nov 2002
Pierce, Samuel R. Jr. obit Feb 2001
Pifer, Alan J. obit Yrbk 2006
Pincay, Laffit Sep 2001
Pineda Lindo, Allan see Black Eyed Peas
Pingree, Chellie Jan 2005
Pinochet, Augusto obit Yrbk 2007
Pitt, Harvey Nov 2002
Pitts, Leonard J. Oct 2004
Plater-Zyberk, Elizabeth see Duany, Andrés and Plater-Zyberk, Elizabeth
Plimpton, George obit Jan 2004
Plimpton, Martha Apr 2002
Poletti, Charles obit Yrbk 2002
Pollan, Michael Oct 2007
Pollitt, Katha Oct 2002
Pomeroy, Wardell B. obit Yrbk 2001
Popeil, Ron Mar 2001
Posen, Zac Jul 2006
Posey, Parker Mar 2003
Poston, Tom obit Yrbk 2007
Potok, Chaim obit Yrbk 2002
Potter, Myrtle S. Aug 2004
Poujade, Pierre obit Yrbk 2004
Powell, Colin L. Nov 2001
Powell, Kevin Jan 2004
Powell, Michael K. May 2003
Prada, Miuccia Feb 2006
Prado, Edgar Sep 2007
Pressel, Morgan Nov 2007
Prigogine, Ilya obit Yrbk 2003
Prince, Charles O. III Jan 2007
Prince-Hughes, Dawn Apr 2005
Prinze, Freddie Jr. Jan 2003
Profumo, John obit Jun 2006
Prosper, Pierre-Richard Aug 2005
Proxmire, William obit Mar 2006
Pryor, Richard obit Apr 2006
Pujols, Albert Sep 2004
Pusey, Nathan M. obit Feb 2002

Queloz, Didier Feb 2002

Query, Nate *see* Decemberists
Quine, W. V. obit Mar 2001
Quine, Willard Van Orman
  see Quine, W. V.
Quinn, Aidan Apr 2005
Quinn, Anthony obit Sep
  2001
Quinn, William F. obit Yrbk
  2006

Rabassa, Gregory Jan 2005
Racette, Patricia Feb 2003
Radiohead Jun 2001
Raimi, Sam Jul 2002
Rainier III, Prince of Monaco
  obit Yrbk 2005
Rakic, Patricia Goldman *see*
  Goldman-Rakic, Patricia
Rakoff, David Nov 2007
Rall, Ted May 2002
Ralston, Joseph W. Jan 2001
Ramirez, Manny Jun 2002
Ramirez, Tina Nov 2004
Ramos, Jorge Mar 2004
Rampling, Charlotte Jun 2002
Rampone, Christie Oct 2004
Randall, Lisa May 2006
Randall, Tony obit Yrbk 2004
Randolph, Willie Sep 2005
Rania Feb 2001
Rao, P. V. Narasimha obit
  Yrbk 2005
Rascal Flatts Aug 2003
Ratzinger, Joseph *see*
  Benedict XVI
Rau, Johannes obit Yrbk 2006
Rawl, Lawrence obit Yrbk
  2005
Rawls, Lou obit Oct 2006
Ray, Rachael Aug 2005
Reagan, Ronald obit Sep 2004
Redd, Michael Mar 2005
Redgrave, Vanessa Sep 2003
Redlener, Irwin Nov 2007
Reeve, Christopher obit Jan
  2005
Reeves, Dan Oct 2001
Reeves, Dianne Jul 2006
Regan, Donald T. obit Yrbk
  2003
Rehnquist, William H. Nov
  2003 obit Yrbk 2005
Reich, Walter Aug 2005
Reichs, Kathy Oct 2006
Reid, Antonio *see* Reid, L. A.
Reid, Harry Mar 2003
Reid, L. A. Aug 2001
Reilly, John C. Oct 2004
Reilly, Rick Feb 2005
Reinhardt, Uwe E. Mar 2004
Reinking, Ann Jun 2004
Reitman, Ivan Mar 2001
Rell, M. Jodi Sep 2005

Ressler, Robert K. Feb 2002
Reuss, Henry S. obit Mar
  2002
Reuther, Victor obit Yrbk
  2004
Revel, Jean Francois obit Yrbk
  2006
Reyes, Silvestre Sep 2007
Reynolds, Glenn Harlan Oct
  2007
Reynolds, John W. Jr. obit
  Mar 2002
Reynoso, Cruz Mar 2002
Rhodes, James A. obit Jul
  2001
Rhodes, John J. obit Yrbk
  2004
Rhodes, Randi Feb 2005
Rhyne, Charles S. obit Yrbk
  2003
Rice, Condoleezza Apr 2001
Richards, Ann obit Yrbk 2007
Richards, Cecile May 2007
Richards, Lloyd obit Yrbk
  2007
Richler, Mordecai obit Oct
  2001
Richter, Gerhard Jun 2002
Rickey, George W. obit Yrbk
  2002
Ricks, Thomas E. Nov 2007
Ridge, Tom Feb 2001
Riefenstahl, Leni obit Yrbk
  2004
Riesman, David obit Yrbk
  2002
Rihanna Nov 2007
Riley, Terry Apr 2002
Rimm, Sylvia B. Feb 2002
Rimsza, Skip Jul 2002
Rines, Robert H. Jan 2003
Rinfret, Pierre A. obit Yrbk
  2006
Riopelle, Jean-Paul obit Yrbk
  2002
Ripley, Alexandra obit Yrbk
  2004
Ripley, S. Dillon obit Aug
  2001
Risen, James Aug 2007
Ritchie, Robert James *see* Kid
  Rock
Ritter, John obit Yrbk 2004
Rivers, Larry obit Nov 2002
Rizzuto, Phil obit Yrbk 2007
Roach, Max obit Nov 2007
Robards, Jason Jr. obit Mar
  2001
Robb, J. D. *see* Roberts, Nora
Robbins, Anthony *see*
  Robbins, Tony
Robbins, Frederick C. obit
  Yrbk 2003

Robbins, Tony Jul 2001
Roberts, John G. Feb 2006
Roberts, John G. Jr. *see*
  Roberts, John G.
Roberts, Nora Sep 2001
Roberts, Tony Oct 2006
Robinson, Arthur H. obit
  Yrbk 2005
Robinson, Eddie obit Yrbk
  2007
Robinson, Janet L. Mar 2003
Robinson, Marilynne Oct
  2005
Robinson, Peter Sep 2007
Rochberg, George obit Yrbk
  2005
Roche, James M. obit Yrbk
  2004
Rockefeller, Laurance S. obit
  Yrbk 2004
Rockwell, Llewellyn H. Jr.
  Jun 2007
Roddick, Andy Jan 2004
Roddick, Anita obit Yrbk
  2007
Rodino, Peter W. obit Yrbk
  2005
Rodriguez, Alex Apr 2003
Rodriguez, Arturo Mar 2001
Rogers, Fred obit Jul 2003
Rogers, William P. obit Mar
  2001
Rojas, Rudy Jan 2006
Rollins, Edward J. Mar 2001
Rollins, Henry Sep 2001
Romenesko, Jim Feb 2004
Romer, John Jul 2003
Romero, Anthony Jul 2002
Romney, Mitt Sep 2006
Rooney, Joe Don *see* Rascal
  Flatts
Rosas, Cesar *see* Los Lobos
Rose, Jalen Mar 2004
Rose, Jim Mar 2003
Rosenfeld, Irene B. Jul 2007
Rosenthal, A. M. obit Sep
  2006
Rosenthal, Joe obit Yrbk 2007
Ross, Alex Nov 2007
Ross, Gary May 2004
Ross, Herbert obit Feb 2002
Ross, Robert Oct 2002
Rostow, Eugene V. obit Yrbk
  2003
Rostow, Walt W. obit Jul 2003
Rostropovich, Mstislav obit
  Aug 2007
Rotblat, Joseph obit Feb 2006
Rote, Kyle obit Yrbk 2002
Roth, William V. Jr. obit Yrbk
  2004
Rothschild, Baron Guy de
  obit Yrbk 2007

Rothschild, Miriam obit Yrbk 2005
Rounds, Michael Jun 2006
Rowan, Carl T. obit Jan 2001
Rowland, Kelly see Destiny's Child
Rowley, Janet D. Mar 2001
Rowntree, David see Blur
Rubenstein, Atoosa Oct 2004
Rubin, Edward M. Jan 2006
Rubin, Rick Sep 2007
Rubin, William S. obit Yrbk 2007
Rudd, Phil see AC/DC
Rukeyser, Louis obit Nov 2006
Rule, Ja see Ja Rule
Rumsfeld, Donald H. Mar 2002
Rus, Daniela Feb 2004
Rusesabagina, Paul May 2005
Rush Feb 2001
Russell, Anna obit Yrbk 2007
Russell, Harold obit Apr 2002
Russell, Kurt Nov 2004
Rutan, Burt Jun 2005
Ryan, George H. Sep 2001
Ryder, Jonathan see Ludlum, Robert
Ryer, Jonathan see Ludlum, Robert

Saab, Elie Aug 2004
Sabah, Jaber Al-Ahmad Al-Jaber Al-, Sheik obit Yrbk 2006
Safina, Carl Apr 2005
Sagan, Francoise obit Feb 2005
Said, Edward W. obit Feb 2004
Salinger, Pierre obit Feb 2005
Sánchez, David Nov 2001
Sanders, Ric see Fairport Convention
Sandford, John Mar 2002
Sándor, György obit Yrbk 2006
Sandoval, Jesse see Shins
Sanger, Stephen Mar 2004
Santana, Johan Jul 2006
Santos, José Nov 2003
Sapolsky, Robert Jan 2004
Sapp, Warren Sep 2003
Saramago, José Jun 2002
Sarris, Andrew Jan 2007
Savage, Rick see Def Leppard
Savimbi, Jonas obit Jun 2002
Sayles Belton, Sharon Jan 2001
Scammon, Richard M. obit Sep 2001

Scaturro, Pasquale V. Oct 2005
Scavullo, Francesco obit Yrbk 2004
Scdoris, Rachael Jul 2005
Scelsa, Vin May 2006
Scelsa, Vincent see Scelsa, Vin
Schaap, Phil Sep 2001
Schakowsky, Jan Jul 2004
Schell, Maria obit Yrbk 2005
Scheuer, James obit Apr 2006
Schieffer, Bob Aug 2006
Schilling, Curt Oct 2001
Schindler, Alexander M. obit Feb 2001
Schirra, Walter M. obit Yrbk 2007
Schjeldahl, Peter Oct 2005
Schlein, Miriam obit Yrbk 2005
Schlesinger, Arthur M. Jr. obit Aug 2007
Schlesinger, John obit Yrbk 2003
Schoenberg, Loren Feb 2005
Scholder, Fritz obit Yrbk 2005
Schott, Marge obit Yrbk 2004
Schriever, Bernard obit Yrbk 2005
Schroeder, Frederick R. obit Yrbk 2006
Schroeder, Ted see Schroeder, Frederick R.
Schultes, Richard Evans obit Sep 2001
Schultz, Ed Aug 2005
Schwartz, Gil Aug 2007
Schwarzenegger, Arnold Aug 2004
Schwarzkopf, Elisabeth obit Yrbk 2006
Scorsese, Martin Jun 2007
Scott, George obit Yrbk 2005 see Blind Boys of Alabama
Scott, H. Lee Oct 2006
Scott, Jill Jan 2002
Scott, Robert L. Jr. obit Yrbk 2006
Scott, Tony Nov 2004
Scottoline, Lisa Jul 2001
Scully, Vin Oct 2001
Sean Paul Jan 2007
Sears, Martha see Sears, William and Martha
Sears, William and Martha Aug 2001
Seau, Junior Sep 2001
Sebelius, Kathleen Nov 2004
Sedaris, Amy Apr 2002
Selway, Phil see Radiohead

Sembène, Ousmane obit Yrbk 2007
Semel, Terry Jul 2006
Senghor, Léopold Sédar obit Mar 2002
Serrano Súñer, Ramón obit Yrbk 2004
Servan-Schreiber, Jean-Jacques obit Yrbk 2007
Settle, Mary Lee obit Yrbk 2006
Setzer, Philip see Emerson String Quartet
Seymour, Lesley Jane Nov 2001
Seymour, Stephanie Oct 2002
Shahade, Jennifer Sep 2005
Shaheen, Jeanne Jan 2001
Shalhoub, Tony Nov 2002
Shapiro, Irving S. obit Nov 2001
Shapiro, Neal May 2003
Shaw, Artie obit Apr 2005
Shawcross, Hartley obit Yrbk 2003
Shearer, Harry Jun 2001
Shearer, Moira obit Yrbk 2006
Sheehan, Cindy May 2007
Sheldon, Sidney obit Yrbk 2007
Shepherd, Michael see Ludlum, Robert
Shields, Mark May 2005
Shinoda, Mike see Linkin Park
Shins Jun 2007
Shoemaker, Willie obit Apr 2004
Short, Bobby obit Nov 2005
Shriver, Lionel Sep 2005
Shubin, Neil Apr 2007
Shumway, Norman E. obit Yrbk 2006
Shyamalan, M. Night Mar 2003
Siddons, Anne Rivers Jan 2005
Sills, Beverly obit Oct 2007
Silva, Daniel Apr 2007
Silver, Joel Nov 2003
Silverman, Sarah Jul 2006
Simmons, Earl see DMX
Simon, Claude obit Yrbk 2005
Simon, Herbert A. obit May 2001
Simon, Paul obit Yrbk 2004
Simone, Nina obit Yrbk 2003
Simpson, Lorna Nov 2004
Sin, Jaime obit Yrbk 2005
Sinegal, James D. Aug 2007
Singer, Bryan Apr 2005
Sinopoli, Giuseppe obit Sep 2001

Sisco, Joseph obit Yrbk 2005
Sissi Jun 2001
Sklansky, David Apr 2007
Slater, Kelly Jul 2001
Slaughter, Frank obit Yrbk 2006
Slavenska, Mia obit Apr 2003
Smathers, George A. obit Jun 2007
Smiley, Tavis Apr 2003
Smith, Ali Jun 2006
Smith, Amy Jun 2005
Smith, Chesterfield H. obit Yrbk 2003
Smith, Dante Terrell see Mos Def
Smith, Elinor Mar 2001
Smith, Howard K. obit Aug 2002
Smith, Jeff obit Yrbk 2004
Smith, Kiki Mar 2005
Smith, Lovie Sep 2007
Smith, Maggie Jul 2002
Smith, Orin C. Nov 2003
Smith, Steve Sep 2006
Smits, Jimmy May 2006
Smuin, Michael obit Yrbk 2007
Smylie, Robert E. obit Yrbk 2004
Snead, Sam obit Yrbk 2002
Snow, John Aug 2003
Snow, Tony Sep 2006
Snyder, Tom obit Yrbk 2007
Soffer, Olga Jul 2002
Solomon, Phil Oct 2007
Solomon, Susan Jul 2005
Sontag, Susan obit May 2005
Sothern, Ann obit Aug 2001
Souzay, Gérard obit Yrbk 2004
Spade, Kate Apr 2007
Spahn, Warren obit Yrbk 2004
Spark, Muriel obit Yrbk 2007
Sparks, Nicholas Feb 2001
Spektor, Regina Jul 2007
Spelke, Elizabeth Apr 2006
Spelling, Aaron obit Yrbk 2006
Spellings, Margaret Jun 2005
Spence, Hartzell obit Yrbk 2001
Spencer, John Jan 2001 obit Yrbk 2006
Spencer, Scott Jul 2003
Spergel, David Jan 2005
Spillane, Mickey obit Nov 2006
Spiropulu, Maria May 2004
Spitzer, Eliot Mar 2003
Sprewell, Latrell Feb 2001
Squyres, Steven Nov 2006

St. John, Robert obit Yrbk 2003
St. Louis, Martin Feb 2007
Stabenow, Debbie Feb 2006
Stackhouse, Jerry Nov 2001
Staley, Dawn Apr 2005
Stanfield, Robert Lorne obit Yrbk 2004
Stanley, Kim obit Jan 2002
Stanton, Andrew Feb 2004
Stanton, Bill May 2001
Stanton, Frank obit Yrbk 2007
Stapleton, Maureen obit Nov 2006
Stapp, Scott see Creed
Stargell, Willie obit Sep 2001
Starr, Chauncey obit Yrbk 2007
Stassen, Harold E. obit May 2001
Steele, Claude M. Feb 2001
Steele, Michael S. Jul 2004
Steig, William obit Apr 2004
Steiger, Rod obit Yrbk 2002
Stein, Benjamin J. Sep 2001
Stein, Janice Gross Aug 2006
Steingraber, Sandra Sep 2003
Steitz, Joan A. Jun 2007
Stephens, John see Legend, John
Stern, Isaac obit Jan 2002
Stern, Jessica May 2006
Stevens, Ted Oct 2001
Stew Sep 2007
Steward, David L. Nov 2004
Stewart, Alice obit Yrbk 2002
Stewart, James "Bubba" Feb 2005
Stewart, Jon Jul 2004
Stewart, Mark see Stew
Stewart, Thomas obit Yrbk 2007
Stewart, Tony Nov 2006
Stiefel, Ethan Apr 2004
Stoller, Debbie Aug 2007
Stoltenberg, Gerhard obit Mar 2002
Stolz, Mary obit Yrbk 2007
Stone, W. Clement obit Yrbk 2002
Storch, Gerald L. Jun 2007
Storr, Anthony obit Sep 2001
Stott, John May 2005
Straight, Michael obit Yrbk 2004
Stratton, Dorothy obit Yrbk 2006
Stratton, William G. obit Aug 2001
Straus, Roger W. Jr. obit Yrbk 2004
Streb, Elizabeth Apr 2003
Stringer, Howard Jan 2006

Stroessner, Alfredo obit Yrbk 2007
Strokes Feb 2007
Stroman, Susan Jul 2002
Struzan, Drew Mar 2005
Stutz, Geraldine obit Yrbk 2005
Styron, William obit Yrbk 2007
Subandrio obit Apr 2005
Sucksdorff, Arne obit Sep 2001
Sugar, Bert Randolph Nov 2002
Sullivan, Daniel Feb 2003
Sullivan, Leon H. obit Sep 2001
Summers, Lawrence H. Jul 2002
Summitt, Pat Jun 2005
Sun Wen Apr 2001
Sutherland, Kiefer Mar 2002
Suzuki, Ichiro Jul 2002
Suzuki, Zenko obit Yrbk 2004
Swearingen, John obit Yrbk 2007
Sweeney, Anne Jun 2003
Swinton, Tilda Nov 2001
Syal, Meera Feb 2001

Taboo Nawasha see Black Eyed Peas
Taintor, Anne Jun 2005
Tajiri, Satoshi Nov 2001
Talese, Nan Sep 2006
Talley, André Leon Jul 2003
Talmadge, Herman E. obit Jun 2002
Tange, Kenzo obit Yrbk 2005
Tangerine Dream Jan 2005
Tao, Terence Sep 2007
Tarter, Jill Cornell Feb 2001
Tartt, Donna Feb 2003
Tarver, Antonio Jun 2006
Tattersall, Ian Aug 2007
Taufa'ahau, Tupou IV obit Yrbk 2007
Taurasi, Diana Nov 2007
Tauscher, Ellen O. Mar 2001
Taylor, Herman A. Jun 2006
Taylor, Jermain Apr 2006
Taylor, John W. obit Apr 2002
Taylor, Koko Jul 2002
Taylor, Lili Jul 2005
Taylor, Theodore obit Feb 2005
Tebaldi, Renata obit Apr 2005
Tebbel, John obit Mar 2005
Tejada, Miguel Jun 2003
Teller, Edward obit Sep 2004
Tetley, Glen obit Yrbk 2007
Thain, John A. May 2004

Thaler, William J. obit Yrbk 2005
Theron, Charlize Nov 2004
Thieu, Nguyen Van obit Jan 2002
Thomas, Dave see Thomas, R. David
Thomas, R. David obit Apr 2002
Thomas, William H. Jan 2006
Thome, Jim Jun 2007
Thompson, Hunter S. obit Yrbk 2005
Thompson, John III Nov 2007
Thompson, John W. Mar 2005
Thompson, Lonnie Jan 2004
Thomson, James A. Nov 2001
Thomson, Kenneth R. obit Yrbk 2006
Thomson, Meldrim Jr. obit Sep 2001
Thurmond, Strom obit Nov 2003
Thyssen-Bornemisza de Kaszan, Baron Hans Heinrich obit Yrbk 2002
Tice, George A. Nov 2003
Tierney, John Aug 2005
Tigerman, Stanley Feb 2001
Tilghman, Shirley M. Jun 2006
Tillerson, Rex Sep 2006
Timbaland Mar 2003
Tisch, Laurence A. obit Yrbk 2004
Titov, Gherman obit Jan 2001
Tobin, James obit May 2002
Toledano, Ralph de obit Yrbk 2007
Toledo, Alejandro Nov 2001
Toles, Thomas G. see Toles, Tom
Toles, Tom Nov 2002
Tolle, Eckhart Feb 2005
Tomlinson, LaDainian Oct 2006
Tre Cool see Green Day
Tremonti, Mark see Creed
Trenet, Charles obit Sep 2001
Trenkler, Freddie obit Yrbk 2001
Trethewey, Natasha Aug 2007
Trevor-Roper, H. R. obit Jul 2003
Tridish, Pete Apr 2004
Trigère, Pauline obit Jul 2002
Tritt, Travis Feb 2004
Trotter, Lloyd Jul 2005
Trout Powell, Eve May 2004
Trout, Robert obit Jan 2001
Trowbridge, Alexander B. obit Yrbk 2006
Troyat, Henri obit Yrbk 2007

Trudeau, Pierre Elliott obit Jan 2001
Truman, David B. obit Yrbk 2004
Truss, Lynne Jul 2006
Tsui Hark Oct 2001
Tufte, Edward R. Nov 2007
Tull, Tanya Nov 2004
Tureck, Rosalyn obit Yrbk 2003
Turner, Mark Nov 2002
Turre, Steve Apr 2001
Tweet Nov 2002
Tyler, Steven see Aerosmith
Tyson, John H. Aug 2001

Underwood, Carrie Mar 2007
Unitas, Johnny obit Yrbk 2002
Uris, Leon obit Yrbk 2003
Urquidez, Benny Nov 2001
Urrea, Luis Alberto Nov 2005
Ustinov, Peter obit Aug 2004

Valdes-Rodriguez, Alisa Jan 2006
Valensi, Nick see Strokes
Valenti, Jack obit Yrbk 2007
Valentine, Bobby Jul 2001
Van Allen, James A. obit Yrbk 2007
Van den Haag, Ernest obit Jul 2002
Van Duyn, Mona obit Nov 2005
Van Exel, Nick Mar 2002
Van Gundy, Jeff May 2001
Van Zandt, Steven Feb 2006
Vance, Cyrus R. obit Apr 2002
Vandiver, S. Ernest obit Yrbk 2005
Vandross, Luther obit Yrbk 2005
Vane, John R. obit Yrbk 2005
Vargas, Elizabeth Apr 2006
Varnay, Astrid obit Yrbk 2007
Varnedoe, Kirk obit Yrbk 2003
Vaughn, Vince Sep 2006
Verdon, Gwen obit Jan 2001
Vick, Michael Nov 2003
Vickrey, Dan see Counting Crows
Vieira, Meredith Apr 2002
Viereck, Peter obit Yrbk 2006
Villaraigosa, Antonio Aug 2007
Vinatieri, Adam Sep 2004
Virilio, Paul Jul 2005
Viscardi, Henry Jr. obit Yrbk 2004

Visser, Lesley Apr 2007
Vitale, Dick Jan 2005
Volokhonsky, Larissa see Pevear, Richard and Volokhonsky, Larissa
Vonnegut, Kurt obit Aug 2007
Voulkos, Peter obit Aug 2002

Wachowski, Andy see Wachowski, Andy and Larry
Wachowski, Andy and Larry Sep 2003
Wachowski, Larry see Wachowski, Andy and Larry
Wade, Dwyane Apr 2006
Waldheim, Kurt obit Oct 2007
Wales, Jimmy Oct 2006
Walker, Mort Feb 2002
Walker, Olene S. Apr 2005
Wall, Art obit Feb 2002
Wallace, Ben Apr 2004
Wallis, Jim Jul 2005
Walsh, Bill obit Yrbk 2007
Walsh, John Jul 2001
Walters, Barbara Feb 2003
Walters, Vernon A. obit Jul 2002
Walworth, Arthur C. obit Yrbk 2005
Ward, Benjamin obit Yrbk 2002
Ward, Paul L. obit Yrbk 2006
Ward, William E. Nov 2005
Ware, David S. Sep 2003
Warner, Mark R. Oct 2006
Warnke, Paul C. obit Feb 2002
Warren, Rick Oct 2006
Washburn, Bradford obit Yrbk 2007
Washington, Walter E. obit Yrbk 2004
Wasserman, Lew R. obit Yrbk 2002
Wasserstein, Wendy obit Yrbk 2006
Waters, Alice Jan 2004
Watkins, Donald Jan 2003
Watkins, Levi Jr. Mar 2003
Watson, Arthel Lane see Watson, Doc
Watson, Doc Feb 2003
Watson, Emily May 2007
Watts, Naomi Mar 2007
Waugh, Auberon obit May 2001
Wayans, Marlon see Wayans, Shawn and Marlon
Wayans, Shawn and Marlon May 2001

Weaver, Dennis obit Yrbk
2006
Weaver, Pat obit Yrbk 2002
Weaver, Sylvester *see*
Weaver, Pat
Webb, Jim Nov 2007
Webb, Karrie Aug 2001
Webber, Chris May 2003
Weber, Dick obit Yrbk 2005
Weinberg, Alvin M. obit Yrbk
2006
Weinberger, Caspar W. obit
Jul 2006
Weinrig, Gary Lee *see* Rush
Weinstein, Allen Jun 2006
Weis, Charlie Nov 2007
Weisberg, Jacob Oct 2007
Weiss, Paul obit Yrbk 2002
Weisskopf, Victor F. obit
Yrbk 2002
Weitz, John obit Apr 2003
Weizman, Ezer obit Aug 2005
Weizsäcker, Carl F. von obit
Yrbk 2007
Wek, Alek Jun 2001
Welch, Stanton Jul 2007
Wells, David May 2004
Wellstone, Paul D. obit Yrbk
2003
Welty, Eudora obit Nov 2001
Wendel, Johnathan Apr 2007
Wendrich, Willeke Jan 2007
Wesley, Valerie Wilson Jun
2002
West, Kanye Aug 2006
Westmoreland, William C.
obit Nov 2005
Wexler, Haskell Aug 2007
Wexler, Jerry Jan 2001
Weyrich, Paul Feb 2005
Wheeldon, Christopher Mar
2004
Whipple, Fred L. obit Yrbk
2005
Whitaker, Mark Aug 2003
White, Armond Oct 2006
White, Byron Raymond obit
Jul 2002
White, Gilbert F. obit Yrbk
2006
White, Jack *see* White Stripes
White, John F. obit Yrbk 2005
White, Meg *see* White Stripes
White, Reggie obit Yrbk 2005
White Stripes Sep 2003
Whitehead, Colson Nov 2001
Whitford, Brad *see* Aerosmith
Whitford, Bradley Apr 2003
Whitson, Peggy Sep 2003
Wiesenthal, Simon obit Yrbk
2005
Wiggins, James Russell obit
Mar 2001

Wilber, Ken Apr 2002
Wilder, Billy obit Yrbk 2002
Wiley, Kehinde Aug 2007
Wilhelm, Hoyt obit Yrbk 2002
Wilkins, Maurice H. F. obit
Yrbk 2005
Wilkins, Robert W. obit Yrbk
2003
will.i.am *see* Black Eyed Peas
Williams, Armstrong May
2004
Williams, Cliff *see* AC/DC
Williams, Harrison A. Jr. obit
Mar 2002
Williams, Michelle *see*
Destiny's Child
Williams, Pharrell *see*
Neptunes
Williams, Preston Warren II
May 2007
Williams, Roy Mar 2007
Williams, Serena *see*
Williams, Venus and
Williams, Serena
Williams, Tad Sep 2006
Williams, Ted obit Oct 2002
Williams, Venus *see*
Williams, Venus and
Williams, Serena
Williams, Venus and
Williams, Serena Feb 2003
Willingham, Tyrone Nov
2002
Willis, Deborah Sep 2004
Willis, Dontrelle Aug 2006
Wilmore, Larry Nov 2007
Wilson, August obit Feb 2006
Wilson, Heather Jul 2006
Wilson, James Q. Aug 2002
Wilson, Kemmons obit Yrbk
2003
Wilson, Luke Feb 2005
Wilson, Marie C. Sep 2004
Wilson, Owen Feb 2003
Wilson, Sloan obit Yrbk 2003
Winchester, Simon Oct 2006
Winsor, Kathleen obit Yrbk
2003
Winston, Stan Jul 2002
Winters, Shelley obit Apr
2006
Wise, Robert obit Apr 2006
Witherspoon, Reese Jan 2004
Woertz, Patricia A. Mar 2007
Woese, Carl R. Jun 2003
Wojciechowska, Maia obit
Yrbk 2002
Wolfe, Art Jun 2005
Wolfe, Julia Oct 2003
Wolff, Maritta M. obit Yrbk
2002
Wolfowitz, Paul Feb 2003
Wolfram, Stephen Feb 2005

Wolpoff, Milford Jul 2006
Wong, Andrea Sep 2007
Wong-Staal, Flossie Apr 2001
Wood, Elijah Aug 2002
Wood, Kerry May 2005
Woodcock, Leonard obit Apr
2001
Woods, Donald obit Nov 2001
Woodson, Rod Oct 2004
Woodward, Robert F. obit
Yrbk 2001
Wooldridge, Anna Marie *see*
Lincoln, Abbey
Wooldridge, Dean E. obit
Yrbk 2007
Worth, Irene obit Aug 2002
Wright, Jeffrey May 2002
Wright, Steven May 2003
Wright, Teresa obit Yrbk 2005
Wright, Will Feb 2004
Wright, Winky Jul 2004
Wriston, Walter B. obit Aug
2005
Wrynn, Dylan *see* Tridish,
Pete
Wyatt, Jane obit Yrbk 2006
Wylde, Zakk Oct 2004
Wyman, Jane obit Yrbk 2007
Wyman, Thomas obit Yrbk
2003

Xenakis, Iannis obit Jul 2001

Yagudin, Alexei Feb 2004
Yard, Molly obit Apr 2006
Yashin, Aleksei *see* Yashin,
Alexei
Yashin, Alexei Jan 2003
Yassin, Ahmed obit Yrbk
2004
Yates, Elizabeth obit Nov
2001
Yates, Sidney R. obit Jan 2001
Yeltsin, Boris obit Jun 2007
Yokich, Stephen P. obit Yrbk
2002
Yorke, Thom *see* Radiohead
Young, Angus *see* AC/DC
Young, Kimberly S. Jan 2006
Young, Malcolm *see* AC/DC
Yusuf, Hamza Mar 2007

Zahir Shah, Mohammed obit
Yrbk 2007
Zahn, Paula Feb 2002
Zaillian, Steven Oct 2001
Zambello, Francesca May
2003
Zatopek, Emil obit Feb 2001
Zellweger, Renee Feb 2004
Zerhouni, Elias Oct 2003

Zeta-Jones, Catherine Apr 2003
Zhao Ziyang obit Yrbk 2005
Zhu Rongji Jul 2001
Ziegler, Ronald L. obit Jul 2003

Zimmer, Hans Mar 2002
Zindel, Paul obit Yrbk 2007
Zinni, Anthony C. May 2002
Zito, Barry Jul 2004
Zittel, Andrea Aug 2006
Zivojinovich, Alex *see* Rush

Zollar, Jawole Willa Jo Jul 2003
Zorina, Vera obit Yrbk 2003
Zucker, Jeff Jan 2002
Zukerman, Eugenia Jan 2004